D1272473

CHILTON®

CHRYSLER
SERVICE MANUAL
2010 EDITION
VOLUME II

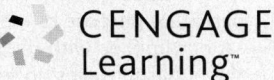

CENGAGE
Learning™

Australia • Brazil • Japan • Korea • Mexico • Singapore • Spain • United Kingdom • United States

CENGAGE
Learning™

CHILTON®
Chrysler Service Manual
2010 Edition
Volume II

Vice President,
Technology Professional
Business Unit:
Gregory L. Clayton

Publisher,
Technology Professional
Business Unit:
David Koontz

Director of Marketing:
Beth A. Lutz

Production Director:
Carolyn Miller

Production Manager:
Andrew Crouth

Marketing Manager:
Jennifer Barbic

Marketing Coordinator:
Rachael Conover

Editorial Assistant:
Tracey Gates

Chilton Content Specialist:
Paula Baillie

Graphical Designer:
Melinda Possinger

Art Director:
Benj Gleeksman

Sr. Content Project Manager:
Elizabeth C. Hough

Managing Editor:
Terry L. Blomquist

Senior Editor:
Christine L. Sheeky

Editors:
Jim Bailey
Ken Burdette
Sherry Burdette
John Howard, A.S.E.
David G. Olson

Printed in the United States of America
1 2 3 4 5 6 7 13 12 11 10 09

For product information and technology assistance, contact us at
Professional & Career Group Customer Support, 1-800-648-7450
For permission to use material from this text or product,
submit all requests online at
www.cengage.com/permissions.
Further permissions questions can be e-mailed to
permissionrequest@cengage.com.

ISBN-13: 978-1-1110-3653-9
ISBN-10: 1-1110-3653-5
ISSN: 1939-621X

Delmar
5 Maxwell Drive
Clifton Park, NY 12065-2919
USA

Cengage Learning is a leading provider of customized learning solutions with office locations around the globe, including Singapore, the United Kingdom, Australia, Mexico, Brazil, and Japan. Locate your local office at: **international.cengage.com/region**

Cengage Learning products are represented in Canada by Nelson Education, Ltd.

NOTICE TO THE READER

Publisher does not warrant or guarantee any of the products described herein or perform any independent analysis in connection with any of the product information contained herein. Publisher does not assume, and expressly disclaims, any obligation to obtain and include information other than that provided to it by the manufacturer.

The reader is expressly warned to consider and adopt all safety precautions that might be indicated by the activities described herein and to avoid all potential hazards. By following the instructions contained herein, the reader willingly assumes all risks in connection with such instructions.

The publisher makes no representations or warranties of any kind, including but not limited to, the warranties of fitness for particular purpose or merchantability, nor are any such representations implied with respect to the material set forth herein, and the publisher takes no responsibility with respect to such material. The publisher shall not be liable for any special, consequential, or exemplary damages resulting, in whole or part, from the readers' use of, or reliance upon, this material.

Table of Contents

Sections

Model Index

USING THIS INFORMATION

Organization

To find where a particular model section or procedure is located, look in the Table of Contents. Main topics are listed with the page number on which they may be found. Following the main topics is an alphabetical listing of all of the procedures within the section and their page numbers.

Manufacturer and Model Coverage

This product covers 2008–2010 Chrysler models that are produced in sufficient quantities to warrant coverage, and which have technical content available from the vehicle manufacturers before our publication date. Although this information is as complete as possible at the time of publication, some manufacturers may make changes which cannot be included here. While striving for total accuracy, the publisher cannot assume responsibility for any errors, changes, or omissions that may occur in the compilation of this data.

Part Numbers & Special Tools

Part numbers and special tools are recommended by the publisher and vehicle manufacturer to perform specific jobs. Before substituting any part or tool for the one recommended, you must be completely satisfied that neither your personal safety, nor the performance of the vehicle will be endangered.

ACKNOWLEDGEMENT

Portions of materials contained herein are sourced from Chrysler Group LLC.

PRECAUTIONS

Before servicing any vehicle, please be sure to read all of the following precautions, which deal with personal safety, prevention of component damage, and important points to take into consideration when servicing a motor vehicle:

- Always wear safety glasses or goggles when drilling, cutting, grinding or prying.
- Steel-toed work shoes should be worn when working with heavy parts. Pockets should not be used for carrying tools. A slip or fall can drive a screwdriver into your body.
- Work surfaces, including tools and the floor should be kept clean of grease, oil or other slippery material.
- When working around moving parts, don't wear loose clothing. Long hair should be tied back under a hat or cap, or in a hair net.
- Always use tools only for the purpose for which they were designed. Never pry with a screwdriver.
- Keep a fire extinguisher and first aid kit handy.
- Always properly support the vehicle with approved stands or lift.
- Always have adequate ventilation when working with chemicals or hazardous material.
- Carbon monoxide is colorless, odorless and dangerous. If it is necessary to operate the engine with vehicle in a closed area such as a garage, always use an exhaust collector to vent the exhaust gases outside the closed area.
- When draining coolant, keep in mind that small children and some pets are attracted by ethylene glycol antifreeze, and

are quite likely to drink any left in an open container, or in puddles on the ground. This will prove fatal in sufficient quantity. Always drain the coolant into a sealable container.

- To avoid personal injury, do not remove the coolant pressure relief cap while the engine is operating or hot. The cooling system is under pressure; steam and hot liquid can come out forcefully when the cap is loosened slightly. Failure to follow these instructions may result in personal injury. The coolant must be recovered in a suitable, clean container for reuse. If the coolant is contaminated it must be recycled or disposed of correctly.
- When carrying out maintenance on the starting system be aware that heavy gauge leads are connected directly to the battery. Make sure the protective caps are in place when maintenance is completed. Failure to follow these instructions may result in personal injury.
- Do not remove any part of the engine emission control system. Operating the engine without the engine emission control system will reduce fuel economy and engine ventilation. This will weaken engine performance and shorten engine life. It is also a violation of Federal law.
- Due to environmental concerns, when the air conditioning system is drained, the refrigerant must be collected using refrigerant recovery/recycling equipment. Federal law requires that refrigerant be recovered into appropriate recovery equipment and the process be conducted by qualified technicians

who have been certified by an approved organization, such as MACS, ASI, etc. Use of a recovery machine dedicated to the appropriate refrigerant is necessary to reduce the possibility of oil and refrigerant incompatibility concerns. Refer to the instructions provided by the equipment manufacturer when removing refrigerant from or charging the air conditioning system.

- Always disconnect the battery ground when working on or around the electrical system.
- Batteries contain sulfuric acid. Avoid contact with skin, eyes, or clothing. Also, shield your eyes when working near batteries to protect against possible splashing of the acid solution. In case of acid contact with skin or eyes, flush immediately with water for a minimum of 15 minutes and get prompt medical attention. If acid is swallowed, call a physician immediately. Failure to follow these instructions may result in personal injury.
- Batteries normally produce explosive gases. Therefore, do not allow flames, sparks or lighted substances to come near the battery. When charging or working near a battery, always shield your face and protect your eyes. Always provide ventilation. Failure to follow these instructions may result in personal injury.
- When lifting a battery, excessive pressure on the end walls could cause acid to spew through the vent caps, resulting in personal injury, damage to the vehicle or battery. Lift with a battery carrier or with your hands on opposite corners. Failure to follow

these instructions may result in personal injury.

• Observe all applicable safety precautions when working around fuel. Whenever servicing the fuel system, always work in a well-ventilated area. Do not allow fuel spray or vapors to come in contact with a spark, open flame, or excessive heat (a hot drop light, for example). Keep a dry chemical fire extinguisher near the work area. Always keep fuel in a container specifically designed for fuel storage; also, always properly seal fuel containers to avoid the possibility of fire or explosion. Do not smoke or carry lighted tobacco or open flame of any type when working on or near any fuel-related components.

• Fuel injection systems often remain pressurized, even after the engine has been turned OFF. The fuel system pressure must be relieved before disconnecting any fuel lines. Failure to do so may result in fire and/or personal injury.

• The evaporative emissions system contains fuel vapor and condensed fuel vapor. Although not present in large quantities, it still presents the danger of explosion or fire. Disconnect the battery ground cable from the battery to minimize the possibility of an electrical spark occurring, possibly causing a fire or explosion if fuel vapor or liquid fuel is present in the area. Failure to follow these instructions can result in personal injury.

• The EPA warns that prolonged contact with used engine oil may cause a number of skin disorders, including cancer! You should make every effort to minimize your exposure to used engine oil. Protective gloves should be worn when changing oil. Wash your hands and any other exposed skin areas as soon as possible after exposure to used engine oil. Soap and water, or waterless hand cleaner should be used.

• Some vehicles are equipped with an air bag system, often referred to as a Supplemental Restraint System (SRS) or Supplemental Inflatable Restraint (SIR) system. The system must be disabled before performing service on or around system components, steering column, instrument panel components, wiring and sensors. Failure to follow safety and disabling procedures could result in accidental air bag deployment, possible personal injury and unnecessary system repairs.

• Always wear safety goggles when working with, or around, the air bag system. When carrying a non-deployed air bag, be sure the bag and trim cover are pointed away from your body. When placing a non-deployed air bag on a work surface, always face the bag and trim cover upward, away from the surface. This will reduce the motion of the module if it is accidentally deployed.

• Electronic modules are sensitive to electrical charges. The ABS module can be damaged if exposed to these charges.

• Brake pads and shoes may contain asbestos, which has been determined to be a cancer-causing agent. Never clean brake surfaces with compressed air. Avoid inhaling brake dust. Clean all brake surfaces with a commercially available brake cleaning fluid.

• When replacing brake pads, shoes, discs or drums, replace them as complete axle sets.

• When servicing drum brakes, disassemble and assemble one side at a time, leaving the remaining side intact for reference.

• Brake fluid often contains polyglycol ethers and polyglycols. Avoid contact with the eyes and wash your hands thoroughly after handling brake fluid. If you do get brake fluid in your eyes, flush your eyes with clean, running water for 15 minutes. If eye irritation persists, or if you have taken brake fluid internally, immediately seek medical assistance.

• Clean, high quality brake fluid from a sealed container is essential to the safe and proper operation of the brake system. You should always buy the correct type of brake fluid for your vehicle. If the brake fluid becomes contaminated, completely flush the system with new fluid. Never reuse any brake fluid. Any brake fluid that is removed from the system should be discarded. Also, do not allow any brake fluid to come in contact with a painted or plastic surface; it will damage the paint.

• Never operate the engine without the proper amount and type of engine oil; doing so will result in severe engine damage.

• Timing belt maintenance is extremely important! Many models utilize an interference-type, non-freewheeling engine. If the timing belt breaks, the valves in the cylinder head may strike the pistons, causing potentially serious (also time-consuming and expensive) engine damage.

• Disconnecting the negative battery cable on some vehicles may interfere with the functions of the on-board computer system (s) and may require the computer to undergo a relearning process once the negative battery cable is reconnected.

• Steering and suspension fasteners are critical parts because they affect performance of vital components and systems and their failure can result in major service expense. They must be replaced with the same grade or part number or an equivalent part if replacement is necessary. Do not use a replacement part of lesser quality or substitute design. Torque values must be used as specified during reassembly.

DODGE

Dakota

SPECIFICATIONS AND MAINTENANCE CHARTS

ENGINE AND VEHICLE IDENTIFICATION

Code ①	Liters (cc)	Cu. In.	Cyl.	Fuel Sys.	Engine Type	Eng. Mfg.	Code ②	Year
			Engine				Model Year	
K	3.7 (3,701)	226	6	MFI	SOHC	Chrysler	8	2008
N	4.7 (4,701)	287	8	MFI	SOHC	Chrysler	9	2009
P	4.7 (4,701)	287	8	FFV	SOHC	Chrysler		

SOHC: Single Overhead Camshaft

MFI: Multi-port Fuel Injection

FFV: Flexible Fuel Vehicle

① Engine Code/8th digit of Vehicle Identification Number (VIN)

② 10th digit of the VIN

36543_DAKO_C0001

GENERAL ENGINE SPECIFICATIONS
All measurements are given in inches.

Year	Model	Engine Displacement Liters	Engine Series ID/VIN	Net Horsepower @ rpm	Net Torque @ rpm (ft. lbs.)	Bore x Stroke (in.)	Com-pression Ratio	Oil Pressure @ rpm
2008	Dakota	3.7	K	211@5200	236@4000	3.66 x 3.40	9.6:1	25-110@3000
	Dakota	4.7	N	302@5650	329@3950	3.66 x 3.40	9.6:1	35-105@3000
2009	Dakota	3.7	K	211@5200	236@4000	3.66 x 3.40	9.6:1	25-110@3000
	Dakota	4.7	P	302@5650	329@3950	3.66 x 3.40	9.6:1	35-105@3000

36543_DAKO_C0002

GASOLINE ENGINE TUNE-UP SPECIFICATIONS

Year	Engine Displacement Liters	Engine VIN	Spark Plug Gap (in.)	Ignition Timing (deg.)	Fuel Pump (psi)	Idle Speed (rpm)	Valve Clearance Intake	Valve Clearance Exhaust
2008	3.7	K	0.043	①	56-60	②	HYD	HYD
	4.7	N	③	①	56-60	②	HYD	HYD
2009	3.7	K	0.043	①	56-60	②	HYD	HYD
	4.7	P	③	①	56-60	②	HYD	HYD

NOTE: The Vehicle Emission Control Information label reflects specification changes made during production.

Follow the figures on the label if they differ from those in this chart.

HYD: Hydraulic

① Ignition timing is controlled by the PCM and is not adjustable

② Idle speed is controlled by the PCM and is not adjustable

③ The 4.7L has 2 spark plugs per cylinder:

    Intake/upper row (FR8TE2): 0.040 inch

    Exhaust/lower row (FR8T1332): 0.050 inch

36543_DAKO_C0003

CAPACITIES

Year	Model	Engine Displacement Liters	Engine VIN	Engine Oil with Filter (qts.)	Transmission (pts.) Manual	Transmission (pts.) Auto. ①	Transfer Case (pts.)	Drive Axle Front (pts.)	Drive Axle Rear (pts.) ①	Fuel Tank (gal.)	Cooling System (qts.)
2008	Dakota	3.7	K	5.0	4.7	②	③	3.5	④	22.0	13.3
	Dakota	4.7	N	6.0	—	②	③	3.5	④	22.0	13.3
2009	Dakota	3.7	K	5.0	4.7	②	③	3.5	④	22.0	13.3
	Dakota	4.7	P	6.0	—	②	③	3.5	④	22.0	13.3

NOTE: All capacities are approximate. Add fluid gradually and check to be sure a proper fluid level is obtained.

① Drain and refill

② 42RLE: 8.0 pts.

    545RFE 2WD: 11.0 pts.

    545RFE 4WD: 13.0 pts.

③ NV233: 2.5 pts.

    NV244: 2.85 pts.

④ Add 0.25 pts. limited slip additive with LSD axles

    8.25 inch axle: 4.3 pts.

    9.25 inch axle: 4.5 pts.

36543_DAKO_C0004

FLUID SPECIFICATIONS

Year	Model	Engine Displacement Liters	Engine VIN	Engine Oil	Manual Trans.	Auto. Trans.	Drive Axle Front	Drive Axle Rear	Transfer Case	Power Steering Fluid	Brake Master Cylinder	Cooling System
2008	Dakota	3.7	K	5W-20	①	①	②	③	①	①	④	⑤
	Dakota	4.7	N	5W-20	—	①	②	③	①	①	④	⑤
2009	Dakota	3.7	K	5W-20	①	①	②	③	①	①	④	⑤
	Dakota	4.7	P	5W-20	—	①	②	③	①	①	④	⑤

DOT: Department Of Transportation

① MOPAR ATF+4 Automatic Transmission Fluid

② SAE 75W-90 Multi-Purpose Type, GL-5 Gear Lubricant (MS-9763)

③ SAE 75W-140 Synthetic Gear Lubricant (MS-8985). Limited-slip rear axles require MOPAR limited-slip additive (MS-10111).

   Whenever a fluid change is made, 0.25 pts. (4 oz) of LSD additive must be added to the gear lubricant for limited-slip axles.

④ MOPAR DOT 3 and SAE J1703 should be used. If DOT 3 brake fluid is not available, DOT 4 is acceptable.

⑤ MOPAR Antifreeze/Coolant 5-Year/100,000 Mile Formula HOAT (Hybrid Organic Additive Technology)

36543_DAKO_C0005

VALVE SPECIFICATIONS

Year	Engine Displacement Liters	Engine VIN	Seat Angle (deg.)	Face Angle (deg.)	Spring Test Pressure (lbs. @ in.)	Spring Installed Height (in.)	Stem-to-Guide Clearance (in.) Intake	Stem-to-Guide Clearance (in.) Exhaust	Stem Diameter (in.) Intake	Stem Diameter (in.) Exhaust
2008	3.7	K	44.5-45.0	45.0-45.5	①	②	0.0008-0.0028	0.0019-0.0039	0.2729-0.2739	0.2717-0.2728
	4.7	N	44.5-45.0	45.0-45.5	174.5-195.6 @1.1370	1.5795	0.0008-0.0028	0.0019-0.0039	0.2729-0.2739	0.2717-0.2728
2009	3.7	K	44.5-45.0	45.0-45.5	①	②	0.0008-0.0028	0.0019-0.0039	0.2729-0.2739	0.2717-0.2728
	4.7	P	44.5-45.0	45.0-45.5	174.5-195.6 @1.1370	1.5795	0.0008-0.0028	0.0019-0.0039	0.2729-0.2739	0.2717-0.2728

① Intake: 213.2-233.8 lbs. @ 1.107 in.
   Exhaust: 196.5-214.9 lbs. @ 1.067 in.

② Intake: 1.5795 in.
   Exhaust: 1.5400 in.

36543_DAKO_C0006

CAMSHAFT AND BEARING SPECIFICATIONS CHART

All measurements are given in inches.

Year	Engine Displ. Liters	Engine VIN	Journal Dia.	Brg. Oil Clearance	Shaft End-play	Runout	Journal Bore	Lobe Height Intake	Lobe Height Exhaust
2008	3.7	K	1.0227-1.0235	0.0010-0.0026	0.0030-0.0079	NA	1.0245-1.0252	NA	NA
	4.7	N	1.0227-1.0235	0.0010-0.0026	0.0030-0.0079	NA	1.0245-1.0252	NA	NA
2009	3.7	K	1.0227-1.0235	0.0010-0.0026	0.0030-0.0079	NA	1.0245-1.0252	NA	NA
	4.7	P	1.0227-1.0235	0.0010-0.0026	0.0030-0.0079	NA	1.0245-1.0252	NA	NA

NA: Information not available

36543_DAKO_C0007

CRANKSHAFT AND CONNECTING ROD SPECIFICATIONS

All measurements are given in inches.

Year	Engine Displacement Liters	Engine VIN	Crankshaft Main Brg. Journal Dia.	Crankshaft Main Brg. Oil Clearance	Crankshaft Shaft End-play	Crankshaft Thrust on No.	Connecting Rod Journal Diameter	Connecting Rod Oil Clearance	Connecting Rod Side Clearance
2008	3.7	K	2.4996-2.5005	0.0008-0.0018	0.0021-0.0112	2	2.2792-2.2798	0.0002-0.0011	0.0040-0.0138
	4.7	N	2.4996-2.5005	0.0002-0.0013	0.0021-0.0112	2	2.0076-2.0082	0.0006-0.0022	0.0040-0.0138
2009	3.7	K	2.4996-2.5005	0.0008-0.0018	0.0021-0.0112	2	2.2792-2.2798	0.0002-0.0011	0.0040-0.0138
	4.7	P	2.4996-2.5005	0.0002-0.0013	0.0021-0.0112	2	2.0076-2.0082	0.0006-0.0022	0.0040-0.0138

36543_DAKO_C0008

PISTON AND RING SPECIFICATIONS
All measurements are given in inches.

Year	Engine Displ. Liters	Engine VIN	Piston Clearance	Ring Gap			Ring Side Clearance		
				Top Compression	Bottom Compression	Oil Control	Top Compression	Bottom Compression	Oil Control
2008	3.7	K	0.0014	0.0079-0.0142	0.0146-0.0249	0.0099-0.0300	0.0020-0.0037	0.0016-0.0031	0.0007-0.0091
	4.7	N	0.0014	0.0079-0.0142	0.0146-0.0249	0.0099-0.0300	0.0020-0.0037	0.0016-0.0031	0.0007-0.0091
2009	3.7	K	0.0014	0.0079-0.0142	0.0146-0.0249	0.0099-0.0300	0.0020-0.0037	0.0016-0.0031	0.0007-0.0091
	4.7	P	0.0014	0.0079-0.0142	0.0146-0.0249	0.0099-0.0300	0.0020-0.0037	0.0016-0.0031	0.0007-0.0091

36543_DAKO_C0009

TORQUE SPECIFICATIONS
All readings in ft. lbs.

Year	Engine Displacement Liters	Engine VIN	Cylinder Head Bolts	Main Bearing Bolts	Rod Bearing Bolts	Crankshaft Damper Bolts	Flywheel Bolts	Manifold		Spark Plugs	Oil Pan Drain Plug
								Intake	Exhaust		
2008	3.7	K	①	②	③	130	70	④	18	20	25
	4.7	N	⑤	⑥	③	130	45	④	18	⑦	25
2009	3.7	K	①	②	③	130	70	④	18	20	25
	4.7	P	⑤	⑥	③	130	45	④	18	⑦	25

① See illustration in text section

    Step 1: bolts 1-8 to 20 ft. lbs.

    Step 2: bolts 1-8 verify torque without loosening

    Step 3: bolts 9-12 to 10 ft. lbs.

    Step 4: bolts 1-8 angle tighten 90 degrees

    Step 5: bolts 1-8 angle tighten 90 degrees, again

    Step 6: bolts 9-12 to 19 ft. lbs.

② See the illustration

    Step 1: Hand tighten bolts 1D, 1G and 1F until bedplate contacts the block

    Step 2: Tighten bolts 1A-1J to 40 ft. lbs.

    Step 3: Tighten bolts 1-8 to 60 inch lbs.

    Step 4: Tighten bolts 1-8 an additional 90 degrees

    Step 5: Tighten bolts A-E to 20 ft. lbs.

③ 20 ft. lbs. plus 90 degrees

④ See illustration in text section. Tighten to 105 inch lbs.

⑤ See illustration in text section

    Step 1: bolts 1-10 to 20 ft. lbs.

    Step 2: bolts 1-10 verify torque without loosening

    Step 3: bolts 11-14 to 89 inch lbs.

    Step 4: bolts 1-10 angle tighten 90 degrees

    Step 5: bolts 1-10 angle tighten 90 degrees, again

    Step 6: bolts 11-14 to 19 ft. lbs.

⑥ Bed plate bolt sequence. Refer to illustration

    Step 1: bolts A-L to 40 ft. lbs.

    Step 2: bolts 1-10 25 inch lbs.

    Step 3: bolts 1-10 plus 90 degrees

    Step 4: bolts A1-A6 20 ft. lbs.

⑦ New plugs/gaskets: 20 ft. lbs.

    Used plugs/gaskets: 16 ft. lbs.

36543_DAKO_C0010

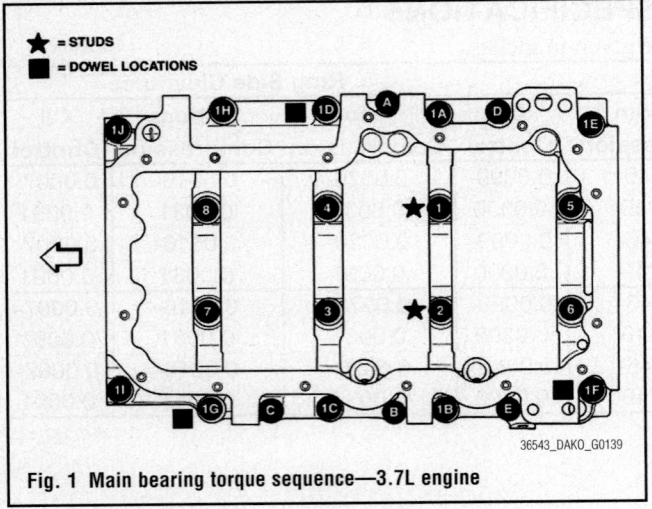

Fig. 1 Main bearing torque sequence—3.7L engine

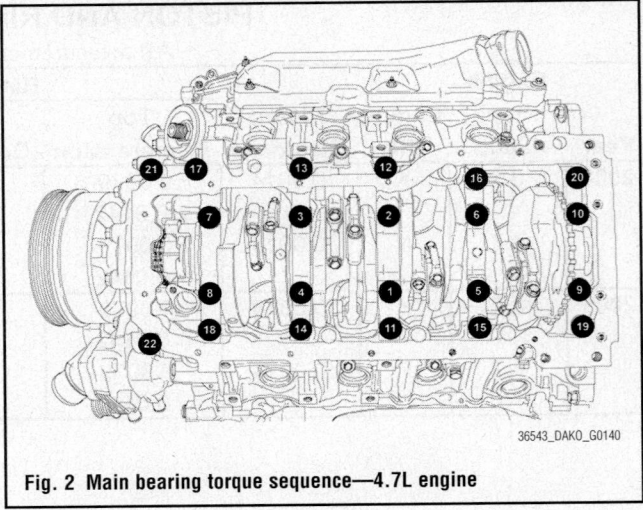

Fig. 2 Main bearing torque sequence—4.7L engine

WHEEL ALIGNMENT

| Year | Model | | Caster | | Camber | | Toe-in |
			Range (+/-Deg.)	Preferred Setting (Deg.)	Range (+/-Deg.)	Preferred Setting (Deg.)	(Deg.)
2008	Dakota	Front	0.50	①	0.50	②	+0.20+/-0.10
		Rear	—	—	0.35	-0.10	0.30+/-0.35
2009	Dakota	Front	0.50	①	0.50	②	+0.20+/-0.10
		Rear	—	—	0.35	-0.10	0.30+/-0.35

NOTE: Measurements are given for unladen vehicle: fuel, coolant & fluid levels are full. Spare tire, jack, hand tools & mats are in designated positions.

① Left wheel: +3.50 degrees

  Right wheel: +3.80 degrees

  Cross-Caster (Maximum Side-To-Side Difference): -0.30 degrees +/- 0.50 degrees

② Left wheel: +0.10 degrees

  Right wheel: -0.10 degrees

  Cross-Camber (Maximum Side-To-Side Difference): +0.20 degrees +/- 0.50 degrees

36543_DAKO_C0011

TIRE, WHEEL AND BALL JOINT SPECIFICATIONS

Year	Model	OEM Tires Standard	OEM Tires Optional	Tire Pressures (psi) Front	Tire Pressures (psi) Rear	Wheel Size	Ball Joint Inspection	Lug Nut Torque (ft. lbs.)
2008	Big Horn/Lone Star	P265/60R18	NA	①	①	8.0 x 18	②	125-145
	Laramie	P265/70R16	NA	①	①	8.0 x 16	②	125-145
	SLT	P245/70R16	NA	①	①	8.0 x 16	②	125-145
	Sport	P265/65R17	NA	①	①	8.0 x 17	②	125-145
	ST 2WD	P245/70R16	NA	①	①	7.0 x 16	②	125-145
	ST 4WD	P265/70R16	NA	①	①	7.0 x 16	②	125-145
	SXT	P245/70R16	NA	①	①	8.0 x 16	②	125-145
	TRX	P265/70R16	NA	①	①	8.0 x 16	②	125-145
2009	Big Horn/Lone Star	P265/65R17	NA	①	①	8.0 x 17	②	125-145
	Laramie	P265/60R18	NA	①	①	8.0 x 18	②	125-145
	ST	P245/70R16	NA	①	①	7.0 x 16	②	125-145
	TRX4-Off Road	P265/70R16	NA	①	①	8.0 x 16	②	125-145

OEM: Original Equipment Manufacturer

PSI: Pounds Per Square Inch

NA: Information not available

① See the tire placard on the vehicle

② If the travel exceeds 0.020 inch, replace the ball joint

36543_DAKO_C0012

BRAKE SPECIFICATIONS

All measurements in inches unless noted

Year	Model		Brake Disc Original Thickness	Brake Disc Minimum Thickness	Brake Disc Maximum Runout	Brake Drum Diameter Original Inside Diameter	Brake Drum Diameter Max. Wear Limit	Brake Drum Diameter Maximum Machine Diameter	Minimum Lining Thickness	Brake Caliper Bracket Bolts (ft. lbs.)	Brake Caliper Mounting Bolts (ft. lbs.)
2008	Dakota	F	1.102	1.039	0.0010	—	—	—	0.040	130	26
		R	—	—	—	11.50	①	11.693	②	—	—
2009	Dakota	F	1.102	1.039	0.0010	—	—	—	0.040	130	26
		R	—	—	—	11.50	①	11.693	②	—	—

F: Front

R: Rear

NA: Information not available

① Always replace the drum if machining would cause the drum diameter to exceed the size limit indicated on the drum.

② Riveted brake shoes: 0.0313 inch from the rivet heads

  Bonded brake shoes: 0.0625 inch thickness

36543_DAKO_C0013

SCHEDULED MAINTENANCE INTERVALS
DODGE—DAKOTA

TO BE SERVICED	TYPE OF SERVICE	VEHICLE MILEAGE INTERVAL (x1000)																								
		6	12	18	24	30	36	42	48	54	60	66	72	78	84	90	96	102	108	114	120	126	132	138	144	150
Accessory drive belts	R																									✓
Air cleaner element (engine)①	R					✓					✓					✓					✓					✓
Air conditioner system	S/I	Inspect system operation annually																								
Automatic transmission fluid	S/I																									
Automatic transmission fluid	R																				✓					
Battery (clean/tighten terminals)	S/I	Once a month																								
Brake fluid level	S/I	Once a month																								
Brake hoses/lines (incl. ABS)	S/I	✓	✓	✓	✓	✓	✓	✓	✓	✓	✓	✓	✓	✓	✓	✓	✓	✓	✓	✓	✓	✓	✓	✓	✓	✓
CV joints	S/I				✓				✓				✓				✓				✓				✓	
Engine coolant	R																	✓								
Engine oil and filter②	R	✓	✓	✓	✓	✓	✓	✓	✓	✓	✓	✓	✓	✓	✓	✓	✓	✓	✓	✓	✓	✓	✓	✓	✓	✓
Engine oil and coolant levels	I	Inspect at each fuel stop																								
Exhaust system	S/I				✓				✓				✓				✓				✓				✓	
Front and rear brake linings	S/I		✓		✓		✓		✓		✓		✓		✓		✓		✓		✓		✓		✓	
Front and rear axle fluid	S/I			✓			✓			✓			✓			✓			✓			✓			✓	
Ignition cables (3.7L engine)	R																		✓							
Ignition cables (4.7L engine)	R																									
Lights	S/I	Once a month																								
Manual transmission fluid	S/I	✓	✓	✓	✓	✓	✓	✓	✓	✓	✓	✓	✓	✓	✓	✓	✓	✓	✓	✓	✓	✓	✓	✓	✓	✓
PCV valve	S/I															✓										
Power steering fluid level	S/I	Once a month																								
Rotate and inspect tires	S/I	✓	✓	✓	✓	✓	✓	✓	✓	✓	✓	✓	✓	✓	✓	✓	✓	✓	✓	✓	✓	✓	✓	✓	✓	✓
Spark plugs (3.7L engine)	R															✓										
Spark plugs (4.7L engine side row)③	R																	✓								
Spark plugs (4.7L engine top row)③	R																				✓					
Suspension components	S/I								✓														✓			
Tire inflation and condition	S/I	Once a month																								
Transfer case fluid	S/I					✓					✓					✓					✓					✓

R: Replace
S/I: Service or Inspect

36543_DAKO_C0014

SCHEDULED MAINTENANCE INTERVALS

DODGE—DAKOTA

FREQUENT OPERATION MAINTENANCE (SEVERE SERVICE)

If a vehicle is operated under any of the following conditions it is considered severe service:

- **Extremely dusty areas.**
- **50% or more of the vehicle operation is in 90°F (32°C) or higher temperatures, or constant operation in temperatures below 32°F (0°C).**
- **Prolonged idling (vehicle operation in stop and go traffic).**
- **Frequent short running periods (engine does not warm to normal operating temperatures).**
- **Police, taxi, delivery usage, or trailer towing usage.**

Air cleaner element (engine) replace every 12,000 miles, if necessary

Automatic transmission fluid replace every 60,000 miles

Engine oil and filter replace every 3,000 miles

Front and rear axle fluid replace every 18,000 miles

Manual transmission replace every 60,000 miles

Transfer case fluid replace every 60,000 miles

① Inspect every 12,000 miles

② ENGINE OIL CHANGE RESET PROCEDURE

The vehicle is equipped with an engine oil change indicator system. The "Oil Change Required" message flashes in the Electronic Vehicle Information Center (EVIC) display for approximately 10 seconds after a single chime has sounded to indicate the next scheduled oil change interval. The engine oil change indicator system is duty cycle based, which means the engine oil change interval may fluctuate depending upon driving habits. Unless reset, this message continues to display each time the ignition switch is turned to the ON/RUN position. To turn off the message temporarily, press and release the Menu button.

To reset the oil change indicator system (after performing the scheduled maintenance) perform the following procedure:

1. Turn the ignition switch to the "ON" position. Do not start the engine.
2. Fully press the accelerator pedal slowly 3 times within 10 seconds.
3. Turn the ignition switch to the "LOCK" position.

NOTE: If the indicator message illuminates when starting the vehicle, the oil change indicator system did not reset. If necessary, repeat the above procedure.

③ The 4.7L engine is equipped with 16 spark plugs; one set is located on the top of the engine under the coils and the second set is located on the side of the engine.

The spark plugs located under the coils are a standard plug and must be changed every 30,000 miles.

The spark plugs located on the side of the engine are a premium plug and must be changed every 102,000 miles.

PRECAUTIONS

Before servicing any vehicle, please be sure to read all of the following precautions, which deal with personal safety, prevention of component damage, and important points to take into consideration when servicing a motor vehicle:

- Never open, service or drain the radiator or cooling system when the engine is hot; serious burns can occur from the steam and hot coolant.

- Observe all applicable safety precautions when working around fuel. Whenever servicing the fuel system, always work in a well-ventilated area. Do not allow fuel spray or vapors to come in contact with a spark, open flame, or excessive heat (a hot drop light, for example). Keep a dry chemical fire extinguisher near the work area. Always keep fuel in a container specifically designed for fuel storage; also, always properly seal fuel containers to avoid the possibility of fire or explosion. Refer to the additional fuel system precautions later in this section.

- Fuel injection systems often remain pressurized, even after the engine has been turned **OFF**. The fuel system pressure must be relieved before disconnecting any fuel lines. Failure to do so may result in fire and/or personal injury.

- Brake fluid often contains polyglycol ethers and polyglycols. Avoid contact with the eyes and wash your hands thoroughly after handling brake fluid. If you do get brake fluid in your eyes, flush your eyes with clean, running water for 15 minutes. If eye irritation persists, or if you have taken

brake fluid internally, IMMEDIATELY seek medical assistance.

- The EPA warns that prolonged contact with used engine oil may cause a number of skin disorders, including cancer. You should make every effort to minimize your exposure to used engine oil. Protective gloves should be worn when changing oil. Wash your hands and any other exposed skin areas as soon as possible after exposure to used engine oil. Soap and water, or waterless hand cleaner should be used.

- All new vehicles are now equipped with an air bag system, often referred to as a Supplemental Restraint System (SRS) or Supplemental Inflatable Restraint (SIR) system. The system must be disabled before performing service on or around system components, steering column, instrument panel components, wiring and sensors. Failure to follow safety and disabling procedures could result in accidental air bag deployment, possible personal injury and unnecessary system repairs.

- Always wear safety goggles when working with, or around, the air bag system. When carrying a non-deployed air bag, be sure the bag and trim cover are pointed away from your body. When placing a non-deployed air bag on a work surface, always face the bag and trim cover upward, away from the surface. This will reduce the motion of the module if it is accidentally deployed. Refer to the additional air bag system precautions later in this section.

- Clean, high quality brake fluid from a sealed container is essential to the safe and

proper operation of the brake system. You should always buy the correct type of brake fluid for your vehicle. If the brake fluid becomes contaminated, completely flush the system with new fluid. Never reuse any brake fluid. Any brake fluid that is removed from the system should be discarded. Also, do not allow any brake fluid to come in contact with a painted surface; it will damage the paint.

- Never operate the engine without the proper amount and type of engine oil; doing so WILL result in severe engine damage.

- Timing belt maintenance is extremely important. Many models utilize an interference-type, non-freewheeling engine. If the timing belt breaks, the valves in the cylinder head may strike the pistons, causing potentially serious (also time-consuming and expensive) engine damage. Refer to the maintenance interval charts for the recommended replacement interval for the timing belt, and to the timing belt section for belt replacement and inspection.

- Disconnecting the negative battery cable on some vehicles may interfere with the functions of the on-board computer system(s) and may require the computer to undergo a relearning process once the negative battery cable is reconnected.

- When servicing drum brakes, only disassemble and assemble one side at a time, leaving the remaining side intact for reference.

- Only an MVAC-trained, EPA-certified automotive technician should service the air conditioning system or its components.

BRAKES

ANTI-LOCK BRAKE SYSTEM (ABS)

GENERAL INFORMATION

PRECAUTIONS

- Certain components within the ABS system are not intended to be serviced or repaired individually.

- Do not use rubber hoses or other parts not specifically specified for and ABS system. When using repair kits, replace all parts included in the kit. Partial or incorrect repair may lead to functional problems and require the replacement of components.

- Lubricate rubber parts with clean, fresh brake fluid to ease assembly. Do not use shop air to clean parts; damage to rubber components may result.

- Use only DOT 3 brake fluid from an unopened container.

- If any hydraulic component or line is

removed or replaced, it may be necessary to bleed the entire system.

- A clean repair area is essential. Always clean the reservoir and cap thoroughly before removing the cap. The slightest amount of dirt in the fluid may plug an orifice and impair the system function. Perform repairs after components have been thoroughly cleaned; use only denatured alcohol to clean components. Do not allow ABS components to come into contact with any substance containing mineral oil; this includes used shop rags.

- The Anti-Lock control unit is a microprocessor similar to other computer units in the vehicle. Ensure that the ignition switch is **OFF** before removing or installing controller harnesses. Avoid static electricity discharge at or near the controller.

- If any arc welding is to be done on the vehicle, the control unit should be unplugged before welding operations begin.

WHEEL SPEED SENSORS

REMOVAL & INSTALLATION

Front Wheel Speed Sensor
See Figure 3.

1. Before servicing the vehicle, refer to the Precautions Section.
2. Raise and safely support the vehicle.
3. Remove the front rotor and caliper adapter.
4. Remove the wheel speed sensor mounting bolt (1) from the hub (3).
5. Remove the wheel speed sensor (2) from the hub (3).

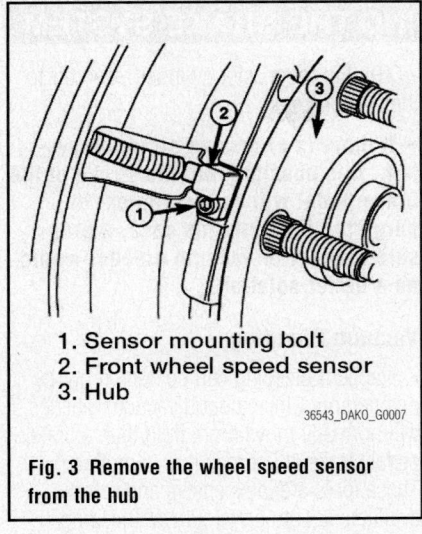

1. Sensor mounting bolt
2. Front wheel speed sensor
3. Hub

36543_DAKO_G0007

Fig. 3 Remove the wheel speed sensor from the hub

6. Remove the wiring from the clips and disconnect the electrical connector.

To install:

7. Install the wiring to the clips and reconnect the electrical connector.

8. Install the wheel speed sensor (2) to the hub (3).

9. Install the wheel speed sensor mounting bolt (1) to the hub (3). Tighten the bolt to 190 inch lbs. (21 Nm).

10. Install the front rotor and brake caliper assembly.

Rear Wheel Speed Sensor

See Figures 4 and 5.

1. Before servicing the vehicle, refer to the Precautions Section.

2. Raise and safely support the vehicle.

3. Remove the brake line mounting nut (4) and remove the brake line (3) from the sensor stud.

4. Remove the park brake cable (2) and bracket (1) from the sensor stud.

5. Disconnect the electrical connector (6).

6. Remove mounting stud (2) from the sensor (5).

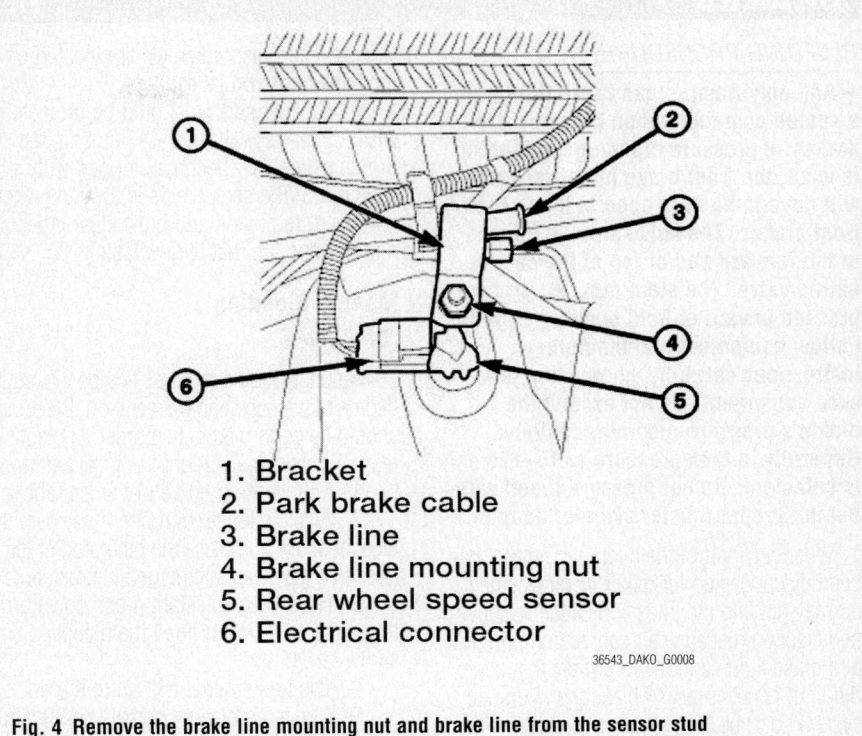

1. Bracket
2. Park brake cable
3. Brake line
4. Brake line mounting nut
5. Rear wheel speed sensor
6. Electrical connector

36543_DAKO_G0008

Fig. 4 Remove the brake line mounting nut and brake line from the sensor stud

7. Remove sensor (1) from differential housing (3).

To install:

8. Connect the harness to the sensor (1).

➡**Be sure the seal is securely in place between the sensor and wiring connector.**

9. Install the O-ring on the sensor (if removed).

10. Insert the sensor (1) in the differential housing (3).

11. Install the sensor mounting stud and tighten to 200 inch lbs. (24 Nm).

12. Connect the electrical connector (6).

13. Install the brake line (3) on the sensor stud.

14. Install the park brake cable (2) and the bracket (1) to the stud and install the nut (4).

15. Lower the vehicle.

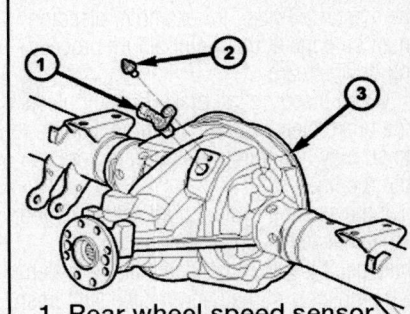

1. Rear wheel speed sensor
2. Mounting stud
3. Differential housing

36543_DAKO_G0009

Fig. 5 Remove sensor from differential housing

BLEEDING PROCEDURE

➡ **Add only fresh, clean brake fluid from a sealed container when bleeding the brakes. If pressure bleeding equipment is used, the front brake metering valve will have to be held open to bleed the front brakes. The valve stem is located in the forward end or top of the combination valve. The stem must either be pressed inward or held outward slightly. Follow equipment manufacturer's instructions carefully when using pressure equipment. Do not exceed the maker's pressure recommendations. Generally, a tank pressure of 15—20 psi is sufficient. Do not pressure bleed without the proper master cylinder adapter.**

When any part of the hydraulic system has been disconnected for repair or replacement, air may get into the lines and cause spongy pedal action (because air can be compressed and brake fluid cannot). To correct this condition, it is necessary to bleed the hydraulic system so to be sure all air is purged.

Bleeding must start where the lines were disconnected. If lines were disconnected at the master cylinder, for example, bleeding must be done at that point before proceeding downstream.

When bleeding the brake system, bleed one brake bleeder point at a time. Failure to do so may result in more air being drawn into the lines.

If the existing system fluid seems dirty or if the vehicle has covered considerable mileage, it is recommended that the system be completely purged and refilled with fresh, clean fluid. The best way to start is to siphon the old fluid out of the master cylinder reservoir and fill it completely with fresh fluid.

Brake fluid tends to darken over time. This does not necessarily indicate contamination. Examine fluid closely for foreign matter.

The primary and secondary hydraulic brake systems are separate and are bled independently. During the bleeding operation, do not allow the reservoir to run dry. Keep the master cylinder reservoir filled with brake fluid. Never use brake fluid that has been drained from the hydraulic system, no matter how clean it seems.

1. Before servicing the vehicle, refer to the Precautions Section.
2. Clean all dirt from around the master cylinder fill cap, remove the cap, and fill the master cylinder with brake fluid until the level is within ¼ inch (6mm) of the top edge of the reservoir.
3. Clean the bleeder screws at all 4

wheels. The bleeder screws are located on the back of the brake calipers.

4. Bleeder screws should be protected with rubber caps. If they are missing, the orifice may easily become clogged with road dirt. If the screw refuses to bleed when loosened, remove it and blow clear. Aftermarket caps are readily available.

Manual Bleeding

See Figure 6.

Manual bleeding requires two people and a degree of patience and cooperation. Bleeding should be performed in this order: (1) Right rear, (2) Left rear, (3) Right front, (4) Left front.

1. Follow the preparatory steps, above.
2. Attach a length of rubber hose over the bleeder screw and place the other end of the hose in a glass jar, submerged in brake fluid.
3. Have your assistant press down on the brake pedal, then open the bleeder screw ½—¾ turn.
4. The brake pedal will go to the floor.
5. Close the bleeder screw—preferably before the pedal reaches the floor. Tell your assistant to allow the brake pedal to return slowly.
6. Repeat these steps to purge all air from the system.
7. When bubbles cease to appear at the end of the bleeder hose, close the bleeder screw and remove the hose. Check that the pedal is firm or at least more firm than it was when you started. If not, continue the procedure.
8. Check the master cylinder fluid level and add fluid accordingly. Do this after bleeding each wheel.
9. Repeat the bleeding operation at the remaining 3 wheels, ending with the one closet to the master cylinder.

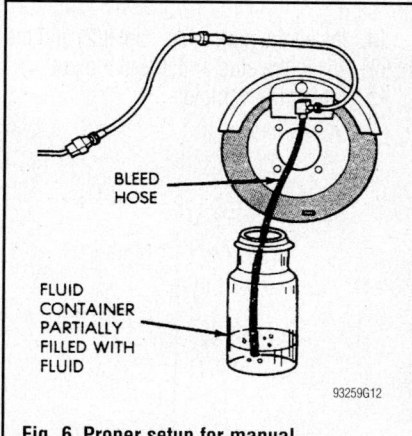

BLEED
HOSE

FLUID
CONTAINER
PARTIALLY
FILLED WITH
FLUID

93259G12

Fig. 6 Proper setup for manual bleeding procedure

10. Fill the master cylinder reservoir to the proper level.

➡ **If there is excessive air in the system, it is possible that the stroke of the brake pedal will be insufficient to purge the lines. In this case, a pressure bleeder or vacuum bleeder would be a better solution.**

Vacuum Bleeding

Vacuum bleeding can be carried out by one person. Since a good vacuum bleeder will normally move more fluid than a brake pedal stroke, this procedure is preferred. These tools are inexpensive and readily available at auto parts outlets. Bleeding should be performed in this order: (1) Right rear, (2) Left rear, (3) Right front, (4) Left front.

1. Follow the preparatory steps, above.
2. Attach the vacuum bleeder according to the manufacturer's recommendations.
3. Pump up the unit until maximum vacuum is reached. Loosen the bleeder screw slightly until bubbles and fluid issue forth. Close the screw before the vacuum is equalized.
4. Repeat the procedure until fluid without bubbles issues from the bleeder screw.
5. Keep a close check on master cylinder fluid level during this procedure as vacuum bleeders move considerable amounts of fluid.

BLEEDING THE ABS SYSTEM

ABS system bleeding requires conventional bleeding methods along with utilizing the scan tool. The procedure involves performing a base brake bleeding, followed by use of the scan tool to cycle and bleed the HCU pump and solenoids. A second base brake bleeding procedure is then required to remove any air remaining in the system.

1. Before servicing the vehicle, refer to the Precautions Section.
2. Perform base brake bleeding. Refer to Bleeding The Brake System.
3. Connect the scan tool to the d Data Link Connector (DLC) beneath the dashboard.
4. Select ANTILOCK BRAKES, followed by MISCELLANEOUS, then ABS BRAKES. Follow the instructions displayed.
5. When the scan tool displays TEST COMPLETE, disconnect the scan tool and proceed.
6. Perform a base brake bleeding a second time.
7. Top off the master cylinder fluid level and verify proper brake operation before moving the vehicle.

BRAKES   **FRONT DISC BRAKES**

❊❊ CAUTION

Dust and dirt accumulating on brake parts during normal use may contain asbestos fibers from production or aftermarket brake linings. Breathing excessive concentrations of asbestos fibers can cause serious bodily harm. Exercise care when servicing brake parts. Do not sand or grind brake lining unless equipment used is designed to contain the dust residue. Do not clean brake parts with compressed air or by dry brushing. Cleaning should be done by dampening the brake components with a fine mist of water, then wiping the brake components clean with a dampened cloth. Dispose of cloth and all residue containing asbestos fibers in an impermeable container with the appropriate label. Follow practices prescribed by the Occupational Safety and Health Administration (OSHA) and the Environmental Protection Agency (EPA) for the handling, processing, and disposing of dust or debris that may contain asbestos fibers.

BRAKE CALIPER

REMOVAL & INSTALLATION
See Figure 7.

❊❊ WARNING

Never allow the disc brake caliper to hang from the brake hose. Damage to the brake hose may result. Provide a suitable support to hang the caliper securely.

1. Before servicing the vehicle, refer to the Precautions Section.
2. Install a prop rod on the brake pedal to keep pressure on the brake system. Holding the pedal in this position will isolate the master cylinder from the hydraulic brake system and will not allow brake fluid to drain out of the brake fluid reservoir while the brake lines are open. This will allow you to bleed out the area of repair instead of the entire system.
3. Raise and safely support the vehicle.
4. Remove the tire and wheel assembly.
5. Compress the disc brake caliper.
6. Remove the banjo bolt and discard the copper washers.
7. Remove the caliper slide pin bolts.

8. Remove the disc brake caliper (1) from the caliper adapter (2).
9. Remove the caliper slide pins from the adapter.

To install:

➡**Petroleum based grease should not be used on any of the rubber components of the caliper. Use only Non-Petroleum based grease. Use grease packets included with the kit or Dow Corning-807® grease.**

10. Clean the slide pin bores thoroughly to remove any old grease.
11. Thoroughly coat the new slide pins on all working surfaces.
12. Install the boot onto the slide pin and then insert into the adapter.
13. Push the pin all the way into the adapter and carefully expel the trapped air by gently pushing on the boot near the slide pin head.

➡**Use new copper washers on the banjo bolt when installing.**

14. Install the disc brake caliper to the brake caliper adapter.
15. Install the banjo bolt with new copper washers to the caliper. Tighten to 250 inch lbs. (28 Nm).
16. Install the caliper slide pin bolts. Tighten to 24 ft. lbs. (32 Nm).
17. Remove the prop rod from the brake pedal.
18. Bleed the area of the repair. If a

proper pedal is not felt during bleeding, then a base bleed system must be performed. Refer to Bleeding the Brake System.
19. Install the tire and wheel assembly.
20. Lower the vehicle.

DISC BRAKE PADS

REMOVAL & INSTALLATION
See Figure 8.

1. Before servicing the vehicle, refer to the Precautions Section.
2. Raise and safely support the vehicle.
3. Remove the wheel and tire assemblies.
4. Compress the caliper.
5. Remove the caliper slide pin bolts.
6. Remove the caliper from the caliper adapter.

❊❊ WARNING

Never allow the disc brake caliper to hang from the brake hose. Damage to the brake hose may result. Provide a suitable support to hang the caliper securely.

7. Support and hang the caliper.
8. Remove the inboard brake pad (4) from the caliper adapter (1).
9. Remove the outboard brake pad from the caliper adapter.
10. Remove the outboard brake pad (2) from the caliper adapter (1).

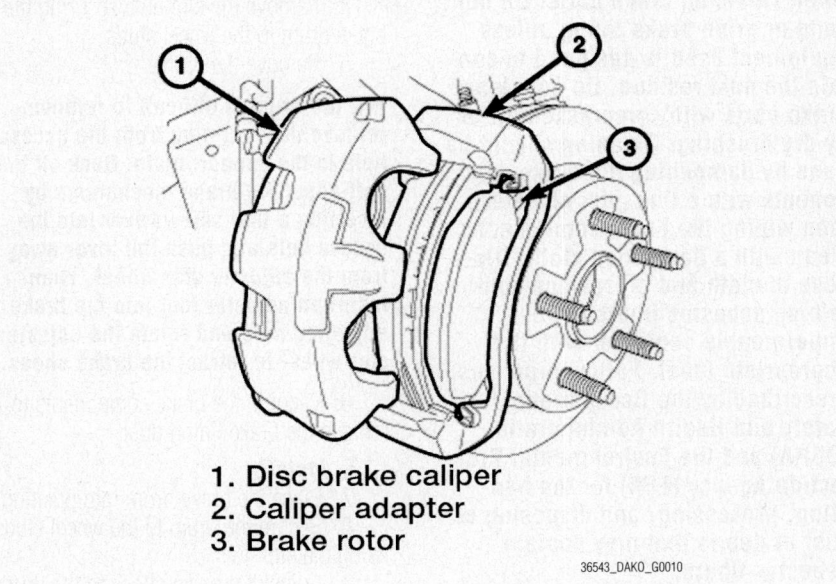

1. Disc brake caliper
2. Caliper adapter
3. Brake rotor

36543_DAKO_G0010

Fig. 7 Remove the disc brake caliper from the caliper adapter

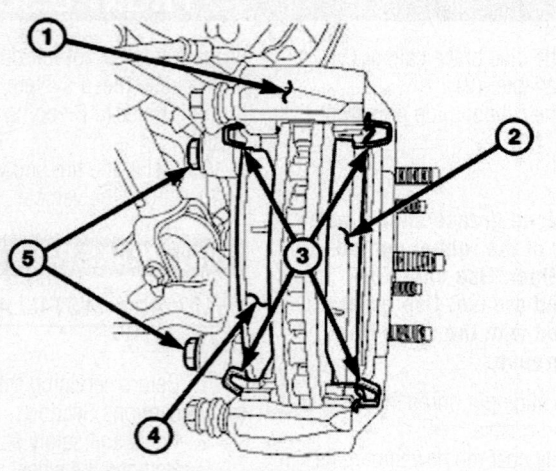

1. Caliper adapter
2. Outboard brake pad
3. Anti-rattle clips
4. Inboard brake pad
5. Caliper mounting bolts

36543_DAKO_G0011

Fig. 8 Remove the brake pads from the caliper adapter

11. Remove the anti-rattle clips from the pad.

To install:

12. Bottom the pistons in the caliper bore with a C-clamp. Place an old brake shoe between the C-clamp and the caliper piston.

13. Clean the caliper mounting adapter.

14. Install new anti-rattle clips to the brake pads.

15. Install the inboard brake pad in adapter.

16. Install the outboard brake pad in adapter.

17. Install the caliper over the brake rotor. Then, push the caliper onto the adapter.

18. Install the caliper slide pin bolts.

19. Install the wheel and tire assemblies and lower the vehicle.

20. Apply the brakes several times to seat the caliper pistons and the brake shoes and obtain a firm pedal.

21. Top off the master cylinder fluid level.

BRAKES

REAR DRUM BRAKES

✳✳ CAUTION

Dust and dirt accumulating on brake parts during normal use may contain asbestos fibers from production or aftermarket brake linings. Breathing excessive concentrations of asbestos fibers can cause serious bodily harm. Exercise care when servicing brake parts. Do not sand or grind brake lining unless equipment used is designed to contain the dust residue. Do not clean brake parts with compressed air or by dry brushing. Cleaning should be done by dampening the brake components with a fine mist of water, then wiping the brake components clean with a dampened cloth. Dispose of cloth and all residue containing asbestos fibers in an impermeable container with the appropriate label. Follow practices prescribed by the Occupational Safety and Health Administration (OSHA) and the Environmental Protection Agency (EPA) for the handling, processing, and disposing of dust or debris that may contain asbestos fibers.

BRAKE DRUM

REMOVAL & INSTALLATION
See Figure 9.

1. Before servicing the vehicle, refer to the Precautions Section.

2. Raise and safely support the vehicle.

3. Remove the wheel and tire assembly.

4. Remove the clip nuts securing the brake drum to the wheel studs.

5. Remove the drum.

➡**If the drum is difficult to remove, remove the rear plug from the access hole in the support plate. Back off the self-adjusting brake mechanism by inserting a thin screwdriver into the access hole and push the lever away from the adjuster star wheel. Then, insert an adjuster tool into the brake adjusting hole and rotate the adjuster star wheel to retract the brake shoes.**

6. Vacuum the brake components to remove the brake lining dust.

To install:

7. Place the brake drum into position.

8. Secure the drum to the wheel studs using the clip nuts.

9. Adjust the brake shoes to the drum with a brake gauge.

10. Install the wheel and tire assembly.

BRAKE SHOES

REMOVAL & INSTALLATION
See Figure 9.

1. Before servicing the vehicle, refer to the Precautions Section.

2. Raise and safely support the vehicle.

3. Remove the wheel and tire assembly.

4. Remove the clip nuts securing the brake drum to the wheel studs.

5. Remove the drum.

➡**If the drum is difficult to remove, remove the rear plug from the access hole in the support plate. Back off the self-adjusting brake mechanism by inserting a thin screwdriver into the access hole and push the lever away from the adjuster star wheel. Then, insert an adjuster tool into the brake adjusting hole and rotate the adjuster star wheel to retract the brake shoes.**

6. Vacuum the brake components to remove the brake lining dust.

7. Remove the shoe return spring (3) with the brake spring pliers tool.

8. Remove the adjuster spring and the lever (5). Disengage the lever from the spring by sliding the lever forward to clear the pivot and work the lever out from under the spring.

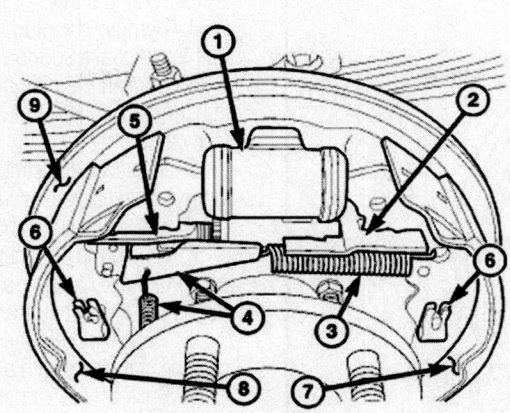

1. Brake cylinder
2. Parking brake lever
3. Parking brake spring
4. Adjuster spring and lever
5. Adjuster strut
6. Hold down clip
7. Rear brake shoe
8. Front brake shoe
9. Support plate

36543_DAKO_G0013

Fig. 9 Illustrated view of the rear drum brake components

9. Disengage and remove the shoe return spring from the brake shoes.

10. Remove the brake shoe hold down clips (6).

11. Remove the rear brake shoe (7) from the support plate (9).

12. Remove the front brake shoe (8) from the support plate (9).

13. Remove the park brake lever (2) from the brake shoe.

To install:

14. Clean and inspect the individual brake components.

15. Lubricate where the brake shoe contacts the support plate with high temperature grease or Lubriplate®.

16. Lubricate the adjuster screw socket, nut, button, and screw thread surfaces with grease or Lubriplate®.

17. Install the parking brake lever (2) to the rear shoe (7) and install the hold down clip (6).

18. Install the adjuster strut (5) onto the shoes and park brake lever (2).

19. Install the front shoe (8) on the support plate (9), and install the hold down clip (6).

20. Install the adjuster spring and lever (4) in the slot in the adjuster strut (7).

21. Install the lower return spring to the shoes.

22. Verify the adjuster operation. Pull both shoes outward to move the adjuster lever (4) to rotate the star wheel. Be sure the adjuster lever properly engages the star wheel teeth.

23. Adjust the brake shoes to the drum with a brake gauge.

24. Install the wheel and tire assembly.

ADJUSTMENT

The rear drum brakes are equipped with a self-adjusting mechanism and require no adjustment under normal circumstances. Adjustment is required when the shoes are replaced, the drums are removed for access to other parts, or when a drum is replaced. Adjustment can be made with a standard brake gauge or with an adjusting tool. Adjustments are performed with the complete brake assembly installed on the backing plate.

Adjustment with a Brake Gauge

See Figures 10 and 11.

1. Before servicing the vehicle, refer to the Precautions Section.

2. Be sure the parking brakes are fully released.

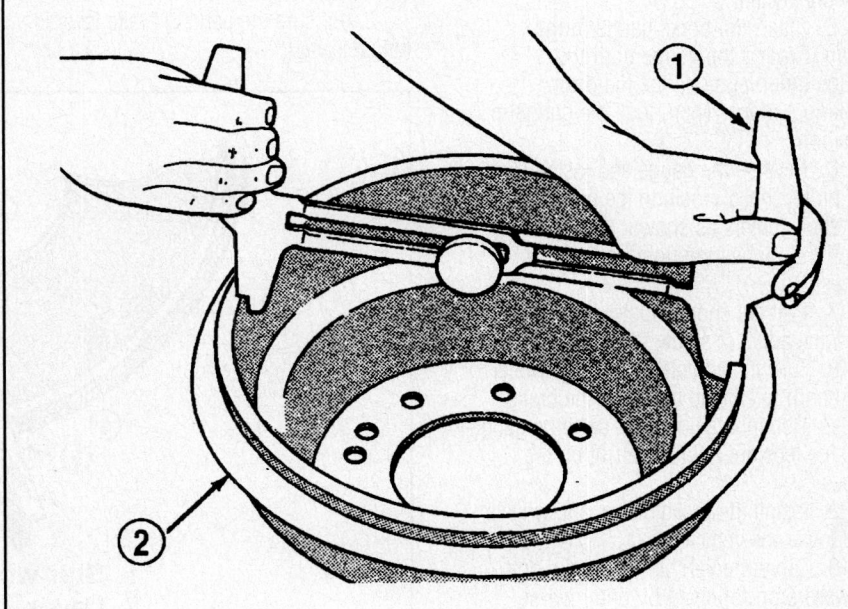

1 - BRAKE GAUGE
2 - BRAKE DRUM

67189-DAKO-G03

Fig. 10 Adjusting gauge on the drum

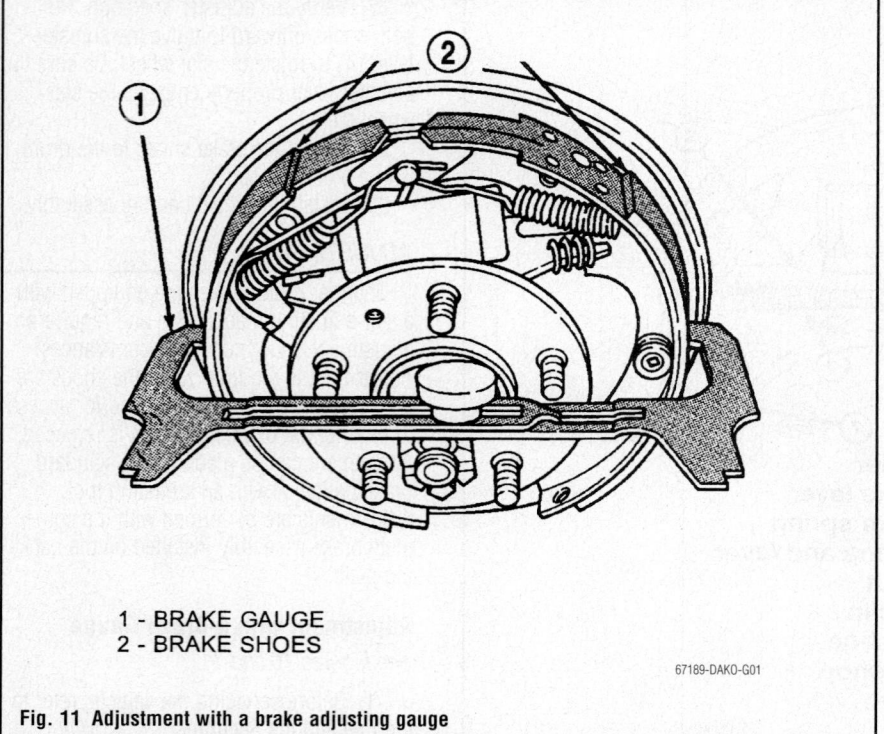

1 - BRAKE GAUGE
2 - BRAKE SHOES

67189-DAKO-G01

Fig. 11 Adjustment with a brake adjusting gauge

3. Raise the rear of the vehicle and remove the wheels and brake drums.

4. Verify that the left and right automatic adjuster levers and cables are properly connected.

5. Insert the brake gauge in the drum. Expand the gauge until the gauge inner legs contact the drum braking surface. Then, lock the gauge in position.

6. Reverse the gauge and install it on the brake shoes. Position the gauge legs at the shoe centers as shown. If gauge does not fit (too loose/too tight), adjust the shoes.

7. Pull the shoe adjuster lever away from the adjuster screw star wheel.

8. Turn the adjuster screw star wheel (by hand) to expand or retract the brake shoes. Continue adjustment until the gauge outside legs are a light drag-fit on the shoes.

9. Install the brake drums and wheels and lower the vehicle.

10. Drive the vehicle and make one forward stop followed by one reverse stop. Repeat this forward/stop process 8–10 times to operate the automatic adjusters and to equalize the adjustment.

➡ **Bring the vehicle to a complete standstill at each stop. Incomplete or rolling stops will not activate the automatic adjusters.**

Adjustment with an Adjusting Tool
See Figure 12.

1. Before servicing the vehicle, refer to the Precautions Section.

2. Be sure the parking brake lever is fully released.

3. Raise the vehicle so the rear wheels can be rotated freely.

4. Remove the plug from each access hole in the brake support plates.

5. Loosen the parking brake cable adjustment nut until there is slack in the front cable.

6. Insert the adjusting tool through the support plate access hole and engage the tool in the teeth of the adjusting screw star wheel.

7. Rotate the adjuster screw star wheel (move the tool handle upward) until a slight drag can be felt when the wheel is rotated.

8. Push and hold the adjuster lever away from the star wheel with a thin screwdriver.

9. Back off the adjuster screw star wheel until the brake drag is eliminated.

10. Repeat the adjustment at the opposite wheel. Be sure the adjustment is equal at both wheels.

11. Install the support plate access hole plugs.

12. Adjust the parking brake cable and lower the vehicle.

13. Drive the vehicle and make one forward stop followed by one reverse stop. Repeat this forward/stop process 8–10 times to operate the automatic adjusters and to equalize the adjustment.

➡ **Bring the vehicle to a complete standstill at each stop. Incomplete or rolling stops will not activate the automatic adjusters.**

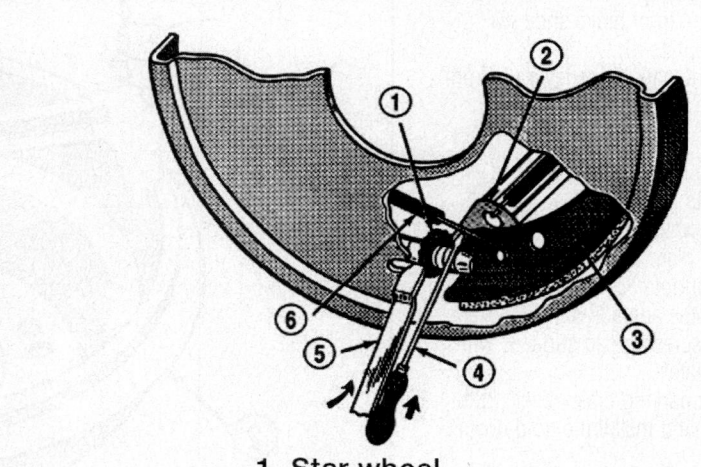

1. Star wheel
2. Lever
3. Brake shoe web
4. Screwdriver
5. Adjusting tool
6. Adjuster spring

36543_DAKO_G0014

Fig. 12 Rear brake shoe adjustment with a brake adjusting tool

BRAKES   PARKING BRAKE

PARKING BRAKE CABLES

ADJUSTMENT

See Figure 13.

➡Adjustment is only needed when the tensioner or a cable has been replaced or disconnected for service. To avoid faulty operation, only the procedure below should be carried out.

1. Before servicing the vehicle, refer to the Precautions Section.
2. The base brakes must be operating correctly and properly adjusted.
3. Check that the parking brake cables operate freely.
4. Raise the vehicle and check that the wheels turn without drag with the parking brake released.
5. Apply the parking brake fully.
6. Mark the tensioner rod ¼inch (6.35mm) from the edge of the tensioner. There may be a factory mark already here.
7. Tighten the adjusting nut on the tensioner until the mark is no longer visible.

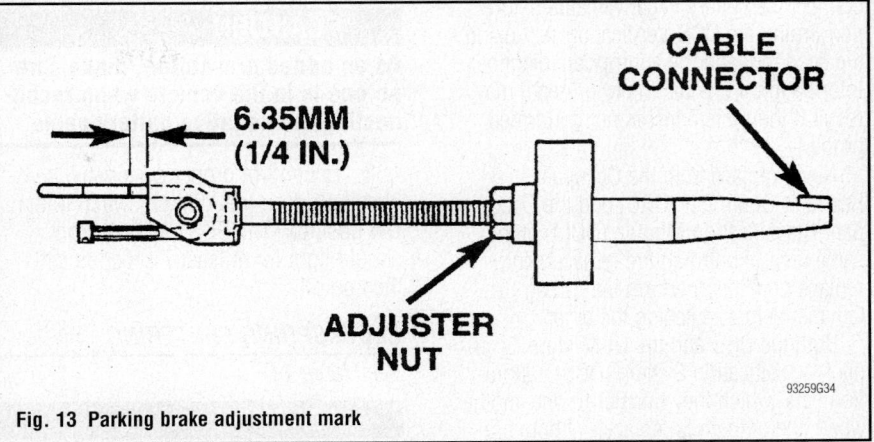

6.35MM (1/4 IN.)

CABLE CONNECTOR

ADJUSTER NUT

93259G34

Fig. 13 Parking brake adjustment mark

8. Release the parking brake and ensure that the wheels turn without drag.

PARKING BRAKE SHOES

REMOVAL & INSTALLATION

The rear drum brake shoes serve as the parking brakes. Refer to the procedures under Rear Drum Brakes for service.

ADJUSTMENT

Refer to the Parking Brake Cable adjustment procedure.

CHASSIS ELECTRICAL   AIR BAG (SUPPLEMENTAL RESTRAINT SYSTEM)

GENERAL INFORMATION

✳✳ CAUTION

These vehicles are equipped with an air bag system. The system must be disarmed before performing service on, or around, system components, the steering column, instrument panel components, wiring and sensors. Failure to follow the safety precautions and the disarming procedure could result in accidental air bag deployment, possible injury and unnecessary system repairs.

SERVICE PRECAUTIONS

Disconnect and isolate the battery negative cable before beginning any airbag system component diagnosis, testing, removal, or installation procedures. Allow system capacitor to discharge for two minutes before beginning any component service. This will disable the airbag system. Failure to disable the airbag system may result in accidental airbag deployment, personal injury, or death.

Do not place an intact undeployed airbag face down on a solid surface. The airbag will propel into the air if accidentally deployed and may result in personal injury or death.

When carrying or handling an undeployed airbag, the trim side (face) of the airbag should be pointing towards the body to minimize possibility of injury if accidental deployment occurs. Failure to do this may result in personal injury or death.

Replace airbag system components with OEM replacement parts. Substitute parts may appear interchangeable, but internal differences may result in inferior occupant protection. Failure to do so may result in occupant personal injury or death.

Wear safety glasses, rubber gloves, and long sleeved clothing when cleaning powder residue from vehicle after an airbag deployment. Powder residue emitted from a deployed airbag can cause skin irritation. Flush affected area with cool water if irritation is experienced. If nasal or throat irritation is experienced, exit the vehicle for fresh air until the irritation ceases. If irritation continues, see a physician.

Do not use a replacement airbag that is not in the original packaging. This may result in improper deployment, personal injury, or death.

The factory installed fasteners, screws and bolts used to fasten airbag components have a special coating and are specifically designed for the airbag system. Do not use substitute fasteners. Use only original equipment fasteners listed in the parts catalog when fastener replacement is required.

During, and following, any child restraint anchor service, due to impact event or vehicle repair, carefully inspect all mounting hardware, tether straps, and anchors for proper installation, operation, or damage. If a child restraint anchor is found damaged in any way, the anchor must be replaced. Failure to do this may result in personal injury or death.

Deployed and non-deployed airbags may or may not have live pyrotechnic material within the airbag inflator.

Do not dispose of driver/passenger/curtain airbags or seat belt tensioners unless you are sure of complete deployment. Refer to the Hazardous Substance Control System for proper disposal.

Dispose of deployed airbags and tensioners consistent with state, provincial, local, and federal regulations.

After any airbag component testing or service, do not connect the battery negative cable. Personal injury or death may result if the system test is not performed first.

If the vehicle is equipped with the Occupant Classification System (OCS), do not connect the battery negative cable before performing the OCS Verification Test using the scan tool and the appropriate diagnostic information. Personal injury or death may result if the system test is not performed properly.

Never replace both the Occupant Restraint Controller (ORC) and the Occupant Classification Module (OCM) at the same time. If both require replacement, replace one, then perform the Airbag System test before replacing the other.

Both the ORC and the OCM store Occupant Classification System (OCS) calibration data, which they transfer to one another when one of them is replaced. If both are replaced at the same time, an irreversible fault will be set in both modules and the OCS may malfunction and cause personal injury or death.

If equipped with OCS, the Seat Weight Sensor is a sensitive, calibrated unit and must be handled carefully. Do not drop or handle roughly. If dropped or damaged, replace with another sensor. Failure to do so may result in occupant injury or death.

If equipped with OCS, the front passenger seat must be handled carefully as well. When removing the seat, be careful when setting on floor not to drop. If dropped, the sensor may be inoperative, could result in occupant injury, or possibly death.

If equipped with OCS, when the passenger front seat is on the floor, no one should sit in the front passenger seat. This uneven force may damage the sensing ability of the seat weight sensors. If sat on and damaged, the sensor may be inoperative, could result in occupant injury, or possibly death.

DISARMING THE SYSTEM

1. Before servicing the vehicle, refer to the Precautions Section.
2. Turn the ignition switch to **OFF**.
3. Disconnect the negative battery cable and isolate it from accidental reconnection. Insulate the cable end with high-quality electrical tape or a similar non-conductive wrapping.
4. Wait at least 2 minutes for the system capacitor to discharge before performing any service. The airbag system is designed to retain enough voltage to deploy the airbag for a short period of time after the battery has been disconnected.

ARMING THE SYSTEM

1. Before servicing the vehicle, refer to the Precautions Section.

2. Reconnect the negative battery cable.

✳✳ CAUTION

As an added precaution, make sure no one is in the vehicle when reconnecting the negative battery cable.

3. To confirm proper system operation, turn the ignition switch to the **ON** position. The SRS indicator light should light for at least 7 seconds and then go off.

CLOCKSPRING CENTERING

See Figure 14.

✳✳ CAUTION

To avoid serious or fatal injury on vehicles equipped with airbags, disable the Supplemental Restraint System (SRS) before attempting any steering wheel, steering column, airbag, seat belt tensioner, impact sensor or instrument panel component diagnosis or service. Disconnect and isolate the negative battery (ground) cable. Wait 2 minutes for the system capacitor to discharge before performing further diagnosis or service. This is the only sure way to disable the SRS. Failure to take

the proper precautions could result in accidental airbag deployment. Failure to follow these instructions may result in possible serious or fatal injury.

1. Turn the steering wheel until the front wheels are in the straight-ahead position.
2. Remove the clockspring from the steering column.
3. Rotate the clockspring rotor (10) clockwise to the end of its travel.

✳✳ WARNING

Do not apply excessive torque.

4. From the end of the clockwise travel, rotate the rotor about 2 ½ turns counterclockwise. The engagement dowel and yellow rubber boot (7) should end up at the bottom, and the arrows on the clockspring rotor and case (9) should be in alignment.
5. The clockspring is now centered. Secure the clockspring rotor to the clockspring case to maintain clockspring centering until it is reinstalled on the steering column.
6. The front wheels should be in the straight-ahead position during reinstallation onto the steering column.

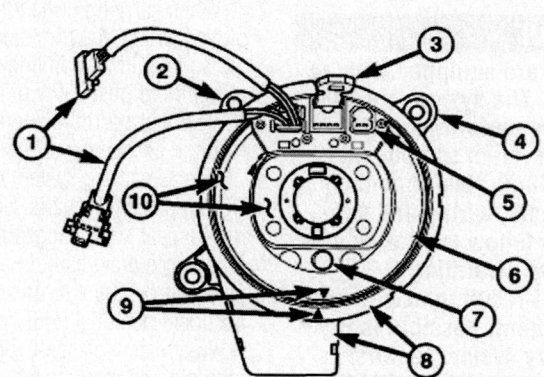

1. Pigtail connectors/wires
2. Mounting tab
3. Clockspring locking pin
4. Mounting tab
5. Connector receptacles
6. Clockspring
7. Yellow rubber boot
8. Molded plastic case
9. Alignment arrows
10. Clockspring rotor

36543_DAKO_G0017

Fig. 14 SRS clockspring view

DRIVE TRAIN

AUTOMATIC TRANSMISSION ASSEMBLY

REMOVAL & INSTALLATION

42RLE Transmission

See Figures 15 through 19.

1. Before servicing the vehicle, refer to the Precautions Section.
2. Disconnect the negative battery cable.
3. Raise and safely support the vehicle.
4. Remove any necessary skid plates.
5. Mark the propeller shaft and axle companion flanges for assembly alignment.
6. Remove the rear propeller shaft.
7. Remove the front propeller shaft, if necessary.
8. Disconnect the input and output speed sensors.
9. Disconnect the transfer case shift motor and mode sensor assembly.
10. Disconnect the variable line pressure connector from the transmission, if equipped.
11. Disconnect the transmission range sensor.
12. Disconnect the wires from the solenoid/pressure switch assembly.
13. Remove the bolts holding the exhaust crossover pipe to the pre-catalytic converter pipe flanges.
14. Remove the bolts holding the exhaust crossover pipe to the catalytic converter flange.
15. Disconnect the gearshift cable from the transmission manual valve lever.
16. Disengage the shift cable from the cable support bracket.
17. Remove the starter motor.
18. Remove the engine to transmission collar.
19. Rotate the crankshaft in a clockwise direction until the converter bolts are accessible. Then remove bolts one at a time. Rotate the crankshaft with a socket wrench on the dampener bolt.
20. Disconnect the transmission vent hose from the transmission.
21. Remove the transfer case.
22. Support the rear of the engine with a safety stand or jack.
23. Raise the transmission slightly with a service jack to relieve the load on the crossmember and supports.
24. Remove the bolts securing the rear support and the cushion to the transmission and crossmember.
25. Remove the bolts attaching the crossmember to the frame and remove the crossmember.
26. Disconnect the transmission fluid cooler lines (1) at the transmission fittings (3) and the clips (2).
27. Remove all remaining converter housing bolts.
28. Carefully work the transmission and the torque converter assembly rearward off the engine block dowels.
29. Hold the torque converter in place during the transmission removal.
30. Lower the transmission and remove the assembly from under the vehicle.

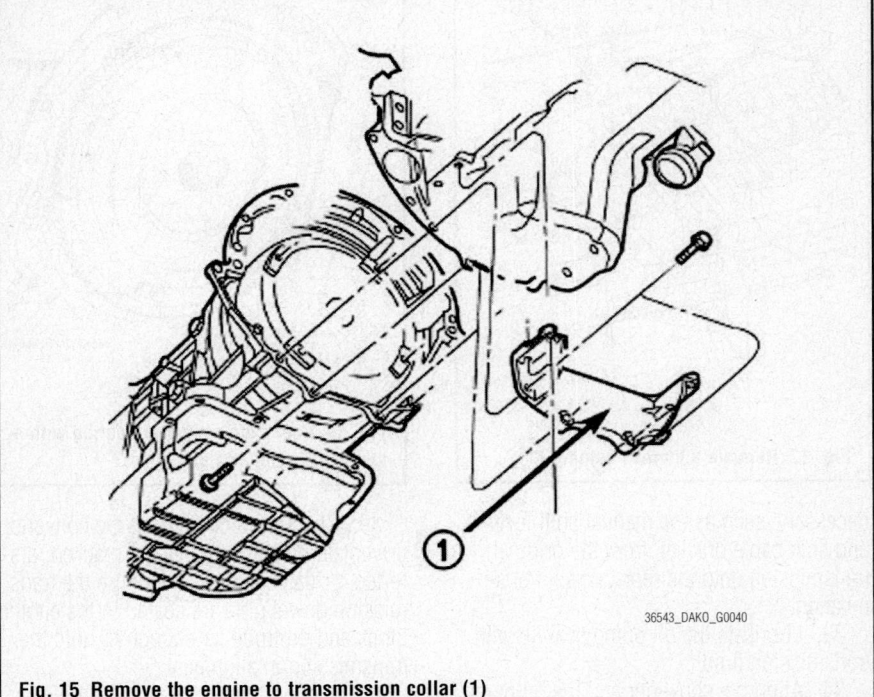

Fig. 15 Remove the engine to transmission collar (1)

36543_DAKO_G0040

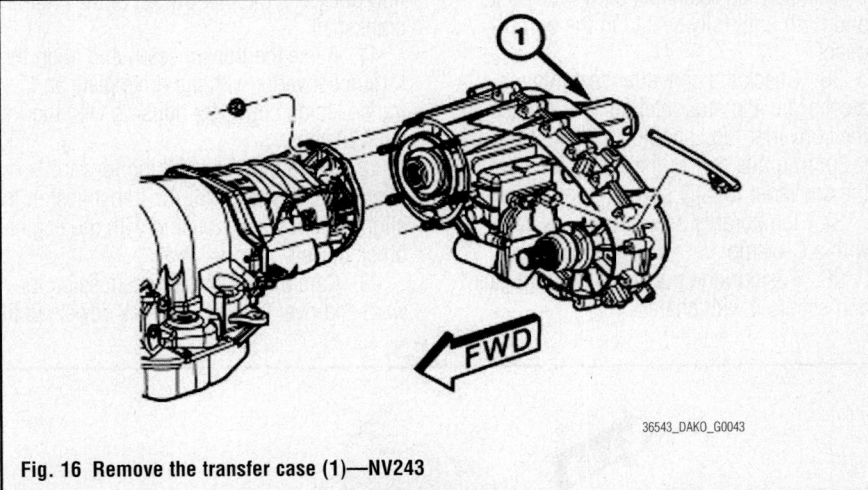

Fig. 16 Remove the transfer case (1)—NV243

36543_DAKO_G0043

31. To remove the torque converter, carefully slide the torque converter out of the transmission.

To install:

➡**Check the torque converter hub and hub drive flats for sharp edges burrs, scratches, or nicks. Polish the hub and flats with 320/400 grit paper and crocus cloth if necessary. The hub must be smooth to avoid damaging the pump seal at installation.**

32. If a replacement transmission is being installed, transfer any components

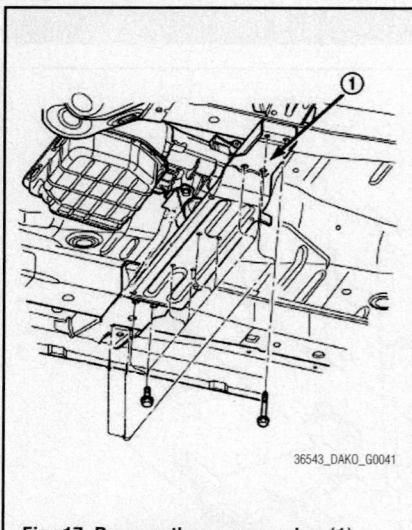

Fig. 17 Remove the crossmember (1)

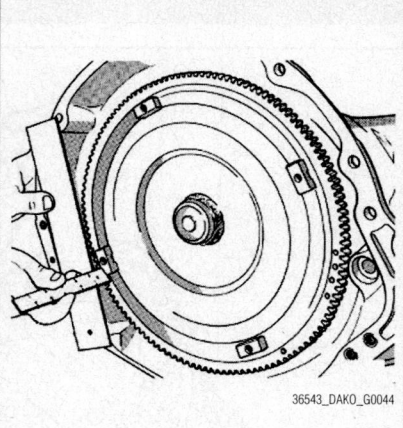

Fig. 19 Check the converter seating with a steel scale and straightedge

necessary, such as the manual shift lever and shift cable bracket, from the original transmission onto the replacement transmission.

33. Lubricate the oil pump seal lip with transmission fluid.

34. Align the converter and the oil pump.

35. Carefully insert the converter in the oil pump. Then rotate the converter back and forth until fully seated in the pump gears.

36. Check the converter seating with a steel scale and straightedge. The surface of the converter lugs should be at least ½ inch (13mm) to the rear of the straightedge when the converter is fully seated.

37. Temporarily secure the converter with a C-clamp.

38. Position the transmission on a jack and secure it with chains.

39. Check the condition of the converter driveplate. Replace the plate if cracked, distorted, or damaged. Also, be sure the transmission dowel pins are seated in the engine block and protrude far enough to hold the transmission in alignment.

40. Apply a light coating of MOPAR® High Temp Grease to the torque converter hub pocket in the rear pocket of the engine crankshaft.

41. Raise the transmission and align the torque converter with the drive plate and transmission converter housing with the engine block.

42. Move the transmission forward. Then raise, lower, or tilt the transmission to align the converter housing with the engine block dowels.

43. Carefully work the transmission forward and over the engine block dowels until

the converter hub is seated in the crankshaft. Verify that no wires, or the transmission vent hose, have become trapped between the engine block and the transmission.

44. Install 2 bolts to attach the transmission to the engine.

45. Install the remaining torque converter housing to engine bolts. Tighten to 50 ft. lbs. (68 Nm).

46. Install the transfer case, if equipped.

47. Install the rear transmission crossmember. Tighten the crossmember-to-frame bolts to 50 ft. lbs. (68 Nm).

48. Install the rear support to the transmission. Tighten the bolts to 35 ft. lbs. (47 Nm).

49. Lower the transmission onto the crossmember and install the bolts attaching the transmission mount to the crossmember. Tighten the clevis bracket to the crossmember bolts to 35 ft. lbs. (47 Nm). Tighten the clevis bracket to rear support bolt to 50 ft. lbs. (68 Nm).

50. Connect the gearshift cable to the support bracket and transmission manual lever.

51. Connect the input and output speed sensor and the transmission range sensor.

52. Connect the variable line pressure connector, if equipped.

53. Connect the wires to the solenoid/pressure switch assembly.

✳✳ WARNING

It is essential that the correct length bolts are used to attach the converter to the driveplate. Bolts that are too long will damage the clutch surface inside the converter.

54. Install the torque converter-to-driveplate bolts. Tighten the bolts to 65 inch lbs. (88 Nm).

55. Install the starter motor and cooler line bracket.

56. Connect the cooler lines to the transmission.

57. Install the transmission fill tube.

58. Install the exhaust components.

59. Align and connect the propeller shaft(s).

60. Adjust the gearshift cable, if necessary.

61. Install any skid plates removed previously.

62. Lower the vehicle.

63. Fill the transmission fluid to the correct level using MOPAR® ATF+4 Automatic Transmission Fluid, or an equivalent.

45RFE & 545RFE Transmissions

See Figures 15, 17, 16, 19 and 20.

1. Before servicing the vehicle, refer to the Precautions Section.

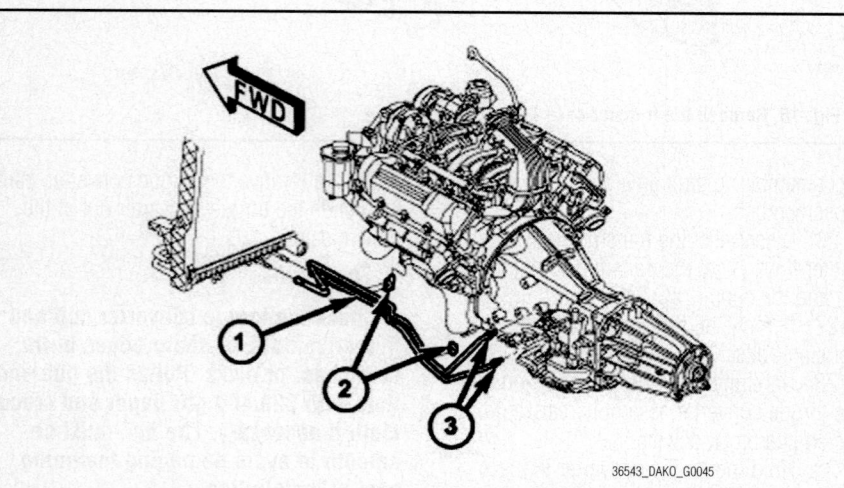

Fig. 18 Disconnect the transmission fluid cooler lines (1) at the transmission fittings (3) and the clips (2)

2. Disconnect the negative battery cable.

3. Raise and safely support the vehicle.

4. Remove any necessary skid plates.

5. Mark the propeller shaft and axle companion flanges for assembly alignment.

6. Remove the rear propeller shaft.

7. Remove the front propeller shaft, if necessary.

8. Remove the exhaust support bracket from the rear of the transmission, if equipped.

9. Disconnect and lower or remove any necessary exhaust components.

10. Remove the front differential support brace, if equipped.

11. Remove the engine to transmission collar.

12. Remove the starter motor.

13. Rotate the crankshaft in a clockwise direction until the converter bolts are accessible. Then remove the bolts one at a time. Rotate the crankshaft with a socket wrench on the dampener bolt.

14. Remove the fill tube bolt at the transmission.

15. Disengage the output speed sensor connector from the output speed sensor.

16. Disengage the input speed sensor connector from the input speed sensor.

17. Disengage the transmission solenoid/TRS assembly connector from the transmission solenoid/TRS assembly.

18. Remove the heat shield, if equipped, and disengage the line pressure sensor connector from the line pressure sensor.

19. Disconnect the fuel line brackets from the transmission case.

20. Disconnect the gearshift cable from the transmission manual valve lever.

21. Remove the gearshift cable from the shift cable support bracket.

22. Disconnect the transmission fluid cooler lines at the transmission fittings and clips.

23. Raise the transmission slightly with a service jack to relieve the load on the crossmember and supports.

24. Remove the bolts securing the rear support and the cushion to the transmission and crossmember.

25. Remove the bolts attaching the crossmember to the frame and remove the crossmember.

26. Remove the transfer case, if equipped.

27. Remove all remaining converter housing bolts

28. While removing the fill tube from the transmission case, carefully work the transmission and the torque converter assembly rearward off the engine block dowels.

29. Hold the torque converter in place during the transmission removal.

30. Lower the transmission and remove the assembly from under the vehicle.

31. To remove the torque converter, carefully slide the torque converter out of the transmission.

To install:

➡ Check the torque converter hub and hub drive flats for sharp edges burrs, scratches, or nicks. Polish the hub and flats with 800/1000 grit paper and crocus cloth if necessary. Verify that the converter hub O-ring is properly installed and is free of any debris. The hub must be smooth to avoid damaging the pump seal at installation.

32. If a replacement transmission is being installed, transfer any components necessary, such as the manual shift lever and shift cable bracket.

33. Lubricate the oil pump seal lip with transmission fluid.

34. Align the converter and the oil pump.

35. Carefully insert the converter in the oil pump. Then, rotate the converter back and forth until fully seated in the pump gears.

36. Check the converter seating with a steel scale and straightedge. The surface of the converter lugs should be at least ½ inch (13mm) to the rear of the straightedge when the converter is fully seated.

37. Temporarily secure the converter with a C-clamp.

38. Position the transmission on a jack and secure it with chains.

39. Check the condition of the converter driveplate. Replace the plate if cracked, distorted, or damaged. Also, be sure the transmission dowel pins are seated in the engine block and protrude far enough to hold the transmission in alignment.

40. Apply a light coating of MOPAR® High Temp Grease to the torque converter hub pocket in the rear pocket of the engine crankshaft.

41. Raise the transmission and align the torque converter with the drive plate, and the transmission converter housing with the engine block.

42. Move the transmission forward. Then raise, lower, or tilt the transmission to align the converter housing with the engine block dowels.

43. While installing the fill tube, carefully work the transmission forward and over the engine block dowels until the converter hub is seated in the crankshaft. Verify that no wires, or the transmission vent hose, have become trapped between the engine block and the transmission.

44. Install 2 bolts to attach the transmission to the engine.

45. Install the remaining torque converter housing to the engine bolts. Tighten to 50 ft. lbs. (68 Nm).

46. Install the transfer case, if equipped. Tighten the transfer case nuts to 26 ft. lbs. (35 Nm).

47. Install the rear support to the transmission. Tighten the bolts to 35 ft. lbs. (47 Nm).

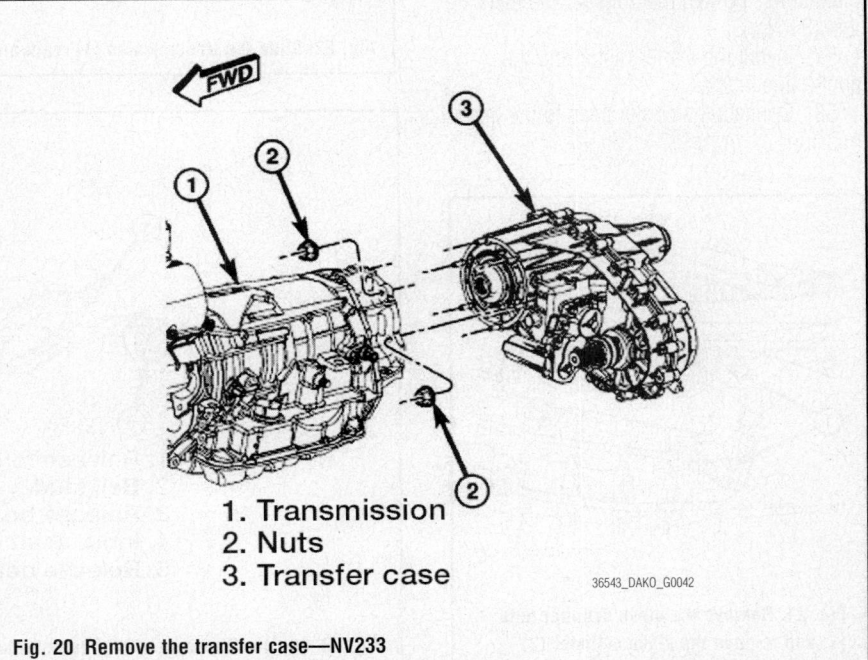

1. Transmission
2. Nuts
3. Transfer case

36543_DAKO_G0042

Fig. 20 Remove the transfer case—NV233

Install the rear transmission crossmember. Tighten the crossmember-to-frame bolts to 50 ft. lbs. (68 Nm).

48. Lower the transmission onto the crossmember and install the bolts attaching the transmission mount to the crossmember. Tighten the clevis bracket to crossmember bolts to 35 ft. lbs. (47 Nm). Tighten the clevis bracket to rear support bolt to 50 ft. lbs. (68 Nm).

49. Connect the gearshift cable to the transmission.

50. Connect the wiring harness connector to the solenoid and the pressure switch assembly connector. Be sure the transmission harnesses are properly routed.

51. Connect the wiring harness connector to the input speed sensor.

52. Connect the wiring harness connector to the output speed sensor.

53. Connect the wiring harness connector to the line pressure sensor.

54. Install the line pressure heat shield, if equipped. Tighten the bolts to 62 inch lbs. (7 Nm).

55. Install the fuel line brackets to the transmission case. Tighten the bolts to 62 inch lbs. (7 Nm).

✵✵ WARNING

It is essential that the correct length bolts are used to attach the converter to the driveplate. Bolts that are too long will damage the clutch surface inside the converter.

56. Install the torque converter-to-driveplate bolts. Tighten the bolts to 270 inch lbs. (31 Nm).

57. Install the starter motor and the cooler line bracket.

58. Connect the cooler lines to the transmission.

59. Install the transmission fill tube bolt. Tighten the bolt to 62 inch lbs. (7 Nm).

60. Install the structural dust cover onto the transmission and the engine.

61. Install the front differential support brace, if equipped.

62. Install the exhaust components that were lowered or removed.

63. Align and install the front propeller shaft, if necessary.

64. Align and install the rear propeller shaft.

65. Adjust the gearshift cable, if necessary.

66. Install any skid plates removed previously.

67. Lower the vehicle.

68. Fill the transmission fluid to the correct level using MOPAR® ATF+4 Automatic Transmission Fluid, or an equivalent.

MANUAL TRANSMISSION ASSEMBLY

REMOVAL & INSTALLATION

See Figures 21 through 25.

1. Before servicing the vehicle, refer to the Precautions Section.

2. Disconnect battery negative cable.

3. Shift the transmission into Neutral and position the vehicle on a hoist.

4. Remove the shift knob, shift lever boot, and shift lever extension.

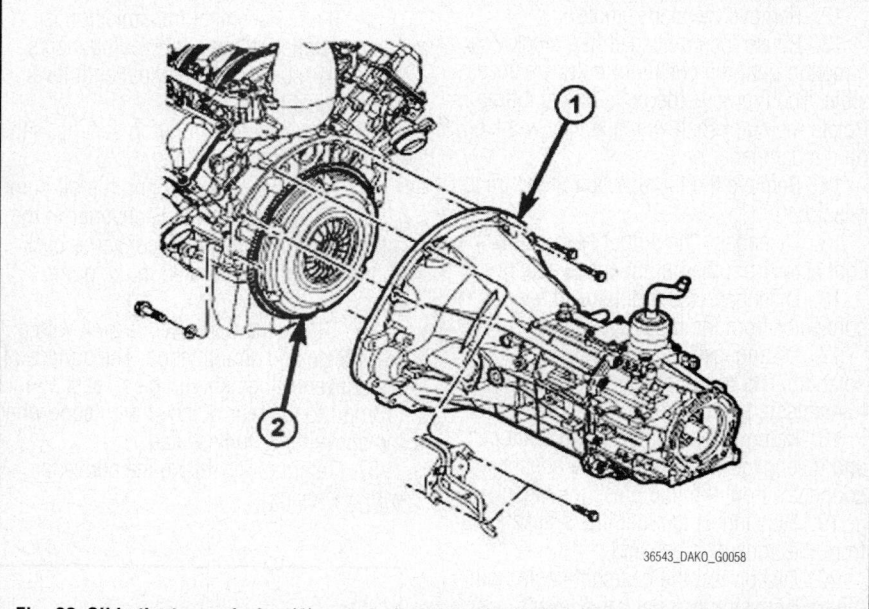

36543_DAKO_G0058

Fig. 22 Slide the transmission (1) rearward until the input shaft clears the clutch assembly (2)

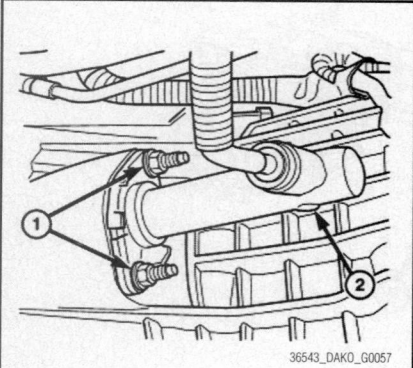

36543_DAKO_G0057

Fig. 21 Remove the slave cylinder nuts (1) and remove the slave cylinder (2)

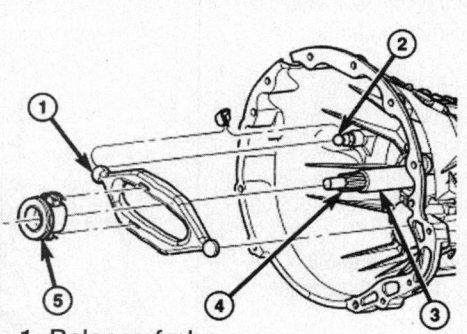

1. Release fork
2. Ball stud
3. Release bearing slide surface
4. Input shaft splines
5. Release bearing bore

36543_DAKO_G0059

Fig. 23 Apply a light coat of high temperature bearing grease to the contact surfaces

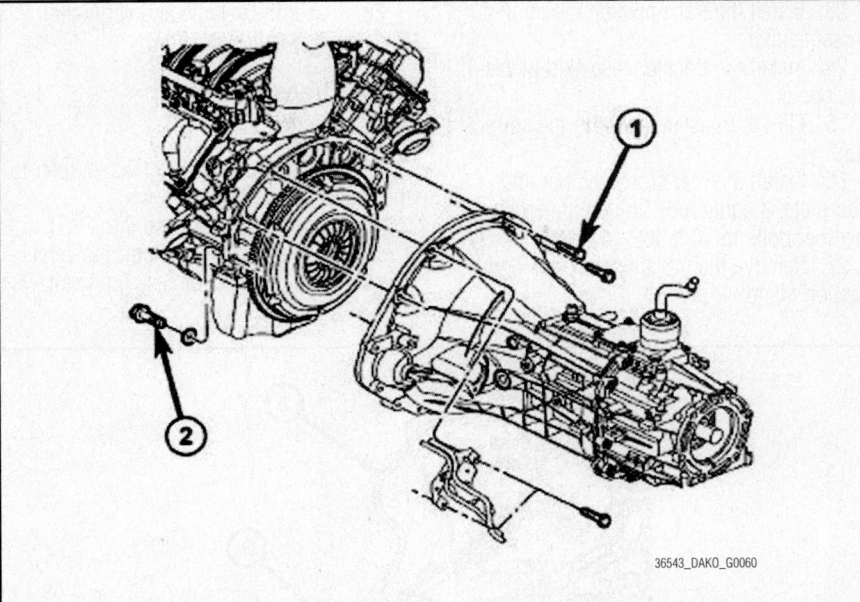

Fig. 24 Install the bolts without washers (1) and bolts with washers (2) to the specified torque

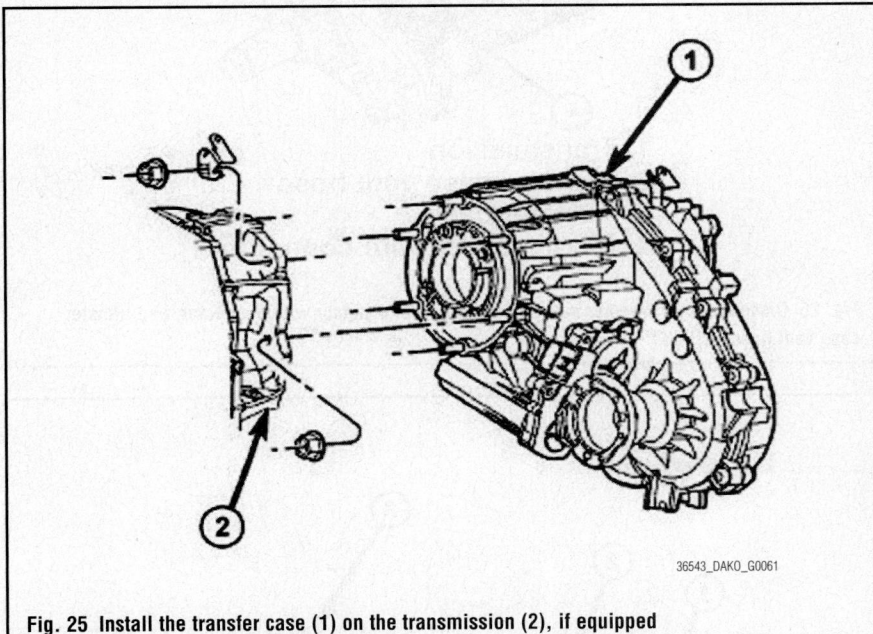

Fig. 25 Install the transfer case (1) on the transmission (2), if equipped

5. Remove the lower shift lever boot assembly from the floorpan.

6. Remove the shift tower bolts through the hole in the floorpan and remove the shift tower from the transmission.

7. Remove the skid plate, if equipped (4WD).

8. Remove the drain plug from the bottom of the transmission and drain the fluid.

9. Mark the propeller shaft and shaft companion flanges for installation reference.

10. Remove the propeller shafts.

11. Remove the Y-pipe from the exhaust manifolds.

12. Lower the exhaust pipes for clearance, as necessary.

13. Remove the backup light switch connector.

14. Remove the clutch slave cylinder splash shield, if equipped.

15. Remove the slave cylinder nuts (1) and remove the slave cylinder (2).

16. Support and secure the transmission to a transmission jack.

17. Remove the transfer from the transmission case, if equipped.

18. Remove the starter.

19. Remove the transmission dust shield.

20. Remove the rear crossmember.

21. Remove the bolts/nuts from the rear transmission mount.

22. Remove the transmission harness wires from the clips on the transmission shift cover.

23. Lower the transmission slightly and remove the transmission bolts.

➡**Do not remove the structural dust cover from the engine block. If the cover is removed, the clutch housing and cover must be aligned with the engine.**

24. Slide the transmission (1) rearward until the input shaft clears the clutch assembly (2).

25. Lower the transmission jack and remove the transmission from the vehicle.

To install:

26. Clean the transmission front housing mounting surface.

27. Apply a light coat of MOPAR high temperature bearing grease, or equivalent, to the contact surfaces of the following components:
- The release fork (1) ball stud (2)
- The release bearing slide surface (3)
- The input shaft splines (4)
- The release bearing bore (5)
- The propeller shaft slip yoke

28. Support and secure the transmission to a jack.

29. Raise and align the transmission input shaft with the clutch disc, then slide the transmission into place.

30. Verify that the front housing is fully seated.

31. Install the transmission bolts without washers (1) and tighten the bolts into the engine to 30 ft. lbs. (41 Nm).

32. Install the transmission bolts with washers (2) into the transmission and tighten to 50 ft. lbs. (68 Nm).

33. Install the dust shield and tighten the bolts to 40 inch lbs. (54 Nm).

34. Install the rear crossmember and tighten the nuts to 75 ft. lbs. (102 Nm).

35. Install the transmission rear mount bolts and tighten to 50 ft. lbs. (68 Nm).

36. Connect the transmission harnesses to the clips on the case and connect the switches.

37. Install the slave cylinder (2) and tighten the cylinder nuts (1) to 200 inch lbs. (23 Nm).

38. Install the transfer case (1) on the transmission (2), if equipped.

39. Remove the transmission jack.

40. Install the propeller shaft/shafts with reference marks aligned.

41. Install the exhaust on the exhaust manifolds.

42. Fill the transmission with lubricant to the bottom edge of the fill plug hole.

43. Install the shift tower and tighten the bolts to 88 inch lbs. (10 Nm).

44. Install the lower shift boot, floor console, shift lever extension, and upper shift boot.

45. Connect the battery negative cable.

TRANSFER CASE ASSEMBLY

REMOVAL & INSTALLATION

NV233 Transfer Case

See Figures 26 and 27.

1. Before servicing the vehicle, refer to the Precautions Section.

2. Shift the transfer case into 2WD.

3. Raise and safely support the vehicle.

4. Drain the transfer case lubricant.

5. Support the transmission with a jack stand.

6. Remove the rear crossmember and skid plate, if equipped.

7. Disconnect the front and rear propeller shafts at the transfer case.

8. Disconnect the transfer case shift motor and mode sensor wire connector (4).

9. Disconnect the transfer case vent hose (2) from the transfer case (3).

10. Support the transfer case with a transmission jack.

11. Secure the transfer case to the jack with chains.

12. Remove the nuts (2) attaching the transfer case (3) to the transmission (1).

13. Pull the transfer case and jack rearward to disengage the transfer case.

14. Remove the transfer case from under the vehicle.

To install:

15. Mount the transfer case on a transmission jack.

16. Secure the transfer case to the jack with chains.

17. Position the transfer case under the vehicle.

18. Align the transfer case and the transmission shafts and install the transfer case (3) onto the transmission (1).

19. Install and tighten the transfer case attaching nuts (2) to 20–25 ft. lbs. (27—34 Nm).

20. Connect the vent hose (2) to the transfer case (3).

21. Connect the shift motor and mode sensor wiring connectors (4). Secure the wire harness to the clips on the transfer case.

22. Align and connect the propeller shafts.

23. Install the transmission mount and crossmember.

24. Install the transfer case skid plates, if equipped.

25. Fill the transfer case with the correct fluid.

26. Install the rear crossmember and skid plate, if equipped. Tighten the crossmember bolts to 30 ft. lbs. (41 Nm).

27. Remove the transmission jack and support stand.

28. Lower the vehicle and verify the transfer case shift operation.

NV243 Transfer Case

See Figure 28.

1. Before servicing the vehicle, refer to the Precautions Section.

2. Shift the transfer case into 2WD.

3. Raise and safely support the vehicle.

4. Drain the transfer case lubricant.

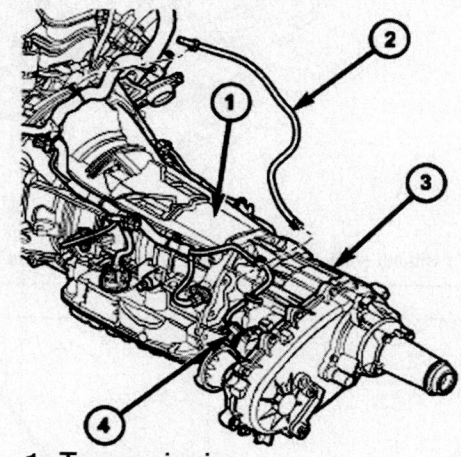

1. Transmission
2. Transfer case vent hose
3. Transfer case
4. Mode sensor wire connector

36543_DAKO_G0066

Fig. 26 Disconnect the transfer case shift motor, mode sensor wire connector, and transfer case vent hose—NV233

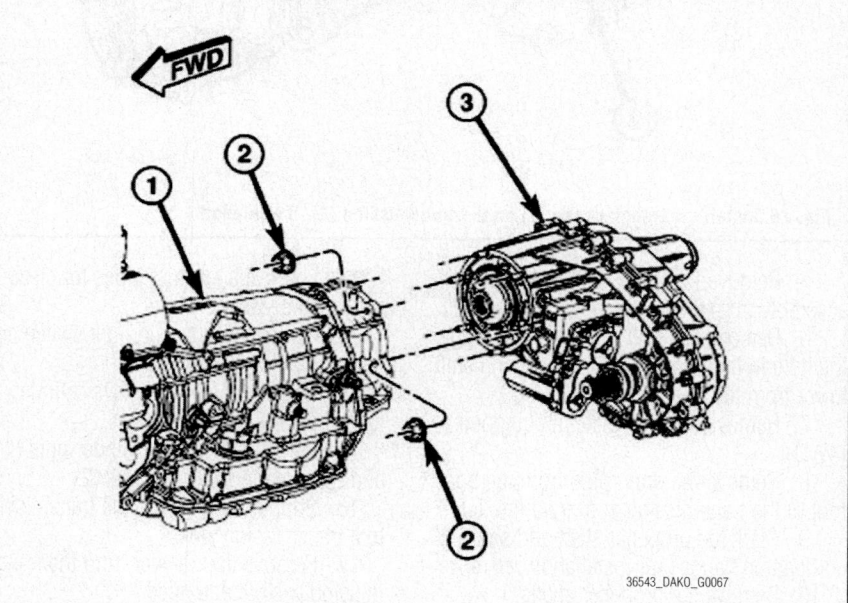

36543_DAKO_G0067

Fig. 27 Remove the nuts (2) attaching the transfer case (3) to the transmission (1)—NV233

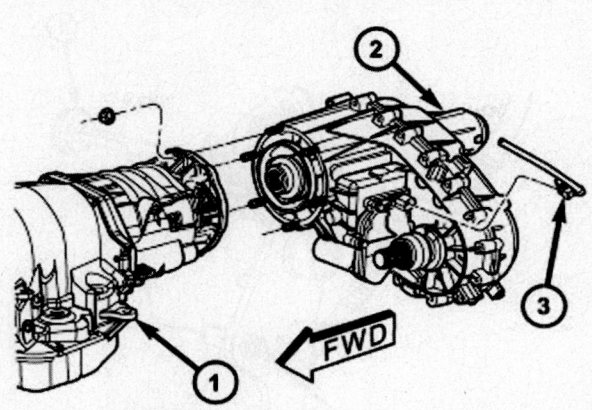

1. Transmission
2. Transfer case
3. Mode sensor wire connectors

36543_DAKO_G0068

Fig. 28 Removal of the transfer case—NV243

5. Remove the transfer case skid plate, if equipped.

6. Support the transmission with a jack stand.

7. Remove the crossmember and the transmission mount.

8. Mark the front and rear propeller shafts for alignment reference.

9. Remove the front and rear propeller shafts.

10. Disconnect the transfer case shift motor and the mode sensor wire connectors (3).

11. Disconnect the transfer case vent hose.

12. Support the transfer case with the transmission jack.

13. Secure the transfer case to the jack with chains.

14. Remove the nuts attaching the transfer case (2) to the transmission (1).

15. Pull the transfer case and the jack rearward to disengage the transfer case.

16. Remove the transfer case from under the vehicle.

To install:

17. Mount the transfer case on a transmission jack.

18. Secure the transfer case to the jack with chains.

19. Position the transfer case under the vehicle.

20. Align the transfer case and the transmission shafts and install the transfer case (3) onto the transmission (1).

21. Install and tighten the transfer case attaching nuts (2) to 20–25 ft. lbs. (27—34 Nm).

22. Connect the vent hose to the transfer case.

23. Connect the shift motor and the mode sensor wiring connectors. Secure the wire harness to the clips on the transfer case.

24. Align and connect the propeller shafts.

25. Install the transmission mount and crossmember.

26. Install the transfer case skid plates, if equipped.

27. Fill the transfer case with the correct fluid.

28. Install the rear crossmember and skid plate, if equipped. Tighten the crossmember bolts to 30 ft. lbs. (41 Nm).

29. Remove the transmission jack and support stand.

30. Lower the vehicle and verify the transfer case shift operation.

CLUTCH DRIVEN DISC & PRESSURE PLATE

REMOVAL & INSTALLATION

See Figures 29 and 30.

1. Before servicing the vehicle, refer to the Precautions Section.

2. Raise and safely support the vehicle.

3. Remove the transmission and clutch housing as an assembly.

4. If the pressure plate is being removed for access to another component, mark the position of the pressure plate cover on the flywheel with small punch marks.

5. Loosen the bolts (2) of the pressure plate (1) evenly and in a rotation to relieve spring tension. Loosen the bolts a few threads at a time to avoid warping the cover.

6. Remove the cover bolts, pressure plate, and clutch disc.

To install:

➡ **Clean the flywheel surface with solvent. Scuff sand the surface with 120/180 grit emery cloth to remove minor scratches and glazing.**

7. Check the new clutch disc for runout and for free operation on the input shaft splines.

8. Lubricate the crankshaft pilot bearing with NLGI-2 rated grease.

9. Verify that the disc hub is positioned correctly. The raised portion of the hub faces away from the flywheel.

10. Position the clutch disc with the pressure plate (2) on the flywheel (1).

11. Insert an alignment tool (3), or spare input shaft, through the clutch disc and into the pilot bearing.

12. Install the cover bolts finger tight.

13. Tighten the cover bolts evenly (and in rotation) a few threads at a time. The cover bolts must be tightened evenly and to the specified torque to avoid distorting the cover.

14. Tighten the cover bolts to:
   a. 5/16 inch bolts: 17 ft. lbs. (23 Nm).
   b. 3/8 inch bolts: 30 ft. lbs. (41 Nm).

15. Apply a light coat of MOPAR® High Temperature Bearing Grease to the splines of the transmission input shaft and to the release bearing slide surface of the front bearing retainer.

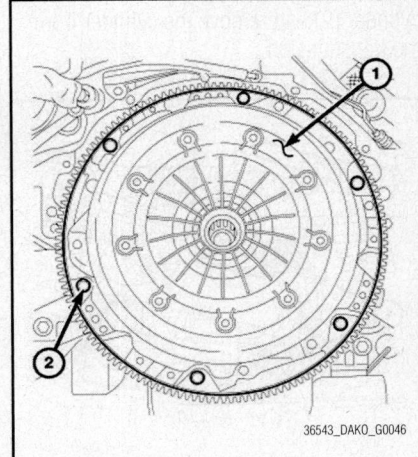

36543_DAKO_G0046

Fig. 29 Loosen the bolts (2) of the pressure plate (1) evenly and in a rotation to relieve spring tension

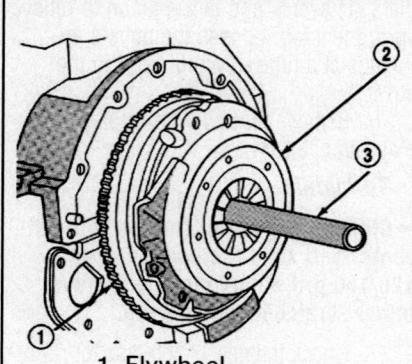

1. Flywheel
2. Pressure plate
3. Alignment tool

36543_DAKO_G0047

Fig. 30 Position the clutch disc with the pressure plate on the flywheel. Insert an alignment tool through the clutch disc and into the pilot bearing

➡Do not over-lubricate the shaft splines as the disc could become contaminated with grease.

16. Install the transmission and clutch housing as an assembly.

CLUTCH SLAVE CYLINDER

REMOVAL & INSTALLATION

See Figures 31 through 33.

The hydraulic linkage is serviced as a complete assembly only. The individual components must not be overhauled or serviced separately.

1. Before servicing the vehicle, refer to the Precautions Section.
2. Raise and safely support the vehicle.
3. Remove the nuts (1) from the slave cylinder (2) and remove the cylinder from the transmission.

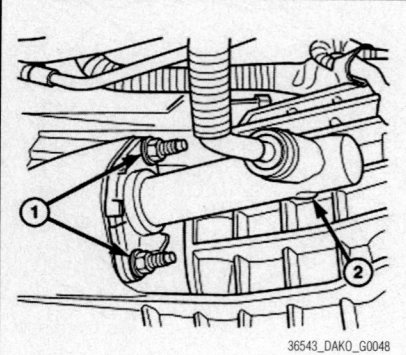

36543_DAKO_G0048

Fig. 31 Remove the nuts (1) from the slave cylinder (2) and remove the cylinder from the transmission

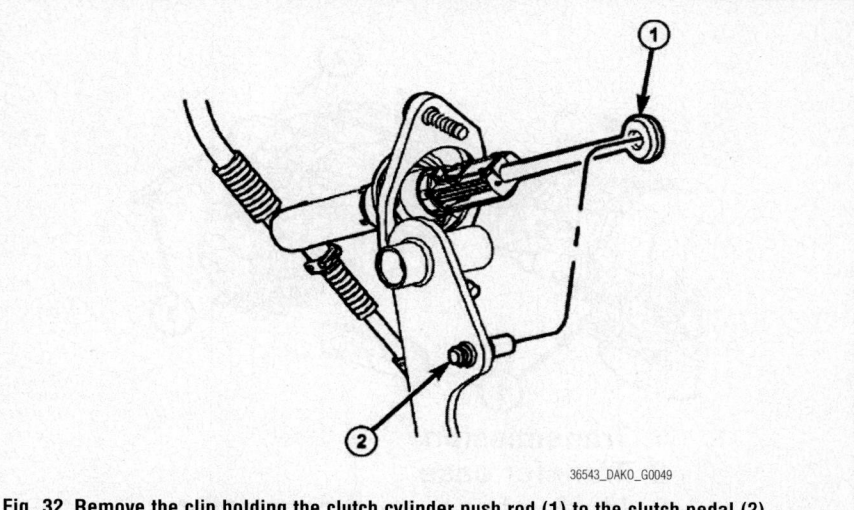

36543_DAKO_G0049

Fig. 32 Remove the clip holding the clutch cylinder push rod (1) to the clutch pedal (2)

✳✳ WARNING

Do not disconnect the slave cylinder quick disconnect. If disconnected, the hydraulic linkage must be replaced.

4. Remove the clip holding the clutch cylinder push rod (1) to the clutch pedal (2).
5. Slide the clutch cylinder push rod (1) off the clutch pedal pin (2).
6. Disconnect the clutch pedal position switch connector (3) from the wiring harness.
7. Remove the hydraulic fluid line clip (4) from the lower dash panel flange.

8. Remove the clutch cylinder nuts (2).
9. Ensure the cap of the clutch reservoir (1) is tight.
10. Remove the nuts from the clutch reservoir (1).
11. Pull the clutch reservoir (1) and cylinder (2) from the dash panel.
12. Remove the hydraulic linkage components from the vehicle as an assembly.

To install:

13. Ensure that the cap of the clutch reservoir is tight.
14. Install the clutch reservoir (1) in the dash panel and tighten the nuts to 40 inch lbs. (5 Nm).

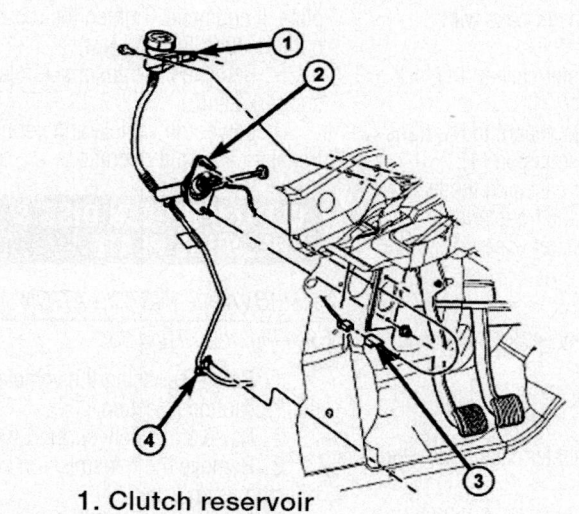

1. Clutch reservoir
2. Slave cylinder
3. Clutch pedal position switch connector
4. Hydraulic fluid line

36543_DAKO_G0050

Fig. 33 Remove the hydraulic linkage components from the vehicle as an assembly

15. Install the clutch cylinder (2) in the dash panel and tighten the nuts to 40 ft. lbs. (54 Nm).

16. Connect the clutch pedal position switch connector (3) to the wiring harness.

17. Install the hydraulic fluid line clip (4) into the hole in the lower dash panel.

18. Apply a light coating of grease to the inner diameter of the clutch cylinder push rod (1) and the outer diameter of the clutch pedal pin (2).

19. Install the clutch cylinder push rod (1) on the clutch pedal pin (2) and install the retaining clip.

20. Install the slave cylinder (2) to the transmission and ensure the rod is securely engaged in the release lever.

➡**If a new clutch linkage is being installed, do not remove the plastic shipping strap from the slave cylinder push rod. The strap will break on its own upon the first clutch application.**

21. Install the slave cylinder nuts (1) and tighten them to 17 ft. lbs. (23 Nm).

22. Verify that the fluid line from the master cylinder to the slave cylinder is properly routed.

HYDRAULIC SYSTEM BLEEDING

➡**It is necessary to bleed the clutch hydraulic release system if the system has lost an excessive amount of fluid and has allowed air into the circuit. Air in the system typically results in a spongy pedal feel and/or improper clutch release. If air cannot be removed from the system using this procedure, it may be necessary to replace both the clutch cylinder assemblies.**

1. Remove the reservoir cap taking care not to damage the diaphragm. If the fluid level is not up to the step in the reservoir, add MOPAR® DOT 3 brake fluid, or equivalent.

2. Slowly depress the clutch pedal while opening the clutch slave cylinder bleed screw.

3. Holding the clutch pedal down and tighten the bleed screw.

4. Repeat Step 2 and Step 3 two times, then check the fluid level in the reservoir.

5. Pump the clutch pedal rapidly a minimum of 10 times. If the clutch pedal still feels spongy, repeat Step 2 through Step 5.

6. If several attempts at purging air from the system are unsuccessful, it may be necessary to replace the clutch cylinder assembly.

7. Top off the clutch reservoir with brake fluid, as necessary.

FRONT AXLE SHAFT, BEARING & SEAL

REMOVAL & INSTALLATION

See Figures 34 through 37.

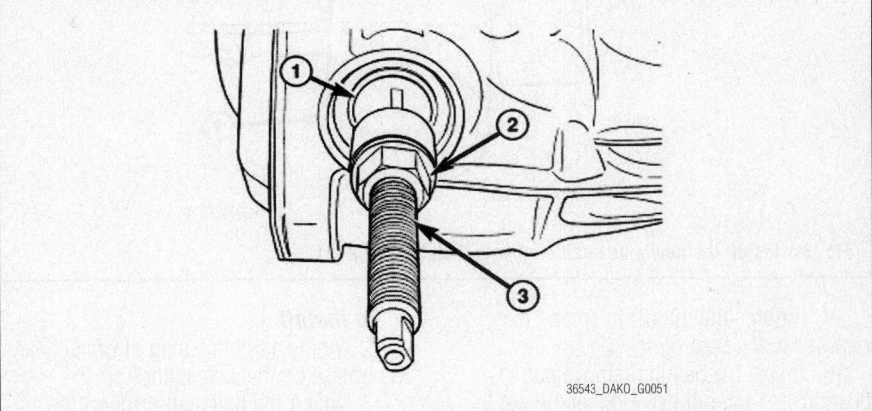

36543_DAKO_G0051

Fig. 34 Install the axle shaft bearing Remover C-4660-A (3) in the bearing (1) and tighten the nut (2)

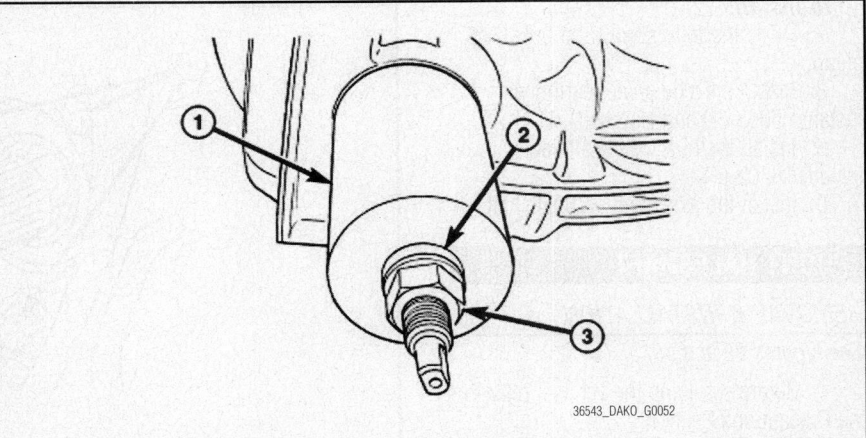

36543_DAKO_G0052

Fig. 35 Install the bearing remove cup (1), bearing (2), and nut (3). Tighten the nut to draw the bearing out

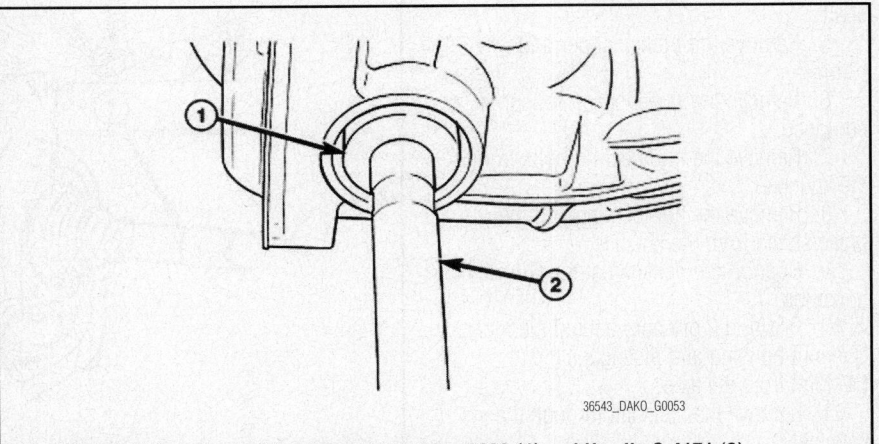

36543_DAKO_G0053

Fig. 36 Install the axle shaft bearing with Installer 5063 (1) and Handle C-4171 (2)

1. Before servicing the vehicle, refer to the Precautions Section.

2. Remove the halfshaft, axle shaft, and seal.

3. Install the axle shaft bearing Remover C-4660-A (3) in the bearing (1).

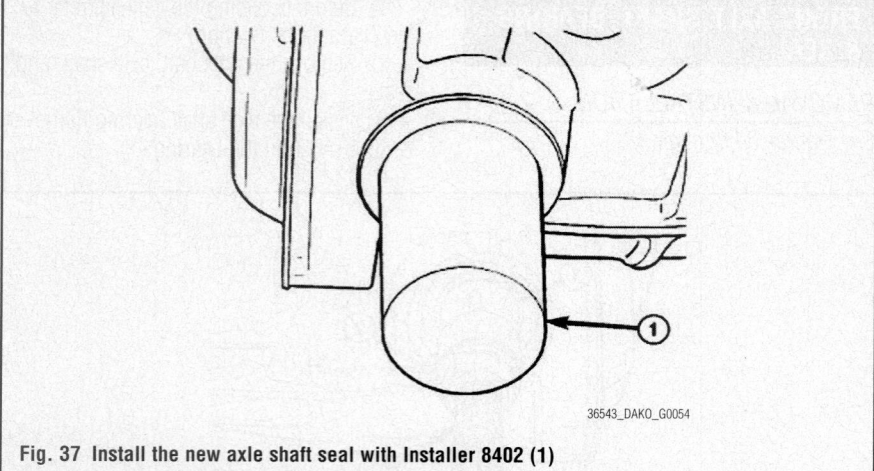

Fig. 37 Install the new axle shaft seal with Installer 8402 (1)

4. Tighten the nut (2) to spread the remover in the bearing.

5. Install the bearing remove cup (1), bearing (2), and nut (3). Tighten the nut to draw the bearing out.

6. Inspect the axle shaft tube bore for roughness and burrs.

To install:

7. Wipe the axle shaft tube bore clean.

8. Install the axle shaft bearing with Installer 5063 (1) and Handle C-4171 (2).

9. Install the new axle shaft seal with Installer 8402 (1).

10. Install the axle shaft and halfshaft.

FRONT HALFSHAFT

REMOVAL & INSTALLATION

See Figures 38 and 39.

1. Before servicing the vehicle, refer to the Precautions Section.

2. With the vehicle in neutral, position the vehicle on a hoist.

3. Remove the skid plate, if equipped.

4. Remove the hub nut from the half-shaft.

5. Remove the brake caliper and rotor.

6. Remove the wheel speed sensor, if equipped.

7. Remove the hub bearing bolts from the knuckle.

8. Remove the hub bearing and the brake shield from the knuckle.

9. Support the halfshaft at the CV-joint housings.

10. Position 2 pry bars behind the inner CV-joint housing and disengage the CV-joint from the axle.

11. Remove the halfshaft through the knuckle.

To install:

12. Apply a light coating of wheel bearing grease on the axle splines.

13. Insert the halfshaft through the steering knuckle and onto the axle. Verify that the shaft snapring engages with the groove on the inside of the joint housing.

14. Clean the hub bearing bore and hub bearing mating surfaces. Lightly coat the mating surfaces with grease.

15. Install the hub bearing onto the axle halfshaft and into the steering knuckle. Tighten the hub bearing bolts to 120 ft. lbs. (163 Nm).

16. Install the wheel speed sensor, if equipped.

17. Install the brake rotor and the caliper adapter with the caliper.

18. Install the halfshaft nut. Apply the brakes and tighten the shaft nut to 185 ft. lbs. (251 Nm).

19. Install the skid plate, if equipped.

FRONT PINION SEAL

REMOVAL & INSTALLATION

See Figures 40 through 43.

1. Before servicing the vehicle, refer to the Precautions Section.

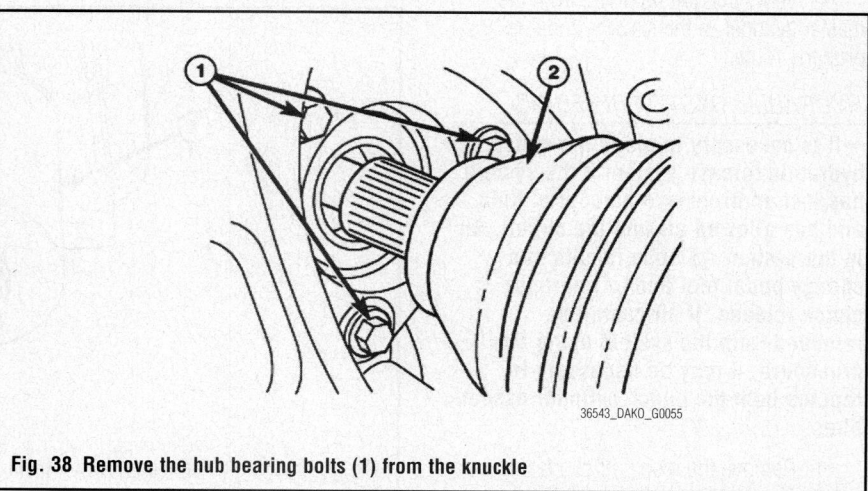

Fig. 38 Remove the hub bearing bolts (1) from the knuckle

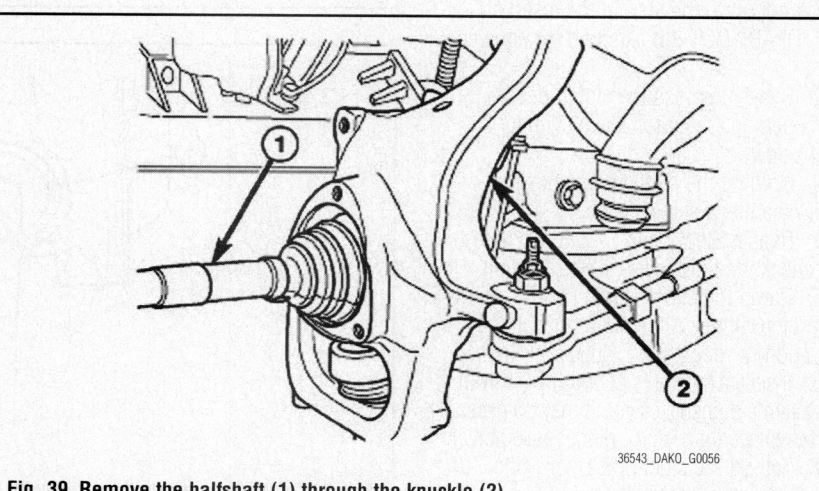

Fig. 39 Remove the halfshaft (1) through the knuckle (2)

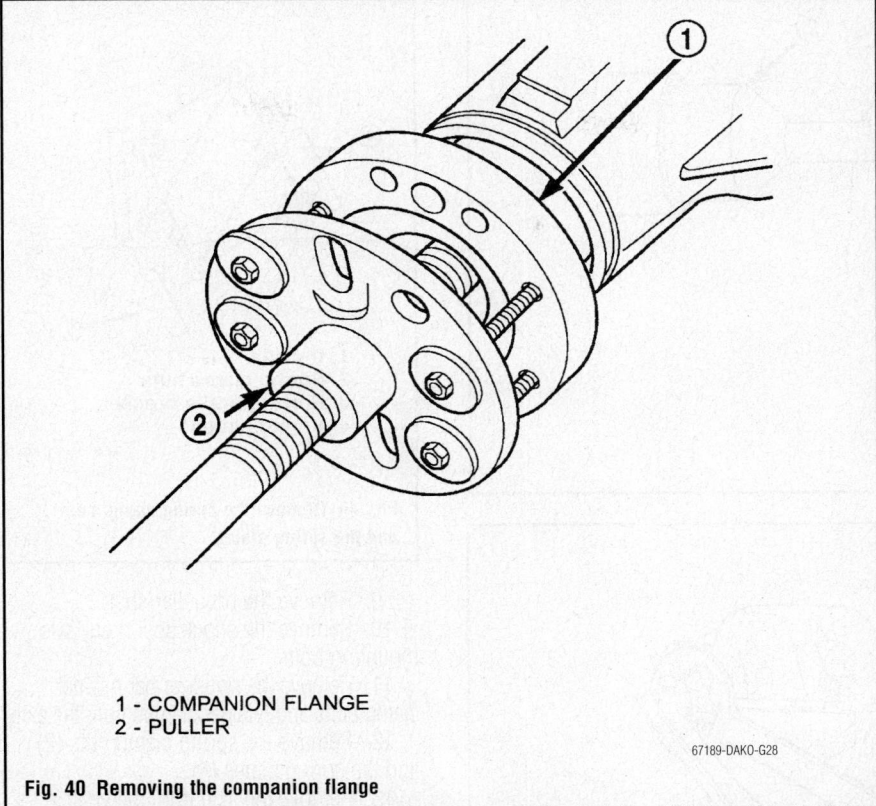

1 - COMPANION FLANGE
2 - PULLER

67189-DAKO-G28

Fig. 40 Removing the companion flange

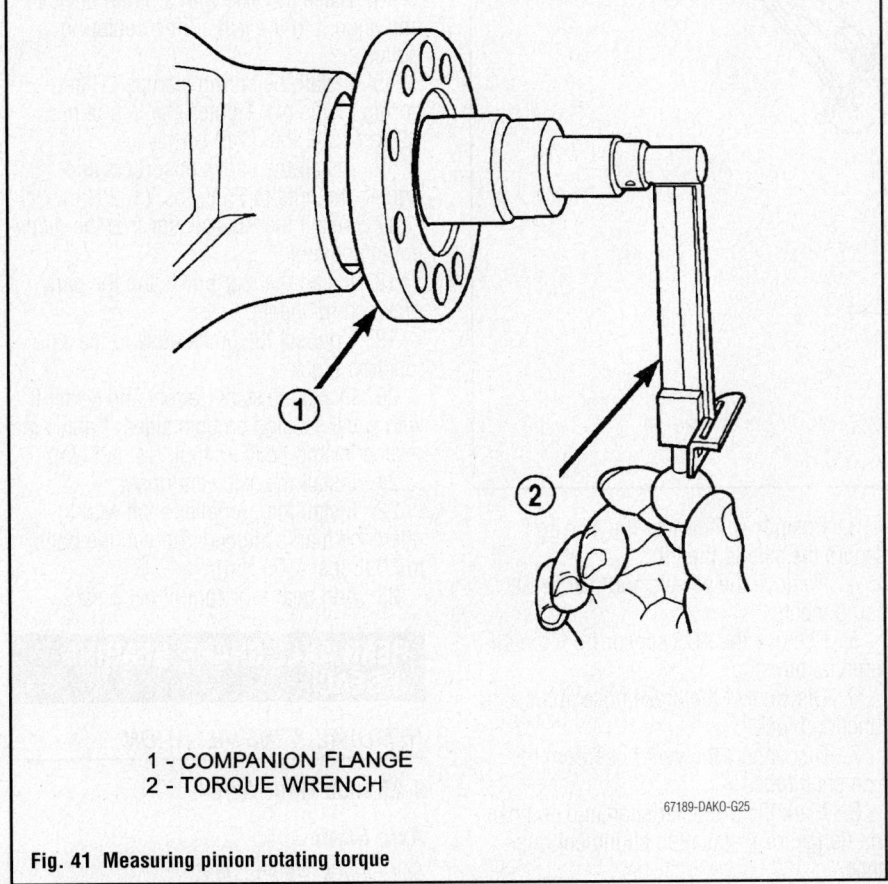

1 - COMPANION FLANGE
2 - TORQUE WRENCH

67189-DAKO-G25

Fig. 41 Measuring pinion rotating torque

2. Remove both halfshafts.

3. Mark the propeller shaft and pinion flange for installation reference.

4. Remove the front propeller shaft.

5. Rotate the pinion gear 3 to 4 times, to verify the pinion rotates smoothly.

6. Record the pinion flange rotating torque with an inch pound torque wrench for installation reference.

7. Hold the flange with the Holder 6719A and the 4 bolts and washers.

8. Remove the pinion nut.

9. Remove the flange with Remover C-452.

10. Remove the pinion seal with a pry tool.

To install:

11. Apply a light coating of gear lubricant on the lip of the pinion seal.

12. Install the seal with Installer C-3972-A and Handle C-4171.

13. Install the pinion flange onto the pinion with Installer C-3718 and holder.

14. Hold the pinion flange with Holder 6719A.

15. Install the new pinion nut and tighten the nut until there is zero bearing end-play.

✳✳ WARNING

Do not exceed the minimum tightening torque when installing the companion flange at this point. Damage to the collapsible spacer or bearings may result.

16. Tighten the pinion nut to 200 ft. lbs. (271 Nm).

✳✳ WARNING

Never loosen the pinion nut to decrease the pinion bearing rotating torque and never exceed the specified preload torque. If the preload torque or rotating torque is exceeded, a new collapsible spacer must be installed.

17. Record the pinion flange rotating torque with a torque wrench. The rotating torque should be equal to the reading recorded during the removal plus an additional 5 inch lbs. (0.56 Nm).

18. If the rotating torque is low, tighten the pinion nut in 5 ft. lbs. (7 Nm) increments until the rotating torque is achieved.

✳✳ WARNING

If the maximum tightening torque is reached prior to reaching the required rotating torque, the collapsible spacer may have been damaged. Replace the collapsible spacer.

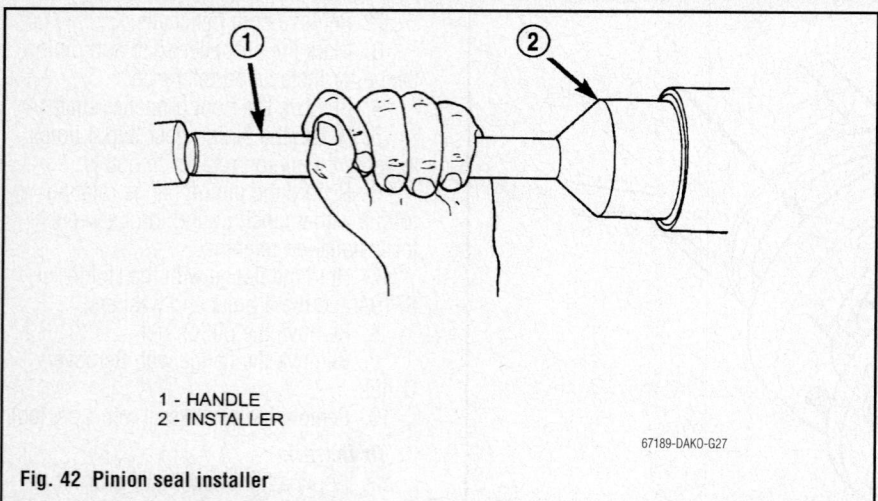

1 - HANDLE
2 - INSTALLER

67189-DAKO-G27

Fig. 42 Pinion seal installer

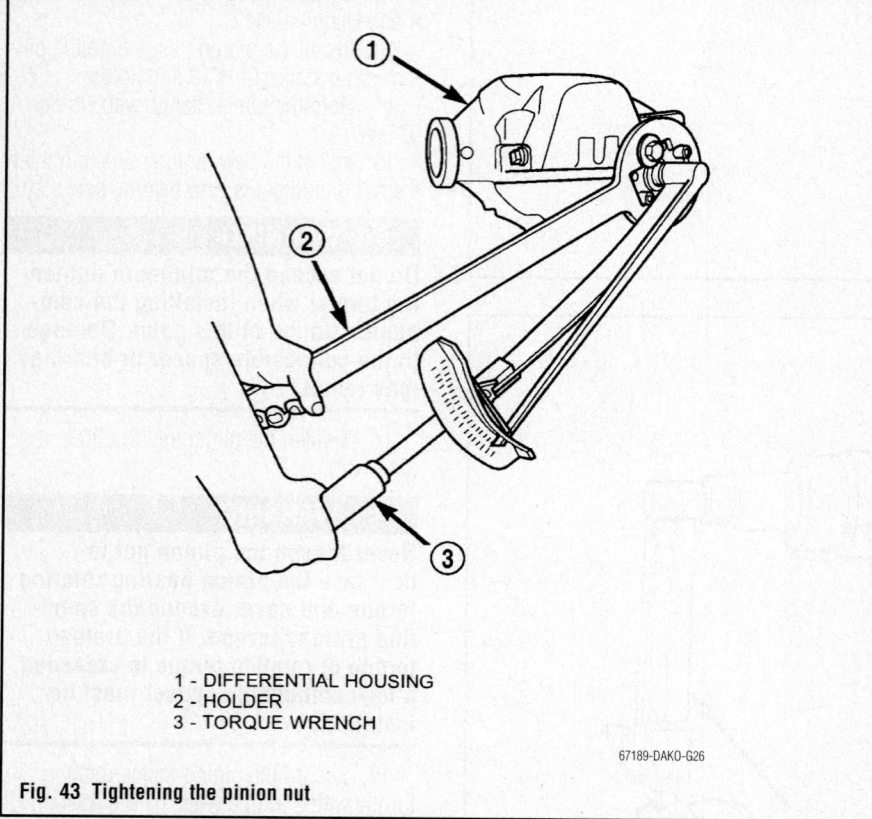

1 - DIFFERENTIAL HOUSING
2 - HOLDER
3 - TORQUE WRENCH

67189-DAKO-G26

Fig. 43 Tightening the pinion nut

19. Install the propeller shaft with the reference marks aligned.
20. Install the halfshafts.

REAR AXLE HOUSING

REMOVAL & INSTALLATION

See Figure 44.

1. Before servicing the vehicle, refer to the Precautions Section.
2. With the vehicle in neutral, carefully position it on a hoist.

3. Position a lift under the axle and secure the axle to the lift.
4. Remove the wheels and rear brake components.
5. Remove the ABS sensor from the differential housing.
6. Disconnect the brake hose at the axle junction block.
7. Disconnect the vent hose from the axle shaft tube.
8. Mark the propeller shaft and companion flange for installation alignment reference.

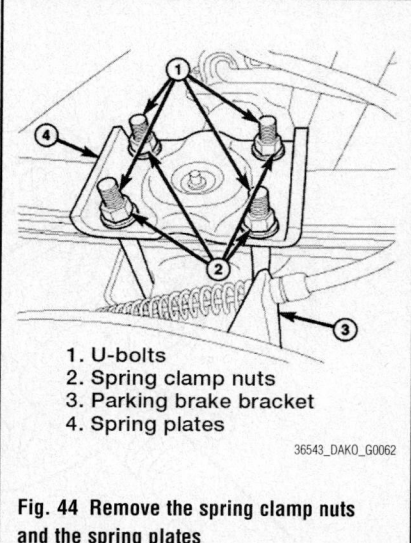

1. U-bolts
2. Spring clamp nuts
3. Parking brake bracket
4. Spring plates

36543_DAKO_G0062

Fig. 44 Remove the spring clamp nuts and the spring plates

9. Remove the propeller shaft.
10. Remove the shock absorbers axle mounting bolts.
11. Remove the stabilizer bar retainer clamp bolts and retainer clamps from the axle.
12. Remove the spring clamp nuts (2) and the spring plates (4).
13. Remove the axle from the vehicle.

To install:

14. Raise the axle with a lifting device and align it to the leaf spring centering bolts.
15. Install the spring clamps (1) and spring plates (4). Tighten the U-bolt nuts (2) to 110 ft. lbs. (149 Nm).
16. Install the shock absorbers and tighten the nuts to 75 ft. lbs. (102 Nm).
17. Install the ABS sensor into the differential housing.
18. Install the rear brake and the park brake components.
19. Connect the brake hose to the axle junction block.
20. Install the stabilizer bar and center it with equal spacing on both sides. Tighten the retainer clamp bolts to 45 ft. lbs. (61 Nm).
21. Install the axle vent hose.
22. Install the propeller shaft with the reference marks aligned. Tighten the bolts to 80 ft. lbs. (108 Nm).
23. Add gear lubricant, if necessary.

REAR AXLE SHAFT, BEARING & SEAL

REMOVAL & INSTALLATION

8.25 Inch Rear Axle

Axle Shaft

See Figures 45 and 46.

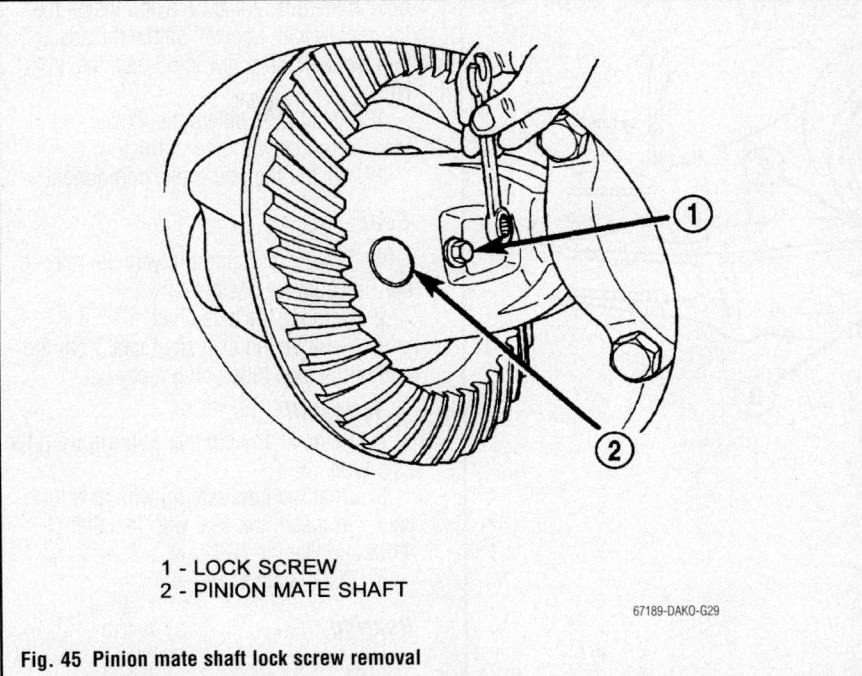

1 - LOCK SCREW
2 - PINION MATE SHAFT

67189-DAKO-G29

Fig. 45 Pinion mate shaft lock screw removal

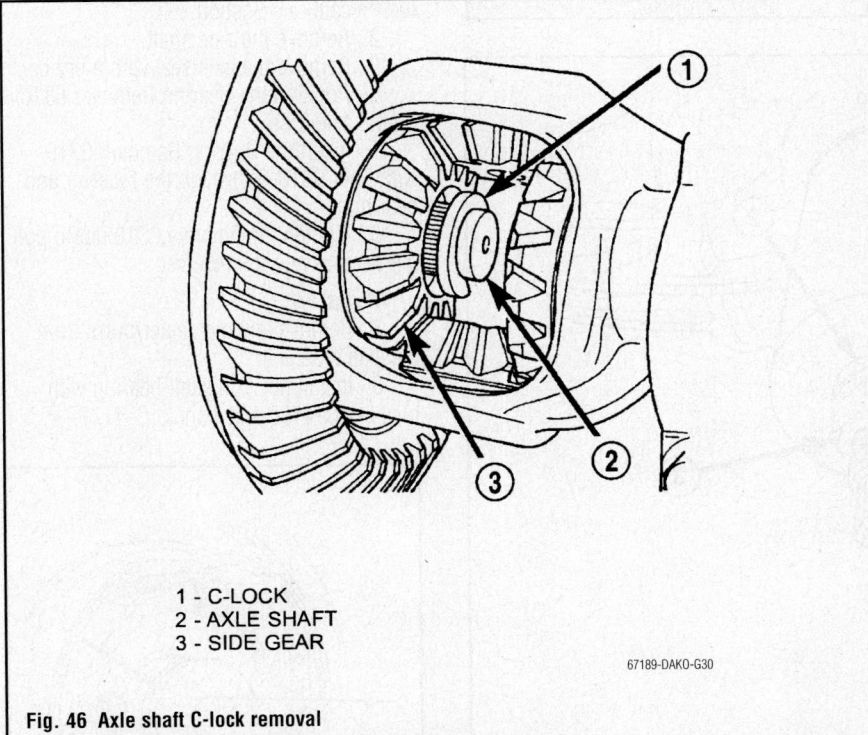

1 - C-LOCK
2 - AXLE SHAFT
3 - SIDE GEAR

67189-DAKO-G30

Fig. 46 Axle shaft C-lock removal

1. Before servicing the vehicle, refer to the Precautions Section.
2. With the vehicle in neutral, carefully position it on a hoist.
3. Remove the rear brake components.
4. Remove the differential housing cover and drain the lubricant.
5. Rotate the differential case to access the pinion mate shaft lock screw.

6. Remove the screw and pinion mate shaft from the differential case.
7. Push the axle shaft inward and remove the axle shaft C-lock.
8. Remove the axle shaft.

To install:
9. Lubricate the bearing bore and seal lip with gear lubricant.

10. Insert the axle shaft through the seal and engage it into the side gear splines.
11. Insert the C-lock in the end of the axle shaft, then push the axle shaft outward to seat the C-lock in the side gear.
12. Insert the pinion shaft into the differential case and through the thrust washers and the differential pinions.
13. Align the hole in the shaft with the hole in the differential case and install the lock screw with Loctite® on the threads. Tighten the lock screw to 96 inch lbs. (11 Nm).
14. Install the differential cover and fill the differential with gear lubricant.
15. Install the rear brake components.

Bearing And Seal

See Figures 47 and 48.

1. Before servicing the vehicle, refer to the Precautions Section.
2. Remove the axle shaft.
3. Remove the axle seal with a pry bar.
4. Position the Bearing Remover 6310 on the axle tube.
5. Insert the Bearing Remover 6310 with Foot 6310-9 through the receiver and bearing.
6. Tighten the Remover 6310 nut to pull the bearing into the receiver.

To install:
7. Remove any old sealer/burrs from the axle tube.
8. Install the axle shaft bearing with Installer C-4198 and Handle C-4171. Drive the bearing in until the tool contacts the axle tube.

➡**The bearing is installed with the bearing part number against the installer.**

9. Coat the new axle seal lip with axle lubricant and install it with Installer C-4198 and Handle C-4171.
10. Install the axle shaft.

9.25 Inch Rear Axle

Axle Shaft

1. Before servicing the vehicle, refer to the Precautions Section.
2. With the vehicle in neutral, carefully position it on a hoist.
3. Remove the rear brake components.
4. Remove the differential housing cover and drain the lubricant.
5. Rotate the differential case, to access the pinion mate shaft lock screw. Remove the screw and the pinion mate shaft from the differential case.
6. Push the axle shaft inward and remove the axle shaft C-lock.

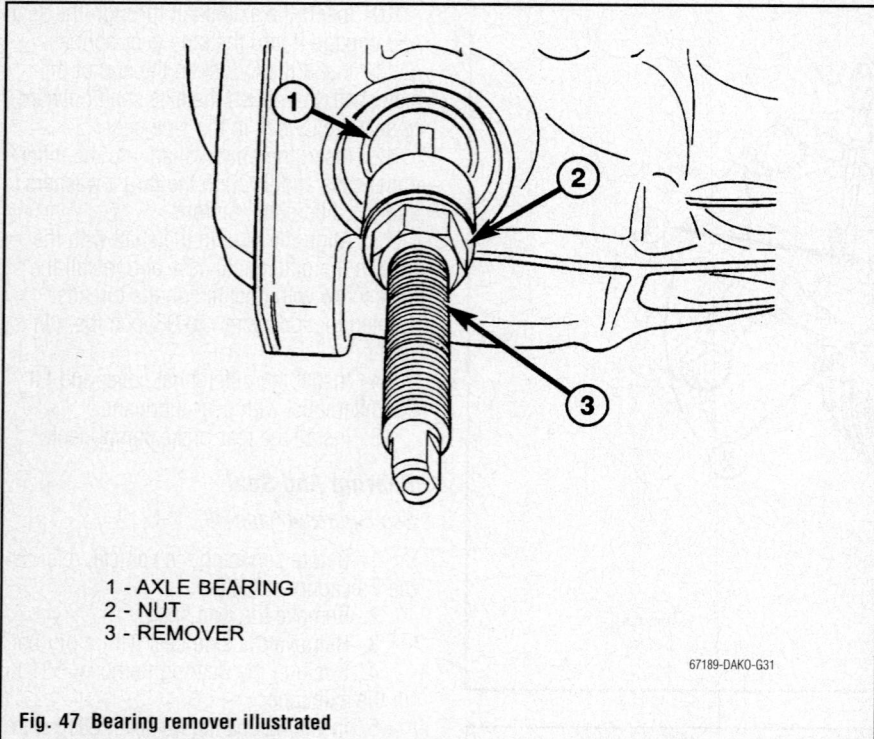

1 - AXLE BEARING
2 - NUT
3 - REMOVER

67189-DAKO-G31

Fig. 47 Bearing remover illustrated

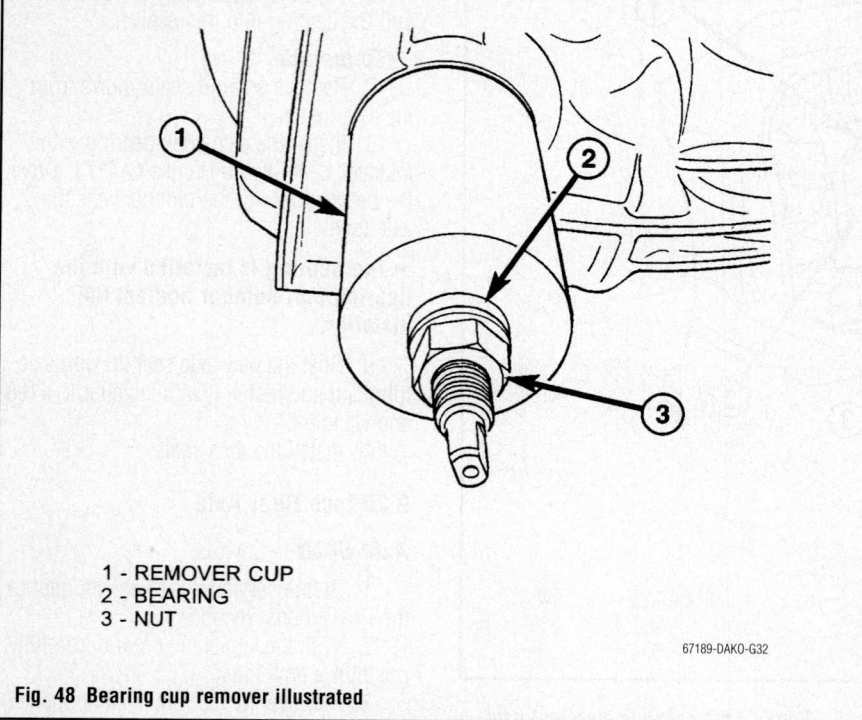

1 - REMOVER CUP
2 - BEARING
3 - NUT

67189-DAKO-G32

Fig. 48 Bearing cup remover illustrated

7. Remove the axle shaft.

To install:

8. Lubricate the bearing bore and seal lip with gear lubricant.

9. Insert the axle shaft through the seal and engage it into the side gear splines.

10. Insert the C-lock in the end of the axle shaft, then push the axle shaft outward to seat the C-lock in the side gear.

11. Insert the pinion shaft into the differential case and through the thrust washers and the differential pinions.

12. Align the hole in the shaft with the

hole in the differential case and install the lock screw with Loctite® on the threads. Tighten the lock screw to 96 inch lbs. (11 Nm).

13. Install the differential cover and fill the differential with gear lubricant.

14. Install the rear brake components.

Seal

1. Before servicing the vehicle, refer to the Precautions Section.

2. Remove the axle shaft.

3. Remove the axle shaft seal from the end of the axle tube using a pry bar.

To install:

4. Remove any old sealer/burrs from the axle tube.

5. Coat the new seal lip with axle lubricant and install the seal with Installer C-4198 and Handle C-4171.

6. Install axle shaft.

Bearing

See Figure 49.

1. Before servicing the vehicle, refer to the Precautions Section.

2. Remove the axle shaft.

3. Remove the axle seal with a pry bar.

4. Position the Bearing Remover 6310 on the axle tube.

5. Insert the Bearing Remover 6310 with Foot 6310-9 through the receiver and bearing.

6. Tighten the Remove 6310 nut to pull the bearing into the receiver.

To install:

7. Remove any old sealer/burrs from the axle tube.

8. Install the axle shaft bearing with Installer C-4198 and Handle C-4171.

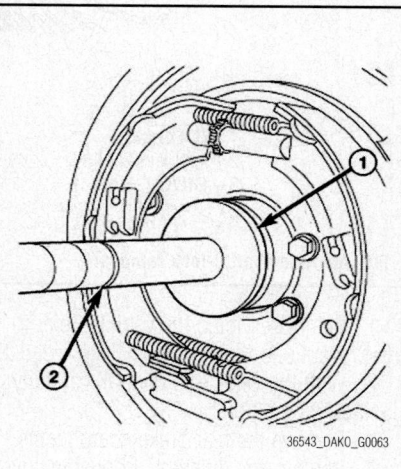

36543_DAKO_G0063

Fig. 49 Using Installer C-4198 and Handle C-4171 to install the rear axle bearing

9. Drive the bearing in until the tool contacts the axle tube.

➡**The bearing is installed with the bearing part number against the installer.**

10. Coat the new axle seal lip with axle lubricant and install with Installer C-4198 and Handle C-4171.

11. Install the axle shaft.

REAR PINION SEAL

REMOVAL & INSTALLATION

See Figures 50 and 51.

1. Before servicing the vehicle, refer to the Precautions Section.

2. With the vehicle in neutral, carefully position it on a hoist.

3. Remove the propeller shaft.

4. Remove the rear brake components to prevent any drag.

5. Rotate the pinion several times to verify the flange rotates smoothly.

6. Record the pinion torque to rotate with an inch pound torque wrench and for installation reference.

7. Install 2 bolts into the companion flange threaded holes, 180° apart. Position the Holder 6719A against the companion flange and install and tighten 2

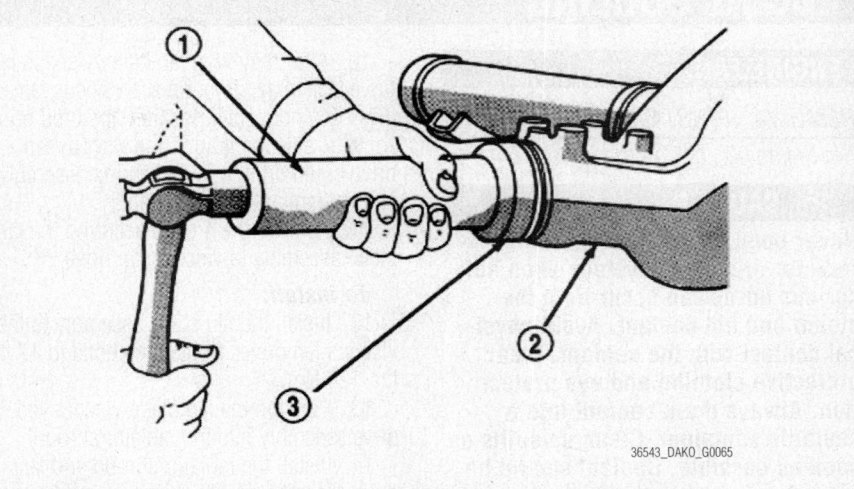

Fig. 51 Install the new pinion seal with Installer C-4076-B and Handle C-4735

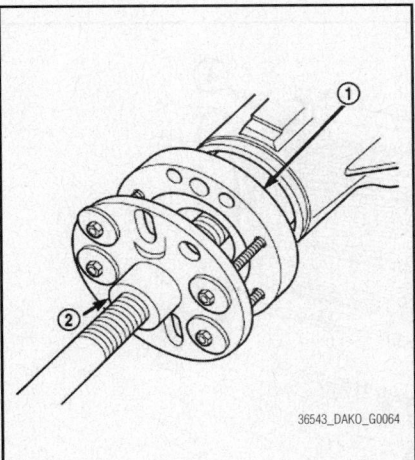

Fig. 50 Remove the companion flange (1) with Puller C-452 (2)

bolts and washers into the remaining holes.

8. Hold the companion flange with Holder 6719A and remove the pinion nut and washer.

9. Mark a line across the pinion shaft and the flange for installation reference.

10. Remove the companion flange (1) with Puller C-452 (2).

11. Remove the pinion seal with a seal puller.

To install:

12. Apply a light coating of gear lubricant on the lip of the pinion seal.

13. Install the new pinion seal with Installer C-4076-B (3) and Handle C-4735 (1) into the rear differential (2).

14. Install the companion flange on the end of the shaft with the reference marks aligned.

15. Install 2 bolts into the threaded holes in the companion flange, 180° apart.

16. Position Holder 6719A against the companion flange and install a bolt and washer into one of the remaining threaded holes. Tighten the bolts so the holder is held to the flange.

17. Install the companion flange on the pinion shaft with Installer C-3718 and Holder 6719A.

18. Install the pinion washer and a new

pinion nut. The convex side of the washer must face outward.

19. Hold the companion flange with Holder 6719A and tighten the pinion nut with a torque wrench to 210 ft. lbs. (285 Nm).

➡**Do not exceed the minimum torque of 210 ft. lbs. (285 Nm) when installing the pinion nut at this point.**

20. Rotate the pinion several times to ensure the pinion bearings are seated.

21. Measure the pinion torque to rotate with an inch pound torque wrench. The pinion torque to rotate should be equal to the recorded reading plus an additional 5 inch lbs. (0.56 Nm). If the pinion torque to rotate is low, tighten the pinion nut in 60 inch lbs. (7 Nm) increments until the proper pinion torque to rotating is achieved.

✳✳ WARNING

Never loosen the pinion nut to decrease the pinion bearing rotating torque. If the pinion torque to rotating is exceeded, a new collapsible spacer must be installed. Failure to follow these instructions will result in damage to the axle.

22. Install the propeller shaft.

23. Install the rear brake rotors components.

ENGINE COOLING

ENGINE FAN

REMOVAL & INSTALLATION
See Figure 52.

✳✳ CAUTION

Never open, service, or drain the radiator or cooling system when hot; serious burns can occur from the steam and hot coolant. Avoid physical contact with the coolant. Wear protective clothing and eye protection. Always drain coolant into a sealable container. Clean up spills as soon as possible. Coolant should be reused unless it is contaminated or is several years old.

1. Before servicing the vehicle, refer to the Precautions Section.
2. Disconnect the negative battery cable.
3. Partially drain the cooling system.
4. Remove the upper radiator hose.
5. Remove the air filter housing assembly.
6. Using Tool 6958 and adapter pins 8346 (1), remove the fan/viscous fan drive assembly from the water pump (2).

➡**Do not attempt to remove the fan/viscous fan drive assembly from vehicle at this time.**

7. Position the fan/viscous fan drive assembly in the radiator shroud.
8. Remove the 2 shroud mounting screws.
9. Remove the radiator shroud and fan drive assembly together.

10. After removing fan blade/viscous fan drive assembly, do not place viscous fan drive in a horizontal position. If stored horizontally, silicone fluid in the viscous fan drive could drain into its bearing assembly and contaminate the lubricant.
11. Remove the 4 bolts securing the fan blade assembly to viscous fan drive.

To install:
12. Install the fan blade assembly to the viscous fan drive. Tighten the bolts to 17 ft. lbs. (23 Nm).
13. Position the fan blade/viscous fan drive assembly into the radiator shroud.
14. Install the radiator shroud and fan drive assembly into the vehicle.
15. Install the fan shroud retaining screws and tighten to 50 inch lbs. (6 Nm).
16. Install the fan blade/viscous fan drive assembly to the water pump shaft.
17. Install the upper radiator hose.
18. Fill cooling system to the proper level with the correct type of fluid.
19. Connect the battery negative cable.

RADIATOR

REMOVAL & INSTALLATION
See Figures 53 and 54.

✳✳ CAUTION

Never open, service, or drain the radiator or cooling system when hot; serious burns can occur from the steam and hot coolant. Avoid physical contact with the coolant. Wear protective clothing and eye protection. Always drain coolant into a sealable container. Clean up spills as soon as possible. Coolant should be reused unless it is contaminated or is several years old.

1. Before servicing the vehicle, refer to the Precautions Section.
2. Disconnect the battery negative cable.
3. Drain the cooling system.
4. Remove the push-pins and the upper condenser/radiator seal (1).
5. Remove the upper radiator hose.
6. Disconnect the power steering hoses from the power steering fluid cooler.
7. If equipped, disconnect the transmission oil cooler lines.
8. Remove the radiator overflow tube.
9. Remove the radiator fan shroud from the radiator and position it over the radiator fan.
10. Raise and safely support the vehicle.

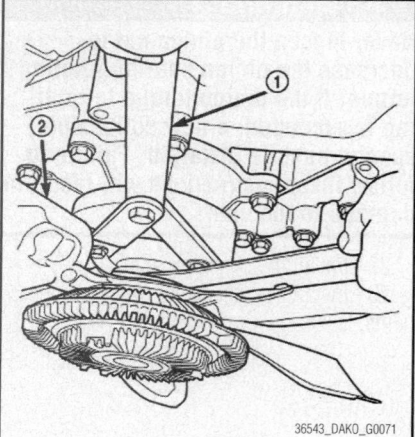

Fig. 52 Using Tool 6958 and adapter pins 8346 (1), remove the fan/viscous fan drive assembly from the water pump (2)

36543_DAKO_G0071

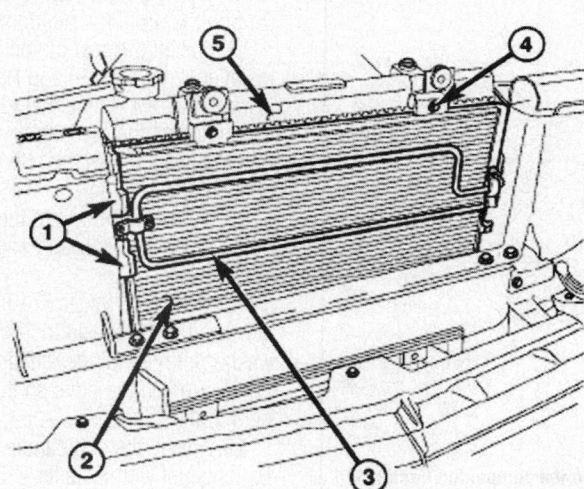

1. Upper condenser/radiator seal
2. Radiator
3. Power steering fluid cooler
4. Upper radiator mounting bolts
5. Upper radiator tank

36543_DAKO_G0072

Fig. 53 Radiator removal

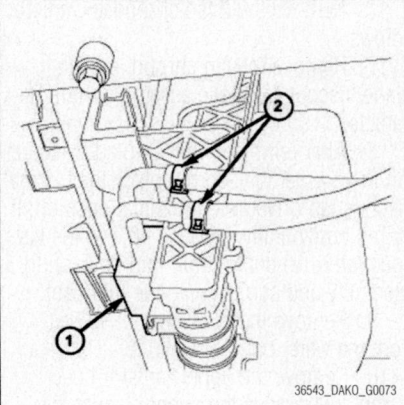

Fig. 54 Disconnect the power steering cooler lines (2) from the fluid cooler (1)

11. Disconnect the power steering cooler lines (2).
12. Remove the lower radiator hose.
13. Lower the vehicle.
14. Remove the upper radiator mounting bolts.
15. Remove the radiator.
16. Remove the power steering fluid oil cooler from the radiator, if necessary.
17. Remove the A/C condenser from the radiator.

To install:

➥The radiator has 2 isolator pins on the bottom of both tanks. These fit into alignment holes in the radiator lower support.

18. Install the A/C condenser, if removed.
19. Install the power steering cooler, if removed.
20. Install the transmission oil cooler, if removed.
21. Install the upper radiator mount.
22. Position the isolator pins into the alignment holes in the radiator lower support.
23. Install the upper radiator support. Tighten the bolts to 200 inch lbs. (23 Nm).
24. Install the LH and the RH radiator side seals.
25. Install the upper radiator hose.
26. Install the radiator overflow tube.
27. Install the radiator shroud.
28. Install the power steering cooler lines.
29. If equipped, install the transmission cooler lines.
30. Install the lower radiator hose.
31. Lower the vehicle.
32. Fill the radiator with the proper amount and type of fluid.

33. Connect the battery negative cable.
34. Start and warm the engine. Check for antifreeze/coolant leaks.

THERMOSTAT

REMOVAL & INSTALLATION

3.7L & 4.7L Engines
See Figure 55.

✽✽ CAUTION

Never open, service, or drain the radiator or cooling system when hot; serious burns can occur from the steam and hot coolant. Avoid physical contact with the coolant. Wear protective clothing and eye protection. Always drain coolant into a sealable container. Clean up spills as soon as possible. Coolant should be reused unless it is contaminated or is several years old.

1. Before servicing the vehicle, refer to the Precautions Section.
2. Disconnect the negative battery cable.
3. Drain the cooling system.
4. Raise and safely support the vehicle.

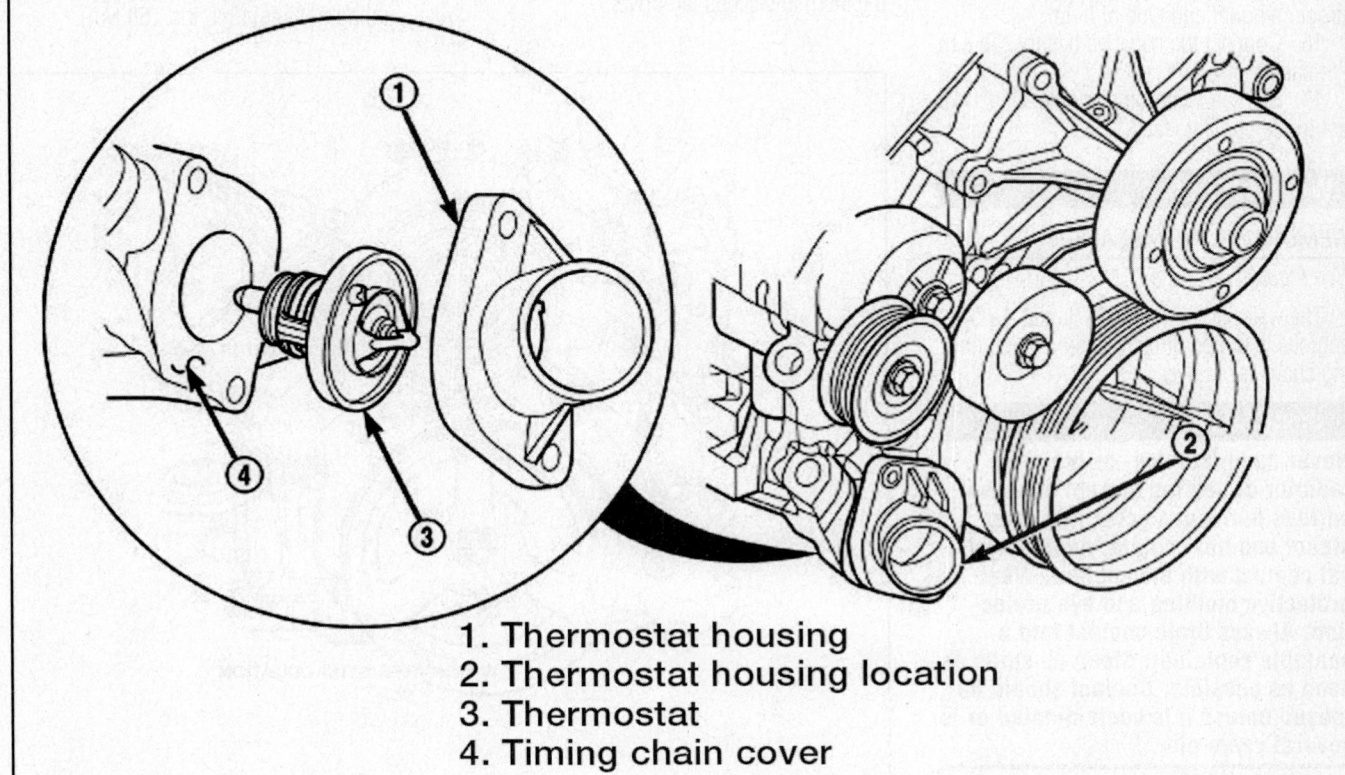

1. Thermostat housing
2. Thermostat housing location
3. Thermostat
4. Timing chain cover

Fig. 55 View of thermostat housing

5. Remove the splash shield (4.7L only).

6. Remove the lower radiator hose from the thermostat housing.

7. Remove the thermostat housing mounting bolts, thermostat housing (1), and thermostat (3).

To install:

8. Clean the mating areas of the timing chain cover and the thermostat housing.

9. Install the thermostat (spring side down) into the recessed machined groove on the timing chain cover.

10. Position the thermostat housing on the timing chain cover.

11. Install the 2 housing-to-timing chain cover bolts. Tighten the bolts to 112 inch lbs. (13 Nm).

❊❊ WARNING

The housing must be tightened evenly and the thermostat must be centered into the recessed groove in the timing chain cover. If not, it may result in a cracked housing, damaged timing chain cover threads, and/or coolant leaks.

12. Install the lower radiator hose on the thermostat housing.

13. Install the splash shield (4.7L only).

14. Lower the vehicle.

15. Fill the cooling system with the proper amount and type of fluid.

16. Connect the negative battery cable to the battery.

17. Start and warm the engine. Check for antifreeze/coolant leaks.

WATER PUMP

REMOVAL & INSTALLATION

See Figures 56 and 57.

The water pump on the 3.7L and 4.7L engines is bolted directly to the engine timing chain case cover.

❊❊ CAUTION

Never open, service, or drain the radiator or cooling system when hot; serious burns can occur from the steam and hot coolant. Avoid physical contact with the coolant. Wear protective clothing and eye protection. Always drain coolant into a sealable container. Clean up spills as soon as possible. Coolant should be reused unless it is contaminated or is several years old.

1. Before servicing the vehicle, refer to the Precautions Section.

Fig. 56 Remove the accessory drive belt from the water pump pulley (2)

2. Disconnect the negative battery cable.

3. Drain the cooling system.

4. Remove the fan/viscous fan drive assembly from the water pump. Refer to Engine Fan, removal & installation.

➡**Do not attempt to remove the fan/viscous fan drive assembly from vehicle at this time.**

5. If the water pump is being replaced, do not unbolt the fan blade assembly from the thermal viscous fan drive.

6. Remove the 2 fan shroud-to-radiator screws.

7. Remove the fan shroud and fan blade/viscous fan drive assembly from the vehicle.

8. After removing the fan blade/viscous fan drive assembly, do not place the thermal viscous fan drive in a horizontal position. If stored horizontally, silicone fluid in the viscous fan drive could drain into its bearing assembly and contaminate the lubricant.

9. Remove the accessory drive belt from the water pump pulley (2).

10. Remove the upper radiator hose clamp and remove the upper hose at the water pump.

11. Remove the 7 water pump mounting bolts and 1 stud bolt.

❊❊ WARNING

Do not pry on the water pump at the timing chain case/cover. The machined surfaces may be damaged resulting in leakage.

12. Remove the water pump and the gasket. Discard the gasket.

To install:

13. Clean the gasket mating surfaces.

14. Using a new gasket, position the water pump (1) and install the mounting bolts as shown. Tighten the water pump mounting bolts to 43 ft. lbs. (58 Nm).

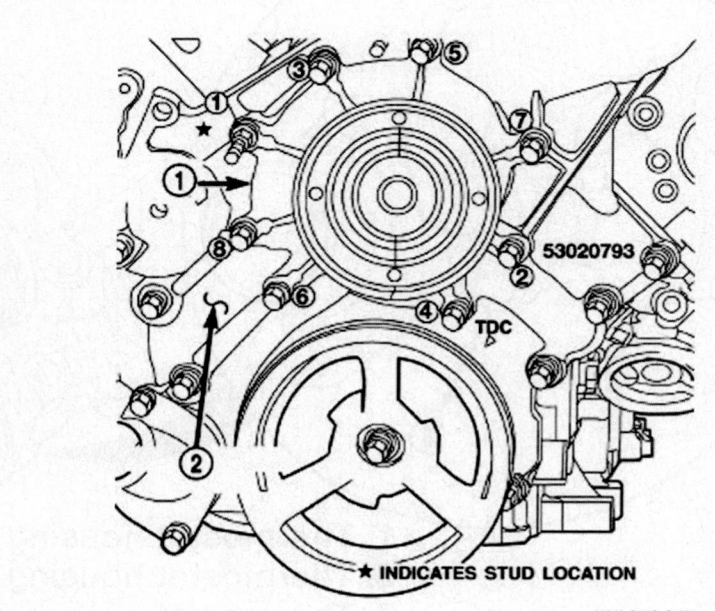

Fig. 57 Position the water pump (1) on the timing chain cover (2). Torque the mounting bolts in the order shown

15. Spin the water pump to be sure that the pump impeller does not rub against the timing chain case/cover.

16. Connect the upper radiator hose to the water pump.

17. Install the accessory drive belt.

18. Position the fan shroud and the fan blade/viscous fan drive assembly.

19. Install the 2 fan shroud-to-radiator screws.

20. Make sure there is 1 inch (25mm) between the tips of the fan blades and the fan shroud.

21. Install the fan blade/viscous fan drive assembly to the water pump shaft.

22. Fill the cooling system with the proper amount and type of fluid.

23. Connect the negative battery cable to the battery.

24. Start and warm the engine. Check for antifreeze/coolant leaks.

ENGINE ELECTRICAL

ALTERNATOR

REMOVAL & INSTALLATION

See Figures 58 and 59.

1. Before servicing the vehicle, refer to the Precautions Section.

✳✳ WARNING

Disconnect the negative cable from the battery before removing the battery output wire (B+) from the alternator. Failure to do so can result in injury or damage to the electrical system.

2. Disconnect the negative battery cable at the battery.

3. Remove the alternator drive belt.

4. Unsnap the plastic insulator cap (3) from the B+ output terminal.

5. Remove the B+ terminal mounting nut (2) at the rear of the alternator. Disconnect the terminal from the alternator.

6. Disconnect the field wire connector (4) at the rear of the alternator by pushing on the connector tab.

7. Remove the 1 rear vertical alternator mounting bolt (2).

8. Remove the 2 front horizontal alternator mounting bolts (1).

CHARGING SYSTEM

9. Remove the alternator from the vehicle.

To install:

10. Position the alternator (3) to the engine and install the 2 horizontal bolts (1) and 1 vertical bolt (2).

11. Tighten all 3 bolts:
- Short horizontal bolt to 55 ft. lbs. (74 Nm)
- Vertical bolt and long horizontal bolt to 40 ft. lbs. (55 Nm)

12. Snap the field wire connector (4) into the rear of the alternator.

13. Install the B+ terminal eyelet to the alternator output stud and tighten to 125 inch lbs. (14 Nm).

✳✳ WARNING

Never force a belt over a pulley rim using a screwdriver. The synthetic fiber of the belt can be damaged.

➥When installing a serpentine accessory drive belt, the belt must be routed correctly. The water pump may be rotating in the wrong direction if the belt is installed incorrectly, causing the engine to overheat. Refer to the belt routing label in the engine compartment.

14. Install the alternator drive belt.

15. Install the negative battery cable to the battery.

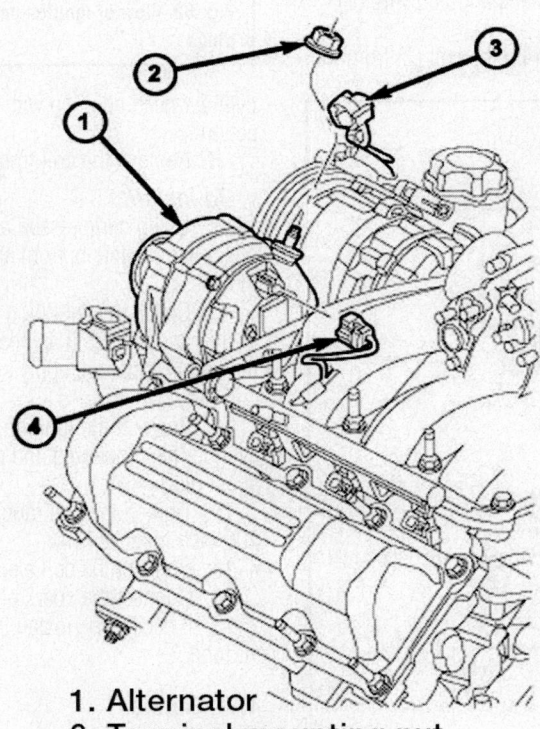

1. Alternator
2. Terminal mounting nut
3. Plastic insulator cap
4. Field wire connector

36543_DAKO_G0077

Fig. 58 Disconnect the electrical connections from the alternator

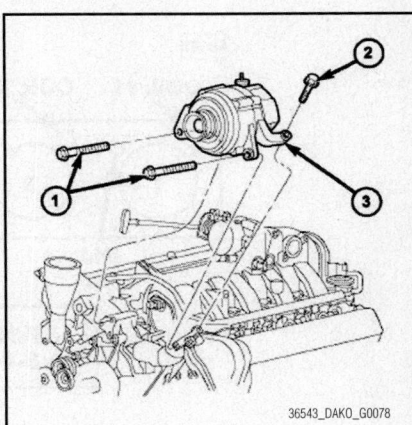

36543_DAKO_G0078

Fig. 59 Remove the alternator mounting bolts

FIRING ORDERS

See Figures 60 and 61.

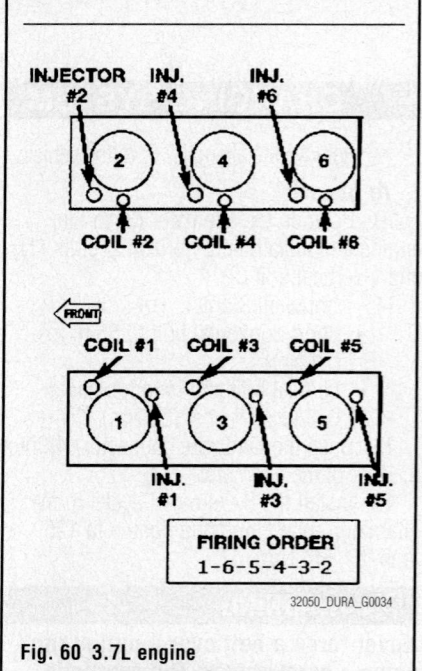

Fig. 60 3.7L engine
FIRING ORDER: 1-6-5-4-3-2

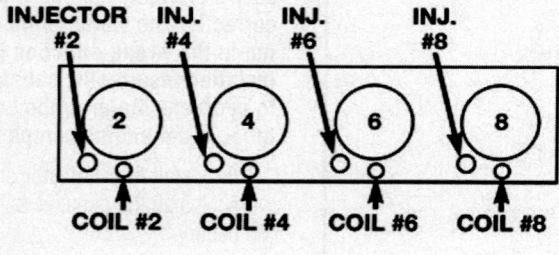

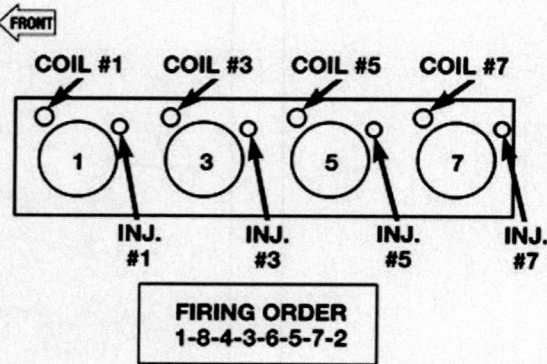

Fig. 61 4.7L engine
FIRING ORDER: 1-8-4-3-6-5-7-2

IGNITION COIL

REMOVAL & INSTALLATION

3.7L Engine

See Figure 62.

An individual ignition coil is used for each pair of spark plugs. Each coil attaches directly to the top of the upper bank of spark plugs. Secondary cables connect each coil to the lower bank of spark plugs. The coils themselves fit into machined holes in the cylinder head. Each coil also has its own individual electrical connector.

1. Before servicing the vehicle, refer to the Precautions Section.
2. Depending on which coil is being removed, the throttle body air intake tube or intake box may need to be removed to gain access to the coil.
3. Disconnect the coil electrical connector(s).
4. Clean the area at the base of the coil with compressed air before removal.
5. Remove the coil mounting bolt (3).
6. Disconnect the spark plug wire (1) from the coil (2).
7. Carefully pull up the coil (2) from the

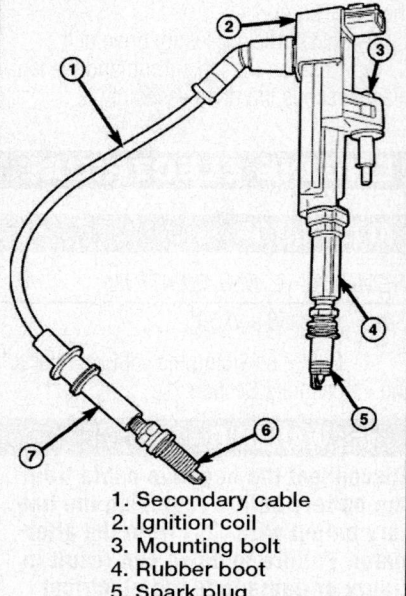

1. Secondary cable
2. Ignition coil
3. Mounting bolt
4. Rubber boot
5. Spark plug
6. Spark plug
7. Rubber boot

Fig. 62 View of ignition coil and spark plugs

cylinder head opening with a slight twisting action.

8. Remove the coil from the vehicle.

To install:

9. Using compressed air, blow out any dirt or contaminants from around the top of the spark plug.
10. Check the condition of the coil O-ring and replace it as necessary. To aid in the coil installation, apply silicone to the coil O-ring.
11. Position the ignition coil (2) into the cylinder head opening and push it onto the spark plug.
12. Tighten the coil mounting bolt to 106 inch lbs. (12 Nm).
13. Connect the coil electrical connector.
14. Connect the spark plug wires.
15. If necessary, install the throttle body air tube.

4.7L Engine

See Figures 62 and 63.

An individual ignition coil (1) is used for each pair of spark plugs. Each coil attaches directly to the top of the 8 upper bank of spark plugs. Secondary cables (3) connect each coil to the 8 lower bank of spark plugs.

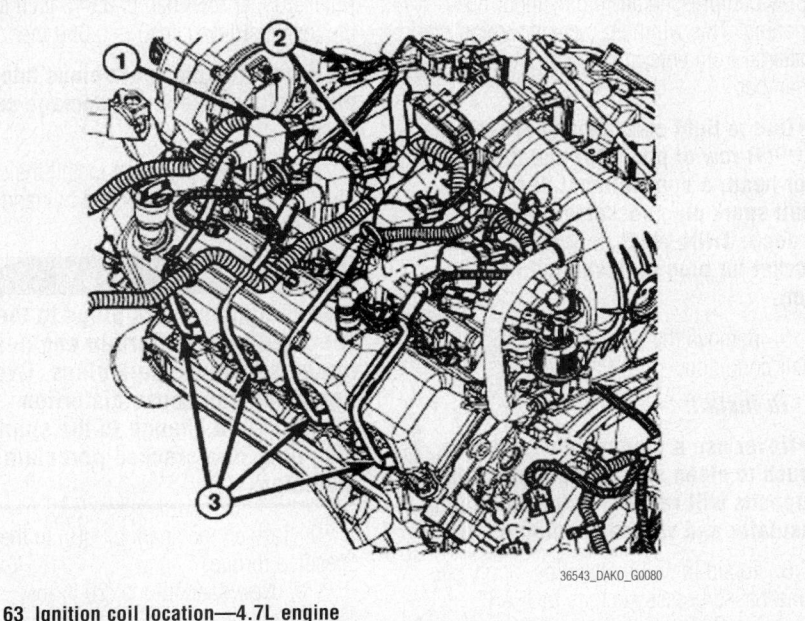

36543_DAKO_G0080

Fig. 63 Ignition coil location—4.7L engine

The coils themselves fit into machined holes in the cylinder head. Each coil also has its own individual electrical connector (2).

A mounting bolt (3) secures each coil assembly to the top of the intake manifold. The bottom of the coil assembly is equipped with a rubber boot (4) to seal the spark plug (5) to the coil. Inside each rubber boot is a spring. The spring is used for a mechanical contact between the coil and the top of the upper bank of spark plugs. These rubber boots and springs are a permanent part of the coil assembly and are not serviced separately. The rubber boot (4) is also used to seal the coil at the opening into the cylinder head.

➡The bolt used to mount the ignition coil assembly is the same bolt used to mount the intake manifold. If replacing either one or all eight coils, check and re-torque all eight bolts.

1. Before servicing the vehicle, refer to the Precautions Section.
2. Depending on which coil assembly is being removed, the throttle body air intake tube or intake box may need to be removed, to gain access to the coil.
3. Disconnect the electrical connector (2) from the coil assembly by pushing downward on the release lock on the top of the connector and pull the connector from the coil.
4. Disconnect the secondary cable (3) at the coil assembly.
5. Clean the area at the base of the coil assembly with compressed air before removal.

6. Remove the coil assembly mounting bolt (3).
7. Carefully pull up the coil assembly (2) from the cylinder head opening with a slight twisting action. This helps to disengage the rubber boot (4) from the spark plug (5).
8. Remove the coil assembly from the engine.

To install:
9. Using compressed air, blow out any dirt or contaminants from around the top of the spark plug.
10. Check the condition of the coil rubber boot (4). To aid in coil installation, apply silicone-based grease such as MOPAR® Dielectric Grease J8126688 into the spark plug end of the rubber boot (4) and to the top of the spark plug (5).
11. Position the ignition coil assembly into the cylinder head opening. Using a twisting action, push the ignition coil assembly onto the spark plug.
12. Tighten the coil assembly mounting bolt (3) to 106 inch lbs. (12 Nm).
13. Connect the electrical connector (2) to the coil assembly by snapping it into position.
14. Connect the secondary cable (3) to the coil assembly (1).
15. If necessary, install the throttle body air intake tube or intake air box to the top of the engine.

IGNITION TIMING

The ignition timing is controlled by the Powertrain Control Module (PCM). No adjustment is necessary or possible.

SPARK PLUGS

REMOVAL & INSTALLATION

3.7L Engine
See Figure 62.

1. Before servicing the vehicle, refer to the Precautions Section.
2. Remove the necessary air filter tubing and air intake components at the top of the engine at the throttle body.

➡The 3 spark plugs located on the left bank of the engine are under 3 individual ignition coils. Each individual ignition coil must be removed to gain access to the spark plug located on the left bank of the engine.

3. Prior to removing the ignition coil, spray compressed air around the coil base at the cylinder head.
4. Remove the ignition coil and check the condition of the ignition coil O-ring and replace as necessary.
5. Prior to removing the spark plug, spray compressed air into the cylinder head opening. This will help prevent foreign material from entering the combustion chamber.
6. Remove the spark plug from the cylinder head using a quality thin wall socket with a rubber or foam insert.
7. Inspect the spark plug condition.

To install:
8. Check and adjust the spark plug gap to specification with a gap gauging tool.

✳✳ WARNING

Special care should be taken when installing spark plugs into the cylinder head spark plug wells. Be sure the plugs do not drop into the plug wells as the electrodes can be damaged.

9. Start the spark plug into the cylinder head by hand to avoid cross threading.
10. Tighten the spark plugs to 20 ft. lbs. (27 Nm).
11. Before installing the ignition coil, check the condition of the coil O-ring and replace as necessary. Apply silicone-based grease such as MOPAR® Dielectric Grease J8126688 into the spark plug end of the rubber boot, coil O-rings, and to the top of spark plugs.
12. Install the ignition coil. Refer to Ignition Coil Pack, removal & installation.
13. Install the necessary air filter tubing

and air intake components at the top of the engine at the throttle body.

4.7L Engine

See Figure 62.

This engine uses TWO DIFFERENT types of spark plugs. A total of 16 plugs are used. The plugs are mounted in 2 rows (banks). The upper row (5) is used on the intake valve side of the cylinder head. The lower row (6) is used on the exhaust valve side of the cylinder head. The upper row (5) uses Bosch Nickel Yttrium plugs. The lower row (6) uses Bosch Iridium plugs. DO NOT INTERCHANGE THESE PLUGS.

1. Before servicing the vehicle, refer to the Precautions Section.

2. Remove the necessary air filter tubing and air intake components at the top of the engine and at the throttle body.

➡**To remove the upper row of spark plugs (5), each individual ignition coil (2) must be removed first.**

3. Remove the ignition coil(s). Refer to Ignition Coil Pack, removal & installation.

4. Prior to removing the spark plug(s), spray compressed air into cylinder head opening. This will help prevent foreign material from entering the combustion chamber.

➡**Due to tight clearances between the UPPER row of plugs (5) and the cylinder head, a conventional deep, thickwall spark plug socket will not fit. Use a deep, THIN-WALL ⅝ inch spark plug socket for plug removal and installation.**

5. Remove the spark plug(s) and inspect their condition.

To install:

➡**Never use a motorized wire wheel brush to clean spark plugs. Metallic deposits will remain on the spark plug insulator and will cause plug misfire.**

6. To aid in coil installation, apply silicone-based grease such as MOPAR® Dielectric Grease into the spark plug end of the rubber boots (4) and (7). Also, apply this grease to the tops of spark plugs (5) and (6).

7. Two different spark plug gaps are used. Check and adjust spark plug gap(s) with a plug gap gauging tool. The 4.7L (intake/upper row) gap is 0.040 inch and the (exhaust/lower row) is 0.050 inch.

➡**Do not drop the spark plugs into the plug wells as electrode damage can occur.**

8. Using special care, install the spark plug(s) into the cylinder head by hand to avoid cross threading.

✳✳ WARNING

Always tighten spark plugs to the specified torque. Certain engines use torque sensitive spark plugs. Overtightening can cause distortion resulting in a change to the spark plug gap, or a cracked porcelain insulator.

9. Tighten the spark plug(s) to the specified torque.
   a. New spark plugs: 20 ft. lbs. (27 Nm).
   b. Used spark plugs: 16 ft. lbs. (22 Nm).

10. Install the ignition coil(s). Refer to Ignition Coil Pack, removal & installation.

11. Install the necessary air filter tubing and air intake components to the top of the engine and to the throttle body.

ENGINE ELECTRICAL

STARTING SYSTEM

STARTER

REMOVAL & INSTALLATION

3.7L and 4.7L Engines

With Manual Transmission

See Figure 64.

1. Before servicing the vehicle, refer to the Precautions Section.

2. Disconnect and isolate the negative battery cable.

3. Raise and safely support the vehicle.

4. If equipped with 4WD and certain transmissions, a support bracket is used between the front axle and the side of the transmission. Remove the 2 support bracket bolts at the transmission. Pry the support bracket slightly to gain access to the lower starter mounting bolt.

5. Remove the mounting bolt (9) and the nut (8) from the starter.

6. Move the starter motor (5) towards the front of the vehicle far enough for the nose of the starter pinion housing to clear the housing.

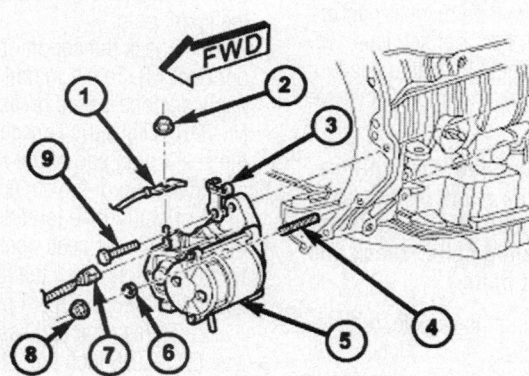

1. Connector eyelet (B+)
2. Nut on connector eyelet (B+)
3. Ground connection
4. Stud
5. Starter motor
6. Lock washer
7. Wire harness connector
8. Mounting nut
9. Mounting bolt

36543_DAKO_G0082

Fig. 64 Starter removal—manual transmission

✳✳ WARNING

Always support the starter motor during this process, do not let the starter motor hang from the wire harness.

7. Tilt the nose downwards and lower the starter motor far enough to access and remove the nut (2) that secures the battery positive cable wire harness connector eyelet to the solenoid battery terminal stud.

8. Remove the battery positive cable wire harness connector eyelet (1) from the solenoid battery terminal stud.

9. Disconnect the battery positive cable wire harness connector (7) from the solenoid terminal connector receptacle.

10. Remove the starter motor.

To install:

11. Connect the solenoid wire to the starter motor (snaps on).

12. Position the battery cable (1) to the solenoid stud. Install the battery cable eyelet nut (2) and tighten to 19 ft. lbs. (25 Nm).

✳✳ WARNING

Do not allow the starter motor to hang from the wire harness.

13. Position the starter motor (5) to the transmission.

14. Install and tighten the lockwasher (6), nut (8), and bolt (9). Tighten the bolt and nut to 50 ft. lbs. (68 Nm).

15. Lower the vehicle.

16. Connect the negative battery cable.

With Automatic Transmission

See Figure 65.

1. Before servicing the vehicle, refer to the Precautions Section.

2. Disconnect and isolate negative battery cable.

3. Raise and safely support the vehicle.

4. If equipped with 4WD and certain transmissions, a support bracket is used

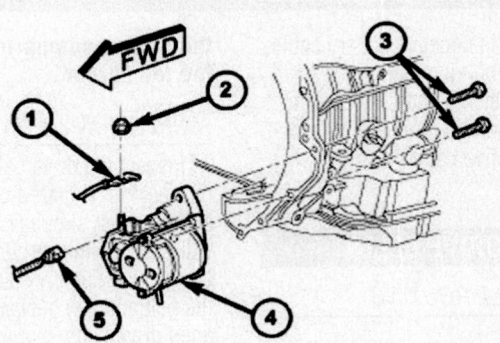

1. Wire harness connector eyelet (B+)
2. Nut on connector eyelet (B+)
3. Mounting bolts
4. Starter motor
5. Solenoid connector eyelet

36543_DAKO_G0083

Fig. 65 Starter removal—automatic transmission

between the front axle and the side of the transmission. Remove the 2 support bracket bolts at the transmission. Pry the support bracket slightly to gain access to the lower starter mounting bolt.

5. Remove the 2 starter mounting bolts (3).

6. Move the starter motor (4) towards the front of the vehicle far enough for the nose of the starter pinion housing to clear the housing.

✳✳ WARNING

Always support starter motor during this process, do not let the starter motor hang from the wire harness.

7. Tilt the nose downwards and lower the starter motor far enough to access and remove the nut (2) that secures the battery positive cable wire harness connector eyelet (1) to the solenoid battery terminal stud.

8. Remove the battery positive cable

wire harness connector eyelet (5) from the solenoid battery terminal stud.

9. Disconnect the battery positive cable wire harness connector from the solenoid terminal connector receptacle.

10. Remove the starter motor.

To install:

11. Connect the solenoid wire to the starter motor (snaps on).

12. Position the battery cable (1) to the solenoid stud. Install and the tighten battery cable eyelet nut (2) and tighten to 19 ft. lbs. (25 Nm).

13. Position the starter motor (4) to the transmission.

14. If equipped with an automatic transmission, slide the cooler tube bracket into position.

15. Install and tighten both bolts (3) to 50 ft. lbs. (68 Nm).

16. Lower the vehicle.

17. Connect the negative battery cable.

ENGINE MECHANICAL

Disconnecting the negative battery cable may interfere with the functions of the on board computer systems and may require the computer to undergo a relearning process once the negative battery cable is reconnected.

ACCESSORY DRIVE BELTS

ACCESSORY BELT ROUTING
See Figure 66.

➡The belt routing schematics are published from the latest information available at the time of publication. If anything differs between these schematics and the Belt Routing Label, use the schematics on Belt Routing Label. This label is located in the engine compartment, usually on the fan shroud.

INSPECTION

Inspect the drive belt for signs of glazing or cracking. A glazed belt will be perfectly smooth from slippage, while a good belt will have a slight texture of fabric visible. Cracks will usually start at the inner edge of the belt and run outward. All worn or damaged drive belts should be replaced immediately.

ADJUSTMENT

It is not necessary to adjust the belt tension on the 3.7L or 4.7L engines. These engines are equipped with an automatic belt tensioner. The tensioner maintains correct belt tension at all times; consequently, do not attempt to use a belt tension gauge on these engines.

REMOVAL & INSTALLATION
See Figures 66 and 67.

1. Before servicing the vehicle, refer to the Precautions Section.
2. Disconnect the negative battery cable.
3. Rotate the belt tensioner until it contacts the stop.

✸✸ WARNING

Do not let the tensioner arm snap back to the free-arm position, severe damage may occur to the tensioner.

4. Remove the accessory drive belt, then slowly rotate the tensioner into the free-arm position.

To install:
5. Check the condition of all the pulleys.

✸✸ WARNING

When installing the serpentine accessory drive belt, the belt MUST be routed correctly. If not, the engine may overheat due to the water pump rotating in the wrong direction.

6. Install the new belt. Route the belt around all the pulleys except the idler pulley. Rotate the tensioner arm until it contacts the stop position. Route the belt around the idler and slowly let the tensioner rotate into the belt. Make sure the belt is seated onto all pulleys.
7. With the drive belt installed, inspect the belt wear indicator on the tensioner (1).
8. On 4.7L engines only, the gap between the tang and the housing stop must

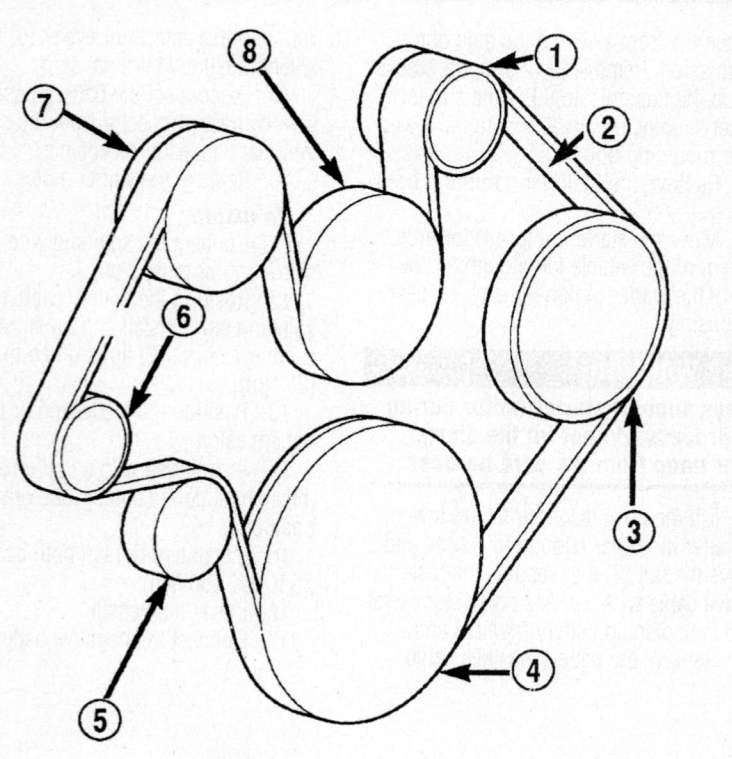

1 - GENERATOR PULLEY
2 - ACCESSORY DRIVE BELT
3 - POWER STEERING PUMP PULLEY
4 - CRANKSHAFT PULLEY
5 - IDLER PULLEY
6 - TENSIONER
7 - A/C COMPRESSOR PULLEY
8 - WATER PUMP PULLEY

67189-DAKO-G51

Fig. 66 Accessory drive belt routing—3.7L and 4.7L engines

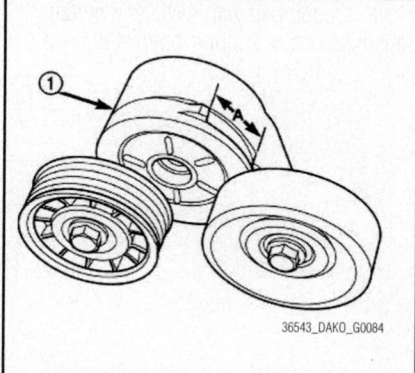

36543_DAKO_G0084

Fig. 67 With the drive belt installed, inspect the belt wear indicator on the tensioner (1)

not exceed .94 inches (24mm). If the measurement exceeds this specification, replace the serpentine accessory drive belt.

CAMSHAFT AND VALVE LIFTERS

REMOVAL & INSTALLATION

3.7L Engine

See Figures 68 through 72.

This procedure shows the left cylinder head camshaft, the right camshaft is similar.

1. Before servicing the vehicle, refer to the Precautions Section.
2. Disconnect the negative battery cable.

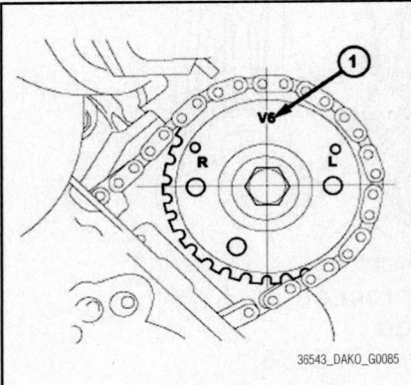

36543_DAKO_G0085

Fig. 68 Camshaft sprocket V6 mark at 12 o'clock position—3.7L engine

※※ **WARNING**

When the timing chain is removed and the cylinder heads are still installed, DO NOT forcefully rotate the camshafts or crankshaft independently of each other. Severe valve and/or piston damage can occur.

➡**When removing the cam sprocket, timing chains, or camshaft, failure to use Wedge Locking Tool 8379 will result in hydraulic tensioner ratchet over-extension, requiring timing chain cover removal to reset the tensioner ratchet.**

3. Remove the cylinder head cover.
4. Set the engine to Top Dead Center (TDC) cylinder No. 1. The camshaft sprocket V6 marks (1) will be at the 12 o'clock position.
5. Mark one link on the secondary timing chain on both sides of the V6 mark on the camshaft sprocket to aid in installation.
6. Loosen but **DO NOT** remove the camshaft sprocket retaining bolt. Leave the bolt snug against the sprocket.
7. Position the Wedge Locking Tool 8379 (1) between the timing chain strands, tap the tool to securely wedge the timing chain against the tensioner arm and guide.

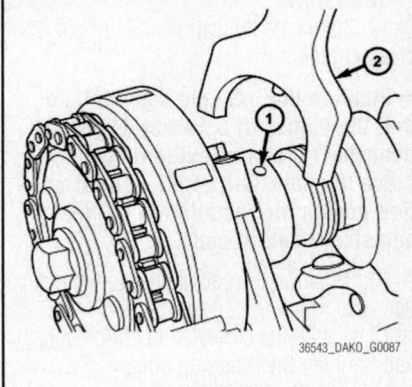

36543_DAKO_G0087

Fig. 70 View of Camshaft Holder 8428 (2) and alignment hole (1)

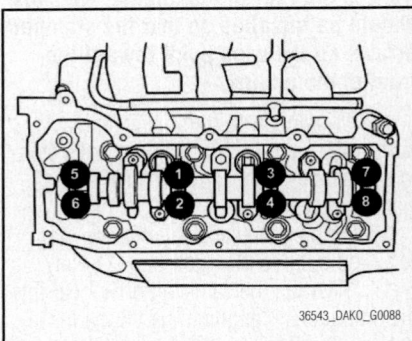

36543_DAKO_G0088

Fig. 71 Camshaft bearing tightening sequence—3.7L engine

※※ **WARNING**

Do not force the wedge past the narrowest point between the chain strands. Damage to the tensioners may occur.

8. Hold the camshaft with the Spanner Wrench 6958 and Adapter Pins 8346 while removing the camshaft sprocket bolt.
9. Using Camshaft Holder 8428 (2), remove the sprocket and gently allow the camshaft to rotate 5° clockwise until the camshaft is in the neutral position (no valve load).
10. Starting at the outside and working inward, loosen the camshaft bearing cap retaining bolts ½ turn at a time. Repeat until all the load is off of the bearing caps.

➡**When the camshaft is removed, the rocker arms may slide downward, mark the rocker arms before removing the camshaft.**

11. Remove the camshaft bearing caps and the camshaft.

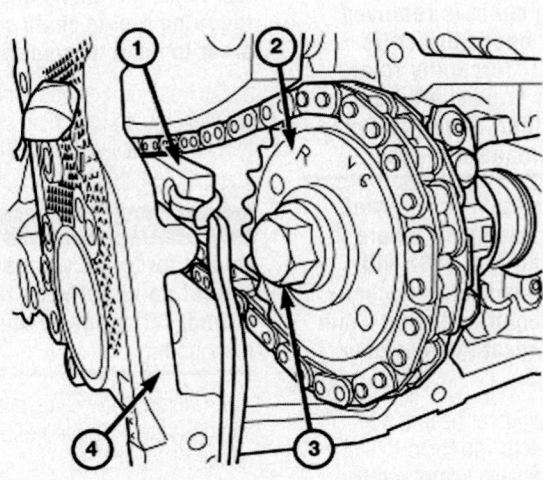

1. Wedge locking tool 8379
2. Camshaft sprocket
3. Camshaft bolt
4. Cylinder head

36543_DAKO_G0086

Fig. 69 Positioning Wedge Locking Tool 8379 (1)

To install:

12. Lubricate the camshaft journals with clean engine oil.

➡️Position the left side camshaft so that the camshaft sprocket dowel is near the 1 o'clock position. This will place the camshaft at the neutral position easing the installation of the camshaft bearing caps.

13. Position the camshaft into the cylinder head.

14. Install the camshaft bearing caps, hand tighten the retaining bolts.

➡️Caps should be installed so that the stamped numbers on the caps are in numerical order, (1 through 4) from the front to the rear of the engine. All caps should be installed so that the stamped arrows on the caps point toward the front of the engine.

15. Working in ½ turn increments, tighten the bearing cap retaining bolts starting with the middle cap and working outward.

16. Tighten the camshaft bearing cap retaining bolts to 100 inch lbs. (11 Nm).

17. Position the camshaft drive gear into the timing chain aligning the V6 mark between the 2 marked chain links (the 2 links marked during removal).

18. Using the Camshaft Holder 8428A, rotate the camshaft until the camshaft sprocket dowel is aligned with the slot in the camshaft sprocket. Install the sprocket onto the camshaft.

19. Remove any excess oil from the camshaft sprocket bolt, then install the camshaft sprocket retaining bolt and hand tighten. Failure to remove any excess oil from the bolt can cause over-torque resulting in bolt failure.

20. Remove the Wedge Locking Tool 8379.

21. Using Spanner Wrench 6958 with adapter pins 8346, tighten the camshaft sprocket retaining bolt to 90 ft. lbs. (122 Nm).

22. Install the cylinder head cover and tighten to 105 inch lbs. (12 Nm).

23. Connect the negative battery cable.

4.7L Engine

See Figures 72 through 77.

This procedure shows the left cylinder head camshaft, the right camshaft is similar.

1. Before servicing the vehicle, refer to the Precautions Section.

2. Disconnect the negative battery cable.

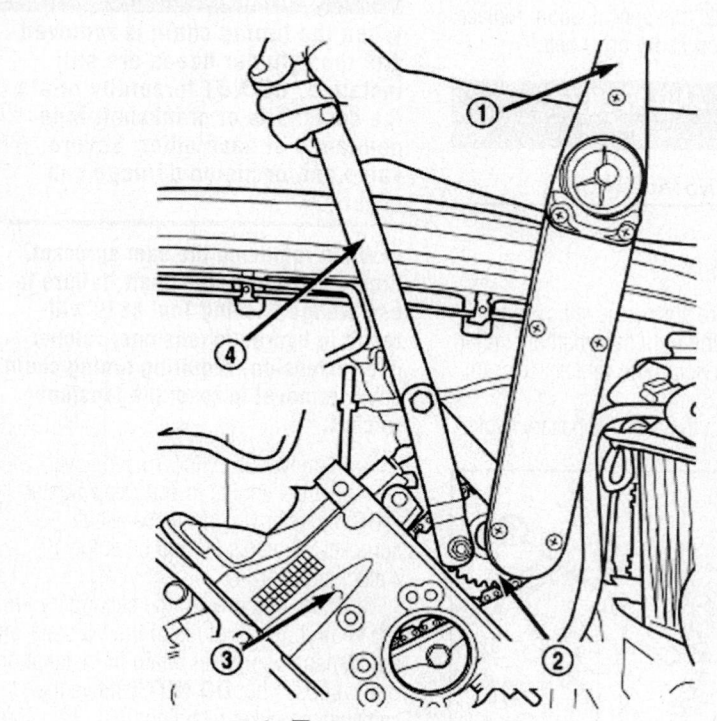

1. Torque wrench
2. Camshaft sprocket
3. Cylinder head
4. Spanner Wrench 6958

36543_DAKO_G0089

Fig. 72 Using Spanner Wrench 6958 with adapter pins 8346

✳️✳️ WARNING

When the timing chain is removed and the cylinder heads are still installed, DO NOT forcefully rotate the camshafts or crankshaft independently of each other. Severe valve and/or piston damage can occur.

➡️When removing the cam sprocket, timing chains, or camshaft, failure to use Wedge Locking Tool 9867 will result in hydraulic tensioner ratchet over-extension, requiring timing chain cover removal to reset the tensioner ratchet.

3. Remove the cylinder head cover.

4. Set the engine to Top Dead Center (TDC) cylinder 1, camshaft sprocket V8 marks at the 12 o'clock position.

5. Mark the link on the secondary timing chain that is aligned with the 2 dots on the cam sprocket, as shown, to aid in installation later.

➡️The timing chain tensioners must be secured prior to removing the camshaft

sprockets. Failure to secure tensioners will allow the tensioners to extend, requiring timing chain cover removal in order to reset tensioners.

6. Position Locking Wedge 9867 between the timing chain strands, tap the tool to securely wedge the timing chain against the tensioner arm and guide.

✳️✳️ WARNING

Do not force the wedge past the narrowest point between the chain strands. Damage to the tensioners may occur.

7. Remove the camshaft sprocket bolt using Spanner Wrench 6958 (4) with Adapter Pins 8346.

8. Install Camshaft Holder 8428A (1) on the camshaft (2).

✳️✳️ WARNING

Do not hold or pry on the camshaft target wheel (located on the right side camshaft sprocket) for any reason. Severe damage will occur to the

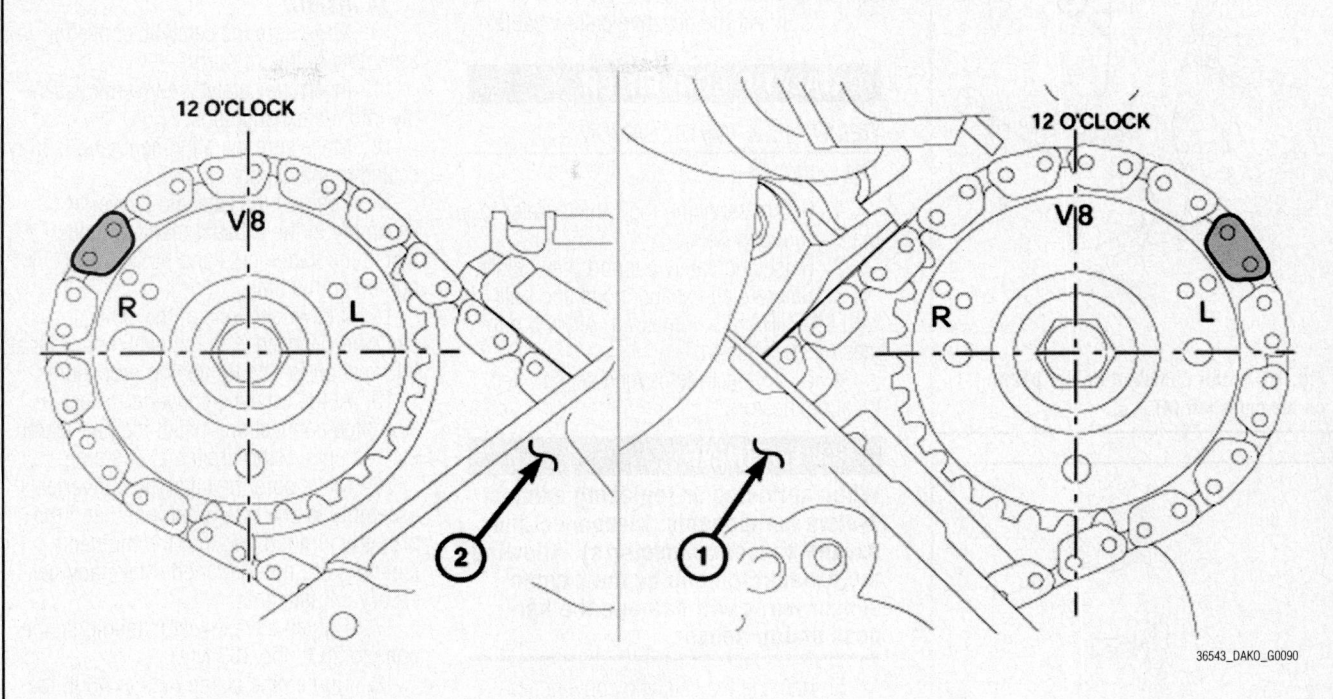

Fig. 73 Mark the link on the secondary timing chain that is aligned with the 2 dots on the cam sprocket to aid in installation

target wheel resulting in a vehicle no start condition.

9. Hold the camshaft with Camshaft Holder 8428A while removing the camshaft sprocket bolt and sprocket.

10. Using Camshaft Holder 8428A gently allow the camshaft to rotate 15° clockwise until the camshaft is in the neutral position (no valve load).

➡When the camshaft is removed the rocker arms may slide downward, mark the rocker arms before removing the camshaft.

11. Loosen the camshaft bearing cap retaining bolts ½ turn at a time. Start at the center and work outward. Repeat until all the load is off of the bearing caps.

12. Remove the camshaft bearing caps and the camshaft.

To install:

13. Lubricate camshaft journals with clean engine oil.

➡Position the left side camshaft so that the camshaft sprocket dowel is near the 1 o'clock position. This will place the camshaft at the neutral position easing the installation of the camshaft bearing caps.

14. Position the camshaft into the cylinder head.

15. Install the camshaft bearing caps, hand tighten the retaining bolts. The camshaft caps are marked for location. The arrow must point towards the front of the engine.

16. Install the camshaft bearing caps, hand tighten the retaining bolts.

17. Working in ½ turn increments, tighten the bearing cap retaining bolts in the sequence shown.

18. Tighten the camshaft bearing cap retaining bolts to 100 inch lbs. (11 Nm) in the sequence shown.

19. Position the camshaft drive gear into the timing chain aligning the 2 painted dots and the colored or painted chain link.

20. Using Camshaft Holder 8428A, rotate the camshaft until the camshaft sprocket dowel is aligned with the slot in the camshaft sprocket. Install the sprocket onto the camshaft.

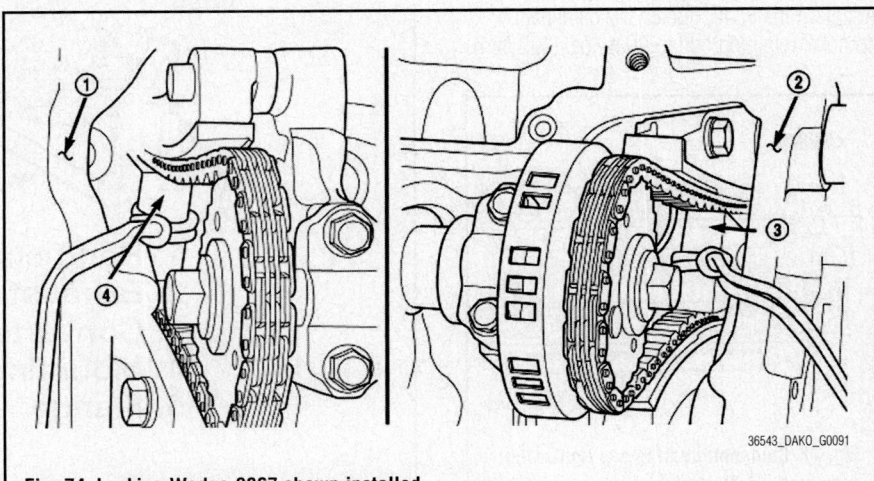

Fig. 74 Locking Wedge 9867 shown installed

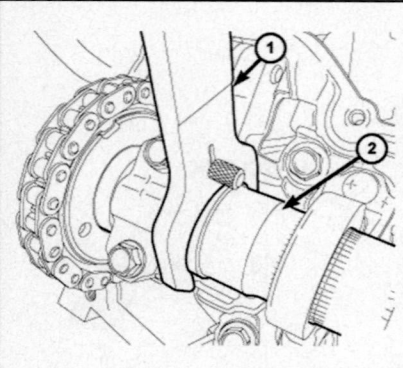

Fig. 75 Install Camshaft Holder 8428A (1) on the camshaft (2)

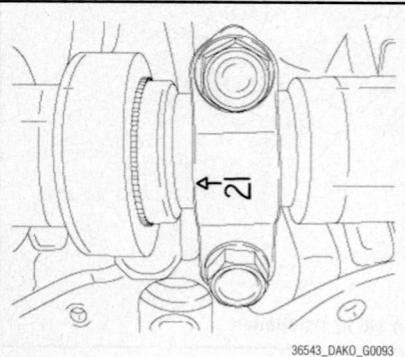

Fig. 76 View of camshaft bearing cap markings

21. Remove any excess oil from the camshaft sprocket bolt, then install the camshaft sprocket retaining bolt and hand tighten. Failure to remove any excess oil from the bolt can cause over-torque resulting in bolt failure.

22. Remove the Wedge Locking Tool 9867.

23. Using Spanner Wrench 6958 with Adapter Pins 8346, tighten the camshaft sprocket retaining bolt to 90 ft. lbs. (122 Nm).

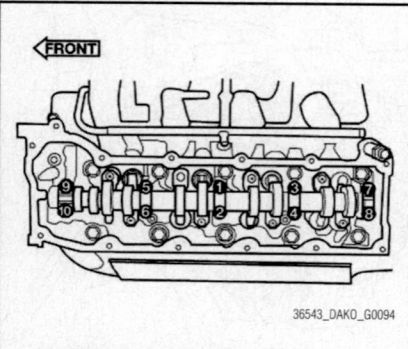

Fig. 77 Camshaft bearing cap tightening sequence—4.7L engine

24. Install the cylinder head cover and tighten to 105 inch. lbs. (12 Nm).

25. Connect the negative battery cable.

CATALYTIC CONVERTER

REMOVAL & INSTALLATION

See Figure 78.

1. Before servicing the vehicle, refer to the Precautions Section.

2. Raise and safely support the vehicle.

3. Saturate all exhaust bolts and nuts with MOPAR® Rust Penetrant. Allow 5 minutes for penetration.

4. Disconnect the oxygen sensor electrical connectors.

✷✷ WARNING

When servicing or replacing exhaust system components, disconnect the oxygen sensor connector(s). Allowing the exhaust to hang by the oxygen sensor wires will damage the harness and/or sensor.

5. Remove the catalytic converter-to-manifold bolts.

6. Remove the clamp holding the catalytic converter to the exhaust pipe(s).

7. If present, grind tack weld.

8. Remove the clamp holding the catalytic converter flange to the muffler or extension pipe.

9. Remove the catalytic converter.

To install:

10. Make sure the catalytic converter assembly is free of burrs.

11. Insert the catalytic converter assembly into the exhaust pipe.

12. Make sure the alignment tang is fully seated in the alignment slot.

13. Position the catalytic converter assembly to the exhaust manifold and install the flange nuts and bolts. Hand tighten at this time.

14. If other sections of the exhaust system where loosened in removal, refer to that information for the tightening procedures.

15. At the catalytic converter-to-extension pipe connection, install the new clamp (1) and nuts. Hand tighten at this time.

16. Make sure the catalytic converter assembly is correctly positioned and the properly aligned and that the muffler isolators are not stretched. Make any necessary adjustments.

17. Tighten the exhaust manifold flange bolts to 25 ft. lbs. (33 Nm).

18. Tighten the clamp nuts to 45 ft. lbs. (61 Nm).

19. Lower the vehicle.

20. Start the engine, inspect for exhaust leaks. Repair exhaust leaks as necessary.

21. Check the exhaust system for contact with the body panels and make any necessary adjustments.

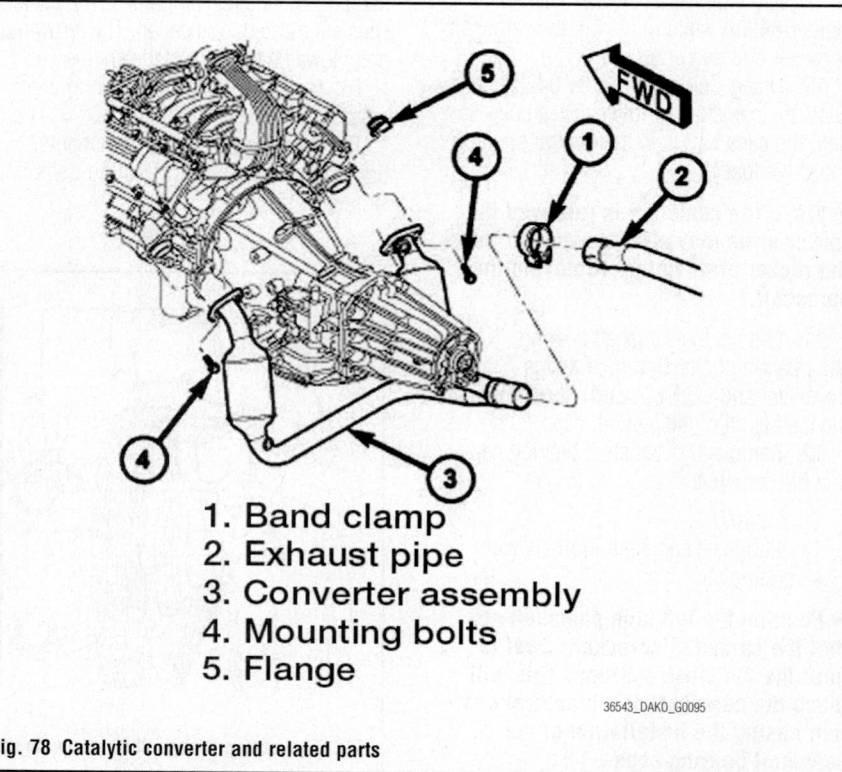

1. Band clamp
2. Exhaust pipe
3. Converter assembly
4. Mounting bolts
5. Flange

Fig. 78 Catalytic converter and related parts

CRANKSHAFT DAMPER

REMOVAL & INSTALLATION

3.7L Engine

See Figures 79 through 81.

1. Before servicing the vehicle, refer to the Precautions Section.
2. Disconnect the negative cable from the battery.
3. Remove the radiator fan.
4. Remove the accessory drive belt.
5. Remove the crankshaft damper bolt.
6. Remove the damper using the Crankshaft Insert 8513A (1) and Three Jaw Puller 1026 (2).

To install:

> ❋❋ **WARNING**
>
> **To prevent severe damage to the crankshaft, damper, or Damper Installer 8512A, thoroughly clean the damper bore and the crankshaft nose before installing the damper.**

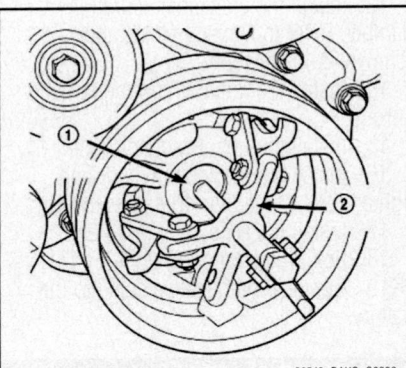

Fig. 79 Remove the damper using Crankshaft Insert 8513A (1) and Three Jaw Puller 1026 (2)

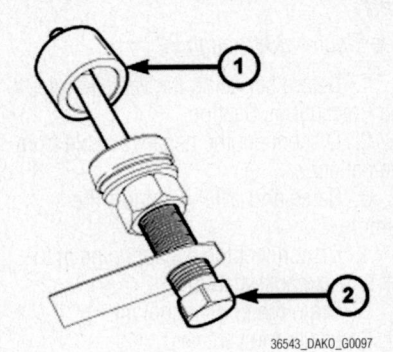

Fig. 80 View of the Damper Installer 8512A (2) and the pressing cup (1) from the A/C hub installer 6871

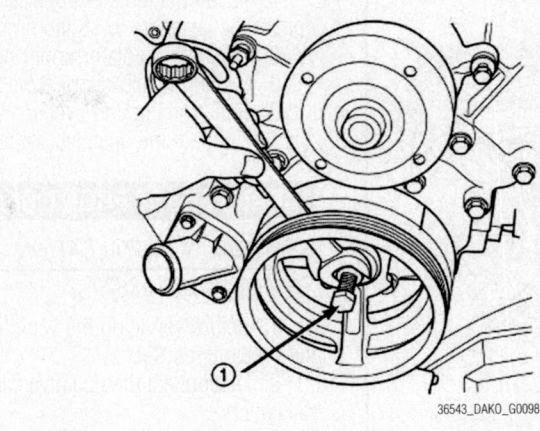

Fig. 81 Using Damper Installer 8512A (1) to press the damper onto the crankshaft

7. Position the damper onto the crankshaft.
8. Assemble the Damper Installer 8512A (2), and the pressing cup (1) from the A/C hub installer 6871.
9. Coat the threads of Damper Installer 8512A with MOPAR® Nickel Anti-Seize or equivalent.
10. Using the Damper Installer 8512A (1), and the pressing cup from the A/C hub installer 6871, press the damper onto the crankshaft.
11. Install and tighten the damper bolt to 130 ft. lbs. (175 Nm).
12. Install the cooling fan.
13. Install the accessory drive belt.
14. Connect the negative cable to the battery.

4.7L Engine

See Figures 82 through 85.

1. Before servicing the vehicle, refer to the Precautions Section.
2. Disconnect the negative cable from the battery.
3. Remove the accessory drive belt.
4. Drain the cooling system.
5. Remove the radiator upper hose.
6. Remove the upper fan shroud.
7. Using Spanner Wrench 6958 with Adapter Pins 8346 (1), loosen the fan and viscous assembly from the water pump.
8. Remove the fan and viscous assembly.
9. Disconnect the electrical connector for the fan mounted inside the radiator shroud.

➡**The transmission cooler line snaps into the shroud lower right hand corner.**

10. Remove the vibration damper bolt.
11. Remove the damper using Special Tools 8513A Insert and Three Jaw Puller 1023 (2).

To install:

> ❋❋ **WARNING**
>
> **To prevent severe damage to the crankshaft, damper, and Damper Installer 8512A, thoroughly clean the damper bore and the crankshaft nose before installing the damper.**

12. Position the damper onto the crankshaft.
13. Assemble the Damper Installer 8512A (2) and the A/C hub installer cup 6871 (1).
14. Using the Damper Installer 8512A (2) and the A/C hub installer cup 6871 (1), press the damper onto the crankshaft.
15. Coat the vibration damper bolt threads with MOPAR® Nickel Anti-Seize or equivalent, install and tighten the bolt to 130 ft. lbs. (175 Nm).
16. Install the cooling fan assembly.

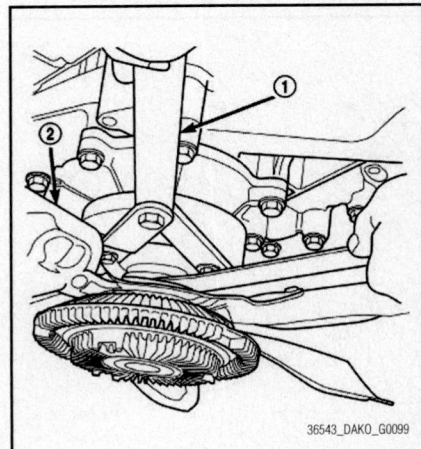

Fig. 82 Using Spanner Wrench 6958 with Adapter Pins 8346 (1), loosen the fan and viscous assembly from the water pump

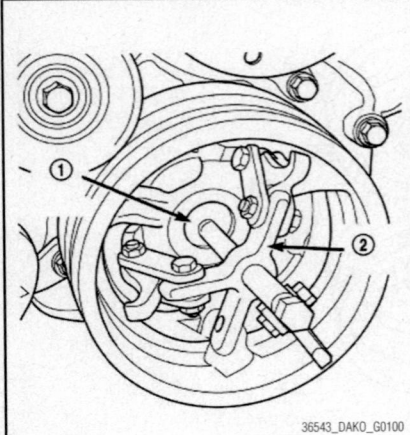

Fig. 83 Remove the damper using Special Tools 8513A Insert (1) and Three Jaw Puller 1023 (2)

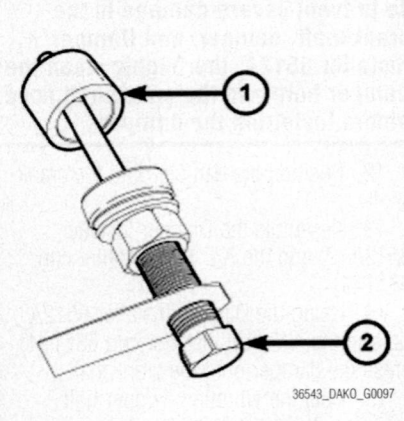

Fig. 84 View of the Damper Installer 8512A (2) and the pressing cup (1) from the A/C hub installer 6871

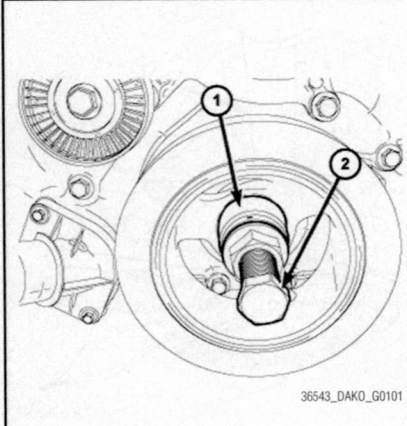

Fig. 85 Using the Damper Installer 8512A (2) and the A/C hub installer cup 6871 (1), press the damper onto the crankshaft

17. Install the radiator upper shroud and tighten the fasteners to 95 inch lbs. (11 Nm).

18. Install the radiator upper hose.

19. Install the accessory drive belt.

20. Refill the cooling system.

21. Connect the negative battery cable.

CRANKSHAFT FRONT SEAL

REMOVAL & INSTALLATION

See Figures 86 and 87.

1. Before servicing the vehicle, refer to the Precautions Section.

2. Disconnect the negative cable from the battery.

3. Remove the accessory drive belt.

4. Remove the A/C compressor mounting fasteners and set the compressor aside.

5. Drain the cooling system.

6. Remove the upper radiator hose.

7. Disconnect the electrical connector for the fan mounted inside the radiator shroud.

8. Remove the radiator shroud attaching fasteners.

➡ **The transmission cooler line snaps into the shroud lower right hand corner.**

9. Remove the radiator cooling fan and shroud.

10. Remove the crankshaft damper. Refer to Crankshaft Damper, removal & installation.

11. Using Crankshaft Front Seal Remover 8511 (1), remove the crankshaft front seal.

To install:

> ❄❄ **WARNING**

To prevent severe damage to the crankshaft, damper, or Special Tool 8512, thoroughly clean the damper

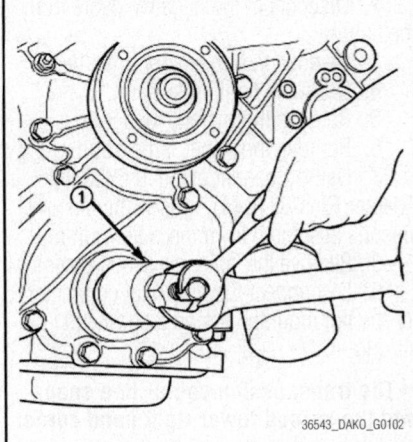

Fig. 86 Using Crankshaft Front Seal Remover 8511 (1), remove the crankshaft front seal

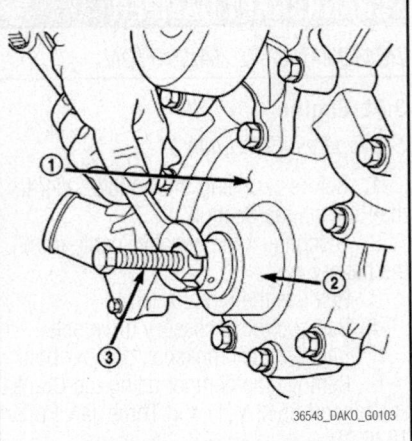

Fig. 87 Using Seal Installer 8348 and Damper Installer 8512A (2, 3), install the crankshaft front seal

bore and the crankshaft nose before installing the damper.

12. Using Seal Installer 8348 and Damper Installer 8512A (2,3), install the crankshaft front seal.

13. Install the crankshaft vibration damper. Refer to Crankshaft Damper, removal & installation.

14. Install the radiator cooling fan and shroud.

15. Install the upper radiator hose.

16. Install the A/C compressor and tighten the fasteners to 40 ft. lbs. (54 Nm).

17. Install the accessory drive belt.

18. Refill the cooling system.

19. Connect the negative cable to the battery.

CYLINDER HEAD

REMOVAL & INSTALLATION

3.7L Engine

Left

See Figures 88 through 92.

1. Before servicing the vehicle, refer to the Precautions Section.

2. Disconnect the negative cable from the battery.

3. Raise and safely support the vehicle.

4. Disconnect the exhaust pipe at the left side exhaust manifold.

5. Drain the engine coolant.

6. Lower the vehicle.

7. Remove the intake manifold.

8. Remove the master cylinder and booster assembly.

9. Remove the cylinder head cover.

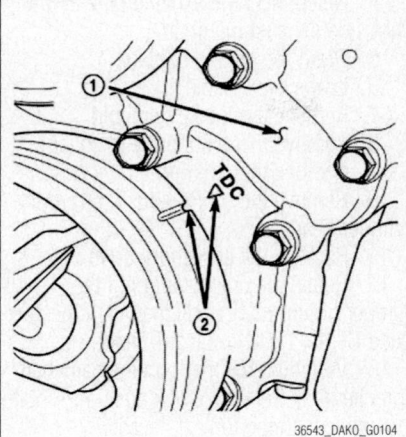

Fig. 88 Align the crankshaft damper to the Top Dead Center (TDC) indicator mark (2) on the timing chain cover (1)

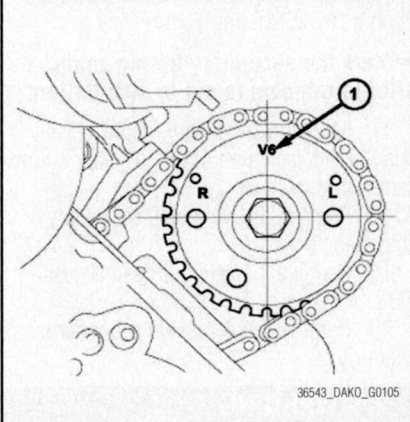

Fig. 89 Verify that the V6 mark (1) on the camshaft sprocket is at the 12 o'clock position

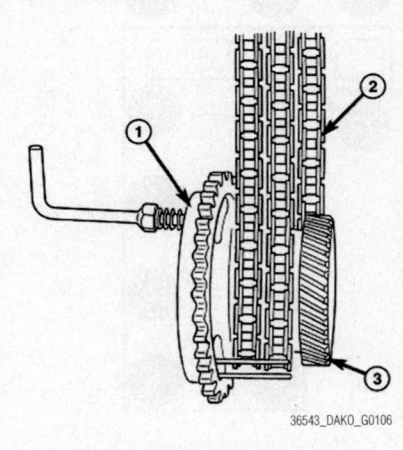

Fig. 90 Lock the secondary timing chains (2) to the idler sprocket using Secondary Camshaft Chain Holder 8429 (1)

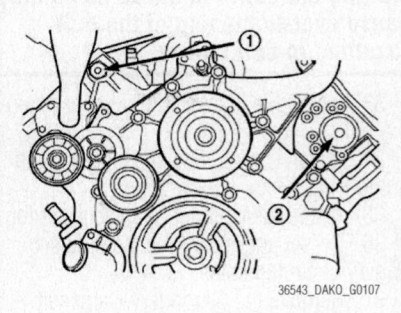

Fig. 91 Remove the cylinder head access plug (1) and (2)

10. Remove the fan shroud and fan blade assembly.

11. Remove the accessory drive belt.

12. Remove the power steering pump and set it aside.

13. Rotate the crankshaft until the damper timing mark is aligned with the Top Dead Center (TDC) indicator mark (2).

14. Verify that the **V6** mark (1) on the camshaft sprocket is at the 12 o'clock position, with the No. 1 cylinder at TDC on the exhaust stroke. Rotate the crankshaft 1 turn if necessary.

15. Remove the vibration damper. Refer to Crankshaft Damper, removal & installation.

16. Remove the timing chain cover.

17. Lock the secondary timing chains (2) to the idler sprocket using Secondary Camshaft Chain Holder 8429 (1).

➡**Mark the secondary timing chain prior to removal to aid in installation.**

18. Mark the secondary timing chain (2), one link on each side of the V6 mark on the camshaft drive gear.

19. Remove the left side secondary chain tensioner.

20. Remove the cylinder head access plug (1) and (2).

21. Remove the left side secondary chain guide.

22. Remove the retaining bolt and the camshaft drive gear.

✳✳ WARNING

Do not allow the engine to rotate. Severe damage to the valve train can occur.

➡**Do not overlook the 4 smaller bolts at the front of the cylinder head. Do not attempt to remove the cylinder head without removing these 4 bolts.**

➡**The cylinder head is attached to the cylinder block with 12 bolts.**

23. Remove the cylinder head retaining bolts.

24. Remove the cylinder head and gasket. Discard the gasket.

✳✳ WARNING

Do not lay the cylinder head on its gasket sealing surface, due to the design of the cylinder head gasket, any distortion to the cylinder head sealing surface may prevent the gasket from properly sealing resulting in leaks.

To install:

➡**The cylinder head bolts are tightened using a torque plus angle procedure. The bolts must be examined BEFORE reuse. If the threads are necked, the bolts should be replaced.**

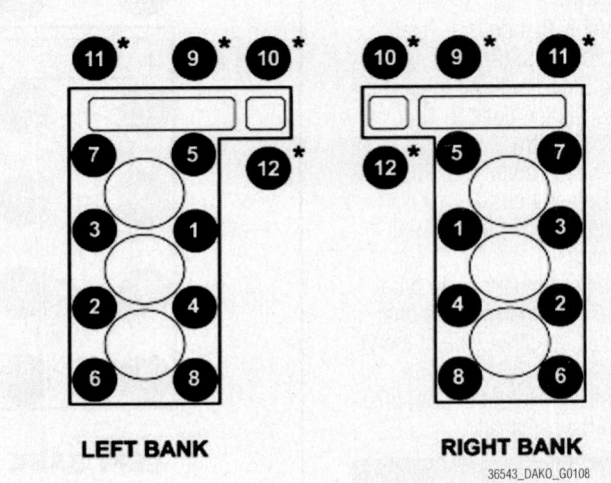

LEFT BANK **RIGHT BANK**

Fig. 92 Smaller cylinder head mounting bolts requiring sealant are marked

25. Clean the cylinder head and cylinder block mating surfaces.

26. Position the new cylinder head gasket on the locating dowels.

27. Position the cylinder head onto the cylinder block. Make sure the cylinder head seats fully over the locating dowels.

➡ **The 4 smaller cylinder head mounting bolts (on each side) require sealant to be added to them before installing. Failure to do so may result in leakage. These locations are identified with an asterisk in the illustration.**

28. Lubricate the cylinder head bolt threads with clean engine oil and install the eight M11 bolts.

29. Coat the four M8 cylinder head bolts with MOPAR® Lock and Seal Adhesive, then install the bolts.

➡ **The cylinder head bolts are tightened using an angle torque procedure, however, the bolts are not a torque-to-yield design.**

30. Tighten the bolts in sequence using the following steps and torque values:
- Step 1: Tighten bolts 1–8, 20 ft. lbs. (27 Nm)
- Step 2: Verify that bolts 1–8, all reached 20 ft. lbs. (27 Nm), by repeating Step 1 without loosening the bolts. Tighten bolts 9–12 to 10 ft. lbs. (14 Nm)
- Step 3: Tighten bolts 1–8, 90°
- Step 4: Tighten bolts 1–8, 90°, again. Tighten bolts 9–12, 19 ft. lbs. (26 Nm)

31. Position the secondary chain onto the camshaft drive gear, making sure one marked chain link is on either side of the V6 mark on the gear.

32. Using Camshaft Holder 8428A, position the gear onto the camshaft.

stalling the bolt. Failure to do so may cause over-tightening of the bolt resulting in bolt failure.

33. Install the camshaft drive gear retaining bolt.

34. Install the left side secondary chain guide.

35. Install the cylinder head access plug.

36. Re-set and install the left side secondary chain tensioner.

37. Remove the Secondary Camshaft Chain Holder 8429A.

38. Install the timing chain cover.

39. Install the crankshaft damper and tighten the bolt to 130 ft. lbs. (175 Nm).

40. Install the power steering pump.

41. Install the fan blade assembly and fan shroud.

42. Install the cylinder head cover.

43. Install the master cylinder and booster assembly.

44. Install the intake manifold.

45. Refill the cooling system.

46. Raise and safely support the vehicle.

47. Install the exhaust pipe onto the left exhaust manifold.

48. Lower the vehicle.

49. Connect the negative cable to the battery.

50. Start the engine and check for leaks.

Right

See Figure 93.

1. Before servicing the vehicle, refer to the Precautions Section.

2. Disconnect the negative cable from the battery.

3. Raise and safely support the vehicle.

4. Disconnect the exhaust pipe at the right side exhaust manifold.

5. Drain the engine coolant.

6. Lower the vehicle.

7. Remove the intake manifold.

8. Remove the cylinder head cover.

9. Remove the radiator fan.

10. Remove the oil fill housing from the cylinder head.

11. Remove the accessory drive belt.

12. Rotate the crankshaft until the damper timing mark is aligned with the Top Dead Center (TDC) indicator mark.

13. Verify the **V6** mark on the camshaft sprocket is at the 12 o'clock position. Rotate the crankshaft one turn, if necessary.

14. Remove the crankshaft damper. Refer to Crankshaft Damper, removal & installation.

15. Remove the timing chain cover.

16. Lock the secondary timing chains to the idler sprocket using Special Tool 8429 Timing Chain Holding Fixture.

➡ **Mark the secondary timing chain prior to removal to aid in installation.**

17. Mark the secondary timing chain, one link on each side of the V6 mark on the camshaft drive gear.

18. Remove the right side secondary chain tensioner.

19. Remove the cylinder head access plug.

20. Remove the right side secondary chain guide.

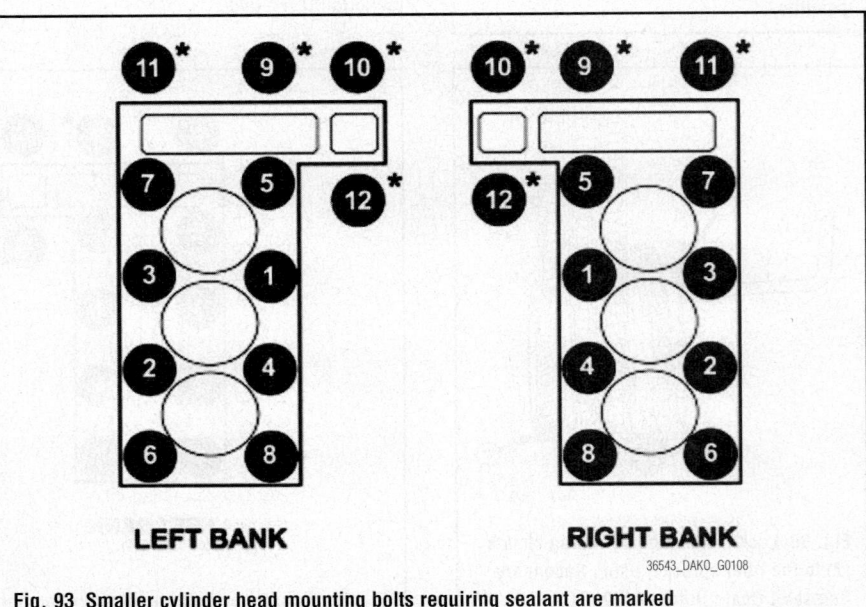

LEFT BANK   **RIGHT BANK**

36543_DAKO_G0108

Fig. 93 Smaller cylinder head mounting bolts requiring sealant are marked

any reason, as the sprocket and camshaft sensor target wheel are serviced as an assembly. If the nut was removed, tighten it to 44 inch lbs. (5 Nm).

21. Remove the retaining bolt and the camshaft drive gear.

✳✳ WARNING

Do not allow the engine to rotate. Severe damage to the valve train can occur.

➡**Do not overlook the 4 smaller bolts at the front of the cylinder head. Do not attempt to remove the cylinder head without removing these 4 bolts.**

✳✳ WARNING

Do not hold or pry on the camshaft target wheel for any reason. A damaged target wheel can result in a vehicle no start condition.

➡**The cylinder head is attached to the cylinder block with 12 bolts.**

22. Remove the cylinder head retaining bolts.
23. Remove the cylinder head and gasket. Discard the gasket.

✳✳ WARNING

Do not lay the cylinder head on its gasket sealing surface, due to the design of the cylinder head gasket, any distortion to the cylinder head sealing surface may prevent the gasket from properly sealing resulting in leakage.

To install:

➡**The cylinder head bolts are tightened using a torque plus angle procedure. The bolts must be examined BEFORE reuse. If the threads are necked, the bolts should be replaced.**

✳✳ WARNING

When cleaning the cylinder head and cylinder block surfaces, DO NOT use a metal scraper or high speed abrasion tool. The surfaces could be cut or ground. Use only a wooden or plastic scraper.

24. Clean the cylinder head and cylinder block mating surfaces.
25. Position the new cylinder head gasket on the locating dowels.

✳✳ WARNING

When installing cylinder head, use care not damage the tensioner arm or the guide arm.

26. Position the cylinder head onto the cylinder block. Make sure the cylinder head seats fully over the locating dowels.

➡**The four M8 cylinder head mounting bolts require sealant to be added to them before installing. Failure to do so may cause leakage.**

27. Lubricate the cylinder head bolt threads with clean engine oil and install the eight M10 bolts.
28. Coat the four M8 cylinder head bolts with MOPAR® Lock and Seal Adhesive then install the bolts.

➡**The cylinder head bolts are tightened using an angle torque procedure, however, the bolts are not a torque-to-yield design.**

29. Tighten the bolts in sequence using the following steps and torque values:
- Step 1: Tighten bolts 1–8, 20 ft. lbs. (27 Nm)
- Step 2: Verify that bolts 1–8, all reached 20 ft. lbs. (27 Nm), by repeating Step 1 without loosening the bolts. Tighten bolts 9–12 to 10 ft. lbs. (14 Nm)
- Step 3: Tighten bolts 1–8, 90°
- Step 4: Tighten bolts 1–8, 90°, again. Tighten bolts 9–12, 19 ft. lbs. (26 Nm)

30. Position the secondary chain onto the camshaft drive gear, making sure one marked chain link is on either side of the V6 mark on the gear.
31. Using Camshaft Holder 8428A, position the gear onto the camshaft.

✳✳ WARNING

Remove excess oil from the camshaft sprocket retaining bolt before reinstalling bolt. Failure to do so may cause over-tightening of the bolt resulting in bolt failure.

32. Install the camshaft drive gear retaining bolt.
33. Install the right side secondary chain guide.
34. Install the cylinder head access plug.
35. Re-set and install the right side secondary chain tensioner.
36. Remove Camshaft Holder 8429A.
37. Install the timing chain cover.

38. Install the crankshaft damper and tighten the bolt to 130 ft. lbs. (175 Nm).
39. Install the accessory drive belt.
40. Install the radiator fan and shroud.
41. Install the cylinder head cover.
42. Install the intake manifold.
43. Install the oil fill housing onto the cylinder head.
44. Refill the cooling system.
45. Raise and safely support the vehicle.
46. Install the exhaust pipe onto the right exhaust manifold.
47. Lower the vehicle.
48. Reconnect the battery negative cable.
49. Start the engine and check for leaks.

4.7L Engine

Left

See Figures 94 through 99.

1. Before servicing the vehicle, refer to the Precautions Section.
2. Disconnect the negative cable from the battery.
3. Raise and safely support the vehicle.
4. Disconnect the exhaust pipe at the left side exhaust manifold.
5. Drain the engine coolant.
6. Lower the vehicle.
7. Remove the intake manifold.
8. Remove the master cylinder and booster assembly.
9. Remove the cylinder head cover.
10. Remove the fan shroud and fan blade assembly.
11. Remove the accessory drive belt.
12. Remove the power steering pump and set it aside.
13. Rotate the crankshaft until the damper timing mark is aligned with the Top Dead Center (TDC) indicator mark.

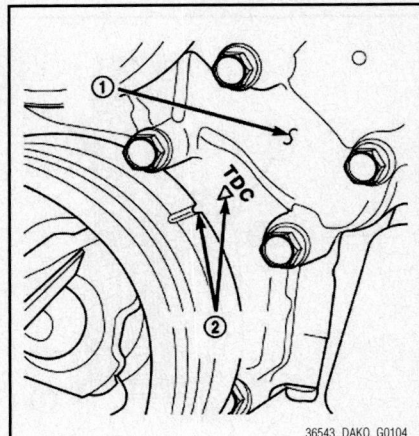

36543_DAKO_G0104

Fig. 94 Align the crankshaft damper to the Top Dead Center (TDC) indicator mark (2) on the timing chain cover (1)

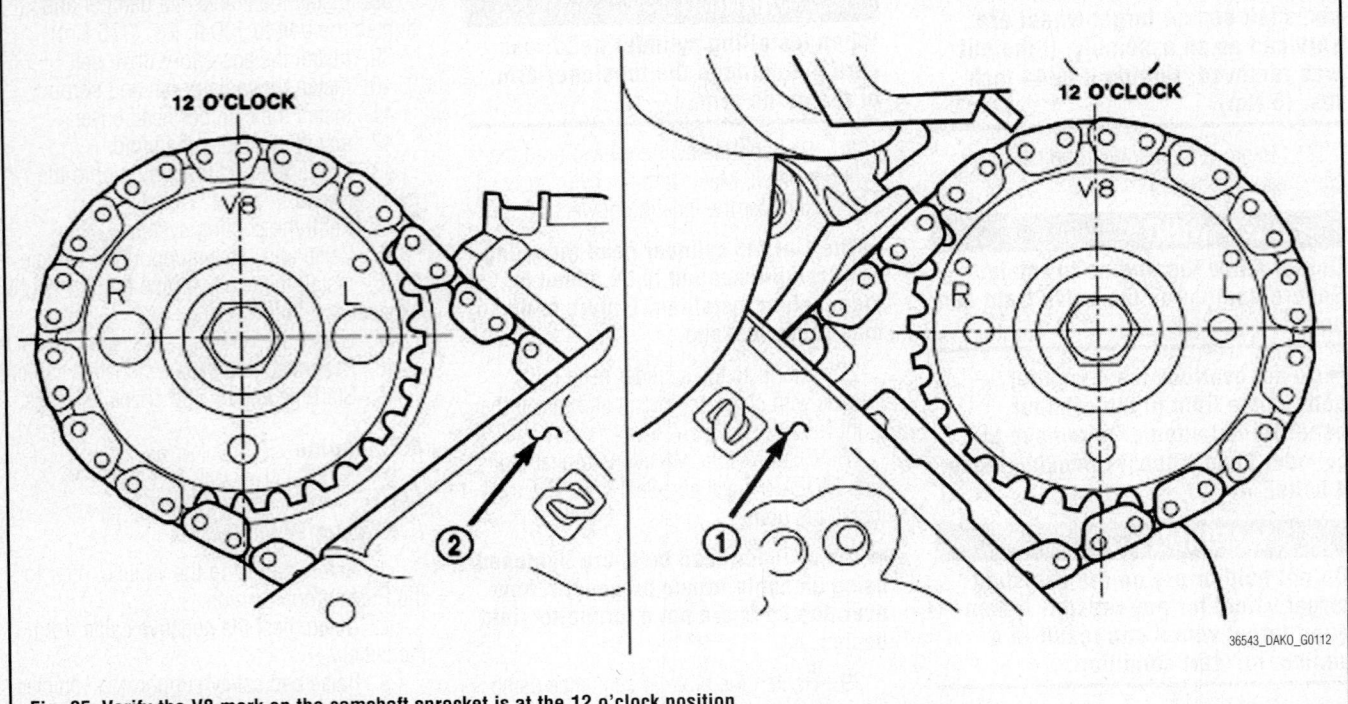

Fig. 95 Verify the V8 mark on the camshaft sprocket is at the 12 o'clock position

14. Verify the V8 mark on the camshaft sprocket is at the 12 o'clock position. Rotate the crankshaft one turn, if necessary.

15. Remove the crankshaft damper. Refer to Crankshaft Damper, removal & installation.

16. Remove the timing chain cover.

17. Lock the secondary timing chains to the idler sprocket using Special Tool 8429.

➡**Mark the secondary timing chain prior to removal to aid in installation.**

18. Mark the secondary timing chain, one link on each side of the V8 mark on the camshaft drive gear.

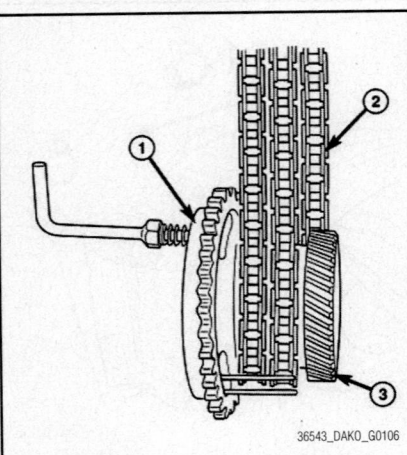

Fig. 96 Lock the secondary timing chains (2) to the idler sprocket using Secondary Camshaft Chain Holder 8429 (1)

19. Remove the left side secondary chain tensioner.

20. Remove the cylinder head access plug (1).

21. Remove the left side secondary chain guide.

22. Remove the retaining bolt and the camshaft drive gear.

※ WARNING

Do not allow the engine to rotate. Severe damage to the valve train can occur.

➡**Do not overlook the 4 smaller bolts at the front of the cylinder head. Do not attempt to remove the cylinder head without removing these 4 bolts.**

➡**The cylinder head is attached to the cylinder block with 14 bolts.**

23. Remove the cylinder head retaining bolts using the sequence illustrated.

24. Remove the cylinder head and gasket. Discard the gasket.

※ WARNING

Do not lay the cylinder head on its gasket sealing surface, due to the design of the cylinder head gasket, any distortion to the cylinder head sealing surface may prevent the gasket from properly sealing resulting in leakage.

To install:

➡**The cylinder head bolts are tightened using a torque plus angle procedure. The bolts must be examined BEFORE reuse. If the threads are necked, the bolts should be replaced.**

※ WARNING

When cleaning cylinder head and cylinder block surfaces, DO NOT use a metal scraper or high speed abrasive tool as the surfaces could be cut or ground. Use only a wooden or plastic scraper.

25. Clean the cylinder head and cylinder block mating surfaces.

26. Position the new cylinder head gasket on the locating dowels.

※ WARNING

When installing cylinder head, use care not damage the tensioner arm or the guide arm.

27. Position the cylinder head onto the cylinder block. Make sure the cylinder head seats fully over the locating dowels.

➡**The four M8 cylinder head mounting bolts (11–14) require sealant to be added to them before installing. Failure to do so may cause leakage. See the illustration.**

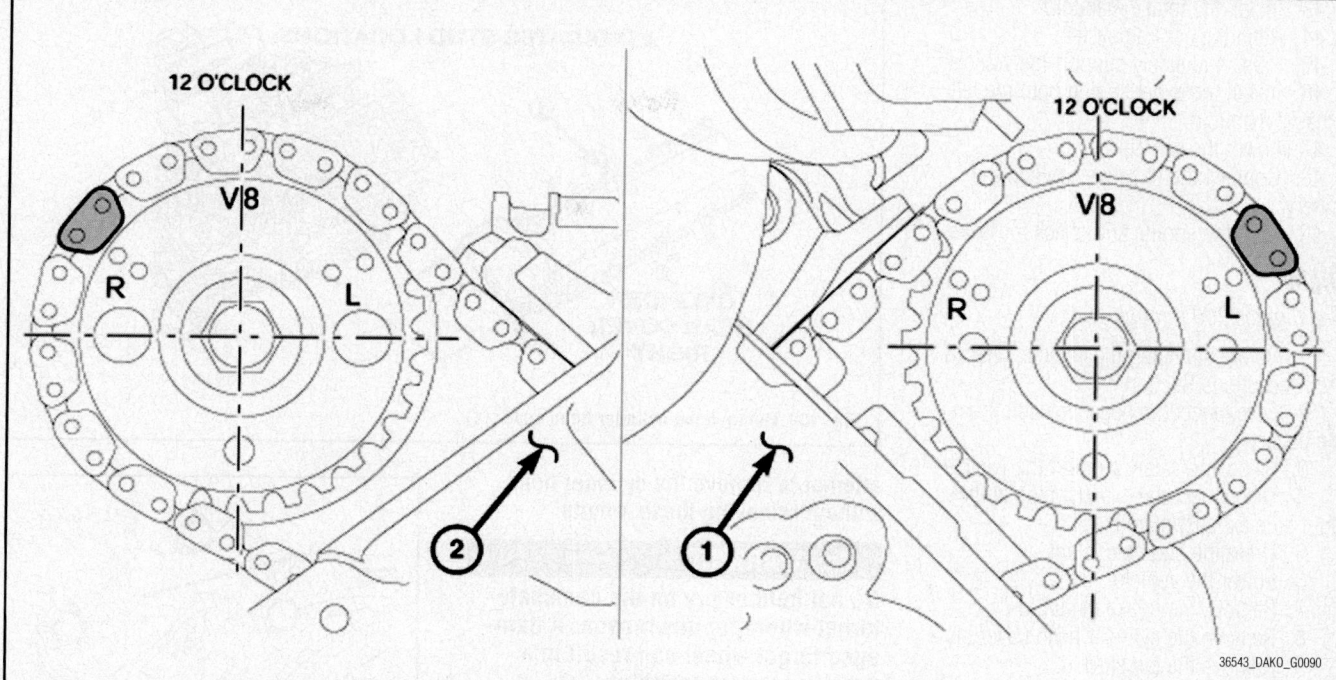

Fig. 97 Mark the link on the secondary timing chain that is aligned with the 2 dots on the cam sprocket to aid in installation

36543_DAKO_G0090

28. Lubricate the cylinder head bolt threads with clean engine oil and install the ten M11 bolts.

29. Coat the four M8 cylinder head bolts with MOPAR® Thread Sealant with PTFE, then install the bolts.

➡ **The cylinder head bolts are tightened using an angle torque procedure.**

30. Tighten the bolts in sequence using the following steps and torque values:

- Step 1: Tighten bolts 1–10 to 20 ft. lbs. (27 Nm)
- Step 2: Verify that bolts 1–10 have all reached 20 ft. lbs. (27 Nm), by repeating Step 1 without loosening the bolts

- Step 3: Tighten bolts 11–14 to 89 inch lbs. (14 Nm)
- Step 4: Tighten bolts 1–10 an additional 90°
- Step 5: Tighten bolts 1–10 an additional 90° again
- Step 6: Tighten bolts 11–14 to 19 ft. lbs. (26 Nm)

31. Position the secondary chain onto the camshaft drive gear, making sure one marked chain link is on either side of the V8 mark on the gear and position the gear onto the camshaft.

32. Install the camshaft drive gear retaining bolt.

33. Install the left side secondary chain guide.

34. Install the cylinder head access plug (1).

35. Re-set and install the left side secondary chain tensioner.

36. Remove Special Tool 8429.

37. Install the timing chain cover.

38. Install the crankshaft damper.

39. Install the power steering pump.

40. Install the fan blade assembly and fan shroud.

41. Install the cylinder head cover.

42. Install the master cylinder and booster assembly.

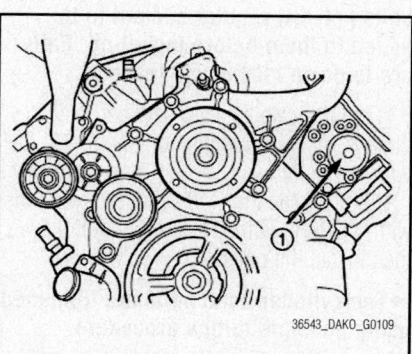

Fig. 98 Remove the cylinder head access plug (1)

36543_DAKO_G0109

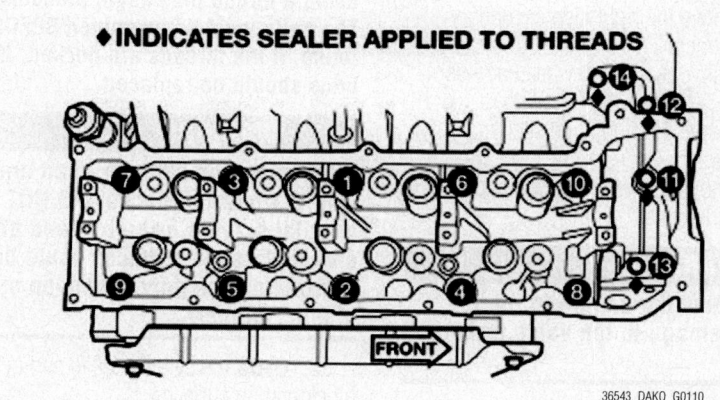

◆ INDICATES SEALER APPLIED TO THREADS

Fig. 99 Cylinder head removal and tightening sequence

36543_DAKO_G0110

43. Install the intake manifold.
44. Refill the cooling system.
45. Raise and safely support the vehicle.
46. Install the exhaust pipe onto the left exhaust manifold.
47. Lower the vehicle.
48. Connect the negative cable to the battery.
49. Start the engine and check for leaks.

Right

See Figures 100 through 104.

1. Before servicing the vehicle, refer to the Precautions Section.
2. Disconnect the negative cable from the battery.
3. Raise and safely support the vehicle.
4. Disconnect the exhaust pipe at the right side exhaust manifold.
5. Drain the engine coolant.
6. Lower the vehicle.
7. Remove the intake manifold.
8. Remove the cylinder head cover (1).
9. Remove the fan shroud.
10. Remove the oil fill housing from the cylinder head.
11. Remove the accessory drive belt.
12. Rotate the crankshaft until the damper timing mark is aligned with the Top Dead Center (TDC) indicator mark (2).
13. Verify the V8 mark on the camshaft sprocket is at the 12 o'clock position. Rotate the crankshaft one turn, if necessary.
14. Remove the crankshaft damper. Refer to Crankshaft Damper, removal & installation.
15. Remove the timing chain cover.
16. Lock the secondary timing chains to the idler sprocket using Special Tool 8429.

➡ **Mark the secondary timing chain prior to removal to aid in installation.**

17. Mark the secondary timing chain, one link on each side of the V8 mark on the camshaft drive gear.
18. Remove the right side secondary chain tensioner.
19. Remove the cylinder head access plug (1).
20. Remove the right side secondary chain guide.
21. Remove the retaining bolt and the camshaft drive gear.

✳✳ WARNING

Do not allow the engine to rotate. Severe damage to the valve train can occur.

➡ **Do not overlook the 4 smaller bolts at the front of the cylinder head. Do not**

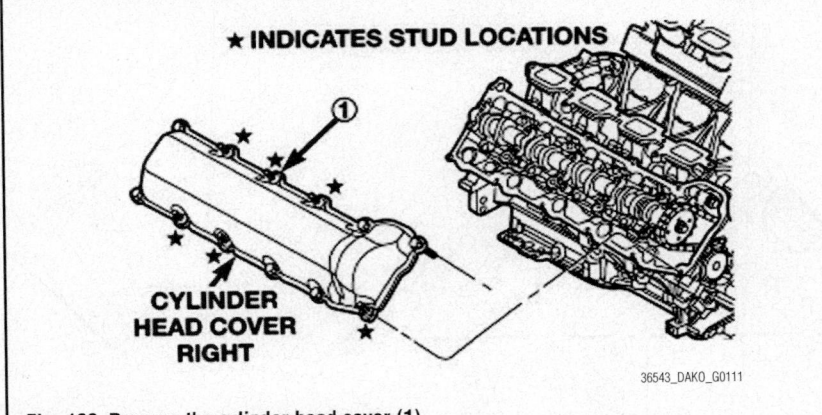

Fig. 100 Remove the cylinder head cover (1)

attempt to remove the cylinder head without removing these 4 bolts.

✳✳ WARNING

Do not hold or pry on the camshaft target wheel for any reason. A damaged target wheel can result in a vehicle no start condition.

➡ **The cylinder head is attached to the cylinder block with 14 bolts.**

22. Remove the cylinder head retaining bolts using the sequence illustrated.
23. Remove the cylinder head and gasket. Discard the gasket.

✳✳ WARNING

Do not lay the cylinder head on its gasket sealing surface, due to the design of the cylinder head gasket, any distortion to the cylinder head sealing surface may prevent the gasket from properly sealing resulting in leakage.

To install:

➡ **The cylinder head bolts are tightened using a torque plus angle procedure. The bolts must be examined BEFORE reuse. If the threads are necked, the bolts should be replaced.**

✳✳ WARNING

When cleaning cylinder head and cylinder block surfaces, DO NOT use a metal scraper or high speed abrasive tool as the surfaces could be cut or ground. Use only a wooden or plastic scraper.

24. Clean the cylinder head and cylinder block mating surfaces.
25. Position the new cylinder head gasket on the locating dowels.

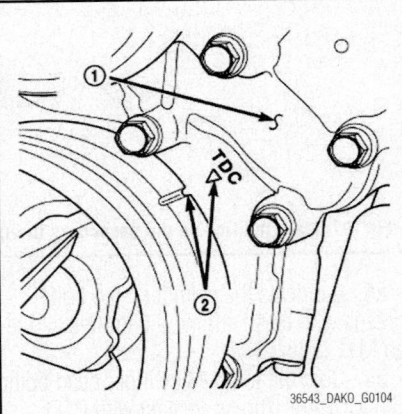

Fig. 101 Align the crankshaft damper to the Top Dead Center (TDC) indicator mark (2) on the timing chain cover (1)

✳✳ WARNING

When installing cylinder head, use care not damage the tensioner arm or the guide arm.

26. Position the cylinder head onto the cylinder block. Make sure the cylinder head seats fully over the locating dowels.

➡ **The four M8 cylinder head mounting bolts (11–14) require sealant to be added to them before installing. Failure to do so may cause leakage.**

27. Lubricate the cylinder head bolt threads with clean engine oil and install the ten M10 bolts.
28. Coat the four M8 cylinder head bolts with MOPAR® Thread Sealant with PTFE, then install the bolts.

➡ **The cylinder head bolts are tightened using an angle torque procedure.**

29. Tighten the bolts in sequence using the following steps and torque values:

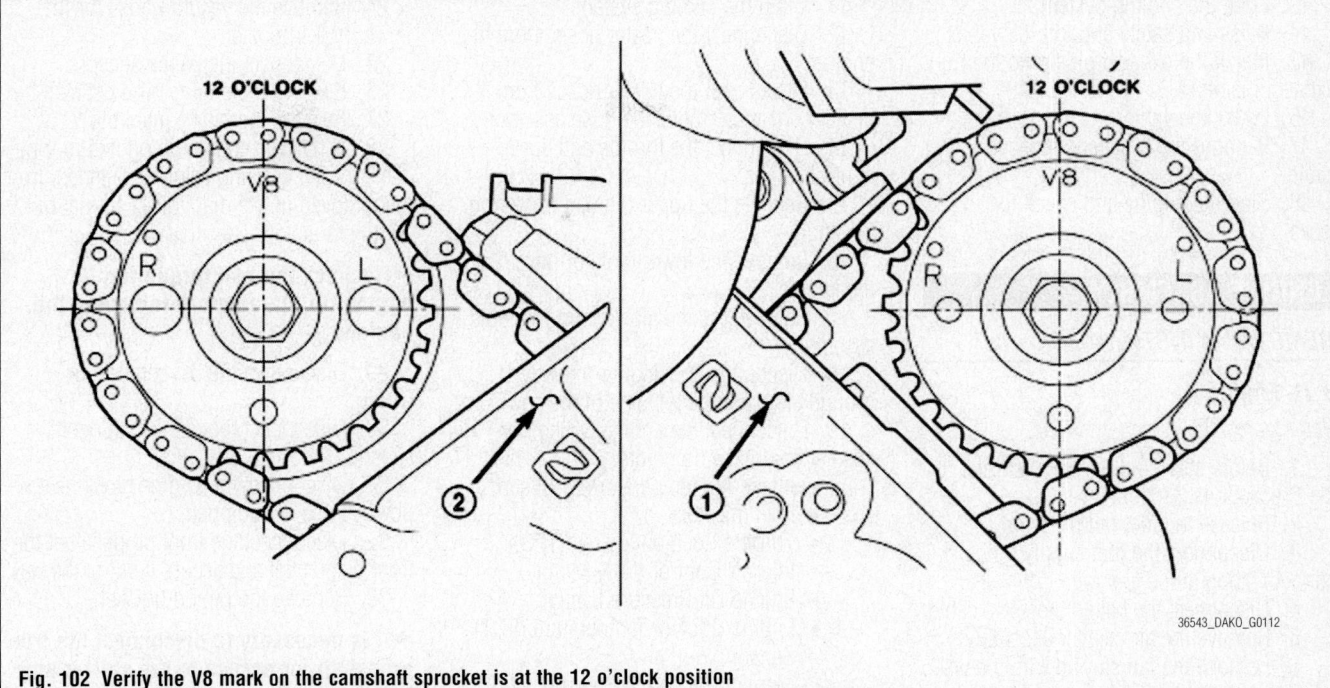

Fig. 102 Verify the V8 mark on the camshaft sprocket is at the 12 o'clock position

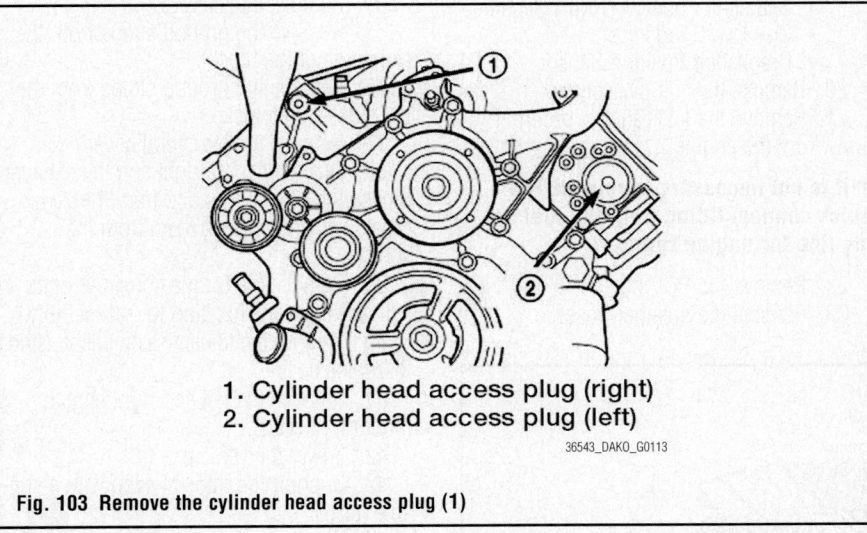

1. Cylinder head access plug (right)
2. Cylinder head access plug (left)

36543_DAKO_G0113

Fig. 103 Remove the cylinder head access plug (1)

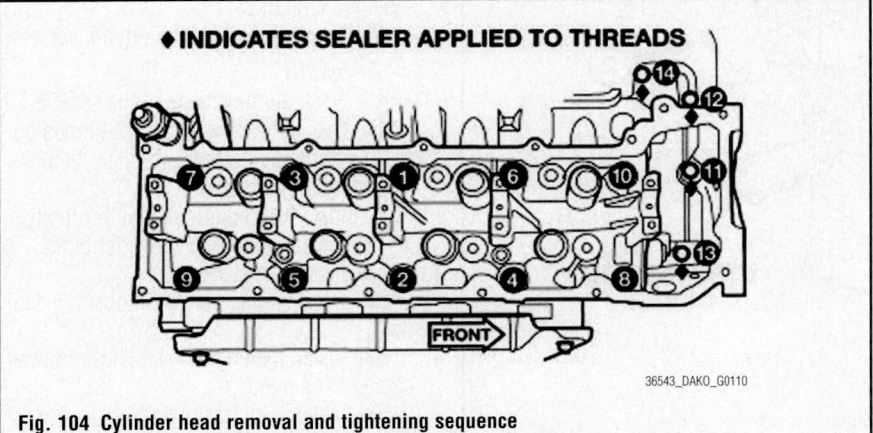

Fig. 104 Cylinder head removal and tightening sequence

- Step 1: Tighten bolts 1–10 to 20 ft. lbs. (27 Nm)
- Step 2: Verify that bolts 1–10 have all reached 20 ft. lbs. (27 Nm), by repeating Step 1 without loosening the bolts
- Step 3: Tighten bolts 11–14 to 89 inch lbs. (14 Nm)
- Step 4: Tighten bolts 1–10 an additional 90°
- Step 5: Tighten bolts 1–10 an additional 90° again
- Step 6: Tighten bolts 11–14 to 19 ft. lbs. (26 Nm)

30. Position the secondary chain onto the camshaft drive gear, making sure one marked chain link is on either side of the V8 mark on the gear and position the gear onto the camshaft.

31. Install the camshaft drive gear retaining bolt.

32. Install the right side secondary chain guide.

33. Install the right side cylinder head access plug (1).

34. Re-set and install the right side secondary chain tensioner.

35. Remove Special Tool 8429.

36. Install the timing chain cover.

37. Install the crankshaft damper.

38. Install the accessory drive belt.

39. Install the fan shroud.

40. Install the cylinder head cover (1).

41. Install the intake manifold.

42. Install the oil fill housing onto the cylinder head.

43. Refill the cooling system.
44. Raise and safely support the vehicle.
45. Install the exhaust pipe onto the right exhaust manifold.
46. Lower the vehicle.
47. Reconnect the battery negative cable.
48. Start the engine and check for leaks.

ENGINE ASSEMBLY

REMOVAL & INSTALLATION

3.7L Engine

See Figure 105.

1. Before servicing the vehicle, refer to the Precautions Section.
2. Release the fuel rail pressure.
3. Disconnect the fuel supply quick connect fitting at the fuel rail.
4. Disconnect the battery negative cable.
5. Remove the air cleaner assembly.
6. Remove the fan shroud with the viscous fan assembly.
7. Remove the accessory drive belt.
8. Remove the A/C compressor and secure it away from the engine.
9. Remove the alternator and secure it away from the engine.

➡**Do NOT remove the phenolic pulley from the P/S pump. It is not required for P/S pump removal.**

10. Remove the power steering pump with the lines attached and secure it away from the engine.

11. Drain the cooling system.
12. Disconnect the heater hoses from the engine.
13. Disconnect the heater hoses from heater core and remove the hose assembly.
14. Disconnect the throttle and speed control cables.
15. Remove the upper radiator hose from the engine.
16. Remove the lower radiator hose from the engine.
17. Remove the radiator/cooling module assembly.
18. Disconnect the engine-to-body ground straps at the left side of the cowl.
19. Disconnect the engine wiring harness at the following points:
   - Intake Air Temperature (IAT) sensor
   - Fuel Injectors
   - Throttle Position Switch (TPS)
   - Idle Air Control (IAC) Motor
   - Engine Oil Pressure Switch
   - Engine Coolant Temperature (ECT) Sensor
   - Manifold Absolute Pressure MAP) Sensor
   - Camshaft Position (CMP) Sensor
   - Coil Over Plugs
   - Crankshaft Position Sensor
20. Remove the coil over plugs.
21. Remove the fuel rail and secure it away from the engine.

➡**It is not necessary to release the quick connect fitting from the fuel supply line for engine removal.**

22. Remove the PCV hose.
23. Remove the breather hoses.

24. Remove the vacuum hose for the power brake booster.
25. Disconnect the knock sensors.
26. Remove the engine oil dipstick tube.
27. Remove the intake manifold.
28. Install the engine lifting fixture, Special Tool 8427, using original fasteners from the removed intake manifold, and fuel rail. Torque to factory specifications.

➡**Recheck the bolt torque for the engine lift plate before removing the engine.**

29. Disconnect the oxygen sensor wiring.
30. Disconnect the crankshaft position sensor.
31. Disconnect the engine block heater power cable, if equipped.
32. Disconnect the front propshaft at the front differential and secure it out of the way.
33. Remove the pinion bracket.

➡**It is necessary to disconnect the front propshaft for access to the starter and left side exhaust flange.**

34. Remove the starter.
35. Remove the ground straps from the right side of the block.
36. Remove the ground straps from the left side of the block.
37. Remove the structural cover.
38. Disconnect the right and left exhaust pipes at the manifolds and from the crossover, and remove them from the vehicle.
39. Remove the torque converter bolts (3), and mark the location for reassembly.
40. Remove the transmission bellhousing-to-engine bolts.
41. Remove the left and right engine mount thru bolts.
42. Lower the vehicle.
43. Support the transmission with a suitable jack.
44. Connect a suitable engine hoist to the engine lift plate.
45. Remove the engine from the vehicle.

To install:
46. Position the engine in the vehicle.
47. Install the transmission bellhousing-to-engine mounting bolts. Tighten the bolts to 30 ft. lbs. (41 Nm).
48. Install the engine mount thru bolts.
49. Install the torque converter bolts.
50. Install the starter.
51. Connect the crankshaft position sensor.
52. Install the engine block heater power cable, if equipped.
53. Install the structural cover.

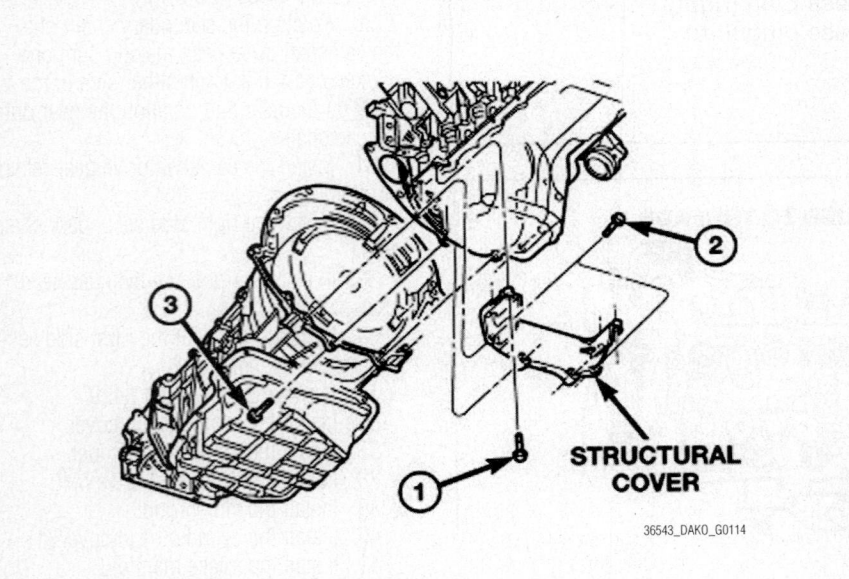

STRUCTURAL COVER

36543_DAKO_G0114

Fig. 105 Structural cover mounting bolt sequence shown

➡**The structural cover requires a specific torque sequence. Failure to follow this sequence may cause severe damage to the cover.**

54. Install the pinion bracket.

55. Install the left and right exhaust pipes.

56. Connect the left and right oxygen sensors.

57. Remove the engine lift plate.

58. Connect the knock sensors.

59. Connect the engine to body ground straps at the left side of the cowl.

60. Install the intake manifold.

61. Install the engine oil dipstick tube.

62. Install the power brake booster vacuum hose.

63. Install the breather hoses.

64. Install the PCV hose.

65. Install the fuel rail.

66. Install the coil over plugs.

67. Connect the engine wiring harness at the following points:
- Intake Air Temperature (IAT) sensor
- Fuel Injectors
- Throttle Position (TPS) Switch
- Idle Air Control (IAC) Motor
- Engine Oil Pressure Switch
- Engine Coolant Temperature (ECT) Sensor
- Manifold Absolute Pressure MAP) Sensor
- Camshaft Position (CMP) Sensor
- Coil Over Plugs
- Crankshaft Position Sensor

68. Connect the ground straps on the right side of the engine.

69. Connect the ground straps on the left side of the engine.

70. Reinstall the radiator/cooling module assembly.

71. Connect the lower radiator hose.

72. Connect the upper radiator hose.

73. Connect the throttle and speed control cables.

74. Install the heater hose assembly.

75. Install the coolant recovery bottle.

76. Install the power steering pump.

77. Install the alternator.

78. Install the A/C compressor.

79. Install the accessory drive belt.

80. Install the fan shroud with the viscous fan assembly.

81. Install the radiator core support bracket.

82. Recharge the A/C system.

83. Install the air cleaner assembly.

84. Refill the engine cooling system.

85. Check and fill the engine oil.

86. Connect the battery negative cable.

87. Start the engine and check for leaks.

4.7L Engine

See Figures 105 and 106.

1. Before servicing the vehicle, refer to the Precautions Section.

2. Release the fuel rail pressure then disconnect the fuel supply quick connect fitting at the fuel rail.

3. Disconnect the battery negative and positive cables.

4. Disconnect the 2 ground straps from the lower left hand side and 1 ground strap from the lower right hand side of the engine.

5. Remove the through bolt retaining nut and bolt from both the left and right side engine mounts.

6. Disconnect the crankshaft position sensor.

7. Remove the exhaust crossover pipe from the exhaust manifolds.

8. Remove the pinion bracket.

9. Remove the structural cover.

10. Remove the starter.

11. Drain the cooling system.

12. Remove the torque converter bolts (automatic transmission).

13. Remove the transmission-to-engine mounting bolts.

14. Disconnect the engine block heater power cable from the block heater, if equipped.

15. Lower the vehicle.

16. Remove the throttle body resonator assembly and air inlet hose.

17. Disconnect the throttle and speed control cables.

18. Disconnect the tube from both the left and right side crankcase breathers. Remove the breathers.

19. Evacuate the A/C system.

20. Remove the A/C compressor.

21. Remove the shroud, fan assembly, and accessory drive belt.

22. Disconnect the transmission oil cooler lines at the radiator.

23. Disconnect the radiator upper and lower hoses.

24. Remove the radiator, A/C condenser, and transmission oil cooler.

25. Remove the alternator.

26. Disconnect the 2 heater hoses from the timing chain cover and heater core.

27. Unclip and remove heater hoses and tubes from the intake manifold.

28. Disconnect the engine harness at the following points:
- Intake Air Temperature (IAT) sensor
- Fuel Injectors
- Throttle Position (TPS) Switch
- Idle Air Control (IAC) Motor
- Engine Oil Pressure Switch
- Engine Coolant Temperature (ECT) Sensor
- Manifold Absolute Pressure (MAP) Sensor
- Camshaft Position (CMP) Sensor
- Coil connectors

29. Disconnect the vacuum lines at the throttle body and intake manifold.

30. Remove the power steering pump and position it out of the way.

31. Remove the intake manifold.

32. Install Engine Lift Plate 10101 in place of the intake manifold.

33. Disconnect the body ground strap at the right side cowl.

34. Disconnect the body ground strap at the left side cowl.

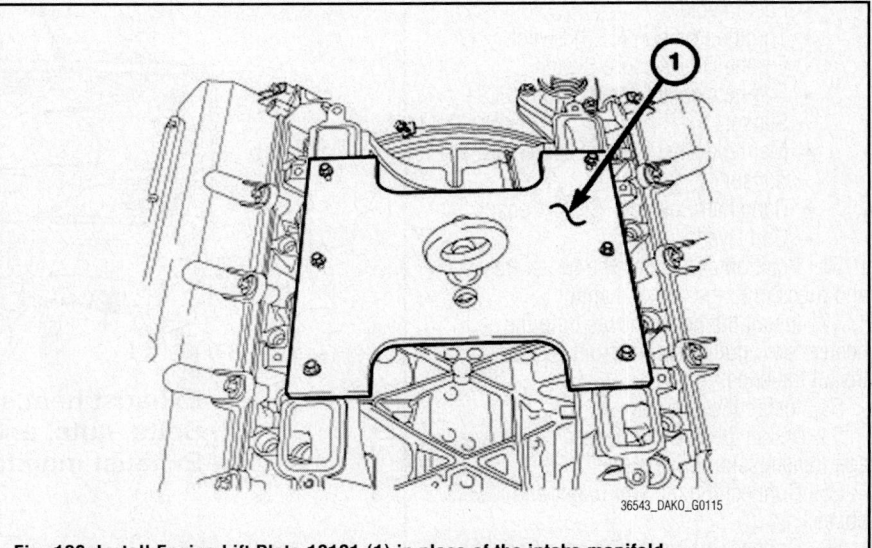

36543_DAKO_G0115

Fig. 106 Install Engine Lift Plate 10101 (1) in place of the intake manifold

➡It will be necessary to support the transmission in order to remove the engine.

35. Position a suitable jack under the transmission.

36. Remove the engine from the vehicle.

To install:

37. Position the engine in the vehicle.

38. Remove the jack from under the transmission.

39. Remove Engine Lifting Plate 10101 (1).

40. Position both the left and right side engine mount brackets and install the through bolts (3) and nuts. Tighten to 70 ft. lbs. (95 Nm).

41. Install the transmission to engine mounting bolts. Tighten the bolts to 30 ft. lbs. (41 Nm).

42. Install the torque converter bolts.

43. Connect the right side body ground strap.

44. Connect the left side body ground strap.

45. Install the intake manifold.

46. Position the alternator wiring behind the oil dipstick tube, then install the oil dipstick tube upper mounting bolt.

47. Install the power steering pump.

48. Connect the fuel supply line quick connect fitting.

49. Connect the vacuum lines at the throttle body and intake manifold.

50. Connect the engine harness at the following points:
- Intake Air Temperature (IAT) Sensor
- Idle Air Control (IAC) Motor
- Fuel Injectors
- Throttle Position (TPS) Switch
- Engine Oil Pressure Switch
- Engine Coolant Temperature (ECT) Sensor
- Manifold Absolute Pressure (MAP) Sensor
- Camshaft Position (CMP) Sensor
- Coil Over Plugs

51. Position and install the heater hoses and tubes onto the intake manifold.

52. Install the heater hoses onto the heater core and the engine front cover, and install the clips.

53. Install the alternator.

54. Install the A/C condenser, radiator, and transmission oil cooler.

55. Connect the radiator upper and lower hoses.

56. Connect the transmission oil cooler lines to the radiator.

57. Install the accessory drive belt, fan assembly, and shroud.

58. Install the A/C compressor.

59. Install both breathers. Connect the tube to both crankcase breathers.

60. Connect the throttle and speed control cables.

61. Install the throttle body resonator assembly and air inlet hose. Tighten the clamps to 35 inch lbs. (4 Nm).

62. Raise and safely support the vehicle.

63. Connect the crankshaft position sensor.

64. Install the starter.

65. Install the structural cover.

✲✲ WARNING

The structural cover requires a specific torque sequence. Failure to follow this sequence may cause severe damage to the cover.

66. Install the pinion bracket.

67. Install the exhaust crossover pipe.

68. Install the engine block heater power cable, if equipped.

69. Check and fill the engine oil to the proper level.

70. Recharge the A/C system.

71. Refill the engine cooling system.

72. Connect the battery positive and negative cables.

73. Start the engine and check for leaks.

EXHAUST MANIFOLD

REMOVAL & INSTALLATION

3.7L Engine

Left

See Figure 107.

1. Before servicing the vehicle, refer to the Precautions Section.

2. Disconnect the negative cable from the battery.

3. Raise and safely support the vehicle.

4. Remove the bolts and nuts attaching the exhaust pipe to the engine exhaust manifold.

5. Lower the vehicle.

6. Remove the exhaust heat shields (1).

7. Remove the bolts, nuts (2), and washers attaching the manifold to the cylinder head.

8. Remove the manifold and gasket from the cylinder head.

To install:

✲✲ WARNING

If the studs came out with the nuts when removing the engine exhaust manifold, install the new studs. Apply sealer on the coarse thread ends. Water leaks may develop at the studs if this precaution is not taken.

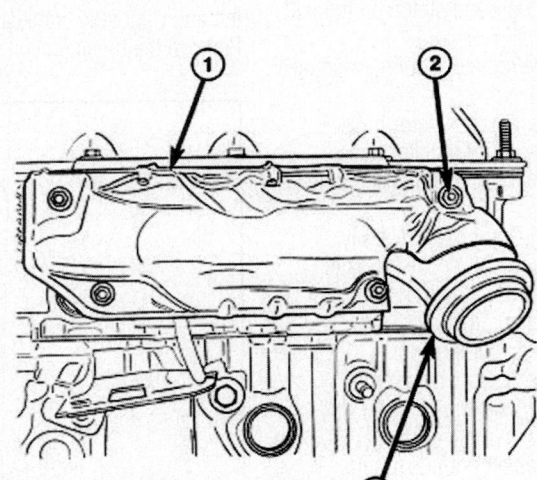

1. Exhaust heat shields
2. Bolts, nuts, and washers
3. Exhaust manifold

36543_DAKO_G0116

Fig. 107 Left exhaust manifold shown—3.7L engine

9. Position the engine exhaust manifold and gasket on the 2 studs located on the cylinder head. Install the conical washers and nuts on these studs.

10. Install the remaining conical washers. Starting at the center arm and working outward, tighten the bolts and nuts to 18 ft. lbs. (25 Nm).

11. Install the exhaust heat shields.

12. Raise and safely support the vehicle.

✳✳ WARNING

Over-tightening the heat shield fasteners may cause the shield to distort and/or crack.

13. Assemble the exhaust pipe to the manifold and secure with the bolts, nuts, and retainers. Tighten the bolts and nuts to 25 ft. lbs. (34 Nm).

Right

See Figure 108.

1. Before servicing the vehicle, refer to the Precautions Section.

2. Disconnect the negative cable from the battery.

3. Raise and safely support the vehicle.

4. Remove the bolts and nuts attaching the exhaust pipe to the engine exhaust manifold.

5. Lower the vehicle.

6. Remove the exhaust heat shield (1).

7. Remove the bolts, nuts (2), and washers attaching the manifold to the cylinder head.

8. Remove the manifold and gasket from the cylinder head.

To install:

✳✳ WARNING

If the studs came out with the nuts when removing the engine exhaust manifold, install the new studs. Apply sealer on the coarse thread ends. Water leaks may develop at the studs if this precaution is not taken.

9. Position the engine exhaust manifold and gasket on the 2 studs located on the cylinder head. Install the conical washers and nuts on these studs.

10. Install the remaining conical washers. Starting at the center arm and working outward, tighten the bolts and nuts to 18 ft. lbs. (25 Nm).

11. Install the exhaust heat shields.

12. Raise and safely support the vehicle.

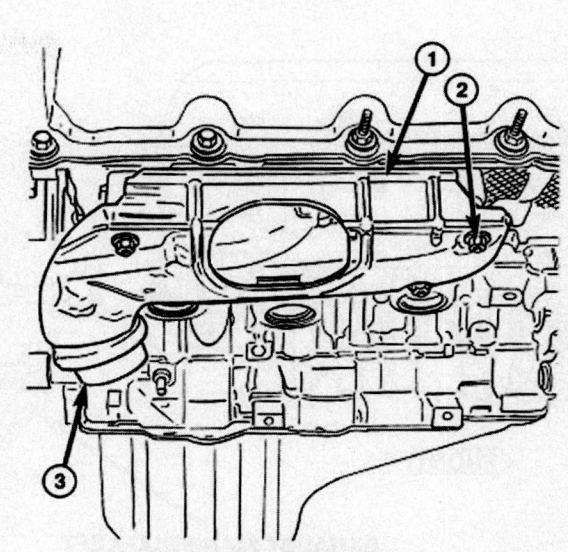

1. **Exhaust heat shield**
2. **Bolts, nuts, and washers**
3. **Exhaust manifold**

36543_DAKO_G0117

Fig. 108 Right exhaust manifold shown—3.7L engine

✳✳ WARNING

Over-tightening the heat shield fasteners may cause the shield to distort and/or crack.

13. Assemble the exhaust pipe to the manifold and secure with the bolts, nuts, and retainers. Tighten the bolts and nuts to 25 ft. lbs. (34 Nm).

4.7L Engine

Left

See Figure 109.

1. Before servicing the vehicle, refer to the Precautions Section.

2. Disconnect the negative battery cable.

3. Raise and safely support the vehicle.

4. Disconnect the exhaust pipe at the manifold.

5. Lower the vehicle.

6. Remove the front 2 exhaust heat shield retaining fasteners. Raise the vehicle and remove the fasteners at the rear of heat shield.

7. Remove the heat shield.

8. Lower the vehicle and remove the upper exhaust manifold retaining bolts.

9. Raise the vehicle and remove the lower exhaust manifold retaining bolts.

10. Remove the exhaust manifold and gasket.

➥**The exhaust manifold is removed from below the engine compartment.**

To install:

11. Install the exhaust manifold and gasket from below the engine compartment.

12. Install the lower exhaust manifold fasteners. DO NOT tighten until all the fasteners are in place.

13. Lower the vehicle and install the upper exhaust manifold fasteners. Tighten all manifold bolts starting at the center and working outward to 18 ft. lbs. (25 Nm).

✳✳ WARNING

Over-tightening the heat shield fasteners may cause the shield to distort and/or crack.

14. Install the exhaust manifold heat shield. Tighten the fasteners to 72 inch lbs. (8 Nm), then loosen 45°.

15. Connect the exhaust pipe to the manifold.

16. Connect the negative cable to the battery.

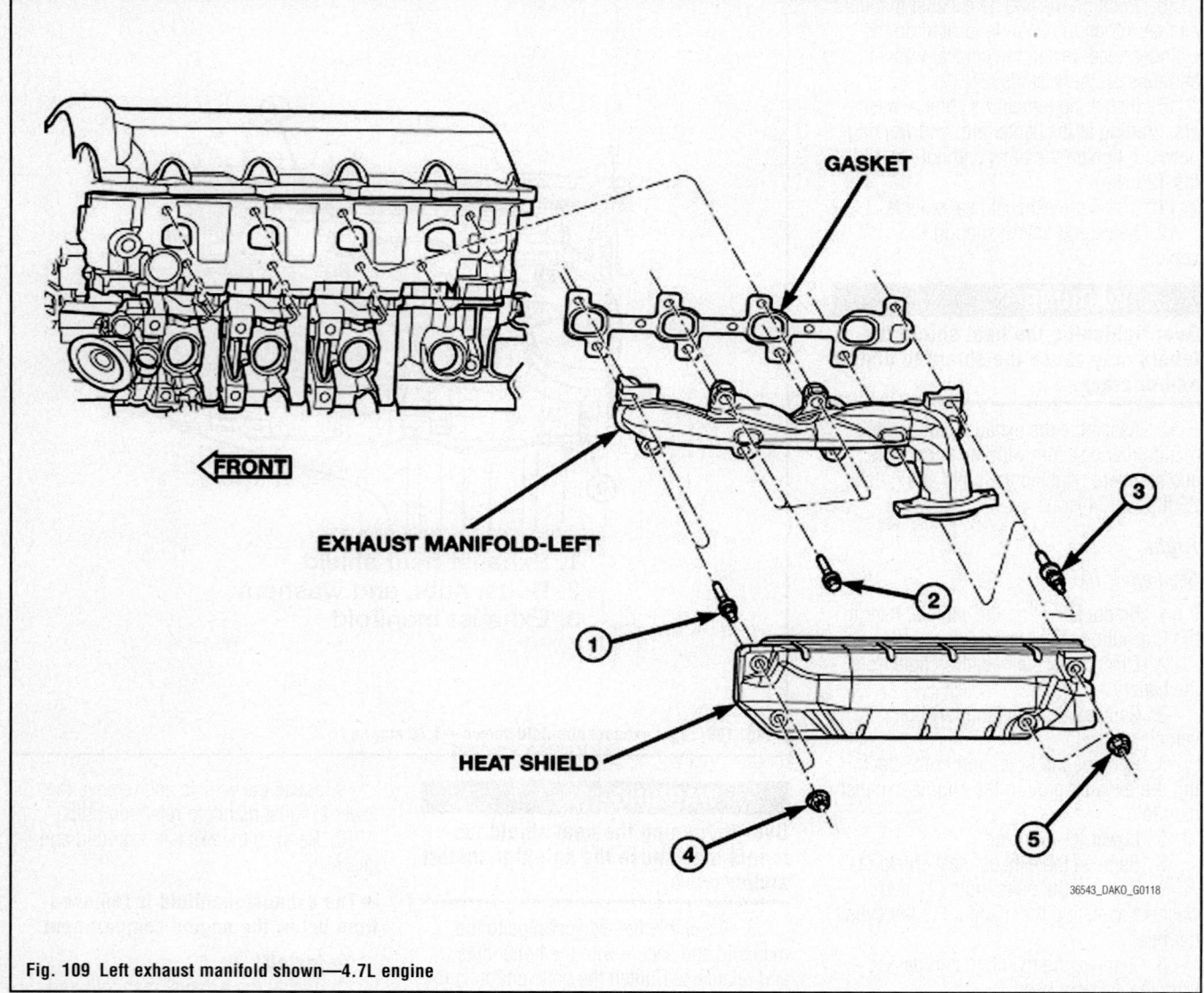

Fig. 109 Left exhaust manifold shown—4.7L engine

Right

See Figure 110.

1. Before servicing the vehicle, refer to the Precautions Section.

2. Disconnect the negative cable from the battery.

3. Remove the air cleaner assembly, resonator assembly, and air inlet hose.

4. Remove the accessory drive belt.

5. Remove the A/C compressor.

6. Remove the A/C accumulator support bracket fastener.

7. Drain the coolant below the heater hose level.

8. Remove the heater hoses at the engine.

9. Remove the fasteners attaching the exhaust manifold heat shield.

10. Remove the heat shield.

11. Remove the upper exhaust manifold attaching fasteners.

12. Raise and safely support the vehicle.

13. Disconnect the exhaust pipe from the manifold.

14. Remove the fasteners attaching the starter. Move the starter aside.

15. Remove the lower exhaust manifold attaching fasteners.

16. Remove the exhaust manifold and gasket.

➡The manifold is removed from below the engine compartment.

To install:

17. Install the exhaust manifold and gasket from below the engine compartment.

18. Install the lower exhaust manifold fasteners. DO NOT tighten until all the fasteners are in place.

19. Lower the vehicle and install the upper exhaust manifold fasteners. Tighten all the manifold bolts starting at center and working outward to 18 ft. lbs. (25 Nm).

✳✳ WARNING

Over-tightening the heat shield fasteners, may cause the shield to distort and/or crack.

20. Install the exhaust manifold heat shield. Tighten the fasteners to 72 inch lbs. (8 Nm), then loosen 45°.

21. Install the starter and fasteners.

22. Connect the exhaust pipe to the manifold.

23. Connect the heater hoses at the engine.

24. Install the fastener attaching the A/C accumulator.

25. Install the A/C compressor and fasteners.

26. Install the accessory drive belt.

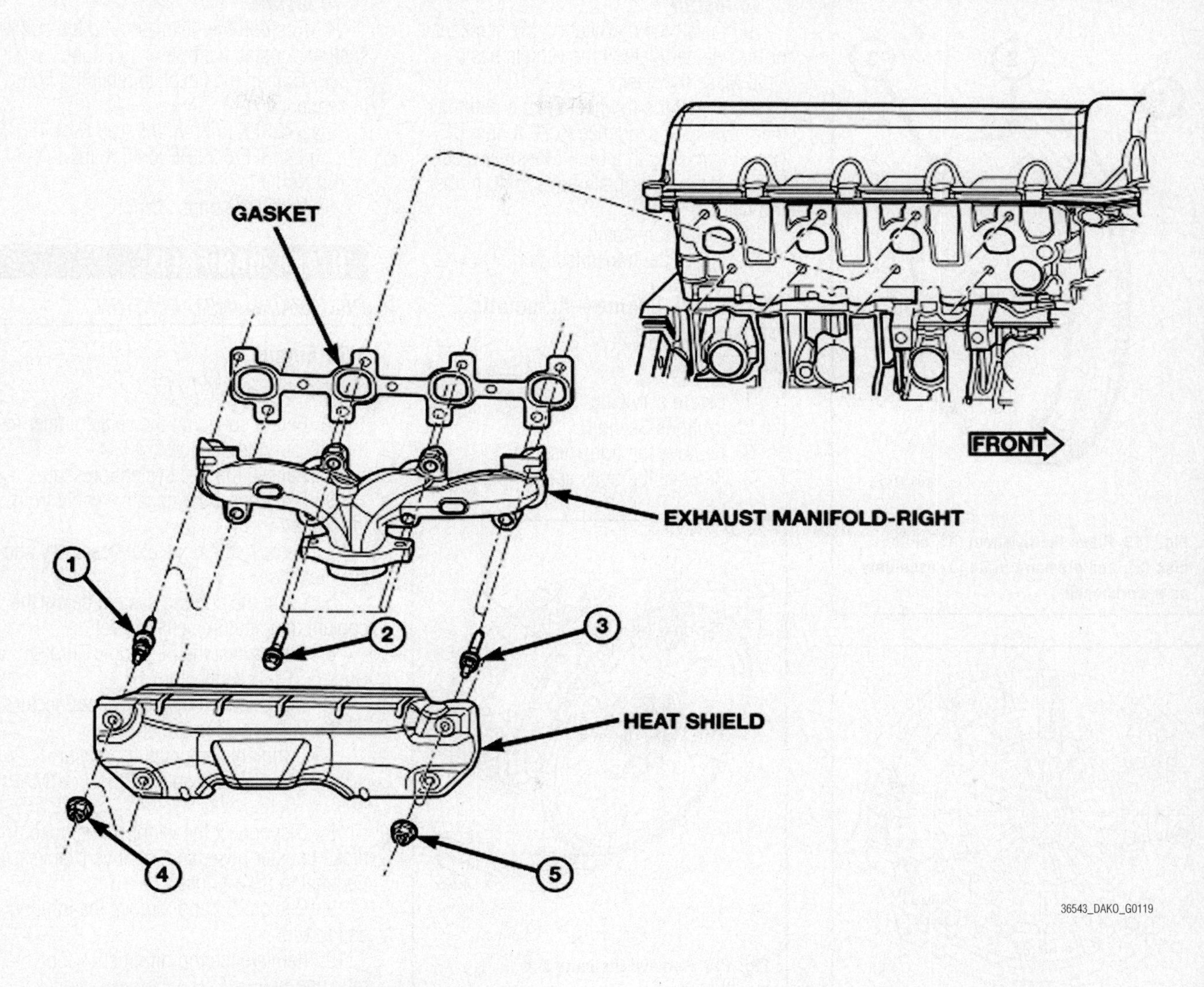

Fig. 110 Right exhaust manifold shown—4.7L engine

27. Install the air cleaner assembly, resonator assembly, and air inlet hose.

28. Install the battery and connect the cables.

29. Fill the cooling system to the proper level.

30. Start the engine and check for leaks.

FLYWHEEL/FLEXPLATE

REMOVAL & INSTALLATION

3.7L Engine—Manual Transmission

See Figures 111 through 114.

1. Before servicing the vehicle, refer to the Precautions Section.

2. Remove the transmission.

→**Vehicles with a Dual Mass Flywheel use an adapter plate between the fly-**

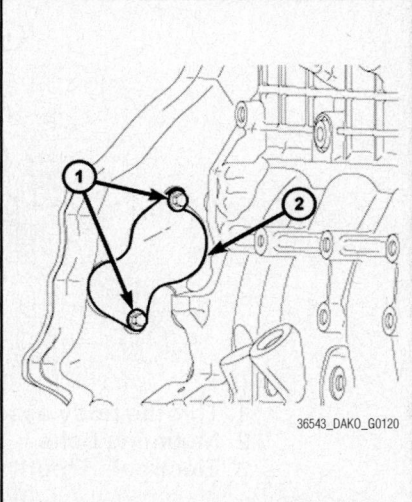

Fig. 111 Remove the dust cover bolts (1) and the dust cover (2)

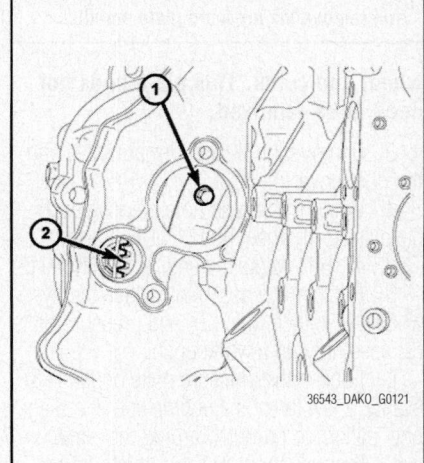

Fig. 112 Using the access hole, remove each flexplate-to-flywheel bolt (1)

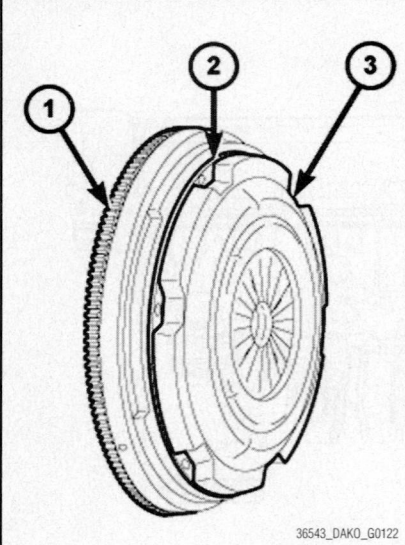

Fig. 113 Place the flywheel (1), clutch disc (2), and pressure plate (3) assembly on a workbench

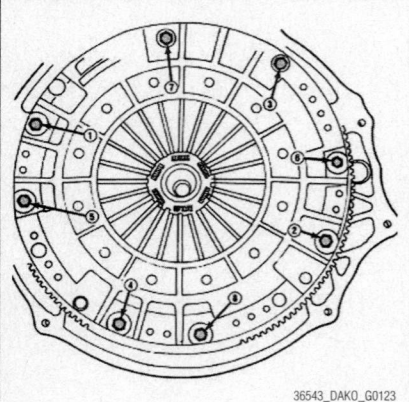

Fig. 114 Remove the pressure plate bolts and remove the pressure plate and disc

wheel and crank. This plate does not need to be removed.

3. Remove the dust cover bolts (1) and the dust cover (2).

4. Using the access hole, remove each flexplate-to-flywheel bolt (1). Use Barring Tool 7471B to rotate the engine and flywheel.

5. Remove the assembly. Place the flywheel (1), clutch disc (2), and pressure plate (3) assembly on a workbench.

6. Loosen the pressure plate bolts (1–8) evenly, a few threads at a time and in a diagonal pattern to prevent warping the plate.

7. Remove the 8 pressure plate bolts (1–8) completely and remove the pressure plate and disc.

8. Remove the flywheel.

To install:

9. Install the flywheel on the crankshaft or the adapter plate, if the vehicle has a Dual Mass flywheel.

10. Install the flywheel bolts and tighten them evenly in sequence to 70 ft. lbs. (95 Nm). Vehicles with a Dual Mass Flywheel, tighten the adapter plate bolts to 40 ft. lbs. (55 Nm).

11. Install the clutch.

12. Install the transmission.

3.7L & 4.7L Engine—Automatic Transmission

See Figure 115.

1. Before servicing the vehicle, refer to the Precautions Section.

2. Remove the transmission.

3. Remove the bolts and flexplate (1).

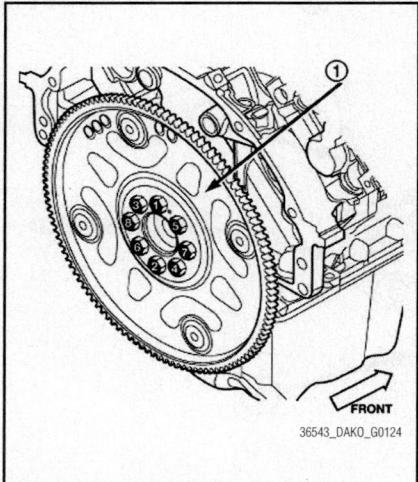

Fig. 115 Remove the bolts and flexplate (1)

To install:

4. Position the flexplate onto the crankshaft and install the bolts hand tight.

5. Tighten the flexplate retaining bolts, in sequence:

    a. 42RLE to 70 ft. lbs. (95 Nm).

    b. 45RFE/545FRE to 45 ft. lbs. (60 Nm).

6. Install the transmission.

INTAKE MANIFOLD

REMOVAL & INSTALLATION

3.7L Engine

See Figures 116 and 117.

1. Before servicing the vehicle, refer to the Precautions Section.

2. Relieve the fuel system pressure.

3. Disconnect the negative cable from the battery.

4. Remove the resonator assembly and air inlet hose.

5. Drain the cooling system below the coolant temperature sensor level.

6. Disconnect the Electronic Throttle Control (ETC) connector (3).

7. Disconnect the electrical connectors for the following components:
- Coolant Temperature Sensor
- Manifold Absolute Pressure (MAP) Sensor

8. Disconnect the vapor purge hose, brake booster hose, and Positive Crankcase Ventilation (PCV) hose.

9. Disconnect and remove the ignition coil towers.

10. Remove the top oil dipstick tube retaining bolt.

11. Remove the EGR tube.

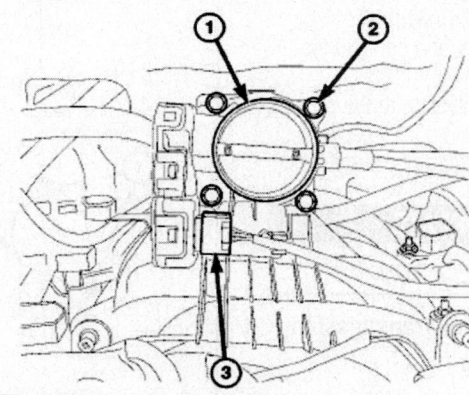

1. **Throttle body assembly**
2. **Mounting bolts**
3. **Electronic Throttle Control (ECT) connector**

Fig. 116 Disconnect the Electronic Throttle Control (ETC)

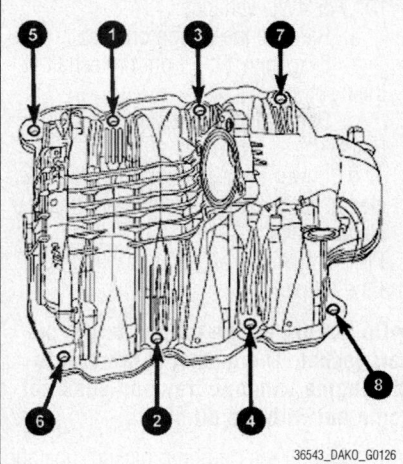

Fig. 117 Intake manifold tightening sequence

12. Remove the fuel rail.
13. Remove the throttle body assembly (1).
14. Remove the intake manifold retaining fasteners in reverse order of the tightening sequence.
15. Remove the intake manifold.

To install:
16. Install the intake manifold seals.
17. Install the intake manifold.
18. Install the intake manifold retaining bolts and tighten in sequence to 105 inch lbs. (12 Nm).

✳✳ WARNING

The proper torque of the throttle body is critical to normal operation. If the throttle body is over-torqued, damage to the throttle body can occur resulting in throttle plate malfunction.

19. Install the throttle body-to-intake manifold O-ring.
20. Install the throttle body (1) to the intake manifold.
21. Install the 4 mounting bolts (2) and tighten to 60 inch lbs. (7 Nm).
22. Install the ECT electrical connector (3).
23. Install the fuel rail.
24. Install the EGR tube.
25. Install the ignition coil towers.
26. Connect the electrical connectors for the following components:
  • Manifold Absolute Pressure (MAP) Sensor
  • Coolant Temperature Sensor
  • Ignition coil towers
27. Install the top oil dipstick tube retaining bolt.
28. Connect the vapor purge hose, brake booster hose, and PCV hose.

29. Fill the cooling system.
30. Install the resonator assembly and air inlet hose.
31. Connect the negative cable to the battery.
32. Using the scan tool, perform the ETC Relearn function.

4.7L Engine

See Figures 118 and 119.

1. Before servicing the vehicle, refer to the Precautions Section.
2. Remove the resonator assembly and air inlet hose.
3. Relieve the fuel system pressure.
4. Disconnect the negative cable from the battery.
5. Disconnect the electrical connectors for the following components:
  • Electronic Throttle Control (ETC) (2)
  • Coolant Temperature Sensor
6. Remove the spark plug wires (3).
7. Disconnect the alternator electrical connections.
8. Disconnect and remove the ignition coils (1, 2) and manifold retaining bolts.
9. Remove the top oil dipstick tube retaining bolt and ground strap.

10. Remove the fuel rail.
11. Remove the intake manifold.

To install:
12. Install the intake manifold gaskets.
13. Position the intake manifold.
14. Install the ignition coils and manifold retaining bolts. Tighten the bolts from the center bolts to the front and to the back in a crisscross pattern to a torque of 106 inch lbs. (12 Nm).
15. Install the throttle body assembly (3), if removed.
16. Install the fuel rail.
17. Connect the electrical connectors for the following components:
  • Manifold Absolute Pressure (MAP) Sensor
  • Electronic Throttle Control (ETC) (2)
  • Coolant Temperature (CTS) Sensor
  • Ignition coils
  • Fuel injectors
18. Install the top oil dipstick tube retaining bolt and ground strap.
19. Install the spark plug wires (3).
20. Connect the alternator electrical connections.
21. Install the resonator assembly and air inlet hose.
22. Connect the negative cable to battery.

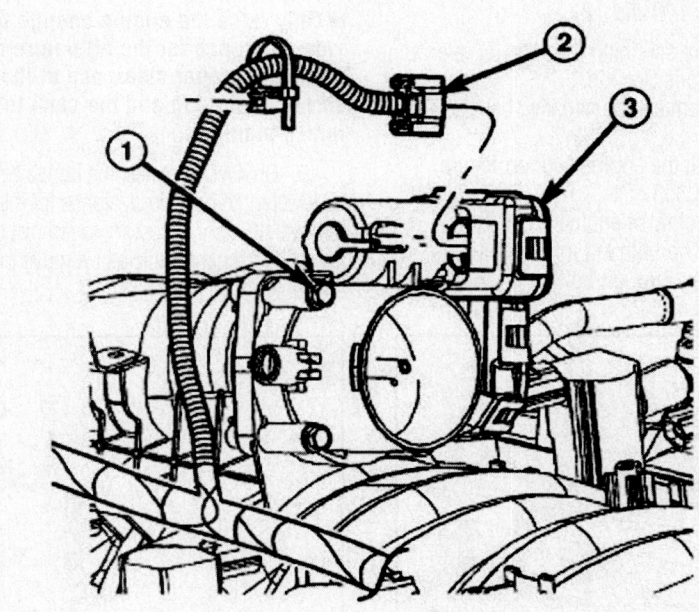

1. Mounting bolts
2. ECT connector
3. Throttle body assembly

36543_DAKO_G0127

Fig. 118 Disconnect the Electronic Throttle Control (ETC) connection

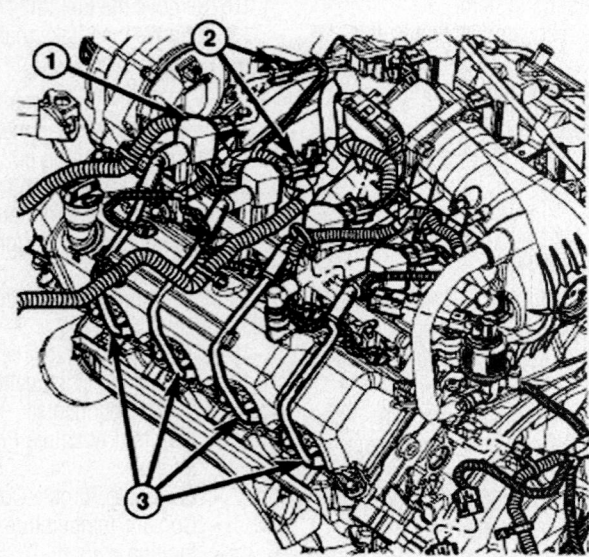

1. Ignition coils
2. Manifold retaining bolts
3. Spark plug wires

36543_DAKO_G0128

Fig. 119 Remove the spark plug wires and ignition coils

OIL PAN

REMOVAL & INSTALLATION

3.7L Engine

See Figures 120 and 121.

1. Before servicing the vehicle, refer to the Precautions Section.
2. Disconnect the negative battery cable.
3. Install the engine support fixture Special Tool 853
4. Do not raise engine at this time.
5. Remove both left and right side engine mount through bolts.

6. Remove the structural dust cover.
7. Drain the engine oil.
8. Raise the engine using Special Tool 8534 (1) to provide clearance to remove the oil pan.

➥**Only raise the engine enough to provide clearance for the oil pan removal. Check for proper clearance at the fan shroud to the fan and the cowl to the intake manifold.**

9. On 4WD vehicles, the front axle must be lowered, to provide clearance for the oil pan removal. It is not necessary to remove the front axle from the vehicle or remove the axle shafts.

10. For 4WD vehicles:
   a. Remove the pinion bracket.
   b. Disconnect the front driveshaft at the front axle.
   c. Remove the front axle mounting bolts.
   d. Lower the axle enough to provide clearance to remove the oil pan, using a suitable jack.
11. Remove the oil pan mounting bolts and the oil pan.

➥**Do not pry on the oil pan or the oil pan gasket. The gasket is integral to the engine windage tray and does not come out with the oil pan.**

12. Unbolt the oil pump pickup tube and remove the tube.
13. Inspect the integral windage tray and the gasket. Replace as needed.

To install:

14. Clean the oil pan gasket mating surface of the bedplate and oil pan.
15. Position the oil pan gasket and pickup tube with new O-ring.
16. Install the mounting bolt and nuts. Tighten the bolt and nuts to 20 ft. lbs. (28 Nm).
17. Position the oil pan and install the mounting bolts. Tighten the mounting bolts to 140 inch lbs. (16 Nm) in the sequence shown.
18. Lower the engine into the mounts using Special Tool 8534 (1).
19. Install both the left and right side engine mount through bolts. Tighten the bolts to 50 ft. lbs. (68 Nm).
20. Remove Special Tool 8534.
21. Install the structural dust cover.
22. For 4WD Vehicles:
   a. Raise the axle using a suitable jack.
   b. Install the front axle mounting bolts.

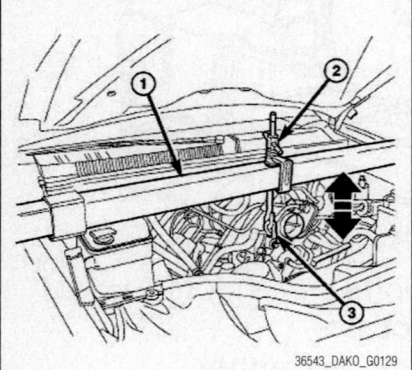

36543_DAKO_G0129

Fig. 120 Raise the engine using Special Tool 8534 to provide clearance to remove the oil pan

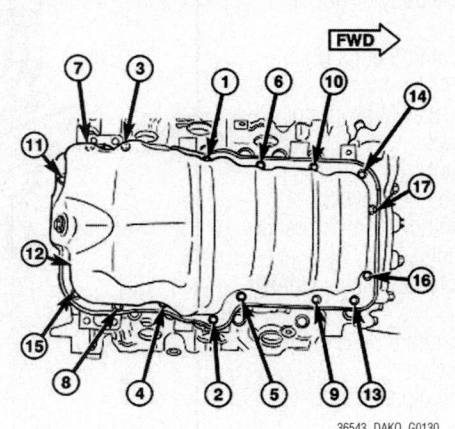

36543_DAKO_G0130

Fig. 121 Oil pan bolt tightening sequence—3.7L engine

c. Install the pinion bracket.

d. Install the front driveshaft to the front axle.

23. Fill the engine oil to the proper level.

24. Reconnect the negative battery cable.

25. Start the engine and check for leaks.

4.7L Engine

See Figures 120 and 122.

1. Before servicing the vehicle, refer to the Precautions Section.

2. Disconnect the negative battery cable.

3. Install the engine support fixture Special Tool 8534 (1). Do not raise the engine at this time.

4. Remove both left and right side engine mount through bolts.

5. Remove the structural dust cover.

6. Drain the engine oil.

➡**Only raise the engine enough to provide clearance for the oil pan removal. Check for proper clearance at the fan shroud to the fan and the cowl to the intake manifold.**

7. Raise the engine using Special Tool 8534 (1) to provide clearance to remove the oil pan.

➡**On 4WD vehicles, the front axle must be lowered, to provide clearance for the oil pan removal. It is not necessary to remove the front axle from the vehicle, or remove the axle shafts.**

8. For 4WD Vehicles:

a. Remove the pinion bracket.

b. Disconnect the front driveshaft at the front axle.

c. Remove the front axle mounting bolts.

d. Lower the axle enough to provide clearance to remove the oil pan, using a suitable jack.

❄❄ WARNING

Do not pry on the oil pan or oil pan gasket. The gasket is integral to the engine windage tray and does not come out with the oil pan.

9. Remove the oil pan mounting bolts and the oil pan.

10. Unbolt the oil pump pickup tube and remove the tube.

11. Inspect the integral windage tray and gasket and replace as needed.

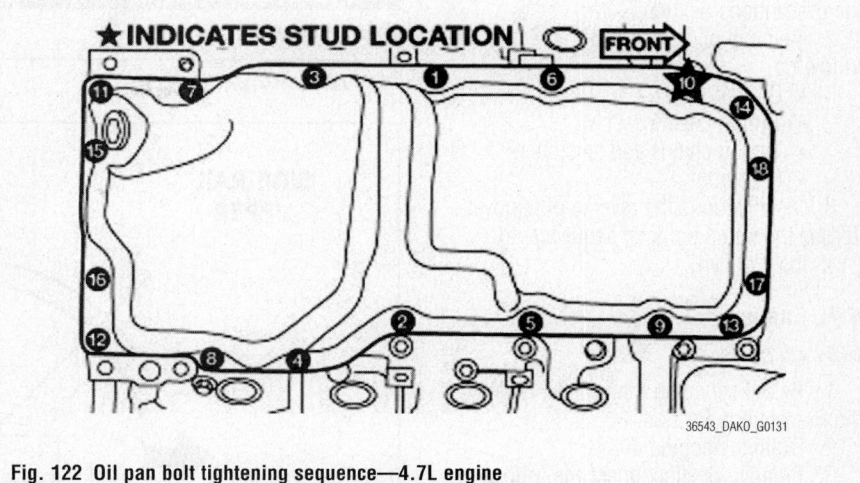

Fig. 122 Oil pan bolt tightening sequence—4.7L engine

To install:

12. Clean the oil pan gasket mating surface of the bedplate and the oil pan.

13. Position the oil pan gasket and pickup tube with a new O-ring.

14. Install the mounting bolt and nuts. Tighten the bolt and nuts to 20 ft. lbs. (28 Nm).

15. Position the oil pan and install the mounting bolts. Tighten the mounting bolts to 11 ft. lbs. (15 Nm) in the sequence shown.

16. Lower the engine into the mounts using Special Tool 8534 (1).

17. Install both the left and right side engine mount through bolts. Tighten the bolts to 50 ft. lbs. (68 Nm).

18. Remove the Special Tool 8534 (1).

19. Install the structural dust cover.

20. For 4WD Vehicles;

a. Raise the axle using a suitable jack.

b. Install the front axle mounting bolts.

c. Install the pinion bracket.

d. Install the front driveshaft to the front axle.

21. Fill the engine oil to the proper level.

22. Connect the negative battery cable.

23. Start the engine and check for leaks.

OIL PUMP

REMOVAL & INSTALLATION

3.7L Engine

See Figure 123.

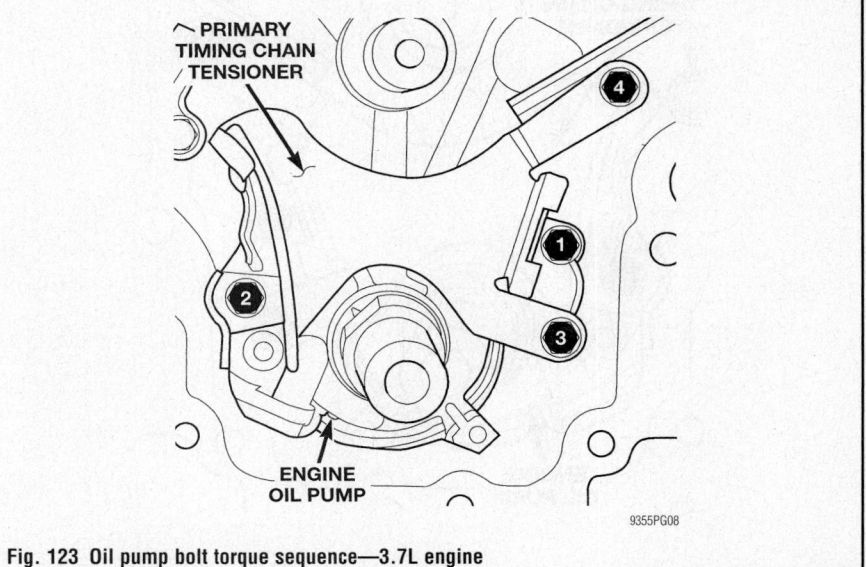

Fig. 123 Oil pump bolt torque sequence—3.7L engine

1. Before servicing the vehicle, refer to the Precautions Section.

2. Remove or disconnect the following:
- Oil Pan
- Timing chain cover
- Timing chains and tensioners
- Oil pump

3. Installation is the reverse of removal. Torque the pump bolts, in sequence, to 21 ft. lbs. (28 Nm).

4.7L Engine

See Figure 124.

1. Before servicing the vehicle, refer to the Precautions Section.

2. Drain the engine oil.

3. Remove or disconnect the following:
- Negative battery cable
- Oil pan
- Oil pump pick-up tube
- Timing chains and tensioners
- Oil pump

To install:

4. Install or connect the following:
- Oil pump. Tighten the bolts to 21 ft. lbs. (28 Nm)
- Timing chains and tensioners
- Oil pump pick-up tube
- Oil pan
- Negative battery cable

5. Fill the crankcase to the correct level.

6. Start the engine and check for leaks.

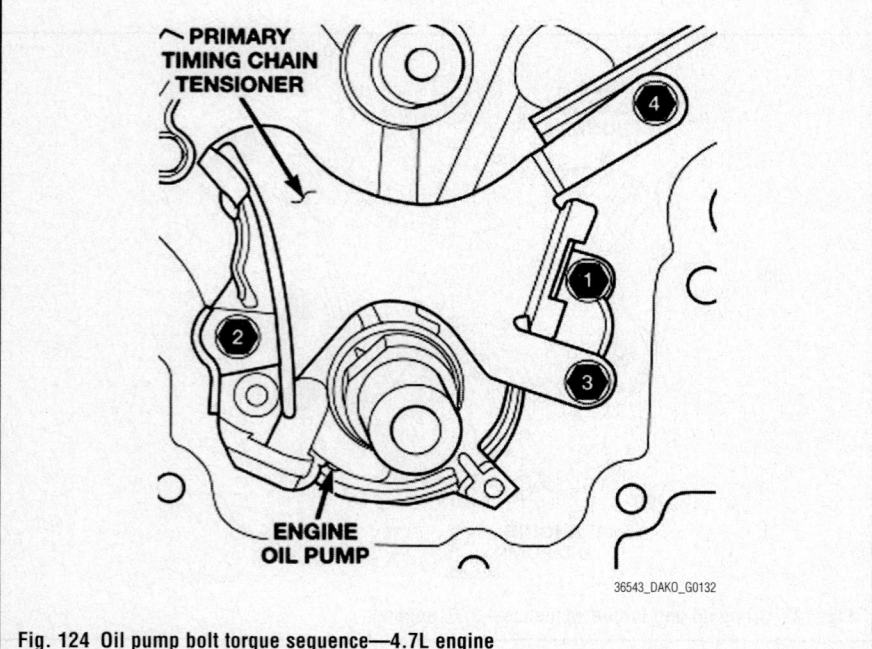

Fig. 124 Oil pump bolt torque sequence—4.7L engine

PISTON AND RING

POSITIONING

See Figure 125.

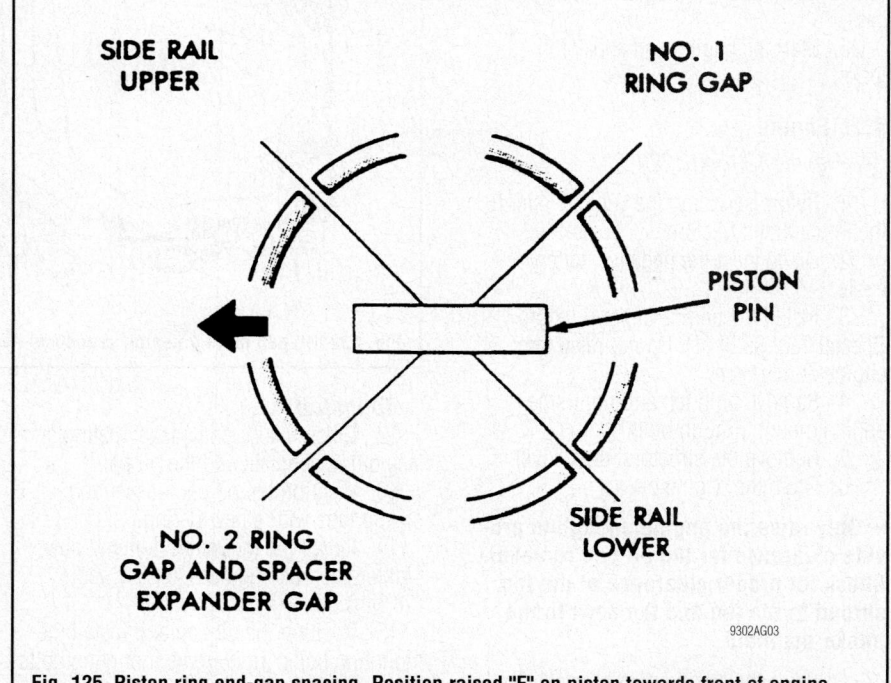

Fig. 125 Piston ring end-gap spacing. Position raised "F" on piston towards front of engine

REAR MAIN SEAL

REMOVAL & INSTALLATION

See Figures 126 through 128.

1. Before servicing the vehicle, refer to the Precautions Section.

➡**This procedure can be performed while the engine is in the vehicle.**

2. If being preformed while the engine is in the vehicle, remove the transmission.

3. Remove the flexplate.

➡**The crankshaft oil seal (1) CAN NOT be reused after removal.**

➡**The Seal Remover 8506 (2) must be installed deeply into the seal. Continue to tighten the removal tool into the seal until the tool cannot be turned farther. Failure to install the tool correctly the first time will cause the tool to pull free**

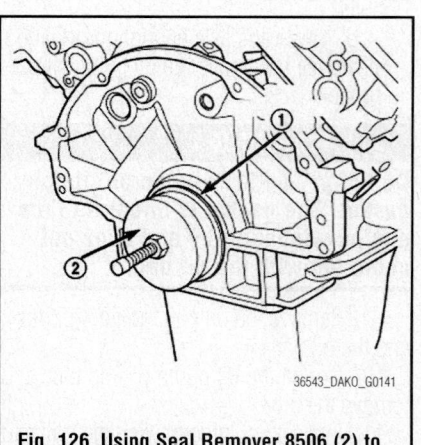

Fig. 126 Using Seal Remover 8506 (2) to remove the crankshaft rear oil seal (1)

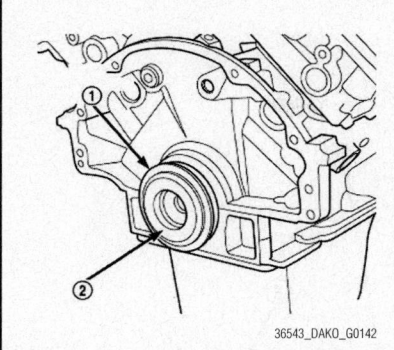

Fig. 127 Position the Seal Installer 8349-2 (2) onto the crankshaft rear face and the crankshaft rear oil seal (1) onto the guide

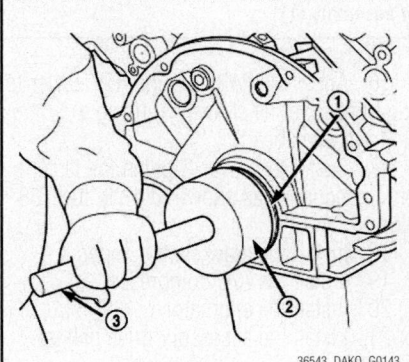

Fig. 128 Using the Seal Installer 8349 (2) and Universal Drive Handle C-4171 (3), with a hammer, tap the seal (1) into place

of seal without removing the seal from the engine.

4. Using Seal Remover 8506 (2), remove the crankshaft rear oil seal (1).

To install:

5. Lubricate the crankshaft flange with engine oil.

6. Position the Seal Installer 8349-2 (2) onto the crankshaft rear face. Then, position the crankshaft rear oil seal (1) onto the guide.

7. Using the Seal Installer 8349 (2) and Universal Drive Handle C-4171 (3), with a hammer, tap the seal (1) into place. Continue to tap on the driver handle until the seal installer seats against the cylinder block crankshaft bore.

8. Install the flexplate.

9. Install the transmission.

ROCKER ARMS/SHAFTS

REMOVAL & INSTALLATION

3.7L Engine

See Figure 129.

1. Before servicing the vehicle, refer to the Precautions Section.

2. Disconnect the battery negative cable to prevent accidental starter engagement.

3. Remove the cylinder head cover.

4. For rocker arm removal on cylinder No. 4, rotate the crankshaft until cylinder No. 1 is at BDC intake stroke.

5. For rocker arm removal on cylinder No. 1, rotate the crankshaft until cylinder No. 1 is at BDC combustion stroke.

6. For rocker arm removal on cylinders No. 3 and No. 5, rotate the crankshaft until cylinder No. 1 is at TDC exhaust stroke.

7. For rocker arm removal on cylinders No. 2 and No. 6, rotate the crankshaft until cylinder No. 1 is at TDC ignition stroke.

8. Using the Remover/Installer 8516 (2), press downward on the valve spring, remove the rocker arm.

To install:

9. Using the Remover/Installer 8516 (2) press downward on the valve spring and install the rocker arm.

> ❄❄ **WARNING**
>
> **Make sure the rocker arms are installed with the concave pocket over the lash adjusters. Failure to do so may cause severe damage to the rocker arms and/or lash adjusters.**

➡Coat the rocker arms with clean engine oil prior to installation.

10. For rocker arm installation on cylinder No. 4, rotate the crankshaft until cylinder No. 1 is at BDC intake stroke.

11. For rocker arm installation on cylinder No. 1, rotate the crankshaft until cylinder No. 1 is at BDC combustion stroke.

12. For rocker arm installation on cylin-

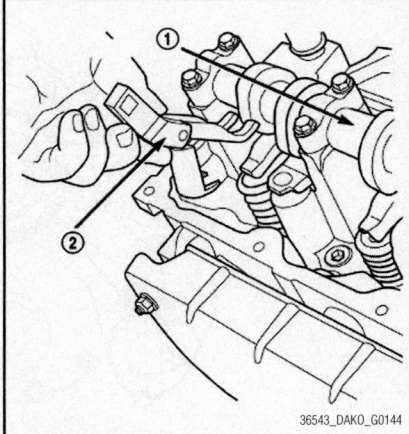

Fig. 129 Rocker arm service using Remover/Installer 8516 (2)

ders No. 3 and No. 5, rotate the crankshaft until cylinder No. 1 is at TDC exhaust stroke.

13. For rocker arm installation on cylinders No. 2 and No. 6, rotate the crankshaft until cylinder No. 1 is at TDC ignition stroke.

14. Install the cylinder head cover.

15. Connect the negative battery cable.

4.7L Engine

See Figure 129.

1. Before servicing the vehicle, refer to the Precautions Section.

2. Disconnect the battery negative cable to prevent accidental starter engagement.

3. Remove the cylinder head cover.

4. For rocker arm removal on cylinders No. 3 and No. 5, rotate the crankshaft until cylinder No. 1 is at TDC exhaust stroke.

5. For rocker arm removal on cylinders No. 2 and No. 8, rotate the crankshaft until cylinder No. 1 is at TDC compression stroke.

6. For rocker arm removal on cylinders No. 4 and No. 6, rotate the crankshaft until cylinder No. 3 is at TDC compression stroke.

7. For rocker arm removal on cylinders No. 1 and No. 7, rotate the crankshaft until cylinder No. 2 is at TDC compression stroke.

8. Using Special Tool 8516 Rocker Arm Remover (2), press downward on the valve spring and remove the rocker arm.

To install:

> ❄❄ **WARNING**
>
> **Make sure the rocker arms are installed with the concave pocket over the lash adjusters. Failure to do so may cause severe damage to the rocker arms and/or lash adjusters.**

➡Coat the rocker arms with clean engine oil prior to installation.

9. For rocker arm installation on cylinders No. 3 and No. 5, rotate the crankshaft until cylinder No. 1 is at TDC exhaust stroke.

10. For rocker arm installation on cylinders No. 2 and No. 8, rotate the crankshaft until cylinder No. 1 is at TDC compression stroke.

11. For rocker arm installation on cylinders No. 4 and No. 6, rotate the crankshaft until cylinder No. 3 is at TDC compression stroke.

12. For rocker arm installation on cylinders No. 1 and No. 7, rotate the crankshaft until cylinder No. 2 is at TDC compression stroke.

13. Using valve spring compressor 10102 press downward on the valve spring and install the rocker arm.

14. Install the cylinder head cover.

15. Connect the negative battery cable.

TIMING CHAIN COVER AND SEAL

REMOVAL & INSTALLATION

3.7L Engine

See Figures 130 through 132.

1. Before servicing the vehicle, refer to the Precautions Section.

2. Disconnect the battery negative cable.

3. Drain the cooling system.

4. Remove the electric cooling fan and fan shroud assembly.

5. Remove radiator fan.

6. Disconnect both heater hoses at the timing cover.

7. Disconnect the lower radiator hose at the engine.

8. Remove the accessory drive belt tensioner assembly (1).

9. Remove crankshaft damper.

10. Remove the alternator.

11. Remove the A/C compressor.

➡ It is not necessary to remove the water pump for timing cover removal.

12. Remove the bolts holding the timing cover to engine block.

13. Remove the timing cover.

To install:

➡ The 3.7L engine uses an anaerobic sealer instead of a gasket to seal the front cover to the engine block, from the factory. For service, MOPAR® Grey Engine RTV sealant must be substituted.

14. Clean the timing chain cover and block surface using rubbing alcohol. Do not use oil based liquids to clean the timing cover or block surfaces.

❈❈ WARNING

Use only rubbing alcohol along with plastic or wooden scrapers. Use no wire brushes, abrasive wheels, or metal scrapers as damage to surfaces could result.

15. Inspect the water passage O-rings (2) for any damage, and replace as necessary.

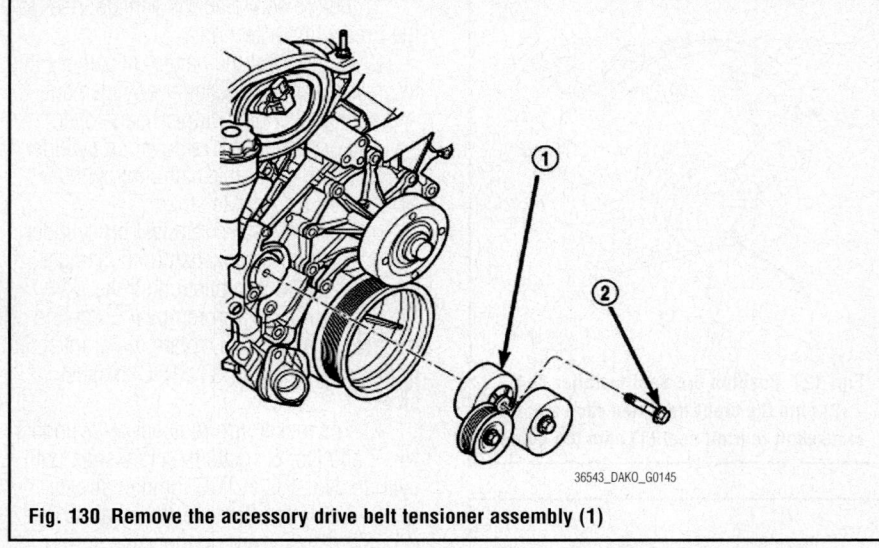

Fig. 130 Remove the accessory drive belt tensioner assembly (1)

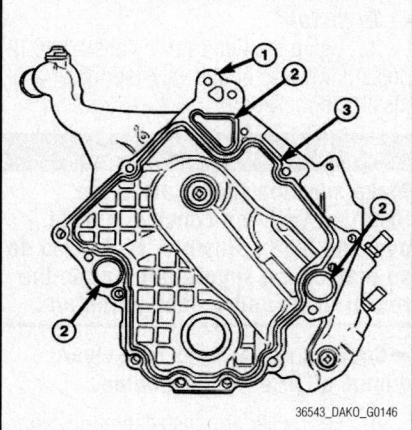

Fig. 131 Inspect the water passage O-rings (2) for any damage. Apply RTV sealer to the front cover as shown (3)

16. Apply MOPAR® Engine RTV sealer to the front cover as shown (3) using a 3–4mm thick bead.

17. Install the cover. Tighten the fasteners in sequence as shown to 43 ft. lbs. (58 Nm).

18. Install the crankshaft damper.

19. Install the A/C compressor.

20. Install the alternator.

21. Install the accessory drive belt tensioner.

22. Install the radiator upper and lower hoses.

23. Install both heater hoses.

24. Install the radiator fan.

25. Connect the battery negative cable.

26. Fill and bleed the cooling system.

27. Start the engine and check for leaks.

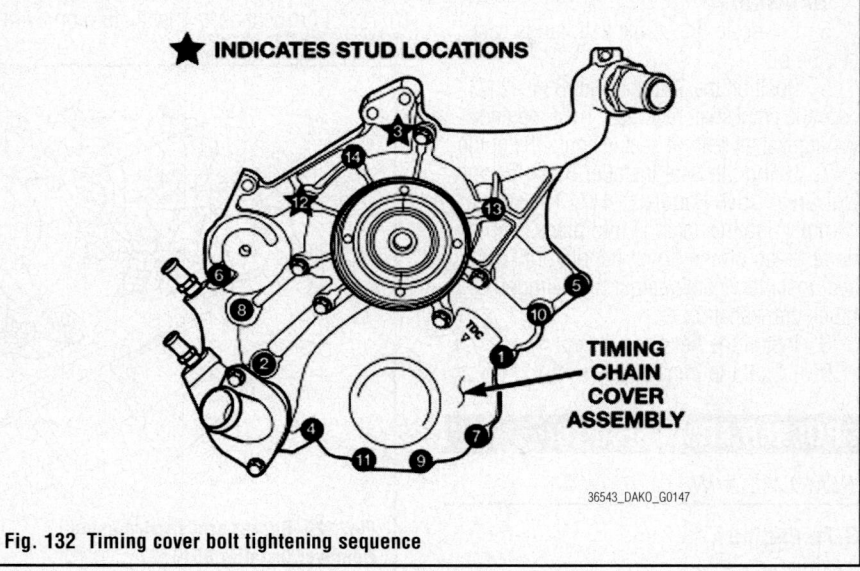

★ INDICATES STUD LOCATIONS

TIMING CHAIN COVER ASSEMBLY

Fig. 132 Timing cover bolt tightening sequence

4.7L Engine

See Figures 130 through 132.

1. Before servicing the vehicle, refer to the Precautions Section.
2. Disconnect the battery negative cable.
3. Disconnect the battery negative cable.
4. Drain cooling system.
5. Disconnect both heater hoses at the timing cover.
6. Disconnect the lower radiator hose at the engine.
7. Remove the crankshaft damper.
8. Remove the accessory drive belt tensioner assembly (1).
9. Remove the alternator and A/C compressor.

➡**It is not necessary to remove the water pump for the timing cover removal.**

10. Remove the bolts holding the timing cover to the engine block.
11. Remove the timing chain cover.

To install:

➡**The 4.7L engine uses an RTV sealer instead of a gasket to seal the front cover to the engine block, from the factory. For service, MOPAR® Grey Engine RTV sealant must be substi-** tuted. If the front cover being used has no provisions for the water passage O-rings, then MOPAR® Grey Engine RTV sealant must be applied around the water passages.

> ❊❊ **WARNING**
>
> **Do not use oil based liquids to clean the timing cover or block surfaces. Use only rubbing alcohol along with plastic or wooden scrapers. Use no wire brushes, abrasive wheels, or metal scrapers, as damage to the surfaces could result.**

12. Clean the timing chain cover and block surface using rubbing alcohol.
13. Inspect the water passage O-rings (2), if equipped, for damage and replace as necessary.
14. Apply MOPAR® Engine RTV sealer to the front cover as shown (3) using a 3–4mm thick bead.
15. Install the cover. Tighten the flange head fasteners in sequence as shown to 43 ft. lbs. (58 Nm).
16. Install the A/C compressor and alternator.
17. Install the crankshaft damper.

18. Install the accessory drive belt tensioner assembly. Tighten the fastener to 40 ft. lbs. (54 Nm).
19. Install the lower radiator hose.
20. Install both heater hoses.
21. Fill the cooling system.
22. Connect the battery negative cable.
23. Start the engine and check for leaks.

TIMING CHAIN AND SPROCKETS

REMOVAL & INSTALLATION

3.7L Engine

See Figures 133 through 143.

1. Before servicing the vehicle, refer to the Precautions Section.
2. Drain the cooling system.
3. Remove or disconnect the following:
   - Negative battery cable
   - Valve covers
   - Radiator fan
4. Rotate the crankshaft so that the crankshaft timing mark aligns with the Top Dead Center (TDC) mark on the front cover, and the **V6** marks on the camshaft sprockets are at 12 o'clock.
5. Remove the power steering pump.

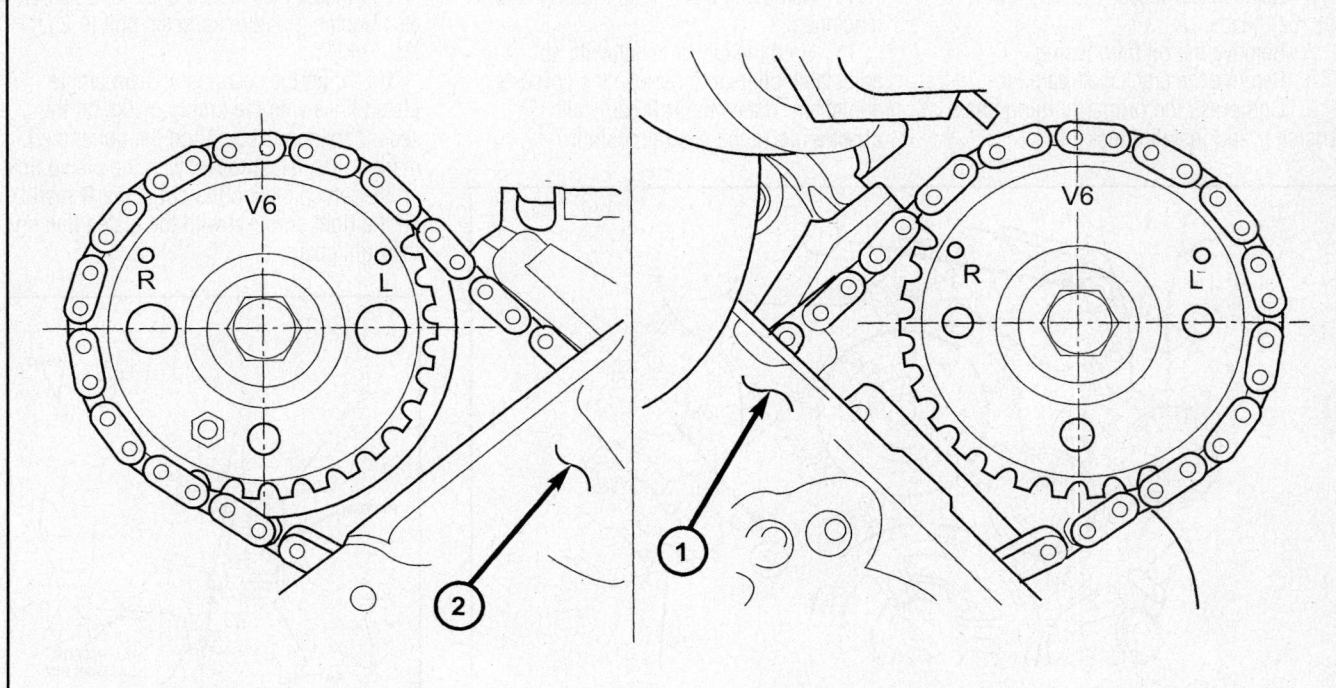

1 - LEFT CYLINDER HEAD
2 - RIGHT CYLINDER HEAD

9355PG09

Fig. 133 Camshaft sprocket timing marks—3.7L engine

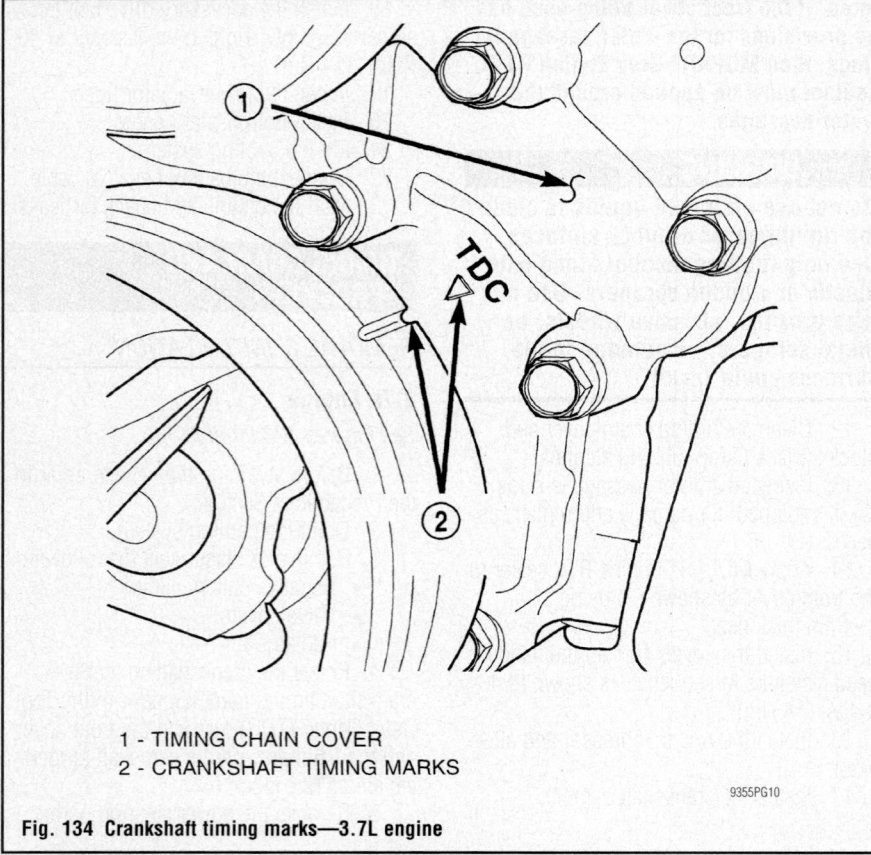

1 - TIMING CHAIN COVER
2 - CRANKSHAFT TIMING MARKS

9355PG10

Fig. 134 Crankshaft timing marks—3.7L engine

6. Remove the access plugs from the cylinder heads.
7. Remove the oil fill housing.
8. Remove the crankshaft damper.
9. Compress the primary timing chain tensioner and install a lock-pin.

10. Remove the secondary timing chain tensioners.
11. Hold the left camshaft with an adjustable pliers and remove the sprocket and chain. Rotate the **left** camshaft 15° **clockwise** to the neutral position.

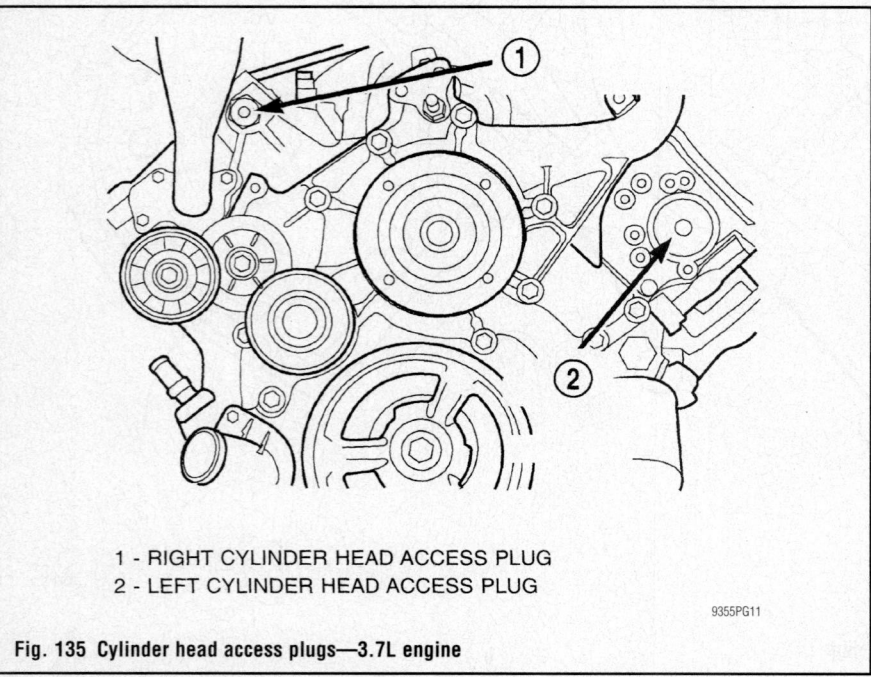

1 - RIGHT CYLINDER HEAD ACCESS PLUG
2 - LEFT CYLINDER HEAD ACCESS PLUG

9355PG11

Fig. 135 Cylinder head access plugs—3.7L engine

12. Hold the right camshaft with an adjustable pliers and remove the camshaft sprocket. Rotate the **right** camshaft 45° **counterclockwise** to the neutral position.
13. Remove the primary timing chain and sprockets.

To install:

14. Use a small prytool to hold the ratchet pawl and compress the secondary timing chain tensioners in a vise and install locking pins.

➡ **The black bolts fasten the guide to the engine block and the silver bolts fasten the guide to the cylinder head.**

15. Install or connect the following:
   • Secondary timing chain guides. Tighten the bolts to 21 ft. lbs. (28 Nm)
   • Secondary timing chains to the idler sprocket so that the double plated links on each chain are visible through the slots in the primary idler sprocket
16. Lock the secondary timing chains to the idler sprocket with a Timing Chain Locking tool as shown.
17. Align the primary chain double plated links with the idler sprocket timing mark and the single plated link with the crankshaft sprocket timing mark.
18. Install the primary chain and sprockets. Tighten the idler sprocket bolt to 25 ft. lbs. (34 Nm).
19. Align the secondary chain single plated links with the timing marks on the secondary sprockets. Align the dot at the **L** mark on the left sprocket with the plated link on the left chain and the dot at the **R** mark on the right sprocket with the plated link on the right chain.

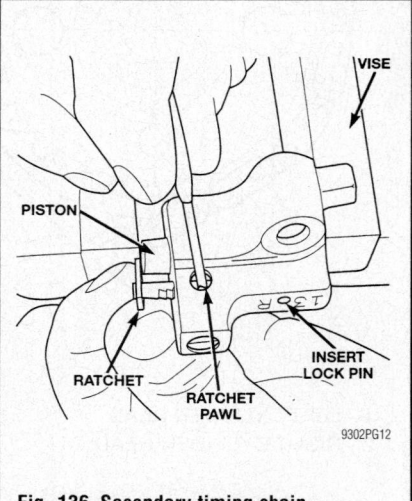

VISE

PISTON

INSERT LOCK PIN

RATCHET

RATCHET PAWL

9302PG12

Fig. 136 Secondary timing chain tensioner preparation—3.7L engine

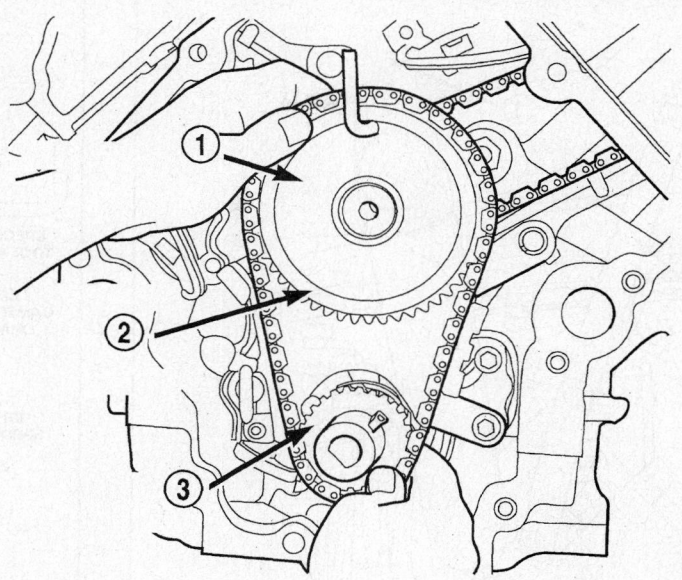

1 - SPECIAL TOOL 8429
2 - PRIMARY CHAIN IDLER SPROCKET
3 - CRANKSHAFT SPROCKET

9355PG12

Fig. 137 Installing the idler gear and timing chain—3.7L engine

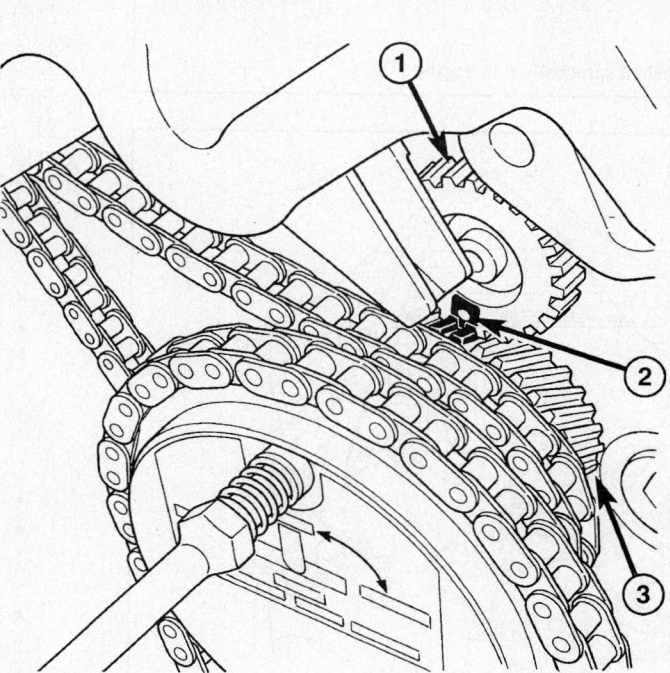

1 - COUNTERBALANCE SHAFT

2 - TIMING MARKS

3 - IDLER SPROCKET

9355PG13

Fig. 138 Counterbalance shaft timing marks—3.7L engine

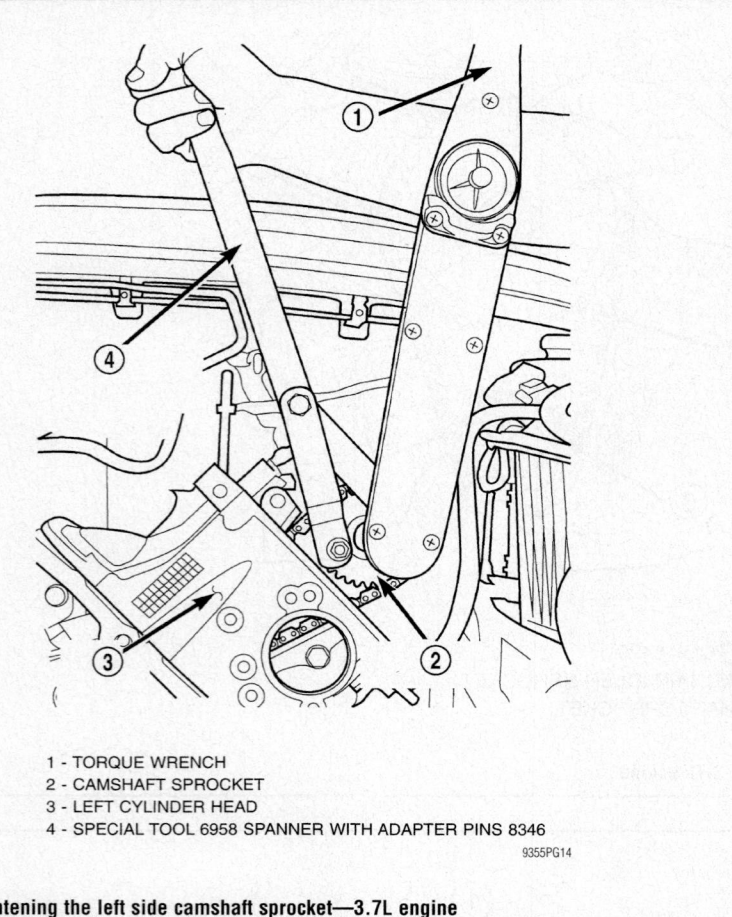

1 - TORQUE WRENCH
2 - CAMSHAFT SPROCKET
3 - LEFT CYLINDER HEAD
4 - SPECIAL TOOL 6958 SPANNER WITH ADAPTER PINS 8346

9355PG14

Fig. 139 Tightening the left side camshaft sprocket—3.7L engine

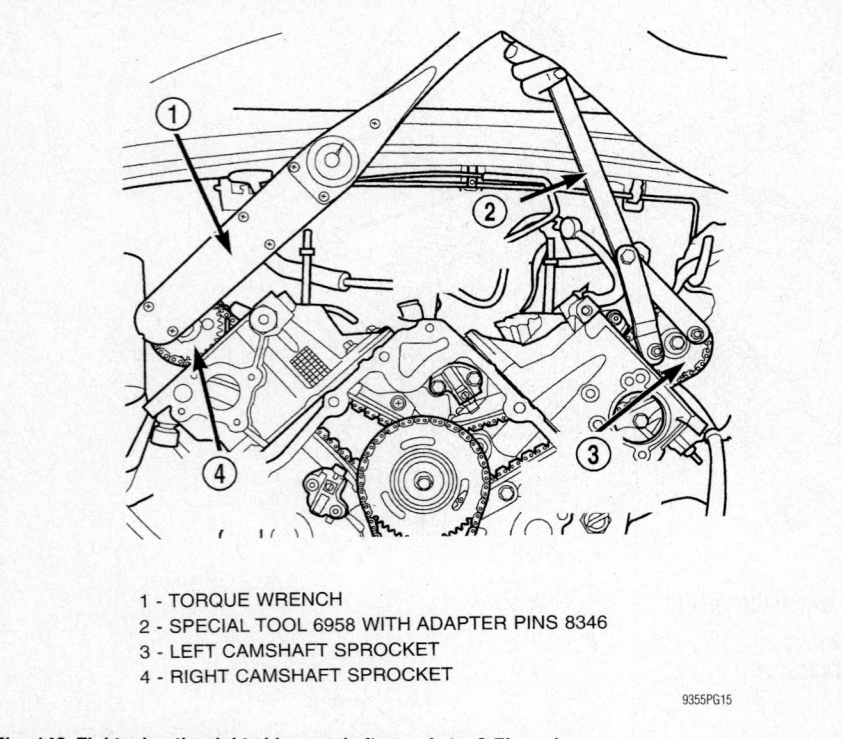

1 - TORQUE WRENCH
2 - SPECIAL TOOL 6958 WITH ADAPTER PINS 8346
3 - LEFT CAMSHAFT SPROCKET
4 - RIGHT CAMSHAFT SPROCKET

9355PG15

Fig. 140 Tightening the right side camshaft sprocket—3.7L engine

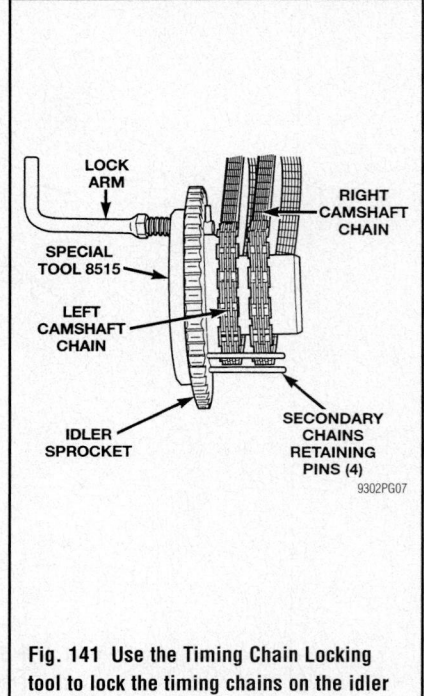

9302PG07

Fig. 141 Use the Timing Chain Locking tool to lock the timing chains on the idler gear—3.7L engine

20. Rotate the camshafts back from the neutral position and install the camshaft sprockets.

21. Remove the secondary chain locking tool.

22. Remove the primary and secondary timing chain tensioner locking pins.

23. Hold the camshaft sprockets with a spanner wrench and tighten the retaining bolts to 90 ft. lbs. (122 Nm).

24. Install or connect the following:
- Front cover. Tighten the bolts, in sequence, to 40 ft. lbs. (54 Nm)
- Front crankshaft seal
- Cylinder head access plugs
- A/C compressor
- Alternator
- Accessory drive belt tensioner. Tighten the bolt to 40 ft. lbs. (54 Nm)
- Oil fill housing
- Crankshaft damper. Tighten the bolt to 130 ft. lbs. (175 Nm)
- Power steering pump
- Lower radiator hose
- Heater hoses
- Accessory drive belt
- Engine cooling fan and shroud
- Camshaft Position (CMP) sensor
- Valve covers
- Negative battery cable

25. Fill and bleed the cooling system.

26. Start the engine, check for leaks and repair if necessary.

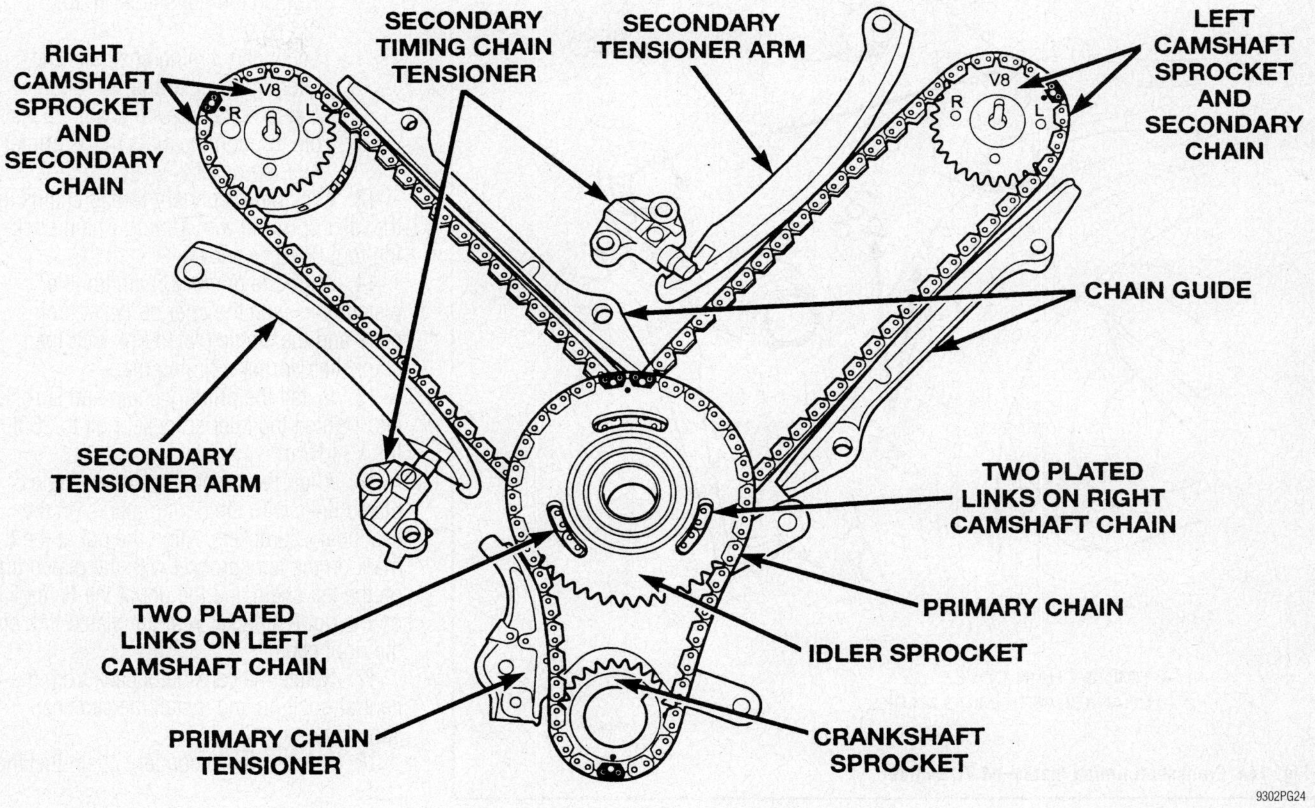

RIGHT CAMSHAFT SPROCKET AND SECONDARY CHAIN

SECONDARY TIMING CHAIN TENSIONER

SECONDARY TENSIONER ARM

LEFT CAMSHAFT SPROCKET AND SECONDARY CHAIN

CHAIN GUIDE

SECONDARY TENSIONER ARM

TWO PLATED LINKS ON RIGHT CAMSHAFT CHAIN

TWO PLATED LINKS ON LEFT CAMSHAFT CHAIN

PRIMARY CHAIN

IDLER SPROCKET

PRIMARY CHAIN TENSIONER

CRANKSHAFT SPROCKET

9302PG24

Fig. 142 Timing chain system and alignment marks—3.7L engine

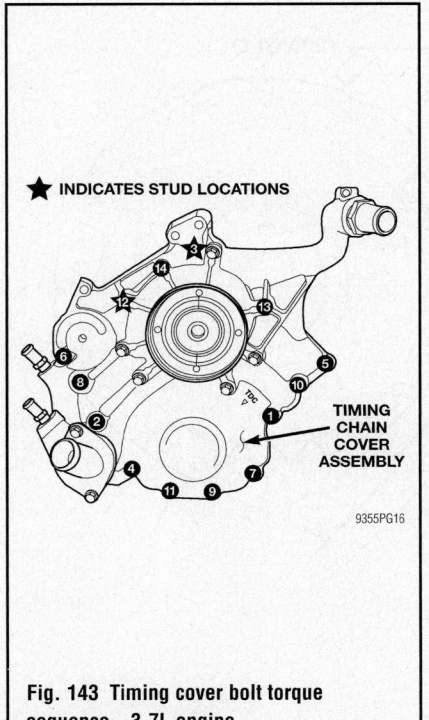

★ **INDICATES STUD LOCATIONS**

TIMING CHAIN COVER ASSEMBLY

9355PG16

Fig. 143 Timing cover bolt torque sequence—3.7L engine

4.7L Engine

See Figures 144 through 151.

1. Before servicing the vehicle, refer to the Precautions Section.
2. Drain the cooling system.
3. Remove or disconnect the following:
   - Negative battery cable
   - Valve covers
   - Camshaft Position (CMP) sensor
   - Engine cooling fan and shroud
   - Accessory drive belt
   - Heater hoses
   - Lower radiator hose
   - Power steering pump
4. Rotate the crankshaft so that the crankshaft timing mark aligns with the Top Dead Center (TDC) mark on the front cover, and the **V8** marks on the camshaft sprockets are at 12 o'clock.
5. Remove or disconnect the following:
   - Crankshaft damper
   - Oil fill housing
   - Accessory drive belt tensioner
   - Alternator
   - A/C compressor
   - Front cover

   - Front crankshaft seal
   - Cylinder head access plugs
   - Secondary timing chain guides
6. Compress the primary timing chain tensioner and install a lock-pin.
7. Remove the secondary timing chain tensioners.
8. Hold the left camshaft with an adjustable pliers and remove the sprocket and chain. Rotate the **left** camshaft 15° **clockwise** to the neutral position.
9. Hold the right camshaft with an adjustable pliers and remove the camshaft sprocket. Rotate the **right** camshaft 45° **counterclockwise** to the neutral position.
10. Remove the primary timing chain and sprockets.

To install:

11. Use a small prytool to hold the ratchet pawl and compress the secondary timing chain tensioners in a vise and install locking pins.

➡ **The black bolts fasten the guide to the engine block and the silver bolts fasten the guide to the cylinder head.**

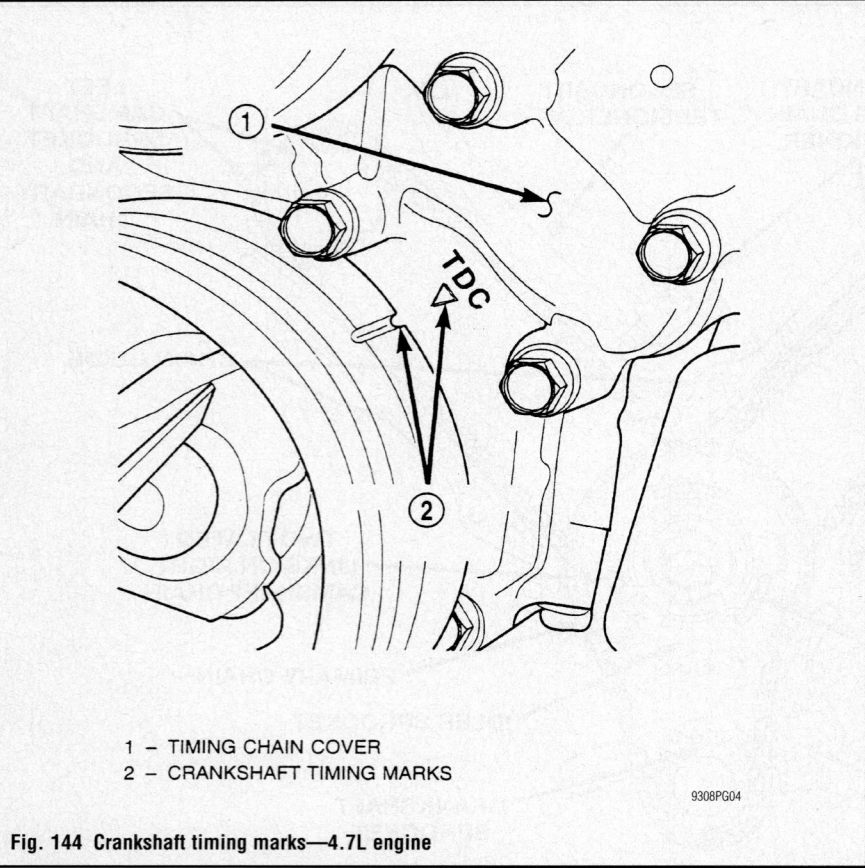

1 – TIMING CHAIN COVER
2 – CRANKSHAFT TIMING MARKS

9308PG04

Fig. 144 Crankshaft timing marks—4.7L engine

12. Install or connect the following:
- Secondary timing chain guides. Tighten the bolts to 21 ft. lbs. (28 Nm)
- Secondary timing chains to the idler sprocket so that the double plated links on each chain are visible through the slots in the primary idler sprocket

13. Lock the secondary timing chains to the idler sprocket with Timing Chain Locking tool 8515 as shown.

14. Align the primary chain double plated links with the idler sprocket timing mark and the single plated link with the crankshaft sprocket timing mark.

15. Install the primary chain and sprockets. Tighten the idler sprocket bolt to 25 ft. lbs. (34 Nm).

16. Align the secondary chain single plated links with the timing marks on the secondary sprockets. Align the dot at the **L** mark on the left sprocket with the plated link on the left chain and the dot at the **R** mark on the right sprocket with the plated link on the right chain.

17. Rotate the camshafts back from the neutral position and install the camshaft sprockets.

18. Remove the secondary chain locking tool.

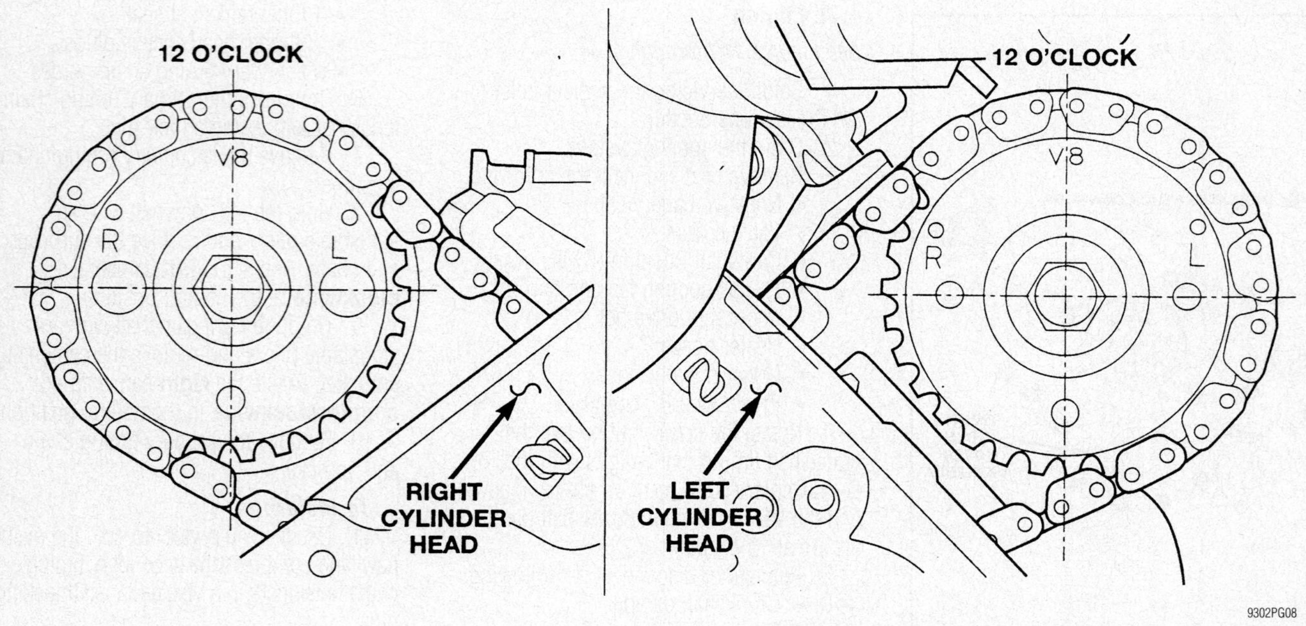

12 O'CLOCK   12 O'CLOCK

V8   V8

R   L   R   L

RIGHT CYLINDER HEAD   **LEFT CYLINDER HEAD**

9302PG08

Fig. 145 Camshaft positioning—4.7L engine

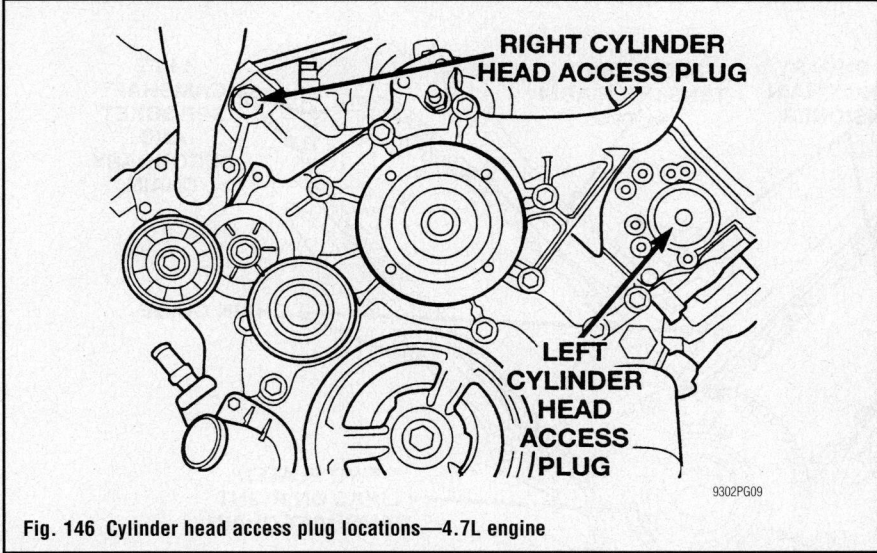

Fig. 146 Cylinder head access plug locations—4.7L engine

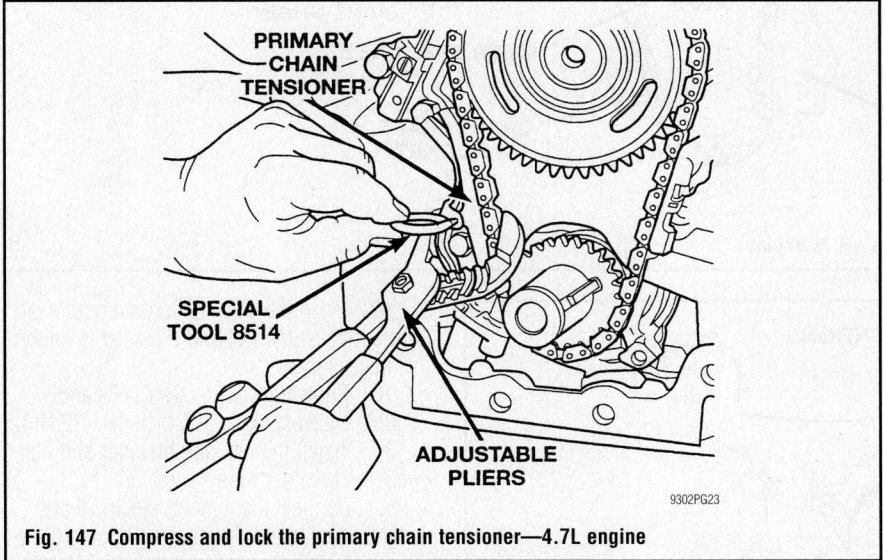

Fig. 147 Compress and lock the primary chain tensioner—4.7L engine

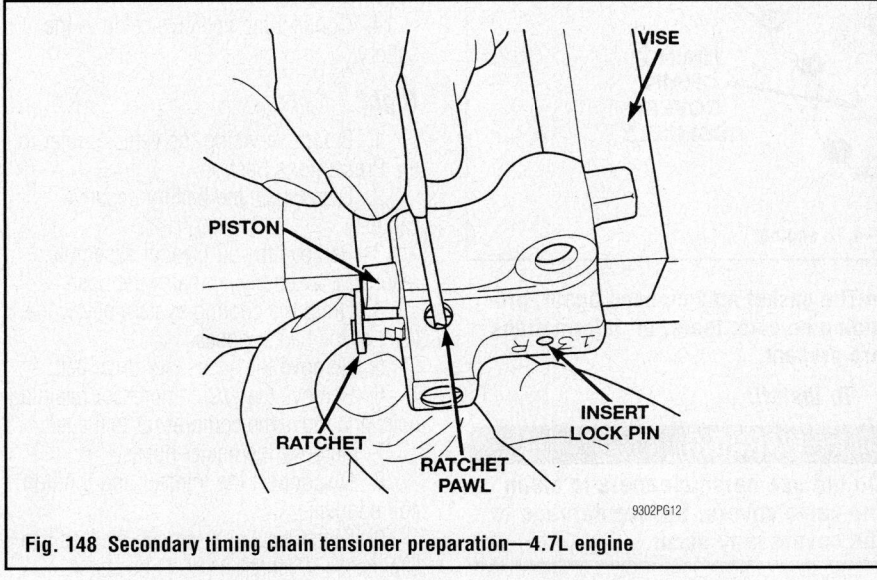

Fig. 148 Secondary timing chain tensioner preparation—4.7L engine

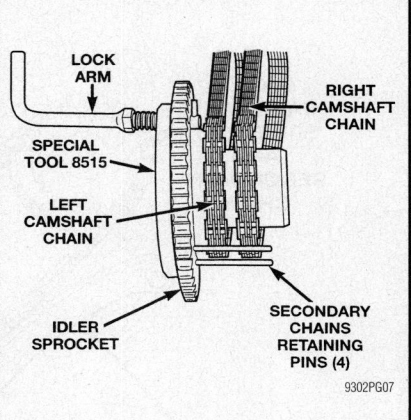

Fig. 149 Use the Timing Chain Locking tool to lock the timing chains on the idler gear—4.7L engine

19. Remove the primary and secondary timing chain tensioner locking pins.

20. Hold the camshaft sprockets with a spanner wrench and tighten the retaining bolts to 90 ft. lbs. (122 Nm).

21. Install or connect the following:
- Front cover. Tighten the bolts, in sequence, to 40 ft. lbs. (54 Nm)
- Front crankshaft seal
- Cylinder head access plugs
- A/C compressor
- Alternator
- Accessory drive belt tensioner. Tighten the bolt to 40 ft. lbs. (54 Nm)
- Oil fill housing
- Crankshaft damper. Tighten the bolt to 130 ft. lbs. (175 Nm)
- Power steering pump
- Lower radiator hose
- Heater hoses
- Accessory drive belt
- Engine cooling fan and shroud
- Camshaft Position (CMP) sensor
- Valve covers
- Negative battery cable

22. Fill the cooling system.

23. Start the engine and check for leaks.

VALVE COVERS

REMOVAL & INSTALLATION

3.7L Engine

Left

1. Before servicing the vehicle, refer to the Precautions Section.

2. Disconnect the negative cable from the battery.

3. Remove the resonator assembly and air inlet hose.

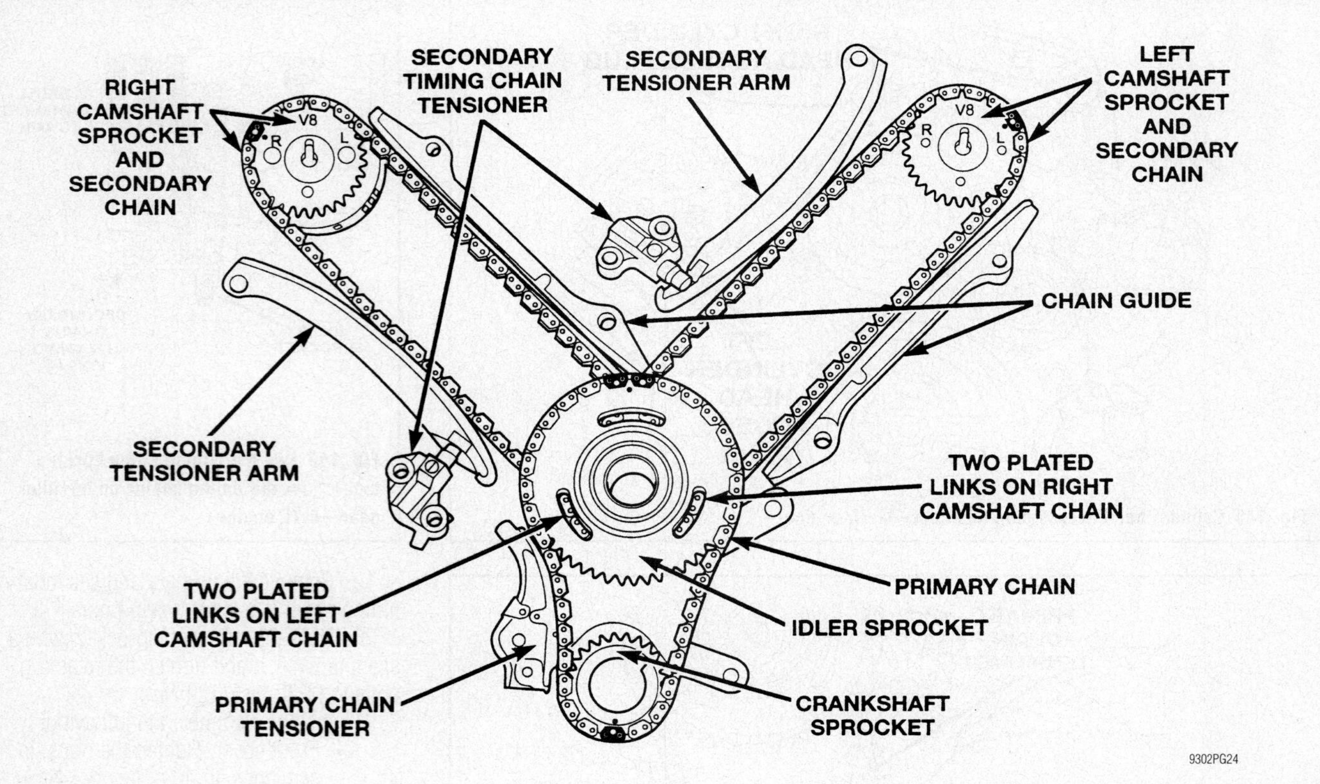

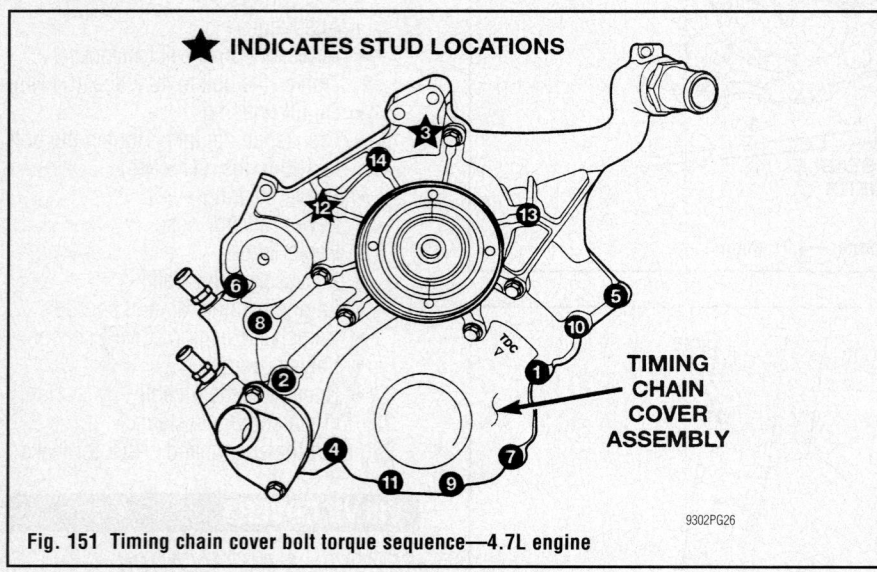

RIGHT CAMSHAFT SPROCKET AND SECONDARY CHAIN

SECONDARY TIMING CHAIN TENSIONER

SECONDARY TENSIONER ARM

LEFT CAMSHAFT SPROCKET AND SECONDARY CHAIN

CHAIN GUIDE

SECONDARY TENSIONER ARM

TWO PLATED LINKS ON RIGHT CAMSHAFT CHAIN

TWO PLATED LINKS ON LEFT CAMSHAFT CHAIN

PRIMARY CHAIN

IDLER SPROCKET

PRIMARY CHAIN TENSIONER

CRANKSHAFT SPROCKET

9302PG24

Fig. 150 Timing chain system and alignment marks—4.7L engine

★ **INDICATES STUD LOCATIONS**

TIMING CHAIN COVER ASSEMBLY

9302PG26

Fig. 151 Timing chain cover bolt torque sequence—4.7L engine

4. Disconnect the injector connectors and unclip the injector harness.

5. Route the injector harness in front of the valve cover.

6. Disconnect the left side breather tube and remove the breather tube.

7. Remove the valve cover mounting bolts.

8. Remove the valve cover and gasket.

➡The gasket may be used again, providing no cuts, tears, or deformations are present.

To install:

✳✳ WARNING

Do not use harsh cleaners to clean the valve covers. Severe damage to the covers may occur.

9. Clean the valve cover and both sealing surfaces. Inspect and replace the gasket as necessary.

10. Tighten the valve cover bolts and double ended studs to 105 inch lbs. (12 Nm).

11. Install the left side breather and connect the breather tube.

12. Connect the injector electrical connectors and injector harness retaining clips.

13. Install the resonator and air inlet hose.

14. Connect the negative cable to the battery.

Right

1. Before servicing the vehicle, refer to the Precautions Section.

2. Disconnect the battery negative cable.

3. Remove the air cleaner assembly, resonator assembly, and air inlet hose.

4. Drain the cooling system below the level of the heater hoses.

5. Remove the accessory drive belt.

6. Remove the A/C compressor retaining bolts and move the compressor to the left.

7. Remove the heater hoses.

8. Disconnect the injector and ignition coil connectors.

9. Disconnect and remove the Positive Crankcase Ventilation (PCV) hose.

10. Remove the oil fill tube.

11. Unclip the injector and ignition coil harness and move it away from the valve cover.

12. Remove the right rear breather tube and filter assembly.

13. Remove the valve cover retaining bolts.

14. Remove the valve cover and gasket.

➡**The gasket may be used again, providing no cuts, tears, or deformations are present.**

To install:

❊❊ **WARNING**

Do not use harsh cleaners to clean the valve covers. Severe damage to the covers may occur.

15. Clean the valve cover and both sealing surfaces. Inspect and replace the gasket, as necessary.

16. Tighten the valve cover bolts and double ended studs to 105 inch lbs. (12 Nm).

17. Install the right rear breather tube and filter assembly.

18. Connect the injector, ignition coil electrical connectors, and harness retaining clips.

19. Install the oil fill tube.

20. Install the PCV hose.

21. Install the heater hoses.

22. Install A/C compressor retaining bolts.

23. Install the accessory drive belt.

24. Fill the cooling system.

25. Install the air cleaner assembly, resonator assembly, and air inlet hose.

26. Connect the battery negative cable.

4.7L Engine

Left

1. Before servicing the vehicle, refer to the Precautions Section.

2. Disconnect the negative cable from the battery.

3. Remove the resonator assembly and air inlet hose.

4. Disconnect the injector connectors and unclip the injector harness.

5. Remove the spark plug wires.

6. Route the injector harness in front of the valve cover.

7. Disconnect the left side breather tube and remove the breather tube.

8. Remove the valve cover mounting bolts.

9. Remove the valve cover and gasket.

➡**The gasket may be used again, provided no cuts, tears, or deformations are present.**

To install:

❊❊ **WARNING**

Do not use harsh cleaners to clean the valve covers. Severe damage to the covers may occur.

10. Clean the valve cover and both sealing surfaces. Inspect and replace the gasket, as necessary.

11. Install the valve cover and hand start all the fasteners. Verify that all studs are in the correct location.

12. Tighten the valve cover bolts and double ended studs to 105 inch lbs. (12 Nm).

13. Install the left side breather and connect the breather tube.

14. Install the spark plug wires.

15. Connect the injector electrical connectors and the injector harness retaining clips.

16. Install the resonator and air inlet hose.

17. Connect the negative cable to the battery.

Right

1. Before servicing the vehicle, refer to the Precautions Section.

2. Disconnect the battery negative cable.

3. Remove the air cleaner assembly, resonator assembly, and air inlet hose.

4. Drain the cooling system.

5. Remove the accessory drive belt.

6. Remove the A/C compressor retaining bolts and move the compressor to the left.

7. Remove the heater hoses.

8. Disconnect the injector and ignition coil connectors.

9. Disconnect and remove the Positive Crankcase Ventilation (PCV) hose.

10. Remove the oil fill tube.

11. Unclip the injector and the ignition coil harness and move them away from the valve cover.

12. Remove the right rear breather tube and filter assembly.

13. Remove the valve cover retaining bolts.

14. Remove the valve cover.

➡**The gasket may be used again, provided no cuts, tears, or deformations are present.**

To install:

❊❊ **WARNING**

Do not use harsh cleaners to clean the valve covers. Severe damage to the covers may occur.

15. Clean the valve cover and both sealing surfaces. Inspect and replace the gasket, as necessary.

16. Install the valve cover and hand start all the fasteners. Verify that all double ended studs are in the correct location.

17. Tighten the valve cover bolts and double ended studs to 105 inch lbs. (12 Nm).

18. Install the right rear breather tube and filter assembly.

19. Connect the injector, ignition coil electrical connectors, and harness retaining clips.

20. Install the oil fill tube.

21. Install the PCV hose.

22. Install the heater hoses.

23. Install the A/C compressor retaining bolts.

24. Install the accessory drive belt.

25. Fill the cooling system.

26. Install the air cleaner assembly, resonator assembly, and air inlet hose.

27. Connect the battery negative cable.

VALVE LASH

ADJUSTMENT

These engines use hydraulic lifters. No maintenance or periodic adjustment is required.

ENGINE PERFORMANCE & EMISSION CONTROLS

CAMSHAFT POSITION (CMP) SENSOR

LOCATION

See Figure 152.

The Camshaft Position (CMP) sensor is bolted to the right-front side of the right cylinder head on the 3.7L and 4.7L engines.

REMOVAL & INSTALLATION

1. Before servicing the vehicle, refer to the Precautions Section.
2. Disconnect the CMP electrical connector.
3. Remove the CMP sensor mounting bolt.
4. Carefully twist the sensor from the cylinder head.

To install:

5. Check the condition of the sensor O-ring.
6. Clean out the machined hole in the cylinder head.
7. Apply a small amount of clean engine oil to the sensor O-ring.
8. Install the CMP sensor into the cylinder head with a slight rocking and twisting action.

❋❋ WARNING

Before tightening the CMP sensor mounting bolt (2), be sure the sensor is completely flush to the cylinder head. If the sensor is not flush, damage to the sensor mounting tang may result.

9. Install the mounting bolt and tighten to 106 inch lbs. (12 Nm).
10. Connect the electrical connector.

CRANKSHAFT POSITION (CKP) SENSOR

LOCATION

3.7L Engine

See Figure 153.

The Crankshaft Position (CKP) sensor is mounted into the right rear side of the cylinder block. It is positioned and bolted into a machined hole.

4.7L Engine

See Figure 154.

The Crankshaft Position (CKP) sensor is mounted into the right rear side of the cylin-

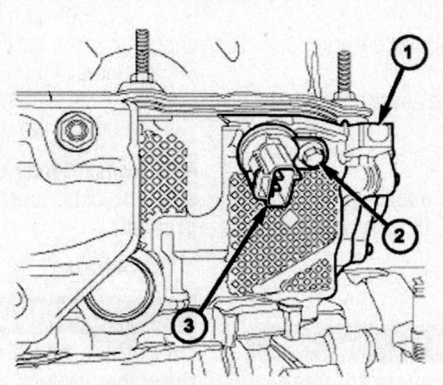

1. Right cylinder head
2. Mounting bolt
3. CMP sensor

36543_DAKO_G0149

Fig. 152 Camshaft Position (CMP) sensor location

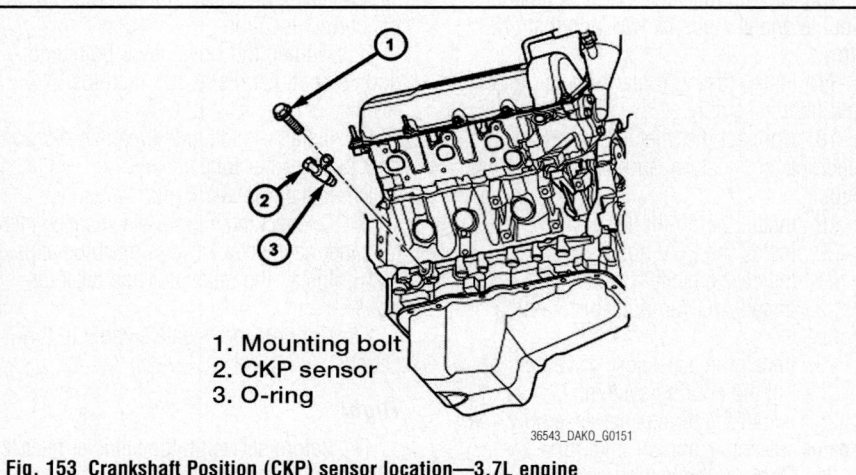

1. Mounting bolt
2. CKP sensor
3. O-ring

36543_DAKO_G0151

Fig. 153 Crankshaft Position (CKP) sensor location—3.7L engine

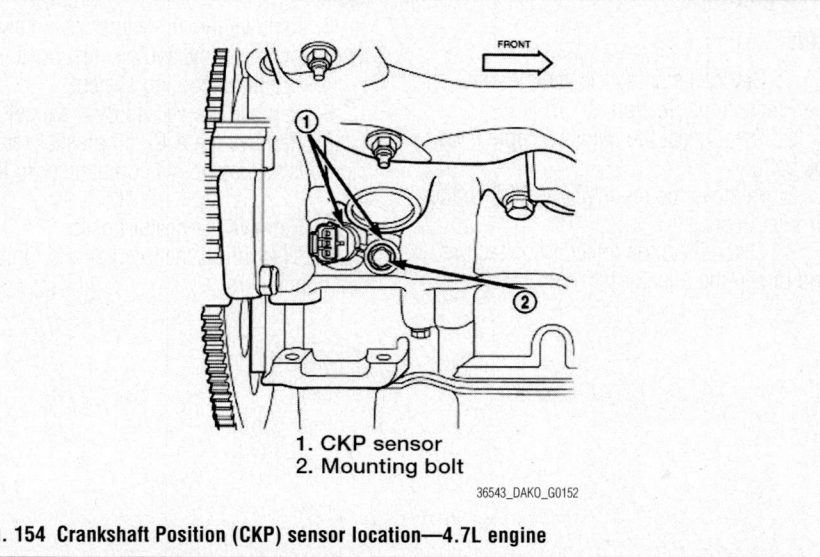

1. CKP sensor
2. Mounting bolt

36543_DAKO_G0152

Fig. 154 Crankshaft Position (CKP) sensor location—4.7L engine

der block. It is positioned and bolted into a machined hole.

REMOVAL & INSTALLATION

1. Before servicing the vehicle, refer to the Precautions Section.
2. Raise and safely support the vehicle.
3. Disconnect the sensor electrical connector.
4. Remove the Crankshaft Position (CKP) sensor mounting bolt.
5. Carefully twist the CKP sensor from the cylinder block.

To install:

6. Check the condition of the O-ring.
7. Clean out the machined hole in the engine block.
8. Apply a small amount of clean engine oil to the sensor O-ring.
9. Install the CKP sensor into the engine block with a slight rocking and twisting action.

❊❊ WARNING

Before tightening the sensor mounting bolt, be sure the sensor is completely flush to the cylinder block. If the sensor is not flush, damage to the sensor mounting tang may result.

10. Install the mounting bolt and tighten to 21 ft. lbs. (28 Nm).
11. Connect the electrical connector to the CKP sensor.
12. Lower the vehicle.

EVAPORATIVE EMISSION (EVAP) CANISTER

LOCATION

See Figure 155.

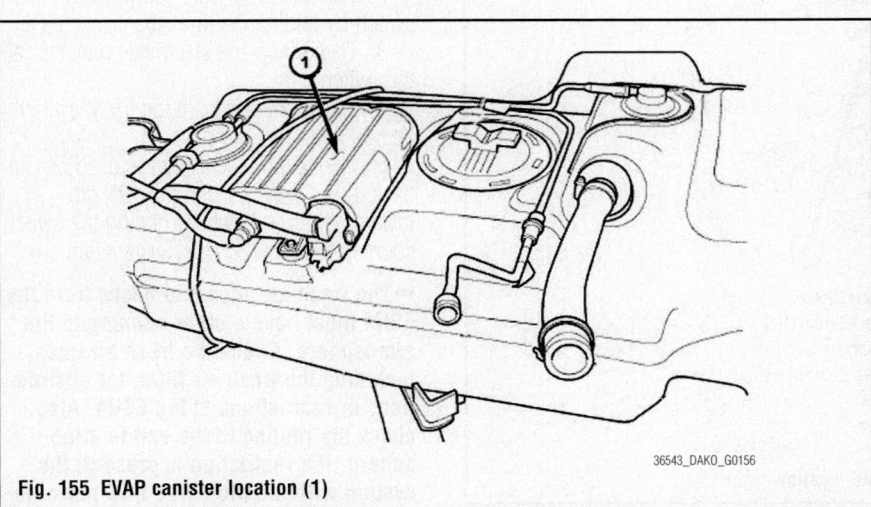

Fig. 155 EVAP canister location (1)

The maintenance free, EVAP canister (1) is mounted to the top of the fuel tank.

REMOVAL & INSTALLATION

Club Cab

See Figure 156.

The EVAP canister is mounted to the top of the fuel tank. Both the EVAP canister and the ESIM switch can be removed without removing the fuel tank.

1. Before servicing the vehicle, refer to the Precautions Section.
2. Raise and safely support the vehicle.
3. Remove the left-rear tire.
4. Remove the plastic shield in front of the left-rear tire. Access to both the EVAP canister and the ESIM switch can be achieved from the area in front of the removed tire and plastic shield.
5. Remove the vapor hose at the ESIM switch.
6. Remove the vapor line (5) from the EVAP canister (3) by pressing on both the tabs (2) simultaneously.
7. Using a screwdriver, pry up and remove the plastic mounting clip and remove the EVAP canister from the top of fuel tank.

➡**The opposite end of the canister is supported by 2 plastic legs.**

To install:

8. Guide the 2 plastic canister locating legs into the top of the fuel tank.
9. Install the plastic mounting clip and press down.
10. Install the electrical connector to the ESIM switch.
11. Install all the vapor hoses and lines to both the EVAP canister and the ESIM switch.

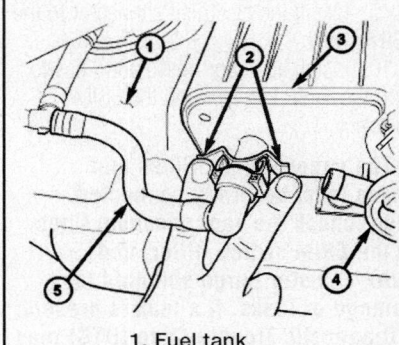

1. Fuel tank
2. Locking tabs
3. EVAP canister
4. ESIM switch
5. Vapor line

36543_DAKO_G0157

Fig. 156 Remove the vapor line from the EVAP canister by pressing on the locking tabs

➡**The vapor/vacuum lines and hoses must be firmly connected. Also, check the vapor/vacuum lines at the ESIM switch, filter, and EVAP canister purge solenoid for damage or leaks. If a leak is present, a Diagnostic Trouble Code (DTC) may be set.**

12. Install the plastic shield in front of the left-rear tire.
13. Install the left-rear tire.

4-Door Quad Cab

See Figure 156.

On 4-door Quad Cab models, the fuel tank must be lowered for EVAP canister removal. The EVAP canister is mounted to the top of the fuel tank.

1. Before servicing the vehicle, refer to the Precautions Section.
2. Lower the fuel tank.
3. Remove the vapor hose at the ESIM switch.
4. Remove the vapor line (5) from the EVAP canister (3) by pressing on both tabs (2) simultaneously.
5. Using a screwdriver, pry up and remove the plastic mounting clip and remove the canister from the top of fuel tank.

➡**The opposite end of the canister is supported by 2 plastic legs.**

To install:

6. Guide the 2 plastic canister locating legs into the top of the fuel tank.
7. Install plastic mounting clip and press down.

36543_DAKO_G0156

8. Raise the fuel tank.

9. Install the electrical connector to the ESIM switch.

10. Install all vapor hoses and lines to both the EVAP canister and the ESIM switch.

➡**The vapor/vacuum lines and hoses must be firmly connected. Also, check the vapor/vacuum lines at the ESIM switch, filter, and EVAP canister purge solenoid for damage or leaks. If a leak is present, a Diagnostic Trouble Code (DTC) may be set.**

11. Install the fuel tank.

EVAPORATIVE EMISSION (EVAP) PURGE SOLENOID

LOCATION

See Figure 157.

The duty cycle EVAP canister purge solenoid is located in the engine compartment. It is attached to a tongue-type bracket near the brake power booster.

REMOVAL & INSTALLATION

See Figure 157.

1. Before servicing the vehicle, refer to the Precautions Section.

2. Disconnect the electrical wiring connector (3) at the solenoid.

3. Disconnect the vacuum lines (5) and (6) at the solenoid.

4. Remove the solenoid moving it straight up from the mounting bracket.

To install:

5. Install the solenoid assembly (2) to the mounting bracket (1).

6. Connect the vacuum lines (5) and (6).

7. Connect the electrical connector (3).

➡**The vapor/vacuum lines and hoses must be firmly connected. Check the vapor/vacuum lines at the ESIM switch, pump filter, and EVAP canister purge solenoid for damage or leaks. If a leak is present, a Diagnostic Trouble Code (DTC) may be set.**

EVAP SYSTEM INTEGRITY MONITOR (ESIM)

LOCATION

See Figure 158.

The EVAP System Integrity Monitor (ESIM) switch is attached to the EVAP canister.

REMOVAL & INSTALLATION

See Figures 158 and 159.

The EVAP System Integrity Monitor (ESIM) switch is attached to the EVAP canister and is usually not serviceable. Replace the switch by replacing the EVAP canister. Refer to Evaporative Emission (EVAP) Canister, removal & installation.

If servicing the ESIM switch separately, refer to the following:

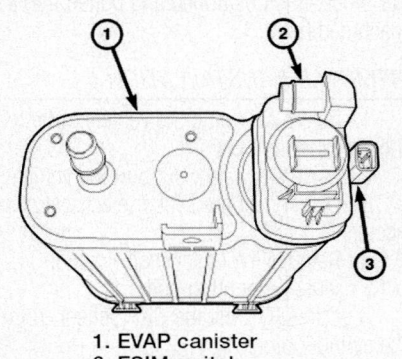

1. EVAP canister
2. ESIM switch
3. ESIM switch connector

36543_DAKO_G0160

Fig. 158 EVAP System Integrity Monitor (ESIM) switch location

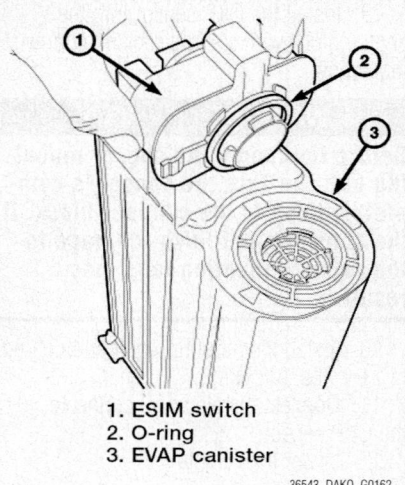

1. ESIM switch
2. O-ring
3. EVAP canister

36543_DAKO_G0162

Fig. 159 Be sure the O-ring and the EVAP canister opening are clean

1. Before servicing the vehicle, refer to the Precautions Section.

2. Remove both plastic lines from the switch by folding the line tabs.

3. Disconnect the electrical connector at the switch.

4. Clean any dirt from the ESIM switch and its lines.

5. A lock tab (see arrow) is used on the back of the switch. Push the lock tab towards the switch while rotating the switch counterclockwise ¼ turn for removal.

➡**The fresh air lines and hoses from the ESIM must have a clear opening to the atmosphere. Check the fresh air lines, including the fresh air filter, for obstructions or restrictions at the ESIM. Also, check the routing to the exit to atmosphere. If a restriction is present, the system will not allow free flow passage**

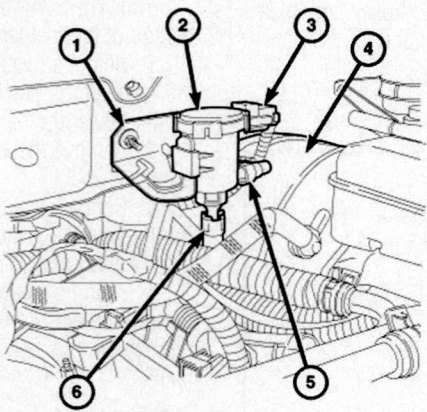

1. Mounting bracket
2. EVAP purge solenoid
3. Electrical connector
4. Brake power booster
5. Vacuum line
6. Vacuum line

36543_DAKO_G0158

Fig. 157 Evaporative Emission (EVAP) purge solenoid location

of clean air, and an early shut-off of the fuel fill nozzle may occur during fuel fill.

To install:

The following graphics display a TYPICAL EVAP Canister and a typical ESIM switch. After installing any ESIM switch, the electrical connector on the switch must be in the 3 o'clock position. This step must be done for proper ESIM switch operation.

6. The fresh air lines and hoses from the ESIM must have a clear opening to the atmosphere. Check the fresh air lines, including the fresh air filter, for obstructions or restrictions at the ESIM. Also, check the routing to the exit to atmosphere. If a restriction is present, the system will not allow free flow passage of clean air, and an early shut-off of the fuel fill nozzle may occur during fuel fill.

7. Be sure the O-ring (2) and the EVAP canister (3) opening are clean.

➡ **The electrical connector (3) on the ESIM switch must be in 3 o'clock position after installation. This step must be done for proper switch operation.**

8. Position the ESIM switch (2) into the EVAP canister (1) and rotate it until the electrical connector is in the 3 o'clock position (3).

9. Connect the electrical connector.

10. Connect the plastic lines to the ESIM switch.

EXHAUST GAS RECIRCULATION (EGR) VALVE

LOCATION

3.7L Engine

See Figure 160.

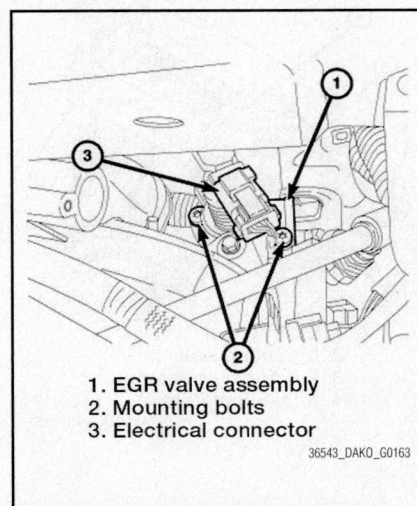

1. EGR valve assembly
2. Mounting bolts
3. Electrical connector

36543_DAKO_G0163

Fig. 160 Exhaust Gas Recirculation (EGR) valve location—3.7L engine

The electronic EGR valve and solenoid assembly (1) is attached to the rear of the left cylinder head. An exhaust gas routing tube connects the EGR valve to the intake manifold.

4.7L Engine

See Figure 161.

The electronic EGR valve and solenoid assembly (4) is attached to the rear of the left cylinder head. An exhaust gas routing tube (3) connects the EGR valve to the intake manifold.

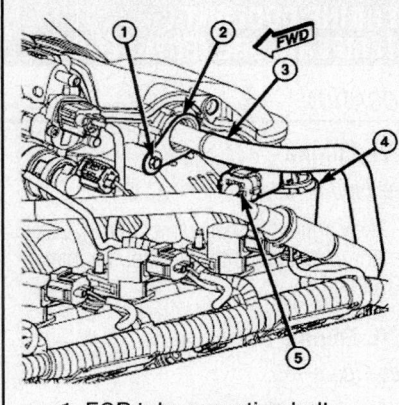

1. EGR tube mounting bolt
2. Intake manifold
3. EGR tube
4. EGR solenoid assembly
5. Electrical connector

36543_DAKO_G0164

Fig. 161 Exhaust Gas Recirculation (EGR) valve location—4.7L engine

REMOVAL & INSTALLATION

3.7L Engine

See Figures 157 and 162.

1. Before servicing the vehicle, refer to the Precautions Section.

2. Use a diagnostic scan tool to record any Diagnostic Trouble Codes (DTC's).

3. Disconnect and isolate the negative battery cable.

4. Remove the EVAP purge solenoid (2). The solenoid lifts from a tongue-type bracket (1).

5. Remove the 2 tube mounting bolts (2) from the EGR assembly.

6. Remove the tube (1) from the solenoid (4). Slip the opposite end of the tube (6) from the intake manifold.

7. Remove the gasket (3) located between the EGR valve solenoid and the tube flange.

8. Disconnect the electrical connector at the solenoid.

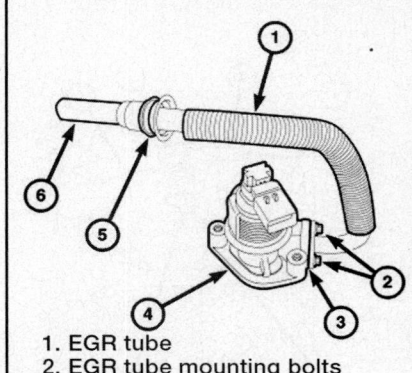

1. EGR tube
2. EGR tube mounting bolts
3. Gasket
4. EGR solenoid assembly
5. Seal to intake manifold
6. EGR tube

36543_DAKO_G0165

Fig. 162 View of EGR valve assembly

9. Remove the 2 EGR valve solenoid mounting bolts.

10. Remove the solenoid from the engine.

11. Remove and discard the gasket located under the EGR solenoid.

To install:

12. Clean the gasket area at the rear of the left cylinder head.

13. Clean the EGR tube where it joins the EGR valve.

14. Position the new gasket between the EGR valve and the cylinder head.

15. Position the EGR valve to the cylinder head. Install and tighten the 2 bolts (2) to 80 inch lbs. (9 Nm).

16. Position the new gasket (3) between the EGR tube flange and the EGR valve assembly.

17. Position the EGR tube (1) to the side of the EGR valve. Position the end of the tube (6) into the intake manifold. Install the 2 bolts (2) that connect the EGR tube to the EGR assembly. Torque the bolts to 102 inch lbs. (11 Nm).

18. Connect the electrical connector (3) to the top of the EGR valve solenoid (1).

19. Install the EVAP canister purge solenoid (2) by slipping the assembly onto the tongue-type bracket (1).

20. Connect the negative battery cable.

21. Using a diagnostic scan tool, erase any previously recorded Diagnostic Trouble Codes (DTC's).

4.7L Engine

See Figures 161 and 163.

The electronic EGR valve and solenoid assembly is attached to the rear of the left cylinder head. An exhaust gas routing tube connects the EGR valve to the intake manifold.

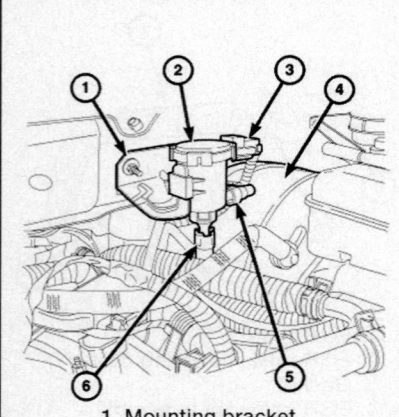

1. Mounting bracket
2. EVAP purge solenoid
3. Electrical connector
4. Brake power booster
5. Vacuum line
6. Vacuum line

36543_DAKO_G0158

Fig. 163 Evaporative Emission (EVAP) purge solenoid location

1. Before servicing the vehicle, refer to the Precautions Section.

2. Use a diagnostic scan tool to record any Diagnostic Trouble Codes (DTC's) that are present.

3. Disconnect and isolate the negative battery cable.

4. Remove the EVAP solenoid (2).

5. Remove the electrical connector (5) at the top of the EGR valve solenoid.

6. Remove the tube mounting bolt (1) at the intake manifold.

7. Remove the 2 bolts connecting the EGR tube to the valve assembly.

8. Remove the gasket located between the EGR tube flange and the EGR valve assembly.

9. Remove the 2 EGR valve mounting bolts.

10. Separate the valve assembly from the engine.

11. Remove and discard the metal gasket located between the cylinder head and the valve assembly.

To install:

12. Clean the area at the rear of the left cylinder head where it joins base of EGR valve.

13. Clean the EGR tube where it joins the EGR valve.

14. Position the new gasket between the EGR valve and the cylinder head.

15. Position the EGR valve onto the cylinder head. Install and tighten the 2 bolts. Torque to 80 inch lbs. (9 Nm).

16. Position the new gasket between the EGR tube flange and the EGR valve assembly.

17. Position the EGR tube (1) to the side of the EGR valve and into the intake manifold. Install the 2 bolts (4) finger tight.

18. Install EGR tube flange bolt (1) at the intake manifold. Torque to 102 inch lbs. (11 Nm).

19. Connect the electrical connector (5) to the top of the EGR valve solenoid (4).

20. Do a final tightening of the 2 EGR tube bolts. Torque to 102 inch lbs. (11 Nm).

21. Install the EVAP solenoid.

22. Connect the negative battery cable.

23. Using a diagnostic scan tool, erase any previously recorded DTC's.

ENGINE COOLANT TEMPERATURE (ECT) SENSOR

LOCATION

3.7L Engine

See Figure 164.

The Engine Coolant Temperature (ECT) sensor is located at the front of the intake manifold.

4.7L Engine

See Figure 165.

The Engine Coolant Temperature (ECT) sensor is located at the front of the intake manifold.

REMOVAL & INSTALLATION

3.7L Engine

See Figure 164.

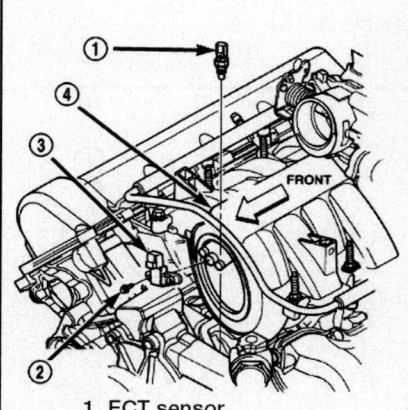

1. Mounting bolts
2. ECT electrical connector
3. ECT sensor
4. Intake manifold

36543_DAKO_G0166

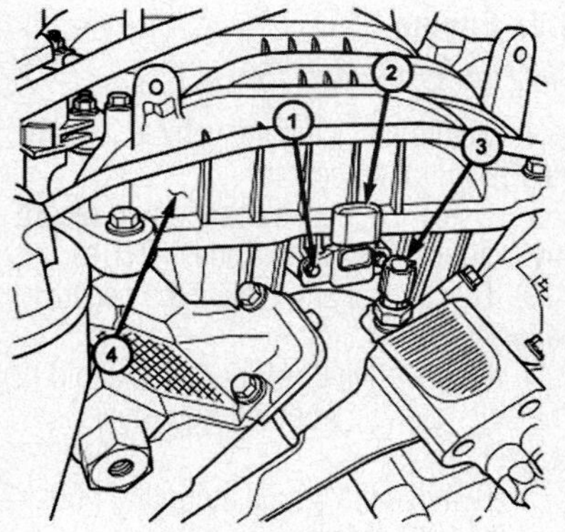

Fig. 164 Engine Coolant Temperature (ECT) sensor location—3.7L engine

1. Before servicing the vehicle, refer to the Precautions Section.

> ※※ **CAUTION**
>
> **Hot, pressurized coolant can cause injury by scalding. The cooling system must be partially drained before removing the ECT sensor.**

2. Partially drain the cooling system.

3. Disconnect the ECT sensor electrical connector.

4. Remove the ECT sensor from the intake manifold.

To install:

5. Apply thread sealant to the ECT sensor threads.

6. Install the ECT sensor and tighten to 20 ft. lbs. (27 Nm).

7. Connect the electrical connector.

8. Refill the cooling system to the correct level

4.7L Engine

See Figure 165.

1. Before servicing the vehicle, refer to the Precautions Section.

> ※※ **CAUTION**
>
> **Hot, pressurized coolant can cause injury by scalding. The cooling system must be partially drained before removing the ECT sensor.**

2. Partially drain the cooling system.

1. ECT sensor
2. Mounting bolt
3. Electrical connector
4. Intake manifold

36543_DAKO_G0167

Fig. 165 Engine Coolant Temperature (ECT) sensor location—4.7L engine

3. Disconnect the sensor electrical connector.

4. Remove the ECT sensor from the intake manifold.

To install:

5. Apply thread sealant to the sensor threads.

6. Install the ECT and tighten to 20 ft. lbs. (27 Nm).

7. Connect the electrical connector.

8. Refill the cooling system to the correct level.

HEATED OXYGEN SENSOR (HO2S)

LOCATION

See Figures 166 and 167.

The Heated Oxygen Sensors (HO2S) are attached to, and protrude into the vehicle exhaust system. Depending on the engine or emission package, the vehicle may use a total of either 2 or 4 sensors.

Federal Emission Packages: Two sensors are used—upstream (referred to as 1/1) and downstream (referred to as 1/2). With this emission package, the upstream

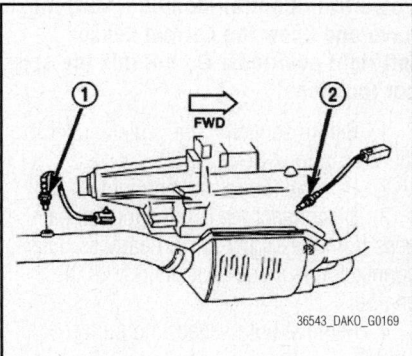

Fig. 166 Heated Oxygen Sensor (HO2S)—Federal Emission package

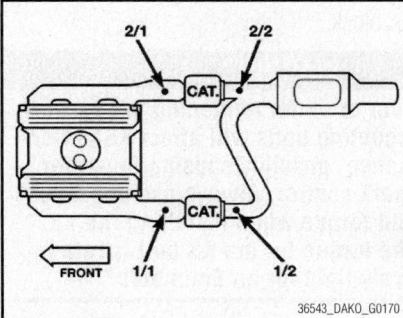

Fig. 167 Heated Oxygen Sensor (HO2S)—California Emission package

sensor (1/1) is located just before the main catalytic converter. The downstream sensor (1/2) is located just after the main catalytic converter.

California Emission Packages: On this emissions package, 4 sensors are used—2 upstream (referred to as 1/1 and 2/1) and 2 downstream (referred to as 1/2 and 2/2). With this emission package, the right upstream sensor (2/1) is located in the right exhaust downpipe just before the mini-catalytic converter. The left upstream sensor (1/1) is located in the left exhaust downpipe just before the mini-catalytic converter. The right downstream sensor (2/2) is located in the right exhaust downpipe just after the mini-catalytic converter, and before the main catalytic converter. The left downstream sensor (1/2) is located in the left exhaust downpipe just after the mini-catalytic converter, and before the main catalytic converter.

REMOVAL & INSTALLATION

Refer to graphics for typical Heated Oxygen Sensor (HO2S) locations if equipped with 2 or 4 oxygen sensors.

1. Before servicing the vehicle, refer to the Precautions Section.

✳✳ WARNING

Never apply any type of grease to the oxygen sensor electrical connector or attempt any soldering of the sensor wiring harness.

✳✳ CAUTION

The exhaust manifold, exhaust pipes, and catalytic converter become very hot during engine operation. Allow the engine to cool before removing the oxygen sensor(s).

2. Raise and safely support the vehicle.

3. On a 4-sensor system, to remove the right upstream (2/1) sensor:

   a. Remove the right front tire/wheel.

   b. Remove the plastic inner fender liner.

4. Disconnect the wire connector from HO2S.

✳✳ WARNING

When disconnecting the sensor electrical connector, do not pull directly on the wire going into the sensor.

5. Remove the HO2S with an oxygen sensor removal and installation tool.

To install:

➡ **The threads of new oxygen sensors are factory coated with an anti-seize compound to aid in removal. DO NOT add any additional anti-seize compound to the threads of a new oxygen sensor.**

6. Clean the threads in the exhaust pipe using an appropriate tap.

7. Install the HO2S sensor. Tighten to 30 ft. lbs. (41 Nm).

8. Connect the HO2S sensor wire connector.

9. On a 4-sensor system, to install the right upstream (2/1) sensor:

   a. Install the plastic inner fender liner.

   b. Install the right front tire/wheel.

10. Lower the vehicle.

INTAKE AIR TEMPERATURE (IAT) SENSOR

LOCATION

3.7L Engine

See Figure 168.

The Intake Air Temperature (IAT) sensor (1) is installed into the air intake tube near the throttle body (2).

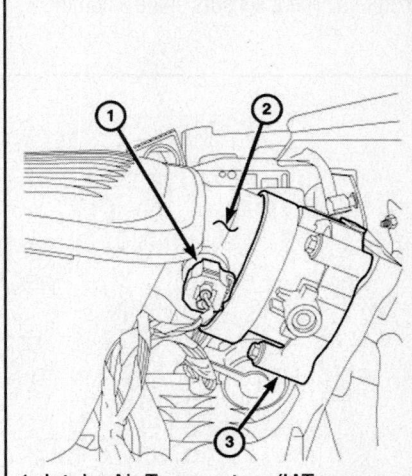

1. Intake Air Temperature (IAT. sensor
2. Throttle body
3. Throttle body mounting bolts

Fig. 168 Intake Air Temperature (IAT) sensor location—3.7L engine

4.7L Engine

See Figure 169.

The Intake Air Temperature (IAT) sensor (1) is located near the throttle body.

REMOVAL & INSTALLATION

See Figure 170.

1. Before servicing the vehicle, refer to the Precautions Section.

2. Disconnect the electrical connector form the Intake Air Temperature (IAT) sensor.

3. Clean any dirt from the air inlet tube at the sensor base.

4. Gently lift the small plastic release tab and rotate the sensor about ¼ turn counterclockwise to remove.

To install:

5. Check the condition of the sensor O-ring (2).

6. Clean the sensor mounting hole.

7. Position the sensor into the intake air tube and rotate clockwise until the release tab clicks into place.

8. Install the electrical connector.

KNOCK SENSOR (KS)

LOCATION

3.7L Engine

See Figure 171.

Two Knock Sensors (KS) (1) are bolted into the cylinder block under the intake manifold. The 2 sensors share a common

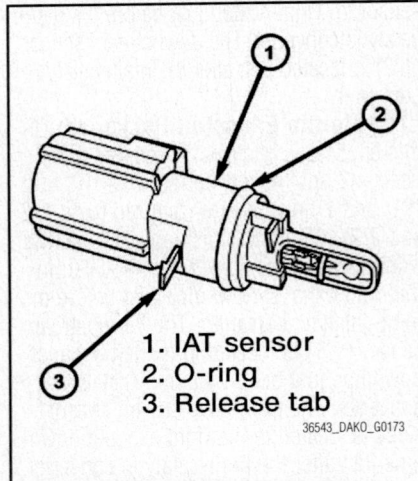

1. IAT sensor
2. O-ring
3. Release tab

36543_DAKO_G0173

Fig. 170 Gently lift the small plastic release tab and rotate the sensor to remove

wiring harness using 1 electrical connector (3). Because of this, they must be replaced as a pair.

4.7L Engine

See Figure 172

One Knock Sensor (KS) (1) is bolted to the cylinder block under the intake manifold.

REMOVAL & INSTALLATION

3.7L Engine

See Figure 171.

The 2 Knock Sensors (KS) (1) are bolted into the cylinder block under the intake

1. Knock sensors
2. Wire identification tag
3. Electrical connector

36543_DAKO_G0175

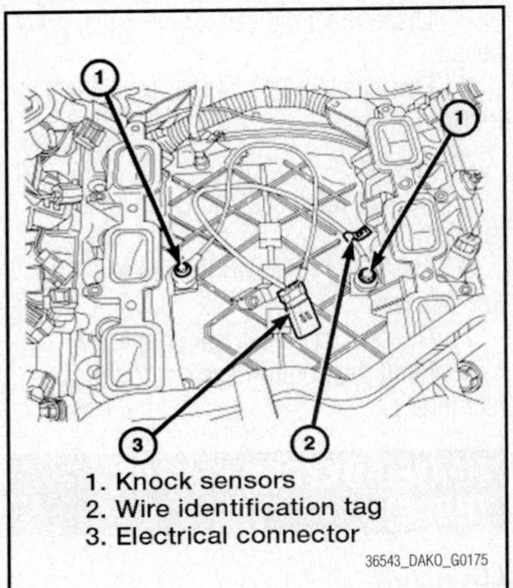

Fig. 171 Knock Sensor (KS) location—3.7L engine

manifold. The 2 sensors share a common wiring harness using 1 electrical connector (3). Because of this, they must be replaced as a pair.

➡The left sensor is identified by an identification tag (LEFT) (2). It is also identified by a larger bolt head. The Powertrain Control Module (PCM) must have and know the correct sensor left/right positions. Do not mix the sensor locations.

1. Before servicing the vehicle, refer to the Precautions Section.

2. Remove the intake manifold.

3. Disconnect the KS dual pigtail harness from the engine wiring harness. This connection is made near the rear of the engine.

4. Remove both sensor mounting bolts.

5. Remove the sensors from the engine.

To install:

6. Thoroughly clean the KS mounting holes.

7. Install the sensors (1) into the cylinder block.

✴✴ WARNING

Over or under tightening the sensor mounting bolts will affect KS performance, possibly causing improper spark control. Always use the specified torque when installing the KS. The torque for the KS bolt is relatively light for an 8mm bolt.

➡There is a foam strip on the bolt threads. This foam is used only to retain the bolts to the sensors for plant

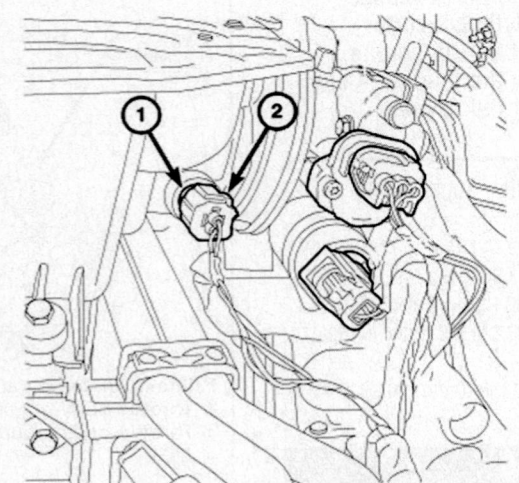

1. Intake Air Temperature (IAT. sensor
2. Electrical connector

36543_DAKO_G0172

Fig. 169 Intake Air Temperature (IAT) sensor location—4.7 engine

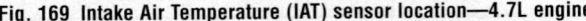

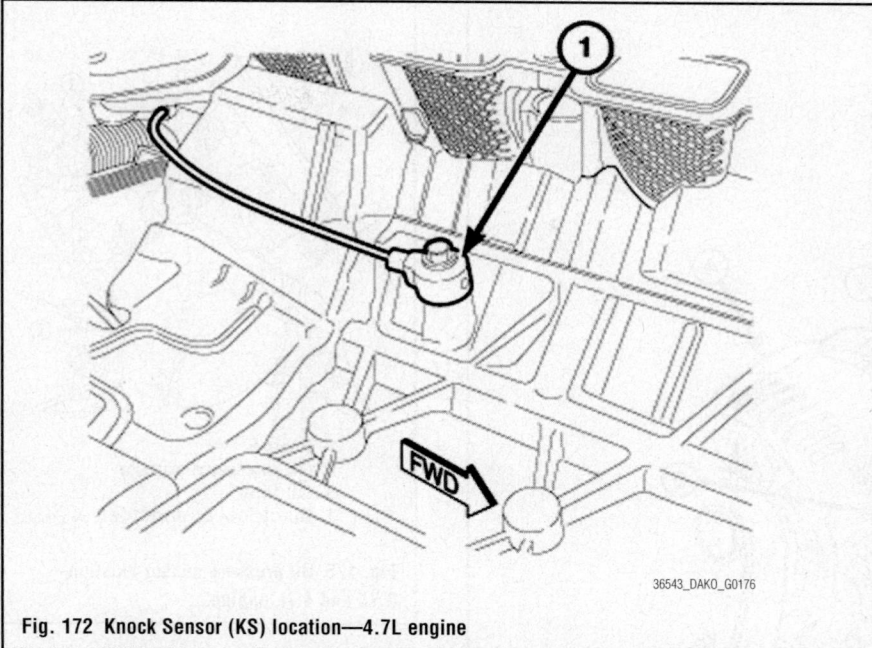

Fig. 172 Knock Sensor (KS) location—4.7L engine

assembly. It is not used as a sealant. Do not apply any adhesive, sealant, or thread-locking compound to these bolts.

8. Install and tighten the mounting bolts. Tighten to 13–17 ft. lbs. (20 Nm).

9. Connect the KS wiring harness to the engine harness at the rear of the intake manifold.

10. Install the intake manifold.

4.7L Engine

See Figure 172.

1. Before servicing the vehicle, refer to the Precautions Section.

2. Remove the intake manifold.

3. Remove the Knock Sensor (KS) bolt.

4. Remove the KS (1).

5. Disconnect the KS wiring harness to the engine harness at the rear of the intake manifold by pressing on the lock tab.

To install:

6. Thoroughly clean the KS mounting hole.

7. Position the KS (1) in place.

✳✳ WARNING

Over or under tightening the sensor mounting bolts will affect KS performance, possibly causing improper spark control. Always use the specified torque when installing the KS.

➥There is a foam strip on the bolt threads. This foam is used only to retain the bolts to the sensors for plant

assembly. It is not used as a sealant. Do not apply any adhesive, sealant, or thread-locking compound to these bolts.

8. Tighten the KS to 15 ft. lbs. (20 Nm).

9. Connect the KS wiring harness to the engine harness at the rear of the intake manifold.

10. Install the intake manifold.

MALFUNCTION INDICATOR LIGHT (MIL)

RESET PROCEDURES

1. Proper operation of the Malfunction Indicator Light (MIL):
   - The MIL will illuminate with the ignition switch ON and the engine OFF
   - The MIL will turn OFF when the engine is started
   - The MIL will remain ON if the self-diagnostic system has detected a malfunction
   - The MIL may turn OFF if the malfunction is no longer present
   - If the MIL is illuminated and then the engine stalls, the MIL will remain illuminated as long as the ignition switch is ON
   - If the MIL is not illuminated and the engine stalls, the MIL will not illuminate until the ignition switch is cycled OFF, then ON
2. Resetting the MIL:
   - The control module turns OFF the MIL after 3 consecutive ignition

cycles that the diagnostic system runs and does not fail
- The control module turns OFF the MIL after a current Diagnostic Trouble Code (DTC) clears when the diagnostic cycle runs and passes
- There may still be a history of DTC's stored in the system. These will clear after 40 consecutive warm-up cycles, if no failures are reported by any other related diagnostic system
- Manual resetting of the MIL and any DTC stored in the system, requires the use of an OBD2 scan tool connected to the Data Link Connector (DLC) for communication with the vehicle. Follow the instructions of the scan tool for both retrieval and resetting of DTC's. The scan tool can be used to command the MIL off.

➥If the error symptoms causing the MIL to illuminate have been corrected, the MIL will return to normal operation.

MANIFOLD ABSOLUTE PRESSURE (MAP) SENSOR

LOCATION

See Figure 173.

The Manifold Absolute Pressure (MAP) sensor (7) is mounted into the front of the intake manifold (1).

REMOVAL & INSTALLATION

See Figures 173 and 174.

The Manifold Absolute Pressure (MAP) sensor (7) is mounted into the front of the intake manifold (1).

1. Before servicing the vehicle, refer to the Precautions Section.

2. Disconnect the electrical connector (2) at the sensor.

3. Clean the area around the MAP sensor.

4. Remove the sensor mounting screw (8).

5. Remove the MAP sensor from the intake manifold by slipping it from the locating pin (6).

To install:

6. Clean the MAP sensor mounting hole at the intake manifold.

7. Check the MAP sensor (1) O-ring seal (2) for cuts or tears.

8. Position the MAP sensor into the manifold by sliding the sensor over the locating pin (6).

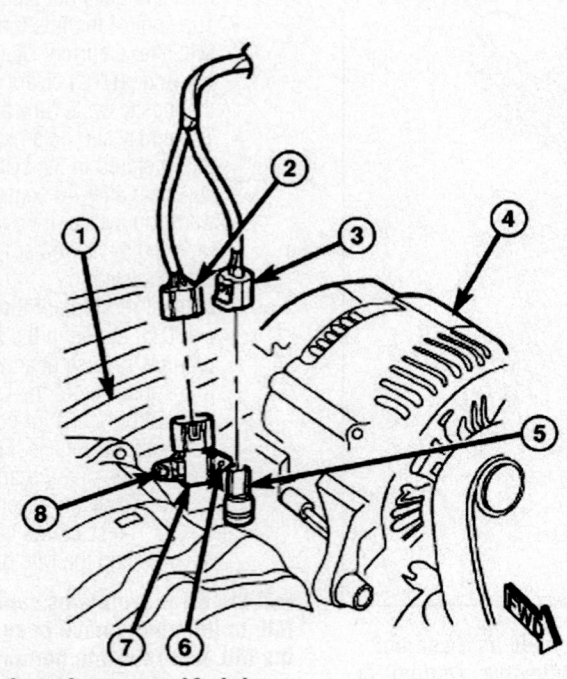

1. Intake manifold
2. MAP connector
3. ECT connector
4. Alternator
5. Engine Coolant Temperature (ECT. sensor
6. Locating pin
7. Manifold Absolute Pressure (MAP. sensor
8. Mounting screw

36543_DAKO_G0177

Fig. 173 Manifold Absolute Pressure (MAP) sensor location—3.7L and 4.7L engines

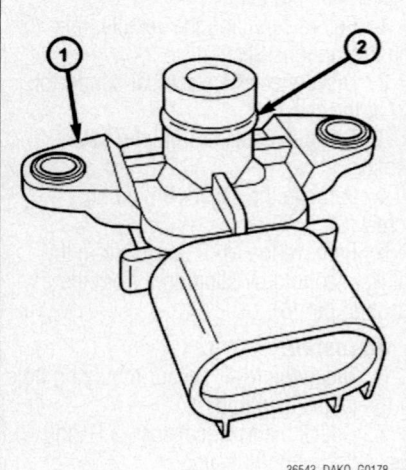

36543_DAKO_G0178

Fig. 174 Check the MAP sensor O-ring seal for cuts or tears

9. Install mounting the bolt (8). Tighten to 25 inch lbs. (3 Nm).
10. Connect the electrical connector (2).

OIL PRESSURE SENSOR

LOCATION
See Figure 175.

REMOVAL & INSTALLATION
See Figure 175.

1. Before servicing the vehicle, refer to the Precautions Section.
2. Disconnect the negative cable from the battery.
3. Raise and safely support the vehicle.
4. Remove the front splash shield.

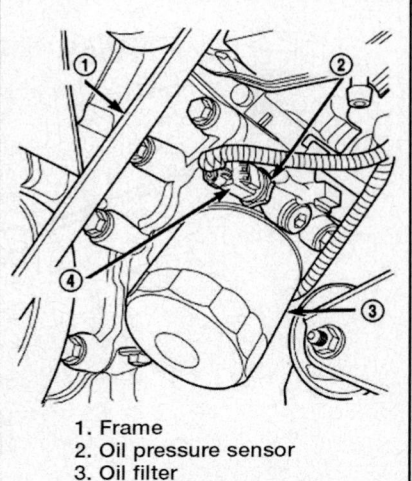

1. Frame
2. Oil pressure sensor
3. Oil filter
4. Electrical connector

36543_DAKO_G0180

Fig. 175 Oil pressure sensor location—3.7L and 4.7L engines

5. Disconnect the oil pressure sensor wire (4).
6. Remove the pressure sensor (2).

To install:
7. Install the oil pressure sensor (2).
8. Connect the oil pressure sensor wire (4).
9. Install the front splash shield.
10. Lower the vehicle.
11. Connect the negative battery cable.
12. Start the engine and ensure there are no oil leaks from the oil pressure sender.

POSITIVE CRANKCASE VENTILATION (PCV) VALVE

LOCATION

3.7L Engine
See Figure 176.

The PCV valve is located at the rear of the left cylinder head.

4.7L Engine
See Figure 177.

The PCV valve (2) is mounted into the top/rear of the left valve cover.

REMOVAL & INSTALLATION

3.7L Engine
See Figures 176 through 178.

The PCV valve is located at the rear of the left cylinder head.
1. Before servicing the vehicle, refer to the Precautions Section.

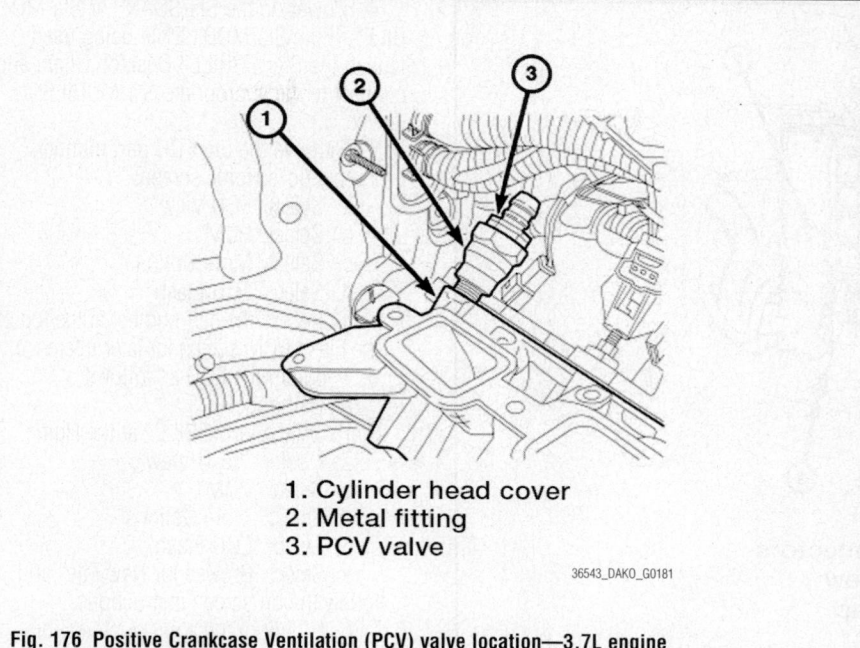

1. Cylinder head cover
2. Metal fitting
3. PCV valve

36543_DAKO_G0181

Fig. 176 Positive Crankcase Ventilation (PCV) valve location—3.7L engine

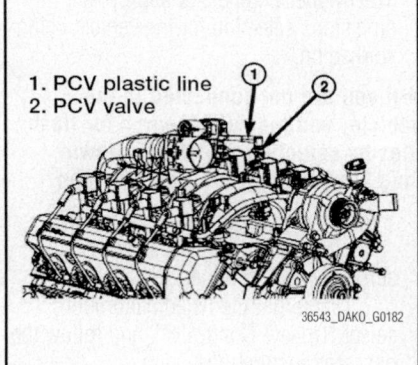

1. PCV plastic line
2. PCV valve

36543_DAKO_G0182

Fig. 177 Positive Crankcase Ventilation (PCV) valve location—4.7L engine

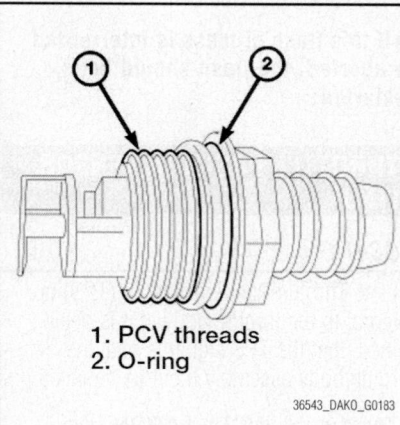

1. PCV threads
2. O-ring

36543_DAKO_G0183

Fig. 178 Check the condition of the PCV valve rubber O-ring

2. Remove the line and the rubber connector hose from the PCV valve.

3. Unscrew the PCV valve (3) from the metal fitting (2).

To install:

4. Check the condition of the PCV valve rubber O-ring (2).

5. Clean the fitting (2).

6. Install the PCV valve (3) into the fitting (2).

7. Install the PCV line and the rubber connector to the valve.

4.7L Engine

See Figure 177.

The PCV valve (2) is mounted into the top/rear of the left valve cover.

1. Before servicing the vehicle, refer to the Precautions Section.

2. Disconnect the plastic line (1) from the end of the PCV valve.

3. Use a small screwdriver to disengage the PCV valve from the valve cover.

To install:

4. Clean out the PCV valve opening at the valve cover.

5. Check the condition of the PCV valve O-ring.

6. Apply engine oil to the O-ring.

7. Place the PCV valve (2) into the valve cover.

8. Attach the plastic line (1) to the valve.

POWERTRAIN CONTROL MODULE (PCM)

LOCATION

See Figure 179.

REMOVAL & INSTALLATION

See Figures 179 and 180.

Certain ABS systems rely on having the Powertrain Control Module (PCM) broadcast the Vehicle Identification Number (VIN) over the bus network. To prevent problems of DTC's and other items related to the VIN broadcast, it is recommend that you disconnect the ABS CAB (controller) temporarily when replacing the PCM. Once the PCM is replaced, write the VIN to the PCM using a diagnostic scan tool. This is done from the engine main menu. Arrow over to the second page to 1. MISCELLANEOUS. Select CHECK VIN from the choices. Make sure it has the correct VIN entered before continuing. When the VIN is complete, turn OFF the ignition key and reconnect the ABS module connector. This will prevent the setting of DTC's and other items associated with the lack of a VIN detected when you turn the key ON after replacing the PCM.

Use a diagnostic scan tool to reprogram the new PCM with the vehicle's original identification number (VIN) and the vehicle's original mileage. If this step is not done, a Diagnostic Trouble Code (DTC) may be set.

The PCM (1) is attached to the right-inner corner of the engine compartment.

✳✳ WARNING

To avoid possible voltage spike damage to the PCM, the ignition key must be OFF, and the negative battery cable must be disconnected before unplugging the PCM connectors.

1. Before servicing the vehicle, refer to the Precautions Section.

2. Disconnect and isolate the negative battery cable.

3. Carefully unplug the four 38-way connectors (2) from the PCM.

4. Remove the 3 PCM mounting bolts (2), and reposition the ground strap (4).

5. Remove the PCM from the vehicle.

To install:

6. Position the PCM (3) to the vehicle.

7. Install the 3 PCM mounting bolts (2). Tighten the bolts to 30–40 inch lbs. (3–5 Nm).

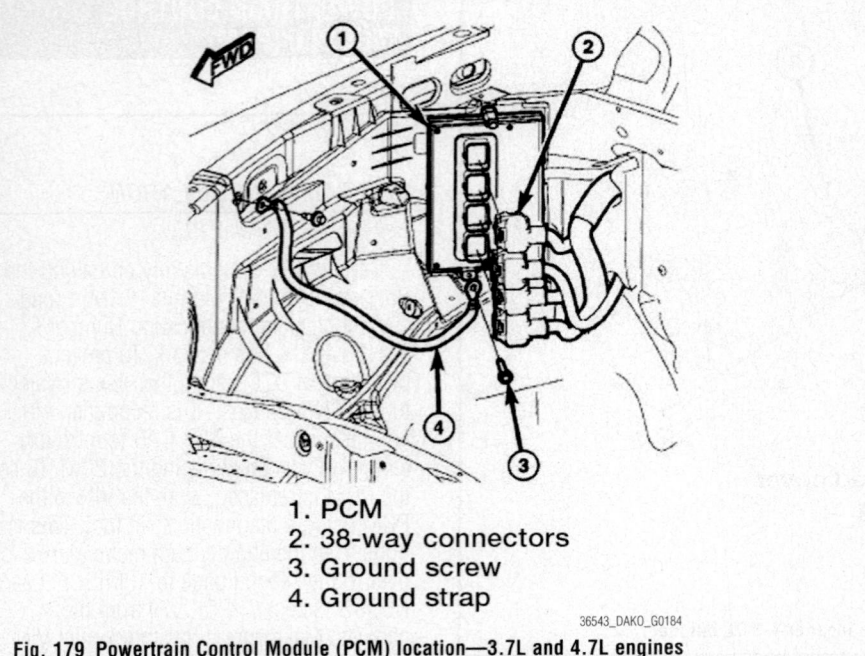

1. PCM
2. 38-way connectors
3. Ground screw
4. Ground strap

36543_DAKO_G0184

Fig. 179 Powertrain Control Module (PCM) location—3.7L and 4.7L engines

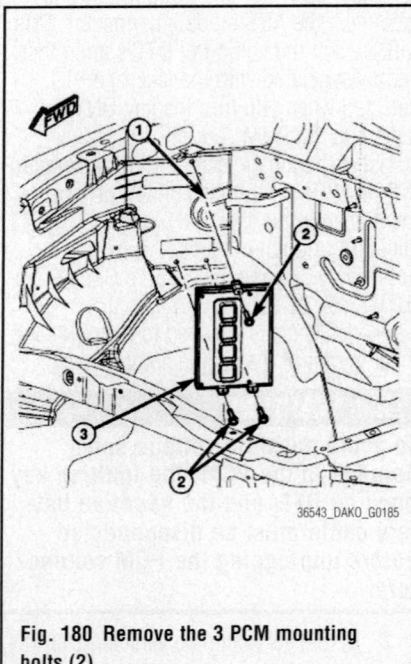

36543_DAKO_G0185

Fig. 180 Remove the 3 PCM mounting bolts (2)

8. Be sure the ground strap (4) is secured at the bottom of the PCM and at the inner-fender.

9. Check the pin connectors in the PCM. Also, check the four 38-way connectors (2) for corrosion or damage. Repair as necessary.

10. Install the four 38-way connectors (2) to the PCM.

11. Connect the negative battery cable.

12. Use the diagnostic scan tool to reset/reprogram the new PCM with the vehicle's original Identification Number (VIN) and the original vehicle mileage. If this step is not done, a Diagnostic Trouble Code (DTC) may be set. Refer to Reset Procedure.

RESET PROCEDURE

This procedure will need to be done when one or more of the following situations are true:

• A vehicle's Powertrain Control Module (PCM) has been replaced

• A Diagnostic Trouble Code (DTC) is set "P1602-PCM Not Programmed."

• An updated calibration or software release is available for either the PCM or TCM ECU.

This procedure assumes that the StarSCAN® and StarMOBILE® devices are configured to with either a wired or wireless connection. The StarSCAN® and StarMO-BILE® must also be running at the latest operating system and software release level.

➡**If this flash process is interrupted or aborted, the flash should be restarted.**

1. Before servicing the vehicle, refer to the Precautions Section.

2. Open the hood of the vehicle and install a battery charger. Verify that the charging rate provides a continuous charge of 13.2–13.5 volts.

3. Connect the StarSCAN® or StarMO-BILE® to the vehicle Data Link Connector (DLC) located under the steering column and turn the ignition key to the RUN position.

4. Power on the StarSCAN® or StarMO-BILE®. If the StarMOBILE® is being used, launch the StarMOBILE® Desktop Client and connect to the appropriate StarMOBILE® device.

5. Retrieve the old ECU part number. From the tool's Home screen:

   a. Select "ECU View"

   b. Select "PCM"

   c. Select "More Options"

   d. Select "ECU Flash"

   e. Record the part number at the top of the Flash PCM screen for later reference.

6. Program the ECU as follows:

   a. Using the StarSCAN®/StarMOBILE® at the Home screen, select "ECU View".

   b. Select "PCM".

   c. Select "More Options".

   d. Select "ECU Flash".

   e. Select "Browse for New File" and follow the on screen instructions.

   f. Highlight the appropriate calibration based on the part number recorded in Step 4e, or by using Year/Model/Engine and appropriate emissions selection for the vehicle being worked on.

➡**If you are not connected to the vehicle, you may also search for flash files by selecting the "Flash Download" button from the Home screen.**

   g. Select "Download to Scantool".

   h. Once the download is complete, select "Close" and then "Back".

   i. Highlight the listed calibration, select "Update Controller", and follow the onscreen instructions.

   j. When the PCM update is complete, select "OK".

   k. Verify that the part number at the top of the Flash PCM screen has updated to the new part number.

➡**If this flash process is interrupted or aborted, the flash should be restarted.**

THROTTLE POSITION SENSOR (TPS)

LOCATION

The Throttle Position Sensor (TPS) is integral to the throttle body. If it is determined, that the TPS signal is bad, the throttle body assembly must be replaced.

REMOVAL & INSTALLATION

The Throttle Position Sensor (TPS) is integral to the throttle body. If it is determined, that the TPS signal is bad, the throttle body assembly must be replaced. Refer to Throttle Body, removal & installation.

VEHICLE SPEED SENSOR (VSS)

LOCATION

3.7L Engine—42RLE Transmission

See Figure 181.

The Vehicle Speed Sensors (VSS) are located on the left side of the transmission case.

4.7L Engine—45RFE and 545RFE Transmissions

See Figure 182.

The Vehicle Speed Sensors (VSS) are located on the left side of the transmission case.

REMOVAL & INSTALLATION

See Figures 181 and 182.

The Vehicle Speed Sensors (VSS) are located on the left side of the transmission case.

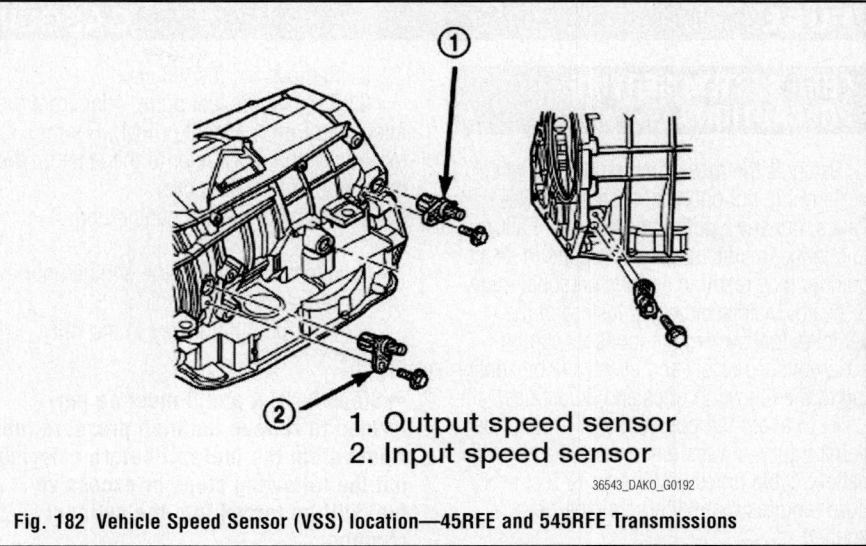

1. Output speed sensor
2. Input speed sensor

36543_DAKO_G0192

Fig. 182 Vehicle Speed Sensor (VSS) location—45RFE and 545RFE Transmissions

1. Before servicing the vehicle, refer to the Precautions Section.
2. Raise and safely support the vehicle.
3. Place a suitable fluid catch pan under the transmission.
4. Remove the wiring connector from the output speed sensor.

5. Remove the bolt holding the speed sensor to the transmission case.
6. Remove the speed sensor from the transmission case.

To install:

➡**The speed sensor bolt has a sealing patch applied from the factory. Be sure to reuse the same bolt.**

➡**Before installing the speed sensor bolt, replenish the sealing patch on the bolt using MOPAR® Lock And Seal Adhesive.**

7. Install the speed sensor into the transmission case.
8. Install the bolt to hold the speed sensor into the transmission case.
   a. Tighten the bolt to 80 inch lbs. (9 Nm)—42RLE transmission.
   b. Tighten the bolt to 105 inch lbs. (12 Nm)—45RFE and 545RFE transmissions.
9. Install the wiring connector onto the speed sensor.
10. Verify the transmission fluid level. Add fluid as necessary.
11. Lower the vehicle.

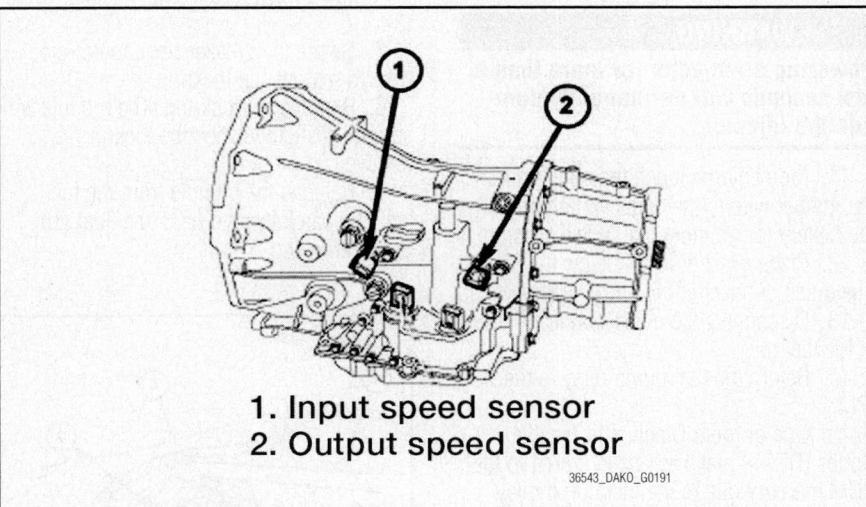

1. Input speed sensor
2. Output speed sensor

36543_DAKO_G0191

Fig. 181 Vehicle Speed Sensor (VSS) location—42RLE Transmission

FUEL SYSTEM SERVICE PRECAUTIONS

Safety is the most important factor when performing, not only fuel system maintenance, but any type of maintenance. Failure to conduct maintenance and repairs in a safe manner may result in serious personal injury or death. Maintenance and testing of the vehicle's fuel system components can be accomplished safely and effectively by adhering to the following rules and guidelines.

• To avoid the possibility of fire and personal injury, always disconnect the negative battery cable unless the repair or test procedure requires that battery voltage be applied.

• Always relieve the fuel system pressure prior to disconnecting any fuel system component (injector, fuel rail, pressure regulator, etc.), fitting, or fuel line connection. Exercise extreme caution whenever relieving fuel system pressure to avoid exposing skin, face, and eyes to fuel spray. Please be advised that fuel under pressure may penetrate the skin or any part of the body that it contacts.

• Always place a shop towel or cloth around the fitting or connection prior to loosening to absorb any excess fuel due to spillage. Ensure that all fuel spillage (should it occur) is quickly removed from the engine surfaces. Ensure that all fuel soaked cloths or towels are deposited into a suitable waste container.

• Always keep a dry chemical (Class B) fire extinguisher near the work area.

• Do not allow fuel spray or fuel vapors to come into contact with a spark or an open flame.

• Always use a back-up wrench when loosening and tightening fuel line connection fittings. This will prevent unnecessary stress and torsion to the fuel line piping.

• Always replace worn fuel fitting O-rings with new. Do not substitute fuel hose or equivalent where fuel pipe is installed.

Before servicing the vehicle, make sure to also refer to the precautions in the beginning of this section as well.

RELIEVING FUEL SYSTEM PRESSURE

Use following procedure if the fuel injector rail is or is not equipped with a fuel pressure test port.

1. Before servicing the vehicle, refer to the Precautions Section.

2. Remove the fuel fill cap.

3. Remove the fuel pump relay from the Integrated Power Module (IPM). For the location of the relay, refer to the label on the underside of the IPM cover.

4. Start and run the engine until it stalls.

5. Attempt restarting the engine until it will no longer run.

6. Turn the ignition key to the OFF position.

➡ **Steps 2, 3, 4 and 5 must be performed to relieve the high pressure fuel from within the fuel rail before carrying out the following steps or excessive fuel will be forced into the cylinder chamber.**

7. Unplug the connector from any the fuel injector.

8. Attach one end of a jumper wire with alligator clips (18 gauge or smaller) to either injector terminal.

9. Connect the other end of the jumper wire to the positive side of the battery.

10. Connect one end of a second jumper wire to the remaining injector terminal.

✸✸ WARNING

Powering an injector for more than a few seconds will permanently damage the injector.

11. Momentarily touch the other end of the jumper wire to the negative terminal of the battery for no more than a few seconds.

12. Place a rag or towel below the fuel line quick-connect fitting at the fuel rail.

13. Disconnect the quick-connect fitting at the fuel rail.

14. Return the fuel pump relay to the IPM.

15. One or more Diagnostic Trouble Codes (DTC's) may have been stored in the PCM memory due to the fuel pump relay removal. A diagnostic scan tool must be used to erase a DTC.

FUEL FILTER

REMOVAL & INSTALLATION

Two fuel filters are used. One is located at the bottom of the fuel pump module and the other is located inside the module. A separate frame mounted fuel filter is not used. Both fuel filters are designed for extended service and do not require normal scheduled maintenance. Filters should only be replaced if a diagnostic procedure indicates to do so.

FUEL PUMP

REMOVAL & INSTALLATION

See Figure 183.

✸✸ CAUTION

The fuel system is under a constant pressure, even with the engine OFF. Before servicing the fuel pump module, the fuel system pressure must be released.

1. Release the fuel system pressure. Refer to Relieving Fuel System Pressure.

2. Before servicing the vehicle, refer to the Precautions Section.

3. Drain and remove the fuel tank.

4. Note the rotational position of the fuel pump module before attempting removal. An indexing arrow is located on the top of the module for this purpose.

5. Position the Lockring Remover/Installer 9340 (3) into the notches on the outside edge of the lockring (5).

6. Install a ½ inch drive breaker bar (1) to the Lockring Remover/Installer 9340 (3).

7. Rotate the breaker bar counter-clockwise to remove the lockring.

8. Remove the lockring. The module will spring up slightly when the lockring is removed.

9. Remove the module from the fuel tank. Be careful not to bend the float arm while removing.

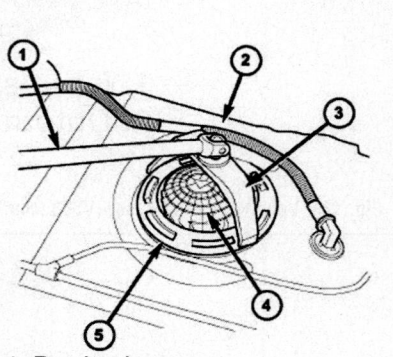

1. Breaker bar
2. Fuel return line
3. Lockring Remover/Installer 9340
4. Fuel pump module
5. Lockring

36543_DAKO_G0194

Fig. 183 Remove the fuel pump module from the fuel tank

To install:

➡️**Whenever the fuel pump module is serviced, the rubber seal (gasket) must be replaced.**

10. Using a new seal (gasket), position the fuel pump module into the opening in the fuel tank.

11. Position the lockring (5) over the top of the fuel pump module.

12. Rotate the module until the embossed alignment arrow points to the center alignment mark. This step must be performed to prevent the float from contacting the side of the fuel tank. Also, be sure the fuel fitting on the top of the pump module is pointed to the driver's side of the vehicle.

13. Install the Lockring Remover/Installer 9340 (3) to the lockring.

14. Install a ½ inch drive breaker (1) into the Lockring Remover/Installer 9340 (3).

15. Tighten the lockring (clockwise) until all 7 notches have engaged.

16. Install the fuel tank.

FUEL RAIL & INJECTORS

REMOVAL & INSTALLATION

3.7L Engine

See Figures 184 and 185.

❋❋ CAUTION

The fuel system is under constant pressure even with engine OFF. Before servicing the fuel rail, the fuel system pressure must be released.

❋❋ WARNING

The left and right fuel rails are replaced as an assembly. Do not attempt to separate the rail halves at the connector tube. Due to the design of the tube, it does not use any clamps. Never attempt to install a clamping device of any kind to the tube. When removing the fuel rail assembly for any reason, be careful not to bend or kink the tube.

1. Before servicing the vehicle, refer to the Precautions Section.

2. Remove the fuel tank filler tube cap.

3. Release the fuel system pressure. Refer to Relieving Fuel System Pressure.

4. Remove the negative battery cable at the battery.

5. Remove the air duct at the throttle body air box.

6. Remove the air box at the throttle body.

7. Disconnect the fuel line latch clip and the fuel line at the fuel rail. A special tool will be necessary for fuel line disconnection.

8. Remove the necessary vacuum lines at the throttle body.

9. Disconnect the electrical connectors at all 6 fuel injectors. To remove connector:

   a. Push the red colored slider away from the injector.

   b. While pushing the slider, depress the tab and remove the connector from the injector.

➡️**The factory fuel injection wiring harness is numerically tagged (INJ 1, INJ 2, etc.) for injector position**

identification. **If the harness is not tagged, note the wiring location before removal.**

10. Disconnect the electrical connectors at the throttle body sensors.

11. Remove the 6 ignition coils.

12. Remove the 4 fuel rail mounting bolts.

13. Gently rock and pull the left side of the fuel rail until the fuel injectors just start to clear the machined holes in the cylinder head. Gently rock and pull the right side of the rail until the injectors just start to clear the cylinder head holes. Repeat this procedure (left/right) until all injectors have cleared the cylinder head holes.

14. Remove the fuel rail (with the injectors attached) from the engine.

15. Disconnect the clip(s) that retain the fuel injector(s) to the fuel rail.

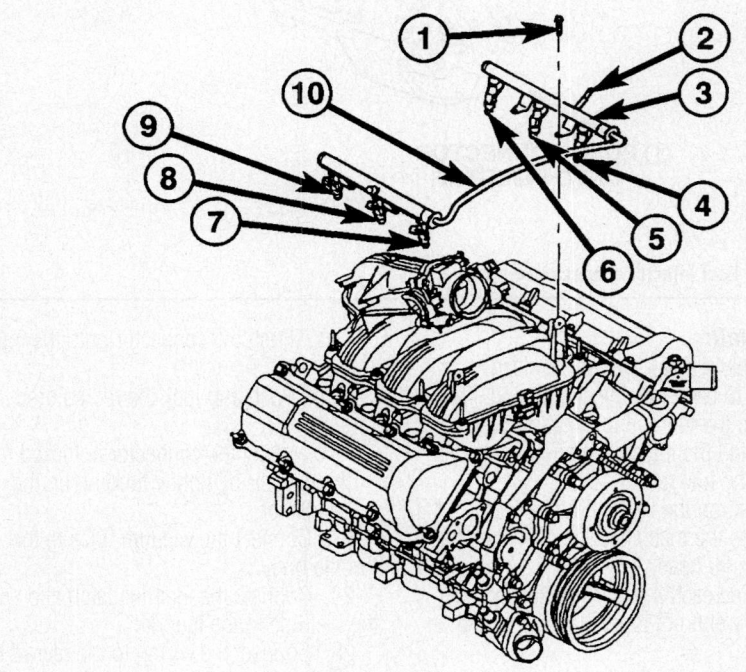

1 - MOUNTING BOLTS (4)
2 - QUICK-CONNECT FITTING
3 - FUEL RAIL
4 - INJ. #1
5 - INJ. #3
6 - INJ. #5
7 - INJ. #2
8 - INJ. #4
9 - INJ. #6
10 - CONNECTOR TUBE

67189-DAKO-G42

Fig. 184 Fuel rail components—3.7L engine

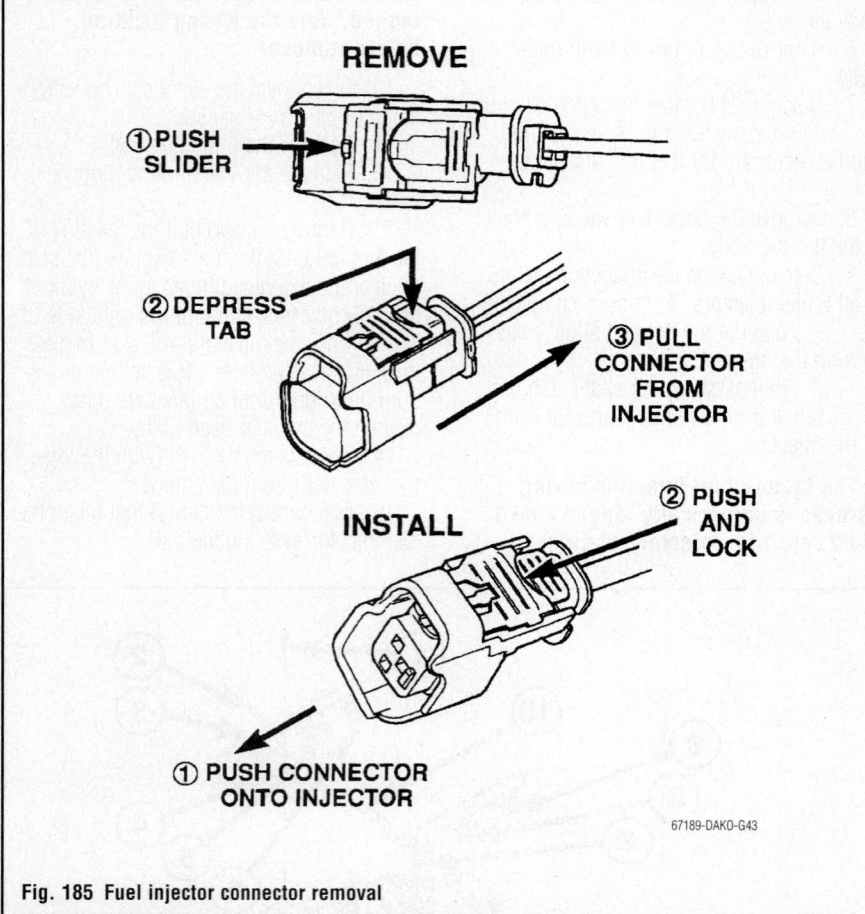

REMOVE

①PUSH
SLIDER

②DEPRESS
TAB

③ PULL
CONNECTOR
FROM
INJECTOR

INSTALL

② PUSH
AND
LOCK

① PUSH CONNECTOR
ONTO INJECTOR

67189-DAKO-G43

Fig. 185 Fuel injector connector removal

To install:

16. Apply a small amount of clean engine oil to each fuel injector O-ring. This will help in the fuel rail installation.

17. Install the injector(s) and the injector clip(s) to the fuel rail.

18. Position the fuel rail/fuel injector assembly to the machined injector openings in the cylinder head.

19. Guide each injector into the cylinder head. Be careful not to tear the injector O-rings.

20. Push the right side of the fuel rail down until the fuel injectors have bottomed on the cylinder head shoulder.

21. Push the left fuel rail down until the injectors have bottomed on the cylinder head shoulder.

22. Install the 4 fuel rail mounting bolts and tighten to 20 ft. lbs. (27 Nm).

23. Install the ignition coils.

24. Connect the electrical connectors to the throttle body.

25. Connect the electrical connectors to the MAP and IAT sensors.

26. Connect the electrical connectors at all the fuel injectors. To install the connector:

a. Push the connector onto the injector.

b. Push and lock the red colored slider.

c. Verify the connector is locked to the injector by lightly tugging on the connector.

27. Connect the vacuum lines to the throttle body.

28. Connect the fuel line latch clip and the fuel line to the fuel rail.

29. Connect the wiring to the rear of the alternator.

30. Install the air box to the throttle body.

31. Install the air duct to the air box.

32. Connect the battery cable to the battery.

33. Start the engine and check for leaks.

4.7L Engine

See Figure 186.

✳✳ CAUTION

The fuel system is under constant pressure even with engine OFF. Before servicing the fuel rail, the fuel system pressure must be released.

✳✳ WARNING

The left and right fuel rails are replaced as an assembly. Do not attempt to separate the rail halves at the connector tube. Due to the design of the tube, it does not use any clamps. Never attempt to install a clamping device of any kind to the tube. When removing the fuel rail assembly for any reason, be careful not to bend or kink the tube.

1. Before servicing the vehicle, refer to the Precautions Section.

2. Remove the fuel tank filler tube cap.

3. Release the fuel system pressure. Refer to Relieving Fuel System Pressure.

4. Remove the negative battery cable at the battery.

5. Remove the air duct at the throttle body air box.

6. Remove the air box at the throttle body.

7. Remove the wiring at the rear of the alternator.

8. Disconnect the fuel line latch clip and the fuel line at the fuel rail. A special tool will be necessary for fuel line disconnection.

9. Remove the vacuum lines at the throttle body.

10. Disconnect the electrical connectors at all 8 fuel injectors. To remove:

a. Push the red colored slider away from the injector.

b. While pushing the slider, depress the tab and remove the connector from the injector.

➡The factory fuel injection wiring harness is numerically tagged (INJ 1, INJ 2, etc.) for injector position identification. If the harness is not tagged, note the wiring location before removal.

11. Disconnect the electrical connectors at the throttle body.

12. Disconnect the electrical connectors at the MAP and IAT sensors.

13. Remove first 3 ignition coils on each bank.

14. Remove the 4 fuel rail mounting bolts.

15. Gently rock and pull the left side of the fuel rail until the fuel injectors just start to clear the machined holes in the cylinder head.

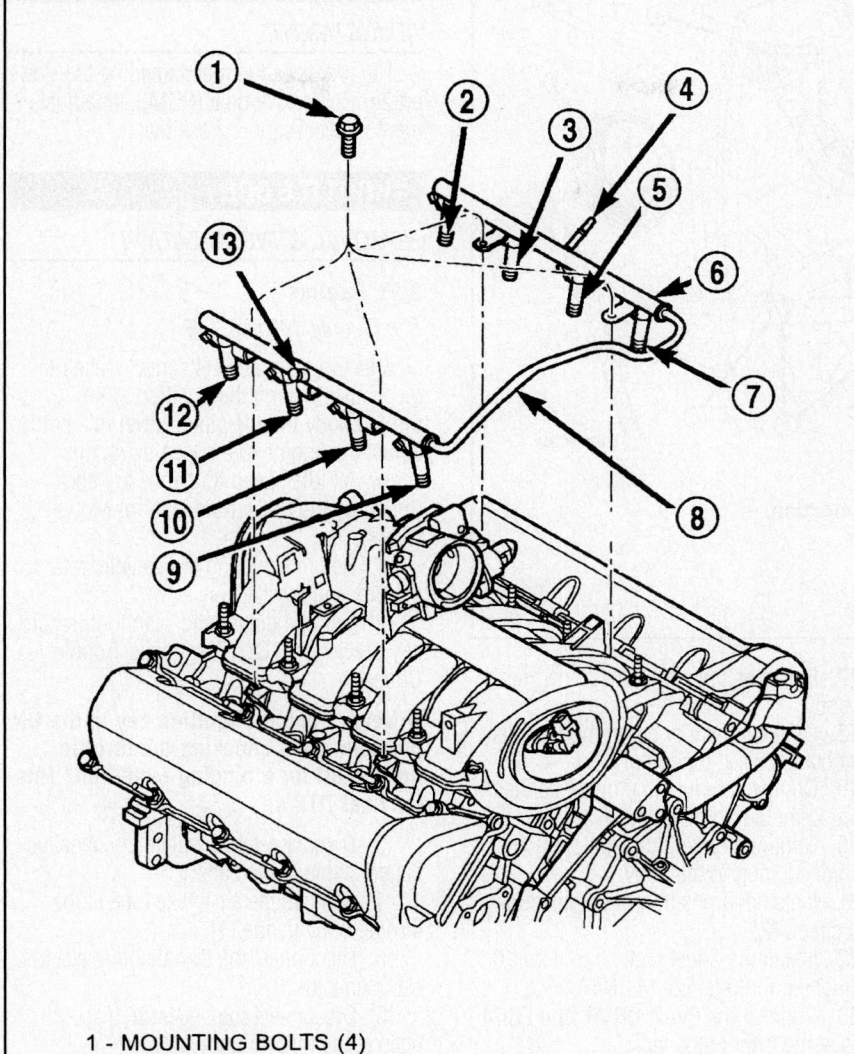

1 - MOUNTING BOLTS (4)
2 - INJ.#7
3 - INJ.#5
4 - QUICK-CONNECT FITTING
5 - INJ.#3

67189-DAKO-G44

Fig. 186 Fuel rail components—4.7L engine

16. Gently rock and pull the right side of the rail until the injectors just start to clear the cylinder head holes. Repeat this procedure (left/right) until all the injectors have cleared the cylinder head holes.

17. Remove the fuel rail (with the injectors attached) from the engine.

18. Disconnect the clip(s) that retain the fuel injector(s) to the fuel rail.

To install:

19. Apply a small amount of clean engine oil to each fuel injector O-ring. This will help in the fuel rail installation.

20. Install the injector(s) and the injector clip(s) to the fuel rail.

21. Position the fuel rail/fuel injector assembly to the machined injector openings in the cylinder head.

22. Guide each injector into the cylinder head. Be careful not to tear the injector O-rings.

23. Push the right side of the fuel rail down until the fuel injectors have bottomed on the cylinder head shoulder.

24. Push the left fuel rail down until the injectors have bottomed on the cylinder head shoulder.

25. Install the 4 fuel rail mounting bolts and tighten to 20 ft. lbs. (27 Nm).

26. Install the ignition coils.

27. Connect the electrical connectors to the throttle body.

28. Connect the electrical connectors to the MAP and IAT sensors.

29. Connect the electrical connectors at all the fuel injectors. To install the connector:

    a. Push the connector onto the injector.

    b. Push and lock the red colored slider. Verify the connector is locked to the injector by lightly tugging on the connector.

30. Connect the vacuum lines to the throttle body.

31. Connect the fuel line latch clip and the fuel line to the fuel rail.

32. Connect the wiring to the rear of the alternator.

33. Install the air box to the throttle body.

34. Install the air duct to the air box.

35. Connect the battery cable to the battery.

36. Start the engine and check for leaks.

FUEL TANK

REMOVAL & INSTALLATION

See Figures 187 and 188.

1. Before servicing the vehicle, refer to the Precautions Section.

2. Release the fuel system pressure. Refer to Relieving Fuel System Pressure.

3. Drain the fuel tank.

4. Disconnect the vent line (3) from the tank.

5. Remove the clamp (7) and disconnect the fill hose (6) at the fuel fill tube.

6. If equipped, remove the fuel tank skid plate.

7. Disconnect the electrical connector at the ESIM switch (9).

8. Disconnect the ESIM, ORVR, and EVAP lines at the front of the tank.

9. Support the tank with a suitable hydraulic jack.

10. Remove the 2 fuel tank strap nuts (3) and remove both tank support straps (2).

11. Carefully lower the tank a few inches and disconnect the fuel pump module electrical connector at the top of the tank. To disconnect the electrical connector:

    a. Push upward on the red colored tab to unlock.

    b. Push on the black colored tab while removing the connector.

12. Disconnect the fuel line at the fuel pump module fitting by pressing on the

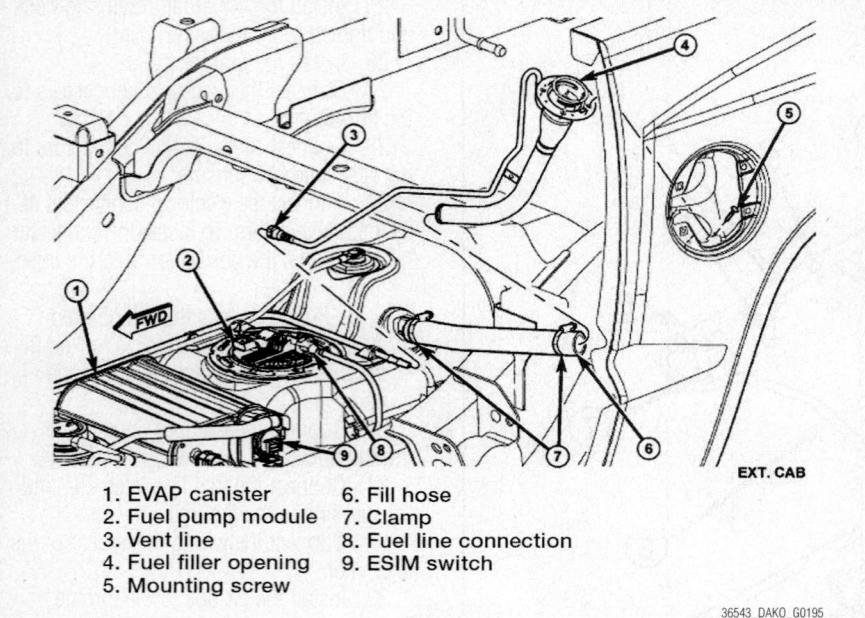

1. EVAP canister
2. Fuel pump module
3. Vent line
4. Fuel filler opening
5. Mounting screw
6. Fill hose
7. Clamp
8. Fuel line connection
9. ESIM switch

36543_DAKO_G0195

Fig. 187 View of fuel tank connections—extended cab

tabs at the side of the quick-connect fitting.

13. Continue to lower the tank for removal.

14. If the fuel tank is to be replaced, remove the fuel pump module from the tank.

To install:

15. If the fuel tank is to be replaced, install the fuel pump module into the tank.

16. Position the fuel tank to the hydraulic jack.

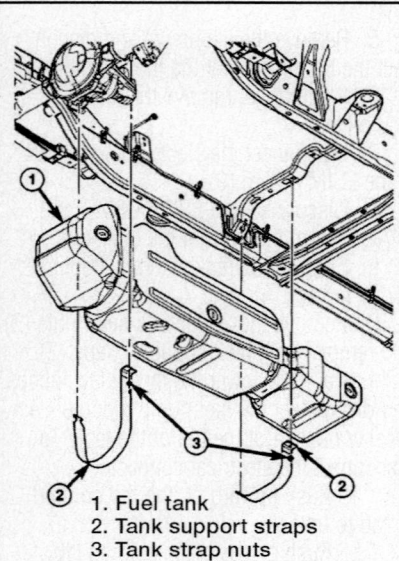

1. Fuel tank
2. Tank support straps
3. Tank strap nuts

36543_DAKO_G0196

Fig. 188 Lower the fuel tank for removal

17. Raise the tank until positioned near the body.

18. Connect the fuel pump module electrical connector at the top of the tank.

19. Connect the fuel line quick-connect fitting to the pump module.

20. Continue raising the tank until it is positioned snug to the body.

21. Install and position both tank support straps (2).

22. Install the 2 fuel tank strap nuts (3) and tighten to 30 ft. lbs. (41 Nm).

23. Connect the EVAP, ORVR, and ESIM lines at the front of the tank.

24. Connect the electrical connector to the ESIM switch (9).

25. Connect the vent line (3).

26. Connect the rubber fill hose (6) to the fuel tank fitting and tighten the hose clamps (7).

27. The vapor/vacuum lines and hoses must be firmly connected. Also, check the vapor/vacuum lines at the ESIM switch, filter, and EVAP canister purge solenoid for damage or leaks. If a leak is present, a Diagnostic Trouble Code (DTC) may be set.

28. If equipped, install the fuel tank skid plate.

29. Install the plastic liner in front of the left-rear tire/wheel.

30. Install the left-rear tire/wheel.

31. Lower the vehicle.

32. Fill the fuel tank with fuel.

33. Start the engine and check for fuel leaks near the top of the module.

IDLE SPEED

ADJUSTMENT

The idle speed is maintained by the Powertrain Control Module (PCM). No adjustment is necessary or possible.

THROTTLE BODY

REMOVAL & INSTALLATION

3.7L Engine

See Figures 189 and 190.

A factory adjusted set screw is used to mechanically limit the position of the throttle body throttle plate. Never attempt to adjust the engine idle speed using this screw. All idle speed functions are controlled by the Powertrain Control Module (PCM).

1. Before servicing the vehicle, refer to the Precautions Section.

2. Using a diagnostic scan tool, record any previous DTC's (Diagnostic Trouble Codes).

➡**Never have the ignition key in the ON position when checking the throttle body shaft for a binding condition. This may set DTC's.**

3. Disconnect and isolate the negative battery cable at the battery.

4. Remove the air intake tube at the throttle body flange (1).

5. Disconnect the throttle body electrical connector (3).

6. Disconnect the necessary vacuum lines at the throttle body.

7. Remove the 4 throttle body mounting bolts (2).

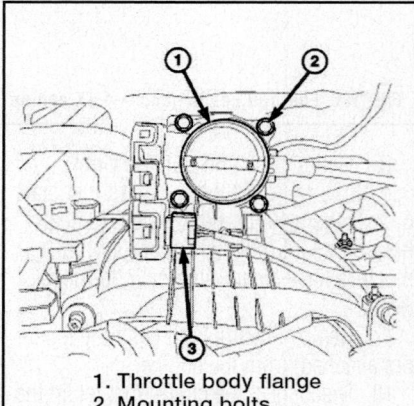

1. Throttle body flange
2. Mounting bolts
3. Electrical connector

36543_DAKO_G0197

Fig. 189 Remove the throttle body from the intake manifold—3.7L engine

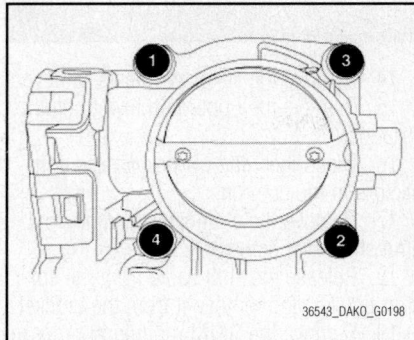

Fig. 190 Throttle body bolt torque sequence

8. Remove the throttle body from the intake manifold.

To install:

9. Check the condition of the throttle body-to-intake manifold O-ring. Replace as necessary.

10. Clean the mating surfaces of the throttle body and the intake manifold.

11. Install the O-ring between the throttle body and the intake manifold.

12. Position the throttle body (1) to the intake manifold.

13. Install all the throttle body mounting bolts (2) finger tight.

✷✷ WARNING

The throttle body mounting bolts MUST be tightened to specifications. Over-tightening can cause damage to the throttle body or the intake manifold.

14. Tighten throttle body mounting bolts, in the sequence shown, to 65 inch lbs. (8 Nm).

15. Install the electrical connector (3).

16. Install the necessary vacuum lines.

17. Install the air cleaner duct at the throttle body.

18. Connect the negative battery cable.

19. Using the diagnostic scan tool, erase all previous DTC's and perform the ETC Relearn function.

4.7L Engine

See Figures 190 and 191.

1. Before servicing the vehicle, refer to the Precautions Section.

2. Using a diagnostic scan tool, record any previous DTC's (Diagnostic Trouble Codes).

➡ **Never have the ignition key in the ON position when checking the throttle body shaft for a binding condition. This may set DTC's.**

3. Disconnect and isolate the negative battery cable at the battery.

4. Remove the air duct and the air resonator box at the throttle body (3).

5. Disconnect the throttle body electrical connector (2).

6. Disconnect the necessary vacuum lines at the throttle body.

7. Remove the 4 throttle body mounting bolts (1).

8. Remove the throttle body from the intake manifold.

To install:

9. Check the condition of the throttle body-to-intake manifold O-ring. Replace as necessary.

10. Clean the mating surfaces of the throttle body and the intake manifold.

11. Install the throttle body-to-intake manifold O-ring.

12. Install all the throttle body mounting bolts (1) finger tight.

✷✷ WARNING

The throttle body mounting bolts MUST be tightened to specifications. Over-tightening can cause damage to the throttle body or the intake manifold.

13. Tighten throttle body mounting bolts, in the sequence shown, to 65 inch lbs. (8 Nm).

14. Install the electrical connector (2).

15. Install the necessary vacuum lines.

16. Install the air cleaner duct and plenum at the throttle body.

17. Connect the negative battery cable.

18. Using the diagnostic scan tool, erase all previous DTC's and perform the ETC Relearn function.

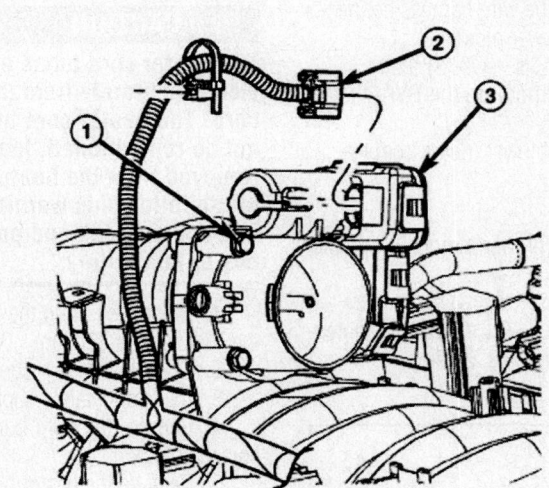

1. Mounting bolts
2. Electrical connector
3. Throttle body

Fig. 191 Remove the throttle body from the intake manifold—4.7L engine

HEATING & AIR CONDITIONING SYSTEM

BLOWER MOTOR

REMOVAL & INSTALLATION

See Figure 192.

> ❋ **CAUTION**
>
> **Disable the airbag system before attempting any steering wheel, steering column, or instrument panel component diagnosis or service. Disconnect and isolate the negative battery (ground) cable, then wait 2 minutes for the airbag system capacitor to discharge before performing further diagnosis or service. This is the only sure way to disable the airbag system. Failure to follow these instructions may result in accidental airbag deployment and possible serious or fatal injury.**

1. Before servicing the vehicle, refer to the Precautions Section.
2. Disconnect and isolate the negative battery cable.
3. Disconnect the wire harness connector (1) from the blower motor (2).
4. Remove the 3 screws (3) that secure the blower motor to the HVAC housing (4).
5. Remove the blower motor from the HVAC housing.

To install:

6. Position the blower motor (2) into the HVAC housing (4).
7. Install the 3 screws (3) that secure the blower motor to the HVAC housing. Tighten the screws to 17 inch lbs. (2 Nm).

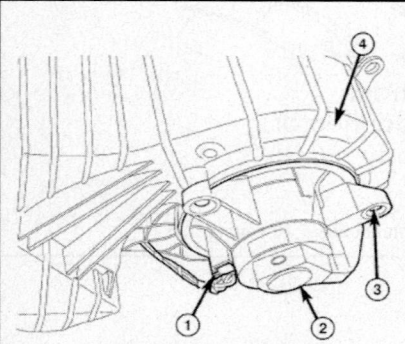

1. Wire harness connector
2. Blower motor
3. Mounting screws
4. HVAC housing

36543_DAKO_G0205

Fig. 192 Remove the blower motor from the HVAC housing

8. Connect the wire harness connector (1) to the blower motor.
9. Reconnect the negative battery cable.

HEATER CORE

REMOVAL & INSTALLATION

See Figures 193 through 196.

> ❋ **CAUTION**
>
> **Disable the airbag system before attempting any steering wheel, steering column, or instrument panel component diagnosis or service. Disconnect and isolate the negative battery (ground) cable, then wait 2 minutes for the airbag system capacitor to discharge before performing further diagnosis or service. This is the only sure way to disable the airbag system. Failure to follow these instructions may result in accidental airbag deployment and possible serious or fatal injury.**

> ❋ **CAUTION**
>
> **The heater core tubes are not serviced separately from the heater core. The heater core tubes should not be repositioned, loosened or removed from the heater core. Failure to follow this warning may result in a coolant leak and possible serious or fatal injury.**

1. Before servicing the vehicle, refer to the Precautions Section.
2. Drain the engine cooling system.
3. Raise and safely support the vehicle.
4. Remove the right front wheelhouse splash shield.
5. Remove the heater hoses from the heater core tubes in the engine compartment.
6. Lower the vehicle.
7. Disconnect and isolate the battery negative cable.
8. Using trim stick C-4755, or equivalent, remove the left door sill trim cover.
9. Remove the screw and remove the left cowl trim cover.
10. Remove the left instrument panel end cap.
11. Remove the 2 screws and remove the steering column opening cover.
12. Remove the screws and position aside the hood release handle.
13. Remove the 4 screws and remove the steering column opening reinforcement.

14. Remove the steering column tilt lever.
15. Remove the upper and lower column shrouds.
16. Disconnect the wiring harness connectors to the column.
17. Remove the shift cable from the column shift lever actuator.
18. Release the shift cable from the column bracket and remove it from the bracket.
19. Remove the SKIM module in order to disconnect the electrical connector.
20. Remove the upper steering shaft coupler bolt and slide the shaft down.
21. Remove the brake light switch and discard.
22. Remove the 4 steering column mounting nuts.
23. Lower the column from the mounting studs.
24. Remove the steering column assembly from the vehicle.
25. Remove the pedal support bracket bolts.
26. Disengage the release rod from the arm on the pedal assembly.
27. Disconnect the electrical connectors from the fuse block.
28. Remove the bolt and remove the ground wire.
29. Open the trim covers in the driver's side A-pillar grab handle and remove the bolts.
30. Remove the A-pillar trim panel.
31. Remove the floor console.
32. Disconnect the 2 body wire harness connectors from the Occupant Restraint Controller (ORC) connector receptacles located on the forward facing side of the module. To disconnect the wire harness connectors from the ORC, depress the

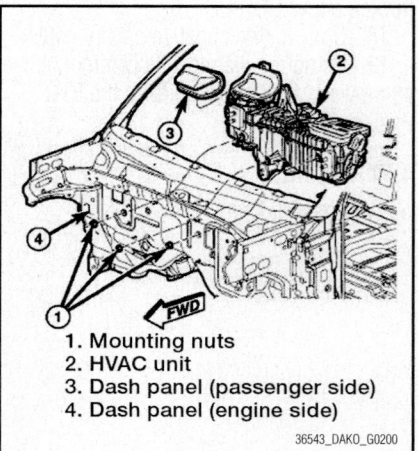

1. Mounting nuts
2. HVAC unit
3. Dash panel (passenger side)
4. Dash panel (engine side)

36543_DAKO_G0200

Fig. 193 HVAC unit location

release tab and lift the lever arm on each connector.

33. Position the carpet aside and remove the center harness screws. Pull instrument panel wiring harness from under the carpet.

34. Remove the center support bolts.

35. Remove the driver's seat.

36. Remove the driver's side floor duct.

37. Remove the driver's side support bolts.

38. Remove the right instrument panel end cap.

39. Remove the passenger side support bolts.

40. Using trim stick C-4755, or equivalent, remove the right door sill trim cover.

41. Remove the screw and remove the right cowl trim cover.

42. Remove the bolts and remove the amplifier.

43. Disconnect the amplifier and antenna electrical connectors.

44. Remove the harness bolt and the ground wire bolt.

45. Remove the passenger side rear floor duct.

46. Open the trim covers in the passenger side A-pillar grab handle and remove the bolts.

47. Remove the A-pillar trim panel.

48. Using trim stick C-4755, or equivalent, remove the instrument panel defroster grille.

49. Disconnect the sensor electrical connector.

50. Remove the 4 fenceline bolts.

51. Lift the instrument panel assembly off the side support pins and remove the assembly through the driver's door.

52. Remove the bolt that secures the HVAC housing bracket to the dash panel.

   a. On the 3.7L engine equipped with an automatic transmission, remove the No. 6 cylinder ignition coil and retaining stud to gain access to the center HVAC housing nut in the engine compartment.

   b. On the 4.7L engine, remove the intake manifold to gain access to the center HVAC housing nut in the engine compartment.

53. Remove the 2 screws that secure the HVAC housing bracket to the top of the HVAC housing.

54. Remove the HVAC housing bracket from the vehicle.

55. Remove the screw that secures the heater core tube retaining bracket to the top of the HVAC housing.

56. Remove the heater core tube retaining bracket from the HVAC housing.

57. Remove the screw that secures the heater core tubes to the heater core.

58. Remove the heater core tubes from the heater core and the dash panel. Remove the O-ring seals from the heater core tube fittings and discard.

59. Remove the 2 screws that secure the heater core retaining bracket to the top of the HVAC housing.

60. Remove the heater core retaining bracket from the top of the HVAC housing.

61. Carefully lift the heater core out of the HVAC housing.

To install:

62. Carefully install the heater core and the heater core retaining bracket to the top of the HVAC housing. Make sure that the heater core insulator is properly positioned.

63. Install the 2 screws that secure the heater core and retaining bracket to the HVAC housing. Tighten the screws to 20 inch lbs. (2 Nm).

64. Lubricate new rubber O-ring seals with clean engine coolant and install them onto the heater core tube fittings. Use only the specified O-ring as it is made of a special material for the engine cooling system.

65. Install the heater core tubes through the dash panel and to the heater core.

66. Install the screw that secures the heater core tubes to the heater core. Tighten the screw securely.

67. Install the heater core tube retaining bracket to the top of the HVAC housing.

68. Install the screw that secures the heater core tube retaining bracket to the HVAC housing. Tighten the screw to 20 inch lbs. (2 Nm).

69. Install the HVAC housing bracket to the top of the HVAC housing and to the dash panel.

70. Install the 2 screws that secure the HVAC housing bracket to the HVAC housing. Tighten the screws to 20 inch lbs. (2 Nm).

71. Install the bolt that secures the HVAC housing bracket to the dash panel. Tighten the bolt to 26 inch lbs. (3 Nm).

72. Position the instrument panel assembly into the vehicle through the driver's side door and install onto the side support pins.

73. Install the 4 fenceline bolts and tighten to 70 inch lbs. (8 Nm).

74. Connect the sensor electrical connector.

75. Install the instrument panel defroster grille and seat fully.

76. Position the passenger side A-pillar trim panel into place and seat fully.

77. Install the bolts and tighten to 55 inch lbs. (6 Nm).

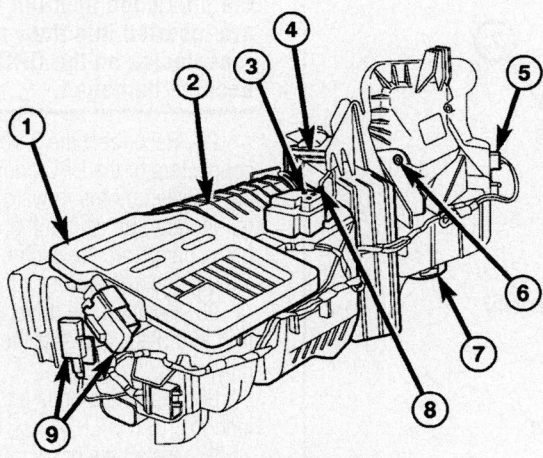

1. HVAC housing assembly
2. Heater core
3. Blend-air doors and actuator
4. A/C evaporator
5. Blower motor resistor
6. Recirculation-air door and actuator
7. Blower motor
8. Evaporator temperature sensor
9. Mode-air doors and actuators and wire harness

36543_DAKO_G0201

Fig. 194 HVAC components illustrated—passenger compartment

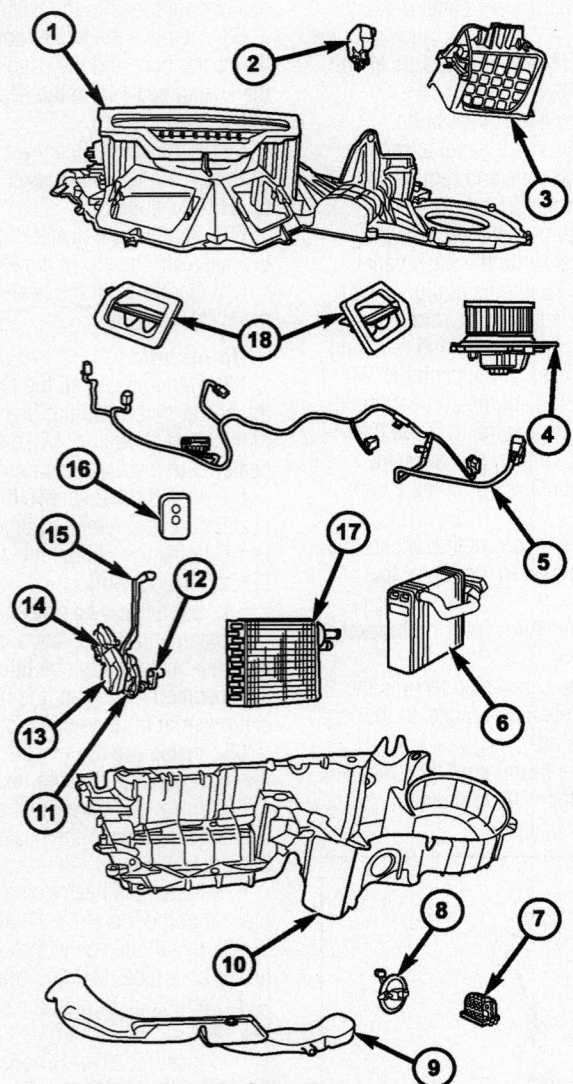

1. Upper HVAC housing
2. Recirculation door actuator
3. Air inlet housing
4. Blower motor and wheel assembly
5. HVAC wire harness
6. A/C evaporator
7. Blower motor resistor block
8. Evaporator temperature sensor
9. Floor distribution duct
10. Lower HVAC housing
11. Mode cam
12. Panel door lever
13. Mode door actuator
14. Blend door actuator
15. Defroster door lever
16. Foam seal
17. Heater core
18. Panel doors

36543_DAKO_G0202

Fig. 195 Expanded view of HVAC unit components—passenger compartment

78. Install the passenger side rear floor duct.

79. Install the screws for the ground wire and passenger side wire harness.

80. Tighten the ground wire and harness bolts to 10 ft. lbs. (14 Nm).

81. Connect the amplifier and antenna electrical connectors.

82. Install the amplifier and install the bolts.

83. Tighten the bolts to 50 inch lbs. (6 Nm).

84. Install the right cowl trim cover and install the screw.

85. Install the right door sill trim cover.

86. Install the passenger side support bolts and tighten to 20 ft. lbs. (27 Nm).

87. Install the right instrument panel end cap.

88. Install the driver's side support bolts and tighten to 20 ft. lbs. (27 Nm).

89. Install the driver's side floor duct.

90. Install the driver's seat.

91. Install the center support bolts and tighten to 95 inch lbs. (11 Nm).

92. Position the center instrument panel wiring harness under the carpet and install the bolts.

⁂ **WARNING**

The lever arms of the wire harness connectors for the ORC MUST be in the unlatched position before they are inserted into their connector receptacles on the ORC or they may become damaged.

93. Reconnect the 2 body wire harness connectors to the ORC connector receptacles located on the forward facing side of the module. Be certain that the latches on both connectors are each fully engaged.

94. Install the floor console.

95. Position the driver's side A-pillar trim into place and seat the retaining clips fully.

96. Install the bolts and tighten to 55 inch lbs. (6 Nm).

97. Install the ground wire and install the bolt.

98. Tighten the ground wire bolts to 10 ft. lbs. (14 Nm).

99. Connect the electrical connectors at the fuse block.

100. Connect the brake release rod to the arm on the pedal assembly.

101. Install the pedal support bolts and tighten to 10 ft. lbs. (14 Nm).

➡**All fasteners must be tightened to specification to ensure proper operation of the steering column.**

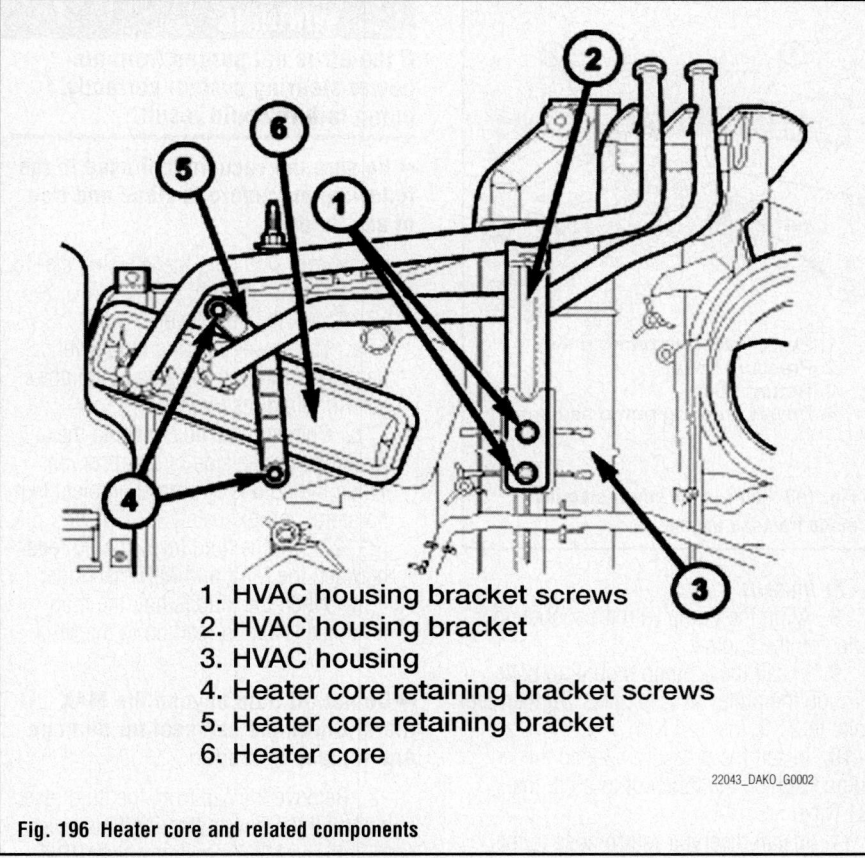

1. HVAC housing bracket screws
2. HVAC housing bracket
3. HVAC housing
4. Heater core retaining bracket screws
5. Heater core retaining bracket
6. Heater core

22043_DAKO_G0002

Fig. 196 Heater core and related components

102. Position the steering column on the dash panel support and loosely install the mounting nuts.

103. Firmly slide the steering column upward against the studs in dash panel and hand tighten the nuts.

104. Install the steering shaft coupler on the steering shaft and loosely install a new bolt.

105. Center steering column in dash opening and tighten mounting nuts to 21 ft. lbs. (28 Nm).

➡**Torque the upper left nut first then the lower right nut. Then torque the lower left nut then the upper right nut.**

➡**A new bolt must be used for reinstallation.**

106. Tighten the coupler bolt to 28 ft. lbs. (38 Nm).

107. Install a new brake light switch.

108. Install the shifter cable.

109. Connect the wiring harness to the column.

110. Install the SKIM module.

111. Install the upper and lower column shrouds and install the screws.

112. Install the column tilt lever.

113. Install the steering column opening reinforcement and install the four screws.

114. Install the hood release handle and install the screws.

115. Install the steering column opening cover and install the two screws.

116. Install the left instrument panel end cap.

117. Install the left cowl trim cover and install the screw.

118. Install the left door sill trim cover and seat fully.

119. Do not reconnect the battery negative cable at this time. The supplemental restraint system verification test procedure should be performed following service of any supplemental restraint system component.

120. Raise and safely support the vehicle.

121. Install the heater hoses to the heater core tubes in the engine compartment.

122. Install the right front wheelhouse splash shield.

123. Lower the vehicle.

124. Refill the engine cooling system.

125. Run the engine until warmed while checking for any leakage.

STEERING

POWER RACK & PINION STEERING GEAR

REMOVAL & INSTALLATION

See Figure 197.

1. Before servicing the vehicle, refer to the Precautions Section.

2. Siphon out as much power steering fluid as possible from the pump.

3. Lock the steering wheel.

4. Raise and safely support the vehicle.

5. Remove the front tires.

6. Remove the nuts from the tie rod ends.

7. Separate tie rod ends from the knuckles with Puller C3894-A.

8. Remove the steering gear pinch bolt.

9. Remove the lower steering coupling from the steering gear.

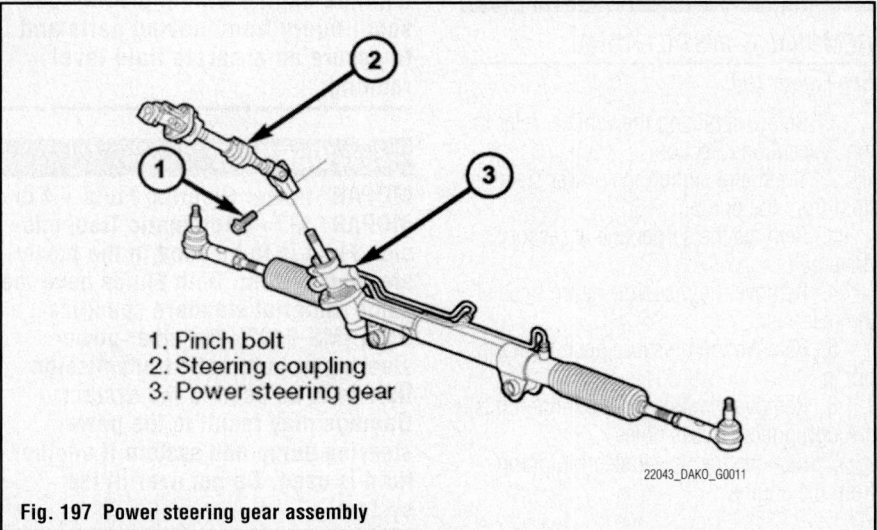

1. Pinch bolt
2. Steering coupling
3. Power steering gear

22043_DAKO_G0011

Fig. 197 Power steering gear assembly

10. Turn the steering gear to the full right position.

➡**Protect the end of hoses to prevent contamination to the system and damage to the O-rings.**

11. Remove the power steering lines from the gear.

12. Remove the steering gear mounting bolts and nuts.

13. Tip the gear forward to allow clearance and move to the right then tip the gear downward on the left side to remove from the vehicle.

To install:

➡**Before installing the power steering gear, inspect the bushings and replace if worn or damaged.**

14. Install the gear to the vehicle and tighten the mounting nuts and bolts to 190 ft. lbs. (258 Nm).

15. Install the power steering lines to the steering gear and tighten the pressure hose to 23 ft. lbs. (31 Nm) and tighten the return hose to 27 ft. lbs. (37 Nm).

16. Slide the shaft coupler onto the gear. Install a new bolt and tighten to 42 ft. lbs. (57 Nm).

17. Clean the tie rod end studs and the knuckle tapers.

18. Install the tie rod ends into the steering knuckles and tighten the nuts to 60 ft. lbs. (81 Nm).

19. Install the front tires.

20. Remove the support and lower the vehicle.

21. Unlock the steering wheel.

22. Fill the power steering system with fluid.

23. Adjust the toe position, as necessary.

POWER STEERING PUMP

REMOVAL & INSTALLATION

See Figure 198.

1. Before servicing the vehicle, refer to the Precautions Section.

2. Drain and siphon the power steering fluid from the pump.

3. Remove the serpentine accessory drive belt.

4. Remove the reservoir return hose at the reservoir.

5. Remove the pressure hose from the pump.

6. Remove the 3 pump mounting bolts through pulley access holes.

7. Remove the power steering pump from the engine.

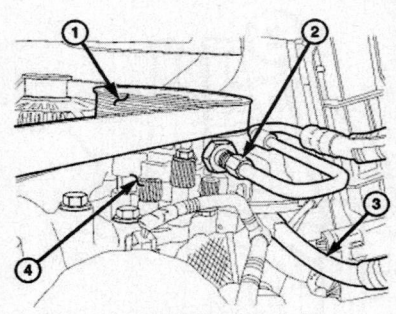

1. Power steering pump pulley
2. Pressure hose
3. Return hose
4. Power steering pump assembly

36543_DAKO_G0209

Fig. 198 Remove the power steering pump from the engine

To install:

8. Align the pump with the mounting holes on the engine.

9. Install the 3 pump mounting bolts through the pulley access holes. Tighten the bolts to 21 ft. lbs. (28 Nm).

10. Install the pressure hose to the pump. Tighten the tube nut to 23 ft. lbs. (31 Nm).

11. Install reservoir return hose to the reservoir.

12. Install the serpentine accessory drive belt.

13. Fill the power steering pump.

14. Bleed the power steering system. Refer to Power Steering Pump, Bleeding.

BLEEDING

See Figure 199.

❋❋ CAUTION

Fluid level should be checked with the engine OFF to prevent personal injury from moving parts and to assure an accurate fluid level reading.

❋❋ WARNING

MOPAR® Power Steering Fluid + 4 or MOPAR® ATF+4 Automatic Transmission Fluid is to be used in the power steering system. Both Fluids have the same material standard specifications (MS-9602). No other power steering or automatic transmission fluid is to be used in the system. Damage may result to the power steering pump and system if another fluid is used. Do not overfill the system.

❋❋ WARNING

If the air is not purged from the power steering system correctly, pump failure could result.

➡**Be sure the vacuum tool used in the following procedure is clean and free of any fluids.**

1. Before servicing the vehicle, refer to the Precautions Section.

2. Check the fluid level.

  a. The power steering fluid level can be viewed through the side of the power steering fluid reservoir.

  b. Compare the fluid level to the markings on the side of the reservoir. When the fluid is at normal ambient temperature, approximately 70–80° F (21–27° C), the fluid level should read between the MAX and MIN markings.

  c. When the fluid is hot, the fluid level is allowed to read up to the MAX line.

➡**Do not fill fluid beyond the MAX mark. Check the cap seal for damage and replace if needed.**

3. Remove the cap from the fluid reservoir and fill the power steering fluid reservoir up to the MAX marking with MOPAR® Power Steering Fluid + 4 or MOPAR® ATF+4 Automatic Transmission Fluid.

4. Tightly insert the Power Steering Cap Adapter (4), Special Tool 9688, into the mouth of the reservoir (3).

➡**Failure to use a vacuum pump reservoir (1) may allow power steering fluid to be sucked into the hand vacuum pump.**

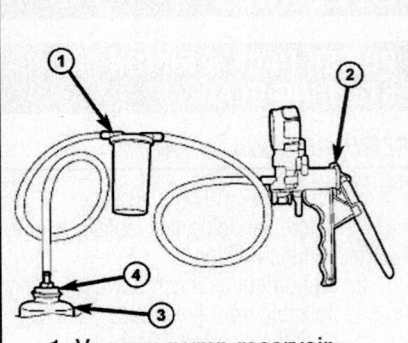

1. Vacuum pump reservoir
2. Hand vacuum pump
3. Reservoir
4. Power steering cap adaptor

36543_DAKO_G0210

Fig. 199 Hand Vacuum Pump, Special Tool C-4207 illustrated

5. Attach the Hand Vacuum Pump (2), Special Tool C-4207, or equivalent, with reservoir (1) attached, to the Power Steering Cap Adapter (4).

❋❋ WARNING

Do not run the vehicle while vacuum is applied to the power steering system. Damage to the power steering pump can occur.

➡ **When performing the following step make sure the vacuum level is maintained during the entire time period.**

6. Using Hand Vacuum Pump (2), apply 20–25 inches Hg (68–85 kPa) of vacuum to the system for a minimum of 3 minutes.

7. Slowly release the vacuum and remove the special tools.

8. Adjust the fluid level as necessary.

9. Repeat above steps until the fluid no longer drops when vacuum is applied.

10. Start the engine and cycle the steering wheel lock-to-lock 3 times.

➡ **Do not hold the steering wheel at the stops.**

11. Stop the engine and check for leaks at all connections.

12. Check for any signs of air in the reservoir and check the fluid level. If air is present, repeat the procedure as necessary.

❋❋ WARNING

Do not run a vehicle with foamy fluid for an extended period. This may cause pump damage.

SUSPENSION

COIL SPRING

REMOVAL & INSTALLATION

See Figures 200 and 201.

1. Before servicing the vehicle, refer to the Precautions Section.
2. Remove the shock absorber. Refer to Shock Absorbers, removal & installation.
3. Install the shock assembly in the Branick 7200® spring removal/installation tool (1), or equivalent.
4. Compress the spring (2).
5. Position the shock nut wrench 9362 (2) on the shock shaft retaining nut. Insert an 8mm socket through the Wrench onto the hex located on the end of the shock shaft.
6. While holding the shock shaft from turning, remove the nut from the shock shaft using the wrench.
7. Remove the upper shock nut.
8. Remove the shock.
9. Remove the shock upper mounting plate.
10. Remove the coil spring.

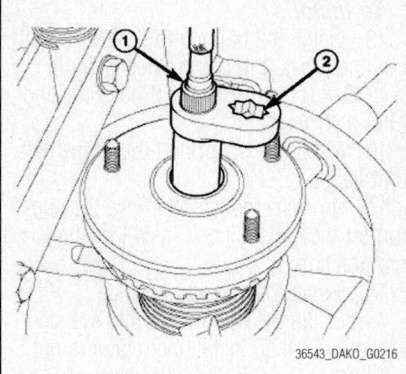

Fig. 201 Position the shock nut wrench 9362 (2) on the shock shaft retaining nut

11. Remove and inspect the upper and lower spring isolators.

To install:

12. Install the lower and upper isolator.
13. Position the shock into the coil spring.
14. Install the upper shock mounting plate.
15. Install the shock nut wrench 9362 (2) (on the end of a torque wrench) on the shock shaft retaining nut.
16. Insert an 8mm socket though the wrench onto the hex located on the end of the shock shaft. While holding the shock shaft from turning, tighten the nut to 33 ft. lbs. (45 Nm).
17. Install the shock upper mounting nut.
18. Decompress the spring (2).
19. Remove the shock assembly from the spring compressor tool (1).
20. Install the shock assembly. Refer to Shock Absorbers, removal & installation.

FRONT SUSPENSION

CONTROL LINKS

REMOVAL & INSTALLATION

See Figure 202

1. Before servicing the vehicle, refer to the Precautions Section.
2. Raise and safely support the vehicle.
3. Remove the lower nut (5) from the stabilizer control link.
4. Remove the upper nut, retainers, and grommets from the stabilizer bar (3).
5. Remove the stabilizer control link (1) from the vehicle.

To install:

6. Install the stabilizer link (1) to the vehicle.
7. Install the retainers, grommets, and upper nut to the stabilizer bar (3). Tighten nut to 17 ft. lbs. (23 Nm).
8. Install the lower nut (5). Tighten to 75 ft. lbs. (102 Nm).
9. Remove the support and lower the vehicle.

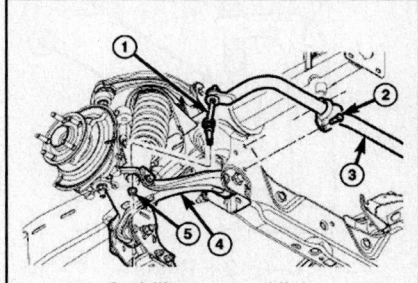

1. Stabilizer control link
2. Stabilizer bar bracket bolt
3. Stabilizer bar
4. Lower control arm
5. Lower control link nut

36543_DAKO_G0217

Fig. 202 Removing the stabilizer control link

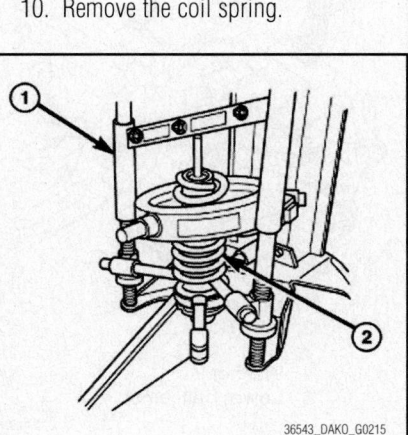

36543_DAKO_G0215

Fig. 200 Using the Branick 7200® spring removal/installation tool

LOWER BALL JOINT

REMOVAL & INSTALLATION

See Figures 203 and 204.

1. Before servicing the vehicle, refer to the Precautions Section.

2. Remove the tire and wheel assembly.

3. Remove the brake caliper and rotor.

4. Remove the outer tie rod retaining nut from the knuckle.

5. Separate the tie rod from the steering knuckle using Special Tool C-3894-A.

6. Remove the upper ball joint nut, then separate the upper ball joint from the knuckle using Special Tool 8677, or equivalent.

7. Remove the lower ball joint nut, then separate the lower ball joint from the steering knuckle using Special Tool 8677.

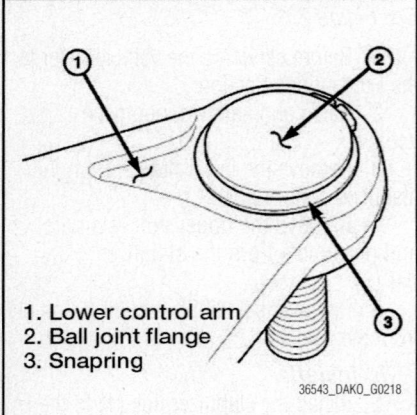

1. Lower control arm
2. Ball joint flange
3. Snapring

36543_DAKO_G0218

Fig. 203 Remove the snapring from the ball joint flange

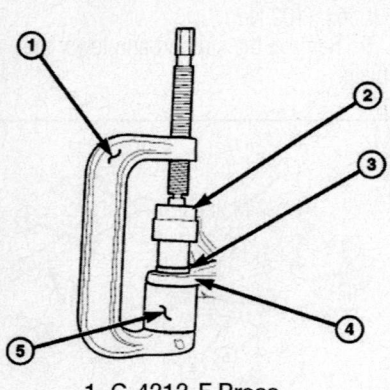

1. C-4212-F Press
2. 8445-3 Driver
3. Ball joint
4. Lower control arm
5. 9604 Receiver

36543_DAKO_G0219

Fig. 204 Removing the lower ball joint from the control arm

8. Remove the steering knuckle.

9. On 4WD models: Move the halfshaft to the side and support the halfshaft out of the way.

10. Remove the snapring from the ball joint flange.

➡**Extreme pressure lubrication must be used on the threaded portions of the tool. This will increase the longevity of the tool and insure proper operation during the removal and installation process.**

11. Press the ball joint (3) from the lower control arm (4) using Special Tools C-4212-F (Press) (1), 8445-3 (Driver) (2), and 9604 (Receiver) (5).

To install:

12. Install the ball joint into the control arm and press it in using Special Tools C-4212-F (press), 8441-4 (Receiver), and 9654-1 (Driver).

13. Install the snapring around the ball joint flange.

14. On 4WD models: Remove the support for the halfshaft and install the halfshaft into position.

15. Install the steering knuckle.

16. Install the tie rod end into the steering knuckle, then install the retaining nut and tighten to 80 ft. lbs. (108 Nm).

17. Install and tighten the halfshaft nut (if equipped) to 185 ft. lbs. (251 Nm).

18. Install the brake caliper and rotor.

19. Install the tire and wheel assembly.

20. Check the vehicle ride height.

LOWER CONTROL ARM

REMOVAL & INSTALLATION

See Figure 205.

1. Before servicing the vehicle, refer to the Precautions Section.

2. Raise and safely support the vehicle.

3. Remove the wheel and tire assembly.

4. Remove the disc brake caliper assembly.

5. Remove the disc brake rotor.

6. Disconnect the wheel speed sensor at the wheel well.

7. Remove the tie rod end jam nut.

8. Disconnect the tie rod from the knuckle using Special Tool C-3894-A, or equivalent.

9. Remove the front halfshaft nut (4WD models).

10. Remove the upper ball joint nut. Separate the upper ball joint from the steering knuckle with a remover.

11. Remove the lower ball joint nut. Separate the lower ball joint from the steering knuckle with Special Tool 8677.

12. Remove the steering knuckle.

13. Remove the stabilizer bar link

14. Remove the shock absorber lower bolt and nut.

15. Remove the lower control arm bolts, nuts, and washers.

16. Remove the lower control arm from the vehicle.

To install:

➡**All suspension components should be tightened with the weight of the vehicle bearing down on them (curb height).**

17. Position the lower control arm at the frame rail brackets. Install the pivot bolts, washers, and nuts. Tighten the nuts finger-tight.

✴✥ WARNING

The ball joint stud taper must be CLEAN and DRY before installing the knuckle. Clean the stud taper with mineral spirits to remove dirt and grease.

18. Install the steering knuckle.

19. Insert the lower ball joint into the steering knuckle. Install and tighten the retaining nut to 95 ft. lbs. (129 Nm).

20. Install the shock absorber lower bolt and nut. Tighten to 155 ft. lbs. (210 Nm).

21. Install the front halfshaft nut (4WD models).

22. Insert the upper ball joint into the steering knuckle. Install and tighten the retaining nut to 70 ft. lbs. (95 Nm).

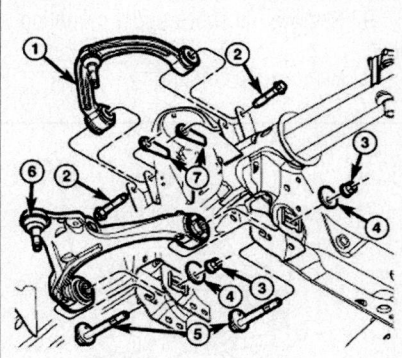

1. Upper control arm
2, 5, 7. Bolts
3. Nut
4. Washer
6. Lower ball joint

36543_DAKO_G0220

Fig. 205 Exploded view of lower and upper control arms

23. Install the stabilizer bar control link and tighten to 75 ft. lbs. (102 Nm).

24. Tighten the lower control arm pivot nut and bolts to 110 ft. lbs. (149 Nm).

25. Insert the outer tie rod end into the steering knuckle. Install and tighten the retaining nut to 80 ft. lbs. (108 Nm).

26. Install the disc brake rotor.

27. Install the disc brake caliper and adapter assembly and tighten to 100 ft. lbs. (135 Nm).

28. Install the wheel and tire assembly.

29. Remove the support and lower the vehicle.

30. Perform a wheel alignment.

SHOCK ABSORBERS

REMOVAL & INSTALLATION

See Figures 206 through 208.

1. Before servicing the vehicle, refer to the Precautions Section.

2. Remove the upper shock nuts (1).

3. Raise and safely support the vehicle.

4. Remove the tire and wheel assembly.

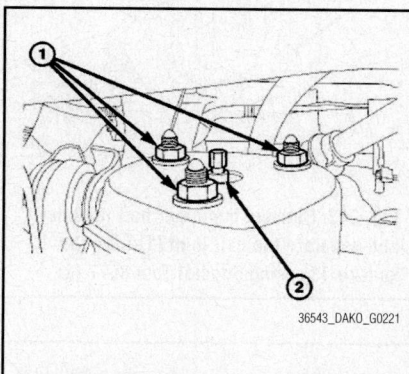

Fig. 206 Remove the upper shock nuts (1)

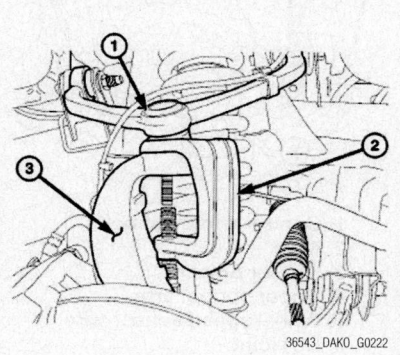

Fig. 207 Remove the upper ball joint nut and separate the ball joint (1) from the knuckle (3) using Special Tool 8677 (2)

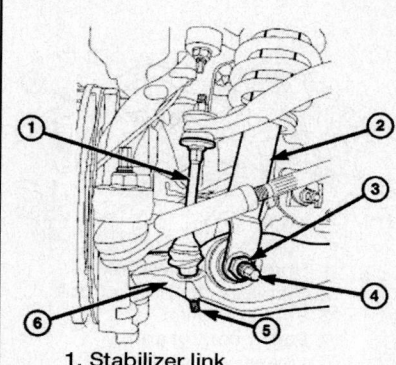

1. Stabilizer link
2. Shock
3. Nut
4. Lower shock bolt
5. Stabilizer link lower nut
6. Lower control arm

36543_DAKO_G0223

Fig. 208 View of lower shock and related components

5. Remove the disc brake caliper mounting bolts.

6. Remove the wheel speed sensor routing clip.

7. Remove the upper ball joint nut and separate the ball joint (1) from the knuckle (3) using Special Tool 8677 (2).

8. Support the lower control arm outboard end.

9. Remove the stabilizer link lower nut (5) and then separate the stabilizer link (1) from the lower control arm (6) to gain access to the lower shock nut (3).

10. Remove the lower shock bolt (4) and nut (3).

11. Remove the shock (2).

To install:

➡ **All suspension components should be tighten with the weight of the vehicle on them (curb height).**

12. Install the upper part of the shock (2) into the frame bracket.

13. Install the upper shock module nuts (1). Tighten to 45 ft. lbs. (61 Nm).

14. Install the lower part of the shock module (2) into the lower control arm shock bushing.

15. Position the shock module (2) to the lower control (6).

16. Install the bolt (4) so the head of the bolt is facing the rear of the vehicle and hand start the nut (3). Tighten the bolt (4) and nut (3) to 155 ft. lbs. (210 Nm).

17. Install the stabilizer link lower nut (5) to the lower control arm (6). Tighten the nut to 75 ft. lbs. (102 Nm).

18. Insert the ball joint in the steering knuckle and tighten the ball joint nut to 70 ft. lbs. (95 Nm).

19. Reposition the wheel speed wire into the retaining brackets.

20. Install the caliper slide pin bolts. Tighten to 24 ft. lbs. (32 Nm).

21. Remove the support from the lower control arm outboard end.

22. Install the tire and wheel assembly.

23. Remove the support and lower the vehicle.

STEERING KNUCKLE

REMOVAL & INSTALLATION

See Figure 209.

1. Before servicing the vehicle, refer to the Precautions Section.

2. Raise and safely support the vehicle.

3. Remove the wheel and tire assembly.

4. Remove the brake caliper, rotor, shield, and ABS wheel speed sensor, if equipped.

5. Remove the front halfshaft nut on 4WD models.

6. Remove the tie rod end nut.

7. Separate the tie rod from the knuckle with puller C-3894-A, or equivalent.

❊❊ WARNING

When installing puller 8677 to separate the ball joint, be careful not to damage the ball joint seal.

8. Remove the upper ball joint nut.

9. Separate the ball joint from the knuckle with puller 8677, or equivalent.

10. Install an hydraulic jack to support the lower control arm.

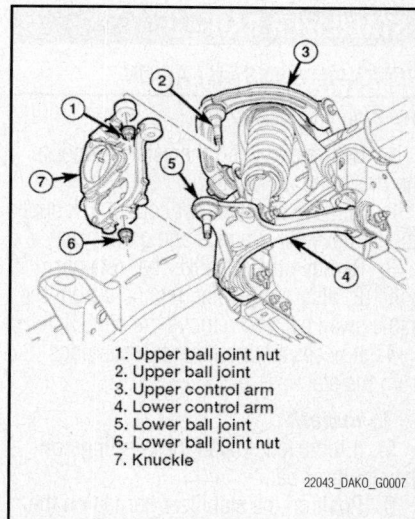

1. Upper ball joint nut
2. Upper ball joint
3. Upper control arm
4. Lower control arm
5. Lower ball joint
6. Lower ball joint nut
7. Knuckle

22043_DAKO_G0007

Fig. 209 Exploded view of the steering knuckle assembly

11. Remove the lower ball joint nut.

12. Separate the ball joint from the knuckle with puller 8677, or equivalent, and remove the knuckle.

13. Remove the hub/bearing bolts from the knuckle.

14. Remove the hub/bearing from the steering knuckle.

15. Remove the steering knuckle.

To install:

❄ CAUTION

The ball joint stud tapers must be CLEAN and DRY before installing the knuckle. Clean the stud tapers with mineral spirits to remove dirt and grease.

16. Install the hub/bearing to the steering knuckle and tighten the bolts to 120 ft. lbs. (163 Nm).

17. Install the knuckle onto the upper and lower ball joints.

18. Install the upper ball joint nut. Tighten the nut to 70 ft. lbs. (95 Nm).

19. Install the lower ball joint nut. Tighten the nut to 95 ft. lbs. (129 Nm).

20. Remove the hydraulic jack from the lower control arm.

21. Install the tie rod end and tighten the nut to 80 ft. lbs. (108 Nm).

22. Install the front halfshaft into the hub/bearing on 4WD models. Tighten the halfshaft nut to 185 ft. lbs. (251 Nm).

23. Install the ABS wheel speed sensor, if equipped, brake shield, rotor, and caliper.

24. Install the wheel and tire assembly.

25. Remove the support and lower the vehicle.

26. Perform a wheel alignment.

STABILIZER BAR

REMOVAL & INSTALLATION

See Figures 210 and 211.

1. Before servicing the vehicle, refer to the Precautions Section.

2. Remove the stabilizer control link upper nut. Remove the retainers and grommets.

3. Remove the stabilizer bar retainer bolts (2) also remove the retainers from the frame sway bar and remove the bar (3).

4. If necessary, remove the bushings from the stabilizer bar.

To install:

5. If removed, install the bushings on the stabilizer bar.

6. Position the stabilizer bar (1) on the frame crossmember brackets and install the bracket (3) and bolts (2) finger-tight.

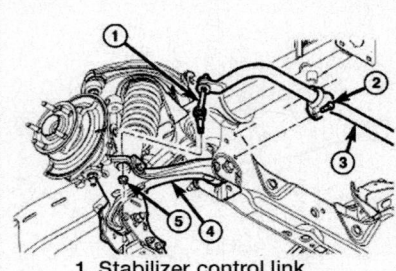

1. Stabilizer control link
2. Stabilizer bar bracket bolt
3. Stabilizer bar
4. Lower control arm
5. Lower control link nut

36543_DAKO_G0224

Fig. 210 View of stabilizer bar and related components

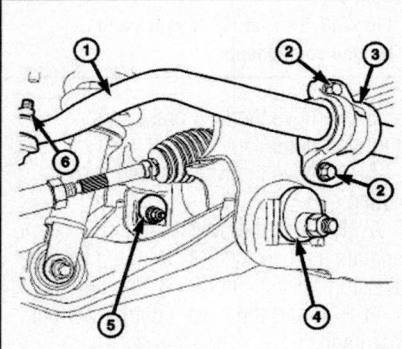

1. Stabilizer bar
2. Bracket bolts
3. Crossmember bracket
4, 5. Control arm fasteners
6. Stabilizer control link nut

36543_DAKO_G0225

Fig. 211 View of stabilizer bar and related components

➡ Check the alignment of the bar to ensure there is no interference with the either frame rail or chassis components. The spacing should be equal on both sides.

7. Install the stabilizer bar (1) to the stabilizer link and install the grommets and retainers.

8. Install the nuts (6) to the stabilizer link and tighten to 17 ft. lbs. (23 Nm).

9. Tighten the bracket bolts (2) to the frame to 45 ft. lbs. (61 Nm).

UPPER BALL JOINT

REMOVAL & INSTALLATION

These models utilize an upper control arm with an integral ball joint. If the upper ball joint is damaged or worn, the upper control arm must be replaced.

UPPER CONTROL ARM

REMOVAL & INSTALLATION

See Figures 212 and 213.

1. Before servicing the vehicle, refer to the Precautions Section.

2. Raise and safely support the vehicle.

3. Remove the wheel and tire assembly.

4. Remove the nut from the upper ball joint.

5. Separate the upper ball joint (1) from the steering knuckle (3) with puller 8677 (2).

❄ WARNING

When installing puller 8677 (2) to separate the ball joint, be careful not to damage the ball joint seal.

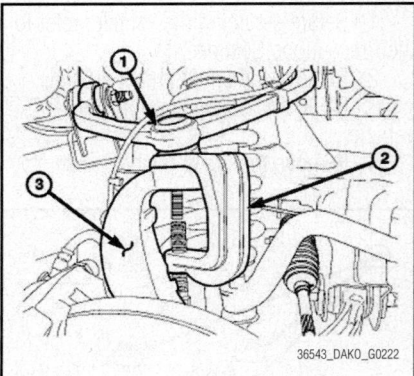

36543_DAKO_G0222

Fig. 212 Remove the upper ball joint nut and separate the ball joint (1) from the knuckle (3) using Special Tool 8677 (2)

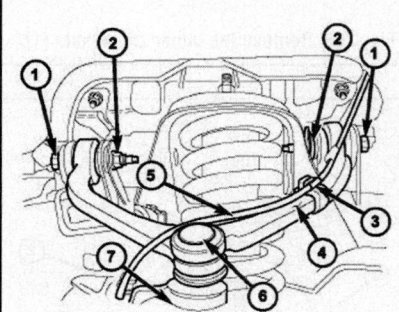

1. Control arm pivot bolts
2. Nuts
3. Sensor bracket
4. Upper control arm
5. Wheel speed sensor wire
6. Ball joint
7. Steering knuckle

36543_DAKO_G0226

Fig. 213 View of the upper control arm

6. Remove the wheel speed sensor wire (5) from the retaining brackets (3) to the upper control arm (4).

7. Remove the control arm pivot bolts (1) and nuts (2) and remove control arm (4).

To install:

➡ **All suspension components should be tightened with the weight of the vehicle on them (curb height).**

8. Position the control arm (4) into the frame brackets. Install the bolts (1) and nuts (2) and tighten to 130 ft. lbs. (176 Nm).

9. Position the wheel speed wire (5) into the retaining brackets (3).

10. Insert the ball joint (6) in the steering knuckle (7) and tighten the ball joint nut to 70 ft. lbs. (95 Nm).

11. Install the wheel and tire assembly.

12. Remove the support and lower the vehicle.

13. Perform a wheel alignment.

WHEEL HUB & BEARING

REMOVAL & INSTALLATION

See Figure 214.

1. Before servicing the vehicle, refer to the Precautions Section.

SUSPENSION

LEAF SPRING

REMOVAL & INSTALLATION

See Figure 215.

❊❊ WARNING

The rear of the vehicle must be raised with a jack or hoist. The lift must be placed under the frame rail crossmember located aft of the rear axle. Use care to avoid bending the side rail flange.

1. Before servicing the vehicle, refer to the Precautions Section.

2. Raise the vehicle at the frame.

3. Use an hydraulic jack to relieve the axle weight.

4. Remove the wheel and tire assemblies.

5. Remove the nuts, the U-bolts, and the spring plate from the axle.

6. Loosen and remove the bolt and then remove the flag nut through the access hole in the bracket from the spring front eye.

7. Remove the nut and bolt (3) that attaches the spring shackle (5) to the rear frame bracket (4).

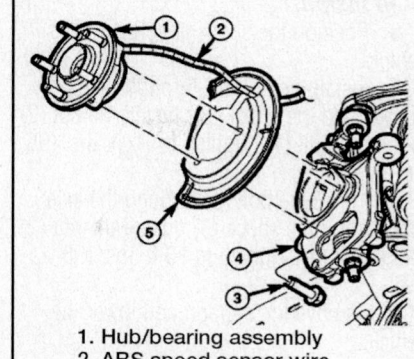

1. Hub/bearing assembly
2. ABS speed sensor wire
3. Mounting bolts
4. Steering knuckle
5. Brake dust shield

36543_DAKO_G0227

Fig. 214 Exploded view of front hub

2. Raise and safely support the vehicle.

3. Remove the wheel and tire assembly.

4. Remove the brake caliper and rotor.

5. Remove the ABS wheel speed sensor, if equipped.

6. Remove the halfshaft nut, on 4WD models.

❊❊ WARNING

Do not strike the knuckle with a hammer to remove the tie rod end or the

8. Remove the spring (6) from the vehicle.

9. Remove the shackle (2) from the spring (6).

To install:

10. Install the spring shackle on the spring finger tight.

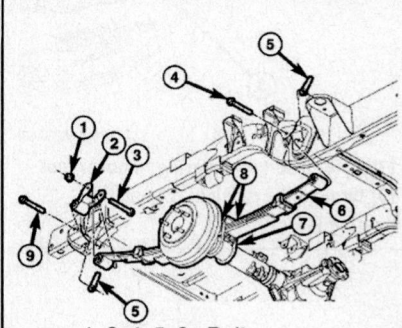

1, 3, 4, 5, 9. Bolts
2. Spring shackle
6. Leaf spring
7. U-bolt
8. Nuts and spring plate

36543_DAKO_G0228

Fig. 215 Exploded view of rear leaf spring

ball joint. Damage to the steering knuckle will occur.

7. Pull down on the steering knuckle to separate the halfshaft from the hub/bearing, on 4WD models.

8. Remove the 3 hub/bearing mounting bolts (3) from the steering knuckle (4).

9. Slide the hub/bearing (1) out of the steering knuckle (4).

10. Remove the brake dust shield (5).

To install:

11. Install the brake dust shield (5).

12. Install the hub/bearing (1) into the steering knuckle (4) and tighten the bolts (3) to 120 ft. lbs. (163 Nm).

13. Install the brake rotor and caliper.

14. Install the ABS wheel speed sensor (2) if equipped.

15. Install the halfshaft nut and tighten to 185 ft. lbs. (251 Nm), on 4WD models.

16. Install the wheel and tire assembly.

17. Remove the support and lower the vehicle.

ADJUSTMENT

These models utilize a hub/bearing assembly which is not adjustable.

REAR SUSPENSION

11. Position the spring on the rear axle pad. Make sure the spring center bolt is inserted in the pad locating hole.

12. Align the front spring eye with the bolt hole in the front frame bracket. Install the spring eye bolt and flag nut through the access hole in the frame and tighten the bolt finger-tight.

13. Align the spring shackle eye with the bolt hole in the rear frame bracket. Install the bolt and nut and tighten the spring shackle eye nut finger-tight.

14. Install the U-bolts, spring plate, and nuts. Tighten the U-bolt nuts to 110 ft. lbs. (149 Nm).

15. Install the wheel and tire assemblies.

16. Remove the support stands from under the frame rails. Lower the vehicle until the springs are supporting the weight of the vehicle.

17. Tighten the front spring eye bolt and flag nut to 125 ft. lbs. (170 Nm).

18. Tighten the rear spring eye-to-shackle bolt and nut and the shackle-to-frame bolt and nut to 125 ft. lbs. (170 Nm).

SHOCK ABSORBER

REMOVAL & INSTALLATION

See Figures 216 and 217.

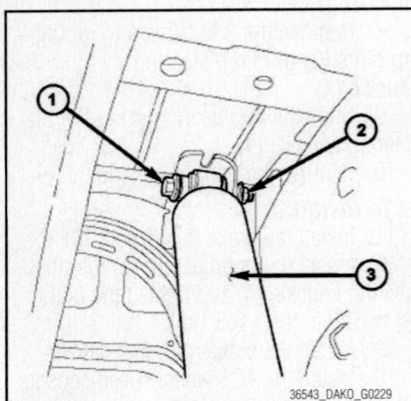

Fig. 216 Remove the upper shock bolt (1) and nut (2)

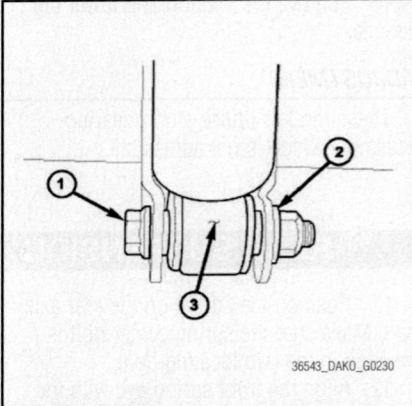

Fig. 217 Remove the lower shock bolt (1) and nut (2)

1. Before servicing the vehicle, refer to the Precautions Section.
2. Raise the vehicle and support the axle.
3. Remove the upper shock bolt (1) and nut (2).
4. Remove the lower shock bolt (1) and nut (2).
5. Remove the rear shock absorber from the vehicle.

To install:

6. Position the shock absorber to the vehicle.
7. Install the bolt (1) through the frame bracket and the shock (3). Install the nut (2) to the top bolt (1). Tighten to 70 ft. lbs. (95 Nm).
8. Install the bolt (1) through the axle bracket and the shock (3). Install the nut (2) to the bolt (1). Tighten to 70 ft. lbs. (95 Nm).
9. Remove the support and lower the vehicle.

WHEEL BEARINGS

REMOVAL & INSTALLATION

See Figures 218 through 220.

1. Before servicing the vehicle, refer to the Precautions Section.
2. Raise and safely support the vehicle.

➡ **Remove the bearing with Bearing Remover 6310 and Foot 6310-9.**

3. Remove the axle shaft.
4. Remove the axle seal with a seal pick.
5. Position the bearing receiver on the axle tube.
6. Insert the bearing remover foot (3) through the receiver (2) and the bearing (1).
7. Tighten the nut (1) to pull the bearing (2) into the receiver (3).

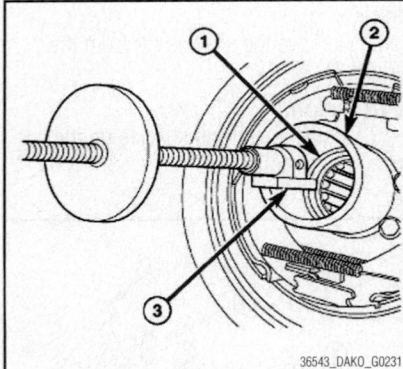

Fig. 218 Insert the bearing remover foot (3) through the receiver (2) and the bearing (1)

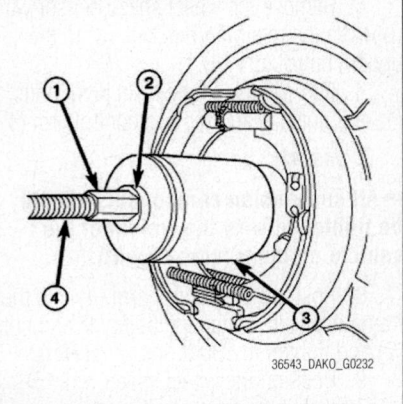

Fig. 219 Tighten the nut (1) to pull the bearing (2) into the receiver (3)

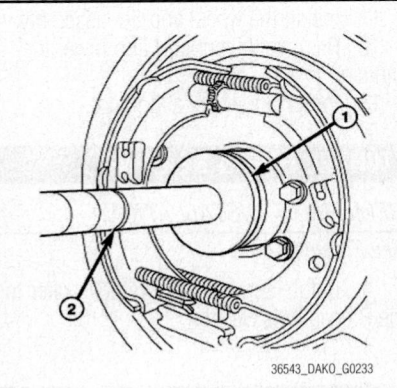

Fig. 220 Using Installer C-4198 (1) and Handle C-4171 (2) to install the rear axle bearing

8. Remove the wheel bearing from the axle.

To install:

9. Remove any old sealer/burrs from axle tube.
10. Install axle shaft bearing with Installer C-4198 (1) and Handle C-4171 (2).
11. Drive the bearing with the bearing part number against the installer until the tool contacts the axle tube.
12. Coat the new axle seal lip with axle lubricant and install it with Installer C-4198 (1) and Handle C-4171 (2).
13. Install the axle shaft.

JEEP

Grand Cherokee

SPECIFICATIONS AND MAINTENANCE CHARTS

ENGINE AND VEHICLE IDENTIFICATION

		Engine						Model Year	
Code	Liters (cc)	Cu. In.	Cyl.	Fuel Sys.	Engine Type	Eng. Mfg.		Code	Year
M	3.0 (3001)	183	6	MFI	OHV	Chrysler		8	2008
K	3.7 (3701)	226	6	MFI	SOHC	Chrysler		9	2009
N	4.7 (4701)	287	8	MFI	SOHC	Chrysler			
2	5.7 (5653)	345	8	MFI	OHV	Chrysler			
3	6.1 (6063)	370	8	MFI	OHV	Chrysler			

SOHC: Single overhead camshaft

OHV: Overhead Valve

MFI: Multi-port Fuel Injection

36543_CHER_C0001

GENERAL ENGINE SPECIFICATIONS

Year	Model	Engine Displ. Liters	Engine VIN	Net Horsepower @ rpm	Net Torque @ rpm (ft. lbs.)	Bore x Stroke (in.)	Compression Ratio	Oil Pressure @ rpm
2008	Grand Cherokee	3.7	K	210@5200	225@4200	3.66x3.40	9.1:1	25-110@3000
		4.7	N	235@4800	295@3200	3.66x3.40	9.0:1	25-110@3000
		5.7	2	335@5200	370@4200	3.91x3.58	9.6:1	25-110@3000
		6.1	3	420@5200	420@4000	4.06x3.58	10.3:1	25-110@3000
		3.0	M	215@4200	376@1800	3.26x3.62	18.0:1	25-110@3000
2009	Grand Cherokee	3.7	K	210@5200	225@4200	3.66x3.40	9.1:1	25-110@3000
		4.7	N	235@4800	295@3200	3.66x3.40	9.0:1	25-110@3000
		5.7	2	335@5200	370@4200	3.91x3.58	9.6:1	25-110@3000
		6.1	3	420@5200	420@4000	4.06x3.58	10.3:1	25-110@3000
		3.0	M	215@4200	376@1800	3.26x3.62	18.0:1	25-110@3000

36543_CHER_C0002

GASOLINE ENGINE TUNE-UP SPECIFICATIONS

Year	Engine Displacement Liters	Engine VIN	Spark Plug Gap (in.)	Ignition Timing (deg.)	Fuel Pump (psi)	Idle Speed (rpm)	Valve Clearance Intake	Exhaust
2008	3.7	K	0.043	①	56-60	②	HYD	HYD
	4.7	N	③	①	56-60	②	HYD	HYD
	5.7	2	0.040	①	56-60	②	HYD	HYD
	6.1	3	0.040	①	56-60	②	HYD	HYD
	3.0	M	NA	①	57-61	②	HYD	HYD
2009	3.7	K	0.043	①	56-60	②	HYD	HYD
	4.7	N	③	①	56-60	②	HYD	HYD
	5.7	2	0.040	①	56-60	②	HYD	HYD
	6.1	3	0.040	①	56-60	②	HYD	HYD
	3.0	M	NA	①	57-61	②	HYD	HYD

NOTE: The Vehicle Emission Control Information (VECI) label often reflects specification changes made during production.

The label figures must be used if they differ from those in this chart.

HYD: Hydraulic

NA: Not Available

① Ignition timing is controlled by the PCM and is not adjustable.

② Idle speed is controlled by the PCM and is not adjustable

③ Upper row 0.040 inches/Lower row 0.050 inches

36543_CHER_C0003

CAPACITIES

Year	Model	Engine Displ. Liters	Engine VIN	Engine Oil with Filter (qts.)	Transmission (pts.)	Transfer Case (pts.)	Drive Axle Front (pts.)	Rear (pts.)	Fuel Tank (gal.)	Cooling System (qts.)
2008	Grand Cherokee	3.7	K	5.0	①	②	3.6	③	21.0	9.0
		4.7	N	6.0	①	②	3.6	③	21.0	14.5
		5.7	2	7.0	①	②	3.6	③	21.0	14.5
		6.1	3	7.0	①	②	3.6	③	21.0	14.8
		3.0	M	10.0	①	②	3.6	③	22.0	14.0
2009	Grand Cherokee	3.7	K	5.0	①	②	3.6	③	21.0	9.0
		4.7	N	6.0	①	②	3.6	③	21.0	14.5
		5.7	2	7.0	①	②	3.6	③	21.0	14.5
		6.1	3	7.0	①	②	3.6	③	21.0	14.8
		3.0	M	10.0	①	②	3.6	③	22.0	14.0

NOTE: All capacities are approximate. Add fluid gradually and check to be sure a proper fluid level is obtained.

① 545RFE Fluid drain/filter service, 2wd: 11 pts.; 4wd: 13 pts.; Overhaul: 28 pts.

② NV140/146: 1.4 pts.; NV245: 3.8 pts.

③ The following values include 0.25 pt. of friction modifier for LSD axles.

C213R axle: 4.4 pts.

C213RE axle: 4.7 pts.

36543_CHER_C0004

FLUID SPECIFICATIONS

Year	Model	Engine Displacement Liters	Engine ID/VIN	Engine Oil	Auto. Trans.	Drive Axle	Power Steering Fluid	Brake Master Cylinder
2008	Grand Cherokee	3.7	K	5W-20	Mopar ATF+4	①	Mopar ATF+4	DOT-3
		4.7	N	5W-20	Mopar ATF+4	①	Mopar ATF+4	DOT-3
		5.7	2	5W-20	Mopar ATF+4	①	Mopar ATF+4	DOT-3
		6.1	3	0W-40	Mopar ATF+4	①	Mopar ATF+4	DOT-3
		3.0	M	5W-30	Mopar ATF+4	①	Mopar ATF+4	DOT-3
2009	Grand Cherokee	3.7	K	5W-20	Mopar ATF+4	①	Mopar ATF+4	DOT-3
		4.7	N	5W-20	Mopar ATF+4	①	Mopar ATF+4	DOT-3
		5.7	2	5W-20	Mopar ATF+4	①	Mopar ATF+4	DOT-3
		6.1	3	0W-40	Mopar ATF+4	①	Mopar ATF+4	DOT-3
		3.0	M	5W-30	Mopar ATF+4	①	Mopar ATF+4	DOT-3

DOT: Department Of Transpotation

① Mopar Synthetic Gear Lube 75W-140

36543_CHER_C0005

VALVE SPECIFICATIONS

Year	Engine Displ. Liters	Engine VIN	Seat Angle (deg.)	Face Angle (deg.)	Spring Test Pressure (lbs. @ in.)	Spring Installed Height (in.)	Stem-to-Guide Clearance (in.) Intake	Stem-to-Guide Clearance (in.) Exhaust	Stem Diameter (in.) Intake	Stem Diameter (in.) Exhaust
2008	3.7	K	44.5-45	45-45.5	213-234@ 1.107	1.579	0.0008-0.0028	0.0019-0.0039	0.2729-0.2739	0.2717-0.2728
	4.7	N	44.5-45	45-45.5	174.5-195.6 @1.1370	1.579	0.0008-0.0028	0.0019-0.0039	0.2729-0.2739	0.2717-0.2728
	5.7	2	44.5-45	45-45.5	231-253@ 1.283	1.81	0.0008-0.0025	0.0009-0.0025	0.3120-0.3130	0.3120-0.3130
	6.1	3	44.5-45	①	②	③	0.0008-0.0025	0.0010-0.0028	0.3120-0.3130	0.3120-0.3130
	3	M	44.5-45.5	44.5-45.5	NA	1.81	NA	NA	0.2347-0.2353	0.2341-0.2353
2009	3.7	K	44.5-45	44.5-45.5	213-234@ 1.107	1.579	0.0008-0.0028	0.0019-0.0039	0.2729-0.2739	0.2717-0.2728
	4.7	N	44.5-45	45-45.5	174.5-195.6 @1.1370	1.579	0.0008-0.0028	0.0019-0.0039	0.2729-0.2739	0.2717-0.2728
	5.7	2	44.5-45	45-45.5	231-253@ 1.283	1.81	0.0008-0.0025	0.0009-0.0025	0.3120-0.3130	0.3120-0.3130
	6.1	3	44.5-45	①	②	③	0.0008-0.0025	0.0010-0.0028	0.3120-0.3130	0.3120-0.3130
	3	M	44.5-45.5	44.5-45.5	NA	1.81	NA	NA	0.2347-0.2353	0.2341-0.2353

NA Not available

① Intake 45.5-46.0; Exhaust 45.0-45.5

② Intake 310.2-340.8@1.30 inches; Exhaust 310.2-340.6@1.22 inches

③ Intake 1.870 inches; Exhaust 1.772 inches

36543_CHER_C0006

CAMSHAFT AND BEARING SPECIFICATIONS CHART

All measurements are given in inches.

Year	Engine Displacement Liters	Engine VIN	Journal Diameter	Brg. Oil Clearance	Shaft End-play	Runout	Journal Bore	Lobe Lift	
								Intake	Exhaust
2008	3.7	K	1.0227-1.0235	0.0010-0.0026	0.0030-0.0079	NA	1.0245-1.0252	NA	NA
	4.7	N	1.0227-1.0235	0.0010-0.0026	0.0030-0.0079	NA	1.0245-1.0252	NA	NA
	5.7	2	①	②	0.0031-0.0114	NA	NA	NA	NA
	6.1	3	①	②	0.0031-0.0114	NA	NA	NA	NA
	3	M	NA	NA	NA	NA	NA	NA	NA
2009	3.7	K	1.0227-1.0235	0.0010-0.0026	0.0030-0.0079	NA	1.0245-1.0252	NA	NA
	4.7	N	1.0227-1.0235	0.0010-0.0026	0.0030-0.0079	NA	1.0245-1.0252	NA	NA
	5.7	2	①	②	0.0031-0.0114	NA	NA	NA	NA
	6.1	3	①	②	0.0030-0.0079	NA	NA	NA	NA
	3	M	NA	NA	NA	NA	NA	NA	NA

NA: Not Available

① No. 1: 2.29 in.
  No. 2: 2.28 in.
  No. 3: 2.26 in.
  No. 4: 2.24 in.
  No. 5: 1.72 in.

② No. 1: 0.0015-0.0030 in.
  No. 2: 0.0019-0.0035 in.
  No. 3: 0.0015-0.0030 in.
  No. 4: 0.0019-0.0035 in.
  No. 5: 0.0015-0.0030 in.

36543_CHER_C0007

CRANKSHAFT AND CONNECTING ROD SPECIFICATIONS

All measurements are given in inches.

Year	Engine Displ. Liters	Engine VIN	Crankshaft				Connecting Rod		
			Main Brg. Journal Dia.	Main Brg. Oil Clearance	Shaft End-play	Thrust on No.	Journal Diameter	Oil Clearance	Side Clearance
2008	3.7	K	2.4996-2.5005	0.00008-0.0018	0.0021-0.0112	2	2.2798-2.2792	0.0002-0.0011	0.0040-0.0138
	4.7	N	2.4996-2.5005	0.0002-0.0013	0.0021-0.0112	2	2.0076-2.0082	0.0004-0.0019	0.0040-0.0138
	5.7	2	2.5585-2.5595	0.0009-0.0020	0.0020-0.0110	3	2.1250-2.1260	0.0007-0.0023	0.0030-0.0137
	6.1	3	2.5585-2.5595	0.0009-0.0020	0.0020-0.0110	3	2.1250-2.1260	0.0007-0.0029	0.0030-0.0137
	3	M	2.9800-2.9900	0.0012-0.0023	0.0040-0.0100	3	2.6615-2.6620	0.0008-0.0040	NA
2009	3.7	K	2.4996-2.5005	0.00008-0.0018	0.0021-0.0112	2	2.2798-2.2792	0.0002-0.0011	0.0040-0.0138
	4.7	N	2.4996-2.5005	0.0002-0.0013	0.0021-0.0112	2	2.0076-2.0082	0.0004-0.0019	0.0040-0.0138
	5.7	2	2.5585-2.5595	0.0009-0.0020	0.0020-0.0110	3	2.1250-2.1260	0.0007-0.0023	0.0030-0.0137
	6.1	3	2.5585-2.5595	0.0009-0.0020	0.0020-0.0110	3	2.1250-2.1260	0.0007-0.0029	0.0030-0.0137
	3	M	2.9800-2.9900	0.0012-0.0023	0.0040-0.0100	3	2.6615-2.6620	0.0008-0.0040	NA

NA: Not available

36543_CHER_C0008

PISTON AND RING SPECIFICATIONS

All measurements are given in inches.

Year	Engine Displ. Liters	Engine VIN	Piston Clearance	Ring Gap			Ring Side Clearance		
				Top Comp.	Bottom Comp.	Oil Control	Top Comp.	Bottom Comp.	Oil Control
2008	3.7	K	0.0014	0.0079-0.0142	0.0146-0.0249	0.0099-0.0300	0.0020-0.0037	0.0016-0.0031	0.0007-0.0091
	4.7	N	0.0014	0.0079-0.0142	0.0146-0.0249	0.0099-0.0300	0.0020-0.0037	0.0016-0.0031	0.0007-0.0091
	5.7	2	0.0120-0.0230	0.0150-0.0210	0.0090-0.0200	0.0059-0.0259	0.0010-0.0035	0.0010-0.0031	0.0020-0.0080
	6.1	3	0.00096-0.0020	0.0118-0.0157	0.0137-0.0236	0.0079-0.0280	0.0007-0.0026	0.0007-0.0022	0.0007-0.0091
	3	M	0.0008-0.0019	0.0048-0.0063	0.0026-0.0044	0.0012-0.0028	0.0048-0.0063	0.0026-0.0044	0.0012-0.0028
2009	3.7	K	0.0014	0.0079-0.0142	0.0146-0.0249	0.0099-0.0300	0.0020-0.0037	0.0016-0.0031	0.0007-0.0091
	4.7	N	0.0014	0.0079-0.0142	0.0146-0.0249	0.0099-0.0300	0.0020-0.0037	0.0016-0.0031	0.0007-0.0091
	5.7	2	0.0120-0.0230	0.0150-0.0210	0.0090-0.0200	0.0059-0.0259	0.0010-0.0035	0.0010-0.0031	0.0020-0.0080
	6.1	3	0.00096-0.0020	0.0118-0.0157	0.0137-0.0236	0.0079-0.0280	0.0007-0.0026	0.0007-0.0022	0.0007-0.0091
	3	M	0.0008-0.0019	0.0048-0.0063	0.0026-0.0044	0.0012-0.0028	0.0048-0.0063	0.0026-0.0044	0.0012-0.0028

36543_CHER_C0009

TORQUE SPECIFICATIONS

All readings in ft. lbs.

Year	Engine Displ. Liters	Engine VIN	Cylinder Head Bolts	Main Bearing Bolts	Rod Bearing Bolts	Crankshaft Damper Bolts	Flexplate Bolts	Manifold Intake	Manifold Exhaust	Spark Plugs	Oil Pan Drain Plug
2008	3.7	K	①	②	③	130	70	④	18	20	25
	4.7	N	⑤	⑥	③	130	45	④	18	20	25
	5.7	2	⑦	⑧	⑨	130	70	9	18	NA	20
	6.1	3	⑦	⑧	⑩	129	70	9	23	NA	20
	3.0	M	⑪	⑫	⑬	N	O	12	18	NA	22
2009	3.7	K	①	②	③	130	70	④	18	20	25
	4.7	N	①	⑤	③	130	45	④	18	20	25
	5.7	2	⑦	⑧	⑨	130	70	9	18	NA	20
	6.1	3	⑦	⑧	⑩	129	70	9	23	NA	20
	3.0	M	⑪	⑫	⑬	N	O	12	18	NA	22

① Step 1: Tighten bolts 1-8 to 20 ft. lbs.

Step 2: Repeat Step 1 for bolts 1-8;Tighten bolts 9-12 to 10 ft. lbs.

Step 3: Tighten bolts 1-8 90 degrees

Step 4: Tighten bolts 1-8 another 90 degrees; Tighten bolts 9-12 to 19 ft. lbs.

② See the illustration

Step 1: Hand tighten bolts 1D, 1G and 1F until bedplate contacts the block

Step 2: tighten bolts 1A-1J to 40 ft. lbs.

Step 3: Tighten bolts 1-8 to 60 inch lbs.

Step 4: Tighten bolts 1-8 an additional 90 degrees

Step 5: Tighten bolts A-E to 20 ft. lbs.

③ 20 ft. lbs. plus 90 degrees

④ 105 inch lbs.

⑤ Step 1: Tighten bolts 1-10 to 20 ft. lbs.

Step 2: Repeat Step 1 for bolts 1-10; verify 10 ft. lbs.

Step 3: Tighten bolts 11-14 to 89 inch lbs.

Step 4: Tighten bolts 1-10 90 degrees

Step 5: Tighten bolts 1-10 an additional 90 degrees

Step 6: Tighten bolts 11-14 to 19 ft. lbs.

⑥ Bed plate bolt sequence. Refer to illustrations

Step 1: Bolts 1-22 to 26 inch lbs.

Step 2: Bolts 1-12 40 ft. lbs.

Step 3: Bolts 1-10 plus 90 degrees

Step 4: Side Bolts 1-6 20 ft. lbs.

⑦ M8:

Step 1: 15 ft. lbs.

Step 2: 25 ft. lbs.

M12:

Step 1: 25 ft. lbs.

Step 2: 40 ft. lbs.

Step 3: plus 90 degree turn

⑧ See the illustration

Step 1: M12 Bolts to 20 ft. lbs.

Step 2: M12 bolts an additional 90 degrees

Step 3: M8 Cross Bolts to 21 ft. lbs.

⑨ 15 ft. lbs. Plus 90 degrees

⑩ 33 ft. lbs. Plus 60 degrees

⑪ Step 1: Tighten M10 bolts to 10 ft. lbs.

Step 2: Tighten M10 bolts to 44 ft. lbs.

Step 3: Tighten M10 bolts 90 degrees

Step 4: Tighten M10 bolts an additional 90 degrees

Step 5: Tighten M10 bolts an additional 90 degrees again

Step 6: Tighten M8 bolts to 15 ft. lbs.

⑫ Step 1: 25 ft. lbs.

Step 2: Tighten 95 degrees

Step 3: plus 95 degrees again

⑬ Step 1: Tighten bolts to 11 ft. lbs. using short arm

Step 2: Tighten bolts to 15 ft. lbs. using long arm

Step 3: Tighten bolts to 22 ft. lbs. using short arm

Step 4: Tighten bolts to 29 ft. lbs. using long arm

Step 5: Tighten bolts to 36 ft. lbs. using short arm

Step 6: Tighten bolts 90 degrees using long arm

Step 7: Tighten bolts 90 degrees using short arm

Step 8: Tighten bolts 90 degrees using long arm

⑭ 154 ft. lbs. Plus 180 degrees

⑮ 33 ft. lbs. Plus 90 degrees

36543_CHER_C0010

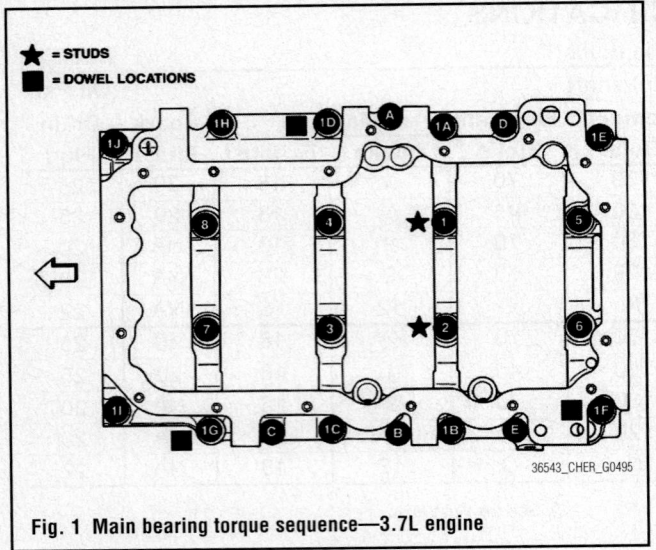

★ = STUDS
■ = DOWEL LOCATIONS

Fig. 1 Main bearing torque sequence—3.7L engine

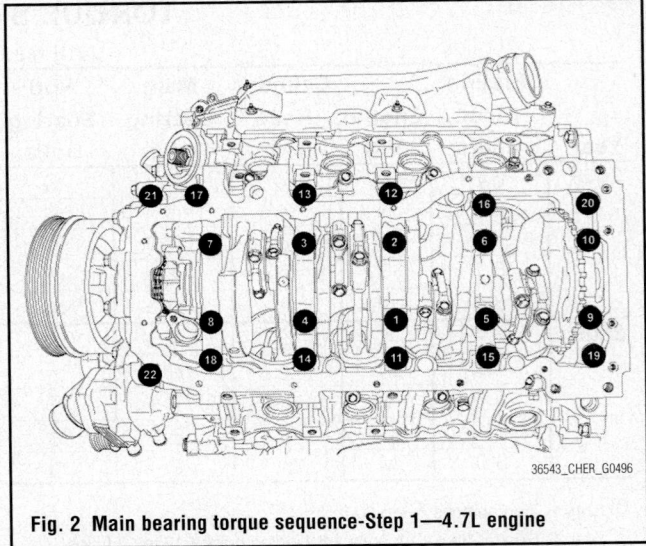

Fig. 2 Main bearing torque sequence-Step 1—4.7L engine

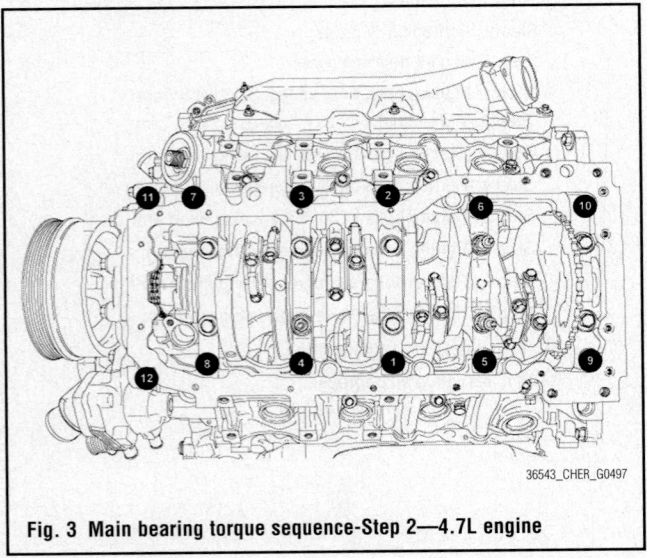

Fig. 3 Main bearing torque sequence-Step 2—4.7L engine

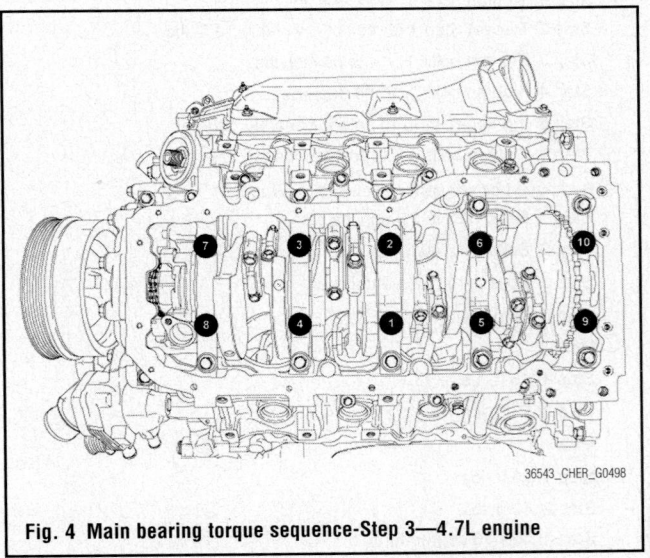

Fig. 4 Main bearing torque sequence-Step 3—4.7L engine

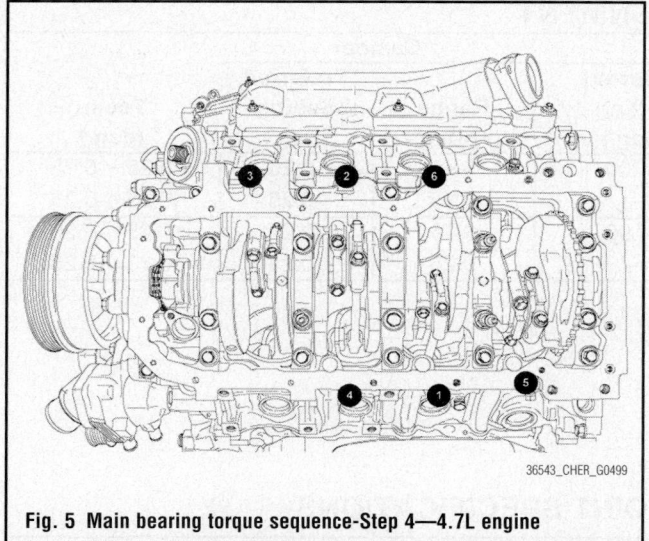

Fig. 5 Main bearing torque sequence-Step 4—4.7L engine

36543_CHER_G0499

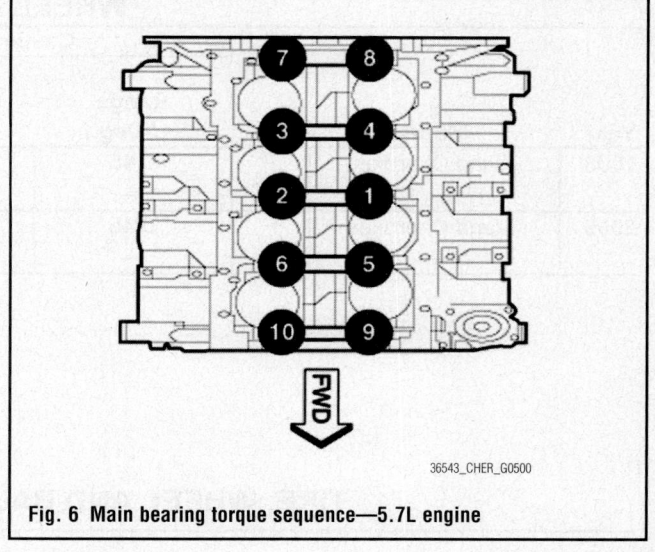

Fig. 6 Main bearing torque sequence—5.7L engine

36543_CHER_G0500

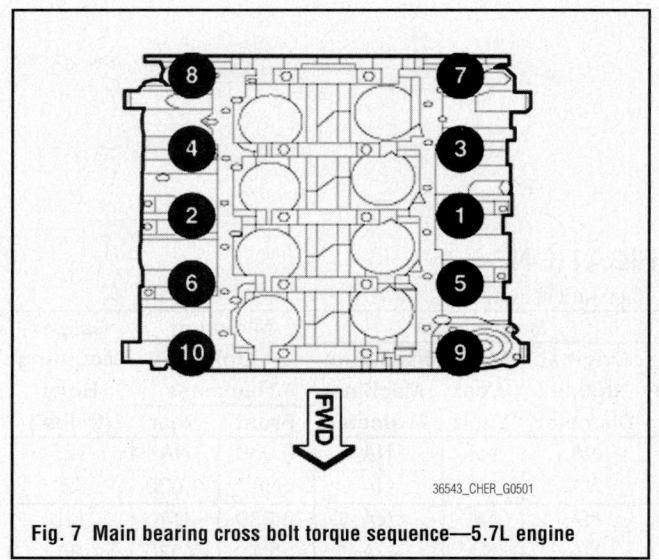

Fig. 7 Main bearing cross bolt torque sequence—5.7L engine

36543_CHER_G0501

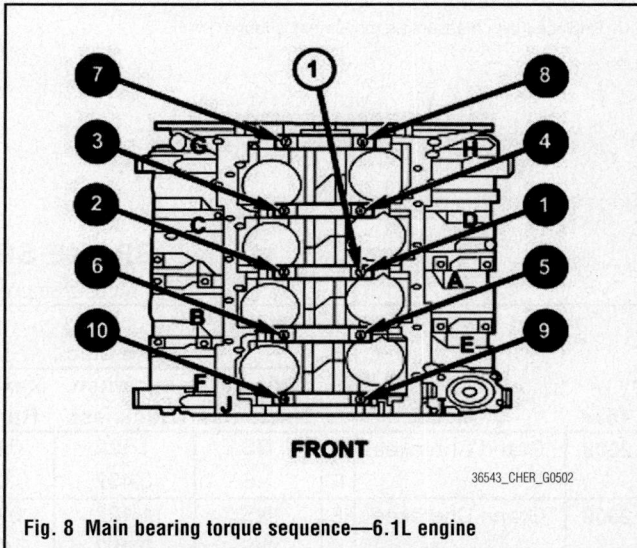

Fig. 8 Main bearing torque sequence—6.1L engine

36543_CHER_G0502

WHEEL ALIGNMENT

Year	Model		Caster		Camber		Toe-in (deg.)
			Range (+/-Deg.)	Preferred Setting (Deg.)	Range (+/-Deg.)	Preferred Setting (Deg.)	
2008	Grand Cherokee	F	0.45	+4.00	0.45	-0.25	0.25+/-0.25
		R	—	—	0.25	-0.25	0.25+/-0.25
2009	Grand Cherokee	F	0.45	+4.00	0.45	-0.25	0.25+/-0.25
		R	—	—	0.25	-0.25	0.25+/-0.25

36543_CHER_C0011

TIRE, WHEEL AND BALL JOINT SPECIFICATIONS

Year	Model	OEM Tires		Tire Pressures (psi)		Wheel Size	Ball Joint Inspection	Lug Nut Torque (ft. lbs.)
		Standard*	Optional	Front	Rear			
2008	Grand Cherokee	P235/65R17	P245/65R17	①	①	①	②	85-115
2009	Grand Cherokee	P235/65R17	P245/65R17	①	①	①	②	85-115

* Vehicles with the 6.1L V8 engine STD: Front: P255/45R20 Rear: P285/40R20

OEM: Original Equipment Manufacturer

STD: Standard

OPT: Optional

① See placard on vehicle

② Replace if any measurable movement is found.

36543_CHER_C0012

BRAKE SPECIFICATIONS

All measurements in inches unless noted

Year	Model		Brake Disc			Brake Drum			Minimum Lining Thickness		Caliper Mounting Bolts (ft. lbs.)
			Original Thickness	Minimum Thickness	Maximum Run-out	Original Inside Diameter	Max. Wear Limit	Maximum Machine Diameter	Front	Rear	
2008	Grand Cherokee	F	NS	1.122	0.002	NA	NA	NA	0.030	NA	125
		R	NS	0.492	0.0008	NA	NA	NA	NA	0.030	85
2009	Grand Cherokee	F	NS	1.122	0.002	NA	NA	NA	0.030	NA	125
		R	NS	0.492	0.0008	NA	NA	NA	NA	0.030	85

F - Front

R - Rear

NS: Not Specified by manufacturer

NA: Not Appicable

36543_CHER_C0013

SCHEDULED MAINTENANCE INTERVALS
Grand Cheerokee

TO BE SERVICED	TYPE OF SERVICE	VEHICLE MILEAGE INTERVAL (x1000)												
		6	12	18	24	30	36	42	48	54	60	66	72	78
Engine oil & filter	R	✓	✓	✓	✓	✓	✓	✓	✓	✓	✓	✓	✓	✓
Tires	Rotate		✓		✓		✓		✓		✓		✓	
Brake linings	I/R						✓		✓		✓		✓	
Brake hoses and lines	I	✓	✓	✓	✓	✓	✓	✓	✓	✓	✓	✓	✓	✓
Manual transmission fluid level	I	✓	✓	✓	✓	✓	✓	✓	✓	✓	✓	✓	✓	✓
Drive axle fluid	R			✓			✓			✓			✓	
Parking brake	Adj					✓					✓			
CV-joints	I								✓					
Air filter	R					✓					✓			
Exhaust system	I								✓					
Transfer case fluid level	I					✓					✓			
Front suspension components	I								✓					
PCV valve	I/R										✓			
Windshield washer fluid	I/F	At every fuel stop												
Tire pressure	I/Adj	Once a month												
Brake fluid level	I/Adj	Once a month												
Power Steering fluid	I/Adj	Once a month												
Automatic transmission fluid	I/Adj	Once a month												
Engine coolant level	I/Adj	Once a month												
Transfer case fluid	R	Every 90,000 miles												
Engine coolant	R	Every 102,000 miles												
Ignition cables	I/R	Every 102,000 miles												
Spark plugs	R	Every 102,000 miles												
Automatic trans. Fluid & filter	R	Every 120,000 miles												

R: Replace   S/I: Service or Inspect   I/R: Inspect and replace if necessary   L: Lubricate   I/F Inspect and fill as needed   I/Adj: Inspect and adjust

If driving in dusty or off-road conditions:
…inspect, and if necessary, replace, the air cleaner every 12,000 miles
…inspect the brake pads, replace if necessary every 12,000 miles.
…inspect the CV-joints every 12,000 miles
…inspect the exhaust system every 12,000 miles
…inspect all front suspension components every 24,000 miles

If used for police, taxi, fleet, off-road, or frequent trailer towing:
…change the front and rear axle fluid every 18,000 miles
…change the automatic transmission fluid and filter every 60,000 miles
…change the transfer case fluid every 60,000 miles

If using your vehicle for any of the following: trailer towing, snow plowing, heavy loading, taxi, police, delivery service (commercial service), off-road, desert operation or more then 50% of your driving is at sustained high speeds during hot weather, above 90°F (32°C):
…change the manual transmission fluid every 30,000 miles

36543_CHER_C0014

SCHEDULED MAINTENANCE INTERVALS
Grand Cheerokee

Oil Change Indicator System

On Electronic Vehicle Information Center (EVIC) equipped vehicles, "Oil Change Require" is displayed in the EVIC and a single chime sounds indicating that an oil change is necessary.

On non-EVIC equipped vehicles, "Change Oil" flashes in the instrument cluster and a single chime sounds indicating that an oil change is necessary.

Illumination of the oil change message is based on the operating conditions of the vehicle. When the message is illuminated, the vehicle must be serviced within 500 miles.

The oil change indicator will not monitor the time since the last oil change. Change the oil if it has been more than 6 months since the last oil change, even if the oil change indicator message is not illuminated.

Under no circumstances should oil change intervals exceed 6,000 miles or 6 months, whichever comes first.

To reset the oil change indicator, refer to the following procedure:

Oil Change Indicator Reset Procedure
1. Turn the ignition switch to the ON position. Do not start the engine.
2. Fully press the accelerator pedal 3 times within 10 seconds.
3. Turn the ignition switch to the LOCK position.

If the indicator message illuminates when the vehicle is started, repeat the procedure.

36543_CHER_C0015

PRECAUTIONS

Before servicing any vehicle, please be sure to read all of the following precautions, which deal with personal safety, prevention of component damage, and important points to take into consideration when servicing a motor vehicle:

• Never open, service or drain the radiator or cooling system when the engine is hot; serious burns can occur from the steam and hot coolant.

• Observe all applicable safety precautions when working around fuel. Whenever servicing the fuel system, always work in a well-ventilated area. Do not allow fuel spray or vapors to come in contact with a spark, open flame, or excessive heat (a hot drop light, for example). Keep a dry chemical fire extinguisher near the work area. Always keep fuel in a container specifically designed for fuel storage; also, always properly seal fuel containers to avoid the possibility of fire or explosion. Refer to the additional fuel system precautions later in this section.

• Fuel injection systems often remain pressurized, even after the engine has been turned **OFF**. The fuel system pressure must be relieved before disconnecting any fuel lines. Failure to do so may result in fire and/or personal injury.

• Brake fluid often contains polyglycol ethers and polyglycols. Avoid contact with the eyes and wash your hands thoroughly after handling brake fluid. If you do get brake fluid in your eyes, flush your eyes with clean, running water for 15 minutes. If eye irritation persists, or if you have taken brake fluid internally, IMMEDIATELY seek medical assistance.

• The EPA warns that prolonged contact with used engine oil may cause a number of skin disorders, including cancer. You should make every effort to minimize your exposure to used engine oil. Protective gloves should be worn when changing oil. Wash your hands and any other exposed skin areas as soon as possible after exposure to used engine oil. Soap and water, or waterless hand cleaner should be used.

• All new vehicles are now equipped with an air bag system, often referred to as a Supplemental Restraint System (SRS) or Supplemental Inflatable Restraint (SIR) system. The system must be disabled before performing service on or around system components, steering column, instrument panel components, wiring and sensors. Failure to follow safety and disabling procedures could result in accidental air bag deployment, possible personal injury and unnecessary system repairs.

• Always wear safety goggles when working with, or around, the air bag system. When carrying a non-deployed air bag, be sure the bag and trim cover are pointed away from your body. When placing a non-deployed air bag on a work surface, always face the bag and trim cover upward, away from the surface. This will reduce the motion of the module if it is accidentally deployed. Refer to the additional air bag system precautions later in this section.

• Clean, high quality brake fluid from a sealed container is essential to the safe and proper operation of the brake system. You should always buy the correct type of brake fluid for your vehicle. If the brake fluid becomes contaminated, completely flush the system with new fluid. Never reuse any brake fluid. Any brake fluid that is removed from the system should be discarded. Also, do not allow any brake fluid to come in contact with a painted surface; it will damage the paint.

• Never operate the engine without the proper amount and type of engine oil; doing so WILL result in severe engine damage.

• Timing belt maintenance is extremely important. Many models utilize an interference-type, non-freewheeling engine. If the timing belt breaks, the valves in the cylinder head may strike the pistons, causing potentially serious (also time-consuming and expensive) engine damage. Refer to the maintenance interval charts for the recommended replacement interval for the timing belt, and to the timing belt section for belt replacement and inspection.

• Disconnecting the negative battery cable on some vehicles may interfere with the functions of the on-board computer system(s) and may require the computer to undergo a relearning process once the negative battery cable is reconnected.

• When servicing drum brakes, only disassemble and assemble one side at a time, leaving the remaining side intact for reference.

• Only an MVAC-trained, EPA-certified automotive technician should service the air conditioning system or its components.

BRAKES

GENERAL INFORMATION

PRECAUTIONS

• Certain components within the ABS system are not intended to be serviced or repaired individually.

• Do not use rubber hoses or other parts not specifically specified for and ABS system. When using repair kits, replace all parts included in the kit. Partial or incorrect repair may lead to functional problems and require the replacement of components.

• Lubricate rubber parts with clean, fresh brake fluid to ease assembly. Do not use shop air to clean parts; damage to rubber components may result.

• Use only DOT 3 brake fluid from an unopened container.

• If any hydraulic component or line is removed or replaced, it may be necessary to bleed the entire system.

• A clean repair area is essential. Always clean the reservoir and cap thoroughly before removing the cap. The slightest amount of dirt in the fluid may plug an orifice and impair the system function. Perform repairs after components have been thoroughly cleaned; use only denatured alcohol to clean components. Do not allow ABS components to come into contact with any substance containing mineral oil; this includes used shop rags.

ANTI-LOCK BRAKE SYSTEM (ABS)

• The Anti-Lock control unit is a microprocessor similar to other computer units in the vehicle. Ensure that the ignition switch is **OFF** before removing or installing controller harnesses. Avoid static electricity discharge at or near the controller.

• If any arc welding is to be done on the vehicle, the control unit should be unplugged before welding operations begin.

WHEEL SPEED SENSORS

REMOVAL & INSTALLATION

Front

See Figures 9 and 10.

1. Raise and support the vehicle.
2. Remove the tire and wheel assembly.
3. Remove the caliper adaptor bolts. Support the caliper and adaptor assembly.

➡ **Do Not let assembly hang by the hose.**

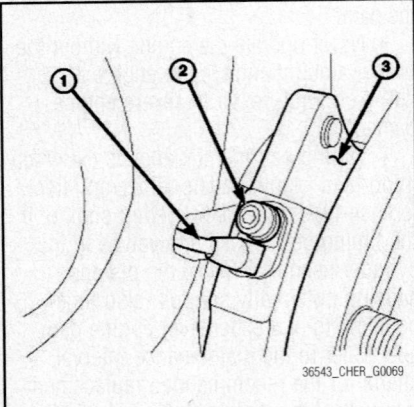

Fig. 9 Remove the front wheel sensor mounting nut (2) to the hub (3)

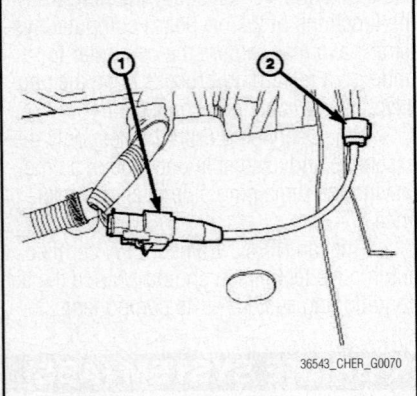

Fig. 10 Disconnect the wire sensor routing clips (2)

4. Remove the disc brake rotor.
5. Remove the front wheel sensor mounting nut (2) to the hub (3).
6. Remove the wheel speed sensor (1) from the hub (3).
7. Disconnect the wire sensor routing clips (2).
8. Disconnect the wheel speed sensor wire connector (1).
9. Remove the sensor and wire.

To install:

10. Reconnect the wheel speed sensor wire connector.
11. Reroute and connect the wheel speed sensor wire to the routing clips.
12. Install the wheel speed sensor into the hub and then install the mounting bolt. Tighten the nut to 106–124 inch lbs. (12–14 Nm).
13. Check the sensor wire routing. Be sure the wire is clear of all chassis components and is not twisted or kinked at any spot.
14. Install the disc brake rotor.
15. Install the caliper adaptor over the rotor.
16. Install the caliper adaptor bolts and tighten to 66–85 ft. lbs. (90–115 Nm).
17. Install the tire and wheel assembly.
18. Remove the support and lower vehicle.

Rear

See Figures 11 and 12.

1. Raise and support the vehicle.
2. Remove the wheel speed sensor mounting bolt (2) from the rear support plate (1).
3. Remove the wheel speed sensor (3) from the support plate.
4. Disconnect the wheel speed sensor electrical connector (3).

To install:

5. Insert the wheel speed sensor through the support plate.

6. Tighten the wheel speed sensor bolt to 106–124 inch lbs. (12–14 Nm).
7. Secure the wheel speed sensor wire to the routing clips. Verify that the sensor wire is secure and clear of the rotating components.
8. Reconnect the wheel speed sensor electrical connector.
9. Lower the vehicle.

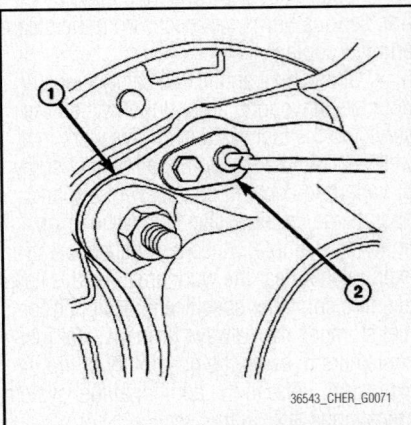

Fig. 11 Remove the wheel speed sensor mounting bolt (2)

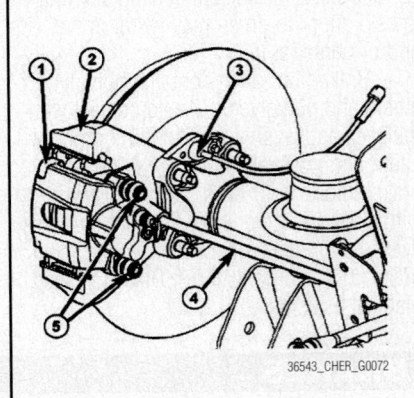

Fig. 12 Remove the wheel speed sensor (3) from the support plate

BRAKES   **BLEEDING THE BRAKE SYSTEM**

BLEEDING PROCEDURE

MANUAL BLEEDING

Use Mopar® brake fluid, or an equivalent quality fluid meeting SAE J1703-F and DOT 3 standards only. Use fresh, clean fluid from a sealed container at all times.

Do not pump the brake pedal at any time while bleeding. Air in the system will be compressed into small bubbles that are distributed throughout the hydraulic system. This will make additional bleeding operations necessary.

Do not allow the master cylinder to run out of fluid during bleed operations. An empty cylinder will allow additional air to be drawn into the system. Check the cylinder fluid level frequently and add fluid as needed.

Bleed only one brake component at a time in the following sequence:

1. Fill the master cylinder reservoir with brake fluid.

2. If calipers are overhauled, open all caliper bleed screws. Then close each bleed screw as fluid starts to drip from it. Top off master cylinder reservoir once more before proceeding.

3. Attach one end of bleed hose (1) to bleed screw and insert opposite end in glass container (2) partially filled with brake fluid. Be sure end of bleed hose is immersed in fluid.

4. Open up bleeder, then have a helper press down the brake pedal. Once the pedal is down close the bleeder. Repeat bleeding until fluid stream is clear and free of bubbles. Then move to the next wheel.

PRESSURE BLEEDING

Use Mopar brake fluid, or an equivalent quality fluid meeting SAE J1703-F and DOT 3 standards only. Use fresh, clean fluid from a sealed container at all times.

Do not pump the brake pedal at any time while bleeding. Air in the system will be compressed into small bubbles that are distributed throughout the hydraulic system. This will make additional bleeding operations necessary.

Do not allow the master cylinder to run out of fluid during bleed operations. An empty cylinder will allow additional air to be drawn into the system. Check the cylinder fluid level frequently and add fluid as needed.

Bleed only one brake component at a time in the following sequence:

Follow the manufacturer's instructions carefully when using pressure equipment. Do not exceed the tank manufacturers pressure recommendations. Generally, a tank pressure of 51-67 kPa (15-20 psi) is sufficient for bleeding.

Fill the bleeder tank with recommended fluid and purge air from the tank lines before bleeding.

Do not pressure bleed without a proper master cylinder adapter. The wrong adapter can lead to leakage, or drawing air back into the system. Use adapter provided with the equipment or Adapter 6921.

BLEEDING THE ABS SYSTEM

ABS system bleeding requires conventional bleeding methods plus use of a scan tool. The procedure involves performing a base brake bleeding, followed by use of the scan tool to cycle and bleed the HCU pump and solenoids. A second base brake bleeding procedure is then required to remove any air remaining in the system.

1. Perform base brake bleeding.

2. Connect scan tool to the Data Link Connector.

3. Select ANTILOCK BRAKES, followed by MISCELLANEOUS, then ABS BRAKES. Follow the instructions displayed. When scan tool displays TEST COMPLETE, disconnect scan tool and proceed.

4. Perform base brake bleeding a second time.

5. Top off master cylinder fluid level and verify proper brake operation before moving vehicle.

BRAKES   **FRONT DISC BRAKES**

✳✳ CAUTION

Dust and dirt accumulating on brake parts during normal use may contain asbestos fibers from production or aftermarket brake linings. Breathing excessive concentrations of asbestos fibers can cause serious bodily harm. Exercise care when servicing brake parts. Do not sand or grind brake lining unless equipment used is designed to contain the dust residue. Do not clean brake parts with compressed air or by dry brushing. Cleaning should be done by dampening the brake components with a fine mist of water, then wiping the brake components clean with a dampened cloth. Dispose of cloth and all residue containing asbestos fibers in an impermeable container with the appropriate label. Follow practices prescribed by the Occupational Safety and Health Administration (OSHA) and the Environmental Protection Agency (EPA) for the handling, processing, and disposing of dust or debris that may contain asbestos fibers.

BRAKE CALIPER

REMOVAL & INSTALLATION

All Except 6.1L Engine

See Figure 13.

1. Install prop rod on the brake pedal to keep pressure on the brake system, Holding pedal in this position will isolate master cylinder from hydraulic brake system and will not allow brake fluid to drain out of brake fluid reservoir while brake lines are open. This will allow you to bleed out the area of repair instead of the entire system.

2. Raise and support vehicle.

3. Remove front wheel and tire assembly.

4. Drain small amount of fluid from master cylinder brake reservoir with clean suction gun.

5. Bottom caliper pistons into the caliper by prying the caliper over.

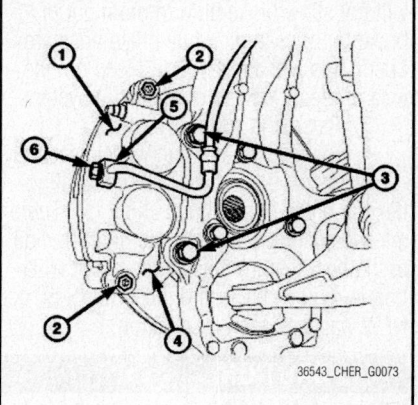

36543_CHER_G0073

Fig. 13 Remove brake hose banjo bolt and gasket washers (6)

6. Remove brake hose banjo bolt and gasket washers (6). Discard gasket washers.

7. Remove the caliper slide bolts (2).

8. Remove the caliper (1) from the adapter (4).

To install:

9. Install the caliper on the adapter.

10. Caliper slide pins should be free from debris and lightly lubricated.

11. Install the caliper slide pin bolts and tighten to 32 ft. lbs. (44 Nm).

12. Gently lift one end of the slide pin boot to equalize air pressure, then release the boot and verify that the boot is fully covering the slide pin.

❄❄ CAUTION

Verify brake hose is not twisted or kinked before tightening banjo bolt.

13. Install brake hose to caliper with new copper washers. Tighten banjo bolt to 23 ft. lbs. (31 Nm).

14. Remove the prop rod from the brake pedal.

15. Bleed the area of repair for the brake system. If a proper pedal is not felt during bleeding an area of repair then a base bleed system must be performed.

16. Install wheel and tire assemblies.

17. Remove supports and lower vehicle.

18. Verify brake fluid level.

6.1L Engine

See Figure 14.

➡ **These calipers are not serviceable. Do not attempt disassembly.**

1. Disconnect and isolate battery negative cable.

2. Install prop rod on the brake pedal to keep pressure on the brake system, Holding pedal in this position will isolate master cylinder from hydraulic brake system and will not allow brake fluid to drain out of brake fluid reservoir while brake lines are open. This will allow you to bleed out the area of repair instead of the entire system.

3. Raise and support vehicle.

4. Remove the tire and wheel assembly.

5. Remove banjo bolt (3) connecting flexible brake hose (2) to caliper (1). There are two sealing washers (one on each side of the hose fitting) that will come off when bolt is removed. Discard these washers; use NEW washers upon installation.

❄❄ CAUTION

When pushing pistons back into caliper bores, use only a trim stick or other suitable soft tool. Never use a

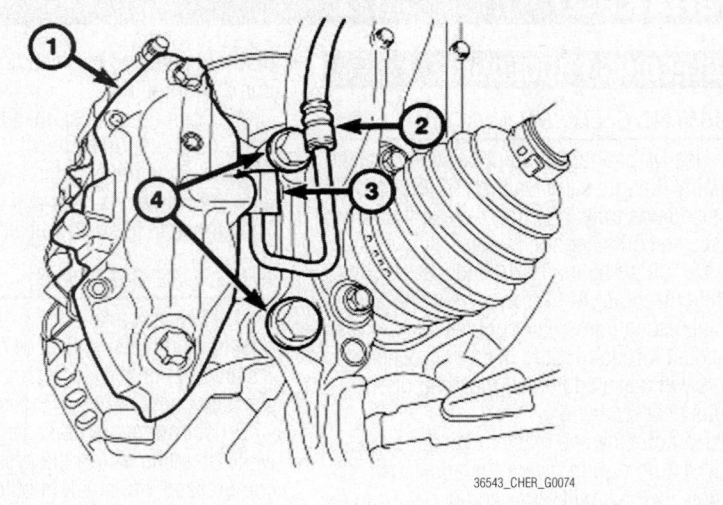

Fig. 14 Remove banjo bolt (3) connecting flexible brake hose (2) to caliper (1)

screwdriver or other metal pry bar due to potential damage to braking surface of rotor, caliper, pistons or dust boots.

6. Place trim stick between brake pad and outer edge of rotor.

7. Using trim stick, slowly apply pressure against brake pad until both pistons (on that side of caliper) are completely bottomed in bores of caliper half.

➡ **Repeat above procedure to opposite brake pad and pistons as necessary.**

8. Remove caliper mounting bolts (4).

9. Remove brake caliper (1) with pads from knuckle and brake rotor.

To install:

❄❄ CAUTION

Always inspect brake pads before installing disc brake caliper and replace as necessary.

10. Completely retract caliper pistons back into bores of caliper. Use hand pressure or a C-clamp may also be used to retract pistons, first placing a wood block or used brake pad (not to be reused) over pistons before installing C-clamp to avoid damaging piston.

11. If brake pads need to be replace install in caliper before installation.

12. Slide caliper with pads over brake rotor and align with knuckle.

13. Install caliper mounting bolts. Tighten bolts to 140 ft. lbs. (190 Nm).

14. Install banjo bolt attaching brake hose to caliper. Install NEW washers on each side of hose fitting as banjo bolt is placed through banjo fitting. Thread banjo bolt into caliper and tighten to 24 ft. lbs. (33 Nm).

15. Install tire and wheel assembly.

16. Lower vehicle.

17. Remove brake pedal holding tool.

18. Connect battery negative cable to battery.

19. Remove the prop rod from the brake pedal.

20. Bleed the area of repair for the brake system. If a proper pedal is not felt during bleeding an area of repair then a base bleed system must be performed.

DISC BRAKE PADS

REMOVAL & INSTALLATION

All Except 6.1L Engine

See Figures 15 and 16.

1. Raise and support vehicle.

2. Remove wheel and tire assembly.

3. Drain small amount of fluid from master cylinder brake reservoir with clean suction gun.

4. Remove the 2 caliper mounting bolts (2).

5. Compress the caliper and remove from the adaptor (4).

6. Secure caliper (1) to nearby suspension part with wire. Do not allow brake hose to support caliper weight.

7. Remove the inboard and outboard brake pads (4) from the caliper adapter (2).

8. Remove the anti-rattle clips (3) from the brake caliper adapter (2).

To install:

9. Remove and clean all rust and debris from the anti-rattle clip mounting surfaces on the brake caliper adapter.

10. Install new anti-rattle clips into the caliper adapter.

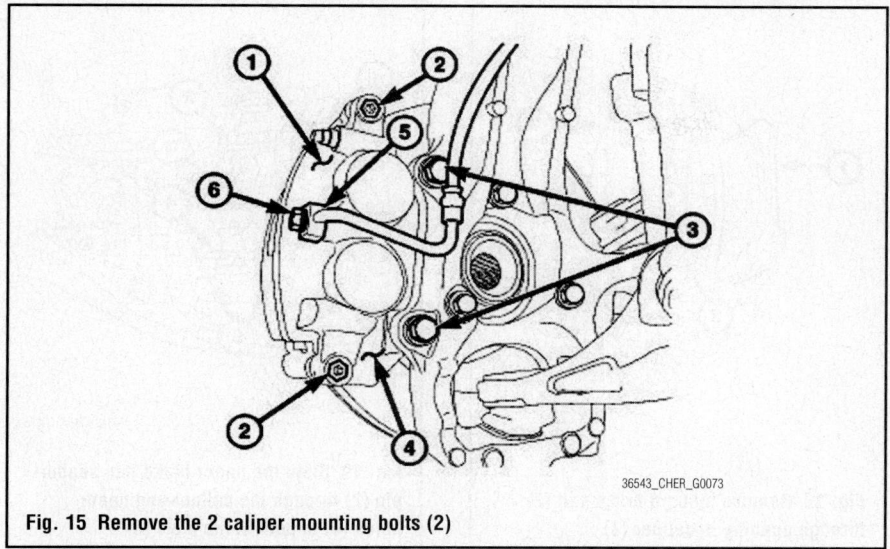

Fig. 15 Remove the 2 caliper mounting bolts (2)

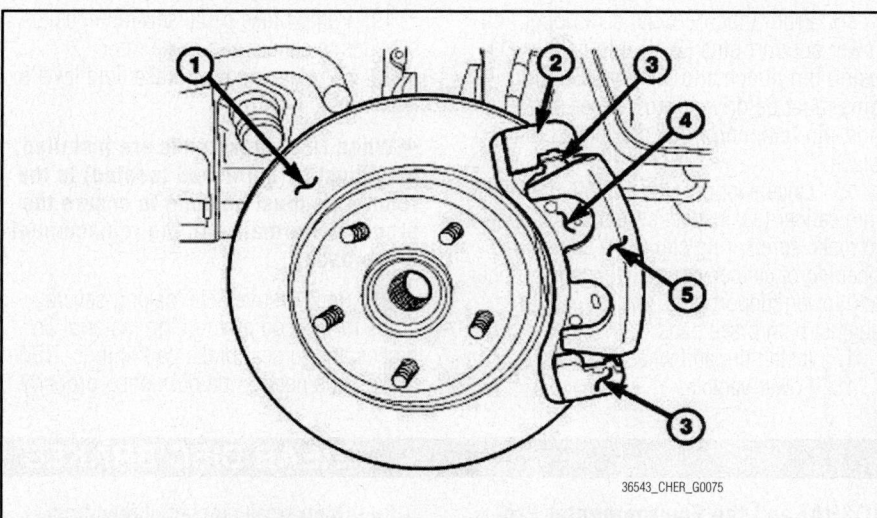

Fig. 16 Remove the inboard and outboard brake pads (4) from the caliper adapter (2)

4. Remove brake pad spring clip (4) out from under the upper support pin (3) still in caliper.

5. Using pin punch (2) and hammer (1), remove upper brake pad support pin (3) in same manner used on lower support pin.

✳✳ CAUTION

When pushing pistons back into caliper bores, if hand pressure is not sufficient, use only a trim stick or other suitable soft tool to do so. Never use a screwdriver or other metal pry bar due to potential damage to braking surface of rotor or pads.

6. Using hand pressure, pull pads back to seat caliper pistons into bores if possible. If not possible, perform the following to do this correctly without damaging the caliper, pistons, dust boots or brake rotor disc.

　a. Place trim stick between inboard brake pad and outer edge of rotor.

　b. Using trim stick, apply pressure against the inboard brake pad until both pistons are completely bottomed in bores of inboard caliper half. Leave trim stick in place to hold pistons in place.

　c. Place second trim stick between outboard brake pad and rotor, then repeat above step on outboard pad and pistons.

➡**Once brake pads are removed from caliper, inspect all four caliper pistons and dust boots for evidence of brake fluid leakage. Also inspect dust boots on all caliper pistons for any cuts, tears or heat cracks and brake pad supports (if equipped) for excess wear or damage. If caliper fails inspection, it should be replaced.**

11. Install the inboard and outboard brake pads onto the caliper adapter.

12. Install caliper on the caliper adapter.

13. Install the caliper slide pin bolts and tighten to 32 ft. lbs. (44 Nm).

14. Install wheel and tire assembly.

15. Remove support and lower vehicle.

16. Pump brake pedal until caliper pistons and brake pads are seated and a firm brake pedal is obtained.

17. Fill brake fluid.

6.1L Engine

See Figures 17 through 19.

1. Raise and support vehicle.

2. Remove the front tire and wheel assembly.

3. Using hammer (1) and pin punch (2) on outboard end, tap the lower brake pad support pin (3) out of caliper (5).

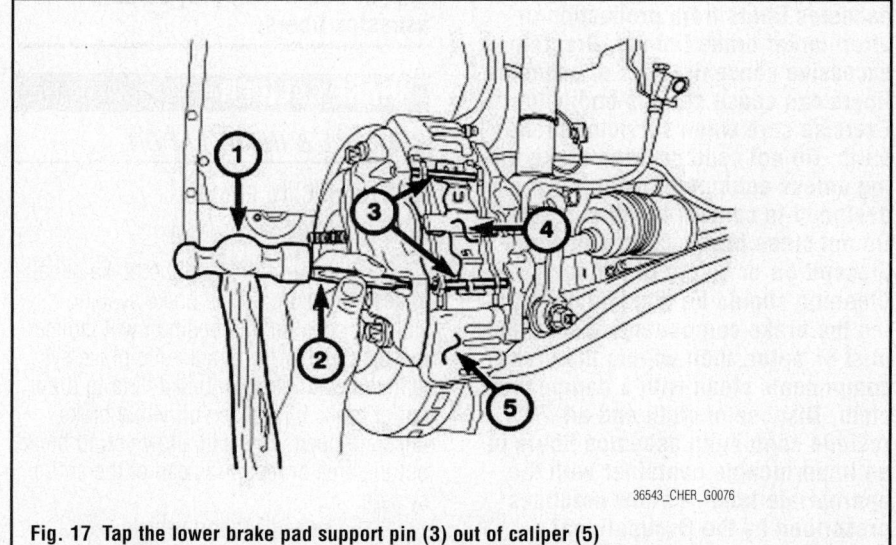

Fig. 17 Tap the lower brake pad support pin (3) out of caliper (5)

7. Remove inboard brake pad (2) through opening in caliper (3). Remove outboard brake pad (1) in same manner.

To install:

8. Make sure all caliper pistons are fully seated (bottomed) in bores.

➡**Brake pads need to have the shims and cooper paste applied. Paste is applied between the shim and the backing plate of the pads, and along the edges of the pads.**

9. Slide the NEW inboard and outboard brake pads and shims into the opening of the disc brake caliper.

10. From the inboard side, slide the upper brake pad support pin (2) through the caliper and upper holes (6) in both brake pads (5). Ensure that the small end of the support pin is in hole (6) in outboard half of caliper.

11. Install the upper end of brake pad spring clip (3) under upper brake pad support pin (2).

12. Press on lower end of spring clip (3) until it touches brake rotor.

13. Slide lower brake pad support pin (4) through caliper and lower holes (6) in both brake pads (5) in the same manner the upper pin was installed. Ensure small end of support pin is in hole (6) in outboard half of caliper.

14. Release the spring clip (3) allowing it to engage lower support pin (4).

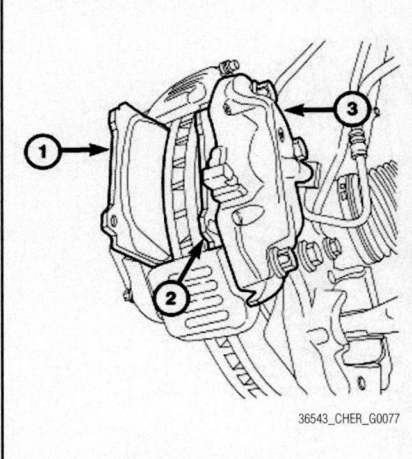

36543_CHER_G0077

Fig. 18 Remove inboard brake pad (2) through opening in caliper (3)

15. From inboard side, seat upper and lower support pins (2, 4) into caliper (1) using pin punch and hammer. Support pins must be driven into caliper until support pin retaining rings are locked into place.

16. Once support pins are fully installed into caliper (1), inspect assembled caliper to make sure spring clip (3) is centered in opening of caliper, correctly engaging upper and lower support pins, and is resting against both brake pads.

17. Install tire and wheel assembly.

18. Lower vehicle.

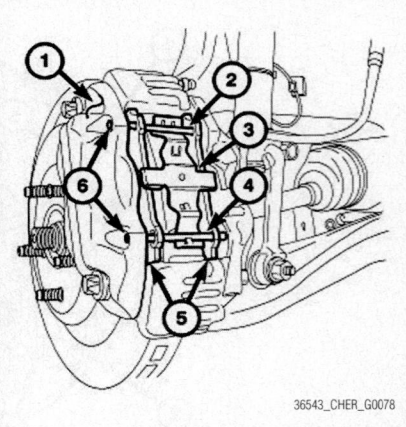

36543_CHER_G0078

Fig. 19 Slide the upper brake pad support pin (2) through the caliper and upper holes (6) in both brake pads (5)

19. Pump brake pedal several times to set pads to caliper and brake rotor.

20. Check and adjust brake fluid level in reservoir.

➡**When NEW brake pads are installed, they must be burnished (seated) to the rotor. This must be done to ensure the proper performance of the replacement brake pads.**

21. Road test vehicle making several stops to wear off any foreign material on brakes and to seat brake pad linings. NEW brake pads need to be burnished properly.

BRAKES

REAR DISC BRAKES

✹✹ CAUTION

Dust and dirt accumulating on brake parts during normal use may contain asbestos fibers from production or aftermarket brake linings. Breathing excessive concentrations of asbestos fibers can cause serious bodily harm. Exercise care when servicing brake parts. Do not sand or grind brake lining unless equipment used is designed to contain the dust residue. Do not clean brake parts with compressed air or by dry brushing. Cleaning should be done by dampening the brake components with a fine mist of water, then wiping the brake components clean with a dampened cloth. Dispose of cloth and all residue containing asbestos fibers in an impermeable container with the appropriate label. Follow practices prescribed by the Occupational Safety and Health Administration (OSHA) and the Environmental Protection Agency (EPA) for the handling, processing, and disposing of dust or debris that may contain asbestos fibers.

BRAKE CALIPER

REMOVAL & INSTALLATION

All Except 6.1L Engine
See Figure 20.

1. Install prop rod on the brake pedal to keep pressure on the brake system, Holding pedal in this position will isolate master cylinder from hydraulic brake system and will not allow brake fluid to drain out of brake fluid reservoir while brake lines are open. This will allow you to bleed out the area of repair instead of the entire system.

2. Raise and support vehicle.

3. Remove rear wheel and tire assembly.

4. Drain small amount of fluid from master cylinder brake reservoir with a clean suction gun.

5. Bottom caliper pistons into the caliper by prying the caliper over.

6. Remove brake hose (3) banjo bolt (5) and discard gasket washers.

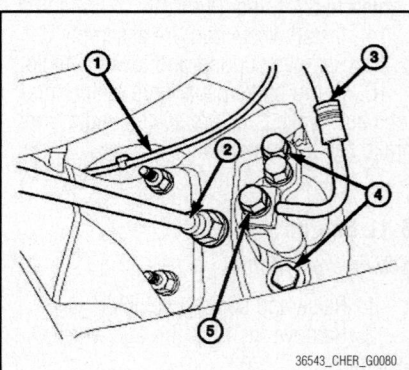

36543_CHER_G0080

Fig. 20 View of the brake hose (3) banjo bolt (5), and slide pins (4)

7. Remove the caliper slide pins (4).

8. Remove caliper (1) from the anchor.

To install:

9. Lubricate the slide pins and slide pin bushings with caliper slide grease or the grease provided with the caliper.

10. Install the caliper on the anchor.

11. Install the caliper slide pin bolts and tighten to 18 ft. lbs. (25 Nm).

✳✳ CAUTION

Verify that the brake hose is not twisted or kinked before tightening the fitting bolt.

12. Install brake hose to caliper with a new gasket washers and tighten banjo bolt to 23 ft. lbs. (31 Nm).

13. Remove the prop rod from the brake pedal.

14. Bleed the area of repair for the brake system, If a proper pedal is not felt during bleeding an area of repair then a base bleed system must be performed.

15. Install wheel and tire assemblies.

16. Remove supports and lower vehicle.

6.1L Engine

See Figure 21.

➡ **These calipers are not serviceable. Do not attempt disassembly.**

1. Disconnect and isolate battery negative cable.

2. Install prop rod on the brake pedal to keep pressure on the brake system, Holding pedal in this position will isolate master cylinder from hydraulic brake system and will not allow brake fluid to drain out of brake fluid reservoir while brake lines are open. This will allow you to bleed out the area of repair instead of the entire system.

3. Raise and support vehicle.

4. Remove the tire and wheel assembly.

5. Remove banjo bolt (2) connecting flexible brake hose (3) to caliper (4). There are two sealing washers (one on each side of hose fitting) that will come off when bolt is removed. Discard these washers; install NEW washers on installation.

✳✳ CAUTION

When pushing pistons back into caliper bores, use only a trim stick or other suitable soft tool. Never use a screwdriver or other metal pry bar due to potential damage to braking surface of rotor, caliper, pistons or dust boots.

6. Place trim stick between brake pad and outer edge of rotor.

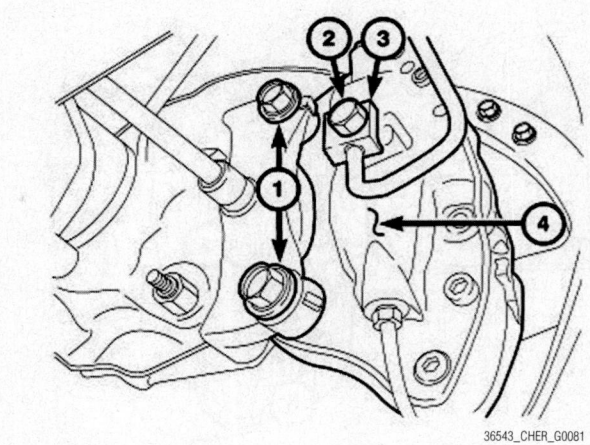

36543_CHER_G0081

Fig. 21 Remove banjo bolt (2) connecting flexible brake hose (3) to caliper (4)

7. Using trim stick, slowly apply pressure against brake pad until both pistons (on that side of caliper) are completely bottomed in bores of caliper half.

8. Remove the lower and upper caliper mounting bolts (1).

9. Remove brake caliper (4) with pads from mount and brake rotor.

To install:

10. Slide caliper with pads over brake rotor and align with knuckle.

11. Install caliper mounting bolts. Tighten bolts to 85 ft. lbs. (115 Nm).

12. Install banjo bolt attaching brake hose to caliper. Install NEW washers on each side of hose fitting as banjo bolt is placed through banjo fitting. Thread banjo bolt into caliper and tighten to 23 ft. lbs. (31 Nm).

13. Install tire and wheel assembly.

✳✳ CAUTION

If NEW brake pads have been installed, keep in mind that braking effectiveness might be somewhat reduced during the first brake applications.

14. Lower vehicle.

15. Connect battery negative cable.

16. Remove the prop rod from the brake pedal.

17. Bleed the area of repair for the brake system, If a proper pedal is not felt during bleeding an area of repair then a base bleed system must be performed.

DISC BRAKE PADS

REMOVAL & INSTALLATION

All Except 6.1L Engine

See Figure 20.

1. Raise and support vehicle.

2. Remove rear wheel and tire assembly.

3. Drain small amount of fluid from master cylinder brake reservoir with a clean suction gun.

4. Bottom caliper pistons into the caliper by prying the caliper over.

5. Remove the caliper slide pins (4).

6. Remove caliper (1) from the anchor.

7. Secure caliper (1) to nearby suspension part with wire. Do not allow brake hose to support caliper weight.

8. Remove the inboard and outboard brake pads from the caliper.

To install:

9. Install the inboard and outboard brake pads onto the caliper.

10. Lubricate the slide pins and slide pin bushings with caliper slide grease or the grease provided with the brake pads.

11. Install caliper on the anchor.

12. Install the caliper slide pin bolts and tighten to 18 ft. lbs. (25 Nm).

13. Install wheel and tire assembly.

14. Remove support and lower vehicle.

15. Pump brake pedal until caliper piston and brake pads are seated and a firm brake pedal is obtained.

16. Fill brake fluid level if necessary.

6.1L Engine

See Figures 22 and 23.

1. Raise and support vehicle.

2. Remove the tire and wheel assembly.

3. Using hammer and pin punch on outboard end, tap upper brake pad support pin (1) out of caliper (2).

4. Remove brake pad spring clip (3) out from under the lower support pin (4) still in caliper.

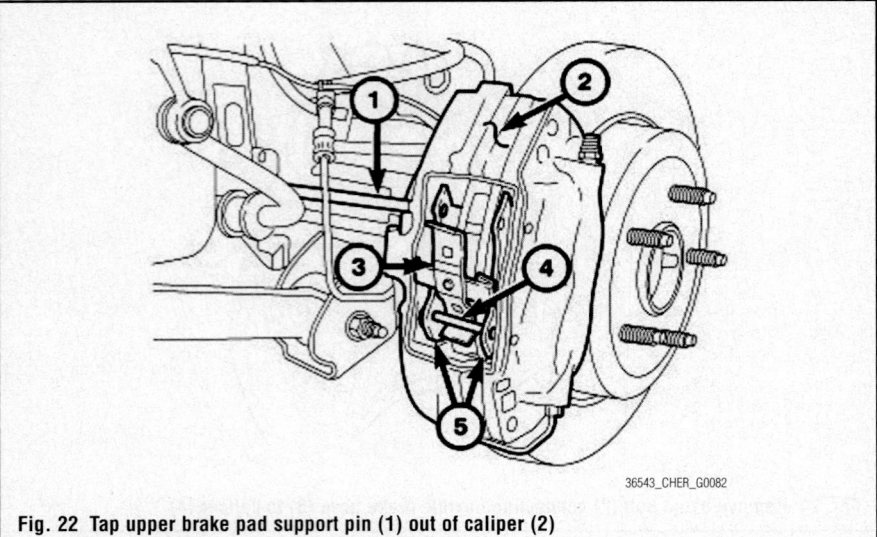

Fig. 22 Tap upper brake pad support pin (1) out of caliper (2)

5. Using pin punch and hammer, remove lower brake pad support pin (4) in same manner used on upper support pin.

❊❊ CAUTION

When pushing pistons back into caliper bores, if hand pressure is not sufficient, use only a trim stick or other suitable soft tool to do so. Never use a screwdriver or other metal pry bar due to potential damage to braking surface of rotor or pads.

6. Using hand pressure, pull pads back to seat caliper pistons into bores if possible. If not possible, perform the following to do this correctly without damaging the caliper, pistons, dust boots or brake rotor disc.

   a. Place trim stick between inboard brake pad and outer edge of rotor.

   b. Using trim stick, apply pressure against the inboard brake pad until both pistons are completely bottomed in bores of inboard caliper half. Leave trim stick in place to hold pistons in place.

   c. Place second trim stick between outboard brake pad and rotor, then repeat above step on outboard pad and pistons.

7. Remove inboard and outboard brake pads (2) through opening in caliper (1).

8. Once brake pads are removed from caliper (1), inspect all four caliper pistons and dust boots for evidence of brake fluid leakage. Also inspect dust boots on all caliper pistons for any cuts, tears or heat cracks and brake pad supports (if equipped)

for excess wear or damage. If caliper fails inspection, it should be replaced.

To install:

9. Make sure all caliper pistons are fully seated (bottomed) in bores.

➡**Brake pads need to have cooper paste applied. Paste is applied along the edges of the pads.**

10. Slide the NEW inboard and outboard brake pads into the opening of the disc brake caliper.

11. From the inboard side, slide the lower brake pad support pin through caliper and lower holes in both brake pads. Ensure

that small end of support pin is in hole in outboard half of caliper.

12. Install lower end of brake pad spring clip under lower brake pad support pin.

13. Press on upper end of spring clip until it touches brake rotor.

14. Slide upper brake pad support pin through caliper and upper holes in both brake pads in the same manner the lower pin was installed. Ensure small end of support pin is in hole in outboard half of caliper.

15. Release the spring clip allowing it to engage upper support pin.

16. From inboard side, seat upper and lower support pins into caliper using pin punch and hammer. Support pins must be driven into caliper until support pin retaining rings are locked into place.

17. Once support pins are fully installed into caliper, inspect assembled caliper to make sure spring clip is centered in opening of caliper, correctly engaging upper and lower support pins, and is resting against both brake pads.

18. Install tire and wheel assembly.

19. Lower vehicle.

➡**When NEW brake pads are installed, they must be burnished (seated) to the rotor. This must be done to ensure the proper performance of the replacement brake pads.**

20. Pump brake pedal several times to set pads to caliper and brake rotor.

21. Check and adjust brake fluid level in reservoir.

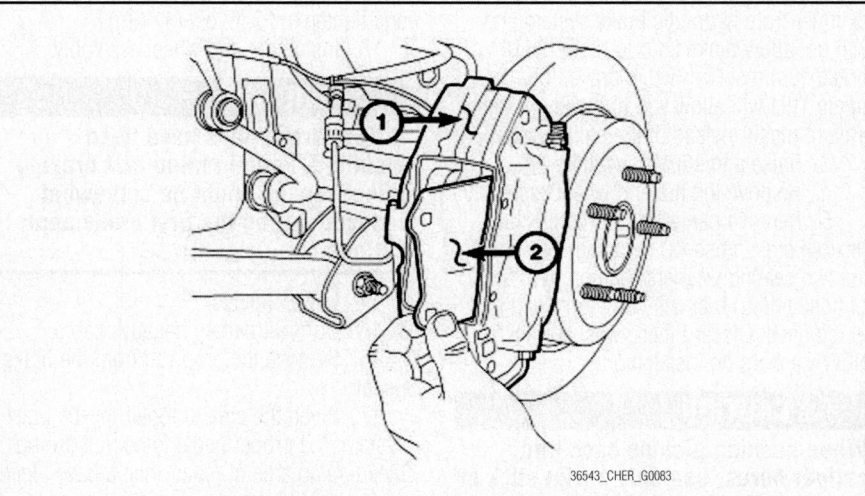

Fig. 23 Remove inboard and outboard brake pads (2) through opening in caliper (1)

BRAKES   **PARKING BRAKE**

PARKING BRAKE CABLES

ADJUSTMENT

The parking brakes are operated by an automatic tensioner mechanism built into the hand lever and cable system. The front cable is connected to the hand lever and the equalizer. The rear cables are attached to the equalizer and the parking brake shoe actuator.

A set of drum type brake shoes are used for parking brakes. The shoes are mounted to the rear disc brake adaptor. The parking brake drum is integrated into the rear disc brake rotor.

Parking brake cable adjustment is controlled by an automatic tensioner mechanism. The only adjustment if necessary is to the park brake shoes if the linings are worn.

PARKING BRAKE SHOES

REMOVAL & INSTALLATION

See Figures 24 and 25.

1. Raise and safely support the vehicle.
2. Remove the rear wheel and tire assembly.
3. Remove the 2 caliper bolts then remove the caliper. Support the caliper. Do not let the caliper hang by the brake hose.
4. Remove the rubber access plug (1) from the back of rear disc brake support plate (3).

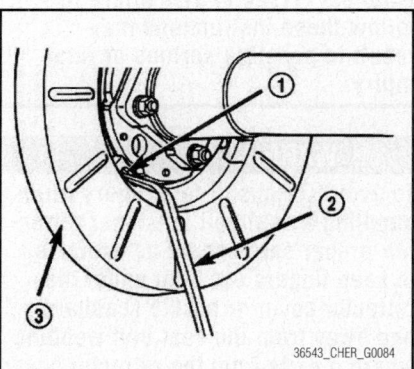

Fig. 24 Remove the rubber access plug (1) from the back of rear disc brake support plate (3)

5. If necessary, retract the parking brake shoes with a brake adjuster tool (2). Position the tool at the top of star wheel and rotate the wheel.
6. Remove the rotor from the axle hub flange.
7. Remove the four axle flange nuts.
8. Remove the axle shaft from the rear differential.
9. Remove the shoe to shoe return spring (6) with needle nose pliers and then remove the adjuster (5).
10. Remove the shoe to shoe return spring (3) with brake pliers.
11. Remove the shoe hold-down clips (4) and pins. The clip is held in place by a pin which fits into the clip notch. To remove the clip, first push the clip ends together and slide the clip until the head of pin clears the narrow part of the notch. Then remove clip (4) and pin.
12. Remove the shoes (1) off the actuator lever (2) for the parking brake then remove the shoes (1).

To install:

13. Install the park brake shoes onto the actuator lever.
14. Install shoes on support plate with hold down clips and pins. Be sure shoes are properly engaged in the park brake actuator lever.
15. Install the return spring.
16. Lubricate and install adjuster screw assembly. Be sure notched ends of screw

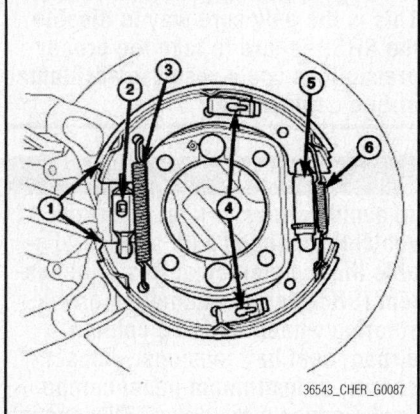

Fig. 25 Parking brake assembly

assembly are properly seated on shoes and that star wheel is aligned with access hole in the support plate.

17. Install shoe to shoe adjuster spring. Needle nose pliers can be used to connect spring to each shoe.
18. Install the axle shaft to the rear differential.
19. Install and tighten the axle flange nuts.
20. Install rotor to the axle hub.
21. Install the caliper and the 2 mounting bolts to 32 ft. lbs. (44 Nm).
22. Adjust the parking brake shoes.
23. Install wheel and tire assembly.
24. Lower vehicle and verify correct parking brake operation.

ADJUSTMENT

Adjustment can be made with a standard brake gauge or with adjusting tool. Adjustment is performed with the complete brake assembly installed on the backing plate.

1. Be sure parking brake lever is fully released.
2. Raise vehicle so rear wheels can be rotated freely.
3. Remove plug from each access hole in brake support plates.
4. Loosen parking brake cable adjustment nut until there is slack in front cable.
5. Insert adjusting tool through support plate access hole and engage tool in teeth of adjusting screw star wheel.
6. Rotate adjuster screw star wheel (move tool handle upward) until slight drag can be felt when wheel is rotated.
7. Push and hold adjuster lever away from star wheel with thin screwdriver.
8. Back off adjuster screw star wheel until brake drag is eliminated.
9. Repeat adjustment at opposite wheel. Be sure adjustment is equal at both wheels.
10. Install support plate access hole plugs.
11. Adjust parking brake cable and lower vehicle.
12. Depress park brake lever and make sure park brakes hold the vehicle stationary.
13. Release park brake lever.

CHASSIS ELECTRICAL — AIR BAG (SUPPLEMENTAL RESTRAINT SYSTEM)

✳ CAUTION

These vehicles are equipped with an air bag system. The system must be disarmed before performing service on, or around, system components, the steering column, instrument panel components, wiring and sensors. Failure to follow the safety precautions and the disarming procedure could result in accidental air bag deployment, possible injury and unnecessary system repairs.

GENERAL INFORMATION

SERVICE PRECAUTIONS

✳ WARNING

To avoid serious or fatal injury on vehicles equipped with the Supplemental Restraint System (SRS), never attempt to repair the electrically conductive circuits or wiring components related to the SRS. Such repairs can compromise the conductivity and current carrying capacity of those critical electrical circuits, which may cause the SRS components not to deploy when required, or to deploy when not required. Any wire harness containing broken, cut, burned or otherwise damaged electrically conductive SRS wiring, terminals or connector components must be removed and replaced with an entire new wire harness. Only minor cuts or abrasions of wire and terminal insulation where the conductive material has not been damaged, or connector insulators where the integrity of the latching and locking mechanisms have not been compromised may be repaired using appropriate methods. Failure to follow these instructions may result in possible serious or fatal injury.

✳ WARNING

To avoid serious or fatal injury during and following any seat belt or child restraint anchor service, carefully inspect all seat belts, buckles, mounting hardware, retractors, tether straps, and anchors for proper installation, operation, or damage. Replace any belt that is cut, frayed, or torn. Straighten any belt that is twisted. Tighten any loose fasteners. Replace any belt that has a damaged or ineffective buckle or retractor. Replace any belt that has a bent or damaged latch plate or anchor plate. Replace any child restraint anchor or the unit to which the anchor is integral that has been bent or damaged. Never attempt to repair a seat belt or child restraint component. Always replace damaged or ineffective seat belt and child restraint components with the correct, new and unused replacement parts listed in the Chrysler Mopar® Parts Catalog.

✳ WARNING

To avoid serious or fatal injury on vehicles equipped with side curtain airbags, disable the Supplemental Restraint System (SRS) before attempting any Occupant Restraint Controller (ORC) diagnosis or service. The ORC contains a rollover sensor, which enables the system to deploy the side curtains in the event of a vehicle rollover event. If an ORC is accidentally rolled during service while still connected to battery power, the side curtain airbags will deploy. Disconnect and isolate the battery negative (ground) cable, then wait two minutes for the system capacitor to discharge before performing further diagnosis or service. This is the only sure way to disable the SRS. Failure to take the proper precautions could result in accidental airbag deployment.

✳ WARNING

To avoid serious or fatal injury on vehicles equipped with airbags, disable the Supplemental Restraint System (SRS) before attempting any steering wheel, steering column, airbag, seat belt tensioner, impact sensor, or instrument panel component diagnosis or service. Disconnect and isolate the battery negative (ground) cable, then wait two minutes for the system capacitor to discharge before performing further diagnosis or service. This is the only sure way to disable the SRS. Failure to take the proper precautions could result in accidental airbag deployment.

✳ WARNING

To avoid serious or fatal injury on vehicles equipped with airbags, before performing any welding operations disconnect and isolate the battery negative (ground) cable and disconnect all wire harness connectors from the Occupant Restraint Controller (ORC). Failure to take the proper precautions could result in accidental airbag deployment and other possible damage to the Supplemental Restraint System (SRS) circuits and components.

✳ WARNING

To avoid serious or fatal injury, do not attempt to dismantle an airbag unit or tamper with its inflator. Do not puncture, incinerate or bring into contact with electricity. Do not store at temperatures exceeding 200°F (93°C). An airbag inflator unit may contain sodium azide and potassium nitrate. These materials are poisonous and extremely flammable. Contact with acid, water, or heavy metals may produce harmful and irritating gases (sodium hydroxide is formed in the presence of moisture) or combustible compounds. An airbag inflator unit may also contain a gas canister pressurized to over 2500 psi (17.24 kPa). Failure to follow these instructions may result in possible serious or fatal injury.

✳ WARNING

To avoid serious or fatal injury when handling a seat belt tensioner retractor, proper care should be exercised to keep fingers out from under the retractor cover or buckle scabbard and away from the seat belt webbing where it exits from the retractor cover or buckle cable where it exits from the scabbard.

✳ WARNING

To avoid serious or fatal injury, replace all Supplemental Restraint System (SRS) components only with parts specified in the Chrysler Mopar® Parts Catalog. Substitute parts may appear interchangeable, but internal differences may result in inferior occupant protection.

DISARMING THE SYSTEM

To avoid serious or fatal injury on vehicles equipped with airbags, disable the Supplemental Restraint System (SRS) before attempting any steering wheel, steering column, airbag, seat belt tensioner, impact sensor, or instrument panel component diagnosis or service.

Disconnect and isolate the battery negative (ground) cable, then wait two minutes for the system capacitor to discharge before performing further diagnosis or service. This is the only sure way to disable the SRS. Failure to take the proper precautions could result in accidental airbag deployment.

ARMING THE SYSTEM

1. During the following test, the battery negative cable remains disconnected and isolated, as it was during the Supplemental Restraint System (SRS) component removal and installation procedures.

2. Be certain that the diagnostic scan tool contains the latest version of the proper diagnostic software. Connect the scan tool to the 16-way Data Link Connector (DLC) (1). The DLC is located on the driver side lower edge of the instrument panel (2), outboard of the steering column.

3. Turn the ignition switch to the ON position and exit the vehicle with the scan tool.

4. Check to be certain that nobody is in the vehicle, then reconnect the battery negative cable.

5. Using the scan tool, read and record the active (current) Diagnostic Trouble Code (DTC) data.

6. Next, use the scan tool to read and record any stored (historical) DTC data.

7. If any DTC is found, refer to the appropriate diagnostic information.

8. Use the scan tool to erase the stored DTC data. If any problems remain, the stored DTC data will not erase. Refer to the appropriate diagnostic information to diagnose any stored DTC that will not erase. If the stored DTC information is successfully erased, go to the next step.

9. Turn the ignition switch to the OFF position for about 15 seconds, and then back to the ON position. Observe the airbag indicator in the instrument cluster. It should light for six to eight seconds, and then go out. This indicates that the SRS is functioning normally and that the repairs are complete. If the airbag indicator fails to light, or lights and stays ON, there is still an active SRS fault or malfunction. Refer to the appropriate diagnostic information to diagnose the problem.

CLOCKSPRING CENTERING

See Figure 26.

➡ A service replacement clockspring is shipped with the clockspring pre-centered and with a molded plastic locking pin installed. This locking pin should not be removed until the steering wheel has been installed on the steering column. If the locking pin is removed before the steering wheel is installed, the clockspring centering procedure must be performed.

➡ When a clockspring is installed into a vehicle without properly centering and locking the entire steering system, the Steering Angle Sensor (SAS) data does not agree with the true position of the steering system and causes the Electronic Stability Program (ESP) system to shut down. This may also damage the clockspring without any immediate malfunction. Unlike some other Chrysler vehicles, this SAS never requires calibration. However, upon each new ignition ON cycle, the steering wheel must be rotated slightly to initialize the SAS.

➡ Determining if the clockspring/SAS is centered is also possible electrically using the diagnostic scan tool. Steering wheel position is displayed as ANGLE with a range of up to 900 degrees. Refer to the appropriate menu item on the diagnostic scan tool.

➡ Before starting this procedure, be certain to turn the steering wheel until the front wheels are in the straight-ahead position and that the entire steering system is locked or inhibited from rotation.

➡ The clockspring may be centered and the rotor may be rotated freely once the steering wheel has been removed.

1. Place the front wheels in the straight-ahead position and inhibit the steering column shaft from rotation.

2. Remove the steering wheel from the steering shaft.

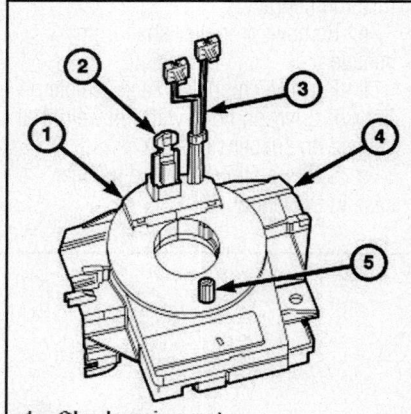

1. Clockspring rotor
2. Locking pin
3. Clockspring airbag pigtail wires
4. Clockspring housing
5. Dowel or drive pin

36543_CHER_G0089

Fig. 26 Rotate the clockspring rotor (1) clockwise

3. Rotate the clockspring rotor (1) clockwise to the end of its travel. Do not apply excessive torque.

4. From the end of the clockwise travel, rotate the rotor about two and one-half turns counterclockwise. Turn the rotor slightly clockwise or counterclockwise as necessary so that the clockspring airbag pigtail wires (3) and connector receptacle are at the top and the dowel or drive pin (5) is at the bottom.

5. The clockspring is now centered.

Secure the clockspring rotor to the clockspring case using a locking pin (2) or some similar device to maintain clockspring centering until the steering wheel is reinstalled on the steering column.

DRIVE TRAIN

AUTOMATIC TRANSMISSION ASSEMBLY

REMOVAL & INSTALLATION

NAG1 Transmission

See Figures 27 through 36.

➡This transmission is used in vehicles equipped with the 3.0L diesel engine or the 3.7L and 6.1L gasoline engines.

1. Disconnect the negative battery cable.
2. Raise and support the vehicle.
3. Remove the propeller shafts.

➡The propeller shaft slip joint boot can be replaced. Place reference marks on both sections of the shaft to ensure proper assemble.

   a. With vehicle in neutral, position vehicle on hoist.

   b. Mark propeller shaft (1) pinion flange (2) and transmission/transfer case flanges for installation reference.

   c. Remove propeller shaft (1) from axle pinion flange (2).

   d. Remove propeller shaft (1) from vehicle transfer case flange (2) or transmission flange (3).

   e. Remove propeller shaft from vehicle.

   f. For 4WD models, place vehicle on floor or drive-on hoist with full weight of vehicle on suspension.

   g. Shift transmission and transfer case in to Neutral.

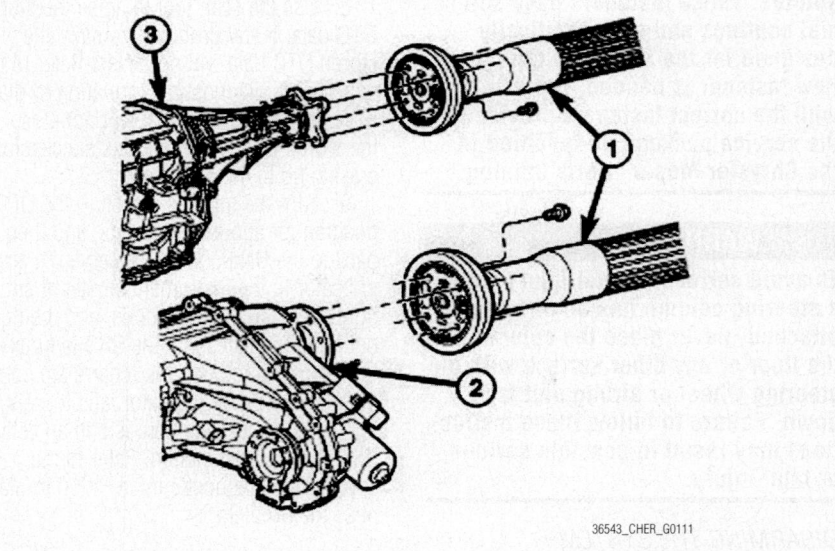

Fig. 28 Remove propeller shaft (1) from vehicle transfer case flange (2) or transmission flange (3)

36543_CHER_G0111

   h. Mark a line across the C/V joints and companion flanges (3) (4) for installation reference.

   i. Remove bolts from C/V joints.

   j. Push propeller shaft forward to clear transfer case companion flange and remove the shaft.

✳✳ CAUTION

Failure to follow these instructions may result in a driveline vibration.

4. Remove the bolts holding the starter motor to the transmission.

➡**For 3.0L diesel engines:**

   a. Remove positive battery cable at battery.

   b. Remove battery.

   c. Remove battery tray (three bolts - one nut).

   d. Remove plastic dress-up cover at top of engine.

   e. Raise vehicle.

   f. If equipped, remove skid plate below starter.

   g. Remove starter mounting bolts. These are located at rear of transmission bellhousing.

➡**For 3.7L and 6.1L engines**

   h. Note: If equipped with 4WD and certain transmissions, a support bracket is used between front axle and side of transmission. Remove 2 support bracket bolts at transmission. Pry support bracket slightly to gain access to lower starter mounting bolt.

   i. Remove two starter bolts.

5. Remove the starter from the transmission starter pocket and safely relocate.

6. Remove the bolts (1, 2, 3) holding the structural cover to the transmission and engine.

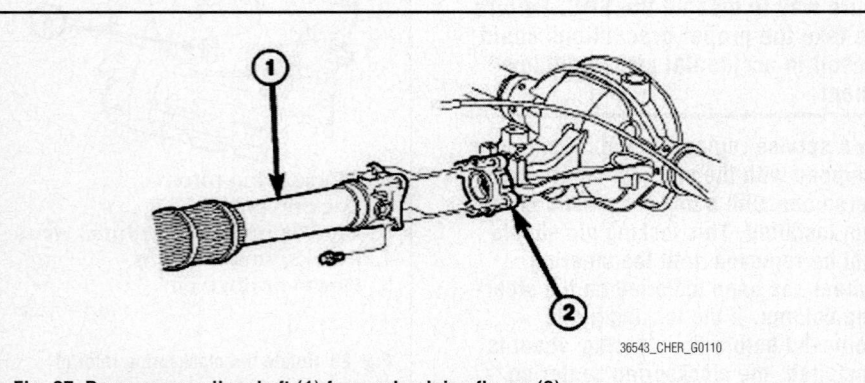

Fig. 27 Remove propeller shaft (1) from axle pinion flange (2)

36543_CHER_G0110

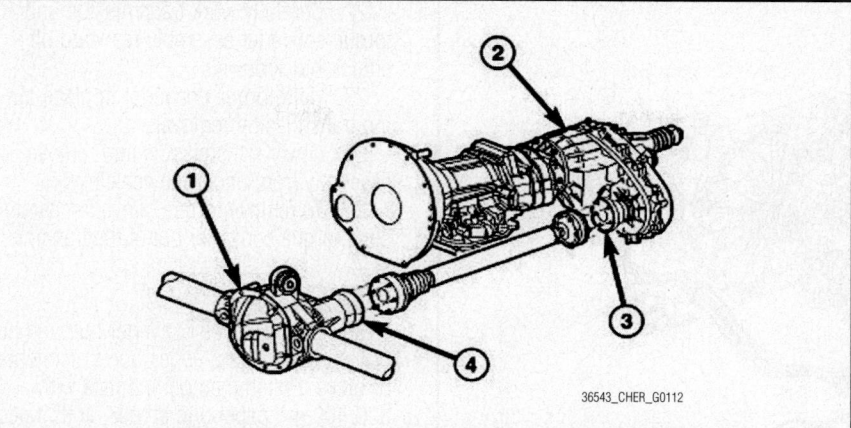

Fig. 29 Mark a line across the C/V joints and companion flanges (3) (4) for installation reference

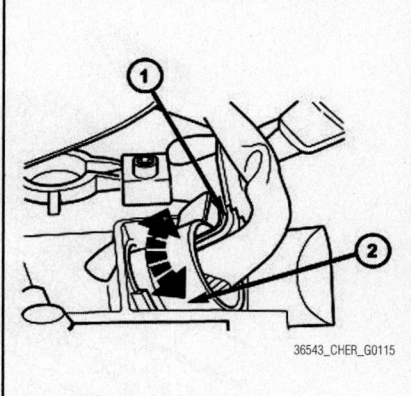

Fig. 32 Disconnect 13-pin plug connector (1)

14. Disconnect transmission fluid cooler lines (2) at transmission (1).

15. Disconnect the transmission vent hose from the transmission.

16. Remove the bolts (4) holding the transmission fill tube (2) to the transmission (1).

17. Support rear of engine with safety stand or jack.

18. Raise transmission slightly with service jack to relieve load on crossmember and supports.

19. Remove bolts securing rear support and cushion to transmission crossmember.

20. Remove bolts attaching crossmember to frame and remove crossmember.

21. Remove all remaining bolts (3) holding the engine (1) to the transmission (2). Note the location of any wiring harness clips (4).

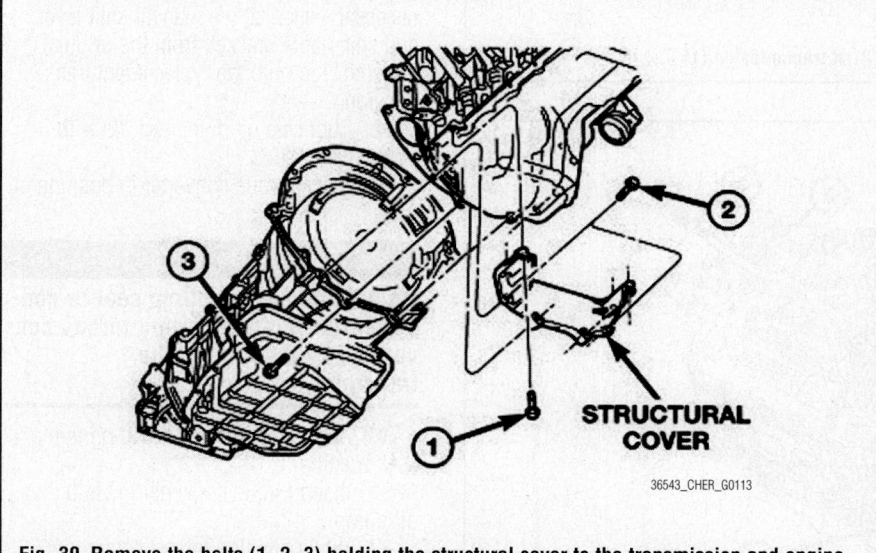

Fig. 30 Remove the bolts (1, 2, 3) holding the structural cover to the transmission and engine

7. Remove the structural cover from the vehicle.

8. For gas engines, rotate crankshaft in clockwise direction until converter bolts are accessible. Then remove bolts one at a time. Rotate crankshaft with socket wrench on dampener bolt.

9. For diesel engines, rotate crankshaft in clockwise direction until converter bolts are accessible. Then remove bolts one at a time. Rotate crankshaft with socket wrench on dampener bolt.

10. Disconnect the gearshift cable (3) from the transmission manual valve lever.

11. Remove the shift cable (3) from the gearshift cable bracket (4).

12. Disconnect 13-pin plug connector (1). Turn bayonet lock of the adapter plug (2) anti-clockwise.

13. Remove the 13-pin connector (1) from the transmission.

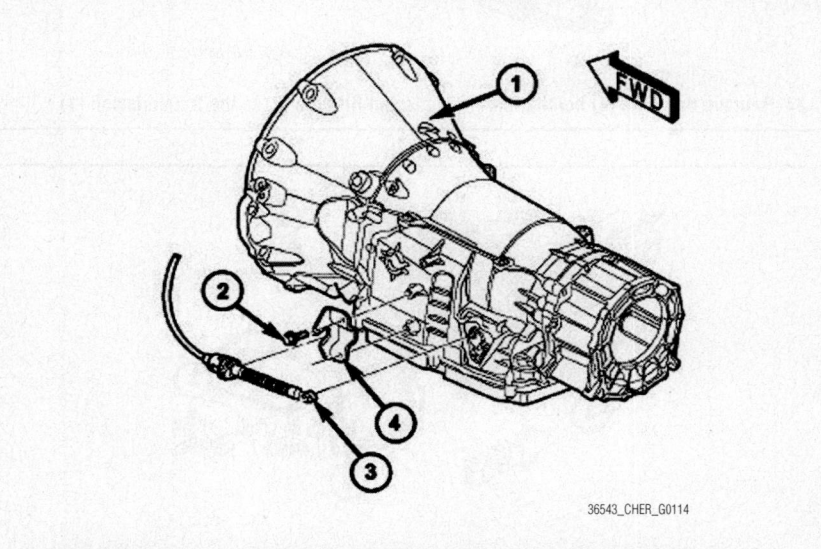

Fig. 31 Disconnect the gearshift cable (3) from the transmission manual valve lever

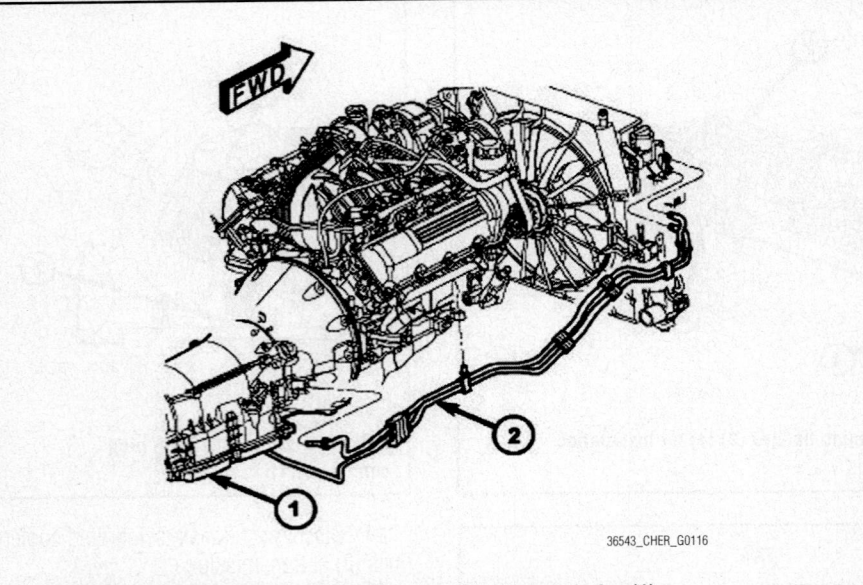

Fig. 33 Disconnect transmission fluid cooler lines (2) at transmission (1)

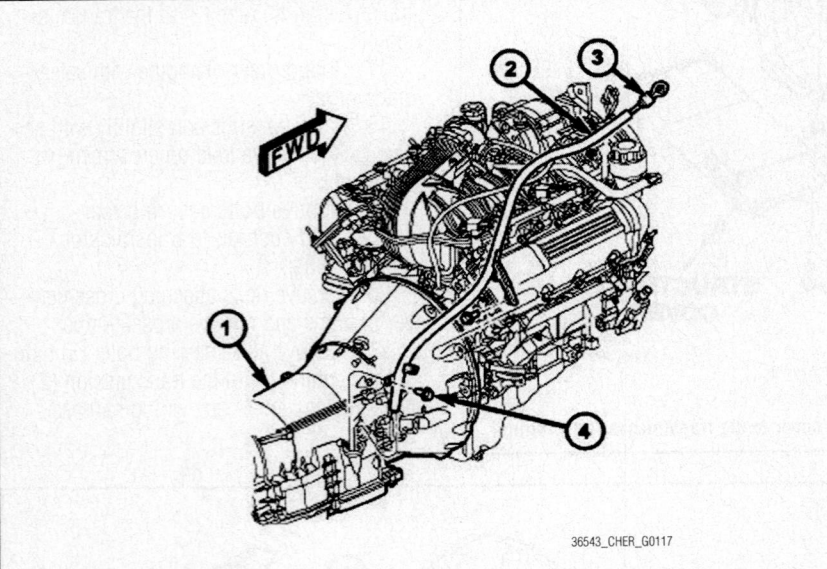

Fig. 34 Remove the bolts (4) holding the transmission fill tube (2) to the transmission (1)

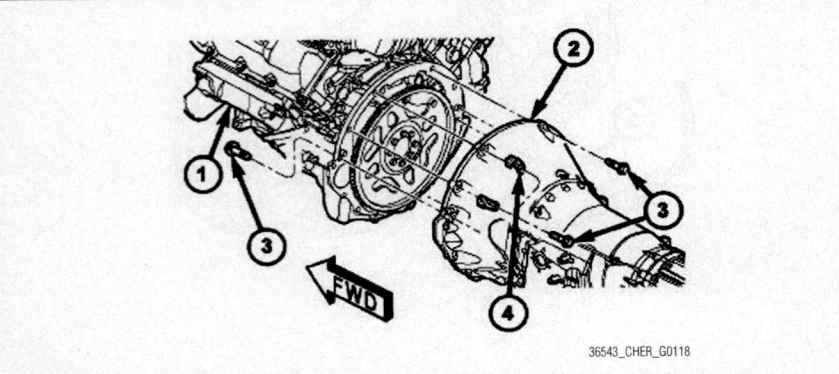

Fig. 35 Remove all remaining bolts (3) holding the engine (1) to the transmission (2)

22. Carefully work transmission and torque converter assembly rearward off engine block dowels.

23. Hold torque converter in place during transmission removal.

24. Lower transmission and remove assembly from under the vehicle.

25. To remove torque converter, carefully slide torque converter out of the transmission.

To install:

26. Check torque converter hub and hub drive flats for sharp edges burrs, scratches, or nicks. Polish the hub and flats with 320/400 grit paper and crocus cloth if necessary. The hub must be smooth to avoid damaging pump seal at installation.

27. If a replacement transmission is being installed, transfer any components necessary, such as the manual shift lever and shift cable bracket, from the original transmission onto the replacement transmission.

28. Lubricate oil pump seal lip with transmission fluid.

29. Place torque converter in position on transmission.

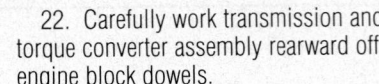

Do not damage oil pump seal or converter hub while inserting torque converter into the front of the transmission.

30. Align torque converter to oil pump seal opening.

31. Insert torque converter (1) hub into oil pump.

32. While pushing torque converter inward, rotate converter until converter is fully seated in the oil pump gears.

33. Check converter seating with a scale and straightedge. Surface of converter lugs should be at least ¾ inches (19 mm) to rear of straightedge when converter is fully seated.

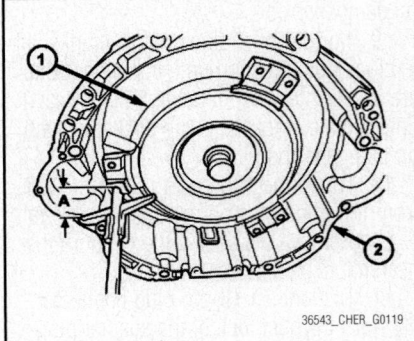

Fig. 36 Insert torque converter(1) hub into oil pump

34. If necessary, temporarily secure converter with C-clamp attached to the converter housing.

35. Check condition of converter driveplate. Replace the plate if cracked, distorted or damaged. Also be sure transmission dowel pins are seated in engine block and protrude far enough to hold transmission in alignment.

36. Apply a light coating of Mopar® High Temp Grease to the torque converter hub pocket in the rear pocket of the engine's crankshaft.

37. Raise transmission and align the torque converter with the drive plate and the transmission converter housing with the engine block.

38. Move transmission forward. Then raise, lower, or tilt transmission to align the converter housing with the engine block dowels.

39. Carefully work transmission forward and over engine block dowels until converter hub is seated in crankshaft. Verify that no wires, or the transmission vent hose, have become trapped between the engine block and the transmission.

40. Install two bolts to attach the transmission to the engine.

41. Install remaining torque converter housing to engine bolts. Tighten to 29 ft. lbs. (39 Nm).

42. Install rear transmission crossmember. Tighten crossmember to frame bolts to 50 ft. lbs. (68 Nm).

43. Install rear support to transmission. Tighten bolts to 35 ft. lbs. (47 Nm).

44. Lower transmission onto crossmember and install bolts attaching transmission mount to crossmember. Tighten clevis bracket to crossmember bolts to 39 ft. lbs. (47 Nm). Tighten the clevis bracket to rear support bolt to 50 ft. lbs. (68 Nm).

45. Remove engine support fixture.

46. Install the engine to transmission structural cover.

47. Connect gearshift cable to the gearshift cable bracket and transmission.

48. Check O-ring on plug connector, and replace if necessary.

49. Install the plug connector into the adapter plug. Turn bayonet lock of the adapter plug clockwise to connect plug connector.

✳✳ CAUTION

It is essential that the correct length bolts are used to attach the converter to the driveplate. Bolts that are too long will damage the clutch surface inside the converter.

50. For gas engines, install all torque converter-to-driveplate bolts by hand.

51. Verify that the torque converter is pulled flush to the driveplate. Tighten bolts to 31 ft. lbs. (42 Nm).

✳✳ CAUTION

It is essential that the correct length bolts are used to attach the converter to the driveplate. Bolts that are too long will damage the clutch surface inside the converter.

52. For diesel engines, install all torque converter-to-driveplate bolts by hand.

53. Verify that the torque converter is pulled flush to the driveplate. Tighten bolts to 31 ft. lbs. (42 Nm).

54. Install starter motor.

55. Install transmission fill tube.

56. Connect cooler lines to transmission.

57. Install exhaust components.

58. Install transfer case, if necessary.

59. Align and connect propeller shafts.

60. Adjust gearshift cable if necessary.

61. Lower vehicle.

62. Connect negative battery cable.

63. Fill transmission with the appropriate fluid.

64. Verify proper operation.

45RFE/545RFE Transmission

See Figures 27 through 29, 37 through 47.

➡ **This transmission is used in vehicles equipped with the 4.7L and 5.7L gasoline engines.**

✳✳ CAUTION

The transmission and torque converter must be removed as an assembly to avoid component damage. The converter driveplate, oil pump, or oil seal can be damaged if the converter is left attached to the driveplate during removal. Be sure to remove the transmission and converter as an assembly.

1. Disconnect the negative battery cable.

2. Raise and support the vehicle

3. Remove the rear propeller shaft.

➡ **The propeller shaft slip joint boot can be replaced. Place reference marks on both sections of the shaft to ensure proper assemble.**

a. With vehicle in neutral, position vehicle on hoist.

b. Mark propeller shaft (1) pinion flange (2) and transmission/transfer case flanges for installation reference.

c. Remove propeller shaft (1) from axle pinion flange (2).

d. Remove propeller shaft (1) from vehicle transfer case flange (2) or transmission flange (3).

e. Remove propeller shaft from vehicle.

4. Remove the front propeller shaft.

a. Place vehicle on floor or drive-on hoist with full weight of vehicle on suspension.

b. Shift transmission and transfer case in to Neutral.

c. Mark a line across the C/V joints and companion flanges (3) (4) for installation reference.

d. Remove bolts from C/V joints.

e. Push propeller shaft forward to clear transfer case companion flange and remove the shaft.

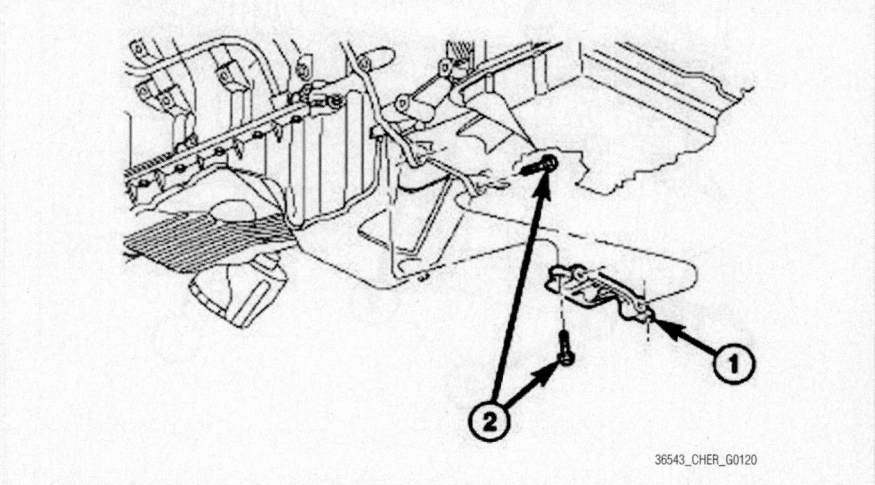

36543_CHER_G0120

Fig. 37 Remove the engine to transmission structural cover (1), 5.7L shown

> ✷✷ **CAUTION**
>
> **Failure to follow these instructions may result in a driveline vibration.**

5. Remove the engine to transmission structural cover (1), 5.7L shown.

   a. Remove the left hand exhaust pipe from exhaust manifold.

   b. Loosen the right hand exhaust manifold-to-exhaust pipe retaining bolts.

   c. Remove the eight bolts retaining structural cover.

   d. Pivot the exhaust pipe downward and remove the structural cover.

6. Remove the torque converter bolts (3).

7. Remove the exhaust support bracket from the rear of the transmission.

8. Disconnect and lower or remove any necessary exhaust components.

9. Remove the starter motor.

10. Rotate crankshaft in clockwise direction until converter bolts are accessible. Then remove bolts one at a time. Rotate crankshaft with socket wrench on dampener bolt.

11. Disconnect the input speed sensor (2) connector.

12. Disconnect the output speed sensor (2) connector.

13. Disconnect the solenoid and pressure switch assembly (2) connector.

14. Disconnect the line pressure sensor (2) connector.

15. Disconnect gearshift cable (3) from transmission manual valve lever (2) and shift cable bracket (4).

16. If necessary, remove the NV245 transfer case (1) from the transmission (3).

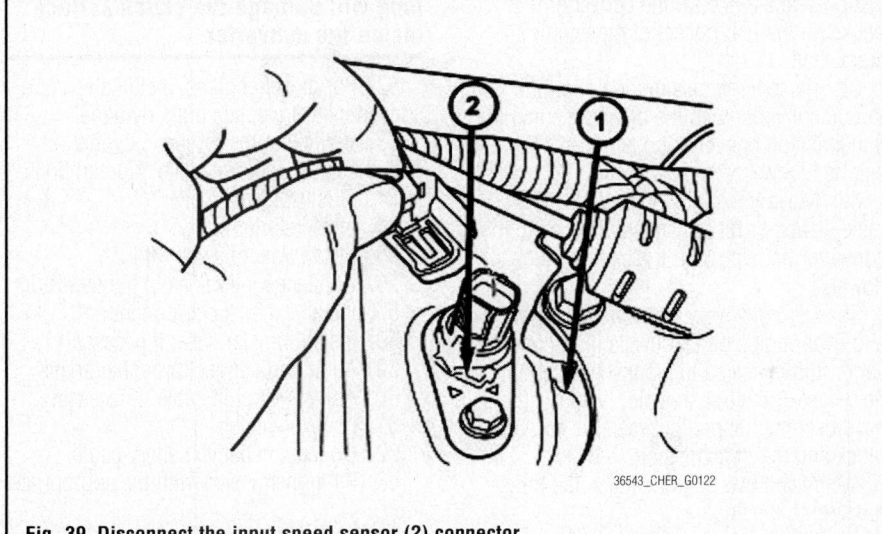

Fig. 39 Disconnect the input speed sensor (2) connector

17. Remove the engine oil pan to transmission bolts (1), 5.7L only.

18. Remove the bolt (4) holding the transmission fill tube (2) to the transmission (1) and remove the fill tube.

19. Disconnect transmission fluid cooler lines (2) at transmission (1) fittings and clips.

20. Disconnect the transmission vent hose from the transmission.

21. Support rear of engine with safety stand or jack.

22. Raise transmission slightly with service jack to relieve load on crossmember and supports.

23. Remove bolts attaching crossmember to frame and remove crossmember.

24. Remove all remaining transmission to engine bolts.

25. Carefully work transmission and torque converter assembly rearward off engine block dowels.

26. Hold torque converter in place during transmission removal.

27. Lower transmission and remove assembly from under the vehicle.

28. To remove torque converter, carefully slide torque converter out of the transmission.

To install:

29. Check torque converter hub and hub drive flats for sharp edges burrs, scratches, or nicks. Polish the hub and flats with 320/400 grit paper and crocus cloth if necessary. Verify that the converter hub O-ring is properly installed and is free of any debris. The hub must be smooth to avoid damaging pump seal at installation.

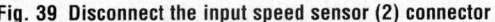

Fig. 38 Remove the torque converter bolts (3)

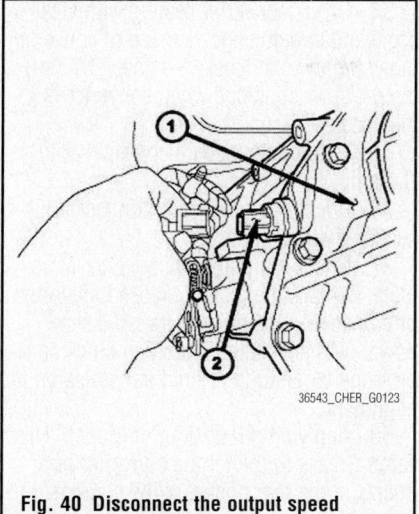

36543_CHER_G0123

Fig. 40 Disconnect the output speed sensor (2) connector

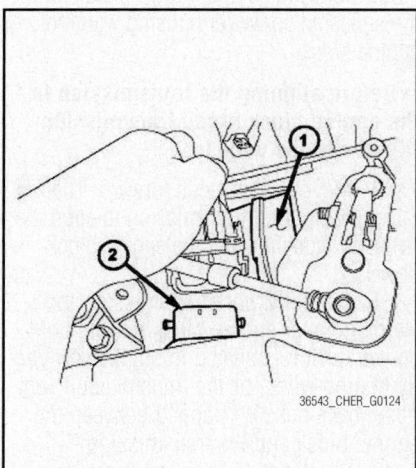

36543_CHER_G0124

Fig. 41 Disconnect the solenoid and pressure switch assembly (2) connector

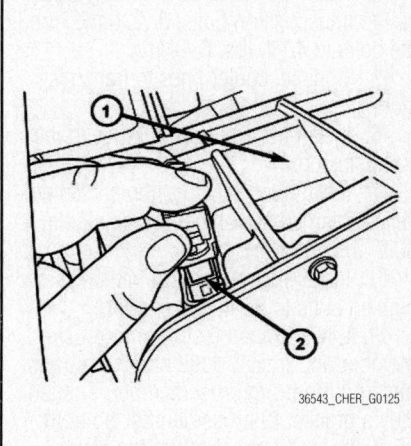

36543_CHER_G0125

Fig. 42 Disconnect the line pressure sensor (2) connector

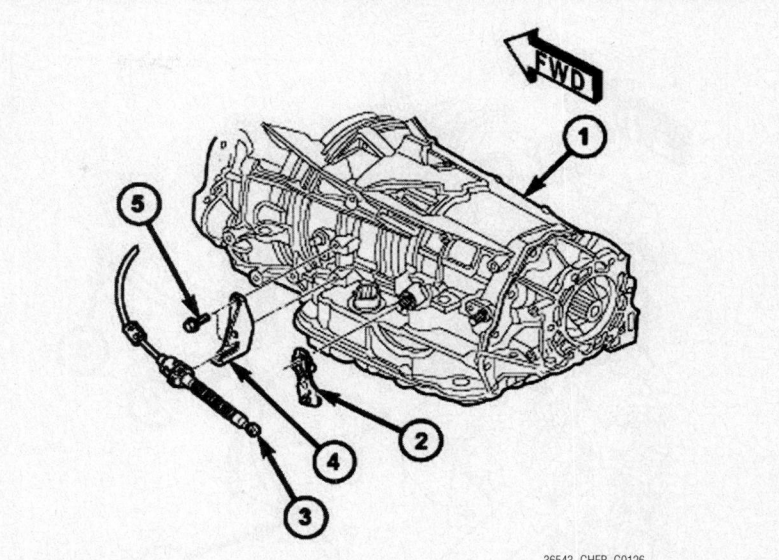

36543_CHER_G0126

Fig. 43 Disconnect gearshift cable (3) from transmission manual valve lever (2) and shift cable bracket (4)

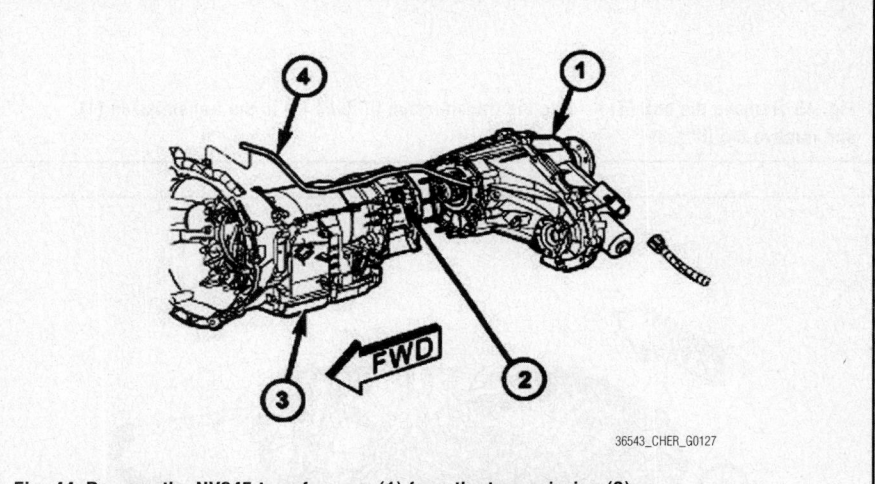

36543_CHER_G0127

Fig. 44 Remove the NV245 transfer case (1) from the transmission (3)

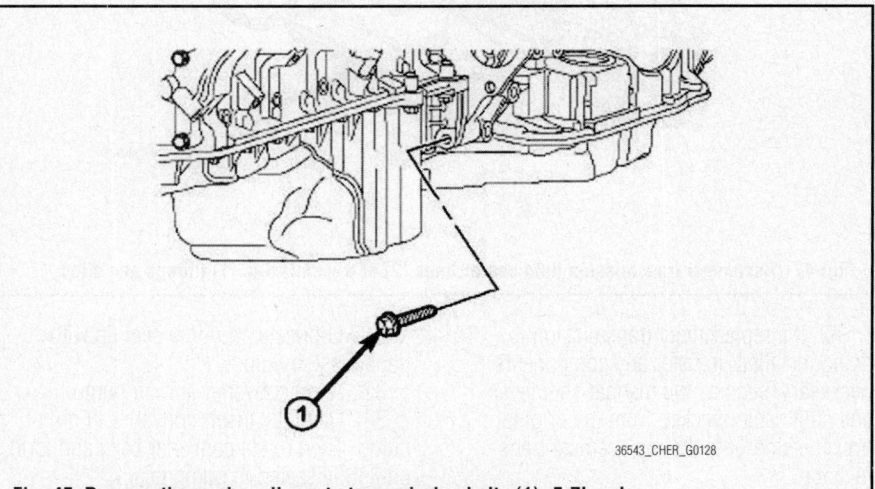

36543_CHER_G0128

Fig. 45 Remove the engine oil pan to transmission bolts (1), 5.7L only

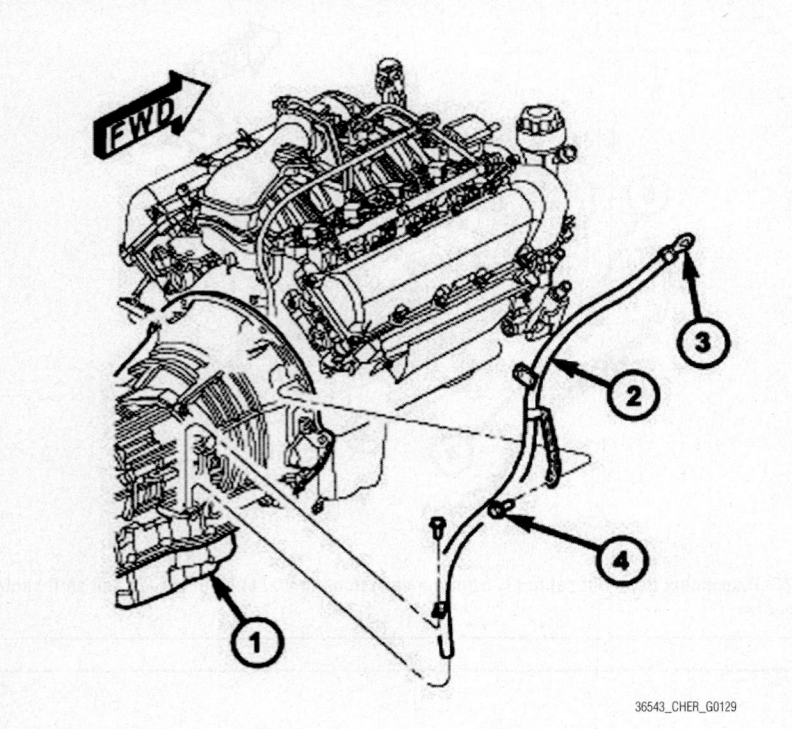

Fig. 46 Remove the bolt (4) holding the transmission fill tube (2) to the transmission (1) and remove the fill tube

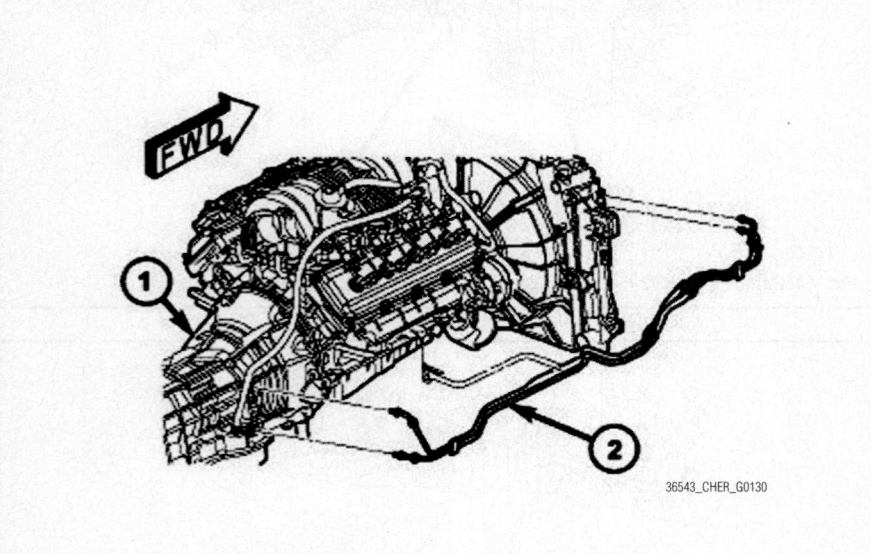

Fig. 47 Disconnect transmission fluid cooler lines (2) at transmission (1) fittings and clips

30. If a replacement transmission is being installed, transfer any components necessary, such as the manual shift lever and shift cable bracket, from the original transmission onto the replacement transmission.

31. Lubricate oil pump seal lip with transmission fluid.

32. Align converter and oil pump.

33. Carefully insert converter in oil pump. Then rotate converter back and forth until fully seated in pump gears.

34. Check converter seating with steel scale and straightedge. Surface of converter lugs should be at least ½ inches (13 mm) to rear of straightedge when converter is fully seated.

35. Temporarily secure converter with C-clamp.

36. Position transmission on jack and secure it with chains.

37. Check condition of converter drive-plate. Replace the plate if cracked, distorted or damaged. Also be sure transmission dowel pins are seated in engine block and protrude far enough to hold transmission in alignment.

38. Apply a light coating of Mopar® High Temp Grease to the torque converter hub pocket in the rear pocket of the engine's crankshaft.

39. Raise transmission and align the torque converter with the drive plate and the transmission converter housing with the engine block.

➡**Before aligning the transmission to the engine block fit the transmission fill tube to the vehicle.**

40. Move transmission forward. Then raise, lower, or tilt transmission to align the converter housing with the engine block dowels.

41. Carefully work transmission forward and over engine block dowels until converter hub is seated in crankshaft. Verify that no wires, or the transmission vent hose, have become trapped between the engine block and the transmission.

42. Install two bolts to attach the transmission to the engine.

43. Install remaining torque converter housing to engine bolts. Tighten to 50 ft. lbs. (68 Nm).

44. Install both the left and right side oil pan to transmission bolts, 5.7L only. Torque the bolts to 40 ft. lbs. (54 Nm).

45. Connect cooler lines to transmission.

46. Install transmission fill tube to the transmission.

47. Install rear transmission crossmember. Tighten crossmember to frame bolts to 50 ft. lbs. (68 Nm).

48. Install rear support to transmission. Tighten bolts to 35 ft. lbs. (47 Nm).

49. Lower transmission onto crossmember and install bolts attaching transmission mount to crossmember. Tighten clevis bracket to crossmember bolts to 35 ft. lbs. (47 Nm). Tighten the clevis bracket to rear support bolt to 50 ft. lbs. (68 Nm).

50. Remove engine support fixture.

51. Install new plastic retainer grommet on any shift cable that was disconnected. Grommets should not be reused. Use pry tool to remove rod from grommet and cut away old grommet. Use pliers to snap new grommet into cable and to snap grommet onto lever.

52. Connect gearshift cable to the shift cable bracket and the transmission manual lever.

53. Connect wires to the input speed sensor. Be sure transmission harnesses are properly routed.

54. Connect wires to the output speed sensor. Be sure transmission harnesses are properly routed.

55. Connect wires to the transmission solenoid/TRS assembly. Be sure transmission harnesses are properly routed.

56. Connect wires to the line pressure sensor. Be sure transmission harnesses are properly routed.

☀☀ CAUTION

It is essential that the correct length bolts are used to attach the converter to the driveplate. Bolts that are too long will damage the clutch surface inside the converter.

57. Install all torque converter-to-driveplate bolts by hand.

58. Verify that the torque converter is pulled flush to the driveplate. Tighten bolts to 270 inch lbs. (31 Nm).

59. Install the structural cover, 5.7L shown.

60. If necessary, install the NV245 transfer case.

61. Install starter motor.

62. Install exhaust components.

63. Align and connect propeller shaft(s).

64. Adjust gearshift cable if necessary.

65. Lower vehicle.

66. Fill transmission with appropriate fluid.

TRANSFER CASE ASSEMBLY

REMOVAL & INSTALLATION

NV140 & NV146 Transfer Case

See Figures 48 and 49.

1. Raise vehicle.

☀☀ CAUTION

Do not allow propeller shafts to hang at attached end. Damage to joint can result.

2. Remove the front and rear propeller shafts.

3. Support transmission with jack stand.

4. Remove rear crossmember and skid plate, if equipped.

5. Disconnect transfer case vent hose (4).

6. Disconnect the wiring connector from the shift motor, if necessary.

7. Support transfer case with transmission jack and secure with chains.

8. Remove nuts (2) attaching transfer case (1) to transmission (3).

9. Pull transfer case and jack rearward to disengage transfer case.

10. Remove transfer case from under vehicle.

To install:

11. Mount transfer case on a transmission jack.

12. Secure transfer case to jack with chains.

13. Position transfer case under vehicle.

14. Align transfer case and transmission shafts and install transfer case onto the transmission.

15. Install and tighten transfer case attaching nuts to 26 ft. lbs. (35 Nm).

16. Connect the transfer case vent hose.

17. Connect front propeller shaft and install rear propeller shaft.

18. For NV140, fill transfer case with correct fluid. Correct as necessary.

19. Install the transfer case fill plug. Tighten the plug to 15–25 ft. lbs. (20–34 Nm).

20. Install rear crossmember and skid plate, if equipped. Tighten crossmember bolts to 30 ft. lbs. (41 Nm).

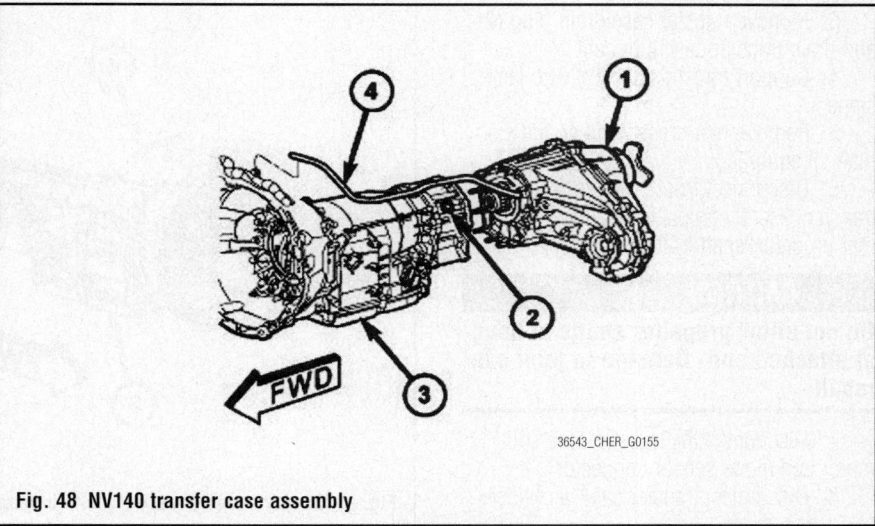

36543_CHER_G0155

Fig. 48 NV140 transfer case assembly

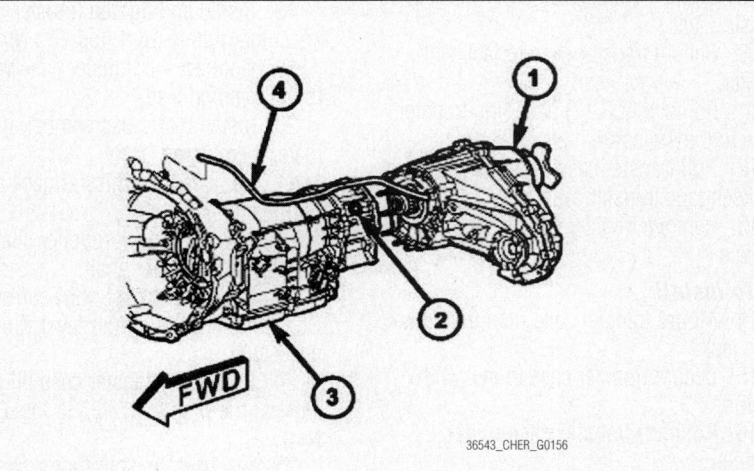

36543_CHER_G0156

Fig. 49 NV146 transfer case assembly

21. Remove transmission jack and support stand.

22. Lower vehicle and verify transfer case shift operation.

23. For NV146, fill transfer case with correct fluid. Correct as necessary.

24. Install the transfer case fill plug. 15–25 ft. lbs. (20–34 Nm).

25. Install rear crossmember and skid plate, if equipped. Tighten crossmember bolts to 30 ft. lbs. (41 Nm).

26. Connect the wiring connector to the shift motor.

27. Remove transmission jack and support stand.

28. Lower vehicle and verify transfer case shift operation.

NV245 Transfer Case

See Figures 50 and 51.

1. Shift transfer case into NEUTRAL.
2. Raise vehicle.
3. Remove transfer case drain plug (2) and drain transfer case lubricant.
4. Support transmission (3) with jack stand.
5. Remove rear crossmember and skid plate, if equipped.
6. Disconnect front propeller shaft from transfer case at companion flange. Remove rear propeller shaft from vehicle.

❊❊ CAUTION

Do not allow propeller shafts to hang at attached end. Damage to joint can result.

7. Disconnect the transfer case shift motor and mode sensor connector.
8. Disconnect transfer case vent hose (4).
9. Support transfer case (1) with transmission jack.
10. Secure transfer case to jack with chains.
11. Remove nuts (2) attaching transfer case to transmission.
12. Pull transfer case and jack rearward to disengage transfer case.
13. Remove transfer case from under vehicle.

To install:

14. Mount transfer case on a transmission jack.
15. Secure transfer case to jack with chains.
16. Position transfer case under vehicle.
17. Align transfer case and transmission shafts and install transfer case onto transmission.

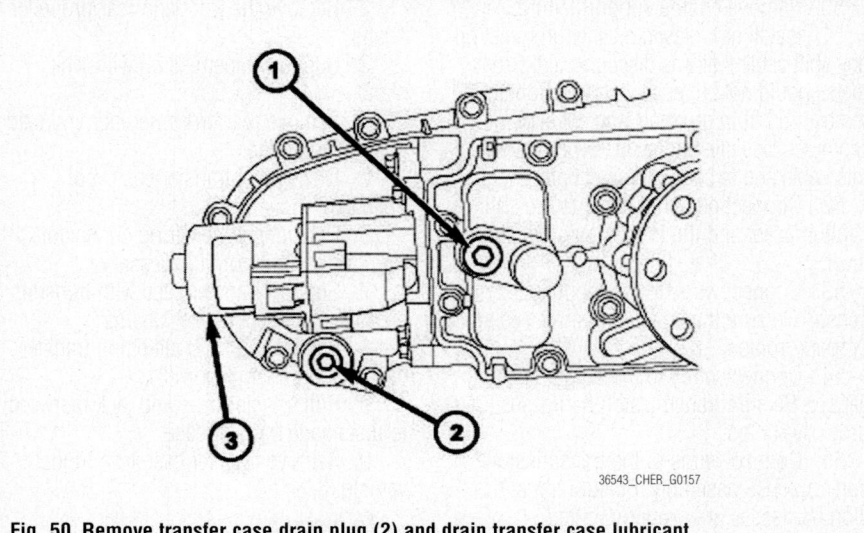

Fig. 50 Remove transfer case drain plug (2) and drain transfer case lubricant

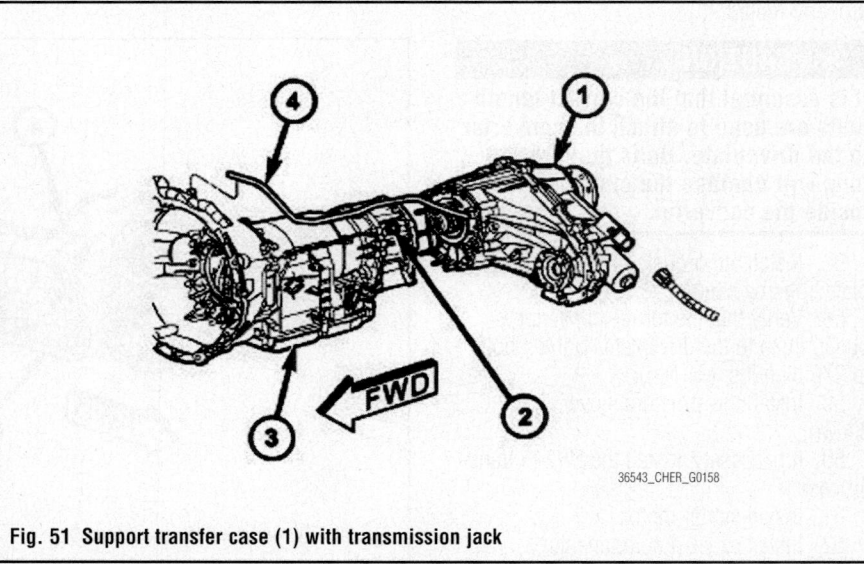

Fig. 51 Support transfer case (1) with transmission jack

18. Install and tighten transfer case attaching nuts to 26 ft. lbs. (35 Nm).
19. Connect the transfer case vent hose to the transfer case.
20. Install rear crossmember and skid plate, if equipped.
21. Remove transmission jack and support stand.
22. Connect front propeller shaft and install rear propeller shaft.
23. Fill transfer case with correct fluid. Check transmission fluid level. Correct as necessary.
24. Install the transfer case fill plug. Tighten the plug to 15–25 ft. lbs. (20–34 Nm).
25. Connect the shift motor and mode sensor wiring connector.
26. Lower vehicle and verify transfer case shift operation.

FRONT AXLE SHAFT, BEARING & SEAL

REMOVAL & INSTALLATION

Axle Shaft

See Figures 52 through 55.

1. With vehicle in neutral, position vehicle on hoist.
2. Remove half shaft hub/bearing nut.
3. Remove wheel speed sensor nut from hub/bearing and remove sensor.
4. Remove brake calipers bolts and remove calipers from caliper adapters.
5. Remove lower stabilizer link (3) bolt (6) from control arm.
6. Remove outer tie rod end nuts and separate tie rods (3) from knuckles (4) with Remover 8677 (5).

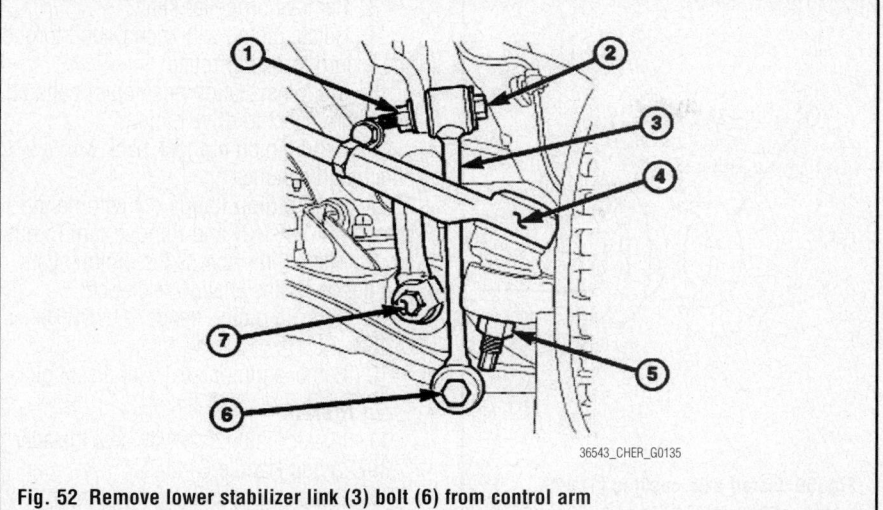

Fig. 52 Remove lower stabilizer link (3) bolt (6) from control arm

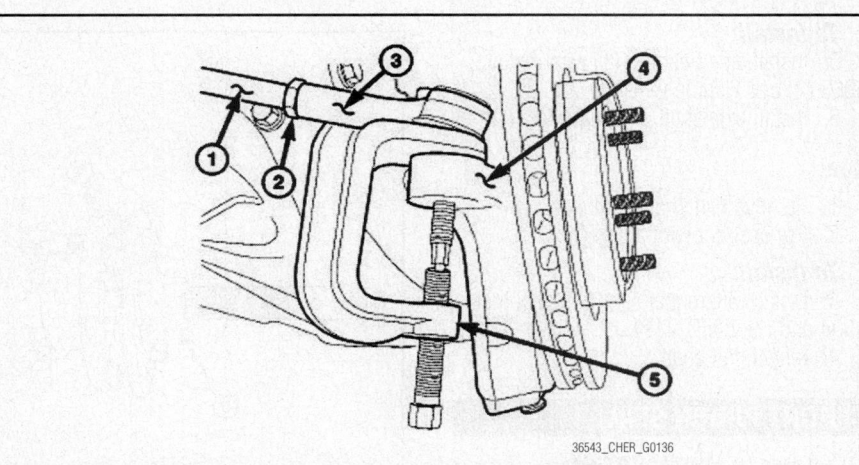

Fig. 53 Remove outer tie rod end nuts and separate tie rods (3) from knuckles (4) with Remover 8677 (5)

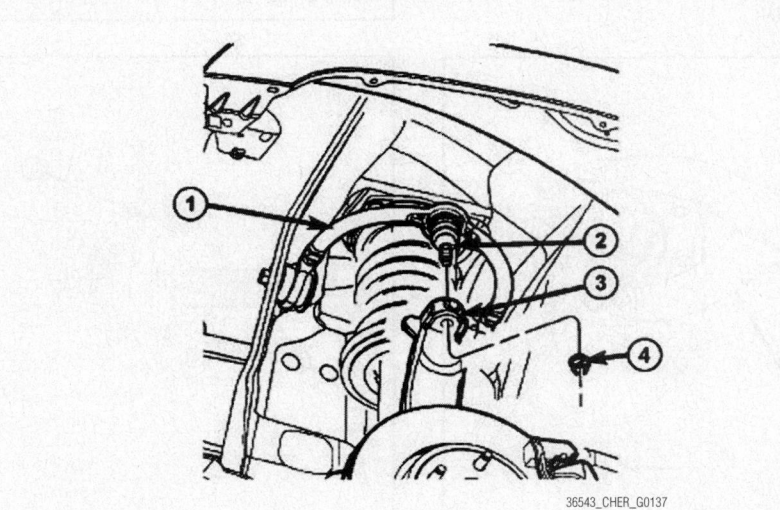

Fig. 54 Remove upper ball joint nuts (4) and separate ball joints (2) from knuckles (3) with Remover 8677

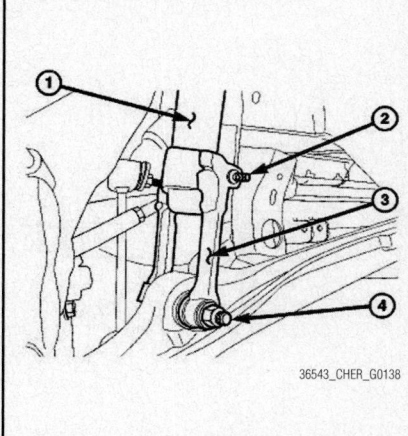

Fig. 55 Remove shock clevis (3) bolt and nut (4) from lower control arm

7. Remove upper ball joint nuts (4) and separate ball joints (2) from knuckles (3) with Remover 8677.

8. Remove shock clevis (3) bolt and nut (4) from lower control arm.

9. Lean the knuckle out and push half shaft out of the hub/bearing.

10. Pry half shafts from axle/axle tube with pry bar.

To install:

11. Install half shaft on the axle and through the hub/bearing. Verify half shaft has engaged.

12. Install shock clevis on lower control arm and tighten nut.

13. Install upper control arm on knuckle and tighten ball joint nut.

14. Install tie rod end on knuckle and tighten.

15. Install stabilizer link on lower control arm and tighten.

16. Install caliper on caliper adapter and tighten.

17. Install wheel speed sensor on the hub/bearing.

18. Install half shaft hub/bearing nut and tighten to 100 ft. lbs. (135 Nm).

Bearing

See Figures 56 through 59.

1. Remove axle shaft.

2. Remove axle shaft tube (1) seal with seal Remover 7794-A (2) and slide hammer.

3. Install axle bearing remover C-4660-A (1) into the axle bearing (2) in the axle tube (3) and tighten remover nut (4).

4. Install bearing receiver C-4660-A (1) washer and nut (2) on remover. Tighten nut (2) and draw bearing into receiver (1).

➡**Do not re-use bearing.**

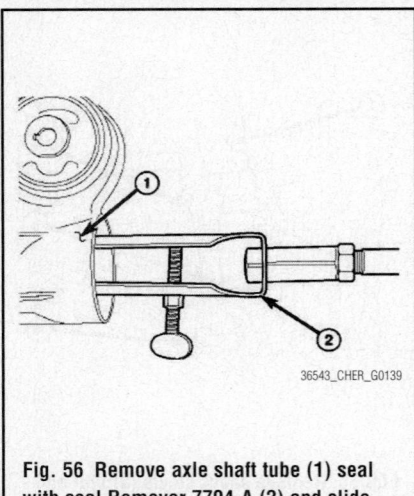

Fig. 56 Remove axle shaft tube (1) seal with seal Remover 7794-A (2) and slide hammer

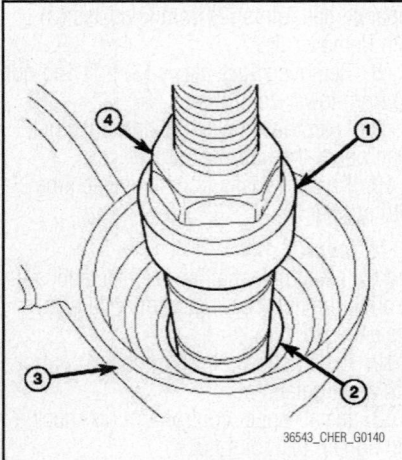

Fig. 57 Install axle bearing remover C-4660-A (1) into the axle bearing (2) in the axle tube (3)

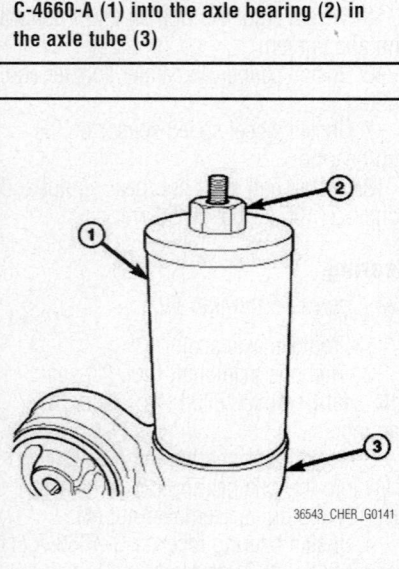

Fig. 58 Install bearing receiver C-4660-A (1) washer and nut (2) on remover

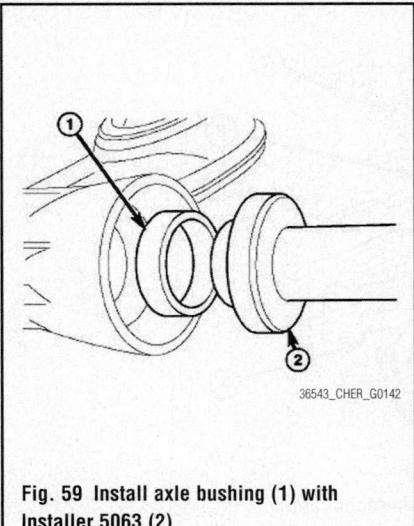
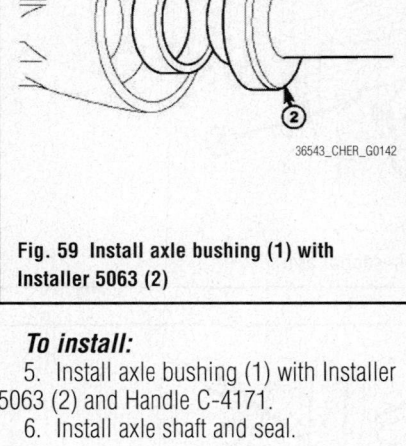

Fig. 59 Install axle bushing (1) with Installer 5063 (2)

To install:

5. Install axle bushing (1) with Installer 5063 (2) and Handle C-4171.
6. Install axle shaft and seal.

Seal

1. Remove half shaft from axle.
2. Pry seal out with a seal pick.

To install:

3. Install differential seal with seal Install 9504 and Handle C-4171.
4. Install half shaft.

FRONT PINION SEAL

REMOVAL & INSTALLATION

See Figures 60 through 63.

1. Remove wheels.
2. Push back brake pads and release hand brake.

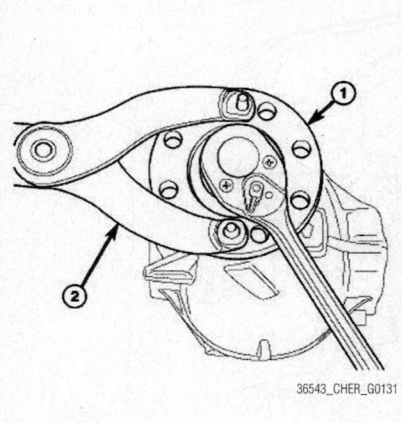

Fig. 60 Hold pinion flange (1) with flange Wrench C-3281(2)

3. Remove propeller shaft.
4. Rotate pinion with inch pound torque and record torque to rotate.
5. Mark installation position of collared nut with respect to drive pinion.
6. Bend pinion nut lock back with a punch and hammer.
7. Hold pinion flange (1) with flange Wrench C-3281(2) and remove pinion nut.
8. Mark a line across the pinion shaft and flange for installation reference.
9. Remove pinion flange (1) with Puller C-452 (2).
10. Remove pinion seal with a seal pick.

To install:

11. Install pinion seal with seal Installer C-3972A and Handle C-4171.
12. Position pinion flange on pinion shaft with reference mark aligned.

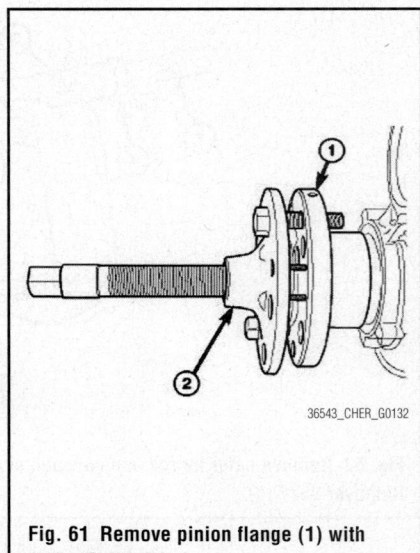

Fig. 61 Remove pinion flange (1) with Puller C-452 (2)

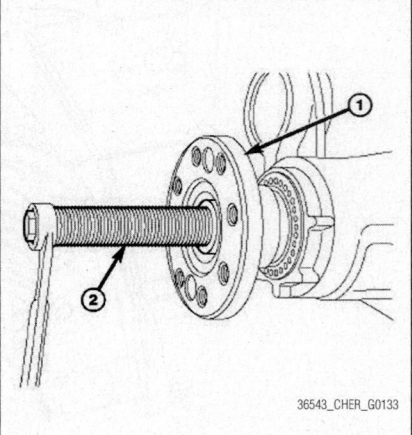

Fig. 62 Install pinion flange (1) on pinion with flange Installer 9616 (2)

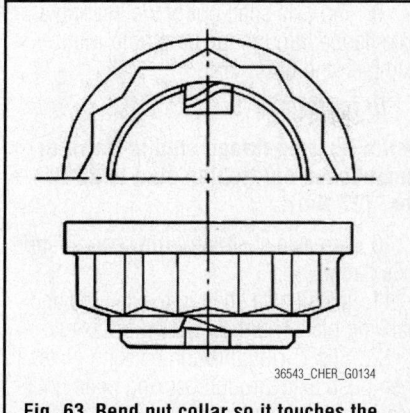

Fig. 63 Bend nut collar so it touches the wall of the slot in the pinion shaft

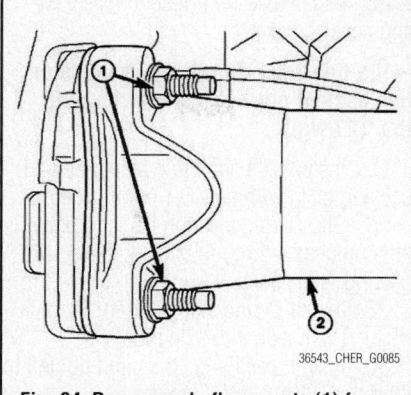

Fig. 64 Remove axle flange nuts (1) from axle (2)

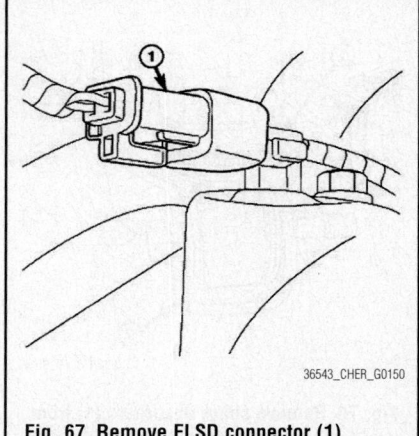

Fig. 67 Remove ELSD connector (1)

13. Install pinion flange (1) on pinion with flange Installer 9616 (2). Tap flange on pinion, then thread installer center bolt on pinion shaft and draw flange onto the pinion.

14. Install new pinion collared nut and carefully tighten nut in stages holding flange with flange Wrench C-3281. Check torque to rotate after each stage, until previously value of torque to rotate is exceeded by 4.4 inch lbs. (0.5 Nm).

15. Cut the pinion nut collar.

16. Bend nut collar so it touches the wall of the slot in the pinion shaft.

17. Connect propeller shaft to pinion flange.

18. Install wheel and tires.

19. Operate brake pedal several times until brake pads contact brake discs (brake pressure built up).

REAR AXLE HOUSING

REMOVAL & INSTALLATION

See Figures 64 through 72.

1. With vehicle in neutral, position on hoist.

2. Remove differential cover (1) and drain fluid.

3. Remove calipers and rotors.

4. Remove speed sensors from axle tube flange.

5. Remove axle flange nuts (1) from axle (2).

6. Pull axle shaft and backing plate out of axle tube until axle bearing (1) is exposed.

7. Remove O-ring (2) from the axle bearing.

8. Remove axle shaft (1) from axle tube and backing plate.

9. Remove ELSD connector (1) if equipped.

10. Remove axle vent hose (1) from axle vent (2) and cover bracket.

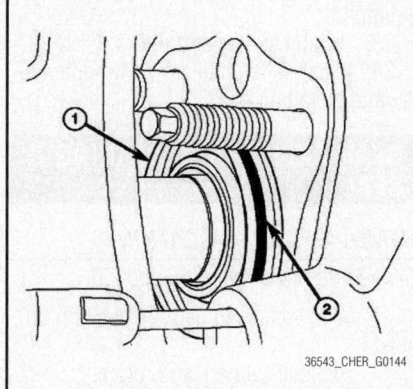

Fig. 65 Remove O-ring (2) from the axle bearing

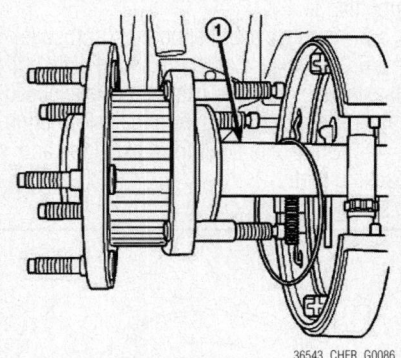

Fig. 66 Remove axle shaft (1) from axle tube and backing plate

11. Remove propeller shaft.

12. Remove stabilizer bar (1) clamp (2) from axle.

13. Support axle with jack.

14. Remove track bar from axle.

15. Remove shock absorbers (1) from axle brackets (2).

16. Remove upper control arms (2) from axle brackets (1).

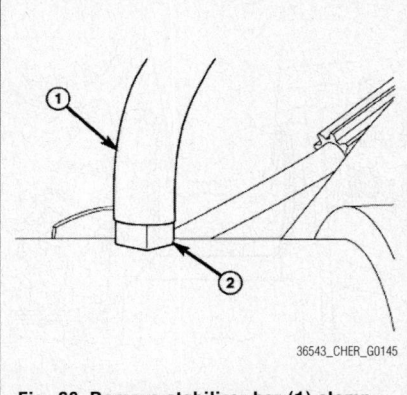

Fig. 68 Remove stabilizer bar (1) clamp (2) from axle

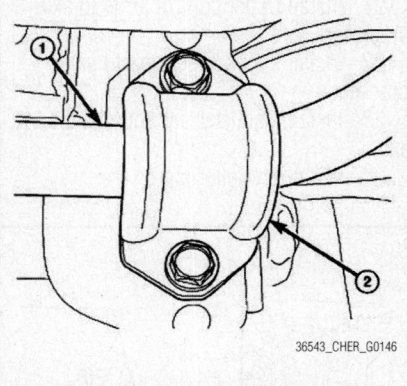

Fig. 69 Remove stabilizer bar (1) clamp (2) from axle

17. Remove lower control arms (1) from axle brackets (2).

18. Lower axle from vehicle and remove coil springs and insulators.

To install:

19. Install coil springs and insulators. Raise axle into place.

20. Install lower control arms to axle brackets.

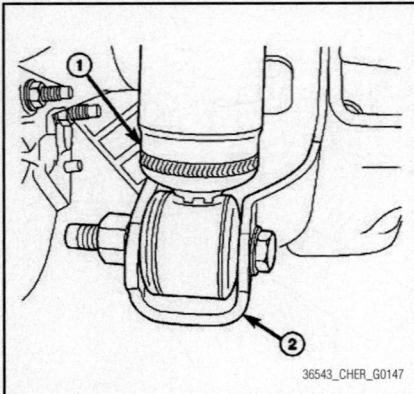

Fig. 70 Remove shock absorbers (1) from axle brackets (2)

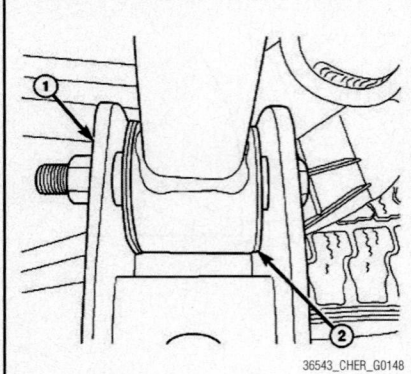

Fig. 71 Remove upper control arms (2) from axle brackets (1)

21. Install upper control arms to axle brackets.
22. Install shock absorbers to axle brackets.
23. Install stabilizer bar and clamps to axle.
24. Install propeller shaft.

25. Install axle vent hose to axle vent and cover bracket.

➡**If a bearing flange stud is loose or has backed out tighten stud to 20 ft. lbs. (27 Nm).**

26. Install axle shaft into axle tube and backing plate with new O-ring on axle.
27. Slip O-ring through backing plate, then push axle through backing plate until bearing is exposed.
28. Install O-ring axle bearing.
29. Push axle into axle tube.
30. Install axle flange nuts and tighten to 88 ft. lbs. (119 Nm).
31. Install speed sensors in axle tube flange.
32. Install the ELDS connector, if equipped.
33. Install calipers and rotors.
34. Install differential cover, fill differential and install fill plug.

REAR AXLE SHAFT, BEARING & SEAL

REMOVAL & INSTALLATION

See Figures 64 through 66 and 73.

1. With vehicle in neutral, position on hoist.
2. Remove calipers and rotors.
3. Tap axle end plug (1) loose from the axle flange (2) with a hammer and punch. Pull plug (1) out of axle flange (2).
4. Remove speed sensors from axle tube flange.
5. Remove axle flange nuts from axle.
6. Pull axle shaft and backing plate out of axle tube until axle bearing (1) is exposed.
7. Remove O-ring from the axle bearing.
8. Slide axle shaft from axle tube and backing plate.

9. Tap axle shaft out of the bearing and axle flange through the plug hole with a hammer and brass drift.

To install:

➡**If a bearing flange stud is loose or has backed out tighten stud to 20 ft. lbs. (27 Nm).**

10. Tap axle shaft into axle bearing and axle flange.
11. Install axle shaft into axle tube and backing plate with new O-ring on axle.
12. Slip O-ring through backing plate, then push axle through backing plate until bearing is exposed.
13. Install O-ring axle bearing.
14. Push axle into axle tube.
15. Install axle flange nuts and tighten to 88 ft. lbs. (119 Nm).
16. Install speed sensors in axle tube flange.
17. Coat new axle flange plug with Mopar® Stud N' Bearing Mount Adhesive or equivalent and install plug with freeze plug installer.
18. Install calipers and rotors.

REAR PINION SEAL

REMOVAL & INSTALLATION

See Figures 74 through 76.

1. With vehicle in neutral, position vehicle on hoist.
2. Mark a reference line across the axle flange (3) and propeller shaft flange (4).
3. Remove propeller shaft
4. Remove brake calipers and rotors to prevent any drag.
5. Rotate flange three or four times and verify flange rotates smoothly.
6. Measure torque to rotating pinion flange (1) with a inch pound torque wrench (2). Record reading for installation reference.

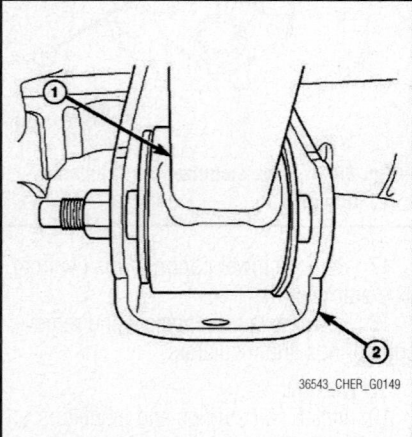

Fig. 72 Remove lower control arms (1) from axle brackets (2)

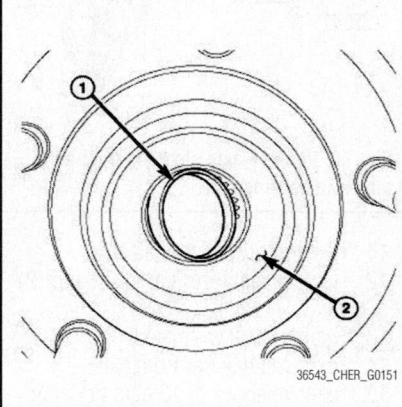

Fig. 73 Tap axle end plug (1) loose from the axle flange (2)

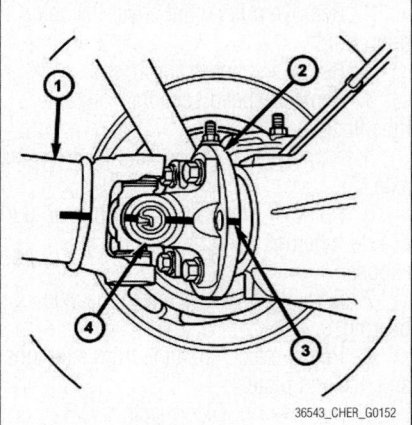

Fig. 74 Mark a reference line across the axle flange (3) and propeller shaft flange (4)

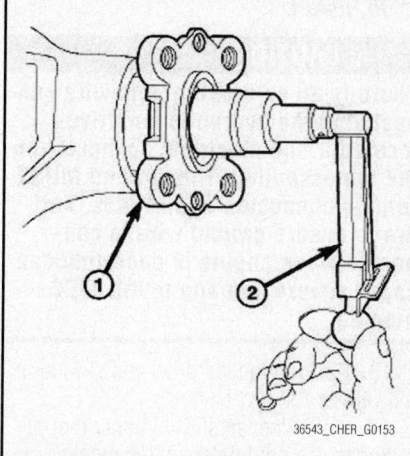

Fig. 75 Measure torque to rotating pinion flange (1) with a inch pound torque wrench (2)

7. Hold pinion flange with Wrench C-3281 and remove pinion nut and washer.

8. Mark line on pinion shaft and flange for installation reference.

9. Remove flange with two jaw puller.

10. Remove pinion seal with a seal puller.

To install:

11. Apply a light coating of gear lubricant on the lip of pinion seal.

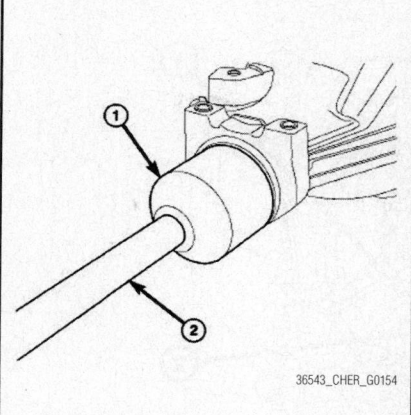

Fig. 76 Install new pinion seal with Installer C-3972A (1) and Handle C-4171 (2)

12. Install new pinion seal with Installer C-3972A (1) and Handle C-4171 (2).

13. Position flange on pinion shaft with the reference marks aligned.

14. Install flange on pinion shaft with Installer C-3718 and Wrench C-3281.

15. Install pinion washer and a new pinion nut. The convex side of the washer must face outward.

16. Hold flange with Wrench C-3281and tighten pinion nut to 210 ft. lbs. (285 Nm). Rotate pinion several revolutions to ensure bearing rollers are seated.

➡ **Do not exceed the minimum tightening torque 210 ft. lbs. (285 Nm) when installing the companion flange retaining nut at this point.**

17. Rotate pinion several times to ensure bearings are seated.

18. Measure pinion torque to rotate with an inch pound torque wrench. Pinion torque to rotate should be equal to recorded reading plus an additional 5 inch lbs. (0.56 Nm).

➡ **If pinion torque to rotate is low, tighten pinion nut in 5 ft. lbs (6.8 Nm) increments until pinion torque to rotate is achieved.**

✳ CAUTION

Never loosen pinion nut to decrease pinion bearing rotating torque. If pinion torque to rotate is exceeded, a new collapsible spacer must be installed. Failure to follow these instructions will result in damage to the axle.

19. Install propeller shaft.
20. Install rear brake components.

ENGINE COOLING

ENGINE FAN

REMOVAL & INSTALLATION

3.7L & 4.7L Engines

See Figure 77.

1. Disconnect electric fan connector (3).
2. Remove shroud mounting bolts.

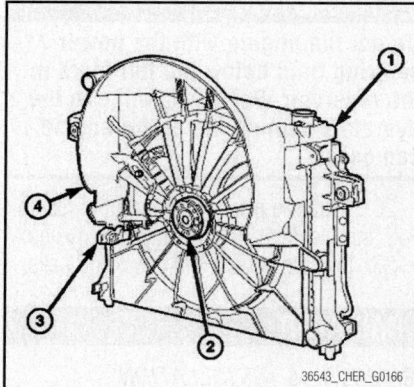

Fig. 77 Disconnect electric fan connector (3)

3. Remove shroud (4) and fan assembly from vehicle.

4. Remove fan assembly mounting bolts and remove fan from shroud (4).

To install:

5. Position fan assembly on shroud.

6. Install fan to fan shroud mounting nuts.

7. Position fan and shroud assembly in vehicle.

8. Install shroud mounting bolts.

9. Connect electric fan electrical connector.

10. Start engine and check fan operation.

5.7L Engine & 3.0L Diesel Engine

See Figures 78 through 80.

1. Raise vehicle on hoist.
2. Drain cooling system.

➡ **The hydraulic fan drive is driven by the power steering pump. When removing lines or hoses from fan drive assembly use a drain pan to catch any power steering fluid that may exit the fan drive or the lines and hoses.**

➡ **Whenever the high pressure line fittings are removed from the hydraulic fan drive the O-rings must be replaced.**

3. Disconnect two high pressure lines at hydraulic fan drive.

4. Remove and discard O-rings from line fittings.

5. Disconnect low pressure return hose at hydraulic fan drive.

➡ **The lower mounting bolts can only be accessed from under vehicle.**

6. Remove two lower mounting bolts from the shroud.

7. Lower vehicle.

8. Disconnect the electrical connector for the fan control solenoid.

9. Disconnect the upper radiator hose at the radiator and position out of the way.

10. Disconnect the power steering gear outlet hose and fluid return hose at the cooler.

11. Remove two upper mounting bolts from the shroud.

12. Remove the shroud and fan drive from vehicle.

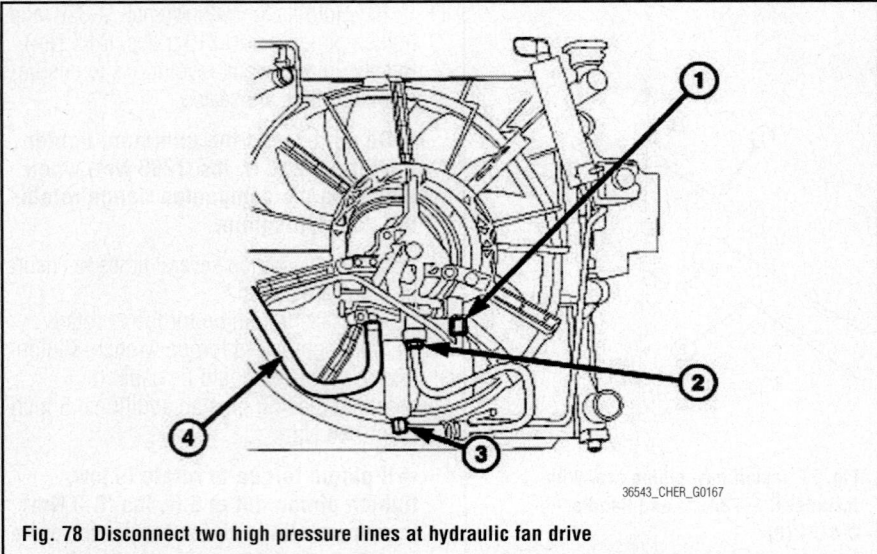

Fig. 78 Disconnect two high pressure lines at hydraulic fan drive

36543_CHER_G0167

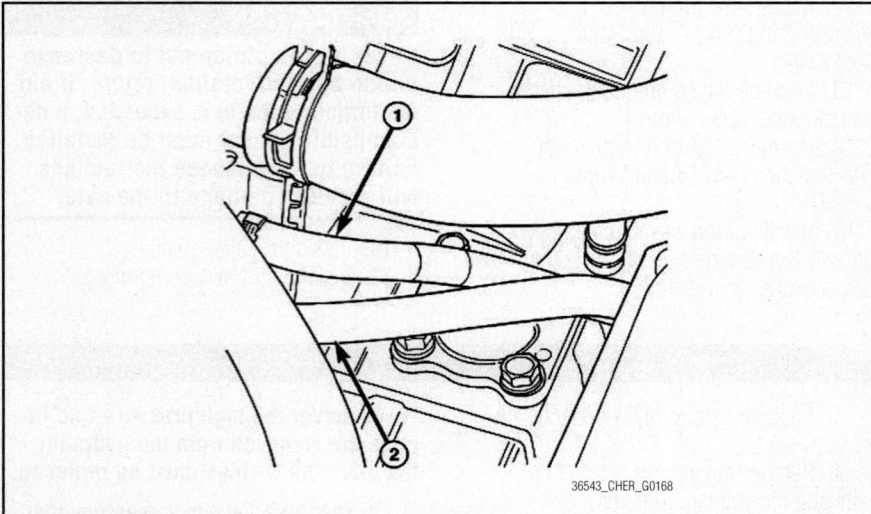

Fig. 79 Disconnect the power steering gear outlet hose and fluid return hose at the cooler

36543_CHER_G0168

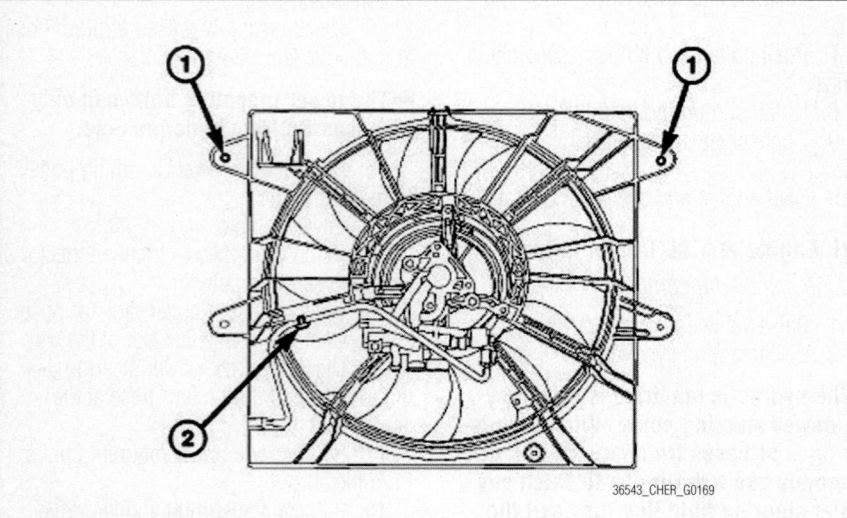

Fig. 80 Remove two upper mounting bolts from the shroud

36543_CHER_G0169

To install:

❋❋ CAUTION

There is an external ground wire connected to the hydraulic fan drive located at the electrical connector on the fan assembly. This ground MUST remain connected at all times. Failure to ensure ground wire is connected when engine is operating can cause severe damage to the JTEC module.

13. Position the fan drive and shroud in the vehicle.

14. Install the fan shroud upper mounting bolts. Do not tighten at this time.

15. Install the upper radiator hose onto the radiator.

16. Connect the power steering cooler hoses.

17. Raise the vehicle on a hoist.

18. Install the fan shroud lower mounting bolts.

➡Whenever the high pressure line fittings are removed from the hydraulic fan drive the O-rings located on the fittings must be replaced.

19. Lubricate the O-rings on the fittings with power steering fluid then connect the inlet and outlet high pressure lines to fan drive. Tighten the inlet line to 36 ft. lbs. (49 Nm). Tighten the outlet line to 22 ft. lbs. (29 Nm).

20. Connect the low pressure return hose to the fan drive.

21. Lower the vehicle.

22. Install the upper radiator hose.

23. Connect the electrical connector for the hydraulic fan control solenoid.

24. Tighten the fan shroud upper mounting bolts.

25. Refill the cooling system.

❋❋ CAUTION

Do not run engine with the power steering fluid below the full mark in the reservoir. Severe damage to the hydraulic cooling fan or the engine can occur.

26. Refill the power steering fluid reservoir and bleed air from the steering system.

27. Run the engine and check for leaks.

RADIATOR

REMOVAL & INSTALLATION

All Gasoline Engines

See Figures 81 through 83.

Do not remove the cylinder block drain plugs or loosen the radiator draincock with the system hot and under pressure. Serious burns from coolant can occur.

Do not waste reusable coolant. If the solution is clean, drain the coolant into a clean container for reuse.

Constant tension hose clamps are used on most cooling system hoses. When removing or installing, use only tools designed for servicing this type of clamp. Always wear safety glasses when servicing constant tension clamps.

A number or letter is stamped into the tongue (2) of constant tension clamps (1). If replacement is necessary, use only an original equipment clamp with matching number or letter.

When removing the radiator or A/C condenser for any reason, note the location of all radiator-to-body and radiator-to-A/C condenser rubber air seals. These are used at the top, bottom and sides of the radiator and A/C condenser. To prevent overheating, these seals must be installed to their original positions.

1. Disconnect the negative battery cable at battery.
2. 5.7L/6.1L - Drain power steering fluid from reservoir.
3. Drain coolant from radiator.
4. Remove the front grille.
   a. Remove the 6 upper push pins (1).
   b. Tip grill forward and remove grill (2).
5. Remove two radiator mounting bolts.
6. 5.7L/6.1L - Disconnect the low pressure hose to the hydraulic fan drive. Reposition the spring clamp.
7. Disconnect both transmission cooler lines from radiator.
8. Disconnect the line from power steering cooler (3) and filter.
9. Disconnect the radiator upper and lower hoses.
10. Disconnect the overflow hose from radiator.

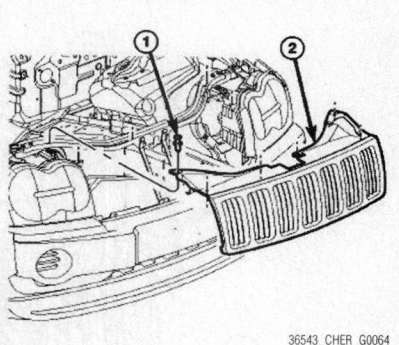

Fig. 80 Remove the grille from the front of the vehicle

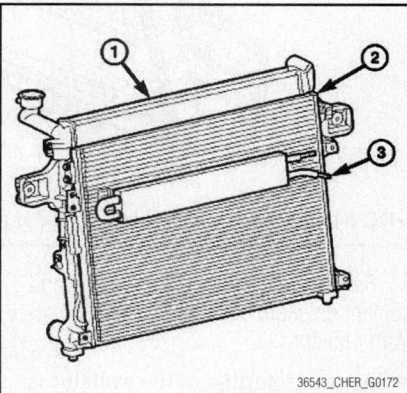

Fig. 82 Disconnect the line from power steering cooler (3) and filter

11. 5.7L/6.1L - Disconnect electric connector for hydraulic fan control solenoid.
12. Remove the air inlet duct at the grille.
13. Disconnect radiator fan electrical connector.
14. The lower part of radiator (1) is equipped with two alignment dowel pins (2). They are located on the bottom of radiator tank and fit into rubber grommets (3). These rubber grommets are pressed into the radiator lower crossmember (4).

The air conditioning system (if equipped) is under a constant pressure even with the engine off. Refer to refrigerant Warnings in, Heating And Air Conditioning before handling any air conditioning component.

➡The radiator and radiator cooling fan can be removed as an assembly. It is not necessary to remove the cooling fan before removing or installing the radiator.

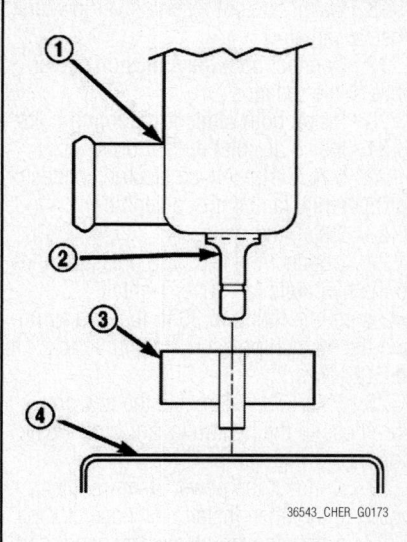

Fig. 83 The lower part of radiator (1) is equipped with two alignment dowel pins (2)

15. Gently lift up and remove radiator from vehicle. Be careful not to scrape the radiator fins against any other component. Also be careful not to disturb the air conditioning condenser (if equipped)

To install:

Before installing the radiator or A/C condenser, be sure the radiator-to-body and radiator-to-A/C condenser rubber air seals are properly fastened to their original positions. These are used at the top, bottom and sides of the radiator and A/C condenser. To prevent overheating, these seals must be installed to their original positions.

16. Equipped with air conditioning: Gently lower the radiator and fan shroud into the vehicle. Guide the two radiator alignment dowels through the holes in the rubber air seals first and then through the A/C support brackets. Continue to guide the alignment dowels into the rubber grommets located in lower radiator crossmember. The holes in the L-shaped brackets (located on bottom of A/C condenser) must be positioned between bottom of rubber air seals and top of rubber grommets.
17. Connect the radiator upper and lower hoses and hose clamps to radiator.

The tangs on the hose clamps must be positioned straight down.

18. Install coolant reserve/overflow tank hose at radiator.

19. Connect both transmission cooler lines at the radiator.

20. Install both radiator mounting bolts.

21. Install air inlet duct at grille.

22. 5.7L/6.1L - Attach electric connector for hydraulic fan control solenoid.

23. Install the grille.

24. Connect the two high pressure lines to the hydraulic fan drive. Tighten 1/2 in. pressure line fitting to 36 ft. lbs. (49 Nm). and the ⅜ inch pressure line fitting to 21 ft. lbs. (29 Nm).

25. 5.7L/6.1L - Connect the low pressure hose to the hydraulic fan drive. Position the spring clamp.

26. Connect the power steering filter hoses to the filter. Install new hose clamps.

27. Rotate the fan blades (by hand) and check for interference at fan shroud.

28. Refill cooling system.

29. 5.7L/6.1L - Refill the power steering reservoir and bleed air from system.

30. Connect battery cable at battery.

31. Start and warm engine. Check for leaks.

3.0L Diesel Engine

See Figure 84.

> ※※ **WARNING**
>
> **Risk of injury to skin and eyes from scalding coolant. Do not open cooling system unless temperature is below 194°F (90°C). Open cap slowly to release pressure. Store coolant in approved and appropriately marked container. Wear protective gloves, clothing and eye wear.**

➡ **When removing the radiator, note the location of the rubber radiator-to-body air seals. These seals are used to prevent overheating and must remain in their original positions.**

Do Not waste usable coolant. If solution is clean, drain into a clean container for reuse.

1. Disconnect negative battery cable.
2. Drain coolant from radiator.

➡ **Whenever the high pressure line fittings are removed from the hydraulic fan drive the O-rings must be replaced.**

3. Disconnect both pressure lines at hydraulic fan drive.
4. Disconnect low pressure return hose at hydraulic fan drive.
5. Disconnect fan electrical connector (4) and set aside.

6. Remove lower, upper radiator, and coolant pressure container hoses (2, 3, 5, 6) from radiator (1).

➡ **The lower portion of the radiator is equipped with two alignment dowel pins that are seated in rubber grommets. These grommets are pressed into the lower cross member and must remain present to prevent radiator tank damage.**

7. Remove radiator retaining bolts, and carefully remove radiator (1) from vehicle.
8. Separate coolant fan from radiator (1).

To install:

➡ **Care must be taken when installing the radiator not to damage the fins of the radiator or other ancillary components. Note the location and proper installation of the radiator to charge air cooler and radiator to body rubber air seals. These must be installed correctly to prevent engine overheating and provide proper A/C efficiency.**

9. Position the radiator assembly.
10. Carefully lower the radiator tank alignment dowels into the rubber grommets in the lower crossmember and secure the radiator assembly.
11. Connect the upper and lower radiator hoses and the coolant pressure container hose, then secure.

12. Connect the coolant fan electrical connector and assure a good ECM ground to the fan assembly.

➡ **Whenever the pressure line fittings are installed at the hydraulic fan drive, the O-rings must be replaced.**

13. Connect the low pressure return hose at the hydraulic fan.
14. Connect both high pressure hoses at the hydraulic fan.

➡ **Do Not waste usable coolant. If the solution is clean and the mixture is correct, reuse original coolant.**

15. Refill the cooling system with the correct mixture to the proper level.
16. Reconnect the negative battery cable.
17. Start the engine and inspect for leaks.

THERMOSTAT

REMOVAL & INSTALLATION

3.7L & 4.7L Engines
See Figure 85.

> ※※ **WARNING**
>
> **Do not loosen the radiator draincock with the system hot and pressurized. Serious burns from the coolant can occur.**

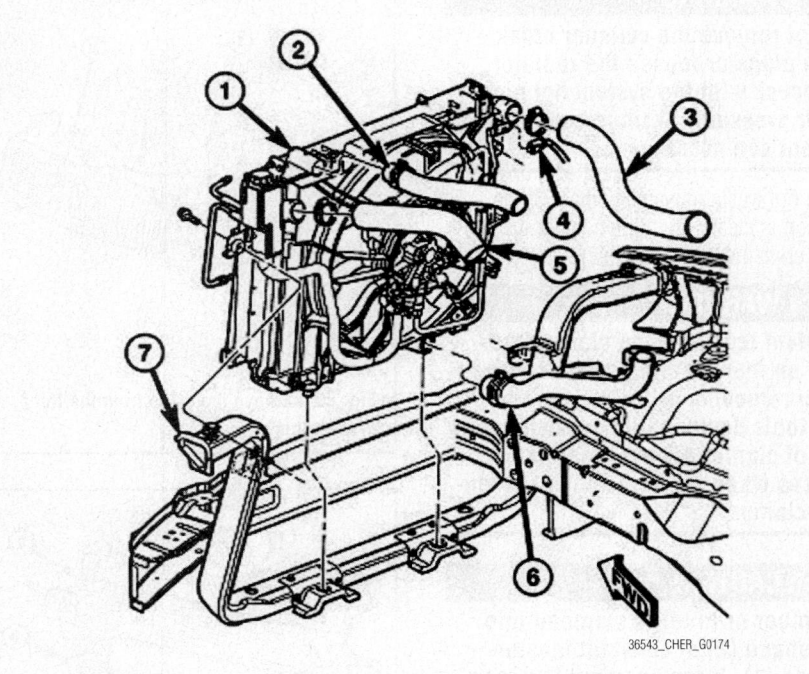

36543_CHER_G0174

Fig. 84 Disconnect fan electrical connector (4) and set aside

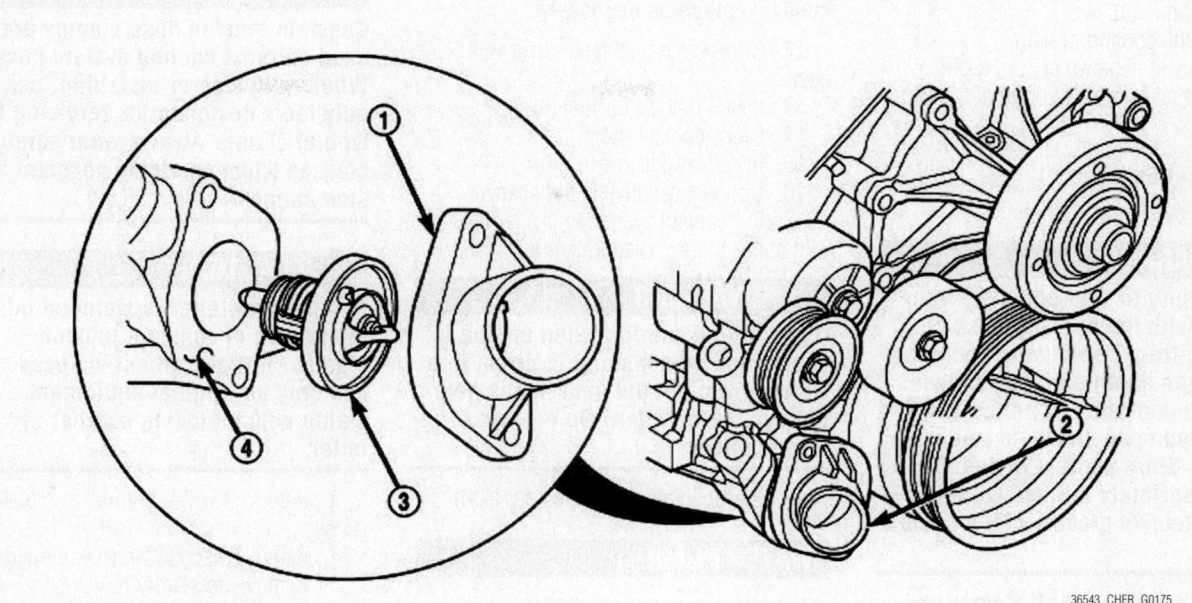

Fig. 85 Thermostat housing location

Do not waste the reusable coolant. If the solution is clean, drain the coolant into a clean container for reuse.

If the thermostat is being replaced, be sure that the replacement is the specified thermostat for the vehicle model and engine type.

1. Disconnect the negative battery cable.
2. Drain the cooling system.
3. Raise the vehicle on a hoist.
4. Remove the splash shield.
5. Remove the lower radiator hose clamp and the lower radiator hose at the thermostat housing (1).
6. Remove the thermostat housing mounting bolts, the thermostat housing (1) and the thermostat (3).

To install:

7. Clean the mating areas of the timing chain cover and thermostat housing.
8. Install the thermostat with the spring side down into the recessed machined groove on the timing chain cover.
9. Position the thermostat housing on the timing chain cover.
10. Install the two housing-to-timing chain cover bolts. Tighten the bolts to 115 inch lbs. (13 Nm).

❊❊ CAUTION

Housing must be tightened evenly and the thermostat must be centered into the recessed groove in the tim-

ing chain cover. If not, it may result in a cracked housing, damaged timing chain cover threads or coolant leaks.

11. Install the lower radiator hose on the thermostat housing.
12. Install the splash shield.
13. Lower vehicle.
14. Fill the cooling system.
15. Connect the negative battery cable to battery.
16. Start and warm the engine. Check for leaks.

5.7L & 6.1L Engines

See Figure 86.

❊❊ WARNING

Do not loosen the radiator draincock with the cooling system hot and pressurized. Serious burns from the coolant can occur.

Do not waste reusable coolant. If the solution is clean, drain the coolant into a clean container for reuse.

If the thermostat is being replaced, be sure that the replacement is the specified thermostat for the vehicle model and engine type.

1. Disconnect the negative battery cable.
2. Drain the cooling system

3. Remove the radiator hose clamp (3) and radiator hose (4) at the thermostat housing (2).
4. Remove the thermostat housing mounting bolts (1), thermostat housing (2) and thermostat.

To install:

5. Position the thermostat and housing on the front cover.
6. Install thermostat housing bolts. Tighten the bolts to 115 inch lbs. (13 Nm).

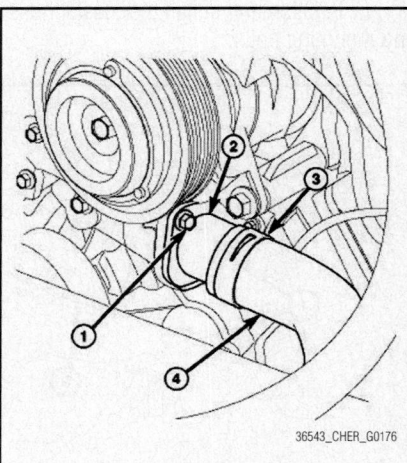

Fig. 86 Remove the radiator hose clamp (3) and radiator hose (4) at the thermostat housing (2)

7. Install the radiator hose onto the thermostat housing.

8. Fill the cooling system.

9. Connect negative battery cable.

10. Start and warm the engine. Check for leaks

3.0L Diesel Engine

See Figure 87.

> ❊❊ **WARNING**
>
> **Risk of injury to skin and eyes from scalding with hot coolant. Risk of poisoning from swallowing coolant. Do not open cooling system unless coolant temperature is below 194°F (90°C). Open cap slowly to release pressure. Store coolant in suitable and appropriately marked container. Wear protective gloves, clothes and eye wear.**

➡️**Inspect condition of all clamps and hoses, replace as necessary.**

1. Disconnect negative battery cable.

2. Remove engine cover.

3. Drain engine coolant.

4. Remove bracket for fuel line.

5. Remove coolant hoses and vent hose from thermostat housing (2).

6. Remove mounting bolts (1) from thermostat housing.

7. Pull thermostat housing (2) back and remove thermostat and sealing ring. Discard sealing ring.

8. Clean all sealing surfaces.

To install:

9. Clean all sealing surfaces.

10. Position and install thermostat with new sealing ring.

11. Position and install thermostat housing mounting bolts.

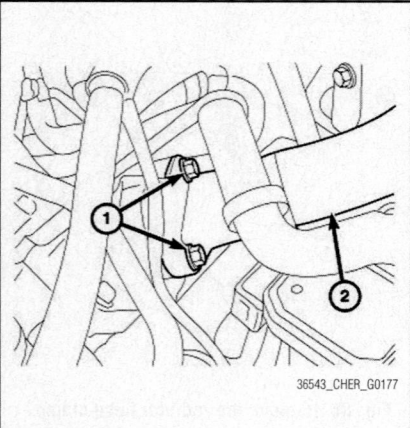

36543_CHER_G0177

Fig. 87 Remove coolant hoses and vent hose from thermostat housing (2)

➡️**Inspect condition of all clamps and hoses, replace as necessary.**

12. Connect coolant hoses and vent hose.

13. Install bracket for fuel line.

14. Close coolant drain.

15. Install engine cover.

16. Connect negative battery cable.

17. Fill coolant system to proper level with appropriate coolant mixture.

> ❊❊ **WARNING**
>
> **Use extreme caution when engine is operating. Do not stand in direct line with fan. Do not put your hands near pulleys, belts or fan. Do not wear loose clothes.**

18. Start engine and inspect for leaks.

WATER PUMP

REMOVAL & INSTALLATION

3.7L & 4.7L Engines

See Figures 88 and 89.

The water pump on 3.7L engines is bolted directly to the engine timing chain case cover (2).

1. Disconnect negative battery cable from battery.

2. Drain cooling system.

> ❊❊ **WARNING**
>
> **Constant tension hose clamps are used on most cooling system hoses. When removing or installing, use only tools designed for servicing this type of clamp. Always wear safety glasses when servicing constant tension clamps.**

> ❊❊ **CAUTION**
>
> **A number or letter is stamped into the tongue of constant tension clamps. If replacement is necessary, use only an original equipment clamp with matching number or letter.**

3. Remove two fan shroud-to-radiator screws.

4. Remove viscous fan (if equipped).

5. Remove accessory drive belt.

6. Remove accessory drive belt tensioner.

7. Remove seven water pump mounting bolts and one stud bolt.

> ❊❊ **CAUTION**
>
> **Do not pry on the water pump at the timing chain case/cover. The machined surfaces may be damaged resulting in leaks.**

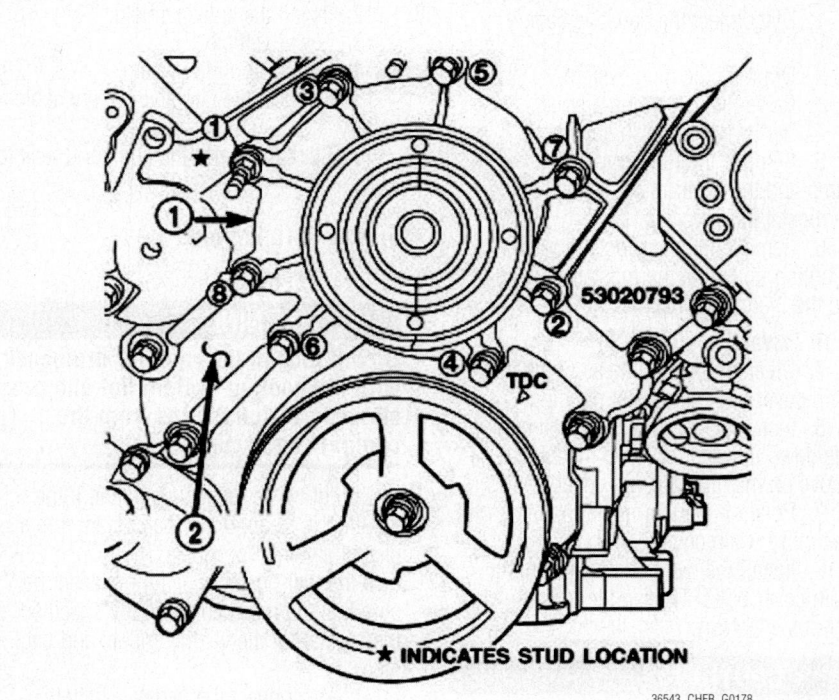

53020793

★ INDICATES STUD LOCATION

36543_CHER_G0178

Fig. 88 Water pump on 3.7L engines

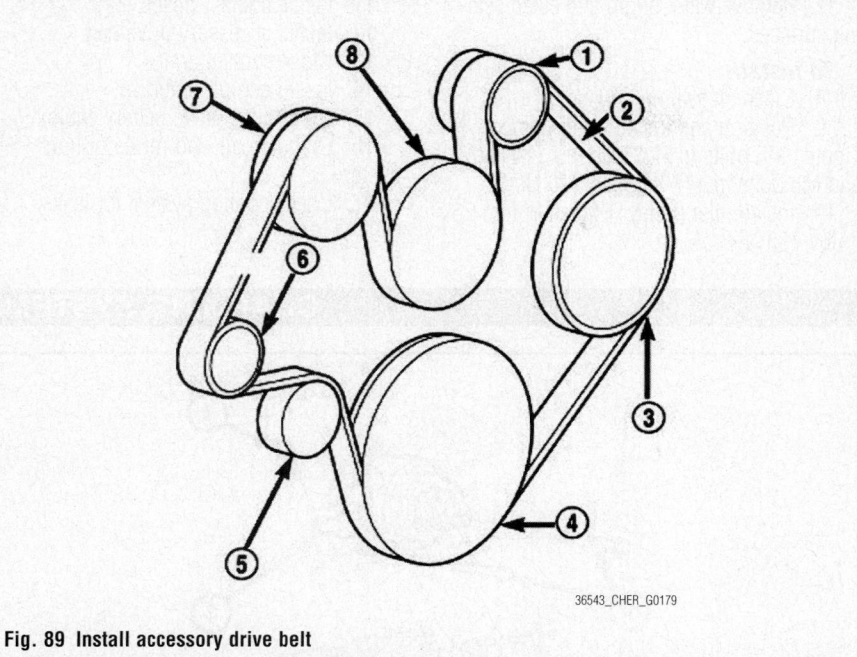

Fig. 89 Install accessory drive belt

8. Remove water pump (1) and gasket. Discard gasket.

To install:

9. Clean gasket mating surfaces.

10. Using a new gasket, position water pump and install mounting bolts and stud. Tighten water pump mounting bolts to 43 ft. lbs. (58 Nm).

11. Spin water pump to be sure that pump impeller does not rub against timing chain case/cover.

12. Install accessory drive belt tensioner.

13. Install accessory drive belt.

❈❈ CAUTION

When installing the serpentine accessory drive belt, belt must be routed correctly. If not, engine may overheat due to water pump rotating in wrong direction.

14. Be sure the upper and lower portions of the fan shroud are firmly connected. All air must flow through the radiator.

15. Install two fan shroud-to-radiator screws.

16. Install viscous fan (if originally equipped).

17. Be sure there is clearance of at least 1.0 inches (25 mm) between tips of fan blades and fan shroud.

18. Evacuate air and refill cooling system.

19. Connect negative battery cable.

20. Check the cooling system for leaks.

5.7L & 6.1L Engines

See Figure 90.

1. Disconnect negative battery cable.

2. Drain coolant.

3. Remove serpentine belt.

  a. Remove the air intake tube between intake manifold and air filter assembly.

  b. Using a suitable square drive tool, release the belt tension by rotating the tensioner (8)clockwise.

  c. Rotate belt tensioner until belt (2) can be removed from pulleys.

  d. Remove belt.

  e. Gently release tensioner.

4. Remove fan clutch assembly.

5. Remove coolant fill bottle.

6. Disconnect washer bottle wiring and hose.

7. Remove fan shroud assembly.

8. Remove A/C compressor and alternator brace.

9. Remove idler pulleys.

10. Remove belt tensioner assembly.

11. Remove upper and lower radiator hoses.

12. Remove heater hoses.

13. Remove water pump mounting bolts and remove pump (3).

To install:

14. Install water pump and mounting bolts. Tighten mounting bolts to 18 ft. lbs. (24 Nm).

15. Install heater hoses.

16. Install upper and lower radiator hoses.

17. Install belt tensioner assembly.

18. Install idler pulleys.

19. Install A/C compressor and alternator brace. Tighten bolt and nuts to 21 ft. lbs. (28 Nm).

20. Install fan shroud assembly.

21. Connect washer bottle wiring and hose.

22. Install coolant fill bottle.

23. Install fan clutch assembly.

24. Install serpentine belt.

25. Connect negative battery cable.

26. Evacuate air and refill cooling system.

27. Check cooling system for leaks.

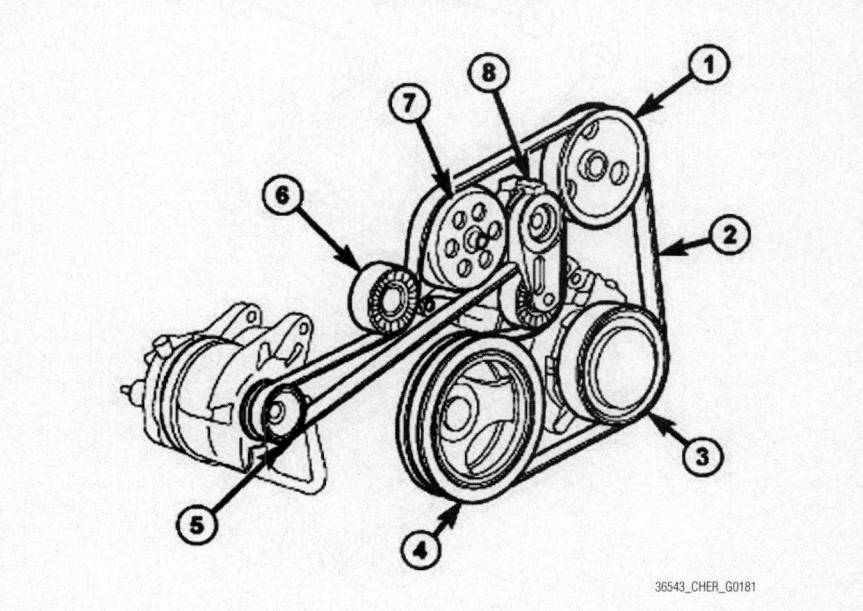

Fig. 90 Release the belt tension by rotating the tensioner (8) clockwise

3.0L Diesel Engine

1. Disconnect negative battery cable.
2. Remove engine cover.
3. Drain engine coolant.
4. Remove accessory drive belt.
5. Disconnect coolant hoses at water pump.
6. Remove idler pulley.
7. Remove water pump and clean sealing surfaces.

To install:

8. Clean all sealing surfaces.
9. Position and install water pump. Tighten M6 bolts to 124 inch lbs. (14 Nm) and M8 bolts to 177 inch lbs. (20 Nm).
10. Install idler pulley. Tighten bolt to 26 ft. lbs. (35 Nm).
11. Install coolant hoses.
12. Install accessory drive belt.
13. Close coolant drain.
14. Install engine cover.
15. Connect negative battery cable.
16. Evacuate air and refill cooling system.
17. Check cooling system for leaks.

ENGINE ELECTRICAL   CHARGING SYSTEM

ALTERNATOR

REMOVAL & INSTALLATION

3.7L & 4.7L Engines

See Figures 91 and 92.

☀☀ WARNING

Disconnect negative cable from battery before removing battery output wire (B+ wire) from alternator. Failure to do so can result in injury or damage to electrical system.

1. Disconnect negative battery cable at battery.
2. Remove alternator drive belt.
3. Unsnap plastic insulator cap (3) from B+ output terminal.
4. Remove B+ terminal mounting nut (2) at rear of alternator. Disconnect terminal from alternator.

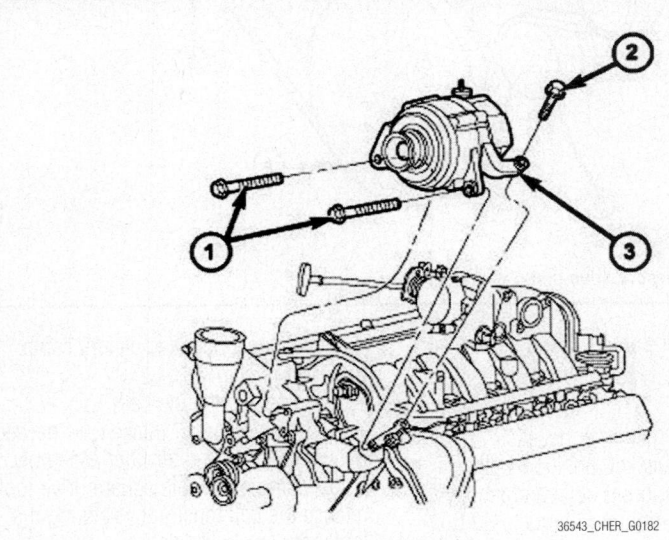

36543_CHER_G0182

Fig. 92 Position alternator (3) to engine and install 2 horizontal bolts (1) and 1 vertical bolt (2)

5. Disconnect field wire connector (4) at rear of alternator by pushing on connector tab.

To install:

6. Position alternator (3) to engine and install 2 horizontal bolts (1) and 1 vertical bolt (2).
7. Tighten all 3 bolts to 40 ft. lbs. (55 Nm).
8. Snap field wire connector into rear of alternator.
9. Install B+ terminal eyelet to alternator output stud. Tighten mounting nut to 108 inch lbs. (12 Nm).

☀☀ CAUTION

Never force a belt over a pulley rim using a screwdriver. The synthetic fiber of the belt can be damaged.

☀☀ CAUTION

When installing a serpentine accessory drive belt, the belt must be routed correctly. The water pump may be rotating in the wrong direc-

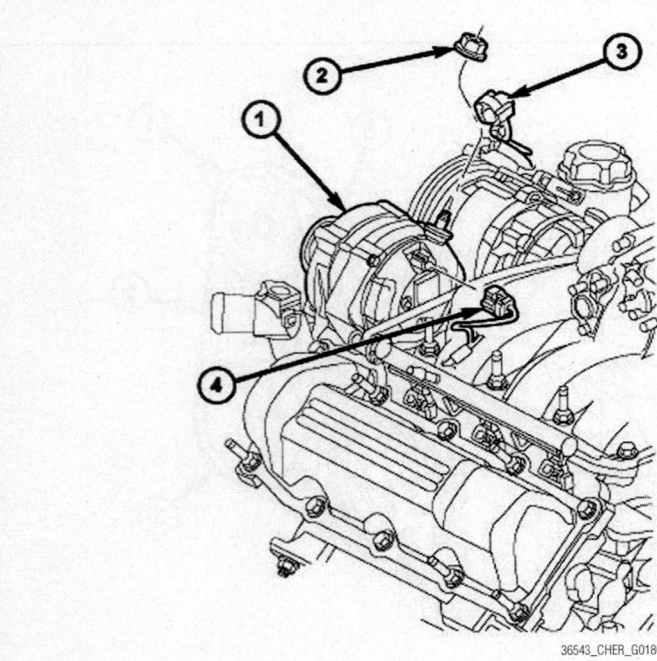

36543_CHER_G0180

Fig. 91 Unsnap plastic insulator cap (3) from B+ output terminal

tion if the belt is installed incorrectly, causing the engine to overheat.

10. Install alternator drive belt.
11. Install negative battery cable to battery.

5.7L & 6.1L Engines

See Figure 93.

✳ WARNING

Disconnect negative cable from battery before removing battery output wire (B+ wire) from alternator. Failure to do so can result in injury or damage to electrical system.

1. Disconnect negative battery cable at battery.
2. Remove alternator drive belt.
3. Unsnap plastic insulator cap from B+ output terminal.
4. Remove B+ terminal mounting nut at rear of alternator. Disconnect terminal from alternator.
5. Disconnect field wire connector (3) at rear of alternator by pushing on connector tab.
6. Remove 2 alternator mounting bolts (1).
7. Remove alternator (2) from vehicle.

To install:

8. Position alternator to engine and install 2 mounting bolts.
9. Torque bolts to 30 ft. lbs. (41 Nm).
10. Snap field wire connector into rear of alternator.

11. Install B+ terminal eyelet to alternator output stud. Tighten mounting nut to 108 inch lbs. (12 Nm).

✳ CAUTION

Never force a belt over a pulley rim using a screwdriver. The synthetic fiber of the belt can be damaged.

✳ CAUTION

When installing a serpentine accessory drive belt, the belt must be routed correctly. The water pump may be rotating in the wrong direction if the belt is installed incorrectly, causing the engine to overheat.

12. Install alternator drive belt.
13. Install negative battery cable to battery.

3.0L Diesel Engine

See Figures 94 through 96.

✳ WARNING

Disconnect negative cable from battery before removing battery output wire (B+ wire) from alternator. Failure to do so can result in injury or damage to electrical system.

1. Disconnect negative battery cable at battery.
2. Remove plastic dress-up cover at top of engine.
3. Remove coolant reservoir tank

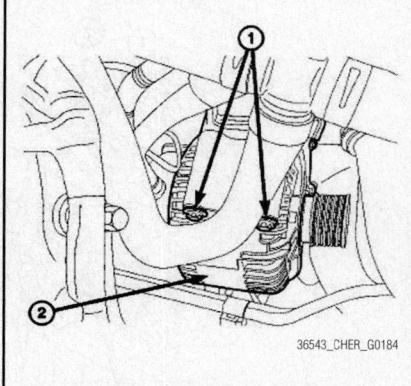
36543_CHER_G0184

Fig. 94 Remove two alternator upper mounting bolts (1)

mounting bolt and position tank toward rear of engine compartment.
4. Remove air filter cover and air filter element.
5. Remove air filter housing (one bolt).
6. Remove alternator drive belt.
7. Remove two alternator upper mounting bolts (1).
8. Raise vehicle.
9. If equipped, remove skid plate below alternator.
10. Disconnect field wire connector (5) at rear of alternator (4) by pushing on connector tab.
11. Remove two alternator lower mounting bolts (2).
12. Lower vehicle.
13. Remove throttle body-to-cylinder head support bracket (four bolts).
14. Remove throttle body (four bolts).
15. Unsnap plastic insulator cap from B+ output terminal.
16. Remove B+ terminal mounting nut (2) at top/rear of alternator and remove cable eye (1) from mounting stud (3).
17. Remove alternator from vehicle.

To install:

18. Position alternator to engine.
19. Install battery B+ cable eyelet and nut to alternator mounting stud.
20. Snap plastic insulator cap to B+ output terminal mounting stud.
21. Install two upper mounting bolts finger tight only.
22. Install throttle body (four bolts).
23. Install throttle body-to-cylinder head support bracket (four bolts).
24. Raise vehicle.
25. Install two lower mounting bolts and tighten.
26. Connect field wire connector to alternator.
27. If equipped, install skid plate below alternator.

36543_CHER_G0183

Fig. 93 Disconnect field wire connector (3) at rear of alternator by pushing on connector tab

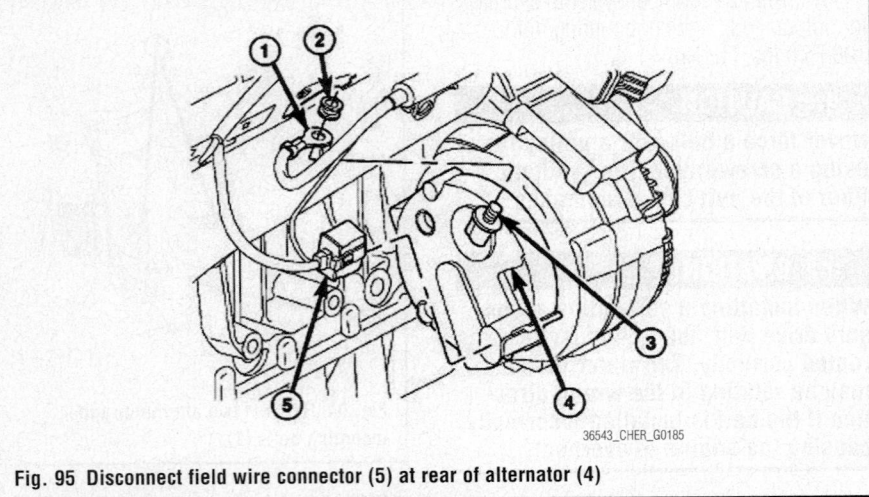

Fig. 95 Disconnect field wire connector (5) at rear of alternator (4)

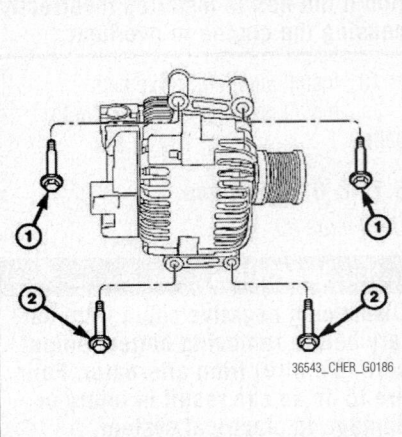

Fig. 96 Remove two alternator lower mounting bolts (2)

28. Lower vehicle.
29. Tighten two alternator upper mounting bolts.
30. Install alternator drive belt.
31. Install air filter housing (one bolt).

32. Install air filter element and air filter housing cover.
33. Install coolant reservoir tank mounting bolt and coolant tank.

34. Install plastic dress-up cover at top of engine.
35. Connect negative battery cable to battery.

ENGINE ELECTRICAL

FIRING ORDER

The firing order for the 3.7L V6 engine is 1-6-5-4-3-2.
The firing order for the 4.7L, 5.7 L and 6.1L V8 engines is 1-8-4-3-6-5-7-2.

IGNITION COIL

REMOVAL & INSTALLATION

3.7L Engine

See Figure 97.

➡An ignition coil (2) with a spark plug wire (1) attached is used for two cylinders. The three coils fits into machined holes in the cylinder head for cylinders 1, 3, and 5. A mounting stud/nut secures each coil to the top of the intake manifold. The bottom of the coil is equipped with a rubber boot (4) to seal the spark plug (5) to the coil. Inside each rubber boot is a spring. The spring is used for a mechanical contact between the coil and the top of the spark plug. These rubber boots and springs are a permanent part of the coil and are not serviced separately. An O-ring is used to seal the coil at the opening into the cylinder head.

1. Depending on which coil is being removed, the throttle body air intake tube or intake box may need to be removed to gain access to coil.

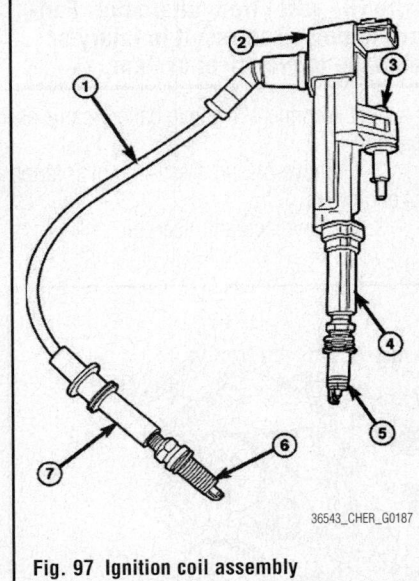

Fig. 97 Ignition coil assembly

2. Disconnect electrical connector from coil by pushing downward on release lock on top of connector and pull connector from coil.
3. Disconnect spark plug wire from coil (1).
4. Clean area at base of coil with compressed air before removal.
5. Remove coil mounting bolt.
6. Carefully pull up coil from cylinder head opening with a slight twisting action.
7. Remove coil from vehicle.

IGNITION SYSTEM

To install:

8. Using compressed air, blow out any dirt or contaminants from around top of spark plug.
9. Check the condition of the coil rubber boot. To aid in coil installation, apply silicone based grease such as Mopar® Dielectric Grease J8126688 into the spark plug end of the rubber boot and to the top of the spark plug.
10. Position the ignition coil assembly into the cylinder head opening. Using a twisting action, push the ignition coil assembly onto the spark plug.
11. Install coil mounting bolt. Tighten to 70 inch lbs. (8 Nm).
12. Connect the electrical connector to the ignition coil assembly by snapping into position.
13. Install the spark plug wires.
14. If necessary, install the throttle body air intake tube, or intake air box.

4.7L Engine

See Figures 98 and 99.

An individual ignition coil (1) is used for each pair of spark plugs. Each coil attaches directly to the top of the eight upper bank of spark plugs. Secondary cables (3) connect each coil to the eight lower bank of spark plugs. The coils themselves fit into machined holes in the cylinder head. Each coil also has its own individual electrical connector (2).

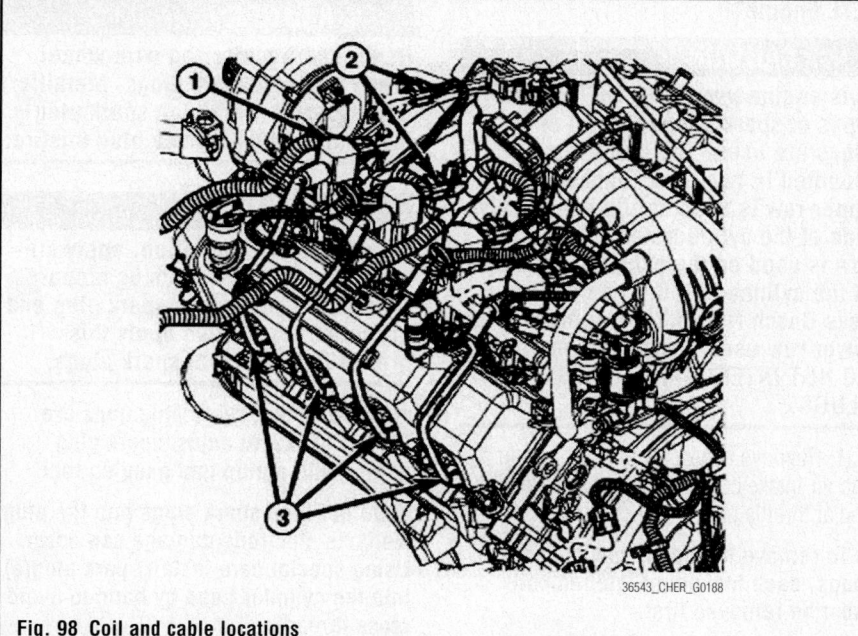

Fig. 98 Coil and cable locations

➡ **The bolt used to mount the ignition coil assembly is the same bolt used to mount the intake manifold. If replacing either one or all eight coils, check and re-torque all eight bolts.**

A mounting bolt (3) secures each coil assembly to the top of the intake manifold. The bottom of the coil assembly is equipped with a rubber boot (4) to seal the spark plug (5) to the coil. Inside each rubber boot is a spring. The spring is used for a mechanical contact between the coil and the top of the upper bank of spark plugs. These rubber boots and springs are a permanent part of the coil assembly and are not serviced separately. The rubber boot (4) is also used to seal the coil at the opening into the cylinder head.

1. Depending on which coil assembly is being removed, the throttle body air intake tube or intake box may need to be removed, to gain access to the coil.
2. Disconnect the electrical connector (2) from the coil assembly by pushing downward on the release lock on the top of the connector and pull connector from the coil.
3. Disconnect the secondary cable (3) at the coil assembly.
4. Clean the area at the base of the coil assembly with compressed air before removal.
5. Remove the coil assembly mounting bolt (3).
6. Carefully pull up the coil assembly (2) from the cylinder head opening with a slight twisting action. This helps to disengage the rubber boot (4) from the spark plug (5).
7. Remove the coil assembly from the engine.

To install:
8. Using compressed air, blow out any dirt or contaminants from around the top of the spark plug.
9. Check the condition of the coil rubber boot. To aid in coil installation, apply silicone based grease such as Mopar® Dielectric Grease J8126688 into the spark plug end of the rubber boot and to the top of the spark plug.
10. Position the ignition coil assembly into the cylinder head opening. Using a twisting action, push the ignition coil assembly onto the spark plug.

➡ **The bolt used to mount the ignition coil assembly is also the same bolt**

used to mount the intake manifold. If replacing either one or all eight coils, check and re-torque all eight bolts.

11. Tighten the coil assembly mounting bolt to 9 ft. lbs. (12 Nm).
12. Connect the electrical connector to the coil assembly by snapping into position.
13. Connect the secondary cable to the coil assembly.
14. If necessary, install the throttle body air intake tube or intake air box to the top of the engine.

5.7L & 6.1L Engines

See Figures 99 and 100.

1. Disconnect the electrical connector (1) from the coil (3).
2. Clean the area at the base of the coil with compressed air before removal.

➡ **The ignition coil mounting bolts are retained in the ignition coil.**

3. Remove the two ignition coil mounting bolts (2).
4. Carefully pull up the ignition coil (1) from the valve cover.
5. Remove ignition coil (1) from vehicle.

To install:
6. Using compressed air, blow out any dirt or contaminants from around top of spark plug.

➡ **Use dielectric grease on each of the spark plug boots before installing the coil.**

7. Position ignition coil into valve cover and push onto spark plugs.
8. Install 2 ignition coil mounting bolts. Tighten to 62 inch lbs. (7 Nm).
9. Connect electrical connector to the ignition coil by snapping into position.

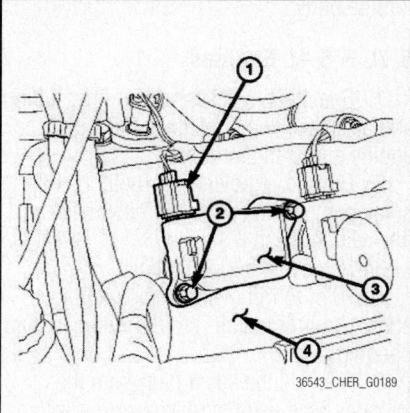

Fig. 99 Disconnect the electrical connector (1) from the coil (3)

Fig. 100 Pull up the ignition coil (1) from the valve cover

IGNITION TIMING

ADJUSTMENT

Ignition timing is not adjustable on any of the available engines.

SPARK PLUGS

REMOVAL & INSTALLATION

3.7L Engine

1. Remove the necessary air filter tubing and air intake components at the top of the engine at the throttle body.

➡The three spark plugs located on the left bank of the engine are under three individual ignition coils. Each individual ignition coil must be removed to gain access to each spark plug located on the left bank of the engine.

2. Prior to removing the ignition coil, spray compressed air around the coil base at the cylinder head.
3. Remove the ignition coil.
4. Check the condition of ignition coil O-ring and replace as necessary.
5. Prior to removing the spark plug, spray compressed air into the cylinder head opening. This will help prevent foreign material from entering combustion chamber.
6. Remove the spark plug from the cylinder head using a quality thin wall socket with a rubber or foam insert.
7. Inspect the spark plug condition.

To install:

8. Check and adjust the spark plug gap with a gap gauging tool.

✷✷ CAUTION

Special care should be taken when installing spark plugs into the cylinder head spark plug wells. Be sure the plugs do not drop into the plug wells as electrodes can be damaged.

9. Start the spark plug into the cylinder head by hand to avoid cross threading.
10. Tighten the spark plugs to 20 ft. lbs. (27 Nm).
11. Before installing the ignition coil, check the condition of the coil O-ring and replace as necessary. Apply silicone based grease such as Mopar® Dielectric Grease J8126688 into the spark plug end of the rubber boot, coil O-rings and to the top of spark plugs.
12. Install the ignition coil.
13. Install the necessary air filter tubing and air intake components at the top of the engine at the throttle body.

4.7L Engine

✷✷ CAUTION

This engine uses TWO DIFFERENT types of spark plugs. A total of 16 plugs are used. The plugs are mounted in two rows (banks). The upper row is used on the intake valve side of the cylinder head. The lower row is used on the exhaust valve side of the cylinder head. The upper row uses Bosch Nickel Yttrium plugs. The lower row uses Bosch Iridium plugs. DO NOT INTERCHANGE THESE PLUGS.

1. Remove necessary air filter tubing and air intake components at top of engine and at throttle body.

➡To remove the upper row of spark plugs, each individual ignition coil must be removed first.

2. Remove the ignition coil(s).
3. Prior to removing the spark plug(s), spray compressed air into cylinder head opening. This will help prevent foreign material from entering combustion chamber.

✷✷ CAUTION

Due to tight clearances between UPPER row of plugs and cylinder head, a conventional deep, thick-wall spark plug socket will not fit. Use a deep, THIN-WALL ⅝ inches spark plug socket for plug removal and installation.

✷✷ CAUTION

Do not attempt to clean any of the spark plugs. Replace only.

4. Remove the spark plug(s) and inspect their condition.

To install:

✷✷ CAUTION

This engine uses TWO DIFFERENT types of spark plugs. A total of 16 plugs are used. The plugs are mounted in two rows (banks). The upper row is used on the intake valve side of the cylinder head. The lower row is used on the exhaust valve side of the cylinder head. The upper row uses Bosch Nickel Yttrium plugs. The lower row uses Bosch Iridium plugs. DO NOT INTERCHANGE THESE PLUGS.

✷✷ CAUTION

Never use a motorized wire wheel brush to clean spark plugs. Metallic deposits will remain on spark plug insulator and will cause plug misfire.

✷✷ CAUTION

To aid in coil installation, apply silicone based grease such as Mopar® Dielectric Grease into spark plug end of rubber boots. Also apply this grease to the tops of spark plugs.

➡Two different spark plug gaps are used. Check and adjust spark plug gap(s) with a plug gap gauging tool.

➡Do not drop spark plugs into the plug wells as electrode damage can occur. Using special care install spark plug(s) into the cylinder head by hand to avoid cross threading.

➡Always tighten spark plugs to the specified torque. Certain engines use torque sensitive spark plugs. Over tightening can cause distortion resulting in a change to the spark plug gap, or a cracked porcelain insulator. s

✷✷ CAUTION

Due to tight clearances between upper row of plugs and cylinder head, a conventional deep, thick-wall spark plug socket will not fit. Use a deep, THIN-WALL ⅝ inches spark plug socket for plug removal and installation.

5. Tighten spark plug(s) to the specified torque.
6. Install ignition coil(s).
7. Install necessary air filter tubing and air intake components to top of engine and to throttle body.

5.7L & 6.1L Engines

1. Remove the necessary air filter tubing and air intake components at the top of the engine and at the throttle body.
2. Prior to removing the ignition coil, spray compressed air around coil base at the cylinder head.
3. Remove the ignition coil.
4. Prior to removing the spark plug, spray compressed air into the cylinder head opening.
5. Remove the spark plug from the cylinder head using a quality socket with a rubber or foam insert.
6. Inspect spark plug condition.

To install:

> ※※ **CAUTION**
>
> **Never use a motorized wire wheel brush to clean spark plugs. Metallic deposits will remain on spark plug insulator and will cause plug misfire.**

> ※※ **CAUTION**
>
> **Do not attempt to clean any of the spark plugs. Replace only.**

7. To aid in the coil installation, apply silicone based grease such as Mopar® Dielectric Grease into the spark plug end of the ignition coil rubber boots. Also apply this grease to the tops of spark plugs.

8. Check and adjust the spark plug gap with a gap gauging tool.

9. Start the spark plug into the cylinder head by hand to avoid cross threading. Special care should be taken when installing spark plugs into the cylinder head spark plug wells. Be sure the plugs do not drop into the plug wells as electrodes can be damaged.

➡ **Always tighten spark plugs to the specified torque. Certain engines use torque sensitive spark plugs. It is a good practice to always tighten spark plugs to a specific torque. Over tightening can cause distortion resulting in a change in the spark plug gap, or a cracked porcelain insulator.**

10. Install the ignition coil.

11. Install necessary air filter tubing and air intake components to the top of the engine and to the throttle body.

ENGINE ELECTRICAL

STARTER

REMOVAL & INSTALLATION

3.7L & 4.7L Engines

See Figure 101.

1. Disconnect and isolate negative battery cable.

2. Raise and support vehicle.

3. If equipped with 4WD, remove front drive shaft.

4. If equipped with 4WD and certain transmissions, a support bracket is used between front axle and side of transmission. Remove 2 support bracket bolts at transmission. Pry support bracket slightly to gain access to lower starter mounting bolt.

5. Remove two bolts (3).

6. Move starter motor (4) towards front of vehicle far enough for nose of starter pinion housing to clear housing. Always support starter motor during this process, do not let starter motor hang from wire harness.

7. Tilt nose downwards and lower starter motor far enough to access and remove nut (2) that secures battery

positive cable wire harness connector eyelet (1) to solenoid battery terminal stud. Do not let starter motor hang from wire harness.

8. Remove battery positive cable wire harness connector eyelet (5) from solenoid battery terminal stud.

9. Disconnect battery positive cable wire harness connector from solenoid terminal connector receptacle.

10. Remove starter motor.

To install:

11. Connect solenoid wire to starter motor (snaps on).

12. Position battery cable to solenoid stud. Install and tighten battery cable eyelet nut. Torque nut to 19 ft. lbs. (25 Nm). Do not allow starter motor to hang from wire harness.

13. Position starter motor to transmission.

14. Slide the automatic transmission cooler tube bracket into position.

15. Install and tighten both bolts. Torque bolts to 50 ft. lbs. (68 Nm).

16. If equipped with 4WD and certain transmissions, a support bracket is used

STARTING SYSTEM

between front axle and side of transmission. Install 2 support bracket bolts at transmission.

17. If equipped with 4WD, install front drive shaft.

18. Lower vehicle.

19. Connect negative battery cable.

5.7L & 6.1L Engines

See Figure 102.

1. Disconnect and isolate negative battery cable.

2. Raise and support vehicle.

3. If equipped with 4WD and certain transmissions, a support bracket is used between front axle and side of transmission. Remove 2 support bracket bolts at transmission. Pry support bracket slightly to gain access to lower starter mounting bolt.

4. Remove two mounting bolts (2).

5. Move starter motor towards front of vehicle far enough for nose of starter pinion housing to clear housing. Always support starter motor (1) during this process, do not let starter motor hang from wire harness.

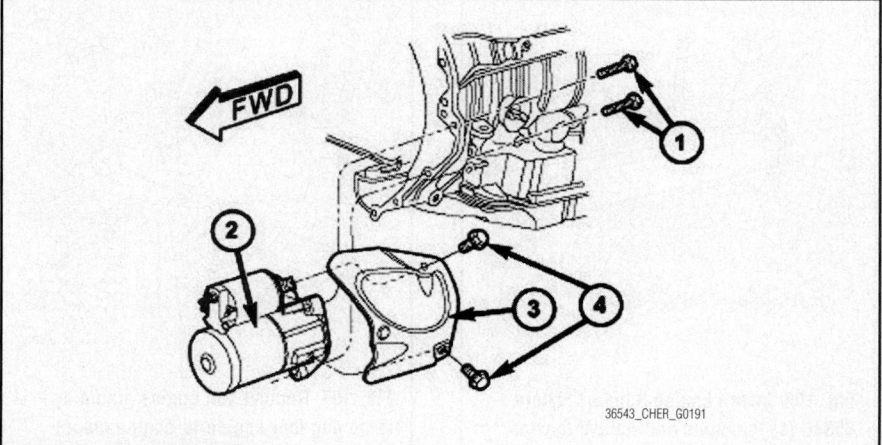

36543_CHER_G0191

Fig. 101 Remove two bolts (3)

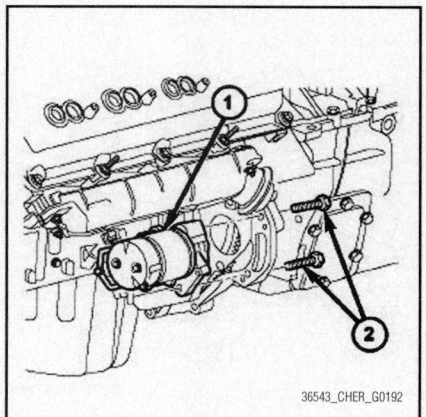

36543_CHER_G0192

Fig. 102 Remove two mounting bolts (2)

6. Tilt nose downwards and lower starter motor far enough to access and remove nut that secures battery positive cable wire harness connector eyelet to solenoid battery terminal stud. Do not let starter motor hang from wire harness.

7. Remove battery positive cable wire harness connector eyelet from solenoid battery terminal stud.

8. Disconnect battery positive cable wire harness connector from solenoid terminal connector receptacle.

9. Remove starter motor.

To install:

10. Connect solenoid wire to starter motor (snaps on).

11. Position battery cable to solenoid stud. Install and tighten battery cable eyelet nut. Torque nut to 19 ft. lbs. (25 Nm). Do not allow starter motor to hang from wire harness.

12. Position starter motor to engine.

13. Slide the automatic transmission cooler tube bracket into position.

14. Install and tighten both mounting bolts. Torque bolts to 50 ft. lbs. (68 Nm).

15. Lower vehicle.

16. Connect negative battery cable.

3.0L Diesel Engine

See Figures 103 through 107.

1. Disconnect and isolate negative battery cable.

2. Remove positive battery cable at battery.

3. Remove battery.

4. Remove battery tray (three bolts—one nut).

5. Remove plastic dress-up cover at top of engine.

6. Raise vehicle.

7. If equipped, remove skid plate below starter.

8. Remove starter mounting bolts (2). These are located at rear of transmission bellhousing (3).

9. Lower vehicle.

10. Remove Power Distribution Center and Fuse/Relay Center (1) from left inner fender. Tie them back and reposition them over the left valve cover. It may be necessary to remove both B+ cables at both Centers.

11. Install Engine Support Fixture 8534B (1) to engine and relieve tension from left engine mount.

12. Remove frame-to-engine mount nut (4) and through-bolt (5).

13. Remove left engine mount by removing four engine-to-engine mount bolts (2). Use a long extension (3) and swivel socket.

14. Remove engine mount (1) from vehicle.

15. Remove battery cable nut at starter solenoid and disconnect cable eyelet from starter.

16. Disconnect solenoid wire at solenoid.

17. Remove starter from vehicle.

To install:

18. While working from engine compartment, position starter to transmission bellhousing.

19. Connect solenoid wire to solenoid.

20. Position battery cable eyelet to starter. Install battery cable nut.

21. Position left engine mount to engine and install four bolts.

22. Tighten four engine-to-engine mount bolts using a long extension and swivel socket.

23. Install and tighten frame-to-engine mount nut and through-bolt.

24. Remove Engine Support Fixture 8534B from engine.

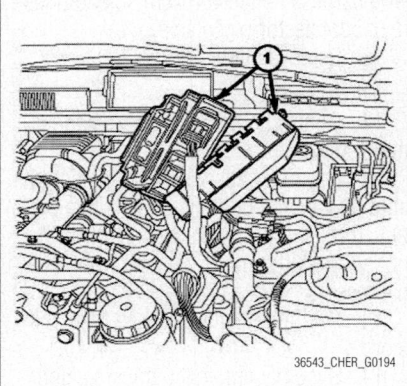

Fig. 104 Remove Power Distribution Center and Fuse/Relay Center (1) from left inner fender

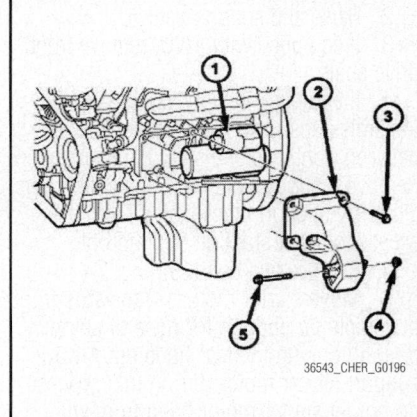

Fig. 106 Remove frame-to-engine mount nut (4) and through-bolt (5)

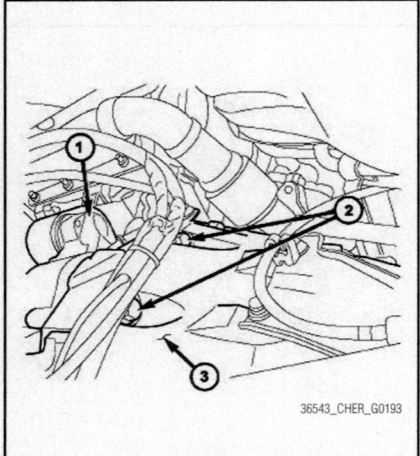

Fig. 103 Remove starter mounting bolts (2)

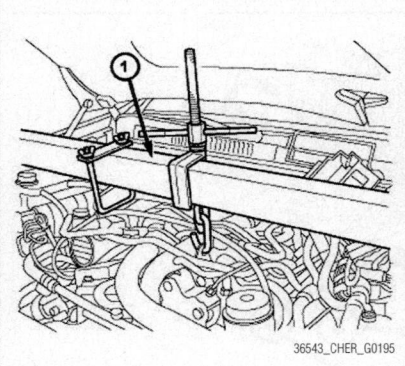

Fig. 105 Install Engine Support Fixture 8534B (1) to engine and relieve tension from left engine mount

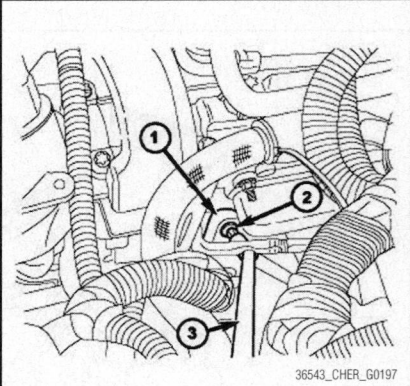

Fig. 107 Remove left engine mount by removing four engine-to-engine mount bolts (2)

25. Install Power Distribution Center and Fuse/Relay Center to left inner fender. Connect both B+ cables to both Centers.

26. Raise vehicle.

27. Install and tighten starter mounting bolts.

28. If equipped, install skid plate below starter.

29. Lower vehicle.

30. Install plastic dress-up cover to top of engine.

31. Install battery tray (three bolts—one nut).

32. Install battery.

33. Install positive battery cable to battery.

34. Install negative battery cable to battery.

ENGINE MECHANICAL

ACCESSORY DRIVE BELTS

ACCESSORY BELT ROUTING

3.7L & 4.7L Engines
See Figure 108.

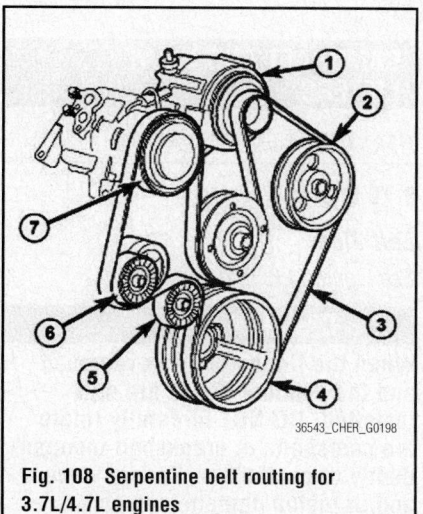

Fig. 108 Serpentine belt routing for 3.7L/4.7L engines

36543_CHER_G0198

5.7L & 6.1L Engines
See Figure 109.

3.0L Diesel Engine
See Figure 110.

INSPECTION

Inspect the drive belt for signs of glazing or cracking. A glazed belt will be perfectly smooth from slippage, while a good belt will have a slight texture of fabric visible. Cracks will usually start at the inner edge of the belt and run outward. All worn or damaged drive belts should be replaced immediately.

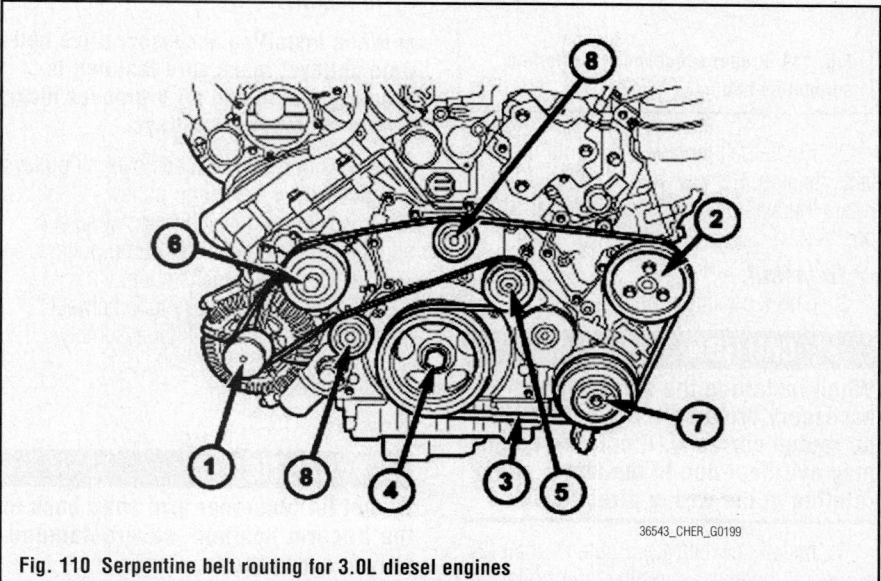

Fig. 110 Serpentine belt routing for 3.0L diesel engines

36543_CHER_G0199

ADJUSTMENT

It is not necessary to adjust belt tension on the 3.0L diesel engine or on the 3.7L, 4.7L, 5.7L, or 6.1L engines. These engines are equipped with an automatic belt tensioner. The tensioner maintains correct belt tension at all times; consequently, do not attempt to use a belt tension gauge on these engines.

REMOVAL & INSTALLATION

3.7L & 4.7L Engines
See Figures 108, 111 and 112.

✳✳ CAUTION

Do not let tensioner arm snap back to the freearm position, severe damage may occur to the tensioner.

1. Disconnect negative battery cable from battery.

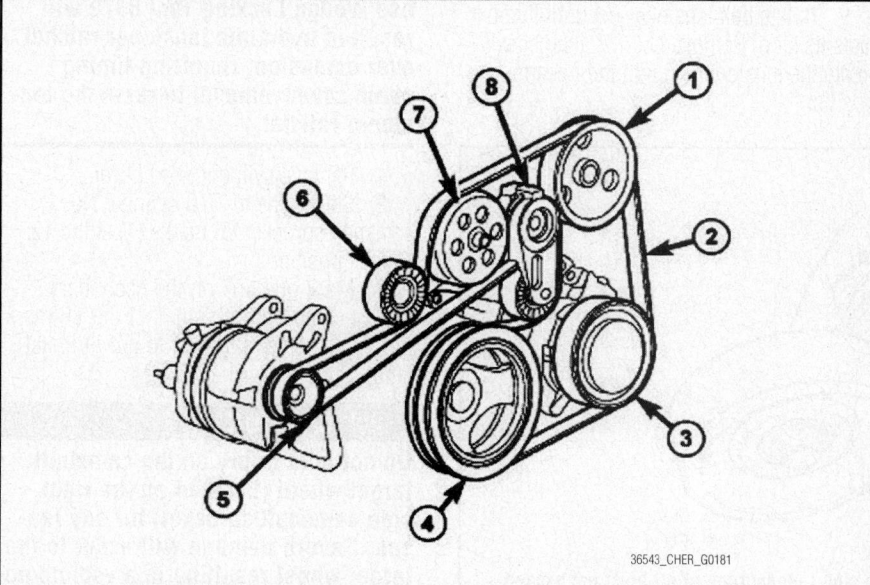

Fig. 109 Serpentine belt routing for 5.7L/6.1L engines

36543_CHER_G0181

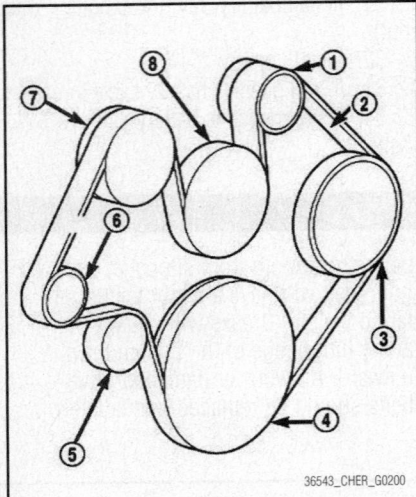

Fig. 111 Proper sequence for installing serpentine belt

2. Rotate belt tensioner (6) until it contacts its stop. Remove belt (3), then slowly rotate the tensioner (6) into the freearm position.

To install:

3. Check condition of all pulleys.

✳✳ CAUTION

When installing the serpentine accessory drive belt, the belt MUST be routed correctly. If not, the engine may overheat due to the water pump rotating in the wrong direction.

4. Install new belt (2). Route the belt (2) around all pulleys except the idler pulley (5). Rotate the tensioner arm (6) until it contacts its stop position. Route the belt (2) around the idler (5) and slowly let the tensioner (6) rotate into the belt. Make sure the belt (2) is seated onto all pulleys.

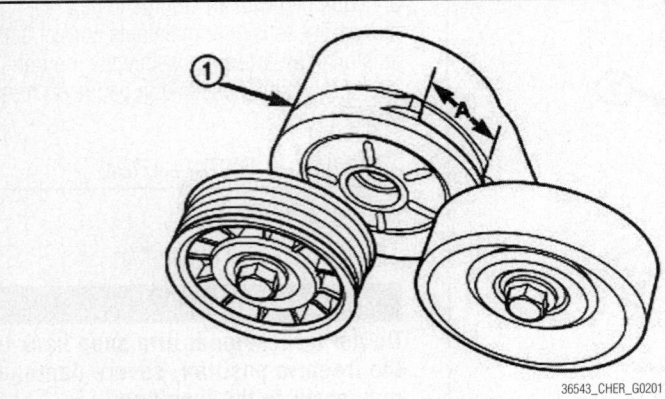

Fig. 112 The gap between the tang and the housing stop (measurement A) must not exceed .94 inches (4 mm)

5. With the drive belt (2) installed, inspect the belt wear indicator. The gap between the tang and the housing stop (measurement A) must not exceed .94 inches (4 mm).

5.7L & 6.1L Engines

See Figure 90.

1. Remove the air intake tube between intake manifold and air filter assembly.
2. Using a suitable square drive tool, release the belt tension by rotating the tensioner (8) clockwise. Rotate belt tensioner (8) until belt (2) can be removed from pulleys .
3. Remove belt (2).
4. Gently release tensioner (8).

To install:

➡**When installing accessory drive belt onto pulleys, make sure that belt is properly routed and all V-grooves make proper contact with pulleys.**

5. Position the drive belt over all pulleys except for the water pump pulley.
6. Rotate tensioner (8) clockwise and slip the belt over the water pump pulley.
7. Gently release tensioner.
8. Install the air intake tube between intake manifold and air filter assembly.

3.0L Diesel Engine

See Figure 110.

✳✳ CAUTION

Do not let tensioner arm snap back to the freearm position, severe damage may occur to the tensioner.

1. Disconnect negative battery cable.
2. Rotate belt tensioner (5) until it contacts its stop. Remove belt (3), then slowly rotate the tensioner (5) into the freearm position.

To install:

3. Check condition of all pulleys.

✳✳ CAUTION

When installing the accessory drive belt, the belt MUST be routed correctly. If not, the engine may overheat due to the water pump rotating in the wrong direction.

4. Install new belt. Route the belt around all pulleys except the idler pulley. Rotate the tensioner arm until it contacts its stop position. Route the belt around the idler and slowly let the tensioner rotate into the belt. Make sure the belt is seated onto all pulleys.

CAMSHAFT AND VALVE LIFTERS

REMOVAL & INSTALLATION

3.7L Engine

Left Side

See Figures 113 through 116.

✳✳ CAUTION

When the timing chain is removed and the cylinder heads are still installed, DO NOT forcefully rotate the camshafts or crankshaft independently of each other. Severe valve and/or piston damage can occur.

✳✳ CAUTION

When removing the cam sprocket, timing chains or camshaft, Failure to use Wedge Locking Tool 8379 will result in hydraulic tensioner ratchet over extension, requiring timing chain cover removal to reset the tensioner ratchet.

1. Remove cylinder head cover.
2. Set engine to TDC cylinder No. 1, camshaft sprocket V6 marks (1) at the 12 o'clock position.
3. Mark one link on the secondary timing chain on both sides of the V6 mark on the camshaft sprocket to aid in installation.

✳✳ CAUTION

Do not hold or pry on the camshaft target wheel (Located on the right side camshaft sprocket) for any reason, Severe damage will occur to the target wheel resulting in a vehicle no start condition.

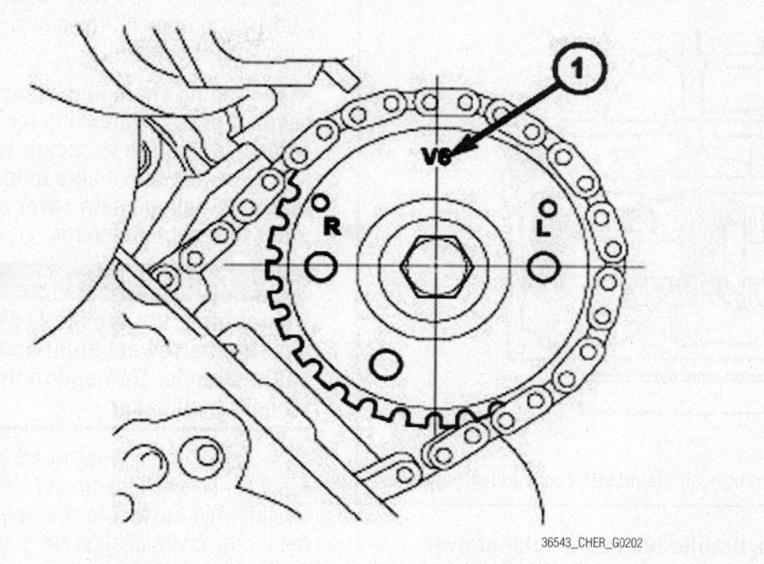

Fig. 113 Set engine to TDC cylinder No. 1, camshaft sprocket V6 marks (1) at the 12 o'clock position

4. Loosen but DO NOT remove the camshaft sprocket retaining bolt. Leave the bolt snug against the sprocket.

➡ **The timing chain tensioners must be secured prior to removing the camshaft sprockets. Failure to secure tensioners will allow the tensioners to extend, requiring timing chain cover removal in order to reset tensioners.**

※※ CAUTION

Do not force the wedge past the narrowest point between the chain strands. Damage to the tensioners may occur.

5. Position Wedge Locking Tool 8379 (1) between the timing chain strands, tap the tool to securely wedge the timing chain against the tensioner arm and guide.

6. Hold the camshaft with the Spanner Wrench 6958 and Adapter Pins 8346 while removing the camshaft sprocket bolt.

7. Using Camshaft Holder 8428 (2), remove the sprocket and gently allow the camshaft to rotate 5° clockwise until the camshaft is in the neutral position (no valve load).

8. Starting at the outside working inward, loosen the camshaft bearing cap retaining bolts 1/2 turn at a time. Repeat until all load is off the bearing caps.

※※ CAUTION

Do not stamp or strike the camshaft bearing caps. Severe damage will occur to the bearing caps.

➡ **When the camshaft is removed the rocker arms may slide downward, mark the rocker arms before removing camshaft.**

9. Remove the camshaft bearing caps and the camshaft.

To install:

10. Lubricate the camshaft journals with clean engine oil.

➡ **Position the left side camshaft so that the camshaft sprocket dowel is near the 1 o'clock position, This will place the camshaft at the neutral position easing the installation of the camshaft bearing caps.**

11. Position the camshaft into the cylinder head.

12. Install the camshaft bearing caps, hand tighten the retaining bolts.

➡ **Caps should be installed so that the stamped numbers on the caps are in numerical order, (1 through 4) from the front to the rear of the engine. All caps should be installed so that the stamped arrows on the caps point toward the front of the engine.**

13. Working in ½ turn increments, tighten the bearing cap retaining bolts starting with the middle cap working outward.

14. Tighten the camshaft bearing cap retaining bolts to 100 inch lbs. (11 Nm).

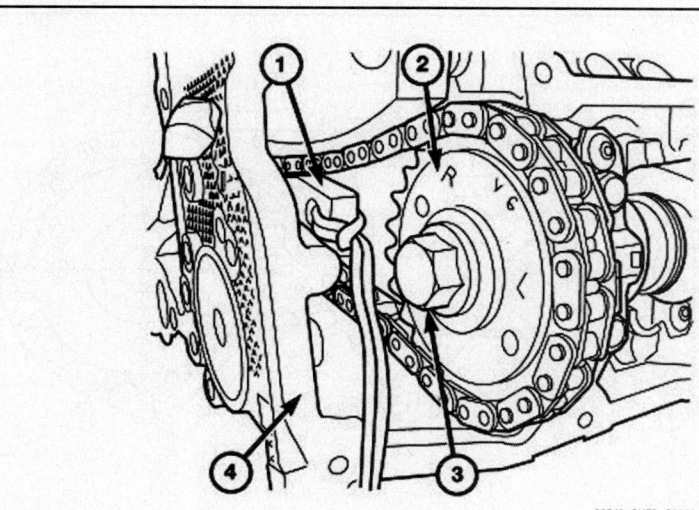

Fig. 114 Position Wedge Locking Tool 8379 (1) between the timing chain strands

Fig. 115 Using Camshaft Holder 8428 (2)

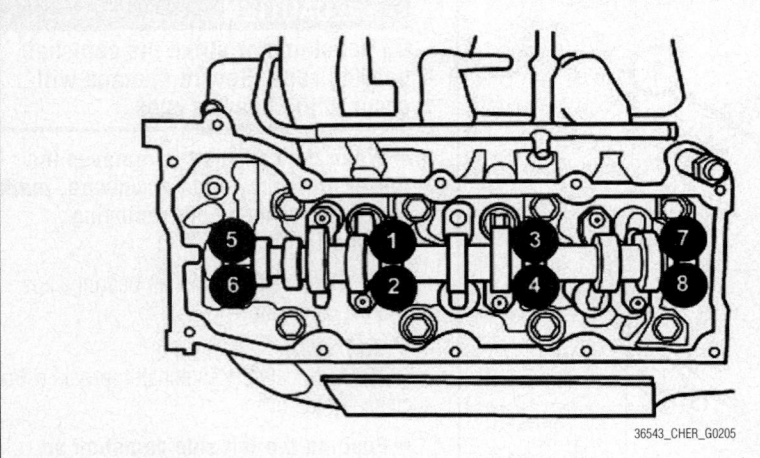

Fig. 116 Tighten the bearing cap retaining bolts starting with the middle cap working outward

15. Position the camshaft drive gear into the timing chain aligning the V6 mark between the two marked chain links (Two links marked during removal).

16. Using the Camshaft Holder 8428A, rotate the camshaft until the camshaft sprocket dowel is aligned with the slot in the camshaft sprocket. Install the sprocket onto the camshaft.

✳✳ CAUTION

Remove excess oil from the camshaft sprocket bolt. Failure to do so can cause bolt over-torque resulting in bolt failure.

17. Remove excess oil from bolt, then install the camshaft sprocket retaining bolt and hand tighten.

18. Remove the Wedge Locking Tool 8379.

19. Using Spanner Wrench 6958 with adapter pins 8346, tighten the camshaft sprocket retaining bolt to 90 ft. lbs. (122 Nm).

20. Install the cylinder head cover.

Right Side

See Figures 114, 116 through 118.

✳✳ CAUTION

When the timing chain is removed and the cylinder heads are still installed, DO NOT forcefully rotate the camshafts or crankshaft independently of each other. Severe valve and/or piston damage can occur.

✳✳ CAUTION

When removing the cam sprocket, timing chains or camshaft, failure to use special tool 8379 will result in

hydraulic tensioner ratchet over extension, requiring timing chain cover removal to re-set the tensioner ratchet.

1. Remove the cylinder head cover.
2. Set engine to TDC cylinder No. 1, camshaft sprocket V6 marks at the 12 o'clock position (1).
3. Mark one link on the secondary timing chain on both sides of the V6 mark on the camshaft sprocket to aid in installation.

✳✳ CAUTION

Do not hold or pry on the camshaft target wheel for any reason, Severe damage will occur to the target wheel. A damaged target wheel could cause a vehicle no start condition.

4. Loosen but DO NOT remove the camshaft sprocket retaining bolt. Leave bolt snug against sprocket.

➡ The timing chain tensioners must be secured prior to removing the camshaft sprockets. Failure to secure tensioners will allow the tensioners to extend, requiring timing chain cover removal in order to reset tensioners.

✳✳ CAUTION

Do not force the Wedge Locking Tool past the narrowest point between the chain strands. Damage to the tensioners may occur.

5. Position the Wedge Locking Tool 8379 (1) between the timing chain strands. Tap the tool to securely wedge the timing chain against the tensioner arm and guide.

6. Remove the camshaft position sensor.

7. Hold the camshaft with Spanner Wrench 8428 (2), while removing the camshaft sprocket bolt and sprocket.

8. Starting at the outside working inward, loosen the camshaft bearing cap retaining bolts ½ turn at a time. Repeat until all load is off the bearing caps.

✳✳ CAUTION

Do not stamp or strike the camshaft bearing caps. Severe damage will occur to the bearing caps.

➡ When the camshaft is removed the rocker arms may slide downward, mark the rocker arms before removing camshaft.

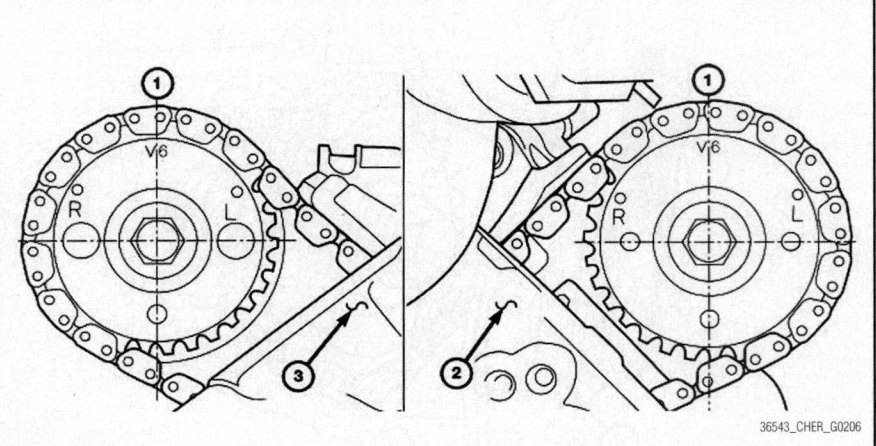

Fig. 117 Set engine to TDC cylinder No. 1, camshaft sprocket V6 marks at the 12 o'clock position (1)

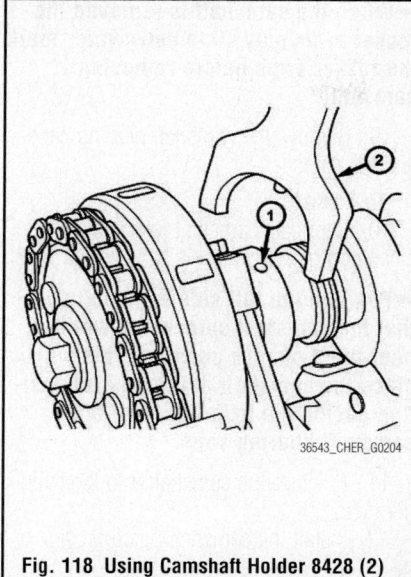

Fig. 118 Using Camshaft Holder 8428 (2)

9. Remove the camshaft bearing caps and the camshaft.

To install:

10. Lubricate camshaft journals with clean engine oil.

➡**Position the right side camshaft so that the camshaft sprocket dowel is near the 10 o'clock position, This will place the camshaft at the neutral position easing the installation of the camshaft bearing caps.**

11. Position the camshaft into the cylinder head.

12. Install the camshaft bearing caps, hand tighten the retaining bolts.

➡**Caps should be installed so that the stamped numbers on the caps are in numerical order (1 through 4) from the front to the rear of the engine. All caps should be installed so that the stamped arrows on the caps point toward the front of the engine.**

13. Working in ½ turn increments, tighten the bearing cap retaining bolts starting with the middle cap working outward.

14. Tighten the camshaft bearing cap retaining bolts to 100 inch lbs. (11 Nm).

15. Position the camshaft drive gear into the timing chain aligning the V6 mark between the two marked chain links (Two links marked during removal).

16. Using Camshaft Holder 8428, rotate the camshaft until the camshaft sprocket dowel is aligned with the slot in the camshaft sprocket. Install the sprocket onto the camshaft.

✳✳ CAUTION

Remove excess oil from the camshaft sprocket bolt. Failure to do so can cause bolt over-torque resulting in bolt failure.

17. Remove excess oil from camshaft sprocket bolt, then install the camshaft sprocket retaining bolt and hand tighten.

18. Remove the Wedge Locking Tool 8379.

19. Using Spanner Wrench 6958 with adapter pins 8346, tighten the camshaft sprocket retaining bolt to 90 ft. lbs. (122 Nm).

20. Install the camshaft position sensor.

21. Install the cylinder head cover.

4.7L Engine

Left Side

See Figures 119 through 124.

1. Remove cylinder head cover.

✳✳ CAUTION

When the timing chain is removed and the cylinder heads are still installed, DO NOT forcefully rotate the camshafts or crankshaft independently of each other. Severe valve and/or piston damage can occur.

✳✳ CAUTION

When removing the cam sprocket, timing chains or camshaft, Failure to use Locking Wedge 9867 will result in hydraulic tensioner ratchet over extension, requiring timing chain cover removal to reset the tensioner ratchet.

2. Set engine to TDC cylinder 1, camshaft sprocket V8 marks at the 12 o'clock position.

3. Mark one link on the secondary timing chain on both sides of the V8 mark on the camshaft sprocket to aid in installation.

✳✳ CAUTION

Do not hold or pry on the camshaft target wheel (Located on the right side camshaft sprocket) for any reason, Severe damage will occur to the target wheel resulting in a vehicle no start condition.

4. Loosen but DO NOT remove the camshaft sprocket retaining bolt. Leave the bolt snug against the sprocket.

➡**The timing chain tensioners must be secured prior to removing the camshaft sprockets. Failure to secure tensioners will allow the tensioners to extend, requiring timing chain cover removal in order to reset tensioners.**

✳✳ CAUTION

Do not force wedge past the narrowest point between the chain strands. Damage to the tensioners may occur.

5. Position Locking Wedge Tool 9867 (4) timing chain wedge between the timing chain strands, tap the tool to securely wedge the timing chain against the tensioner arm and guide.

➡**When gripping the camshaft, place the pliers on the tube portion of the camshaft only. Do not grip the lobes or the sprocket areas.**

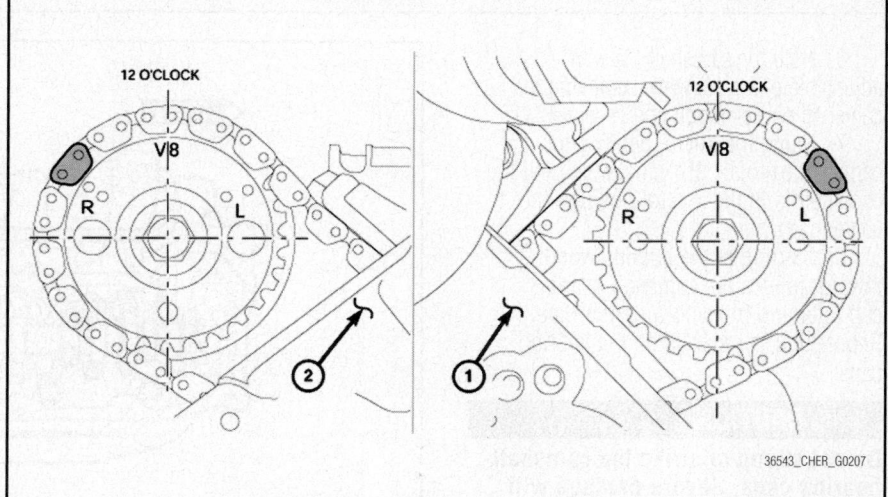

Fig. 119 Set engine to TDC cylinder 1, camshaft sprocket V8 marks at the 12 o'clock position

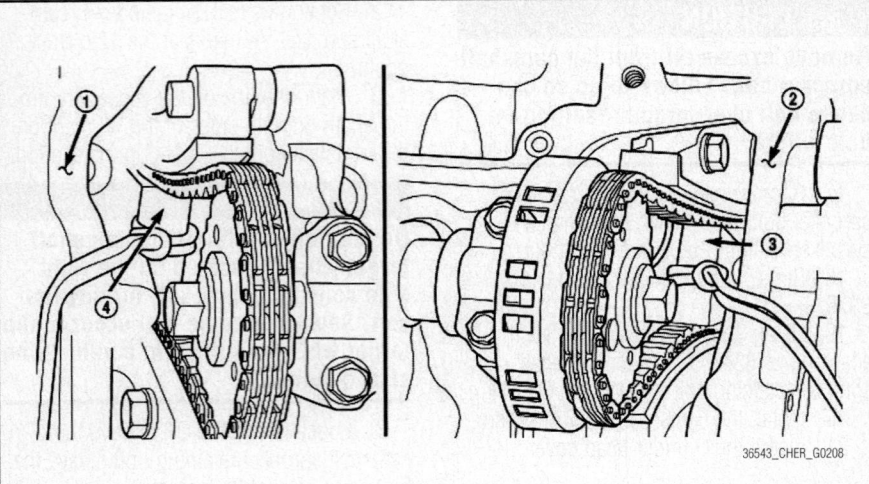

Fig. 120 Position Locking Wedge Tool 9867 (4) timing chain wedge between the timing chain strands

➡When the camshaft is removed the rocker arms may slide downward, mark the rocker arms before removing camshaft.

9. Remove the camshaft bearing caps and the camshaft.

To install:

10. Lubricate camshaft journals with clean engine oil.

➡Position the left side camshaft so that the camshaft sprocket dowel is near the 1 o'clock position, This will place the camshaft at the neutral position easing the installation of the camshaft bearing caps.

11. Position the camshaft into the cylinder head.

12. Install the camshaft bearing caps, hand tighten the retaining bolts.

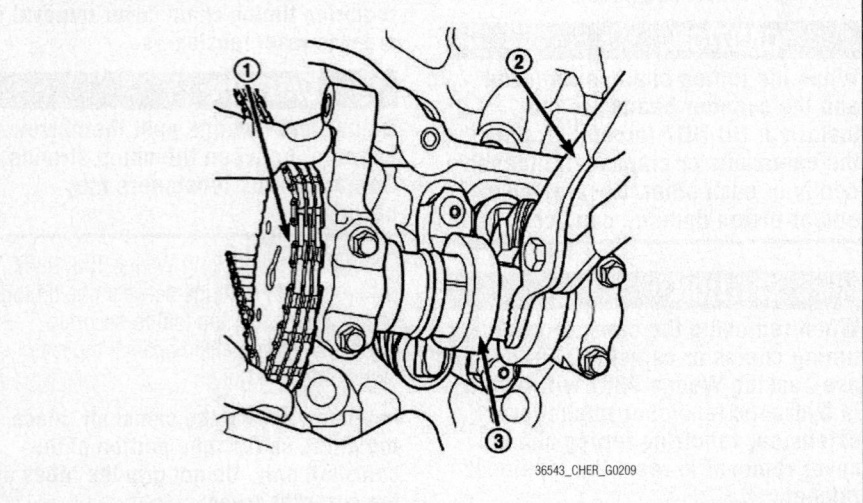

Fig. 121 Hold the camshaft (3) with adjustable pliers (2) while removing the camshaft sprocket bolt and sprocket (1)

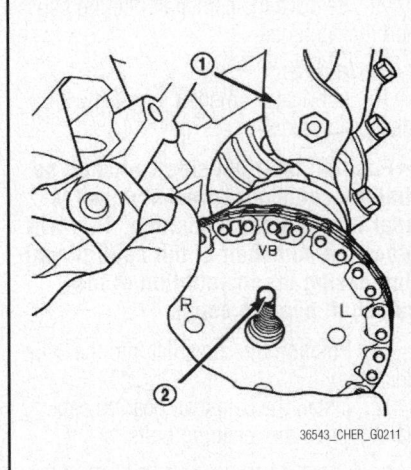

Fig. 123 Rotate the camshaft until the camshaft sprocket dowel is aligned with the slot in the camshaft sprocket

6. Hold the camshaft (3) with adjustable pliers (2) while removing the camshaft sprocket bolt and sprocket (1).

7. Using the pliers, gently allow the camshaft to rotate 15° clockwise until the camshaft is in the neutral position (no valve load).

8. Starting at the outside working inward, loosen the camshaft bearing cap retaining bolts ½ turn at a time. Repeat until all load is off the bearing caps.

✷✷ CAUTION

Do not stamp or strike the camshaft bearing caps. Severe damage will occur to the bearing caps.

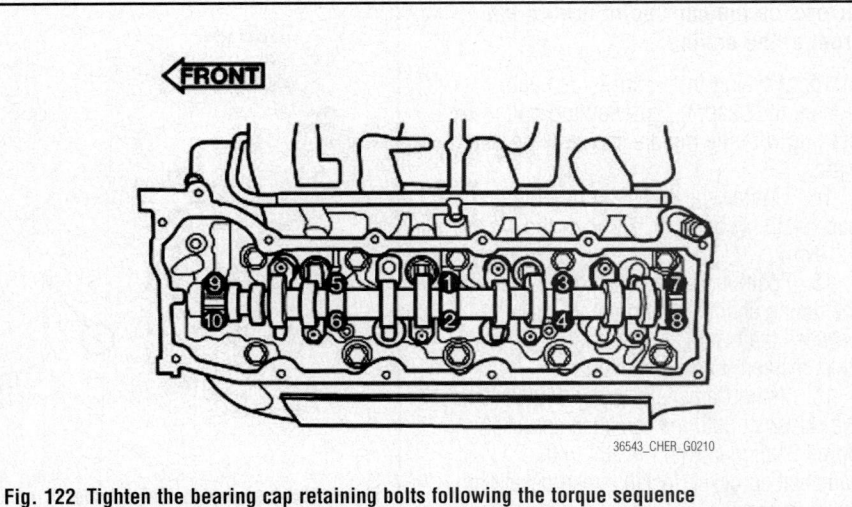

Fig. 122 Tighten the bearing cap retaining bolts following the torque sequence

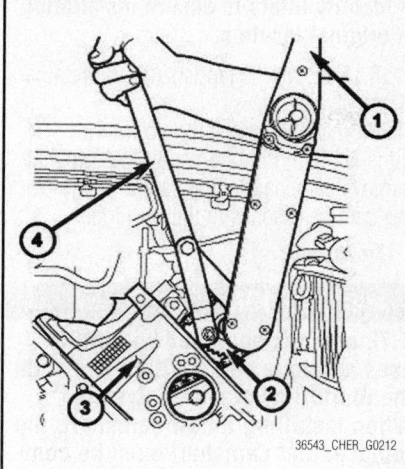

Fig. 124 Tighten the camshaft sprocket retaining bolt

13. Working in ½ turn increments, tighten the bearing cap retaining bolts following the torque sequence.

14. Tighten the camshaft bearing cap retaining bolts to 100 inch lbs. (11 Nm).

15. Position the camshaft drive gear into the timing chain aligning the V8 mark between the two marked chain links (Two links marked during removal).

➡**When gripping the camshaft, place the pliers on the tube portion of the camshaft only. Do not grip the lobes or the sprocket areas.**

16. Using the adjustable pliers (1), rotate the camshaft until the camshaft sprocket dowel (2) is aligned with the slot in the camshaft sprocket. Install the sprocket onto the camshaft.

✳✳ **CAUTION**

Remove excess oil from the camshaft sprocket bolt. Failure to do so can cause bolt over-torque resulting in bolt failure.

17. Remove excess oil from bolt, then install the camshaft sprocket retaining bolt and hand tighten.

18. Remove Locking Wedge Tool 9867 timing chain wedge.

19. Using Spanner Wrench 6958 (4) with adapter pins 8346, tighten the camshaft sprocket retaining bolt (2) to 90 ft. lbs. (122 Nm).

20. Install the cylinder head cover.

Right Side

See Figures 119 through 120, 122, 123, 125 through 127.

1. Remove the cylinder head.

✳✳ **CAUTION**

When the timing chain is removed and the cylinder heads are still installed, DO NOT forcefully rotate the camshafts or crankshaft independently of each other. Severe valve and/or piston damage can occur.

✳✳ **CAUTION**

When removing the cam sprocket, timing chains or camshaft, Failure to use locking wedge tool 9867 will result in hydraulic tensioner ratchet over extension, Requiring timing chain cover removal to re-set the tensioner ratchet.

2. Set engine to TDC cylinder 1, camshaft sprocket V8 marks at the 12 o'clock position.

3. Mark one link on the secondary timing chain on both sides of the V8 mark on the camshaft sprocket to aid in installation.

✳✳ **CAUTION**

Do not hold or pry on the camshaft target wheel for any reason, Severe damage will occur to the target wheel. A damaged target wheel could cause a vehicle no start condition.

4. Loosen but DO NOT remove the camshaft sprocket retaining bolt (2). Leave bolt snug against sprocket (3).

➡**The timing chain tensioners must be secured prior to removing the camshaft sprockets. Failure to secure tensioners will allow the tensioners to extend, requiring timing chain cover removal in order to reset tensioners.**

✳✳ **CAUTION**

Do not force wedge (3) past the narrowest point between the chain strands. Damage to the tensioners may occur.

5. Position Locking Wedge Tool 9867 timing chain wedge (3) between the timing chain strands. Tap the tool to securely wedge the timing chain against the tensioner arm and guide.

6. Remove the camshaft position sensor (3).

➡**When gripping the camshaft, place the pliers (1) on the tube portion of the**

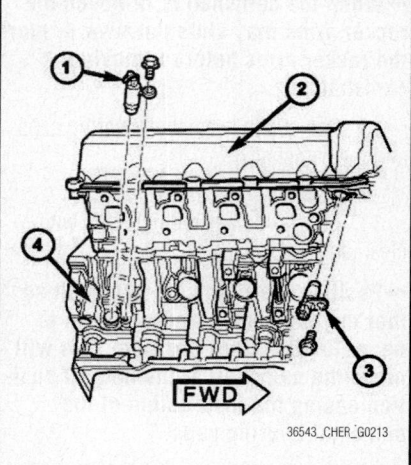

Fig. 125 Remove the camshaft position sensor (3)

camshaft only. Do not grip the lobes or the sprocket areas.

7. Hold the camshaft with adjustable pliers (1) while removing the camshaft sprocket bolt (2) and sprocket (3).

8. Using the pliers (1), gently allow the camshaft to rotate 45° counter-clockwise until the camshaft is in the neutral position (no valve load).

9. Starting at the outside working inward, loosen the camshaft bearing cap retaining bolts ½ turn at a time. Repeat until all load is off the bearing caps.

✳✳ **CAUTION**

Do not stamp or strike the camshaft bearing caps. Severe damage will occur to the bearing caps.

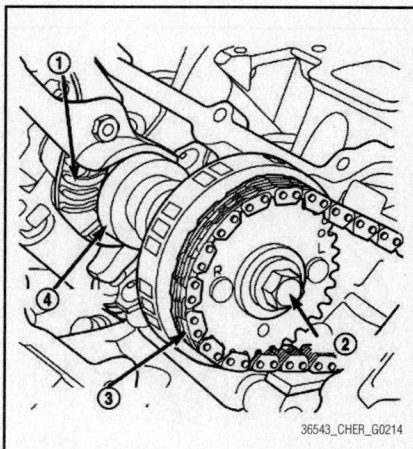

Fig. 126 Hold the camshaft with adjustable pliers (1) while removing the camshaft sprocket bolt (2) and sprocket (3)

➥**When the camshaft is removed the rocker arms may slide downward, mark the rocker arms before removing camshaft.**

10. Remove the camshaft bearing caps and the camshaft.

To install:

11. Lubricate camshaft journals with clean engine oil.

➥**Position the right side camshaft so that the camshaft sprocket dowel is near the 10 o'clock position, This will place the camshaft at the neutral position easing the installation of the camshaft bearing caps.**

12. Position the camshaft into the cylinder head.

13. Install the camshaft bearing caps, hand tighten the retaining bolts.

14. Working in ½ turn increments, tighten the bearing cap retaining bolts starting with the middle cap working outward.

15. Torque the camshaft bearing cap retaining bolts to 100 inch lbs. (11 Nm).

16. Position the camshaft drive gear into the timing chain aligning the V8 mark between the two marked chain links (Two links marked during removal).

➥**When gripping the camshaft, place the pliers on the tube portion of the camshaft only. Do not grip the lobes or the sprocket areas.**

17. Using the adjustable pliers, rotate the camshaft until the camshaft sprocket dowel is aligned with the slot in the camshaft sprocket. Install the sprocket onto the camshaft.

❋❋ CAUTION

Remove excess oil from the camshaft sprocket bolt. Failure to do so can cause bolt over-torque resulting in bolt failure.

18. Remove excess oil from camshaft sprocket bolt, then install the camshaft sprocket retaining bolt and hand tighten.

19. Remove locking wedge tool 9867.

20. Using spanner wrench 6958 with adapter pins 8346 (2), tighten the camshaft sprocket retaining bolt (4) to 90 ft. lbs. (122 Nm).

21. Install the camshaft position sensor.

22. Install the cylinder head cover.

5.7L & 6.1L Engines

See Figures 128 through 130.

1. Remove the battery negative cable.
2. Remove the air cleaner assembly.
3. Drain the coolant.
4. Remove the accessory drive belt.
5. Remove the alternator.
6. Remove the A/C compressor, and set aside.
7. Remove the radiator.
8. Remove intake manifold.
9. Remove cylinder head covers.
10. Remove both left and right cylinder heads.
11. Remove the rocker arms.
12. Remove the push rods.
13. Remove timing case cover.
14. Remove the oil pan.
15. Remove the oil pick up tube.
16. Remove the oil pump.
17. Remove timing chain.
18. Remove camshaft tensioner/thrust plate assembly.

➥**Identify lifters to ensure installation in original location.**

19. Remove the tappets (2) and retainer (1) assembly.

20. Install a long bolt into front of camshaft to aid in removal of the camshaft. Remove camshaft, being careful not to damage cam bearings with the cam lobes.

To install:

❋❋ CAUTION

5.7L engines equipped with MDS uses a unique camshaft for use with the Multi Displacement System. When installing a new camshaft, the replacement camshaft must be compatible with the Multi Displacement System.

21. Lubricate camshaft lobes and camshaft bearing journals and insert the camshaft.

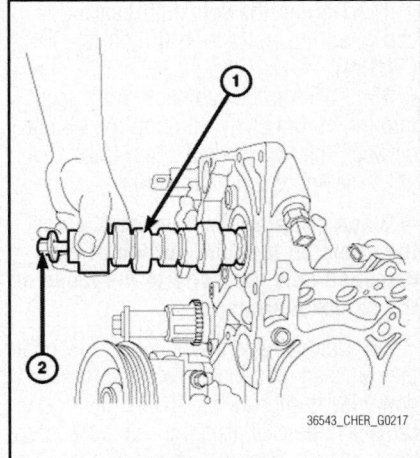

36543_CHER_G0217

Fig. 129 Remove camshaft

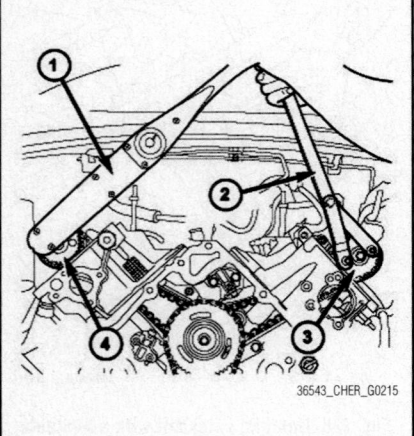

36543_CHER_G0215

Fig. 127 Using spanner wrench 6958 with adapter pins 8346 (2)

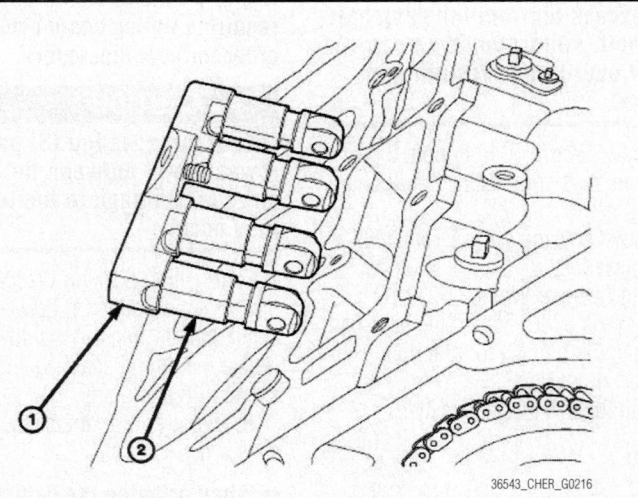

36543_CHER_G0216

Fig. 128 Remove the tappets (2) and retainer (1) assembly

22. Install camshaft Tensioner plate assembly. Tighten bolts to 250 inch lbs. (28 Nm).

23. Install timing chain and sprockets.

24. Measure camshaft end play. If not within limits install a new thrust plate.

25. Install the oil pump.

26. Install the oil pick up tube.

27. Each tappet reused must be installed in the same position from which it was removed. When camshaft is replaced, all of the tappets must be replaced.

❋❋ CAUTION

5.7L engines equipped with MDS uses both standard roller tappets (2) and deactivating roller tappets (1). The deactivating roller tappets must be used in cylinders 1,4,6,7. The deactivating tappets can be identified by the two holes in the side of the tappet body (3), for the latching pins.

28. Install tappets (2) and retaining yoke assembly (1).

29. Install both left and right cylinder heads (4).

30. Install push rods.

31. Install rocker arms.

32. Install timing case cover.

33. Install the oil pan.

34. Install cylinder head covers.

35. Install intake manifold.

36. Install the A/C compressor (2).

37. Install the alternator (2).

38. Install the accessory drive belt.

39. Install the radiator.

40. Install the air cleaner assembly.

41. Install the battery negative cable.

42. Refill coolant.

43. Refill engine oil.

44. Start engine and check for leaks.

CATALYTIC CONVERTER

REMOVAL & INSTALLATION

3.7L Engine

See Figures 131 through 133.

1. Raise and support the vehicle.

2. Saturate the bolts and nuts with heat valve lubricant. Allow 5 minutes for penetration.

3. Remove the transmission cross-member.

   a. Remove the skid plate.

   b. Support the transmission with a suitable lifting device.

   c. Remove the four transmission mount bolts (1).

   d. Remove the eight crossmember bolts (2) and remove the crossmember.

4. Disconnect and mark oxygen sensor electrical connectors.

5. Remove steady rest bracket mounting bolt (5) from transmission.

6. Remove the nuts from the front exhaust pipe/catalytic converter assembly to muffler flange.

7. Remove bolts (2) and flanged nuts (1) at the exhaust manifold.

8. Remove the front exhaust pipe/catalytic converter assembly (3) from the vehicle.

9. Remove steady rest bracket (4) from front exhaust pipe/catalytic converter assembly (3).

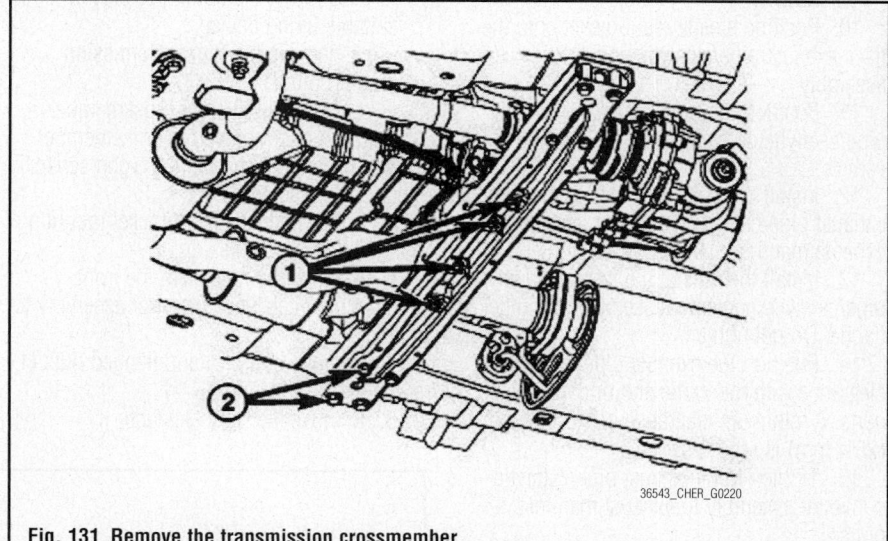

Fig. 131 Remove the transmission crossmember

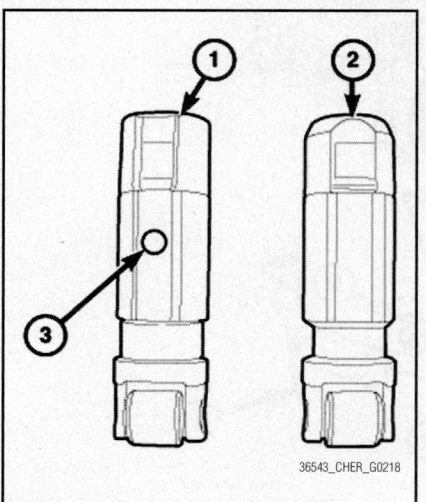

Fig. 130 Standard roller tappets (2) and deactivating roller tappets (1)

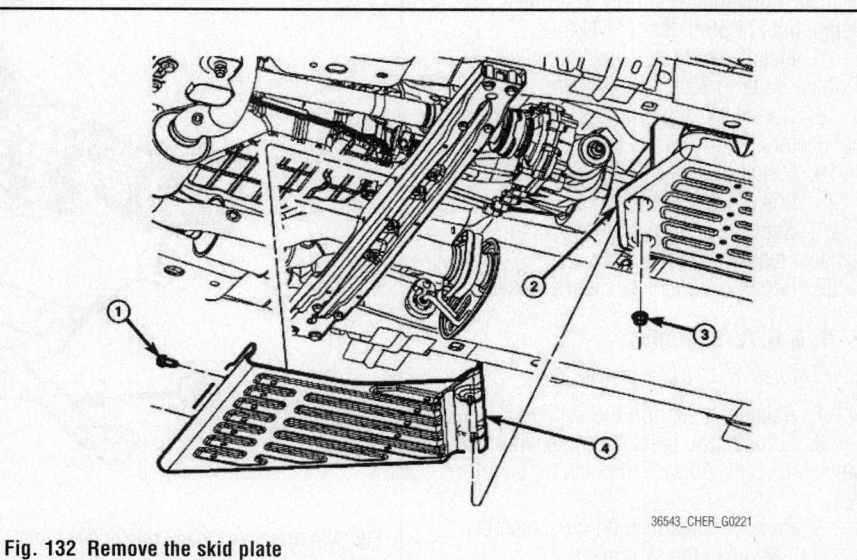

Fig. 132 Remove the skid plate

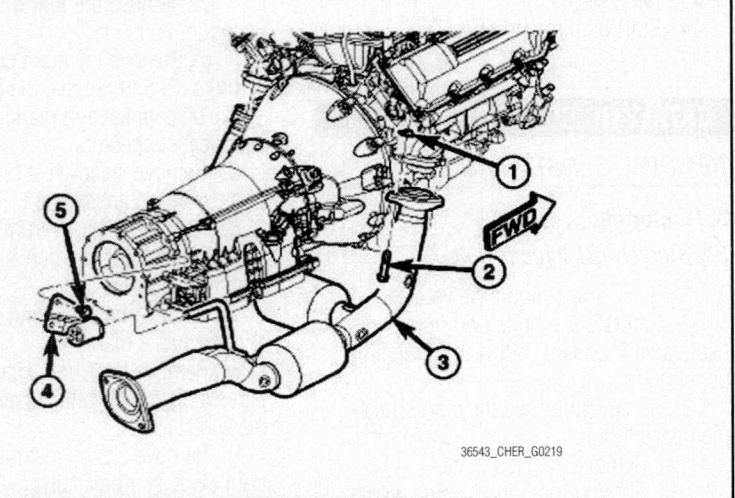

36543_CHER_G0219

Fig. 133 Remove steady rest bracket mounting bolt (5) from transmission

To install:

10. Position steady rest bracket onto the front exhaust pipe/catalytic converter assembly.

11. Position the front exhaust pipe/catalytic converter assembly into vehicle.

12. Install the bolts and nuts at the front exhaust pipe/catalytic converter assembly to exhaust manifold flange. Do not tighten.

13. Install the nuts at the front exhaust pipe/catalytic converter assembly to muffler flange. Do not tighten.

14. Position the exhaust pipe for proper clearance with the frame and underbody parts. A minimum clearance of 1.0 inches (25.4 mm) is required.

15. Tighten front exhaust pipe/catalytic converter assembly to exhaust manifold bolts.

16. Tighten the front exhaust pipe and catalytic converter assembly to muffler flange nuts to 35 ft. lbs. (47 Nm).

17. Install steady rest bracket bolts. Tighten bolts to 35 ft. lbs. (47 Nm).

18. Connect oxygen sensor electrical connectors.

19. Install transmission crossmember.

20. Lower vehicle.

21. Start the vehicle and inspect for exhaust leaks.

22. Repair exhaust leaks as necessary.

4.7L & 5.7L Engines

See Figures 131, 132 and 134.

1. Raise and support the vehicle.

2. Saturate the bolts and nuts with heat valve lubricant. Allow 5 minutes for penetration.

3. Remove transmission crossmember.
   a. Remove the skid plate.

b. Support the transmission with a suitable lifting device.

c. Remove the four transmission mount bolts (1).

d. Remove the eight crossmember bolts (2) and remove the crossmember.

4. Disconnect and mark oxygen sensor electrical connectors.

5. Remove steady rest bracket mounting bolt (5) from transmission.

6. Remove the nuts from the front exhaust pipe/catalytic converter assembly to muffler flange.

7. Remove bolts (2) and flanged nuts (1) at the exhaust manifold.

8. Remove the front exhaust

pipe/catalytic converter assembly (3) from the vehicle.

9. Remove steady rest bracket (4) from front exhaust pipe/catalytic converter assembly (3).

To install:

10. Position steady rest bracket onto the front exhaust pipe/catalytic converter assembly.

11. Position the front exhaust pipe/catalytic converter assembly into vehicle.

12. Install the bolts and nuts at the front exhaust pipe/catalytic converter assembly to exhaust manifold flange. Do not tighten.

13. Install the nuts at the front exhaust pipe/catalytic converter assembly to muffler flange. Do not tighten.

14. Position the exhaust pipe for proper clearance with the frame and underbody parts. A minimum clearance of 1.0 inches (25.4 mm) is required.

15. Tighten front exhaust pipe/catalytic converter assembly to exhaust manifold bolts.

16. Tighten the front exhaust pipe and catalytic converter assembly to muffler flange nuts to 35 ft. lbs. (47 Nm).

17. Install steady rest bracket bolts. Tighten bolts to 35 ft. lbs. (47 Nm).

18. Connect oxygen sensor electrical connectors.

19. Install transmission crossmember.

20. Lower vehicle.

21. Start the vehicle and inspect for exhaust leaks.

22. Repair exhaust leaks as necessary.

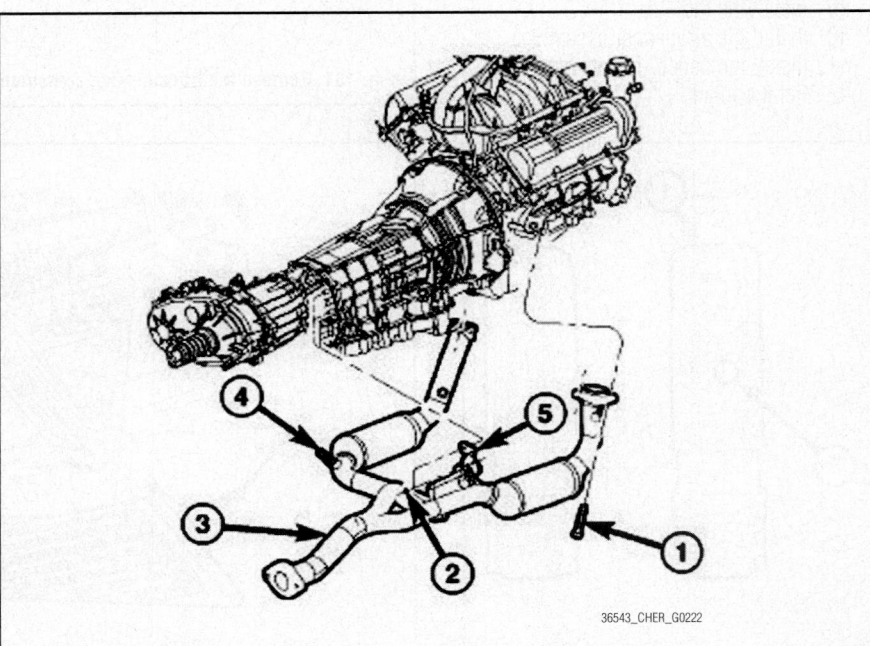

36543_CHER_G0222

Fig. 134 Remove steady rest bracket mounting bolt (5) from transmission

6.1L Engine

See Figures 131, 132 and 135.

1. Raise and support the vehicle.
2. Saturate the bolts and nuts with heat valve lubricant. Allow 5 minutes for penetration.
3. Remove transmission crossmember.

   a. Remove the skid plate.

   b. Support the transmission with a suitable lifting device.

   c. Remove the four transmission mount bolts (1).

   d. Remove the eight crossmember bolts (2) and remove the crossmember.

4. Disconnect and mark oxygen sensor electrical connectors.
5. Remove steady rest bracket mounting bolt (5) from transmission.
6. Remove the nuts from the front exhaust pipe/catalytic converter assembly to muffler flange.
7. Remove bolts (2) and flanged nuts (1) at the exhaust manifold.
8. Remove the front exhaust pipe/catalytic converter assembly (3) from the vehicle.
9. Remove steady rest bracket (4) from front exhaust pipe/catalytic converter assembly (3).

To install:

10. Position steady rest bracket onto the front exhaust pipe/catalytic converter assembly.
11. Position the front exhaust pipe/catalytic converter assembly into vehicle.
12. Install the bolts and nuts at the front exhaust pipe/catalytic converter assembly to exhaust manifold flange. Do not tighten.
13. Install the nuts at the front exhaust pipe/catalytic converter assembly to muffler flange. Do not tighten.
14. Position the exhaust pipe for proper clearance with the frame and underbody parts. A minimum clearance of 1.0 inches (25.4 mm) is required.
15. Tighten front exhaust pipe/catalytic converter assembly to exhaust manifold bolts.
16. Tighten the front exhaust pipe and catalytic converter assembly to muffler flange nuts to 35 ft. lbs. (47 Nm).
17. Install steady rest bracket bolts. Tighten bolts to 35 ft. lbs. (47 Nm).
18. Connect oxygen sensor electrical connectors.
19. Install transmission crossmember.
20. Lower vehicle.

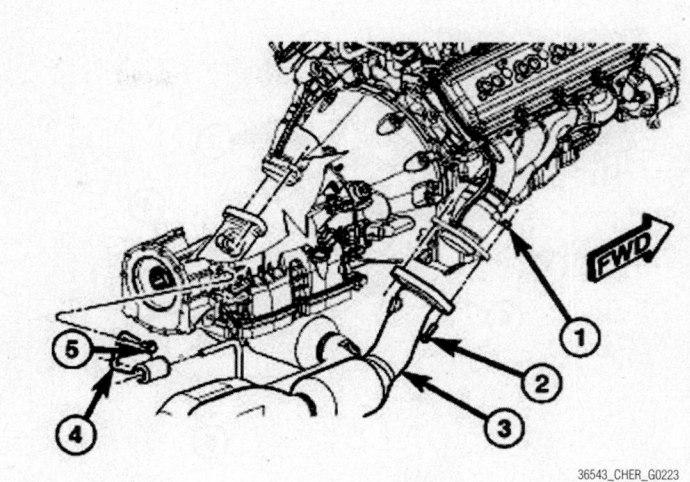

Fig. 135 Remove steady rest bracket mounting bolt (5) from transmission

36543_CHER_G0223

21. Start the vehicle and inspect for exhaust leaks.
22. Repair exhaust leaks as necessary.

3.0L Diesel Engine

See Figures 136 and 137.

1. Disconnect negative battery cable.
2. Raise vehicle on hoist.
3. Disconnect differential pressure ports (2).
4. Disconnect exhaust temperature sensors (3).
5. Disconnect downstream oxygen sensor connectors (4).
6. Remove exhaust from the diesel particulate filter (5).

7. Remove mounting bolts (4) and (7).
8. Remove the nuts from the down pipe (2).
9. Remove the catalyst assembly.

To install:

10. Install the catalyst assembly.
11. Install the nuts to the down pipe.
12. Install mounting bolts.
13. Install exhaust onto the diesel particulate filter.
14. Connect downstream oxygen sensor connectors.
15. Connect exhaust temperature sensors.

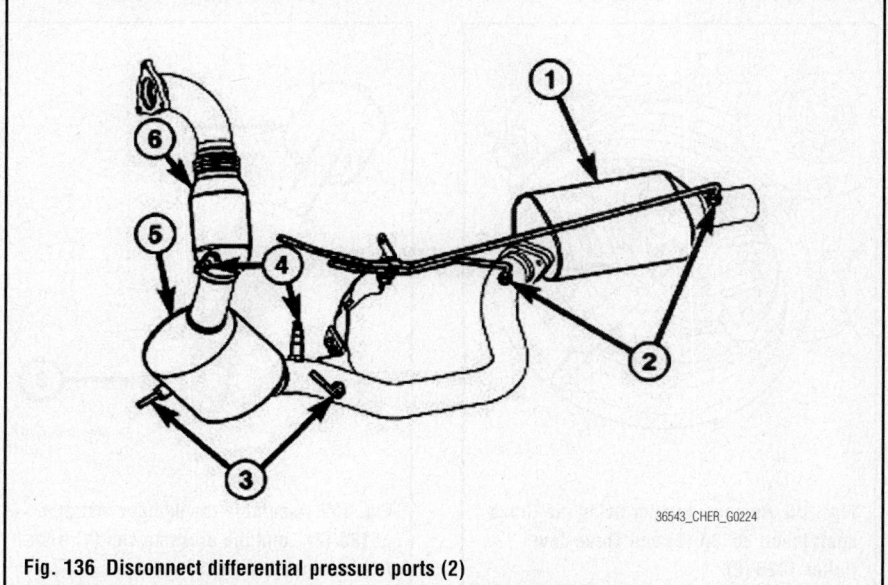

36543_CHER_G0224

Fig. 136 Disconnect differential pressure ports (2)

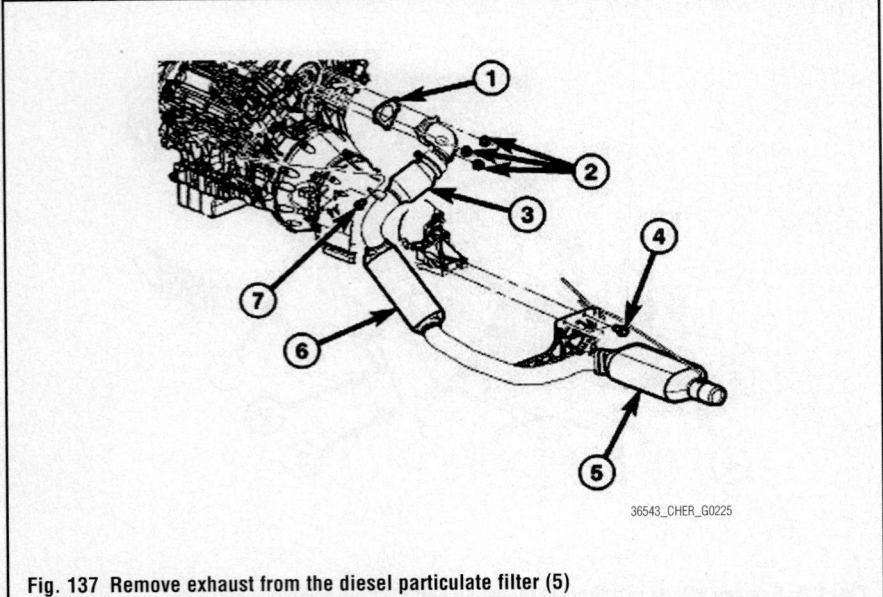

Fig. 137 Remove exhaust from the diesel particulate filter (5)

16. Connect differential pressure ports.
17. Connect negative battery cable.

CRANKSHAFT DAMPER

REMOVAL & INSTALLATION

3.7L Engine

See Figures 138 through 140.

1. Disconnect the negative cable from battery.
2. Remove the radiator fan.
3. Remove accessory drive belt.
4. Remove the vibration damper bolt.
5. Remove damper using the Crankshaft Insert 8513A (1) and Three Jaw Puller 1026 (2).

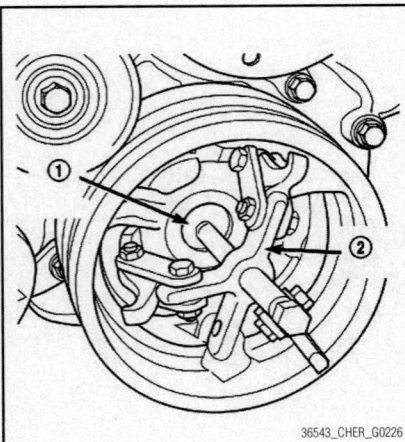

Fig. 138 Remove damper using the Crankshaft Insert 8513A (1) and Three Jaw Puller 1026 (2)

To install:

> ### ✳✳ CAUTION
> To prevent severe damage to the Crankshaft, Damper or Damper Installer 8512A, thoroughly clean the damper bore and the crankshaft nose before installing Damper.

6. Position the damper onto crankshaft.
7. Assemble the damper installer 8512A (2), and the pressing cup (1) from A/C hub installer 6871.
8. Coat the threads of damper installer 8512A with Mopar® Nickel Anti-Seize or equivalent.
9. Using the damper installer 8512A (1), and the pressing cup from the A/C hub

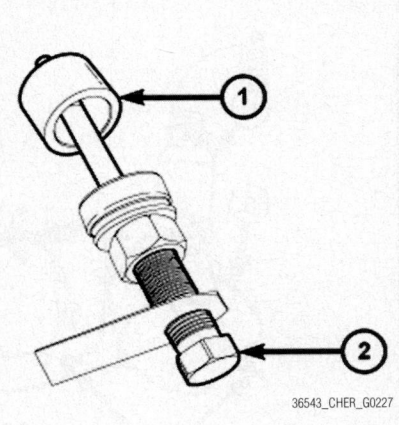

Fig. 139 Assemble the damper installer 8512A (2), and the pressing cup (1) from A/C hub installer 6871

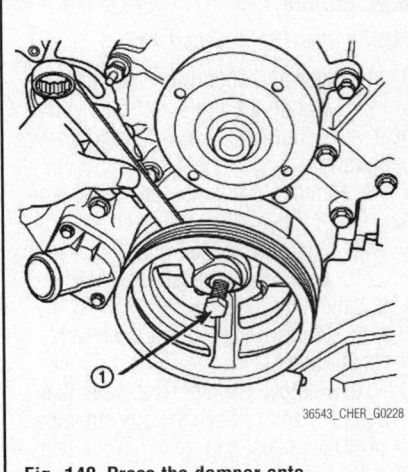

Fig. 140 Press the damper onto crankshaft

installer 6871, press the damper onto crankshaft.

10. Install and tighten the vibration damper bolt to 130 ft. lbs. (175 Nm).
11. Install the cooling fan.
12. Install the accessory drive belt.
13. Connect the negative cable to battery.

4.7L Engine

See Figures 139, 141 through 143.

1. Disconnect and isolate the negative battery cable.

> ### ✳✳ CAUTION
> Do not let the tensioner arm snap back to the freearm position, severe damage may occur to the tensioner.

2. Rotate the belt tensioner until it contacts its stop and remove the belt, then slowly rotate the tensioner into the freearm position.
3. Raise and support the vehicle.

> ### ✳✳ WARNING
> Do not remove the radiator pressure cap, cylinder block drain plugs or loosen the radiator draincock with the system hot and under pressure. Serious burns from coolant can occur.

4. Drain the cooling system.
5. Lower the vehicle.
6. Remove the upper radiator hose.

➡ The thermal viscous fan drive/fan blade assembly is attached (threaded) to the water pump hub shaft.

➡ The transmission cooler line snaps onto the lower right hand corner of the fan shroud.

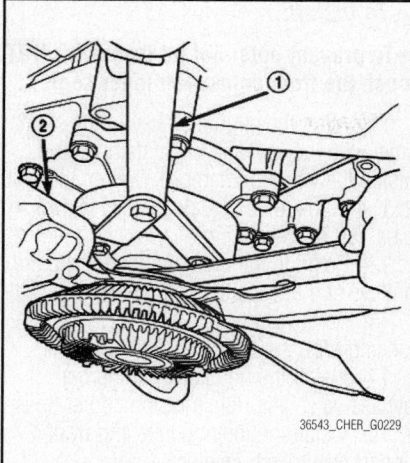

Fig. 141 Remove fan blade/viscous fan drive assembly (2) from water pump

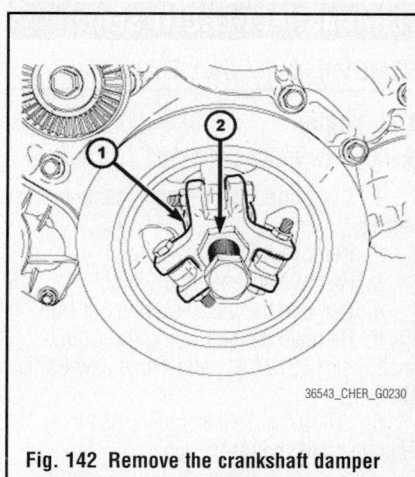

Fig. 142 Remove the crankshaft damper

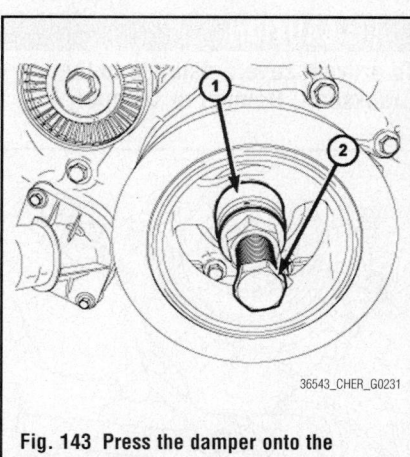

Fig. 143 Press the damper onto the crankshaft

❋❋ **CAUTION**

After removing fan blade/viscous fan drive assembly, do not place viscous fan drive in horizontal position. If stored horizontally, silicone fluid in

the viscous fan drive could drain into the bearing assembly and contaminate the bearing lubricant.

7. Remove the fan shroud and fan blade/viscous fan drive assembly as a complete unit from the vehicle.

a. Remove fan blade/viscous fan drive assembly (2) from water pump using special tool 6958 spanner wrench and 8346 adapters (1), by turning mounting nut counterclockwise as viewed from front. Threads on viscous fan drive are RIGHT HAND.

b. Do not attempt to remove fan/viscous fan drive assembly (2) from vehicle at this time.

c. Do not unbolt fan blade assembly from viscous fan drive at this time.

d. Remove fan shroud to radiator bolts.

e. Remove fan shroud and fan blade/viscous fan drive assembly as a complete unit from vehicle.

8. Remove the vibration damper retaining bolt.

9. Using the crankshaft insert 8513A (1) and the three jaw puller 8454 (2) remove the crankshaft damper.

To install:

❋❋ **CAUTION**

To prevent severe damage to the crankshaft, damper, and damper installer 8512A, thoroughly clean the damper bore and the crankshaft nose before installing damper.

10. Position the damper onto the crankshaft.

11. Assemble the damper installer 8512A (2) and the A/C hub installer cup 6871 (1).

12. Using the damper installer 8512A (2) and the A/C hub installer cup 6871 (1), press the damper onto the crankshaft.

13. Coat the vibration damper bolt threads with Mopar® Nickel Anti-Seize or equivalent, install and tighten the bolt to 130 ft. lbs. (175 Nm).

14. Install the cooling fan assembly.

15. Install the radiator upper shroud and tighten fasteners to 95 inch lbs. (11 Nm).

16. Install the radiator upper hose.

17. Install the accessory drive belt

18. Refill the cooling system

19. Connect the negative battery cable.

5.7L & 6.1L Engines

See Figures 144 and 145.

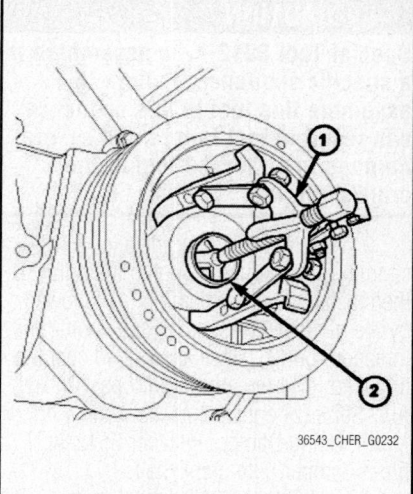

Fig. 144 Remove damper using Crankshaft Insert 8513A and Three Jaw Puller 1023

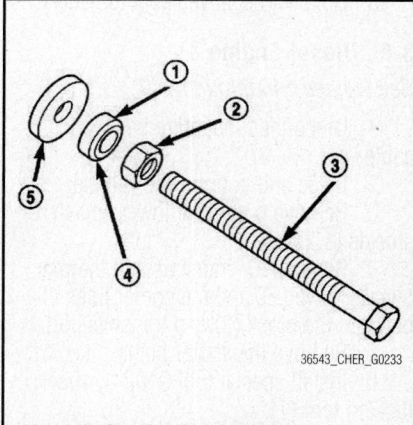

Fig. 145 Special Tool 8512-A, is assembled in a specific sequence

1. Disconnect negative cable from battery.

2. Remove accessory drive belt.

3. Drain cooling system.

4. Remove radiator upper hose.

5. Remove fan shroud.

6. Remove crankshaft damper bolt.

7. Remove damper using Crankshaft Insert 8513A and Three Jaw Puller 1023.

To install:

❋❋ **CAUTION**

To prevent severe damage to the Crankshaft, Damper or Damper Installer 8512A, thoroughly clean the damper bore and the crankshaft nose before installing Damper.

8. Slide damper onto crankshaft slightly.

⁂ CAUTION

Special Tool 8512-A, is assembled in a specific sequence. Failure to assemble this tool in this sequence can result in tool failure and severe damage to either the tool or the crankshaft.

9. Assemble Damper Installer 8512-A as follows, thread nut (2) onto the bolt (3) then install the roller bearing (1) followed by the hardened washer (5) slides onto the threaded rod (3). Once assembled coat the threaded rod's threads with Mopar® Nickel Anti-Seize (or equivalent).

10. Using Damper Installer 8512-A, press damper onto crankshaft.

11. Install then tighten crankshaft damper bolt to 130 ft. lbs. (175 Nm).

12. Install radiator upper hose.

13. Install accessory drive belt.

14. Refill cooling system.

15. Connect negative cable to battery.

3.0L Diesel Engine

See Figures 146 through 149.

1. Disconnect negative battery cable.

2. Raise and support the vehicle.

3. Remove both front lower splash shields (1,2).

4. Remove the transmission thermal bypass valve (2), and the cooler lines (1) between the block (2) and transmission.

5. Remove the starter blank.

6. Install special tool 9102 flywheel locking tool (1).

7. Release the accessory drive belt tension by resetting the drive belt tensioner (1) and installing a retaining pin.

8. Remove the vibration damper bolt.

9. Install special tool 9544 vibration damper puller (1).

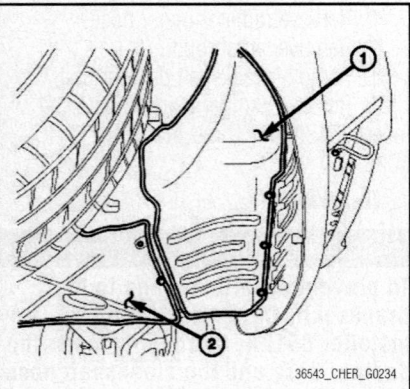

Fig. 146 Remove both front lower splash shields (1,2)

⁂ CAUTION

Care must be taken when removing the damper. DO NOT damage or gouge the front crankshaft seal.

10. Remove the vibration damper (2).

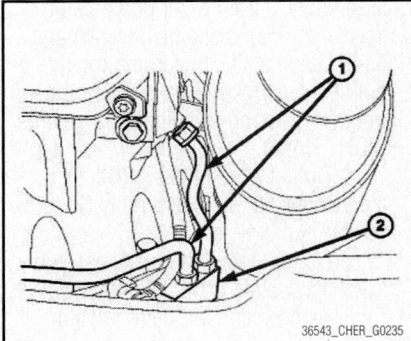

Fig. 147 Remove the transmission thermal bypass valve (2), and the cooler lines (1) between the block (2) and transmission

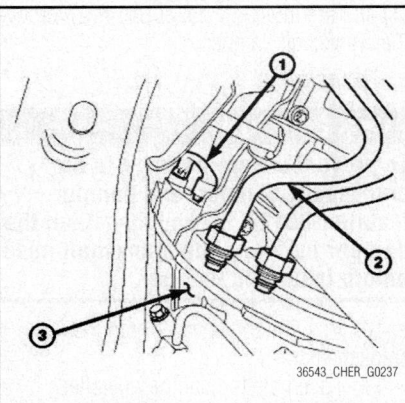

Fig. 148 Install special tool 9102 flywheel locking tool (1)

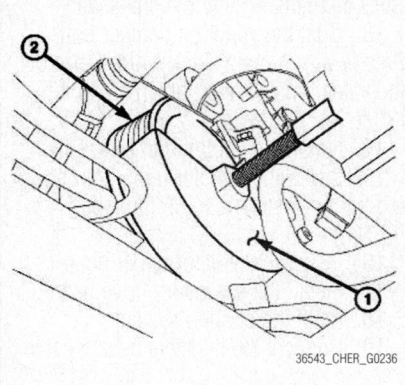

Fig. 149 Install special tool 9544 vibration damper puller (1)

To install:

➡ To prevent potential oil leaks, DO NOT touch the front crankshaft inner seal.

11. Align the alignment key in the crankshaft with the key way in the damper and install the vibration damper. Tighten the bolt to 154 ft. lbs. plus 180 degrees (210 Nm, plus 180 degrees).

12. Position the drive belt back onto the pulleys and release the belt tensioner.

13. Remove special tool 9102 flywheel locking tool.

14. Install the transmission thermal bypass valve and transmission cooler lines.

15. Install the intermediate and front underbody splash shields.

16. Lower the vehicle.

17. Connect negative battery cable.

CRANKSHAFT FRONT SEAL

REMOVAL & INSTALLATION

3.7L Engine

See Figures 138 through 140, 150 and 151.

1. Disconnect the negative cable from battery.

2. Remove the radiator fan.

3. Remove accessory drive belt.

4. Remove the vibration damper bolt.

5. Remove damper using the Crankshaft Insert 8513A (1) and Three Jaw Puller 1026 (2).

6. Using the Seal Remover 8511 (1), remove crankshaft front seal.

To install:

⁂ CAUTION

To prevent severe damage to the Crankshaft, Damper or Damper

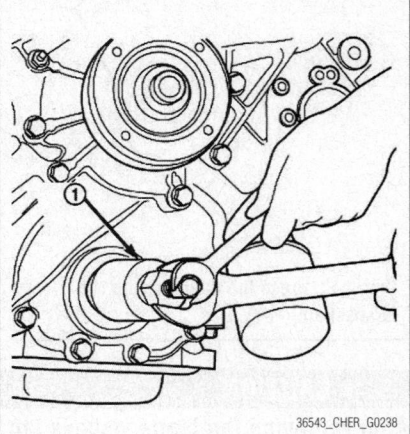

Fig. 150 Using the Seal Remover 8511 (1), remove crankshaft front seal

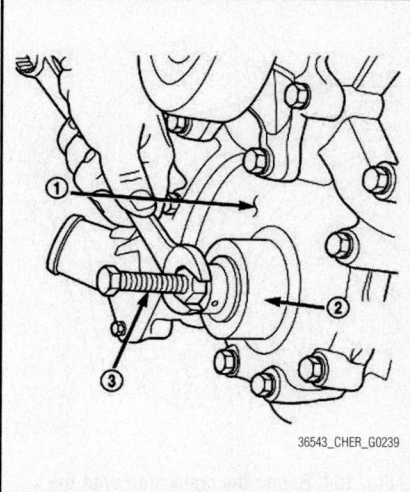

Fig. 151 Install the crankshaft front seal

Installer 8512A, thoroughly clean the damper bore and the crankshaft nose before installing Damper.

7. Using the Seal Installer 8348 (2) and Damper Installer 8512A (3), install the crankshaft front seal.

8. Position the damper onto crankshaft.

9. Assemble the damper installer 8512A (2) , and the pressing cup (1) from A/C hub installer 6871.

10. Coat the threads of damper installer 8512A with Mopar® Nickel Anti-Seize or equivalent.

11. Using the damper installer 8512A (1), and the pressing cup from the A/C hub installer 6871, press the damper onto crankshaft.

12. Install and tighten the vibration damper bolt to 130 ft. lbs. (175 Nm).

13. Install the cooling fan.

14. Install the accessory drive belt.

15. Connect the negative cable to battery.

4.7L Engine

See Figures 139, 141, 142, 143, 150 and 151.

1. Disconnect and isolate the negative battery cable.

✳✳ CAUTION

Do not let the tensioner arm snap back to the freearm position, severe damage may occur to the tensioner.

2. Rotate the belt tensioner until it contacts its stop and remove the belt, then slowly rotate the tensioner into the freearm position.

3. Raise and support the vehicle.

✳✳ WARNING

Do not remove the radiator pressure cap, cylinder block drain plugs or loosen the radiator draincock with the system hot and under pressure. Serious burns from coolant can occur.

4. Drain the cooling system.

5. Lower the vehicle.

6. Remove the upper radiator hose.

➡**The thermal viscous fan drive/fan blade assembly is attached (threaded) to the water pump hub shaft.**

➡**The transmission cooler line snaps onto the lower right hand corner of the fan shroud.**

✳✳ CAUTION

After removing fan blade/viscous fan drive assembly, do not place viscous fan drive in horizontal position. If stored horizontally, silicone fluid in the viscous fan drive could drain into the bearing assembly and contaminate the bearing lubricant.

7. Remove the fan shroud and fan blade/viscous fan drive assembly as a complete unit from the vehicle.

a. Remove fan blade/viscous fan drive assembly (2) from water pump using special tool 6958 spanner wrench and 8346 adapters (1), by turning mounting nut counterclockwise as viewed from front. Threads on viscous fan drive are RIGHT HAND.

b. Do not attempt to remove fan/viscous fan drive assembly (2) from vehicle at this time.

c. Do not unbolt fan blade assembly from viscous fan drive at this time.

d. Remove fan shroud to radiator bolts.

e. Remove fan shroud and fan blade/viscous fan drive assembly as a complete unit from vehicle.

8. Remove the vibration damper retaining bolt.

9. Using the crankshaft insert 8513A (1) and the three jaw puller 8454 (2) remove the crankshaft damper.

10. Using the Seal Remover 8511 (1), remove crankshaft front seal.

To install:

✳✳ CAUTION

To prevent severe damage to the crankshaft, damper, and damper installer 8512A, thoroughly clean the damper bore and the crankshaft nose before installing damper.

11. Using the Seal Installer 8348 (2) and Damper Installer 8512A (3), install the crankshaft front seal.

12. Position the damper onto the crankshaft.

13. Assemble the damper installer 8512A (2) and the A/C hub installer cup 6871 (1).

14. Using the damper installer 8512A (2) and the A/C hub installer cup 6871 (1), press the damper onto the crankshaft.

15. Coat the vibration damper bolt threads with Mopar® Nickel Anti-Seize or equivalent, install and tighten the bolt to 130 ft. lbs. (175 Nm).

16. Install the cooling fan assembly.

17. Install the radiator upper shroud and tighten fasteners to 95 inch lbs. (11 Nm).

18. Install the radiator upper hose.

19. Install the accessory drive belt

20. Refill the cooling system

21. Connect the negative battery cable.

5.7L & 6.1L Engines

See Figures 144, 145, 152 and 153.

1. Disconnect negative cable from battery.

2. Remove accessory drive belt.

3. Drain cooling system.

4. Remove radiator upper hose.

5. Remove fan shroud.

6. Remove crankshaft damper bolt.

7. Remove damper using Crankshaft Insert 8513A and Three Jaw Puller 1023.

8. Using Crankshaft Front Seal Remover 9071 (1), remove crankshaft front seal (2).

To install:

✳✳ CAUTION

The front crankshaft seal must be installed dry. Do not apply lubricant to the sealing lip or the outer edge.

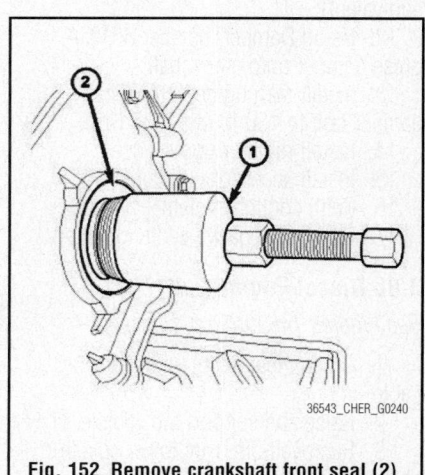

Fig. 152 Remove crankshaft front seal (2)

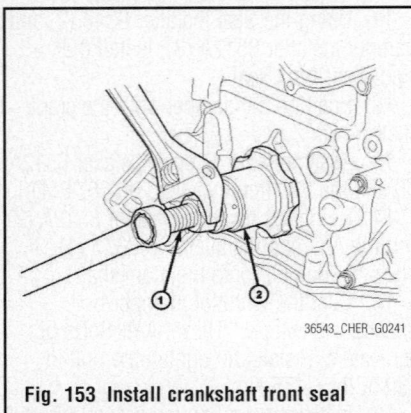

Fig. 153 Install crankshaft front seal

9. Using Crankshaft Front Oil Seal Installer 9072 (2) and Damper Installer 8512A (1), install crankshaft front seal.

> ✳✳ **CAUTION**
>
> **To prevent severe damage to the Crankshaft, Damper or Damper Installer 8512A, thoroughly clean the damper bore and the crankshaft nose before installing Damper.**

10. Slide damper onto crankshaft slightly.

> ✳✳ **CAUTION**
>
> **Special Tool 8512-A, is assembled in a specific sequence. Failure to assemble this tool in this sequence can result in tool failure and severe damage to either the tool or the crankshaft.**

11. Assemble Damper Installer 8512-A as follows, thread nut (2) onto the bolt (3) then install the roller bearing (1) followed by the hardened washer (5) slides onto the threaded rod (3). Once assembled coat the threaded rod's threads with Mopar® Nickel Anti-Seize (or equivalent).
12. Using Damper Installer 8512-A, press damper onto crankshaft.
13. Install then tighten crankshaft damper bolt to 130 ft. lbs. (175 Nm).
14. Install radiator upper hose.
15. Install accessory drive belt.
16. Refill cooling system.
17. Connect negative cable to battery.

3.0L Diesel Engine

See Figures 146 through 149.

1. Disconnect negative battery cable.
2. Raise and support the vehicle.
3. Remove both front lower splash shields (1,2).

4. Remove the transmission thermal bypass valve (2), and the cooler lines (1) between the block (2) and transmission.
5. Remove the starter blank.
6. Install special tool 9102 flywheel locking tool (1).
7. Release the accessory drive belt tension by resetting the drive belt tensioner (1) and installing a retaining pin.
8. Remove the vibration damper bolt.
9. Install special tool 9544 vibration damper puller (1).

> ✳✳ **CAUTION**
>
> **Care must be taken when removing the damper. DO NOT damage or gouge the front crankshaft seal.**

10. Remove the vibration damper (2).
11. Using suitable seal puller, remove the front crankshaft seal.

To install:

➠**To prevent potential oil leaks, DO NOT touch the front crankshaft inner seal.**

12. Clean timing chain cover seal surface.

➠**Keep seal centered in the timing chain cover at all times.**

13. Install crankshaft oil seal using Installer 8936A.
14. Align the alignment key in the crankshaft with the key way in the damper and install the vibration damper. Tighten the bolt to 154 ft. lbs. plus 180 degrees (210 Nm, plus 180 degrees).
15. Position the drive belt back onto the pulleys and release the belt tensioner.
16. Remove special tool 9102 flywheel locking tool.
17. Install the transmission thermal bypass valve and transmission cooler lines.
18. Install the intermediate and front underbody splash shields.
19. Lower the vehicle.
20. Connect negative battery cable.

CYLINDER HEAD

REMOVAL & INSTALLATION

3.7L Engine

See Figures 154 through 158.

1. Disconnect the negative cable from the battery.
2. Raise the vehicle on a hoist.
3. Disconnect the exhaust pipe at the left side exhaust manifold.
4. Drain the engine coolant.
5. Lower the vehicle.
6. Remove the intake manifold.

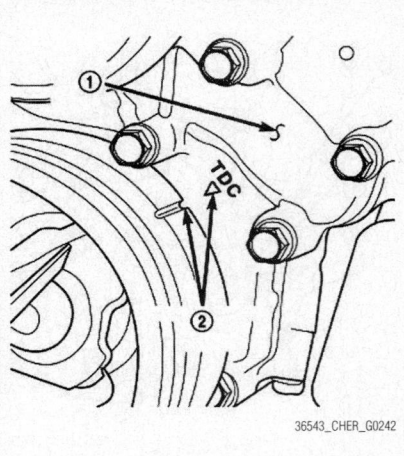

Fig. 154 Rotate the crankshaft until the damper timing mark is aligned with TDC indicator mark (2)

7. Remove the master cylinder and booster assembly.
8. Remove the cylinder head cover.
9. Remove the fan shroud and fan blade assembly.
10. Remove the accessory drive belt.
11. Remove the power steering pump and set aside.
12. Rotate the crankshaft until the damper timing mark is aligned with TDC indicator mark (2).
13. Verify the V6 mark (1) on the camshaft sprocket is at the 12 o'clock position, with the No. 1 cylinder at TDC on the exhaust stroke. Rotate the crankshaft one turn if necessary.
14. Remove the vibration damper.
15. Remove the timing chain cover.
16. Lock the secondary timing chains (2) to the idler sprocket using Secondary Camshaft Chain Holder 8429 (1).

➠**Mark the secondary timing chain prior to removal to aid in installation.**

17. Mark the secondary timing chain (2), one link on each side of the V6 mark on the camshaft drive gear.
18. Remove the left side secondary chain tensioner.
19. Remove the cylinder head access plug (1) and (2).
20. Remove the left side secondary chain guide.
21. Remove the retaining bolt and the camshaft drive gear.

> ✳✳ **CAUTION**
>
> **Do not allow the engine to rotate. Severe damage to the valve train can occur.**

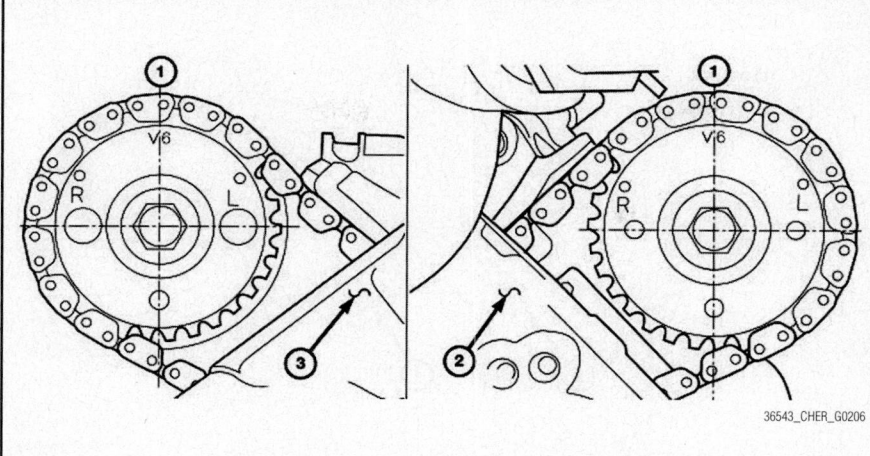

Fig. 155 Verify the V6 mark (1) on the camshaft sprocket is at the 12 o'clock position

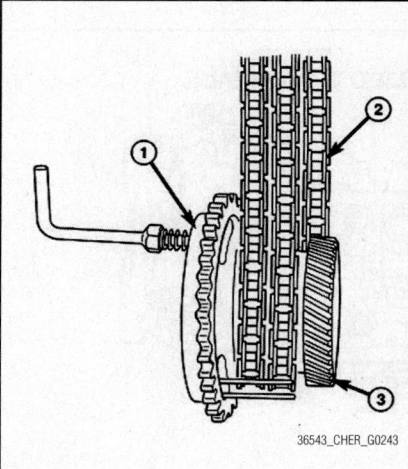

Fig. 156 Lock the secondary timing chains (2) to the idler sprocket using Secondary Camshaft Chain Holder 8429 (1)

> ✳✳ **CAUTION**
>
> **Do not overlook the four smaller bolts at the front of the cylinder head. Do not attempt to remove the cylinder head without removing these four bolts.**

➡ **The cylinder head is attached to the cylinder block with twelve bolts.**

22. Remove the cylinder head retaining bolts.
23. Remove the cylinder head and gasket. Discard the gasket.

> ✳✳ **CAUTION**
>
> **Do not lay the cylinder head on its gasket sealing surface, due to the design of the cylinder head gasket any distortion to the cylinder head**

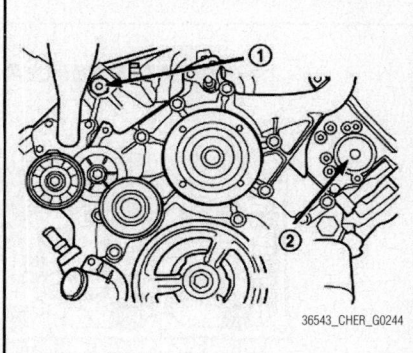

Fig. 157 Remove the cylinder head access plug (1 and 2)

sealing surface may prevent the gasket from properly sealing resulting in leaks.

To install:

➡ **The cylinder head bolts are tightened using a torque plus angle procedure. The bolts must be examined BEFORE reuse. If the threads are necked down the bolts should be replaced.**

Necking can be checked by holding a straight edge against the threads (2). If all the threads do not contact the scale, the bolt should be replaced.

> ✳✳ **CAUTION**
>
> **When cleaning cylinder head and cylinder block surfaces, use only a wooden or plastic scraper.**

24. Clean the cylinder head and cylinder block mating surfaces.
25. Position the new cylinder head gasket on the locating dowels.

> ✳✳ **CAUTION**
>
> **When installing cylinder head, use care not damage the tensioner arm or the guide arm.**

26. Position the cylinder head onto the cylinder block. Make sure the cylinder head seats fully over the locating dowels.

➡ **The four smaller cylinder head mounting bolts require sealant to be added to them before installing. Failure to do so may cause leaks. The locations are identified with an *.**

27. Lubricate the cylinder head bolt threads with clean engine oil and install the eight M11 bolts.
28. Coat the four M8 cylinder head bolts with Mopar® Lock and Seal Adhesive then install the bolts.

➡ **The cylinder head bolts are tightened using an angle torque procedure, however, the bolts are not a torque-to-yield design.**

29. Tighten the bolts in sequence using the following steps and torque values:
   - Step 1: Tighten bolts 1-8, 20 ft. lbs. (27 Nm).
   - Step 2: Verify that bolts 1-8, all reached 20 ft. lbs. (27 Nm), by repeating step 1 without loosening the bolts. Tighten bolts 9 thru 12 to 10 ft. lbs. (14 Nm).
   - Step 3: Tighten bolts 1-8, 90 degrees.
   - Step 4: Tighten bolts 1-8, 90 degrees, again. Tighten bolts 9-12, 19 ft. lbs. (26 Nm)

30. Position the secondary chain onto the camshaft drive gear, making sure one marked chain link is on either side of the V6 mark on the gear then using Camshaft Holder 8428 position the gear onto the camshaft.

> ✳✳ **CAUTION**
>
> **Remove excess oil from camshaft sprocket retaining bolt before reinstalling bolt. Failure to do so may cause over-torquing of bolt resulting in bolt failure.**

31. Install the camshaft drive gear retaining bolt.
32. Install the left side secondary chain guide.
33. Install the cylinder head access plug.
34. Re-set and install the left side secondary chain tensioner.
35. Remove Secondary Camshaft Chain Holder 8429.
36. Install the timing chain cover.

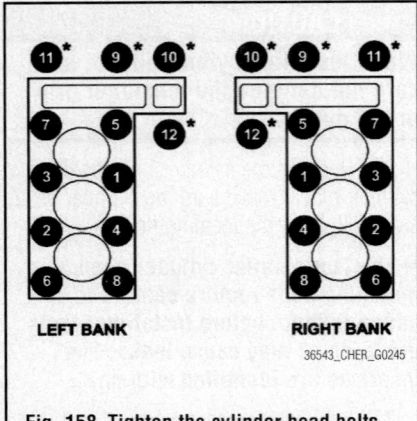

Fig. 158 Tighten the cylinder head bolts in sequence

37. Install the crankshaft damper. Tighten damper bolt 130 ft. lbs. (175 Nm).
38. Install the power steering pump.
39. Install the fan blade assembly and fan shroud.
40. Install the cylinder head cover.
41. Install the master cylinder and booster assembly.
42. Install the intake manifold.
43. Refill the cooling system.
44. Raise the vehicle.
45. Install the exhaust pipe onto the left exhaust manifold.
46. Lower the vehicle.
47. Connect the negative cable to the battery.
48. Start the engine and check for leaks.

4.7L Engine

See Figures 154, 156, 157, 159 through 161.

1. Disconnect the negative cable from the battery.
2. Raise the vehicle on a hoist.
3. Disconnect the exhaust pipe at the exhaust manifold.
4. Drain the engine coolant.
5. Lower the vehicle.
6. Remove the intake manifold.
7. Remove the master cylinder and booster assembly, if removing the left cylinder head.
8. Remove the cylinder head cover.
9. Remove the fan shroud and fan blade assembly.
10. Remove the oil fill housing from right cylinder head.
11. Remove accessory drive belt.
12. Remove the power steering pump and set aside.
13. Rotate the crankshaft until the damper timing marks are aligned (2).

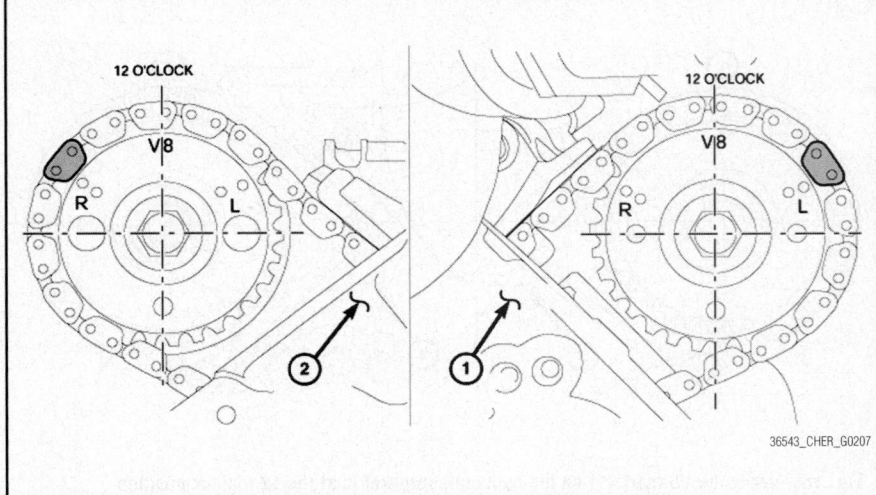

Fig. 159 Verify the V8 mark on the camshaft sprocket is at the 12 o'clock position

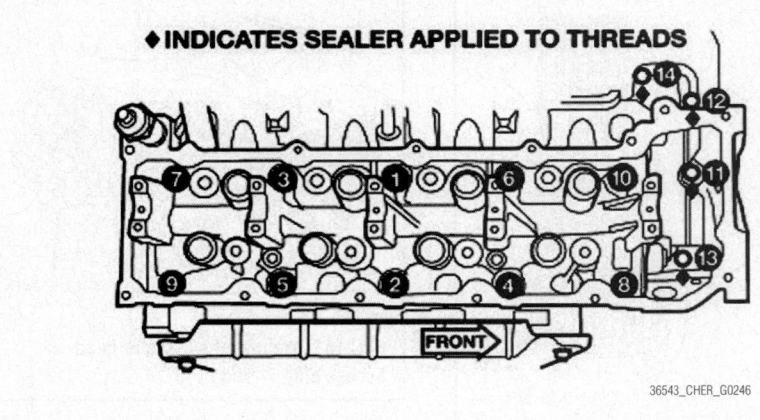

Fig. 160 Cylinder head bolt loosening and tightening sequence

14. Verify the V8 mark on the camshaft sprocket is at the 12 o'clock position. Rotate the crankshaft one turn if necessary.
15. Remove the crankshaft damper.
16. Remove the timing chain cover.
17. Lock the secondary timing chains to the idler sprocket using secondary camshaft chain holder 8429.

➡ **Mark the secondary timing chain prior to removal to aid in installation.**

18. Mark the secondary timing chain, one link on each side of the V8 mark on the camshaft drive gear.
19. Remove the secondary chain tensioner.

✳✳ CAUTION

Do not allow the engine to rotate. Severe damage to the valve train can occur.

20. Remove the cylinder head access plug.
21. Remove the secondary chain guide.
22. Remove the retaining bolt and the camshaft drive gear.

✳✳ CAUTION

Do not overlook the four smaller bolts at the front of the cylinder head. Do not attempt to remove the cylinder head without removing these four bolts.

➡ **The cylinder head is attached to the cylinder block with fourteen bolts.**

23. Remove the cylinder head retaining bolts in sequence.

✳✳ CAUTION

Do not lay the cylinder head on its gasket sealing surface, due to the design of the cylinder head gasket any distortion to the cylinder head

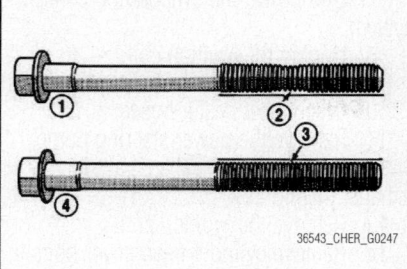

Fig. 161 If the threads are necked down (2) the bolts should be replaced

sealing surface may prevent the gasket from properly sealing resulting in leaks.

24. Remove the cylinder head and gasket. Discard the gasket.

To install:

➡ **The cylinder head bolts are tightened using a torque plus angle procedure. The bolts must be examined BEFORE reuse. If the threads are necked down (2) the bolts should be replaced.**

Necking can be checked by holding a straight edge against the threads. If all the threads do not contact the scale, the bolt should be replaced.

✱✱ CAUTION

When cleaning cylinder head and cylinder block surfaces, use only a wooden or plastic scraper.

25. Clean the cylinder head and cylinder block mating surfaces.

26. Position the new cylinder head gasket on the locating dowels.

✱✱ CAUTION

When installing cylinder head, use care not damage the tensioner arm or the guide arm.

27. Position the cylinder head onto the cylinder block. Make sure the cylinder head seats fully over the locating dowels.

➡ **The four M8 cylinder head mounting bolts (11–14) require sealant to be added to them before installing. Failure to do so may cause leaks.**

28. Lubricate the cylinder head bolt threads with clean engine oil and install the ten M11 bolts.

29. Coat the four M8 cylinder head bolts with Mopar® Thread Sealant with PTFE then install the bolts.

➡ **The cylinder head bolts are tightened using an torque angle procedure.**

30. Tighten the bolts in sequence using the following steps and torque values:
- Tighten bolts 1–10 to 20 ft. lbs. (27 Nm).
- Verify that bolts 1–10 have all reached 20 ft. lbs. (27 Nm), by repeating step 1 without loosening the bolts.
- Tighten bolts 11–14 to 89 inch lbs. (14 Nm).
- Rotate bolts 1–10 an additional 90°.
- Rotate bolts 1–10 an additional 90° again.
- Tighten bolts 11–14 to 19 ft. lbs. (26 Nm).

31. Position the secondary chain onto the camshaft drive gear, making sure one marked chain link is on either side of the V8 mark on the gear and position the gear onto the camshaft.

32. Install the camshaft drive gear retaining bolt.

33. Install the left side secondary chain guide.

34. Install the cylinder head access plug.

35. Re-set and Install the left side secondary chain tensioner.

36. Remove Secondary Camshaft Chain Holder 8429.

37. Install the timing chain cover.

38. Install the crankshaft damper.

39. Install the power steering pump.

40. Install the fan blade assembly and fan shroud.

41. Install the cylinder head cover.

42. Reinstall the master cylinder and booster assembly.

43. Install the intake manifold.

44. Fill the cooling system.

45. Raise the vehicle.

46. Install the exhaust pipe onto the left exhaust manifold.

47. Lower the vehicle.

48. Fill with oil.

49. Connect the negative cable to the battery.

50. Start the engine and check for leaks.

5.7L Engine

See Figures 162 through 166.

1. Perform the Fuel System Pressure Release procedure.

2. Disconnect the fuel supply line.

3. Disconnect the battery negative cable.

4. Drain cooling system.

5. Remove the air cleaner resonator and duct work.

6. Remove closed crankcase ventilation system.

7. Disconnect the exhaust at the exhaust manifolds.

8. Disconnect the evaporation control system.

9. Disconnect heater hoses.

10. Remove the power steering pump.

11. Remove cylinder head cover bolts in sequence.

12. Remove cylinder head covers and gaskets.

13. Remove intake manifold and throttle body as an assembly.

14. Remove rocker arm assemblies and push rods. Identify to ensure installation in original locations.

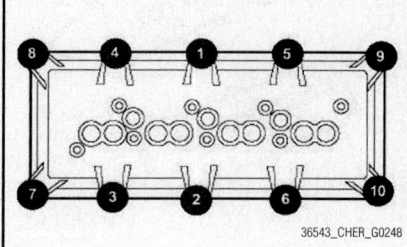

Fig. 162 Cylinder head cover bolts loosening and tightening sequence

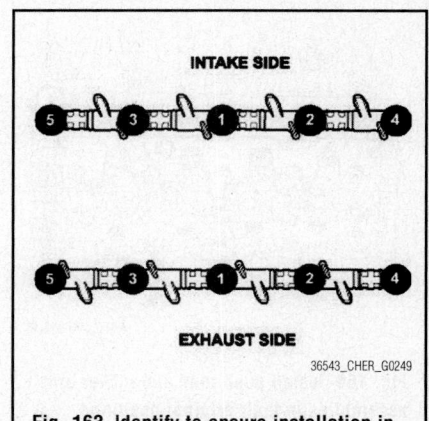

Fig. 163 Identify to ensure installation in original locations

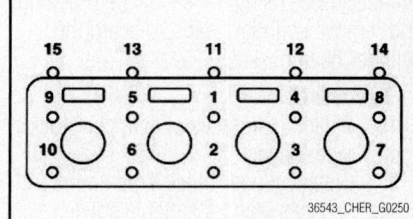

Fig. 164 Cylinder head bolt loosening and tightening sequence

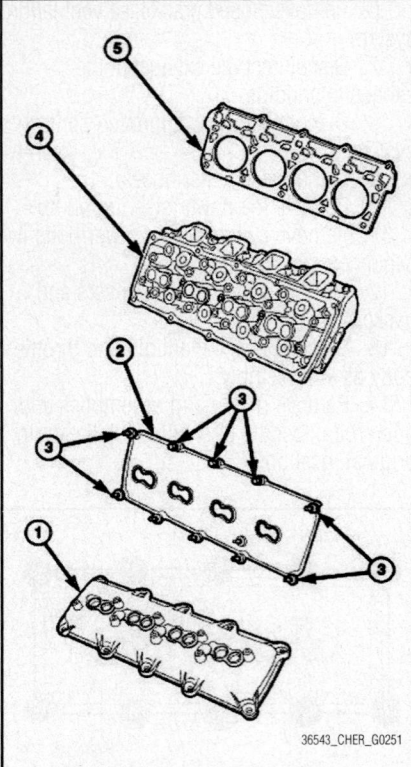

Fig. 165 Position new cylinder head gaskets (5) onto the cylinder block

Fig. 166 Install push rods and rocker arm assemblies in their original position, using push rod retainer 9070 (1)

15. Remove the head bolts from each cylinder head, using the sequence provided, and remove cylinder heads. Discard the cylinder head gasket.

To install:

16. Clean all surfaces of cylinder block and cylinder heads.

17. Clean cylinder block front and rear gasket surfaces using a suitable solvent.

✳✳ CAUTION

The cylinder head gaskets are not interchangeable between the left

and right sides. They are marked with an "L" and "R" to indicate the left or right side and they are marked "TOP" to indicate which side goes up.

✳✳ CAUTION

The head gaskets are marked "TOP" to indicate which side goes up.

18. Position new cylinder head gaskets (5) onto the cylinder block.

19. Position cylinder heads (4) onto head gaskets (5) and cylinder block.

20. Tighten the cylinder head bolts in three steps using the sequence provided:
  - Step 1: Snug tighten M12 cylinder head bolts, in sequence, to 25 ft. lbs. (34 Nm) and M8 bolts to 15 ft. lbs. (20 Nm).
  - Step 2: Tighten M12 cylinder head bolts, in sequence, to 40 ft. lbs. (54 Nm) and verify M8 bolts to 15 ft. lbs. (20 Nm).
  - Step 3: Turn M12 cylinder head bolts, in sequence, 90 degrees and tighten M8 bolts to 25 ft. lbs. (34 Nm).

21. Install push rods and rocker arm assemblies in their original position, using push rod retainer 9070 (1).

22. Install the intake manifold and throttle body assembly.

23. If required, adjust spark plugs to specifications. Install the plugs.

24. Connect the heater hoses.

25. Install the fuel supply line.

26. Install the power steering pump.

27. Install the drive belt.

28. Install cylinder head covers.

29. Connect the evaporation control system.

30. Install the air cleaner.

31. Fill cooling system.

32. Connect the negative cable to the battery.

33. Start engine check for leaks.

6.1L Engine

See Figures 162 through 166.

1. Perform the Fuel System Pressure Release procedure.

2. Disconnect the fuel supply line.

3. Disconnect the battery negative cable.

4. Drain cooling system.

5. Remove the air cleaner resonator and duct work.

6. Remove closed crankcase ventilation system.

7. Disconnect the evaporation control system.

8. Unplug the ignition coil.

9. Remove ignition coil mounting bolts.

10. Disconnect heater hoses.

11. Remove the power steering pump.

12. Disconnect the exhaust at the exhaust manifolds.

13. Remove the ignition coils.

14. Remove cylinder head cover bolts in sequence.

15. Remove cylinder head covers and gaskets.

16. Remove intake manifold and throttle body as an assembly.

17. Remove rocker arm assemblies and push rods. Identify to ensure installation in original locations.

18. Remove the head bolts from each cylinder head, using the sequence provided, and remove cylinder heads. Discard the cylinder head gasket.

To install:

19. Clean all surfaces of cylinder block and cylinder heads.

20. Clean cylinder block front and rear gasket surfaces using a suitable solvent.

✳✳ CAUTION

The cylinder head gaskets are not interchangeable between the left and right sides. They are marked with an "L" and "R" to indicate the left or right side and they are marked "TOP" to indicate which side goes up.

➡ Rotate crankshaft at 45°, so that all pistons are ½ the way down the cylinder bore to avoid piston to valve contact.

21. Position new cylinder head gaskets (5) onto the cylinder block.

22. Position cylinder heads (4) onto head gaskets (5) and cylinder block.

23. Tighten the cylinder head bolts in three steps using the sequence provided:
  - Step 1: Snug tighten M12 cylinder head bolts, in sequence, to 25 ft. lbs. (34 Nm) and M8 bolts to 15 ft. lbs. (20 Nm).
  - Step 2: Tighten M12 cylinder head bolts, in sequence, to 40 ft. lbs. (54 Nm) and verify M8 bolts to 15 ft. lbs. (20 Nm).
  - Step 3: Turn M12 cylinder head bolts, in sequence, 90 degrees and tighten M8 bolts to 25 ft. lbs. (34 Nm).

24. Install push rods and rocker arm assemblies in their original position, using push rod retainer 9070 (1).

25. Install the intake manifold and throttle body assembly.

26. If required, adjust spark plugs to specifications. Install the plugs.

27. Connect the heater hoses.

28. Install the fuel supply line.

29. Install the power steering pump.

30. Install the accessory drive belt.

31. Install cylinder head covers.

32. Install the ignition coils.

33. Reconnect the ignition coil wiring.

34. Connect the evaporation control system.

35. Install the air cleaner.

36. Fill cooling system.

37. Connect the negative cable to the battery.

38. Start engine check for leaks.

ENGINE ASSEMBLY

REMOVAL & INSTALLATION

3.7L Engine

See Figures 167 through 170.

1. Release fuel rail pressure then disconnect the fuel supply quick connect fitting at the fuel rail.

2. Remove the strut tower support (1).

3. Disconnect the battery negative cable.

4. Remove air cleaner assembly.

5. Remove fan shroud with viscous fan assembly.

6. Remove drive belt.

7. Remove A/C compressor and secure away from engine.

8. Remove alternator and secure away from engine.

➡**Do NOT remove the phenolic pulley from the P/S pump. It is not required for P/S pump removal.**

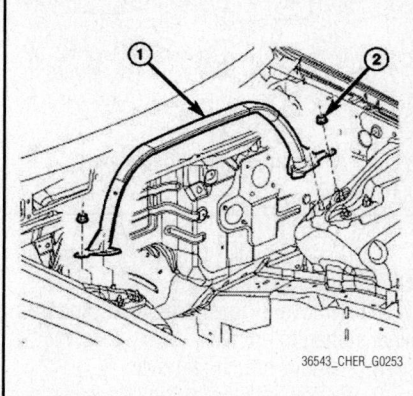

Fig. 167 Remove the strut tower support (1)

9. Remove power steering pump with lines attached and secure away from engine.

10. Drain cooling system.

11. Disconnect the heater hoses from the engine.

12. Disconnect heater hoses from heater core and remove hose assembly.

13. Remove upper radiator hose from engine.

14. Remove lower radiator hose from engine.

15. Remove radiator/cooling module assembly.

16. Disconnect the engine to body ground straps at the left side of cowl.

17. Disconnect the engine wiring harness at the following points:

- Intake Air Temperature (IAT) sensor (4)
- Fuel injectors
- Throttle body (2)
- Idle Air Control (IAC) motor (3)
- Engine oil pressure switch
- Engine Coolant Temperature (ECT) sensor
- Manifold Absolute Pressure MAP) sensor
- Camshaft Position (CMP) sensor
- Coil over plugs
- Crankshaft Position (CKP) sensor

18. Remove coil over plugs.

19. Remove fuel rail and secure away from engine.

➡**It is NOT necessary to release the quick connect fitting from the fuel supply line for engine removal.**

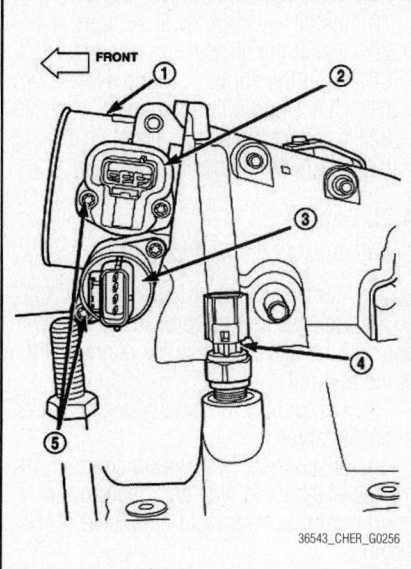

Fig. 168 Disconnect the engine wiring harness at the following points

20. Remove the PCV hose.

21. Remove the breather hoses.

22. Remove the vacuum hose for the power brake booster.

23. Disconnect knock sensors.

24. Remove engine oil dipstick tube.

25. Remove the intake manifold.

26. Install Engine Lifting Fixture 8427 using original fasteners from the removed intake manifold, and fuel rail. Torque to factory specifications.

➡**Recheck bolt torque on the Engine Lift Fixture before removing engine.**

27. Disconnect oxygen sensor wiring.

28. Disconnect Crankshaft Position (CKP) sensor.

29. Disconnect the engine block heater power cable, if equipped.

30. Disconnect the front propeller shaft at the front differential and secure out of way.

➡**It is necessary to disconnect the front propeller shaft for access to the starter and left side exhaust flange.**

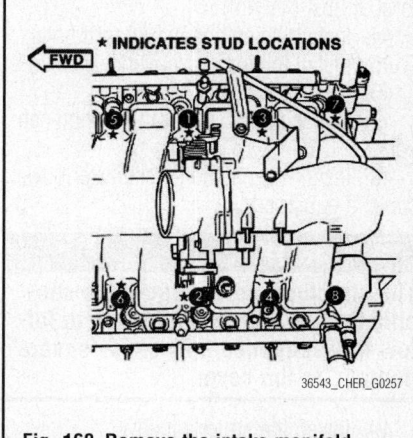

Fig. 169 Remove the intake manifold

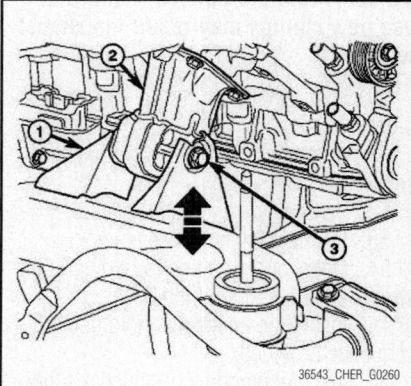

Fig. 170 Remove left and right engine mount thru bolts (3)

31. Remove the starter.

32. Remove the ground straps from the left and right side of the block.

33. Remove the structural cover.

34. Disconnect the right and left exhaust pipes at the manifolds and from the crossover, and remove from the vehicle.

➡**The exhaust clamps at the manifolds cannot be reused. New clamps must be used or leaks may occur.**

35. Remove torque converter bolts, marking their locations for reassembly.

36. Remove transmission bellhousing to engine bolts.

37. Remove left and right engine mount thru bolts (3).

38. Lower the vehicle.

39. Support the transmission with a suitable jack.

40. Connect a suitable engine hoist to the Engine Lifting Fixture 8427.

41. Remove engine from vehicle.

To install:

42. Position the engine in the vehicle.

43. Install the transmission bellhousing to engine mounting bolts. Tighten the bolts to 30 ft. lbs. (41 Nm)

44. Install the engine mount thru bolts.

45. Install the torque converter bolts.

46. Install the starter.

47. Connect the crankshaft position sensor.

48. Install the engine block heater power cable, if equipped.

✳✳ CAUTION

The structural cover requires a specific torque sequence. Failure to follow this sequence may cause severe damage to the cover.

49. Install the structural cover.

➡**New clamps must be used on exhaust manifold flanges. Failure to use new clamps may result in exhaust leaks.**

50. Install the left and right exhaust pipes.

51. Connect the left and right oxygen sensors.

52. Remove the engine lift plate.

53. Connect the knock sensors.

54. Connect the engine to body ground straps at the left side of the cowl.

55. Install the intake manifold using the sequence provided.

56. Install the engine oil dipstick tube.

57. Install the power brake booster vacuum hose.

58. Install the breather hoses.

59. Install the PCV hose.

60. Install the fuel rail.

61. Install the coil over plugs.

62. Connect the engine wiring harness at the following points:
- Intake Air Temperature (IAT) sensor
- Fuel injectors
- Throttle Position Switch (TPS)
- Idle Air Control (IAC) motor
- Engine Oil Pressure switch
- Engine Coolant Temperature (ECT) sensor
- Manifold Absolute Pressure MAP) sensor
- Camshaft Position (CMP) sensor
- Coil Over Plugs
- Crankshaft Position (CKP) sensor

63. Connect the ground straps on the right side of the engine.

64. Connect the ground straps on the left side of the engine.

65. Reinstall the radiator/cooling module assembly.

66. Connect lower radiator hose.

67. Connect upper radiator hose.

68. Connect throttle and speed control cables.

69. Install the heater hose assembly.

70. Install coolant recovery bottle.

71. Install the power steering pump.

72. Install the alternator.

73. Install the A/C compressor.

74. Install the drive belt.

75. Install the fan shroud with the viscous fan assembly.

76. Install the radiator core support bracket.

77. Recharge the A/C system.

78. Install the strut tower support.

79. Install the air cleaner assembly.

80. Refill the engine cooling system.

81. Check and fill engine oil.

82. Connect the battery negative cable.

83. Start the engine and check for leaks.

4.7L Engine

See Figures 167, 170 through 173.

1. Remove the strut tower support (1).

2. Release fuel rail pressure then disconnect the fuel supply quick connect fitting at the fuel rail.

3. Disconnect the battery negative and positive cables.

4. Disconnect two ground straps from the lower left hand side and one ground strap from the lower right hand side of the engine.

5. Remove the through bolt retaining nut and bolt (3) from both the left and right side engine mounts.

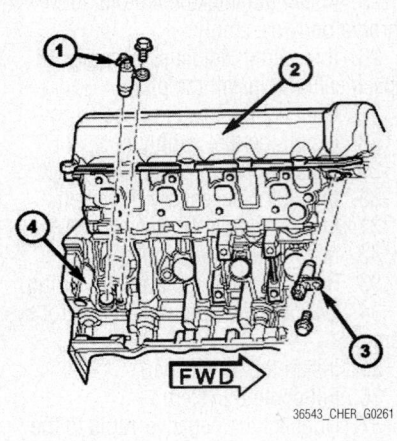

Fig. 171 Disconnect the Crankshaft Position (CKP) sensor (1)

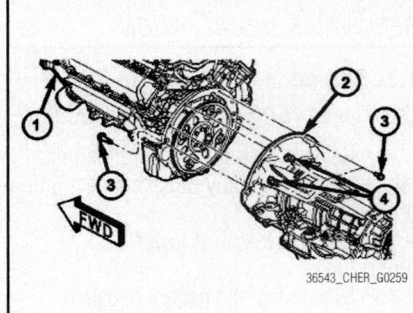

Fig. 172 Remove transmission bellhousing to engine bolts (3)

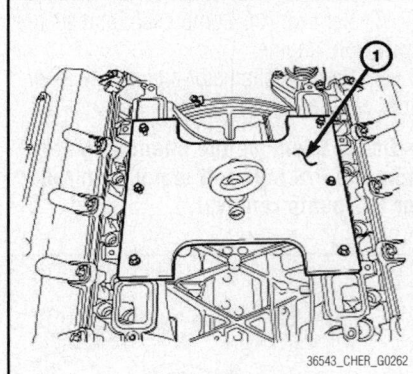

Fig. 173 Install engine lifting plate 10101 (1)

6. Disconnect the Crankshaft Position (CKP) sensor (1).

7. Remove exhaust crossover pipe from exhaust manifolds.

8. Remove structural cover.

9. Remove starter.

10. Drain cooling system.

11. Remove torque converter bolts.

12. Remove the transmission bellhousing bolts (3).

13. Disconnect the engine block heater power cable from the block heater, if equipped.

14. Lower vehicle.

15. Discharge A/C system.

16. Remove A/C compressor.

17. Remove shroud, fan assembly and accessory drive belt.

18. Disconnect transmission oil cooler lines at the radiator.

19. Disconnect radiator upper and lower hoses.

20. Remove radiator, A/C condenser and transmission oil cooler.

21. Remove alternator.

22. Remove power steering pump and position out of the way.

23. Disconnect body ground strap at the right side cowl.

24. Disconnect body ground strap at the left side cowl.

25. Remove intake manifold.

26. Install engine lifting plate 10101 (1).

➡ **It will be necessary to support the transmission in order to remove the engine.**

27. Position a suitable jack under the transmission.

28. Remove engine from the vehicle.

To install:

29. Position engine in the vehicle.

30. Remove jack from under the transmission.

31. Remove Engine Lifting Fixture 10101.

32. Position both the left and right side engine mount brackets and install the through bolts and nuts. Tighten to 70 ft. lbs. (95 Nm)

33. Install transmission to bellhousing bolts. Tighten the bolts to 30 ft. lbs. (41 Nm).

34. Install torque converter bolts.

35. Connect right side body ground strap.

36. Connect left side body ground straps.

37. Install intake manifold.

38. Position alternator wiring behind the oil dipstick tube, then install the oil dipstick tube upper mounting bolt.

39. Install power steering pump.

40. Position and install heater hoses and tubes onto intake manifold.

41. Install the heater hoses onto the heater core and the engine front cover, and install clips.

42. Install the alternator.

43. Install A/C condenser, radiator and transmission oil cooler.

44. Connect radiator upper and lower hoses.

45. Connect the transmission oil cooler lines to the radiator.

46. Install accessory drive belt, fan assembly and shroud.

47. Install A/C compressor.

48. Install throttle body resonator assembly and air inlet hose.

49. Raise vehicle.

50. Connect crankshaft position sensor.

51. Install the starter.

> ※※ **CAUTION**
>
> **The structural cover requires a specific torque sequence. Failure to follow this sequence may cause severe damage to the cover.**

52. Install structural cover.

53. Install exhaust crossover pipe.

54. Install engine block heater power cable, if equipped.

55. Install the strut tower support.

56. Check and fill engine oil.

57. Recharge the A/C system.

58. Refill the engine cooling system.

59. Connect the battery positive and negative cables.

60. Start the engine and check for leaks.

5.7L & 6.1L Engines

See Figures 167, 170, 174 through 177.

1. Remove the strut tower support (1).

2. Remove the engine cover.

3. Perform the Fuel System Pressure Release procedure.

4. Disconnect the battery negative cable.

5. Remove the air cleaner resonator and duct work as an assembly.

6. Drain cooling system.

7. Remove the accessory drive belt.

8. Remove radiator fan shroud.

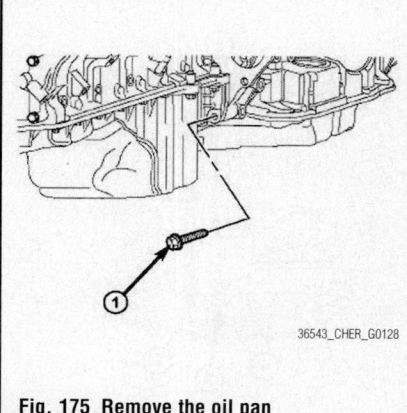

Fig. 175 Remove the oil pan to transmission bolts (1)

9. Remove the A/C compressor with the lines attached. Secure compressor out of the way.

10. Remove alternator assembly.

11. Remove the intake manifold and IAFM as an assembly.

12. Remove the ground wires from the rear of each cylinder head.

13. Disconnect the heater hoses from the engine.

➡ **It is NOT necessary to disconnect P/S hoses from pump, for P/S pump removal.**

14. Remove the power steering pump and set aside.

15. Disconnect the fuel supply line.

16. Raise and support the vehicle on a hoist and drain the engine oil.

17. Remove engine front mount to frame bolts (3) and nuts.

18. Disconnect the transmission oil cooler lines from their retainers at the oil pan bolts.

19. Disconnect exhaust pipe at manifolds.

20. Disconnect the starter wires. Remove starter motor.

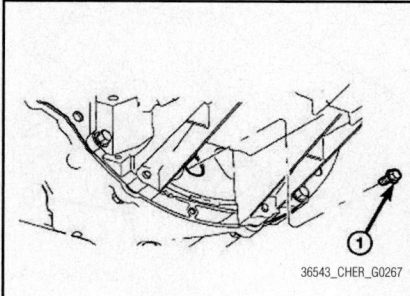

Fig. 174 Remove drive plate to converter bolts

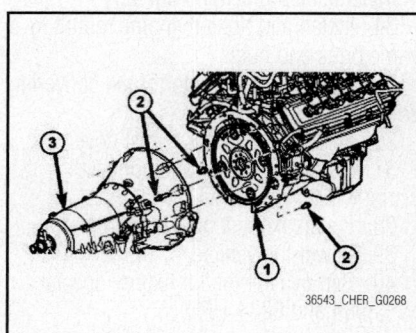

Fig. 176 Remove transmission bellhousing to engine block bolts (2)

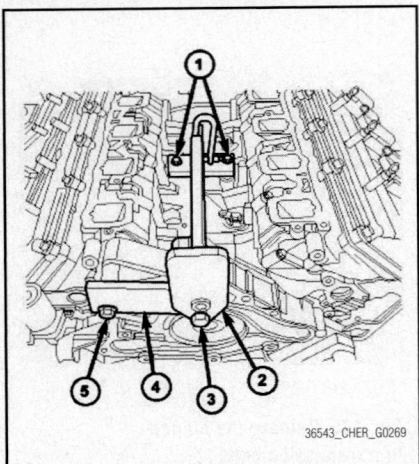

Fig. 177 Install engine lift fixture, special tool 8984 (2) and 8984-UPD (1)

21. Remove the structural dust cover.
22. Remove drive plate to converter bolts.
23. Remove the oil pan to transmission bolts (1).
24. Remove transmission bellhousing to engine block bolts (2).
25. Lower the vehicle.
26. Install engine lift fixture, special tool 8984 (2) and 8984-UPD (1).
27. Separate engine from transmission, remove engine from vehicle, and install engine assembly on a repair stand.

To install:

28. Install engine lift fixture Special tool 8984 and 8984-UPD.
29. Position the engine in the engine compartment.
30. Lower engine into compartment and align engine with transmission.
31. Mate engine and transmission and install two transmission to engine block mounting bolts finger tight.
32. Lower engine assembly until the engine mounts rests in frame perches.
33. Install remaining transmission to engine block mounting bolts and the oil pan to transmission bolts and tighten.
34. Install and tighten engine mount to frame bolts and nuts.
35. Install drive plate to torque converter bolts.
36. Install the structural dust cover.
37. Install the starter and connect the starter wires.
38. Install exhaust pipe to manifold.
39. Lower the vehicle.
40. Remove engine lift fixture, special tool 8984 and 8984-UPD.
41. Connect the fuel supply line.
42. Reinstall the power steering pump.
43. Connect the heater hoses.

44. Reconnect the ground wires to the rear of each cylinder head.
45. Install the intake manifold.
46. Install the alternator, and wire connections.
47. Install A/C compressor.
48. Install the accessory drive belt.
49. Install the radiator fan shroud.
50. Connect the radiator lower hose.
51. Connect the transmission oil cooler lines to the radiator.
52. Connect the radiator upper hose.
53. Install the air cleaner resonator and duct work.
54. Add engine oil to crankcase.
55. Fill cooling system.
56. Install the engine cover.
57. Install the strut tower support.
58. Connect battery negative cable.
59. Start engine and inspect for leaks.
60. Road test vehicle.

3.0L Diesel Engine

See Figures 178 through 184.

1. Disconnect negative battery cable.

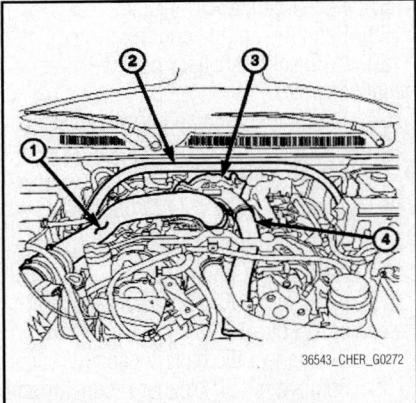

Fig. 178 Remove the strut tower support (2)

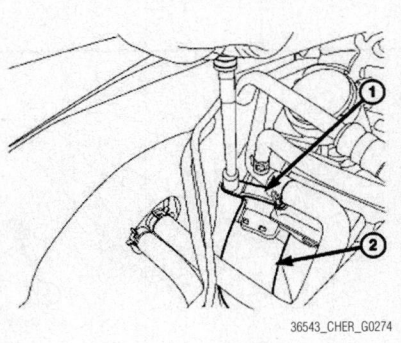

Fig. 179 Remove lower catalytic converter to upper catalytic converter clamp (1) behind right cylinder head

2. Drain cooling system.
3. Evacuate air conditioning.
4. Remove the strut tower support (2).
5. Remove engine cover.
6. Remove air cleaner housing.
7. Remove lower catalytic converter to upper catalytic converter clamp (1) behind right cylinder head.
8. Raise and support the vehicle.
9. Remove front splash shield.
10. Drain power steering at cooling fan, cap lines and set aside.
11. Remove catalytic converter clamp from exhaust pipe.
12. Remove transfer case splash shield.
13. Disconnect the front exhaust pipe at muffler.
14. Remove the catalytic converter and front exhaust pipe.
15. Paint mark the flex plate to torque converter relationship and remove the torque converter bolts (1) through the access hole.
16. Support the transmission with a transmission jack and remove the transfer case cross over bolts from frame.

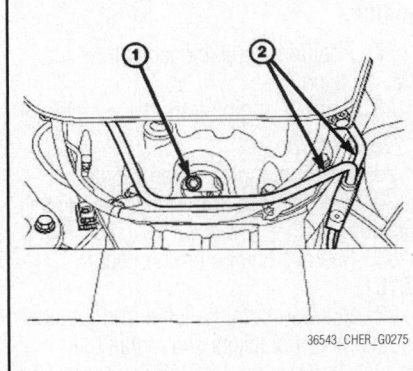

Fig. 180 Remove the torque converter bolts (1) through the access hole

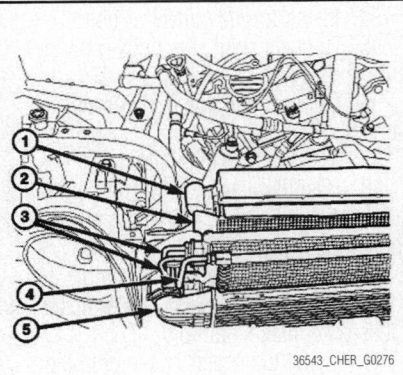

Fig. 181 Remove the charge air inlet hose (5)

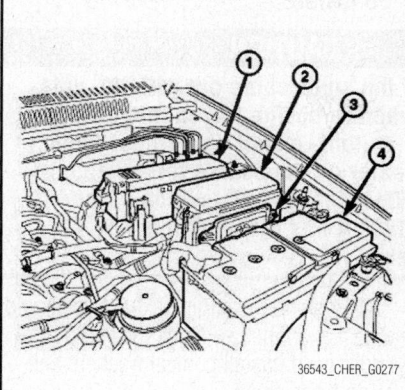

Fig. 182 Remove the Power Distribution Center (PDC) (1) from the bracket and remove the bracket

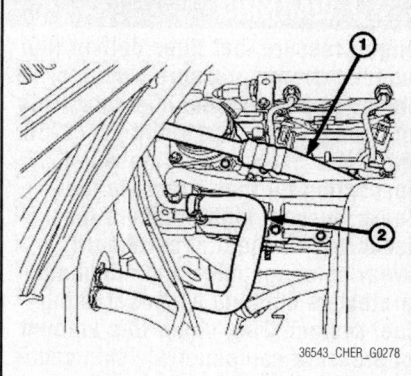

Fig. 183 Disconnect the heater hose (2) at cooler tube on the right cylinder head

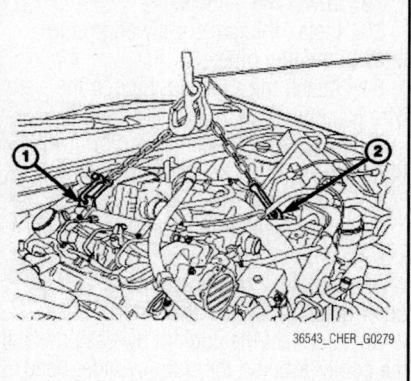

Fig. 184 Lift the weight of the engine off of the engine mounts (1,2)

17. Carefully lower the transmission enough to gain access to the upper transmission to engine mounting bolts, and remove accessible bolts.

18. Raise transmission, install the transfer case cross over bolts, and remove transmission jack.

19. Disconnect the transmission wiring harness at transmission and route wiring harness toward the starter.

20. Remove remaining transmission to engine bolts.

21. Disconnect the engine ground strap in front of the starter.

22. Loosen both engine mount through bolts.

23. Remove the lower radiator hose.

24. Remove the front axle housing.

25. Lower the vehicle.

26. Remove the front grille and radiator upper core support.

27. Remove the hood latch and position aside.

28. Remove the front core support brackets.

29. Remove the charge air inlet hose (5).

30. Remove the charge air outlet hose (5).

31. Disconnect the power steering reservoir hose to pump, at the reservoir.

32. Disconnect the suction/discharge lines at the condenser and accumulator.

33. Disconnect the transmission cooler (3) and power steering cooler lines (4) at the coolant module.

34. Position the radiator (1) deflectors aside and remove coolant module to core support fasteners.

35. Remove cooler module assembly.

36. Remove the battery and tray.

37. Remove the Power Distribution Center (PDC) (1) from the bracket and remove the bracket.

38. Disconnect the Power Control Module (PCM) (3) and route the engine wiring harness on top of the engine.

39. Route engine wiring aside and disconnect the starter wiring.

40. Unplug air conditioning (A/C) compressor wiring at compressor, route the transmission harness forward, and place the harness on top of the engine.

41. Disconnect the alternator wiring harness, and position aside.

42. Disconnect the vacuum hose at the vacuum pump, and set aside.

43. Disconnect the wiring harness connectors from the PDC.

44. Disconnect the heater hose (2) at cooler tube on the right cylinder head.

45. Disconnect the coolant by-pass hose (2) at the cooler tube on the right cylinder head.

46. Disconnect the coolant hose, at the outer housing, by the alternator.

47. Disconnect the A/C lines (1) at the expansion valve.

48. Remove the engine cover mounting bracket.

49. Remove the transmission oil level indicator tube retaining bolt.

50. Loosen front axle vent tube from wiring harness and position aside.

51. Disconnect the fuel lines from the fuel pipe using special tool 6507.

52. Remove upper turbocharger heat shield.

53. Connect engine lift chain to engine lift fixtures.

54. Support the transmission with a floor jack.

55. Lift the weight of the engine off of the engine mounts (1,2).

56. Remove right engine mount from engine.

57. Remove left engine mount from engine.

58. Remove engine from vehicle.

To install:

59. Carefully align the engine assembly in the engine bay area and align with the transmission, Do Not lower the engine.

60. Install left engine mount to engine. Tighten bolts to 26 ft. lbs. (35 Nm).

61. Install right engine mount to engine. Tighten bolts to 26 ft. lbs. (35 Nm).

62. Align the engine to transmission, and lower the engine mounts into position.

63. Remove engine lifting device.

64. Route the transmission wiring harness through to the rear of the engine.

65. Raise and support the vehicle.

66. Install accessible engine to transmission housing bolts. Tighten bolts to 50 ft. lbs. (68 Nm).

67. Support the transmission and remove the rear transmission crossmember retaining bolts.

68. Lower the transmission and install the upper transmission to engine fasteners. Tighten bolts to 50 ft. lbs. (68 Nm).

69. Raise the transmission and install the transmission crossmember.

70. Install the flex plate to torque converter bolts.

71. Tighten engine mount through bolts to 22 ft. lbs. (30 Nm).

72. Install the engine ground wire above the starter. Tighten bolt to 10 ft. lbs. (14 Nm).

73. Install the starter wiring.

74. Connect the Crankshaft Position (CKP) sensor wiring harness connector.

75. Route the transmission wiring harness and make necessary sensor connections at the transmission.

76. Install the front axle housing.

77. Install the catalytic converter and front exhaust pipe.

78. Install the transfer case shield.

79. Lower the vehicle.
80. Install the fuel supply and return lines to the fuel pipe.
81. Attach the axle vent tube to the wiring harness.
82. Secure the transmission oil level indicator.
83. Install the engine cover bracket.
84. Connect the A/C lines at the expansion valve.
85. Connect the coolant hose, at the outer housing, by the alternator.
86. Connect the coolant by-pass hose at the cooler tube on the right cylinder head.
87. Connect the heater hose, at the cooler tube on the right cylinder head.
88. Connect the wiring harness connectors to the PDC.
89. Connect the vacuum hose to the vacuum pump.
90. Connect the alternator wiring.
91. Connect the A/C compressor wiring harness connector.
92. Connect the PCM wiring harness connectors.
93. Install the PDC bracket and mount the PDC.

➡ **Do Not connect the negative battery cable when installing the battery.**

94. Install the battery and tray.
95. Install the coolant module assembly.
96. Connect the transmission cooler and power steering cooler lines to the coolant module.
97. Connect the suction/discharge lines at the A/C condenser and accumulator.
98. Connect the power steering reservoir hose to pump, at the reservoir.
99. Install the charge air inlet and outlet hoses at cooler.
100. Install the front core support bracket.
101. Install the front grille and upper radiator core support bracket with the hood latch.
102. Raise and support the vehicle.
103. Install the power steering hydraulic lines at cooling fan.
104. Install the lower radiator hose.
105. Lower the vehicle.
106. Install lower catalytic converter exhaust clamp behind right cylinder head.
107. Install the turbocharger upper heat shield.
108. Install air cleaner housing and connect the air cleaner outlet tube to the turbocharger.
109. Install the strut tower support.
110. Fill all appropriate fluid levels.
111. Evacuate and recharge air conditioning.
112. Connect the negative battery cable.

High-pressure fuel lines deliver fuel under extreme pressure from the injection pump to the injectors. This may be as high as 19,580 psi (1350 bar). Use extreme caution when inspecting for high-pressure fuel leaks. Inspect high-pressure fuel leaks with a sheet of cardboard. Wear safety goggles and adequate protective clothing when servicing fuel system. Fuel under this amount of pressure can penetrate skin causing serious or fatal injury.

113. Start engine, allow to warm, turn engine off and inspect for leaks.
114. Bleed power steering system using the scan tool procedure.
115. Install lower splash shields.
116. Install engine cover.

EXHAUST MANIFOLD

REMOVAL & INSTALLATION

3.7L Engine

Right Exhaust Manifold

See Figure 185.

1. Disconnect the negative cable from the battery.
2. Raise and support the vehicle.
3. Remove the bolts and nuts attaching the exhaust pipe to the engine exhaust manifold.
4. Lower the vehicle.
5. Remove the exhaust heat shield (1).
6. Remove bolts, nuts (2) and washers attaching manifold to cylinder head.
7. Remove manifold and gasket from the cylinder head.

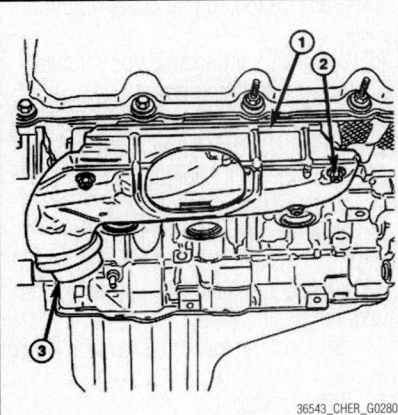

Fig. 185 Remove the exhaust heat shield (1)

36543_CHER_G0280

To install:

❋❋ **CAUTION**

If the studs came out with the nuts when removing the engine exhaust manifold, install new studs. Apply sealer on the coarse thread ends. Water leaks may develop at the studs if this precaution is not taken.

8. Position the engine exhaust manifold and gasket on the two studs located on the cylinder head. Install conical washers and nuts on these studs.
9. Install remaining conical washers. Starting at the center arm and working outward, tighten the bolts and nuts to 18 ft. lbs. (25 Nm).
10. Install the exhaust heat shields.
11. Raise and support the vehicle.

❋❋ **CAUTION**

Over tightening heat shield fasteners, may cause shield to distort and/or crack.

12. Assemble exhaust pipe to manifold and secure with bolts, nuts and retainers. Tighten the bolts and nuts to 25 ft. lbs. (34 Nm).

Left Exhaust Manifold

See Figure 186.

1. Disconnect the negative cable from the battery.
2. Raise and support the vehicle.
3. Remove the bolts and nuts attaching the exhaust pipe to the engine exhaust manifold.
4. Lower the vehicle.
5. Remove the exhaust heat shields (1).

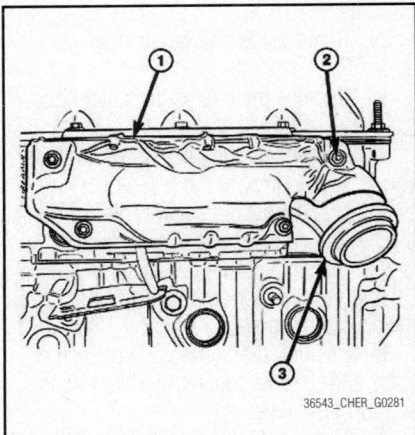

Fig. 186 Remove the exhaust heat shields (1)

36543_CHER_G0281

6. Remove bolts, nuts (2) and washers attaching manifold to cylinder head.

7. Remove manifold and gasket from the cylinder head.

To install:

☀ CAUTION

If the studs came out with the nuts when removing the engine exhaust manifold, install new studs. Apply sealer on the coarse thread ends. Water leaks may develop at the studs if this precaution is not taken.

8. Position the engine exhaust manifold and gasket on the two studs located on the cylinder head. Install conical washers and nuts on these studs.

9. Install remaining conical washers. Starting at the center arm and working outward, tighten the bolts and nuts to 18 ft. lbs. (25 Nm).

10. Install the exhaust heat shields.

11. Raise and support the vehicle.

☀ CAUTION

Over tightening heat shield fasteners, may cause shield to distort and/or crack.

12. Assemble exhaust pipe to manifold and secure with bolts, nuts and retainers. Tighten the bolts and nuts to 25 ft. lbs. (34 Nm).

4.7L Engine

Right Exhaust Manifold

See Figure 187.

1. Disconnect the negative cable from the battery.

2. Remove the battery from vehicle.

3. Remove the Power Distribution Center (PDC) fasteners and set aside.

4. Remove the battery tray assembly.

5. Remove the washer bottle assembly.

6. Remove the accessory drive belt.

7. Remove the A/C compressor from mounting and set aside.

8. Remove the A/C accumulator support bracket fastener.

9. Drain the coolant.

10. Remove the heater hoses at the engine.

11. Remove the fasteners attaching the exhaust manifold heat shield.

12. Remove the heat shield.

13. Remove the upper exhaust manifold attaching fasteners.

14. Raise the vehicle on a hoist.

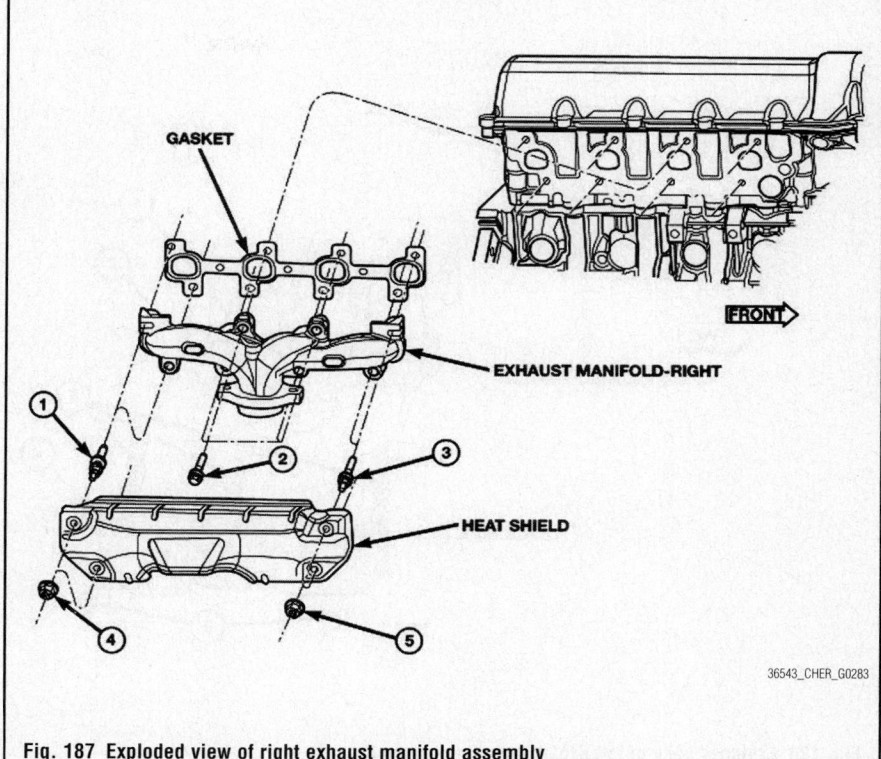

Fig. 187 Exploded view of right exhaust manifold assembly

36543_CHER_G0283

15. Disconnect the exhaust pipe from the manifold.

16. Remove the bolts attaching the starter. Move the starter aside.

17. Remove the lower exhaust manifold attaching fasteners.

18. Remove the exhaust manifold and gasket. The manifold is removed from below the engine compartment.

To install:

19. Install the exhaust manifold and gasket from below the engine compartment.

20. Install the lower exhaust manifold fasteners (1,2,3,). DO NOT tighten until all fasteners are in place.

21. Lower the vehicle and install the upper exhaust manifold fasteners (1,2,3,). Tighten all manifold bolts starting at center and working outward to 18 ft. lbs. (25 Nm).

☀ CAUTION

Over tightening heat shield fasteners, may cause shield to distort and/or crack.

22. Install the exhaust manifold heat shield. Tighten fasteners (4,5) to 72 inch lbs. (8 Nm), then loosen 45 degrees.

23. Install the starter.

24. Connect the exhaust pipe to the manifold.

25. Connect the heater hoses at the engine.

26. Install the fastener attaching the A/C accumulator.

27. Install the A/C compressor and fasteners.

28. Install the accessory drive belt.

29. Install the washer bottle and battery tray assembly.

30. Install the PDC.

31. Install the battery and connect the cables.

32. Fill the cooling system.

Left Exhaust Manifold

See Figure 188.

1. Disconnect the negative battery cable.

2. Remove the air cleaner housing and clean air tube.

3. Remove the front two exhaust manifold heat shield retaining nuts (5).

4. Raise and support the vehicle.

5. Disconnect the exhaust pipe at the exhaust manifold.

6. Remove the rear two exhaust manifold heat shield retaining nuts (5) and remove the heat shield (4).

7. Remove the lower exhaust manifold retaining bolts (3).

8. Lower the vehicle.

9. Remove the upper exhaust manifold retaining bolts (3).

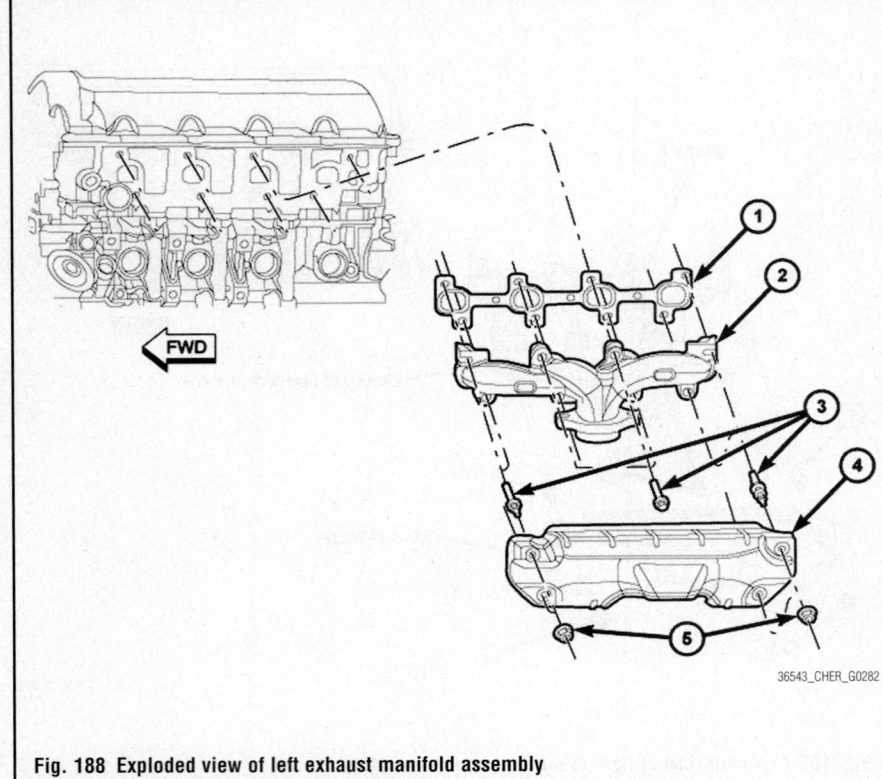

Fig. 188 Exploded view of left exhaust manifold assembly

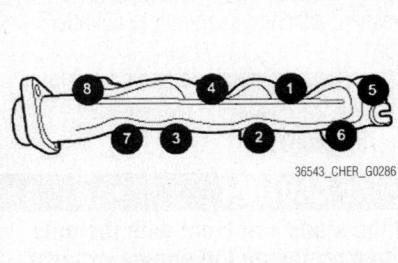

Fig. 189 Remove the eight bolts/studs from the exhaust manifold

➡ **The Exhaust manifold is removed from below the engine compartment.**

10. Raise and support the vehicle.

11. Remove the exhaust manifold (2) and gasket (1).

To install:

12. Position the exhaust manifold (2) and gasket (1) from below the engine compartment.

13. Install the lower exhaust manifold retaining bolts (3) hand tight.

14. Lower the vehicle.

15. Install the upper exhaust manifold retaining bolts (3) and tighten all manifold bolts starting at center and working outward to 18 ft. lbs. (25 Nm).

⁂ **CAUTION**

Over tightening heat shield fasteners, may cause shield to distort and/or crack.

16. Position the exhaust manifold heat shield (4) and install the front two heat shield retaining nuts hand tight.

17. Raise and support the vehicle.

18. Install the back two exhaust manifold heat shield retaining nuts (5) and tighten to 72 inch lbs. (8 Nm), then loosen 45 degrees.

19. Connect the exhaust pipe to the exhaust manifold.

20. Lower the vehicle.

21. Tighten the front two exhaust manifold heat shield retaining nuts (5) to 72 inch lbs. (8 Nm), then loosen 45 degrees.

22. Install the air cleaner housing and clean air tube.

23. Connect the negative battery cable.

5.7L Engine

Right Exhaust Manifold

See Figure 189.

1. Partially drain the engine coolant.

2. Remove the engine cover.

3. Disconnect the negative battery terminal.

4. Remove the air box assembly (2).

5. Remove the coolant recovery bottle (1).

6. Disconnect and re-position the upper right side engine harness.

⁂ **CAUTION**

Use caution when connecting, disconnecting or repositioning any wiring harness. Damage could occur to the wiring harness due to vehicle mileage, vehicle age and environmental conditions.

7. If required, disconnect and re-position the heater hoses from the heater core tubes in the engine compartment.

8. Raise and secure the vehicle.

9. Remove any skid plates (if equipped).

10. Saturate the front exhaust pipe/catalytic converter assembly bolts and nuts with heat valve lubricant. Allow 5 minutes for penetration.

11. Disconnect and remove the upstream O2 sensor from the exhaust pipe/catalytic converter assembly.

12. Remove the bolts from the front right exhaust pipe/catalytic converter assembly.

13. Loosen the bolts from the front left exhaust pipe/catalytic converter assembly. Do not remove the bolts.

14. Remove the front right tire and wheel assembly.

15. Remove the front right side wheelhouse splash shield.

16. Lower the vehicle.

17. Remove the right side exhaust manifold heat shield.

18. Remove the eight bolts/studs from the exhaust manifold using the sequence provided.

19. Remove the exhaust manifold and gasket from the front of the vehicle.

20. Inspect the exhaust manifold for any damage.

21. Clean the mating surfaces.

To install:

22. Prior to installation, make sure all gasket mating surfaces are clean and free of any debris.

23. Inspect the exhaust manifold for any damage.

24. Install manifold gasket and manifold through the front of the vehicle.

➡ **Make sure gasket is properly seated before tightening the manifold stud/bolts.**

25. Install the eight manifold studs/bolts using the sequence provided. Tighten the studs/bolts to 18 ft. lbs. (25 Nm).

26. Install the exhaust manifold heat shield. Tighten the nuts to 71 inch lbs. (8 Nm).

27. Raise and secure the vehicle.

28. Install the bolts and nuts at the right front exhaust pipe/catalytic converter assembly to exhaust manifold flange. Do not tighten.

29. Position the exhaust pipe for proper clearance with the frame and underbody parts. A minimum clearance of 1.0 inches (25.4 mm) is required.

30. Once properly aligned, tighten the right front exhaust pipe/catalytic converter assembly to exhaust manifold bolts to 19 ft. lbs. (26 Nm).

31. Tighten the left front exhaust pipe/catalytic converter assembly to the exhaust manifold bolts to 19 ft. lbs. (26 Nm).

32. Connect and install the upstream O2 sensor to the exhaust pipe/catalytic converter assembly.

33. Install the front right side wheelhouse splash shield.

34. Install any skid plates (if equipped).

35. Install the front tire and wheel.

36. Lower the vehicle.

37. If required, connect and position the heater hoses from the heater core tubes in the engine compartment.

✳✳ CAUTION

Use caution when connecting, disconnecting or repositioning any wiring harness. Damage could occur to the wiring harness due to vehicle mileage, vehicle age and environmental conditions.

38. Connect and position the upper right side engine harness.

39. Install the coolant recovery bottle.

40. Install the air box assembly.

41. Fill the engine coolant.

42. Connect the negative battery terminal.

43. Install the engine cover.

44. Start the engine and check for any leaks.

Left Exhaust Manifold

See Figures 190 through 194.

1. Lock the steering wheel in the center position.

✳✳ CAUTION

Steering column module is centered to the vehicle's steering system. Failure to keep the system and steering column module centered and locked/inhibited from rotating can result in steering column module damage.

2. Remove the engine cover.

3. Disconnect the battery terminals.

4. Remove the battery and battery tray.

✳✳ CAUTION

Use caution when connecting, disconnecting or repositioning any wiring harness. Damage could occur to the wiring harness due to vehicle mileage, vehicle age and environmental conditions.

5. Disconnect the bulk connector (4).

6. Disconnect the tail lamp harness.

7. Remove the nut from the bulk connector retaining bracket (3) and reposition the bracket.

8. Disconnect the power steering switch (1) and reposition the harness.

9. Disconnect power distribution center (PDC) connector and reposition harness.

10. Remove the lower coupling pinch bolt (1) from the intermediate steering shaft (2) at the rack and pinion assembly (3).

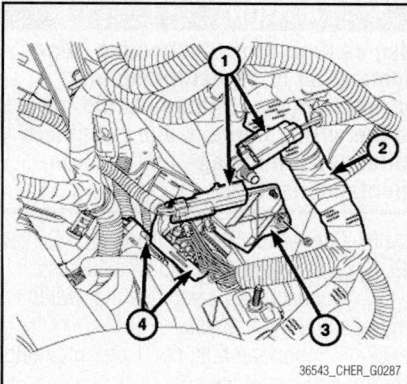

36543_CHER_G0287

Fig. 190 Disconnect the bulk connector (4)

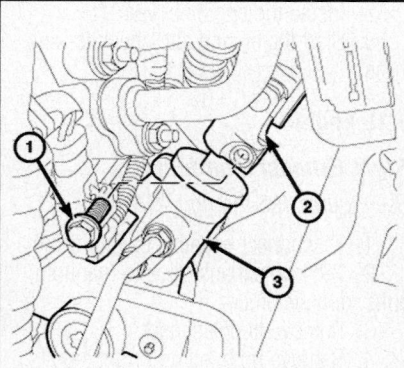

36543_CHER_G0288

Fig. 191 Remove the lower coupling pinch bolt (1) from the intermediate steering shaft (2) at the rack and pinion assembly (3)

11. Remove upper mounting bolt from dipstick tube.

12. Remove the two left front exhaust manifold heat shield nuts.

13. Lift and secure the vehicle.

14. Remove any skid plates (if equipped).

15. Remove the front propeller shaft (4 X 4 equipped vehicles).

16. Remove the front left side tire and wheel.

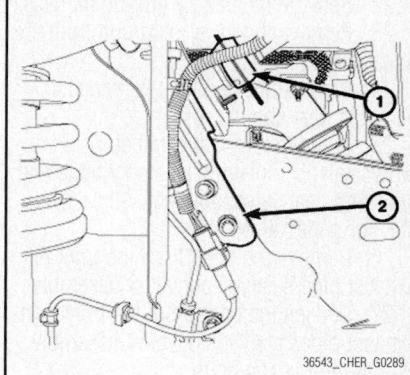

36543_CHER_G0289

Fig. 192 Remove the two bolts and two nuts from the intermediate steering shaft support bracket (2)

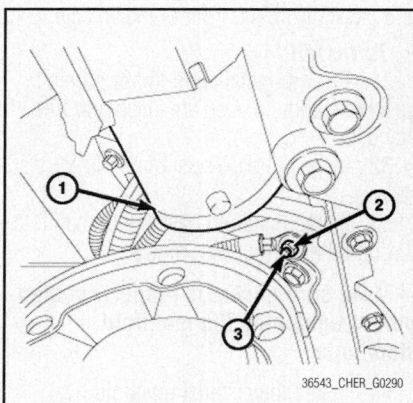

36543_CHER_G0290

Fig. 193 Remove the nut (2) from the battery ground harness, located in front of the starter (1)

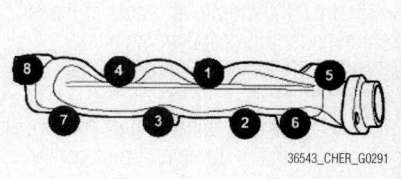

36543_CHER_G0291

Fig. 194 Remove the eight bolts/studs from the exhaust manifold using the sequence provided

17. Remove the front left side wheel-house splash shield.

18. Reposition any harnesses as needed.

19. Remove the two bolts and two nuts from the intermediate steering shaft support bracket (2).

20. Remove the intermediate steering shaft support bracket (2).

21. Remove the nut (2) from the battery ground harness, located in front of the starter (1).

22. Remove the battery ground harness.

23. Remove the lower stud/bolt from the dipstick tube.

24. Remove the two left rear exhaust manifold heat shield nuts.

25. Saturate the front exhaust pipe/catalytic converter assembly bolts and nuts with heat valve lubricant. Allow 5 minutes for penetration.

26. Remove the bolts from the front left exhaust pipe/catalytic converter assembly.

27. Loosen the bolts from the front right exhaust pipe/catalytic converter assembly. Do not remove the bolts.

28. Lower the vehicle.

29. Remove the eight bolts/studs from the exhaust manifold using the sequence provided.

30. Remove the exhaust manifold (2) and gasket from the front of the vehicle.

To install:

31. Prior to installation, make sure all gasket mating surfaces are clean and free of any debris.

32. Inspect the exhaust manifold for any damage.

33. Install manifold gasket and manifold through the front of the vehicle.

➡**Make sure gasket is properly seated before tightening the manifold stud/bolts.**

34. Install the exhaust manifold heat shield. Tighten the nuts to 71 inch lbs. (8 Nm).

35. Install the dipstick tube upper mounting bolt. Tighten the bolt to 9 ft. lbs. (12 Nm).

36. Raise and secure the vehicle.

37. Install the bolts and nuts at the left front exhaust pipe/catalytic converter assembly to exhaust manifold flange. Do not tighten.

38. Position the exhaust pipe for proper clearance with the frame and underbody parts. A minimum clearance of 1.0 inches (25.4 mm) is required.

39. Once properly aligned, tighten the left front exhaust pipe/catalytic converter assembly to exhaust manifold bolts.

40. Tighten the right front exhaust pipe/catalytic converter assembly to the exhaust manifold bolts.

41. Install the lower dipstick stud/bolt located in front of the starter. Tighten the stud/bolt to 9 ft. lbs. (12 Nm).

42. Install the battery ground harness to the lower dipstick stud/bolt. Tighten the nut to 8 ft. lbs. (11 Nm).

43. Install the front propeller shaft (4WD equipped vehicles).

44. Install the two bolts and two nuts from the intermediate steering shaft support bracket to the frame. Tighten the bolts to 9 ft. lbs. (12 Nm).

45. Install the front left side wheelhouse splash shield.

46. Install any skid plates (if equipped).

47. Install the front tire and wheel.

48. Lower the vehicle.

49. Install the lower coupling pinch bolt through the intermediate steering shaft to the rack and pinion assembly. Tighten the bolt to 36 ft. lbs. (49 Nm).

✷✷ CAUTION

Use caution when connecting, disconnecting or repositioning any wiring harness. Damage could occur to the wiring harness due to vehicle mileage, vehicle age and environmental conditions.

50. Connect the Power Distribution Center (PDC) connector and position the harness.

51. Connect the power steering switch and position the harness.

52. Position the bulk connector retaining bracket and install the nut.

53. Connect the tail lamp harness.

54. Connect the bulk connector.

55. Install the battery tray.

56. Install the battery.

57. Install the engine cover.

58. Start the engine and check for any leaks.

6.1L Engine

Right Exhaust Manifold

See Figures 195 through 197.

1. Disconnect negative battery cable.

2. Remove exhaust pipe to manifold bolts, remove pipe.

3. Remove knock sensor.

4. Remove both left and right side engine mount to frame bolts (3).

5. Install engine support fixture special tool 8534 (1). Do not use the third leg.

6. Raise engine using special tool 8534 to provide clearance to remove the exhaust manifold.

7. Remove the top row of bolts from manifold from under the hood.

8. Remove the bottom row of bolts from manifold from under vehicle.

9. Remove the manifold from under vehicle.

To install:

10. Install manifold gasket and manifold.

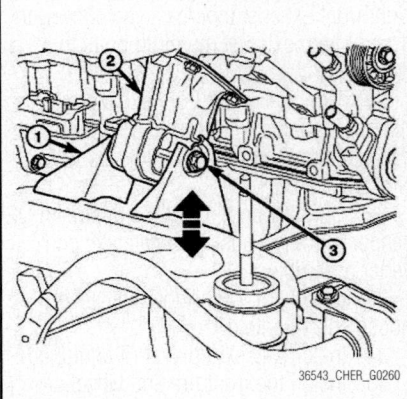

Fig. 195 Remove left and right engine mount through bolts (3)

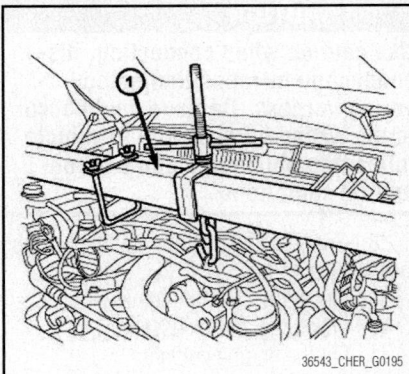

Fig. 196 Install engine support fixture special tool 8534 (1)

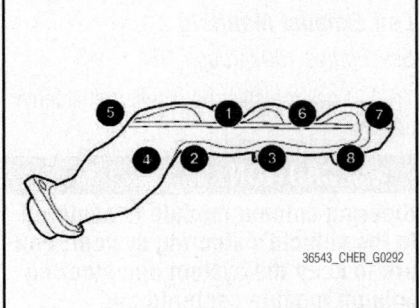

Fig. 197 Install manifold bolts and tighten using the sequence provided

11. Install manifold bolts and tighten to 23 ft. lbs. (31 Nm) using the sequence provided.

12. Lower the engine using Engine Support Fixture 8534.

13. Install both left and right side engine mount to frame bolts.

14. Remove Engine Support Fixture 8534.

15. Install the air cleaner housing.

16. Install the knock sensor.

17. Install the exhaust pipe to manifold bolts.

18. Reconnect negative battery cable.

Left Exhaust Manifold

See Figures 105, 170, 198 and 199.

1. Remove air cleaner housing.

2. Disconnect negative battery cable.

3. Remove exhaust pipe to manifold bolts, remove pipe.

4. Remove starter (1) and heat shield (3).

5. Remove knock sensor.

6. Remove the front propeller shaft at the front axle, and position out of the way.

7. Remove both left and right side engine mount to frame bolts (3).

8. Install engine support fixture special tool 8534 (1). Do not use the third leg.

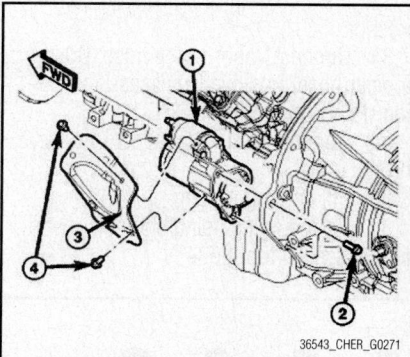

36543_CHER_G0271

Fig. 198 Remove starter (1) and heat shield (3)

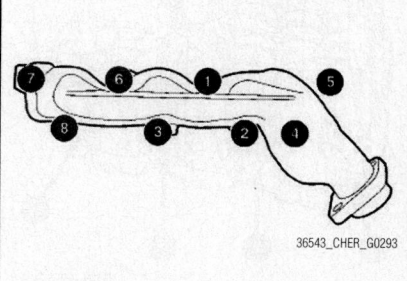

36543_CHER_G0293

Fig. 199 Install manifold bolts and tighten using the sequence provided

9. Raise engine using special tool 8534 to provide clearance to remove the exhaust manifold.

10. Remove the top row of bolts from manifold from under the hood.

11. Remove the bottom row of bolts from manifold from under vehicle.

12. Remove manifold from under vehicle.

To install:

13. Install manifold gasket and manifold.

14. Install manifold bolts and tighten to 23 ft. lbs. (31 Nm) using the sequence provided.

15. Install the knock sensor.

16. Install starter and heat shield.

17. Lower the engine using Engine Support 8534.

18. Install both left and right side engine mount to frame bolts.

19. Remove Engine Support fixture 8534.

20. Install the front propeller shaft.

21. Install the exhaust pipe to manifold bolts.

22. Reconnect negative battery cable.

3.0L Diesel Engine

Right Exhaust Manifold

1. Disconnect negative battery cable.

2. Remove the engine cover.

3. Remove the turbo heat shield.

4. Remove the exhaust elbow at the turbo.

5. Remove the right exhaust manifold.

To install:

6. Discard the old gasket and clean the cylinder head and manifold sealing surfaces.

7. Install a new exhaust manifold gasket.

8. Install the right exhaust manifold to cylinder head nuts. Torque the nuts to 222 inch lbs. (25 Nm)

9. Install the exhaust elbow to turbocharger bolts. Torque to 177 inch lbs. (20 Nm). and then add another 90° of rotation.

10. Install the strut tower brace.

11. Install the engine cowl.

12. Install the engine cover.

13. Connect the negative battery cable.

Left Exhaust Manifold

1. Disconnect negative battery cable.

2. Remove the engine cover.

3. Remove the turbo heat shield.

4. Remove the EGR tube.

5. Remove the exhaust elbow at the turbo.

6. Remove the left exhaust manifold.

To install:

7. Discard the old gasket and clean the cylinder head and manifold sealing surfaces.

8. Install a new exhaust manifold gasket.

9. Install the left exhaust manifold to cylinder head nuts. Tighten the nuts to 222 inch lbs. (25 Nm).

10. Install the exhaust elbow to turbocharger bolts. Tighten to 177 inch lbs. (20 Nm) and then add another 90° of rotation.

11. Install the turbocharger heat shield. Tighten to 88 inch lbs. (10 Nm).

12. Install the engine cover.

13. Connect the negative battery cable.

FLEXPLATE

REMOVAL & INSTALLATION

See Figures 200 and 201.

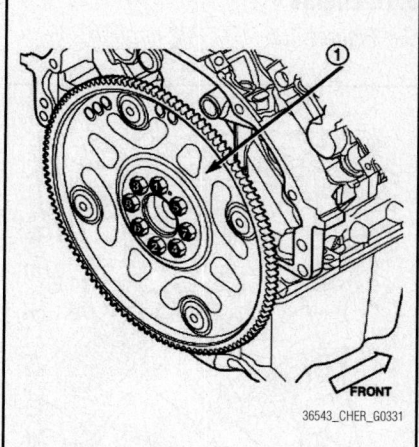

36543_CHER_G0331

Fig. 200 Remove the bolts using the sequence provided

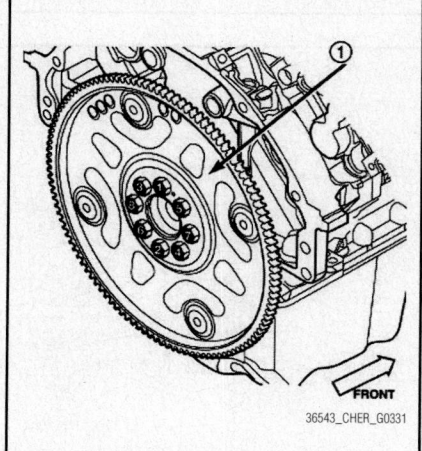

36543_CHER_G0331

Fig. 201 Install the bolts using the sequence shown

1. Remove the transmission.
2. Remove the bolts using the sequence provided.
3. Remove the flexplate.

To install:

4. Position the flexplate onto the crankshaft and install the bolts hand tight.
5. For 3.7L/5.7L6.1L engines, tighten the flexplate retaining bolts to 70 ft. lbs. (95 Nm) in the sequence shown.
6. For 4.7L engines, tighten the flexplate retaining bolts to 45 ft. lbs. (70 Nm) in the sequence shown.
7. For 3.0L diesel engines, tighten the flexplate retaining bolts to 35 ft. lbs. (44 Nm) in the sequence shown.
8. Install the transmission.

INTAKE MANIFOLD

REMOVAL & INSTALLATION

3.7L Engine

See Figures 105, 170, 202 through 205.

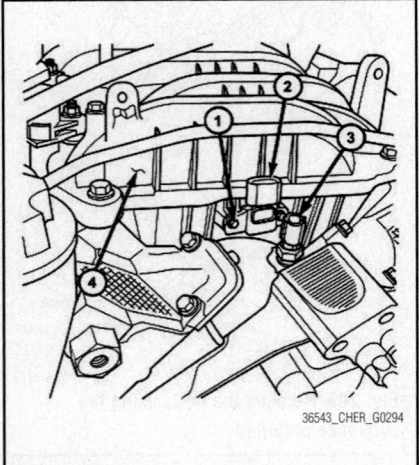

Fig. 202 Disconnect electrical connectors

Fig. 203 Disconnect the ETC connector from the throttle body (3)

1. Perform the Fuel System Pressure Release procedure.
2. Disconnect negative cable from battery.
3. Remove resonator assembly and air inlet hose.
4. Disconnect electrical connectors for the following components:
   • Manifold Absolute Pressure (MAP) sensor (2)
   • Engine Coolant Temperature (ECT) sensor (3)
   • Ignition coil towers
5. Disconnect vapor purge hose, brake booster hose, Positive Crankcase Ventilation (PCV) hose.
6. Remove the alternator.
7. Remove the air conditioning compressor.
8. Disconnect the ETC connector from the throttle body (3).
9. Disconnect and remove ignition coil towers.
10. Remove top oil dipstick tube retaining bolt.
11. Remove the EGR tube (1).
12. Remove the fuel rail.
13. Remove throttle body assembly.
14. Drain cooling system below coolant temperature level.
15. Support engine using engine support fixture (1), special tool 8534.
16. Remove the right side engine mount to frame bolt (3).
17. With the bolt removed, lower engine until engine mount rests in frame mount.
18. Remove intake manifold retaining fasteners in reverse order of tightening sequence.
19. Remove intake manifold.

To install:

20. Install intake manifold gaskets.
21. Install intake manifold.
22. Install intake manifold retaining bolts and tighten in sequence shown to 105 inch lbs. (12 Nm).
23. Install fuel rail.
24. Install the EGR tube.
25. Install top oil dipstick tube retaining bolt.

✳✳ CAUTION

Proper torque of the throttle body is critical to normal operation. If the throttle body is over-torqued, damage to the throttle body can occur resulting in throttle plate malfunction.

26. Install throttle body-to-intake manifold O-ring.

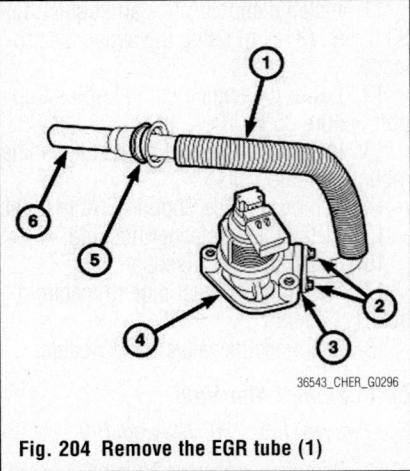

Fig. 204 Remove the EGR tube (1)

27. Install throttle body to intake manifold.
28. Install four mounting bolts.
29. Install ignition coil towers.
30. Connect electrical connectors for the following components:
   • Manifold Absolute Pressure (MAP) sensor
   • Engine Coolant Temperature (ECT) sensor
   • Ignition coil towers
31. Install alternator.
32. Install the air conditioning compressor.
33. Connect Vapor purge hose, Brake booster hose, Positive Crankcase Ventilation (PCV) hose.
34. Connect the ETC connector to the throttle body).
35. Fill cooling system.
36. Raise engine using engine support fixture, special tool 8534.

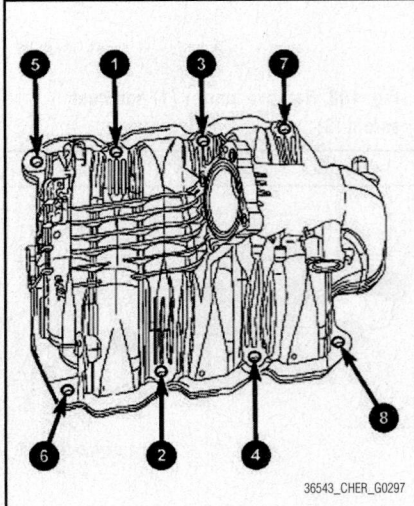

Fig. 205 Remove intake manifold retaining fasteners in reverse order

37. Install the right side engine mount to frame bolt.

38. Remove engine support fixture, special tool 8534.

39. Install resonator assembly and air inlet hose.

40. Connect negative cable to battery.

41. Using the scan tool, perform the ETC Relearn function.

4.7L Engine

See Figure 206.

1. Perform the Fuel System Pressure Release procedure.

2. Disconnect negative cable from battery.

3. Remove air cleaner housing and throttle body resonator.

4. Disconnect throttle and speed control cables.

5. Disconnect electrical connectors for the following components:
   • Manifold Absolute Pressure (MAP) sensor
   • Electronic Throttle Control (ETC)
   • Intake Air Temperature (IAT) sensor
   • Engine Coolant Temperature (ECT) sensor
   • Ignition coils
   • Fuel injectors

6. Disconnect vapor purge hose, brake booster hose, speed control servo hose, positive crankcase ventilation (PCV) hose.

7. Remove accessory drive belt.

8. Disconnect alternator electrical connections.

9. Unbolt the alternator and move it away from the intake manifold for clearance.

10. Disconnect air conditioning compressor electrical connections.

11. Unbolt the air conditioning compressor and move it away from the intake manifold for clearance.

12. Disconnect left and right radio suppressor straps.

13. Disconnect and remove ignition coil towers.

14. Remove top oil dipstick tube retaining bolt and ground strap.

15. Remove fuel rail.

16. Remove throttle body assembly and mounting bracket.

17. Drain cooling system.

18. Remove intake manifold retaining fasteners, in reverse order of tightening sequence.

➡**Intake must be lifted upward and level in the front and rear to clear the cowl. Interference with the cowl will occur during removal.**

19. Remove intake manifold.

To install:

20. Install intake manifold gaskets.

21. Install intake manifold.

22. Install intake manifold retaining bolts and tighten in sequence shown in to 105 inch lbs. (12 Nm).

23. Install left and right radio suppressor straps.

24. Install throttle body assembly.

25. Install fuel rail.

26. Install ignition coils.

27. Install coolant temperature sensor.

28. Connect electrical connectors for the following components:
   • Manifold Absolute Pressure (MAP) sensor
   • Electronic Throttle Control (ETC)
   • Intake Air Temperature (IAT) sensor
   • Engine Coolant Temperature (ECT) sensor
   • Ignition coils
   • Fuel injectors

29. Install top oil dipstick tube retaining bolt and ground strap.

30. Install alternator including electrical connections.

31. Connect Vapor purge hose, Brake booster hose, Positive Crankcase Ventilation (PCV) hose.

32. Install air conditioning compressor including electrical connections.

33. Fill cooling system.

34. Install accessory drive belt.

35. Install air cleaner housing and throttle body resonator.

36. Connect negative cable to battery.

5.7L Engine

1. Remove engine cover.

2. Bleed fuel system.

3. Disconnect negative cable from battery.

4. Remove air inlet hose.

5. Remove ignition wires from on top of intake manifold.

6. Disconnect electrical connectors for the following components:
   • Manifold Absolute Pressure (MAP) Sensor
   • Fuel Injectors
   • Electric Throttle Control (ETC)

7. Remove wire harness from intake manifold.

8. Disconnect brake booster hose, purge hose, and Make Up Air (MUA) hose.

9. Remove EGR tube from intake manifold.

10. Remove intake manifold retaining fasteners in a crisscross pattern starting from the outside bolts and ending at the middle bolts.

11. Remove intake manifold as an assembly.

To install:

12. Position intake manifold.

13. Install intake manifold retaining bolts, and tighten in sequence from the middle bolts towards the outside in a crisscross pattern. Torque fasteners to 105 inch lbs. (12 Nm).

14. Install EGR tube.

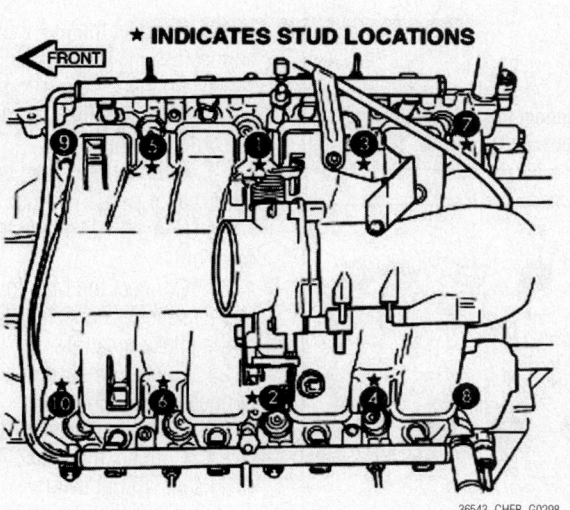

★ INDICATES STUD LOCATIONS

FRONT

36543_CHER_G0298

Fig. 206 Remove intake manifold retaining fasteners, in reverse order

15. Install wire harness on intake manifold.

16. Connect electrical connectors for the following components:

- Manifold Absolute Pressure (MAP) sensor
- Fuel Injectors
- Electronic Throttle Control (ETC)

17. Install ignition wires.

18. Connect Brake booster hose, purge hose, and MUA hose (Make Up Air hose).

19. Install air inlet hose.

20. Connect negative cable to battery.

21. Install engine cover.

6.1L Engine

See Figures 207 through 211.

1. Remove the engine covers, they snap off of the fuel rail ball studs.

✳✳ WARNING

The fuel system is under constant pressure even with engine off. Before servicing the fuel rail, fuel system pressure must be released.

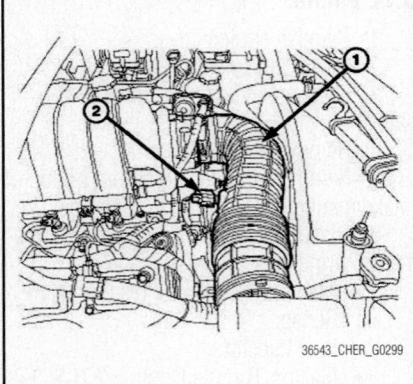

Fig. 207 Disconnect the Intake Air Temperature (IAT) sensor connector (2)

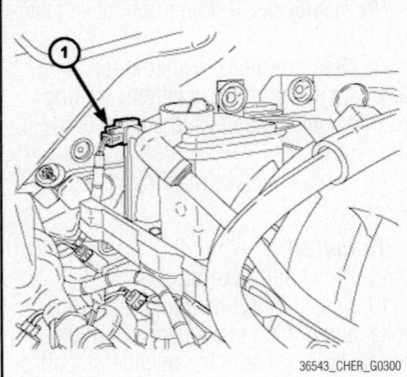

Fig. 208 Disconnect the Manifold Air Pressure (MAP) sensor connector (1)

2. Perform the fuel pressure release procedure.

3. Disconnect the negative battery cable.

4. Disconnect the Intake Air Temperature (IAT) sensor connector (2).

5. Remove the clean air tube (1).

6. Disconnect the Manifold Air Pressure (MAP) sensor connector (1) located at the back of the intake manifold.

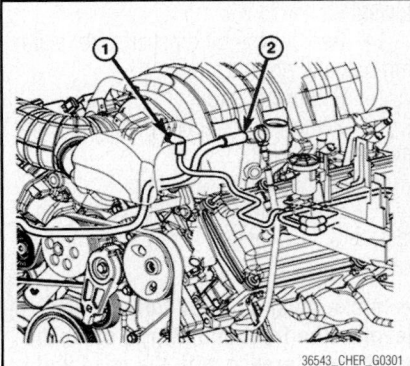

Fig. 209 Disconnect the brake booster vacuum hose, vapor purge vacuum hose (2), and the Make Up Air (MUA) hose (1) to the Intake manifold

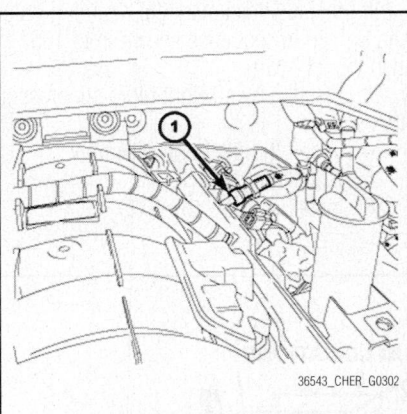

Fig. 210 Disconnect the fuel supply line quick connect fitting (1)

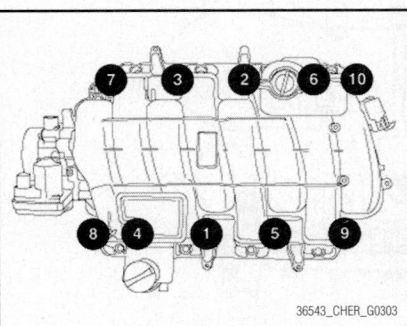

Fig. 211 Removing and installing of the intake manifold fasteners

7. Disconnect the throttle body electrical connector.

8. Disconnect the brake booster vacuum hose, (it may be easier to disconnect the vacuum hose at the booster), vapor purge vacuum hose (2), and the Make Up Air (MUA) hose (1) to the Intake manifold.

9. Remove the safety retainer clip at the fuel supply line.

10. Disconnect the fuel supply line quick connect fitting (1) at the fuel rail and disconnect the fuel supply line to the fuel rail (1).

➡ **The factory fuel injection wiring harness is numerically tagged (INJ 1, INJ 2, etc.) for injector position identification. If the harness is not tagged, note wiring location before removal.**

11. Disconnect the fuel injector electrical connectors.

12. Using the sequence shown, remove the intake manifold retaining fasteners.

13. Remove the intake manifold and throttle body as an assembly.

To install:

14. Install the intake manifold seals.

15. Carefully position the intake manifold without disturbing the seals.

16. Apply Mopar® Lock & Seal Adhesive to the intake manifold retaining bolts.

17. Using the sequence shown, install the intake manifold retaining fasteners and tighten to 9 ft. lbs. (12 Nm).

➡ **The factory fuel injection wiring harness is numerically tagged (INJ 1, INJ 2, etc.) for injector position identification. If the harness was not tagged, note the wiring location previously marked before removal.**

18. Connect the fuel injector electrical connectors.

19. Connect the fuel supply line quick connect fitting at the fuel rail and install the safety retainer clip.

20. Connect the brake booster vacuum hose, vapor purge vacuum hose, and the Make Up Air (MUA) hose to the Intake manifold.

21. Connect the Manifold Air Pressure (MAP) sensor connector located at the back of the intake manifold.

22. Connect the throttle body electrical connector.

23. Install the clean air tube.

24. Connect the Intake Air Temperature (IAT) sensor connector.

25. Install the engine covers, they snap on the fuel rail ball studs.

26. Connect the negative battery cable.

3.0L Diesel Engine

See Figures 212 and 213.

1. Disconnect negative battery cable.
2. Remove the engine cover.
3. Drain the cooling system.
4. Remove the coolant reservoir an position aside.
5. Remove the strut tower support (2).
6. Remove the air cleaner housing cover and air inlet tube (1).
7. Remove the charge air outlet tube (4).
8. Remove the right rear engine cover bracket and disconnect the transmission oil level indicator tube retaining bolt.
9. Remove the turbocharger.

✳✳ CAUTION

Observe the position of the turbocharger oil passage housing and gasket. Failure to properly position the gasket during assembly will result in immediate turbocharger failure after assembly.

10. Remove the turbocharger oil housing adaptor (1) and gasket.
11. Remove the EGR tube to the left cylinder head.
12. Disconnect the coolant hose at the EGR housing.
13. Disconnect the EGR and EGR temperature sensor wiring harness connectors.
14. Disconnect the swirl valve module wiring harness connector.
15. Remove the left fuel rail and high pressure lines.
16. Remove the right fuel rail and high pressure lines.
17. Disconnect the fuel return hoses at the injectors.
18. Disconnect the return fuel hose harness and position aside.
19. Remove fuel rail transfer line.

20. Remove the fuel filter assembly.
21. Remove the fuel filter supply and return pipe harness and position aside.
22. Remove the glow plug module.
23. Remove the EGR air control valve assembly.

✳✳ CAUTION

Do Not rest the intake manifold on the swirl valve actuator. Care must be taken when handling the swirl valve assembly.

24. Remove the intake manifold and gasket.

To install:

➡**Before installation, clean cylinder heads and intake manifold surfaces.**

25. Properly position the intake manifold gasket and install the intake manifold.

✳✳ CAUTION

The right intake manifold upper thermostat housing bolts should be tightened to 74 inch lbs. (8.4 Nm).

26. Tighten bolts to 142 inch lbs. (16 Nm), starting in the middle and tightening in a cross pattern outward until reaching the upper thermostat bolts on the right front manifold.
27. Tighten the upper thermostat bolts on the right cylinder head to 74 inch lbs. (8.4 Nm).
28. Install the fuel filter.
29. Position and install the fuel filter supply and return pipe harness.
30. Position and install the fuel injector return fuel hose harness.
31. Position and properly route the engine wiring harness.
32. Install the left fuel rail. Tighten bolts to 20 ft. lbs. (27 Nm).

➡**Inspect the fuel lines, especially around the barrel ends for damage. Replace as necessary.**

33. Install the fuel rail transfer line along with the right fuel rail. Tighten fuel rail bolts to 20 ft. lbs. (27 Nm), and fuel pipe to 24 ft. lbs. (33Nm).
34. Install the fuel injector high pressure lines. Tighten lines to 20 ft. lbs. (27 Nm).
35. Connect the swirl valve motor electrical connector.
36. Connect the EGR and EGR temperature sensor wiring harness connectors.
37. Connect the coolant hose at the EGR housing.
38. Install the EGR tube to the EGR housing.

✳✳ CAUTION

Observe the positioning of the oil housing to block gasket. This gasket must be attached to the housing and both oil passages aligned properly. Failure to do so will result in immediate turbocharger damage upon start up.

39. Install the turbocharger oil housing adaptor.
40. Install the turbocharger.
41. Install the right rear engine cover bracket and connect the transmission oil level indicator tube.
42. Install the charge air outlet tube.
43. Install the EGR air control valve assembly.
44. Install the glow plug module.
45. Install the air cleaner cover and air inlet tube.
46. Install the engine cover.
47. Install the strut tower support.
48. Fill the engine with coolant.
49. Connect the negative battery cable.

✳✳ WARNING

High-pressure fuel lines deliver fuel under extreme pressure from the injection pump to the injectors. This may be as high as 19,580 psi (1350 bar). Use extreme caution when inspecting for high-pressure fuel leaks. Inspect high-pressure fuel leaks with a sheet of cardboard. Wear safety goggles and adequate protective clothing when servicing fuel system. Fuel under this amount of pressure can penetrate skin causing serious or fatal injury.

50. Start the engine, allow to warm, turn the engine off and inspect for leaks.

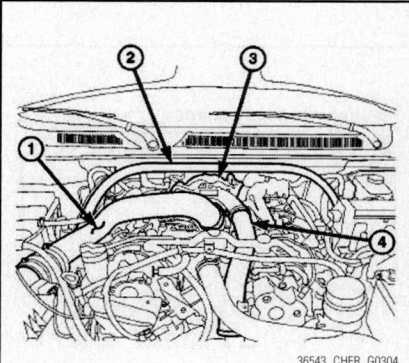

36543_CHER_G0304

Fig. 212 Remove the air cleaner housing cover and air inlet tube (1)

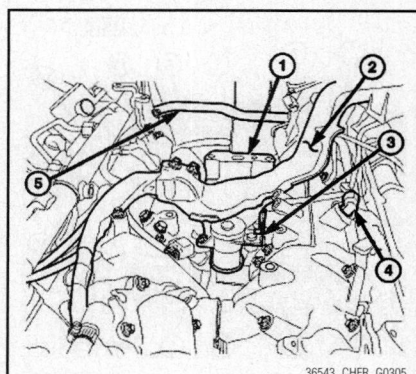

36543_CHER_G0305

Fig. 213 Remove the turbocharger oil housing adaptor (1) and gasket

OIL PAN

REMOVAL & INSTALLATION

3.7L Engine

See Figures 170, 214 through 216.

1. Disconnect negative battery cable.

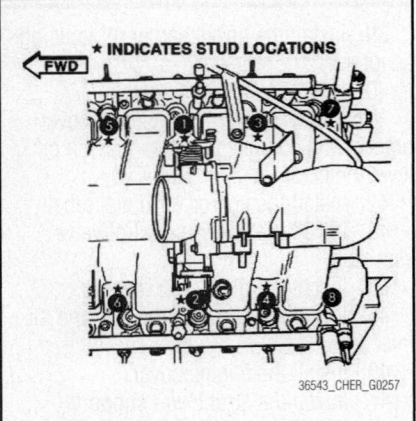

Fig. 214 Remove the intake manifold

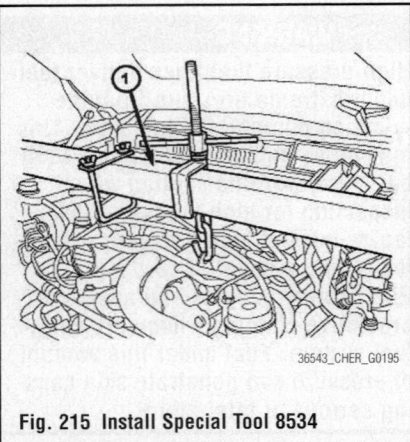

Fig. 215 Install Special Tool 8534

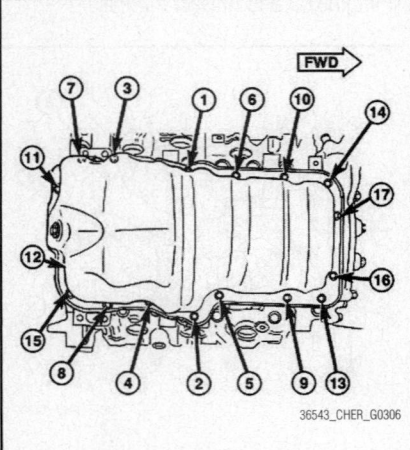

Fig. 216 Install stud at position No. 9

2. Remove the radiator fan.
3. Remove the intake manifold.
4. Install Special Tool 8534. Do not raise engine at this time.
5. Remove the structural cover.
6. Remove both left and right side engine mount through bolts (3).
7. Raise engine using Engine Support 8534, to provide clearance to remove oil pan.
8. Drain engine oil and remove oil filter.

➡**Do not pry on oil pan or oil pan gasket. Gasket is mounted to engine and does not come out with oil pan.**

9. Remove the oil pan mounting bolts and oil pan.
10. Unbolt oil pump pickup tube and remove tube and oil pan gasket from engine.

To install:

11. Clean the oil pan gasket mating surface of the bedplate and oil pan.
12. Inspect integrated oil pan gasket, and replace as necessary.
13. Position the integrated oil pan gasket/windage tray assembly.
14. Install the oil pickup tube.
15. If removed, install stud at position No. 9.
16. Install the mounting bolt and nuts. Tighten nuts to 20 ft. lbs. (28 Nm).
17. Position the oil pan and install the mounting bolts. Tighten the mounting bolts to 140 inch lbs. (16 Nm) in the sequence shown.
18. Install structural dust cover.
19. Lower the engine into mounts using Engine Support 8534.
20. Remove Engine Support 8534.
21. Install both the left and right side engine mount through bolts. Tighten the nuts to 50 ft. lbs. (68 Nm).
22. Install the intake manifold.
23. Fill engine oil.
24. Reconnect the negative battery cable.
25. Start engine and check for leaks.

4.7L Engine

See Figures 105, 170 and 217.

1. Disconnect the negative battery cable.
2. Install engine support fixture (1) special tool 8534. Do not raise engine at this time.
3. Loosen both left and right side engine mount through bolts (3). Do not remove bolts.
4. Remove the structural dust cover.
5. Drain engine oil.

✳✳ CAUTION

Only raise the engine enough to provide clearance for oil pan removal. Check for proper clearance at fan shroud to fan and cowl to intake manifold.

6. Raise engine using special tool 8534 to provide clearance to remove oil pan.
7. Remove the front axle.

➡**Do not pry on oil pan or oil pan gasket. Gasket is integral to engine windage tray and does not come out with oil pan.**

8. Remove the oil pan mounting bolts and oil pan.
9. Unbolt oil pump pickup tube and remove tube.
10. Inspect the integral windage tray and gasket and replace as needed.

To install:

11. Clean the oil pan gasket mating surface of the bedplate and oil pan.
12. Position the oil pan gasket and pickup tube with new O-ring. Install the mounting bolt and nuts. Tighten bolt and nuts to 20 ft. lbs. (28 Nm).
13. Position the oil pan and install the mounting bolts. Tighten the mounting bolts to 11 ft. lbs. (15 Nm) in the sequence shown.
14. Lower the engine into mounts using special tool 8534.
15. Install both the left and right side engine mount through bolts Tighten the nuts to 50 ft. lbs. (68 Nm).
16. Remove special tool 8534.
17. Install structural dust cover.
18. Install the front axle.
19. Fill engine oil.
20. Reconnect the negative battery cable.
21. Start engine and check for leaks.

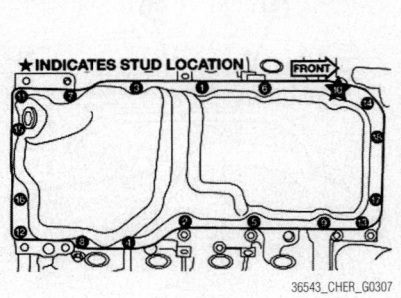

Fig. 217 Position the oil pan and install the mounting bolts

5.7L Engine

See Figures 104, 170, 218 through 220.

1. Disconnect the negative battery cable.
2. Remove the engine cover.
3. Raise vehicle.
4. Remove both left and right side engine mount to frame bolts (3).
5. Drain engine oil and remove the oil filter.
6. Remove the engine oil dipstick and tube from the oil pan.
7. Lower the vehicle.
8. Install Engine Support Fixture 8534 (1). Do not use the third leg.
9. Raise engine using Engine Support Fixture 8534 to provide clearance to remove oil pan.
10. Raise the vehicle.
11. Remove the front axle.
12. Remove the structural dust cover.

➡**Do not pry on oil pan or oil pan gasket. Gasket is integral to engine windage tray and does not come out with oil pan.**

➡**The horizontal M10 fasteners are 5 mm longer in length, and must be reinstalled in original locations.**

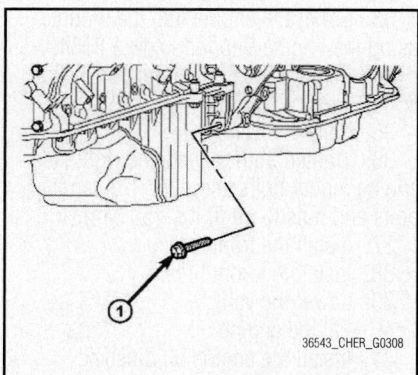

36543_CHER_G0308

Fig. 218 Remove the M10 fasteners (1) (vertical and horizontal) from the rear of the oil pan

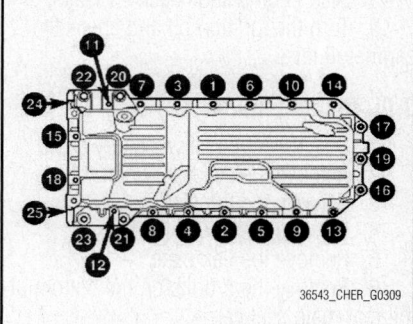

36543_CHER_G0309

Fig. 219 Oil pan mounting bolts removal and tightening sequence

13. Remove the M10 fasteners (1) (vertical and horizontal) from the rear of the oil pan to the transmission and engine.
14. Remove the oil pan mounting bolts using the sequence provided, and oil pan.

➡**When the oil pan is removed, a new oil pan gasket/windage tray assembly must be installed. The old gasket cannot be reused.**

15. Discard the integral windage tray and gasket and replace.

To install:

16. Clean the oil pan gasket mating surface of the block and oil pan.

➡**Mopar® Engine RTV must be applied to the 4 T-joints, (area where front cover, rear retainer, block, and oil pan gasket meet). The bead of RTV should cover the bottom of the gasket. This area is approximately 4.5 mm x 25 mm in each of the 4 T-joint locations.**

17. Apply Mopar® Engine RTV at the 4 T-joints.

➡**When the oil pan is removed, a new oil pan gasket/windage tray assembly must be installed. The old gasket cannot be reused.**

18. Install a new oil pan gasket/windage tray assembly.

19. If removed, reinstall the oil pump pickup tube with new O-ring. Tighten tube to pump fasteners to 250 inch lbs. (28 Nm).

➡**The horizontal M10 fasteners are 5 mm longer in length, and must be reinstalled in original locations.**

➡**New M6 fasteners must be used when reinstalling the oil pan. Do not reuse the old M6 fasteners.**

20. Align the rear of the oil pan with the rear face of the engine block, and install the M10 and M6 oil pan fasteners finger tight. Using the following torque sequence, torque the M6 mounting bolts to 44 inch lbs. (5 Nm).
21. Using the following torque sequence, tighten the M10 oil pan fasteners to 39 ft. lbs. (54 Nm).
22. Using the following torque sequence, tighten the M6 oil pan fasteners to 106 inch lbs. (12 Nm).
23. Install both the left and right side oil pan to transmission bolts. Tighten the bolts to 39 ft. lbs. (54 Nm).
24. Lower the engine into mounts using Engine Support Fixture 8534.
25. Install both the left and right side engine mount bolts and nuts. Tighten the studs and nuts to 39 ft. lbs. (54 Nm).
26. Install the engine oil dipstick and tube.

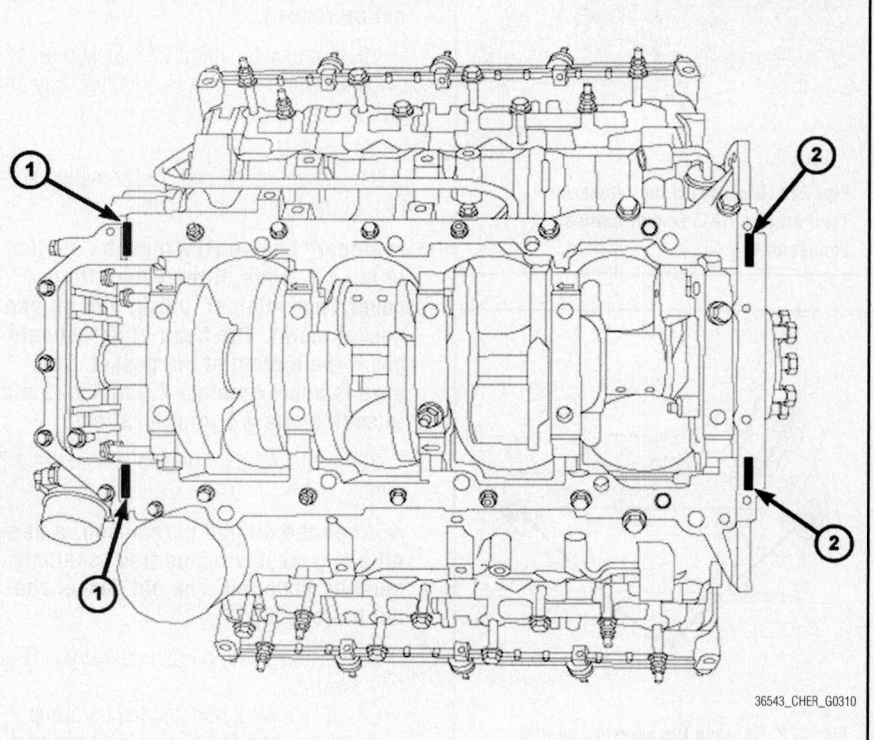

36543_CHER_G0310

Fig. 220 Apply Mopar® Engine RTV at the 4 T- joints

27. Remove Engine Support Fixture 8534.
28. Install the front axle.
29. Install the engine cover.
30. Fill engine oil.
31. Install oil filter, if removed.
32. Connect the negative battery cable.
33. Start engine and check for leaks.

6.1L Engine

See Figures 105, 218 through 222.

1. Disconnect the Negative Battery cable from the batter.
2. Remove the engine oil dipstick.
3. Disconnect the Intake Air Temperature (IAT) sensor harness connector (2).
4. Remove the Inlet Air hose (1).
5. Raise the vehicle on a hoist and drain the engine oil.
6. Remove the front tires.
7. Remove the front axle assembly.
8. Loosen the left and right side engine mount to frame bolts (3).

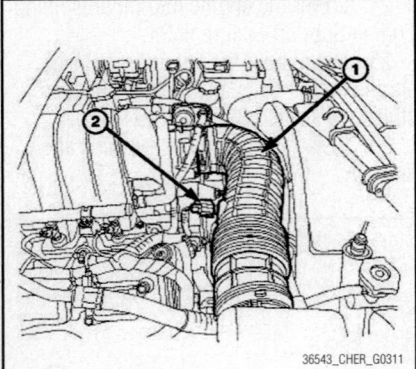

Fig. 221 Disconnect the Intake Air Temperature (IAT) sensor harness connector (2)

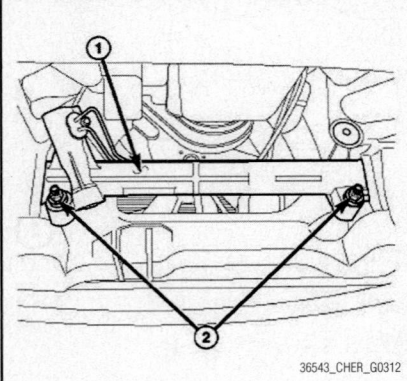

Fig. 222 Remove the steering gear to frame mounting bolts

9. Lower the vehicle.
10. Install the Engine Support Fixture 8534 (1) and connect the lifting adapter (2) to the water pump bolt stud (3). Do not use the third leg.
11. Raise engine using Engine Support Fixture 8534 (1) to provide clearance to remove engine oil pan.
12. Raise the vehicle.
13. Remove the structural dust cover.
14. Remove the steering gear to frame mounting bolts, and lower the gear. Do not remove from vehicle, or disconnect hoses.

➡**Do not pry on oil pan or oil pan gasket. Gasket is integral to engine windage tray and does not come out with oil pan.**

➡**The horizontal M10 fasteners are 5 mm longer in length, and must be reinstalled in original locations.**

15. Lower the engine wire harness and retainers from the oil pan bolts.
16. Lower the transmission cooler line retainers from the oil pan bolts.
17. Remove the M10 fasteners (1) (vertical and horizontal) from the rear of the oil pan to the transmission and engine.
18. Remove the oil pan mounting bolts using the sequence provided, and oil pan.

➡**When the oil pan is removed, a new oil pan gasket/windage tray assembly must be installed. The old gasket cannot be reused.**

19. Remove the engine oil pickup tube.
20. Discard the integral windage tray and gasket and replace.

To install:
21. Clean the oil pan gasket mating surface of the block and oil pan.

➡**Mopar® Engine RTV must be applied to the 4 T-joints, (area where front cover, rear retainer, block, and oil pan gasket meet). The bead of RTV should cover the bottom of the gasket. This area is approximately 4.5 mm x 25 mm in each of the 4 T-joint locations.**

22. Apply Mopar® Engine RTV at the 4 T-joints.

➡**When the oil pan is removed, a new oil pan gasket/windage tray assembly must be installed. The old gasket cannot be reused.**

23. Install a new oil pan gasket/windage tray assembly.
24. If removed, reinstall the oil pump pickup tube with new O-ring. Tighten tube to pump fasteners to 250 inch lbs. (28 Nm).

➡**The horizontal M10 fasteners are 5 mm longer in length, and must be reinstalled in original locations.**

➡**New M6 fasteners must be used when reinstalling the oil pan. Do not reuse the old M6 fasteners.**

25. Align the rear of the oil pan with the rear face of the engine block, and install the M10 and M6 oil pan fasteners finger tight. Using the following torque sequence, torque the M6 mounting bolts to 44 inch lbs. (5 Nm).
26. Using the following torque sequence, tighten the M10 oil pan fasteners to 39 ft. lbs. (54 Nm).
27. Using the following torque sequence, tighten the M6 oil pan fasteners to 106 inch lbs. (12 Nm).
28. Install both the left and right side engine mount bolts and nuts. Tighten the studs and nuts to 39 ft. lbs. (54 Nm).
29. Install the structural dust cover.
30. Install the engine oil filter, if removed.
31. Position the steering gear and install the Steering gear mounting nuts. Tighten to 180 ft. lbs. (244 Nm).
32. Lower the vehicle.
33. Lower the engine into the mounts using the Engine Support Fixture 8534.
34. Remove the Engine Support Fixture 8534.
35. Raise the vehicle.
36. Tighten both the left and right side engine mount bolts and nuts. Tighten the bolts and nuts to 39 ft. lbs. (54 Nm).
37. Install the front axle.
38. Install the front tires.
39. Lower the vehicle
40. Fill the engine oil.
41. Install the engine oil dipstick.
42. Install the Inlet Air hose.
43. Connect the Intake Air Temperature (IAT) sensor harness connector.
44. Reconnect the negative battery cable.
45. Start engine and check for leaks.
46. Turn the Ignition off and check the engine oil level.

3.0L Diesel Engine

1. Disconnect negative battery cable.
2. Remove the accessory belt.
3. Remove the transfer case.
4. Remove the transmission.
5. Remove the flex plate.
6. Remove the 5 bolts on the bottom of the rear main seal carrier.
7. Remove oil pan bolts.
8. Remove the oil pan.

To install:

➡Sealing surfaces must be free of a gasket material and oil residue.

➡If installing a new oil pan, exchange the oil temperature sensor and the oil level sensor.

9. Position the oil pan to engine block and install the oil pan bolts. Tighten the oil pan bolts to 106 inch lbs. (12 Nm).

10. Install the bolts holding the rear main seal carrier to the oil pan. Tighten the bolts to 7 ft. lbs. (9 Nm).

11. Install the flex plate.

12. Install the transmission.

13. Install the lower A/C compressor bolt to oil pan. Tighten the bolt to 15 ft. lbs. (20 Nm).

14. Install the oil level indicator tube.

15. Fill the oil pan to the appropriate level with the correct viscosity engine oil.

16. Connect the negative battery cable.

17. Start the engine, allow to warm.

❋❋ WARNING

Any time the oil is drained and filled it is very important to wait 15 minutes before starting the engine.

❋❋ WARNING

Before checking the engine oil level turn the engine off and wait 15 minutes for the oil to return to the oil pan.

18. Turn engine off and inspect for leaks.

19. Install the skid plate.

OIL PUMP

REMOVAL & INSTALLATION

3.7L & 4.7L Engines

See Figure 223.

1. Remove the oil pan and pick-up tube.

2. Remove the timing chain cover.

3. Remove the timing chains and tensioners.

4. Remove the four bolts, primary timing chain tensioner and the oil pump.

To install:

5. Position the oil pump onto the crankshaft and install one oil pump retaining bolt.

6. Position the primary timing chain tensioner and install three retaining bolts.

7. Tighten the oil pump and primary timing chain tensioner retaining bolts to 250 inch lbs. (28 Nm) in the sequence shown.

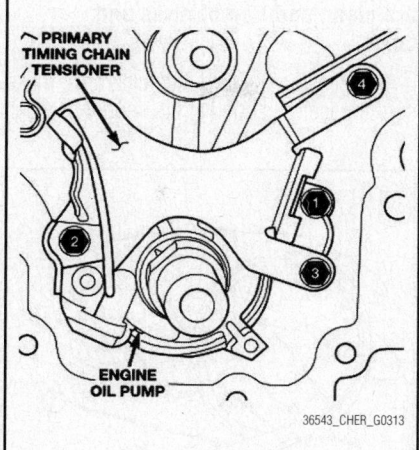

Fig. 223 Engine oil pump tightening sequence

8. Install the secondary timing chain tensioners and timing chains.

9. Install the timing chain cover.

10. Install the pick-up tube and oil pan.

5.7L & 6.1L Engines

See Figures 224 and 225.

1. Remove the oil pan and pick-up tube.

2. Remove the timing chain cover.

3. Remove the four bolts(2) and the oil pump (1).

To install:

4. Position the oil pump onto the crankshaft and install the 4 oil pump retaining bolts.

5. Tighten the oil pump retaining bolts to 250 inch lbs. (28 Nm) in the sequence shown.

6. Install the timing chain cover.

7. Install the pick-up tube and oil pan.

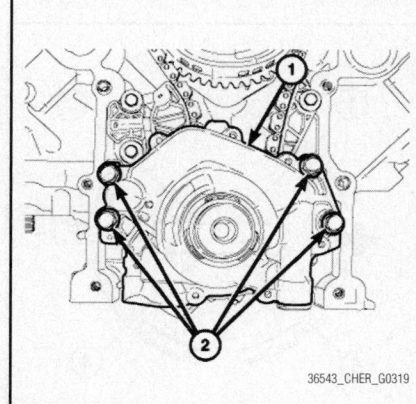

Fig. 224 Remove the four bolts (2) and the oil pump (1)

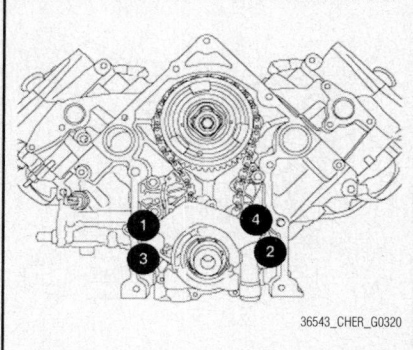

Fig. 225 Tighten the oil pump retaining bolts to 250 inch lbs. (28 Nm) in the sequence shown

3.0L Diesel Engine

See Figures 226 and 227.

1. Remove oil pan.

2. Remove fasteners at the oil pump cover.

3. Remove oil pump fasteners (1).

4. Remove oil pump from the crankcase.

To install:

5. Clean the strainer of the oil pump and replace sealing ring. Fill oil pump with engine oil so that oil is delivered when first starting engine.

6. Install the oil pump.

7. Install fastener for oil pump. Tighten fastener to 14 ft. lbs. (19 Nm).

8. Install fastener for oil pump cover with oil pipe to oil pump. Tighten fastener to 9 ft. lbs. (12 Nm).

9. Install bracket to the oil pump. Tighten fastener to 7 ft. lbs. (9 Nm).

❋❋ WARNING

Any time the oil is drained and filled it is critical to wait 15 minutes before starting the engine.

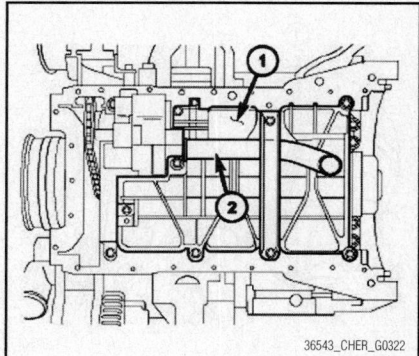

Fig. 226 Remove fasteners at the oil pump cover

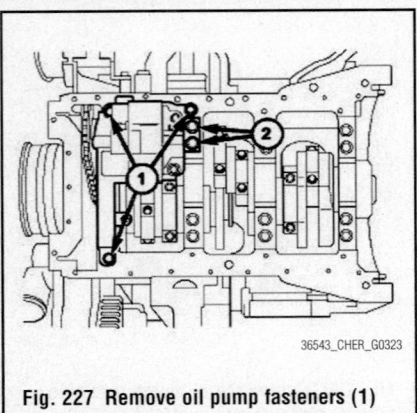

Fig. 227 Remove oil pump fasteners (1)

❄❄ WARNING

Before checking the engine oil level turn the engine off and wait 15 minutes for the oil to return to the oil pan.

10. Install oil pan.

PISTON AND RING

POSITIONING

See Figures 228 through 231.

Before reinstalling used rings or installing new rings, the ring clearances must be checked.

1. Wipe the cylinder bore clean.
2. Insert the ring in the cylinder bore.

➡**The ring gap measurement must be made with the ring positioned at least 0.50 inches (12 mm) from bottom of cylinder bore.**

3. Using a piston, to ensure that the ring is squared in the cylinder bore, slide the ring downward into the cylinder.
4. Using a feeler gauge (1), check the ring end gap. Replace any rings not within specification.

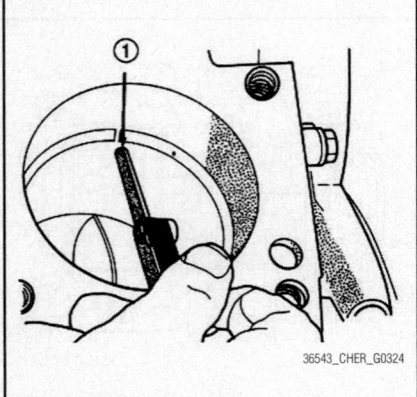

Fig. 228 Using a feeler gauge (1), check the ring end gap

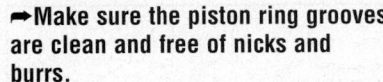

➡**Make sure the piston ring grooves are clean and free of nicks and burrs.**

5. Measure the ring side clearance make sure the feeler gauge (1) fits snugly between

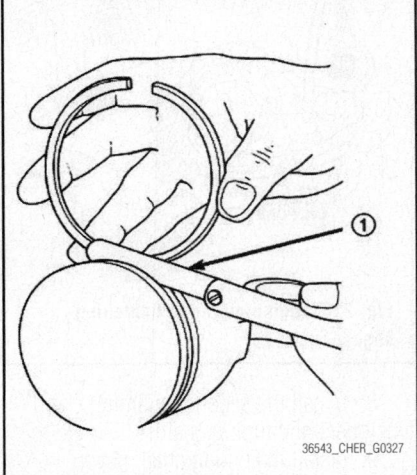

Fig. 229 Measure the ring side clearance make sure the feeler gauge (1)

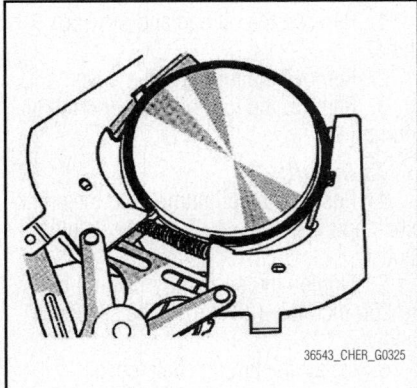

Fig. 230 Using a piston ring installer

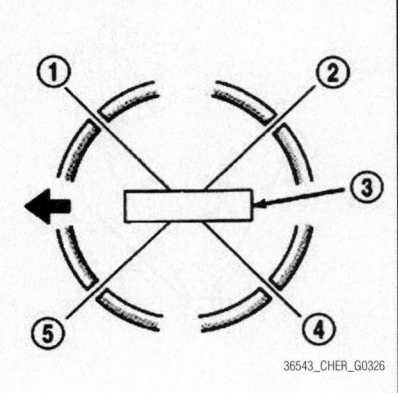

Fig. 231 Position piston ring end gaps

the ring land and the ring. Replace any ring not within specification.

6. Rotate the ring around the piston, the ring must rotate in the groove without binding.

7. The No. 1 and No. 2 piston rings have a different cross section. Ensure No. 2 ring is installed with manufacturers I.D. mark (Dot) facing up, towards top of the piston.

➡**Piston rings are installed in the following order:**

- Oil ring expander.
- Upper oil ring side rail.
- Lower oil ring side rail.
- No. 2 Intermediate piston ring.
- No. 1 Upper piston ring.

8. Install the oil ring expander.
9. Install the upper side rail by placing one end between the piston ring groove and the expander ring. Hold the end firmly and press down the portion to be installed until side rail is in position. Repeat this step for the lower side rail.
10. Install No. 2 intermediate piston ring using a piston ring installer.
11. Install No. 1 upper piston ring using a piston ring installer.
12. Position piston ring end gaps. It is important that expander ring gap is at least 45° from the side rail gaps, but not on the piston pin center or on the thrust direction.

REAR MAIN SEAL

REMOVAL & INSTALLATION

Gasoline Engines
See Figures 232 through 234.

➡**This procedure can be performed in vehicle.**

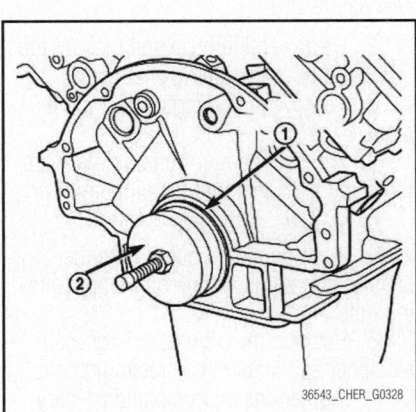

Fig. 232 Using Seal Remover 8506 (2), remove the crankshaft rear oil seal (1)

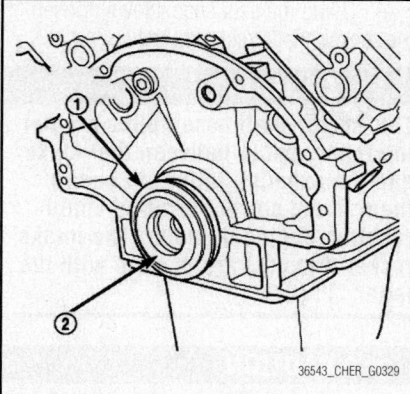

Fig. 233 Position the Seal Installer 8349-2 (2) onto the crankshaft rear face

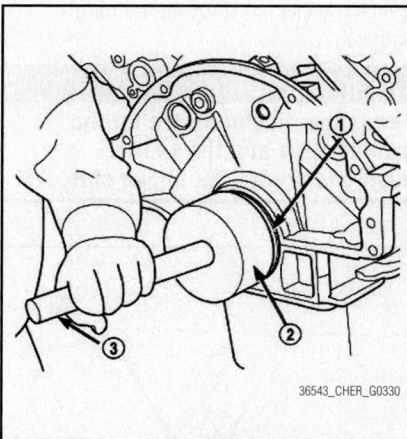

Fig. 234 Using the Seal Installer 8349 (2) and Universal Drive Handle C-4171 (3)

1. If being performed in vehicle, remove the transmission.
2. Remove the flexplate.

➡ **The crankshaft oil seal (1) CANNOT be reused after removal.**

➡ **The Seal Remover 8506 (2) must be installed deeply into the seal. Continue to tighten the removal tool into the seal until the tool cannot be turned farther. Failure to install tool correctly the first time will cause tool to pull free of seal without removing seal from engine.**

3. Using Seal Remover 8506 (2), remove the crankshaft rear oil seal (1).

To install:
4. Lubricate the crankshaft flange with engine oil.
5. Position the Seal Installer 8349-2 (2) onto the crankshaft rear face. Then position the crankshaft rear oil seal (1) onto the guide.
6. Using the Seal Installer 8349 (2) and Universal Drive Handle C-4171 (3), with a

hammer, tap the seal (1) into place. Continue to tap on the driver handle until the seal installer seats against the cylinder block crankshaft bore.
7. Install the flexplate.
8. Install the transmission.

Diesel Engine
See Figure 235.

1. Remove the transmission.
2. Remove the bolts holding the flex plate to the crankshaft (3).
3. Remove the flex plate.
4. Remove the bolts holding the rear main seal carrier (1) to the engine block and oil pan.
5. Remove the rear main seal carrier (1) from the engine block and oil pan.
6. Clean sealant residue from the engine block and oil pan.

To install:
7. Apply sealant 0.059 inches (1.5 mm) wide, MOPAR Engine Sealant / RTV Silicone Rubber Adhesive to the rear main seal carrier. Install the rear oil seal cover within 10 minutes after applying sealing compound. Do not spread the sealing bead.
8. Install the rear main seal carrier to the engine block and oil pan.
9. Install the bolts holding the rear main seal carrier to the engine block and oil pan. Torque the bolts to 70 inch lbs. (8 Nm) and then to 88 inch lbs. (10 Nm).
10. Install the flex plate.
11. Install the transmission.

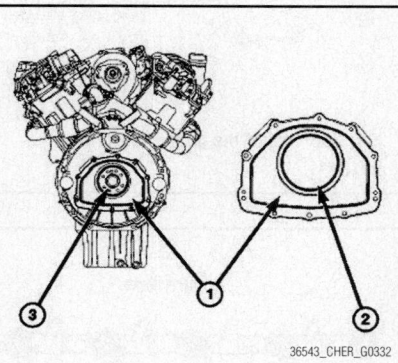

Fig. 235 Remove the bolts holding the rear main seal carrier (1) to the engine block and oil pan

ROCKER ARMS/SHAFTS

REMOVAL & INSTALLATION

3.7L Engine
See Figure 236.

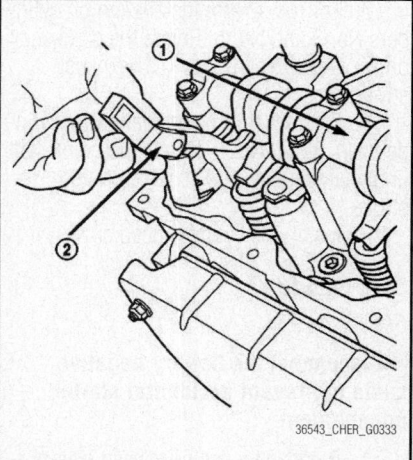

Fig. 236 Using the Remover/Installer 8516 (2), press downward on the valve spring, remove rocker arm

➡ **Disconnect the battery negative cable to prevent accidental starter engagement.**

1. Remove the cylinder head cover.
2. For rocker arm removal on cylinder No. 4, Rotate the crankshaft until cylinder No. 1 is at BDC intake stroke.
3. For rocker arm removal on cylinder No. 1, Rotate the crankshaft until cylinder No. 1 is at BDC combustion stroke.
4. For rocker arm removal on cylinders No. 3 and No. 5, Rotate the crankshaft until cylinder No. 1 is at TDC exhaust stroke.
5. For rocker arm removal on cylinders No. 2 and No. 6, Rotate the crankshaft until cylinder No. 1 is at TDC ignition stroke.
6. Using the Remover/Installer 8516 (2), press downward on the valve spring, remove rocker arm.

To install:
7. Using the Remover/Installer 8516 press downward on the valve spring and install the rocker arm.

⁂ **CAUTION**

Make sure the rocker arms are installed with the concave pocket over the lash adjusters. Failure to do so may cause severe damage to the rocker arms and/or lash adjusters.

➡ **Coat the rocker arms with clean engine oil prior to installation.**

8. For rocker arm installation on cylinders No. 4, Rotate the crankshaft until cylinder No. 1 is at BDC intake stroke.
9. For rocker arm installation on cylinder No. 1, Rotate the crankshaft until cylinder No. 1 is at BDC combustion stroke.

10. For rocker arm installation on cylinders No. 3 and No. 5, Rotate the crankshaft until cylinder No. 1 is at TDC exhaust stroke.

11. For rocker arm installation on cylinders No. 2 and No. 6, Rotate the crankshaft until cylinder No. 1 is at TDC ignition stroke.

12. Install the cylinder head cover.

4.7L Engine

See Figure 236.

➥**Disconnect the battery negative cable to prevent accidental starter engagement.**

1. Remove the cylinder head cover.
2. For rocker arm removal on cylinders 3 and 5 Rotate the crankshaft until cylinder 1 is at TDC exhaust stroke.
3. For rocker arm removal on cylinders 2 and 8 Rotate the crankshaft until cylinder 1 is at TDC compression stroke.
4. For rocker arm removal on cylinders 4 and 6 Rotate the crankshaft until cylinder 3 is at TDC compression stroke.
5. For rocker arm removal on cylinders 1 and 7 Rotate the crankshaft until cylinder 2 is at TDC compression stroke.
6. Using special tool 8516 Rocker Arm Remover (2), press downward on the valve spring, remove rocker arm.

To install:

✳✳ CAUTION

Make sure the rocker arms are installed with the concave pocket over the lash adjusters. Failure to do so may cause severe damage to the rocker arms and/or lash adjusters.

➥**Coat the rocker arms with clean engine oil prior to installation.**

7. For rocker arm installation on cylinders 3 and 5 Rotate the crankshaft until cylinder 1 is at TDC exhaust stroke.

8. For rocker arm installation on cylinders 2 and 8 Rotate the crankshaft until cylinder 1 is at TDC compression stroke.

9. For rocker arm installation on cylinders 4 and 6 Rotate the crankshaft until cylinder 3 is at TDC compression stroke.

10. For rocker arm installation on cylinders 1 and 7 Rotate the crankshaft until cylinder 2 is at TDC compression stroke.

11. Using valve spring compressor 10102 press downward on the valve spring, install rocker arm.

12. Install the cylinder head cover.

5.7L Engine

See Figures 237 through 241.

1. Disconnect the negative battery cable.
2. Remove the engine cover.
3. Remove the ignition coils.
4. Using the sequence shown, remove the cylinder head cover.
5. Install the pushrod retainer 9070 (1).

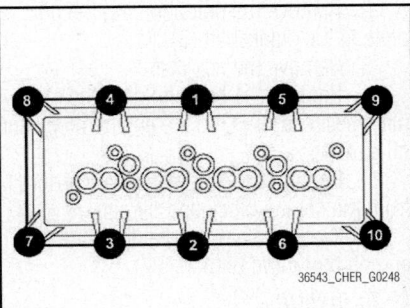

Fig. 237 Using the sequence shown, remove the cylinder head cover

Fig. 238 Install the pushrod retainer 9070 (1)

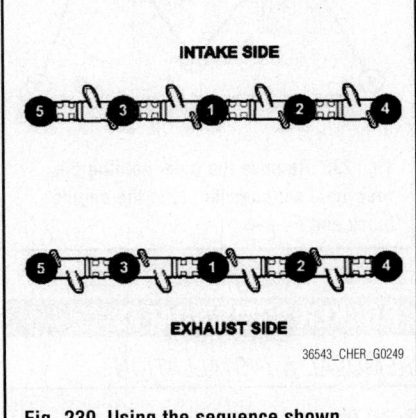

Fig. 239 Using the sequence shown, loosen the rocker shafts retaining bolts

6. Using the sequence shown, loosen the rocker shafts retaining bolts.

✳✳ CAUTION

The rocker shaft assemblies are not interchangeable between the intake and the exhaust, failure to install them in the correct location could result in engine damage. The intake rocker arms (1) are marked with the letter "I" (2).

✳✳ CAUTION

Do not remove the retainers (1) from the rocker shaft (3).

7. Remove the rocker shaft (3). Note the rocker shaft location during removal.

✳✳ CAUTION

The longer pushrods are for the exhaust side and the shorter pushrods are for the intake side.

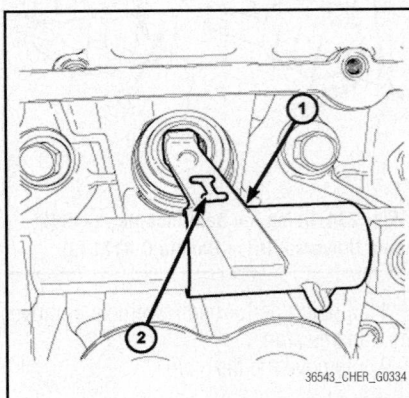

Fig. 240 The intake rocker arms (1) are marked with the letter "I" (2)

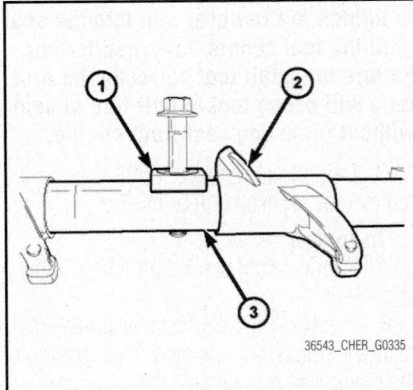

Fig. 241 Do not remove the retainers (1) from the rocker shaft (3)

8. Remove the pushrods. Note the pushrod location during removal.

To install:

> ✳✳ **CAUTION**
>
> **The longer pushrods are for the exhaust side and the shorter pushrods are for the intake side.**

9. Install the pushrods in the same order as removed.
10. Install the pushrod retainer 9070.

> ✳✳ **CAUTION**
>
> **Make sure that the retainers and the rocker arms are not overlapped when tightening bolts or engine damage could result.**

> ✳✳ **CAUTION**
>
> **Verify the pushrod(s) are installed into the rocker arm(s) properly and using a suitable light, looking down through the push rod hole, verify the pushrod(s) are installed into the tappet(s) correctly while installing the rocker shaft assembly or engine damage could result. Recheck after the rocker shaft has been tightened to specification.**

> ✳✳ **CAUTION**
>
> **The rocker shaft assemblies are not interchangeable between the intake and the exhaust, failure to install them in the correct location could result in engine damage. The intake rocker arms are marked with the letter "I".**

11. Install the rocker shaft assemblies in the same order as removed.
12. Using the sequence shown, tighten the rocker shaft bolts to 16 ft. lbs. (22 Nm).

> ✳✳ **CAUTION**
>
> **Do NOT rotate or crank the engine during or immediately after rocker arm installation. Allow the hydraulic roller tappets adequate time to bleed down (about five minutes).**

13. Remove pushrod retainer 9070.
14. Using the sequence shown, install the cylinder head cover.
15. Install the ignition coils.
16. Install the engine cover.
17. Connect the negative battery cable.

6.1L Engine

See Figures 163, 166 and 242.

1. Remove cylinder head cover.
2. Install Push Rod Retaining Plate 9070 (1).
3. Loosen the rocker shafts using the sequence provided.

> ✳✳ **CAUTION**
>
> **The rocker shaft assemblies are not interchangeable between intake and exhaust. The intake rocker arms are marked with an "I".**

4. Remove the rocker shafts. Note location for reassembly.

> ✳✳ **CAUTION**
>
> **The longer push rods are for the exhaust side, and the shorter push rods are for intake side.**

5. Remove the push rods. Note push rod location for reassembly.

> ✳✳ **CAUTION**
>
> **Do not remove the retainers (1) from the rocker shaft (3).**

To install:

> ✳✳ **CAUTION**
>
> **The longer push rods are for the exhaust side, and the shorter push rods are for intake side.**

6. Install the push rods in the same order as removed.
7. Install the Push Rod Retaining Plate 9070.

> ✳✳ **CAUTION**
>
> **Ensure that retainers and rocker arms are not overlapped when torquing bolts.**

> ✳✳ **CAUTION**
>
> **Verify that push rod is installed into rocker arm and tappet correctly while installing rocker shaft assembly. Recheck after rocker shaft has been torqued to specification.**

> ✳✳ **CAUTION**
>
> **The rocker shaft assemblies are not interchangeable between intake and exhaust. The intake rocker arms are marked with the letter "I".**

8. Install rocker shaft assemblies in the same order as removed.
9. Tighten the rocker shaft bolts to 195 inch lbs. (22 Nm) using the sequence provided.

> ✳✳ **CAUTION**
>
> **Do Not rotate or crank the engine during or immediately after rocker arm installation. Allow the hydraulic roller tappets adequate time to bleed down (about five minutes).**

10. Remove Push Rod Retaining Plate 9070.
11. Install cylinder head cover.

3.0L Diesel Engine

See Figure 243.

1. Remove the appropriate camshafts.
2. Remove the rocker arm (1) and lifter (2) assembly.

➡ **When the hydraulic lifters are removed from the engine, they must be stored upright and in clean conditions.**

3. Separate the rocker arm from the lifter.

To install:

4. Assemble the rocker arm to the hydraulic lifter with the retaining clip.

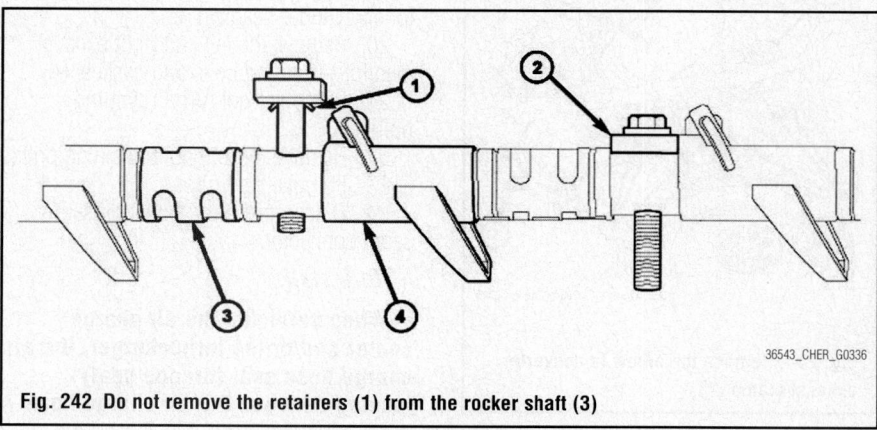

36543_CHER_G0336

Fig. 242 Do not remove the retainers (1) from the rocker shaft (3)

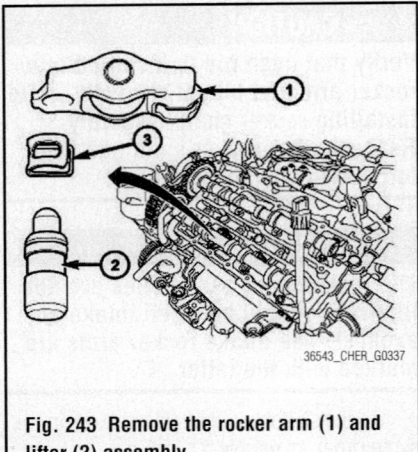

Fig. 243 Remove the rocker arm (1) and lifter (2) assembly

5. Install the rocker arm and lifter assembly onto the cylinder head.
6. Install the camshaft(s).

TURBOCHARGER

REMOVAL & INSTALLATION

3.0L Diesel Engine

See Figures 212, 244 through 246.

➡When servicing the air charge cooler and/or the turbocharger, the air charge hose seal (orange seal) located between the air charge hose and the turbocharger must be replaced.

➡There is no procedure for repairing the turbocharger. If damage is found during inspection, the turbocharger must be replaced.

1. Disconnect the negative battery cable.
2. Remove the engine trim cover.
3. Remove the air intake tube (air cleaner to turbo) (1).

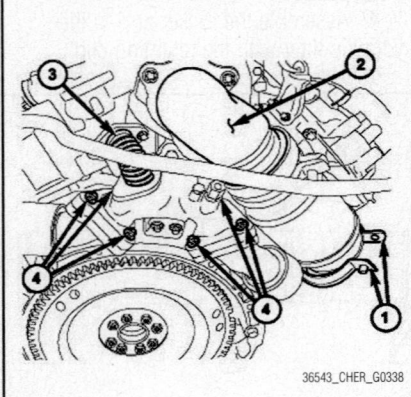

Fig. 244 Remove the elbow to converter exhaust clamp (1)

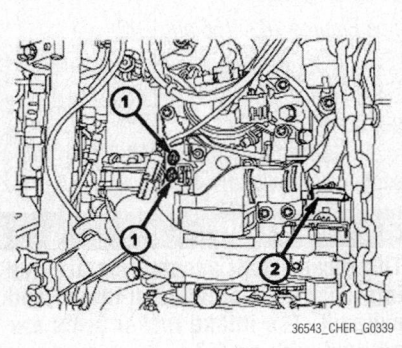

Fig. 245 Remove the turbo front bracket retaining bolts (1)

4. Remove the engine cover front bracket.
5. Remove air tube (turbo to cooler) (4).
6. Remove the turbo heat shield (3).
7. Remove the elbow to converter exhaust clamp (1).
8. Remove the turbo front bracket retaining bolts (1).
9. Raise the vehicle and remove the front splash shield.
10. Drain the cooling system.
11. Disconnect the downstream catalytic converter at the extension pipe.
12. Disconnect the extension pipe to muffler.
13. Disconnect the O2 sensor wire connector.
14. Reposition the extension pipe and catalytic converter.
15. Lower the vehicle and disconnect the catalytic converter to downstream catalytic converter clamp.
16. Remove the upstream catalytic converter.
17. Disconnect transmission fill tube and trim cover bracket and set aside.
18. Disconnect the exhaust elbow at turbo.
19. Disconnect the EGR tube at manifold to left cylinder head (3).
20. Remove the left and right exhaust manifold retaining bolts and gaskets (4).
21. Remove front turbo retaining bolts (1).
22. Remove turbo mount retaining bolts.
23. Remove the turbo.
24. Disconnect turbo boost pressure servo connector.

To install:

➡When servicing the air charge cooler and/or the turbocharger, the air charge hose seal (orange seal) located between the air charge hose

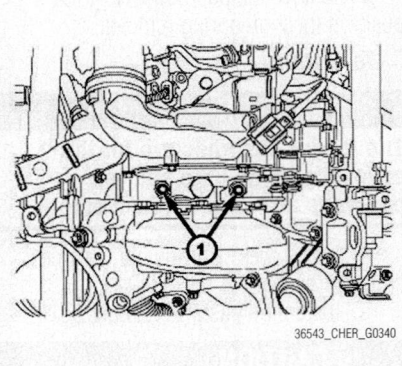

Fig. 246 Remove front turbo retaining bolts (1)

and the turbocharger must be replaced.

25. Connect the turbo boost pressure servo connector.
26. Position the turbocharger and gasket onto the exhaust manifold.

❋❋ CAUTION

Make sure the gasket is installed properly or the turbo oil feed hole will be blocked.

27. Install the front turbo retaining bolts and gasket. Tighten the bolts to 22 ft. lbs. (30 Nm).
28. Install the left and right exhaust manifold retaining bolts and gaskets. Tighten the bolts to 89 inch lbs. (10 Nm).
29. Reconnect the EGR tube at manifold to the left cylinder head.
30. Reconnect the transmission fill tube and trim cover bracket and set aside.
31. Install the upstream catalytic converter.
32. Raise the vehicle and reconnect the catalytic converter to the downstream catalytic converter clamp.
33. Install extension pipe and catalytic converter.
34. Reconnect O2 sensor wire connector.
35. Reconnect the extension pipe to muffler.
36. Reconnect the downstream catalytic converter at the extension pipe.
37. Refill cooling system.
38. Install front splash shield.
39. Install the exhaust clamp (elbow to converter).
40. Lower vehicle, install the turbo front bracket retaining bolts.
41. Install the turbo heat shield.
42. Install air tube (turbo to cooler).
43. Install engine cover front bracket.
44. Install air intake tube (air cleaner to turbo).

45. Install the engine trim cover.
46. Reconnect the negative battery cable.

TIMING CHAIN COVER AND SEAL

REMOVAL & INSTALLATION

3.7L Engine

See Figures 247 and 248.

1. Disconnect the battery negative cable.
2. Drain the cooling system.
3. Remove electric cooling fan and fan shroud assembly.
4. Remove the radiator fan.
5. Disconnect both heater hoses at timing cover.
6. Disconnect lower radiator hose at engine.
7. Remove accessory drive belt tensioner assembly (1).

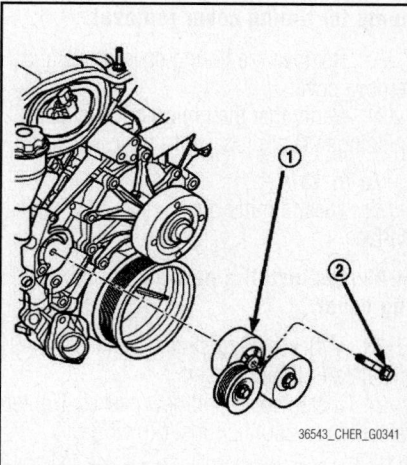

Fig. 247 Remove accessory drive belt tensioner assembly (1)

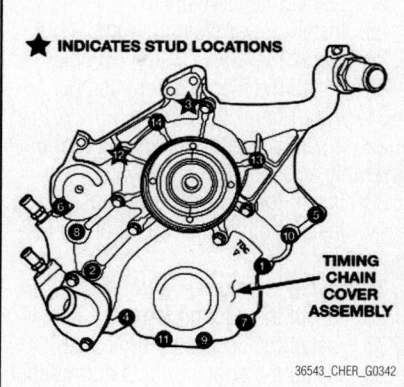

★ **INDICATES STUD LOCATIONS**

TIMING CHAIN COVER ASSEMBLY

Fig. 248 View of the bolts holding the timing cover to engine block

8. Remove crankshaft damper.
9. Remove the alternator.
10. Remove the A/C compressor.

> ✳✳ **CAUTION**
>
> **The 3.7L engine uses an anaerobic sealer instead of a gasket to seal the front cover to the engine block, from the factory. For service, Mopar® Grey Engine RTV sealant must be substituted.**

➡ It is not necessary to remove the water pump for timing cover removal.

11. Remove the bolts holding the timing cover to engine block.
12. Remove the timing cover.

To install:

> ✳✳ **CAUTION**
>
> **Do not use oil based liquids to clean timing cover or block surfaces. Use only rubbing alcohol, along with plastic or wooden scrapers. Use no wire brushes or abrasive wheels or metal scrapers, or damage to surfaces could result.**

13. Clean timing chain cover and block surface using rubbing alcohol.

> ✳✳ **CAUTION**
>
> **The 3.7L uses a special anaerobic sealer instead of a gasket to seal the timing cover to the engine block, from the factory. For service repairs, Mopar® Engine RTV must be used as a substitute.**

14. Inspect the water passage O-rings for any damage, and replace as necessary.
15. Apply Mopar® Engine RTV sealer to front cover using a 3 to 4 mm thick bead.
16. Install cover. Tighten fasteners in sequence to 43 ft. lbs. (58 Nm).
17. Install crankshaft damper.
18. Install the A/C compressor.
19. Install the alternator.
20. Install accessory drive belt tensioner.
21. Install radiator upper and lower hoses.
22. Install both heater hoses.
23. Install the radiator fan.
24. Fill the cooling system.
25. Connect the battery negative cable.

4.7L Engine

See Figures 247 and 248.

1. Disconnect the battery negative cable.
2. Drain cooling system.

3. Disconnect both heater hoses at timing cover.
4. Disconnect lower radiator hose at engine.
5. Remove crankshaft damper.
6. Remove accessory drive belt tensioner assembly (1).
7. Remove the alternator and A/C compressor.

> ✳✳ **CAUTION**
>
> **The 4.7L engine uses an RTV sealer instead of a gasket to seal the front cover to the engine block, from the factory. For service, Mopar® Grey Engine RTV sealant must be substituted.**

➡ It is not necessary to remove the water pump for timing cover removal.

8. Remove the bolts holding the timing cover to engine block.
9. Remove cover.

To install:

> ✳✳ **CAUTION**
>
> **Do not use oil based liquids to clean timing cover or block surfaces. Use only rubbing alcohol, along with plastic or wooden scrapers. Use no wire brushes or abrasive wheels or metal scrapers, or damage to surfaces could result.**

10. Clean timing chain cover and block surface using rubbing alcohol.

> ✳✳ **CAUTION**
>
> **The 4.7L can use a special RTV sealer instead of a carrier gasket to seal the timing cover to the engine block, from the factory. For service repairs, Mopar® Grey Engine RTV must be used as a substitute, if RTV is present. If the front cover being used has no provisions for the water passage O-rings, then Mopar® Grey Engine RTV must be applied around the water passages.**

11. Inspect the water passage O-rings, if equipped for any damage, and replace as necessary.
12. Apply Mopar® Grey Engine RTV sealer to the front cover following the path above, using a 3 to 4mm thick bead.
13. Install cover. Tighten flange head fasteners in sequence to 43 ft. lbs. (58 Nm).
14. Install the A/C compressor and alternator.
15. Install crankshaft damper.

16. Install accessory drive belt tensioner assembly. Tighten fastener to 40 ft. lbs. (54 Nm).
17. Install lower radiator hose.
18. Install both heater hoses.
19. Fill cooling system.
20. Connect the battery negative cable.

5.7L Engine

See Figure 249.

1. Disconnect the battery negative cable.
2. Remove the engine cover.
3. Remove air cleaner assembly.
4. Drain cooling system.
5. Remove accessory drive belt.
6. Remove the cooling fan.
7. Remove coolant bottle and washer bottle.
8. Remove fan shroud.

➡**It is not necessary to disconnect A/C lines or discharge Freon.**

9. Remove A/C compressor and set aside.
10. Remove the alternator.
11. Remove upper radiator hose.
12. Disconnect both heater hoses at timing cover.
13. Disconnect lower radiator hose at engine.
14. Remove accessory drive belt tensioner and both idler pulleys.
15. Remove crankshaft damper.

➡**Do not remove the hoses from the power steering pump.**

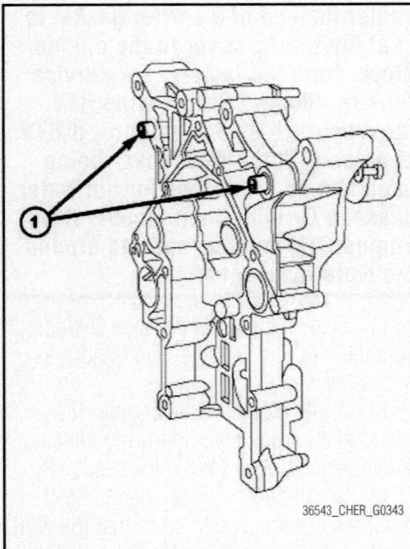

Fig. 249 Verify that timing cover slide bushings (1) are located in timing cover

36543_CHER_G0343

16. Remove power steering pump and set aside.
17. Remove the dipstick support bolt.
18. Drain the engine oil.
19. Remove the oil pan and pick up tube.

➡**It is not necessary to remove water pump for timing cover removal.**

20. Remove timing cover bolts and remove cover.
21. Verify that timing cover slide bushings (1) are located in timing cover.

To install:

22. Clean timing chain cover and block surface.

➡**Always install a new gasket on timing cover.**

23. Verify that the slide bushings are installed in timing cover.
24. Install cover and new gasket. Tighten fasteners to 250 inch lbs. (28 Nm).

➡**The large lifting stud is torqued to 40 ft. lbs. (55 Nm).**

25. Install the oil pan and pick up tube.
26. Install the A/C compressor.
27. Install the alternator.
28. Install power steering pump.
29. Install the dipstick support bolt.
30. Install the thermostat housing.
31. Install crankshaft damper.
32. Install accessory drive belt tensioner assembly and both idler pulleys.
33. Install radiator lower hose.
34. Install both heater hoses.
35. Install radiator fan shroud.
36. Install the cooling fan.
37. Install the accessory drive belt.
38. Install the coolant bottle and washer bottle.
39. Install the upper radiator hose.
40. Install the air cleaner assembly.
41. Fill cooling system.
42. Refill engine oil.
43. Connect the battery negative cable.
44. Install the engine cover.

6.1L Engine

See Figure 249.

1. Disconnect the battery negative cable.
2. Remove the engine cover.
3. Remove the air cleaner assembly.
4. Drain the cooling system.
5. Remove the accessory drive belt.
6. Remove the cooling fan.
7. Remove the coolant bottle and washer bottle.
8. Remove the fan shroud.

➡**It is not necessary to disconnect A/C lines or discharge Freon.**

9. Remove A/C compressor and set aside.
10. Remove the alternator.
11. Remove the upper radiator hose.
12. Disconnect both heater hoses at the timing cover.
13. Disconnect the lower radiator hose at engine.
14. Remove accessory drive belt tensioner and both idler pulleys.
15. Remove the crankshaft damper.

➡**Do not remove the hoses from the power steering pump.**

16. Remove power steering pump and set aside.
17. Remove the dipstick support bolt.
18. Drain the engine oil.
19. Remove the oil pan and pick up tube.

➡**It is not necessary to remove water pump for timing cover removal.**

20. Remove the timing cover bolts and remove cover.
21. Verify that the timing cover slide bushings (1) are located in timing cover.

To install:

22. Clean timing chain cover and block surface.

➡**Always install a new gasket on timing cover.**

23. Verify that the slide bushings are installed in timing cover.
24. Install cover and new gasket. Tighten fasteners to 250 inch lbs. (28 Nm).

➡**The large lifting stud is torqued to 40 ft. lbs. (55 Nm).**

25. Install the oil pan and pick up tube.
26. Install the A/C compressor.
27. Install the alternator.
28. Install power steering pump.
29. Install the dipstick support bolt.
30. Install the thermostat housing.
31. Install crankshaft damper.
32. Install accessory drive belt tensioner assembly and both idler pulleys.
33. Install the radiator lower hose.
34. Install both heater hoses at the timing cover.
35. Install radiator fan shroud.
36. Install the cooling fan.
37. Install the accessory drive belt.
38. Install the coolant bottle and washer bottle.
39. Install the upper radiator hose.
40. Install the air cleaner assembly.

41. Fill cooling system.
42. Refill engine oil.
43. Connect the battery negative cable.
44. Install the engine covers.

3.0L Diesel Engine

See Figures 250 through 252.

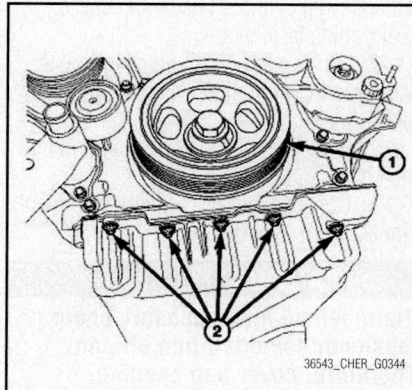

36543_CHER_G0344

Fig. 250 Remove the front oil pan to timing cover bolts

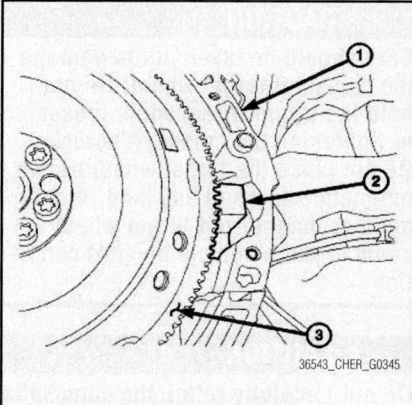

36543_CHER_G0345

Fig. 251 Install special tool 9102 crankshaft lock

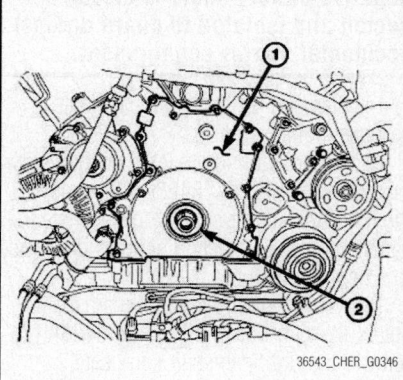

36543_CHER_G0346

Fig. 252 Remove the front timing cover bolts and cover

1. Disconnect negative battery cable.
2. Remove the engine cover.
3. Remove the front engine cover bracket.
4. Raise and support the vehicle.
5. Drain the power steering into a suitable and appropriately marked container.
6. Remove the power steering hose between the pump and cooling fan.
7. Remove the power steering hose between the cooling fan and suspension.
8. Remove the lower cooling fan module retaining bolts.
9. Disconnect the cooling fan wiring harness connector.
10. Remove the power steering line between the retainer and cooling fan module.
11. Remove the front splash shield.
12. Remove the front oil pan to timing cover bolts.
13. Lower the vehicle.
14. Remove the hoses at the power steering reservoir.
15. Remove the cooling fan module upper bolts and remove the fan assembly.
16. Remove the charge air outlet tube.
17. Remove the accessory drive belt.
18. Disconnect the charge air inlet hose at the EGR air control valve.
19. Remove the glow plug module.
20. Remove the EGR air control valve.
21. Remove both accessory drive belt idler pulleys.
22. Remove the accessory drive belt tensioner.
23. Rotate the engine to TDC by the crankshaft bolt.
24. Raise and support the vehicle.
25. Remove the starter blank.
26. Install special tool 9102 crankshaft lock.
27. Lower the vehicle.
28. Remove the vibration damper and pulley.
29. Remove the front timing cover seal.
30. Remove the front timing cover bolts and cover.

To install:

➡**Component mating surfaces must be clean and free of all oil residue.**

31. Install the front crankshaft seal in the timing cover.
32. Install the timing cover. Tighten bolts to 7 ft. lbs. (9 Nm).
33. Raise and support the vehicle.
34. Install the front oil pan bolts. Tighten bolts to 10 ft. lbs. (14 Nm).
35. Lower the vehicle.

36. Install the vibration damper and pulley. Tighten bolt to 154 ft. lbs (210 Nm), and then an additional 180 degrees.
37. Install the accessory drive belt tensioner. Tighten bolt to 43 ft. lbs. (58 Nm).
38. Install the idler pulleys. Tighten bolts to 43 ft. lbs. (58 Nm).
39. Install the accessory drive belt.
40. Install the EGR air control valve assembly.
41. Install the glow plug module.
42. Install the charge air outlet tube.
43. Install the cooling fan module. Tighten upper bolts to 10 ft. lbs. (14 Nm).
44. Raise and support the vehicle.
45. Remove special tool 9102 crankshaft lock.
46. Install the starter blank.
47. Install the lower cooling fan module bolts. Tighten lower bolts to 10 ft. lbs. (14 Nm).
48. Install the power steering line between the retainer and cooling fan module.
49. Connect the cooling fan wiring harness connector.
50. Install the power steering hose between the cooling fan and suspension.
51. Install the power steering hose between the pump and cooling fan.
52. Install the front skid plate.
53. Lower the vehicle.
54. Install the hoses at the power steering reservoir.
55. Fill the power steering reservoir.
56. Install the front engine cover bracket.
57. Install the engine cover.
58. Connect the negative battery cable.
59. Purge the air from the power steering system before starting by raising the vehicle and rotating the steering wheel back and forth 20 times.
60. Start the engine and follow the bleed procedure with the scan tool.
61. Turn engine off and inspect for leaks.

TIMING CHAIN AND SPROCKETS

REMOVAL & INSTALLATION

3.7L Engine

See Figures 253 through 262.

1. Disconnect negative cable from battery.
2. Drain cooling system.
3. Remove right and left cylinder head covers.
4. Remove radiator fan.

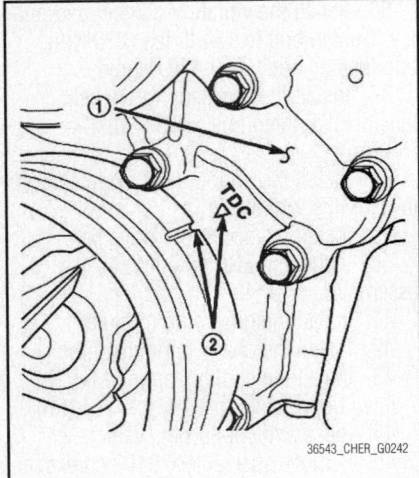

Fig. 253 Rotate engine until timing mark (2) on crankshaft damper aligns with TDC mark on timing chain cover (1)

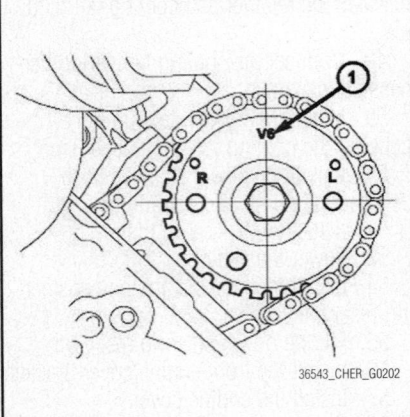

Fig. 254 Make sure the camshaft sprocket "V6" marks (1) are at the 12 o'clock position

Fig. 255 Remove access plugs (1 and 2) from left and right cylinder heads for access to chain guide fasteners

Fig. 256 Using Camshaft Holder 8428 (2)

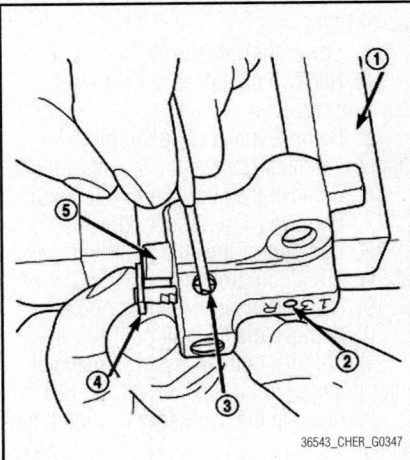

Fig. 257 Using a vise, lightly compress the secondary chain tensioner piston until the piston step (5) is flush with the tensioner body

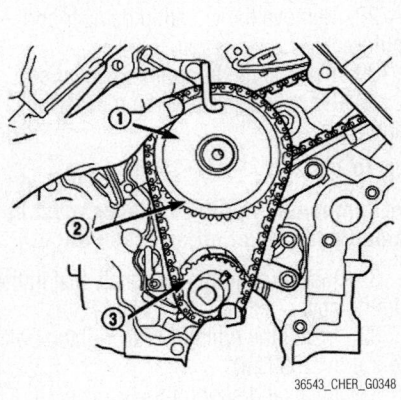

Fig. 258 Install both secondary chains onto the idler sprocket (2)

5. Rotate engine until timing mark (2) on crankshaft damper aligns with TDC mark on timing chain cover (1).

6. Make sure the camshaft sprocket "V6" marks (1) are at the 12 o'clock position (No. 1 TDC exhaust stroke).

7. Remove power steering pump.

8. Remove access plugs (1 and 2) from left and right cylinder heads for access to chain guide fasteners.

9. Remove the oil fill housing to gain access to the right side tensioner arm fastener.

10. Remove crankshaft damper and timing chain cover.

11. Collapse and pin primary chain tensioner.

✳✳ CAUTION

Plate behind left secondary chain tensioner could fall into oil pan. Therefore, cover pan opening.

12. Remove secondary chain tensioners.
13. Remove Camshaft Position (CMP) sensor.

✳✳ CAUTION

Care should be taken not to damage the camshaft target wheel. Do not hold the target wheel while loosening or tightening the camshaft sprocket. Do not place the target wheel near a magnetic source of any kind. A damaged or magnetized target wheel could cause a vehicle no start condition.

✳✳ CAUTION

Do not forcefully rotate the camshafts or crankshaft independently of each other. Damaging intake valve to piston contact will occur. Ensure the negative battery cable is disconnected and isolated to guard against accidental starter engagement.

14. Remove left and right camshaft sprocket bolts.

15. While holding the left camshaft steel tube Camshaft Holder 8428A (2), remove the left camshaft sprocket. Slowly rotate the camshaft approximately 5 degrees clockwise to a neutral position.

16. While holding the right camshaft steel tube with Camshaft Holder 8428A (2), remove the right camshaft sprocket.

17. Remove idler sprocket assembly bolt.

18. Slide the idler sprocket assembly and crank sprocket forward simultaneously

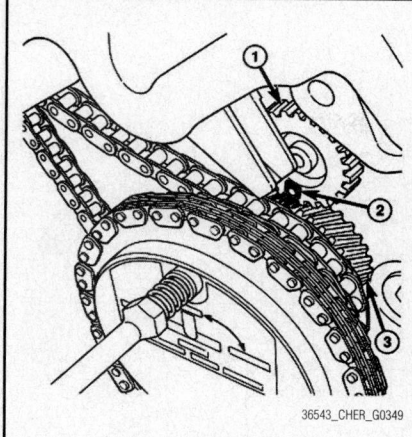

Fig. 259 Install all chains, crankshaft sprocket, and idler sprocket as an assembly

to remove the primary and secondary chains.

19. Remove both pivoting tensioner arms and chain guides.

20. Remove primary chain tensioner.

To install:

21. Using a vise, lightly compress the secondary chain tensioner piston until the piston step (5) is flush with the tensioner body. Using a pin or suitable tool, release ratchet pawl (4) by pulling pawl back against spring force through access hole on side of tensioner. While continuing to hold pawl back, Push ratchet device to approximately 2 mm from the tensioner body. Install Tensioner Pins 8514 (2) into hole on front of tensioner. Slowly open vise to transfer piston spring force to lock pin.

22. Position primary chain tensioner over oil pump and insert bolts into lower two holes on tensioner bracket. Tighten bolts to 250 inch lbs. (28 Nm).

23. Install right side chain tensioner arm. Install Torx® bolt. Tighten Torx® bolt to 250 inch lbs. (28 Nm).

✳✳ CAUTION

The silver bolts retain the guides to the cylinder heads and the black bolts retain the guides to the engine block.

24. Install the left side chain guide. Tighten the bolts to 250 inch lbs. (28 Nm).

25. Install left side chain tensioner arm, and Torx® bolt. Tighten Torx® bolt to 250 inch lbs. (28 Nm).

26. Install the right side chain guide. Tighten the bolts to 250 inch lbs. (28 Nm).

27. Install both secondary chains onto the idler sprocket (2). Align two plated links

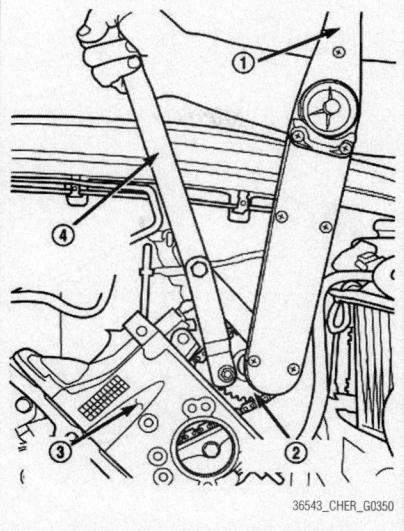

Fig. 260 Using Spanner Wrench 6958, with Adaptor Pins 8346 (4)

on the secondary chains to be visible through the two lower openings on the idler sprocket (4 o'clock and 8 o'clock). Once the secondary timing chains are installed, Secondary Camshaft Chain Holder 8429 (1) to hold chains in place for installation.

28. Align primary chain double plated links with the timing mark at 12 o'clock on the idler sprocket. Align the primary chain single plated link with the timing mark at 6 o'clock on the crankshaft sprocket.

29. Lubricate idler shaft and bushings with clean engine oil.

➥**The idler sprocket must be timed to the counterbalance shaft drive gear before the idler sprocket is fully seated.**

30. Install all chains, crankshaft sprocket, and idler sprocket as an assembly. After guiding both secondary chains through the block and cylinder head openings, affix chains with a elastic strap or equivalent. This will maintain tension on chains to aid in installation. Align the timing mark (2) on the idler sprocket gear (3) to the timing mark on the counterbalance shaft drive gear (1), then seat idler sprocket fully. Before installing idler sprocket bolt, lubricate washer with oil, and tighten idler sprocket assembly retaining bolt to 25 ft. lbs. (34 Nm).

➥**It will be necessary to slightly rotate camshafts for sprocket installation.**

31. Align left camshaft sprocket "L" dot to plated link on chain.

32. Align right camshaft sprocket "R" dot to plated link on chain.

Fig. 261 Using Spanner Wrench 6958, with Adaptor Pins 8346 (2)

✳✳ CAUTION

Remove excess oil from the camshaft sprocket bolt. Failure to do so can result in over-torque of bolt resulting in bolt failure.

33. Remove Secondary Camshaft Chain Holder 8429, then attach both sprockets to camshafts. Remove excess oil from bolts, then Install sprocket bolts, but do not tighten at this time.

34. Verify that all plated links are aligned with the marks on all sprockets and the "V6" marks on camshaft sprockets are at the 12 o'clock position.

✳✳ CAUTION

Ensure the plate between the left secondary chain tensioner and block is correctly installed.

35. Install both secondary chain tensioners. Tighten bolts to 250 inch lbs. (28 Nm).

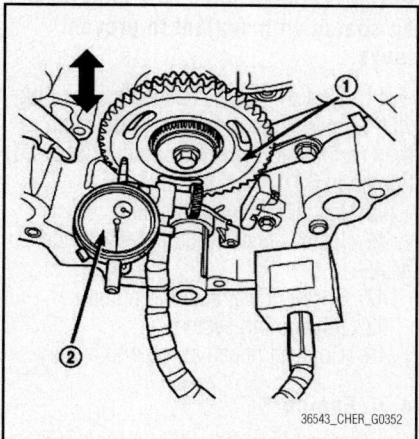

Fig. 262 The idler gear end play being checked

➡ **Left and right secondary chain tensioners are not common.**

36. Remove all locking pins from tensioners.

✳✳ CAUTION

After pulling locking pins out of each tensioner, DO NOT manually extend the tensioner(s) ratchet. Doing so will over tension the chains, resulting in noise and/or high timing chain loads.

37. Using Spanner Wrench 6958, with Adaptor Pins 8346 (4), tighten left camshaft sprocket bolts to 90 ft. lbs. (122 Nm).

38. Using Spanner Wrench 6958, with Adaptor Pins 8346 (2), tighten right camshaft sprocket bolts to 90 ft. lbs. (122 Nm).

39. Rotate engine two full revolutions. Verify timing marks are at the follow locations:
- primary chain idler sprocket dot is at 12 o'clock
- primary chain crankshaft sprocket dot is at 6 o'clock
- secondary chain camshaft sprockets "V6" marks are at 12 o'clock
- balance shaft drive gear dot is aligned to the idler sprocket gear dot

40. Lubricate all three chains with engine oil.

41. After installing all chains, it is recommended that the idler gear end play be checked. The end play must be within 0.004–0.010 inches (0.10–0.25 mm). If not within specification, the idler gear (1) must be replaced.

42. Install timing chain cover and crankshaft damper.

43. Install cylinder head covers.

➡ **Before installing threaded plug in right cylinder head, the plug must be coated with sealant to prevent leaks.**

44. Coat the large threaded access plug with Mopar® Thread Sealant with Teflon, then install into the right cylinder head and tighten to 60 ft. lbs. (81 Nm).

45. Install the oil fill housing.

46. Install access plug in left cylinder head.

47. Install power steering pump.

48. Fill cooling system.

49. Connect negative cable to battery.

4.7L Engine

See Figures 154, 260, 262 through 268.

1. Disconnect negative cable from battery.

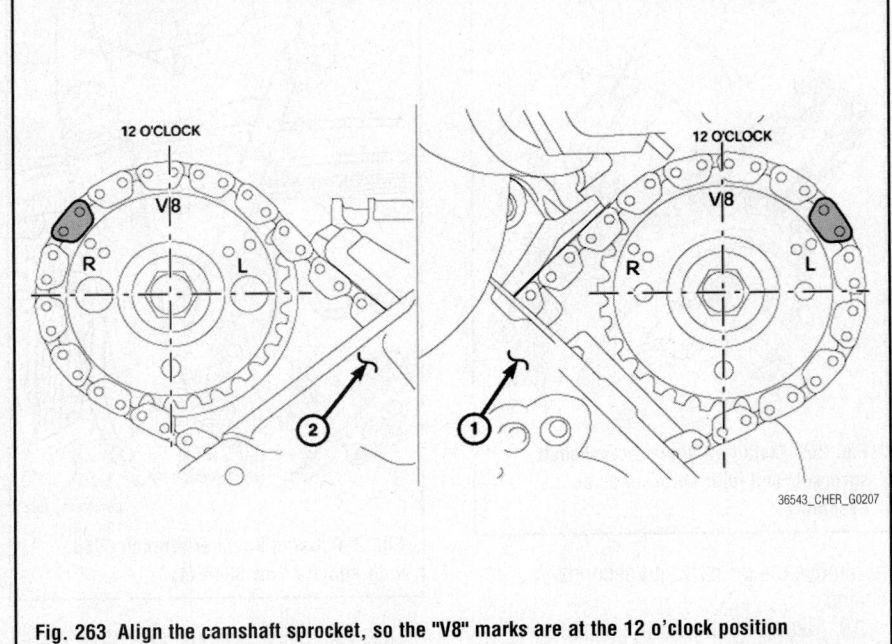

Fig. 263 Align the camshaft sprocket, so the "V8" marks are at the 12 o'clock position

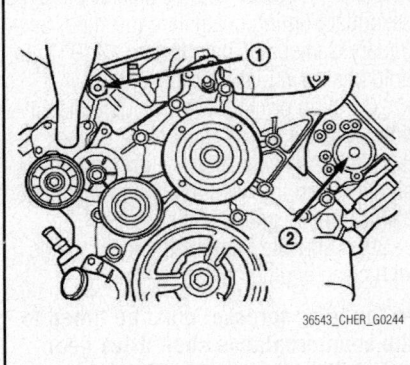

Fig. 264 Remove access plugs (1 and 2) from left and right cylinder heads for access to chain guide fasteners

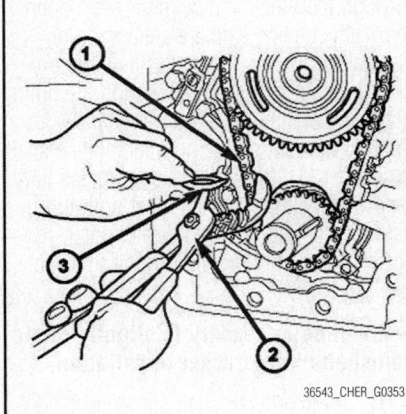

Fig. 265 Collapse and pin primary chain tensioner

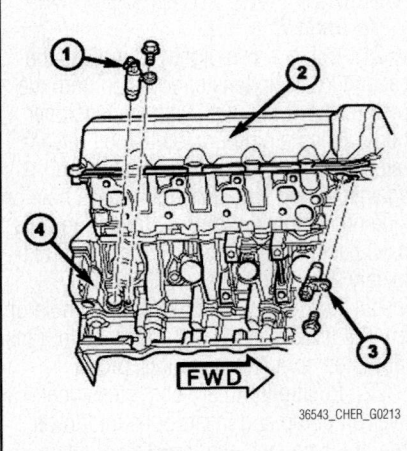

Fig. 266 Remove Camshaft Position (CMP) sensor from right cylinder head

2. Drain cooling system.

3. Remove right and left cylinder head covers.

4. Remove radiator fan.

5. Rotate engine until timing mark on crankshaft damper aligns with TDC mark on timing chain cover (1 cylinder exhaust stroke).

6. Align the camshaft sprocket, so the "V8" marks are at the 12 o'clock position.

7. Remove power steering pump.

8. Remove access plugs (2) from left and right cylinder heads for access to chain guide fasteners.

9. Remove the oil fill housing to gain access to the right side tensioner arm fastener.

10. Remove crankshaft damper and timing chain cover.

11. Collapse and pin primary chain tensioner.

> ❊❊ **CAUTION**
>
> **Plate behind left secondary chain tensioner could fall into oil pan. Therefore, cover pan opening.**

12. Remove secondary chain tensioners.

13. Remove Camshaft Position (CMP) sensor from right cylinder head.

> ❊❊ **CAUTION**
>
> **Care should be taken not to damage the camshaft target wheel. Do not hold the target wheel while loosening or tightening the camshaft sprocket. Do not place the target wheel near a magnetic source of any kind. A damaged or magnetized target wheel could cause a vehicle no start condition.**

> ❊❊ **CAUTION**
>
> **Do not forcefully rotate the camshafts or crankshaft independently of each other. Damaging intake valve to piston contact will occur. Ensure the negative battery cable is disconnected and isolated to guard against accidental starter engagement.**

14. Remove left and right camshaft sprocket bolts.

15. While holding the left camshaft steel tube with adjustable pliers, remove the left camshaft sprocket. Slowly rotate the camshaft approximately 15 degrees clockwise to a neutral position.

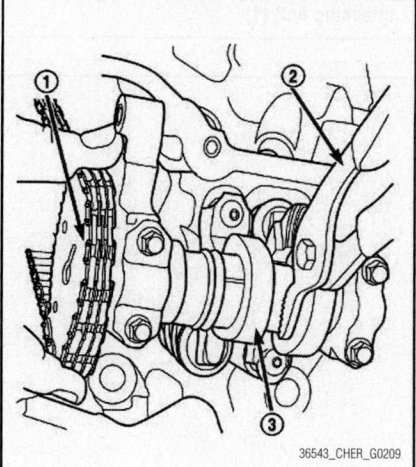

Fig. 267 Remove the left camshaft sprocket

36543_CHER_G0209

16. While holding the right camshaft steel tube with adjustable pliers, remove the right camshaft sprocket. Slowly rotate the camshaft approximately 45 degrees counterclockwise to a neutral position.

17. Remove idler sprocket assembly bolt.

18. Slide the idler sprocket assembly and crank sprocket forward simultaneously to remove the primary and secondary chains.

19. Remove both pivoting tensioner arms and chain guides.

20. Remove chain tensioner.

To install:

21. Using a vise, lightly compress the secondary chain tensioner piston until the piston step is flush with the tensioner body. Using a pin or suitable tool, release ratchet pawl by pulling pawl back against spring force through access hole on side of tensioner. While continuing to hold pawl back, Push ratchet device to approximately 2 mm from the tensioner body. Install Special Tool 8514 lock pin into hole on front of tensioner. Slowly open vise to transfer piston spring force to lock pin.

22. Position primary chain tensioner over oil pump and insert bolts into lower two holes on tensioner bracket. Tighten bolts to 250 inch lbs. (28 Nm).

23. Install right side chain tensioner arm. Apply Mopar® Lock N, Seal to Torx® bolt, tighten bolt to 250 inch lbs. (28 Nm).

➡The silver bolts retain the guides to the cylinder heads and the black bolts retain the guides to the engine block.

24. Install the left side chain guide. Tighten the bolts to 250 inch lbs. (28 Nm).

> ❊❊ **CAUTION**
>
> **Over-tightening the tensioner arm Torx® bolt can cause severe damage to the cylinder head. Tighten Torx® bolt to specified torque only.**

25. Install left side chain tensioner arm. Apply Mopar® Lock N, Seal to Torx® bolt, tighten bolt to 250 inch lbs. (28 Nm).

26. Install the right side chain guide. Tighten the bolts to 250 inch lbs. (28 Nm).

27. Install both secondary chains onto the idler sprocket. Align two plated links on the secondary chains to be visible through the two lower openings on the idler sprocket (4 o'clock and 8 o'clock). Once the secondary timing chains are installed, position special tool 8429 to hold chains in place for installation.

28. Align primary chain double plated links with the timing mark at 12 o'clock on

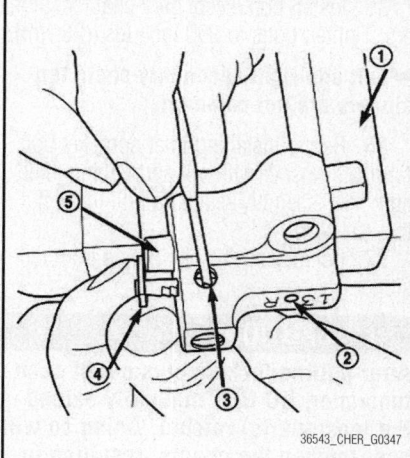

Fig. 268 Using a vise, lightly compress the secondary chain tensioner piston until the piston step (5) is flush with the tensioner body

36543_CHER_G0347

the idler sprocket. Align the primary chain single plated link with the timing mark at 6 o'clock on the crankshaft sprocket.

29. Lubricate idler shaft and bushings with clean engine oil.

30. Install all chains, crankshaft sprocket, and idler sprocket as an assembly. After guiding both secondary chains through the block and cylinder head openings, affix chains with a elastic strap or the equivalent, This will maintain tension on chains to aid in installation.

➡It will be necessary to slightly rotate camshafts for sprocket installation.

31. Align left camshaft sprocket "L" dot to plated link on chain.

32. Align right camshaft sprocket "R" dot to plated link on chain.

> ❊❊ **CAUTION**
>
> **Remove excess oil from the camshaft sprocket bolt. Failure to do so can result in over-torque of bolt resulting in bolt failure.**

33. Remove Special Tool 8429, then attach both sprockets to camshafts. Remove excess oil from bolts, then Install sprocket bolts, but do not tighten at this time.

34. Verify that all plated links are aligned with the marks on all sprockets and the "V8" marks on camshaft sprockets are at the 12 o'clock position.

> ❊❊ **CAUTION**
>
> **Ensure the plate between the left secondary chain tensioner and block is correctly installed.**

35. Install both secondary chain tensioners. Tighten bolts to 250 inch lbs. (28 Nm).

➡**Left and right secondary chain tensioners are not common.**

36. Before installing idler sprocket bolt, lubricate washer with oil, and tighten idler sprocket assembly retaining bolt to 25 ft. lbs. (34 Nm).

37. Remove all 3 locking pins from tensioners.

✳✳ CAUTION

After pulling locking pins out of each tensioner, DO NOT manually extend the tensioner(s) ratchet. Doing so will over tension the chains, resulting in noise and/or high timing chain loads.

38. Using Special Tool 6958, Spanner with Adaptor Pins 8346, tighten left and right camshaft sprocket bolts to 90 ft. lbs. (122 Nm).

39. Rotate engine two full revolutions. Verify timing marks are at the following locations:
- primary chain idler sprocket dot is at 12 o'clock.
- primary chain crankshaft sprocket dot is at 6 o'clock.
- secondary chain camshaft sprockets "V8" marks are at 12 o'clock.

40. Lubricate all three chains with engine oil.

41. After installing all chains, it is recommended that the idler gear end play be checked . The end play must be within 0.004–0.010 inches (0.10–0.25 mm). If not within specification, the idler gear and idler shaft must be replaced.

42. Install timing chain cover and crankshaft damper.

43. Install cylinder head covers.

➡**Before installing threaded plug in right cylinder head, the plug must be coated with sealant to prevent leaks.**

44. Coat the large threaded access plug with Mopar® Thread Sealant with Teflon, then install into the right cylinder head and tighten to 60 ft. lbs. (81 Nm).

45. Install the oil fill housing.

46. Install access plug in left cylinder head.

47. Install power steering pump.

48. Install radiator fan.

49. Fill cooling system.

50. Connect negative cable to battery.

5.7L Engine

See Figures 269 through 276.

1. Disconnect the negative battery cable.

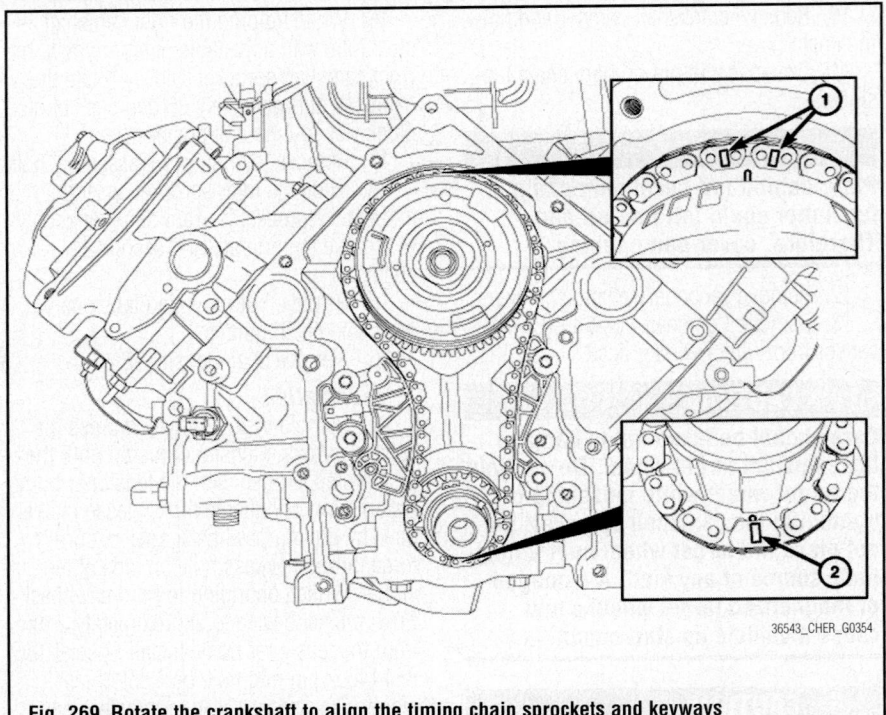

Fig. 269 Rotate the crankshaft to align the timing chain sprockets and keyways

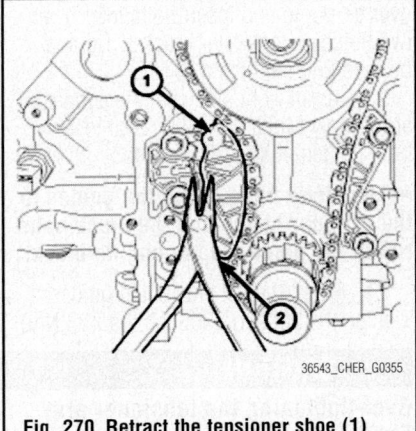

Fig. 270 Retract the tensioner shoe (1)

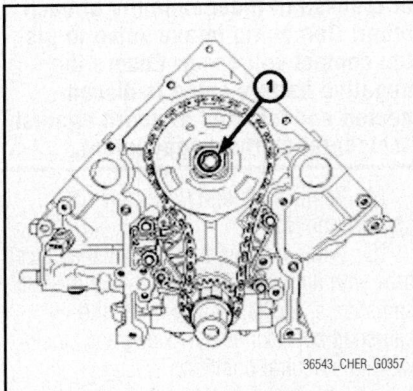

Fig. 272 Remove the camshaft sprocket attaching bolt (1)

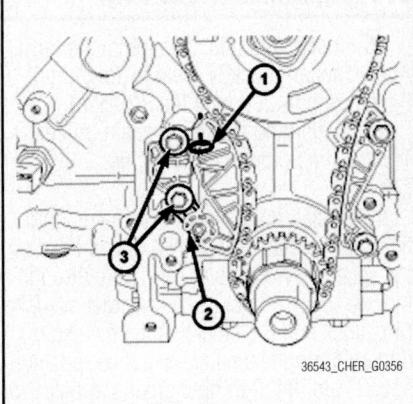
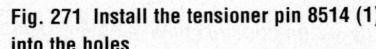

Fig. 271 Install the tensioner pin 8514 (1) into the holes

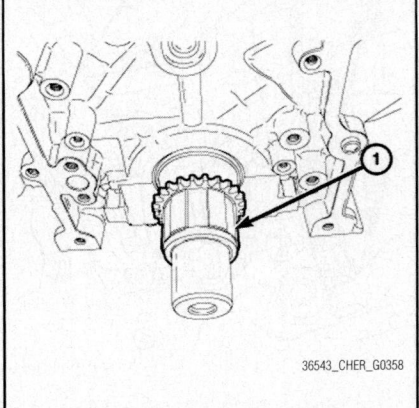

Fig. 273 Slide crankshaft sprocket (1) on the crankshaft

2. Drain the cooling system.

3. Remove the timing chain cover.

4. Remove the oil pump retaining bolts and pump.

5. Install the vibration damper bolt finger tight. Using a suitable socket and breaker bar, rotate the crankshaft to align the timing chain sprockets and keyways as shown.

6. Retract the tensioner shoe (1) until the hole in the shoe lines up with the hole in the bracket.

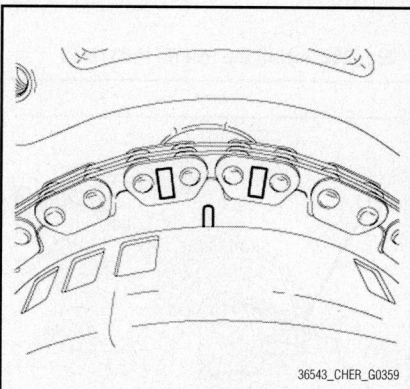

Fig. 274 Align camshaft timing marks and install sprocket on camshaft

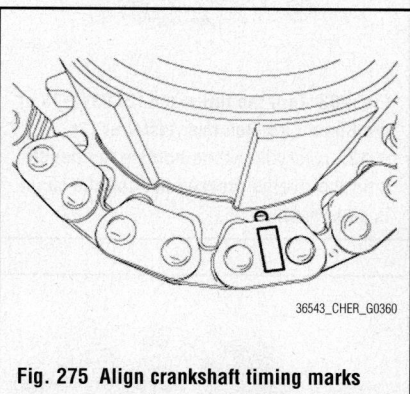

Fig. 275 Align crankshaft timing marks

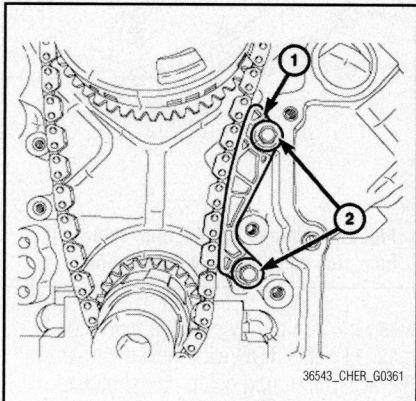

Fig. 276 Install timing chain guide (1) and tighten bolts (2)

7. Install the tensioner pin 8514 (1) into the holes.

8. Remove the camshaft sprocket attaching bolt (1).

9. Remove the timing chain with the camshaft and crankshaft sprockets.

To install:

10. Slide crankshaft sprocket (1) on the crankshaft.

11. Align camshaft timing marks and install sprocket on camshaft.

12. Install camshaft retaining bolt finger tight.

13. Align crankshaft timing marks.

14. Install timing chain guide (1) and tighten bolts (2) to 106 inch lbs. (12 Nm).

15. Verify timing marks (1,2).

16. Remove Tensioner Pin 8514.

17. Tighten camshaft sprocket bolt to 90 ft. lbs. (122 Nm).

18. Install the oil pump.

19. Install the timing chain cover.

20. Fill engine with oil.

21. Fill cooling system.

22. Connect negative battery cable.

23. Start engine and check for leaks.

6.1L Engine

See Figures 277 through 281

1. Disconnect battery negative cable.

2. Drain cooling system.

3. Remove Timing Chain Cover.

4. Re-install the vibration damper bolt finger tight. Using a suitable socket and breaker bar, rotate the crankshaft to align timing chain sprockets and keyways.

✷✷ CAUTION

The camshaft pin and the slot in the cam sprocket must be at 12:00 o'clock (2). The crankshaft keyway

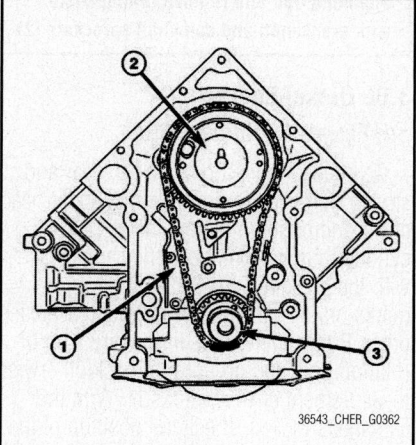

Fig. 277 Rotate the crankshaft to align timing chain sprockets and keyways

must be at 2:00 o'clock (3). The crankshaft sprocket must be installed so that the dots and or paint marking is at 6:00 o'clock.

5. Remove oil pump.

6. Retract tensioner shoe (1) until hole in shoe lines up with hole in bracket.

7. Slide a suitable pin (2) into the holes.

8. Remove camshaft sprocket attaching bolt and remove timing chain with crankshaft and camshaft sprockets (2).

To install:

✷✷ CAUTION

The timing chain must be installed with the single plated link aligned with the dot and or paint marking on the camshaft sprocket. The crankshaft sprocket is aligned with the dot and or paint marking on the sprocket between two plated timing chain links.

✷✷ CAUTION

The camshaft pin and the slot in the cam sprocket must be at 12:00 o'clock. The crankshaft keyway must be at 2:00 o'clock. The crankshaft sprocket must be installed so that the dots and or paint marking is at 6:00 o'clock.

9. Place both camshaft sprocket and crankshaft sprocket on the bench with timing marks on exact imaginary center line through both camshaft and crankshaft bores.

10. Place timing chain around both sprockets.

11. Lift sprockets and chain (keep sprockets tight against the chain in position).

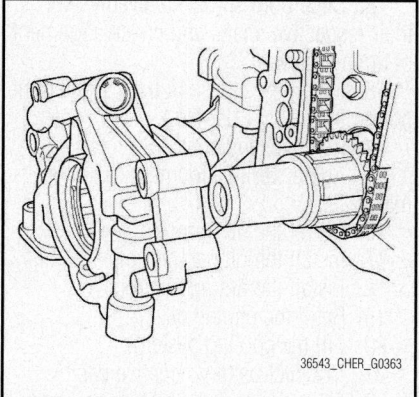

Fig. 278 Remove oil pump

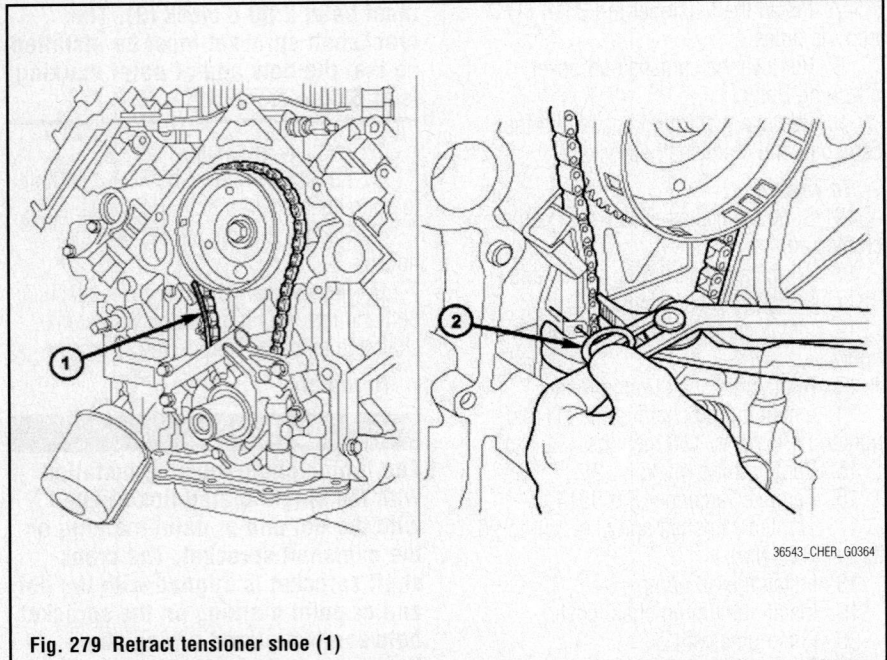

Fig. 279 Retract tensioner shoe (1)

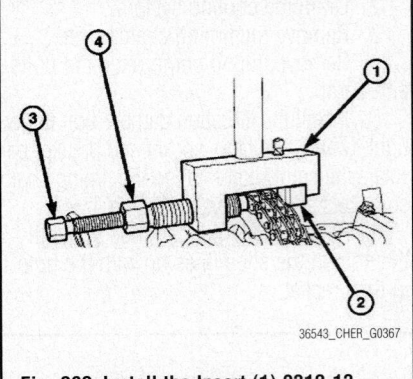

36543_CHER_G0367

Fig. 282 Install the Insert (1) 9312-13

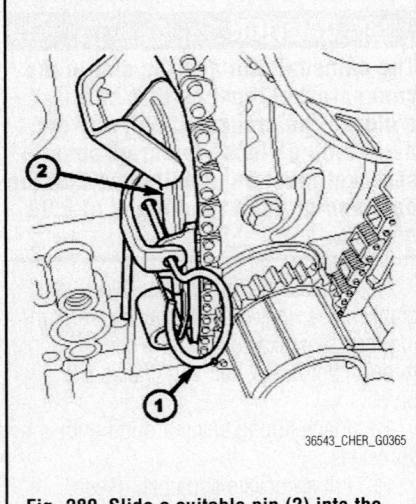

36543_CHER_G0365

Fig. 280 Slide a suitable pin (2) into the holes

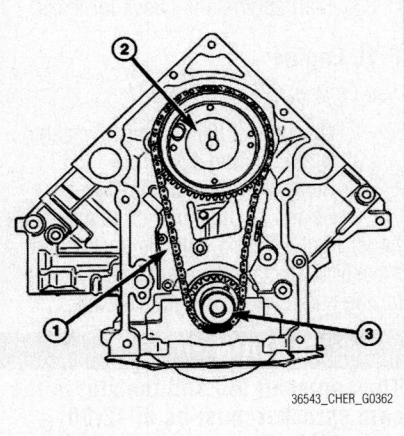

36543_CHER_G0362

Fig. 281 Remove camshaft sprocket attaching bolt and remove timing chain with crankshaft and camshaft sprockets (2)

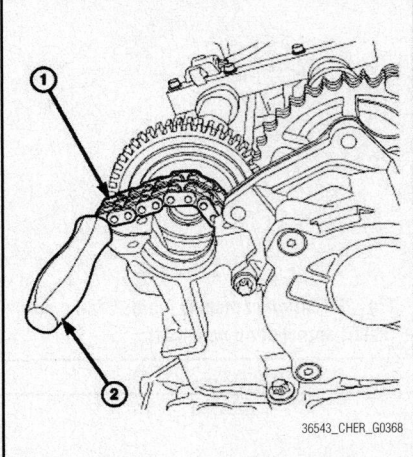

36543_CHER_G0368

Fig. 283 Turn the thrust pin (2) 9312-13 of the Chain Link Remover/Installer (1) 9312A clockwise while holding the handle until the rivet is pressed out and the chain is separated.

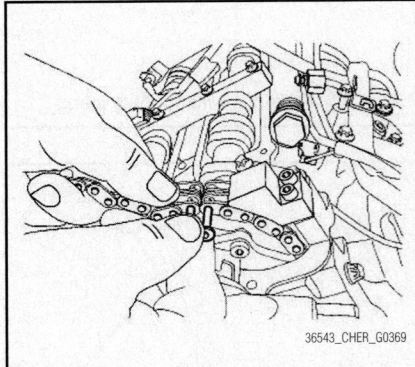

36543_CHER_G0369

Fig. 284 Connect NEW timing chain, oil hole side up with the assembly link

12. Slide both sprockets evenly over their respective shafts and check alignment of timing marks.

13. Install the camshaft bolt. Tighten the bolt to 90 ft. lbs. (122 Nm).

14. Remove tensioner pin.

15. Again, verify alignment of timing marks.

16. Install the oil pump.

17. Install the oil pan and pick up.

18. Install the timing chain cover.

19. Refill the engine oil.

20. Fill the cooling system.

21. Connect battery negative cable.

22. Start engine and check for oil and coolant leaks.

3.0L Diesel Engine

See Figures 282 through 291.

To check the timing chain for wear and stretch, remove the right-bank cylinder head cover and position the engine at TDC of cylinder number one Lock the camshafts with the Locking Pins 8929. The timing marks on the camshaft gears must face each other. Rotate the engine in the direction of rotation only and do not turn back otherwise measurement errors can result. With the camshafts locked, check the position of the vibration damper. The chain stretch is measured by the number of crankshaft degrees past the TDC mark. The timing chain is OK

when the belt pulley is at the marking at max. 11° after TDC with locked camshafts. Replace the timing chain has stretched beyond specifications.

1. Disconnect negative battery cable.

2. Remove the right cylinder head cover.

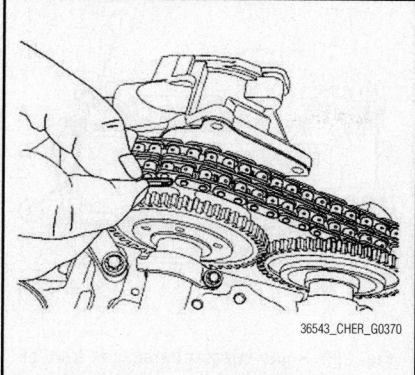

Fig. 285 Place the baking plate on the back side of the master link

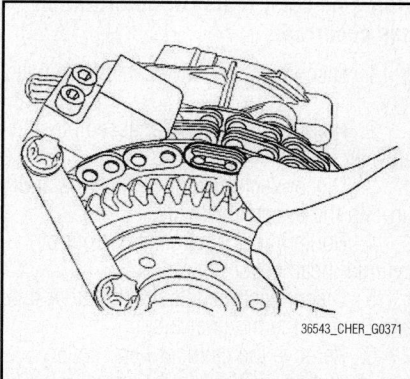

Fig. 286 Place the master link clip on the master link

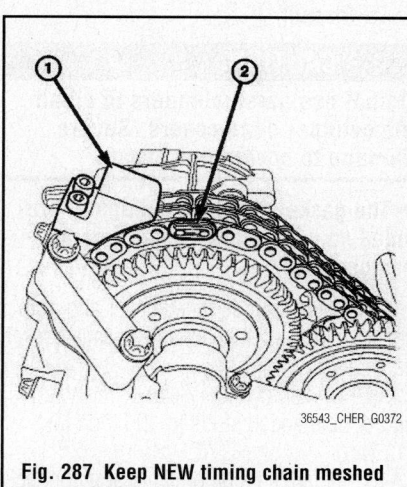

Fig. 287 Keep NEW timing chain meshed with camshaft sprocket

3. Make sure the crankshaft is turned to the TDC. Verify TDC of the crankshaft by lining up the mark on the front cover with the mark on the crankshaft damper.

4. Make sure that the timing marks on the back of the camshafts are horizontal and pointing at each other.

5. Remove the timing chain tensioner.

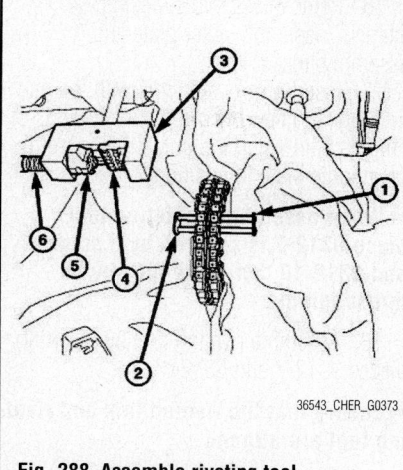

Fig. 288 Assemble riveting tool

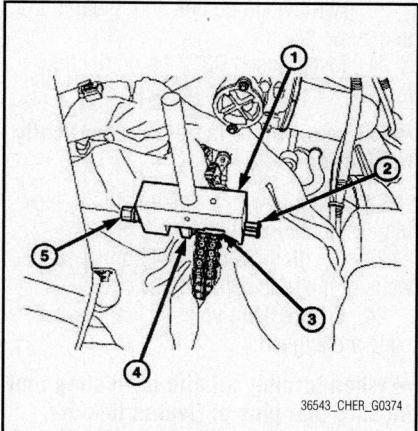

Fig. 289 Screw in spindle of riveting tool until firm resistance is felt

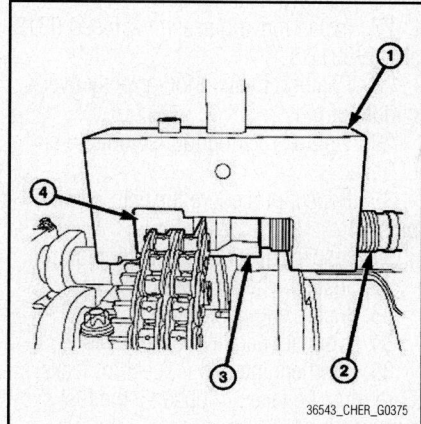

Fig. 290 Position riveting tool exactly over middle of pin

➡Cover the timing chain area. Care must be taken not to drop any repair debris or pieces into the engine when separating the timing chain links.

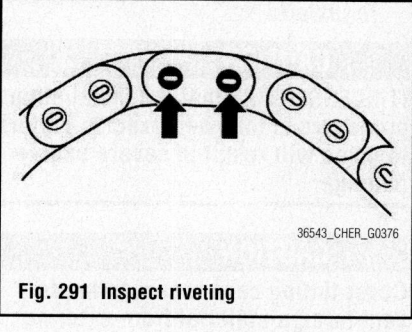

Fig. 291 Inspect riveting

6. Install the Timing Chain Holder 9554 using two of the cylinder head cover bolts.

7. Assemble the Chain Link Remover/Installer (1) 9312A using the Thrust Pin (3) 9312-3 and Thrust Spindle (4) 9312-4. Install the Insert (1) 9312-13 and retain with screw provided.

❋❋ CAUTION

Care must be taken not to drop the timing chain plates into the engine once the timing chain is separated.

➡When installing the Chain Link Remover/Installer 9312A onto timing chain link, be sure to back off the smaller nut of the thrust pin 9312-3 until the pin is recessed inside of the Thrust Spindle, 9312-4. Screw the Thrust Spindle 9312-4 in until it is seated and aligned properly over the rivet of the timing chain.

➡When fitting the thrust spindle, ensure that the thrust pin is positioned at the left timing chain pin of a chain link.

➡Cover the timing chain area. Care must be taken not to drop any repair debris or pieces into the engine when separating the timing chain links.

8. Carefully turn the thrust pin (2) 9312-13 of the Chain Link Remover/Installer (1) 9312A clockwise while holding the handle until the rivet is pressed out and the chain is separated. Discard the loose link and plates.

9. Use a small screwdriver to prevent the timing chain from slipping into the engine.

➡One whole timing chain link must be removed.

❋❋ CAUTION.

IT IS ESSENTIAL that the installation procedure for the timing chain is followed exactly. Failure to do so will result in severe engine damage.

To install:

> ❋❋ **CAUTION**
>
> IT IS ESSENTIAL that the installation procedure is followed exactly. Failure to do so will result in severe engine damage.

> ❋❋ **CAUTION**
>
> Cover timing case recesses to prevent foreign material from entering engine.

10. Use a small screwdriver to prevent the timing chain from slipping down into the engine.

> ❋❋ **CAUTION**
>
> Always install the NEW timing chain with the oil holes pointing up. Failure to do so will result in severe engine damage.

11. Connect NEW timing chain, oil hole side up and OLD timing chain with the assembly link.
12. Place the baking plate on the back side of the master link.
13. Place the master link clip on the master link.

➡ **Always keep NEW timing chain meshed with camshaft sprocket.**

> ❋❋ **CAUTION**
>
> DO NOT CRANK ENGINE and DO NOT ROTATE ENGINE BACKWARD. Engine rotation is clockwise, as you are looking at the engine. Rotate engine at crankshaft only.

➡ **With the timing cover and special tools in place, the timing chain cannot jump time while being fed through the engine. As the engine is rotated the timing chain may appear to slip as the valve springs move the camshafts.**

➡ **Draw out the end of OLD timing chain evenly as it becomes free, to the same extent that NEW timing chain is drawn in.**

14. Draw in NEW timing chain with the oil holes facing up, by rotating the crankshaft slowly in direction of rotation of engine.
15. Rotate the engine until the ends of the NEW timing chain meet and can be connected.

➡ **Assembly link is only an assembly aid and NOT designed for engine running.**

16. Remove assembly locking element, assembly outer plate and assembly link.
17. Insert new riveted link with the oil hole up, and new middle plate into ends of timing chain using the guide link to hold the middle plate in position.

➡ **When assembling riveting tool, piece 9312-7 is secured by a screw and 9312-10 can move loosely on thrust spindle**

18. Assemble riveting tool by inserting pieces 9312-7 and 9312-10.

➡ **Ensure that the riveted link and riveting tool are aligned.**

19. Press in new riveted link as far as the stop.
20. Remove guide link and riveting tool to change inserts.
21. Install insert 9312-8a on riveting tool.

➡ **The outer plate is held magnetically by riveting tool.**

22. Insert new outer plate into the moving assembly insert.
23. Position riveting tool so that spacer webs of the guide are side by side.
24. Ensure that riveted link and outer plate are aligned.

➡ **When turning spindle of riveting tool, be sure that pins of riveted link are inserted into holes of outer plate.**

25. Screw in spindle of riveting tool until firm resistance is felt.
26. Remove riveting tool.
27. Install moving assembly insert 9312-a11 to 9312-1.
28. Position riveting tool exactly over middle of pin.
29. Tighten riveting tool spindle to end of travel.
30. Repeat procedure for both riveting pins.
31. Inspect riveting, re-rivet if required.
32. Install cylinder head cover.
33. Install engine cover.
34. Connect negative battery cable.
35. Start engine and inspect for leaks. Care must be taken to observe the fuel system warnings.

VALVE (CYLINDER HEAD) COVERS

REMOVAL & INSTALLATION

3.7L Engine
See Figure 292.

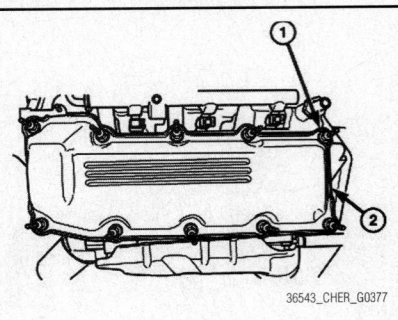

Fig. 292 Route injector harness in front of cylinder head cover (2)

➡ **The gasket may be used again, providing no cuts, tears, or deformation has occurred.**

1. Disconnect negative cable from battery.
2. Remove the resonator assemble and air inlet hose.
3. Disconnect injector connectors and un-clip the injector harness.
4. Route injector harness in front of cylinder head cover (2).
5. Disconnect the left side breather tube and remove the breather tube.
6. Remove the cylinder head cover mounting bolts (1).
7. Remove cylinder head cover and gasket.

To install:

> ❋❋ **CAUTION**
>
> Do not use harsh cleaners to clean the cylinder head covers. Severe damage to covers may occur.

➡ **The gasket may be used again, provided no cuts, tears, or deformation has occurred.**

8. Clean cylinder head cover and both sealing surfaces. Inspect and replace gasket as necessary.
9. Tighten cylinder head cover bolts and double ended studs to 105 inch lbs. (12 Nm).
10. Install left side breather and connect breather tube.
11. Connect injector electrical connectors and injector harness retaining clips.
12. Install the resonator and air inlet hose.
13. Connect negative cable to battery.

4.7L Engine

Left Side
See Figure 293.

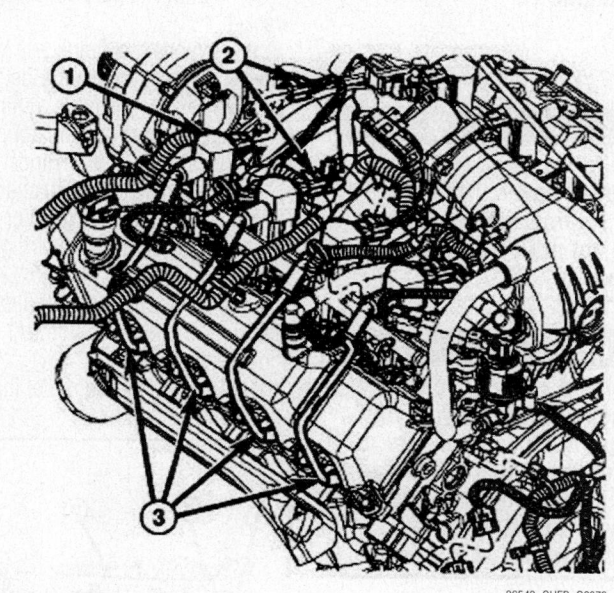

Fig. 293 Remove the spark plug wires (3)

1. Disconnect negative cable from battery.

2. Remove the resonator assemble and air inlet hose.

3. Remove the spark plug wires (3).

4. Route injector harness in front of cylinder head cover.

5. Disconnect the left side breather tube and remove the breather tube.

6. Remove the cylinder head cover mounting bolts.

7. Remove cylinder head cover and gasket.

➡ **The gasket may be used again, provided no cuts, tears, or deformation has occurred.**

To install:

✳✳ CAUTION

Do not use harsh cleaners to clean the cylinder head covers. Severe damage to covers may occur.

8. Clean cylinder head cover and both sealing surfaces. Inspect and replace gasket as necessary.

9. Install cylinder head cover and hand start all fasteners. Verify that all studs are in the correct location.

10. Tighten cylinder head cover bolts and double ended studs to 105 inch lbs. (12 Nm).

11. Install left side breather and connect breather tube.

12. Install the spark plug wires.

13. Install the resonator and air inlet hose.

14. Connect negative cable to battery.

Right Side

1. Disconnect battery negative cable.

2. Disconnect battery positive cable.

3. Remove the battery tray.

4. Drain cooling system.

5. Remove accessory drive belt.

6. Remove air conditioning compressor retaining bolts and move compressor to the left.

7. Remove heater hoses.

8. Disconnect injector and ignition coil connectors.

9. Disconnect and remove positive crankcase ventilation (PCV) hose.

10. Remove oil fill tube.

11. Un-clip injector and ignition coil harness and move away from cylinder head cover.

12. Remove right rear breather tube and filter assembly.

13. Remove cylinder head cover retaining bolts.

14. Remove cylinder head cover.

➡ **The gasket may be used again, provided no cuts, tears, or deformation has occurred.**

To install:

✳✳ CAUTION

Do not use harsh cleaners to clean the cylinder head covers. Severe damage to covers may occur.

15. Clean cylinder head cover and both sealing surfaces. Inspect and replace gasket as necessary.

16. Install cylinder head cover and hand start all fasteners.

17. Tighten cylinder head cover bolts and double ended studs to 105 inch lbs. (12 Nm).

18. Install right rear breather tube and filter assembly.

19. Install spark plug wires.

20. Install the oil fill tube.

21. Install PCV hose.

22. Install heater hoses.

23. Install air conditioning compressor retaining bolts.

24. Install accessory drive belt.

25. Fill Cooling system.

26. Install air cleaner assembly, resonator assembly and air inlet hose.

27. Connect battery negative cable.

5.7L & 6.1L Engines

See Figures 294 and 295.

1. Disconnect negative battery cable.

2. Disconnect ignition coil connector (1).

3. Remove ignition coil retaining bolts (3).

4. Remove ignition coil (1).

5. Remove cylinder head cover retaining bolts.

6. Remove cylinder head cover (1).

➡ **The gasket (2) may be used again, provided no cuts, tears, or deformation have occurred.**

To install:

✳✳ CAUTION

Do not use harsh cleaners to clean the cylinder head covers. Severe damage to covers may occur.

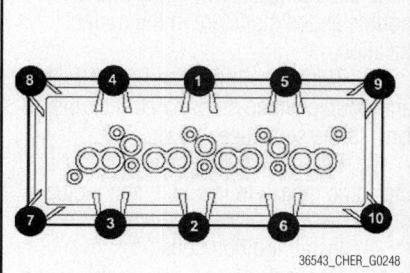

Fig. 294 Cylinder head cover retaining bolts and studs loosening and tightening sequence

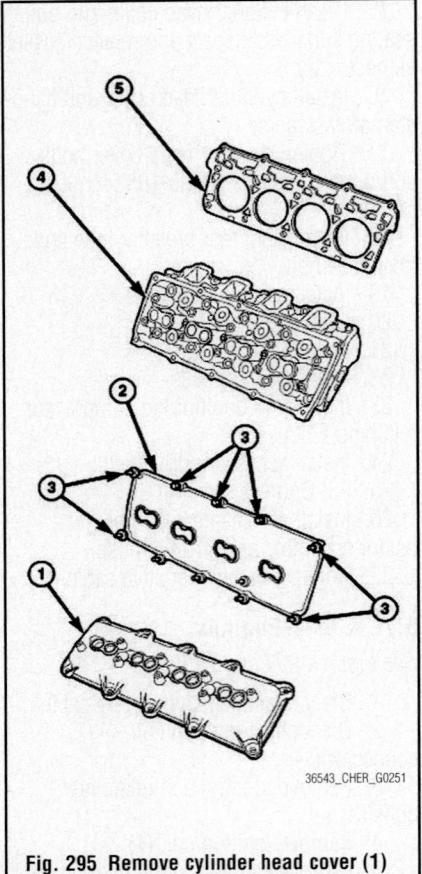

36543_CHER_G0251

Fig. 295 Remove cylinder head cover (1)

> ✳✳ **CAUTION**
>
> Do not allow other components including the wire harness to rest on or against the engine cylinder head cover. Prolonged contact with other objects may wear a hole in the cylinder head cover.

7. Clean cylinder head cover and both sealing surface.

8. Inspect and replace gasket as necessary.

9. Install cylinder head cover and hand start all fasteners. Verify that all double ended studs are in the correct location.

10. Tighten cylinder head cover bolts and double ended studs to 70 inch lbs. (8 Nm) in the sequence shown.

11. Before installing coil(s), apply dielectric grease to inside of spark plug boots.

12. Install ignition coils.

13. Connect ignition coil electrical connectors.

14. Install PCV hose.

15. Install the engine cover.

16. Connect the negative battery cable.

3.0L Diesel Engine

Right Side

See Figures 296 through 298.

> ✳✳ **CAUTION**
>
> Care must be taken when removing the cylinder head cover. The cover is the camshaft retainer and end play interface. Do not pry on the cylinder head cover tabs.

> ✳✳ **CAUTION**
>
> The cylinder head cover is sealed with Mopar sealant that may be difficult when separating components. If the component are difficult to separate heat the sealed edges or area with a heat gun. DO NOT use any heat source that works with flame.

➡Note the different length cylinder head cover bolts and their position for assembly purposes.

1. Disconnect the negative battery cable.

2. Position the coolant reservoir aside.

3. Remove the strut tower support.

4. Remove engine cover.

5. Remove engine cover front bracket.

6. Remove air cleaner cover (2) and inlet tube (1) to turbocharger.

7. Remove engine cover right rear bracket.

8. Remove the Crankcase Ventilation Valve (CCV) and breather tube.

9. Disconnect the fuel return line.

10. Disconnect the fuel supply and return lines at the right cylinder head cover.

11. Disconnect the Camshaft Position (CMP) sensor and fuel injector wiring and position the right engine wiring harness aside.

12. Pull out on the fuel injector return fuel hose retainers, disconnect the hoses and position aside.

13. Remove the right fuel injectors.

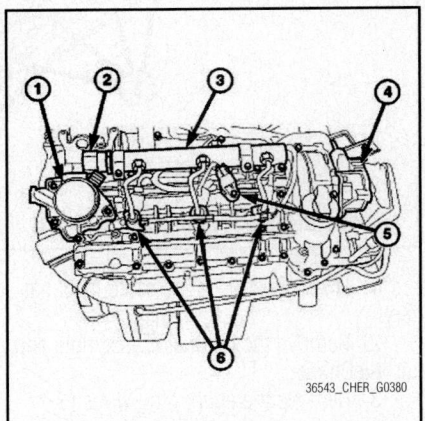

36543_CHER_G0380

Fig. 297 Remove the vacuum pump (4)

36543_CHER_G0379

Fig. 296 Remove air cleaner cover (2) and inlet tube (1) to turbocharger

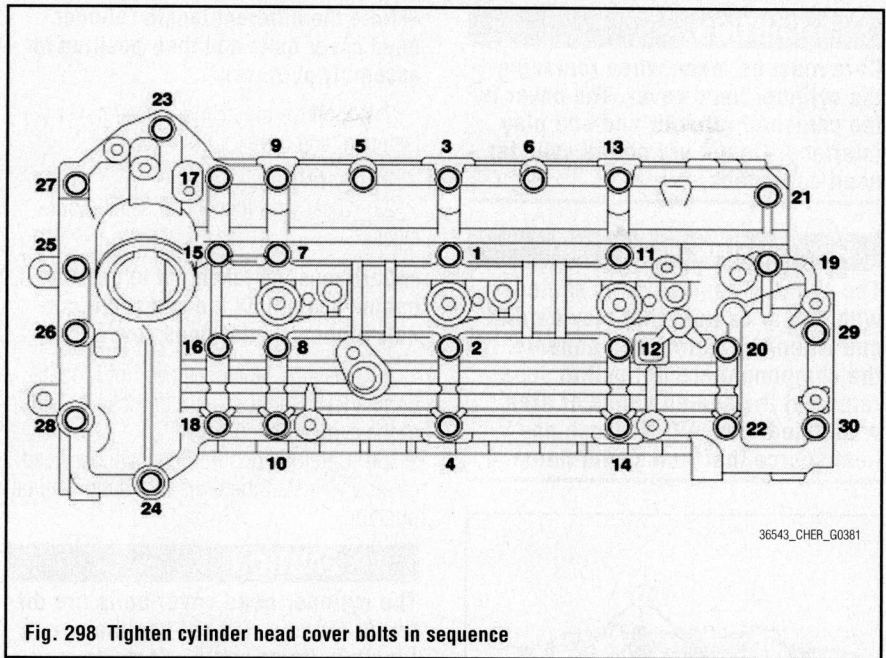

Fig. 298 Tighten cylinder head cover bolts in sequence

14. Remove the Air Conditioning (A/C) / heater hose bracket.

15. Remove the oil level indicator tube retaining bolt.

16. Remove the EGR air control valve assembly resonator.

17. Remove the vacuum pump (4).

18. Remove the cylinder head cover retaining bolts and remove cover.

To install:

19. Clean and inspect all sealing surfaces.

➡**Care must be taken not to get any engine sealant on the camshaft journals of the cylinder head cover.**

20. Install a ⅛ inches bead of Mopar Engine RTV Gen II sealant to the underside of the cylinder head cover.

⁂ **CAUTION**

The cylinder head cover bolts are different lengths. Make sure to install the bolts into their original position.

21. Carefully position the cylinder head cover and install the bolts into their original position.

22. Tighten cylinder head cover bolts in sequence, first to 35 inch lbs. (4 Nm), and then repeat the sequence to 75 inch lbs. (8.4 Nm).

⁂ **CAUTION**

Make sure to replace the lower copper washer seal on the injector. DO NOT re-use the old seal, DO NOT double the seals.

23. Install the fuel injectors. Tighten the retaining claw bolts to 5 ft. lbs. (7 Nm) and then an additional 180 degrees.

24. Install the CCV housing. Tighten the fasteners to 124 inch lbs. (14 Nm).

25. Install the vacuum pump. Tighten the fasteners to 80 inch lbs. (9 Nm).

26. Install the EGR air control valve resonator. Tighten the fasteners to 80 inch lbs. (9 Nm).

27. Install the oil level indicator tube fastener. Tighten the bolt to 97 inch lbs. (11 Nm).

28. Install the AC / heater hose bracket. Tighten the bolts to 80 inch lbs. (9 Nm).

29. Install the fuel rail. Tighten bolts to 80 inch lbs. (9 Nm).

➡**Inspect all fuel lines for damage or wear. Replace as necessary. DO NOT over tighten the fuel line nuts.**

30. Install the fuel injector high pressure lines. Tighten line nuts to 24 ft. lbs. (33 Nm).

31. Position the engine wiring harness and connect the CMP, fuel rail pressure sensor and fuel injectors.

32. Connect the fuel return hoses to fuel injectors, pushing down on the hose retainers.

33. Install the air cleaner cover and inlet tube.

34. Install the rear engine cover bracket.

35. Connect the CCV hose to air inlet tube and connect the CCV heater wiring harness connector.

36. Install the engine cover.

37. Install the strut tower support.

38. Install the coolant reservoir.

39. Connect the negative battery cable.

⁂ **WARNING**

High-pressure fuel lines deliver fuel under extreme pressure from the injection pump to the injectors. This may be as high as 19,580 psi (1350 bar). Use extreme caution when inspecting for high-pressure fuel leaks. Inspect high-pressure fuel leaks with a sheet of cardboard. Wear safety goggles and adequate protective clothing when servicing fuel system. Fuel under this amount of pressure can penetrate skin causing serious or fatal injury.

40. Start engine, allow to warm, turn engine off and inspect for leaks.

Left Side

See Figures 296, 299 through 303.

1. Disconnect negative battery cable.

2. Remove engine cover and bracket.

3. Remove air cleaner cover (2) and inlet tube to turbocharger.

4. Remove the high pressure line (2) from the fuel pump and the fuel rail.

5. Remove the bracket (3) from the oil filter housing.

6. Disconnect the fuel temperature sensor connector (4).

7. Disconnect the fuel quantity solenoid connector.

8. Remove the wiring harness retaining bolts and position the engine harness aside.

9. Remove the bolts from the intercooler air chamber.

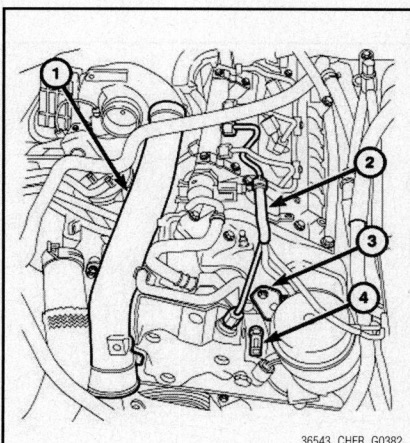

Fig. 299 Remove the high pressure line (2) from the fuel pump and the fuel rail

10. Remove the turbo outlet to intercooler inlet air tube (1).

11. Remove the power brake booster vacuum line (2) from the vacuum pump and position aside.

12. Disconnect the power feed line from the alternator and position aside.

13. Remove the supply and return fuel lines (1).

14. Disconnect the EGR solenoid connector.

15. Remove the EGR valve (2).

16. Disconnect the fuel injector electrical connectors.

17. Remove the fuel injector wiring harness from the cylinder head cover and position aside.

18. Remove the left cylinder head fuel return line.

19. Remove the high pressure fuel lines from the fuel injectors.

20. Remove the fuel injectors (1).

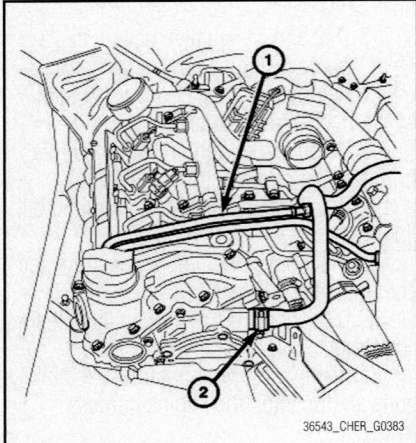

Fig. 300 Remove the power brake booster vacuum line (2) from the vacuum pump

Fig. 301 Remove the EGR valve (2)

✲✲ CAUTION

Care must be taken when removing the cylinder head cover. The cover is the camshaft retainer and end play interface. Do not pry on the cylinder head cover tabs.

✲✲ CAUTION

The cylinder head cover is sealed with Mopar sealant that may be difficult when separating components. If the component are difficult to separate heat the sealed edges or area with a heat gun. DO NOT use any heat source that works with flame.

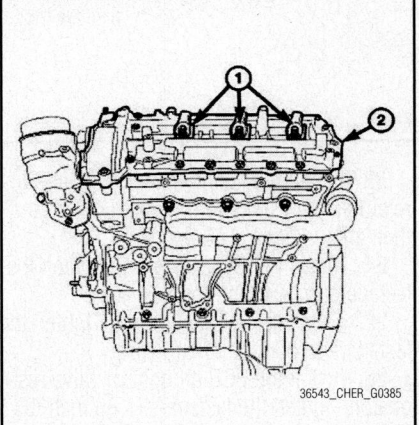

Fig. 302 Remove the cylinder head cover (2) fasteners and cover

➡Note the different length cylinder head cover bolts and their position for assembly purposes.

21. Remove the cylinder head cover (2) fasteners and cover.

To install:

22. Clean and inspect all sealing surfaces.

➡Care must be taken not to get any engine sealant on the camshaft journals of the cylinder head cover.

23. Install a ⅛ inches bead of Mopar® Engine RTV Gen II sealant to the underside of the cylinder head cover.

24. Carefully position the cylinder head cover and install the bolts into their original position.

✲✲ CAUTION

The cylinder head cover bolts are different lengths. Do not use the wrong length bolts or engine damage may result.

25. Tighten cylinder head cover bolts in sequence, first to 35 inch lbs. (4 Nm), and then repeat the sequence to 75 inch lbs. (8.4 Nm).

26. Install the EGR valve.

✲✲ CAUTION

The fuel injector sealing washers MUST be replaced. DO NOT use the old sealing washers or double the sealing washers.

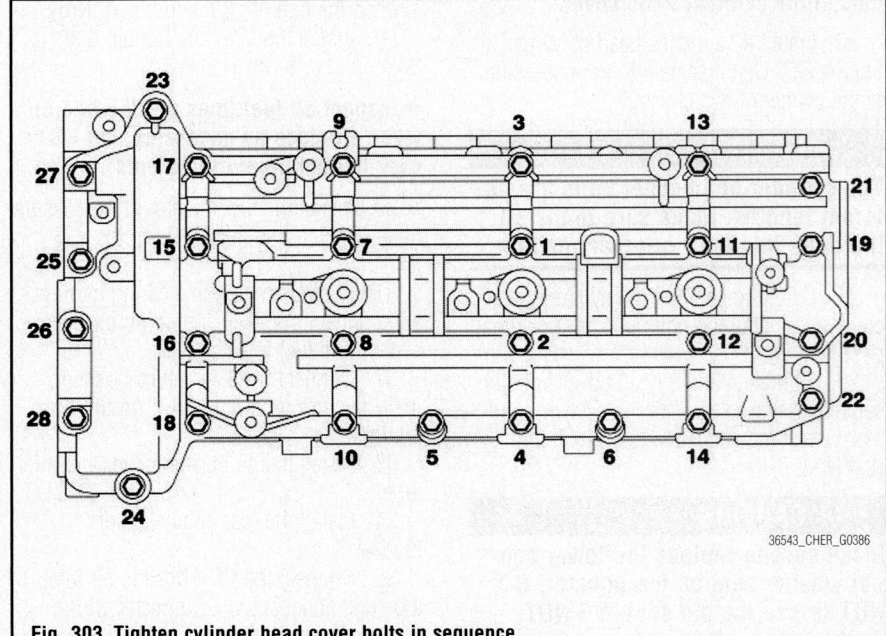

Fig. 303 Tighten cylinder head cover bolts in sequence

➡**Care must be taken not to apply any lubricant to the fuel injector nozzles.**

27. Install the fuel injectors. Tighten the injector retaining claw bolt to 5 ft. lbs. (7 Nm) and then an additional 180 degrees.

28. Re-position and secure the engine harness.

29. Install the left fuel rail. Tighten the fuel rail bolts to 8 ft. lbs. (11 Nm).

30. Position the return fuel lines and secure to the injectors. Push down on the release lock tab to secure.

31. Connect the fuel injector electrical connectors.

32. Install the left rear engine cover bracket.

33. Install the high pressure fuel lines from the fuel rail to injectors. Tighten the line connections to 20 ft. lbs. (27 Nm).

34. Install the fuel line from the high pressure pump to the left fuel rail. Tighten the retaining bolt to 22 ft. lbs. (30 Nm).

35. Install the fuel supply line to the fuel filter and high pressure pump.

36. Connect both fuel lines at the high pressure pump.

37. Install the air filter housing and tube.

38. Connect the negative battery cable.

39. Start the engine, run until warm, turn engine off and inspect for leaks).

✳✳ WARNING

Under no circumstances should gasoline be mixed with diesel fuel (not even during winter). The high pres- sure pump is lubricated by diesel fuel. Immediate fuel system damage may occur causing replacement and flushing of the complete diesel fuel system. High pressure pump seizure will cause metal particles to spread throughout the fuel circuit. All CDI fuel system components connected to the fuel circuit will have to be exchanged and the lines flushed.

VALVE LASH

ADJUSTMENT

The 3.7L and 4.7L engines use hydraulic valve lash adjusters. No adjustment is possible. If the hydraulic lash adjuster is not operating properly it must be replaced.

ENGINE PERFORMANCE & EMISSION CONTROLS

ACCELERATOR PEDAL POSITION SENSOR (APPS)

LOCATION

The Accelerator Pedal Position Sensor (APPS) is attached to the accelerator pedal assembly under the instrument panel.

The APPS is used only with the 5.7L and the 6.1L V-8 engines. The 5.7L/6.1L engines do not use a mechanical throttle cable.

REMOVAL & INSTALLATION

See Figure 304.

The accelerator pedal is serviced as a complete assembly including the bracket.

1. Disconnect electrical connector (3) at APPS (6).

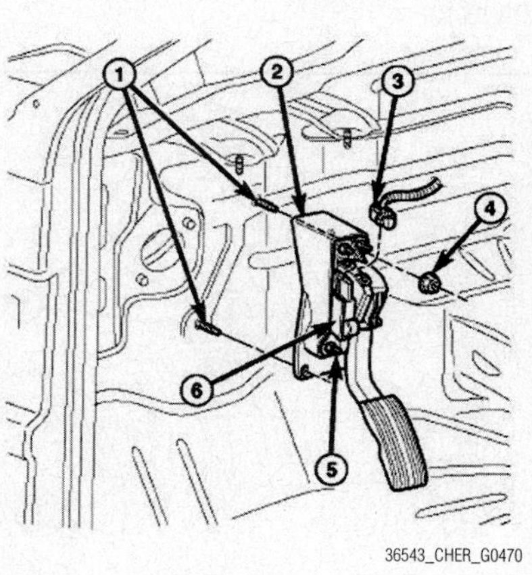

Fig. 304 Disconnect electrical connector (3) at APPS (6)

36543_CHER_G0470

2. Remove two accelerator pedal mounting bracket nuts (4). Remove accelerator pedal assembly.

3. Remove three sensor-to-pedal nuts (5). Remove APPS from accelerator pedal assembly.

To install:

4. Install APPS to pedal assembly and install three nuts.

5. Place accelerator pedal assembly over two mounting studs.

6. Install and tighten two mounting nuts.

7. Install electrical connector to APPS.

8. Use a scan tool may to learn electrical parameters. Go to the Miscellaneous menu, and then select ETC Learn.

9. If the previous step is not performed, a Diagnostic Trouble Code (DTC) will be set.

10. If necessary, also use a scan tool to erase any Diagnostic Trouble Codes (DTC's) from PCM.

11. Before starting engine, operate accelerator pedal to check for any binding.

CAMSHAFT POSITION (CMP) SENSOR

LOCATION

The Camshaft Position (CMP) sensor is bolted to the right-front side of the right cylinder head on 3.7L and 4.7L engines. On 5.7L and 6.1L engines, it is located below the alternator on the timing chain cover. On the 3.0L diesel engine the CMP is mounted on the right cylinder head cover.

REMOVAL & INSTALLATION

1. Raise and safely support the vehicle.

2. Disconnect the CMP electrical connector.

3. Remove the CMP sensor mounting bolts.

4. Carefully twist the sensor from the cylinder.

To install:

5. Check the condition of the sensor O-ring.

6. Clean out the machined hole in the cylinder head.

7. Apply a small amount of clean engine oil to the sensor O-ring.

8. Install the CMP sensor into the cylinder head with a slight rocking and twisting action.

9. Install the mounting bolt and tighten to 106 inch lbs. (12 Nm).

10. Connect the electrical connector.

11. Lower the vehicle.

CRANKSHAFT POSITION (CKP) SENSOR

LOCATION

The Crankshaft Position (CKP) sensor is mounted into the right rear side of the cylinder block. It is positioned and bolted into a machined hole.

REMOVAL & INSTALLATION

3.7L Engine

See Figure 305.

1. Raise vehicle.

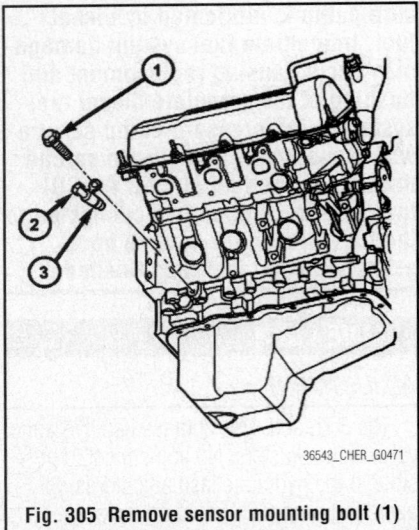

Fig. 305 Remove sensor mounting bolt (1)

2. Disconnect sensor electrical connector.

3. Remove sensor mounting bolt (1).

4. Carefully twist sensor from cylinder block.

5. Check condition of sensor O-ring (3).

To install:

6. Clean out machined hole in engine block.

7. Apply a small amount of engine oil to sensor O-ring.

8. Install sensor into engine block with a slight rocking and twisting action.

❊❊ CAUTION

Before tightening the sensor mounting bolt, be sure the sensor is completely flush to the cylinder block. If the sensor is not flush, damage to the sensor mounting tang may result.

9. Install mounting bolt tighten to 21 ft. lbs. (28 Nm) torque.

10. Connect electrical connector to sensor.

11. Lower vehicle.

4.7L Engine

See Figure 306.

1. Raise vehicle.

2. Disconnect CKP electrical connector at sensor.

3. Remove CKP mounting bolt (2).

4. Carefully twist sensor from cylinder block.

5. Remove sensor from vehicle.

6. Check condition of sensor O-ring.

To install:

7. Clean out machined hole in engine block.

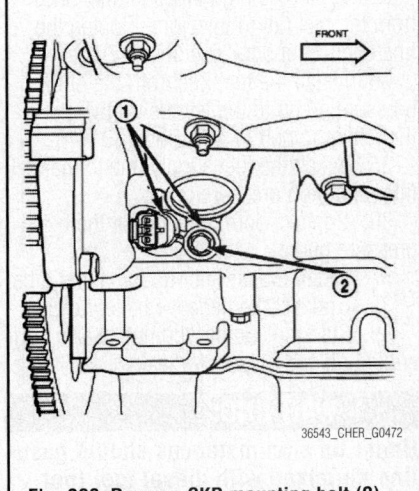

Fig. 306 Remove CKP mounting bolt (2)

8. Apply a small amount of engine oil to sensor O-ring.

9. Install sensor into engine block with a slight rocking and twisting action.

❊❊ CAUTION

Before tightening the sensor mounting bolt, be sure the sensor is completely flush to the cylinder block. If the sensor is not flush, damage to the sensor mounting tang may result.

10. Install mounting bolt tighten to 21 ft. lbs. (28 Nm) torque.

11. Connect electrical connector to sensor.

12. Lower vehicle.

5.7L Engine

See Figure 307.

1. Raise vehicle.

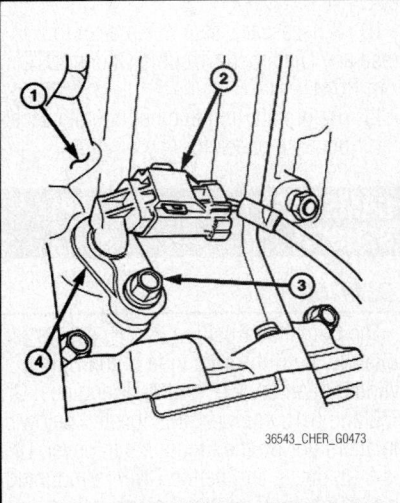

Fig. 307 Remove CKP mounting bolt (3)

2. Disconnect CKP electrical connector (2) at sensor.

3. Remove CKP mounting bolt (3).

4. Carefully twist sensor from cylinder block.

5. Remove sensor from vehicle.

6. Check condition of sensor O-ring.

To install:

7. Clean out machined hole in engine block.

8. Apply a small amount of engine oil to sensor O-ring.

9. Install sensor into engine block with a slight rocking and twisting action.

❊❊ CAUTION

Before tightening the sensor mounting bolt, be sure the sensor is completely flush to the cylinder block. If the sensor is not flush, damage to the sensor mounting tang may result.

10. Install mounting bolt tighten to 21 ft. lbs. (28 Nm) torque.

11. Connect electrical connector to sensor.

12. Lower vehicle.

3.0L Diesel Engine

See Figure 308.

1. Disconnect the negative battery cable.

2. Raise and support the vehicle.

3. Remove the Crankshaft Position (CKP) sensor heat shield (1).

4. Disconnect the CKP wiring harness connector.

5. Remove the bolt and sensor (2).

To install:

6. Clean the CKP sensor bore and install the sensor. Tighten the bolt to 80 inch lbs. (9 Nm).

7. Connect the engine harness connector.

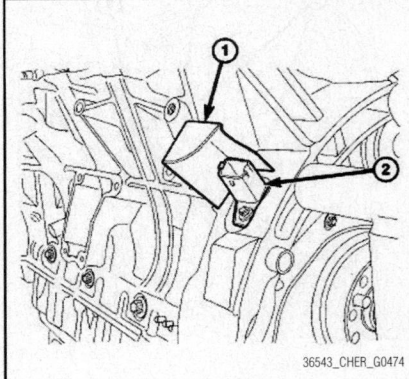

Fig. 308 Remove the Crankshaft Position (CKP) sensor heat shield (1)

8. Install the heat shield.
9. Lower the vehicle.
10. Connect the negative battery cable.

EVAPORATIVE EMISSION (EVAP) CANISTER

LOCATION

The Evaporative System Vapor Canister is located in the left-rear quarter-panel behind the left-rear tire.

REMOVAL & INSTALLATION

See Figures 309 through 312.

The Natural Vacuum Leak Detection (NVLD) pump (2) is attached to the Evaporative System Vapor Canister (3). This assembly is located in the left-rear quarter-panel behind the left-rear tire.

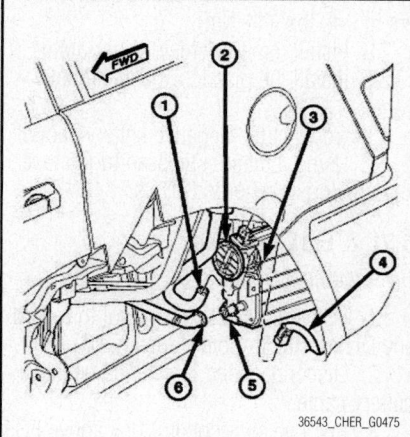

36543_CHER_G0475

Fig. 309 The Natural Vacuum Leak Detection (NVLD) pump (2) is attached to the Evaporative System Vapor Canister (3)

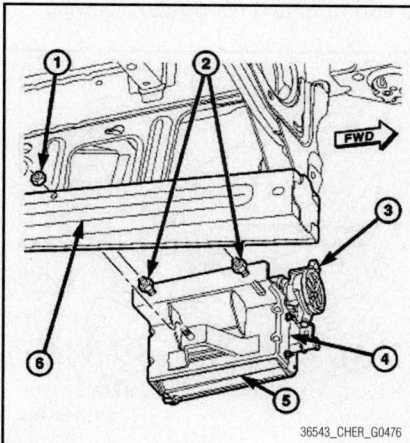

36543_CHER_G0476

Fig. 310 Remove three canister bracket-to-body nuts (1) and (2)

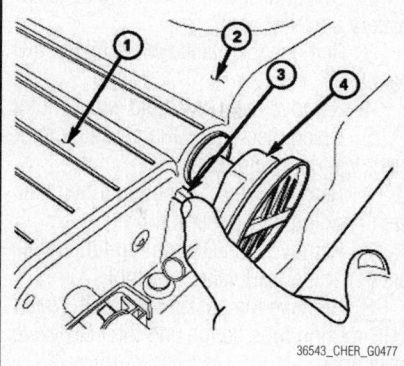

36543_CHER_G0477

Fig. 311 Pry outward on tab (3) and rotate pump clockwise about 70 degrees for removal

1. Raise and support vehicle.
2. Remove left-rear tire.
3. To access EVAP canister or NVLD pump, remove plastic splash shield at rear of left-rear tire.
4. Disconnect electrical connector (4) at pump.
5. Carefully remove vapor/vacuum hoses (1) and (6) at pump.
6. Remove three canister bracket-to-body nuts (1) and (2).
7. Separate canister from mounting bracket by removing two canister-to-bracket nuts at front of canister (4). The opposite end of canister is equipped with two alignment pins. Remove canister from support bracket by pulling these two pins from the two rubber grommets
8. To Separate NVLD Pump from EVAP canister:

   a. Pry outward on tab (3) and rotate pump clockwise about 70 degrees for removal.

   b. Remove NVLD pump O-ring (2) from EVAP canister (1).

To install:

9. Install new NVLD pump O-ring to EVAP canister.
10. Position NVLD pump into EVAP canister.
11. Rotate pump until tab aligns with notch in EVAP canister.
12. Position canister into mounting bracket. Install and tighten two canister-to-mounting bracket nuts.
13. Position canister/pump assembly to body. Install and tighten three mounting bracket-to-body nuts.
14. Carefully install vapor/vacuum lines and to NVLD pump and EVAP canister. The vapor/vacuum lines and hoses must be firmly connected. Check the vapor/vacuum lines at the NVLD pump, filter and EVAP

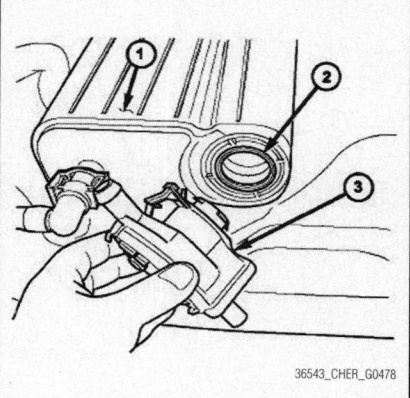

36543_CHER_G0478

Fig. 312 Remove NVLD pump O-ring (2) from EVAP canister (1)

canister purge solenoid for damage or leaks. If a leak is present, a Diagnostic Trouble Code (DTC) may be set.

15. Connect electrical connector to pump.
16. Install plastic splash shield at rear of left-rear tire.
17. Install left-rear tire.

EXHAUST GAS RECIRCULATION (EGR) VALVE

LOCATION

The electronic EGR valve and solenoid assembly is attached to the rear of the left cylinder head.

REMOVAL & INSTALLATION

3.7L Engine

See Figures 313 and 314.

1. Use a diagnostic scan tool to record any Diagnostic Trouble Codes (DTC).
2. Disconnect and isolate the negative battery cable.

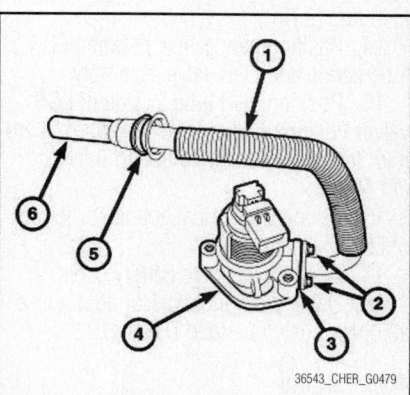

36543_CHER_G0479

Fig. 313 An exhaust gas routing tube (1) connects the EGR valve (4) to the intake manifold

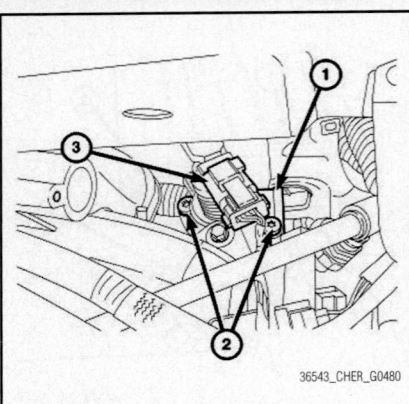

Fig. 314 Disconnect electrical connector (3) at solenoid (1)

➡**An exhaust gas routing tube (1) connects the EGR valve (4) to the intake manifold.**

3. Remove two tube mounting bolts (2).
4. Remove tube (1) from solenoid (4). Slip opposite end of tube (6) from intake manifold.
5. Remove gasket (3) located between EGR valve solenoid and tube flange.
6. Disconnect electrical connector (3) at solenoid (1).
7. Remove two EGR valve solenoid mounting bolts (2).
8. Remove solenoid (1) from engine.
9. Remove and discard gasket (1) located under EGR solenoid.

To install:

10. Clean gasket area at rear of left cylinder head where it joins base of EGR valve.
11. Clean EGR tube where it joins EGR valve.
12. Position new gasket between EGR valve and cylinder head.
13. Position EGR valve to cylinder head. Install and tighten two bolts. Torque to 80 inch lbs. (9 Nm).
14. Position new gasket between EGR tube flange and EGR valve assembly.
15. Position EGR tube to side of EGR valve. Position end of tube into intake manifold. Install two bolts. Torque to 9 ft. lbs. (11 Nm).
16. Connect electrical connector to top of EGR valve solenoid.
17. Connect negative battery cable.
18. Using a diagnostic scan tool, erase any previously recorded DTCs.

4.7L Engine

See Figures 315 and 316.

1. Use a diagnostic scan tool to record any Diagnostic Trouble Codes (DTC).

2. Disconnect and isolate the negative battery cable.
3. Remove the plastic windshield cowl panel.
4. Remove the windshield wiper motor.
5. Disconnect the EGR valve solenoid electrical connector (5).
6. Remove the EGR routing tube retainers (1) at the intake manifold.
7. Remove the EGR routing tube retainers (4) at the EGR valve assembly.
8. Remove the gasket located between EGR routing tube flange and the EGR valve assembly.
9. Remove the EGR valve assembly retainers (5).
10. Remove the EGR valve assembly (3) from the engine.
11. Remove and discard the metal gasket located between the cylinder head and the EGR valve assembly.

To install:

12. Clean the area at the rear of the left

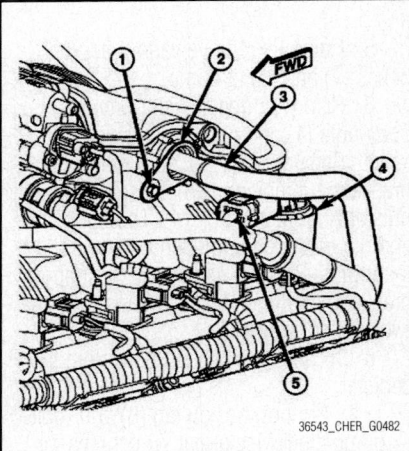

Fig. 315 Disconnect the EGR valve solenoid electrical connector (5)

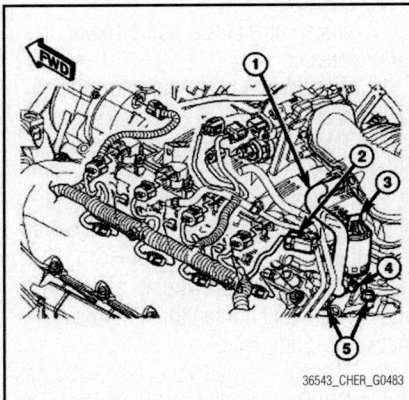

Fig. 316 Remove the EGR routing tube retainers (4) at the EGR valve assembly

cylinder head where it joins the base of the EGR valve.
13. Clean the EGR routing tube where it joins the EGR valve.
14. Position the new gasket between the EGR valve and the cylinder head.
15. Position the EGR valve to the cylinder head and install the retainers and tighten to 80 inch lbs. (9 Nm).
16. Position a new gasket between the EGR routing tube flange and the EGR valve assembly.
17. Position the EGR routing tube to the side of the EGR valve and into the intake manifold and install the retainers hand tight.
18. Install the EGR routing tube flange retainers at the intake manifold and tighten to 9 ft. lbs. (11 Nm).
19. Connect the electrical connector to the EGR valve solenoid.
20. Tighten the EGR routing tube retainers to 9 ft. lbs. (11 Nm).
21. Install the windshield wiper motor.
22. Install the plastic windshield cowl panel.
23. Connect the negative battery cable.
24. Using a diagnostic scan tool, erase any previously recorded DTCs.

5.7L & 6.1L Engines

See Figures 317 and 318.

1. Use a diagnostic scan tool to record any Diagnostic Trouble Codes (DTC).
2. Disconnect and isolate the negative battery cable.
3. Remove air resonator box above EGR valve/solenoid.
4. Remove accessory serpentine drive belt.
5. Remove alternator mounting bolts.
6. Reposition alternator to gain access to EGR valve-to-cylinder head mounting

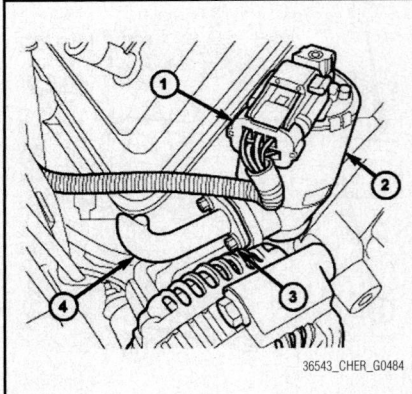

Fig. 317 Disconnect electrical connector (1) from EGR solenoid (2)

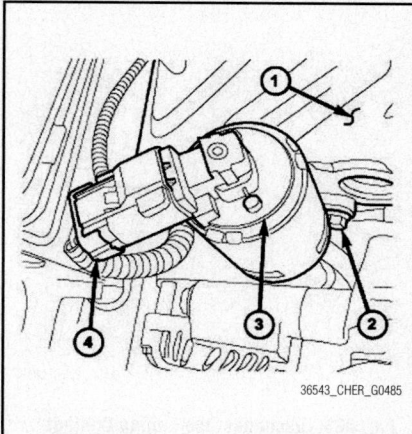

Fig. 318 Remove two mounting bolts (2)

bolts. No need to remove alternator wiring from alternator.

7. Disconnect electrical connector (1) from EGR solenoid (2).

8. Remove two bolts (3) connecting EGR tube (4) to valve assembly.

9. Remove gasket located between EGR tube flange and EGR valve assembly.

10. Remove two mounting bolts (2).

11. Separate valve assembly (3) from cylinder head (1).

12. Remove and discard metal gasket located between cylinder head and valve assembly.

To install:

13. Position a new metal gasket between cylinder head and valve assembly.

14. Install two mounting bolts and tighten to 20 ft. lbs. (27 Nm).

15. Clean EGR tube where it joins EGR valve.

16. Position new gasket between EGR tube flange and EGR valve assembly.

17. Install two bolts connecting EGR tube to valve assembly. Tighten bolts to 20 ft. lbs. (27 Nm).

18. Connect electrical connector to EGR solenoid.

19. Position alternator to alternator mounting bracket.

20. Install alternator mounting bolts. Tighten alternator mounting bolts to 30 ft. lbs. (41 Nm).

✳✳ CAUTION

Never force a belt over a pulley rim using a screwdriver. The synthetic fiber of the belt can be damaged.

✳✳ CAUTION

When installing a serpentine accessory drive belt, the belt must be routed correctly. The water pump

may be rotating in the wrong direction if the belt is installed incorrectly, causing the engine to overheat.

21. Install accessory serpentine drive belt.

22. Install air resonator box above EGR valve/solenoid.

23. Connect negative battery cable to battery.

24. Using a diagnostic scan tool, erase any previously recorded DTCs.

3.0L Diesel Engine

See Figure 319.

1. Disconnect the negative battery cable.

2. Remove engine cover.

3. Disconnect the EGR valve harness connector (1).

4. Remove EGR valve retaining bolts (2) and valve (3), discard the gasket.

To install:

5. Clean EGR valve sealing surfaces.

6. Lubricate the seal and install the EGR valve in intake manifold. Tighten EGR valve retaining bolts to 80 inch lbs. (9 Nm).

7. Connect the EGR valve harness connector.

8. Install engine cover.

9. Connect the negative battery cable.

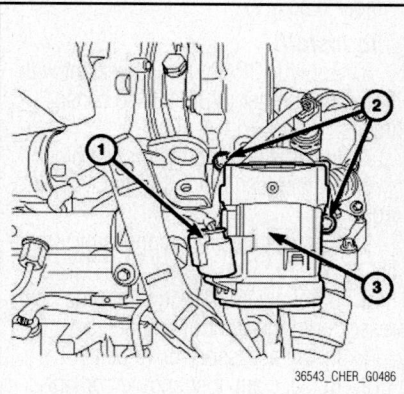

Fig. 319 Disconnect the EGR valve harness connector (1)

ENGINE COOLANT TEMPERATURE (ECT) SENSOR

LOCATION

The Engine Coolant Temperature (ECT) sensor is used to sense engine coolant temperature. The sensor protrudes into an engine water jacket.

The Engine Coolant Temperature (ECT) sensor on the 3.7L engine is installed into a

water jacket at front of intake manifold near rear of alternator.

On the 4.7L engine, the ECT sensor is located near the front of the intake manifold.

The Engine Coolant Temperature (ECT) sensor on the 5.7L/6.1L engine is located under the air conditioning compressor. It is installed into a water jacket at the front of the cylinder block.

REMOVAL & INSTALLATION

3.7L Engine

See Figure 320.

✳✳ WARNING

Hot, pressurized coolant can cause injury by scalding. Cooling system must be partially drained before removing the Engine Coolant Temperature (ECT) sensor.

➡**Do not waste reusable coolant. If solution is clean, drain coolant into a clean container for reuse.**

1. Partially drain the cooling system.

2. Disconnect the electrical connector from the sensor (3).

3. Remove the sensor (3) from the intake manifold (4).

To install:

4. Apply MOPAR® thread sealant with PFTE part number 04318034 to sensor threads.

5. Install sensor to engine.

6. Tighten sensor to 8 ft. lbs. (11 Nm) torque.

7. Connect electrical connector to sensor.

8. Replace any lost engine coolant.

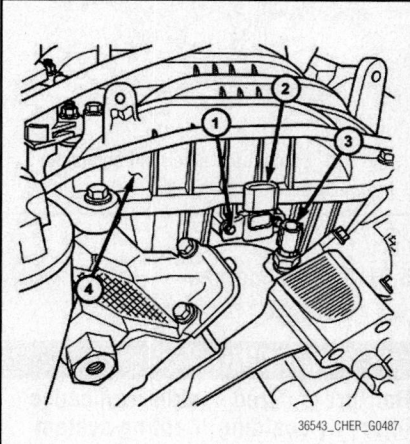

Fig. 320 Disconnect the electrical connector from the sensor (3)

4.7L Engine

See Figure 321.

> **⁕⁕ WARNING**
>
> Hot, pressurized coolant can cause injury by scalding. Cooling system must be partially drained before removing the Engine Coolant Temperature (ECT) sensor.

➡ Do not waste reusable coolant. If solution is clean, drain coolant into a clean container for reuse.

1. Partially drain cooling system.
2. Disconnect electrical connector from ECT sensor (1).
3. Remove sensor (1) from intake manifold.

To install:

4. Apply MOPAR® thread sealant with PFTE part number 04318034 to sensor threads.
5. Install sensor to engine.
6. Tighten sensor to 8 ft. lbs. (11 Nm) torque.
7. Connect electrical connector to sensor.
8. Replace any lost engine coolant.

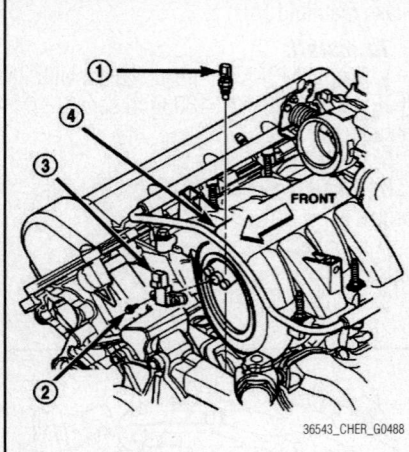

Fig. 321 Disconnect electrical connector from ECT sensor (1)

5.7L & 6.1L Engines

See Figure 322.

> **⁕⁕ WARNING**
>
> Hot, pressurized coolant can cause injury by scalding. Cooling system must be partially drained before removing the coolant temperature sensor.

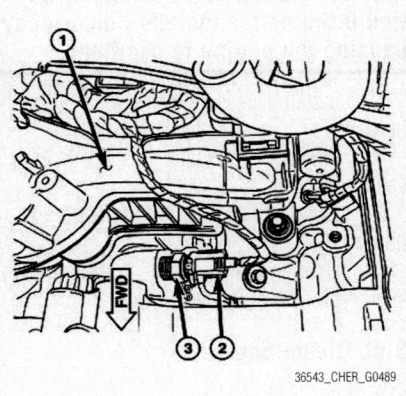

Fig. 322 Disconnect electrical connector (2) from sensor (3)

➡ Do not waste reusable coolant. If solution is clean, drain coolant into a clean container for reuse.

1. Partially drain the cooling system.
2. Remove accessory drive belt.
3. Carefully unbolt air conditioning compressor from front of engine. Do not disconnect any A/C hoses from compressor. Temporarily support compressor to gain access to ECT sensor (3).
4. Disconnect electrical connector (2) from sensor (3).
5. Remove sensor (3) from engine cylinder block (1).

To install:

6. Apply MOPAR® thread sealant with PFTE part number 04318034 to sensor threads.
7. Install sensor to the engine block.
8. Tighten sensor to 8 ft. lbs. (11 Nm) torque.
9. Connect electrical connector to sensor.
10. Carefully bolt air conditioning compressor onto the front of engine.
11. Install accessory drive belt.
12. Replace any lost engine coolant.

3.0L Diesel Engine

See Figure 323.

> **⁕⁕ WARNING**
>
> Risk of injury to skin and eyes from scalding with hot coolant. Risk of poisoning from swallowing coolant. Do not open cooling system unless coolant temperature is below 194°F (90°C). Open cap slowly to release pressure. Store coolant in suitable and appropriately marked container. Wear protective gloves, clothes and eye wear.

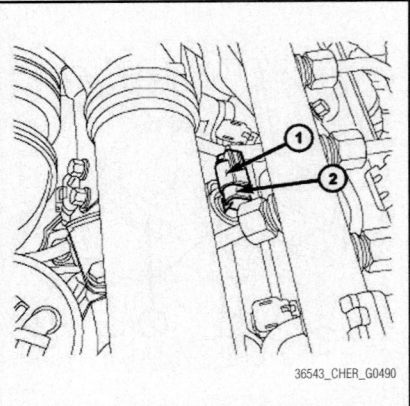

Fig. 323 Disconnect the Engine Coolant Temperature (ECT) sensor electrical connector (1)

➡ Do not waste reusable coolant. If solution is clean, drain coolant into a clean container for reuse.

1. Disconnect negative battery cable.
2. Remove engine cover.
3. Partially drain coolant system.
4. Disconnect the Engine Coolant Temperature (ECT) sensor electrical connector (1).

➡ Capture any residual coolant that may flow.

5. Remove coolant temperature sensor (2).

To install:

6. Apply MOPAR® thread sealant with PFTE part number 04318034 to sensor threads.
7. Position and install coolant temperature sensor to engine.
8. Connect coolant temperature sensor electrical connector.
9. Refill coolant system to proper level with proper mixture of coolant.
10. Install engine cover.
11. Connect negative battery cable.

> **⁕⁕ WARNING**
>
> Use extreme caution when engine is operating. Do not stand in a direct line with fan. Do not put your hands near pulleys, belts or fan. Do not wear loose clothes.

12. Start engine and inspect area for leaks.

HEATED OXYGEN (HO2S) SENSOR

LOCATION

See Figure 324.

If equipped with a Federal Emission Package, two sensors are used: upstream

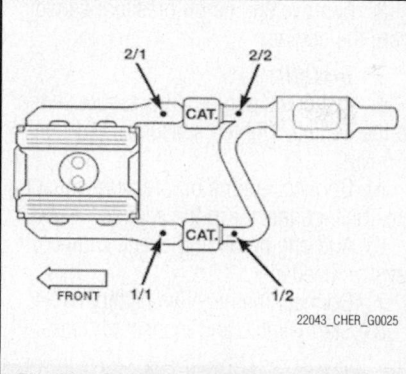

Fig. 324 Oxygen sensor mounting points

(referred to as 1/1) and downstream (referred to as 1/2). With this emission package, the upstream sensor (1/1) is located just before the main catalytic converter. The downstream sensor (1/2) is located just after the main catalytic converter.

If equipped with a California Emission Package, 4 sensors are used: 2 upstream (referred to as 1/1 and 2/1) and 2 downstream (referred to as 1/2 and 2/2). With this emission package, the right upstream sensor (2/1) is located in the right exhaust downpipe just before the mini-catalytic converter. The left upstream sensor (1/1) is located in the left exhaust downpipe just before the mini-catalytic converter. The right downstream sensor (2/2) is located in the right exhaust downpipe just after the mini-catalytic converter, and before the main catalytic converter. The left downstream sensor (1/2) is located in the left exhaust downpipe just after the mini-catalytic converter, and before the main catalytic converter.

REMOVAL & INSTALLATION

1. Raise and safely support the vehicle.
2. Disconnect the wire connector from oxygen sensor.

✳✳ WARNING
When disconnecting sensor electrical connector, do not pull directly on wire going into sensor.

3. Remove the sensor with an oxygen sensor removal and installation tool.
4. Clean threads in exhaust pipe using appropriate tap.

To install:

➡**Threads of new oxygen sensors are factory coated with anti-seize compound.**

✳✳ WARNING
Do not add any additional anti-seize compound to the threads of a new oxygen sensor.

5. Install the oxygen sensor and tighten to 22 ft. lbs. (30 Nm).
6. Connect the electrical connector.
7. Lower the vehicle.

IDLE AIR CONTROL (IAC) VALVE

LOCATION

➡**An IAC valve/motor is not used with the 5.7L engine.**

The IAC motor is mounted to the throttle body.

REMOVAL & INSTALLATION
See Figure 325.

1. Remove air resonator box at throttle body.
2. Disconnect electrical connector from IAC motor.
3. Remove two mounting bolts (screws).
4. Remove IAC motor from throttle body.

To install:
5. Install IAC motor to throttle body.
6. Install and tighten two mounting bolts (screws) to 60 inch lbs. (7 Nm).
7. Install electrical connector.
8. Install air resonator to throttle body.

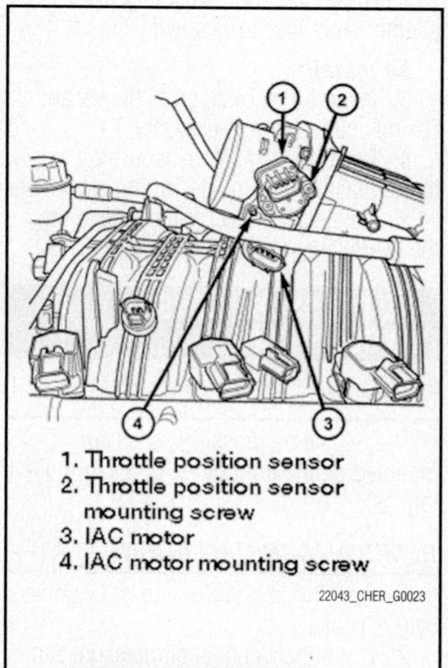

1. Throttle position sensor
2. Throttle position sensor mounting screw
3. IAC motor
4. IAC motor mounting screw

22043_CHER_G0023

Fig. 325 IAC motor mounting

INTAKE AIR TEMPERATURE (IAT) SENSOR

LOCATION

The Intake Air Temperature (IAT) sensor is installed in the air inlet tube.

REMOVAL & INSTALLATION
See Figure 326.

1. Disconnect the electrical connector form the Intake Air Temperature (IAT) sensor.
2. Clean any dirt from the air inlet tube at the sensor base.
3. Gently lift the small plastic release tab and rotate the sensor about ¼ turn counter-clockwise to remove.

To install:
4. Check the condition of the sensor O-ring.
5. Clean the sensor mounting hole.
6. Position the sensor into the intake air tube and rotate clockwise until the release tab clicks into place.
7. Install the electrical connector.

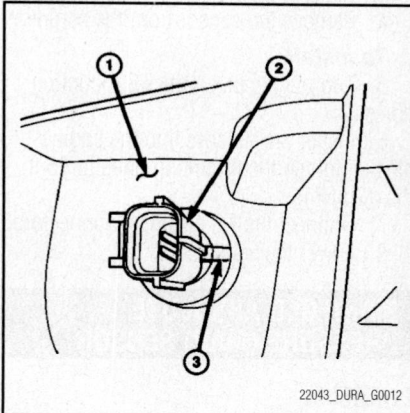

Fig. 326 The IAT sensor (2) is located in the air inlet (1). Lift the tab (3) to remove it

KNOCK SENSOR (KS)

LOCATION

3.7L & 4.7L Engines

Two Knock Sensors (KS) are bolted into the engine block under the intake manifold.

5.7L & 6.1L Engines

Two Knock Sensors (KS) are bolted into each side of the engine block under the exhaust manifolds.

REMOVAL & INSTALLATION

3.7L & 4.7L Engines

1. Disconnect the knock sensor dual pigtail harness from engine wiring harness. This connection is made near rear of engine.
2. Remove the intake manifold
3. Remove the Knock Sensor (KS) mounting bolts.
4. Remove the sensors from engine.

To install:

5. Thoroughly clean the KS mounting holes.
6. Install the sensors into the engine block. Tighten the mounting bolts to 15 ft. lbs. (20 Nm).
7. Install the intake manifold.
8. Connect the KS wiring harness to the engine wiring harness at the rear of the engine.

5.7L & 6.1L Engines

1. Raise and safely support the vehicle.
2. Disconnect the Knock Sensor (KS) electrical connector.
3. Remove the KS mounting bolt.
4. Remove the sensor from the engine.

To install:

5. Thoroughly clean the KS mounting holes.
6. Install the sensors into the engine block. Tighten the mounting bolts to 15 ft. lbs. (20 Nm).
7. Connect the KS electrical connectors.
8. Lower the vehicle.

MANIFOLD ABSOLUTE PRESSURE (MAP) SENSOR

LOCATION

3.7L & 4.7L Engines

The Manifold Absolute Pressure (MAP) sensor is mounted to the front of the intake manifold with two bolts.

5.7L & 6.1L Engines

The Manifold Absolute Pressure (MAP) sensor is mounted to the back of the intake manifold by a quarter turn fastener.

REMOVAL & INSTALLATION

3.7L & 4.7L Engines

See Figure 327.

1. Disconnect the sensor electrical connector.
2. Clean the area around the Manifold Absolute Pressure (MAP) sensor.

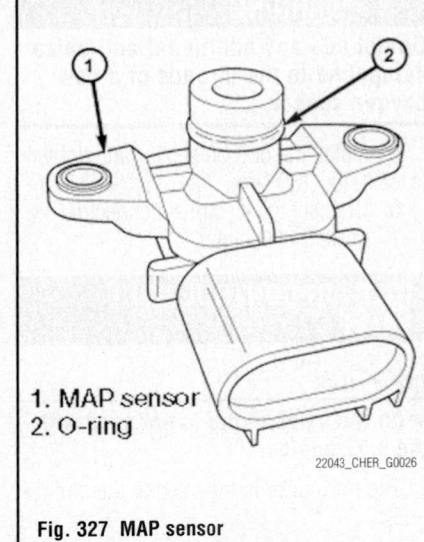

1. MAP sensor
2. O-ring

22043_CHER_G0026

Fig. 327 MAP sensor

3. Remove the two mounting screws.
4. Remove the MAP sensor from the intake manifold.

To install:

5. Inspect the condition of the sensor O-ring and replace if necessary.
6. Position the MAP sensor into the manifold and install the two mounting screws.
7. Connect the electrical connector.

5.7L & 6.1L Engines

1. Disconnect the electrical connector at the Manifold Absolute Pressure (MAP) sensor by sliding the release lock out. Then press down on the lock tab.
2. Rotate the MAP sensor ¼ turn counter-clockwise to remove.

To install:

3. Inspect the condition of the sensor O-ring and replace if necessary.
4. Position the MAP sensor into the intake manifold and rotate ¼ turn clockwise.
5. Connect the electrical connector to the MAP sensor until it clicks into place.

OIL PRESSURE SENSOR – DIESEL ENGINES

LOCATION

The engine oil pressure sensor is mounted on the front of the oil filter housing.

REMOVAL & INSTALLATION

1. Open hood and disconnect negative battery cable.
2. Disconnect engine oil pressure sensor connector.

3. Remove engine oil pressure sensor from the engine.

To install:

4. Install the engine oil pressure sensor to the engine. Tighten sensor to 11 ft. lbs. (15 Nm).
5. Connect engine oil pressure sensor electrical connector to the sensor.
6. Add engine oil and check engine oil level as needed.
7. Connect the negative battery cable.
8. Start vehicle and inspect for leaks.

OIL PRESSURE SWITCH – GASOLINE ENGINES

LOCATION

The oil pressure switch is a pressure sensitive switch that is activated by the engine's oil pressure (in the main oil gallery). The switch is a two terminal device (one terminal is provided to the wiring harness and the other terminal is the switch's metal housing that screws into the engine block).

REMOVAL & INSTALLATION

See Figure 328.

1. Disconnect the negative cable from the battery.
2. Raise vehicle on hoist.
3. Remove front splash shield.
4. Disconnect oil pressure switch connector (4).
5. Remove the pressure switch (2).

To install:

6. Install the oil pressure switch.
7. Connect oil pressure switch connector.
8. Install front splash shield.

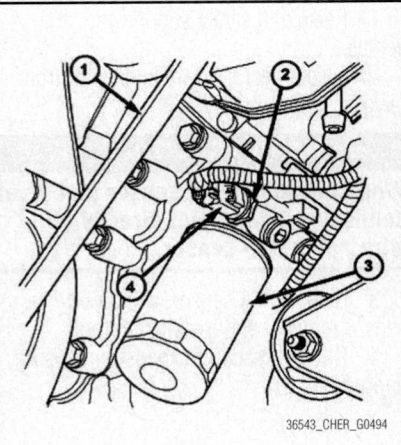

36543_CHER_G0494

Fig. 328 Disconnect oil pressure switch connector (4)

9. Lower vehicle.
10. Connect the negative battery cable.
11. Start the engine and ensure there are no oil leaks from the oil pressure switch.

POWERTRAIN CONTROL MODULE (PCM)

LOCATION

The Powertrain control Module (PCM) is attached to the right-front inner fender located in the engine compartment.

REMOVAL & INSTALLATION

See Figures 329 and 330.

➡**To avoid possible voltage spike damage to the PCM, ignition key must be off, and negative battery cable must be disconnected before unplugging PCM connectors.**

1. Disconnect and isolate negative battery cable.
2. Carefully unplug the 38-way connectors (2) from PCM.
3. A locating pin (5) is used in place of one of the PCM mounting bolts. Pry clip (4) from pin (5).
4. Remove two PCM mounting bolts (2), and remove PCM from vehicle.
5. Position ground strap (3) to the side.

To install:

✳✳ CAUTION

Certain ABS systems rely on having the Powertrain Control Module (PCM) broadcast the Vehicle Identification Number (VIN) over the bus network. To prevent problems of DTCs and other items related to the VIN broadcast, it is recommend that you dis-

connect the ABS CAB (controller) temporarily when replacing the PCM. Once the PCM is replaced, write the VIN to the PCM using a diagnostic scan tool. This is done from the engine main menu. Arrow over to the second page to "1. Miscellaneous". Select "Check VIN" from the choices. Make sure it has the correct VIN entered before continuing. When the VIN is complete, turn off the ignition key and reconnect the ABS module connector. This will prevent the setting of DTCs and other items associated with the lack of a VIN detected when you turn the key ON after replacing the PCM.

✳✳ CAUTION

Use a diagnostic scan tool to reprogram the new PCM with the vehicles original identification number (VIN) and the vehicles original mileage. If this step is not done, a Diagnostic Trouble Code (DTC) may be set.

6. Install clip to pin.
7. Position PCM to body and install two bolts. Be sure to position ground strap before installing bolt.
8. Check pin connectors in PCM. Also check the 38-way connectors for corrosion or damage. Repair as necessary.
9. Carefully plug the 38–way connectors into PCM.
10. Connect negative battery cable.
11. Use a diagnostic scan tool to reprogram new PCM with vehicles original Identification number (VIN) and original vehicle mileage. If this step is not done, a Diagnostic Trouble Code (DTC) may be set.

RESET PROCEDURE

This procedure will need to be done when one or more of the following situations are true:

1. A vehicle's Powertrain Control Module/Engine Control Module (PCM/ECM) has been replaced.
2. A diagnostic trouble code (DTC) is set P1602 - PCM/ECM Not Programmed.
3. An updated calibration or software release is available for either the PCM/ECM or TCM ECUs.

Check PCM/ECM VIN

4. From the "Home" screen, select "ECU View"
   a. Select "PCM/ECM"
   b. Select "Misc. Functions"
   c. Select "Check PCM/ECM VIN" and follow the on screen instructions.

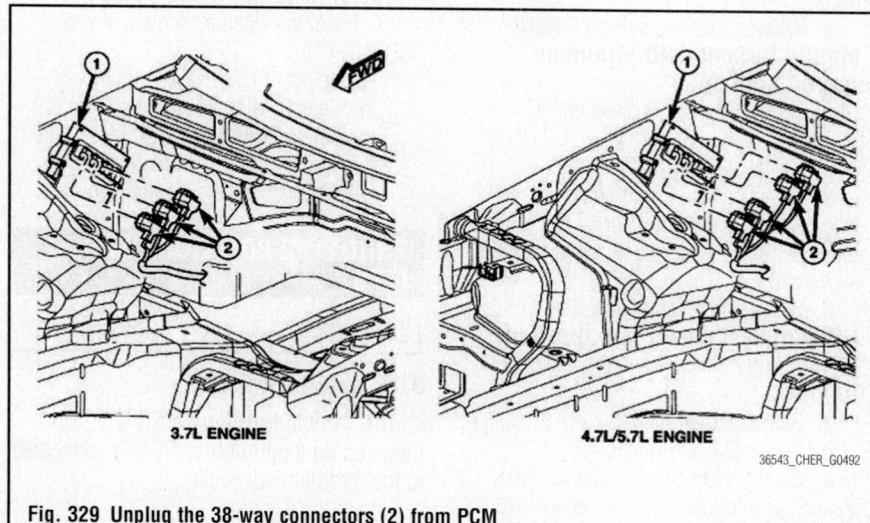

3.7L ENGINE

4.7L/5.7L ENGINE

36543_CHER_G0492

Fig. 329 Unplug the 38-way connectors (2) from PCM

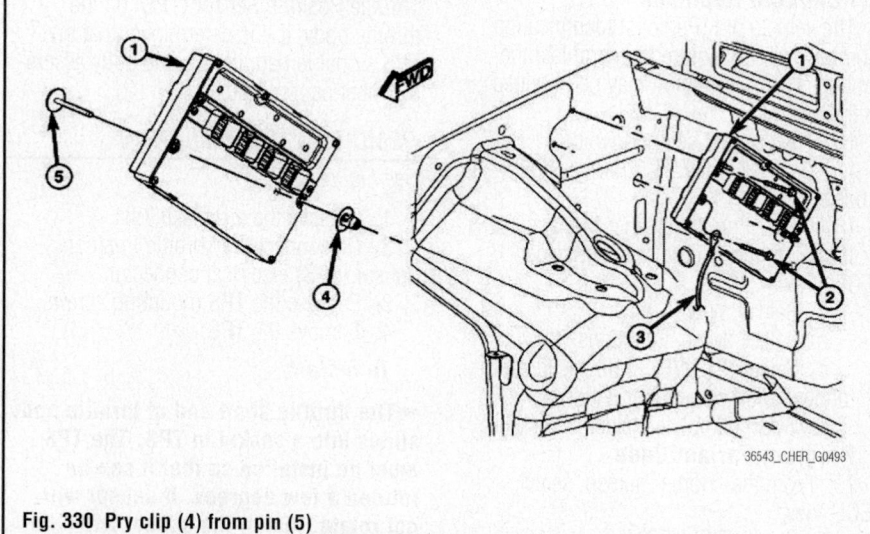

36543_CHER_G0493

Fig. 330 Pry clip (4) from pin (5)

d. When complete, select "Finish"

Diesel Particulate Filter (Used) Learning

5. From the "Home" screen, select "ECU View"

    a. Select "PCM/ECM"

    b. Select "Misc. Functions"

    c. Select "Diesel Particulate Filter (Used) Learning" and follow the on screen instructions.

    d. When complete, select "Finish"

ECU Replacement with Value Transfer

6. From the "Home" screen, select "ECU View"

    a. Select "PCM/ECM"

    b. Select "Misc. Functions"

    c. Select "ECU Replacement with Value Transfer" and follow the on screen instructions.

    d. When complete, select "Finish"

ECU Replacement without Value Transfer

7. From the "Home" screen, select "ECU View"

    a. Select "PCM/ECM"

    b. Select "Misc. Functions"

    c. Select "ECU Replacement without Value Transfer" and follow the on screen instructions.

    d. When complete, select "Finish"

Enable / Disable Vehicle Features

8. From the "Home" screen, select "ECU View"

    a. Select "PCM/ECM"

    b. Select "Misc. Functions"

    c. Select "Enable / Disable Vehicle Features" and follow the on screen instructions.

    d. When complete, select "Finish"

Exhaust Throttle Plate Adaptive Learn Position

9. From the "Home" screen, select "ECU View"

    a. Select "PCM/ECM"

    b. Select "Misc. Functions"

    c. Select "Exhaust Throttle Plate Adaptive Learn Position" and follow the on screen instructions.

    d. When complete, select "Finish"

Fuel Mean Value Adaptation Initialization

10. From the "Home" screen, select "ECU View"

    a. Select "PCM/ECM"

    b. Select "Misc. Functions"

    c. Select "Fuel Mean Value Adaptation Initialization" and follow the on screen instructions.

    d. When complete, select "Finish"

IMA Rapid Calibration

11. From the "Home" screen, select "ECU View"

    a. Select "PCM/ECM"

    b. Select "Misc. Functions"

    c. Select "IMA Rapid Calibration Test" and follow the on screen instructions.

    d. When complete, select "Finish"

Initialize EGS

12. From the "Home" screen, select "ECU View"

    a. Select "PCM/ECM"

    b. Select "Misc. Functions"

    c. Select "Initialize EGS" and follow the on screen instructions.

    d. When complete, select "Finish"

Injector Quantity Adjustment

13. From the "Home" screen, select "ECU View"

    a. Select "PCM/ECM"

    b. Select "Misc. Functions"

    c. Select "Injector Quantity Adjustment" and follow the on screen instructions.

    d. When complete, select "Finish"

Mobile DeSoot - NO Minimum Required Soot Load

14. From the "Home" screen, select "ECU View"

    a. Select "PCM/ECM"

    b. Select "Misc. Functions"

    c. Select "Mobile DeSoot - NO Minimum Required Soot Load" and follow the on screen instructions.

    d. When complete, select "Finish"

NOx Catalyst (New) Initialization

15. From the "Home" screen, select "ECU View"

    a. Select "PCM/ECM"

    b. Select "Misc. Functions"

    c. Select "NOx Catalyst (New) Initialization" and follow the on screen instructions.

    d. When complete, select "Finish"

PCM/ECM Replaced

The vehicle pin (Personal Identification Number) will be required to complete the routine. This information may be obtained in three ways:

16. The original selling invoice

17. Dealer CONNECT > Parts > Key Codes

18. Contacting the District Manager.

19. From the "Home" screen, select "ECU View"

    a. Select "WIN"

    b. Select "Misc. Functions"

    c. Select "PCM/ECM Replaced" and follow the on screen instructions.

    d. When complete, select "Finish"

Program Variant Code

20. From the "Home" screen, select "ECU View"

    a. Select "PCM/ECM"

    b. Select "Misc. Functions"

    c. Select "Program Variant Code" and follow the on screen instructions.

    d. When complete, select "Finish"

Quicklearn

21. From the "Home" screen, select "ECU View"

    a. Select "PCM/ECM"

    b. Select "Misc. Functions"

    c. Select "Quicklearn" and follow the on screen instructions.

    d. When complete, select "Finish"

Reset Regenerative Filter Timers

22. From the "Home" screen, select "ECU View"

    a. Select "PCM/ECM"

    b. Select "Misc. Functions"

    c. Select "Reset Regenerative Filter Times" and follow the on screen instructions.

    d. When complete, select "Finish"

Set Oil Dilution Mass Value

23. From the "Home" screen, select "ECU View"

    a. Select "PCM/ECM"

    b. Select "Misc. Functions"

    c. Select "Set Oil Dilution Mass Value" and follow the on screen instructions.

    d. When complete, select "Finish"

THROTTLE POSITION SENSOR (TPS)

LOCATION

3.7L & 4.7L Engines

The Throttle Position Sensor (TPS) is mounted on the throttle body and connected to the throttle blade shaft.

5.7L & 6.1L Engines

The 5.7L engine does not use a separate Throttle Position Sensor (TPS) on the throttle body. If it is determined, that the TPS signal is bad, the throttle body assembly must be replaced.

REMOVAL & INSTALLATION

See Figure 331.

1. Remove the air intake tube.

2. Disconnect the Throttle Position Sensor (TPS) electrical connector.

3. Remove the TPS mounting screws.

4. Remove the TPS.

To install:

➡ **The throttle shaft end of throttle body slides into a socket in TPS. The TPS must be installed so that it can be rotated a few degrees. If sensor will not rotate, install the sensor with**

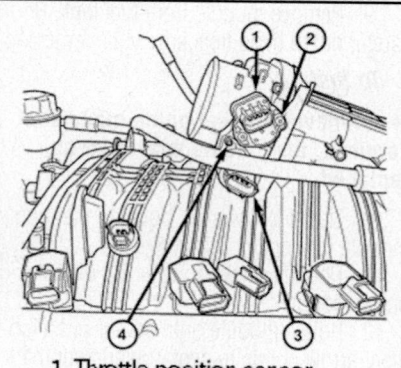

1. Throttle position sensor
2. Throttle position sensor mounting screw
3. IAC motor
4. IAC motor mounting screw

22043_CHER_G0023

Fig. 331 Throttle position sensor mounting

throttle shaft on other side of socket tangs. The TPS will be under slight tension when rotated.

5. Install the TPS and tighten the mounting screws to 60 inch lbs. (7 Nm).
6. Connect the TPS electrical connector.
7. Manually operate the throttle by hand to check for any TPS binding before starting the engine.
8. Install the air intake tube.

VEHICLE SPEED SENSOR (VSS)

LOCATION

The Vehicle Speed Sensor (VSS) is located on the left side of the transmission case.

REMOVAL & INSTALLATION

1. Raise and safely support the vehicle.
2. Place a suitable catch pan under the transmission for any fluid.
3. Remove the wiring connector from the output speed sensor.
4. Remove the mounting bolt and remove the speed sensor from the transmission case.

To install:

5. Install the speed sensor into the transmission case and tighten the bolt to 105 inch lbs. (12 Nm).
6. Install the wiring connector to the speed sensor.
7. Verify the proper transmission fluid level and refill as necessary.
8. Lower the vehicle.

FUEL
GASOLINE FUEL INJECTION SYSTEM

FUEL SYSTEM SERVICE PRECAUTIONS

✳ WARNING

High-pressure fuel lines deliver fuel under extreme pressure from the injection pump to the injectors. This may be as high as 19,580 psi (1350 bar). Use extreme caution when inspecting for high-pressure fuel leaks. Inspect high-pressure fuel leaks with a sheet of cardboard. Wear safety goggles and adequate protective clothing when servicing fuel system. Fuel under this amount of pressure can penetrate skin causing serious or fatal injury.

Safety is the most important factor when performing not only fuel system maintenance but any type of maintenance. Failure to conduct maintenance and repairs in a safe manner may result in serious personal injury or death. Maintenance and testing of the vehicle's fuel system components can be accomplished safely and effectively by adhering to the following rules and guidelines.

• To avoid the possibility of fire and personal injury, always disconnect the negative battery cable unless the repair or test procedure requires that battery voltage be applied.

• Always relieve the fuel system pressure prior to disconnecting any fuel system component (injector, fuel rail, pressure regulator, etc.), fitting or fuel line connection. Exercise extreme caution whenever relieving fuel system pressure to avoid exposing

skin, face and eyes to fuel spray. Please be advised that fuel under pressure may penetrate the skin or any part of the body that it contacts.

• Always place a shop towel or cloth around the fitting or connection prior to loosening to absorb any excess fuel due to spillage. Ensure that all fuel spillage (should it occur) is quickly removed from engine surfaces. Ensure that all fuel soaked cloths or towels are deposited into a suitable waste container.

• Always keep a dry chemical (Class B) fire extinguisher near the work area.

• Do not allow fuel spray or fuel vapors to come into contact with a spark or open flame.

• Always use a back-up wrench when loosening and tightening fuel line connection fittings. This will prevent unnecessary stress and torsion to fuel line piping.

• Always replace worn fuel fitting O-rings with new. Do not substitute fuel hose or equivalent where fuel pipe is installed.

RELIEVING FUEL SYSTEM PRESSURE

Use following procedure if the fuel injector rail is, or is not equipped with a fuel pressure test port.

1. Remove fuel fill cap.
2. Remove fuel pump relay from Power Distribution Center (PDC). For location of relay, refer to label on underside of PDC cover.
3. Start and run engine until it stalls.
4. Attempt restarting engine until it will no longer run.

5. Turn ignition key to OFF position.

✳ CAUTION

Steps 1, 2, 3, and 4 must be performed to relieve high pressure fuel from within fuel rail. Do not attempt to use following steps to relieve this pressure as excessive fuel will be forced into a cylinder chamber.

6. Unplug connector from any fuel injector.
7. Attach one end of a jumper wire with alligator clips (18 gauge or smaller) to either injector terminal.
8. Connect other end of jumper wire to positive side of battery.
9. Connect one end of a second jumper wire to remaining injector terminal.

✳ CAUTION

Powering an injector for more than a few seconds will permanently damage the injector.

10. Momentarily touch other end of jumper wire to negative terminal of battery for no more than a few seconds.
11. Place a rag or towel below fuel line quick-connect fitting at fuel rail.
12. Disconnect quick-connect fitting at fuel rail.
13. Return fuel pump relay to PDC.
14. One or more Diagnostic Trouble Codes (DTC's) may have been stored in Powertrain Control Module (PCM) memory due to fuel pump relay removal. A diagnostic scan tool must be used to erase a DTC.

FUEL FILTER

REMOVAL & INSTALLATION

Two fuel filters are used. One is located at the bottom of the fuel pump module. The other is located inside the module. A separate frame mounted fuel filter is not used with any engine.

Both fuel filters are designed for extended service. They do not require normal scheduled maintenance. Filters should only be replaced if a diagnostic procedure indicates to do so.

FUEL PUMP MODULE

REMOVAL & INSTALLATION

See Figures 332 through 334.

The electric fuel pump is located inside of the fuel pump module. A 12 volt, permanent magnet, electric motor powers the fuel pump. The electric fuel pump is not a separate, serviceable component.

The fuel pump module assembly (3) is located on top of fuel tank.

The module assembly (5) contains the following components:

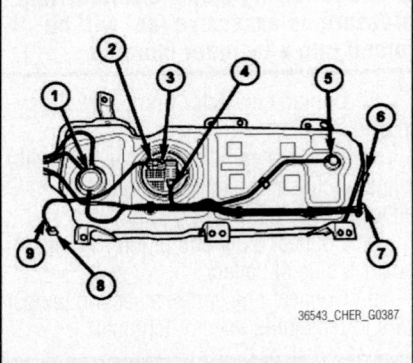

Fig. 332 The fuel pump module assembly (3)

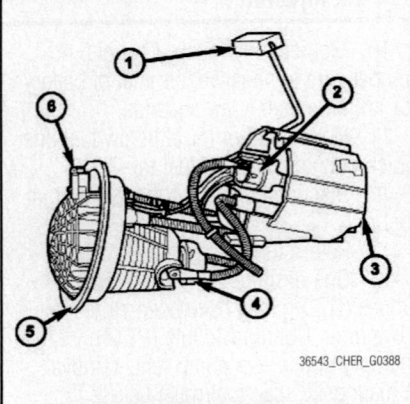

Fig. 333 The module assembly (5)

- An internal fuel filter
- A separate fuel pick-up, or inlet filter (3)
- A fuel pressure regulator (4)
- An electric fuel pump (2)
- A lock-ring to retain pump module to tank
- A soft gasket between tank flange and module
- A fuel gauge sending unit (fuel level sensor) (1)
- Fuel line connection (6)

If the fuel gauge sending unit, electrical fuel pump, primary inlet filter, fuel filter, or fuel pressure regulator require service, the fuel pump module must be replaced.

✳✳ WARNING

The fuel system is under a constant pressure, even with the engine off. Before servicing the fuel system, the fuel pressure must be released.

1. Perform the fuel pressure release procedure.
2. Disconnect the negative battery cable.
3. Drain and remove fuel tank.
4. Note rotational position of module before attempting removal. An indexing arrow is located on top of module for this purpose.
5. Position SAE Fuel Pump Lock Ring Wrench 9340 (3) into notches on outside edge of lockring (5).
6. Install ½ inch drive breaker bar (1) to SAE Fuel Pump Lock Ring Wrench 9340 (3).
7. Rotate breaker bar counter-clockwise to remove lockring.
8. Remove lockring. The module will spring up slightly when lockring is removed.

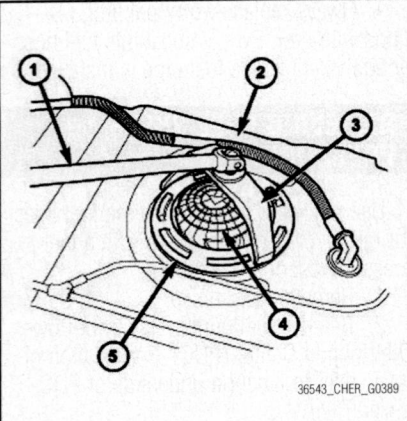

Fig. 334 Position SAE Fuel Pump Lock Ring Wrench 9340 (3)

9. Remove module from fuel tank. Be careful not to bend float arm while removing.

To install:

➡ **Whenever the fuel pump module is serviced, the module seal must be replaced.**

10. Using a new seal, position fuel pump module into opening in fuel tank.
11. Position lockring over top of fuel pump module.
12. Rotate module until embossed alignment arrow points to center alignment mark. This step must be performed to prevent float from contacting side of fuel tank. Also be sure fuel fitting on top of pump module is pointed to drivers side of vehicle.
13. Install SAE Fuel Pump Lock Ring Wrench 9340 to lockring.
14. Tighten lockring until all seven notches have engaged.
15. Install fuel tank.

FUEL RAIL & INJECTORS

REMOVAL & INSTALLATION

3.7L Engine

See Figures 335 and 336.

✳✳ WARNING

The fuel system is under constant pressure even with engine off. Before servicing the fuel rail, fuel system pressure must be released.

✳✳ CAUTION

The left and right fuel rails are replaced as an assembly. Do not

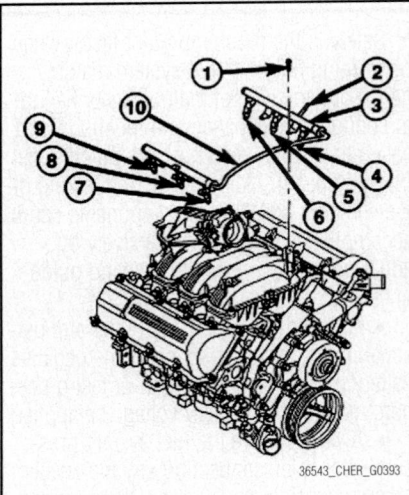

Fig. 335 Remove four fuel rail mounting bolts (1)

attempt to separate rail halves at connector tubes. Due to design of tubes, it does not use any clamps. Never attempt to install a clamping device of any kind to tubes. When removing fuel rail assembly for any reason, be careful not to bend or kink tubes.

1. Remove fuel tank filler tube cap.
2. Perform Fuel System Pressure Release Procedure.
3. Remove negative battery cable at battery.
4. Remove air duct at throttle body air box.
5. Remove air box at throttle body.
6. Remove air resonator mounting bracket at front of throttle body (2 bolts).
7. Disconnect fuel line latch clip and fuel line at fuel rail. A tool, Snap-On number FIH 9055-1 or equivalent, will be necessary for fuel line disconnection.
8. Remove necessary vacuum lines at throttle body.
9. Disconnect electrical connectors at all 6 fuel injectors. Push red colored slider away from injector. While pushing slider, depress tab and remove connector from injector. The factory fuel injection wiring harness is numerically tagged (INJ 1, INJ 2, etc.) for injector position identification. If harness is not tagged, note wiring location before removal.
10. Disconnect electrical connectors at all throttle body sensors.
11. Remove 6 ignition coils.
12. Remove four fuel rail mounting bolts (1).
13. Gently rock and pull left side of fuel rail until fuel injectors just start to clear machined holes in cylinder head. Gently

rock and pull right side of rail until injectors just start to clear cylinder head holes. Repeat this procedure (left/right) until all injectors have cleared cylinder head holes.
14. Remove fuel rail (with injectors attached) from engine.
15. Using suitable pliers, remove the fuel injector retaining clip (2).
16. Remove the fuel injector (3) from the fuel rail (4) using a side to side motion while pulling the injector out of the fuel rail assembly.

To install:

➡If the same fuel injector is to be reinstalled, install new O-rings.

➡Apply a small amount of clean engine oil to each injector O-ring. This will aid in the installation.

17. Install the fuel injector into the fuel rail using a side to side motion while pushing injector into the fuel rail assembly.
18. Using suitable pliers, install the fuel injector retaining clip.
19. Clean out fuel injector machined bores in intake manifold.
20. Apply a small amount of engine oil to each fuel injector O-ring. This will help in fuel rail installation.
21. Position fuel rail/fuel injector assembly to machined injector openings in cylinder head.
22. Guide each injector into cylinder head. Be careful not to tear injector O-rings.
23. Push right side of fuel rail down until fuel injectors have bottomed on cylinder head shoulder. Push left fuel rail down until injectors have bottomed on cylinder head shoulder.
24. Install 4 fuel rail mounting bolts and tighten. Tighten to 100 inch lbs. (11 Nm).
25. Install 6 ignition coils.
26. Connect electrical connectors to throttle body.
27. Connect electrical connectors at all fuel injectors. Push connector onto injector and then push and lock red colored slider. Verify connector is locked to injector by lightly tugging on connector.
28. Connect necessary vacuum lines to throttle body.
29. Install air resonator mounting bracket near front of throttle body (2 bolts).
30. Connect fuel line latch clip and fuel line to fuel rail.
31. Install air box to throttle body.
32. Install air duct to air box.
33. Connect battery cable to battery.
34. Start engine and check for leaks.

4.7L Engine

See Figures 336 through 337.

✳✳ **WARNING**

The fuel system is under constant pressure even with engine off. Before servicing the fuel rail, fuel system pressure must be released.

✳✳ **CAUTION**

The left and right fuel rails are replaced as an assembly. Do not attempt to separate rail halves at connector tubes. Due to design of tubes, it does not use any clamps. Never attempt to install a clamping device of any kind to tubes. When removing fuel rail assembly for any reason, be careful not to bend or kink tubes.

1. Remove fuel tank filler tube cap.
2. Perform Fuel System Pressure Release Procedure.
3. Remove negative battery cable at battery.
4. Remove air duct at throttle body air box.
5. Remove air box at throttle body.
6. Remove air resonator mounting bracket at front of throttle body (2 bolts).
7. Disconnect fuel line latch clip and fuel line at fuel rail . A tool will be necessary for fuel line disconnection.
8. Remove necessary vacuum lines at throttle body.

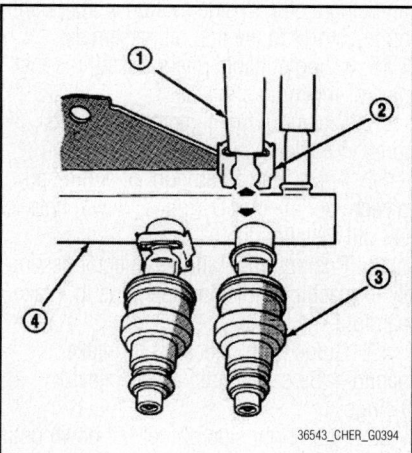

Fig. 336 Remove the fuel injector retaining clip (2)

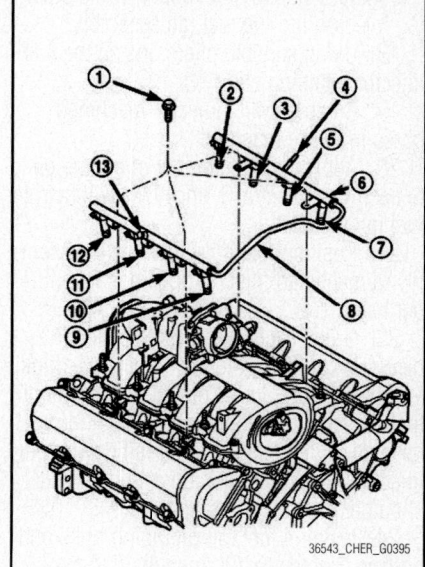

Fig. 337 Remove 4 fuel rail mounting bolts (1)

36543_CHER_G0394

36543_CHER_G0395

9. Disconnect electrical connectors at all 8 fuel injectors. Push red colored slider away from injector. While pushing slider, depress tab and remove connector from injector. The factory fuel injection wiring harness is numerically tagged (INJ 1, INJ 2, etc.) for injector position identification. If harness is not tagged, note wiring location before removal.

10. Disconnect electrical connectors at all throttle body sensors.

11. Remove 8 ignition coils.

12. Remove 4 fuel rail mounting bolts (1).

13. Gently rock and pull left side of fuel rail until fuel injectors just start to clear machined holes in cylinder head. Gently rock and pull right side of rail until injectors just start to clear cylinder head holes. Repeat this procedure (left/right) until all injectors have cleared cylinder head holes.

14. Remove fuel rail (with injectors attached) from engine.

15. Using suitable pliers, remove the fuel injector retaining clip (2).

16. Remove the fuel injector (3) from the fuel rail (4) using a side to side motion while pulling the injector out of the fuel rail assembly.

To install:

➡️ If the same fuel injector is to be reinstalled, install new O-rings.

➡️ Apply a small amount of clean engine oil to each injector O-ring. This will aid in the installation.

17. Install the fuel injector into the fuel rail using a side to side motion while pushing injector into the fuel rail assembly.

18. Using suitable pliers, install the fuel injector retaining clip.

19. Clean out fuel injector machined bores in intake manifold.

20. Apply a small amount of engine oil to each fuel injector O-ring. This will help in fuel rail installation.

21. Position fuel rail/fuel injector assembly to machined injector openings in cylinder head.

22. Guide each injector into cylinder head. Be careful not to tear injector O-rings.

23. Push right side of fuel rail down until fuel injectors have bottomed on cylinder head shoulder. Push left fuel rail down until injectors have bottomed on cylinder head shoulder.

24. Install 4 fuel rail mounting bolts and tighten. Tighten to 100 inch lbs. (11 Nm).

25. Install 8 ignition coils.

26. Connect electrical connectors to throttle body.

27. Connect electrical connectors at fuel injectors. Push connector onto injector and then push and lock red colored slider. Verify connector is locked to injector by lightly tugging on connector.

28. Connect necessary vacuum lines to throttle body.

29. Install air resonator mounting bracket near front of throttle body (2 bolts).

30. Connect fuel line latch clip and fuel line to fuel rail.

31. Install air box to throttle body.

32. Install air duct to air box.

33. Connect battery cable to battery.

34. Start engine and check for leaks.

5.7L & 6.1L Engines

See Figures 336 and 338.

✳✳ WARNING

The fuel system is under constant pressure even with engine off. Before servicing the fuel rail, fuel system pressure must be released.

✳✳ CAUTION

The left and right fuel rails are replaced as an assembly. Do not attempt to separate rail halves at connector tube. Due to design of tube, it does not use any clamps. Never attempt to install a clamping device of any kind to tube. When removing fuel rail assembly for any reason, be careful not to bend or kink tube.

1. Remove fuel tank filler tube cap.

2. Perform fuel system pressure release procedure.

3. Remove negative battery cable at battery.

4. Remove flex tube (air cleaner housing to engine).

5. Remove air resonator box at throttle body.

6. Disconnect electrical connectors at all 8 fuel injectors. Push red colored slider away from injector. While pushing slider, depress tab and remove connector from injector. The factory fuel injection wiring harness is numerically tagged (INJ 1, INJ 2, etc.) for injector position identification. If harness is not tagged, note wiring location before removal.

7. Disconnect electrical connectors at all throttle body sensors.

8. Disconnect fuel supply tube quick connect fitting at the fuel rail.

9. Remove four fuel rail mounting bolts (1) and hold-down clamps.

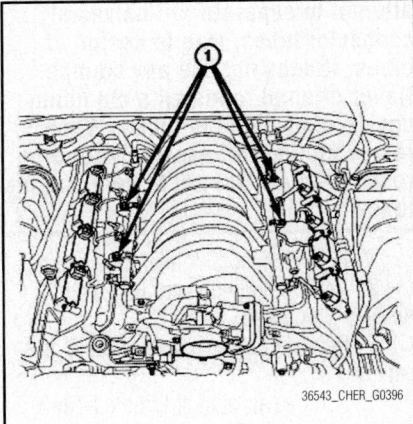

Fig. 338 Remove four fuel rail mounting bolts (1) and hold-down clamps

10. Gently rock and pull left side of fuel rail until fuel injectors just start to clear machined holes in intake manifold. Gently rock and pull right side of rail until injectors just start to clear intake manifold head holes. Repeat this procedure (left/right) until all injectors have cleared machined holes.

11. Remove fuel rail (with injectors attached) from engine.

12. Using suitable pliers, remove the fuel injector retaining clip (2).

13. Remove the fuel injector (3) from the fuel rail (4) using a side to side motion while pulling the injector out of the fuel rail assembly.

To install:

➡️ If the same fuel injector is to be reinstalled, install new O-rings.

➡️ Apply a small amount of clean engine oil to each injector O-ring. This will aid in the installation.

14. Install the fuel injector into the fuel rail using a side to side motion while pushing injector into the fuel rail assembly.

15. Using suitable pliers, install the fuel injector retaining clip.

16. Clean out fuel injector machined bores in intake manifold.

17. Apply a small amount of engine oil to each fuel injector O-ring. This will help in fuel rail installation.

18. Position fuel rail/fuel injector assembly to machined injector openings in intake manifold.

19. Guide each injector into intake manifold. Be careful not to tear injector O-rings.

20. Push right side of fuel rail down until fuel injectors have bottomed on shoulders. Push left fuel rail down until injectors have bottomed on shoulders.

21. Install 4 fuel rail hold-down clamps and 4 mounting bolts. Tighten bolts to 71 inch lbs. (8 Nm).

22. Connect electrical connector to throttle body.

23. Connect electrical connectors at all fuel injectors. Push connector onto injector and then push and lock red colored slider. Verify connector is locked to injector by lightly tugging on connector.

24. Connect fuel line latch clip and fuel line to fuel rail.

25. Install air resonator to throttle body (2 bolts).

26. Install flexible air duct to air box.

27. Connect battery cable to battery.

28. Start engine and check for leaks.

FUEL TANK

REMOVAL & INSTALLATION

See Figures 339 through 341.

1. Release fuel system pressure.

2. Drain fuel tank.

3. Loosen clamp (9) and disconnect rubber fill hose (3) at tank fitting (7).

4. At rear of tank, disconnect fuel pump module electrical jumper connector (5) from body connector (6).

5. At rear of tank, disconnect EVAP lines (2) and (3) from lines (1) and (4).

6. At front of tank, disconnect fuel and EVAP lines (9) and (10) from lines (11) and (12).

7. Support tank with a hydraulic jack.

8. Remove bolts (1) and (2) at right side of fuel tank.

9. Remove bolts (3) at left side of fuel tank.

10. Lower tank for removal.

11. If fuel tank is to be replaced, remove fuel pump module from tank.

To install:

12. Position fuel tank to hydraulic jack.

13. Raise tank until positioned to body.

14. Install fuel tank mounting bolts and tighten to 50 ft. lbs. (68 Nm).

15. Remove hydraulic jack.

16. Connect EVAP, ORVR, fuel and NVLD lines at front and rear of tank.

17. Connect fuel pump module electrical jumper connector to body connector.

18. Connect rubber fill hose to tank fitting and tighten clamp.

19. Lower vehicle.

20. Fill fuel tank with fuel.

21. Start engine and check for fuel leaks near top of module.

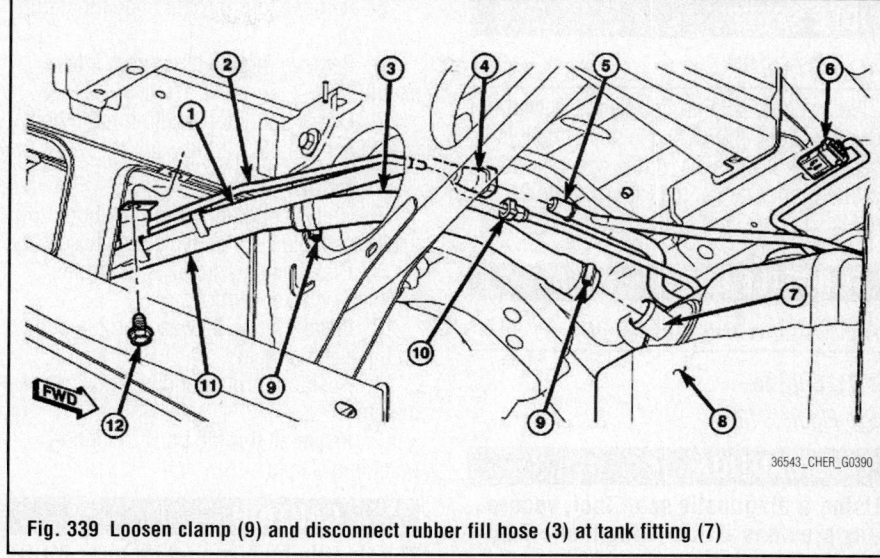

Fig. 339 Loosen clamp (9) and disconnect rubber fill hose (3) at tank fitting (7)

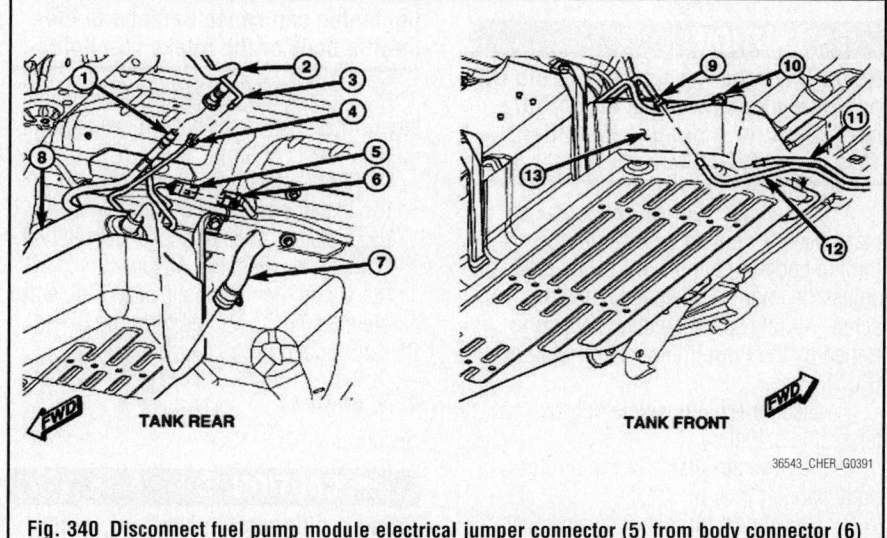

Fig. 340 Disconnect fuel pump module electrical jumper connector (5) from body connector (6)

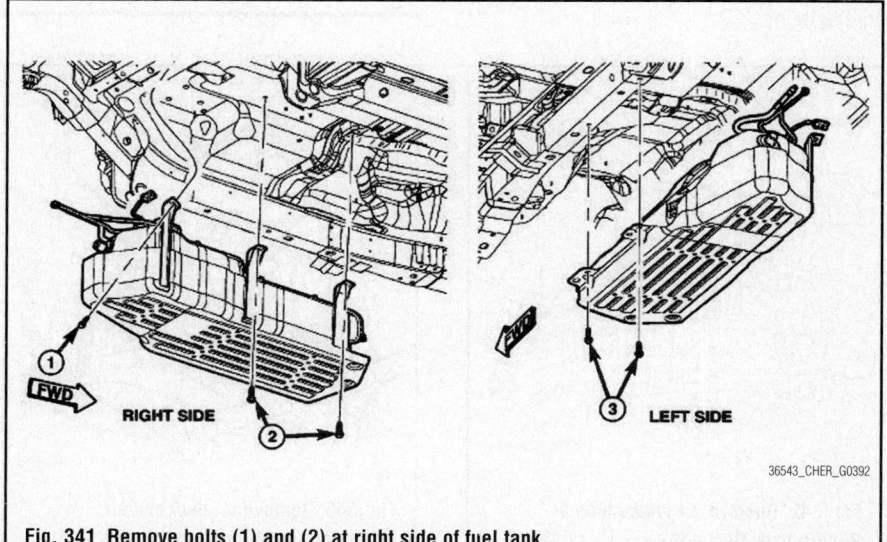

Fig. 341 Remove bolts (1) and (2) at right side of fuel tank

IDLE SPEED

ADJUSTMENT

Idle speed is controlled by the Powertrain Control Module (PCM). No adjustment is necessary or possible. If idle speed is not within proper range, the PCM should be replaced.

THROTTLE BODY

REMOVAL & INSTALLATION

3.7L Engine

See Figure 342.

> **CAUTION**
>
> Using a diagnostic scan tool, record any previous DTC's (Diagnostic Trouble Codes).

> **CAUTION**
>
> Never have the ignition key in the ON position when checking the throttle body shaft for a binding condition. This may set DTC's.

A (factory adjusted) set screw is used to mechanically limit the position of the throttle body throttle plate. Never attempt to adjust the engine idle speed using this screw. All idle speed functions are controlled by the Powertrain Control Module (PCM).

1. Disconnect and isolate negative battery cable at battery.
2. Remove air intake tube at throttle body flange (1).
3. Disconnect throttle body electrical connector (3).
4. Disconnect necessary vacuum lines at throttle body.

5. Remove four throttle body mounting bolts (2).
6. Remove throttle body from intake manifold.
7. Check condition of old throttle body-to-intake manifold O-ring.

To install:

8. Check condition of throttle body-to-intake manifold O-ring. Replace as necessary.
9. Clean mating surfaces of throttle body and intake manifold.
10. Install O-ring between throttle body and intake manifold.
11. Position throttle body to intake manifold.
12. Install all throttle body mounting bolts finger tight.

> **CAUTION**
>
> The throttle body mounting bolts MUST be tightened to specifications. Over tightening can cause damage to the throttle body or the intake manifold.

13. Tighten mounting bolts in a mandatory torque criss-cross pattern sequence to 65 inch lbs. (7.5 Nm).
14. Install electrical connector.
15. Install necessary vacuum lines.
16. Install air cleaner duct at throttle body.
17. Connect negative battery cable.
18. Using the diagnostic scan tool, erase all previous DTC's and perform the ETC Relearn function.

4.7L Engine

See Figure 343.

> **CAUTION**
>
> Using a diagnostic scan tool, record any previous DTC's (Diagnostic Trouble Codes).

> **CAUTION**
>
> Never have the ignition key in the ON position when checking the throttle body shaft for a binding condition. This may set DTC's.

1. Disconnect and isolate negative battery cable at battery.
2. Remove air duct and air resonator box at throttle body (3).
3. Disconnect throttle body electrical connector (2).
4. Disconnect necessary vacuum lines at throttle body.
5. Remove four throttle body mounting bolts (1).
6. Remove throttle body from intake manifold.
7. Check condition of old throttle body-to-intake manifold O-ring.

To install:

8. Check condition of throttle body-to-intake manifold O-ring. Replace as necessary.
9. Clean mating surfaces of throttle body and intake manifold.
10. Install throttle body-to-intake manifold O-ring.
11. Install all throttle body mounting bolts finger tight.

> **CAUTION**
>
> The throttle body mounting bolts MUST be tightened to specifications. Over tightening can cause damage to the throttle body or the intake manifold.

12. Tighten mounting bolts in a mandatory torque criss-cross pattern sequence to 65 inch lbs. (7.5 Nm).
13. Install electrical connector.
14. Install necessary vacuum lines.
15. Install air cleaner duct and plenum at throttle body.
16. Connect negative battery cable.
17. Using the diagnostic scan tool, erase all previous DTC's and perform the ETC Relearn function.

5.7L & 6.1L Engines

See Figures 344 and 345.

1. Disconnect and isolate negative battery cable from battery.
2. Remove air duct and air resonator box at throttle body.
3. Disconnect electrical connector at throttle body (3).
4. Remove four throttle body mounting bolts (2).
5. Remove throttle body from intake manifold.

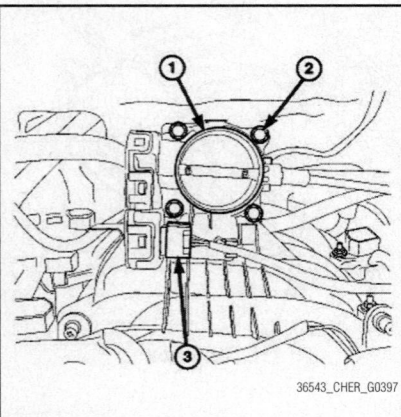

36543_CHER_G0397

Fig. 342 Remove air intake tube at throttle body flange (1)

36543_CHER_G0398

Fig. 343 Remove air duct and air resonator box at throttle body (3)

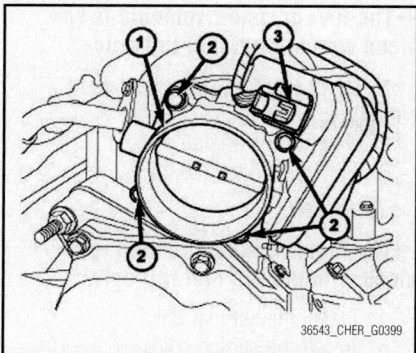

Fig. 344 Disconnect electrical connector at throttle body (3)

6. Check condition of throttle body O-ring (2).

To install:

7. Clean and check condition of throttle body-to-intake manifold O-ring.

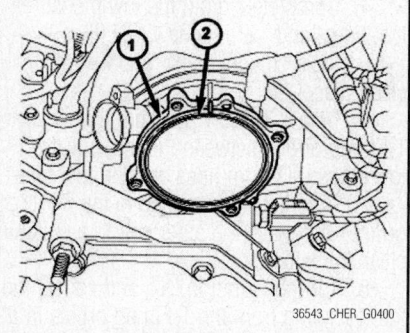

Fig. 345 Check condition of throttle body O-ring (2)

8. Clean mating surfaces of throttle body and intake manifold.

9. Install throttle body to intake manifold by positioning throttle body to manifold alignment pins.

10. Install all throttle body mounting bolts finger tight.

❈❈ CAUTION

The throttle body mounting bolts MUST be tightened to specifications. Over tightening can cause damage to the throttle body or the intake manifold.

11. Tighten mounting bolts in a mandatory torque criss-cross pattern sequence to 50 inch lbs. (5.6 Nm).

12. Install electrical connector.

13. Install air plenum to flange.

14. Connect negative battery cable.

15. Using the diagnostic scan tool, perform the ETC Relearn function.

FUEL | DIESEL FUEL INJECTION SYSTEM

FUEL SYSTEM SERVICE PRECAUTIONS

❈❈ WARNING

High-pressure fuel lines deliver fuel under extreme pressure from the injection pump to the injectors. This may be as high as 19,580 psi (1350 bar). Use extreme caution when inspecting for high-pressure fuel leaks. Inspect high-pressure fuel leaks with a sheet of cardboard. Wear safety goggles and adequate protective clothing when servicing fuel system. Fuel under this amount of pressure can penetrate skin causing serious or fatal injury.

❈❈ WARNING

No sparks, open flames or smoking. Risk of poisoning from inhaling and swallowing fuel. Risk of injury to eyes and skin from contact with fuel. Pour fuels only into suitable and appropriately marked containers. Wear protective clothing.

RELIEVING FUEL SYSTEM PRESSURE

1. Turn the ignition off.
2. Remove engine cover.
3. Connect a hose to the fuel filter water drain and insert the remaining end into a

approved and appropriately marked container.

4. Turn the water drain counterclockwise to bleed air.

❈❈ CAUTION

Turning the ignition to the on position will engage the in tank fuel pump. Be sure that the bleed hose and the fuel capture container is secure.

5. Turn the ignition to the on position and observe the container until fuel flows free of bubbles.

6. Turn the ignition off.

7. Tighten the water drain valve on the fuel filter.

8. Remove the bleed hose and container.

9. Install engine cover.

FUEL FILTER

REMOVAL & INSTALLATION

See Figure 346.

❈❈ WARNING

No sparks, open flames or smoking. Risk of poisoning from inhaling and swallowing fuel. Risk of injury to eyes and skin from contact with fuel. Pour fuels only into suitable and appropriately marked containers. Wear protective clothing.

1. Disconnect negative battery cable.
2. Insert a suitable hose into the fuel drain port (9), turn drain port counterclock-

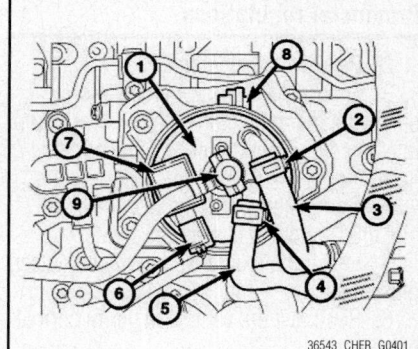

Fig. 346 Insert a suitable hose into the fuel drain port (9)

wise and drain fuel into a suitable and appropriately marked container.

3. Disconnect fuel feed (5) and return lines (3) at fuel filter and set aside.

4. Disconnect Water In Fuel (WIF) sensor electrical connector (6) at fuel filter.

5. Remove fuel filter retaining bracket bolt and remove fuel filter (1).

To install:

➥Assure fuel filter drain port is closed.

6. Connect WIF sensor electrical connector (6).

7. Position fuel filter (1) in bracket and tighten retaining bolt to 44 inch lbs. (5 Nm).

8. Connect fuel feed (5) and return lines (3).

9. Connect negative battery cable.

10. Start engine and inspect for leaks.

DRAINING WATER FROM THE SYSTEM

➡ **Fuel system damage that was caused by incorrect or contaminated fuel that was introduced into the fuel system by the customer is not covered under warranty.**

If The Engine Was Not Started After Incorrect Or Contaminated Fuel Was Used During Refueling

If the fuel system has been contaminated (with gasoline, water, etc.) AND the engine WAS NOT STARTED, the following procedure must be followed:

1. Remove all fuel from the fuel tank. Use an appropriate fuel container. Dispose of the contaminated fuel using the proper procedures.

❋❋ CAUTION

Dispose of petroleum based products in a manner consistent with all applicable Local, State, Federal, and Provincial regulations.

2. Remove the fuel tank.
3. Ensure the swirl pot indentation below the in the fuel tank electric fuel pump inlet is completely drained of any contaminated fuel.
4. Completely drain the low pressure fuel lines, and install a new fuel filter.
5. Install the fuel tank, and fill with clean diesel fuel.
6. Road test the vehicle to verify normal operation.

If The Engine Was Started After Incorrect Or Contaminated Fuel Was Used During Refueling

If the fuel system has been contaminated (with gasoline, water, etc.) AND the engine WAS STARTED, the following procedure must be followed:

1. Remove all fuel from the fuel tank. Use an appropriate fuel container. Dispose of the contaminated fuel using the proper procedures.

❋❋ CAUTION

Dispose of petroleum based products in a manner consistent with all applicable Local, State, Federal, and Provincial regulations.

2. Remove the fuel tank.
3. Ensure the swirl pot indentation below the in the fuel tank electric fuel pump inlet is completely drained of any contaminated fuel.

4. Completely drain the low pressure fuel lines, and install a new fuel filter.
5. Install the fuel tank, and fill with clean diesel fuel.
6. Detach the low pressure line at the T-Fitting orifice between the fuel injector low pressure return lines and the fuel filter
7. Connect a clean hose to the T-Fitting orifice, and place the other end in a suitable clean container.
8. Turn the ignition ON, and collect the fuel escaping from the T-Fitting orifice in a clean container. Check the fuel sample for metal chips, dirt, or other foreign matter.
9. If any dirt or metal chips are present in the fuel sample, completely clean the high pressure side of the fuel injection system, then install new the fuel injectors, and the high pressure fuel pump.
10. If there are no metal chips or dirt present in the fuel sample, the fuel system is ok. Reconnect the T-Fitting orifice, and road test the vehicle to verify normal operation.

FUEL PRESSURE SENSOR

REMOVAL & INSTALLATION

➡ **To avoid leakage problems, the fuel pressure sensor should not be removed unless it is to be replaced.**

1. Disconnect the negative battery cable.
2. Remove the engine cover.
3. Unplug the electrical connector at the fuel pressure sensor.
4. Remove the right fuel rail.
5. Position the fuel rail in a soft jawed vise.
6. Remove the fuel pressure sensor.

To install:

➡ **The installation of the fuel pressure sensor must be performed out of vehicle so that the sensor can be tightened properly.**

7. Install the fuel pressure sensor and new seal. Tighten to 123 inch lbs. (14 Nm).
8. Install the fuel rail.
9. Connect the fuel pressure sensor electrical connector.
10. Connect the negative battery cable.
11. Start the engine, allow it to warm. Turn the engine off and inspect for leaks.
12. Install the engine cover.

FUEL PRESSURE SOLENOID

REMOVAL & INSTALLATION

The fuel pressure solenoid is attached to the rear of the left fuel rail.

➡ **The fuel pressure solenoid is serviced with the left fuel rail only.**

1. Disconnect the negative battery cable.
2. Remove the engine cover.
3. Remove the left fuel rail.

To install:

➡ **The fuel pressure solenoid is serviced with the left fuel rail only.**

4. Install the left fuel rail.
5. Install the engine cover.
6. Reconnect the negative battery cable.

FUEL SUPPLY PUMP

REMOVAL & INSTALLATION

See Figures 334 and 347.

1. Drain and remove fuel tank.
2. Note rotational position of pump module before attempting removal. An indexing arrow (4) is located on top of module for this purpose.
3. Disconnect pigtail harness connector (2) at pump module (7).
4. Disconnect fittings (3) and (6) from pump module.
5. Position Lockring Remover/Installer 9340 (3) into notches on outside edge of lockring (5).
6. Install ½ inch drive breaker bar (1) to tool 9340 (3).
7. Rotate breaker bar counter-clockwise to remove lockring.
8. Remove lockring. The module will spring up slightly when lockring is removed.
9. Remove module from fuel tank. Be careful not to bend float arm while removing.

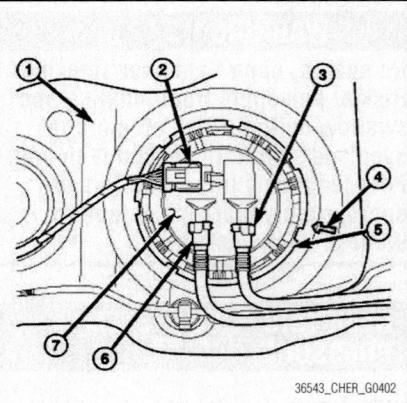

Fig. 347 Note rotational position of pump module before attempting removal

To install:

> ✳✳ **CAUTION**
>
> **Whenever the fuel pump module is serviced, the rubber seal (gasket) must be replaced.**

10. Using a new seal (gasket), position fuel pump module into opening in fuel tank.

11. Position lockring over top of fuel pump module.

12. Rotate module until embossed alignment arrow points to center alignment mark. This step must be performed to prevent float from contacting side of fuel tank. Also be sure fuel fittings on top of pump module are pointed to right side of vehicle.

13. Install Lockring Remover/Installer 9340 to lockring.

14. Install ½ inch drive breaker into Lockring Remover/Installer 9340.

15. Tighten lockring (clockwise) until all seven notches have engaged.

16. Connect pigtail harness connector to pump module.

17. Connect fittings and to pump module.

18. Install fuel tank.

FUEL SYSTEM PURGING

BLEEDING

1. Turn the ignition off.
2. Remove engine cover.
3. Connect a hose to the fuel filter water drain and insert the remaining end into a approved and appropriately marked container.
4. Turn the water drain counterclockwise to bleed air.

> ✳✳ **CAUTION**
>
> **Turning the ignition to the on position will engage the in tank fuel pump. Be sure that the bleed hose and the fuel capture container is secure.**

5. Turn the ignition to the on position and observe the container until fuel flows free of bubbles.

6. Turn the ignition off.

7. Tighten the water drain valve on the fuel filter.

8. Remove the bleed hose and container.

9. Install engine cover.

GLOW PLUGS

REMOVAL & INSTALLATION

> ✳✳ **CAUTION**
>
> **Engine temperature must be at least 194°F (90°C) before removing glow**

plugs. If cylinder head is already removed, warm cylinder head to 194°F (90°C) before removing glow plugs.

1. Disconnect negative battery cable.

2. Remove the engine cover.

3. Disconnect the glow plug electrical connector.

> ✳✳ **WARNING**
>
> **Risk of injury to skin and eyes from handling hot or glowing objects. Wear protective gloves, clothing and eye wear.**

4. Clean the glow plug bay.
5. Remove the glow plugs.

To install:

6. Install the glow plug. Tighten the glow plugs to 106 inch lbs. (12 Nm).

7. Connect the glow plug electrical connector.

8. Install the engine cover.

9. Connect the negative battery cable.

HIGH PRESSURE FUEL INJECTION PUMP

REMOVAL & INSTALLATION
See Figure 348.

> ✳✳ **WARNING**
>
> **High pressure fuel lines deliver diesel fuel under extreme pressure from the injection pump to the fuel injectors. This may be as high as 23,200 psi (1600 bar). Use extreme caution when inspecting for high pressure fuel leaks. Fuel under this amount of pressure can penetrate skin causing personal injury or death. Inspect for high pressure fuel leaks with a sheet of cardboard. Wear safety goggles and adequate protective clothing when servicing fuel system.**

1. Remove engine cover.
2. Remove negative battery cable.
3. Release fuel pressure.
4. Remove high pressure line support bracket.
5. Remove high pressure line retaining nut.
6. Remove the return line clamp using Fuel Line Pliers 9539.
7. Remove the inlet supply clamp using Fuel Line Pliers 9539.

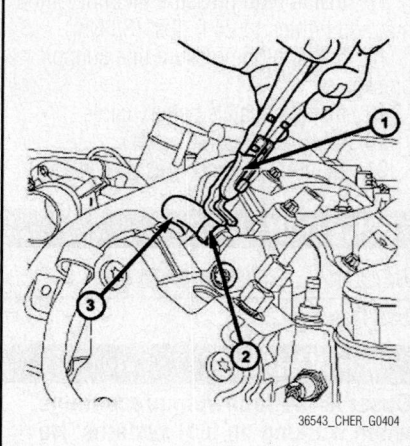

36543_CHER_G0404

Fig. 348 Remove the return line clamp using Fuel Line Pliers 9539

8. Remove both rubber lines at the pump.

9. Disconnect the pump electrical connectors.

10. Remove the pump mounting bolts.

11. Remove the pump assembly.

> ✳✳ **CAUTION**
>
> **Do not crimp or bend fuel line. Capture all fluids that flow out of connections.**

To install:

> ✳✳ **CAUTION**
>
> **Do not force the high pressure pump into the left cylinder head, or attempt to seat it by drawing it in with the bolts. The pump gears must be aligned with the drive gear on the cam before the high pressure pump will seat on the cylinder head mounting surface. Otherwise, damage to the high pressure pump or camshaft drive gear can result.**

12. Install high pressure pump to the left cylinder head. Torque mounting bolts to 10 ft. lbs. (14 Nm).

13. Connect the pump electrical connectors.

14. Install fuel lines at pump.

15. Install inlet supply line clamp using Fuel Line Pliers 9539.

16. Install return line clamp using Fuel Line Pliers 9539.

> ✳✳ **CAUTION**
>
> **Do not crimp or bend fuel line. Inspect sealing cone at line; replace line if compression exists.**

17. Install high pressure fuel line union nut, and tighten to 24 ft. lbs. (33 Nm).

18. Install high pressure line support bracket.

19. Install negative battery cable.

20. Install the engine cover.

21. Start engine and check for leaks.

INJECTION LINES

REMOVAL & INSTALLATION

See Figure 349.

❉❉ WARNING

Observe the following precautions when working on fuel systems: No sparks, open flames or smoking. Avoid inhaling and swallowing fuel. Avoid eye and skin contact with fuel. Pour fuels only into suitable and appropriately marked containers. Wear protective clothing. Failure to observe these precautions may result in fire, explosion, property damage, and serious or fatal injury.

❉❉ WARNING

High-pressure fuel lines deliver fuel under extreme pressure from the injection pump to the injectors. This may be as high as 19,580 psi (1350 bar). Use extreme caution when inspecting for high-pressure fuel leaks. Inspect high-pressure fuel leaks with a sheet of cardboard. Wear safety goggles and adequate protective clothing when servicing fuel system. Fuel under this amount of pressure can penetrate skin causing serious or fatal injury.

1. Disconnect negative battery cable.
2. Remove engine cover.

❉❉ CAUTION

Counterhold with wrench at threaded connections of injectors. DO NOT EXCEED the tightening torque in order to avoid damaging the threaded connection.

❉❉ CAUTION

Do not crimp or bend lines.

➡**After removing injection lines, seal connections and ensure cleanliness.**

3. Unscrew union nuts of injection lines.

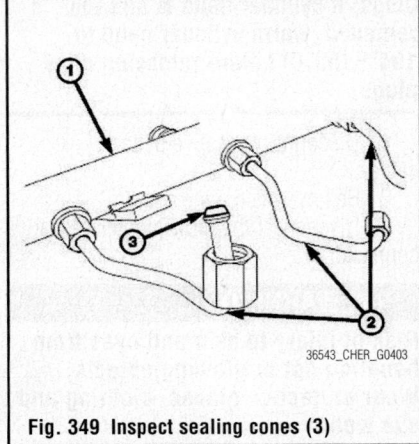

Fig. 349 Inspect sealing cones (3)

4. Remove injection lines.

To install:

5. Loosen the fuel rail mounting bolts to allow stress-free installation of high pressure fuel lines (2).

➡**Inspect sealing cones (3). Replace if damaged.**

6. Position and install fuel lines (2). Tighten to 20 ft. lbs. (27 Nm).

7. Tighten fuel rail mounting bolts to 124 inch lbs. (14 Nm).

8. Install engine cover.

9. Connect negative battery cable.

10. Start engine, allow to warm, turn engine off and inspect for leaks.

INJECTION TIMING

ADJUSTMENT

The high pressure fuel injection pump is driven by the camshaft and requires no timing.

Fuel that enters the high pressure pump is pressurized between 2,900–23,205 psi (200–1600 bar). The pressurized fuel is then supplied to the fuel rail. The high pressure pump and flange located behind the pump are supplied as an assembly.

Fuel passages and control elements in the flange regulate the flow of fuel to the high pressure pumping chambers, and control the lubrication of the pump.

INJECTORS

REMOVAL & INSTALLATION

1. Disconnect negative battery cable.
2. Remove engine cover.
3. Disconnect the fuel return hose at the injector by lifting up on retaining tab and wiggling hose free.

4. Loosen the high pressure fuel lines at the fuel rail.

5. Disconnect the high pressure line at the fuel injector.

6. Disconnect the fuel injector electrical connector.

7. Remove the fuel injector hold down.

➡**If injectors are tight, remove with tool 9552.**

8. Remove injectors and discard lower sealing washer.

To install:

➡**Any time a new injector is installed, or if an existing injector is installed in any location other than its original location, the injector quantity adjustment procedure must be performed.**

9. Clean injectors and recesses.

➡**Do Not apply any lubricant to the fuel injector nozzle. Care must be taken not to restrict the discharge orifices in the nozzle.**

10. Coat injector body with anti seize lubricant then install injectors with new sealing washers.

11. Install tensioning claws. Tighten fasteners in two stages, 62 inch lbs. (7 Nm) then 180 degrees.

❉❉ CAUTION

Inspect both ends of the fuel line and fittings. If there is any damage to the sealing surface, replace the fuel line.

12. Position fuel return line at injectors, hand tighten the high pressure fuel line at the fuel rail and at the injector.

13. Tighten the fuel line fitting at the fuel rail to 20 ft. lbs. (27 Nm), and tighten the fuel line at the injector to 24 ft. lbs. (33 Nm).

14. Reconnect the fuel injector electrical connector.

➡**For the left rear injector, position the engine wiring harness and tighten the harness fasteners to 75 inch lbs. (8.5 Nm).**

15. Install the return fuel hose on the injector and push down on the retaining ring.

16. Connect negative battery cable.

17. Install engine cover.

18. Start engine, allow to warm, turn engine off and inspect for leaks.

HEATING & AIR CONDITIONING SYSTEM

BLOWER MOTOR

REMOVAL & INSTALLATION

See Figure 350.

1. Disconnect and isolate the negative battery cable.
2. If equipped, remove the instrument panel silencer from the passenger side of the instrument panel.
3. Remove the glove box from the instrument panel.
4. Disconnect the blower motor wire harness connector (1) from the blower motor power module or resistor (2), depending on how equipped.
5. Remove the three screws (3) that secure the blower motor (4) to the HVAC housing (5).
6. Remove the blower motor from the HVAC housing.

To install:

7. Position the blower motor into the HVAC housing.
8. Install the three screws that secure the blower motor to the HVAC housing.
9. Connect the wire harness connector to the blower motor power module or resistor, depending on how equipped.
10. Install the glove box into the instrument panel.
11. If equipped, install the instrument panel silencer onto the passenger side of the instrument panel.
12. Reconnect the negative battery cable.

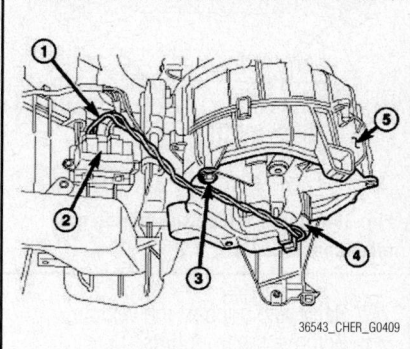

Fig. 350 Disconnect the blower motor wire harness connector (1) from the blower motor power module or resistor (2)

HEATER CORE

REMOVAL & INSTALLATION

See Figures 351 and 352.

✳✳ WARNING

Refer to the applicable warnings and cautions for this system before performing the following operation. Failure to follow these instructions may result in possible serious or fatal injury.

✳✳ WARNING

Disable the airbag system before attempting any steering wheel, steering column or instrument panel component diagnosis or service. Disconnect and isolate the negative battery (ground) cable, then wait two minutes for the airbag system capacitor to discharge before performing further diagnosis or service. This is the only sure way to disable the airbag system. Failure to follow these instructions may result in acci-

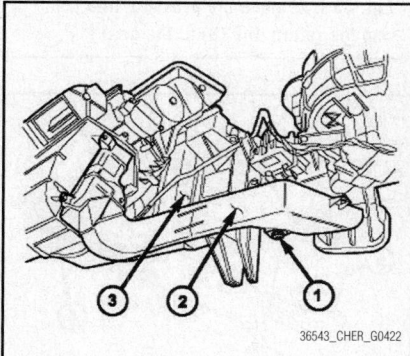

Fig. 351 Remove the five screws (1) that secure the heater core and tube cover (2) to the HVAC housing (3)

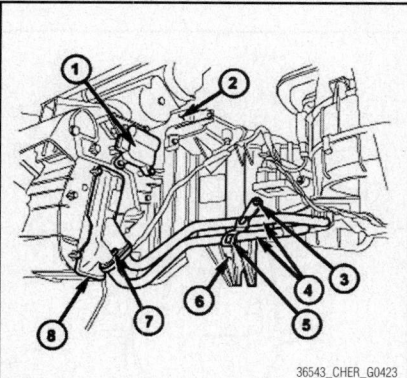

Fig. 352 Remove the blend door actuator (1) from the passenger side of the HVAC air distribution housing (2)

dental airbag deployment and possible serious or fatal injury.

➡ Take the proper precautions to protect the front face of the instrument panel from cosmetic damage while performing this procedure.

1. Drain the engine cooling system.
2. Disconnect and isolate the negative battery cable.
3. If required, disconnect the heater hoses from the heater core tubes in the engine compartment.
4. Remove the instrument panel.
5. Remove the five screws (1) that secure the heater core and tube cover (2) to the HVAC housing (3).
6. Remove the heater core and tube cover from the HVAC housing.
7. If equipped with dual zone heating-A/C, remove the blend door actuator (1) from the passenger side of the HVAC air distribution housing (2).
8. Remove the screw (3) that secure the heater core tubes (4) and retaining bracket (5) to the HVAC housing (6).

➡ Take proper precautions to protect the carpeting from engine coolant. Have absorbent toweling readily available to clean up any spills.

9. Remove the bolt (7) that secures the heater tubes to the heater core (8).
10. Disconnect the heater core tubes from the heater core and remove and discard the O-ring seals.
11. Install plugs in, or tape over the opened heater core ports.
12. Carefully pull the heater core out of the HVAC air distribution housing.
13. If required, remove the heater core tubes from the vehicle.

To install:

14. Carefully install the heater core into the passenger side of the HVAC air distribution housing.
15. Remove the tape or plugs from the heater core ports.
16. If removed, position the heater core tubes into the vehicle.
17. Lubricate new rubber O-ring seals with clean engine coolant and install them onto the heater core tubes. Use only the specified O-ring as they are made of a special material for the engine cooling system.
18. Connect the heater core tubes to the heater core.

19. Install the bolt that secures the heater core tubes to the heater core. Tighten the bolt securely.

20. Install the screw that secures the heater core tube retaining bracket to the HVAC housing.

21. If equipped with dual zone heating-A/C, install the blend door actuator onto the passenger side of the HVAC air distribution housing.

22. Install the heater core and tube cover onto the HVAC housing.

23. Install the five screws that secure the heater core and tube cover to the HVAC housing.

24. Install the instrument panel.

25. If disconnected, connect the heater hoses to the heater core tubes in the engine compartment.

26. Connect the negative battery cable.

27. If the heater core is being replaced, flush the cooling system.

28. Refill the engine cooling system.

STEERING

POWER RACK & PINION STEERING GEAR

REMOVAL & INSTALLATION

See Figures 353 through 359.

✷✷ CAUTION

Steering column module is centered to the vehicles steering system. Failure to keep the system and steering column module centered and locked/inhibited from rotating can result in steering column module damage.

1. Place the front wheels in the straight ahead position with the steering wheel centered and locked with a steering wheel lock.

2. Drain or siphon the power steering system.

3. Remove the column coupler shaft bolt (2) and remove the shaft from the gear (3).

➡ **The power steering lines on the 8 cylinder engines are removed from below the vehicle.**

4. **6 Cylinder engine only**—Remove the pressure line (2), and the return line (3) at the gear (1).

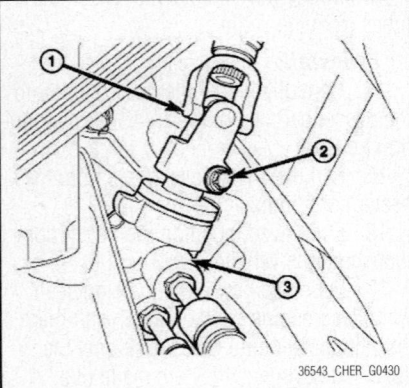

Fig. 353 Remove the column coupler shaft bolt (2) and remove the shaft from the gear (3)

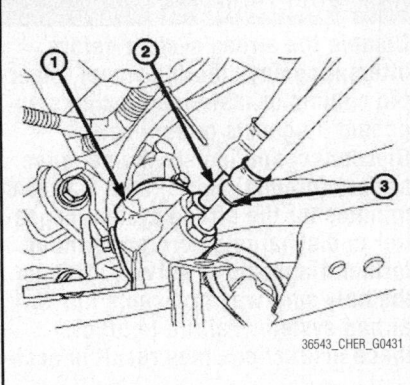

Fig. 354 Remove the pressure line (2), and the return line (3) at the gear (1)

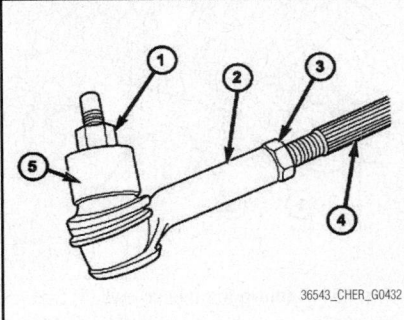

Fig. 355 Loosen the tie rod end jam nuts (3)

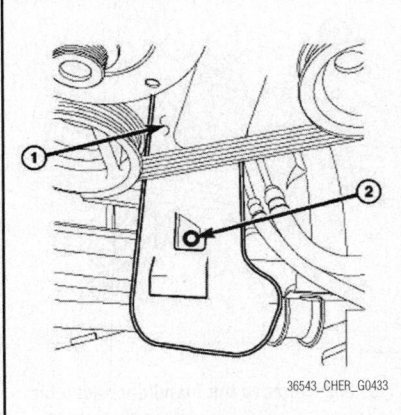

Fig. 356 Remove the oil drip tray (1)

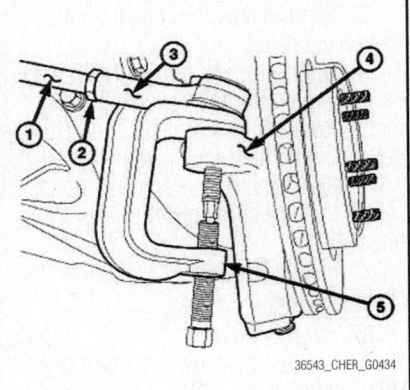

Fig. 357 Remove the outer tie rod end nut and separate the tie rod (3) from the knuckle (4)

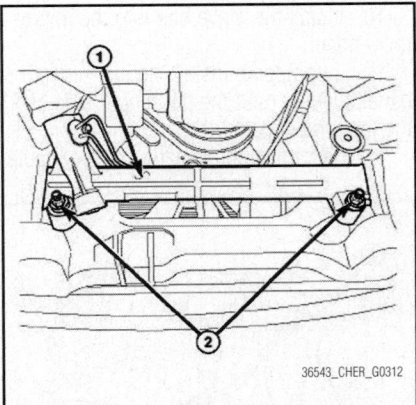

Fig. 358 Remove the two steering gear mounting bolts (2)

5. Raise and support the vehicle,.

6. Remove the front tires.

7. Loosen the tie rod end jam nuts (3).

8. Remove the oil drip tray (1), if equipped.

9. Remove the outer tie rod end nut and separate the tie rod (3) from the knuckle (4) using Ball Joint Remover 8677 (5).

10. Remove the front skid plate, (if equipped).

11. Remove the front splash shield (if equipped).

12. **4WD Only**—Remove the front axle.

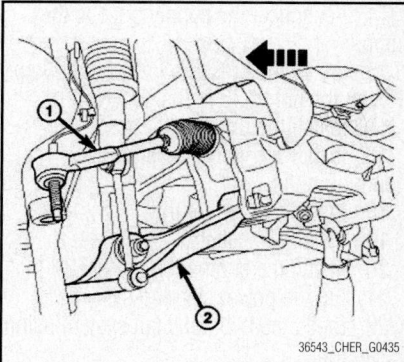

Fig. 359 Turn the steering gear to the full left position to allow clearance from the control arms (2)

13. **8 Cylinder engine only**—Remove the pressure line (2), and the return line (3) at the gear (1).

14. Remove the two steering gear mounting bolts (2).

➡ **The tie rods would move to the right when turning the steering gear to the left.**

15. Move the steering gear to the right side of the vehicle, then turn the steering gear to the full left position to allow clearance from the control arms (2) and remove the gear by lowering the left side first.

16. Remove the outer tie rod ends from the steering gear (if needed).

To install:

17. Install the outer tie rod ends. (if removed).

18. Position the steering gear back into the vehicle the same way it was removed.

19. Install the steering gear mounting nuts and tighten to 180 ft. lbs. (244 Nm). After tightening the nuts, re-center the steering gear.

20. **8 Cylinder engine only**—Install the pressure and return lines to the steering gear and tighten to 21 ft. lbs. (28 Nm).

21. **4WD ONLY**—Install the front axle.

22. Install the front splash shield (if removed).

23. Install the front skid plate (if removed).

24. Install the oil filter drip tray.

25. Install the outer tie rod ends to the knuckles and tighten the tie rod end nuts to 70 ft. lbs. (95 Nm).

26. Install the wheel and tire assembly.

27. Remove the support and lower the vehicle.

28. **6 Cylinder engine only**—Install the pressure and return hoses to the steering gear and tighten to 21 ft. lbs. (28 Nm).

✳✳ CAUTION

The steering gear must be centered prior to installing the coupler to prevent clockspring damage.

29. Install the column coupler shaft into the lower coupling, install a new bolt, and tighten to 36 ft. lbs. (49 Nm).

30. Remove the steering wheel lock.

31. Fill the power steering pump.

POWER STEERING PUMP

REMOVAL & INSTALLATION

3.7L & 4.7L Engines

1. Siphon power steering reservoir.

2. Remove the cooler return hose at the reservoir.

3. Disconnect the pressure hose nut at the pump.

4. Remove the pressure hose at the pump.

5. Remove serpentine drive belt.

6. Remove 3 pump mounting bolts.

7. Remove pulley from pump if necessary.

To install:

8. Install pulley on pump if removed.

9. Install 3 pump mounting bolts and tighten to 21 ft. lbs. (28 Nm).

10. Install the drive belt.

11. Install the pressure hose on the pump and tighten the nut to 21 ft. lbs. (28 Nm).

12. Install the cooler return hose at the reservoir.

13. Add power steering fluid.

5.7L Engine

See Figure 360.

1. Siphon power steering reservoir.

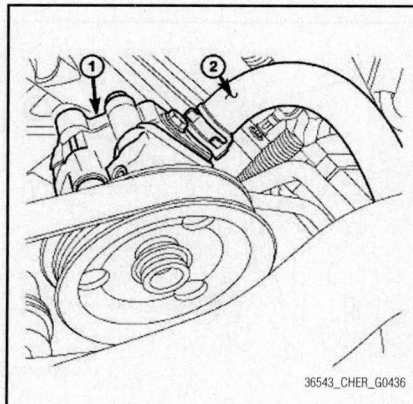

Fig. 360 Disconnect the supply hose (2) at the pump (1)

2. Remove the air intake tube.

3. Remove the drive belt.

4. Disconnect the supply hose (2) at the pump (1).

5. Disconnect the pressure line at the pump.

6. Remove the three pump mounting bolts.

To install:

7. Install pulley on pump if removed.

8. Install 3 pump mounting bolts and tighten to 21 ft. lbs. (28 Nm).

9. Install the pressure hose on the pump and tighten the nut to 35 ft. lbs. (47 Nm).

10. Reconnect the supply hose at the pump.

11. Install the drive belt.

12. Install the air intake tube.

13. Fill the system with power steering fluid.

14. Bleed the hydraulic fan system using a scan tool.

6.1L Engine

See Figure 361.

1. Remove the air inlet tube from the throttle body.

2. Remove serpentine drive belt.

3. Siphon power steering reservoir.

4. Remove the cooler return hose (2) at the reservoir (1).

5. Disconnect the pressure hose nut (3) at the pump (4).

6. Remove 3 pump mounting bolts.

7. Remove pulley from pump if necessary.

To install:

8. Install pulley on pump if removed.

9. Install 3 pump mounting bolts and tighten to 21 ft. lbs. (28 Nm).

10. Install the drive belt.

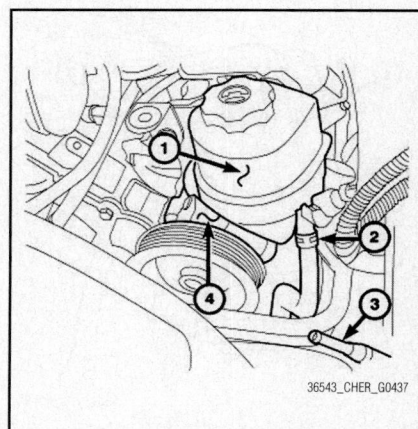

Fig. 361 Remove the cooler return hose (2) at the reservoir (1)

11. Install the pressure hose on the pump and tighten the nut to 21 ft. lbs. (28 Nm).

12. Install the cooler return hose at the reservoir.

13. Add power steering fluid.

14. Install the air inlet tube.

3.0L Diesel Engine

1. Remove the engine top cover.
2. Remove the battery.
3. Remove the battery tray.
4. Remove the inner cooler muffler mounting bolts.

5. Remove the drive belt.
6. Siphon the power steering system.
7. Remove the pressure line at the pump.
8. Remove the supply line at the pump.
9. Remove the pump mounting bolts.
10. Remove the pump from the vehicle.
11. Transfer the brackets if necessary.

To install:

12. Install the pump to the vehicle.
13. Install the pump mounting bracket bolts. Tighten to 21 ft. lbs. (28 Nm).

14. Reconnect the supply hose at the pump.
15. Install the pressure line at the pump. Tighten the nut to 35 ft. lbs. (47 Nm).
16. Install the drive belt.
17. Install the inner cooler muffler mounting bolts.
18. Install the battery tray.
19. Install the battery.
20. Install the engine top cover.
21. Fill the power steering system.
22. Bleed the hydraulic fan system using a scan tool.

SUSPENSION   FRONT SUSPENSION

LOWER BALL JOINT

REMOVAL & INSTALLATION

See Figures 362 through 366.

1. Remove the tire and wheel assembly.
2. Remove the brake caliper and rotor.
3. Disconnect the tie rod (2) from the steering knuckle (4) using special tool C-3894-A (1).
4. Separate the upper ball joint (2) from the knuckle (3) using special tool 8677 (1).
5. Separate the lower ball joint (3) from the steering knuckle (1) using special tool 8677 (2).

6. Remove the steering knuckle.
7. **4WD only:** Remove the clevis bracket and move the halfshaft to the side and support the halfshaft out of the way.

   a. Remove the clevis bolt (2) at the shock (1).
   b. Remove the lower clevis bolt/nut (4) at the lower control arm.

➡**Extreme pressure lubrication must be used on the threaded portions of the tool. This will increase the longevity of the tool and insure proper operation during the removal and installation process.**

8. Press the ball joint from the lower control arm (3) using special tools C-4212-F (Press) (1), C-4212-3 (Driver) (2) and 9654-3 (Receiver) (4).

To install:

➡**Extreme pressure lubrication must be used on the threaded portions of the tool. This will increase the longevity of the tool and insure proper operation**

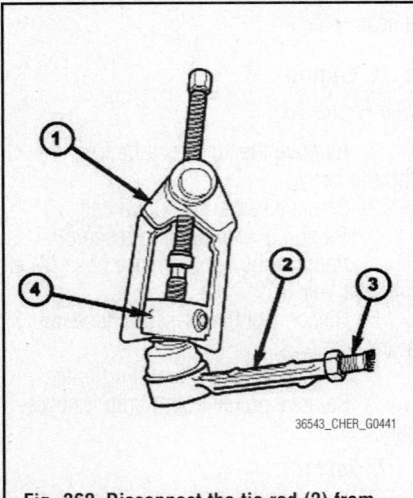

Fig. 362 Disconnect the tie rod (2) from the steering knuckle (4)

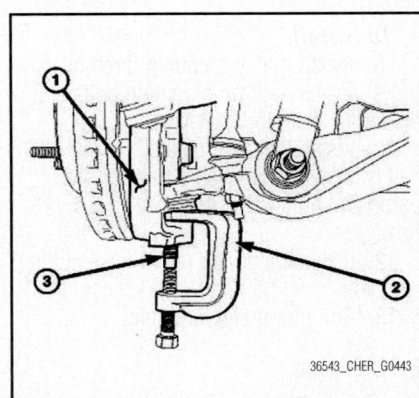

Fig. 364 Separate the lower ball joint (3) from the steering knuckle (1)

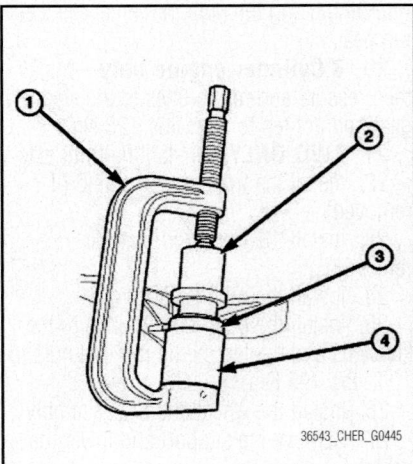

Fig. 366 Press the ball joint from the lower control arm (3)

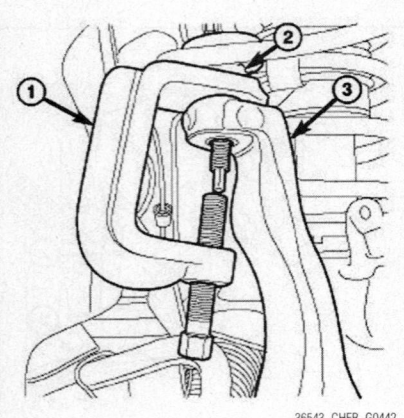

Fig. 363 Separate the upper ball joint (2) from the knuckle (3)

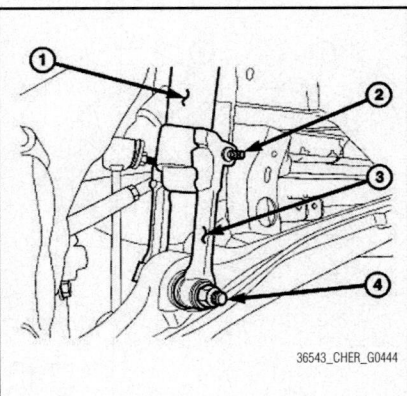

Fig. 365 Remove the clevis bolt (2) at the shock (1)

during the removal and installation process.

9. Install the ball joint into the control arm and press in using special tools C-4212-F (Press), 9654-1 (Driver) and 9654-2 (Receiver).

10. Stake the ball joint flange in four evenly spaced places around the ball joint flange, using a chisel and hammer.

11. **4WD only:** Remove the support for the halfshaft and install into position, then install the clevis bracket.

12. Install the steering knuckle.

13. Install the tie rod end into the steering knuckle.

14. Install and tighten the halfshaft nut to 185 ft. lbs. (251 Nm). (If equipped).

15. Install the brake caliper and rotor.

16. Install the tire and wheel assembly.

17. Check the vehicle ride height.

18. Perform a wheel alignment.

LOWER CONTROL ARM

REMOVAL & INSTALLATION

See Figures 367 through 370.

1. Raise and support the vehicle.
2. Remove the tire and wheel assembly.
3. Remove the steering knuckle (3).
4. Remove the shock clevis bracket (3) from the lower control arm.
5. Remove the stabilizer link (2) at the lower control arm.
6. Remove the nut and bolt from the front of the lower control arm.
7. Remove the rear bolts (2) and flag nuts (3) from the lower control arm (1).
8. Remove the lower control arm from the vehicle.

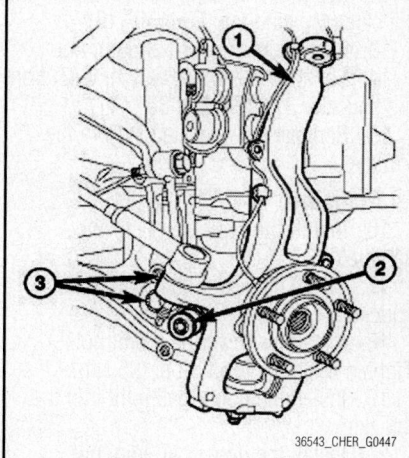

Fig. 368 Remove the shock clevis bracket (3) from the lower control arm

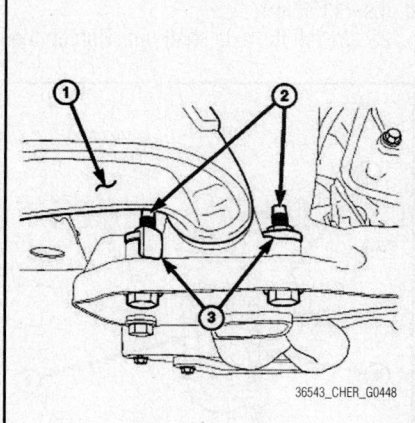

Fig. 369 Remove the rear bolts (2) and flag nuts (3) from the lower control arm (1)

To install:

9. Position the lower suspension arm into the cradle.

10. Install the rear bolts and flag nuts to secure the lower control arm to the frame, Tighten the bolts to 65 ft. lbs. (88 Nm).

11. Install the nut and bolt for the front of the lower control arm Tighten to 125 ft. lbs. (169 Nm).

➡**Orientation of the flag bolt is critical. Flag and head of the bolt (7) must be installed on the forward side of the lower control arm.**

12. Install the lower clevis bolt at the lower control arm and tighten to 125 ft. lbs. (169 Nm).

13. Install the stabilizer link (6) at the lower control arm and tighten to 85 ft. lbs. (115 Nm).

14. Install the steering knuckle to the upper ball joint and tighten the nut to 70 ft. lbs. (95 Nm).

15. Install the tire and wheel assembly.

16. Lower the vehicle.

17. Perform wheel alignment.

STABILIZER BAR CONTROL LINKS

REMOVAL & INSTALLATION

See Figure 371.

1. Raise and support the vehicle.
2. Remove the tire and wheel assembly.
3. Remove the upper link bolt and nut (1 and 2).
4. Remove the lower link bolt (6).
5. Remove the stabilizer link (3).

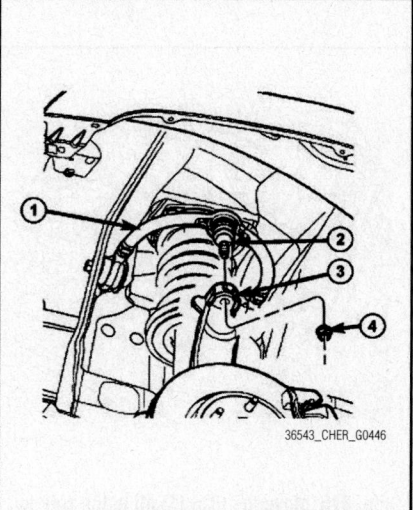

Fig. 367 Remove the steering knuckle (3)

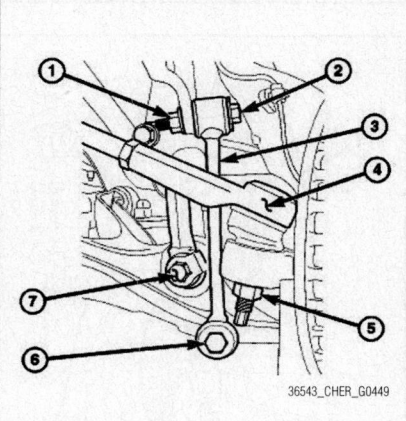

Fig. 370 Flag and head of the bolt (7) must be installed on the forward side of the lower control arm

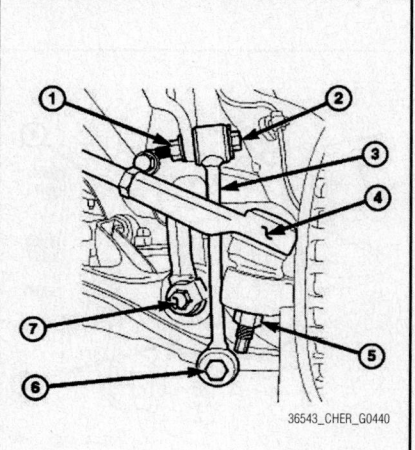

Fig. 371 Remove the upper link bolt and nut (1 and 2)

To install:

6. Install the stabilizer link to the vehicle.

7. Install the lower link bolt and tighten to 85 ft. lbs. (115 Nm).

8. Install the upper link bolt and nut and tighten to 80 ft. lbs. (108 Nm).

9. Install the tire and wheel assembly.

10. lower the vehicle.

STEERING KNUCKLE

REMOVAL & INSTALLATION

See Figures 367 and 368, 372 through 374.

1. Raise and support the vehicle.
2. Remove the tire and wheel assembly.

❋❋ CAUTION

Never allow the disc brake caliper to hang from the brake hose. Damage to the brake hose will result. Provide a suitable support to hang the caliper securely.

3. Remove the brake caliper.

4. Remove the caliper adapter.

5. Remove the O-ring (2) and discard then remove disc brake rotor (1).

6. Remove the wheel speed sensor bolt and disconnect the wire from the retaining clips from the knuckle.

7. Remove the axle shaft nut. (if equipped with 4WD)

8. Remove the hub/bearing.

9. Remove the outer tie rod end retaining nut.

10. Separate the outer tie rod end (3) from the steering knuckle using special tool 8677 (5).

11. Remove the lower ball joint nut.

12. Separate the lower ball joint from the knuckle (1) using tool C-4150A (2).

13. Remove the upper ball joint nut.

14. Separate the upper ball joint (2) from the knuckle (3) using tool 8677 (1).

15. Remove the knuckle (3) from the vehicle.

To install:

16. Install the knuckle (1) to the vehicle.

17. Install the lower ball joint into the knuckle.

18. Install the lower ball joint nut. Tighten the nut to 70 ft. lbs. (95 Nm).

19. Install the upper ball joint into the knuckle.

20. Install the upper ball joint nut. Tighten the nut to 70 ft. lbs. (95 Nm).

21. Install the outer tie rod end to the steering knuckle.

22. Install the hub/bearing. Tighten to 85 ft. lbs. (115 Nm).

23. Install the axle shaft nut. Tighten the

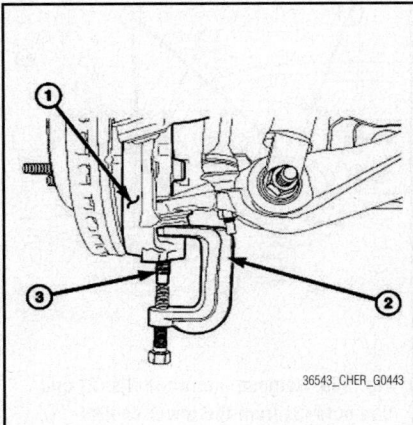

Fig. 373 Separate the lower ball joint from the knuckle (1)

nut to 96 ft. lbs. (135 Nm).(if equipped with 4WD).

➡**Check the sensor wire routing. Be sure the wire is clear of all chassis components and is not twisted or kinked at any spot.**

24. Install the wheel speed sensor into the hub and then install the mounting bolt and tighten to 106–124 inch lbs. (12–14 Nm).

25. Install the disc brake rotor.

26. Install the caliper adapter.

27. Install the tire and wheel assembly.

28. Perform wheel alignment.

STRUT

REMOVAL & INSTALLATION

Left

See Figures 368, 374 through 376.

1. Remove the air box cover and air intake hose.

2. Remove the 3 Power Distribution Center (PDC) bracket nuts.

3. Move the PDC (1) off to the side to access the four upper strut mount nuts (2).

4. Remove the four upper strut mount nuts (2).

5. Raise and support the vehicle.

6. Remove the tire.

7. Remove the two brake caliper adapter bolts.

8. Support the brake caliper adaptor and caliper. Do not allow the caliper to hang by the brake hose.

9. Remove the disc brake rotor.

10. Remove the upper ball joint nut.

11. Separate the upper ball joint (2) from the knuckle (3) using special tool 8677 (1).

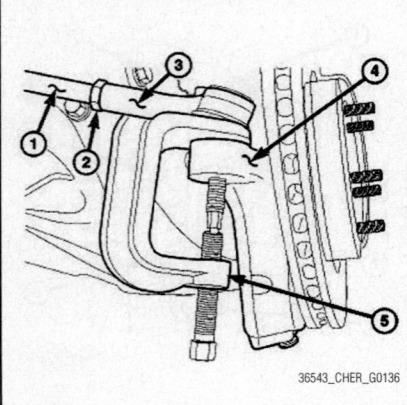

Fig. 372 Separate the outer tie rod end (3) from the steering knuckle

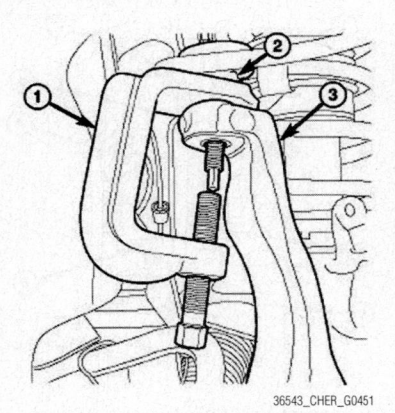

Fig. 374 Separate the upper ball joint (2) from the knuckle (3)

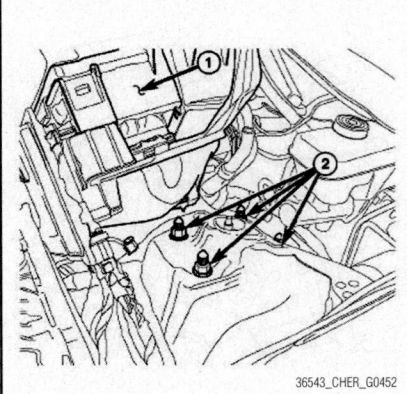

Fig. 375 Move the PDC (1) off to the side to access the four upper strut mount nuts (2)

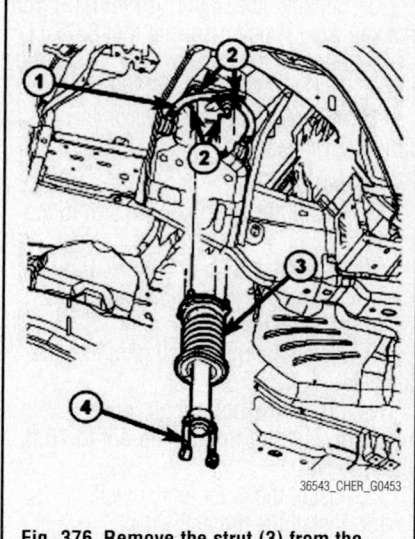

Fig. 376 Remove the strut (3) from the vehicle

12. Remove the lower clevis bolt (3) at the lower control arm.

13. Remove the lower stabilizer bolt (2) at the lower control arm.

14. Remove the strut (3) from the vehicle.

To install:

15. Install the strut assembly to the vehicle.

16. Install the four upper strut nuts. Tighten to 70 ft. lbs. (95 Nm).

17. Install the 3 PDC bracket nuts.

18. Raise the vehicle up.

19. Install the lower stabilizer bolt at the lower control arm and tighten to 85 ft. lbs. (115 Nm).

20. Install the lower clevis bolt at the lower control arm and tighten to 125 ft. lbs. (169 Nm).

21. Install the upper ball joint into the knuckle and tighten the nut to 55 ft. lbs. (75 Nm).

22. Install the disc brake rotor.

23. Install the caliper adaptor mounting bolts to 130 ft. lbs. (176 Nm).

24. Install the tire and wheel assembly.

25. Lower the vehicle.

Right

See Figures 374, 376 through 378.

1. Remove the air box cover and air intake hose.

2. Disconnect the cruise control servo electrical connector.

3. Remove the coolant reservoir mounting bolt and move the coolant reservoir off to the side.

4. Remove the four upper strut mounting nuts (1).

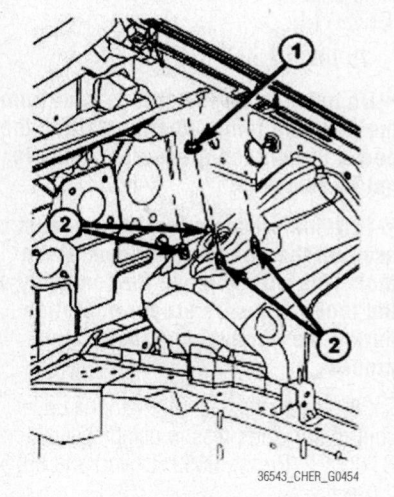

Fig. 377 Remove the four upper strut mounting nuts (1)

5. Raise and support the vehicle.

6. Remove the tire.

7. Remove the two brake caliper adapter bolts.

8. Support the brake caliper adaptor and caliper. Do not allow the caliper to hang by the brake hose.

9. Remove the disc brake rotor.

10. Remove the upper ball joint nut.

11. Separate the upper ball joint (2) from the knuckle (3) using special tool 8677(1).

12. Remove the lower clevis bolt (3) at the lower control arm.

13. Remove the lower stabilizer bolt (2) at the lower control arm.

14. Remove the strut (3) from the vehicle.

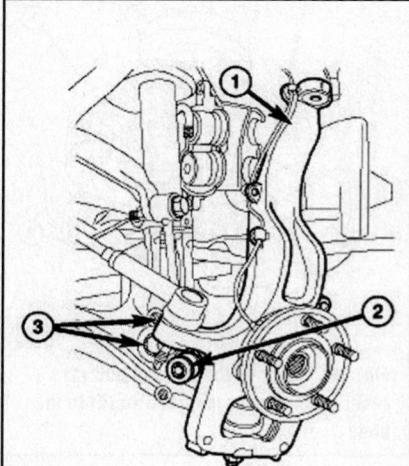

Fig. 378 Remove the lower clevis bolt (3) at the lower control arm

To install:

15. Install the strut assembly to the vehicle.

16. Install the four upper strut nuts. Tighten to 70 ft. lbs. (95 Nm).

17. Install the coolant reservoir bolt.

18. Reconnect the cruise control servo wiring connector.

19. Install the air box cover and air intake hose.

20. Raise the vehicle up.

21. Install the lower stabilizer bolt at the lower control arm.

22. Install the lower clevis bolt at the lower control arm and tighten to 125 ft. lbs. (169 Nm).

23. Install the upper ball joint into the knuckle and tighten the nut to 55 ft. lbs. (75 Nm).

24. Install the disc brake rotor.

25. Install the caliper adaptor mounting bolts to 130 ft. lbs. (176 Nm).

26. Install the tire and wheel assembly.

27. Lower the vehicle.

STABILIZER BAR

REMOVAL & INSTALLATION

See Figures 369 through 378.

1. Raise and support the vehicle.

2. Remove the front splash shield.

3. Remove the stabilizer bar link upper nut (1) and bolt (2).

4. Remove the two stabilizer bushing clamp (2) bolts.

5. Remove the stabilizer bar (1).

To install:

6. Install the stabilizer bar to the vehicle.

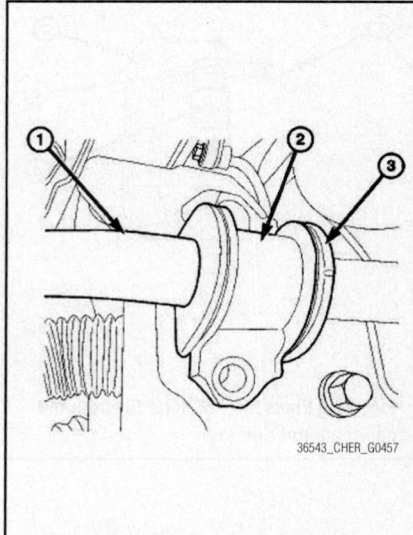

Fig. 379 Remove the two stabilizer bushing clamp (2) bolts

7. Install the stabilizer bushing clamp and tighten the bolts to 95 ft. lbs. (129 Nm).

8. Install the upper stabilizer link and tighten nut and bolt to 80 ft. lbs. (108 Nm).

9. Install the front splash shield.

10. Lower the vehicle.

UPPER BALL JOINT

REMOVAL & INSTALLATION

See Figures 374 and 380.

1. Raise vehicle and support the axle.

2. Remove the tire and wheel.

3. Remove the upper ball joint retaining nut.

4. Separate the upper ball joint (2) from the knuckle (3) using special tool 8677 (1).

5. Move the knuckle (3) out of the way to allow ball joint removal tool access.

➡**When installing a new ball joint, Do not remove the rubber grease boot on the new ball joint during installation.**

6. Remove the rubber grease boot from the ball joint in the control arm. This will allow better fit of the ball joint tool when removing.

➡**Extreme pressure lubrication must be used on the threaded portions of the tool. This will increase the longevity of the tool and insure proper operation during the removal and installation process.**

7. Press the ball joint (3) from the upper control arm (1) using special tools C-4212-F (Press) (2) and 9652 (Driver) (4).

To install:

➡**Do not remove the grease boot from the new ball joint. When installing the new ball joint the grease boot should not be removed.**

➡**Extreme pressure lubrication must be used on the threaded portions of the tool. This will increase the longevity of the tool and insure proper operation during the removal and installation process.**

8. Install the ball joint into the upper control arm and press in using special tools C-4212-F (Press), 9652 (Driver) and 8975-2 (Receiver).

9. Install the upper ball joint into the knuckle.

10. Install the upper ball joint retaining nut and tighten to 70 ft. lbs. (95 Nm).

11. Install the tire and wheel.

12. Remove the supports and lower the vehicle.

13. Perform a wheel alignment.

UPPER CONTROL ARM

REMOVAL & INSTALLATION

See Figures 374 and 381.

1. Raise vehicle and support the axle.

2. Remove the tire and wheel.

3. Remove the inner fender well (2).

4. Remove the upper ball joint retaining nut.

5. Separate the upper ball joint (2) from the knuckle (3) using special tool 8677 (1).

6. Remove the nut and bolt (1) securing the upper control arm (5) to the body.

7. Remove the upper control arm (5) from the vehicle.

To install:

8. Install the upper control arm to the vehicle.

9. Install the nut and bolt securing the upper control arm to the body and tighten to 80 ft. lbs. (108 Nm.

10. Install the upper ball joint into the knuckle.

11. Install the upper ball joint retaining nut and tighten the nut to 70 ft. lbs. (95 Nm).

12. Install the inner fender well.

13. Install the tire and wheel.

14. Remove the supports and lower the vehicle.

15. Perform a wheel alignment.

WHEEL HUB & BEARING

REMOVAL & INSTALLATION

1. Raise and support the vehicle.

2. Remove the wheel and tire assembly.

➡**Support the caliper, Do not let the caliper hang by the hose.**

3. Remove the disc brake caliper.

4. Remove the brake caliper adaptor.

5. Remove and discard the O-ring and then remove the disc brake rotor.

6. Remove the wheel speed sensor nut.

7. Remove the wheel speed sensor.

8. Remove the 3 hub bearing mounting bolts from the back of the steering knuckle.

9. Remove hub bearing from the steering knuckle.

To install:

10. Install the hub bearing to the knuckle then tighten the 3 bolts to 85 ft. lbs. (115 Nm).

11. Install the wheel speed sensor into the hub. Install the mounting bolt and tighten to 106–124 inch lbs. (12–14 Nm).

12. Install the brake rotor.

13. Install the brake caliper adaptor.

14. Install the caliper.

15. Install the wheel and tire assembly.

16. Remove the support and lower the vehicle.

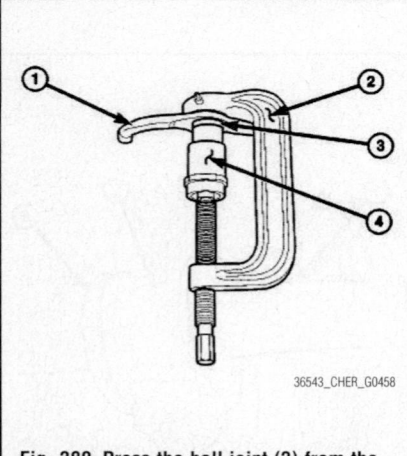

36543_CHER_G0458

Fig. 380 Press the ball joint (3) from the upper control arm (1)

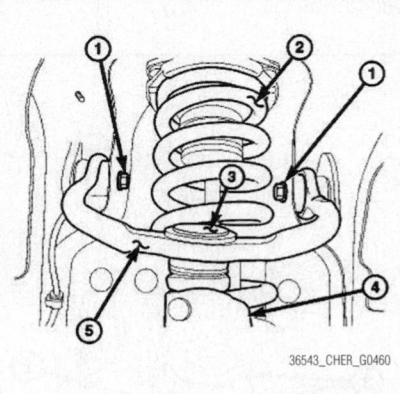

36543_CHER_G0460

Fig. 381 Remove the nut and bolt (1) securing the upper control arm (5) to the body

SUSPENSION **REAR SUSPENSION**

COIL SPRING

REMOVAL & INSTALLATION

See Figures 382 and 383.

1. Raise and support the vehicle. Position a hydraulic jack under the axle to support the axle.
2. Remove the wheel and tire assembly on the side of the repair.
3. Remove the lower shock bolt (3) from the axle bracket.
4. If the left spring is being serviced, remove the left rear bolt securing the fuel tank skid plate in place. This will allow clearance for the suspension when the spring is removed.
5. Remove the stabilizer bar link from the body rail.
6. Lower the hydraulic jack and tilt the axle.
7. Pull down on the axle as necessary and remove the coil spring (4) by lifting it up and off the lower perch first.
8. Remove and inspect the spring isolators.

To install:

9. Install the upper isolator on the spring seat on body.
10. Install the lower isolator (3) on the axle bracket.
11. Pull down on the axle and position the coil spring (1), ID tag end up, over the upper perch, then lower it onto the lower perch.
12. Raise the axle with the hydraulic jack.

Fig. 382 Remove the lower shock bolt (3) from the axle bracket

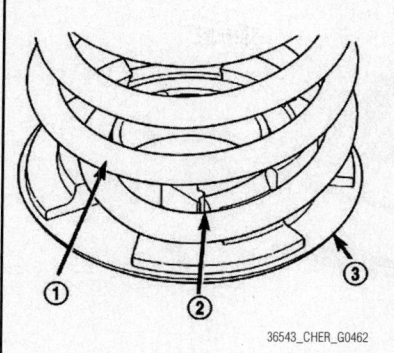

Fig. 383 Install the lower isolator (3) on the axle bracket

13. Install the shock absorber to the axle bracket and tighten the bolt to 85 ft. lbs. (115 Nm).
14. If the left spring is being serviced, install the previously removed fuel tank skid plate bolt and tighten to 50ft. lbs. (68 Nm).
15. Install the stabilizer bar link to the body rail and tighten the bolt to 75 ft. lbs. (102 Nm).
16. Install the wheel and tire assembly.
17. Remove the supports and lower the vehicle.

CONTROL ARMS/LINKS

REMOVAL & INSTALLATION

Stabilizer Link-Base Vehicle

1. Raise and support the vehicle.
2. Remove the rear tire.
3. Support the rear axle with a jack.
4. Remove the upper link bolt at the frame.
5. Remove the lower link nut at the stabilizer bar.
6. Remove stabilizer link.

To install:

7. Install the upper bolt for the stabilizer link to the frame and tighten to 75 ft. lbs. (102 Nm).
8. Install the stabilizer link to the stabilizer bar.
9. Install the nut and tighten to 65 ft. lbs. (88 Nm).
10. Remove the jack and lower the vehicle.

Stabilizer Link-Vehicles with 6.1L Engine

See Figure 384.

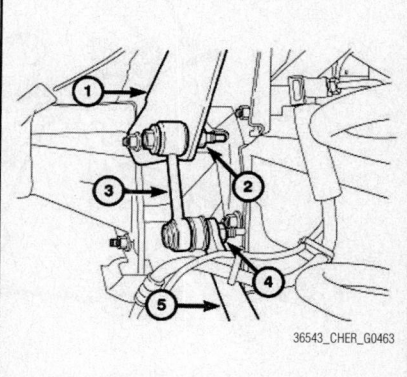

Fig. 384 Remove the upper link bolt and nut (2) at the bracket (1)

1. Raise and support the vehicle.
2. Remove the tire and wheel assembly.
3. Remove the upper link bolt and nut (2) at the bracket (1).
4. Remove the lower stabilizer link nut (4) from the stabilizer bar (5).
5. Remove the link (3).

To install:

6. Install the upper bolt and nut for the stabilizer link to the bracket. Tighten to 75 ft. lbs. (102 Nm).
7. Install the stabilizer link to the stabilizer bar.
8. Install the nut and tighten to 65 ft. lbs. (88 Nm).
9. Install the tire and wheel assembly.
10. Lower the vehicle.

Lower Control Arm

Left Side

See Figures 385 and 386.

1. Raise the vehicle and support the rear axle.
2. Remove the fuel tank.
3. Remove the lower suspension arm nut (2) and bolt (1) from the axle bracket.
4. Remove the nut (1) and bolt (8) from the frame rail and remove the lower suspension arm (9).

To install:

➡**All torques should be done with vehicle on the ground with full vehicle weight.**

5. Position the lower suspension arm in the frame rail.
6. Install the frame rail bracket bolt and nut. Tighten to 130 ft. lbs. (176 Nm).
7. Position the lower suspension arm in the axle bracket.

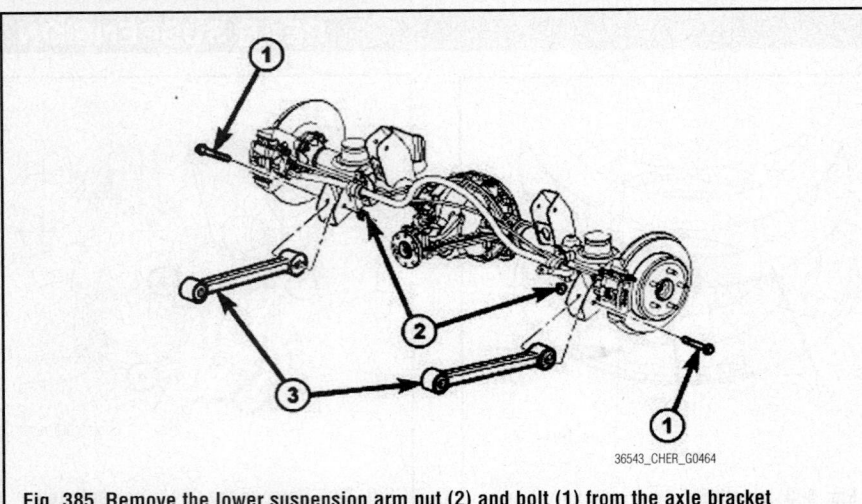

Fig. 385 Remove the lower suspension arm nut (2) and bolt (1) from the axle bracket

36543_CHER_G0464

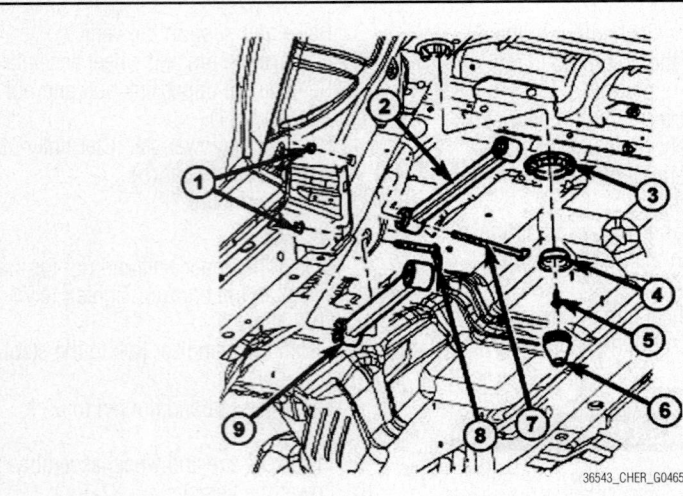

Fig. 386 Remove the nut (1) and bolt (8) from the frame rail and remove the lower suspension arm (9)

36543_CHER_G0465

8. Install the axle bracket bolt and nut. Tighten to 155 ft. lbs. (210 Nm).

9. Install the fuel tank.

10. Remove the supports and lower the vehicle.

Right Side

See Figures 385 through 386.

1. Raise the vehicle and support the rear axle.

2. Remove the lower suspension arm nut (2) and bolt (1) from the axle bracket.

3. Remove the nut (1) and bolt (8) from the frame rail and remove the lower suspension arm (9).

To install:

➡**All torques should be done with vehicle on the ground with full vehicle weight.**

4. Position the lower suspension arm in the frame rail.

5. Install the frame rail bracket bolt and nut. Tighten to 130 ft. lbs. (176 Nm).

6. Position the lower suspension arm in the axle bracket.

7. Install the axle bracket bolt and nut. Tighten to 155 ft. lbs. (210 Nm).

8. Remove the supports and lower the vehicle.

Upper Control Arm

Left Side

See Figures 386 through 387.

1. Raise and support the vehicle.

2. Support the rear axle.

3. Lower the fuel tank in order to gain access to the bolt.

4. Remove the upper suspension arm nut (2) and bolt (3) from the axle bracket.

5. Remove the nut (1) and bolt (7) from the frame rail and remove the upper suspension arm (2).

To install:

➡**All torques should be done with vehicle on the ground with full vehicle weight.**

6. Position the upper suspension arm in the frame rail bracket.

7. Install the mounting bolt and nut tighten to 95 ft. lbs. (129 Nm).

8. Position the upper suspension arm in the axle bracket.

9. Install the mounting bolt and nut tighten to 100 ft. lbs. (136 Nm).

10. Raise the fuel tank back into place and secure.

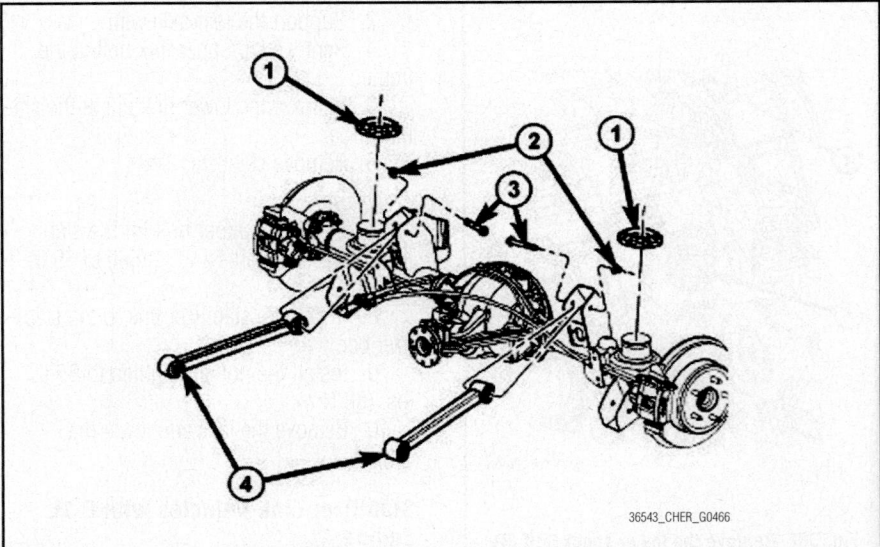

Fig. 387 Remove the upper suspension arm nut (2) and bolt (3) from the axle bracket

36543_CHER_G0466

11. Remove the supports and lower the vehicle.

Right Side

See Figures 386 and 387.

1. Raise and support the vehicle.
2. Support the rear axle.
3. Remove the upper suspension arm nut (2) and bolt (3) from the axle bracket.
4. Remove the nut (1) and bolt (7) from the frame rail and remove the upper suspension arm (2).

To install:

➡**All torques should be done with vehicle on the ground with full vehicle weight.**

5. Position the upper suspension arm in the frame rail bracket.
6. Install the mounting bolt and nut tighten to 95 ft. lbs. (129 Nm).
7. Position the upper suspension arm in the axle bracket.
8. Install the mounting bolt and nut tighten to 100 ft. lbs. (136 Nm).
9. Remove the supports and lower the vehicle.

SHOCK ABSORBER

REMOVAL & INSTALLATION

See Figures 382 and 388.

1. Raise and support the vehicle. Position a hydraulic jack under the axle to support the axle.
2. Remove the upper bolt (1) from the frame bracket.
3. Remove the lower bolt from the axle bracket (2).
4. Remove the shock absorber (1).

To install:

5. Install the shock absorber in the frame bracket and install the bolt.
6. Install the shock absorber in the axle bracket and install the bolt.
7. Tighten the upper mounting bolt and nut to 70 ft. lbs. (95 Nm).
8. Tighten the lower mounting bolt and nut to 85 ft. lbs. (115 Nm).
9. Remove the supports and lower the vehicle.

STABILIZER BAR

REMOVAL & INSTALLATION

See Figures 389 and 390.

1. Raise and support the vehicle.
2. Remove both rear tire assemblies.
3. Remove the stabilizer bar links from stabilizer bar.
4. Remove the stabilizer bar retainer bolts from the retainer (2).
5. Remove the stabilizer bar (1) by twisting it out and around the rotor and caliper from the right rear side of the vehicle.

To install:

6. Twist and rotate to position the stabilizer bar on the axle from the right rear side of the vehicle.
7. Install the retainers and bolts. Ensure the bar is centered with equal spacing on both sides. Tighten the bolts to 31 ft. lbs. (42 Nm).
8. Install the links to the stabilizer bar.
9. Tighten the nuts at the stabilizer bar to 90 ft. lbs. (122 Nm).
10. Install the tire and wheel assemblies.
11. Remove support and lower the vehicle.

36543_CHER_G0469

Fig. 390 Remove the stabilizer bar (1) by twisting it out and around the rotor and caliper

TRACK BAR

REMOVAL & INSTALLATION

See Figures 391 and 392.

1. Raise and support the vehicle. Position a hydraulic jack under the axle to support the axle.
2. Remove the track bar bolt (3) and nut (2) from the frame bracket.
3. Remove the left lower shock bolt at the axle.
4. Pry in between the coil springs to remove track bar bolt.
5. Remove the track bar bolt (3) and nut (2) from the axle bracket.

To install:

6. Install the track bar to the vehicle.
7. Pry in between the coil springs to install track bar bolt.

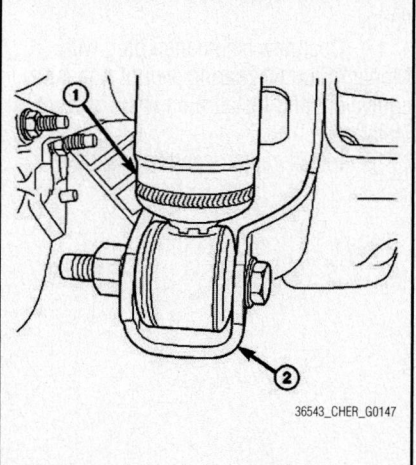

36543_CHER_G0147

Fig. 388 Remove the lower bolt from the axle bracket (2)

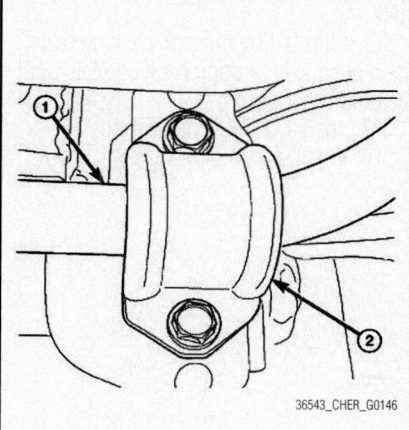

36543_CHER_G0146

Fig. 389 Remove the stabilizer bar retainer bolts from the retainer (2)

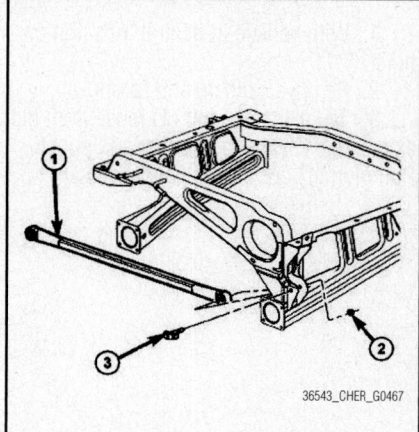

36543_CHER_G0467

Fig. 391 Remove the track bar bolt (3) and nut (2) from the frame bracket

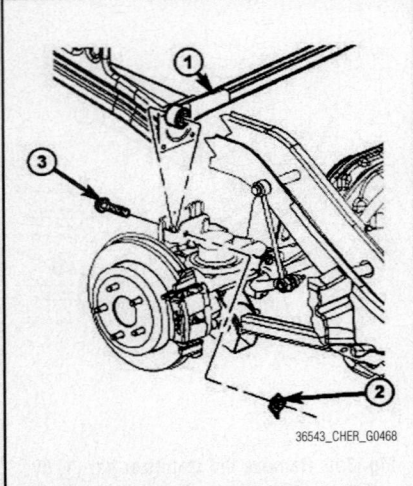

Fig. 392 Remove the track bar bolt (3) and nut (2) from the axle bracket

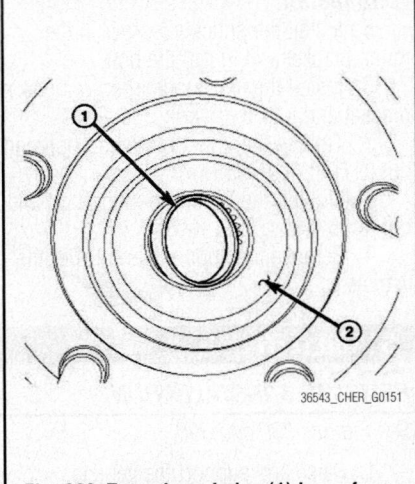

Fig. 393 Tap axle end plug (1) loose from the axle flange (2)

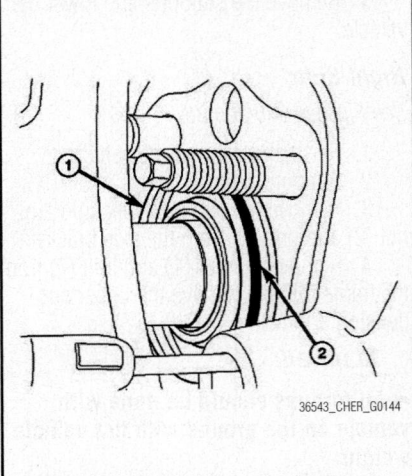

Fig. 394 Remove O-ring (2) from the axle bearing

8. Install the track bar bolt and nut in the frame bracket.

9. Install the track bar into the axle bracket.

10. Install the track bar bolt and nut in the axle bracket.

11. Install the left lower shock bolt to the axle Tighten to 85 ft. lbs. (115 Nm).

12. Remove the supports and lower the vehicle.

➡**Torques should be done with vehicle on the ground with full vehicle weight.**

13. Tighten the upper mounting bolt/nut to 140 ft. lbs. (190 Nm).

14. Tighten the lower mounting bolt/nut to 140 ft. lbs. (190 Nm).

WHEEL HUB AND BEARING

REMOVAL & INSTALLATION

See Figures 393 through 395.

1. With vehicle in neutral, position on hoist.

2. Remove calipers and rotors.

3. Tap axle end plug (1) loose from the axle flange (2) with a hammer and punch. Pull plug (1) out of axle flange (2).

4. Remove speed sensors from axle tube flange.

5. Remove axle flange nuts from axle.

6. Pull axle shaft and backing plate out of axle tube until axle bearing (1) is exposed.

7. Remove O-ring (2) from the axle bearing.

8. Slide axle shaft (1) from axle tube and backing plate.

9. Tap axle shaft out of the bearing and axle flange through the plug hole with a hammer and brass drift.

To install:

➡**If a bearing flange stud is loose or has backed out tighten stud to 20 ft. lbs. (27 Nm).**

10. Tap axle shaft into axle bearing and axle flange.

11. Install axle shaft into axle tube and backing plate with new O-ring on axle.

12. Slip O-ring through backing plate, then push axle through backing plate until bearing is exposed.

13. Install O-ring axle bearing.

14. Push axle into axle tube.

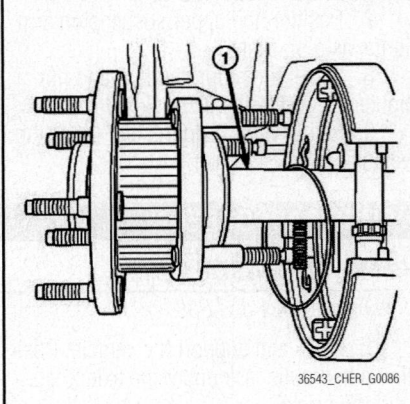

Fig. 395 Slide axle shaft (1) from axle tube and backing plate

15. Install axle flange nuts and tighten to 88 ft. lbs. (119 Nm).

16. Install speed sensors in axle tube flange.

17. Coat new axle flange plug with Mopar® Stud N' Bearing Mount Adhesive or equivalent and install plug with freeze plug installer.

18. Install calipers and rotors.

DODGE

Journey

12

SPECIFICATIONS AND MAINTENANCE CHARTS

ENGINE AND VEHICLE IDENTIFICATION

Code ①	Liters	Cu. In.	Cyl.	Fuel Sys.	Engine Type	Eng. Mfg.	Code ②	Year
B	2.4	148	I4	MFI	DOHC	Chrysler	9	2009
B PZEV	2.4	148	I4	MFI	DOHC	Chrysler		
D	2.7	167	V6	MFI	DOHC	Chrysler		
V	3.5	214	V6	MFI	SOHC	Chrysler		

MFI: Multi-point Fuel Injection

SOHC: Single Overhead Camshaft

DOHC: Double Overhead Camshaft

PZEV: Partially Zero Emissions Vehicle (California)

① 8th position of VIN

② 10th position of VIN

36543_JOUR_C0001

GENERAL ENGINE SPECIFICATIONS

All measurements are given in inches.

Year	Model	Engine Displacement Liters	Engine Series (ID/VIN)	Fuel System	Net Horsepower @ rpm	Net Torque @ rpm (ft. lbs.)	Bore x Stroke (in.)	Com- pression Ratio	Oil Pressure @ rpm
2009	Journey	2.4	B	MFI	173@6000	166@4400	3.47x3.82	10.5:1	25-80@3000
		2.4	B PZEV	MFI	173@6000	166@4400	3.47x3.82	10.5:1	25-80@3000
		2.7	D	MFI	190@6400	190@4000	3.39x3.09	9.67:1	45-105@3000
		3.5	V	MFI	235@6400	232@4000	3.78x3.19	10.0:1	45-105@3000

MFI: Multi-point Fuel Injection

36543_JOUR_C0002

GASOLINE ENGINE TUNE-UP SPECIFICATIONS

Year	Engine Displacement Liters	Engine ID/VIN	Spark Plug Gap (in.)	Ignition Timing (deg.) MT	AT	Fuel Pump (psi) ①	Idle Speed (rpm) MT	AT	Valve Clearance In.	Ex.
2009	2.4	B	0.043	—	①	58	—	②	HYD	HYD
	2.4	B PZEV	0.031	—	①	58	—	②	HYD	HYD
	2.7	D	0.05	—	①	58	—	②	HYD	HYD
	3.5	R	0.05	—	①	58	—	②	HYD	HYD

NOTE: The Vehicle Emission Control Information label often reflects specification changes made during production.

The label figures must be used if they differ from those in this chart.

HYD: Hydraulic

① Ignition timing cannot be adjusted. Base engine timing is set at TDC during assembly.

② Refer to the Vehicle Emission Control Information label for correct specifications.

36543_JOUR_C0003

CAPACITIES

Year	Model	Engine Displacement Liters	Engine ID/VIN	Engine Oil with Filter (qts.)	Transmission (pts.) 5-Spd	Transmission (pts.) Auto.	Fuel Tank (gal.)	Cooling System (qts.)
2009	Journey	2.4	B	4.5	5	8.0 ①	20.5	7.7
		2.4	B PZEV	4.5	5	8.0 ①	18.5	7.7
		2.7	D	5.5	NA	11.0 ①	20.5	9.8
		3.5	V	5.5	NA	11.0 ①	21.1	11.6

NOTE: All capacities are approximate. Add fluid gradually and ensure a proper fluid level is obtained.

NA: Not Applicable

① Overhaul fill capacity with torque converter empty: 18.4 qts.

36543_JOUR_C0004

FLUID SPECIFICATIONS

Year	Model	Engine Displacement Liters	Engine ID/VIN	Engine Oil	Auto. Trans.	Manual Trans.	Power Steering Fluid	Brake Master Cylinder
2009	Journey	2.4	B	5W-30	①	①	②	③
		2.4	B PZEV	5W-30	①	①	②	③
		2.7	D	5W-30	①	①	②	③
		3.5	V	10W-30	①	①	②	③

DOT: Department Of Transportation

① Mopar® ATF+4 Automatic Transmission Fluid or equivalent.

② Mopar® Power Steering Fluid+4, Mopar® ATF+4 Automatic Transmission Fluid or equivalent.

③ Mopar® DOT 3, SAE J1703 should be used. If DOT 3, SAE J1703 brake fluid isn't available, then DOT 4 is acceptable. Use only recommended brake fluids.

36543_JOUR_C0005

VALVE SPECIFICATIONS

Year	Engine Displacement Liters	Engine ID/VIN	Seat Angle (deg.)	Face Angle (deg.)	Spring Test Pressure (lbs. @ in.)	Spring Installed Height (in.)	Stem-to-Guide Clearance (in.) Intake	Stem-to-Guide Clearance (in.) Exhaust	Stem Diameter (in.) Intake	Stem Diameter (in.) Exhaust
2009	2.4	B	44.75-45.10	44.25-45.75	40.35@1.38	1.378	0.0008-0.0021	0.0012-0.0024	0.2151-0.2157	0.2148-0.2153
	2.4	B PZEV	44.75-45.10	44.25-45.75	40.35@1.38	1.378	0.0008-0.0021	0.0012-0.0024	0.2151-0.2157	0.2148-0.2153
	2.7	D	45-45.5	44.5-45.5	56-64@1.50	1.496	0.0009-0.0026	0.002-0.0037	0.2337-0.2344	0.2326-0.2333
	3.5	V	45-45.5	44.5-45	①	1.496	0.0009-0.0026	0.0020-0.0037	0.2730-0.2737	0.2719-0.2726

① 70.5-79.5 @1.49 (INT)
  69.5-80.5 @1.49 (EXT)

36543_JOUR_C0006

CAMSHAFT AND BEARING SPECIFICATIONS CHART

All measurements are given in inches.

Year	Engine Displacement Liters	Engine ID/VIN	Journal Dia.	Brg. Oil Clearance	Shaft End-play	Runout	Journal Bore	Lobe Height Intake	Lobe Height Exhaust
2009	2.4	B	①	②	0.004-0.0090	NA	NA	NA	NA
	2.4	B PZEV	①	②	0.004-0.0090	NA	NA	NA	NA
	2.7	D	0.9449-0.9441	0.0020-0.0035	0.0051-0.0110	NA	0.9469-0.9476	NA	NA
	3.5	V	1.6905-1.6913	0.003-0.0047	0.001-0.0140	NA	1.6944-1.6853	NA	NA

NA: Not Available

① Front intake - 1.1797 - 1.1803 in.

Front exhaust - 1.4166 - 1.4173 in.

Cam Journal Diameter No. 1-4 - 0.943 - 0.944 in.

② Front intake journal - 0.0008 - 0.0022 in.

Front exhaust journal - 0.0007 - 0.0020 in.

All others - 0.0008 - 0.0026 in.

36543_JOUR_C0007

CRANKSHAFT AND CONNECTING ROD SPECIFICATIONS

All measurements are given in inches.

Year	Engine Displacement Liters	Engine ID/VIN	Crankshaft Main Brg. Journal Dia.	Crankshaft Main Brg. Oil Clearance	Crankshaft Shaft End-play	Crankshaft Thrust on No.	Connecting Rod Journal Diameter	Connecting Rod Oil Clearance	Connecting Rod Side Clearance
2009	2.4	B	①	0.0011-0.0018	0.0019-0.0098	3	②	0.0012-0.0023	0.0039-0.0010
	2.4	B PZEV	①	0.0011-0.0018	0.0019-0.0098	3	②	0.0012-0.0023	0.0039-0.0010
	2.7	D	2.4997-2.5004	0.0014-0.0021	0.0019-0.0108	3	2.1067-2.1060	0.0010-0.0026	0.0052-0.0150
	3.5	V	2.5192-2.5202	0.0013-0.0024	0.002-0.0100	3	2.282-2.2830	0.0009-0.0021	0.0153 Max.

① 0: 2.0466 - 2.0467 in.

1: 2.0465 - 2.0466 in.

2: 2.0464 - 2.0465 in.

3: 2.0462 - 2.0464 in.

4: 2.0461 - 2.0462 in.

② 1: 1.8884 - 1.8886 in.

2: 1.8884 - 1.8881 in.

3: 1.8879 - 1.8881 in.

36543_JOUR_C0008

PISTON AND RING SPECIFICATIONS

All measurements are given in inches.

Year	Engine Displacement Liters	Engine ID/VIN	Piston Clearance	Ring Gap			Ring Side Clearance		
				Top Compression	Bottom Compression	Oil Control	Top Compression	Bottom Compression	Oil Control
2009	2.4	B	0.0006-0.0006	0.0059-0.0118	0.0118-0.0177	0.0079-0.0276	0.1182-0.0028	0.1182-0.0028	0.0024-0.0059
	2.4	B PZEV	0.0006-0.0006	0.0059-0.0118	0.0118-0.0177	0.0079-0.0276	0.1182-0.0028	0.1182-0.0028	0.0024-0.0059
	2.7	D	0.0003-0.0016	0.008-0.0140	0.0146-0.0249	0.010-0.0300	0.0013-0.0032	0.0016-0.0031	0.0022-0.008
	3.5	V	0.0003-0.0018	0.008-0.0140	0.0078-0.0157	0.010-0.0300	0.0016-0.0031	0.0016-0.0031	0.0015-0.0073

36543_JOUR_C0009

TORQUE SPECIFICATIONS

All readings in ft. lbs.

Year	Engine Displacement Liters	Engine ID/VIN	Cylinder Head Bolts	Main Bearing Bolts	Rod Bearing Bolts	Crankshaft Damper Bolts	Flywheel Bolts	Manifold		Spark Plug	Oil Pan Drain Plug
								Intake	Exhaust		
2009	2.4	B	①	②	③	155	④	17	25	20	30
	2.4	B PZEV	①	②	③	155	④	17	25	20	30
	2.7	D	⑤	⑥	⑦	125	70	9	17	13	20
	3.5	V	⑧	⑨	⑦	70	70	⑩	⑪	20	20

① Short head bolt

  Step 1: 25 ft. lbs.

  Step 2: 45 ft. lbs.

  Step 3: 45 ft. lbs. again

  Step 4: Plus 1/4 turn

① Long head bolt

  Step 1: 25 ft. lbs.

  Step 2: 54 ft. lbs.

  Step 3: 54 ft. lbs. again

  Step 4: Plus 1/4 turn

② For bolts identified in procedure

  Step 1: 11 ft. lbs.

  Step 2: 20 ft. lbs.

  Step 3: Plus 1/8 turn

② For bolts not identified in procedure

  Step 1: 11 ft. lbs.

  Step 2: 33 ft. lbs.

  Step 3: Plus 1/8 turn

③ Step 1: 15 ft. lbs.

  Step 2: Plus 1/4 turn

④ Step 1: 22 ft. lbs.

  Step 2: Plus 55 degrees rotation

⑤ Step 1: Bolts 1-8 35 ft. lbs.

  Step 2: Bolts 1-8 55 ft. lbs.

  Step 3: Bolts 1-8 55 ft. lbs. again

  Step 4: Bolts 1-8 Plus 1/4 turn do not use torque wrench

  Step 5: Bolts 9-11 250 inch lbs.

⑥ Step 1: Main cap inner bolts 15 ft. lbs.

  Step 2: Main cap inner bolts Plus 1/4 turn

  Step 3: Windage tray bolts 20 ft. lbs.

  Step 4: Windage tray bolts Plus 1/4 turn

  Step 5: Main cap tie (horizontal) bolts 250 inch lbs.

⑦ Step 1: 20 ft. lbs.

  Step 2: Plus 1/4 turn

⑧ Step 1: 45 ft. lbs.

  Step 2: 65 ft. lbs.

  Step 3: 65 ft. lbs. again

  Step 4: Plus 1/4 turn do not use torque wrench

⑨ Step 1: Main cap inner bolts 15 ft. lbs.

  Step 2: Main cap inner bolts Plus 1/4 turn

  Step 3: Windage tray bolts 20 ft. lbs.

  Step 4: Windage tray bolts Plus 1/4 turn

  Step 5: Main cap tie (horizontal) bolts 20 ft. lbs.

⑩ Lower: 250 inch lbs. Upper: 105 inch lbs.

⑪ 200 inch lbs.

36543_JOUR_C0010

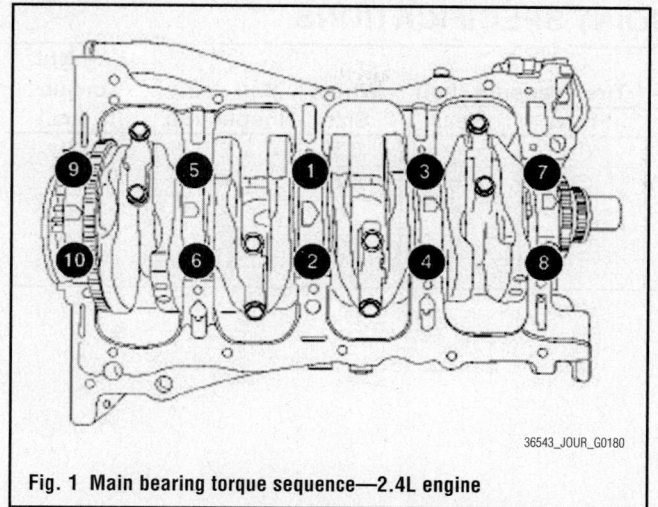

36543_JOUR_G0180

Fig. 1 Main bearing torque sequence—2.4L engine

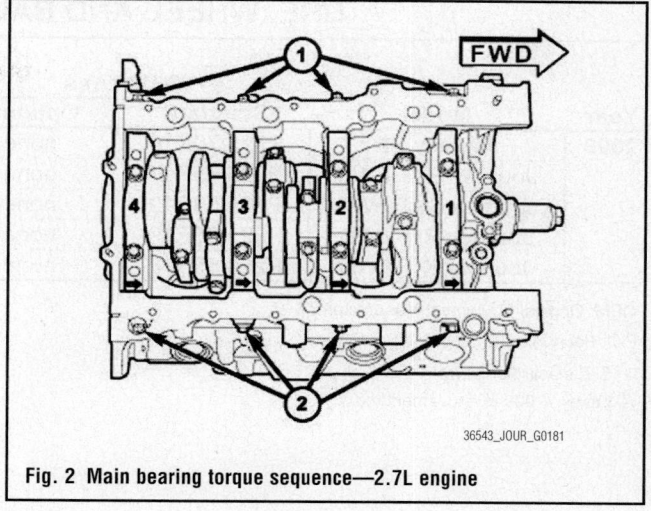

36543_JOUR_G0181

Fig. 2 Main bearing torque sequence—2.7L engine

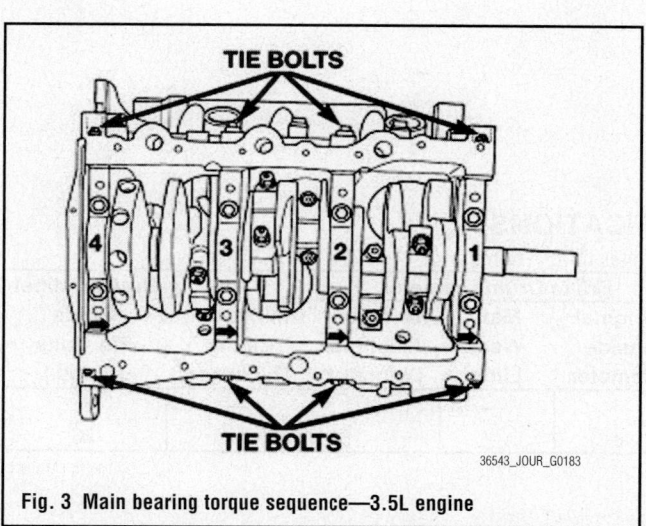

36543_JOUR_G0183

Fig. 3 Main bearing torque sequence—3.5L engine

WHEEL ALIGNMENT

Year	Model		Caster Range (+/-Deg.)	Caster Preferred Setting (Deg.)	Camber Range (+/-Deg.)	Camber Preferred Setting (Deg.)	Toe-in (Deg.)
2009	Journey	F	+2.00 to +4.00	+3.00	-0.65 to +0.45	-0.10	-0.25 + 0.45
		R	—	—	-1.25 to +0.05	-0.60	-0.30 + 0.30

36543_JOUR_C0011

TIRE, WHEEL AND BALL JOINT SPECIFICATIONS

| Year | Model | OEM Tires | | Tire Pressure (psi) | | Wheel Size | Ball Joint Inspection | Lug Nut Torque (ft. lbs.) |
		Standard	Optional	Front	Rear			
2009	Journey SE	P225/70R16	none	①	①	6.5	②	100
	Journey SXT FWD	P225/65R17	none	①	①	6.5	②	100
	Journey SXT AWD	P225/55R19	none	①	①	7	②	100
	Journey R/T FWD	P225/55R19	none	①	①	7	②	100
	Journey R/T AWD	P225/55R19	none	①	①	7.0	②	100

OEM: Original Equipment Manufacturer

PSI: Pounds Per Square Inch

① See placard on vehicle

② Lower: 0.039 in. movement max.

36543_JOUR_C0012

BRAKE SPECIFICATIONS

All measurements in inches unless noted

| Year | Model | | Brake Disc | | | Brake Drum Diameter | | | Minimum Lining Thickness | Brake Caliper Guide Pin Bolts (ft. lbs.) |
			Original Thickness	Minimum Thickness	Maximum Run-out	Original Inside Diameter	Max. Wear Limit	Maximum Machine Diameter		
2009	Journey	F	1.107	1.040	0.002	—	—	—	—	26
		R	0.482	0.409	0.002	—	—	—	—	26

36543_JOUR_C0013

SCHEDULED MAINTENANCE INTERVALS
Dodge Journey

TO BE SERVICED	SERVICE	VEHICLE MILEAGE INTERVAL (x1000)												
		7.5	15	22.5	30	37.5	45	52.5	60	67.5	75	82.5	90	97.5
Engine oil & filter*	R	✓	✓	✓	✓	✓	✓	✓	✓	✓	✓	✓	✓	✓
Brake hoses	S/I	✓	✓	✓	✓	✓	✓	✓	✓	✓	✓	✓	✓	✓
Coolant level, hoses & clamps	S/I	✓	✓	✓	✓	✓	✓	✓	✓	✓	✓	✓	✓	✓
CV joints & front suspension components	S/I	✓	✓	✓	✓	✓	✓	✓	✓	✓	✓	✓	✓	✓
Exhaust system	S/I	✓	✓	✓	✓	✓	✓	✓	✓	✓	✓	✓	✓	✓
Rotate tires	S/I	✓	✓	✓	✓	✓	✓	✓	✓	✓	✓	✓	✓	✓
Accessory drive belts	S/I		✓			✓	✓		✓		✓		✓	
Brake linings	S/I			✓			✓			✓			✓	
Air filter element	R					✓			✓				✓	
Spark plugs ① ②	R													
Lubricate front & rear ball joints	S/I				✓				✓				✓	
Engine coolant	R						✓				✓			
PCV valve	S/I								✓				✓	
Ignition cables ② ③	R													
Camshaft timing belt ④	R													

R: Replace   S/I: Service or Inspect

① 4-cylinder: every 30,000 miles.

② 6-cylinder: 100,000 miles.

③ 4-cylinder: 60,000 miles.

④ Replace at 105,000 miles for normal service; replace at 102,000 miles for severe service

FREQUENT OPERATION MAINTENANCE (SEVERE SERVICE)

If a vehicle is operated under any of the following conditions it is considered severe service:

- Extremely dusty areas.
- 50% or more of vehicle operatiing in 32°C (90°F) or higher temperatures, or constant operation in temperatures below 0°C (32°F).
- Prolonged idling (vehicle operation in stop and go traffic).
- Frequent short running periods (engine does not warm to normal operating temperatures).
- Police, taxi, delivery usage or trailer towing usage.

Oil & oil filter change: change every 3,000 miles.

Rotate tires every 6,000 miles.

Brake linings: check every 12,000 miles.

Air filter element: change every 15,000 miles.

Automatic transaxle fluid: service or inspect every 15,000 miles.

PCV valve: check every 30,000 miles.

Engine coolant, replace at 36,000, 51,000 & 81,000 miles.

*Oil Change Indicator System

On Electronic Vehicle Information Center (EVIC) equipped vehicles, "Oil Change Required" is displayed in the EVIC and a single chime sounds, indicating that an oil change is necessary. On non-EVIC equipped vehicles, "Change Oil" flashes in the instrument cluster and a single chime sounds indicating that an oil change is necessary. Illumination of the oil change message is based on the operating conditions of the vehicle. When the message is illuminated, the vehicle must be serviced within 500 miles.

The oil change indicator will not monitor the time since the last oil change. Change the oil if it has been more than 6 months since the last oil change, even if the oil change indicator message is not illuminated.

Under no circumstances should oil change intervals exceed 6,000 miles or 6 months, whichever comes first.

To reset the oil change indicator, perform the following procedure:

1. Turn the ignition switch to the ON position. Do not start the engine.
2. Fully press the accelerator pedal 3 times within 10 seconds.
3. Turn the ignition switch to the LOCK position.

If the indicator message illuminates when the vehicle is started, repeat the procedure.

PRECAUTIONS

Before servicing any vehicle, please be sure to read all of the following precautions, which deal with personal safety, prevention of component damage, and important points to take into consideration when servicing a motor vehicle:

• Never open, service or drain the radiator or cooling system when the engine is hot; serious burns can occur from the steam and hot coolant.

• Observe all applicable safety precautions when working around fuel. Whenever servicing the fuel system, always work in a well-ventilated area. Do not allow fuel spray or vapors to come in contact with a spark, open flame, or excessive heat (a hot drop light, for example). Keep a dry chemical fire extinguisher near the work area. Always keep fuel in a container specifically designed for fuel storage; also, always properly seal fuel containers to avoid the possibility of fire or explosion. Refer to the additional fuel system precautions later in this section.

• Fuel injection systems often remain pressurized, even after the engine has been turned **OFF**. The fuel system pressure must be relieved before disconnecting any fuel lines. Failure to do so may result in fire and/or personal injury.

• Brake fluid often contains polyglycol ethers and polyglycols. Avoid contact with the eyes and wash your hands thoroughly after handling brake fluid. If you do get brake fluid in your eyes, flush your eyes with clean, running water for 15 minutes. If eye irritation persists, or if you have taken brake fluid internally, IMMEDIATELY seek medical assistance.

• The EPA warns that prolonged contact with used engine oil may cause a number of skin disorders, including cancer. You should make every effort to minimize your exposure to used engine oil. Protective gloves should be worn when changing oil. Wash your hands and any other exposed skin areas as soon as possible after exposure to used engine oil. Soap and water, or waterless hand cleaner should be used.

• All new vehicles are now equipped with an air bag system, often referred to as a Supplemental Restraint System (SRS) or Supplemental Inflatable Restraint (SIR) system. The system must be disabled before performing service on or around system components, steering column, instrument panel components, wiring and sensors. Failure to follow safety and disabling procedures could result in accidental air bag deployment, possible personal injury and unnecessary system repairs.

• Always wear safety goggles when working with, or around, the air bag system. When carrying a non-deployed air bag, be sure the bag and trim cover are pointed away from your body. When placing a non-deployed air bag on a work surface, always face the bag and trim cover upward, away from the surface. This will reduce the motion of the module if it is accidentally deployed. Refer to the additional air bag system precautions later in this section.

• Clean, high quality brake fluid from a sealed container is essential to the safe and proper operation of the brake system. You should always buy the correct type of brake fluid for your vehicle. If the brake fluid becomes contaminated, completely flush the system with new fluid. Never reuse any brake fluid. Any brake fluid that is removed from the system should be discarded. Also, do not allow any brake fluid to come in contact with a painted surface; it will damage the paint.

• Never operate the engine without the proper amount and type of engine oil; doing so WILL result in severe engine damage.

• Timing belt maintenance is extremely important. Many models utilize an interference-type, non-freewheeling engine. If the timing belt breaks, the valves in the cylinder head may strike the pistons, causing potentially serious (also time-consuming and expensive) engine damage. Refer to the maintenance interval charts for the recommended replacement interval for the timing belt, and to the timing belt section for belt replacement and inspection.

• Disconnecting the negative battery cable on some vehicles may interfere with the functions of the on-board computer system(s) and may require the computer to undergo a relearning process once the negative battery cable is reconnected.

• When servicing drum brakes, only disassemble and assemble one side at a time, leaving the remaining side intact for reference.

• Only an MVAC-trained, EPA-certified automotive technician should service the air conditioning system or its components.

BRAKES

GENERAL INFORMATION

PRECAUTIONS

• Certain components within the ABS system are not intended to be serviced or repaired individually.

• Do not use rubber hoses or other parts not specifically specified for and ABS system. When using repair kits, replace all parts included in the kit. Partial or incorrect repair may lead to functional problems and require the replacement of components.

• Lubricate rubber parts with clean, fresh brake fluid to ease assembly. Do not use shop air to clean parts; damage to rubber components may result.

• Use only DOT 3 brake fluid from an unopened container.

• If any hydraulic component or line is removed or replaced, it may be necessary to bleed the entire system.

• A clean repair area is essential. Always clean the reservoir and cap thoroughly before removing the cap. The slightest amount of dirt in the fluid may plug an orifice and impair the system function. Perform repairs after components have been thoroughly cleaned; use only denatured alcohol to clean components. Do not allow ABS components to come into contact with any substance containing mineral oil; this includes used shop rags.

ANTI-LOCK BRAKE SYSTEM (ABS)

• The Anti-Lock control unit is a microprocessor similar to other computer units in the vehicle. Ensure that the ignition switch is **OFF** before removing or installing controller harnesses. Avoid static electricity discharge at or near the controller.

• If any arc welding is to be done on the vehicle, the control unit should be unplugged before welding operations begin.

WHEEL SPEED SENSORS

REMOVAL & INSTALLATION

➡**See front knuckle or rear hub and bearing.**

BLEEDING PROCEDURE

➡**This bleeding procedure is only for the vehicle's base brakes hydraulic system. For bleeding the antilock brakes hydraulic system, refer to Bleeding the ABS System.**

❋❋ CAUTION

Before removing the master cylinder reservoir cap, thoroughly clean the cap and master cylinder fluid reservoir to prevent dirt and other foreign matter from dropping into the master cylinder fluid reservoir.

➡**The following wheel sequence should be used when bleeding the brake hydraulic system. The use of this wheel sequence will ensure adequate removal of all trapped air from the brake hydraulic system.**

- Left Rear Wheel
- Right Front Wheel
- Right Rear Wheel
- Left Front Wheel

➡**When bleeding the brake system, some air may be trapped in the brake lines far upstream, as much as ten feet from the bleeder screw. Therefore, it is essential to have a fast flow of a large volume of brake fluid when bleeding the brakes to ensure all the air gets out.**

Pressure bleeding the brakes is recommended, although the brakes may be manually bled or pressure bled. Refer to the appropriate following procedure.

Pressure Bleeding Procedure

Follow the pressure bleeder manufacturer's instructions for use of the pressure bleeding equipment.

1. Install Master Cylinder Pressure Bleed Cap, Special Tool 6921, or equivalent on the master cylinder fluid reservoir. Attach the fluid hose from the pressure bleeder to the fitting on Special Tool 6921.

2. Attach a clear plastic hose to the bleeder screw and feed the hose into a clear jar containing enough fresh brake fluid to submerge the end of the hose.

3. Open the bleeder screw at least one full turn or more to obtain a steady stream of brake fluid.

4. After approximately 120-240 ml (4-8 ounces) of fluid have been bled through the brake circuit and an air-free flow is maintained in the clear plastic hose and jar, close the bleeder screw.

5. Repeat this procedure at all the remaining bleeder screws.

6. Check and adjust brake fluid level to the FULL mark on the reservoir.

7. Check brake pedal travel and feel. If pedal travel is excessive or if the pedal feels excessively spongy, some air may still be trapped in the system. Re-bleed the brakes as necessary including the IPB Caliper Brake Bleeding Procedure on the rear calipers as listed below.

8. Test drive the vehicle to verify the brakes are operating properly and pedal feel is correct.

Manual Bleeding Procedure

➡**To bleed the brakes manually, the aid of a helper will be required.**

1. Attach a clear plastic hose to the bleeder screw and feed the hose into a clear jar containing enough fresh brake fluid to submerge the end of the hose.

2. Have a helper pump the brake pedal three or four times and hold it in the down position.

3. With the pedal in the down position, open the bleeder screw at least one full turn.

4. Once the brake pedal has dropped, close the bleeder screw. After the bleeder screw is closed, release the brake pedal.

5. Repeat the above steps until all trapped air is removed from that wheel circuit (usually four or five times).

6. Bleed the remaining wheel circuits in the same manner until all air is removed from the brake system. Monitor the fluid level in the master cylinder reservoir to make sure it does not go dry.

7. Check and adjust brake fluid level to the FULL mark.

8. Check brake pedal travel and feel. If pedal travel is excessive or if the pedal feels excessively spongy, some air may still be trapped in the system. Re-bleed the brakes as necessary including the IPB Caliper Brake Bleeding Procedure on the rear calipers as listed below.

9. Test drive the vehicle to verify the brakes are operating properly and pedal feel is correct.

IPB Caliper Brake Bleeding Procedure

➡**The following procedure is normally only necessary if a rear brake caliper has been removed and installed, or replaced.**

Perform the following procedure on each rear brake caliper as necessary.

1. Raise and support vehicle.

2. Remove the wheel mounting nuts, then the tire and wheel assembly.

3. Remove the brake caliper lower guide pin bolt.

4. Swing the caliper assembly upward, pivoting off the upper guide pin, until clear of the adapter bracket.

5. Remove the outboard pad from the adapter bracket.

6. Return the caliper back down over the adapter bracket into mounted position and install the lower guide pin bolt finger tight.

7. Slowly pump the brake pedal until the caliper fingers touch the outboard surface of the brake rotor. Release the pedal.

8. Remove the brake caliper lower guide pin bolt.

9. Swing the caliper assembly upward, pivoting off the upper guide pin, until clear of the adapter bracket.

10. Reinstall the outboard pad in the adapter bracket.

11. Open the caliper bleeder screw at least one full turn.

12. If necessary, seat (bottom) the caliper piston in the bore as follows:

   a. Assemble a 3/8 in. drive ratchet handle and an extension.

   b. Insert the extension through Special Tool 8807-1.

   c. Place Special Tool 8807-2 on the end of the extension.

   d. Insert lugs on Special Tool 8807-2 into notches in face of caliper piston.

   e. Thread the screw drive on 8807-1 down until it contacts the top of 8807-2 which is against the caliper piston. Do not over tighten the screw-drive. Damage to the piston can occur.

   f. Turn 8807-2 with the ratchet, rotating the piston in a clockwise direction until fully seated (bottomed) in the bore. It may be necessary to turn 8807-1 with 8807-2 to start the process of piston retraction.

13. Close the bleeder screw.

14. Return the caliper back down over the adapter bracket into mounted position and install the lower guide pin bolt finger tight.

15. Have a helper pump the brake pedal three or four times and hold it in the down position.

16. With the pedal in the down position, open the bleeder screw at least one full turn and let out fluid and air, if any.

17. Once the brake pedal has dropped, close the bleeder screw. Once the bleeder screw is closed, release the brake pedal.

18. Repeat the previous three steps until all trapped air is removed.

19. Tighten the guide pin bolt to 26 ft. lbs. (35 Nm).

20. Repeat the above procedure on the opposite rear brake caliper as necessary.

21. Check brake pedal travel and feel. If pedal travel is still excessive or if the pedal feels excessively spongy, repeat the entire procedure as necessary.

22. Install the tire and wheel assembly. Install and tighten wheel mounting nuts to 100 ft. lbs. (135 Nm).

23. Lower the vehicle.

24. Test drive the vehicle to verify the brakes are operating properly and pedal feel is correct.

BLEEDING THE ABS SYSTEM

The base brake's hydraulic system must be bled anytime air enters the hydraulic system. The ABS must always be bled anytime it is suspected that the HCU has ingested air.

Brake systems with ABS must be bled as two independent braking systems. The non-ABS portion of the brake system with ABS is to be bled the same as any non-ABS system.

The ABS portion of the brake system must be bled separately. Use the following procedure to properly bleed the brake hydraulic system including the ABS.

➡**During the brake bleeding procedure, be sure the brake fluid level remains close to the FULL level in the master cylinder fluid reservoir. Check the fluid level periodically during the bleeding procedure and add Mopar® DOT 3 brake fluid as required.**

When bleeding the ABS system, the following bleeding sequence must be followed to insure complete and adequate bleeding.

1. Make sure all hydraulic fluid lines are installed and properly torqued.

2. Connect the scan tool to the diagnostics connector. The diagnostic connector is located under the lower steering column cover to the left of the steering column.

3. Using the scan tool, check to make sure the ABM does not have any fault codes stored. If it does, clear them.

❄ **WARNING**

When bleeding the brake system wear safety glasses. A clear bleed tube (1) must be attached to the bleeder screws and submerged in a clear container filled part way with clean brake fluid (2). Direct the flow of brake fluid away from yourself and the painted surfaces of the vehicle. Brake fluid at high pressure may come out of the bleeder screws when opened.

➡**Pressure bleeding is recommended to bleed the base brake system to ensure all air is removed from system. Manual bleeding may also be used, but additional time is needed to remove all air from system.**

4. Bleed the base brake system.

5. Using the scan tool, select ECU VIEW, followed by ABS MISCELLANEOUS FUNCTIONS to access bleeding. Follow the instructions displayed. When finished, disconnect the scan tool and proceed.

6. Bleed the base brake system a second time. Check brake fluid level in the reservoir periodically to prevent emptying, causing air to enter the hydraulic system.

7. Fill the master cylinder fluid reservoir to the FULL level.

8. Test drive the vehicle to be sure the brakes are operating correctly and that the brake pedal does not feel spongy.

BRAKES   **FRONT DISC BRAKES**

❄ **CAUTION**

Dust and dirt accumulating on brake parts during normal use may contain asbestos fibers from production or aftermarket brake linings. Breathing excessive concentrations of asbestos fibers can cause serious bodily harm. Exercise care when servicing brake parts. Do not sand or grind brake lining unless equipment used is designed to contain the dust residue. Do not clean brake parts with compressed air or by dry brushing. Cleaning should be done by dampening the brake components with a fine mist of water, then wiping the brake components clean with a dampened cloth. Dispose of cloth and all residue containing asbestos fibers in an impermeable container with the appropriate label. Follow practices prescribed by the Occupational Safety and Health Administration (OSHA) and the Environmental Protection Agency (EPA) for the handling, processing, and disposing of dust or debris that may contain asbestos fibers.

BRAKE CALIPER

REMOVAL & INSTALLATION
See Figures 4 and 5.

1. Using a brake pedal holding tool, depress the brake pedal past its first one inch (25 mm) of travel and hold it in this position. This will isolate the master cylinder from the brake hydraulic system and will not allow the brake fluid to drain out of the master cylinder reservoir when the lines are opened.

2. Raise and support the vehicle.

3. Remove the wheel mounting nuts, then the tire and wheel assembly.

4. Remove the banjo bolt (3) connecting the brake flex hose (2) to the brake caliper

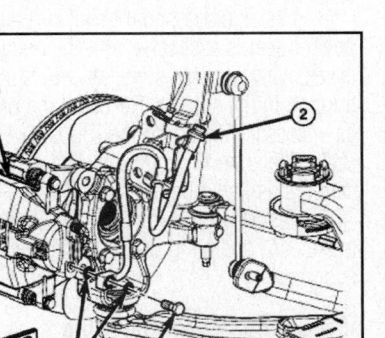

36543_JOUR_G0021

Fig. 4 Caliper hose components

36543_JOUR_G0022

Fig. 5 Caliper components

(1). There are two washers (4) that will come off with the banjo bolt. Discard the washers. They should not be reused.

> ✳✳ **CAUTION**
>
> **When removing or installing a caliper guide pin bolt, it is necessary to hold the guide pin stationary while turning the bolt. Hold the guide pin stationary using a wrench placed upon the pin's hex-shaped head.**

5. Remove the two brake caliper guide pin bolts (2, 3).

6. Slide the disc brake caliper (4) from the disc brake adapter bracket (1) and brake pads and remove.

To install:

7. Completely retract the caliper piston back into the bore of the caliper. Use a C-clamp to retract the piston. Place a wood block over the piston before installing the C-clamp to avoid damaging the piston.

> ✳✳ **CAUTION**
>
> **Use care when installing the caliper (4) onto the adapter bracket (1) to avoid damaging the guide pin boots.**

8. Install the disc brake caliper over the brake pads on the brake caliper adapter bracket.

> ✳✳ **CAUTION**
>
> **When removing or installing a caliper guide pin bolt, it is necessary to hold the guide pin stationary while turning the bolt. Hold the guide pin stationary using a wrench placed upon the pin's hex-shaped head.**

9. Align the caliper guide pin bolt holes with the adapter bracket. Install the upper (2) and lower (3) caliper guide pin bolts. Tighten the guide pin bolts to 26 ft. lbs. (35 Nm).

10. Install the banjo bolt (3) connecting the brake flex hose (2) to the brake caliper (1). Install NEW brake hose washers (4) on each side of the hose fitting as the banjo bolt is guided through the fitting. Thread the banjo bolt into the caliper and tighten it to 19 ft. lbs. (26 Nm).

11. Install the tire and wheel assembly. Install and tighten the wheel mounting nuts to 100 ft. lbs. (135 Nm).

12. Lower the vehicle.

13. Remove the brake pedal holding tool.

14. Bleed the caliper as necessary.

15. Road test the vehicle and make several stops to wear off any foreign material on the brakes and to seat the brake shoes.

DISC BRAKE PADS

REMOVAL & INSTALLATION

See Figure 6.

1. Raise and support the vehicle.

2. Remove the wheel mounting nuts, then the tire and wheel assembly.

3. Remove the disc brake caliper from the disc brake adapter bracket and brake pads.

4. Remove the brake pads (4, 5) from the caliper adapter bracket (2).

To install:

➡ **Make sure that the audible wear indicator (if equipped) is placed toward the top when the inboard brake pad is installed on each side of the vehicle.**

➡ **If the brake pads have a protective paper on the rear face of the brake pad plate, it must be removed before pad installation.**

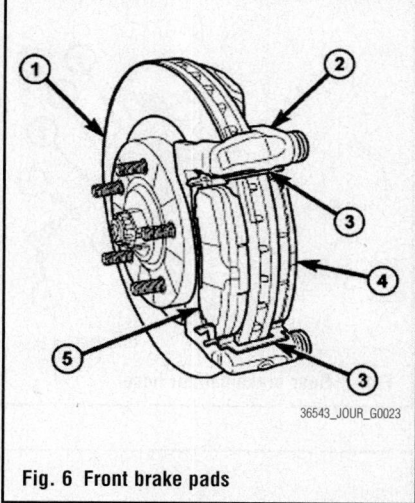

Fig. 6 Front brake pads

5. Place the brake pads (4, 5) in the abutment shims (3) clipped into the disc brake caliper adapter bracket (2). Place the pad with the wear indicator (if equipped) attached on the inboard side (2).

6. Completely retract the caliper piston back into the bore of the caliper.

> ✳✳ **CAUTION**
>
> **Use care when installing the caliper (4) onto the adapter bracket (1) to avoid damaging the boots.**

7. Install the disc brake caliper over the brake pads on the brake caliper adapter bracket.

8. Pump the brake pedal several times before moving the vehicle to set the pads to the brake rotor.

9. Check and adjust the brake fluid level in the reservoir as necessary.

10. Road test the vehicle and make several stops to wear off any foreign material on the brakes and to seat the brake pads.

BRAKES

> ✳✳ **CAUTION**
>
> **Dust and dirt accumulating on brake parts during normal use may contain asbestos fibers from production or aftermarket brake linings. Breathing excessive concentrations of asbestos fibers can cause serious bodily harm. Exercise care when servicing brake parts. Do not sand or grind brake lining unless equipment used is designed to contain the dust residue. Do not clean brake parts with compressed air or by dry brushing. Cleaning should be done by dampen-ing the brake components with a fine mist of water, then wiping the brake components clean with a dampened cloth. Dispose of cloth and all residue containing asbestos fibers in an impermeable container with the appropriate label. Follow practices prescribed by the Occupational Safety and Health Administration (OSHA) and the Environmental Protection Agency (EPA) for the handling, processing, and disposing of dust or debris that may contain asbestos fibers.**

REAR DISC BRAKES

BRAKE CALIPER

REMOVAL & INSTALLATION

See Figures 7 and 8.

1. Disconnect and isolate battery negative cable from battery post.

2. Using a brake pedal holding tool as shown, depress brake pedal past its first inch of travel and hold it in this position. Holding pedal in this position will isolate master cylinder from hydraulic brake system and will not allow brake fluid to drain out of brake fluid reservoir while brake lines are open.

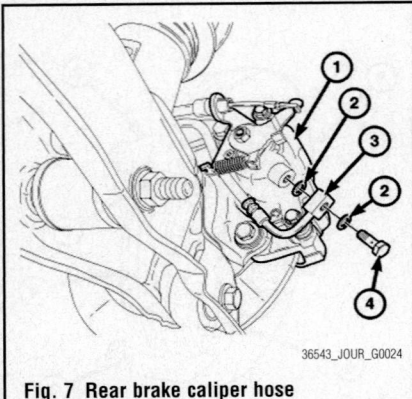

Fig. 7 Rear brake caliper hose

36543_JOUR_G0024

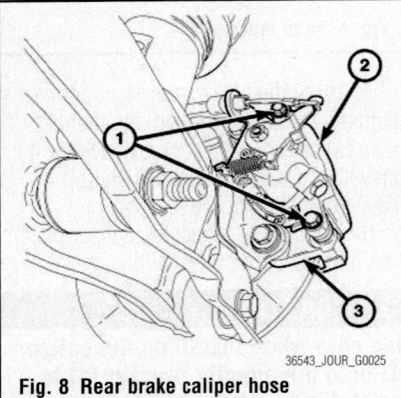

Fig. 8 Rear brake caliper hose

36543_JOUR_G0025

3. Raise and support vehicle.

4. Remove wheel mounting nuts (3), then tire and wheel assembly (1).

5. Manually release the parking brake cable tension.

6. Collapse the cable retainer fingers (2) at the end of the cable housing (3), then pull the cable housing out of the mounting bracket (1).

7. Slide the cable strand out of the mounting bracket, then pull the parking brake cable strand (1) upward and unhook it from the caliper lever (2).

8. Remove the banjo bolt (4) connecting the brake flex hose (3) to the brake caliper (1). There are two washers (2) that will come off with the banjo bolt. Discard the washers. They should not be reused.

※※ CAUTION

When removing or installing a caliper guide pin bolt, it is necessary to hold the guide pin stationary while turning the bolt. Hold the guide pin stationary using a wrench placed upon the pin's hex-shaped head.

9. Remove two caliper guide pin bolts (1).

10. Slide the disc brake caliper (2) from the disc brake adapter bracket (3) and brake pads.

To install:

※※ CAUTION

When installing a NEW brake caliper it is necessary to bleed the brakes using a special procedure which has been integrated to this installation procedure.

11. Remove the outboard pad (5) from the adapter bracket.

※※ CAUTION

Use care when installing the caliper (2) onto the adapter bracket to avoid damaging the guide pin boots.

12. Install the disc brake caliper (2) over the inboard brake pad on the brake caliper adapter bracket and the brake rotor.

※※ CAUTION

When removing or installing a caliper guide pin bolt, it is necessary to hold the guide pin stationary while turning the bolt. Hold the guide pin stationary using a wrench placed upon the pin's hex-shaped head.

13. Align the caliper guide pin bolt holes with the adapter bracket. Install the upper and lower caliper guide pin bolts (1). Lightly tighten the guide pin bolts at this time.

14. Install the banjo bolt (4) connecting the brake flex hose (3) to the brake caliper (1). Be sure to install a NEW brake hose washer (2) on each side of the hose fitting as the banjo bolt is guided through the fitting. Thread the banjo bolt into the caliper and tighten it to 19 ft. lbs. (26 Nm).

15. Access the interior of the vehicle, remove the brake pedal holder, then slowly pump the brake pedal until the rear caliper fingers touch the outboard surface of the brake rotor where the brake pad was removed. Release the pedal.

※※ CAUTION

When removing or installing a caliper guide pin bolt, it is necessary to hold the guide pin stationary while turning the bolt. Hold the guide pin stationary using a wrench placed upon the pin's hex-shaped head.

16. Remove two caliper guide pin bolts (1).

17. Slide the disc brake caliper (2) from the disc brake adapter bracket (3).

18. Reinstall the outboard pad (5) in the adapter bracket (3).

19. Open the caliper bleeder screw at least one full turn.

20. Seat (bottom) the caliper piston in the bore as follows:

a. Assemble a 3/8 in. drive ratchet handle and an extension (3).

b. Insert the extension through Special Tool 8807–1 (2).

c. Place Special Tool 8807–2 (1) on the end of the extension.

d. Insert lugs on Special Tool 8807–2 into notches in face of caliper piston (5).

e. Thread the screw drive on 8807–1 down until it contacts the top of 8807–2 which is against the caliper piston. Do not over tighten the screw-drive. Damage to the piston can occur.

f. Turn 8807–2 with the ratchet, rotating the piston in a clockwise direction until fully seated (bottomed) in the bore. It may be necessary to turn 8807–1 with 8807–2 to start the process of piston retraction.

21. Close the bleeder screw.

※※ CAUTION

Use care when installing the caliper onto the adapter bracket to avoid damaging the guide pin boots.

※※ CAUTION

When removing or installing a caliper guide pin bolt, it is necessary to hold the guide pin stationary while turning the bolt. Hold the guide pin stationary using a wrench placed upon the pin's hex-shaped head.

22. Return the brake caliper back down over the adapter bracket into mounted position and install the guide pin bolts (1). Tighten both guide pin bolts to 26 ft. lbs. (35 Nm).

➡**While bleeding air from the brake caliper in the following steps, be sure to monitor the fluid level in the master cylinder reservoir making sure it does not go dry.**

23. Have a helper pump the brake pedal three or four times and hold it in the down position.

24. With the pedal in the down position, open the bleeder screw at least one full turn and let out fluid and air, if any.

25. Once the brake pedal has dropped, close the bleeder screw. Once the bleeder screw is closed, release the brake pedal.

26. Repeat the previous three steps as necessary until all trapped air is removed.

27. If necessary, bleed remaining wheel circuits as necessary using normal bleeding procedure. Refer to bleeding.

28. Pull the parking brake cable strand (1) outward from the cable housing and hook it onto the caliper lever (2).

29. Push the excess cable strand back into the cable housing, then insert the cable housing (3) into the mounting bracket (1) until the retainer fingers (2) lock into place. Make sure both fingers are engaged preventing removal of the cable from the bracket.

30. Install tire and wheel assembly (1). Install and tighten wheel mounting nuts (3) to 100 ft. lbs. (135 Nm).

31. Reconnect the parking brake cable equalizer and reset the cable tension.

32. Lower vehicle.

33. Connect battery negative (-) cable to battery post.

34. Road test vehicle making several stops to wear off any foreign material on brakes and to seat brake pads.

DISC BRAKE PADS

REMOVAL & INSTALLATION

See Figure 9.

1. Remove the disc brake caliper from the disc brake adapter bracket and brake pads.

2. Remove the brake pads (2, 5) from the caliper adapter bracket (3).

To install:

✳✳ CAUTION

Anytime the brake rotor or brake pads are being replaced, the rear caliper piston must be seated (bottomed) to compensate for the new brake rotor or lining. Because the parking brake self-adjuster mechanism is attached to the piston, a special seating

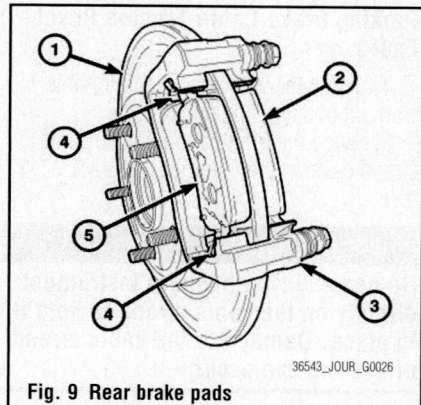

Fig. 9 Rear brake pads

method is required. The only acceptable method is by rotating the piston back into the bore using Retractor, Special Tool 8807, as described below. Any other seating method will damage the self-adjuster mechanism.

3. If necessary, seat (bottom) the caliper piston in the bore as follows:

a. Assemble a 3/8 in. drive ratchet handle and an extension (3).

b. Insert the extension through Special Tool 8807–1 (2).

c. Place Special Tool 8807–2 (1) on the end of the extension.

d. Insert lugs on Special Tool 8807–2 into notches in face of caliper piston (5).

e. Thread the screw drive on 8807–1 down until it contacts the top of 8807–2 which is against the caliper piston. Do not over tighten the screw-drive. Damage to the piston can occur.

f. Turn 8807–2 with the ratchet, rotating the piston in a clockwise direction until fully seated (bottomed) in the bore. It may be necessary to turn 8807–1 with 8807–2 to start the process of piston retraction.

4. Make sure abutment shims (4) are in

place on both upper and lower slide abutments of caliper adapter (3).

➡**If the brake pads have a protective paper on the rear face of the brake pad plate, it must be removed before pad installation.**

5. Place the brake pads (2, 5) in the abutment shims (3) clipped into the disc brake caliper adapter bracket (3).

✳✳ CAUTION

Use care when installing the caliper (2) onto the adapter bracket to avoid damaging the guide pin boots.

6. Install the disc brake caliper (2) over the brake pads on the brake caliper adapter bracket (3).

✳✳ CAUTION

When removing or installing a caliper guide pin bolt, it is necessary to hold the guide pin stationary while turning the bolt. Hold the guide pin stationary using a wrench placed upon the pin's hex-shaped head.

7. Align the caliper guide pin bolt holes with the adapter bracket. Install the upper and lower caliper guide pin bolts (1). Tighten the guide pin bolts to 26 ft. lbs. (35 Nm).

8. Install tire and wheel assembly (1). Install and tighten wheel mounting nuts (3) to 100 ft. lbs. (135 Nm).

9. Lower vehicle.

10. Pump brake pedal several times to ensure vehicle has a firm brake pedal before moving vehicle.

11. Check and adjust brake fluid level as necessary.

12. Road test vehicle and make several stops to wear off any foreign material on brakes and to seat brake pads.

BRAKES   PARKING BRAKE

PARKING BRAKE CABLES

ADJUSTMENT

Parking Brake Cable Tension Release - Foot Lever

See Figure 10.

Use the following procedure to release the tension from the parking brake cables and the automatic adjuster in the parking brake lever (pedal) mechanism when required.

1. Release the parking brake.

2. Raise the vehicle to a comfortable working position and support.

3. Wipe the parking brake cable strands (front and both rear) clean where visible at the intermediate bracket.

✳✳ CAUTION

Do not use any type of sharp instrument to hold the cable strand in place. Damage to the cable strand or coating can occur.

4. Pull rearward on the equalizer (4) until the front cable stops, then grasp the front cable (5) strand and hold it in this position. Disconnect the equalizer from the front cable strand.

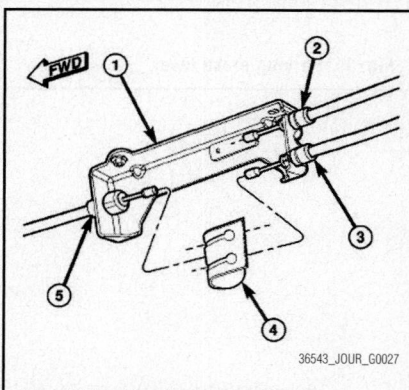

Fig. 10 Parking brake equalizer

5. Release the front cable strand allowing the lever automatic self-adjusting mechanism to pull the front cable strand forward. This action allows the adjuster mechanism to rotate around to its stop, removing tension from the adjuster and front parking brake cable.

Parking Brake Cable Tension Release - Hand Lever

See Figure 11.

1. Release the parking brake.
2. Block the tire and wheel assemblies so the vehicle does not move once the parking brake lever is released.
3. Release the parking brake.
4. Remove the cover from the side of the parking brake lever. To remove the cover, unclip it at the top and rotate it counter-clockwise.
5. Place the parking brake lever (1) in the fully released (down) position.
6. Loosen the adjusting nut (2) on the end of the front parking brake cable. Back it off to the end of the cable.
7. If the cable equalizer/bent nail tensioner needs to be removed, perform the following:
   a. Raise the vehicle to a comfortable working position and support.
   b. Remove the parking brake cable equalizer/bent nail tensioner (4) from the three parking brake cables (2, 3, 5).

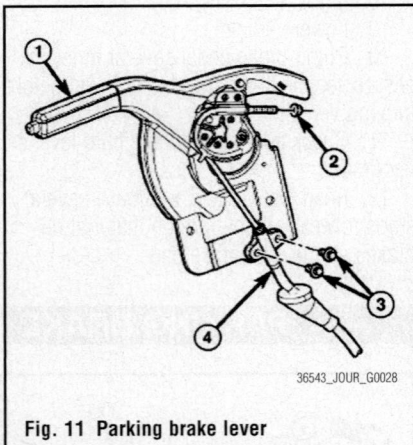

Fig. 11 Parking brake lever

36543_JOUR_G0028

Parking Brake Cable Tension Reset - Foot Lever

1. Raise the vehicle to a comfortable working position and support.
2. Wipe the front parking brake cable strand clean at the intermediate bracket (1) area.

✳✳ CAUTION

Do use any type of sharp instrument directly on the cable strand to hold it in place. Damage to the cable strand or coating can occur.

3. Clamp an appropriate pair of pliers on the front parking brake cable button (2) only and pull the cable stand rearward until it stops, then grasp the front cable strand and hold it in this position. Remove the pliers from the button.
4. While holding the front cable in this position, install the equalizer (2) (attached to both rear cables) on the front parking brake cable.
5. Release the grasp on the front parking brake cable.
6. Lower the vehicle.
7. Apply and release the parking brake lever one time. This will seat the parking brake cables and allow the auto adjuster in the parking brake lever mechanism to correctly tension the parking brake cables.

Parking Brake Cable Tension Reset - Hand Lever

1. If the cable equalizer/bent nail tensioner needs to be installed on the cables, perform the following:
   a. Raise the vehicle to a comfortable working position and support.
   b. Connect the parking brake cable equalizer/bent nail tensioner (4) to the three parking brake cables (2, 3, 5).
   c. Remove any slack from the parking brake cables by pushing the front cable strand forward into the housing until slack is removed.
   d. Lower the vehicle.
2. If not installed during Step 1, make sure the parking brake cable equalizer/bent nail tensioner is attached to all three parking brake cables

3. Make sure that the front parking brake cable is properly aligned and installed on the cable track of the parking brake lever.

➡**Actuating the parking brake lever to its fully applied position one time after tightening the adjustment nut will yield (stretch) the bent nail portion of the equalizer approximately ¼ inch (6 mm). This process will correctly set the parking brake cable tension.**

4. Adjust parking brake cable tension using the following steps:
   a. Make sure the parking brake lever in the fully released (down) position.
   b. While maintaining tension on the cable, tighten the adjusting nut (2) on the front parking brake cable until 34 millimeters (1.34 in.) of thread (1) is out past the end of the adjustment nut.
   c. Actuate the parking brake lever to its fully applied position one time, then reposition it to its fully released (down) position.
5. Raise the vehicle to a point where the rear wheels just clear the floor.
6. Check the rear wheels of the vehicle; they should rotate freely without dragging.
7. Apply the parking brake. Check the rear wheels of the vehicle. They should not rotate.
8. Return the parking brake lever to its fully released (down) position and check the rear wheels. They should rotate freely without dragging.
9. Apply the parking brake.
10. Lower the vehicle.
11. Install the cover on the side of the parking brake lever.

PARKING BRAKE SHOES

REMOVAL & INSTALLATION

Refer to the Rear Disc Brake Pads procedure.

CHASSIS ELECTRICAL | AIR BAG (SUPPLEMENTAL RESTRAINT SYSTEM)

GENERAL INFORMATION

✳✳ CAUTION

These vehicles are equipped with an air bag system. The system must be disarmed before performing service on, or around, system components, the steering column, instrument panel components, wiring and sensors. Failure to follow the safety precautions and the disarming procedure could result in accidental air bag deployment, possible injury and unnecessary system repairs.

SERVICE PRECAUTIONS

To avoid serious or fatal injury on vehicles equipped with the Supplemental Restraint System (SRS), never attempt to repair the electrically conductive circuits or wiring components related to the SRS. Such repairs can compromise the conductivity and current carrying capacity of those critical electrical circuits, which may cause SRS components not to deploy when required, or to deploy when not required. Any wire harness containing broken, cut, burned or otherwise damaged electrically conductive SRS wiring, terminals or connector components must be removed and replaced with an entire new wire harness. Only minor cuts or abrasions of wire and terminal insulation where the conductive material has not been damaged, or connector insulators where the integrity of the latching and locking mechanisms have not been compromised may be repaired using appropriate methods. Disconnect and isolate the battery negative (ground) cable, then wait two minutes for the system capacitor to discharge before performing further diagnosis or service. This is the only sure way to disable the SRS. Failure to take the proper precautions could result in accidental airbag deployment.

To avoid serious or fatal injury during and following any seat belt or child restraint anchor service, carefully inspect all seat belts, buckles, mounting hardware, retractors, tether straps, and anchors for proper installation, operation, or damage. Replace any belt that is cut, frayed, or torn. Straighten any belt that is twisted. Tighten any loose fasteners. Replace any belt that has a damaged or ineffective buckle or retractor. Replace any belt that has a bent or damaged latch plate or anchor plate. Replace any child restraint anchor or the unit to which the anchor is integral that has been

bent or damaged. Never attempt to repair a seat belt or child restraint component. Always replace damaged or ineffective seat belt and child restraint components with the correct, new and unused replacement parts listed in the Chrysler Mopar® Parts Catalog. Failure to follow these instructions may result in possible serious or fatal injury.

To avoid serious or fatal injury on vehicles equipped with side curtain or seat (thorax) airbags, disable the Supplemental Restraint System (SRS) before attempting any Occupant Restraint Controller (ORC) diagnosis or service. The ORC contains a rollover sensor, which enables the system to deploy the side curtains or seat airbags in the event of a vehicle rollover event. If an ORC is accidentally rolled during service while still connected to battery power, the side curtain and seat airbags will deploy. Disconnect and isolate the battery negative (ground) cable, then wait two minutes for the system capacitor to discharge before performing further diagnosis or service. This is the only sure way to disable the SRS. Failure to take the proper precautions could result in accidental airbag deployment.

To avoid serious or fatal injury on vehicles equipped with airbags, disable the Supplemental Restraint System (SRS) before attempting any steering wheel, steering column, airbag, seat belt tensioner, impact sensor, or instrument panel component diagnosis or service. Disconnect and isolate the battery negative (ground) cable, then wait two minutes for the system capacitor to discharge before performing further diagnosis or service. This is the only sure way to disable the SRS. Failure to take the proper precautions could result in accidental airbag deployment.

To avoid serious or fatal injury on vehicles equipped with airbags, before performing any welding operations disconnect and isolate the battery negative (ground) cable and disconnect all wire harness connectors from the Occupant Restraint Controller (ORC). Failure to take the proper precautions could result in accidental airbag deployment and other possible damage to the Supplemental Restraint System (SRS) circuits and components.

To avoid serious or fatal injury, do not attempt to dismantle an airbag unit or tamper with its inflator. Do not puncture, incinerate or bring into contact with electricity. Do not store at temperatures exceeding 93° C (200° F). An airbag inflator unit may contain sodium azide and potassium nitrate. These materials are poisonous and

extremely flammable. Contact with acid, water, or heavy metals may produce harmful and irritating gases (sodium hydroxide is formed in the presence of moisture) or combustible compounds. An airbag inflator unit may also contain a gas canister pressurized to over 17.24 kPa (2500 psi). Failure to follow these instructions may result in possible serious or fatal injury.

To avoid serious or fatal injury when handling a seat belt tensioner retractor or buckle, proper care should be exercised to keep fingers out from under the retractor or buckle cover and away from the seat belt webbing or cable where it exits from the retractor or buckle cover.

To avoid serious or fatal injury, replace all Supplemental Restraint System (SRS) components only with parts specified in the Chrysler Mopar® Parts Catalog. Substitute parts may appear interchangeable, but internal differences may result in inferior occupant protection. Failure to follow these instructions may result in possible serious or fatal injury.

To avoid serious or fatal injury, the fasteners, screws, and bolts originally used for the Supplemental Restraint System (SRS) components must never be replaced with any substitutes. These fasteners have special coatings and are specifically designed for the SRS. Anytime a new fastener is needed, replace it with the correct fasteners provided in the service package or specified in the Chrysler Mopar® Parts Catalog. Failure to follow these instructions may result in possible serious or fatal injury.

To avoid serious or fatal injury when a steering column has an airbag unit attached, never place the column on the floor or any other surface with the steering wheel or airbag unit face down. Failure to follow these instructions may result in possible serious or fatal injury.

DISARMING THE SYSTEM

Disconnect and isolate the battery negative (ground) cable, then wait two minutes for the system capacitor to discharge before performing further diagnosis or service. This is the only sure way to disable the SRS.

ARMING THE SYSTEM

Supplemental Restraints Verification Test

➡**The following procedure should be performed using a diagnostic scan tool to verify proper Supplemental Restraint**

System (SRS) operation following the service or replacement of any SRS component. Refer to the appropriate diagnostic procedures.

❉ CAUTION

To avoid serious or fatal injury on vehicles equipped with airbags, disable the Supplemental Restraint System (SRS) before attempting any steering wheel, steering column, airbag, seat belt tensioner, impact sensor, or instrument panel component diagnosis or service. Disconnect and isolate the battery negative (ground) cable, then wait two minutes for the system capacitor to discharge before performing further diagnosis or service. This is the only sure way to disable the SRS. Failure to take the proper precautions could result in accidental airbag deployment.

1. During the following test, the battery negative cable remains disconnected and isolated, as it was during the Supplemental Restraint System (SRS) component removal and installation procedures.

2. Be certain that the diagnostic scan tool contains the latest version of the proper diagnostic software. Connect the scan tool to the 16-way Data Link Connector (DLC) (2). The DLC is located on the driver side lower edge of the instrument panel within a rectangular cutout in the lower instrument panel reinforcement, just forward of the instrument panel steering column opening cover (1).

3. Turn the ignition switch to the ON position and exit the vehicle with the scan tool.

4. Check to be certain that nobody is in the vehicle, then reconnect the battery negative cable.

5. Using the scan tool, read and record the active (current) Diagnostic Trouble Code (DTC) data.

6. Next, use the scan tool to read and record any stored (historical) DTC data.

7. If any DTC is found in Step #5 or Step #6 , refer to the appropriate diagnostic information.

8. Use the scan tool to erase the stored DTC data. If any problems remain, the stored DTC data will not erase. Refer to the appropriate diagnostic information to diagnose any stored DTC that will not erase. If the stored DTC information is successfully erased, go to Step #9 .

9. Turn the ignition switch to the OFF position for about 15 seconds, and then back to the ON position. Observe the airbag indicator in the instrument cluster. It should light from four to six seconds, and then go out. This indicates that the SRS is functioning normally and that the repairs are complete. If the airbag indicator fails to light, or lights and stays ON, there is still an active SRS fault or malfunction. Refer to the appropriate diagnostic information to diagnose the problem.

CLOCKSPRING CENTERING

A service replacement clockspring is shipped with the clockspring pre-centered and with a molded plastic locking pin installed. This locking pin should not be removed until the steering wheel has been installed on the steering column. If the locking pin is removed before the steering wheel is installed, the clockspring centering procedure must be performed.

➡ When a clockspring is installed into a vehicle without properly centering and locking the entire steering system, the Steering Angle Sensor (SAS) data does not agree with the true position of the steering system and causes the Electronic Stability Program (ESP) system to shut down. This may also damage the clockspring without any immediate malfunction. Unlike some other Chrysler vehicles, this SAS never requires calibration. However, upon each new ignition ON cycle, the steering wheel must be rotated slightly to initialize the SAS.

➡ Determining if the clockspring/SAS is centered is also possible electrically using the diagnostic scan tool. Steering wheel position is displayed as ANGLE with a range of up to 900 degrees. Refer to the appropriate menu item on the diagnostic scan tool.

➡ Before starting this procedure, be certain to turn the steering wheel until the front wheels are in the straight-ahead position and that the entire steering system is locked or inhibited from rotation.

➡ The clockspring may be centered and the rotor may be rotated freely once the steering wheel has been removed.

1. Place the front wheels in the straight-ahead position and inhibit the steering column shaft from rotation.

2. Remove the steering wheel from the steering shaft.

3. Rotate the clockspring rotor clockwise to the end of its travel. Do not apply excessive torque.

4. From the end of the clockwise travel, rotate the rotor about two and one-half turns counterclockwise. Turn the rotor slightly clockwise or counterclockwise as necessary so that the clockspring airbag pigtail wires and connector receptacle are at the top and the dowel or drive pin is at the bottom.

5. The clockspring is now centered. Secure the clockspring rotor to the clockspring case using a locking pin or some similar device to maintain clockspring centering until the steering wheel is reinstalled on the steering column.

DRIVE TRAIN

AUTOMATIC TRANSAXLE

REMOVAL & INSTALLATION

41TE Transaxle

See Figures 12 and 13.

➡ **The 41TE transaxle is on vehicles with the 2.4L engine.**

➡ **If transaxle assembly is being replaced or overhauled (clutch and/or seal replacement), it is necessary to perform the TCM Quick Learn Procedure.**

Refer to the exploded view as necessary when performing the following steps.

1. Disconnect battery cable.
2. Remove the engine cover.
3. Remove air cleaner assembly.
4. Remove dipstick tube. Plug hole to prevent debris from entering transaxle.
5. Using Disconnect Release Tool 8875A, disconnect the transmission cooler line quick-connect fittings.
6. Unplug the transaxle electrical connector at the Powertrain Control Module (PCM).
7. Disconnect shift cable from manual valve lever and bracket.
8. Remove throttle body support bracket.
9. Disconnect Oxygen Sensor harness retainer from transaxle case.
10. Remove rear mount bracket-to-transaxle case bolts.
11. Remove starter upper bracket-to-block bolt.

12. Raise and safely support the vehicle.
13. Remove side and lower shields.
14. Remove halfshafts.
15. Remove rear mount bracket lower bolt.
16. Remove rear mount thru-bolt.
17. Remove rear mount-to-cross member bolts.
18. Remove rear mount and bracket.
19. Support engine/transaxle with screw jack and wood block on engine oil pan.
20. Remove front mount thru-bolt.
21. Remove crossmember bolts and remove the crossmember.
22. Remove front mount bracket to block and transaxle.
23. Remove front mount bracket and mount.
24. Remove starter.
25. Remove converter dust shield.
26. Remove torque converter bolts.
27. Remove left mount bracket-to-transaxle bolts.
28. Carefully lower engine/transaxle assembly to gain access to and remove transaxle-to-engine bolts.
29. With aid of helper or transmission jack, remove transaxle assembly from vehicle.

To install:

30. Install transaxle to engine. Install and transaxle-to-engine bolts and tighten to 70 ft. lbs. (95 Nm).
31. Install upper mount to transaxle.
32. Raise engine/transaxle assembly into position, install through bolt at rear mount and tighten to 55 ft. lbs. (70 Nm).

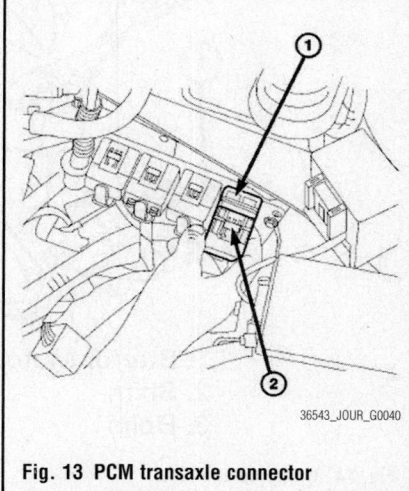

36543_JOUR_G0040

Fig. 13 PCM transaxle connector

33. Remove transmission jack and screw jack.
34. Install torque converter bolts and tighten to 65 ft. lbs. (88 Nm).
35. Install torque converter dust shield.
36. Install starter motor assembly and lower bolt.
37. Install crossmember assembly.
38. Install rear mount/bracket assembly.
39. Install halfshafts.
40. Lower vehicle.
41. Install starter upper bracket-to-block bolt.
42. Install throttle body support bracket (if equipped).
43. Connect gearshift cable to manual valve lever.
44. Connect the powertrain control module electrical connector.
45. Connect oil cooler lines to the transaxle. Verify connection by pulling outward.
46. Install dipstick tube.
47. Install air cleaner assembly.
48. Install splash shields.
49. Connect battery negative cable.

62TE Transaxle

See Figures 14 and 15.

➡ **This transaxle is found on vehicles with 2.7L and 3.5L engines.**

1. Open hood.
2. Disconnect negative battery cable.
3. Unplug the electrical connector to the Inlet Air Temperature sensor at the air box.
4. Remove the hold-down bolt and hose clamp at the air box.
5. Remove the air box.

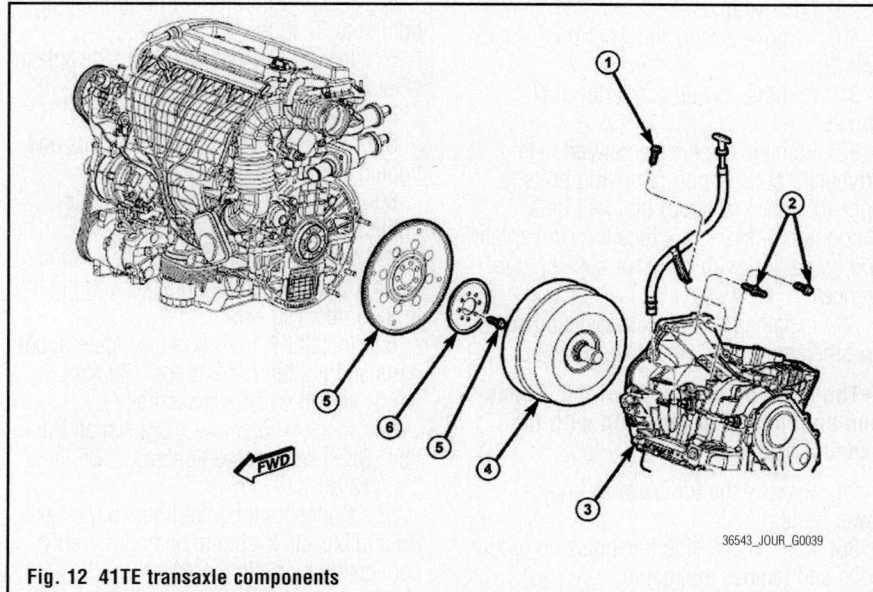

36543_JOUR_G0039

Fig. 12 41TE transaxle components

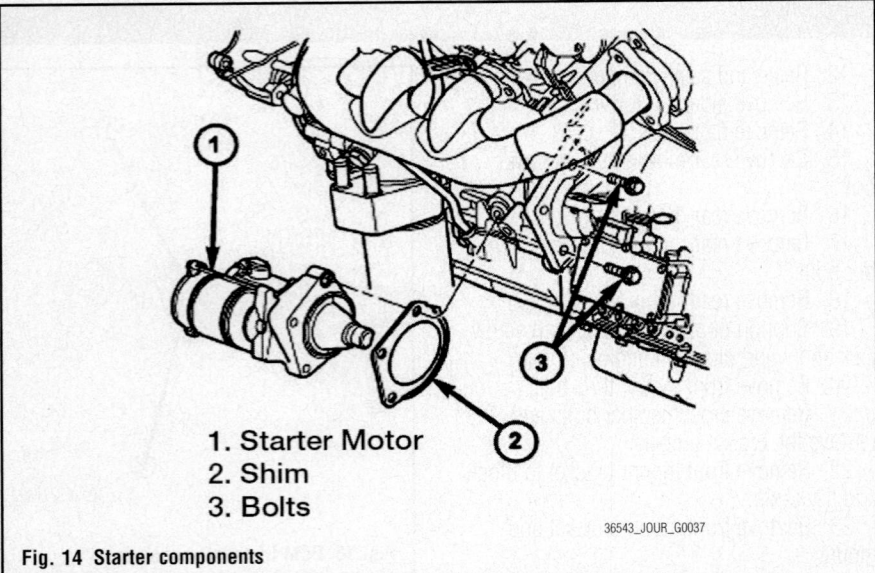

1. Starter Motor
2. Shim
3. Bolts

36543_JOUR_G0037

Fig. 14 Starter components

6. Disconnect gearshift cable from transaxle manual valve lever.

7. Disconnect gearshift cable from the bracket.

8. Disconnect the electrical connector at the Crankshaft Position (CKP) sensor.

9. Remove hold-down bolt at the Crankshaft Position (CKP) sensor.

10. Remove the Crankshaft Position (CKP) sensor.

11. Disconnect oil cooler lines from transaxle using Disconnect Tool 8875A.

➡**The transmission harness will be removed with the transaxle.**

12. Unplug the transaxle electrical connector at the powertrain control module.

13. Remove the transaxle upper bell-housing-to-block bolts.

14. Remove rear transaxle mount bracket bolts (1).

15. Remove the bolt holding the ground cable to the front mount bracket.

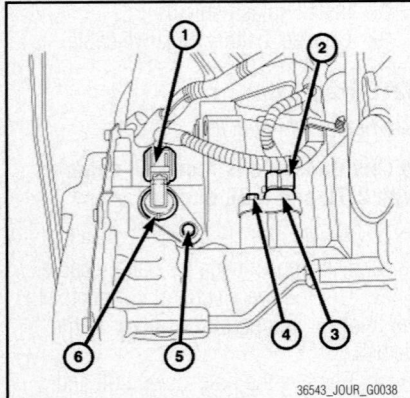

36543_JOUR_G0038

Fig. 15 Transaxle connectors

16. Raise the vehicle on the hoist.

17. Remove both halfshafts.

18. Remove the front and both side splash shields.

19. Remove the PTU if equipped.

20. Remove the mount through bolt.

21. Remove the transmission crossmember bolts.

22. Remove the transmission crossmember.

23. Remove the front mount bracket bolts.

24. Remove the front mount bracket.

25. Disconnect starter motor electrical connectors. Remove starter motor and shim.

26. Remove bolts to exhaust bracket.

27. Remove cross under pipe.

28. Remove bolts to stand off bracket.

29. Remove bracket.

30. Remove torque converter dust shield bolt (3).

31. Remove torque converter dust shield.

32. Remove the torque converter-to-driveplate bolts. Upon removing bolts, a tight-tolerance (slotted) bolt will be encountered. Mark this location (driveplate and converter) with paint for assembly reference.

33. Install a transmission jack and support the engine. Secure transaxle to jack.

➡**The bolts on each side of the inspection opening were removed with the exhaust bracket.**

34. Remove the transaxle-to-engine lower bolts.

35. Remove left side transmission mount bolts and remove the mount.

36. Lower transaxle from engine compartment.

37. Disconnect solenoid/pressure switch assembly connector (2).

38. Disconnect both output speed sensor connectors (1, 2).

39. Disconnect input speed sensor connector.

40. Remove the harness from transaxle.

To install:

41. Install the wiring harness onto the transaxle.

42. Connect input speed sensor connector.

43. Connect both output speed sensor connectors (1, 2).

44. Connect solenoid/pressure switch assembly connector (2).

➡**The two transaxle-to-engine bolts next to the inspection cover will have a exhaust bracket under them.**

45. Install transaxle into position. Install the transaxle-to-engine two outer lower bolts and torque to 52 ft. lbs. (70 Nm).

46. Install torque converter-to-driveplate bolts and tighten to 65 ft. lbs. (88 Nm).

47. Install torque converter dust shield and bolt tighten to 53 inch lbs. (6 Nm).

48. Install bolts to stand off bracket and tighten to 70 ft. lbs. (95 Nm).

49. Install bolts (3) to exhaust bracket.

50. Install the cross under pipe.

51. Install the starter motor.

52. Install the PTU if equipped.

53. Install the front mount bracket.

54. Install the front mount bracket bolts and tighten to 74 ft. lbs. (100 Nm).

55. Install the transmission crossmember and tighten to 37 ft. lbs. (50 Nm).

56. Install front mount through bolt and tighten to 37 ft. lbs. (50 Nm)

57. Install the front and both side splash shields.

58. Lower the vehicle.

59. Install the left side mount bolts and tighten to 74 ft. lbs. (100 Nm)

60. Install the rear mount and bolts, tighten to 74 ft. lbs. (100 Nm).

61. Install the bolt holding the ground cable to the front mount bracket and tighten to 37 ft. lbs. (50 Nm)

62. Install the transaxle-to-engine upper bolts and tighten to 52 ft. lbs. (70 Nm).

63. Install halfshaft assemblies.

64. Install and connect Crankshaft Position (CKP) sensor and tighten to 105 inch lbs. (12 Nm).

65. Connect oil cooler lines to transaxle. An audible 'click' should be heard. Verify connection by pulling outward.

66. Connect gearshift cable to the bracket

67. Connect gearshift cable to transaxle manual valve lever. Verify adjustment.

68. Connect the powertrain control module electrical connector.

69. Install the air box and the engine cover.

70. Connect the intake air tempter sensor electrical connector.

71. Connect negative battery cable.

MANUAL TRANSAXLE ASSEMBLY

REMOVAL & INSTALLATION

1. Raise hood.
2. Remove engine cover.
3. Remove air cleaner assembly.
4. Disconnect negative battery cable.
5. Unplug the speed sensor connector (if equipped).
6. Disconnect back-up lamp switch connector.
7. Remove shift cable-to-bracket clips.
8. Disconnect shift selector and crossover cable from levers. Remove cables and secure out of the way.
9. Remove the slave cylinder hydraulic line bolt at bracket.
10. Remove the clip at the hydraulic line and separate the line.
11. Remove the air inlet tube by loosening the screw at the throttle body.
12. Remove the throttle body support bracket bolts.
13. Remove the throttle body support bracket.
14. Remove upper bell housing bolts.
15. Remove the starter bolts and slide the starter back.
16. Remove the upper transmission mount-to-bracket bolts.
17. Raise vehicle on hoist.
18. Remove the splash shields.
19. Remove transaxle oil drain plug and drain oil into a suitable container. Reinstall drain plug and tighten to 120 inch lbs. (14 Nm).
20. Remove both halfshafts.
21. Support the engine with a screw jack.
22. Remove bell housing dust cover.
23. Remove four modular clutch-to-drive plate bolts. While removing bolts, one tight-tolerance (slotted) drive plate hole will be encountered. When this bolt is removed, mark drive plate and modular clutch assembly at this location, and be sure to align marks upon reassembly.
24. Remove the transmission crossmember.
25. Install a transmission jack.

26. Remove the rear transmission through bolt.

27. Remove the rear transmission mount bolts and mount from the frame.

28. Remove the rear transmission mount bracket bolts and bracket from transmission.

29. Remove the remaining transmission bell housing bolts.

30. Carefully lower engine and transaxle on screw jack and transmission jack until proper removal clearance is obtained.

31. Obtain a helper to assist in holding transaxle while removing transaxle-to-engine mounting bolts.

32. Remove transaxle from vehicle.

33. Remove clutch module from transaxle input shaft.

34. Remove front mount bracket and hydraulics from transaxle.

To install:

35. Install clutch module (if equipped) onto input shaft.

36. Install transaxle into position.

37. Install the transmission crossmember.

38. Install the rear transmission mount bracket and bolts, tighten to 50 ft. lbs. (68 Nm).

39. Install the rear transmission mount and bolts, tighten to 50 ft. lbs. (68 Nm).

40. Install the rear transmission mount through bolt at this time and tighten to 50 ft. lbs. (68 Nm).

41. Install transaxle-to-engine mounting bolts and tighten to 35 ft. lbs. (48 Nm).

42. Raise engine and transaxle with screw jack and transmission jack until upper mount bracket aligns with upper mount. Install mount bolts and tighten to 50 ft. lbs. (68 Nm).

43. Remove screw jack.

44. Install four modular clutch-to-drive plate bolts. Align drive plate and modular clutch alignment marks placed upon disassembly. Start with tight-tolerance (slotted) hole, install and torque bolts to 65 ft. lbs. (88 Nm).

45. Install starter motor and tighten bolts to 40 ft. lbs. (54 Nm). Make sure to fasten ground cable to upper starter bolt.

46. Install bell housing dust cover.

47. Install both front axle driveshafts.

48. Fill transaxle with suitable amount of fluid (2.7 liters).

49. Lower the vehicle.

50. Install the remaining bell housing bolts and tighten to 35 ft. lbs. (48 Nm).

51. Connect the hydraulic clutch slave cylinder lines and clip, verify connection by pushing and pulling connection.

52. Bleed slave cylinder.

53. Connect shift and selector cables to shift lever. Install cables to bracket.

54. Connect back-up lamp switch connector.

55. Connect the vehicle speed sensor connector if equipped.

56. Install the air cleaner assembly.

57. Connect the negative battery cable.

58. Road test vehicle and inspect for leaks.

CLUTCH DRIVEN DISC & PRESSURE PLATE

REMOVAL & INSTALLATION

See Figures 16 and 17.

✳✳ WARNING

Chrysler does not manufacture any vehicles or replacement parts that contain asbestos. Aftermarket products may or may not contain asbestos. Refer to aftermarket product packaging for product information. Whether the product contains asbestos or not, dust and dirt can accumulate on manual clutch parts during normal use. Follow practices prescribed by appropriate regulations for the handling, processing and disposing of dust and debris

1. Remove transaxle (3) from vehicle.
2. Remove modular clutch assembly (1) from transaxle input shaft.

To install:
3. Install clutch module onto input shaft.
4. Install transaxle into vehicle.

CLUTCH MASTER CYLINDER

REMOVAL & INSTALLATION

See Figure 18.

1. Remove the engine cover.
2. Remove air cleaner assembly.
3. Disconnect battery negative cable.
4. Remove lower instrument panel bezel.
5. Disconnect the pushrod (3) at the clutch pedal.
6. Disconnect hydraulic supply tube (2) at clutch master cylinder by pulling retaining clip then pulling out on tube. To completely drain clutch master cylinder and tubing, remove brake master cylinder cap band drain fluid into suitable container.
7. Disconnect clutch master cylinder supply line from brake master cylinder reservoir (1). Cap off or collect fluid spillage from reservoir port.

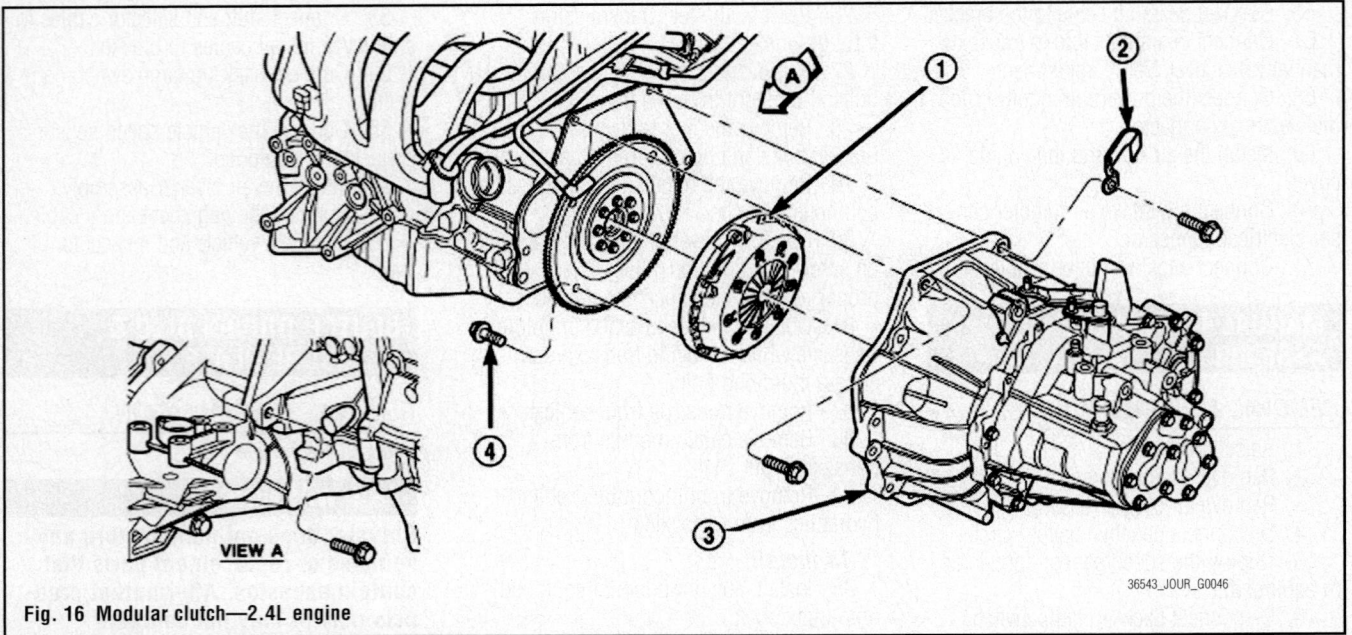

Fig. 16 Modular clutch—2.4L engine

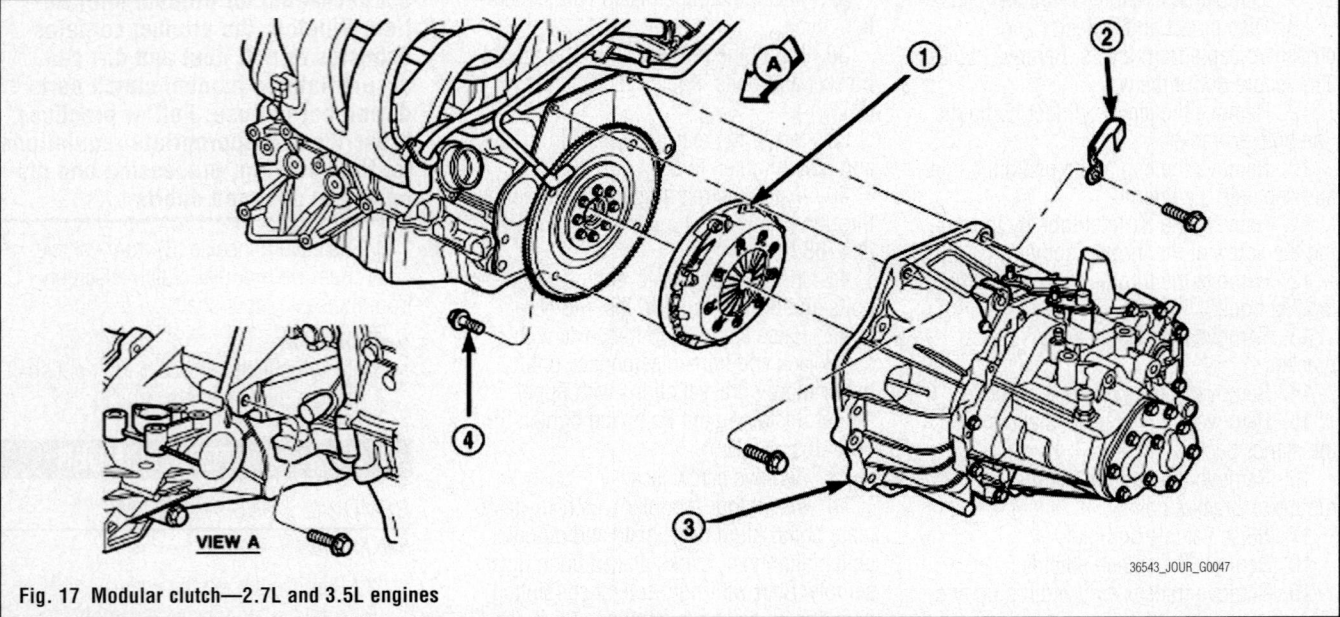

Fig. 17 Modular clutch—2.7L and 3.5L engines

❋❋ CAUTION

Use care when removing clutch master cylinder from engine compartment. Aggressive handling can result in a damaged hydraulic tube and improper clutch release operation upon reassembly.

❋❋ CAUTION

Brake fluid will damage painted surfaces. If brake fluid is spilled on any painted surfaces, wash it off immediately with water.

8. Remove master cylinder assembly (4) from mounting position by turning ¼ turn and carefully work hydraulic pipe from out of left rail retainer and engine compartment.

To install:

9. Install clutch master cylinder (4).

10. Insert tube (2) into master cylinder port and install retaining clip.

11. Connect clutch master cylinder supply hose (2) to brake master cylinder reservoir (1).

12. Verify that brake master cylinder reservoir is full and cap is off.

13. Install clutch master cylinder body to clutch pedal and ¼ turn to secure.

14. Connect clutch master cylinder rod (3) to clutch pedal pin. An audible "click" should be heard.

15. Install lower instrument panel bezel.

16. Connect battery negative cable.

17. Install air cleaner assembly.

18. Verify that brake master cylinder reservoir is full. Top off with DOT 3 brake fluid if necessary.

19. Bleed clutch system.

20. Actuate clutch pedal a minimum of fifteen times to allow any air ingested into the system to vent to the master cylinder reservoir. If residual air becomes trapped in

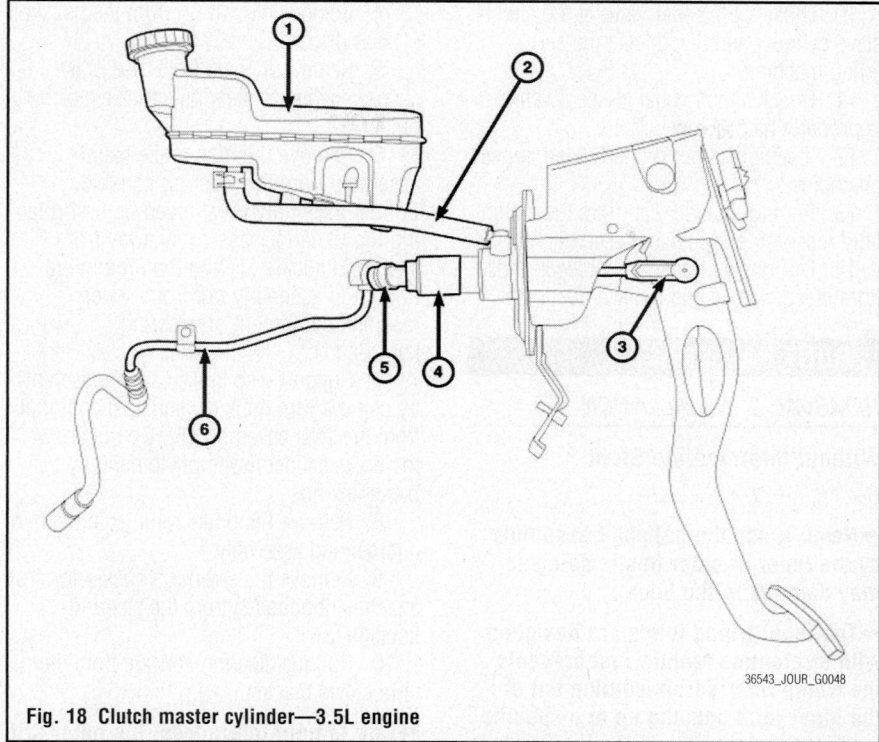

Fig. 18 Clutch master cylinder—3.5L engine

the system, it is necessary to bleed the clutch hydraulic system.

21. Verify proper clutch release system operation.

CLUTCH SLAVE CYLINDER

REMOVAL & INSTALLATION

See Figure 19.

➡ **To prevent drainage of clutch master cylinder assembly upon slave cylinder removal, it is necessary to make sure brake master cylinder fluid level is full and reservoir cap is installed tight.**

1. Remove transaxle from vehicle.
2. Disconnect the clutch hydraulic line (6) from the bleeder assembly (2).

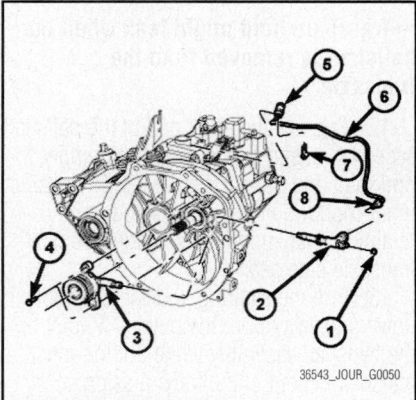

Fig. 19 Clutch slave cylinder

3. Disconnect and remove bleeder assembly (2) from the clutch master cylinder (3).
4. Remove the slave cylinder-to-clutch bellhousing bolts (4) and remove slave cylinder (3) from transaxle.

To install:

5. Install slave cylinder (3) to transaxle using new bolts (4).

➡ **Torque three CSC body screws first, then torque the fluid tube attachment.**

6. Torque slave cylinder-to-case bolts in three steps:
   • Step 1: 18 inch lbs. (2 Nm)
   • Step 2: 44 inch lbs. (5 Nm)
   • Step 3: 88 inch lbs. (10 Nm)
7. Install the bleeder (2).
8. Reconnect the clutch hydraulic line (6) to the bleeder (2).
9. Install transaxle.
10. Bleed clutch hydraulic system

CLUTCH HYDRAULIC SYSTEM BLEEDING

BLEEDING PROCEDURE

Manual Bleeding Clutch Hydraulic Circuit

See Figure 20.

➡ **An assistant is required to perform this procedure**

1. Verify fluid level in clutch/brake cylinder. Top off with DOT 3 brake fluid as necessary. Leave cap off.
2. Raise vehicle on hoist.

➡ **The container must be positioned at a lower level than the bleeder valve on the clutch slave cylinder**

3. Remove the dust cap from the bleed port on the clutch slave cylinder and install suitable size and length of clear hose (4) to monitor and divert fluid into a suitable container.
4. Lower vehicle, but only enough to gain access to and fill the brake master cylinder.
5. Have the assistant press down and hold the clutch pedal until it reaches the floor.

➡ **Do not allow clutch/brake fluid reservoir to run dry while fluid exits bleed port. If the reservoir runs dry during this procedure, it must be refilled. and this step must be repeated.**

➡ **Ensure the assistant does not release the clutch pedal from the floor while the bleed port on the clutch slave cylinder is open. Otherwise, air will enter the clutch hydraulic circuit.**

6. Open the bleed port on the clutch slave cylinder enough to allow hydraulic fluid to drain. Any air in the system will escape at this time.
7. Close the bleed port on the clutch slave cylinder, and have the assistant release the clutch pedal to the full up position.
8. Repeat steps 5 through 7 at least 15 times or until air bubbles are no longer present in the clutch hydraulic fluid.
9. Slowly actuate the clutch pedal 10 times between the full up and pedal stop position.

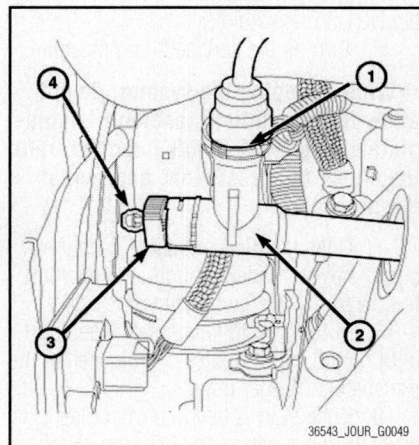

Fig. 20 Bleeding clutch master cylinder

10. Apply parking brake. Start engine and verify clutch operation and pedal feel. If the clutch pedal feels fine and the transaxle can be easily shifted from neutral to any gear, the clutch is operating correctly. If pedal still feels spongy or clutch does not fully disengage, excessive air is still trapped within the system, most likely at the master cylinder.

11. Disconnect the hose from the bleed port on the clutch master cylinder and install the dust cap.

12. Top off brake master cylinder fluid level with DOT 3 brake fluid as necessary.

Power Manual Bleeding Clutch Hydraulic Circuit

1. Remove reservoir cap and connect bleeder cap to clutch/brake fluid reservoir.

➥Use Bleeder Cap/Modified reservoir cap adapter Snap-on #901-059 or equivalent.

2. Connect service filling machine to bleeder cap.

➥Use Service Filling Machine/Brake power bleeder or equivalent.

3. Service filling machine should be pressurized between 2.0 and 2.5 bar (29 - 36 PSI).

4. Remove dust cap from bleeder valve and connect the transparent bleeder hose to bleeder valve.

➥Use Bleeder Container to capture hydraulic fluid and the Transparent Bleeder Hose to route fluid to container.

➥The Container must be at a lower level than the bleeder valve on the clutch slave cylinder.

5. Place the other end of hose in the bleeder container to capture the used fluid. The end of the hose MUST be submerged in the DOT 3 brake fluid.

6. Turn on the service filling machine.

➥While bleeding the system, do not allow the clutch fluid reservoir to completely empty out. If this happens, refill the clutch fluid reservoir, and repeat the procedure.

7. Open the bleeder valve (3) on the clutch slave cylinder enough to allow fluid to flow from the clutch hydraulic system.

8. Allow fluid to flow out of bleed port until no more air bubbles can be seen in the transparent bleeder hose.

9. Once fluid is free of air bubbles; make 15 quick actuations between clutch pedal stop positions.

10. Close the bleeder valve at the clutch slave cylinder and disconnect the service filling machine.

11. Check clutch pedal to see if vehicle is properly bled.

12. If vehicle is not properly bled, repeat procedure.

13. Remove bleeder cap from the clutch fluid reservoir and replace reservoir cap.

14. Disconnect transparent bleeder hose from bleeder valve and replace dust cap.

FRONT HALFSHAFT

REMOVAL & INSTALLATION

Without Intermediate Shaft

See Figure 21.

➥Never grasp the halfshaft assembly by the inner or outer boots; doing so may damage to the boot.

➥The inner tripod joints are designed with a retention feature that prevents the tripod rollers from coming out of the inner joint housing up to a specific load. If this feature is overcome and any of the rollers are pulled past the retention feature the joint will "lock-up" and no longer function properly. The entire halfshaft assembly must be replaced if this occurs.

➥Some halfshafts use a tuned rubber damper weight. When replacing a half-shaft assembly, be sure the replacement halfshaft has a damper weight.

1. Raise and safely support the vehicle.
2. Remove the wheel and tire assembly from the vehicle.
3. Apply the service brakes to keep hub from turning, then loosen the halfshaft nut (2).

➥Do not re-use the hub nut. The hub nut is a single-use type. A new hub nut is required for reassembly.

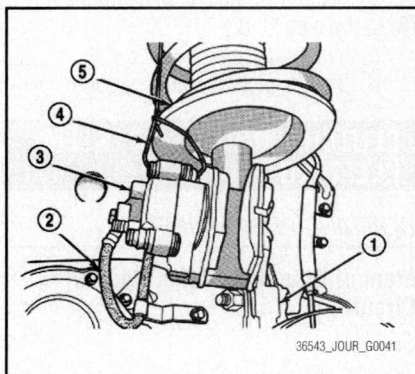

Fig. 21 Knuckle and strut assembly

36543_JOUR_G0041

4. Remove the nut (2) from the halfshaft (1) and discard it.

5. Remove the two front disc brake caliper adapter to steering knuckle attaching bolts (4) .

6. Remove the disc brake caliper assembly from the steering knuckle. Caliper assembly is removed by first rotating top of caliper assembly away from steering knuckle (1) and then removing bottom of assembly out from under machined abutment on steering knuckle (1).

7. Support disc brake caliper assembly by using a wire hook (4) and suspending it from the strut assembly (5). Do not allow the brake caliper assembly to hang by the brake flex hose (2).

8. Remove the brake rotor from the hub and bearing assembly.

9. Remove the steering knuckle-to-strut attachment bolts (2) from the steering knuckle (3).

10. Pull the steering knuckle from the strut clevis bracket.

➥Due to tight tolerances, the outer C/V joint might have to be forced apart from the bearing hub. To avoid damaging the axle halfshaft threads during removal, install the hub nut (4) so that approximately half the threads are engaged on the shaft, and use a soft faced hammer (1) to tap the shaft (2) out of the hub.

➥Care must be taken not to separate the inner C/V joint during this operation. Do not allow halfshaft to hang by inner C/V joint after removing outer C/V Joint from the hub/bearing assembly in steering knuckle, end of halfshaft must be supported.

11. Pull steering knuckle assembly down and away from the outer C/V joint of the halfshaft assembly while pulling the joint out of the hub bearing.

➥Transaxle fluid might leak when the halfshaft is removed from the transaxle.

12. Support the outer end of the halfshaft assembly. Insert a pry bar between inner tripod joint and transaxle case (2). Pry against inner tripod joint (1), until tripod joint retaining snap-ring is disengaged from transaxle side gear.

13. Pull the steering knuckle assembly down and away from the outer C/V joint of the halfshaft assembly while pulling the halfshaft (1) out of the transmission.

14. Remove the halfshaft.

To install:

15. Position the left or right halfshafts for installation.

➡The inner tripod joints are designed with a retention feature that prevents the tripod rollers from coming out of the inner joint housing up to a specific load. If this feature is overcome and any of the rollers are pulled past the retention feature the joint will "lock-up" and no longer function properly. The entire halfshaft assembly must be replaced if this occurs.

➡Some halfshafts use a tuned rubber damper weight. When replacing a half-shaft assembly, be sure the replacement halfshaft has the same damper weight as the original.

16. Thoroughly clean spline and oil seal sealing surface, on tripod joint. Lightly lubricate oil seal sealing surface on tripod joint with fresh clean transmission lubricant.

17. Holding halfshaft assembly by tripod joint and interconnecting shaft, install tripod joint into transaxle side gear as far as possible by hand. Be sure to engage splines prior to applying force.

18. Install the one piece halfshaft (1) into the transmission Test that snap-ring is fully engaged by attempting to remove tripod joint by hand. If snap-ring is fully engaged, tripod joint will not be removable by hand.

19. Forcefully push the tripod joint into the transaxle side gear, until snap-ring is engaged. Test that snap-ring is fully engaged by attempting to remove tripod joint by hand. If snap-ring is fully engaged, tripod joint will not be removable by hand.

20. Clean all debris and moisture out of steering knuckle, in the area were outer CV joint will be installed into steering knuckle.

21. Ensure that front of outer CV joint (1) which fits against the face of the hub and bearing is free of debris and moisture before installing outer CV joint into hub and bearing assembly.

22. Slide halfshaft back into front hub and bearing assembly.

✳✳ CAUTION

The steering knuckle to strut assembly attaching bolts are serrated and must not be turned during installation. Install nuts while holding bolts stationary in the steering knuckle.

✳✳ CAUTION

If the vehicle being serviced is equipped with eccentric strut assem-

bly attaching bolts, the eccentric bolt must be installed in the bottom (slotted) hole on the strut clevis bracket.

23. Install steering knuckle in clevis bracket of strut damper assembly. Install the strut damper to steering knuckle attaching bolts. Tighten both bolts to 65 ft. lbs. (88 Nm) plus an additional ¼ turn.

24. Install braking disc on hub and bearing assembly.

25. Install disc brake caliper assembly on steering knuckle. Caliper is installed by first sliding bottom of caliper assembly under abutment on steering knuckle, and then rotating top of caliper against top abutment.

26. Install disc brake caliper adapter to steering knuckle attaching bolts. Tighten the disc brake caliper adapter attaching bolts to 125 ft. lbs. (169 Nm).

➡Install a new hub nut, the original hub nut is one-time use only, and must be discarded when removed.

27. Clean all foreign matter from the threads of the outer CV joint. Install the halfshaft to hub/bearing assembly nut on halfshaft and securely tighten nut.

28. With the brakes applied to keep hub from turning, tighten the hub nut to 118 ft. lbs. (160 Nm).

29. Install front wheel and tire assembly. Install and tighten the wheel mounting stud nuts in proper sequence until all nuts are torqued (1) to half the required specification. Then repeat the tightening sequence to the full specified torque of 100 ft. lbs. (135 Nm).

30. Lower vehicle.

31. Check for correct fluid level in transaxle assembly.

With Intermediate Shaft

See Figure 22.

➡Never grasp the halfshaft assembly by the inner or outer boots. This can cause damage to the boot, which will allow contaminants to enter the C/V joint.

➡The inner tripod joints are designed with a retention feature that prevents the tripod rollers from coming out of the inner joint housing up to a specific load. If this feature is overcome and any of the rollers are pulled past the retention feature the joint will "lock-up" and no longer function properly. The entire halfshaft assembly must be replaced if this occurs.

➡Some halfshafts use a tuned rubber damper weight to cancel vibration. When replacing a halfshaft assembly, be sure the replacement halfshaft has a damper.

1. Raise and safely support the vehicle.

2. Remove the wheel and tire assembly from the vehicle.

3. With the vehicle's brakes applied to keep hub from turning, loosen the halfshaft nut.

➡The hub nut is a single use type. A new nut is required for reassembly. Do not re-use the hub nut.

4. Remove the nut from the halfshaft.

5. Remove the two front disc brake caliper adapter to steering knuckle attaching bolts.

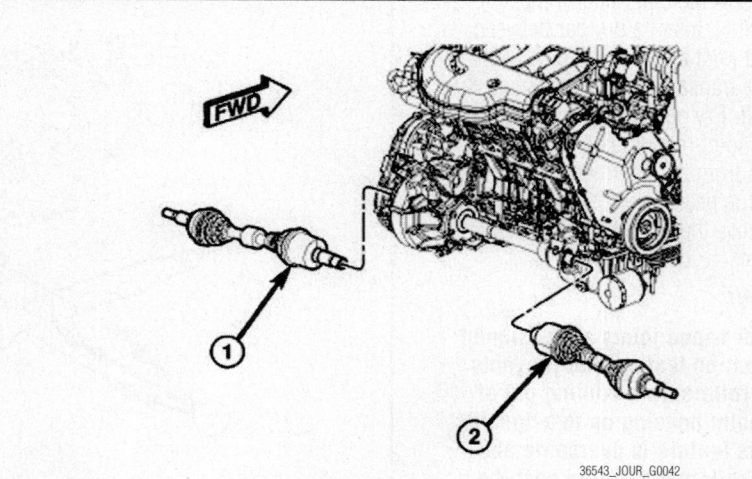

36543_JOUR_G0042

Fig. 22 Halfshafts, with intermediate shaft—3.5L engine shown, all others equipped with intermediate shaft are similar

6. Remove the disc brake caliper assembly from the steering knuckle. Caliper assembly is removed by first rotating top of caliper assembly away from steering knuckle and then removing bottom of assembly out from under machined abutment on steering knuckle.

7. Support disc brake caliper assembly by using a wire hook and suspending it from the strut assembly. Do not allow the brake caliper assembly to hang by the brake flex hose.

8. Remove the brake rotor from the hub and bearing assembly.

9. Remove the steering knuckle-to-strut attachment bolts from the steering knuckle.

10. Pull the steering knuckle from the strut clevis bracket.

➡ Due to tight tolerances, the outer C/V Joint might have to be forced apart from the bearing hub. To avoid damaging the axle halfshaft threads during removal, install the hub nut so that approximately half of the threads are engaged on the shaft, and use a soft faced hammer to tap the shaft out of the hub.

➡ Care must be taken not to separate the inner C/V joint during this operation. Do not allow halfshaft to hang by inner C/V joint after removing outer C/V Joint from the hub/bearing assembly in steering knuckle, end of halfshaft must be supported.

11. Pull steering knuckle assembly down and away from the outer C/V joint of the halfshaft assembly while pulling the joint out of the hub bearing.

12. Support the outer end of the halfshaft assembly. Insert a pry bar between inner tripod joint and the intermediate shaft, or the transaxle case if removing the left halfshaft. Pry against inner tripod joint, until tripod joint retaining snap-ring is disengaged from the intermediate shaft or transaxle side gear.

13. Remove the left axle halfshaft or right axle halfshaft.

To install:

➡ The inner tripod joints are designed with a retention feature that prevents the tripod rollers from coming out of the inner joint housing up to a specific load. If this feature is overcome and any of the rollers are pulled past the retention feature the joint will "lock-up" and no longer function properly.

The entire halfshaft assembly must be replaced if this occurs.

➡ Some halfshafts use a tuned rubber damper weight. When replacing a halfshaft assembly, be sure the replacement halfshaft has the same damper weight as the original.

➡ Care must be taken not to separate the inner C/V joint during this operation. Do not allow halfshaft to hang by inner C/V joint after removing outer C/V Joint from the hub/bearing assembly in steering knuckle, end of halfshaft must be supported.

14. Thoroughly clean spline and oil seal sealing surface, on tripod joint. Lightly lubricate oil seal sealing surface on tripod joint with fresh clean transmission lubricant.

➡ Verify the snap ring is fully engaged by attempting to remove tripod joint by hand. If snap ring is fully engaged, tripod joint will not be removable by hand.

15. Holding halfshaft assembly or by tripod joint and interconnecting shaft, install tripod joint into transaxle side gear (left side) or the intermediate shaft (right side) as far as possible by hand. Be sure to engage splines prior to applying force.

16. Install the outer C/V joint into the hub while moving the steering knuckle as necessary to align the axle halfshaft end with the splined hole in the hub.

17. Install the steering knuckle to the strut clevis bracket.

18. Install the steering knuckle-to-strut attachment bolts. Install the nuts. While holding the bolts in place, tighten the nuts to 103 ft. lbs. (140 Nm).

19. Install the brake rotor to the hub and bearing assembly.

20. Install the disc brake caliper assembly to the steering knuckle.

21. Install the two front disc brake caliper adapter to steering knuckle guide pin bolts. Tighten the guide pin bolts to 26 ft. lbs. (35 Nm)

➡ The hub nut is a single use type. A new nut is required for reassembly. Do not re-use the hub nut.

22. Install a new hub nut nut and snug it. Do not torque it at this time

23. While a helper applies the brakes to keep the hub from rotating, tighten the hub nut to 118 ft. lbs. (160 Nm).

24. Install the wheel and tire assembly.

INTERMEDIATE SHAFT

REMOVAL & INSTALLATION

2.4L Engine

See Figure 23.

1. Remove the right halfshaft.
2. Remove the three intermediate shaft bolts (1).
3. Remove the intermediate shaft (2).

To install:

4. Install the intermediate shaft (2).
5. Install the three intermediate shaft bolts (1).
6. Install the right halfshaft.

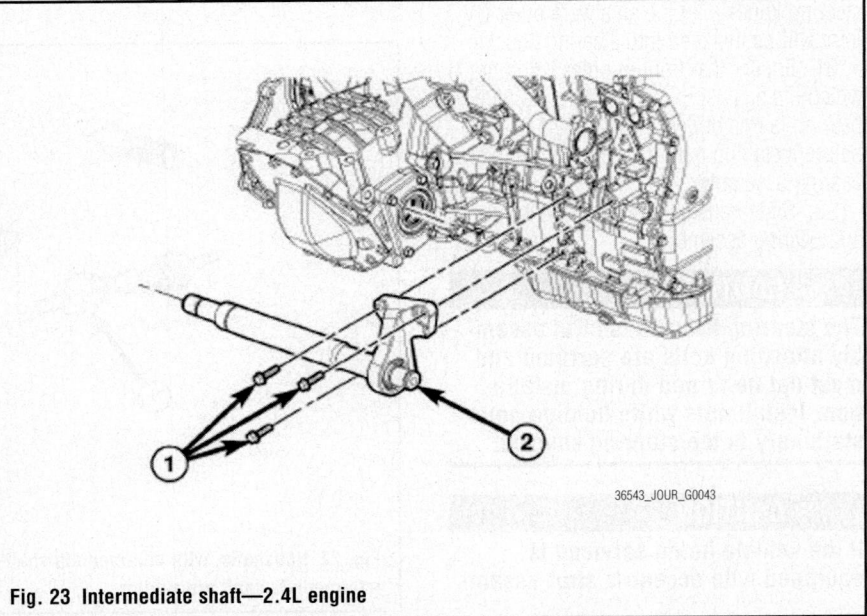

36543_JOUR_G0043

Fig. 23 Intermediate shaft—2.4L engine

2.7L Engine

See Figure 24.

1. Remove the right halfshaft.
2. Remove the heat shield bolts (2).
3. Remove the heat shield (3).
4. Remove the intermediate shaft bolts (1) and (5).
5. Remove the intermediate shaft (4).

To install:

6. Install the intermediate shaft (4).
7. Install the intermediate shaft bolts (1) and (5). Tighten bolt (1) to 38 Nm (28 ft. lb.) and bolts (5) to 23 Nm (17 ft. lb.).
8. Install the heat shield (3).
9. Install the heat shield bolts (2).
10. Install the right halfshaft.

3.5L Engine

See Figure 25.

1. Remove the right halfshaft.
2. Remove the intermediate shaft bolts (1).
3. Remove the heat shield bolts (2).
4. Remove the heat shield (3).
5. Remove the intermediate shaft (4).

To install:

6. Install the intermediate shaft (4).
7. Install the intermediate shaft bolts (1) and tighten to 38 Nm (28 ft. lb.).
8. Install the heat shield (3).
9. Install the heat shield bolts (2) and tighten to 10 Nm (7 ft. lb).
10. Install the right halfshaft.

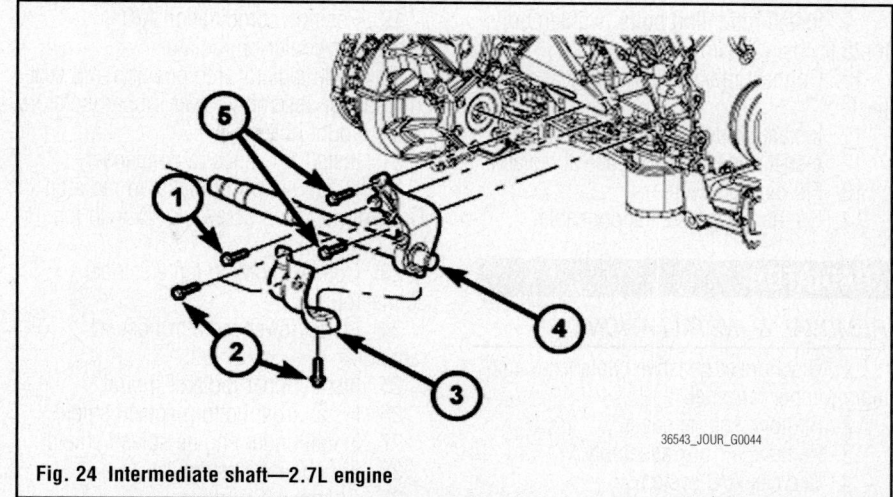

Fig. 24 Intermediate shaft—2.7L engine

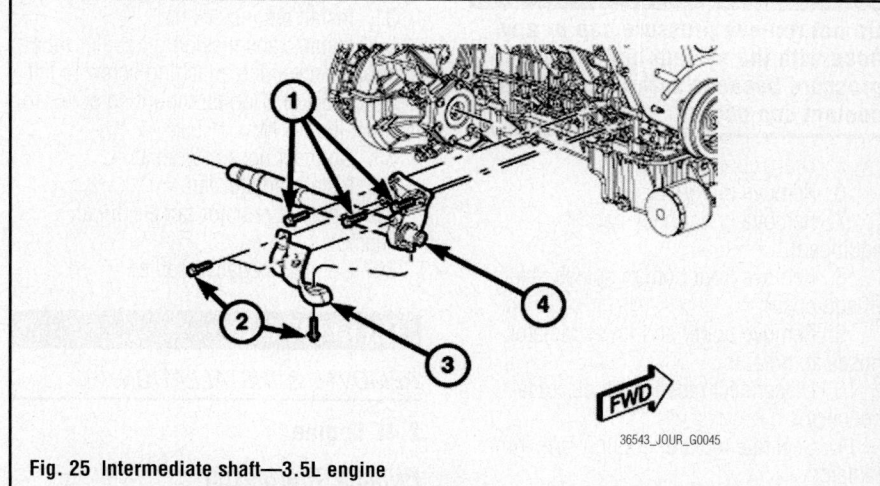

Fig. 25 Intermediate shaft—3.5L engine

ENGINE COOLING

ENGINE FAN

REMOVAL & INSTALLATION

See Figure 26.

1. Disconnect and isolate the negative battery cable.
2. Remove windshield washer reservoir.
3. Drain cooling system below level of the upper radiator hose.
4. Remove upper radiator hose at radiator and position aside.
5. Disconnect radiator fan electrical connector.
6. Remove fasteners and un-clip radiator fan assembly from radiator.
7. Remove radiator fan assembly by lifting upward.

To install:

8. Position radiator fan into retaining clips.

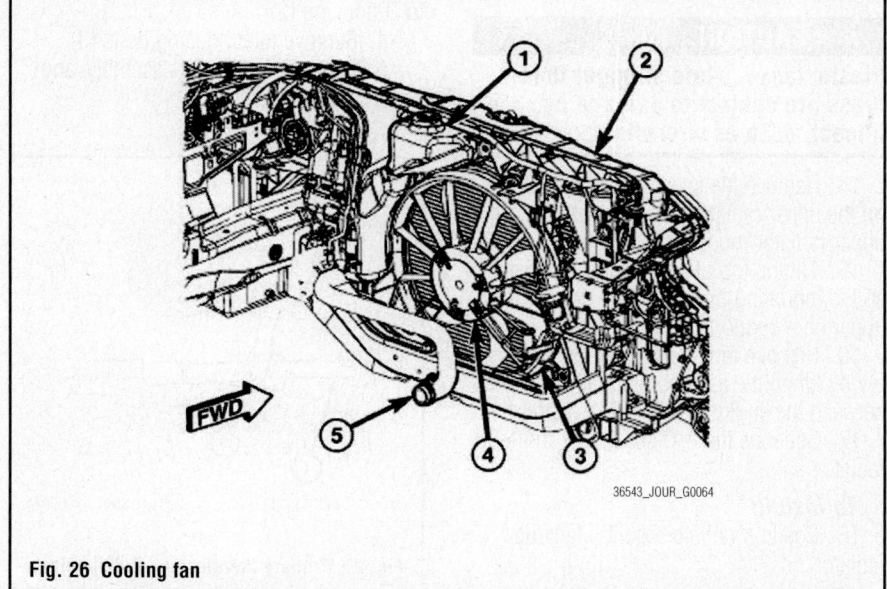

Fig. 26 Cooling fan

9. Install mounting bolts. Tighten bolts to 25 ft. lbs. (35 Nm).

10. Connect radiator fan electrical connector.

11. Install windshield washer reservoir.

12. Install upper radiator hose at radiator.

13. Fill cooling system.

14. Connect negative battery cable.

RADIATOR

REMOVAL & INSTALLATION

1. Disconnect negative cable from auxiliary jumper terminal.

2. Remove engine cover.

3. Remove air box assembly.

4. Recover A/C system.

✳✳ WARNING

Do not remove pressure cap or any hose with the system hot and under pressure because serious burns from coolant can occur.

5. Drain cooling system.

6. Remove the grille.

7. Remove under belly pan (if equipped).

8. Remove front bottom splash shield (if equipped).

9. Remove upper and lower radiator hoses at radiator.

10. Disconnect radiator fan electrical connector.

11. Separate radiator cooling fans from radiator.

12. Disconnect A/C line at condenser/cooler.

13. Remove transmission oil cooler tubes support bracket at left side of radiator (if equipped).

✳✳ CAUTION

Plastic tanks, while stronger than brass are subject to damage by impact, such as wrenches.

14. Remove the two Torx screws located on the upper radiator support that hold the upper radiator mounting brackets.

15. Tilt the top of the radiator rearward so the mounting brackets slide out of the upper core support.

16. Remove radiator/condenser assembly by lifting the assembly out of the vehicle between the engine and the core support.

17. Separate the A/C condenser from the radiator.

To install:

18. Position radiator cooling fans on radiator.

19. Position combination A/C condenser/cooler on radiator.

20. Slide radiator into position and seat the radiator assembly lower rubber isolators in the mount holes.

21. Install A/C lines to condenser.

22. Install support bracket to radiator. Tighten mounting screws to 45 inch lbs. (5 Nm).

23. Connect cooling fan electrical connector.

24. Install lower radiator hose at radiator.

25. Install upper radiator mount.

26. Install front bottom splash shield.

27. Install under engine splash shield.

28. Fill cooling system.

29. Charge A/C system.

30. Install air filter housing.

31. Install engine cover.

32. Install transmission oil cooler tube support bracket and attaching screw to left side of radiator. Tighten mounting screw to 45 inch lbs. (5 Nm).

33. Connect hoses to radiator.

34. Install radiator fan.

35. Connect radiator fan electrical connector.

36. Connect negative cable.

THERMOSTAT

REMOVAL & INSTALLATION

2.4L Engine

Primary Thermostat

See Figure 27.

1. Partially drain cooling system.

2. Remove air filter housing.

3. Disconnect coolant hose (1) from inlet housing (2).

4. Remove inlet housing bolts (3).

5. Remove thermostat assembly, and clean sealing surfaces.

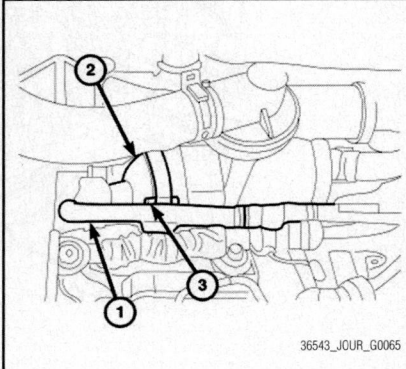

Fig. 27 Primary thermostat—2.4L engine

To install:

6. Position thermostat into the water plenum, aligning air bleed with the location notch on inlet housing (2).

7. Install inlet housing (2) onto coolant adapter. Tighten bolts to 79 inch lbs. (9 Nm).

8. Connect coolant hose (1).

9. Install air filter housing.

10. Fill cooling system.

Secondary Thermostat

See Figure 28.

1. Partially drain cooling system.

2. Remove air filter housing .

3. Disconnect coolant hoses from rear of coolant adapter .

4. Remove radiator hose.

5. Remove radiator hose from front of coolant adapter.

6. Remove coolant adapter mounting bolts.

7. Carefully slide coolant adapter off water pump inlet tube and remove coolant adapter (2) and secondary thermostat.

To install:

8. Position thermostat into the cylinder head.

9. Inspect the water pump inlet tube O-rings for damage before installing the tube in the coolant adapter. Replace O-ring as necessary.

10. Lubricate O-rings with soapy water.

11. Position coolant adapter on water pump inlet tube and cylinder head.

12. Install coolant adapter mounting bolts. Tighten bolts to 13 ft. lbs. (18 Nm).

13. Connect front coolant hose.

14. Connect two rear coolant hoses.

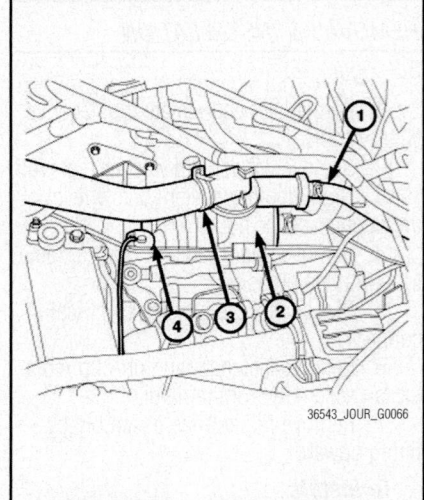

Fig. 28 Secondary thermostat—2.4L engine

15. Connect radiator hose.
16. Install air filter housing.
17. Fill cooling system.

2.7L Engine

See Figure 29.

1. Disconnect negative cable from remote jumper terminal.
2. Drain cooling system.
3. Raise vehicle on hoist.
4. Remove right front wheel and belt splash shield.
5. Remove accessory drive belts.
6. Remove lower generator mounting bolt.
7. Lower vehicle.
8. Disconnect generator electrical connectors.
9. Disconnect AC clutch and AC pressure sensor electrical connectors. Reposition wiring harness.
10. Remove oil dipstick and tube. Plug hole in oil pan where dipstick tube mounts with water tight stopper.

✳✳ WARNING

If hole for dipstick tube in oil pan is not plugged, coolant will enter oil pan. Serious engine damage can occur.

11. Remove remaining generator mounting bolts. Remove generator.
12. Remove radiator hose tube mounting bolt (3).
13. Disconnect hose clamps (1) at thermostat housing.
14. Remove thermostat housing bolts.
15. Remove thermostat and housing.

To install:

16. Clean gasket sealing surfaces.

➡ **Install thermostat with the bleed valve located at the 12 o'clock position.**

17. Install thermostat and gasket into the thermostat housing.
18. Install thermostat and housing to cylinder block. Tighten attaching bolts to 105 inch lbs. (12 Nm).
19. Connect hoses at thermostat housing.
20. Install generator and attaching bolts.

✳✳ CAUTION

Before removing plug in oil pan, clean residual coolant from area.

21. Remove plug in oil pan and install engine oil dipstick tube.
22. Reconnect AC clutch and AC pressure sensor connectors.
23. Reconnect generator connectors.
24. Raise vehicle on hoist.
25. Install accessory drive belts.
26. Install belt splash shield and right front wheel.
27. Lower vehicle.
28. Reconnect negative battery cable.
29. Fill cooling system.

3.5L Engine

See Figure 30.

✳✳ WARNING

Do not remove pressure cap with the system hot and under pressure because serious burns from coolant can occur.

1. Disconnect negative battery cable.
2. Drain cooling system.
3. Remove engine cover.
4. Disconnect radiator upper hose from thermostat housing.
5. Remove thermostat housing bolts.
6. Remove housing, thermostat, and gasket.

To install:

7. Clean gasket sealing surfaces.
8. Install thermostat and gasket into thermostat housing. For ease of installation, install bolts in housing for thermostat and gasket retention.
9. Install thermostat and housing to Intake manifold. Tighten bolts to 105 inch lbs. (12 Nm).
10. Connect radiator hoses and install hose clamp.
11. Install engine cover.
12. Refill cooling system.
13. Connect negative cable.

WATER PUMP

REMOVAL & INSTALLATION

2.4L Engine

See Figure 31.

1. Remove the accessory drive belt.
2. Raise and safely support the vehicle.
3. Remove accessory drive belt splash shield.
4. Drain cooling system.
5. Remove screws attaching water pump pulley (1). Remove pulley (1).
6. Remove water pump mounting bolts (2).
7. Remove water pump (3).

To install:

8. Position water pump assembly (1) and gasket onto cylinder block.
9. Position water inlet tube (4) and gasket onto water pump (1).
10. Install mounting bolts (2). Tighten bolts to 19 ft. lbs. (25 Nm).
11. Install drive belt splash shield.
12. Lower vehicle.
13. Install accessory drive belt.
14. Fill cooling system

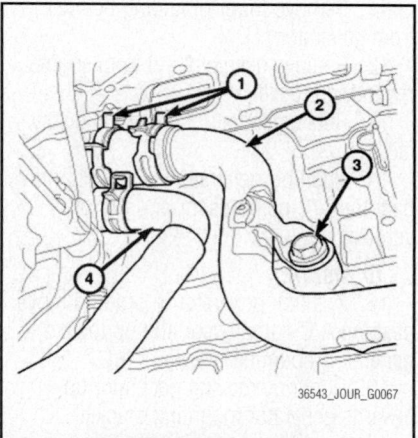

36543_JOUR_G0067

Fig. 29 Thermostat—2.7L engine

36543_JOUR_G0068

Fig. 30 Thermostat—3.5L engine

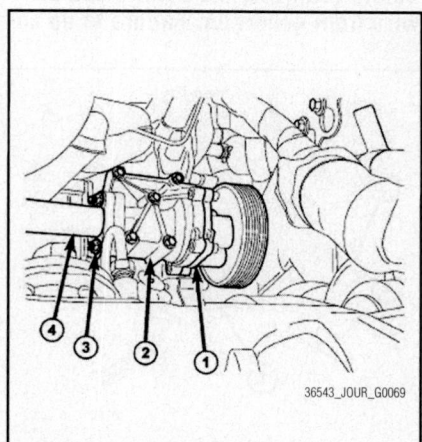

36543_JOUR_G0069

Fig. 31 Water pump—2.4L engine

2.7L Engine

See Figure 32.

✳✳ WARNING

Do not remove pressure cap with the system hot and pressurized. Serious burns from coolant can result.

1. Disconnect negative battery cable.
2. Drain cooling system.

➡**The water pump is driven by the primary timing chain.**

3. Remove the timing chain cover, timing chain, and all chain guides.

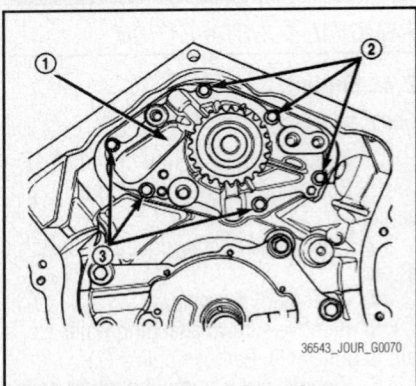

Fig. 32 Water pump—2.7L engine

4. Remove bolts attaching water pump to block.
5. Remove water pump and gasket.

To install:

6. Clean all sealing surfaces.
7. Install water pump and gasket. Tighten mounting bolts to 105 inch lbs. (12 Nm).
8. Install timing chain guides, timing chain, and timing chain cover.
9. Reconnect negative battery cable.
10. Fill cooling system

3.5L Engine

See Figure 33.

➡**It is normal for the water pump to weep a small amount of coolant from the weep hole (black stain on water pump body). Do not replace the water pump if this condition exists. Replace the water pump if a heavy deposit or a steady flow of engine coolant is evident on water pump body from the weep hole (shaft seal failure). Be sure to perform a thorough analysis before replacing water pump.**

1. Drain cooling system.
2. Remove engine timing belt.
3. Remove water pump mounting bolts.

Note position of longer bolt for proper re-installation.

4. Remove water pump body from engine.
5. Clean water pump mounting surface.

To install:

6. Clean all O-ring surfaces on pump and cover.
7. Install new O-ring on water pump.
8. Position water pump to engine.
9. Install mounting bolts and tighten to 105 inch lbs. (12 Nm).
10. Install timing belt.
11. Fill cooling system.

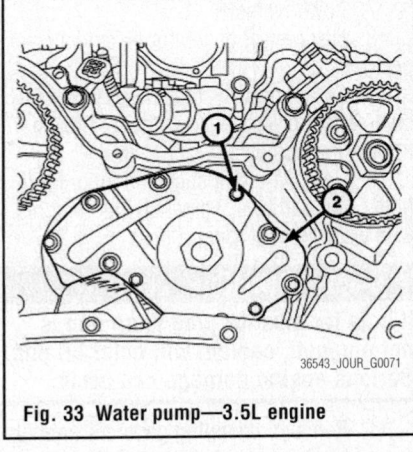

Fig. 33 Water pump—3.5L engine

ENGINE ELECTRICAL

ALTERNATOR

REMOVAL & INSTALLATION

2.4L Engine

See Figure 34.

✳✳ CAUTION

Disconnect the negative battery cable before removing the battery output wire from generator. Failure to do so

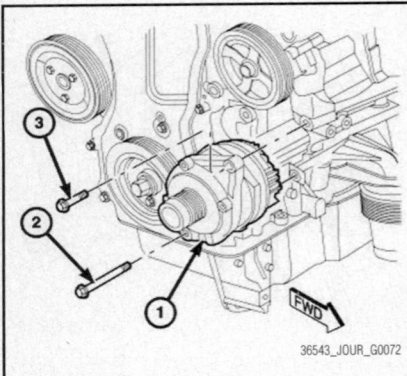

Fig. 34 Alternator—2.4L engine

can result in injury or damage to electrical system.

1. Disconnect and isolate the negative battery cable.
2. Remove underbody air dam.
3. Remove right front wheelhouse splash shield.
4. Remove generator drive belt.

➡**Do not disconnect the A/C lines when relocating the A/C compressor.**

✳✳ CAUTION

Support the A/C compressor when relocating. Failure to properly support the A/C compressor can cause damage to the lines and or seals. This can cause a leak in the A/C system.

5. Relocate A/C compressor.

✳✳ CAUTION

Never force a belt over a pulley rim using a screwdriver. The synthetic fiber of the belt can be damaged.

CHARGING SYSTEM

6. Unsnap plastic protective cover from B+ mounting stud.
7. Remove B+ terminal mounting nut and B+ terminal from generator.
8. Disconnect field wire electrical connector by pushing on connector tab.
9. Remove bolt and lower idler pulley.
10. Remove upper mounting bolt (3) from generator (1).
11. Remove lower mounting bolt (2) from generator (1).
12. Remove generator (1) from engine mounting bracket.
13. Rotate generator so that the pulley faces down.
14. Position generator in order to move past the A/C compressor and out of vehicle.

To install:

15. Position generator in order to move past the A/C compressor and up toward generator mounting bracket.
16. Continue moving generator up towards generator mounting bracket.
17. Install generator (1) to engine mounting bracket.

18. Install lower mounting bolt (2) and upper mounting bolt (3) to generator (1). Tighten bolts to 45 ft. lbs. (61 Nm).

19. Install lower idler pulley and bolt. Tighten bolt to 37 ft. lbs. (50 Nm).

20. Connect field wire connector into generator.

21. Install B+ terminal and nut to generator mounting stud. Tighten nut to 89 inch lbs. (10 Nm).

22. Snap plastic protective cover to B+ terminal.

23. Install A/C compressor.

✳✳ CAUTION
Never force a belt over a pulley rim using a screwdriver. The synthetic fiber of the belt can be damaged.

✳✳ CAUTION
When installing a serpentine accessory drive belt, the belt MUST be routed correctly. The water pump will be rotating in the wrong direction if the belt is installed incorrectly, causing the engine to overheat.

24. Install drive belt.

25. Install right front wheelhouse splash shield.

26. Install underbody air dam.

27. Connect negative battery cable, tighten nut to 40 inch lbs. (4.5 Nm).

2.7L Engine
See Figure 35.

✳✳ CAUTION
Disconnect the negative battery cable before removing the battery output wire from generator. Failure to do so can result in injury or damage to electrical system.

1. Disconnect and isolate the negative battery cable.

✳✳ CAUTION
Never force a belt over a pulley rim using a screwdriver. The synthetic fiber of the belt can be damaged.

2. Remove generator drive belt.

3. Unsnap plastic protective cover from B+ mounting stud.

4. Remove B+ terminal mounting nut and B+ terminal at top of generator.

5. Disconnect field wire electrical connector by pushing on connector tab.

6. Remove upper mounting bolts (3) from generator (1).

7. Remove lower mounting bolt (2) from generator (1).

8. Remove generator (1) from engine mounting bracket.

To install:

9. Install generator (1) to engine mounting bracket.

10. Install lower mounting bolt (2) and upper mounting bolt (3) to generator (1). Tighten bolts to 20 ft. lbs. (27 Nm).

11. Connect field wire connector into generator.

12. Install B+ terminal and nut to generator mounting stud. Tighten nut to 89 inch lbs. (10 Nm)

13. Snap plastic protective cover to B+ terminal.

✳✳ CAUTION
Never force a belt over a pulley rim using a screwdriver. The synthetic fiber of the belt can be damaged.

✳✳ CAUTION
When installing a serpentine accessory drive belt, the belt MUST be routed correctly. The water pump will be rotating in the wrong direction if the belt is installed incorrectly, causing the engine to overheat.

14. Install drive belt.

15. Connect negative battery cable, tighten nut to 40 inch lbs. (4.5 Nm).

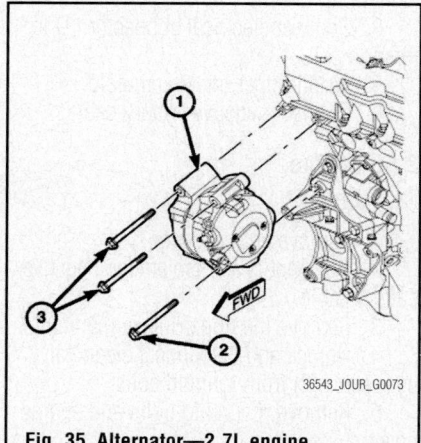

Fig. 35 Alternator—2.7L engine

36543_JOUR_G0073

3.5L Engine
See Figure 36.

✳✳ CAUTION
Never force a belt over a pulley rim using a screwdriver. The synthetic fiber of the belt can be damaged.

1. Disconnect and isolate the negative battery cable.

2. Remove generator drive belt.

3. Unsnap plastic protective cover from B+ mounting stud.

4. Remove B+ terminal mounting nut and B+ terminal at top of generator.

5. Disconnect field wire electrical connector by pushing on connector tab.

6. Remove short mounting bolt (3) from generator (1).

7. Remove long mounting bolt (2) from generator (1).

8. Remove generator (1) from engine mounting bracket.

To install:

9. Install generator (1) to engine mounting bracket.

10. Install long mounting bolt (2) and short mounting bolt (3) to generator (1). Tighten bolts to 31 ft. lbs. (42 Nm).

11. Connect field wire connector into generator.

12. Install B+ terminal and nut to generator mounting stud. Tighten nut to 89 inch lbs. (10 Nm)

13. Snap plastic protective cover to B+ terminal.

14. Install drive belt.

15. Connect negative battery cable, tighten nut to 40 inch lbs. (4.5 Nm).

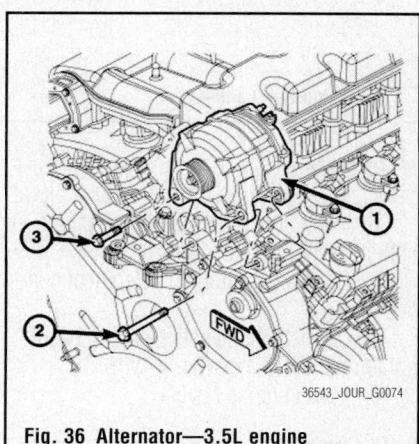

Fig. 36 Alternator—3.5L engine

36543_JOUR_G0074

FIRING ORDERS

For the 2.4L engine, the firing order is:
- 1–3–4–2

For the 2.7L and 3.5L engines, the firing order is:
- 1–2–3–4–5–6

IGNITION COIL

REMOVAL & INSTALLATION

2.4L Engine

See Figure 37.

➡️**Prior to removing coil, spray compressed air around coil top to make sure no dirt drops into the spark plug tube.**

The electronic ignition coil attaches directly to the valve cover.

1. Disconnect and isolate the negative battery cable.
2. Remove engine cover.
3. Disconnect electrical connector from ignition coil.
4. Remove ignition coil mounting bolts.
5. Twist the ignition coil then pull straight up.

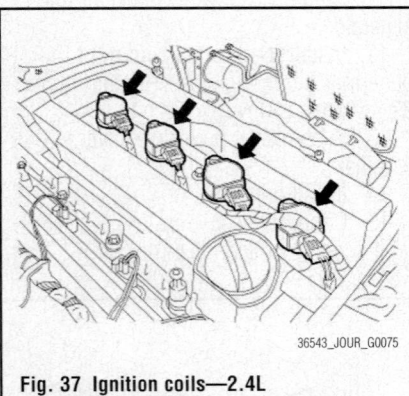

Fig. 37 Ignition coils—2.4L

To install:

6. Install ignition coil onto spark plug.
7. Install ignition coil mounting bolt, tighten to 80 inch lbs. (9 Nm).
8. Connect ignition coil electrical connectors.
9. Connect the negative battery cable, tighten nut to 45 inch lbs. (5 Nm).
10. Install engine cover.

2.7L Engine

See Figure 38.

➡️**Always remove the ignition coil assembly by turning the assembly 1/2 turn and pulling up in a steady motion.**

1. Disconnect the negative battery cable.
2. Remove the upper intake manifold.
3. Disconnect electrical connector (1) from ignition coil.
4. Remove mounting bolt (2) from ignition coil.

✳✳ CAUTION

Prior to removing the ignition coils, spray compressed air around the coils and spark plugs. If dirt and debris enter the engine, this may cause internal engine damage.

5. Remove the ignition coils.

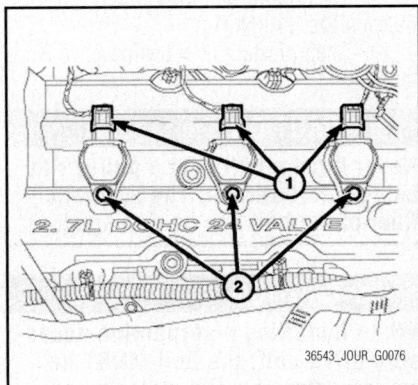

Fig. 38 Ignition coils—2.7L engine

To install:

6. Align ignition coil with top of spark plug.
7. Twist and push down ignition coil assembly onto spark plug and valve cover. Install mounting bolt (2) and tighten to 65 inch lbs. (7.5 Nm).
8. Connect electrical connector (1) to ignition coil.
9. Install upper intake manifold.
10. Connect negative battery cable.

3.5L Engine

See Figure 39.

1. Remove engine cover.
2. Disconnect and isolate the negative battery cable.
3. Remove the upper intake manifold.
4. Unlock and disconnect electrical connector (2) from ignition coils.
5. Remove mounting bolts and engine cover studs (1).

✳✳ CAUTION

Prior to removing the ignition coils, spray compressed air around the coils and spark plugs. If dirt and

debris enter the engine, this may cause internal engine damage.

6. Twist, lift and remove ignition coil from engine.

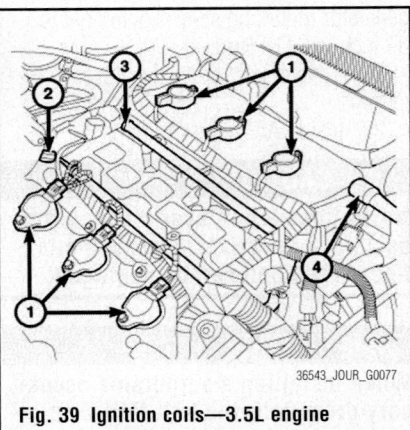

Fig. 39 Ignition coils—3.5L engine

To install:

7. Install ignition coil (1).
8. Install engine cover studs (1) in the two outside ignition coils on the front of the engine. Install bolts on the other ignition coils.
9. Tighten studs and bolts to 71 inch lbs. (8 Nm).
10. Connect electrical connector and lock (2).
11. Install intake manifold.
12. Connect negative battery cable and tighten nut to 45 inch lbs. (5 Nm).
13. Install engine cover.

IGNITION TIMING

ADJUSTMENT

All engines use a fixed ignition timing system. Basic ignition timing is not adjustable. All spark advance is determined by the Powertrain Control Module (PCM).

SPARK PLUGS

REMOVAL & INSTALLATION

➡️**Prior to loosening the spark plug, use compressed air to blow out any debris that might be in the spark plug tube.**

1. Remove the spark plug using a quality socket with a rubber or foam insert.
2. Inspect the spark plug condition.

To install:

✳✳ CAUTION

Handle the spark plugs with care. Do not drop or force the spark plugs into

the wells, damage to the electrodes and/or porcelain body may occur. Always start each spark plug by hand in order to avoid cross-threading the spark plug in the cylinder head. Always tighten spark plugs to the specified torque. Too much or not enough torque will cause damage to the cylinder head and/or spark plug and may lead to poor engine performance.

3. Install each spark plug to the cylinder head. On 2.4L and 3.5L engines, tighten spark plugs to 20 ft. lbs. (27 Nm). On 2.7L, tighten spark plugs to 13 ft. lbs. (17 Nm).

4. Install ignition coil onto spark plug.

ENGINE ELECTRICAL

STARTER

REMOVAL & INSTALLATION

2.4L Engine

See Figure 40.

1. Disconnect and isolate the negative battery cable.
2. Remove throttle body.
3. Remove starter mounting bolts (1) and negative battery cable (2) from transmission housing (3).
4. Remove starter motor (4) from transmission housing (3).
5. Position starter to move past the intake manifold.
6. Remove battery cable nut (5), ignition sense wire (4) and battery cable (1) from solenoid stud.
7. Disconnect electrical connector (3) from starter solenoid (2).
8. Remove starter from vehicle.

To install:

9. Install starter to vehicle.
10. Connect electrical connector (3) to starter solenoid (2).
11. Install battery cable (1), ignition sense wire (4) and battery cable nut (5) to solenoid stud. Tighten nut to 90 inch lbs. (10 Nm).
12. Position starter motor past the intake manifold.
13. Install starter motor (4) to transmission housing (3).
14. Install negative battery cable (2) and starter mounting bolts (1) to transmission

housing (3). Tighten bolts to 40 ft. lbs. (54 Nm).
15. Install throttle body.
16. Connect negative battery cable, tighten nut to 40 inch lbs. (4.5 Nm).

2.7L Engine

See Figure 41.

1. Disconnect and isolate the negative battery cable.
2. Remove the front mount through bolt.
3. Remove lower engine anti-roll mount bolt.
4. Remove crossmember mounting bolts.
5. Remove crossmember mounting bolts.
6. Remove crossmember from vehicle.
7. Remove torque reaction bracket transmission to starter bolt.
8. Remove negative battery cable.
9. Remove torque reaction bracket to transmission bolt.
10. Remove torque reaction bracket to engine bolt.
11. Remove torque reaction bracket from vehicle.
12. Remove battery cable nut, ignition sense wire and battery cable from solenoid stud.
13. Disconnect electrical connector from starter solenoid.
14. Remove starter mounting bolts (1) from transmission housing (2).

STARTING SYSTEM

15. Remove starter motor (4) and dust shield (3) from transmission housing (2).
16. Remove starter motor (4) from vehicle.

To install:

17. Install starter motor (4) and dust shield (3) to transmission housing (2).
18. Install starter mounting bolts (1) to transmission housing (2). Tighten bolts to 40 ft. lbs. (54 Nm).
19. Install battery cable, ignition sense wire and battery cable nut to solenoid stud. Tighten nut to 90 inch lbs. (10 Nm).
20. Connect electrical connector to starter solenoid.
21. Install torque reaction bracket to vehicle.
22. Install torque reaction bracket to engine bolt. Hand tighten bolt.
23. Install torque reaction bracket to transmission bolt. Hand tighten bolt.
24. Install negative battery cable.
25. Install torque reaction bracket transmission to starter bolt. Hand tighten bolt.

✳✳ CAUTION

The torque reaction bracket bolts need to be tightened using a mandatory torque sequence. Failure to tighten bolts using the mandatory torque sequence provided may result in damage to the fasteners, bracket, and threaded bolts holes for the engine and transmission.

26. Tighten bolts in a mandatory torque sequence to 40 ft. lbs. (54 Nm).
27. Install crossmember to vehicle. Tighten bolts to 37 ft. lbs. (50 Nm).
28. Install lower engine anti-roll mount bolt and tighten bolt to 35 ft. lbs. (47 Nm).
29. Install crossmember bolts and tighten bolts to 41 ft. lbs. (55 Nm).
30. Install mount through bolt and tighten to 35 ft. lbs. (47 Nm).
31. Connect negative battery cable, tighten nut to 40 inch lbs. (4.5 Nm).

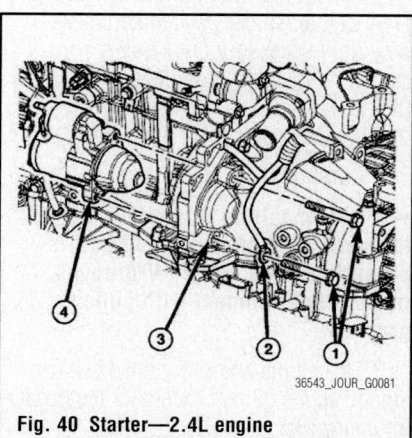

36543_JOUR_G0081

Fig. 40 Starter—2.4L engine

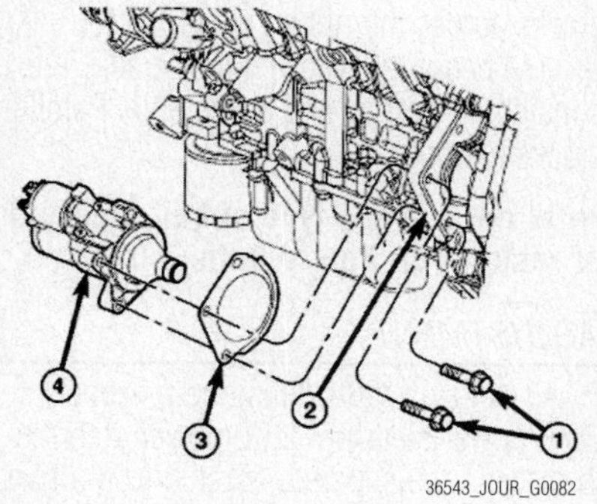

36543_JOUR_G0082

Fig. 41 Starter—2.7L engine

3.5L Engine

See Figure 42.

1. Disconnect and isolate the negative battery cable.

2. Remove heat shield nuts and position heat shield (2) aside.

3. Remove belly pan, if equipped.

4. Remove front mount through bolt from transmission bracket and mount.

5. Remove rear bolts from transmission crossmember.

6. Remove front bolts from transmission crossmember.

7. Remove transmission crossmember.

8. Remove heat shield bolts and remove heat shield.

9. Remove oxygen sensor and position aside.

10. Remove bolt from transmission bracket.

11. Remove bolts and transmission bracket from transmission housing.

12. Remove battery cable nut, ignition wire and battery cable from starter solenoid stud.

13. Disconnect electrical connector from starter solenoid.

14. Remove starter mounting bolts and ground wire and remove the starter from the transmission housing.

15. Remove starter motor dust shield (2) from starter (1).

➡**If the flywheel is damaged refer to the transmission section for flywheel replacement.**

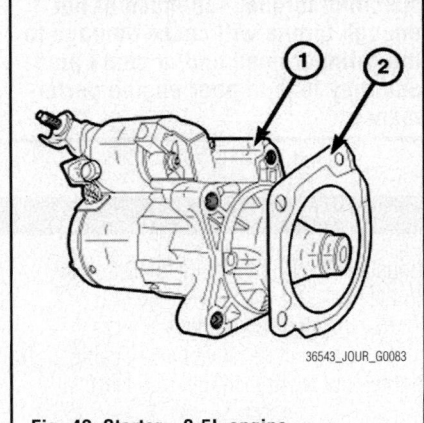

Fig. 42 Starter—3.5L engine

36543_JOUR_G0083

16. Rotate and fully inspect flywheel gears and wields for damage.

To install:

17. Install starter motor dust shield (2) to starter (1).

18. Position starter into transmission housing, install ground wire and starter mounting bolts. Tighten bolts to 40 ft. lbs. (54 Nm).

19. Install battery cable, ignition wire and battery cable nut to starter solenoid stud. Tighten nut to 90 inch lbs. (10 Nm).

20. Connect electrical connector to starter solenoid.

21. Install transmission bracket and bolts to transmission housing. Hand tighten bolts.

22. Install bolt to transmission bracket. Hand tighten bolt.

※※ **CAUTION**

The torque reaction bracket bolts need to be tightened using a mandatory torque sequence. Failure to tighten bolts using the mandatory torque sequence provided may result in damage to the fasteners, bracket, and threaded bolts holes for the engine and transmission.

23. Tighten bolts in a mandatory torque sequence to 37 ft. lbs. (50 Nm).

24. Install oxygen sensor and tighten to 30 ft. lbs. (41 Nm).

25. Install heat shield and bolts. Tighten bolts to 106 inch lbs. (12 Nm).

26. Install bolts to transmission crossmember. Tighten bolts to 41 ft. lbs. (55 Nm).

27. Install bolts to transmission crossmember. Tighten bolts to 37 ft. lbs. (50 Nm).

28. Install front mount through bolt to transmission bracket and mount. Tighten bolt to 35 ft. lbs. (47 Nm).

29. If equipped, install belly pan.

➡**Make sure the lower heat shield is installed to the lower stud before the upper heat shield is install. The upper heat shield stacks on top of the lower heat shield, and both shields are held together by the lower nut.**

30. Position heat shield (2) over the studs and install heat shield nuts. Tighten nuts to 106 inch lbs. (12 Nm).

31. Connect the negative battery cable, tighten nut to 45 inch lbs. (5 Nm).

ENGINE MECHANICAL

➡**Disconnecting the negative battery cable may interfere with the functions of the on board computer systems and may require the computer to undergo a relearning process, once the negative battery cable is reconnected.**

ACCESSORY DRIVE BELTS

ACCESSORY BELT ROUTING

2.4L Engine

See Figure 43.

2.7L Engine

See Figure 44.

3.5L Engine

See Figure 45.

INSPECTION

Belt replacement under any or all of the following conditions is required:

• Excessive wear
• Frayed cords
• Severe glazing

Poly-V Belt system may develop minor cracks across the ribbed side (due to reverse bending). These minor cracks are considered normal and acceptable. Parallel cracks are not .

➡**Do not use any type of belt dressing or restorer on Poly-V Belts.**

ADJUSTMENT

All belts are auto-tensioned, except 2.7L power steering. 2.7L power steering is driven by a separate, stretch to fit drive belt.

REMOVAL & INSTALLATION

2.4L Engine

See Figure 43.

1. Using a wrench, rotate accessory drive belt tensioner (8) counterclockwise until accessory drive belt (2) can be removed from pulleys (5 and 9).

2. Remove accessory drive belt (2).

To install:

➡**When installing drive belt on the pulleys, make sure that belt is properly routed and all V-grooves make proper contact with pulley grooves.**

3. Install the accessory drive belt (2) around all the pulleys except for the generator pulley (3).

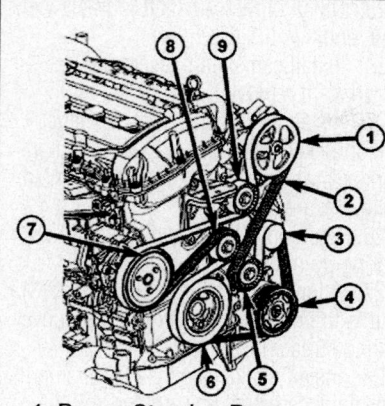

1. Power Steering Pump
2. Accessory Drive Belt
3. Generator
4. Crankshaft Pulley
5. Lower Idler Pulley
6. Crankshaft Pulley
7. Water Pump Pulley
8. Accessory Drive Belt Tensioner
9. Upper Idler Pulley

36543_JOUR_G0084

Fig. 43 Belt routing—2.4L engine

4. Using a wrench, rotate accessory drive belt tensioner (8) counterclockwise until accessory drive belt (2) can be installed on the generator pulley (3). Release spring tension onto accessory drive belt (2).

2.7L Engine

Serpentine

See Figure 44.

1. Raise vehicle on hoist.
2. Remove RH wheelhouse splash shield.
3. Rotate accessory drive belt tensioner (5) clockwise to allow enough slack to remove accessory drive belt (3).

To install:

➡️**When installing drive belt onto pulleys, make sure that belt is properly routed and all V-grooves make proper contact with pulley.**

4. Position accessory drive belt (3) on all pulleys except generator (1).

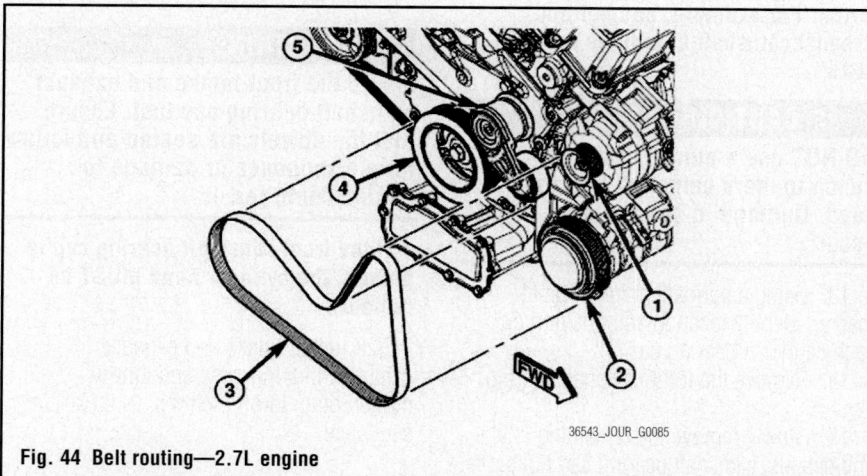

36543_JOUR_G0085

Fig. 44 Belt routing—2.7L engine

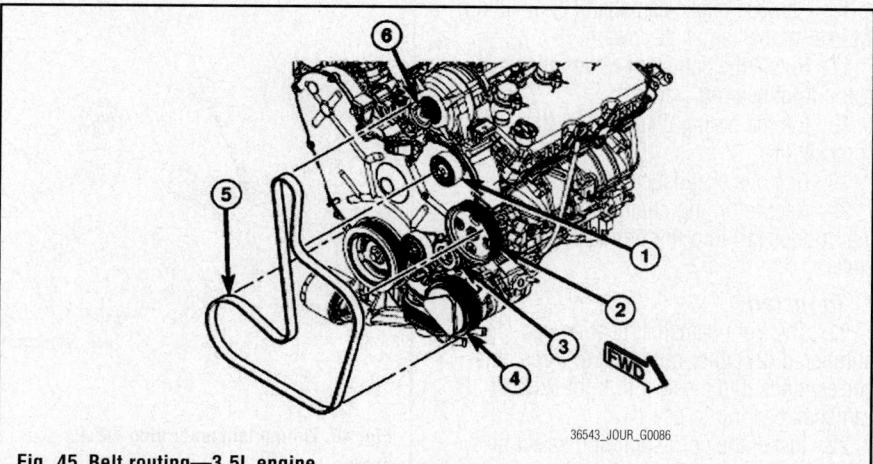

36543_JOUR_G0086

Fig. 45 Belt routing—3.5L engine

5. Rotate accessory drive belt tensioner (5) clockwise.
6. Position accessory drive belt (3) on generator pulley (1).
7. Slowly release accessory drive belt tensioner (5).
8. Install RH wheelhouse splash shield.
9. Lower vehicle.

Power Steering

See Figure 46.

1. Raise and support the vehicle.
2. Remove RH wheelhouse splash shield.
3. Use a socket and ratchet to rotate the crankshaft clockwise.
4. While rotating the crankshaft clockwise, walk the power steering drive belt (2) off of the power steering pulley (1).
5. Remove the power steering drive belt (2).

To install:

6. Position the power steering drive belt (2) on the crankshaft pulley. Make sure the belt (2) is fully seated in the crankshaft pulley grooves.
7. Position the bottom of the drive belt (2) on the bottom of the power steering pulley (1).

➡️**Use only wire ties with nylon locks, not metal.**

8. Working from the back side of the power steering pulley (1), insert a nylon wire tie (3), 7.75 × ⅛ × 0.050 in. through one of the holes in the pulley (1).
9. Tighten the wire tie to hold the drive belt (2) in position.
10. While holding the drive belt (2) to make sure it stays in position, slowly rotate the engine clockwise.
11. Once the belt is in position on the pulley (1), continue rotating the engine until the wire tie snaps (3).

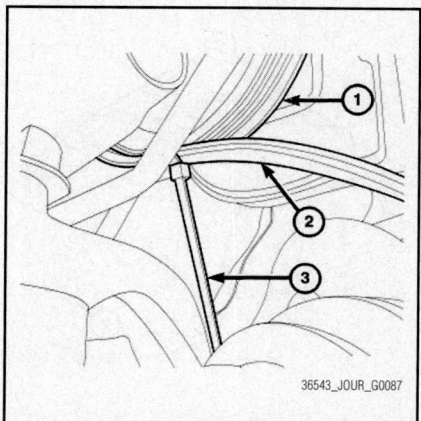

36543_JOUR_G0087

Fig. 46 Power steering belt installation—2.7L engine

12. Remove the wire tie (3) from the vehicle.

13. Install the RH wheelhouse splash shield.

3.5L Engine

See Figure 45.

1. Raise vehicle on hoist.
2. Remove RH wheelhouse splash shield.
3. Rotate accessory drive belt tensioner (3) clockwise to allow enough slack to remove accessory drive belt (5).

To install:

4. Position accessory drive belt (5) on all pulleys except generator (6).
5. Rotate accessory drive belt tensioner (3) clockwise.
6. Position accessory drive belt (5) on generator pulley (6).
7. Slowly release accessory drive belt tensioner (3).
8. Install RH wheelhouse splash shield.
9. Lower vehicle.

BALANCE SHAFT

REMOVAL & INSTALLATION

2.4L Engine

Refer to the Oil Pump procedure in this section.

CAMSHAFT AND VALVE LIFTERS

REMOVAL & INSTALLATION

2.4L Engine

See Figures 47 through 52.

1. Remove engine cover by pulling upward.

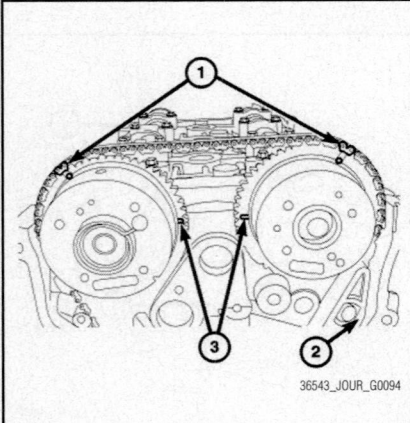

Fig. 47 Aligning camshaft marks—2.4L engine

2. Disconnect and isolate the negative battery cable.
3. Remove cylinder head cover.
4. Raise and support the vehicle.
5. Remove the frame cover portion of the right splash shield.
6. Rotate engine to TDC (1).
7. Make sure camshaft timing marks (3) are in line with the cylinder head cover sealing surface.
8. Mark the chain link corresponding to timing marks (1) with a paint marker.
9. Remove timing tensioner plug (1) from front cover.
10. Insert small Allen wrench through timing tensioner plug hole and lift ratchet (2) upward to release the tensioner and push Allen wrench inward. Leave the Allen wrench installed during the remainder of this procedure.
11. Insert Locking Wedge 9701 (1) between camshaft phasers.
12. Lightly tap Locking Wedge 9701 (2) into place until it will no longer sink down.

➡**Camshaft bearing caps should have been marked during engine manufacturing. For example, number one exhaust camshaft bearing is marked "E1>".**

✳✳ CAUTION

DO NOT use a number stamp or a punch to mark camshaft bearing caps. Damage to bearing caps could occur.

13. Using a permanent ink or paint marker, identify location and position on each camshaft bearing cap.
14. Remove the front camshaft bearing cap.
15. Slowly remove the remaining intake and exhaust camshaft bearing cap bolts one turn at a time.
16. Remove intake camshaft (1) by lifting the rear of the camshaft upward.
17. Rotate the camshaft while lifting out of the front bearing cradle.
18. Lift the timing chain (2) off the sprocket (1).
19. Remove exhaust camshaft.
20. Secure timing chain with wire so that it does fall into the timing chain cover.

To install:

21. The front camshaft bearing cap (1) is numbered (2) either one, two, or three, this corresponds to the select fit front exhaust camshaft bearing to use.
22. Install the corresponding select fit front exhaust camshaft bearing (1).

23. Oil all of the camshaft journals with clean engine oil.
24. Install camshaft phasers on camshafts if removed.
25. Install timing chain onto exhaust cam sprocket making sure that the timing marks (1) on the sprocket and the painted chain link are aligned.
26. Position exhaust camshaft and on bearing journals in the cylinder head.
27. Align exhaust cam timing mark (3) so it is in line with the cylinder head cover sealing surface (2).
28. Install intake camshaft by raising the rear of the camshaft upward and roll the sprocket into the chain.
29. Align the timing marks (1) on the intake cam sprocket with the painted chain link.
30. Position the intake camshaft into the bearing journals in the cylinder head.
31. Verify that the timing marks (1) are aligned on both camshafts and that the timing marks (3) are facing each other and are in line with the cylinder head cover sealing surface (2).

✳✳ CAUTION

Install the front intake and exhaust camshaft bearing cap last. Ensure that the dowels are seated and follow torque sequence or damage to engine could result.

➡**If the front camshaft bearing cap is broken, the cylinder head MUST be replaced.**

32. Install intake and exhaust camshaft bearing caps and slowly tighten bolts to 85 inch lbs. (9.5 Nm) in sequence.

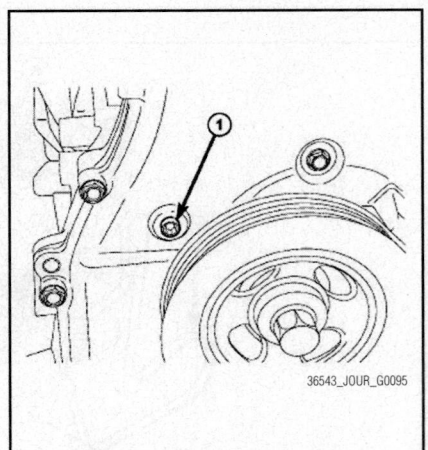

Fig. 48 Timing tensioner plug—2.4L engine

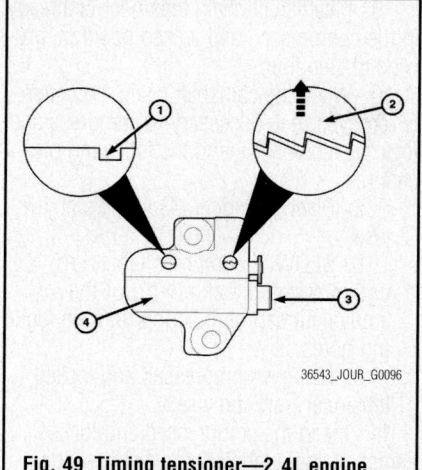

Fig. 49 Timing tensioner—2.4L engine

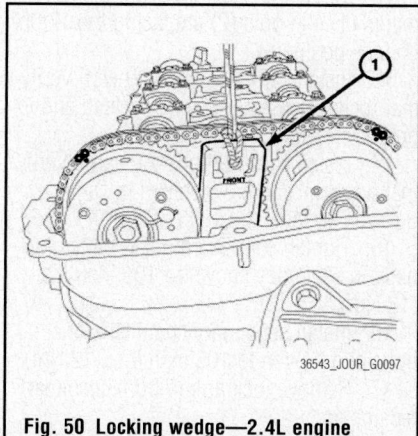

Fig. 50 Locking wedge—2.4L engine

➡️ **Verify that the exhaust bearing shells are correctly installed, and the dowels are seated in the head, prior to torquing bolts.**

33. Install the front intake and exhaust bearing cap and tighten bolts to 18 ft. lbs. (25 Nm) in sequence.

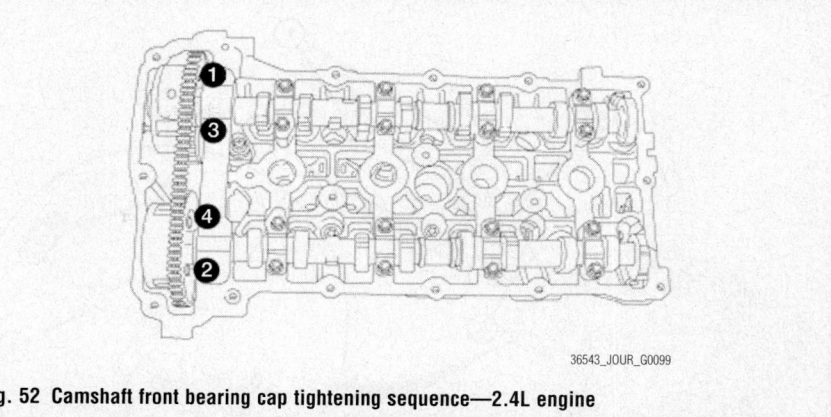

Fig. 52 Camshaft front bearing cap tightening sequence—2.4L engine

34. Verify that all timing marks (1,3) are aligned.

35. Remove Allen wrench from timing chain tensioner.

36. Remove Locking Wedge 9701 (1) by pulling straight upward on pull rope.

37. Apply MOPAR® thread sealant to timing tensioner plug (1) and Install.

38. Rotate the crankshaft CLOCKWISE two complete revolutions until the crankshaft is repositioned at the TDC position.

39. Verify that the camshafts timing marks (3) are in the proper position and in line with the cylinder head cover sealing surface. If the marks do not line up, the timing chain is not correctly installed.

40. Install right splash shield.

41. Remove RTV from gasket (1).

42. Inspect cylinder head cover gaskets (1,2) for damage. If no damage is present, gaskets can be reinstalled.

43. Install cylinder head cover.

44. Connect negative battery cable.

45. Fill cooling system.

46. Fill with oil.

47. Operate engine until it reaches

normal operating temperature. Check oil and cooling systems for correct fluid levels.

48. Install engine cover.

2.7L Engine

See Figures 53 through 57.

➡️ **The engine can be equipped with either conventional roller-type (early production) or silent type (late production) secondary timing chains.**

1. Remove the primary timing chain Refer to Timing Chain and Sprockets.

2. Remove secondary chain tensioner mounting bolts.

➡️ **Camshaft bearing caps should have been marked during engine manufacturing. For example, number one exhaust camshaft bearing is marked "1E>"**

3. Slowly loosen camshaft bearing cap bolts in the sequence shown.

4. Remove camshaft bearing caps (1).

5. Remove intake camshaft (7), exhaust camshaft (2), secondary timing chain (8), and secondary timing chain tensioner (6) together as an assembly.

6. Remove secondary timing chain tensioner (6) and secondary timing chain (8) from camshafts (2) and (7).

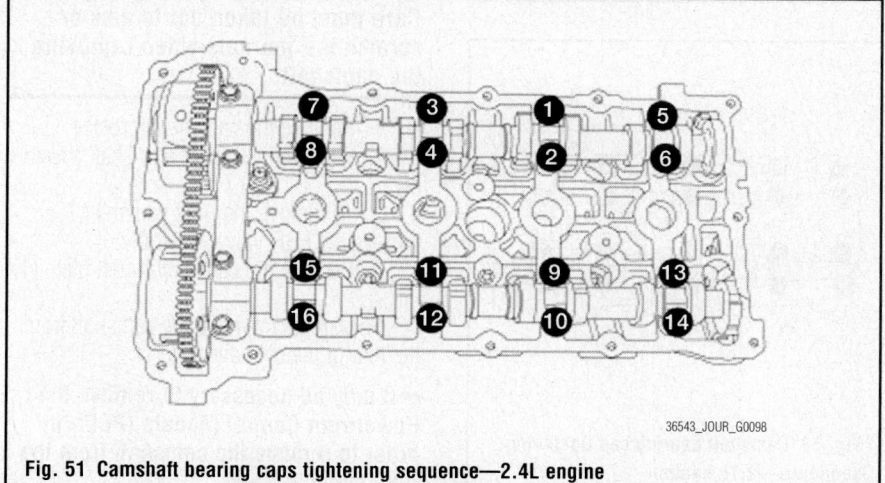

Fig. 51 Camshaft bearing caps tightening sequence—2.4L engine

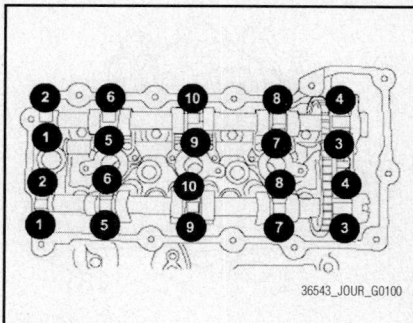

Fig. 53 Camshaft bearing cap loosening sequence—2.7L engine

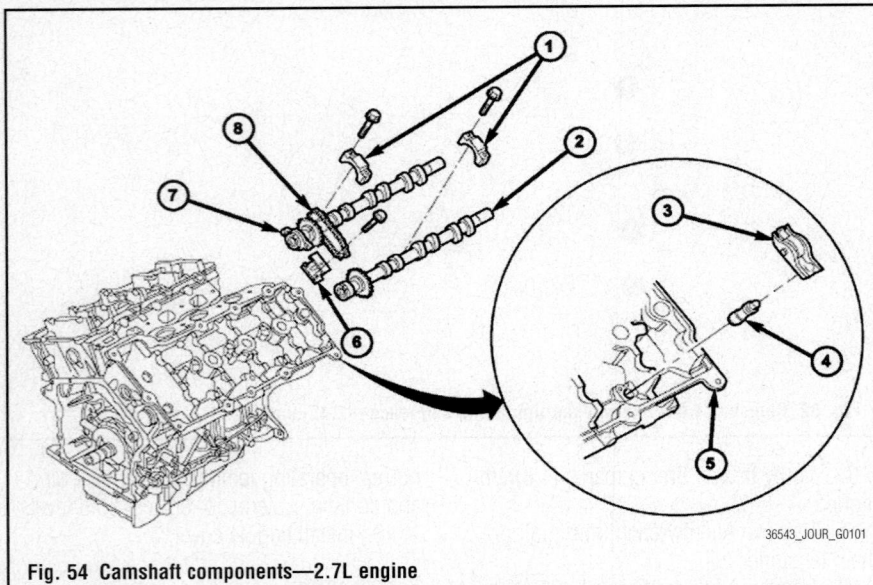

Fig. 54 Camshaft components—2.7L engine

7. Inspect camshafts Refer to Inspection.

To install:

➡**The engine can be equipped with either conventional roller-type (early production) or silent type (late production) secondary timing chains.**

When the timing chain is removed and the cylinder heads are installed, DO NOT rotate the camshafts or crankshaft without first locating the proper crankshaft position. Failure to do so will result in valve and/or piston damage.

8. Assemble camshaft chain on the cams. If equipped with roller chains (early production), ensure that plated links (1) are aligned with the timing dot (2)

on the camshaft sprockets. If equipped with silent chains (late production), ensure that marked links (1) are aligned with the timing dot (2) on the camshaft sprockets.

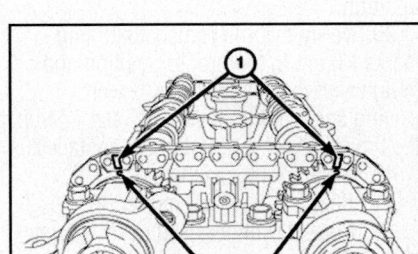

Fig. 56 Camshaft chain alignment (late production)—2.7L engine

Fig. 55 Camshaft chain alignment (early production)—2.7L engine

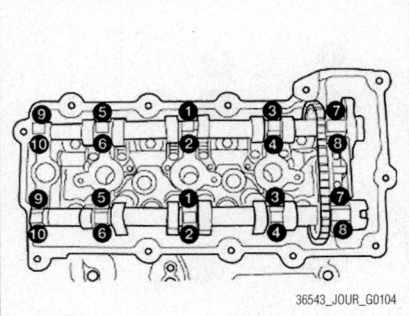

Fig. 57 Camshaft bearing cap tightening sequence—2.7L engine

9. If camshaft chain tensioner is already in the compressed and locked position, proceed to step four.

10. When the camshaft chain tensioner is removed, it is necessary to compress and lock the tensioner using the following procedures:

a. Place tensioner (1) into a soft jaw vise.

b. SLOWLY compress tensioner until fabricated lock pin (2) or the equivalent can be inserted into the locking holes.

c. Remove compressed and locked tensioner from the vise.

11. Insert the compressed and locked camshaft chain tensioner in-between the camshafts and chain.

12. Rotate the cams so that the timing marks (1) and dots (2) are facing the 12:00 O'clock position.

13. Install cams to cylinder head. Verify that rocker arms are correctly seated and in proper positions.

14. Install camshaft bearing caps. Verify that bearing caps are installed in same position as removed.

15. Tighten cam bearing cap bolts gradually in sequence shown to 105 inch lbs. (12 Nm).

16. Install secondary chain tensioner bolts and tighten to 105 inch lbs. (12 Nm).

17. Remove locking pin from secondary tensioners.

18. Verify end play of camshafts are within specification Refer to inspection.

19. Install the primary timing chain.

3.5L Engine

See Figure 58.

➡**Camshafts are removed from the rear of each cylinder head.**

Care must be taken not to nick or scratch the journals when removing the camshaft.

1. Remove the camshaft sprocket.

2. Remove the rocker arm shaft assembly.

3. To remove the right camshaft, remove the EGR Valve assembly.

4. Remove the camshaft thrust plate (1) or (2).

5. Carefully remove the camshaft from the rear of the cylinder head.

➡**It may be necessary to remove the Powertrain Control Module (PCM) in order to remove the camshaft from the right cylinder head.**

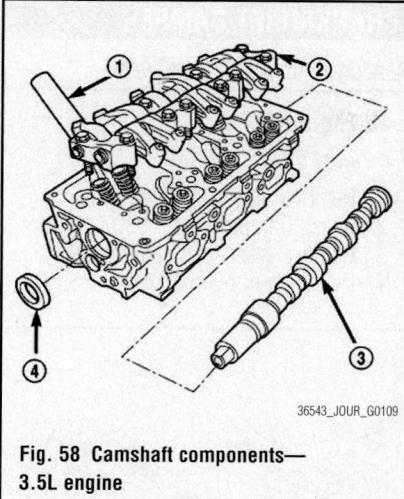

**Fig. 58 Camshaft components—
3.5L engine**

To install:

➡**Care must be taken not to scrape or
nick the camshaft journals when
installing the camshaft into position.**

6. Lubricate camshaft bearing journals,
camshaft lobes and camshaft seal with clean
engine oil and install camshaft into cylinder
head.

7. Install the camshaft sprocket.

8. Install the camshaft thrust plate (1)
or (2). Clean the mating surfaces and apply
the appropriate sealer as necessary. Torque
fasteners to 21 ft. lbs. (28 Nm).

9. If necessary, install the EGR Valve
assembly and Powertrain Control Module
(PCM).

10. Install the rocker arm assembly.

CATALYTIC CONVERTER

REMOVAL & INSTALLATION

2.4L Engine

See Figure 59.

❋❋ WARNING

**The normal operating temperature of
the exhaust system is very high.
Therefore, never work around or
attempt to service any part of the
exhaust system until it is cooled.
Special care should be taken
when working near the catalytic
converter. The temperature of the
converter rises to a high level after
a short period of engine operating
time.**

➡**When replacement is required on
any component of the exhaust system,
you must use original equipment parts
(or their equivalent).**

1. Raise and support vehicle.

2. Apply penetrating oil to band clamp
nut and bolt.

3. Disconnect oxygen sensor connector
(1) .

4. Remove oxygen sensor.

5. Loosen resonator and muffler
assembly to catalytic converter band clamp.

6. Pull muffler and resonator assembly
rearward to remove from catalytic converter.

7. Remove flange nuts (2) at exhaust
manifold.

8. Remove catalytic converter from
vehicle (3).

9. Remove and discard gasket.

To install:

➡**Always work from the front to rear of
exhaust system when aligning and
tightening exhaust system components.**

10. Clean manifold to converter sealing
surfaces.

11. Using a new gasket, position catalytic converter to exhaust manifold.

12. Install catalytic converter mounting
bolts (2). Tighten to 21 ft. lbs. (28 Nm).

13. Position a new band clamp onto the
resonator and muffler assembly.

14. Install resonator and muffler assembly onto catalytic converter.

15. Align exhaust system to maintain
position and proper clearance with underbody parts. All support isolators should
have equal load on them.

16. Tighten resonator and muffler
assembly band clamp to 40 ft. lbs. (54 Nm).

17. Lower vehicle.

18. Start the engine and inspect for
exhaust leaks. Repair exhaust leaks as necessary.

19. Check the exhaust system for contact
with the body panels. Make the necessary
adjustments, if needed.

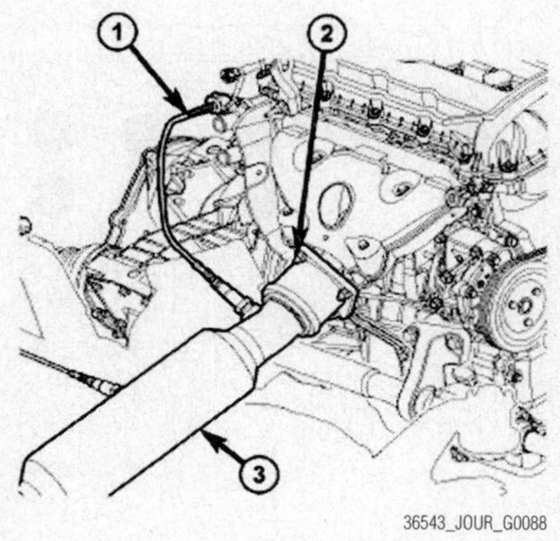

2.7L Engine

Front

See Figure 60.

For removal of the front catalytic converter, remove exhaust manifold.

1. Remove engine cover.

2. Disconnect negative cable from
battery.

3. Remove bolts attaching upper heat
shield.

4. Remove upper heat shield.

5. Disconnect exhaust pipe from manifold.

6. Disconnect oxygen sensor electrical
connector.

7. Remove manifold support bracket.

8. Remove lower exhaust manifold heat
shield.

9. Remove exhaust manifold retaining
fasteners.

10. Remove and discard manifold
gasket.

To install:

11. Install a new exhaust manifold gasket. DO NOT APPLY SEALER.

12. Position exhaust manifold in place.

13. Tighten the exhaust manifold bolts to
25 ft. lbs. (34 Nm), in sequence.

14. Install exhaust manifold heat
shields. Tighten bolts to 105 inch lbs.
(12 Nm).

15. Install exhaust manifold support
bracket.

16. Install new catalytic converter
gasket.

17. Install exhaust pipe to manifold. Tighten fasteners to 21 ft. lbs. (28
Nm).

18. Connect oxygen sensor electrical
connector.

19. Connect negative battery cable.

20. Install engine cover.

Fig. 59 Catalytic converter—2.4L engine

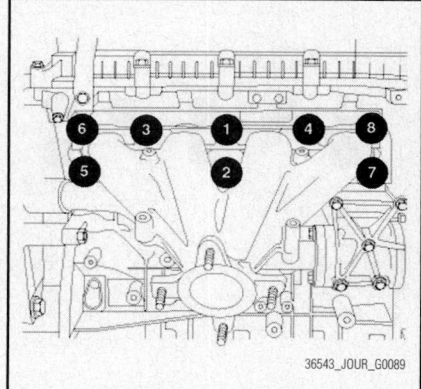

**Fig. 60 Front catalytic converter—
2.7L engine**

Rear

See Figure 61.

For removal of the catalytic converter, remove exhaust manifold.

1. Remove engine cover.
2. Disconnect negative cable from battery.
3. Remove bolts attaching upper heat shield.
4. Remove upper heat shield.
5. Disconnect exhaust pipe from manifold.
6. Disconnect oxygen sensor electrical connector.
7. Remove manifold support bracket.
8. Remove lower exhaust manifold heat shield.
9. Remove exhaust manifold retaining fasteners.
10. Remove and discard manifold gasket.

To install:

11. Install a new exhaust manifold gasket. DO NOT APPLY SEALER.
12. Position exhaust manifold in place.
13. Tighten the exhaust manifold bolts to 25 ft. lbs. (34 Nm), in sequence.
14. Install exhaust manifold heat shields. Tighten bolts to 105 inch lbs. (12 Nm).
15. Install exhaust manifold support bracket.
16. Install new catalytic converter gasket.
17. Install exhaust pipe to manifold. Tighten fasteners to 21 ft. lbs. (28 Nm).
18. Connect oxygen sensor electrical connector.
19. Connect negative battery cable.
20. Install engine cover.

3.5L Engine

See Figure 62.

For removal of the catalytic converters, remove exhaust manifolds.

1. Remove engine cover.
2. Disconnect negative cable from battery.
3. Remove bolts attaching upper heat shield.
4. Remove upper heat shield.
5. Disconnect exhaust pipe from manifold.
6. Disconnect oxygen sensor electrical connector.
7. Remove manifold support bracket.
8. Remove lower exhaust manifold heat shield.
9. Remove exhaust manifold retaining fasteners.
10. Remove and discard manifold gasket.

To install:

11. Install a new exhaust manifold gasket. DO NOT APPLY SEALER.
12. Position exhaust manifold in place.
13. Tighten the exhaust manifold bolts to 25 ft. lbs. (34 Nm).
14. Install exhaust manifold heat shields (1). Tighten bolts to 105 inch lbs. (12 Nm).
15. Install exhaust manifold support bracket.
16. Install new catalytic converter gasket.
17. Install exhaust pipe to manifold. Tighten fasteners to 21 ft. lbs. (28 Nm).
18. Connect oxygen sensor electrical connector.
19. Connect negative battery cable.
20. Install engine cover.

CRANKSHAFT DAMPER

REMOVAL & INSTALLATION

2.4L Engine

See Figure 63.

1. Remove accessory drive belts.
2. Install Damper holder 9707 (1).
3. Remove crankshaft damper bolt.
4. Pull damper off crankshaft.

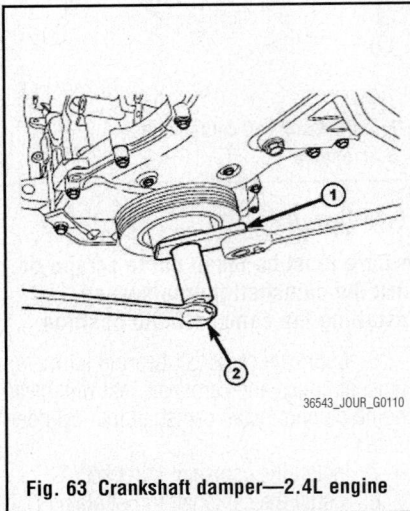

Fig. 63 Crankshaft damper—2.4L engine

To install:

5. Install crankshaft damper.
6. Apply clean engine oil crankshaft damper bolt threads and between bolt head and washer. Tighten bolt to 155 ft. lbs. (210 Nm).
7. Install accessory drive belts.

2.7L Engine

See Figure 64.

1. Disconnect negative battery cable.
2. Remove right front wheel and belt splash shield.
3. Remove accessory drive belts.
4. Remove damper bolt.
5. Remove damper by using Special Tools 8194 Insert and 8454 Puller (1).

To install:

6. Install damper using Special Tools 8179 (3) Screw, with Nut and Thrust Bearing from 6792, and 6792-1 Installer (2).
7. Install damper center bolt. Tighten center bolt to 125 ft. lbs. (170 Nm).
8. Install accessory drive belts.
9. Install belt splash shield and right front wheel.
10. Lower vehicle.
11. Connect negative battery cable.

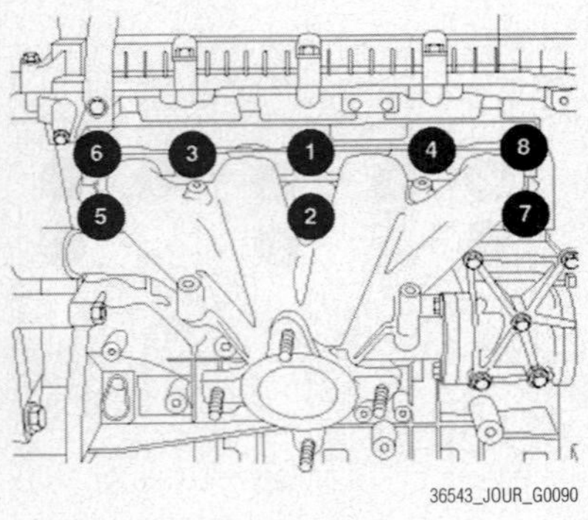

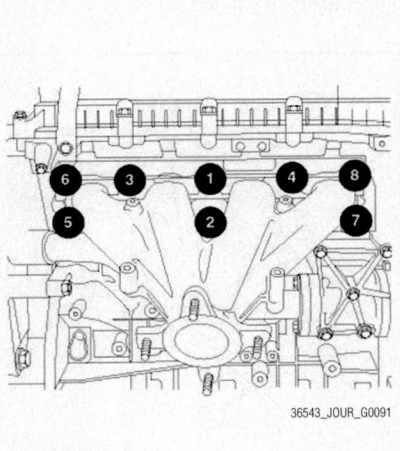

Fig. 61 Rear catalytic converter—2.7L engine

36543_JOUR_G0090

Fig. 62 Catalytic converter—3.5L engine

36543_JOUR_G0091

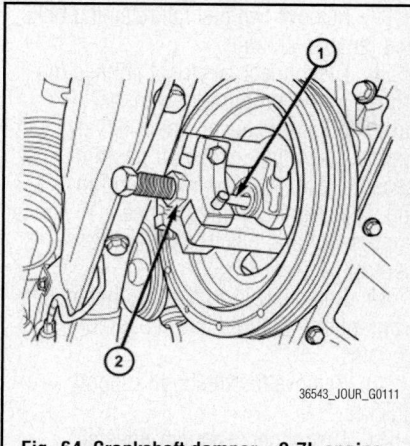

Fig. 64 Crankshaft damper—2.7L engine

3.5L Engine

See Figure 65.

1. Disconnect negative battery cable.
2. Raise vehicle on hoist.
3. Remove the right engine mount.
4. Remove the right front wheel and accessory drive belt splash shield.
5. Remove accessory drive belt.
6. Suitably support the engine.
7. Remove the lower crossmember.
8. Low the engine.
9. Remove vibration damper bolt.
10. Use Special Tool 1023 puller (1), and insert 9020-R (2), remove crankshaft damper.

To install:

11. Install crankshaft damper using Special Tools C-4685-C1 (5.9 in.) Bolt (2), with Nut and Thrust Bearing from 6792, and 6792-1 (1) Installer.
12. Install vibration damper bolt. Torque bolt to 70 ft. lbs. (95 Nm).
13. Install the lower crossmember.
14. Install accessory drive belt.

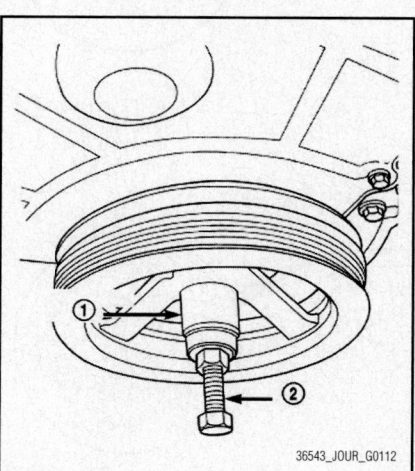

Fig. 65 Crankshaft damper—3.5L engine

15. Install the accessory drive belt splash shield and right front wheel.
16. Lower vehicle.
17. Install the right engine mount.
18. Connect the negative battery cable.

CRANKSHAFT FRONT SEAL

REMOVAL & INSTALLATION

2.4L Engine

See Figure 66.

1. Remove accessory drive belt.
2. Install damper holder 9707 and remove damper retaining bolt.
3. Pull damper off crankshaft.
4. Remove front crankshaft oil seal (1) by prying out with a screwdriver. Be careful not to damage the cover seal surface.

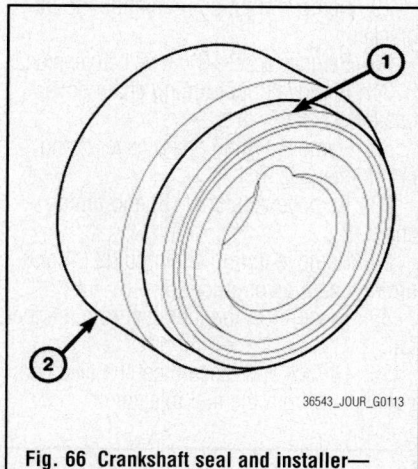

Fig. 66 Crankshaft seal and installer—2.4L engine

To install:

5. Place seal (1) onto Seal installer 9506 (2) with seal spring towards the inside of engine.
6. Install new seal (1) by using Seal installer 9506 (2) and crankshaft damper bolt (3).
7. Press seal into front cover until Seal Installer 9506 seats against timing chain cover.
8. Remove seal installer 9506.
9. Install crankshaft vibration damper.
10. Oil the bolt threads and between the bolt head and washer.
11. Install damper retaining bolt and damper holder 9707. Tighten bolt to 155 ft. lbs. (210 Nm).

2.7L Engine

See Figures 67 and 68.

1. Remove crankshaft vibration damper.
2. Install Special Tool 8194, Insert into

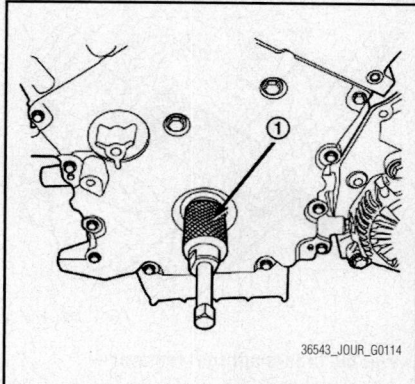

Fig. 67 Crankshaft seal remover—2.7L engine

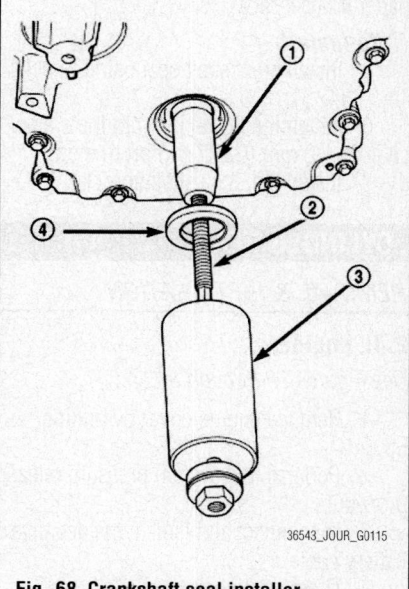

Fig. 68 Crankshaft seal installer—2.7L engine

crankshaft nose. Remove seal using Special Tool 6771, Remover (1).

To install:

3. Install new seal using Special Tools 6780-2 Sleeve, 6780-1 Installer, and 8179 Stud (2).
4. Install crankshaft vibration damper.

3.5L Engine

See Figure 69.

1. Remove the crankshaft sprocket.
2. Tap the dowel pin (2) out of the crankshaft.
3. Remove crankshaft seal using Special Tool 6341A (1).

✳✳ CAUTION

Do not nick shaft seal surface or seal bore.

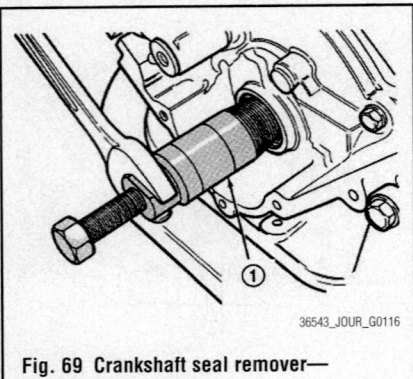

Fig. 69 Crankshaft seal remover—3.5L engine

4. Shaft seal lip surface must be free of varnish, dirt or nicks. Polish with 400 grit paper if necessary.

To install:

5. Install crankshaft seal using Special Tool 6342 (1).

6. Install the dowel pin into the crankshaft to 1.2 mm (0.047 in.) protrusion.

7. Install the crankshaft sprocket.

CYLINDER HEAD

REMOVAL & INSTALLATION

2.4L Engine

See Figures 70 through 81.

1. Remove engine cover by pulling upward.

2. Perform fuel system pressure release procedure.

3. Disconnect and isolate the negative battery cable.

4. Drain cooling system.

5. Remove clean air hose and air cleaner housing.

6. Remove coolant recovery bottle.

7. Remove and reposition power steering reservoir.

8. Remove accessory drive belt.

9. Remove power steering hose hold-down.

10. Remove the three power steering pump mounting bolts through the openings in the pulley and reposition the pump.

11. Remove the cylinder head cover.

12. Remove ignition coils from the cylinder head cover.

13. Raise and support the vehicle.

14. Remove the frame cover portion of the right splash shield.

15. Set engine to TDC.

16. Remove lower A/C compressor bolts if equipped.

17. Remove lower A/C compressor mount if equipped.

18. Remove accessory drive belt lower idler pulley.

19. Remove crankshaft damper.

20. Remove three bolts and water pump pulley from water pump.

21. Remove lower bolt from right side engine mount bracket.

22. Remove timing chain cover lower bolts at front of oil pan.

23. Remove exhaust manifold.

24. Lower vehicle.

25. Support engine with suitable jack.

26. Remove right engine mount bracket retaining bolts.

27. Remove retaining nuts and reposition mount bracket.

28. Remove accessory drive upper idler pulley.

29. Remove right upper engine mount bracket.

30. Remove accessory drive belt tensioner.

31. Remove upper timing chain cover retaining bolts.

32. Remove timing chain cover using pry points (1,2,3).

33. Remove tensioner (5) and timing chain (2).

34. Remove timing chain guide (4) and timing chain pivot guide (6).

35. Disconnect the fuel line from the fuel rail.

36. Unlock and disconnect the electrical connectors from the fuel injectors.

37. Remove two fuel rail retaining bolts and remove fuel rail.

38. Disconnect electrical connectors from coolant temperature sensor, oil temperature sensor, variable valve timing solenoids, camshaft position sensors, MAP sensor, manifold tuning valve, ignition interference suppressor and electronic throttle control.

39. Remove wiring harness retainer from intake manifold and reposition harness.

40. Remove throttle body support bracket.

41. Disconnect vacuum lines at intake.

42. Remove intake manifold retaining bolts and remove intake manifold.

43. Remove four bolts and reposition coolant adapter (3).

44. Remove ground strap at right rear of cylinder head if equipped.

➡Camshaft bearing caps should have been marked during engine manufacturing. For example, number one exhaust camshaft bearing is marked "E1>".

✳✳ CAUTION

DO NOT use a number stamp or a punch to mark camshaft bearing caps. Damage to bearing caps could occur.

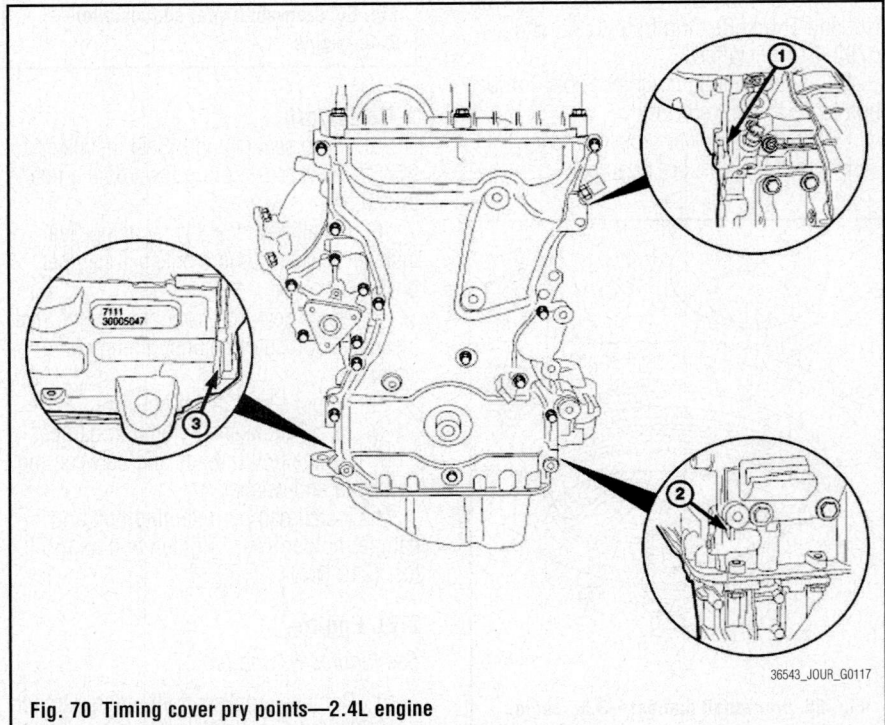

Fig. 70 Timing cover pry points—2.4L engine

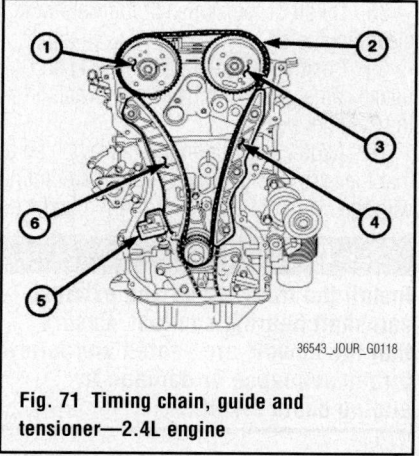

Fig. 71 Timing chain, guide and tensioner—2.4L engine

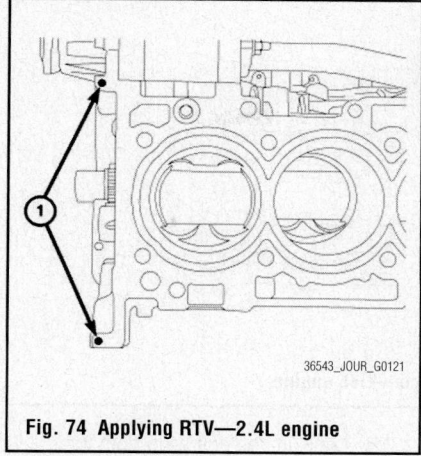

Fig. 74 Applying RTV—2.4L engine

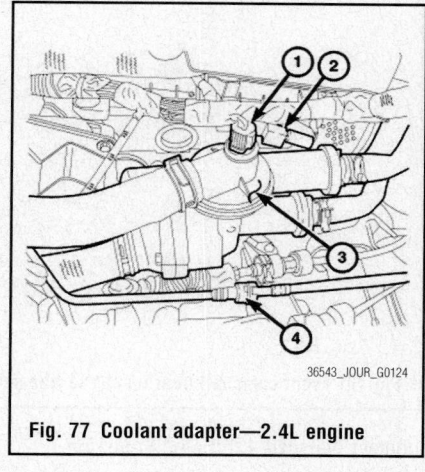

Fig. 77 Coolant adapter—2.4L engine

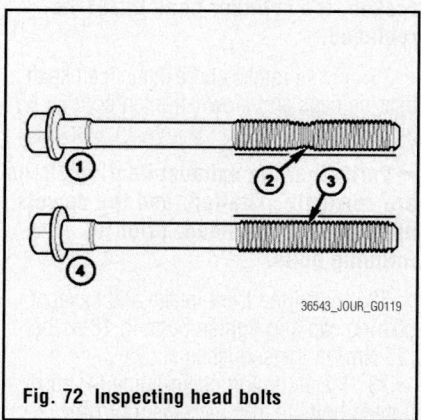

Fig. 72 Inspecting head bolts

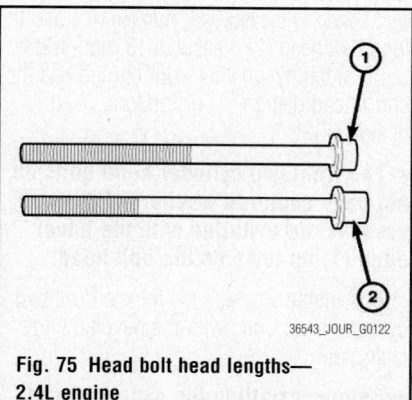

Fig. 75 Head bolt head lengths—2.4L engine

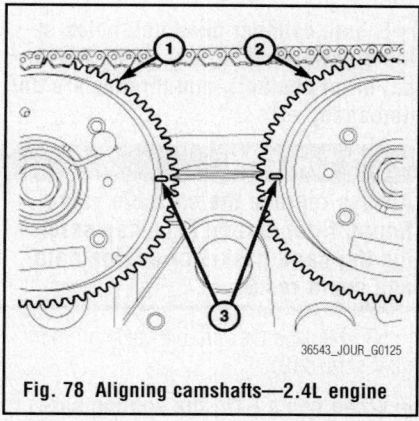

Fig. 78 Aligning camshafts—2.4L engine

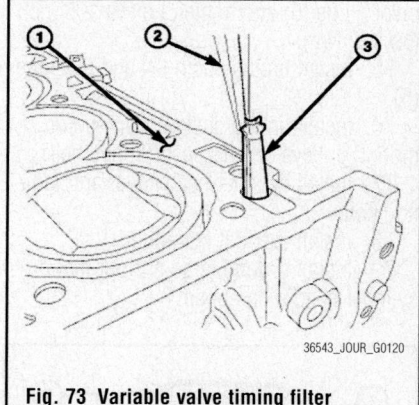

Fig. 73 Variable valve timing filter screen—2.4L

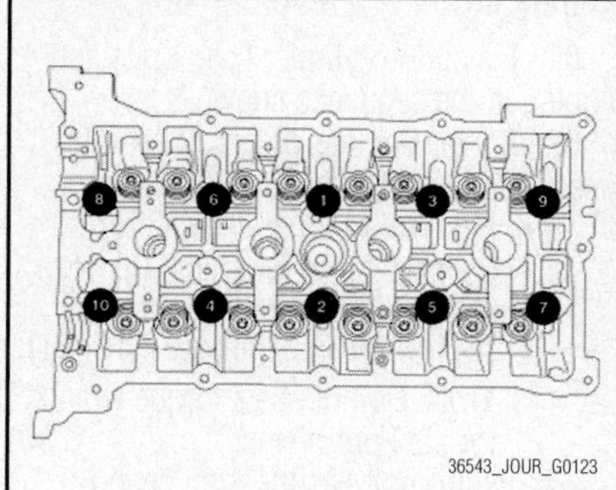

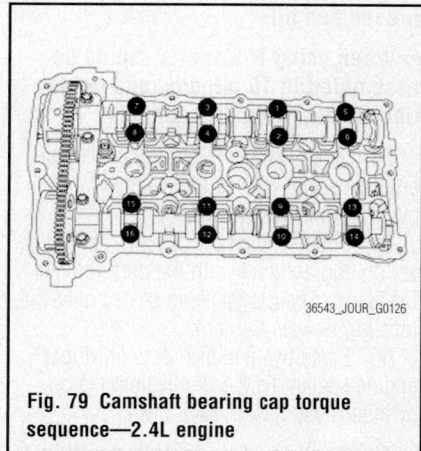

Fig. 76 Head bolt torque sequence—2.4L engine

Fig. 79 Camshaft bearing cap torque sequence—2.4L engine

45. Using a permanent ink or paint marker, identify location and position on each camshaft bearing cap.

46. Remove the front camshaft bearing cap.

47. Slowly remove the remaining intake and exhaust camshaft bearing cap bolts one turn at a time.

48. Remove the camshafts.

➡All of the cylinder head bolts have captured washers EXCEPT the front two (1).

49. Remove cylinder head bolts and two uncaptured washers.

50. Remove cylinder head from engine block.

51. Inspect and clean cylinder head and block sealing surfaces.

➡Ensure cylinder head bolt holes in the block are clean, dry (free of residual oil or coolant), and threads are not damaged.

To install:

※※ **CAUTION**

The cylinder head bolts are tightened using a torque plus angle procedure. The bolts must be examined BEFORE reuse. If the threads are necked down the bolts must be replaced.

52. Check cylinder head bolts for necking by holding a scale or straight edge against the threads. If all the threads do not

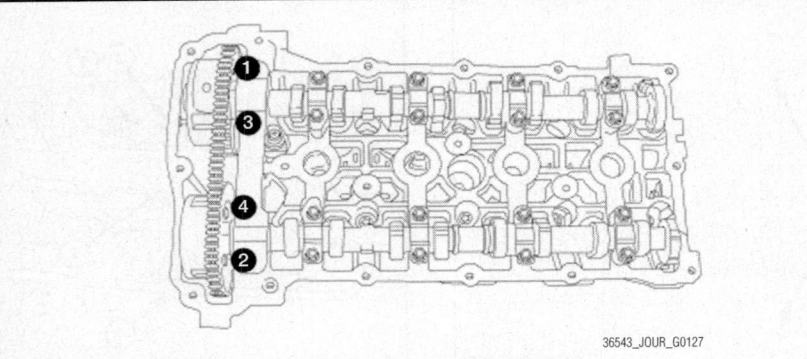

Fig. 80 Front camshaft bearing cap torque sequence—2.4L engine

contact the scale (2) the bolt must be replaced.

➡**Ensure cylinder head bolt holes in the block are clean, dry (free of residual oil or coolant), and threads are not damaged.**

✳✳ CAUTION

Always replace the variable valve timing filter screen (3) when servicing the head gasket or engine damage could result.

53. Replace the variable valve timing filter screen (3).

➡**When using RTV, the sealing surfaces must be clean and free from grease and oil.**

➡**When using RTV, parts should be assembled in 10 minutes and tighten to final torque within 45 minutes.**

54. Place two pea size dots of Mopar® engine sealant RTV or equivalent (1) on cylinder block as shown.

55. Position the new cylinder head gasket on engine block with the part number facing up. Ensure gasket is seated over the locating dowels in block.

56. Place two pea size dots of Mopar® engine sealant RTV or equivalent (1) on cylinder head gasket as shown.

➡**The head must be installed within 15 minutes before the RTV skins.**

57. Position cylinder head onto engine block.

✳✳ CAUTION

This engine was built with 2 different style cylinder head bolts. Each style bolt requires a different torque value. The bolts can be identified by the short bolt head (1) and the long bolt head (2).

58. Measure the bolt head from the washer to the top of the bolt head. The short bolt head (1) measures 8 mm (5/16") and the long bolt head (2) measures 13 mm (1/2").

59. Identify whether your engine has the short head design (1) or the long head design (2).

➡**The front two cylinder head bolts do not have captured washers. The washers must be installed with the bevel edge (1) up towards the bolt head.**

60. Install washers (1) for the front two cylinder head bolts with the beveled edge facing up.

➡**Before installing the cylinder head bolts, lubricate the threads with clean engine oil.**

61. Install the cylinder head bolts and tighten in the sequence shown.

62. If your bolt has the short head (1), use the following torque specifications:
- First: All to 25 ft. lbs. (30 Nm)
- Second: All to 45 ft. lbs. (61 Nm)
- Third: All to 45 ft. lbs. (61 Nm)
- Fourth: All an additional 90° CAUTION: Do not use a torque wrench for the Fourth step.

63. If your bolt has the long head (2), use the following torque specifications:
- First: All to 25 ft. lbs. (30 Nm)
- Second: All to 54 ft. lbs. (73 Nm)
- Third: All to 54 ft. lbs. (73 Nm)
- Fourth: All an additional 90° CAUTION: Do not use a torque wrench for the Fourth step.

64. Clean excess RTV from the timing chain cover sealing surface.

65. Install coolant adapter (3) with new seals. Tighten bolts to 13 ft. lbs. (18 Nm).

66. The front camshaft bearing cap (1) is numbered (2) either one, two, or three, this corresponds to the select fit front exhaust camshaft bearing to use.

67. Install the corresponding select fit front exhaust camshaft bearing (1).

68. Oil all of the camshaft journals with clean engine oil.

69. Position exhaust camshaft (1) and intake camshaft (2) on bearing journals in the cylinder head.

70. Align camshaft timing marks (3) so that they are facing each other and are in line with the cylinder head cover sealing surface.

✳✳ CAUTION

Install the front intake and exhaust camshaft bearing cap last. Ensure that the dowels are seated and follow torque sequence or damage to engine could result.

➡**If the front camshaft bearing cap is broken, the cylinder head MUST be replaced.**

71. Install intake and exhaust camshaft bearing caps and slowly tighten bolts to 85 inch lbs. (9.5 Nm) in the sequence shown.

➡**Verify that the exhaust bearing shells are correctly installed, and the dowels are seated in the head, prior to torquing bolts.**

72. Install the front intake and exhaust bearing cap and tighten bolts to 18 ft. lbs. (25 Nm) in the sequence shown.

73. Install timing chain guide (4) and tighten bolts to 105 inch lbs. (12 Nm).

74. Install the moveable timing chain pivot guide (6) and tighten bolt to 105 inch lbs. (12 Nm).

75. Install timing chain (2) and tensioner (5).

76. Install timing chain cover, engine mount, pulleys and accessory drive belt.

77. Install cylinder head cover and ignition coils.

78. Install exhaust manifold.

79. Install ground strap at right rear of cylinder head if equipped.

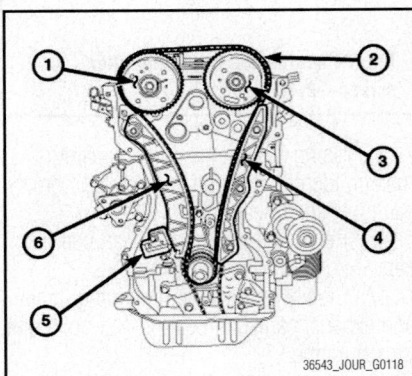

Fig. 81 Timing chain, guide and tensioner—2.4L engine

80. Install intake manifold, vacuum lines and fuel rail.

81. Connect coil and injector electrical connectors.

82. Connect electrical connectors to coolant temperature sensor, camshaft position sensors, oil temperature sensor, variable valve timing solenoids, MAP sensor, manifold tuning valve, ignition interference suppressor and electronic throttle control.

83. Install power steering pump reservoir. Tighten mounting screw to 106 inch lbs. (12 Nm).

84. Install coolant recovery reservoir. Tighten mounting bolts to 89 inch lbs. (10 Nm).

85. Install clean air hose and air cleaner housing.

86. Fill cooling system.

87. Install new oil filter and fill engine with oil.

88. Connect negative battery cable.

89. Operate engine until it reaches normal operating temperature. Check oil and cooling systems for leaks and correct fluid levels.

90. Install engine cover.

2.7L Engine

See Figures 82 through 90.

1. Perform fuel pressure release procedure before attempting any repairs.

2. Disconnect negative cable from remote jumper terminal.

3. Drain cooling system.

4. Remove accessory drive belts.

5. Remove the vibration damper.

6. Remove exhaust cross-under pipe.

7. Remove the manifold/converter.

8. Remove oil pressure sensor heat shield. Disconnect oil pressure sensor connector.

9. Remove upper and lower intake manifolds.

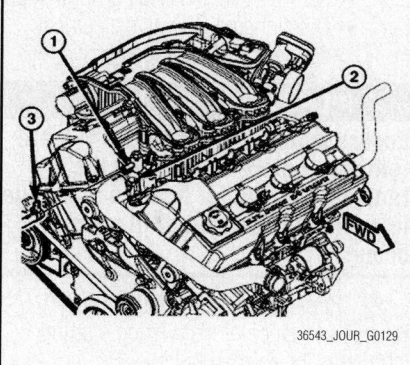

Fig. 83 Coolant outlet connector—2.7L engine

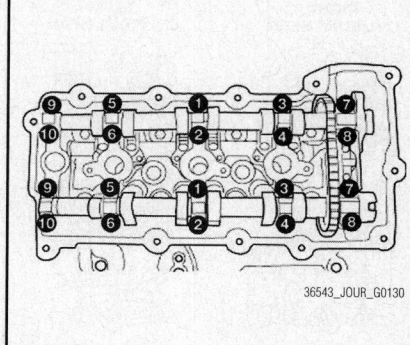

Fig. 84 Camshaft bearing cap torque sequence—2.7L engine

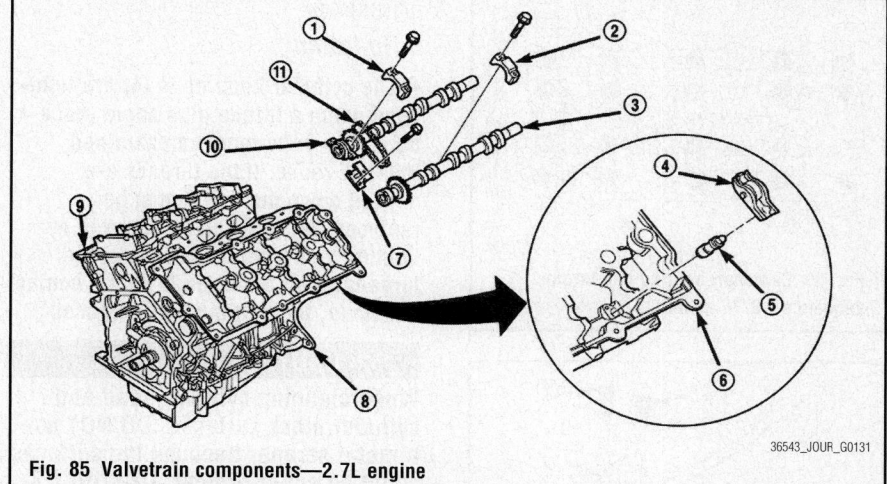

Fig. 85 Valvetrain components—2.7L engine

10. Remove cylinder head covers.

11. Disconnect camshaft position sensor and Crankshaft Position (CKP) sensor connectors.

12. Reposition engine wiring harness to left side of vehicle.

13. Remove coolant outlet connector (3).

14. Remove timing chain cover.

15. Rotate crankshaft until crankshaft sprocket timing mark aligns with timing mark on oil pump housing.

16. Remove primary timing chain.

17. Remove upper primary timing chain guides.

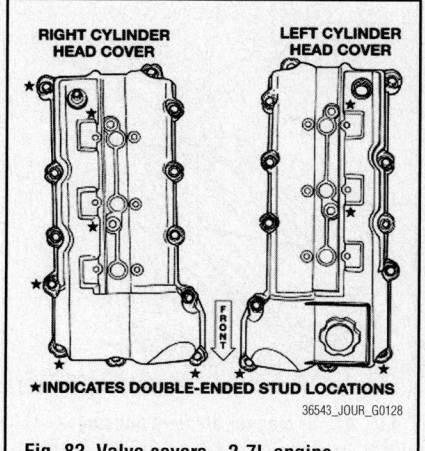

Fig. 82 Valve covers—2.7L engine

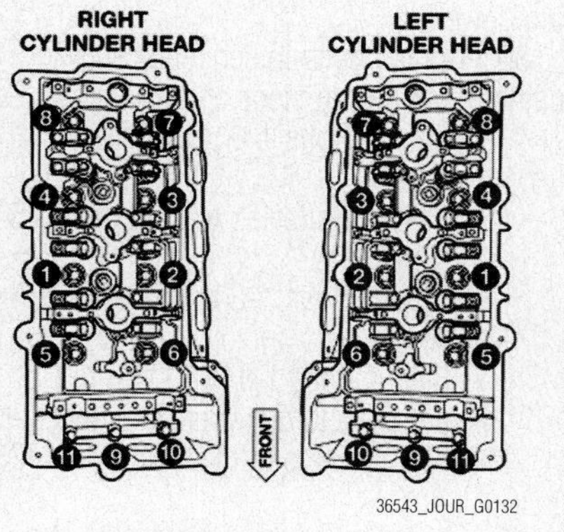

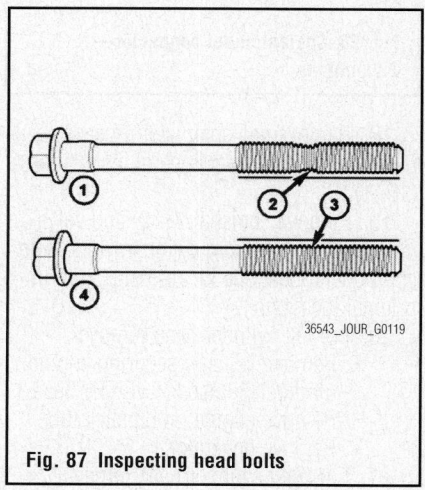

Fig. 86 Head bolt torque sequence—2.7L engine

Fig. 87 Inspecting head bolts

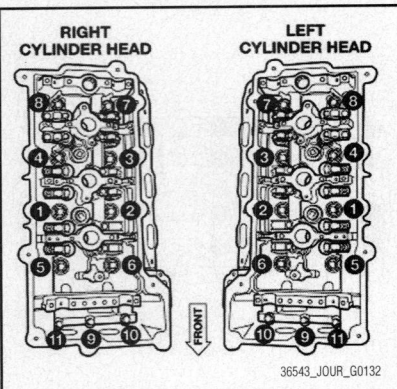

Fig. 88 Head bolt torque sequence—2.7L engine

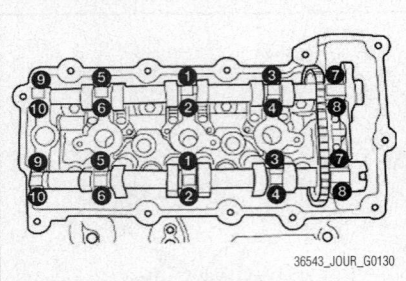

Fig. 89 Camshaft bearing cap torque sequence—2.7L engine

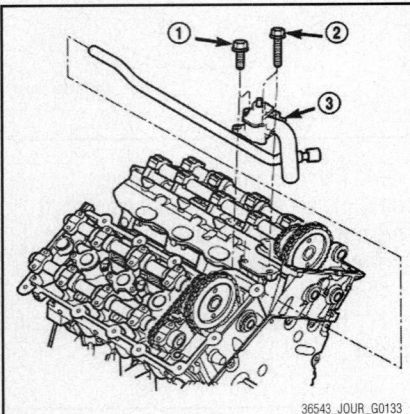

Fig. 90 Coolant outlet connector—2.7L engine

18. Remove camshaft bearing caps gradually in REVERSE sequence of installation (10–1).

19. Remove camshafts (10) and valvetrain components from cylinder head. Note component locations for re-installation in original locations.

20. For left cylinder head removal:
- Remove fastener securing engine oil dipstick tube to cylinder head. Remove engine oil dipstick tube.
- Remove generator.

21. For right cylinder head removal:

- Remove cylinder head ground strap.
- Disconnect EGR valve electrical connector (if equipped).

> **✳✳ CAUTION**
>
> **Ensure cylinder head bolts 11–9 are removed before attempting the removal of cylinder head, as damage to cylinder head and/or block may occur.**

22. Remove cylinder head bolts in reverse sequence of installation starting with bolts 11–9, then bolts 8–1.

23. Remove cylinder head(s).

24. Remove and discard cylinder head gasket.

25. Clean cylinder head and block sealing surfaces.

To install:

➡ **The cylinder head bolts (4) are tightened using a torque plus angle procedure. The bolts must be examined BEFORE reuse. If the threads are necked down the bolts must be replaced Necking can be checked by holding a straight edge against the threads. If all the threads do not contact the scale, the bolt must be replaced.**

> **✳✳ CAUTION**
>
> **When cleaning cylinder head and cylinder block surfaces, DO NOT use a metal scraper because the surfaces could be cut or ground. Use ONLY a wooden or plastic scraper.**

26. Clean sealing surfaces of cylinder head and block.

27. Lubricate bolt threads with clean engine oil and install bolts.

28. Install new head gasket over locating dowels.

29. Install cylinder head to block, assuring head is properly positioned over locating dowels.

30. Tighten bolts in sequence shown, using the following steps and torque values:
- Step 1: Bolts 1-8 to 35 ft. lbs. (48 Nm)
- Step 2: Bolts 1-8 to 55 ft. lbs. (75 Nm)
- Step 3: Bolts 1-8 to 55 ft. lbs. (75 Nm)
- Step 4: Bolts 1-8 to +90° Turn Do not use a torque wrench for this step.
- Step 5: Bolts 9-11 to 21 ft. lbs. (28 Nm)

31. For left cylinder head installation:
- Install engine oil dipstick tube.
- Install generator.

32. For right cylinder head installation:
- Install cylinder head ground strap.
- Connect EGR valve electrical connector (if equipped).

33. Install all valvetrain components and camshafts. Tighten camshaft bearing caps in sequence shown to 105 inch lbs. (12 Nm).

34. Install primary timing chain, guides and sprockets.

35. Install coolant outlet connector (3).

36. Install cylinder head covers.

37. Connect camshaft position sensor and Crankshaft Position (CKP) sensor connectors.

38. Install timing chain cover.

39. Install crankshaft vibration damper.

40. Install lower and upper intake manifolds.

41. Connect oil pressure sensor connector. Install oil pressure sensor heat shield.

42. Install the manifold/converter.

43. Install exhaust cross-under pipe.

44. Install accessory drive belts.

45. Fill cooling system.

46. Connect negative cable to remote jumper terminal.

3.5L Engine

Left Cylinder Head

See Figures 91 through 99.

1. Remove the engine cover.

2. Perform the fuel pressure release procedure.

3. Disconnect the negative battery cable.

4. Drain cooling system.

5. Remove air cleaner element housing.

6. Remove radiator fan assembly.

7. Remove the coolant recovery container.

8. Remove the generator.

9. Disconnect the fuel line (1) at the fuel rail (2).

10. Remove the upper intake manifold.

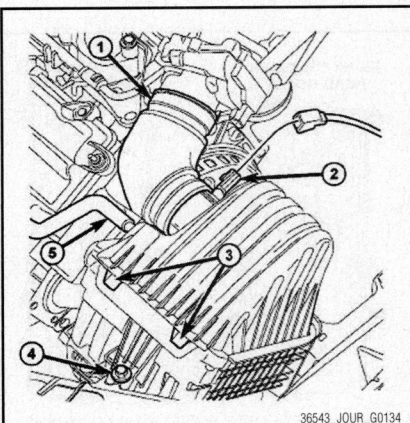

Fig. 91 Air cleaner element housing—3.5L engine

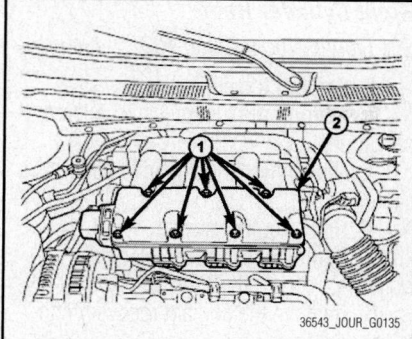

Fig. 92 Upper intake manifold—3.5L engine

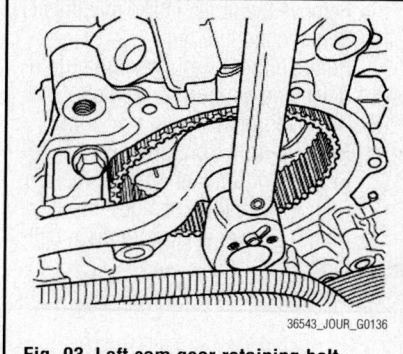

Fig. 93 Left cam gear retaining bolt—3.5L engine

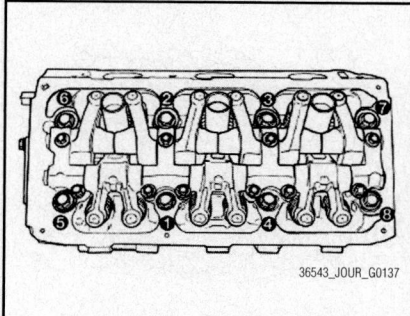

Fig. 94 Left cylinder head bolt torque sequence—3.5L engine

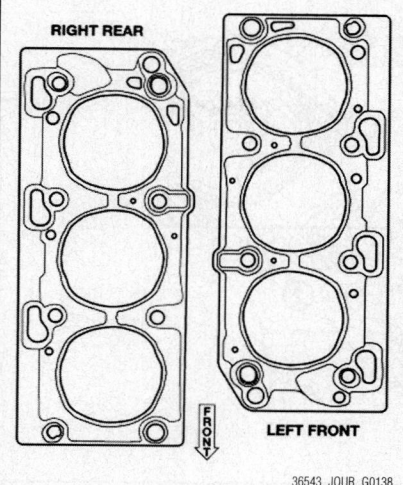

Fig. 95 Cylinder head gasket identification—3.5L engine

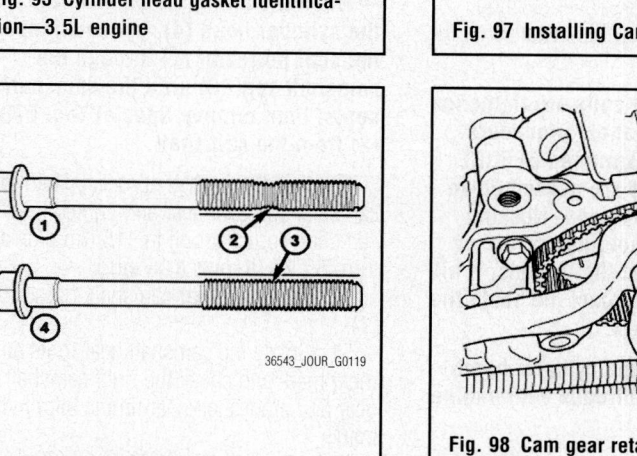

Fig. 96 Inspecting head bolts

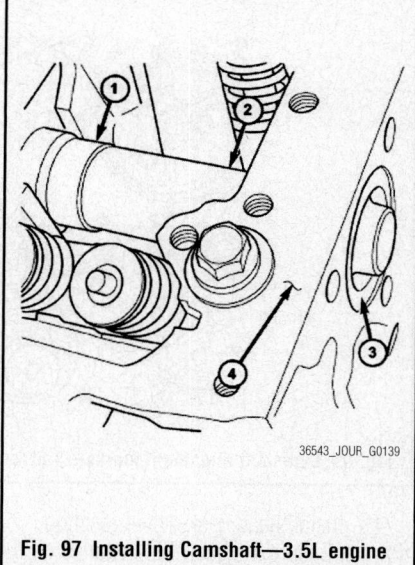

Fig. 97 Installing Camshaft—3.5L engine

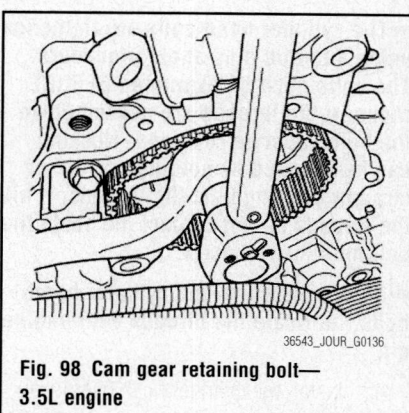

Fig. 98 Cam gear retaining bolt—3.5L engine

11. Remove the fuel rail.
12. Remove the lower intake manifold.
13. Raise and support the vehicle.
14. Remove the left exhaust manifold.
15. Remove right front tire.
16. Remove right inner splash shield.
17. Remove vibration damper (5).
18. Remove lower accessory drive belt idler pulley (6).
19. Remove the power steering mounting bolts and set the pump aside.
20. Remove lower outer timing belt cover bolts.
21. Remove the support and lower vehicle.
22. Remove the upper accessory drive belt idler pulley (2).

23. Remove the belt tensioner.
24. Support the engine with a block of wood and a floor jack.
25. Remove the upper engine mount.
26. Remove the power steering reservoir bolts and set reservoir aside.
27. Remove the remaining outer timing belt cover bolts and remove cover.
28. Remove the timing belt.
29. Remove the left cylinder head cover to cylinder head ground strap.
30. Remove the left cylinder head cover.
31. Remove the left rocker arm assembly (2).
32. Hold the left cam gear and loosen the cam gear retaining bolt.
33. Remove the front timing belt housing to cylinder head bolts.
34. Remove the left camshaft thrust plate.
35. Carefully push the camshaft out of the back of the cylinder head approximately 3.5 inches. Remove the camshaft sprocket and bolt.
36. NOTE: It may be necessary to raise

the engine slightly in order to remove the camshaft sprocket bolt.
37. Remove the cylinder head bolts in REVERSE of tightening sequence.
38. Remove the cylinder head.
39. Clean and inspect all mating surfaces.

To install:

※※ **CAUTION**

When cleaning cylinder head and cylinder block surfaces, DO NOT use a metal scraper because the surfaces could be cut or ground. Use ONLY a wooden or plastic scraper.

40. Clean sealing surfaces of cylinder head and block.

※※ **CAUTION**

The cylinder head gaskets are not interchangeable between cylinder heads and are clearly marked right or left.

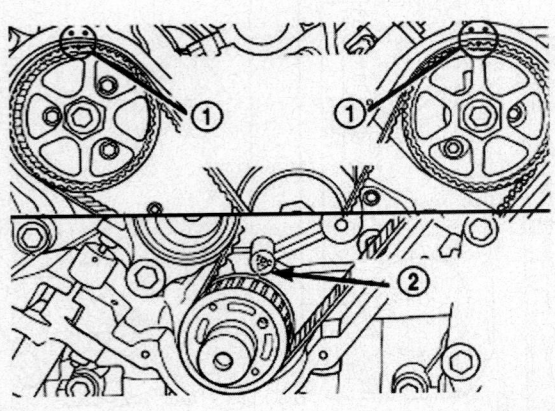

Fig. 99 Camshaft alignment marks—3.5L engine

41. Install head gasket over locating dowels. Ensure the gasket is installed on the correct side of engine.

➡The cylinder head bolts are tightened using a torque plus angle procedure. The bolts must be examined BEFORE reuse. If the threads are necked down the bolts must be replaced. Necking can be checked by holding a scale or straight edge against the threads. If all the threads do not contact the scale the bolt must be replaced.

➡Before installing the cylinder head bolts, lubricate the threads with engine oil.

42. Install the cylinder head over locating dowels and finger tighten the head bolts.

43. Tighten the cylinder head bolts in the sequence shown.

44. Using the 4 step torque-turn method, tighten according to the following torque values:
- Step 1: All to 45 ft. lbs. (61 Nm)
- Step 2: All to 65 ft. lbs. (88 Nm)
- Step 3: All (again) to 65 ft. lbs. (88 Nm)
- Step 4: + 90° Turn Do not use a torque wrench for this step.

45. Bolt torque after 90° turn should be over 90 ft. lbs. (122 Nm) in the tightening direction. If not, replace the bolt.

46. Install the inner timing cover to cylinder head bolts. Tighten bolts to 40 ft. lbs. (54 Nm).

47. Apply light coat of clean engine oil to the camshaft oil seal lip and Special Tool 6788 Seal Protector Sleeve.

48. Install oil seal Special Tool 6788 Seal Protector Sleeve onto the camshaft and install the camshaft into the cylinder head.

➡When installing the camshaft (1) into the cylinder head (4), you must insert the seal protector (2) through the camshaft seal (3) until the camshaft seats, then remove Special Tool 6788 (2) from the camshaft.

49. Install camshaft sprocket. Hold the camshaft sprocket gear and tighten the camshaft sprocket bolt to 115 Nm plus a ¼ turn (85 lbs. ft. plus a ¼ turn).

50. Install the rear camshaft thrust plate (1).

51. Rotate the camshaft gear to its alignment mark and check the right camshaft gear and crankshaft gear timing alignment marks.

52. Install the timing belt and tensioner.

53. Install the timing belt front cover.

54. Install the power steering reservoir.

55. Install the vibration damper (5).

56. Install the upper engine mount.

57. Install the accessory drive belt tensioner.

58. Install the lower accessory drive belt idler pulley.

59. Install the left exhaust manifold.

60. Install the exhaust cross over pipe.

61. Install the left rocker arm assembly (2).

62. Install the left cylinder head cover and ground strap.

63. Install lower intake manifold.

64. Install the fuel rail.

65. Install the upper intake manifold.

66. Connect the fuel line (1) to the fuel rail.

67. Install the radiator cooling fan assembly.

68. Install the radiator core support.

69. Install the radiator close out panel.

70. Install the air cleaner housing.

71. Install the engine cover.

72. Fill the coolant system.

73. Connect the negative battery cable.

Right Cylinder Head

See Figures 100 through 107.

1. Remove the engine cover.
2. Perform the fuel pressure release procedure.
3. Disconnect the negative battery cable.
4. Drain cooling system.
5. Remove air cleaner element housing.
6. Remove the coolant recovery container.
7. Remove the generator.
8. Disconnect the fuel line at the fuel rail.
9. Remove the upper intake manifold (2).
10. Remove the fuel rail.
11. Remove the lower intake manifold.
12. Raise and support the vehicle.
13. Remove right exhaust manifold.
14. Remove right front tire.
15. Remove right inner splash shield.
16. Remove vibration damper.
17. Remove lower accessory drive belt idler pulley.

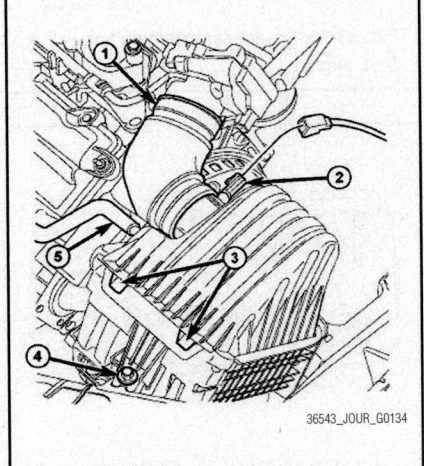

Fig. 100 Air cleaner element housing—3.5L engine

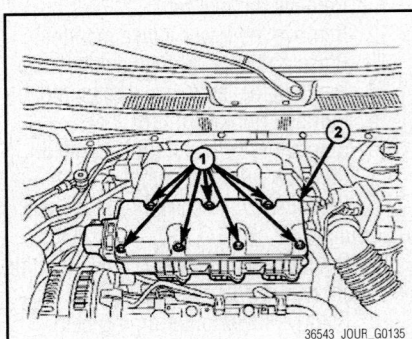

Fig. 101 Upper intake manifold—3.5L engine

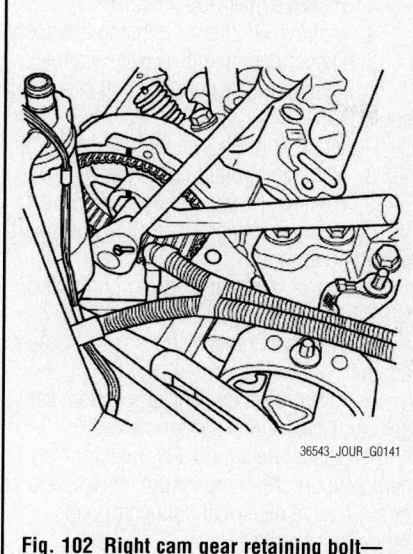

Fig. 102 Right cam gear retaining bolt—3.5L engine

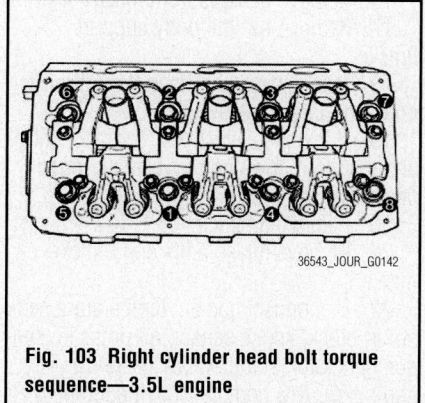

Fig. 103 Right cylinder head bolt torque sequence—3.5L engine

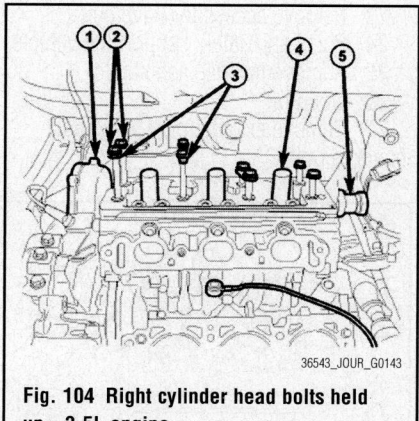

Fig. 104 Right cylinder head bolts held up—3.5L engine

18. Remove lower outer timing belt cover bolts.

19. Remove the supports and lower the vehicle.

20. Remove the upper accessory drive belt idler pulley.

21. Remove the belt tensioner.

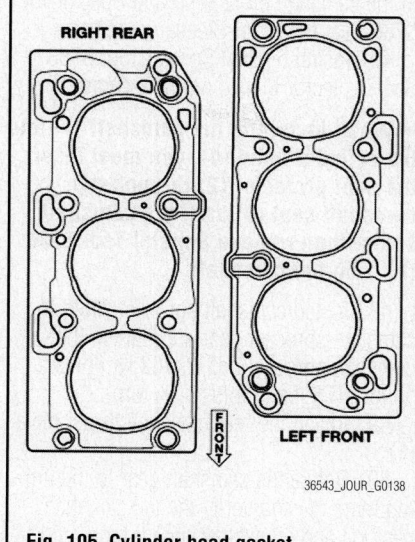

Fig. 105 Cylinder head gasket identification—3.5L engine

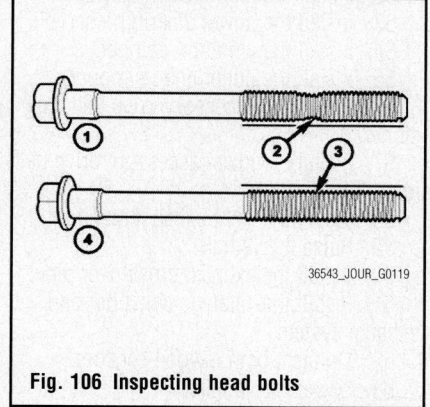

Fig. 106 Inspecting head bolts

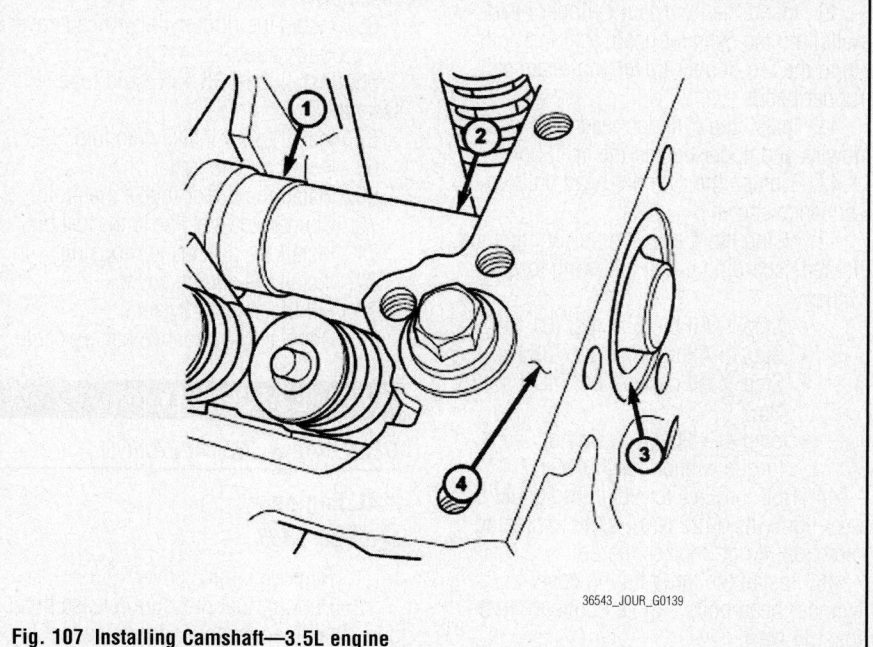

Fig. 107 Installing Camshaft—3.5L engine

22. Support the engine with a block of wood and a floor jack.

23. Remove the upper engine mount.

24. Remove the power steering reservoir bolts and set reservoir aside.

25. Remove the remaining outer timing belt cover bolts and cover.

26. Remove the timing belt.

27. Remove the right valve cover to cylinder head ground strap.

28. Remove the EGR valve and tube assembly.

29. Remove the right cylinder head cover.

30. Remove the right rocker arm and shaft assembly.

31. Hold the cam gear and loosen the right cam gear retaining bolt.

32. Remove the inner timing cover to right cylinder head retaining bolts.

33. Remove the right rear camshaft thrust plate.

34. Carefully push the camshaft out of the back of the cylinder head approximately 3.5 inches. Remove the camshaft sprocket and bolt.

➡It may be necessary to raise the engine slightly in order to remove the camshaft sprocket bolt.

35. Remove the cylinder head bolts in REVERSE of tightening sequence.

➡Because of clearance restrictions when removing the right cylinder head, the front four cylinder head bolts must be loosened, raised and supported with rubber bands before the cylinder head can be removed.

36. Remove the cylinder head.
37. Clean and inspect all mating surfaces

To install:

✳✳ CAUTION

When cleaning cylinder head and cylinder block surfaces, DO NOT use a metal scraper because the surfaces could be cut or ground. Use ONLY a wooden or plastic scraper

38. Clean sealing surfaces of cylinder head and block.

✳✳ CAUTION

The cylinder head gaskets are not interchangeable between cylinder heads and are clearly marked right or left.

39. Install head gasket over locating dowels. Ensure the gasket is installed on the correct side of engine.

The cylinder head bolts are tightened using a torque plus angle procedure. The bolts must be examined BEFORE reuse. If the threads are necked down the bolts must be replaced.

Necking can be checked by holding a scale or straight edge against the threads. If all the threads do not contact the scale the bolt must be replaced.

➡**Before installing the cylinder head bolts, lubricate the threads with engine oil.**

40. Insert the front four cylinder head bolts into the cylinder head. Pull the bolts up to the top of their travel and retain with rubber bands.
41. Install the cylinder head over locating dowels and finger tighten the head bolts.
42. Tighten the cylinder head bolts in the sequence shown.
43. Using the 4 step torque-turn method, tighten according to the following torque values:
   - Step 1: All to 45 ft. lbs. (61 Nm)
   - Step 2: All to 65 ft. lbs. (88 Nm)
   - Step 3: All (again) to 65 ft. lbs. (88 Nm)
   - Step 4: + 90° Turn Do not use a torque wrench for this step.
44. Bolt torque after 90° turn should be over 90 ft. lbs. (122 Nm) in the tightening direction. If not, replace the bolt.
45. Install the inner timing cover to cylinder head bolts. Tighten bolts to 40 ft. lbs. (54 Nm).
46. Apply light coat of clean engine oil

to the camshaft oil seal lip and Special Tool 6788 Seal Protector Sleeve.
47. Install oil seal Special Tool 6788 Seal Protector Sleeve onto the camshaft.

➡**When installing the camshaft (1) into the cylinder head (4), you must insert the seal protector (2) through the camshaft seal (3) until the camshaft seats, then remove Special Tool 6788 (2) from the camshaft.**

48. Install camshaft sprocket. Hold the camshaft sprocket gear and tighten the camshaft sprocket bolt to 102 Nm plus a ¼ turn (75 lbs. ft. plus a ¼ turn).
49. Install the rear camshaft thrust plate (1).
50. Rotate the camshaft gear to the timing mark (1) and verify the left camshaft gear (1) and crankshaft gear timing marks (2) are aligned.
51. Install the timing belt and tensioner.
52. Install the timing belt outer cover.
53. Install the power steering reservoir.
54. Install the vibration damper.
55. Install the upper engine mount.
56. Install the accessory drive belt tensioner.
57. Install the lower accessory drive belt idler pulley.
58. Install the right exhaust manifold.
59. Raise the vehicle.
60. Install the exhaust cross over pipe.
61. Install the catalytic converter and exhaust system.
62. Connect both oxygen sensors.
63. Lower the vehicle.
64. Install the right rocker arm assembly.
65. Install the right cylinder head cover and ground strap.
66. Install the EGR valve and tube assembly.
67. Install lower intake manifold.
68. Install the fuel rail.
69. Install the upper intake manifold.
70. Connect the fuel line to the fuel rail.
71. Install the air cleaner housing.
72. Install the engine cover.
73. Fill the coolant system.
74. Connect the negative battery cable.

ENGINE ASSEMBLY

REMOVAL & INSTALLATION

2.4L Engine

See Figure 108.

1. Remove engine cover.
2. Perform fuel pressure release procedure, then disconnect and remove fuel line (3).

3. Remove make-up air hose (2).
4. Remove air cleaner housing assembly.
5. Disconnect negative battery cable.
6. Discharge air conditioning system, if equipped.
7. Drain cooling system.
8. Remove coolant reservoir.
9. Remove power steering reservoir.
10. Remove power steering line support at engine mount.
11. Remove power steering pump and set aside.
12. Remove coolant hoses from coolant adapter.
13. Disconnect coolant temperature sensor connector and capacitor connector.
14. Disconnect coils (1), injectors (4), cam sensors, oil temperature sensor, and oil control valve electrical connectors and reposition harness.
15. Remove PCV hose (5) from valve cover.
16. Remove harness from intake.
17. Remove throttle body support bracket.
18. Remove vacuum lines from throttle body and intake manifold.
19. Disconnect electronic throttle control and manifold flow control valve electrical connectors.
20. Remove dipstick.
21. Remove intake bolts and remove intake.
22. Disconnect coolant temperature sensor at block, knock sensor, oil pressure sensor, generator, starter, block heater (if equipped), A/C compressor (if equipped), and block ground.
23. Remove accessory drive belt.
24. Raise and safely support the vehicle.
25. Remove front splash shield.
26. Drain oil.
27. Remove exhaust pipe to exhaust manifold bolts.

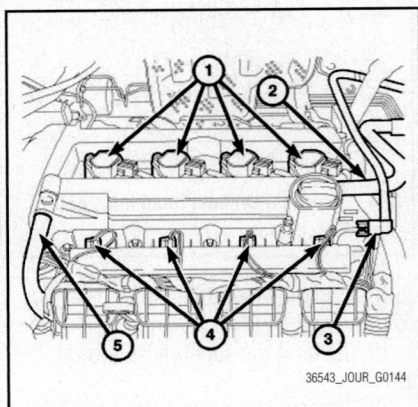

36543_JOUR_G0144

Fig. 108 Fuel lines and make-up air hose—3.5L engine

28. Disconnect oxygen sensor connector.

29. Remove exhaust manifold heat shield.

30. Remove exhaust manifold.

31. Remove inspection cover and mark torque converter to flywheel.

32. On vehicles equipped with an automatic transaxle, remove torque converter bolts.

33. On vehicles equipped with an manual transaxle, remove modular clutch bolts.

34. Remove lower bellhousing bolts.

35. Remove A/C compressor from engine and set aside.

36. Remove generator and lower idler pulley.

37. Disconnect CKP sensor electrical connector.

38. Remove right engine mount bracket retaining bolts.

39. Remove power steering hose hold-down.

40. Remove retaining nuts and position mount bracket aside.

41. Remove intake oil control valve to prevent damage.

42. Install engine lift chain to rear lift bracket and bolt to cylinder head in the front.

43. Hoist engine from vehicle.

44. Separate engine and transmission.

To install:

45. Connect engine lift chain to engine.

46. Slowly lower engine assembly in to position.

47. Position right mount bracket and install bolts.

48. Install retaining nuts and tighten nuts to 22 ft. lbs. (30 Nm).

49. Tighten bolts to 37 ft. lbs. (50 Nm).

50. Install A/C compressor mounting bracket.

51. Install A/C compressor and connect lines.

52. Install exhaust manifold and upper lower heat shields.

53. Install oxygen sensor and connect electrical connector.

54. Install Ground strap near right strut tower.

55. Raise vehicle.

56. Install Crankshaft Position (CKP) sensor (CKP).

57. Connect CKP electrical connector.

58. Install manifold to exhaust pipe bolts and tighten bolts.

59. Install generator.

60. Install lower bell housing bolts and tighten.

61. Align torque converter and flex plate

mark. Install torque converter bolts and tighten.

62. Install inspection cover.

63. Install new oil filter.

64. Lower vehicle.

65. Install upper idler pulley.

66. Install power steering pump.

67. Install power steering line support bracket.

68. Install power steering pump.

69. Install accessory drive belt.

70. Connect electrical connectors at block ground, starter, A/C compressor, knock sensor, oil pressure sensor, generator, coolant temperature sensor at block, and block heater.

71. Install intake manifold and tighten bolts to 18 ft. lbs. (25 Nm) as shown.

72. Install throttle body support bracket.

73. Connect manifold flow control valve and electronic throttle control electrical connectors.

74. Insert wiring harness retainer into intake manifold.

75. Install engine oil dip stick.

76. Install PCV hose.

77. Install vacuum lines at throttle body and intake manifold.

78. Install intake air tube on throttle body.

79. Connect engine harness electrical connectors.

80. Install coolant hoses at coolant adapter.

81. Install coolant reservoir and connect hose.

82. Connect fuel line to fuel rail.

83. Connect negative battery cable.

84. Install air cleaner housing and connect inlet air hose.

85. Fill with coolant.

86. Fill with oil.

❊❊ CAUTION

Do NOT run the engine with a vacuum pump in operation or with a vacuum present within the A/C system. Failure to follow this caution will result in serious A/C compressor damage.

---

87. Evacuate the refrigerant system.

88. Charge the refrigerant system.

89. Start engine and check for leaks.

90. Install engine cover.

2.7L Engine

See Figures 109 through 114.

1. Remove the engine cover.

2. Release fuel pressure.

3. Disconnect negative battery cable.

4. Drain cooling system .

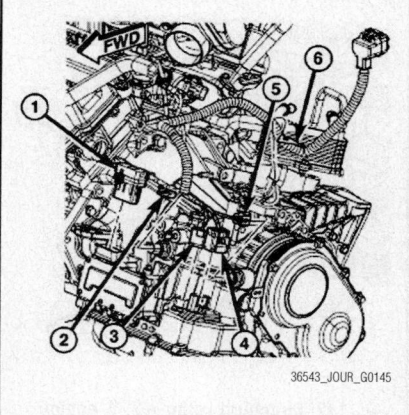

Fig. 109 Transmission connectors— 2.7L engine

Fig. 110 Engine connectors—2.7L engine

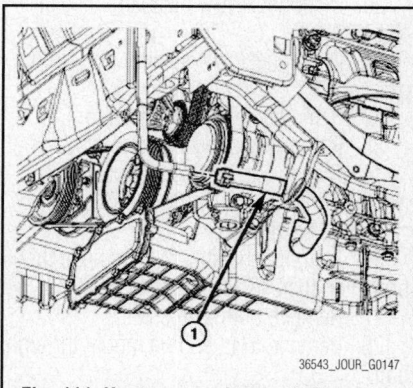

Fig. 111 Heater return hose—2.7L engine

5. Evacuate the A/C system using a suitable refrigerant recovery machine.

6. Remove throttle body air inlet hose and air cleaner housing assembly.

7. Raise vehicle on hoist.

8. Remove both front wheels.

9. Remove fasteners, and remove the belly pan.

10. Remove the left lower splash shield.

11. Remove the right lower splash shield.

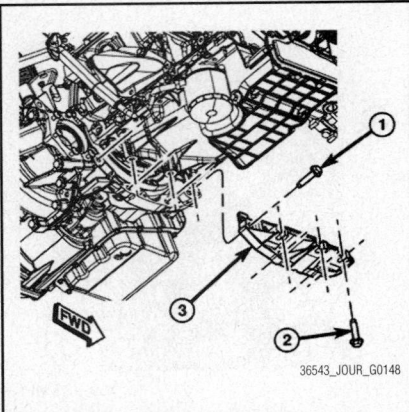

Fig. 112 Structural collar—2.7L engine

12. Remove the lower fascia closeout panel.

13. Lower vehicle.

14. Disconnect upper and lower radiator hoses at the thermostat housing and at the water pump fitting.

15. Disconnect transmission control module harness connector (1).

16. Disconnect transmission solenoid harness connectors (3) and (4).

17. Disconnect transmission input shaft speed sensor (2) and the output shaft speed sensor (5).

18. Disconnect transmission shift cable.

19. Disconnect the transaxle oil cooler lines at the transaxle.

20. Disconnect A/C discharge line at compressor.

21. Disconnect A/C suction line at compressor.

22. Remove the A/C compressor.

23. Remove cooling fan assembly.

24. Disconnect engine electrical harnesses connectors (1), (2) and (3).

25. Raise vehicle.

26. If equipped with AWD, remove the propeller shaft-to-PTU fasteners.

27. Remove both axle shafts.

28. Remove front engine mount through bolt.

29. Remove accessory drive belts.

30. Remove power steering pump and bracket as an assembly. Do not disconnect power steering lines from pump. Reposition pump and support with suitable retaining strap.

31. Disconnect heater return hose (1) from pipe connection at right front frame rail area.

32. Remove structural collar.

33. Remove the exhaust cross-under pipe.

34. Remove rear engine mount and transaxle bracket.

35. Drain engine oil.

36. Remove transaxle torque converter housing cover.

37. Mark flex plate to torque converter position. Remove torque converter bolts.

38. Lower vehicle.

39. Disconnect positive cable from battery and TIPM.

40. Disconnect ground cable from left side transaxle mount bracket.

41. Disconnect ETC harness connector from throttle body.

42. Disconnect coolant pressure bottle coolant hose from engine coolant outlet connector.

43. Disconnect heater hose from engine coolant outlet below the ETC.

44. If equipped, disconnect the oil cooler lines from the engine oil cooler.

45. Disconnect ground strap at right shock tower.

46. Disconnect fuel line from fuel rail inlet.

47. Disconnect vapor purge vacuum hose.

48. Disconnect brake booster vacuum hose.

49. Disconnect all ground straps attaching to engine.

50. Position vehicle height to allow engine dolly 6135 and cradle 6710 with posts 6848 to be installed under vehicle.

51. Loosen cradle engine mounts to allow movement for positioning onto engine locating holes on the engine block, compressor mount bracket and oil pan rail. Lower vehicle and position cradle until the engine is resting on posts. Tighten post mounts to cradle frame to prevent movement when removing or installing engine/transaxle assembly. Secure engine/transaxle assembly to dolly/cradle with safety straps.

52. Lower vehicle so weight of the engine and transmission ONLY is on the cradle.

53. Remove right and left side engine mount bolts.

54. Slowly raise vehicle in short length spans. Inspect at each interval for potential engine or transaxle contact to vehicle components. Move the cradle/dolly fixture as necessary to allow for removal clearance.

To install:

55. Position engine/transaxle assembly under vehicle and slowly lower vehicle in short length spans. Inspect at each interval for potential engine or transaxle contact to vehicle components. Move the cradle/dolly fixture as necessary to allow for installation clearance.

Fig. 113 Engine connectors—2.7L engine

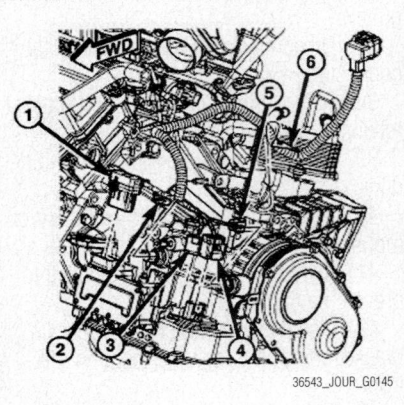

Fig. 114 Transmission connectors—2.7L engine

56. Continue lowering vehicle until right side engine mount and left side transaxle mount align to their mounting locations. Install mounting bolts and torque to 45 ft. lbs. (61 Nm).

57. Remove safety straps from engine/transaxle assembly. Slowly raise vehicle enough to remove the engine dolly and cradle.

58. Reattach all ground straps to engine.

59. Connect brake booster vacuum hose.

60. Connect vapor purge vacuum hose.

61. Connect fuel line.

62. Connect ground strap to right shock tower.

63. Connect the heater hose to the engine coolant outlet below the ETC.

64. If equipped, reconnect the oil cooler lines from the engine oil cooler.

65. Connect coolant pressure bottle coolant hose to coolant outlet connector.

66. Connect ETC harness connector.

67. Connect ground cable to right engine mount bracket.

68. Connect positive cable to battery and TIPM.

69. Raise vehicle.

70. Automatic Transaxle Equipped Vehicles:
- Install torque converter bolts.
- Install torque converter housing cover.

71. Manual Transaxle Equipped Vehicles:
- Install modular clutch assembly-to-drive plate bolts.
- Install clutch/drive plate inspection cover.

72. Connect clutch hydraulic circuit quick connect fitting.

73. Install rear engine mount and transaxle bracket.

74. Install exhaust cross-under pipe.

75. Install structural collar.

76. Reconnect the heater return hose (1) from the pipe connection at the right front frame rail area.

77. Install A/C compressor to bracket.

78. Connect A/C compressor clutch electrical connector.

79. Install power steering pump and bracket assembly.

80. Install accessory drive belts and (5).

81. Install the fore-aft crossmember.

82. Install front engine mount through bolt.

83. Connect the propeller shaft to the PTU.

84. Install both axle shafts.

85. Lower vehicle.

86. Install the cooling fan assembly.

87. Connect engine electrical harness connectors (1), (2), and (3) to PCM and bulkhead connectors.

88. Automatic Transmission Equipped Vehicles:
- Connect transmission shift cable.
- Connect transmission electrical harness connectors (1), (2), (3), (4) and (5).
- Connect transmission oil cooler lines.

89. Manual Transaxle Equipped Vehicles:
- Connect transmission shift cables.
- Connect back up lamp switch connector.

90. Connect upper and lower radiator hoses.

91. Raise and safely support the vehicle.

92. Ensure oil pan drain plug is installed. Install new oil filter.

93. Install left lower splash shield.

94. Install the right splash shield.

95. Install both front wheels.

96. Lower vehicle.

97. Install throttle body air inlet hose and air cleaner housing assembly.

98. Fill engine crankcase with proper oil to correct level.

99. Evacuate and recharge Air Conditioning system.

100. Fill cooling system.

101. Connect negative battery cable.

102. Start engine and run until operating temperature is reached. Inspect for leaks, and verify normal operation.

3.5L Engine

See Figures 115 through 123.

➡**Capture and store any residual fluid drainage, or leakage from disconnected components or systems in appropriately marked containers. Dispose of residual fluid in accordance with all applicable environmental regulations.**

1. Remove the engine cover.

2. Disconnect and isolate the negative battery cable.

3. Drain the cooling system.

4. Evacuate and recover the air conditioning system.

5. Perform the fuel pressure release procedure.

6. Disconnect fuel line from the fuel rail inlet and position aside.

7. Remove the Air Cleaner Housing.

8. Remove the Upper Intake Manifold (2).

9. Raise the vehicle.

10. Remove the 12 belly pan fasteners and remove the belly pan.

11. Remove the Right Forward Splash Shield.

12. Remove the Left Forward Splash Shield.

13. Remove the Front Closeout Panel.

14. Remove the accessory drive belt.

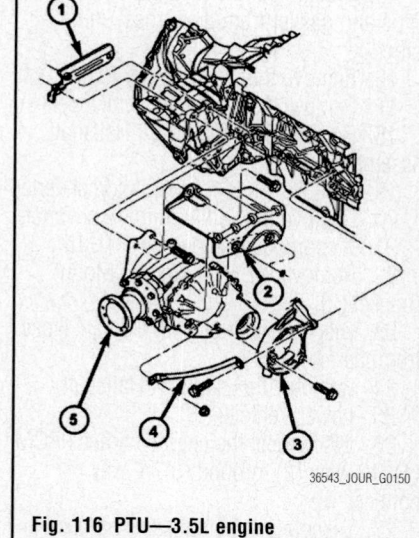

Fig. 116 PTU—3.5L engine

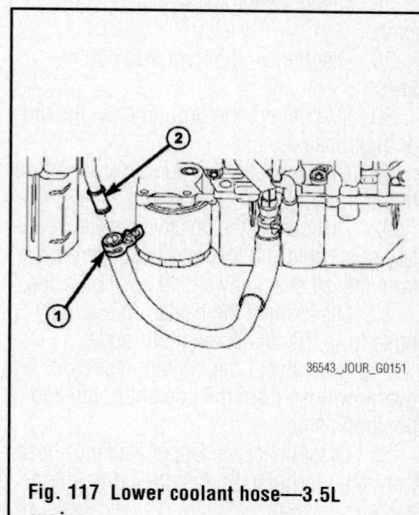

Fig. 117 Lower coolant hose—3.5L engine

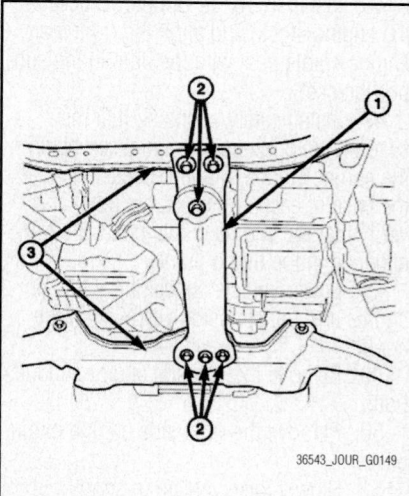

Fig. 115 Crossmember—3.5L engine

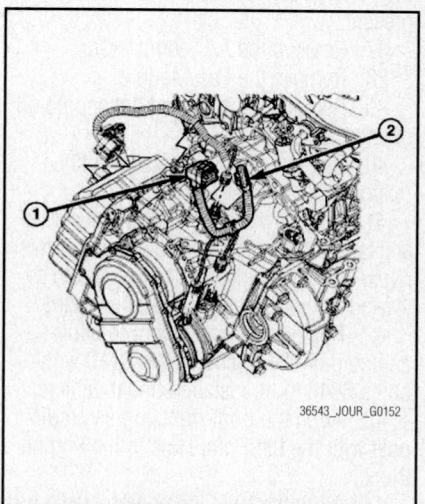

Fig. 118 Engine harness PCM connectors—3.5L engine

15. Disconnect the Exhaust Extension Pipe and gasket from the Cross-under pipe.

16. Remove the Cross Under Pipe.

17. Remove the fore-aft crossmember.

18. Remove the Right Front Halfshaft assembly.

19. Remove the Right Manifold/converter.

20. Remove the Left Manifold/converter.

21. If equipped, remove the PTU (5).

22. Remove the Front Engine Mount Bracket (2).

23. Disconnect the Lower Coolant Hose from the return tube.

24. Remove the Left Front Halfshaft.

25. Lower Vehicle.

26. Disconnect the engine harness PCM (1), 12–way (2), ground (3), 8–way (4) connectors.

27. Disconnect the transaxle harness PCM (1), and 6-way (2) connectors.

28. Disconnect the transaxle shifter cable.

29. Disconnect the transaxle cooler lines.

30. Disconnect the ground from the side of the transaxle.

31. Disconnect the ground from the front of the transaxle.

32. Disconnect the positive auxiliary battery post cable and the negative battery cable from the left shock tower and position aside.

33. Disconnect the heater core supply hose from the intake manifold outlet.

34. Disconnect the coolant reservoir overflow hose from the coolant bottle and position aside.

35. Disconnect the Upper Radiator hose from the thermostat housing and position aside.

36. Disconnect both A/C lines and and the harness connector from the A/C compressor.

37. Remove the A/C compressor.

38. Remove the Fan Module.

39. Remove the bolt, and the engine oil dipstick tube.

40. Remove the power steering line retainer bolt.

41. Position the power steering pump (2) and reservoir aside in the engine compartment. Avoid opening the power steering system by leaving the power steering lines connected.

42. Position vehicle height to allow engine dolly 6135 and cradle 6710 with posts 6848 to be installed under vehicle.

43. Align the front right engine cradle post with the Lift Point Hole in the Engine Block.

44. Align the front left engine cradle post and 8130 support bracket with the lift point hole in the engine block.

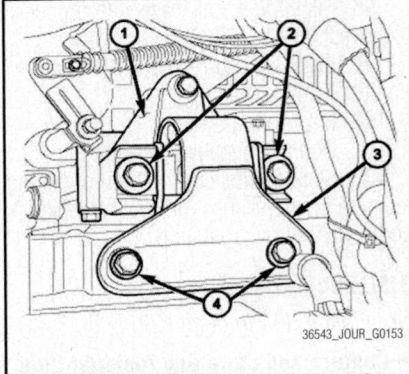

Fig. 119 Left engine mount—3.5L engine

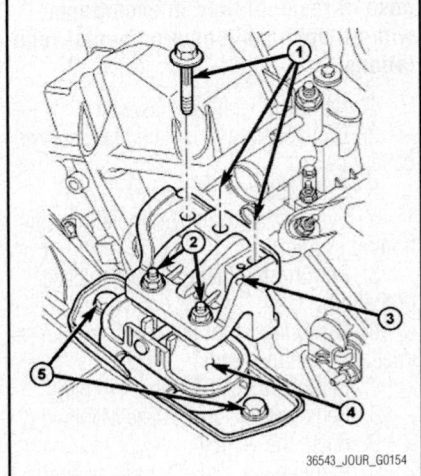

Fig. 120 Right engine mount—3.5L engine

45. Install 10107–1 Support Bracket in the engine block, and align the left rear engine cradle post with the hole in the support bracket.

46. Install 10107–2 Support Bracket in the engine block, and align the right rear engine cradle post with the hole in the support bracket.

47. Install safety straps so that they securely hold the powertrain assembly in the engine cradle. Tighten the fasteners at the base of each engine cradle post, and verify that the engine cradle posts are fully engaged in the lifting points.

48. Lower vehicle so weight of the engine and transmission ONLY is on the cradle.

49. Remove the left side engine mount bolts.

50. Remove the right side engine mount bolts.

51. Slowly raise vehicle in short length spans. Inspect at each interval for potential engine or transaxle contact to

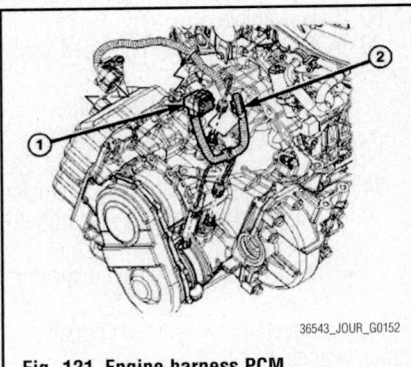

Fig. 121 Engine harness PCM connectors—3.5L engine

vehicle components. Move the cradle/dolly fixture as necessary to allow for removal clearance.

To install:

52. Align the front right engine cradle post with the Lift Point Hole in the Engine Block.

53. Align the front left engine cradle post and 8130 support bracket with the lift point hole in the engine block.

54. Install 10107–1 Support Bracket in the engine block, and align the left rear engine cradle post with the hole in the support bracket.

55. Install 10107–2 Support Bracket in the engine block, and align the right rear engine cradle post with the hole in the support bracket.

56. Install safety straps so that they securely hold the powertrain assembly in the engine cradle. Tighten the fasteners at the base of each engine cradle post, and verify that the engine cradle posts are fully engaged in the lifting points.

57. Raise the vehicle body on a hoist.

58. Position the engine cradle and powertrain beneath the vehicle.

59. Slowly lower the vehicle body in short length spans. Inspect at each interval for potential engine or transaxle contact to body or suspension components. Move the cradle/dolly fixture as necessary.

60. Install ground strap to the hood and position the hood back.

61. Install 3 right engine mount bolts (1). Tighten bolts to 37 ft. lbs. (50 Nm).

62. Install the left side engine mount bolts (2). Tighten bolts to 72 ft. lbs. (98 Nm).

63. Install the power steering pump.

64. Install the power steering line retainer bolt.

65. Install the fan module.

66. Install the engine oil dipstick tube and the bolt.

67. Install the A/C compressor.

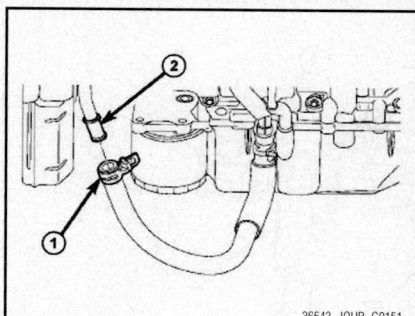

**Fig. 122 Lower coolant hose—
3.5L engine**

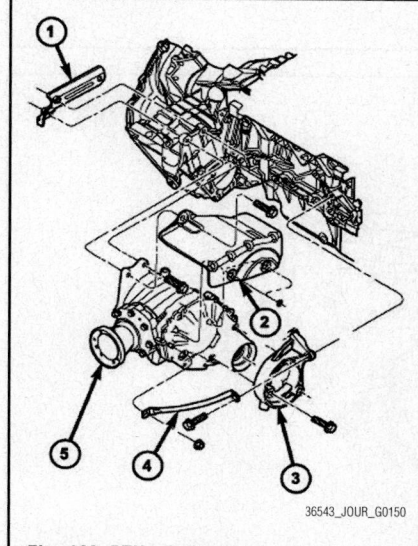

Fig. 123 PTU—3.5L engine

68. Reconnect both A/C lines and and the harness connector to the A/C compressor.

69. Reconnect the Upper Radiator hose (1) to the thermostat housing and position aside.

70. Reconnect the coolant reservoir overflow hose to the coolant bottle and position aside.

71. Reconnect the heater core supply hose to the intake manifold outlet.

72. Reconnect the positive auxiliary battery post cable and the negative battery cable to the left shock tower and position aside.

73. Reconnect the ground to the front of the transaxle.

74. Reconnect the ground to the side of the transaxle.

75. Reconnect the transaxle cooler lines.

76. Reconnect the transaxle shifter cable.

77. Reconnect the transaxle harness PCM (1), and 6-way (2) connectors.

78. Reconnect the engine harness PCM (1), 12–way (2), ground (3), 8–way (4) connectors.

79. Raise and safely support the vehicle.

80. Install the left front halfshaft.

81. Reconnect the Lower Coolant Hose (1) from the return tube (2).

82. Install the Front Engine Mount Bracket (2).

83. If equipped, install the PTU (5).

84. Install the left manifold/converter.

85. Install the right manifold/converter.

86. Install the right front halfshaft assembly.

87. Install the fore-aft crossmember.

88. Install the cross under pipe.

89. Install the exhaust extension pipe and gasket to the cross-under pipe.

90. Install the accessory drive belt.

91. Install the front closeout panel.

92. Install the left forward splash shield.

93. Install the right forward splash shield.

94. Install the belly pan and install the 12 belly pan fasteners.

95. Install the upper intake manifold.

96. Install the air cleaner housing.

97. Reconnect the fuel line to the fuel rail inlet.

98. Recharge the air conditioning system.

99. Fill the cooling system.

100. Reconnect the negative battery cable.

101. Start the engine and allow it to reach normal operating temperature. Inspect for leaks, and verify normal operation.

102. Install the engine cover.

EXHAUST MANIFOLD

REMOVAL & INSTALLATION

2.4L Engine
See Figure 124.

1. Remove engine cover.
2. Disconnect negative cable from battery.
3. Remove bolts attaching upper heat shield.
4. Remove upper heat shield.
5. Disconnect exhaust pipe from manifold.
6. Disconnect oxygen sensor electrical connector.
7. Remove manifold support bracket.
8. Remove lower exhaust manifold heat shield.
9. Remove exhaust manifold retaining fasteners.
10. Remove and discard manifold gasket.

To install:
11. Install a new exhaust manifold gasket. DO NOT APPLY SEALER.
12. Position exhaust manifold in place.
13. Tighten the exhaust manifold bolts, in sequence, to 25 ft. lbs. (34 Nm).
14. Install exhaust manifold heat shields. Tighten bolts to 105 inch lbs. (12 Nm).
15. Install exhaust manifold support bracket.
16. Install new catalytic converter gasket.
17. Install exhaust pipe to manifold. Tighten fasteners to 21 ft. lbs. (28 Nm).
18. Connect oxygen sensor electrical connector.
19. Connect negative battery cable.
20. Install engine cover.

2.7L Engine

Cross-Under Pipe

1. Remove the belly pan.
2. Remove the fasteners, and remove the exhaust extension pipe from the cross under pipe.
3. Remove the rear manifold/converter-to-cross under pipe fasteners and.
4. Remove the front manifold/converter-to-cross under fasteners, and remove the cross under pipe.

To install:
5. Install the cross under pipe. and the front manifold/converter-to-cross under fasteners. Tighten to 20 ft. lbs. (27 Nm).
6. Install the rear manifold/converter-to-cross under pipe fasteners. Tighten to 21 ft. lbs. (29 Nm).
7. Install the exhaust extension pipe to the cross under pipe, and install the fasteners. Tighten to 20 ft. lbs. (27 Nm)
8. Install the belly pan.

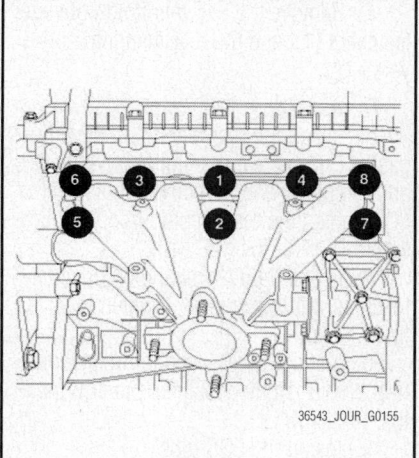

Fig. 124 Exhaust manifold bolt torque sequence—2.4L engine

Front Exhaust Manifold

See Figure 125.

1. Disconnect negative battery cable.
2. Remove the engine cover.
3. Disconnect and remove oxygen sensors.
4. Remove the upper manifold/converter heat shield.
5. Remove the belly pan.
6. Remove the front manifold/converter-to-cross-under fasteners.
7. Remove front exhaust manifold/converter attaching bolts (1) and remove the front manifold/converter (2).

To install:

8. Clean gasket mounting surfaces.
9. Install a new gasket (3), the front manifold/converter (2), and the front exhaust manifold/converter attaching bolts (1). Tighten bolts to 17 ft. lbs. (23 Nm).
10. Install the front manifold/converter-to-cross-under fasteners. Tighten to 20 ft. lbs. (27 Nm).
11. Install the upper manifold/converter heat shield and the heat shield fasteners. Tighten fasteners to 106 inch lbs. (12 Nm).
12. Install the oxygen sensors. Tighten to 30 ft. lbs. (41 Nm).
13. Install the belly pan.
14. Install the negative battery cable.
15. Install the engine cover.

Rear Exhaust Manifold

See Figure 126.

1. Remove the belly pan.
2. Remove the oxygen sensors.
3. Remove the EGR tube.
4. Remove the rear manifold/converter heat shield.
5. Remove the rear manifold/converter-to-cross-under fasteners.
6. Remove the rear manifold/converter fasteners (1), and the rear manifold/converter (2).

To install:

7. Install the rear manifold/converter gasket (3), the rear manifold/converter (2), and the rear manifold/converter fasteners (1). Tighten the rear manifold/converter fasteners to 17 ft. lbs. (23 Nm)
8. Install the rear manifold/converter-to-cross-under fasteners. Tighten to 21 ft. lbs. (29 Nm).
9. Install the rear manifold/converter heat shield. Tighten fasteners to 106 inch lbs. (12 Nm).
10. Install the EGR tube.
11. Install the oxygen sensors. Tighten to 30 ft. lbs. (41 Nm).
12. Install the belly pan.

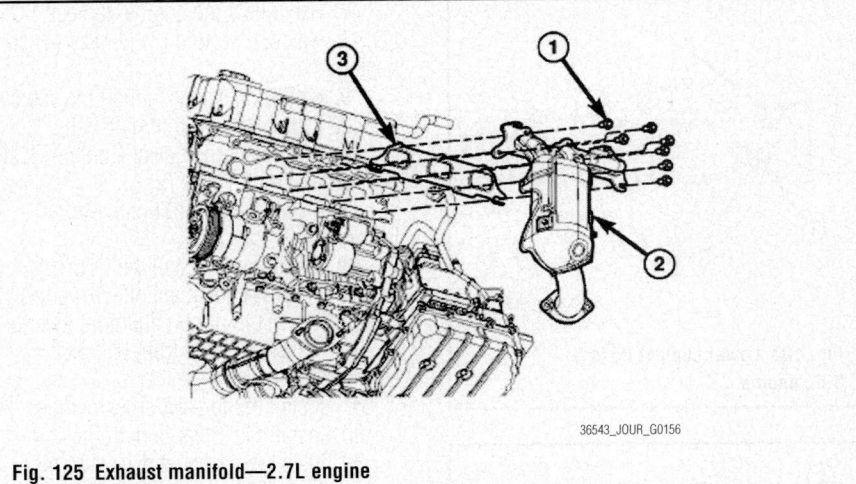

Fig. 125 Exhaust manifold—2.7L engine

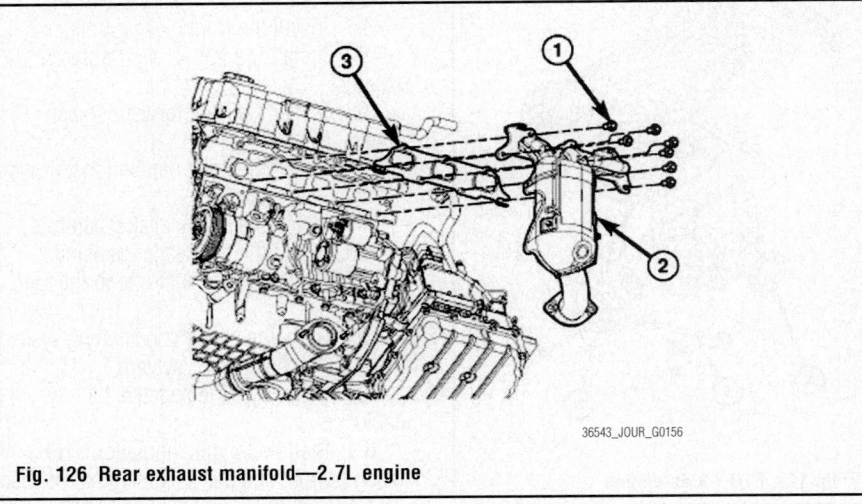

Fig. 126 Rear exhaust manifold—2.7L engine

3.5L Engine

Cross-Under Pipe

See Figure 127.

1. Remove the fasteners and remove the belly pan.
2. Remove the front engine mount through bolt.
3. Remove the rear torque mount through bolt.
4. Remove the cross-under-to-transmission bracket bolt.
5. Remove the right manifold/converter-to-cross-under fasteners.
6. Remove the left manifold/converter-to-cross-under fasteners.
7. Remove the exhaust extension pipe from the cross-under.
8. Rotate the engine forward or backward as needed to gain enough clearance to remove the cross-under pipe.
9. If necessary, remove the bracket fasteners and the cross-under transmission bracket.

To install:

10. If the cross-under transmission bracket was removed, install the bracket and the fasteners. Tighten to 40 ft. lbs. (54 Nm).

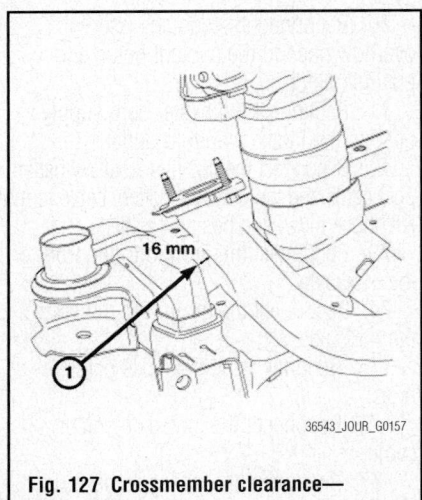

Fig. 127 Crossmember clearance—3.5L engine

11. Rotate the engine forward or backward as needed to gain enough clearance to install the cross-under pipe.

12. Install the left manifold/converter-to-cross-under fasteners. Tighten to 21 ft. lbs. (29 Nm).

➡**Verify that there is at least 16 mm (0.62 in.) of clearance between the indentation in the cross-under pipe near the extension pipe flange and the fore-aft crossmember. Otherwise, the cross-under pipe can contact the fore-aft crossmember due to engine torquing, causing a noise/vibration during acceleration.**

13. Install the right manifold/converter-to-cross-under fasteners. Tighten to 21 ft. lbs. (29 Nm).

14. Install the cross-under-to-transmission bracket bolt. Tighten to 21 ft. lbs. (29 Nm).

15. Install the rear torque mount through bolt. Tighten to 37 ft. lbs. (50 Nm).

16. Install the front engine mount through bolt.

17. Position new gasket on crossover and install the exhaust extension pipe and fasteners. Tighten fasteners to 20 ft. lbs. (27 Nm)

18. Install the belly pan and the fasteners.

Front Exhaust Manifold

See Figure 128.

1. Disconnect and isolate the negative battery cable.

2. Remove the fasteners, and remove the upper heat shield.

3. Loosen the oil level indicator tube retaining bolt and position the dipstick tube aside.

4. Remove the 12 belly pan fasteners and remove the belly pan.

5. Remove the left manifold/converter-to-cross-under pipe fasteners.

6. Disconnect the harness connector and remove the front lower manifold/converter oxygen sensor.

7. Disconnect the harness connector (3) and remove the front upper manifold/converter oxygen sensor.

8. Remove the manifold/converter retaining bolts (1), the manifold/converter (2), and gasket (3).

To install:

9. Position the manifold/converter (2) and gasket (3). Install the retaining bolts (1). Tighten bolts starting at the center working outward to 17 ft. lbs. (23 Nm).

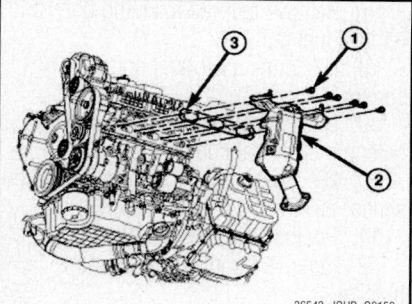

Fig. 128 Front exhaust manifold—3.5L engine

10. Install the upper heat shield, and torque nuts to 105 inch lbs. (12 Nm).

11. Install the oil level indicator tube and the retaining bolt.

12. Install the left upstream oxygen sensor and connect the harness connector.

13. Install the left downstream oxygen sensor and connect the harness connector.

14. Install the left manifold/converter cross under pipe retaining bolts. Tighten bolts to 23 ft. lbs. (31 Nm).

15. Install the belly pan and the 12 belly pan fasteners.

16. Connect the negative battery cable.

Rear Exhaust Manifold

See Figure 129.

1. Disconnect the negative battery cable.

2. Raise and support the vehicle.

3. Remove the 12 belly pan fasteners and remove the belly pan.

4. Disconnect the exhaust extension pipe from the cross-under.

5. Disconnect the harness connector and remove right manifold/converter downstream oxygen sensor.

6. Disconnect the harness connector

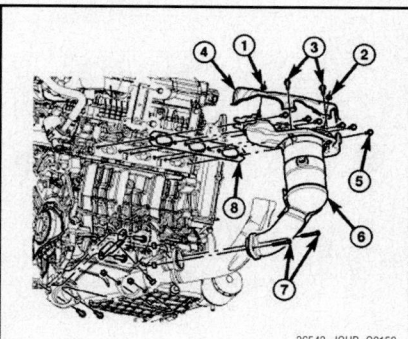

Fig. 129 Rear exhaust manifold—3.5L engine

and remove the right manifold/converter upstream oxygen sensor.

7. Remove the heat shield retainers (1), (2), and (3).

8. Remove the right manifold/converter retaining bolts (5) and (7), the right manifold/converter (6), and the gasket (8).

To install:

9. Clean right manifold/converter gasket sealing surfaces with an appropriate tool.

10. Position the right manifold/converter and gasket. Install the retaining bolts. Tighten bolts starting at the center working outward to 17 ft. lbs. (23 Nm).

11. Install the right manifold/converter upper heat shield (4).

12. Install the right manifold/converter upstream oxygen sensor and reconnect the harness connector.

13. Install the right manifold/converter downstream oxygen sensor and reconnect the harness connector.

14. Install the exhaust extension pipe. Tighten the fasteners to 20 ft. lbs. (27 Nm).

15. Install the belly pan and the 12 belly pan fasteners.

16. Lower the vehicle.

17. Connect the negative battery cable.

FLYWHEEL

REMOVAL & INSTALLATION

2.4L Engine

See Figures 130 and 131.

❋❋ WARNING

Chrysler does not manufacture any vehicles or replacement parts that contain asbestos. Aftermarket products may or may not contain asbestos. Refer to aftermarket product packaging for product information. Whether the product contains

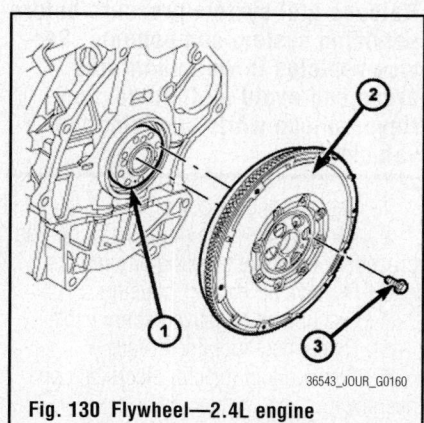

Fig. 130 Flywheel—2.4L engine

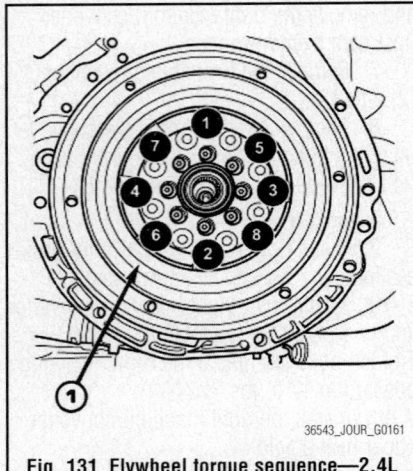

Fig. 131 Flywheel torque sequence—2.4L

asbestos or not, dust and dirt can accumulate on manual clutch parts during normal use. Follow practices prescribed by appropriate regulations for the handling, processing and disposing of dust and debris

1. Remove transaxle.
2. Remove clutch pressure plate and disc.
3. Remove the six flywheel-to-crankshaft bolts (3) and remove flywheel assembly (2).

To install:

4. Clean the surfaces of the flywheel and pressure plate to make certain that all oil, grease, and rust have been removed.
5. Install and torque the flywheel-to-crankshaft bolts to 70 ft. lbs. (95 Nm).
6. Install clutch pressure plate and disc.
7. Install transaxle assembly

INTAKE MANIFOLD

REMOVAL & INSTALLATION

2.4L Engine

See Figure 132.

✳✳ WARNING

Release fuel system pressure before servicing system components. Service vehicles in well ventilated areas and avoid ignition sources. Never smoke while servicing the vehicle.

1. Remove engine cover.
2. Perform fuel system pressure release procedure before attempting any repairs
3. Remove air cleaner housing.
4. Disconnect negative battery cable.
5. Disconnect fuel line at rail.
6. Remove fuel injector electrical connectors.

7. Remove fuel rail retaining bolts and remove fuel rail.
8. Disconnect oil temperature sensor.
9. Disconnect variable valve timing solenoid electrical connector.
10. Disconnect intake camshaft position sensor electrical connector.
11. Position harness out of the way.
12. Remove throttle body support bracket.
13. Disconnect electronic throttle control electrical connector.
14. Remove wiring harness retainer from the intake manifold.
15. Disconnect MAP sensor electrical connector.
16. Disconnect vacuum lines at intake.
17. Remove intake manifold retaining bolts.
18. Remove intake manifold.

To install:

19. Clean all gasket surfaces.
20. Replace intake manifold gasket.
21. Install intake manifold, tighten bolts to 18 ft. lbs. (25 Nm).
22. Install the fuel rail assembly to intake manifold. Tighten bolts to 17 ft. lbs. (23 Nm).
23. Connect fuel injector electrical connectors.
24. Inspect quick connect fittings for damage, replace if necessary.
25. Connect fuel supply hose to fuel rail assembly. Check connection by pulling on connector to make sure it is locked into position.
26. Install air cleaner housing.
27. Connect negative battery cable.
28. Fill the cooling system.
29. Start engine and check for leaks.
30. Install engine cover.

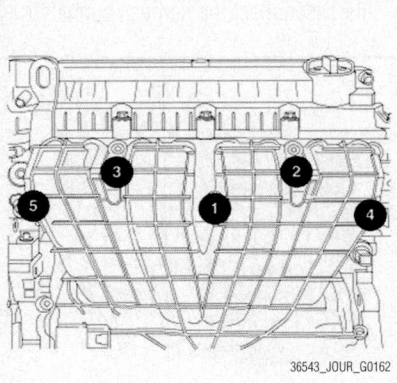

Fig. 132 Intake manifold torque sequence—2.4L engine

2.7L Engine

Lower

See Figure 133.

1. Release fuel system pressure.
2. Remove upper intake manifold.
3. Disconnect electrical connectors from the fuel injectors.
4. Remove fuel supply hose from fuel rail.
5. Remove screw attaching fuel rail support bracket to the throttle body support bracket.
6. Remove bolts attaching fuel rail.
7. Remove fuel rail and injectors as an assembly.
8. Remove manifold attaching bolts.
9. Remove lower manifold.
10. Inspect manifold.

To install:

11. Clean and inspect sealing surfaces of cylinder head and manifold. Gaskets can be reused provided they are free of cuts or tears.
12. Position manifold on cylinder head surfaces.

➡ **For ease of installing upper intake manifold, install a bolt 2–3 turns to the rearmost attaching hole of intake. This will properly position lower manifold.**

13. Install manifold attaching bolts and tighten in sequence shown, to 105 inch lbs. (12 Nm). Remove bolt used for aligning manifold.
14. Install fuel rail with injectors.
15. Connect the fuel injector electrical connectors.

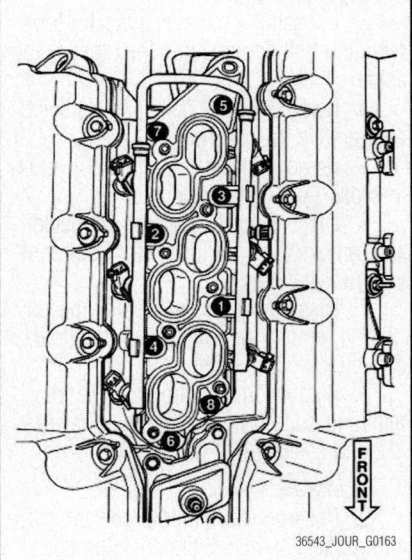

Fig. 133 Lower intake manifold torque sequence—3.5L engine

➡**Make sure fuel injectors are located in the correct location and position, as upper intake manifold interference could occur.**

16. Install screw attaching fuel rail support bracket to the throttle body support bracket.

17. Connect fuel supply hose to fuel rail.

18. Install upper intake manifold.

Upper

See Figure 134.

1. Disconnect negative battery cable.

2. Remove throttle body air inlet hose (1) and air cleaner housing assembly.

3. Disconnect electrical connectors from the following components:

- Manifold Absolute Pressure (MAP) Sensor
- Throttle Position Sensor (TPS) Sensor
- Idle Air Control (IAC) Motor
- Inlet Air Temperature (IAT) sensor (IAT)

4. Disconnect Vapor Purge hose, Brake Booster hose, Positive Crankcase Ventilation (PCV) hose.

5. Remove EGR tube.

6. Disconnect the electronic throttle control (ETC).

7. Remove lower throttle body support bracket.

8. Remove rear support bracket fasteners.

9. Remove manifold attaching bolts.

10. Remove upper manifold.

To install:

11. Clean and inspect sealing surfaces. Gaskets can be reused, if free of cuts or tears.

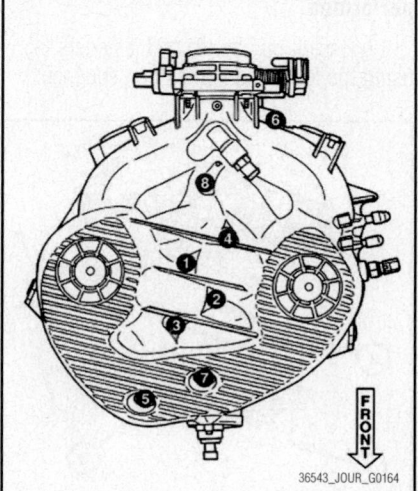

Fig. 134 Upper intake manifold torque sequence—3.5L engine

➡**Make sure fuel injectors and wiring harnesses are in correct position to not interfere with upper manifold installation.**

12. Position upper manifold onto lower manifold.

13. Install manifold attaching bolts and tighten in sequence shown, to 105 inch lbs. (12 Nm).

14. Install lower throttle body support bracket.

15. Connect PCV, brake booster, and vapor purge hoses.

16. Connect electrical connectors to the following components:

- Manifold Absolute Pressure (MAP) Sensor
- Throttle Position Sensor (TPS) Sensor
- Idle Air Control (IAC) Motor
- Inlet Air Temperature (IAT) sensor (IAT)

17. Install EGR tube.

18. Connect electronic throttle control connector (ETC).

19. Install throttle body air inlet hose and air cleaner housing assembly.

20. Connect negative battery cable.

3.5L Engine

Lower

See Figure 135.

1. Disconnect the negative battery cable.

2. Perform fuel pressure release procedure.

3. Drain the cooling system.

4. Disconnect the upper radiator hose from the thermostat housing.

5. Remove the upper intake manifold.

6. Disconnect the electrical connectors to fuel injectors and coolant temperature sensor.

7. Disconnect heater supply and return hoses from the thermostat housing.

8. Disconnect the fuel line from the fuel rail.

9. Remove the 4 bolts attaching fuel rail.

10. Remove fuel rail and injectors as an assembly.

11. Remove lower intake 4 bolts and position the ignition coil capacitor aside.

12. Remove the lower intake manifold.

To install:

13. Clean all sealing surfaces.

14. Position new gaskets and intake manifold on cylinder head surfaces.

15. Position the ignition coil capacitor and install the intake manifold bolts.

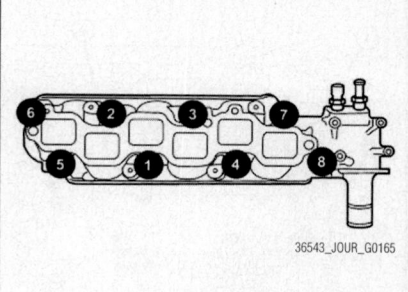

Fig. 135 Lower intake manifold torque sequence—3.5L engine

Gradually tighten in sequence shown until a torque of 21 ft. lbs. (28 Nm) is obtained.

16. Install fuel rail and injectors as an assembly.

17. Connect fuel supply hose to fuel rail.

18. Connect heater supply and return hoses to the intake manifold.

19. Connect electrical connectors to fuel injectors and coolant temperature sensor.

20. Install upper intake manifold.

21. Connect the upper radiator hose to the thermostat housing.

22. Fill the cooling system.

23. Connect negative battery cable.

Upper

See Figures 136 and 137.

1. Remove engine cover.

2. Disconnect negative battery cable.

3. Remove air cleaner housing and inlet hose.

4. Disconnect the EGR tube.

5. Disconnect the following vacuum hoses from the upper intake manifold:

- Positive Crankcase Ventilation (PCV) Valve (1)
- EVAP Purge Solenoid (2)
- EGR Tube (3)
- Power Brake Booster (4)

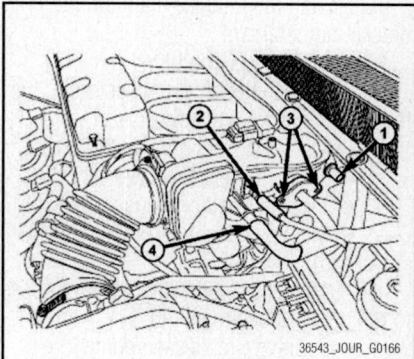

Fig. 136 Vacuum Hoses—3.5L engine

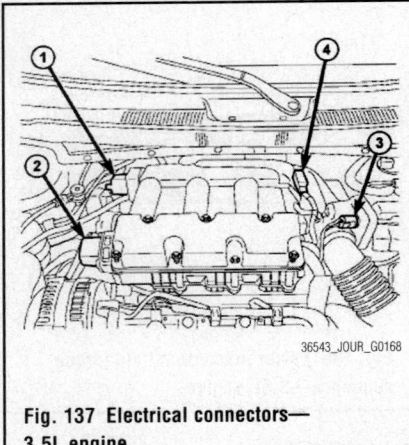

Fig. 137 Electrical connectors— 3.5L engine

6. Disconnect electrical connectors from the following sensors and actuators:
- Manifold Tuning Valve (MTV) (1)
- Short Runner Valve (2)
- Throttle Position Sensor (TPS) (3)
- Manifold Absolute Pressure (MAP) (4)

7. Remove the Manifold Tuning Valve, then remove the 2 nuts from the rear intake manifold brackets.

8. Loosen the 2 bolts from rear intake manifold brackets and position brackets aside.

9. Remove the 7 upper intake manifold retaining bolts and the upper intake manifold. Clean all gasket sealing surfaces.

To install:

10. Clean and inspect gasket sealing surfaces.

11. Position new gasket.

12. Install the throttle body on the upper intake (if required).

13. Install upper intake manifold and hand start all attaching bolts.

14. Tighten bolts gradually starting in the center working outward until a torque of 105 inch lbs. (12 Nm) is obtained.

15. Install the rear intake manifold brackets to the head.

16. Install the 2 intake manifold to bracket nut retainers.

17. Install the EGR tube.

18. Connect electrical connectors to the following sensors and actuators:
- Manifold Tuning Valve (MTV) (1)
- Short Runner Valve (2)
- Throttle Position Sensor (TPS) (3)
- Manifold Absolute Pressure (MAP) (4)

19. Connect the following vacuum hoses to the upper intake manifold:
- Positive Crankcase Ventilation (PCV) Valve (1)
- EVAP Purge Solenoid (2)

- EGR Tube (3)
- Power Brake Booster (4)

20. Install air cleaner housing and inlet hose.

21. Connect negative battery cable.

22. Install the engine cover.

OIL PAN

REMOVAL & INSTALLATION

2.4L Engine

See Figure 138.

1. Raise vehicle on hoist.

2. Remove oil drain plug and drain the engine oil.

3. Remove accessory drive belt splash shield.

4. Remove lower A/C compressor mounting bolt (if equipped).

5. Remove A/C mounting bracket.

➡**Do not use pry points in block to remove oil pan.**

6. Remove oil pan retaining bolts.

7. Using a putty knife, loosen seal around oil pan.

8. Remove oil pan.

To install:

➡**Oil pan sealing surfaces must be free of grease or oil.**

➡**Parts must be assembled within 10 minutes of applying RTV.**

9. Apply Mopar® Engine RTV GEN II at the front cover to engine block parting lines.

10. Apply a 2 mm bead of Mopar® Engine RTV GEN II around the oil pan as shown.

11. Position oil pan and install bolts. Tighten bolts to 105 inch lbs. (12 Nm).

➡**The 2 long bolts must be tightened to 16 ft. lbs. (22 Nm).**

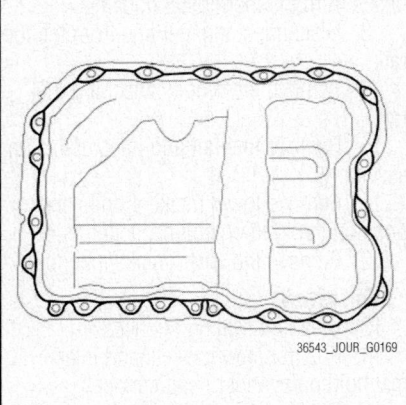

Fig. 138 RTV on oil pan—2.4L engine

12. Install oil drain plug.

13. Lower vehicle and fill engine crankcase with proper oil to correct level.

14. Start engine and check for leaks.

2.7L Engine

See Figure 139.

1. Disconnect and isolate the negative battery cable.

2. Remove engine oil dipstick and tube.

3. Drain engine oil and remove oil filter.

4. Remove structural collar.

5. Remove exhaust cross-under pipe.

6. Remove torque converter housing cover.

7. Remove lower bolt attaching the A/C compressor to oil pan.

✳✳ CAUTION

Assure removal of the two bolts attaching the timing cover to the oil pan, as damage to the timing cover and/or oil pan may occur.

8. Remove oil pan attaching fasteners (1). Remove oil pan (3) and gasket (2).

To install:

9. Clean oil pan and sealing surfaces. Inspect oil pan and timing chain cover gaskets. Replace as necessary.

10. Apply an ⅛ inch bead of Mopar® Engine RTV GEN II to the front T-joints (oil pan gasket to timing cover gasket interface) and the rear T-joints (oil pan gasket to crankshaft rear oil seal retainer gasket interface).

11. Install oil pan gasket (2) to block.

➡**To prevent oil leaks at oil pan to timing chain cover, the following tightening sequence procedure must be performed.**

12. Install oil pan (3) and fasteners (1) using the following tightening sequence:

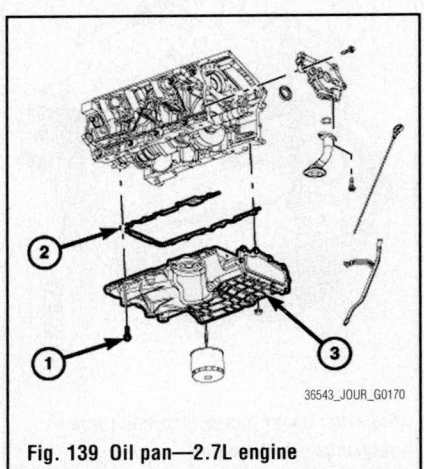

Fig. 139 Oil pan—2.7L engine

- Install oil pan bolts and nuts finger tight only-just tight enough to compress the gasket's rubber seal.
- Install timing chain cover to pan bolts and tighten to 105 inch lbs. (12 Nm).
- Tighten oil pan bolts to 21 ft. lbs. (28 Nm).
- Tighten oil pan nuts to 105 inch lbs. (12 Nm).

13. Install lower bolt attaching the A/C compressor to oil pan. Tighten bolt to 21 ft. lbs. (28 Nm).
14. Install torque converter housing cover.
15. Install oil filter and drain plug.
16. Install exhaust cross-under pipe.
17. Install structural collar.
18. Install engine oil dipstick and tube.
19. Fill engine crankcase with proper oil to correct level.
20. Connect negative battery cable.

3.5L Engine

1. Disconnect negative battery cable.
2. Remove the engine oil indicator.
3. Remove the engine oil indicator tube bolt.
4. Remove the engine oil indicator tube.
5. Raise and support the vehicle.
6. Remove the front crossmember.
7. Remove the crossover pipe.
8. Loosen the front exhaust manifold.
9. Remove the oil pan bell housing bolts.
10. Drain the engine oil.
11. Remove the engine oil filter.
12. Remove the oil pan fasteners. Remove the oil pan.

➡**A small amount of oil will remain in the oil pan. Use care when removing the oil pan from the engine.**

13. Remove oil pan gasket.

To install:

14. Clean oil pan and all gasket surfaces.
15. Apply a ⅛ inch bead of Mopar® Engine RTV GEN II at the parting line of the oil pump housing and the rear seal retainer.
16. Install oil pan gasket to the engine block.
17. Install the oil pan and tighten the oil pan bolts to 21 ft. lbs. (28 Nm).
18. Tighten the oil pan bell housing bolts to 40 ft. lbs. (55 Nm).
19. All engines are equipped with a high quality full-flow, disposable type oil filter. When replacing oil filter, use a Mopar® filter or equivalent.
20. Wipe base clean, then inspect gasket contact surface.

21. Lubricate gasket of new filter with clean engine oil.
22. Install and tighten oil filter to 12 ft. lbs. (16 Nm) of torque after gasket contacts base. Use filter wrench if necessary.
23. Lower vehicle.
24. Install and tighten the oil pan drain bolt to 20 ft. lbs. (27 Nm).
25. Tighten the front manifold/converter bolts.
26. Install the crossover pipe.
27. Install the front crossmember.
28. Lower vehicle.
29. Install the oil level indicator tube.
30. Tighten the oil level indicator tube bolt.
31. Install the oil indicator.
32. Fill engine crankcase with proper oil to correct level.
33. Connect negative battery cable.

OIL PUMP

REMOVAL & INSTALLATION

2.4L Engine

See Figures 140 through 142.

1. Rotate engine to TDC (1,2) on #1 compression stroke.
2. Remove oil pan.
3. Mark the chain (6) and the sprocket (5) for reassembly.
4. Push tensioner piston back into the tensioner body.
5. With piston held back insert tensioner pin 9703 into the tensioner body to hold the piston in the retracted position.

➡**Do not remove sprocket from BSM.**

6. Remove BSM mounting bolts. Discard 180 mm bolts, 185 mm bolts can be reused.
7. Lower the back of the BSM and remove the chain from the sprocket.
8. Remove BSM from the engine.

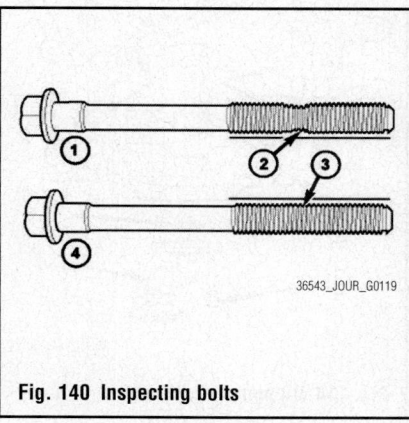

Fig. 140 Inspecting bolts

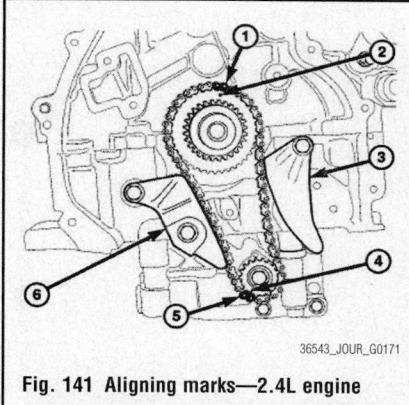

36543_JOUR_G0171

Fig. 141 Aligning marks—2.4L engine

To install:

❋❋ CAUTION

There are two different Balance Shaft Module (BSM) to engine block bolts used. 180 mm bolts with a lock-patch on the threads or 185 mm bolts without lock-patch. Do not reuse the 180 mm bolts. Always discard 180 mm bolts after removing. Failure to replace these bolts can result in engine damage. The 185 mm bolts are reusable. Install the same length bolts that were removed and use either four new 180 mm bolts or four 185 mm bolts.

9. The 185 mm (7.283 in.) length bolts must be checked for stretching. Check the bolts with a straight edge for necking (2). If the bolts are necked down, they must be replaced.
10. Clean BSM mounting holes with Mopar® brake parts cleaner.
11. If chain was removed, align marks on crankshaft sprocket (2) and chain (1).
12. Align marks on oil pump sprocket (5) and chain (4).
13. Install chain on sprocket.
14. Pivot BSM assembly upwards and position on ladder frame.
15. Start BSM mounting bolts by hand.

➡**Use a three step procedure when tightening BSM mounting bolts. For new 180 mm bolts, go to step 8. For 185 mm bolts, go to step 9.**

16. Tighten new 180 mm BSM mounting bolts as follows:
   a. Tighten to 11 ft. lbs. (15 Nm) in the sequence shown.
   b. Tighten to 24 ft. lbs. (33 Nm) in the sequence shown.
   c. Rotate bolts an additional 90° in the sequence shown.

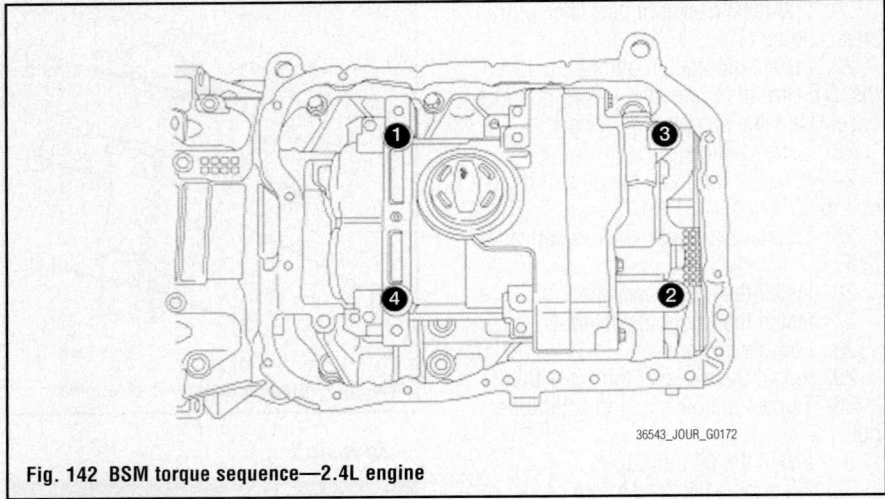

Fig. 142 BSM torque sequence—2.4L engine

17. Tighten 185 mm BSM mounting bolts as follows:

a. Tighten to 11 ft. lbs. (15 Nm) in the sequence shown.

b. Tighten to 22 ft. lbs. (29 Nm) in the sequence shown.

c. Rotate bolts an additional 90° in the sequence shown.

18. Remove tensioner pin 9703 (4).
19. Install oil pan.
20. Fill with oil.
21. Start engine and check for leaks.

2.7L Engine

See Figures 143 and 144.

➡The oil pump pressure relief valve can be serviced by removing the oil pan.

1. Remove crankshaft vibration damper.
2. Remove timing chain cover.
3. Remove timing chain and sprockets.
4. Remove oil pan.
5. Ensure that crankshaft position is at 60° ATDC of No.1 cylinder, or crankshaft sprocket mark aligns with mark on oil pump (1). This position will properly locate oil pump upon installation.

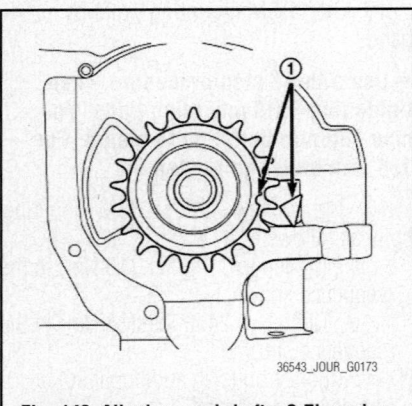

Fig. 143 Aligning crankshaft—2.7L engine

6. Remove oil pick-up tube (3) and O-ring.
7. Remove oil pump attaching bolts (1).
8. Remove oil pump.

To install:

✴✴ CAUTION

Crankshaft position must be at 60° ATDC of No.1 cylinder before installing oil pump. This position will properly locate oil pump. If not properly located, severe damage to oil pump can occur.

9. Prime oil pump before installation by filling rotor cavity with engine oil.

10. If crankshaft has been rotated, it must be repositioned to 60° ATDC of No.1 cylinder prior to oil pump installation.

11. Install oil pump carefully over crankshaft and into position.

12. Install oil pump attaching bolts (1). Tighten bolts to 21 ft. lbs. (28 Nm).

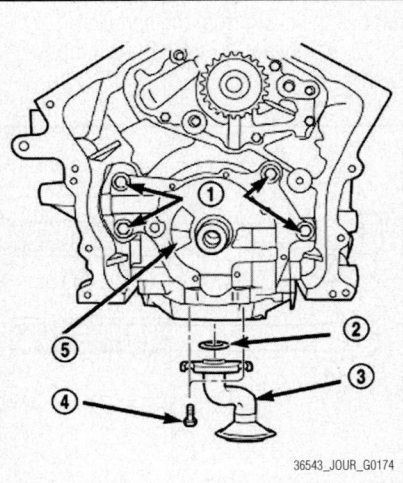

Fig. 144 Oil pump—2.7L engine

13. Install oil pick-up tube (3) with new O-ring. Lubricate O-ring before installation. Tighten attaching bolts to 21 ft. lbs. (28 Nm).

14. Install oil pan.
15. Install timing chain and sprockets.
16. Install timing chain cover.
17. Install crankshaft vibration damper.
18. Fill crankcase with engine oil to correct level.

3.5L Engine

➡It is necessary to remove the oil pump body to service the oil pump rotors.

➡The oil pump pressure relief valve can be serviced by removing the oil pan.

1. Drain the cooling system.
2. Remove the timing belt.
3. Remove the crankshaft sprocket.
4. Remove the oil pan.
5. Remove the oil pickup tube.
6. Remove the oil pump fasteners. Remove pump and gasket from engine.

To install:

➡Thoroughly clean all bolt threads and threaded area in the engine, removing all oil residue, before assembly.

7. Prime oil pump before installation by filling rotor cavity with clean engine oil.

8. Install oil pump and gasket carefully over the crankshaft and position pump onto block.

➡DO NOT apply the thread sealant to the underside of the bolt head.

9. Apply Mopar Thread Sealant as directed on the package to the oil pump cover bolts where indicated. The sealant must be applied from the tip to approximately 10 mm of the thread length. Tighten the oil pump cover bolts to 105 inch lbs. (12 Nm). Tighten oil pump to block bolts to 21 ft. lbs. (28 Nm)

10. Install new O-ring on oil pickup tube.
11. Install oil pickup tube.
12. Install oil pan.
13. Install crankshaft sprocket.
14. Install timing belt.
15. Install the timing belt covers.
16. Install the crankshaft vibration damper.
17. Install the accessory drive belts.
18. Fill the cooling system.
19. Fill engine crankcase with proper oil to the correct level.

PISTON AND RING

POSITIONING

2.4L Engine

See Figure 145.

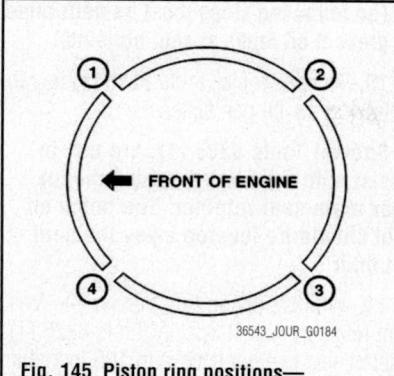

**Fig. 145 Piston ring positions—
2.4L engine**

2.7L & 3.5L Engines

See Figure 146.

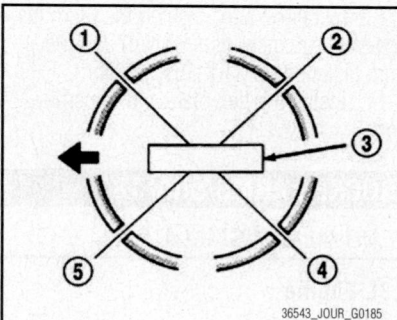

**Fig. 146 Piston ring positions—2.7L and
3.5L engines**

REAR MAIN SEAL

REMOVAL & INSTALLATION

2.4L Engine

See Figure 147.

1. Remove transaxle.
2. Remove flex plate bolts and discard.

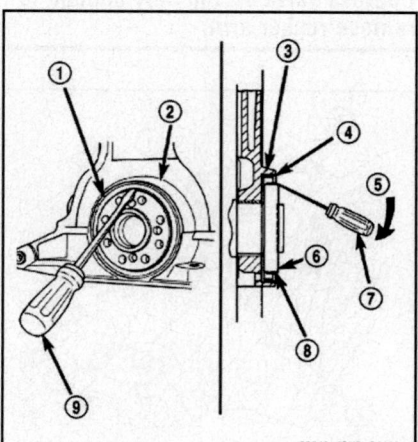

Fig. 147 Rear main seal—2.4L engine

3. Remove flex plate (1).
4. Insert a 3/16 flat bladed screwdriver (7) between the dust lip (8) and the metal case (4) of the crankshaft seal (1). Angle the screwdriver through the dust lip against metal case of the seal. Pry out seal.

> ✳✳ **CAUTION**
>
> **Do not permit the screwdriver blade to contact crankshaft seal surface. Contact of the screwdriver blade against crankshaft edge (chamfer) is permitted.**

5. Check to make sure the seals garter spring is not on the crankshaft.

To install:

> ✳✳ **CAUTION**
>
> **If a burr or scratch is present on the crankshaft edge (chamfer), cleanup with 800 emery cloth to prevent seal damage during installation of new seal. If emery cloth is used, the crankshaft must be cleaned off Mopar® brake parts cleaner.**

➡**When installing seal, lubricate Seal Guide 9509 with clean engine oil.**

6. Place Seal Guide 9509 (3) on crankshaft.
7. Position seal (2) over guide tool. Guide tool should remain on crankshaft during installation of seal. Ensure that the lip of the seal is facing towards the crankcase during installation.
8. Drive the seal into the block using Seal Driver 9706 (1) and Driver Handle C-4171 (4) until Seal Driver 9706 bottoms out against the block.
9. Install flex plate (1).
10. Install washer (2).
11. Install new flex plate bolts (3) and tighten to 70 ft. lbs. (95 Nm).
12. Install transaxle.

2.7L Engine

See Figures 148 and 149.

➡**The crankshaft rear oil seal is incorporated in the seal adapter (2) and cannot be removed from the adapter. The crankshaft rear oil seal/seal adapter (2) are serviced as an assembly.**

1. Remove transmission.
2. Remove flex plate attaching bolts (2), backing plate (3), and flex plate (1).
3. Remove oil pan.

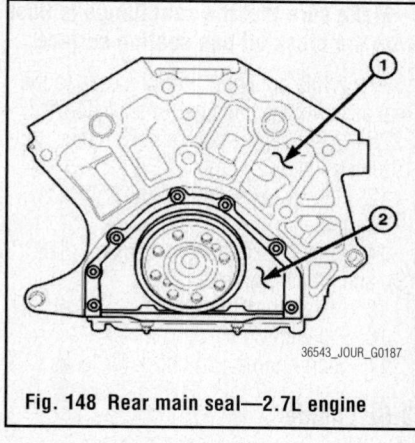

Fig. 148 Rear main seal—2.7L engine

4. Remove seal retainer attaching screws.
5. Remove crankshaft rear oil seal/adapter (2).

To install:

➡Inspect the crankshaft to make sure no nicks or burrs are on the seal surface.

6. Clean sealing surfaces thoroughly.
7. Apply engine oil to the seal lip inside diameter.

➡**The seal lip (2) on the retainer must always uniformly curl inward toward the engine on the crankshaft (1).**

8. Position the special tool 6926 (1) onto the crankshaft and gently slide the seal (2) over the crankshaft.
9. Install seal retaining bolts finger tight.

➡**The following steps must be performed to prevent oil leaks at sealing joints.**

10. Attach Special Tools 8225 (1) to pan rail using the oil pan fasteners.

➡**Make sure that the "2.7L" stamped on the special tool is facing the cylinder block (flat side of tools against pan rail).**

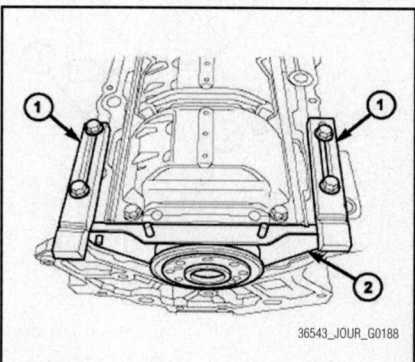

Fig. 149 Rear main seal tool—2.7L engine

➡Make sure that the seal flange is flush with the block oil pan sealing surface.

11. While applying firm pressure to the seal assembly (2) against Special Tools 8225 (1), tighten seal assembly screws to 105 inch lbs. (12 Nm).

12. Remove special tool 8225.

13. Install oil pan.

14. Install flex plate (1), backing plate (3), and attaching bolts (2).

15. Install transmission.

16. Fill with oil (5).

17. Start engine and check for leaks.

3.5L Engine

See Figures 150 and 151.

1. Remove the engine oil pan.

2. Lower the weight of the engine back onto the engine mounts.

➡Before separating the transmission from the engine, use an appropriate

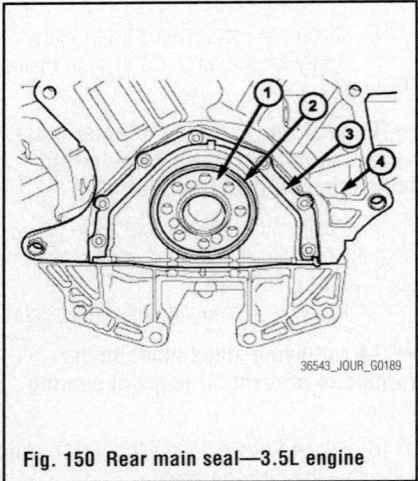

Fig. 150 Rear main seal—3.5L engine

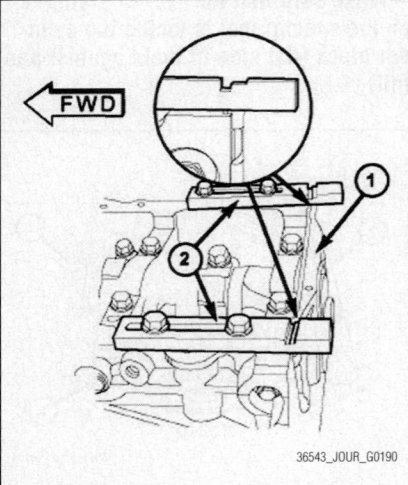

Fig. 151 Rear main seal tool—3.5L engine

support fixture or lifting device to support the weight of the engine.

3. Remove transmission from vehicle.

4. Remove the flex plate.

5. Remove the rear crankshaft oil seal retainer bolts.

6. Remove the crankshaft oil seal and clean all mating surfaces.

To install:

✳✳ CAUTION

If a burr or scratch is present on the crankshaft edge (chamfer), clean surface using 400 grit sand paper to prevent seal damage during installation. Make sure the rear crankshaft oil seal surface is clean and free of any abrasive materials.

➡The rear crankshaft oil seal and retainer are an assembly. DO NOT separate the seal protector from the rear crankshaft oil seal before installation on engine. Damage to the seal lip will occur if the seal protector is removed and installed prior to installation on engine.

7. Apply engine oil to crankshaft seal surface.

8. If the seal protector (1) is missing or was accidentally dislodged, go to Step 3 . Otherwise, carefully position the oil seal retainer assembly (3), and seal protector (1) on crankshaft and push firmly into place on engine block (during this step, the seal protector will be pushed from the rear oil seal assembly as a result of installing the rear oil seal). Hand tighten the rear oil seal fasteners, and go to Step 4 .

➡The seal lip (2) must always uniformly curl inward toward the engine on the crankshaft (1).

✳✳ CAUTION

If for any reason the installation sleeve is missing or dislodged from rear crankshaft oil seal prior to installation, the following procedure must be performed.

9. Using the chamfered seal guide from Special Tool 6926, insert the tapered end (1) into the transmission side of the rear crankshaft oil seal assembly (2), and push the seal guide through the seal assembly. This will ensure the seal lip is positioned toward the engine when the seal assembly is installed. When the seal lip is correctly positioned, go to Step #2 .

➡The following steps must be performed to prevent oil leaks at sealing joints.

10. Attach Special Tools 8225 (1) to pan rail using the oil pan fasteners

➡Special Tools 8225 (1), are use to assist with the fit of the flush mount rear main seal retainer. The notch on tool should be located away the seal retainer.

11. While applying firm pressure to the seal retainer against Special Tools 8225 (1), tighten seal retainer screws to 105 inch lbs. (12 Nm).

12. Remove special tool #8225 (1).

➡Make sure that the seal flange is flush with the block oil pan sealing surface.

13. Install oil pan. Tighten the 6mm fasteners to 105 inch lbs. (12 Nm) and the 8mm fasteners to 21 ft. lbs. (28 Nm).

14. Install the flex plate and transmission.

ROCKER ARMS/SHAFTS

REMOVAL & INSTALLATION

2.7L Engine

See Figure 152.

1. Remove cylinder head cover(s).

✳✳ CAUTION

Always rotate engine by turning the crankshaft. Failure to do so will result in valve and/or piston damage.

2. Rotate engine until the cam lobe is on its base circle (heel), on the rocker arm being removed.

✳✳ CAUTION

Depress valve spring only enough to remove rocker arm.

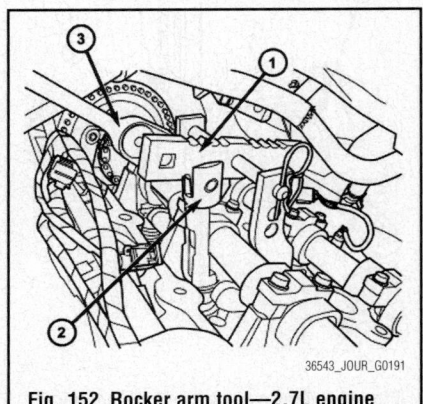

Fig. 152 Rocker arm tool—2.7L engine

3. Using Special Tools 8215-A (1) and 8216-A (2) Adaptor, depress valve spring only enough to release tension on rocker arm.

4. Remove rocker arm from cylinder head.

> ※※ **CAUTION**
>
> **If rocker arms are to be reused, identify position of rocker arms for reassembly in their original positions.**

5. Repeat procedure for each rocker arm removed.

6. Inspect the rocker arm for wear or damage.

To install:

7. Lubricate rocker arms with clean engine oil before installation.

8. Rotate engine until cam lobe is on its base circle (heel) of rocker arm being installed.

9. Using Special Tools 8215-A (1) and 8216-A Adaptor, depress valve spring only enough to install rocker arm.

10. Install rocker arm in original position (if reused) over valve and lash adjuster. Release tension on valve spring.

➡ **Inspect rocker arm for proper engagement into lash adjuster and valve tip.**

11. Repeat procedure for each rocker arm being installed.

12. Install cylinder head cover(s).

3.5L Engine

See Figure 153.

> ※※ **CAUTION**
>
> **The rocker arm shafts are hollow and are used as lubrication oil passages. The rocker arm and shaft assembly on the RIGHT side of the engine has an oil passage hole from the cylinder**

head to the third rocker shaft support. The rocker arm shaft assembly on the LEFT side of the engine has an oil passage hole from the cylinder head to the second rocker shaft support.

1. Remove cylinder head covers.

2. Identify the rocker arm assembly and rocker arms before disassembly.

3. Remove rocker arm assembly bolts.

4. Remove rocker arm assembly.

➡ **To prevent air induction into lash adjusters, avoid turning rocker arm assembly upside down.**

> ※※ **CAUTION**
>
> **Do not allow rocker arm assembly to rest on lash adjusters, as damage may occur to lash adjusters and/or plastic retainers.**

To install:

➡ **Rocker arm and shaft assembly can be installed either prior to or after (preferred) cylinder head installation.**

5. Rotate camshaft gears clockwise to where the number one cylinder intake valves would just start to open. The camshaft lobes are now in a neutral position (no load to the valve). This will allow the rocker arm shaft assembly to be tightened into position with little or no valve spring load on it.

6. Install the rocker arm and shaft assembly making sure that the identification marks face toward the front of engine for left head and toward the rear of the engine for right head.

7. Tighten rocker arm/shaft assembly bolts in the sequence shown to 23 ft. lbs. (31 Nm).

8. Install cylinder head covers.

TIMING BELT FRONT COVER

REMOVAL & INSTALLATION

2.4L Engine

See Figures 154 through 156.

1. Remove engine cover by pulling upward.

2. Perform fuel pressure bleed procedure.

3. Disconnect and isolate the negative battery cable.

4. Remove coolant recovery bottle.

5. Remove and reposition power steering reservoir.

6. Remove accessory drive belt.

7. Remove power steering hose hold-down.

8. Remove the three power steering pump mounting bolts through the openings in the pulley and reposition the pump.

9. Remove the cylinder head cover.

10. Remove ignition coils from the cylinder head cover.

11. Raise and support the vehicle.

12. Remove the frame cover portion of the right splash shield.

13. Set engine to TDC.

14. Remove lower A/C compressor bolts if equipped.

15. Remove lower A/C compressor mount if equipped.

16. Remove accessory drive belt lower idler pulley.

17. Remove crankshaft damper (2).

18. Remove three bolts and water pump pulley (4) from water pump.

19. Remove lower bolt from right side engine mount bracket (1).

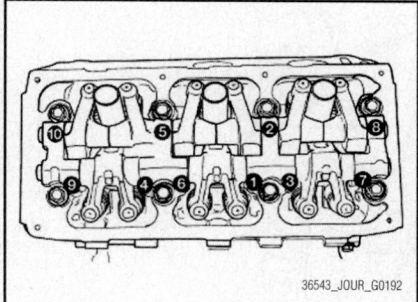

36543_JOUR_G0192

Fig. 153 Rocker arm torque sequence—3.5L engine

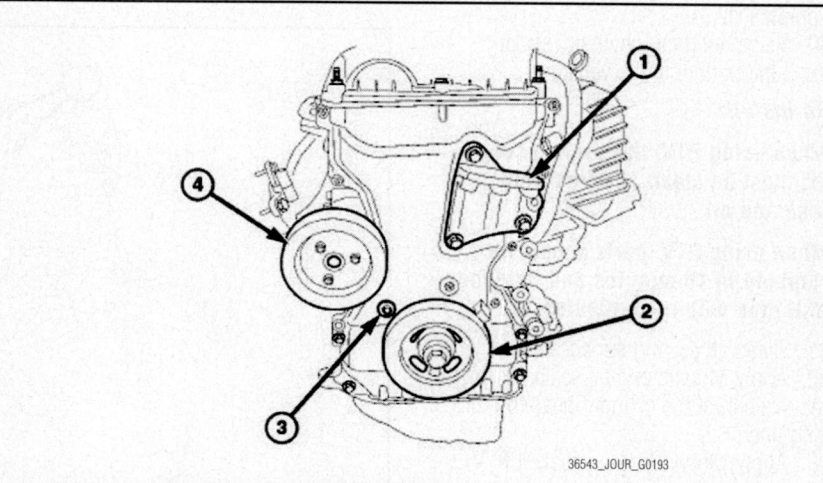

36543_JOUR_G0193

Fig. 154 Engine mount and water pump—2.4L engine

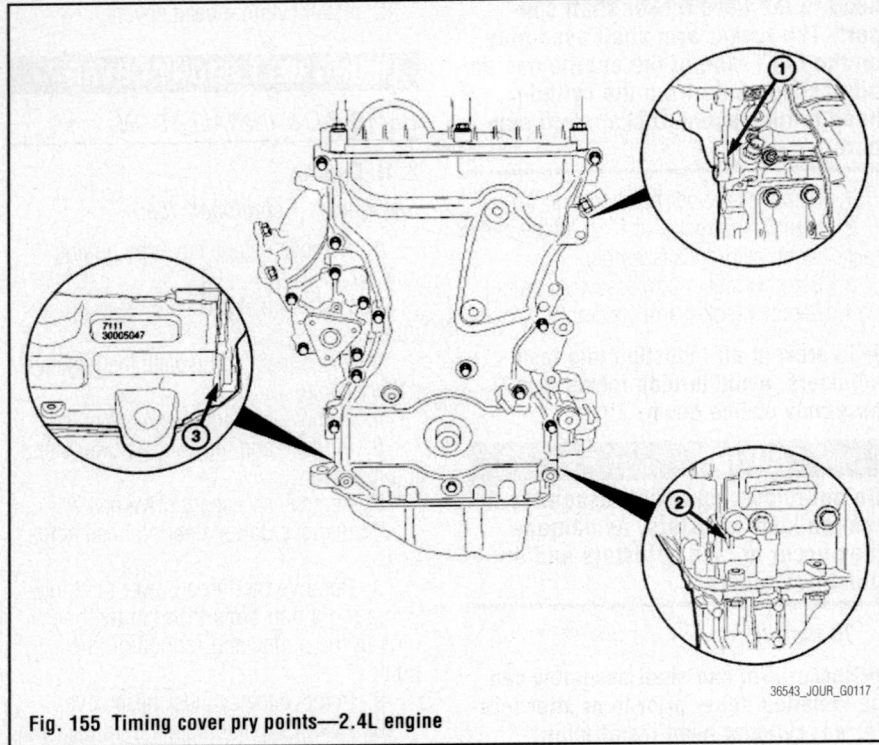

Fig. 155 Timing cover pry points—2.4L engine

20. Remove timing chain cover lower bolts from oil pan.

21. Lower vehicle.

22. Support engine with suitable jack.

23. Remove right engine mount bracket retaining bolts.

24. Remove retaining nuts and reposition mount bracket.

25. Remove accessory drive upper idler pulley.

26. Remove right upper engine mount bracket.

27. Remove accessory drive belt tensioner.

28. Remove upper timing chain cover retaining bolts.

29. Remove timing chain cover using pry points (1,2,3).

30. Remove timing chain cover out through the bottom of the vehicle.

To install:

➡When using RTV, the sealing surfaces must be clean and free from grease and oil.

➡When using RTV, parts should be assembled in 10 minutes and tighten to final torque within 45 minutes.

31. Clean all sealing surfaces.

32. Apply Mopar® engine sealant RTV (or equivalent) at the cylinder head to block parting line (1,2).

33. Apply Mopar® engine sealant RTV (or equivalent) at the ladder frame to block parting line (1,2).

34. Apply Mopar® engine sealant RTV (or equivalent) in the corner of the oil pan and block.

35. Apply 2 mm bead of Mopar® engine sealant RTV (or equivalent) to the oil pan.

36. Apply 2 mm bead of Mopar® engine sealant RTV (or equivalent) to the engine block (1,2).

37. Install timing chain cover upwards from under the vehicle.

38. Install timing chain cover upper retaining bolts and tighten M6 bolts to 80 inch lbs. (9 Nm) and M8 bolts to 19 ft. lbs. (26 Nm).

39. Install accessory drive belt tensioner. Tighten bolt to 17 ft. lbs. (24 Nm).

40. Install right engine mount bracket. Tighten bolts to 37 ft. lbs. (50 Nm).

41. Install accessory drive belt upper idler pulley. Tighten bolt to 35 ft. lbs. (48 Nm).

42. Position engine mount adapter and install bolts.

43. Install retaining nuts and tighten nuts to 22 ft. lbs. (30 Nm).

44. Tighten bolts to 37 ft. lbs. (50 Nm).

45. Remove jack from under engine.

46. Raise and support the vehicle.

47. Install oil pan to timing chain cover lower retaining bolts and tighten M6 bolts to 80 inch lbs. (9 Nm).

48. Install water pump pulley (4) and tighten three bolts to 80 inch lbs. (9 Nm).

49. Install crankshaft damper (2).

50. Install accessory drive belt lower idler pulley. Tighten bolt to 35 ft. lbs. (48 Nm).

51. Install lower A/C compressor mounting bracket. Tighten the bolts to 18 ft. lbs. (25 Nm).

52. Install A/C compressor. Tighten the bolts to 18 ft. lbs. (25 Nm).

53. Install right lower splash shield.

54. Lower vehicle.

55. Install cylinder head cover and ignition coils.

56. Place the power steering pump in mounting position. Install the three bolts through openings in the pulley. Tighten the mounting bolts to 19 ft. lbs. (26 Nm).

57. Install the power steering hose holddown.

58. Install accessory drive belt.

59. Install power steering pump reservoir. Tighten mounting screw to 106 inch lbs. (12 Nm).

60. Install coolant recovery reservoir. Tighten mounting bolts to 89 inch lbs. (10 Nm).

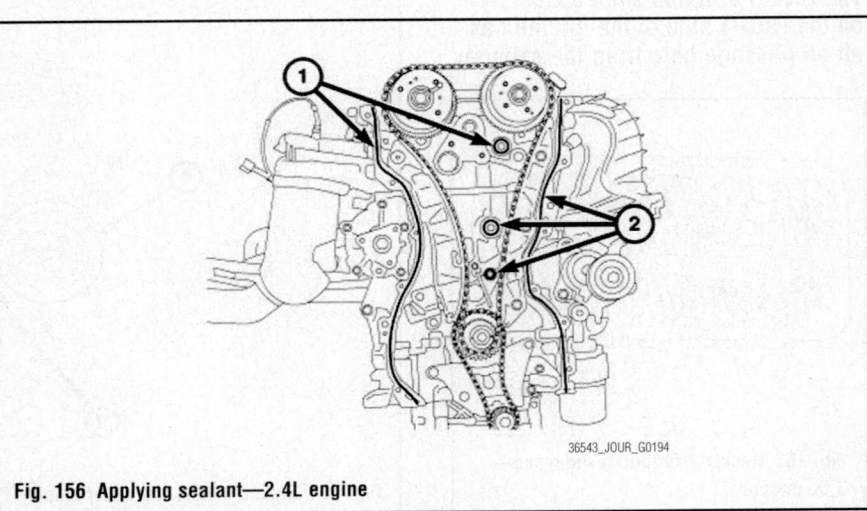

Fig. 156 Applying sealant—2.4L engine

61. Install clean air hose and air cleaner housing.

62. Connect negative battery cable.

63. Operate engine until it reaches normal operating temperature. Check oil system for leaks and correct fluid level.

64. Install engine cover.

2.7L Engine

See Figure 157.

1. Disconnect and isolate the negative battery cable.

2. Drain cooling system.

3. Remove coolant pressure container.

4. Remove right front wheel and belt splash shield.

5. Remove accessory drive belts.

6. Remove crankshaft vibration damper.

7. Remove AC/Generator belt tensioner/bracket assembly.

8. Disconnect heater hose from tube at right front frame rail area.

9. Remove screws securing heater supply tube to right frame rail. Reposition heater supply tube.

10. Place a floor jack with wooden block under oil pan to support engine.

11. Remove right engine mount.

12. Remove upper timing chain cover bolts.

13. Remove remaining bolts securing timing chain cover to engine.

14. Remove timing chain cover (2).

15. Discard timing chain cover gasket (1). Remove front crankshaft oil seal from cover.

To install:

16. Inspect and clean timing chain cover sealing surfaces.

17. Before installing timing cover gasket

apply a ⅛ inch bead of Mopar® Engine RTV GEN II to the parting lines between the oil pan and cylinder block.

18. Install timing cover (2) and gasket (1). Tighten M10 cover bolts to 40 ft. lbs. (54 Nm) and M6 bolts to 105 inch lbs. (12 Nm).

19. Install front crankshaft oil seal using Special Tool 6780-2 sleeve and 6780-1 installer.

20. Lower vehicle.

21. Install right engine mount.

22. Install screws attaching heater supply tube to right front frame rail area.

23. Raise vehicle on hoist.

24. Connect heater hose to supply tube at right front frame rail area.

25. Install AC/Generator belt tensioner/bracket assembly.

26. Install crankshaft vibration damper.

27. Install accessory drive belts.

28. Install belt splash shield and right front wheel.

29. Lower vehicle.

30. Install coolant pressure container.

31. Fill cooling system.

32. Connect negative battery cable.

3.5L Engine

See Figure 158.

1. Perform fuel pressure release procedure.

2. Disconnect negative battery cable.

3. Raise the vehicle.

4. Remove the accessory drive belt.

5. Remove accessory drive belt tensioner.

6. Remove bolts for power steering pump. Reposition power steering pump aside.

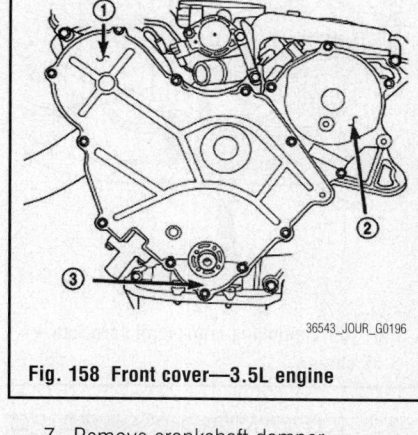

Fig. 158 Front cover—3.5L engine

7. Remove crankshaft damper.

8. Remove the lower front timing belt cover fasteners.

9. Lower the vehicle.

10. Support the engine with a floor jack.

11. Remove the front engine mount.

12. Disconnect the fuel supply line at the fuel rail.

13. Remove the upper timing belt cover bolts and remove front timing belt cover.

To install:

➡ **The timing cover bolts and both holes to the engine block must be thoroughly cleaned and free of oil residue before assembly. IN ADDITION, add thread sealant to the timing cover bolts that mount to the oil pump.**

14. Install front timing belt cover.

15. Install the upper engine mount.

16. Connect fuel supply line at fuel rail.

17. Raise the vehicle.

18. Install power steering pump fasteners. Tighten bolts to 16 ft. lbs. (23 Nm).

19. Install crankshaft damper.

20. Install accessory drive belt tensioner. Torque fastener to 21 ft. lbs. (28 Nm).

21. Install accessory drive belt.

22. Lower the vehicle.

23. Connect negative battery cable.

TIMING BELT AND SPROCKETS

REMOVAL & INSTALLATION

3.5L Engine

See Figures 159 through 161.

1. Perform fuel pressure release procedure.

2. Disconnect negative battery cable.

3. Remove both cylinder head covers.

4. Remove the front timing belt cover.

5. Mark belt running direction, if timing belt is to be reused.

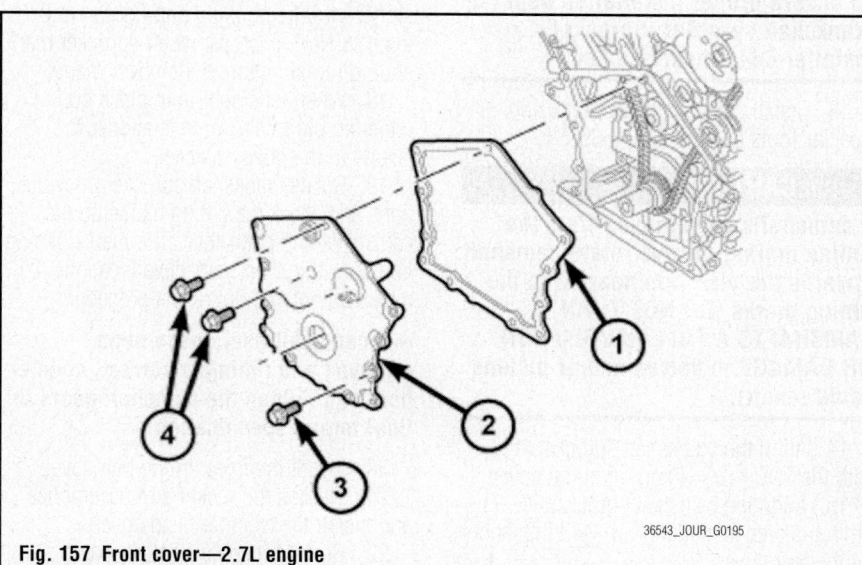

Fig. 157 Front cover—2.7L engine

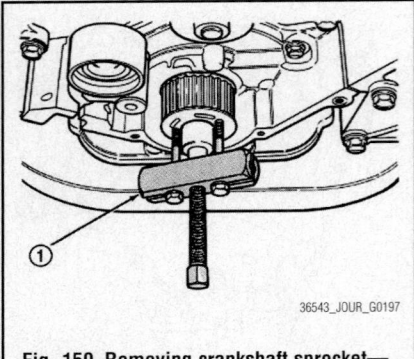

Fig. 159 Removing crankshaft sprocket—3.5L engine

✻✻ CAUTION

When aligning timing marks, always rotate engine by turning the crankshaft. Failure to do so will result in valve and/or piston damage.

6. Rotate engine clockwise until crankshaft mark aligns with the TDC mark on oil pump housing and the camshaft sprocket timing marks are aligned with the marks on the rear cover.

7. Remove the timing belt tensioner and remove timing belt.

8. Inspect the tensioner for fluid leakage.

9. Inspect the pivot and bolt for free movement, bearing grease leakage, and smooth rotation. If not rotating freely, replace the arm and pulley assembly.

10. When tensioner is removed from the engine it is necessary to compress the plunger into the tensioner body.

✻✻ CAUTION

Index the tensioner in the vise the same way it is installed on the engine. This ensures proper pin orientation when tensioner is installed on the engine.

a. Place the tensioner into a vise and SLOWLY compress the plunger. Total

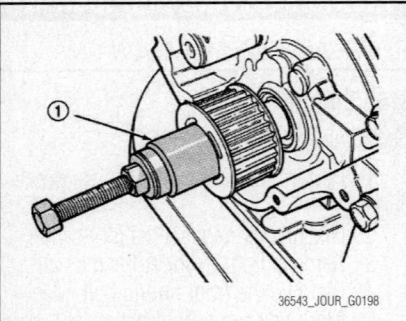

Fig. 160 Installing crankshaft sprocket—3.5L engine

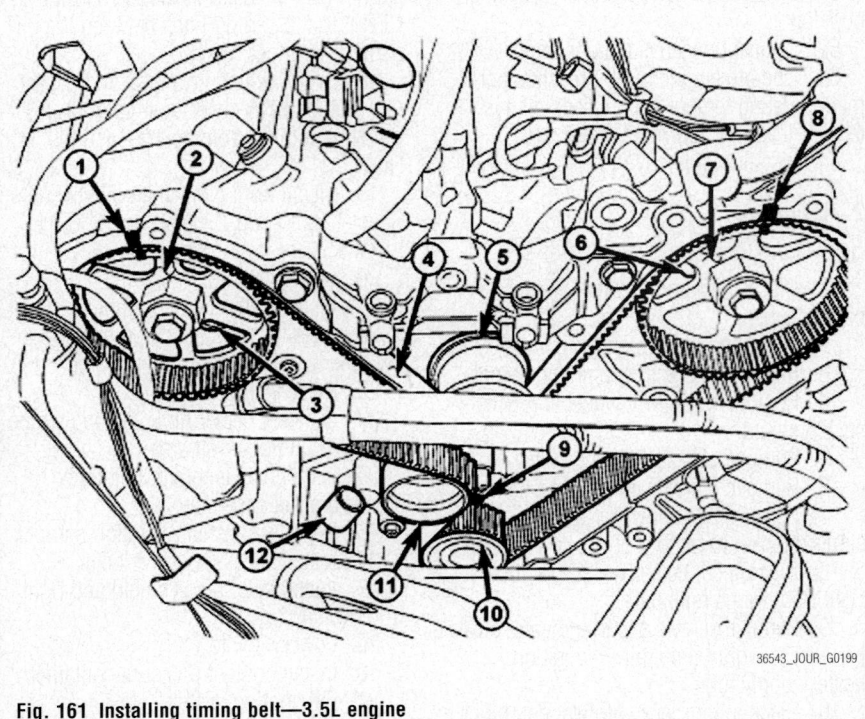

Fig. 161 Installing timing belt—3.5L engine

bleed down of tensioner should take about 5 minutes.

b. When plunger is compressed into the tensioner body install a pin through the body and plunger to retain plunger in place until tensioner is installed.

11. Remove crankshaft sprocket using Special Tool L-4407-A.

12. To remove camshaft sprocket, see camshaft.

To install:

✻✻ CAUTION

To ensure proper installation depth of crankshaft sprocket, Sprocket Installer 6641 must be used.

13. Install crankshaft sprocket using Special Tools 6641 and C-4685-C1.

✻✻ CAUTION

If camshafts have moved from the timing marks, always rotate camshaft towards the direction nearest to the timing marks (DO NOT TURN CAMSHAFTS A FULL REVOLUTION OR DAMAGE to valves and/or pistons could result).

14. Align the crankshaft sprocket (10) with the TDC mark (9) on oil pump cover.

15. Align the camshaft sprockets (2, 7) timing reference marks (1, 8) with the marks on the rear cover.

16. Install the timing belt starting at the crankshaft sprocket (10) going in a counterclockwise direction. Install the belt around the last sprocket. Maintain tension on the belt as it is positioned around the tensioner pulley (11).

➡**If the camshaft gears have been removed it is only necessary to have the camshaft gear retaining bolts installed to a snug torque at this time.**

17. Holding the tensioner pulley (11) against the belt, install the tensioner into the housing and tighten to 21 ft. lbs. (28 Nm). Each camshaft sprocket mark should remain aligned the cover marks.

18. When tensioner is in place pull retaining pin to allow the tensioner to extend to the pulley bracket.

19. Rotate crankshaft sprocket 2 revolutions and check the timing marks on the camshafts and crankshaft. The marks should line up within their respective locations. If marks do not line up, repeat procedure.

➡**If camshaft gears have been removed and timing is correct, counterhold and tighten the camshaft gears to final torque specification.**

20. Install the front timing belt cover.

21. Tighten the rocker arm assemblies and install the cylinder head covers.

22. Connect negative battery cable.

TIMING BELT REAR COVER

REMOVAL & INSTALLATION

3.5L Engine

See Figures 162 through 164.

1. Perform fuel pressure release procedure.
2. Disconnect the negative battery cable.
3. Remove timing belt.
4. Remove camshaft sprockets.
5. Remove rear timing belt cover bolts.
6. Remove the rear cover.

➡The rear timing belt cover has O-rings to seal the water pump passages to cylinder block. Do not reuse the O-rings.

To install:

7. Clean rear timing belt cover O-ring sealing surfaces and grooves. Lubricate new O-rings with Mopar® Dielectric Grease or equivalent to facilitate assembly.
8. Position NEW O-rings on cover.
9. Install rear timing belt cover. Tighten bolts to the following specified torque:
   - M10: 40 ft. lbs. (54 Nm)
   - M8: 20 ft. lbs. (28 Nm)
   - M6: 105 inch lbs. (12 Nm)

10. Install camshaft sprockets.
11. Install timing belt.

TIMING CHAIN COVER AND SEAL

REMOVAL & INSTALLATION

2.4L Engine

See Figure 165.

1. Remove engine cover by pulling upward.
2. Perform fuel pressure bleed procedure.

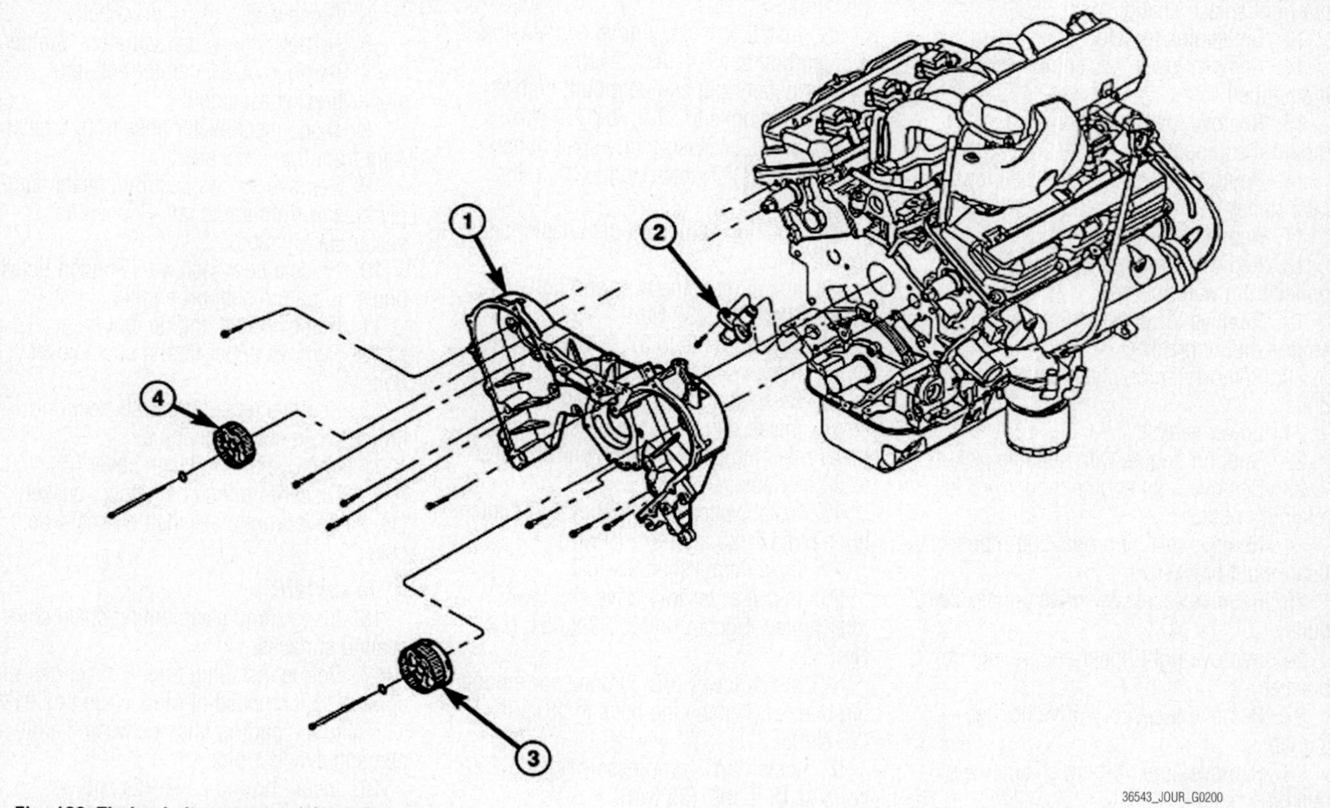

Fig. 162 Timing belt rear cover (1)—3.5L engine

36543_JOUR_G0200

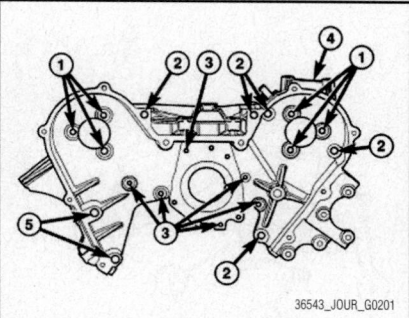

Fig. 163 Timing belt rear cover bolts—3.5L engine

36543_JOUR_G0201

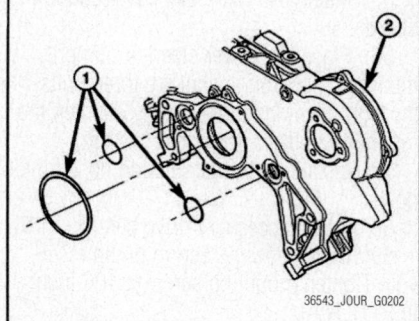

Fig. 164 Timing belt rear cover (2) O-rings (1)—3.5L engine

36543_JOUR_G0202

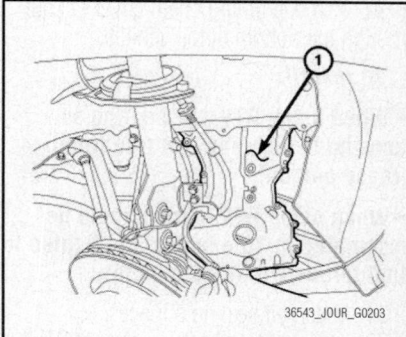

Fig. 165 Timing chain cover (1)—2.4L engine

36543_JOUR_G0203

3. Disconnect and isolate the negative battery cable.

4. Remove coolant recovery bottle.

5. Remove and reposition power steering reservoir.

6. Remove accessory drive belt.

7. Remove power steering hose hold-down.

8. Remove the three power steering pump mounting bolts through the openings in the pulley and reposition the pump.

9. Remove the cylinder head cover.

10. Remove ignition coils from the cylinder head cover.

11. Raise and support the vehicle.

12. Remove the frame cover portion of the right splash shield.

13. Set engine to TDC.

14. Remove lower A/C compressor bolts if equipped.

15. Remove lower A/C compressor mount if equipped.

16. Remove accessory drive belt lower idler pulley.

17. Remove crankshaft damper.

18. Remove three bolts and water pump pulley from water pump.

19. Remove lower bolt from right side engine mount bracket.

20. Remove timing chain cover lower bolts.

21. Lower vehicle.

22. Support engine with suitable jack.

23. Remove right engine mount bracket retaining bolts.

24. Remove retaining nuts and reposition mount bracket.

25. Remove accessory drive upper idler pulley.

26. Remove right upper engine mount bracket.

27. Remove accessory drive belt tensioner.

28. Remove upper timing chain cover retaining bolts.

29. Remove timing chain cover using pry points (1,2,3).

30. Remove timing chain cover (1) out through the bottom of the vehicle.

To install:

➡ When using RTV, the sealing surfaces must be clean and free from grease and oil.

➡ When using RTV, parts should be assembled in 10 minutes and tighten to final torque within 45 minutes.

31. Clean all sealing surfaces.

32. Apply Mopar® engine sealant RTV (or equivalent) at the cylinder head to block parting line.

33. Apply Mopar® engine sealant RTV (or equivalent) at the ladder frame to block parting line.

34. Apply Mopar® engine sealant RTV (or equivalent) in the corner of the oil pan and block.

35. Apply 2 mm bead of Mopar® engine sealant RTV (or equivalent) to the oil pan.

36. Apply 2 mm bead of Mopar® engine sealant RTV (or equivalent) to the engine block.

37. Install timing chain cover (1) upwards from under the vehicle.

38. Install timing chain cover upper retaining bolts and tighten M6 bolts to 80 inch lbs. (9 Nm) and M8 bolts to 19 ft. lbs. (26 Nm).

39. Install accessory drive belt tensioner. Tighten bolt to 17 ft. lbs. (24 Nm).

40. Install right engine mount bracket (1). Tighten bolts to 37 ft. lbs. (50 Nm).

41. Install accessory drive belt upper idler pulley (1). Tighten bolt to 35 ft. lbs. (48 Nm).

42. Position engine mount adapter and install bolts.

43. Install retaining nuts and tighten nuts to 22 ft. lbs. (30 Nm).

44. Tighten bolts to 37 ft. lbs. (50 Nm).

45. Remove jack from under engine.

46. Raise and support the vehicle.

47. Install oil pan to timing chain cover lower retaining bolts and tighten M6 bolts to 80 inch lbs. (9 Nm).

48. Install water pump pulley and tighten three bolts to 80 inch lbs. (9 Nm).

49. Install crankshaft damper.

50. Install accessory drive belt lower idler pulley. Tighten bolt to 35 ft. lbs. (48 Nm).

51. Install lower A/C compressor mounting bracket. Tighten the bolts to 18 ft. lbs. (25 Nm).

52. Install A/C compressor. Tighten the bolts to 18 ft. lbs. (25 Nm).

53. Install right lower splash shield.

54. Lower vehicle.

55. Install cylinder head cover and ignition coils.

56. Place the power steering pump in mounting position. Install the three bolts through openings in the pulley. Tighten the mounting bolts to 19 ft. lbs. (26 Nm).

57. Install the power steering hose hold-down.

58. Install accessory drive belt.

59. Install power steering pump reservoir. Tighten mounting screw to 106 inch lbs. (12 Nm).

60. Install coolant recovery reservoir. Tighten mounting bolts to 89 inch lbs. (10 Nm).

61. Install clean air hose and air cleaner housing.

62. Connect negative battery cable.

63. Operate engine until it reaches normal operating temperature. Check oil system for leaks and correct fluid level.

64. Install engine cover.

2.7L Engine

See Figure 166.

1. Disconnect and isolate the negative battery cable.

2. Drain cooling system.

3. Remove coolant pressure container.

4. Remove right front wheel and belt splash shield.

5. Remove accessory drive belts.

6. Remove crankshaft vibration damper.

7. Remove AC/Generator belt tensioner/bracket assembly.

8. Disconnect heater hose from tube at right front frame rail area.

9. Remove screws securing heater supply tube to right frame rail. Reposition heater supply tube.

10. Place a floor jack with wooden block under oil pan to support engine.

11. Remove right engine mount.

12. Remove upper timing chain cover bolts.

13. Remove remaining bolts securing timing chain cover to engine.

14. Remove timing chain cover (2).

15. Discard timing chain cover gasket (1). Remove front crankshaft oil seal from cover.

To install:

16. Inspect and clean timing chain cover sealing surfaces.

17. Before installing timing cover gasket apply a ⅛ inch bead of Mopar® Engine RTV GEN II to the parting lines between the oil pan and cylinder block.

18. Install timing cover (2) and gasket (1). Tighten M10 cover bolts to 40 ft.

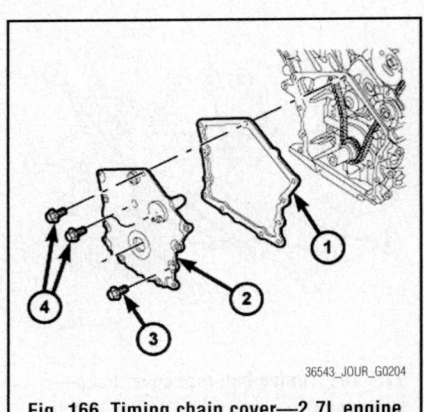

36543_JOUR_G0204

Fig. 166 Timing chain cover—2.7L engine

lbs. (54 Nm) and M6 bolts to 105 inch lbs. (12 Nm).

19. Install front crankshaft oil seal using Special Tool 6780-2 sleeve and 6780-1 installer.

20. Lower vehicle.

21. Install right engine mount.

22. Install screws attaching heater supply tube to right front frame rail area.

23. Raise vehicle on hoist.

24. Connect heater hose to supply tube at right front frame rail area.

25. Install AC/Generator belt tensioner/bracket assembly.

26. Install crankshaft vibration damper.

27. Install accessory drive belts.

28. Install belt splash shield and right front wheel.

29. Lower vehicle.

30. Install coolant pressure container.

31. Fill cooling system.

32. Connect negative battery cable.

TIMING CHAIN AND SPROCKETS

REMOVAL & INSTALLATION

2.4L Engine

See Figures 165, 167 and 168.

1. Remove timing chain cover, as outlined in this section.

➡The crankshaft timing mark (3) or (5) can be in one of two locations depending on whether the engine is early production (5), late production (3) or assembled with service parts (3). In all cases the keyway (2) will always be in the 9:00 position, in line with the ladder frame mounting surface (1) when the engine is at TDC.

2. Verify that the engine is still set to TDC.

➡If the timing chain plated links can no longer be seen, the timing chain

links corresponding to the timing marks must be marked prior to removal if the chain is to be reused.

3. Mark chain link (4) corresponding to crankshaft timing mark (3) or (5).

4. With the engine still set to TDC, verify that the marks on the camshaft sprockets (3) are in line with the cylinder head cover sealing surface (2). If the marks do not line up, the timing chain is not correctly installed.

5. Mark chain link (1) corresponding to camshaft timing mark.

6. Remove timing chain tensioner (5).

7. Remove timing chain (2).

➡Camshaft phasers and camshaft sprockets are supplied as an assembly, do not attempt to disassemble.

8. Remove oil pan.

9. Remove oil pump drive chain tensioner.

10. Remove oil pump drive chain.

11. Remove crankshaft sprocket.

To install:

➡The crankshaft timing mark (3) or (5) can be in one of two locations depending on whether the engine is early production (5), late production (3) or assembled with service parts (3). In all cases the keyway (2) will always be in the 9:00 position, in line with the ladder frame mounting surface (1) when the engine is at TDC.

12. Verify that the engine is still set to TDC.

13. Align camshaft timing marks (3) so they are facing each other and in line with the cylinder head cover sealing surface (2).

14. Install timing chain so plated (or marked) links on chain align with timing marks on camshaft sprockets (1).

15. Align timing mark on the crankshaft sprocket (3) or (5) with the plated (or

marked) link (4) on the timing chain. Position chain so slack will be on the tensioner side.

➡**Keep the slack in the timing chain on the tensioner side.**

16. Install the timing chain tensioner (5).

17. Rotate the crankshaft CLOCKWISE two complete revolutions until the crankshaft is repositioned at the TDC position with the key way at the 9 o'clock position.

18. Verify that the camshafts timing marks (3) are in the proper position and in line with the cylinder head cover sealing surface. If the marks do not line up, the timing chain is not correctly installed.

19. Install front timing chain cover.

20. Connect negative battery cable.

21. Operate engine until it reaches normal operating temperature. Check oil and cooling systems for correct fluid levels.

2.7L Engine

1. Disconnect negative battery cable.

2. Drain cooling system.

3. Remove upper intake manifold, as outlined in this section.

4. Remove cylinder head covers, crankshaft vibration damper, and timing chain cover.

✳✳ CAUTION

When aligning timing marks, always rotate engine by turning the crankshaft. Failure to do so will result in valve and/or piston damage.

5. Align crankshaft sprocket timing mark to mark on oil pump housing. The mark on oil pump housing is 60° ATDC of #1 cylinder.

✳✳ CAUTION

When the timing chain is removed and the cylinder heads are still installed, DO NOT rotate the camshafts or crankshaft without first locating the proper crankshaft position. Failure to do so will result in valve and/or piston damage.

6. Remove power steering pump and bracket as an assembly. Do not disconnect power steering lines from pump. Reposition pump and support with suitable retaining strap.

7. Remove primary timing chain tensioner retainer cap and tensioner from right cylinder head.

8. Disconnect and remove camshaft position sensor from left cylinder head.

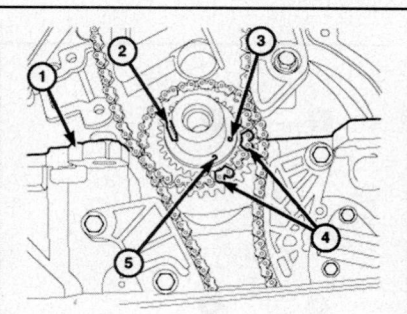

36543_JOUR_G0311

Fig. 167 Aligning crankshaft marks— 2.4L engine

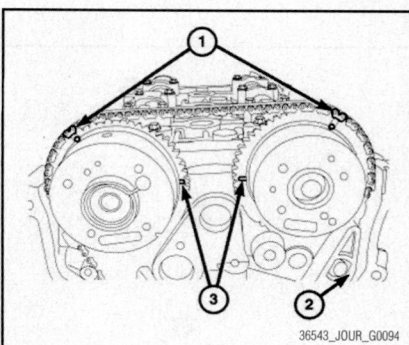

36543_JOUR_G0094

Fig. 168 Aligning camshaft marks— 2.4L engine

9. Remove timing chain guide access plugs from cylinder heads.

➡ **When camshaft sprocket bolts are removed, the camshafts will rotate in a clockwise direction.**

10. Starting with the right camshaft sprocket, remove the sprocket attaching bolts. Remove camshaft damper (if equipped) and sprocket.

11. Remove left side camshaft sprocket attaching bolts and remove sprocket .

12. Remove lower chain guide and tensioner arm.

13. Remove the primary timing chain.

14. For removal of crankshaft sprocket.

To install:

15. Inspect all sprockets and chain guides. Replace if worn.

16. For crankshaft sprocket installation procedures.

17. If removed, install right and left side short chain guides. Tighten attaching bolts to 21 ft. lbs. (28 Nm).

18. Align crankshaft sprocket timing mark to the mark on oil pump housing.

➡ **Lubricate timing chain and guides with engine oil before installation.**

19. Place left side primary chain sprocket onto the chain so that the timing mark is located in-between the two (plated) timing links.

20. Lower the primary chain with left side sprocket through the left cylinder head opening.

➡ **The camshaft sprockets can be allowed to float on the camshaft hub during installation.**

21. Loosely position left side camshaft sprocket over camshaft hub.

22. Align timing (plated) link to the crankshaft sprocket timing mark.

23. Position primary chain onto water pump drive sprocket.

24. Align right camshaft sprocket timing mark to the timing (plated) link on the timing chain and loosely position over camshaft hub.

25. Verify that all chain timing (plated) links are properly aligned to the timing marks on all sprockets.

26. Install left side lower chain guide and tensioner arm. Tighten attaching bolts to 21 ft. lbs. (28 Nm).

➡ **Inspect O-ring on chain guide access plugs before installing. Replace O-ring as necessary.**

27. Install chain guide access plugs to cylinder heads. Tighten plugs to 15 ft. lbs. (20 Nm).

➡ **To reset the primary timing chain tensioner, engine oil will first need to be purged from the tensioner.**

28. Purge oil from timing chain tensioner using the following procedure:

a. Place the check ball end of tensioner into the shallow end of Special Tool 8186.

b. Using hand pressure, slowly depress tensioner until oil is purged from tensioner.

29. Reset timing chain tensioner using the following procedure:

a. Position cylinder plunger into the deeper end of Special Tool 8186.

b. Apply a downward force until tensioner is reset.

➡ **If oil was not first purged from the tensioner, use slight finger pressure to assist the center arm pin of Special Tool 8186 to unseat the tensioner's check ball.**

✳ CAUTION

Ensure the tensioner is properly reset. The tensioner body must bottom against the top edge of Special Tool 8186. Failure to properly perform the resetting procedure may cause tensioner jamming.

30. Install the reset chain tensioner into the right cylinder head.

31. Position tensioner retaining plate and tighten bolts to 105 inch lbs. (12 Nm).

32. Starting at the right cylinder bank, first position the camshaft damper (if equipped) on camshaft hub, then insert a 3/8" square drive extension with a breaker bar into intake camshaft drive hub. Rotate camshaft until the camshaft hub aligns to the camshaft sprocket and damper attaching holes. Install the sprocket attaching bolts and tighten to 21 ft. lbs. (28 Nm).

33. Turn the left side camshaft by inserting a 3/8" square drive extension with a breaker bar into intake camshaft drive hub and rotate camshaft until the sprocket attaching bolts can be installed. Tighten sprocket bolts to 21 ft. lbs. (28 Nm).

34. Rotate engine slightly clockwise to remove timing chain slack, if necessary.

35. Activate the timing chain tensioner by using a flat bladed pry tool to gently pry tensioner arm towards the tensioner slightly. Then release the tensioner arm. Verify the tensioner is activated (extends).

36. Install power steering pump and bracket assembly.

37. Install camshaft position sensor and connect electrical connector.

38. Install the timing chain cover, crankshaft vibration damper, and cylinder head covers.

39. Install upper intake manifold.

➡ **After installation of a reset tensioner, engine noise will occur after initial start-up. This noise will normally disappear within 5-10 seconds.**

40. Fill cooling system.

41. Connect negative battery cable.

VALVE COVERS

REMOVAL & INSTALLATION

2.4L Engine

See Figures 169 and 170.

1. Remove engine cover by pulling upward.

2. Disconnect and isolate the negative battery cable.

3. Remove make up air hose.

4. Remove PCV hose.

5. Disconnect ignition coil electrical connectors.

6. Use compressed air to blow dirt and debris off the cylinder head cover prior to removal.

7. Remove cylinder head cover bolts.

8. Remove cylinder head cover from cylinder head.

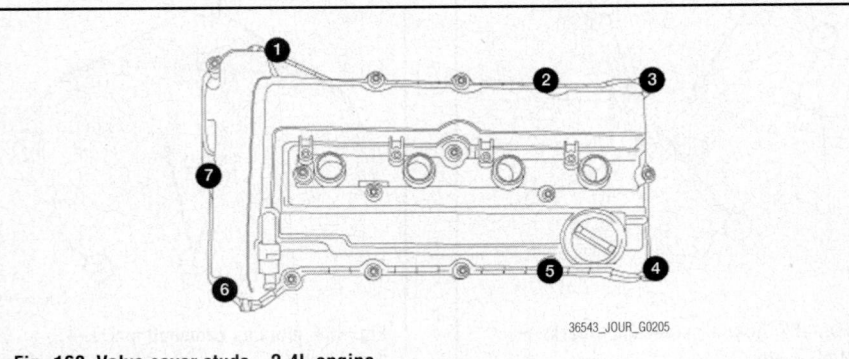

36543_JOUR_G0205

Fig. 169 Valve cover studs—2.4L engine

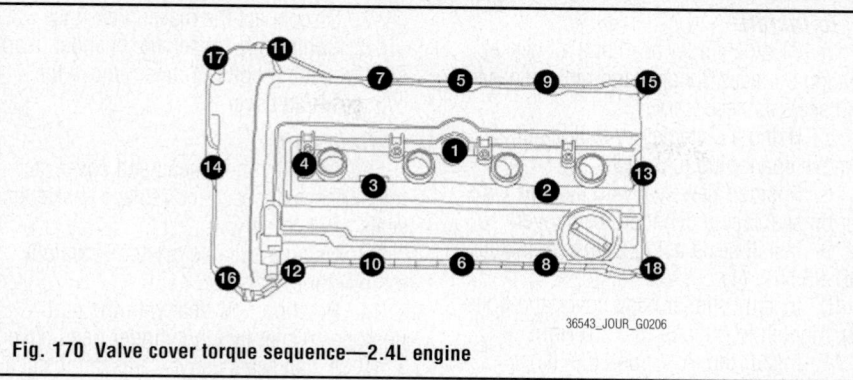

Fig. 170 Valve cover torque sequence—2.4L engine

To install:

9. Install new cylinder head cover gaskets.
10. Install studs in cover as shown.
11. Clean all RTV from cylinder head.

➡**When using RTV, the sealing surfaces must be clean and free from grease and oil.**

➡**When using RTV, parts should be assembled in 10 minutes and tighten to final torque within 45 minutes.**

12. Apply a dot of Mopar® engine sealant RTV or equivalent to cylinder head/front cover T-joint.
13. Install cylinder head cover assembly to cylinder head and install all bolts, ensuring the studs are located as shown.
14. Tighten bolts in sequence shown using a 2 step torque method as follows:
    a. Tighten all bolts to 44 inch lbs. (5 Nm).
    b. Tighten all bolts to 90 inch lbs. (10 Nm).
15. Install ignition coils. Tighten fasteners to 70 inch lbs. (8 Nm).
16. If the PCV valve was removed, tighten PCV valve to 44 inch lbs. (5 Nm).
17. Connect coil electrical connectors.
18. Connect PCV hose to PCV valve.
19. Connect make up air hose.
20. Connect negative battery cable.
21. Install engine cover by pressing the rear of the cover down first.

2.7L Engine

Left

See Figures 171 and 172.

1. Disconnect negative battery cable.
2. Disconnect electrical connectors from ignition coils and capacitor. Reposition electrical harness.
3. Remove ground strap from cylinder head cover stud.
4. Disconnect engine harness retaining clips (1) from cylinder head cover studs. Position the engine harness (3) aside.

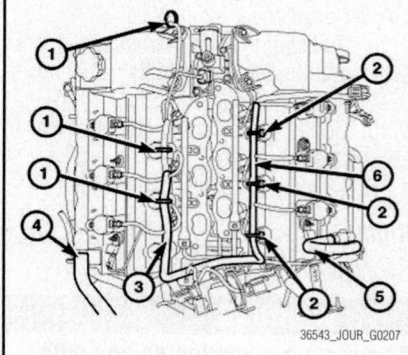

Fig. 171 Retaining clips and harness—2.7L engine

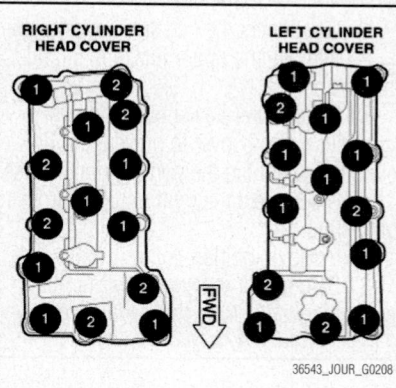

Fig. 172 Valve cover fasteners—2.7L engine

5. Remove fastener attaching ignition coil capacitor.
6. Remove ignition coils.
7. Loosen all left cylinder head cover fasteners.
8. Disconnect the makeup air hose (4).

➡**Cylinder head cover attaching bolts are captured to the cover.**

✴✴ CAUTION

Make certain the double ended studs in the center of the cylinder head

cover are loose before attempting to remove cover .

9. Remove the left cylinder head cover.

To install:

10. Clean cylinder head cover and both sealing surfaces. Inspect and replace gaskets as necessary.
11. Install cylinder head cover and hand start all fasteners. Verify that all double-ended studs are in the correct locations (1).
12. Tighten cylinder head cover attaching bolts and double-ended studs to 105 inch lbs. (12 Nm).
13. Reposition the left engine harness (3), and install the left engine harness retainers (1) to the double-ended studs.
14. Install the ignition coils.
15. Install ignition coil capacitor and fastener.
16. Reconnect all electrical connectors.
17. Install ground strap to cylinder head cover stud.
18. Install the makeup air hose.
19. Connect negative battery cable.

Right

See Figures 171 through 172.

1. Disconnect negative battery cable.
2. Disconnect electrical connectors from ignition coils and capacitor.
3. Disconnect right engine harness retaining clips (2) from cylinder head cover studs. Position the engine harness (6) aside.
4. Disconnect the PCV hose (5) from the upper intake manifold.
5. Remove upper intake manifold.
6. Remove ground strap from cylinder head cover stud.
7. Disconnect electrical harness retaining clips from cylinder head cover studs. Reposition electrical harness.
8. Remove fastener attaching ignition coil capacitor.
9. Remove ignition coils.
10. Loosen all cylinder head cover fasteners.

To install:

11. Clean cylinder head cover and both sealing surfaces. Inspect and replace gaskets as necessary.
12. Install cylinder head cover and hand start all fasteners. Verify that all double-ended studs are in the correct locations.
13. Tighten cylinder head cover attaching bolts and double-ended studs (1) to 105 inch lbs. (12 Nm).
14. Install ignition coils.
15. Install ignition coil capacitor and fastener.

16. Connect ground strap to cylinder head cover stud.

17. Reposition the right engine harness (6), and install the right engine harness retainers (2) to the double-ended studs.

18. Install upper intake manifold.

19. Reconnect the PCV to the upper intake manifold.

3.5L Engine

Left

See Figures 173 and 174.

> ❊❊ **WARNING**
>
> **Do not start or run the engine with the cylinder head cover removed. Damage or personal injury may occur.**

1. Disconnect and isolate the negative battery cable.

2. Disconnect and remove the three ignition coils.

3. Disconnect engine harness retaining clips (2) from cylinder head cover studs. Position the engine harness aside.

4. Disconnect the PCV hose (3) from the valve cover assembly (if required).

5. Completely loosen the eight cylinder head cover retaining bolts (4) and remove the cylinder head cover.

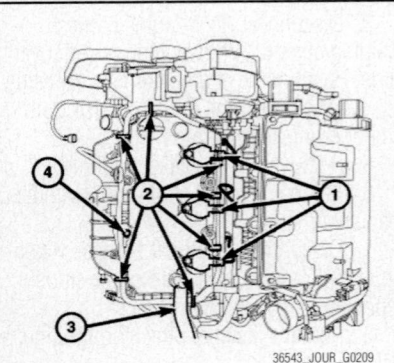

Fig. 173 Retaining clips and harness—3.5L engine

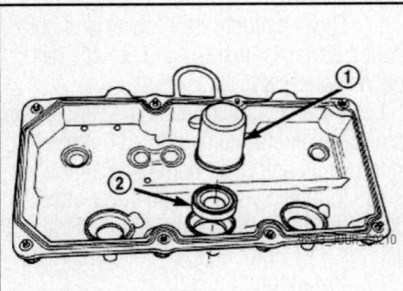

Fig. 174 Installing seal—3.5L engine

To install:

6. Clean cylinder head and all gasket sealing surfaces. Inspect and replace gasket and seals as necessary.

7. Using a suitable pry tool, carefully remove spark plug tube seals (2).

8. Position new seal with the part number on seal facing cylinder head cover.

9. Install seals using Camshaft Installer MD-998306 (1).

10. Install cylinder head cover and bolts (4). Tighten to 90 inch lbs. (10 Nm).

11. Install the PCV hose (3) (if required).

12. Position the wiring harness on the cylinder head cover.

13. Reinstall the wire harness retainers (2) around the perimeter of the valve cover.

14. Install the ignition coils.

15. Connect the ignition coil electrical connectors (1).

16. Connect negative battery cable.

Right

See Figures 174 and 175.

> ❊❊ **WARNING**
>
> **Do not start or run the engine with the cylinder head cover removed. Damage or personal injury may occur.**

1. Disconnect the negative battery cable.

2. Remove the upper intake manifold from the engine.

3. Cover lower intake manifold intake ports with a clean cover to prevent dirt or debris from entering the ports during service.

4. Disconnect the ignition coil harness connectors (2).

5. Remove ignition coils.

6. Disconnect the engine wiring harness retainers (1) from the valve cover.

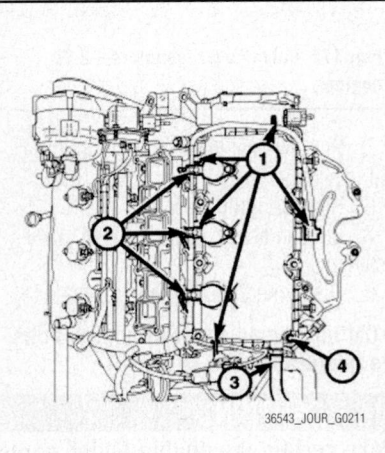

Fig. 175 Right valve cover—3.5L engine

7. Disconnect the makeup air hose (3).

8. Completely loosen the cylinder head cover retaining bolts (4) and remove the cylinder head cover.

To install:

9. Clean cylinder head and cover mating surfaces. Inspect and replace gasket and seals as necessary.

10. Using a suitable pry tool, carefully remove tube seals (2).

11. Position new seal with the part number on seal facing cylinder head cover.

12. Install seals using Camshaft Installer MD-998306 (1).

13. Install cylinder head cover bolts (4) and tighten to 90 inch lbs. (10 Nm).

14. Reconnect the wire harness retainers (1) to the valve cover.

15. Install the ignition coils.

16. Connect the ignition coil electrical connectors (2).

17. Reconnect the makeup air hose (3).

18. Install upper intake manifold.

19. Connect negative battery cable.

VALVE LASH

ADJUSTMENT

2.4L Engine

Measuring Valve Lash

See Figure 176.

➡ **The engine must be cold to measure valve lash.**

1. Remove engine cover.

2. Remove cylinder head cover.

3. Rotate camshaft so lobes are vertical (1).

4. Check clearance using feeler gauges.

5. Repeat for all tappets and record readings.

6. If clearance was too small, refer to Clearance too Small .

7. If clearance was too large, refer to Clearance too Large .

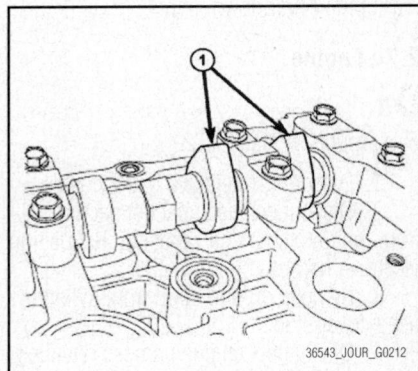

Fig. 176 Rotating camshaft—2.4L engine

Clearance Too Small

See Figure 177.

1. Remove camshafts.
2. Specification – clearance = change.
3. Decrease tappet thickness by change figure.
4. Install camshafts.
5. Verify that valve lash is correct.

Clearance Too Large

See Figure 177.

1. Remove camshafts.
2. Clearance – specification = change.
3. Increase tappet thickness by change figure.
4. Install camshafts.
5. Verify that valve lash is correct.

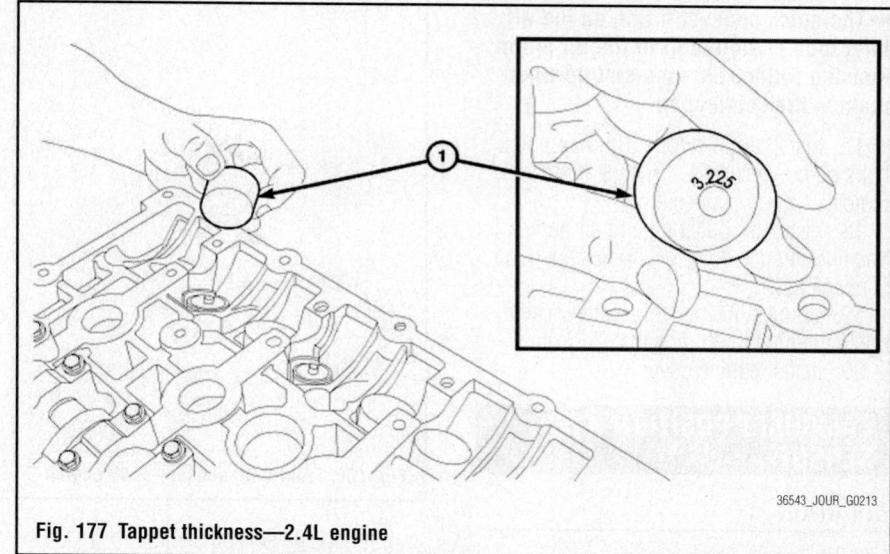

Fig. 177 Tappet thickness—2.4L engine

36543_JOUR_G0213

ENGINE PERFORMANCE & EMISSION CONTROLS

ACCELERATOR PEDAL POSITION (APP) SENSOR

LOCATION

The Accelerator Pedal Position (APP) sensor is built into accelerator pedal.

REMOVAL & INSTALLATION

See Figure 178.

1. Disconnect and isolate negative battery cable at battery.
2. Disconnect the electrical connector from accelerator pedal.
3. Remove mounting nuts and remove accelerator pedal from the mounting studs.

To install:

✳✳ CAUTION

The accelerator pedal and mounting nuts need to be torque in a mandatory torque sequence or

damage could result to the pedal assembly.

4. Install the accelerator pedal and mounting nuts to the mounting studs. Tighten the nuts in a mandatory torque sequence to 12 ft. lbs. (16 Nm).
5. Connect the electrical connector from accelerator pedal.
6. Connect the negative battery cable, tighten nut to 45 inch lbs. (5 Nm).
7. Use a scan tool and perform the APPS RELEARN function.

AIR INJECTION (AIR) PUMP

LOCATION

The Air Injection (AIR) Pump is located on the left side of the engine compartment.

REMOVAL & INSTALLATION

See Figure 179.

1. Disconnect and isolate negative battery.
2. Remove engine cover.
3. Remove air inlet tube (3) by pushing the ends (1) together while pulling the air inlet tube (3) away from air pump housing connection (2).
4. Remove air outlet tube by pushing the coupling ends together while pulling the air outlet tube away from the air pump.
5. Remove bolt (1) from heat shield (2) and air pump bracket (3).
6. Remove heat shield bolt (1) and heat shield (3) from air pump bracket (2).
7. Disconnect electrical harness

connector (1) from the air pump electrical connector (2).
8. Remove air pump and bracket assembly from vehicle.
9. Remove air pump mounting nuts (5) from bracket (4).
10. Remove air pump (3) from bracket (4).

To install:

11. Install air pump (3) to bracket (4).
12. Install air pump mounting nuts (5) to bracket (4). Tighten the nuts to 71 inch lbs. (8 Nm).
13. Position air pump and bracket assembly in vehicle.
14. Connect electrical harness connector (1) to the air pump electrical connector (2).
15. Install heat shield (3) and bolt (1) to air pump bracket (2). Tighten the bolt to 71 inch lbs. (8 Nm).
16. Install relay, heat shield (2) and bolt (1) to air pump bracket (3). Tighten the bolt to 71 inch lbs. (8 Nm).

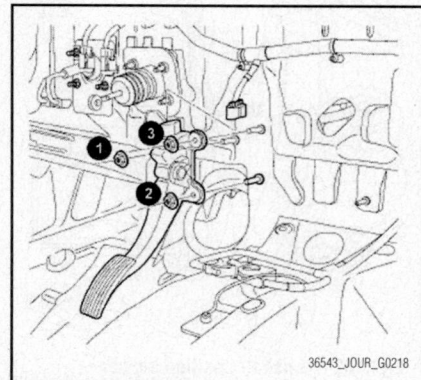

Fig. 178 Accelerator Pedal

36543_JOUR_G0218

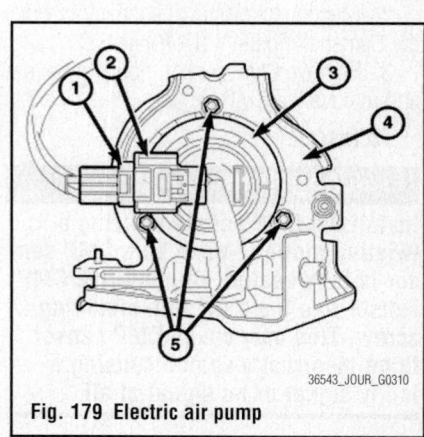

Fig. 179 Electric air pump

36543_JOUR_G0310

➡The quick connect fitting on the air inlet tube is slotted to fit the air pump housing fitting. Line the slot up when making the connection.

17. Install air inlet tube (3) to air pump housing connection (2). A click noise will indicate a good connection.

18. Install air outlet tube to air pump housing. A click noise will indicate a good connection.

19. Connect the negative battery cable, tighten the nut to 45 inch lbs. (5 Nm).

20. Install engine cover.

CAMSHAFT POSITION (CMP) SENSOR

LOCATION

2.4L Engine

Front

On the 2.4L engine, the front CMP sensor is located at the front of the cylinder head.

Rear

On the 2.4L engine, the rear CMP sensor is located at the rear of the cylinder head.

2.7L Engine

The camshaft position sensor is mounted in the front of the head.

3.5L Engine

The CMP sensor is mounted in the front of the head.

REMOVAL & INSTALLATION

2.4L Engine

Front

See Figure 180.

1. Disconnect and isolate the negative battery cable.

2. Disconnect electrical connector from the Camshaft Position (CMP) sensor.

3. Remove CMP sensor mounting screw and remove the CMP sensor.

To install:

✳✳ CAUTION

Install the CMP sensor utilizing a twisting motion. Make sure CMP sensor is fully seated. Do not drive CMP sensor into the bore with mounting screw. This may cause CMP sensor to be incorrectly seated causing a faulty signal or no signal at all.

Fig. 180 Front CMP sensor—2.4L engine

4. Lubricate sensor O-ring.

5. Install CMP sensor and mounting bolt, tighten to 80 inch lbs. (9 Nm).

6. Connect electrical connector to camshaft position sensor.

7. Connect the negative battery cable, tighten nut to 45 inch lbs. (5 Nm).

Rear

See Figure 181.

1. Disconnect and isolate the negative battery cable.

2. Disconnect electrical connector at sensor.

3. Remove nut retaining heat shield.

4. Pull heat shield out to uncover sensor.

5. Remove mounting bolt.

6. Remove sensor.

To install:

7. Lubricate sensor O-ring.

8. Install CMP sensor and mount-

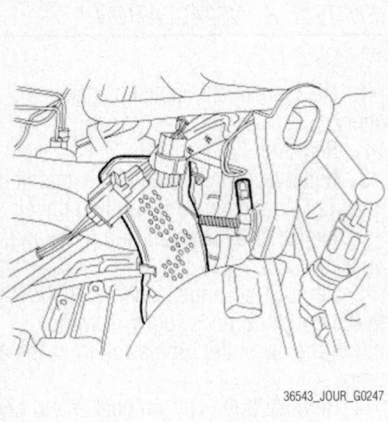

Fig. 181 Rear camshaft position sensor— 2.4L engine

ing bolt, tighten to 80 inch lbs. (9 Nm).

9. Connect electrical connector to camshaft position sensor.

10. Install heat shield onto mounting stud.

11. Install heat shield retaining nut and tighten.

12. Connect the electrical connector.

13. Connect the negative battery cable, tighten nut to 45 inch lbs. (5 Nm).

2.7L Engine

See Figure 182.

1. Disconnect electrical connector from the Camshaft Position (CMP) sensor.

2. Remove the CMP sensor screw.

3. Without pulling on the connector, pull the sensor out of the chain case cover.

To install:

✳✳ CAUTION

Install the CMP sensor utilizing twisting motion. Make sure CMP sensor is fully seated. Do not drive CMP sensor into the bore with mounting screw. This may cause CMP sensor to be incorrectly seated causing a faulty signal or no signal at all.

4. Install CMP sensor in the chain case cover and push sensor in until contact is made with the boss on the head. While holding the sensor in this position, install and tighten the retaining bolt to 106 inch lbs. (12 Nm).

5. Attach electrical connector to CMP sensor.

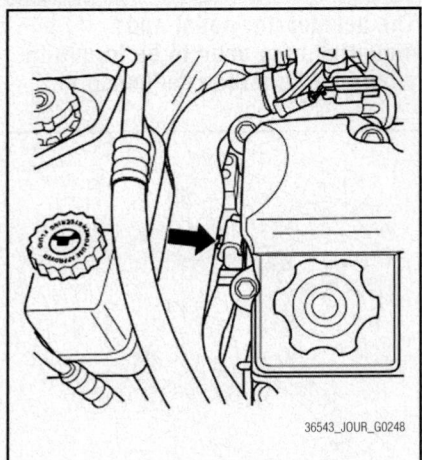

Fig. 182 Camshaft position sensor— 2.7L engine

3.5L Engine

See Figure 183.

1. Disconnect and isolate the negative battery cable at battery.
2. Disconnect electrical connector (3) from Camshaft Position (CMP) sensor (2).
3. Remove bolt (1) and CMP sensor (2).

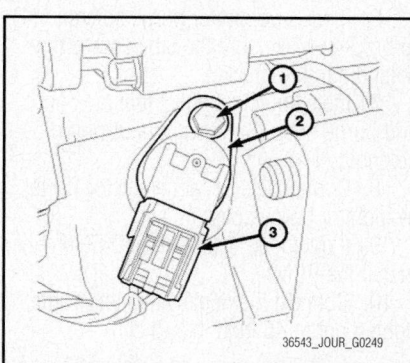

Fig. 183 Camshaft position sensor—3.5L engine

To install:

✷✷ CAUTION

Install camshaft position (CMP) sensor utilizing twisting motion. Make sure CMP sensor is fully seated. Do not drive CMP sensor into the bore with mounting screw. This may cause CMP sensor to be incorrectly seated causing a faulty signal or no signal at all.

4. Install camshaft position (CMP) sensor (2) and mounting bolt (1).
5. Tighten bolt to 106 inch lbs. (12 Nm).
6. Connect electrical connector (3) to camshaft position CMP sensor (2).
7. Connect negative battery cable and tighten nut to 45 inch lbs. (5 Nm).

CRANKSHAFT POSITION (CKP) SENSOR

LOCATION

2.4L Engine

The Crankshaft Position (CKP) sensor is in the rear of the engine block near the transmission.

2.7L Engine

The Crankshaft Position (CKP) sensor is in the transmission housing.

3.5L Engine

The Crankshaft Position (CKP) sensor is

located on the driver side of the vehicle, above the differential housing. The bottom of the sensor sits above the drive plate.

REMOVAL & INSTALLATION

2.4L Engine

See Figure 184.

1. Remove the engine cover.
2. Disconnect and isolate the negative battery cable.
3. Remove the air cleaner body.
4. Disengage the upstream O2 sensor wire harness retainer and Crankshaft Position (CKP) sensor wire harness retainer from the heat shield.
5. Remove one nut (1) and two heat shield retaining bolts (2).
6. Remove heat shield (3).
7. Remove the Crankshaft Position (CKP) sensor mounting bolt.
8. Remove sensor with the wire harness attached.
9. Unlock and disconnect the electrical connector from the CKP sensor.

To install:

10. Check O-ring for damage and lubricate the O-ring with engine oil before installing sensor.
11. Using a twisting motion, install the CKP sensor.
12. Install the CKP sensor bolt. Tighten the bolt to 80 inch lbs. (9 Nm).
13. Connect and lock the electrical connector to the CKP sensor.
14. Install the heat shield with one nut and two heat shield retaining bolts.
15. Install the upstream O2 sensor wire harness retainer and Crankshaft Position (CKP) sensor wire harness retainer to the heat shield.
16. Install the air cleaner body.
17. Connect the negative battery cable.
18. Install the engine cover.

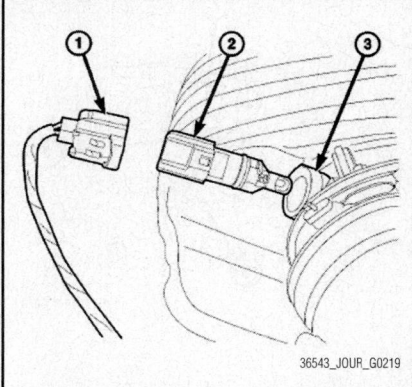

Fig. 184 CKP sensor—2.4L engine

2.7L Engine

See Figure 185.

➡**If the CKP sensor (3) is difficult to remove twist side to side during removal.**

1. Disconnect and isolate the negative battery cable.
2. Disconnect electrical connector (1) from Crankshaft Position (CKP) sensor (3).
3. Remove bolt (2) and remove CKP sensor (3) from transmission housing.

To install:

➡**If reinstalling the sensor, check O-ring on the sensor for damage, replace if necessary. Lubricate the O-ring with clean engine oil before installing sensor.**

4. Install Crankshaft Position (CKP) sensor (3) into the transmission housing.
5. Install bolt (2) to CKP sensor (3) and tighten the bolt to 80 inch lbs. (9 Nm).
6. Connect electrical connector (1) to CKP sensor (3).
7. Connect the negative battery cable, tighten nut to 45 inch lbs. (5 Nm).

3.5L Engine

1. Disconnect and isolate the negative battery cable.
2. Unlock and disconnect electrical connector from Crankshaft Position (CKP) sensor.
3. Remove sensor mounting screw. Remove sensor.

To install:

4. Install sensor and push sensor down until contact is made with the transmission case. While holding the sensor in this position, install and tighten the retaining bolt to 105 inch lbs. (12 Nm) torque.
5. Connect electrical connector and lock to Crankshaft Position (CKP) sensor.

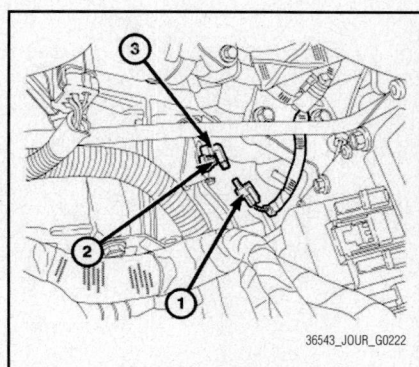

Fig. 185 Crankshaft Position (CKP) sensor—2.7L engine

6. Connect the negative battery cable, tighten nut to 45 inch lbs. (5 Nm).

EVAPORATIVE EMISSION (EVAP) CANISTER

LOCATION

The Evaporative Emission (EVAP) canister is location under the rear of the vehicle.

REMOVAL & INSTALLATION

See Figures 186 and 187.

1. Disconnect and isolate the negative battery cable.
2. Remove the spare tire, refer to the owner's manual.
3. Raise and support vehicle.
4. Remove the 4 nuts (1) and the spare tire well (2).
5. Remove 2 nuts from EVAP canister mounting brackets and reposition EVAP canister assembly.
6. Disconnect purge line (4) from EVAP canister (1).

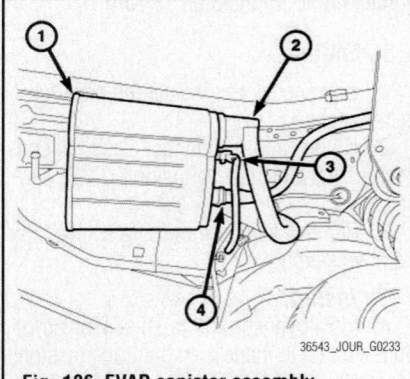

36543_JOUR_G0233

Fig. 186 EVAP canister assembly

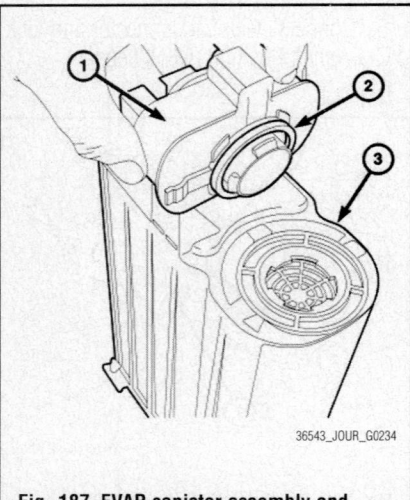

36543_JOUR_G0234

Fig. 187 EVAP canister assembly and ESIM switch

7. Remove fresh air hose (2) and electrical connector (3) from the ESIM.
8. Remove EVAP canister assembly from vehicle.
9. A lock tab (see arrow) is used on the back of the switch. Push lock tab towards switch while rotating switch counterclockwise ¼ turn for removal.

To install:

The picture displays a typical EVAP Canister and a typical ESIM switch. After installing any ESIM switch, the electrical connector on the switch must be in the 3 O'clock position. This step must be done for proper ESIM switch operation.

10. The fresh air hose that attaches to the ESIM must have a clear opening to the atmosphere. Check the fresh air hose, including the fresh air filter, for obstructions or restrictions at the ESIM. If a restriction is present, the system will not allow free flow passage of clean air, and an early shut off of the fuel fill nozzle may occur during fuel fill.
11. Be sure O-ring (2) and EVAP canister opening are clean.
12. Install ESIM (1) to the EVAP canister (3).
13. Install mounting brackets to EVAP canister assembly.

EVAPORATIVE EMISSION (EVAP) PURGE SOLENOID

REMOVAL & INSTALLATION

See Figure 188.

1. Disconnect and isolate negative battery cable at battery.
2. If equipped with 2.7L or 3.5L engine, remove the PCM.

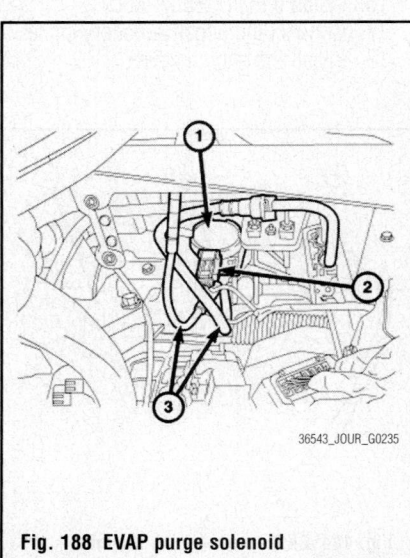

36543_JOUR_G0235

Fig. 188 EVAP purge solenoid

3. Disconnect electrical connector (2) from evaporator purge solenoid (1).
4. Remove purge hose and quick connect fuel tank hose (3) from evaporator purge solenoid (1).
5. Release tab to remove evaporator purge solenoid (1) from bracket.

To install:

6. Install evaporator purge solenoid (1) to bracket. Make sure the tab secures the solenoid to the bracket.
7. Install quick connect fuel tank hose and purge hose (3) to evaporator purge solenoid (1).
8. Connect electrical connector (2) to evaporator purge solenoid (1).
9. If equipped with 2.7L or 3.5L engine, install the PCM.
10. Connect the negative battery cable, tighten nut to 45 inch lbs. (5 Nm).

EVAPORATIVE EMISSION SYSTEM MONITOR SWITCH

LOCATION

The Evaporative Emission system monitor switch is located under the rear of the vehicle.

REMOVAL & INSTALLATION

See Figures 187 and 189.

1. Disconnect and isolate the negative battery cable.
2. Remove the spare tire, refer to the owner's manual.
3. Raise and support vehicle.
4. Remove the 4 nuts (1) and the spare tire well (2).
5. Remove fresh air hose (2) and electrical connector (3) from the ESIM.

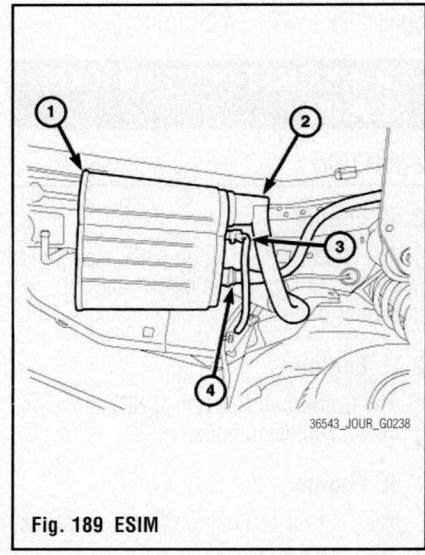

36543_JOUR_G0238

Fig. 189 ESIM

6. A lock tab (see arrow) is used on the back of the switch. Push lock tab towards switch while rotating switch counterclockwise ¼ turn for removal.

7. Remove ESIM (1) from the EVAP canister (3).

To install:

8. The fresh air hose that attaches to the ESIM must have a clear opening to the atmosphere. Check the fresh air hose, including the fresh air filter, for obstructions or restrictions at the ESIM. If a restriction is present, the system will not allow free flow passage of clean air, and an early shut off of the fuel fill nozzle may occur during fuel fill.

9. Be sure O-ring (2) and EVAP canister opening are clean.

10. Install ESIM (1) to the EVAP canister (3).

11. Install fresh air hose (2) and electrical connector (3) to the ESIM.

12. Install the spare tire well (2) with 4 nuts (1).

13. Lower vehicle.

14. Install the spare tire, refer to the owner's manual.

15. Connect the negative battery cable, tighten nut to 45 inch lbs. (5 Nm).

ENGINE COOLANT TEMPERATURE (ECT) SENSOR

LOCATION

2.4L Engine

There are two Engine Coolant Temperature (ECT) sensors. One of the sensors threads into the block. The other sensor is located at the top of the coolant adapter housing.

2.7L Engine

The Engine Coolant Temperature (ECT) sensor threads into the coolant outlet connector.

3.5L Engine

The Engine Coolant Temperature (ECT) sensor threads into the lower intake manifold.

REMOVAL & INSTALLATION

2.4L Engine

Cylinder Block Mounted

See Figure 190.

1. Disconnect negative battery cable.
2. Partially drain cooling system below level of ECT sensor.
3. Disconnect ECT sensor electrical connector.

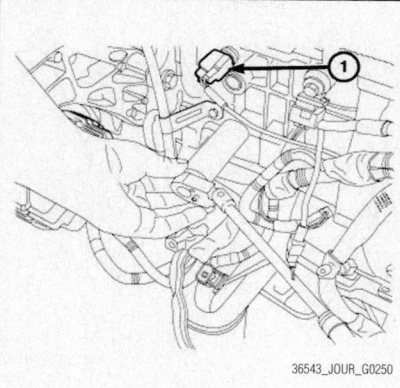

Fig. 190 Cylinder block mounted ECT sensor—2.4L engine

4. Remove ECT sensor.

To install:

5. Install ECT sensor (1). Make sure the sensor is locked in place
6. Reconnect ECT sensor electrical connector.
7. Fill cooling system.
8. Connect negative battery cable.

Coolant Adapter Mounted

See Figure 191.

1. Disconnect negative battery cable.
2. Partially drain cooling system below level of ECT sensor (1).
3. Disconnect ECT sensor electrical connector.
4. Remove ECT sensor (1).

To install:

5. Install ECT sensor. Tighten sensor to 14 ft. lbs. (19 Nm).
6. Reconnect ECT sensor electrical connector.

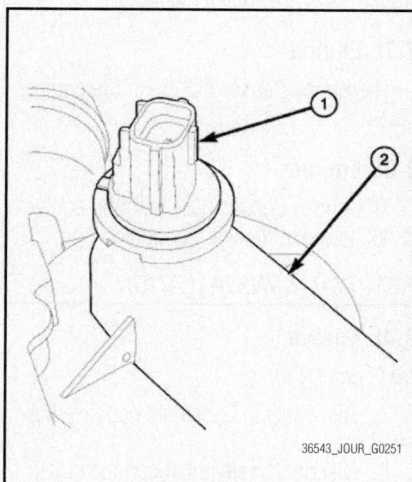

Fig. 191 Coolant adapter mounted ECT sensor—2.4L engine

7. Fill cooling system.
8. Connect negative battery cable.

2.7L Engine

See Figure 192.

1. Partially drain cooling system below level of ECT sensor.
2. Remove upper intake manifold.
3. Disconnect ECT sensor electrical connector.
4. Remove ECT sensor.

To install:

5. Install ECT sensor. Tighten sensor to 14 ft. lbs. (19 Nm).
6. Reconnect ECT sensor electrical sensor.
7. Fill cooling system.

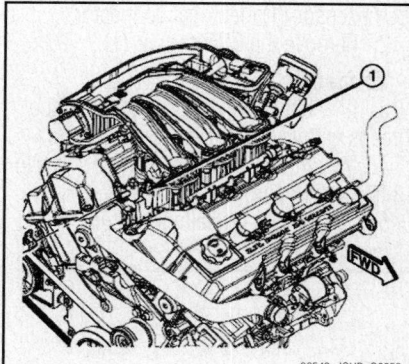

Fig. 192 Engine coolant temperature sensor—2.7L engine

3.5L Engine

See Figure 193.

1. Disconnect negative battery cable.
2. Partially drain cooling system.

Fig. 193 Engine coolant temperature sensor—3.5L engine

3. Disconnect coolant sensor electrical connector.

4. Remove coolant temperature sensor.

To install:

5. Install engine coolant temperature sensor. Tighten sensor to 20 ft. lbs. (28 Nm) torque.

6. Attach electrical connector to sensor.

7. Fill cooling system.

8. Connect negative battery cable.

ENGINE OIL TEMPERATURE (EOT) SENSOR

REMOVAL & INSTALLATION

See Figure 194.

1. Disconnect Engine Oil Temperature (EOT) sensor (1) electrical connector.

2. Remove the EOT sensor (1).

To install:

3. If re-using the EOT sensor, coat the threads with Mopar® thread sealant.

4. Install the EOT sensor (1). Tighten to 13 ft. lbs. (18 Nm).

5. Connect electrical connector.

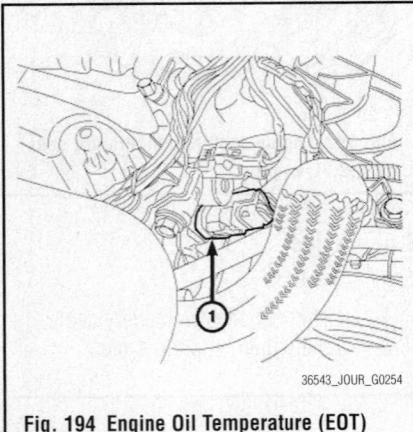

Fig. 194 Engine Oil Temperature (EOT) sensor

INLET AIR TEMPERATURE (IAT) SENSOR

LOCATION

The Inlet Air Temperature (IAT) sensor is located in air box.

REMOVAL & INSTALLATION

See Figure 195.

1. Disconnect and isolate the negative battery cable.

➡**Clean dirt from sensor area prior to removal from air box.**

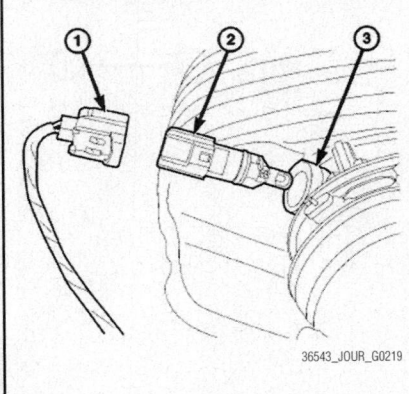

Fig. 195 Inlet Air Temperature (IAT) sensor

2. Disconnect the Inlet Air Temperature (IAT) sensor electrical connector (1).

3. Remove the Inlet Air Temperature (IAT) sensor (2) from the air box (3) by turning the sensor 1/4 turn in the counter-clockwise direction.

To install:

4. Install the Inlet Air Temperature (IAT) sensor (2) to the air box (3) by turning the sensor 1/4 turn in the clockwise direction.

5. Connect the Inlet Air Temperature (IAT) sensor electrical connector (1).

6. Connect the negative battery cable, tighten nut to 45 inch lbs. (5 Nm).

KNOCK SENSOR (KS)

LOCATION

2.4L Engine

The Knock Sensor (KS) bolts into the side of the cylinder block in front of the starter under the intake manifold.

2.7L Engine

The Knock Sensor (KS) is in the engine block.

3.5L Engine

The Knock Sensor (KS) is in the engine block between the cylinder banks.

REMOVAL & INSTALLATION

2.4L Engine

See Figure 196.

1. Disconnect and isolate negative battery cable.

2. Disconnect electrical connector (3) from the Knock Sensor (KS) (2).

3. Remove bolt (1) and KS (2) from engine block.

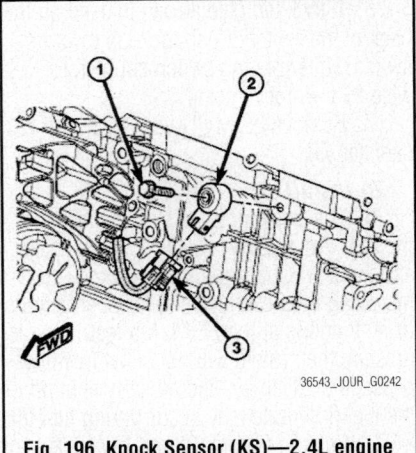

Fig. 196 Knock Sensor (KS)—2.4L engine

To install:

❋❋ CAUTION

Always torque knock sensors to the correct torque specification. Over or under-tightening effects knock sensor performance. Ensure the electrical connector orientation is at the sic O'clock position to the engine block.

4. Install the KS (2) and bolt (1) to engine block. Tighten bolt to 16 ft. lbs. (22 Nm).

5. Connect electrical connector (3) to the KS (2).

6. Connect negative battery cable, tighten nut to 40 inch lbs. (4.5 Nm).

2.7L Engine

See Figures 197 and 198.

❋❋ WARNING

Do not remove pressure cap with the system hot and under pressure because serious burns from coolant can occur.

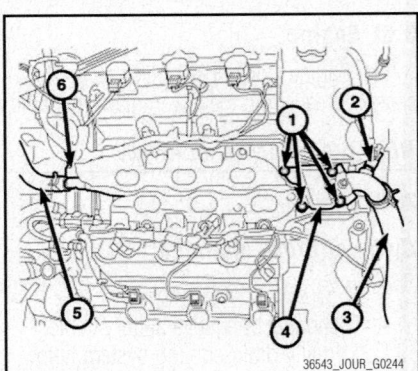

Fig. 197 Water housing outlet tube— 2.7L engine

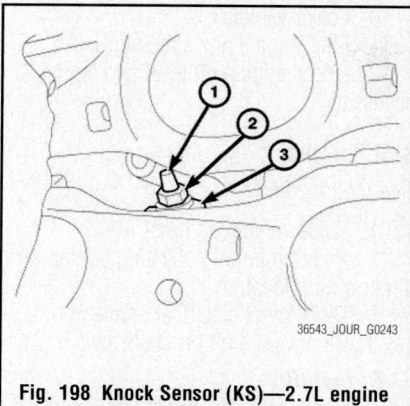

Fig. 198 Knock Sensor (KS)—2.7L engine

1. Drain cooling system.
2. Disconnect and isolate the negative battery cable.
3. Remove lower intake manifold.
4. Remove radiator upper hose (3) at water housing outlet tube (4).
5. Remove heater hose (5) from water housing outlet tube (4) at rear of engine.
6. Disconnect water housing outlet tube (4) from retaining clip (6) at rear of engine.
7. Disconnect electrical connector (2) from coolant temperature sensor.
8. Remove 4 bolts (1) attaching water housing outlet tube (4) to cylinder heads.
9. Disconnect electrical connector from the Knock Sensor (KS).
10. Reposition the water housing outlet tube and remove nut (2) from the KS mounting stud (1).
11. Remove the KS (3) from engine block.

To install:

⁕⁕ CAUTION

Over or under-tightening affects Knock Sensor (KS) performance resulting in possible improper spark control.

12. Install KS (3) and nut (2) onto stud (1).
13. Tighten the KS nut to 11 ft. lbs. (15 Nm).
14. Attach electrical connector to the KS.
15. Position the water housing outlet tube (4) to the cylinder heads and loosely install four bolts (1).
16. Attach water housing outlet tube (4) to the retaining clip (6) at rear of engine.
17. Tighten the four bolts (1) to 30 inch lbs. (3 Nm).
18. Connect electrical connector (2) to the coolant temperature sensor.
19. Install heater hose (5) to water housing outlet tube (4) at rear of engine.
20. Install radiator upper hose (3) to water housing outlet tube (4).

21. Install intake manifold.
22. Connect the negative battery cable, tighten nut to 45 inch lbs. (5 Nm).
23. Fill cooling system.
24. Operate engine until it reaches normal operating temperature. Check cooling system for correct fluid levels.

3.5L Engine

See Figure 199.

1. Disconnect the negative battery cable.
2. Remove the upper intake manifold.
3. Disconnect the electrical connector from the Knock Sensor (KS).
4. Remove the KS.

To install:

⁕⁕ CAUTION

Always use the specified torque when installing the knock sensor bolt. Over or under-tightening the sensor mounting bolt will affect knock sensor performance, possibly causing improper spark control.

5. Install the KS and tighten to 15 ft. lbs. (20 Nm).
6. Route the KS wire in the proper location.
7. Install upper intake manifold,
8. Connect the electrical connector.
9. Connect the negative battery cable.

Fig. 199 Knock Sensor (KS)—3.5L engine

MANIFOLD ABSOLUTE PRESSURE (MAP) SENSOR

LOCATION

The Manifold Absolute Pressure (MAP) sensor is located in the intake manifold.

REMOVAL & INSTALLATION

2.4L Engine

See Figure 200.

1. Disconnect and isolate the negative battery cable.
2. Disconnect electrical connector from Manifold Absolute Pressure (MAP) sensor.
3. Remove screw from MAP sensor.
4. Remove MAP sensor.

To install:

5. Install Manifold Absolute Pressure (MAP) sensor to intake manifold.
6. Tighten screw to 40 inch lbs. (4.5 Nm).
7. Connect electrical connector to sensor.
8. Connect the negative battery cable, tighten nut to 45 inch lbs. (5 Nm).

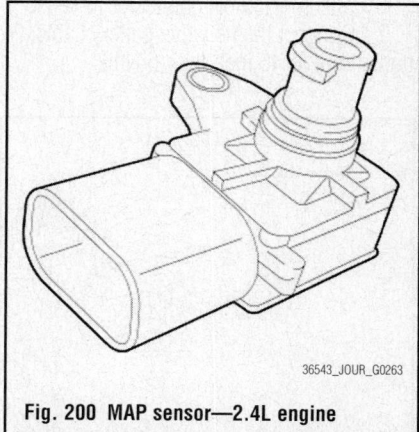

Fig. 200 MAP sensor—2.4L engine

2.7L Engine

See Figure 201.

1. Disconnect and isolate the negative battery cable.
2. Disconnect electrical connector from Manifold Absolute Pressure (MAP) sensor.

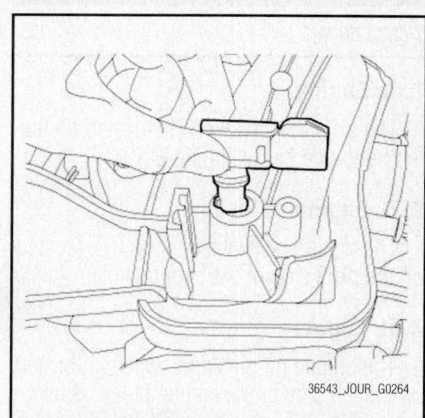

Fig. 201 MAP sensor—2.7L engine

3. Remove screw from MAP sensor.
4. Lift sensor to remove.

To install:

5. Install sensor to intake manifold plenum and turn clockwise to tighten.
6. Attach electrical connector to sensor.
7. Connect the negative battery cable, tighten nut to 45 inch lbs. (5 Nm).

3.5L Engine

See Figure 202.

1. Disconnect and isolate the negative battery cable.
2. Disconnect electrical connector from Manifold Absolute Pressure (MAP) sensor.
3. Remove screw from MAP sensor.
4. Lift sensor to remove.

To install:

5. Install sensor to intake manifold plenum and turn clockwise to tighten.
6. Attach electrical connector to sensor.
7. Connect the negative battery cable, tighten nut to 45 inch lbs. (5 Nm).

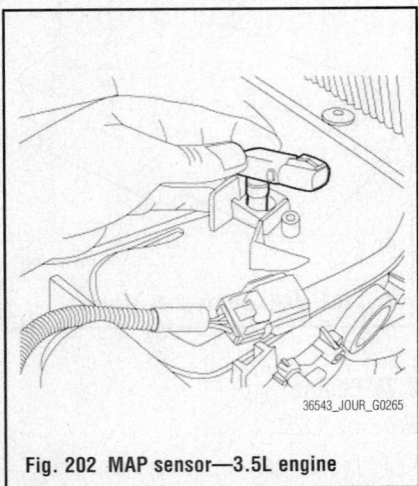

Fig. 202 MAP sensor—3.5L engine

OIL PRESSURE SENSOR

LOCATION

2.4L Engine

The oil pressure switch is located on the left front side of the engine block.

2.7L Engine

The engine oil pressure switch is located on the right side of the engine block.

3.5L Engine

The engine oil pressure switch is located on the left side of the engine block, above the oil filter.

REMOVAL & INSTALLATION

2.4L Engine

1. Raise and safely support the vehicle.
2. Disconnect electrical connector.
3. Remove oil pressure sensor using oil pressure socket C-4597 and discard sensor.

To install:

➡**If the oil pressure sensor is removed, it must be replaced with a new sensor.**

⁑ **CAUTION**

The oil pressure sensor has tapered threads, Over-tightening could crack the engine block.

4. Install oil pressure sensor using oil pressure socket C-4597 and tighten to 71 inch lbs. (8 Nm).
5. Connect electrical connector.

2.7L Engine

1. Raise vehicle on hoist.
2. Remove heat shield that covers oil pressure switch.
3. Disconnect oil pressure switch electrical connector.
4. Position an oil collecting container under switch location.
5. Remove switch by unscrewing from the engine block.

To install:

6. Apply Mopar® Thread Sealant to the switch threads.
7. Install oil pressure switch.
8. Connect electrical connector.
9. Install oil pressure switch heat shield.

10. Lower vehicle.
11. Start engine and check for leaks.
12. Check engine oil level and adjust as necessary.

3.5L Engine

See Figure 204.

1. Raise vehicle on hoist.
2. Position an oil collecting container under switch location.
3. Disconnect electrical connector (1).
4. Remove the oil pressure switch (2).

To install:

5. Apply Mopar® Thread Sealant to the switch threads.
6. Install oil pressure switch (2).
7. Connect electrical connector (1).
8. Lower vehicle.
9. Start engine and check for leaks.
10. Check engine oil level and adjust as necessary.

OXYGEN (O2) SENSOR

LOCATION

The Oxygen (O2) sensors are located in exhaust system.

REMOVAL & INSTALLATION

2.4L Engine

Upstream Oxygen Sensor (1/1)

See Figure 205.

⁑ **CAUTION**

The exhaust manifold, exhaust pipes and catalytic converter(s) become very hot during engine operation. Allow engine to cool before removing

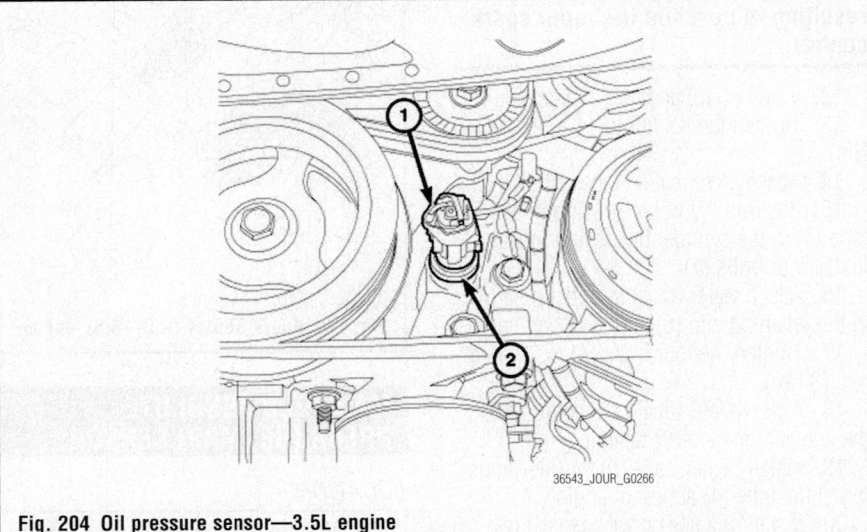

Fig. 204 Oil pressure sensor—3.5L engine

oxygen sensor. Failure to allow engine to cool before removal may result in personal injury caused by burns.

✳✳ CAUTION

When disconnecting sensor electrical connector, do not pull directly on wires going into oxygen sensor (O2S). Damage to the oxygen sensor may occur.

➡Use an O2S removal tool for this procedure.

1. Raise and support vehicle.
2. Disconnect O2S wire harness mounting clips from engine or body, if equipped.
3. Disconnect O2S pigtail harness from engine wiring harness (6).
4. Remove O2S (2) from exhaust pipe (1).

To install:

✳✳ CAUTION

When Equipped: The oxygen sensor (O2S) pigtail harness must be clipped and/or bolted back to their original positions on engine or body to prevent mechanical damage to wiring.

➡Use an O2S removal tool for this procedure.

Threads of new oxygen sensors are factory coated with anti-seize compound to aid in removal. DO NOT add any additional anti-seize compound to threads of a new O2S.

5. Install the O2S (2) to exhaust pipe (1). Tighten to 30 ft. lbs. (41 Nm).
6. Connect O2S pigtail harness to engine wiring harness (6).
7. Connect O2S wire harness mounting clips to engine or body, if equipped.

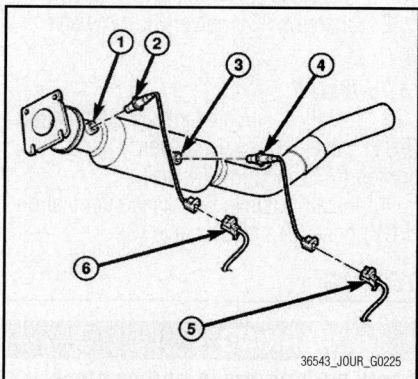

Fig. 205 Oxygen sensors—2.4L engine

Downstream Oxygen Sensor (1/2)

✳✳ CAUTION

The exhaust manifold, exhaust pipes and catalytic converter(s) become very hot during engine operation. Allow engine to cool before removing oxygen sensor. Failure to allow engine to cool before removal may result in personal injury caused by burns.

✳✳ CAUTION

When disconnecting sensor electrical connector, do not pull directly on wires going into oxygen sensor (O2S). Damage to the oxygen sensor may occur.

➡Use an O2S removal tool for this procedure.

1. Raise and support vehicle.
2. Disconnect O2S wire harness mounting clips from engine or body, if equipped.
3. Disconnect O2S pigtail harness from engine wiring harness (5).
4. Remove O2S (4) from catalytic converter (3).

To install:

➡Use an O2S removal tool for this procedure.

Threads of new oxygen sensors are factory coated with anti-seize compound to aid in removal. DO NOT add any additional anti-seize compound to threads of a new O2S.

5. Install the O2S (4) to catalytic converter (3). Tighten to 30 ft. lbs. (41 Nm).
6. Connect O2S pigtail harness to engine wiring harness (5).
7. Connect O2S wire harness mounting clips to engine or body, if equipped.

2.7L and 3.5L Engines

Downstream Oxygen Sensor (1/2) And Upstream Oxygen Sensor (1/1)
See Figure 206.

✳✳ CAUTION

The exhaust manifold, exhaust pipes and catalytic converter(s) become very hot during engine operation. Allow engine to cool before removing oxygen sensor. Failure to allow engine to cool before removal may result in personal injury caused by burns.

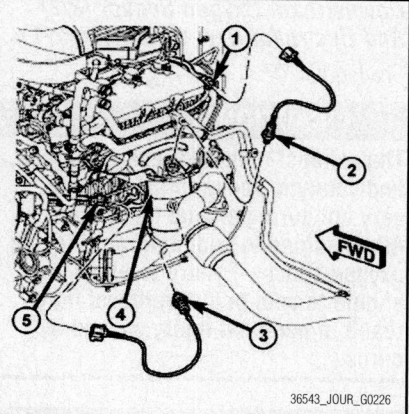

Fig. 206 Oxygen sensors 1/1 and 1/2—2.7L and 3.5L engines

✳✳ CAUTION

When disconnecting sensor electrical connector, do not pull directly on wires going into oxygen sensor (O2S). Damage to the oxygen sensor may occur.

➡Use an O2S removal tool for this procedure.

1. Raise and support vehicle.
2. Disconnect O2S wire harness mounting clips from engine or body, if equipped.
3. Disconnect O2S pigtail harness from engine wiring harness (1).
4. Remove O2S (2) from catalytic converter (4).
5. Disconnect O2S pigtail harness from engine wiring harness (5).
6. Remove O2S (3) from catalytic converter (4).

To install:

➡Use an O2S removal tool for this procedure. Threads of new oxygen sensors are factory coated with anti-seize compound to aid in removal. DO NOT add any additional anti-seize compound to threads of a new O2S.

7. Install O2S (3) to catalytic converter (4).
8. Connect O2S pigtail harness to engine wiring harness (2).
9. Install the O2S (2) to catalytic converter (4). Tighten to 30 ft. lbs. (41 Nm).
10. Connect O2S pigtail harness to engine wiring harness (1).
11. Connect O2S wire harness mounting clips to engine or body, if equipped.

Downstream Oxygen Sensor (2/2) And Upstream Oxygen Sensor (2/1)

See Figure 207.

> ### ❄ CAUTION
>
> **The exhaust manifold, exhaust pipes and catalytic converter(s) become very hot during engine operation. Allow engine to cool before removing oxygen sensor. Failure to allow engine to cool before removal may result in personal injury caused by burns.**

> ### ❄ CAUTION
>
> **When disconnecting sensor electrical connector, do not pull directly on wires going into oxygen sensor (O2S). Damage to the oxygen sensor may occur.**

➡ **Use an O2S removal tool for this procedure.**

1. Raise and support vehicle.
2. Disconnect O2S wire harness mounting clips from engine or body, if equipped.
3. Disconnect O2S pigtail harness from engine wiring harness (1).
4. Remove the O2S (5) from catalytic converter (4).
5. Disconnect O2S pigtail harness from engine wiring harness (2).
6. Remove O2S (3) from catalytic converter (4).

To install:

➡ **Use an O2S removal tool for this procedure. Threads of new oxygen sensors are factory coated with anti-seize compound to aid in removal. DO NOT add**

any additional anti-seize compound to threads of a new O2S.

7. Install O2S (3) to catalytic converter (4).
8. Connect O2S pigtail harness to engine wiring harness (5).
9. Install O2S (2) to catalytic converter (4). Tighten to 30 ft. lbs. (41 Nm).
10. Connect O2S pigtail harness to engine wiring harness (1).
11. Connect O2S wire harness mounting clips to engine or body, if equipped.

POSITIVE CRANKCASE VENTILATION (PCV) VALVE

LOCATION

2.4L Engine

The Positive Crankcase Ventilation (PCV) valve is located in the valve cover.

2.7L Engine

The Positive Crankcase Ventilation (PCV) valve is located under the intake manifold on the right rear bank of the engine.

3.5L Engine

The Positive Crankcase Ventilation (PCV) valve is located on the end of the rear valve cover.

REMOVAL & INSTALLATION

2.4L Engine

See Figure 208.

1. Remove the engine cover.
2. Remove the hose from the PCV valve.
3. Unscrew the PCV valve.

To install:

4. Lubricate the O-ring on the valve.
5. Install the PCV valve and tighten the valve to 72 inch lbs. (8 Nm).
6. Install the hose.
7. Install engine cover.

2.7L Engine

See Figure 209.

1. Remove the Positive Crankcase Ventilation (PCV) hose (3) from PCV valve (2).
2. Unscrew PCV valve (2) from valve cover (1).

To install:

3. Install the Positive Crankcase Ventilation (PCV) valve (2) to valve cover (1) and tighten to 35 inch lbs. (4 Nm).
4. Install Positive Crankcase Ventilation (PCV) hose (3) to PCV valve (2).

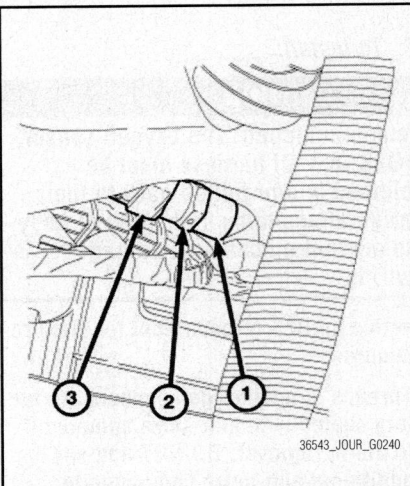

Fig. 209 Positive Crankcase Ventilation (PCV) valve—2.7L engine

3.5L Engine

See Figure 210.

1. Remove Positive Crankcase Ventilation (PCV) hose (2) from PCV valve (3).
2. Unscrew PCV valve (3) from valve cover (1).

To install:

3. Install Positive Crankcase Ventilation (PCV) valve (3) to valve cover (1) and tighten to 35 inch lbs. (4 Nm).
4. Install Positive Crankcase Ventilation (PCV) hose (2) to PCV valve (3).

TESTING

> ### ❄ WARNING
>
> **Apply parking brake and/or block wheels before performing any test**

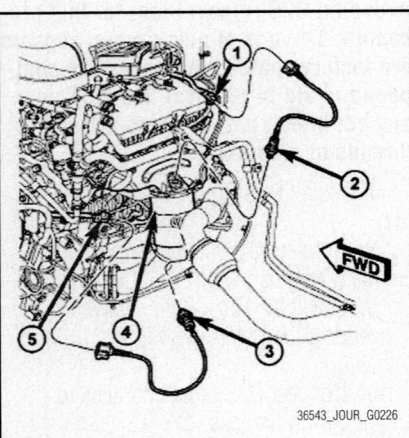

Fig. 207 Oxygen sensors 2/1 and 2/2— 2.7L and 3.5L engines

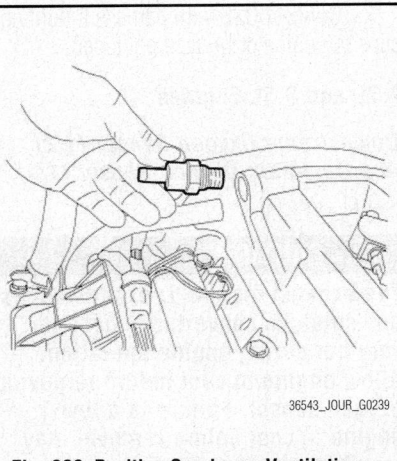

Fig. 208 Positive Crankcase Ventilation (PCV) valve—2.4L engine

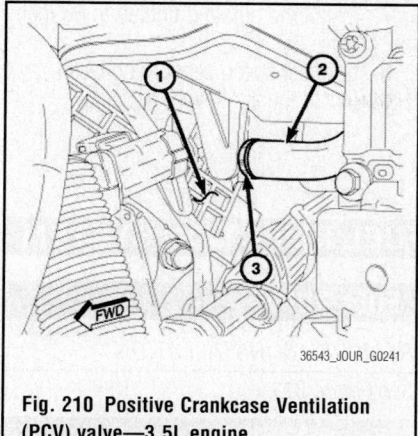

Fig. 210 Positive Crankcase Ventilation (PCV) valve—3.5L engine

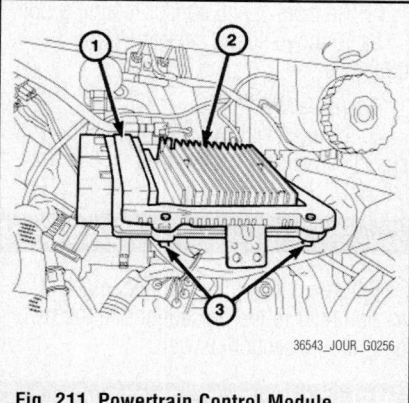

Fig. 211 Powertrain Control Module (PCM)—GPEC

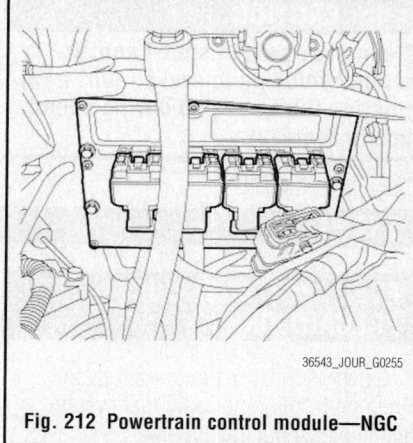

Fig. 212 Powertrain control module—NGC

or adjustment with the engine operating.

1. With engine idling, remove the hose from the PCV valve. If the valve is not plugged, a hissing noise will be heard as air passes through the valve. A strong vacuum should also be felt when a finger is placed over the valve inlet.

2. Install hose on PCV valve. Remove the make-up air hose from the air plenum at the rear of the engine. Hold a piece of stiff paper (parts tag) loosely over the end of the make-up air hose.

3. After allowing approximately one minute for crankcase pressure to reduce, the paper should draw up against the hose with noticeable force. If the engine does not draw the paper against the grommet after installing a new valve, replace the PCV valve hose.

4. Turn the engine off. Remove the PCV valve from intake manifold. The valve should rattle when shaken.

5. Replace the PCV valve and retest the system if it does not operate as described in the preceding tests. Do not attempt to clean the old PCV valve.

POWERTRAIN CONTROL MODULE (PCM)

LOCATION

The Powertrain Control Module (PCM) is located underhood, on the firewall.

REMOVAL & INSTALLATION

GPEC CONTROLLER—2.4L engine

See Figure 211.

➡Use the scan tool to reprogram the new Powertrain Control module (PCM) with the original Vehicle Identification Number (VIN) and the vehicles original

mileage. If this step is not done, a Diagnostic Trouble Code (DTC) may be set.

To avoid possible voltage spike damage to PCM, ignition key must be off, and the negative battery cable must be disconnected before unplugging the PCM connectors.

1. Disconnect and isolate the negative battery cable.

2. Unlock and disconnect the 2 electrical connectors (1) at the PCM (2).

3. Remove the 4 bolts (3) holding the PCM (2) to the bracket (1) and remove the PCM (2) from the vehicle.

To install:

➡Use the scan tool to reprogram the new Powertrain Control module (PCM) with the original Vehicle Identification Number (VIN) and the vehicles original mileage. If this step is not done, a Diagnostic Trouble Code (DTC) may be set.

4. Install PCM (2) to bracket (1) with 4 bolts (3).

5. Install and lock the 2 electrical connectors (1) to the PCM (2).

6. Connect the negative battery cable, tighten nut to 45 inch lbs. (5 Nm).

7. Use the scan tool to reprogram new PCM with vehicles original Identification Number (VIN) and original vehicle mileage.

NGC CONTROLLER

See Figure 212.

➡Use the scan tool to reprogram the new Powertrain Control module (PCM) with the original Vehicle Identification Number (VIN) and the vehicles original mileage. If this step is not done, a Diagnostic Trouble Code (DTC) may be set.

To avoid possible voltage spike damage to PCM, ignition key must be off, and the

negative battery cable must be disconnected before unplugging the PCM connectors.

1. Disconnect and isolate the negative battery cable.

2. Unlock and disconnect the 4 electrical connectors at the PCM.

3. Remove the 3 fasteners (1) holding the PCM to the bracket.

To install:

➡Use the scan tool to reprogram the new Powertrain Control module (PCM) with the original Vehicle Identification Number (VIN) and the vehicles original mileage. If this step is not done, a Diagnostic Trouble Code (DTC) may be set.

4. Install PCM to bracket with 3 fasteners (1).

5. Install and lock the 4 electrical connectors to the PCM.

6. Connect the negative battery cable, tighten nut to 45 inch lbs. (5 Nm).

7. Use the scan tool to reprogram new PCM with vehicles original Identification Number (VIN) and original vehicle mileage.

VEHICLE SPEED SENSOR (VSS)

LOCATION

The Vehicle Speed Sensor (VSS) is sensor mounted above the transaxle differential.

REMOVAL & INSTALLATION

➡This procedure is for manual transaxle applications only.

1. Open hood.
2. Remove the air cleaner housing.
3. Disconnect the speed sensor connector.

4. Remove speed sensor retaining bolt.
5. Remove speed sensor from transaxle.

To install:

6. Using a NEW O-ring, install the speed sensor to the transaxle.

7. Install the bolt and tighten to 60 inch lbs. (7 Nm).
8. Connect speed sensor connector.
9. Install the air cleaner housing.

FUEL   GASOLINE FUEL INJECTION SYSTEM

FUEL SYSTEM SERVICE PRECAUTIONS

Safety is the most important factor when performing not only fuel system maintenance but any type of maintenance. Failure to conduct maintenance and repairs in a safe manner may result in serious personal injury or death. Maintenance and testing of the vehicle's fuel system components can be accomplished safely and effectively by adhering to the following rules and guidelines.

• To avoid the possibility of fire and personal injury, always disconnect the negative battery cable unless the repair or test procedure requires that battery voltage be applied.

• Always relieve the fuel system pressure prior to disconnecting any fuel system component (injector, fuel rail, pressure regulator, etc.), fitting or fuel line connection. Exercise extreme caution whenever relieving fuel system pressure to avoid exposing skin, face and eyes to fuel spray. Please be advised that fuel under pressure may penetrate the skin or any part of the body that it contacts.

• Always place a shop towel or cloth around the fitting or connection prior to loosening to absorb any excess fuel due to spillage. Ensure that all fuel spillage (should it occur) is quickly removed from engine surfaces. Ensure that all fuel soaked cloths or towels are deposited into a suitable waste container.

• Always keep a dry chemical (Class B) fire extinguisher near the work area.

• Do not allow fuel spray or fuel vapors to come into contact with a spark or open flame.

• Always use a back-up wrench when loosening and tightening fuel line connection fittings. This will prevent unnecessary stress and torsion to fuel line piping.

• Always replace worn fuel fitting O-rings with new Do not substitute fuel hose or equivalent where fuel pipe is installed.

Before servicing the vehicle, make sure to also refer to the precautions in the beginning of this section as well.

RELIEVING FUEL SYSTEM PRESSURE

1. Remove fuel fill cap.
2. Remove fuel pump fuse from Totally Integrated Power Module (TIPM). For location of fuse, refer to label on underside of TIPM cover.
3. Start and run engine until it stalls.
4. Attempt restarting engine until it will no longer run.
5. Turn ignition key to OFF position.
6. Place a rag or towel below fuel line quick-connect fitting at fuel rail.
7. Disconnect quick-connect fitting at fuel rail.
8. When the repair is complete, reconnect fuel fittings and return fuel pump fuse to TIPM.
9. One or more Diagnostic Trouble Codes (DTC's) may have been stored in PCM memory due to fuel pump fuse removal. A diagnostic scan tool must be used to erase a DTC.

DRAINING FUEL TANK

1. Disconnect and isolate the negative battery cable.
2. Remove fuel fill cap.
3. Raise and support vehicle.
4. Remove fuel fill hose clamp at rear of tank.
5. Remove fuel fill hose from fuel tank fitting.
6. Position a drain hose into the fuel fill hose opening.
7. Drain fuel tank using an approved gasoline draining station.

FUEL FILTER

REMOVAL & INSTALLATION

The fuel filter and fuel pressure regulator are combined within the fuel pump module assembly. They are not serviceable.

FUEL PUMP

REMOVAL & INSTALLATION

See Figure 213.

⁜ WARNING

The fuel system is under a constant pressure (even with the engine off). Before servicing the fuel pump module, the fuel system pressure must be released.

1. Drain and remove fuel tank.
2. Note rotational position of module before attempting removal.
3. Install 1/2 inch drive breaker bar to special Lockring Remover/Installer tool 9340 and position special Lockring Remover/Installer tool 9340 into notches on outside edge of lockring.
4. Rotate breaker bar counter-clockwise to remove lockring. The module will spring up slightly when lockring is removed.
5. If equipped with AWD, disconnect fuel line between fuel pump module (1) and fuel level unit (2).

⁜ WARNING

The fuel reservoir of the fuel pump module does not empty out when the tank is drained. The fuel in the reservoir will spill out when the module is removed.

6. Remove module from fuel tank. Be careful not to bend float arm while removing.

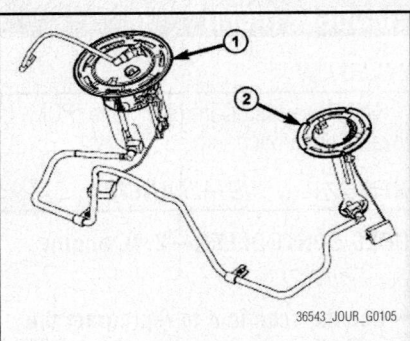

Fig. 213 Fuel pump module and fuel level unit—AWD shown

7. Remove fuel pump module O-ring seal from fuel tank.

To install:

✳✳ CAUTION

Whenever the fuel pump module is serviced, the rubber seal (gasket) must be replaced.

8. Wipe seal area of tank clean and install a new seal (gasket) to fuel tank.

9. If equipped with AWD, connect fuel line between fuel pump module (1) and fuel level unit (2).

10. Install fuel pump module to fuel tank.

11. Position fuel pump module in fuel tank and install fuel pump module lock-ring using Lockring Remover/Installer 9340. Tighten (clockwise) until the lockring and fuel pump module are fully seated.

12. Install fuel tank.

FUEL RAIL & INJECTORS

REMOVAL & INSTALLATION

2.4L Engine

See Figure 214.

✳✳ WARNING

Release fuel system pressure before servicing fuel system components. Service vehicles in well ventilated areas and avoid ignition sources. Never smoke while servicing the vehicle. This may result in personal injury or death.

1. Release the fuel pressure.
2. Disconnect and isolate the negative battery cable.
3. Remove engine cover.
4. Unlock and disconnect the electrical connectors from the fuel injectors.

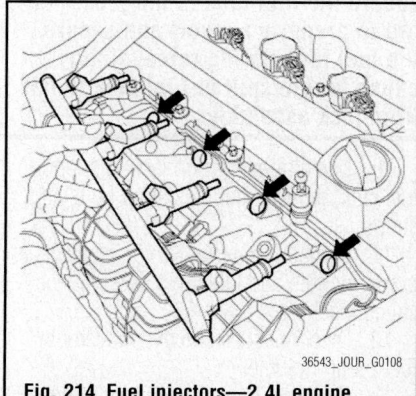

Fig. 214 Fuel injectors—2.4L engine

5. Disconnect the fuel line from the fuel rail.
6. Remove wire harness from fuel rail mounting studs.
7. Remove the 2 bolts from the fuel rail at the lower manifold.
8. Remove the fuel rail and injectors from the intake manifold.
9. Remove fuel injector clip holding fuel injector to fuel rail.
10. Remove fuel injector from fuel rail.

To install:

11. Apply a light coating of clean engine oil to the O-ring on the nozzle end of each injector.
12. Install injector into cup of fuel rail.
13. Install retaining clip and check to ensure injector is properly captured in the fuel rail assembly.
14. Insert fuel injector nozzles into openings in intake manifold. Seat the injectors in place.
15. Install the 2 bolts to the fuel rail. Tighten fuel rail bolts to 20 ft. lbs. (27 Nm).
16. Install wiring harness clips to the fuel rail mounting studs.
17. Connect and lock the electrical connectors to the fuel injectors.
18. Connect the fuel line to the fuel rail.
19. Connect the negative battery cable, tighten nut to 45 inch lbs. (5 Nm).
20. Use the scan tool ASD Fuel System Test to pressurize the fuel system. Check for leaks.
21. Install engine cover.

2.7L Engine

See Figure 215.

✳✳ WARNING

Release fuel system pressure before servicing fuel rail. Service vehicles in well ventilated areas and avoid ignition sources. Never smoke while servicing the vehicle.

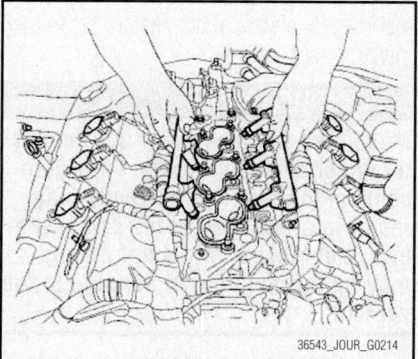

Fig. 215 Fuel injectors—2.7L engine

1. Release fuel system pressure.
2. Disconnect and isolate the negative battery cable.
3. Remove upper intake manifold.
4. Cover intake manifold to prevent foreign material from entering engine.
5. Disconnect fuel supply tube quick connect fitting at the rear of the fuel rail.
6. If the injector connectors are not tagged with their cylinder number, tag them to identify the correct cylinder .
7. Remove electrical connectors from the fuel injectors.
8. Remove mounting bolts on both sides of fuel rail.
9. Lift fuel rail straight up off of cylinder head.
10. Remove retaining clips from fuel injectors at fuel rail.
11. Remove fuel injector from fuel rail.

To install:

12. Lightly lubricate the fuel injector O-rings with a couple drops of clean engine oil.
13. Install retaining clips on fuel injectors.
14. Push injectors into fuel injector rail until clips are in the correct position.
15. Position fuel rail over cylinder heads, and push rail into place. Tighten fuel rail mounting bolts to 105 inch lbs. (12 Nm).
16. Connect the fuel supply tube quick connect fitting to the fuel rail.
17. Connect the electrical connectors to the fuel injectors.
18. Install intake manifold.
19. Connect the negative battery cable, tighten the nut to 45 inch lbs. (5 Nm).
20. Use the scan tool ASD Fuel System Test to pressurize the fuel system. Check for leaks.

3.5L Engine

See Figures 216 through 218.

✳✳ WARNING

The fuel system is under a constant pressure (even with the engine off). Before servicing any part on the fuel system, the fuel system pressure must be released.

1. Release fuel pressure.
2. Disconnect and isolate the negative battery cable.
3. Remove the upper intake manifold.
4. Disconnect the quick connect fuel line from the fuel rail.

➥**Mark fuel injector electrical harness connectors with correct corresponding cylinder numbers.**

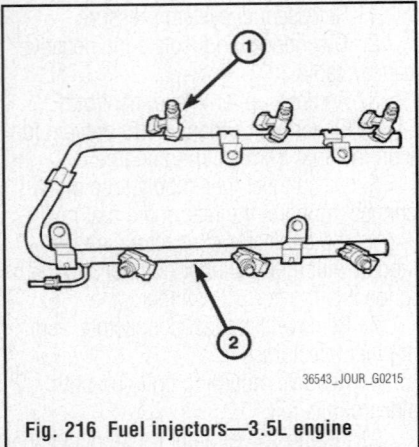

Fig. 216 Fuel injectors—3.5L engine

5. Disconnect all fuel injector electrical connectors (1) from fuel injectors (2).

6. Remove fuel rail mounting bolts from fuel rail and lower intake manifold.

➡ **Gently rock the fuel rail and injectors back and forth to loosen the seals on the fuel injectors from the cylinder heads.**

✳✳ CAUTION

Do Not use excessive force or prying tools to remove fuel rail and injectors. Damage to the fuel rail and injectors may result.

7. Lift fuel rail straight up off of the cylinder heads.

8. Drain any excess fuel from the fuel rail into an approved fuel storage container.

➡ **Mark or tag each fuel injector with correct corresponding cylinder numbers**

9. Remove retaining clips (5) from fuel injectors (2) at fuel rail (4).

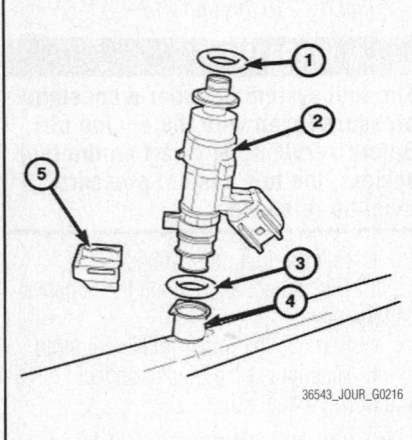

Fig. 217 Fuel injector components— 3.5L engine

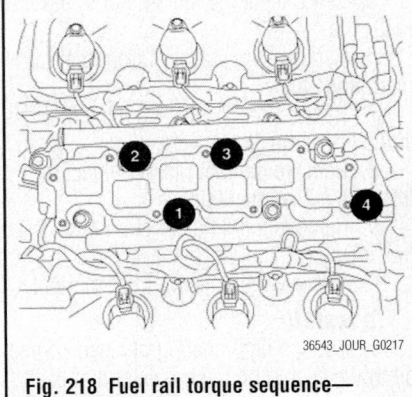

Fig. 218 Fuel rail torque sequence— 3.5L engine

To install:

➡ **Inspect each O-ring seal on all the fuel injectors, replace O-ring seals if any damaged is noted. Note the fuel injector O-rings are color coded. The Blue colored O-ring is for the fuel rail side and the Green colored O-ring is cylinder head side.**

10. Install and lubricate each fuel injector O-rings (1), (3) with a light drop of clean engine oil.

11. Install all of the fuel injectors (2) to the fuel rail (4), then install the retaining clips (5) to the fuel rail (4).

12. Inspect each fuel injector for proper installation. Note how the retaining clip (3) secures the fuel injector (1) to the fuel rail (2).

✳✳ CAUTION

The fuel rail bolts are actually lower intake manifold bolts. These bolts must be torqued in a mandatory torque sequence.

13. Insert fuel injector nozzles into openings in the cylinder heads. Seat the injectors in place. Install the fuel rail bolts and tighten bolts in a mandatory torque sequence to 21 ft. lbs. (28 Nm).

14. Correctly position and connect all fuel injector electrical connectors (1) to fuel injectors (2).

✳✳ CAUTION

Make sure the fuel line quick connector is connected properly. Failure to connect the fuel line correctly may result in a fuel leak at the rail assembly. Fuel leaked onto a hot engine may ignite resulting in damage to the vehicle.

15. Connect quick connect fuel line to fuel rail.

16. Install upper intake manifold.

17. Connect the negative battery cable, tighten the nut to 45 inch lbs. (5 Nm).

18. Use the scan tool ASD Fuel System Test to pressurize the fuel system. Check for leaks.

FUEL TANK

REMOVAL & INSTALLATION

All Wheel Drive (AWD) Models
See Figure 219.

✳✳ WARNING

The fuel system is under constant pressure even with engine off. Until the fuel pressure has been properly relieved from the system, do not attempt to open the fuel system.

1. Release the fuel system pressure.
2. Drain fuel tank.
3. Remove exhaust system muffler.
4. Remove rear propshaft.
5. Remove one bolt, two nuts and splash shield.
6. Disconnect the fuel pump module quick connect fitting from the body mounted fuel line bundle.
7. Disconnect the purge line quick connect fitting from the body mounted fuel line bundle .
8. Disconnect the purge line quick connect fitting from the fuel tank connection.

➡ **The fuel fill tube vent line quick connect fitting is located at the rear of the fuel tank near the parking brake cable.**

9. Disconnect the fuel fill tube vent line and remove from the fuel tank quick connect fitting.

✳✳ WARNING

Support fuel tank with a transmission jack or equivalent. Use straps to secure the fuel tank to the jack. Failure to properly support and secure the fuel tank during removal may cause fuel to spill or fuel tank to fall from jack assembly.

10. Use a transmission jack to support fuel tank, remove fuel tank strap bolts and straps.

11. Partially lower tank to gain access to pump module and fuel level sensor electrical connectors.

12. Disconnect electrical connector at fuel pump module.

13. Continue lowering tank for removal.

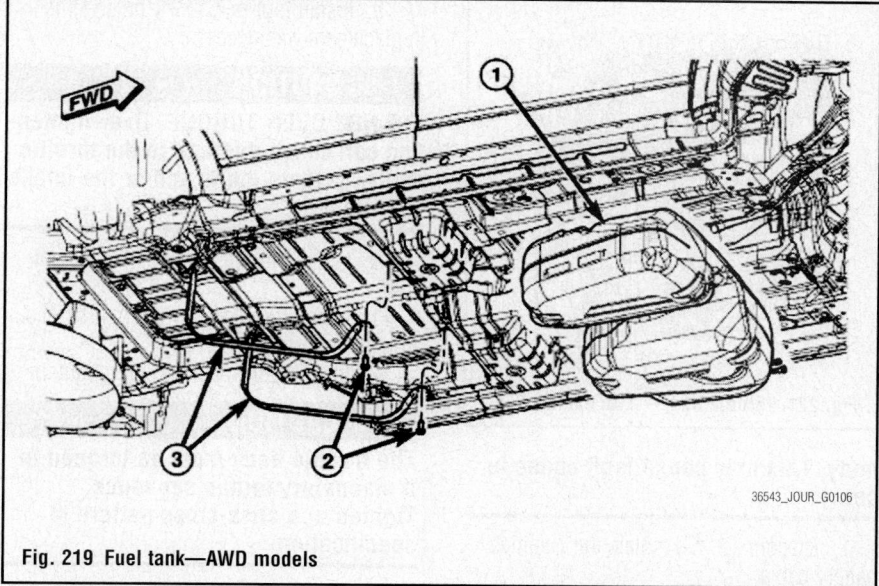

Fig. 219 Fuel tank—AWD models

36543_JOUR_G0106

14. If fuel tank is to be replaced, remove fuel pump module from tank.

15. If fuel tank is to be replaced, remove three fasteners and fuel tank shield (1) from fuel tank (2).

To install:

16. Install fuel tank shield (1) to fuel tank (2).

17. Install fuel pump module to fuel tank.

✷✷ WARNING

Support fuel tank with a transmission jack or equivalent. Use straps to secure the fuel tank to the jack. Failure to properly support and secure the fuel tank during removal may cause fuel to spill or fuel tank to fall from jack assembly.

18. Position fuel tank onto a transmission jack or equivalent and raise the fuel tank into vehicle position.

19. Connect electrical connector to fuel pump module and fuel level sensor.

20. Install fuel tank straps and bolts. Tighten to 35 ft. lbs. (48 Nm).

21. Install fuel tube vent line to fuel tank quick connect fitting.

22. Install purge line quick connect fitting to fuel tank connection.

23. Install fuel filler tube to fuel tank. Tighten hose clamp to 27 inch lbs. (3 Nm).

24. Connect the purge line quick connect fitting to the body mounted fuel line bundle.

25. Connect fuel pump module quick connect fitting to the body mounted fuel line bundle.

26. Install splash shield with one bolt and two nuts.

27. Install rear propshaft.

28. Install exhaust muffler.

29. Connect the negative battery cable, tighten nut to 45 inch lbs. (5 Nm).

30. Fill fuel tank. Use the scan tool to pressurize the fuel system. Check for leaks.

Front Wheel Drive (FWD) Models

See Figure 220.

✷✷ WARNING

The fuel system is under constant pressure even with engine off. Until the fuel pressure has been properly relieved from the system, do not attempt to open the fuel system.

1. Release the fuel system pressure.
2. Drain the fuel tank.
3. Remove exhaust muffler.

4. Remove one bolt, two nuts and splash shield.

5. Disconnect the fuel pump module quick connect fitting from the body mounted fuel line bundle.

6. Disconnect the purge line quick connect fitting from the body mounted fuel line bundle.

7. Disconnect the fuel purge line quick connect fitting from the fuel tank connection.

➡ **The fuel fill tube vent line quick connect fitting is located at the rear of the fuel tank near the parking brake cable (2).**

8. Disconnect the fuel fill tube vent line and remove from the fuel tank quick connect fitting.

✷✷ WARNING

Support fuel tank with a transmission jack or equivalent. Use straps to secure the fuel tank to the jack. Failure to properly support and secure the fuel tank during removal may cause fuel to spill or fuel tank to fall from jack assembly.

9. Use a transmission jack to support fuel tank, remove fuel tank strap bolts and straps.

10. Partially lower tank to gain access to pump module electrical connector.

11. Disconnect electrical connector at fuel pump module.

12. Continue lowering tank for removal.

13. If fuel tank is to be replaced, remove fuel pump module from tank.

14. If fuel tank is to be replaced, remove four fasteners and fuel tank shield (1) from fuel tank (2).

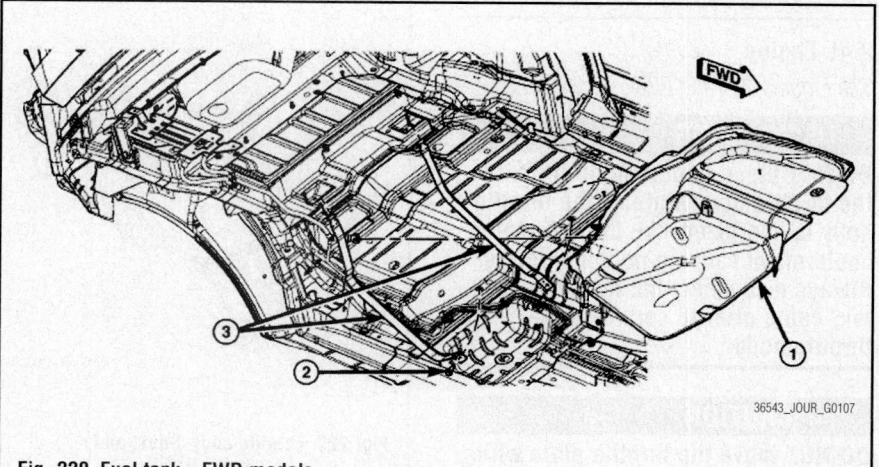

36543_JOUR_G0107

Fig. 220 Fuel tank—FWD models

To install:

15. Install fuel tank shield (1) to fuel tank (2).

16. Install fuel pump module to fuel tank and connect fuel line.

17. Position fuel tank onto a transmission jack or equivalent and raise the fuel tank into vehicle position.

18. Connect electrical connector to fuel pump module.

19. Install fuel tank straps and bolts. Tighten to 35 ft. lbs. (48 Nm).

20. Install fuel fill tube vent line to fuel tank quick connect fitting (3).

21. Install purge line quick connect fitting to fuel tank connection.

22. Install fuel filler tube to fuel tank. Tighten hose clamp to 27 inch lbs. (3 Nm).

23. Connect the purge line quick connect fitting to the body mounted fuel line bundle.

24. Connect the fuel pump module quick connect fitting to the body mounted fuel line bundle.

25. Install splash shield with one bolt and two nuts.

26. Install exhaust muffler.

27. Connect the negative battery cable, tighten nut to 45 inch lbs. (5 Nm).

28. Fill fuel tank. Use the scan tool to pressurize the fuel system. Check for leaks.

THROTTLE BODY

REMOVAL & INSTALLATION

2.4L Engine

See Figures 221 and 222.

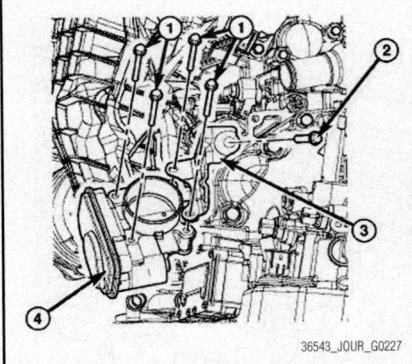

Fig. 221 Throttle body—2.4L engine

body. This may cause fault codes to set.

1. Disconnect and isolate the negative battery cable.

2. Remove throttle body air intake hose.

3. Disconnect throttle body electrical connector from throttle body.

4. Remove throttle body support bracket bolt.

5. Remove four bolts (1), throttle body bracket (3) and throttle body (4) from the intake manifold.

➡Inspect intake manifold to throttle body gasket (2) for damage. Inspect the j-nuts for damage or excessive wear. Replace as necessary.

6. Inspect the four j-nuts (1) for damage or excessive wear, remove if necessary.

7. Inspect intake manifold to throttle body gasket for damage, remove if necessary.

To install:

8. Install a new intake manifold to throttle body gasket (2), if replacement was necessary.

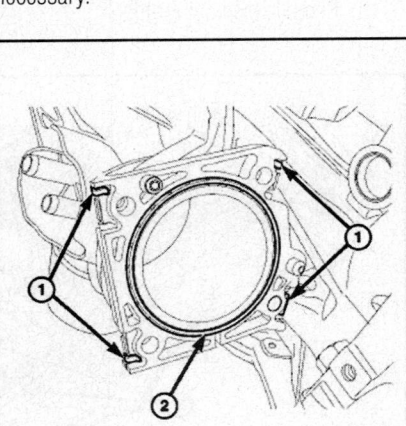

Fig. 222 Throttle body J-nuts and gasket—2.4L engine

9. Install four new four j-nuts (1), if replacement was necessary.

10. Install throttle body to intake manifold.

11. Install throttle body support bracket, bolt and hand tighten.

12. Install four bolts and hand tighten.

13. Tighten the bolts in a mandatory torque criss-cross pattern sequence to 65 inch lbs. (7.5 Nm).

14. Tighten the bracket bolt to 18 ft. lbs. (25 Nm).

15. Connect electrical connector to throttle body.

16. Install clean air hose and tighten clamps to 35 inch lbs. (4 Nm).

17. Connect the negative battery cable, tighten nut to 45 inch lbs. (5 Nm).

18. Use a scan tool and clear all fault codes then perform the ETC RELEARN function.

2.7L Engine

See Figure 223.

1. Disconnect and isolate negative battery cable at battery.

2. Loosen clamp and remove throttle body air intake hose from throttle body.

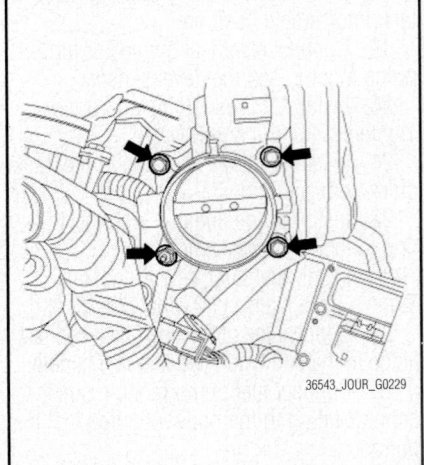

Fig. 223 Throttle body—2.7L engine

3. Disconnect electrical connector from throttle body.

4. Remove lower throttle body bracket nut.

5. Remove upper throttle body bracket nut.

6. Remove the throttle body support bracket from throttle body.

7. Remove three throttle body bolts and one stud.

8. Remove throttle body from intake manifold.

To install:

➡**Make sure the intake gasket is clean and free of debris. Inspect the intake gasket for damage. Replace as necessary.**

✳ CAUTION

DO NOT OVER TORQUE. Over-tightening can cause damage to the throttle body, gaskets, bolts and/or the intake manifold.

9. Install throttle body, gasket and bolts to intake manifold.

✳ CAUTION

The throttle body must be torqued in a mandatory torque sequence. Tighten in a criss-cross pattern to specification.

10. Tighten the three bolts and one stud in a mandatory torque criss-cross pattern sequence to 50 inch lbs. (5.5 Nm).

11. Install throttle body support bracket to the throttle body stud and the stud located on the transmission.

12. Install lower throttle body bracket nut. Tighten to 21 ft. lbs. (28 Nm).

13. Install upper throttle body bracket nut. Tighten to 106 inch lbs. (12 Nm).

14. Connect electrical connector to throttle body.

15. Install throttle body air intake hose and tighten clamp.

16. Connect the negative battery cable, tighten nut to 45 inch lbs. (5 Nm).

17. Use a scan tool and perform the ETC RELEARN function.

3.5L Engine

See Figure 224.

1. Disconnect and isolate negative battery cable at battery.

2. Remove engine cover.

3. Remove clean air hose from throttle body.

4. Disconnect electrical connector (1) from throttle body.

5. Remove nut form throttle body bracket.

6. Remove bolt and throttle body bracket.

7. Remove bolts, stud and remove throttle body from intake manifold.

To install:

➡**Make sure the intake gasket is clean and free of debris. Inspect the intake gasket for damage. Replace as necessary.**

✳ CAUTION

DO NOT OVER TORQUE. Over-tightening can cause damage to the throttle body, gaskets, bolts and/or the intake manifold.

8. Install throttle body, gasket and bolts to intake manifold.

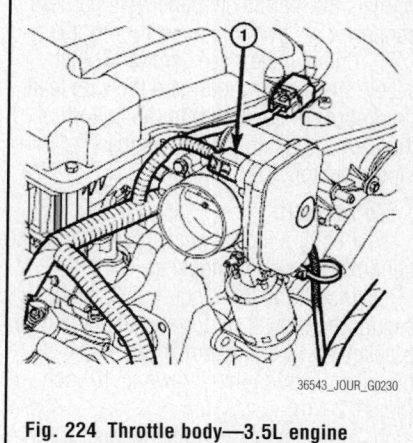

Fig. 224 Throttle body—3.5L engine

9. Install throttle body and three throttle body bolts, and stud. Hand tighten the three bolts and one stud.

✳ CAUTION

The throttle body must be torqued in a mandatory torque sequence. Tighten in a criss-cross pattern to specification.

10. Tighten the three bolts and one stud in a mandatory torque criss-cross pattern sequence to 50 inch lbs. (5.5 Nm).

11. Install throttle body bracket, nut and bolt. Tighten nut to 106 inch lbs. (12 Nm). Tighten bolt to 21 ft. lbs. (28 Nm).

12. Connect electrical connector to throttle body.

13. Install clean air hose to throttle body.

14. Install engine cover.

15. Connect the negative battery cable, tighten nut to 45 inch lbs. (5 Nm).

16. Use a scan tool and perform the ETC RELEARN function.

HEATING & AIR CONDITIONING SYSTEM

BLOWER MOTOR

REMOVAL & INSTALLATION

See Figure 225.

✳ WARNING

Disable the airbag system before attempting any steering wheel, steering column or instrument panel component diagnosis or service. Disconnect and isolate the negative battery (ground) cable, then wait two minutes for the airbag system capacitor to discharge before performing further diagnosis or service. This is the only sure way to disable the

airbag system. Failure to follow these instructions may result in accidental airbag deployment and possible serious or fatal injury.

➡The blower motor is located on the bottom of the passenger side of the HVAC housing. The blower motor can be removed from the vehicle without having to remove the HVAC housing.

1. Disconnect and isolate the negative battery cable.

2. If equipped, remove the silencer from below the passenger side of the instrument panel.

3. From underneath the instrument panel, disengage the connector lock and dis-

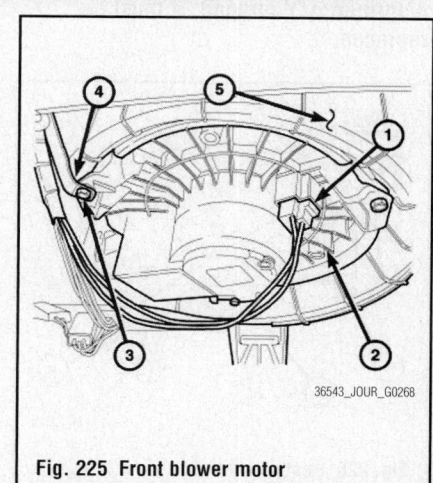

Fig. 225 Front blower motor

connect the instrument panel wire harness connector (1) from the blower motor (2).

4. Remove the three screws (3) that secure the blower motor and the wire lead bracket (4) (if equipped) to the bottom of the HVAC housing (5) and remove the blower motor.

To install:

5. Position the blower motor (2) into the bottom of the HVAC housing (5).

6. Install the three screws (3) that secure the blower motor and the wire lead bracket (4) (if equipped) to the HVAC housing. Tighten the screws to 10 inch lbs. (1.2 Nm).

7. Connect the instrument panel wire harness connector (1) to the blower motor and engage the connector lock.

8. If equipped, install the silencer below the passenger side of the instrument panel.

9. Reconnect the negative battery cable.

HEATER CORE

REMOVAL & INSTALLATION

See Figure 226.

✳✳ WARNING

Refer to the applicable warnings and cautions for this system before performing the following operation. Failure to follow the warnings and cautions may result in possible serious or fatal injury.

➡ The HVAC housing assembly must be removed from vehicle for service of the heater core.

1. Remove the HVAC housing assembly and place it on a workbench.

2. Remove the left side front floor duct.

➡ If the foam seal for the flange is deformed or damaged, it must be replaced.

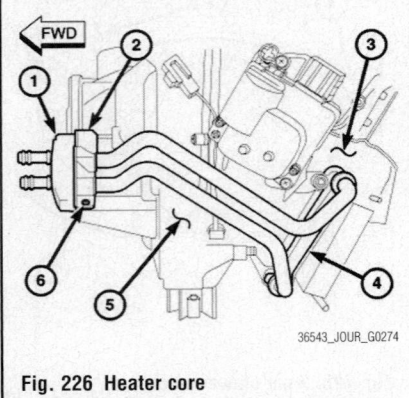

Fig. 226 Heater core

3. Remove the foam seal from the flange located on the front of the HVAC housing.

4. Remove the screw that secures the flange to the front of the HVAC housing and remove the flange.

5. Carefully pull the heater core (4) out of the driver side of the air distribution housing (3).

To install:

6. Carefully install the heater core (4) into the side of the air distribution housing (3).

7. Install the flange that secures the heater core tubes to the front of the HVAC housing.

8. Install the screw that secures the flange to the HVAC housing. Tighten the screw to 10 inch lbs. (1.2 Nm).

➡ If the foam seal for the flange is deformed or damaged, it must be replaced.

9. Install the foam seal onto the flange.
10. Install the left side front floor duct.

➡ If the heater core is being replaced, flush the cooling system.

11. Install the HVAC housing assembly

HVAC HOUSING

REMOVAL & INSTALLATION

See Figure 227.

✳✳ WARNING

Disable the airbag system before attempting any steering wheel, steering column or instrument panel component diagnosis or service. Disconnect and isolate the negative battery (ground) cable, then wait two minutes for the airbag system capacitor to discharge before performing further diagnosis or service. This is the only sure way to disable the airbag system. Failure to follow these instructions may result in accidental airbag deployment and possible serious or fatal injury.

✳✳ WARNING

Refer to the applicable warnings and cautions for this system before performing the following operation. Failure to follow the warnings and cautions may result in possible serious or fatal injury.

➡ The HVAC housing must be removed

from the vehicle and disassembled for service of the heater core, A/C evaporator, air intake housing and the mode-air and blend-air doors.

1. Disconnect and isolate the negative battery cable.

2. Recover the refrigerant from the refrigerant system.

3. Partially drain the engine cooling system.

4. If equipped with heat shield, remove the top nut that secures the heat shield to the stud located on the dash panel.

➡ Two slots are provided at the bottom of the heat shield to aid in heat shield removal, if equipped. Complete removal of the two bottom heat shield retaining nuts is not required.

5. If equipped, reach behind the engine and remove the two bottom nuts the that secure the heat shield to the studs located on the dash panel and remove the heat shield. Rotate and tilt the heat shield as required.

6. Remove the nut that secures the A/C liquid and suction line assembly to the A/C expansion valve.

7. Disconnect the A/C liquid and suction line assembly from the A/C evaporator and remove and discard the dual-plane seals.

8. Install plugs in, or tape over the opened refrigerant line fittings and the evaporator ports.

9. Disconnect the heater hoses from the heater core tubes. Install plugs in, or tape over the opened heater core tubes to prevent coolant spillage during housing removal.

➡ Make sure to remove the five bolts that secure the HVAC housing to the instrument panel support prior to removing the instrument panel from the vehicle.

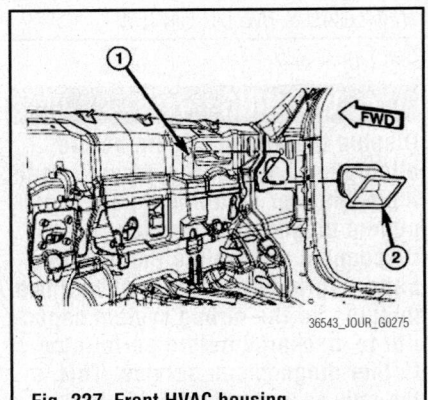

Fig. 227 Front HVAC housing

10. Remove the instrument panel.

11. Remove the rear floor ducts.

12. Remove the condensation drain tube.

13. Remove the nut that secures the passenger side of the HVAC housing to the dash panel.

➡**Use care to ensure that the interior is covered in case of loss of residual fluids from the heater and evaporator cores.**

14. Pull the HVAC housing rearward and remove the HVAC housing assembly from the passenger compartment.

15. If required, remove the HVAC housing air inlet duct (2) from the passenger compartment side of the dash panel (1).

To install:

16. If removed, install the HVAC housing air inlet duct onto the passenger compartment side of the dash panel (1). Make sure the foam seal is not missing or damaged and that the retaining tabs are fully engage to the dash panel.

17. Position the HVAC housing assembly to the dash panel. Be certain that the passenger side of the HVAC housing is cor-

rectly located over the dash panel mounting stud.

18. Install the nut that secures the HVAC housing to the passenger compartment side of dash panel. Tighten the nut to 40 inch lbs. (4.5 Nm).

19. Install the condensation drain tube.

20. Install the rear floor ducts.

21. Install the instrument panel.

22. Remove the previously installed plugs or caps and connect the heater hoses to the heater core tubes.

23. Remove the tape or plugs from the refrigerant line fittings and the expansion valve ports.

24. Lubricate the rubber O-ring seals with clean refrigerant oil and install them onto the liquid and suction line fittings. Use only the specified O-ring seals as they are made of special materials compatible to the R-134a system. Use only refrigerant oil of the type recommended for the A/C compressor in the vehicle.

25. Connect the A/C liquid and suction line assembly to the A/C expansion valve.

26. Install the nut (1) that secures the A/C liquid and suction line assembly to the

A/C expansion valve. Tighten the nut to 15 ft. lbs. (20 Nm).

27. If equipped, position the heat shield onto the studs located on the dash panel in the engine compartment and install the retaining nuts. Tighten the nuts to 10 inch lbs. (1 Nm).

28. Reconnect the negative battery cable.

29. If the heater core is being replaced, flush the cooling system.

30. Refill the engine cooling system.

✳✳ CAUTION

Do NOT run the engine with a vacuum pump in operation or with a vacuum present within the A/C system when equipped with the Denso 6SEU16 variable displacement compressor. Failure to follow this caution will result in serious A/C compressor damage.

31. Evacuate and charge the refrigerant system.

32. Initiate the Actuator Calibration function using a scan tool.

AUXILIARY HEATING & AIR CONDITIONING SYSTEM

BLOWER MOTOR

REMOVAL & INSTALLATION

See Figures 228 and 229.

1. Disconnect and isolate the negative battery cable.

2. Remove right rear quarter trim panel.

3. Disconnect the wire harness connector (3) from the rear blower motor (1).

4. Disengage the locking tab (4) and remove the rear blower motor from the rear heater-A/C housing (2) by turning the blower motor counterclockwise.

To install:

5. Position the rear blower motor (1) into the rear heater-A/C housing (2) and rotate the blower motor clockwise until the blower motor is fully engaged to the housing and the retaining tab (4) is in the locked position.

6. Connect the wire harness connector (3) to the rear blower motor.

7. Install the right rear quarter trim panel.

8. Reconnect the negative battery cable.

HEATER CORE

REMOVAL & INSTALLATION

See Figure 230.

✳✳ WARNING

Refer to the applicable warnings and cautions for this system before performing the following operation. Failure to follow the warnings and cautions may result in serious or fatal injury.

1. Disconnect and isolate the negative battery cable.

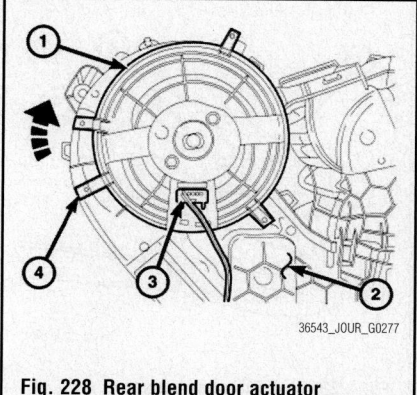

Fig. 228 Rear blend door actuator

36543_JOUR_G0277

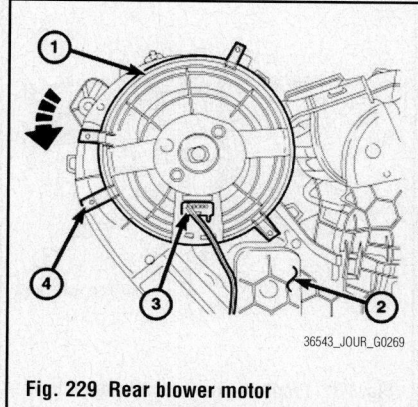

Fig. 229 Rear blower motor

36543_JOUR_G0269

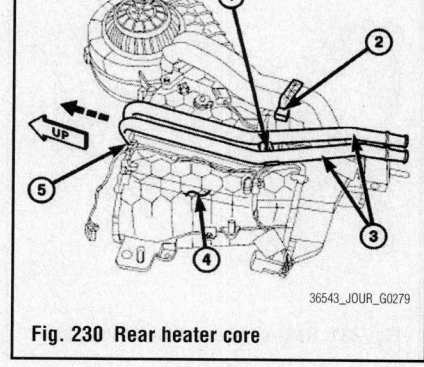

Fig. 230 Rear heater core

36543_JOUR_G0279

2. Remove the rear heater-A/C housing and place it on a workbench.

3. Remove the foam seal from the flange located at the bottom of the rear heater-A/C housing. If the foam seal is deformed or damaged, it must be replaced.

4. Remove the three screws that secure the flange to the bottom of the rear heater-A/C housing and remove the flange.

5. Disconnect the wire harness connector from the rear blend door actuator located on the outboard side of the rear heater-A/C housing.

6. Remove the two screws that secure the rear blend door actuator to the rear heater-A/C housing and remove the actuator.

7. Disconnect the wire harness connector from the rear mode door actuator located on the outboard side of the rear heater-A/C distribution housing.

8. Remove the three metal retaining clips that secure the rear distribution housing to the rear heater-A/C housing.

9. Release the five plastic retaining tabs that secure the rear distribution housing and rear heater-A/C housing together and separate the housings.

10. Remove the screw (1) that secures the rear heater core tubes (3) to the outboard side of the rear heater-A/C housing (4).

⁑ CAUTION

To prevent damage to the plastic evaporator tube bracket, carefully guide the heater core tubes past the bracket during removal of the heater core.

11. Carefully pull the rear heater core (5) out of the top of the rear heater-A/C housing. Guide the heater core tubes past the plastic evaporator tube bracket (2). If the foam seals on the heater core are deformed or damaged, they must be replaced.

To install:

⁑ CAUTION

To prevent damage to the plastic evaporator tube bracket, carefully guide the heater core tubes past the bracket during installation of the heater core.

12. Carefully install the rear heater core (5) into the rear heater-A/C housing (4). Guide the heater core tubes past the plastic evaporator tube bracket (2). Make sure that the foam seals are properly installed.

13. Install the screw (1) that secures the rear heater core tubes (3) to the outboard side of the rear heater-A/C housing. Tighten the screw to 10 inch lbs. (1.2 Nm).

14. Position the rear heater-A/C distribution housing to the rear heater-A/C housing

and engage the five plastic retaining tabs. Make sure the retaining tabs are fully engaged.

15. Install the three metal retaining clips that secure the rear distribution housing to the rear heater-A/C housing.

16. Connect the wire harness connector to the rear mode door actuator.

17. Position the rear blend door actuator onto the rear heater-A/C housing. If necessary, rotate the actuator slightly to align the splines on the actuator output shaft with those on the rear blend-air door pivot shaft.

18. Install the two screws that secure the rear blend door actuator to the rear heater-A/C housing. Tighten the screws to 10 inch lbs. (1.2 Nm).

19. Connect the wire harness connector to the rear blend door actuator.

20. Position the flange to the bottom of the rear heater-A/C housing and install the three retaining screws. Tighten the screws to 10 inch lbs. (1.2 Nm).

21. Install the foam seal onto the flange at the bottom of the rear heater-A/C housing. Make sure that the foam seal is properly installed.

22. Install the rear heater-A/C housing.

23. Reconnect the negative battery cable.

24. If the rear heater core is being replaced, flush the cooling system.

25. Refill the engine cooling system.

26. Evacuate and charge the refrigerant system.

STEERING

POWER RACK & PINION STEERING GEAR

REMOVAL & INSTALLATION

See Figures 231 through 235.

1. Siphon out as much power steering fluid as possible from the reservoir.

2. Place the front wheels of vehicle (and steering wheel) in the STRAIGHT-AHEAD position. Using a steering wheel holder, lock the steering wheel in place to keep it from rotating. This keeps the clockspring in the proper orientation while the intermediate shaft is disconnected.

3. Reposition the floor carpeting and sound deadening insulation to access the intermediate shaft coupling (1) at the base of the column.

4. Remove the intermediate shaft coupling bolt.

5. Separate the intermediate shaft coupling from the steering gear pinion shaft.

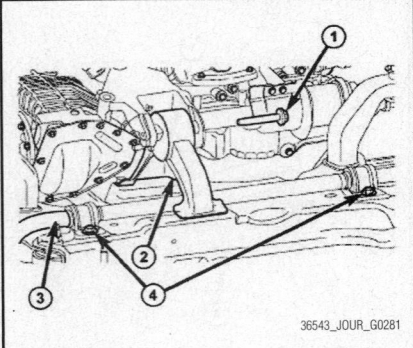

Fig. 231 Rear engine mount through bolt

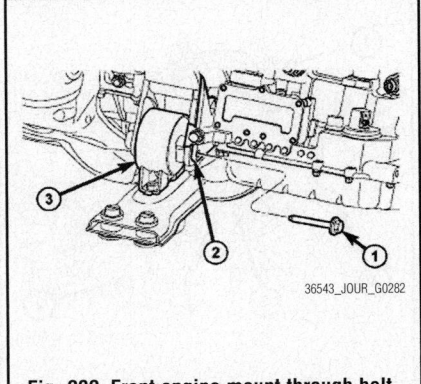

Fig. 232 Front engine mount through bolt

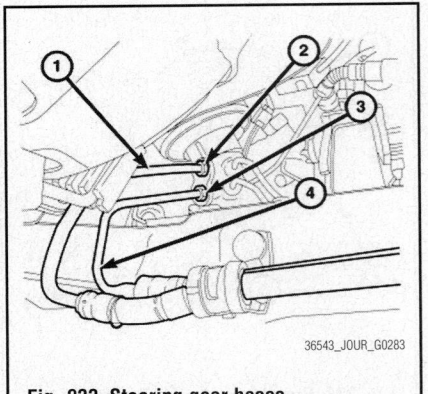

Fig. 233 Steering gear hoses

6. Release the clips securing the dash seal to the dash panel and push the seal away from the dash panel.

7. Raise and support the vehicle.

8. On each side of the vehicle, remove the wheel mounting nuts, then the tire and wheel assembly.

9. On each side of the gear, remove the nut (3) from the out tie rod end (6) at the knuckle.

10. On each side of the gear, separate the outer tie rod end from the knuckle using Remover, Special Tool 9360.

11. If equipped, remove the engine belly pan.

12. Remove the rear engine mount through-bolt (1).

13. Remove the front engine mount through-bolt (1).

14. Remove the screws securing the power steering hose routing clamps to the rear of the crossmember.

15. Unscrew the tube nut (2), then remove the return hose (1) at the steering gear.

16. Unscrew the tube nut (3), then remove the pressure hose (4) at the steering gear.

➡ **Before lowering the front suspension crossmember, the location of the crossmember must be marked on the body of the vehicle. Do this so the crossmember can be relocated, upon reinstallation, against the body of vehicle in the same location as before removal. If the front suspension crossmember is not reinstalled in exactly the same location as before removal, the preset front wheel alignment settings (caster and camber) may be lost.**

17. Using a crayon or marker that will not break the paint surface, mark the location of the front crossmember (1) on the body near each mounting bolt. Do not use any type of sharp instrument that will damage the underbody of the vehicle.

18. Support the crossmember (9) with a transmission jack.

19. Remove the four mounting bolts (6) securing the front crossmember (9) to the body.

20. Remove the mounting screws (8) securing the front crossmember reinforcement brackets (7) (one each side of vehicle) to the body (1). Remove the brackets.

21. Using the jack, slowly lower the crossmember approximately 3 inches (76 mm) (as measured at the rear crossmember mounts). Do not lower the crossmember more than necessary as the fore/aft crossmember is still attached to the radiator support and damage may occur.

22. Remove the screws and push-pins securing the heat shield over the right side of the steering gear. Remove the shield.

23. Remove the two bolts securing the steering gear to the crossmember.

24. Tip the steering gear pinion shaft (3) straight up and remove the dash seal (2) from the steering gear.

25. Slide the steering gear across the crossmember and out through left wheel opening.

26. If necessary, remove outer tie rods from inner tie rod threads. Count how many rotations it takes to remove each outer tie rod for installation reference.

To install:

27. If necessary, install the outer tie rods onto the inner tie rod threads. As the outer tie rods are installed, count out same number rotations as were counted on tie rod removal. This will get the toe setting somewhat close to specification before the vehicle is aligned at end of this procedure. Snug the tie rod jam nuts on both ends of gear. Tighten the tie rod jam nuts to specification while performing the wheel alignment at end of this procedure.

28. Carefully install the steering gear through the left wheel opening using the

reverse of how it was removed. Move it across the crossmember until centered.

29. Tip the steering gear pinion shaft straight up and install the dash seal matching it to the contour of the steering gear housing.

30. Position the steering gear in mounted position on the crossmember.

31. Install the two bolts securing the steering gear to the crossmember. Tighten the gear mounting bolts to 74 ft. lbs. (100 Nm).

32. Install the heat shield over the steering gear. Install the mounting screws and push-pins. Tighten the screws to 53 inch lbs. (6 Nm).

33. Center the power steering gear rack in its travel as necessary.

➡ **When installing the front suspension crossmember it is very important that the crossmember be attached to the body in exactly the same spot as when it was removed. Otherwise, the vehicle's wheel alignment settings (caster and camber) will be lost making wheel alignment more difficult.**

34. Slowly raise the crossmember into mounted position using the transmission jack matching the crossmember to the marked locations on the body made during removal.

35. Position the front crossmember reinforcement brackets (one each side of vehicle) over the crossmember rear mounting bushings and install the mounting screws, but do not tighten at this time.

36. Install the four mounting bolts securing the front crossmember to the body. Tighten the crossmember mounting bolts to 100 ft. lbs. (135 Nm).

37. Tighten the crossmember reinforcement bracket mounting screws (8) to 37 ft. lbs. (50 Nm).

38. Remove the transmission jack.

39. Install the pressure hose tube (4) at the gear. Tighten the tube nut to 24 ft. lbs. (32 Nm).

40. Install the return hose tube (1) at the gear. Tighten the tube nut to 24 ft. lbs. (32 Nm).

41. Position the power steering hose routing clamps on the crossmember. Install and tighten the screws to 71 inch lbs. (8 Nm).

42. Install the rear engine mount through-bolt.

43. Install the front engine mount through-bolt.

44. If equipped, install the engine belly pan.

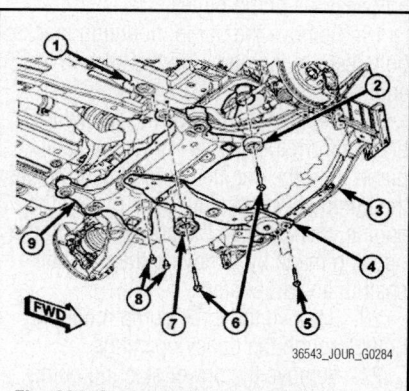

36543_JOUR_G0284

Fig. 234 Crossmember components

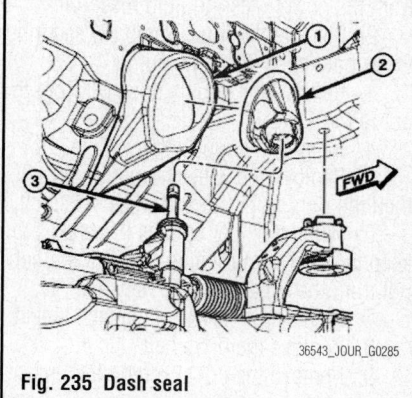

36543_JOUR_G0285

Fig. 235 Dash seal

➡Prior to attaching the outer tie rod end to the knuckle, inspect the tie rod seal boot. If the seal boot is damaged, replace the outer tie rod end.

45. On each side of the gear, install the outer tie rod end into the hole in the knuckle arm. Start a NEW tie rod mounting nut onto the stud. While holding the tie rod end stud with a wrench, tighten the nut with a wrench or crowfoot wrench. Tighten the nut to 63 ft. lbs. (85 Nm).

46. On each side of the vehicle, install the tire and wheel assembly. Install and tighten the wheel mounting nuts to 100 ft. lbs. (135 Nm).

47. Lower the vehicle.

48. Lift the dash seal into position and engage the retaining clips securing the dash seal to the dash panel.

49. Remove the steering wheel holder using care not to rotate the steering wheel.

50. Verify the front wheels of vehicle are in the STRAIGHT-AHEAD position.

51. Center the intermediate shaft coupling over the steering gear pinion shaft, then slide the intermediate shaft onto the steering gear pinion shaft.

52. Install the intermediate shaft coupling bolt. Tighten the bolt to 31 ft. lbs. (42 Nm).

53. Position the sound deadening insulation and floor carpet back into place.

54. Fill and bleed the power steering system.

55. Check for fluid leaks.

56. Perform wheel alignment as necessary.

POWER STEERING PUMP

REMOVAL & INSTALLATION

2.4L Engine

See Figure 236.

1. Siphon as much fluid as possible from the power steering fluid reservoir.

2. Remove the engine appearance cover.

3. Remove the pressure hose routing bracket bolt (2) at the upper mount (8).

4. Remove the pressure hose (3) at the pump pressure port (5).

5. Remove the hose clamp (2) securing the supply hose (1) at the pump.

6. Remove the supply hose (1) from the pump (3).

7. Remove the drive belt (2).

8. Remove the three pump mounting bolts (1) through the pulley (3) openings.

9. Remove the power steering pump.

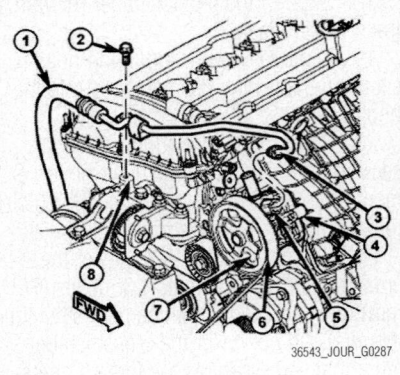

Fig. 236 Power steering pump components—2.4L engine

To install:

10. Using a lint free towel, wipe clean the open power steering pressure hose end and the power steering pump port. Replace any used O-rings with new. Lubricate the O-ring with clean power steering fluid.

11. Place the pump in mounting position. Install the three bolts through the pulley openings. Tighten the mounting bolts to 19 ft. lbs. (26 Nm).

12. Install the drive belt.

13. Install the supply hose (1) at the pump (3).

14. Clamp the hose clamp securing the supply hose to the pump.

15. Install the pressure hose (3) at the pump pressure port (5). Tighten the tube nut to 24 ft. lbs. (32 Nm).

16. Install the pressure hose routing bracket bolt (2) to the engine mount (8). Tighten the bolt to 18 ft. lbs. (25 Nm).

17. Fill and bleed the power steering system.

18. Check for leaks.

19. Install the engine appearance cover.

2.7L Engine

See Figure 237.

1. Siphon as much fluid as possible from the power steering fluid reservoir.

2. Remove the hose clamp (3) securing the supply hose (2) at the pump.

3. Remove the supply hose (2) from the pump (4).

4. Raise and support the vehicle.

5. Remove the wheel mounting nuts, then the right front tire and wheel assembly.

6. While a helper applies the brakes to keep the hub from rotating, remove the hub nut from the right side axle halfshaft.

7. Remove the drive belt splash shield.

8. Remove the drive belt.

9. Remove the nut attaching the outer

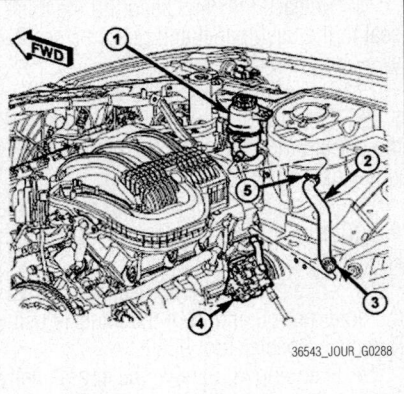

Fig. 237 Power steering pump components—2.7L engine

tie rod to the right knuckle. To do this it might be necessary to hold the tie rod end stud with a wrench while loosening and removing the nut with a standard wrench or crowfoot wrench.

10. Release the outer tie rod end from the knuckle using Remover, Special Tool 9360.

11. Remove the outer tie rod from the knuckle.

12. Remove the nut attaching the lower ball joint to the right lower control arm.

13. Release the lower ball joint from the lower control arm using Remover, Special Tool 9360.

➡Do not allow the halfshaft to hang by the inner C/V joint; it must be supported to keep the joint from separating during this operation.

14. Lift the knuckle out of the lower control arm and pull the knuckle off the halfshaft outer C/V joint splines.

15. Remove the right halfshaft from the vehicle.

16. Remove the pressure hose at the pump.

17. Remove the pump mounting bracket bolt near the pump pulley.

18. Remove the pump mounting bracket bolts behind the pump on the back of the engine.

19. Remove the pump with mounting bracket from the engine. To remove the pump from the engine compartment, rotate the pump so that the pulley is toward the engine, then remove the pump through the opening made by removing the axle halfshaft in an earlier step.

20. Remove the three pump mounting bolts through the pulley openings.

21. Remove the power steering pump from the mounting bracket.

To install:

22. Place the pump in the mounting bracket. Install the three bolts through the pulley openings. Tighten the mounting bolts to 22 ft. lbs. (30 Nm).

23. Install the pump with mounting bracket on the engine. To install the pump into the engine compartment, rotate the pump so that the pulley is toward the engine, then insert the pump up through the opening where the axle halfshaft is usually located. Rotate the pump around and into mounting position.

24. Install the pump mounting bracket bolts behind the pump on the back of the engine. Do not tighten the bolts at this time.

25. Install the pump mounting bracket bolt near the pump pulley.

26. Tighten all three pump mounting bracket bolts to 22 ft. lbs. (30 Nm).

27. Using a lint free towel, wipe clean the open power steering pressure hose end and the power steering pump port. Replace any used O-rings with new. Lubricate the O-ring with clean power steering fluid.

28. Install the pressure hose at the pump pressure port. Tighten the tube nut to 24 ft. lbs. (32 Nm).

29. Install the right axle halfshaft.

30. Insert the axle halfshaft into the rear of the hub and bearing hub and bearing, Insert the lower ball joint stud (of knuckle) into the mounting hole in the lower control arm.

31. Install a NEW ball joint stud nut. Tighten the nut to 70 ft. lbs. (95 Nm).

32. Install the outer tie rod ball stud into the hole in the knuckle arm. Start the tie rod end knuckle nut onto the stud. While holding the tie rod end stud with a wrench, tighten the nut with a wrench or crowfoot wrench to 63 ft. lbs. (85 Nm).

33. Install a NEW power steering pump drive belt.

34. Install the drive belt splash shield.

35. Clean all foreign matter from the threads of the halfshaft outer C/V joint.

36. Install the hub nut on the end of the halfshaft (2) and snug it.

37. While a helper applies the brakes to keep the hub from rotating, tighten the hub nut (3) to 97 ft. lbs. (132 Nm).

38. Install the tire and wheel assembly. Install and tighten wheel mounting nuts to 100 ft. lbs. (135 Nm).

39. Lower the vehicle.

40. Install the supply hose (2) at the pump (4).

41. Install the hose clamp (3) securing the supply hose to the pump.

42. Fill and bleed the power steering system.

43. Check for leaks.

3.5L Engine

See Figure 238.

1. Siphon as much fluid as possible from the power steering fluid reservoir.

2. Remove the engine appearance cover.

3. Unscrew the tube nut, then remove the pressure hose at the pump (4).

4. Remove the pressure hose routing clamp bolt (2) at the engine cylinder head.

5. Remove the clamp (3) securing the supply hose (2) to the power steering pump supply fitting (4), then remove the hose from the supply fitting.

6. Raise and support the vehicle.

7. Remove the wheel mounting nuts, then the right front tire and wheel assembly.

8. Remove the drive belt splash shield.

9. Remove the drive belt.

10. Lower the vehicle.

11. Remove the two nuts securing the right engine mount bracket to the mount.

12. Position a floor jack with an appropriate size block of wood below the engine oil pan. raise the jack until the block of wood just comes into contact with the bottom of the oil pan, but no further.

13. Slowly raise the right side of the engine using the floor jack while viewing the pump drive pulley. Raise the engine until all three power steering pump mounting bolts can be accessed through the openings in the drive pulley.

14. Remove the three pump mounting bolts through the pulley openings.

15. Remove the power steering pump.

To install:

16. Using a lint free towel, wipe clean the open power steering pressure hose end and the power steering pump port. Replace any used O-rings with new. Lubricate the O-ring with clean power steering fluid.

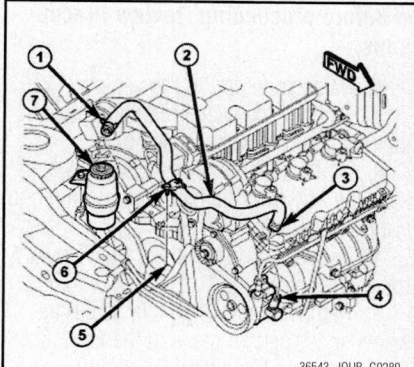

Fig. 238 Power steering pump components—3.5L engine

36543_JOUR_G0289

17. Place the pump in mounted position. Install the three bolts through the pulley openings. Tighten the mounting bolts to 22 ft. lbs. (30 Nm).

18. Slowly lower the right side of the engine using the floor jack, guiding the right engine mount bracket mounting holes over the mounting studs of the right engine mount.

19. Remove the floor jack and block of wood from below engine.

20. Install the two nuts securing the right engine mount bracket to the mount.

21. Raise and support the vehicle.

22. Install the drive belt.

23. Install the drive belt splash shield.

24. Install the tire and wheel assembly. Install and tighten wheel mounting nuts to 100 ft. lbs. (135 Nm).

25. Lower the vehicle.

26. Place the pump end of the supply hose (2) onto the pump supply fitting (4). Expand the hose clamp (3) and slide it over the hose and pump supply fitting. Secure the clamp once it is past the bead formed into the fluid supply fitting.

27. Install the pressure hose at the power steering pump (4). Tighten the tube nut to 24 ft. lbs. (32 Nm).

28. Position the pressure hose routing clamp at the engine cylinder head. Install and tighten the routing clamp bolt (2) to 16 ft. lbs. (22 Nm).

29. Fill and bleed the power steering system.

30. Check for leaks.

31. Install the engine appearance cover.

BLEEDING

See Figure 239.

> ❄❄ **WARNING**
>
> **The fluid level should be checked with engine off to prevent injury from moving components.**

> ❄❄ **CAUTION**
>
> **Mopar® Power Steering Fluid + 4 or Mopar® ATF+4 Automatic Transmission Fluid is to be used in the power steering system. Both Fluids have the same material standard specifications (MS-9602). No other power steering or automatic transmission fluid is to be used in the system. Damage may result to the power steering pump and system if another fluid is used. Do not overfill the system.**

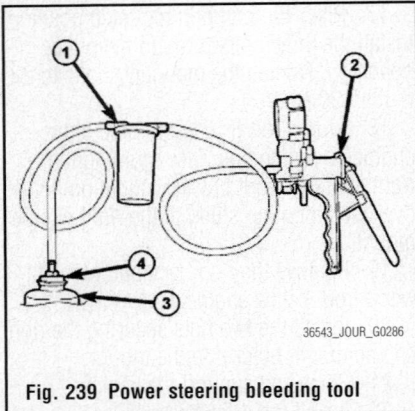

Fig. 239 Power steering bleeding tool

✳✳ CAUTION

If the air is not purged from the power steering system correctly, pump failure could result.

➡️**Be sure the vacuum tool used in the following procedure is clean and free of any fluids.**

1. Check the fluid level. As measured on the side of the reservoir, the level should indicate between MAX and MIN when the fluid is at normal ambient temperature. Adjust the fluid level as necessary.
2. Tightly insert Power Steering Cap Adapter (4), Special Tool 9688, into the mouth of the reservoir (3).

✳✳ CAUTION

Failure to use a vacuum pump reservoir (1) may allow power steering fluid to be sucked into the hand vacuum pump.

3. Attach Hand Vacuum Pump (2), Special Tool C-4207 or equivalent, with reservoir (1) attached, to the Power Steering Cap Adapter (4).

✳✳ CAUTION

Do not run the engine while vacuum is applied to the power steering system. Damage to the power steering pump can occur.

➡️**When performing the following step make sure the vacuum level is maintained during the entire time period.**

4. Using Hand Vacuum Pump (2), apply 68-85 kPa (20-25 in. Hg) of vacuum to the system for a minimum of three minutes.
5. Slowly release the vacuum and remove the special tools.
6. Adjust the fluid level as necessary. Refer to Step 1 .
7. Repeat Step 1 through Step 6 until the fluid no longer drops when vacuum is applied.
8. Start the engine and cycle the steering wheel lock-to-lock three times.

➡️**Do not hold the steering wheel at the stops.**

9. Stop the engine and check for leaks at all connections.
10. Check for any signs of air in the reservoir and check the fluid level. If air is present, repeat the procedure as necessary.

SUSPENSION

PRECAUTIONS

✳✳ WARNING

Chrysler LLC does not manufacture any vehicles or replacement parts that contain asbestos. Aftermarket products may or may not contain asbestos. Refer to aftermarket product packaging for product information.

Whether the product contains asbestos or not, dust and dirt can accumulate on brake parts during normal use. Follow practices prescribed by appropriate regulations for the handling, processing and disposing of dust and debris.

✳✳ WARNING

Do not remove the strut rod nut while strut assembly is installed in vehicle, or before the coil spring is compressed with a compression tool. The spring is held under high pressure.

✳✳ CAUTION

At no time when servicing a vehicle can a sheet metal screw, bolt, or other metal fastener be installed in the shock tower to take the place of an original plastic clip. It may come
into contact with the strut or coil spring.

✳✳ CAUTION

Wheel bearing damage will result if after loosening the axle hub nut, the vehicle is rolled on the ground or the weight of the vehicle is allowed to be supported by the tires for any length of time.

LOWER BALL JOINT

REMOVAL & INSTALLATION
See Figures 240 and 241.

➡️**Before proceeding, review Precautions.**

1. Raise and support the vehicle.
2. Remove the wheel mounting nuts, then the tire and wheel assembly.
3. While a helper applies the brakes to keep the hub from rotating, remove the hub nut from the axle halfshaft.
4. Access and remove the front brake rotor.
5. Remove the routing clip securing wheel speed sensor cable to the knuckle.
6. Remove the screw fastening the wheel speed sensor head to the knuckle. Pull the sensor head out of the knuckle.

FRONT SUSPENSION

7. Remove the nut (4) attaching the lower ball joint to the lower control arm (5).
8. Release the lower ball joint (5) from the lower control arm (1) using Remover (2) 9360. Do not lift the knuckle out of the lower control arm at this time.
9. Lift the knuckle (2) out of the lower control arm (5).

➡️**Do not allow the halfshaft (1) to hang by the inner C/V joint; it must be supported to keep the joint from separating during this operation.**

10. Pull the knuckle (2) off the axle halfshaft (1) outer C/V joint splines and support the halfshaft.

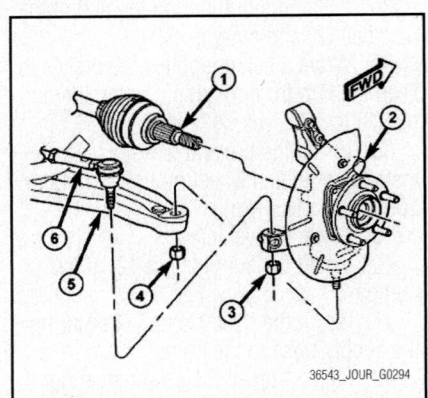

Fig. 240 Lower Ball joint components

11. Through the access hole (1) in the knuckle, tap the ends of the snap-ring (2) with a drift punch and remove it from the ball joint.

12. Install Remover 9964-3, and Remover, Special Tool 9964-4 on Remover/Installer, Special Tool 8441-1. Place the tools over the ball joint, then hand tighten the screw-drive.

13. Using hand-tools, tighten the screw-drive forcing the ball joint out of the knuckle.

14. Loosen the screw-drive and remove the tools and ball joint.

To install:

15. Install Installer, Special Tool 9964-1, and Installer, Special Tool 9964-2 on Remover/Installer, Special Tool 8441-1. Place a new ball joint (stem down) into Installer 9964-2.

16. Position the assembly onto the knuckle as shown, then hand tighten the screw-drive.

17. Using hand-tools, tighten the screw-drive forcing the ball joint into the knuckle. Continue to install the ball joint until the flange on the ball joint comes to a stop against the bottom of the knuckle.

18. Loosen the screw-drive and remove the tools.

19. Install a NEW snap-ring into the groove in the ball joint using a drift punch.

20. Slide the hub and bearing in the knuckle onto the splines of the halfshaft outer C/V joint.

21. Insert the lower ball joint stud into the mounting hole in the lower control arm.

22. Install a NEW ball joint stud nut. Tighten the nut to 70 ft. lbs. (95 Nm).

23. Install the wheel speed sensor head into the knuckle. Install the mounting screw and tighten it to 106 inch lbs. (12 Nm).

24. Install the routing clip securing the wheel speed sensor cable to the knuckle.

25. Install the brake rotor, disc brake caliper and adapter.

26. Clean all foreign matter from the threads of the halfshaft outer C/V joint.

27. Install the hub nut on the end of the halfshaft and snug it.

28. While a helper applies the brakes to keep the hub from rotating, tighten the hub nut to 97 ft. lbs. (132 Nm).

29. Install the tire and wheel assembly. Install and tighten wheel mounting nuts to 100 ft. lbs. (135 Nm).

30. Lower the vehicle.

31. Perform wheel alignment as necessary.

LOWER CONTROL ARM

REMOVAL & INSTALLATION

See Figure 240 and 242.

➡**Before proceeding, review Precautions.**

1. Raise and support the vehicle.
2. Remove the wheel mounting nuts, then the tire and wheel assembly.
3. Remove the nut (4) attaching the lower ball joint to the lower control arm (5).
4. Release the lower ball joint from the lower control arm using Remover (2) 9360. Do not lift the knuckle out of the lower control arm at this time.

✱✱ CAUTION

Upon removing the knuckle from the ball joint stud, do not pull outward on the knuckle. Pulling the knuckle outward at this point can separate the inner C/V joint on the halfshaft thus damaging it.

5. At each end of the stabilizer bar, while holding the stabilizer bar link lower stud stationary, remove the nut securing the link to the stabilizer bar.

6. Rotate the ends of the stabilizer bar upward away from the lower control arm.

7. Remove the front bolt attaching the lower control arm to the front suspension crossmember.

8. Remove the nut on the rear bolt (2) attaching the lower control arm (3) to the front suspension crossmember. Remove the bolt.

9. Remove the lower control arm (3) from the crossmember.

To install:

10. Place the lower control arm (3) into the front suspension crossmember.

11. Insert the rear bolt (2) up through the crossmember and lower control arm (3). Install the nut on the top-end of the bolt, but do not tighten it at this time.

12. Install, but do not fully tighten, the front bolt (1) attaching the lower control arm (3) to the crossmember.

13. With no weight or obstruction on the lower control arm, tighten the lower control arm front mounting bolt (2) to 107 ft. lbs. (145 Nm).

14. With no weight or obstruction on the lower control arm, tighten the lower control arm rear mounting bolt nut to 107 ft. lbs. (145 Nm).

15. Attach the stabilizer bar link at each end of the stabilizer bar. At each link, install and tighten the nut while holding the stabilizer bar link lower stud stationary. Tighten the nuts to 35 ft. lbs. (48 Nm).

➡**If a new or cleaned lower control arm is being installed, it is important to have a film of general purpose grease around the ball joint mounting hole on the lower control arm to avoid any future corrosion issues. Make sure the grease does not get inside the ball joint mounting hole or on the ball joint stud during installation.**

16. Insert the lower ball joint stud into the mounting hole in the lower control arm (5).

17. Install a NEW ball joint stud nut. Tighten the nut to 70 ft. lbs. (95 Nm).

18. Install the tire and wheel assembly. Install and tighten the wheel mounting nuts to 100 ft. lbs. (135 Nm).

19. Lower the vehicle.

20. Perform wheel alignment as necessary.

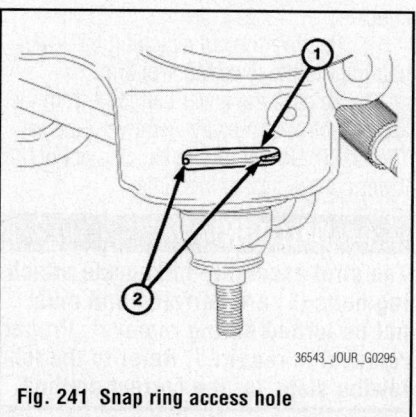

36543_JOUR_G0295

Fig. 241 Snap ring access hole

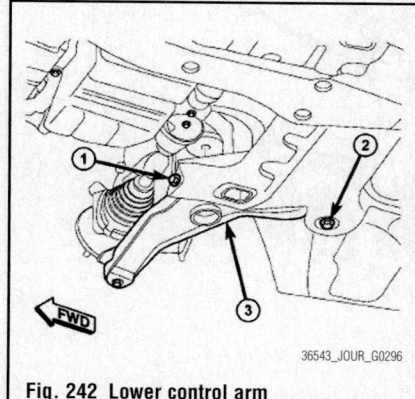

36543_JOUR_G0296

Fig. 242 Lower control arm

MCPHERSON STRUT

REMOVAL & INSTALLATION

See Figure 243.

➡ **Before proceeding, review Precautions.**

1. Remove the engine appearance cover.

2. Remove the two push-pins securing the cowl top screen at the ends. Remove the remaining push-pins. Remove the cowl top screen.

3. Remove the wiper arms.

4. Remove the push-pins securing the cowl screen to the wheelhouse brace and cowl. Rotate the screw in the center of the cowl screen 90° clockwise to release the screen. Remove the cowl screen.

5. Raise and support the vehicle.

6. Remove the wheel mounting nuts, then the tire and wheel assembly.

➡ **If both strut assemblies are to be removed, mark the strut assemblies right or left and keep the parts separated to avoid mix-up. Not all parts of the strut assembly are interchangeable side-to-side.**

7. Remove the screw securing the flex hose routing bracket to the strut.

8. While holding the stabilizer bar link (1) stud stationary, remove the nut (4) securing the link to the strut (3).

✸✸ **CAUTION**

The strut assembly-to-knuckle attaching bolts (5) are serrated and must not be turned during removal. Hold the bolts stationary in the knuckle while removing the nuts, then tap the bolts out using a pin punch.

9. While holding the bolt heads stationary, remove the two nuts (2) from the bolts (5) attaching the strut (3) to the knuckle (6).

10. Remove the two bolts (5) attaching the strut (3) to the knuckle (6) using a pin punch.

11. Lower the vehicle just enough to open the hood without allowing the tires to touch the floor.

12. Remove the three nuts attaching the strut assembly upper mount to the strut tower.

13. Remove the strut assembly from the vehicle.

To install:

14. Raise the strut assembly into the strut tower, aligning the three studs on the strut assembly upper mount with the holes in strut tower. Install the three mounting nuts on the studs. Tighten the three nuts to 41 ft. lbs. (55 Nm).

✸✸ **CAUTION**

The strut clevis-to-knuckle bolts (5) are serrated and must not be turned during installation. Install the nuts while holding the bolts stationary in the knuckle.

15. Position the lower end of the strut assembly (3) in line with the upper end of the knuckle (6), aligning the mounting holes. Install the two attaching bolts (5). Install the nuts (2). While holding the bolts in place, tighten the nuts to 103 ft. lbs. (140 Nm).

16. Attach the stabilizer bar link (1) to the strut (3). Install and tighten the nut (4) while holding the stabilizer bar link stud stationary. Tighten the nut to 35 ft. lbs. (48 Nm).

17. Secure the flex hose routing bracket to the strut with the mounting screw.

Tighten the mounting screw to 10 ft. lbs. (13 Nm).

18. Install tire and wheel assembly. Install and tighten wheel mounting nuts to 100 ft. lbs. (135 Nm).

19. Lower the vehicle.

20. Install the cowl screen. Install the push-pins securing the cowl screen to the wheelhouse brace and cowl. Rotate the screw in the center of the cowl screen 90° counterclockwise to lock the screen in place.

21. Install the wiper arms.

22. Install the cowl top screen. Install the two push-pins securing the cowl top screen at the ends. Install the remaining push-pins.

23. Install the engine appearance cover.

STEERING KNUCKLE

REMOVAL & INSTALLATION

See Figures 243 and 244.

➡ **Before proceeding, review Precautions.**

1. Raise and support the vehicle.

2. Remove the wheel mounting nuts, then the tire and wheel assembly.

3. While a helper applies the brakes to keep the hub from rotating, remove the hub nut from the axle halfshaft.

4. Access and remove the front brake rotor.

5. Remove the routing clip securing wheel speed sensor cable to the knuckle.

6. Remove the screw fastening the wheel speed sensor head to the knuckle. Pull the sensor head out of the knuckle.

7. Remove the nut attaching the outer tie rod to the knuckle. To do this it might be necessary to hold the tie rod end stud with a wrench while loosening and removing the nut with a standard wrench or crowfoot wrench.

8. Release the outer tie rod end from the knuckle using Remover, Special Tool 9360.

9. Remove the outer tie rod from the knuckle.

10. Remove the nut attaching the lower ball joint to the lower control arm.

11. Release the lower ball joint from the lower control arm using Remover, Special Tool 9360. Do not lift the knuckle out of the lower control arm at this time.

✸✸ **CAUTION**

The strut assembly-to-knuckle attaching bolts (5) are serrated and must not be turned during removal. Proper removal is required. Refer to the following steps for the correct method.

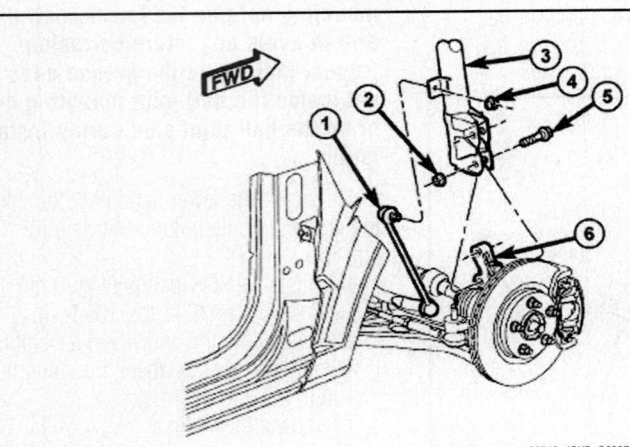

Fig. 243 Strut assembly and stabilizer bar link

36543_JOUR_G0297

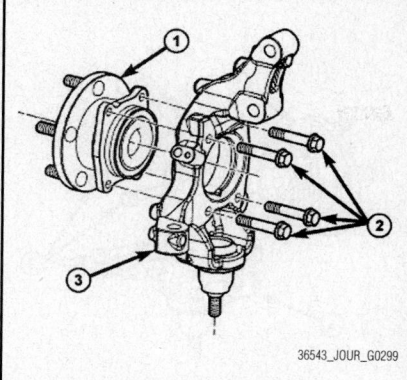

Fig. 244 Knuckle and hub and bearing assembly

12. While holding the bolt heads stationary, remove the two nuts (2) from the bolts (5) attaching the strut (3) to the knuckle (6).

13. Remove the two bolts (5) attaching the strut (3) to the knuckle (6) using a pin punch.

➡ **Do not allow the halfshaft to hang by the inner C/V joint; it must be supported to keep the joint from separating during this operation.**

14. Pull the knuckle off the halfshaft outer C/V joint splines and remove the knuckle from the vehicle.

15. If required, remove the three screws fastening the shield to the knuckle. Remove the shield.

16. If required, remove the four bolts (2) fastening the hub and bearing (1) to the knuckle (3).

17. If required, slide the hub and bearing (1) out of the knuckle.

To install:

18. If required, install the hub and bearing (1) by sliding it into the knuckle.

19. If installing hub and bearing, install the four bolts (2) fastening the hub and bearing (1) to the knuckle (3). Tighten the four bolts to 60 ft. lbs. (82 Nm).

20. If required, install the shield on the knuckle. Install and tighten the three mounting screws to 89 inch lbs. (10 Nm).

21. Slide the hub and bearing in the knuckle onto the splines of the halfshaft outer C/V joint (1).

22. Insert the lower ball joint stud into the mounting hole in the lower control arm.

23. Install a NEW ball joint stud nut. Tighten the nut to 70 ft. lbs. (95 Nm).

✳ CAUTION

The strut clevis-to-knuckle bolts are serrated and must not be turned during installation. Install the nuts while holding the bolts stationary in the steering knuckle. Refer to the following step.

24. Position the lower end of the strut assembly in line with the upper end of the knuckle, aligning the mounting holes. Install the two mounting bolts.

25. Install the nuts on the two bolts. While holding the bolts in place, tighten the nuts to 103 ft. lbs. (140 Nm).

26. Install the outer tie rod ball stud into the hole in the knuckle arm. Start the tie rod end-to-knuckle nut (4) onto the stud. While holding the tie rod end stud with a wrench, tighten the nut with a wrench or crowfoot wrench to 63 ft. lbs. (85 Nm).

27. Install the wheel speed sensor head into the knuckle. Install the mounting screw (1) and tighten it to 106 inch lbs. (12 Nm).

28. Install the routing clip securing the wheel speed sensor cable to the knuckle.

29. Install the brake rotor, disc brake caliper and adapter.

30. Clean all foreign matter from the threads of the halfshaft outer C/V joint.

31. Install the hub nut on the end of the halfshaft and snug it.

32. While a helper applies the brakes to keep the hub from rotating, tighten the hub nut to 97 ft. lbs. (132 Nm).

33. Install the tire and wheel assembly. Install and tighten wheel mounting nuts to 100 ft. lbs. (135 Nm).

34. Lower the vehicle.

35. Perform wheel alignment as necessary.

STABILIZER BAR

REMOVAL & INSTALLATION

See Figure 245.

➡ **Before proceeding, review Precautions.**

1. Raise and support the vehicle.

2. If equipped, remove the engine belly pan.

3. Remove the rear engine mount.

4. Remove the front engine mount through-bolt.

5. At each end of the stabilizer bar, while holding the stabilizer bar link lower stud stationary, remove the nut securing the link to the stabilizer bar.

6. Remove the screws securing the power steering hose routing clamps to the rear of the crossmember.

7. Remove the screws and push-pins securing the heat shield over the right side of the steering gear.

8. Remove the two bolts securing the steering gear to the crossmember.

9. Support the steering gear using a bungee cord or other to keep the steering gear from lowering when the crossmember is lowered.

➡ **Before removing the front suspension crossmember from the vehicle, the location of the crossmember must be marked on the body of the vehicle. Do this so the crossmember can be relocated, upon reinstallation, against the body of vehicle in the same location as before removal. If the front suspension crossmember is not reinstalled in exactly the same location as before removal, the preset front wheel alignment settings (caster and camber) may be lost.**

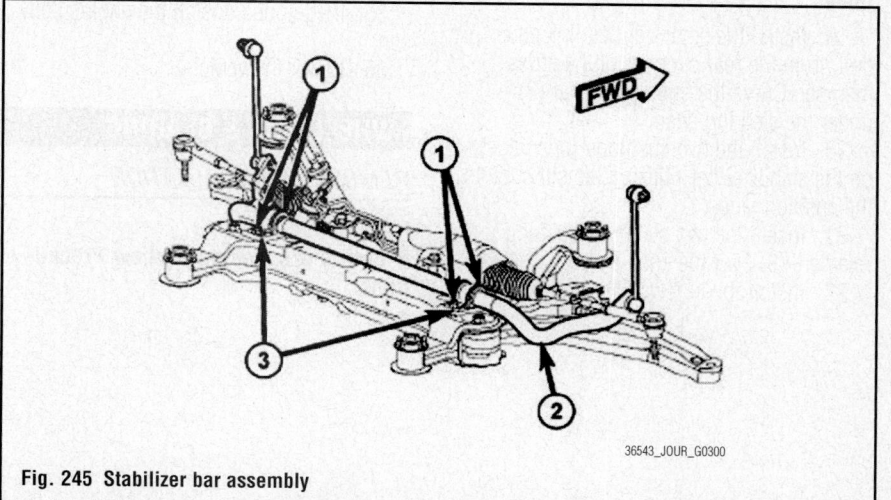

Fig. 245 Stabilizer bar assembly

10. Mark the location of the front crossmember on the body near each mounting bolt.

11. Support the crossmember with a transmission jack.

12. Remove the four mounting bolts securing the front crossmember to the body.

13. Remove the mounting screws securing the front crossmember reinforcement brackets (one each side of vehicle) to the body. Remove the brackets.

14. Slowly lower the crossmember using the jack until there is enough space present to remove the stabilizer bar between the rear of the crossmember and the body. Due to the fact that the fore-and-aft crossmember is still attached, do not lower crossmember any more than necessary to remove the stabilizer bar.

15. Remove the screws (1) securing the stabilizer bushing retainers (3) to the crossmember.

16. Remove the two stabilizer bushing retainers (3).

17. Utilizing the slit cut into the cushions (bushings), remove the two cushions from the stabilizer bar.

18. Remove the stabilizer bar (2) from the vehicle.

To install:

➡Before stabilizer bar installation, inspect the cushions and links for excessive wear, cracks, damage and distortion. Replace any pieces failing inspection.

➡Before installing the stabilizer bar, make sure the bar is not upside down. The stabilizer bar must be installed so that when in mounted position, the ends of the bar curve under the steering gear tie rods, up to the links.

19. Install the stabilizer bar, link ends first, from the rear over top of the crossmember. Curve the ends of the bar (2) under the steering gear.

20. Install the two cushions (bushings) on the stabilizer bar utilizing the slit cut into the cushion sides.

21. Install the two stabilizer bushing retainers (3) over the cushions.

22. Install the screws (1) securing the stabilizer bushing retainers (3) to the crossmember. Tighten all four stabilizer bar cushion retainer screws to 44 ft. lbs. (60 Nm).

23. Slowly raise the crossmember into mounted position using the transmission jack matching the crossmember to the marked locations on the body made during removal.

24. Position the front crossmember reinforcement brackets (one each side of vehicle) over the crossmember rear mounting bushings and install the mounting screws, but do not tighten at this time.

25. Install the four mounting bolts securing the front crossmember to the body. Tighten the crossmember mounting bolts to 100 ft. lbs. (135 Nm).

26. Tighten the crossmember reinforcement bracket mounting screws to 37 ft. lbs. (50 Nm).

27. Remove the transmission jack.

28. Remove the bungee cord or other supporting the steering gear.

29. Install the two bolts securing the steering gear to the crossmember. Tighten the steering gear mounting bolts to 74 ft. lbs. (100 Nm).

30. Position the heat shield over the steering gear. Install the mounting screws and push-pins. Tighten the screws to 53 inch lbs. (6 Nm).

31. Position the power steering hose routing clamps on the crossmember. Install and tighten the screws to 71 inch lbs. (8 Nm).

32. Attach the stabilizer bar link at each end of the stabilizer bar. At each link, install and tighten the nut while holding the stabilizer bar link lower stud stationary. Tighten the nuts to 35 ft. lbs. (48 Nm).

33. Install the rear engine mount.

34. Install the front engine mount through-bolt.

35. If equipped, install the engine belly pan.

36. Lower the vehicle.

WHEEL HUB & BEARING

REMOVAL & INSTALLATION

See Figure 246.

➡Before proceeding, review Precautions.

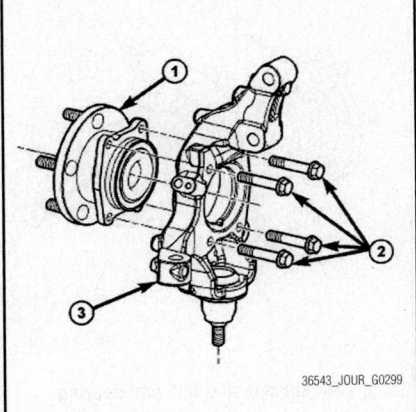

Fig. 246 Knuckle and hub and bearing assembly

1. Raise and support the vehicle.
2. Remove the wheel mounting nuts, then the tire and wheel assembly.
3. While a helper applies the brakes to keep the hub from rotating, remove the hub nut from the axle halfshaft.
4. Access and remove the front brake rotor.
5. Remove the four bolts (2) fastening the hub and bearing to the knuckle (3).
6. Slide the hub and bearing (1) off the halfshaft and out of the knuckle.

To install:

7. Install the hub and bearing (1) by sliding it over the halfshaft and into the knuckle.
8. Install the four bolts (2) fastening the hub and bearing (1) to the knuckle (3). Tighten the four bolts to 60 ft. lbs. (82 Nm).
9. Install the brake rotor, disc brake caliper and adapter.
10. Clean all foreign matter from the threads of the halfshaft outer C/V joint.
11. Install the hub nut on the end of the halfshaft and lightly tighten it.
12. While a helper applies the brakes to keep the hub from rotating, tighten the hub nut (1) to 97 ft. lbs. (132 Nm).
13. Install the tire and wheel assembly. Install and tighten wheel mounting nuts to 100 ft. lbs. (135 Nm).
14. Lower the vehicle.

PRECAUTIONS

✳✳ WARNING

Chrysler LLC does not manufacture any vehicles or replacement parts that contain asbestos. Aftermarket products may or may not contain asbestos. Refer to aftermarket product packaging for product information.

Whether the product contains asbestos or not, dust and dirt can accumulate on brake parts during normal use. Follow practices prescribed by appropriate regulations for the handling, processing and disposing of dust and debris.

✳✳ CAUTION

Only frame contact or wheel lift hoisting equipment can be used on this vehicle. It cannot be hoisted using equipment designed to lift a vehicle by the rear axle. If this type of hoisting equipment is used, damage to rear suspension components will occur.

✳✳ CAUTION

All-Wheel-Drive only - Wheel bearing damage will result if after loosening the hub nut, the vehicle is rolled on the ground or the weight of the vehicle is allowed to be supported by the tires for a length of time.

➡**If a rear suspension component becomes bent, damaged or fails, no attempt should be made to straighten or repair it. Always replace it with a new component.**

CONTROL ARMS/LINKS

REMOVAL & INSTALLATION

Lower Control Arm

See Figure 247.

1. Raise and support the vehicle.
2. Remove the wheel mounting nuts, then the tire and wheel assembly.
3. If equipped, while holding the stabilizer bar link lower stud stationary, remove the nut securing the link to the lower control arm.
4. If equipped with load-leveling shocks, support the lower shock with a jack using just enough force to allow easy removal of

the lower shock mounting bolt in the following step. Lower the jack following bolt removal.
5. Remove the lower shock mounting nut and bolt.
6. Remove the nut (2) and bolt (7) securing the lower control arm (3) to the knuckle (1).
7. Remove the nut (4) and bolt (6) securing the lower control arm (3) to the rear crossmember (5).
8. Remove the lower control arm (3).

To install:

9. Position the lower control arm (3) and install the bolt (6) and nut (4) securing the lower control arm to the crossmember (5). Do not tighten at this time.
10. Install the bolt (7) and nut (2) securing the lower control arm (3) to the knuckle (1). Do not tighten at this time.
11. If equipped with load-leveling shocks, place a jack against the lower shock eye and support the lower end of the shock assembly. Lift the shock assembly using the jack until the hole in the lower shock eye lines up with that in the lower control arm.
12. Install the mounting bolt and nut fastening the shock assembly to the lower control arm. Do not tighten at this time.

➡**When attaching a stabilizer bar link to the lower control arm it is important that the lower mounting stud be positioned properly. The lower mounting stud on the right side link needs to point toward the front of the vehicle when inserted through the lower control arm mounting flange. The left side link lower stud needs to point toward the rear of the vehicle. Otherwise the**

suspension geometry will not function properly.

✳✳ CAUTION

Before installing the nut in the following step, it is especially important to clean the threads and apply Mopar® Lock AND Seal Adhesive or equivalent.

13. If equipped, attach the stabilizer bar link to the lower control arm. Install the nut and while holding the stabilizer bar link lower stud stationary, tighten the nut to 35 ft. lbs. (48 Nm).
14. Install the tire and wheel assembly
15. Lower the vehicle.
16. Position the vehicle on an alignment rack/drive-on lift. Raise the vehicle as necessary to access mounting bolts and nuts.
17. Tighten the lower control arm mounting bolt nut at the crossmember to 77 ft. lbs. (105 Nm).
18. Tighten the lower control arm mounting bolt nut at the knuckle to 77 ft. lbs. (105 Nm).
19. Tighten the shock assembly lower mounting bolt nut to 73 ft. lbs. (99 Nm).
20. Perform wheel alignment as necessary.

Upper Control Arm

See Figure 248.

1. Raise and support the vehicle.
2. Remove the wheel mounting nuts, then the tire and wheel assembly.
3. Remove the nut (3) and bolt (4) securing the upper control arm (5) to the knuckle.
4. Remove the nut (2) and bolt (1) securing the upper control arm (5) to the crossmember.

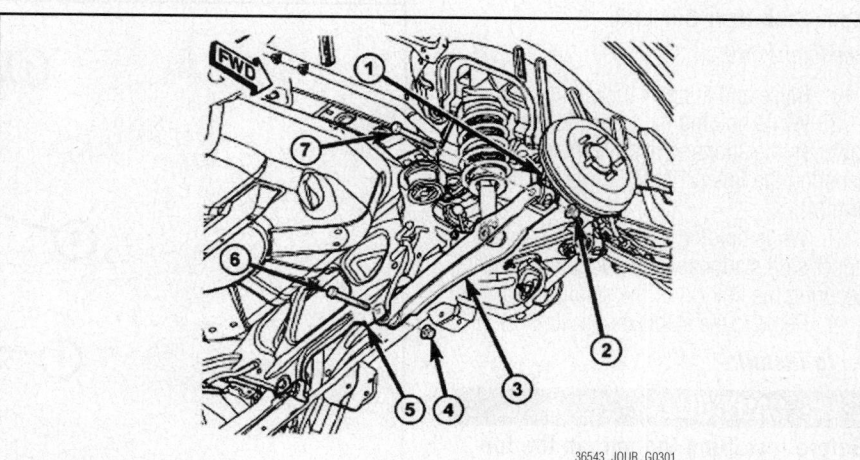

36543_JOUR_G0301

Fig. 247 Lower control arm

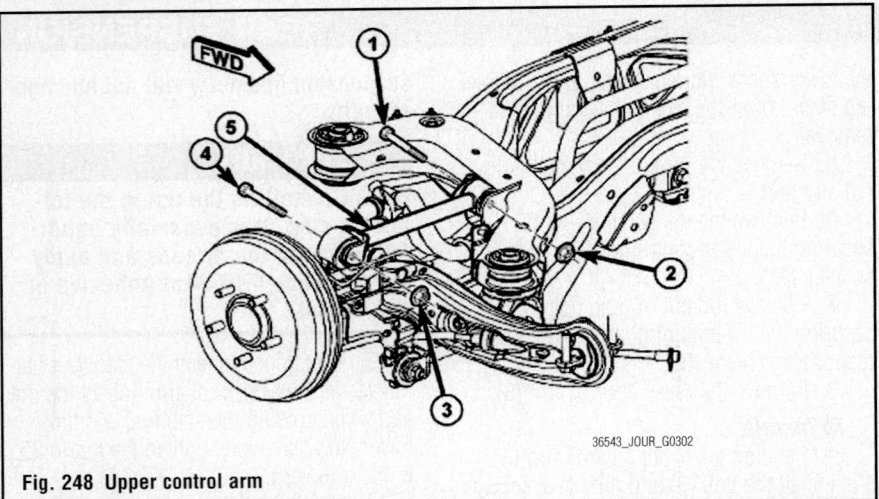

Fig. 248 Upper control arm

5. Remove the upper control arm (5).

To install:

6. Position the upper control arm (5) and install the bolt (1) and nut (2) securing the arm to the crossmember. Do not tighten at this time.

7. Install the bolt (4) and nut (3) securing the upper control arm (5) to the knuckle. Do not tighten at this time.

8. Install the tire and wheel assembly. Install and tighten the wheel mounting nuts (3) to 100 ft. lbs. (135 Nm).

9. Lower the vehicle.

10. Position the vehicle on an alignment rack/drive-on lift. Raise the vehicle as necessary to access mounting bolts and nuts.

11. Tighten the upper control arm mounting bolt nut at the crossmember to 77 ft. lbs. (105 Nm).

12. Tighten the upper control arm mounting bolt nut at the knuckle to 77 ft. lbs. (105 Nm).

13. Perform wheel alignment as necessary.

Rear Stabilizer Bar Link

See Figure 249.

1. Raise and support the vehicle.

2. While holding the stabilizer bar link lower stud stationary, remove the nut (3) securing the link (2) to the lower control arm (4).

3. While holding the stabilizer bar link upper stud stationary, remove the nut (5) securing the link (2) to the stabilizer bar (1).

4. Remove the stabilizer bar link (2).

To install:

✲✲ CAUTION

Before installing the nuts in the following steps, it is especially important to clean the threads and apply

Mopar® Lock AND Seal Adhesive or equivalent.

5. Install the stabilizer link (2) upper stud in the end of the stabilizer bar (1) from the inboard side. Install the nut (5) on the upper stud and while holding the stabilizer link stud stationary, tighten the nut to 35 ft. lbs. (48 Nm).

➡ When attaching a stabilizer bar link to the lower control arm it is important that the lower mounting stud be positioned properly. The lower mounting stud on the right side link needs to point toward the front of the vehicle when inserted through the lower control arm mounting flange. The left side link lower stud needs to point toward the rear of the vehicle. Otherwise the suspension geometry will not function properly.

6. Attach the stabilizer bar link (2) to the lower control arm (4). Install the nut (3) and while holding the stabilizer bar link lower

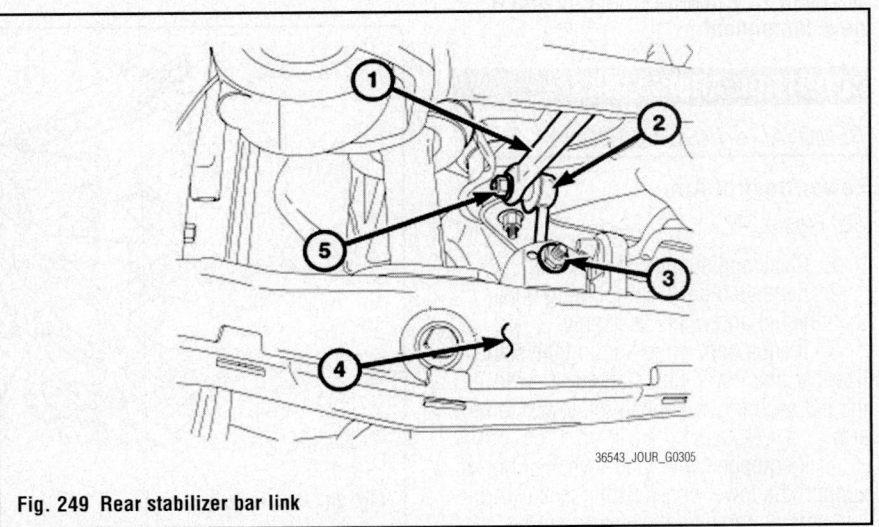

Fig. 249 Rear stabilizer bar link

stud stationary, tighten the nut (2) to 35 ft. lbs. (48 Nm).

7. Lower the vehicle.

Rear Toe Link

See Figure 250.

1. Raise and support the vehicle.

2. Remove the mounting bolt (2) and nut securing the toe link (3) to the knuckle.

3. Mark the position of the cam bolt cam on the crossmember using a paint marker or crayon. Do not use any type marker that will scratch or damage the surface of the crossmember.

4. While holding the cam bolt (4) head stationary, loosen and remove the toe link mounting cam bolt nut (3) and washer (1). Remove the cam bolt.

5. Remove the toe link (2).

To install:

✲✲ CAUTION

When installing the cam bolt (4) and washer make sure the cams stay inside the abutments built into the crossmember. Failure to do so can damage the abutments and make toe adjustment difficult.

6. Position the toe link (2) and install the cam bolt (4) from the front through the crossmember and link. Match the cam on the bolt to the marks made during removal or position the top of the cam to the 12 O'clock position.

7. Install the cam washer (1) and nut (3) securing the toe link (2) to the crossmember. Do not tighten at this time.

8. Install the mounting bolt (2) and nut securing the link to the knuckle. To install the bolt it may be necessary to flex the trailing link at the body mount bushing

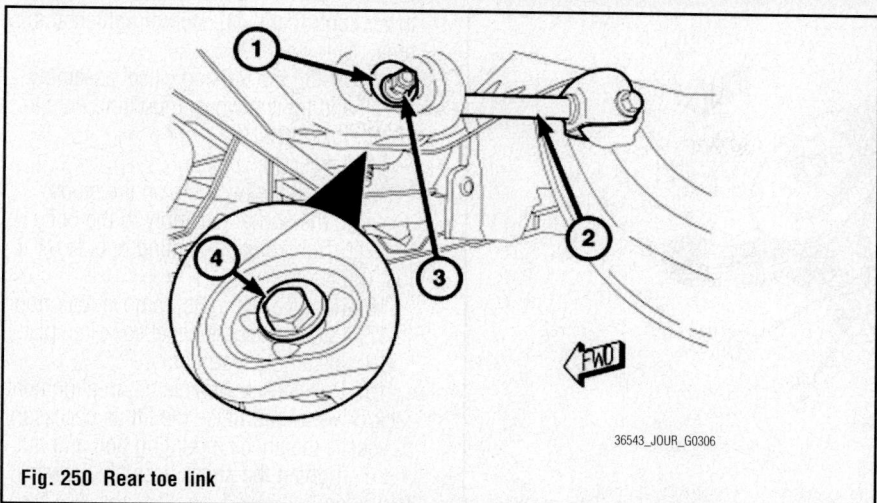

Fig. 250 Rear toe link

inward or outward using an appropriate prying tool. Do not tighten at this time.

9. Lower the vehicle.

10. Position the vehicle on an alignment rack/drive-on lift. Raise the vehicle as necessary to access mounting bolts and nuts.

11. Tighten the toe link mounting bolt nut at the knuckle to 77 ft. lbs. (105 Nm).

12. Perform wheel alignment as necessary.

13. Once rear toe is set, while holding the cam bolt (4) head stationary, tighten the toe link mounting cam bolt nut (3) to 26 ft. lbs. (35 Nm).

Rear Trailing Link

See Figure 251.

1. Raise and support the vehicle.

2. Remove the wheel mounting nuts, then the tire and wheel assembly.

3. Remove the screw securing the brake flex hose and tube bracket to the trailing link.

4. Remove the screw securing the wheel speed sensor routing clip to the trailing link.

5. Remove the three bolts securing the knuckle to the trailing link.

6. Remove the two bolts (2) fastening the leading end of the trailing link (3) to the body (1).

7. Remove the trailing link.

To install:

> ✳✳ **CAUTION**
>
> **Before installing the bolts in the following step, it is especially important to clean the threads and apply Mopar® Lock AND Seal Adhesive or equivalent.**

8. Position the trailing link and install the three bolts securing the trailing link to the knuckle. Be sure to include the parking brake cable routing clamp when installing the top mounting bolt. Tighten the mounting bolts to 44 ft. lbs. (60 Nm).

9. Position the forward end of the trailing link (3) on the body (1) and install the two mounting bolts (2). Do not tighten the bolts at this time.

10. Position the brake flex hose and tube bracket on the trailing link and install the mounting screw. Tighten the screw to 17 ft. lbs. (23 Nm).

11. Attach the wheel speed sensor routing clip to the trailing link using the mounting screw.

12. Install tire and wheel assembly. Install and tighten wheel mounting nuts to 100 ft. lbs. (135 Nm).

13. Lower the vehicle.

14. Position the vehicle on an alignment rack/drive-on lift. Raise the vehicle as necessary to access yet to be tightened mounting bolts.

15. Tighten the two mounting bolts fastening the leading end of the trailing link (3) to the body (1) to 81 ft. lbs. (110 Nm).

16. Perform wheel alignment as necessary.

SHOCK ABSORBER

REMOVAL & INSTALLATION

With Third Row Seating

See Figure 252.

➡ **Before proceeding, refer to Precautions.**

1. Access and remove the rear quarter trim panel.

2. Move insulation out of the way to access the shock assembly upper mounting nuts.

3. Remove the two nuts securing the shock assembly to the body bracket.

4. Raise and support the vehicle.

5. Remove the wheel mounting nuts, then the rear tire and wheel assembly.

6. If equipped with load-leveling shocks, support the lower shock with a jack using just enough force to allow easy removal of the lower shock mounting bolt in the following step. Lower the jack following bolt removal.

7. Remove the lower shock mounting nut (1) and bolt (4).

8. Lower the shock assembly (2) out of the body bracket and lift out over rear suspension.

To install:

➡ **When installing the shock assembly into the body bracket in the following step, be sure to position the upper mounting bracket so that the angular formed side (as viewed from above) of**

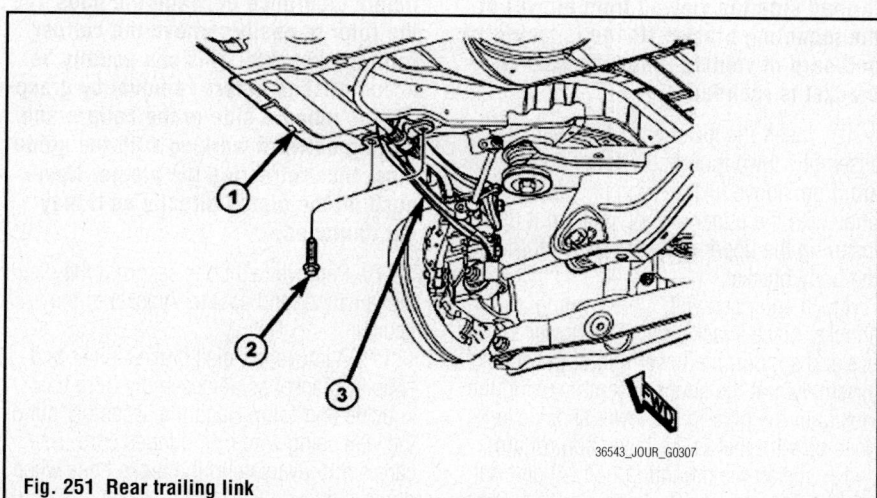

Fig. 251 Rear trailing link

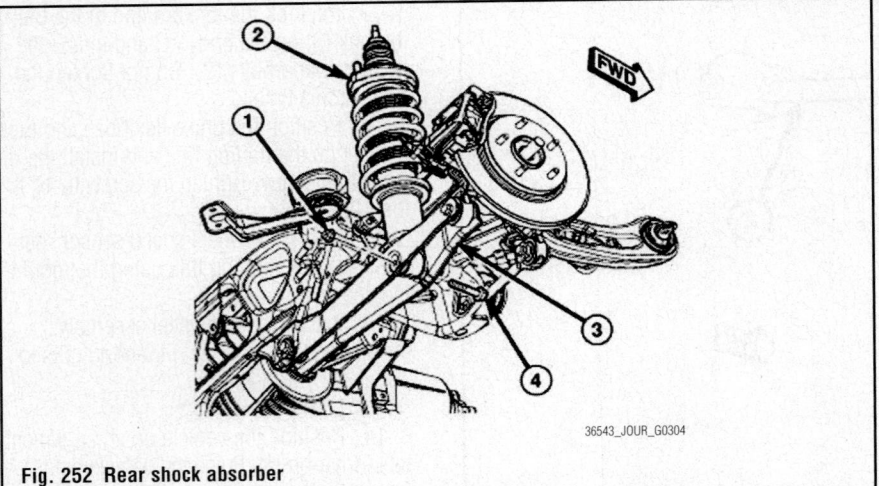

Fig. 252 Rear shock absorber

the mounting bracket flange is facing outboard of vehicle (opposite side of bracket is rounded).

9. Insert the lower end of the shock assembly down though the lower control arm from above just enough to clear the body with the upper mount, then lift it up, inserting the upper mounting studs through the body bracket.

10. If equipped with load-leveling shocks, place a jack against the lower shock eye and support the lower end of the shock assembly. Lift the shock assembly using the jack until the hole in the lower shock eye lines up with that in the lower control arm.

11. Install the mounting bolt (4) and nut (1) fastening the shock assembly (2) to the lower control arm (3). Do not tighten at this time.

12. Install the tire and wheel assembly. Install and tighten wheel mounting nuts to 100 ft. lbs. (135 Nm).

13. Lower the vehicle.

14. Install the two nuts on the studs securing the shock assembly to the body bracket. Tighten the mounting nuts to 41 ft. lbs. (55 Nm).

15. Install the rear quarter trim panel and components removed to access it.

16. Position the vehicle on an alignment rack/drive-on lift. Raise the lift as necessary to access the shock mounting bolt and nut.

17. Tighten the shock assembly lower mounting bolt nut (1) to 73 ft. lbs. (99 Nm).

Without Third Row Seating

➡**Before proceeding, refer to Precautions.**

1. Remove four nuts, remove load floor.

2. Open access panel by breaking perforations along panel, then folding panel upward.

3. Move insulation out of the way to access shock assembly upper mounting nuts.

4. Remove the two nuts securing the shock assembly to the body bracket.

5. Raise and support the vehicle.

6. Remove the wheel mounting nuts, then the rear tire and wheel assembly.

7. If equipped with load-leveling shocks, support the lower shock with a jack using just enough force to allow easy removal of the lower shock mounting bolt in the following step. Lower the jack following bolt removal.

8. Remove the lower shock mounting nut (1) and bolt (4).

9. Lower the shock assembly (2) out of the body bracket and lift out over rear suspension.

To install:

➡**When installing the shock assembly into the body bracket in the following step, be sure to position the upper mounting bracket so that the angular formed side (as viewed from above) of the mounting bracket flange is facing outboard of vehicle (opposite side of bracket is rounded).**

10. Insert the lower end of the shock assembly down though the lower control arm from above just enough to clear the body with the upper mount, then lift it up, inserting the upper mounting studs through the body bracket.

11. If equipped with load-leveling shocks, place a jack against the lower shock eye and support the lower end of the shock assembly. Lift the shock assembly using the jack until the hole in the lower shock eye lines up with that in the lower control arm.

12. Install the mounting bolt (4) and nut (1) fastening the shock assembly (2) to the

lower control arm (3). Do not tighten at this time.

13. Install the tire and wheel assembly. Install and tighten wheel mounting nuts to 100 ft. lbs. (135 Nm).

14. Lower the vehicle.

15. Install the two nuts on the studs securing the shock assembly to the body bracket. Tighten the mounting nuts to 41 ft. lbs. (55 Nm).

16. Remove four nuts, remove load floor.

17. Fold the access panel back into place.

18. Install the load floor.

19. Position the vehicle on an alignment rack/drive-on lift. Raise the lift as necessary to access the shock mounting bolt and nut.

20. Tighten the shock assembly lower mounting bolt nut (1) to 73 ft. lbs. (99 Nm).

WHEEL HUB & BEARING

REMOVAL & INSTALLATION

All Wheel Drive (AWD) Models

See Figure 253.

➡**Before proceeding, refer to Precautions.**

1. Raise and support the vehicle.

2. Remove the wheel mounting nuts, then the tire and wheel assembly.

3. Remove the cotter pin from the hub nut on the end of the axle halfshaft.

4. While a helper applies the brakes to keep the hub from rotating, remove the hub nut and washer from the axle halfshaft.

5. Tap the end of the halfshaft inward, loosening it from the hub and bearing. This will also allow more room to access the hub and bearing mounting bolts in a later step.

➡**In some cases, it may be necessary to retract the caliper piston in its bore a small amount in order to provide sufficient clearance between the pads and the rotor to easily remove the caliper from the knuckle. This can usually be accomplished before removal by grasping the inboard side of the caliper and pulling outward working with the guide pins, thus retracting the piston. Never push on the piston directly as it may get damaged.**

6. Remove two bolts securing the disc brake caliper and adapter bracket to the knuckle.

7. Remove the disc brake caliper and adapter bracket as an assembly from the knuckle and rotor. Hang the assembly out of the way using wire or a bungee cord. Use care not to overextend the brake hose when doing this.

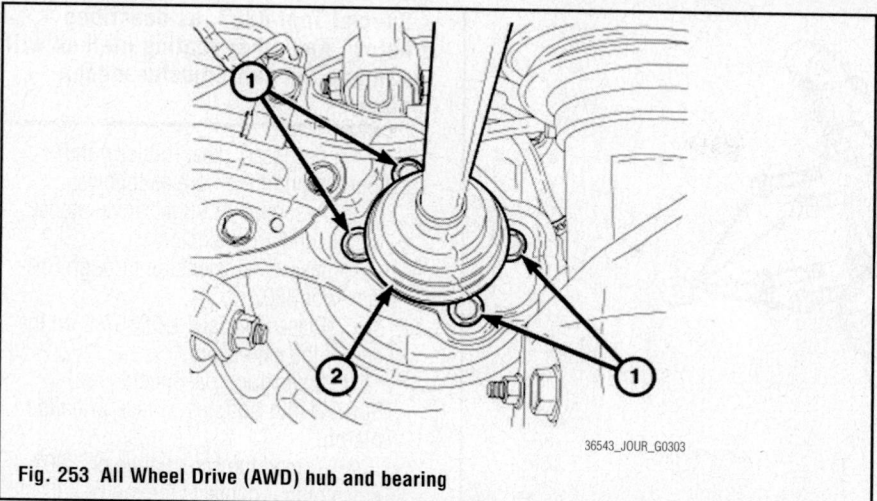

Fig. 253 All Wheel Drive (AWD) hub and bearing

8. Remove any retaining clips, then slide the brake rotor off the hub and bearing.

✳✳ CAUTION

Prior to removal, clean area around sensor head to help prevent contaminants from entering bearing when sensor head is removed.

9. Remove the screw fastening the speed sensor head to the hub and bearing.

10. Remove the wheel speed sensor head from the hub and bearing, then pass it through the brake shield.

11. Remove the four bolts (1) securing the hub and bearing to the knuckle.

12. Remove the hub and bearing from the knuckle and halfshaft (2).

To install:

13. With the brake shield in place on the knuckle, slide the hub and bearing over the axle halfshaft and position it on the knuckle.

14. Install the four bolts (1) securing the hub and bearing to the knuckle. Tighten the bolts to 77 ft. lbs. (105 Nm).

✳✳ CAUTION

Ensure that sensor mounting surface on bearing is clean before sensor installation.

15. Pass the wheel speed sensor head through the hole in the brake shield, then push it into the mounting hole in hub and bearing and align the mounting screw hole.

16. Install a NEW mounting screw. Tighten the mounting screw to 55 inch lbs. (6 Nm).

17. Clean the rotor mounting face of the hub and bearing to remove any dirt or corrosion.

18. Install the brake rotor over the hub and bearing.

✳✳ CAUTION

If the brake rotor or brake pads are being replaced, the rear caliper piston must be seated (bottomed) to compensate for the new brake rotor or lining. Because the parking brake self-adjuster mechanism is attached to the piston, a special seating method is required. The only acceptable method is by rotating the piston back into the bore using Retractor, Special Tool 8807, as described below. Any other seating method will damage the self-adjuster mechanism.

19. If necessary, seat (bottom) the caliper piston in the bore as follows:

a. Assemble a 3/8 in. drive ratchet handle and an extension.

b. Insert the extension through Special Tool 8807-1.

c. Place Special Tool 8807-2 on the end of the extension.

d. Insert lugs on Special Tool 8807-2 into notches in face of caliper piston.

e. Thread the screw drive on 8807-1 down until it contacts the top of 8807-2 which is against the caliper piston. Do not over tighten the screw-drive. Damage to the piston can occur.

f. Turn 8807-2 with the ratchet, rotating the piston in a clockwise direction until fully seated (bottomed) in the bore. It may be necessary to turn 8807-1 with 8807-2 to start the process of piston retraction.

20. Install the disc brake caliper and adapter bracket (2) over the knuckle and rotor as an assembly.

21. Install the two bolts securing the disc brake caliper and adapter bracket to the knuckle. Tighten the mounting bolts to 74 ft. lbs. (100 Nm).

22. Clean all foreign matter from the threads of the halfshaft outer C/V joint.

23. Install the washer and hub nut on the end of the halfshaft and snug it.

24. While a helper applies the brakes to keep the hub from rotating, tighten the hub nut to 181 ft. lbs. (245 Nm).

25. Insert the cotter pin through the notches in the nut and the hole in halfshaft. If the notches in the nut do not line up with the hole in the halfshaft, continue to tighten the nut until they do. Do not loosen the nut.

26. Wrap the cotter pin ends tightly around the lock nut.

27. Install tire and wheel assembly. Install and tighten wheel mounting nuts to 100 ft. lbs. (135 Nm).

28. Lower the vehicle.

29. Pump the brake pedal several times to ensure the vehicle has a firm brake pedal before moving it. Check the brake fluid level.

Front Wheel Drive (FWD) Models
See Figure 254.

➡ **Before proceeding, refer to Precautions.**

1. Raise and support the vehicle.

2. Remove the wheel mounting nuts, then the rear tire and wheel assembly.

➡ **In some cases, it may be necessary to retract the caliper piston in its bore a small amount in order to provide sufficient clearance between the pads and the rotor to easily remove the caliper from the knuckle. This can usually be accomplished before removal by grasping the inboard side of the caliper and pulling outward working with the guide pins, thus retracting the piston. Never push on the piston directly as it may get damaged.**

3. Remove two bolts securing the disc brake caliper and adapter bracket to the knuckle.

4. Remove the disc brake caliper and adapter bracket as an assembly from the knuckle and rotor. Hang the assembly out of the way using wire or a bungee cord. Use care not to overextend the brake hose when doing this.

5. Remove any retaining clips, then slide the brake rotor off the hub and bearing.

✳✳ CAUTION

Prior to removal, clean area around sensor head to help prevent contaminants from entering bearing when sensor head is removed.

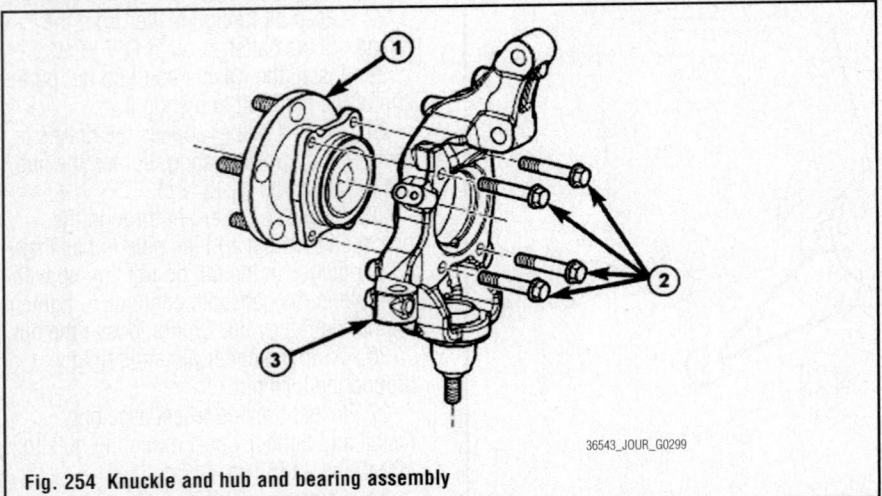

36543_JOUR_G0299

Fig. 254 Knuckle and hub and bearing assembly

6. Remove the screw fastening the speed sensor head to the hub and bearing.

7. Remove the wheel speed sensor head from the hub and bearing, then pass it through the brake shield.

8. Remove the four bolts (2) securing the hub and bearing (1) to the knuckle (3).

9. Remove the hub and bearing.

To install:

10. With the brake shield in place on the knuckle, slide and position the hub and bearing into the knuckle.

11. Install the four bolts securing the hub and bearing to the knuckle. Tighten the bolts to 77 ft. lbs. (105 Nm).

✳✳ CAUTION

Ensure that sensor mounting surface on bearing is clean before sensor installation.

12. Pass the wheel speed sensor head through the hole in the brake shield, then push it into the mounting hole in hub and bearing and align the mounting screw hole.

13. Install a NEW mounting screw. Tighten the mounting screw to 55 inch lbs. (6 Nm).

14. Clean the rotor mounting face of the hub and bearing (1) to remove any dirt or corrosion.

15. Install the brake rotor over the hub and bearing.

✳✳ CAUTION

If the brake rotor or brake pads are being replaced, the rear caliper piston must be seated (bottomed) to compensate for the new brake rotor or lining. Because the parking brake self-adjuster mechanism is attached to the piston, a special seating method is required. The only acceptable method is by rotating the piston back into the bore using Retractor, Special Tool 8807, as described below. Any other seating method will damage the self-adjuster mechanism.

16. If necessary, seat (bottom) the caliper piston in the bore as follows:

a. Assemble a 3/8 in. drive ratchet handle and an extension.

b. Insert the extension through Special Tool 8807-1.

c. Place Special Tool 8807-2 on the end of the extension.

d. Insert lugs on Special Tool 8807-2 into notches in face of caliper piston.

e. Thread the screw drive on 8807-1 down until it contacts the top of 8807-2 which is against the caliper piston. Do not over tighten the screw-drive. Damage to the piston can occur.

f. Turn 8807-2 with the ratchet, rotating the piston in a clockwise direction until fully seated (bottomed) in the bore. It may be necessary to turn 8807-1 with 8807-2 to start the process of piston retraction.

17. Install the disc brake caliper and adapter bracket over the knuckle and rotor as an assembly.

18. Install the two bolts securing the disc brake caliper and adapter bracket to the knuckle. Tighten the mounting bolts to 74 ft. lbs. (100 Nm).

19. Install the tire and wheel assembly. Install and tighten the wheel mounting nuts (3) to 100 ft. lbs. (135 Nm).

20. Lower the vehicle.

21. Pump the brake pedal several times to ensure the vehicle has a firm brake pedal before moving it. Check the brake fluid level.

DODGE AND JEEP

13

Liberty • Nitro

SPECIFICATIONS AND MAINTENANCE CHARTS

ENGINE AND VEHICLE IDENTIFICATION

		Engine						Model Year	
Code	Liters (cc)	Cu. In.	Cyl.	Fuel Sys.	Engine Type	Eng. Mfg.	Code	Year
K	3.7 (3701)	226	6	MFI	SOHC	Chrysler	8	2008
X	4.0 (3966)	244	6	MFI	SOHC	Chrysler	9	2009

MFI: Multi-port Fuel Injection

SOHC: Single Overhead Camshaft

36543_LIBE_C0001

GENERAL ENGINE SPECIFICATIONS

Year	Model	Engine Displ. Liters	Engine VIN	Net Horsepower @ rpm	Net Torque @ rpm (ft. lbs.)	Bore x Stroke (in.)	Comp. Ratio	Oil Pressure @ rpm
2008	Liberty	3.7	K	210@5200	235@4000	3.66x3.40	9.1:1	25-110@3000
	Nitro	3.7	K	210@5200	235@4000	3.66x3.40	9.1:1	25-110@3000
		4.0	X	255@5800	265@4200	3.78x3.58	10.3:1	45-105@3000
2009	Liberty	3.7	K	210@5200	235@4000	3.66x3.40	9.1:1	25-110@3000
	Nitro	3.7	K	210@5200	235@4000	3.66x3.40	9.1:1	25-110@3000
		4.0	X	255@5800	265@4200	3.78x3.58	10.3:1	45-105@3000

36543_LIBE_C0002

GASOLINE ENGINE TUNE-UP SPECIFICATIONS

Year	Engine Displacement Liters	Engine VIN	Spark Plug Gap (in.)	Ignition Timing (deg.)	Fuel Pump (psi)	Idle Speed (rpm)	Valve Clearance Intake	Valve Clearance Exhaust
2008	3.7	K	0.042	①	53-63	①	HYD	HYD
	4.0	X	0.050	①	53-63	①	HYD	HYD
2009	3.7	K	0.042	①	53-63	①	HYD	HYD
	4.0	X	0.050	①	53-63	①	HYD	HYD

Note: The information on the Vehicle Emission Control label must be used, if different from the figures in this chart.

HYD: Hydraulic

① Ignition timing and idle speed are controlled by the PCM. No adjustment is necessary.

36543_LIBE_C0003

CAPACITIES

Year	Model	Engine Displ. Liters	Engine VIN	Engine Oil with Filter	Transmission (pts.) Man.	Transmission (pts.) Auto.	Transfer Case (pts.)	Drive Axle Front (pts.)	Drive Axle Rear (pts.)	Fuel Tank (gal.)	Cooling System (qts.)
2008	Liberty	3.7	K	5.0	3.17	①	②	2.6	4.4	19.5	14.0
	Nitro	3.7	K	5.0	3.17	①	②	2.6	4.4	19.5	14.0
		4.0	X	5.5	3.17	①	②	2.6	4.4	19.5	14.0
2009	Liberty	3.7	K	5.0	3.17	①	②	2.6	4.4	19.5	14.0
	Nitro	3.7	K	5.0	3.17	①	②	2.6	4.4	19.5	14.0
		4.0	X	5.5	3.17	①	②	2.6	4.4	19.5	14.0

NOTE: All capacities are approximate. Add fluid gradually and check to be sure a proper fluid level is obtained.

For rear axles, when equipped with Trac Lok, add 4 oz. of limited slip additive.

Capacities for automatic trnasmissions is for service.

① NAG1: 10.6
42RLE: 8.0

② MP1522: 3.8 pts.
MP3022: 4.0 pts.

36543_LIBE_C0004

FLUID SPECIFICATIONS

Year	Model	Engine Displacement Liters	Engine ID/VIN	Engine Oil	Auto. Trans.	Transfer Case	Drive Axle	Power Steering Fluid	Brake Master Cylinder
2008	Liberty	3.7	K	5W-20	Mopar ATF+4	Mopar ATF+4	①	Mopar ATF+4	DOT-3
	Nitro	3.7	K	5W-20	Mopar ATF+4	Mopar ATF+4	①	Mopar ATF+4	DOT-3
		4.0	X	10W-30	Mopar ATF+4	Mopar ATF+4	①	Mopar ATF+4	DOT-3
2009	Liberty	3.7	K	5W-20	Mopar ATF+4	Mopar ATF+4	①	Mopar ATF+4	DOT-3
	Nitro	3.7	K	5W-20	Mopar ATF+4	Mopar ATF+4	①	Mopar ATF+4	DOT-3
		4.0	X	10W-30	Mopar ATF+4	Mopar ATF+4	①	Mopar ATF+4	DOT-3

DOT: Department Of Transpotation

① Front axle: GL5 80W-90

Rear axle: 75W-140 Synthetic

36543_LIBE_C0005

VALVE SPECIFICATIONS

Year	Engine Displ. Liters	Engine VIN	Seat Angle (deg.)	Face Angle (deg.)	Spring Test Pressure (lbs. @ in.)	Spring Installed Height (in.)	Stem-to-Guide Clearance (in.)		Stem Diameter (in.)	
							Intake	Exhaust	Intake	Exhaust
2008	3.7	K	44.5-45	44.5-45	221-242@ 1.107	1.619	0.0008-0.0028	0.0019-0.0039	0.2729-0.2739	0.2717-0.2728
	4.0	X	44.5-45	44.5-45	①	1.496	0.0009-0.0026	0.0020-0.0037	0.2730-0.2737	0.2719-0.2726
2009	3.7	K	44.5-45	44.5-45	221-242@ 1.107	1.619	0.0008-0.0028	0.0019-0.0039	0.2729-0.2739	0.2717-0.2728
	4.0	X	44.5-45	44.5-45	①	1.496	0.0009-0.0026	0.0020-0.0037	0.2730-0.2737	0.2719-0.2726

① Intake Valve Closed: 69.5-80.5 lbs. @ 1.496 in.

Exhaust Valve Closed: 79.9-90.1 @ 1.496 in

Inake Valve Open: 145.3-160.7 @ 122 in.

Exhaust Valve Closed: 195.8-212.2 @ 1.22 in.

36543_LIBE_C0006

CAMSHAFT AND BEARING SPECIFICATIONS CHART

All measurements are given in inches.

Year	Engine Displacement Liters	Engine VIN	Journal Diameter	Brg. Oil Clearance	Shaft End-play	Runout	Journal Bore	Lobe Lift	
								Intake	Exhaust
2008	3.7	K	1.0227-1.0235	0.0010-0.0026	0.0030-0.0079	NS	NS	NS	NS
	4.0	X	1.6905-1.6913	0.0010-0.0040	0.002-0.0020	NS	NS	NS	NS
2009	3.7	K	1.0227-1.0235	0.0010-0.0026	0.0030-0.0079	NS	NS	NS	NS
	4.0	X	1.6905-1.6913	0.0010-0.0040	0.002-0.0020	NS	NS	NS	NS

NS: Not Supplied by manufacturer

36543_LIBE_C0007

CRANKSHAFT AND CONNECTING ROD SPECIFICATIONS

All measurements are given in inches.

Year	Engine Displ. Liters	Engine VIN	Crankshaft				Connecting Rod		
			Main Brg. Journal Dia.	Main Brg. Oil Clearance	Shaft End-play	Thrust on No.	Journal Diameter	Oil Clearance	Side Clearance
2008	3.7	K	2.4996-2.5005	0.0020-0.0034	0.0021-0.0112	2	2.2794-2.2797	0.0004-0.0019	0.0040-0.0138
	4.0	X	2.7170-2.7160	0.0013-0.0024	0.002-0.010	2	2.2828-2.2835	0.0009-0.0021	0.0153
2009	3.7	K	2.4996-2.5005	0.0020-0.0034	0.0021-0.0112	2	2.2794-2.2797	0.0004-0.0019	0.0040-0.0138
	4.0	X	2.7170-2.7160	0.0013-0.0024	0.002-0.010	2	2.2828-2.2835	0.0009-0.0021	0.0153

36543_LIBE_C0008

PISTON AND RING SPECIFICATIONS

All measurements are given in inches.

Year	Engine Displ. Liters	Engine VIN	Piston Clearance	Ring Gap			Ring Side Clearance		
				Top Compression	Bottom Compression	Oil Control	Top Compression	Bottom Compression	Oil Control
2008	3.7	K	0.0014	0.0146-0.0249	0.0146-0.0249	0.0100-0.0300	0.0020-0.0037	0.0016-0.0031	0.0007-0.0091
	4.0	X	0.0030-0.0018	0.008-0.014	0.008-0.016	0.010-0.030	0.0016-0.0031	0.0016-0.0031	0.0015-0.0073
2009	3.7	K	0.0014	0.0146-0.0249	0.0146-0.0249	0.0100-0.0300	0.0020-0.0037	0.0016-0.0031	0.0007-0.0091
	4.0	X	0.0030-0.0018	0.008-0.014	0.008-0.016	0.010-0.030	0.0016-0.0031	0.0016-0.0031	0.0015-0.0073

36543_LIBE_C0009

TORQUE SPECIFICATIONS

All readings in ft. lbs.

Year	Engine Displ. Liters	Engine VIN	Cylinder Head Bolts	Main Bearing Bolts	Rod Bearing Bolts	Crankshaft Damper Bolts	Flywheel Bolts	Manifold		Spark Plugs	Oil Pan Drain Plug
								Intake	Exhaust		
2008	3.7	K	①	②	③	130	70	9	18	20	25
	4.0	X	④	⑤	⑥	70	70	⑦	⑧	20	20
2009	3.7	K	①	②	③	130	70	9	18	20	25
	4.0	X	④	⑤	⑥	70	70	⑦	⑧	20	20

① Step 1: Bolts 1-8 to 20 ft. lbs.
  Step 2: Bolts 1-10, verify torque
  Step 3: Bolts 9-12 to 10 ft. lbs.
  Step 4: Bolts 1-8, plus 90 degrees
  Step 5: Bolts 9-12 to 19 ft. lbs.

② Bed plate bolt sequence. Refer to illustration
  Step 1: Hand tighten bolts 1D,1G, 1F until bedplate contacts block.
  Step 2: Tighten bolts 1A - 1J to 40 ft. lbs.
  Step 3: Tighten bolts 1 - 8 to 5 ft. lbs.
  Step 4: Turn bolts 1 - 8 an additional 90 degrees
  Step 5: Tighten bolts A - E to 20 ft. lbs.

③ 20 ft. lbs. plus 90 degrees

④ Step 1: 45 ft. lbs.
  Step 2: 65 ft. lbs.
  Step 3: 65 ft. lbs.
  Step 4: Plus 90 degrees

⑤ Refer to the procedure.
  Step 1: Inner 15 ft. lbs. plus 1/4 turn
  Step 2: Outer 20 ft. lbs. plus 1/4 turn
  Step 3: Lateral bolts 250 inch lbs.

⑥ Step 1: 20 ft. lbs.
  Step 2: plus 90 degrees

⑦ Lower manifold:
  Step 1: 250 inch lbs.
  Upper manifold: 105 inch lbs.
  Step 1: 105 inch lbs.

⑧ 250 inch. lbs.

36543_LIBE_C0010

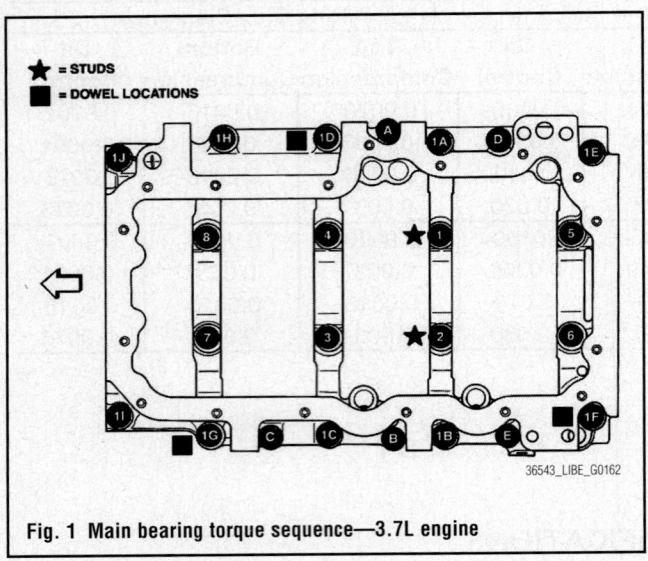

Fig. 1 Main bearing torque sequence—3.7L engine

36543_LIBE_G0162

WHEEL ALIGNMENT

| Year | Model | | Caster | | Camber | | Toe-in (deg.) |
			Range (+/-Deg.)	Preferred Setting (Deg.)	Range (+/-Deg.)	Preferred Setting (Deg.)	
2008	Liberty	F	0.50	3.300	-0.375	-0.20	0.075-0.325
		R	NA	NA	-0.625-+0.125	-0.25	-0.16-+0.66
	Nitro	F	0.50	3.300	-0.375	-0.20	0.075-0.325
		R	NA	NA	-0.625-+0.125	-0.25	-0.16-+0.66
2009	Liberty	F	0.50	3.300	-0.375	-0.20	0.075-0.325
		R	NA	NA	-0.625-+0.125	-0.25	-0.16-+0.66
	Nitro	F	0.50	3.300	-0.375	-0.20	0.075-0.325
		R	NA	NA	-0.625-+0.125	-0.25	-0.16-+0.66

NA: Not Available

36543_LIBE_C0011

TIRE, WHEEL AND BALL JOINT SPECIFICATIONS

Year	Model	OEM Tires Standard	OEM Tires Optional	Tire Pressures (psi) Front	Tire Pressures (psi) Rear	Wheel Size	Ball Joint Inspection	Lug Nut Torque (ft. lbs.)
2008	Liberty	P225/75R16	P235/65R17 P245/50R20	①	①	NS	②	85-115
	Nitro	P225/75R16	P235/65R17 P245/50R20	①	①	NS	②	85-115
2009	Liberty	P225/75R16	P235/65R17 P245/50R20	①	①	NS	②	85-115
	Nitro	P225/75R16	P235/65R17 P245/50R20	①	①	NS	②	85-115

NS: Not supplied

OEM: Original Equipment Manufacturer

STD: Standard

OPT: Optional

① See placard on vehicle

② Replace if any measurable movement is found.

36543_LIBE_C0012

BRAKE SPECIFICATIONS

All measurements in inches unless noted

Year	Model		Brake Disc Original Thickness	Brake Disc Minimum Thickness	Brake Disc Maximum Run-out	Brake Drum Original Inside Diameter	Brake Drum Max. Wear Limit	Brake Drum Maximum Machine Diameter	Minimum Lining Thickness	Caliper Mounting Bolts (ft. lbs.)
2008	Liberty	F	1.100	1.039	0.004	NA	NA	NA	0.04	28
		R	0.472	0.409	0.004	NA	NA	NA	0.04	28
	Nitro	F	1.100	1.039	0.004	NA	NA	NA	0.04	28
		R	0.472	0.409	0.004	NA	NA	NA	0.04	28
2009	Liberty	F	1.100	1.039	0.004	NA	NA	NA	0.04	28
		R	0.472	0.409	0.004	NA	NA	NA	0.04	28
	Nitro	F	1.100	1.039	0.004	NA	NA	NA	0.04	28
		R	0.472	0.409	0.004	NA	NA	NA	0.04	28

F- Front

R - Rear

NA Not applicable

36543_LIBE_C0013

SCHEDULED MAINTENANCE INTERVALS
Jeep Liberty & Dodge Nitro

TO BE SERVICED	TYPE OF SERVICE	VEHICLE MILEAGE INTERVAL (x1000)												
		6	12	18	24	30	36	42	48	54	60	66	72	84
Engine oil & filter ①	R	✓	✓	✓	✓	✓	✓	✓	✓	✓	✓	✓	✓	✓
Tires	Rotate	✓	✓	✓	✓	✓	✓	✓	✓	✓	✓	✓	✓	✓
A/C filter	R								✓					
Brake linings	I		✓		✓		✓		✓		✓		✓	
Engine air filter	S/I	✓	✓	✓	✓		✓	✓	✓	✓		✓	✓	✓
Engine air filter	R					✓					✓			
CV joints	I		✓		✓		✓		✓		✓		✓	
Exhaust system	I		✓		✓		✓		✓		✓		✓	
Suspension componets	I		✓		✓		✓		✓		✓		✓	
Spark plugs (3.7L)	R					✓					✓			
PCV valve	I/R										✓			
Rear axle fluid	R	Every 48,000 miles												
Front axle fluid *	R	Every 48,000 miles												
Transfer case fluid *	R	Every 60,000 miles												
Engine coolant	R	Every 60,000 miles												
Ignition cables	R	Every 60,000 miles												
Power steering fluid	R	Every 60,000 miles												
Auto. trans. fluid and filter *	R	Every 60,000 miles												
Accessory drive belt	I/R	Every 72,000 miles												
Spark plugs (4.0L)	R	Every 102,000 miles												
Timing belt (4.0L)	R	Every 102,000 miles												

R: Replace   S: Service   I: Inspect   Adj: Adjust

* Inspect every 24K miles. For police, taxi, fleet, off-road, or frequent trailer towing.

The above schedule is to be used if you drive under any of the following conditions:

Driving in temperatures under 32 degrees F

Stop and go traffic

Extensive engine idling

Driving in dusty conditions

Frequent trips under 10 miles

More than 50 % of your driving is in hot weather (90 deg. F) above 50 miles per hour

Trailer towing

Taxi, police or delivery service

If none of these conditions is met, double the maintenance intervals

① Oil Change Indicator System

On Electronic Vehicle Information Center (EVIC) equipped vehicles, "Oil Change Required" is displayed in the EVIC and a single chime sounds, indicating that an oil change is necessary. On non-EVIC equipped vehicles, "Change Oil" flashes in the instrument cluster and a single chime sounds indicating that an oil change is necessary. Illumination of the oil change message is based on the operating conditions of the vehicle. When the message is illuminated, the vehicle must be serviced within 500 miles.

The oil change indicator will not monitor the time since the last oil change. Change the oil if it has been more than 6 months since the last oil change, even if the oil change indicator message is not illuminated.

Under no circumstances should oil change intervals exceed 6,000 miles or 6 months, whichever comes first.

To reset the oil change indicator, perform the following procedure:

1. Turn the ignition switch to the ON position. Do not start the engine.

2. Fully press the accelerator pedal 3 times within 10 seconds.

3. Turn the ignition switch to the LOCK position.

If the indicator message illuminates when the vehicle is started, repeat the procedure.

36543_LIBE_C0014

PRECAUTIONS

Before servicing any vehicle, please be sure to read all of the following precautions, which deal with personal safety, prevention of component damage, and important points to take into consideration when servicing a motor vehicle:

• Never open, service or drain the radiator or cooling system when the engine is hot; serious burns can occur from the steam and hot coolant.

• Observe all applicable safety precautions when working around fuel. Whenever servicing the fuel system, always work in a well-ventilated area. Do not allow fuel spray or vapors to come in contact with a spark, open flame, or excessive heat (a hot drop light, for example). Keep a dry chemical fire extinguisher near the work area. Always keep fuel in a container specifically designed for fuel storage; also, always properly seal fuel containers to avoid the possibility of fire or explosion. Refer to the additional fuel system precautions later in this section.

• Fuel injection systems often remain pressurized, even after the engine has been turned **OFF**. The fuel system pressure must be relieved before disconnecting any fuel lines. Failure to do so may result in fire and/or personal injury.

• Brake fluid often contains polyglycol ethers and polyglycols. Avoid contact with the eyes and wash your hands thoroughly after handling brake fluid. If you do get brake fluid in your eyes, flush your eyes with clean, running water for 15 minutes. If eye irritation persists, or if you have taken brake fluid internally, IMMEDIATELY seek medical assistance.

• The EPA warns that prolonged contact with used engine oil may cause a number of skin disorders, including cancer. You should make every effort to minimize your exposure to used engine oil. Protective gloves should be worn when changing oil. Wash your hands and any other exposed skin areas as soon as possible after exposure to used engine oil. Soap and water, or waterless hand cleaner should be used.

• All new vehicles are now equipped with an air bag system, often referred to as a Supplemental Restraint System (SRS) or Supplemental Inflatable Restraint (SIR) system. The system must be disabled before performing service on or around system components, steering column, instrument panel components, wiring and sensors. Failure to follow safety and disabling procedures could result in accidental air bag deployment, possible personal injury and unnecessary system repairs.

• Always wear safety goggles when working with, or around, the air bag system. When carrying a non-deployed air bag, be sure the bag and trim cover are pointed away from your body. When placing a non-deployed air bag on a work surface, always face the bag and trim cover upward, away from the surface. This will reduce the motion of the module if it is accidentally deployed. Refer to the additional air bag system precautions later in this section.

• Clean, high quality brake fluid from a sealed container is essential to the safe and proper operation of the brake system. You should always buy the correct type of brake fluid for your vehicle. If the brake fluid becomes contaminated, completely flush the system with new fluid. Never reuse any brake fluid. Any brake fluid that is removed from the system should be discarded. Also, do not allow any brake fluid to come in contact with a painted surface; it will damage the paint.

• Never operate the engine without the proper amount and type of engine oil; doing so WILL result in severe engine damage.

• Timing belt maintenance is extremely important. Many models utilize an interference-type, non-freewheeling engine. If the timing belt breaks, the valves in the cylinder head may strike the pistons, causing potentially serious (also time-consuming and expensive) engine damage. Refer to the maintenance interval charts for the recommended replacement interval for the timing belt, and to the timing belt section for belt replacement and inspection.

• Disconnecting the negative battery cable on some vehicles may interfere with the functions of the on-board computer system(s) and may require the computer to undergo a relearning process once the negative battery cable is reconnected.

• When servicing drum brakes, only disassemble and assemble one side at a time, leaving the remaining side intact for reference.

• Only an MVAC-trained, EPA-certified automotive technician should service the air conditioning system or its components.

BRAKES

GENERAL INFORMATION

PRECAUTIONS

• Certain components within the ABS system are not intended to be serviced or repaired individually.

• Do not use rubber hoses or other parts not specifically specified for and ABS system. When using repair kits, replace all parts included in the kit. Partial or incorrect repair may lead to functional problems and require the replacement of components.

• Lubricate rubber parts with clean, fresh brake fluid to ease assembly. Do not use shop air to clean parts; damage to rubber components may result.

• Use only DOT 3 brake fluid from an unopened container.

• If any hydraulic component or line is removed or replaced, it may be necessary to bleed the entire system.

• A clean repair area is essential. Always clean the reservoir and cap thoroughly before removing the cap. The slightest amount of dirt in the fluid may plug an orifice and impair the system function. Perform repairs after components have been thoroughly cleaned; use only denatured alcohol to clean components. Do not allow ABS components to come into contact with any substance containing mineral oil; this includes used shop rags.

• The Anti-Lock control unit is a microprocessor similar to other computer units in the vehicle. Ensure that the ignition switch is **OFF** before removing or installing controller harnesses. Avoid static electricity discharge at or near the controller.

• If any arc welding is to be done on the vehicle, the control unit should be unplugged before welding operations begin.

ANTI-LOCK BRAKE SYSTEM (ABS)

WHEEL SPEED SENSORS

REMOVAL & INSTALLATION

Front

See Figure 2.

1. See all applicable precautions before beginning service procedures.
2. Raise and support the vehicle.
3. Remove the tire and wheel assembly.
4. Remove the caliper adapter.

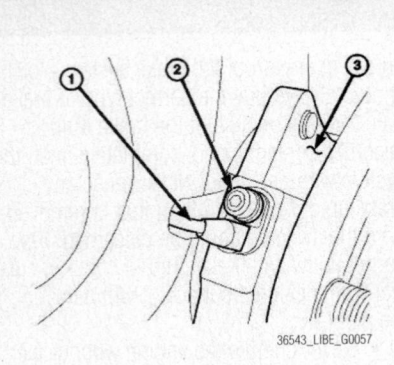

Fig. 2 Remove the bolt (2) mounting the wheel speed sensor to the hub (3), remove the wheel speed sensor wire (1) from the hub/bearing, and remove the wheel speed sensor

❋❋ WARNING

Never allow the disc brake caliper to hang from the brake hose. Damage to the brake hose with result. Provide a suitable support to hang the caliper securely.

5. Remove the disc brake rotor.
6. Remove the bolt (2) mounting the wheel speed sensor to the hub (3).
7. Remove the wheel speed sensor wire (1) from the hub/bearing and through the brake shield.
8. Remove the wheel speed sensor wire hold down clips.

9. Remove the locking connector at the wheel liner from the sensor connector.
10. Remove the wheel speed sensor from the vehicle.

To install:

❋❋ WARNING

When installing, do not rotate sensor, as this may cause the sensor to rub on the tone ring and be damaged.

11. Install the wheel speed sensor to the vehicle.
12. Install the wheel speed sensor through the brake shield and to the hub/bearing.
13. Install the wheel speed sensor wire hold down routing clips.
14. Install the wheel speed sensor mounting bolt to the hub. Tighten the mounting bolt to 71 inch lbs. (8 Nm).
15. Install the disc brake rotor.
16. Install the disc brake caliper adapter.
17. Install the tire and wheel assembly.

Rear
See Figure 3.

1. See all applicable precautions before beginning service procedures.
2. Raise and support the vehicle.
3. Disengage the locking tab connector.
4. Disconnect the wheel speed sensor electrical connector (1).
5. Remove the wheel speed sensor mounting bolt (2) from the rear support plate.

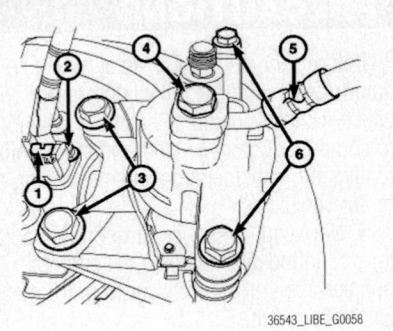

Fig. 3 Disengage the locking tab connector, disconnect the electrical connector (1), remove the mounting bolt (2), and remove the wheel speed sensor

6. Remove the wheel speed sensor from the support plate.

To install:

7. Insert the wheel speed sensor through the support plate.
8. Tighten the wheel speed sensor bolt to 80 inch lbs. (9 Nm).
9. Secure the wheel speed sensor wire to the routing clips. Verify that the sensor wire is secure and clear of the rotating components.
10. Reconnect the wheel speed sensor electrical connector.

➥**Make sure the connector locking tab is fully engaged and locked in position.**

11. Lower the vehicle.

BRAKES   BLEEDING THE BRAKE SYSTEM

BLEEDING PROCEDURE

Manual Bleeding
See Figure 4.

1. See all applicable precautions before beginning service procedures.

❋❋ WARNING

Use Mopar® brake fluid, or an equivalent quality fluid meeting SAE J1703-F and DOT 3 standards only. Use fresh, clean fluid from a sealed container at all times.

➥Do not pump the brake pedal at any time while bleeding. Air in the system will be compressed into small bubbles that are distributed throughout the hydraulic system. This will make additional bleeding operations necessary.

➥Do not allow the master cylinder to run out of fluid during bleed opera-

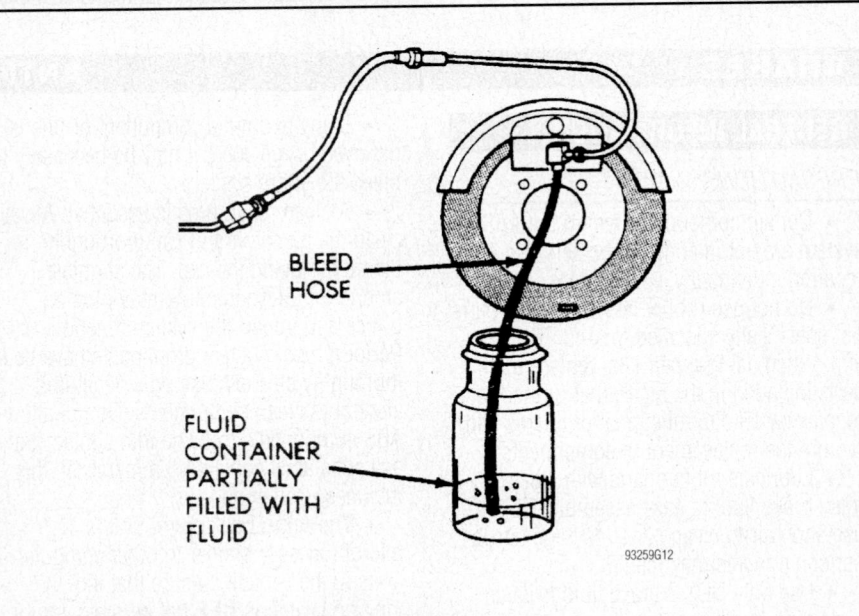

BLEED HOSE

FLUID CONTAINER PARTIALLY FILLED WITH FLUID

Fig. 4 Proper setup for manual bleeding procedure

tions. An empty cylinder will allow additional air to be drawn into the system. Check the cylinder fluid level frequently and add fluid as needed.

2. Bleed only one brake component at a time in the following sequence:
   a. Master Cylinder
   b. Junction Block
   c. Right Rear Wheel
   d. Left Rear Wheel
   e. Right Front Wheel
   f. Left Front Wheel

3. Remove reservoir filler caps and fill reservoir.

4. If calipers were overhauled, open all caliper bleed screws. Then close each bleed screw as fluid starts to drip from it. Top off master cylinder reservoir once more before proceeding.

5. Attach one end of bleed hose to bleed screw and insert opposite end in glass container partially filled with brake fluid. Be sure end of bleed hose is immersed in fluid.

6. Open up bleeder, then have a helper press down the brake pedal. Once the pedal is down close the bleeder. Repeat bleeding until fluid stream is clear and free of bubbles. Then move to the next wheel.

Pressure Bleeding

1. See all applicable precautions before beginning service procedures.

❋❋ WARNING

Use Mopar® brake fluid, or an equivalent quality fluid meeting SAE J1703-F and DOT 3 standards only. Use fresh, clean fluid from a sealed container at all times.

➡ **Do not pump the brake pedal at any time while bleeding. Air in the system will be compressed into small bubbles that are distributed throughout the hydraulic system. This will make additional bleeding operations necessary.**

➡ **Do not allow the master cylinder to run out of fluid during bleed operations. An empty cylinder will allow additional air to be drawn into the system. Check the cylinder fluid level frequently and add fluid as needed.**

❋❋ WARNING

Follow the manufacturer's instructions carefully when using pressure equipment. Do not exceed the tank manufacturers pressure recommendations. Generally, a tank pressure of 15–20 psi (103–139 kPa) is sufficient for bleeding.

➡ **Fill the bleeder tank with recommended fluid and purge air from the tank lines before bleeding.**

❋❋ WARNING

Do not pressure bleed without a proper master cylinder adapter. The wrong adapter can lead to leakage, or drawing air back into the system.

Use adapter provided with the equipment or Adapter 6921.

2. Bleed only one brake component at a time in the following sequence:
   a. Master Cylinder
   b. Right Rear Wheel
   c. Left Rear Wheel
   d. Right Front Wheel
   e. Left Front Wheel

BLEEDING THE ABS SYSTEM

1. See all applicable precautions before beginning service procedures.

ABS system bleeding requires conventional bleeding methods plus use of a scan tool. The procedure involves performing a base brake bleeding, followed by use of the scan tool to cycle and bleed the HCU pump and solenoids. A second base brake bleeding procedure is then required to remove any air remaining in the system.

2. Perform base brake bleeding. Refer to Bleeding the Brake System.

3. Connect scan tool to the Data Link Connector (DLC).

4. Select ANTI-LOCK BRAKES, followed by MISCELLANEOUS, then ABS BRAKES. Follow the instructions displayed. When scan tool displays TEST COMPLETE, disconnect scan tool and proceed.

5. Perform base brake bleeding a second time.

6. Top off master cylinder fluid level and verify proper brake operation before moving vehicle.

BRAKES

❋❋ WARNING

Dust and dirt accumulating on brake parts during normal use may contain asbestos fibers from production or aftermarket brake linings. Breathing excessive concentrations of asbestos fibers can cause serious bodily harm. Exercise care when servicing brake parts. Do not sand or grind brake lining unless equipment used is designed to contain the dust residue. Do not clean brake parts with compressed air or by dry brushing. Cleaning should be done by dampening the brake components with a fine mist of water, then wiping the brake components clean with a dampened cloth. Dispose of cloth and all residue containing asbestos fibers in an impermeable container with the appropriate label. **Follow practices prescribed by the Occupational Safety and Health Administration (OSHA) and the Environmental Protection Agency (EPA) for the handling, processing, and disposing of dust or debris that may contain asbestos fibers.**

BRAKE CALIPER

REMOVAL & INSTALLATION

See Figure 5.

1. See all applicable precautions before beginning service procedures.

2. Install prop rod on the brake pedal to keep pressure on the brake system, Holding pedal in this position will isolate master cylinder from hydraulic brake system and will not allow brake fluid to drain out of

FRONT DISC BRAKES

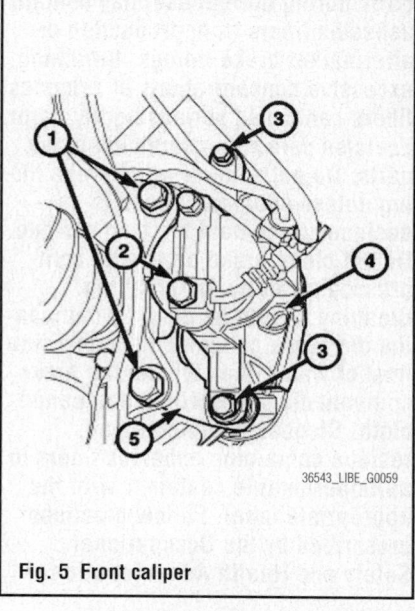

36543_LIBE_G0059

Fig. 5 Front caliper

brake fluid reservoir while brake lines are open. This will allow you to bleed out the area of repair instead of the entire system.

3. Raise and support vehicle.

4. Remove front wheel and tire assembly.

5. Remove the brake hose banjo bolt (2) if replacing caliper.

6. Remove the caliper mounting bolts (3).

7. Remove the caliper (4) from vehicle.

To install:

8. Install caliper (4) to the caliper adapter (5).

9. Coat the caliper mounting bolts (3) with silicone grease. Begin with the bolt closet to the bleeder screws (top), Then install and tighten the bolts to 28 ft. lbs. (37 Nm).

✷✷ WARNING

Verify that the brake hose is not twisted or kinked before tightening the fitting bolt.

10. Install the brake hose banjo bolt (2) and brake hose to the caliper (4) with **NEW** seal washers and tighten fitting bolt to 23 ft. lbs. (31 Nm) if removed.

11. Remove the prop rod from the vehicle.

12. Bleed the brake system.

✷✷ WARNING

If a proper pedal is not felt during bleeding an area of repair then a base bleed system must be performed.

13. Install the wheel and tire assemblies.

14. Remove the supports and lower the vehicle.

15. Verify a firm pedal before moving the vehicle.

DISC BRAKE PADS

REMOVAL & INSTALLATION

See Figure 6.

1. See all applicable precautions before beginning service procedures.

2. Raise and safely support the vehicle.

3. Remove the front wheel and tire assembly.

4. Drain a small amount of fluid from the master cylinder brake reservoir with a clean suction gun.

5. Bottom the caliper pistons into the caliper by prying the caliper over.

6. Remove the caliper mounting bolts (1).

7. Remove the disc brake caliper (2) from the adapter (4). Refer to Front Disc Brake Caliper Removal & Installation.

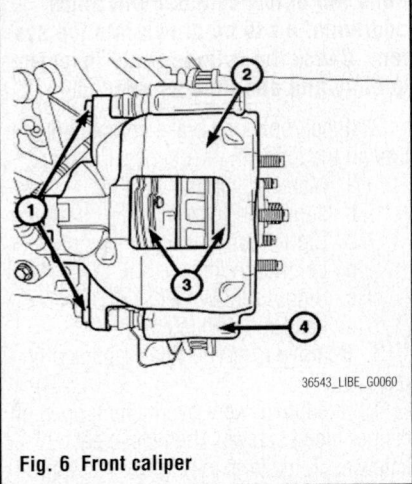

36543_LIBE_G0060

Fig. 6 Front caliper

✷✷ WARNING

Never allow the disc brake caliper to hang from the brake hose. Damage to the brake hose will result. Provide a suitable support to hang the caliper securely.

8. Remove the inboard and outboard pads (3).

To install:

9. Install the inboard and outboard pads (3).

10. Install the caliper (2).

11. Install the tire and wheel assembly.

BRAKES

✷✷ WARNING

Dust and dirt accumulating on brake parts during normal use may contain asbestos fibers from production or aftermarket brake linings. Breathing excessive concentrations of asbestos fibers can cause serious bodily harm. Exercise care when servicing brake parts. Do not sand or grind brake lining unless equipment used is designed to contain the dust residue. Do not clean brake parts with compressed air or by dry brushing. Cleaning should be done by dampening the brake components with a fine mist of water, then wiping the brake components clean with a dampened cloth. Dispose of cloth and all residue containing asbestos fibers in an impermeable container with the appropriate label. Follow practices prescribed by the Occupational Safety and Health Administration

(OSHA) and the Environmental Protection Agency (EPA) for the handling, processing, and disposing of dust or debris that may contain asbestos fibers.

BRAKE CALIPER

REMOVAL & INSTALLATION

See Figure 7.

1. See all applicable precautions before beginning service procedures.

2. Install prop rod on the brake pedal to keep pressure on the brake system, Holding pedal in this position will isolate master cylinder from hydraulic brake system and will not allow brake fluid to drain out of brake fluid reservoir while brake lines are open. This will allow you to bleed out the area of repair instead of the entire system.

3. Raise and support the vehicle.

4. Remove the tire and wheel assembly.

REAR DISC BRAKES

5. Remove the brake hose banjo bolt (4) if replacing caliper.

6. Remove the caliper mounting bolts (6).

7. Remove the caliper from vehicle.

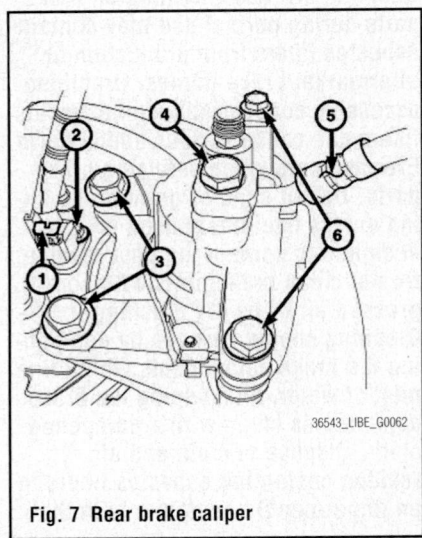

36543_LIBE_G0062

Fig. 7 Rear brake caliper

To install:

8. Install the caliper and tighten the bolts to 28 ft. lbs. (37 Nm).

❊❊ WARNING

Verify that the brake hose (5) is not twisted or kinked before tightening the fitting bolt.

9. Install the brake hose (5) to the caliper with **NEW** seal washers and install the brake hose banjo bolt (4). Tighten fitting bolt to 23 ft. lbs. (31 Nm).
10. Remove the prop rod from the vehicle.
11. Bleed the area of repair for the brake system.

❊❊ WARNING

If a proper pedal is not felt during bleeding an area of repair then a base bleed system must be performed.

12. Install the wheel and tire assemblies.
13. Remove the supports and lower the vehicle.
14. Verify a firm pedal before moving the vehicle.

DISC BRAKE PADS

REMOVAL & INSTALLATION
See Figure 8.

1. See all applicable precautions before beginning service procedures.
2. Raise and support vehicle.
3. Remove the wheel and tire assemblies.
4. Compress the caliper (1).
5. Remove the rear caliper mounting bolts (4).

➥**Do not allow brake hose to support caliper assembly.**

6. Remove the caliper by tilting the top up and off the caliper adapter.
7. Support and hang the caliper.
8. Remove the brake pads (2) from the caliper (1).

To install:
9. Install the brake pads (2) to the caliper adapter.
10. Install caliper (1) to the rotor and then install the caliper mounting bolts (4).

11. Install wheel and tire assemblies and lower vehicle.
12. Apply brakes several times to seat caliper pistons and brake shoes and obtain firm pedal.
13. Top off master cylinder fluid level.

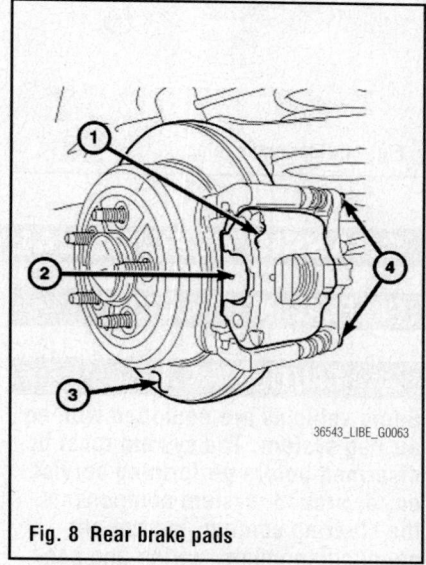

36543_LIBE_G0063

Fig. 8 Rear brake pads

BRAKES

PARKING BRAKE CABLES

ADJUSTMENT

No adjustment is needed, as the parking brake cables are self-adjusting. If the cables have been replaced, follow the parking shoe replacement procedure to set the shoes correctly.

LOCK OUT
See Figure 9.

➥**The parking brake is self-adjusting, it cannot be adjusted.**

1. See all applicable precautions before beginning service procedures.
2. Remove the center floor console. Refer to Floor Console Removal & Installation in Body Interior section.
3. With lever in DOWN position, pull up on the core cable (4) rotating the drum (5) until the drum cut-out aligns with hole on lever tab (3), then install a punch (2) in this hole and drum cut-out. Release grasp on core cable.
4. The park brake system is now locked out to perform necessary repairs

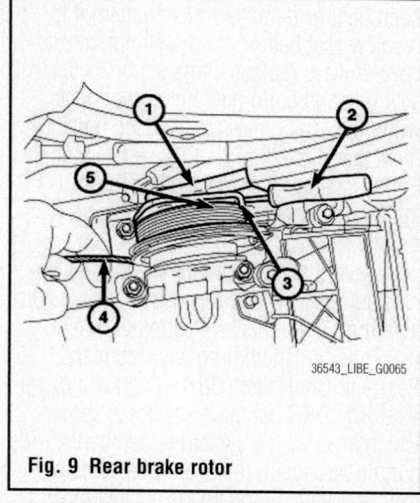

36543_LIBE_G0065

Fig. 9 Rear brake rotor

PARKING BRAKE SHOES

REMOVAL & INSTALLATION
See Figures 10 and 11.

1. See all applicable precautions before beginning service procedures.
2. Raise and support the vehicle.
3. Remove the tire and wheel assembly.
4. Remove the disc brake caliper.

PARKING BRAKE

5. Remove the disc brake rotor.
6. Remove the axle shaft (2).
7. Disassemble the rear park brake shoes (1).

To install:
8. Reassemble the rear park brake shoes.
9. Adjust the rear brake shoes:
   a. Measure the drum diameter with the gauge and lock it into position.

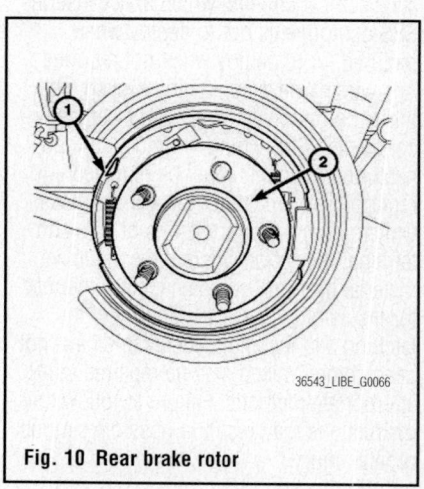

36543_LIBE_G0066

Fig. 10 Rear brake rotor

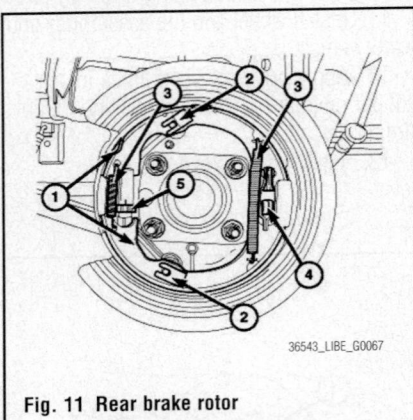

Fig. 11 Rear brake rotor

b. Turn the gauge around and check the shoe diameter diagonally across at the top of one shoe and bottom of the opposite shoe (widest point). The gauge should be a light drag fit over the shoes.

c. If the gauge is not a light drag fit over the shoes, turn the star wheel by hand to move the shoes in or out so that the correct clearance can be achieved.

10. Install axle shaft.
11. Install the disc brake rotor.
12. Install the disc brake caliper.
13. Install the tire and wheel assembly.

14. Lower the vehicle.

➡On a new vehicle or after parking brake lining replacement, it is recommended that the parking brake system be conditioned prior to use. This is done by making one stop from 25 mph on dry pavement or concrete using light to moderate force on the parking brake foot pedal.

ADJUSTMENT

The parking brake is self-adjusting, it cannot be adjusted.

CHASSIS ELECTRICAL — AIR BAG (SUPPLEMENTAL RESTRAINT SYSTEM)

GENERAL INFORMATION

✷✷ CAUTION

Some vehicles are equipped with an air bag system. The system must be disarmed before performing service on, or around, system components, the steering column, instrument panel components, wiring and sensors. Failure to follow the safety precautions and the disarming procedure could result in accidental air bag deployment, possible injury and unnecessary system repairs.

SERVICE PRECAUTIONS

To avoid serious or fatal injury on vehicles equipped with the Supplemental Restraint System (SRS), never attempt to repair the electrically conductive circuits or wiring components related to the SRS. Such repairs can compromise the conductivity and current carrying capacity of those critical electrical circuits, which may cause the SRS components not to deploy when required, or to deploy when not required. Any wire harness containing broken, cut, burned or otherwise damaged electrically conductive SRS wiring, terminals or connector components must be removed and replaced with an entire new wire harness. Only minor cuts or abrasions of wire and terminal insulation where the conductive material has not been damaged, or connector insulators where the integrity of the latching and locking mechanisms have not been compromised may be repaired using appropriate methods. Failure to follow these instructions may result in possible serious or fatal injury.

To avoid serious or fatal injury during and following any seat belt or child restraint anchor service, carefully inspect all seat belts, buckles, mounting hardware, retractors, tether straps, and anchors for proper installation, operation, or damage. Replace any belt that is cut, frayed, or torn. Straighten any belt that is twisted. Tighten any loose fasteners. Replace any belt that has a damaged or ineffective buckle or retractor. Replace any belt that has a bent or damaged latch plate or anchor plate. Replace any child restraint anchor or the unit to which the anchor is integral that has been bent or damaged. Never attempt to repair a seat belt or child restraint component. Always replace damaged or ineffective seat belt and child restraint components with the correct, new and unused replacement parts listed in the Chrysler Mopar ® Parts Catalog. Failure to follow these instructions may result in possible serious or fatal injury.

To avoid serious or fatal injury on vehicles equipped with side curtain airbags, disable the Supplemental Restraint System (SRS) before attempting any Occupant Restraint Controller (ORC) diagnosis or service. The ORC contains a rollover sensor, which enables the system to deploy the side curtain airbags in the event of a vehicle rollover event. If an ORC is accidentally rolled during service while still connected to battery power, the side curtain airbags will deploy. Disconnect and isolate the battery negative (ground) cable, then wait two minutes for the system capacitor to discharge before performing further diagnosis or service. This is the only sure way to disable the SRS. Failure to take the proper precautions could result in accidental airbag deployment.

To avoid serious or fatal injury on vehi-

cles equipped with airbags, disable the Supplemental Restraint System (SRS) before attempting any steering wheel, steering column, airbag, Occupant Classification System (OCS), seat belt tensioner, impact sensor, or instrument panel component diagnosis or service. Disconnect and isolate the battery negative (ground) cable, then wait two minutes for the system capacitor to discharge before performing further diagnosis or service. This is the only sure way to disable the SRS. Failure to take the proper precautions could result in accidental airbag deployment.

To avoid serious or fatal injury on vehicles equipped with airbags, before performing any welding operations disconnect and isolate the battery negative (ground) cable and disconnect all wire harness connectors from the Occupant Restraint Controller (ORC). Failure to take the proper precautions could result in accidental airbag deployment and other possible damage to the Supplemental Restraint System (SRS) circuits and components.

To avoid serious or fatal injury, do not attempt to dismantle an airbag unit or tamper with its inflator. Do not puncture, incinerate or bring into contact with electricity. Do not store at temperatures exceeding 93° C (200° F). An airbag inflator unit may contain sodium azide and potassium nitrate. These materials are poisonous and extremely flammable. Contact with acid, water, or heavy metals may produce harmful and irritating gases (sodium hydroxide is formed in the presence of moisture) or combustible compounds. An airbag inflator unit may also contain a gas canister pressurized to over 2500 psi (17.24 kPa). Failure to follow these instructions may result in possible serious or fatal injury.

To avoid serious or fatal injury, replace all Supplemental Restraint System (SRS) components only with parts specified in the Chrysler Mopar® Parts Catalog. Substitute parts may appear interchangeable, but internal differences may result in inferior occupant protection. Failure to follow these instructions may result in possible serious or fatal injury.

To avoid serious or fatal injury, the fasteners, screws, and bolts originally used for the Supplemental Restraint System (SRS) components must never be replaced with any substitutes. These fasteners have special coatings and are specifically designed for the SRS. Anytime a new fastener is needed, replace it with the correct fasteners provided in the service package or specified in the Chrysler Mopar® Parts Catalog. Failure to follow these instructions may result in possible serious or fatal injury.

To avoid serious or fatal injury when a steering column has an airbag unit attached, never place the column on the floor or any other surface with the steering wheel or airbag unit face down. Failure to follow these instructions may result in possible serious or fatal injury.

At no time should any source of electricity be permitted near the inflator on the back of a non-deployed airbag or seat belt tensioner. When carrying a non-deployed airbag, the trim cover or airbag cushion side of the unit should be pointed away from the body to minimize injury in the event of an accidental deployment. If the airbag unit is placed on a bench or any other surface, the trim cover or airbag cushion side of the unit should be face up to minimize movement in the event of an accidental deployment.

Wear safety glasses, rubber gloves, and long sleeved clothing when cleaning powder residue from vehicle after an airbag deployment. Powder residue emitted from a deployed airbag can cause skin irritation. Flush affected area with cool water if irritation is experienced. If nasal or throat irritation is experienced, exit the vehicle for fresh air until the irritation ceases. If irritation continues, see a physician.

Do not use a replacement airbag that is not in the original packaging. This may result in improper deployment, personal injury, or death.

During, and following, any child restraint anchor service, due to impact event or vehicle repair, carefully inspect all mounting hardware, tether straps, and anchors for proper installation, operation, or damage. If a child restraint anchor is found damaged in

any way, the anchor must be replaced. Failure to do this may result in personal injury or death.

Deployed and non-deployed airbags may or may not have live pyrotechnic material within the airbag inflator.

Do not dispose of driver/passenger/curtain airbags or seat belt tensioners unless you are sure of complete deployment.

Never replace both the Occupant Restraint Controller (ORC) and the Occupant Classification Module (OCM) at the same time. If both require replacement, replace one, then perform the Airbag System test before replacing the other. Both the ORC and the OCM store Occupant Classification System (OCS) calibration data, which they transfer to one another when one of them is replaced. If both are replaced at the same time, an irreversible fault will be set in both modules and the OCS may malfunction and cause personal injury or death.

If equipped with OCS, the Seat Weight Sensor is a sensitive, calibrated unit and must be handled carefully. Do not drop or handle roughly. If dropped or damaged, replace with another sensor. Failure to do so may result in occupant injury or death.

If equipped with OCS, the front passenger seat must be handled carefully as well. When removing the seat, be careful when setting on floor not to drop. If dropped, the sensor may be inoperative, could result in occupant injury, or possibly death.

If equipped with OCS, when the passenger front seat is on the floor, no one should sit in the front passenger seat. This uneven force may damage the sensing ability of the seat weight sensors. If sat on and damaged, the sensor may be inoperative, could result in occupant injury, or possibly death.

Airbags and seat belt tensioners must be stored in their original, special container until they are used for service. Also, they must be stored in a clean, dry environment; away from sources of extreme heat, sparks, and high electrical energy. Always place or store any airbag on a surface with its trim cover or airbag cushion side facing up, to minimize movement in case of an accidental deployment.

All damaged, ineffective or non-deployed airbags and seat belt tensioners which are replaced on vehicles are to be handled and disposed of properly. If an airbag or seat belt tensioner unit is ineffective or damaged and non-deployed, refer to the Hazardous Substance Control System for information

regarding the potentially hazardous properties of the subject component and the proper safe handling procedures. Then dispose of all non-deployed and deployed airbags and seat belt tensioners in a manner consistent with state, provincial, local and federal regulations.

The Supplemental Restraint System (SRS) should be disarmed whenever any steering wheel, steering column, seat belt tensioner, airbag, impact sensor Occupant Classification System (OCS), or instrument panel components require diagnosis or service. Failure to observe this warning could result in accidental airbag deployment and possible personal injury.

DISARMING THE SYSTEM

Disconnect and isolate the negative battery cable. Wait 2 minutes for the system capacitor to discharge before performing any service.

ARMING THE SYSTEM

To arm the system, connect the negative battery cable.

CLOCKSPRING CENTERING

See Figure 12.

✳✳ CAUTION

To avoid serious or fatal injury on vehicles equipped with airbags, disable the Supplemental Restraint System (SRS) before attempting any steering wheel, steering column, airbag, Occupant Classification System (OCS), seat belt tensioner, impact sensor, or instrument panel component diagnosis or service. Disconnect and isolate the battery negative (ground) cable, then wait two minutes for the system capacitor to discharge before performing further diagnosis or service. This is the only sure way to disable the SRS. Failure to take the proper precautions could result in accidental airbag deployment.

➡**A service replacement clockspring is shipped with the clockspring pre-centered and with a molded plastic locking pin installed. This locking pin should not be removed until the steering wheel has been installed on the steering column. If the locking pin is removed before the steering wheel is installed, the clockspring centering procedure must be performed.**

✳✳ WARNING

When a clockspring is installed into a vehicle without properly centering and locking the entire steering system, the Steering Angle Sensor (SAS) data does not agree with the true position of the steering system and causes the Electronic Stability Program (ESP) system to shut down. This may also damage the clockspring without any immediate malfunction. Unlike some other Chrysler vehicles, this SAS never requires calibration. However, upon each new ignition ON cycle, the steering wheel must be rotated slightly to initialize the SAS.

➡ Determining if the clockspring/SAS is centered is also possible electrically using the diagnostic scan tool. Steering wheel position is displayed as ANGLE with a range of up to 900 degrees. Refer to the appropriate menu item on the diagnostic scan tool.

➡ Before starting this procedure, be certain to turn the steering wheel until the front wheels are in the straight-ahead position and that the entire steering system is locked or inhibited from rotation.

➡ The clockspring may be centered and the rotor may be rotated freely once the steering wheel has been removed.

1. Place the front wheels in the straight-ahead position and inhibit the steering column shaft from rotation.
2. Remove the steering wheel from the steering shaft.
3. Rotate the clockspring rotor (1) clockwise to the end of its travel. Do not apply excessive torque.
4. From the end of the clockwise travel, rotate the rotor about two and one-half turns counterclockwise. Turn the rotor slightly clockwise or counterclockwise as necessary so that the clockspring airbag pigtail wires (3) and connector receptacle are at the top and the dowel or drive pin (5) is at the bottom.

5. The clockspring is now centered. Secure the clockspring rotor to the clockspring case using a locking pin (2) or some similar device to maintain clockspring centering until the steering wheel is reinstalled on the steering column.

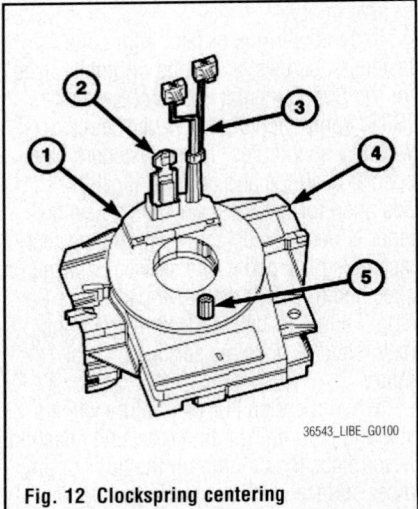

36543_LIBE_G0100

Fig. 12 Clockspring centering

DRIVE TRAIN

AUTOMATIC TRANSMISSION ASSEMBLY

REMOVAL & INSTALLATION

See Figures 13 through 15.

1. See all applicable precautions before beginning service procedures.
2. Disconnect the negative battery cable.
3. Raise and support the vehicle.
4. Remove any necessary skid plates.
5. Mark propeller shaft and axle companion flanges for assembly alignment.
6. Remove the rear propeller shaft.
7. Remove the front propeller shaft, if necessary.
8. Remove the crossmember.
9. Remove the transfer case, if equipped.
10. Disconnect wires from the input and output speed sensors.
11. Disconnect wires from the transmission range sensor, the Variable Line Pressure (VLP) electrical connector, and the solenoid/pressure switch assembly.
12. Disconnect gearshift cable from transmission manual valve lever.
13. Disengage the shift cable from the cable support bracket.
14. Remove the starter motor.

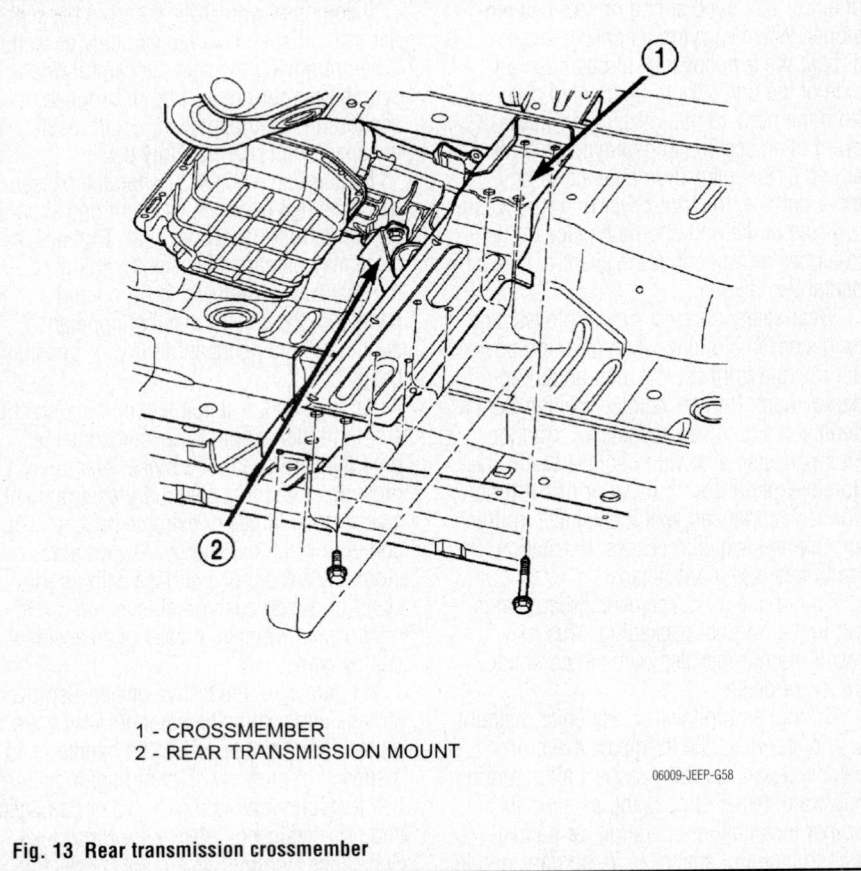

1 - CROSSMEMBER
2 - REAR TRANSMISSION MOUNT

06009-JEEP-G58

Fig. 13 Rear transmission crossmember

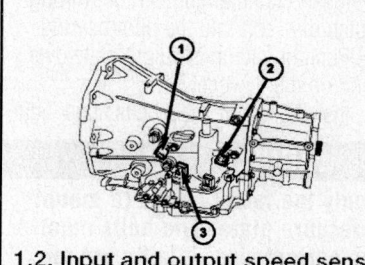

1,2. Input and output speed sensors
3. Transmission range sensor

36543_LIBE_G0097

Fig. 14 Disconnect wires and connectors

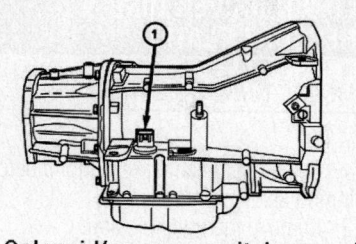

. Solenoid/pressure switch assembl

36543_LIBE_G0098

Fig. 15 Disconnect wires and connectors, cont.

15. Remove the engine to transmission collar.

16. Rotate crankshaft in clockwise direction until converter bolts are accessible. Then remove bolts one at a time. Rotate crankshaft with socket wrench on dampener bolt.

17. Disconnect the transmission vent hose from the transmission.

18. Raise transmission slightly with service jack to relieve load on crossmember and supports.

19. Remove all remaining converter housing bolts.

20. Remove fill tube bolt at transmission.

21. Carefully work transmission and torque converter assembly rearward off engine block dowels.

22. Hold torque converter in place during transmission removal.

23. Lower transmission and remove assembly from under the vehicle.

24. To remove torque converter, carefully slide torque converter out of the transmission.

To install:

25. Check torque converter hub and hub drive flats for sharp edges burrs, scratches, or nicks. Polish the hub and flats with 800/1000 grit paper and crocus cloth if necessary. Verify that the converter hub O-ring is properly installed and is free of any debris. The hub must be smooth to avoid damaging pump seal at installation.

26. If a replacement transmission is being installed, transfer any components necessary, such as the manual shift lever and shift cable bracket, from the original transmission onto the replacement transmission.

27. Lubricate oil pump seal lip with transmission fluid.

28. Align converter and oil pump.

29. Carefully insert converter in oil pump. Then rotate converter back and forth until fully seated in pump gears.

30. Check converter seating with steel scale and straightedge. Surface of converter lugs should be at least ½ in. (13mm) to rear of straightedge when converter is fully seated.

31. Temporarily secure converter with C-clamp.

32. Position transmission on jack and secure it with chains.

33. Check condition of converter driveplate. Replace the plate if cracked, distorted or damaged.

➡**Be sure transmission dowel pins are seated in engine block and protrude far enough to hold transmission in alignment.**

34. Apply a light coating of Mopar® High Temp Grease to the torque converter hub pocket in the rear pocket of the engine's crankshaft.

35. Raise transmission and align the torque converter with the drive plate and transmission converter housing with the engine block.

36. Move transmission forward. Then raise, lower or tilt transmission to align the converter housing with engine block dowels.

37. Carefully work transmission forward and over engine block dowels until converter hub is seated in crankshaft. Verify that no wires, or the transmission vent hose, have become trapped between the engine block and the transmission.

38. Install two bolts to attach the transmission to the engine.

39. Install remaining torque converter housing to engine bolts. Tighten to 50 ft. lbs. (68 Nm).

40. Install transmission fill tube bolt. Tighten bolt to 45 inch lbs. (5 Nm).

41. Install transfer case, if equipped. Tighten transfer case nuts to 26 ft. lbs. (35 Nm).

42. Connect gearshift cable to support bracket and transmission manual lever.

43. Connect input and output speed sensor wires.

44. Connect wires to the Variable Line Pressure (VLP) electrical connector.

45. Connect wires to the transmission range sensor and the solenoid/pressure switch assembly.

46. Install torque converter-to-driveplate bolts. Tighten bolts to 65 ft. lbs. (88 Nm).

47. Install starter motor and cooler line bracket, if equipped.

48. Install structural cover.

49. Connect cooler lines to transmission.

50. Install exhaust components.

51. Install front propeller shaft.

52. Install rear support to transmission. Tighten bolts to 35 ft. lbs. (47 Nm).

53. Install rear transmission crossmember. Tighten crossmember to frame bolts to 50 ft. lbs. (68 Nm).

54. Lower transmission onto crossmember and install bolts attaching transmission mount to crossmember. Tighten clevis bracket to crossmember bolts to 35 ft. lbs. (47 Nm). Tighten the clevis bracket to rear support bolt to 50 ft. lbs. (68 Nm).

55. Remove engine support fixture.

56. Install the rear propeller shaft.

57. Adjust gearshift cable if necessary.

58. Install any skid plates removed previously.

59. Lower vehicle.

60. Fill transmission with Mopar® ATF +4, Automatic Transmission Fluid.

MANUAL TRANSMISSION ASSEMBLY

REMOVAL & INSTALLATION

3.7L Engine

See Figure 16.

1. See all applicable precautions before beginning service procedures.

2. Disconnect negative battery cable.

3. With vehicle in neutral, position vehicle on hoist.

4. Remove drain plug and drain fluid.

5. Mark installation reference marks on propeller shaft/shafts and remove shafts.

6. Remove transfer case shift cable bracket nuts, cable, wiring connector, and vent hose, if equipped.

7. Remove transfer case, if equipped.

8. Support transmission with jack.

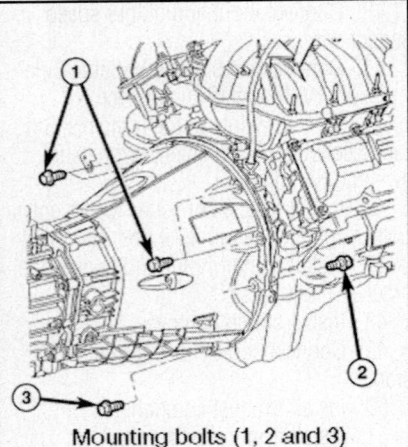

Mounting bolts (1, 2 and 3)

22043_LIBE_G0007

Fig. 16 Exploded view of the transmission mounting—3.7L engine

9. Remove transmission mount and crossmember.

10. Remove clutch slave cylinder nuts and remove cylinder.

11. Remove backup lamp switch wiring connector.

12. Remove shift lever tower bolts and remove shift lever housing.

13. Remove starter bolts and remove starter.

14. Remove transmission bolt and remove transmission.

To install:

15. Install transmission on engine.

16. On 3.7L engine, tighten bolts to 30 ft. lbs. (41 Nm). Tighten bolts to 50 ft. lbs. (67 Nm). Tighten bolts to 40 ft. lbs. (54 Nm).

17. Clean shift tower and mating surface then apply Mopar® Gasket Maker to shift tower.

18. Install shift tower and tighten bolts to 7 ft. lbs. (10 Nm).

19. Install back-up lamp wiring connector.

20. Install clutch slave cylinder and mounting nuts.

21. Install transmission crossmember and tighten bolts to 35 ft. lbs. (47 Nm). Install transmission mount bolts and tighten to 35 ft. lbs. (47 Nm).

22. Install transfer case, if equipped.

23. For 3.7L engine, install transfer case shift linkage.

24. Install transfer case wiring connector and vent hose.

25. Install propeller shaft/shafts with reference marks aligned.

26. Remove fill plug and fill transmission with lubricant.

CLUTCH DRIVEN DISC & PRESSURE PLATE

REMOVAL & INSTALLATION

See Figure 17.

1. See all applicable precautions before beginning service procedures.

2. Remove the transmission.

3. Mark position of pressure plate on flywheel with paint or a scriber for assembly reference, if clutch is not being replaced.

4. Loosen pressure plate bolts evenly and in rotation to relieve spring tension and avoid warping the plate.

5. Remove pressure plate bolts and pressure plate and disc.

To install:

6. Lightly scuff sand flywheel face with 180 grit emery cloth, then clean with a wax and grease remover.

7. Lubricate pilot bearing with Mopar® high temperature bearing grease or equivalent.

8. Check runout and operation of a new clutch disc.

➡**Disc must slide freely on transmission input shaft splines.**

9. With the disc on the input shaft, check face runout with dial indicator. Check runout at disc hub ¼ in. (6mm) from outer edge of facing. Obtain another clutch disc if runout exceeds 0.020 in. (0.5mm).

10. Position clutch disc on flywheel with side marked flywheel against the flywheel.

➡**If not marked, the flat side of disc hub goes towards the flywheel on the 3.7L engine.**

11. Insert clutch alignment tool through the clutch disc and into the pilot bearing.

12. Position clutch pressure plate over disc and on the flywheel.

13. Install pressure plate bolts finger tight.

✳✳ WARNING

Use only the factory bolts to mount the pressure plate. The bolts must be the correct size. If bolts are too short, there isn't enough thread engagement. If too long, bolts interfere with the Dual Mass Flywheel.

14. Tighten pressure plate bolts evenly and in rotation a few threads at a time.

✳✳ WARNING

The bolts must be tightened evenly and to specified torque. Failure to follow these instructions will distort the pressure plate.

15. For 3.7L engines, tighten pressure plate bolts to 24 ft. lbs. (37 Nm).

16. Apply light coat of Mopar® high temperature bearing grease or equivalent to clutch disc hub and splines of transmission input shaft.

➡**Do not over lubricate shaft splines. This will result in grease contamination of disc.**

17. Install the transmission.

CLUTCH MASTER CYLINDER

REMOVAL & INSTALLATION

See Figure 18.

1. Pry actuator rod off clutch pedal pin.

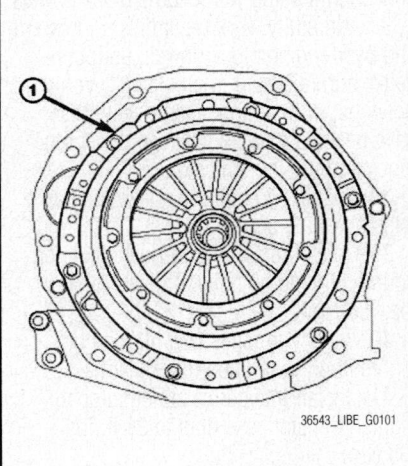

36543_LIBE_G0101

Fig. 17 Pressure plate positioning

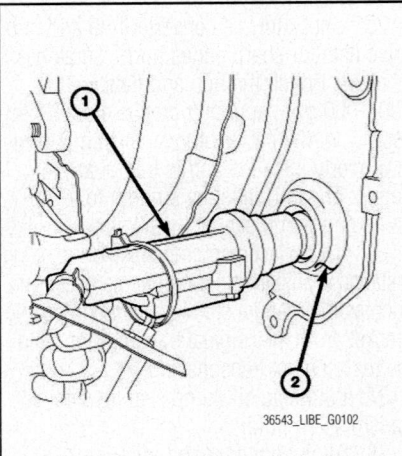

36543_LIBE_G0102

Fig. 18 Turn clutch master cylinder assembly clockwise to remove

2. Remove hose from clutch master cylinder and plug hose to prevent fluid loss.

3. Disconnect wiring harness from pedal position switch.

4. Pull the hydraulic line clip and remove line from bottom of clutch master cylinder.

5. Turn clutch master cylinder assembly (1) clockwise a quarter turn and remove from brake booster mounting plate (2).

To install:

6. Install clutch master cylinder through brake booster mounting plate and turn counter clockwise a quarter turn.

7. Install actuator hose to clutch master cylinder.

8. Install hydraulic line to the bottom of clutch master cylinder.

➡**Verify O-ring is on hydraulic line.**

9. Connect wiring harness to pedal position switch.

10. Install actuator rod on clutch pedal pin.

11. Bleed clutch hydraulic circuit.

CLUTCH SLAVE CYLINDER

REMOVAL & INSTALLATION

See Figure 19.

1. With transmission in neutral, position vehicle on hoist.

2. Pull clip from hydraulic line (1) at the slave cylinder (2) and remove the line.

3. Remove mounting nuts (3) from slave cylinder (2).

4. Remove the slave cylinder.

To install:

5. Install slave cylinder (2) in transmission.

6. Install slave cylinder nuts (3) and tighten to 17 ft. lbs. (23 Nm).

7. Install hydraulic line (1) to slave cylinder (2). NOTE: Verify O-ring is on hydraulic line.

8. Bleed hydraulic system

TRANSFER CASE ASSEMBLY

REMOVAL & INSTALLATION

See Figure 20.

1. See all applicable precautions before beginning service procedures.

2. Raise vehicle.

➡**Do not allow propshafts to hang at attached end. Damage to joint can result.**

3. Remove the front and rear propeller shafts.

4. Support transmission with jack stand.

5. Remove rear crossmember and skid plate, if equipped.

6. Disconnect transfer case vent hose (4).

7. Disconnect the wiring connector from the shift motor, if necessary.

8. Support transfer case with transmission jack and secure with chains.

9. Remove nuts (2) attaching transfer case (1) to transmission (3).

10. Pull transfer case and jack rearward to disengage transfer case.

11. Remove transfer case from under vehicle.

To install:

12. Mount transfer case on a transmission jack.

13. Secure transfer case to jack with chains.

14. Position transfer case under vehicle.

15. Align transfer case and transmission shafts and install transfer case onto the transmission.

16. Install and tighten transfer case attaching nuts to 26 ft. lbs. (35 Nm) torque.

17. Connect the transfer case vent hose.

18. Connect front propeller shaft and install rear propeller shaft.

19. Fill transfer case with correct fluid.

20. Install the transfer case fill plug. Tighten the plug to 15–25 ft. lbs. (20–34 Nm).

21. Install rear crossmember and skid plate, if equipped.

22. Remove transmission jack and support stand.

23. Lower vehicle and verify transfer case shift operation.

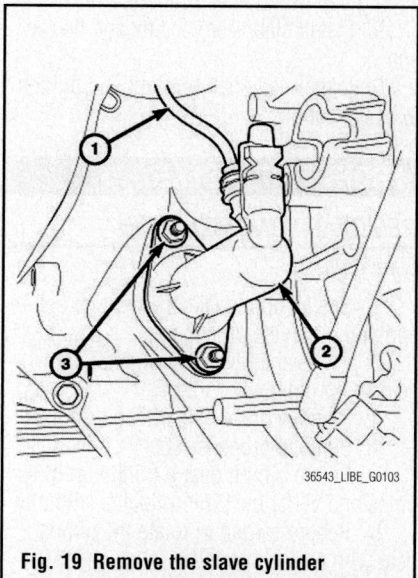

36543_LIBE_G0103

Fig. 19 Remove the slave cylinder

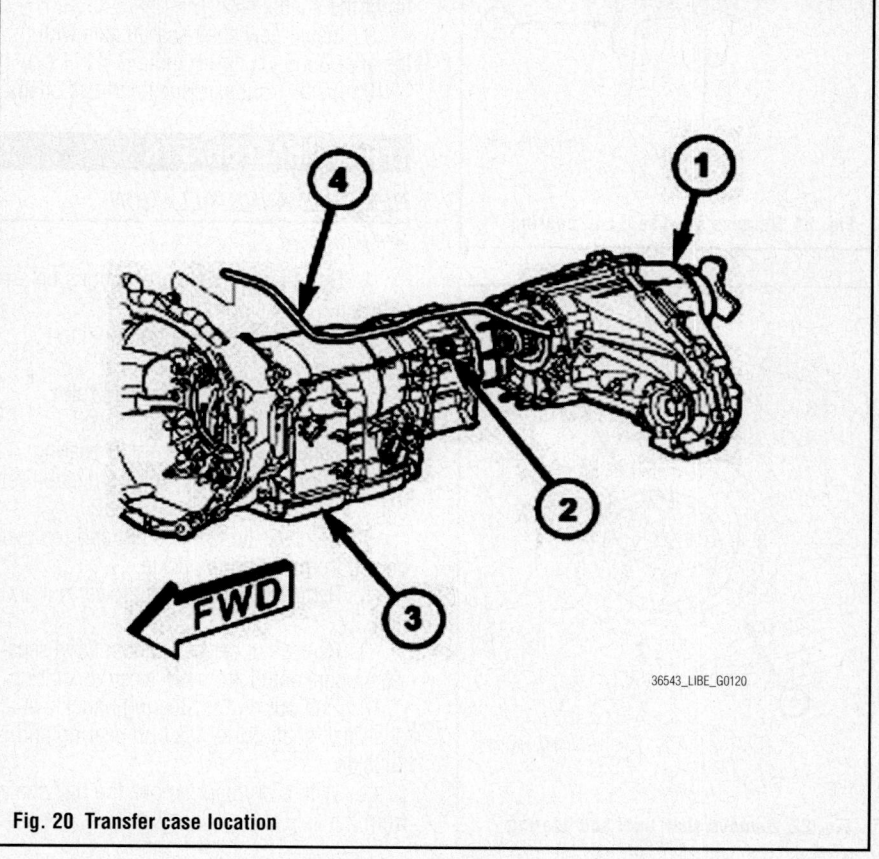

36543_LIBE_G0120

Fig. 20 Transfer case location

FRONT AXLE SHAFT, BEARING & SEAL

REMOVAL & INSTALLATION

Inner Bearing

See Figures 21 through 23.

1. Remove haft shafts.
2. On the right side, remove axle shaft with Remover 8420A and Slide Hammer C-3752.
3. Remove shaft seal (1) with Remover 7794-A (2) and a Slide Hammer C-637.
4. Remove shaft bearing/bushing (1) with Remover 7794-A (2) and a Slide Hammer C-637.

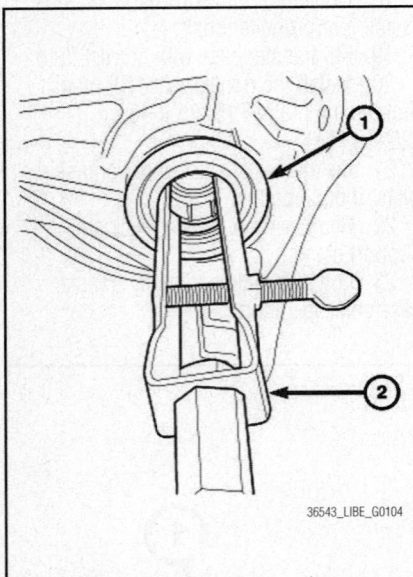

Fig. 21 Remove shaft seal and bearing

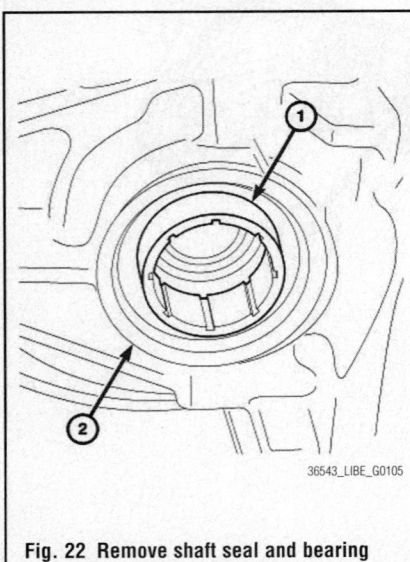

Fig. 22 Remove shaft seal and bearing

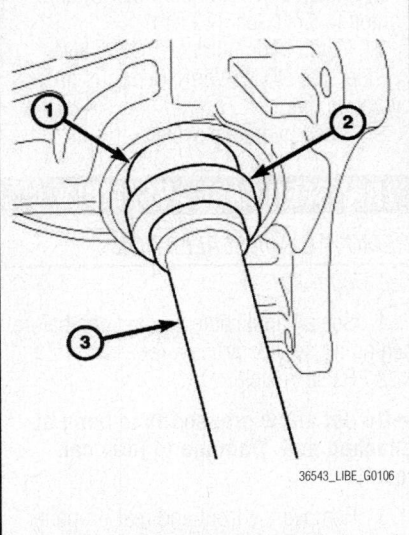

Fig. 23 Drive bearing/bushing in flush with housing bore

To install:

5. Position bearing/bushing (1) in the housing (2) bore.
6. Install shaft bearing/bushing (1) with large diameter end of Installer 8805 (2) and Handle C-4171 (3).
7. Drive bearing/bushing in flush with housing bore.
8. Apply a light coat of lubricant on the lip of the shaft seal.
9. Install new shaft seal in axle with Installer 8806 (1) and Handle C-4171 (2).
10. Install right axle shaft and half shafts.

FRONT HALFSHAFTS

REMOVAL & INSTALLATION

See Figure 24.

1. See all applicable precautions before beginning service procedures.
2. With vehicle in neutral, position vehicle on hoist.
3. Remove brake caliper and rotor.
4. Remove nut from half shaft.
5. Remove sensor from hub bearing.
6. Remove stabilizer link from stabilizer bar.
7. Remover tie rod end nut and remove tie rod from steering knuckle.
8. Remove clevis bracket lower nut and bolt.
9. Remove upper ball joint nut and separate upper control arm from steering knuckle.
10. Pull out on the steering knuckle and push half shaft out of the hub bearing and knuckle.
11. With a pry bar, remove the half shaft from the axle.

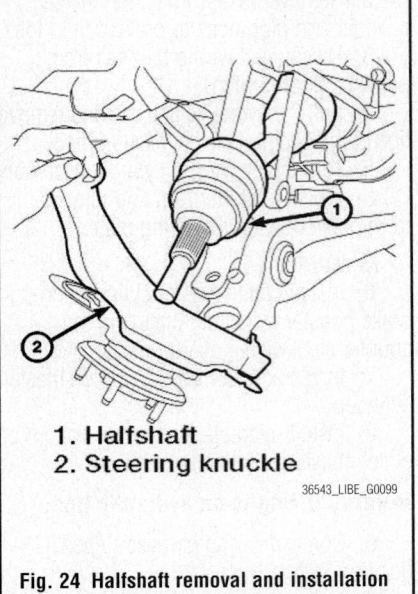

1. Halfshaft
2. Steering knuckle

Fig. 24 Halfshaft removal and installation

To install:

12. Apply a light coat of wheel bearing grease on the female splines of the inner C/V joint.
13. Clean hub bearing bore and apply a light coat of wheel bearing grease.
14. Install half shaft in axle and push firmly to engage the snap ring.
15. Pull out on the steering knuckle and push the half shaft through the knuckle and hub bearing.
16. Install upper control arm on steering knuckle and tighten ball joint nut to specifications.
17. Align clevis with lower control arm. Install lower clevis and tighten nut to specifications.
18. Install tie rod end in steering knuckle and tighten nut to specifications.
19. Install stabilizer bar link and tie rod end.
20. Install half shaft hub nut and tighten to specifications.

FRONT PINION SEAL

REMOVAL & INSTALLATION

See Figure 25.

1. See all applicable precautions before beginning service procedures.
2. With vehicle in neutral, position vehicle on hoist.
3. Remove brake calipers and rotors.
4. Remove propeller shaft.
5. Rotate pinion gear a minimum of ten times and verify the pinion rotates smoothly.
6. Record torque to rotate the pinion gear with an inch pound torque wrench.

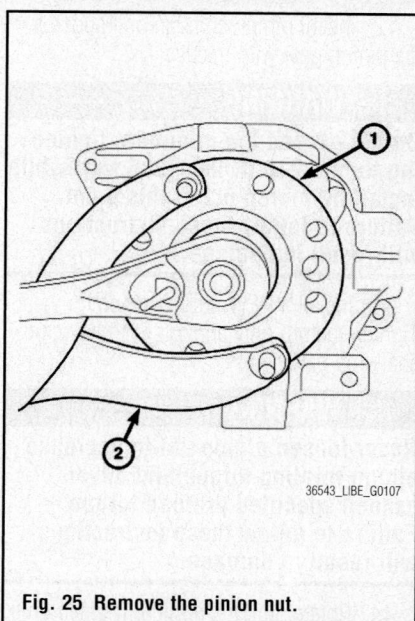

Fig. 25 Remove the pinion nut.

7. Using a short piece of pipe and Spanner Wrench to hold the pinion companion flange and remove the pinion nut.

8. Mark a line on the pinion shaft and flange for installation reference.

9. Remove pinion companion flange with Remover and Spanner Wrench.

10. Remove pinion seal with a seal puller.

To install:

11. Apply a light coating of gear lubricant on the lip of pinion seal. Install seal with a seal driver.

12. Install pinion companion flange on the pinion gear with Installer.

✳✳ WARNING

Do not exceed the minimum tightening torque 160 ft. lbs. (216 Nm) while installing pinion nut at this point. Failure to follow these instructions will result in damage.

13. Install a NEW nut on the pinion gear. Tighten the nut only enough to remove the shaft end play.

✳✳ WARNING

Never loosen pinion nut to decrease pinion rotating torque and never exceed specified preload torque. Failure to follow these instructions will result in damage.

14. Rotate pinion a minimum of ten time and verify pinion rotates smoothly. Rotate the pinion shaft with an inch pound torque wrench. Rotating torque should be equal to the reading recorded during removal plus 5 inch lbs. (0.56 Nm).

15. If rotating torque is low, use Spanner Wrench to hold the pinion companion flange and tighten the pinion nut in 5 ft. lbs. (6.8 Nm) increments until proper rotating torque is achieved.

✳✳ WARNING

If maximum tightening torque is reached 260 ft. lbs. (352 Nm) prior to reaching required rotating torque, the collapsible spacer may have been damaged. Never loosen pinion nut to decrease pinion rotating torque and never exceed specified preload torque. Failure to follow these instructions will result in damage.

16. Install brake rotors, calipers and propeller shaft

17. Fill differential with gear lubricant.

REAR AXLE HOUSING

REMOVAL & INSTALLATION

1. See all applicable precautions before beginning service procedures.

2. Remove or disconnect the following:
- Rear wheels
- Brake rotors
- Parking brake cables
- Wheel speed sensors, if equipped
- Brake hose
- Vent hose
- Driveshaft
- Stabilizer bar links
- Shock absorbers
- Track bar
- Upper and lower control arms
- Coil springs
- Axle housing

To install:

➡**The weight of the vehicle must be supported by the springs when the control arm and track bar fasteners are tightened.**

3. Install or connect the following:
- Axle housing and coil springs to the vehicle
- Upper and lower control arms
- Track bar
- Shock absorbers
- Stabilizer bar links. Tighten the nuts to 40 ft. lbs. (54 Nm).
- Driveshaft
- Vent hose
- Brake hose
- Wheel speed sensors, if equipped
- Parking brake cables
- Brake rotors or drums
- Rear wheels

4. Tighten the upper control arm bolts to 55 ft. lbs. (75 Nm), the lower control arm bolts to 130 ft. lbs. (177 Nm) and the track bar bolts to 74 ft. lbs. (100 Nm).

REAR AXLE SHAFT, BEARING & SEAL

REMOVAL & INSTALLATION

See Figures 26 through 28.

1. Remove axle shaft.

2. Remove axle seal with seal pick.

3. Position bearing (2) receiver (1) on axle tube.

4. Insert bearing remover Foot 6310-9 (3) through receiver (2) and bearing (1).

5. Tighten remove nut (1) on the shaft (4) to pull bearing into the receiver (3).

To install:

6. Remove any old sealer/burrs from axle tube.

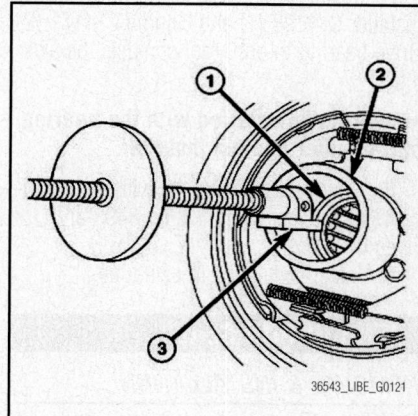

Fig. 26 Position bearing (2) receiver (1) on axle tube

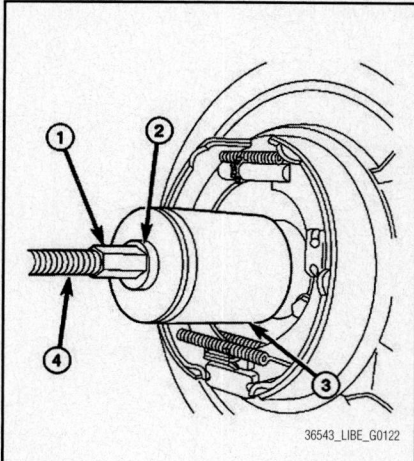

Fig. 27 Insert bearing remover Foot 6310-9 (3) through receiver (2) and bearing (1).

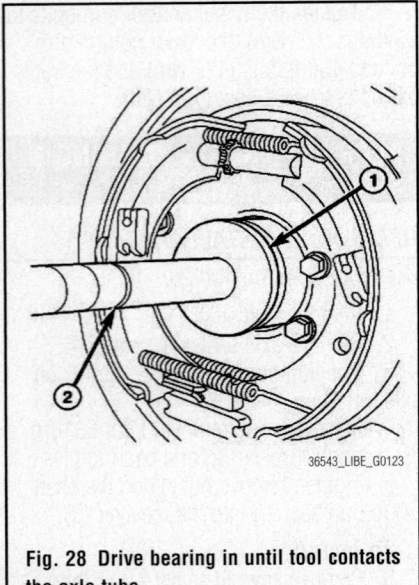

Fig. 28 Drive bearing in until tool contacts the axle tube.

7. Install axle shaft bearing with Installer C-4198 (1) and Handle C-4171 (2). Drive bearing in until tool contacts the axle tube.

➡**Bearing is installed with the bearing part number against installer.**

8. Coat new axle seal lip with axle lubricant. Install seal with Installer 8493 and Handle C-4171.

9. Install axle shaft in axle tube.

REAR PINION SEAL

REMOVAL & INSTALLATION

See Figure 29.

1. See all applicable precautions before beginning service procedures.

2. With vehicle in neutral, position vehicle on hoist.

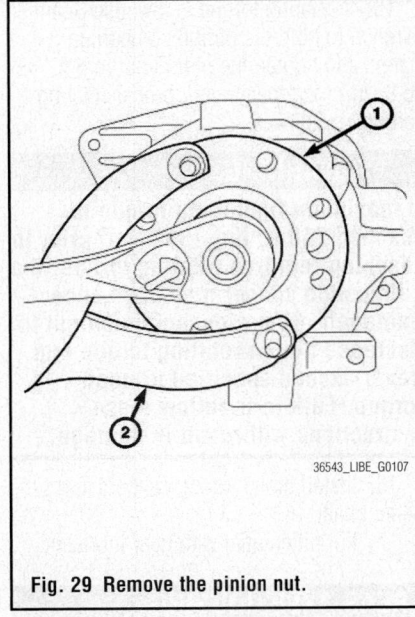

Fig. 29 Remove the pinion nut.

3. Remove brake calipers and rotors.

4. Remove propeller shaft.

5. Rotate pinion gear a minimum of ten times and verify the pinion rotates smoothly.

6. Record torque to rotate the pinion gear with an inch pound torque wrench.

7. Using a short piece of pipe and Spanner Wrench to hold the pinion companion flange and remove the pinion nut.

8. Mark a line on the pinion shaft and flange for installation reference.

9. Remove pinion companion flange with Remover and Spanner Wrench.

10. Remove pinion seal with a seal puller.

To install:

11. Apply a light coating of gear lubricant on the lip of pinion seal. Install seal with a seal driver.

12. Install pinion companion flange on the pinion gear with Installer.

✳✳ WARNING

Do not exceed the minimum tightening torque 210 ft. lbs. (285 Nm) while installing pinion nut at this point. Failure to follow these instructions will result in damage.

13. Install a NEW nut on the pinion gear. Tighten the nut only enough to remove the shaft end play.

✳✳ WARNING

Never loosen pinion nut to decrease pinion rotating torque and never exceed specified preload torque. Failure to follow these instructions will result in damage.

14. Rotate pinion a minimum of ten time and verify pinion rotates smoothly. Rotate the pinion shaft with an inch pound torque wrench. Rotating torque should be equal to the reading recorded during removal plus 5 inch lbs. (0.56 Nm).

15. If rotating torque is low, use Spanner Wrench to hold the pinion companion flange and tighten the pinion nut in 5 ft. lbs. (6.8 Nm) increments until proper rotating torque is achieved.

✳✳ CAUTION

Never loosen pinion nut to decrease pinion rotating torque and never exceed specified preload torque. Failure to follow these instructions will result in damage.

16. Install brake rotors, calipers and propeller shaft

17. Fill differential with gear lubricant.

ENGINE COOLING

ENGINE FAN

REMOVAL & INSTALLATION

3.7L & 4.0L Engines—Viscous & Electric Fans

1. See all applicable precautions before beginning service procedures.

➡If the fan blade is bent, warped, cracked or damaged in any way, it must be replaced only with a replacement fan blade. Do not attempt to repair a damaged fan blade.

➡For 3.7L Heavy Duty/Max Cool/Trailer Tow cooling package, the viscous fan cannot be removed separate from the shroud. Both fan and shroud must be removed together.

2. Disconnect battery negative cable.
3. Using special tool 6958 wrench and 8346 adapters, remove the viscous fan from the water pump.
4. Gently lay fan into shroud.
5. Disconnect the electrical connector for the electric fan, then disconnect connector from shroud.
6. Remove the two fan shroud mounting bolts connecting the fan shroud to the radiator.
7. Remove the shroud and fan from the vehicle.

To install:

➡For 3.7L Heavy Duty/Max Cool/Trailer Tow cooling package, the viscous fan cannot be installed separate from the shroud. Both fan and shroud must be installed together.

8. Gently lay viscous fan into shroud.
9. Install fan shroud assembly into the vehicle.
10. Tighten fan shroud to radiator bolts to 50 inch lbs. (5.5 Nm).
11. Using special tool 6958 wrench and 8346 adapters, install the viscous fan on the water pump.
12. Connect fan motor wire connector to harness connector, and attach connector to shroud.
13. Connect battery negative cable.
14. Start engine and check fan operation.

4.0L Engine—Viscous Fan Only

See Figure 30.

1. See all applicable precautions before beginning service procedures.
2. Partially drain the cooling system.

3. Remove the upper radiator hose.
4. Remove the air filter housing assembly.
5. Using Tool 6958 and adapter pins 8346, remove fan/viscous fan drive assembly from water pump.
6. Do not attempt to remove fan/viscous fan drive assembly from vehicle at this time.
7. Position the fan/fan drive assembly in the radiator shroud.
8. Remove the two shroud mounting screws.
9. Remove the radiator shroud and fan drive assembly.

➡After removing fan blade/viscous fan drive assembly, do not place viscous fan drive in horizontal position. If stored horizontally, silicone fluid in the viscous fan drive could drain into its bearing assembly and contaminate lubricant.

10. Remove four bolts securing fan blade assembly to viscous fan drive .

To install:

11. Install fan blade assembly to viscous fan drive. Tighten bolts to 17 ft. lbs. (23 Nm).
12. Position fan blade/viscous fan drive assembly into the radiator shroud.
13. Install the radiator shroud and fan drive assembly into the vehicle.
14. Install fan shroud retaining screws. Tighten screws to 50 inch lbs. (6 Nm).
15. Using Tool 6958, install the fan blade/viscous fan drive assembly to the

water pump shaft. Tighten mounting nut to 37 ft. lbs. (50 Nm).
16. Install the upper radiator hose.
17. Fill cooling system.
18. Connect battery negative cable.

RADIATOR

REMOVAL & INSTALLATION

See Figure 31.

1. See all applicable precautions before beginning service procedures.
2. Disconnect the negative battery cable at battery.
3. Drain coolant from radiator.
4. Remove combination coolant recovery/washer fluid reservoir assembly.
5. Remove the front grill.
6. Remove the cooling fan from the engine, if equipped.
7. Remove the two radiator mounting bolts.
8. Disconnect the connector for the electric fan.
9. Disconnect the power steering cooler line from cooler.
10. Disconnect the radiator upper and lower hoses.
11. Disconnect the overflow hose from radiator.
12. The lower part of radiator is equipped with two alignment dowel pins (2). They are located on the bottom of radiator tank and fit into rubber grommets (3). These rubber grommets (3) are pressed into the radiator lower crossmember (4).

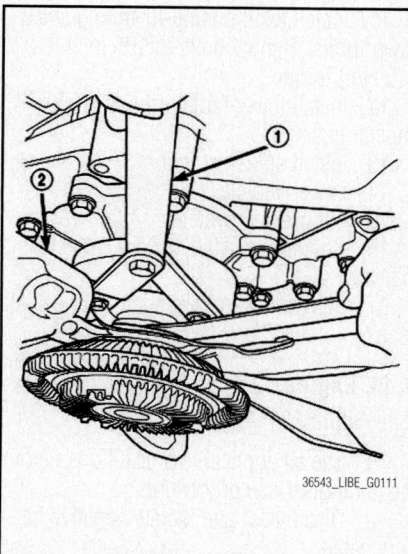

Fig. 30 Removing fan blade/viscous fan drive assembly

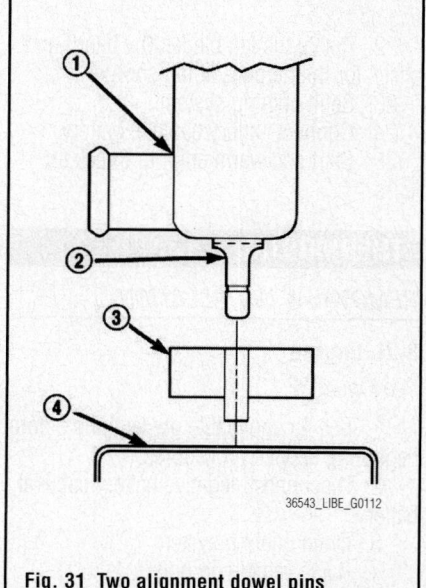

Fig. 31 Two alignment dowel pins

※※ WARNING

The air conditioning system (if equipped) is under a constant pressure even with the engine off.

→The radiator and radiator cooling fan can be removed as an assembly. It is not necessary to remove the cooling fan before removing or installing the radiator.

13. Gently lift up and remove radiator from vehicle.

※※ WARNING

Be careful not to scrape the radiator fins against any other component. Also be careful not to disturb the air conditioning condenser (if equipped).

To install:

14. Gently lower the radiator and fan shroud into the vehicle. Guide the two radiator alignment dowels into the rubber grommets located in lower radiator crossmember.

15. Connect the radiator upper and lower hoses and hose clamps to radiator.

※※ WARNING

The tangs on the hose clamps must be positioned straight down.

16. Install coolant reserve/overflow tank hose at radiator.
17. Install both radiator mounting bolts.
18. Reconnect the electric cooling fan.
19. Install the grill.
20. Install combination coolant recovery/washer fluid reservoir assembly.
21. Reinstall the cooling fan to the engine.
22. Rotate the fan blades (by hand) and check for interference at fan shroud.
23. Refill cooling system.
24. Connect battery cable at battery.
25. Start and warm engine. Check for leaks.

THERMOSTAT

REMOVAL & INSTALLATION

3.7L Engine

See Figure 32.

1. See all applicable precautions before beginning service procedures.
2. Disconnect negative battery cable at battery.
3. Drain cooling system.
4. Raise vehicle on hoist.

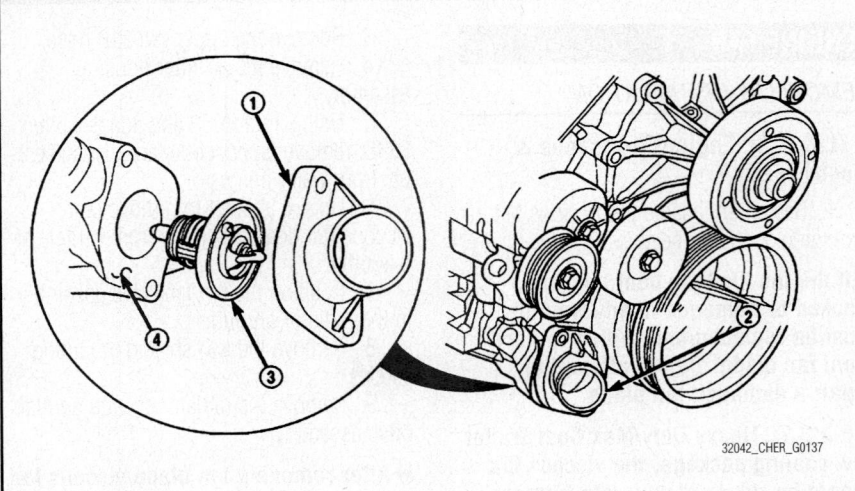

Fig. 32 The location of the thermostat (3) and its housing (1) on the 3.7L engine

5. Remove splash shield.
6. Remove lower radiator hose clamp and lower radiator hose at thermostat housing.
7. Remove thermostat housing mounting bolts, thermostat housing and thermostat.

To install:

8. Clean mating areas of timing chain cover and thermostat housing.
9. Install thermostat (spring side down) into recessed machined groove on housing assembly. Make sure rubber seal locating tab is positioned in the corresponding notch in the housing.
10. Position thermostat housing on timing chain cover.
11. Install two housing-to-timing chain cover bolts. Tighten bolts to 105 inch lbs. (12 Nm) torque.
12. Install lower radiator hose on thermostat housing.
13. Install splash shield.
14. Lower vehicle.
15. Fill cooling system.
16. Connect negative battery cable to battery.
17. Start and warm the engine. Check for leaks.

4.0L Engine

See Figure 33.

1. See all applicable precautions before beginning service procedures.
2. Disconnect and isolate negative battery cable.
3. Drain cooling system.
4. Remove air housing.

5. Remove upper intake manifold.
6. Remove radiator tube mounting nuts (6).
7. Remove radiator hose (1) at thermostat housing (4).
8. Remove thermostat housing bolts (3), thermostat housing (4) and thermostat.
9. Clean thermostat housing mating surface on lower intake manifold.

To install:

10. Make sure jiggle pin is at the 12 o'clock position. Position thermostat and thermostat housing onto the lower intake manifold.
11. Install thermostat housing bolts. Tighten bolts to 25 ft. lbs. (35 Nm).
12. Install upper radiator hose onto thermostat housing.

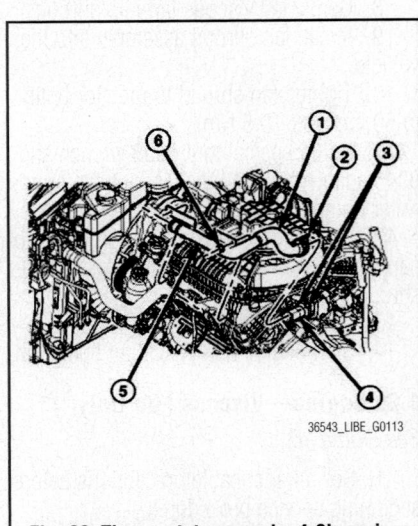

Fig. 33 Thermostat removal—4.0L engine

13. Position upper radiator hose tube and install mounting nuts. Tighten nuts to 85 inch lbs. (9 Nm).

14. Install upper intake manifold.

15. Install air cleaner housing.

16. Fill cooling system.

WATER PUMP

REMOVAL & INSTALLATION

3.7L Engine

See Figure 34.

1. See all applicable precautions before beginning service procedures.

2. Drain the cooling system.

3. Remove or disconnect the following:
   • Negative battery cable
   • Fan and clutch assembly from the pump
   • Fan shroud and fan assembly.

❄❄ WARNING

If you're reusing the fan clutch, keep it upright to avoid silicone fluid loss.

   • Lower hose
   • Water pump (8 bolts)

4. Installation is the reverse of removal. Tighten the bolts, in sequence, to 40 ft. lbs. (54 Nm).

4.0L Engine

See Figure 35.

1. See all applicable precautions before beginning service procedures.

2. Disconnect negative battery cable.

3. Remove air filter housing.

4. Drain cooling system.

5. Remove coolant recover container.

6. Remove viscous radiator fan.

7. Remove RH engine mount through bolt.

8. Raise engine assembly.

9. Carefully unbolt the air conditioning compressor from the front of engine. Do not disconnect any A/C hoses from the compressor. Temporarily support the compressor.

10. Remove accessory drive belt bracket.

11. Remove engine timing belt.

12. Remove water pump mounting bolts (3).

13. Remove water pump.

14. Clean mounting surface.

To install:

15. Position water pump and new gasket.

16. Install water pump mounting bolts. Tighten to 105 inch lbs. (12 Nm).

17. Install engine timing belt.

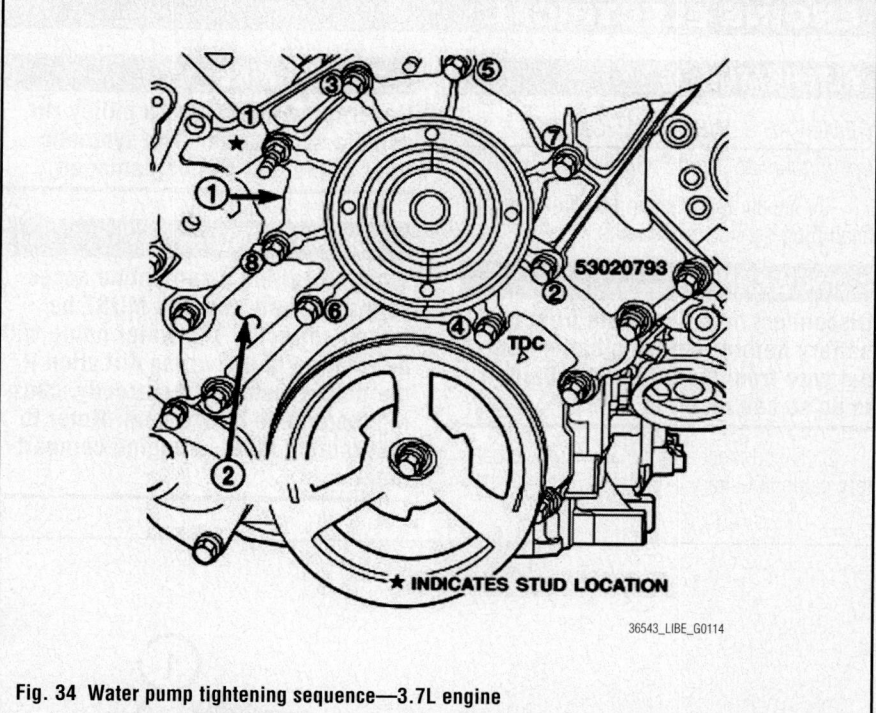

Fig. 34 Water pump tightening sequence—3.7L engine

★ INDICATES STUD LOCATION

53020793

36543_LIBE_G0114

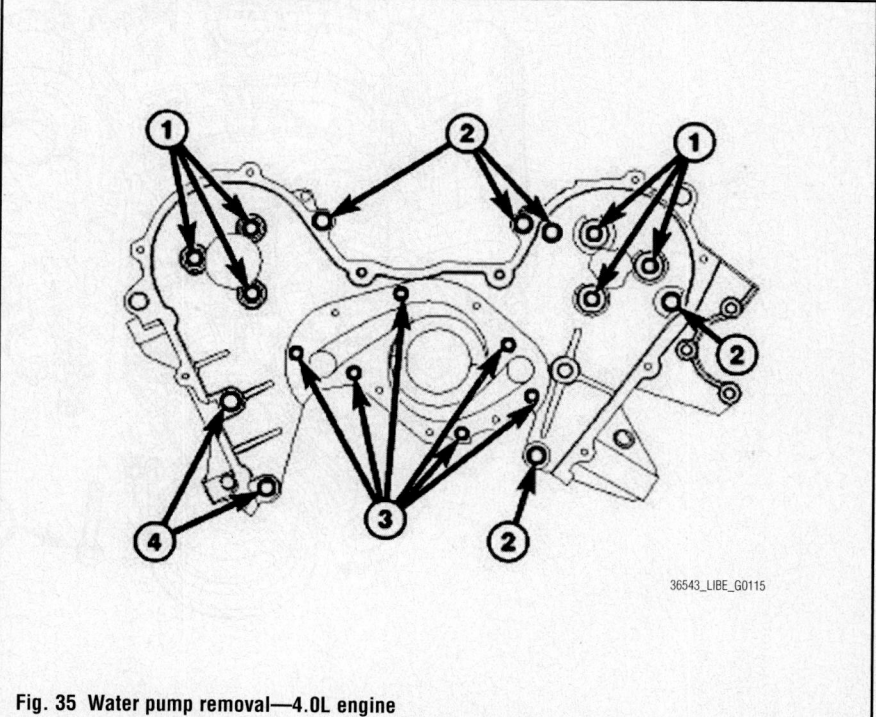

Fig. 35 Water pump removal—4.0L engine

36543_LIBE_G0115

18. Install accessory drive bracket. Tighten bolts to 40 ft. lbs. (54 Nm).

19. Position A/C compressor and install A/C compressor mounting nuts. Tighten nuts to 21 ft. lbs. (28 Nm).

20. Lower engine and install right-hand engine mount through bolt. Tighten bolt to 40 lbs. ft. (54 Nm).

21. Install accessory drive belt.

22. Install viscous radiator fan.

23. Install coolant recover container.

24. Install air filter assembly.

25. Connect negative battery cable.

26. Fill cooling system.

ALTERNATOR

REMOVAL & INSTALLATION

See Figures 36 through 38.

1. See all applicable precautions before beginning service procedures.

❋❋ WARNING

Disconnect negative cable from the battery before removing battery output wire from the alternator. Failure to do so can result in injury.

2. Disconnect and isolate negative battery cable at battery.

❋❋ WARNING

Never force a belt over a pulley rim using a screwdriver. The synthetic fiber of the belt can be damaged.

❋❋ WARNING

When installing a serpentine accessory drive belt, the belt MUST be routed correctly. The water pump will be rotating in the wrong direction if the belt is installed incorrectly, causing the engine to overheat. Refer to belt routing label in engine compartment.

3. Remove alternator drive belt.
4. Unsnap plastic protective cover from B+ mounting stud.
5. Remove B+ terminal mounting nut at top of alternator.
6. Disconnect field wire electrical connector at rear of alternator by pushing on connector tab.
7. Remove generator mounting bolts.
8. Remove alternator from vehicle.

To install:

9. Position alternator to engine and install mounting bolts. Tighten horizontal mounting bolt(s) followed by vertical mounting bolt(s).

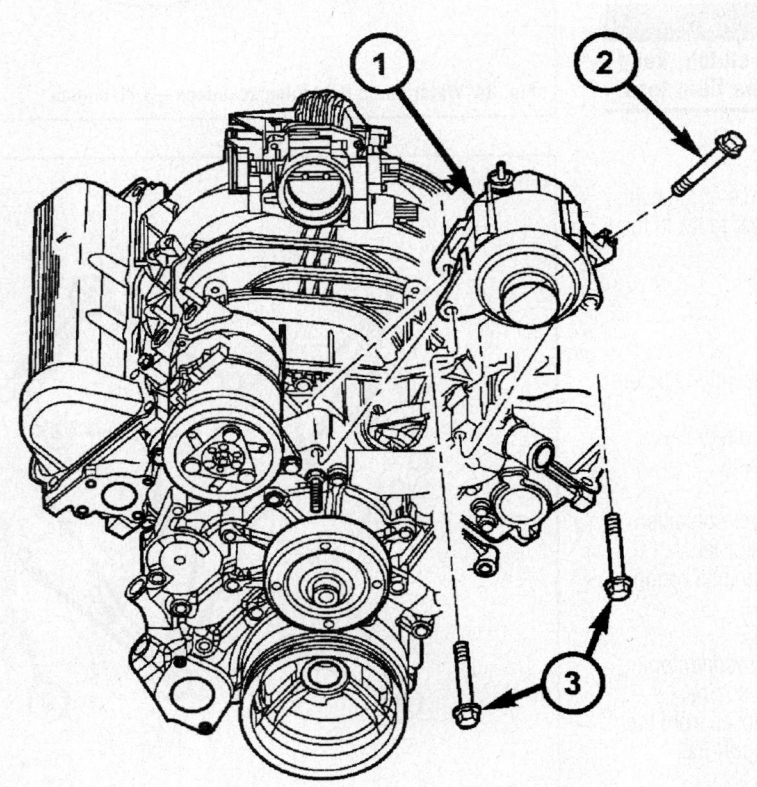

1 - GENERATOR
2 - VERTICAL MOUNTING BOLT
3 - HORIZONTAL MOUNTING BOLTS

06009-JEEP-G11

Fig. 36 Alternator mounting—3.7L engine

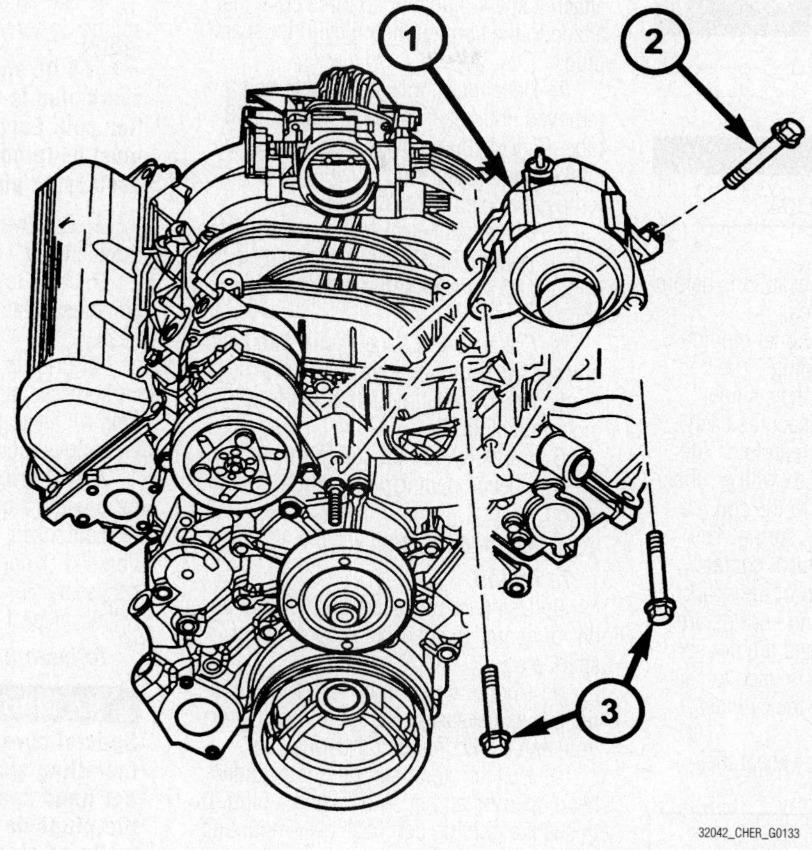

Fig. 37 The alternator for the 3.7L engine

10. Snap field wire connector into rear of generator.

11. Install B+ terminal and nut to alternator mounting stud.

12. Snap plastic protective cover to B+ terminal.

❋❋ WARNING

Never force a belt over a pulley rim using a screwdriver. The synthetic fiber of the belt can be damaged.

❋❋ WARNING

When installing a serpentine accessory drive belt, the belt MUST be routed correctly. The water pump will be rotating in the wrong direction if the belt is installed incorrectly, causing the engine to overheat. Refer to belt routing label in engine compartment.

13. Install drive belt.

14. Install negative battery cable to battery.

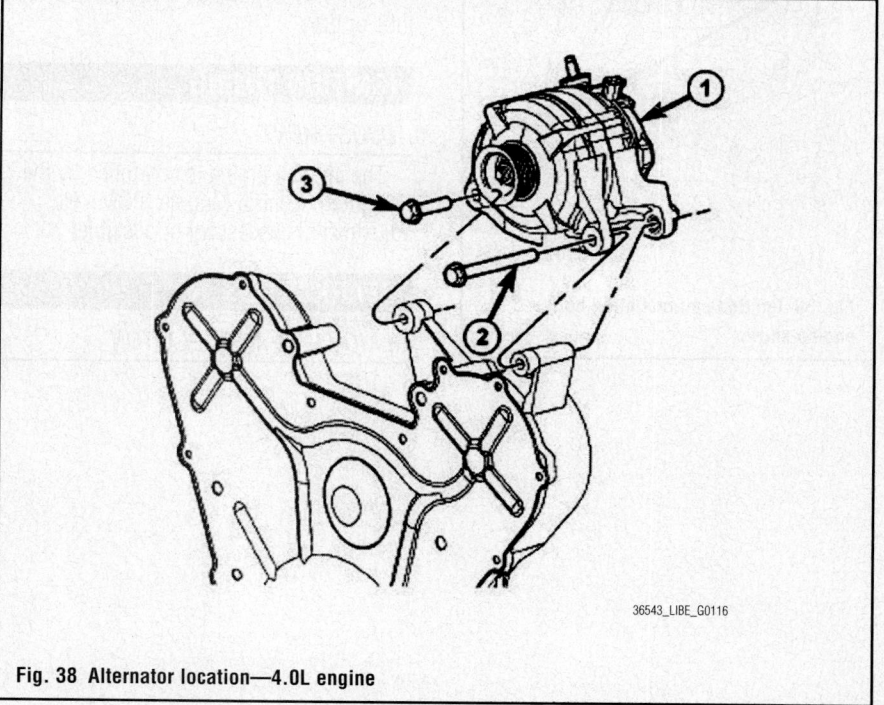

Fig. 38 Alternator location—4.0L engine

FIRING ORDERS

3.7L Engine Firing order: 1–6–5–4–3–2
4.0L Engine Firing order: 1–2–3–4–5–6

IGNITION COIL

REMOVAL & INSTALLATION

See Figure 39.

1. See all applicable precautions before beginning service procedures.

On 4.0L engines an individual ignition coil is used for each spark plug . The coil fits into machined holes in the cylinder head. A mounting stud/nut secures each coil to the top of the intake manifold. The bottom of the coil is equipped with a rubber boot to seal the spark plug to the coil. Inside each rubber boot is a spring. The spring is used for a mechanical contact between the coil and the top of the spark plug. These rubber boots and springs are a permanent part of the coil and are not serviced separately. An O-ring is used to seal the coil at the opening into the cylinder head.

3.7L engines are similar, except they

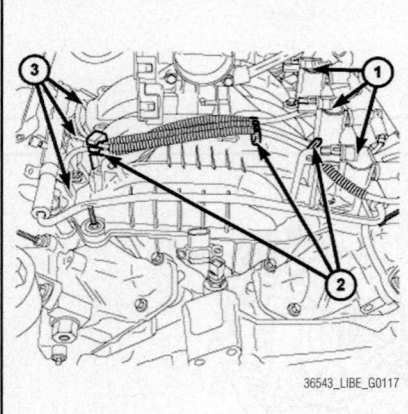

Fig. 39 Ignition coil mounting bolts—3.7L engine shown

36543_LIBE_G0117

attach a spark plug wire to three coils that attach to the corresponding cylinder spark plug.

2. Depending on which coil is being removed, the upper intake manifold, EGR tube, PCV vacuum hoses, throttle body air intake tube or intake box may need to be removed to gain access to coil.

3. Disconnect electrical connector from coil by pushing downward on release lock on top of connector and pull connector from coil.

4. Clean area at base of coil with compressed air before removal.

5. Remove coil mounting nut from mounting stud.

6. Carefully pull up coil from cylinder head opening with a slight twisting action.

7. Remove coil from vehicle.

To install:

8. Using compressed air, blow out any dirt or contaminants from around top of spark plug.

9. Check condition of coil O-ring and replace as necessary. To aid in coil installation, apply silicone to coil O-ring.

10. Position ignition coil into cylinder head opening and push onto spark plug. Do this while guiding coil base over mounting stud.

11. Install coil mounting stud nut.

12. Connect electrical connector to coil by snapping into position.

13. If necessary, install throttle body air tube or box.

IGNITION TIMING

ADJUSTMENT

The ignition timing is controlled by the Powertrain Control Module (PCM). No adjustment is necessary or possible.

SPARK PLUGS

REMOVAL & INSTALLATION

1. See all applicable precautions before beginning service procedures.

➡️**For 4.0L engines, each individual spark plug is located under each ignition coil. Each individual ignition coil must be removed to gain access to each spark plug.**

2. Remove necessary air filter tubing at throttle body.

3. Prior to removing ignition coil, spray compressed air around coil base at cylinder head.

4. Prior to removing spark plug, spray compressed air into cylinder head opening. This will help prevent foreign material from entering combustion chamber.

5. Remove spark plug from cylinder head using a quality socket with a rubber or foam insert. Also check condition of ignition coil O-ring and replace as necessary.

6. Inspect spark plug condition.

To install:

✸✸ WARNING

Special care should be taken when installing spark plugs into the cylinder head spark plug wells. Be sure the plugs do not drop into the plug wells as electrodes can be damaged.

✸✸ WARNING

Always tighten spark plugs to the specified torque. Over tightening can cause distortion resulting in a change in the spark plug gap or a cracked porcelain insulator.

7. Start the spark plug into the cylinder head by hand to avoid cross threading.

8. Tighten spark plugs.

9. Before installing coil(s), check condition of coil O-ring and replace as necessary. To aid in coil installation, apply silicone to coil O-ring.

10. Install ignition coil(s).

STARTER

REMOVAL & INSTALLATION

3.7L Engine

See Figure 40.

1. See all applicable precautions before beginning service procedures.
2. Disconnect and isolate negative battery cable.
3. Raise and support vehicle.
4. Remove 2 flange bolts securing left exhaust downpipe to crossover pipe. Lower pipe slightly to allow front propeller shaft removal.
5. Remove front propeller shaft.
6. Remove 2 starter heat shield bolts at side of starter.
7. Remove starter heat shield nut at front of starter.
8. Remove starter heat shield.
9. Remove solenoid wire from solenoid terminal.
10. Remove battery cable from stud on starter solenoid.
11. Remove 2 starter mounting bolts.
12. Position front of starter to face rear of vehicle. Rotate starter until solenoid position is located below starter.
13. Remove starter from vehicle by passing it between exhaust pipe and transmission bell housing.

To install:

14. Position front of starter towards rear of vehicle with solenoid position rotated

until it is located below starter. Install starter by passing it between exhaust pipe and transmission bell housing.

15. Position starter into bell housing and install 2 bolts.
16. Install battery cable and nut to stud on starter solenoid.
17. Install solenoid wire connector to solenoid terminal.
18. Position starter heat shield and install nut at front of starter.
19. Install 2 starter heat shield bolts at side of starter.
20. Install front propeller shaft.
21. Install 2 flange bolts securing left exhaust down-pipe to crossover pipe.

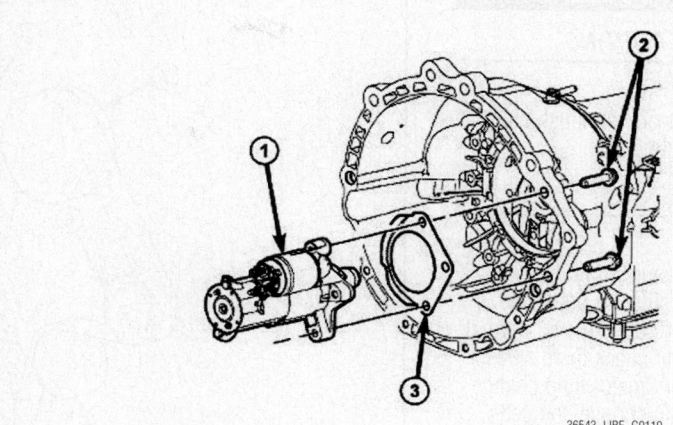

Fig. 41 Starter location—4.0L engine

36543_LIBE_G0119

22. Lower vehicle.
23. Connect negative battery cable.

4.0L Engine

See Figure 41.

1. See all applicable precautions before beginning service procedures.
2. Disconnect and isolate negative battery cable.
3. Raise and support vehicle.
4. Four Wheel Drive Equipped: Remove front propeller shaft.
5. Remove solenoid nut from mounting stud.
6. After nut has been removed, pull battery cable from mounting stud while removing electrical connector from solenoid terminal.
7. Remove two starter mounting bolts (2).
8. Remove starter assembly (1) from transmission.
9. Remove plate (3) from transmission.
10. Rotate starter assembly (1) to allow removal from vehicle.

To install:

11. Rotate starter assembly to allow positioning into transmission.
12. Install two starter mounting bolts and tighten.
13. Position battery cable assembly onto stud while pushing solenoid connector onto solenoid terminal.
14. Install nut and tighten.
15. Four Wheel Drive Equipped: Install front propeller shaft.
16. Lower vehicle.
17. Connect negative battery cable.

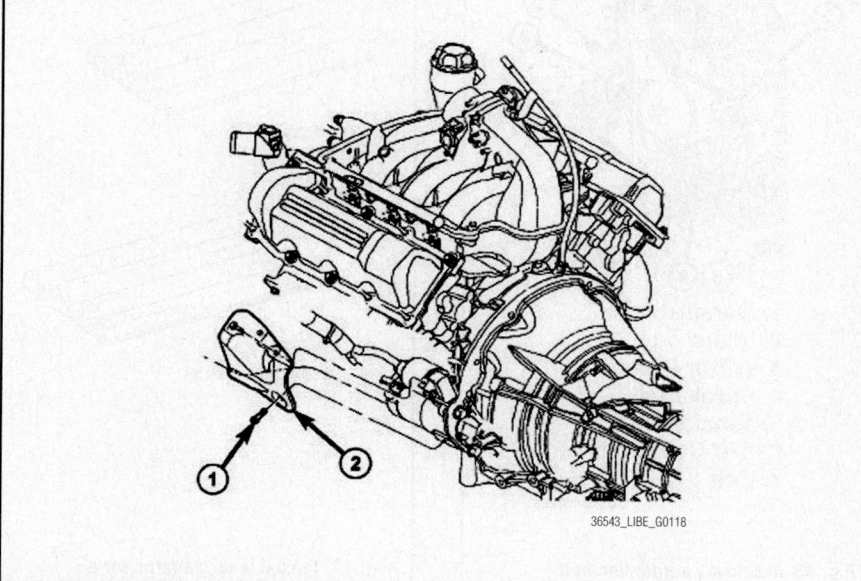

36543_LIBE_G0118

Fig. 40 Starter position—3.7L engine

ENGINE MECHANICAL

ACCESSORY DRIVE BELTS

ACCESSORY BELT ROUTING

See Figures 42 and 43.

Refer to the accompanying illustrations for accessory belt routing.

INSPECTION

See Figure 44.

Although many manufacturers recommend that the drive belt(s) be inspected every 30,000 miles (48,000 km) or more, it is really a good idea to check them at least once a year, or at every major fluid change. Whichever interval you choose, the belts should be checked for wear or damage. Obviously, a damaged drive belt can cause problems should it give way while the vehicle is in operation. But, improper length belts (too short or long), as well as excessively worn belts, can also cause problems. Loose accessory drive belts can lead to poor engine cooling and diminished output from the alternator, air conditioning compressor or power steering pump. A belt that is too tight places a severe strain on the driven unit and can wear out bearings quickly.

Serpentine drive belts should be inspected for rib chunking (pieces of the ribs breaking off), severe glazing, frayed cords or other visible damage. Any belt which is missing sections of 2 or more adjacent ribs which are ½ in. (13mm) or longer must be replaced. You might want to note that serpentine belts do tend to form small cracks across the backing. If the only wear you find is in the form of one or more cracks are across the backing and NOT parallel to the ribs, the belt is still good and does not need to be replaced.

ADJUSTMENT

See Figure 45.

Periodic drive belt tensioning is not necessary, because an automatic spring-loaded tensioner is used with these belts to maintain proper adjustment at all times. The tensioner is also useful as a wear indicator. When the belt is properly installed, the arrow on the tensioner housing must point within the acceptable range lines on the tensioners face. If the arrow falls outside the range, either an improper belt has been installed or the belt is worn beyond its useful life span. In either case, a new belt must be installed immediately to assure proper engine operation and to prevent possible accessory damage.

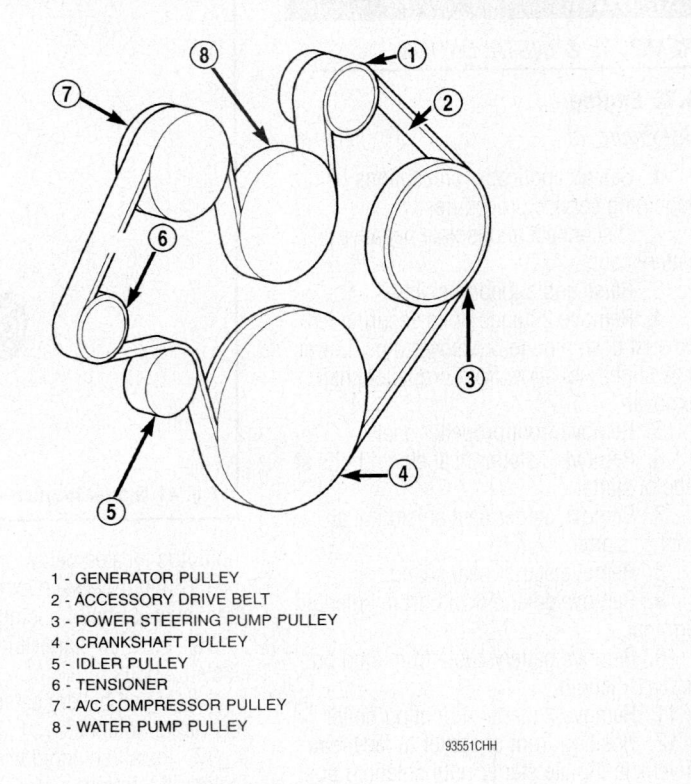

1 - GENERATOR PULLEY
2 - ACCESSORY DRIVE BELT
3 - POWER STEERING PUMP PULLEY
4 - CRANKSHAFT PULLEY
5 - IDLER PULLEY
6 - TENSIONER
7 - A/C COMPRESSOR PULLEY
8 - WATER PUMP PULLEY

93551CHH

Fig. 42 Accessory serpentine belt routing—3.7L engine

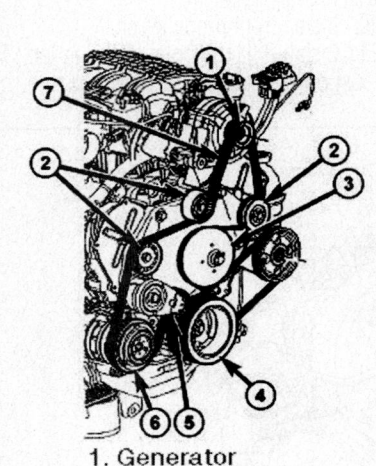

1. Generator
2. Idlers
3. Water Pump
4. Crankshaft
5. Tensioner
6. A/C Compressor
7. Belt

36543_LIBE_G0124

Fig. 43 Accessory serpentine belt routing—4.0L engine

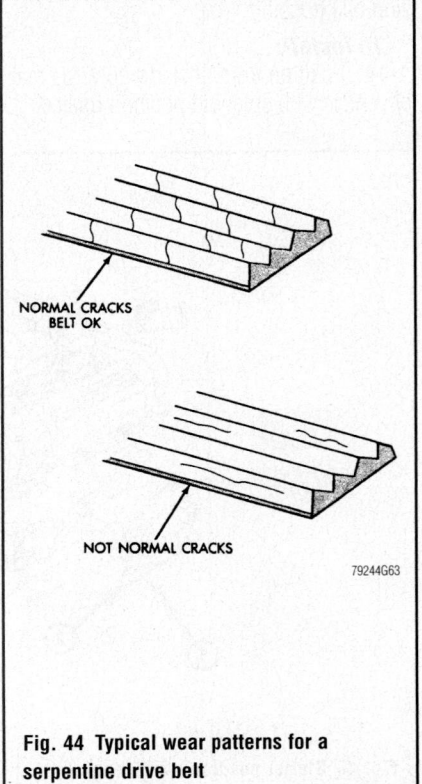

NORMAL CRACKS BELT OK

NOT NORMAL CRACKS

79244G63

Fig. 44 Typical wear patterns for a serpentine drive belt

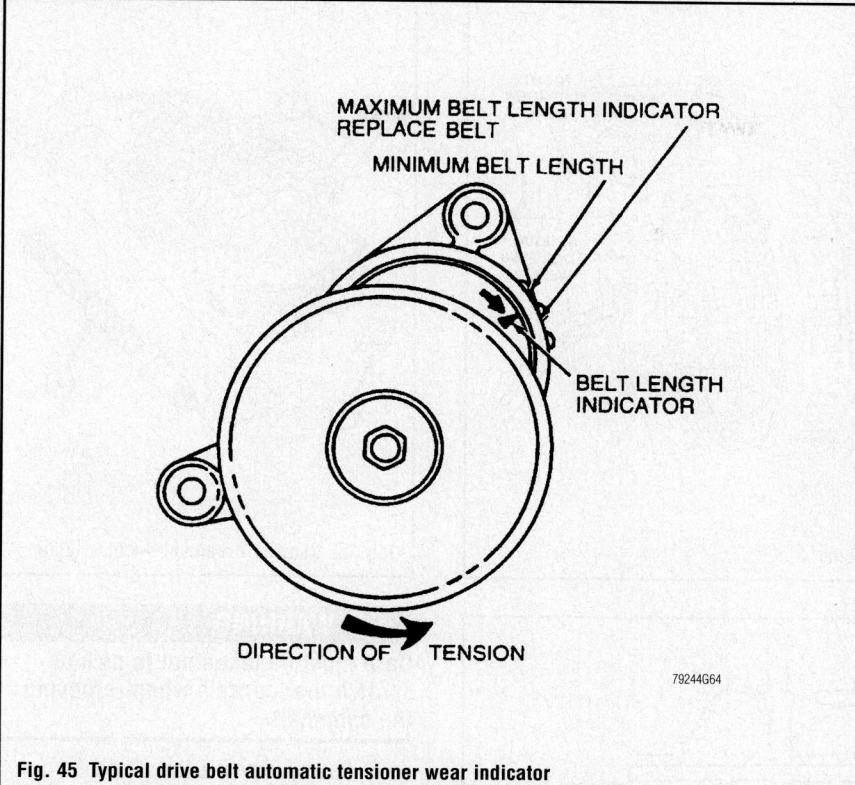

Fig. 45 Typical drive belt automatic tensioner wear indicator

REMOVAL & INSTALLATION

3.7L Engine

See Figure 42.

1. See all applicable precautions before beginning service procedures.
2. Disconnect negative battery cable from battery.
3. Rotate belt tensioner until it contacts its stop.
4. Remove belt, then slowly rotate the tensioner into the free arm position.

To install:

5. Check condition of all pulleys.

❄❄ WARNING

When installing the serpentine accessory drive belt, the belt MUST be routed correctly. If not, the engine may overheat due to the water pump rotating in the wrong direction.

6. Install new belt . Route the belt around all pulleys except the idler pulley. Rotate the tensioner arm until it contacts its stop position. Route the belt around the idler and slowly let the tensioner rotate into the belt. Make sure the belt is seated onto all pulleys.
7. With the drive belt installed, inspect the belt wear indicator. On 3.7L engines, the gap between the tang and the housing stop must not exceed 24 mm (.94 in.).

4.0L Engine

See Figure 43.

1. See all applicable precautions before beginning service procedures.
2. Remove combination coolant recovery/washer reservoir.
3. Insert a suitable square drive ratchet into the square hole on belt tensioner arm.
4. Rotate accessory drive belt tensioner clockwise to release belt tension.

5. Remove accessory drive belt.

To install:

➡ **When installing accessory drive belt onto pulleys, make sure that belt is properly routed and all V-grooves make proper contact with pulleys.**

6. Rotate tensioner clockwise and position accessory drive belt over all pulleys.
7. Gently release tensioner.
8. Install combination coolant recovery/washer reservoir.

CAMSHAFT AND VALVE LIFTERS

REMOVAL & INSTALLATION

3.7L Engine

See Figures 46 through 48.

1. See all applicable precautions before beginning service procedures.
2. Remove or disconnect the following:
   - Negative battery cable
   - Cylinder head covers
   - Rocker arms
   - Hydraulic lash adjusters

➡ **Keep all valvetrain components in order for assembly.**

3. Set the engine at Top Dead Center (TDC) of the compression stroke for the No. 1 cylinder.
4. Install Timing Chain Wedge 8379 to retain the chain tensioners.
5. Remove the camshaft position sensor, if necessary.
6. Matchmark the timing chains to the camshaft sprockets.
7. Install Camshaft Holding Tool 8428 to the left camshaft sprocket.
8. Remove or disconnect the following:

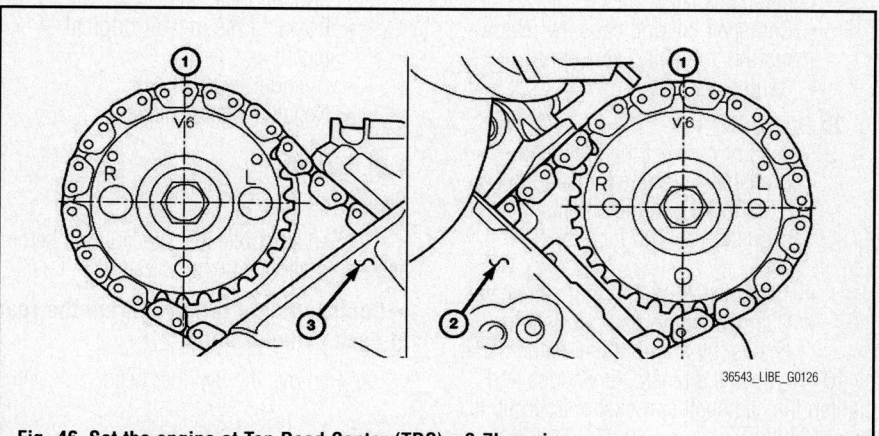

Fig. 46 Set the engine at Top Dead Center (TDC)—3.7L engine

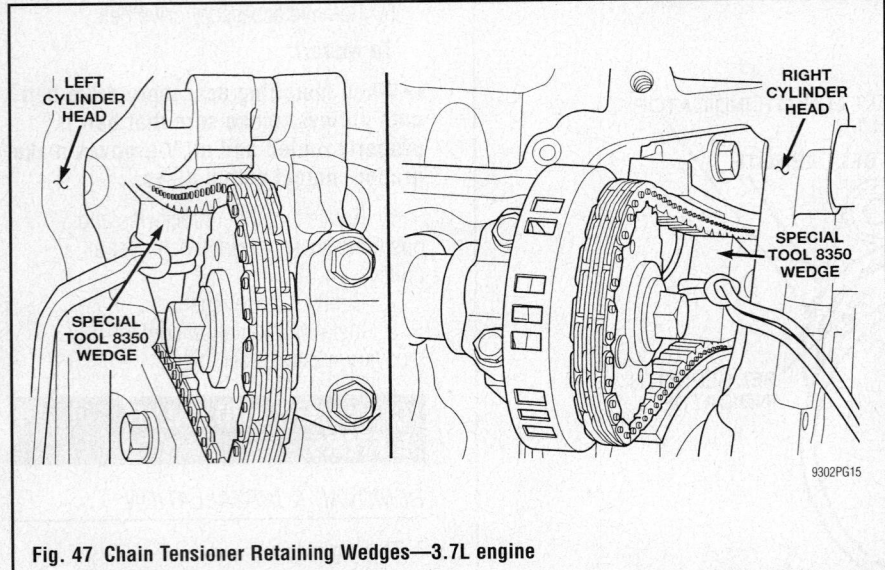

Fig. 47 Chain Tensioner Retaining Wedges—3.7L engine

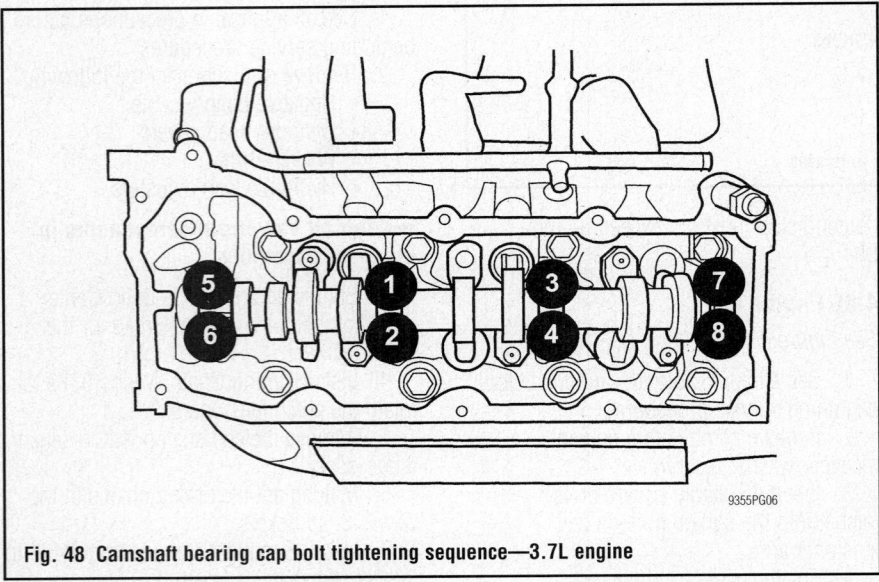

Fig. 48 Camshaft bearing cap bolt tightening sequence—3.7L engine

- Right camshaft timing sprocket and target wheel
- Left camshaft sprocket
- Camshaft bearing caps, by reversing the tightening sequence
- Camshafts

To install:
9. Install or connect the following:
- Camshafts. Torque the bearing cap bolts in ½ turn increments, in sequence, to 100 inch lbs. (11 Nm).
- Target wheel to the right camshaft
- Camshaft timing sprockets and chains, by aligning the matchmarks
10. Remove the tensioner wedges and tighten the camshaft sprocket bolts to 90 ft. lbs. (122 Nm).

11. Install or connect the following:
- Hydraulic lash adjusters in their original locations
- Rocker arms in their original locations
- Cylinder head covers
- Negative battery cable

4.0L Engine
See Figure 49.

1. See all applicable precautions before beginning service procedures.

➡**Camshafts are removed from the rear of each cylinder head.**

2. Remove the cylinder head.

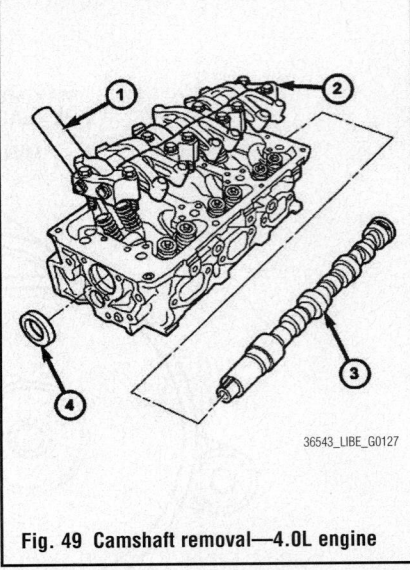

Fig. 49 Camshaft removal—4.0L engine

✳✳ WARNING
Care must be taken not to nick or scratch the journals when removing the camshaft.

3. Carefully remove the camshaft from the rear of the cylinder head.

To install:

✳✳ WARNING
Care must be taken not to scrape or nick the camshaft journals when installing the camshaft into position.

4. Lubricate camshaft bearing journals, camshaft lobes and camshaft seal with clean engine oil and install camshaft into cylinder head.
5. Install the cylinder head.

CATALYTIC CONVERTER

REMOVAL & INSTALLATION

3.7L Engine
See Figure 50.

1. See all applicable precautions before beginning service procedures.

✳✳ CAUTION
If torches are used when working on the exhaust system, do not allow the flame near the fuel lines.

2. Raise and support the vehicle.
3. Saturate the bolts (1) and nuts with heat valve lubricant. Allow 5 minutes for penetration.

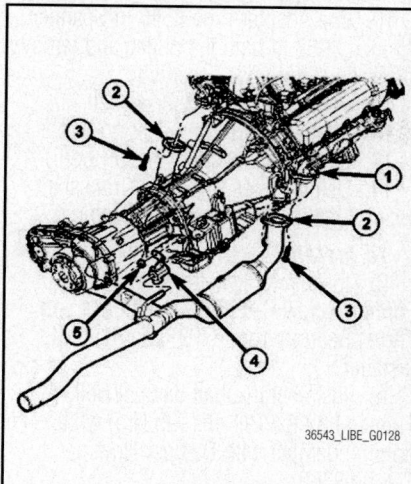

Fig. 50 Catalytic Converter removal—3.7L engine

4. Disconnect oxygen sensor electrical connectors.

5. Remove the nuts from the front exhaust pipe and catalytic converter assembly to muffler flange.

6. Remove bolts (1) and flanged nuts at the manifold.

7. Lower the front exhaust pipe/catalytic converter assembly (3) and slide out of the mount at the transmission (if equipped).

8. Remove the front exhaust pipe/catalytic converter assembly from the vehicle.

To install:

9. Position the front exhaust pipe and catalytic converter assembly into the mount at the transmission (if equipped) and onto the exhaust manifold flange connection.

10. Install the nuts at the front exhaust pipe and catalytic converter assembly to muffler flange. Do not tighten.

11. Position the exhaust pipe for proper clearance with the frame and underbody parts. A minimum clearance of 1.0 in. (25.4mm) is required.

12. Tighten the bolt at exhaust manifold to 19 inch lbs. (27 Nm).

13. Tighten the front exhaust pipe and catalytic converter assembly to muffler flange nuts to 19 ft. lbs. (27 Nm).

14. Position the front pipe onto the exhaust manifold flange connection. Tighten the clamp to 95 inch lbs. (10 Nm).

15. Connect oxygen sensor electrical connectors.

16. Lower the vehicle.

17. Start the vehicle and inspect for exhaust leaks. Repair exhaust leaks as necessary.

18. Check the exhaust system for contact with the body panels. Make adjustments, if necessary.

4.0L Engine

See Figure 51.

1. See all applicable precautions before beginning service procedures.

⁂ CAUTION

If torches are used when working on the exhaust system, do not allow the flame near the fuel lines.

2. Disconnect and isolate the negative battery cable.

3. Raise and support the vehicle.

4. Remove the nuts from the front exhaust pipe and catalytic converter assembly to muffler flange.

5. Saturate the bolts and nuts with heat valve lubricant. Allow 5 minutes for penetration.

6. Disconnect oxygen sensor electrical connectors.

7. Separate the front exhaust pipe to manifold flange connection.

8. Lower the front exhaust pipe/catalytic converter assembly and slide the isolator out of the mount at the transmission (if equipped).

9. Remove the front exhaust pipe/catalytic converter assembly from the vehicle.

To install:

10. Position the front exhaust pipe and catalytic converter assembly isolator into the mount at the transmission (if equipped) and onto the exhaust manifold flange connection.

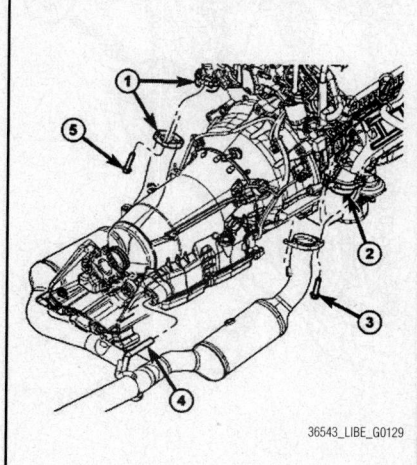

Fig. 51 Catalytic Converter removal—4.0L engine

11. Install the nuts at the front exhaust pipe and catalytic converter assembly to muffler flange. Do not tighten.

12. Position the exhaust pipe for proper clearance with the frame and underbody parts. A minimum clearance of 1.0 in. (25.4 mm) is required.

13. Tighten the bolt at exhaust manifold to 28 ft. lbs. (36 Nm).

14. Tighten the front exhaust pipe and catalytic converter assembly to muffler flange nuts to 28 ft. lbs (36 Nm).

15. Position the front pipe onto the exhaust manifold flange connection. Tighten the clamp to 95 inch lbs. (10 Nm).

16. Connect oxygen sensor electrical connectors.

17. Lower the vehicle.

18. Connect the negative battery cable.

19. Start the vehicle and inspect for exhaust leaks. Repair exhaust leaks as necessary.

20. Check the exhaust system for any contact with the body panels. Make adjustments, if necessary.

CRANKSHAFT DAMPER

REMOVAL & INSTALLATION

3.7L Engine

See Figure 52.

1. See all applicable precautions before beginning service procedures.

2. Disconnect negative cable from battery.

3. Remove accessory drive belt.

➡**Transmission cooler line snaps into shroud lower right hand corner.**

4. Remove crankshaft damper bolt.

5. Remove damper using Special Tools 8513 Insert and 1026 Three Jaw Puller.

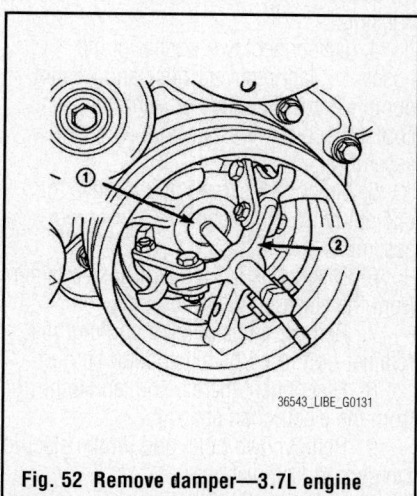

Fig. 52 Remove damper—3.7L engine

To install:

> **⁜ WARNING**
>
> **To prevent severe damage to the crankshaft, damper or Special Tool 8512, thoroughly clean the damper bore and the crankshaft nose before installing damper.**

6. Align crankshaft damper slot with key in crankshaft. Slide damper onto crankshaft slightly.

> **⁜ WARNING**
>
> **Special Tool 8512A, is assembled in a specific sequence. Failure to assemble this tool in this sequence can result in tool failure and severe damage to either the tool or the crankshaft.**

7. Assemble Special Tool 8512-A as follows, The nut is threaded onto the shaft first. Then the roller bearing is placed onto the threaded rod (The hardened bearing surface of the bearing MUST face the nut). Then the hardened washer slides onto the threaded rod. Once assembled coat the threaded rod's threads with Mopar® Nickel Anti- Seize or (Loctite No. 771).

8. Using Special Tool 8512A, press damper onto crankshaft.

9. Install then tighten crankshaft damper bolt to 130 ft. lbs. (175 Nm).

10. Install accessory drive belt.

11. Connect negative cable to battery.

4.0L Engine

See Figures 53 and 54.

1. See all applicable precautions before beginning service procedures.

2. Disconnect and isolate the negative battery cable.

3. Remove the air cleaner element housing.

4. Disconnect two washer pump hoses, coolant recovery hose and washer pump electrical connector from the coolant recovery/washer fluid reservoir assembly.

5. Remove 5 screws and remove the coolant recovery/washer fluid reservoir assembly.

6. Disengage the radiator hose retainer from the electric fan shroud.

7. Remove transmission cooling line retainer bolt from the electric fan shroud.

8. Disconnect the electric fan connector from the electric fan shroud.

9. Remove two bolts and lift the electric fan shroud from vehicle.

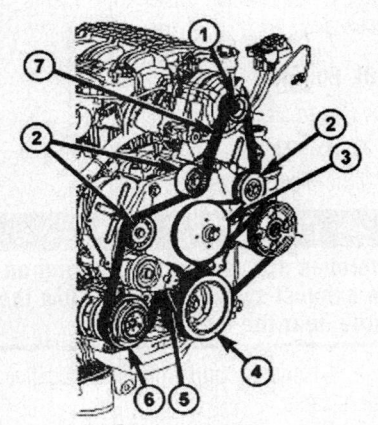

1. Generator
2. Idlers
3. Water Pump
4. Crankshaft
5. Tensioner
6. A/C Compressor
7. Belt

36543_LIBE_G0124

Fig. 53 Accessory serpentine belt routing—4.0L engine

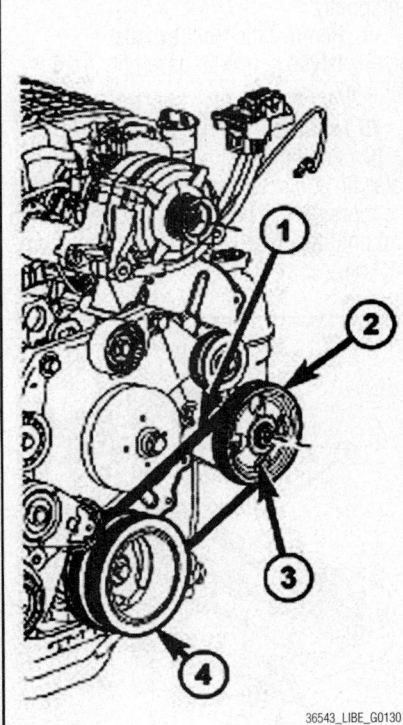

36543_LIBE_G0130

Fig. 54 Power steering belt routing — 4.0L engine

10. Use Adapter Pins 8346 in Spanner Wrench 6958 to hold the pulley and remove fan/viscous fan drive assembly.

11. Remove accessory drive belt.

12. Remove the power steering belt.

13. Remove crankshaft damper bolt.

14. Using Puller 1023 and Crankshaft Insert 9020, remove crankshaft damper.

To install:

15. Install crankshaft damper using Forcing Screw C-4685-C1, with Nut and Thrust Bearing from 6792, and 6792-1 Installer.

16. Install crankshaft damper bolt. Tighten bolt to 70 ft. lbs (95 Nm) while holding damper with Damper Holding Fixture 9365.

17. Install the power steering belt.

18. Install the accessory drive belt.

19. Use Adapter Pins 8346 in Spanner Wrench 6958 to hold the pulley while installing the fan blade/viscous fan drive assembly. Tighten mounting nut to 37 ft. lbs. (50 Nm).

20. Install electric fan shroud with two screws. Tighten screws to 50 inch lbs. (6 Nm).

21. Connect and lock the electric fan connector.

22. Install transmission cooler line retainer to electric fan shroud with one screw.

23. Install radiator hose retainer to electric fan shroud.

24. Install the coolant recovery/washer fluid reservoir assembly with five screws. Connect two washer pump hoses, coolant recovery hose, and washer pump electrical connector.

25. Install and connect the air cleaner element housing.

26. Connect the negative battery cable. Tighten nut to 40 inch lbs. (4.5 Nm).

CRANKSHAFT FRONT SEAL

REMOVAL & INSTALLATION

3.7L Engine

See Figure 55.

1. See all applicable precautions before beginning service procedures.

2. Disconnect the negative battery cable.

3. Drain the cooling system.

4. Remove the accessory drive belt.

5. Remove the A/C compressor mounting bolts and set the compressor aside.

➡It is not necessary to disconnect the A/C lines from the compressor.

Fig. 55 A special tool is required to remove and install the seal without removing the front timing cover

6. Remove the upper radiator hose.
7. Disconnect the engine fan electrical connector, located inside the radiator shroud.
8. Remove the engine fan.
9. Remove the camshaft damper bolt.
10. Using Special Tool 8513 Insert and 1026 three-jaw puller, remove the crankshaft damper.
11. Remove the seal using Special Tool 8511.

To install:

12. Using Special Tools 8348 and 8512, install the crankshaft front seal.
13. Install the crankshaft damper as follows:
   a. Align the crankshaft damper slot with the key in the crankshaft. Slide the damper onto the crankshaft.
   b. Assemble Special Tool 8512-A. The nut is threaded onto the threaded rod first. Then the roller bearing is placed onto the threaded rod (The hardened bearing surface of the bearing MUST face the nut). Then the hardened washer slides onto the threaded rod. Once assembled coat the threaded rod's threads with Mopar® Nickel Anti-Seize or equivalent.
   c. Using Special Tool 8512-A, press the damper onto the crankshaft.
14. Install the crankshaft damper bolt and tighten to 130 ft. lbs. (175 Nm).
15. Install the engine fan.
16. Install the upper radiator hose.
17. Install the A/C compressor and tighten the mounting bolts to 40 ft. lbs. (54 Nm).
18. Install the accessory drive belt.
19. Refill the cooling system to the correct level.
20. Connect the negative battery cable.

21. Start the engine and check for leaks.

4.0L Engine

See Figure 56
1. See all applicable precautions before beginning service procedures.

> ✷✷ **WARNING**
>
> **The 4.0L engine is NOT a free-wheeling design. Therefore, care should be taken not to rotate the camshafts or crankshaft with the timing belt removed.**

2. Remove the crankshaft sprocket.
   a. Remove the timing belt
   b. Remove crankshaft sprocket using Gear Puller L-4407-A (1).
3. Tap the dowel pin (2) out of the crankshaft .
4. Remove crankshaft seal using Tool 6341A

> ✷✷ **WARNING**
>
> **Do not nick shaft seal surface or seal bore**

➡**Shaft seal lip surface must be free of varnish, dirt or nicks. Polish with 400 grit paper if necessary.**

To install:

5. Install crankshaft seal using Special Tool 6342.
6. Install the dowel pin into the crankshaft to 0.047 in. (1.2mm) protrusion.

➡**To ensure proper installation depth of crankshaft sprocket, Sprocket Installer 6641 must be used.**

7. Install the crankshaft sprocket.
   a. Install crankshaft sprocket using Forcing Screw C-4685-C1, with Nut and

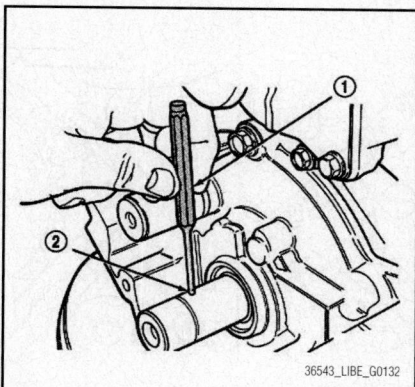

Fig. 56 Dowel pin removal—4.0L engine

Thrust Bearing from 6792, and Sprocket Installer 6641.
   b. Install timing belt.

CYLINDER HEAD

REMOVAL & INSTALLATION

3.7L Engine

Left Side

See Figures 57 through 61.

1. See all applicable precautions before beginning service procedures.
2. Drain the cooling system.
3. Properly relieve the fuel system pressure.
4. Remove or disconnect the following:
   • Negative battery cable
   • Exhaust Y-pipe
   • Intake manifold
   • Cylinder head cover
   • Engine cooling fan and shroud
   • Accessory drive belt
   • Power steering pump
5. Rotate the crankshaft so that the crankshaft timing mark aligns with the Top Dead Center (TDC) mark on the front cover, and the **V6** marks on the camshaft sprockets are at 12 o'clock as shown.
   • Crankshaft damper
   • Front cover
6. Lock the secondary timing chain to the idler sprocket with Timing Chain Locking tool 8429.
7. Matchmark the secondary timing chain one link on each side of the V6 mark to the camshaft sprocket.
   • Left secondary timing chain tensioner
   • Cylinder head access plug
   • Secondary timing chain guide
   • Camshaft sprocket
   • Cylinder head

➡**The cylinder head is retained by twelve bolts. Four of the bolts are smaller and are at the front of the head.**

To install:

8. Check the cylinder head bolts for signs of stretching and replace as necessary.
9. Lubricate the threads of the 11mm bolts with clean engine oil.
10. Coat the threads of the 8mm bolts with Mopar® Lock and Seal Adhesive.
11. Install the cylinder heads. Use new gaskets and tighten the bolts, in sequence, as follows:
   a. Step 1: Bolts 1–8 to 20 ft. lbs. (27 Nm)

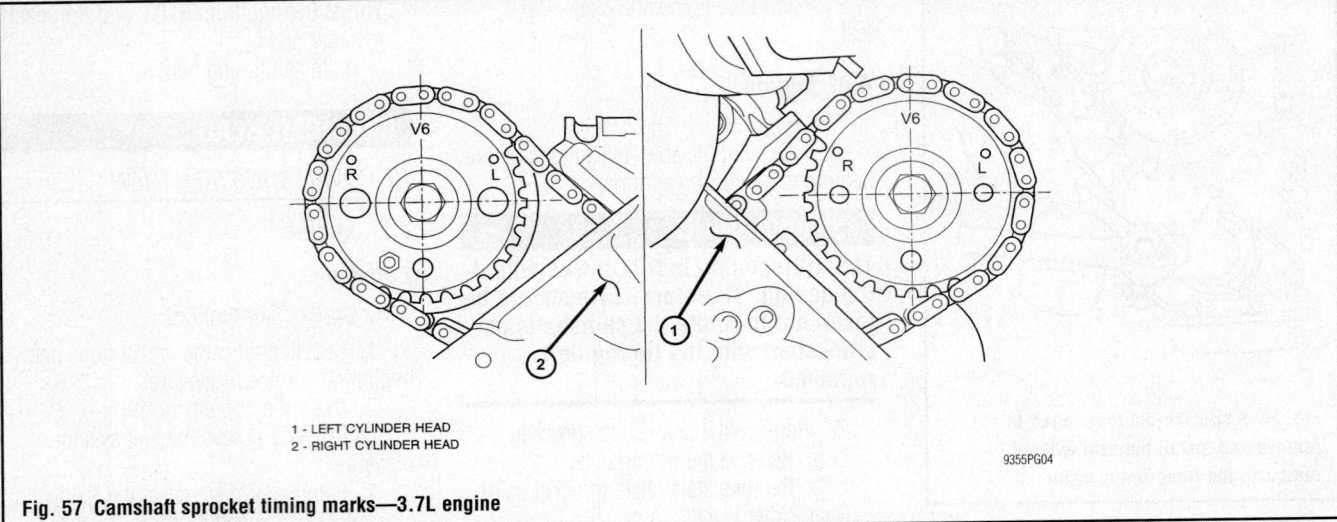

1 - LEFT CYLINDER HEAD
2 - RIGHT CYLINDER HEAD

9355PG04

Fig. 57 Camshaft sprocket timing marks—3.7L engine

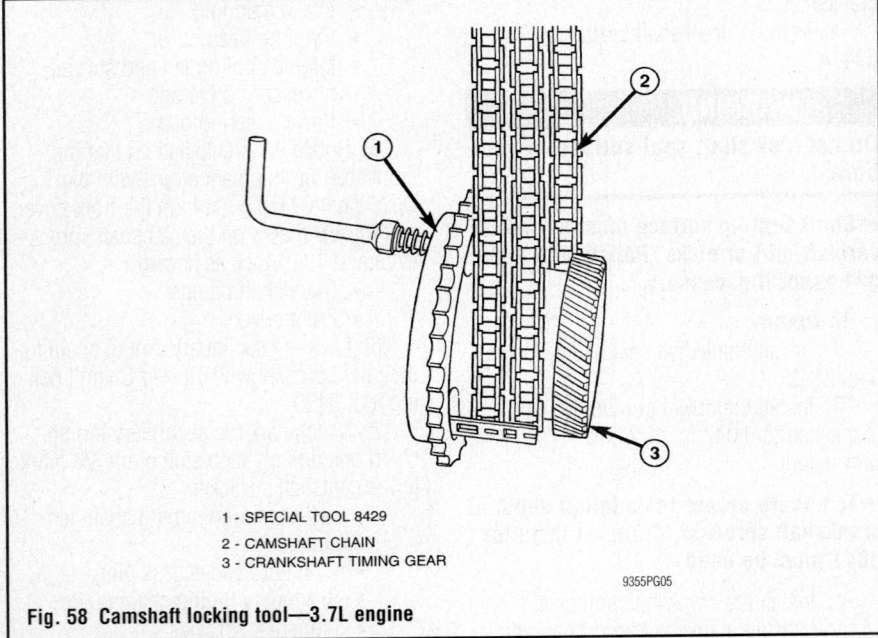

1 - SPECIAL TOOL 8429
2 - CAMSHAFT CHAIN
3 - CRANKSHAFT TIMING GEAR

9355PG05

Fig. 58 Camshaft locking tool—3.7L engine

b. Step 2: Bolts 1–8 verify torque without loosening

c. Step 3: Bolts 9–12 to 10 ft. lbs. (14 Nm)

d. Step 4: Bolts 1–8 plus ¼ (90°) turn

e. Step 5: Bolts 1–8 plus ¼ (90°) turn again

f. Step 6: Bolts 9–12 to 19 ft. lbs. (26 Nm)

12. Install or connect the following:
   - Camshaft sprocket. Align the secondary chain matchmarks and tighten the bolt to 90 ft. lbs. (122 Nm).
   - Secondary timing chain guide
   - Cylinder head access plug
   - Secondary timing chain tensioner

13. Remove the Timing Chain Locking tool.

14. Install or connect the following:
   - Front cover

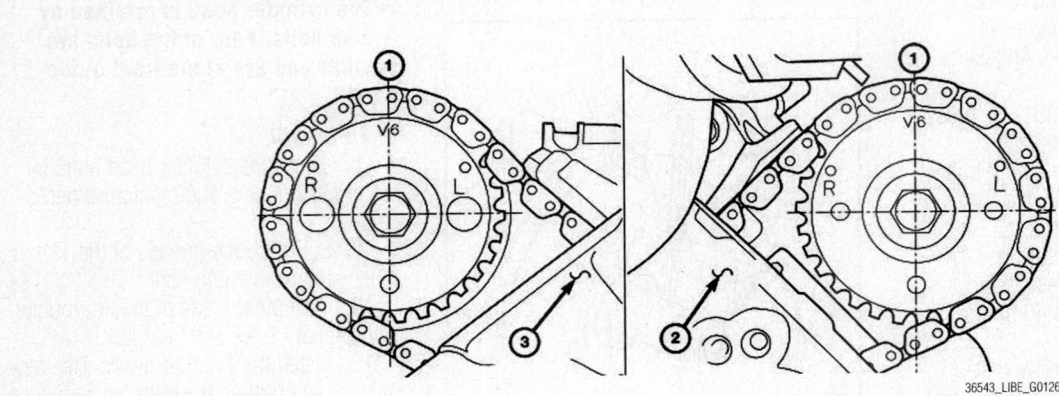

36543_LIBE_G0126

Fig. 59 Matchmark the secondary timing chain one link on each side of the V6 mark to the camshaft sprocket—3.7L engine

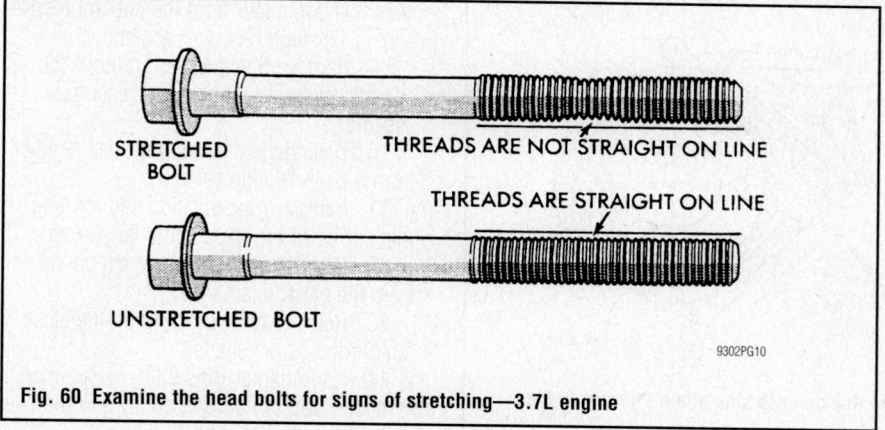

Fig. 60 Examine the head bolts for signs of stretching—3.7L engine

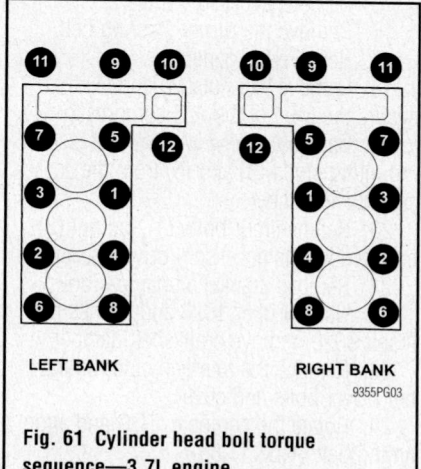

Fig. 61 Cylinder head bolt torque sequence—3.7L engine

LEFT BANK   RIGHT BANK

- Crankshaft damper, and torque the bolt to 130 ft. lbs. (175 Nm)
- Power steering pump
- Accessory drive belt
- Engine cooling fan and shroud
- Cover
- Intake manifold
- Exhaust Y-pipe
- Negative battery cable

15. Fill and bleed the cooling system.
16. Start the engine, check for leaks and repair if necessary.

Right Side

See Figures 62 and 63.

1. See all applicable precautions before beginning service procedures.
2. Drain the cooling system.
3. Properly relieve the fuel system pressure.
4. Remove or disconnect the following:
- Negative battery cable
- Exhaust Y-pipe
- Intake manifold
- Valve cover
- Engine cooling fan and shroud
- Accessory drive belt

- Oil fill housing
- Power steering pump
5. Rotate the crankshaft so that the crankshaft timing mark aligns with the Top

Dead Center (TDC) mark on the front cover, and the **V6** marks on the camshaft sprockets are at 12 o'clock as shown.
6. Remove or disconnect the following:
- Crankshaft damper
- Front cover
7. Lock the secondary timing chains to the idler sprocket with Timing Chain Locking tool 8429.
8. Matchmark the secondary timing chains to the camshaft sprockets.
9. Remove or disconnect the following:
- Secondary timing chain tensioners
- Cylinder head access plugs
- Secondary timing chain guides
- Camshaft sprockets
- Cylinder heads

➡**Each cylinder head is retained by eight 11mm bolts and four 8mm bolts.**

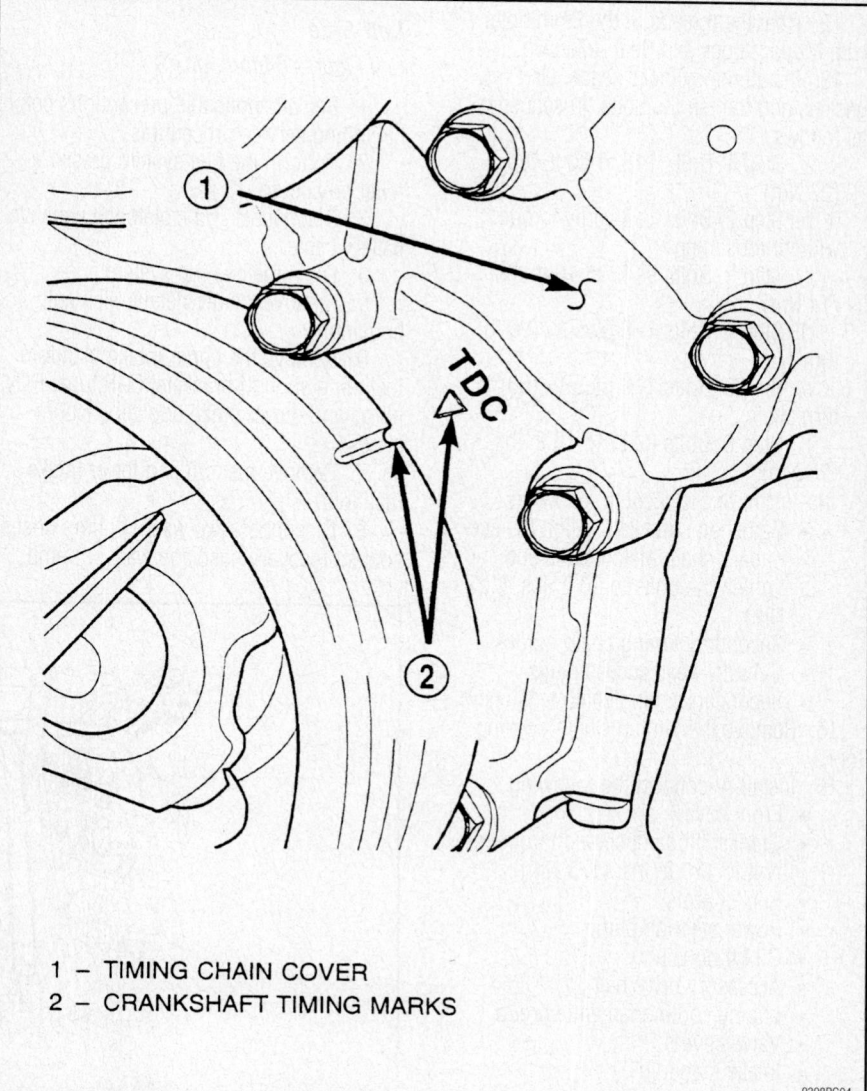

1 – TIMING CHAIN COVER
2 – CRANKSHAFT TIMING MARKS

Fig. 62 Crankshaft timing marks—3.7L engine

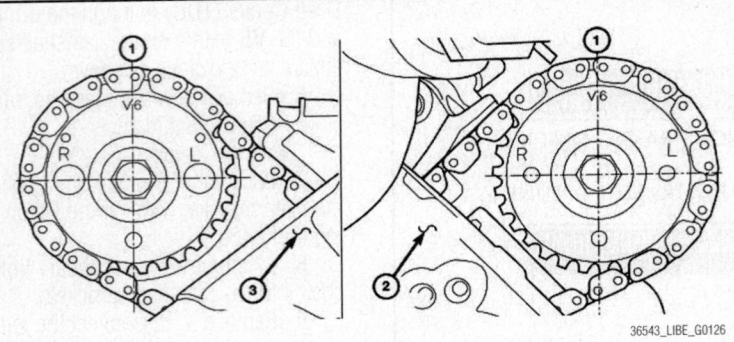

Fig. 63 Matchmark the secondary timing chain one link on each side of the V6 mark to the camshaft sprocket.—3.7L engine

To install:

10. Check the cylinder head bolts for signs of stretching and replace as necessary.

11. Lubricate the threads of the 11mm bolts with clean engine oil.

12. Coat the threads of the 8mm bolts with Mopar® Lock and Seal Adhesive.

13. Install the cylinder heads. Use new gaskets and tighten the bolts, in sequence, as follows:

    a. Step 1: Bolts 1–8 to 20 ft. lbs. (27 Nm)

    b. Step 2: Bolts 1–8 verify torque without loosening

    c. Step 3: Bolts 9–12 to 10 ft. lbs. (14 Nm)

    d. Step 4: Bolts 1–8 plus ¼ (90 °) turn

    e. Step 5: Bolts 1–8 plus ¼ (90 °) turn again

    f. Step 6: Bolts 9–12 to 19 ft. lbs. (26 Nm)

14. Install or connect the following:
- Camshaft sprockets. Align the secondary chain matchmarks and tighten the bolts to 90 ft. lbs. (122 Nm).
- Secondary timing chain guides
- Cylinder head access plugs
- Secondary timing chain tensioners.

15. Remove the Timing Chain Locking tool.

16. Install or connect the following:
- Front cover
- Crankshaft damper, and torque the bolt to 130 ft. lbs. (175 Nm)
- Rocker arms
- Power steering pump
- Oil fill housing
- Accessory drive belt
- Engine cooling fan and shroud
- Valve covers
- Intake manifold
- Exhaust Y-pipe
- Negative battery cable

17. Fill and bleed the cooling system.

18. Start the engine, check for leaks and repair if necessary.

4.0L Engine

Left Side

See Figures 64 through 73.

1. See all applicable precautions before beginning service procedures.

2. Perform the fuel system pressure relief procedure.

3. Disconnect and isolate the negative battery cable.

4. Drain the cooling system.

5. Remove the air cleaner element housing

6. Remove the upper intake manifold including support brackets, EGR tube, PCV, purge and power brake booster vacuum hoses.

7. Remove fuel rail and lower intake manifold.

8. Disconnect two washer pump hoses, coolant recovery hose and washer pump electrical connector from the coolant recovery/washer fluid reservoir assembly.

9. Remove 5 screws and remove the coolant recovery/washer fluid reservoir assembly.

10. Disengage the radiator hose retainer from the electric fan shroud.

11. Remove transmission cooling line retainer bolt from the electric fan shroud.

12. Disconnect the electric fan connector from the electric fan shroud.

13. Remove two bolts and lift the electric fan shroud from vehicle.

14. Use Adapter Pins 8346 in Spanner Wrench 6958 to hold the pulley and remove fan/viscous fan drive assembly.

15. Remove accessory drive.

16. Remove the power steering belt.

17. Remove the generator.

18. Remove two nuts (4) and (6) that secure the front of the A/C compressor (1).

19. Back out the two A/C compressor mounting studs (3) and (5) from the accessory drive bracket.

20. Remove four bolts (1) and nut (3) and remove the accessory drive bracket (2).

21. Remove crankshaft damper bolt.

22. Using Puller 1023 and Crankshaft Insert 9020, remove crankshaft damper.

23. Remove the fourteen outer timing belt cover bolts and cover.

24. Rotate the engine to TDC and align timing belt marks (1,8,9).

25. Raise and support the vehicle.

26. Remove front exhaust pipe to exhaust manifold mounting bolts.

27. Remove bolt and reposition oil cooler hose.

28. Remove the timing belt tensioner and reset the tensioner.

29. Lower vehicle.

30. Remove the timing belt.

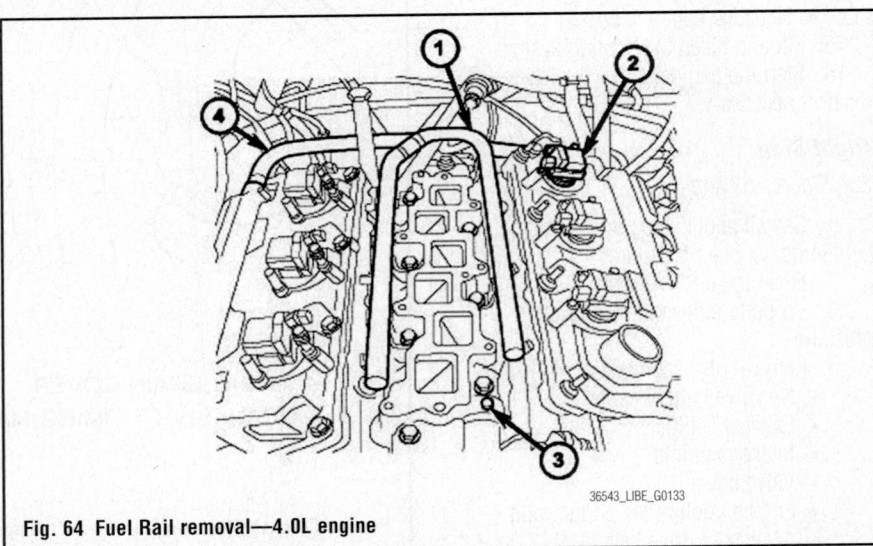

Fig. 64 Fuel Rail removal—4.0L engine

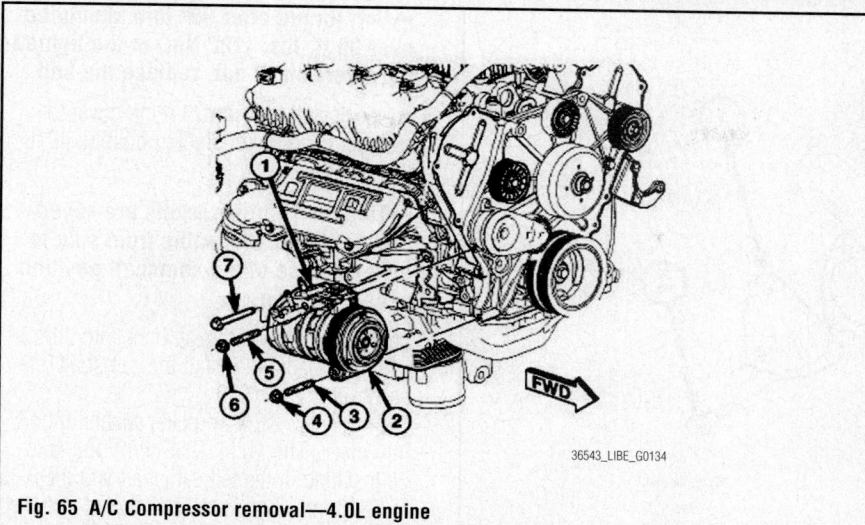

Fig. 65 A/C Compressor removal—4.0L engine

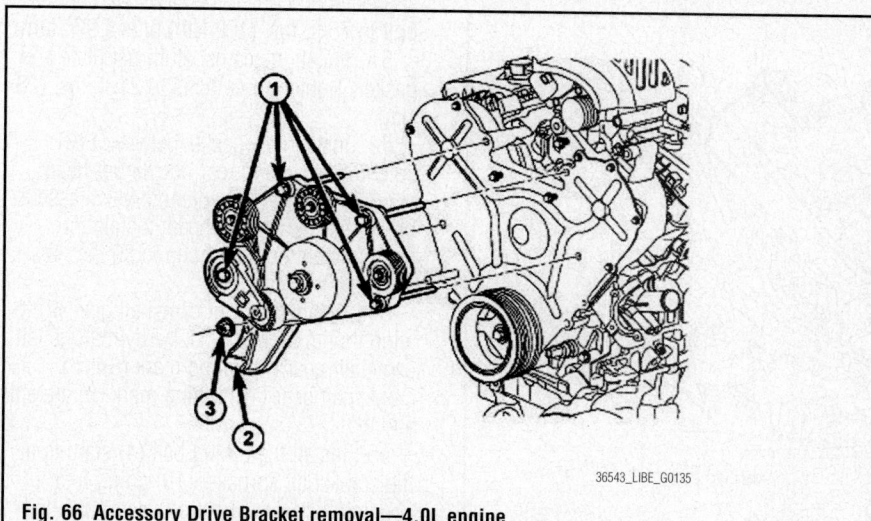

Fig. 66 Accessory Drive Bracket removal—4.0L engine

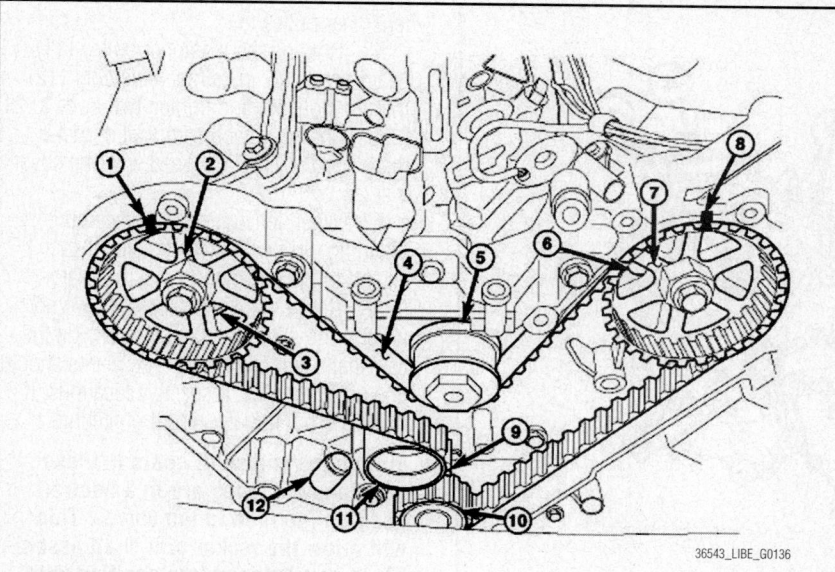

Fig. 67 Timing Belt alignment—4.0L engine

31. Disconnect wire harness connectors from knock sensor and ignition.

32. Remove ignition coils.

33. Remove spark plugs.

34. Remove dipstick retaining bolt and remove dipstick tube.

35. Remove eight bolts and left cylinder head cover.

36. Remove ten bolts and left rocker arm assembly.

37. Remove three bolts (2) and the left camshaft thrust plate (1).

38. Counter-hold the left cam gear and remove the cam gear retaining bolt.

39. Remove the cam gear.

40. Remove the four inner timing cover to left cylinder head retaining bolts (1) and (2).

41. Remove the cylinder head bolts in REVERSE of tightening sequence shown.

42. Push the camshaft out of the back of the cylinder head approximately 3.5 inches and remove the cylinder head.

43. Clean and inspect all mating surfaces. If replacing cylinder head, transfer exhaust manifold.

To install:

➡The cylinder head bolts are tightened using a torque plus angle procedure. The bolts must be examined BEFORE reuse. If the threads are necked down the bolts must be replaced.

44. Install camshaft in cylinder head. Push camshaft out of the back of the cylinder head approximately 3.5 inches. Install head gasket and cylinder head over locating dowels.

✳✳ WARNING

The cylinder head gaskets are not interchangeable between cylinder heads and are clearly marked right or left.

45. Ensure that the correct head gaskets are used and are oriented correctly on cylinder block.

46. Install and finger tighten eight head bolts.

47. Tighten the cylinder head bolts in the following sequence, using the 4 step torque-turn method. Tighten according to the following torque values:

   a. Step 1: All to 45 ft. lbs. (61 Nm)

   b. Step 2: All to 65 ft. lbs. (88 Nm)

   c. Step 3: All (again) to 65 ft. lbs. (88 Nm)

   d. Step 4: Plus 90° turn. Do not use a torque wrench for this step.

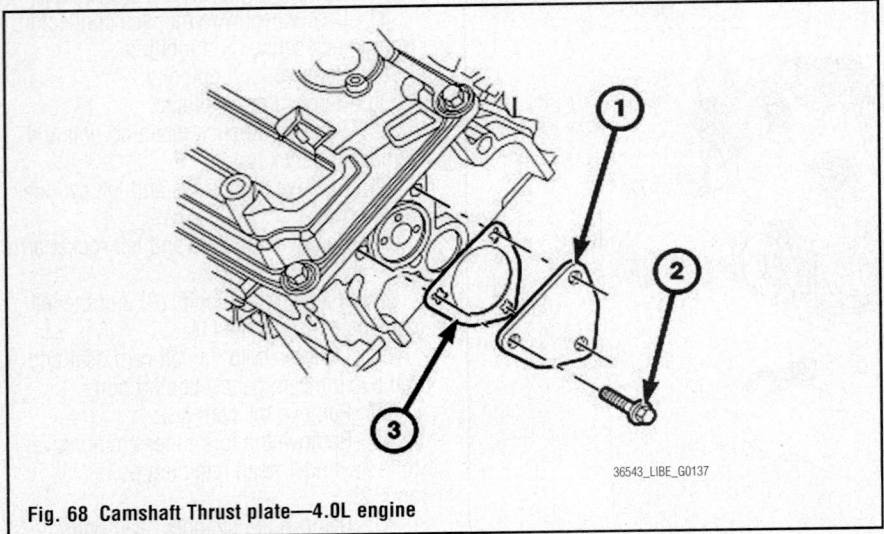

Fig. 68 Camshaft Thrust plate—4.0L engine

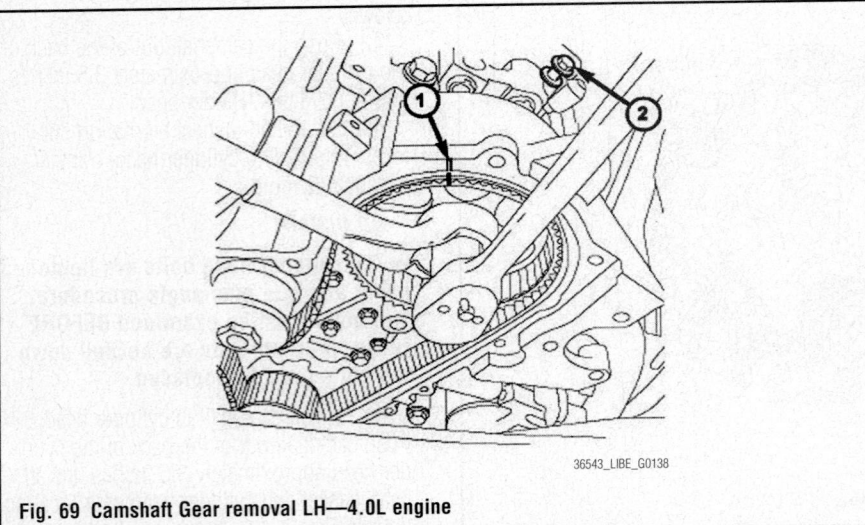

Fig. 69 Camshaft Gear removal LH—4.0L engine

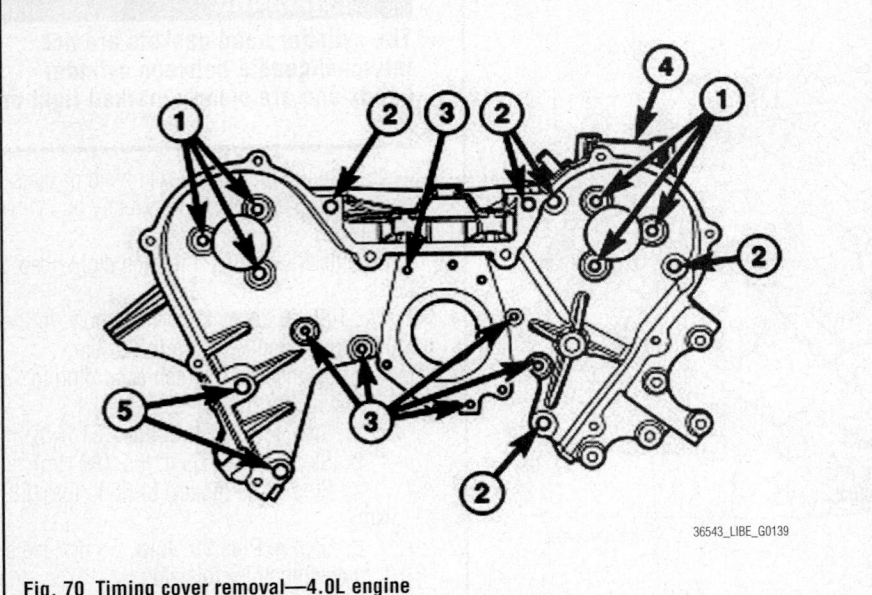

Fig. 70 Timing cover removal—4.0L engine

➡**Bolt torque after 90° turn should be over 90 ft. lbs. (122 Nm) in the tightening direction. If not, replace the bolt.**

48. Install four inner timing cover to cylinder head bolts. Tighten bolts to 40 ft. lbs. (54 Nm).

➡**The camshaft sprockets are keyed and not interchangeable from side to side because of the camshaft position sensor pick-up.**

49. Push the camshaft back into the cylinder head and install the camshaft sprocket.

50. Install NEW sprocket attaching bolt into place. The 10 in. (255 mm) bolt is to be installed in the left camshaft and the 8 ⅜ in. (213 mm) bolt is to be installed into the right camshaft. Counter-hold the camshaft sprocket and tighten the camshaft sprocket bolt to 75 ft. lbs. (102 Nm) plus a 90° turn.

51. Install the camshaft thrust plate and gasket. Tighten three bolts to 21 ft. lbs. (28 Nm).

52. Install new gasket between EGR solenoid/valve and rear of cylinder head.

53. Position EGR solenoid/valve assembly to rear of cylinder head. Install and tighten two mounting bolts to 80 inch lbs. (8 Nm).

54. Rotate the right camshaft gear (2) to align its timing mark (1). Verify that the left camshaft gear (7) timing mark (8) and crankshaft gear (10) timing mark (9) are still aligned.

55. Install the timing belt (4) starting at the crankshaft sprocket (10) going in a counterclockwise direction. Install the belt around the last sprocket. Maintain tension on the belt as it is positioned around the tensioner pulley (11).

56. Holding the tensioner pulley (11) against the belt, install the tensioner (12) into the housing and tighten two bolts to 21 ft. lbs. (28 Nm). Each camshaft sprocket mark should remain aligned with the cover marks.

57. When tensioner is in place pull retaining pin to allow the tensioner to extend to the tensioner pulley bracket.

58. Rotate crankshaft sprocket two revolutions and check the timing marks on the camshafts and crankshaft. The marks should line up within their respective locations. If marks do not line up, repeat procedure.

➡**With the camshaft gears in these positions the lobes are in a neutral position (no load to the valve). This will allow the rocker arm shaft assembly to be tightened into position with little or no valve spring load on it.**

Fig. 71 Cylinder Head tightening sequence—4.0L engine

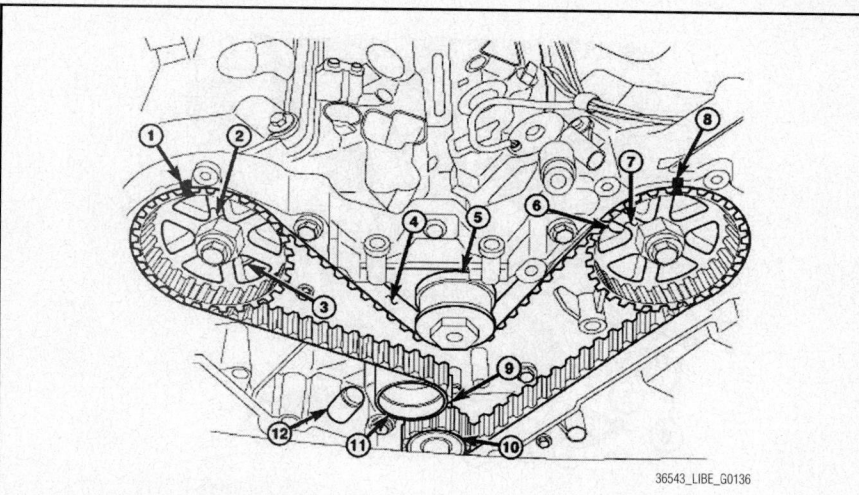

Fig. 72 Timing belt alignment—4.0L engine

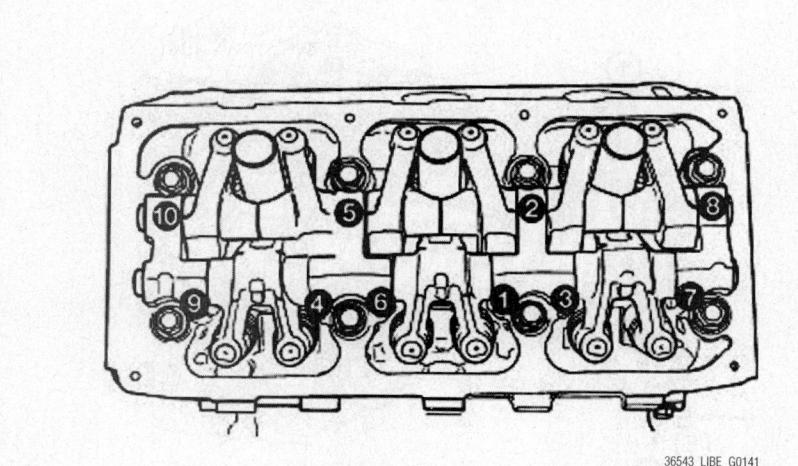

Fig. 73 Rocker arm tightening sequence—4.0L engine

59. Install the rocker arm and shaft assembly and ten bolts making sure that the identification marks face toward the front of engine for left head and toward the rear of the engine for right head.

60. Tighten the ten rocker arm/shaft assembly bolts in sequence to 23 ft. lbs. (31 Nm).

61. Clean cylinder head and cover mating surfaces. Inspect and replace gasket and seals as necessary.

62. Install cylinder head cover and eight bolts. Tighten bolts to 105 inch lbs. (12 Nm).

63. Install the spark plugs. Tighten to 20 ft. lbs. (28 Nm).

64. Install ignition coils into cylinder head.

65. Install and tighten coil mounting bolts to 60 inch lbs. (6.7 Nm).

66. Reposition engine wire harness and install retainers to cylinder head cover. Connect and lock electrical connectors to ignition coils (1) and knock sensor.

67. Install dipstick tube and bolt.

68. Connect the front exhaust pipe to exhaust manifold. Tighten the fasteners to 300 inch lbs. (34 Nm).

69. Reposition oil cooler hose retainer bracket near timing belt tensioner and install bolt.

70. Install the front timing belt outer cover and 14 bolts.

71. Tighten the timing cover bolts as follows:

- M6 bolts: 105 inch lbs. (12 Nm)
- M8 bolts: 21 ft. lbs. (28 Nm)
- M10 bolts: 40 ft. lbs. (54 Nm)

72. Install crankshaft damper using Forcing Screw C-4685-C1, with Nut and Thrust Bearing from 6792, and 6792-1 Installer.

73. Install crankshaft damper bolt. Tighten bolt to 70 ft. lbs. (95 Nm) while holding damper with Damper Holding Fixture 9365.

74. Install the accessory drive bracket. Tighten four bolts and nut to 40 ft. lbs. (54 Nm).

75. Install the lower stud and upper stud that secures the front of the A/C compressor to the accessory drive bracket. Tighten studs securely.

76. Install the lower nut and upper nut that secures the front of the A/C compressor to the accessory drive bracket. Tighten nuts to 21 ft. lbs. (28 Nm).

77. Position generator to engine and install two mounting bolts and. Tighten both bolts to 42 ft. lbs. (57 Nm).

78. Snap field wire connector into rear of generator.

79. Install B+ terminal and nut to generator mounting stud. Tighten nut to 115 inch lbs. (13 Nm).

80. Snap plastic protective cover to B+ terminal.

81. Install the power steering belt.

82. Install the accessory drive belt.

83. Use Adapter Pins 8346 in Spanner Wrench 6958 to hold the pulley while installing the fan blade/viscous fan drive assembly. Tighten mounting nut to 37 ft. lbs. (50 Nm).

84. Install electric fan shroud with two screws. Tighten screws to 50 inch lbs. (6 Nm).

85. Connect and lock the electric fan connector.

86. Install transmission cooler line retainer to electric fan shroud with one screw.

87. Install radiator hose retainer to electric fan shroud.

88. Install the coolant recovery/washer fluid reservoir assembly with five screws. Connect two washer pump hoses, coolant recovery hose, and washer pump electrical connector.

89. Install lower intake manifold and fuel rail.

90. Install the upper intake manifold, EGR tube, PCV, Purge and power brake booster vacuum hoses.

91. Install and connect the air cleaner element housing.

92. Fill the coolant system.

93. Connect the negative battery cable. Tighten nut to 40 inch lbs. (4.5 Nm).

Right Side

See Figures 74 through 84.

1. See all applicable precautions before beginning service procedures.

2. Perform the fuel system pressure relief procedure.

3. Disconnect and isolate the negative battery cable.

4. Drain the cooling system.

5. Remove the air cleaner element housing

6. Remove the upper intake manifold including support brackets, EGR tube, PCV, purge and power brake booster vacuum hoses.

7. Remove fuel rail and lower intake manifold.

8. Disconnect two washer pump hoses, coolant recovery hose and washer pump electrical connector from the coolant recovery/washer fluid reservoir assembly.

9. Remove 5 screws and remove the coolant recovery/washer fluid reservoir assembly.

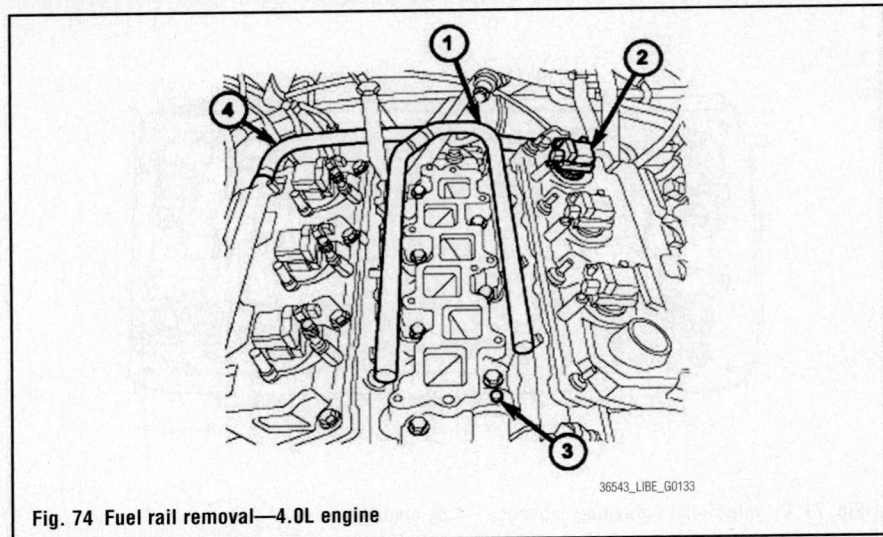

Fig. 74 Fuel rail removal—4.0L engine

36543_LIBE_G0133

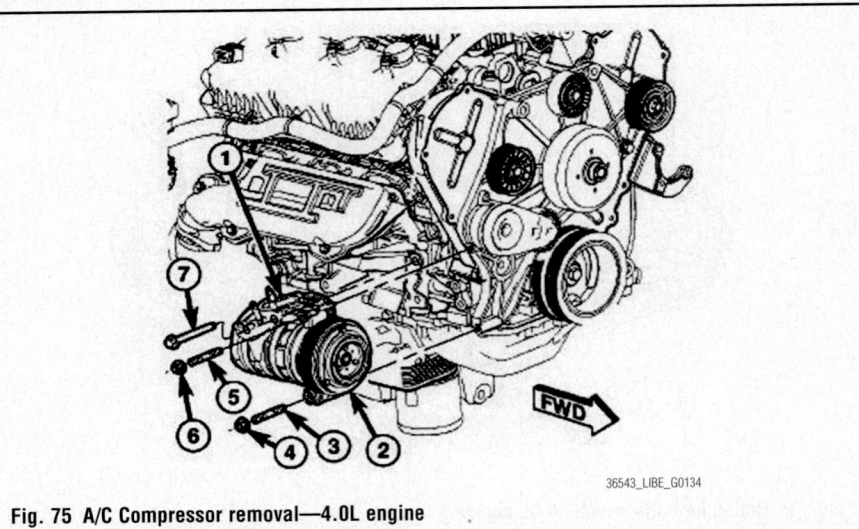

Fig. 75 A/C Compressor removal—4.0L engine

36543_LIBE_G0134

Fig. 76 Accessory Drive Bracket removal—4.0L engine

36543_LIBE_G0135

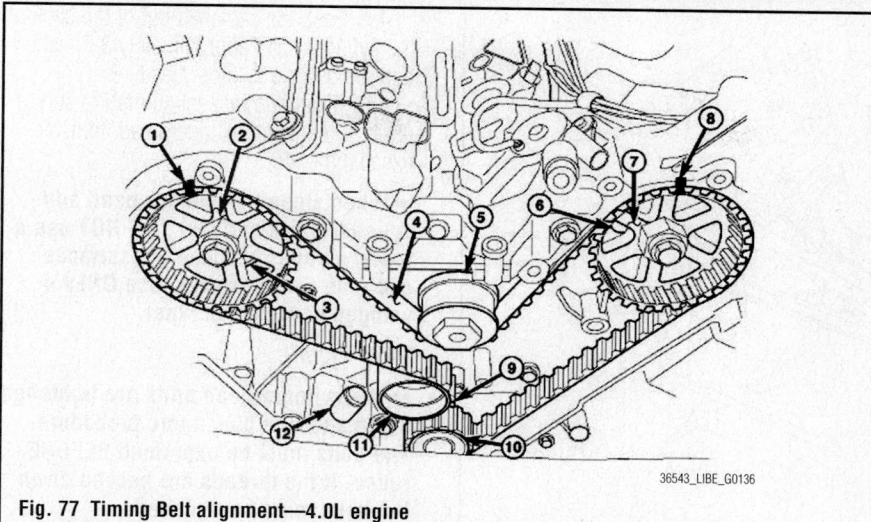

Fig. 77 Timing Belt alignment—4.0L engine

36543_LIBE_G0136

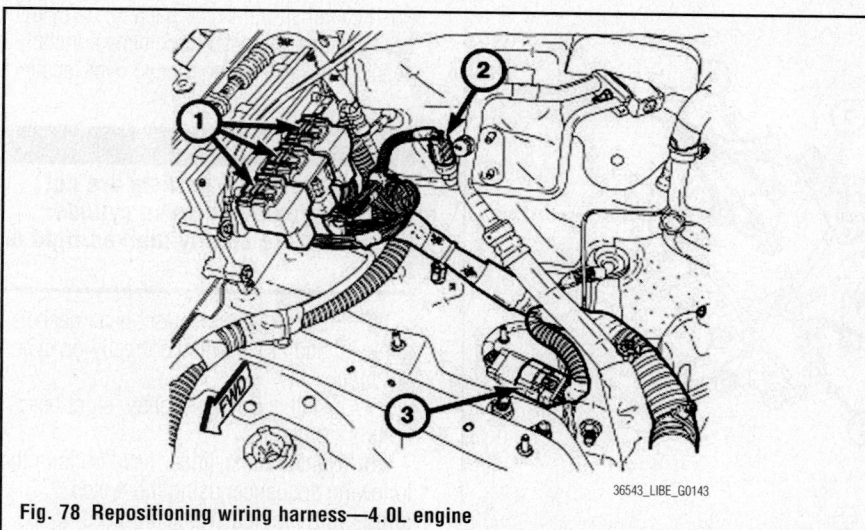

Fig. 78 Repositioning wiring harness—4.0L engine

36543_LIBE_G0143

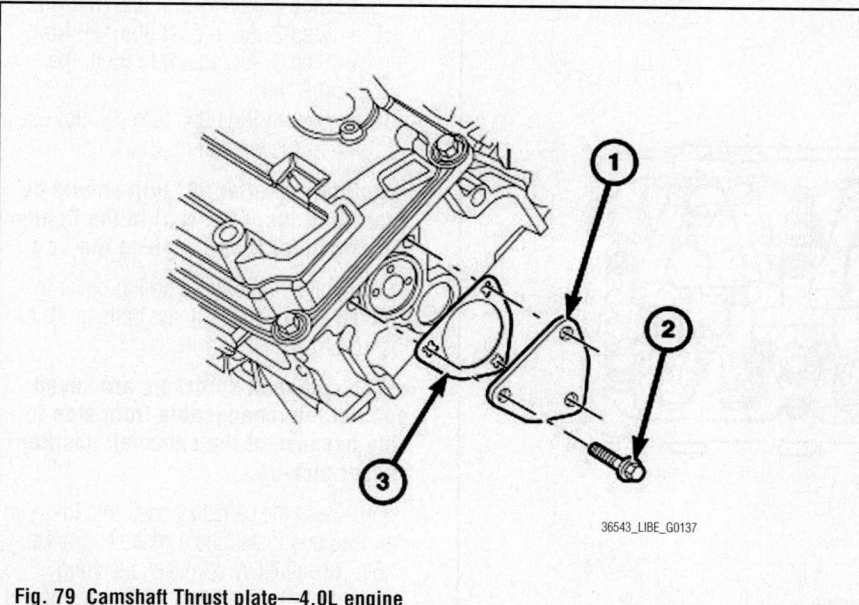

36543_LIBE_G0137

Fig. 79 Camshaft Thrust plate—4.0L engine

10. Disengage the radiator hose retainer from the electric fan shroud.

11. Remove transmission cooling line retainer bolt from the electric fan shroud.

12. Disconnect the electric fan connector from the electric fan shroud.

13. Remove two bolts and lift the electric fan shroud from vehicle.

14. Use Adapter Pins 8346 in Spanner Wrench 6958 to hold the pulley and remove fan/viscous fan drive assembly.

15. Remove accessory drive.

16. Remove the power steering belt.

17. Remove the generator.

18. Remove two nuts (4) and (6) that secure the front of the A/C compressor (1).

19. Back out the two A/C compressor mounting studs (3) and (5) from the accessory drive bracket.

20. Remove four bolts (1) and nut (3) and remove the accessory drive bracket (2).

21. Remove crankshaft damper bolt.

22. Using Puller 1023 and Crankshaft Insert 9020, remove crankshaft damper.

23. Remove the fourteen outer timing belt cover bolts and cover.

24. Rotate the engine to TDC and align timing belt marks (1,8,9).

25. Raise and support the vehicle.

26. Remove front exhaust pipe to exhaust manifold mounting bolts.

27. Remove bolt and reposition oil cooler hose.

28. Remove the timing belt tensioner and reset the tensioner.

29. Lower vehicle.

30. Remove the timing belt.

31. Disconnect wire harness connectors from EGR valve, capacitor, and ignition coils. Release wire harness track retainer tabs from cylinder head cover.

32. Disconnect electrical connectors from PCM (1), A/C high pressure switch (2), body harness (3), A/C compressor clutch and reposition engine wire harness.

33. Remove the EGR valve with two bolts and gasket.

34. Remove ignition coils.

35. Remove spark plugs.

36. Remove eight bolts and right cylinder head cover.

37. Remove ten bolts and right rocker arm assembly.

38. Remove three bolts (2) and the left camshaft thrust plate (1).

39. Counter-hold the right cam gear and remove the cam gear retaining bolt.

40. Remove the cam gear.

41. Remove the three inner timing cover to right cylinder head retaining bolts (1).

42. Remove the cylinder head bolts in REVERSE of tightening sequence shown.

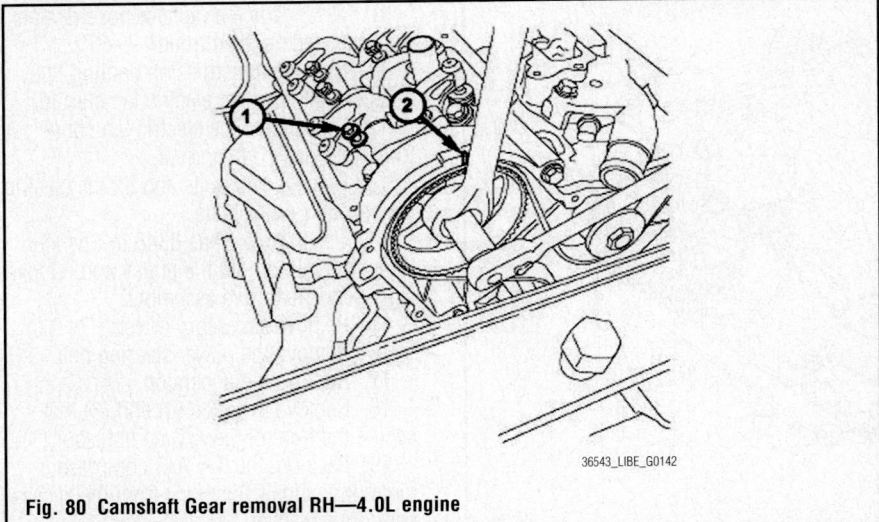

36543_LIBE_G0142

Fig. 80 Camshaft Gear removal RH—4.0L engine

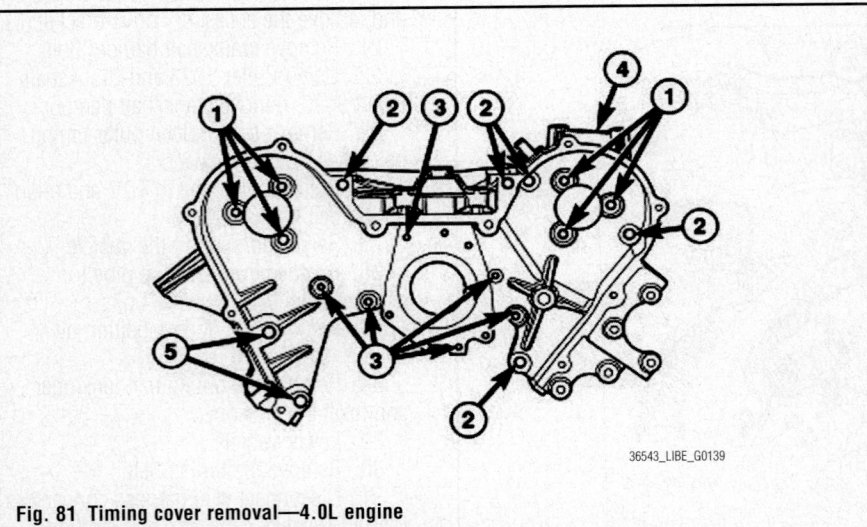

36543_LIBE_G0139

Fig. 81 Timing cover removal—4.0L engine

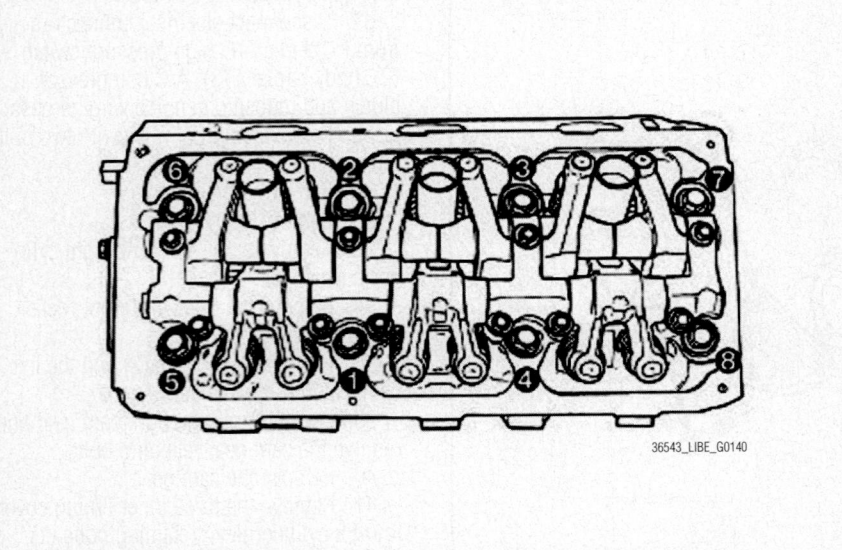

36543_LIBE_G0140

Fig. 82 Cylinder Head tightening sequence—4.0L engine

43. Push the camshaft out of the back of the cylinder head approximately 3.5 inches and remove the cylinder head.

44. Clean and inspect all mating surfaces. If replacing cylinder head, transfer exhaust manifold.

➡When cleaning cylinder head and cylinder block surfaces, **DO NOT** use a metal scraper because the surfaces could be cut or ground. Use **ONLY** a wooden or plastic scraper.

To install:

➡The cylinder head bolts are tightened using a torque plus angle procedure. The bolts must be examined **BEFORE** reuse. If the threads are necked down the bolts must be replaced.

45. Install camshaft in cylinder head. Push camshaft out of the back of the cylinder head approximately 3.5 inches. Install head gasket and cylinder head over locating dowels.

✴✴ WARNING

The cylinder head gaskets are not interchangeable between cylinder heads and are clearly marked right or left.

46. Ensure that the correct head gaskets are used and are oriented correctly on cylinder block.

47. Install and finger tighten eight head bolts

48. Tighten the cylinder head bolts in the following sequence, using the 4 step torque-turn method. Tighten according to the following torque values:

- Step 1: All to 45 ft. lbs. (61 Nm)
- Step 2: All to 65 ft. lbs. (88 Nm)
- Step 3: All (again) to 65 ft. lbs. (88 Nm)
- Step 4: Plus 90° turn. Do not use a torque wrench for this step.

➡Bolt torque after 90° turn should be over 90 ft. lbs. (122 Nm) in the tightening direction. If not, replace the bolt.

49. Install three inner timing cover to cylinder head bolts. Tighten bolts to 40 ft. lbs. (54 Nm).

➡The camshaft sprockets are keyed and not interchangeable from side to side because of the camshaft position sensor pick-up.

50. Push the camshaft back into the cylinder head and install the camshaft sprocket.

51. Install NEW sprocket attaching bolt into place. The 10 in. (255 mm) bolt is

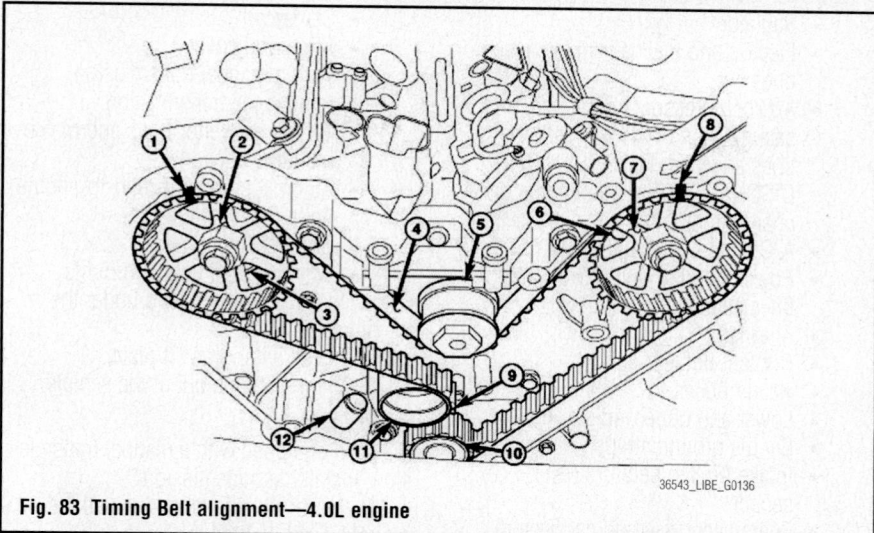

Fig. 83 Timing Belt alignment—4.0L engine

36543_LIBE_G0136

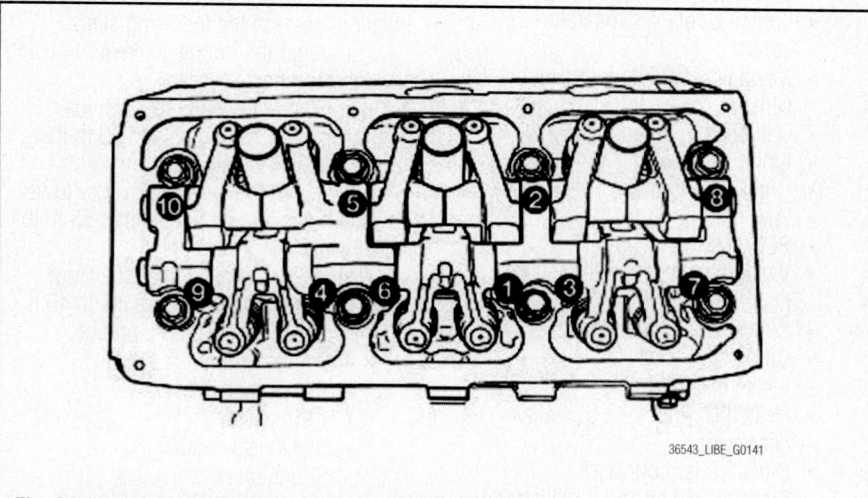

Fig. 84 Rocker Arm tightening sequence—4.0L engine

36543_LIBE_G0141

to be installed in the left camshaft and the 8 ⅜ in. (213 mm) bolt is to be installed into the right camshaft. Counter-hold the camshaft sprocket and tighten the camshaft sprocket bolt to 75 ft. lbs. (102 Nm) plus a 90° turn.

52. Install the camshaft thrust plate and gasket. Tighten three bolts to 21 ft. lbs. (28 Nm).

53. Install new gasket between EGR solenoid/valve and rear of cylinder head.

54. Position EGR solenoid/valve assembly to rear of cylinder head. Install and tighten two mounting bolts to 80 inch lbs. (8 Nm).

55. Rotate the right camshaft gear (2) to align its timing mark (1). Verify that the left camshaft gear (7) timing mark (8) and crankshaft gear (10) timing mark (9) are still aligned.

56. Install the timing belt (4) starting at the crankshaft sprocket (10) going in a counterclockwise direction. Install the belt around the last sprocket. Maintain tension on the belt as it is positioned around the tensioner pulley (11).

57. Holding the tensioner pulley (11) against the belt, install the tensioner (12) into the housing and tighten two bolts to 21 ft. lbs. (28 Nm). Each camshaft sprocket mark should remain aligned with the cover marks.

58. When tensioner is in place, pull retaining pin to allow the tensioner to extend to the tensioner pulley bracket.

59. Rotate crankshaft sprocket two revolutions and check the timing marks on the camshafts and crankshaft. The marks should line up within their respective locations. If marks do not line up, repeat procedure.

➡**With the camshaft gears in these positions the lobes are in a neutral**

position (no load to the valve). This will allow the rocker arm shaft assembly to be tightened into position with little or no valve spring load on it.

60. Install the rocker arm and shaft assembly and ten bolts making sure that the identification marks face toward the front of engine for left head and toward the rear of the engine for right head.

61. Tighten the ten rocker arm/shaft assembly bolts in sequence to 275 inch lbs. (31 Nm).

62. Clean cylinder head and cover mating surfaces. Inspect and replace gasket and seals as necessary.

63. Install cylinder head cover and eight bolts. Tighten bolts to 105 inch lbs. (12 Nm).

64. Install the spark plugs. Tighten to 20 ft. lbs. (28 Nm).

65. Install ignition coils into cylinder head.

66. Install and tighten coil mounting bolts to 60 inch lbs. (6.7 Nm).

67. Reposition engine wire harness and install retainers to cylinder head cover. Connect and lock electrical connectors to ignition coils, capacitor and EGR valve.

68. Reposition engine wire harness, connect and lock electrical connectors to PCM, body harness, A/C high pressure switch and A/C compressor clutch.

69. Connect the front exhaust pipe to exhaust manifold. Tighten the fasteners to 300 inch lbs. (34 Nm).

70. Reposition oil cooler hose retainer bracket near timing belt tensioner and install bolt.

71. Install the front timing belt outer cover and 14 bolts.

72. Tighten the timing cover bolts as follows:
- M6 bolts: 105 inch lbs. (12 Nm)
- M8 bolts: 21 ft. lbs. (28 Nm)
- M10 bolts: 40 ft. lbs. (54 Nm)

73. Install crankshaft damper using Forcing Screw C-4685-C1, with Nut and Thrust Bearing from 6792, and 6792-1 Installer.

74. Install crankshaft damper bolt. Tighten bolt to 70 ft. lbs. (95 Nm) while holding damper with Damper Holding Fixture 9365.

75. Install the accessory drive bracket. Tighten four bolts and nut to 40 ft. lbs. (54 Nm).

76. Install the lower stud and upper stud that secures the front of the A/C compressor to the accessory drive bracket. Tighten studs securely.

77. Install the lower nut and upper nut that secures the front of the A/C compressor to the accessory drive bracket. Tighten nuts to 21 ft. lbs. (28 Nm).

78. Position generator to engine and install two mounting bolts and. Tighten both bolts to 42 ft. lbs. (57 Nm).

79. Snap field wire connector into rear of generator.

80. Install B+ terminal and nut to generator mounting stud. Tighten nut to 115 inch lbs. (13 Nm).

81. Snap plastic protective cover to B+ terminal.

82. Install the power steering belt.

83. Install the accessory drive belt.

84. Use Adapter Pins 8346 in Spanner Wrench 6958 to hold the pulley while installing the fan blade/viscous fan drive assembly. Tighten mounting nut to 37 ft. lbs. (50 Nm).

85. Install electric fan shroud with two screws. Tighten screws to 50 inch lbs. (6 Nm).

86. Connect and lock the electric fan connector.

87. Install transmission cooler line retainer to electric fan shroud with one screw.

88. Install radiator hose retainer to electric fan shroud.

89. Install the coolant recovery/washer fluid reservoir assembly with five screws. Connect two washer pump hoses, coolant recovery hose, and washer pump electrical connector.

90. Install lower intake manifold and fuel rail.

91. Install the upper intake manifold, EGR tube, PCV, Purge and power brake booster vacuum hoses.

92. Install and connect the air cleaner element housing.

93. Fill the coolant system.

94. Connect the negative battery cable. Tighten nut to 40 inch lbs. (4.5 Nm).

ENGINE ASSEMBLY

REMOVAL & INSTALLATION

See Figure 85.

1. See all applicable precautions before beginning service procedures.

2. Properly relieve the fuel system pressure.

3. Drain the cooling system.

4. Drain the engine oil.

5. Remove or disconnect the following:
- Negative battery cable
- Hood
- Air cleaner assembly
- Radiator
- Electric and mechanical fan assemblies
- A/C compressor, if equipped, and secure it out of the way with the lines attached. For 3.7L DO NOT DISCHARGE. For 4.0L engine discharge is required.
- A/C lines 4.0L Engine ONLY.
- Power steering pump, with the lines attached
- Alternator
- Coolant bottle
- Heater hoses
- Lower and upper radiator hoses
- Engine ground straps
- Intake Air Temperature (IAT) sensor
- Fuel injection wiring connectors
- Oil pressure sender connector
- Engine Coolant Temperature (ECT) sensor
- Manifold Absolute Pressure (MAP) sensor
- Camshaft Position (CMP) sensor
- Ignition coil wiring connector
- Crankshaft Position (CKP) sensor
- Fuel rail
- PCV hose
- Vacuum hoses from the intake manifold
- Knock sensor connectors
- Oil dipstick tube
- Intake manifold
- Heated Oxygen (HO$_2$S) sensor connector
- Block heater connector
- Front driveshaft at the differential
- Starter
- Structural cover
- With a manual transmission, remove the transmission
- Torque converter bolts and match-mark the converter
- Automatic transmission-to-engine bolts
- Exhaust front pipes
- Left and right engine mounts

6. Place a support stand under the transmission.

7. Install an engine lift plate.

8. Lift the engine out of the vehicle.

To install:

9. If equipped with a manual transmission, install the transmission.

10. Lower the engine and install the mounts. Don't tighten the bolts yet.

11. If equipped with an automatic transmission, perform the following steps:

a. Align the torque converter housing to the engine.

b. Torque the bolts to 30 ft. lbs. (41 Nm)—3.7L engine and 50 ft. lbs. (68 Nm)—4.0L engine.

c. Install the torque converter to flex-plate bolts. Torque the bolts to 55 ft. lbs. (75 Nm).

12. Install or connect the following:
- Torque the through bolts to 45 ft. lbs. (61 Nm)—3.7L engine.
- Engine ground strap
- Starter motor
- CKP sensor
- Block heater cable
- Structural cover

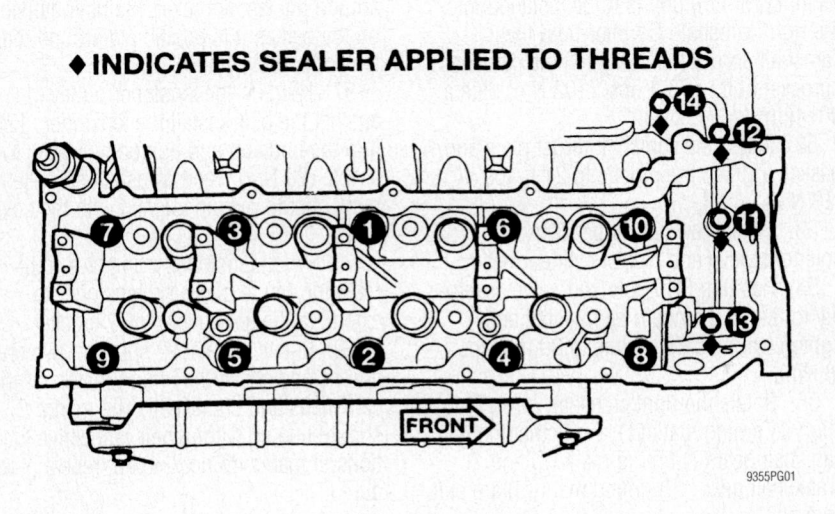

Fig. 85 Tighten the structural cover bolts in this order—3.7L engine

⁑ **WARNING**

The structural cover must be held tightly against the engine and bellhousing during tightening. The torque for all bolts is 40 ft. lbs. (54 Nm). The bolts must be tightened in the order shown.

- Exhaust pipes. New flange clamps MUST be used.
- HO2S sensor connectors
- KS sensors
- Intake Manifold
- Dipstick tube
- Vacuum hoses to the intake manifold
- PCV and breather hoses
- Fuel rail
- IAT sensor
- Fuel injector connectors
- Oil pressure sender
- ECT sensor electrical connector
- MAP sensor
- CMP sensor
- Radiator hoses
- Heater hoses
- Coolant bottle
- Power steering pump
- Alternator
- A/C compressor
- A/C lines 4.0L Engine ONLY.
- Radiator
- Fan assemblies
- Air cleaner assembly
- Negative battery cable

13. Fill and bleed the power steering system.
14. Fill the engine with clean oil.
15. Recharge A/C system—4.0L engine.
16. Start the engine and check for leaks, repair if necessary.

EXHAUST MANIFOLD

REMOVAL & INSTALLATION

3.7L Engines

See Figures 86 and 87.

1. See all applicable precautions before beginning service procedures.
2. Disconnect the negative battery cable.
3. Raise and support the vehicle.
4. Remove the bolts and nuts attaching the exhaust pipe to the engine exhaust manifold.
5. Lower the vehicle.
6. Remove the exhaust heat shield (1).
7. Remove bolts, nuts and washers attaching manifold to cylinder head.

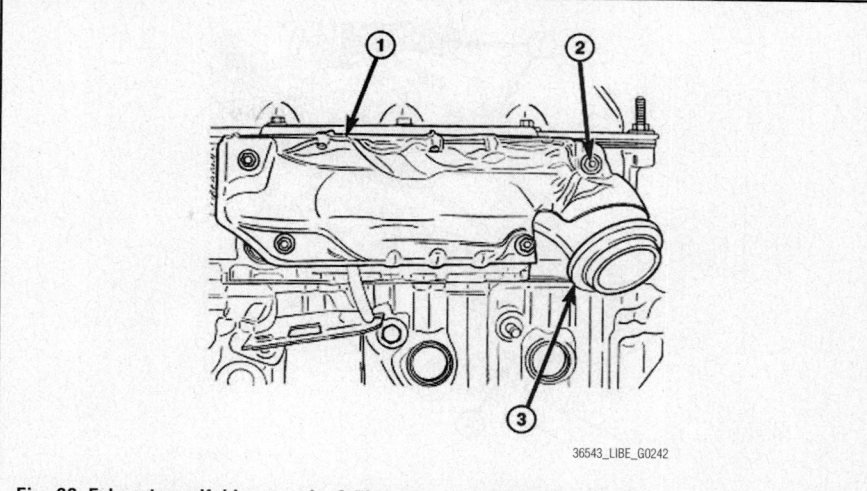

Fig. 86 Exhaust manifold removal—3.7L engine, left exhaust manifold

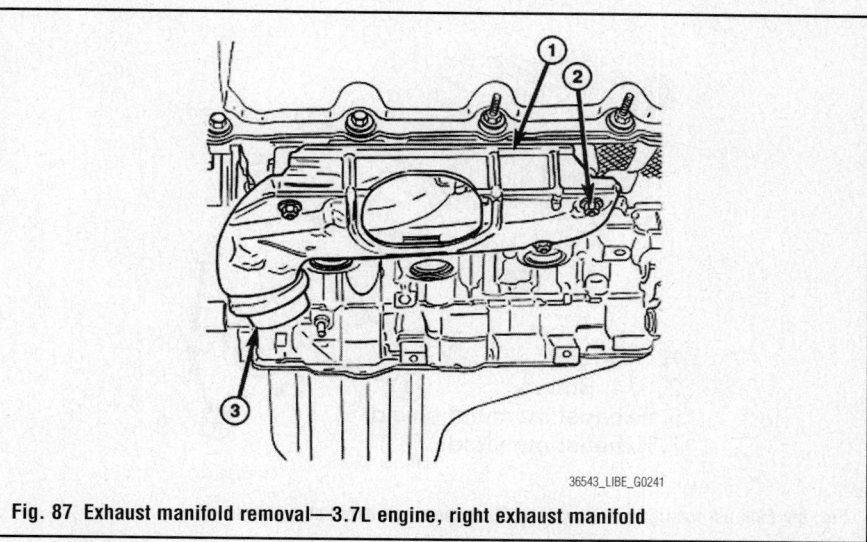

Fig. 87 Exhaust manifold removal—3.7L engine, right exhaust manifold

8. Remove manifold and gasket from the cylinder head.

To install:

➡️ **If the studs came out with the nuts when removing the engine exhaust manifold, install new studs. Apply sealer on the coarse thread ends. Water leaks may develop at the studs if this precaution is not taken.**

9. Position the engine exhaust manifold and gasket on the two studs located on the cylinder head. Install conical washers and nuts on these studs .
10. Install remaining conical washers. Starting at the center arm and working outward, tighten the bolts and nuts to 18 ft. lbs. (25 Nm).
11. Install the exhaust heat shields.
12. Raise and support the vehicle.

⁑ **WARNING**

Over-tightening heat shield fasteners may cause shield to distort and/or crack.

13. Assemble exhaust pipe to manifold and secure with bolts, nuts and retainers. Tighten the bolts and nuts to 25 ft. lbs. (34 Nm).

4.0L Engine

See Figures 88 through 90.

1. See all applicable precautions before beginning service procedures.
2. Disconnect and isolate the negative battery cable.
3. Disconnect the upstream oxygen sensor electrical connector, if necessary.
4. Raise and support the vehicle.
5. Separate the front exhaust pipe to manifold union (2).

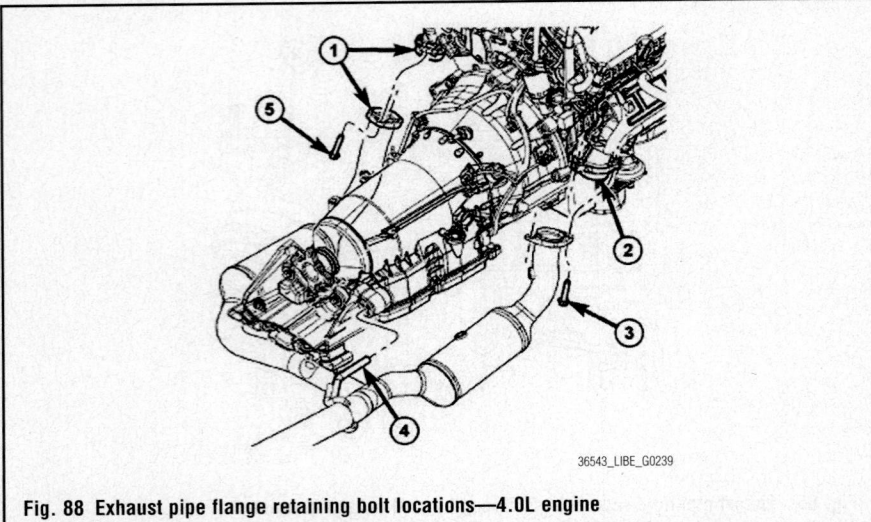

Fig. 88 Exhaust pipe flange retaining bolt locations—4.0L engine

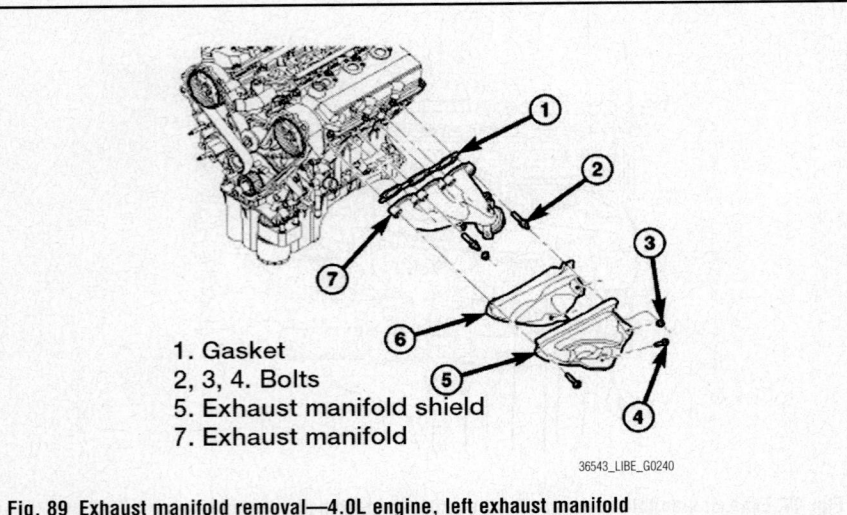

1. Gasket
2, 3, 4. Bolts
5. Exhaust manifold shield
7. Exhaust manifold

Fig. 89 Exhaust manifold removal—4.0L engine, left exhaust manifold

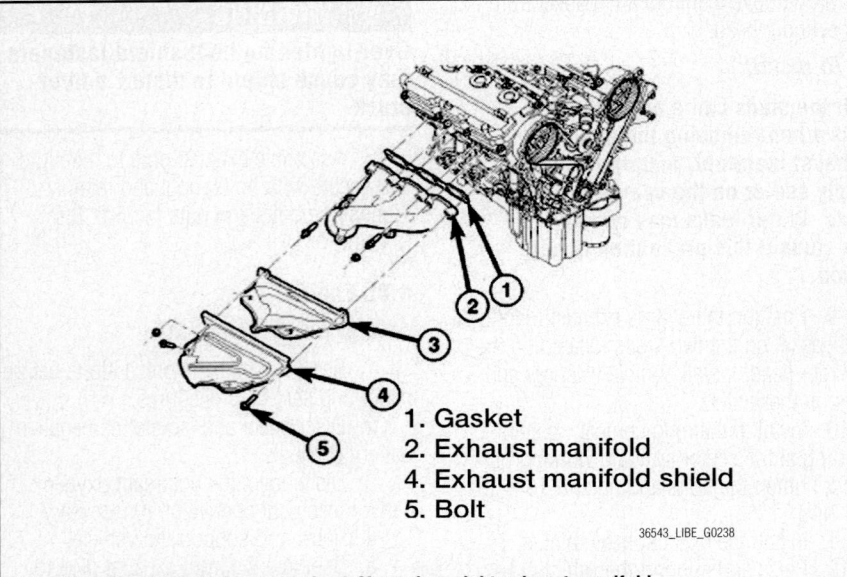

1. Gasket
2. Exhaust manifold
4. Exhaust manifold shield
5. Bolt

Fig. 90 Exhaust manifold removal—4.0L engine, right exhaust manifold

6. Lower the vehicle.

7. Disconnect and remove the oxygen sensor from the exhaust manifold (7).

8. Remove the exhaust manifold shield (5) retaining bolts, exhaust manifold (7), and discard gasket (1).

To install:

9. Clean gasket surfaces.

➡**If replacing the exhaust manifold, tighten the exhaust outlet studs to 29 ft. lbs. (39 Nm).**

10. Position the exhaust manifold and gasket. Install the retaining bolts. Tighten 4 bolts starting at the center working outward to 17 ft. lbs. (23 Nm).

11. Install the heat shields. Tighten the heat shield fasteners to 105 inch lbs. (12 Nm).

12. Tighten the 2 out most nuts to 73 inch lbs. (8 Nm).

13. Connect the oxygen sensor.

14. Raise and support the vehicle.

15. Connect the front exhaust pipe to exhaust manifold. Tighten the fasteners to 25 ft. lbs. (34 Nm).

16. Connect the negative battery cable.

FLYWHEEL/FLEXPLATE

REMOVAL & INSTALLATION

1. See all applicable precautions before beginning service procedures.

2. Remove the transmission.

3. Remove the clutch disc and pressure plate.

4. Remove the flywheel-to-crankshaft bolts and remove flywheel assembly.

To install:

5. Clean the surfaces of the flywheel and pressure plate.

6. Install the flywheel with new bolts and tighten the bolts in a crisscross pattern to 70 ft. lbs. (95 Nm).

7. Install the clutch disc and pressure plate.

8. Install the transmission.

9. The remaining installation is the reverse of removal.

INTAKE MANIFOLD

REMOVAL & INSTALLATION

3.7L Engine

See Figure 91.

1. See all applicable precautions before beginning service procedures.

2. Properly relieve the fuel system pressure.

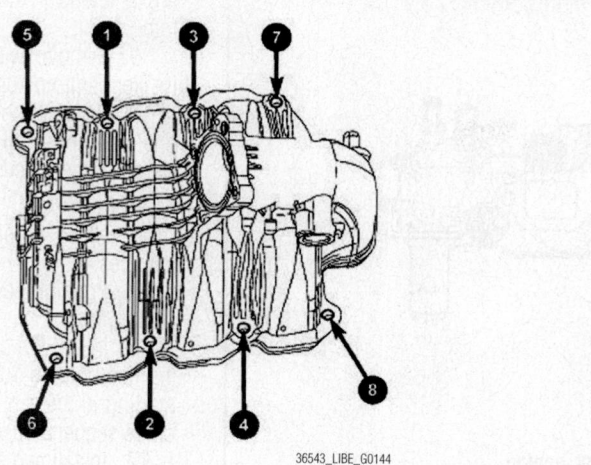

Fig. 91 Remove the intake manifold—3.7L engine

3. Disconnect the negative cable from battery.

4. Remove the resonator assembly and air inlet hose.

5. Drain the cooling system below coolant temperature sensor level.

6. Disconnect the electronic throttle control (ETC) connector.

7. Disconnect electrical connectors for the following components:

    a. Coolant Temperature Sensor.

    b. Manifold Absolute Pressure (MAP) Sensor.

8. Disconnect vapor purge hose, brake booster hose, and positive crankcase ventilation (PCV) hose.

9. Disconnect and remove ignition coil towers.

10. Remove the top oil dipstick tube retaining bolt.

11. Remove the EGR tube.

12. Remove fuel rail.

13. Remove throttle body assembly.

14. Remove the intake manifold retaining fasteners in reverse order of tightening sequence.

15. Remove the intake manifold.

To install:

16. Install the intake manifold seals.

17. Install the intake manifold.

18. Install the intake manifold retaining bolts and tighten in sequence shown to 105 inch lbs. (12 Nm).

▬ **✷✷ WARNING** ▬

Proper torque of the throttle body is critical to normal operation. If the throttle body is over-torqued, damage to the throttle body can occur resulting in throttle plate malfunction.

19. Install the throttle body-to-intake manifold O-ring.

20. Install the throttle body to intake manifold.

21. Install the four mounting bolts. Tighten bolts to 60 inch lbs. (7 Nm).

22. Install electrical connector.

23. Install the fuel rail.

24. Install the EGR tube

25. Install ignition coil towers.

26. Connect electrical connectors for the following components:

27. Manifold Absolute Pressure (MAP) Sensor

28. Coolant Temperature (CTS) Sensor

29. Ignition coil towers

30. Install top oil dipstick tube retaining bolt.

31. Connect Vapor purge hose, Brake booster hose, Positive crankcase ventilation (PCV) hose.

32. Fill the cooling system.

33. Install the resonator assembly and air inlet hose.

34. Connect the negative cable to battery.

35. Using the scan tool, perform the ETC Relearn function.

4.0L Engine

Lower

See Figures 92 through 94.

1. See all applicable precautions before beginning service procedures.

2. Perform fuel pressure release procedure.

3. Remove and isolate negative battery cable at battery.

4. Drain the cooling system.

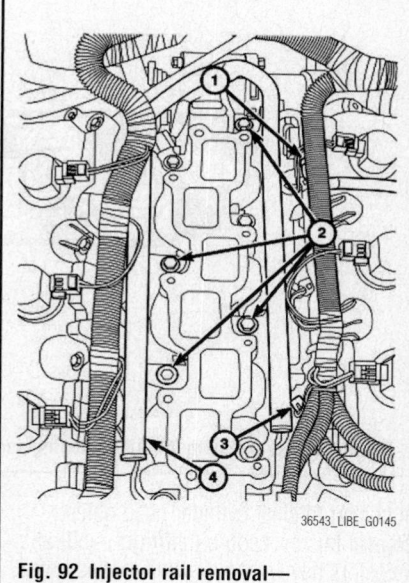

Fig. 92 Injector rail removal— 4.0L engine

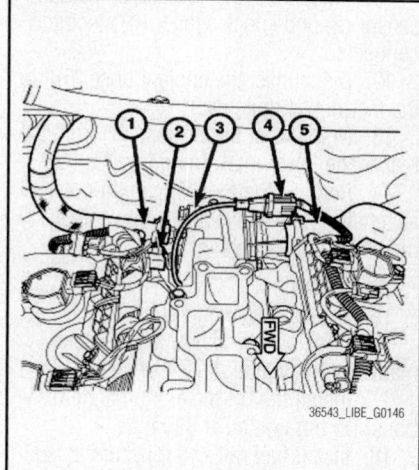

Fig. 93 Sensor and hose removal— 4.0L engine

5. Remove the upper intake manifold including EGR tube, PCV, purge and power brake booster vacuum hoses.

6. Disconnect the fuel supply hose from fuel rail (1).

7. Disconnect electrical connectors (3) at all six fuel injectors. The factory fuel injection wiring harness is numerically tagged (INJ 1, INJ 2, etc.) for injector position identification. If harness is not tagged, note wiring location before removal.

8. Remove four fuel rail mounting bolts (2).

9. Gently rock and pull left side of fuel rail until fuel injectors just start to clear machined holes in cylinder head. Gently rock and pull right side of rail until injectors

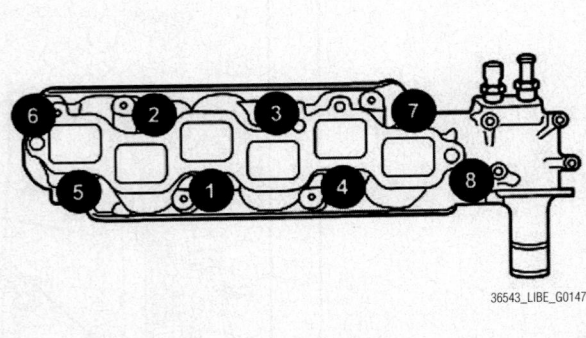

Fig. 94 Lower intake manifold tightening sequence—4.0L engine

just start to clear cylinder head holes. Repeat this procedure (left/right) until all injectors have cleared cylinder head holes.

10. Remove fuel rail (with injectors attached) from engine.

11. Disconnect the coolant temperature sensor (2) and knock sensor (4) electrical connectors.

12. Disconnect the coolant hose (5) from the thermostat housing.

13. Disconnect heater hose (1) from the rear of the lower intake manifold (3).

14. Remove the four remaining bolts attaching lower intake and remove intake manifold and gaskets.

To install:

15. Clean all sealing surfaces.

16. Position new gaskets and intake manifold on cylinder head surfaces.

17. Install four of the eight manifold bolts. Do not tighten at this time.

18. Install fuel rail and injectors as an assembly.

19. Install the four remaining intake manifold bolts and gradually tighten in sequence shown until a torque of 21 ft. lbs. (28 Nm) is obtained.

20. Connect fuel supply hose to fuel rail.

21. Connect fuel injector electrical connectors.

22. Connect heater hose to rear lower intake manifold.

23. Connect coolant hose to thermostat housing.

24. Connect coolant temperature sensor and knock sensor electrical connectors.

25. Install upper intake manifold, EGR tube, PVC, purge and power brake booster vacuum hoses.

26. Fill the cooling system.

27. Connect the negative battery cable. Tighten nut to 40 inch lbs. (4.5 Nm).

Upper

See Figures 95 and 96.

1. See all applicable precautions before beginning service procedures.

2. Disconnect and isolate the negative battery cable.

3. Disconnect the Intake Air Temperature (IAT) sensor (5), Manifold Absolute Pressure (MAP) sensor (3), electronic throttle control (2) and manifold tuning valve (4) electrical connectors.

4. Loosen clamps (1) and remove air inlet hose (6) from the throttle body .

5. Disconnect the PCV, purge and power brake booster vacuum hoses from the upper intake manifold.

6. Remove two EGR tube mounting flange bolts at the intake manifold.

7. Remove two EGR tube mounting flange bolts (3) at the EGR solenoid/valve (2).

8. Separate the EGR tube (4) and gasket (5) from the EGR solenoid/valve (2). Slip

opposite end of tube (4) from intake manifold.

9. Remove two nuts from studs on left intake manifold support brackets.

10. Remove the upper intake manifold retaining bolts and manifold. Clean all gasket sealing surfaces.

To install:

11. Clean and inspect gasket sealing surfaces.

12. Position new upper intake manifold gasket.

13. Install the upper intake manifold. Tighten bolts to 105 inch lbs. (12 Nm), starting in the center working outward in a cross sequence pattern.

14. Install two nuts to the left manifold support brackets. Tighten nuts to 105 inch lbs. (12 Nm).

15. Install new O-ring to intake manifold end of EGR tube.

16. Install two flange mounting bolts at the intake manifold. Do not tighten at this time.

17. Install new gasket between EGR solenoid/valve and tube flange.

18. Position tube to solenoid/valve. Install and tighten two flange bolts at solenoid/valve to 80 inch lbs. (8 Nm).

19. Tighten two flange bolts at intake manifold to 35 inch lbs. (4 Nm).

20. Connect the PVC, purge and power brake booster vacuum hoses to the intake manifold.

21. Connect the manifold tuning valve, electronic throttle control, MAP sensor and IAT sensor electrical connectors.

22. Install the inlet hose tighten clamps.

23. Connect negative battery cable. Tighten nut to 45 inch lbs. (5 Nm).

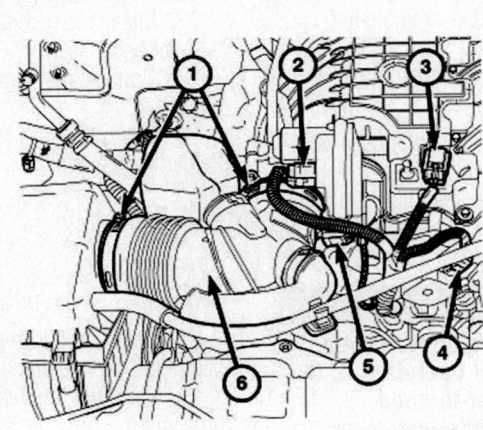

Fig. 95 Sensor connector removal—4.0L engine

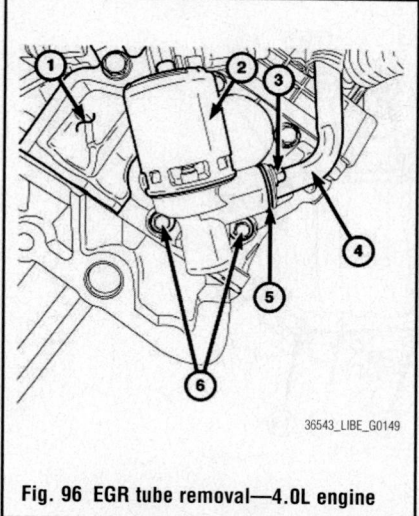

Fig. 96 EGR tube removal—4.0L engine

OIL PAN

REMOVAL & INSTALLATION

3.7L Engine

2WD Models

See Figures 97 and 98.

1. See all applicable precautions before beginning service procedures.
2. Disconnect and isolate negative battery cable.
3. Install engine support fixture.
4. Raise and support vehicle.
5. Remove the front wheel assemblies.
6. Remove the skid plate (if equipped).
7. Drain engine oil.

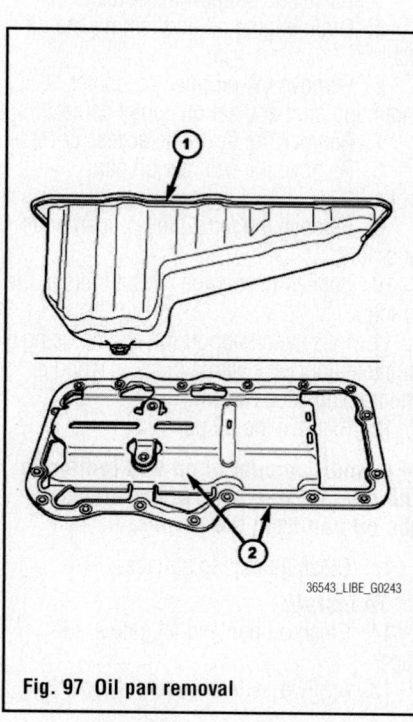

Fig. 97 Oil pan removal

8. Mark adjustment cam position of front lower control arm bolts.
9. Remove the front lower control arm bolts.
10. Disconnect the left-hand tie rod.
11. Disconnect the left-hand lower ball joint.
12. Disconnect the left-hand strut clevis.
13. Remove the left-hand front axle.
14. Remove the front axle brace bolts.
15. Remove the front prop shaft.
16. Drain front axle.
17. Using a transmission jack, support the front axle.
18. Remove the axle bracket bolts.
19. With the right-hand axle still in place, remove front differential.
20. Remove the transmission oil cooler line bracket.
21. Remove the engine to transmission stiffening bracket.
22. Position Engine Support 8534 on the fender lip and align the slots in the brackets with the fender mounting holes.
23. Secure brackets to the fender using four M6 X 1.0 X 25 MM flanged cap screws.
24. Tighten the thumbscrews to secure the sleeves to the support tube.
25. Secure the support tube in an upright position.
26. Assemble the flat washer, thrust bearing, hook and T handle.
27. Using the M10 X 1.75 mm flanged nut supplied with the support fixture, secure the chain to the front engine lifting stud.
28. Loosen the engine mounts.
29. Remove the oil pan bolts.
30. Separate the oil pan (1) from engine.
31. Move the oil pan to one side, remove oils sump bolt and windage tray bolts.

➡ **Do not pry on oil pan or oil pan gasket. Gasket is integral to engine windage tray and does not come out with oil pan.**

32. Move the oil pan and windage tray (2) toward front of vehicle and remove from vehicle.

To install:

33. Clean the oil pan gasket mating surface of the bedplate and oil pan.
34. Clean the oil pan and block gasket mating surfaces.
35. Inspect integrated oil pan gasket, and replace as necessary.
36. Drop the oil pump pick-up tube into the oil pan, and install the oil pan, pick-up tube, and the windage tray, as an assembly, from the front of the vehicle.
37. Install the windage tray, then the oil pump pick-up tube, and the (2) nuts and (1) bolt holding the oil pump pick-up tube, in place.

➡ **It will be necessary to move the oil pan from side to side to gain access to these fasteners.**

38. Tighten the pick-up tube fasteners.
39. Install the oil pan.
40. Install and tighten the oil pan bolts.
41. Install the engine to transmission structural cover, (if equipped).
42. Lower engine, and remove Engine Support 8534.
43. Lower the vehicle.
44. Lower the engine using Engine Support Fixture 8534.
45. Remove the Engine Support Fixture 8534.
46. Raise the vehicle.
47. Tighten both engine mount through bolts.

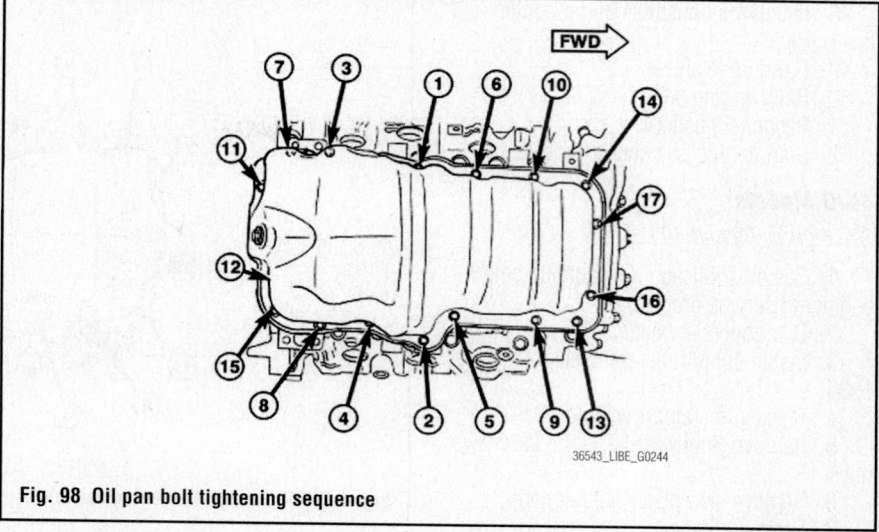

Fig. 98 Oil pan bolt tightening sequence

48. Install the transmission oil cooler line bracket.

49. Lower the vehicle.

50. Refill engine oil.

51. Reconnect battery.

52. Start engine and check for leaks.

4WD Models

See Figures 99 and 100.

1. See all applicable precautions before beginning service procedures.

2. Disconnect the battery.

3. Install support fixture special tool 8534.

4. Raise and support vehicle.

5. Remove front wheel and tire assemblies.

6. Remove skid plate (if equipped).

7. Drain engine oil.

8. Remove engine to transmission structural cover (if equipped).

9. Remove transmission oil cooler line bracket.

10. Remove the front axle assembly from the vehicle.

11. Loosen both engine mount through bolts.

12. Lower the vehicle.

➡**It is not necessary to remove the viscous fan, or fan shroud, for oil pan removal.**

13. Raise the engine using support fixture special tool 8534, until the viscous fan almost touches the fan shroud.

14. Raise the vehicle.

15. Remove the oil pan bolts.

16. Separate the oil pan from the engine.

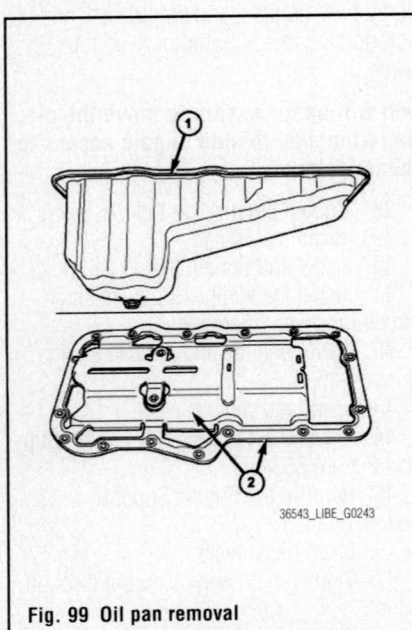

Fig. 99 Oil pan removal

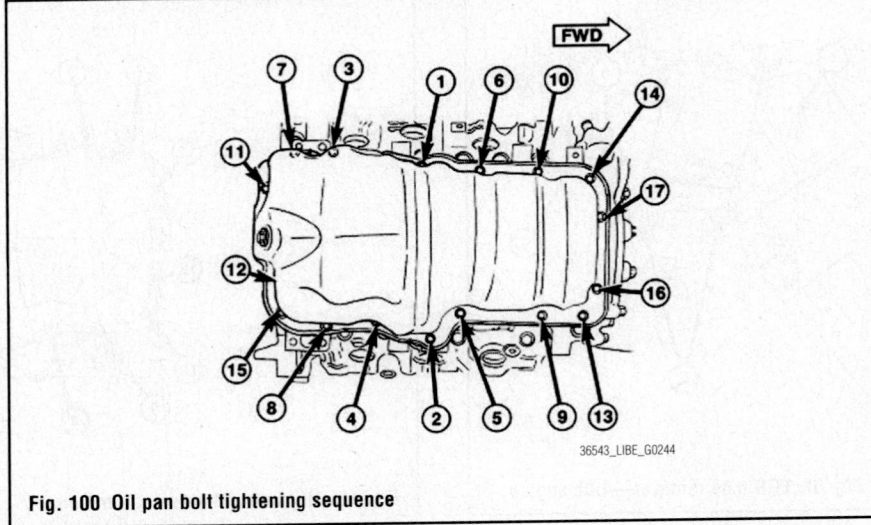

Fig. 100 Oil pan bolt tightening sequence

36543_LIBE_G0244

17. Remove the nuts and bolt holding the oil pump pick-up tube, and windage tray in place.

➡**It will be necessary to move the oil pan from side to side to gain access to these fasteners.**

18. Drop the oil pump pick-up tube into the oil pan, and remove the oil pan, pick-up tube, and the windage tray, as an assembly, from the front of the vehicle.

To install:

19. Inspect oil pan gasket for defects, and replace if necessary.

20. Clean the oil pan and block gasket mating surfaces.

21. Drop the oil pump pick-up tube into the oil pan and install the oil pan, pick-up tube, and the windage tray, as an assembly, from the front of the vehicle.

22. Install the windage tray, then the oil pump pick-up tube, and the nuts and bolt holding the oil pump pick-up tube, in place.

➡**It will be necessary to move the oil pan from side to side to gain access to these fasteners.**

23. Torque the pick-up tube fasteners.

24. Install the oil pan.

25. Install and tighten the oil pan bolts.

26. Install the engine to transmission structural cover, (if equipped).

27. Lower the vehicle.

28. Lower the engine using Engine Support Fixture 8534.

29. Remove the Engine Support Fixture 8534.

30. Raise the vehicle.

31. Tighten both engine mount through bolts.

32. Install the transmission oil cooler line bracket.

33. Install the front axle assembly to the vehicle.

34. Install the skid plate (if equipped).

35. Install the front wheel and tire assemblies.

36. Lower the vehicle.

37. Refill engine oil.

38. Reconnect battery.

39. Start engine, and check for leaks.

4.0L Engine

See Figures 101 through 104.

1. See all applicable precautions before beginning service procedures.

2. Disconnect negative battery cable.

3. Remove engine oil indicator.

4. Raise and support the vehicle.

5. Drain engine oil and remove the oil filter.

6. Remove the oil filter, oil cooler mounting stud and set oil cooler aside.

7. Remove the flex plate access cover.

8. Remove the two rear oil pan bolts (3).

9. Remove the remaining oil pan bolts and nuts.

10. Loosen the engine mount bolts at the cradle.

11. Raise and support the engine using a suitable floor jack with a block of wood at the transmission housing.

12. Remove the oil pan.

➡**A small amount of oil will remain in the oil pan. Use care when removing the oil pan from the engine.**

13. Clean all mating surfaces.

To install:

14. Clean oil pan and all gasket surfaces.

15. Apply a ⅛ inch bead of Mopar®

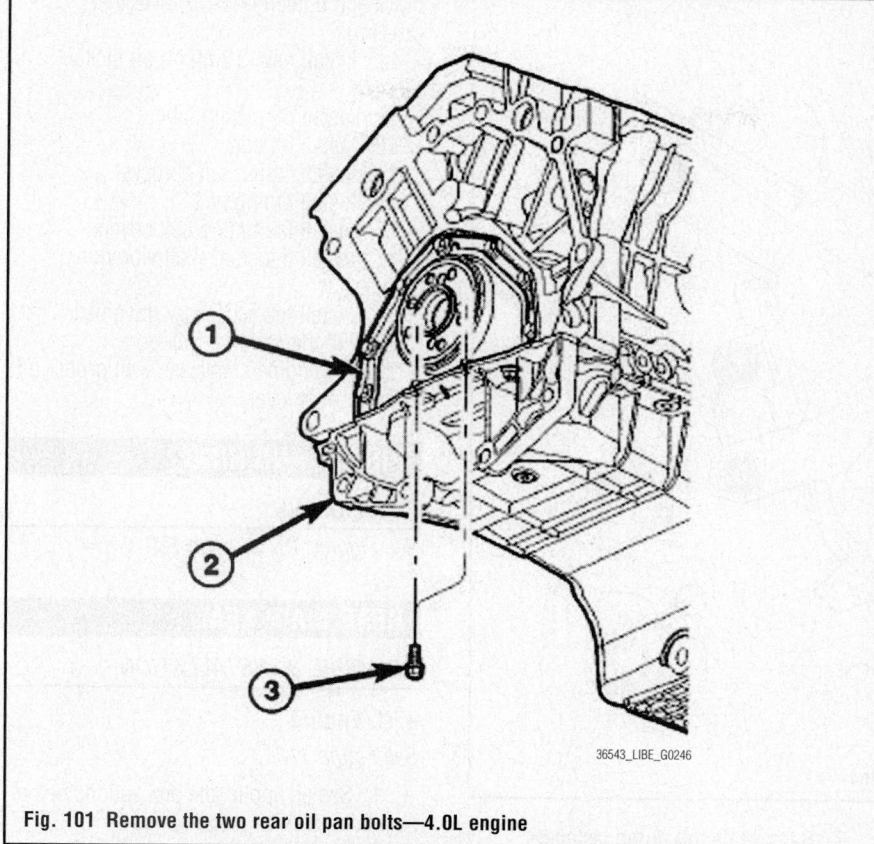

Fig. 101 Remove the two rear oil pan bolts—4.0L engine

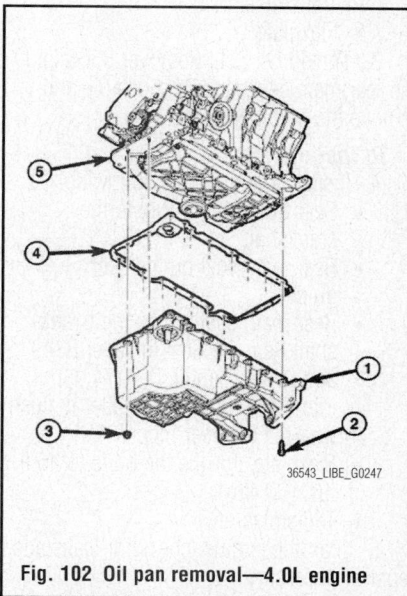

Fig. 102 Oil pan removal—4.0L engine

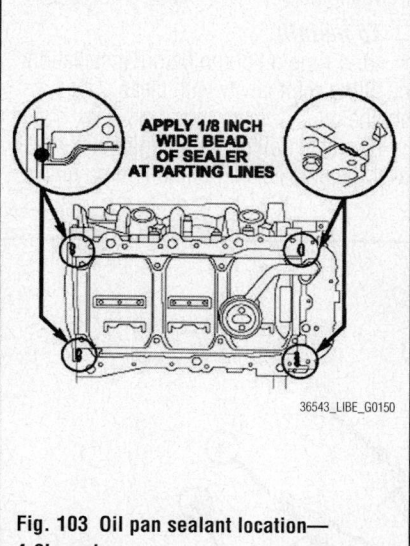

Fig. 103 Oil pan sealant location— 4.0L engine

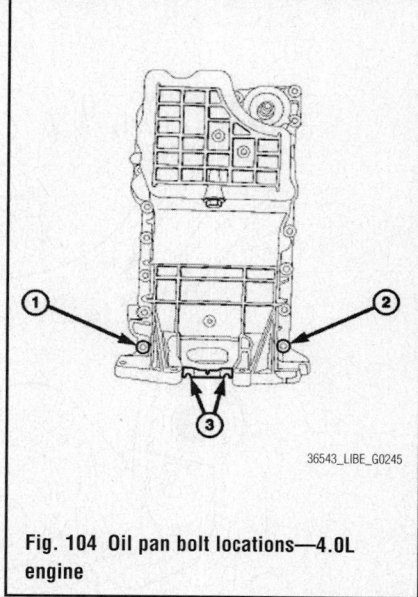

Fig. 104 Oil pan bolt locations—4.0L engine

Engine RTV GEN II at the parting line of the oil pump housing and the rear seal retainer.

16. Install oil pan gasket to the engine block.

17. Install the oil pan while aligning the oil level indicator tube and attach fasteners finger tight.

➡**Assure that the rear face of the oil pan is flush to the transmission bell housing when installing the oil pan.**

18. Pre-torque the horizontal rear oil pan to transmission bolts to 12 inch lbs. (1.4 Nm).

19. First tighten the M8 (1) oil pan alignment bolt to 21 ft. lbs. (28 Nm), then tighten bolt (2) to 21 ft. lbs. (28 Nm).

20. Tighten the remaining M8 bolts and M8 nuts to 21 ft. lbs. (28 Nm), and the M6 bolts to 105 inch lbs. (12 Nm).

21. Tighten the four M10 oil pan to transmission bolts to 40 ft. lbs. (55 Nm).

22. Lower the engine and remove the lifting fixture. Tighten the engine mount to cradle fasteners to 55 lbs. ft. (75 Nm).

23. Install the flex plate inspection cover and tighten the fastener to 97 inch lbs. (11 Nm).

24. Install the oil cooler. Align the oil cooler notch to oil pan tab.

25. Install the engine oil filter. Tighten filter to 106 inch lbs. (12 Nm).

26. Fill engine crankcase with proper oil to correct level.

27. Connect negative battery cable.

OIL PUMP

REMOVAL & INSTALLATION

3.7L Engine

See Figure 105.

1. See all applicable precautions before beginning service procedures.

2. Remove or disconnect the following:
- Oil Pan
- Timing chain cover
- Timing chains and tensioners
- Oil pump

To install:

3. Installation is the reverse of removal. Torque the pump bolts, in sequence, to 21 ft. lbs. (28 Nm).

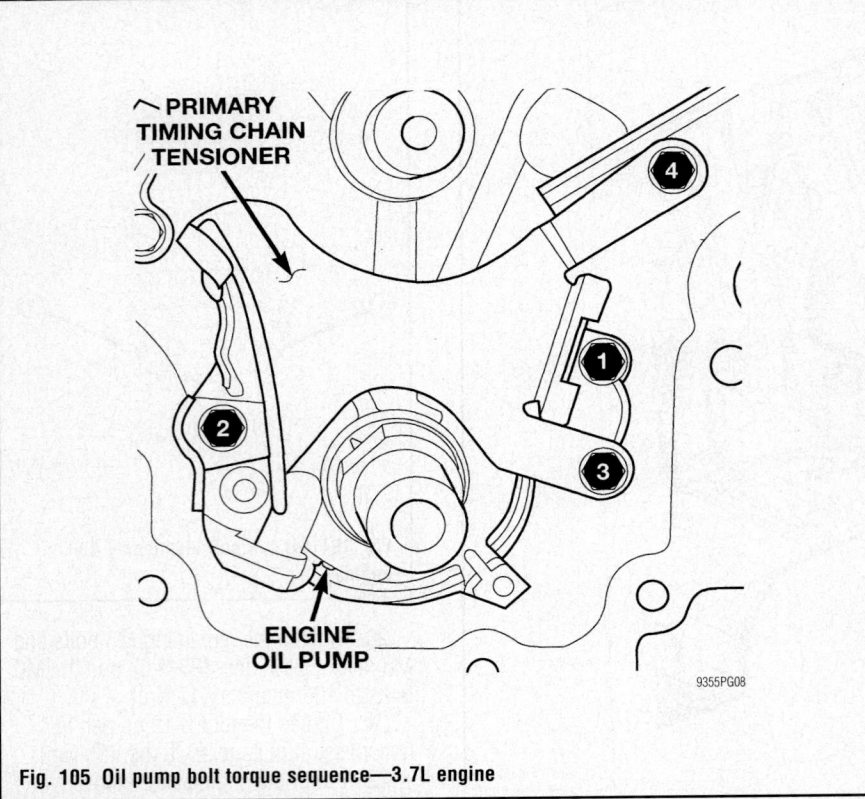

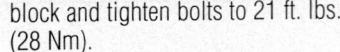

Fig. 105 Oil pump bolt torque sequence—3.7L engine

4.0L Engine

See Figure 106.

1. See all applicable precautions before beginning service procedures.
2. Drain the cooling system.
3. Remove the timing belt.
4. Remove the crankshaft sprocket.
5. Remove the oil pan.
6. Remove the oil pickup tube.
7. Remove the oil pump fasteners.
8. Remove the oil pump and gasket from engine.

To install:

9. Prime oil pump before installation by filling rotor cavity with clean engine oil.
10. Install oil pump and gasket carefully over the crankshaft. Position pump onto

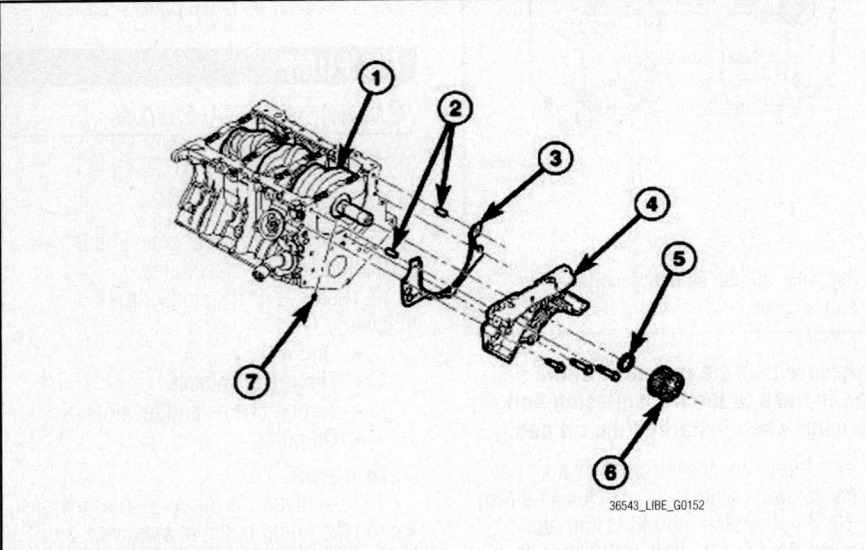

Fig. 106 Oil pump removal—4.0L engine

block and tighten bolts to 21 ft. lbs. (28 Nm).

11. Install new O-ring on oil pickup tube.
12. Install oil pickup tube.
13. Install oil pan.
14. Install crankshaft sprocket.
15. Install timing belt.
16. Install the timing belt covers.
17. Install the crankshaft vibration damper.
18. Install the accessory drive belt.
19. Fill the cooling system.
20. Fill engine crankcase with proper oil to the correct level.

PISTON AND RING

POSITIONING

See Figures 107 through 109.

REAR MAIN SEAL

REMOVAL & INSTALLATION

3.7L Engine

See Figure 110.

1. See all applicable precautions before beginning service procedures.
2. Remove or disconnect the following:
   - Transmission
   - Flexplate
3. Thread Oil Seal Remover 8506 into the rear main seal as far as possible and remove the rear main seal.

To install:

4. Install or connect the following:
   - Seal Guide 8349-2 onto the crankshaft
   - Rear main seal on the seal guide
   - Rear main seal, using the Crankshaft Rear Oil Seal Installer 8349 and Driver Handle C-4171; tap it into place until the installer is flush with the cylinder block.
   - Flexplate. Torque the bolts to 45 ft. lbs. (60 Nm).
   - Transmission
5. Start the engine, check for leaks and repair if necessary.

4.0L Engine

See Figures 111 through 115.

1. See all applicable precautions before beginning service procedures.
2. Remove the engine oil pan.
3. Lower the weight of the engine back onto the engine mounts.

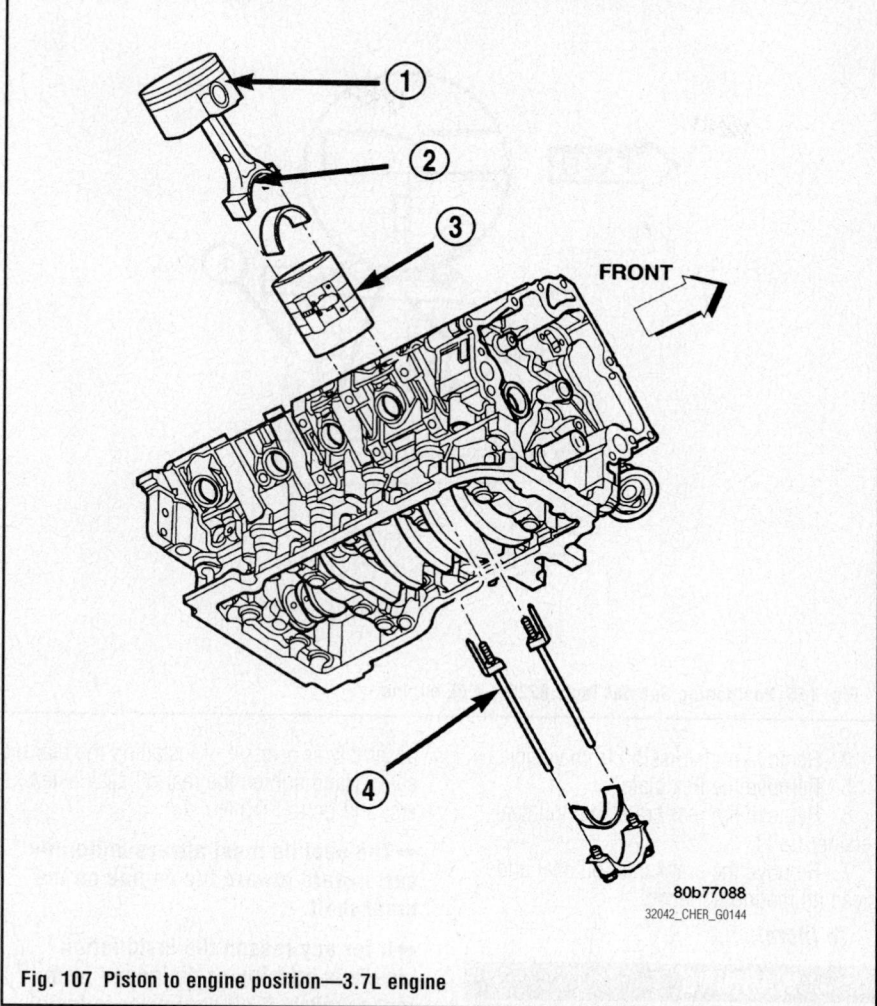

FRONT

80b77088
32042_CHER_G0144

Fig. 107 Piston to engine position—3.7L engine

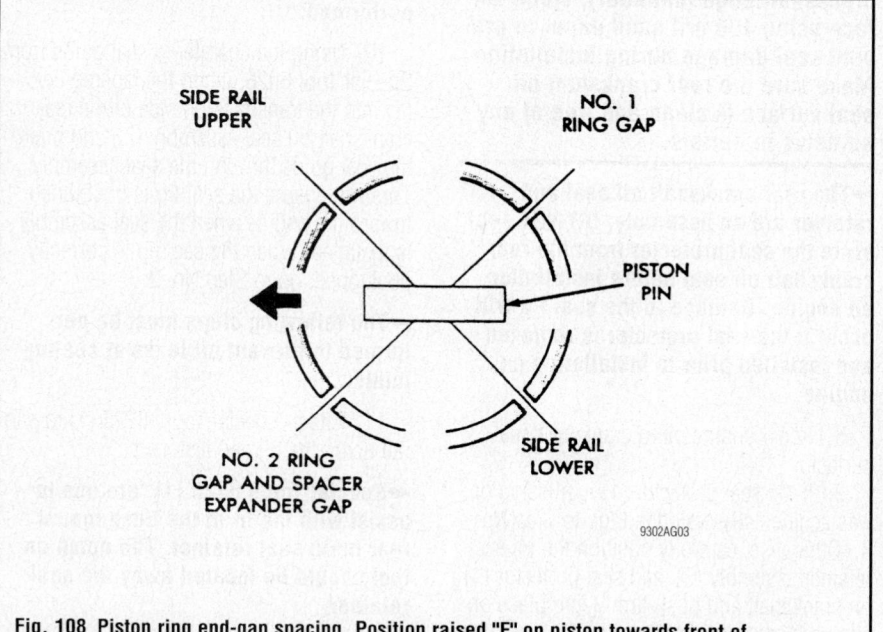

SIDE RAIL
UPPER

NO. 1
RING GAP

PISTON
PIN

NO. 2 RING
GAP AND SPACER
EXPANDER GAP

SIDE RAIL
LOWER

9302AG03

Fig. 108 Piston ring end-gap spacing. Position raised "F" on piston towards front of engine—3.7L engine

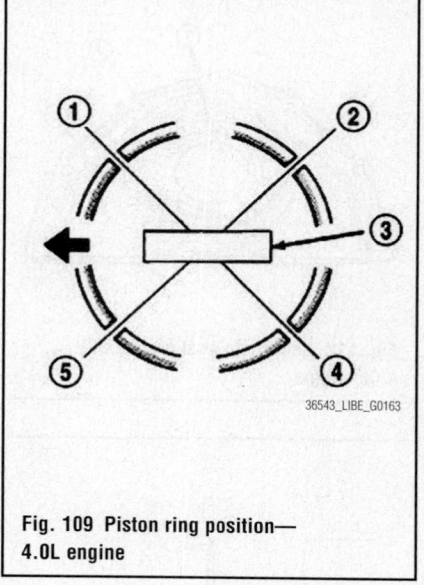

36543_LIBE_G0163

Fig. 109 Piston ring position—
4.0L engine

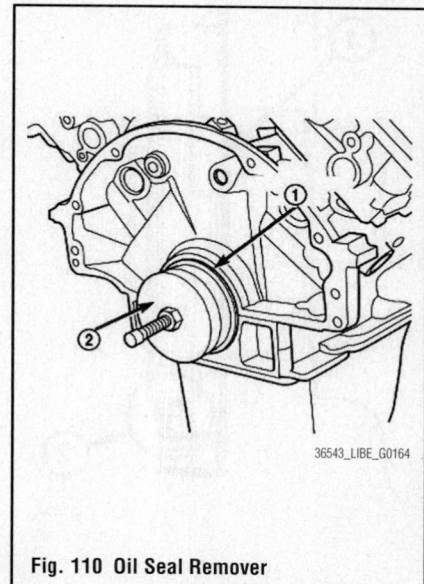

36543_LIBE_G0164

Fig. 110 Oil Seal Remover

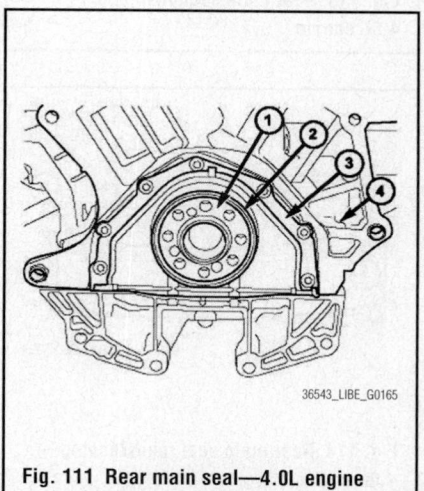

36543_LIBE_G0165

Fig. 111 Rear main seal—4.0L engine

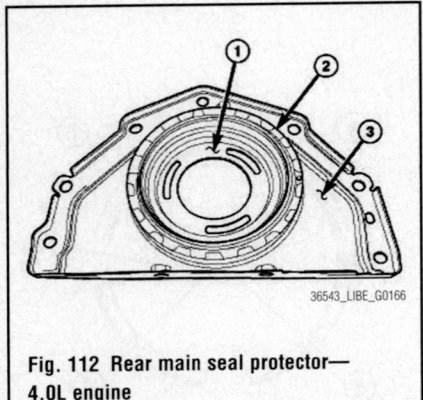

Fig. 112 Rear main seal protector— 4.0L engine

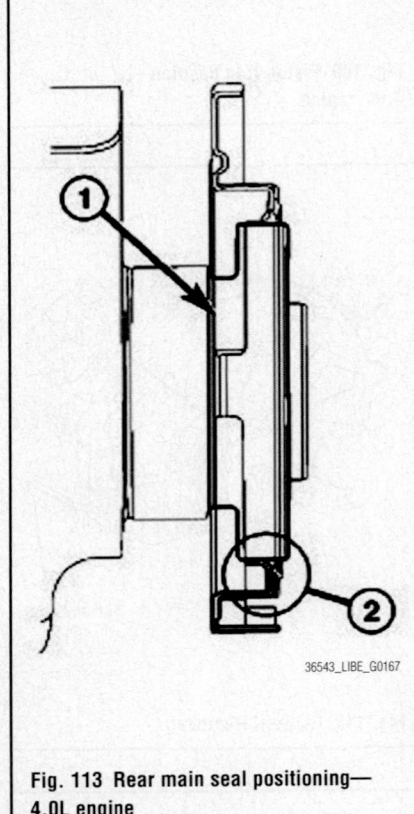

Fig. 113 Rear main seal positioning— 4.0L engine

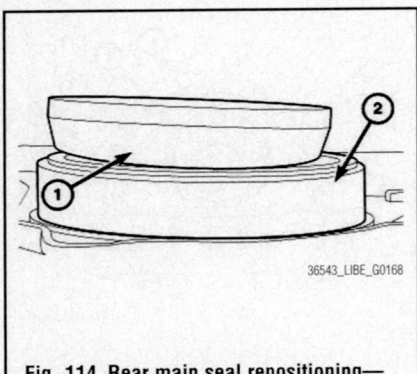

Fig. 114 Rear main seal repositioning— 4.0L engine

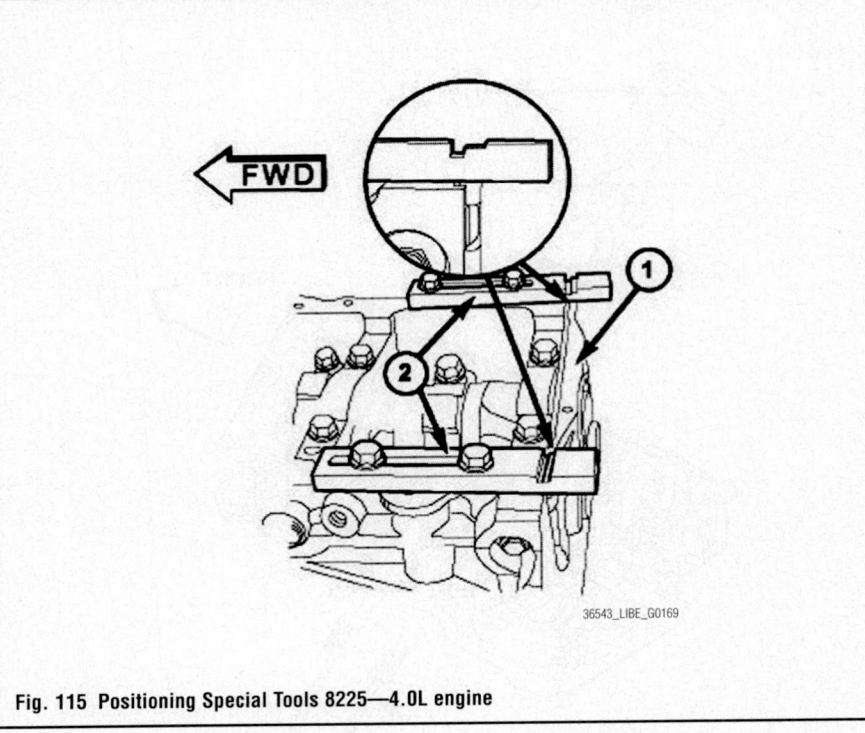

Fig. 115 Positioning Special Tools 8225—4.0L engine

4. Remove transmission from vehicle.
5. Remove the flex plate.
6. Remove the rear crankshaft oil seal retainer bolts.
7. Remove the crankshaft oil seal and clean all mating surfaces.

To install:

※※ WARNING

If a burr or scratch is present on the crankshaft edge (chamfer), clean surface using 400 grit sand paper to prevent seal damage during installation. Make sure the rear crankshaft oil seal surface is clean and free of any abrasive materials.

➥The rear crankshaft oil seal and retainer are an assembly. DO NOT separate the seal protector from the rear crankshaft oil seal before installation on engine. Damage to the seal lip will occur if the seal protector is removed and installed prior to installation on engine.

8. Apply engine oil to crankshaft seal surface.
9. If the seal protector (1) is missing or was accidentally dislodged, go to Step No. 3 . Otherwise, carefully position the oil seal retainer assembly (3), and seal protector (1) on crankshaft and push firmly into place on engine block (during this step, the seal protector will be pushed from the rear oil seal

assembly as a result of installing the rear oil seal). Hand tighten the rear oil seal fasteners, and go to Step No. 4 .

➥The seal lip must always uniformly curl inward toward the engine on the crankshaft.

➥If for any reason the installation sleeve is missing or dislodged from rear crankshaft oil seal prior to installation, the following procedure must be performed:

10. Using the chamfered seal guide from Special Tool 6926, insert the tapered end (1) into the transmission side of the rear crankshaft oil seal assembly (2), and push the seal guide through the seal assembly. This will ensure the seal lip is positioned toward the engine when the seal assembly is installed. When the seal lip is correctly positioned, go to Step No. 2 .

➥The following steps must be performed to prevent oil leaks at sealing joints:

11. Attach Special Tools 8225 (1) to pan rail using the oil pan fasteners.

➥Special Tools 8225 (1), are use to assist with the fit of the flush mount rear main seal retainer. The notch on tool should be located away the seal retainer.

12. While applying firm pressure to the seal retainer against Special Tools 8225 (1),

tighten seal retainer screws to 105 inch lbs. (12 Nm).

13. Remove special tool No. 8225 (1).

14. Install oil pan. Tighten the 6mm fasteners to 105 inch lbs. (12 Nm) and the 8mm fasteners to 21 ft. lbs. (28 Nm).

15. Install the flex plate and transmission.

ROCKER ARMS/SHAFTS

REMOVAL & INSTALLATION

3.7L Engine

See Figure 116.

1. See all applicable precautions before beginning service procedures.

2. Remove or disconnect the following:
   - Negative battery cable
   - Valve covers

3. Rotate the crankshaft so that the piston of the cylinder to be serviced is at Top Dead Center (TDC) and both valves are closed.

4. Use special tool 8516 to depress the valve and remove the rocker arm.

5. Repeat for each rocker arm to be serviced.

➡ **Keep valvetrain components in order for reassembly.**

To install:

6. Rotate the crankshaft so that the piston of the cylinder to be serviced is at BDC.

7. Compress the valve spring and install each rocker arm in its original position.

8. Repeat for each rocker arm to be installed.

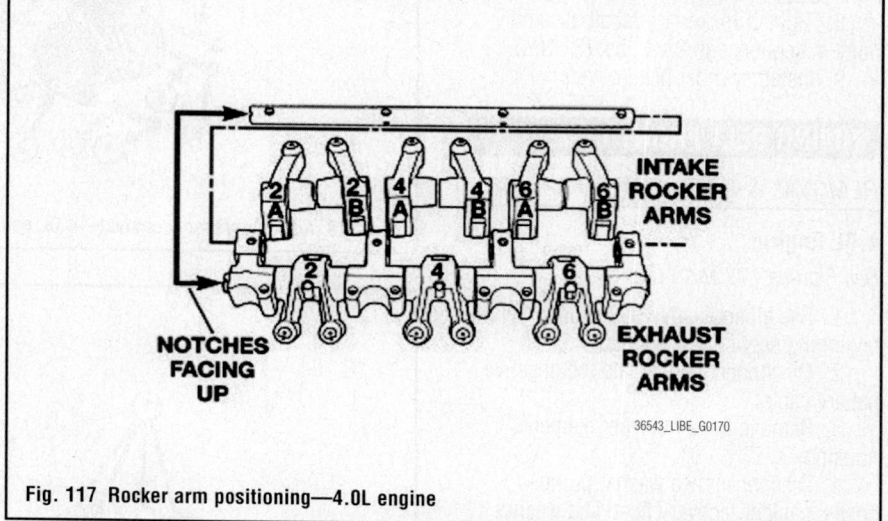

Fig. 117 Rocker arm positioning—4.0L engine

9. Install or connect the following:
   - Cylinder head cover
   - Negative battery cable

4.0L Engine

See Figure 117.

1. See all applicable precautions before beginning service procedures.

➡ The rocker arm shafts are hollow and are used as lubrication oil passages. The rocker arm and shaft assembly on the RIGHT side of the engine has an oil passage hole from the cylinder head to the third rocker shaft support. The rocker arm shaft assembly on the LEFT side of the engine has an oil passage hole from the cylinder head to the second rocker shaft support.

2. Remove cylinder head covers.

3. Identify the rocker arm assembly and rocker arms before disassembly.

4. Remove rocker arm assembly bolts.

5. Remove rocker arm assembly.

➡ To prevent air ingestion into lash adjusters, avoid turning rocker arm assembly upside down.

✷✷ WARNING

Do not allow rocker arm assembly to rest on lash adjusters, as damage may occur to lash adjusters and/or plastic retainers.

To install:

➡ Rocker arm and shaft assembly can be installed either prior to or after (preferred) cylinder head installation.

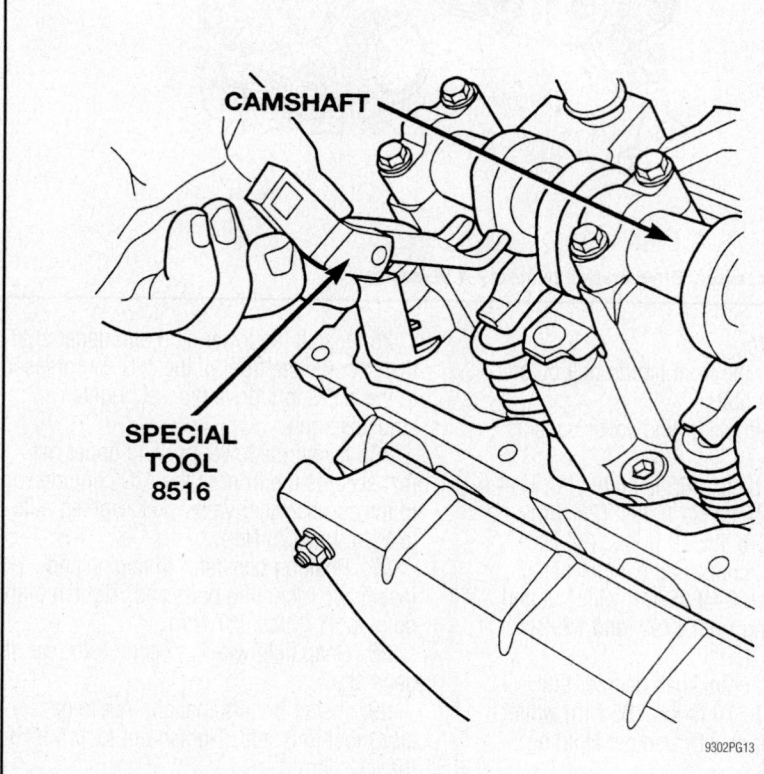

Fig. 116 Rocker arm service—3.7L engine

6. Rotate camshaft gears to a neutral position (no load to the valve). This will allow the rocker arm shaft assembly to be tightened into position with little or no valve spring load on it.

7. Install the rocker arm and shaft assembly making sure that the identification marks face toward the front of engine for left head and toward the rear of the engine for right head.

8. Tighten rocker arm/shaft assembly bolts in sequence to 23 ft. lbs. (31 Nm).

9. Install cylinder head covers

TIMING BELT FRONT COVER

REMOVAL & INSTALLATION

4.0L Engine

See Figures 118 and 119.

1. See all applicable precautions before beginning service procedures.

2. Disconnect and isolate the negative battery cable.

3. Remove the air cleaner element housing.

4. Disconnect two washer pump hoses, coolant recovery hose and washer pump electrical connector from the coolant recovery/washer fluid reservoir assembly.

5. Remove 5 screws and remove the coolant recovery/washer fluid reservoir assembly.

6. Disengage the radiator hose retainer from the electric fan shroud.

7. Remove transmission cooling line retainer bolt from the electric fan shroud.

8. Disconnect the electric fan connector from the electric fan shroud.

9. Remove two bolts and lift the electric fan shroud from vehicle.

10. Use Adapter Pins 8346 in Spanner Wrench 6958 to hold the pulley and remove fan/viscous fan drive assembly.

11. Remove accessory drive.

12. Remove the power steering belt.

13. Remove generator.

14. Remove two nuts (4) and (6) that secure the front of the A/C compressor (1).

15. Back out the two A/C compressor mounting studs (3) and (5) from the accessory drive bracket.

16. Remove four bolts (1) and nut (3) and remove the accessory drive bracket (2).

17. Remove crankshaft damper bolt.

18. Using Puller 1023 and Crankshaft Insert 9020, remove crankshaft damper.

19. Remove the fourteen outer timing belt cover bolts and cover.

Fig. 118 A/C Compressor removal—4.0L engine

36543_LIBE_G0134

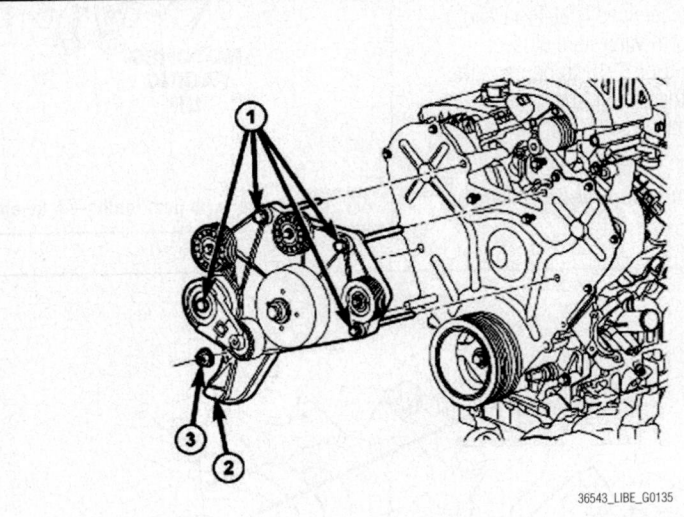

Fig. 119 Accessory Drive Bracket removal—4.0L engine

36543_LIBE_G0135

To install:

20. Install the front timing belt outer cover and 14 bolts.

21. Tighten the timing cover bolts as follows:
- M6 bolts: 105 inch lbs. (12 Nm)
- M8 bolts: 21 ft. lbs. (28 Nm)
- M10 bolts: 40 ft. lbs. (54 Nm)

22. Install crankshaft damper using Forcing Screw C-4685-C1, with Nut and Thrust Bearing from 6792, and 6792-1 Installer.

23. Install crankshaft damper bolt. Tighten bolt to 70 ft. lbs. (95 Nm) while holding damper with Damper Holding Fixture 9365.

24. Install the accessory drive bracket. Tighten four bolts and nut to 40 ft. lbs. (54 Nm).

25. Install the lower stud and upper stud that secures the front of the A/C compressor to the accessory drive bracket. Tighten studs securely.

26. Install the lower nut and upper nut that secures the front of the A/C compressor to the accessory drive bracket. Tighten nuts to 21 ft. lbs. (28 Nm).

27. Position generator to engine and install two mounting bolts and. Tighten both bolts to 42 ft. lbs. (57 Nm).

28. Snap field wire connector into rear of generator.

29. Install B+ terminal and nut to generator mounting stud. Tighten nut to 115 inch lbs. (13 Nm).

30. Snap plastic protective cover to B+ terminal.

31. Install the power steering belt.

32. Install the accessory drive belt.

33. Use Adapter Pins 8346 in Spanner Wrench 6958 to hold the pulley while installing the fan blade/viscous fan drive assembly. Tighten mounting nut to 37 ft. lbs. (50 Nm).

34. Install electric fan shroud with two screws. Tighten screws to 50 inch lbs. (6 Nm).

35. Connect and lock the electric fan connector.

36. Install transmission cooler line retainer to electric fan shroud with one screw.

37. Install radiator hose retainer to electric fan shroud.

38. Install the coolant recovery/washer fluid reservoir assembly with five screws. Connect two washer pump hoses, coolant recovery hose, and washer pump electrical connector.

39. Install lower intake manifold and fuel rail.

40. Install the upper intake manifold, EGR tube, PCV, Purge and power brake booster vacuum hoses.

41. Install and connect the air cleaner element housing.

42. Fill the coolant system.

43. Connect the negative battery cable. Tighten nut to 40 inch lbs. (4.5 Nm).

TIMING BELT AND SPROCKETS

REMOVAL & INSTALLATION

4.0L Engine

See Figures 120 through 124.

1. See all applicable precautions before beginning service procedures.

2. Disconnect and isolate the negative battery cable.

3. Remove the front timing belt cover.

4. Mark belt running direction, if timing belt is to be reused.

❋❋ WARNING

When aligning timing marks, always rotate engine by turning the crankshaft. Failure to do so will result in valve and/or piston damage.

5. Rotate engine clockwise until crankshaft (10) mark aligns with the TDC mark on oil pump housing (9) and the camshaft sprocket (2, 7) timing marks (1, 8) are aligned with the marks on the rear cover.

6. Raise and support the vehicle.

7. Remove bolt (2) and reposition oil cooler hose (1).

8. Remove the timing belt tensioner (12).

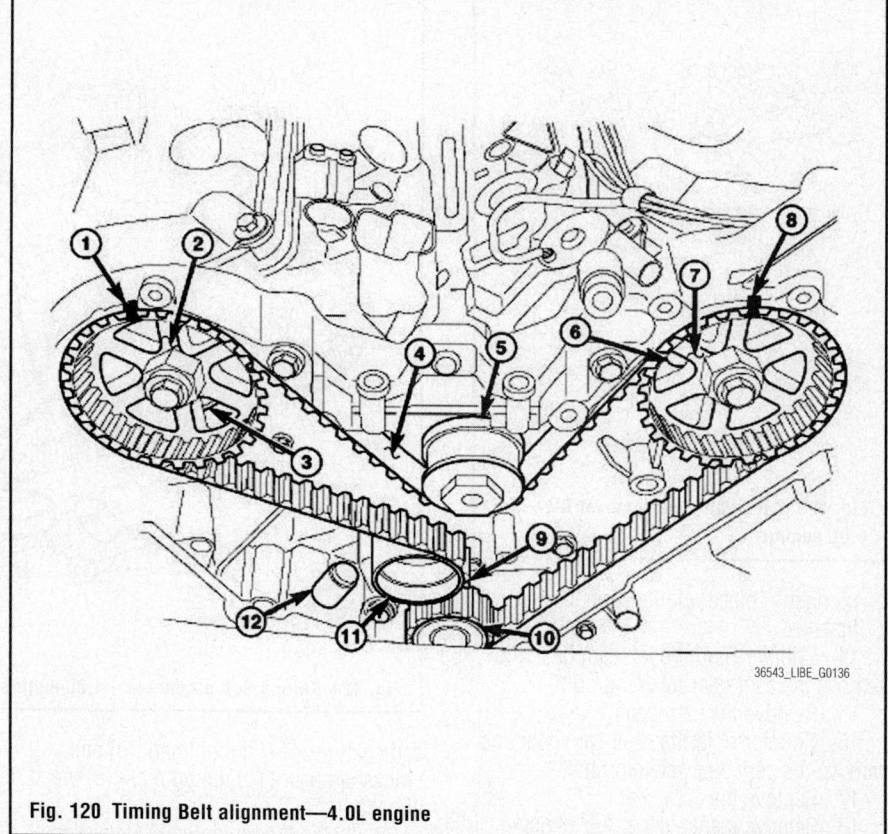

Fig. 120 Timing Belt alignment—4.0L engine

36543_LIBE_G0136

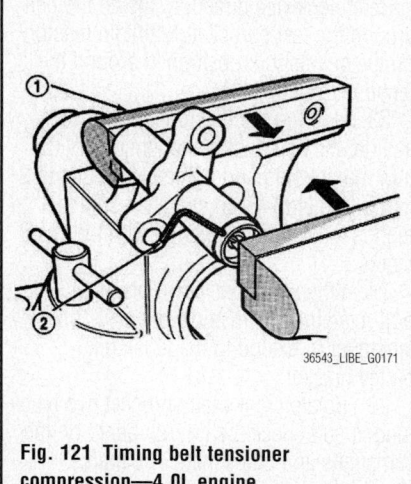

Fig. 121 Timing belt tensioner compression—4.0L engine

36543_LIBE_G0171

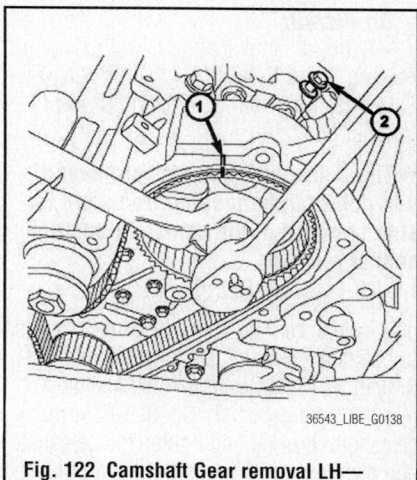

Fig. 122 Camshaft Gear removal LH—4.0L engine

36543_LIBE_G0138

9. Lower vehicle.

10. Remove the timing belt (4).

11. Inspect the tensioner for fluid leakage.

12. Inspect the pivot and bolt for free movement, bearing grease leakage, and smooth rotation. If not rotating freely, replace the arm and pulley assembly.

➡**When tensioner is removed from the engine it is necessary to compress the plunger into the tensioner body.**

13. Index the tensioner in the vise the same way it is installed on the engine. This ensures proper pin orientation when tensioner is installed on the engine.

a. Place the tensioner into a vise (1) and SLOWLY compress the plunger. Total bleed down of tensioner should take approximately two minutes.

b. When plunger is compressed into the tensioner body install a pin (2) through the body and plunger to retain

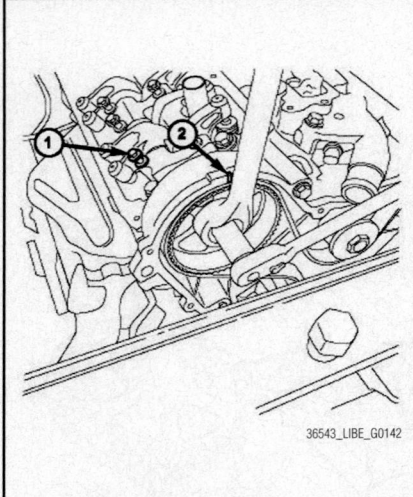

Fig. 123 Camshaft Gear removal RH—4.0L engine

plunger in place until tensioner is installed.

14. Counter-hold the left cam gear and remove the cam gear retaining bolt.

15. Remove the cam gear.

16. Counter-hold the right cam gear and remove the cam gear retaining bolt.

17. Remove the cam gear.

18. Remove crankshaft sprocket using Gear Puller L-4407-A (1).

To install:

19. Install crankshaft sprocket using Forcing Screw C-4685-C1, with Nut and Thrust Bearing from 6792, and Sprocket Installer 6641 (1).

➡ **The camshaft sprockets are keyed and not interchangeable from side to side because of the camshaft position sensor pick-up.**

20. Install NEW sprocket attaching bolt into place. The 10 in. (255 mm) bolt is to be installed in the left camshaft and the 8 3/8 in. (213 mm) bolt is to be installed into the right camshaft. Counter-hold the camshaft sprocket and tighten the camshaft sprocket bolt to 75 ft. lbs. (102 Nm) plus a 90° turn.

❊❊ WARNING

If camshafts have moved from the timing marks, always rotate camshaft towards the direction nearest to the timing marks (DO NOT TURN CAMSHAFTS A FULL REVOLUTION OR DAMAGE to valves and/or pistons could result).

21. Rotate the right camshaft gear (2) to align its timing mark (1). Verify that the left

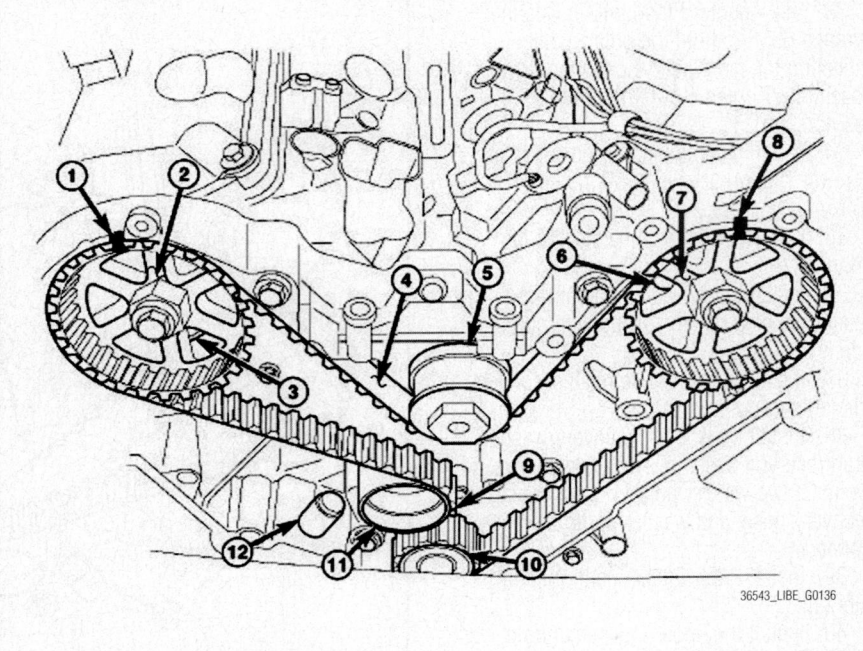

Fig. 124 Timing Belt alignment—4.0L engine

camshaft gear (7) timing mark (8) and crankshaft gear (10) timing mark (9) are still aligned.

22. Install the timing belt (4) starting at the crankshaft sprocket (10) going in a counterclockwise direction. Install the belt around the last sprocket. Maintain tension on the belt as it is positioned around the tensioner pulley (11).

23. Holding the tensioner pulley (11) against the belt, install the tensioner (12) into the housing and tighten two bolts to 21 ft. lbs. (28 Nm) (Each camshaft sprocket mark should remain aligned with the cover marks.

24. When tensioner is in place, pull retaining pin to allow the tensioner to extend to the tensioner pulley bracket.

25. Rotate crankshaft sprocket two revolutions and check the timing marks on the camshafts and crankshaft. The marks should line up within their respective locations. If marks do not line up, repeat procedure.

➡ **With the camshaft gears in these positions the lobes are in a neutral position (no load to the valve).**

26. Install the front timing belt cover.

27. Connect negative battery cable. Tighten nut to 40 inch lbs. (4.5 Nm).

TIMING BELT REAR COVER

REMOVAL & INSTALLATION

4.0L Engine

See Figures 125 and 126.

1. See all applicable precautions before beginning service procedures.

➡ **The rear timing belt cover has O-rings to seal the water pump passages to cylinder block. Do not reuse the O-rings.**

2. Perform fuel pressure release procedure.

3. Disconnect and isolate the negative battery cable.

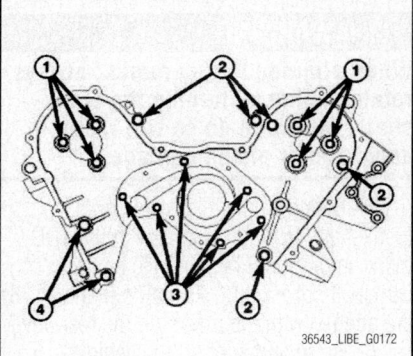

Fig. 125 Timing belt rear cover bolt positions—4.0L engine

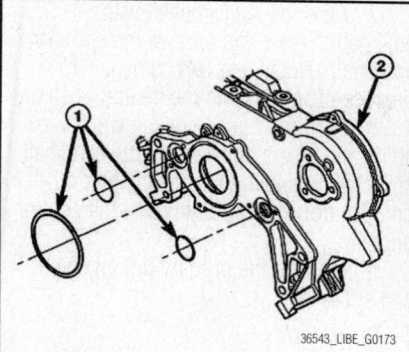

Fig. 126 Timing belt rear cover seal positions—4.0L engine

4. Drain the cooling system.
5. Remove timing belt.
6. Remove camshaft sprockets.
7. Remove the generator.
8. Remove three pump mounting bolts through pump pulley and reposition the power steering pump.
9. Remove rear timing belt cover bolts (1, 2, 4).
10. Remove the rear cover.

To install:

11. Clean rear timing belt cover O-ring sealing surfaces and grooves. Lubricate new O-rings (1) with Mopar® Dielectric Grease or equivalent to facilitate assembly.
12. Position NEW O-rings (1) on cover (2).
13. Install rear timing belt cover. Tighten nuts and bolts to the following specified torque:
 • M10 (2, 4): 40 ft. lbs. (54 Nm)
 • M8 (1): 20 ft. lbs. (28 Nm)
14. Position water pump and new gasket.
15. Install water pump mounting bolts (3). Tighten to 105 inch lbs. (12 Nm).
16. Install three power steering pump mounting bolts through pulley. Tighten pump mounting bolts to 21 ft. lbs. (28 Nm).
17. Position generator to engine and install two mounting bolts and tighten both bolts to 42 ft. lbs. (57 Nm).
18. Snap field wire connector into rear of generator.
19. Install B+ terminal and nut to generator mounting stud. Tighten nut to 115 inch lbs. (13 Nm).
20. Snap plastic protective cover to B+ terminal.
21. Install camshaft sprockets.
22. Install timing belt.
23. Connect negative battery cable. Tighten nut to 45 inch lbs. (5 Nm).

24. Fill cooling system.
25. Operate engine until it reaches normal operating temperature. Check cooling system for correct fluid level.

TIMING CHAIN COVER AND SEAL

REMOVAL & INSTALLATION

3.7L Engine
See Figure 127.

1. See all applicable precautions before beginning service procedures.
2. Disconnect the battery negative cable.
3. Drain the cooling system.
4. Remove electric cooling fan and fan shroud assembly.
5. Remove radiator fan.
6. Disconnect both heater hoses at timing cover.
7. Disconnect lower radiator hose at engine.

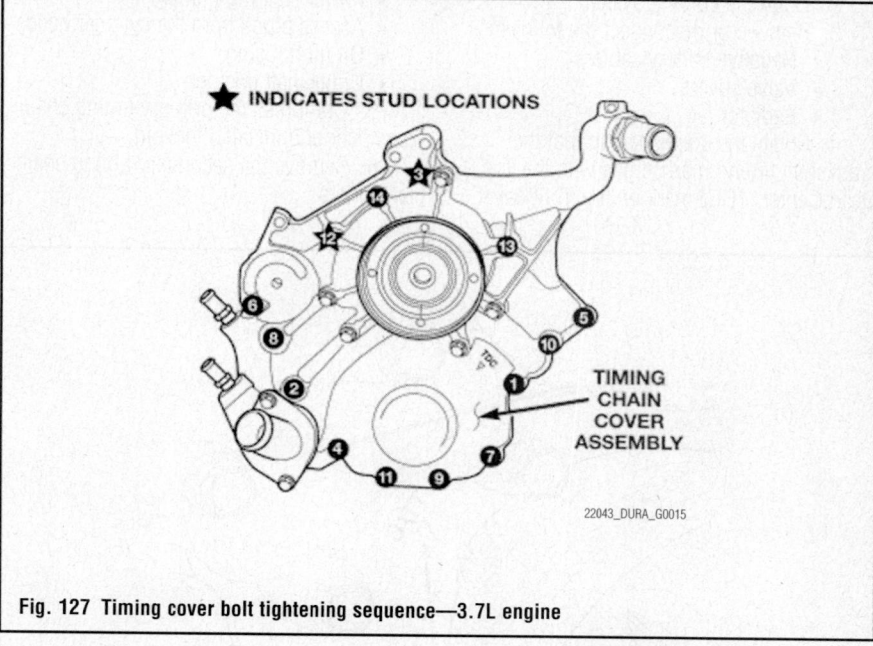

Fig. 127 Timing cover bolt tightening sequence—3.7L engine

8. Remove accessory drive belt tensioner assembly.
9. Remove crankshaft damper.
10. Remove the generator.
11. Remove A/C compressor.

➥It is not necessary to remove the water pump for timing cover removal.

12. Remove the bolts holding the timing cover to engine block.
13. Remove the timing cover.

To install:
14. Clean timing chain cover and block

surface using rubbing alcohol. Do not use oil based liquids to clean timing cover or block surfaces.

✳✳ WARNING

Use only rubbing alcohol, along with plastic or wooden scrapers. Use no wire brushes or abrasive wheels or metal scrapers, or damage to surfaces could result.

15. Inspect the water passage o-rings for any damage, and replace as necessary.
16. Apply Mopar® Engine RTV sealer to front cover as shown using a 3 to 4mm thick bead.
17. Install cover. Tighten fasteners in sequence as shown in to 43 ft. lbs. (58 Nm).
18. Install crankshaft damper.
19. Install the A/C compressor.
20. Install the generator.
21. Install accessory drive belt tensioner.

22. Install radiator upper and lower hoses.
23. Install both heater hoses.
24. Install radiator fan.
25. Fill cooling system.

TIMING CHAIN AND SPROCKETS

REMOVAL & INSTALLATION

3.7L Engine
See Figures 128 through 138.

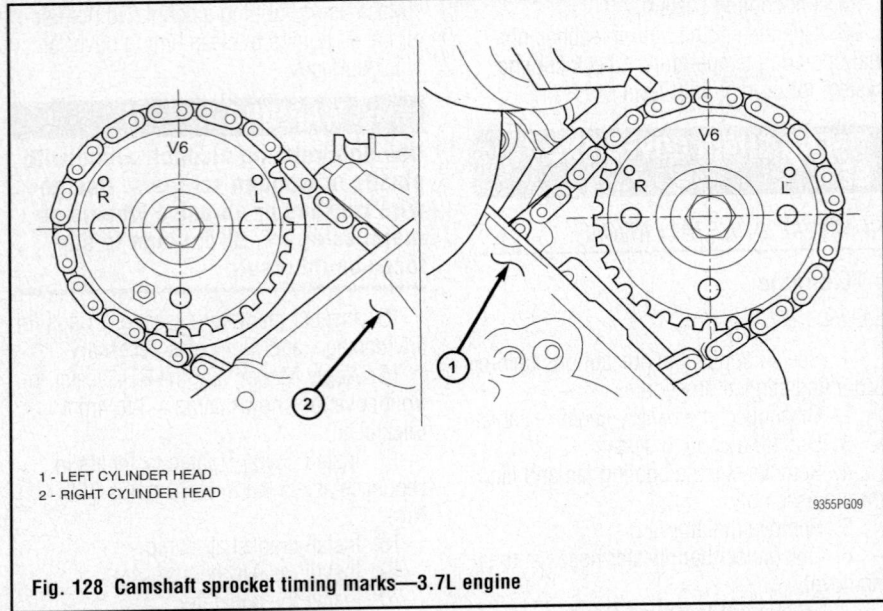

1 - LEFT CYLINDER HEAD
2 - RIGHT CYLINDER HEAD

9355PG09

Fig. 128 Camshaft sprocket timing marks—3.7L engine

1. See all applicable precautions before beginning service procedures.
2. Drain the cooling system.
3. Remove or disconnect the following:
   • Negative battery cable
   • Valve covers
   • Radiator fan
4. Rotate the crankshaft so that the crankshaft timing mark aligns with the Top Dead Center (TDC) mark on the front cover, and the **V6** marks on the camshaft sprockets are at 12 o'clock.
   • Power steering pump
   • Access plugs from the cylinder heads
   • Oil fill housing
   • Crankshaft damper
5. Compress the primary timing chain tensioner and install a lockpin.
6. Remove the secondary timing chain tensioners.

7. Hold the left camshaft with adjustable pliers and remove the sprocket and chain. Rotate the **left** camshaft 15 degrees **clockwise** to the neutral position.
8. Hold the right camshaft with adjustable pliers and remove the camshaft sprocket. Rotate the **right** camshaft 45 degrees **counterclockwise** to the neutral position.
9. Remove the primary timing chain and sprockets.

To install:

10. Use a small prytool to hold the ratchet pawl and compress the secondary timing chain tensioners in a vise and install locking pins.

➡ The black bolts fasten the guide to the engine block and the silver bolts fasten the guide to the cylinder head.

11. Install or connect the following:
   • Secondary timing chain guides. Tighten the bolts to 21 ft. lbs. (28 Nm).
   • Secondary timing chains to the idler sprocket so that the double plated links on each chain are visible through the slots in the primary idler sprocket
12. Lock the secondary timing chains to the idler sprocket with Timing Chain Locking tool as shown.
13. Align the primary chain double plated links with the idler sprocket timing mark and the single plated link with the crankshaft sprocket timing mark.
14. Install the primary chain and sprockets. Tighten the idler sprocket bolt to 25 ft. lbs. (34 Nm).
15. Align the secondary chain single plated links with the timing marks on the secondary sprockets. Align the dot at the **L** mark on the left sprocket with the plated link on the left chain and the dot at the **R** mark on the right sprocket with the plated link on the right chain.
16. Rotate the camshafts back from the neutral position and install the camshaft sprockets.
17. Remove the secondary chain locking tool.
18. Remove the primary and secondary timing chain tensioner locking pins.
19. Hold the camshaft sprockets with a spanner wrench and tighten the retaining bolts to 90 ft. lbs. (122 Nm).
20. Install or connect the following:
   • Front cover. Tighten the bolts, in sequence, to 40 ft. lbs. (54 Nm).
   • Front crankshaft seal
   • Cylinder head access plugs

1 - TIMING CHAIN COVER
2 - CRANKSHAFT TIMING MARKS

TDC

9355PG10

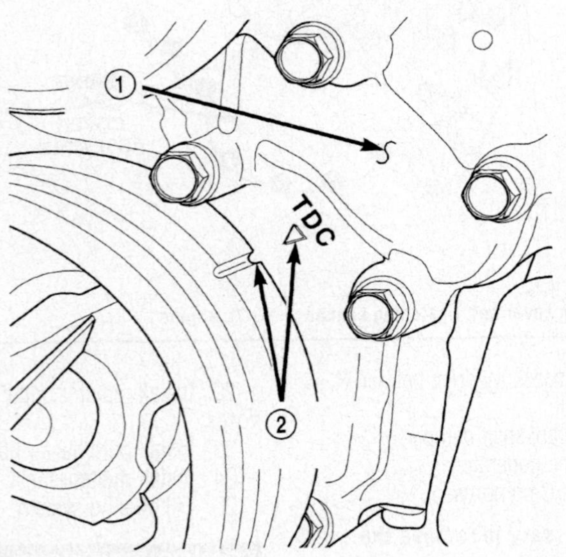

Fig. 129 Crankshaft timing marks—3.7L engine

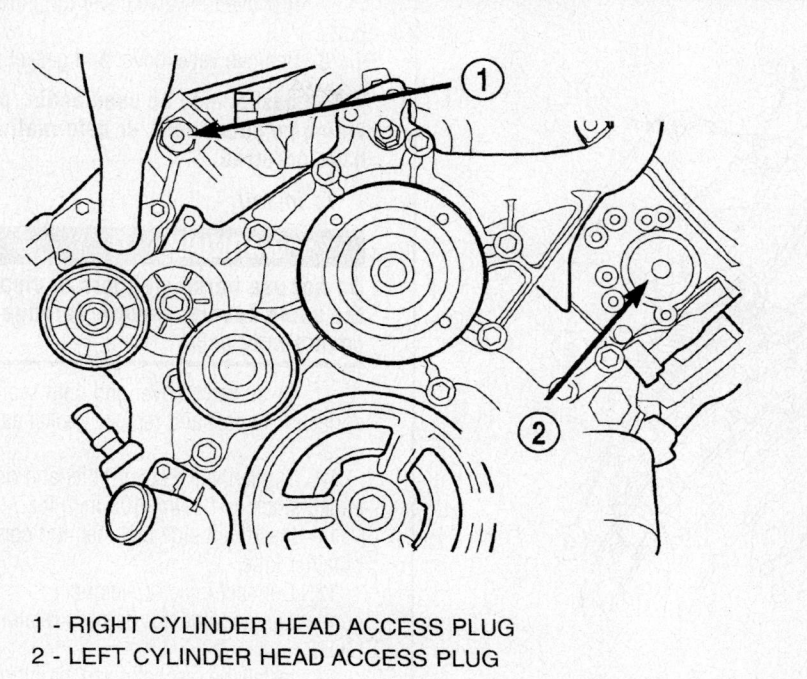

1 - RIGHT CYLINDER HEAD ACCESS PLUG
2 - LEFT CYLINDER HEAD ACCESS PLUG

9355PG11

Fig. 130 Cylinder head access plugs—3.7L engine

- Accessory drive belt
- Engine cooling fan and shroud
- Camshaft Position (CMP) sensor
- Valve covers
- Negative battery cable

21. Fill and bleed the cooling system.
22. Start the engine, check for leaks and repair if necessary.

VALVE COVERS

REMOVAL & INSTALLATION

3.7L Engine

Left Side

See Figure 139.

1. See all applicable precautions before beginning service procedures.
2. Disconnect negative cable from battery.
3. Remove the resonator assembly and air inlet hose.
4. Disconnect injector connectors and unclip the injector harness.
5. Route injector harness in front of valve cover.
6. Disconnect the left side breather tube and remove the breather tube.

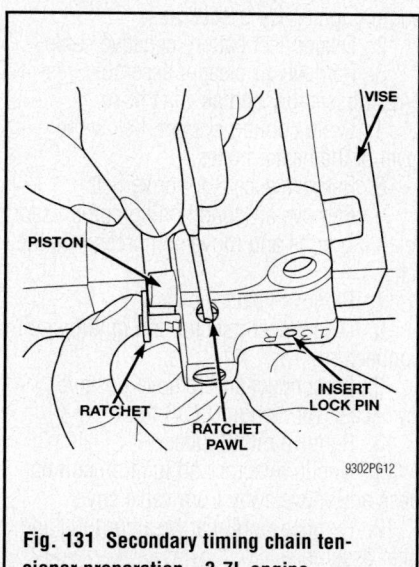

Fig. 131 Secondary timing chain tensioner preparation—3.7L engine

9302PG12

- A/C compressor
- Alternator
- Accessory drive belt tensioner. Tighten the bolt to 40 ft. lbs. (54 Nm).
- Oil fill housing
- Crankshaft damper. Tighten the bolt to 130 ft. lbs. (175 Nm).
- Power steering pump
- Lower radiator hose
- Heater hoses

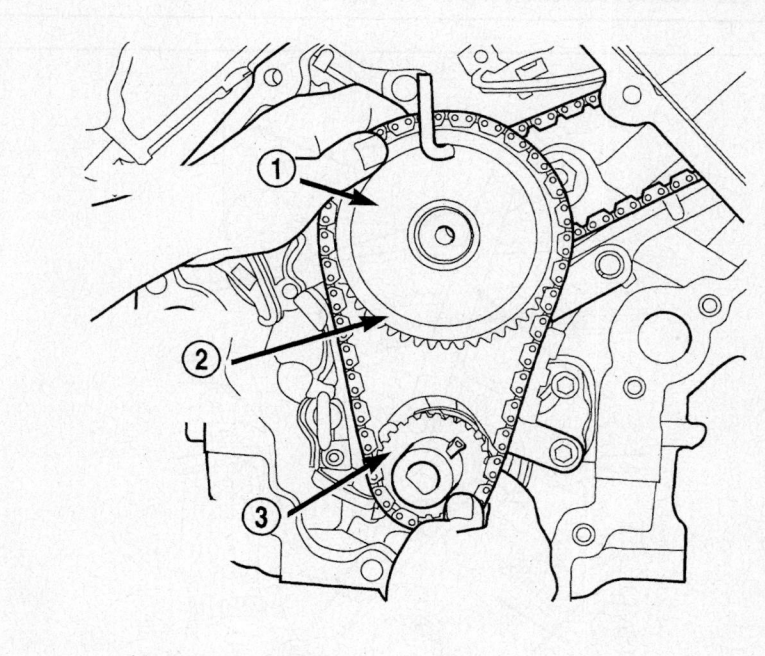

1 - SPECIAL TOOL 8429
2 - PRIMARY CHAIN IDLER SPROCKET
3 - CRANKSHAFT SPROCKET

9355PG12

Fig. 132 Installing the idler gear and timing chain—3.7L engine

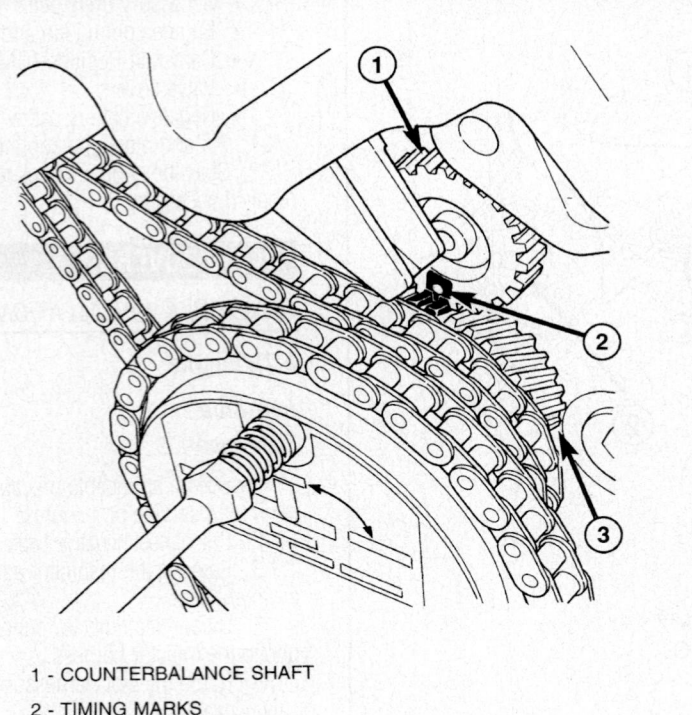

1 - COUNTERBALANCE SHAFT

2 - TIMING MARKS

3 - IDLER SPROCKET

9355PG13

Fig. 133 Counterbalance shaft timing marks—3.7L engine

1 - TORQUE WRENCH
2 - CAMSHAFT SPROCKET
3 - LEFT CYLINDER HEAD
4 - SPECIAL TOOL 6958 SPANNER WITH ADAPTER PINS 8346
9355PG14

Fig. 134 Tightening the left side camshaft sprocket—3.7L engine

7. Remove the valve cover mounting bolts.

8. Remove valve cover and gasket.

➡The gasket may be used again, providing no cuts, tears, or deformations have occurred.

To install:

✳✳ WARNING

Do not use harsh cleaners to clean the valve covers. Severe damage to covers may occur.

9. Clean valve cover and both sealing surfaces. Inspect and replace gasket as necessary.

10. Tighten valve cover bolts and double ended studs to 12 Nm (105 inch lbs.).

11. Install left side breather and connect breather tube.

12. Connect injector electrical connectors and injector harness retaining clips.

13. Install the resonator and air inlet hose.

14. Connect negative cable to battery.

Right Side

1. See all applicable precautions before beginning service procedures.

2. Disconnect battery negative cable.

3. Remove air cleaner assembly, resonator assembly and air inlet hose.

4. Drain cooling system, below the level of the heater hoses.

5. Remove accessory drive belt.

6. Remove air conditioning compressor retaining bolts and move compressor to the left.

7. Remove heater hoses.

8. Disconnect injector and ignition coil connectors.

9. Disconnect and remove positive crankcase ventilation (PCV) hose.

10. Remove oil fill tube.

11. Unclip injector and ignition coil harness and move away from valve cover.

12. Remove right rear breather tube and filter assembly.

13. Remove valve cover retaining bolts.

14. Remove valve cover and gasket.

➡The gasket may be used again, providing no cuts, tears, or deformations have occurred.

To install:

✳✳ WARNING

Do not use harsh cleaners to clean the valve covers. Severe damage to covers may occur.

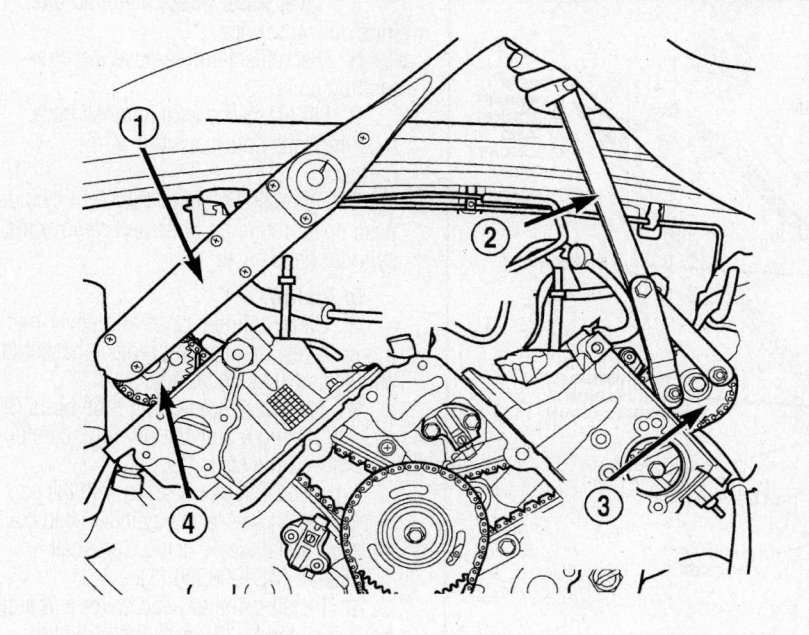

1 - TORQUE WRENCH
2 - SPECIAL TOOL 6958 WITH ADAPTER PINS 8346
3 - LEFT CAMSHAFT SPROCKET
4 - RIGHT CAMSHAFT SPROCKET

9355PG15

Fig. 135 Tightening the right side camshaft sprocket—3.7L engine

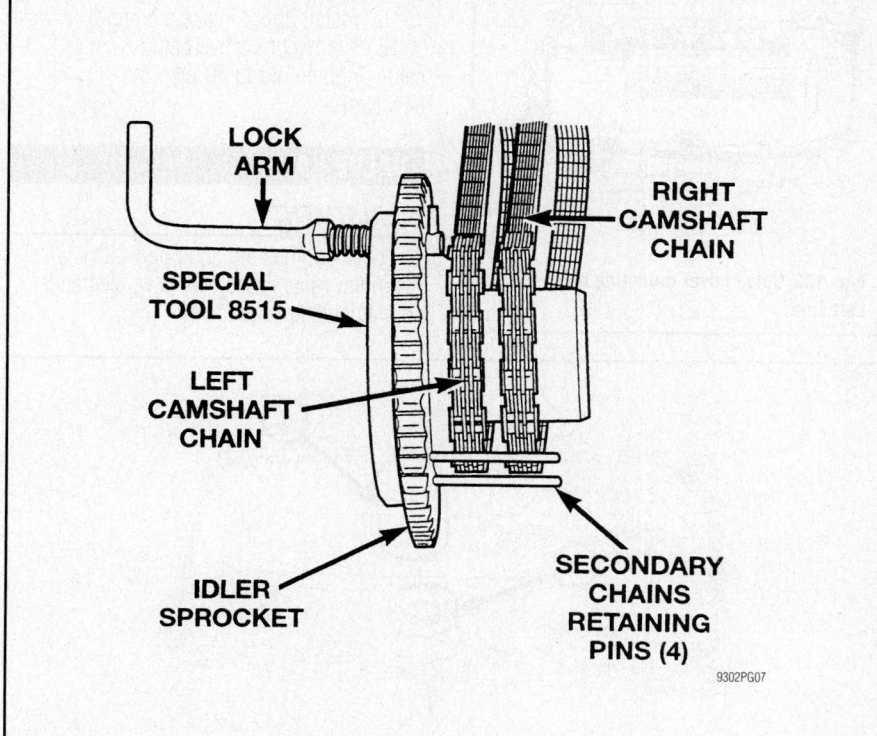

9302PG07

Fig. 136 Use the Timing Chain Locking tool to lock the timing chains on the idler gear—3.7L engine

15. Clean valve cover and both sealing surfaces. Inspect and replace gasket as necessary.

16. Tighten valve cover bolts and double ended studs to 105 in. lbs (12 Nm).

17. Install right rear breather tube and filter assembly.

18. Connect injector, ignition coil electrical connectors and harness retaining clips.

19. Install the oil fill tube.

20. Install PCV hose.

21. Install heater hoses.

22. Install air conditioning compressor retaining bolts.

23. Install accessory drive belt.

24. Fill cooling system.

25. Install air cleaner assembly, resonator assembly and air inlet hose.

26. Connect battery negative cable.

4.0L Engine

Left Side

See Figure 140.

1. See all applicable precautions before beginning service procedures.

2. Disconnect and isolate the negative battery cable.

3. Remove the upper intake manifold from the engine.

4. Cover lower intake manifold with a suitable cover during service.

5. Disconnect and remove the three ignition coils.

6. Lift up on the wire harness track retaining tabs and reposition wire harness.

7. Completely loosen eight cylinder head cover retaining bolts and remove the cylinder head cover.

To install:

8. Clean cylinder head and cover mating surfaces. Inspect and replace gasket (1) and seals (2) as necessary.

9. To replace spark plug tube seals (2):

   a. Using a suitable pry tool, carefully remove tube seals (2).

   b. Position new seal (2) with the part number on seal facing cylinder head cover.

   c. Install seals using Camshaft Installer MD-998306 (1).

10. Install cylinder head cover and eight bolts. Tighten to 105 inch lbs. (12 Nm).

11. Position the wiring harness on the cylinder head cover.

12. Reinstall the wire harness track retaining tabs into the cover.

13. Install the ignition coils. Tighten mounting screws to 60 inch lbs. (6.7 Nm).

14. Connect the ignition coil electrical connectors.

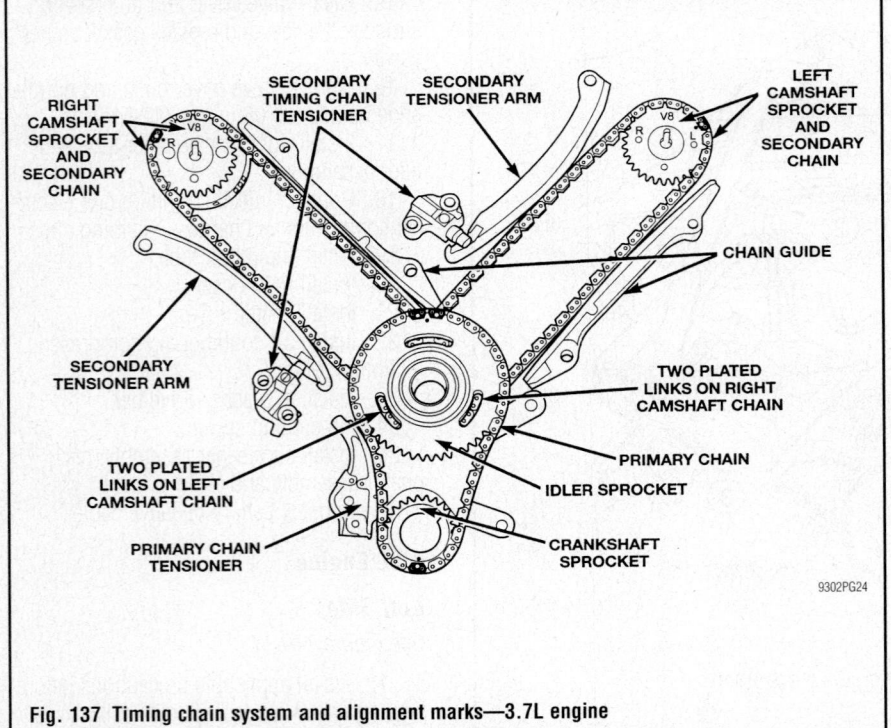

Fig. 137 Timing chain system and alignment marks—3.7L engine

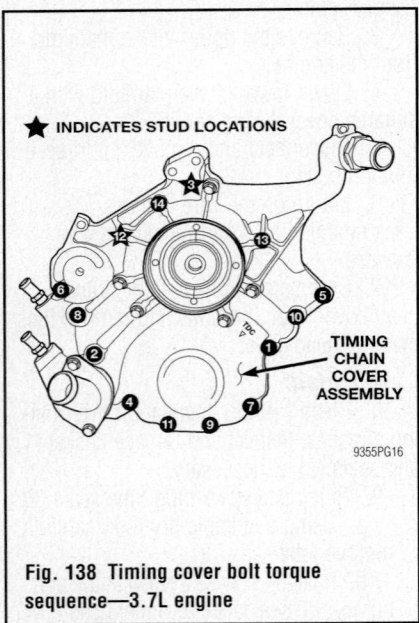

★ INDICATES STUD LOCATIONS

TIMING CHAIN COVER ASSEMBLY

Fig. 138 Timing cover bolt torque sequence—3.7L engine

15. Install upper intake manifold.
16. Connect negative battery cable. Tighten nut to 40 inch lbs. (4.5 Nm).

Right Side

See Figure 140.

1. See all applicable precautions before beginning service procedures.
2. Disconnect and isolate the negative battery cable.
3. Remove the upper intake manifold.

4. Cover lower intake manifold openings during service.
5. Disconnect and remove the three ignition coils.
6. Lift up on the wire harness track retaining tabs and reposition wire harness.
7. Completely loosen the eight cylinder head cover retaining bolts and remove the cylinder head cover.

To install:

8. Clean cylinder head and cover mating surfaces. Inspect and replace gasket (1) and seals (2) as necessary.
9. To replace spark plug tube seals (2):
   a. Using a suitable pry tool, carefully remove tube seals (2).
   b. Position new seal (2) with the part number on seal facing cylinder head cover.
   c. Install seals using Camshaft Installer MD-998306 (1).
10. Install cylinder head cover and eight bolts. Tighten to 105 inch lbs. (12 Nm).
11. Position the wiring harness on the cylinder head cover.
12. Reinstall the wire harness track retaining tabs into the cover.
13. Install the ignition coils. Tighten mounting screws to 60 inch lbs. (6.7 Nm).
14. Connect the ignition coil electrical connectors.
15. Install upper intake manifold.
16. Connect negative battery cable. Tighten nut to 40 inch lbs. (4.5 Nm).

VALVE LASH

ADJUSTMENT

These engines are equipped with hydraulic valve lifters. No valve clearance adjustments are necessary.

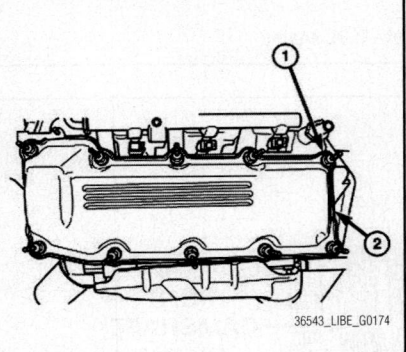

Fig. 139 Valve cover mounting bolts—Left side

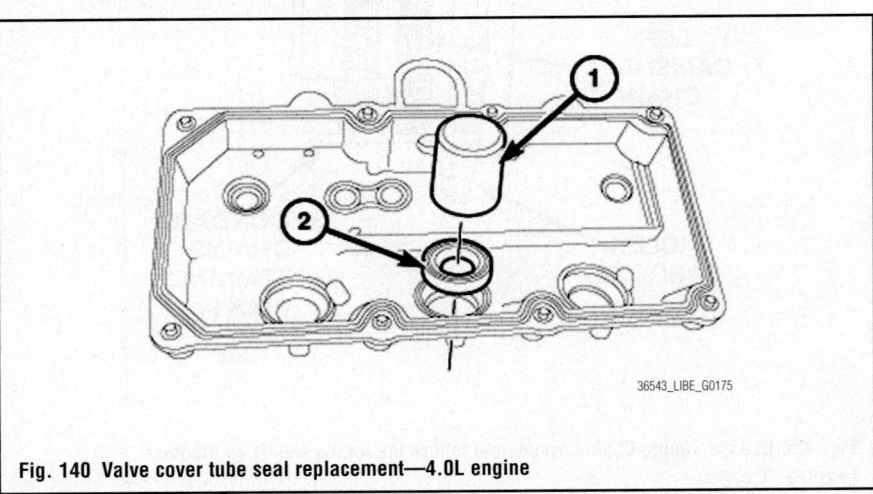

Fig. 140 Valve cover tube seal replacement—4.0L engine

ENGINE PERFORMANCE & EMISSION CONTROLS

ACCELERATOR PEDAL POSITION (APP) SENSOR

LOCATION

The accelerator pedal and Accelerator Pedal Position (APP) sensor are serviced as a complete assembly including the bracket.

REMOVAL & INSTALLATION

1. See all applicable precautions before beginning service procedures.
2. Disconnect electrical connector at Accelerator Pedal Position (APP) sensor.
3. Remove two accelerator pedal mounting bracket nuts.
4. Remove accelerator pedal/APP sensor assembly from vehicle.

To install:

5. Position accelerator pedal/APP sensor assembly over two mounting studs.
6. Install two accelerator pedal mounting bracket nuts.
7. Connect electrical connector at APP sensor.
8. Before starting engine, operate accelerator pedal to check for any binding.

CAMSHAFT POSITION (CMP) SENSOR

LOCATION

See Figure 141.

On 3.7L engines, the Camshaft Position (CMP) sensor is located on the front/top of the right cylinder head.

REMOVAL & INSTALLATION

3.7L Engine

See Figure 142.

1. See all applicable precautions before beginning service procedures.
2. Disconnect electrical connector at Camshaft Position (CMP) sensor.
3. Remove sensor mounting bolt.
4. Carefully remove sensor from cylinder head in a rocking and twisting action. Twisting sensor eases removal.

To install:

5. Check condition of sensor O-ring.
6. Clean out machined hole in cylinder head.
7. Apply a small amount of engine oil to sensor O-ring.
8. Install sensor into cylinder head with a slight rocking and twisting action.

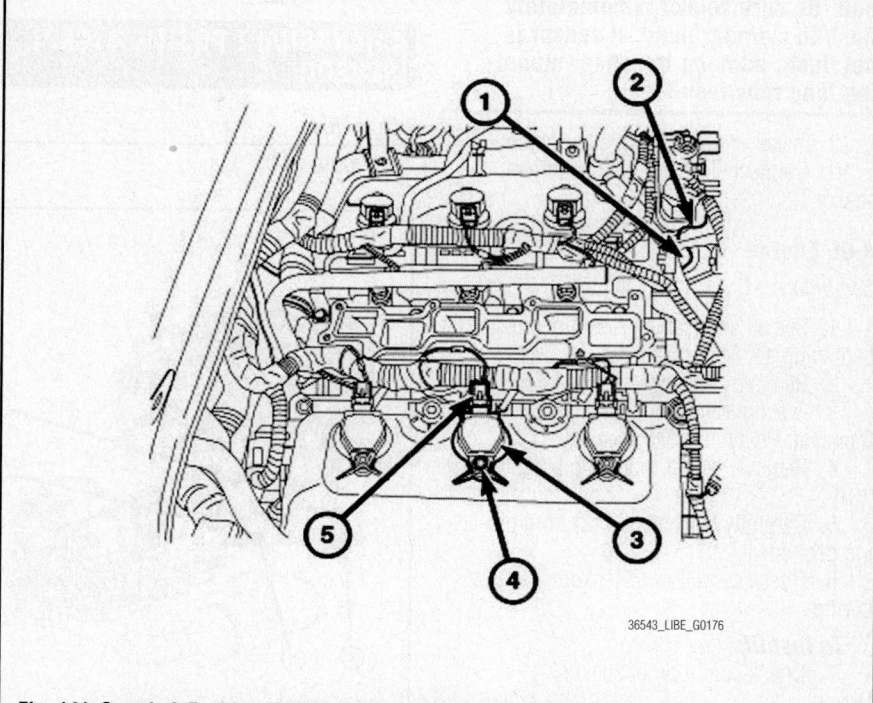

36543_LIBE_G0176

Fig. 141 Camshaft Position (CMP) sensor location—4.0L engine

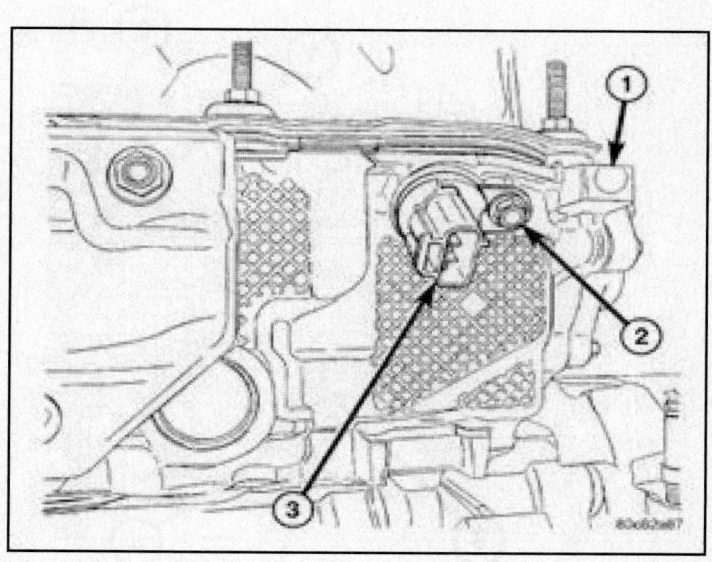

21180_CDIA_G484

Fig. 142 Showing the CMP sensor (3) and mounting bolt (2) on the right front cylinder head (1) on the 3.7L engine

✳✳ **WARNING**

Before tightening sensor mounting bolt, be sure sensor is completely flush to cylinder head. If sensor is not flush, damage to sensor mounting tang may result.

9. Install mounting bolt and tighten.
10. Connect electrical connector to sensor.

4.0L Engine

See Figure 143.

1. See all applicable precautions before beginning service procedures.
2. Remove generator.
3. Disconnect electrical connector (1) at Camshaft Position (CMP) sensor.
4. Remove sensor mounting bolt (3).
5. Carefully twist sensor (2) from timing gear cover.
6. Check condition of sensor O-ring.

To install:

7. Check condition of sensor O-ring.
8. Carefully twist sensor (2) into timing gear cover (4).
9. Install sensor mounting bolt (3) and tighten to 106 inch lbs. (12 Nm).

10. Connect electrical connector (1) to CMP sensor.
11. Install generator.

CRANKSHAFT POSITION (CKP) SENSOR

LOCATION

See Figure 144.

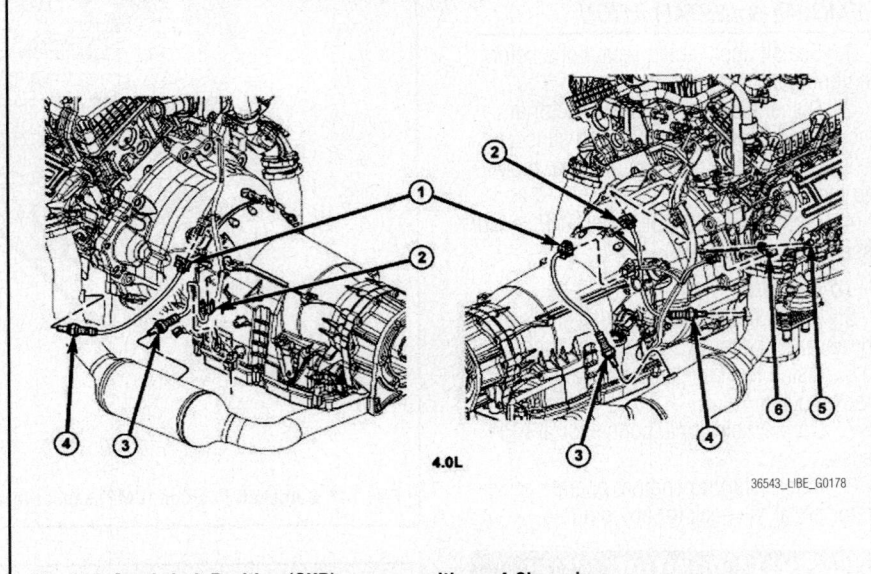

Fig. 144 Crankshaft Position (CKP) sensor position—4.0L engine

On 3.7L engines, the Crankshaft Position (CKP) sensor is mounted into the right rear side of the cylinder block.

REMOVAL & INSTALLATION

3.7L Engine

See Figure 145.

1. See all applicable precautions before beginning service procedures.
2. Raise vehicle.
3. Disconnect sensor electrical connector.
4. Remove sensor mounting bolt.
5. Carefully remove sensor from cylinder block in a rocking and twisting action.
6. Check condition of sensor O-ring.

To install:

7. Clean out machined hole in engine block.
8. Apply a small amount of engine oil to sensor O-ring.
9. Install sensor into engine block with a slight rocking and twisting action.

✳✳ **WARNING**

Before tightening sensor mounting bolt, be sure sensor is completely flush to cylinder block. If sensor is not flush, damage to sensor mounting tang may result.

10. Install mounting bolt and tighten to 21 ft. lbs. (28 Nm).
11. Connect electrical connector to sensor.

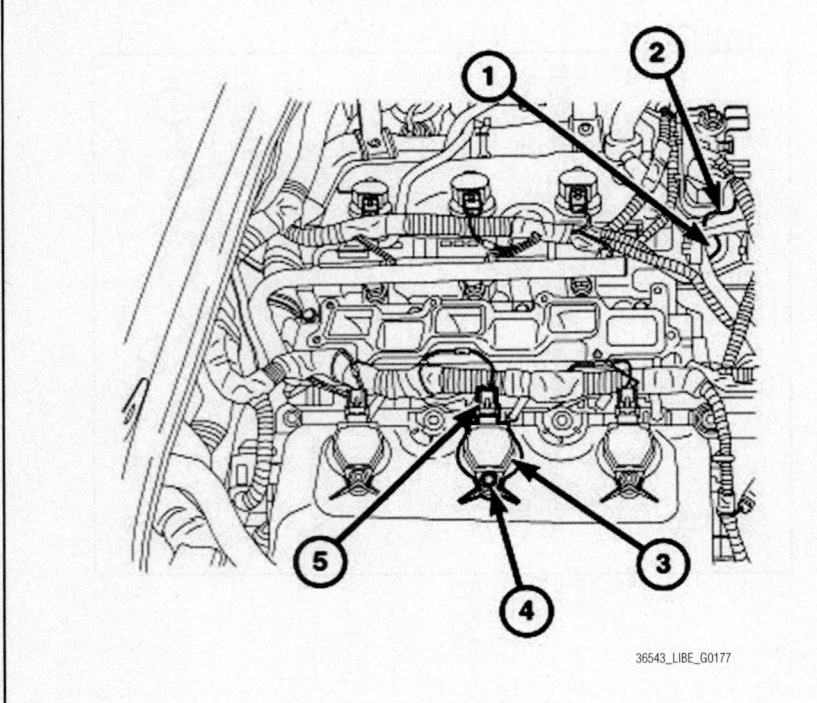

Fig. 143 Camshaft Position (CMP) sensor removal—4.0L engine

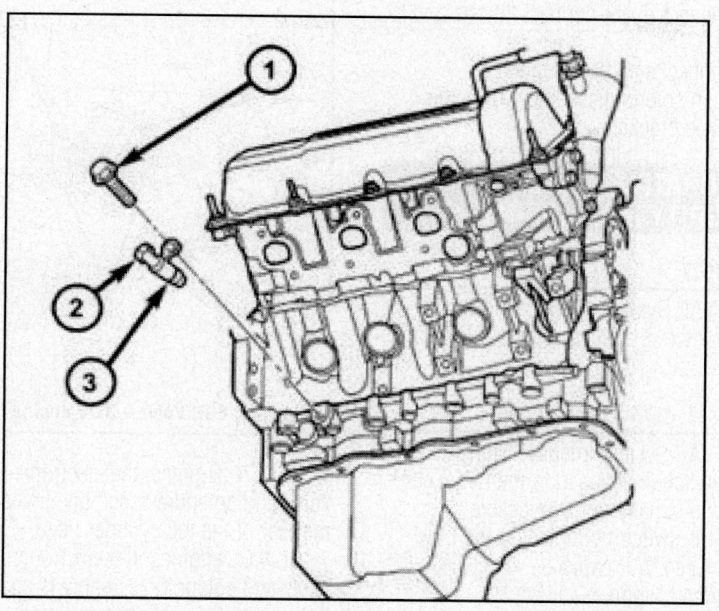

Fig. 145 Mounting bolt (1) CKP sensor (2) O-ring (3) on the 3.7L engine

EVAPORATIVE EMISSION (EVAP) CANISTER

LOCATION

The EVAP canister is located under the vehicle behind the plastic splash shield used for the left/rear tire. The EVAP System Integrity Monitor (ESIM) switch is attached to the EVAP canister.

REMOVAL & INSTALLATION

See Figure 146.

1. See all applicable precautions before beginning service procedures.
2. Raise and support vehicle.
3. Clean dirt or debris from canister vacuum lines.
4. Disconnect electrical connector (3) at ESIM switch (2).
5. Disconnect rubber hose (6) from ESIM switch (2).
6. Disconnect quick-connect fitting (5) at EVAP canister.
7. Remove nut/bolt at front of canister mounting bracket.
8. To remove canister, pull straight forward until pins have cleared bracket.

4.0L Engine

1. See all applicable precautions before beginning service procedures.

➡**The Crankshaft Position (CKP) sensor is mounted into the right side of the transmission bellhousing. It is positioned and bolted into a machined hole.**

2. Raise vehicle.
3. Disconnect sensor electrical connector.
4. Remove sensor mounting bolt.
5. Carefully twist sensor from transmission.

To install:

6. Clean out machined hole in transmission bellhousing.
7. Install sensor into transmission.

➡**Before tightening sensor mounting bolt, be sure sensor is completely flush to transmission. If sensor is not flush, damage to sensor mounting tang may result.**

8. Install mounting bolt.
9. Connect electrical connector to sensor.
10. Lower vehicle.

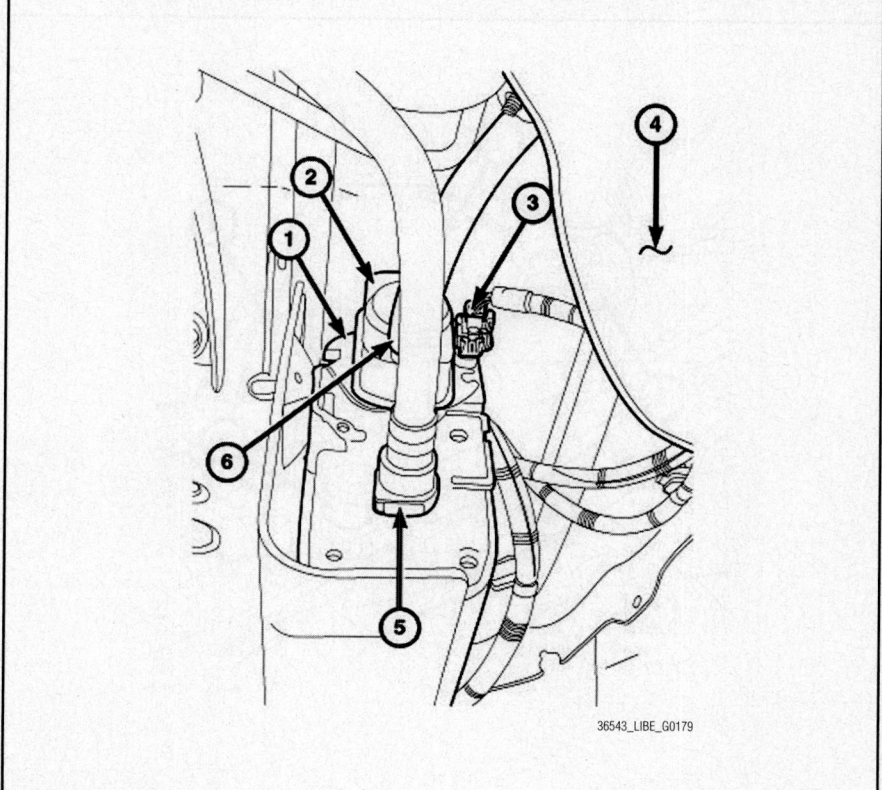

Fig. 146 EVAP canister location

To install:

9. Position canister locating pins into bracket.

10. Install nut/bolt at front of canister mounting bracket.

11. Clean dirt or debris from canister vacuum lines.

12. Connect electrical connector to ESIM switch.

13. Connect rubber hose to ESIM switch.

14. Connect quick-connect fitting to EVAP canister.

15. Lower vehicle.

EVAPORATIVE EMISSION (EVAP) PURGE SOLENOID

LOCATION

The EVAP canister purge solenoid is located near the battery.

REMOVAL & INSTALLATION

See Figure 147.

1. See all applicable precautions before beginning service procedures.

2. Lift the solenoid assembly (1) from the tongue-type bracket (2).

3. Disconnect electrical connector (5).

4. Disconnect quick-connect fittings (3) and (4) from solenoid.

To install:

5. Connect quick-connect fittings and to solenoid.

6. Connect electrical connector.

7. Push solenoid assembly onto the tongue-type bracket.

EVAPORATIVE SYSTEM INTEGRITY MONITOR (ESIM)

LOCATION

The EVAP System Integrity Monitor (ESIM) switch is attached to the EVAP canister.

REMOVAL & INSTALLATION

The EVAP System Integrity Monitor (ESIM) switch is attached to the EVAP canister and is usually not serviceable. Replace the switch by replacing the EVAP canister. See EVAP canister removal/installation.

EXHAUST GAS RECIRCULATION (EGR) VALVE

LOCATION

See Figures 148 and 149.

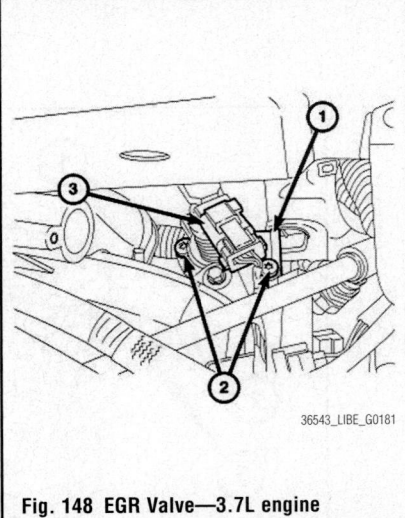

36543_LIBE_G0181

Fig. 148 EGR Valve—3.7L engine

On 3.7L engines, the electronic EGR valve and solenoid assembly is attached to the rear of the left cylinder head.

On 4.0L engines, the electronic EGR valve and solenoid assembly is attached to the rear of the right cylinder head.

REMOVAL & INSTALLATION

3.7L Engine

See Figure 150.

1. See all applicable precautions before beginning service procedures.

2. Use a diagnostic scan tool to record any DTC's (Diagnostic Trouble Codes).

3. Disconnect and isolate the negative battery cable.

4. An exhaust gas routing tube (1) connects the EGR valve (4) to the intake manifold.

5. Remove two tube mounting bolts (2).

6. Remove tube (1) from solenoid (4). Slip opposite end of tube (6) from intake manifold.

7. Remove gasket (3) located between EGR valve solenoid and tube flange.

8. Disconnect electrical connector at solenoid.

9. Remove two EGR valve solenoid mounting bolts.

10. Remove solenoid from engine.

11. Remove and discard gasket located under EGR solenoid.

To install:

12. Clean gasket area at rear of left cylinder head where it joins base of EGR valve.

13. Clean EGR tube where it joins EGR valve.

14. Position new gasket between EGR valve and cylinder head.

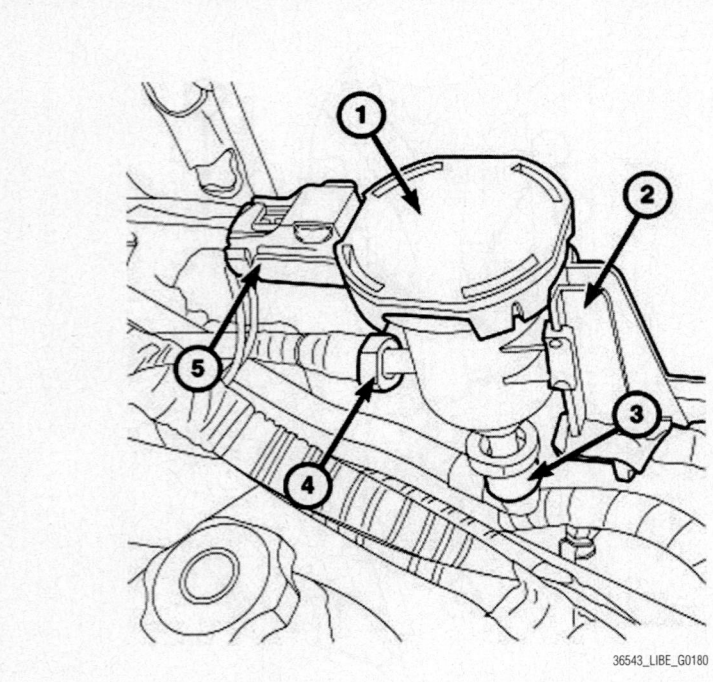

36543_LIBE_G0180

Fig. 147 EVAP Purge Solenoid removal

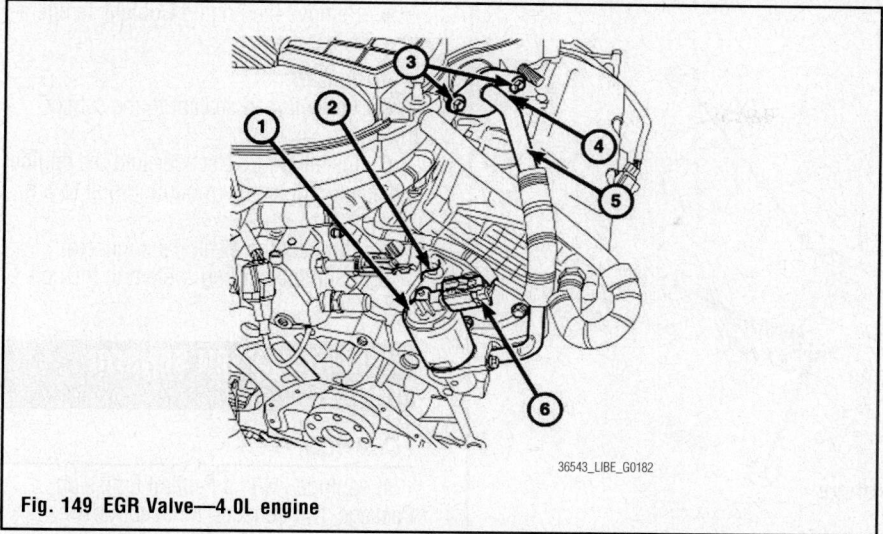

Fig. 149 EGR Valve—4.0L engine

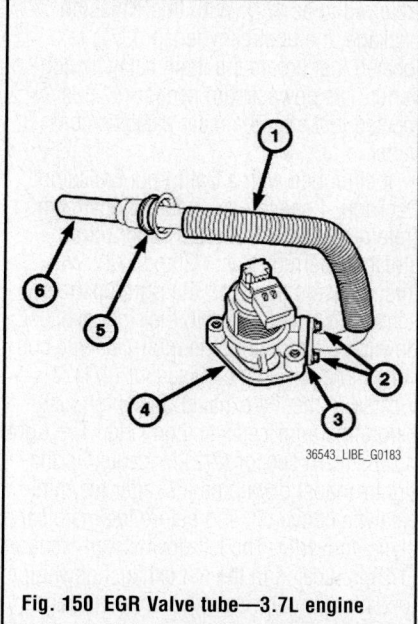

Fig. 150 EGR Valve tube—3.7L engine

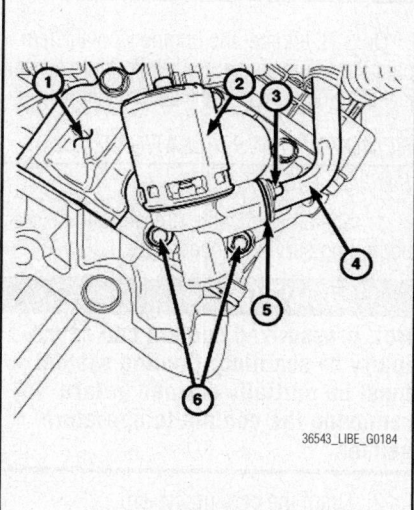

Fig. 151 EGR Valve removal—4.0L engine

15. Position EGR valve to cylinder head. Install and tighten two bolts. Tighten to 80 inch lbs. (9 Nm).

16. Position new gasket between EGR tube flange and EGR valve assembly.

17. Position EGR tube to side of EGR valve. Position end of tube into intake manifold. Install two bolts. Tighten to 97 inch lbs. (11 Nm).

18. Connect electrical connector to top of EGR valve solenoid.

19. Connect negative battery cable.

20. Using a diagnostic scan tool, erase any previously recorded Diagnostic Trouble Codes.

4.0L Engine

See Figures 149 and 151.

1. See all applicable precautions before beginning service procedures.

2. Use a diagnostic scan tool to record any DTC's (Diagnostic Trouble Codes).

3. Disconnect and isolate the negative battery cable.

4. An exhaust gas routing tube (5) connects the EGR valve (1) to the intake manifold.

5. Remove two flange mounting bolts at intake manifold.

6. Remove two flange bolts (3) at solenoid (2).

7. Separate tube (4) from solenoid (2). Slip opposite end of tube (4) from intake manifold.

8. Remove and discard gasket (5) located between EGR valve solenoid and tube flange.

9. Disconnect electrical connector at solenoid.

10. Remove two EGR solenoid/valve mounting bolts (6).

11. Remove solenoid/valve assembly (2) from rear of cylinder head.

12. Remove and discard gasket located between EGR solenoid/valve and cylinder head.

To install:

13. Install new gasket between EGR solenoid/valve (2) and rear of cylinder head.

14. Position EGR solenoid/valve assembly to rear of cylinder head. Install and tighten two mounting bolts (6).

15. Install new O-ring to intake manifold end of tube (5).

16. Install two flange mounting bolts (3) at intake manifold. Do not tighten bolts at this time.

17. Install new gasket (5) between EGR valve solenoid and tube flange.

18. Position tube (4) to solenoid (2). Slip opposite end of tube (4) into intake manifold.

19. Install and tighten two flange bolts (3) at solenoid.

ELECTRONIC CONTROL MODULE (ECM)

LOCATION

The Electronic Control Module (ECM) is attached to the inner fender located in the engine compartment.

REMOVAL & INSTALLATION

See Figure 152.

1. See all applicable precautions before beginning service procedures.

✷✷ WARNING

The use of a diagnostic scan tool is required the Electronic Control Module (ECM) is being in order to reprogram the new ECM.

2. Disconnect the negative battery cable.

3. Unplug the 38-way connectors from the ECM.

➡**A locating pin is used in place of one of the mounting bolts.**

4. Pry the clip from the locating pin.

5. Remove the two remaining mounting bolts.

6. Remove the ECM from the vehicle.

To install:

7. Position the ECM to the body and install the two mounting bolts.

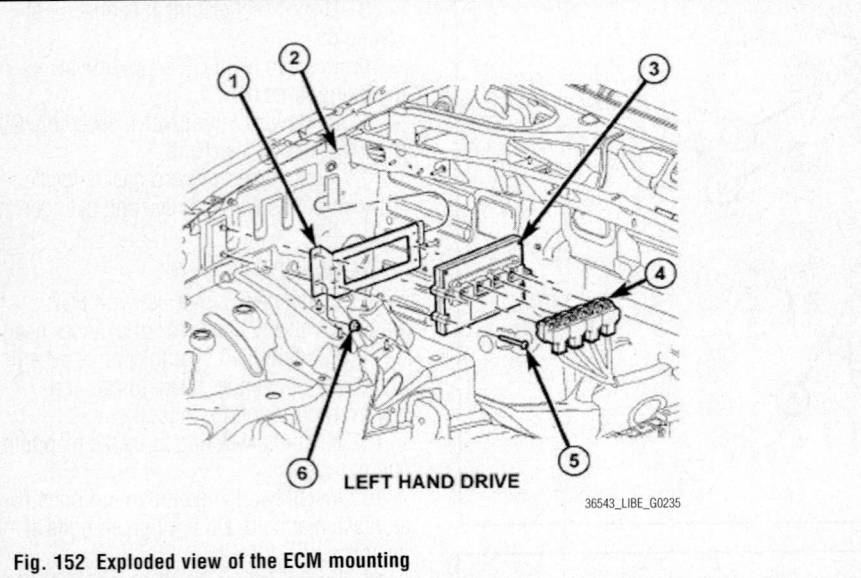

LEFT HAND DRIVE

36543_LIBE_G0235

Fig. 152 Exploded view of the ECM mounting

➡**Position the ground strap in place before tightening the mounting bolts.**

8. Install the clip to the locating pin.

9. Tighten the mounting bolts to 35 inch lbs. (4 Nm).

10. Carefully plug in the 38-way connectors to the ECM.

11. Connect the negative battery cable.

12. Use a diagnostic scan tool to reprogram the ECM with the VIN and original mileage if ECM has been replaced.

ENGINE COOLANT TEMPERATURE (ECT) SENSOR

LOCATION

See Figure 153.

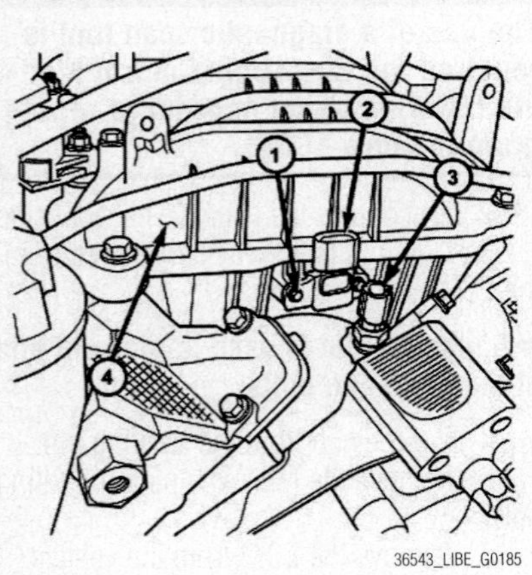

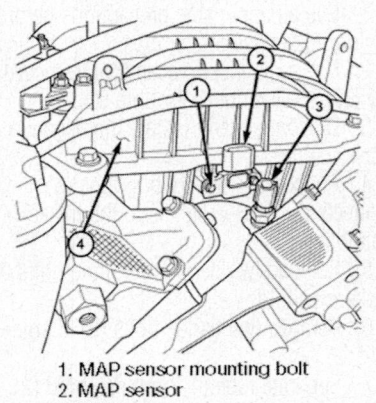

Fig. 153 Engine Coolant Temperature (ECT) sensor location—4.0L engine

36543_LIBE_G0185

On 3.7L engine, the Engine Coolant Temperature (ECT) sensor is installed into a water jacket at the front of the intake manifold.

REMOVAL & INSTALLATION

See Figure 154.

1. See all applicable precautions before beginning service procedures.

❋❋ CAUTION

Hot, pressurized coolant can cause injury by scalding. Cooling system must be partially drained before removing the coolant temperature sensor.

2. Drain the cooling system.

3. Disconnect the sensor electrical connector.

1. MAP sensor mounting bolt
2. MAP sensor
3. ECT sensor

22043_DAKO_G0019

Fig. 154 ECT sensor location on the 3.7L engines

4. Remove the Engine Coolant Temperature (ECT) sensor.

To install:

5. Apply thread sealant to the sensor threads.

6. Install the ECT sensor into the engine block and tighten the mounting bolt to 8 ft. lbs. (11 Nm).

7. Connect the electrical connector.

8. Refill the cooling system to the correct level.

HEATED OXYGEN SENSOR (HO2S)

LOCATION

If equipped with a Federal Emission Package, two sensors are used: upstream (referred to as 1/1) and downstream (referred to as 1/2). With this emission package, the upstream sensor (1/1) is located just before the main catalytic converter. The downstream sensor (1/2) is located just after the main catalytic converter.

If equipped with a California Emission Package, 4 sensors are used: 2 upstream (referred to as 1/1 and 2/1) and 2 downstream (referred to as 1/2 and 2/2). With this emission package, the right upstream sensor (2/1) is located in the right exhaust downpipe just before the mini-catalytic converter. The left upstream sensor (1/1) is located in the left exhaust downpipe just before the mini-catalytic converter. The right downstream sensor (2/2) is located in the right exhaust downpipe just after the mini-catalytic converter, and before the main catalytic converter. The left downstream sensor (1/2) is located in the left exhaust downpipe just after the mini-catalytic converter, and before the main catalytic converter.

REMOVAL & INSTALLATION

1. See all applicable precautions before beginning service procedures.

2. Raise and safely support the vehicle.

3. Disconnect the wire connector from oxygen sensor.

❋❋ WARNING

When disconnecting sensor electrical connector, do not pull directly on wire going into sensor.

4. Remove the sensor with an oxygen sensor removal and installation tool.

5. Clean threads in exhaust pipe using appropriate tap.

To install:

➡Threads of new oxygen sensors are factory coated with anti-seize compound.

✳✳ WARNING

Do not add any additional anti-seize compound to the threads of a new oxygen sensor.

6. Install the oxygen sensor and tighten to 22 ft. lbs. (30 Nm).
7. Connect the electrical connector.
8. Lower the vehicle.

INTAKE AIR TEMPERATURE (IAT) SENSOR

LOCATION

For 3.7L engine, the Intake Air Temperature (IAT) sensor is installed in the intake manifold with the sensor element extending into the air stream.

For 4.0L engine, the Intake Air Temperature (IAT) sensor is installed into the rubber air intake tube near the throttle body.

REMOVAL & INSTALLATION

3.7L Engine

See Figure 155.

1. See all applicable precautions before beginning service procedures.
2. Disconnect electrical connector from Intake Air Temperature (IAT) sensor. Clean dirt from intake manifold at sensor base.
3. Gently lift on small plastic release tab and rotate sensor about ¼ turn counterclockwise. Check condition of sensor O-ring.

To install:
4. Clean the sensor mounting hole in the intake manifold.
5. Position the sensor into intake manifold and rotate clockwise until past release tab.
6. Install electrical connector.

4.0L Engine

1. See all applicable precautions before beginning service procedures.
2. Disconnect electrical connector from Intake Air Temperature (IAT) sensor.
3. Clean dirt from IAT sensor base.
4. Pull out on IAT sensor while rotating for removal.
5. Check condition of sensor O-ring.

To install:
6. Clean mounting hole.
7. Check condition of sensor O-ring.

8. Push IAT sensor into rubber intake tube while rotating for installation.
9. Connect electrical connector to IAT sensor.

KNOCK SENSOR (KS)

LOCATION

The Knock (KS) sensors are bolted into the cylinder block under the intake manifold.

REMOVAL & INSTALLATION

3.7L Engine

See Figure 156.

1. See all applicable precautions before beginning service procedures.

➡The left sensor is identified by an identification tag (LEFT). It is also identified by a larger bolt head. The Powertrain Control Module (PCM) must have and know the correct sensor left/right positions. Do not mix the sensor locations.

2. Disconnect knock sensor dual pigtail harness from engine wiring harness. This connection is made near rear of left valve cover.
3. Remove intake manifold.
4. Remove sensor mounting bolts. Remove sensors from engine.

➡Note the foam strip on bolt threads. This foam is used only to retain the bolts to sensors for plant assembly. It is not used as a sealant. Do not apply any adhesive, sealant or thread locking compound to these bolts.

To install:

✳✳ WARNING

Over or under tightening the sensor mounting bolts will affect knock sensor performance, possibly causing improper spark control. Always use the specified torque when installing the knock sensors. The torque for the knock sensor bolt is relatively light for an 8mm bolt.

5. Thoroughly clean knock sensor mounting holes.
6. Install sensors into cylinder block.
7. Install and tighten mounting bolts to 15 ft. lbs. (20 Nm).
8. Install intake manifold.
9. Connect knock sensor wiring harness to engine harness at rear of intake manifold.

4.0L Engine

1. See all applicable precautions before beginning service procedures.
2. Perform the fuel system pressure relief procedure.

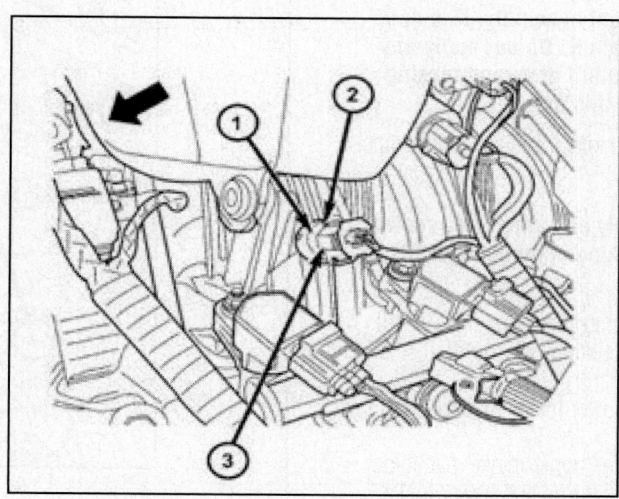

21180_CDIA_G511

Fig. 155 IAT sensor (1), release tab (2), and electrical connector (3) on 3.7L engines

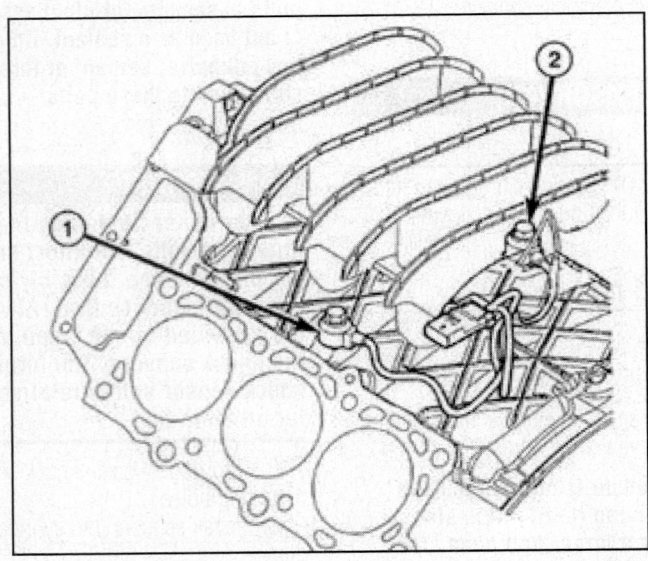

Fig. 156 Knock sensor locations (1) and mounting bolts (2)—3.7L engine

3. Disconnect and isolate the negative battery cable.

4. Drain the cooling system.

5. Remove the upper intake manifold including EGR tube, PCV, purge and power brake booster vacuum hoses.

6. Remove fuel rail and lower intake manifold.

7. Remove sensor mounting bolt.

➡**Note foam strip on bolt threads. This foam is used only to retain the bolt to sensor for plant assembly. It is not used as a sealant. Do not apply any adhesive, sealant or thread locking compound to this bolt.**

8. Remove knock sensor from engine.

To install:

➡**Do not apply any adhesive, sealant or thread locking compound to this bolt.**

9. Position sensor to engine. Install and tighten mounting bolt to 7 ft. lbs. (10 Nm).

10. Install lower intake manifold and fuel rail.

11. Install the upper intake manifold, EGR tube, PCV, Purge and power brake booster vacuum hoses.

12. Fill the coolant system.

13. Connect the negative battery cable. Tighten nut to 40 inch lbs. (4.5 Nm).

MALFUNCTION INDICATOR LIGHT (MIL)

RESET PROCEDURES

Clear Diagnostic Trouble Codes.

MANIFOLD ABSOLUTE PRESSURE (MAP) SENSOR

LOCATION

The Manifold Absolute Pressure (MAP) sensor is located on the front of the intake manifold.

REMOVAL & INSTALLATION

3.7L Engine

See Figure 157.

1. See all applicable precautions before beginning service procedures.

2. Disconnect and isolate the negative battery cable at battery.

3. Disconnect electrical connector at sensor.

4. Clean area around Manifold Absolute Pressure (MAP) sensor.

5. Remove 2 sensor mounting screws.

6. Remove MAP sensor from intake manifold.

To install:

7. Check condition of sensor O-ring.

8. Clean MAP sensor mounting hole at intake manifold.

9. Check MAP sensor O-ring seal for cuts or tears.

10. Position sensor into manifold.

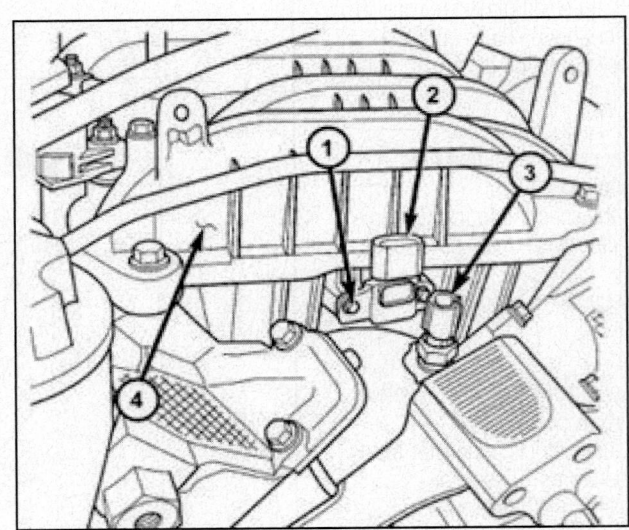

Fig. 157 Indicating the location of the MAP sensor mounting screws: MAP sensor screws (1), MAP sensor (2), ECT sensor (3), and intake manifold (4)

11. Install MAP sensor mounting bolts (screws). Tighten screws to 25 inch lbs. (3 Nm).

12. Connect electrical connector.

13. Reconnect the negative battery cable at battery.

4.0L Engine

See Figure 158.

1. See all applicable precautions before beginning service procedures.

➤**An O-ring is used to seal the sensor to the intake manifold.**

2. Disconnect and isolate the negative battery cable at battery.

3. Disconnect electrical connector at sensor.

4. Clean area around Manifold Absolute Pressure (MAP) sensor.

5. Rotate sensor ¼ turn counter-clockwise until tangs align.

6. Pull MAP sensor from intake manifold.

7. Check condition of sensor O-ring.

To install:

8. Check condition of sensor O-ring.

9. Position MAP sensor into intake manifold. Note locating tangs.

10. Rotate sensor ¼ turn clockwise.

11. Connect electrical connector at sensor.

12. Connect negative battery cable. Tighten nut to 45 inch lbs. (5 Nm).

OIL PRESSURE SENSOR

LOCATION

Switch is located in a main oil galley near the oil filter.

REMOVAL & INSTALLATION

1. See all applicable precautions before beginning service procedures.

2. Raise vehicle on hoist.

3. Position an oil collecting container under switch location.

4. Disconnect electrical connector.

5. Unscrew oil pressure switch.

To install:

6. Apply Mopar® Thread Sealant to the switch threads.

7. Install oil pressure switch to fitting.

8. Connect electrical connector.

9. Lower vehicle.

10. Start engine and check for leaks.

11. Check engine oil level and adjust as necessary.

POSITIVE CRANKCASE VENTILATION (PCV) VALVE

LOCATION

See Figures 159 and 160.

REMOVAL & INSTALLATION

3.7L Engine

1. See all applicable precautions before beginning service procedures.

2. Remove line (1) and rubber connector hose from PCV valve.

3. Unthread PCV valve from metal fitting.

To install:

4. Check condition of PCV valve rubber O-ring.

5. Clean fitting.

6. Install PCV valve into fitting.

7. Install PCV line and rubber connector to valve.

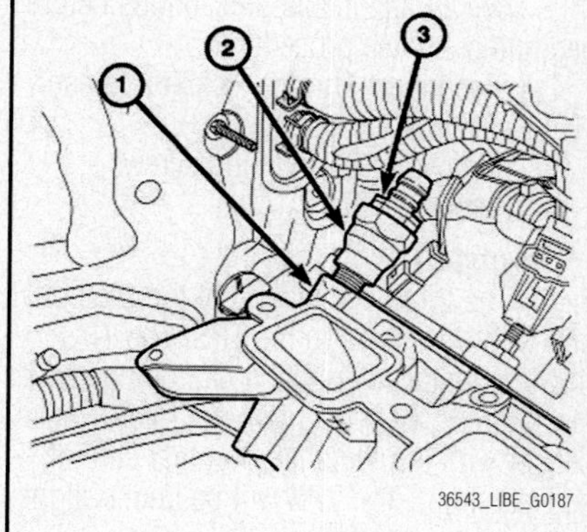

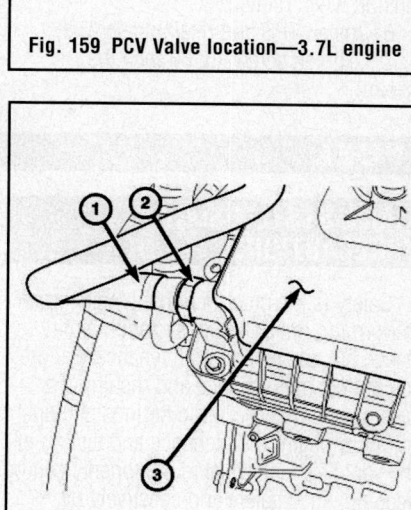

36543_LIBE_G0187

Fig. 159 PCV Valve location—3.7L engine

36543_LIBE_G0188

Fig. 160 PCV Valve location—4.0L engine

4.0L Engine

1. See all applicable precautions before beginning service procedures.

2. Remove hose clamp and rubber hose from PCV valve.

3. Unthread PCV valve from rear of valve cover.

To install:

4. Check condition of PCV valve rubber O-ring.

5. Clean PCV fitting.

6. Thread and tighten PCV valve into rear of valve cover.

7. Install rubber PCV hose and hose clamp to PCV valve.

THROTTLE POSITION SENSOR (TPS)

LOCATION

The Throttle Position Sensor (TPS) is mounted on the throttle body and is connected to the throttle blade.

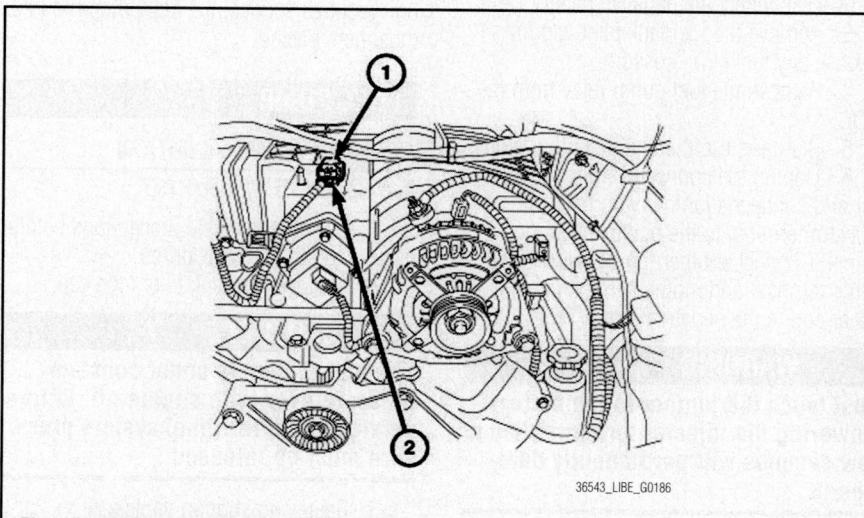

36543_LIBE_G0186

Fig. 158 MAP sensor location—4.0L engine

REMOVAL & INSTALLATION

1. See all applicable precautions before beginning service procedures.
2. Disconnect Throttle Position Sensor (TPS) electrical connector.
3. Remove TPS mounting screws.
4. Remove TPS.

To install:

5. The throttle shaft end of throttle body slides into a socket in the TPS. The TPS must be installed so that it can be rotated a few degrees. (If sensor will not rotate, install sensor with throttle shaft on other side of socket tangs). The TPS will be under slight tension when rotated.
6. Install TPS and retaining screws.
7. Tighten screws to 60 inch lbs. (7 Nm).

8. Connect TPS electrical connector to TPS.
9. Manually operate throttle (by hand) to check for any TPS binding before starting engine.

VEHICLE SPEED SENSOR (VSS)

LOCATION

The Vehicle Speed Sensor (VSS) is located on the left side of the transmission case.

REMOVAL & INSTALLATION

1. See all applicable precautions before beginning service procedures.
2. Raise and safely support the vehicle.

3. Place a suitable catch pan under the transmission for any fluid.
4. Remove the wiring connector from the output speed sensor.
5. Remove the mounting bolt and remove the speed sensor from the transmission case.

To install:

6. Install the speed sensor into the transmission case and tighten the bolt to 105 inch lbs. (12 Nm).
7. Install the wiring connector to the speed sensor.
8. Verify the proper transmission fluid level and refill as necessary.
9. Lower the vehicle.

FUEL

FUEL SYSTEM SERVICE PRECAUTIONS

Safety is the most important factor when performing not only fuel system maintenance but any type of maintenance. Failure to conduct maintenance and repairs in a safe manner may result in serious personal injury or death. Maintenance and testing of the vehicle's fuel system components can be accomplished safely and effectively by adhering to the following rules and guidelines.

• To avoid the possibility of fire and personal injury, always disconnect the negative battery cable unless the repair or test procedure requires that battery voltage be applied.
• Always relieve the fuel system pressure prior to disconnecting any fuel system component (injector, fuel rail, pressure regulator, etc.), fitting or fuel line connection. Exercise extreme caution whenever relieving fuel system pressure to avoid exposing skin, face and eyes to fuel spray. Please be advised that fuel under pressure may penetrate the skin or any part of the body that it contacts.
• Always place a shop towel or cloth around the fitting or connection prior to loosening to absorb any excess fuel due to spillage. Ensure that all fuel spillage (should it occur) is quickly removed from engine surfaces. Ensure that all fuel soaked cloths or towels are deposited into a suitable waste container.
• Always keep a dry chemical (Class B) fire extinguisher near the work area.

• Do not allow fuel spray or fuel vapors to come into contact with a spark or open flame.
• Always use a back-up wrench when loosening and tightening fuel line connection fittings. This will prevent unnecessary stress and torsion to fuel line piping.
• Always replace worn fuel fitting O-rings with new. Do not substitute fuel hose or equivalent where fuel pipe is installed.

Before servicing the vehicle, make sure to also refer to the precautions in the beginning of this section as well.

RELIEVING FUEL SYSTEM PRESSURE

1. See all applicable precautions before beginning service procedures.
2. Disconnect the negative battery cable.
3. Remove the fuel tank filler cap to release any fuel tank pressure.
4. Remove the fuel pump relay from the PDC.
5. Start and run the engine until it stops.
6. Unplug the connector from any injector and connect a jumper wire from either injector terminal to the positive battery terminal. Connect another jumper wire to the other terminal and momentarily touch the other end to the negative battery terminal.

✷✷ WARNING

Just touch the jumper to the battery. Powering the injector for more than a few seconds will permanently damage it.

7. Place a rag below the quick-disconnect coupling at the fuel rail and disconnect it.

FUEL FILTER

REMOVAL & INSTALLATION

1. See all applicable precautions before beginning service procedures.
See Fuel Pump for Removal and Installation instructions.
These vehicles incorporate the use of a fuel pump module which comprises:
• An internal fuel filter
• A separate fuel pick-up, or inlet filter
• A fuel pressure regulator
• An electric fuel pump
• A fuel gauge sending unit (fuel level sensor)
If the filter(s), regulator, pump or sending unit requires service, the fuel pump module must be replaced.

FUEL PUMP

REMOVAL & INSTALLATION

See Figures 161 through 163.

1. See all applicable precautions before beginning service procedures.
2. Remove fuel tank filler tube cap.

✷✷ CAUTION

The fuel system is under constant pressure even with engine off. Before servicing fuel rail, fuel system pressure must be released.

3. Raise and support vehicle.

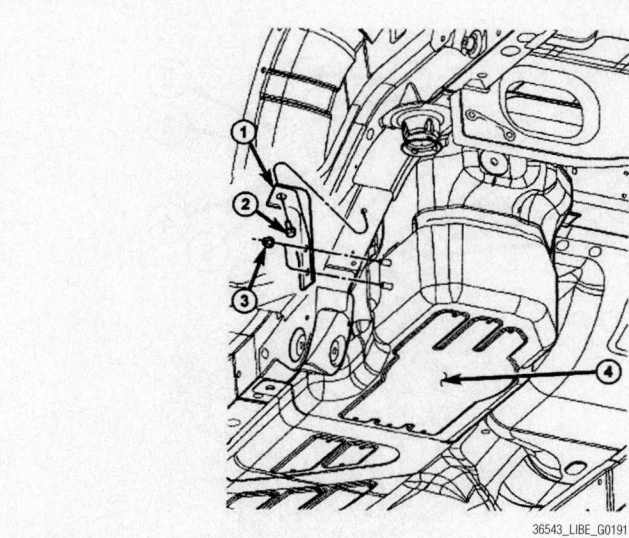

Fig. 161 Fuel tank bracket removal

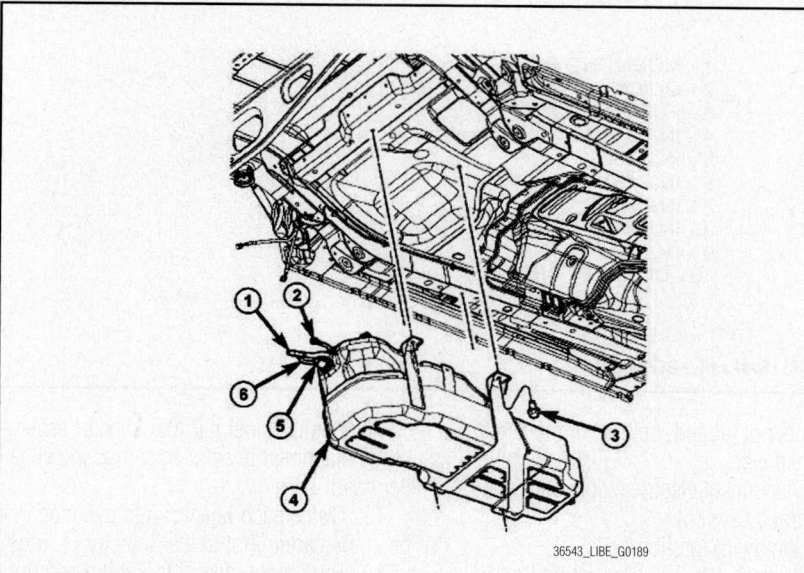

Fig. 162 Fuel tank removal

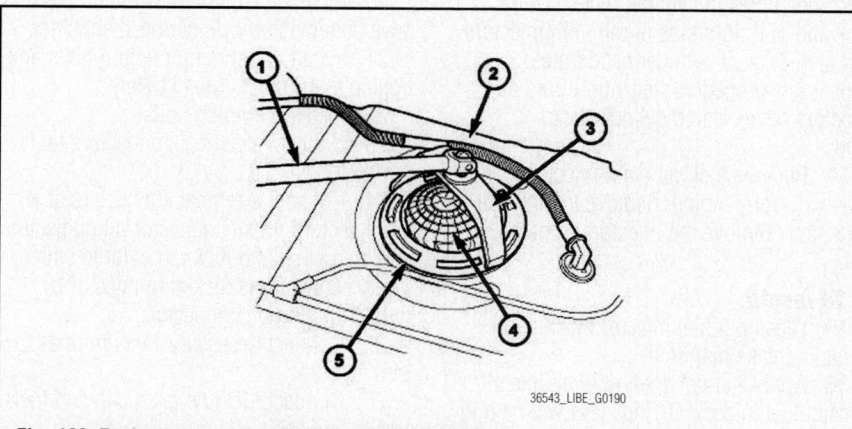

Fig. 163 Fuel pump module removal and installation

4. Disconnect fuel line quick connect fittings and at front of fuel tank.

5. Remove fuel fill hose and clamp at rear of tank.

6. Position a drain hose into the fuel fill hose opening. Note that a small flapper valve is installed into the opening. Drain tank.

7. Disconnect vapor lines and at rear of tank.

8. Remove rear propeller shaft.

9. Support tank with a hydraulic jack.

10. Loosen two nuts (3) at tank support bracket (1).

11. Remove bolt (2) from tank support bracket (1).

12. Remove tank mounting bolts at both sides of tank.

13. Partially lower tank to gain access to pump module electrical connector.

14. Disconnect electrical connector at fuel pump module.

15. Continue lowering tank for removal.

16. Note rotational position of module before attempting removal. An indexing arrow is located on top of module for this purpose.

17. Position special Lockring Remover/Installer tool 9340 (3) into notches on outside edge of lockring (5).

18. Install ½ inch drive breaker bar (1) to special Lockring Remover/Installer tool 9340 (3).

19. Rotate breaker bar counter-clockwise to remove lockring.

20. Remove lockring. The module will spring up slightly when lockring is removed.

21. Remove module from fuel tank. Be careful not to bend float arm while removing.

To install:

22. Install the fuel pump module in the tank.

23. Using a new seal (gasket), position fuel pump module into opening in fuel tank.

24. Position lockring (5) over top of fuel pump module.

25. Rotate module until embossed alignment arrow points to center alignment mark. This step must be performed to prevent float from contacting side of fuel tank.

26. Install Lockring Remover/Installer 9340 (3) to lockring.

27. Install ½ inch drive breaker (1) into Lockring Remover/Installer 9340 (3).

28. Tighten lockring (clockwise) until all seven notches have engaged.

29. Place tank to a hydraulic jack and raise just enough to connect fuel pump module electrical connector.

30. Continue raising tank until snug to body.

31. Install tank mounting bolts at both sides of tank. Tighten to 45 ft. lbs. (61 Nm).

32. Tighten two nuts at tank support bracket to 45 ft. lbs. (61 Nm).

33. Install bolt. Tighten to 45 ft. lbs. (61 Nm).

34. Install rear propeller shaft.

35. Connect vapor lines and at rear of tank.

36. Connect fuel fill hose and clamp at rear of tank.

37. Connect fuel line quick connect fittings at front of fuel tank.

38. Lower vehicle, fill tank with fuel and install fuel fill cap.

39. Check for fuel leaks.

FUEL RAIL & INJECTORS

REMOVAL & INSTALLATION

3.7L Engine

See Figure 165.

1. See all applicable precautions before beginning service procedures.

✳✳ CAUTION

The fuel system is under constant pressure even with engine off. Before servicing fuel rail, fuel system pressure must be released.

➡**The left and right fuel rails are replaced as an assembly. Do not attempt to separate rail halves at connector tube. Due to design of tube, it does not use any clamps. Never attempt to install a clamping device of any kind to tube. When removing fuel rail assembly for any reason, be careful not to bend or kink tube.**

2. Remove fuel tank filler tube cap.

3. Perform Fuel System Pressure Release Procedure.

4. Remove negative battery cable at battery.

5. Remove air duct at throttle body air box.

6. Remove air box at throttle body.

7. Disconnect fuel line latch clip and fuel line at fuel rail. A special tool will be necessary for fuel line disconnection.

8. Remove necessary vacuum lines at throttle body.

9. Disconnect electrical connectors at all 6 fuel injectors. Push red colored slider away from injector. While pushing slider, depress tab and remove connector from injector. The factory fuel injection wiring harness is numerically tagged (INJ 1, INJ 2, etc.) for injector position identification. If

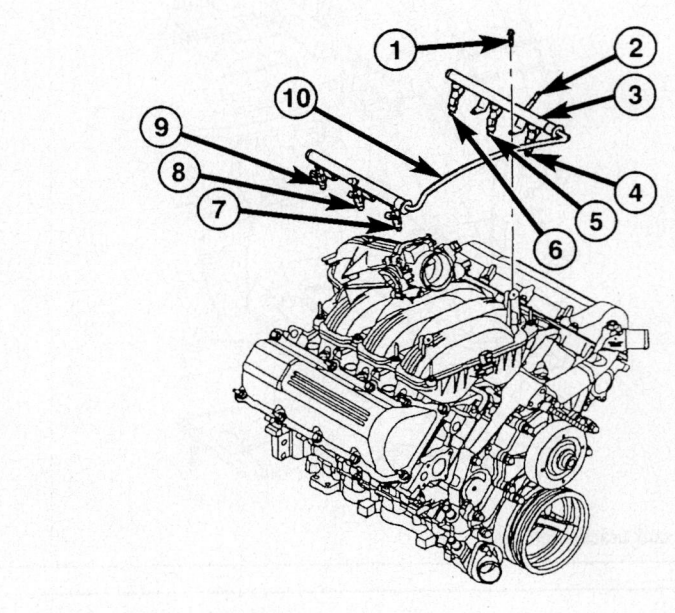

1 - MOUNTING BOLTS (4)
2 - QUICK-CONNECT FITTING
3 - FUEL RAIL
4 - INJ. #1
5 - INJ. #3
6 - INJ. #5
7 - INJ. #2
8 - INJ. #4
9 - INJ. #6
10 - CONNECTOR TUBE

67189-JEEP-G52

Fig. 165 Fuel rail—3.7L engines

harness is not tagged, note wiring location before removal.

10. Disconnect electrical connectors at throttle body sensors.

11. Remove 6 ignition coils.

12. Remove 4 fuel rail mounting bolts.

13. Gently rock and pull left side of fuel rail until fuel injectors just start to clear machined holes in cylinder head. Gently rock and pull right side of rail until injectors just start to clear cylinder head holes. Repeat this procedure (left/right) until all injectors have cleared cylinder head holes.

14. Remove fuel rail (with injectors attached) from engine. Remove the injector clips, then remove the injectors from the rail.

To install:

15. Clean out fuel injector machined bores in intake manifold.

16. Apply a small amount of engine oil to each fuel injector O-ring. This will help in fuel rail installation.

17. Position fuel rail/fuel injector assembly to machined injector openings in cylinder head.

18. Guide each injector into cylinder head. Be careful not to tear injector O-rings.

19. Push right side of fuel rail down until fuel injectors have bottomed on cylinder head shoulder.

20. Push left fuel rail down until injectors have bottomed on cylinder head shoulder.

21. Install 4 fuel rail mounting bolts and tighten to 100 inch lbs. (11 Nm).

22. Install 6 ignition coils.

23. Connect electrical connectors to throttle body.

24. Connect electrical connectors at all fuel injectors. Push connector onto injector and then push and lock red colored slider. Verify connector is locked to injector by lightly tugging on connector.

25. Connect necessary vacuum lines to throttle body.

26. Connect fuel line latch clip and fuel line to fuel rail.

27. Install air box to throttle body.
28. Install air duct to air box.
29. Connect battery cable to battery.
30. Start engine and check for leaks.

4.0L Engine

1. See all applicable precautions before beginning service procedures.
2. Perform Fuel System Pressure Release Procedure.
3. Remove and isolate negative battery cable at battery.
4. Remove upper intake manifold including EGR tube, PVC, purge and power brake booster vacuum.
5. Disconnect fuel supply hose from fuel rail.
6. Disconnect electrical connectors at all six fuel injectors. The factory fuel injection wiring harness is numerically tagged (INJ 1, INJ 2, etc.) for injector position identification. If harness is not tagged, note wiring location before removal.
7. Remove four fuel rail mounting bolts.
8. Gently rock and pull left side of fuel rail until fuel injectors just start to clear machined holes in cylinder head. Gently rock and pull right side of rail until injectors just start to clear cylinder head holes. Repeat this procedure (left/right) until all injectors have cleared cylinder head holes.
9. Remove fuel rail (with injectors attached) from engine.
10. Disconnect clip(s) that retain fuel injector(s) to fuel rail.

To install:

11. Install fuel injector(s) into fuel rail assembly and install retaining clip(s).
12. If same injector(s) is being reinstalled, install new O-ring(s). Two different O-rings are being used. These can be easily identified by color. Install black O-ring at intake manifold end of injector. Install red/rust colored O-ring at fuel rail end of injector.
13. Apply a small amount of clean engine oil to each injector O-ring. This will aid in installation.
14. Clean out fuel injector machined bores in intake manifold.
15. Apply a small amount of engine oil to each fuel injector O-ring. This will help in fuel rail installation.
16. Position fuel rail/fuel injector assembly to machined injector openings in cylinder head.
17. Guide each injector into cylinder head. Be careful not to tear injector O-rings.
18. Push right side of fuel rail down until fuel injectors have bottomed on cylinder

head shoulder. Push left fuel rail down until injectors have bottomed on cylinder head shoulder.
19. Install four fuel rail mounting bolts and tighten to 21 ft. lbs. (28 Nm).
20. Connect fuel supply hose to fuel rail.
21. Connect fuel injector electrical connectors.
22. Install upper intake manifold, EGR tube, PVC, purge and power brake booster vacuum hoses.
23. Connect battery cable to battery. Tighten nut to 40 inch lbs. (4.5 Nm).
24. Start engine and check for leaks.

FUEL TANK

REMOVAL & INSTALLATION

See Figures 166 and 167.

1. See all applicable precautions before beginning service procedures.
2. Remove fuel tank filler tube cap.

✳✳ CAUTION

The fuel system is under constant pressure even with engine off. Before servicing fuel rail, fuel system pressure must be released.

3. Raise and support vehicle.
4. Disconnect fuel line quick connect fittings and at front of fuel tank.

5. Remove fuel fill hose and clamp at rear of tank.
6. Position a drain hose into the fuel fill hose opening. Note that a small flapper valve is installed into the opening. Drain tank.
7. Disconnect vapor lines and at rear of tank.
8. Remove rear propeller shaft.
9. Support tank with a hydraulic jack.
10. Loosen two nuts (3) at tank support bracket (1).
11. Remove bolt (2) from tank support bracket (1).
12. Remove tank mounting bolts at both sides of tank.
13. Partially lower tank to gain access to pump module electrical connector.
14. Disconnect electrical connector at fuel pump module.
15. Continue lowering tank for removal.

To install:

16. Place tank to a hydraulic jack and raise just enough to connect fuel pump module electrical connector.
17. Continue raising tank until snug to body.
18. Install tank mounting bolts at both sides of tank. Tighten to 45 ft. lbs. (61 Nm).
19. Tighten two nuts at tank support bracket to 45 ft. lbs. (61 Nm).
20. Install bolt. Tighten to 45 ft. lbs. (61 Nm).

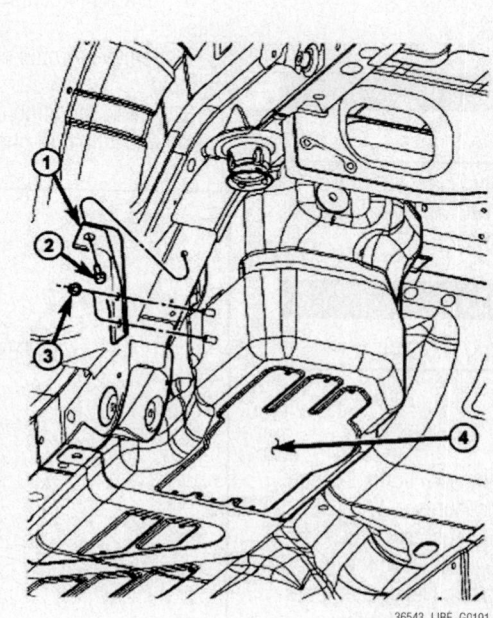

36543_LIBE_G0191

Fig. 166 Fuel tank bracket removal

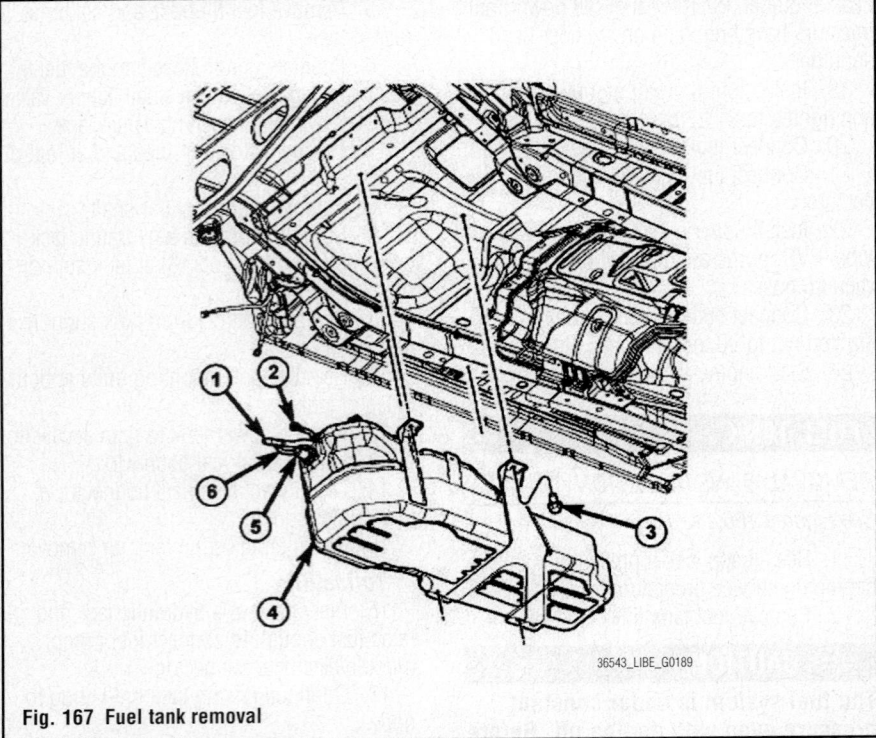

Fig. 167 Fuel tank removal

21. Install rear propeller shaft.
22. Connect vapor lines and at rear of tank.
23. Connect fuel fill hose and clamp at rear of tank.
24. Connect fuel line quick connect fittings at front of fuel tank.
25. Lower vehicle, fill tank with fuel and install fuel fill cap.
26. Check for fuel leaks.

IDLE SPEED

ADJUSTMENT

Idle speed is maintained by the Powertrain Control Module (PCM). No adjustment is necessary or possible.

THROTTLE BODY

REMOVAL & INSTALLATION

3.7L Engine

See Figure 168.

1. See all applicable precautions before beginning service procedures.

A (factory adjusted) set screw is used to mechanically limit the position of the throttle body throttle plate. Never attempt to adjust the engine idle speed using this screw. All idle speed functions are controlled by the Powertrain Control Module (PCM).

2. Remove air cleaner tube at throttle body.
3. Disconnect throttle body electrical connectors at IAC motor and TPS.
4. Remove all control cables from throttle body (lever) arm.
5. Disconnect necessary vacuum lines at throttle body.
6. Remove three throttle body mounting bolts.
7. Remove throttle body from intake manifold.
8. Check condition of old throttle body-to-intake manifold O-ring.

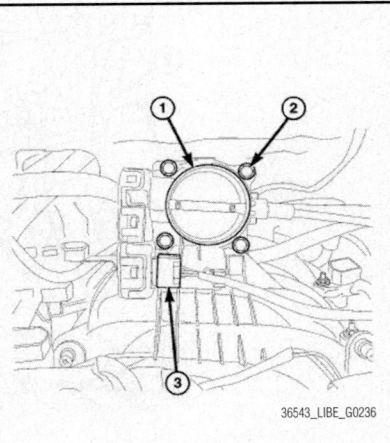

Fig. 168 Throttle body mount bolts on the 3.7L engine

To install:

9. Check condition of throttle body-to-intake manifold O-ring. Replace as necessary.
10. Clean mating surfaces of throttle body and intake manifold.
11. Install throttle body-to-intake manifold O-ring.
12. Install throttle body to intake manifold.
13. Install 3 mounting bolts. Tighten bolts to 105 inch lbs. (12 Nm) torque.
14. Install control cables.
15. Install electrical connectors.
16. Install necessary vacuum lines.
17. Install air plenum.

4.0L Engine

See Figure 169.

1. See all applicable precautions before beginning service procedures.

➡A (factory adjusted) set screw is used to mechanically limit the position of the throttle body throttle plate. Never attempt to adjust the engine idle speed using this screw. All idle speed functions are controlled by the Powertrain Control Module (PCM).

2. Disconnect and isolate negative battery cable at battery.
3. Loosen clamps and reposition the air inlet hose.
4. Disconnect throttle body electrical connector.
5. Remove four throttle body mounting bolts.
6. Remove throttle body from intake manifold.

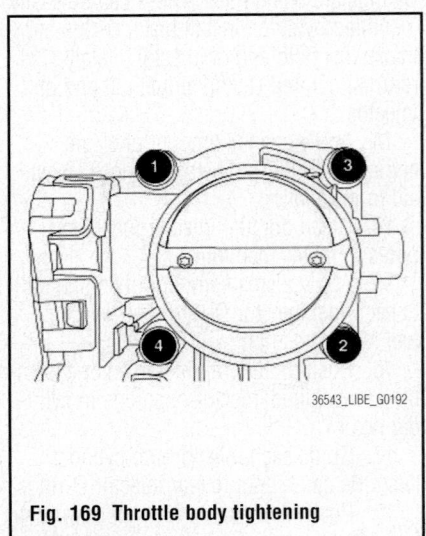

Fig. 169 Throttle body tightening sequence

7. Check condition of old throttle body-to-intake manifold O-ring.

To install:

8. Check condition of throttle body-to-intake manifold O-ring. Replace as necessary.

9. Clean mating surfaces of throttle body and intake manifold.

10. Install O-ring between throttle body and intake manifold.

11. Position throttle body to intake manifold.

12. Install all throttle body mounting bolts finger tight.

➡The throttle body mounting bolts **MUST be tightened to specifications. Over tightening can cause damage to the throttle body or the intake manifold.**

13. Obtain a torque wrench. Tighten mounting bolts in a mandatory torque criss-cross pattern sequence to 65 inch lbs. (7.5 Nm).

14. Connect the electronic throttle control, MAP sensor and IAT sensor electrical connectors.

15. Install the inlet hose tighten clamps.

16. Connect negative battery cable. Tighten nut to 45 inch lbs. (5 Nm).

17. Using the diagnostic scan tool, erase all previous DTC's.

HEATING & AIR CONDITIONING SYSTEM

BLOWER MOTOR

REMOVAL & INSTALLATION

1. See all applicable precautions before beginning service procedures.

✳✳ CAUTION

Disable the airbag system before attempting any steering wheel, steering column, or instrument panel component diagnosis or service. Failure to take the proper precautions could result in accidental airbag deployment and possible personal injury or death.

➡**The blower motor is located on the passenger side of the vehicle under the instrument panel. The blower motor can be removed without having to remove the instrument panel or the HVAC housing.**

2. Disconnect and isolate the negative battery cable.

3. Disconnect the wire harness connector from the blower motor.

4. Release the locking tab that secures the blower motor to the HVAC housing and rotate blower motor counterclockwise.

5. Rotate and tilt the blower motor as needed for clearance to remove the blower motor and wheel from the HVAC housing.

To install:

➡**Failure to install the blower motor assembly correctly could result in an air leak or the blower motor assembly becoming completely disengaged from the HVAC housing.**

6. Align and install the blower motor into the HVAC housing.

7. Rotate the blower motor until all of the locking tabs have secured the blower motor assembly to the HVAC housing.

8. Connect the wire harness connector to the blower motor.

9. Reconnect the battery negative cable.

10. Test the blower motor for proper installation by turning the blower motor speed to its fastest position and checking around the outer edges of the blower assembly for air leaks. If any air leaks are found, remove and reinstall the blower motor.

HEATER CORE

REMOVAL & INSTALLATION

See Figures 170 through 172.

1. See all applicable precautions before beginning service procedures.

2. Disconnect and remove the negative battery.

✳✳ CAUTION

After disconnecting the negative battery cable, wait 2 minutes for the driver's/passenger's air bag system capacitor to discharge before attempting to do any work around the steering column or instrument.

3. If equipped, remove the silencer from below the driver side of the instrument panel.

4. Disconnect the wire harness connector from the mode door actuator (2) and the blend door actuator (6) located on the driver side of the air distribution housing.

5. Carefully disengage the retaining tabs (3) that secure the mode door actuator and the blend door actuator to the actuator

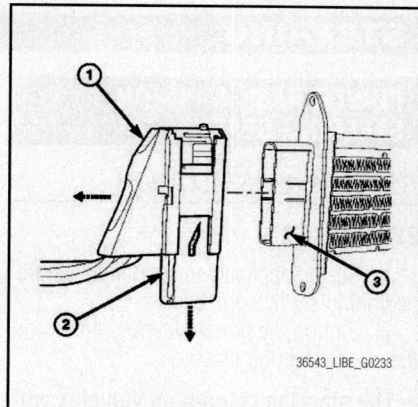

Fig. 171 Disconnect the wire harness connector

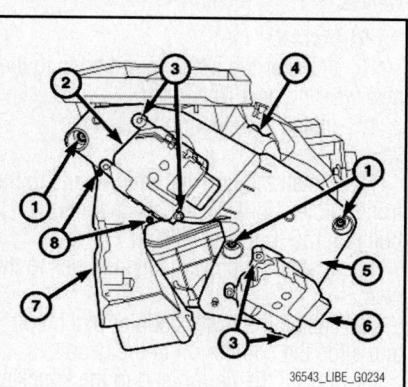

Fig. 170 Heater housing connector locations

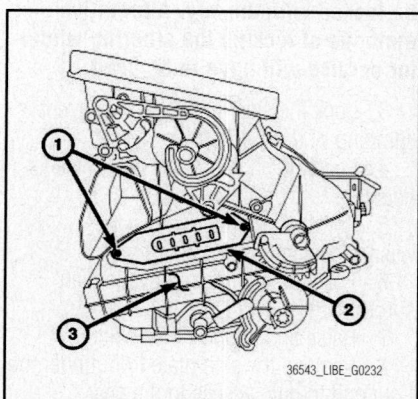

Fig. 172 Positive temperature coefficient (PTC) heater unit location

mounting bracket (5) and remove the actuators.

6. Remove the three screws (1) that secure the actuator mounting bracket to the air distribution housing and remove the bracket.

7. Remove the screw (8) that secures the driver side front floor duct (7) to the air distribution housing and remove the duct

➡**PTC heater shown removed from distribution housing for clarity.**

➡**To disconnect the wire harness connector from the PTC heater, disengage the connector lock while pulling the connector away from the heater unit.**

8. Disengage the wire connector lock (2) that secures the wire harness connector (1) to the positive temperature coefficient (PTC) heater unit (3) and disconnect the connector from the heater.

To install:

9. Carefully install the positive temperature coefficient (PTC) heater unit into the driver side of the air distribution housing. Make sure to position the two locator tabs

on the end of the heater unit into the molded locator indentations on the right side of the air distribution housing.

10. Install the two screws that secure the PTC heater unit to the air distribution housing. Tighten the screws to 10 inch lbs. (1.2 Nm).

➡**PTC heater shown removed from distribution housing for clarity.**

11. Connect the wire harness connector to the PTC heater unit while pushing inward on the connector lock. Make sure the wire harness connector and lock are fully engaged.

12. Install the driver side front floor duct onto the driver side of the air distribution housing and install the retaining screw. Tighten the screw to 10 inch lbs. (1.2 Nm).

13. Position the actuator mounting bracket onto the air distribution housing and install the three retaining screws. Tighten the screws to 10 inch lbs. (1.2 Nm).

14. Position the mode door actuator and the blend door actuator onto the actuator mounting bracket. If necessary, rotate the actuator slightly to align the splines on the

actuator output shaft with those on the door linkage.

➡**If the retaining tabs on the actuator mounting bracket become broken during service, the alignment pins on the bracket bosses can be removed and screws can be used to retain the actuator to the bracket. Once the alignment pins are removed, pre-made holes can be found the center of the bosses, exactly where the pins were. This assures correct actuator alignment to the bracket. Use care not to overtighten the screws and damage the bosses.**

15. Engage the retaining tabs that secure the mode and blend door actuators to the actuator mounting bracket. Make sure the retaining tabs are fully engaged.

16. Connect the wire harness connector to the mode and blend door actuators.

17. If equipped, install the silencer below the driver side of the instrument panel.

18. Reconnect the negative battery cable.

STEERING

POWER RACK & PINION STEERING GEAR

REMOVAL & INSTALLATION

2WD Models

1. See all applicable precautions before beginning service procedures.

2. Siphon the power steering fluid from the power steering reservoir.

➡**The steering column on vehicles with an automatic transmission may not be equipped with an internal locking shaft that allows the ignition key cylinder to be locked with the key. Alternative methods of locking the steering wheel for service will have to be used.**

3. Lock the steering wheel to prevent spinning of the clockspring.

4. For 4.0L engine, remove air cleaner housing.

5. For 4.0L engine, remove the washer/coolant reservoir assembly.

6. For 4.0L engine, remove the fan shroud.

7. Raise and support the vehicle.

8. Remove the skid plate from under the front end to gain access to the gear.

9. Remove the tire and wheel assembly.

➡**Mark the alignment adjusting cams and tie rod end jam nuts on the steering gear for easier installation.**

10. Remove the tie rod end nuts.

11. Separate tie rod ends from the knuckles with Puller C-3894-A.

12. Remove the lower intermediate shaft coupler pinch bolt and slide the coupler off the gear.

13. Remove the power steering lines from the gear.

14. Remove the mounting bolts from the gear to the front cradle.

15. Remove the steering gear from the vehicle.

To install:

16. Transfer the outer tie rod ends to the new steering gear (if needed).

17. Install the steering gear to the vehicle.

18. Install the gear mounting bolts to the front cradle. Tighten the gear mounting bolts to 130 ft. lbs. (176 Nm).

19. Install the power steering lines to the gear.

20. Install the lower coupler pinch bolt and slide the coupler on to the gear.

21. Install the tie rod end to the knuckle and tighten the nuts to 30 ft. lbs (41 Nm) plus an additional 90° turn.

22. Install the tire and wheel assembly.

23. Install the skid plate.

24. Lower the vehicle.

25. For 4.0L engine, install air cleaner housing.

26. For 4.0L engine, install the washer/coolant reservoir assembly.

27. For 4.0L engine, install the fan shroud.

28. Unlock the steering wheel.

29. Fill the power steering fluid.

30. Reset the toe and center the steering wheel.

4WD Models

See Figure 173.

1. See all applicable precautions before beginning service procedures.

2. Siphon the power steering fluid from the power steering reservoir.

➡**The steering column on vehicles with an automatic transmission may not be equipped with an internal locking shaft that allows the ignition key cylinder to be locked with the key. Alternative methods of locking the steering wheel for service will have to be used.**

3. Lock the steering wheel to prevent spinning of the clockspring.

4. Disconnect the battery (3).

5. Remove the battery.

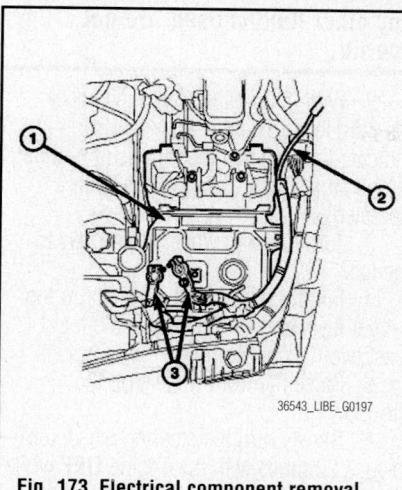

Fig. 173 Electrical component removal

6. Unclip the power center (2) and move it to the side out of the way to access the battery tray (1).

7. Remove the battery tray (1).

8. Remove the lower intermediate shaft coupler pinch bolt and slide the coupler off the gear.

9. Raise and support the vehicle.

10. Remove the skid plate from under the front end to gain access to the gear.

11. Remove the front tire and wheel assemblies.

➡**Mark the alignment adjusting cams for easier installation.**

12. Remove the tie rod end nuts.

13. Separate tie rod ends from the knuckles with Puller C-3894-A.

14. Remove the power steering lines.

15. Remove the mounting bolts from the gear to the front cradle.

16. Remove the left front lower suspension arm cam/bolt and lower the control arm enough to get the axle mounting bracket bolt out. This must be done to remove the axle mounting bracket.

17. Remove the axle mounting bracket.

18. Remove the oil filter and trough.

19. Put the steering gear in the full right position and lower the gear out of the vehicle.

20. Remove the steering gear from the vehicle.

To install:

21. Transfer the tie rod ends to the new steering gear (if needed).

22. Install the steering gear to the vehicle.

23. Install the gear mounting bolts to the front cradle. Tighten the gear mounting bolts to 130 ft. lbs. (176 Nm).

24. Install the power steering lines to the gear and tighten to 20 ft. lbs. (27 Nm).

25. Install the oil filter trough and filter.

26. Install the axle mounting bracket.

27. Install the left lower control arm into position and install the cam/bolt.

28. Install the tie rod end to the knuckle and tighten the nuts to 30 ft. lbs (41 Nm). plus an additional 90° turn.

29. Install the tire and wheel assembly.

30. Lower the vehicle.

31. Install the lower coupler pinch bolt and slide the coupler on to the gear. Tighten to 39 ft. lbs. (53 Nm).

32. Install the battery tray.

33. Install the battery.

34. Reinstall the power center back into place.

35. Reconnect the battery cables.

36. Unlock the steering wheel.

37. Fill the power steering fluid.

38. Perform a wheel alignment.

POWER STEERING PUMP

REMOVAL & INSTALLATION

3.7L Engine

See Figure 174.

1. See all applicable precautions before beginning service procedures.

2. Siphon out as much power steering fluid as possible.

3. Remove the radiator cross member.

4. Remove the engine cooling fan.

5. Remove the fan shroud.

6. Remove the serpentine drive belt.

7. Remove the power steering high pressure hose at the pump.

8. Remove the return hose at the pump.

9. Remove the three bolts securing the pump to the bracket thru the holes in the pulley.

10. Remove the pump from the vehicle.

To install:

11. Install the pump to the vehicle.

12. Install the three bolts securing the pump to the engine. Tighten the bolts to 35 ft. lbs. (47 Nm).

13. Install the power steering hoses.

14. Install the serpentine belt.

15. Install the fan shroud.

16. Install the engine cooling fan.

17. Install the radiator crossmember.

18. Refill the power steering fluid and check for leaks.

4.0L Engine

See Figure 175.

1. See all applicable precautions before beginning service procedures.

2. Siphon out as much power steering fluid as possible.

3. Remove air cleaner housing.

4. Remove the washer/coolant reservoir assembly .

5. Remove the fan shroud.

6. Remove power steering belt.

7. Remove pressure line at the pump.

8. Remove return line at the reservoir.

9. Remove three pump mounting bolts through pump pulley.

10. Remove pump from the vehicle.

To install:

11. Install power steering pump back in engine compartment using reverse order of its removal.

12. Install three power steering pump mounting bolts through pulley. Tighten pump mounting bolts to 21 ft. lbs. (28 Nm).

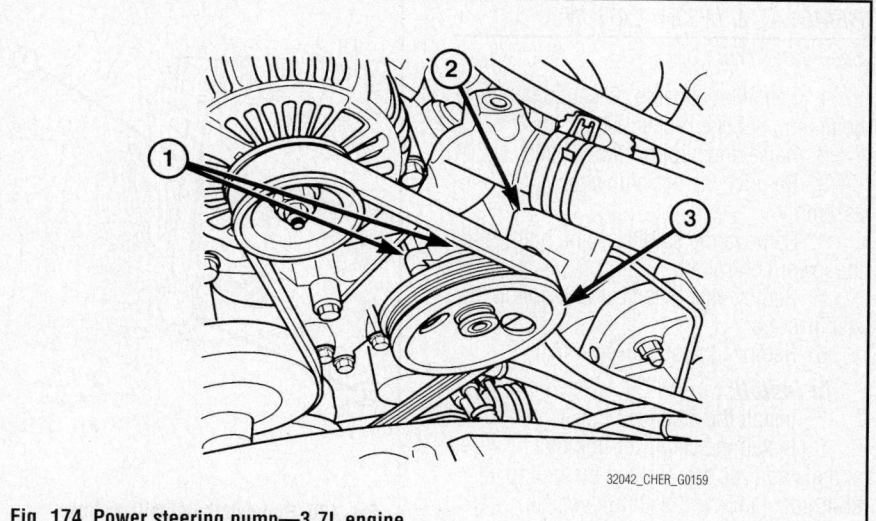

Fig. 174 Power steering pump—3.7L engine

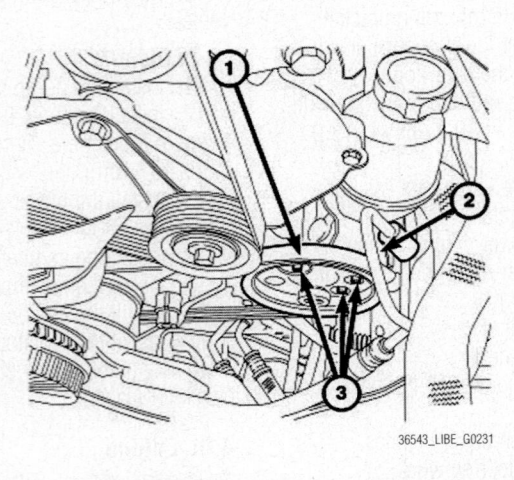

Fig. 175 Remove three pump mounting bolts through pump pulley

➥Before installing power steering pressure hose on power steering pump, replace O-ring on end of power steering pressure hose. Lubricate O-ring using clean power steering fluid.

13. Install pressure line into pump. Thread pressure line tube nut into pump and tighten to 20 ft. lbs (27 Nm).

14. Install return line into the reservoir.

15. Install power steering belt.

16. Install the fan shroud.

17. Install the washer/coolant reservoir assembly.

18. Install air cleaner housing.

19. Fill and bleed power steering system.

20. Inspect for leaks.

BLEEDING

1. See all applicable precautions before beginning service procedures.

✳✳ WARNING

The fluid level should be checked with engine OFF to prevent injury from moving components.

✳✳ WARNING

MOPAR® ATF+4 is to be used in the power steering system. No other power steering or automatic transmission fluid is to be used in the system. Damage may result to the power steering pump and system if

any other fluid is used. Do not overfill.

2. Wipe filler cap clean, then check the fluid level. The dipstick should indicate COLD when the fluid is at normal temperature (before engine has been operated).

3. Turn steering wheel all the way to the left.

4. Fill the pump fluid reservoir to the proper level and let the fluid settle for at least two (2) minutes.

5. Raise the front wheels off the ground.

6. Slowly turn the steering wheel lock-to-lock 20 times with the engine **OFF** while checking the fluid level.

➥Vehicles with long return lines or oil coolers turn wheel 40 times.

7. Start the engine. With the engine idling maintain the fluid level.

8. Lower the front wheels and let the engine idle for two minutes.

9. Turn the steering wheel in both direction and verify power assist and quiet operation of the pump.

10. If the fluid is extremely foamy or milky looking, allow the vehicle to stand a few minutes and repeat the procedure.

✳✳ WARNING

Do not run a vehicle with foamy fluid for an extended period. This may cause pump damage.

SUSPENSION

CONTROL LINKS

REMOVAL & INSTALLATION

See Figure 176.

1. See all applicable precautions before beginning service procedures.

2. Raise and support the vehicle.

3. Remove the tire and wheel assembly.

4. Remove the stabilizer link bolt (2) at the lower control arm.

5. Remove the stabilizer link bolt at the stabilizer bar.

6. Remove the stabilizer link (1).

To install:

7. Install the stabilizer link.

8. Install the stabilizer link bolt at the stabilizer bar. Tighten the bolt to 85 ft. lbs. (115 Nm) with full vehicle weight.

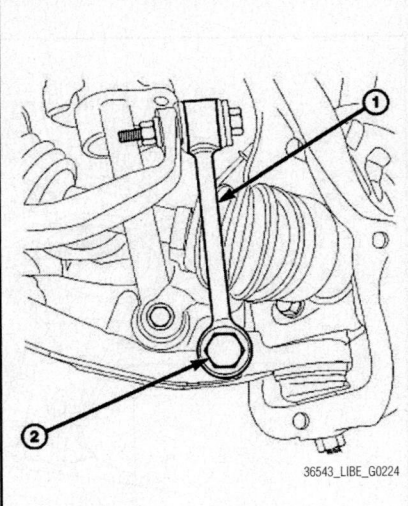

Fig. 176 Remove the stabilizer link

FRONT SUSPENSION

9. Install the stabilizer link bolt at the lower control arm. Tighten the bolt to 75 ft. lbs. (102 Nm) with full vehicle weight.

10. Install the tire and wheel assembly.

LOWER BALL JOINT

REMOVAL & INSTALLATION

See Figure 177.

1. See all applicable precautions before beginning service procedures.

2. Remove the tire and wheel assembly.

3. Remove the brake caliper and rotor.

4. Separate the tie rod from the steering knuckle using special tool 9360.

5. Separate the upper ball joint from the knuckle using special tool 9360.

6. Separate the lower ball joint from the steering knuckle using special tool 8677.

7. Remove the steering knuckle.

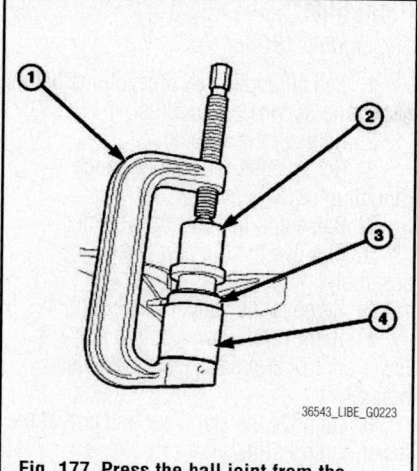

Fig. 177 Press the ball joint from the lower control arm

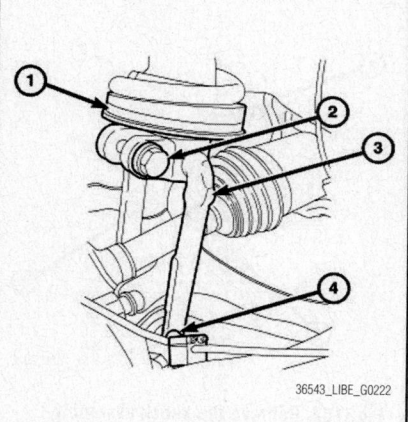

Fig. 178 Shock absorber lower clevis bolt/nut (4)

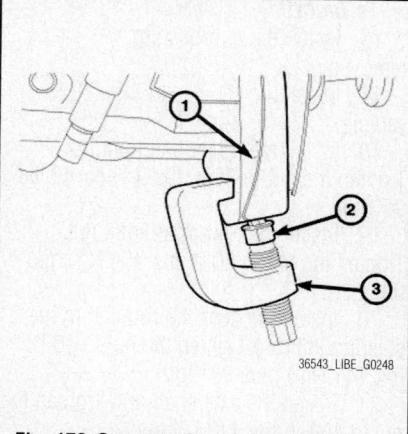

Fig. 179 Separate the lower ball joint from the suspension arm using tool C-4150A

➥**Extreme pressure lubrication must be used on the threaded portions of the tool. This will increase the longevity of the tool and insure proper operation during the removal and installation process.**

8. Press the ball joint from the lower control arm (3) using special tools C-4212-F (PRESS) (1), C-4212-3 (Driver) (2) and 9654-3 (Receiver) (4).

To install:

9. Install the ball joint into the lower control arm using special tools C-4212-F (PRESS), C-4212-3 (Driver) and 9654-3 (Receiver).

10. Stake the ball joint flange in four evenly spaced places around the ball joint flange, using a chisel and hammer.

11. Install the steering knuckle.

12. Install the tie rod end into the steering knuckle.

13. Install and tighten the halfshaft nut to 100 ft. lbs. (136 Nm).

14. Install the brake caliper and rotor.

15. Install the tire and wheel assembly.

16. Check the vehicle ride height.

17. Perform a wheel alignment.

LOWER CONTROL ARM

REMOVAL & INSTALLATION

See Figure 178.

1. See all applicable precautions before beginning service procedures.

2. Remove or disconnect the following:
   • Front wheel
   • Lower clevis bracket bolt from the control arm (4)
   • Stabilizer link at the control arm
   • Lower ball joint nut

   • Control arm from lower ball joint with tool C4150A

➥**Matchmark the front and rear control arm pivot bolts.**

   • Front pivot bolt
   • Rear pivot bolt
   • Control arm

To install:

3. Install or connect the following:
   • Lower control arm
   • Rear pivot bolt
   • Front pivot bolt
   • Ball joint nut and tighten to 40 ft. lbs. (54 Nm) plus 90° turn.

4. Align the matchmarks and tighten the pivot bolts to 125 ft. lbs. (170 Nm).

5. The remainder of the installation is the reverse of removal. Torque the stabilizer link bolt to 75 ft. lbs. (102 Nm); the lower clevis bracket bolt to 110 ft. lbs. (150 Nm).

STEERING KNUCKLE

REMOVAL & INSTALLATION

See Figures 179 and 180.

1. See all applicable precautions before beginning service procedures.

2. Raise and support the vehicle.

3. Remove the tire and wheel assembly.

4. Remove the caliper adapter.

❊❊ WARNING

Never allow the disc brake caliper to hang from the brake hose. Damage to the brake hose will result. Provide a suitable support to hang the caliper securely.

5. Remove the disc brake rotor.

6. Remove the wheel speed sensor.

7. Remove the axle shaft nut (if equipped with 4WD).

8. Remove the outer tie rod nut.

9. Separate the outer tie rod end from the steering knuckle using tool 9360.

10. Remove the lower ball joint nut.

11. Separate the lower ball joint from the suspension arm using tool C-4150A.

12. Remove the upper ball joint nut.

13. Separate the upper ball joint from the knuckle using tool 9360.

➥**Inspect the seal side surface of the upper ball joint, lower ball joint AND outer tie rod knuckle bosses. If any significant grooves or gouges are present (or heavily scratched) replace the steering knuckle.**

14. Remove the knuckle from the vehicle.

15. Remove the hub/bearing, if necessary.

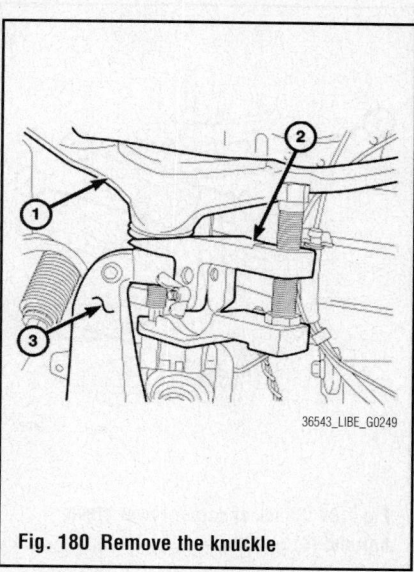

Fig. 180 Remove the knuckle

To install:

16. Install the hub/bearing, if removed.

17. Install the knuckle to the vehicle.

18. Install the upper ball joint nut. Tighten the nut to 30 ft. lbs. (41 Nm) plus 90° turn.

19. Install the lower ball joint nut. Tighten the nut to 40 ft. lbs. (54 Nm) plus 90° turn.

20. Install the outer tie rod end to the steering knuckle Tighten the nut to 30 ft. lbs. (41 Nm) plus 90° turn.

21. Install the axle shaft nut. Tighten the nut to 100 ft. lbs. (136 Nm).

22. Install the wheel speed sensor.

23. Install the disc brake rotor.

24. Install the caliper adapter.

25. Install the tire and wheel assembly.

26. Perform the set toe procedure.

STRUT

REMOVAL & INSTALLATION

Left Side

See Figures 181 and 182.

1. See all applicable precautions before beginning service procedures.

2. Disconnect the battery.

3. Remove the battery.

4. Unclip the power center and move it to the side out of the way to access the battery tray.

5. Remove the battery tray.

6. Remove the four upper shock mounting nuts.

7. Raise and support the vehicle.

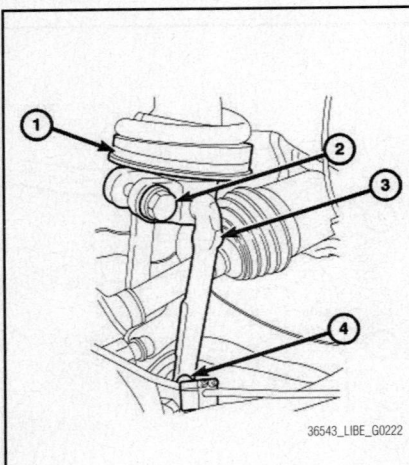

Fig. 181 Shock absorber lower clevis bolt/nut (4)

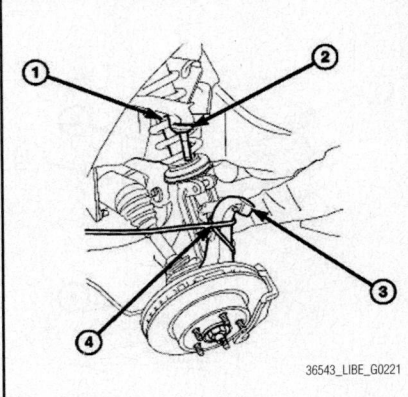

Fig. 182 Remove the shock assembly from the vehicle

8. Remove the tire and wheel assembly.

9. Remove the caliper and support.

10. Remove the lower bolt at the lower control arm securing the clevis bracket.

11. Remove the stabilizer link bolt at the lower control arm.

12. Remove the upper ball joint nut.

13. Separate the upper ball joint from the knuckle using remover 9360 (2).

14. Push downward on the steering knuckle (3) and support the knuckle (4) this will allow access to remove the shock.

15. Remove the shock assembly (1) from the vehicle.

To install:

16. Install the shock assembly to the vehicle.

17. Install the four upper shock mounting nuts. Tighten the nuts to 80 ft. lbs. (108 Nm).

18. Raise the knuckle into place and reconnect the upper ball joint nut. Tighten the nut to 30 ft. lbs (41 Nm) plus an additional 90° turn.

19. Install the clevis bracket bolt at the lower control arm. Tighten the bolt to 110 ft. lbs. (150 Nm) with full vehicle weight.

20. Install the caliper.

21. Install the lower stabilizer link at the lower control arm. Tighten the bolt to 75 ft. lbs. (102 Nm) with full vehicle weight.

22. Install the tire and wheel assembly.

23. Lower the vehicle.

24. Install the battery tray.

25. Install the battery.

26. Reinstall the power center back into place.

27. Reconnect the battery cables.

Right Side

See Figures 181 and 182.

1. See all applicable precautions before beginning service procedures.

2. Remove the air box.

3. Remove the four upper shock mounting nuts.

4. Raise and support the vehicle.

5. Remove the tire and wheel assembly.

6. Remove the caliper and support.

7. Remove the lower bolt at the lower control arm securing the clevis bracket.

8. Remove the stabilizer link bolt at the lower control arm.

9. Remove the upper ball joint nut.

10. Separate the upper ball joint from the knuckle using remover 9360.

11. Push downward on the steering knuckle and support the knuckle this will allow access to remove the shock.

12. Remove the shock assembly from the vehicle.

To install:

13. Install the shock assembly to the vehicle.

14. Install the four upper shock mounting nuts. Tighten the nuts to 80 ft. lbs. (108 Nm).

15. Raise the knuckle into place and reconnect the upper ball joint nut. Tighten the nut to 30 ft. lbs (41 Nm) plus an additional 90° turn.

16. Install the clevis bracket bolt at the lower control arm. Tighten the bolt to 110 ft. lbs. (150 Nm) with full vehicle weight.

17. Install the caliper.

18. Install the lower stabilizer link at the lower control arm. Tighten the bolt to 75 ft. lbs. (102 Nm) with full vehicle weight.

19. Install the tire and wheel assembly.

20. Lower the vehicle.

21. Install the air box.

STABILIZER BAR

REMOVAL & INSTALLATION

See Figure 183.

1. See all applicable precautions before beginning service procedures.

2. Raise and support the vehicle.

3. Remove the tire and wheel assembly.

4. Remove the upper stabilizer link bolts at the stabilizer bar.

5. Remove the stabilizer bar bushing clamps from the frame.

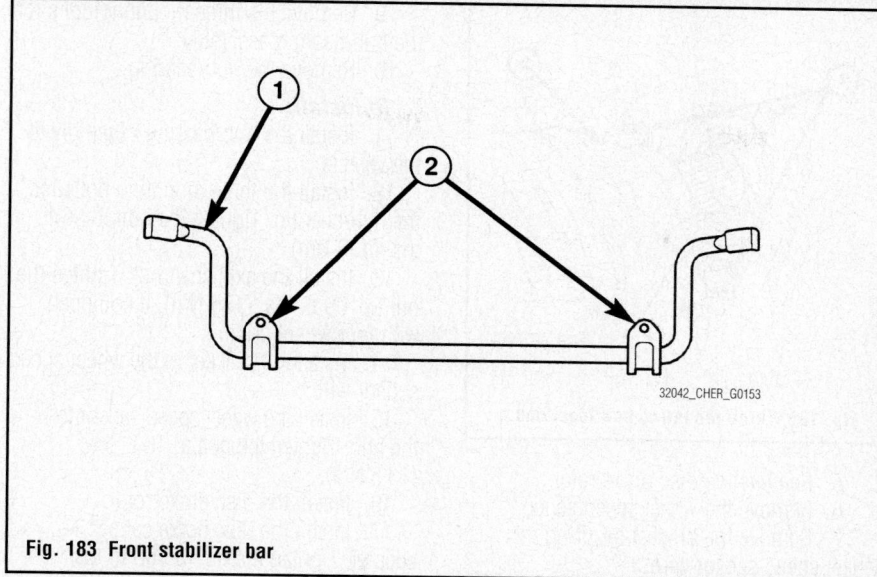

Fig. 183 Front stabilizer bar

6. Remove the stabilizer bar from the vehicle.

To install:

7. Install the stabilizer bar to the vehicle.

8. Install the stabilizer bar bushing clamps. Tighten the nuts to 110 ft. lbs. (149 Nm).

9. Install the upper stabilizer link bolts and washer at the stabilizer bar. Tighten the bolt to 85 ft. lbs. (115 Nm).

10. Install the tire and wheel assembly.

11. Lower the vehicle.

UPPER BALL JOINT

REMOVAL & INSTALLATION

The upper ball joint is serviced as an assembly with the control arm.

UPPER CONTROL ARM

REMOVAL & INSTALLATION

Right

See Figure 184.

1. See all applicable precautions before beginning service procedures.

2. Raise and support the vehicle.

3. Remove the right side tire and wheel assembly.

4. Remove the upper ball joint nut.

5. Separate the upper ball joint from the steering knuckle using remover 9360.

6. Lower the vehicle.

7. Remove the air box assembly.

8. Remove the upper control arm rear bolt/nut.

9. Remove the upper control arm front bolt/nut.

10. Remove the upper control arm from the vehicle.

To install:

11. Install the upper control arm to the vehicle.

12. Install the upper control arm front flag bolt. Tighten the nut to 90 ft. lbs (122 Nm). with full vehicle weight.

13. Install the upper control arm rear flag bolt. Tighten the nut to 90 ft. lbs (122 Nm). with full vehicle weight.

14. Install the air box.

15. Install the upper ball joint nut. Tighten the nut to 30 ft. lbs. (41 Nm) plus an additional 90° turn.

16. Install the right side tire and wheel assembly.

17. Lower the vehicle.

18. Set the toe

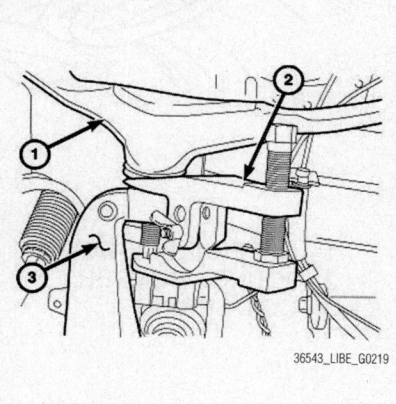

Fig. 184 Separate the upper ball joint from the steering knuckle

Left

See Figure 185.

1. See all applicable precautions before beginning service procedures.

2. Raise and support the vehicle.

3. Remove the left side tire and wheel assembly.

4. Remove the upper ball joint nut.

5. Separate the upper ball joint from the steering knuckle using remover 9360.

6. Lower the vehicle.

7. Remove the battery.

8. Unclip the power center and move it to the side out of the way.

9. Remove the battery tray.

10. Remove the upper control arm rear nut by using a ratchet and extension under the steering shaft.

11. Remove the upper control arm front bolt.

12. Remove the upper control arm from the vehicle.

To install:

13. Install the upper control arm to the vehicle.

14. Install the upper control arm front flag bolt. Tighten the nut to 90 ft. lbs. (122 Nm) with full vehicle weight.

15. Install the upper control arm rear flag bolt. Tighten the nut to 90 ft. lbs. (122 Nm) with full vehicle weight.

16. Install the battery tray.

17. Install the battery.

18. Re-clip and mount the power center.

19. Install the upper ball joint nut. Tighten the nut to 30 ft. lbs. (41 Nm) plus an additional 90° turn.

20. Install the left side tire and wheel assembly.

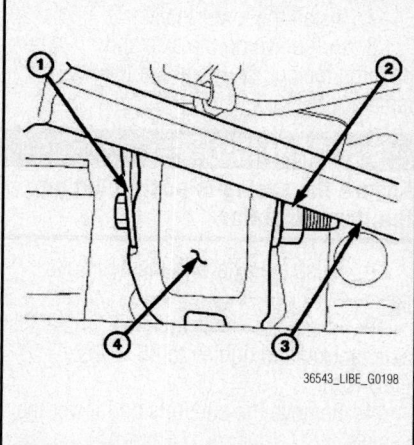

Fig. 185 Upper Control Arm removal— Front

21. Lower the vehicle.
22. Set the toe.

WHEEL HUB & BEARING

REMOVAL & INSTALLATION

See Figure 186.

1. See all applicable precautions before beginning service procedures.
2. Raise and support the vehicle.
3. Remove the tire and wheel assembly.
4. Remove the caliper adapter.

❊❊ WARNING

Never allow the disc brake caliper to hang from the brake hose. Damage to the brake hose will result. Provide a suitable support to hang the caliper securely.

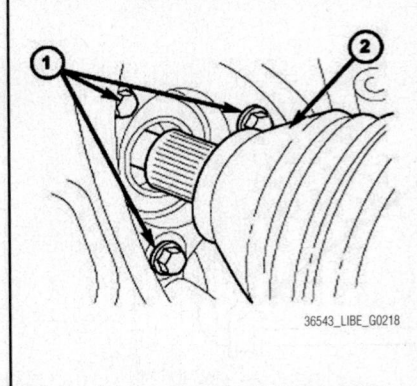

Fig. 186 Three mounting bolt locations

5. Remove the disc brake rotor.
6. Remove the wheel speed sensor.
7. Remove the bracket securing the wheel speed sensor wire.
8. Remove the axle shaft nut, if equipped with four wheel drive.

9. Remove the three mounting bolts for the hub/bearing assembly.
10. Remove the hub/bearing.

To install:

11. Install the hub/bearing assembly to the vehicle.
12. Install the three mounting bolts for the hub/bearing. Tighten the bolt to 96 ft. lbs. (130 Nm).
13. Install the axle shaft nut. Tighten the nut to 100 ft. lbs. (135 Nm), if equipped with four wheel drive.
14. Install the bracket to the wheel speed sensor wire.
15. Install the wheel speed sensor to the hub. Tighten the bolt to 10 ft. lbs. (13.5 Nm).
16. Install the disc brake rotor.
17. Install the disc brake caliper adapter. Tighten the nut to 100 ft. lbs. (135 Nm).
18. Install the tire and wheel assembly.

SUSPENSION

COIL SPRING

REMOVAL & INSTALLATION

See Figure 187.

1. See all applicable precautions before beginning service procedures.
2. Raise and support the vehicle. Position a hydraulic jack under the axle to support the axle.
3. Remove the shock absorber lower bolt from the axle bracket.
4. Lower the hydraulic jack and tilt the axle and remove the coil spring.
5. Remove and inspect the upper and lower spring isolators.

To install:

6. Install the upper isolator.
7. Install the lower isolator.
8. Pull down on the axle and position the coil spring in the lower isolator.

❊❊ WARNING

Ensure the spring is positioned on the lower isolator.

9. Raise the axle with the hydraulic jack.
10. Install the shock absorber to the axle bracket and tighten to 85 ft. lbs. (115 Nm).
11. Remove the supports and lower the vehicle.
12. Tighten the stabilizer bar links to 73 ft. lbs. (99 Nm).

REAR SUSPENSION

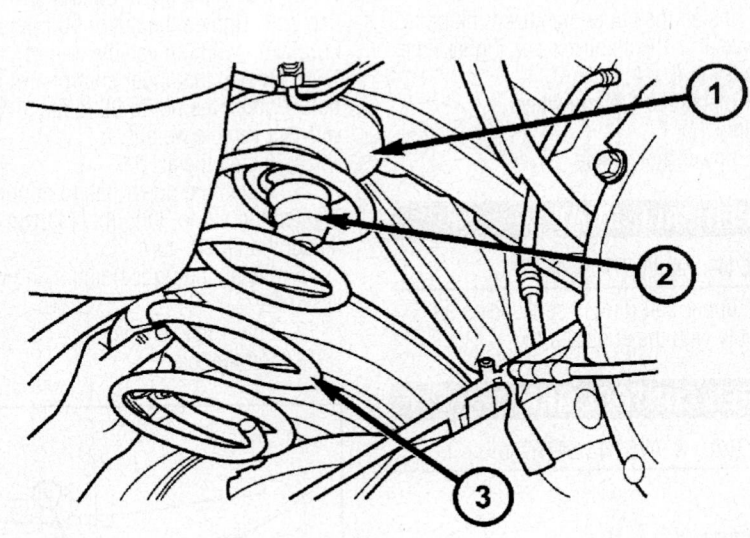

1 - UPPER INSULATOR
2 - JOUNCE BUMPER
3 - COIL SPRING

Fig. 187 Rear coil spring

CONTROL LINKS

REMOVAL & INSTALLATION

See Figure 188.

1. Raise and support the vehicle.
2. Support the rear axle with a jack.
3. Remove the rear tire right side only.
4. Remove the upper link (2) bolt at the frame.
5. Remove the lower link nut at the stabilizer bar.
6. Remove stabilizer link.

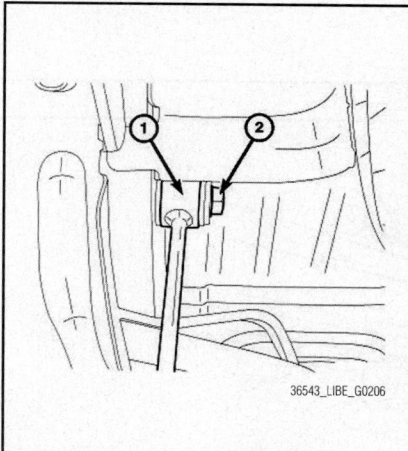

Fig. 188 Remove the upper link bolt

To install:

7. Install the upper bolt for the stabilizer link to the frame and tighten to 75 ft. lbs. (102 Nm).
8. Install the stabilizer link to the stabilizer bar.
9. Install the nut and tighten to 85 ft. lbs. (115 Nm) with full vehicle weight.
10. Install the spare tire right side only.
11. Remove the jack and lower the vehicle.

LOWER CONTROL ARMS

REMOVAL & INSTALLATION

Left Side

See Figure 189.

1. See all applicable precautions before beginning service procedures.
2. Raise the vehicle and support the rear axle.
3. Remove the fuel tank.
4. Remove the lower suspension arm nut and bolt from the axle bracket.

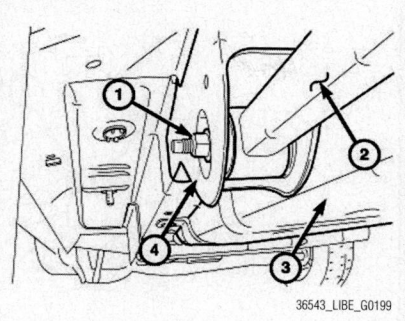

Fig. 189 Lower Control Arm removal— Left Rear

5. Remove the nut and bolt from the frame rail and remove the lower suspension arm.

To install:

➥**All torques should be done with vehicle on the ground with full vehicle weight.**

6. Position the lower suspension arm in the frame rail.
7. Install the frame rail bracket bolt and nut. Tighten to 120 ft. lbs. (163 Nm) with full vehicle weight.
8. Position the lower suspension arm in the axle bracket.
9. Install the axle bracket bolt and nut. Tighten to 150 ft. lbs. (203 Nm) with full vehicle weight.
10. Install the fuel tank.
11. Remove the supports and lower the vehicle.

Right Side

See Figure 190.

1. See all applicable precautions before beginning service procedures.

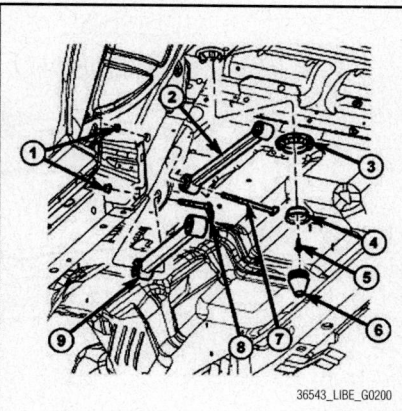

Fig. 190 Lower Control Arm removal— Right Rear

2. Raise the vehicle and support the rear axle.
3. Remove the lower suspension arm nut and bolt from the axle bracket.
4. Remove the exhaust from the mid and rear hanger rubber isolators to allow the exhaust system to lower enough to remove the bolt at the frame rail.
5. Remove the nut (1) and bolt (8) from the frame rail and remove the lower suspension arm (9).

To install:

➥**All torques should be done with vehicle on the ground with full vehicle weight.**

6. Position the lower suspension arm in the frame rail.
7. Install the frame rail bracket bolt and nut. Tighten to 120 ft. lbs. (163 Nm). with full vehicle weight.
8. Install the exhaust back in the mid and rear hanger rubber isolators.
9. Position the lower suspension arm in the axle bracket.
10. Install the axle bracket bolt and nut. Tighten to 150 ft. lbs. (203 Nm). with full vehicle weight.
11. Remove the supports and lower the vehicle.

SHOCK ABSORBER

REMOVAL & INSTALLATION

See Figure 191.

1. See all applicable precautions before beginning service procedures.
2. Raise and support the vehicle. Position a hydraulic jack under the axle to support the axle.

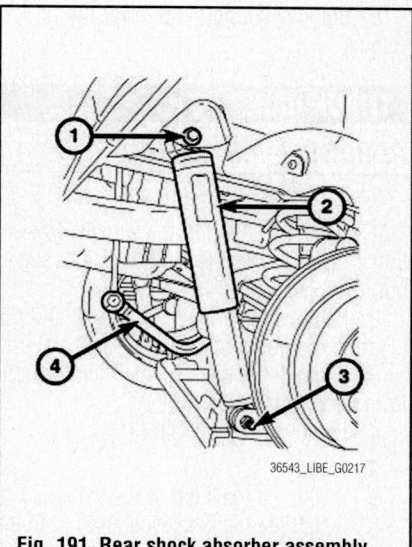

Fig. 191 Rear shock absorber assembly

Do not allow the axle to hang from the upper suspension arm ball joint.

3. Remove the upper nut and bolt from the frame bracket .

4. Remove the lower nut and bolt from the axle bracket. Remove the shock absorber.

To install:

5. Install the shock absorber in the frame bracket and install the bolt and nut.

6. Install the shock absorber in the axle bracket and install the bolt and nut.

7. Remove the supports and lower the vehicle.

8. Tighten the upper mounting nuts to 80 ft. lbs. (108 Nm). Tighten the lower mounting nuts to 85 ft. lbs. (115 Nm).

STABILIZER BAR

REMOVAL & INSTALLATION

See Figure 192.

1. Raise and support the vehicle.

2. Remove the stabilizer nut (3) at the bar (5).

3. Remove the stabilizer links (4) from the stabilizer bar (5).

4. Remove the stabilizer bar bolts (1) from the axle.

5. Remove the stabilizer bar (5).

To install:

6. Position the stabilizer bar on the axle. Ensure the bar is centered with equal spacing on both sides. Tighten the bolts to 35 ft. lbs. (47 Nm).

7. Install the stabilizer links to the bar. Tighten the nuts to 65 ft. lbs. (88 Nm) with full vehicle weight.

8. Remove support and lower the vehicle.

TRACK BAR

REMOVAL & INSTALLATION

See Figures 193 and 194.

1. Raise and support the vehicle. Position a hydraulic jack under the axle to support the axle.

2. Remove the track bar flag bolt and nut (1) from the frame bracket (2).

3. Remove the track bar bolt and nut (2) from the axle bracket (3).

4. Remove the track bar (1).

To install:

5. Install the track bar to the vehicle.

6. Install the track bar bolt and nut in the frame bracket.

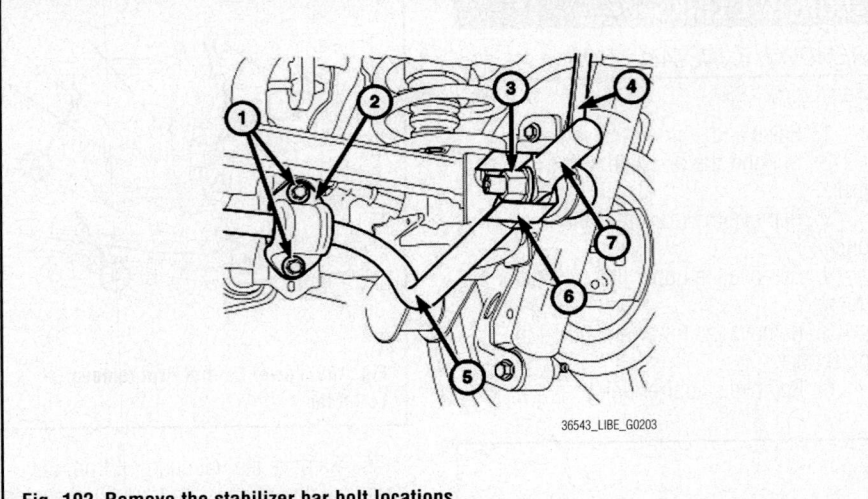

Fig. 192 Remove the stabilizer bar bolt locations

36543_LIBE_G0203

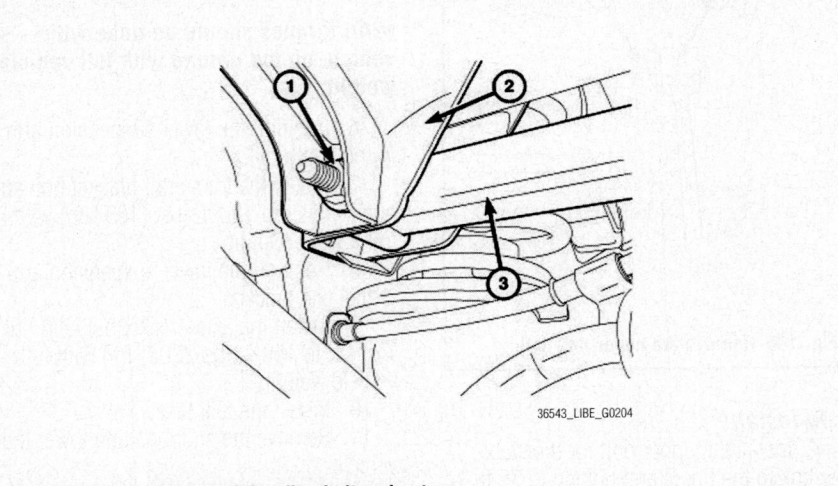

Fig. 193 Remove the track bar flag bolt and nut

36543_LIBE_G0204

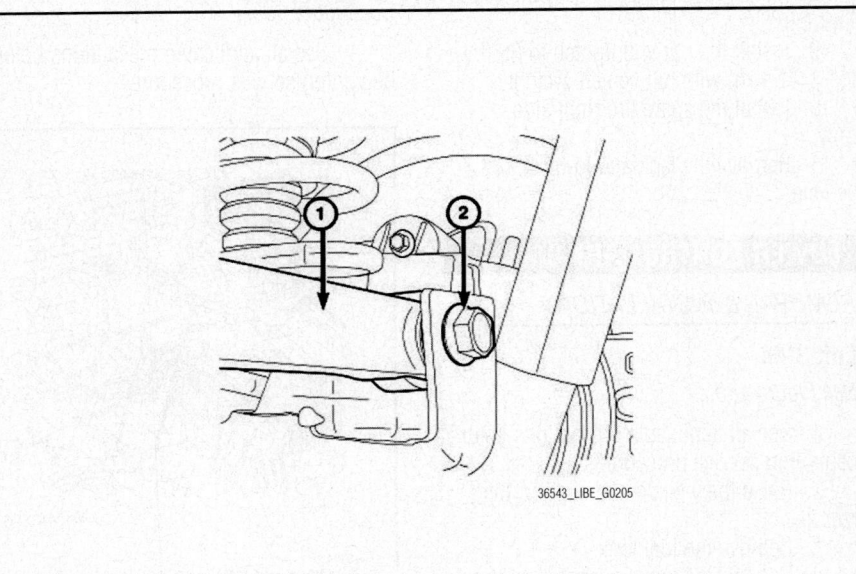

Fig. 194 Remove the track bar bolt and nut

36543_LIBE_G0205

7. Install the track bar into the axle bracket.

8. Install the track bar bolt and nut in the axle bracket.

9. Remove the supports and lower the vehicle.

10. Tighten the body side mounting bolt/nut to 135 ft. lbs. (183 Nm).

11. Tighten the axle side mounting bolt/nut to 130 ft. lbs. (176 Nm).

UPPER CONTROL ARMS

REMOVAL & INSTALLATION

Left Side

See Figure 195.

1. See all applicable precautions before beginning service procedures.

2. Raise and support the vehicle.

3. Support the rear axle.

4. Lower the fuel tank in order to gain access to the bolt.

5. Remove the upper suspension arm nut and bolt from the axle bracket.

6. Remove the nut and bolt (1) from the frame rail and remove the upper suspension arm (2).

To install:

➡**All torques should be done with vehicle on the ground with full vehicle weight.**

7. Position the upper suspension arm in the frame rail bracket.

8. Install the mounting bolt and nut. Tighten to 70 ft. lbs. (95 Nm) with full vehicle weight.

9. Position the upper suspension arm in the axle bracket.

10. Install the mounting bolt and nut. Tighten to 85 ft. lbs. (115 Nm) with full vehicle weight.

11. Raise the fuel tank back into place and secure.

12. Remove the supports and lower the vehicle.

Right Side

See Figure 196.

1. See all applicable precautions before beginning service procedures.

2. Raise and support the vehicle.

3. Support the rear axle.

4. Remove the upper suspension arm nut and bolt (1) from the axle bracket.

5. Remove the nut (3) and flag bolt from the frame rail and remove the upper suspension arm (2).

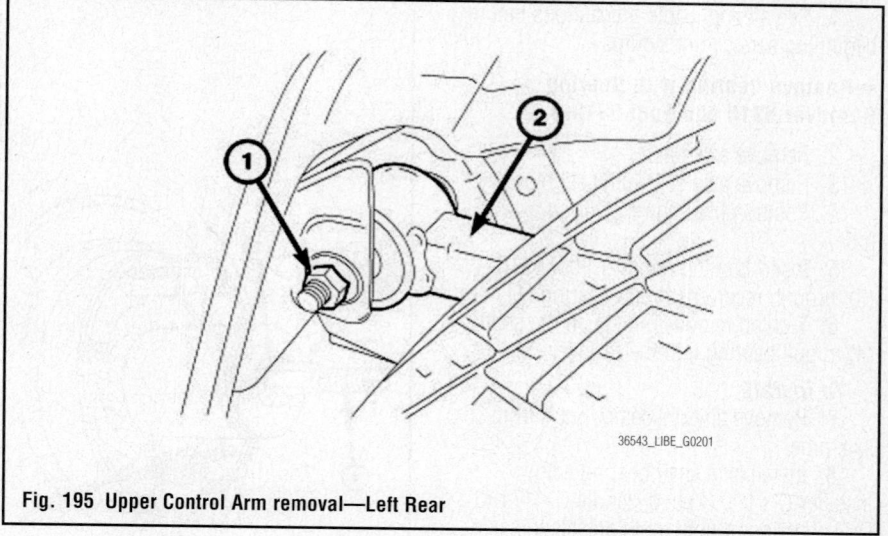

Fig. 195 Upper Control Arm removal—Left Rear

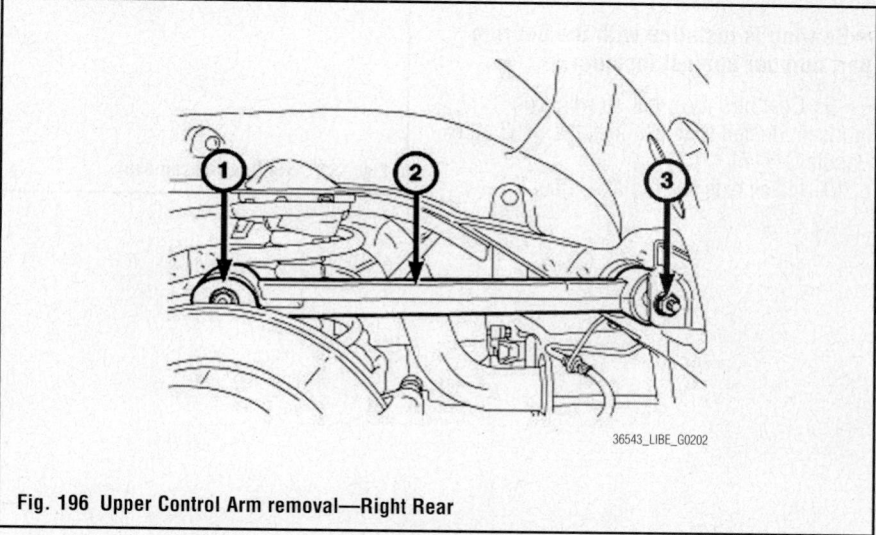

Fig. 196 Upper Control Arm removal—Right Rear

To install:

➡**All torques should be done with vehicle on the ground with full vehicle weight.**

6. Position the upper suspension arm in the frame rail bracket.

7. Install the mounting flag bolt and nut. Tighten to 70 ft. lbs. (95 Nm) with full vehicle weight.

8. Position the upper suspension arm in the axle bracket.

9. Install the mounting bolt and nut. Tighten to 85 ft. lbs. (115 Nm) with full vehicle weight.

10. Remove the supports and lower the vehicle.

WHEEL BEARINGS

REMOVAL & INSTALLATION

See Figures 197 through 199.

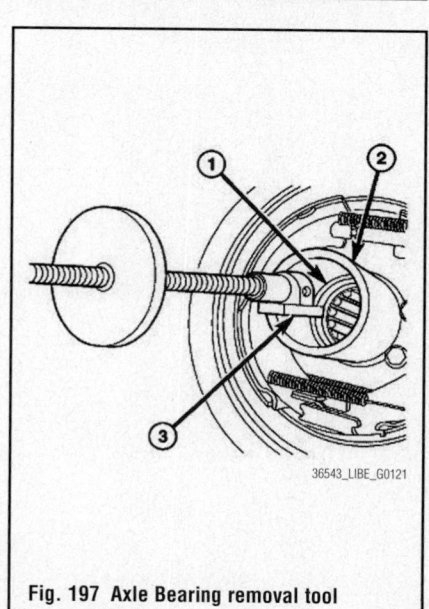

Fig. 197 Axle Bearing removal tool positioning

1. See all applicable precautions before beginning service procedures.

➡**Remove bearing with Bearing Remover 6310 and Foot 6310-9.**

2. Remove axle shaft.

3. Remove axle seal with seal pick.

4. Position bearing receiver on axle tube.

5. Insert bearing remover Foot 6310-9 (3) through receiver (2) and bearing (1).

6. Tighten remove nut (1) on the shaft (4) to pull bearing into the receiver (3).

To install:

7. Remove any old sealer/burrs from axle tube.

8. Install axle shaft bearing with Installer C-4198 (1) and Handle C-4171 (2). Drive bearing in until tool contacts the axle tube.

➡**Bearing is installed with the bearing part number against installer.**

9. Coat new axle seal lip with axle lubricant. Install seal with Installer 8493 and Handle C-4171.

10. Install axle shaft in axle tube.

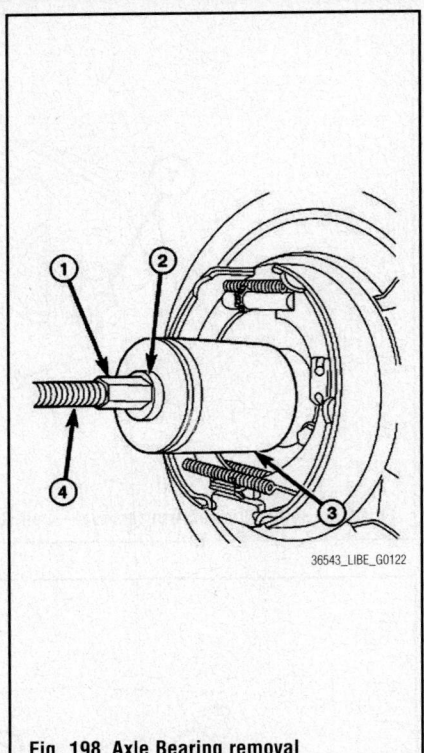

36543_LIBE_G0122

Fig. 198 Axle Bearing removal

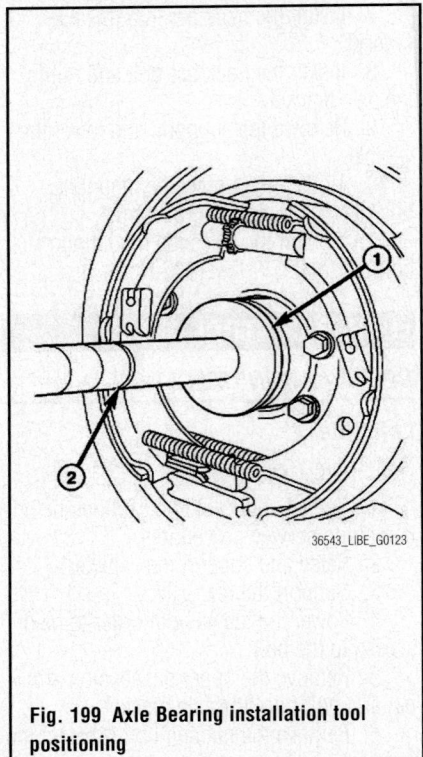

36543_LIBE_G0123

Fig. 199 Axle Bearing installation tool positioning

SPECIFICATIONS AND MAINTENANCE CHARTS

ENGINE AND VEHICLE IDENTIFICATION

		Engine						Model Year	
Code ①	Liters (cc)	Cu. In.	Cyl.	Fuel Sys.	Engine Type	Eng. Mfg.	Code ②		Year
③	2.4 (2429)	148	L4	SMPI	DOHC	Chrysler	8		2008
④	2.4 (2429)	148	L4	SMPI	DOHC	Chrysler	9		2009

DOHC: Double Overhead Camshaft

SMFI: Sequential Multi-port Fuel Injection

① 8th position of VIN

② 10th position of VIN

③ Non-Turbocharged model
  2008 VIN B, 2009 VIN 9

④ Turbocharged model
  2008 VIN 8 or E, 2009 VIN 8

36543_PTCR_C0001

GENERAL ENGINE SPECIFICATIONS

Year	Model	Engine Displacement Liters	Net Horsepower @ rpm	Net Torque @ rpm (ft. lbs.)	Bore x Stroke (in.)	Com- pression Ratio	Oil Pressure @ rpm
2008	PT Cruiser LX	2.4	150@5,100	165@4,000	3.445x3.976	9.5:1	25-80@3000
	PT Cruiser Touring	2.4	150@5,100	165@4,000	3.445x3.976	9.5:1	25-80@3000
2009	PT Cruiser LX	2.4	150@5,100	165@4,000	3.445x3.976	9.5:1	25-80@3000
	PT Cruiser Touring	2.4	150@5,100	165@4,000	3.445x3.976	9.5:1	25-80@3000
	PT Cruiser Limited	2.4	①	①	3.445x3.976	8.1:1	25-80@3000

① Turbocharged: 180 HP @ 5200 rpm, 210 ft. lbs. TQ @ 2,800 - 4,000 rpm.

36543_PTCR_C0002

ENGINE TUNE-UP SPECIFICATIONS

Year	Engine Displacement Liters	Spark Plug Gap (in.)	Ignition Timing (deg.)	Fuel Pump (psi)	Idle Speed (rpm)	Valve Clearance In.	Valve Clearance Ex.
2008	2.4	①	②	53-63	③	HYD	HYD
2009	2.4	①	②	53-63	③	HYD	HYD

NOTE: The Vehicle Emission Control Information label often reflects specification changes made during production.

The label figures must be used if they differ from those in this chart.

HYD: Hydraulic

① 2.4L Turbo 0.050, 2.4L Non-turbo 0.040

② Ignition timing is regulated by the Powertrain Control Module (PCM), and cannot be adjusted.

③ Idle speed is controlled by the Powertrain Control Module (PCM), and cannot be adjusted.

36543_PTCR_C0003

CAPACITIES

Year	Model	Engine Displacemen Liters	Engine ID/VIN	Engine Oil with Filter (qts.)	Transaxle (pts.) 5-Spd	Transaxle (pts.) Auto.	Fuel Tank (gal.)	Cooling System (qts.)
2008	PT Cruiser	2.4	All	5.0	①	②	15.0	6.5
2009	PT Cruiser	2.4	All	5.0	①	②	15.0	6.5

NOTE: All capacities are approximate. Add fluid gradually and ensure a proper fluid level is obtained.

① Manual transaxle NV T350: 5.0 - 5.6 pts.

② Automatic transaxle estimated service fill: 8.0 pts.

  Automatic transaxle overhaul fill capacity with torque converter empty: 17.2 pts.

36543_PTCR_C0004

FLUID SPECIFICATIONS

Year	Model	Engine Displacement Liters	Engine ID/VIN	Engine Oil	Auto. Trans.	Manual Trans.	Power Steering Fluid	Brake Master Cylinder
2008	PT Cruiser	2.4	All	5W-30	①	①	②	③
2009	PT Cruiser	2.4	All	5W-30	①	①	②	③

DOT: Department Of Transportation

① MOPAR® ATF+4 Automatic Transmission Fluid or equivalent.

② MOPAR® Power Steering Fluid+4, MOPAR® ATF+4 Automatic Transmission Fluid or equivalent.

③ MOPAR® DOT 3, SAE J1703 should be used. If DOT 3, SAE J1703 brake fluid is not available, then DOT 4 is acceptable. Use only recommended brake fluids.

36543_PTCR_C0005

VALVE SPECIFICATIONS

Year	Engine Displacement Liters	Seat Angle (deg.)	Face Angle (deg.)	Spring Test Pressure (lbs. @ in.)	Spring Installed Height (in.)	Stem-to-Guide Clearance (in.) Intake	Stem-to-Guide Clearance (in.) Exhaust	Stem Diameter (in.) Intake	Stem Diameter (in.) Exhaust
2008	2.4	44.5-45.0	44.5-45.0	134@ 1.152	1.496	0.0018-0.0025	0.0029-0.0037	0.2337-0.2344	0.2326-0.2333
2009	2.4	44.5-45.0	44.5-45.0	134@ 1.152	1.496	0.0018-0.0025	0.0029-0.0037	0.2337-0.2344	0.2326-0.2333

36543_PTCR_C0006

CAMSHAFT AND BEARING SPECIFICATIONS CHART

All measurements are given in inches.

Year	Engine Displ. Liters	Engine ID/VIN	Journal Dia.	Brg. Oil Clearance	Shaft End-play	Runout	Journal Bore	Lobe Height Intake	Exhaust
2008	2.4	All	1.0220-1.0230	0.0009-0.0025	0.0019-0.0066	NS	NS	0.3240	0.2590
2009	2.4	All	1.0220-1.0230	0.0009-0.0025	0.0019-0.0066	NS	NS	0.3240	0.2590

NS: Manufacturer does not supply information.

36543_PTCR_C0007

CRANKSHAFT AND CONNECTING ROD SPECIFICATIONS

All measurements are given in inches.

Year	Engine Displacement Liters	Crankshaft Main Brg. Journal Dia.	Main Brg. Oil Clearance	Shaft End-play	Thrust on No.	Connecting Rod Journal Diameter	Oil Clearance	Side Clearance
2008	2.4	2.3620-2.3625	0.0007-0.0024	0.0035-0.0094	3	1.9680-1.9685	0.0009-0.0027	0.0050-0.0150
2009	2.4	2.3610-2.3625	0.0007-0.0023	0.0035-0.0094	3	1.9670-1.9685	0.0009-0.0027	0.0051-0.0150

36543_PTCR_C0008

PISTON AND RING SPECIFICATIONS

All measurements are given in inches.

Year	Engine Displacement Liters	Piston Clearance	Ring Gap Top Compression	Bottom Compression	Oil Control	Ring Side Clearance Top Compression	Bottom Compression	Oil Control
2008	2.4 ①	0.0007-0.0020 ②	0.0090-0.0200	0.009-0.018	0.009-0.025	0.0011-0.0031	0.0011-0.0031	0.0004-0.007
	2.4 ③	0.0018-0.0025 ②	0.0078-0.0157	0.0070-0.0150	0.0050-0.0250	0.0011-0.0031	0.0011-0.0031	0.0010-0.0060
2009	2.4 ①	0.0007-0.0020 ②	0.0090-0.0200	0.009-0.018	0.009-0.025	0.0011-0.0031	0.0011-0.0031	0.0004-0.007
	2.4 ③	0.0018-0.0025 ②	0.0078-0.0157	0.0070-0.0150	0.0050-0.0250	0.0011-0.0031	0.0011-0.0031	0.0010-0.0060

① Non-turbocharged engine.

② Non-turbocharged engine measured at 0.551 inches from bottom of skirt.

  Turbocharged engine measured at 0.886 inches from bottom of skirt.

③ Turbocharged engine.

36543_PTCR_C0009

TORQUE SPECIFICATIONS

All readings in ft. lbs.

Year	Engine Displacement Liters	Cylinder Head Bolts	Main Bearing Bolts	Rod Bearing Bolts	Crankshaft Damper Bolts	Flywheel Bolts	Manifold		Spark Plugs	Oil Pan Drain Plug
							Intake	Exhaust		
2008	2.4	①	②	③	100	70	④	17	13	20
2009	2.4	①	②	③	100	70	④	17	13	20

① Step 1: With bearing cap bed plate installed and No. 4 piston journal at TDC, move crank forward and reverse and wedge crank in forward position.

Step 2: Tighten bolts 1-10 to 30 ft. lbs. in sequence.

Step 3: Remove wedge tool and retighten bolts 1-10 to 30 ft. lbs.

Step 4: Tighten bolts 11-20 to 21 ft. lbs. in sequence.

Step 5: Tighten bolts 1-10 to 55 ft. lbs. in sequence.

Step 6: Retighten bolts 11-20 to 21 ft. lbs. in sequence.

After the main bearing bed plate is installed, check the crankshaft turning torque. The turning torque should not exceed 50 inch lbs.

② M8 bolts: 21 ft. lbs.
M11 bolts: 55 ft. lbs.

③ Step 1: 20 ft. lbs.
Step 2: Plus 1/4 turn

④ Lower manifold: non turbo models 105 inch lbs.
Lower manifold: turbo models aluminum 250 inch lbs, plastic 105 inch lbs.
Upper manifold: non turbo models 105 inch lbs.
Upper manifold: turbo models aluminum 250 inch lbs, plastic 105 inch lbs.

36543_PTCR_C0010

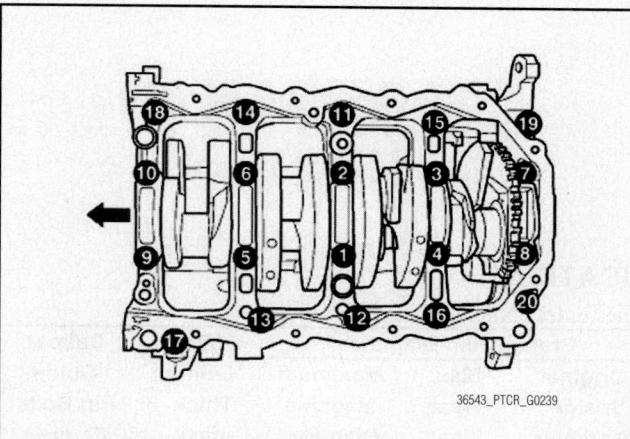

36543_PTCR_G0239

Fig. 1 Main bearing torque sequence

WHEEL ALIGNMENT SPECIFICATIONS

Year	Model		Caster Range (+/-Deg.)	Caster Preferred Setting (Deg.)	Camber Range (+/-Deg.)	Camber Preferred Setting (Deg.)	Toe-in (+/-Deg.)
2008	PT Cruiser	F	1.00	+2.45	0.40	0.00	+0.10 +/-0.10
		R	—	—	0.25	0.00	+0.30 +/-0.20
2009	PT Cruiser	F	1.00	+2.45	0.40	0.00	+0.10 +/-0.10
		R	—	—	0.25	0.00	+0.30 +/-0.20

F: Front

R: Rear

36543_PTCR_C0011

TIRE, WHEEL AND BALL JOINT SPECIFICATIONS

Year	Model	OEM Tires Standard	OEM Tires Optional	Tire Pressures (psi) Front	Tire Pressures (psi) Rear	Wheel Size	Ball Joint Inspection	Lug Nuts (ft. lbs.)
2008	PT Cruiser LX	P195/65R15	P205/55R16	①	①	15 inch	②	100
	PT Cruiser Special	P205/55R16	None	①	①	16 inch	②	100
	PT Cruiser Touring	P205/55R16	P205/50R17	①	①	16 inch	②	100
2009	PT Cruiser LX	P195/65R15	None	①	①	15 inch	②	100
	PT Cruiser Touring	P205/55R16	P205/50R17	①	①	16 inch	②	100
	PT Cruiser Limited	P205/50R17	None	①	①	17 inch	②	100

OEM: Original Equipment Manufacturer

PSI: Pounds Per Square Inch

① See placard on vehicle

② Replace if any measurable movement is found

36543_PTCR_C0012

BRAKE SPECIFICATIONS

All measurements in inches unless noted

Year	Model		Brake Disc Original Thickness	Brake Disc Minimum Thickness	Brake Disc Maximum Run-out	Brake Drum Diameter Original Inside Diameter	Brake Drum Diameter Max. Wear Limit	Brake Drum Diameter Maximum Machine Diameter	Min. Lining Thickness	Caliper Guide Pin Bolts (ft. lbs.)
2008	PT Cruiser	F	0.902-0.909	0.843	0.004	NA	NA	NA	0.040	26
	Base	R	0.344-0.364	0.285	0.005	①	①	①	NS	16
	PT Cruiser	F	1.099-1.106	1.039	0.004	NA	NA	NA	0.040	26
	Performance	R	0.463-0.482	0.404	0.005	NA	NA	NA	0.040	16
2009	PT Cruiser	F	0.902-0.909	0.843	0.004	NA	NA	NA	0.040	26
	Base	R	0.344-0.364	0.285	0.005	①	①	①	NS	16
	PT Cruiser	F	1.099-1.106	1.039	0.004	NA	NA	NA	0.040	26
	Performance	R	0.463-0.482	0.404	0.005	NA	NA	NA	0.040	16

NA: Does not apply

NS: Manufacturer does not supply information.

F: Front

R: Rear

① Check drum face for specifications

36543_PTCR_C0013

SCHEDULED MAINTENANCE INTERVALS
Chrysler—PT Cruiser

TO BE SERVICED	TYPE OF SERVICE	VEHICLE MILEAGE INTERVAL (x1000)														
		6	12	18	24	30	36	42	48	54	60	66	72	78	84	90
Engine oil & filter* ①	R	✓	✓	✓	✓	✓	✓	✓	✓	✓	✓	✓	✓	✓	✓	✓
Rotate tires	I/Adj	✓	✓	✓	✓	✓	✓	✓	✓	✓	✓	✓	✓	✓	✓	✓
Brake linings	S/I			✓			✓			✓			✓			✓
Engine air cleaner filter	R					✓					✓					✓
Make-up air filter	R					✓					✓					✓
Spark plugs	R					✓					✓					✓
Tie rod ends & boot seals	I					✓					✓					✓
Generator drive belt tension	I/Adj					✓					✓					✓
Parking brake ②	Adj					✓										
PCV valve ③	S/I										✓					✓
Engine coolant ④	R										✓					
Ignition cables	R										✓					
Engine timing belt	R	Every 102,000 miles														
Power Steering fluid	I/F	Once a month														
Transaxle fluid	I/F	Once a month														
Windshield washer fluid	I/F	At every fuel stop														
Tire pressure	I/Adj	Once a month														
Brake fluid level	I/F	Once a month														
Brake hoses & lines	S/I	At each oil change														
Coolant level, hoses, clamps	I/F	Once a month and at each oil change														
Engine oil level	I/F	At every fuel stop														
Battery & terminals	S/I	Once a month														
Lights & electrical items	S/I	Once a month														
Radiator seals	S/I	Once a month														
Exhaust system	S/I	At each oil change														
CV joints & front suspension	S/I	At each oil change														

R: Replace   S/I: Service or Inspect   I/R: Inspect and replace if necessary   L: Lubricate   I/F Inspect and fill as needed   I/Adj: Inspect and adjust

① Turbocharged model Engine oil and filter change every 5,000 miles.

② On vehicles equipped with four-wheel disc brakes, adjust parking brake every 30,000 miles.

③ I/R PCV valve at 60,000 miles, then every 30,000 miles after that and replace if necessary. Not required if replaced at previous inspection.

④ Engine coolant: flush and replace at 60 months or 102,000 miles, whichever occurs first.

Engine oil & filter change: change every 6,000 miles.

Rotate tires every 6,000 miles. Turbocharged every 5,000 miles.

Brake linings: inspect every 18,000 miles. Turbocharged every 20,000 miles.

Air filters: inspect every 30,000 miles. Replace as necessary.

Spark plugs: replace every 30,000 miles.

Ignition cables: replace every 60,000 miles.

36543_PTCR_C0014

SCHEDULED MAINTENANCE INTERVALS
Chrysler—PT Cruiser

ALTERNATIVE SPECIFICATIONS (These driving conditions apply to most vehicles): day and night temperatures below 32 degrees F (0 degrees C); stop and go driving; extensive engine idling; driving in dusty conditions; more than 50% of driving is at sustained high speeds during hot weather; above 90 degrees F (32 degrees C); trailer towing; E85 fuel; commercial service.

...change the oil every 3,000 miles or every 3 months, whichever comes first.

...inspect the brake linings every 12,000 miles.

...inspect the air filters every 1,000 miles. Replace as necessary.

...automatic transaxle fluid replaced every 60,000 miles, manual transaxle fluid replaced every 48,000 miles for trailer towing or commercial use.

*Oil Change Indicator System

On Electronic Vehicle Information Center (EVIC) equipped vehicles, "Oil Change Required" is displayed in the EVIC and a single chime sounds, indicating that an oil change is necessary. On non-EVIC equipped vehicles, "Change Oil" flashes in the instrument cluster and a single chime sounds indicating that an oil change is necessary. Illumination of the oil change message is based on the operating conditions of the vehicle. When the message is illuminated, the vehicle must be serviced within 500 miles.

The oil change indicator will not monitor the time since the last oil change. Change the oil if it has been more than 6 months since the last oil change, even if the oil change indicator message is not illuminated.

Under no circumstances should oil change intervals exceed 6,000 miles or 6 months, whichever comes first.

To reset the oil change indicator, perform the following procedure:

1. Turn the ignition switch to the ON position. Do not start the engine.

2. Fully press the accelerator pedal 3 times within 10 seconds.

3. Turn the ignition switch to the LOCK position.

If the indicator message illuminates when the vehicle is started, repeat the procedure.

36543_PTCR_C0015

PRECAUTIONS

Before servicing any vehicle, please be sure to read all of the following precautions, which deal with personal safety, prevention of component damage, and important points to take into consideration when servicing a motor vehicle:

• Never open, service or drain the radiator or cooling system when the engine is hot; serious burns can occur from the steam and hot coolant.

• Observe all applicable safety precautions when working around fuel. Whenever servicing the fuel system, always work in a well-ventilated area. Do not allow fuel spray or vapors to come in contact with a spark, open flame, or excessive heat (a hot drop light, for example). Keep a dry chemical fire extinguisher near the work area. Always keep fuel in a container specifically designed for fuel storage; also, always properly seal fuel containers to avoid the possibility of fire or explosion. Refer to the additional fuel system precautions later in this section.

• Fuel injection systems often remain pressurized, even after the engine has been turned **OFF**. The fuel system pressure must be relieved before disconnecting any fuel lines. Failure to do so may result in fire and/or personal injury.

• Brake fluid often contains polyglycol ethers and polyglycols. Avoid contact with the eyes and wash your hands thoroughly after handling brake fluid. If you do get brake fluid in your eyes, flush your eyes with clean, running water for 15 minutes. If eye irritation persists, or if you have taken

brake fluid internally, IMMEDIATELY seek medical assistance.

• The EPA warns that prolonged contact with used engine oil may cause a number of skin disorders, including cancer. You should make every effort to minimize your exposure to used engine oil. Protective gloves should be worn when changing oil. Wash your hands and any other exposed skin areas as soon as possible after exposure to used engine oil. Soap and water, or waterless hand cleaner should be used.

• All new vehicles are now equipped with an air bag system, often referred to as a Supplemental Restraint System (SRS) or Supplemental Inflatable Restraint (SIR) system. The system must be disabled before performing service on or around system components, steering column, instrument panel components, wiring and sensors. Failure to follow safety and disabling procedures could result in accidental air bag deployment, possible personal injury and unnecessary system repairs.

• Always wear safety goggles when working with, or around, the air bag system. When carrying a non-deployed air bag, be sure the bag and trim cover are pointed away from your body. When placing a non-deployed air bag on a work surface, always face the bag and trim cover upward, away from the surface. This will reduce the motion of the module if it is accidentally deployed. Refer to the additional air bag system precautions later in this section.

• Clean, high quality brake fluid from a sealed container is essential to the safe and

proper operation of the brake system. You should always buy the correct type of brake fluid for your vehicle. If the brake fluid becomes contaminated, completely flush the system with new fluid. Never reuse any brake fluid. Any brake fluid that is removed from the system should be discarded. Also, do not allow any brake fluid to come in contact with a painted surface; it will damage the paint.

• Never operate the engine without the proper amount and type of engine oil; doing so WILL result in severe engine damage.

• Timing belt maintenance is extremely important. Many models utilize an interference-type, non-freewheeling engine. If the timing belt breaks, the valves in the cylinder head may strike the pistons, causing potentially serious (also time-consuming and expensive) engine damage. Refer to the maintenance interval charts for the recommended replacement interval for the timing belt, and to the timing belt section for belt replacement and inspection.

• Disconnecting the negative battery cable on some vehicles may interfere with the functions of the on-board computer system(s) and may require the computer to undergo a relearning process once the negative battery cable is reconnected.

• When servicing drum brakes, only disassemble and assemble one side at a time, leaving the remaining side intact for reference.

• Only an MVAC-trained, EPA-certified automotive technician should service the air conditioning system or its components.

BRAKES

GENERAL INFORMATION

PRECAUTIONS

• The antilock brake system uses an electronic control module known as the Antilock Brake Module (ABM). This module is designed to withstand normal current draws associated with vehicle operation. Care must be taken to avoid overloading the circuits.

• In testing for open or short circuits, do not ground or apply voltage to any of the circuits unless instructed to do so for a diagnostic procedure.

• These circuits should only be tested using a high impedance multi-meter or the designated scan tool as described in this section. Power should never be removed or

applied to any control module with the ignition in the ON position. Before removing or connecting battery cables, fuses, or connectors, always turn the ignition to the OFF position.

• The ABM 47-way connector should never be connected or disconnected with the ignition switch in the ON position.

• This vehicle utilizes active wheel speed sensors. Do not apply voltage to wheel speed sensors at any time.

• Use only factory wiring harnesses. Do not cut or splice wiring to the brake circuits. The addition of aftermarket electrical equipment (car phone, radar detector, citizen band radio, trailer lighting, trailer brakes, etc.) on a vehicle equipped with antilock brakes may

ANTI-LOCK BRAKE SYSTEM (ABS)

affect the function of the antilock brake system.

• Do not use rubber hoses or other parts not specifically specified for and ABS system. When using repair kits, replace all parts included in the kit. Partial or incorrect repair may lead to functional problems and require the replacement of components.

• When performing any service procedure on a vehicle equipped with ABS, do not apply a 12-volt power source to the ground circuit of the pump motor in the HCU. Doing this will damage the pump motor and will require replacement of the entire HCU.

• An attempt to remove or disconnect certain system components may result in improper system operation. Only those components with approved removal and installation procedures in this manual should be serviced.

• If welding work is to be performed on the vehicle using an electric arc welder, the ABM connector should be disconnected during the welding operation.

• Many components of the ABS are not serviceable and must be replaced as an assembly. Do not disassemble any component which is not designed to be serviced.

• Brake fluid will damage painted surfaces. If brake fluid is spilled on any painted surface, wash off with water immediately.

• Only the recommended jacking or hoisting positions for this vehicle are to be used whenever it is necessary to lift a vehicle.

• Lubricate rubber parts with clean, fresh brake fluid to ease assembly. Do not use shop air to clean parts; damage to rubber components may result.

• Use only DOT 3 brake fluid from an unopened container.

• If any hydraulic component or line is removed or replaced, it may be necessary to bleed the entire system.

• A clean repair area is essential. Always clean the reservoir and cap thoroughly before removing the cap. The slightest amount of dirt in the fluid may plug an orifice and impair the system function. Perform repairs after components have been thoroughly cleaned; use only denatured alcohol to clean components. Do not allow ABS components to come into contact with any substance containing mineral oil; this includes used shop rags.

WHEEL SPEED SENSORS

REMOVAL & INSTALLATION

Front

See Figures 2 through 5.

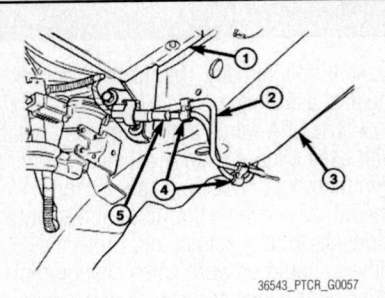

Fig. 3 Disconnect the wheel speed sensor cable connector (5) and routing clips (4)—left side

1. Before servicing the vehicle, refer to the Precautions Section.
2. Raise and safely support the vehicle.
3. For right side sensor, disconnect the wheel speed sensor cable connector (1) from the wiring harness on the inside of the frame rail above the front suspension crossmember. The connector has a locking tab which that must be pulled back before the connector release tab can be depressed, releasing the connection.
4. For left side sensor, disconnect the wheel speed sensor cable connector (5) from the wiring harness on the inside of the frame rail above the front suspension crossmember. The connector has a locking tab which must be pulled back before the connector release tab can be depressed, releasing the connection.
5. For left side sensor, remove the speed sensor cable routing clips (4) from the brake tube (2) on the inside of and under the frame rail (3).
6. Remove the wheel speed sensor cable (3) from the retainer on the brake hose bracket (2) mounted to the frame rail (6).

7. Remove the screw (3) fastening the wheel speed sensor (1) head to the knuckle (4).

✳✳ CAUTION

When removing a wheel speed sensor from the knuckle, do not use pliers on the sensor head. This may damage the sensor head. If the sensor has seized, use a hammer and a punch to tap the edge of the sensor head ear, rocking the sensor side-to-side until free.

8. Carefully pull the sensor head with heat shield (2) out of the knuckle. Separate the shield from the sensor head.
9. Remove the screw (5) securing the wheel speed sensor routing bracket to the rear of the strut (6). Remove the wheel speed sensor (1) from the vehicle.

To install:

✳✳ WARNING

Failure to install speed sensor cables properly may result in contact with moving parts or an over extension of cables causing an open circuit. Be sure that cables are installed, routed, and clipped properly.

10. Place the routing bracket of the wheel speed sensor against the mounting flange (rearward ear) on the rear of the strut. Install and tighten the mounting screw to 105 inch lbs. (12 Nm).
11. Place the heat shield on the wheel speed sensor head.
12. Install the wheel speed sensor head with heat shield on the knuckle. Install and

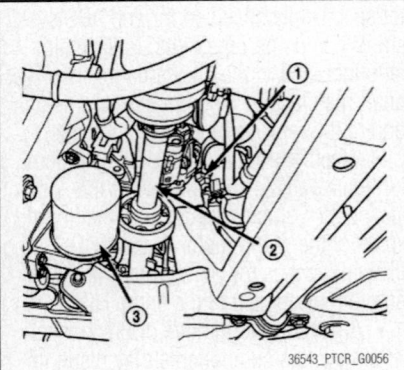

Fig. 2 Disconnect the wheel speed sensor cable connector (1)—right side

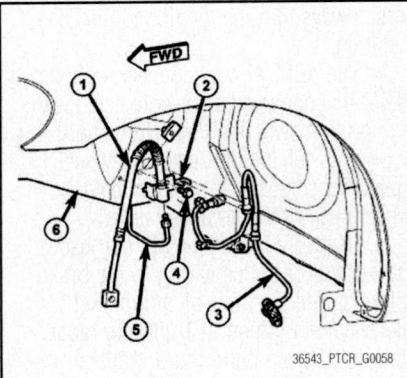

Fig. 4 Remove wheel speed sensor cable (3)

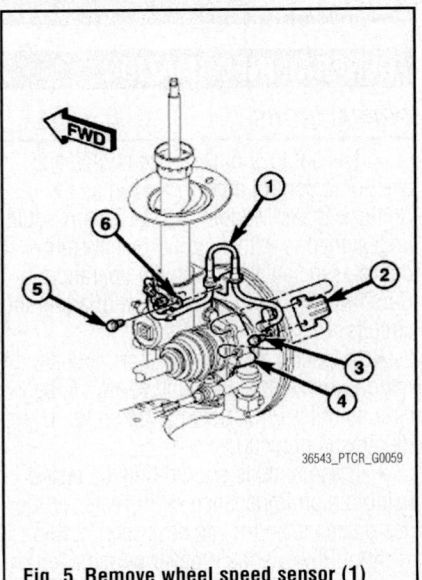

Fig. 5 Remove wheel speed sensor (1)

tighten the mounting screw to 105 inch lbs. (12 Nm).

13. From the sensor bracket on the strut, loop the harness end of the sensor cable (3) upward, then downward at the outside of the frame rail. Install the speed sensor cable grommet into the retainer on the brake hose bracket on the frame rail.

14. Right side sensor: Route the wheel speed sensor cable around the bottom of the frame rail and connect it to the wiring harness connector on the inside of the frame rail. Remember to push in the locking tab on the connector.

15. Left side sensor: Route the wheel speed sensor cable around the bottom of the frame rail and connect it to the wiring harness connector on the inside of the frame rail. Remember to push in the locking tab on the connector. Attach the speed sensor cable routing clips to the brake tube on the inside of and under the frame rail.

16. Lower the vehicle.

17. Perform the Diagnostic Verification Test and clear any faults.

Rear

See Figures 6 through 8.

1. Before servicing the vehicle, refer to the Precautions Section.

2. Raise and safely support the vehicle.

3. Disconnect the wheel speed sensor cable (5) connector at the body wiring harness (1). The connector has a locking tab which must be pulled back before the connector release tab can be depressed, releasing the connection.

4. Remove the wheel speed sensor cable connector from the body (4) mounted clip (2).

5. Remove the speed sensor cable routing clips (3) from the brake tube (6).

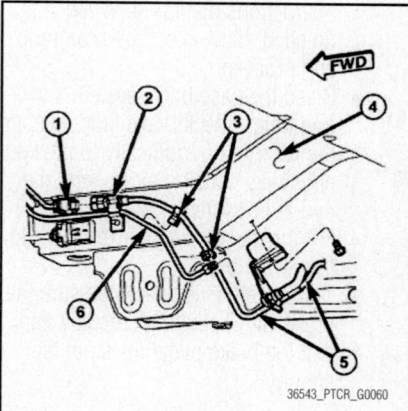

36543_PTCR_G0060

Fig. 6 Remove the wheel speed sensor cable connector (5) and routing clips (3)

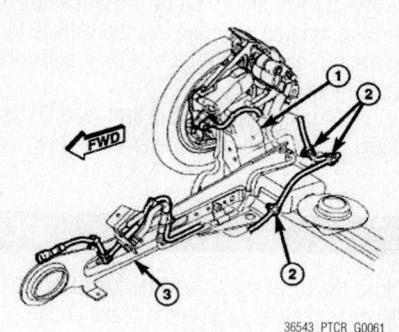

36543_PTCR_G0061

Fig. 7 Remove the wheel speed sensor routing clips (2) from the axle (1) and trailing arm (3)

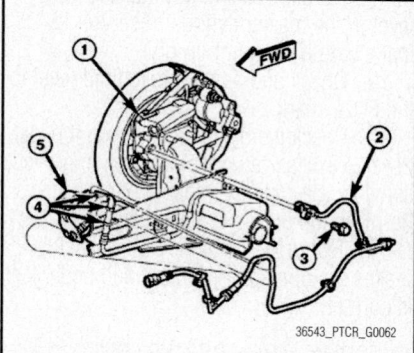

36543_PTCR_G0062

Fig. 8 Remove the wheel speed sensor

6. Remove the wheel speed sensor routing clips (2) from the axle (1) and trailing arm (3).

7. Remove the wheel speed sensor cable (2) from the retainer on the brake hose bracket (5).

8. Remove the wheel speed sensor cable from the routing clips (4) running along the brake hose.

9. Remove the screw (3) securing the antilock brake wheel speed sensor (2) head to the disc brake adapter (1) or drum brake support plate. Remove the sensor head from the adapter/support plate and remove sensor from vehicle.

To install:

※ WARNING

Failure to install speed sensor cables properly may result in contact with moving parts or an over extension of cables causing an open circuit. Be sure that cables are installed, routed, and clipped properly.

10. Insert the wheel speed sensor head into the disc brake adapter or drum brake support plate.

11. Install the mounting screw securing the wheel speed sensor in place. Tighten the mounting screw to 105 inch lbs. (12 Nm).

12. Install the routing clips securing the wheel speed sensor to the axle and its trailing arm.

13. Install wheel speed sensor cable into the routing clips on the brake hose.

14. Install the speed sensor cable grommet into the retainer on the brake hose bracket.

15. Install the speed sensor cable routing clips on the brake tube.

16. Connect the wheel speed sensor cable connector at the body wiring harness.

17. Install the wheel speed sensor cable connector into the routing clip mounting it to the vehicle's body.

18. Lower the vehicle.

19. Perform the Diagnostic Verification Test and clear any faults.

ABS VERIFICATION TEST

1. Before servicing the vehicle, refer to the Precautions Section.

※ CAUTION

To avoid possible serious or fatal injury, check brake capability is available before road testing.

➡ If the ABM (Anti-Lock Brake Module), SAS (Steering Angle Sensor), Dynamics Sensor was replaced, it must be initialized using the scan tool. If not initialized, the ABS indicator will flash continuously with no DTCs. To initialize the ABM and clear offsets have wheels pointing straight ahead and follow the directions on the scan tool. The drive test requires a 90 degree turn. If the Dynamics Sensor was replaced, test drive the vehicle by turning the vehicle left or right in a curving manner at a velocity between 6 and 15 mph (10 and 25 km/h).

2. Turn the ignition off.

3. Connect all previously disconnected components and connectors.

4. Verify all accessories are turned off and the battery is fully charged.

5. Verify that the ignition is on, with the scan tool, erase all Diagnostic Trouble Codes from All modules. Start the engine and allow it to run for 2 minutes and fully operate the system that was indicating the failure.

6. Turn the ignition off and wait 5 seconds. Turn the ignition on and using the scan tool, read DTCs from all modules.

7. If any Diagnostic Trouble Codes are

present, return to symptom list and trouble shoot new or recurring symptom.

➡ **For Sensor Signal and Pump Motor faults, the ABM must sense all 4 wheels at 7.5 mph (12 km/h) before it will extinguish the ABS indicator.**

8. If there are no DTCs present after turning ignition on, road test the vehicle for at least 5 minutes. Perform several anti-lock braking stops.

9. Again, with the scan tool read DTCs. If any DTCs are present, refer to the diag-

nostic test procedures and troubleshoot the new or recurring symptom.

10. If there are no Diagnostic Trouble Codes (DTCs) present, and the customer's concern can no longer be duplicated, the repair is complete.

BRAKES   BLEEDING THE BRAKE SYSTEM

BLEEDING PROCEDURE

1. Before servicing the vehicle, refer to the Precautions Section.

※ WARNING

Before removing the master cylinder cap, wipe it clean to prevent dirt and other foreign matter from dropping into the master cylinder reservoir.

※ WARNING

Use only Mopar® brake fluid, or equivalent, from a fresh, tightly sealed container. Brake fluid must conform to DOT 3 specifications.

Do not pump the brake pedal at any time while having a bleeder screw open during the bleeding process. This will only increase the amount of air in the system and make additional bleeding necessary.

Do not allow the master cylinder reservoir to run out of brake fluid while bleeding the system. An empty reservoir will allow additional air into the brake system. Check the fluid level frequently and add fluid as needed.

The following wheel circuit sequence for bleeding the brake hydraulic system should be used to ensure adequate removal of all trapped air from the hydraulic system:

- The Left rear wheel
- The Right front wheel
- The Right rear wheel
- The Left front wheel

2. Before servicing the vehicle, refer to the Precautions Section.

3. Attach a clear plastic hose to the bleeder screw and feed the hose into a clear jar containing enough fresh brake fluid to submerge the end of the hose.

4. Have a helper pump the brake pedal 3–4 times and hold it in the down position.

5. With the pedal in the down position, open the bleeder screw at least 1 full turn.

6. Once the brake pedal has dropped,

close the bleeder screw. After the bleeder screw is closed, release the brake pedal.

7. Repeat the above steps until all trapped air is removed from that wheel circuit (usually 4–5 times).

8. Bleed the remaining wheel circuits in the same manner until all air is removed from the brake system. Monitor the fluid level in the master cylinder reservoir to make sure it does not go dry.

9. Check and adjust brake fluid level to the FULL mark.

10. Check the brake pedal travel. If pedal travel is excessive or has not been improved, some air may still be trapped in the system. Re-bleed the brakes as necessary.

11. Test drive the vehicle to verify the brakes are operating properly and pedal feel is correct.

BLEEDING THE ABS SYSTEM

1. Before servicing the vehicle, refer to the Precautions Section.

➡ **The base brake hydraulic system must be bled anytime air enters the hydraulic system. The ABS must always be bled anytime it is suspected that the HCU has ingested air.**

➡ **Brake systems with ABS must be bled as two independent braking systems. The non-ABS portion of the brake system with ABS is to be bled the same as any non-ABS system.**

➡ **The ABS portion of the brake system must be bled separately. Use the following procedure to properly bleed the brake hydraulic system including the ABS.**

※ WARNING

During the brake bleeding procedure, be sure the brake fluid level remains close to the FULL level in the master cylinder fluid reservoir. Check the fluid level periodically during the bleeding procedure and add Mopar® DOT 3 brake fluid as required.

When bleeding the ABS system, the following bleeding sequence must be followed to insure complete and adequate bleeding:

- Make sure all hydraulic fluid lines are installed and properly tightened
- Connect the scan tool to the diagnostics connector. The connector is located under the lower steering column cover to the left of the steering column.
- Using the scan tool, check to make sure the ABS does not have any fault codes stored. If it does, clear them.

※ WARNING

When bleeding the brake system, wear safety glasses. A clear bleed tube must be attached to the bleeder screws and submerged in a clear container filled part way with clean brake fluid. Direct the flow of the brake fluid away from yourself and the painted surfaces of the vehicle. Brake fluid at high pressure may come out of the bleeder screws when opened.

- Bleed the base brake system using the standard pressure or manual bleeding procedure.
- Using the scan tool, select ECU VIEW, followed by ABS MISCELLANEOUS FUNCTIONS to access bleeding.. Follow the instructions displayed. When finished, disconnect the scan tool and proceed.
- Bleed the base brake system a second time. Check brake fluid level in the reservoir periodically to prevent emptying, causing air to enter the hydraulic system.
- Fill the master cylinder reservoir to the FULL level.
- Test drive the vehicle to be sure the brakes are operating correctly and that the brake pedal does not feel spongy

BRAKES   **FRONT DISC BRAKES**

✳✳ CAUTION

Dust and dirt accumulating on brake parts during normal use may contain asbestos fibers from production or aftermarket brake linings. Breathing excessive concentrations of asbestos fibers can cause serious bodily harm. Exercise care when servicing brake parts. Do not sand or grind brake lining unless equipment used is designed to contain the dust residue. Do not clean brake parts with compressed air or by dry brushing. Cleaning should be done by dampening the brake components with a fine mist of water, then wiping the brake components clean with a dampened cloth. Dispose of cloth and all residue containing asbestos fibers in an impermeable container with the appropriate label. Follow practices prescribed by the Occupational Safety and Health Administration (OSHA) and the Environmental Protection Agency (EPA) for the handling, processing, and disposing of dust or debris that may contain asbestos fibers.

BRAKE CALIPER

REMOVAL & INSTALLATION

See Figure 9.

1. Before servicing the vehicle, refer to the Precautions Section.
2. Isolate the master cylinder. Use a brake pedal holding tool and depress the brake pedal past its first 1 inch of travel and hold it in this position. (This will keep brake

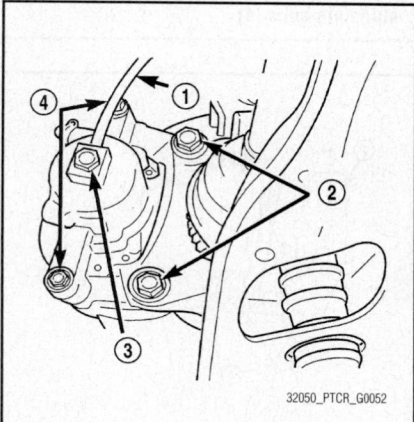

Fig. 9 Front brake caliper mounting point

fluid from draining from the master cylinder).
3. Raise and support the vehicle.
4. Remove the tire and wheel assembly.
5. Remove the banjo bolt (3) connecting the brake hose (1) to the brake caliper. There are two washers (one on each side of the flex hose fitting) that will come off with the banjo bolt. Discard the washers.
6. Remove the two brake caliper guide pin bolts (4).
7. Slide the disc brake caliper off the disc brake adapter and pads.

To install:

✳✳ WARNING

When installing new brake components, be sure to use correct parts. Parts designed for BR4 Performance Brake System must not be mixed with other brake systems.

8. Completely retract the caliper piston back into the bore of the caliper. Use a C-clamp to retract the piston. Place a wood block over the piston before installing the C-clamp to avoid damaging the piston.

✳✳ WARNING

Use care when installing the caliper onto the disc brake adapter to avoid damaging the boots on the caliper guide pins.

9. Install the disc brake caliper over the brake pads on the brake caliper adapter. Make sure the springs on the pads do not get caught in the hole formed into the center of the caliper housing.
10. Align the caliper guide pin bolt holes with the guide pins. Install the caliper guide pin bolts and tighten them to 26 ft. lbs. (35 Nm).
11. Install the banjo bolt connecting the brake hose to the brake caliper. Install NEW washers on each side of the hose fitting as the banjo bolt is guided through the fitting. Thread the banjo bolt into the caliper and tighten it to 18 ft. lbs. (24 Nm).
12. Install the tire and wheel assembly. Tighten the wheel mounting nuts to 100 ft. lbs. (135 Nm).
13. Lower the vehicle.
14. Remove the brake pedal holding tool.
15. Bleed the caliper as necessary.
16. Road test the vehicle and make several stops to wear off any foreign material on the brakes and to seat the brake shoes.

DISC BRAKE PADS

REMOVAL & INSTALLATION

See Figures 10 and 11.

1. Before servicing the vehicle, refer to the Precautions Section.
2. Raise and support the vehicle.
3. Remove the tire and wheel assembly.
4. Remove the two brake caliper guide pin bolts (4).
5. Remove the disc brake caliper from the disc brake adapter and hang it out of the way using wire or a bungee cord. Use care not to overextend the brake hose (1) when doing this.
6. Remove the brake pads from the disc brake caliper adapter.

To install:

➡Inboard brake pads are not identical side-to-side. This is due to placement

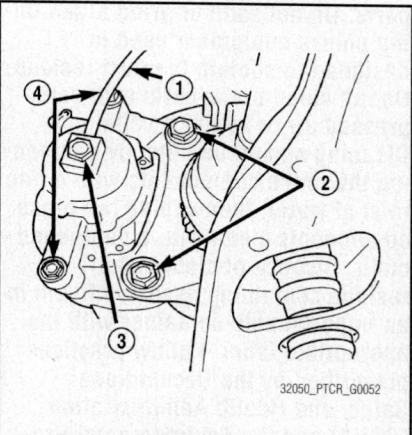

Fig. 10 Front brake caliper and guide pin bolts

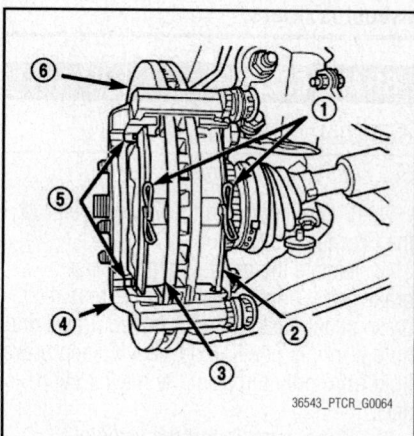

Fig. 11 Brake pad and caliper positioning

of the audible wear indicator on the end of each inboard pad. Make sure that the audible wear indicators are placed toward the top when the inboard pads are installed on each side of the vehicle.

7. Place the brake pads (2, 3) in the abutment shims (5) clipped into the disc brake caliper adapter (4) as shown. Place the pad with the wear indicator attached on the inboard side (2).

8. Completely retract the caliper piston back into the bore of the caliper.

※※ WARNING

Use care when installing the caliper onto the disc brake adapter to avoid damaging the boots on the caliper guide pins.

9. Install the disc brake caliper over the brake pads on the brake caliper adapter. Make sure the springs (1) on the pads do not get caught in the hole formed into the center of the caliper housing.

10. Align the caliper guide pin bolt holes with the guide pins. Install the caliper guide

pin bolts and tighten them to 26 ft. lbs. (35 Nm).

11. Install tire and wheel assembly. Tighten the wheel mounting nuts to 100 ft. lbs. (135 Nm).

12. Lower the vehicle.

13. Pump the brake pedal several times before moving the vehicle to set the pads to the brake rotor.

14. Check and adjust the brake fluid level as necessary.

15. Road test the vehicle and make several stops to wear off any foreign material on the brakes and to seat the brake pads.

BRAKES

REAR DISC BRAKES

※※ CAUTION

Dust and dirt accumulating on brake parts during normal use may contain asbestos fibers from production or aftermarket brake linings. Breathing excessive concentrations of asbestos fibers can cause serious bodily harm. Exercise care when servicing brake parts. Do not sand or grind brake lining unless equipment used is designed to contain the dust residue. Do not clean brake parts with compressed air or by dry brushing. Cleaning should be done by dampening the brake components with a fine mist of water, then wiping the brake components clean with a dampened cloth. Dispose of cloth and all residue containing asbestos fibers in an impermeable container with the appropriate label. Follow practices prescribed by the Occupational Safety and Health Administration (OSHA) and the Environmental Protection Agency (EPA) for the handling, processing, and disposing of dust or debris that may contain asbestos fibers.

BRAKE CALIPER

REMOVAL & INSTALLATION

See Figures 12 through 17.

1. Before servicing the vehicle, refer to the Precautions Section.

2. Isolate the master cylinder. Use a brake pedal holding tool and depress the brake pedal past its first 1 inch of travel and hold it in this position. (This will keep brake fluid from draining from the master cylinder).

3. Raise and support the vehicle.

4. Remove the tire and wheel assembly.

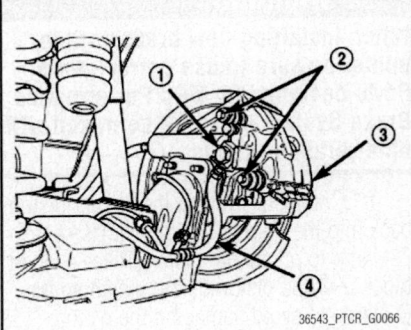

Fig. 12 Remove the banjo bolt (1) connecting the brake hose (4) to the brake caliper (3)

5. Remove the banjo bolt (1) connecting the brake hose (4) to the brake caliper (3). There are two washers (one on each side of the flex hose fitting) that will come off with the banjo bolt. Discard the washers; install new washers upon installation.

※※ WARNING

In some cases, it may be necessary to retract the caliper piston in its bore a small amount in order to provide sufficient clearance between the shoes and the rotor to easily remove the caliper from the knuckle. This can usually be accomplished before the guide pin bolts are removed, by grasping the rear of the caliper and pulling outward working with the guide pins, thus retracting the piston. Never push on the piston directly as it may get damaged.

6. Remove the 2 brake caliper guide pin bolts (4).

7. Remove the caliper assembly (1) from the brake adapter by first rotating the

top of the caliper away from the rotor (2), and then lifting the caliper assembly off the lower machined abutment (4) on the adapter.

8. Remove the outboard brake pad from the caliper by prying the brake pad retaining

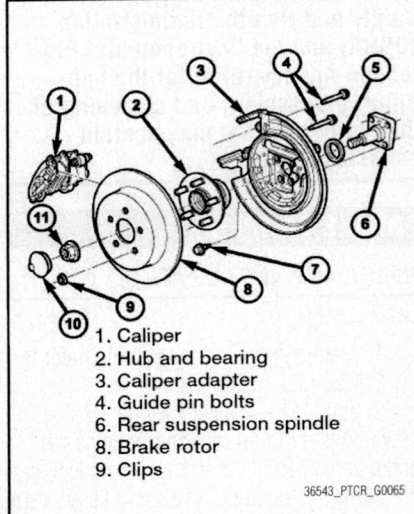

1. Caliper
2. Hub and bearing
3. Caliper adapter
4. Guide pin bolts
5. Rear suspension spindle
8. Brake rotor
9. Clips

Fig. 13 Rear brake assembly, showing guide pin bolts (4)

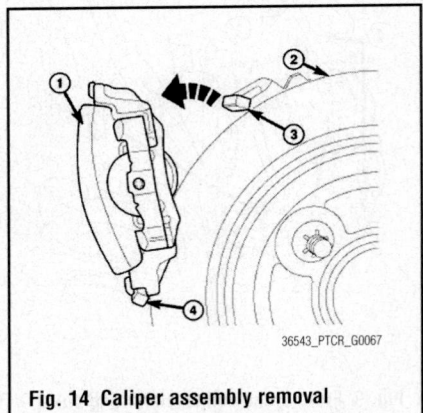

Fig. 14 Caliper assembly removal

clip over the raised area on the caliper. Slide the brake pad off of the brake caliper.

9. Pull the inboard brake pad away from caliper piston until the retaining clip is free from the cavity in the piston. Remove the pad.

To install:

✳✳ WARNING

When installing new brake components, be sure to use correct parts. Parts designed for the BR4 Performance Brake System must not be mixed with other brake systems.

10. If not already present, completely retract the caliper piston back into the piston bore of the caliper. Use a C-clamp to retract the piston. Place a wood block over the piston before installing the C-clamp to avoid damaging the piston.

11. Install the inboard brake pad into the caliper piston (2) by firmly pressing the pad in with the thumbs. Be sure the inboard brake pad is positioned squarely against the face of the caliper piston once installed.

12. Slide the outboard brake pad (2) onto the caliper. Be sure the retaining clip

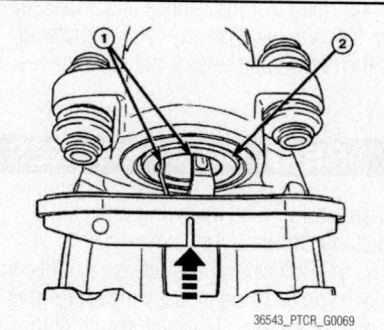

Fig. 15 Install inboard brake pad into caliper piston

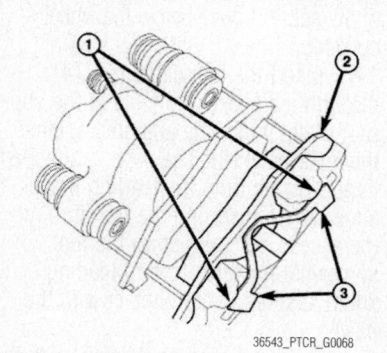

Fig. 16 Slide outboard brake pad onto caliper

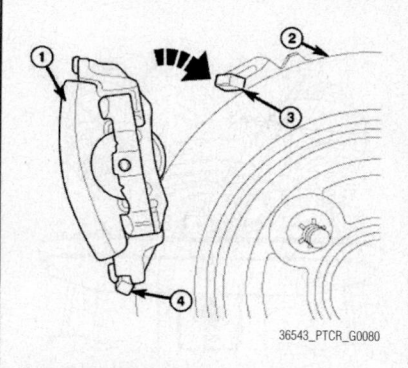

Fig. 17 Caliper assembly installation

(3) is squarely seated in the depressed areas on the caliper beyond the raised retaining bead (1).

13. Lubricate both adapter caliper slide abutments (3, 4) with a liberal amount of Mopar® Multipurpose Lubricant or equivalent.

✳✳ WARNING

Use care when installing the caliper assembly onto adapter so the guide pin bushings and sleeves do not get damaged by the mounting bosses on adapter.

14. Starting with the lower end, carefully guide the caliper (1) and brake pads over the brake rotor (2). First catch the caliper's bottom edge behind the caliper slide abutment (4), then rotate the top of the caliper into mounted position on the upper abutment (3).

✳✳ WARNING

Extreme caution should be taken not to cross-thread the caliper uide pin bolts (4) when they are installed.

15. Carefully install the caliper guide pin bolts. Tighten the bolts to 16 ft. lbs. (22 Nm).

16. Install the banjo bolt connecting the brake hose to the brake caliper. Install NEW washers on each side of the hose fitting as the banjo bolt is guided through the fitting. Thread the banjo bolt into the caliper and tighten it to 18 ft. lbs. (24 Nm).

17. Install the tire and wheel assembly. Tighten the wheel mounting nuts to 100 ft. lbs. (135 Nm).

18. Lower the vehicle.

19. Remove the brake pedal holding tool.

20. Bleed the caliper as necessary.

21. Road test the vehicle and make several stops to wear off any foreign material on the brakes and to seat the brake shoes.

DISC BRAKE PADS

REMOVAL & INSTALLATION
See Figures 13, 17 through 19.

1. Before servicing the vehicle, refer to the Precautions Section.

2. Raise and safely support the vehicle.

3. Remove the tire and wheel assembly.

✳✳ WARNING

In some cases, it may be necessary to retract the caliper piston in its bore a small amount in order to provide sufficient clearance between the pads and the rotor to easily remove the caliper from the knuckle. This can usually be accomplished before the guide pin bolts are removed, by grasping the inboard side of the caliper and pulling outward working with the guide pins, thus retracting the piston. Never push on the piston directly as it may get damaged.

4. Remove the 2 caliper guide pin bolts (4).

5. Remove the caliper assembly (1) from the brake adapter by first rotating the top of the caliper away from the rotor (2), and then lifting the caliper assembly off the lower machined abutment (4) on the adapter.

6. Hang the brake caliper from rear strut using wire or cord to prevent the weight of the caliper from damaging the brake hose.

7. Remove the outboard brake pad from the caliper by prying the brake pad retaining clip over the raised area on the caliper. Slide the brake pad off of the brake caliper.

8. Pull the inboard brake pad away from caliper piston until the retaining clip is free from the cavity in the piston. Remove the pad.

To install:

✳✳ WARNING

When installing new brake components, be sure to use correct parts. Parts designed for the BR4 Performance Brake System must not be mixed with other brake systems.

9. Completely retract the caliper piston back into the piston bore of the caliper. This is required to gain the necessary pad-to-rotor clearance for the caliper installation onto the steering knuckle.

10. Install the inboard brake pad into the caliper piston (2) by firmly pressing the pad in with the thumbs. Be sure the inboard brake pad is positioned squarely against the face of the caliper piston once installed.

11. Slide the outboard brake pad (2) onto the caliper. Be sure the retaining clip (3) is squarely seated in the depressed areas on the caliper beyond the raised retaining bead (1).

12. Lubricate both adapter caliper slide abutments (3, 4) with a liberal amount of Mopar® Multipurpose Lubricant or equivalent.

✳✳ WARNING

Use care when installing the caliper assembly onto adapter so the guide pin bushings and sleeves do not get damaged by the mounting bosses on adapter.

13. Starting with the lower end, carefully guide the caliper (1) and brake pads over the brake rotor (2). First catch the caliper's bottom edge behind the caliper slide abut-

36543_PTCR_G0069

Fig. 18 Install inboard brake pad into caliper piston

ment (4), then rotate the top of the caliper into mounted position on the upper abutment (3).

✳✳ WARNING

Extreme caution should be taken not to cross-thread the caliper guide pin bolts (4) when they are installed.

14. Carefully install the caliper guide pin bolts. Tighten the bolts to 16 ft. lbs. (22 Nm).

15. Install the banjo bolt connecting the brake hose to the brake caliper. Install NEW

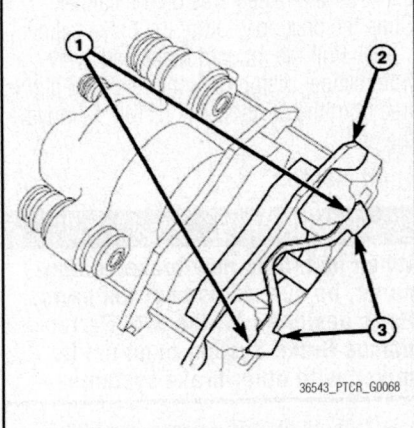

36543_PTCR_G0068

Fig. 19 Slide outboard brake pad onto caliper

washers on each side of the hose fitting as the banjo bolt is guided through the fitting. Thread the banjo bolt into the caliper and tighten it to 18 ft. lbs. (24 Nm).

16. Install the tire and wheel assembly. Tighten the wheel mounting nuts to 100 ft. lbs. (135 Nm).

17. Lower the vehicle.

18. Remove the brake pedal holding tool.

19. Bleed the caliper as necessary.

20. Road test the vehicle and make several stops to wear off any foreign material on the brakes and to seat the brake shoes.

BRAKES   REAR DRUM BRAKES

✳✳ CAUTION

Dust and dirt accumulating on brake parts during normal use may contain asbestos fibers from production or aftermarket brake linings. Breathing excessive concentrations of asbestos fibers can cause serious bodily harm. Exercise care when servicing brake parts. Do not sand or grind brake lining unless equipment used is designed to contain the dust residue. Do not clean brake parts with compressed air or by dry brushing. Cleaning should be done by dampening the brake components with a fine mist of water, then wiping the brake components clean with a dampened cloth. Dispose of cloth and all residue containing asbestos fibers in an impermeable container with the appropriate label. Follow practices prescribed by the Occupational Safety and Health Administration

(OSHA) and the Environmental Protection Agency (EPA) for the handling, processing, and disposing of dust or debris that may contain asbestos fibers.

BRAKE DRUM

REMOVAL & INSTALLATION
See Figures 20 and 21.

1. Before servicing the vehicle, refer to the Precautions Section.

2. Raise and safely support the vehicle.

3. Remove the tire and wheel assembly.

4. Remove the brake drum retaining clips (if equipped).

5. Slide the brake drum off the wheel mounting studs of the hub and remove it from the vehicle. If the drum does not come off, further brake clearance can be obtained by backing off the brake adjuster screw. To

do so, perform the following procedure (Backing Off Shoe Adjustment):

a. Fabricate a pawl release tool like the one shown using a coat hanger or heavy mechanics wire. Make the length of the overall tool about 6 inches (15 cm) (1). The (2) end is the end to be inserted into the brake assembly in the upcoming step.

b. Remove the plug from the rear of the support plate below the wheel cylinder.

c. Insert the fabricated tool (4) through the access hole (1) in the support plate, under the adjuster, against the lever pawl (3). The pawl is attached to and pivots from the leading brake shoe. When inserting the tool through the access hole, directing the tool somewhat forward (toward leading shoe) assures better contact with the pawl.

d. While pushing on the pawl with the fabricated tool (4) to disengage it from the adjuster star-wheel teeth, rotate the

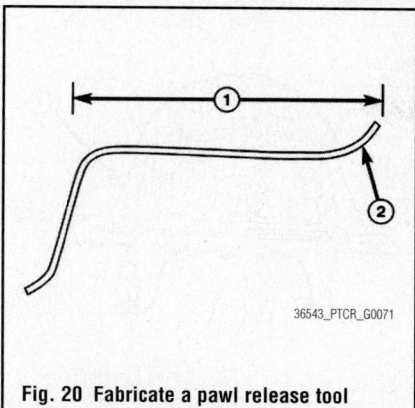

Fig. 20 Fabricate a pawl release tool

star-wheel (2) downward to back off the adjustment using a small screwdriver or a brake adjuster tool.

e. Once the adjuster screw is backed off a sufficient amount, the drum should slide off the wheel mounting studs.

To install:

6. Before installing drum, inspect brake shoe linings for wear, alignment, and contamination. Repair or replace as necessary.

➡ **If rust or any foreign material is present on hub, drum or wheel mating surfaces, wet wire brush these areas to remove prior to assembly of parts.**

7. Properly remove any buildup formed along outer edge of drum's machined braking surface.

8. Adjust the brake shoes-to-drum diameter using a brake shoe gauge. Refer to Brake Shoes, Adjustment.

9. Slide the brake drum onto the wheel mounting studs on the hub and bearing.

10. Install the tire and wheel assembly. Tighten the wheel mounting nuts to 100 ft. lbs. (135 Nm).

11. Lower the vehicle.

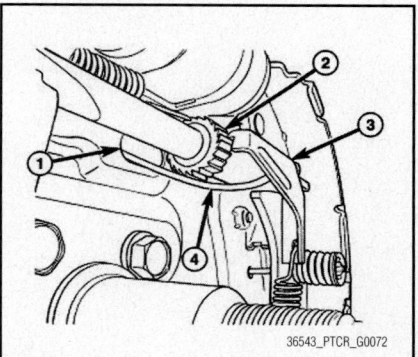

Fig. 21 Backing Off Shoe Adjustment

12. Road test the vehicle stopping in both forward and reverse directions. The automatic-adjuster will continue to adjust the brakes as necessary during the road test.

BRAKE SHOES

REMOVAL & INSTALLATION

See Figures 22 through 24.

1. Before servicing the vehicle, refer to the Precautions Section.

➡ **Make sure parking brake is in "Released" position before raising vehicle.**

2. Raise and support the vehicle.

➡ **Perform all of the following steps on each side of the vehicle to complete shoe set removal. It may be easier to install the new components on the first side of the vehicle before disassembling the opposite side, so it may be used as a reference guide for proper installation.**

3. Remove the tire and wheel assembly.

4. Remove any brake drum retaining clips, then the drum.

5. Remove the dust cap from the hub and bearing.

6. Remove the hub nut (2), then slide the hub and bearing (4) from the spindle.

7. Compress the cable return spring, then remove the parking brake cable from the parking brake lever.

8. Remove the lower return spring (4).

9. Compress and remove both shoe hold-down spring clips (1).

10. Remove both shoes and remaining parts as an assembly from the anchor (3) and the wheel cylinder (2).

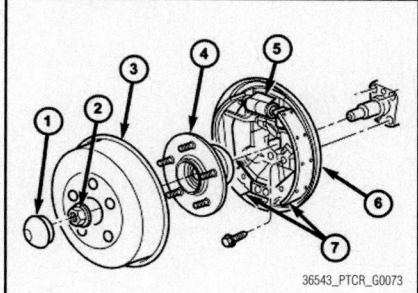

Fig. 22 Remove the hub nut (2), then slide the hub and bearing (4) from the spindle

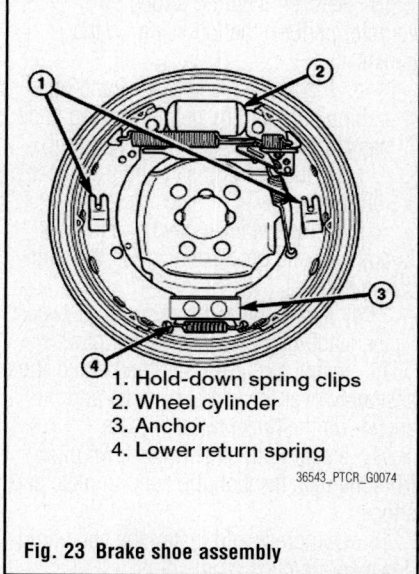

1. Hold-down spring clips
2. Wheel cylinder
3. Anchor
4. Lower return spring

Fig. 23 Brake shoe assembly

11. Remove the adjuster spring from the leading shoe and the lever pawl.

12. Remove the lever pawl from the pivot on the leading shoe and slide it out from under the adjuster.

13. Remove the adjuster and the upper return spring from the shoes.

To install:

➡ **Perform Step No. 1 through Step No. 13 on each side of vehicle to complete shoe set installation, then proceed to Step No. 14.**

14. Lubricate shoe contact areas on support plate and anchor using Mopar® Brake Lubricant or equivalent.

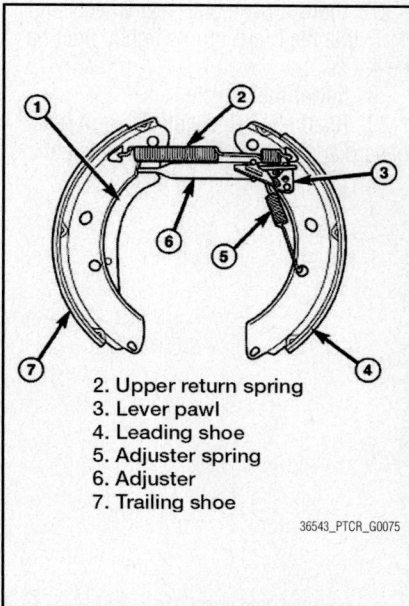

2. Upper return spring
3. Lever pawl
4. Leading shoe
5. Adjuster spring
6. Adjuster
7. Trailing shoe

Fig. 24 Brake shoe adjustment assembly

15. Before installing shoes on vehicle, perform the following on the bench:

    a. Place one leading shoe and one trailing shoe on the bench (trailing shoe has parking brake lever attached to it).

    b. Install the adjuster and the upper return spring.

    c. Slide the lever pawl under the adjuster and onto the pivot on the leading shoe.

    d. Install the adjuster spring between the leading shoe and the lever pawl.

16. Install the pre-assembled brake shoe assembly over the wheel cylinder and the anchor on the brake support plate.

17. Install both shoe hold-down pins from the rear, through the support plate and shoes.

18. Compress and install the shoe hold-down spring clips on the pins.

19. Install the lower return spring.

20. Compress the parking brake cable return spring, then install the cable on the parking brake lever. Release the spring guiding it beneath the retaining tab on the lever.

21. Slide the hub and bearing onto the spindle.

22. Install a NEW hub nut on the spindle. Tighten the nut to 160 ft. lbs. (217 Nm).

23. Install the hub and bearing dust cap.

24. Adjust the brake shoes-to-drum diameter using a brake shoe gauge. Refer to Brake Shoes, Adjustment.

25. Install the brake drum.

26. Install the tire and wheel assembly. Tighten the wheel mounting nuts to 100 ft. lbs. (135 Nm).

27. Slowly rotate both rear wheels and verify that the brake drums lightly drag on the shoes.

28. Lower the vehicle.

29. Road test vehicle stopping in both forward and reverse directions. Automatic-adjuster will continue to adjust brakes as necessary during the road test.

ADJUSTMENT

See Figures 25 and 26.

1. Before servicing the vehicle, refer to the Precautions Section.

2. Verify the parking brake lever is in the fully released position.

3. Raise and safely support the vehicle.

4. Remove the tire and wheel assembly.

5. Remove any brake drum retaining clips the brake drum.

6. Using a brake shoe gauge, Special Tool C-3919 or equivalent, measure the inside diameter of the brake drum at the center of the shoe contact area. Tighten the gauge set-screw at this measurement.

7. Place the other side of the brake shoe gauge on the brake shoes as shown.

8. Adjust the shoe diameter to the setting on the gauge. To adjust the shoe diameter, turn the adjuster-screw star-wheel using a screwdriver inserted through the adjusting hole in the rear of the shoe sup-

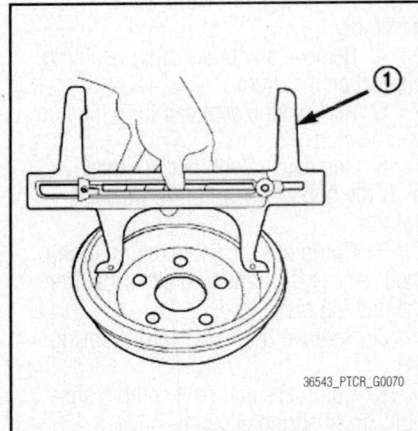

Fig. 25 Measure the inside diameter of the brake drum

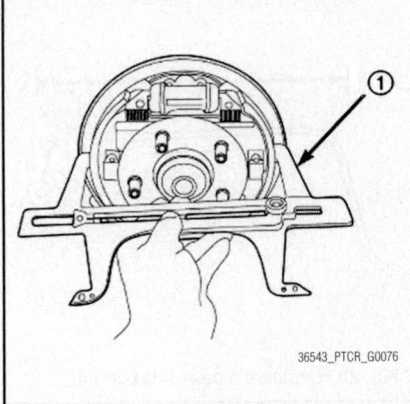

Fig. 26 Place the brake shoe gauge on the brake shoes

port plate. Once the tip of the screwdriver contacts the star-wheel teeth, move the handle of tool downward using the support plate as a pivot to adjust the shoes outward.

9. Once the shoe diameter is set, remove the tool and install the brake drum. Refer to Brake Drum Removal & Installation.

10. Turn the drum. A slight drag should be felt while rotating the drum. If not, repeat the above procedure.

11. Install the tire and wheel assembly. Tighten the wheel mounting nuts to 100 ft. lbs. (135 Nm).

12. After adjusting both rear drum brakes as necessary, lower the vehicle.

13. Apply and release the parking brake lever one time after the adjustment process is completed so the parking brake can readjust itself to the new brake shoe adjustment.

14. Road test the vehicle stopping in both forward and reverse directions. The automatic-adjuster will continue to adjust brakes as necessary during the road test.

BRAKES

PARKING BRAKE CABLES

ADJUSTMENT

See Figures 27 and 28.

1. Before servicing the vehicle, refer to the Precautions Section.

> ✳✳ **CAUTION**
>
> **The airbag system is a complex electromechanical unit. Before attempting to service any component near the occupant restraint controller (ORC), first disconnect and isolate the battery negative cable. Allow the system capacitor to discharge for two (2) minutes. Failure to do this could result in accidental airbag deployment and possible personal injury.**

> ✳✳ **CAUTION**
>
> **The automatic adjusting feature of this parking brake lever contains a clock spring loaded to approximately 19 pounds. Do not release the automatic adjuster lockout device unless the rear parking brake cables and equalizer are connected to the lever output cable. Keep hands out of automatic adjuster sector and pawl area. Failure to observe caution in handling this mechanism could lead to serious injury.**

2. Disconnect the negative battery cable.

3. Block the tire and wheels so the vehicle does not move once the vehicle parking brake lever is released.

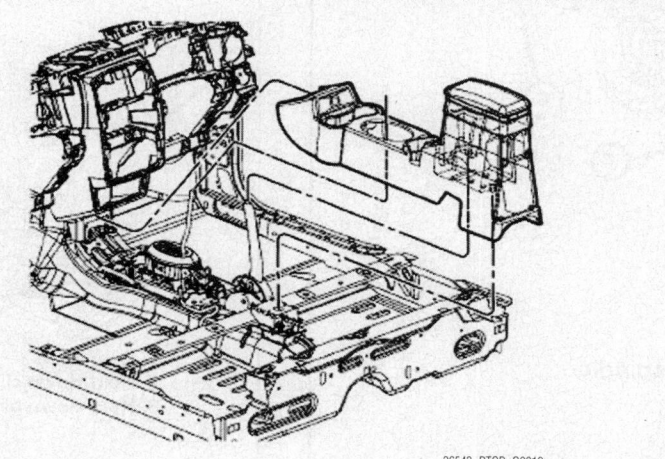

Fig. 27 Center console

36543_PTCR_G0019

4. Remove the center console, as follows:

   a. Remove the four screws located inside the storage bin.

   b. Remove the two screws located under the cup holder lining.

   c. Disconnect the electrical connectors.

   d. Remove the center console from the vehicle.

5. Raise parking brake lever (1) to full upright (applied) position.

6. Keeping hands clear of the automatic adjuster sector and pawl area, firmly grasp the pin punch (3) (drill bit or locking pin) installed in the parking brake lever (1), then quickly remove it from the lever mechanism. This will allow the parking brake lever mechanism to automatically adjust the parking brake cables.

7. Cycle the parking brake lever once to position the parking brake cables, then fully apply the parking brake.

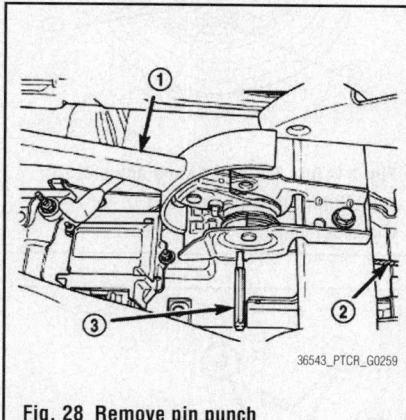

36543_PTCR_G0259

Fig. 28 Remove pin punch

8. Raise the vehicle to a point where the rear wheels just clear the floor. Check the rear wheels of the vehicle. They should not rotate with the lever in its full upright (applied) position.

9. Return the parking brake lever to its released position.

10. Check the rear wheels of the vehicle. They should rotate freely without excessive dragging with the lever in its released position. If excessive drag is present, adjust the rear brake shoes and repeat above parking brake test.

11. Apply the parking brake.

12. Lower the vehicle.

13. Install the center console, as follows:

   a. Position the center console into the vehicle.

   b. Connect the electrical connectors.

   c. Install the two screws in the cup holder.

   d. Install the four screws in the storage bin.

14. Remove the blocks from the tires and wheels.

15. Connect the negative battery cable.

PARKING BRAKE SHOES

REMOVAL & INSTALLATION

See Figures 29 through 33.

1. Before servicing the vehicle, refer to the Precautions Section.

2. Raise and safely support the vehicle.

3. Remove the tire and wheel assembly.

> ✳✳ **WARNING**
>
> **In some cases, it may be necessary to retract the caliper piston in its bore a small amount in order to provide sufficient clearance between the pads and the rotor to easily remove the caliper from the knuckle. This can usually be accomplished before the guide pin bolts are removed, by grasping the inboard side of the caliper and pulling outward working with the guide pins, thus retracting the piston. Never push on the piston directly as it may get damaged.**

4. Remove the two caliper guide pin bolts.

5. Remove the caliper assembly (1) from the brake adapter by first rotating the top of the caliper away from the rotor (2), and then lifting the caliper assembly off the lower machined abutment (4) on the adapter.

6. Hang the brake caliper from rear strut using wire or cord to prevent the weight of the caliper from damaging the brake hose.

7. Remove any clips (9) retaining the brake rotor (8) to the wheel studs.

8. Slide the brake rotor (8) off the hub and bearing (2).

9. Remove the dust cap (10) from the rear hub and bearing (2).

10. Remove the rear hub and bearing retaining nut (11).

11. Remove the rear hub and bearing (2) from the rear spindle (6).

12. Remove the rear brake shoe hold-down clip from the hold-down pin.

13. Turn the brake shoe adjuster (3) wheel until the adjuster is at shortest length.

14. Remove the adjuster from the parking brake shoes.

15. Remove the lower return spring.

16. Pull the rear brake shoe away from the anchor and disconnect the upper return spring. Remove both from the vehicle.

17. Remove the front brake shoe (1) hold-down clip (2) from the hold-down pin (3).

18. Remove the front brake shoe.

To install:

➡ If replacing parking brake shoes on both sides of vehicle, perform Step No. 1

through Step No. 13 on each side of the vehicle to complete shoe set installation, then proceed to Step No. 14.

19. Install the front brake shoe on the adapter. Insert the hold-down pin (from the rear) through the shoe and install the hold-down clip securing the shoe in place. Position the clip as shown to avoid contact with other components.

20. Attach the upper shoe return spring on the two shoes. Pull the rear brake shoe over the anchor block until it is properly located on the adapter. Make sure the parking brake actuator lever is properly installed between the front and rear shoes.

21. Install the lower return spring on the shoes.

22. Install the brake shoe adjuster between the front and rear shoes. The star wheel mounts toward the rear of the vehicle.

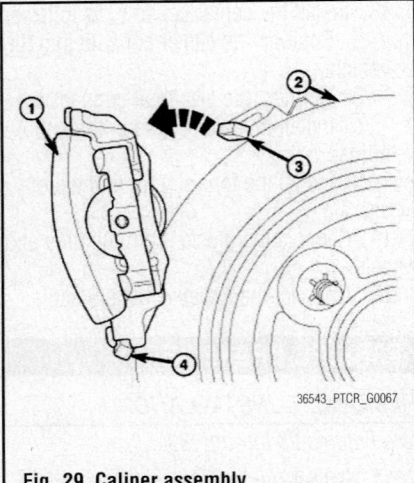

Fig. 29 Caliper assembly

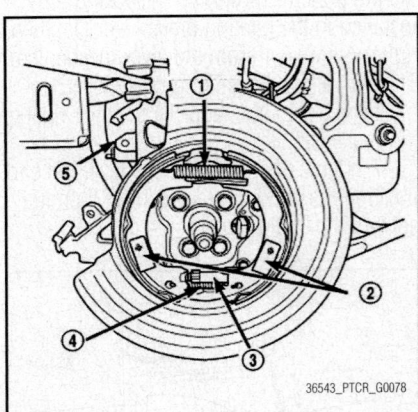

Fig. 31 Turn the brake shoe adjuster (3) wheel until the adjuster is at shortest length

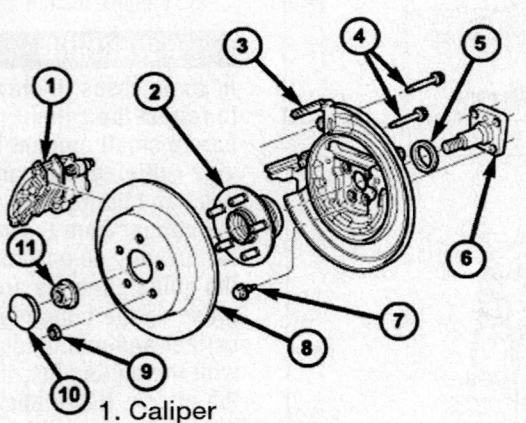

1. Caliper
2. Hub and bearing
3. Caliper adapter
4. Guide pin bolts
6. Rear suspension spindle
8. Brake rotor
9. Clips

Fig. 30 Rear brake assembly

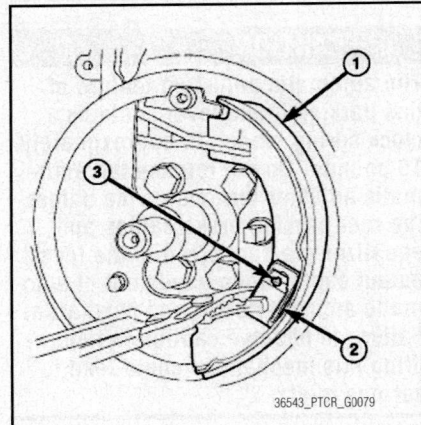

Fig. 32 Remove the front brake shoe (1) hold-down clip (2) from the hold-down pin (3)

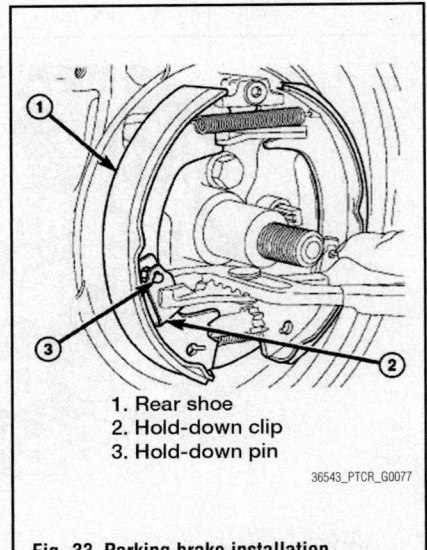

1. Rear shoe
2. Hold-down clip
3. Hold-down pin

Fig. 33 Parking brake installation

23. Insert the hold-down pin (from the rear) through the rear shoe and install the hold-down clip securing the shoe in place. Position the clip as shown to avoid contact with other components.

24. Using a brake shoe gauge, adjust the parking brake shoes to a diameter of 6.75 in. (171 mm).

25. Slide the hub and bearing onto the rear spindle.

26. Install a NEW hub and bearing retaining nut. Tighten the hub nut to 160 ft. lbs. (217 Nm).

27. Install the hub and bearing dust cap.

28. Install the brake rotor.

29. Install the disc brake caliper over the rotor and onto the brake adapter as indicated.

30. Install the two caliper guide pin bolts securing the caliper. Tighten the bolts to 192 inch lbs. (22 Nm).

31. Install the tire and wheel assembly. Tighten the wheel mounting nuts to 100 ft. lbs. (135 Nm).

32. Adjust the parking brake shoes as necessary.

33. Lower the vehicle.

ADJUSTMENT

➡ **The parking brake shoes used in the drum-in-hat park brake system do not automatically adjust to compensate for brake shoe lining wear. Therefore, it is necessary to manually adjust the parking brake shoes.**

1. Before proceeding, verify the parking brake lever is in the released position.

2. Raise the vehicle.

3. Remove the rubber plug from the adjusting hole in the disc brake caliper adapter.

4. Adjust the parking brakes. Use the first bullet point for the adjustment of the left side parking brake shoes. Use the second bullet point for the adjustment of the right side parking brake shoes.

• Insert a medium size screwdriver through adjustment hole in the left backing plate. Position the screwdriver against the star wheel on the parking brake shoe adjuster. Using the screwdriver, rotate the star wheel downward until a slight drag is noticed when turning the rear tire and wheel assembly. Then, using the screwdriver, slowly rotate the star wheel upward, backing off the adjuster, just enough to allow the rear tire and wheel assembly to rotate without the parking brake shoes dragging. Do not back off the adjuster star wheel more than 2 clicks past the point of no drag. The parking brake shoe-to-drum clearance is now properly set.

• Insert a medium size screwdriver through adjustment hole in the right backing plate. Position the screwdriver against the star wheel

on the parking brake shoe adjuster. Using the screwdriver, rotate the star wheel upward until a slight drag is noticed when turning the rear tire and wheel assembly. Then, using the screwdriver, slowly rotate the star wheel downward, backing off the adjuster, just enough to allow the rear tire and wheel assembly to rotate without the parking brake shoes dragging. Do not back off the adjuster star wheel more that 2 clicks past the point of no drag. The parking brake shoe-to-drum clearance is now properly set.

5. Install the rubber plug in the adjusting holes of the disc brake caliper adapter.

6. Lower the vehicle until the rear tires are just clearing the floor.

7. Reach inside the vehicle and fully apply and release the park brakes 2 times after adjusting the parking brake shoes.

8. With the parking brake lever in the fully applied position, attempt to hand rotate each rear tire and wheel assembly to ensure that the parking brake shoes are working.

9. With the parking brake lever in the released position, hand rotate each rear tire and wheel assembly to ensure that the parking brake shoes are not dragging.

10. Lower the vehicle.

CHASSIS ELECTRICAL

AIR BAG (SUPPLEMENTAL RESTRAINT SYSTEM)

GENERAL INFORMATION

✳✳ CAUTION

These vehicles are equipped with an air bag system. The system must be disarmed before performing service on, or around, system components, the steering column, instrument panel components, wiring and sensors. Failure to follow the safety precautions and the disarming procedure could result in accidental air bag deployment, possible injury and unnecessary system repairs.

SERVICE PRECAUTIONS

This system contains a sensitive, complex electronic unit. Disconnect and isolate the battery negative remote cable before beginning airbag system component removal or installation procedures. Allow system capacitor to discharge for two minutes before removing airbag components. This will dis-

able the airbag system. Failure to disconnect the battery could result in accidental airbag deployment, serious or fatal injury.

To avoid serious or fatal injury on vehicles equipped with the Supplemental Restraint System (SRS), never attempt to repair the electrically conductive circuits or wiring components related to the SRS. Such repairs can compromise the conductivity and current carrying capacity of those critical electrical circuits, which may cause SRS components not to deploy when required, or to deploy when not required. Any wire harness containing broken, cut, burned or otherwise damaged electrically conductive SRS wiring, terminals or connector components must be removed and replaced with an entire new wire harness. Only minor cuts or abrasions of wire and terminal insulation where the conductive material has not been damaged, or connector insulators where the integrity of the latching and locking mechanisms have not been compromised may be repaired using appropriate methods.

Do not place an intact undeployed airbag face down on a solid surface. The airbag will propel into the air if accidentally deployed and may result in personal injury or death.

When carrying or handling an undeployed airbag, the trim side (face) of the airbag should be pointing away from the body to minimize possibility of serious or fatal injury if accidental deployment occurs..

Replace airbag system components with OEM replacement parts. Substitute parts may appear interchangeable, but internal differences may result in inferior occupant protection. Failure to do so may result in occupant personal injury or death.

Wear safety glasses, rubber gloves, and long sleeved clothing when cleaning powder residue from vehicle after an airbag deployment. Powder residue emitted from a deployed airbag can cause skin irritation. Flush affected area with cool water if irritation is experienced. If nasal or throat irritation is experienced, exit the vehicle for fresh air until the irritation ceases. If irritation continues, see a physician.

Do not use a replacement airbag that is not in the original packaging. This may result in improper deployment, personal injury, or death.

The factory installed fasteners, screws and bolts used to fasten airbag components are specifically designed for the airbag system. Do not use substitute fasteners, use only original equipment fasteners listed in the parts catalog when fastener replacement is required.

Airbags should be stored in a cool, dry place, away from excessive heat and static electrical activity with the fabric airbag facing up. If not, a premature deployment can result in serious or fatal injury.

The side impact airbag system contains sensitive, complex electronic units. Before attempting to diagnose or service any side impact airbag system components, you must first disconnect and isolate the battery negative remote cable. This is the only sure way to disable the side impact airbag system. Allow system capacitor to discharge for two minutes before removing airbag components. Failure to do this could result in accidental side impact airbag module deployment and possible serious or fatal injury.

Do not attempt to dismantle a side impact airbag or tamper with its inflator. Do not puncture, incinerate, or bring into contact with electricity. Do not store at temperatures exceeding 200° F (93° C).

The fasteners, screws, and bolts originally used for the side impact airbag system components are specifically designed for the side impact airbag system. They must never be replaced with any substitutes. Any time a new fastener is needed, replace it with the correct fasteners provided in the service package or specified in the Mopar® parts catalog.

During, and following, any child restraint anchor service, due to impact event or vehicle repair, carefully inspect all mounting hardware, tether straps, and anchors for proper installation, operation, or damage. If a child restraint anchor is found damaged in any way, the anchor must be replaced. Failure to do this may result in personal injury or death.

Deployed and non-deployed airbags may or may not have live pyrotechnic material within the airbag inflator. Do not dispose of driver, passenger, or side airbags unless you are sure of complete deployment. Please refer to the Hazardous Substance Control System for proper disposal. Dispose of deployed air bags in a manner consistent with state, provincial, local, and federal regulations.

After any airbag component testing or service, do not connect the battery negative cable. Personal injury or death may result if the system test is not performed first.

If the vehicle is equipped with the Occupant Classification System (OCS), do not connect the battery negative cable before performing the OCS Verification Test using the scan tool and the appropriate diagnostic information. Personal injury or death may result if the system test is not performed properly.

Never replace both the Occupant Restraint Controller (ORC) and the Occupant Classification Module (OCM) at the same time. If both require replacement, replace one, then perform the Airbag System test before replacing the other.

Both the ORC and the OCM store Occupant Classification System (OCS) calibration data, which they transfer to one another when one of them is replaced. If both are replaced at the same time, an irreversible fault will be set in both modules and the OCS may malfunction and cause personal injury or death.

If equipped with OCS, the Seat Weight Sensor is a sensitive, calibrated unit and must be handled carefully. Do not drop or handle roughly. If dropped or damaged, replace with another sensor. Failure to do so may result in occupant injury or death.

If equipped with OCS, the front passenger seat must be handled carefully as well. When removing the seat, be careful when setting on floor not to drop. If dropped, the sensor may be inoperative, could result in occupant injury, or possibly death.

If equipped with OCS, when the passenger front seat is on the floor, no one should sit in the front passenger seat. This uneven force may damage the sensing ability of the seat weight sensors. If sat on and damaged, the sensor may be inoperative, could result in occupant injury, or possibly death.

DISARMING THE SYSTEM

Disconnect and isolate the negative battery cable. Wait 2 minutes to allow the system capacitor to fully discharge before servicing the vehicle.

ARMING THE SYSTEM

Reconnect the negative battery cable.

CLOCKSPRING CENTERING

➡ If the rotating tape within the clock spring is not positioned properly with the steering wheel and the front wheels, the clock spring may fail during use. The following procedure MUST BE USED to center the clock spring if:

- The clock spring is not known to be properly positioned
- The front wheels were moved
- The steering wheel was moved from the half turn (180 degrees) to the right (clockwise) position

1. Place the wheels in the straight ahead position.
2. Open hood.
3. Disconnect and isolate the battery negative cable. Allow system capacitor to discharge for 2 minutes before beginning.

✳✳ CAUTION

Wait two minutes for the airbag system reserve capacitor to discharge before beginning any airbag system or component service. Failure to do so may result in accidental airbag deployment, serious or fatal injury.

4. Remove the steering wheel. Refer to the Steering Wheel Removal & Installation procedure in the Steering Section.

➡ Once the driver airbag and steering wheel are removed, the clockspring doesn't have to be removed to center it. The clockspring rotor moves freely once the steering wheel is removed.

5. Rotate the clockspring rotor in the CLOCKWISE DIRECTION to the end of travel. Do not apply excessive torque.

6. From the end of travel, rotate counterclockwise more than 180 degrees so the connector and squib wire are at the twelve o'clock position (top). Rotate counter clockwise two additional full turns. Engage clockspring locking mechanism.

7. Install the steering wheel. Refer to the Steering Wheel Removal & Installation procedure in the Steering Section.

8. Install the driver airbag. Refer to Driver Side Airbag Removal & Installation.

✳✳ CAUTION

Do not connect the negative battery cable at this time. Perform the Air Bag System Test prior to connecting the negative battery cable. Failure to follow this warning may result in accidental air bag deployment and possible serious or fatal injury.

DRIVE TRAIN

AUTOMATIC TRANSAXLE ASSEMBLY

REMOVAL & INSTALLATION

40/41TE Transaxle

See Figures 34 through 38.

1. Before servicing the vehicle, refer to the Precautions Section.
2. Disconnect battery cables.
3. Remove air cleaner assembly. Refer to Air Cleaner Assembly Removal & Installation, in the Engine Mechanical section.
4. Remove battery and battery tray.
5. Remove uppermost starter-to-transaxle bellhousing bolt and remove transaxle dipstick AND tube. Plug hole to prevent debris from entering transaxle.

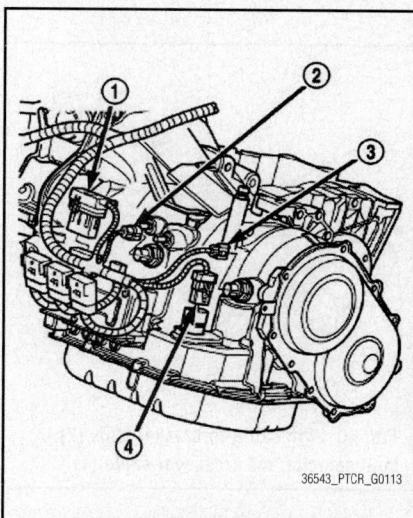

Fig. 34 Disconnect sensor connectors

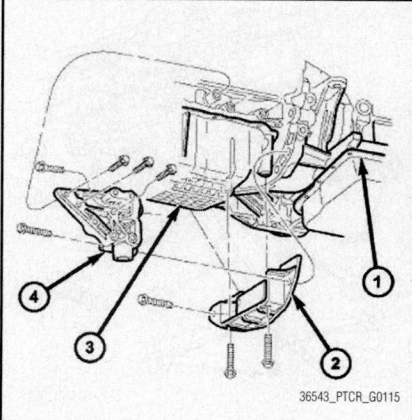

Fig. 35 Remove the left engine-to-transaxle lateral bending brace and structural collar (2)

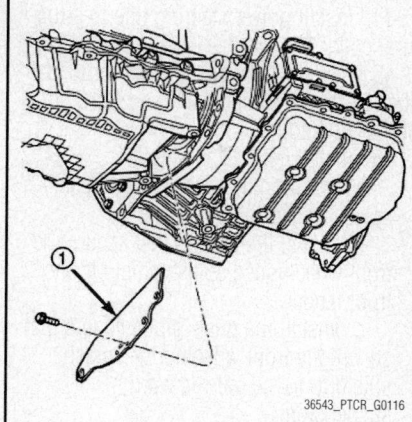

Fig. 36 Remove bellhousing dust cover (1)

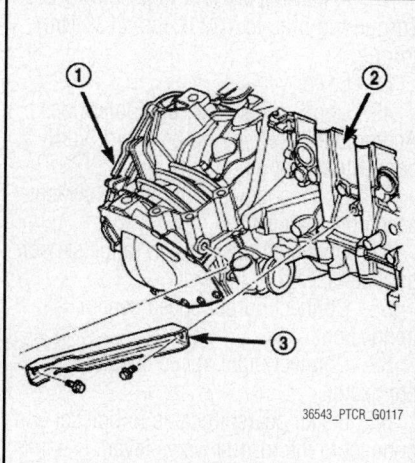

Fig. 37 Remove the right engine-to-transaxle lateral bending brace (3)

6. Disconnect gearshift cable from manual valve lever. Remove gearshift cable from trans mount bracket and position cable out of the way.
7. Using Release Tool 8875A, disconnect transaxle oil cooler lines.
8. Disconnect input speed sensor connector (2).
9. Disconnect output speed sensor connector (3).
10. Disconnect transmission range sensor connector (4).
11. Disconnect solenoid/pressure switch assembly connector (1).
12. Raise vehicle on hoist.
13. Remove front wheel covers (if equipped) and front wheel/tire assemblies.
14. Remove left splash shield:
    a. Remove the push-pin fasteners that secure the front wheelhouse splash shield to the frame rail forward of suspension.
    b. Remove the push-pin fasteners that secure the front wheelhouse splash shield to frame rail rearward of suspension.
    c. Remove the screws that secure the front wheelhouse splash shield to the front fender and remove the splash shield.
15. Remove left and right halfshaft assemblies. Refer to Halfshaft Removal & Installation section for proper procedures.
16. Disconnect power steering hose from structural collar.
17. Remove the left engine-to-transaxle lateral bending brace and structural collar (2).
18. Remove bellhousing dust cover (1).

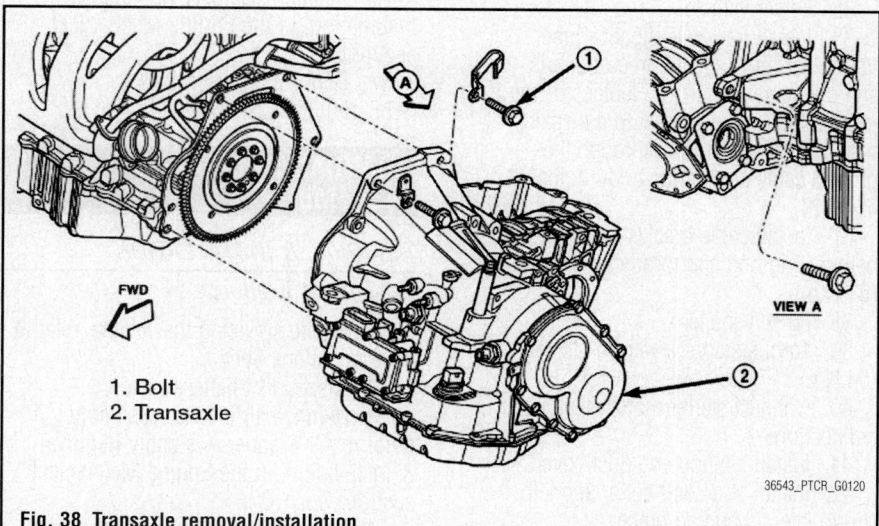

1. Bolt
2. Transaxle

Fig. 38 Transaxle removal/installation

19. Remove the right engine-to-transaxle lateral bending brace (3).

20. Disconnect starter motor electrical connections.

21. Remove starter motor. Refer to Starter Removal & Installation in the Engine Electrical section.

22. Remove lower starter-to-transaxle bellhousing lower bolt and position starter motor out of the way.

23. Remove gearshift cable bracket. Position cable out of the way.

24. Remove four drive plate-to-torque converter bolts.

25. Support engine assembly with screw jack and wood block.

26. Remove transmission upper mount to bracket bolts.

27. Lower engine/transaxle to gain access to and remove transaxle-to-engine bolts (1).

28. Remove transaxle (2) from vehicle.

29. If replacing transaxle, remove upper mount bracket and gearshift cable bracket and transfer to new/replacement transaxle.

To install:

30. Install transaxle to engine. Install and torque transaxle-to-engine bolts to 80 ft. lbs. (108 Nm).

31. Raise engine/transaxle assembly enough line up transaxle mount bracket. Install two mount-to-transaxle bracket bolts and torque to 50 ft. lbs. (68 Nm).

32. Remove screw jack support.

33. Install four drive plate-to-torque converter bolts and torque to 65 ft. lbs. (88 Nm) torque.

34. Position starter into place and hand-tighten lower bolt. Refer to Starter Removal & Installation in the Engine Electrical section..

35. Lower vehicle.

36. Install transaxle dipstick tube. Verify that openings are free of debris and o-ring seal is intact. Replace o-ring if necessary. Secure bracket to transaxle. Install starter upper bolt through the ground cable and torque to 40 ft. lbs. (54 Nm).

37. Install cable bracket-to-transaxle bellhousing bolt and torque to 45 ft. lbs. (61 Nm).

38. Raise vehicle.

39. Torque starter lower bolt to 40 ft. lbs. (54 Nm).

40. Connect starter motor electrical connections.

41. Install bellhousing dust cover.

42. Install structural collar and left (front) lateral bending brace.

43. Install right (rear) lateral bending brace. Torque bolts to 60 ft. lbs. (81 Nm) torque.

44. Install power steering line to structural collar.

45. Install front halfshafts. Refer to Half-shaft Removal & Installation section for proper procedures.

46. Install left splash shield:

   a. Position the front wheelhouse splash shield to the vehicle.

   b. Install the screws that secure the front wheelhouse splash shield to the front fender.

   c. Install the push-pin fasteners that secure the front wheelhouse splash shield to frame rail rearward of suspension.

   d. Install the push-pin fasteners that secure the front wheelhouse splash shield to the frame rail forward of suspension.

47. Install left wheel/tire assembly. Torque lug nuts to 100 ft. lbs. (136 Nm) torque.

48. Lower vehicle.

49. Connect transaxle oil cooler lines. An audible 'click' should be heard. Verify connection by pulling outward.

50. Connect solenoid/pressure switch assembly connector.

51. Connect transmission range sensor connector.

52. Connect output speed sensor connector.

53. Connect input speed sensor connector.

54. Install gearshift cable to bracket and connect to the manual valve lever.

55. Install the battery tray, battery, and hold-down clamp.

56. Install air cleaner assembly. Refer to Air Cleaner Assembly Removal & Installation, in the Engine Mechanical section.

57. Connect battery cables.

58. Fill transaxle with fluid.

MANUAL TRANSAXLE ASSEMBLY

REMOVAL & INSTALLATION

See Figures 39 through 44.

1. Before servicing the vehicle, refer to the Precautions Section.

2. Disconnect battery cables.

3. Remove air cleaner assembly. Refer to Air Cleaner Assembly Removal & Installation, in the Engine Mechanical section.

4. Remove battery and battery tray.

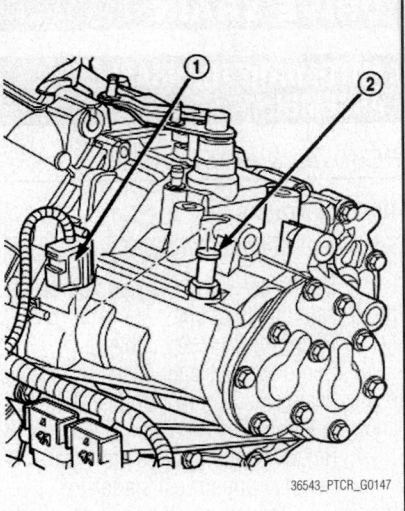

Fig. 39 Disconnect back-up lamp switch connector (1)

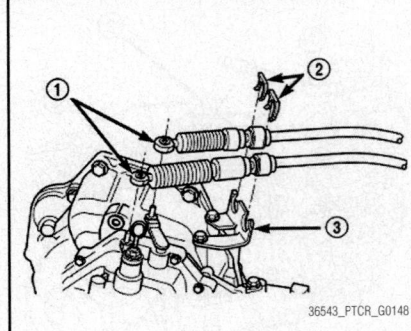

Fig. 40 Shift cable-to-bracket clips (2), shift selector and crossover cable (1)

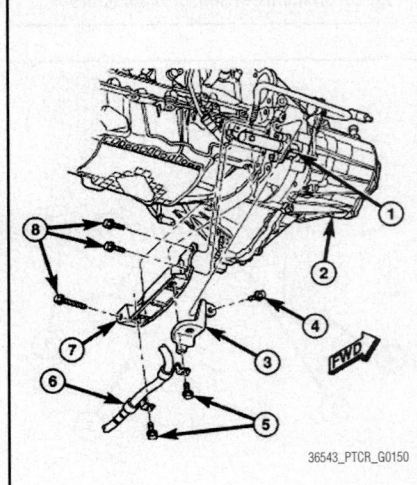

Fig. 41 Engine-to-transaxle lateral bending braces and structural collar

5. Disconnect back-up lamp switch connector (1).

6. Remove shift cable-to-bracket clips (2).

7. Disconnect shift selector and crossover cable (1) from levers. Remove cables and secure out of the way.

8. Disconnect the vehicle speed sensor connector.

9. Raise and safely support the vehicle.

10. Remove transaxle oil drain plug and drain oil into a suitable container. Reinstall drain plug and torque to 10 ft. lbs. (14 Nm) torque.

11. Remove clutch slave cylinder from transaxle. Refer to Slave Cylinder Removal & Installation in the Clutch section.

12. Remove both axle halfshafts. Refer to Halfshaft Removal & Installation.

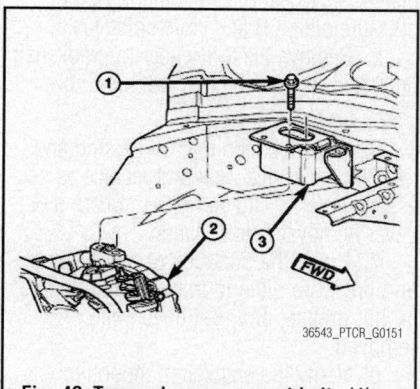

36543_PTCR_G0151

Fig. 42 Transaxle upper mount bolts (1)

13. Disconnect power steering hose from structural collar.

14. Remove the left engine-to-transaxle lateral bending brace (3) and structural collar (7).

15. Remove bellhousing dust cover if equipped.

16. Remove the right engine-to-transaxle lateral bending brace (3).

17. Remove starter motor. Refer to Starter Removal & Installation in the Engine Electrical, Starting System section.

18. Support engine at oil pan with screw jack and wood block.

19. Remove transaxle upper mount bolts (1).

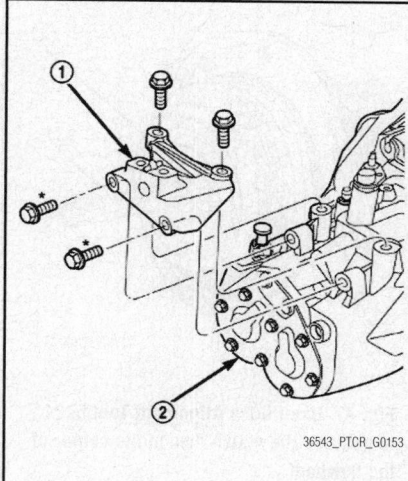

36543_PTCR_G0153

Fig. 44 Transaxle upper mount

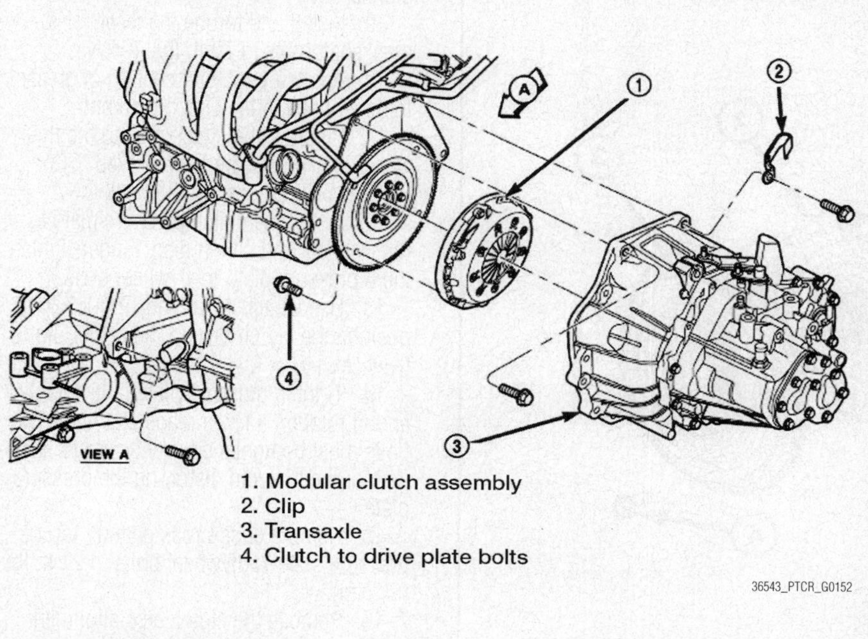

20. Remove four modular clutch-to-drive plate bolts (4). While removing bolts, one tight-tolerance (slotted) drive plate hole will be encountered. When this bolt is removed, mark driveplate and modular clutch assembly (1) at this location, and be sure to align marks upon reassembly.

21. Carefully lower engine and transaxle on screw jack until proper removal clearance is obtained.

22. Obtain a helper to assist in holding transaxle while removing transaxle-to-engine mounting bolts.

23. Remove transaxle from vehicle (3).

24. Remove clutch module (1) from transaxle input shaft (if equipped).

25. If installing a new or replacement transaxle, remove the upper mount (1), transfer to the replacement unit and torque all bolts to 45 ft. lbs. (62 Nm) torque.

To install:

26. Install clutch module (if equipped) onto input shaft. Install transaxle into position.

27. Install transaxle-to-engine mounting bolts and tighten to 80 ft. lbs. (108 Nm) torque.

28. Raise engine and transaxle with screw jack until upper mount bracket aligns with upper mount. Install mount bolts and tighten to 50 ft. lbs. (68 Nm) torque.

29. Remove screwjack.

30. Install 4 modular clutch-to-driveplate bolts (4) Fig. 2. Align drive plate and modular clutch alignment marks placed upon disassembly. Start with tight-tolerance (slotted) hole, install and torque bolts to 65 ft. lbs. (88 Nm) torque.

31. Install starter motor and tighten bolts to 40 ft. lbs. (54 Nm) torque. Make sure to fasten ground cable to upper starter bolt. Refer to Starter Removal & Installation in the Engine Electrical, Starting System section.

32. Connect starter electrical harness and tighten positive cable nut to 90 in. lbs. (10 Nm) torque.

33. Install bellhousing dust cover.

34. Install left engine-to-transaxle bending brace and structural collar. Refer to Engine Structural Collar, in the Engine Mechanical section.

35. Install power steering hose to structural collar.

36. Install the right lateral bending brace and tighten bolts to 60 ft. lbs. (81 Nm) torque.

37. Install bolts to hold slave cylinder to transaxle. Refer to Slave Cylinder Removal & Installation in the Clutch section.

1. Modular clutch assembly
2. Clip
3. Transaxle
4. Clutch to drive plate bolts

36543_PTCR_G0152

Fig. 43 Manual transaxle

38. Install both axle halfshafts. Refer to Halfshaft Removal & Installation..

39. Fill transaxle with suitable amount of fluid.

40. Connect clutch master cylinder tube to the hydraulic clutch slave cylinder. An audible click should be heard. Verify connection by pushing and pulling quick connect.

41. Lower vehicle.

42. Connect vehicle speed sensor connector.

43. Connect shift crossover and selector cables to shift lever. Install cables to bracket and install retaining clips.

44. Connect back-up lamp switch connector.

45. Install the battery tray, battery, and hold-down clamp.

46. Install air cleaner assembly. Refer to Air Cleaner Assembly Removal & Installation, in Engine Mechanical section.

47. Connect battery cables.

48. Road test vehicle and inspect for leaks.

CLUTCH DRIVEN DISC & PRESSURE PLATE

REMOVAL & INSTALLATION

See Figures 45 through 47.

⁂ CAUTION

Chrysler does not manufacture any vehicles or replacement parts that contain asbestos. Aftermarket products may or may not contain asbestos. Refer to aftermarket product packaging for product information. Whether the product contains asbestos or not, dust and dirt can accumulate on manual clutch parts during normal use. Follow practices prescribed by appropriate regulations for the handling, processing and disposing of dust and debris.

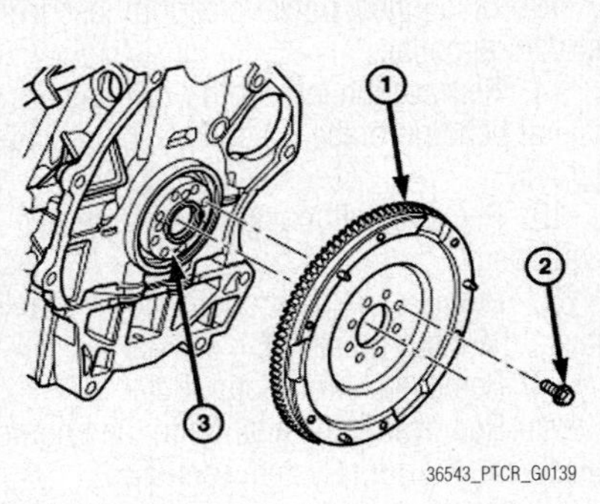

Fig. 46 Flywheel bolt location

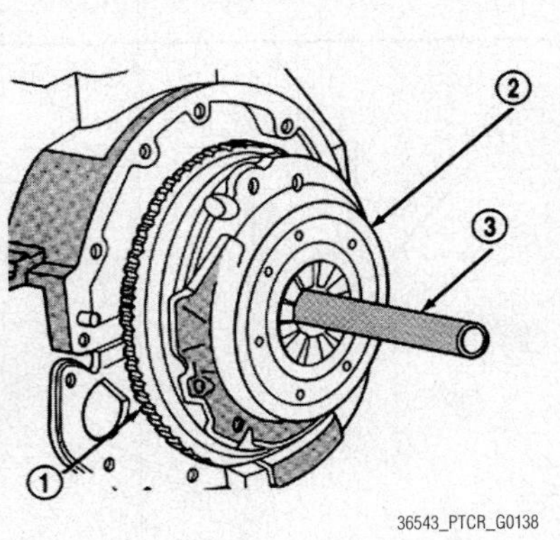

Fig. 47 Use Clutch Alignment Tool 6724 to position the clutch disc to the center of the flywheel

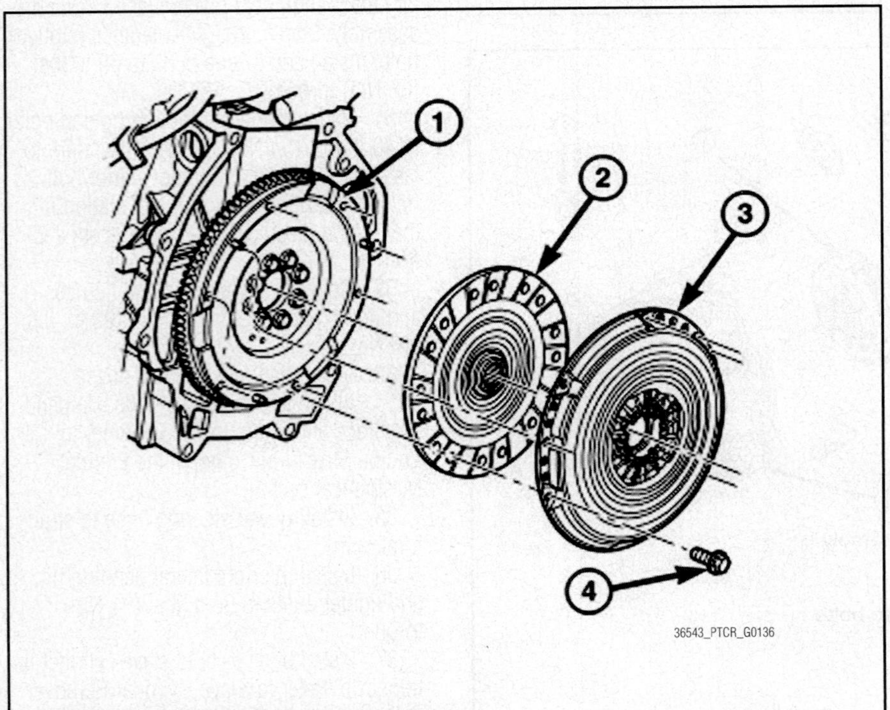

Fig. 45 Flywheel, clutch disc, and pressure plate

1. Before servicing the vehicle, refer to the Precautions Section.

2. Remove transaxle assembly. Refer to Manual Transaxle Removal & Installation.

3. Mark position of pressure plate on flywheel (1) with paint or a scriber for assembly reference.

4. Loosen and remove the 6 pressure plate-to-flywheel bolts (4). Remove the pressure plate (3) and clutch disc (2).

5. Remove the 8 flywheel-to-crankshaft bolts and remove the flywheel assembly.

To install:

6. Inspect clutch release bearing and lever for excessive wear and replace as necessary. Refer to Clutch Release Bearing & Lever Removal & Installation.

7. Clean the surfaces of the flywheel and pressure plate to make certain that all oil, grease, and rust have been removed.

8. Verify the crankshaft mounting flange is free of debris, oil, grease, etc. Position the flywheel onto the engine crankshaft.

9. Install and torque the flywheel-to-crankshaft bolts to 70 ft. lbs. (95 Nm).

10. Apply a very light coating of grease to the splines in the clutch disc hub.

11. Position the clutch disc to the flywheel. Make sure the side marked "FLYWHEEL SIDE" faces the flywheel.

12. Install the clutch pressure plate to the flywheel and clutch disc. Finger-tighten the 6 pressure plate-to-flywheel bolts.

13. Use Clutch Alignment Tool 6724 to position the clutch disc to the center of the flywheel.

14. Tighten pressure plate bolts evenly and in rotation a few threads at a time. The bolts must be tightened evenly and to specified torque to avoid distorting the pressure plate.

15. Using a criss-cross pattern, torque pressure plate-to-flywheel bolts to 21 ft. lbs. (28 Nm).

16. Remove the clutch disc alignment tool.

17. Apply light coat of Mopar® High Temperature Bearing Grease or equivalent to clutch disc hub and splines of transaxle input shaft.

✳✳ WARNING

Do not over lubricate shaft splines. This will result in grease contamination of disc.

18. Install the transaxle. Refer to Manual Transaxle Removal & Installation.

ADJUSTMENTS

This vehicle utilizes a modular clutch, which is serviced as an assembly and is self-adjusting.

CLUTCH MASTER CYLINDER

REMOVAL & INSTALLATION

See Figures 48 through 53.

➡Vehicles equipped with a non-turbocharged engine have one-piece master/slave cylinder assemblies. If the master cylinder requires replacement, the master AND slave cylinders must be replaced with a two-piece "quick-connect" system. If the slave cylinder requires replacement, the slave cylinder is serviced separately.

➡Replacement master cylinder assemblies come pre-filled with fluid. No fluid service or system bleeding should be required, unless the hydraulic system has lost an excessive amount of fluid and has ingested air into the master or slave cylinder assembly.

1. Before servicing the vehicle, refer to the Precautions Section.

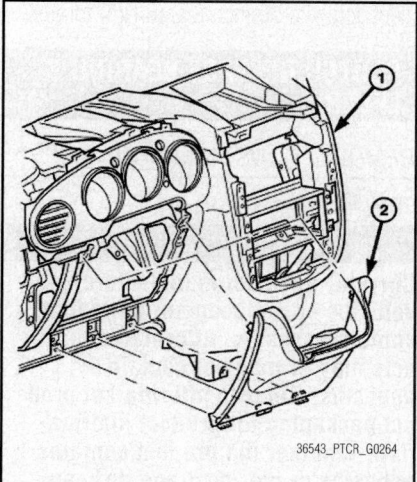

Fig. 48 Lower instrument panel bezel

2. Remove the air cleaner assembly.
3. Disconnect the battery negative cable.
4. Remove lower instrument panel bezel.
5. Remove clip and disconnect the brake booster input rod from the brake pedal pin (1).
6. Remove the brake booster mounting nuts (2).
7. Slide brake booster forward enough to gain access to and remove clutch master cylinder.
8. Disconnect clutch master cylinder pushrod from clutch pedal. Inspect retainer bushing and replace if damaged in any way.
9. Remove the 2 clutch master cylinder retaining nuts (2).
10. Remove Totally Integrated Power Module (TIPM) bracket and position out of way.
11. Raise and support the vehicle, as necessary.

➡To completely drain clutch master cylinder and tubing, remove brake master cylinder cap.

12. Disconnect hydraulic supply tube at clutch slave cylinder. Using suitable screw-

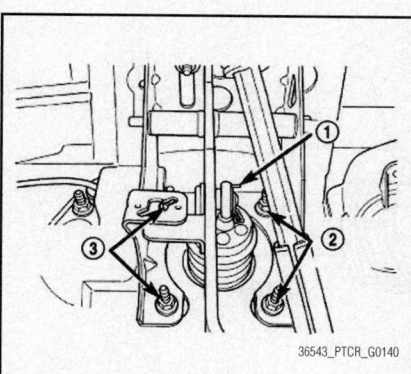

Fig. 49 Brake booster

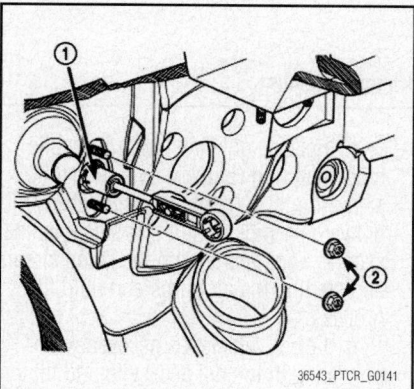

Fig. 50 Clutch master cylinder retaining nuts

driver, release both hydraulic tube retaining clips. Disconnect tube and drain fluid into suitable container.

13. Remove the support and lower the vehicle, as necessary.

14. Disconnect clutch master cylinder supply line (3) from brake master cylinder reservoir (1). Cap off or collect fluid spillage from reservoir port.

✳✳ WARNING

Use care when removing clutch master cylinder from engine compartment. Aggressive handling can result in a damaged hydraulic tube and improper clutch release operation upon reassembly.

✳✳ WARNING

Brake fluid will damage painted surfaces. If brake fluid is spilled on any painted surfaces, wash it off immediately with water.

15. Remove master cylinder assembly from mounting position and carefully work hydraulic pipe from out of left rail retainer and engine compartment.

To install:

16. Install clutch master cylinder into position but do not fasten to dash panel at this time. Carefully route hydraulic pipe into position as removed.

17. Connect hydraulic supply tube to clutch slave cylinder as follows:

a. Raise vehicle as necessary, depress both retaining clips to secure and insert tube into slave cylinder port and verify connection by pulling outward. Lower vehicle as necessary.

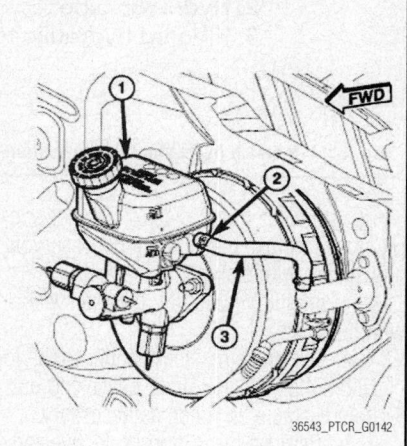

Fig. 51 Clutch master cylinder supply line (3) and brake master cylinder reservoir (1)

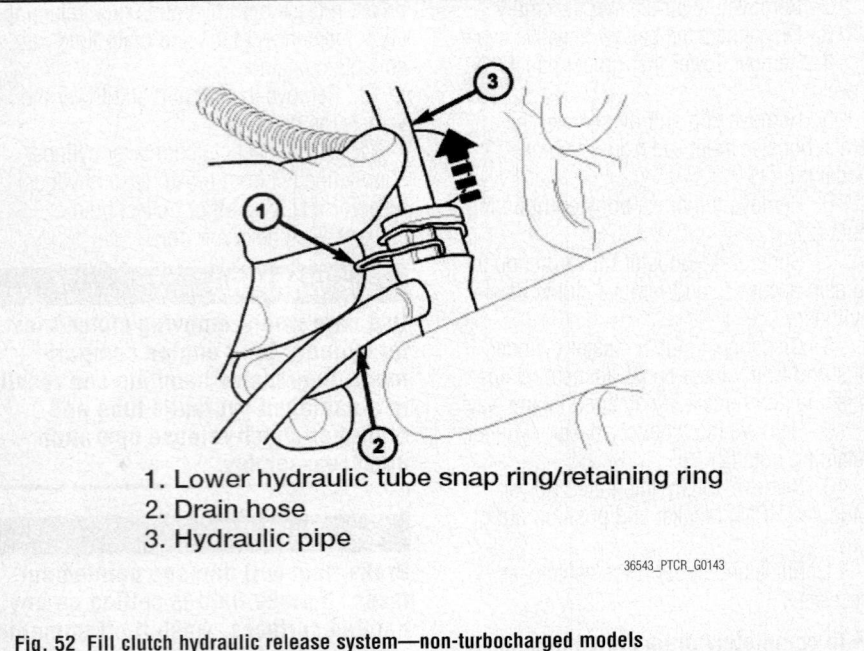

1. Lower hydraulic tube snap ring/retaining ring
2. Drain hose
3. Hydraulic pipe

36543_PTCR_G0143

Fig. 52 Fill clutch hydraulic release system—non-turbocharged models

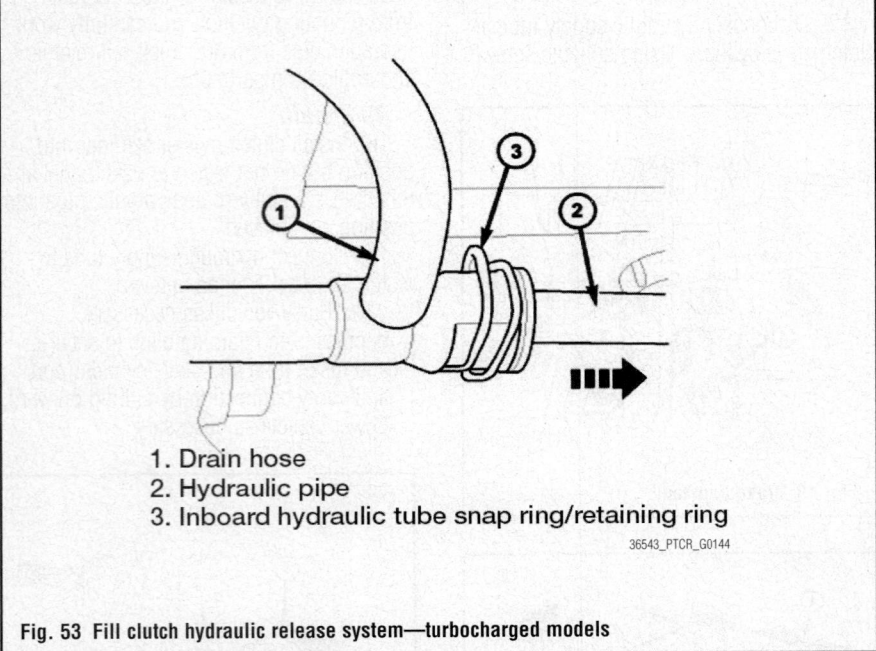

1. Drain hose
2. Hydraulic pipe
3. Inboard hydraulic tube snap ring/retaining ring

36543_PTCR_G0144

Fig. 53 Fill clutch hydraulic release system—turbocharged models

18. Connect clutch master cylinder supply hose to brake master cylinder reservoir and secure with clamp.

19. Fill clutch hydraulic release system with fluid by:

a. Fill brake master cylinder to the top with suitable DOT3 fluid. Leave cap off. Raise vehicle on hoist, as necessary.

b. Remove bleed port protective cap, and install suitable size and length of clear hose to monitor and divert fluid into suitable container.

c. Release only the lower hydraulic tube snap ring (inboard hydraulic tube snap ring for turbocharged models), pull outward on pipe until it stops against the second ring, opening up the bleed circuit and starting the air purge and fluid fill process.

d. Lower vehicle, as necessary, but only enough to gain access to and fill the brake master cylinder.

e. Top off brake master cylinder fluid level while air is purged and fluid drains

from bleed port. Continue this until no air bubbles are seen and a solid column of fluid exists.

f. Close hydraulic bleed circuit. Insert hydraulic pipe fully into slave cylinder and depress retaining ring. Remove drain hose. Replace bleed port protective cap.

20. Verify that brake master cylinder reservoir is full and cap is off.

✱✱ CAUTION

Due to clutch master cylinder design and placement, the master cylinder body traps a significant amount of air which does not purge by means of normal methods. It is necessary to position master cylinder body vertical, with pushrod pointing down, for about ten seconds to purge air trapped from end of cylinder. Failure to perform this step upon assembly will result in inadequate system bleeding and poor release system functionality.

21. Position clutch master cylinder body vertically, with pushrod pointing down, for about ten seconds to purge air trapped from end of cylinder. Install brake master cylinder cap.

22. Install clutch master cylinder body to dash panel. From inside vehicle, install and torque two clutch master cylinder-to-dash panel retaining nuts to 11 ft. lbs. (15 Nm) torque.

23. Loosen master cylinder pushrod adjustment screw.

24. Connect clutch master cylinder rod to clutch pedal pin. An audible "click" should be heard. If damaged, replace nylon retainer.

25. Adjust clutch pedal position. Gently lift upward on clutch pedal. Tighten adjustment screw to 55 inch lbs. (6 Nm) torque.

CLUTCH RELEASE BEARING & LEVER

REMOVAL & INSTALLATION

See Figure 54.

✱✱ CAUTION

Chrysler does not manufacture any vehicles or replacement parts that contain asbestos. Aftermarket products may or may not contain asbestos. Refer to aftermarket product packaging for product information. Whether the product contains asbestos or not, dust and dirt can accumulate on manual clutch parts

during normal use. Follow practices prescribed by appropriate regulations for the handling, processing and disposing of dust and debris.

➡ Models equipped with the turbocharged engine option utilize a release bearing that is integral to the Concentric Slave Cylinder (CSC).

1. Before servicing the vehicle, refer to the Precautions Section.

2. Remove transaxle assembly. Refer to Manual Transaxle Removal & Installation.

3. Move the lever (1) and bearing assembly (2) to a vertical in-line position. Grasp the release lever (2) with two hands in the pivot stud socket area. Pull with even pressure and the lever will pop off the pivot-stud. Do not use a screwdriver or pry bar to pop off the lever. This may damage the spring clip on the lever.

4. As a unit, remove the lever from the bearing thrust plate. Be careful not to damage retention tabs on bearing.

5. Examine the condition of the bearing. It is pre-lubricated and sealed and should not be immersed in oil or solvent.

6. The bearing should turn smoothly when held in the hand under a light thrust load. A light drag caused by the lubricant fill is normal. If the bearing is noisy, rough, or dry, replace the complete bearing assembly with a new bearing.

7. Check the condition of the pivot stud spring clips on back side of clutch release lever. If the clips are broken or distorted, replace the clutch release lever.

To install:

8. The pivot ball pocket in the lever, as well as the lever arms should be lubricated with grease prior to installation.

9. Assemble the lever to the bearing. The small pegs on the bearing must go over the lever arms.

10. Slide the bearing and lever assembly onto the input shaft bearing retainer, as a unit.

11. Snap the clutch release lever onto the pivot ball.

12. Reinstall transaxle assembly. Refer to Manual Transaxle Removal & Installation.

CLUTCH SLAVE CYLINDER

REMOVAL & INSTALLATION

Non-Turbocharged Models

See Figure 55.

➡ To prevent drainage of clutch master cylinder assembly upon slave cylinder removal, it is necessary to make sure brake master cylinder fluid level is full and reservoir cap is installed tight.

1. Verify proper brake fluid level and top off if necessary. Install and tighten brake master cylinder cap to prevent clutch hydraulic system drainage.

2. Raise and safely support the vehicle.

3. Using a suitable screwdriver, release both slave cylinder hydraulic line snap ring retainers. Do not separate at this time.

4. Remove slave cylinder-to-transaxle mounting bolts.

5. Have the replacement slave cylinder ready. Remove the slave cylinder (1) from the transaxle and separate it from the hydraulic tube. Quickly attach the replacement slave cylinder to the plumbing and secure it with both the retaining clips.

To install:

6. Connect slave cylinder to hydraulic tube. Press both retainer clips to secure tube in cylinder.

7. Install the slave cylinder assembly into position on transaxle and tighten bolts to 14 ft. lbs. (19 Nm).

8. Carefully lower the vehicle.

9. Verify clutch master cylinder reservoir is full. Top off with DOT 3 brake fluid if necessary.

10. Bleed clutch hydraulic system. Refer to Hydraulic System Bleeding, in this section.

11. Verify proper clutch release system operation.

Turbocharged Models

See Figures 56 and 57.

1. Remove transaxle from vehicle.

2. Remove 4 slave cylinder-to-clutch bellhousing bolts and remove slave cylinder from transaxle.

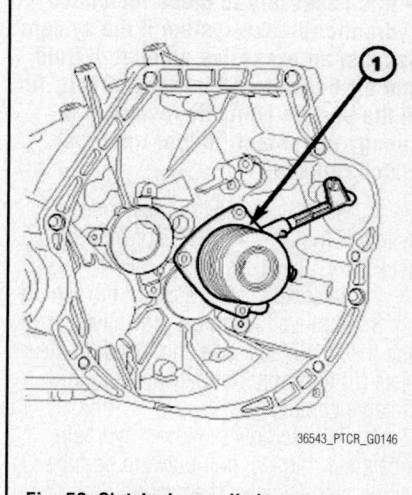

36543_PTCR_G0146

Fig. 56 Clutch slave cylinder—turbocharged models

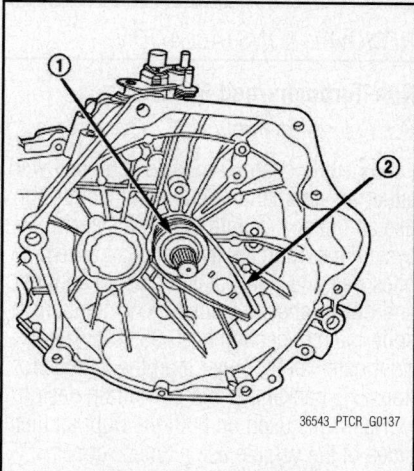

36543_PTCR_G0137

Fig. 54 Lever and bearing assembly

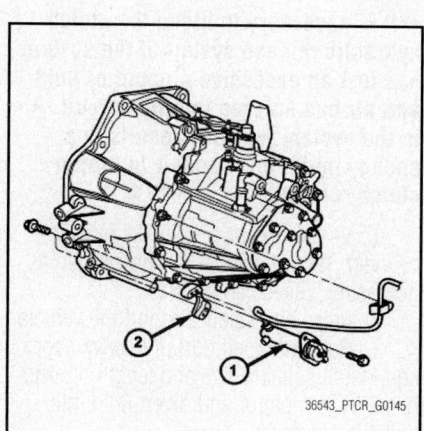

36543_PTCR_G0145

Fig. 55 Clutch slave cylinder—non-turbocharged models

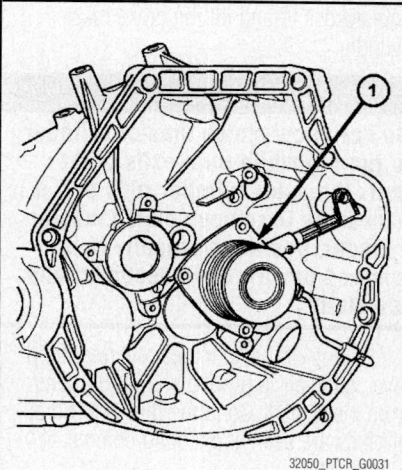

32050_PTCR_G0031

Fig. 57 Clutch slave cylinder installation location—turbocharged models

To install:

3. Install slave cylinder to transaxle using new bolts.

➡Torque the 3 CSC body screws first, then the fluid tube attachment.

4. Torque the slave cylinder-to-case bolts in three steps:
- 18 inch lbs. (2 Nm)
- 44 inch lbs. (5 Nm)
- 74 inch lbs. (8 Nm)
5. Install the transaxle.

CLUTCH HYDRAULIC SYSTEM BLEEDING

BLEEDING PROCEDURE

Non-Turbocharged Models

See Figures 52 and 55.

➡It is necessary to bleed the clutch hydraulic release system if the system has lost an excessive amount of fluid and air has entered into the circuit. Air in the system typically results in a spongy pedal feel, and/or improper clutch release.

1. Verify fluid level in brake master cylinder. Top off with DOT 3 brake fluid as necessary. Leave cap off.
2. Raise and safely support the vehicle.
3. Remove bleed port protective cap, and install suitable size and length of clear hose (2) to monitor and divert fluid into suitable container.
4. Release only the lower hydraulic tube snap ring (1), pull outward on tube (3) until it stops against the second ring, opening up the bleed circuit and starting the air purge and fluid fill process.
5. Lower vehicle, but only enough to gain access to and fill the brake master cylinder.

✳✳ WARNING

Do not allow clutch master cylinder to run dry while fluid exits bleed port. If master cylinder runs dry, it is necessary to remove clutch master cylinder, position vertically (with pushrod down) for 10 seconds, and reinstall.

6. Top off brake master cylinder fluid level while air is purged and fluid drains from bleed port. Continue this until no air bubbles are seen and a solid column of fluid exists.
7. Close hydraulic bleed circuit. Insert hydraulic pipe fully into slave cylinder and depress retaining ring so both are closed, securing tube. Pull outward to verify connection. Remove drain hose.
8. From driver's seat, actuate clutch pedal 60–100 times. Replace dust cap onto bleed port.
9. Apply parking brake. Start engine and verify clutch operation and pedal feel. If pedal feels fine and clutch operates as designed, stop here. If pedal still feels spongy or clutch does not fully disengage, excessive air is still trapped within the system.
10. Verify fluid level in clutch master cylinder reservoir. Top off with DOT 3 brake fluid as necessary.
11. Raise vehicle on hoist.
12. Remove clutch slave cylinder assembly from the transaxle case (1), but do not disconnect from the system. Allow the slave cylinder to hang, making it the lowest part of the system.

✳✳ WARNING

While slave cylinder is detached from the transaxle, DO NOT actuate the clutch master cylinder. Damage to the slave cylinder will result.

13. Depress slave cylinder pushrod until it bottoms and then release. Repeat this at least 50 times, forcing trapped air upwards and out of the system.
14. Re-install slave cylinder (1) into position. Torque slave cylinder-to-case bolt to 14 ft. lbs. (19 Nm).
15. Lower vehicle.
16. Verify clutch operation. Repeat procedure if necessary.
17. Top off brake master cylinder fluid level with DOT 3 brake fluid as necessary.

Turbocharged Models

See Figure 54.

➡It is necessary to bleed the clutch hydraulic release system if the system has lost an excessive amount of fluid and air has entered into the circuit. Air in the system typically results in a spongy pedal feel, and/or improper clutch release.

1. Verify fluid level in brake master cylinder. Top off with DOT 3 brake fluid as necessary. Leave cap off.
2. Raise and safely support the vehicle.
3. Remove bleed port protective cap, and install suitable size and length of clear hose (1) to monitor and divert fluid into suitable container.
4. Release only the inner (closest to bleed port) hydraulic tube snap ring (3), pull outward on tube (2) until it stops against the second ring, opening up the bleed circuit and starting the air purge and fluid fill process.
5. Lower vehicle, but only enough to gain access to and fill the brake master cylinder.

➡Do not allow clutch master cylinder to run dry while fluid exits bleed port. If master cylinder runs dry, it is necessary to remove clutch master cylinder, position vertically (with pushrod down) for 10 seconds, and reinstall.

6. Top off brake master cylinder fluid level while air is purged and fluid drains from bleed port. Continue this until no air bubbles are seen and a solid column of fluid exists.
7. Close hydraulic bleed circuit. Insert hydraulic pipe fully into slave cylinder and depress retaining ring so both are closed, securing tube. Pull outward to verify connection. Remove drain hose. Replace dust cap on bleed port.
8. From driver's seat, actuate clutch pedal 60–100 times.
9. Apply parking brake. Start engine and verify clutch operation and pedal feel. If pedal feels fine and clutch operates as designed, stop here. If pedal still feels spongy or clutch does not fully disengage, excessive air is still trapped within the system, most likely at the master cylinder.
10. Remove clutch master cylinder body from dash panel or pedal bracket. Position cylinder body vertical (pushrod pointing down) for 10 seconds. Air bubbles will be seen escaping master cylinder.
11. Verify clutch operation. Repeat procedure if necessary.
12. Top off brake master cylinder fluid level with DOT 3 brake fluid as necessary.

FRONT HALFSHAFTS

REMOVAL & INSTALLATION

Non-Turbocharged Models

See Figures 58 through 65.

Non-turbocharged models equipped with either an automatic or manual transmission use an unequal-length halfshaft system. The system incorporates two halfshaft assemblies (left and right) that consist of an inner and outer constant velocity (CV) joint and a solid interconnecting shaft 95, 14). The right halfshaft is longer than the left due to transaxle packaging and powertrain design.

Halfshafts used on both the right and left sides of the vehicle use a tuned rubber damper weight (4) mounted to the intercon-

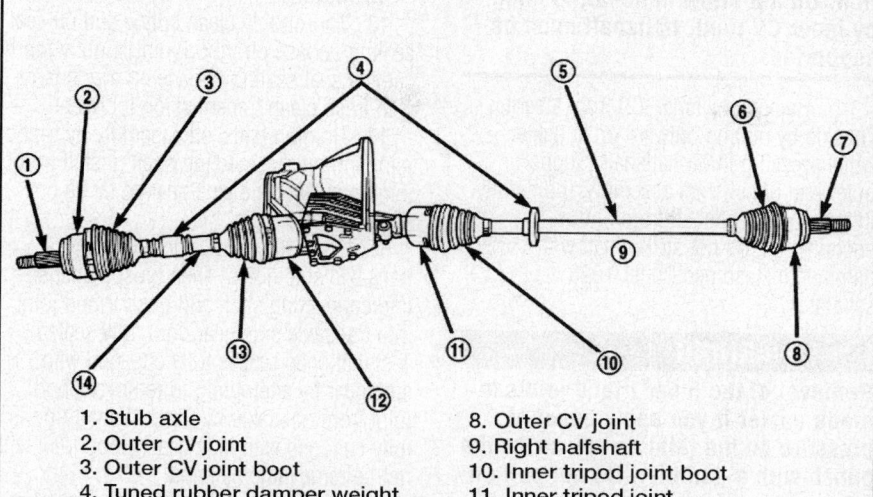

1. Stub axle
2. Outer CV joint
3. Outer CV joint boot
4. Tuned rubber damper weight
5. Interconnecting shaft, right-hand
6. Outer CV joint boot
7. Stub axle
8. Outer CV joint
9. Right halfshaft
10. Inner tripod joint boot
11. Inner tripod joint
12. Inner tripod joint
13. Inner tripod joint boot
14. Interconnecting shaft, left-hand

36543_PTCR_G0155

Fig. 58 Unequal length halfshaft system—non-turbocharged models

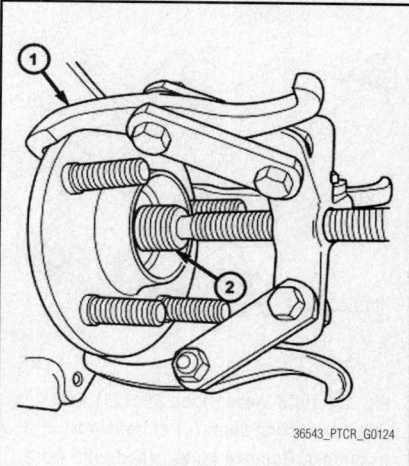

36543_PTCR_G0124

Fig. 62 Remove halfshaft (2) from steering knuckle by pulling outward on knuckle while pressing in on halfshaft

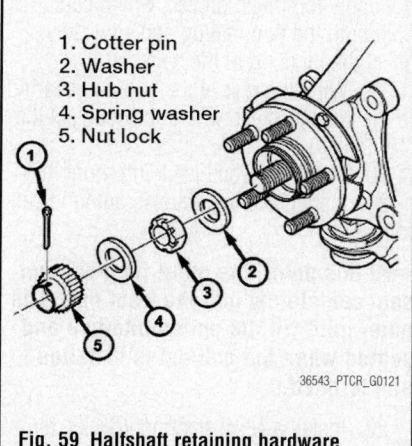

1. Cotter pin
2. Washer
3. Hub nut
4. Spring washer
5. Nut lock

36543_PTCR_G0121

Fig. 59 Halfshaft retaining hardware

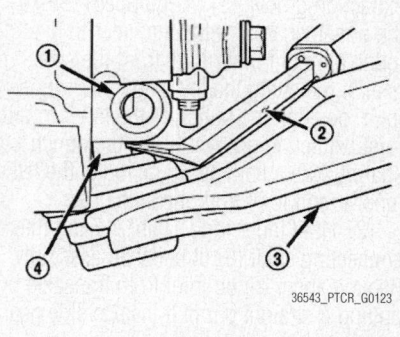

36543_PTCR_G0123

Fig. 61 Separate ball joint stud (4) from steering knuckle (1) by prying down on lower control arm (3)

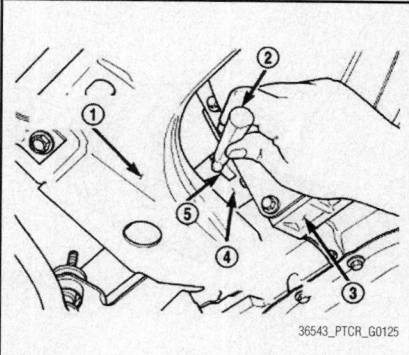

36543_PTCR_G0125

Fig. 63 Remove the inner tripod joints (4) from the side gears of the transaxle using a punch (2) to dislodge the inner tripod joint retaining ring from the transaxle side gear

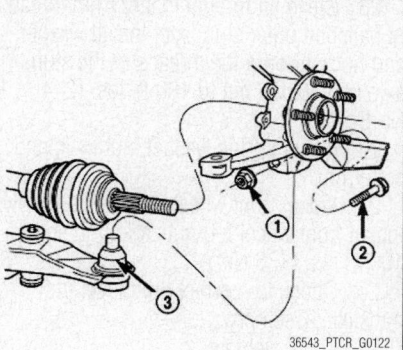

36543_PTCR_G0122

Fig. 60 Remove nut and bolt (1,2) retaining ball joint stud (3) into steering knuckle

necting shaft (5,14). The damper weight applications vary by which side of the vehicle the halfshaft is located on and the transmission application of the vehicle. When replacing a halfshaft, be sure the replacement halfshaft has the same damper weight as the original.

1. Before servicing the vehicle, refer to the Precautions Section.

✻✻ WARNING

Boot sealing is vital to retain special lubricants and to prevent foreign contaminants from entering the CV joint. Mishandling, such as allowing the assemblies to dangle unsupported, or pulling or pushing the ends can cut boots or damage CV joints. During removal and installation procedures, always support both ends of the halfshaft to prevent damage.

✻✻ CAUTION

The halfshaft, when installed, acts as a bolt and secures the front hub/bearing assembly. If vehicle is to be supported or moved on its wheels with a halfshaft removed, install a PROPER-SIZED BOLT AND NUT through front hub. Tighten bolt and nut to 180 ft. lbs. (244 Nm). This will ensure that the hub bearing cannot loosen.

2. Disconnect battery negative cable.
3. Place transaxle in gated park.
4. Raise vehicle on hoist.

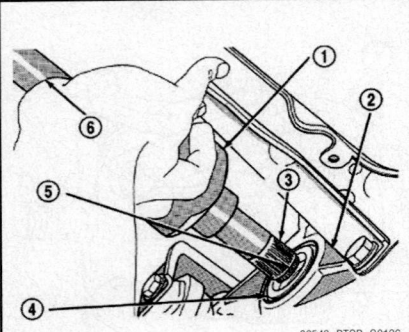

Fig. 64 Hold inner tripod joint (1) and interconnecting shaft (6) of halfshaft assembly. Remove inner tripod joint from transaxle by pulling it straight out of transaxle side gear and transaxle oil seal (4)

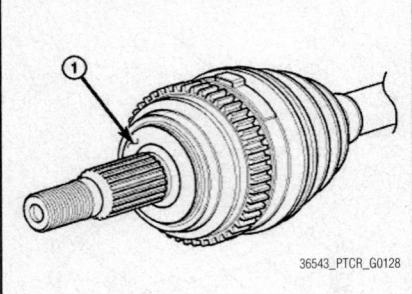

Fig. 65 Apply a light coating of Mopar® multi-purpose wheel bearing grease around the circumference of the flat surface (1)

5. Remove wheel and tire assembly.
6. Remove the cotter pin (1), nut lock (5), spring washer (4), and hub nut (3) from the end of the outer C/V joint stub axle.
7. If equipped with ABS, disconnect the front wheel speed sensor and secure harness out of the way.
8. Remove nut and bolt (1,2) retaining ball joint stud (3) into steering knuckle.

❊❊ WARNING
Use caution when separating ball joint stud from steering knuckle, so ball joint seal does not get damaged.

9. Separate ball joint stud (4) from steering knuckle (1) by prying down on lower control arm (3).

❊❊ WARNING
Care must be taken not to separate the inner CV joint during this opera-

tion. Do not allow halfshaft to hang by inner CV joint, halfshaft must be supported.

10. Remove halfshaft (2) from steering knuckle by pulling outward on knuckle while pressing in on halfshaft. Support outer end of halfshaft assembly. If difficulty in separating halfshaft from hub is encountered, do not strike shaft with hammer, instead use Puller 1026 (1) to separate.

❊❊ WARNING
Removal of the inner tripod joints is made easier if you apply outward pressure on the joint as you strike the punch with a hammer. Do not pull on interconnecting shaft to remove, as the inner joint will become separated.

11. Remove the inner tripod joints (4) from the side gears of the transaxle using a punch (2) to dislodge the inner tripod joint retaining ring from the transaxle side gear. If removing the right side inner tripod joint, position the punch to the inner tripod joint extraction groove (5) (if equipped). Strike the punch sharply with a hammer to dislodge the right inner joint from the side gear. If removing the left side inner tripod joint, position the punch to the inner tripod joint extraction groove. Strike the punch sharply with a hammer to dislodge the left inner tripod joint from the side gear.
12. Hold inner tripod joint (1) and interconnecting shaft (6) of halfshaft assembly. Remove inner tripod joint from transaxle by pulling it straight out of transaxle side gear and transaxle oil seal (4).

❊❊ WARNING
When removing tripod joint, do not let spline or snap ring drag across sealing lip of the transaxle to tripod joint oil seal. When tripod joint is removed from transaxle, some fluid will leak out.

❊❊ CAUTION
The halfshaft, when installed, acts as a bolt and secures the front hub/bearing assembly. If vehicle is to be supported or moved on its wheels with a halfshaft removed, install a PROPER-SIZED BOLT AND NUT through front hub. Tighten bolt and nut to 180 ft. lbs. (244 Nm). This will ensure that the hub bearing cannot loosen.

To install:

13. Thoroughly clean spline and oil seal sealing surface on tripod joint. Lightly lubricate oil seal sealing surface on tripod joint with fresh clean transmission lubricant.
14. Holding halfshaft assembly by tripod joint and interconnecting shaft, install tripod joint into transaxle side gear as far as possible by hand.
15. Carefully align tripod joint with transaxle side gears. Then grasp halfshaft interconnecting shaft and push tripod joint into transaxle side gear until fully seated. Test that snap ring is fully engaged with side gear by attempting to remove tripod joint from transaxle by hand. If snap ring is fully engaged with side gear, tripod joint will not be removable by hand.
16. Clean all debris and moisture out of steering knuckle.
17. Ensure that front of outer CV joint which fits into steering knuckle, is free of debris and moisture before assembling into steering knuckle.
18. Apply a light coating of Mopar® multi-purpose wheel bearing grease around the circumference of the flat surface (1). Do not apply too much grease, which could spill onto the non mating and adversely affect the function of the halfshaft.
19. Wipe the rear of the hub and bearing in the knuckle clean where they contact the C/V joint.
20. Install halfshaft back into front hub.
21. Install steering knuckle onto the ball joint stud.

➡**At this point, the outer joint will not seat completely into the front hub. The outer joint will be pulled into hub and seated when the hub nut is installed and torqued.**

22. Install a NEW steering knuckle to ball joint stud bolt and nut. Tighten the nut and bolt to 70 ft. lbs. (95 Nm).
23. Clean all foreign matter from threads of halfshaft outer stub axle. Install washer and hub nut onto the threads of the stub axle and tighten nut to 180 ft. lbs. (244 Nm).
24. Install spring washer, nut lock, and cotter pin.
25. Install front wheel and tire assembly. Install front wheel lug nuts and tighten to 100 ft. lbs. (136 Nm).
26. Check for correct fluid level in transaxle assembly.
27. Lower vehicle.
28. Connect battery negative cable.

Turbocharged Models
See Figures 59 through 62, 66 through 68.

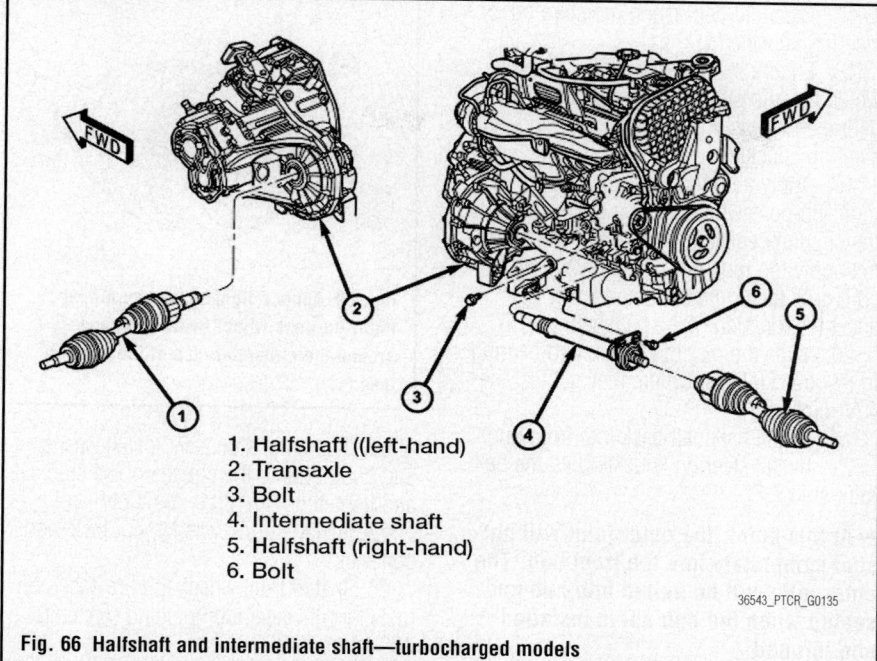

1. Halfshaft ((left-hand)
2. Transaxle
3. Bolt
4. Intermediate shaft
5. Halfshaft (right-hand)
6. Bolt

36543_PTCR_G0135

Fig. 66 Halfshaft and intermediate shaft—turbocharged models

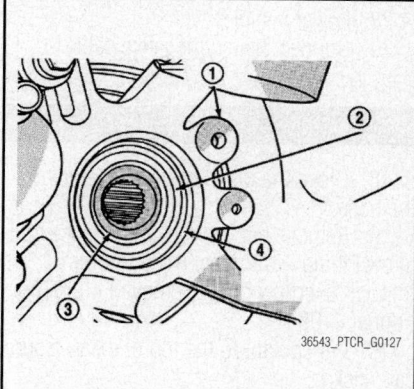

36543_PTCR_G0127

Fig. 68 Clean all debris and moisture out of steering knuckle (4)

Vehicles equipped with the 2.4L turbocharger utilize an equal-length halfshaft system. The system incorporates two halfshaft assemblies (left and right) that consist of an inner and outer constant velocity (CV) joint and a solid interconnecting shaft, and an intermediate shaft/bearing assembly.

The left halfshaft uses a tuned-rubber damper weight mounted to the interconnecting shaft. When replacing a halfshaft, be sure the replacement halfshaft has the same damper weight as the original.

1. Before servicing the vehicle, refer to the Precautions Section.

✳✳ WARNING

Boot sealing is vital to retain special lubricants and to prevent foreign contaminants from entering the CV joint.

Mishandling, such as allowing the assemblies to dangle unsupported, or pulling or pushing the ends can cut boots or damage CV joints. During removal and installation procedures, always support both ends of the halfshaft to prevent damage.

✳✳ CAUTION

The halfshaft, when installed, acts as a bolt and secures the front hub/bearing assembly. If vehicle is to be supported or moved on its wheels with a halfshaft removed, install a PROPER-SIZED BOLT AND NUT through front hub. Tighten bolt and nut to 180 ft. lbs. (244 Nm). This will ensure that the hub bearing cannot loosen.

2. Disconnect battery negative cable.
3. Place transaxle in gated park.
4. Raise vehicle on hoist.
5. Remove wheel and tire assembly.
6. Remove the cotter pin (1), nut lock (5), spring washer (4), and hub nut (3) from the end of the outer C/V joint stub axle.
7. If equipped with ABS, disconnect the front wheel speed sensor and secure harness out of the way.
8. Remove nut and bolt (1,2) retaining ball joint stud (3) into steering knuckle.

✳✳ WARNING

Use caution when separating ball joint stud from steering knuckle, so ball joint seal does not get damaged.

9. Separate ball joint stud (4) from steering knuckle (1) by prying down on lower control arm (3).

✳✳ WARNING

Care must be taken not to separate the inner CV joint during this operation. Do not allow halfshaft to hang by inner CV joint, halfshaft must be supported.

10. Remove halfshaft (2) from steering knuckle by pulling outward on knuckle while pressing in on halfshaft. Support outer end of halfshaft assembly. If difficulty in separating halfshaft from hub is encountered, do not strike shaft with hammer, instead use Puller 1026 (1) to separate.

✳✳ WARNING

Removal of the inner tripod joints is made easier if you apply outward pressure on the joint as you strike the punch with a hammer. Do not pull on interconnecting shaft to remove, as the inner joint will become separated.

➡ When left halfshaft is removed from transaxle, some fluid may leak out.

11. Remove left halfshaft: While applying outward pressure on joint by hand, dislodge inner tripod joint from differential side gear by striking outward with a punch at extraction groove. When removing tripod joint and halfshaft, do not let spline or snap ring drag across sealing lip of the transaxle to tripod joint oil seal.

12. Remove right halfshaft: Slide inner tripod joint off of intermediate shaft. If difficulty is encountered, dislodge joint from intermediate shaft using punch.

13. If intermediate shaft is to be removed, remove three intermediate shaft bearing-to-bracket bolts. 2.4L turbocharged models utilize two (2) intermediate shaft bearing-to-bracket bolts. Remove intermediate shaft bearing/shaft assembly from transaxle.

✳✳ CAUTION

The halfshaft, when installed, acts as a bolt and secures the front hub/bearing assembly. If vehicle is to be supported or moved on its wheels with a halfshaft removed, install a PROPER-SIZED BOLT AND NUT through front hub. Tighten bolt and nut to 180 ft. lbs. (244 Nm). This will ensure that the hub bearing cannot loosen.

To install:

14. If removed, install intermediate shaft/bearing assembly. Install and torque bearing-to-bracket bolts to 21 ft. lbs. (28 Nm).

15. Install left halfshaft: Thoroughly clean spline and oil seal sealing surface on left tripod joint. Lightly lubricate oil seal sealing surface on tripod joint with fresh clean transmission lubricant. While holding halfshaft assembly by tripod joint and interconnecting shaft, install tripod joint into transaxle as far as possible by hand. Carefully align tripod joint with transaxle side gears. Then grasp halfshaft interconnecting shaft and push tripod joint into transaxle side gear until fully seated. Test that snap ring is fully engaged with the female spline by attempting to remove tripod joint from intermediate shaft by hand. If snap ring is fully engaged with side gear, tripod joint will not be removable by hand.

16. Install right halfshaft: Thoroughly clean right halfshaft tripod joint spline, as well as intermediate shaft spline. While holding halfshaft assembly by tripod joint and interconnecting shaft, install tripod joint onto intermediate shaft as far as possible by hand.

17. Clean all debris and moisture out of steering knuckle (4).

18. Ensure that front of outer CV joint which fits into steering knuckle, is free of debris and moisture before assembling into steering knuckle.

19. Apply a light coating of Mopar® multi-purpose wheel bearing grease around the circumference of the flat surface (1). Do not apply too much grease, which could spill onto the non mating and adversely affect the function of the halfshaft.

20. Wipe the rear of the hub and bearing in the knuckle clean where they contact the C/V joint.

21. Install halfshaft back into front hub.

22. Install steering knuckle onto the ball joint stud.

➡ **At this point, the outer joint will not seat completely into the front hub. The outer joint will be pulled into hub and seated when the hub nut is installed and torqued.**

23. Install a NEW steering knuckle to ball joint stud bolt and nut. Tighten the nut and bolt to 70 ft. lbs. (95 Nm).

24. Clean all foreign matter from threads

Fig. 69 Apply a light coating of Mopar® multi-purpose wheel bearing grease around the circumference of the flat surface (1)

of halfshaft outer stub axle. Install washer and hub nut onto the threads of the stub axle and tighten nut to 180 ft. lbs. (244 Nm).

25. Install spring washer, nut lock, and cotter pin.

26. Install front wheel and tire assembly. Install front wheel lug nuts and tighten to 100 ft. lbs. (136 Nm).

27. Check for correct fluid level in transaxle assembly.

28. Lower vehicle.

29. Connect battery negative cable.

ENGINE COOLING

COOLANT DRAINING & REFILLING

COOLANT DRAIN PROCEDURE

1. Before servicing the vehicle, refer to the Precautions Section.

✳✳ CAUTION

Do not open the radiator draincock with the system hot and under pressure. Serious burns from coolant can occur.

2. Position a clean collecting container under draincock location.

3. Without removing the pressure cap and with system not under pressure, turn draincock counterclockwise to open.

4. The coolant reserve bottle should empty first, then remove the pressure cap.

5. If coolant reserve bottle does not empty first:
   a. Check condition of the pressure cap and cap seals.
   b. Check for kinked/torn overflow hose from filler neck to reserve bottle.

6. Allow cooling system to drain completely.

COOLANT FILL PROCEDURE

1. Before servicing the vehicle, refer to the Precautions Section.

2. Close radiator draincock. Hand tighten only.

3. Open, but do not remove cooling system bleed valve.

4. Attach a 0.250 in. (6.35 mm) inside diameter clear hose that is 48 in. (120.0 cm) long to the bleed valve. Route the hose away from the accessory drive belts and radiator fan. Position the other end of the hose into a clean collecting container. The hose will prevent coolant from contacting the accessory drive belts, A/C compressor, and other components.

➡ **Be careful not to spill coolant on drive belts or the alternator.**

➡ **While filling the cooling system, pour coolant into the larger section of the Filling Aid Funnel 8195.**

5. Remove the cooling system pressure cap. Install Special Tool 8195 Filling Aid Funnel.

6. Use the supplied clip to pinch overflow hose.

7. Slowly fill the cooling system until a steady stream of coolant flows from the attached hose on the bleed valve.

8. Close the bleed valve and remove the hose.

9. Remove clip from overflow hose and allow Filling Aid Funnel 8195 to drain through overflow hose. Remove Filling Aid Funnel 8195.

10. Fill coolant to the top of the pressure cap neck.

11. Install cooling system pressure cap.

✳✳ WARNING

Coolant may leak out of the bottle overflow tube if filling too rapidly.

12. Slowly fill coolant recovery container to at least the FULL HOT mark with the recommended coolant. It may be necessary to add additional coolant to the reserve/recovery bottle after three or four warm up/cool down cycles to maintain coolant level between the FULL HOT and ADD marks. This is due to the removal of trapped air from the system.

ENGINE FAN

REMOVAL & INSTALLATION

See Figure 69.

1. Before servicing the vehicle, refer to the Precautions Section.

➡The fan motor, fan, and the shroud are serviced as an assembly.

✳✳ CAUTION

Do not open the radiator draincock with the system hot and under pressure, because serious burns from coolant can occur.

2. Disconnect negative cable from battery.

3. Remove battery and battery tray.

4. Drain cooling system below upper radiator hose level. See Coolant section, Drain Procedure.

5. Remove grille.

6. Remove upper radiator closure panel and center brace.

7. Disconnect upper radiator hose from radiator.

8. For turbocharger equipped vehicles: Remove radiator inlet neck.

9. Raise and safely support the vehicle.

10. Disconnect radiator fan electrical connector.

11. Remove the 2 lower and left side radiator fan screws.

12. Lower the vehicle and remove the remaining radiator fan attaching screws.

✳✳ WARNING

Care should be taken not to damage the radiator cooling fins and tubes during fan removal.

13. Remove the radiator fan by lifting up from the engine compartment.

To install:

14. Install the radiator fan into position on the radiator.

15. Hand-start all radiator fan fasteners.

16. Tighten all radiator fan retaining screws to 55 inch lbs. (6 Nm).

17. Connect the radiator fan electrical connector.

18. Carefully lower the vehicle.

19. For turbocharger equipped vehicles: Inspect radiator inlet neck O-ring. Replace if necessary. Install radiator inlet neck. Torque fasteners to 55 inch lbs. (6 Nm).

20. Connect the upper radiator hose to radiator. Align hose and position clamp so it will not interfere with the engine or the hood.

21. Install upper radiator closure panel and center brace.

22. Install grille.

23. Install battery tray and battery.

24. Connect cables to battery.

25. Fill cooling system. See Coolant section, Fill Procedure.

RADIATOR

REMOVAL & INSTALLATION

See Figures 70 and 71.

1. Before servicing the vehicle, refer to the Precautions Section.

2. Disconnect battery cables.

✳✳ CAUTION

Do not open the radiator draincock with the system hot and under pressure, because serious burns from coolant can occur.

3. Drain the cooling system. See Coolant section, Drain Procedure.

4. Remove air cleaner assembly. Refer to Air Cleaner Assembly Removal & Installation, in the Engine Mechanical section.

5. Remove battery and battery tray.

6. Remove grille.

➡It is not necessary to discharge the air conditioning system to remove the radiator.

7. Remove upper radiator closure panel and center brace.

8. Disconnect the upper radiator hose.

9. Remove the radiator fan. See Engine Fan Removal & Installation.

10. Turbocharged models: Disconnect and cap the power steering hoses.

11. Disconnect lower radiator hose.

12. Non-turbocharged models with automatic transaxle: Remove the 2 fasteners attaching transaxle oil cooler to radiator.

13. Non-turbocharged models: Remove lower radiator air seal from side radiator air seals.

14. Remove the fasteners (2) attaching A/C condenser to radiator. Reposition A/C condenser.

15. Turbocharged models: Remove fasteners (5) attaching charge air cooler to radiator.

16. Remove the radiator assembly by lifting it up from the engine compartment. Care should be taken not to damage the cooling fins and tubes during removal.

17. Non-turbocharged models: Remove the lower air seal from radiator.

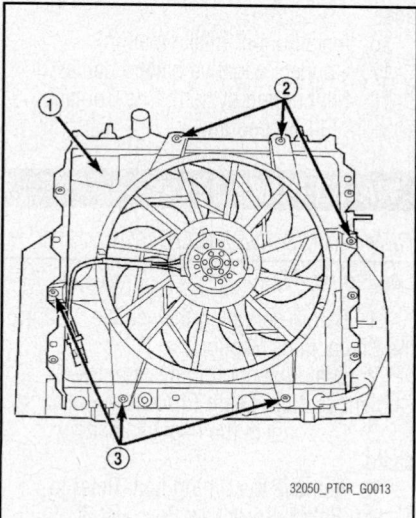

32050_PTCR_G0013

Fig. 69 Radiator fan mounting points

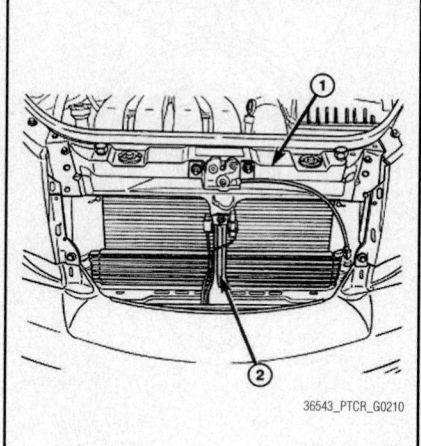

36543_PTCR_G0210

Fig. 70 Remove upper radiator closure panel and center brace

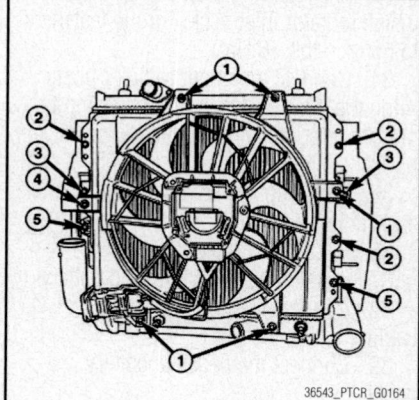

36543_PTCR_G0164

Fig. 71 Remove the fasteners (2) attaching A/C condenser to radiator; and for turbocharged models, remove fasteners (5) attaching charge air cooler to radiator

To install:

18. Non-turbocharged models: Install the lower air seal to radiator.

➡**Turbocharged models: When lowering the radiator, make sure lower radiator pins engage properly through charge air cooler locating tabs.**

19. Position radiator into mounting position.

20. Position A/C condenser against radiator. Hand start fasteners.

21. Turbocharged models: Install fasteners attaching charge air cooler to radiator. Torque fasteners to 70 inch lbs. (8 Nm).

22. Install the radiator fan/shroud assembly. Hand start fasteners.

23. Torque all condenser fasteners to 70 inch lbs. (8 Nm).

24. Torque all radiator fan fasteners to 55 inch lbs. (6 Nm).

25. Non-turbocharged models with automatic transaxle: Install fasteners attaching transaxle oil cooler to radiator. Torque fasteners to 70 inch lbs. (8 Nm).

26. Raise and safely support the vehicle.

27. Non-turbocharged models: Connect the lower air seal to the side air seals.

28. Connect lower radiator hose. Align the hose and position the clamp so it will not interfere with engine components.

29. Connect the radiator fan electrical connector.

30. Turbocharged models: Connect the power steering hoses.

31. Close radiator draincock.

32. Carefully lower the vehicle.

33. Turbocharged models: Inspect radiator inlet neck O-ring. Replace if necessary. Install radiator inlet neck. Torque fasteners to 55 inch lbs. (6 Nm).

34. Connect the upper radiator hose. Align the hose and position the clamp to prevent interference with the engine or hood.

35. Install upper radiator closure panel and center brace.

36. Install the grille.

37. Install the battery tray and battery.

38. Connect the positive battery cable.

39. Connect the negative battery cable.

40. Install air cleaner housing assembly. Refer to Air Cleaner Assembly Removal & Installation, in the Engine Mechanical section.

41. Fill the cooling system with coolant. See Coolant section, Fill Procedure.

42. Operate engine until it reaches normal operating temperature. Check cooling system for correct fluid level.

43. Turbocharged models: Check power steering fluid level. Fill as needed.

THERMOSTAT

REMOVAL & INSTALLATION

See Figures 72 and 73.

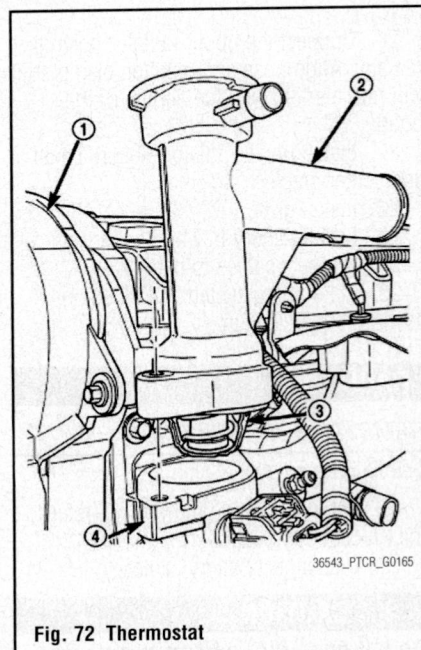

36543_PTCR_G0165

Fig. 72 Thermostat

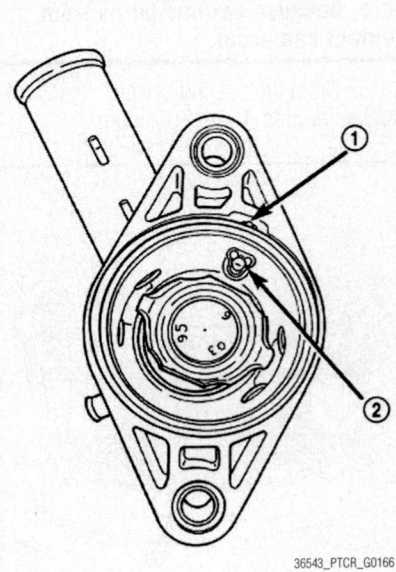

36543_PTCR_G0166

Fig. 73 Place the new thermostat assembly into the coolant outlet connector, aligning air bleed (2) with the location notch on outlet connector

1. Before servicing the vehicle, refer to the Precautions Section.

2. Disconnect negative battery cable.

3. Remove upper intake manifold. Refer to Intake Manifold Removal & Installation, in the Engine Mechanical section.

4. Partially drain the cooling system below thermostat housing level. See Coolant section, Drain Procedure.

5. Disconnect upper radiator hose from outlet connector.

6. Disconnect coolant recovery system hose from outlet connector.

7. Turbocharger equipped vehicles:
   a. Remove fastener securing A/C suction line support bracket to coolant outlet connector stud.
   b. Unclip A/C suction line support bracket from A/C suction line. Reposition bracket.

8. Remove coolant outlet connector bolts.

9. Remove thermostat assembly.

To install:

10. Clean all gasket sealing surfaces.

11. Place the new thermostat assembly into the coolant outlet connector, aligning air bleed (2) with the location notch on outlet connector.

12. Install coolant outlet connector with thermostat in position onto thermostat housing. Tighten bolts to 9 ft. lbs. (12.5 Nm).

13. Turbocharger equipped vehicles:
   a. Attach A/C suction line support bracket to A/C suction line.
   b. Install fastener securing A/C suction line support bracket to coolant outlet connector.

14. Connect upper radiator hose.

15. Connect the coolant recovery system hose.

16. Install upper intake manifold.

17. Connect negative battery cable.

18. Fill cooling system. See Coolant section, Fill Procedure.

WATER PUMP

REMOVAL & INSTALLATION

See Figure 74.

1. Before servicing the vehicle, refer to the Precautions Section.

2. Drain the cooling system. See Coolant section, Drain Procedure.

3. Disconnect the negative battery cable.

4. Remove the timing belt. Refer to Timing Belt & Sprockets Removal & Installation, in the Engine Mechanical section.

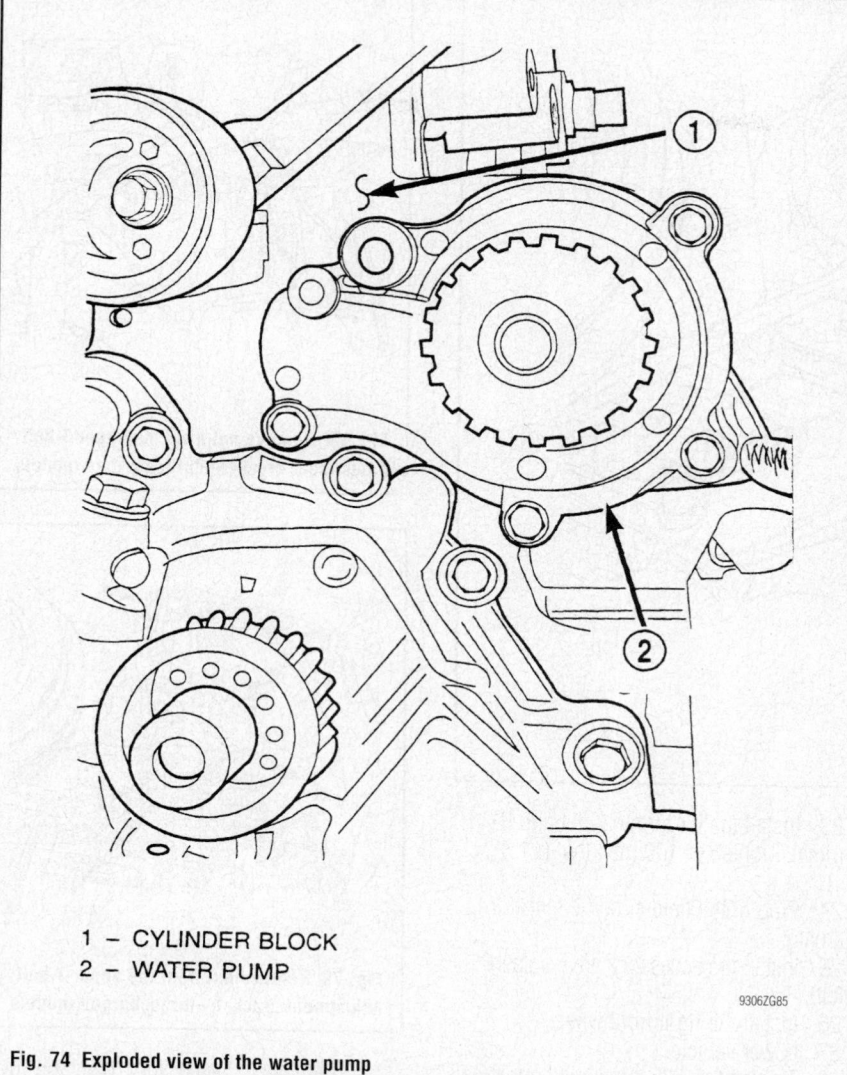

1 – CYLINDER BLOCK
2 – WATER PUMP

9306ZG85

Fig. 74 Exploded view of the water pump

5. Remove the camshaft sprockets and rear timing belt cover. Refer to Timing Belt Rear Cover Removal & Installation, in the Engine Mechanical section.

6. Remove screws attaching water pump to engine. Remove pump.

To install:

7. Apply Mopar® dielectric grease to new O-ring before installation.

8. Install O-ring gasket in water pump body groove.

✳✳ WARNING

Make sure O-ring gasket is properly seated in water pump groove before tightening screws. An improperly located O-ring may cause damage to the O-ring, resulting in a coolant leak.

9. Assemble pump body to block and tighten screws to 105 inch lbs. (12 Nm).

10. Rotate pump by hand to check for freedom of movement.

11. Evacuate air and refill cooling system. See Coolant section, Fill Procedure.

12. Pressurize cooling system to 15 psi (103 Kpa) with pressure tester and check water pump shaft seal and O-ring for leaks.

13. Install rear timing belt cover and camshaft sprockets. Refer to Timing Belt Rear Cover Removal & Installation, in the Engine Mechanical section.

14. Install timing belt. Refer to Timing Belt & Sprockets Removal & Installation, in the Engine Mechanical section.

15. Connect the negative battery cable.

16. Start the vehicle and check for leaks, repair if necessary.

ENGINE ELECTRICAL

ALTERNATOR

REMOVAL & INSTALLATION

Non-Turbocharged Models

See Figures 75 through 77.

1. Before servicing the vehicle, refer to the Precautions Section.

2. Disconnect the negative battery cable.

3. Remove the air cleaner lid.

4. Disconnect the Inlet Air Temperature (IAT) sensor and make-up hose.

5. Loosen the upper alternator T-bolt lock nut.

6. Raise and safely support the vehicle.

7. Remove the right front wheel.

8. Remove the accessory drive splash shield:

9. Remove the pencil strut. Refer to Engine Torque Struts in the Engine Mechanical section.

10. Loosen the lower pivot bolt.

11. Loosen the accessory drive belt T-bolt.

12. Unplug field circuit connector from alternator.

13. Remove the B+ terminal nut and B+ terminal.

14. Remove the alternator belt. Refer to Accessory Drive Belt Removal & Installation.

15. Remove the axle shaft. Refer to Half-shaft Removal & Installation.

16. Remove the alternator lower mounting bolt and nut from the upper T-bolt.

17. Remove the alternator.

CHARGING SYSTEM

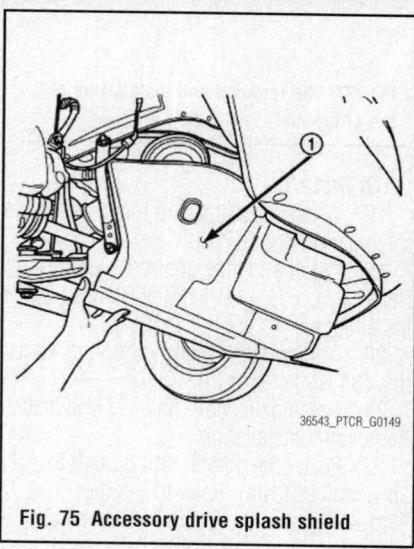

36543_PTCR_G0149

Fig. 75 Accessory drive splash shield

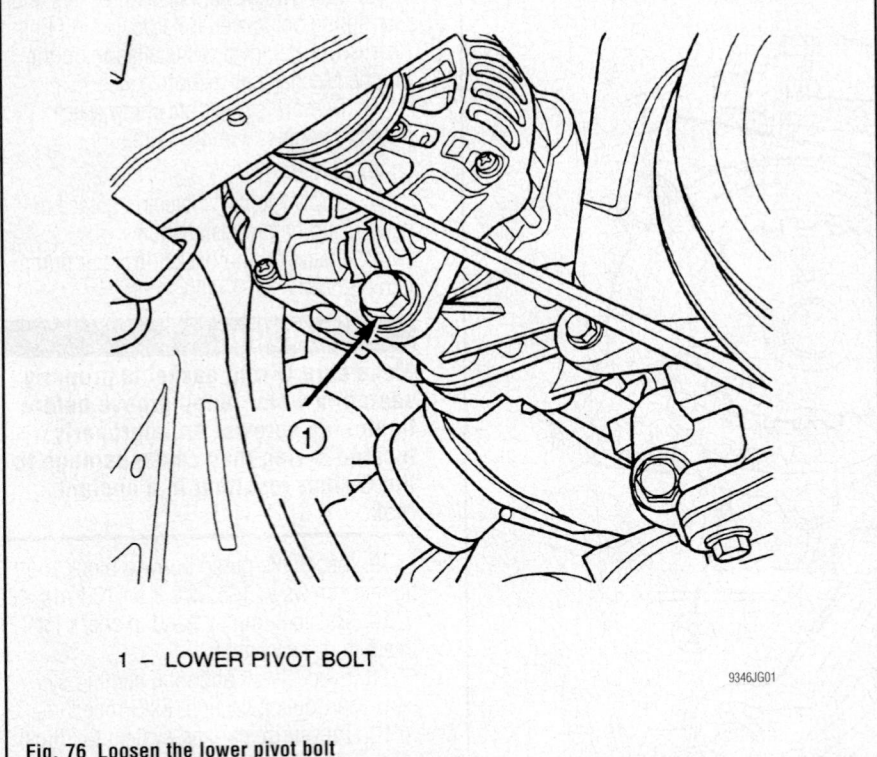

1 – LOWER PIVOT BOLT

9346JG01

Fig. 76 Loosen the lower pivot bolt

32050_PTCR_G0008

Fig. 77 The removal and installation of the alternator

To install:

18. Install alternator and loose assemble the bolt and nut.

19. Install and tension the alternator belt. Refer to Accessory Drive Belt Removal & Installation.

20. Tighten the lower pivot bolt to 40 ft. lbs. (54 Nm).

21. Install axle shaft. Refer to Halfshaft Removal & Installation.

22. Install the pencil strut tighten to 38 ft. lbs. (52 Nm). Refer to Engine Torque Struts in the Engine Mechanical section.

23. Install the B+ terminal nut and B+ terminal. Tighten to 100 inch lbs. (11.3 Nm).

24. Plug in the field circuit connector to alternator.

25. Install the accessory drive splash shield.

26. Install the right front wheel.

27. Lower vehicle.

28. Tighten the T-bolt locknut and tighten to 40 ft. lbs. (54 Nm).

29. Connect the negative battery cable.

30. Install the air cleaner lid and connect the inlet air temperature sensor and makeup hose.

31. Check the transmission fluid.

Turbocharged Models

See Figures 78 and 79.

1. Before servicing the vehicle, refer to the Precautions Section.

➡**The alternator is located above the oil filter and axle shaft.**

2. Disconnect the negative battery cable.

3. Remove the 2 bolts from the top of the heat shield on the alternator.

4. Remove nut from the upper T-bolt adjustment bracket.

5. Raise and safely support the vehicle.

6. Remove the right front wheel.

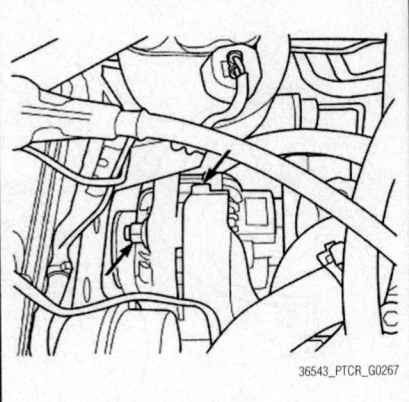

36543_PTCR_G0267

Fig. 78 Remove nut from the upper T-bolt adjustment bracket—turbocharged models

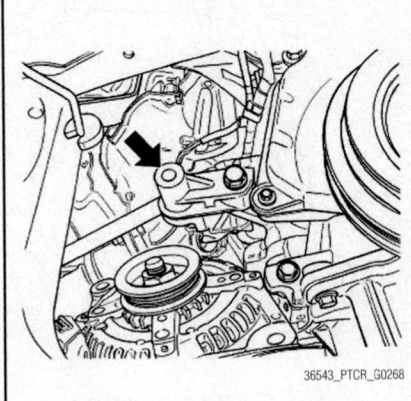

36543_PTCR_G0268

Fig. 79 Remove nut from the upper T-bolt adjustment bracket—turbocharged models

7. Remove the accessory drive splash shield.

8. Remove the lower heat shield bolt.

9. Remove the alternator heat shield.

10. Unplug field circuit connector from alternator.

11. Remove the B+ terminal nut and B+ terminal.

12. Remove the pencil strut. Refer to Engine Torque Struts in the Engine Mechanical section.

13. Loosen the lower alternator pivot bolt.

14. Loosen the accessory drive belt T-bolt.

15. Remove the alternator belt.

16. Remove the axle shaft assembly.

17. Remove the alternator from the lower mounting bracket and set alternator to the side.

18. Remove the lower mounting bracket for the alternator.

19. Remove alternator through the axle shaft hole.

To install:

20. Install alternator through the axle shaft hole in wheel well.

21. Put alternator on upper T-bolt and loosen install the nut.

22. Install the lower mounting bracket for the alternator to the block and tighten bolts to 40 ft. lbs. (54 Nm).

23. Loose install the lower pivot bolt for the alternator.

24. Install the B+ terminal nut and B+ terminal. Tighten nut to 100 inch lbs. (11.3 Nm).

25. Plug in the field circuit connector to alternator.

26. Install the axle shaft assembly.

27. Install alternator belt.

28. Tighten the accessory drive belt t-bolt and tighten nut to 40 ft. lbs. (54 Nm).

29. Tighten the lower alternator pivot bolt and tighten bolts to 40 ft. lbs. (54 Nm).

30. Install the pencil strut and tighten to 38 ft. lbs. (52 Nm). Refer to Engine Torque Struts in the Engine Mechanical section.

31. Install the alternator heat shield.

32. Install the lower heat shield bolt and tighten bolt to 40 ft. lbs. (54 Nm).

33. Install the accessory drive splash shield.

34. Install the right front wheel.

35. Lower vehicle.

36. Install nut to the upper adjustment bracket and tighten to 18 ft. lbs. (25 Nm).

37. Install the 2 bolts to the heat shield on the alternator and tighten bolts to 40 inch lbs. (4.5 Nm).

38. Connect the negative battery cable.

ENGINE ELECTRICAL

IGNITION SYSTEM

FIRING ORDER

See Figure 80.

IGNITION COIL

REMOVAL & INSTALLATION

Non-Turbocharged Models

See Figure 81.

1. Before servicing the vehicle, refer to the Precautions Section.

2. Remove the negative battery cable.

3. Disconnect electrical connector from coil pack.

4. Remove spark plug cables from coil pack.

5. Remove coil pack mounting nuts.

6. Remove coil pack.

To install:

7. Install coil pack on valve cover. Tighten the bolts to 105 inch lbs. (12 Nm)

8. Transfer spark plug cables to new coil pack. The coil pack towers are numbered with the cylinder identification. Be sure the ignition cables snap onto the towers.

9. Install the negative battery cable.

Turbocharged Models

See Figures 82 and 83.

1. Before servicing the vehicle, refer to the Precautions Section.

2. Disconnect the negative battery cable.

3. Remove the throttle control shield.

4. Remove the throttle cables from the throttle body lever.

5. Remove the throttle cable bracket and relocate.

6. Remove the spark plug cables from the ignition coil.

7. Unlock and disconnect the electrical connector from the ignition coil.

8. Remove bolts from ignition coil.

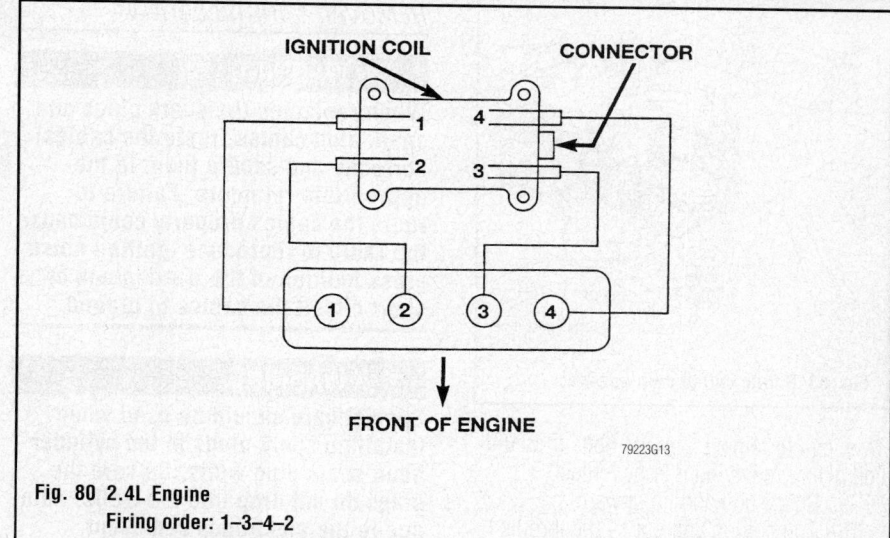

Fig. 80 2.4L Engine
Firing order: 1–3–4–2
Distributorless Ignition System

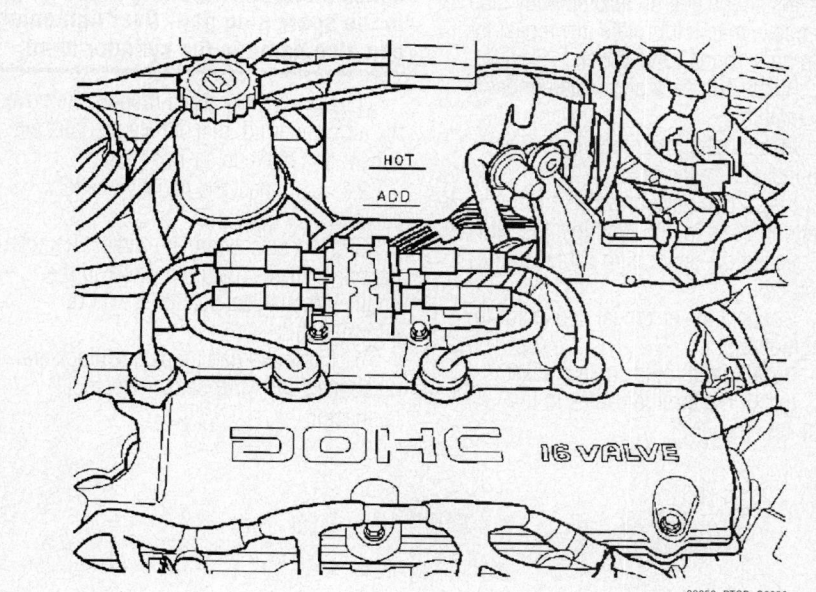

Fig. 81 The electronic ignition coil pack attaches directly to the valve cover

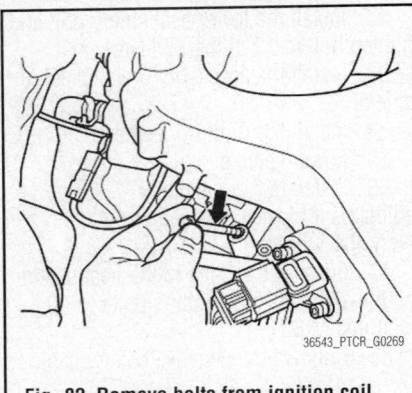

Fig. 82 Remove bolts from ignition coil

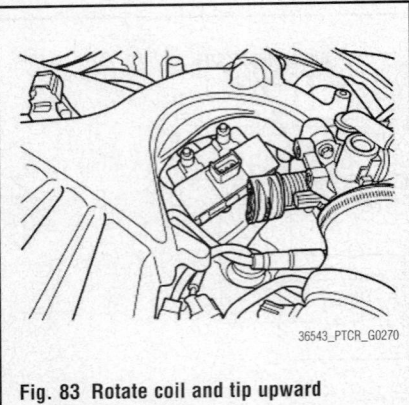

Fig. 83 Rotate coil and tip upward

Twist coil to remove 2 of the bolts from the coil before removing it from vehicle.

9. Rotate coil and tip upward.

10. Pull coil up and out by the throttle body side of the intake manifold.

To install:

11. Install the coil on throttle body side of the intake manifold, rotate down past the throttle body to the valve cover.

12. Rotate coil pack and install under intake manifold.

13. Install bolts to ignition coil. Twist coil to install 2 of the bolts.

14. Install coil pack on valve cover. Tighten the bolts to 105 inch lbs. (12 Nm).

15. Install the spark plug cables to the ignition coil.

16. Connect the electrical connector to the ignition coil.

17. Install the throttle cable bracket.

18. Install the throttle cables to the throttle body lever.

19. Connect the negative battery cable.

➡**Check and make sure that throttle body and attachments will not contact ignition cables.**

20. Install the throttle control shield.

IGNITION TIMING

ADJUSTMENT

The ignition timing is controlled by the Powertrain Control Module (PCM). No adjustment is necessary or possible.

SPARK PLUGS

REMOVAL & INSTALLATION

❋❋ WARNING

When replacing the spark plugs and spark plug cables, route the cables correctly and secure them in the appropriate retainers. Failure to route the cables properly could cause the radio to reproduce ignition noise, cross ignition of the spark plugs or short circuit the cables to ground.

❋❋ WARNING

Special care should be used when installing spark plugs in the cylinder head spark plug wells. Be sure the plugs do not drop into the wells, damage to the electrodes can occur. Always tighten spark plugs to the specified torque. Over tightening can cause distortion resulting in a change in the spark plug gap. Over tightening can also damage the cylinder head.

1. Non-turbocharged models: Remove the air cleaner lid, disconnect the inlet air sensor and makeup air hose.

2. Disconnect the negative battery cable.

3. Non-turbocharged models: Remove the upper intake manifold. Refer to the Engine Mechanical section for more information.

4. Turbocharged models: Unlock and disconnect the MAP sensor electrical connector.

5. Turbocharged models: Remove the throttle control shield.

6. Disconnect the cable from the ignition coil first.

7. Always remove cables by grasping at the boot, rotating the boot ½ turn, and pulling straight back in a steady motion.

8. Prior to removing the spark plug, spray compressed air around the spark plug hole and the area around the spark plug.

9. Remove the spark plug using a quality socket with a rubber or foam insert.

10. Inspect the spark plug condition.

To install:

❋❋ WARNING

Do not over apply anti-seize compound. Only use enough to lightly coat threads on the spark plug.

11. Apply a small amount of anti-seize to threads of each spark plug.

12. Check and adjust spark plug gap.

13. Start each spark plug by hand to avoid cross threading and plug damage, use a quality socket with a rubber insert and start each spark plug into the cylinder head by hand.

❋❋ WARNING

The tapered seat plugs for this application are torque-critical! It is imperative that 13 ft. lbs. (17.5 Nm) is NOT exceeded.

14. Install and tighten spark plugs to 13 ft. lbs. (17.5 Nm).

15. Install ignition cables over spark plugs. An audible click noise can be heard and felt when the ignition cable is properly attached to spark plug.

16. Turbocharged models: Install the throttle control shield.

17. Turbocharged models: Connect and lock the MAP sensor electrical connector.

18. Non-turbocharged models: Install the upper intake manifold. Refer to the Engine section for more information.

19. Connect the negative battery cable.

20. Non-turbocharged models: Install the air cleaner lid and connect the inlet air temperature sensor and makeup hose.

ENGINE ELECTRICAL

STARTER

REMOVAL & INSTALLATION

Non-Turbocharged Models

See Figure 84.

1. Before servicing the vehicle, refer to the Precautions Section.
2. Remove or disconnect the following:
   - The negative battery cable
   - The air cleaner assembly cover
3. Raise and safely support the vehicle.
   - The engine structural collar, refer to Engine Structural Collar Removal & Installation in the Engine Mechanical section.
   - The starter electrical connectors
   - The starter motor mounting bolts
   - The starter

To install:

4. Install the starter and torque the bolts to 40 ft. lbs. (54 Nm).
5. Connect starter motor wiring. Torque solenoid battery cable nut to 90 inch lbs. (10 Nm).

6. Install the engine structural collar. Refer to Engine Structural Collar Removal & Installation in the Engine Mechanical section.
7. Lower the vehicle.
8. Install the air cleaner assembly cover.
9. Connect the negative battery cable.
10. Verify operation of vehicle and systems.

Turbocharged Models

See Figure 85.

1. Before servicing the vehicle, refer to the Precautions Section.
2. Remove or disconnect the following:
   - The negative battery cable
   - The air cleaner assembly cover
   - The upper starter bolt and ground wire, by pushing the inner cooler up and out of the way
3. Raise and safely support the vehicle.
   - The inner cooler lower hose from the inner cooler
   - The nuts retaining the inner cooler tube

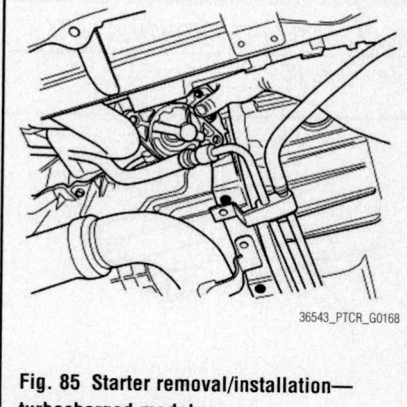

Fig. 85 Starter removal/installation—turbocharged models

   - The studs retaining the power steering lines
   - Position the power steering lines aside
   - The engine structural collar, refer to Engine Structural Collar Removal & Installation in the Engine Mechanical section
   - The starter electrical connectors
   - The positive battery cable
   - The lower starter bolt
   - The starter

To install:

4. Install the starter and torque the bolts to 40 ft. lbs. (54 Nm). Attach the starter electrical connectors.
5. Install the engine structural collar. Refer to Engine Structural Collar Removal & Installation in the Engine Mechanical section

6. Install or connect the following:
   - The power steering lines aside
   - The studs retaining the power steering lines and tighten to 45 ft. lbs. (61 Nm)
   - The nuts retaining the inner cooler tube
   - The inner cooler lower hose to the inner cooler
   - The upper starter bolt by pushing the inner cooler up and out of the way. Tighten to 40 ft. lbs. (54 Nm).
   - The air cleaner assembly cover
   - The negative battery cable

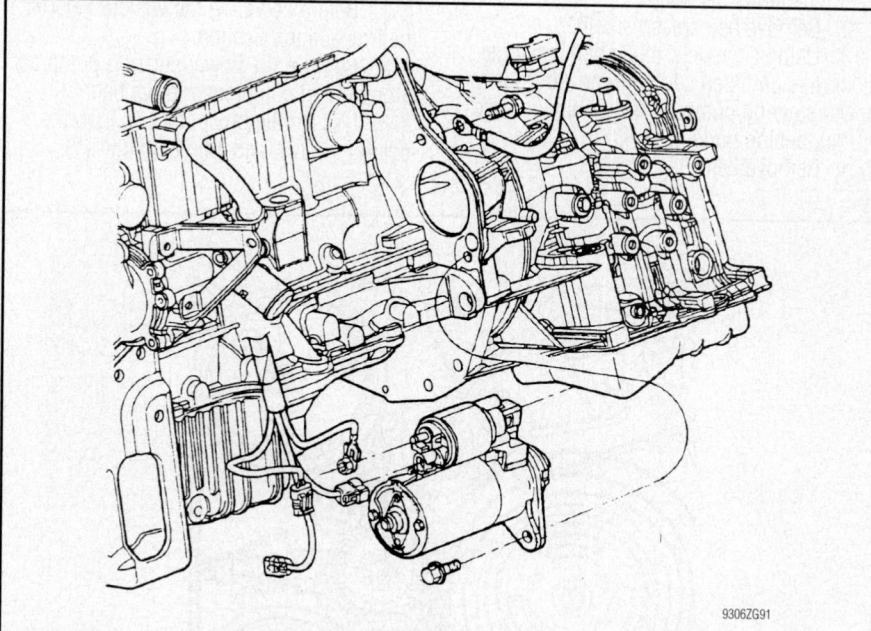

Fig. 84 Removal of the starter motor mounting—non-turbocharged models

ENGINE MECHANICAL

ACCESSORY DRIVE BELTS

ACCESSORY BELT ROUTING

See Figure 86.

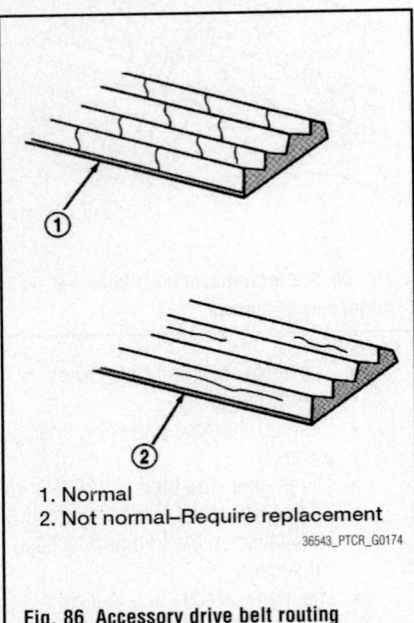

1. Normal
2. Not normal–Require replacement

36543_PTCR_G0174

Fig. 86 Accessory drive belt routing

INSPECTION

Noises generated by the accessory drive belt are most noticeable at idle. Before replacing a belt to resolve a noise condition, inspect all of the accessory drive pulleys for contamination, alignment, glazing, or excessive end play.

When inspecting serpentine accessory drive belts, small cracks that run across the ribbed surface of the belt from rib to rib, are considered normal. These are not a reason to replace the belt. However, cracks running along a rib (not across) are not normal. Any belt with cracks running along a rib must be replaced. Also replace the belt if it has excessive wear, frayed cords or severe glazing.

ADJUSTMENT

Power Steering and Air Conditioning Compressor Belt

The power steering and air conditioning belt is automatically adjusted with a spring tensioner.

Alternator Belt

The alternator belt must be adjusted manually for proper tension.

1. Before servicing the vehicle, refer to the Precautions Section.
2. Check belt tension using Special Tool 8371—Belt Tension Gauge Adapter, and the scan tool using the following procedures:
3. Connect 8371 to the scan tool following the instructions provided in tool kit.
4. Place end of microphone probe approximately 1 in. (2.54cm) from belt at one of the belt center span locations.
5. Pluck the belt a minimum of 3 times. (Use your finger or other suitable object.)
6. The frequency of the belt in hertz (Hz) will display on the scan tool screen.
7. Adjust belt to obtain proper frequency (tension), as follows:
   - New: 135 lbs./235–247 Hz
   - Used: 100 lbs./207–217 Hz

REMOVAL & INSTALLATION

Power Steering Pump & Air Conditioning Compressor Belt

See Figures 87 through 89.

1. Before servicing the vehicle, refer to the Precautions Section.
2. Remove belt splash shield.
3. Using a wrench, rotate belt tensioner clockwise until belt can be removed from power steering pump pulley. Gently, release spring tension on tensioner.
4. Remove belt (8).

To install:

✳✳ CAUTION
Do not check belt tension with engine running.

➡**When installing drive belt onto pulleys, make sure that belt is properly routed and all V-grooves make proper contact with pulley grooves.**

5. Install belt over all pulleys except for the power steering pump pulley.
6. Using a wrench, rotate belt tensioner clockwise until belt can be installed onto power steering pump pulley. Release spring tension onto belt.
7. After belt is installed, inspect belt length indicator marks (2,3 and 5). The indicator mark should be within the minimum belt length and maximum belt length marks. On a new belt, the indicator mark should align approximately with the nominal belt length mark.
8. Install the belt splash shield.

Alternator Belt

See Figure 90.

1. Before servicing the vehicle, refer to the Precautions Section.
2. Remove the power steering pump/air conditioning compressor drive belt.
3. Loosen the pivot bolt (3), then the locking nut (2), and adjusting bolt (1).

36543_PTCR_G0172

Fig. 87 Belt tensioner

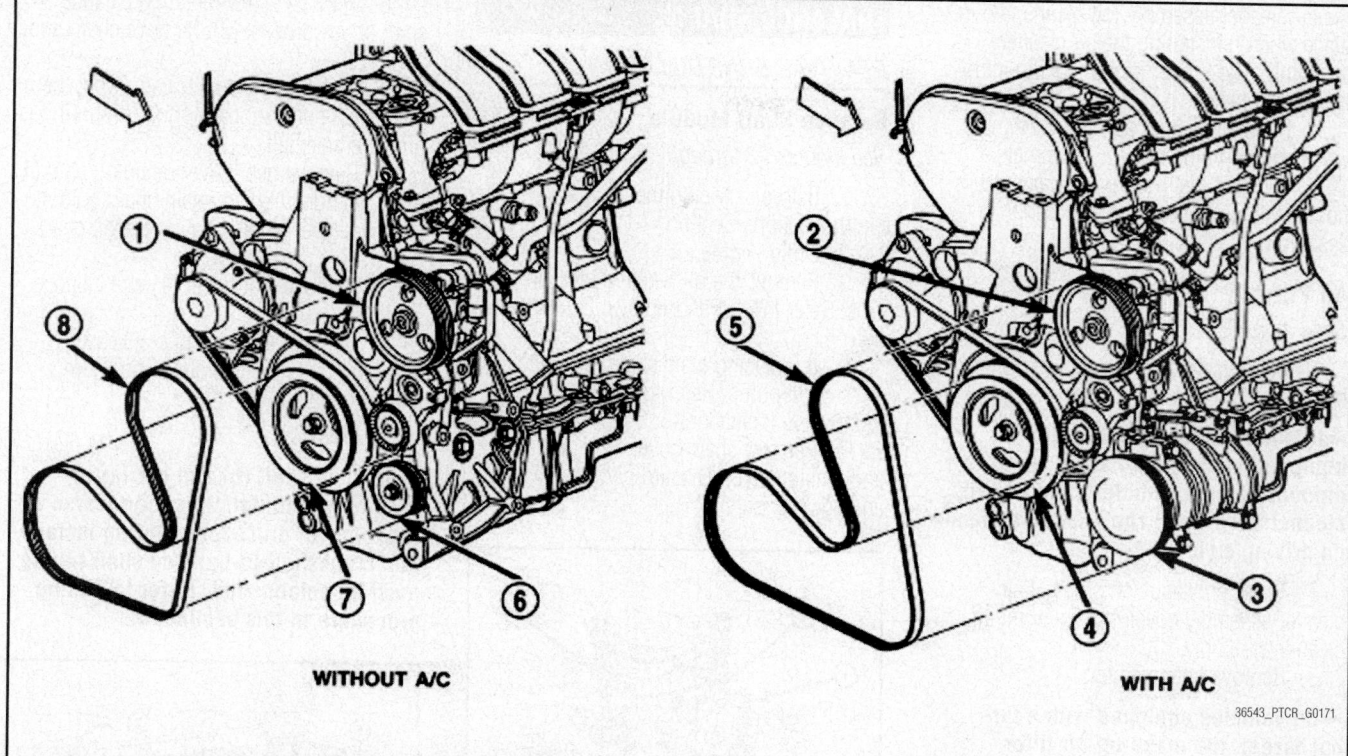

WITHOUT A/C

WITH A/C

36543_PTCR_G0171

Fig. 88 Power steering pump/air conditioning compressor belt

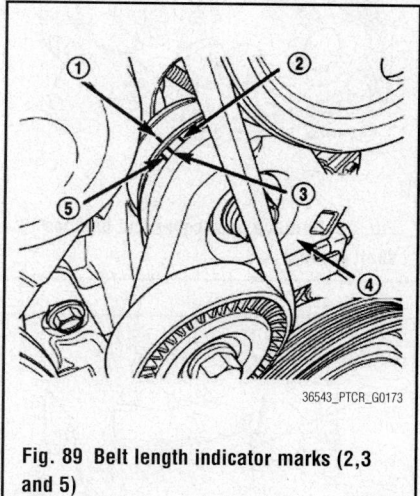

36543_PTCR_G0173

Fig. 89 Belt length indicator marks (2,3 and 5)

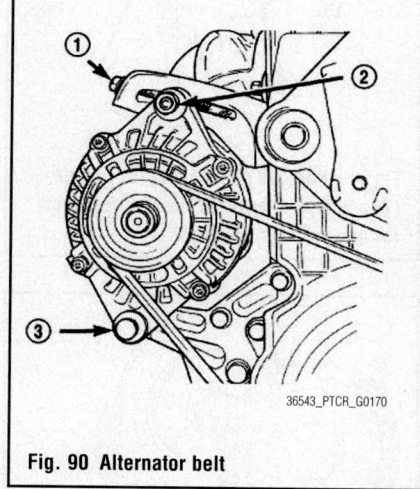

36543_PTCR_G0170

Fig. 90 Alternator belt

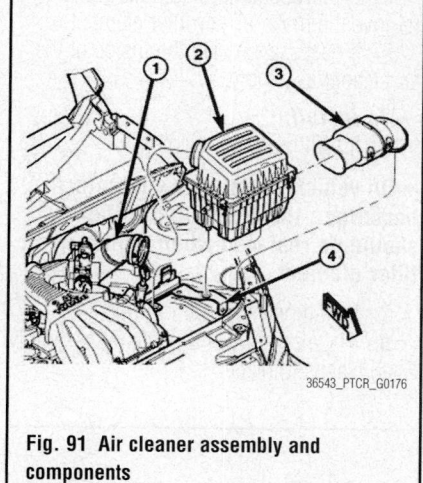

36543_PTCR_G0176

Fig. 91 Air cleaner assembly and components

4. Remove the alternator belt.

To install:

✳✳ CAUTION

Do not check belt tension with engine running.

➡When installing drive belt onto pulleys, make sure that belt is properly routed and all V-grooves make proper contact with pulley grooves.

5. Install belt and/or adjust belt tension by tightening adjusting bolt. Adjust belt to

specification shown in Belt Tension Chart.

6. Tighten pivot bolt to 40 ft. lbs. (54 Nm) and locking nut to 40 ft. lbs. (54 Nm).

7. Install the power steering pump/air conditioning compressor drive belt.

AIR CLEANER

REMOVAL & INSTALLATION

Air Cleaner Assembly
See Figure 91.

1. Before servicing the vehicle, refer to the Precautions Section.

2. Disconnect the throttle body air inlet hose/clean air hose (1) from the air cleaner assembly (2).

3. Pull air cleaner assembly straight up to remove.

4. Remove the inlet duct (3) from the air cleaner assembly (2).

To install:

5. Install inlet duct to the air cleaner assembly.

6. Make sure the rubber grommets, for

the air cleaner assembly lower pins, are in place when reinstalling the air cleaner assembly. The rubber grommets mount to the TIPM bracket.

7. Push air cleaner assembly down while aligning pins into the grommets.

8. Connect the throttle body air inlet hose/clean air hose to the air cleaner assembly.

Air Filter

See Figure 92.

1. Before servicing the vehicle, refer to the Precautions Section.

➡ **It is normal for turbocharger equipped vehicles to have a small amount of oil accumulation in the air cleaner assembly. The amount depends on driving style.**

2. Unfasten clasps on sides of air cleaner assembly cover. Lift cover off air cleaner assembly.

3. Remove filter element.

➡ **On vehicles equipped with a turbocharger, the make-up-air filter should be replaced when replacing air filter element.**

4. On turbocharger equipped vehicles remove the make-up-air filter element.

5. If necessary, clean the inside of the air cleaner assembly.

To install:
6. Install new filter element.

➡ **On vehicles equipped with a turbocharger, the make-up-air filter should be replaced when replacing air filter element.**

7. Install new make-up-air filter.

8. Place cover over air cleaner assembly. Snap clasps in place.

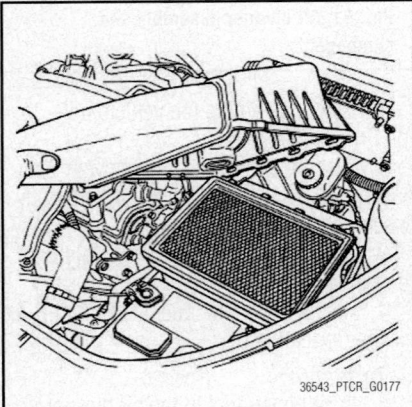

36543_PTCR_G0177

Fig. 92 Air cleaner and filter

BALANCE SHAFT

REMOVAL & INSTALLATION

Balance Shaft Module

See Figures 93 through 102.

1. Before servicing the vehicle, refer to the Precautions Section.

2. Drain engine oil.

3. Remove the oil pan and pick-up tube. Refer to Oil Pan Removal & Installation.

4. If replacing crankshaft sprocket, remove oil pump. Refer to Oil Pump Removal & Installation.

5. Remove chain cover (6), guide (7) and tensioner (2). Discard pivot screw (5) and adjuster screw (4).

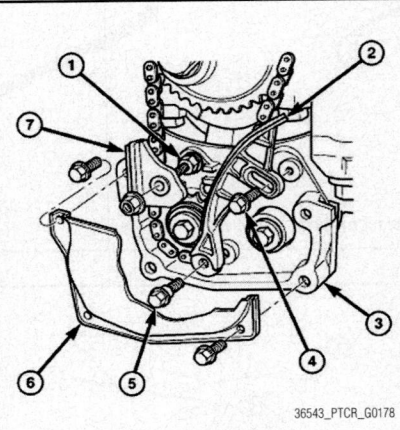

36543_PTCR_G0178

Fig. 93 Remove chain cover (6), guide (7) and tensioner (2), discard pivot screw (5) and adjuster screw (4)

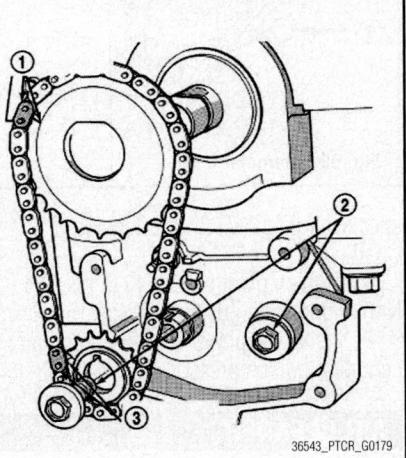

36543_PTCR_G0179

Fig. 94 Remove screw retaining balance shaft drive sprocket (2), remove chain and sprocket

6. Remove screw retaining balance shaft drive sprocket (2). Remove chain and sprocket.

7. Using two wide pry bars, work the crankshaft sprocket back and forth until it is off the crankshaft.

8. Remove gear cover retaining stud (1) (double ended to also retain chain guide). Remove cover (6) and balance shaft gears (5).

9. Remove rear cover (1) and balance shafts (3).

10. Remove 4 carrier to crankcase attaching bolts to separate carrier from engine bedplate.

To install:

➡ **Balance shaft (6) and carrier (4) assembly installation is the reverse of the removal procedure. During installation crankshaft-to-balance shaft timing must be established. Refer to Timing procedure in this section.**

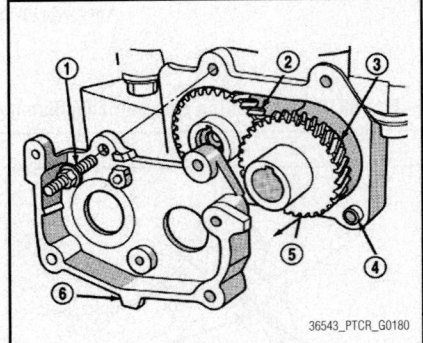

36543_PTCR_G0180

Fig. 95 Remove gear cover and balance shaft gears

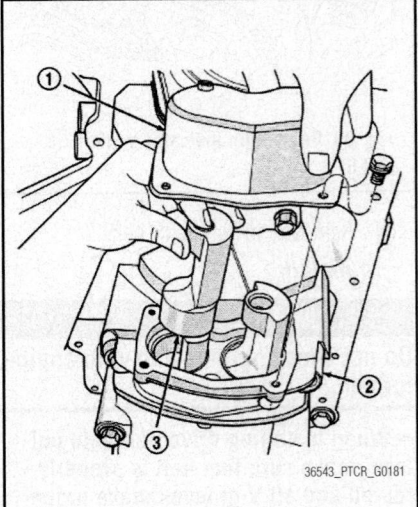

36543_PTCR_G0181

Fig. 96 Remove rear cover and balance shafts

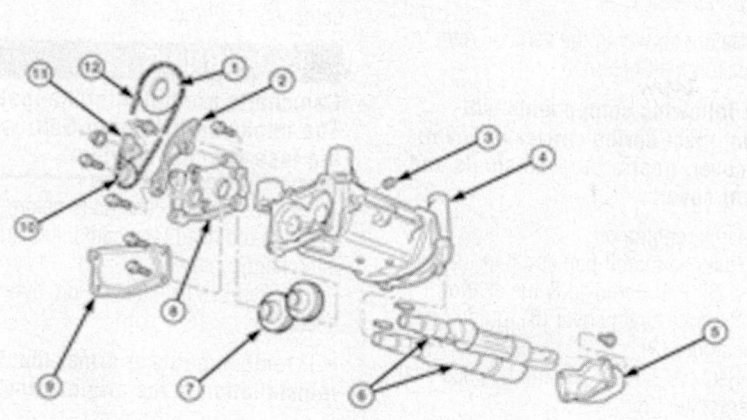

1. SPROCKET
2. TENSIONER
3. PLUG
4. CARRIER
5. REAR COVER
6. BALANCE SHAFTS

7. GEARS
8. GEAR COVER
9. CHAIN COVER
10. SPROCKET
11. GUIDE
12. CHAIN

22043_PTCR_G0062

Fig. 97 Exploded view of the balance shafts and carrier assembly

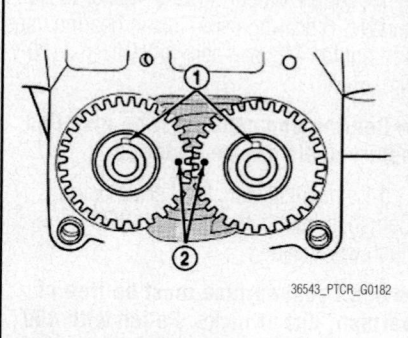

36543_PTCR_G0182

Fig. 98 Balance shaft and gear positioning

11. With balance shafts installed in carrier position carrier on crankcase and install four attaching bolts and tighten to 40 ft. lbs. (54 Nm).

12. Turn balance shafts until both shaft key ways are up (1), parallel to vertical centerline of engine. Install short hub drive gear on sprocket driven shaft and long hub gear on gear driven shaft. After installation of the gear and balance shaft keyways, these must be up (1) with gear timing marks meshed (2) as shown.

13. Install gear cover and tighten double

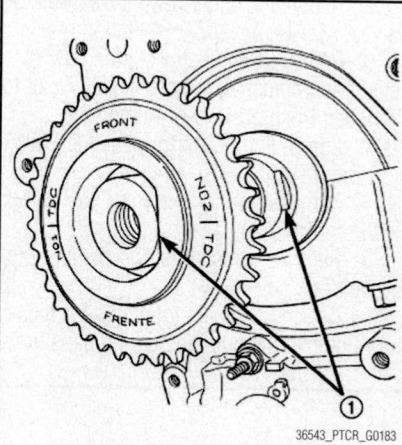

36543_PTCR_G0183

Fig. 99 Align the flat on the balance shaft drive sprocket to the flat on the crankshaft (1)

ended stud/washer fastener to 105 inch lbs. (12 Nm).

14. Align the flat on the balance shaft drive sprocket to the flat on the crankshaft (1).

15. Install balance shaft drive sprocket on crankshaft using Balance Shaft Installer 6052 (2).

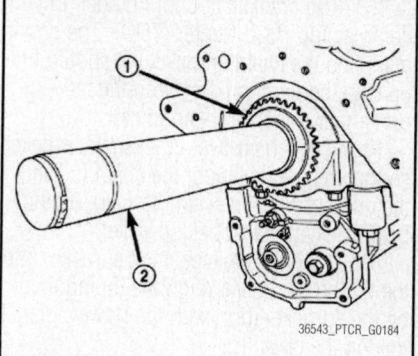

36543_PTCR_G0184

Fig. 100 Install balance shaft drive sprocket on crankshaft using Balance Shaft Sprocket Installer 6052 (2)

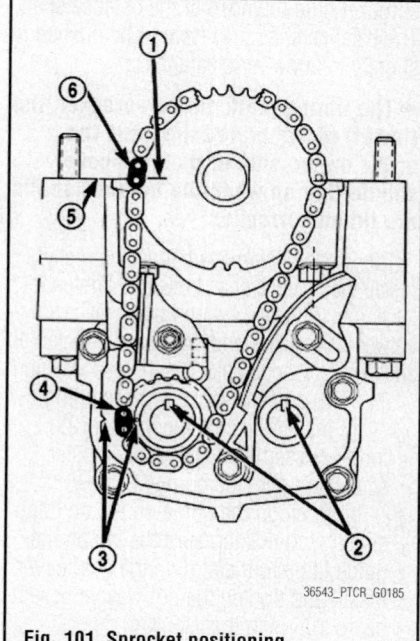

36543_PTCR_G0185

Fig. 101 Sprocket positioning

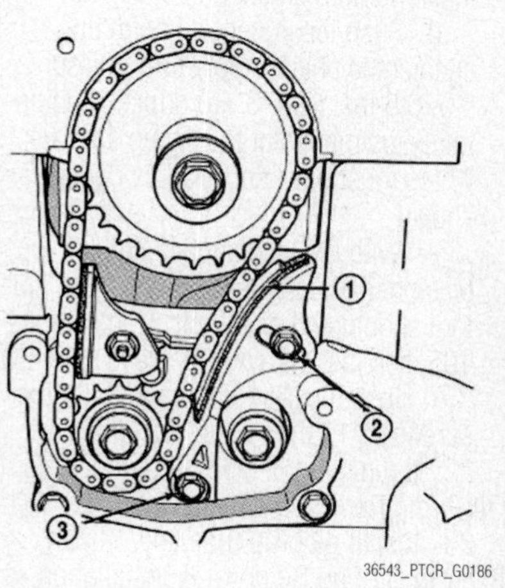

36543_PTCR_G0186

Fig. 102 Chain tensioning

16. Turn crankshaft until number 1 cylinder is at Top Dead Center (TDC). The timing marks on the chain sprocket (1) should line up with the parting line (5) on the left side of number one main bearing cap.

17. Place chain over crankshaft sprocket so that the plated link of the chain is over the number 1 cylinder timing mark on the balance shaft crankshaft sprocket.

18. Place the balance shaft sprocket into the timing chain and align the timing mark on the sprocket (dot) with the (lower) plated link on the chain.

➡The lower plated link (4) is 8 links from the upper link (6).

19. With balance shaft keyways pointing up (2) (12 o'clock) slide the balance shaft sprocket onto the nose of the balance shaft. The balance shaft may have to be pushed in slightly to allow for clearance.

➡The timing mark on the sprocket, the (lower) nickel plated link, and the arrow on the side of the gear cover should line up when the balance shafts are timed correctly.

20. If the sprockets are timed correctly, install the balance shaft bolts and tighten to 21 ft. lbs. (28 Nm). A wood block placed between crankcase and crankshaft counterbalance will prevent crankshaft and gear rotation.

21. The process for chain tensioning:

a. Install the chain tensioner (2) loosely assembled with new adjuster screw and shouldered pivot screw.

b. Position the guide on the double-ended stud making sure the tab on the guide fits into the slot on the gear cover. Install and tighten the nut/washer assembly to 105 inch lbs. (12 Nm).

c. Place a shim (1) 0.039 in. (1mm) thick x 2.75 in. (70mm) long between tensioner and chain.

d. Push tensioner and shim up against the chain. Apply firm pressure 5.5–6.6 lbs. (2.5–3 Kg) directly behind the adjustment slot to take up all slack. Chain must have shoe radius contact as shown.

e. With the load applied, tighten top tensioner adjuster bolt (2) first, then bottom shouldered pivot bolt. Tighten bolts to 105 inch lbs. (12 Nm). Remove shim (1).

f. Install carrier covers and tighten screws to 105 inch lbs. (12 Nm).

22. If removed, install oil pump. Refer to Oil Pump Removal & Installation.

23. Install pick-up tube and oil pan. Refer to Oil Pan Removal & Installation.

24. Fill engine crankcase with proper oil to correct level.

Balance Shaft Carrier

See Figures 94 and 95.

1. Before servicing the vehicle, refer to the Precautions Section.

➡The following components will remain intact during carrier removal: Gear cover, gears, balance shafts and the rear cover.

2. Drain engine oil.

3. Remove the oil pan and pick-up tube. Refer to Oil Pan Removal & Installation.

4. Remove chain cover (6), guide (7), and tensioner (2).

5. Remove screw retaining balance shaft drive sprocket (2).

6. Move balance shaft inboard through drive chain sprocket. Sprocket will hang in lower chain loop.

7. Remove carrier to crankcase attaching bolts to remove carrier.

To install:

8. Installation is the reverse of removal.

CAMSHAFT AND VALVE LIFTERS

REMOVAL & INSTALLATION

See Figures 103 through 109.

1. Before servicing the vehicle, refer to the Precautions Section.

2. Remove cylinder head cover. Refer to Valve Cover Removal & Installation.

3. Remove Camshaft Position (CMP) sensor and camshaft target magnet. Refer to Camshaft Position Sensor Removal & Installation in Engine Performance & Emission Controls.

4. Remove timing belt. Refer to Timing Belt Removal & Installation.

5. Remove camshaft sprockets and timing belt rear cover.

6. Bearing caps are identified for location. Remove the outside bearing caps first.

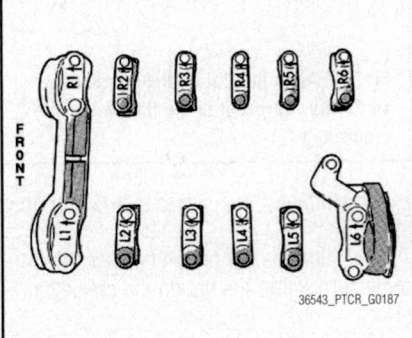

Fig. 103 Bearing caps location

7. Loosen the camshaft bearing cap attaching fasteners in sequence shown one camshaft at a time.

✳✳ WARNING

Camshafts are not interchangeable. The intake cam number 6 thrust bearing face spacing is wider.

8. Identify the camshafts before removing from the head. The camshafts are not interchangeable.

9. Remove camshafts from cylinder head.

➡If removing rocker arms, identify for reinstallation in the original position.

To install:

✳✳ WARNING

Ensure that NONE of the pistons are at top dead center when installing the camshafts.

10. Lubricate all camshaft bearing journals, rocker arms and camshaft lobes.

11. Install all rocker arms in original positions, if reused.

12. Position camshafts on cylinder head bearing journals. Install right and left camshaft bearing caps No. 2–5 and right No. 6. Tighten M6 fasteners to 105 inch lbs. (12 Nm) in the sequence shown.

13. Apply Mopar® Gasket Maker to No. 1 and No. 6 bearing caps. Install bearing caps and tighten M8 fasteners to 21 ft. lbs. (28 Nm).

➡Bearing end caps must be installed before seals can be installed.

14. Install camshaft oil seals using Camshaft Seal Installer MD-998306 until flush with head.

➡Shaft seal surface must be free of varnish, dirt or nicks. Polish with 400 grit paper if necessary.

15. Install camshaft target magnet and CMP (3). Refer to Camshaft Position Sensor Removal & Installation in Engine Performance & Emission Controls.

16. Install cylinder head cover. Refer to Valve Cover Removal & Installation.

17. Install timing belt rear cover and tighten fasteners (1,2) and install timing belt tensioner (3). Refer to Timing Belt Rear Cover Removal & Installation.

18. Install camshaft sprockets. Hold sprockets with camshaft sprocket holder 6847 while tightening center bolt to 85 ft. lbs. (115 Nm). Refer to Timing Belt & Sprockets Removal & Installation.

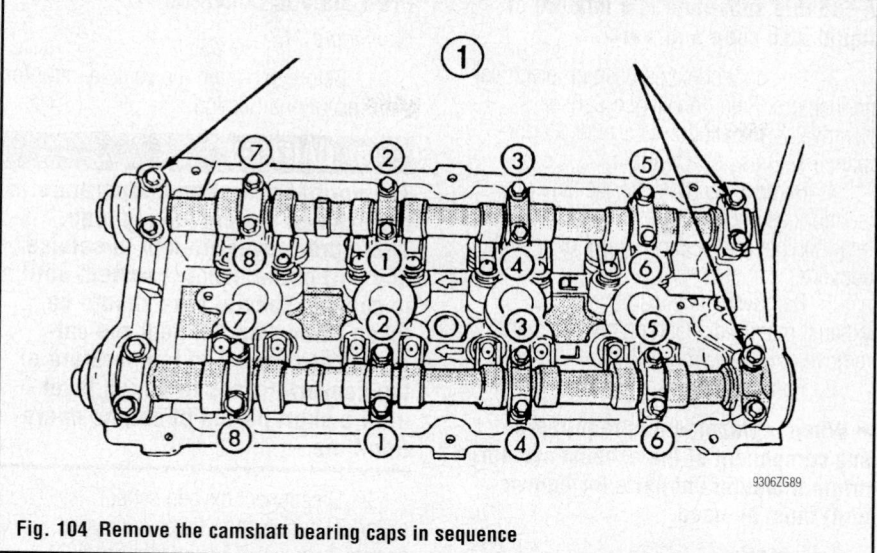

Fig. 104 Remove the camshaft bearing caps in sequence

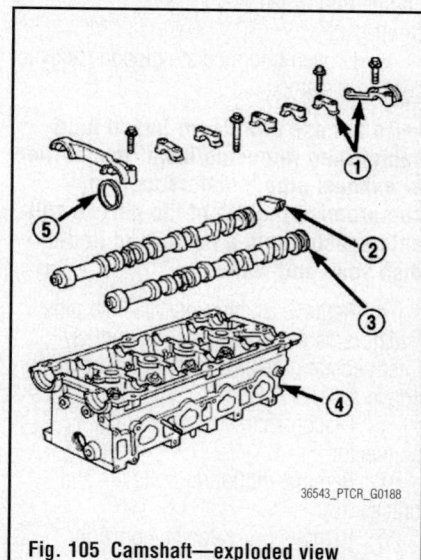

Fig. 105 Camshaft—exploded view

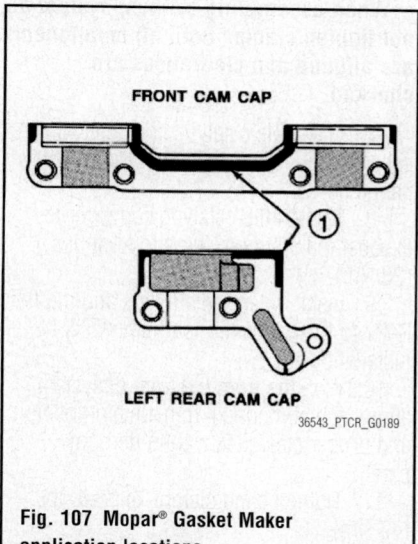

Fig. 107 Mopar® Gasket Maker application locations

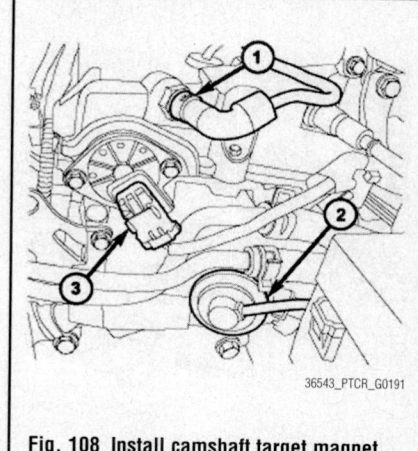

Fig. 108 Install camshaft target magnet and CMP (3)

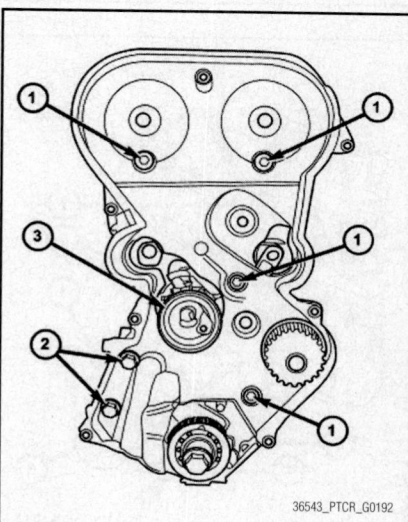

Fig. 109 Install timing belt rear cover and tighten fasteners (1,2) and install timing belt tensioner (3)

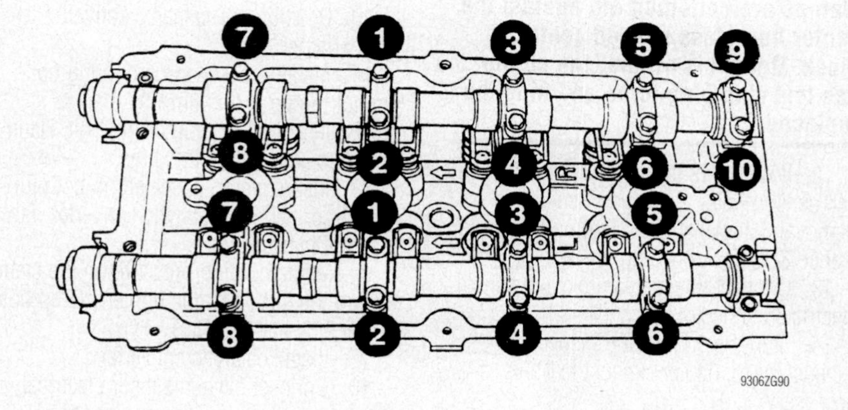

✳✳ WARNING

Do not use an impact wrench to tighten camshaft sprocket bolts. Damage to the camshaft-to-sprocket locating dowel pin may occur.

19. Install timing belt. Refer to Timing Belt & Sprockets Removal & Installation.

CATALYTIC CONVERTER

REMOVAL & INSTALLATION

Catalytic Converter

See Figures 110 and 111.

1. Before servicing the vehicle, refer to the Precautions Section.

Fig. 106 Camshaft bearing cap tightening sequence

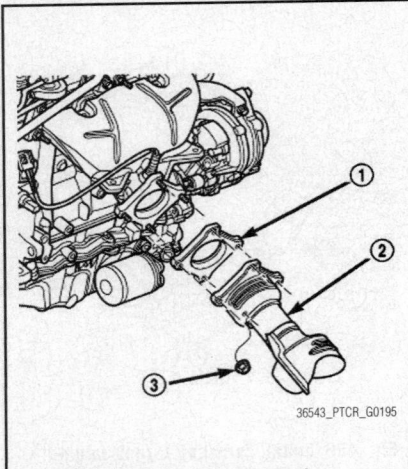

Fig. 110 Catalytic converter and fasteners—non-turbocharged models

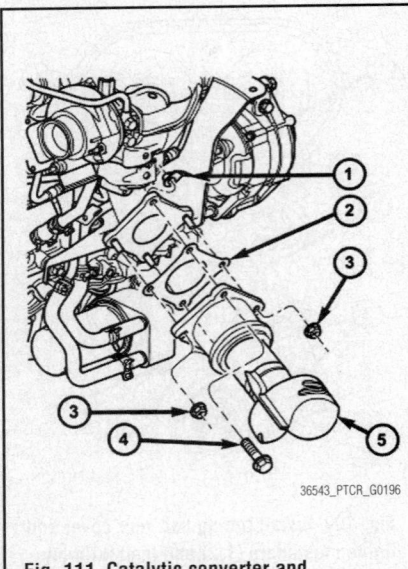

Fig. 111 Catalytic converter and fasteners—turbocharged models

❊❊ CAUTION

The normal operating temperature of the exhaust system is very high. Therefore, never attempt to service any part of the exhaust system until it is cooled. Special care should be taken when working near the catalytic converter. The temperature of the converter rises to a high level after a short period of engine operation time.

   2. Loosen intermediate pipe to catalytic converter clamp.

➡**Do not use petroleum-based lubricants when removing/installing muffler or exhaust pipe isolators as it may compromise the life of the part.**

A suitable substitute is a mixture of liquid dish soap and water.

   3. Disconnect oxygen sensor electrical connectors. Refer to Oxygen Sensor Removal & Installation in Engine Performance & Emission Controls.
   4. Remove muffler/intermediate pipe isolators as necessary to slide muffler/intermediate pipe assembly out of catalytic converter.
   5. Remove catalytic converter to exhaust manifold attaching fasteners and remove converter from vehicle.
   6. Remove and discard flange gasket.

➡**When replacement is required on any component of the exhaust system, original equipment parts (or equivalent) must be used.**

   To install:

➡**When assembling exhaust system do not tighten clamps until all components are aligned and clearances are checked.**

   7. Assemble catalytic converter to exhaust manifold connection. Use a new flange gasket.
   8. Tighten the catalytic converter to exhaust manifold fasteners to 21 ft. lbs. (28 Nm).
   9. Install intermediate pipe and muffler. Refer to Intermediate Pipe Removal & Installation.
   10. Working from the front of system, align each component to maintain position and proper clearance with underbody parts.
   11. Tighten band clamps to 35 ft. lbs. (47 Nm).

❊❊ WARNING

Band clamps should never be tightened such that the two sides of the clamps are bottomed out against the center hourglass shaped center block. Once this occurs, the clamp has lost clamping force and must be replaced.

   12. If removed, install downstream oxygen sensor. Refer to Oxygen Sensor Removal & Installation in Engine Performance & Emission Controls.
   13. Connect downstream oxygen sensor electrical connector.
   14. Start the engine and inspect for exhaust leaks. Repair exhaust leaks as necessary.
   15. Check the exhaust system for contact with the body panels. Make the necessary adjustments, if needed.

Pre-Catalytic Converter
See Figure 112.

   1. Before servicing the vehicle, refer to the Precautions Section.

❊❊ CAUTION

The normal operating temperature of the exhaust system is very high. Therefore, never attempt to service any part of the exhaust system until it is cooled. Special care should be taken when working near the catalytic converter. The temperature of the converter rises to a high level after a short period of engine operation time.

   2. Disconnect oxygen sensor electrical connectors. Refer to Oxygen Sensor Removal & Installation in Engine Performance & Emission Controls.
   3. Loosen intermediate pipe to catalytic converter clamp.

➡**Do not use petroleum-based lubricants when removing/installing muffler or exhaust pipe isolators as it may compromise the life of the part. A suitable substitute is a mixture of liquid dish soap and water.**

   4. Remove muffler/intermediate pipe isolators as necessary to slide muffler/intermediate pipe assembly out of catalytic converter.
   5. Disconnect sensor electrical connector.
   6. Remove mounting bolts (7) and bracket (6).
   7. Remove pre-catalytic converter clamp (4).
   8. Remove pre-catalytic converter (5).

   To install:
   9. Position gasket on turbocharger.
   10. Position pre-catalytic converter to turbocharger.
   11. Install bracket and mounting bolts. Do not torque at this time.
   12. Install clamp and clamp bolt. Hand tighten clamp bolt at this time.
   13. Insure clamp is seated on both turbocharger and pre-catalytic converter. Tap clamp if necessary.
   14. While holding pressure on the clamp toward the turbocharger, tighten clamp bolt to 8.8 inch lbs. (15 Nm).
   15. Install catalytic converter.
   16. Connect oxygen sensor electrical connectors. Refer to Oxygen Sensor Removal & Installation in Engine Performance & Emission Controls.

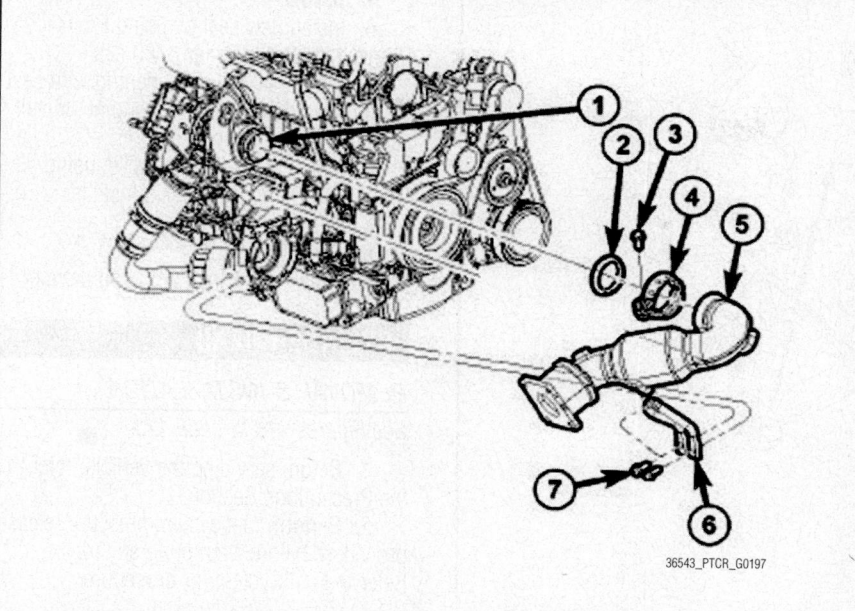

Fig. 112 Pre-catalytic converter and components

CRANKSHAFT DAMPER

REMOVAL & INSTALLATION

See Figures 113 and 114.

1. Before servicing the vehicle, refer to the Precautions Section.
2. Remove the accessory drive belts.
3. Remove lower splash shield.
4. Remove the crankshaft damper bolt.
5. Remove the damper by using Special Tool 1026 and Insert 6827A.

To install:

6. Install crankshaft damper using Special Tool 6792 (M12 1.75 x 150mm bolt, washer, thrust bearing and nut).

➡**Lubricate the threads of the M12 1.75 x 150mm bolt using Mopar® Nickel Anti-seize Compound or equivalent, before beginning to press the damper on.**

7. Apply Mopar® Lock and Seal Adhesive (Medium Strength Threadlocker) to

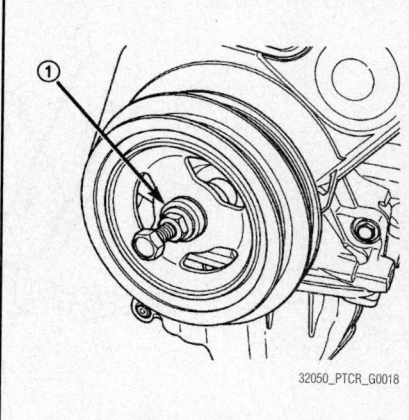

Fig. 114 Installation of the crankshaft damper

crankshaft damper bolt and tighten to 100 ft. lbs. (136 Nm).

8. Install the accessory drive belts.

CRANKSHAFT FRONT SEAL

REMOVAL & INSTALLATION

See Figures 115 through 117.

1. Before servicing the vehicle, refer to the Precautions Section.
2. Remove the crankshaft vibration damper. Refer to Crankshaft Damper Removal & Installation.
3. Remove timing belt. Refer to Timing Belt Removal & Installation.
4. Remove crankshaft sprocket (3) using Crankshaft Sprocket Remover 6793 (1) and Crankshaft Sprocket Remover Insert C-4685-C2 (2).

✳✳ WARNING

Do not nick shaft seal surface or seal bore.

5. Use Crankshaft Front Seal Remover 6771 (1) to remove front crankshaft oil seal. Be careful not to damage the seal surface of cover.

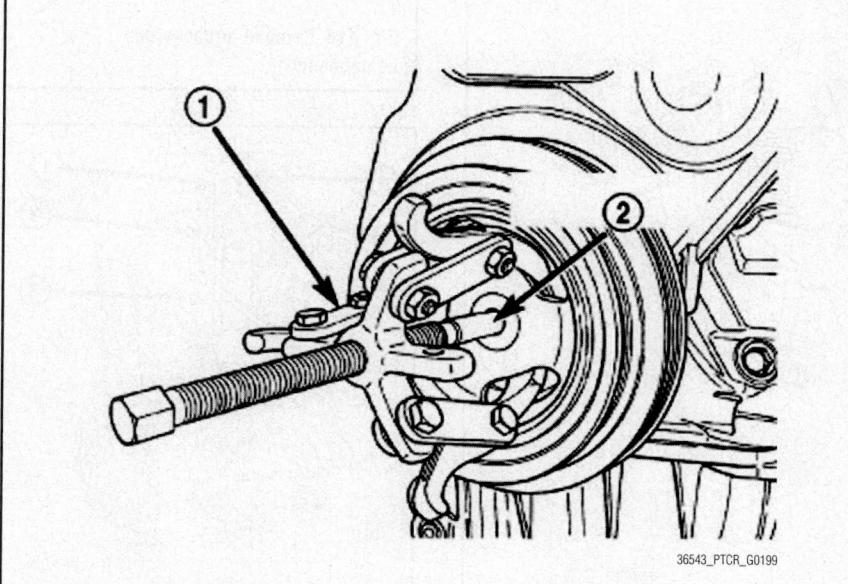

Fig. 113 Remove crankshaft damper

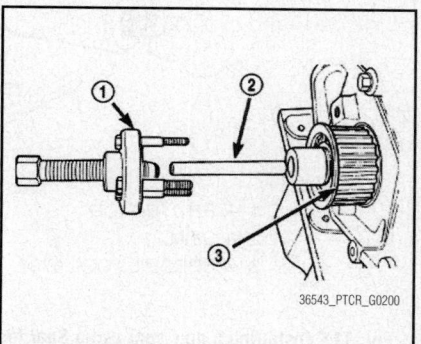

Fig. 115 Remove crankshaft sprocket

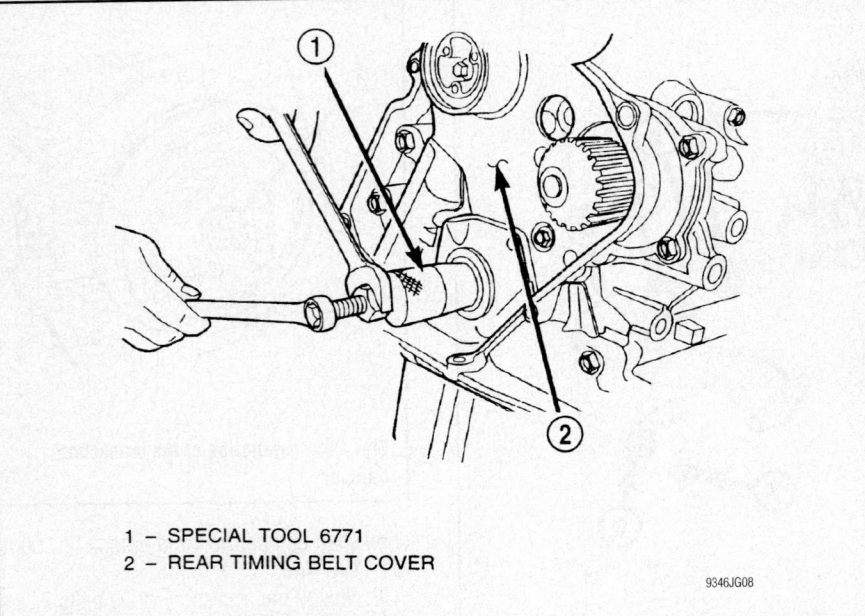

1 – SPECIAL TOOL 6771
2 – REAR TIMING BELT COVER

9346JG08

Fig. 116 Removing the front crankshaft oil seal

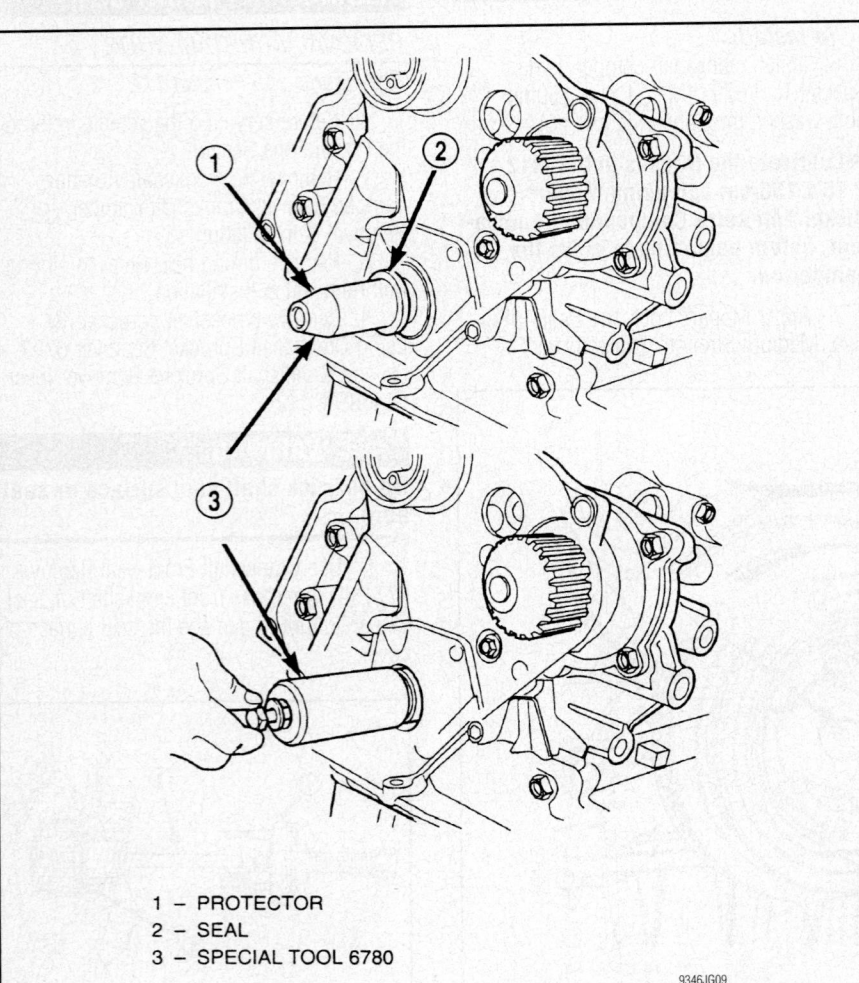

1 – PROTECTOR
2 – SEAL
3 – SPECIAL TOOL 6780

9346JG09

Fig. 117 Installing a new seal using Seal Installer 6780-1; proceed with caution if using substitute tools

To install:

6. Install new seal by using Front Crankshaft Seal Installer 6780 (3).

7. Place seal (2) into opening with seal spring towards the inside of engine. Install seal until flush with cover.

8. Install crankshaft sprocket using Crankshaft Damper/Sprocket Installer 6792 (1).

9. Install timing belt.

10. Install crankshaft vibration damper.

CYLINDER HEAD

REMOVAL & INSTALLATION

See Figures 118 through 123.

1. Before servicing the vehicle, refer to the Precautions Section.

2. Perform fuel system pressure release procedure before attempting any repairs. Refer to Fuel System for procedure.

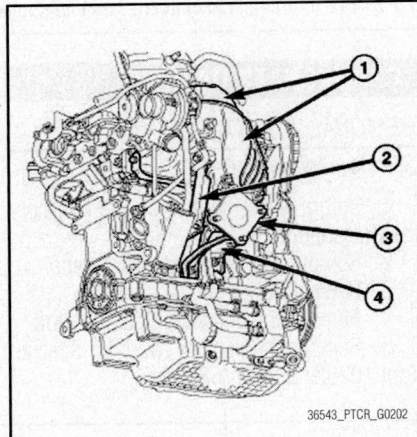

36543_PTCR_G0202

Fig. 118 Remove turbocharger components

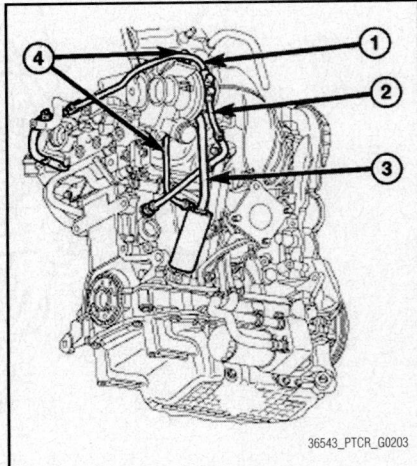

36543_PTCR_G0203

Fig. 119 Oil and coolant lines—turbocharged models

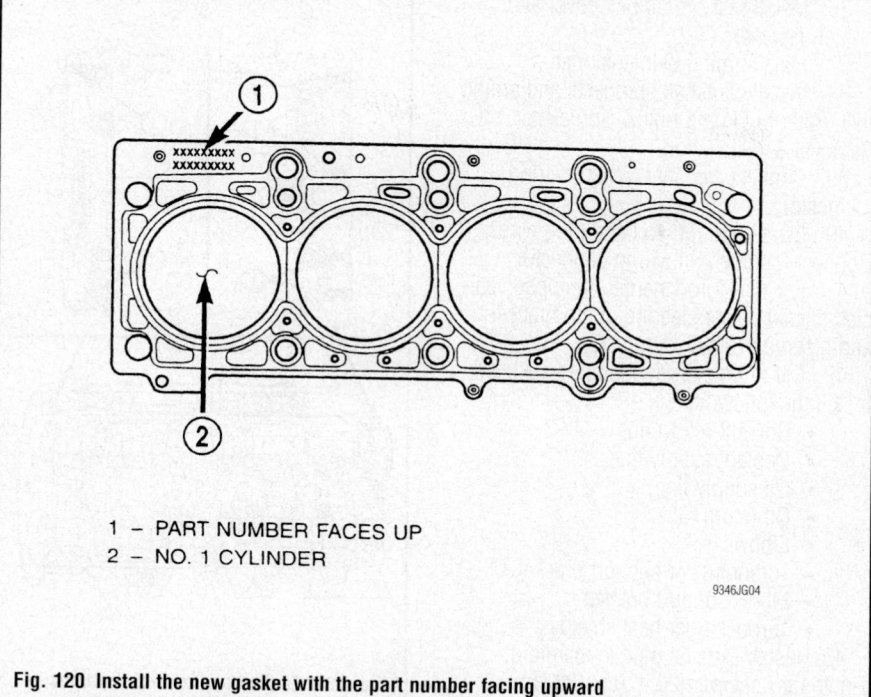

1 – PART NUMBER FACES UP
2 – NO. 1 CYLINDER

9346JG04

Fig. 120 Install the new gasket with the part number facing upward

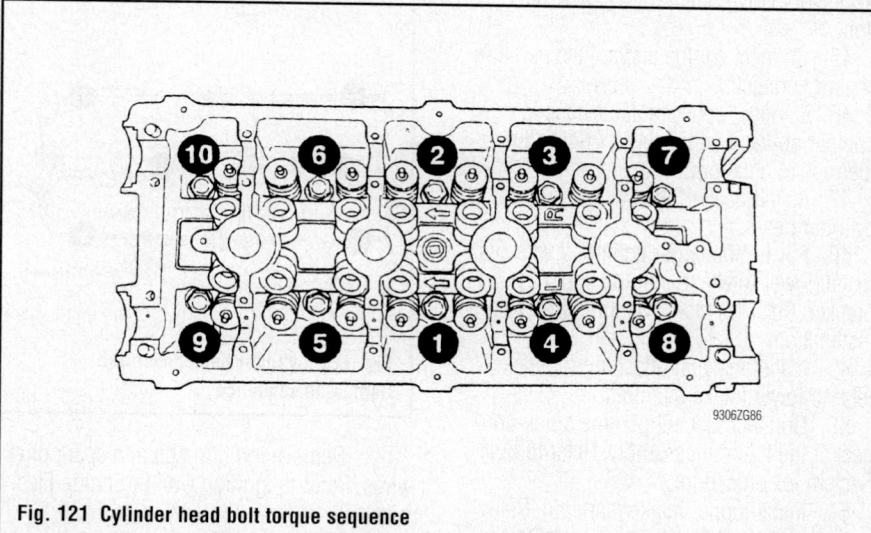

9306ZG86

Fig. 121 Cylinder head bolt torque sequence

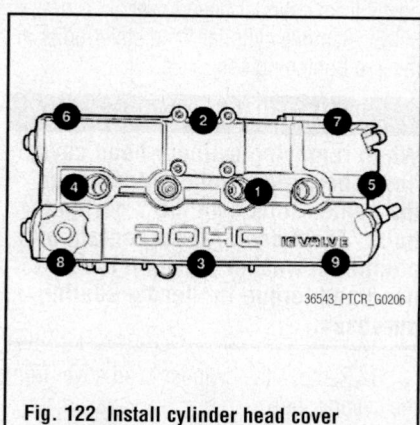

36543_PTCR_G0206

Fig. 122 Install cylinder head cover

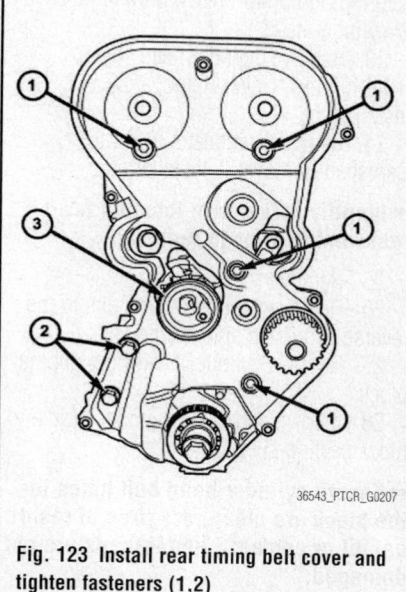

36543_PTCR_G0207

Fig. 123 Install rear timing belt cover and tighten fasteners (1,2)

3. Remove clean air hose and air cleaner housing. Refer to Air Cleaner Removal & Installation.

4. Disconnect negative cable from battery.

5. Open drain cock to drain cooling system into a clean container.

6. Remove upper intake manifold. Refer to Intake Manifold Removal & Installation.

7. Remove fastener attaching dipstick tube to lower intake manifold.

8. For turbocharger equipped vehicles, remove lower intake manifold support bracket.

9. Disconnect the fuel supply line quick-connect at the fuel rail assembly. Refer to Fuel System for procedure.

10. Remove heater tube support bracket from cylinder head.

11. Remove upper radiator hose. Disconnect heater hoses from thermostat housing.

12. Disconnect engine coolant temperature sensor connector.

13. Remove accessory drive belts. Refer to Accessory Drive Belt Removal & Installation.

14. Raise and safely support the vehicle.

15. Disconnect exhaust pipe from manifold.

16. For turbocharger equipped vehicles, remove the following:
   - Turbocharger heat shields (1)
   - Elbow support bracket (4)
   - Turbocharger support bracket (2)
   - Elbow (3)

17. For turbocharger equipped vehicles, remove the following:
   - Oil return tube (4)
   - Oil supply line (1)
   - Coolant supply line (3)
   - Coolant return line (2)

18. Disconnect ignition coil wiring connector. Remove ignition coil and plug wires from engine.

19. Disconnect camshaft position sensor wiring connector.

20. Remove timing belt and camshaft sprockets. Refer to Timing Belt & Sprockets Removal & Installation.

21. Remove timing belt idler pulley and rear timing belt cover.

22. For non-turbocharger equipped vehicles, remove the fasteners securing power

steering pump fluid reservoir and bracket to cylinder head.

23. Remove cylinder head cover. Refer to Valve Cover Removal & Installation.

24. Remove camshafts. Refer to Camshaft Removal & Installation.

➡**Identify rocker arm location for reassembly prior to removal.**

25. Remove rocker arms.

26. Remove cylinder head bolts in the reverse sequence of tightening.

27. Remove cylinder head from engine block.

28. Inspect and clean cylinder head and block sealing surfaces.

➡**Ensure cylinder head bolt holes in the block are clean, dry (free of residual oil or coolant), and threads are not damaged.**

To install:

➡**The Cylinder head bolts should be examined BEFORE reuse. If the threads are necked down, the bolts should be replaced. Necking can be checked by holding a scale or straight edge against the threads. If all the threads do not contact the scale, the bolt should be replaced.**

➡**Cylinder head should be cleaned and inspected prior to replacement.**

29. Position the new cylinder head gasket on engine block with the part number (1) facing up. Ensure gasket is seated over the locating dowels in block.

30. Position cylinder head onto engine block.

31. Before installing the bolts, the threads should be lightly coated with engine oil.

32. Tighten the cylinder head bolts in the sequence shown. Using the 4 step torque-turn method, tighten according to the following values:

    a. Step 1: All to 25 ft. lbs. (34 Nm).
    b. Step 2: All to 60 ft. lbs. (82 Nm).
    c. Step 3: All to 60 ft. lbs. (82 Nm).

❄ WARNING

Do not use a torque wrench for the Fourth step.

    d. Step 4: Turn all bolts an additional ¼ turn.

33. Install rocker arms.

34. Install camshafts. Refer to Camshaft Removal & Installation.

35. Install cylinder head cover. Refer to Valve Cover Removal & Installation.

36. Install rear timing belt cover and tighten fasteners (1,2).

37. Install timing belt tensioner.

38. Install camshaft sprockets and timing belt. Refer to Timing Belt & Sprockets Removal & Installation.

39. Connect camshaft sensor wiring connector.

40. Install ignition coil and plug wires. Connect ignition coil wiring connector.

41. For non-turbocharger equipped vehicles, install power steering pump bracket and reservoir to cylinder head.

42. For turbocharger equipped vehicles, install the following:

- Coolant return line
- Coolant supply line
- Oil supply line
- Oil return tube
- Elbow
- Turbocharger support bracket
- Elbow support bracket
- Turbocharger heat shields

43. Install exhaust pipe to manifold. Tighten fasteners to 20 ft. lbs. (28 Nm).

44. Install accessory drive belts. Refer to Accessory Drive Belt Removal & Installation.

45. Connect engine coolant temperature sensor connector.

46. Connect upper radiator hose to coolant outlet. Connect heater hoses to thermostat housing.

47. Install heater tube support bracket to cylinder head.

48. For turbocharger equipped vehicles, install lower intake manifold support bracket. Refer to Intake Manifold Removal & Installation.

49. Install fastener attaching dipstick tube to lower intake manifold.

50. Connect fuel supply line quick-connect at the fuel rail assembly. Refer to Fuel System for procedure.

51. Install upper intake manifold. Refer to Intake Manifold Removal & Installation.

52. Remove radiator pressure cap and fill the cooling system.

53. Connect negative cable to battery.

54. Install clean air hose and air cleaner housing. Refer to Air Cleaner Removal & Installation.

CYLINDER HEAD COVERS

REMOVAL & INSTALLATION

See Figures 124 and 125.

1. Before servicing the vehicle, refer to the Precautions Section.

2. Remove upper intake manifold. Refer to Intake Manifold.

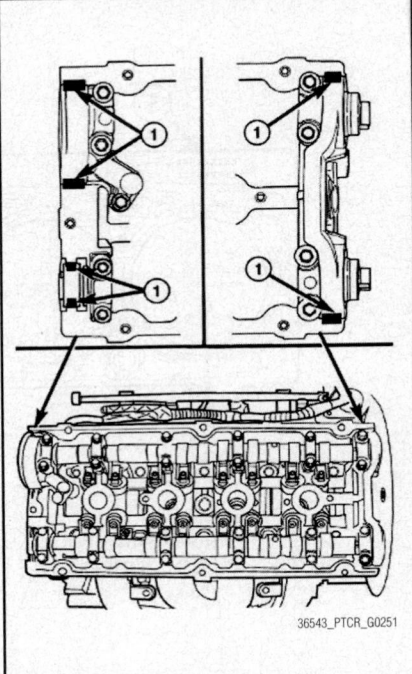

36543_PTCR_G0251

Fig. 124 Sealant application locations

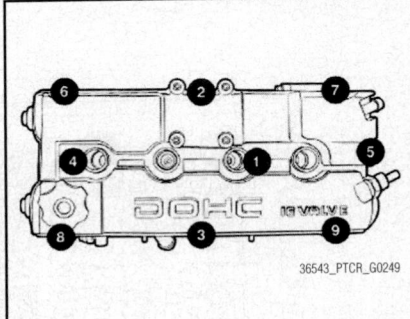

36543_PTCR_G0249

Fig. 125 Cylinder head cover bolt tightening sequence

3. Remove ignition coil and spark plug wires. Refer to Ignition Coil in Engine Electrical.

4. Disconnect PCV and make-up air hoses from cylinder head cover.

5. Remove cylinder head cover bolts in reverse tightening sequence.

❄ WARNING

When removing cylinder head cover bolts, be careful not to interchange the center bolts with the 7 perimeter bolts. The 2 center bolts contain an aluminum washer between the bolt head and torque limiter for sealing purposes.

6. Remove the cylinder head cover from the cylinder head.

To install:

➡ **Replace spark plug well seals and bolt seals when installing a new cylinder head cover gasket.**

7. Install new cylinder head cover gaskets and spark plug well seals.

8. Replace cylinder head cover bolt seals.

✳✳ CAUTION

Do not allow oil or solvents to contact the timing belt as they can deteriorate the rubber and cause tooth skipping.

9. Apply Mopar® Engine RTV GEN II at the camshaft cap corners and at the top edges of the ½ round seal.

✳✳ WARNING

When installing cylinder head cover bolts, be careful not to interchange the 2 center bolts with the 7 perimeter bolts. The 2 center bolts contain an aluminum washer between the bolt head and torque limiter for sealing purposes.

10. Install the cylinder head cover assembly to cylinder head. Install all bolts, ensuring the 2 bolts containing the sealing washer are located in the center locations of cover.

11. Tighten bolts in sequence using a 3 step torque method as follows:
- Tighten all bolts to 40 inch lbs. (5 Nm)
- Tighten all bolts to 80 inch lbs. (9 Nm)
- Tighten all bolts to 105 inch lbs. (12 Nm)

12. Install ignition coil and spark plug wires. Tighten fasteners to 105 inch lbs. (12 Nm).

13. If the PCV valve was removed, apply Mopar® Thread Sealant with Teflon to threads and install valve to cylinder head cover. Tighten PCV valve to 70 inch lbs. (8 Nm).

14. Connect PCV and make-up air hoses to cylinder head cover.

15. Install the upper intake manifold.

ENGINE ASSEMBLY

REMOVAL & INSTALLATION

See Figures 118, 126 through 128.

1. Perform fuel pressure release procedure, then disconnect and remove fuel line. Refer to Fuel System for procedure.

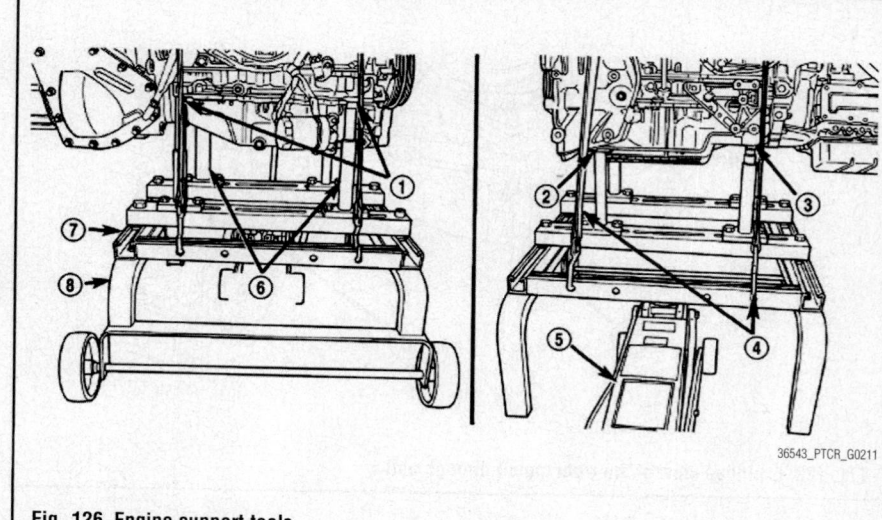

Fig. 126 Engine support tools

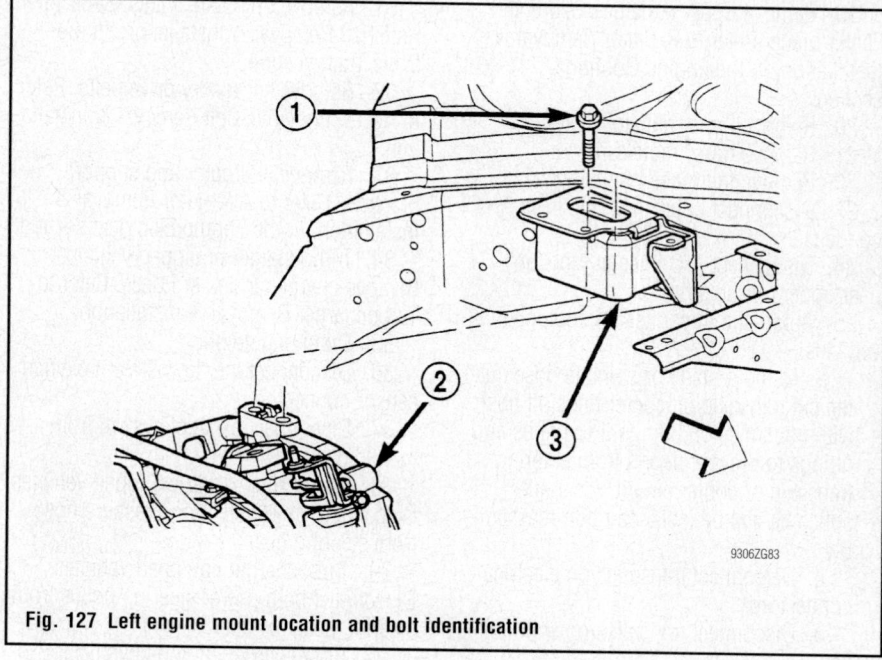

Fig. 127 Left engine mount location and bolt identification

2. Remove air cleaner housing assembly and clean air hose. Refer to Air Cleaner Removal & Installation.

3. Disconnect both cables from battery.

4. Remove battery and battery tray.

5. Disconnect battery temperature sensor.

6. Drain cooling system. Refer to Coolant Drain Procedure, in the Engine Cooling section.

7. Discharge air conditioning system, if equipped.

8. Remove throttle cable cover.

9. Disconnect throttle and speed control cables from throttle body.

10. Disconnect engine wiring harness at Powertrain Control Module (PCM).

11. Disconnect positive cable from Totally Integrated Power Module (TIPM)(1) and ground wire from vehicle body. Remove bolts attaching TIPM (2) and set aside.

12. Disconnect wiring connectors at lower battery tray support.

13. Disconnect ground wire (1) from the vehicle body-to-engine at the right side strut tower.

14. Disconnect brake booster vacuum hose from intake manifold.

15. Disconnect the proportional purge hose from throttle body.

16. Disconnect coolant reserve/recovery hose from coolant outlet connector.

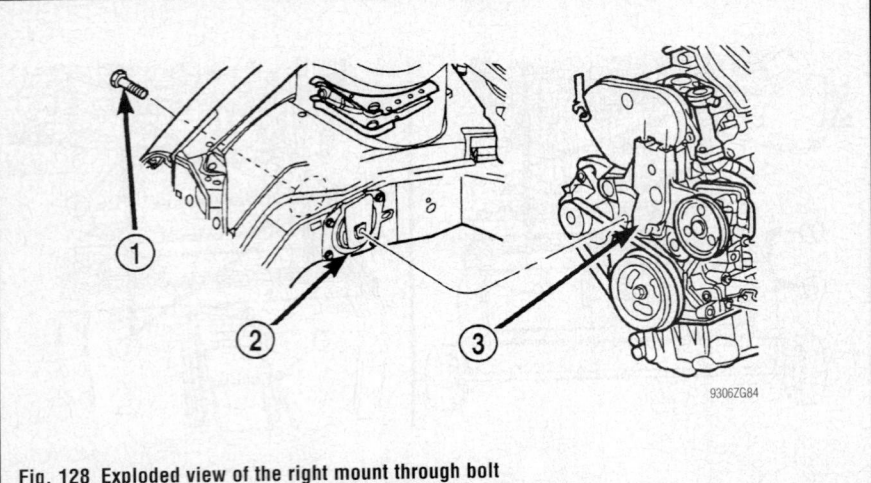

Fig. 128 Exploded view of the right mount through bolt

17. Disconnect heater hoses.
18. Remove grille.
19. Remove upper radiator closure and center brace. Refer to Radiator Removal & Installation, in the Engine Cooling section.
20. Remove upper radiator hose.
21. Remove lower radiator hose.
22. Remove thermostat housing.
23. Disconnect upper A/C line from A/C condenser.
24. Disconnect A/C lines at junction near upper torque strut.
25. Automatic transmission equipped vehicles:
   a. Using a blade or suitable hose cutter, cut transaxle oil cooler lines off flush with transmission fittings. Plug lines and fittings to prevent debris from entering transaxle or cooler circuit. A service splice kit will be installed upon reassembly.
   b. Disconnect transmission electrical connectors.
   c. Disconnect transmission shift linkage.
26. Manual Transmission equipped vehicles:
   a. Using Special Tool 6638A, disconnect clutch hydraulic line.
   b. Disconnect transmission shift linkage.
   c. Disconnect transmission electrical connectors.
27. Turbocharger equipped vehicles: Disconnect power steering hoses from radiator.
28. Disconnect radiator fan electrical connector and remove cooling module assembly (fan, radiator, A/C condenser, transmission oil cooler).
29. Hoist vehicle and remove front wheels.

30. Remove right and left inner splash shields.
31. Remove both axle shafts. Refer to Halfshaft Removal & Installation, in the Drive Train section.
32. Remove accessory drive belts. Refer to Accessory Drive Belt Removal & Installation.
33. Remove alternator and support brackets. Refer to Alternator Removal & Installation, in the Engine Electrical section.
34. Turbocharger equipped vehicles: Remove charge air cooler hoses. Refer to Turbocharger Removal & Installation.
35. Drain engine oil.
36. Disconnect the downstream oxygen sensor connector.
37. Disconnect exhaust system from manifold.
38. Non-turbocharger equipped vehicles: Disconnect power steering pressure hose from steering gear.
39. Turbocharger equipped vehicles: Disconnect both power steering hoses from steering gear.
40. Turbocharger equipped vehicles: Remove upper and lower heat shields (1), elbow support bracket (4), turbocharger support bracket (2), and elbow (3).
41. Remove structural collar. Refer to Engine Structural Collar Removal & Installation.
42. Automatic Transmission equipped vehicles: Remove torque converter bolts and mark converter to flex plate orientation for reassembly.
43. Manual Transmission equipped vehicles: Remove drive plate to clutch module bolts and mark plate orientation for reassembly.
44. Remove lower engine torque strut (5). Refer to Engine Torque Strut Removal & Installation.

45. Lower the vehicle and remove A/C compressor.
46. Disconnect power steering lines from power steering pump.
47. Remove power steering pump.
48. Raise vehicle enough to allow engine dolly (7), cradle (8), and posts (6) to be installed under vehicle. (Using the following Special Tools: Dolly 6135, Cradle 6710, Post Kit Engine Cradle 6848.)
49. Loosen engine support posts (6) to allow movement for positioning onto engine locating holes and flange on the engine bedplate. Lower vehicle and position cradle (8) until the engine is resting on support posts (6). Tighten mounts to cradle (8) frame. This will keep support posts (6) from moving when removing or installing engine and transmission.
50. Install safety straps (4) around the engine to cradle (8). Tighten safety straps (4) and lock them into position.

✳✳ CAUTION

Safety straps MUST be used.

51. Raise vehicle enough to determine if safety straps (4) are secure enough to hold cradle (8) assembly to engine.
52. Lower vehicle so weight of the engine and transmission ONLY is on the cradle (8) assembly.
53. Remove the upper engine torque strut.
54. Remove right mount through bolt.
55. Remove left mount attaching bolts.
56. Raise the vehicle slowly until engine/transaxle assembly clears engine compartment. It may be necessary to move the engine/transmission assembly with the cradle to allow for removal around body flanges.

To install:
57. Position the engine and transmission assembly under vehicle and slowly lower the vehicle over the engine/transaxle assembly.

✳✳ WARNING

To prevent possible damage to engine mount bracket (3) or mount (2), the through bolt (1) must be started by hand to prevent cross threading.

58. Continue lowering vehicle until the engine/transaxle aligns to mounting locations. Install the mounting bolts at the right engine mount. Tighten bolts (1) to 87 ft. lbs. (118 Nm).
59. Install the left transaxle mount. Tighten bolts to 87 ft. lbs. (118 Nm).
60. Install upper engine torque strut. Refer to Engine Torque Strut Removal & Installation.

61. Remove safety straps from engine/ transaxle assembly. Slowly raise vehicle enough to remove the engine dolly and cradle.

62. Install the power steering pump.

63. Connect the power steering lines to the power steering pump.

64. Install the A/C compressor.

65. Install lower engine torque strut. Refer to Engine Torque Strut Removal & Installation.

66. Automatic Transmission equipped vehicles: Install torque converter bolts.

67. Manual Transmission equipped vehicles: Install drive plate to clutch module bolts.

68. Install structural collar. Refer to Engine Structural Collar Removal & Installation.

69. Turbocharger equipped vehicles: Install elbow, turbocharger support bracket, elbow support bracket, and upper and lower heat shields.

70. Non-turbocharger equipped vehicles: Connect power steering pressure hose to steering gear.

71. Turbocharger equipped vehicles: Connect both power steering hoses to steering gear.

72. Connect the exhaust system to manifold.

73. Connect the downstream oxygen sensor.

74. Turbocharger equipped vehicles: Install charge air cooler to throttle body hose.

75. Install charge air cooler to turbocharger hose.

76. Install the alternator and mounting brackets.

77. Install the accessory drive belts.

78. Install the axle shafts. Refer to Halfshaft Removal & Installation, in the Drive Train section.

79. Install the right inner splash shield.

80. Install wheels and lower vehicle.

81. Install the cooling module assembly (fan, radiator, A/C condenser, transmission oil cooler). Connect radiator fan electrical connector.

82. Turbocharger equipped vehicles: Connect power steering hoses to radiator.

83. Manual transmission equipped vehicles:

   a. Connect the clutch hydraulic line.

   b. Connect the transmission shift linkage.

   c. Connect the transmission electrical connectors.

→**It is not necessary to bleed the clutch hydraulic system. The quick-connect fittings close immediately after disconnection; allowing no fluid to escape.**

84. Automatic transmission equipped vehicles:

   a. Connect the transmission oil cooler lines using service splice kit. Refer to instructions provided with kit.

   b. Connect the transmission electrical connectors.

   c. Connect the transmission shift linkage.

85. Connect the A/C lines at junction near upper torque strut.

86. Connect the upper A/C line to A/C condenser.

87. Install the upper and lower radiator hoses.

88. Install the upper radiator closure panel and center brace. Refer to Radiator Removal & Installation, in the Engine Cooling section.

89. Install the grille and tighten grille retaining fasteners.

90. Connect the fuel line and heater hoses.

91. Connect the coolant reserve/recovery hose to coolant outlet connector.

92. Connect the brake booster vacuum hose to intake manifold.

93. Connect the proportional purge hose to throttle body.

94. Install all ground straps and connect engine wiring harness.

95. Position Totally Integrated Power Module (TIPM) and install bolts Connect the positive battery cable to TIPM and ground wire to vehicle body.

96. Connect the engine wiring harness at Powertrain Control Module (PCM).

97. Connect the throttle and speed control cables.

98. Install battery tray and battery.

99. Connect cables to battery.

100. Install air cleaner housing assembly and connect clean air hose.

101. Install oil filter. Fill engine crankcase with proper oil to correct level.

102. Fill power steering system.

103. Fill cooling system. Refer to Coolant Fill Procedure, in the Engine Cooling section.

104. Evacuate and recharge A/C system.

105. Start engine and run until operating temperature is reached. Check for leaks.

106. Perform torque strut adjustment procedure. Refer to Engine Torque Strut Adjustment.

107. Adjust transmission linkage, if necessary.

ENGINE STRUCTURAL COLLAR

REMOVAL & INSTALLATION

Automatic Transaxle

See Figures 129 through 131.

1. Before servicing the vehicle, refer to the Precautions Section.

2. Raise and safely support the vehicle.

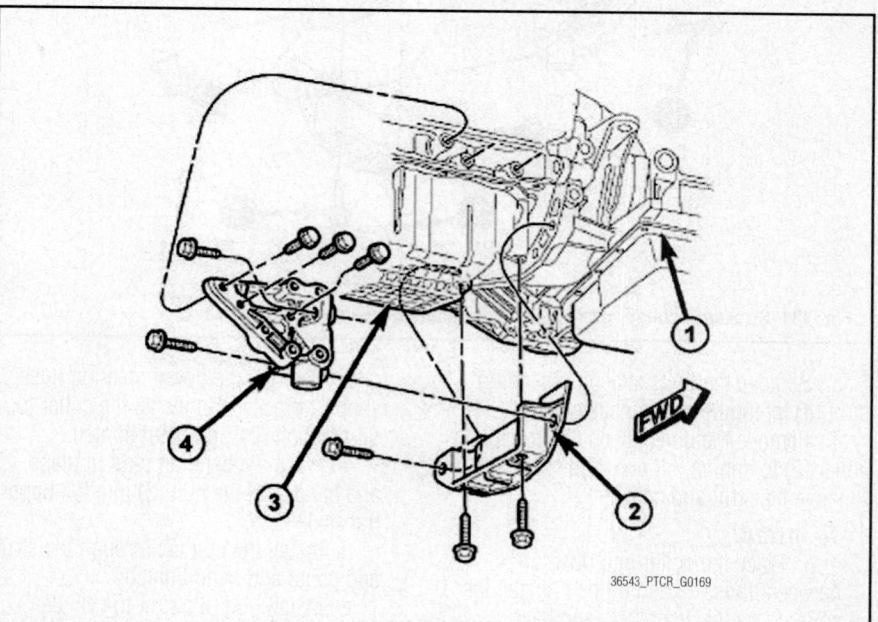

Fig. 129 Structural collar removal component locations—automatic transaxle

36543_PTCR_G0169

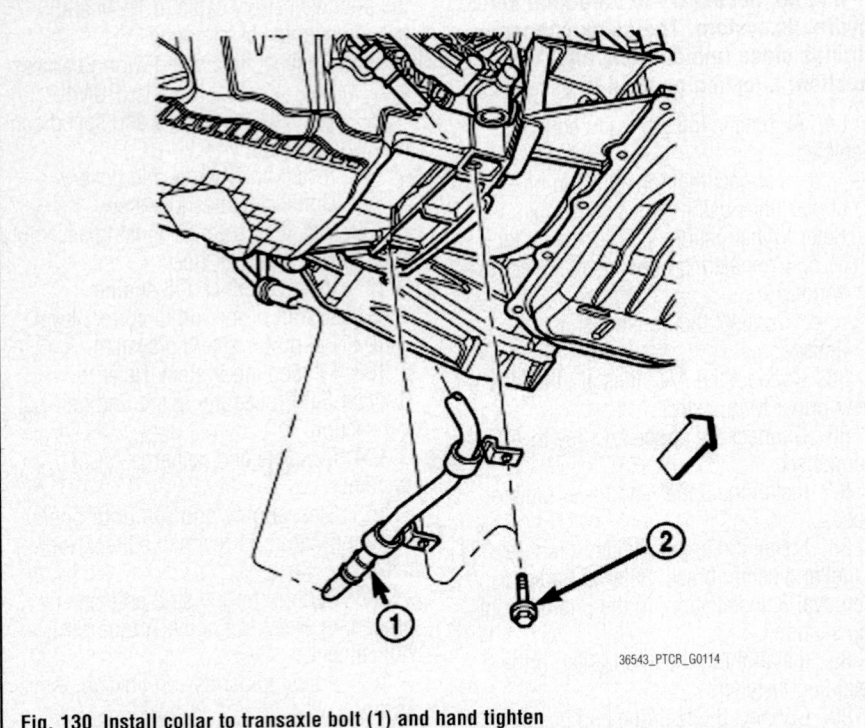

Fig. 130 Install collar to transaxle bolt (1) and hand tighten

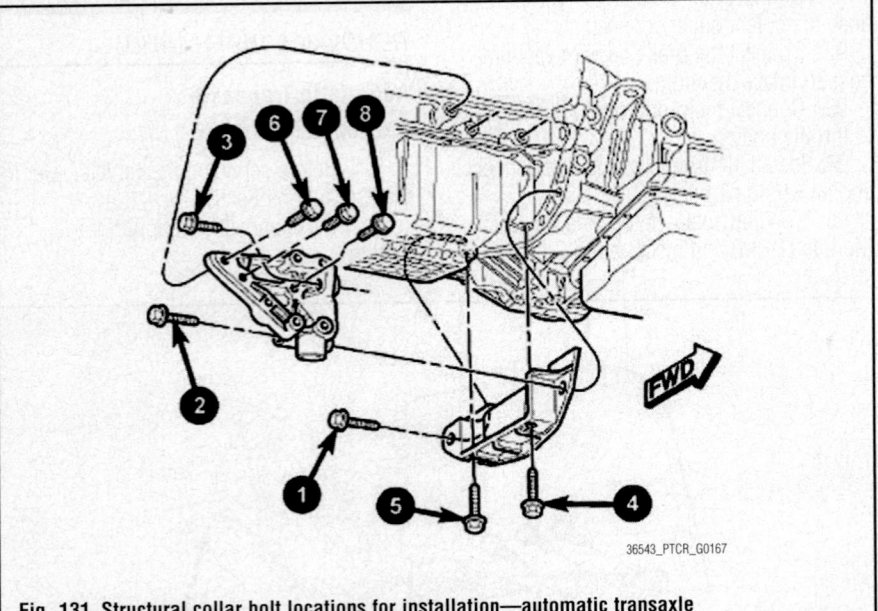

Fig. 131 Structural collar bolt locations for installation—automatic transaxle

3. Remove the bolts attaching bending strut (4) to engine and transaxle (1).

4. Remove the bolts attaching structural collar (2) to engine, oil pan, and transaxle. Remove the strut and collar.

To install:

a. Place the collar into position between transaxle and oil pan. Install the collar to transaxle bolt (1) and hand tighten.

b. Position the power steering hose support bracket and install the collar to oil pan bolt (2), and hand tighten.

c. Place the bending strut in place and hand start the bolt (3) into the upper transaxle hole.

d. Install the bolt (2) through the strut and collar and hand tighten.

e. Install bolt (6), strut to cylinder block, and hand tighten.

f. Place the power steering hose support bracket in position and install the remaining collar to oil pan bolt (5), and then hand tighten the remaining bolts.

g. Tighten the collar-to-transaxle bolts (1–3) to 75 ft. lbs. (101 Nm).

h. Install the bolts (7 and 8) through the strut and into the block.

i. Tighten the remaining bolts (4–8) to 45 ft. lbs. (61 Nm).

Manual Transaxle

See Figure 132.

1. Before servicing the vehicle, refer to the Precautions Section.

2. Raise and safely support the vehicle.

3. Remove bolts attaching collar and clutch slave cylinder (6) to transaxle (7).

4. Remove remaining bolts attaching structural collar (9) to oil pan and transaxle. Remove structural collar (9).

5. Lower the vehicle.

To install:

a. Place the collar in position and hand tighten the collar to transaxle bolt.

b. Position the power steering hose support bracket and install the collar to oil pan bolt. Hand tighten.

c. Position the clutch slave cylinder into position and hand start the bolts.

d. Position power steering hose support bracket and install the remaining collar to oil pan bolt. Hand tighten.

e. Final torque all bolts in sequence shown in to the following torque values:
- Tighten bolts (1) to 75 ft. lbs. (101 Nm)
- Tighten bolts (2 and 5) to 45 ft. lbs. (61 Nm)
- Tighten bolts (3 and 4) to 20 ft. lbs. (28 Nm)

6. Lower the vehicle.

ENGINE TORQUE STRUTS

REMOVAL & INSTALLATION

Upper Torque Strut

See Figure 133.

1. Before servicing the vehicle, refer to the Precautions Section.

2. Remove the bolts attaching upper torque strut (6) to shock tower bracket and engine mount bracket.

3. Remove the timing belt front upper cover (if A/C equipped).

4. Remove the upper torque strut (6).

To install:

5. Position the upper torque strut into mounting location.

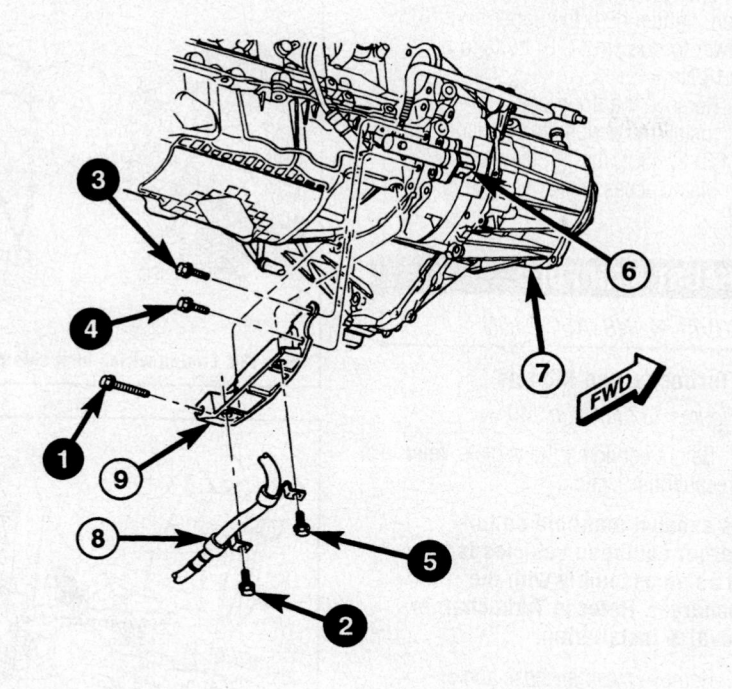

1–5 – BOLT TIGHTENING SEQUENCE
6 – HYDRAULIC CLUTCH SLAVE CYLINDER
7 – TRANSAXLE
8 – POWER STEERING HOSE
9 – COLLAR

67189-PTCR-G08

Fig. 132 Structural collar assembly—manual transaxle

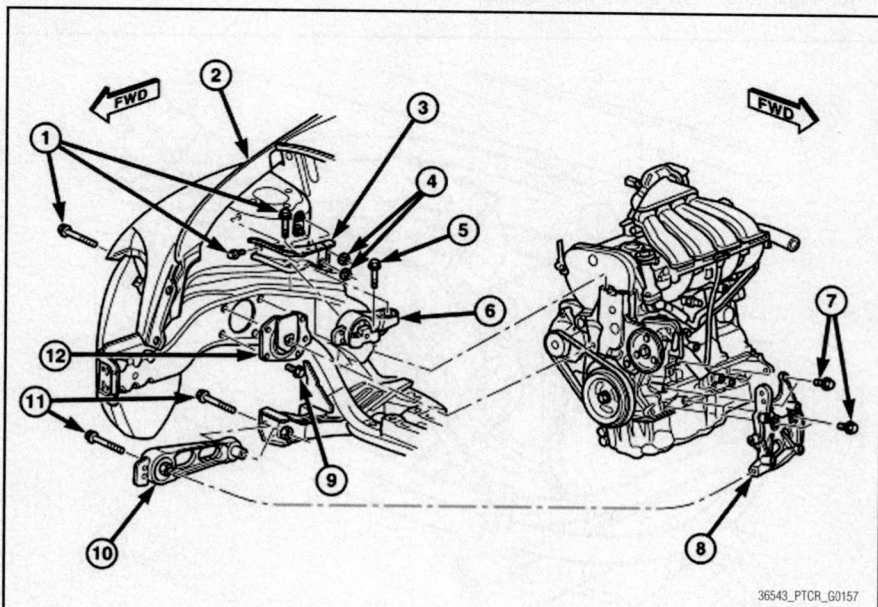

36543_PTCR_G0157

Fig. 133 Upper torque strut (6) location

6. Move torque strut aside (towards right fender) and install timing belt front upper cover (if A/C equipped).

7. Install the torque strut mounting bolts and perform the torque strut adjustment procedure, described in this section.

Lower Torque Strut

See Figure 134.

1. Before servicing the vehicle, refer to the Precautions Section.

2. Raise and safely support the vehicle.

3. Remove the accessory drive belt splash shield.

4. Remove the pencil strut (2).

5. Remove the bolts attaching lower torque strut to crossmember and strut bracket.

6. Remove the lower torque strut (5).

To install:

7. Position the lower torque strut into mounting locations.

8. Install the mounting bolts and perform torque strut adjustment procedure, described in this section.

9. Install the pencil strut and tighten nuts to 43 ft. lbs. (58 Nm).

10. Install the accessory belt splash shield and lower vehicle.

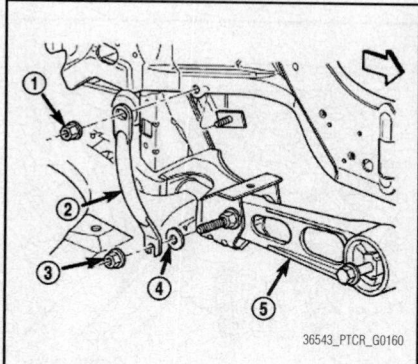

36543_PTCR_G0160

Fig. 134 Pencil strut (2) and lower torque strut (5)

AJUSTMENT

See Figures 133 through 136.

1. Before servicing the vehicle, refer to the Precautions Section.

➡**The upper and lower torque struts need to be adjusted together to assure proper engine positioning and engine mount loading. Whenever a torque strut bolt(s) is loosened, this procedure must be performed.**

2. Remove accessory drive belt splash shield.

3. Remove pencil strut (2).

4. Loosen the upper (6) and lower torque strut (10) attaching bolt at the suspension crossmember and shock tower bracket.

5. The engine position may now be adjusted by positioning a suitable floor jack on the forward edge of the transmission bell housing.

➡The floor jack must be positioned as shown to prevent minimal upward lifting of the engine.

6. With the engine supported, remove the upper (6) and lower torque strut (10) attachment bolt(s) at shock tower bracket and suspension crossmember. Verify that the torque struts are free to move within the shock tower bracket and crossmember. Reinstall the torque strut bolt(s), but do not tighten.

7. Carefully apply upward force, allowing the upper engine to rotate rearward.

8. Adjust until the distance between the center of the rearmost attaching bolt on the engine mount bracket (point "A") and the center of the hole on the shock tower bracket (point "B") is 4.70 in. (119 mm).

❋❋ CAUTION

The engine must be held in position with jack until both the upper and lower torque strut bolts are tightened.

Fig. 135 Floor jack positioning

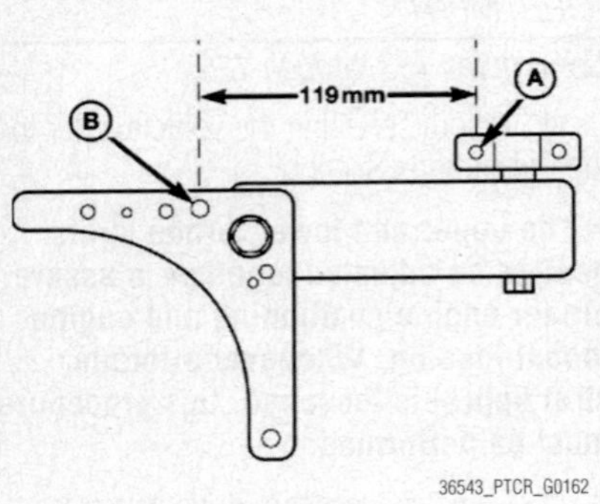

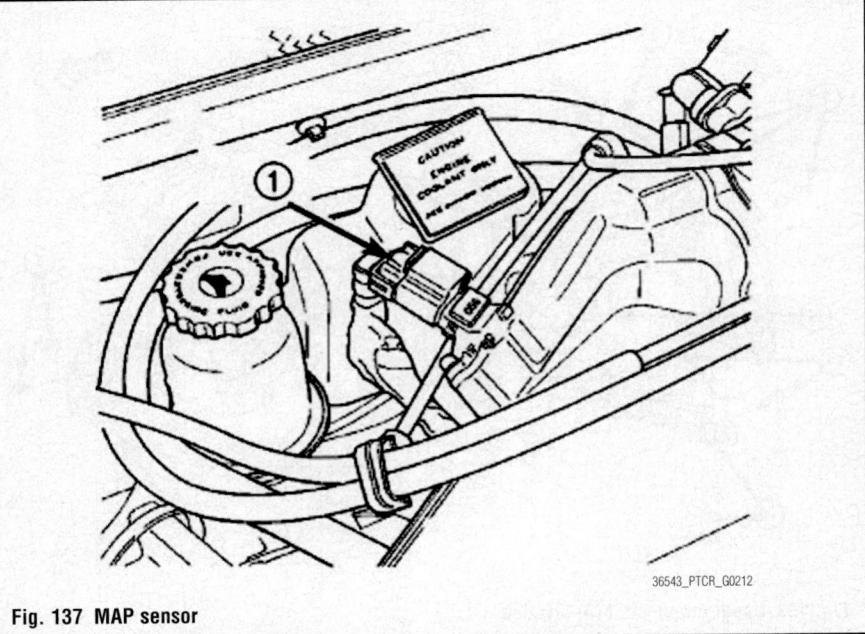

Fig. 136 Strut tightening position

9. With the engine held at the proper position, tighten both the upper strut (6) and lower torque strut (10) bolts to 85 ft. lbs. (115 Nm).

10. Remove the floor jack.

11. Install the pencil strut (2) and tighten nuts (1,3) to 43 ft. lbs. (58 Nm).

12. Install accessory drive belt splash shield.

EXHAUST MANIFOLD

REMOVAL & INSTALLATION

Non-Turbocharged Models

See Figures 137 through 140.

1. Before servicing the vehicle, refer to the Precautions Section.

➡The exhaust manifold on turbocharger equipped vehicles is serviced as an assembly with the turbocharger. Refer to Turbocharger Removal & Installation.

2. Remove clean air hose and air cleaner housing.

3. Disconnect the negative battery cable.

4. Disconnect the throttle and speed control cables from the throttle lever and bracket.

5. Disconnect the Manifold Absolute Pressure (MAP) sensor electrical connector.

6. Remove fasteners securing power steering fluid reservoir to cylinder head.

7. The coolant recovery container.

8. Remove bolts attaching upper heat shield.

9. Remove the upper heat shield.

10. Raise and safely support the vehicle.

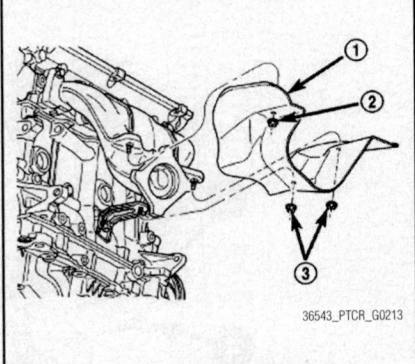

Fig. 138 Engine wiring heat shield

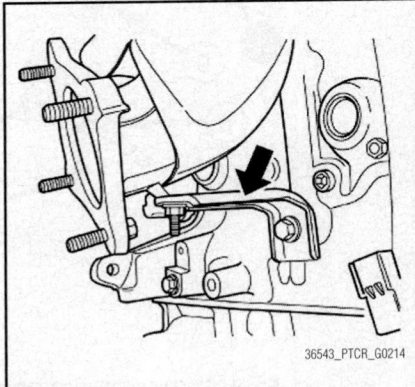

Fig. 139 Manifold support bracket

11. Disconnect the exhaust pipe from the manifold.

12. Remove the engine wiring heat shield.

13. Remove the manifold support bracket.

14. Remove the lower exhaust manifold heat shield.

Fig. 137 MAP sensor

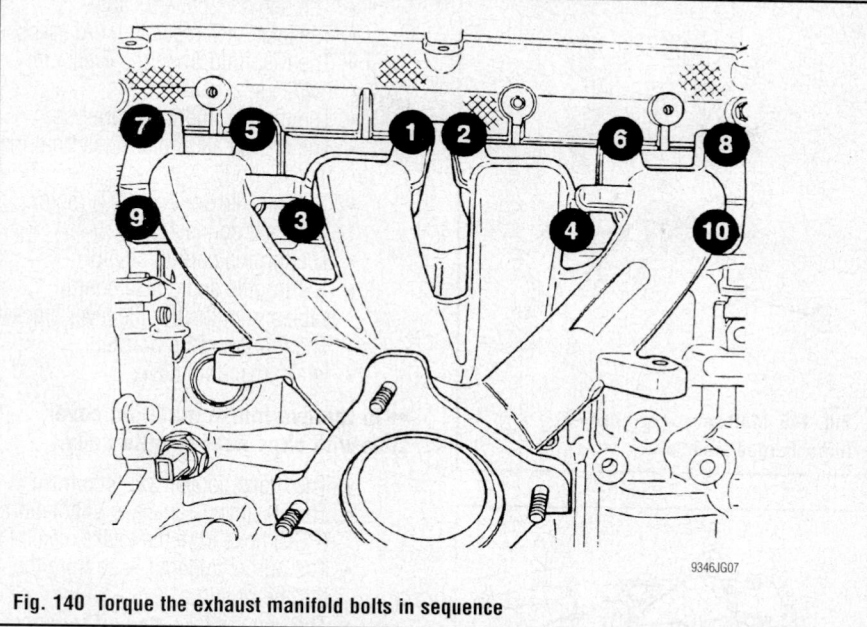

Fig. 140 Torque the exhaust manifold bolts in sequence

15. Disconnect oxygen sensor electrical connector.

16. Remove exhaust manifold lower retaining fasteners.

17. Lower vehicle and remove the upper exhaust manifold retaining fasteners.

18. Remove exhaust manifold from above/between the engine and cowl panel.

19. Remove and discard manifold gasket.

To install:

20. Install a new exhaust manifold gasket. DO NOT APPLY SEALER.

21. Position exhaust manifold in place. Tighten fasteners in the sequence shown to 17 ft. lbs. (23 Nm). Raise and lower vehicle for fastener access as necessary. Repeat tightening procedure until all fasteners are at specified torque.

22. Install exhaust manifold heat shields. Tighten bolts to 105 inch lbs. (12 Nm).

23. Install exhaust manifold support bracket.

24. Install engine wiring heat shield.

25. Connect oxygen sensor electrical connector.

26. Install exhaust pipe to manifold with a new gasket. Tighten fasteners to 21 ft. lbs. (28 Nm).

27. Install coolant recovery container.

28. Install fasteners securing power steering fluid reservoir to cylinder head.

29. Connect MAP sensor electrical connector.

30. Connect throttle and speed control cables to the throttle lever and bracket.

31. Connect negative cable to battery.

32. Install clean air hose and air cleaner housing.

Turbocharged Models

The exhaust manifold on turbocharged model is removed as an assembly with the turbocharger. For service information, refer to Turbocharger, Removal & Installation.

FLEXPLATE

REMOVAL & INSTALLATION

See Figure 141.

1. Before servicing the vehicle, refer to the Precautions Section.

2. Remove the transaxle.

3. Remove the flexplate retaining bolts (3).

4. Remove the shim (4) and flexplate (2).

To install:

5. Install the flexplate and shim.

6. Install the bolts and torque to 70 ft. lbs. (95 Nm).

7. Install the transaxle assembly.

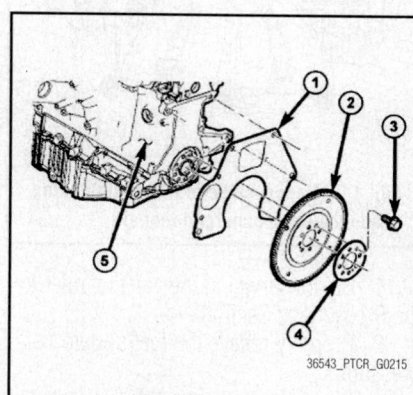

Fig. 141 Flexplate

INTAKE MANIFOLD

REMOVAL & INSTALLATION

Upper

Non-Turbocharged Models

See Figures 142 through 144.

1. Before servicing the vehicle, refer to the Precautions Section.

2. Properly relieve the fuel system pressure.

3. Remove the negative battery cable.

4. Disconnect inlet air temperature sensor and make-up air hose (1) from clean air hose.

5. Remove air cleaner housing and clean air hose assembly.

6. Disconnect negative cable from battery.

7. Remove throttle and speed control cables from throttle lever and bracket.

8. Disconnect Manifold Absolute Pressure (MAP) sensor (1).

9. Disconnect Idle Air Control (IAC) motor (1) and Throttle Position (TPS) sensor (3) wiring connectors.

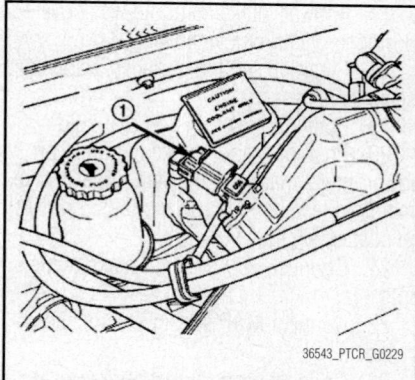

Fig. 142 MAP sensor location—non-turbocharged models

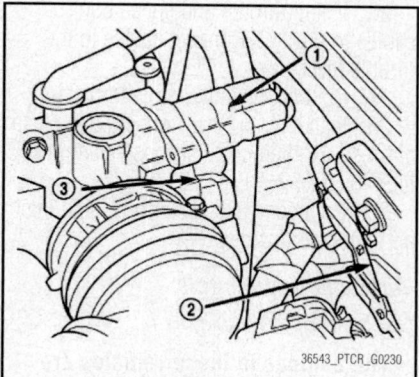

Fig. 143 IAC and TPS locations—non-turbocharged models

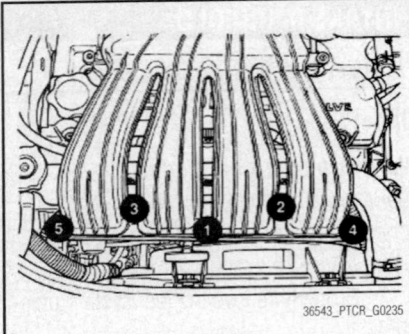

Fig. 144 Upper intake manifold tightening sequence—non-turbocharged engines

10. Disconnect proportional purge hoses.

11. Disconnect brake booster hose.

12. Disconnect PCV hose from intake manifold.

13. Remove rear intake manifold support bracket.

14. Remove upper intake manifold fasteners.

15. Remove upper intake manifold.

16. If further service is required, cover the lower intake manifold openings to prevent foreign materials from entering the engine.

To install:

17. If lower intake manifold was covered during service, remove cover.

18. Clean all sealing surfaces. Replace seals as necessary.

19. Position new seals on manifold.

20. Position upper intake manifold on lower intake manifold. Tighten upper intake manifold fasteners to 105 inch lbs. (12 Nm). in sequence shown.

21. Connect PCV hose to intake manifold.

22. Connect MAP sensor electrical connector.

23. Connect proportional purge hoses.

24. Connect brake booster hose.

25. Connect IAC motor and TPS wiring connectors.

26. Install throttle and speed control cables to bracket. Connect cables to the throttle lever.

27. Connect negative cable to battery.

28. Install air cleaner housing and clean air hose. Tighten clean air hose clamp to 15 inch lbs. (1.7 Nm).

29. Connect make-up air hose and inlet air temperature sensor.

Turbocharged Models

See Figures 145 through 147.

➡ **The engines in these vehicles are equipped with either an aluminum or plastic manifold.**

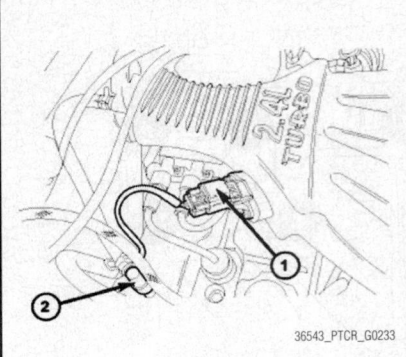

Fig. 145 MAP sensor location— turbocharged models

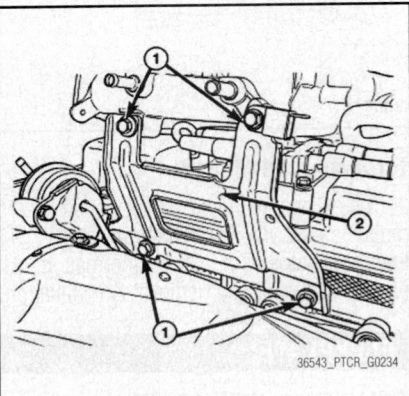

Fig. 146 Upper intake manifold support bracket location—turbocharged models

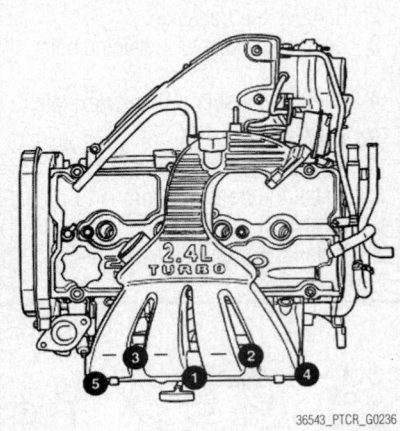

Fig. 147 Upper intake manifold tightening sequence—turbocharged models

1. Before servicing the vehicle, refer to the Precautions Section.

2. Properly relieve the fuel system pressure.

3. Remove or disconnect the following:

- The negative battery cable
- The Inlet Air Temperature (IAT) sensor
- The Manifold Absolute Pressure (MAP) sensor
- The throttle inlet pressure hose
- The charge air cooler hose from the throttle body
- The Idle Air Control (IAC) motor electrical connector
- The throttle control shield
- The throttle and cruise control cables from the throttle lever bracket
- The throttle cable bracket
- Intake manifold cover

➡ **To remove intake manifold cover, start with clips near throttle body.**

- The brake booster vacuum hose
- The Positive Crankcase Ventilation (PCV) hose from the intake manifold
- The purge solenoid hose from the throttle body
- The upper intake manifold support bracket and manifold

➡ **Cover the lower intake manifold to avoid dirt and other objects from entering.**

4. Clean the mating surfaces.

To install:

5. Remove the cover from the lower intake manifold.

6. Install or connect the following:

- The new gasket
- The intake manifold on the lower intake manifold. If equipped with an aluminum manifold, torque the bolts in sequence to 250 inch lbs. (28 Nm). If equipped with a plastic manifold, torque the bolts in sequence to 105 inch lbs. (12 Nm).
- The upper intake manifold support bracket. Torque the retainers to 21 ft. lbs. (28 Nm).
- The purge solenoid hose to the throttle body
- The brake booster vacuum hose
- The PCV hose
- The throttle cable bracket and tighten the screws to 105 inch lbs. (12 Nm)
- The throttle and cruise control cables to the throttle lever bracket
- The throttle control shield
- The IAC motor electrical connector
- The MAP sensor
- The charge air cooler hose to the throttle body
- The IAT sensor
- The throttle inlet pressure hose
- The negative battery cable

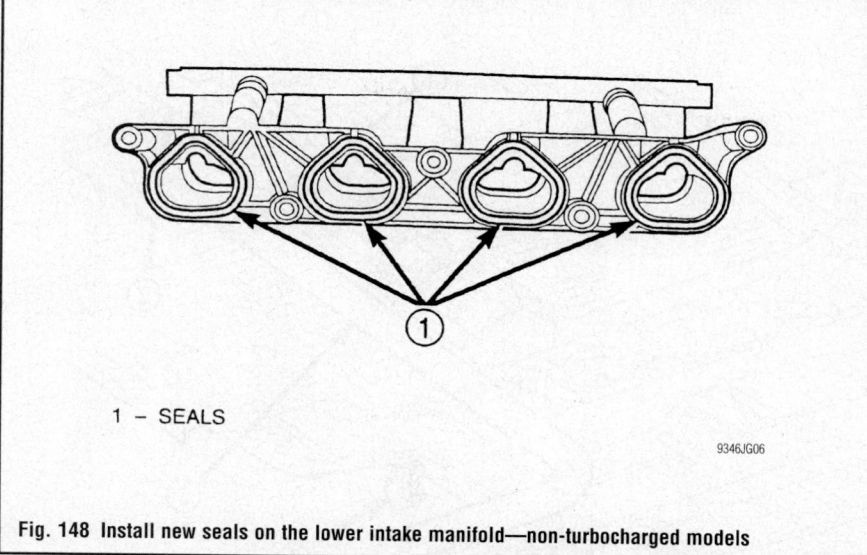

1 – SEALS

9346JG06

Fig. 148 Install new seals on the lower intake manifold—non-turbocharged models

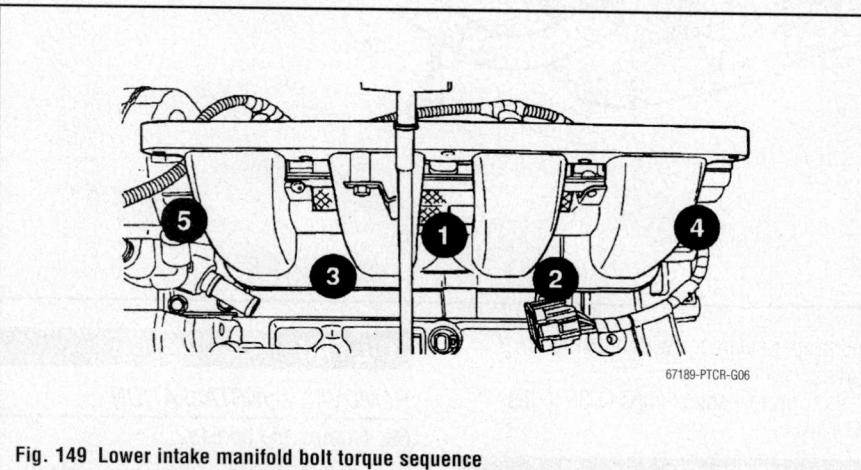

67189-PTCR-G06

Fig. 149 Lower intake manifold bolt torque sequence

Lower

See Figures 148 and 149.

➡**The engines in these vehicles are equipped with either an aluminum or plastic manifold.**

1. Before servicing the vehicle, refer to the Precautions Section.
2. Properly relieve the fuel system pressure.
3. Drain the coolant system. Refer to Coolant Fill Procedure, in the Engine Cooling section.
4. Remove or disconnect the following:
   - The negative battery cable
   - The Inlet Air Temperature (IAT) sensor and make-up hose
   - The air cleaner
   - The upper intake manifold, refer to Upper Intake Manifold
   - The upper radiator hose and coolant outlet connector, refer to Refer to Radiator in Engine Cooling
   - The fuel supply line quick-connect from the fuel rail, refer to Fuel Rail & Injectors in Fuel Systems
   - The fuel injector wiring harness
   - The oil dipstick tube from the lower intake manifold
   - The intake manifold and discard the gaskets and seals
5. Thoroughly clean the gasket mating surfaces.

To install:

6. Install or connect the following:
   - New seals on non-turbocharged models
   - The intake manifold and torque the bolts in sequence to 105 inch lbs. (12 Nm) on non-turbocharged models
   - New gaskets on turbocharged models

   - The intake manifold. If equipped with an aluminum manifold, torque the bolts in sequence to 21 ft. lbs. (28 Nm). If equipped with a plastic manifold, torque the bolts in sequence to 12.5 ft. lbs. (12 Nm) on turbocharged models.
   - The lower intake manifold support bracket. If equipped with an aluminum manifold, torque fasteners to 40 ft. lbs. (54 Nm), if equipped with a plastic manifold, torque manifold fasteners to 55 inch lbs. (6 Nm).
   - The fuel injector wiring harness
   - The fuel supply line quick-connect to the fuel tube assembly
   - The oil dipstick tube to the lower intake manifold
   - The upper radiator hose
   - The upper intake manifold
   - The IAT sensor
   - The air cleaner assembly
   - The negative battery cable
7. Fill the coolant system. Refer to Coolant Fill Procedure, in the Engine Cooling section.
8. Pressurize the fuel system. Refer to Fuel System section.
9. Start the vehicle and check for leaks, repair if necessary.

INTERMEDIATE PIPE

REMOVAL & INSTALLATION

See Figure 150.

1. Before servicing the vehicle, refer to the Precautions Section.

✳✳ CAUTION

The normal operating temperature of the exhaust system is very high. Therefore, never work around or attempt to service any part of the exhaust system until it is cooled. Special care should be taken when working near the catalytic converter. The temperature of the converter rises to a high level after a short period of engine operating time.

2. Raise vehicle on hoist and apply penetrating oil to band clamp fastener of component being removed.

✳✳ WARNING

Do not use petroleum-based lubricants when removing/installing muffler or exhaust pipe isolators as it may compromise the life of the part. A suitable substitute is a

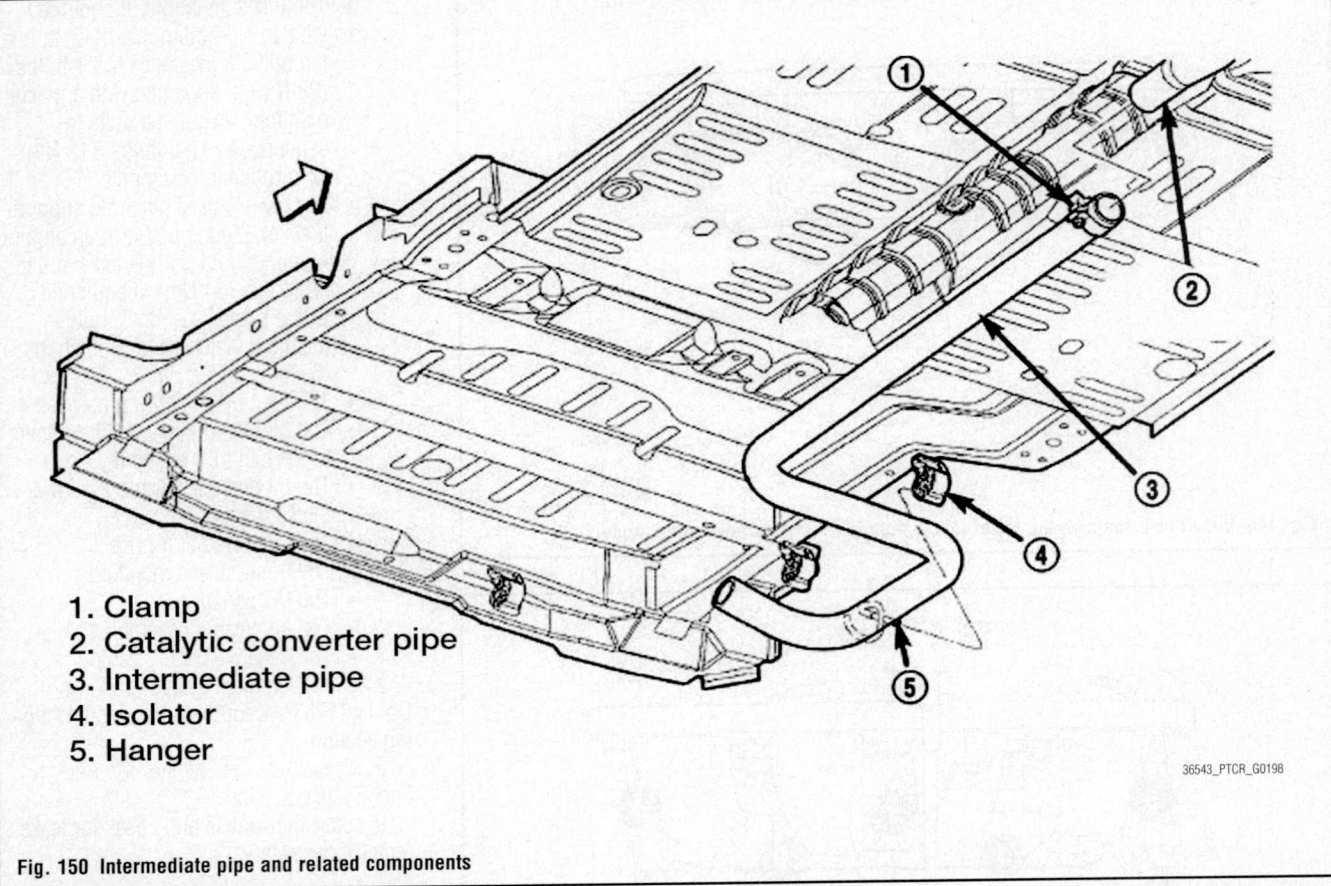

1. Clamp
2. Catalytic converter pipe
3. Intermediate pipe
4. Isolator
5. Hanger

36543_PTCR_G0198

Fig. 150 Intermediate pipe and related components

mixture of liquid dish soap and water.

3. Remove muffler.
4. Loosen band clamp and remove support isolator. Remove intermediate pipe from catalytic converter pipe (2).
5. Clean ends of pipes and muffler to assure mating of all parts. Discard broken or worn isolators, rusted or overused clamps, supports, and attaching parts.

➡**When replacement is required on any component of the exhaust system, you must use original equipment parts (or their equivalent).**

To install:

✳✳ WARNING

When assembling exhaust system do not tighten clamps until components are aligned and clearances are checked.

6. Install intermediate pipe and the isolator supports to the underbody.
7. Install muffler.
8. Working from the front of system; align each component to maintain position

and proper clearance with underbody parts.

9. Tighten band clamps to 35 ft. lbs. (47 Nm).

✳✳ WARNING

Band clamps should never be tightened such that the two sides of the clamps are bottomed out against the center hourglass shaped center block. Once this occurs, the clamp band has been stretched and has lost its clamping force and must be replaced. To replace the band clamp; remove the nut and peel back the ends of the clamp until spot weld breaks. File or grind remaining weld material until pipe surface is smooth.

➡**Maintain proper clamp orientation when replacing with new clamp.**

10. Start the engine and inspect for exhaust leaks. Repair exhaust leaks as necessary.
11. Check the exhaust system for contact with the body panels. Make the necessary adjustments, if needed.

OIL PAN

REMOVAL & INSTALLATION
See Figures 151 and 152.

1. Before servicing the vehicle, refer to the Precautions Section.
2. Drain the engine oil and remove the oil filter.
3. Support the powertrain assembly.
4. Remove or disconnect the following:

- The negative battery cable
- The right inner splash shield
- The turbocharger-to-charge air cooler hose assembly, if equipped
- The oil cooler connector bolt, if equipped with a turbocharger. Do not disconnect the coolant lines from the oil cooler and reposition the cooler.
- The engine structural collar, refer to Engine Structural Collar.
- The lower torque strut, refer to Engine Torque Struts.
- The oil filter adapter
- The oil pan and gasket

5. Thoroughly clean all gasket mating surfaces.

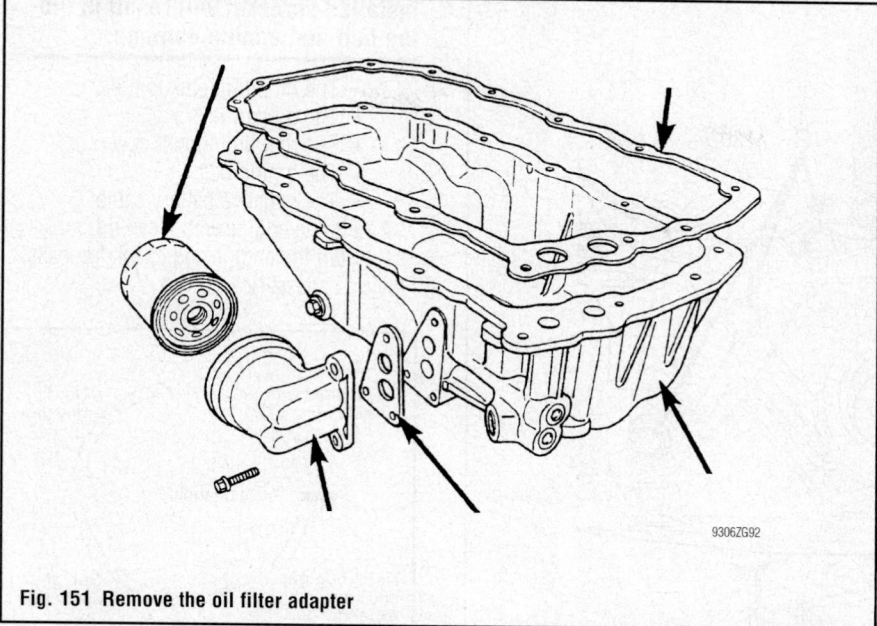

Fig. 151 Remove the oil filter adapter

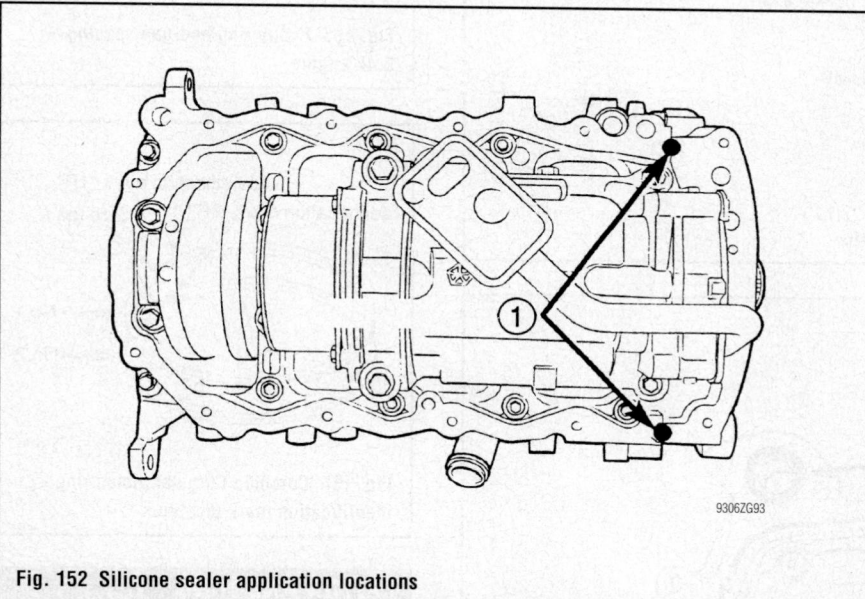

Fig. 152 Silicone sealer application locations

To install:

6. Apply silicone sealer to the oil pump-to-engine block parting line.

7. Install or connect the following:
- The new gasket on the oil pan
- The oil pan and torque the bolts to 105 inch lbs. (12 Nm)
- The oil filter and adapter and torque the screws to 105 inch lbs. (12 Nm)

8. If equipped with a turbocharger, replace the oil cooler seal. Lubricate the seal with and place the oil cooler-to-oil filter adapter in position making sure to align the notch on the tab. Install the oil cooler connector bolt and tighten to 41 ft. lbs. (55 Nm).

✳✳ WARNING

Follow the proper tightening sequence for the structural collar or damage to the collar or oil pan may occur.

9. Install the engine structural collar. Refer to Engine Structural Collar.

10. Install or connect the following:
- The lower torque strut, refer to Engine Torque Struts
- The turbocharger-to-charge air cooler hose assembly, if equipped
- The right inner splash shield
- The negative battery cable

11. Fill the engine with clean oil and a new filter.

12. Start the vehicle and check for leaks, repair if necessary.

OIL PUMP

REMOVAL & INSTALLATION

See Figures 153 and 154.

1. Before servicing the vehicle, refer to the Precautions Section.

2. Drain the engine oil.

3. Remove or disconnect the following:
- The negative battery cable
- The timing belt and rear cover, refer to Timing Belt and Sprockets
- The oil pan, refer to Oil Pan
- The crankshaft sprocket, using Tool 6793 and Insert Tool C-4685-C2
- The crankshaft key
- The oil pickup tube
- The oil pump

To install:

4. Wash all parts in a solvent; then, inspect carefully for damage or wear, as follows:

a. Inspect the mating surface of the oil pump should be smooth. Replace the pump cover, if scratched or grooved.

b. Apply Mopar® gasket maker to the oil pump.

c. Install the O-ring into the oil pump body discharge passage.

5. Prime the oil pump before installation by filling the rotor cavity with engine oil.

6. Install or connect the following:
- The oil pump, align the rotor flats with the crankshaft flats and torque the bolts to 21 ft. lbs. (28 Nm).

✳✳ WARNING

The front crankshaft seal MUST be out of the pump to align or damage may result.

- The new front crankshaft seal, using Seal Driver Tool 6780
- The crankshaft key
- The crankshaft sprocket, using a Crankshaft Sprocket Installer Tool 6792

✳✳ WARNING

The crankshaft sprocket is set to a predetermined depth from the factory for correct timing belt tracking. If removed, use of Special Tool 6792 is required to set the sprocket to original installation depth. An incorrectly

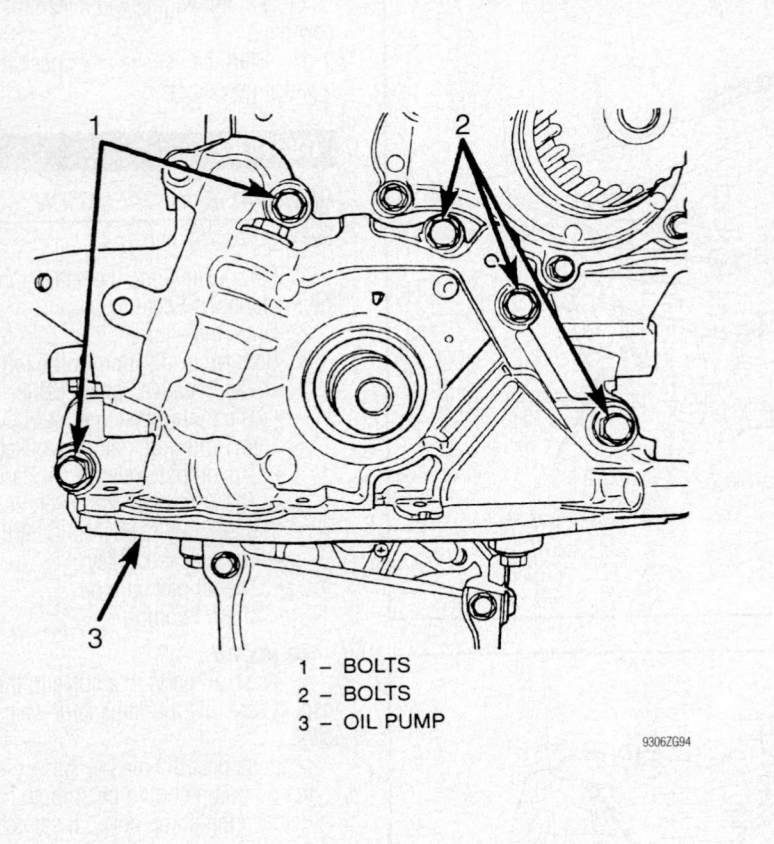

1 – BOLTS
2 – BOLTS
3 – OIL PUMP

9306ZG94

Fig. 153 Exploded view of the oil pump mounting bolts

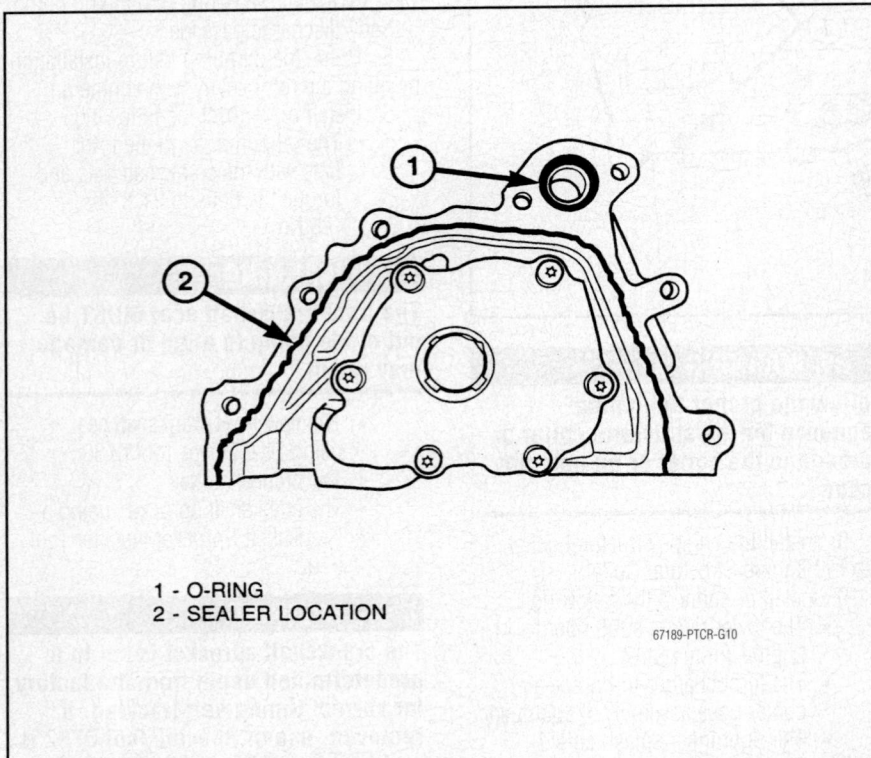

1 - O-RING
2 - SEALER LOCATION

67189-PTCR-G10

Fig. 154 Apply a small amount of gasket maker to the pump body cover mounting surface

installed sprocket will result in timing belt and engine damage.

- The oil pump pickup tube
- The oil pan
- The rear timing belt cover
- The timing belt
- The negative battery cable

7. Fill the engine with clean oil.
8. Start the engine and check for leaks; repair if necessary.

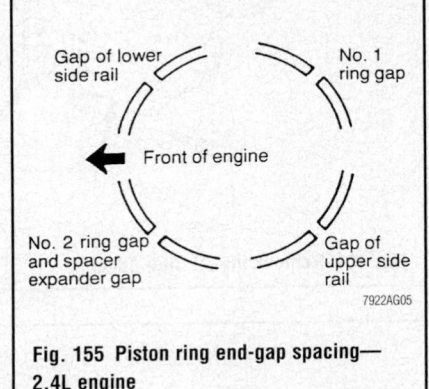

Fig. 155 Piston ring end-gap spacing—2.4L engine

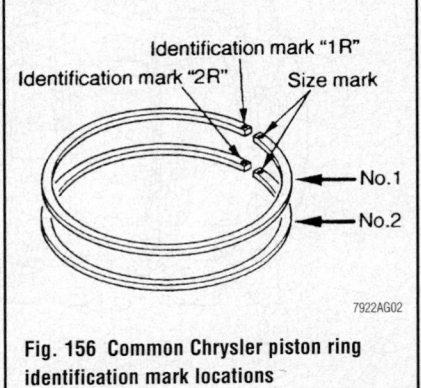

Fig. 156 Common Chrysler piston ring identification mark locations

PISTON AND RING

POSITIONING

See Figures 155 and 156.

REAR MAIN SEAL

REMOVAL & INSTALLATION

See Figures 157 and 158.

1. Before servicing the vehicle, refer to the Precautions Section.
2. Remove or disconnect the following:
   - The transaxle, refer to Transaxle in Drivetrain
   - The flexplate/flywheel, refer to Flexplate
   - The rear main seal

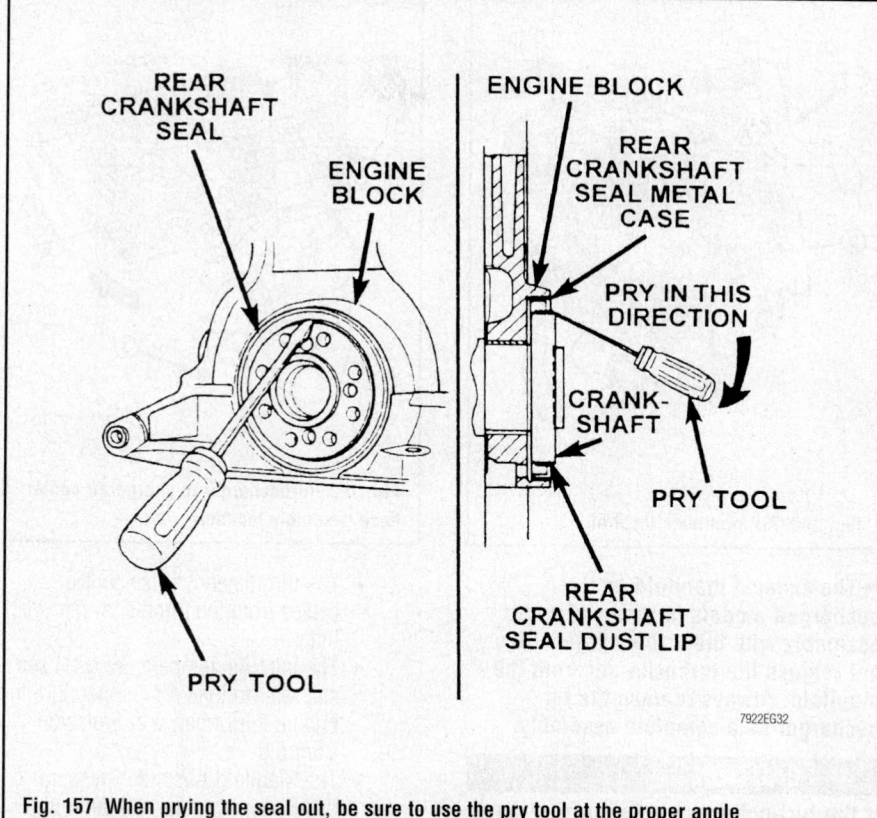

Fig. 157 When prying the seal out, be sure to use the pry tool at the proper angle

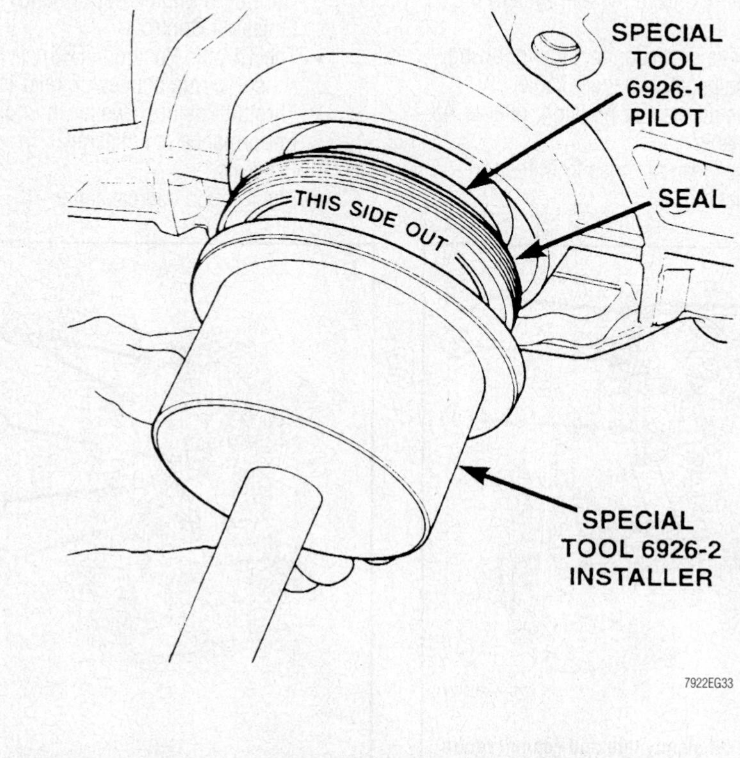

7922EG32

Fig. 158 Place a proper size pilot tool with a magnetic base on the crankshaft

7922EG33

3. Insert a seal remover between the dust lip and the metal case of the crankshaft seal. Angle the tool through the dust lip against the metal case of the seal. Pry out the seal.

❋❋ WARNING

DO NOT let the pry tool contact the crankshaft seal surface. Contact of the tool blade against the crankshaft edge (chamfer) is permitted.

To install:

❋❋ WARNING

If the crankshaft edge (chamfer) has any burrs or scratches on the edge, clean it up with 400 grit sand paper to prevent seal damage during installation of the new seal.

➡ **No lubrication is necessary when installing the seal.**

4. Place Crankcase Seal Pilot Tool 6926-1 on the crankshaft; this is a pilot tool with a magnetic base.
5. Position the seal over the pilot Tool; be sure the words THIS SIDE OUT on the seal can be read.

➡ **The pilot tool should stay on the crankshaft during installation of the seal. Be sure the seal lip faces the crankcase during installation.**

❋❋ WARNING

If the seal is driven in the block past flush, this may cause an oil leak.

6. Drive the seal into the block, using Crankshaft Seal Tool 6926-2 and handle C-4171, until the tool bottoms out against the block.
7. Install or connect the following:
   • The flexplate/flywheel. Apply Lock & Seal Adhesive® to the bolt treads and torque the bolts in a star pattern, to 70 ft. lbs. (95 Nm).
   • The transaxle
   • The negative battery cable
8. Start the vehicle and check for leaks, repair if necessary.

ROCKER ARMS/SHAFTS

REMOVAL & INSTALLATION

See Figure 159.

➡ **This procedure is for in-vehicle service with camshafts installed.**

1. Before servicing the vehicle, refer to the Precautions Section.

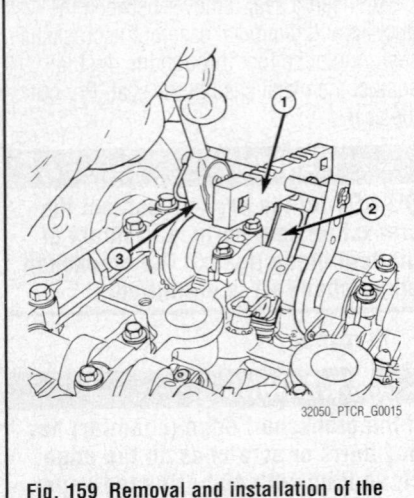

Fig. 159 Removal and installation of the rocker arms

2. Remove cylinder head cover. Refer to Cylinder Head Cover.

3. Remove spark plugs. Refer to Spark Plugs.

4. Rotate engine until the camshaft lobe, on the follower being removed, is positioned on its base circle (heel). Also, the piston should be a minimum of 0.25 inch (6.3mm) below Top Dead Center (TDC) position.

✳✳ WARNING

If cam follower assemblies are to be reused, always mark position for reassembly in their original positions.

5. Using Special Tools 8215A and 8436 slowly depress valve assembly until rocker arm can be removed.

6. Repeat removal procedure for each rocker arm.

To install:

7. Lubricate rocker arm with clean engine oil.

8. Using Special Tools 8215A and 8436 slowly depress valve assembly until rocker arm can be installed on the hydraulic lifter and valve stem.

9. Repeat installation procedure for each rocker arm.

10. Install spark plugs.

11. Install cylinder head cover.

TURBOCHARGER

REMOVAL & INSTALLATION

See Figures 160 through 164.

1. Before servicing the vehicle, refer to the Precautions Section.

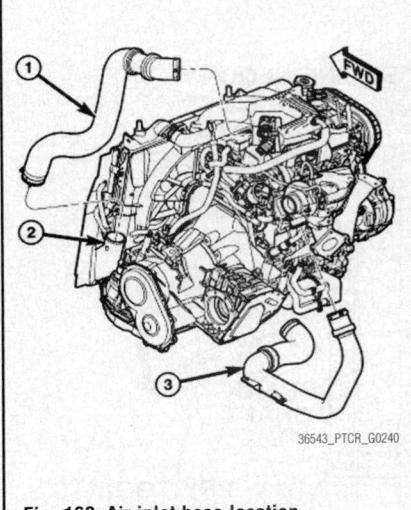

Fig. 160 Air inlet hose location

➡️**The exhaust manifold on turbocharged models is removed as an assembly with the turbocharger. Do not remove the turbocharger from the manifold. Always replace the turbocharger as a complete assembly.**

✳✳ CAUTION

If the turbocharger is being replaced due to bearing failure, the oil pressure feed line has to be replaced and the return tube should be cleaned.

2. Properly relieve the fuel system pressure.

3. Remove or disconnect the following:
- The negative battery cable
- The air cleaner housing, refer to Air cleaner
- The clean air hose from the turbocharger

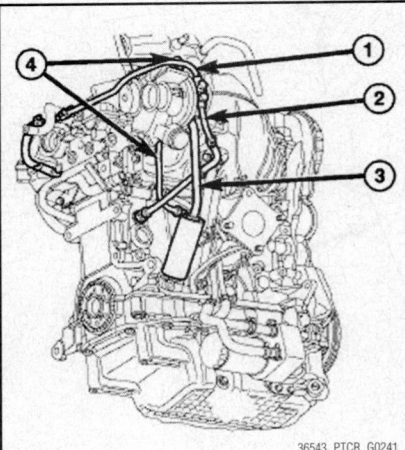

Fig. 161 Oil supply line and coolant return line locations

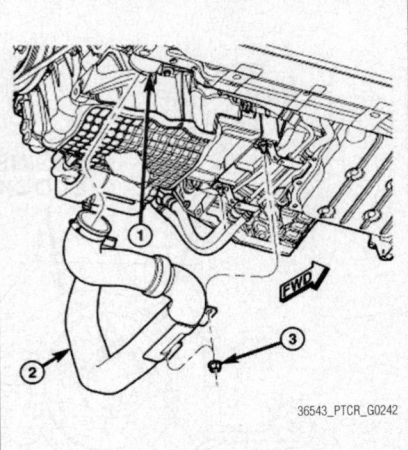

Fig. 162 Turbocharger to charge air cooler hose assembly location

- The throttle and cruise control cables from the throttle lever bracket
- The Inlet Air Temperature (IAT) sensor, refer to Inlet Air Temperature in Engine Performance & Emission Controls
- The Manifold Absolute Pressure (MAP) sensor, refer to Manifold Absolute Pressure in Engine Performance & Emission Controls
- The Idle Air Control (IAC) motor electrical connector, refer to Idle Air Control in Engine Performance & Emission Controls
- The Throttle Position (TPS) sensor wiring connector, refer to Throttle Position Sensor in Engine Performance & Emission Controls
- The ignition coil capacitor

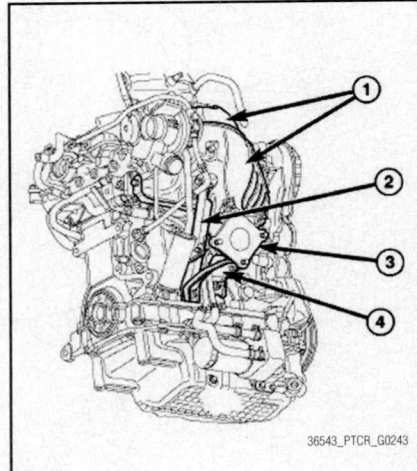

Fig. 163 Turbocharger component location

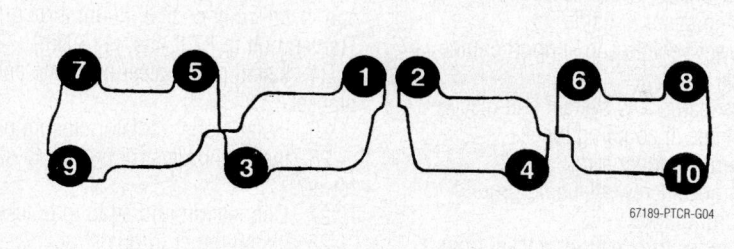

67189-PTCR-G04

Fig. 164 Exhaust manifold torque sequence—turbocharged models

- The upstream Oxygen Sensor (O2S) connector
- The air inlet hose from the throttle body
- The vacuum hoses from the throttle body and upper intake manifold
- The upper intake manifold support bracket and manifold, refer to Intake Manifold

➡ **Cover the lower intake manifold to avoid dirt and other objects from entering.**

- The turbocharger lower heat shield
- The oil supply line from the turbocharger
- The coolant return line
- The vacuum hoses
- The muffler ground strap
- The downstream O2S connector
- The catalytic converter and intermediate pipe as an assembly, refer to Catalytic Converter
- The turbocharger to charge air cooler hose assembly
- The turbocharger, elbow support and support brackets
- The oil return tube
- The turbocharger coolant supply line and upper heat shield
- The turbocharger elbow
- The lower exhaust manifold fasteners from below, then lower the vehicle and remove the upper manifold fasteners
- The turbocharger/manifold assembly from between the engine and cowl panel.

4. Discard the gasket.
5. Clean the mating surfaces.

➡ **The turbocharger and exhaust manifold are serviced as an assembly. Do Not attempt to remove the turbocharger from the exhaust manifold. Exhaust leaks will result. It is recommended that the turbocharger elbow be replaced along with the turbocharger/exhaust manifold assembly.**

To install:

6. Install or connect the following:
- The new gasket. Use no sealer when installing the gasket.

➡ **Stainless steel layer of exhaust manifold gasket goes against cylinder head, graphite layer of gasket goes against manifold surface.**

- The turbocharger/manifold assembly between the engine and cowl panel. Tighten the fasteners working from the center out in progressing in both directions to 21 ft. lbs. (28 Nm).
- The turbocharger elbow. Tighten the fasteners to 21 ft. lbs. (28 Nm).
- The turbocharger upper heat shield. Tighten the fasteners to 21 ft. lbs. (28 Nm).
- The coolant supply line using new washers. Tighten the banjo bolt to 22 ft. lbs. (30 Nm) and the flared fitting to 23 ft. lbs. (31 Nm).
- The new oil return tube gasket, return tub and tighten to 105 inch lbs. (12 Nm). Make sure the heat shield for the oil return line is installed properly.
- The turbocharger support bracket. Tighten the M8 fasteners to 21 ft. lbs. (28 Nm) and the M10 fasteners to 40 ft. lbs. (54 Nm).
- The turbocharger elbow support bracket
- The turbocharger to charge air cooler hose assembly
- The catalytic converter and intermediate pipe as an assembly
- The muffler ground strap
- The downstream O2S connector
- The vacuum hose
- The coolant return line using new washers. Tighten the banjo bolt to 22 ft. lbs. (30 Nm).
- The oil supply line and tighten the flared fitting to 23 ft. lbs. (31 Nm)

➡ **The lower heat shield tabs must overlap the upper heat shield to prevent fatigue and premature union failure.**

- The turbocharger lower heat shield. Tighten the fasteners to 21 ft. lbs. (28 Nm)

7. Remove the cover placed on the lower intake manifold.
- The upper intake manifold and support bracket
- The vacuum hoses to the throttle body and upper intake manifold
- The air inlet hose to the throttle body
- The IAT sensor connector
- The MAP sensor
- The TPS sensor wiring connector
- The IAC motor electrical connector
- The ignition coil capacitor
- The upstream O2S connector
- The throttle and cruise control cables to the throttle lever bracket
- The clean air hose to the turbocharger
- The air cleaner housing
- The negative battery cable

8. Fill the cooling system.
9. Chain the oil and filter.
10. Start the vehicle and check for exhaust system leaks and also check the system is not contacting any body panels. Adjust the system as necessary to avoid panel contact.

TIMING BELT FRONT COVER

REMOVAL & INSTALLATION

Upper

See Figure 165.

1. Before servicing the vehicle, refer to the Precautions Section.
2. Disconnect negative battery cable.
3. Remove upper torque strut attaching bolts and set strut aside. Refer to Engine Torque Struts.
4. Turbocharger equipped vehicles, discharge and evacuate the A/C system. Refer to the Heating & Air Conditioning.
5. Disconnect air conditioning lines at junction block near upper timing belt cover.
6. Remove upper timing belt cover fasteners and remove cover.

To install:

7. Install timing belt cover and tighten fasteners to 50 inch lbs. (6 Nm).
8. Install upper torque strut.
9. Turbocharger equipped vehicles:
   a. Connect air conditioning lines at junction block near upper timing belt cover.

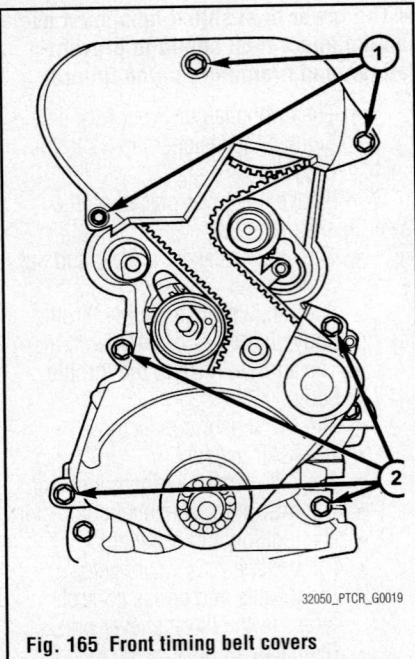

Fig. 165 Front timing belt covers

b. Recharge the A/C as outlined in the Heating & Air Conditioning Section.

10. Perform torque strut adjustment procedure.

Lower

See Figure 166.

1. Before servicing the vehicle, refer to the Precautions Section.

2. Disconnect negative battery cable.

3. Raise and safely support the vehicle. Remove right front wheel.

4. Remove the right splash shield.

5. Remove accessory drive belts.

6. Remove crankshaft damper. Refer to Crankshaft Damper.

7. Remove the lower torque strut. Refer to Engine Torque Struts.

8. Disconnect exhaust system from manifold. Refer to Catalytic Converter.

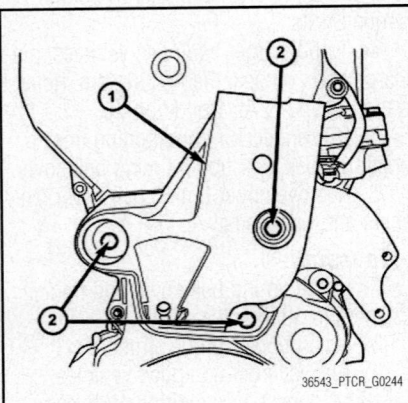

Fig. 166 Engine support bracket location

9. Disconnect A/C pressure switch at rear of compressor housing.

10. Lower vehicle and support engine with a jack.

11. Discharge A/C system and disconnect A/C lines at coupling block.

12. Remove upper torque strut.

13. Remove screw attaching ground strap to strut bracket.

14. Remove torque strut bracket from strut tower.

15. Remove upper radiator closure panel.

16. Remove power steering pump and bracket. Set pump aside. Do not disconnect lines from pump. Refer to Power Steering Pump in Steering.

17. With engine properly supported, remove right engine mount through bolt.

18. Raise engine with jack until engine support bracket bolts are accessible.

19. Remove engine support bracket.

20. Remove timing belt cover fasteners and remove cover.

To install:

21. Install lower timing belt cover and tighten fasteners to 50 inch lbs. (6 Nm).

22. Install right engine support bracket. Ensure the power steering pump is properly located in mounting location on bracket. Tighten mount bracket bolts to 45 ft. lbs. (61 Nm).

23. Lower engine into mounting position and install right engine mount through bolt. Tighten bolt to 87 ft. lbs. (118 Nm).

24. Install power steering pump and bracket.

25. Install upper radiator closure panel.

26. Install torque strut bracket to strut tower.

27. Connect ground strap to bracket.

28. Install upper torque strut.

29. Connect A/C lines and charge A/C system.

30. Raise and safely support the vehicle.

31. Connect exhaust system to manifold.

32. Connect A/C pressure switch connector.

33. Install crankshaft damper.

34. Install accessory drive belts.

35. Install lower torque strut.

36. Perform torque strut adjustment procedure.

37. Install right splash shield.

38. Install right front wheel. Tighten the wheel lug nuts to 100 ft. lbs. (136 Nm).

39. Connect the negative cable to the battery.

TIMING BELT AND SPROCKETS

REMOVAL & INSTALLATION

Timing Belt

See Figures 167 through 172.

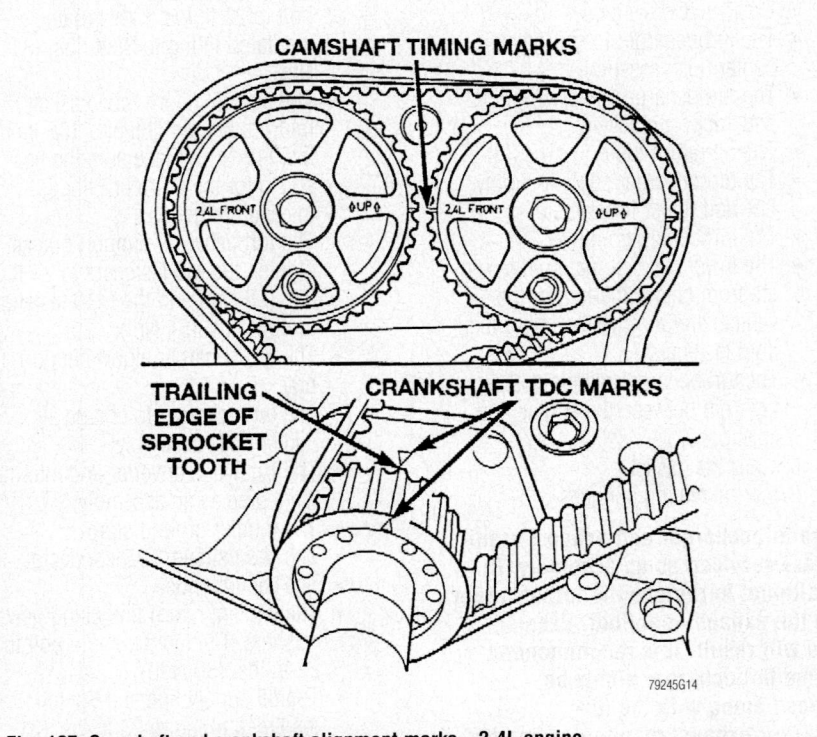

Fig. 167 Camshaft and crankshaft alignment marks—2.4L engine

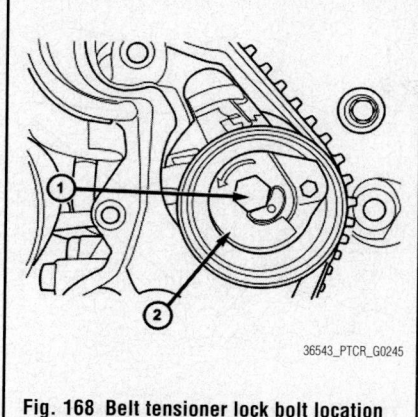

Fig. 168 Belt tensioner lock bolt location

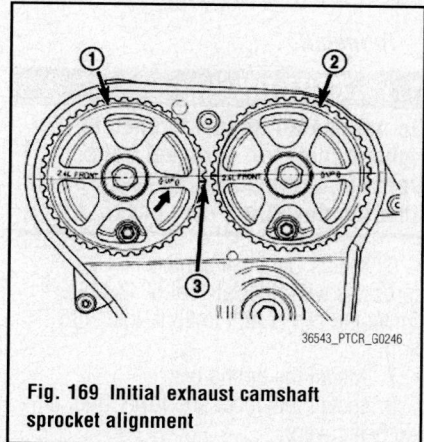

Fig. 169 Initial exhaust camshaft sprocket alignment

1. Before servicing the vehicle, refer to the Precautions Section.

2. Remove timing belt front cover. Refer to Timing Belt Front Cover.

❄❄ WARNING

When aligning crankshaft and camshaft timing marks always rotate engine from crankshaft. Camshaft should not be rotated after timing belt is removed. Damage to valve components may occur. Always align timing marks before removing timing belt.

3. Rotate the crankshaft until the Top Dead Center (TDC) mark on the oil pump housing aligns with the TDC mark on the crankshaft sprocket.

➡ **The crankshaft sprocket TDC mark (2) is located on the trailing edge of the sprocket tooth. Failure to align trailing edge of sprocket tooth to TDC mark on oil pump housing will cause the camshaft timing marks to be mis-aligned.**

4. Loosen the belt tensioner lock bolt.

5. Install a 6mm Allen wrench into the

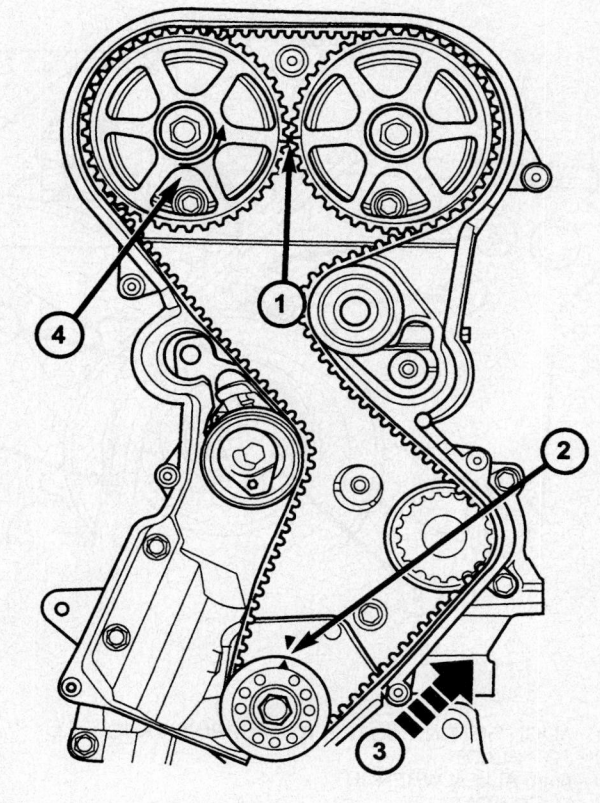

1 - CAMSHAFT TIMING MARKS 1/2 NOTCH LOCATION
2 - CRANKSHAFT AT TDC
3 - INSTALL BELT IN THIS DIRECTION
4 - ROTATE CAMSHAFT SPROCKET TO TAKE UP BELT SLACK

67189-PTCR-G12

Fig. 170 Proper timing belt routing

tensioner. Rotate the tensioner counter-clockwise while pushing on the wrench until it slides into the locking hole.

6. Remove the timing belt.

❄❄ WARNING

If timing belt was damaged due to incorrect tracking (alignment), the belt tensioner pulley and bracket must be replaced as an assembly.

To install:

7. Set the crankshaft sprocket at TDC by aligning the sprocket with the arrow on the oil pump housing.

8. Set the camshafts timing marks so that the exhaust camshaft sprocket is a ½ notch below the intake camshaft sprocket.

9. Install the timing belt by starting at the crankshaft. Go around the water pump sprocket, idler pulley, camshaft sprockets and the tensioner.

10. Move the exhaust camshaft sprocket counterclockwise to align the marks and to remove any slack.

11. Insert a 6mm Allen wrench into the tensioner opening on the top plate of the tensioner pulley.

12. Rotate the top plate counterclockwise. The pulley will move against the belt and the tensioner setting notch will start to move clockwise. Continue to move the top plate counterclockwise until the setting notch is aligned with the spring tang.

13. Using the Allen wrench, to prevent the top plate from moving, tighten the tensioner lock bolt to 220 inch lbs. (25 Nm). Make sure the setting notch and spring tang are still aligned after the lock nut is tighten (if not repeat the procedure).

14. Remove the wrench from the belt tensioner.

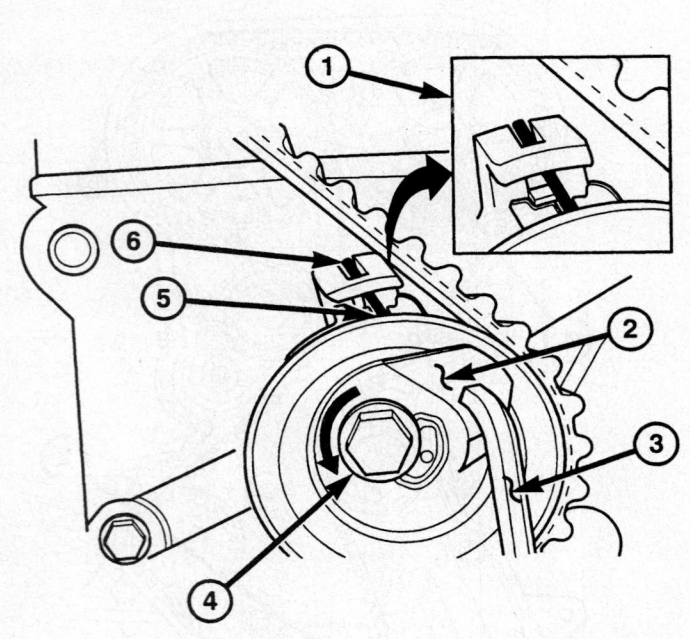

1 - ALIGN SETTING NOTCH WITH SPRING TANG
2 - TOP PLATE
3 - 6mm ALLEN WRENCH
4 - LOCK BOLT
5 - SETTING NOTCH
6 - SPRING TANG

67189-PTCR-G11

Fig. 171 Aligning the belt tensioner

➡When repositioning the crankshaft to the TDC position, this must be done only during the clockwise rotation movement. If the TDC is missed, rotate a further two full turns until TDC is

reached. Do not rotate the crankshaft counterclockwise as this will result in improper tensioner settings.

15. Rotate the crankshaft 2 full revolutions and verify that the TDC marks are properly aligned.

16. Check the spring tang is within the tolerance window, if not repeat the previous two steps.

17. Install timing belt front covers.

Camshaft Sprockets

See Figure 173.

1. Before servicing the vehicle, refer to the Precautions Section.

2. Remove upper and lower front timing belt covers. Refer to Timing Belt Front Cover.

3. Remove timing belt. Refer to Timing Belt.

4. Use Special Tool 6847 to hold camshaft sprockets while removing the sprocket bolt(s).

5. Remove camshaft sprocket(s).

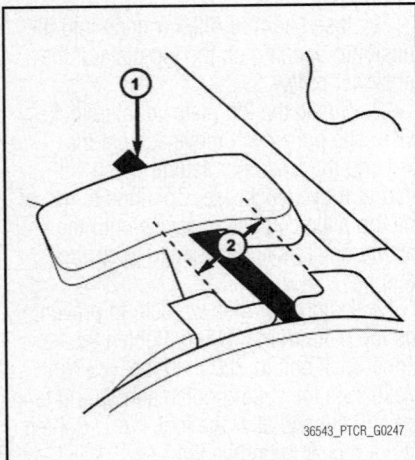

36543_PTCR_G0247

Fig. 172 Spring tang tolerance window alignment

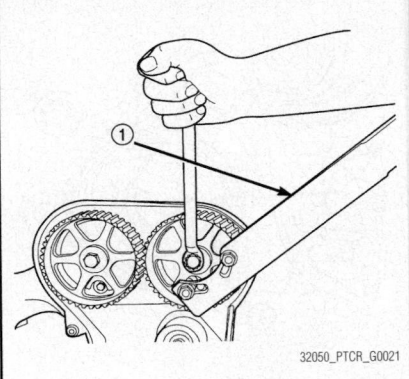

32050_PTCR_G0021

Fig. 173 Camshaft sprocket removal and installation

To install:

✳✳ CAUTION

Do not use an impact wrench to tighten camshaft sprocket bolts. Damage to the camshaft-to-sprocket locating dowel pin may occur.

6. Install camshaft sprockets. Hold sprockets with Special Tool 6847 while tightening center bolt to 85 ft. lbs. (115 Nm).

7. Install the timing belt.

8. Install the upper and lower front timing belt covers.

Crankshaft Sprocket

See Figure 174.

1. Before servicing the vehicle, refer to the Precautions Section.

2. Remove upper and lower front timing belt covers. Refer to Timing Belt Front Cover.

3. Remove the timing belt. Refer to Timing Belt.

4. Remove the crankshaft sprocket using Special Tool 6793 and insert C-4685-C2.

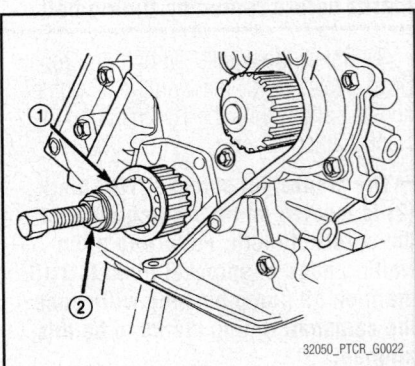

32050_PTCR_G0022

Fig. 174 Crankshaft sprockets removal and installation

To install:

✳✳ WARNING

The crankshaft sprocket is set to a predetermined depth from the factory for correct timing belt tracking. If removed, use of Special Tool 6792 is required to set the sprocket to original installation depth. An incorrectly installed sprocket will result in timing belt and engine damage.

5. Install the crankshaft sprocket using Special Tool 6792.
6. Install the timing belt.
7. Install the upper and lower front timing belt covers.

Timing Belt Tensioner

See Figures 175 and 176.

1. Remove timing belt. Refer to Timing Belt.
2. Remove timing belt idler pulley.
3. Remove camshaft sprockets. Refer to Camshaft Sprockets.
4. Remove rear timing belt cover fasteners (1,2) and remove cover from engine.
5. Remove lower bolt (1) attaching timing belt tensioner assembly to engine and remove tensioner (2) as an assembly.

To install:

6. Align timing belt tensioner assembly (2) to engine and install lower mounting bolt (1), but do not tighten. To properly align tensioner assembly to engine; temporarily install one of the engine bracket mounting bolts (M10) 5–7 turns into the tensioner assembly upper mounting location (3).
7. Torque the tensioners lower mounting bolt (1) to 45 ft. lbs. (61 Nm) and remove the upper bolt used for tensioner alignment (3).
8. Install rear timing belt cover and fasteners.
9. Install timing belt idler pulley and torque mounting bolt to 45 ft. lbs. (61 Nm).

✳✳ WARNING

Do not use an impact wrench to tighten camshaft sprocket bolts. Damage to the camshaft-to-sprocket locating dowel pin may occur.

10. Install camshaft sprockets.
11. Install timing belt.

VALVE LASH

ADJUSTMENT

The engine in this vehicle does not require periodic valve lash adjustment.

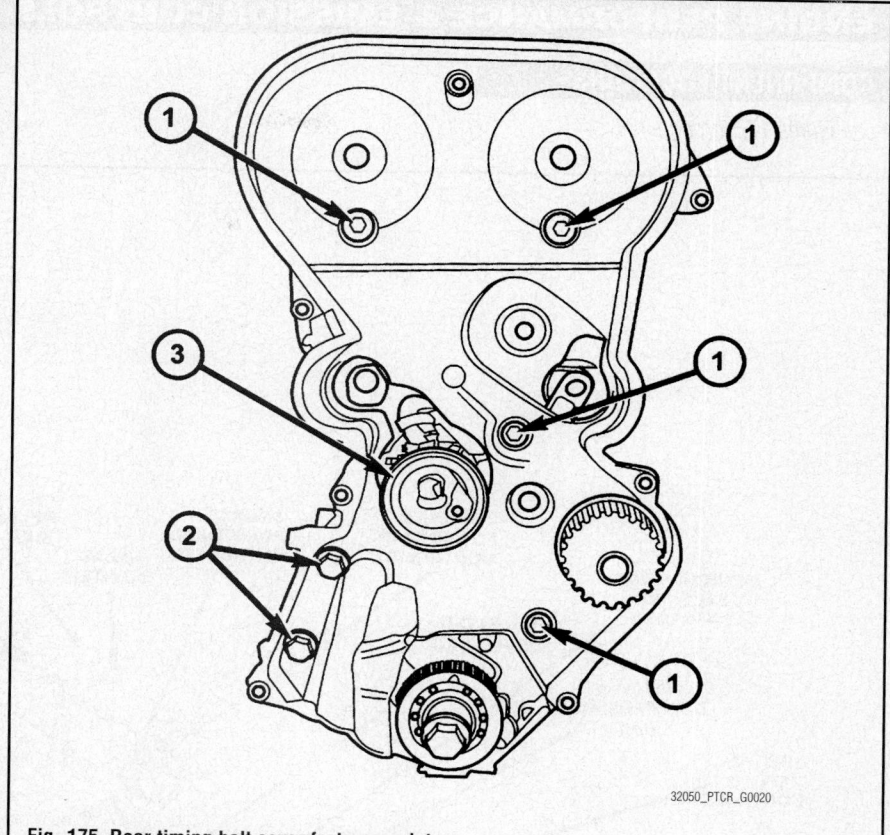

Fig. 175 Rear timing belt cover fastener points

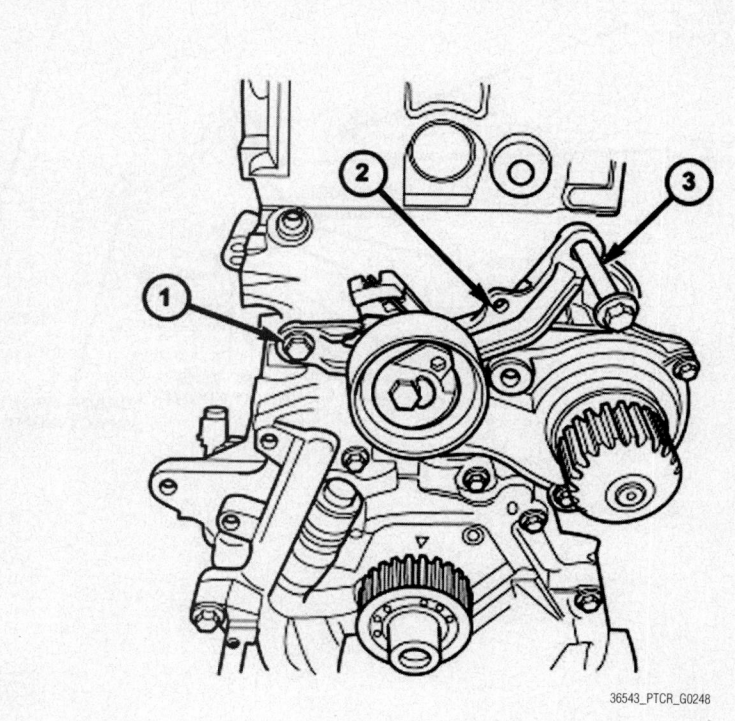

Fig. 176 Timing belt tensioner assembly

ENGINE PERFORMANCE & EMISSION CONTROLS

COMPONENT LOCATIONS

See Figures 177 through 181.

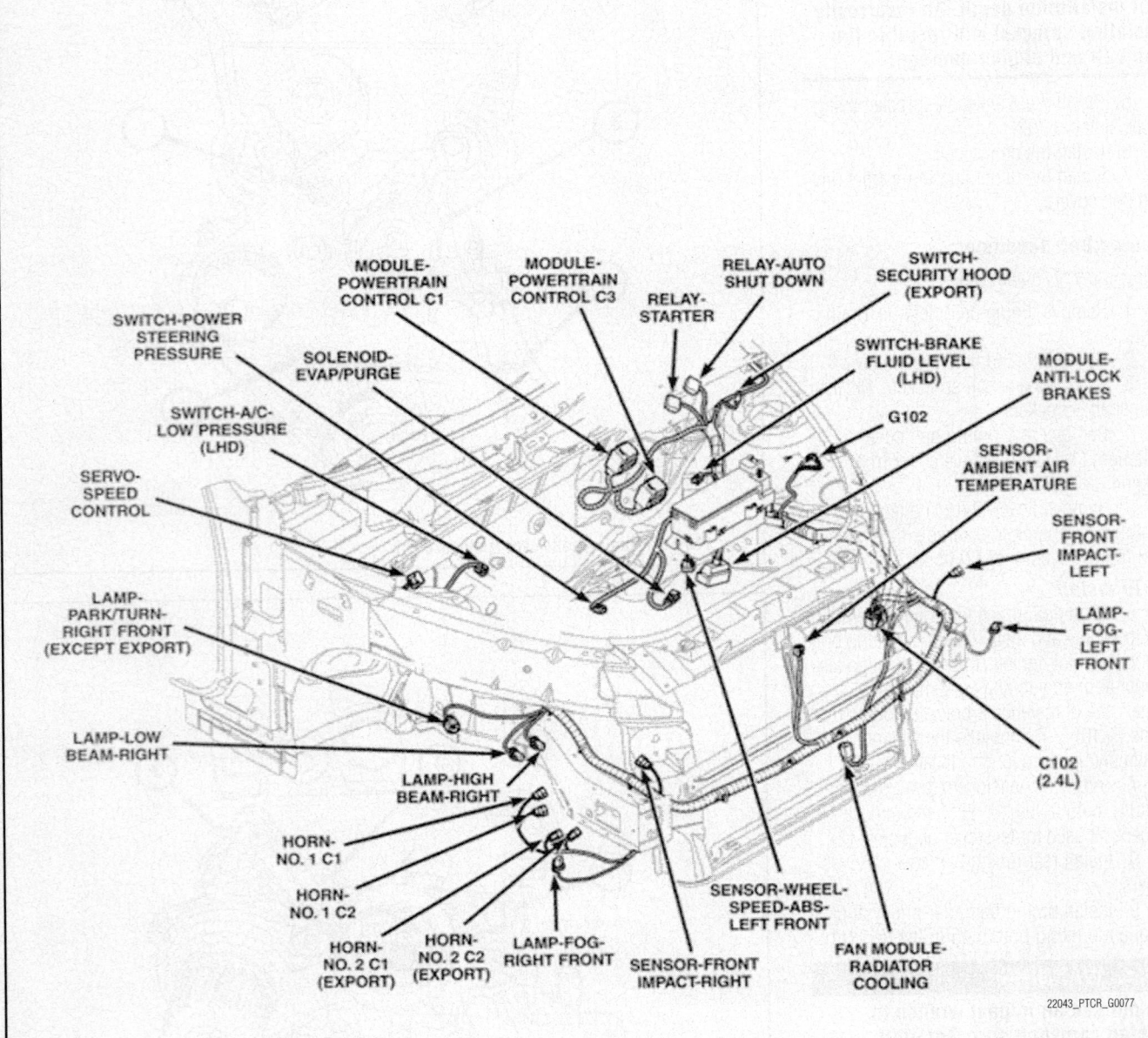

Fig. 177 Engine compartment component connections

22043_PTCR_G0077

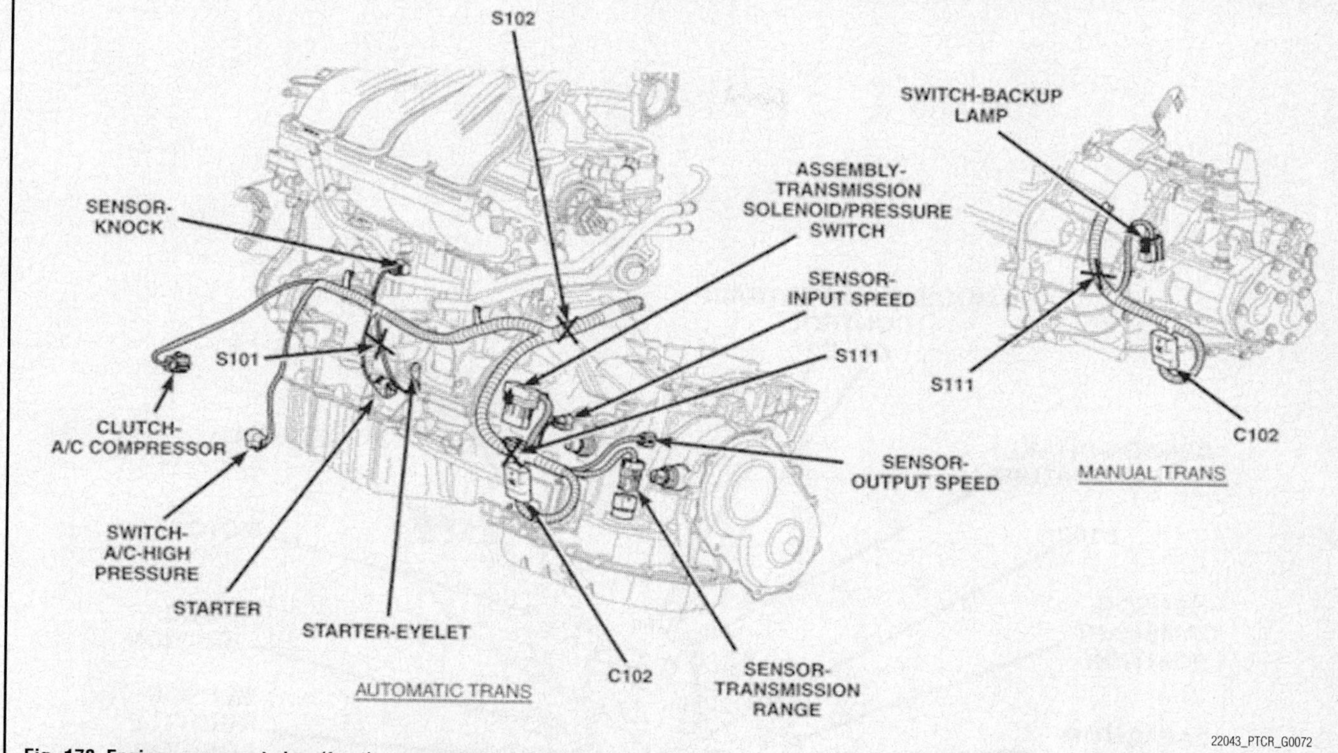

Fig. 178 Engine component view (front)—non-turbocharged models

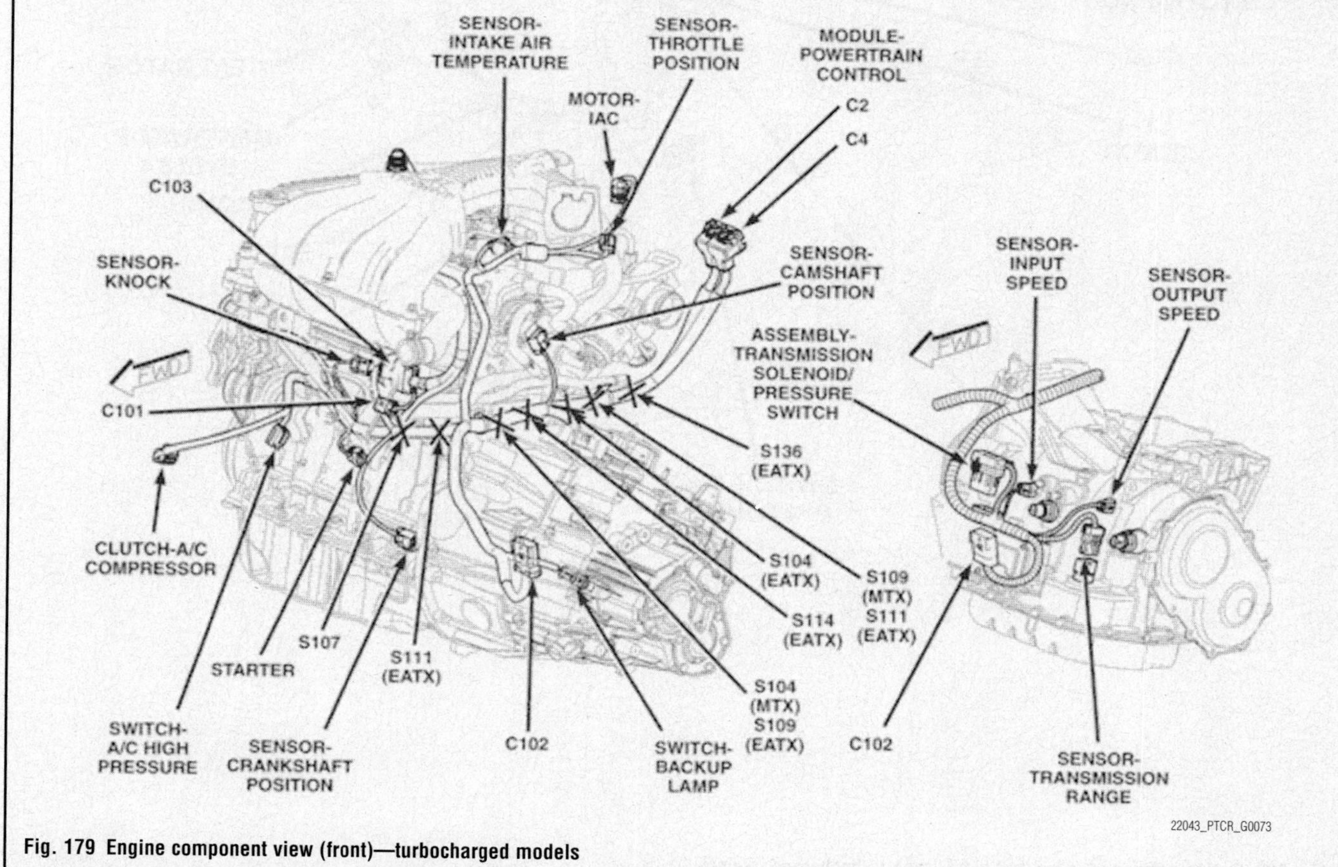

22043_PTCR_G0072

Fig. 179 Engine component view (front)—turbocharged models

22043_PTCR_G0073

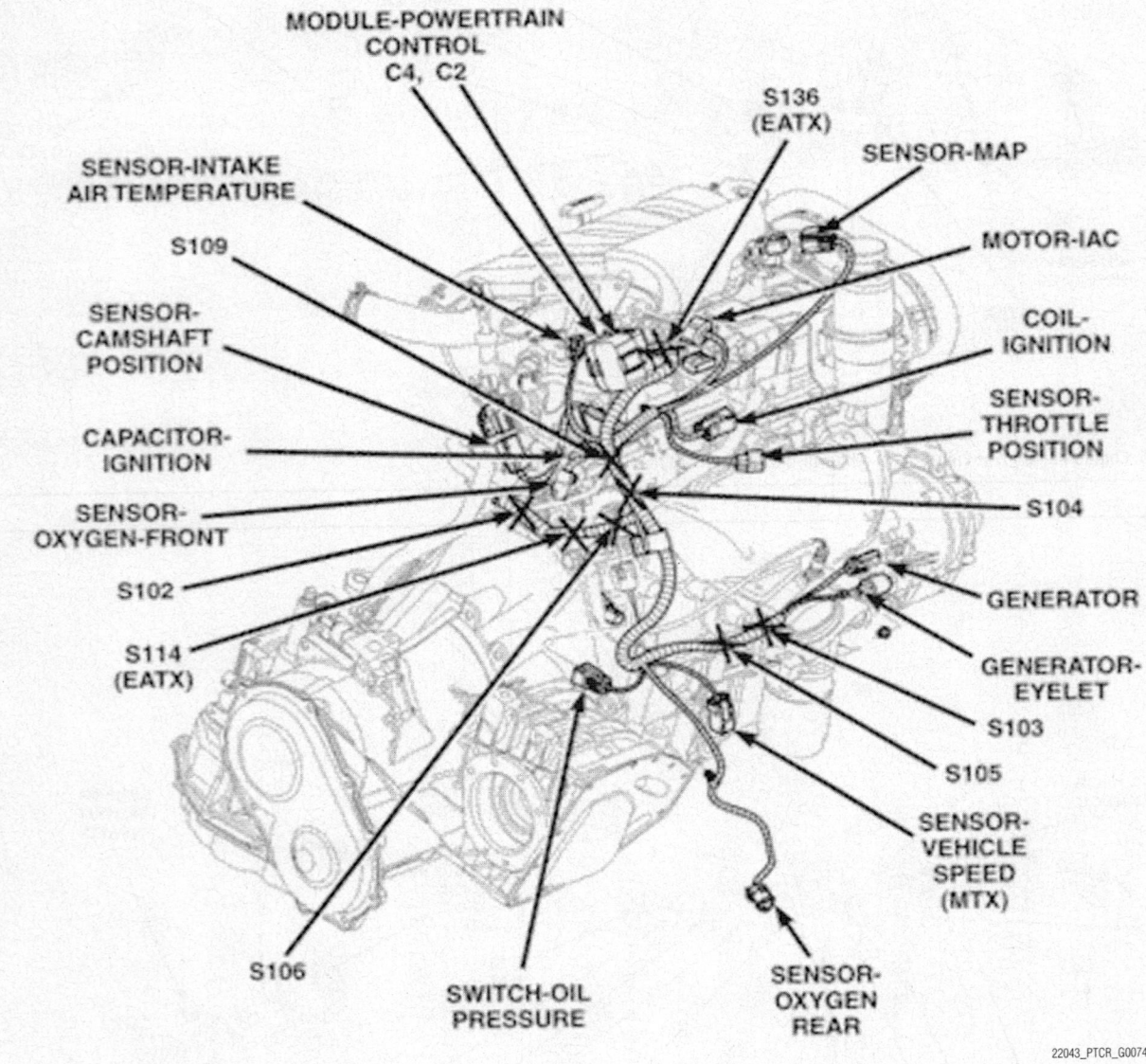

MODULE-POWERTRAIN
CONTROL
C4, C2

S136
(EATX)

SENSOR-MAP

SENSOR-INTAKE
AIR TEMPERATURE

MOTOR-IAC

S109

COIL-
IGNITION

SENSOR-
CAMSHAFT
POSITION

SENSOR-
THROTTLE
POSITION

CAPACITOR-
IGNITION

S104

SENSOR-
OXYGEN-FRONT

GENERATOR

S102

GENERATOR-
EYELET

S114
(EATX)

S103

S105

S106

SENSOR-
VEHICLE
SPEED
(MTX)

SWITCH-OIL
PRESSURE

SENSOR-
OXYGEN
REAR

22043_PTCR_G0074

Fig. 180 Engine component view (left side)—non-turbocharged models

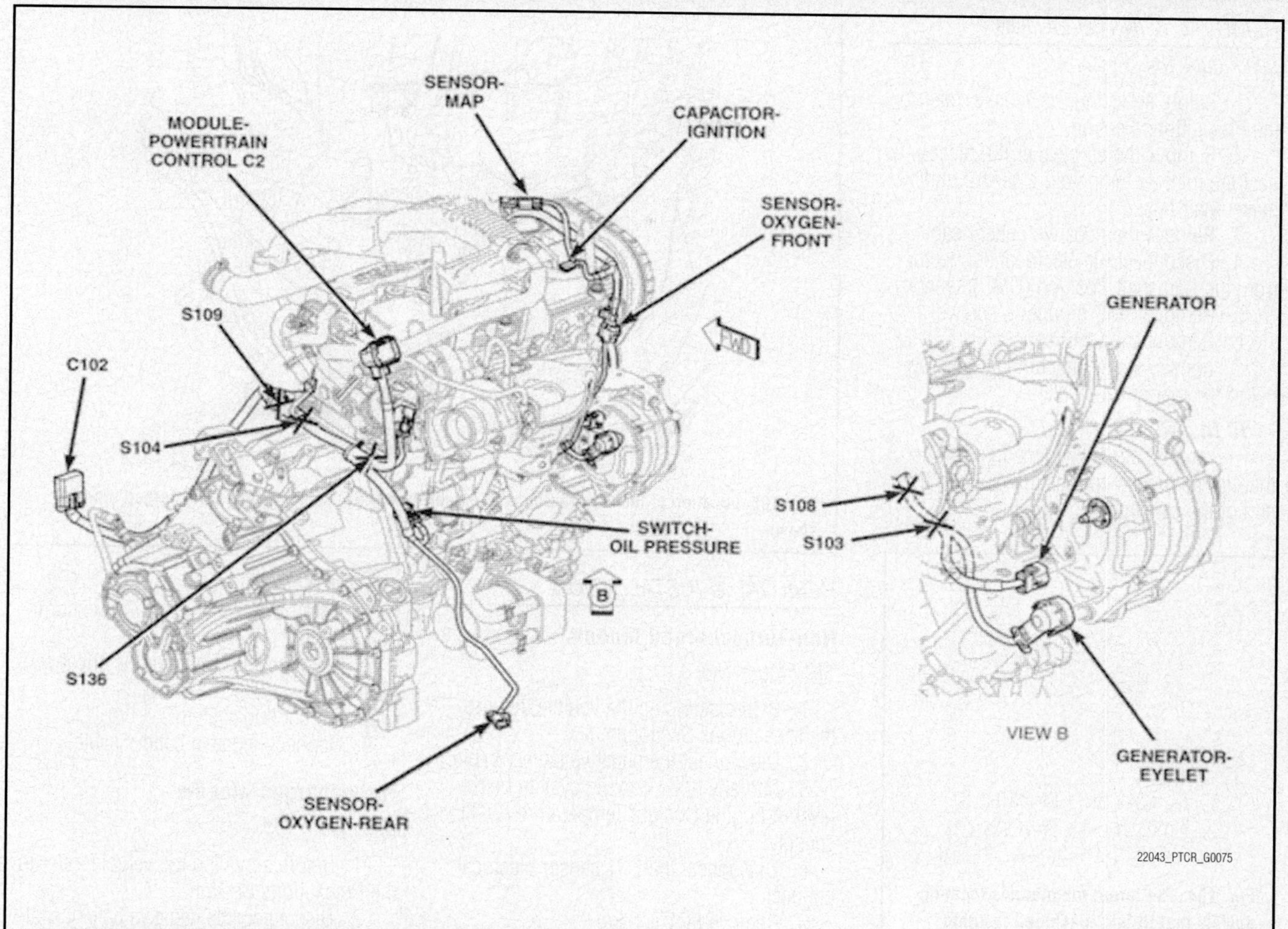

Fig. 181 Engine component view (left side)—turbocharged models

The following labels appear in Fig. 181: MODULE-POWERTRAIN CONTROL C2, SENSOR-MAP, CAPACITOR-IGNITION, SENSOR-OXYGEN-FRONT, GENERATOR, C102, S109, S104, S136, SWITCH-OIL PRESSURE, SENSOR-OXYGEN-REAR, S108, S103, VIEW B, GENERATOR-EYELET, AWD, B

22043_PTCR_G0075

ACCELERATOR PEDAL POSITION (APP) SENSOR

LOCATION

See Figure 182.

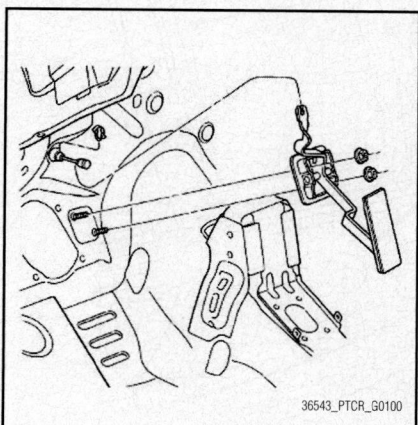

Fig. 182 Accelerator pedal position (APP) sensor location

36543_PTCR_G0100

REMOVAL & INSTALLATION

1. Remove the throttle cable from the throttle body cam.

2. Reach behind the top of the pedal shaft and push the retainer toward rear of vehicle. It may be necessary to squeeze retainer ears together on dash side of pedal shaft.

3. Lift cable up through slot in top of pedal shaft.

4. Remove nuts from accelerator pedal assembly studs. Remove assembly from vehicle.

To install:

5. Position accelerator pedal assembly on dash panel. Install retaining nuts. Tighten retaining nuts to 105 inch lbs. (12 Nm).

6. Place cable through slot in top of pedal shaft.

7. While holding pedal lever, push retainer clip forward in vehicle engaging it into the pedal lever.

8. Hold the throttle body lever in the wide open position and install the throttle cable.

CAMSHAFT POSITION (CMP) SENSOR

LOCATION

See Figure 183.

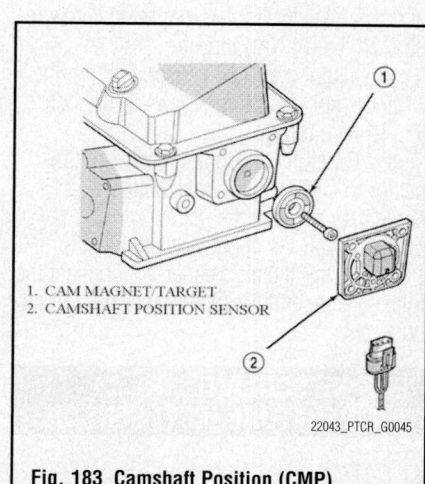

1. CAM MAGNET/TARGET
2. CAMSHAFT POSITION SENSOR

22043_PTCR_G0045

Fig. 183 Camshaft Position (CMP) sensor location

REMOVAL & INSTALLATION

See Figure 184.

1. Before servicing the vehicle, refer to the Precautions Section.
2. Remove the air cleaner lid, disconnect the inlet air temperature sensor and makeup air hose.
3. Remove the negative battery cable.
4. Disconnect the electrical connector from the Camshaft Position (CMP) sensor.
5. Remove CMP mounting screws.
6. Remove the CMP sensor.
7. Loosen screw attaching target magnet to the rear of camshaft.

To install:

The target magnet has locating dowels that fit into machined locating holes in the end of the camshaft.

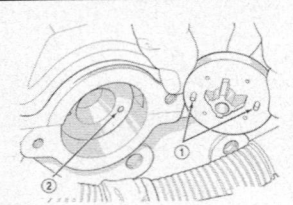

1. LOCATING DOWELS
2. LOCATING HOLES (2)

22043_PTCR_G0044

Fig. 184 The target magnet has locating dowels that fit into machined locating holes in the end of the camshaft

✳✳ WARNING

Over tightening could cause cracks in the target magnet. If the magnet cracks, replace it.

8. Install the target magnet in the end of the camshaft. Tighten mounting screw to 35 inch lbs. (4 Nm) torque.
9. Install the CMP sensor. Tighten the CMP sensor mounting screws to 80 inch lbs. (9 Nm) torque.
10. Carefully attach the electrical connector to CMP sensor. Installation at an angle may damage the sensor pins.
11. Install the negative battery cable.
12. Install the air cleaner lid, connect the inlet air temperature sensor and makeup air hose.

ENGINE COOLANT TEMPERATURE (ECT) SENSOR

LOCATION

See Figure 185 and 186.

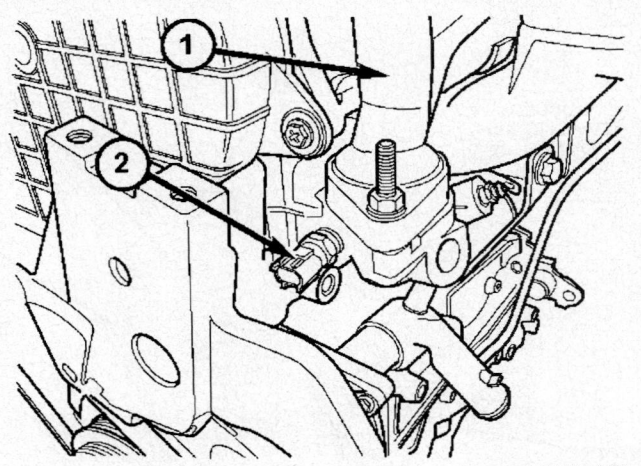

32050_PTCR_G0010

Fig. 185 Location of the Engine Coolant Temperature (ECT) sensor (2)—turbocharged models shown

REMOVAL & INSTALLATION

Non-Turbocharged Models

See Figure 186.

1. Before servicing the vehicle, refer to the Precautions Section.
2. Disconnect the negative battery cable.
3. Partially drain cooling system below level of Engine Coolant Temperature (ECT) sensor.
4. Disconnect the ECT sensor electrical connector.
5. Remove ECT sensor.

To install:

6. Install ECT sensor. Torque sensor to 168 inch lbs. (19 Nm).
7. Reconnect ECT sensor electrical connector.
8. Fill cooling system.
9. Connect negative battery cable.

Turbocharged Models

See Figure 185.

1. Before servicing the vehicle, refer to the Precautions Section.
2. Disconnect the negative battery cable.

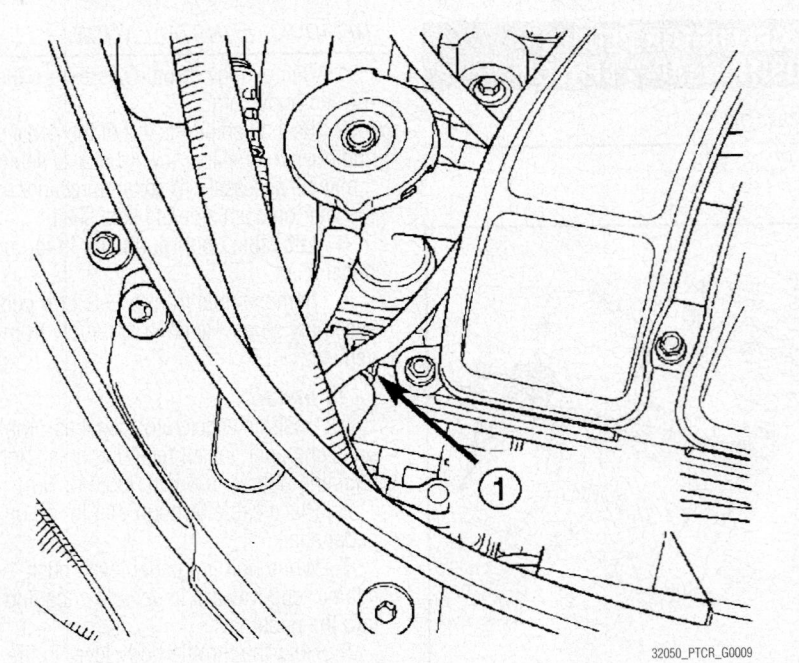

32050_PTCR_G0009

Fig. 186 Location of the Engine Coolant Temperature (ECT) sensor—non-turbocharged models

3. Partially drain cooling system below level of ECT sensor.

4. Remove upper torque strut. Refer to Engine Torque Struts in Engine Mechanical.

5. Disconnect ECT sensor electrical connector.

6. Remove ECT sensor.

To install:

7. Install ECT sensor. Torque sensor to 168 inch lbs. (19 Nm).

8. Reconnect ECT sensor electrical connector.

9. Install upper torque strut.

10. Fill cooling system.

11. Connect negative battery cable.

CRANKSHAFT POSITION (CKP) SENSOR

LOCATION

See Figure 187.

The Crankshaft Position (CKP) sensor is in the front of the engine block just under the starter motor.

REMOVAL & INSTALLATION

1. Before servicing the vehicle, refer to the Precautions Section.

2. Disconnect the negative battery cable.

3. Raise and support the vehicle.

4. Unlock and disconnect the electrical connector to the Crankshaft Position (CKP) sensor.

5. Remove the CKP sensor bolt.

6. Remove the CKP.

To install:

7. Lubricate the CKP sensor O-ring with clean engine oil.

8. Install the CKP sensor using a twisting motion. Make sure the sensor is fully seated.

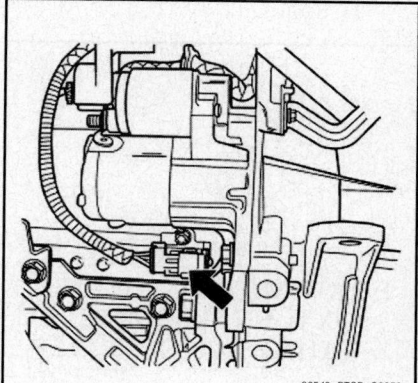

36543_PTCR_G0252

Fig. 187 Crankshaft Position (CKP) sensor location

✳ WARNING

Do not drive the senor into the bore with the mounting bolt.

9. Tighten the mounting bolt to 80 inch lbs. (9 Nm).

10. Connect the electrical connector to the CKP sensor.

11. Lower the vehicle.

12. Connect the negative battery cable.

EVAPORATIVE EMISSION (EVAP) CANISTER

LOCATION

See Figure 188.

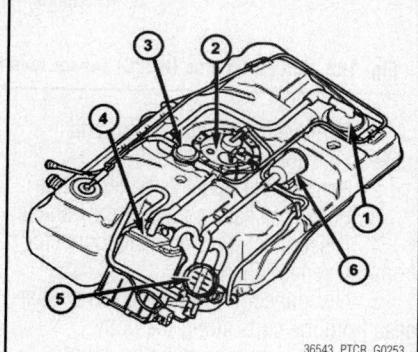

36543_PTCR_G0253

Fig. 188 Evaporative Emission (EVAP) Canister (4) location

REMOVAL & INSTALLATION

1. Remove fuel tank.

2. Remove the push pin.

3. Remove hoses from EVAP canister.

4. Spread spring clips on the side of EVAP canister and tip canister out and away from bracket tabs.

To install:

5. Install EVAP canister over bracket tabs.

6. Push canister back and into the bracket until the spring clips snap over the edge of the canister.

7. Install the push pin through the EVAP canister and the bracket and into the fuel tank.

8. Install hoses and lines.

9. Install the fuel tank and EVAP system.

EVAPORATIVE EMISSIONS (EVAP) PURGE CONTROL SOLENOID

LOCATION

See Figure 189.

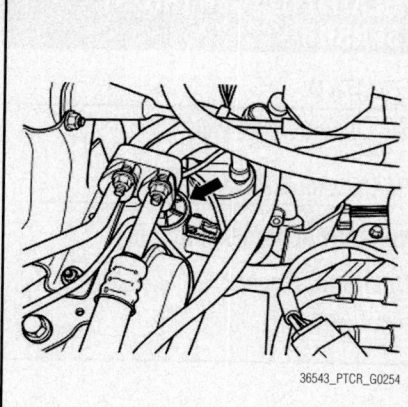

36543_PTCR_G0254

Fig. 189 Evaporative Emission (EVAP) Purge Solenoid location

REMOVAL & INSTALLATION

See Figure 190.

1. Disconnect the negative battery cable.

2. Remove solenoid from mounting bracket by pressing tab and pulling of the solenoid from bracket.

3. Unlock and disconnect the electrical connector from the purge solenoid (1).

4. Remove the 2 vacuum lines (2).

5. Remove solenoid.

To install:

6. Install the 2 vacuum lines.

7. Connect and lock the electrical connector to the purge solenoid.

8. Install solenoid to the mounting bracket.

9. Connect the negative battery cable.

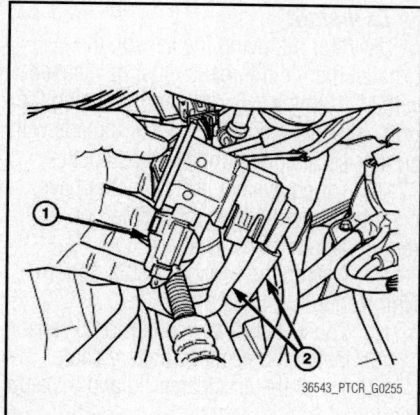

36543_PTCR_G0255

Fig. 190 Evaporative Emission (EVAP) purge solenoid removal

HEATED OXYGEN (HO2S) SENSOR

LOCATION

See Figures 191 through 193.

REMOVAL & INSTALLATION

Non-Turbocharged Models

Upstream Sensor

See Figure 191.

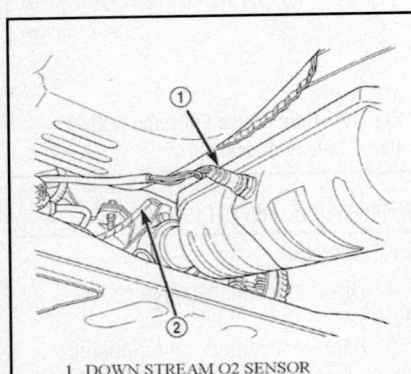

1. DOWN STREAM O2 SENSOR
2. UP STREAM O2 SENSOR

22043_PTCR_G0049

Fig. 191 Heated Oxygen (HO2S) sensor location (sensors 1 & 2)—non-turbocharged models

1. Before servicing the vehicle, refer to the Precautions Section.
2. Remove the air cleaner lid and makeup air hose.
3. Remove the negative battery cable.
4. Disconnect the electrical connector from the sensor.
5. Remove the sensor using an oxygen sensor special tool C-4907.

To install:

6. After removing the sensor, the exhaust manifold threads must be cleaned with an 18mm x 1.5 + 6E tap. If reusing the original sensor, coat the sensor threads with an anti-seize compound such as Loctite® 771-64, or equivalent. New sensors have compound on the threads and do not require an additional coating.
7. Tighten the sensor to 30 ft. lbs. (41 Nm) torque.
8. Connect electrical connector to sensor.
9. Install the negative battery cable.
10. Install the air cleaner lid and makeup air hose.

Downstream Sensor

The downstream heated oxygen sensor threads into the exhaust pipe behind the catalytic converter.

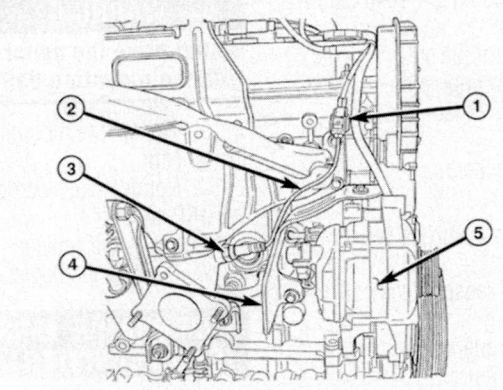

1. O2 Sensor Electrical Connector
2. Wire routing
3. O2 Sensor
4. Heat Shield
5. Alternator

22043_PTCR_G0050

Fig. 192 Heated Oxygen (HO2S) sensor location (sensor 1, up stream)—turbocharged models

1. Remove the air cleaner lid and makeup air hose.
2. Remove the negative battery cable.
3. Raise and safely support the vehicle.
4. Disconnect the electrical connector from the sensor.
5. Disconnect the sensor electrical harness from the clips along the body.
6. Remove sensor using an oxygen sensor crow foot wrench such as Snap-On® tool YA8875, or equivalent.

To install:

The downstream oxygen sensor threads into the exhaust pipe behind the catalytic converter.

7. After removing the sensor, the exhaust manifold threads must be cleaned with an 18mm x 1.5 + 6E tap. If reusing the original sensor, coat the sensor threads with an anti-seize compound such as Loctite® 771-64, or equivalent. New sensors have compound on the threads and do not require an additional coating.
8. Tighten the sensor to 30 ft. lbs. (41 Nm) torque.
9. Connect sensor electrical harness to clips along body.
10. Connect electrical connector to sensor.
11. Lower vehicle.
12. Install the negative battery cable.
13. Install the air cleaner lid and makeup air hose.

Turbocharged Models

Upstream Sensor

See Figure 192.

1. Before servicing the vehicle, refer to the Precautions Section.

2. Disconnect the negative battery cable.
3. Unlock and disconnect the electrical connector. It is on the passenger side near the EVAP purge solenoid.
4. Raise and safely support the vehicle.
5. Remove sensor using an oxygen sensor crow foot wrench such as Snap-On® tool YA8875, or equivalent.

To install:

6. Install HO2S (3) using an oxygen sensor crow foot wrench such as Snap-On® tool YA8875, or equivalent and tighten to 30 ft. lbs. (41 Nm).
7. Route HO2S sensor wire above the heat shield (4) for the alternator and away from the exhaust manifold.
8. Lower vehicle.
9. Connect and lock the HO2S connector (1). It is on the passenger side near the EVAP purge solenoid.
10. Connect the negative battery cable.

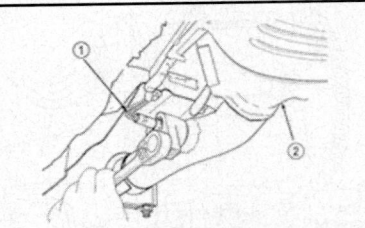

1. DOWNSTREAM HEATED OXYGEN SENSOR
2. CATALYTIC CONVERTER

22043_PTCR_G0051

Fig. 193 Heated Oxygen (HO2S) sensor location (sensor 2, downstream)—turbocharged models

Downstream Sensor

The downstream oxygen sensor threads into the exhaust pipe behind the catalytic converter.

1. Remove the air cleaner lid and makeup air hose.
2. Remove the negative battery cable.
3. Raise and safely support the vehicle.
4. Disconnect the electrical connector from the sensor.
5. Disconnect the sensor electrical harness from the clips along the body.
6. Remove sensor using an oxygen sensor crow foot wrench such as Snap-On® tool YA8875, or equivalent.

To install:

The downstream oxygen sensor threads into the exhaust pipe behind the catalytic converter.

7. After removing the sensor, the exhaust manifold threads must be cleaned with an 18mm x 1.5 + 6E tap. If reusing the original sensor, coat the sensor threads with an anti-seize compound such as Loctite® 771-64, or equivalent. New sensors have compound on the threads and do not require an additional coating.
8. Tighten the sensor to 30 ft. lbs. (41 Nm) torque.
9. Connect sensor electrical harness to clips along body.
10. Connect electrical connector to sensor.
11. Lower vehicle.
12. Install the negative battery cable.
13. Install the air cleaner lid and makeup air hose.

IDLE AIR CONTROL (IAC) VALVE

LOCATION

See Figure 194.

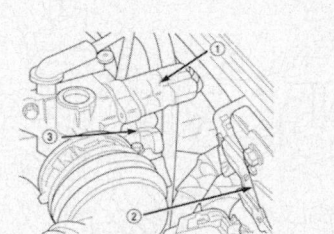

1. Idle Air Control (IAC) Valve
2. Powertrain Control Module (PCM)
3. Throttle Position Sensor (TPS)

22043_PTCR_G0057

Fig. 194 Idle Air Control (IAC) Valve location

REMOVAL & INSTALLATION

See Figure 195.

1. Before servicing the vehicle, refer to the Precautions Section.
2. Disconnect the negative cable from the battery.
3. Remove the electrical connector from the Idle Air Control (IAC) valve.
4. Remove the IAC valve mounting screws.
5. Remove the valve from the throttle body. Ensure the O-rings are removed with the valve.

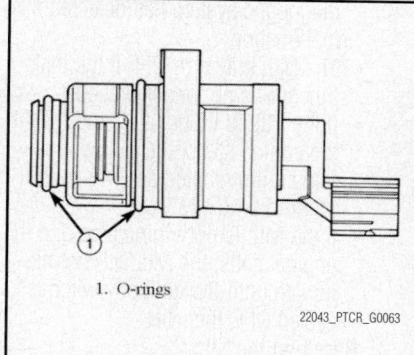

1. O-rings

22043_PTCR_G0063

Fig. 195 Ensure the O-rings are removed with the Idle Air Control (IAC) valve

To install:

When servicing throttle body components, always reassemble components with new O-rings and seals where applicable. Never use lubricants on O-rings or seals, damage may result. If assembly of component is difficult, a light coat of engine oil may be applied to the O-RINGS ONLY to aid assembly.

6. The new IAC valve has a new O-ring installed on it.
7. Carefully place the IAC valve into the throttle body.
8. Install the mounting screw. Tighten the screw to 62 inch lbs. (7 Nm).
9. Connect the electrical connector to the IAC valve.
10. Connect the negative cable to battery.

INJECTION PRESSURE REGULATOR (IPR)

LOCATION

See Figure 196.

REMOVAL & INSTALLATION

1. Remove the fuel pump module. Refer to Fuel Pump Module in Fuel Systems
2. Remove the fuel pressure regulator.

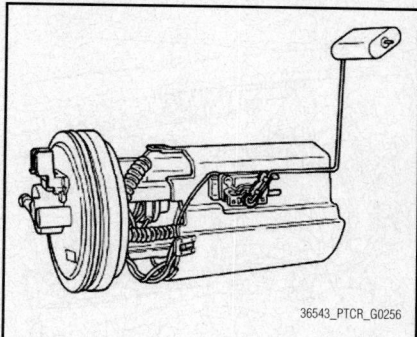

36543_PTCR_G0256

Fig. 196 Fuel pump module with fuel pressure regulator

To install:

3. Installation is reverse of removal.

INTAKE AIR TEMPERATURE (IAT) SENSOR

LOCATION

See Figures 197 and 198.

REMOVAL & INSTALLATION

➡**The sensor is located in the clean air duct.**

1. Unlatch or unbolt the air cleaner lid.
2. Lift air cleaner lid and reposition.
3. Disconnect the negative battery cable.
4. Disconnect electrical connector from the sensor.
5. Remove the sensor.

To install:

6. Install sensor.
7. Attach electrical connector to sensor.

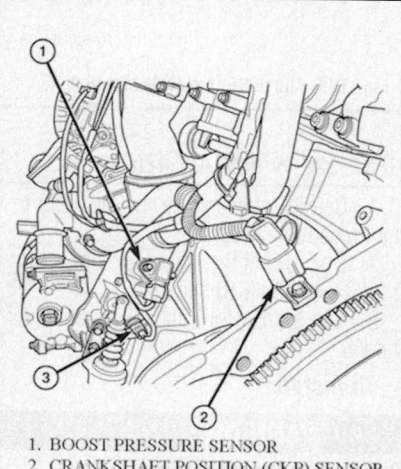

1. BOOST PRESSURE SENSOR
2. CRANKSHAFT POSITION (CKP) SENSOR
3. INTAKE AIR TEMPERATURE SENSOR

22043_PTCR_G0055

Fig. 197 Intake Air Temperature (IAT) sensor location—turbocharged models

Fig. 198 Intake Air Temperature (IAT) sensor location—non-turbocharged models

8. Connect the negative battery cable.
9. Install the air cleaner lid.

KNOCK SENSOR (KS)

LOCATION

See Figure 199.

The knock sensor threads into the side of the cylinder block in front of the starter.

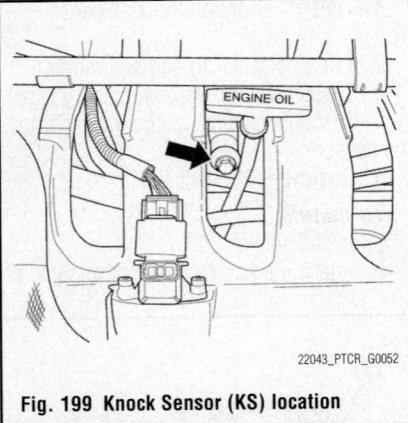

Fig. 199 Knock Sensor (KS) location

REMOVAL & INSTALLATION

1. Before servicing the vehicle, refer to the Precautions Section.
2. Disconnect the electrical connector from the Knock (KS) sensor.
3. Use a crow foot socket to remove the KS.

To install:

✳✳ WARNING

Over or under tightening the KS effects KS performance, possibly causing improper spark control.

4. Install the KS. Tighten KS to 88 inch lbs. (10 Nm) torque.

5. Attach electrical connector to knock sensor.

MALFUNCTION INDICATOR LIGHT (MIL)

RESET PROCEDURES

1. Proper operation of the Malfunction Indicator Lamp (MIL):
   - The MIL will illuminate with the ignition switch ON and the engine OFF
   - The MIL will turn OFF when the engine is started
   - The MIL will remain ON if the self-diagnostic system has detected a malfunction
   - The MIL may turn OFF if the malfunction is no longer present
   - If the MIL is illuminated and then the engine stalls, the MIL will remain illuminated as long as the ignition switch is ON
   - If the MIL is not illuminated and the engine stalls, the MIL will not illuminate until the ignition switch is cycled OFF, then ON
2. Resetting the MIL:
   - The control module turns OFF the MIL after 3 consecutive ignition cycles that the diagnostic system runs and does not fail
   - A current Diagnostic Trouble Code (DTC) clears when the diagnostic cycle runs and passes
   - There may still be a history of DTC's stored in the system. These will clear after 40 consecutive warm-up cycles, if no failures are reported by any other related diagnostic system
   - Manual resetting of the MIL and any DTC stored in the system, requires the use of an OBD2 scan tool connected to the data link connector for communication with the vehicle. Follow the instructions of the scan tool for both retrieval and resetting of DTC's.

➡**If the error symptoms causing the MIL to illuminate have been corrected, the MIL will return to normal operation.**

MANIFOLD ABSOLUTE PRESSURE (MAP) SENSOR

LOCATION

See Figure 200.

REMOVAL & INSTALLATION

1. Before servicing the vehicle, refer to the Precautions Section.

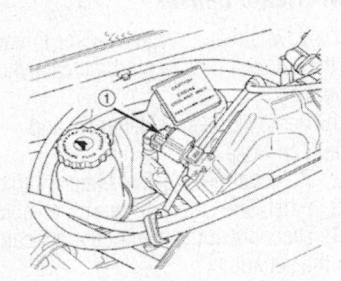

1. MAP SENSOR

Fig. 200 Manifold Absolute Pressure (MAP) sensor location

2. Disconnect the negative battery cable.
3. Disconnect the electrical connector from Manifold Absolute Pressure (MAP) sensor.
4. Remove 2 screws holding the MAP sensor to the intake manifold.

To install:

5. Install the MAP sensor. Install and tighten the 2 screws.
6. Connect the electrical connector to the MAP sensor.
7. Connect the negative battery cable.

POSITIVE CRANKCASE VENTILATION (PCV) VALVE

LOCATION

See Figure 201.

REMOVAL & INSTALLATION

1. Remove PCV hose.
2. Remove PCV valve from camshaft cover.

To install:

3. Installation is reverse of removal.

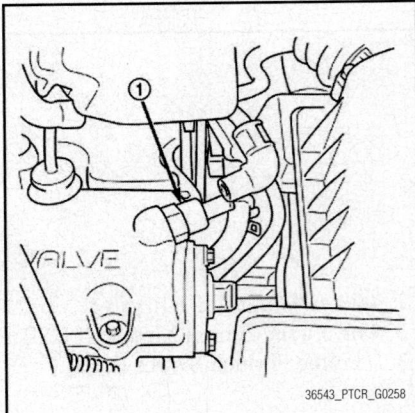

Fig. 201 Positive Crankcase Ventilation (PCV) Valve location

POWERTRAIN CONTROL MODULE (PCM)

LOCATION
See Figure 202.

The Powertrain Control Module (PCM), used in this vehicle, is located on the driver's side engine compartment and is forward of the shock suspension mounting where it is fastened to the inner fender.

REMOVAL & INSTALLATION
See Figures 202 through 205.

The Powertrain Control Module (PCM) engine control strategy prevents reduced idle speeds until after the engine operates for 200 miles (320 km). If the PCM is replaced after 200 miles (320 km) of usage, update the mileage and Vehicle Identification Number (VIN) in the new PCM. Use the scan tool to change the mileage and VIN in the PCM. If this step is not done, a Diagnostic Trouble Code (DTC) may be set and SKIM must be done or car will not start if it is a SKIM equipped car. With a SKIM car, you must do a secret key transfer also. Refer

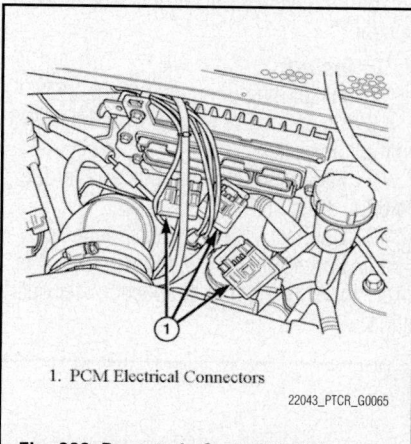

1. PCM Electrical Connectors

22043_PTCR_G0065

Fig. 202 Powertrain Control Module (PCM) location

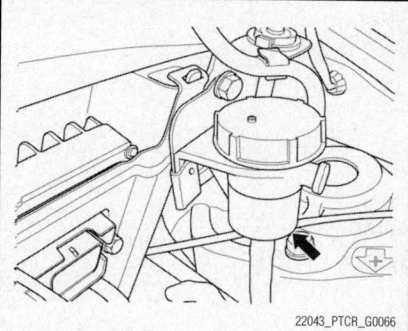

22043_PTCR_G0066

Fig. 203 Remove the clutch reservoir and relocate

to the appropriate Powertrain Diagnostic Manual and the scan tool.

❋❋ WARNING

To avoid possible voltage spike damage to the PCM, the ignition key must be off, and the negative battery cable must be disconnected before unplugging the PCM connectors.

➡ Take note of any radio presets before disconnecting the negative battery cable.

1. Before servicing the vehicle, refer to the Precautions Section.
2. Disconnect the negative battery cable and isolate the cable from making a connection unintentionally.

❋❋ WARNING

If the negative battery cable is not disconnected properly, there is the possibility of damaging the PCM by contacting the positive battery cable at the Total Integrated Power Module (TIPM).

3. Remove plastic clips that hold the wiring harness to the support bracket.
4. Unlock and disconnect the electrical connectors (1) from the Powertrain Control Module (PCM).
5. Remove the clutch reservoir and relocate.
6. Remove the 4 mounting bolts from the PCM mounting bracket.
7. Remove PCM and mounting bracket.
8. Remove the 3 mounting bolts from the PCM bracket to PCM.

To install:

9. Install the PCM bracket and the 3 mounting bolts to the PCM. Tighten the bolts to 106 inch lbs. (12 Nm).
10. Tip the PCM and bracket assembly into the bracket.
11. Locate the PCM and bracket assembly on the tab (2).

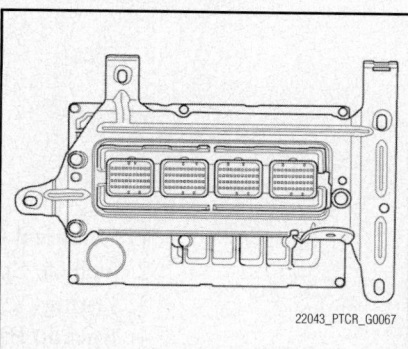

22043_PTCR_G0067

Fig. 204 Remove the PCM and PCM mounting bracket

1. Mounting Bolt
2. Bracket Tab

22043_PTCR_G0068

Fig. 205 Locate the PCM and bracket assembly on the tab

12. Install the 4 mounting bolts to the PCM mounting bracket and tighten to 97 inch lbs. (11 Nm).
13. Relocate and install the clutch reservoir.

➡ The electrical connectors for the PCM are COLOR coded.

14. Connect and lock the electrical connectors to the PCM.
15. Install the plastic clips that hold the wiring harness to the support bracket.
16. Connect the negative battery cable.
17. Use the scan tool to reprogram the new PCM with the original Vehicle Identification Number (VIN) and the vehicle's actual mileage. If this step is not done, a Diagnostic Trouble Code (DTC) may be set.

THROTTLE POSITION SENSOR (TPS)

LOCATION
See Figure 206.

REMOVAL & INSTALLATION
See Figures 206 through 208.

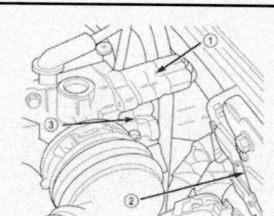

1. Idle Air Control (IAC) Valve
2. Powertrain Control Module (PCM)
3. Throttle Position Sensor (TPS)

22043_PTCR_G0056

Fig. 206 Throttle Position Sensor (TPS) location

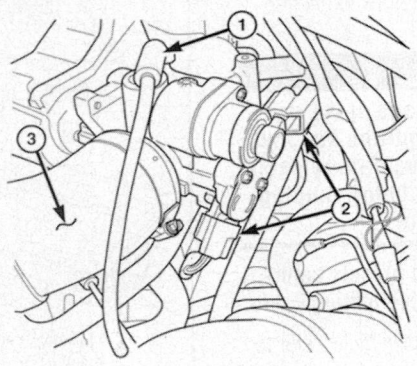

1. Purge Hose
2. Electrical Connection
3. Inlet Hose

22043_PTCR_G0058

Fig. 207 Disconnect the electrical connector from the TPS

The Throttle Position (TPS) sensor attaches to the side of the throttle body.

1. Before servicing the vehicle, refer to the Precautions Section.
2. Remove the air cleaner lid and makeup air hose. Loosen the clamp and relocate the assembly.
3. Remove the negative battery cable.
4. Disconnect the electrical connector from the TPS (2).
5. Remove the TPS mounting screws.
6. Remove the TPS.

To install:
The TPS attaches to the side of the throttle body (1).

7. The throttle shaft end of the throttle body slides into a socket in the TPS (2). Note to make sure that the rubber O-ring is in place and seated around the TPS rotor housing surface. The socket has 2 tabs inside it. The throttle shaft rests against the tabs. When indexed correctly, the TPS can rotate clockwise a few degrees to line up the mounting screw holes with the screw holes in the throttle body. The TPS has slight ten-

sion when rotated into position. If it is difficult to rotate the TPS into position, reinstall the sensor with the throttle shaft on the other side of the tabs in the socket of the TPS. Tighten the mounting screws to 53 inch lbs. (6 Nm) torque.

8. After installing the TPS, the throttle plate should be closed. If the throttle plate is open, install the sensor on the other side of the tabs in the socket.
9. Attach the electrical connectors to the TPS.
10. Install the negative battery cable.
11. Install the air cleaner lid and makeup air hose and tighten the clamp.

VEHICLE SPEED SENSOR (VSS)

LOCATION
See Figure 209.

1. Throttle Shaft
2. Tabs

22043_PTCR_G0059

Fig. 208 The TPS attaches to the side of the throttle body

The Vehicle Speed Sensor (VSS) is mounted into the transaxle assembly.

REMOVAL & INSTALLATION
1. Before servicing the vehicle, refer to the Precautions Section.
2. Raise and support the vehicle on a hoist.
3. Disconnect the Vehicle Speed (VSS) sensor connector.

✳✳ WARNING
Clean the area around the VSS before removing in order to prevent dirt from entering the transaxle during the VSS removal.

4. Remove the VSS retaining bolt.
5. Remove the VSS from transaxle.

✳✳ WARNING
Carefully remove the VSS so that the sensor drive gear does not fall into the transaxle. Should the sensor drive gear fall into the transaxle during sensor removal, the drive gear must be reattached to the sensor.

6. Remove VSS drive gear from speed sensor.

To install:
7. Install the pinion gear to the VSS.
8. Using a NEW O-ring, install the VSS to the transaxle.
9. Install the retaining bolt and torque to 62 inch lbs. (7 Nm).
10. Connect VSS electrical connector.
11. Lower the vehicle and road test it in order to verify the proper speedometer operation.

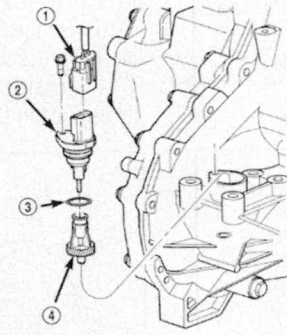

1. Electrical Connector
2. Vehicle Speed Sensor (VSS)
3. O-ring
4. Speedo Pinion

22043_PTCR_G0060

Fig. 209 Vehicle Speed (VSS) sensor location

FUEL   **GASOLINE FUEL INJECTION SYSTEM**

FUEL SYSTEM SERVICE PRECAUTIONS

Safety is the most important factor when performing not only fuel system maintenance but any type of maintenance. Failure to conduct maintenance and repairs in a safe manner may result in serious personal injury or death. Maintenance and testing of the vehicle's fuel system components can be accomplished safely and effectively by adhering to the following rules and guidelines.

• To avoid the possibility of fire and personal injury, always disconnect the negative battery cable unless the repair or test procedure requires that battery voltage be applied.

• Always relieve the fuel system pressure prior to disconnecting any fuel system component (injector, fuel rail, pressure regulator, etc.), fitting or fuel line connection. Exercise extreme caution whenever relieving fuel system pressure to avoid exposing skin, face and eyes to fuel spray. Please be advised that fuel under pressure may penetrate the skin or any part of the body that it contacts.

• Always place a shop towel or cloth around the fitting or connection prior to loosening to absorb any excess fuel due to spillage. Ensure that all fuel spillage (should it occur) is quickly removed from engine surfaces. Ensure that all fuel soaked cloths or towels are deposited into a suitable waste container.

• Always keep a dry chemical (Class B) fire extinguisher near the work area.

• Do not allow fuel spray or fuel vapors to come into contact with a spark or open flame.

• Always use a back-up wrench when loosening and tightening fuel line connection fittings. This will prevent unnecessary stress and torsion to fuel line piping.

• Always replace worn fuel fitting O-rings with new. Do not substitute fuel hose or equivalent where fuel pipe is installed.

Before servicing the vehicle, make sure to also refer to the precautions in the beginning of this section as well.

RELIEVING FUEL SYSTEM PRESSURE

1. Before servicing the vehicle, refer to the Precautions Section.

✳✳ CAUTION

Relieve the fuel system pressure before servicing any components of the fuel system. Service vehicles in well ventilated areas and avoid

ignition sources. **NEVER smoke while servicing the vehicle!**

2. Before servicing the vehicle, refer to the Precautions Section.
3. Raise and safely support the vehicle.
4. With vehicle on a hoist, disconnect the fuel pump module harness connector.
5. Lower the vehicle.
6. Start and run the engine until it stalls.
7. Attempt to restart the engine until it will no longer run.
8. Turn the ignition key to the OFF position.
9. One or more Diagnostic Trouble Codes (DTC's) may have been stored in PCM memory due to fuel pump module being removed. When the repair is complete use the scan tool to erase the DTC(s).

FUEL FILTER

REMOVAL & INSTALLATION

The fuel filter is part of the fuel pump module located in the fuel tank. It is serviced as part of the fuel pump module.

FUEL PUMP

REMOVAL & INSTALLATION
See Figure 210.

1. Before servicing the vehicle, refer to the Precautions Section.

✳✳ CAUTION

Release fuel system pressure before servicing fuel system components. Service vehicles in well ventilated areas and avoid ignition sources. Never smoke while servicing the vehicle. This may result in personal injury or death.

2. Remove fuel filler cap and relieve fuel system pressure. Refer to Relieving Fuel System Pressure, in this section.
3. Remove the air cleaner lid, disconnect the inlet air temperature sensor and makeup air hose. Refer to Air Cleaner Removal & Installation, in the Engine Mechanical section.
4. Remove the negative battery cable.
5. Raise and safely support the vehicle.
6. Remove fuel tank. Refer to Fuel Tank Removal & Installation, in this section.

✳✳ WARNING

Clean top of fuel tank around the fuel pump module to remove loose dirt

and debris. Failure to clean the fuel tank properly can cause dirt and debris in enter and the fuel system causing damage to the fuel system and/or engine components.

7. Disconnect fuel filter lines from fuel pump module.

✳✳ WARNING

Mark the position of the fuel pump module on the top of the fuel tank prior to removal. The pump has to be properly aligned in the tank for the fuel gauge to work properly.

8. Using Special Tool No. 9340, remove lock ring to release pump module.

✳✳ CAUTION

The fuel reservoir of the fuel pump module does not empty out when the tank is drained. The fuel in the reservoir may spill out when the module is removed. Use caution to avoid personal injury.

9. Remove fuel pump module and seal from tank. Discard seal.

To install:

10. Wipe seal area of tank clean. Place a new seal between the tank threads and the pump module opening.

➡**The pump has to properly located to the tank for the fuel gauge to work properly.**

11. Position fuel pump module in tank. Make sure the alignment tab line up on the fuel tank and pump module for Gas or Diesel fuel tanks.

12. While holding the pump module in position, install lock ring and use special tool No. 9340 to tighten lock ring.

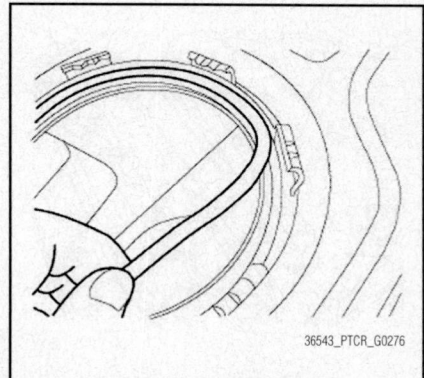

36543_PTCR_G0276

Fig. 210 Fuel pump seal positioning

13. Install fuel tank. Refer to Fuel Tank Removal & Installation, in this section.

14. Lower the vehicle.

15. Install the negative battery cable.

16. Install the air cleaner lid, connect the inlet air temperature sensor and makeup air hose. Refer to Air Cleaner Removal & Installation, in the Engine Mechanical section.

17. Fill fuel tank with clean fuel. Use the Scan Tool to pressurize the system and check for leaks.

FUEL RAIL & INJECTORS

REMOVAL & INSTALLATION

See Figures 211 through 214.

1. Before servicing the vehicle, refer to the Precautions Section.

✳✳ CAUTION

Release fuel system pressure before servicing fuel system components. Service vehicles in well ventilated areas and avoid ignition sources. Never smoke while servicing the vehicle. This may result in personal injury or death.

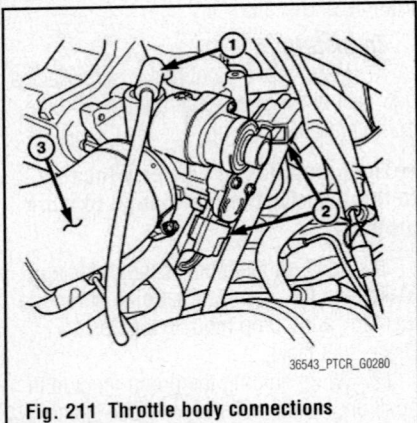

Fig. 211 Throttle body connections

Fig. 212 Intake manifold ports

2. Release fuel system pressure. Refer to Relieving Fuel System Pressure, in this section.

3. Disconnect the negative battery cable.

4. Disconnect the throttle body inlet hose (3) and remove from throttle body.

5. Disconnect the purge hose from the throttle body (1).

6. Unlock and disconnect the electrical connection at the throttle body (2).

7. Remove the throttle control shield.

8. Remove the throttle and speed control cables from the throttle body.

9. Remove the cables from the throttle body bracket.

10. Unlock and disconnect the MAP sensor electrical connector.

11. Remove the vacuum lines from the rear of the intake manifold.

12. Remove the 5 bolts from the front of the intake manifold.

13. Remove the 2 bolts from the rear of the intake manifold.

14. Remove the intake manifold. Cover the lower intake manifold openings.

15. Drain the Coolant system. Refer to Coolant Drain Procedure, in the Engine Cooling section.

16. Remove the upper radiator hose clamp.

17. Remove the 2 small hoses from the thermostat housing.

18. Remove the 2 bolts from the thermostat housing and rotate the assembly up and out of the way.

19. Rotate upper radiator hose up and out of the way.

➡**Wrap shop towels around hose to catch any gasoline spillage.**

20. Disconnect the fuel line from the fuel rail.

21. Unlock and disconnect the electrical connectors from the fuel injectors.

22. Remove the wiring harness from the fuel rail.

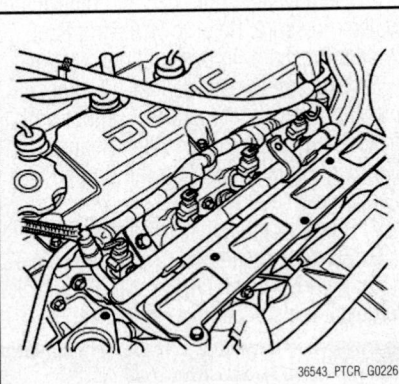

Fig. 213 Fuel injection rail location.

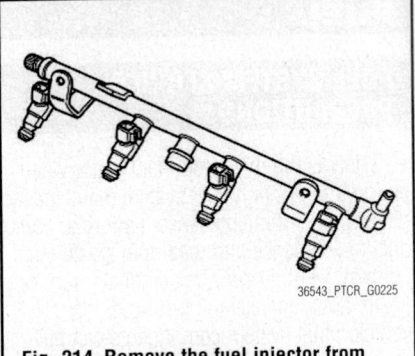

Fig. 214 Remove the fuel injector from the fuel rail

23. Remove the 2 bolts from the fuel rail.

24. Remove the fuel rail and injectors from the intake manifold.

25. To remove fuel injectors, remove the fuel injectors from the fuel rail.

To install:

26. Install the fuel injectors to the fuel rail.

27. Apply a light coating of clean engine oil to the O-ring on the nozzle end of each injector.

28. Install injector into cup of fuel rail.

29. Install retaining clip and check to ensure injector is properly captured.

30. Insert fuel injector nozzles into openings in intake manifold. Seat the injectors in place.

31. Install the 2 bolts to the fuel rail. Tighten fuel rail bolts to 16.5 ft. lbs. (22.5 Nm).

32. Install the wiring harness to the fuel rail.

33. Connect and lock the electrical connectors to the fuel injectors.

34. Connect the fuel line to the fuel rail.

35. Rotate the assembly back into place.

36. Install the 2 bolts to the thermostat housing, and tighten to 110 inch lbs. (12.5 Nm).

37. Move the upper radiator house clamp back into place.

38. Install the 2 small hoses to the thermostat housing.

39. Fill the Coolant system. Refer to Coolant Fill Procedure, in the Engine Cooling section.

40. Install the intake manifold. Refer to Intake Manifold Removal & Installation, in the Engine Mechanical section.

41. Install the 2 bolts to the rear of the intake manifold tighten to 21 ft. lbs. (28 Nm).

42. Install the 5 bolts to the front of the intake manifold and tighten to 21 ft. lbs. (28 Nm).

43. Install the vacuum lines to the rear of the intake manifold.

44. Connect and lock the MAP sensor electrical connector.

45. Install the cables to the throttle body bracket.

46. Install the throttle and speed control cables to the throttle body.

47. Install the throttle control shield.

48. Connect and lock the electrical connections at the throttle body.

49. Connect the purge hose to the throttle body.

50. Connect the throttle body inlet hose to the throttle body and tighten clamps to 20–30 inch lbs. (2–4 Nm) torque.

51. Connect the negative battery cable.

52. Use the San Tool ASD Fuel System Test to pressurize the fuel system. Check for leaks.

FUEL TANK

REMOVAL & INSTALLATION

✳✳ CAUTION

Release fuel system pressure before servicing fuel system components. Service vehicles in well ventilated areas and avoid ignition sources. Never smoke while servicing the vehicle. This may result in personal injury or death.

1. Before servicing the vehicle, refer to the Precautions Section.

2. Release fuel system pressure. Refer to Relieving Fuel System Pressure, in this section.

3. Remove the air cleaner lid, disconnect the inlet air temperature sensor and makeup air hose.

4. Remove the negative battery cable.

5. Remove fuel cap slowly to release tank pressure.

6. Raise and support the vehicle.

7. With vehicle on a hoist, drain fuel from tank.

✳✳ CAUTION

There may be fuel in the fill tube. Remove hose carefully to reduce fuel splash.

8. Disconnect fuel tank from rubber fill hose.

➡Wrap shop towels around hoses to catch any gasoline spillage.

9. Remove bolts from the fuel tank straps.

10. Disconnect fuel line, in the front of the fuel tank. This is a quick connect fitting.

11. Lower fuel tank and remove the EVAP line and recirculation line.

12. Remove vacuum line from the Leak Detection Pump.

13. Unlock the electrical connector and disconnect the electrical connector.

14. Remove hoses from EVAP canister.

15. Remove fuel tank from vehicle.

To install:

16. Position fuel tank on a transmission jack.

17. Raise fuel tank into position.

18. Connect vacuum line to the Leak Detection Pump.

19. Install EVAP line and recirculation line.

20. Connect electrical connector and lock the connector.

21. Connect the fuel line.

22. Connect fuel fill tube to tank inlet. Tighten hose clamp to 38 inch lbs. (4 Nm) torque.

23. Position fuel tank straps. Tighten fuel tank strap bolts to 17 ft. lbs. (23 Nm) torque.

24. Remove transmission jack. Ensure straps are not twisted or bent.

25. Lower vehicle.

26. Fill fuel tank, install filler cap.

27. Install the negative battery cable.

28. Install the air cleaner lid, connect the inlet air temperature sensor and makeup air hose.

29. Use the scan tool ASD Fuel System Test to pressurize the fuel system. Check for leaks.

IDLE SPEED

ADJUSTMENT

The Powertrain Control Module (PCM) adjusts engine idle speed through the idle air control valve to compensate for engine load, coolant temperature, or barometric pressure changes. No adjustment is necessary or possible.

THROTTLE BODY

REMOVAL & INSTALLATION

Non-Turbocharged Models

See Figure 215.

1. Before servicing the vehicle, refer to the Precautions Section.

2. Remove the air cleaner lid, disconnect the inlet air temperature sensor and makeup air hose.

3. Remove the negative battery cable.

4. Remove the engine cover or throttle control shield if equipped.

5. Remove throttle cable from the throttle body cam.

6. Lift the retaining tabs on the cable and slide cable out of bracket.

7. If equipped with speed control, remove speed control cable from throttle

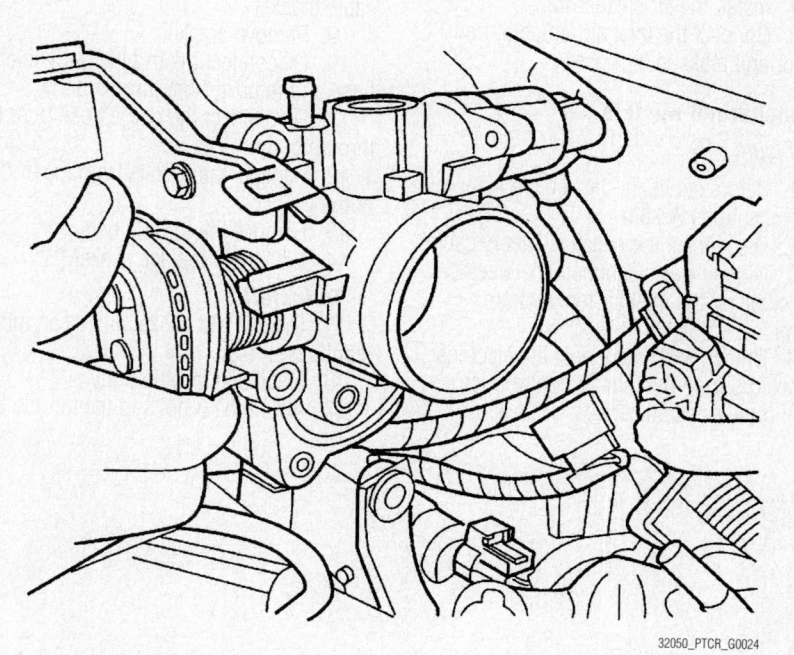

32050_PTCR_G0024

Fig. 215 Installation of the throttle body—non-turbocharged engine

lever by sliding clasp out hole used for throttle cable.

8. Remove EVAP purge hose from nipple on throttle body.

9. Remove the electrical connectors from the throttle position sensor and idle air control motor.

10. Remove 2 screws holding cable mounting bracket and support bracket.

11. Remove throttle body mounting bolts.

12. Lift throttle body straight up and away to remove the throttle body.

To install:

13. Attach electrical connectors to idle air control motor and throttle position sensor.

14. Make sure that the throttle body gasket is in place in the manifold.

15. Position throttle body on intake and install mounting bolts. Do not tighten bolts at this time.

16. Install throttle cable bracket. Do not tighten bolts at this time.

17. Tighten throttle body bolts to 85–125 inch lbs. (10–14 Nm).

18. Tighten throttle cable bracket bolts to 85–125 inch lbs. (10–14 Nm).

19. Install EVAP purge hose to throttle body nipple.

20. Install cable housing(s) retainer tabs into bracket.

21. Install throttle body cables by rotating the throttle cam forward to the wide open position.

22. Install throttle control shield.

23. Install the negative battery cable.

24. Install the air cleaner lid.

25. Connect the inlet air temperature sensor and makeup air hose.

Turbocharged Models

See Figure 216.

1. Before servicing the vehicle, refer to the Precautions Section.

2. Disconnect the negative battery cable.

3. Unlock and disconnect the electrical connector for the inlet air temperature sensor.

4. Unlock and disconnect the electrical connectors from the idle air control motor and throttle position sensor.

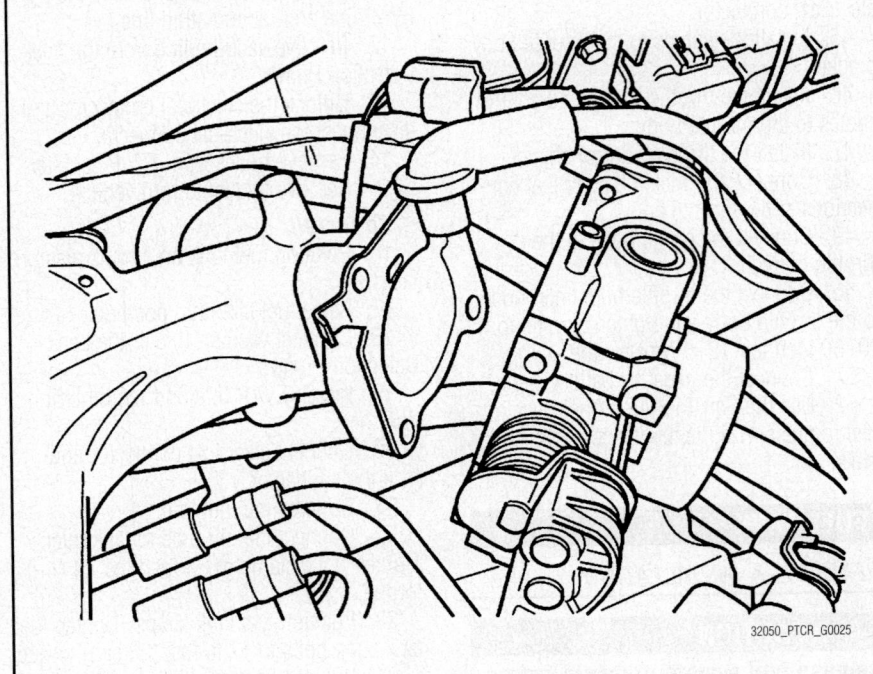

Fig. 216 Installation of the throttle body—turbocharged model

5. Remove the throttle control shield.

6. Remove the throttle cable from the throttle body cam.

7. If equipped with speed control, remove speed control cable from the throttle cam by sliding clasp out hole used for throttle cable.

8. Remove the 2 screws for the throttle cable bracket.

9. Remove bracket.

10. Disconnect the throttle body inlet hose and remove from throttle body.

11. Disconnect the purge hose from the throttle body.

12. Remove the 3 bolts from the throttle body.

13. Remove the throttle body.

14. Clean and replace gasket.

To install:

15. Discard old gasket and clean intake manifold surface.

16. Install the throttle body.

17. Install the 3 bolts to the throttle body and tighten to 85–125 inch lbs. (10–14 Nm).

18. Connect the purge hose to the throttle body.

19. Connect the throttle body inlet hose to the throttle body and tighten clamp.

20. Install bracket.

21. Install the 2 screws for the throttle cable bracket and tighten to 85–125 inch lbs. (10–14 Nm).

22. If equipped with speed control, install speed control cable to the throttle cam by sliding clasp in the hole used for throttle cable.

23. Install the throttle cable to the throttle body cam.

24. Install the throttle control shield.

25. Connect and lock the electrical connectors from the idle air control motor and throttle position sensor.

26. Connect and lock the electrical connector for the inlet air temperature sensor.

27. Connect the negative battery cable.

HEATING & AIR CONDITIONING SYSTEM

BLOWER MOTOR

REMOVAL & INSTALLATION

See Figure 217.

1. See all applicable precautions before beginning service procedures.

➡The blower motor is located on the bottom right side of the HVAC housing. The blower motor can be removed from the vehicle without having to remove the HVAC housing.

2. Disconnect and isolate the negative battery cable.
3. Remove the passenger side instrument panel silencer.
4. Remove the glove box.
5. Reach through the glove box opening and disengage the connector lock and disconnect the instrument panel wire harness connector from the connector of the blower motor wire harness (3).
6. Disengage the blower motor connector from the retainer located on the HVAC housing.
7. From underneath of the instrument panel, remove the 3 screws (2) that secure the blower motor (1) to the bottom of the HVAC housing and remove the blower motor.

To install:

8. Position the blower motor into the bottom of the HVAC housing.
9. Install the three screws that secure the blower motor to the HVAC housing. Tighten the screws to 17 inch lbs. (2 Nm).
10. Reach through the glove box opening and engage the connector for the blower motor wire harness leads to the retainer located on the HVAC housing.
11. Connect the instrument panel wire harness connector to the blower motor wire

harness connector and engage the connector lock.

12. Install the glove box.
13. Install the passenger side instrument panel silencer.
14. Reconnect the negative battery cable.

HEATER CORE

REMOVAL & INSTALLATION

See Figures 218 and 219.

1. Before servicing the vehicle, refer to the Precautions Section.

➡The HVAC housing assembly must be removed from vehicle for service of the heater core.

2. Remove the HVAC housing assembly and place it on a workbench.
3. Remove the left floor distribution duct.
4. Remove the three screws (1) that secure the heater core cover (2) to the driver side of the air distribution housing (3) and the HVAC housing (4) and remove the cover.

➡If the foam seal for the flange is deformed or damaged, it must be replaced.

5. Remove the foam seal (1) from the flange (2) located on the driver side of the HVAC housing (6).
6. Remove the two screws (4) that secure the heater core (5) to the driver side of the air distribution housing (3).
7. Carefully pull the heater core out of the driver side of the air distribution housing.
8. If required, remove the retaining clips that secure the heater core tubes to the heater core and disconnect the tubes from

the heater core and remove and discard the O-ring seals.

To install:

9. If removed, lubricate new O-rings with clean engine coolant and install them onto the heater core tubes. Connect the tubes to the heater core and install the retaining clips.
10. Carefully install the heater core into the driver side of the air distribution housing.
11. Install the two screws that secure the heater core to the air distribution housing. Tighten the screws to 17 inch lbs. (2 Nm).

➡If the foam seal for the flange is deformed or damaged, it must be replaced.

12. Install the foam seal onto the flange located on the driver side of the HVAC housing.
13. Position the heater core cover onto the driver side of the air distribution housing and HVAC housing.
14. Install the three screws that secure the heater core cover to the air distribution housing and HVAC housing. Tighten the screws to 17 inch lbs. (2 Nm).
15. Install the left floor distribution duct.

➡If the heater core is being replaced, flush the cooling system.

16. Install the HVAC housing assembly.

HVAC HOUSING

REMOVAL & INSTALLATION

See Figures 220 through 223.

1. Before servicing the vehicle, refer to the Precautions Section.

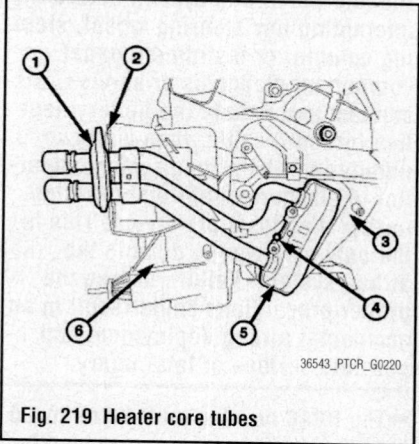

36543_PTCR_G0220

Fig. 219 Heater core tubes

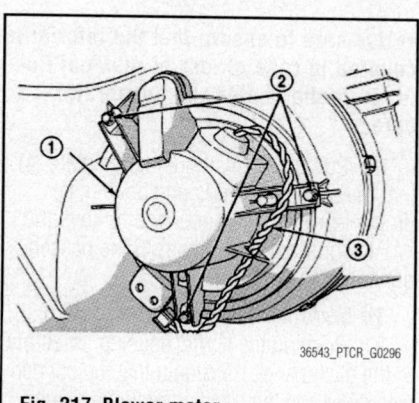

36543_PTCR_G0296

Fig. 217 Blower motor

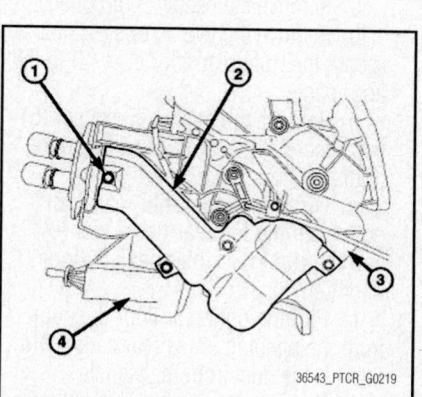

36543_PTCR_G0219

Fig. 218 Heater core cover

➡The HVAC housing must be removed from the vehicle and disassembled for service of the heater core, A/C evaporator, air intake housing and the mode-air and blend-air doors.

2. Disconnect and isolate the negative battery cable.

3. If equipped, remove the engine cover.

4. Recover the refrigerant from the refrigerant system.

5. Partially drain the engine cooling system. Refer to Coolant Drain Procedure, in the Engine Cooling section.

6. Remove the coolant recovery container.

7. Remove the air intake tube and air filter housing cover. Refer to Air Cleaner Removal & Installation, in the Engine Mechanical section.

8. Remove the two bolts that secure the accumulator tubes to the evaporator tube tapping block and disconnect the accumulator tubes from the tapping block. Refer to Accumulator in this section.

9. Disengage the accumulator mounting bracket from the rubber grommet located on the right frame and position the A/C accumulator out of the way.

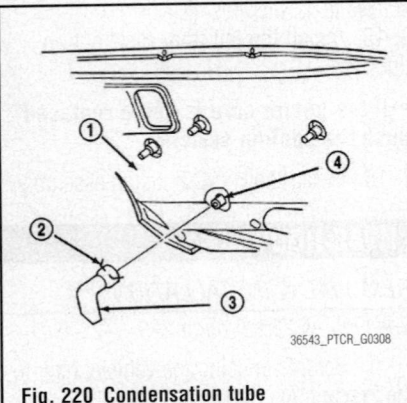

Fig. 220 Condensation tube

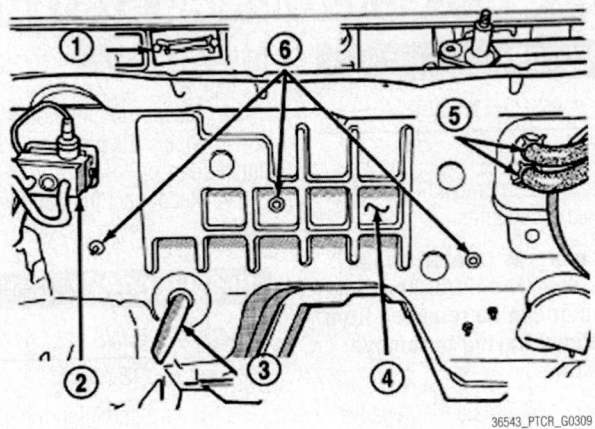

Fig. 221 Heater hoses (5), heater core tubes, and HVAC housing retaining nuts (6)

10. Remove and discard the O-ring seals and install plugs in, or tape over all of the opened refrigerant line fittings and the evaporator ports.

11. Remove the condensation drain tube (3), as follows:

   a. Raise and safely support the vehicle.

   b. Disengage the retaining clamp (2) that secures the condensate drain tube (3) to the HVAC housing drain (4) located at the passenger side of the dash panel (1) in the engine compartment.

12. Disconnect the heater hoses (5) from the heater core tubes. Install plugs in, or tape over the opened heater core tubes to prevent coolant spillage during housing removal.

13. Remove three HVAC housing retaining nuts (6) located on the engine compartment side of the dash panel (4).

14. Remove the instrument panel.

15. Remove the right rear floor duct, as follows:

➡Illustration shown with front floor carpet removed for clarity.

   a. Remove the center floor console.

   b. Remove the two screws (4) that secure the right rear floor duct (3) to the floor panel.

   c. Remove the push-pin retainer (5) that secures the rear floor carpet to the right rear floor duct.

   d. Disengage the right rear floor duct from the left rear floor duct (6) and the right rear intermediate floor duct (2).

   e. Pull the right rear floor duct out from the opening in the rear carpet and remove the duct from the vehicle.

   f. If required, disengage the right rear intermediate floor duct from the

right floor distribution duct (1) and remove the intermediate duct from the vehicle.

16. Position the dash panel insulator (1) out of the way and remove the bolt (3) that secures the HVAC housing (4) to the passenger compartment side of the dash panel (2).

17. Remove the bolt (5) that secures the HVAC housing to the floor bracket (6).

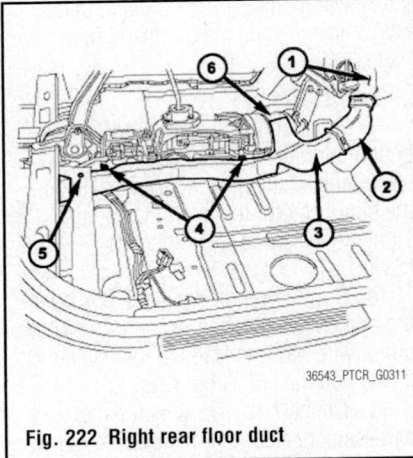

Fig. 222 Right rear floor duct

➡Use care to ensure that the interior is covered in case of loss of residual fluids from the heater and evaporator cores.

18. Pull the HVAC housing rearward so that the mounting studs and condensate drain clear the dash panel and remove the HVAC housing assembly from the passenger compartment.

To install:

19. Position the HVAC housing assembly to the dash panel. Be certain that the condensate drain and the housing mounting studs are inserted into their correct locations.

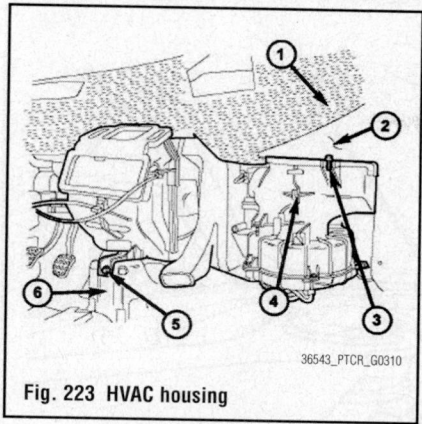

Fig. 223 HVAC housing

36543_PTCR_G0310

20. Install the bolt that secures the air inlet housing to the passenger compartment side of dash panel. Tighten the bolt to 40 inch lbs. (4.5 Nm).

21. Install the bolt that secures the HVAC housing to the floor bracket. Tighten the bolt to 40 inch lbs. (4.5 Nm).

22. Install the right rear floor duct, as follows:

   a. If removed, position the right rear intermediate floor duct into the vehicle and engage it to the right floor distribution duct.

   b. Position the right rear floor duct onto the vehicle and install the rear of the duct into the opening in the rear carpet.

   c. Engage the right rear floor duct to the right rear intermediate floor duct and to the left rear floor duct.

   d. Install the two screws that secure the right rear floor duct to the floor panel. Tighten the screws to 17 inch lbs. (2 Nm).

   e. Install the push-pin retainer that secures the rear carpet to the right rear floor duct.

   f. Install the center floor console.

23. Reposition the dash panel insulator and install the instrument panel.

24. Install the three nuts that secure the HVAC housing to the engine compartment side of the dash panel. Tighten the nuts to 40 inch lbs. (4.5 Nm).

25. Remove the previously installed plugs or caps and connect the heater hoses to the heater core tubes.

26. Install the condensation drain tube, as follows:

   a. Position the condensate drain tube onto the HVAC housing drain located on the passenger side of the dash panel in the engine compartment.

   b. Engage the retaining clamp that secures the condensate drain tube onto the HVAC housing drain.

27. Remove the tape or plugs from the opened refrigerant line fittings and the evaporator ports.

28. Lubricate new rubber O-ring seals with clean refrigerant oil and install them onto the refrigerant line and tube fittings. Use only the specified O-rings as they are made of a special material for the R-134a system. Use only refrigerant oil of the type recommended for the A/C compressor in the vehicle.

29. Engage the accumulator mounting bracket onto the rubber grommet located on the right frame rail.

30. Connect the accumulator tubes to the evaporator tube tapping block and install the two retaining bolts. Tighten the bolts to 100 inch lbs. (11 Nm). Refer to Accumulator in this section.

31. Install the air intake tube and air filter housing cover. Refer to Air Cleaner Removal & Installation, in the Engine Mechanical section.

32. Install the coolant recovery container.

33. Reconnect the negative battery cable.

34. If the heater core is being replaced, flush the cooling system.

35. Refill the engine cooling system. Refer to Coolant Fill Procedure, in the Engine Cooling section.

36. Evacuate the refrigerant system.

37. Charge the refrigerant system.

38. If equipped, install the engine cover.

STEERING

POWER RACK & PINION STEERING GEAR

REMOVAL & INSTALLATION

See Figures 224 through 227.

1. Before servicing the vehicle, refer to the Precautions Section.

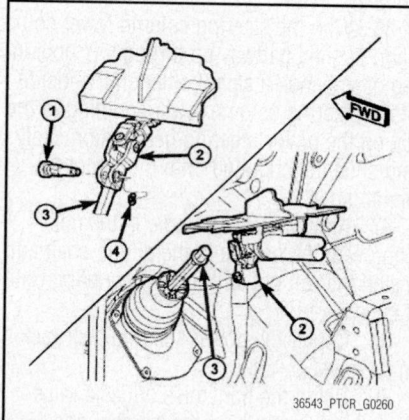

Fig. 224 Steering couplings

36543_PTCR_G0260

2. Place the steering wheel in the straight ahead position. Using a steering wheel holder, lock the steering wheel in place to keep it from rotating. This keeps the clockspring in the proper orientation.

3. Remove the silencer pad below the knee blocker panel below the steering column.

4. Fold down and remove the knee blocker.

5. Remove the steering column coupling retainer pin, back off the pinch bolt nut, and remove the steering column coupling pinch bolt (the pinch bolt nut is caged to the coupling and is not removable).

6. Separate the upper and lower steering column couplings.

7. Raise and safely support the vehicle.

8. Remove both front tire and wheel assemblies from the vehicle.

9. Remove nuts attaching both outer tie rods to the steering knuckles. Remove each nut by holding the tie rod stud stationary while loosening and removing the nut with a crowfoot wrench (or open-end wrench).

10. Remove the outer tie rods from the steering knuckles using Remover, Special Tool MB991113.

11. Remove the tie rod heat shields.

12. On vehicles equipped with a power steering fluid pressure switch, release the locking tab on the wiring harness connector for the power steering fluid pressure switch, then remove the wiring harness connector from the power steering fluid pressure switch.

13. Back out the tube nut securing the power steering fluid pressure hose to the gear.

14. Disconnect the cooler or return hose at the power steering gear outlet port fitting.

15. On turbocharged engine vehicles, back out the tube nut (3) securing the pressure hose to the gear.

16. On turbocharged engine vehicles, open the routing clip (2) and remove the pressure hose from the clip and gear.

17. On turbocharged engine vehicles, remove the return hose clamp (4), then remove the return hose at the power steering gear outlet port fitting.

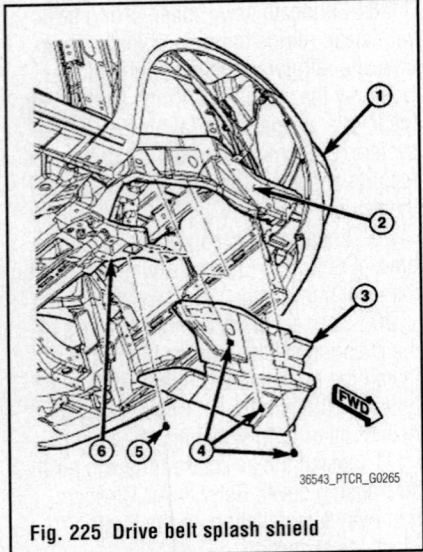

Fig. 225 Drive belt splash shield

18. On vehicles equipped with crossmember mounted power steering fluid coolers:

a. Remove the cooler tube from the right routing clip.

b. Remove the 2 screws securing the cooler to the front suspension crossmember. Allow the cooler to hang out of the way.

19. Remove the pencil strut from the right front corner of the crossmember and body of the vehicle. Refer to Engine Torque Struts in Engine Mechanical.

20. Remove the washer behind the strut from the torque strut bolt.

21. Remove the screws fastening the front fascia to the reinforcement as necessary in order to access the drive belt splash shield forward fastener screw.

22. Remove the drive belt splash shield fasteners. Remove the shield.

23. Remove the bolt mounting the engine torque strut to the right forward corner of the front suspension crossmember. Refer to Engine Torque Struts in Engine Mechanical.

➡ **Before removing the front suspension crossmember from the vehicle, the location of the crossmember must be scribed on the body of the vehicle. Do this so the crossmember can be relocated, upon reinstallation, against the body of vehicle in the same location as before removal. If the front suspension crossmember is not reinstalled in exactly the same location as before removal, the preset front wheel alignment settings (caster and camber) will be lost.**

24. Using an awl, scribe a line marking the location of where the front suspension

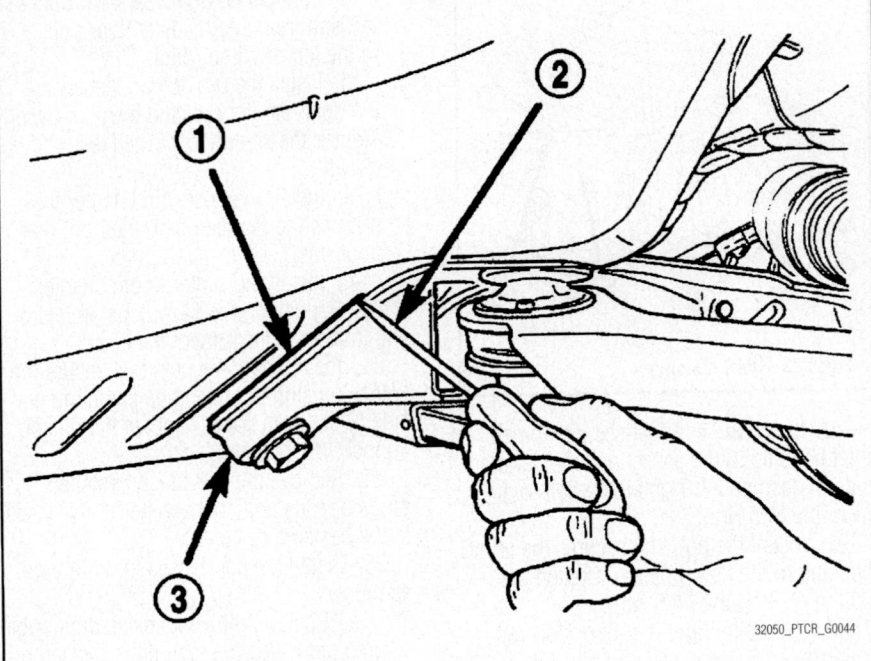

Fig. 226 Marking the location of the crossmember as it is mounted against the body of the vehicle

crossmember is mounted against the body of the vehicle.

25. Position a transmission jack under the center of the front suspension crossmember and raise it to support the bottom of the crossmember.

26. Loosen all 6 bolts attaching the front suspension crossmember to the frame rails of vehicle. Do not completely remove the 2 mounting bolts going through the lower control arm rear isolator bushings. They are designed to disengage from the body threads yet stay within the lower control arm rear isolator bushing. Back the 2 bolts out just enough to disengage the threaded tapping plates in the body of the vehicle. Completely remove the other 4 bolts.

27. Lower the front suspension crossmember using the transmission jack enough to allow the power steering gear to be removed from the rear of the crossmember. When lowering front suspension crossmember, do not let the crossmember hang from the lower control arms. The weight should be supported by the transmission jack.

28. Remove the roll pin securing the steering column lower coupling to the power steering gear pinion shaft using a roll pin punch.

29. Push the steering column lower coupling up and off of the power steering gear pinion shaft.

30. Release the pinion shaft dash cover seal from the tabs cast into the power steer-

ing gear housing and remove the seal from the power steering gear.

31. Loosen and remove the 4 bolts attaching the power steering gear to the front suspension crossmember.

32. Remove the power steering gear from the front suspension crossmember.

To install:

33. Install the steering gear on the front suspension crossmember.

34. Install the 4 power steering gear mounting bolts. Tighten the mounting bolts to a torque of 45 ft. lbs. (61 Nm).

35. Install the pinion shaft dash cover seal over the power steering pinion shaft and onto the power steering gear housing. Align the holes on each side of the seal with the tabs cast into the power steering gear housing.

36. With the steering column lower coupling pushed partway up through its hole in the dash panel, match the flat on the inside of the steering column lower coupling to the flat on the power steering gear pinion shaft and slide the coupling onto the top of the pinion shaft.

37. Align the roll pin hole in the coupling with the groove in the pinion shaft and install the roll pin through the coupling until it is centered.

38. Center the power steering gear rack in its travel.

39. Using the transmission jack, raise the front suspension crossmember and power steering gear until the crossmember

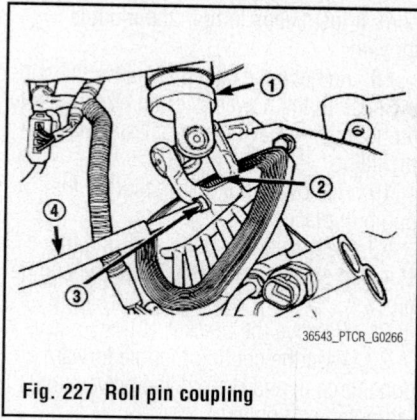

Fig. 227 Roll pin coupling

contacts its mounting spot against the body and frame rails of the vehicle. As the crossmember is raised, carefully guide the steering column lower coupling up through its hole in the dash panel.

40. Start the 2 crossmember mounting bolts through the lower control arm rear isolator bushings into the tapping plates mounted in the body.

41. Install the 2 front and the 2 rear mounting bolts attaching the front suspension crossmember to the frame rails of the vehicle. Lightly tighten all 6 mounting bolts to approximately 20 inch lbs. (2 Nm) to hold the front suspension crossmember in position at this time.

➡**When reinstalling the front suspension crossmember back in the vehicle, it is very important that the crossmember be attached to the body in exactly the same spot as when it was removed. Otherwise, the vehicle wheel alignment settings (caster and camber) will be lost.**

42. Using a soft face hammer, tap the front suspension crossmember back-and-forth or side-to-side until it is aligned with the previously scribed positioning marks on the body of the vehicle.

43. Once the front suspension crossmember is correctly positioned, tighten the 2 crossmember mounting bolts through the lower control arm rear isolator bushings to a torque of 185 ft. lbs. (250 Nm), then tighten the 4 remaining crossmember mounting bolts to a torque of 113 ft. lbs. (153 Nm).

44. Fasten the engine torque strut to the right forward corner of the front suspension crossmember using its mounting bolt.

45. Install the washer on the end of the stud extending from the torque strut bolt.

46. Install the pencil strut to the right front corner of the crossmember and body of the vehicle. Tighten the pencil strut nuts to a torque of 38 ft. lbs. (52 Nm).

47. Install the drive belt splash shield and fasteners.

48. Install the screws fastening the front fascia to the reinforcement.

49. Using a lint free towel, wipe clean the open power steering hose ends and the power steering gear ports.

50. Replace the pressure hose used O-ring with a new one. Lubricate the O-ring with power steering fluid.

51. On vehicles equipped with crossmember mounted power steering fluid coolers:

a. Place the cooler in mounting position and snap the cooler tube going to the gear into the right routing clip on the front of the gear. Close the routing clip.

b. Install the 2 screws securing the cooler to the front suspension crossmember. Tighten the screws to a torque of 90 inch lbs. (10 Nm).

52. Slide the cooler or return hose onto the steel gear outlet port fitting. Secure the clamp on the hose past the bead on the steel fitting.

➡**On vehicles equipped with crossmember mounted power steering fluid coolers, forward of the steering gear, the power steering fluid pressure hose routes between the front suspension crossmember and the driveshaft. When tightening the pressure hose tube nut to the steering gear, the pressure hose must be positioned (clocked) such that its final routing after tightened to 23 ft. lbs. (31 Nm) offers 4–10mm clearance to the front suspension crossmember (measured at the pressure hose steel-to-rubber coupling). There should be a clocking donut on the hose to preset this distance.**

53. Attach the power steering fluid pressure hose to its port on the power steering gear.

54. On turbocharged vehicles, install the routing clip up from gear outlet tube onto the fluid pressure hose tube.

55. While making sure the pressure hose is not in contact with any vehicle components, tighten the pressure hose tube nut at the gear to 23 ft. lbs. (31 Nm).

56. On vehicles equipped with a power steering fluid pressure switch, reconnect the wiring harness connector at the power steering fluid pressure switch. Be sure the locking tab on the wiring harness connector is securely latched.

57. Perform the following to each outer tie rod:

• Place the tie rod heat shield on the knuckle steering arm, aligning the hole in the shield with the hole in the knuckle and the tangs on the outside of the shield with the outside configuration of the steering arm. The shield should now be facing outboard, away from the power steering gear and tie rod

• Attach the outer tie rod end to its steering knuckle

• Start the attaching nut onto the stud of the outer tie rod

• While holding the stud of the tie rod stationary with a wrench, tighten the attaching nut

• Using a crowfoot wrench attached to a torque wrench, tighten the attaching nut to 40 ft. lbs. (54 Nm)

58. Install the tire and wheel assemblies back on vehicle. Tighten the wheel mounting nuts to 100 ft. lbs. (135 Nm).

59. Lower the vehicle to ground level.

60. Install the dash-to-lower coupling seal in place over the lower coupling plastic collar.

➡**Verify that grease is present on the lip of the dash-to-coupling seal where it contacts the coupling plastic collar.**

61. Verify the front wheels of vehicle are in the STRAIGHT-AHEAD position.

➡**Do not tighten the coupling pinch bolt anytime the vehicle is not at curb riding height. It may cause unwanted conditions within the steering column if the vehicle is suspended in any manner when the pinch bolt is tightened.**

62. Inside the passenger compartment, reconnect the steering column lower coupling to the steering column upper coupling. Install the coupling pinch bolt and tighten the pinch bolt nut to a torque of 21 ft. lbs. (28 Nm). Install the pinch bolt retainer pin.

63. Remove the steering wheel holder.

64. While looking under the instrument panel at the lower coupling, rotate the steering wheel back-and-forth to verify that the lower coupling does not squeak against the dash-to-coupling seal.

65. Install the knee blocker.

66. Install the silencer pad below the knee blocker panel below the steering column.

67. Fill and bleed the power steering system. Refer to Power Steering Bleeding Procedure.

68. Check for fluid leaks.

69. Adjust the front toe setting on the vehicle.

POWER STEERING PUMP

REMOVAL & INSTALLATION

Non-Turbocharged Models

See Figures 228 through 231.

1. Before servicing the vehicle, refer to the Precautions Section.
2. Siphon as much fluid as possible from the power steering fluid reservoir.
3. Raise and safely support the vehicle.
4. Remove the right front tire and wheel assembly.
5. Remove the screws fastening the front fascia to the reinforcement as necessary in order to access the drive belt splash shield forward fastener screw.
6. Remove the drive belt splash shield fasteners. Remove the shield.
7. Remove the accessory drive belt from the A/C compressor and power steering pump. Refer to the Accessory Drive Belt in Engine Mechanical.
8. Remove the electrical connectors from the A/C compressor.
9. Remove the 4 bolts fastening the A/C compressor to the engine, then move the compressor toward the center of the vehicle, allowing the compressor to settle in place.
10. Remove the pressure hose from the pump in the following fashion:
   a. From below, place a crowfoot wrench on a long extension onto the pressure hose tube nut at the pump.
   b. Place a shop towel between the crowfoot and the pump pulley to avoid slipping and possibly damaging the pulley.
   c. Unthread the tube nut from the pump.
11. Lower the vehicle.
12. Remove the grille from the front of the vehicle.
13. Remove the hood-opening weatherstrip from across the radiator closure panel.

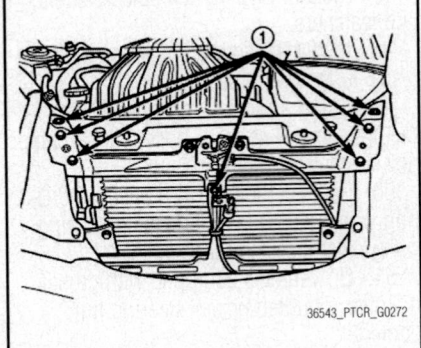

Fig. 229 Fasteners securing the upper radiator closure panel

14. Remove the ambient temperature sensor from the radiator closure panel.
15. Remove the fasteners securing the upper radiator closure panel in place, then remove the panel.
16. Lift the cooling module out of its lower mounts and carefully move it toward the left side of the vehicle. It will move only a limited amount with the hoses still connected. Do not force it.

➡ **For additional room, the right side bolts securing the lower radiator closure panel in front of the cooling module can be removed.**

17. Using a bungee cord, tie the cooling module forward. Be sure to attach the cord in a location that will not damage the vehicle. Do not over tighten the bungee

cord. It just needs to hold the module forward.

18. Remove the clamp securing the supply hose to the power steering pump supply fitting, then remove the hose from the supply fitting.
19. Remove the 3 bolts securing the pump in place.
20. Remove the 2 bolts securing the stamped steel support bracket to the engine block.
21. Remove the bracket.
22. Ease the cooling module forward, don't force it, and remove the power steering pump and pulley.

To install:

23. Using a lint free towel, wipe clean the open power steering pressure hose end and the power steering pump port. Replace any used O-rings with new. Lubricate the O-ring with clean power steering fluid.
24. Ease the cooling module forward, don't force it, and install the power steering pump and pulley into its mounting area in the same fashion it was removed.
25. Place the pump in mounting position with the stamped steel support bracket behind it. Install the 3 bolts through the bracket and pump, into the threaded engine cover. Do not tighten the bolts at this time.
26. Install the 2 bolts fastening the bracket to the engine block. Tighten the 2 bolts to a torque of 40 ft. lbs. (54 Nm).

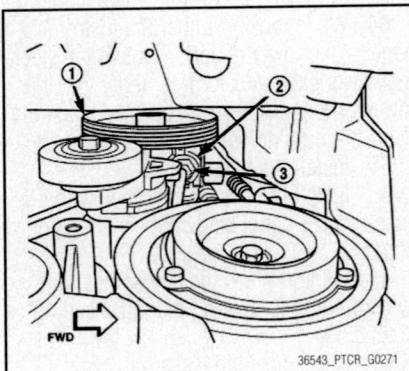

Fig. 228 Crowfoot wrench positioning

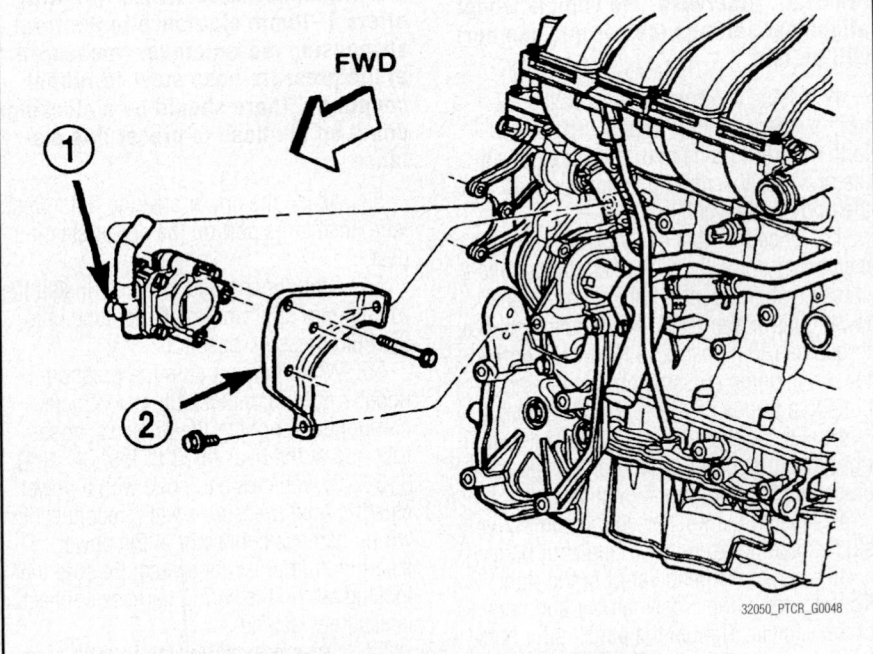

Fig. 230 Power steering pump mounting bolts—non-turbocharged models

Fig. 231 Power steering pump removal—non-turbocharged models

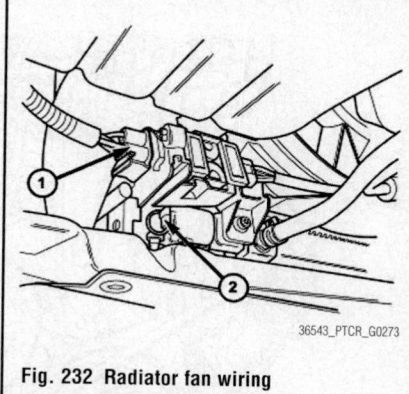

Fig. 232 Radiator fan wiring connector location

27. Tighten the 3 pump mounting bolts previously installed to a torque of 21 ft. lbs. (28 Nm).

28. Push the fluid supply hose onto the pump supply fitting. Expand the hose clamp and slide it over the hose and pump supply fitting. Secure the clamp once it is past the bead formed into the fluid reservoir fitting.

❊❊ WARNING

Make sure the supply hose is routed above the engine timing chain cover. The power steering fluid supply hose must remain clear of any unfriendly surface that can cause possible damage to it.

29. Raise and safely support the vehicle.

30. Thread the fluid pressure hose tube nut into the pump.

31. Using a crowfoot wrench on a long extension with a torque wrench, tighten the pressure hose tube nut at the power steering pump to a torque of 23 ft. lbs. (31 Nm).

32. Install the four bolts fastening the A/C compressor to the engine. Tighten the mounting bolts to a torque of 21 ft. lbs (28 Nm).

33. Install the A/C compressor electrical connectors.

34. Install the A/C drive belt. Refer to Accessory Drive Belt in Engine Mechanical.

35. Install the drive belt splash shield and fasteners.

36. Install the screws fastening the front fascia to the reinforcement.

37. Install the right front tire and wheel assembly. Install and tighten the wheel mounting nuts to a torque of 100 ft. lbs. (135 Nm).

38. Lower the vehicle.

39. Remove the bungee cord and move the cooling module back into is lower mounts.

40. If previously removed, install the right side bolts securing the lower radiator closure panel in front of the cooling module.

41. Install the radiator closure panel and fasten it in place.

42. Install the ambient temperature sensor on the radiator closure panel.

43. Install the hood-opening weather-strip across the radiator closure panel.

44. Install the grille on the front of the vehicle.

45. Fill and bleed the power steering system. Refer to Power Steering Bleeding Procedure.

46. Check for leaks.

Turbocharged Models

See Figures 229, 232 through 236.

1. Before servicing the vehicle, refer to the Precautions Section.

2. Siphon as much fluid as possible from power steering fluid reservoir.

3. Raise and safely support the vehicle.

4. Drain engine coolant.

5. Remove right front tire and wheel assembly.

6. Disconnect radiator fan wiring connector.

7. Remove two lower fan mounting screws.

8. Remove accessory drive belt splash shield.

9. Remove accessory drive belt. Refer to the Accessory Drive Belt in Engine Mechanical.

10. Carefully lower the vehicle.

11. Remove grille from front of vehicle.

12. Remove hood-opening weather-strip from across radiator closure panel.

13. Remove ambient temperature sensors from radiator closure panel.

14. Remove fasteners securing upper radiator closure panel in place, then remove the panel and lay it out of way.

15. Remove the 2 screws fastening upper radiator hose inlet neck to radiator, then separate inlet neck from radiator.

16. Carefully tip the top of the cooling module toward the front of the vehicle. DO NOT FORCE IT.

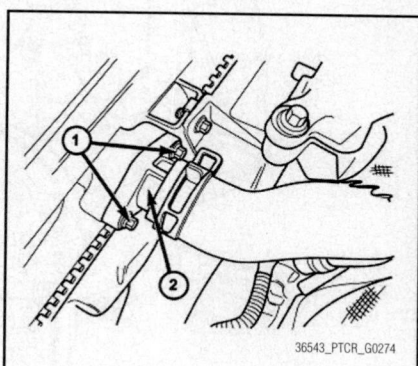

Fig. 233 Upper radiator hose inlet neck bolt location

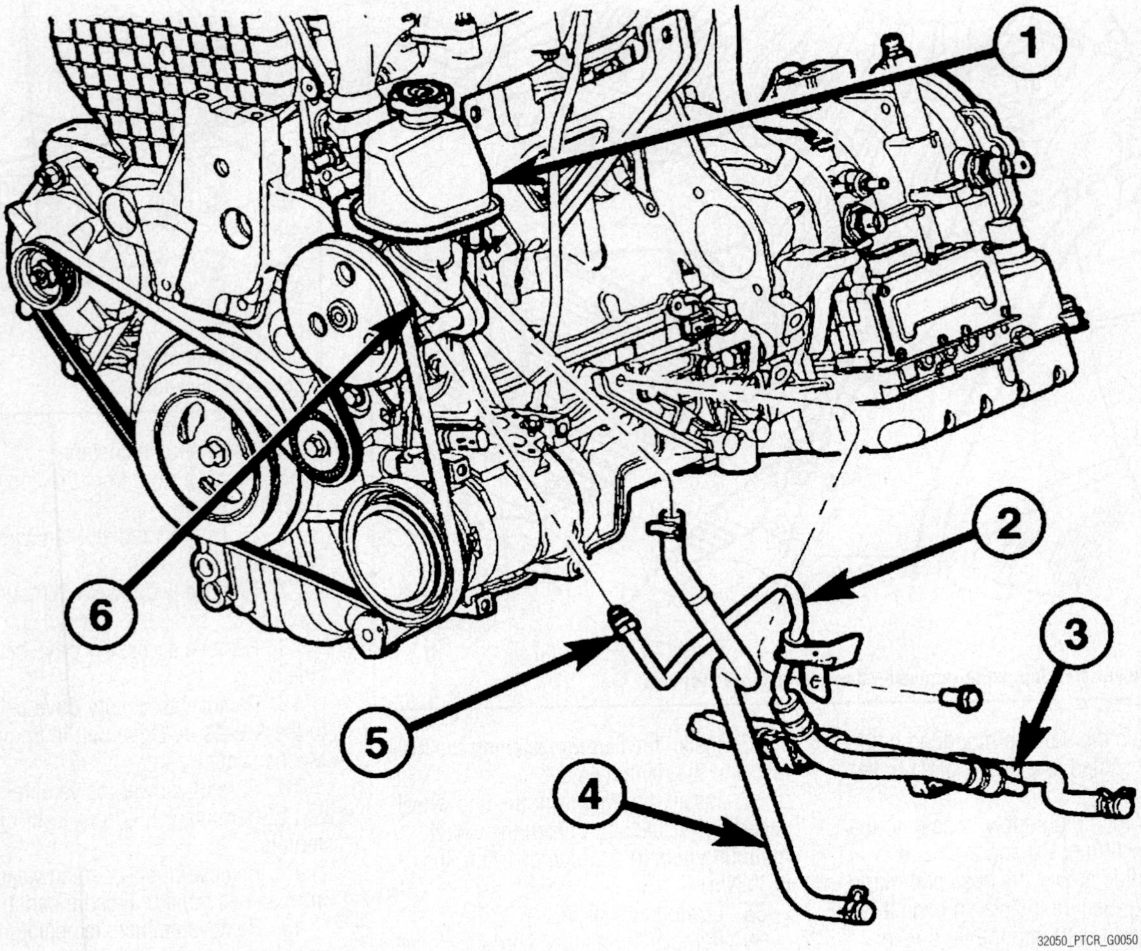

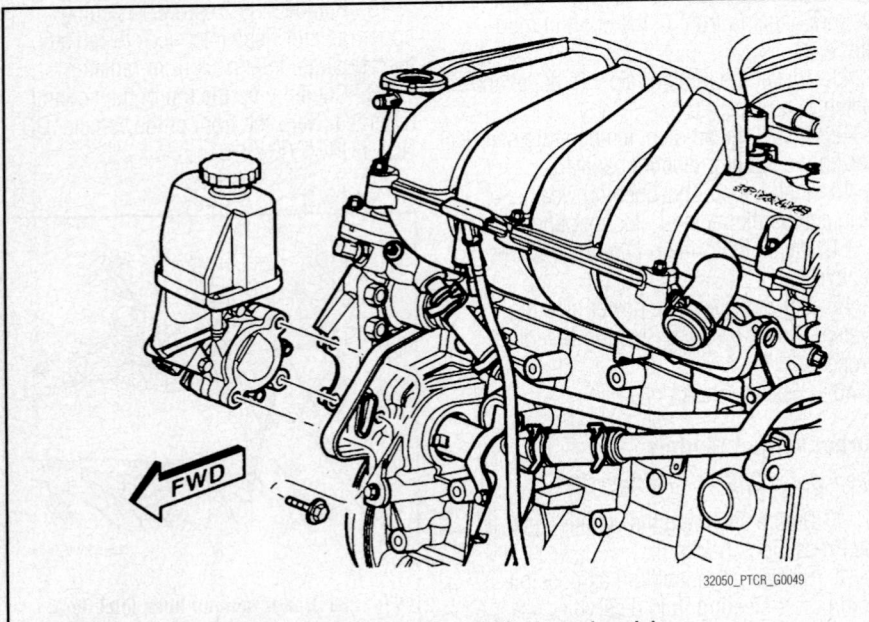

Fig. 234 Power steering pump hose connection locations—turbocharged models

32050_PTCR_G0050

Fig. 235 Power steering pump mounting location—turbocharged models

32050_PTCR_G0049

17. Using a bungee cord or equivalent, tie the module forward in this position. Be sure to attach the cord in a location that will not damage the vehicle. Do not over tighten the bungee cord. It just needs to hold the module forward.

18. Remove the remaining 4 screws fastening radiator fan to cooling module.

19. Remove the fan.

20. Remove clamp securing fluid return hose to pump reservoir, then remove hose from reservoir fitting. Cap off hose end and reservoir fitting.

21. Back out tube nut securing fluid pressure hose to power steering pump and remove hose from pump. Cap off hose end and pump pressure port.

22. Remove the 3 mounting bolts securing the power steering pump in place.

23. Remove the 2 bolts securing the stamped steel support bracket to engine block. Remove bracket.

24. Remove power steering pump with pulley and reservoir attached.

To install:

25. Using a lint free towel, wipe clean open power steering pressure hose end and power steering pump pressure port. Replace any used O-rings with new. Lubricate O-ring with clean power steering fluid.

26. Install power steering pump with pulley and reservoir into its mounting area in same fashion it was removed.

27. Place pump in mounting position with stamped steel support bracket behind it. Install three pump mounting bolts through bracket and pump, into threaded engine cover. DO NOT TIGHTEN BOLTS AT THIS TIME.

28. Install 2 bolts fastening support bracket to engine block. Tighten the 2 bolts to 40 ft. lbs. (54 Nm).

29. Tighten the 3 pump mounting bolts previously installed to 21 ft. lbs. (28 Nm).

30. Thread pressure hose tube nut into pump pressure fitting. Tighten tube nut to 23 ft. lbs. (31 Nm).

31. Install the fluid return hose onto power steering fluid reservoir return fitting. Expand hose clamp and slide it over hose and pump return fitting. Secure the clamp once it is past the bead formed into the fluid reservoir fitting.

32. Position the radiator fan and install the 2 upper and the 2 side mounting screws. DO NOT TIGHTEN SCREWS AT THIS TIME. Tighten screws to 55 inch lbs. (6 Nm).

33. Position the cooling module back into its lower mounts.

34. Clean and inspect or replace upper radiator hose inlet neck O-ring, then install inlet neck to radiator and install and tighten 2 mounting screws.

35. Install radiator closure panel and fasten it in place.

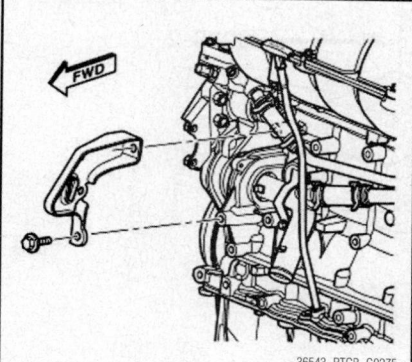

Fig. 236 Support bracket bolt locations

36. Install ambient temperature sensors on radiator closure panel.

37. Install hood-opening weather-strip across radiator closure panel.

38. Install grilld on front of vehicle.

39. Raise and safely support vehicle.

40. Install accessory drive belt. Refer to the Accessory Drive Belt in Engine Mechanical.

41. Install accessory drive belt splash shield.

42. Install the 2 remaining lower fan mounting screws. Tighten the screws to 55 inch lbs. (6 Nm).

43. Connect the radiator fan wiring connector.

44. Install the right front tire and wheel assembly. Install and tighten the wheel mounting nuts to 100 ft. lbs. (135 Nm).

45. Carefully lower the vehicle.

46. Tighten the 2 upper and the 2 side radiator fan mounting screws to 55 inch lbs. (6 Nm).

47. Fill the cooling system to the proper level.

48. Perform the Power Steering Pump Initial Operation procedure to properly fill and bleed the power steering system.

49. Check for leaks.

BLEEDING PROCEDURE

Vacuum Bleeding

✳✳ CAUTION

The fluid level should be checked with engine off to prevent injury from moving components.

✳✳ WARNING

Mopar® Power Steering Fluid+4 or Mopar® ATF+4 Automatic Transmission Fluid is to be used in the power steering system. Both fluids have the same material standard specifications (MS-9602). No other power steering or automatic transmission fluid is to be used in the system. Damage may result to the power steering pump and system if another fluid is used. Do not overfill the system.

✳✳ WARNING

If the air is not purged from the power steering system correctly, pump failure could result.

➡**Be sure the vacuum tool used in the following procedure is clean and free of any fluids.**

1. Check the fluid level. As measured on the side of the reservoir, the level should indicate between FULL and ADD (or MAX. COLD and MIN. COLD) when the fluid is at normal ambient temperature. Adjust the fluid level as necessary.

2. Tightly insert Power Steering Cap Adapter, Special Tool 9688, into the mouth of the reservoir.

✳✳ WARNING

Failure to use a vacuum pump reservoir may allow power steering fluid to be sucked into the hand vacuum pump.

3. Attach Hand Vacuum Pump, Special Tool C-4207 or equivalent, with reservoir attached, to the power steering cap adapter.

✳✳ WARNING

Do not run the vehicle while vacuum is applied to the power steering system. Damage to the power steering pump can occur.

➡**When performing the following step make sure the vacuum level is maintained during the entire time period.**

4. Using Hand Vacuum Pump, apply 68–85 kPa (20–25 in. Hg) of vacuum to the system for a minimum of three minutes.

5. Slowly release the vacuum and remove the special tools.

6. Adjust the fluid level as necessary. Refer to Step No. 1 .

7. Repeat Step No. 1 through Step No. 6 until the fluid no longer drops when vacuum is applied.

8. Start the engine and cycle the steering wheel lock-to-lock three times.

➡**Do not hold the steering wheel at the stops.**

9. Stop the engine and check for leaks at all connections.

10. Check for any signs of air in the reservoir and check the fluid level. If air is present, repeat the procedure as necessary.

Standard Bleeding

✳✳ WARNING

The fluid level should be check and adjusted with the engine off to prevent injury from moving the engine components.

✳✳ CAUTION

Use only Mopar® ATF+4 Automatic Transmission Fluid (MS-9602) in the power steering system. Do not overfill.

1. Fill the power steering fluid reservoir to the proper level, then let the fluid settle for at least 2 minutes.

2. Start the engine and let run for a few seconds, then turn the engine OFF.

3. Add fluid if necessary. Repeat the above procedure until the fluid level remains constant after running the engine.

4. Raise the front wheels off the ground.

5. Start the engine. Slowly turn the steering wheel right and left, lightly contacting the wheel stops.

6. Add power steering fluid if necessary.

7. Lower the vehicle and turn the steering wheel slowly from lock to lock.

8. Stop the engine. Check the fluid level and refill as required.

9. If the fluid is extremely foamy, allow the vehicle to stand a few minutes and repeat the above procedure.

SUSPENSION

LOWER BALL JOINT

REMOVAL & INSTALLATION

See Figures 237 through 240.

The front suspension ball joints operate with no free-play. The ball joints are replaceable ONLY as an assembly. Do not attempt any type of repair on the ball joint assembly. The ball joint is a press fit into the lower control arm with the joint stud retained in the steering knuckle by the clamp bolt. To check the ball joint, with the weight of the vehicle resting on the road wheels, grasp the grease fitting and without using any tools, attempt to move the grease fitting. If the ball joint is worn the grease fitting will move easily. If movement is noted, replacement of the ball joint is recommended.

1. Before servicing the vehicle, refer to the Precautions Section.

2. Remove the wheel.

3. Remove the stabilizer bar-to-lower control arm links.

4. Loosen, but do not remove the bolts holding the stabilizer bar retainers to the crossmember. Then, rotate the stabilizer bar and attaching links away from the lower control arms.

✳✳ WARNING

Pulling the steering knuckle outward after releasing the ball joint can separate the inner CV-joint.

5. Remove the steering knuckle-to-ball joint stud pinch bolt and nut.

6. Remove the ball joint from the steering knuckle using appropriate tool.

✳✳ WARNING

Be careful when separating the ball joint stud from the knuckle, so the seal does not become damaged.

7. If removing the right lower control arm, perform the following steps:
   a. Remove the drive belt splash shield.

b. Remove the pencil strut from the right front corner of the crossmember.

c. Remove the engine torque strut.

8. Remove the pivot bolts attaching the lower control arm to the front crossmember.

9. Remove the lower control arm.

10. Remove the ball joint using a pry tool.

11. Using a hydraulic press, press the ball joint from the lower control arm using Receiver tool 6908-2 and Adapter Tool 6804.

To install:

12. Install the ball joint into the lower control arm with the notch in the ball joint stud facing the front lower control arm bushing.

13. Using an hydraulic press, press the ball joint into the lower control arm using Receiver Tool 6758 and Adapter tool 6804.

14. Install the ball joint boot seal using a driver tool such as a large socket or suitable sized piece of pipe.

FRONT SUSPENSION

✳✳ WARNING

Do not use a shop press that was used to install the ball joint, for the press exerts too much force.

15. Install the lower control arm into the front crossmember.

16. Install the rear lower control arm-to-crossmember and frame rail bolt.

➡ **DO NOT tighten the rear bolt at this time.**

17. Install the front lower control arm-to-crossmember nut and bolt.

18. Torque the lower control arm to rear pivot bolt to 185 ft. lbs. (250 Nm) and the front pivot bolt 120 ft. lbs. (163 Nm).

19. Install the ball joint stud into the steering knuckle. Torque the steering knuckle-to-ball joint stud pinch bolt/nut to 70 ft. lbs. (95 Nm).

20. If the right side lower control arm has been service, install the following:
   a. Install the engine torque strut.

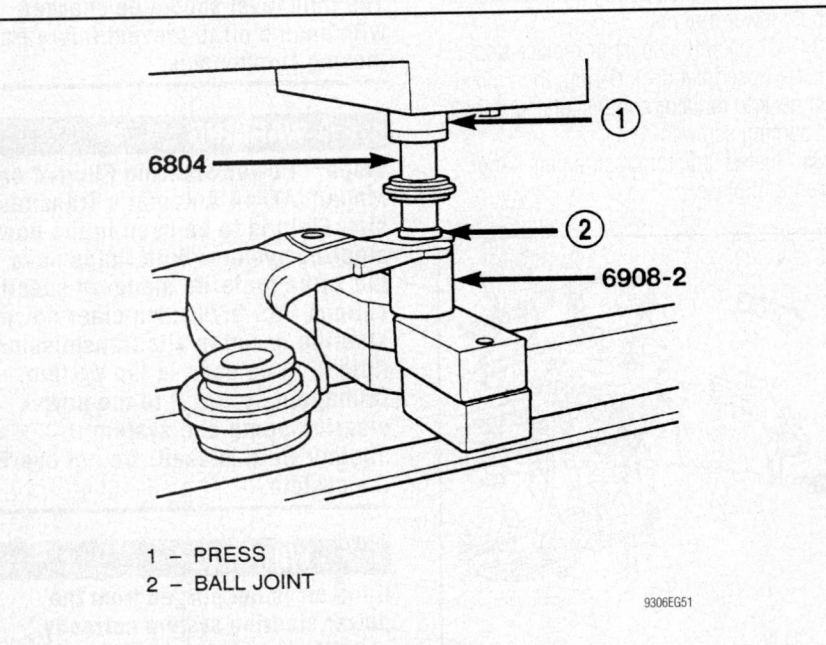

1 – PRESS
2 – BALL JOINT

9306EG51

Fig. 237 Removing the ball joint from the control arm

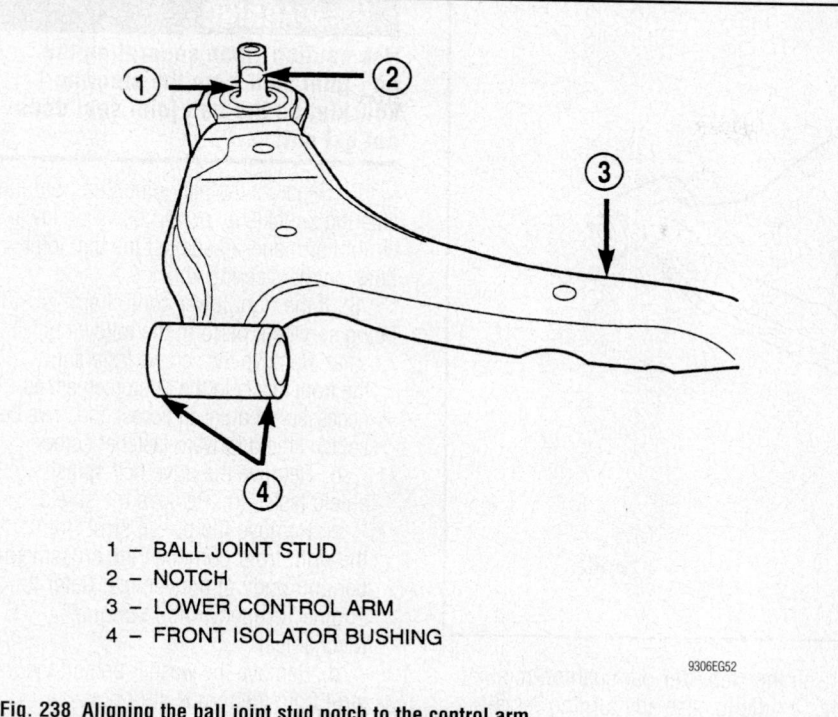

1 – BALL JOINT STUD
2 – NOTCH
3 – LOWER CONTROL ARM
4 – FRONT ISOLATOR BUSHING

9306EG52

Fig. 238 Aligning the ball joint stud notch to the control arm

b. Install the pencil strut to the right front corner of the crossmember and torque the nuts to 43 ft. lbs. (58 Nm).

c. Install the drive belt splash shield.

d. Install the front fascia-to-reinforcement screws.

e. Install the stabilizer bar-to-lower control arm link assemblies and bushings.

f. Rotate the stabilizer bar into position, installing the stabilizer bar links into the lower control arms.

g. Install the top stabilizer bar link bushings and nuts. DO NOT tighten the link yet.

h. Install the wheel.

i. Lower the vehicle so the suspension is supporting the total weight of the vehicle.

j. Torque the stabilizer bar-to-lower control arm links to 21 ft. lbs. (28 Nm).

k. Torque the stabilizer bar bushing retainer-to-crossmember bolts to 21 ft. lbs. (28 Nm).

21. Check and/or adjust the toe, as necessary.

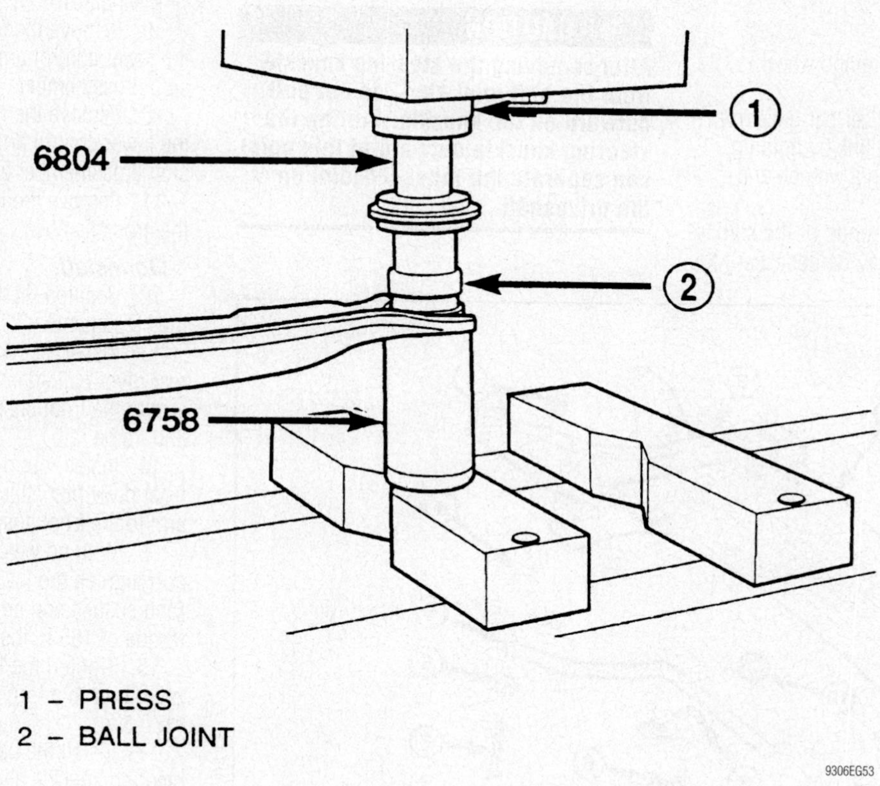

6804

6758

1 – PRESS
2 – BALL JOINT

9306EG53

Fig. 239 Installing the ball joint to the control arm

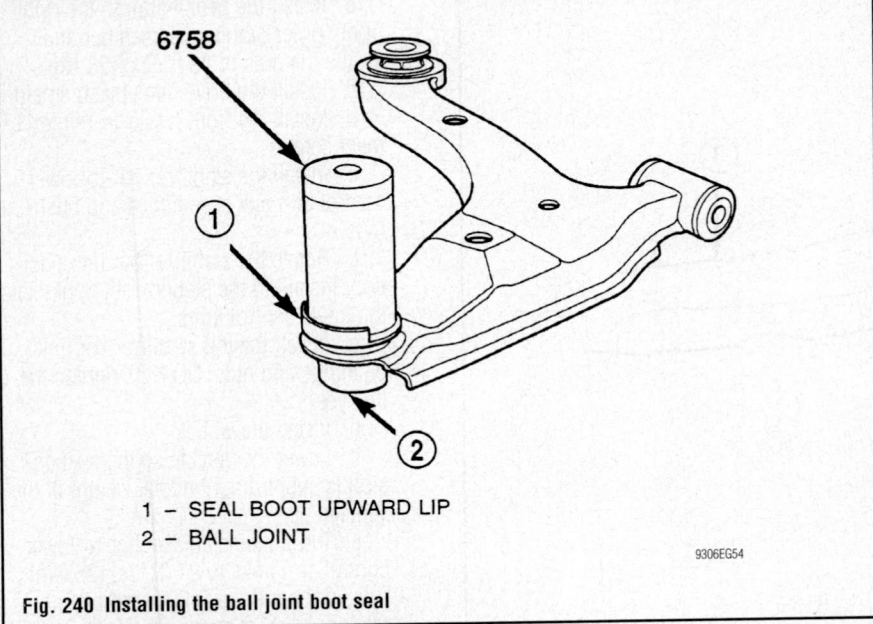

6758

1 – SEAL BOOT UPWARD LIP
2 – BALL JOINT

9306EG54

Fig. 240 Installing the ball joint boot seal

LOWER CONTROL ARM

REMOVAL & INSTALLATION

See Figures 241 and 242.

1. Before servicing the vehicle, refer to the Precautions Section.
2. Raise the vehicle.
3. Remove the front tire and wheel assembly.
4. Remove both stabilizer bar links from the vehicle. Remove each link by holding the upper retainer/nut with a wrench and turning the link bolt.
5. Rotate the forward ends of the stabilizer bar downward. It may be necessary to loosen the stabilizer bar cushion retainer bolts a little to ease any turning resistance.
6. Remove the nut and pinch bolt clamping the ball joint stud to the steering knuckle.

❉❉ CAUTION

After removing the steering knuckle from the ball joint stud, do not pull outward on the knuckle. Pulling the steering knuckle outward at this point can separate the inner CV-joint on the driveshaft.

❉❉ WARNING

Use caution when separating the ball joint stud from the steering knuckle, so the ball joint seal does not get cut.

7. Separate the ball joint stud from the steering knuckle by prying down on lower control arm and up against the ball joint boss on the steering knuckle.
8. If the right lower control arm is being serviced, perform the following:
   a. Remove the screws fastening the front fascia to the reinforcement as necessary in order to access the drive belt splash shield forward fastener screw.
   b. Remove the drive belt splash shield fasteners. Remove the shield.
   c. Remove the pencil strut from the right front corner of the crossmember and body of the vehicle. Refer to Engine Torque Struts in Engine Mechanical.
   d. Remove the washer behind the strut from the torque strut bolt.
   e. Remove the bolts mounting the engine torque strut in place, then remove the engine torque strut from the vehicle. Refer to Engine Torque Struts in Engine Mechanical.
9. Remove the front pivot bolt attaching the lower control arm to the front suspension crossmember.
10. Remove the rear pivot bolt attaching the lower control arm to the front suspension crossmember and frame rail.
11. Remove the lower control arm from the crossmember.

To install:

12. Position the lower control arm into the crossmember.
13. Install, but do not fully tighten, the rear pivot bolt attaching the lower control arm to the front suspension crossmember and frame rail.
14. Install, but do not fully tighten, the front pivot bolt attaching the lower control arm to the front suspension crossmember.
15. With no weight on the lower control arm, tighten the lower control arm rear pivot (and suspension crossmember) bolt to a torque of 185 ft. lbs. (250 Nm).
16. Tighten the lower control arm front pivot bolt to a torque of 125 ft. lbs. (170 Nm).
17. Install the ball joint stud into the steering knuckle aligning the bolt hole in the knuckle boss with the notch formed in the side of the ball joint stud.
18. If the right lower control arm has been serviced, perform the following:

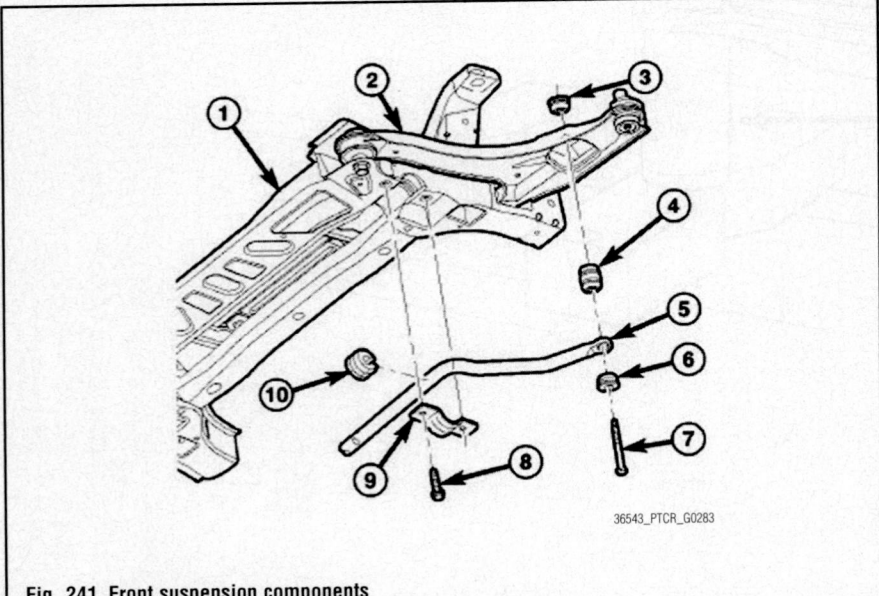

36543_PTCR_G0283

Fig. 241 Front suspension components

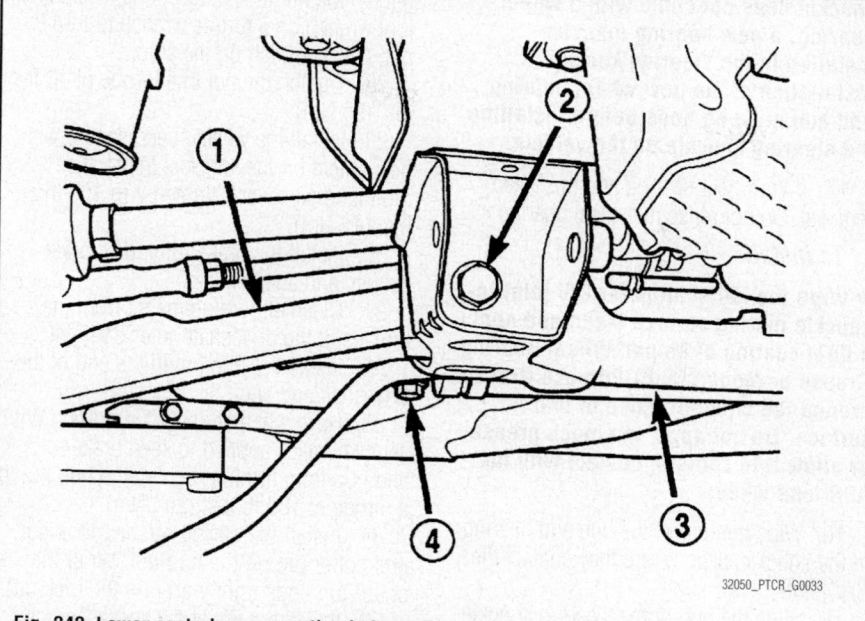

Fig. 242 Lower control arm mounting bolts and location

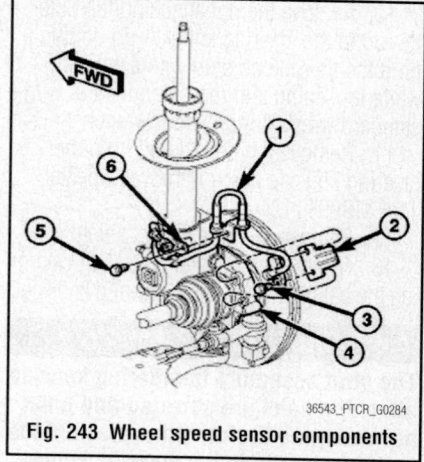

Fig. 243 Wheel speed sensor components

a. Install the engine torque strut. To properly align and tighten the torque strut, install the washer on the end of the stud extending from the torque strut bolt.

b. Install the pencil strut to the right front corner of the crossmember and body of the vehicle. Tighten the pencil strut nuts to a torque of 38 ft. lbs. (52 Nm).

c. Install the drive belt splash shield and fasteners.

d. Install the screws fastening the front fascia to the reinforcement.

19. Install a new ball joint stud pinch bolt and nut. Tighten the nut to a torque of 70 ft. lbs. (95 Nm).

20. Rotate the forward ends of the stabilizer bar into mounting position.

21. Clean the threads of the stabilizer bar link bolts, then apply Mopar® Lock And Seal or equivalent to the threads.

22. Install both stabilizer bar links back on vehicle. Start each stabilizer bar link bolt with bushing from the bottom, through the stabilizer bar, inner link bushings, lower control arm, and into the upper retainer/nut and bushing. Do not fully tighten the link assemblies at this time.

23. Lower the vehicle to ground level.

➡It may be necessary to put the vehicle on a platform hoist or alignment rack to gain access to the stabilizer bar mounting bolts with the vehicle at curb height.

24. Tighten each stabilizer bar link by holding the upper retainer/nut with a wrench and turning the link bolt. Tighten each link bolt to a torque of 22 ft. lbs. (29 Nm).

25. If previously loosened, tighten the stabilizer bar cushion retainer bolts to a torque of 18 ft. lbs. (25 Nm).

26. Perform wheel alignment as necessary.

STEERING KNUCKLE

REMOVAL & INSTALLATION

See Figures 243 through 245.

1. Before servicing the vehicle, refer to the Precautions Section.

2. Apply the brakes and hold in place.

3. Raise and safely support the vehicle.

4. Remove the front tire and wheel assembly.

5. Remove the cotter pin, lock nut and spring washer from the hub nut.

6. While the brakes are applied, loosen and remove the hub nut on the end of the driveshaft.

7. Release the brakes.

8. Remove the front disc brake caliper and adapter as an assembly, and the brake rotor from the steering knuckle. Refer to Front Disc Brake Caliper in Brakes.

9. Remove the screw (5) fastening the wheel speed sensor (1) to the knuckle (4). Pull the sensor head with heat shield (2) out of the knuckle.

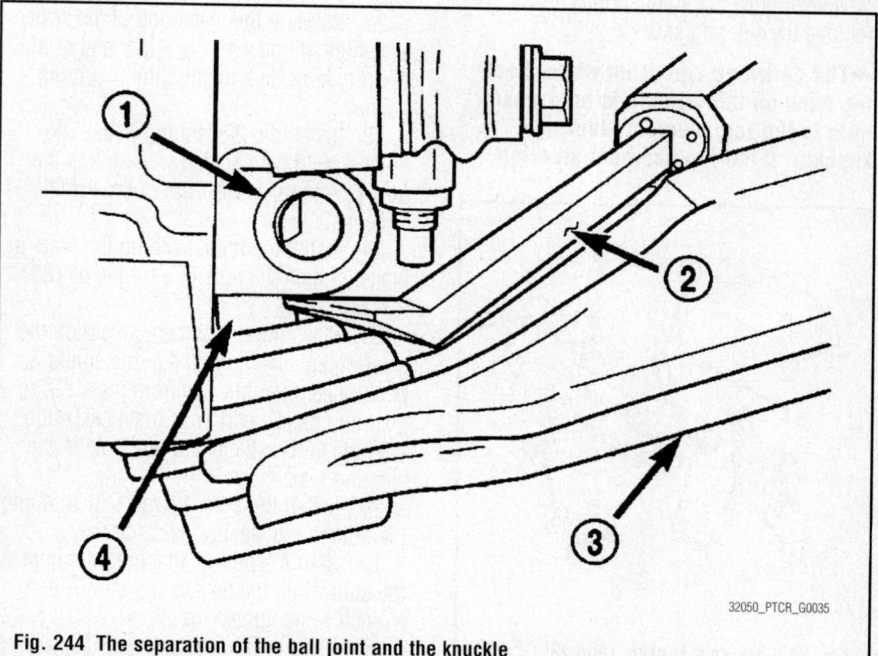

Fig. 244 The separation of the ball joint and the knuckle

10. Remove the nut attaching the outer tie rod to the steering knuckle. To do this, hold the tie rod end stud with a wrench while loosening and removing the nut with a standard wrench or crowfoot wrench.

11. Remove the tie rod end from the steering knuckle using Remover, Special Tool MB991113.

12. Remove the tie rod heat shield.

13. Remove the nut and pinch bolt clamping the ball joint stud to the steering knuckle.

※※ CAUTION

The strut assembly-to-steering knuckle attaching bolts are serrated and must not be turned during removal. Hold the bolts stationary in the steering knuckles while removing the nuts, then tap the bolts out using a pin punch.

14. Remove the 2 bolts attaching the strut to the steering knuckle.

※※ WARNING

Use caution when separating the ball joint stud from the steering knuckle, so the ball joint seal does not get cut.

15. Separate the ball joint stud from the steering knuckle by prying down on lower control arm and up against the ball joint boss on the steering knuckle.

➡ **Do not allow the driveshaft to hang by the inner CV-joint; it must be supported to keep the joint from separating during this operation.**

16. Pull the steering knuckle off the driveshaft outer CV-joint splines and remove the steering knuckle.

➡ **The cartridge type front wheel bearing used on this vehicle is not transferable to the replacement steering knuckle. If the replacement steering**

knuckle does not come with a wheel bearing, a new bearing must be installed in the steering knuckle. Installation of the new wheel bearing and hub must be done before installing the steering knuckle on the vehicle.

17. If the wheel bearing and hub need removal. Do not reuse the wheel bearing.

To install:

➡ **Wipe the halfshaft outer C/V joint-to-knuckle mating surface clean and apply a light coating of Mopar®Wheel Bearing Grease or Mopar®Multi-Purpose Grease around the circumference of that flat surface. Do not apply too much grease or allow it to come in contact with the ABS tone wheel.**

18. Wipe the rear of the hub and bearing in the knuckle clean where they contact the C/V joint.

19. Slide the hub of the steering knuckle onto the splines on the driveshaft C/V joint.

20. Install the steering knuckle onto the ball joint stud aligning the bolt hole in the knuckle boss with the notch formed in the side of the ball joint stud.

21. Install a new ball joint stud pinch bolt and nut. Tighten the nut to a torque of 70 ft. lbs. (95 Nm).

※※ CAUTION

The strut assembly-to-steering knuckle attaching bolts are serrated and must not be turned during installation. Install the nuts while holding the bolts stationary in the steering knuckle.

22. Position the lower end of the strut assembly in line with the upper end of the steering knuckle and align the mounting holes.

23. Install the 2 attaching bolts. The bolts should be installed with so that the nuts face towards the front of the vehicle once installed.

24. Install the nuts. Holding the bolts in place, tighten the nuts to a torque of 120 ft. lbs. (163 Nm).

25. Place the tie rod heat shield on the steering knuckle arm so that the shield is positioned straight away from the steering gear and tie rod end once installed. Align the hole in the shield with the hole in the steering knuckle arm.

26. Install the outer tie rod ball stud into the hole in the steering knuckle arm.

27. Start the tie rod attaching nut onto the stud. Hold the tie rod end stud with a wrench while tightening the nut with a standard wrench or crowfoot wrench. To fully

tighten the nut to specifications, use a crowfoot wrench on a torque wrench to turn the nut, and a wrench on the stud.

28. Tighten the nut to a torque of 40 ft. lbs. (55 Nm).

29. Install the wheel speed sensor with heat shield on the knuckle. Install the mounting screw and tighten it to 105 inch lbs. (12 Nm).

30. Install the brake rotor, disc brake caliper, and adapter.

31. Clean all foreign matter from the threads of the driveshaft outer CV-joint.

32. Install the hub nut in the end of the driveshaft and snug it.

33. Have a helper apply the brakes. With vehicle brakes applied to keep brake rotor and hub from turning, tighten the hub nut to a torque of 180 ft. lbs. (244 Nm).

34. Install the spring washer, lock nut, and cotter pin on the hub nut. Wrap the cotter pin ends tightly around the lock nut.

35. Install the tire and wheel assembly. Install the wheel mounting nuts and tighten them to a torque of 100 ft. lbs. (135 Nm).

36. Lower the vehicle.

37. Set the front toe on the vehicle to required specification.

STRUT

REMOVAL & INSTALLATION
See Figure 246.

1. Before servicing the vehicle, refer to the Precautions Section.

2. Install or connect the following:
   - The negative battery cable
   - The front wheels
   - Mark each strut assembly (right or left), as applicable, if both struts are being removed

36543_PTCR_G0285

Fig. 245 Steering knuckle removal

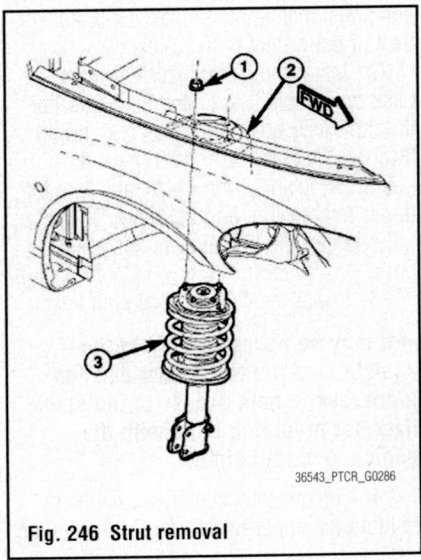

36543_PTCR_G0286

Fig. 246 Strut removal

- The ground strap from the rear of the strut
- The Anti-lock Brake System (ABS) wheel speed sensor from the strut, if equipped

✳✳ WARNING

The steering knuckle-to-strut assembly attaching bolts are serrated and must not be turned during removal.

- The steering knuckle nuts while holding the bolts stationary
- The 3 upper strut mount-to-strut tower nuts
- The strut assembly

To install:

3. Install or connect the following:
- The strut assembly into the strut tower by aligning the 3 upper strut mount studs with the shock tower holes. Torque the 3 upper strut mount nut/washer assemblies to 25 ft. lbs. (34 Nm).

✳✳ WARNING

The steering knuckle-to-strut assembly attaching bolts are serrated and must not be turned during installation.

- The steering knuckle nuts while holding the bolts stationary
- The steering knuckle arm and position it into the strut assembly by aligning the strut assembly-to-steering knuckle holes
- Both strut-to-steering knuckle bolts. Torque both bolts to 120 ft. lbs. (163 Nm).

➡ **The bolts should be installed with the nuts facing the front of the vehicle.**

- The ABS wheel sensor to the rear of the strut and torque the screw to 120 inch lbs. (13 Nm)
- The ground strap to the rear of the strut and torque the screw to 120 inch lbs. (13 Nm)
- The front wheel
- The negative battery cable

STABILIZER BAR

REMOVAL & INSTALLATION

See Figure 247.

1. Raise the vehicle.
2. Remove both stabilizer bar links from the vehicle. Remove each link by holding the upper retainer/nut with a wrench and turning the link bolt.

3. Remove the stabilizer bar cushion retainer bolts and retainers, and remove the stabilizer bar with cushions attached from the vehicle.
4. To remove the cushions from the stabilizer bar, peel back each cushion at the slit and roll it off the bar.

To install:

➡ **Before stabilizer bar installation, inspect the cushions and links for excessive wear, cracks, damage and distortion. Replace any pieces failing inspection.**

5. If removed, install the stabilizer bar cushions on the stabilizer bar utilizing the slit in each cushion. Position the cushions at each end of the bar's straight beam, just before it begins to curve.

➡ **Before installing the stabilizer bar, make sure the bar is not upside-down. The stabilizer bar must be installed with the curve on the outboard ends of the bar facing downward to clear the control arms once fully installed.**

6. Place the stabilizer bar in position on the front suspension crossmember. The slits in each cushion must point toward the front of the vehicle and sit directly on top of the

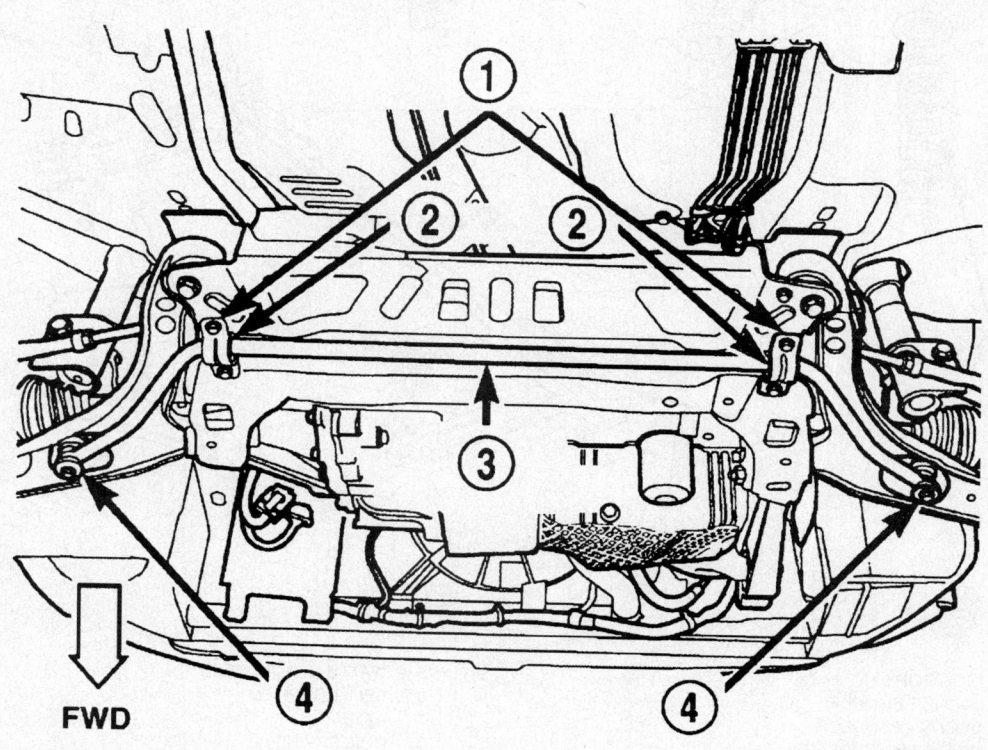

FWD

32050_PTCR_G0034

Fig. 247 Typical view of a stabilizer bar

raised beads formed into the stamping on the crossmember.

7. Install the cushion retainers, matching the raised beads formed into the cushion retainers to the grooves formed into the cushions.

8. Install the cushion retainer bolts, but do not completely tighten them at this time.

9. Clean the threads of the stabilizer bar link bolts, then apply Mopar® Lock And Seal or equivalent to the threads.

10. Install both stabilizer bar links back on vehicle. Start each stabilizer bar link bolt with bushing from the bottom, through the stabilizer bar, inner link bushings, lower control arm, and into the upper retainer/nut and bushing. Do not fully tighten the link assemblies at this time.

11. Lower the vehicle.

➡It may be necessary to put the vehicle on a platform hoist or alignment rack to gain access to the stabilizer bar mounting bolts with the vehicle at curb height.

12. Tighten each stabilizer bar link by holding the upper retainer/nut with a wrench and turning the link bolt. Tighten each link bolt to a torque of 22 ft. lbs. (29 Nm).

13. Tighten the stabilizer bar cushion retainer bolts to a torque of 18 ft. lbs. (25 Nm).

WHEEL HUB & BEARING

REMOVAL & INSTALLATION

The PT Cruiser is equipped with a sealed hub and bearing assemblies. The hub and bearing assembly is non-serviceable. If the assembly is damaged, the complete knuckle must be replaced.

SUSPENSION

COIL SPRING

REMOVAL & INSTALLATION

See Figures 248 through 252.

1. Before servicing the vehicle, refer to the Precautions Section.
2. Remove or disconnect the following:
   • Both rear wheels

REAR SUSPENSION

• The Watts link bell crank from the center of the axle
• The sway bar cushion retainers, refer to Stabilizer Bar

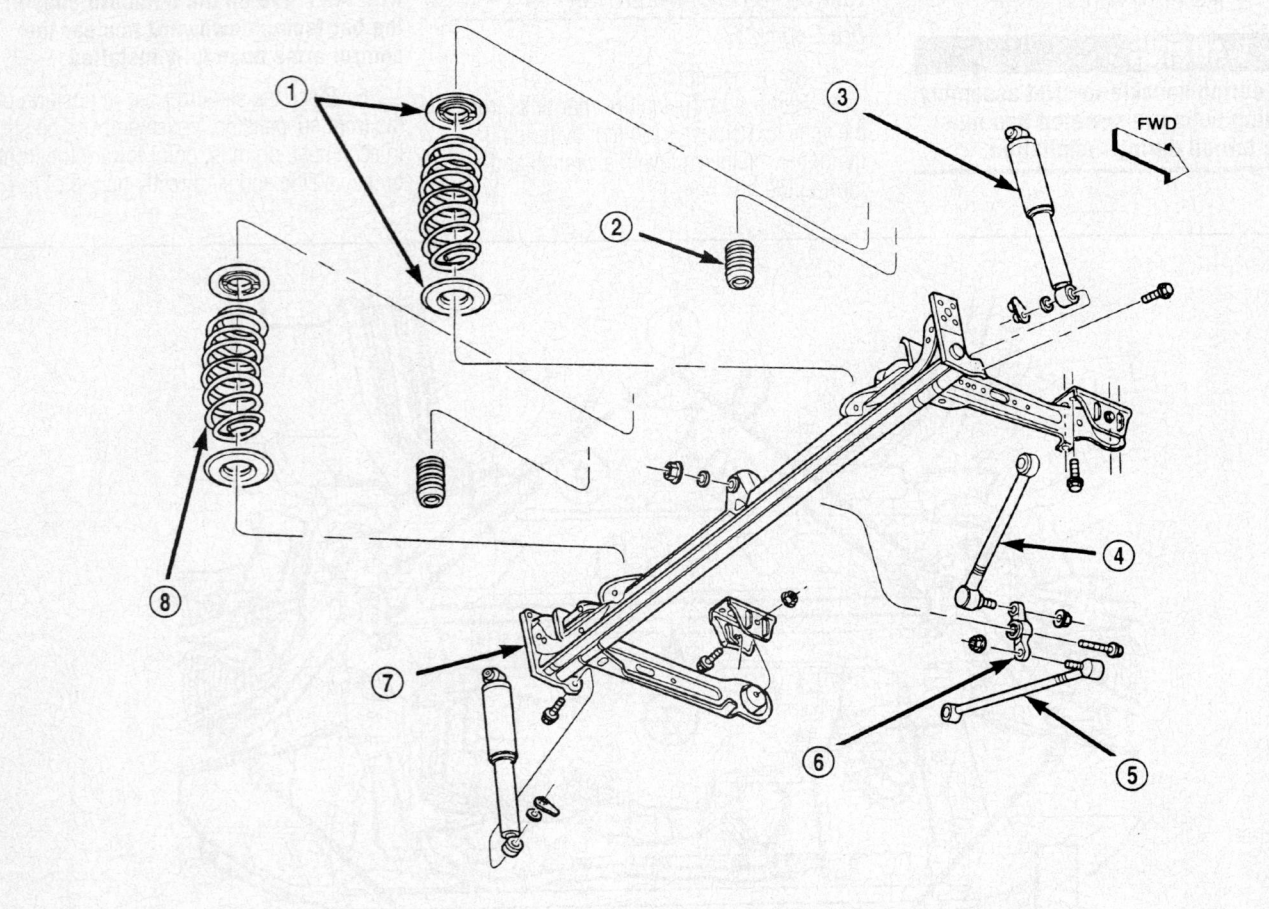

1 – ISOLATORS
2 – JOUNCE BUMPER
3 – SHOCK ABSORBER
4 – WATTS LINK (UPPER)

5 – WATTS LINK (LOWER)
6 – BELL CRANK
7 – AXLE
8 – COIL SPRING

9346JG12

Fig. 248 Exploded view of the rear suspension

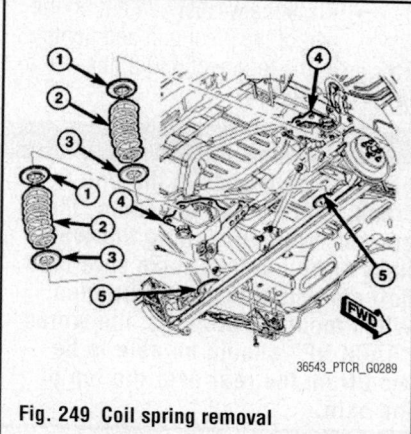

Fig. 249 Coil spring removal

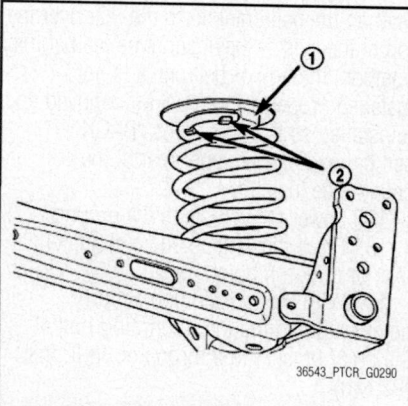

Fig. 250 Rubber isolator positioning

- The sway bar from the rear axle, and place a jack under the rear axle
- The shock absorber and lower the jack, refer to Shock Absorber
- The coil springs and rubber isolators

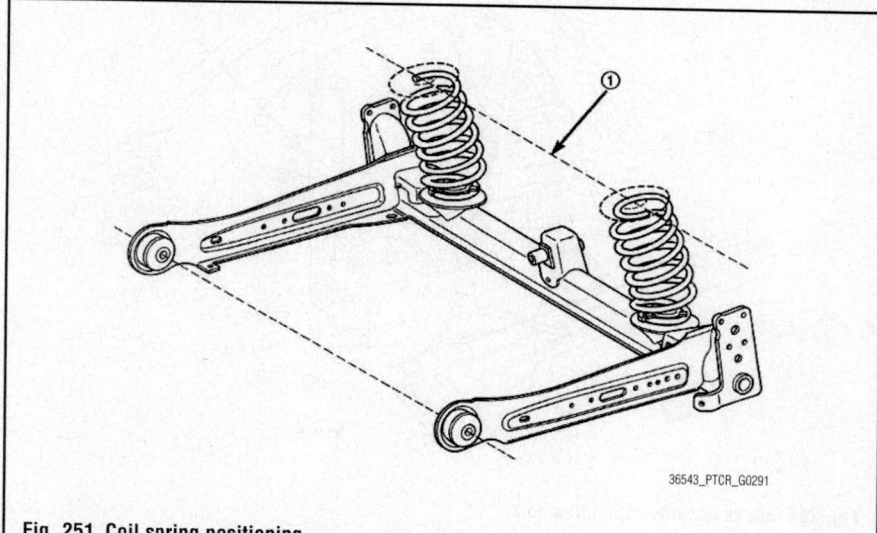

Fig. 251 Coil spring positioning

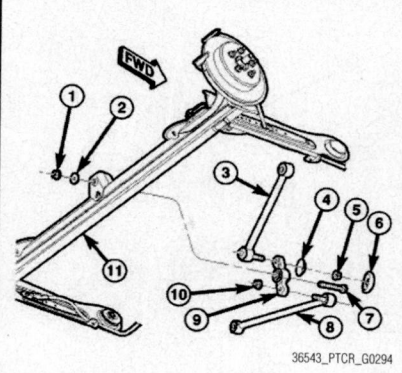

Fig. 252 Watts link bell crank positioning

To install:

3. Install or connect the following:
- The rubber isolator on each end of the coil spring and wrap the finger around the coil
- The coil springs on top of the axle spring perches and make certain that the upper coils end near the outboard sides of the vehicle and not at 180 degrees of that location

➡ **Both ends of the coil spring are identical. Either end of the spring can be the top or bottom.**

- The coil springs into the spring mounting brackets
- The shock washer and nut on the lower mounting bolts and torque the bolts to 65 ft. lbs. (88 Nm)
- The lower end of the sway bar retainers in the slots at the back of the axle

- The stabilizer bar mounting bolt through the cushion retainer and torque to 45 ft. lbs. (61 Nm)

✳✳ WARNING

When installing the watts links and bell crank to the axle, make sure the bell crank is right-side-up. When mounted properly, the words "BACK UP" should be able to be read from the rear over the top of the axle.

- The Watts link bell crank to the center of the axle and torque the bolts to 110 ft. lbs. (149 Nm)
- The rear wheels, tighten wheel mounting nuts to 100 ft. lbs. (135 Nm)

CONTROL ARMS/LINKS

REMOVAL & INSTALLATION

See Figure 253.

This vehicle uses a Watts link assembly which serves the same purpose as a track bar. That is, it is used to control rear axle lateral movement and provides cross-car location of the axle. Unlike a track bar, the Watts link assembly offers more consistent handling and stability at varying suspension heights, either lightly loaded or fully laden. As the suspension lowers or raises, the Watts link assembly compensates by rotating the bell crank in the desired direction. This rotation simulates shortening or lengthening of the links. Since there is one link on each side, the change affects each side of the suspension evenly.

1. Before servicing the vehicle, refer to the Precautions Section.
2. Raise and safely support the vehicle.
3. If the lower Watts link is being removed, perform the following first, otherwise proceed to the next step:
- Remove the nut securing the bell crank pivot bolt in the center of the axle
- With the bolt still installed, slide the bell crank away from the axle just enough to remove the nut securing the lower link to the bell crank

4. Remove the nut securing the ball joint to the bell crank.
5. Install the Remover, Special Tool MB991113, on the link ball joint at the bell crank and release ball joint from the bell crank.

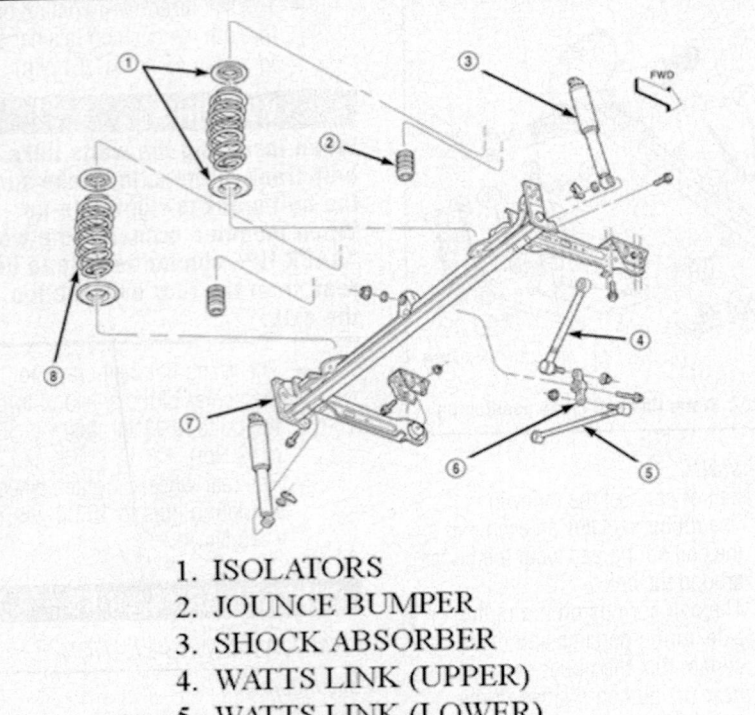

1. ISOLATORS
2. JOUNCE BUMPER
3. SHOCK ABSORBER
4. WATTS LINK (UPPER)
5. WATTS LINK (LOWER)
6. BELL CRANK
7. AXLE
8. COIL SPRING

22043_PTCR_G0004

Fig. 253 Location of the Watts links in relation to the rear suspension

6. Remove the bolt securing the link to the bracket on the body of the vehicle. Remove the link.

To install:

➡ **When installing the link, DO NOT attempt to turn the ball joint end of the link independently.**

7. Making sure the ball joint end is positioned properly for mounting to the bell crank, install the link into the bracket on the body of the vehicle.

8. Install the bolt (and flag nut for upper link) securing the link to the bracket, but do not fully tighten it at this time. It must be tightened when the vehicle is at curb height.

➡ **The upper link extends from the right side of the vehicle to the upper end of the bell crank while the lower link extends from the left side of the vehicle to the lower end of the bell crank.**

9. Install the upper or lower link to the bell crank. Install the nut on the ball joint stud and tighten it to a torque of 10 ft. lbs. (14 Nm) plus an additional 180°.

10. If the lower link is the link being installed, perform the following, otherwise proceed to the next step.
  • Slide the bell crank pivot bolt all the way through the axle

• Place the washer and nut on the end of the pivot bolt and tighten it to a torque of 110 ft. lbs. (149 Nm)

⁂ **CAUTION**

Although both ends of the bell crank appear to be the same, they are not. When installing the Watts links or bell crank, make sure the bell crank is properly positioned. When mounted properly, the words "BACK UP" should be able to be read from the rear over the top of the axle.

11. Verify the words "BACK UP" can be read on the bell crank from the rear over the top of the axle. If they cannot be read at this position, the link or bell crank is not installed properly and must be removed and reinstalled so that the words "BACK UP" can be read on the upper rear of the bell crank once installed.

12. Lower the vehicle to the ground.

13. Place the vehicle on an alignment rack or drive-on hoist.

14. With the suspension at curb height, tighten the link mounting bolt at the body bracket to a torque of 68 ft. lbs. (92 Nm).

SHOCK ABSORBER

REMOVAL & INSTALLATION

See Figure 254.

1. Before servicing the vehicle, refer to the Precautions Section.

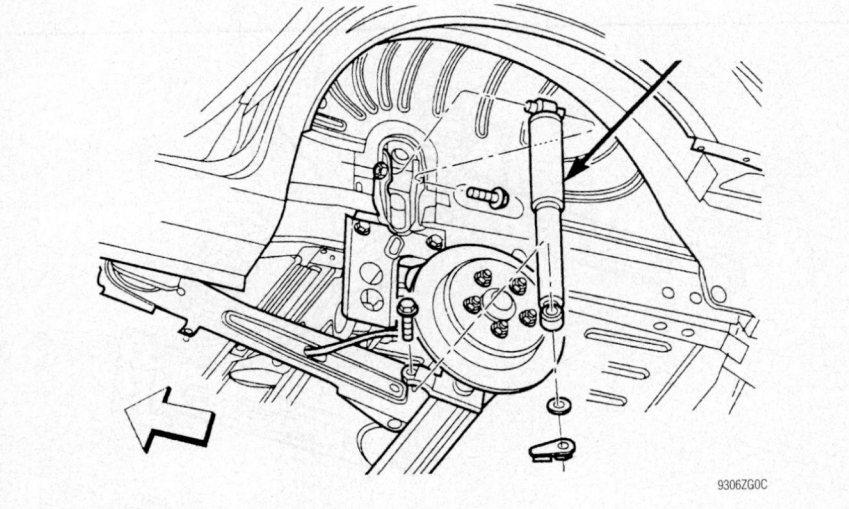

9306ZG0C

Fig. 254 Shock absorber mounting bolts

2. Remove the rear wheel and position a transmission jack under the center of the axle. Raise the jack enough to support the axle.

3. Remove or disconnect the following:
- The shock absorber lower mounting bolt from the axle
- The upper mounting bolt
- The shock absorber

To install:

4. Install or connect the following:
- The shock absorber eye to the body bracket. Hand tighten the upper mounting bolt.
- The lower the jack and install the lower mounting bolt through the axle flange and shock absorber. Torque the bolt to 65 ft. lbs. (88 Nm).
- Torque the upper mounting bolt to 73 ft. lbs. (99 Nm).
- The rear wheel
- The negative battery cable

TESTING

Inspect the shock absorber for damage and evidence of fluid running from the upper end of the fluid reservoir. (Actual leakage will be a stream of fluid running down the side of the reservoir tube and dripping off lower end of unit). A slight amount of seepage between the shaft and shaft seal is not unusual and does not affect performance of the shock absorber.

STABILIZER BAR

REMOVAL & INSTALLATION

See Figures 255 through 257.

1. Before servicing the vehicle, refer to the Precautions Section.

2. Raise and support the vehicle.

3. Remove the wheel mounting nuts (3), then the rear tire and wheel assembly.

4. Remove the nut and bolt from the lower end of the stabilizer bar link (1) attaching it to the stabilizer bar (2).

5. Remove the bolt retaining the link (1) to the frame rail, then remove the stabilizer bar link from the vehicle.

6. Remove the rear stabilizer bar, on each side, remove the bolt (3) securing the stabilizer bar cushion retainer (1) to the rear axle (2). Lift each retainer from the slot in the axle allowing the stabilizer bar to hang free.

7. Remove stabilizer bar.

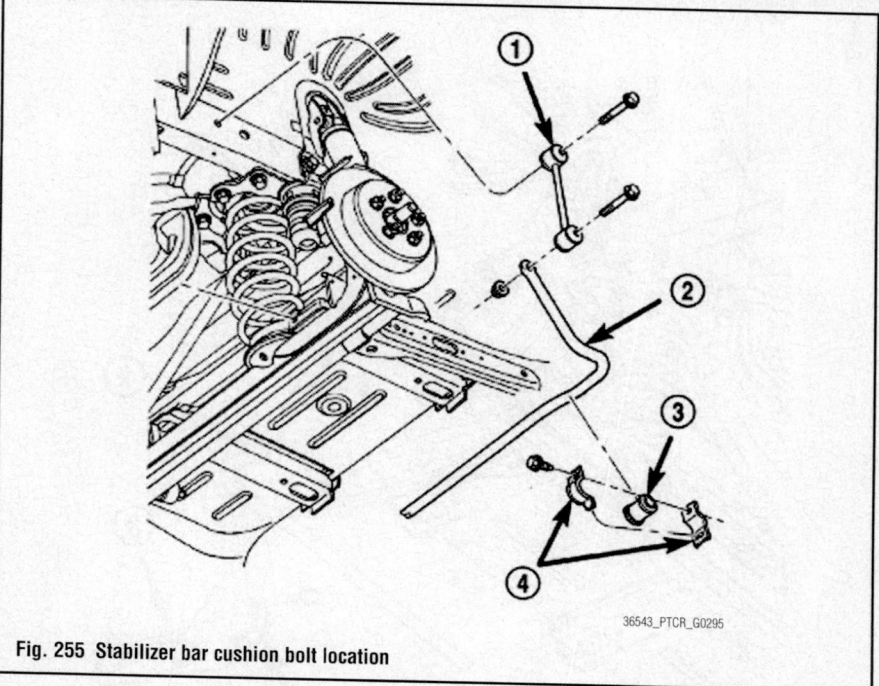

Fig. 255 Stabilizer bar cushion bolt location

36543_PTCR_G0295

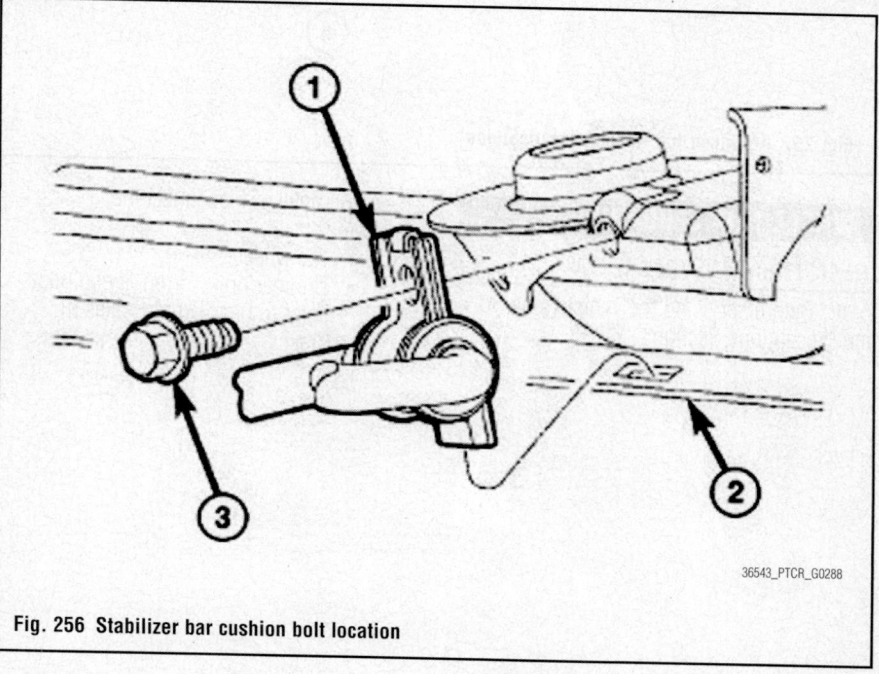

Fig. 256 Stabilizer bar cushion bolt location

36543_PTCR_G0288

To install:

8. Install each cushion (3) on the stabilizer bar (2) by opening the slit in side and wrapping it around the bar. When installed properly, the slit in the cushion should face toward the front of the car once the bar is installed.

9. Perform the following on each stabilizer bar retainer (4):

a. Hook the lower end of each retainer halve to the other.

b. Install the two halves of the retainer (4) over the cushion (3), matching the contour of each retainer with the cushion. The slit in the cushion should face straight toward the forward halve of the retainer.

c. Fold the crimp tab on the forward retainer halve over the rear halve crimping the two halves together.

10. Install the mounting bolts and tighten each to 45 ft. lbs. (61 Nm).

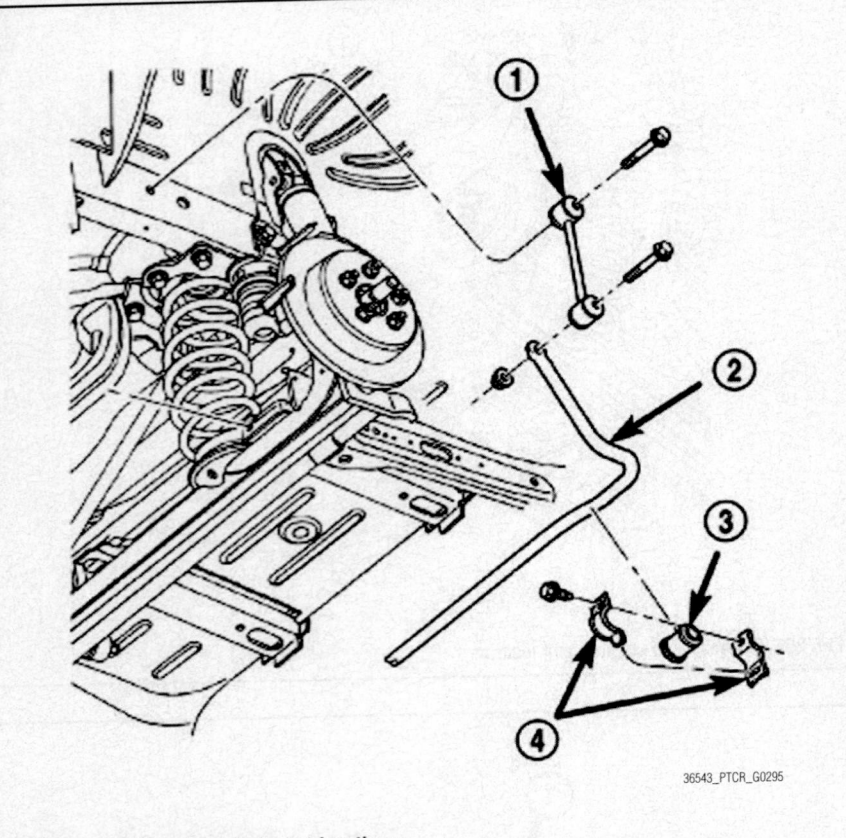

36543_PTCR_G0295

Fig. 257 Stabilizer bar attachment locations

WHEEL HUB & BEARING

REMOVAL & INSTALLATION

1. Before servicing the vehicle, refer to the Precautions Section.

2. Remove or disconnect the following:
- The wheel
- The rear brake drum, if equipped. Refer to Rear Drum Brakes in Brakes.

- The caliper (suspend on a wire) and the rotor, if equipped with rear disc brakes. Refer to Rear Disc Brakes in Brakes.

✳✳ WARNING

DO NOT allow the caliper to hang by the brake hose.

- The dust cap from the rear hub/bearing
- The hub/bearing assembly-to-knuckle/spindle nut

➡ **Discard the hub nut and replace with a new one during installation.**

- The hub/bearing from the spindle by pulling it off the end of the spindle by hand

To install:

✳✳ WARNING

The hub/bearing nut must be tightened to its proper torque value—but NOT over-tightened. The proper specification is crucial to the life of the hub bearing.

3. Position the hub/bearing assembly on the rear spindle/knuckle. Install a NEW hub nut and tighten to 160 ft. lbs. (217 Nm).

4. Install or connect the following:
- The dust cap and seat it using a soft face hammer to carefully tap it into place
- The brake drum, if equipped
- The caliper and rotor, if equipped
- Rear wheel

SPECIFICATIONS AND MAINTENANCE CHARTS

ENGINE AND VEHICLE IDENTIFICATION

Engine							Model Year	
Code ①	Liters (cc)	Cu. In.	Cyl.	Fuel Sys.	Engine Type	Eng. Mfg.	Code ②	Year
K	3.7 (3701)	226	6	MPI	SOHC	Chrysler	9	2009
P	4.7 (4701)	287	8	MPI	SOHC	Chrysler		
T	5.7 (5653)	345	8	MDS VCT	OHV	Chrysler		

OHV: Overhead Valve

MDS: Multi Displacement System

MPI: Multi Point Injection

SOHC: Single Over Head Camshaft

VCT: Variable Cam Timing

① 8th position of VIN

② 10th position of VIN

36543_RAM1_C0001

GENERAL ENGINE SPECIFICATIONS

Year	Model	Engine Displacement Liters	Engine Series (ID/VIN)	Net Horsepower @ rpm	Net Torque @ rpm (ft. lbs.)	Bore x Stroke (in.)	Com-pression Ratio	Oil Pressure @ rpm
2009	Ram Truck 1500	3.7	K	211@5200	236@4000	3.66x3.40	9.6:1	25-110@3000
		4.7	P	235@4800	295@3200	3.66x3.40	9.0:1	35-105@3000
		5.7	T	345@5400	375@4200	3.91x3.58	9.6:1	25-110@3000

36543_RAM1_C0002

GASOLINE ENGINE TUNE-UP SPECIFICATIONS

Year	Engine Displacement Liters	Engine ID/VIN	Spark Plug Gap (in.)	Ignition Timing (deg.)	Fuel Pump (psi)	Idle Speed (rpm)	Valve Clearance	
							Intake	Exhaust
2009	3.7	K	0.042	①	NA	②	HYD	HYD
	4.7	P	0.040	①	NA	②	HYD	HYD
	5.7	T	0.045	①	NA	②	HYD	HYD

NOTE: The Vehicle Emission Control Information (VECI) label often reflects specification changes made during production. The label figures must be used if they differ from those in this chart.

HYD: Hydraulic

① Ignition timing is controlled by the PCM and is not adjustable.

② Idle speed is controlled by the PCM and is not adjustable

36543_RAM1_C0003

CAPACITIES

Year	Model	Engine Displacement Liters	Engine ID/VIN	Oil with Filter (qts.)	Transmission (pts.) Manual	Transmission (pts.) Auto. ①	Transfer Case (pts.)	Drive Axle Front (pts.)	Drive Axle Rear (pts.)	Fuel Tank (gal.)	Cooling System (qts.)
2009	Ram Truck 1500	3.7	K	5.0	—	②	③	④	⑤	⑥	14.0
		4.7	P	6.0	—	②	③	④	⑤	⑥	14.0
		5.7	T	7.0	—	②	③	④	⑤	⑥	16.0

NOTE: All capacities are approximate. Add fluid gradually and check to be sure a proper fluid level is obtained.

① For fluid drain and filter replacement only.

② 48RLE: 8.0 pts.
   45RFE/545RFE:
   4x2: 11.0 pts.
   4x4: 13.0 pts.

③ NV243: 3.4 pts.
   NV 246: 4.0 pts.

④ C205FD: 3.5 pts.

⑤ 9.25: 4.6 pts. W/Trac-Lok + 4 oz. Additive

⑥ Regular cab short bed/Quad cab/Crew cab Standard: 26.0
   Regular cab short bed/Quad cab/Crew cab Optional: 32.0

36543_RAM1_C0005

FLUID SPECIFICATIONS

Year	Model	Engine Displacement Liters	Engine ID/VIN	Engine Oil	Manual Trans.	Auto. Trans. ①	Drive Axle ②	Power Steering Fluid	Brake Master Cylinder	Engine Coolant
2009	Ram 1500	3.7	K	5W-20	—	ATF+4	75W-90 ③	ATF+4	DOT 3	Mopar® (HOAT)
		4.7	P	5W-20	—	ATF+4	75W-90 ③	ATF+4	DOT 3	Mopar® (HOAT)
		5.7	T	5W-20	—	ATF+4	75W-90 ③	ATF+4	DOT 3	Mopar® (HOAT)

NOTE: Check the engines oil cap or owners manual for specific engine oil grade variations.

DOT: Department Of Transpotation

① Transfer case ATF+4 except NVG246: NVG 246 ATF

② Ram 1500 Models rear axle: Synthetic 75W-140 plus 4oz limited slip additive

④ Synthetic is recommended

36543_RAM1_C0006

VALVE SPECIFICATIONS

Year	Engine Displacement Liters	Engine ID/VIN	Seat Angle (deg.)	Face Angle (deg.)	Spring Test Pressure (lbs. @ in.)	Spring Installed Height (in.)	Stem-to-Guide Clearance (in.) Intake	Stem-to-Guide Clearance (in.) Exhaust	Stem Diameter (in.) Intake	Stem Diameter (in.) Exhaust
2009	3.7	K	44.5-45	45-45.5	①	1.579	0.0008-0.0028	0.0019-0.0039	0.2729-0.2739	0.2717-0.2728
	4.7	P	44.5-45	45-45.5	174.4-195.5 @1.137	1.579	0.0008-0.0028	0.0019-0.0039	0.2729-0.2739	0.2717-0.2728
	5.7	T	44.5-45	45-45.5	242 @1.283	1.810	0.0008-0.0025	0.0009-0.0025	0.3120-0.3130	0.3120-0.3130

① Intake 213.2-233.8 @ 1.107
   Exhaust without damper: 196.5-214.9 @ 1.067

36543_RAM1_C0008

CAMSHAFT AND BEARING SPECIFICATIONS CHART

All measurements are given in inches.

Year	Engine Displacement Liters	Engine ID/VIN	Journal Dia.	Brg. Oil Clearance	Shaft End-play	Runout	Journal Bore	Lobe Height	
								Intake	Exhaust
2009	3.7	K	1.0227-1.0235	0.001-0.0026	0.003-0.0079	NA	1.0245-1.0252	NA	NA
	4.7	P	1.0227-1.0235	0.001-0.0026	0.003-0.0079	NA	1.0245-1.0252	NA	NA
	5.7	T	①	②	0.0031-0.0114	NA	NA	NA	NA

NA: Not Available

① No.1: 2.29
  No.2: 2.28
  No.3: 2.26
  No.4: 2.24
  No.5: 1.72
② No.1, 3, 5: (0.0015-.003)
  No.2, 4: (0.0019-.0035)

36543_RAM1_C0007

CRANKSHAFT AND CONNECTING ROD SPECIFICATIONS

All measurements are given in inches.

Year	Engine Displacement Liters	Engine ID/VIN	Crankshaft				Connecting Rod		
			Main Brg. Journal Dia.	Main Brg. Oil Clearance	Shaft End-play	Thrust on No.	Journal Diameter	Oil Clearance	Side Clearance
2009	3.7	K	2.4996-2.5005	0.0008-0.0018	0.0021-0.0112	2	2.2792-2.2798	0.0002-0.0017	0.0040-0.0138
	4.7	P	2.4996-2.5005	0.0002-0.0013	0.0021-0.0112	3	2.0076-2.0082	0.0006-0.0022	0.0040-0.0138
	5.7	T	2.5585-2.5595	0.0009-0.0020	0.0020-0.0110	3	2.1250-2.1260	0.0007-0.0023	0.0030-0.0137

36543_RAM1_C0009

PISTON AND RING SPECIFICATIONS

All measurements are given in inches.

Year	Engine Displacement Liters	Engine ID/VIN	Piston Clearance	Ring Gap			Ring Side Clearance		
				Top Compression	Bottom Compression	Oil Control	Top Compression	Bottom Compression	Oil Control
2009	3.7	K	0.0011-0.0016	0.0079-0.0142	0.0146-0.0249	0.0099-0.0300	0.0020-0.0037	0.0016-0.0043	0.0007-0.0091
	4.7	P	0.0011-0.0016	0.0079-0.0142	0.0146-0.0249	0.0099-0.0300	0.0020-0.0037	0.0016-0.0032	0.0007-0.0091
	5.7	T	0.0012-0.0023	0.015-0.0210	0.009-0.0200	0.0059-0.0259	0.0010-0.0035	0.0010-0.0031	0.0020-0.0080

36543_RAM1_C0010

TORQUE SPECIFICATIONS
All readings in ft. lbs.

Year	Engine Displacement Liters	Engine ID/VIN	Cylinder Head Bolts	Main Bearing Bolts	Rod Bearing Bolts	Crankshaft Damper Bolts	Flywheel Bolts	Manifold Intake	Manifold Exhaust	Spark Plugs	Oil Pan Drain Plug
2009	3.7	K	①	②	③	130	70	④	18	20	25
	4.7	P	⑤	⑥	③	130	45	④	18	20	25
	5.7	T	⑥	⑦	⑧	130	55	④	18	13	25

① Step 1: 1-8 to 20 ft. lbs.

   Step 2: Repeat step 1: and

   tighten bolts 9-12 to 10 ft. lbs.

   Step 3: Tighten bolts 1-8 plus 90 degrees

   Step 4: Repeat step 3: and

   tighten bolts 9-12 to 19 ft. lbs.

② Bed plate: see procedure

③ 20 ft. lbs. plus 90 degrees

④ 105 inch lbs.

⑤ Step 1: 1-10 to 20 ft. lbs.

   Step 2: Repeat step 1 without loosening bolts

   Step 3: Tighten bolts 11-14 89 inch lbs.

   Step 4: Rotate bolts 1-10 plus 90 degrees

   Step 5: Repeat step 4

   Step 6: Tighten bolts 11-14 to 19 ft. lbs.

⑥ Bedplate: see procedure

⑥ Step 1: 1-10 to 25 ft. lbs.

   Step 2: 11-15 to 15 ft. lbs.

   Step 3: 1-10 to 40 ft. lbs.

   Step 4: 11-15 to 15 ft. lbs.

   Step 5: 1-10 plus 90 degrees

   Step 6: 1-10 plus 90 degrees

   Step 7: 11-15 to 25 ft. lbs.

⑦ Step 1: Main bolts to 10 ft. lbs.

   Step 2: Main bolts to 20 ft. lbs.

   Step 3: Main bolts plus 90 degrees

   Step 4: Crossbolts to 21 ft. lbs.

   Step 5: Repeat step 4.

⑧ 15 ft. lbs. plus 90 degrees

36543_RAM1_C0011

WHEEL ALIGNMENT

Year	Model	GVW	Wheel Base (in.)	Caster Range (+/-Deg.)	Caster Preferred Setting (Deg.)	Camber Range (+/-Deg.)	Camber Preferred Setting (Deg.)	Toe-in (in.)
2009	1500 17 inch tire	—	—	①	①	- 0.40 to 0.60	0.10	0.10+/-0.10
	1500 20 inch tire	—	—	②	②	- 0.40 to 0.60	0.10	0.10+/-0.10

① Left side range 3.00 to 4.00 Preferred 3.50

   Right side range 3.25 to 4.25 Preferred 3.75

② Left side range 3.00 to 4.00 Preferred 3.50

   Right side range 3.40 to 4.40 Preferred 3.90

36543_RAM1_C0014

TIRE, WHEEL AND BALL JOINT SPECIFICATIONS

Year	Model	OEM Tires		Tire Pressures (psi)		Wheel Size	Lut Nut (ft. lbs.)
		Standard	Optional	Front	Rear		
2009	1500 ST Regular 2WD Short	P265/70R17	None	①	①	7 or 8	130
	1500 ST Regular 2WD Long	P265/70R17	None	①	①	7 or 8	130
	1500 ST Quad 2WD	P265/70R17	None	①	①	7 or 8	130
	1500 ST Crew 2WD	P265/70R17	P275/60R20	①	①	7-8 or 9	130
	1500 ST Regular 4X4 Short	P265/70R17	None	①	①	7 or 8	130
	1500 ST Regular 4X4 Long	P265/70R17	None	①	①	7 or 8	130
	1500 ST Quad 4X4 Short	P265/70R17	None	①	①	7 or 8	130
	1500 ST Quad 4X4 Long	P265/70R17	None	①	①	7 or 8	130
	1500 ST Crew 4X4	P265/70R17	P275/60R20	①	①	7-8 or 9	130
	1500 SLT Regular 2WD Short	P265/70R17	P275/60R20	①	①	7-8 or 9	130
	1500 SLT Regular 2WD Long	P265/70R17	P275/60R20	①	①	7-8 or 9	130
	1500 SLT Quad 2WD	P265/70R17	P275/60R20	①	①	7-8 or 9	130
	1500 SLT Crew 2WD	P265/70R17	P275/60R20	①	①	7-8 or 9	130
	1500 SLT Regular 4X4 Short	P265/70R17	P275/60R20	①	①	7-8 or 9	130
	1500 SLT Regular 4X4 Long	P265/70R17	P275/60R20	①	①	7-8 or 9	130
	1500 SLT Quad 4X4	P265/70R17	P275/60R20	①	①	7-8 or 9	130
	1500 SLT Crew 4X4	P265/70R17	P275/60R20	①	①	7-8 or 9	130
	1500 TRX Quad 2WD	P265/70R17	None	①	①	7	130
	1500 TRX Crew 2WD	P265/70R17	None	①	①	7	130
	1500 TRX Quad 4X4	P265/70R17	None	①	①	7	130
	1500 TRX Crew 4X4	P265/70R17	None	①	①	7	130
	1500 Sport Quad 2WD	P275/60R20	None	①	①	9	130
	1500 Sport Crew 2WD	P275/60R20	None	①	①	9	130
	1500 Sport Regular4X4 Short	P275/60R20	None	①	①	9	130
	1500 Sport Quad 4X4	P275/60R20	None	①	①	9	130
	1500 Sport Crew 4X4	P275/60R20	None	①	①	9	130
	1500 Sport R/T 2WD Short	P275/60R20	None	①	①	9	130
	1500 Laramie Quad 2WD	P275/60R20	P265/70R17	①	①	8 or 9-8	130
	1500 Laramie Crew 2WD	P275/60R20	P265/70R17	①	①	8 or 9-8	130
	1500 Laramie Quad 4X4	P275/60R20	P265/70R17	①	①	8 or 9-8	130
	1500 Laramie Crew 2WD	P275/60R20	P265/70R17	①	①	8 or 9-8	130
	1500 Laramie Quad 4X4	P275/60R20	P265/70R17	①	①	8 or 9-8	130
	1500 Laramie Crew 4X4	P275/60R20	P265/70R17	①	①	8 or 9-8	130

OEM: Original Equipment Manufacturer

PSI: Pounds Per Square Inch

STD: Standard

OPT: Optional

① See sticker on drivers door

36543_RAM1_C0013

BRAKE SPECIFICATIONS

All measurements in inches unless noted

Year	Model		Brake Disc			Brake Drum			Minimum Lining Thickness		Brake Caliper	
			Original Thickness	Minimum Thickness	Maximum Run-out	Original Inside Diameter	Max. Wear Limit	Max. Machine Diameter	Front	Rear	Bracket Bolts (ft. lbs.)	Mounting Bolts (ft. lbs.)
2009	Ram Pick-up	F	1.1	1.039	0.002	—	—	—	①	①	130	24
	1500	R	.86	.803	0.002	—	—	—	①	①	120	22

① 0.04 in. at thinnest point

36543_RAM1_C0012

SCHEDULED MAINTENANCE INTERVALS
2009 RAM 1500 PICKUP

TO BE SERVICED	TYPE OF SERVICE	6	12	18	24	30	36	42	48	54	60	66	72	78	84	90
Engine oil & filter *	R	✓	✓	✓	✓	✓	✓	✓	✓	✓	✓	✓	✓	✓	✓	✓
Tire pressure, battery & terminals ①	I															
CV joints	I		✓		✓		✓		✓		✓		✓		✓	
Drive axle fluid	I			✓			✓			✓			✓			✓
Engine coolant & hoses ①	I															
Lights & other electrical items ①	I															
Brake, P/S & A/T fluid levels	I	✓	✓	✓	✓	✓	✓	✓	✓	✓	✓	✓	✓	✓		✓
Front suspension components	I				✓				✓				✓			
Brake hoses	I	✓	✓	✓	✓	✓	✓	✓	✓	✓	✓	✓	✓	✓		✓
Exhaust system	I		✓		✓		✓		✓		✓		✓		✓	
Brake linings	I		✓		✓		✓		✓		✓		✓		✓	
Air cleaner element	R					✓					✓					✓
Spark plugs ②	R					✓					✓					✓
Transfer case fluid	I															✓
Tires	Rotate	✓	✓	✓	✓	✓	✓	✓	✓	✓	✓	✓	✓	✓	✓	✓
Engine coolant	R										✓					
Spark plug cables (3.7L)	I										✓					
PCV valve	I															✓

R: Replace   S/I: Service or Inspect   Adj: Adjust   L: Lubricate

① Once a month, inspect tires and check pressure. Check battery and tighten terminals if required. Check fluid levels.

② Vehicle's built with the 4.7L are equipped with sixteen spark plugs.

One set is located on the top of the engine under the coils and the second set is located on the side of the engine.

The spark plugs located under the coils are a standard plug and must be changed every 50 000 km (30,000 miles).

The spark plugs located on the side of the engine are a premium plug and must be changed every 170 000 km (102,000 miles).

3.7L and 5.7L engine, change the plugs at 50,000km, 30,000 miles.

FREQUENT OPERATION MAINTENANCE (SEVERE SERVICE)

If a vehicle is operated under any of the following conditions it is considered severe service:

- Extremely dusty areas.

- 50% or more of the vehicle operation is in 32°C (90°F) or higher temperatures, or constant operation in temperatures below 0°C (32°F).

- Prolonged idling (vehicle operation in stop and go traffic.

- Frequent short running periods (engine does not warm to normal operating temperatures).

- Police, taxi, delivery usage or trailer towing usage.

Oil & oil filter change: change every 3000 miles.

Air filter/air pump air filter: check every 12,000 miles.

Automatic transmission fluid & filter: change every 60,000 miles.

Transfer case fluid: change every 60,000 miles.

Axle fluid: change every 18,000 miles.

*Oil Change Indicator System

On Electronic Vehicle Information Center (EVIC) equipped vehicles, "Oil Change Require" is displayed in the EVIC and a single chime sounds indicating that an oil change is necessary. On non-EVIC equipped vehicles, "Change Oil" flashes in the instrument cluster and a single chime sounds indicating that an oil change is necessary. Illumination of the oil change message is based on the operating conditions of the vehicle. When the message is illuminated, the vehicle must be serviced within 500 miles.

The oil change indicator will not monitor the time since the last oil change. Change the oil if it has been more than 6 months since the last oil change, even if the oil change indicator message is not illuminated.

Under no circumstances should oil change intervals exceed 6,000 miles or 6 months, whichever comes first.

To reset the oil change indicator, refer to the following procedure:

1. Turn the ignition switch to the ON position. Do not start the engine.

2. Fully press the accelerator pedal 3 times within 10 seconds.

3. Turn the ignition switch to the LOCK position.

If the indicator message illuminates when the vehicle is started, repeat the procedure.

PRECAUTIONS

Before servicing any vehicle, please be sure to read all of the following precautions, which deal with personal safety, prevention of component damage, and important points to take into consideration when servicing a motor vehicle:

• Never open, service or drain the radiator or cooling system when the engine is hot; serious burns can occur from the steam and hot coolant.

• Observe all applicable safety precautions when working around fuel. Whenever servicing the fuel system, always work in a well-ventilated area. Do not allow fuel spray or vapors to come in contact with a spark, open flame, or excessive heat (a hot drop light, for example). Keep a dry chemical fire extinguisher near the work area. Always keep fuel in a container specifically designed for fuel storage; also, always properly seal fuel containers to avoid the possibility of fire or explosion. Refer to the additional fuel system precautions later in this section.

• Fuel injection systems often remain pressurized, even after the engine has been turned **OFF**. The fuel system pressure must be relieved before disconnecting any fuel lines. Failure to do so may result in fire and/or personal injury.

• Brake fluid often contains polyglycol ethers and polyglycols. Avoid contact with the eyes and wash your hands thoroughly after handling brake fluid. If you do get brake fluid in your eyes, flush your eyes with clean, running water for 15 minutes. If eye irritation persists, or if you have taken brake fluid internally, IMMEDIATELY seek medical assistance.

• The EPA warns that prolonged contact with used engine oil may cause a number of skin disorders, including cancer. You should make every effort to minimize your exposure to used engine oil. Protective gloves should be worn when changing oil. Wash your hands and any other exposed skin areas as soon as possible after exposure to used engine oil. Soap and water, or waterless hand cleaner should be used.

• All new vehicles are now equipped with an air bag system, often referred to as a Supplemental Restraint System (SRS) or Supplemental Inflatable Restraint (SIR) system. The system must be disabled before performing service on or around system components, steering column, instrument panel components, wiring and sensors. Failure to follow safety and disabling procedures could result in accidental air bag deployment, possible personal injury and unnecessary system repairs.

• Always wear safety goggles when working with, or around, the air bag system. When carrying a non-deployed air bag, be sure the bag and trim cover are pointed away from your body. When placing a non-deployed air bag on a work surface, always face the bag and trim cover upward, away from the surface. This will reduce the motion of the module if it is accidentally deployed. Refer to the additional air bag system precautions later in this section.

• Clean, high quality brake fluid from a sealed container is essential to the safe and proper operation of the brake system. You should always buy the correct type of brake fluid for your vehicle. If the brake fluid becomes contaminated, completely flush the system with new fluid. Never reuse any brake fluid. Any brake fluid that is removed from the system should be discarded. Also, do not allow any brake fluid to come in contact with a painted surface; it will damage the paint.

• Never operate the engine without the proper amount and type of engine oil; doing so WILL result in severe engine damage.

• Timing belt maintenance is extremely important. Many models utilize an interference-type, non-freewheeling engine. If the timing belt breaks, the valves in the cylinder head may strike the pistons, causing potentially serious (also time-consuming and expensive) engine damage. Refer to the maintenance interval charts for the recommended replacement interval for the timing belt, and to the timing belt section for belt replacement and inspection.

• Disconnecting the negative battery cable on some vehicles may interfere with the functions of the on-board computer system(s) and may require the computer to undergo a relearning process once the negative battery cable is reconnected.

• When servicing drum brakes, only disassemble and assemble one side at a time, leaving the remaining side intact for reference.

• Only an MVAC-trained, EPA-certified automotive technician should service the air conditioning system or its components.

BRAKES

GENERAL INFORMATION

PRECAUTIONS

• Certain components within the ABS system are not intended to be serviced or repaired individually.

• Do not use rubber hoses or other parts not specifically specified for and ABS system. When using repair kits, replace all parts included in the kit. Partial or incorrect repair may lead to functional problems and require the replacement of components.

• Lubricate rubber parts with clean, fresh brake fluid to ease assembly. Do not use shop air to clean parts; damage to rubber components may result.

• Use only DOT 3 brake fluid from an unopened container.

• If any hydraulic component or line is removed or replaced, it may be necessary to bleed the entire system.

• A clean repair area is essential. Always clean the reservoir and cap thoroughly before removing the cap. The slightest amount of dirt in the fluid may plug an orifice and impair the system function. Perform repairs after components have been thoroughly cleaned; use only denatured alcohol to clean components. Do not allow ABS components to come into contact with any substance containing mineral oil; this includes used shop rags.

ANTI-LOCK BRAKE SYSTEM (ABS)

• The Anti-Lock control unit is a microprocessor similar to other computer units in the vehicle. Ensure that the ignition switch is **OFF** before removing or installing controller harnesses. Avoid static electricity discharge at or near the controller.

• If any arc welding is to be done on the vehicle, the control unit should be unplugged before welding operations begin.

WHEEL SPEED SENSORS

REMOVAL & INSTALLATION

Front

1. Remove the front rotor.
2. Remove the wheel speed sensor mounting bolt from the hub.

3. Remove the wheel speed sensor from the hub.

4. Remove the wiring from the clips and disconnect the electrical connector.

To install:

5. Install the wiring to the clips and Reconnect the electrical connector.

6. Install the wheel speed sensor to the hub.

7. Install the wheel speed sensor mounting bolt to the hub. Tighten the bolt to 16 ft. lbs. (21 Nm).

8. Install the front rotor and brake caliper assembly

Rear

1. Raise the vehicle on a hoist.

2. Disconnect the wheel speed sensor electrical connector.

3. Remove the mounting bolt from the sensor.

4. Remove the sensor from the brake caliper adapter.

To install:

5. Insert the wheel speed sensor in the brake caliper adapter.

6. Install the sensor mounting bolt and tighten to 17 ft. lbs. (24 Nm).

7. Reconnect the electrical wiring connector (3) to the sensor (4).

8. Lower the vehicle.

WHEEL SPEED SENSOR RINGS (TOOTHED RINGS)

REMOVAL & INSTALLATION

The "tone wheel" works in conjunction with the front wheel speed sensors as part of the ABS. There is one on each wheel.

The tone wheel is located on the hub/bearing , on the axle outer stub shaft or inside the hub/bearing housing, depending on model and equipment.

This component is not serviceable or removable and if damaged, the assembly of which it is a part must be replaced.

BRAKES

BLEEDING THE BRAKE SYSTEM

BLEEDING PROCEDURE

Manual Bleeding

Use Mopar® brake fluid, or an equivalent quality fluid meeting SAE J1703-F and DOT 3 standards only. Use fresh, clean fluid from a sealed container at all times.

1. Remove reservoir filler caps and fill reservoir.

2. If calipers were overhauled, open all caliper bleed screws. Then close each bleed screw as fluid starts to drip from it. Top off master cylinder reservoir once more before proceeding.

3. Attach one end of bleed hose to bleed screw and insert opposite end in glass container partially filled with brake fluid. Be sure end of bleed hose is immersed in fluid.

➡Bleed procedure should be in this order (1) Right rear (2) Left rear (3) Right front (4) Left front.

4. Open up bleeder, then have a helper press down the brake pedal. Once the pedal is down, hold the pedal down while closing the bleeder. Repeat bleeding until fluid

stream is clear and free of bubbles. Then move to the next wheel.

5. Before moving the vehicle verify the pedal is firm and not mushy.

6. Top off the brake fluid and install the reservoir cap.

Pressure Bleeding

Use Mopar® brake fluid, or an equivalent quality fluid meeting SAE J1703-F and DOT 3 standards only. Use fresh, clean fluid from a sealed container at all times.

Follow the manufacturer's instructions carefully when using pressure equipment. Do not exceed the tank manufacturers pressure recommendations. Generally, a tank pressure of 15-20 psi is sufficient for bleeding.

Fill the bleeder tank with recommended fluid and purge air from the tank lines before bleeding.

Do not pressure bleed without a proper master cylinder adapter. The wrong adapter can lead to leakage, or drawing air back into the system.

BLEEDING THE ABS SYSTEM

ABS system bleeding requires conventional bleeding methods plus use of a scan tool. The procedure involves performing a base brake bleeding, followed by use of the scan tool to cycle and bleed the HCU pump and solenoids. A second base brake bleeding procedure is then required to remove any air remaining in the system.

1. Perform base brake bleeding. Refer to Bleeding The Brake System.

2. Connect scan tool to the Data Link Connector.

3. Select ANTILOCK BRAKES, followed by MISCELLANEOUS, then ABS BRAKES. Follow the instructions displayed. When scan tool displays TEST COMPLETE, disconnect scan tool and proceed.

4. Perform base brake bleeding a second time. Refer to Bleeding The Brake System.

5. Top off master cylinder fluid level and verify proper brake operation before moving vehicle.

BRAKES

FRONT DISC BRAKES

❋❋ CAUTION

Dust and dirt accumulating on brake parts during normal use may contain asbestos fibers from production or aftermarket brake linings. Breathing excessive concentrations of asbestos fibers can cause serious bodily harm. Exercise care when servicing brake parts. Do not sand or grind brake lining unless equipment used is designed to contain the dust residue. Do not clean brake parts with compressed air or by dry brushing. Cleaning should be done by dampening the brake components with a fine mist of water, then wiping the brake components clean with a dampened cloth. Dispose of cloth and all residue containing asbestos fibers in an impermeable container with the appropriate label. Follow practices prescribed by the Occupational Safety and Health Administration (OSHA) and the Environmental Protection Agency (EPA) for the handling, processing, and disposing of dust or debris that may contain asbestos fibers.

BRAKE CALIPER

REMOVAL & INSTALLATION

See Figure 1.

1. Raise and support the vehicle.
2. Remove the tire and wheel assembly.
3. Compress the disc brake caliper.
4. Remove the banjo bolt and discard the copper washers.
5. Remove the caliper slide pin bolts.
6. Remove the disc brake caliper from the caliper adapter.
7. Remove the caliper slide pins from the adapter.

To install:

8. Clean slide pin bores thoroughly to remove any old grease.
9. Thoroughly coat the new slide pins on all working surfaces with Dow Corning-807® grease or equivalent.

❋❋ WARNING

Petroleum based grease should not be used on any of the rubber components of the caliper, Use only Non-Petroleum based grease.

10. Install the boot onto the slide pin and then insert into the adapter.

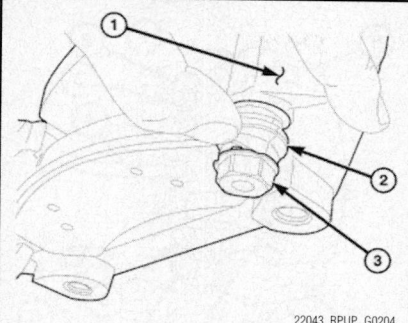

Fig. 1 Caliper adapter (1), boot (2), pin (3)

11. Push the pin all the way into the adapter and carefully expel the trapped air by gently pushing on the boot near the slide pin head.
12. Install the disc brake caliper to the brake caliper adapter.

➥ **Verify brake hose is not twisted or kinked before tightening fitting bolt.**

13. Install the banjo bolt with new copper washers to the caliper. Tighten to 21 ft. lbs. (28 Nm).
14. Install the caliper slide pin bolts. Tighten to 24 ft. lbs. (32 Nm).
15. Remove the prop rod.
16. Bleed the area of repair for the brake system.

➥ **If a proper pedal is not felt during bleeding an area of repair then a base bleed system must be performed.**

17. Install the tire and wheel assembly.
18. Lower the vehicle.

DISC BRAKE PADS

REMOVAL & INSTALLATION

See Figures 2 and 3.

1. Before servicing the vehicle, refer to the Precautions Section.
2. Raise and support vehicle.
3. Remove the wheel and tire assemblies.
4. Compress the caliper.
5. Remove the caliper slide pin bolts.
6. Remove the caliper from the caliper adapter.

❋❋ WARNING

Do not allow brake hose to support caliper assembly.

7. Support and hang the caliper.
8. Remove the inboard brake pad from the caliper adapter

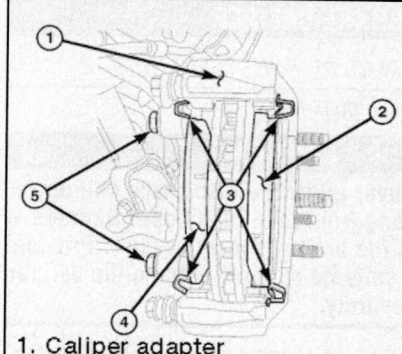

1. Caliper adapter
2. Outboard brake pad
3. Anti-rattle clips
4. Inboard brakepad
5. Caliper adapter mounting bolts

Fig. 2 Brake pad mounting shown

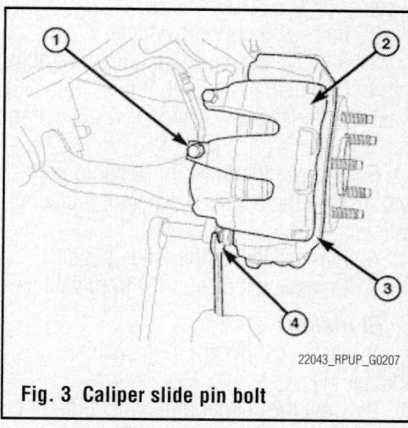

Fig. 3 Caliper slide pin bolt

9. Remove the outboard brake pad from the caliper adapter.
10. Remove the anti-rattle clips from the pad.

To install:

11. Bottom pistons in caliper bore with C-clamp. Place an old brake shoe between a C-clamp and caliper piston.
12. Clean caliper mounting adapter.
13. Install new anti-rattle clips to the brake pads.
14. Install inboard brake pad in adapter.
15. Install outboard brake pad in adapter.
16. Install the caliper over rotor, Then push the caliper onto the adapter.
17. Install the caliper slide pin bolts. tighten to 24 ft. lbs. (32 Nm).
18. Install wheel and tire assemblies and lower vehicle.
19. Apply brakes several times to seat caliper pistons and brake shoes and obtain firm pedal.
20. Top off master cylinder fluid level.

BRAKE CALIPER

REMOVAL & INSTALLATION

See Figure 4.

> ✳✳ **CAUTION**
>
> **Never allow the disc brake caliper to hang from the brake hose. Damage to the brake hose will result. Provide a suitable support to hang the caliper securely.**

1. Install prop rod on the brake pedal to keep pressure on the brake system, Holding pedal in this position will isolate master cylinder from hydraulic brake system and will not allow brake fluid to drain out of brake fluid reservoir while brake lines are open. This will allow you to bleed out the area of repair instead of the entire system.
2. Raise and support vehicle.
3. Remove the wheel and tire assembly.
4. Drain small amount of fluid from master cylinder brake reservoir with suction gun.
5. Remove the brake hose banjo bolt and discard the copper washers if replacing caliper.
6. Remove the caliper slide bolts (3).
7. Remove the caliper (6) from vehicle.

To install:
8. Install caliper (6) to the caliper adapter (1).
9. Coat the caliper mounting slide pin bolts (3) with silicone grease. Then install and tighten the bolts to 30 Nm (22 ft. lbs.).

> ✳✳ **CAUTION**
>
> **Verify that the brake hose is not twisted or kinked before tightening the fitting bolt.**

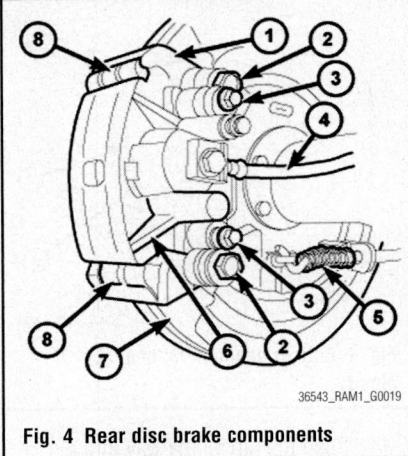

Fig. 4 Rear disc brake components

36543_RAM1_G0019

10. Install the brake hose banjo bolt if removed.
11. Install the brake hose (4) to the caliper (6) with new copper washers and tighten fitting bolt to 28 Nm (245 in. lbs.).
12. Remove the prop rod from the brake pedal.
13. Bleed the area of repair for the brake system. If a proper pedal is not felt during bleeding an area of repair then a base bleed system must be performed. Refer to BLEEDING THE BRAKE SYSTEM.
14. Install the wheel and tire assemblies.
15. Remove the supports and lower the vehicle.
16. Verify a firm pedal before moving the vehicle.

DISC BRAKE PADS

REMOVAL & INSTALLATION

See Figure 4.

1. Raise and support the vehicle.
2. Remove the rear wheel and tire assemblies.

3. Compress the caliper.
4. Remove caliper slide bolts.

➡ **Do not allow brake hose to support caliper assembly.**

5. Remove the caliper, by tilting the top out and off the caliper adapter.
6. Remove inboard brake shoe from the caliper adapter.
7. Remove outboard brake shoe from caliper adapter.

➡ **Anti-rattle springs are not interchangeable.**

8. Remove the top anti-rattle spring from the caliper adapter.
9. Remove the bottom anti-rattle spring from the caliper adapter.

To install:
10. Clean caliper mounting adapter and anti-rattle springs.
11. Lubricate anti-rattle springs with Mopar® brake grease.

➡ **Anti-rattle springs are not interchangeable.**

12. Install new top anti-rattle spring.
13. Install new bottom anti-rattle spring.
14. Install inboard brake shoe in adapter.
15. Install outboard brake shoe in adapter.
16. Tilt the bottom of the caliper over rotor and under adapter. Then push the top of the caliper down onto the adapter.
17. Install caliper. Refer to Brake Caliper.
18. Install wheel and tire assemblies.
19. Remove the supports and lower the vehicle.
20. Apply brakes several times to seat caliper pistons and brake shoes and obtain firm pedal.
21. Top off master cylinder fluid level.

BRAKES

PARKING BRAKE

PARKING BRAKE CABLES

ADJUSTMENT

See Figure 5.

➡Tensioner adjustment is only necessary when the tensioner, or a cable has been replaced or disconnected for service. When adjustment is necessary, perform adjustment only as described in the following procedure. This is necessary to avoid faulty park brake operation.

1. Raise the vehicle.
2. Back off the cable tensioner adjusting nut to create slack in the cables.
3. Remove the rear wheel/tire assemblies. Remove the brake rotors.
4. Verify the brakes are in good condition and operating properly.
5. Verify the park brake cables operate freely and are not binding, or seized.
6. Check the rear brake shoe adjustment with standard brake gauge. Refer to Adjustment.
7. Install the rotors. Verify that the rotors rotate freely without drag.
8. Install the wheel/tire assemblies.
9. Lower the vehicle enough for access to the park brake foot pedal. Then fully apply the park brakes.

➡Leave park brakes applied until adjustment is complete.

10. Raise the vehicle again.
11. Mark the tensioner rod 6.35 mm (1/4 in.) from edge of the tensioner.
12. Tighten the adjusting nut on the tensioner rod until the mark is no longer visible.

❋❋ CAUTION

Do not loosen, or tighten the tensioner adjusting nut for any reason after completing adjustment.

13. Lower the vehicle until the rear wheels are 15-20 cm (6-8 in.) off the shop floor.
14. Release the park brake foot pedal and verify that rear wheels rotate freely without drag. Then lower the vehicle.

PARKING BRAKE SHOES

REMOVAL & INSTALLATION

See Figures 6 through 8.

1. Remove the disc brake rotor.
2. Lockout the parking brake cable (2).
3. Disengage the park brake cable (2) from behind the rotor assembly to allow easier disassembly of the park brake shoes.
4. Remove the axleshaft. Refer to Rear Axle - 9 1/4.
5. Disassemble the rear park brake shoes (4).

To install:

➡**On a new vehicle or after parking brake lining replacement, it is recommended that the parking brake system be conditioned prior to use. This is**

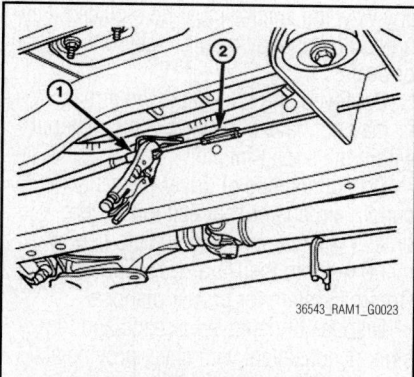

Fig. 6 Locking out parking brake cable

done by making one stop from 25 mph on dry pavement or concrete using light to moderate force on the parking brake foot pedal.

6. Reassemble the rear park brake shoes (4).
7. Install the axleshaft. Refer to Rear Axle - 9 1/4.
8. Install the park brake cable to the lever behind the support plate.
9. Unlock the park brake cable.
10. Install the disc brake rotor.
11. Adjust the rear brake shoes. Refer to Adjustment.
12. Install the tire and wheel assembly.
13. Remove the support and lower the vehicle.

ADJUSTMENT

Adjustment can be made with a standard brake gauge or with adjusting tool . Adjustment is performed with the complete brake assembly installed on the backing plate.

1. Be sure parking brake lever is fully released.
2. Raise vehicle so rear wheels can be rotated freely.
3. Remove plug from each access hole in brake support plates.
4. Loosen parking brake cable adjustment nut until there is slack in front cable.
5. Insert adjusting tool through support plate access hole and engage tool in teeth of adjusting screw star wheel.
6. Rotate adjuster screw star wheel (move tool handle upward) until slight drag can be felt when wheel is rotated.
7. Push and hold adjuster lever away from star wheel with thin screwdriver.

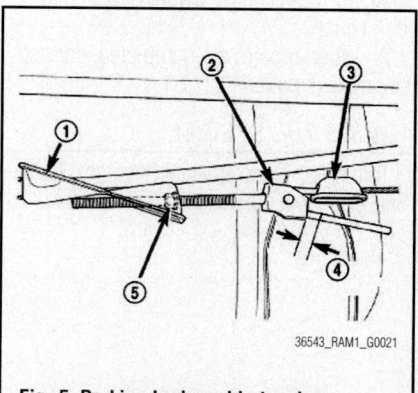

Fig. 5 Parking brake cable tensioner

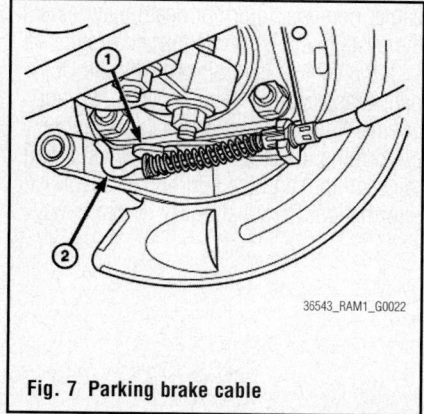

Fig. 7 Parking brake cable

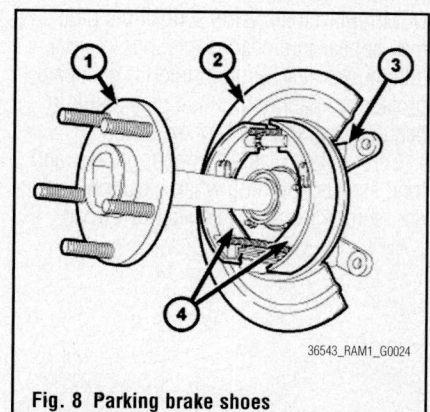

Fig. 8 Parking brake shoes

8. Back off adjuster screw star wheel until brake drag is eliminated.

9. Repeat adjustment at opposite wheel. Be sure adjustment is equal at both wheels.

10. Install support plate access hole plugs.

11. Adjust parking brake cable and lower vehicle.

12. Depress park brake pedal and make sure park brakes hold the vehicle stationary.

13. Release park brake pedal.

CHASSIS ELECTRICAL

AIR BAG (SUPPLEMENTAL RESTRAINT SYSTEM)

GENERAL INFORMATION

✴✴ CAUTION

Vehicles are equipped with an air bag system. The system must be disarmed before performing service on, or around, system components, the steering column, instrument panel components, wiring and sensors. Failure to follow the safety precautions and the disarming procedure could result in accidental air bag deployment, possible injury and unnecessary system repairs.

SERVICE PRECAUTIONS

Disconnect and isolate the battery negative cable before beginning any airbag system component diagnosis, testing, removal, or installation procedures. Allow system capacitor to discharge for two minutes before beginning any component service. This will disable the airbag system. Failure to disable the airbag system may result in accidental airbag deployment, personal injury, or death.

Do not place an intact undeployed airbag face down on a solid surface. The airbag will propel into the air if accidentally deployed and may result in personal injury or death.

When carrying or handling an undeployed airbag, the trim side (face) of the airbag should be pointing towards the body to minimize possibility of injury if accidental deployment occurs. Failure to do this may result in personal injury or death.

Replace airbag system components with OEM replacement parts. Substitute parts may appear interchangeable, but internal differences may result in inferior occupant protection. Failure to do so may result in occupant personal injury or death.

Wear safety glasses, rubber gloves, and long sleeved clothing when cleaning powder residue from vehicle after an airbag deployment. Powder residue emitted from a deployed airbag can cause skin irritation. Flush affected area with cool water if irritation is experienced. If nasal or throat irritation is experienced, exit the vehicle for fresh air until the irritation ceases. If irritation continues, see a physician.

Do not use a replacement airbag that is not in the original packaging. This may result in improper deployment, personal injury, or death.

The factory installed fasteners, screws and bolts used to fasten airbag components have a special coating and are specifically designed for the airbag system. Do not use substitute fasteners. Use only original equipment fasteners listed in the parts catalog when fastener replacement is required.

During, and following, any child restraint anchor service, due to impact event or vehicle repair, carefully inspect all mounting hardware, tether straps, and anchors for proper installation, operation, or damage. If a child restraint anchor is found damaged in any way, the anchor must be replaced. Failure to do this may result in personal injury or death.

Deployed and non-deployed airbags may or may not have live pyrotechnic material within the airbag inflator.

Do not dispose of driver/passenger/curtain airbags or seat belt tensioners unless you are sure of complete deployment. Refer to the Hazardous Substance Control System for proper disposal.

Dispose of deployed airbags and tensioners consistent with state, provincial, local, and federal regulations.

After any airbag component testing or service, do not connect the battery negative cable. Personal injury or death may result if the system test is not performed first.

If the vehicle is equipped with the Occupant Classification System (OCS), do not connect the battery negative cable before performing the OCS Verification Test using the scan tool and the appropriate diagnostic information. Personal injury or death may result if the system test is not performed properly.

Never replace both the Occupant Restraint Controller (ORC) and the Occupant Classification Module (OCM) at the same time. If both require replacement, replace one, then perform the Airbag System test before replacing the other.

Both the ORC and the OCM store Occupant Classification System (OCS) calibration data, which they transfer to one another when one of them is replaced. If both are replaced at the same time, an irreversible fault will be set in both modules and the OCS may malfunction and cause personal injury or death.

If equipped with OCS, the Seat Weight Sensor is a sensitive, calibrated unit and must be handled carefully. Do not drop or handle roughly. If dropped or damaged, replace with another sensor. Failure to do so may result in occupant injury or death.

If equipped with OCS, the front passenger seat must be handled carefully as well. When removing the seat, be careful when setting on floor not to drop. If dropped, the sensor may be inoperative, could result in occupant injury, or possibly death.

If equipped with OCS, when the passenger front seat is on the floor, no one should sit in the front passenger seat. This uneven force may damage the sensing ability of the seat weight sensors. If sat on and damaged, the sensor may be inoperative, could result in occupant injury, or possibly death.

DISARMING THE SYSTEM

1. Disconnect and isolate the negative battery cable. Wait 2 minutes for the system capacitor to discharge before performing any service.

2. When repairs are completed, connect the negative battery cable.

ARMING THE SYSTEM

To arm the Supplemental Restraint System (SRS), connect the negative battery cable.

DRIVE TRAIN

AUTOMATIC TRANSMISSION ASSEMBLY

REMOVAL & INSTALLATION

42RLE

1. Before servicing the vehicle, refer to the Precautions Section.
2. Disconnect the negative battery cable.
3. Raise and support the vehicle.
4. Remove any necessary skid plates.
5. Mark propeller shaft and axle companion flanges for assembly alignment.
6. Remove the rear propeller shaft.
7. Remove the front propeller shaft, if necessary.
8. Disconnect the input and output speed sensors.
9. Disconnect the transfer case shift motor and mode sensor assembly.
10. Disconnect the variable line pressure connector from the transmission, if equipped.
11. Disconnect the transmission range sensor.
12. Disconnect wires from the solenoid/pressure switch assembly.
13. Remove the bolts holding the exhaust crossover pipe to the pre—catalytic converter pipe flanges.
14. Remove the bolts holding the exhaust crossover pipe to the catalytic converter flange.
15. Disconnect gearshift cable from transmission manual valve lever.
16. Disengage the shift cable from the cable support bracket.
17. Remove the starter motor.
18. Remove the engine to transmission collar.
19. Rotate crankshaft in clockwise direction until converter bolts are accessible. Then remove bolts one at a time. Rotate crankshaft with socket wrench on dampener bolt.
20. Disconnect the transmission vent hose from the transmission.
21. Remove transfer case.
22. Support rear of engine with safety stand or jack.
23. Raise transmission slightly with service jack to relieve load on crossmember and supports.
24. Remove bolts securing rear support and cushion to transmission and crossmember.
25. Remove bolts attaching crossmember to frame and remove crossmember.

26. Disconnect transmission fluid cooler line sat transmission fittings and clips.
27. Remove all remaining converter housing bolts.
28. Carefully work transmission and torque converter assembly rearward off engine block dowels.
29. Hold torque converter in place during transmission removal.
30. Lower transmission and remove assembly from under the vehicle.
31. To remove torque converter, carefully slide torque converter out of the transmission.

To install:

→Check torque converter hub and hub drive flats for sharp edges burrs, scratches, or nicks. Polish the hub and flats with 320/400 grit paper and crocus cloth if necessary. The hub must be smooth to avoid damaging pump seal at installation.

32. If a replacement transmission is being installed, transfer any components necessary, such as the manual shift lever and shift cable bracket, from the original transmission onto the replacement transmission.
33. Lubricate oil pump seal lip with transmission fluid.
34. Align converter and oil pump.
35. Carefully insert converter in oil pump. Then rotate converter back and forth until fully seated in pump gears.
36. Check converter seating with steel scale and straightedge. Surface of converter lugs should be at least ½ inch (13mm) to rear of straightedge when converter is fully seated.
37. Temporarily secure converter with C-clamp.
38. Position transmission on jack and secure it with chains.
39. Check condition of converter driveplate. Replace the plate if cracked, distorted or damaged. Also be sure transmission dowel pins are seated in engine block and protrude far enough to hold transmission in alignment.
40. Apply a light coating of Mopar® High Temp Grease to the torque converter hub pocket in the rear pocket of the engine's crankshaft.
41. Raise transmission and align the torque converter with the drive plate and transmission converter housing with the engine block.
42. Move transmission forward. Then

raise, lower or tilt transmission to align the converter housing with engine block dowels.

43. Carefully work transmission forward and over engine block dowels until converter hub is seated in crankshaft. Verify that no wires, or the transmission vent hose, have become trapped between the engine block and the transmission.
44. Install two bolts to attach the transmission to the engine.
45. Install remaining torque converter housing to engine bolts. Tighten to 50 ft. lbs. (68 Nm).
46. Install transfer case, if equipped.
47. Install rear transmission crossmember. Tighten crossmember to frame bolts to 50 ft. lbs. (68 Nm).
48. Install rear support to transmission. Tighten bolts to 35 ft. lbs. (47 Nm).
49. Lower transmission onto crossmember and install bolts attaching transmission mount to crossmember. Tighten clevis bracket to crossmember bolts to 35 ft. lbs. (47 Nm). Tighten the clevis bracket to rear support bolt to 50 ft. lbs. (68 Nm).
50. Connect gearshift cable to support bracket and transmission manual lever.
51. Connect the input and output speed sensor and the transmission range sensor.
52. Connect the variable line pressure connector, if equipped.
53. Connect wires to the solenoid/pressure switch assembly.

✷✷ WARNING

It is essential that correct length bolts be used to attach the converter to the driveplate. Bolts that are too long will damage the clutch surface inside the converter.

54. Install torque converter-to-driveplate bolts. Tighten bolts to 65 inch lbs. (88 Nm).
55. Install starter motor and cooler line bracket.
56. Connect cooler lines to transmission.
57. Install transmission fill tube.
58. Install exhaust components.
59. Align and connect propeller shaft(s).
60. Adjust gearshift cable if necessary.
61. Install any skid plates removed previously.
62. Lower the vehicle.
63. Connect the negative battery cable.
64. Fill transmission with Mopar® ATF +4, Automatic Transmission Fluid.

45RFE/545RFE

1. Before servicing the vehicle, refer to the Precautions Section.
2. Disconnect the negative battery cable.
3. Raise and support the vehicle.
4. Remove any necessary skid plates.
5. Mark propeller shaft and axle companion flanges for assembly alignment.
6. Remove the rear propeller shaft.
7. Remove the front propeller shaft, if necessary.
8. Remove the engine to transmission structural dust cover.
9. Remove the exhaust support bracket from the rear of the transmission.
10. Disconnect and lower or remove any necessary exhaust components.
11. Remove the starter motor.
12. Rotate crankshaft in clockwise direction until converter bolts are accessible. Then remove bolts one at a time. Rotate crankshaft with socket wrench on dampener bolt.
13. Disengage the output speed sensor connector from the output speed sensor.
14. Disengage the input speed sensor connector from the input speed sensor.
15. Disengage the transmission solenoid/TRS assembly connector from the transmission solenoid/TRS assembly.
16. Disengage the line pressure sensor connector from the line pressure sensor.
17. Disconnect gearshift cable from transmission manual valve lever.
18. Disconnect the transmission vent hose from the transmission.
19. Support rear of engine with safety stand or jack.
20. Raise transmission slightly with service jack to relieve load on crossmember and supports.
21. Remove bolts securing rear support and cushion to transmission and crossmember.
22. Remove transfer case, if necessary.
23. Disconnect transmission fluid cooler lines at transmission fittings and clips.
24. Remove all remaining converter housing bolts.
25. Carefully work transmission and torque converter assembly rearward off engine block dowels.
26. Hold torque converter in place during transmission removal.
27. Lower transmission and remove assembly from under the vehicle.
28. To remove torque converter, carefully slide torque converter out of the transmission.

To install:

29. Check torque converter hub and hub drive flats for sharp edges burrs, scratches, or nicks. Polish the hub and flats with 320/400 grit paper and crocus cloth if necessary. Verify that the converter hub o-ring is properly installed and is free of any debris. The hub must be smooth to avoid damaging pump seal at installation.
30. If a replacement transmission is being installed, transfer any components necessary, such as the manual shift lever and shift cable bracket, from the original transmission onto the replacement transmission.
31. Lubricate oil pump seal lip with transmission fluid.
32. Align converter and oil pump.
33. Carefully insert converter in oil pump. Then rotate converter back and forth until fully seated in pump gears.
34. Check converter seating with steel scale and straightedge. Surface of converter lugs should be at least ½ inch (13mm) to rear of straightedge when converter is fully seated.
35. Temporarily secure converter with C-clamp.
36. Position transmission on jack and secure it with chains.
37. Check condition of converter driveplate. Replace the plate if cracked, distorted or damaged. Also be sure transmission dowel pins are seated in engine block and protrude far enough to hold transmission in alignment.
38. Apply a light coating of Mopar® High Temp Grease to the torque converter hub pocket in the rear pocket of the engine's crankshaft.
39. Raise transmission and align the torque converter with the drive plate and transmission converter housing with the engine block.
40. Move transmission forward. Then raise, lower or tilt transmission to align the converter housing with engine block dowels.
41. Carefully work transmission forward and over engine block dowels until converter hub is seated in crankshaft. Verify that no wires, or the transmission vent hose, have become trapped between the engine block and the transmission.
42. Install two bolts to attach the transmission to the engine.
43. Install remaining torque converter housing to engine bolts. Tighten to 50 ft. lbs. 50 ft. lbs (68 Nm).
44. Install transfer case, if equipped. Tighten transfer case nuts to 26 ft. lbs. (35 Nm).

45. Install rear support to transmission. Tighten bolts to 35 ft. lbs. (47 Nm).
46. Lower transmission onto crossmember and install bolts attaching transmission mount to crossmember. Tighten clevis bracket to crossmember bolts to 35 ft. lbs. (47 Nm). Tighten the clevis bracket to rear support bolt to 50 ft. lbs. (68 Nm).
47. Remove engine support fixture.
48. Connect gearshift cable to transmission.
49. Connect wires to solenoid and pressure switch assembly connector.
50. Connect wires to input and output speed sensors.
51. Connect wires to line pressure sensor.

➡ **Be sure transmission harnesses are properly routed.**

❋❋ WARNING

It is essential that correct length bolts be used to attach the converter to the driveplate. Bolts that are too long will damage the clutch surface inside the converter.

52. Install torque converter-to-driveplate bolts. Tighten bolts to 270 inch lbs. (31 Nm).
53. Install starter motor and cooler line bracket.
54. Connect cooler lines to transmission.
55. Install transmission fill tube.
56. Install exhaust components, if necessary.
57. Install the structural dust cover onto the transmission and the engine.
58. Align and connect propeller shaft(s).
59. Adjust gearshift cable if necessary.
60. Install any skid plates removed previously.
61. Lower vehicle.
62. Fill transmission with Mopar® ATF +4, Automatic Transmission Fluid.

TRANSFER CASE ASSEMBLY

REMOVAL & INSTALLATION

NV243

See Figures 9 and 10.

1. Shift transfer case into 2WD.
2. Raise vehicle.
3. Drain transfer case lubricant.
4. Remove the transfer case skid plate, if equipped.
5. Support transmission with jack stand.
6. Remove crossmember and transmission mount.

7. Mark front and rear propeller shafts for alignment reference.

8. Remove front and rear propeller shafts.

9. Disconnect transfer case shift motor and mode sensor wire connectors.

10. Disconnect transfer case vent hose.

11. Support transfer case with transmission jack.

12. Secure transfer case to jack with chains.

13. Remove nuts attaching transfer case to transmission.

14. Pull transfer case and jack rearward to disengage transfer case.

15. Remove transfer case from under vehicle.

To install:

16. Mount transfer case on a transmission jack.

17. Secure transfer case to jack with chains.

18. Position transfer case under vehicle.

19. Align transfer case and transmission shafts and install transfer case onto the transmission.

20. Install and tighten transfer case attaching nuts to 20–25 ft. lbs. (27–34 Nm) torque.

21. Connect the vent hose.

22. Connect the shift motor and mode sensor wiring connectors. Secure wire harness to clips on transfer case.

23. Align and connect the propeller shafts.

➡**The fill and drain plugs are both in the rear case.**

24. Install drain plug. Tighten plug to 15–25 ft. lbs. (20–34 Nm).

25. Fill transfer case to bottom edge of fill plug opening with Mopar® ATF +4, Automatic Transmission fluid.

26. Install and tighten fill plug to 15–25 ft. lbs. (20–34 Nm).

27. Install skid plate, if equipped.

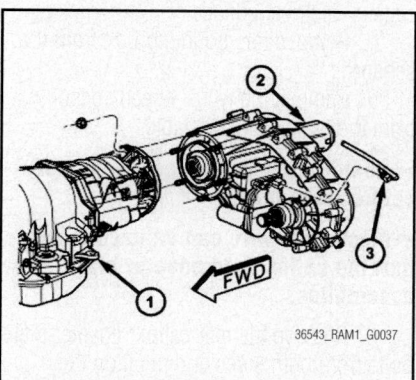

Fig. 9 Transfer case—NV243

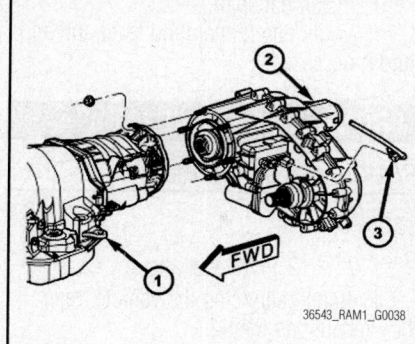

Fig. 10 Transfer case—NV246

28. Remove transmission jack and support stand.

29. Lower vehicle and verify transfer case shift operation.

NV246

1. Raise vehicle.

2. Drain transfer case lubricant.

3. Mark front and rear propeller shafts for alignment reference.

4. Support transmission with jack stand.

5. Remove the transfer case skid plate, if equipped.

6. Disconnect front and rear propeller shafts at transfer case.

7. Disconnect transfer case shift motor and mode sensor wire connectors, front output speed sensor, and rear output speed sensor wire connectors.

8. Disconnect transfer case vent hose.

9. Support transfer case with transmission jack.

10. Secure transfer case to jack with chains.

11. Remove nuts attaching transfer case to transmission.

12. Pull transfer case and jack rearward to disengage transfer case.

13. Remove transfer case from under vehicle.

To install:

✳✳ CAUTION

Make sure that a new transfer case isolator gasket is installed between the transfer case and transmission before installation. Failure to install an isolator gasket could lead to a severe corrosion issue.

14. Mount transfer case on a transmission jack.

15. Secure transfer case to jack with chains.

16. Position transfer case under vehicle.

17. Align transfer case and transmission shafts and install transfer case onto the transmission.

18. Install and tighten transfer case attaching nuts to 20–25 ft. lbs. (27–34 Nm) torque.

19. Connect the vent hose.

20. Connect the shift motor and mode sensor wiring connectors. Secure wire harness to clips on transfer case.

21. Connect the front and rear output speed sensor wire connectors.

22. Align and connect the propeller shafts.

➡**The fill and drain plugs are both in the rear case.**

23. Install drain plug. Tighten plug to 20 ft. lbs. (27 Nm).

24. Fill transfer case to bottom edge of fill plug opening with Mopar® NVG 246 Automatic Transmission Fluid or equivalent.

25. Install and tighten fill plug to 20 ft. lbs. (27 Nm).

26. Install skid plate, if equipped.

27. Remove transmission jack and support stand.

28. Lower vehicle and verify transfer case shift operation.

FRONT AXLE SHAFT, BEARING & SEAL

REMOVAL & INSTALLATION

C205FD

See Figures 11 through 14.

1. Before servicing the vehicle, refer to the Precautions Section.

2. Remove halfshaft from vehicle.

3. Clean axle seal area.

4. Remove O-ring and snap ring from axle shaft.

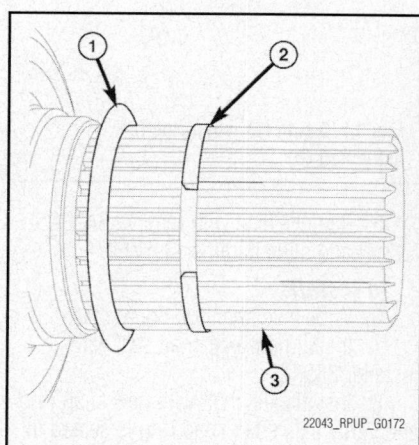

Fig. 11 O-ring (1), snap ring (2), axle shaft (3)

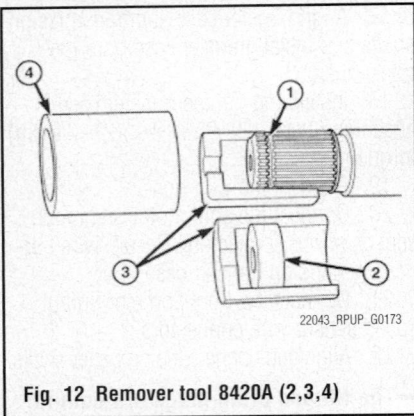

Fig. 12 Remover tool 8420A (2,3,4)

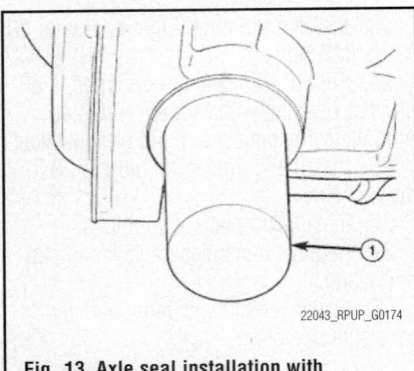

Fig. 13 Axle seal installation with tool 8694

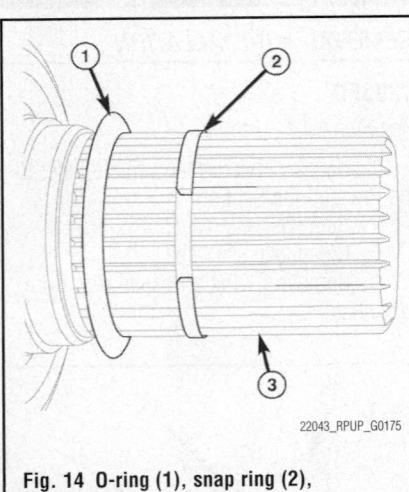

Fig. 14 O-ring (1), snap ring (2), axle shaft (3)

5. Remove axle with remove 8420A (2,3,4) and slide hammer C-3752.

To install:

6. Wipe axle shaft tube bore clean.
7. Install new axle shaft seal with installer 8694.
8. Install axle shaft with new snap ring and verify axle shaft snap ring is seated in side gear.
9. Install O-ring and snap ring on axle shaft.

10. Install halfshaft.
11. Verify differential fluid level and add fluid if necessary.

FRONT PINION SEAL

REMOVAL & INSTALLATION

C205FD

See Figure 15.

1. Before servicing the vehicle, refer to the Precautions Section.
2. With axle in **2WD** remove front propeller shaft and left halfshaft.
3. Rotate pinion gear three or four times and verify pinion rotates smoothly.
4. Record pinion torque to rotate with an inch pound torque wrench, for installation reference.
5. Position Holder 6719 against the companion flange and install a four bolts and washers into the threaded holes and tighten the bolts.
6. Remove pinion nut.
7. Mark a line across the pinion shaft and flange for installation reference.
8. Remove the companion flange with Remover C-452.
9. Remove pinion seal with a seal puller.

To install:

10. Apply a light coating of gear lubricant on the lip of pinion seal
11. Install seal with Installer 8695 and Handle C-4171.
12. Install flange on the pinion shaft with the reference marks aligned.
13. Install companion flange onto the pinion with Installer C-3718 and Holder 6719A.
14. Position holder against the companion flange and install four bolts and washers into the threaded holes. Tighten the bolt and

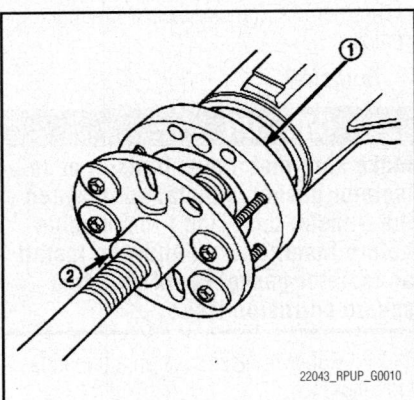

Fig. 15 Pinion flange (1) removal with C—452 (2)

washer so that the holder is held to the flange.
15. Install a new pinion nut onto the pinion shaft and tighten the pinion nut until there is zero bearing end-play

✱✱ WARNING

Do not exceed 200 ft. lbs. (271 Nm) the minimum tightening torque when installing the companion flange at this point. Never loosen pinion nut to decrease pinion bearing rotating torque and never exceed specified preload torque. Failure to follow these instructions will damage the axle.

16. Measure pinion Torque To Rotate with an inch pound torque wrench. Pinion Torque To Rotate should be equal to recorded reading plus an additional 5 inch. lbs. (0.56 Nm).
17. If rotating torque is low, tighten the pinion nut in 5 ft. lbs. (6.8 Nm) increments until pinion Torque To Rotate is achieved.

✱✱ WARNING

If maximum tightening torque 350 ft. lbs. (475 Nm) is reached prior to reaching the required rotating torque, the collapsible spacer may have been damaged. Failure to follow these instructions will damage the axle.

18. Install the propeller shaft and the left halfshaft.
19. Check the fluid level and add as needed.

REAR AXLE HOUSING

REMOVAL & INSTALLATION

9¼ Axle

1. With vehicle in neutral, position vehicle on hoist.
2. Remove the rear wheels.
3. Disconnect the rear wheel speed sensor electrical connector.
4. Remove the mounting bolt from the sensor.
5. Remove the wheel speed sensor from the brake caliper adapter.

➡ **Do not allow brake hose to support caliper assembly.**

➡ **Mechanics wire can be used to support the caliper and adapter plate assemblies.**

6. Remove the rear caliper adapter plate bolts from both sides and position the calipers aside.

7. Disconnect the axle vent hose from the axle.

8. Remove the rear drive shaft.

9. Pull the park brake cable spring back.

➡**A 13mm line wrench can be used to compress the cable tabs. Insert while spring is pulled back and rotate the wrench to compress the tabs.**

10. Compress the cable tabs on each cable end fitting at the brake cable support plate.

11. Remove the park brake cable from the brake cable support plate.

12. Remove the upper park brake cable bolt from the rear axle.

13. Remove the park brake bolt on the upper control arm bracket.

14. Position the park brake cable away from the rear axle.

15. Remove the stabilizer bar bolts and position the stabilizer bar aside.

16. Position a lift under the axle and secure the axle to the lift.

17. Remove both lower shock absorber bolts and position the shock absorbers away from the axle.

18. Remove the track bar bolt and position the track bar away from the rear axle.

19. Remove both the upper control arm to rear axle bolts and position the upper control arms away from the axle.

20. Remove both the lower control arm to rear axle bolts and position the lower control arms away from the axle.

21. Slightly lower the rear axle assembly and remove the rear springs.

22. Remove the rear axle from the vehicle.

To install:

➡**All suspension torques should be made with the full vehicle weight on the ground being supported by the tires.**

23. Position the spring and isolator on the axle and align into the spring upper pocket.

24. Carefully raise the rear axle into place.

25. Position both the lower control arms into the rear axle brackets and loosely install the bolts.

26. Position both the upper control arms into the rear axle brackets and loosely install the bolts.

27. Position the rear track bar to the rear axle bracket and loosely install the bolt.

28. Position both the rear shock absorbers to the axle brackets and loosely install the rear shock absorber bolts.

29. Remove the axle lift.

➡**The stabilizer bar must be centered with equal spacing on both sides.**

30. Position the stabilizer bar to the rear axle and install and tighten the bolts to 65 Nm (48 ft. lbs.).

31. Position the park brake cable back to the rear axle.

32. Install the park brake cable bolt on the upper control arm bracket and tighten to 22 Nm (16 ft. lbs.).

33. Install the upper park brake cable bolt to the rear axle and tighten to 22 Nm (16 ft. lbs.).

34. Install the rear cable into the tensioner rods behind the rear of the brake assemblies.

35. Pull the park brake cable springs back until the cable end fitting tabs lock into place.

➡**Pull on the cable to ensure that it is locked into place.**

36. Install the rear drive shaft.

37. Connect the axle vent hose to the axle.

38. Position the calipers back onto the brake rotors and install and tighten the adapter plate bolts to 135 Nm (100 ft. lbs).

39. Position the rear wheel speed sensors to the brake caliper adapters.

40. Install the mounting bolts to the wheel speed sensor and tighten to 24 Nm (18 ft. lbs).

41. Connect the rear wheel speed sensor electrical connectors.

42. Install the rear wheels.

43. Lower the vehicle.

44. Tighten the upper and lower control arm to 300 Nm (221 ft. lbs.).

45. Tighten the track bar mounting bolt to 155 Nm (114.5 ft. lbs.).

46. Tighten shock bolt to 100 ft. lbs. (136 Nm).

REAR AXLE SHAFT, BEARING & SEAL

REMOVAL & INSTALLATION

9¼ Axle

Shaft

See Figure 16.

1. With vehicle in neutral, position vehicle on hoist.

2. Remove wheel and tire assembly.

3. Remove brake caliper (3), adapter and rotor (1).

4. Remove differential housing cover and drain lubricant.

5. Rotate differential case so pinion

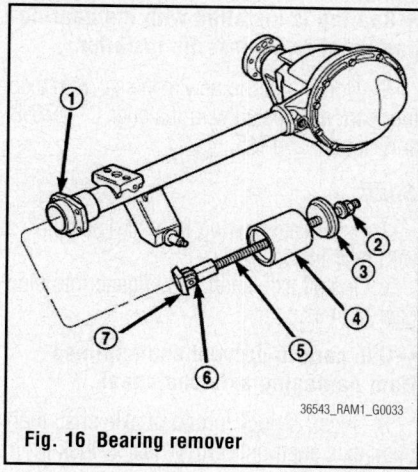

Fig. 16 Bearing remover

mate shaft lock screw is accessible. Remove lock screw and pinion mate shaft from differential case.

6. Push axle shaft inward and remove C-lock from the axle shaft.

7. Remove axle shaft carefully to prevent damage to the shaft bearing and seal in the axle tube.

Bearing & Seal

1. Remove axle shaft seal from axle tube with a small pry bar.

➡**The seal and bearing can be removed at the same time with the bearing removal tool.**

2. Remove axle shaft bearing with Bearing Remover 6310 (4) (5) and Foot 6310-9 (7).

To install:

Bearing & Seal

See Figure 17.

1. Wipe axle tube bore clean and remove any old sealer or burrs from the tube.

2. Install axle shaft bearing with Installer C-4198 and Handle C-4171. Drive bearing in until tool contacts the axle tube.

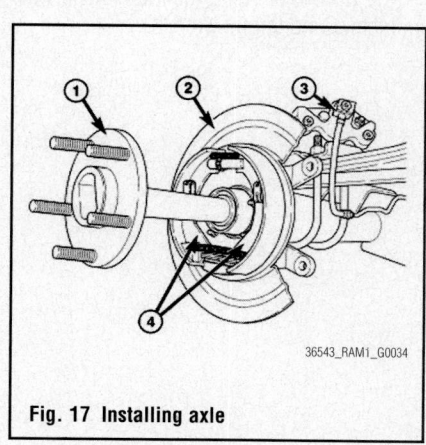

Fig. 17 Installing axle

→Bearing is installed with the bearing part number against the installer.

3. Coat lip of the new axle seal with axle lubricant and install with Installer C-4076-B and Handle C-4735.

Shaft

1. Lubricate bearing bore and seal lip with gear lubricant.
2. Install axle shaft and engage into side gear splines.

→Use care to prevent shaft splines from damaging axle shaft seal.

3. Insert C-lock in end of axle shaft then push axle shaft outward to seat C-lock in side gear (3).
4. Insert pinion shaft into differential case and through thrust washers and differential pinions.
5. Align hole in pinion mate shaft with hole in the differential case and install lock screw with Loctite® on the threads. Tighten lock screw to 11 Nm (8 ft. lbs.).
6. Install differential cover and fill with gear lubricant to the bottom of the fill plug hole.
7. Install brake rotor, caliper adapter and caliper.
8. Install wheel and tire.

REAR PINION SEAL

REMOVAL & INSTALLATION

9¼ Axle

See Figures 18 and 19.

1. Mark universal joint, companion flange and pinion shaft for installation reference.
2. Remove propeller shaft from the companion flange.
3. Remove the brake rotors to prevent any drag.
4. Rotate companion flange three or four times.
5. Record pinion torque to rotating with an inch pound torque wrench.

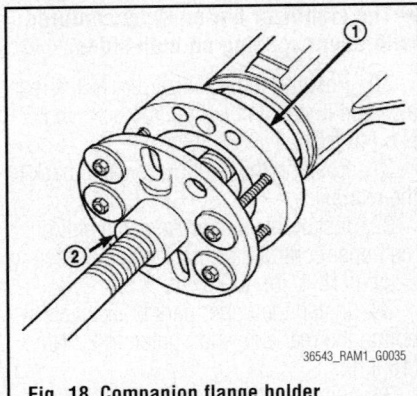

Fig. 18 Companion flange holder

6. Install two bolts into the companion flange threaded holes, 180° apart. Position Holder 6719A against the companion flange and install and tighten two bolts and washers into the remaining holes.
7. Hold the companion flange with Holder 6719A and remove pinion nut and washer.
8. Mark a line across the pinion shaft and flange for installation reference.
9. Remove companion flange with Puller C-452.
10. Remove pinion seal with seal puller or slide-hammer mounted screw.

To install:

11. Apply a light coating of gear lubricant on the lip of pinion seal.
12. Install new pinion seal (3) with Handle C-4735 and Installer C-4076-B (1).
13. Install flange on the pinion shaft with the reference marks aligned.
14. Install two bolts into the threaded holes in the companion flange, 180° apart.
15. Position Holder 6719A (2) against the companion flange and install a bolt and washer into one of the remaining threaded holes. Tighten the bolts so holder is held to the flange.
16. Install companion flange on pinion shaft with Installer C-3718 and Holder 6719A.
17. Install pinion washer and a new pinion

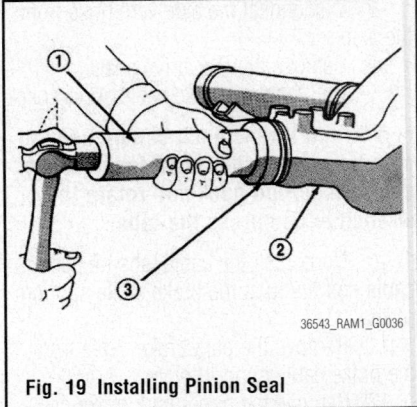

Fig. 19 Installing Pinion Seal

nut. The convex side of the washer must face outward.
18. Hold companion flange with Holder 6719A (2) and tighten pinion nut with a torque wrench (3) to 285 Nm (210 ft. lbs.).

→Do not exceed the minimum torque 285 Nm (210 ft. lbs.) when installing the pinion nut at this point.

19. Rotate pinion several times to ensure pinion bearings are seated.
20. Measure pinion torque to rotate (1) with an inch pound torque wrench (2). Pinion torque to rotate should be equal to recorded reading plus an additional 0.56 Nm (5 in. lbs.). If pinion torque to rotate is low, tighten pinion nut in 6.8 Nm (5 ft. lbs.) increments until pinion torque to rotating is achieved.

✳✳ CAUTION

Never loosen pinion nut to decrease pinion bearing rotating torque. If pinion torque to rotating is exceeded, a new collapsible spacer must be installed. Failure to follow these instructions will result in damage to the axle.

21. Install propeller shaft.
22. Install rear brake rotors components.

ENGINE COOLING

ENGINE FAN

REMOVAL & INSTALLATION

Viscous

See Figure 20.

> ❈❈ **WARNING**
>
> **If the viscous fan drive is replaced because of mechanical damage, the cooling fan blades should also be inspected. Inspect for fatigue cracks, loose blades, or loose rivets that could have resulted from excessive vibration. Replace fan blade assembly if any of these conditions are found. Also inspect water pump bearing and shaft assembly for any related damage due to a viscous fan drive malfunction.**

1. Before servicing the vehicle, refer to the Precautions Section.
2. Disconnect negative battery cable from battery.
3. Remove coolant reserve/overflow container from fan shroud and lay aside. **Do Not** disconnect the hoses or drain coolant from the container.
4. The thermal viscous fan drive/fan blade assembly is attached (threaded) to the water pump hub shaft . Remove the fan blade/viscous fan drive assembly from the water pump by turning the mounting nut counterclockwise as viewed from the front. Threads on the viscous fan drive are **RIGHT-HAND** A 36 MM fan wrench should be used to prevent pulley from rotating.

➥**Do Not unbolt the fan blade assembly from viscous fan drive at this time.**

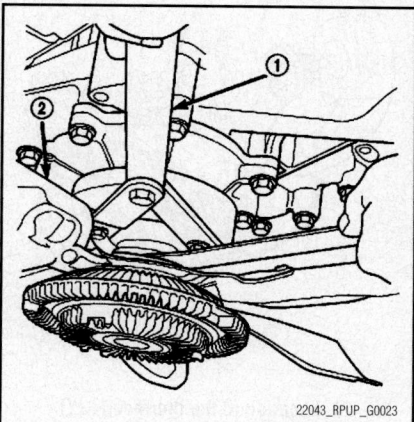

Fig. 20 Viscous fan drive assembly removal

22043_RPUP_G0023

5. Remove the fan shroud-to-radiator mounting bolts.
6. Pull the lower shroud mounts out of the radiator tank clips.
7. Remove the fan shroud and fan blade/viscous fan drive assembly as a complete unit from vehicle.
8. After removing the fan blade/viscous fan drive assembly, **do not** place the viscous fan drive in a horizontal position. If stored horizontally, silicone fluid in the viscous fan drive could drain into its bearing assembly and contaminate lubricant.

> ❈❈ **WARNING**
>
> **Do not remove water pump pulley-to-water pump bolts. This pulley is under spring tension**

9. Remove four bolts securing fan blade assembly to viscous fan drive .

> ❈❈ **WARNING**
>
> **Some engines equipped with serpentine drive belts have reverse rotating fans and viscous fan drives. They are marked with the word REVERSE to designate their usage. Installation of the wrong fan or viscous fan drive can result in engine overheating.**

To install:

➥**Viscous Fan Drive Fluid Pump Out Requirement: After installing a new viscous fan drive, bring the engine speed up to approximately 2000 rpm and hold for approximately two minutes. This will ensure proper fluid distribution within the drive.**

10. Install fan blade assembly to the viscous fan drive. Tighten the bolts to 18 ft. lbs. (24 Nm).
11. Position the fan shroud and the fan blade/viscous fan drive assembly to the vehicle as a complete unit.
12. Install the fan shroud.
13. Install the fan blade/viscous fan drive assembly to the water pump shaft . Tighten mounting nut to 37 ft. lbs. (50 Nm).
14. Install the coolant reserve/overflow container to the fan shroud.
15. Connect the negative battery cable.

Electric

See Figure 21.

1. Disconnect and isolate the negative battery cable.
2. Remove the upper radiator seal push pins.

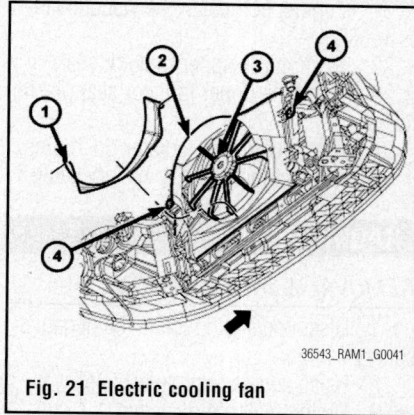

Fig. 21 Electric cooling fan

36543_RAM1_G0041

3. Remove the upper radiator seal plastic rivets.
4. Remove the upper radiator seal.
5. If equipped, remove the viscous fan assembly from the water pump hub shaft.
6. Disconnect the radiator fan electrical connector.
7. Remove the fan shroud to radiator mounting bolts .
8. Disengage the fan shroud's lower retaining clips and position the fan shroud towards the rear of vehicle.
9. Disengage the electric cooling fan to radiator upper retaining clips.
10. Disengage the electric fan to radiator lower retaining clips.
11. Pulling upward remove the viscous fan, radiator fan shroud and the electric cooling fan as an assembly.
12. The lower fan shroud can be removed from the upper fan shroud if needed.
13. If damaged, remove radiator fan resistor from shroud.

To install:

14. If removed, install the electric cooling fan resistor. Tighten the mounting screw securely.
15. If removed, install the lower fan shroud to the upper fan shroud.
16. Position the viscous fan (if equipped), radiator fan shroud and electric cooling fan into the vehicle as an assembly.
17. Install the electric cooling fan by engaging the electric cooling fan's upper and lower retaining clips to the radiator.
18. Install the fan shroud by engaging the fan shroud's lower retaining clips to the radiator/electric cooling fan

➥**Make sure all retaining clips lock into place.**

19. Install the fan shroud mounting bolts. Tighten to 89 inch lbs. (10 Nm).

20. Connect the electric cooling fan electrical connector.

21. If equipped, install the viscous fan assembly.

22. Position the upper radiator seal.

23. Install the upper radiator seal plastic rivets.

24. Install the upper radiator push pins.

25. Connect the negative battery cable.

RADIATOR

REMOVAL & INSTALLATION

1. Disconnect and isolate the negative battery cable.

2. Raise and secure the vehicle.

3. Drain the cooling system.

✳✳ WARNING

Do not remove the cylinder block drain plugs or loosen the radiator draincock with the system hot and under pressure. Serious burns from the coolant can occur.

4. Remove the lower radiator clamp and hose.

5. Remove the lower radiator seal.

6. Remove the lower center electric fan to radiator retaining clip.

7. Lower the vehicle.

8. Remove the upper radiator clamp and hose.

9. Remove the upper radiator seal push pins.

10. Remove the upper radiator seal plastic rivets.

11. Remove the upper radiator seal.

12. If equipped, remove the viscous fan assembly from the water pump hub shaft. Refer to Engine Fan.

13. Remove the grille.

14. Remove the bolt from the transmission cooler line to radiator bracket.

15. Remove the washer reserve tank.

16. Remove the coolant overflow/recovery bottle.

17. Remove the front bolts from the A/C compressor/transmission combination cooler.

18. Remove the upper center electric fan to radiator retaining clip.

19. Disconnect the transmission cooler lines from the transmission cooler, then plug the transmission lines and cooler to prevent leakage.

20. Disengage the two A/C compressor/transmission combination cooler mounting brackets from the left side of the radiator, do not disconnect the A/C lines. After the A/C compressor/transmission

combination cooler is disengaged, secure it to the upper radiator support with a strap, cord or equivalent.

21. Remove the fan shroud mounting bolts and pull up and out of the radiator tank clips. Position the shroud rearward over the fan blades towards engine.

22. Disengage the electric cooling fan to radiator upper retaining clips.

23. Disengage the electric fan to radiator lower retaining clips.

24. Remove the viscous fan, fan shroud and electric cooling fan as an assembly.

25. Remove the two radiator upper mounting bolts.

26. Lift the radiator straight up and out of the engine compartment. Take care not to damage cooling fins or tubes on the radiator and oil coolers when removing.

To install:

27. Position the radiator into the engine compartment. Take care not to damage cooling fins or tubes on the radiator and oil coolers when installing.

28. Install the rubber insulators to the lower radiator mounting features (alignment dowel and support bracket at the lower part of the radiator).

29. Install the two radiator upper mounting bolts. Tighten the bolts to 71 inch lbs. (8 Nm).

30. Install the electric cooling fan. Refer to Engine Fan.

31. Install the fan shroud by engaging the fan shroud's lower retaining clips to the radiator/electric cooling fan.

32. Install the fan shroud to radiator lower center retaining clip.

33. Install the fan shroud mounting bolts. Tighten to 89 inch lbs. (10 Nm).

34. Install the fan shroud to radiator upper center retaining clip.

➡**Make sure all retaining clips lock into place.**

35. Connect the electric cooling fan electrical connector.

36. Engage the two A/C compressor/transmission combination cooler mounting brackets to the left side of the radiator.

37. Connect the transmission cooler lines to the transmission cooler.

38. Install the two bolts that secure the A/C condenser to the right side of the radiator. Tighten the bolts to 2.2 Nm (20 in. lbs.).

39. Install the bolt securing the transmission cooler line to radiator bracket. Tighten the bolt securely.

40. Install the coolant overflow/recovery bottle.

41. Install the windshield washer reserve tank.

42. Install the front grille.

43. If equipped, install the viscous fan. Refer to Engine Fan.

44. Connect the upper radiator hose and install the clamp in its proper position.

45. Install the upper radiator seal plastic rivets.

46. Install the upper radiator seal push pins.

47. Raise and secure the vehicle.

48. Install the lower center electric fan to radiator retaining clip.

49. Install the lower radiator clamp and hose.

50. Install the lower radiator seal.

51. Install battery negative cable.

52. Fill cooling system with coolant.

53. Check the system for any leaks.

54. Operate the engine until it reaches normal operating temperature. Check cooling system fluid levels.

THERMOSTAT

REMOVAL & INSTALLATION

3.7L & 4.7L Engines
See Figure 22.

✳✳ CAUTION

Do not loosen the radiator draincock with the cooling system hot and pressurized. Serious burns from the coolant can occur.

Do not waste reusable coolant. If the solution is clean, drain the coolant into a clean container for reuse.

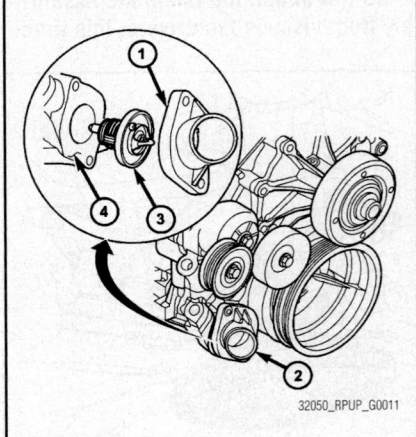

32050_RPUP_G0011

Fig. 22 Location of the thermostat (2), thermostat housing (1), thermostat & gasket (3) and timing chain cover (4)— 3.7L and 4.7L engines

If the thermostat is being replaced, be sure that the replacement is the specified thermostat for the vehicle model and engine type.

1. Before servicing the vehicle, refer to the Precautions Section.
2. Disconnect the negative battery cable.
3. Drain the cooling system.
4. Raise and support the vehicle.
5. Remove the splash shield.
6. Remove the lower radiator hose clamp and the lower radiator hose at the thermostat housing.
7. Remove the thermostat housing mounting bolts, thermostat housing and thermostat.

To install:

8. Clean the mating areas of the timing chain cover and the thermostat housing.
9. Install the thermostat (spring side down) into the recessed machined groove on the timing chain cover.
10. Position the thermostat housing on the timing chain cover.
11. Install the housing-to-timing chain cover bolts. Tighten the bolts to 112 inch lbs. (13 Nm).

✳✳ WARNING

The housing must be tightened evenly and the thermostat must be centered into the recessed groove in the timing chain cover. If not, it may result in a cracked housing, damaged timing chain cover threads or coolant leaks.

12. Install the lower radiator hose on the thermostat housing.
13. Install the splash shield.
14. Lower the vehicle.
15. Fill the cooling system.
16. Connect negative battery cable.
17. Start and warm the engine. Check for leaks.

5.7L Engine

See Figure 23.

✳✳ CAUTION

Do not loosen the radiator draincock with the cooling system hot and pressurized. serious burns from the coolant can occur.

Do not waste reusable coolant. If the solution is clean, drain the coolant into a clean container for reuse.

If the thermostat is being replaced, be sure that the replacement is the specified

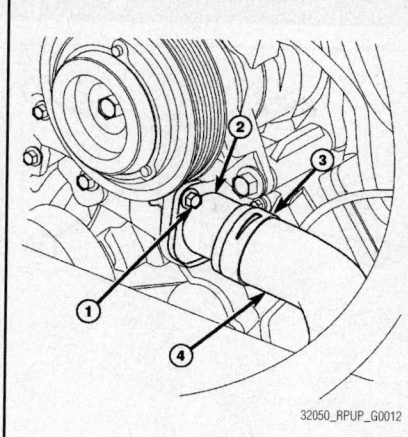

Fig. 23 View of the retaining bolt (1), thermostat housing (2), clamp (3) and radiator hose (4)—5.7L engines

thermostat for the vehicle model and engine type.

1. Before servicing the vehicle, refer to the Precautions Section.
2. Disconnect the negative battery cable.
3. Drain the cooling system
4. Remove the radiator hose clamp and radiator hose at the thermostat housing.
5. Remove the thermostat housing mounting bolts, thermostat housing and thermostat .

To install:

6. Position the thermostat and housing on the front cover.
7. Install the thermostat housing bolts. Tighten the bolts to 112 inch lbs. (13 Nm).
8. Install the radiator hose onto the thermostat housing.
9. Fill the cooling system.
10. Connect negative battery cable.
11. Start and warm the engine. Check for leaks.

WATER PUMP

REMOVAL & INSTALLATION

3.7L & 4.7L Engines

See Figure 24.

1. Before servicing the vehicle, refer to the Precautions Section.
2. Drain the cooling system.
3. Remove or disconnect the following:
   - Negative battery cable
   - Fan and clutch assembly from the pump
   - Fan shroud and fan assembly. If you're reusing the fan clutch, keep it upright to avoid silicone fluid loss!

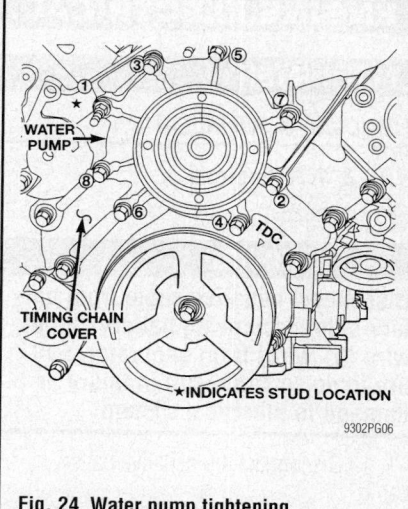

Fig. 24 Water pump tightening sequence—3.7L and 4.7L engines

   - Lower hose
   - 8 water pump bolts
4. Installation is the reverse of removal. Tighten the bolts, in sequence, to 40 ft. lbs. (54 Nm).

5.7L Engine

1. Before servicing the vehicle, refer to the Precautions Section.
2. Drain the cooling system.
3. Remove or disconnect the following:
   - Negative battery cable
   - Accessory drive belt
   - Engine cooling fan
   - Coolant recovery bottle
   - Washer bottle
   - Fan shroud
   - A/C compressor and alternator brace
   - Idler pulleys
   - Belt tensioner
   - Radiator hoses
   - Heater hoses
   - Water pump

To install:

4. Install or connect the following:
   - Water pump and tighten the bolts to 18 ft. lbs. (24 Nm)
   - Heater hoses
   - Radiator hoses
   - Idler pulleys
   - A/C compressor and alternator brace
   - Fan shroud
   - Washer bottle
   - Coolant recovery bottle
   - Accessory drive belt
   - Negative battery cable
   - Negative battery cable
5. Fill the cooling system.
6. Start the engine and check for leaks.

ALTERNATOR

REMOVAL & INSTALLATION

3.7L & 4.7L Engines

See Figure 25.

> **✳✳ WARNING**
>
> **Disconnect negative cable from battery before removing battery output wire (b+ wire) from generator. Failure to do so can result in injury or damage to electrical system.**

1. Disconnect the negative battery cable.
2. Remove the generator drive belt.
3. Unsnap the plastic insulator cap from the B+ output terminal (3) .
4. Remove the B+ terminal mounting nut at the rear of generator (2) . Disconnect the terminal from the generator.
5. Disconnect the field wire connector at the rear of the generator (4) by pushing on the connector tab.
6. Remove the one rear vertical generator mounting bolt (2) .
7. Remove the two front horizontal generator mounting bolts (1) .
8. Remove the generator from vehicle.

To install:

9. Position the generator to the engine and install the two horizontal bolts and the one vertical bolt. Tighten all three bolts to 55 Nm (40 ft. lbs.).
10. Snap the field wire connector into the rear of the generator.
11. Install the B+ terminal eyelet to the generator output stud. Tighten to 12 Nm (8.8 ft. lbs.).
12. Install the accessory drive belt. Refer to Accessory Drive Belts.
13. Connect the negative battery cable.

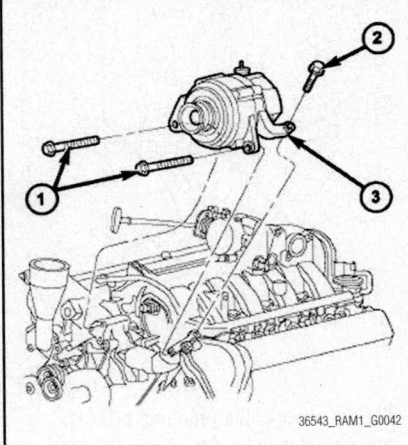

Fig. 25 Generator—3.7L and 4.7L engines

5.7L Engine

See Figure 26.

> **✳✳ WARNING**
>
> **Disconnect negative cable from battery before removing battery output wire (b+ wire) from generator. Failure to do so can result in injury or damage to electrical system.**

1. Disconnect the negative battery cable.
2. Remove the generator drive belt.
3. Unsnap the plastic insulator cap from the B+ output terminal.
4. Remove the B+ terminal mounting nut at the rear of the generator. Disconnect the terminal from the generator.
5. Disconnect the field wire connector at the rear of generator by pushing on the connector tab.

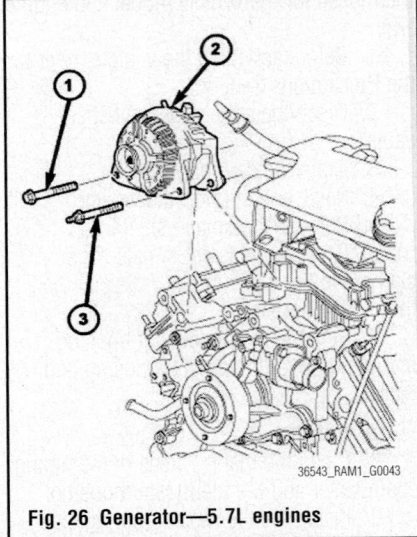

Fig. 26 Generator—5.7L engines

6. Remove the generator support bracket nuts (3) and bolt (4) and remove the support bracket.
7. Remove the two generator mounting bolts (1) and (3) .
8. Remove the generator from the vehicle.

To install:

9. Position the generator to the engine and install the two mounting bolts. Tighten to 41 Nm (30 ft. lbs.).
10. Position the support bracket to the front of the generator and install the bolt and nuts. Tighten to 41 Nm (30 ft. lbs.).
11. Snap the field wire connector into the rear of the generator.
12. Install the B+ terminal eyelet to the generator output stud. Tighten mounting nut to 12 Nm (8.8 ft. lbs.).
13. Install the accessory drive belt. Refer to Accessory Drive Belts.
14. Connect the negative battery cable.

FIRING ORDERS

See Figures 27 through 29.

3.7L firing order 1–6–5–4–3–2

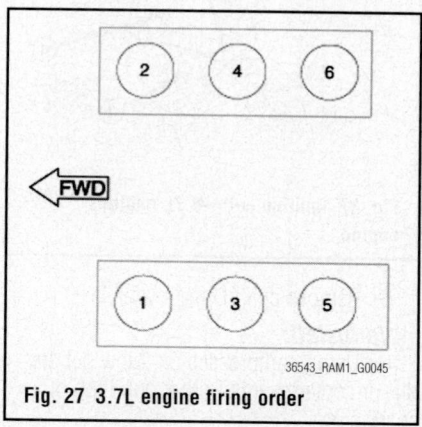

Fig. 27 3.7L engine firing order

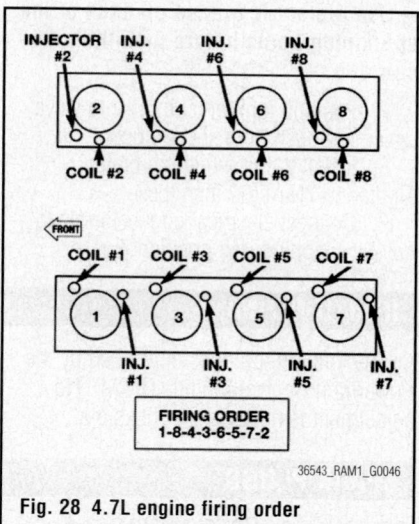

Fig. 28 4.7L engine firing order

IGNITION COIL

REMOVAL & INSTALLATION

3.7L Engine

See Figure 30.

→An ignition coil (2) with a spark plug wire (1) attached is used for two cylinders. The three coils fits into machined holes in the cylinder head for cylinders 1, 3, and 5. A mounting stud/nut secures each coil to the top of the intake manifold . The bottom of the coil is equipped with a rubber boot (4) to seal the spark plug (5) to the coil. Inside each rubber boot is a spring. The spring is used for a mechanical contact between the coil and the top of

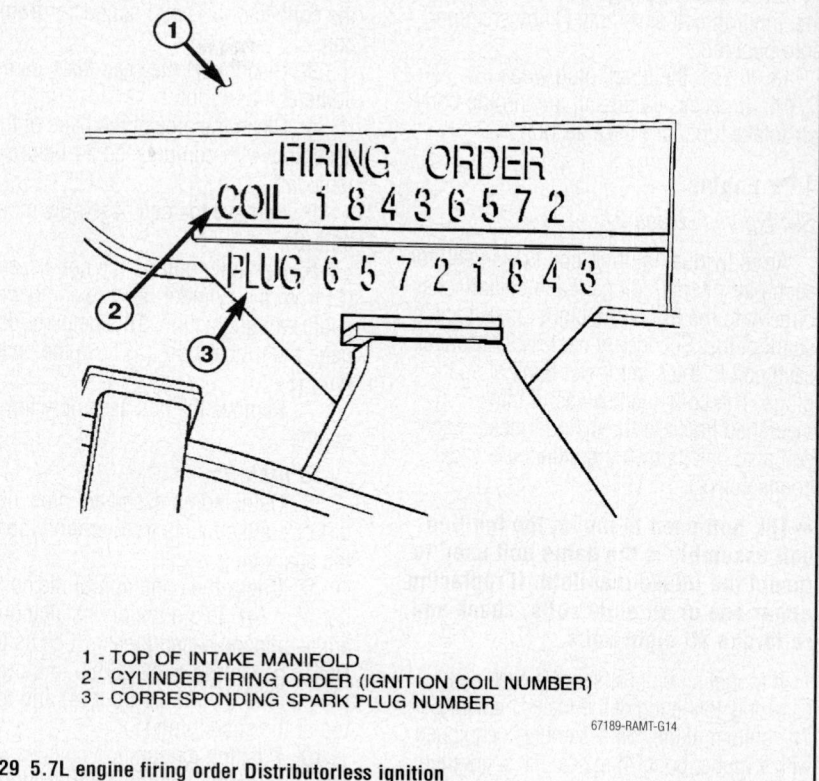

1 - TOP OF INTAKE MANIFOLD
2 - CYLINDER FIRING ORDER (IGNITION COIL NUMBER)
3 - CORRESPONDING SPARK PLUG NUMBER

Fig. 29 5.7L engine firing order Distributorless ignition

the spark plug. These rubber boots and springs are a permanent part of the coil and are not serviced separately. An O-ring is used to seal the coil at the opening into the cylinder head.

1. Depending on which coil is being removed, the throttle body air intake tube or intake box may need to be removed to gain access to coil.

2. Disconnect electrical connector from coil by pushing downward on release lock on top of connector and pull connector from coil.

3. Disconnect spark plug wire from coil (1).

4. Clean area at base of coil with compressed air before removal.

5. Remove coil mounting bolt.

6. Carefully pull up coil (1) from cylinder head opening with a slight twisting action.

7. Remove coil from vehicle.

To install:

8. Using compressed air, blow out any dirt or contaminants from around top of spark plug.

9. Check the condition of the coil rubber boot (4). To aid in coil installation, apply silicone based grease such as Mopar® Dielectric Grease # J8126688 into the spark

plug end of the rubber boot (4) and to the top of the spark plug (5).

10. Position the ignition coil assembly (1) into the cylinder head opening. Using a twisting action, push the ignition coil assembly onto the spark plug.

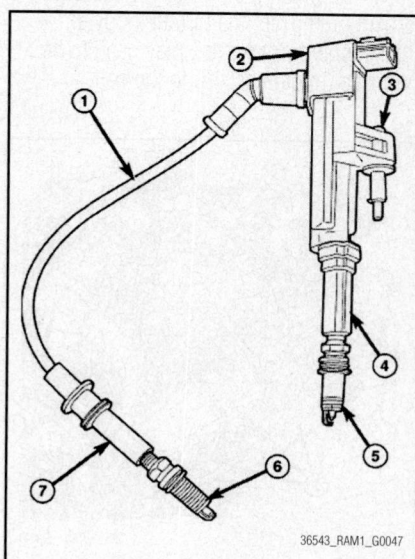

Fig. 30 Ignition coil—3.7L and 4.7L engines

11. Install coil mounting bolt. Tighten to 8 Nm (70 inch lbs).

12. Connect the electrical connector to the ignition coil assembly (1) by snapping into position.

13. Install the spark plug wires (3).

14. If necessary, install the throttle body air intake tube, or intake air box.

4.7L Engine

See Figures 30 and 31.

An individual ignition coil (1) is used for each pair of spark plugs. Each coil attaches directly to the top of the eight upper bank of spark plugs. Secondary cables (3) connect each coil to the eight lower bank of spark plugs. The coils themselves fit into machined holes in the cylinder head. Each coil also has its own individual electrical connector (2).

➡**The bolt used to mount the ignition coil assembly is the same bolt used to mount the intake manifold. If replacing either one or all eight coils, check and re-torque all eight bolts.**

A mounting bolt (3) secures each coil assembly to the top of the intake manifold. The bottom of the coil assembly is equipped with a rubber boot (4) to seal the spark plug (5) to the coil. Inside each rubber boot is a spring. The spring is used for a mechanical contact between the coil and the top of the upper bank of spark plugs. These rubber boots and springs are a permanent part of the coil assembly and are not serviced separately. The rubber boot (4) is also used to seal the coil at the opening into the cylinder head.

1. Depending on which coil assembly is being removed, the throttle body air intake tube or intake box may need to be removed, to gain access to the coil.

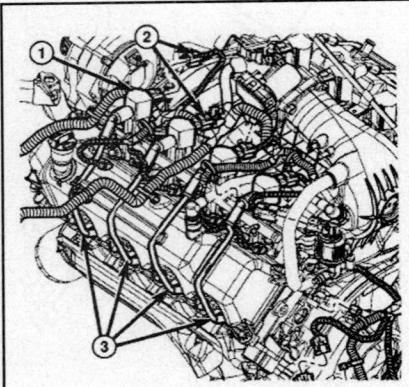

Fig. 31 Ignition coils—4.7L engines engine

2. Disconnect the electrical connector (2) from the coil assembly by pushing downward on the release lock on the top of the connector and pull connector from the coil.

3. Disconnect the secondary cable (3) at the coil assembly.

4. Clean the area at the base of the coil assembly with compressed air before removal.

5. Remove the coil assembly mounting bolt (3).

6. Carefully pull up the coil assembly (2) from the cylinder head opening with a slight twisting action. This helps to disengage the rubber boot (4) from the spark plug (5).

7. Remove the coil assembly from the engine.

To install:

8. Using compressed air, blow out any dirt or contaminants from around the top of the spark plug.

9. Check the condition of the coil rubber boot (4). To aid in coil installation, apply silicone based grease such as Mopar® Dielectric Grease # J8126688 into the spark plug end of the rubber boot (4) and to the top of the spark plug (5).

10. Position the ignition coil assembly into the cylinder head opening. Using a twisting action, push the ignition coil assembly onto the spark plug.

➡**The bolt used to mount the ignition coil assembly is also the same bolt used to mount the intake manifold. If replacing either one or all eight coils, check and re-torque all eight bolts.**

11. Tighten the coil assembly mounting bolt (3) to 12 Nm (9 ft. lbs.).

12. Connect the electrical connector (2) to the coil assembly by snapping into position.

13. Connect the secondary cable (3) to the coil assembly (1).

14. If necessary, install the throttle body air intake tube or intake air box to the top of the engine.

5.7L Engine

See Figure 32.

1. Disconnect the electrical connector (1) from coil (3).

2. Clean area at base of coil with compressed air before removal.

3. Remove two mounting bolts (2) (note that mounting bolts are retained to coil).

4. Carefully pull up coil (1) from valve cover.

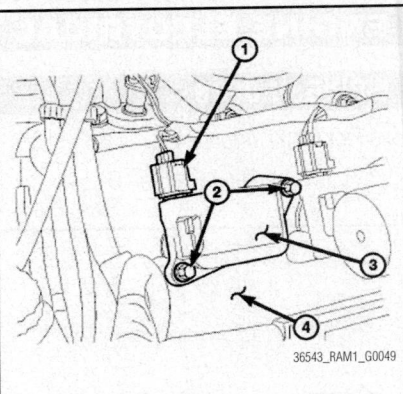

Fig. 32 Ignition coil—5.7L engines engine

5. Remove coil (1) from vehicle.

To install:

6. Using compressed air, blow out any dirt or contaminants from around top of spark plug.

➡**Use dielectric grease on each of the spark plug boots before installing the coil.**

7. Position ignition coil (1) into valve cover and push onto spark plugs.

8. Install 2 coil mounting bolts (2). Tighten to 7N·m (62 inch lbs.).

9. Connect electrical connector (1) to coil by snapping into position.

IGNITION TIMING

The ignition timing is controlled by the Powertrain Control Module (PCM). No adjustment is necessary or possible.

SPARK PLUGS

REMOVAL & INSTALLATION

3.7L Engine

➡**The three spark plugs located on the left bank of the engine are under three individual ignition coils. Each individual ignition coil must be removed to gain access to each spark plug located on the left bank of the engine.**

1. Remove the necessary air filter tubing and air intake components at the top of the engine at the throttle body.

2. Prior to removing the ignition coil, spray compressed air around the coil base at the cylinder head.

3. Remove the ignition coil. Refer to Ignition Coil. Check the condition of ignition coil O-ring and replace as necessary.

4. Prior to removing the spark plug, spray compressed air into the cylinder head opening. This will help prevent foreign material from entering combustion chamber.

5. Remove the spark plug from the cylinder head using a quality thin wall socket with a rubber or foam insert.

6. Inspect the spark plug condition.

To install:

7. Check and adjust the spark plug gap with a gap gauging tool.

✳✳ CAUTION

Special care should be taken when installing spark plugs into the cylinder head spark plug wells. Be sure the plugs do not drop into the plug wells as electrodes can be damaged.

8. Start the spark plug into the cylinder head by hand to avoid cross threading.

9. Tighten the spark plugs to 20 ft. lbs. (27 Nm).

10. Before installing the ignition coil check the condition of the coil O-ring and replace as necessary. Apply silicone based grease such as Mopar® Dielectric Grease J8126688 into the spark plug end of the rubber boot, coil O-rings and to the top of spark plugs.

11. Install the ignition coil. Refer to Ignition Coil.

12. Install the necessary air filter tubing and air intake components at the top of the engine at the throttle body.

4.7L Engine

✳✳ CAUTION

This engine uses TWO DIFFERENT types of spark plugs. A total of 16 plugs are used. The plugs are mounted in two rows (banks). The upper row is used on the intake valve side of the cylinder head. The lower row is used on the exhaust valve side of the cylinder head. The upper row uses Bosch® Nickel Yttrium plugs. The lower row uses Bosch® Iridium plugs. DO NOT INTERCHANGE THESE PLUGS.

1. Remove necessary air filter tubing and air intake components at top of engine and at throttle body.

➡**To remove the upper row of spark plugs, each individual ignition coil must be removed first.**

2. Remove the ignition coil(s). Refer to Ignition Coil.

3. Prior to removing the spark plug(s), spray compressed air into cylinder head opening. This will help prevent foreign material from entering combustion chamber.

✳✳ CAUTION

Due to tight clearances between UPPER row of plugs and cylinder head, a conventional deep, thick-wall spark plug socket will not fit. Use a deep, THIN-WALL 5/8" spark plug socket for plug removal and installation.

✳✳ CAUTION

Do not attempt to clean any of the spark plugs. Replace only.

4. Remove the spark plug(s) and inspect their condition.

To install:

5. To aid in coil installation, apply silicone based grease such as Mopar® Dielectric Grease into spark plug end of rubber boots and. Also apply this grease to the tops of spark plugs.

➡**Two different spark plug gaps are used.**

6. Check and adjust spark plug gap(s) with a plug gap gauging tool.

➡**Do not drop spark plugs into the plug wells as electrode damage can occur.**

7. Using special care install spark plug(s) into the cylinder head by hand to avoid cross threading.

➡**Always tighten spark plugs to the specified torque. Certain engines use torque sensitive spark plugs. Over tightening can cause distortion resulting in a change to the spark plug gap, or a cracked porcelain insulator.**

✳✳ CAUTION

Due to tight clearances between upper row of plugs and cylinder head, a conventional deep, thick-wall spark plug socket will not fit. Use a deep, THIN-WALL 5/8" spark plug socket for plug removal and installation.

8. Tighten spark plug(s) to the specified torque.

9. Install ignition coil(s). Refer to Ignition Coil.

10. Install necessary air filter tubing and air intake components to top of engine and to throttle body.

5.7L Engine

1. Remove the necessary air filter tubing and air intake components at the top of the engine and at the throttle body.

2. Prior to removing the ignition coil, spray compressed air around the base of the ignition coil at the cylinder head.

3. Remove the ignition coil. Refer to Ignition Coil.

4. Prior to removing the spark plug, spray compressed air into the cylinder head opening.

5. Remove the spark plug from the cylinder head using a quality thin wall socket with a rubber or foam insert.

6. Inspect the spark plug condition.

To install:

✳✳ CAUTION

Do not attempt to clean any of the spark plugs. Replace only.

7. Check and adjust spark plug gap with a gap gauging tool.

✳✳ CAUTION

Special care should be taken when installing spark plugs into the cylinder head spark plug wells. Be sure the plugs do not drop into the plug wells as electrodes can be damaged.

8. Start the spark plug into the cylinder head by hand to avoid cross threading.

➡**Always tighten spark plugs to the specified torque. Certain engines use torque sensitive spark plugs. It is a good practice to always tighten spark plugs to a specific torque. Over tightening can cause distortion resulting in a change in the spark plug gap, or a cracked porcelain insulator.**

➡**Spark plugs have a torque critical tapered design. Do not exceed 15 ft. lbs. (20 Nm).**

9. Tighten spark plugs to 13 ft. lbs. (18 Nm).

10. To aid in coil installation, apply silicone based grease such as Mopar® Dielectric Grease into spark plug end of ignition coil rubber boots. Also apply this grease to the tops of spark plugs.

11. Install ignition coil. Refer to Ignition Coil.

12. Install necessary air filter tubing and air intake components to top of engine and to throttle body

ENGINE ELECTRICAL

STARTER

REMOVAL & INSTALLATION

3.7L & 4.7L Engines

1. Remove or disconnect the following:
   - Negative battery cable

➡ **If equipped with 4WD and certain transmissions, a support bracket is used between front axle and side of transmission. Remove 2 support bracket bolts at transmission. Pry support bracket slightly to gain access to lower starter mounting bolt.**

- Starter mounting bolts
- Starter solenoid harness connections
- Starter

To install:

2. Connect the starter solenoid wiring connectors.

3. Install the starter and torque the bolts to 50 ft. lbs. (68 Nm).

4. Install the negative battery cable and check for proper operation.

5.7L Engine

1. Remove or disconnect the following:
   - Negative battery cable

➡ **Depending on drivetrain configuration, a support bracket may be used.**

- Starter mounting bolts
- Starter solenoid harness connections
- Starter

To install:

2. Connect the starter solenoid wiring connectors.

3. Install the starter and torque the bolts to 50 ft. lbs. (68 Nm).

4. Install the negative battery cable and check for proper operation.

ENGINE MECHANICAL

➡ **Disconnecting the negative battery cable may interfere with the functions of the on board computer systems and may require the computer to undergo a relearning process, once the negative battery cable is reconnected.**

ACCESSORY DRIVE BELTS

ACCESSORY BELT ROUTING

See Figures 33 and 34.

INSPECTION

Inspect the drive belt for signs of glazing or cracking. A glazed belt will be perfectly smooth from slippage, while a good belt will have a slight texture of fabric visible. Cracks will usually start at the inner edge of the belt and run outward. All worn or damaged drive belts should be replaced immediately.

ADJUSTMENT

Belt tension is not adjustable. Belt adjustment is maintained by an automatic (spring load) belt tensioner.

REMOVAL & INSTALLATION

3.7L & 4.7L Engines

See Figures 33 and 35.

❋❋ WARNING

Do not let tensioner arm snap back to the free arm position, sever damage may occur to the tensioner.

Belt tension is not adjustable. Belt adjustment is maintained by an automatic (spring load) belt tensioner.

1. Disconnect negative battery cable from battery.

2. Rotate belt tensioner until it contacts its stop. Remove belt, then slowly rotate the tensioner into the free arm position..

3. Check condition of all pulleys.

❋❋ WARNING

When installing the serpentine accessory drive belt, the belt MUST

be routed correctly. If not, the engine may overheat due to the water pump rotating in the wrong direction.

To install:

4. Install new belt. Route the belt around all pulleys except the idler pulley. Rotate the tensioner arm until it contacts its stop position. Route the belt around the idler and slowly let the tensioner rotate into the belt.

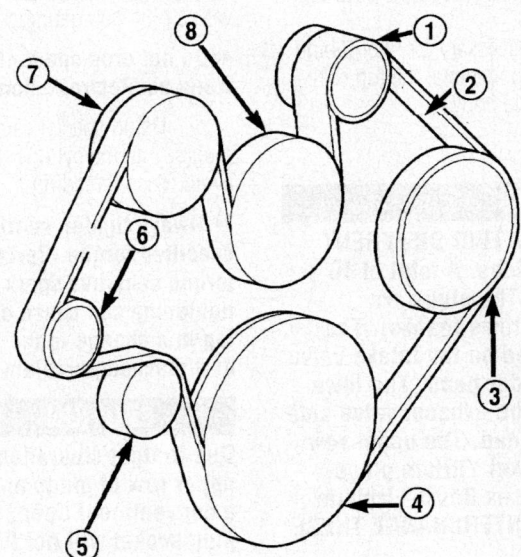

1 - GENERATOR PULLEY
2 - ACCESSORY DRIVE BELT
3 - POWER STEERING PUMP PULLEY
4 - CRANKSHAFT PULLEY
5 - IDLER PULLEY
6 - TENSIONER
7 - A/C COMPRESSOR PULLEY
8 - WATER PUMP PULLEY

67189-RAMT-G15

Fig. 33 Accessory serpentine belt routing—3.7L and 4.7L engines

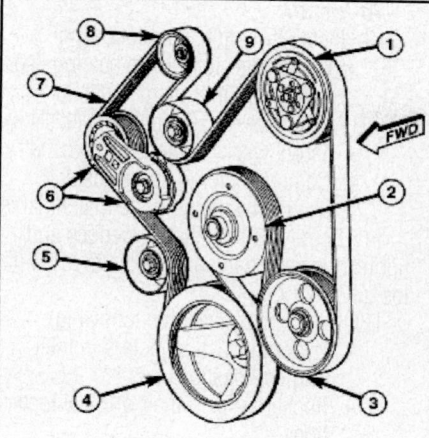

1. A/C COMPRESSOR IDLER PULLEY
2. FAN DRIVE PULLEY
3. POWER STEERING PUMP
4. CRANKSHAFT PULLEY
5. IDLER ASSEMBLY
6. TENSIONER ASSEMBLY
7. ACCESSORY DRIVE BELT
8. Alternator
9. IDLER PULLEY

Fig. 34 Accessory serpentine belt routing—5.7L engines

Make sure the belt is seated onto all pulleys.

5. With the drive belt installed, inspect the belt wear indicator. On 4.7L only, the gap between the tang and the housing stop (measurement A) must not exceed 24 mm (.94 inches). If the measurement exceeds this specification replace the serpentine accessory drive belt.

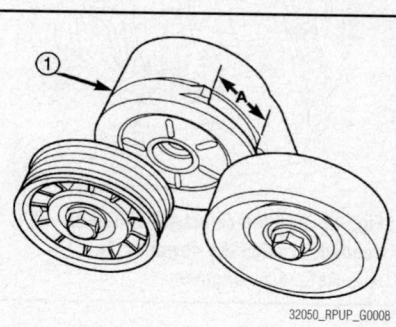

Fig. 35 With the drive belt installed, inspect the belt wear indicator. On 4.7L, the gap between the tang and the housing stop (measurement A) must not exceed 0.94 in. (24mm)

5.7L Engine

1. Remove the air intake tube between intake manifold and air filter assembly.
2. Insert a suitable square drive ratchet into the square hole on belt tensioner arm.
3. Release the belt tension by rotating the tensioner **clockwise**. Rotate belt tensioner until belt can be removed from pulleys.
4. Remove the drive belt.
5. Gently release tensioner.

To install:

➡️When installing accessory drive belt onto pulleys, make sure that belt is properly routed and all V-grooves make proper contact with pulleys.

6. Position the drive belt over all pulleys except for the water pump pulley.
7. Rotate tensioner **clockwise** and slip the belt over the water pump pulley.
8. Gently release tensioner.
9. Install the air intake tube between intake manifold and air filter assembly.

BALANCE SHAFT

REMOVAL & INSTALLATION

3.7L Engine

See Figures 36 and 37.

1. Remove the primary and secondary timing chains. Refer to the TIMING CHAIN and SPROCKET procedures in this section.

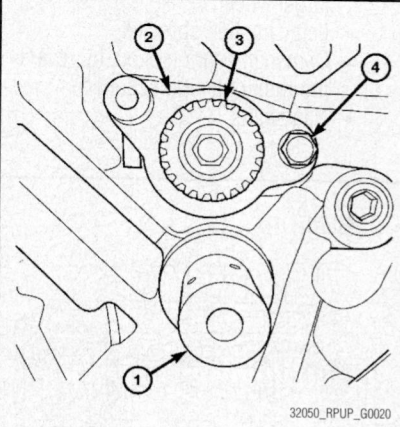

Fig. 36 View of the idler shaft (1), counterbalance shaft thrust plate (2), counterbalance shaft drive gear (3) and retaining bolt (4)

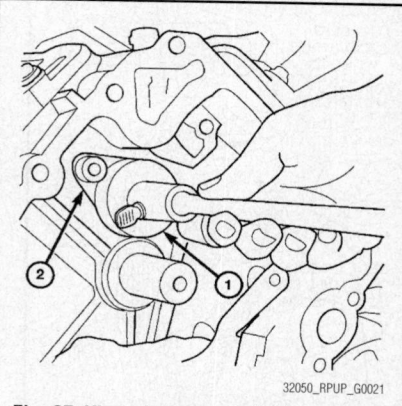

Fig. 37 View of the counterbalance shaft removal & installation tool (1) and the counterbalance shaft thrust plate (2)

➡️The balance shaft and gear are serviced as an assembly. Do not attempt to remove the gear from the balance shaft.

2. Remove the retaining bolt from the counterbalance shaft thrust plate.
3. Using Special Tool 8641 Counterbalance shaft remover/installer tool (1), remove the counterbalance shaft from the engine.

To install:

4. Coat counterbalance shaft bearing journals with clean engine oil.

➡️The balance shaft is heavy, and care should be used when installing shaft, so bearings are not damaged.

5. Using Special Tool 8641 Counterbalance shaft remover/installer tool (1), carefully install counterbalance shaft into engine.
6. Install Counterbalance shaft thrust plate retaining bolt finger-tight. Do not tighten bolt at this time.
7. Position the right side of the thrust plate with the right chain guide bolt, install bolt finger-tight.
8. Torque the thrust plate retaining bolt to 21 ft. lbs. (28 Nm).
9. Remove the chain guide bolt so that guide can be installed.

CAMSHAFT AND VALVE LIFTERS

REMOVAL & INSTALLATION

3.7L & 4.7L Engines

See Figures 38 through 42.

1. Before servicing the vehicle, refer to the Precautions Section.
2. Remove or disconnect the following:
   • Negative battery cable

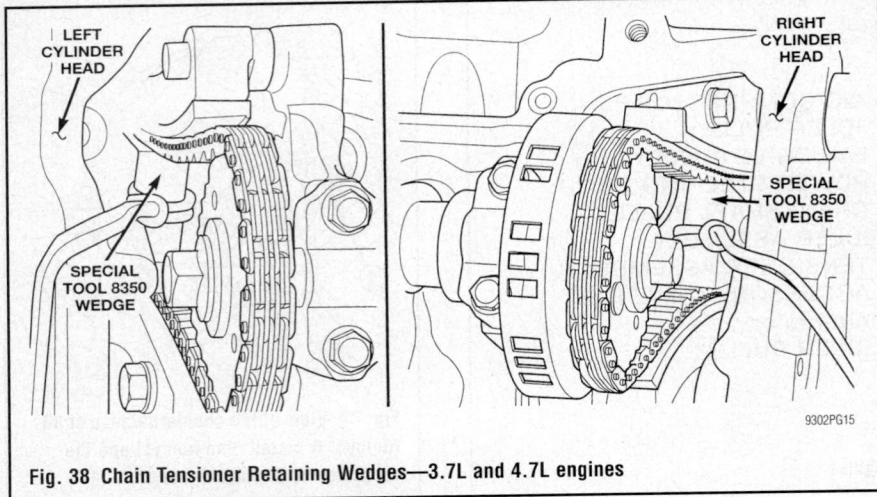

Fig. 38 Chain Tensioner Retaining Wedges—3.7L and 4.7L engines

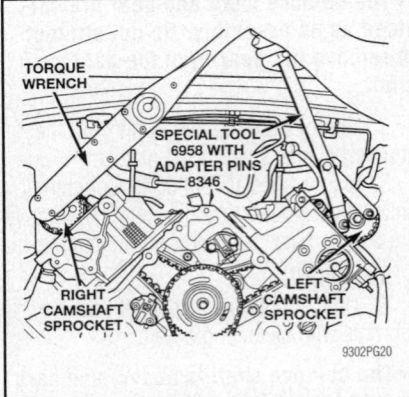

Fig. 39 Hold the left camshaft sprocket with a spanner wrench while removing or installing the camshaft sprocket bolts—4.7L engines

- Cylinder head covers
- Rocker arms
- Hydraulic lash adjusters

➡**Keep all valvetrain components in order for assembly.**

3. Set the engine at Top Dead Center

(TDC) of the compression stroke for the No. 1 cylinder.

4. Install Timing Chain Wedge (8350 4.7L; 8379 3.7L) to retain the chain tensioners.

5. Matchmark the timing chains to the camshaft sprockets.

6. Install Camshaft Holding Tool (6958 and Adapter Pins 8346 4.7L; 8428 3.7L) to the left camshaft sprocket.

7. On 3.7L, use tool 8428 and rotate the camshaft 5 degrees clockwise to eliminate valve load.

8. On 4.7L, use adjustable pliers to rotate the left camshaft 15 degrees clockwise to eliminate valve load. Use adjustable pliers to rotate the right camshaft 45 degrees counterclockwise to eliminate valve load.

9. Remove or disconnect the following:

- Right camshaft timing sprocket and target wheel
- Left camshaft sprocket
- Camshaft bearing caps, by reversing the tightening sequence
- Camshafts

To install:

10. Install or connect the following:
- Camshafts. Torque the bearing cap bolts in ½ turn increments, in sequence, to 100 inch lbs. (11 Nm).
- Target wheel to the right camshaft
- Camshaft timing sprockets and chains, by aligning the matchmarks

11. Remove the tensioner wedges and tighten the camshaft sprocket bolts to 90 ft. lbs. (122 Nm).

12. Install or connect the following:
- Hydraulic lash adjusters in their original locations
- Rocker arms in their original locations
- Cylinder head covers
- Negative battery cable

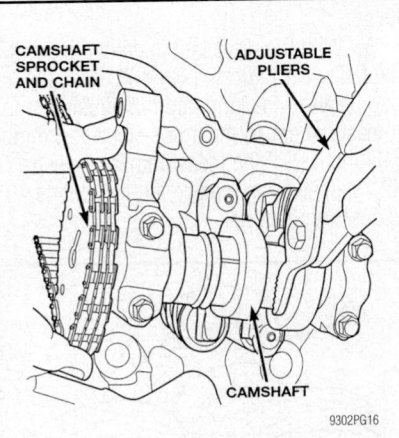

Fig. 42 Turn the camshaft with pliers, if needed, to align the dowel in the sprocket—4.7L engines

5.7L Engine

1. Before servicing the vehicle, refer to the Precautions Section.

2. Drain the cooling system.

3. Recover the A/C refrigerant, if equipped with air conditioning.

4. Set the crankshaft to Top Dead Center (TDC) of the compression stroke for the No. 1 cylinder.

5. Remove or disconnect the following:
- Negative battery cable
- Camshaft rear cam bearing core plug
- Air cleaner
- Accessory drive belt
- Alternator
- A/C compressor
- Radiator
- Intake manifold
- Cylinder head covers
- Cylinder heads

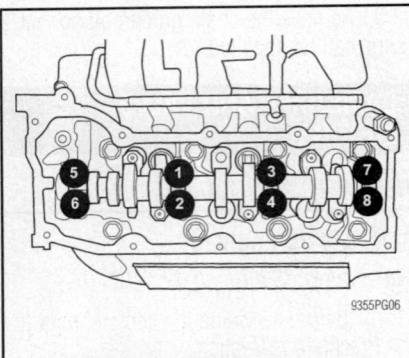

Fig. 40 Camshaft bearing cap bolt tightening sequence—3.7L engines

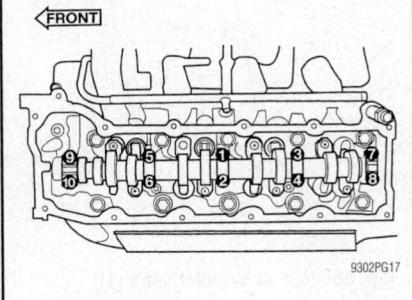

Fig. 41 Camshaft bearing cap bolt tightening sequence—4.7L engines

- Oil pan
- Front cover
- Oil pickup tube
- Oil pump
- Timing chain and sprockets
- Camshaft thrust plate
- Hydraulic lifters
- Camshaft

To install:

6. Install or connect the following:
- Camshaft
- Camshaft thrust plate. Tighten the bolts to 21 ft. lbs. (28 Nm).
- Timing chain and sprockets
- Oil pump
- Oil pickup tube

➥**Lifters must be replaced in their original positions.**

- Hydraulic lifters
- Cylinder heads
- Pushrods
- Rocker arms
- Front cover
- Oil pan
- Cylinder head covers
- Intake manifold
- A/C compressor
- Alternator
- Accessory drive belt
- Radiator
- Air cleaner
- Camshaft rear cam bearing core plug
- Negative battery cable

7. Fill the cooling system.
8. Recharge the A/C system, if equipped.
9. Start the engine and check for leaks.

CATALYTIC CONVERTER

REMOVAL & INSTALLATION

3.7L & 4.7L Engines

1. Raise and support vehicle.
2. Saturate the bolts and nuts with heat valve lubricant. Allow 5 minutes for penetration.
3. Disconnect oxygen sensor electrical connectors.
4. Remove clamp.
5. Remove bolts exhaust to manifold.
6. Remove catalytic converter.

To install:

7. Install RH catalytic converter to exhaust clamp on RH catalytic converter and position into exhaust pipe.
8. Install and hand tighten RH catalytic converter to exhaust manifold bolts.
9. Install c-clip nut and bolt to converter to manifold.

10. Tighten catalytic converter to exhaust manifold bolts to 23 ft. lbs. (31 Nm).
11. Tighten all clamp nuts to 52.2 Nm (40 ft. lbs.) torque.
12. Check the exhaust system for contact with the body panels. A minimum of 25 mm (1.0 in.) is required between the exhaust system components and body/frame parts. Make the necessary adjustments, if needed.
13. Check to ensure you have at least 1 inch (25mm) clearance to oil pan.
14. Plug in O2 sensor wiring.
15. Lower the vehicle.
16. Start the engine and inspect for exhaust leaks. Repair exhaust leaks as necessary.

5.7L Engine

1. Raise and support vehicle.
2. Saturate the bolts and nuts with heat valve lubricant. Allow 5 minutes for penetration.
3. Disconnect oxygen sensor electrical connectors.
4. Remove clamps and nuts.
5. Remove catalytic converter to exhaust manifold bolts and nuts.
6. Remove catalytic converter assembly.

To install:

7. Install catalytic converter to exhaust clamp on catalytic converter and position into exhaust pipe.
8. Make sure the alignment tang on catalytic converter is fully seated in the notch on the exhaust pipe.
9. Install catalytic converter to exhaust manifold bolts and nuts.
10. Tighten catalytic converter to exhaust manifold bolts to 23 ft. lbs. (31 Nm).
11. Tighten catalytic converter to exhaust pipe clamp nuts to 40 ft. lbs. (54 Nm) torque.
12. Check the exhaust system for contact with the body panels. A minimum of 25 mm (1.0 in.) is required between the exhaust system components and body/frame parts. Make the necessary adjustments, if needed.
13. Lower the vehicle.
14. Start the engine and inspect for exhaust leaks. Repair exhaust leaks as necessary.

CRANKSHAFT DAMPER

REMOVAL & INSTALLATION

See Figures 43 through 46.

1. Disconnect the negative battery cable.
2. Remove accessory drive belt, as outlined in Engine Mechanical.
3. Drain cooling system.
4. Remove radiator upper hose.
5. Remove upper fan shroud.

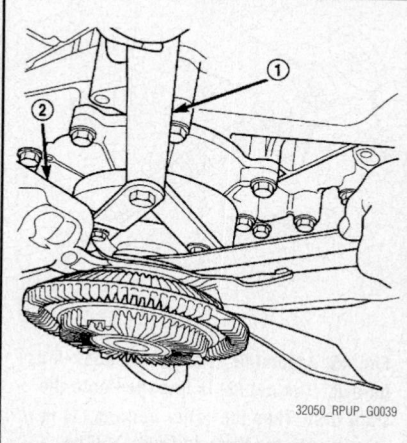

Fig. 43 Using Special Tools 6958 Spanner with Adapter Pins 8346 (1), loosen fan (2) and viscous assembly from water pump

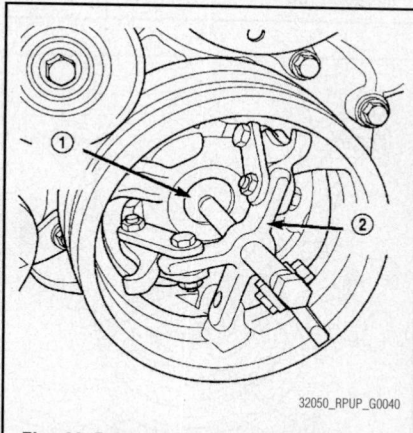

Fig. 44 Remove damper using Special Tools 8513 Insert (1) and 1026 Three Jaw Puller (2)

6. Using Special Tools 6958 Spanner with Adapter Pins 8346 (1), loosen fan (2) and viscous assembly from water pump.
7. Remove fan and viscous assembly.
8. Disconnect electrical connector for fan mounted inside radiator shroud.

➥**Transmission cooler line snaps into shroud lower right hand corner.**

9. Remove crankshaft damper bolt.
10. Remove damper using Special Tools 8513 Insert (1) and 1026 Three Jaw Puller (2).

To install:

❊❊ WARNING

To prevent severe damage to the Crankshaft, Damper or Special Tool 8512-A, thoroughly clean the damper bore and the crankshaft nose before installing Damper.

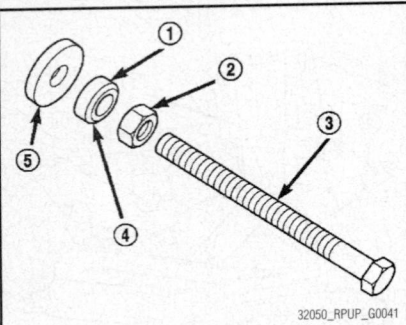

Fig. 45 Assemble Special Tool 8512-A as follows, The nut (2) is threaded onto the shaft first. Then the roller bearing (1) is placed onto the threaded rod (3) (The hardened bearing surface of the bearing (1) MUST face the nut (2). Then the hardened washer (5) slides onto the threaded rod

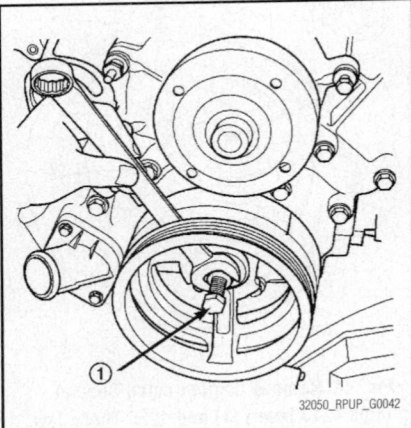

Fig. 46 Using Special Tool 8512-A, press damper onto crankshaft (1)

11. Align crankshaft damper slot with key in crankshaft. Slide damper onto crankshaft slightly.

❊❊ WARNING

Special Tool 8512-A, is assembled in a specific sequence. Failure to assemble this tool in this sequence can result in tool failure and severe damage to either the tool or the crankshaft.

12. Assemble Special Tool 8512-A as follows, The nut (2) is threaded onto the shaft first. Then the roller bearing (1) is placed onto the threaded rod (3) (The hardened bearing surface of the bearing (1) MUST face the nut (2). Then the hardened washer (5) slides onto the threaded rod. Once

assembled coat the threaded rod's threads with Mopar® Nickel Anti-Seize or equivalent.

13. Using Special Tool 8512-A, press damper onto crankshaft (1).
14. Install then tighten crankshaft damper bolt to 130 ft. lbs. (175 Nm).
15. Install fan blade assembly.
16. Install radiator upper shroud and tighten fasteners to 95 inch lbs. (11 Nm).
17. Connect electrical connector for shroud fan.
18. Install radiator upper hose.
19. Install accessory drive belt.
20. Refill cooling system.
21. Connect the negative battery cable.

CRANKSHAFT FRONT SEAL

REMOVAL & INSTALLATION

3.7L & 4.7L Engines

See Figures 47 and 48.

1. Before servicing the vehicle, refer to the Precautions Section.
2. Disconnect negative cable from battery.
3. Remove the accessory drive belt.
4. Remove the A/C compressor mounting fasteners and set compressor aside.
5. Drain the cooling system.
6. Remove the upper radiator hose.
7. Disconnect electrical connector for fan mounted inside radiator shroud.
8. Remove the radiator shroud attaching fasteners.

➥**Transmission cooler line snaps into shroud lower right hand corner.**

9. Remove radiator cooling fan and shroud.
10. Remove the crankshaft damper bolt.
11. Remove the damper using crank-

Fig. 47 Damper removal using crankshaft insert 8513 (1) and 1026 three jaw puller (2).

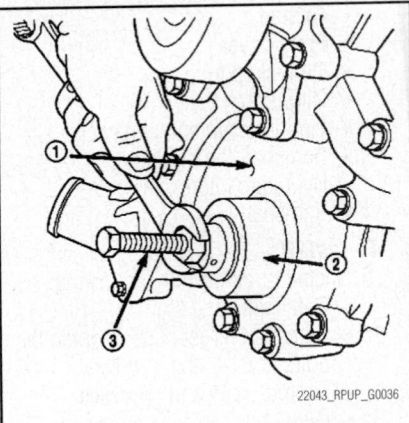

Fig. 48 Using special tools 8348 and 8512 (2,3), install crankshaft front seal.

shaft insert 8513 and 1026 three jaw puller.

12. Using crankshaft front seal remover 8511, remove crankshaft front seal.

To install:

❊❊ WARNING

To prevent severe damage to the crankshaft, damper or special tool 8512, thoroughly clean the damper bore and the crankshaft nose before installing Damper.

13. Using special tool 8348 and 8512, install crankshaft front seal.
14. Install the vibration damper. Tighten the bolt to 130 ft. lbs. (175 Nm).
15. Install the radiator cooling fan and shroud.
16. Install the upper radiator hose.
17. Install A/C compressor and tighten fasteners to 40 ft. lbs. (54 Nm).
18. Install the accessory drive belt.
19. Refill the cooling system.
20. Connect negative cable to battery.

5.7L Engine

See Figures 49 and 50.

1. Before servicing the vehicle, refer to the Precautions Section.
2. Disconnect negative cable from battery.
3. Remove the accessory drive belt.
4. Drain the cooling system.
5. Remove the upper radiator hose.
6. Remove the radiator shroud attaching fasteners.
7. Remove the radiator cooling fan and shroud.
8. Remove the crankshaft damper bolt.
9. Remove the damper using crankshaft insert 8513A and three jaw puller 1023.

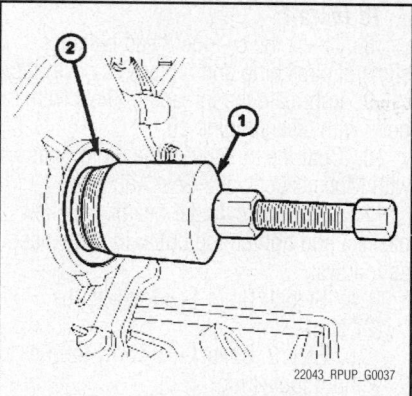

Fig. 49 Using Crankshaft Front Seal Remover 9071 (1), to remove crankshaft front seal (2).

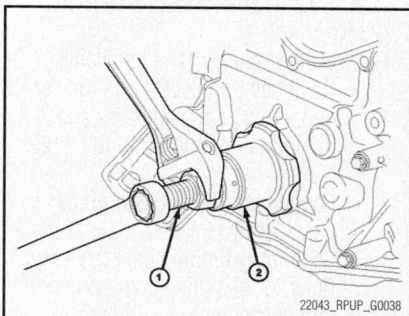

Fig. 50 Using crankshaft front oil seal installer 9072 (2) and damper installer 8512A (1), to install crankshaft front seal.

10. Using crankshaft front seal remover 9071, remove crankshaft front seal.

To install:

> ❊❊ **WARNING**
>
> **The front crankshaft seal must be installed dry. Do not apply lubricant to sealing lip or to outer edge.**

11. Using crankshaft front oil seal installer 9072 and damper installer 8512A, install crankshaft front seal.

> ❊❊ **WARNING**
>
> **To prevent severe damage to the Crankshaft or Damper, thoroughly clean the damper bore and the crankshaft nose before installing Damper.**

12. Install the vibration damper. Tighten bolt to 129 ft. lbs. (176 Nm).
13. Install radiator cooling fan and shroud.
14. Install the upper radiator hose.
15. Install the accessory drive belt refer
16. Refill the cooling system.
17. Connect negative cable to battery.

CYLINDER HEAD

REMOVAL & INSTALLATION

3.7L Engine

Left Side

See Figures 51 through 54.

1. Before servicing the vehicle, refer to the Precautions Section.
2. Drain the cooling system.
3. Properly relieve the fuel system pressure.
4. Remove or disconnect the following:
- Negative battery cable
- Exhaust Y-pipe
- Intake manifold
- Brake booster and master cylinder
- Cylinder head cover
- Engine cooling fan and shroud
- Accessory drive belt
- Power steering pump

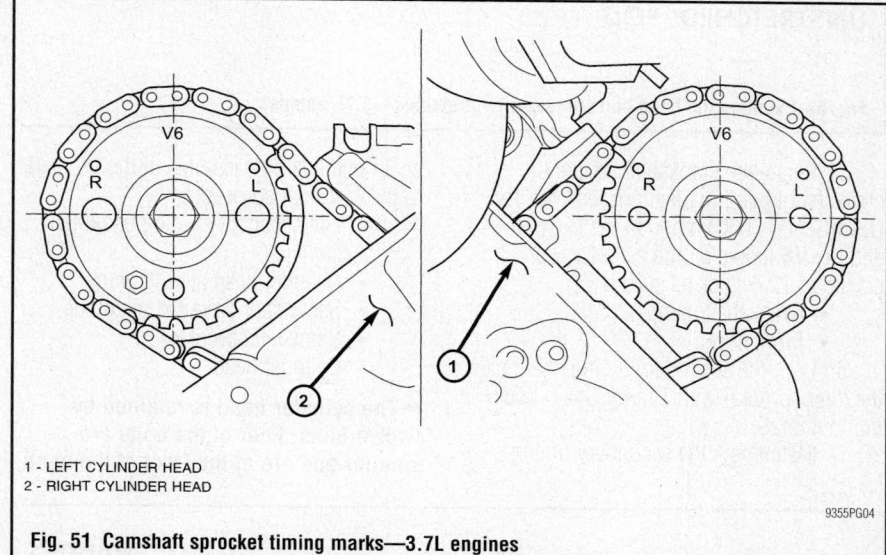

1 - LEFT CYLINDER HEAD
2 - RIGHT CYLINDER HEAD

Fig. 51 Camshaft sprocket timing marks—3.7L engines

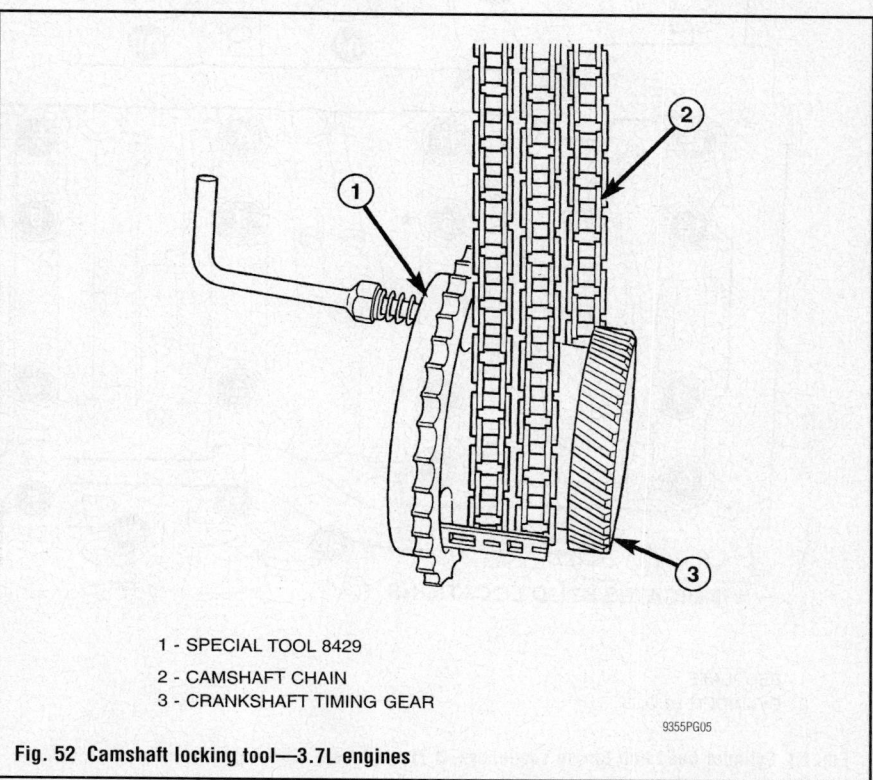

1 - SPECIAL TOOL 8429

2 - CAMSHAFT CHAIN

3 - CRANKSHAFT TIMING GEAR

Fig. 52 Camshaft locking tool—3.7L engines

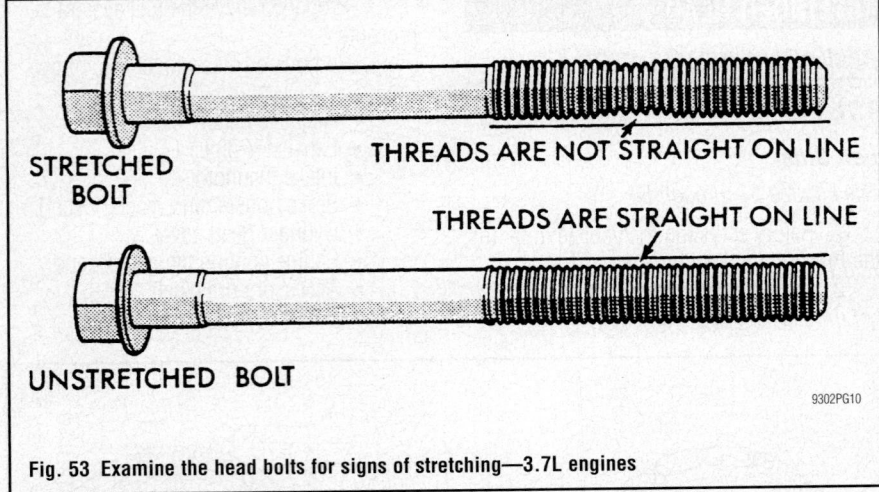

STRETCHED BOLT
THREADS ARE NOT STRAIGHT ON LINE
THREADS ARE STRAIGHT ON LINE
UNSTRETCHED BOLT
9302PG10

Fig. 53 Examine the head bolts for signs of stretching—3.7L engines

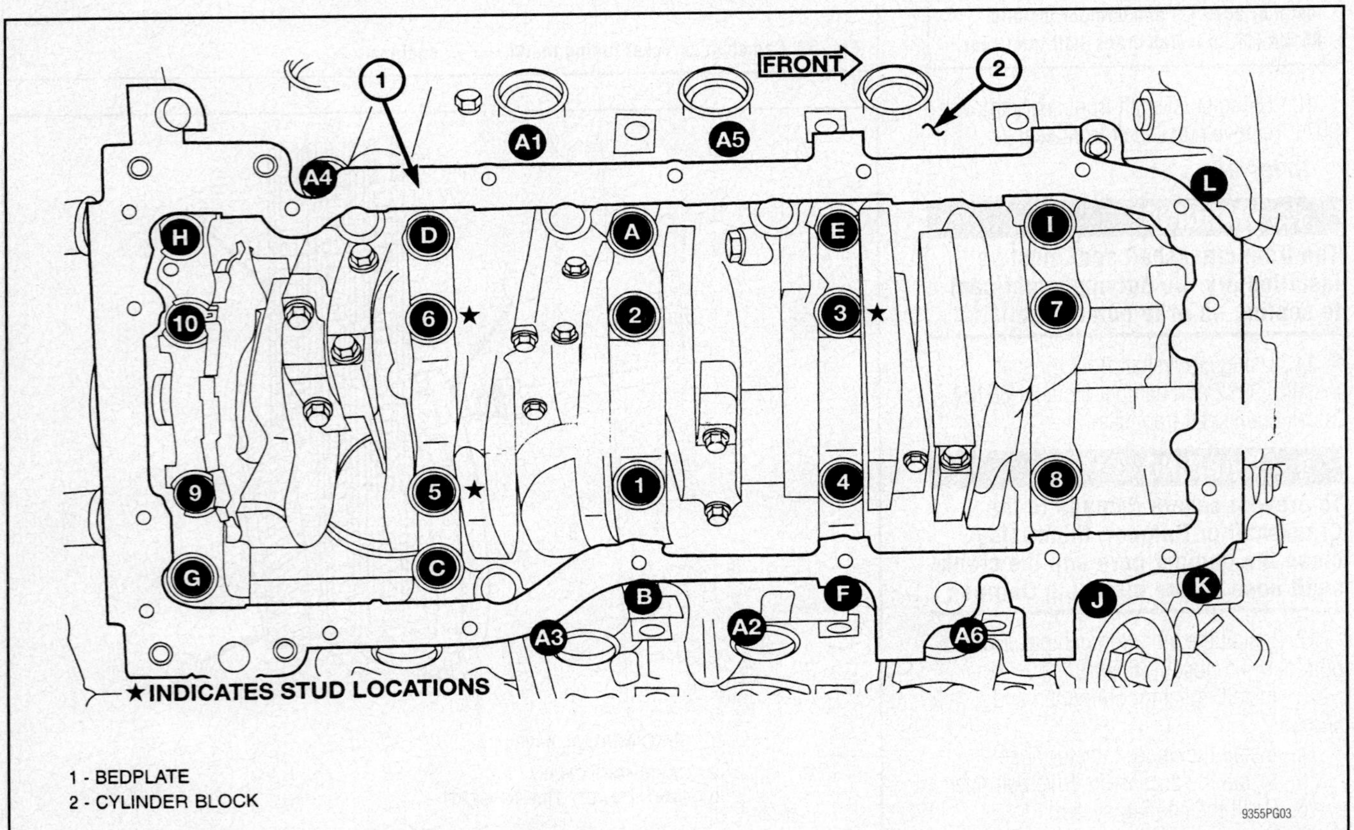

5. Rotate the crankshaft so that the crankshaft timing mark aligns with the Top Dead Center (TDC) mark on the front cover, and the **V6** marks on the camshaft sprockets are at 12 o'clock as shown.
   - Crankshaft damper
   - Front cover
6. Lock the secondary timing chain to the idler sprocket with Timing Chain Locking tool 8429.
7. Matchmark the secondary timing chain one link on each side of the V6 mark to the camshaft sprocket.
   - Left secondary timing chain tensioner
   - Cylinder head access plug
   - Secondary timing chain guide
   - Camshaft sprocket
   - Cylinder head

➡The cylinder head is retained by twelve bolts. Four of the bolts are smaller and are at the front of the head.

To install:

8. Check the cylinder head bolts for signs of stretching and replace as necessary.
9. Lubricate the threads of the 11mm bolts with clean engine oil.
10. Coat the threads of the 8mm bolts with Mopar® Lock and Seal Adhesive.
11. Install the cylinder heads. Use new gaskets and tighten the bolts, in sequence, as follows:
    a. Step 1: Bolts 1–8 to 20 ft. lbs. (27 Nm)
    b. Step 2: Bolts 1–10 verify torque without loosening
    c. Step 3: Bolts 9–12 to 10 ft. lbs. (14 Nm)
    d. Step 4: Bolts 1–8 plus ¼ (90 degree) turn
    e. Step 5: Bolts 9–12 to 19 ft. lbs. (26 Nm)
12. Install or connect the following:
    - Camshaft sprocket. Align the secondary chain matchmarks and tighten the bolt to 90 ft. lbs. (122 Nm).
    - Secondary timing chain guide
    - Cylinder head access plug
    - Secondary timing chain tensioner. Refer to the timing chain procedure in this section.

FRONT
1
2
A1
A5
A4
L
H
D
A
E
I
10
6
2
3
7
9
5
1
4
8
G
C
B
F
J
K
A3
A2
A6
★INDICATES STUD LOCATIONS
1 - BEDPLATE
2 - CYLINDER BLOCK
9355PG03

Fig. 54 Cylinder head bolt torque sequence—3.7L engines

13. Remove the Timing Chain Locking tool.

14. Install or connect the following:
- Front cover
- Crankshaft damper. Torque the bolt to 130 ft. lbs. (175 Nm).
- Power steering pump
- Accessory drive belt
- Engine cooling fan and shroud
- Cover
- Intake manifold
- Exhaust Y-pipe
- Negative battery cable

15. Fill and bleed the cooling system.

16. Start the engine, check for leaks and repair if necessary.

Right Side

See Figures 53 through 56.

1. Before servicing the vehicle, refer to the Precautions Section.

2. Drain the cooling system.

3. Properly relieve the fuel system pressure.

4. Remove or disconnect the following:
- Negative battery cable
- Exhaust Y-pipe
- Intake manifold
- Valve cover
- Engine cooling fan and shroud
- Accessory drive belt
- Oil fill housing
- Power steering pump

5. Rotate the crankshaft so that the crankshaft timing mark aligns with the Top Dead Center (TDC) mark on the front cover, and the **V6** marks on the camshaft sprockets are at 12 o'clock as shown.

6. Remove or disconnect the following:
- Crankshaft damper
- Front cover

7. Lock the secondary timing chains to the idler sprocket with Timing Chain Locking tool 8429.

8. Matchmark the secondary timing chains to the camshaft sprockets.

9. Remove or disconnect the following:
- Secondary timing chain tensioners
- Cylinder head access plugs
- Secondary timing chain guides
- Camshaft sprockets
- Cylinder heads

➥Each cylinder head is retained by 8 11mm bolts and four 8mm bolts.

To install:

10. Check the cylinder head bolts for signs of stretching and replace as necessary.

11. Lubricate the threads of the 11mm bolts with clean engine oil.

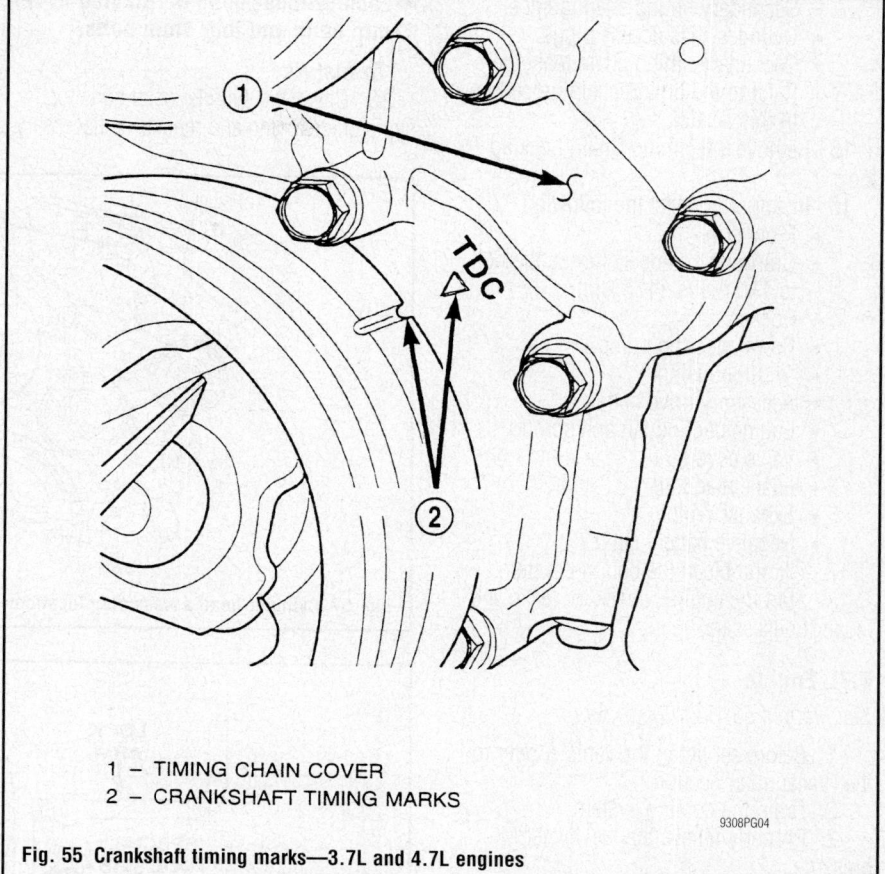

1 – TIMING CHAIN COVER
2 – CRANKSHAFT TIMING MARKS

9308PG04

Fig. 55 Crankshaft timing marks—3.7L and 4.7L engines

12. Coat the threads of the 8mm bolts with Mopar® Lock and Seal Adhesive.

13. Install the cylinder heads. Use new gaskets and tighten the bolts, in sequence, as follows:
   a. Step 1: Bolts 1–8 to 20 ft. lbs. (27 Nm)
   b. Step 2: Bolts 1–10 verify torque without loosening
   c. Step 3: Bolts 9–12 to 10 ft. lbs. (14 Nm)
   d. Step 4: Bolts 1–8 plus ¼ (90 degree) turn
   e. Step 5: Bolts 9–12 to 19 ft. lbs. (26 Nm)

14. Install or connect the following:
- Camshaft sprockets. Align the secondary chain matchmarks and tighten the bolts to 90 ft. lbs. (122 Nm).

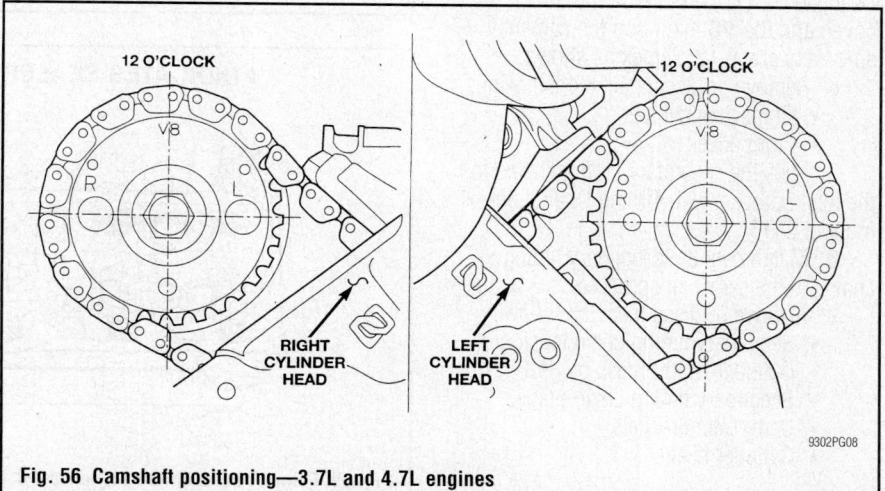

9302PG08

Fig. 56 Camshaft positioning—3.7L and 4.7L engines

- Secondary timing chain guides
- Cylinder head access plugs
- Secondary timing chain tensioners. Refer to the timing chain procedure in this section.

15. Remove the Timing Chain Locking tool.

16. Install or connect the following:
- Front cover
- Crankshaft damper. Torque the bolt to 130 ft. lbs. (175 Nm).
- Rocker arms
- Power steering pump
- Oil fill housing
- Accessory drive belt
- Engine cooling fan and shroud
- Valve covers
- Intake manifold
- Exhaust Y-pipe
- Negative battery cable

17. Fill and bleed the cooling system.

18. Start the engine, check for leaks and repair if necessary.

4.7L Engine

See Figures 53, 55 through 59.

1. Before servicing the vehicle, refer to the Precautions Section.

2. Drain the cooling system.

3. Properly relieve the fuel system pressure.

4. Remove or disconnect the following:
- Negative battery cable
- Exhaust Y-pipe
- Intake manifold
- Valve covers
- Engine cooling fan and shroud
- Accessory drive belt
- Oil fill housing
- Power steering pump
- Rocker arms

5. Rotate the crankshaft so that the crankshaft timing mark aligns with the Top Dead Center (TDC) mark on the front cover, and the **V8** marks on the camshaft sprockets are at 12 o'clock as shown.

6. Remove or disconnect the following:
- Crankshaft damper
- Front cover

7. Lock the secondary timing chains to the idler sprocket with Timing Chain Locking tool 8515.

8. Matchmark the secondary timing chains to the camshaft sprockets.

9. Remove or disconnect the following:
- Secondary timing chain tensioners
- Cylinder head access plugs
- Secondary timing chain guides
- Camshaft sprockets
- Cylinder heads

➡**Each cylinder head is retained by ten 11mm bolts and four 8mm bolts.**

To install:

10. Check the cylinder head bolts for signs of stretching and replace as necessary.

11. Lubricate the threads of the 11mm bolts with clean engine oil.

12. Coat the threads of the 8mm bolts with Mopar® Lock and Seal Adhesive.

13. Install the cylinder heads. Use new

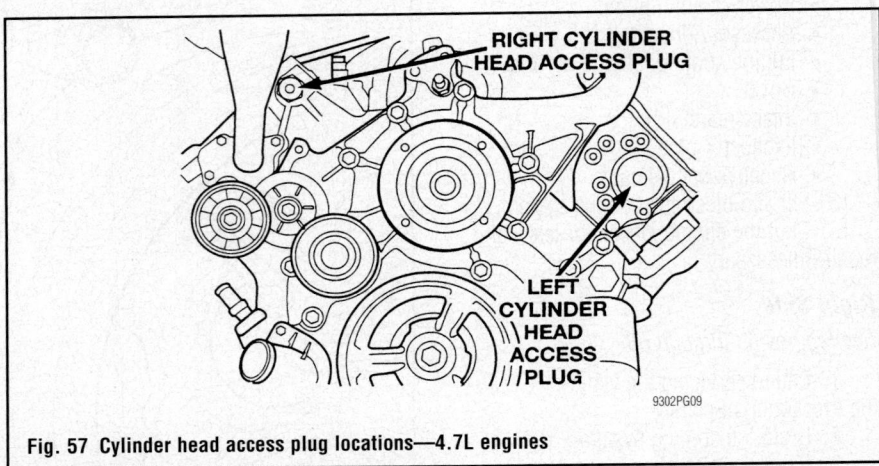

Fig. 57 Cylinder head access plug locations—4.7L engines

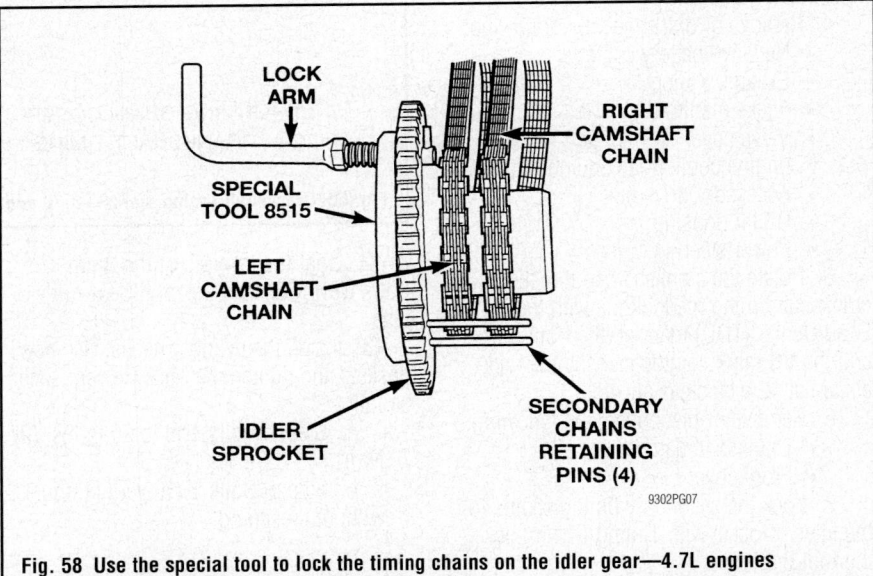

Fig. 58 Use the special tool to lock the timing chains on the idler gear—4.7L engines

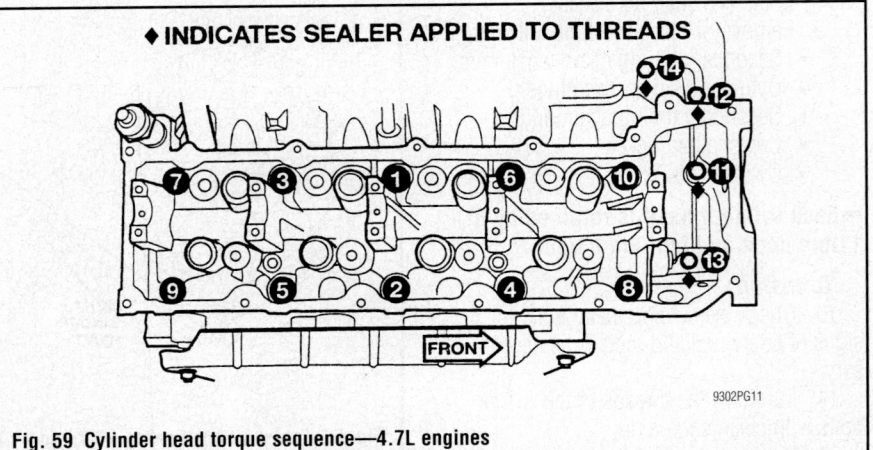

Fig. 59 Cylinder head torque sequence—4.7L engines

gaskets and tighten the bolts, in sequence, as follows:

    a. Step 1: Bolts 1–10 to 15 ft. lbs. (20 Nm)

    b. Step 2: Bolts 1–10 to 35 ft. lbs. (47 Nm)

    c. Step 3: Bolts 11–14 to 18 ft. lbs. (25 Nm)

    d. Step 4: Bolts 1–10 plus ¼ (90 degree) turn

    e. Step 5: Bolts 11–14 to 22 ft. lbs. (30 Nm)

14. Install or connect the following:
- Camshaft sprockets. Align the secondary chain matchmarks and tighten the bolts to 90 ft. lbs. (122 Nm).
- Secondary timing chain guides
- Cylinder head access plugs
- Secondary timing chain tensioners. Refer to the timing chain procedure in this section.

15. Remove the Timing Chain Locking tool 8515.

16. Install or connect the following:
- Front cover
- Crankshaft damper. Torque the bolt to 130 ft. lbs. (175 Nm).
- Rocker arms
- Power steering pump
- Oil fill housing
- Accessory drive belt
- Engine cooling fan and shroud
- Valve covers
- Intake manifold
- Exhaust Y-pipe
- Negative battery cable

17. Fill and bleed the cooling system.

18. Start the engine, check for leaks and repair if necessary.

5.7L Engine

See Figure 60.

1. Before servicing the vehicle, refer to the Precautions Section.

2. Drain the cooling system.

3. Properly relieve the fuel system pressure.

4. Remove or disconnect the following:
- Negative battery cable
- Air cleaner resonator and ducts
- Alternator
- Closed crankcase ventilation system
- EVAP control system
- Heater hoses
- Cylinder head covers
- Intake manifold
- Rocker arms and pushrods
- Cylinder heads

To install:

➡**The head gaskets are not interchangeable. They are marked "L" and "R".**

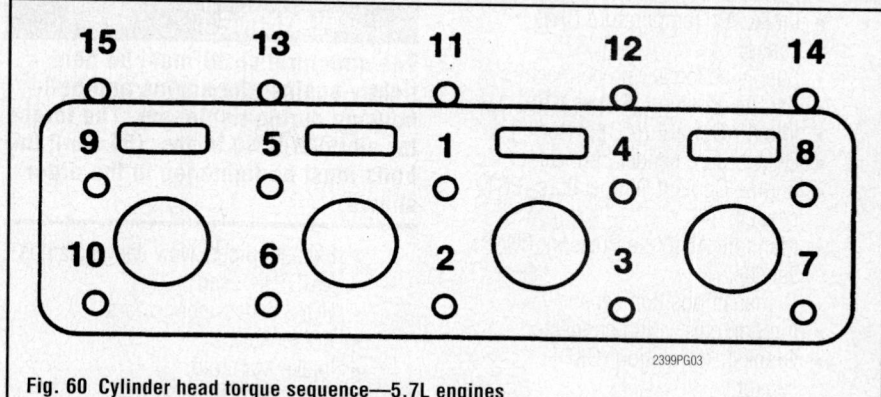

```
15    13    11    12    14
 9  [  ]  5  [  ]  1  [  ]  4  [  ]  8
10        6         2         3        7
```
2399PG03

Fig. 60 Cylinder head torque sequence—5.7L engines

5. Install the cylinder heads. Use new gaskets and tighten the bolts, in sequence, as follows:

    a. Step 1: 12 mm bolts–25 ft. lbs. (34 Nm); 8mm bolts–15 ft. lbs. (20 Nm)

    b. Step 2: 12mm bolts–40 ft. lbs. (54 Nm); 8mm bolts retorque–15 ft. lbs. (20 Nm)

    c. Step 3: 12mm bolts–plus 90 degrees; 8mm bolts–25 ft. lbs. (34 Nm)

6. Install or connect the following:
- Rocker arms and pushrods
- Intake manifold
- Heater hoses
- Alternator
- Cylinder head covers. Torque the studs and bolts to 70 inch lbs.
- Air cleaner resonator and ducts
- Negative battery cable

ENGINE ASSEMBLY

REMOVAL & INSTALLATION

3.7L Engine

See Figure 61.

1. Before servicing the vehicle, refer to the Precautions Section.

2. Properly relieve the fuel system pressure.

3. Drain the cooling system.

4. Drain the engine oil.

5. Remove or disconnect the following:
- Negative battery cable
- Hood
- Air cleaner assembly
- Radiator
- Electric and mechanical fan assemblies
- A/C compressor, if equipped, and secure it out of the way with the lines attached. DO NOT DISCHARGE!
- Power steering pump, with the lines attached

➡**Do NOT remove the phenolic pulley from the P/S pump. It is not required for P/S pump removal.**

- Alternator
- Coolant bottle
- Heater hoses
- Accelerator and speed control cables
- Lower and upper radiator hoses
- Engine ground straps

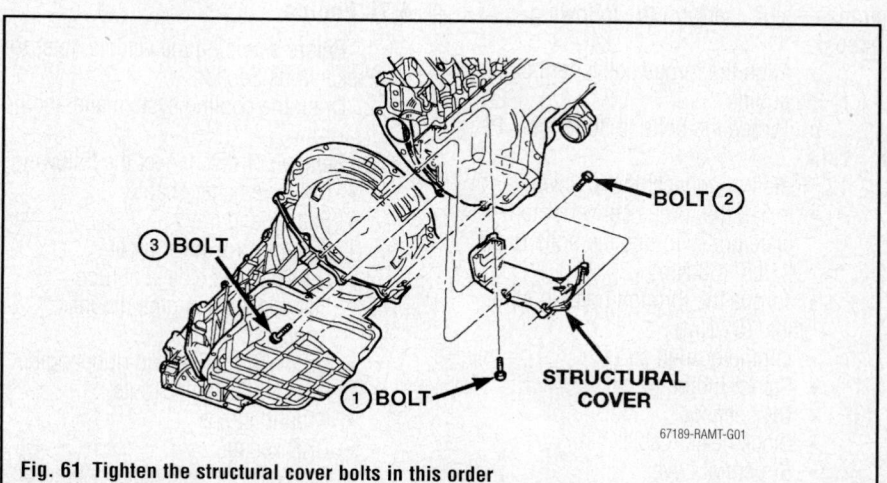

67189-RAMT-G01

Fig. 61 Tighten the structural cover bolts in this order

- Intake Air Temperature (IAT) sensor
- Fuel injection wiring connectors
- Throttle Position (TP) sensor
- Idle Air Control (IAC) motor
- Oil pressure sender connector
- Engine Coolant Temperature (ECT) sensor
- Manifold Absolute Pressure (MAP) sensor
- Camshaft position sensor
- Ignition coil wiring connector
- Crankshaft Position (CKP) sensor
- Coil pack
- Fuel rail
- PCV hose
- Vacuum hoses from the intake manifold
- Knock sensor connectors
- Oil dipstick tube
- Intake manifold
- Heated Oxygen (HO2S) sensor connector
- Block heater connector
- Front driveshaft at the differential
- Starter
- Structural cover
- Torque converter bolts and match-mark the converter
- Automatic transmission-to-engine bolts
- Exhaust front pipes
- Left and right engine mounts

6. Place a support stand under the transmission.

7. Install an engine lift plate

8. Lift the engine out of the vehicle.

To install:

9. If equipped with a manual transmission, install the transmission

10. Lower the engine and install the mounts. Don't tighten the bolts yet.

11. If equipped with an automatic transmission, perform the following steps:

   a. Align the torque converter housing to the engine.

   b. Torque the bolts to 30 ft. lbs. (41 Nm).

12. Install or connect the following:

- Install the torque converter to flex-plate bolts. Torque the bolts to 50 ft. lbs. (68 Nm)
- Torque the through bolts to 45 ft. lbs. (61 Nm)
- Engine ground strap
- Starter motor
- CKP sensor
- Block heater cable
- Structural cover

※ WARNING

The structural cover must be held tightly against the engine and bell-housing during tightening. The torque for all bolts is 40 ft. lbs. (54 Nm); the bolts must be tightened in the order shown.

- Exhaust pipes. New flange clamps MUST be used!
- HO2S sensor connectors
- KS sensors
- Intake Manifold
- Dipstick tube
- Vacuum hoses to the intake manifold
- PCV and breather hoses
- Fuel rail
- Ignition coil
- IAT sensor
- Fuel injector connectors
- TP sensor
- IAC motor
- Oil pressure sender
- ECT sensor electrical connector
- MAP sensor
- CMP sensor
- Radiator hoses
- Cruise control cable, if equipped
- Throttle cable
- Heater hoses
- Coolant bottle
- Power steering pump
- Alternator
- A/C compressor
- Radiator
- Fan assemblies
- Air cleaner assembly
- Negative battery cable

13. Fill and bleed the power steering system.

14. Fill the engine with clean oil.

15. Start the engine and check for leaks, repair if necessary.

4.7L Engine

1. Before servicing the vehicle, refer to the Precautions Section.

2. Drain the cooling system and engine oil.

3. Remove or disconnect the following:

- Negative battery cable
- Battery and tray
- Exhaust crossover pipe
- On 4WD, the axle vent tube
- Left and right engine mount through bolts
- On 4WD, the left and right engine mount bracket locknuts
- Ground straps
- CKP sensor
- On 4WD, the axle isolator bracket

- Structural cover
- Starter
- Torque converter bolts
- Transmission-to-engine bolts
- Engine block heater
- Resonator and air inlet
- Throttle and speed control cables
- Crankcase breathers
- A/C compressor
- Shroud and fan assemblies
- Transmission cooler lines
- Radiator hoses
- Radiator
- Alternator
- Heater hoses
- Engine harness
- Vacuum lines
- Fuel system pressure
- Fuel line at the rail
- Power steering pump

4. Install lifting eyes and take up the weight of the engine with a crane.

5. Support the transmission with a jack.

6. Remove the engine.

To install:

7. Installation is the reverse of removal. Observe the following:

- Left and right engine mount through bolts: 2wd 70 ft. lbs. (95 Nm); 4WD 75 ft. lbs. (102 Nm)
- On 4WD, the bracket locknuts: 30 ft. lbs. (41 Nm)
- Transmission-to-engine bolts: 30 ft. lbs. (41 Nm)

※ WARNING

The structural cover must be held tightly against the engine and bell-housing during tightening. The torque for all bolts is 40 ft. lbs. (54 Nm); the bolts must be tightened in the order shown.

5.7L Engine

1. Before servicing the vehicle, refer to the Precautions Section.

2. Drain the cooling system.

3. Drain the engine oil.

4. Relieve the fuel system pressure.

5. Remove or disconnect the following:

- Negative battery cable
- Hood
- Air cleaner and resonator
- Accessory drive belt
- Engine fan
- Radiator
- A/C compressor, if equipped
- Alternator
- Intake manifold and IAFM as an assembly
- Heater hoses

- Power steering pump
- Fuel line
- Engine front mount thru-bolt nuts
- Transmission oil cooler lines
- Exhaust pipes at the manifolds
- Starter motor
- Structural dust cover and transmission inspection cover
- Torque converter-to-flexplate bolts
- Transmission flange bolts. Support the transmission.
- Engine

To install:

❊❊ WARNING

The structural cover must be held tightly against the engine and bell-housing during tightening. The torque for all bolts is 40 ft. lbs. (54 Nm); the bolts must be tightened in the order shown.

6. Install or connect the following:
   - Engine. Tighten the engine mount thru-bolt finger-tight.
   - Transmission flange bolts. Tighten the bolts to 40–45 ft. lbs. (54–61 Nm). Then, tighten the mount bolt nuts to 70 ft. lbs. (95 Nm)
   - Transmission oil cooler lines
   - Torque converter. Tighten the bolts to 23 ft. lbs. (31 Nm).
   - Structural dust cover and transmission inspection cover
   - Starter motor
   - Fuel line
   - Power steering pump
   - Heater hoses
   - Intake manifold and IAFM as an assembly
   - Alternator
   - A/C compressor, if equipped
   - Radiator
   - Engine fan
   - Accessory drive belt
   - Air cleaner and resonator
   - Hood
   - Negative battery cable
7. Fill the crankcase to the correct level.
8. Fill the cooling system.
9. Start the engine and check for leaks.

EXHAUST MANIFOLD

REMOVAL & INSTALLATION

3.7L & 4.7L Engines

See Figure 62.

1. Before servicing the vehicle, refer to the Precautions Section.
2. Drain the cooling system.

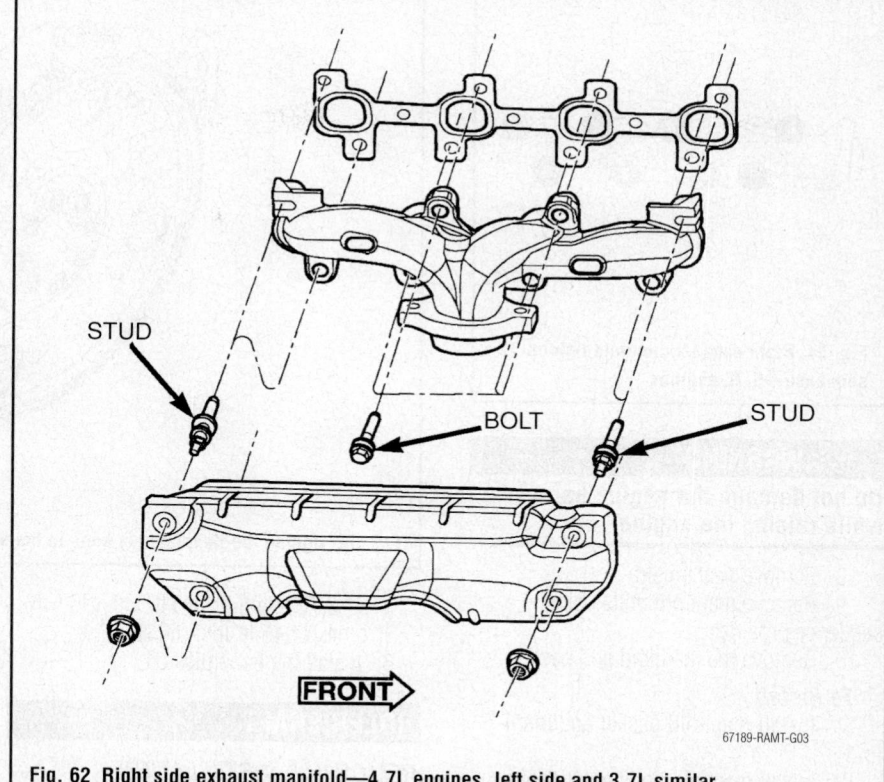

Fig. 62 Right side exhaust manifold—4.7L engines, left side and 3.7L similar

67189-RAMT-G03

3. Remove or disconnect the following:
   - Battery
   - Power distribution center
   - Battery tray
   - Windshield washer fluid bottle
   - Air cleaner assembly
   - Accessory drive belt
   - A/C compressor
   - A/C accumulator bracket
   - Heater hoses
   - Exhaust manifold heat shields
   - Exhaust Y-pipe
   - Starter motor
   - Exhaust manifolds

To install:

4. Install or connect the following:
   - Exhaust manifolds, using new gaskets. Tighten the bolts to 18 ft. lbs. (25 Nm), starting with the inner bolts and work out to the ends.
   - Starter motor
   - Exhaust Y-pipe
   - Exhaust manifold heat shields
   - Heater hoses
   - A/C accumulator bracket
   - A/C compressor
   - Accessory drive belt
   - Air cleaner assembly
   - Windshield washer fluid bottle
   - Battery tray
   - Power distribution center
   - Battery

5. Fill the cooling system.
6. Start the engine and check for leaks.

5.7L Engine

See Figures 63 and 64.

1. Before servicing the vehicle, refer to the Precautions Section.
2. Disconnect negative battery cable.
3. Raise the vehicle.
4. Remove exhaust pipe to manifold bolts.
5. Lower the vehicle.
6. Install engine support fixture special tool number 8534.
7. Raise the engine enough to remove manifolds.

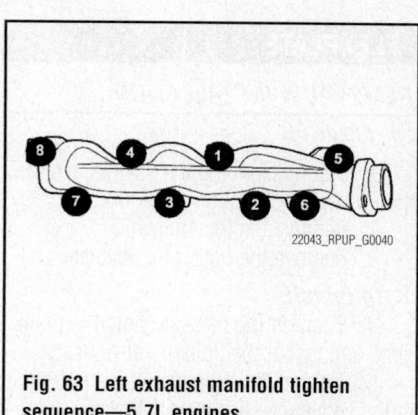

22043_RPUP_G0040

Fig. 63 Left exhaust manifold tighten sequence—5.7L engines

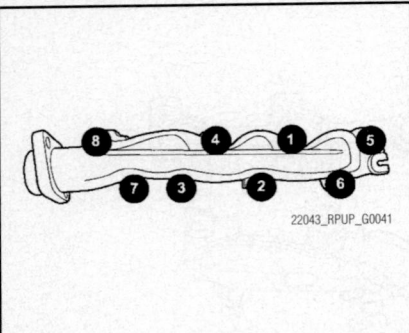

Fig. 64 Right exhaust manifold tighten sequence—5.7L engines

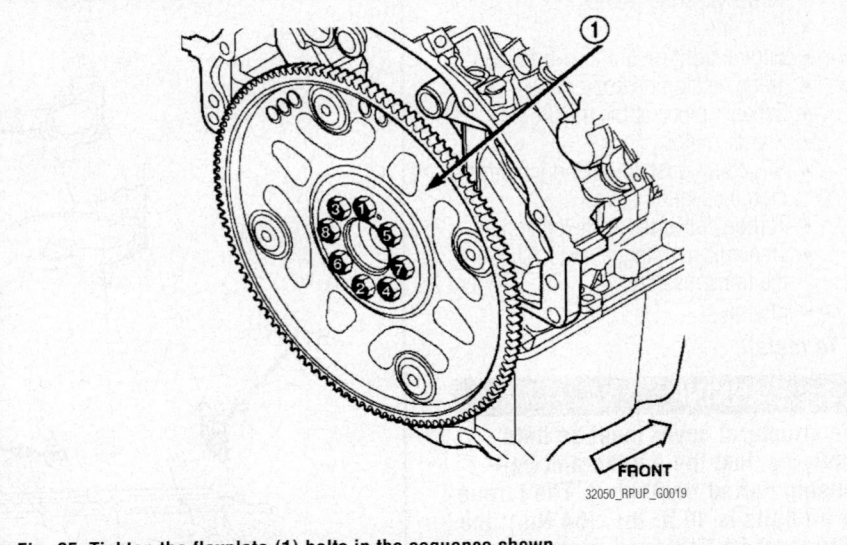

Fig. 65 Tighten the flexplate (1) bolts in the sequence shown

❈❈ WARNING

Do not damage the engine harness while raising the engine.

8. Remove heat shield.
9. Remove manifold bolts using sequence provided.
10. Remove the manifold and gasket.

To install:

11. Install manifold gasket and manifold.
12. Install manifold bolts and tighten using sequence provided to 18 ft. lbs. (25 Nm).
13. Install heat shield and tighten nuts to 11 ft. lbs. (15 Nm).
14. Lower the engine.

❈❈ WARNING

Do not damage the engine harness while lowering the engine.

15. Remove engine support fixture from engine.
16. Raise the vehicle.
17. Tighten right and left side engine mount through bolts.
18. Install exhaust flange to pipe bolts.
19. Lower the vehicle.
20. Connect negative battery cable.

FLEXPLATE

REMOVAL & INSTALLATION

See Figure 65.

1. Before servicing the vehicle, refer to the Precautions Section
2. Remove the transmission.
3. Remove the bolts and flexplate.

To install:

4. Position the flexplate onto the crankshaft and install the bolts hand-tight.
5. Tighten the flexplate retaining bolts, in the sequence shown, as follows:

a. 3.7L and 5.7L: 70 ft. lbs. (95 Nm)
b. 4.7L: 45 ft. lbs. (60 Nm)
6. Install the transmission.

IDLER SHAFT

REMOVAL & INSTALLATION

3.7L & 4.7L Engines

1. Remove the primary and secondary timing chains and sprockets. Refer to procedure in this section.

➡**To remove the idler shaft, it is necessary to tap threads into the shaft, to install the removal tool.**

2. Using a 12mm X 1.75 tap, cut threads in the idler shaft center bore.
3. Cover the radiator core with a suitable cover.

❈❈ WARNING

Be careful when removing the idler shaft, Do not strike the radiator cooling fins with the slide hammer.

4. Using Special Tool 8517 Slide Hammer, remove the idler shaft.
5. Thoroughly clean the idler shaft bore.

To install:

6. Position the idler shaft in the bore.

➡**The two lubrication holes in the idler shaft do not require any special alignment.**

➡**Before using the retaining bolt to install the idler shaft, coat the threads and the pilot on the idler shaft, with clean engine oil.**

7. Using the primary idler sprocket

retaining bolt and washer, carefully draw the idler shaft into the bore until fully seated.
8. Coat the idler shaft with clean engine oil.
9. Install the timing chains and sprockets. Refer to procedure in this section.

INTAKE MANIFOLD

REMOVAL & INSTALLATION

3.7L & 4.7L Engines

See Figure 66.

1. Before servicing the vehicle, refer to the Precautions Section.
2. Drain the cooling system.
3. Properly relieve the fuel system pressure.
4. Remove or disconnect the following:
- Negative battery cable
- Air cleaner assembly
- Accelerator cable
- Cruise control cable
- Manifold Absolute Pressure (MAP) sensor connector
- Intake Air Temperature (IAT) sensor connector
- Throttle Position (TP) sensor connector
- Idle Air Control (IAC) valve connector
- Engine Coolant Temperature (ECT) sensor
- Positive Crankcase Ventilation (PCV) valve and hose
- Canister purge vacuum line
- Brake booster vacuum line
- Cruise control servo hose
- Accessory drive belt
- Alternator

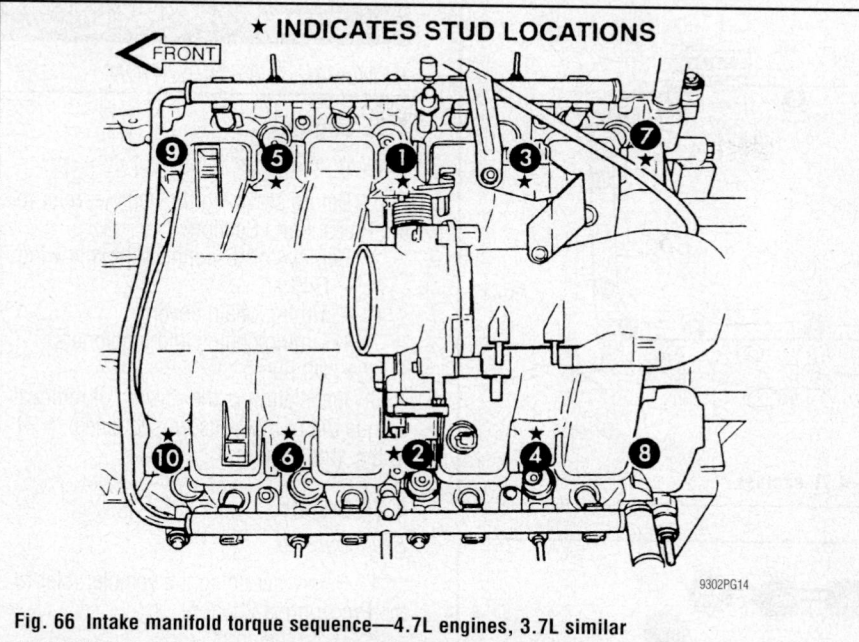

★ INDICATES STUD LOCATIONS

Fig. 66 Intake manifold torque sequence—4.7L engines, 3.7L similar

- A/C compressor
- Engine ground straps
- Ignition coil towers
- Oil dipstick tube
- Fuel line
- Fuel supply manifold
- Throttle body and mounting bracket
- Cowl seal
- Right engine lifting stud
- Intake manifold. Remove the fasteners in reverse of the tightening sequence.

To install:

5. Install or connect the following:
- Intake manifold using new gaskets. Torque the bolts, in sequence, to 105 inch lbs. (12 Nm).
- Right engine lifting stud
- Cowl seal
- Throttle body and mounting bracket
- Fuel supply manifold
- Fuel line
- Oil dipstick tube
- Ignition coil towers
- Engine ground straps
- A/C compressor
- Alternator
- Accessory drive belt
- Cruise control servo hose
- Brake booster vacuum line
- Canister purge vacuum line
- PCV valve and hose
- ECT sensor
- IAC valve connector
- TP sensor connector
- IAT sensor connector
- MAP sensor connector
- Cruise control cable

- Accelerator cable
- Air cleaner assembly
- Negative battery cable
6. Fill and bleed the cooling system.
7. Start the engine, check for leaks and repair if necessary.

5.7L Engine

1. Before servicing the vehicle, refer to the Precautions Section.
2. Drain the cooling system.
3. Relieve the fuel system pressure.
4. Remove or disconnect the following:

- Negative battery cable
- Air cleaner assembly
- Accessory drive belt
- MAP connector
- IAT connector
- TPS connector
- CTS connector
- Brake booster hose
- PCV hose
- Alternator
- A/C compressor
- Intake manifold bolts, in a criss-cross pattern, from the outside to the center
- Intake manifold/IAFM

To install:

5. Position new intake manifold seals.
6. Install the intake manifold. Tighten the bolts in sequence from the center outwards, to 105 inch lbs. (12 Nm).
7. Install or connect the following:

- Electrical connectors
- Alternator
- A/C compressor
- Brake booster hose
- PCV hose
- Accessory drive belt
- Negative battery cable
- Air cleaner assembly

OIL PAN

REMOVAL & INSTALLATION

See Figures 67 through 69.

1. Before servicing the vehicle, refer to the Precautions Section.

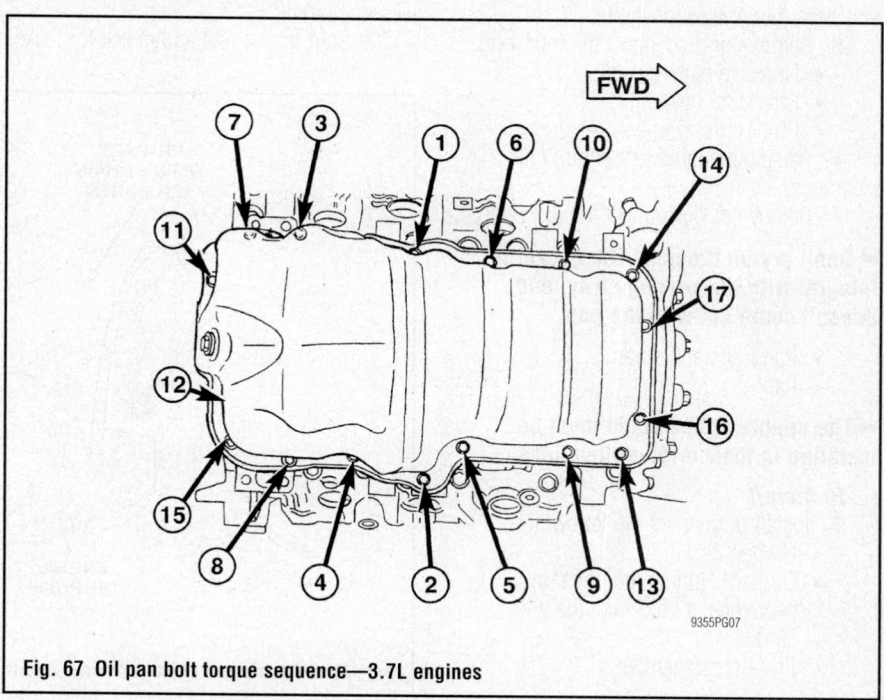

Fig. 67 Oil pan bolt torque sequence—3.7L engines

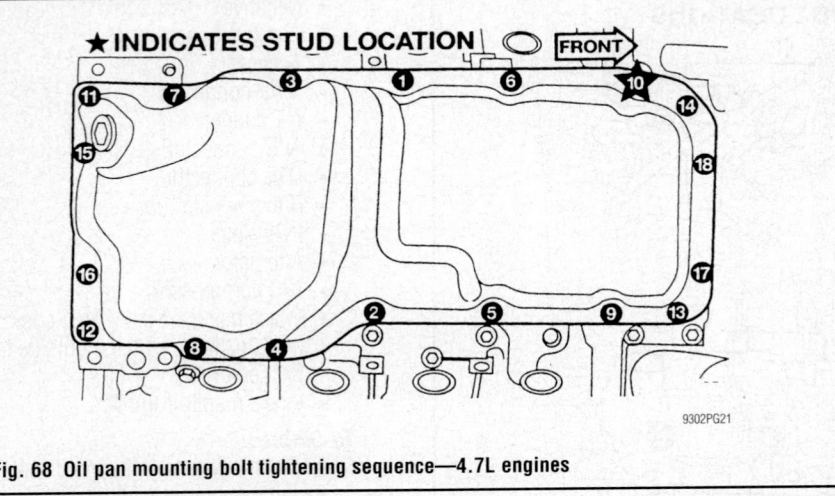

Fig. 68 Oil pan mounting bolt tightening sequence—4.7L engines

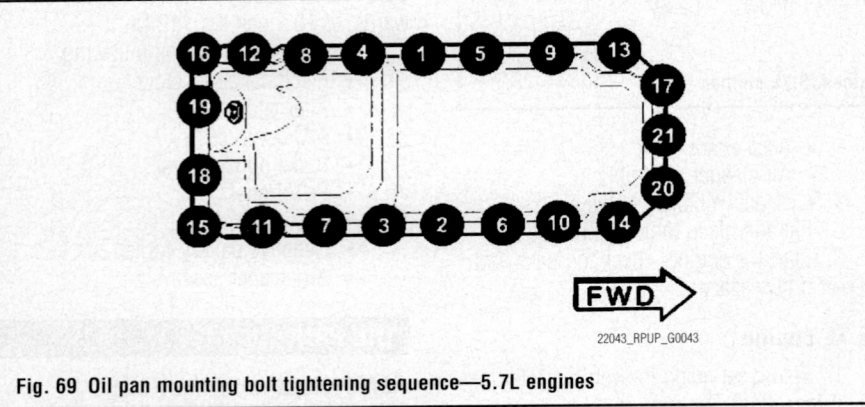

Fig. 69 Oil pan mounting bolt tightening sequence—5.7L engines

2. Drain the engine oil.
3. Attach an engine crane.
4. Loosen, but don't remove, the left and right mount through-bolts.
5. Remove or disconnect the following:
   - Negative battery cable
   - Structural cover
   - Front crossmember
6. Raise the engine just enough for clearance.
7. Remove or disconnect the following:

➡**Don't pry on the pan. The gasket is integral with the windage tray, and doesn't come out with the pan.**

   - Pan bolts and studs
   - Pan

➡**The double ended studs must be installed in their original locations.**

To install:

8. Install or connect the following:
   - Oil pan gasket
   - Oil pan. Tighten the bolts, in sequence, to 105 inch lbs. (12 Nm).
   - Front crossmember

   - Structural cover
   - Negative battery cable
9. Fill the crankcase to the proper level with engine oil.
10. Start the engine and check for leaks.

OIL PUMP

REMOVAL & INSTALLATION

3.7L Engine

See Figure 70.

1. Before servicing the vehicle, refer to the Precautions Section.
2. Remove or disconnect the following:
   - Oil Pan
   - Timing chain cover
   - Timing chains and tensioners
   - Oil pump
3. Installation is the reverse of removal. Torque the pump bolts, in sequence, to 21 ft. lbs. (28 Nm).

4.7L Engine

See Figure 70.

1. Before servicing the vehicle, refer to the Precautions Section.
2. Drain the engine oil.
3. Remove or disconnect the following:
   - Negative battery cable
   - Oil pan
   - Oil pump pick-up tube
   - Timing chains and tensioners
   - Oil pump

To install:

4. Install or connect the following:
   - Oil pump. Tighten the bolts to 21 ft. lbs. (28 Nm).
   - Timing chains and tensioners
   - Oil pump pick-up tube
   - Oil pan
   - Negative battery cable
5. Fill the crankcase to the correct level.
6. Start the engine and check for leaks.

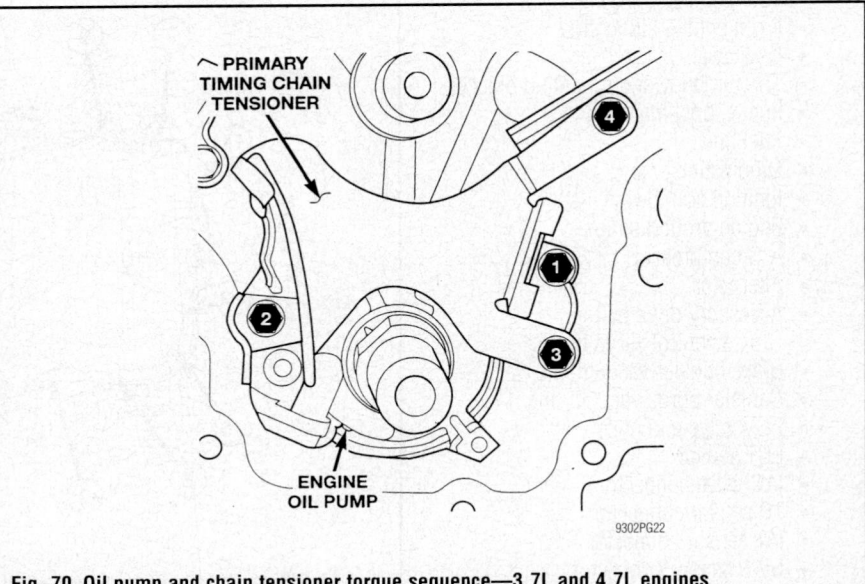

Fig. 70 Oil pump and chain tensioner torque sequence—3.7L and 4.7L engines

5.7L Engine

1. Before servicing the vehicle, refer to the Precautions Section.
2. Drain the engine oil.
3. Remove or disconnect the following:

- Negative battery cable
- Oil pan
- Oil pump pick-up tube
- Timing chains and tensioners
- Oil pump

To install:

4. Install or connect the following:

- Oil pump. Tighten the bolts to 21 ft. lbs. (28 Nm).
- Timing chains and tensioners
- Oil pump pick-up tube
- Oil pan
- Negative battery cable

5. Fill the crankcase to the correct level.
6. Start the engine and check for leaks.

PISTON AND RING

POSITIONING

See Figures 71 and 72.

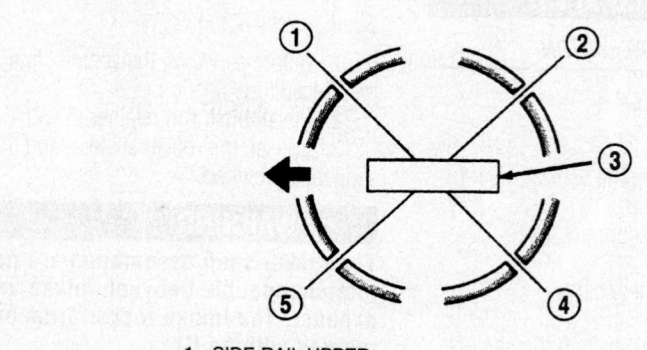

1 - SIDE RAIL UPPER
2 - NO. 1 RING GAP
3 - PISTON PIN
4 - SIDE RAIL LOWER
5 - NO. 2 RING GAP AND SPACER EXPANDER GAP

2399PG02

Fig. 72 Piston ring end-gap spacing—5.7L engines

REAR MAIN SEAL

REMOVAL & INSTALLATION

See Figure 73.

1. Before servicing the vehicle, refer to the Precautions Section.
2. Remove or disconnect the following:

- Transmission
- Flexplate

3. Thread Oil Seal Remover 8506 into the rear main seal as far as possible and remove the rear main seal.

To install:

4. Install or connect the following:

- Seal Guide 8349-2 onto the crankshaft
- Rear main seal on the seal guide
- Rear main seal, using the Crankshaft Rear Oil Seal Installer 8349 and Driver Handle C-4171; tap it into place until the installer is flush with the cylinder block
- Flexplate. Torque the bolts in the sequence shown to 45 ft. lbs. (60 Nm) on auto trans., or 70 ft. lbs. (95 Nm) for man. trans.
- Transmission

5. Start the engine, check for leaks and repair if necessary.

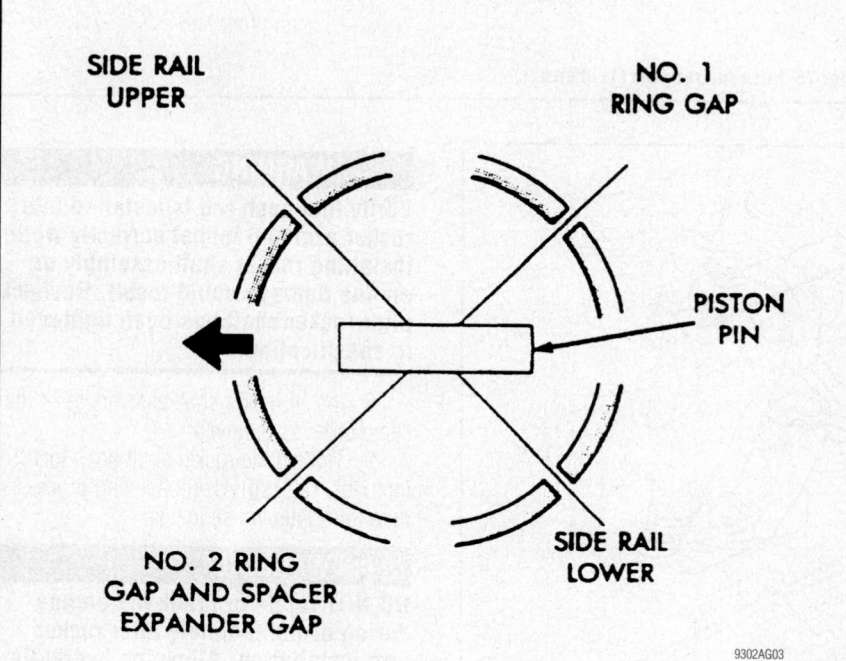

SIDE RAIL UPPER

NO. 1 RING GAP

PISTON PIN

SIDE RAIL LOWER

NO. 2 RING GAP AND SPACER EXPANDER GAP

9302AG03

Fig. 71 Piston ring end-gap spacing. Position raised "F" on piston toward front of engine—3.7L and 4.7L engines

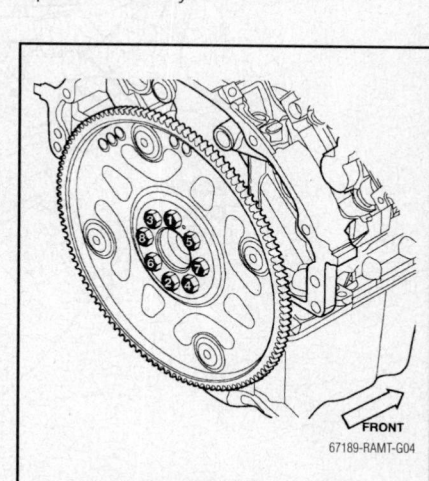

FRONT

67189-RAMT-G04

Fig. 73 Flexplate bolt tightening sequence

ROCKER ARMS/SHAFTS

REMOVAL & INSTALLATION

3.7L & 4.7L Engines

See Figure 74.

1. Before servicing the vehicle, refer to the Precautions Section.
2. Remove or disconnect the following:
   - Negative battery cable
   - Valve covers
3. Rotate the crankshaft so that the piston of the cylinder to be serviced is at Top Dead Center (TDC) and both valves are closed.
4. Use special tool 8516 to depress the valve and remove the rocker arm.
5. Repeat for each rocker arm to be serviced.

➡**Keep valve train components in order for reassembly.**

To install:

6. Rotate the crankshaft so that the piston of the cylinder to be serviced is at BDC.
7. Compress the valve spring and install each rocker arm in its original position.
8. Repeat for each rocker arm to be installed.
9. Install or connect the following:
   - Cylinder head cover
   - Negative battery cable

5.7L Engine

See Figures 75 and 76.

1. Before servicing the vehicle, refer to the Precautions Section.
2. Install push rod retainer (1) 9070.
3. Loosen the rocker shafts using the sequence provided.

❋❋ WARNING
The rocker shaft assemblies are not interchangeable between intake and exhaust. The intake rocker arms are marked with an (I).

4. Remove the rocker shafts. Note location for reassembly.

❋❋ WARNING
The longer push rods are for the exhaust side, and the shorter push rods are for intake side.

5. Remove the push rods. Note push rod location for reassembly.

To install:

6. Install the push rods in the same order as removed.
7. Install the push rod retainer (1) 9070.

❋❋ WARNING
Ensure that retainers and rocker arms are not overlapped when tightening bolts or engine damage could result.

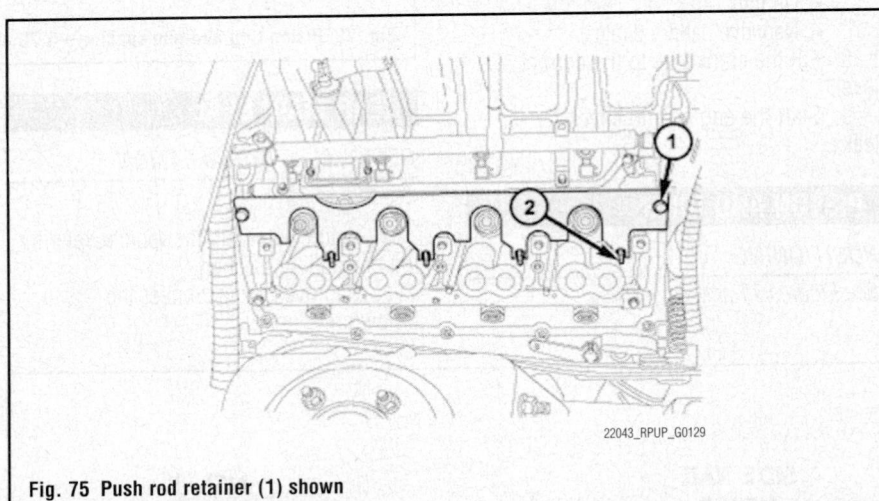

Fig. 75 Push rod retainer (1) shown

❋❋ WARNING
Verify that push rod is installed into rocker arm and tappet correctly while installing rocker shaft assembly or engine damage could result. Recheck after rocker shaft has been tightened to specification.

8. Install rocker shaft assemblies in the same order as removed.
9. Tighten the rocker shaft bolts to 195 inch. lbs. (22 Nm). Use loosening procedure for tightening sequence.

❋❋ WARNING
DO NOT rotate or crank the engine during or immediately after rocker arm installation. Allow the hydraulic roller tappets adequate time to bleed down (about 5 minutes).

10. Remove push rod retainer (1) 9070.
11. Install cylinder head cover.

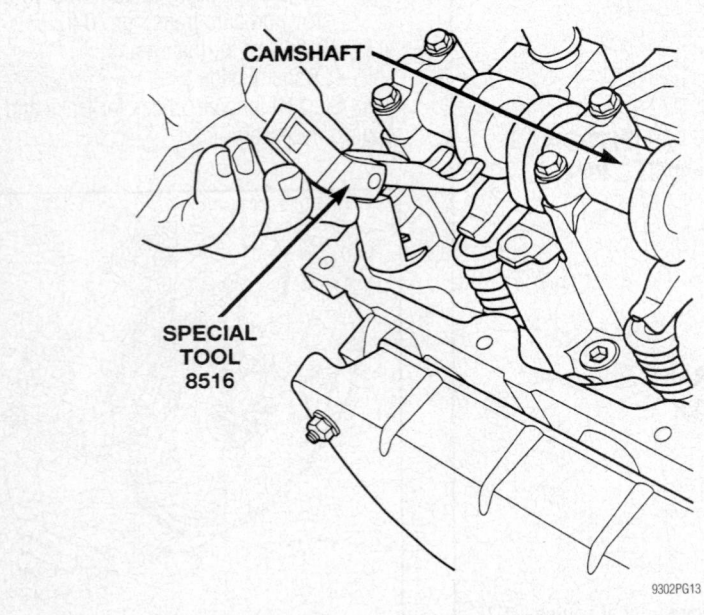

Fig. 74 Rocker arm service—3.7L and 4.7L engines

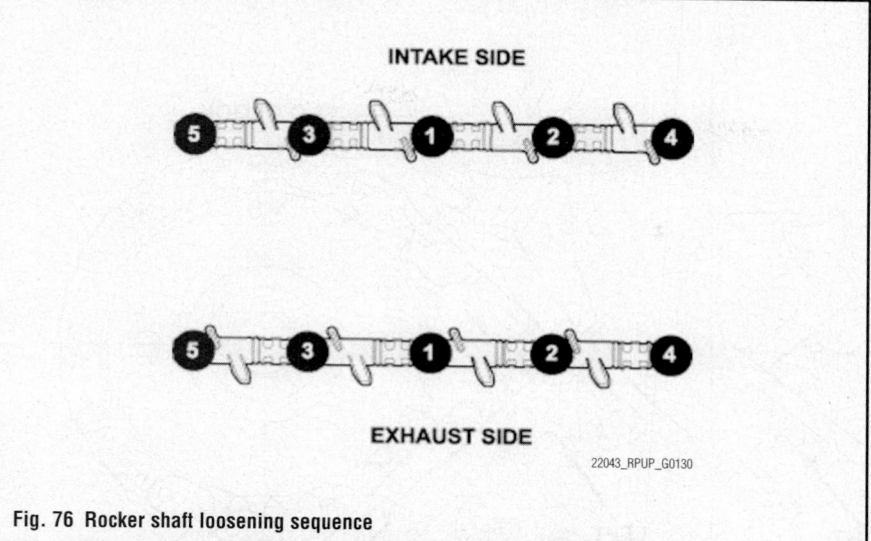

INTAKE SIDE

EXHAUST SIDE

22043_RPUP_G0130

Fig. 76 Rocker shaft loosening sequence

TIMING CHAIN, SPROCKETS, FRONT COVER AND SEAL

REMOVAL & INSTALLATION

3.7L & 4.7L Engines

See Figures 77 through 92.

1. Before servicing the vehicle, refer to the Precautions Section.

2. Drain the cooling system.

3. Remove or disconnect the following:
   - Negative battery cable
   - Valve covers
   - Radiator fan
   - Heater hoses
   - Alternator
   - Air conditioning compressor
   - Power steering pump
   - Front cover

4. Rotate the crankshaft so that the crankshaft timing mark aligns with the Top Dead Center (TDC) mark on the front cover, and the **V8 or V6** marks on the camshaft sprockets are at 12 o'clock.
   - Access plugs from the cylinder heads
   - Oil fill housing
   - Crankshaft damper

5. Compress the primary timing chain tensioner and install a lock pin.

6. Remove the secondary timing chain tensioners.

7. Hold the left camshaft with adjustable pliers and remove the sprocket and chain. Rotate the **left** camshaft 15 degrees **clockwise** to the neutral position.

8. Hold the right camshaft with adjustable pliers and remove the camshaft sprocket. Rotate the **right** camshaft 45

degrees **counterclockwise** to the neutral position.

9. Remove the primary timing chain and sprockets.

To install:

10. Use a small pry tool to hold the ratchet pawl and compress the secondary timing chain tensioners in a vise and install locking pins.

➡ **The black bolts fasten the guide to the engine block and the silver**

bolts fasten the guide to the cylinder head.

11. Install or connect the following:
   - Secondary timing chain guides. Tighten the bolts to 21 ft. lbs. (28 Nm).
   - Secondary timing chains to the idler sprocket so that the double plated links on each chain are visible through the slots in the primary idler sprocket

12. Lock the secondary timing chains to the idler sprocket with Timing Chain Locking tool as shown.

13. Align the primary chain double plated links with the idler sprocket timing mark and the single plated link with the crankshaft sprocket timing mark.

14. Install the primary chain and sprockets. Tighten the idler sprocket bolt to 25 ft. lbs. (34 Nm).

15. Align the secondary chain single plated links with the timing marks on the secondary sprockets. Align the dot at the **L** mark on the left sprocket with the plated link on the left chain and the dot at the **R** mark on the right sprocket with the plated link on the right chain.

16. Rotate the camshafts back from the neutral position and install the camshaft sprockets.

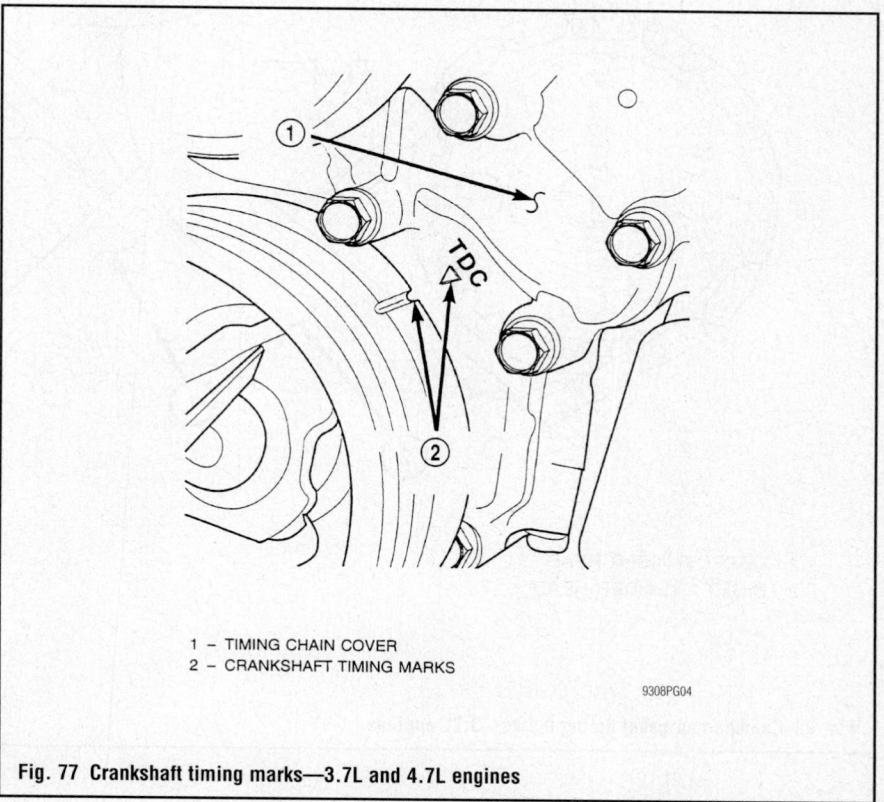

1 – TIMING CHAIN COVER
2 – CRANKSHAFT TIMING MARKS

9308PG04

Fig. 77 Crankshaft timing marks—3.7L and 4.7L engines

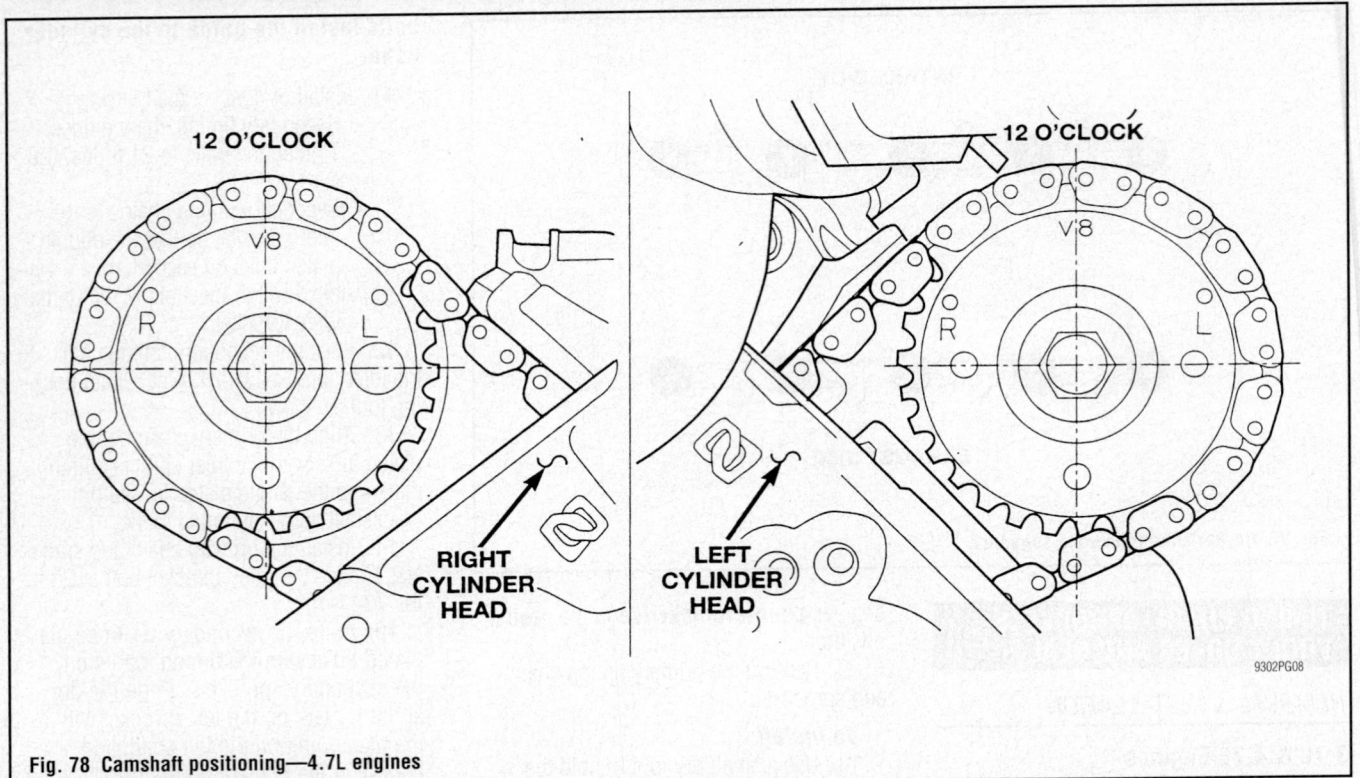

12 O'COCK — V8 — R — L — **RIGHT CYLINDER HEAD** — 2 — **12 O'CLOCK** — V8 — R — L — **LEFT CYLINDER HEAD** — 2

9302PG08

Fig. 78 Camshaft positioning—4.7L engines

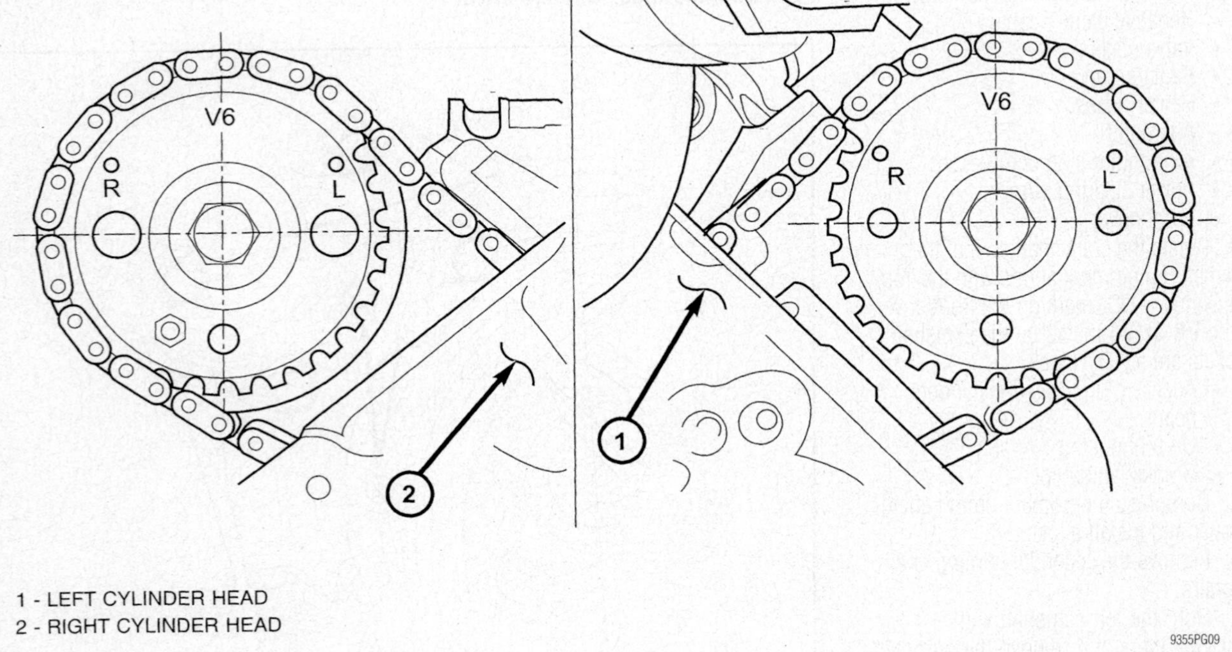

V6 — R — L — 2 — V6 — R — L — 1

1 - LEFT CYLINDER HEAD
2 - RIGHT CYLINDER HEAD

9355PG09

Fig. 79 Camshaft sprocket timing marks—3.7L engines

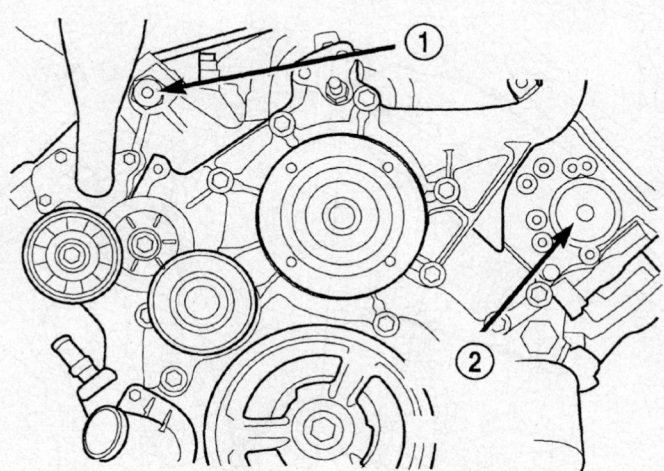

1 - RIGHT CYLINDER HEAD ACCESS PLUG
2 - LEFT CYLINDER HEAD ACCESS PLUG

9355PG11

Fig. 80 Cylinder head access plugs—3.7L engines

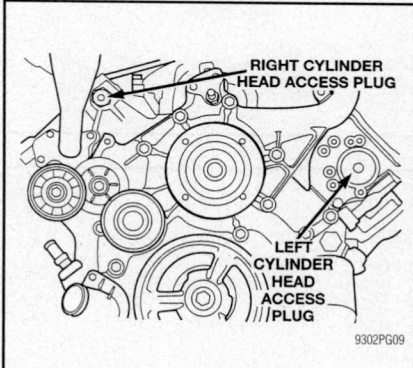

RIGHT CYLINDER HEAD ACCESS PLUG

LEFT CYLINDER HEAD ACCESS PLUG

9302PG09

Fig. 81 Cylinder head access plug locations—4.7L engines

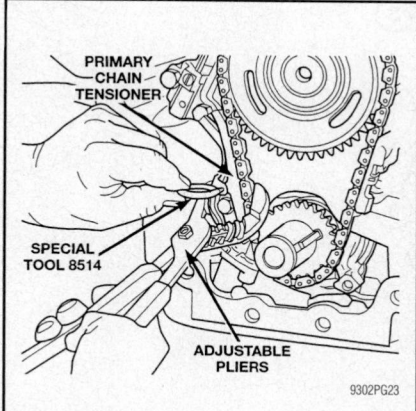

PRIMARY CHAIN TENSIONER

SPECIAL TOOL 8514

ADJUSTABLE PLIERS

9302PG23

Fig. 82 Compress and lock the primary chain tensioner—4.7L engines

17. Remove the secondary chain locking tool.

18. Remove the primary and secondary timing chain tensioner locking pins.

19. Hold the camshaft sprockets with a spanner wrench and tighten the retaining bolts to 90 ft. lbs. (122 Nm).

20. Install or connect the following:
- Front cover. Tighten the bolts, in sequence, to 40 ft. lbs. (54 Nm).
- Front crankshaft seal

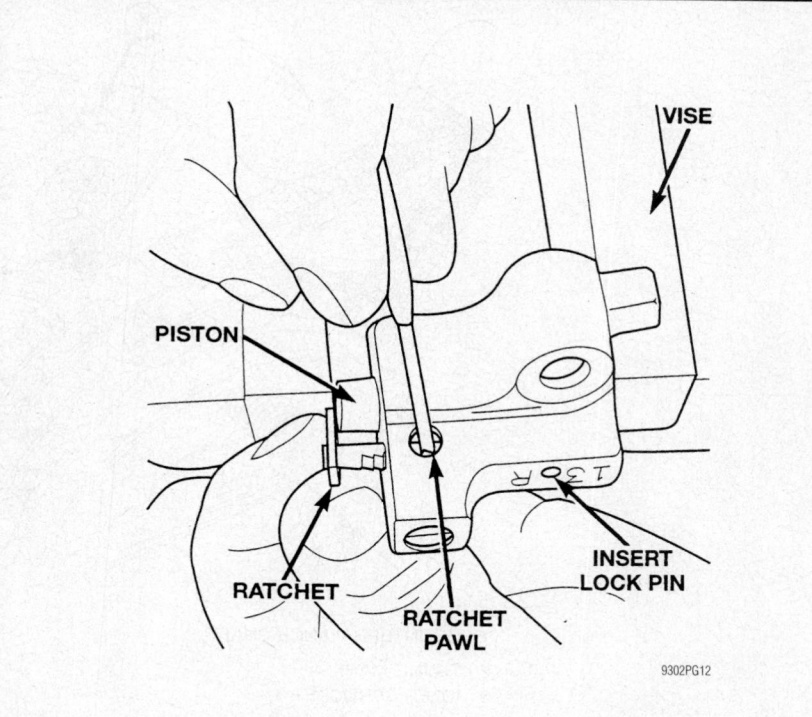

VISE

PISTON

RATCHET

RATCHET PAWL

INSERT LOCK PIN

9302PG12

Fig. 83 Secondary timing chain tensioner preparation—3.7L and 4.7L engines

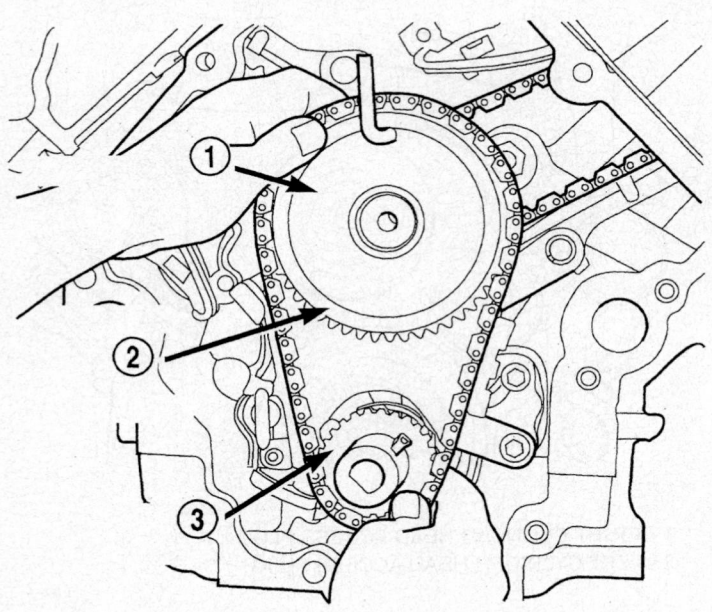

1 - SPECIAL TOOL 8429
2 - PRIMARY CHAIN IDLER SPROCKET
3 - CRANKSHAFT SPROCKET

9355PG12

Fig. 84 Installing the idler gear and timing chains—3.7L and 4.7L engines

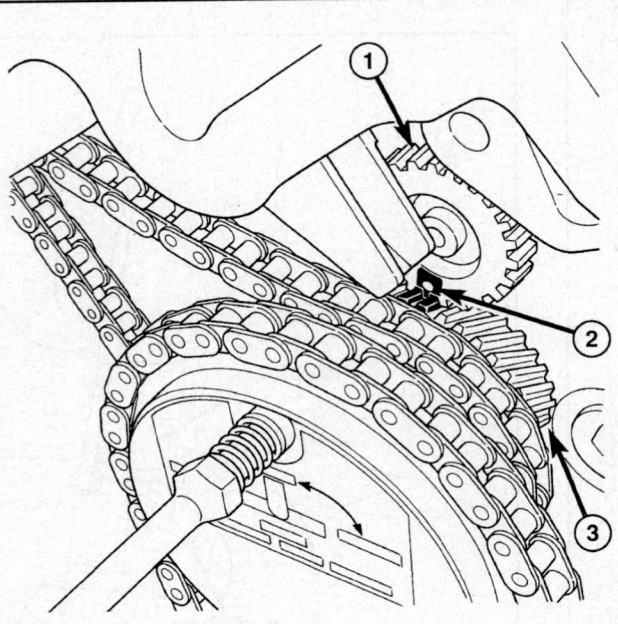

1 - COUNTERBALANCE SHAFT
2 - TIMING MARKS
3 - IDLER SPROCKET

9355PG13

Fig. 85 Counterbalance shaft timing marks—3.7L engines

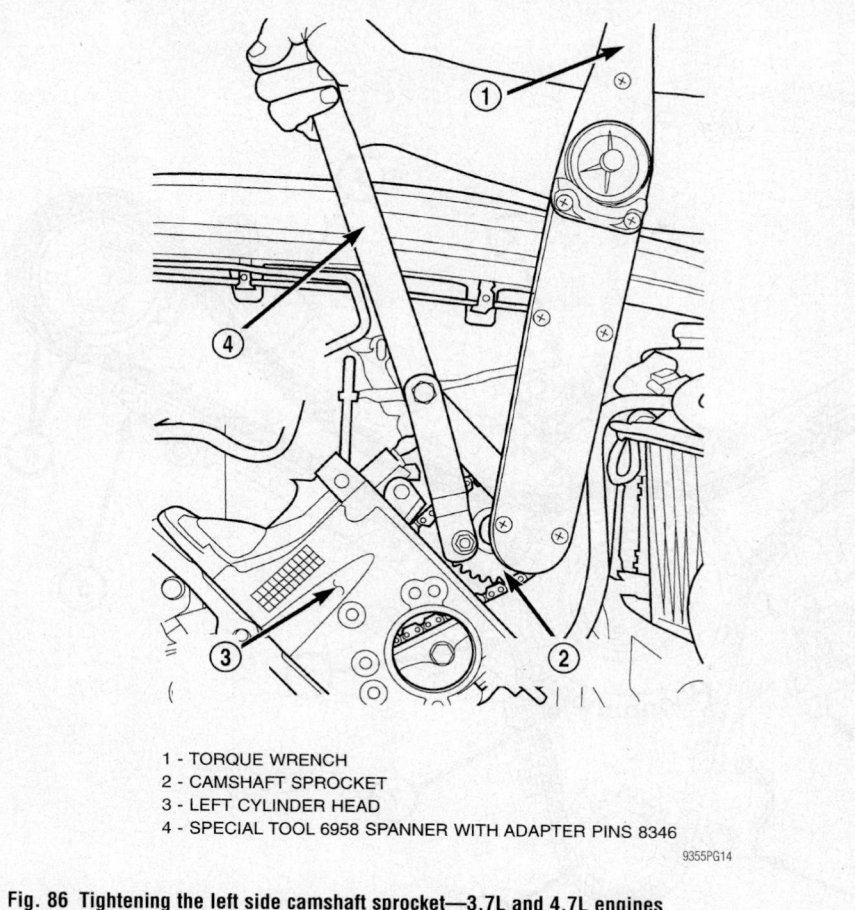

1 - TORQUE WRENCH
2 - CAMSHAFT SPROCKET
3 - LEFT CYLINDER HEAD
4 - SPECIAL TOOL 6958 SPANNER WITH ADAPTER PINS 8346

9355PG14

Fig. 86 Tightening the left side camshaft sprocket—3.7L and 4.7L engines

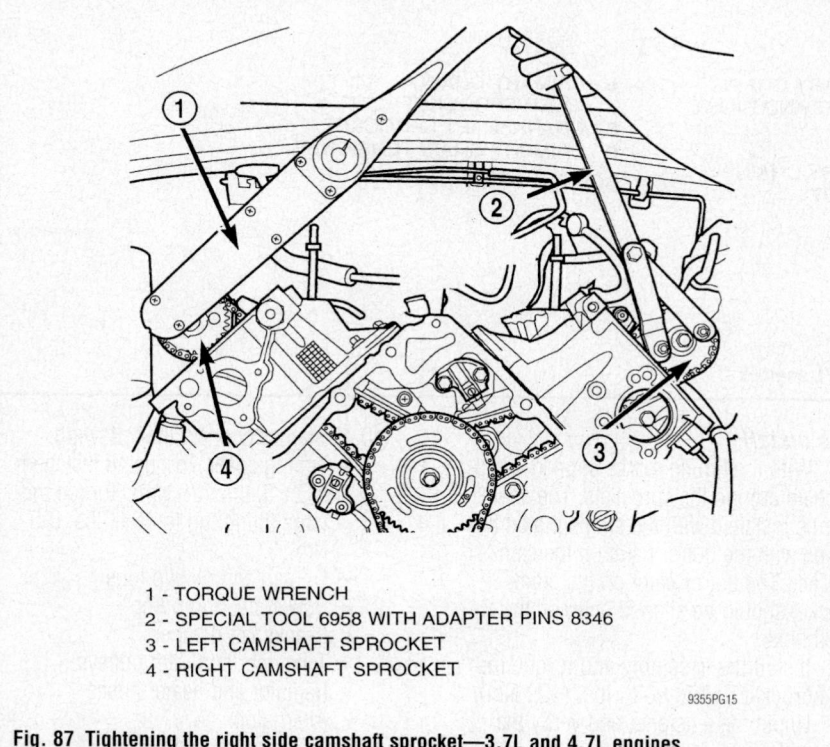

1 - TORQUE WRENCH
2 - SPECIAL TOOL 6958 WITH ADAPTER PINS 8346
3 - LEFT CAMSHAFT SPROCKET
4 - RIGHT CAMSHAFT SPROCKET

9355PG15

Fig. 87 Tightening the right side camshaft sprocket—3.7L and 4.7L engines

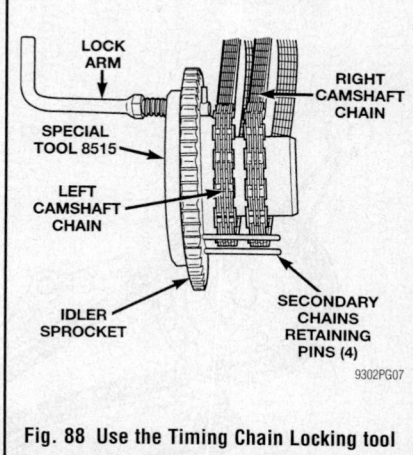

Fig. 88 Use the Timing Chain Locking tool to lock the timing chains on the idler gear—4.7L engines

- Cylinder head access plugs
- A/C compressor
- Alternator
- Accessory drive belt tensioner. Tighten the bolt to 40 ft. lbs. (54 Nm).
- Oil fill housing
- Crankshaft damper. Tighten the bolt to 130 ft. lbs. (175 Nm).
- Power steering pump
- Lower radiator hose
- Heater hoses
- Accessory drive belt
- Engine cooling fan and shroud
- Camshaft Position (CMP) sensor
- Valve covers
- Negative battery cable

21. Fill and bleed the cooling system.

22. Start the engine, check for leaks and repair if necessary.

5.7L Engine

See Figure 92.

1. Before servicing the vehicle, refer to the Precautions Section.

2. Drain the cooling system.

3. Remove or disconnect the following:
- Negative battery cable
- Drive belt
- Radiator and cooling fan
- Coolant and washer bottles
- Fan shroud
- A/C compressor
- Alternator
- Radiator and heater hoses
- Tensioner and idler pulleys
- Crankshaft damper
- Power steering pump
- Oil pan and pickup tube
- Timing cover
- Re-install the damper

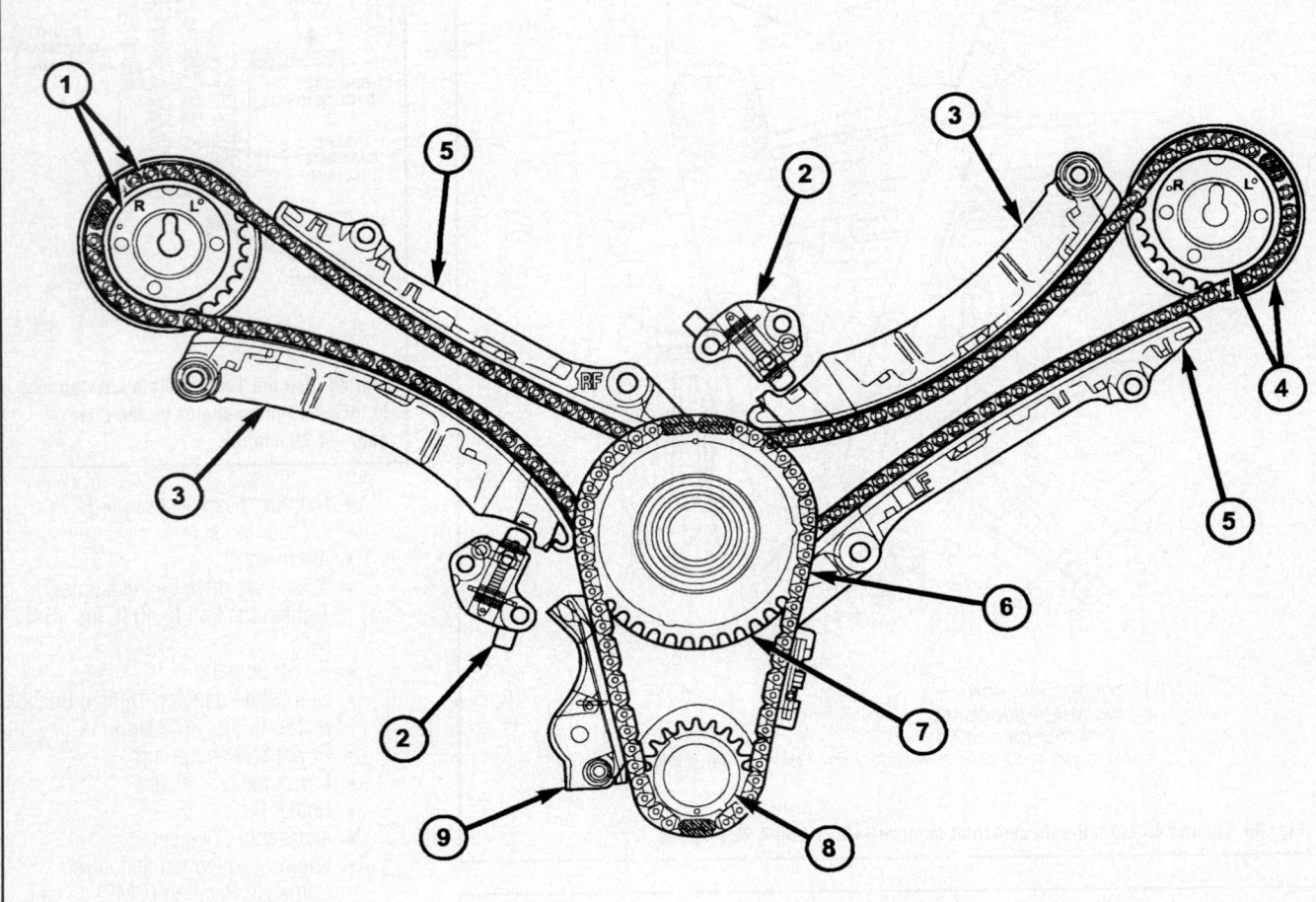

1 - RIGHT CAMSHAFT SPROCKET AND SECONDARY CHAIN
2 - SECONDARY TIMING CHAIN TENSIONER (LEFT AND RIGHT SIDE NOT INTERCHANGEABLE)
3 - SECONDARY TENSIONER ARM
4 - LEFT CAMSHAFT SPROCKET AND SECONDARY CHAIN
5 - CHAIN GUIDE (LEFT AND RIGHT SIDE ARE NOT INTERCHANGEABLE)
6 - PRIMARY CHAIN
7 - IDLER SPROCKET
8 - CRANKSHAFT SPROCKET
9 - PRIMARY CHAIN TENSIONER

67189-RAMT-G05

Fig. 89 Timing chain system and alignment marks—3.7L engines

4. Rotate the crankshaft so that the camshaft sprocket and crankshaft sprocket timing marks are aligned.

➡**The camshaft pin and slot in the cam sprocket must be a 12 o'clock, the crankshaft keyway must be at 2 o'clock, and the dots or paint on the crank sprocket must be at 6 o'clock.**

5. Pin back the tensioner shoe.
6. Remove the timing chain and sprockets.

To install:

7. With the timing marks aligned, wrap the chain around the sprockets. The chain must be installed with the single plated link aligned with the dot or paint on the cam sprocket. The dot or paint on the crank sprocket should be aligned between the 2 plated links.

8. Install the assembly and torque the cam sprocket bolt to 90 ft. lbs. (122 Nm).

9. Unpin the tensioner and verify the alignment.

10. Install or connect the following:
   - Timing cover. Torque all fasteners to 21 ft. lbs. (28 Nm). Torque the large lifting lug to 40 ft. lbs. (55 Nm).
   - Oil pan and pickup tube
   - Power steering pump
   - Crankshaft damper
   - Tensioner and idler pulleys
   - Radiator and heater hoses
   - Alternator
   - A/C compressor

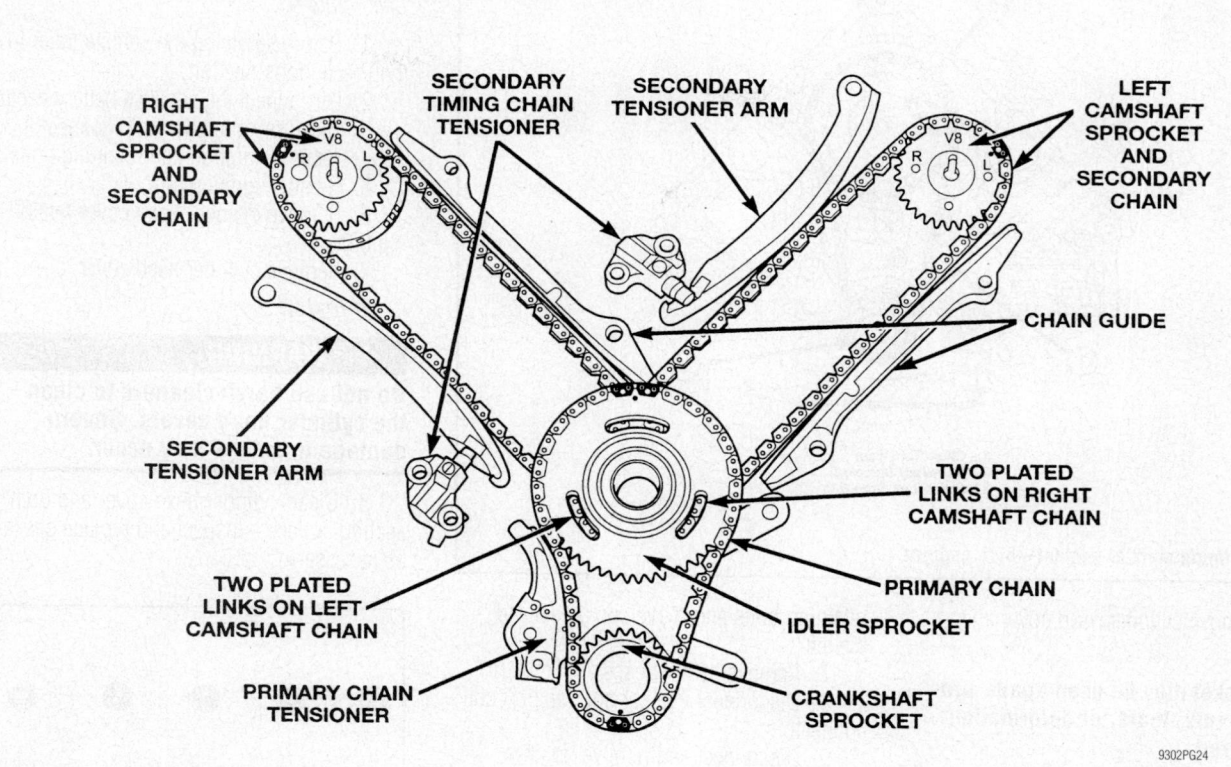

Fig. 90 Timing chain system and alignment marks—4.7L engines

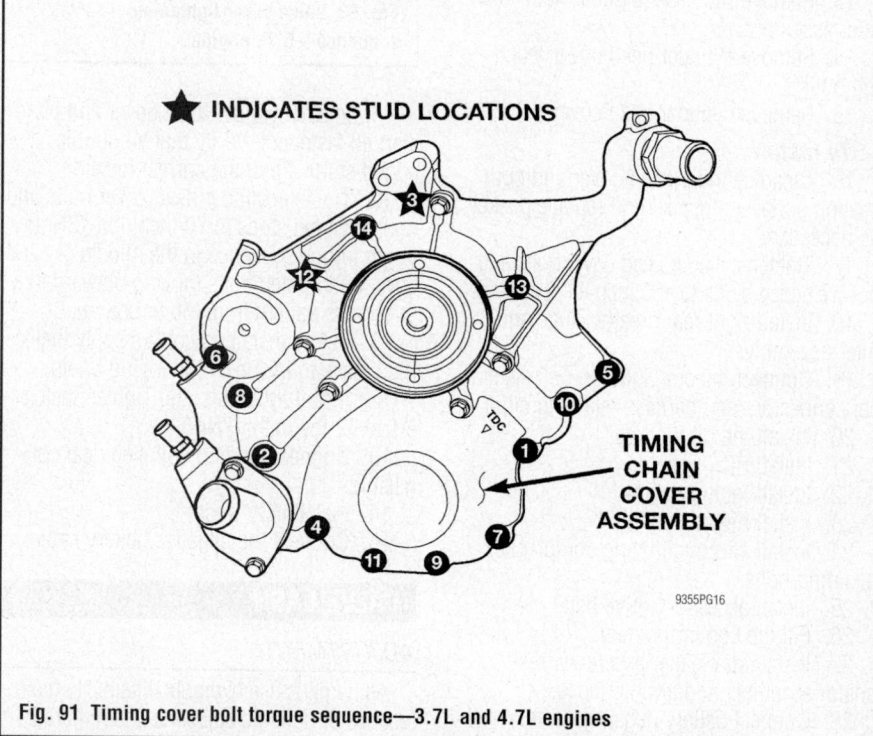

Fig. 91 Timing cover bolt torque sequence—3.7L and 4.7L engines

* Fan shroud
* Coolant and washer bottles
* Radiator fan
* Drive belt
* Negative battery cable

VALVE COVERS

REMOVAL & INSTALLATION

3.7L & 4.7L Engines

Left Side

1. Disconnect the negative battery cable.

2. Before servicing the vehicle, refer to the Precautions Section.

3. Remove the resonator assemble and air inlet hose.

4. Disconnect injector connectors and un-clip the injector harness.

5. Route injector harness in front of cylinder head cover.

6. Disconnect the left side breather tube and remove the breather tube.

7. Remove ignition coils and wires.

8. Remove the cylinder head cover mounting bolts.

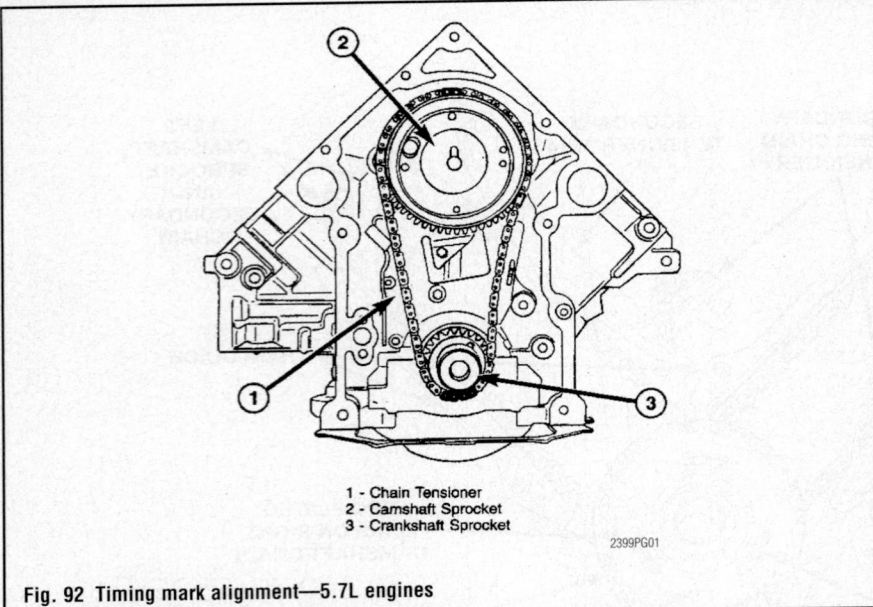

1 - Chain Tensioner
2 - Camshaft Sprocket
3 - Crankshaft Sprocket

2399PG01

Fig. 92 Timing mark alignment—5.7L engines

9. Remove cylinder head cover and gasket.

➡ **The gasket may be used again, providing no cuts, tears, or deformation has occurred.**

To install:

※※ WARNING

Do not use harsh cleaners to clean the cylinder head covers. Severe damage to covers may occur.

10. Clean cylinder head cover and both sealing surfaces. Inspect and replace gasket as necessary.
11. Install cylinder head cover.
12. Tighten cylinder head cover bolts and double ended studs to 105 in. lbs. (12 Nm).
13. Install left side breather and connect breather tube.
14. Install ignition coils and wires.
15. Connect injector electrical connectors and injector harness retaining clips.
16. Install the resonator and air inlet hose.
17. Connect the negative battery cable.

Right Side

1. Before servicing the vehicle, refer to the Precautions Section.
2. Disconnect the negative battery cable.
3. Remove air cleaner assembly, resonator assembly and air inlet hose.
4. Drain cooling system to a level below the heater hoses.
5. Remove accessory drive belt.
6. Remove air conditioning compressor retaining bolts and move compressor to the left.
7. Remove heater hoses.
8. Disconnect injector and ignition coil connectors.
9. Disconnect and remove positive crankcase ventilation (PCV) hose.
10. Remove oil fill tube.
11. Remove ignition wires.
12. Un-clip injector and ignition coil harness and move away from cylinder head cover.
13. Remove right rear breather tube and filter assembly.
14. Remove cylinder head cover retaining bolts.
15. Remove cylinder head cover.

To install:
16. Clean cylinder head cover and both sealing surfaces. Inspect and replace gasket as necessary.
17. Tighten cylinder head cover bolts and double ended studs to 105 inch lbs. (12 Nm).
18. Install right rear breather tube and filter assembly.
19. Connect injector, ignition coil electrical connectors and harness retaining clips.
20. Install the oil fill tube.
21. Install PCV hose.
22. Install ignition wires.
23. Install heater hoses.
24. Install air conditioning compressor retaining bolts.
25. Install accessory drive belt.
26. Fill the cooling system.
27. Install air cleaner assembly, resonator assembly and air inlet hose.
28. Connect battery negative cable.

5.7L Engine

See Figure 93.

1. Before servicing the vehicle, refer to the Precautions Section.
2. Disconnect the negative battery cable.
3. Disconnect ignition coil connector.
4. Remove ignition coil retaining bolts.
5. Remove ignition coil.
6. Remove cylinder head cover retaining bolts.
7. Remove cylinder head cover

To install:

※※ WARNING

Do not use harsh cleaners to clean the cylinder head covers. Severe damage to covers may occur.

8. Clean cylinder head cover and both sealing surfaces. Inspect and replace gasket as necessary.

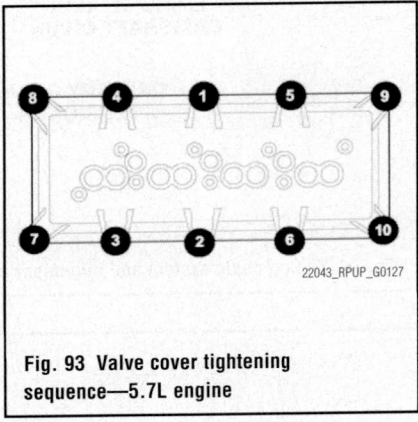

22043_RPUP_G0127

Fig. 93 Valve cover tightening sequence—5.7L engine

9. Install cylinder head cover and hand start all fasteners. Verify that all double ended studs are in the correct location.
10. Tighten cylinder head cover bolts and double ended studs to 70 inch. lbs. (8Nm). Begin torque sequence in the middle of head cover and tighten bolts moving outward in a crisscross pattern from top to bottom.
11. Before installing coil(s), apply dielectric grease to inside of spark plug boots.
12. Install ignition coils. Tighten fasteners to 62 lbs inch. (7Nm).
13. Connect ignition coil electrical connectors.
14. Install PCV hose.
15. Connect the negative battery cable.

VALVE LASH

ADJUSTMENT

All engines use hydraulic lifters. No maintenance or periodic adjustment is required.

ENGINE PERFORMANCE & EMISSION CONTROLS

ACCELERATOR PEDAL POSITION (APP) SENSOR

LOCATION

The APP sensor is located on the accelerator pedal assembly.

REMOVAL & INSTALLATION

1. Disconnect the 6-way electrical connector at the APPS.
2. Remove the upper accelerator pedal mounting bolt.
3. Remove the lower accelerator pedal mounting bolt.
4. Remove the accelerator pedal assembly from the vehicle.

To install:

5. Position the accelerator pedal assembly on the pedal sled.
6. Install the lower accelerator pedal mounting bolt and tighten to 60 inch lbs. (7 Nm).
7. Install the upper accelerator pedal mounting bolt 60 inch lbs. (7 Nm).
8. Connect the 6-way electrical connector at the APPS.
9. If necessary, use a Scan Tool to erase any Diagnostic Trouble Codes (DTC's).

CAMSHAFT POSITION (CMP) SENSOR

LOCATION

3.7L & 4.7L Engines

See Figure 94.

The Camshaft Position Sensor (CMP) is bolted to the right-front side of the right cylinder head.

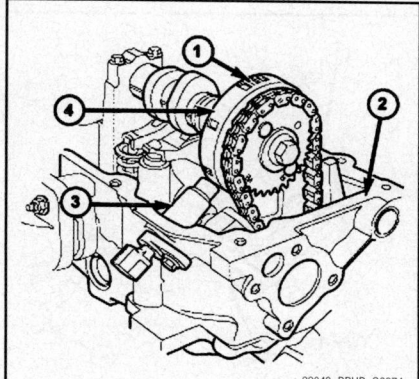

Fig. 94 Camshaft position sensor (3) location—3.7 and 4.7L engine

22043_RPUP_G0074

5.7L Engine

See Figure 95.

The Camshaft Position Sensor (CMP) is located below the generator on the timing chain /case cover on the right/front side of engine.

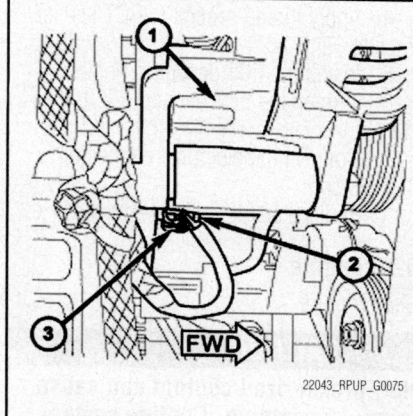

Fig. 95 Camshaft position sensor location—5.7L engines

22043_RPUP_G0075

REMOVAL & INSTALLATION

3.7L & 4.7L Engines

See Figure 94.

1. Before servicing the vehicle, refer to the precautions in the beginning of this section.
2. Disconnect the electrical connector at Camshaft Position (CMP) sensor.
3. Remove the CMP sensor mounting bolt.
4. Carefully twist sensor from cylinder head.
5. Check condition of sensor O-ring.

To install:

6. Clean out the machined hole in the cylinder head.
7. Apply a small amount of engine oil to sensor O-ring.
8. Install the CMP sensor into cylinder head with a slight rocking and twisting action.

✳✳ WARNING

Before tightening sensor mounting bolt, be sure sensor is completely flush to cylinder head. If sensor is not flush, damage to sensor mounting tang may result.

9. Install mounting bolt and tighten to 106 in. lbs. (12 Nm).
10. Connect the electrical connector to sensor.

5.7L Engine

See Figure 95.

1. Before servicing the vehicle, refer to the precautions in the beginning of this section.
2. Disconnect the electrical connector at Camshaft Position (CMP) sensor.
3. Remove the CMP sensor mounting bolt.
4. Carefully twist CMP sensor from timing gear/chain cover.
5. Check condition of sensor O-ring.

To install:

6. Clean out machined hole in timing gear/chain cover.
7. Install the CMP sensor into timing gear/chain cover with a slight rocking action. Do not twist sensor into position as damage to O-ring may result.

✳✳ WARNING

Before tightening sensor mounting bolt, be sure sensor is completely flush to timing gear/chain cover. If sensor is not flush, damage to sensor mounting tang may result.

8. Install the CMP mounting bolt and tighten to 106 in. lbs. (12 Nm).
9. Connect the electrical connector to the CMP sensor.

CRANKSHAFT POSITION (CKP) SENSOR

LOCATION

The Crankshaft Position (CKP) sensor is mounted into the right rear side of the cylinder block. It is positioned and bolted into a machined hole.

REMOVAL & INSTALLATION

1. Raise the vehicle.
2. Disconnect the Crankshaft Position Sensor (CKP) electrical connector.
3. Remove the CKP sensor mounting bolt.
4. Carefully twist sensor from cylinder block.
5. Check condition of sensor O-ring.

To install:

6. Clean out the machined hole in the engine block.
7. Apply a small amount of engine oil to sensor O-ring.
8. Install the CKP sensor into engine block with a slight rocking and twisting action.

✳✳ WARNING

Before tightening sensor mounting bolt, be sure sensor is completely flush to cylinder block. If sensor is not flush, damage to sensor mounting tang may result.

9. Install mounting bolt and tighten to 21 ft. lbs. (28 Nm).
10. Connect the electrical connector to the CKP sensor.
11. Lower the vehicle.

ENGINE COOLANT TEMPERATURE (ECT) SENSOR

LOCATION

3.7L & 4.7L Engines

See Figure 96.

The Engine Coolant Temperature (ECT) sensor is located in the intake manifold toward the front of the engine.

5.7L Engine

See Figure 97.

The Engine Coolant Temperature (ECT) sensor is located directly under the A/C compressor in the engine block. The A/C compressor must be unbolted to gain access to ECT sensor.

REMOVAL & INSTALLATION

3.7L & 4.7L Engines

See Figure 96.

✳✳ CAUTION

Hot, pressurized coolant can cause injury by scalding. Cooling system must be partially drained before removing the coolant temperature sensor.

1. Partially drain the cooling system.
2. Disconnect the electrical connector from the Engine Coolant Temperature (ECT) sensor.
3. Remove the sensor from the intake manifold.

To install:

4. Apply thread sealant to ECT sensor threads.
5. Install the ECT sensor to engine.
6. Tighten the ECT sensor to 8 ft. lbs. (11 Nm).
7. Connect the electrical connector to ETC sensor.
8. Replace any lost engine coolant.

5.7L Engine

See Figure 97.

✳✳ CAUTION

Hot, pressurized coolant can cause injury by scalding. Cooling system must be partially drained before removing the Engine Coolant Temperature (ECT) sensor.

1. Partially drain the cooling system.
2. Remove accessory drive belt
3. Carefully unbolt the air conditioning compressor from front of engine. Do not disconnect any A/C hoses from compressor.
4. Temporarily support the compressor to gain access to ECT sensor.
5. Disconnect the electrical connector from sensor.
6. Remove the ECT sensor from the cylinder block.

To install:

7. Apply thread sealant to ETC sensor threads.

8. Install the ETC sensor into engine.
9. Tighten the sensor to 8 ft. lbs. (11 Nm).
10. Connect the electrical connector to ETC sensor.
11. Install air conditioning compressor onto the front of engine
12. Install the accessory drive belt.
13. Replace any lost engine coolant.

EVAPORATIVE EMISSIONS (EVAP) CANISTER

LOCATION

The EVAP canister is located next to the fuel tank.

REMOVAL & INSTALLATION

Type-1 Canisters

See Figure 98.

A single, vertically mounted EVAP canister (1) is used with Type 1. The ESIM (Emission System Integrity Monitor) switch (3) is mounted to the canister.

1. Raise and support vehicle.
2. If equipped, remove necessary skid plates. Certain models, equipped with a certain fuel tank size, may require the removal of the fuel tank skid plate and/or the transfer case skid plate to gain access to the EVAP canister(s).
3. Disconnect electrical wiring connector from ESIM switch (3).
4. Disconnect vapor line (6) from ESIM switch.
5. Disconnect quick-connect vapor line (5) from canister.
6. Remove canister mounting bracket bolt. This is located below and near the ESIM switch.
7. Pull canister from mounting bracket

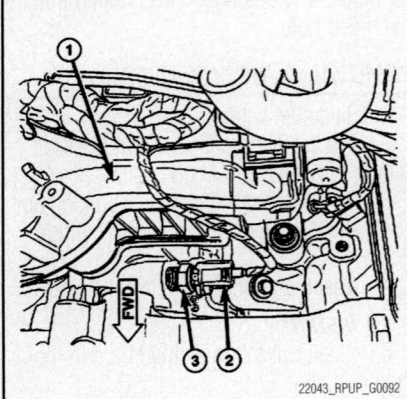

Fig. 96 The Engine Coolant Temperature (ECT) sensor (3) location—4.7L engines shown, 3.7L similar

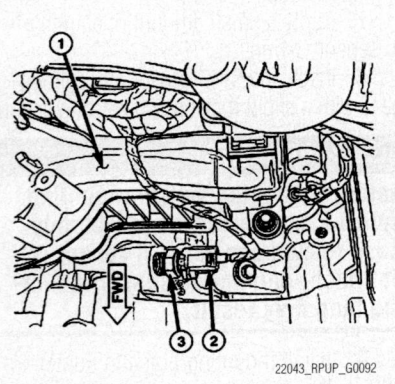

Fig. 97 The Engine Coolant Temperature (ECT) sensor (3) location—5.7L engines

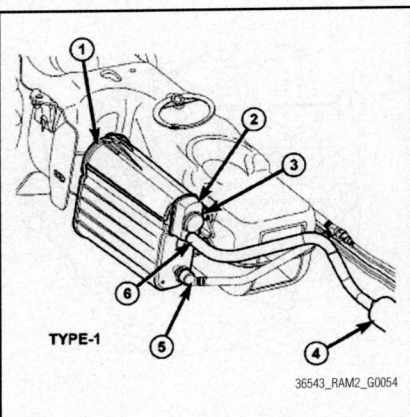

Fig. 98 Evaporative (EVAP) system type 1 canister—5.7L engines

while guiding two canister locating pins from mounting bracket.

To install:

> ⁎⁎ **CAUTION**
>
> **After installing any EVAP canister or ESIM switch, the electrical connector on the switch MUST be in the 3 O'clock position (as viewed from front). This step must be done for proper ESIM switch operation.**

8. Two locating pins are located at rear of canister. Push these two pins into canister mounting bracket.

9. Install canister mounting bracket bolt. This is located below and near the ESIM switch.

10. Connect quick-connect vapor line (5) to canister.

11. Connect vapor line (6) to ESIM switch.

12. Connect electrical wiring connector to ESIM switch (3).

13. If equipped, install necessary skid plates.

14. All vapor/vacuum lines and hoses must be firmly connected. Also check the vapor/vacuum lines at the EVAP canister purge solenoid for damage or leaks. If a leak is present, a Diagnostic Trouble Code (DTC) may be set.

15. Lower vehicle.

Type-2 Canisters

See Figure 99.

A single, vertically mounted EVAP canister (1) is used with Type 2. The ESIM (Emission System Integrity Monitor) switch (2) is mounted to the canister.

1. Raise and support vehicle.
2. If equipped, remove necessary skid

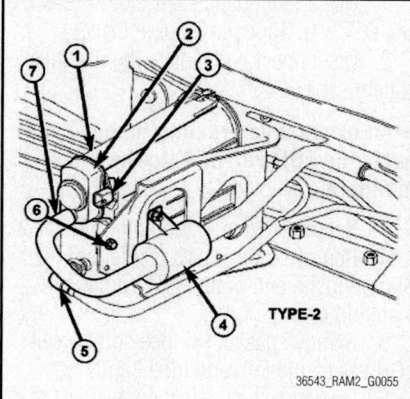

Fig. 99 Evaporative (EVAP) system type 2 canister—5.7L engines

plates. Certain models, equipped with a certain fuel tank size, may require the removal of the fuel tank skid plate and/or the transfer case skid plate to gain access to the EVAP canister(s).

3. Disconnect electrical wiring connector from ESIM switch (3).

4. Disconnect vapor line (7) from ESIM switch.

5. Disconnect quick-connect vapor line (5) at canister.

6. Remove canister mounting bracket bolt (6).

7. Pull canister from mounting bracket while guiding two canister locating pins from mounting bracket.

To install:

> ⁎⁎ **CAUTION**
>
> **After installing any EVAP canister or ESIM switch, the electrical connector on the switch MUST be in the 3 O'clock position (as viewed from front). This step must be done for proper ESIM switch operation.**

8. Two locating pins are located at rear of canister. Push these two pins into canister mounting bracket.

9. Install canister mounting bracket bolt (6).

10. Connect quick-connect vapor line (5) to canister.

11. Connect vapor line (7) to ESIM switch.

12. Connect electrical wiring connector to ESIM switch (3).

13. If equipped, install necessary skid plates.

14. All vapor/vacuum lines and hoses must be firmly connected. Also check the vapor/vacuum lines at the EVAP canister purge solenoid for damage or leaks. If a leak is present, a Diagnostic Trouble Code (DTC) may be set.

15. Lower vehicle.

Type-3 Canisters

See Figure 100.

Dual, vertically mounted EVAP canisters (1) and (4) are used with Type 3. The ESIM (Emission System Integrity Monitor) switch (2) is mounted to the main canister (1). Canister (4) is considered a secondary canister.

1. Raise and support vehicle.

2. If equipped, remove necessary skid plates. Certain models, equipped with a certain fuel tank size, may require the removal of the fuel tank skid plate and/or the transfer case skid plate to gain access to the EVAP canister(s).

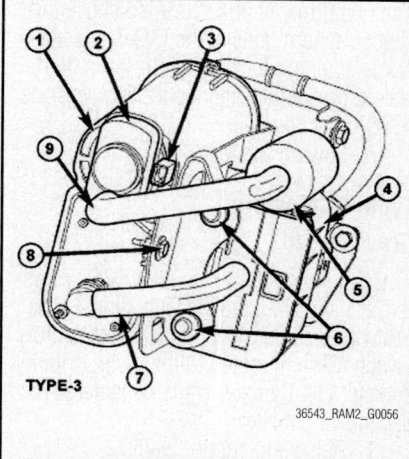

Fig. 100 Evaporative (EVAP) system type 3 canister—5.7L engines

3. Disconnect electrical wiring connector from ESIM switch (3).

4. Disconnect vapor line (9) from ESIM switch.

5. Disconnect quick-connect vapor line (7) at main canister.

6. Remove canister mounting bracket bolt (8).

7. Pull canister from mounting bracket while guiding two canister locating pins from mounting bracket.

8. To remove the secondary canister (4), remove mounting bolt. Pull canister from mounting bracket while guiding two canister locating pins (6) from mounting bracket.

To install:

> ⁎⁎ **CAUTION**
>
> **After installing any EVAP canister or ESIM switch, the electrical connector on the switch MUST be in the 3 O'clock position (as viewed from front). This step must be done for proper ESIM switch operation.**

9. Push secondary canister (4) into mounting bracket while guiding two canister locating pins (6) into mounting bracket. Install mounting bolt.

10. Push main, primary canister (1) into mounting bracket while guiding two canister locating pins into mounting bracket.

11. Install main canister mounting bracket bolt (8).

12. Connect quick-connect vapor line (7) to main canister.

13. Connect vapor line (9) to ESIM switch.

14. Connect electrical wiring connector to ESIM switch (3).

15. If equipped, install necessary skid plates.

16. All vapor/vacuum lines and hoses

must be firmly connected. Also check the vapor/vacuum lines at the EVAP canister purge solenoid for damage or leaks. If a leak is present, a Diagnostic Trouble Code (DTC) may be set.

17. Lower vehicle.

Type-4 Canisters

See Figure 101.

Dual, horizontally mounted EVAP canisters (1) and (7) are used with Type 4. The ESIM (Emission System Integrity Monitor) switch (3) is mounted to the main, primary canister (1). Canister (7) is considered a secondary canister.

1. Raise and support vehicle.
2. If equipped, remove necessary skid plates. Certain models, equipped with a certain fuel tank size, may require the removal of the fuel tank skid plate and/or the transfer case skid plate to gain access to the EVAP canister(s).
3. Disconnect electrical wiring connector from ESIM switch (4).
4. Disconnect vapor line (5) from ESIM switch.
5. Disconnect quick-connect vapor line (8) at main canister.
6. Remove primary canister mounting bracket nut (9).
7. Pull canister from mounting bracket while guiding two canister locating pins from mounting bracket.
8. To remove the secondary canister (7), remove mounting nut (6). Pull canister from mounting bracket while guiding two canister locating pins from mounting bracket.

To install:

✳✳ CAUTION

After installing any EVAP canister or ESIM switch, the electrical connector

on the switch MUST be in the 3 O'clock position (as viewed from front). This step must be done for proper ESIM switch operation.

9. Position two secondary canister locating pins into mounting bracket. Install mounting nut (6).
10. Position two primary canister locating pins into mounting bracket.
11. Install primary canister mounting bracket nut (9).
12. Connect quick-connect vapor line (8) to main canister.
13. Connect vapor line (5) to ESIM switch.
14. Connect electrical wiring connector to ESIM switch (4).
15. If equipped, install necessary skid plates.
16. All vapor/vacuum lines and hoses must be firmly connected. Also check the vapor/vacuum lines at the EVAP canister purge solenoid for damage or leaks. If a leak is present, a Diagnostic Trouble Code (DTC) may be set.
17. Lower vehicle.

EVAPORATIVE EMISSIONS (EVAP) PURGE CONTROL SOLENOID

LOCATION

The duty cycle EVAP canister purge solenoid is located in the engine compartment below and near the battery.

REMOVAL & INSTALLATION

See Figure 102.

1. Carefully pull the solenoid assembly straight up from the tongue-type bracket without bending the two vapor lines.

2. Disconnect electrical wiring connector (2) at solenoid.
3. Disconnect vapor line quick-connect fitting (3) at solenoid.
4. Disconnect vapor line quick-connect fitting (4) at solenoid.

To install:

5. Connect vapor line quick-connect fitting (3) to solenoid.
6. Connect vapor line quick-connect fitting (4) to solenoid.
7. Connect electrical wiring connector (2) to solenoid.
8. Carefully push the solenoid assembly (1) straight down onto the tongue-type bracket without bending the two vapor lines.

EXHAUST GAS RECIRCULATION (EGR) VALVE

LOCATION

3.7L Engine

The electronic EGR valve and solenoid assembly is attached to the rear of the left cylinder head.

4.7L Engine

The electronic EGR valve and solenoid assembly is attached to the rear of the left cylinder head. An exhaust gas routing tube connects the EGR valve to the intake manifold.

5.7L Engine

The electronic EGR valve and solenoid assembly is attached to the front of the right cylinder head. An exhaust gas routing tube connects the EGR valve to the intake manifold.

REMOVAL & INSTALLATION

3.7L Engine

See Figure 103.

1. Use a diagnostic scan tool to record any DTC's (Diagnostic Trouble Codes).
2. Disconnect and isolate the negative battery cable.

➡**An exhaust gas routing tube (1) connects the EGR valve (4) to the intake manifold.**

3. Remove two tube mounting bolts (2).
4. Remove tube (1) from solenoid (4). Slip opposite end of tube (6) from intake manifold.
5. Remove gasket (3) located between EGR valve solenoid and tube flange.
6. Disconnect electrical connector (3) at solenoid (1).
7. Remove two EGR valve solenoid mounting bolts (2).

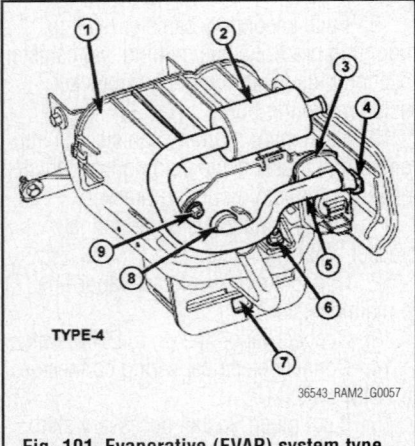

Fig. 101 Evaporative (EVAP) system type 4 canister—5.7L engines

36543_RAM2_G0057

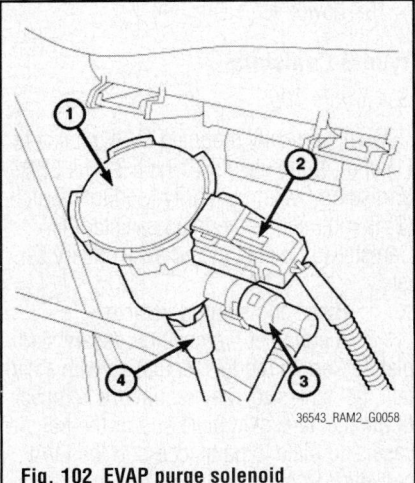

Fig. 102 EVAP purge solenoid

36543_RAM2_G0058

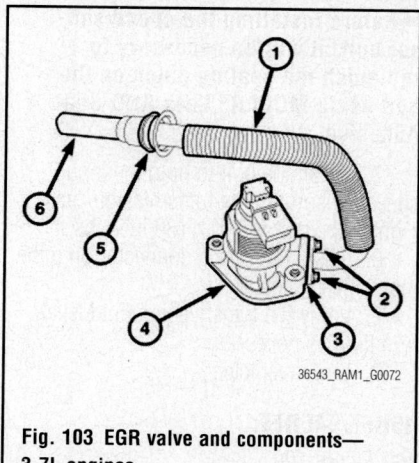

Fig. 103 EGR valve and components—3.7L engines

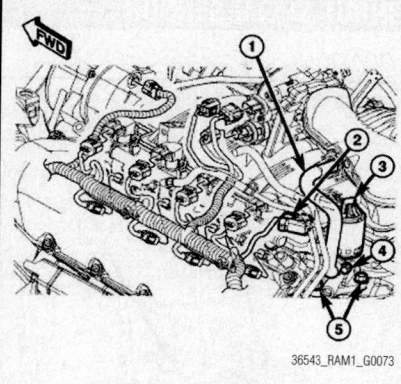

Fig. 104 EGR valve and components—4.7L engines

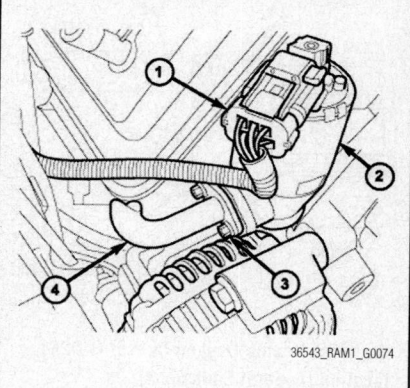

Fig. 105 EGR valve and components—5.7L engines

8. Remove solenoid (1) from engine.

9. Remove and discard gasket (1) located under EGR solenoid.

To install:

10. Clean gasket area (1) at rear of left cylinder head where it joins base of EGR valve.

11. Clean EGR tube where it joins EGR valve.

12. Position new gasket between EGR valve and cylinder head.

13. Position EGR valve to cylinder head. Install and tighten two bolts (2). Torque to 80 inch lbs. (9 Nm).

14. Position new gasket (3) between EGR tube flange and EGR valve assembly.

15. Position EGR tube (1) to side of EGR valve. Position end of tube (6) into intake manifold. Install two bolts (2). Torque to 8.5 ft. lbs. (11 Nm).

16. Connect electrical connector (3) to top of EGR valve solenoid (1).

17. Connect negative battery cable.

18. Using a diagnostic scan tool, erase any previously recorded DTC's (Diagnostic Trouble Codes).

4.7L Engine

See Figure 104.

1. Use a diagnostic scan tool to record any DTC's (Diagnostic Trouble Codes).

2. Disconnect and isolate the negative battery cable.

3. Remove electrical connector (5) at top of EGR valve solenoid.

4. Remove tube mounting bolt (1) at intake manifold.

5. Remove two bolts (4) connecting EGR tube (1) to valve assembly.

6. Remove gasket located between EGR tube flange and EGR valve assembly.

7. Remove two EGR valve mounting bolts (5).

8. Separate valve assembly (3) from engine.

9. Remove and discard metal gasket located between cylinder head and valve assembly.

To install:

10. Clean area at rear of left cylinder head where it joins base of EGR valve.

11. Clean EGR tube where it joins EGR valve.

12. Position new gasket between EGR valve and cylinder head.

13. Position EGR valve to cylinder head. Install and tighten two bolts (5). Torque to 80 inch lbs. (9 Nm).

14. Position new gasket between EGR tube flange and EGR valve assembly.

15. Position EGR tube (1) to side of EGR valve and into intake manifold. Install two bolts (4) finger tight (temporarily).

16. Install EGR tube flange bolt (1) at intake manifold. Torque to 8.5 ft. lbs. (11 Nm).

17. Connect electrical connector (5) to top of EGR valve solenoid (4).

18. Do a final tightening of two EGR tube bolts (4). Torque to 8.5 ft. lbs. (11 Nm).

19. Connect negative battery cable.

20. Using a diagnostic scan tool, erase any previously recorded DTC's (Diagnostic Trouble Codes).

5.7L Engine

See Figure 105.

1. Use a diagnostic scan tool to record any DTC's (Diagnostic Trouble Codes).

2. Disconnect and isolate the negative battery cable.

3. Disconnect electrical connector (1) from EGR solenoid (2).

4. Remove two bolts (3) connecting EGR tube (4) to valve assembly.

5. Remove gasket located between EGR tube flange and EGR valve assembly.

6. Remove two mounting bolts (2).

7. Separate valve assembly (3) from cylinder head (1).

8. Remove and discard metal gasket located between cylinder head and valve assembly.

To install:

9. Position a new metal gasket between cylinder head (1) and valve assembly (3).

10. Install two mounting bolts (2) and tighten to 20 ft. lbs. (27 Nm).

11. Clean EGR tube where it joins EGR valve.

12. Position new gasket between EGR tube flange and EGR valve assembly.

13. Install two bolts (3) connecting EGR tube (4) to valve assembly (2). Tighten bolts to 20 ft. lbs. (27 Nm).

14. Connect electrical connector (1) to EGR solenoid (2).

15. Connect negative battery cable.

16. Using a diagnostic scan tool, erase any previously recorded DTC's (Diagnostic Trouble Codes).

HEATED OXYGEN SENSOR (HO2S)

LOCATION

See Figures 106 and 107.

Refer to the accompanying illustrations for HO2S locations.

REMOVAL & INSTALLATION

See Figures 106 and 107.

❊❊ CAUTION

The exhaust manifold, exhaust pipes and catalytic converter become very hot during the engine operation. Allow engine to cool before removing oxygen sensor.

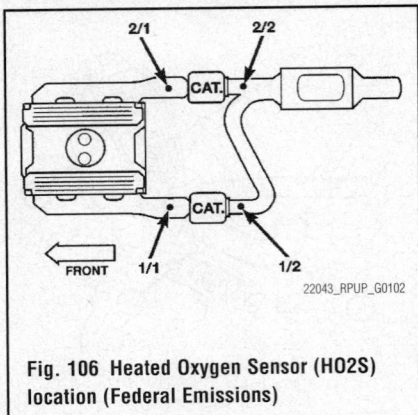

Fig. 106 Heated Oxygen Sensor (HO2S) location (Federal Emissions)

1. Before servicing the vehicle, refer to the precautions in the beginning of this section.
2. Raise and support vehicle.
3. Disconnect wire connector from O2S sensor.

✳✳ WARNING

When disconnecting sensor electrical connector, do not pull directly on wire going into sensor.

4. Remove the HO2S sensor with an oxygen sensor removal and installation tool.
5. Clean threads in exhaust pipe using appropriate tap.

To install:

➡ **Threads of new oxygen sensors are factory coated with anti-seize compound to aid in removal. DO NOT add any additional anti-seize compound to threads of a new oxygen sensor.**

6. Install the HO2S sensor. Tighten to 30 ft. lbs. (41 Nm).
7. Connect the HO2S sensor wire connector.
8. Lower the vehicle.

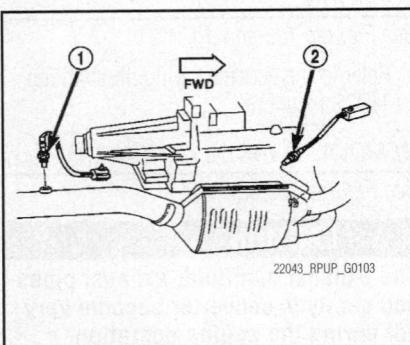

Fig. 107 Heated Oxygen Sensor (HO2S) location (California Emissions)

INPUT SPEED SENSOR

LOCATION

See Figures 108 and 109.

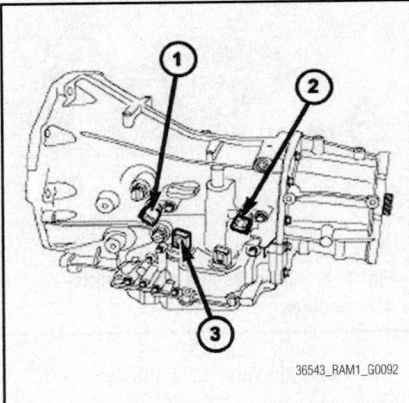

Fig. 108 Input speed sensor location— 42RLE

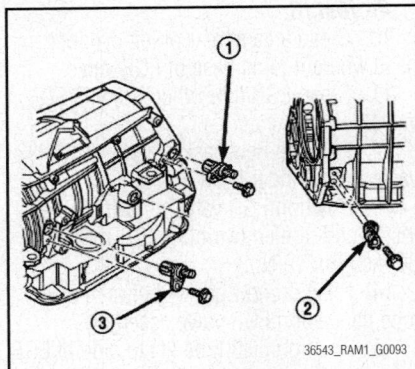

Fig. 109 Input speed sensor location— 45RFE/545RFE

REMOVAL & INSTALLATION

42RLE

See Figure 108.

1. Raise vehicle.
2. Place a suitable fluid catch pan under the transmission.
3. Remove the wiring connector from the input speed sensor.

➡ **The speed sensor bolt has a sealing patch applied from the factory. Be sure to reuse the same bolt.**

4. Remove the bolt holding the input speed sensor to the transmission case.
5. Remove the input speed sensor from the transmission case.

To install:

6. Install the input speed sensor (1) into the transmission case.

➡ **Before installing the speed sensor bolt, it will be necessary to replenish the sealing patch on the bolt using MOPAR® Lock AND Seal Adhesive.**

7. Install the bolt to hold the input speed sensor into the transmission case. Tighten the bolt to 9 Nm (80 inch lbs.).
8. Install the wiring connector onto the input speed sensor
9. Verify the transmission fluid level. Add fluid as necessary.
10. Lower vehicle.

45RFE/545RFE

See Figure 109.

1. Raise vehicle.
2. Place a suitable fluid catch pan under the transmission.
3. Remove the wiring connector from the input speed sensor (3).
4. Remove the bolt holding the input speed sensor to the transmission case.
5. Remove the input speed sensor (3) from the transmission case.

To install:

6. Install the input speed sensor (3) into the transmission case.
7. Install the bolt to hold the input speed sensor (3) into the transmission case. Tighten the bolt to 12 Nm (105 inch lbs.).
8. Install the wiring connector onto the input speed sensor.
9. Verify the transmission fluid level. Add fluid as necessary.
10. Lower vehicle.

INTAKE AIR TEMPERATURE (IAT) SENSOR

LOCATION

3.7L & 4.7L Engines

See Figures 110 and 111.

The Intake Air Temperature (IAT) sensor is installed into the air intake tube near the throttle body.

5.7L Engine

See Figure 112.

The Intake Air Temperature (IAT) sensor is installed into the front of the intake manifold air box plenum.

REMOVAL & INSTALLATION

See Figures 110 through 112.

1. Before servicing the vehicle, refer to the Precautions Section.

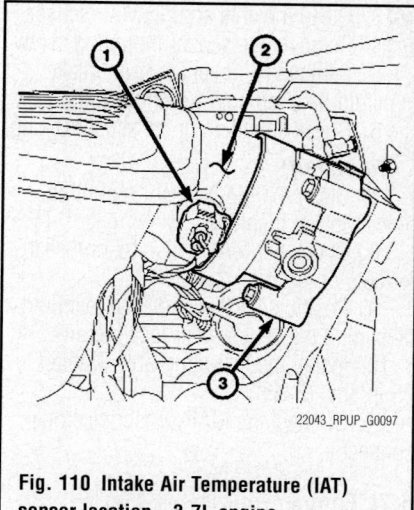

Fig. 110 Intake Air Temperature (IAT) sensor location—3.7L engine

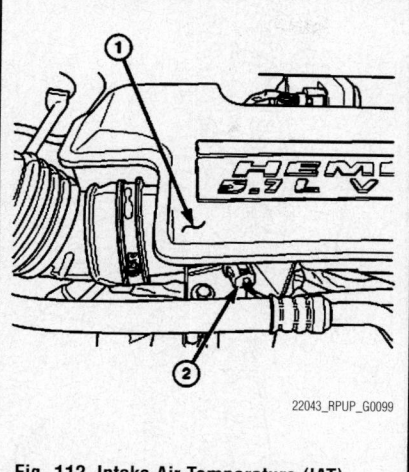

Fig. 112 Intake Air Temperature (IAT) sensor location—5.7L engine

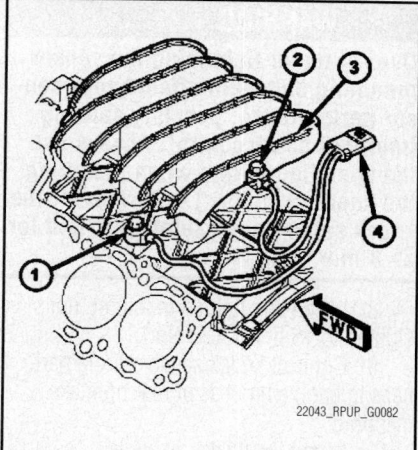

Fig. 113 Knock sensor location view— 4.7L engine shown, 3.7L similar

2. Disconnect the electrical connector from IAT sensor.

3. Clean any dirt from intake tube at the sensor base.

4. Gently lift on small plastic release tab and rotate sensor about ¼ turn counterclockwise for removal.

5. Check the condition of IAT sensor O-ring.

To install:

6. Clean sensor mounting hole in air intake tube.

7. Position sensor into air intake tube and rotate clockwise until past release tab.

8. Install the electrical connector.

KNOCK SENSOR (KS)

LOCATION

3.7L & 4.7L Engine

See Figure 113.

The two Knock Sensors (KS) are bolted into the cylinder block under the intake

manifold. The two sensors share a common wiring harness using one electrical connector. Because of this, they must be replaced as a pair.

5.7L Engine

Two knock sensors are bolted into each side of the cylinder block (outside) under the exhaust manifold.

REMOVAL & INSTALLATION

3.7L & 4.7L Engines

See Figure 113.

➥The left sensor is identified by an identification tag (LEFT) (2). It is also identified by a larger bolt head. The Powertrain Control Module (PCM) must have and know the correct sensor left/right positions. Do not mix the sensor locations.

1. Before servicing the vehicle, refer to the Precautions Section.

2. Remove the intake manifold.

3. Disconnect knock sensor dual pigtail harness from engine wiring harness. This connection is made near rear of engine.

4. Remove both sensor mounting bolts. Note foam strip on bolt threads. This foam is used only to retain the bolts to sensors for plant assembly. It is not used as a sealant. Do not apply any adhesive, sealant or thread locking compound to these bolts.

5. Remove the knock sensors from the engine.

To install:

6. Thoroughly clean the knock sensor mounting holes.

7. Install the sensors into cylinder block.

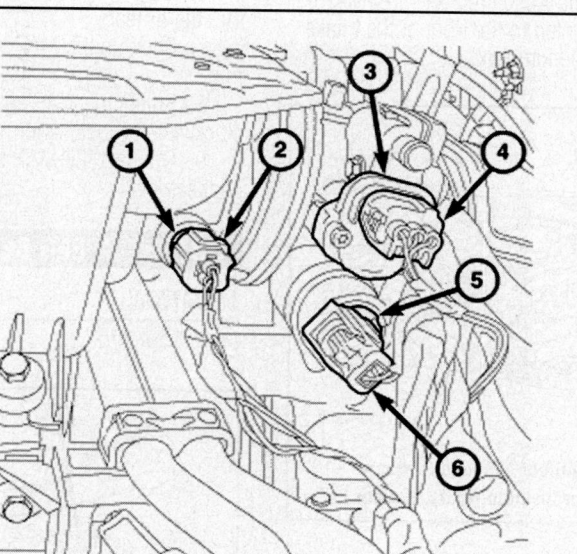

1. IAT sensor
2. IAT sensor electrical connector
3. TPS sensor
4. TPS sensor electrical connector
5. IAC sensor
6. IAC sensor electrical connector

Fig. 111 Intake Air Temperature (IAT) sensor location—4.7L engine

❋❋ WARNING

Over or under tightening the sensor mounting bolts will affect knock sensor performance, possibly causing improper spark control. Always use the specified torque when installing the knock sensors. The torque for the knock senor bolt is relatively light for an 8 mm bolt.

8. Install and tighten mounting bolts. Tighten to 15 ft. lbs. (20 Nm).

9. Connect knock sensor wiring harness to engine harness at rear of intake manifold.

10. Install the intake manifold.

5.7L Engine

1. Before servicing the vehicle, refer to the Precautions Section.

2. Raise the vehicle.

3. Disconnect the knock sensor electrical connector.

4. Remove knock sensor mounting bolt. Note foam strip on bolt threads. This foam is used only to retain the bolts to sensors for plant assembly. It is not used as a sealant. Do not apply any adhesive, sealant or thread locking compound to these bolts.

5. Remove knock sensor from the engine.

To install:

6. Thoroughly clean the knock sensor mounting hole.

7. Install knock sensor into the cylinder block.

❋❋ WARNING

Over or under tightening the sensor mounting bolts will affect knock sensor performance, possibly causing improper spark control. Always use the specified torque when installing the knock sensors. The torque for the knock sensor bolt is relatively light for an 8 mm bolt.

8. Install and tighten mounting bolt. Tighten to 15 ft. lbs. (20 Nm).

MANIFOLD ABSOLUTE PRESSURE (MAP) SENSOR

LOCATION

3.7L & 4.7L Engines

See Figure 114.

The Manifold Absolute Pressure (MAP) sensor is mounted into the front of the intake manifold.

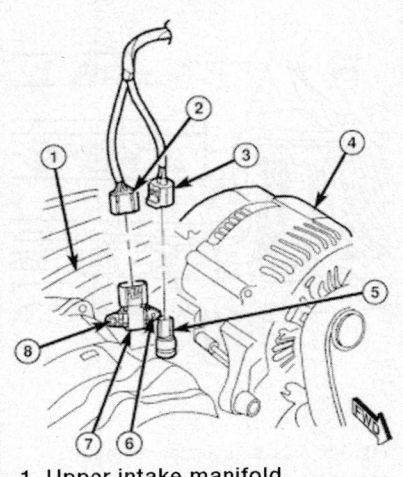

1. Upper intake manifold
2. MAP sensor electrical connector
3. ECT sensor electrical connector
4. Alternator
5. ECT sensor
6. Locating pin
7. MAP sensor
8. Mounting bolt

22043_RPUP_G0094

Fig. 114 Manifold Absolute Pressure (MAP) sensor location—3.7L and 4.7L engines

5.7L Engine

See Figure 115.

The Manifold Absolute Pressure (MAP) sensor is mounted to the front of the intake manifold air plenum box.

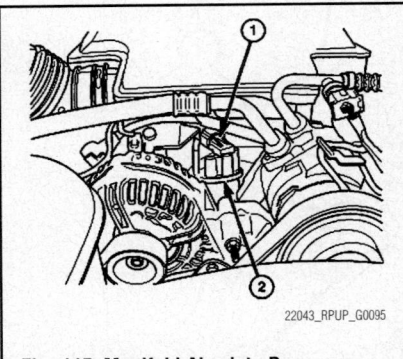

22043_RPUP_G0095

Fig. 115 Manifold Absolute Pressure (MAP) sensor location—5.7L engines

REMOVAL & INSTALLATION

3.7L & 4.7L Engines

See Figure 114.

1. Before servicing the vehicle, refer to the Precautions Section.

2. Disconnect the electrical connector at the Manifold Absolute Pressure (MAP) sensor.

3. Clean the area around MAP sensor.

4. Remove one sensor mounting screw.

5. Remove MAP sensor from intake manifold by slipping it from locating pin.

6. Check condition of the sensor O-ring.

To install:

7. Clean the MAP sensor mounting hole at intake manifold.

8. Check the MAP sensor o-ring seal for cuts or tears.

9. Position MAP sensor into manifold by sliding the sensor over locating pin.

10. Install the mounting bolt. Tighten to 25 in. lbs. (3 Nm).

11. Connect the MAP sensor electrical connector.

5.7L Engine

See Figure 115.

1. Before servicing the vehicle, refer to the Precautions Section.

2. Disconnect electrical connector at Manifold Absolute Pressure (MAP) sensor by sliding release lock out. Press down on lock tab for removal.

3. Rotate the sensor a ¼ turn counterclockwise for removal.

4. Check the condition of sensor O-ring.

To install:

5. Clean the MAP sensor mounting hole at intake manifold.

6. Check the MAP sensor O-ring seal for cuts or tears.

7. Position the MAP sensor into manifold.

8. Rotate the MAP sensor a ¼ turn clockwise for installation.

9. Connect the MAP sensor electrical connector.

OUTPUT SPEED SENSOR (OSS)

LOCATION

See Figure 116.

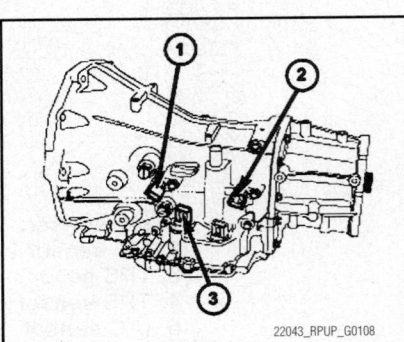

22043_RPUP_G0108

Fig. 116 Input (1) and output (2) speed sensor location

The OSS is mounted in the left side of the transmission case.

REMOVAL & INSTALLATION

See Figure 116.

1. Before servicing the vehicle, refer to the Precautions Section.
2. Raise the vehicle.
3. Place a suitable fluid catch pan under the transmission.
4. Remove the wiring connector from the output speed sensor.

➡**The speed sensor bolt has a sealing patch applied from the factory. Be sure to reuse the same bolt.**

5. Remove the bolt holding the output speed sensor to the transmission case.
6. Remove the output speed sensor (2) from the transmission case.

To install:

7. Install the output speed sensor (2) into the transmission case.

Before installing the speed sensor bolt, it will be necessary to replenish the sealing patch on the bolt using MOPAR® Lock & Seal Adhesive.

8. Install the bolt to hold the output speed sensor into the transmission case. Tighten the bolt to 80 inch lbs. (9 Nm).
9. Install the wiring connector onto the output speed sensor.
10. Verify the transmission fluid level. Add fluid as necessary.
11. Lower the vehicle.

POSITIVE CRANKCASE VENTILATION (PCV) VALVE

LOCATION

3.7L Engine

The PCV valve is located at the rear of the left cylinder head.

4.7L Engine

The PCV valve is mounted into the top/rear of the left valve cover.

5.7L Engine

The PCV valve is mounted into the top of the intake manifold. This is located to the right / rear of the throttle body.

REMOVAL & INSTALLATION

3.7L Engine

See Figure 117.

1. Remove line (1) and rubber connector hose from PCV valve.

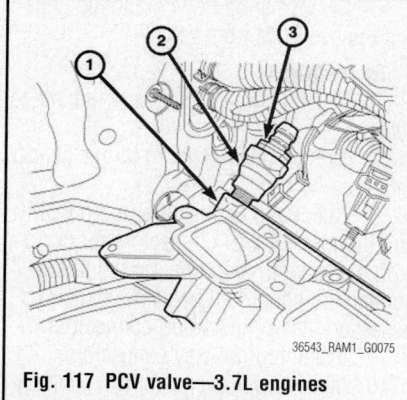
Fig. 117 PCV valve—3.7L engines

2. Unthread PCV valve (3) from metal fitting (2).

To install:

3. Check condition of PCV valve rubber O-ring (2).
4. Clean fitting (2).
5. Install PCV valve (3) into fitting (2).
6. Install PCV line (1) and rubber connector to valve.

4.7L Engine

See Figure 118.

1. Disconnect plastic line (1) from end of PCV valve.
2. Use a small screwdriver to disengage PCV valve from valve cover.

To install:

3. Clean out PCV valve opening at valve cover.
4. Check condition of PCV valve o-ring.
5. Apply engine oil to o-ring.
6. Place PCV valve (2) into valve cover.
7. Attach plastic line (1) to valve.

Fig. 118 PCV valve—4.7L engines

5.7L Engine

See Figure 119.

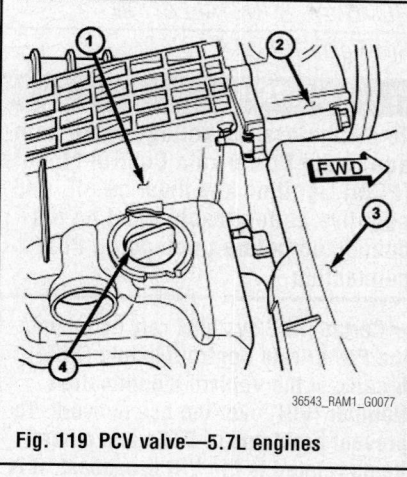
Fig. 119 PCV valve—5.7L engines

1. The PCV valve is sealed to the intake manifold with 2 O-rings (2).
2. Remove PCV valve by rotating counter-clockwise 90 degrees until locating tabs (3) have been freed. After tabs have cleared, pull valve straight up from intake manifold.
3. After valve is removed, check condition of 2 valve O-rings (2).

To install:

4. Clean out intake manifold opening.
5. Check condition of two o-rings on PCV valve.
6. Apply engine oil to two o-rings.
7. Place PCV valve into intake manifold and rotate 90 degrees clockwise for installation.

POWERTRAIN CONTROL MODULE (PCM)

LOCATION

See Figure 120.

The Powertrain Control Module (PCM) is located in the engine compartment attached to the dash panel.

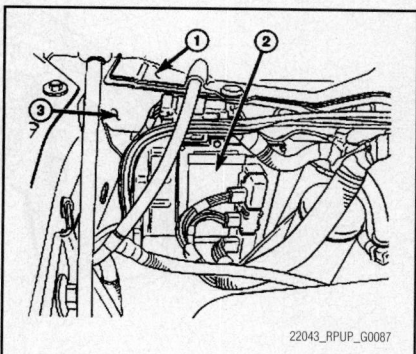
Fig. 120 Powertrain Control Module (PCM) location view

REMOVAL & INSTALLATION

See Figure 121.

✳ WARNING

To avoid possible voltage spike damage to the Powertrain Control Module (PCM), ignition key must be off, and negative battery cable must be disconnected before unplugging PCM connectors.

➡Certain ABS systems rely on having the Powertrain Control Module (PCM) broadcast the Vehicle Identification Number (VIN) over the bus network. To prevent problems of DTCs and other items related to the VIN broadcast, it is recommend that you disconnect the ABS CAB controller temporarily when replacing the PCM. Once the PCM is replaced, write the VIN to the PCM using a scan tool. This is done from the engine main menu. Arrow over to the second page to Miscellaneous. Select (check VIN) from the choices. Make sure it has the correct VIN entered before continuing. When the VIN is complete, turn off the ignition key and reconnect the ABS module connector. This will prevent the setting of DTCs and other items associated with the lack of a VIN detected when you turn the key ON after replacing the PCM.

1. Before servicing the vehicle, refer to the Precautions Section.
2. Disconnect negative battery cable at battery.
3. Remove cover over electrical connectors. Cover snaps onto PCM.
4. Carefully unplug the four 38-way connectors from PCM.

5. Remove three PCM mounting bolts and remove PCM from vehicle.

To install:

6. Install PCM and 3 mounting bolts to vehicle.
7. Tighten bolts. Refer to torque specifications.
8. Check pin connectors in the PCM and the four 38-way connectors for corrosion or damage. Also, the pin heights in connectors should all be same. Repair as necessary before installing connectors.
9. Install four 38-way connectors.
10. Install cover over electrical connectors. Cover snaps onto PCM.
11. Install negative battery cable.
12. The vehicle is equipped with a fully electronic accelerator pedal position sensor. Perform the following 3 steps:
    a. Connect negative battery cable to battery.
    b. Turn ignition switch ON, but do not crank engine.
    c. Leave ignition switch ON for a minimum of 10 seconds. This will allow PCM to learn electrical parameters.
    d. The scan tool may also be used to learn electrical parameters. Go to the Miscellaneous menu, and then select ETC Learn.
13. If the previous step is not performed, a Diagnostic Trouble Code (DTC) will be set.
14. If necessary, use a scan tool to erase any Diagnostic Trouble Codes (DTC's) from PCM. Also use the scan tool to reprogram new PCM with vehicles original Vehicle Identification Number (VIN) and original vehicle mileage.

TRANSMISSION OIL TEMPERATURE (TOT) SENSOR

LOCATION

42RLE

➡**This applies to vehicles with the 3.7L engine.**

The transmission temperature sensor (2) is located in the transmission range sensor (1) and communicates transmission sump temperature to the TCM.

45RFE/545RFE

➡**This applies to vehicles with 4.7L and 5.7L engines.**

The Transmission Range Sensor (TRS) is part of the solenoid module, which is mounted to the top of the valve body inside the transmission.

The TRS also has an integrated temperature sensor (thermistor) that communicates transmission temperature to the TCM and PCM.

REMOVAL & INSTALLATION

42RLE

1. Remove valve body assembly from vehicle. Refer to Transmission.
2. Remove the manual shaft seal.
3. Remove manual shaft/TRS retaining screw.
4. Slide TRS off of manual valve shaft.

To install:

5. Install the TRS to the manual shaft. Make sure TRS locating pin rests in manual valve bore slot.
6. Install the TRS/manual shaft retaining screw and torque to 45 inch lbs. (5 Nm) torque.
7. Install the manual shaft seal.
8. Install valve body to the transmission.

45RFE/545RFE

➡**If the Transmission Solenoid/TRS Assembly is being replaced, the Quick Learn Procedure must be performed.**

1. Remove the valve body from the transmission. Refer to Transmission.
2. Remove the bolts holding the transmission solenoid/TRS assembly onto the valve body.
3. Separate the transmission solenoid/TRS assembly from the valve body.

To install:

4. Place TRS selector plate in the PARK position.

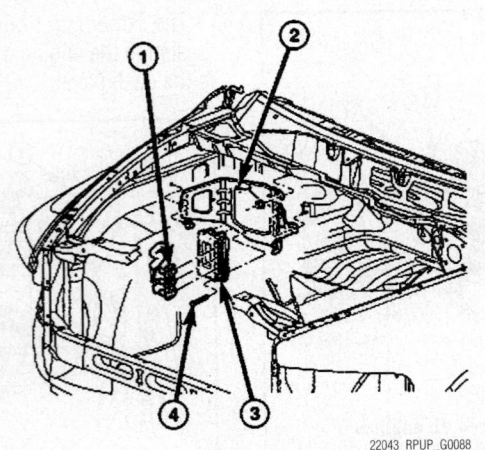

22043_RPUP_G0088

Fig. 121 Powertrain Control Module (PCM) electrical connectors (1), bracket (2), PCM (3), Mounting bolts (4)

5. Position the transmission solenoid/TRS assembly onto the valve body. Be sure that both alignment dowels are fully seated in the valve body and that the TRS switch contacts are properly positioned in the selector plate

6. Install the bolts to hold the transmission solenoid/TRS assembly onto the valve body.

7. Tighten the solenoid assembly screws adjacent to the arrows cast into the bottom of the valve body first. Tighten the screws to 50 inch lbs. (6 Nm).

8. Tighten the remainder of the solenoid assembly screws to 50 inch lbs. (6 Nm).

9. Install the valve body into the transmission.

TCM QUICK LEARN PROCEDURE

The quick learn procedure requires the use of the scan tool.

This program allows the electronic transmission system to recalibrate itself. This will provide the proper transmission operation. The quick learn procedure should be performed if any of the following procedures are performed:

- Transmission Assembly Replacement.
- Transmission Control Module Replacement.
- Solenoid Pack Replacement.
- Clutch Plate and/or Seal Replacement.
- Valve Body Replacement or Recondition.

To perform the Quick Learn Procedure, the following conditions must be met:

- The brakes must be applied.
- The engine speed must be above 500 rpm.
- The throttle angle (TPS) must be less than 3 degrees.
- The shift lever position must stay in PARK until prompted to shift to overdrive.
- The shift lever position must stay in overdrive after the Shift to Overdrive prompt until the scan tool indicates the procedure is complete.
- The calculated oil temperature must be above 60° and below 200°.

TRANSMISSION RANGE (TR) SENSOR

LOCATION

42RLE

➡This applies to vehicles with the 3.7L engine

The Transmission Range Sensor (TRS) is mounted to the top of the valve body inside the transmission and can only be serviced by removing the valve body assembly. The

electrical connector extends through the transmission case.

45RFE/545RFE

➡This applies to vehicles with 4.7L and 5.7L engines.

The Transmission Range Sensor (TRS) is part of the solenoid module, which is mounted to the top of the valve body inside the transmission.

REMOVAL & INSTALLATION

42RLE

1. Remove valve body assembly from vehicle. Refer to Transmission.

2. Remove the manual shaft seal.

3. Remove manual shaft/TRS retaining screw.

4. Slide TRS off of manual valve shaft.

To install:

5. Install the TRS (2) to the manual shaft. Make sure TRS locating pin rests in manual valve bore slot.

6. Install the TRS/manual shaft retaining screw and torque to 45 inch lbs. (5 Nm) torque.

7. Install the manual shaft seal.

8. Install valve body to the transmission.

45RFE/545RFE

➡If the Transmission Solenoid/TRS Assembly is being replaced, the Quick Learn Procedure must be performed.

1. Remove the valve body from the transmission. Refer to Transmission.

2. Remove the bolts holding the transmission solenoid/TRS assembly onto the valve body .

3. Separate the transmission solenoid/TRS assembly from the valve body.

To install:

4. Place TRS selector plate in the PARK position.

5. Position the transmission solenoid/TRS assembly onto the valve body. Be sure that both alignment dowels are fully seated in the valve body and that the TRS switch contacts are properly positioned in the selector plate

6. Install the bolts to hold the transmission solenoid/TRS assembly onto the valve body.

7. Tighten the solenoid assembly screws adjacent to the arrows cast into the bottom of the valve body first. Tighten the screws to 50 inch lbs. (6 Nm).

8. Tighten the remainder of the solenoid assembly screws to 50 inch lbs. (6 Nm).

9. Install the valve body into the transmission.

TCM QUICK LEARN PROCEDURE

The quick learn procedure requires the use of the scan tool.

This program allows the electronic transmission system to recalibrate itself. This will provide the proper transmission operation. The quick learn procedure should be performed if any of the following procedures are performed:

- Transmission Assembly Replacement.
- Transmission Control Module Replacement.
- Solenoid Pack Replacement.
- Clutch Plate and/or Seal Replacement.
- Valve Body Replacement or Recondition.

To perform the Quick Learn Procedure, the following conditions must be met:

- The brakes must be applied.
- The engine speed must be above 500 rpm.
- The throttle angle (TPS) must be less than 3 degrees.
- The shift lever position must stay in PARK until prompted to shift to overdrive.
- The shift lever position must stay in overdrive after the Shift to Overdrive prompt until the scan tool indicates the procedure is complete.
- The calculated oil temperature must be above 60° and below 200°.

VARIABLE LINE PRESSURE SENSOR

LOCATION

42RLE

➡This applies to vehicles with the 3.7L engine.

The line pressure sensor is mounted on the top of the valve body, next to the pressure control solenoid.

45RFE/545RFE

➡This applies to vehicles with 4.7L and 5.7L engines.

The line pressure sensor is mounted in the side of the transmission case.

REMOVAL & INSTALLATION

42RLE

1. Remove valve body assembly from vehicle. Refer to Transmission.

2. Remove the electrical connectors from the pressure control solenoid and the line pressure sensor.

3. Remove the screws holding the pressure control solenoid and line pressure sensor to the valve body.

4. Remove the pressure control solenoid and line pressure sensor from the valve body.

To install:

5. Install the pressure control solenoid and line pressure sensor into the valve body.

6. Install the screws to hold the pressure control solenoid and line pressure sensor to the valve body.

7. Install the electrical connectors to the pressure control solenoid and the line pressure sensor.

8. Install valve body to the transmission.

45RFE/545RFE

See Figure 122.

1. Remove the valve body from the transmission. Refer to Transmission.

2. Raise vehicle.

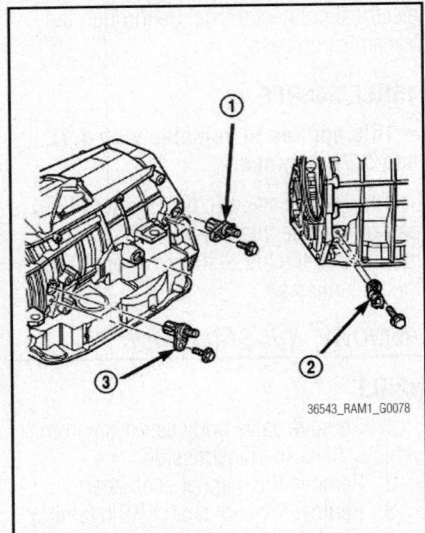

Fig. 122 Variable Line Pressure Sensor—45RFE/545RFE

36543_RAM1_G0078

3. Place a suitable fluid catch pan under the transmission.

4. Remove the wiring connector from the line pressure sensor.

5. Remove the bolt holding the line pressure sensor to the transmission case.

6. Remove the line pressure sensor from the transmission case.

To install:

7. Install the line pressure sensor into the transmission case.

8. Install the bolt to hold the line pressure sensor into the transmission case. Tighten the bolt to 106 inch lbs. (12 Nm).

9. Install the wiring connector onto the line pressure sensor.

10. Verify the transmission fluid level. Add fluid as necessary.

11. Lower vehicle.

FUEL

GASOLINE FUEL INJECTION SYSTEM

FUEL SYSTEM SERVICE PRECAUTIONS

Safety is the most important factor when performing not only fuel system maintenance but any type of maintenance. Failure to conduct maintenance and repairs in a safe manner may result in serious personal injury or death. Maintenance and testing of the vehicle's fuel system components can be accomplished safely and effectively by adhering to the following rules and guidelines.

• To avoid the possibility of fire and personal injury, always disconnect the negative battery cable unless the repair or test procedure requires that battery voltage be applied.

• Always relieve the fuel system pressure prior to disconnecting any fuel system component (injector, fuel rail, pressure regulator, etc.), fitting or fuel line connection. Exercise extreme caution whenever relieving fuel system pressure to avoid exposing skin, face and eyes to fuel spray. Please be advised that fuel under pressure may penetrate the skin or any part of the body that it contacts.

• Always place a shop towel or cloth around the fitting or connection prior to loosening to absorb any excess fuel due to spillage. Ensure that all fuel spillage (should it occur) is quickly removed from engine surfaces. Ensure that all fuel soaked cloths or towels are deposited into a suitable waste container.

• Always keep a dry chemical (Class B) fire extinguisher near the work area.

• Do not allow fuel spray or fuel vapors to come into contact with a spark or open flame.

• Always use a back-up wrench when loosening and tightening fuel line connection fittings. This will prevent unnecessary stress and torsion to fuel line piping.

• Always replace worn fuel fitting O-rings with new. Do not substitute fuel hose or equivalent where fuel pipe is installed.

Before servicing the vehicle, make sure to also refer to the precautions in the beginning of this section as well.

RELIEVING FUEL SYSTEM PRESSURE

➡A separate fuel pump relay is no longer used. A circuit within the Totally Integrated Power Module (TIPM) is used to control the electric fuel pump located within the fuel pump module. The TIPM is located in the engine compartment in front of the battery.

1. Remove fuel fill cap.

2. On bottom of vehicle, disconnect fuel pump module electrical connector. This can be accomplished at either of the two connectors.

3. Start and run engine until it stalls.

4. Attempt restarting engine until it will no longer run.

5. Turn ignition key to OFF position.

6. Place a rag or towel below fuel line quick-connect fitting at fuel rail.

7. Disconnect quick-connect fitting at fuel rail.

8. Reconnect fuel pump module electrical connector on bottom of vehicle.

9. One or more Diagnostic Trouble Codes (DTC's) may have been stored in PCM memory due to disconnecting fuel pump module circuit. A diagnostic scan tool must be used to erase a DTC.

FUEL FILTER

REMOVAL & INSTALLATION

See Figure 123.

The fuel filter is located in the fuel tank. If the electrical fuel pump, primary inlet filter, fuel filter or fuel pressure regulator require service, the fuel pump module must be removed.

1. Before servicing the vehicle, refer to the Precautions Section.

2. Relieve the fuel system pressure.

3. Remove or disconnect the following:
   • Negative battery cable
   • Fuel tank

4. Pull the filter/regulator out of the rubber grommet. Cut the hose clamp and remove the fuel line.

To install:

5. Install the filter/regulator with a new clamp and push it into the rubber grommet.

6. Install or connect the following:
   • Fuel tank
   • Negative battery cable

7. Start the engine and check for leaks.

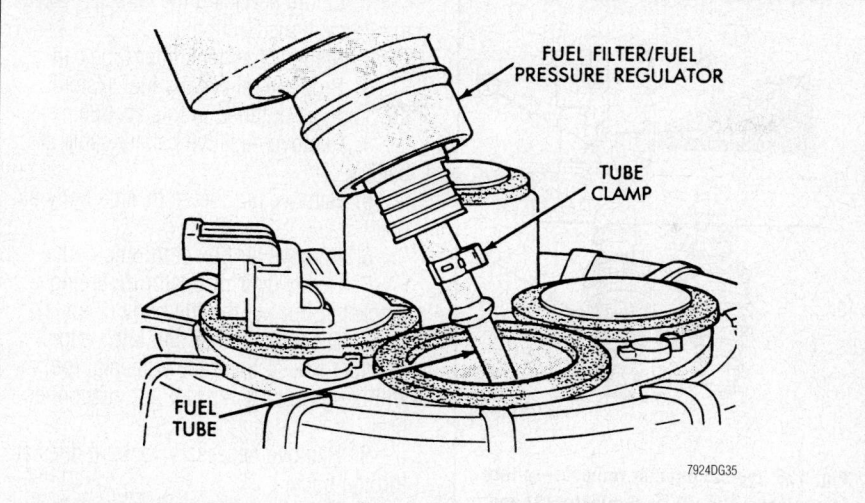

Fig. 123 Pull and twist the filter/regulator to remove it from the top of the fuel pump module

FUEL PRESSURE REGULATOR

REMOVAL & INSTALLATION

The fuel pressure regulator is located in the fuel tank. If the electrical fuel pump, primary inlet filter, fuel filter or fuel pressure regulator require service, the fuel pump module must be removed. Refer to Fuel Pump Module.

FUEL PUMP MODULE

REMOVAL & INSTALLATION
See Figure 124.

✳✳ CAUTION

The fuel system may be under a constant pressure (even with the engine

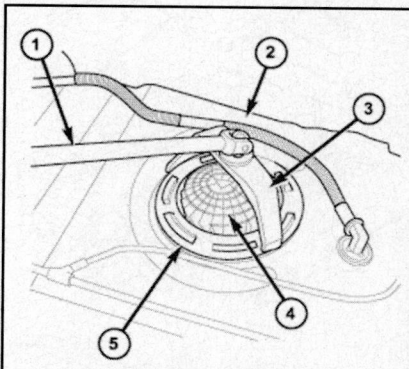

1. 1/2 Drive breaker bar
2. Fuel tank
3. Special tool 9340
4. Fuel pump
5. Lockring

22043_RPUP_G0144

Fig. 124 Lockring removal shown with tool 9340

off). Before servicing the fuel pump module, the fuel system pressure must be released.

1. Before servicing the vehicle, refer to the Precautions Section.
2. Drain and remove fuel tank. Refer to Fuel Tank Removal/Installation.
3. Remove plastic fuel pump module cover by pushing pegs outward.
4. Note rotational position of module before attempting removal. An indexing arrow is located on top of module for this purpose.
5. Position special tool 9340 into notches on outside edge of lockring.
6. Install ½ inch drive breaker bar to tool 9340.
7. Rotate breaker bar counter-clockwise to remove lockring.
8. Remove lockring. The module will spring up slightly when lockring is removed.
9. Remove module from fuel tank. Be careful not to bend float arm while removing.

To install:
10. Using a new seal (gasket), position fuel pump module into opening in fuel tank.
11. Position lockring (5) over top of fuel pump module.
12. Rotate module until embossed alignment arrow points to center alignment mark. This step must be performed to prevent float from contacting side of fuel tank. Also be sure fuel fitting on top of pump module is pointed to drivers side of vehicle.
13. Install Special Tool 9340 (3) to lockring.
14. Install 1/2 inch drive breaker (1) into Special Tool 9340 (3).

15. Tighten lockring (clockwise) until all seven notches have engaged.
16. Snap plastic fuel pump module cover (1) to pump module.
17. Install fuel tank.

FUEL RAIL & INJECTORS

REMOVAL & INSTALLATION

3.7L Engine
See Figures 125 and 126.

✳✳ CAUTION

The fuel system is under constant pressure even with engine off. Before servicing fuel rail, fuel system pressure must be released.

✳✳ WARNING

The left and right fuel rails are replaced as an assembly. Do not attempt to separate rail halves at connector tubes. Due to design of tubes, it does not use any clamps. Never attempt to install a clamping device of any kind to tubes. When removing fuel rail assembly for any reason, be careful not to bend or kink tubes.

1. Before servicing the vehicle, refer to the Precautions Section.
2. Remove fuel tank filler tube cap.
3. Properly relieve the fuel system pressure, as outlined in this section.
4. Remove negative battery cable at battery.

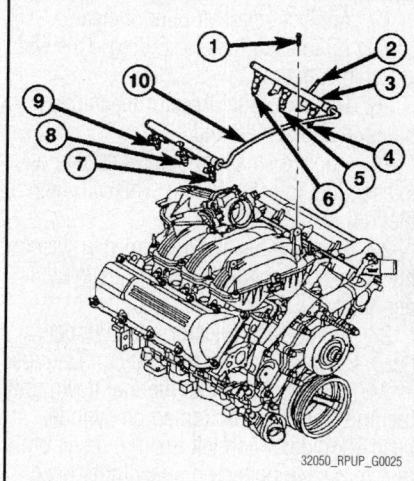

32050_RPUP_G0025

Fig. 125 Exploded view of the fuel rail mounting bolts (1), quick-connect fitting (2), fuel rail (3), injectors (4-9) and connector tube—3.7L engines

5. Remove air duct at throttle body air box.

6. Remove air box at throttle body.

7. Remove air resonator mounting bracket at front of throttle body (2 bolts).

8. Disconnect fuel line latch clip and fuel line at fuel rail. A special tool will be necessary for fuel line disconnection.

9. Remove necessary vacuum lines at throttle body.

10. Disconnect electrical connectors at all 6 fuel injectors. Push the red colored slider away from injector. While pushing slider, depress tab and remove connector from injector. The factory fuel injection wiring harness is numerically tagged (INJ 1, INJ 2, etc.) for injector position identification. If harness is not tagged, note wiring location before removal.

11. Disconnect electrical connectors at all throttle body sensors.

12. Remove 6 ignition coils, as outlined in Engine Electrical.

13. Remove 4 fuel rail mounting bolts.

14. Gently rock and pull left side of fuel rail until fuel injectors just start to clear machined holes in cylinder head. Gently rock and pull right side of rail until injectors just start to clear cylinder head holes. Repeat this procedure (left/right) until all injectors have cleared cylinder head holes.

15. Remove fuel rail (with injectors attached) from engine.

16. Disconnect clip(s) that retain fuel injector(s) to fuel rail.

To install:

17. Install fuel injector(s) into fuel rail assembly and install retaining clip(s).

18. If same injector(s) is being reinstalled, install new O-ring(s).

19. Apply a small amount of clean engine oil to each injector O-ring. This will aid in installation.

20. Clean out fuel injector machined bores in intake manifold.

21. Apply a small amount of engine oil to each fuel injector O-ring. This will help in fuel rail installation.

22. Position fuel rail/fuel injector assembly to machined injector openings in cylinder head.

23. Guide each injector into cylinder head. Be careful not to tear injector O-rings.

24. Push right side of fuel rail down until fuel injectors have bottomed on cylinder head shoulder. Push left fuel rail down until injectors have bottomed on cylinder head shoulder.

25. Install 4 fuel rail mounting bolts and tighten.

26. Install 6 ignition coils.

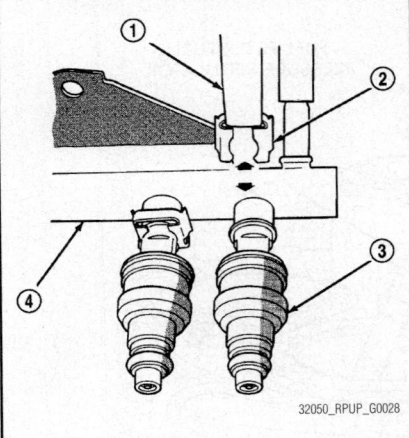

Fig. 126 Typical injector removal—pliers (1), injector clip (2), fuel injector (3) and fuel rail (4)

27. Connect electrical connectors to throttle body.

28. Connect electrical connectors at all fuel injectors. To install connector, push connector onto injector and then push and lock red colored slider. Make sure the connector is locked to the injector by lightly tugging on connector.

29. Connect necessary vacuum lines to throttle body.

30. Install air resonator mounting bracket near front of throttle body (2 bolts).

31. Connect fuel line latch clip and fuel line to fuel rail.

32. Install air box to throttle body.

33. Install air duct to air box.

34. Connect battery cable to battery.

35. Start engine and check for leaks.

4.7L Engine
See Figures 126 and 127.

✳✳ CAUTION

The fuel system is under constant pressure even with engine off. Before servicing fuel rail, fuel system pressure must be released.

✳✳ WARNING

The left and right fuel rails are replaced as an assembly. Do not attempt to separate rail halves at connector tubes. Due to design of tubes, it does not use any clamps. Never attempt to install a clamping device of any kind to tubes. When removing fuel rail assembly for any reason, be careful not to bend or kink tubes.

1. Before servicing the vehicle, refer to the Precautions Section.

2. Remove fuel tank filler tube cap.

3. Properly relieve the fuel system pressure, as outlined in this section.

4. Remove negative battery cable at battery.

5. Remove air duct at throttle body air box.

6. Remove air box at throttle body.

7. Remove air resonator mounting bracket at front of throttle body (2 bolts).

8. Disconnect fuel line latch clip and fuel line at fuel rail. A special tool will be necessary for fuel line disconnection.

9. Remove necessary vacuum lines at throttle body.

10. Disconnect electrical connectors from all 8 fuel injectors. To remove connector, push red colored slider away from injector. While pushing slider, depress tab and remove connector from injector. The factory fuel injection wiring harness is numerically tagged (INJ 1, INJ 2, etc.) for injector position identification. If harness is not tagged, note wiring location before removal.

11. Disconnect electrical connectors at all throttle body sensors.

12. Remove 8 ignition coils, as outlined in Engine Electrical.

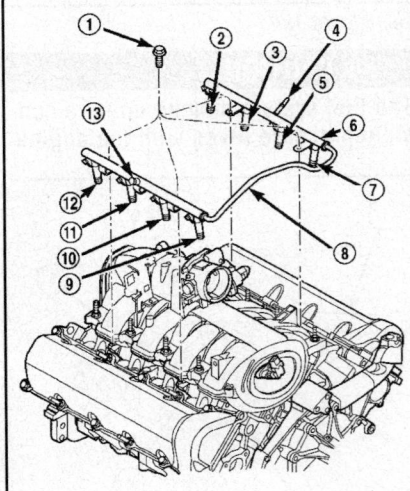

Fig. 127 Exploded view of the fuel rail mounting bolts (1), injector No. 7 (2), injector No. 5 (3), quick connect fitting (4), injector No. 3 (5), fuel rail (6), injector No. 1 (7), connector tube (8), injector No. 2 (9), injector No. 4 (10), injector No. 6 (11), injector No. 8 (12), pressure test port cap (13)—4.7L engines

13. Remove 4 fuel rail mounting bolts.

14. Gently rock and pull left side of fuel rail until fuel injectors just start to clear machined holes in cylinder head. Gently rock and pull right side of rail until injectors just start to clear cylinder head holes. Repeat this procedure (left/right) until all injectors have cleared cylinder head holes.

15. Remove fuel rail (with injectors attached) from engine.

16. Disconnect clip(s) that retain fuel injector(s) to fuel rail.

To install:

17. Install fuel injector(s) into fuel rail assembly and install retaining clip(s).

18. If same injector(s) is being reinstalled, install new O-ring(s).

19. Apply a small amount of clean engine oil to each injector O-ring. This will aid in installation.

20. Clean out fuel injector machined bores in intake manifold.

21. Apply a small amount of engine oil to each fuel injector O-ring. This will help in fuel rail installation.

22. Position fuel rail/fuel injector assembly to machined injector openings in cylinder head.

23. Guide each injector into cylinder head. Be careful not to tear injector O-rings.

24. Push right side of fuel rail down until fuel injectors have bottomed on cylinder head shoulder. Push left fuel rail down until injectors have bottomed on cylinder head shoulder.

25. Install 4 fuel rail mounting bolts and tighten.

26. Install 8 ignition coils.

27. Connect electrical connectors to throttle body.

28. Connect electrical connectors at all fuel injectors. To install connector, push connector onto injector and then push and lock red colored slider. Make sure the connector is locked to the injector by lightly tugging on connector.

29. Connect necessary vacuum lines to throttle body.

30. Install air resonator mounting bracket near front of throttle body (2 bolts).

31. Connect fuel line latch clip and fuel line to fuel rail.

32. Install air box to throttle body.

33. Install air duct to air box.

34. Connect battery cable to battery.

35. Start engine and check for leaks.

5.7L Engine

See Figures 126 and 128.

✲✲ CAUTION

The fuel system is under constant pressure even with engine off. Before servicing fuel rail, fuel system pressure must be released.

✲✲ WARNING

The left and right fuel rails are replaced as an assembly. Do not attempt to separate rail halves at connector tube. Due to design of tube, it does not use any clamps. Never attempt to install a clamping device of any kind to tube. When removing fuel rail assembly for any reason, be careful not to bend or kink tube.

---

1. Before servicing the vehicle, refer to the Precautions Section.

2. Remove fuel tank filler tube cap.

3. Properly relieve the fuel system pressure, as outlined in this section.

4. Remove negative battery cable at battery.

5. Remove flex tube (air cleaner housing to engine).

6. Remove air resonator box at throttle body.

7. Disconnect all spark plug cables from all spark plugs and ignition coils. Do not remove cables from cable routing tray. Note original cable positions while removing.

8. Remove spark plug cable tray from engine by releasing 4 retaining clips. Remove tray and cables from engine as an assembly.

9. Disconnect electrical connectors at all 8 ignition coils. Refer to Ignition Coil Removal/Installation in Engine Electrical.

10. Disconnect fuel line latch clip and fuel line at fuel rail. A special tool will be necessary for fuel line disconnection.

11. Disconnect electrical connectors at all 8 fuel injectors. To remove connector, push red colored slider away from injector. While pushing slider, depress tab and remove connector from injector. The factory fuel injection wiring harness is numerically tagged (INJ 1, INJ 2, etc.) for injector position identification. If harness is not tagged, note wiring location before removal.

12. Disconnect electrical connectors at all throttle body sensors.

13. Remove 4 fuel rail mounting bolts (2) and hold-down clamps (3).

14. Gently rock and pull left side of fuel rail until fuel injectors just start to clear machined holes in intake manifold. Gently rock and pull right side of rail until injectors just start to clear intake manifold head holes.

15. Repeat this procedure (left/right) until all injectors have cleared machined holes.

16. Remove fuel rail (with injectors attached) from engine.

17. Disconnect clip(s) that retain fuel injector(s) to fuel rail.

To install:

18. Install fuel injector(s) into fuel rail assembly and install retaining clip(s).

19. If same injector(s) is being reinstalled, install new O-ring(s).

20. Apply a small amount of clean engine oil to each injector O-ring. This will aid in installation.

21. Apply a small amount of engine oil

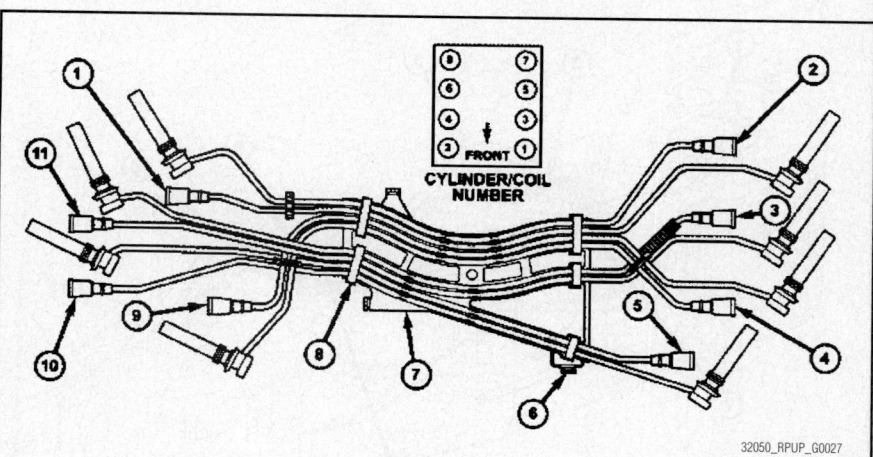

Fig. 128 View of the No. 8 coil to No. 5 spark plug (1), No. 5 coil to No. 8 spark plug (2), No. 7 coil to No. 4 spark plug (3), No. 3 coil to No. 2 spark plug (4), No. 1 coil to No. 6 spark plug (5), clips (6), cable tray (7), clips (8), No. 2 coil to No. 3 spark plug (9), No. 6 coil to No. 1 spark plug (10), No. 4 coil to No. 7 spark plug (11)—5.7L engines

to each fuel injector O-ring. This will help in fuel rail installation.

22. Position fuel rail/fuel injector assembly to machined injector openings in intake manifold.

23. Guide each injector into intake manifold. Be careful not to tear injector O-rings.

24. Push right side of fuel rail down until fuel injectors have bottomed on shoulders. Push left fuel rail down until injectors have bottomed on shoulders.

25. Install 4 fuel rail hold-down clamps and 4 mounting bolts.

26. Position spark plug cable tray and cable assembly to intake manifold. Snap 4 cable tray retaining clips into intake manifold.

27. Install all cables to spark plugs and ignition coils.

28. Connect electrical connector to throttle body.

29. Install electrical connectors to all 8 ignition coils.

30. Connect electrical connector to throttle body.

31. Attach the electrical connectors at all fuel injectors. To install connector, push connector onto injector and then push and lock red colored slider. Make sure the connector is locked to the injector by lightly tugging on connector.

32. Connect the fuel line latch clip and fuel line to fuel rail.

33. Install air resonator to throttle body (2 bolts).

34. Install flexible air duct to air box.

35. Connect battery cable to battery.

36. Start engine and check for leaks.

FUEL TANK

REMOVAL & INSTALLATION

See Figure 129.

1. Release fuel system pressure. Refer to Relieving Fuel System Pressure.

2. Raise and support vehicle.

3. Drain fuel tank. Refer to Draining Fuel Tank.

4. Loosen clamps.

5. Remove hoses from tank.

6. Disconnect electrical connector (1) at top of module.

7. Disconnect fuel supply line (3) and vapor line quick-connect fittings (5).

8. Support tank with a hydraulic jack.

9. Remove nuts (5).

10. Remove both tank straps (4).

11. Lower tank and remove from hydraulic jack.

12. If fuel pump module is being removed, refer to Fuel Pump Module.

To install:

13. If fuel pump module is being installed, refer to Fuel Pump Module. This must be done before installing tank.

14. Place assembly to a hydraulic jack.

15. Raise assembly up to frame.

16. Install tank straps (4).

17. Install strap nuts (5) and tighten to 41 Nm (30 ft. lbs.) torque.

18. Connect fuel supply line (3) and vapor line quick-connect fittings (5).

19. Position hoses to tank fittings.

20. Tighten clamps.

21. Connect electrical connector (1) at top of module.

22. Fill tank and check for leaks.

DRAINING FUEL TANK

❊❊ WARNING

The fuel system may be under constant fuel pressure even with the engine off. This pressure must be released before servicing the fuel tank.

Due to a one-way check valve installed into the fuel fill fitting at the tank, the tank cannot be drained conventionally at the fuel fill cap.

Two different procedures may be used to drain the fuel tank:

• Through the fuel fill fitting on the tank (conventional)

• Using a diagnostic scan tool to activate the fuel pump relay (Alternative)

The quickest draining procedure involves removing the rubber fuel fill hose at the fuel tank.

Conventional Procedure

If the electric fuel pump is not operating, the fuel must be drained through the fuel fill fitting at the tank. Refer to the following procedure:

1. Perform the Fuel System Pressure Release procedure. Refer to Relieving Fuel System Pressure.

2. Raise and support the vehicle.

3. Thoroughly clean the area around the fuel fill fitting and the rubber fuel fill hose at the tank.

4. If the vehicle is equipped with 4 doors and a 6 foot (short) box, remove left-rear wheel/tire assembly.

5. Loosen the clamp and disconnect the rubber fuel fill hose at the fuel tank fitting.

6. Remove the one-way check valve located in the fuel fill opening of the fuel tank.

7. Using an approved gasoline draining station, drain the fuel tank through the fuel fill opening of the fuel tank.

Alternative Procedure

As an alternative procedure, the electric fuel pump may be activated allowing the tank to be drained at the fuel rail connection. Refer to the diagnostic scan tool for fuel pump activation procedures.

1. Perform the Fuel System Pressure Release procedure. Refer to Relieving Fuel System Pressure.

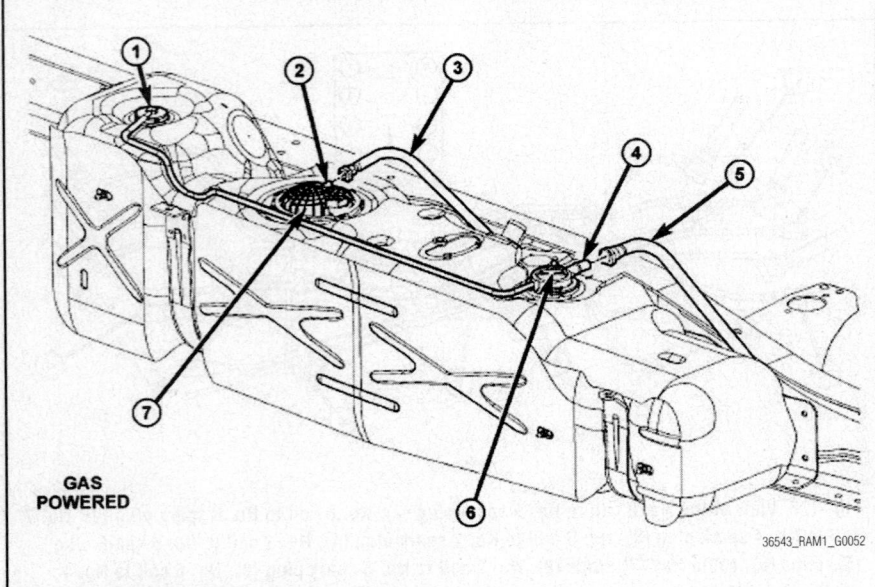

GAS
POWERED

36543_RAM1_G0052

Fig. 129 Fuel tank components

2. Attach one end of the special test hose (6631) or (6539) at the fuel line quick-connect fitting (tool number 6631 is used on 5/16" fuel lines while tool number 6539 is used on 3/8" fuel lines).

3. Position the opposite end of this special test hose to an OSHA approved gasoline caddy.

4. Using the scan tool, activate the fuel pump and drain the tank until empty.

IDLE SPEED

ADJUSTMENT

Idle speed is maintained by the Powertrain Control Module (PCM). No adjustment is necessary or possible.

THROTTLE BODY

REMOVAL & INSTALLATION

3.7L Engine
See Figure 130.

> ※※ **WARNING**
>
> **A (factory adjusted) set screw is used to mechanically limit the position of the throttle body throttle plate. Never attempt to adjust the engine idle speed using this screw. All idle speed functions are controlled by the Powertrain Control Module (PCM).**

1. Before servicing the vehicle, refer to the Precautions Section.

2. Disconnect and isolate negative battery cable at battery.

3. Remove air intake tube at throttle body flange.

4. Disconnect throttle body electrical connector.

5. Disconnect necessary vacuum lines at throttle body.

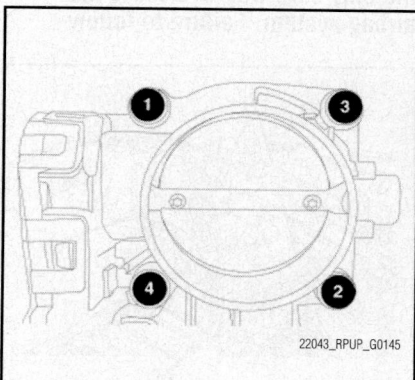

Fig. 130 Throttle body tightening sequence—3.7L engines

6. Remove four throttle body mounting bolts.

7. Remove throttle body from intake manifold.

8. Check condition of old throttle body-to-intake manifold O-ring.

To install:

9. Check condition of throttle body-to-intake manifold O-ring. Replace as necessary.

10. Clean mating surfaces of throttle body and intake manifold.

11. Install O-ring between throttle body and intake manifold.

12. Position throttle body to intake manifold.

13. Install all throttle body mounting bolts finger tight.

> ※※ **WARNING**
>
> **The throttle body mounting bolts MUST be torqued to specifications. DO NOT OVER TIGHTEN MOUNTING BOLTS. Over tightening can cause damage to the throttle body, throttle plate, gaskets, bolts and/or the intake manifold. Proper torque of the mounting bolts is critical to normal operation.**

14. Tighten mounting bolts (as shown) in a mandatory torque criss-cross pattern sequence to 65 inch lbs. (7.5 Nm).

15. Using the diagnostic scan tool, erase all previous DTC's and perform the ETC Relearn Procedure.

16. Install electrical connector.

17. Install necessary vacuum lines.

18. Install air cleaner duct at throttle body.

19. Connect negative battery cable.

20. Using the diagnostic scan tool, erase all previous DTC's and perform the ETC Relearn function.

4.7L Engine
See Figure 131.

> ※※ **WARNING**
>
> **Never have the ignition key in the ON position when/if checking the throttle body shaft for a binding condition. This may set DTC's.**

1. Before servicing the vehicle, refer to the Precautions Section.

2. Disconnect and isolate negative battery cable at battery.

3. Remove air duct and air resonator box at throttle body.

4. Disconnect throttle body electrical connector.

5. Disconnect necessary vacuum lines at throttle body.

6. Remove four throttle body mounting bolts.

7. Remove throttle body from intake manifold.

8. Check condition of old throttle body-to-intake manifold O-ring.

To install:

9. Check condition of throttle body-to-intake manifold O-ring. Replace as necessary.

10. Clean mating surfaces of throttle body and intake manifold.

11. Install throttle body-to-intake manifold O-ring

12. Install all throttle body mounting bolts finger tight.

> ※※ **WARNING**
>
> **The throttle body mounting bolts MUST be torqued to specifications. DO NOT OVER TIGHTEN MOUNTING BOLTS. Over tightening can cause damage to the throttle body, throttle plate, gaskets, bolts and/or the intake manifold. Proper torque of the mounting bolts is critical to normal operation.**

13. Tighten mounting bolts (as shown) in a mandatory torque crisscross pattern sequence to 65 inch lbs. (7.5 Nm).

14. Install electrical connector.

15. Install necessary vacuum lines.

16. Install air cleaner duct and plenum at throttle body.

17. Connect negative battery cable.

18. Using the diagnostic scan tool, erase all previous DTC's and perform the ETC Relearn Procedure.

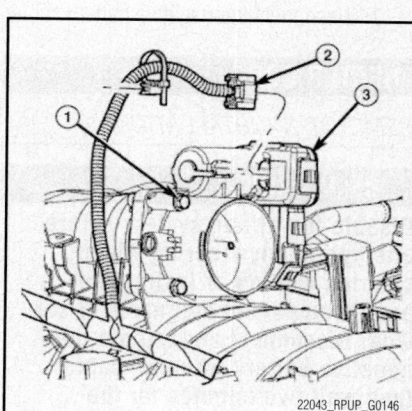

Fig. 131 Throttle body—4.7L engines

5.7L Engine

> ✳✳ **WARNING**
>
> Do not use spray (carb) cleaners on any part of the throttle body. Do not apply silicone lubricants to any part of the throttle body.

1. Before servicing the vehicle, refer to the Precautions Section.
2. Remove air duct and air resonator box at throttle body.
3. Disconnect electrical connector from the throttle body.
4. Remove 4 throttle body mounting bolts.

5. Remove throttle body from intake manifold.
6. Check condition of throttle body O-ring.

To install:

7. Clean and check condition of throttle body-to-intake manifold O-ring.
8. Clean mating surfaces of throttle body and intake manifold.
9. Install the throttle body to the intake manifold by positioning the throttle body to the manifold alignment pins.
10. Install 4 mounting bolts and tighten to 105 inch lbs. (12 Nm).
11. Attach the electrical connector.
12. Install the air plenum.

13. Using the diagnostic scan tool, erase all previous DTC's and perform the ETC Relearn Procedure.

THROTTLE RELEARN PROCEDURE

If the throttle body has been changed, the following procedure must be performed:

1. Disconnect negative battery cable from battery. Leave cable disconnected for approximately 90 seconds.
2. Reconnect cable to battery.
3. Turn ignition switch **ON**, but do not crank engine.
4. Leave ignition switch **ON** for a minimum of 10 seconds. This will allow PCM to learn throttle body electrical parameters.

HEATING & AIR CONDITIONING SYSTEM

BLOWER MOTOR

REMOVAL & INSTALLATION

➡The blower motor is located on the passenger side of the vehicle under the instrument panel. The blower motor can be removed from the vehicle without having to remove the HVAC housing assembly.

1. Disconnect and isolate the negative battery cable.
2. Disconnect the HVAC wire harness lead from the blower motor.
3. Remove the three screws that secure the blower motor to the bottom of the HVAC housing and remove the blower motor.

To install:

4. Position the blower motor into the bottom of the HVAC housing.
5. Install the three screws that secure the blower motor to the HVAC housing. Tighten the screws to 15 inch lbs. (1.7 Nm).
6. Connect the HVAC wire harness lead to the blower motor.
7. Reconnect the negative battery cable.

HEATER CORE

REMOVAL & INSTALLATION

> ✳✳ **WARNING**
>
> Disable the airbag system before attempting any steering wheel, steering column or instrument panel component diagnosis or service. Disconnect and isolate the negative battery (ground) cable, then wait two minutes for the airbag system capacitor to discharge before performing further diagnosis

or service. This is the only sure way to disable the airbag system. Failure to follow these instructions may result in accidental airbag deployment and possible serious or fatal injury.

➡Disassembly of the HVAC housing is not required to remove heater core.

1. Remove the HVAC housing and place it on a workbench. Refer to HVAC Housing.
2. Remove the foam seal from the flange.
3. Remove the two screws that secure the flange to the front of the HVAC housing.
4. Carefully disengage the retaining tab that secures the flange to the HVAC housing and remove the flange.
5. Carefully pull the heater core out of the front of the HVAC housing.
6. Inspect all foam seals and replace as required.

To install:

7. Inspect the foam seals on the heater core and replace as required.
8. Carefully install the heater core into the front of the HVAC housing.
9. Position the flange onto the front of the HVAC housing. Make sure the retaining tab is fully engaged.
10. Install the two screws that secure the flange to the HVAC housing. Tighten the screws to 10 inch lbs. (1.1 Nm).
11. Install the foam seal onto the flange.

➡If the heater core is being replaced, flush the cooling system.

12. Install the HVAC housing. Refer to HVAC Housing.

HVAC HOUSING

REMOVAL & INSTALLATION
See Figure 132.

> ✳✳ **WARNING**
>
> Refer to the applicable warnings and cautions for this system before performing the following operation. Refer to Precautions. Failure to follow these instructions may result in possible serious or fatal injury.

> ✳✳ **WARNING**
>
> Disable the airbag system before attempting any steering wheel, steering column or instrument panel component diagnosis or service. Disconnect and isolate the negative battery (ground) cable, then wait two minutes for the airbag system capacitor to discharge before performing further diagnosis or service. This is the only sure way to disable the airbag system. Failure to follow

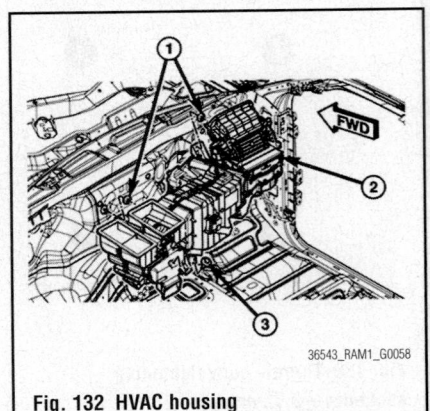

36543_RAM1_G0058

Fig. 132 HVAC housing

these instructions may result in accidental airbag deployment and possible serious or fatal injury.

➡ **The HVAC housing must be removed from the vehicle for service of the A/C evaporator, heater core, mode-air and blend-air doors and air inlet housing.**

1. Disconnect and isolate the negative battery cable.
2. Recover the refrigerant from the refrigerant system.
3. Drain the engine cooling system. Refer to Cooling.
4. Disconnect the A/C liquid line and the A/C suction line from the A/C expansion valve.
5. Disconnect the heater hoses from the heater core tubes.
6. If required, remove the Powertrain Control Module (PCM) to gain access to the two nuts (2) that secure the HVAC housing to the engine compartment side of the dash panel.
7. Remove the two nuts from the studs (1) that secure the HVAC housing to the engine compartment side of the dash panel.
8. If equipped with center floor console, remove the floor console duct.

9. Remove the instrument panel from the passenger compartment.
10. If equipped, remove the rear floor ducts.
11. Remove the bolt (3) that secures the HVAC housing (2) to the floor bracket.
12. Remove the two nuts (1) that secure the HVAC housing to the passenger compartment side of the dash panel.
13. Pull the HVAC housing assembly rearward and remove the housing assembly from the passenger compartment.

To install:

14. Position the HVAC housing assembly (2) into the passenger compartment and over the studs on the dash panel, with the condensate drain tube in its proper location.
15. Install the two nuts (1) that secure the HVAC housing to the passenger compartment side of the dash panel. Tighten the nuts to 6.8 Nm (60 in. lbs.).
16. Install the bolt (3) that secures the HVAC housing to the floor bracket. Tighten the bolt to 6.8 Nm (60 in. lbs.).
17. If equipped, install the rear floor ducts.
18. Install the instrument panel assembly.
19. If equipped with center floor console, install the floor console duct.

20. Install the two nuts (2) onto the two studs (1) that secure the HVAC housing to the engine compartment side of the dash panel. Tighten the nuts to 6.8 Nm (60 in. lbs.).
21. If removed, install the Powertrain control module (PCM).
22. Connect the heater hoses to the heater core tubes.
23. Connect the A/C liquid line and the A/C suction line to the A/C expansion valve.
24. Reconnect the negative battery cable.
25. If the heater core is being replaced, flush the cooling system.
26. Refill the engine cooling system. Refer to Bleeding in Cooling System.
27. Evacuate the refrigerant system.
28. If the A/C evaporator is being replaced, add 60 milliliters (2 fluid ounces) of refrigerant oil to the refrigerant system. When replacing multiple A/C system components, refer to the Refrigerant Oil Capacities chart to determine how much oil should be added to the refrigerant system. Use only refrigerant oil of the type recommended for the A/C compressor in the vehicle.
29. Charge the refrigerant system.
30. Initiate the Actuator Calibration function using a scan tool.

STEERING

POWER RACK & PINION STEERING GEAR

REMOVAL & INSTALLATION

See Figure 133.

➡ **The steering column on vehicles with an automatic transmission is not equipped with an internal locking shaft that allows the ignition key cylinder to be locked with the key. Alternative methods of locking the steering wheel for service will have to be used.**

1. Lock the steering wheel.
2. Drain and siphon the power steering fluid from the reservoir.
3. Raise and support the vehicle.
4. Remove and discard the steering coupler pinch bolt.
5. Remove the power steering hoses from the rack and pinion.
6. Remove the tire and wheel assembly.
7. Remove the tie rod end nuts and separate tie rod ends from the knuckles using Ball Joint Remover 8677.
8. Remove the skid plate.

9. Remove the rack and pinion mounting bolts (1).
10. Remove the rack and pinion (2) from the vehicle.

To install:

➡ **Before installing gear inspect bushings and replace if worn or damaged.**

➡ **In the frame there are two holes for the mounting of the steering gear, one is slotted and one is round. When tightening the gear to specifications make sure to tighten the mounting bolt with the hole first to avoid movement of the steering gear.**

11. Install the gear on the front crossmember and tighten the mounting bolts to 235 ft. lbs. (319 Nm).
12. Slide the shaft coupler onto the gear. Install new pinch bolt and tighten to 36 ft. lbs. (49 Nm).
13. Clean and dry the tie rod end studs and the knuckle tapers.
14. Install the tie rod ends into the steering knuckles and tighten the nuts to 45 ft. lbs. (61 Nm) then an additional 90°.

15. Install the pressure power steering hose to the steering gear and tighten to 23 ft. lbs. (32 Nm).
16. Install the return power steering hose to the steering gear and tighten to 37 ft. lbs. (50 Nm).
17. Install the front skid plate.
18. Install the tire and wheel assembly.
19. Remove the support and lower the vehicle.
20. Fill the system with fluid. Refer to Bleeding under Power Steering Pump.
21. Adjust the toe position.

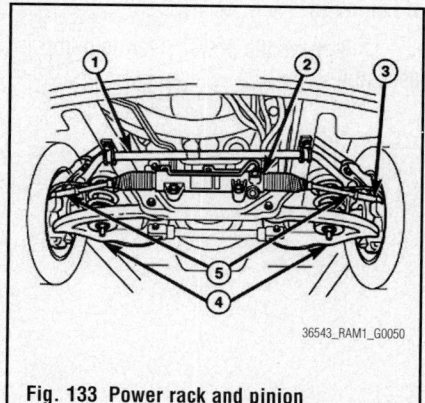

36543_RAM1_G0050

Fig. 133 Power rack and pinion

POWER STEERING PUMP

REMOVAL & INSTALLATION

1. Drain and siphon the power steering fluid from the reservoir.
2. Remove the serpentine belt.

CAUTION

Do not remove the fitting on the pump that the high pressure hose screws into. The fitting may come loose unless it is backed up using another wrench. If the fitting does come loose, it must be retightened before continuing to 40–50 ft. lbs. (57–67 Nm). If this fitting comes out of the pump body, the internal spring and valve parts will fall out of the pump and they cannot be reinstalled properly. If this occurs the pump needs to be replaced with a new pump.

3. Disconnect the return hose.
4. Disconnect the pressure hose.
5. Remove the three bolts securing the pump to the cylinder head thru the pulley holes.

To install:

6. Align the pump with the mounting holes in the left cylinder head.
7. Install 3 pump mounting bolts through the pulley access holes. Tighten the bolts to 21 ft. lbs. (28 Nm).
8. Reconnect the pressure line and return hose to the pump and reservoir. Tighten the pressure line to 23 ft. lbs. (31 Nm).
9. Install the serpentine drive belt. Refer to Accessory Drive Belt.
10. Fill the power steering pump. Refer to Bleeding.

PULLEY REPLACEMENT

➡Do not reuse the old power steering pump pulley it is not intended for reuse. A new pulley must be installed if removed.

1. Remove the power steering pump assembly.
2. Remove the pulley from the pump using (OTC® 7185) power steering pulley removal tool or equivalent.

To install:

3. Replace the pulley if it's bent, cracked, or loose.
4. Install the pulley on the pump using (OTC® 7771) power steering pulley installation tool or equivalent making sure it is flush with the end of the shaft. Ensure the tool and pulley remain aligned with the pump shaft.
5. Install the power steering pump assembly.
6. Run engine until warm (5 min.) and note any belt chirp. If chirp exists, move pulley outward approximately 0.5 mm (0.020 in.). If noise increases, press on 1.0 mm (0.040 in.). Be careful that pulley does not contact mounting bolts.

BLEEDING

WARNING

The fluid level should be checked with engine off to prevent injury from moving components.

CAUTION

Mopar® Power Steering Fluid + 4 or Mopar® ATF+4 Automatic Transmission Fluid is to be used in the power steering system. Both Fluids have the same material standard specifications (MS-9602). No other power steering or automatic transmission fluid is to be used in the system. Damage may result to the power steering pump and system if another fluid is used. Do not overfill the system.

CAUTION

If the air is not purged from the power steering system correctly, pump failure could result.

➡Be sure the vacuum tool used in the following procedure is clean and free of any fluids.

1. Check the fluid level. As measured on the side of the reservoir, the level should indicate between MAX and MIN when the fluid is at normal ambient temperature. Adjust the fluid level as necessary.
2. Tightly insert P/S Cap Adapter 9688 into the mouth of the reservoir.

CAUTION

Failure to use a vacuum pump reservoir may allow power steering fluid to be sucked into the hand vacuum pump.

3. Attach Hand Vacuum Pump C-4207-A, or equivalent, with reservoir attached, to the P/S Cap Adapter 9688.

CAUTION

Do not run the vehicle while vacuum is applied to the power steering system. Damage to the power steering pump can occur.

➡When performing the following step make sure the vacuum level is maintained during the entire time period.

4. Using Hand Vacuum Pump, apply 68-85 kpa (20-25 in. Hg) of vacuum to the system for a minimum of three minutes.
5. Slowly release the vacuum and remove the special tools.
6. Adjust the fluid level as necessary. Refer to Step 1 .
7. Repeat Step 1 through Step 6 until the fluid no longer drops when vacuum is applied.
8. Start the engine and cycle the steering wheel lock-to-lock three times.

➡Do not hold the steering wheel at the stops.

9. Stop the engine and check for leaks at all connections.
10. Check for any signs of air in the reservoir and check the fluid level. If air is present, repeat the procedure as necessary.

See Figures 134 and 135.

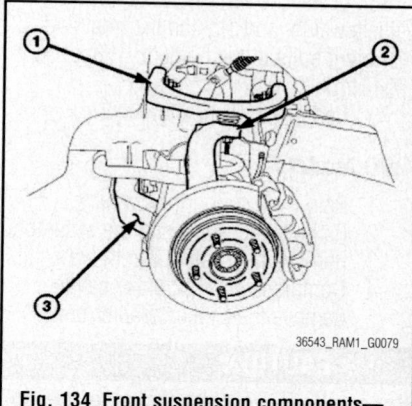

Fig. 134 Front suspension components—2WD models

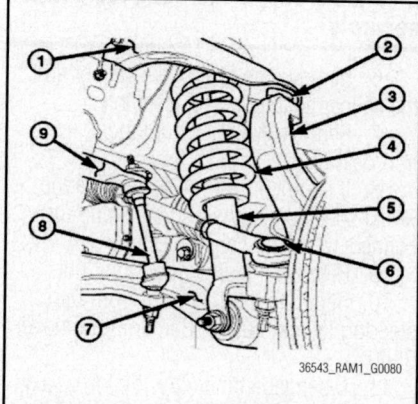

Fig. 135 Front suspension components—4WD

COIL SPRING

REMOVAL & INSTALLATION

2WD Models

See Figure 136.

1. Raise and support vehicle.
2. Remove the front wheel and tire assembly.
3. Support the lower control arm (4) at the outboard side of the lower control arm to support vehicle weight.
4. Remove the shock absorber. Refer to SHOCK ABSORBER.
5. Install Front Spring Compressor DD-1278 (3) up through the lower suspension arm, coil spring and shock hole in the frame. The bell-shaped adapter (3) goes against the lower suspension arm. Install the nut on top of the tool at the shock hole.

6. Tighten the spring compressor nut against bell-shaped adapter finger tight then loosen 1/2 turn.

➡**This will hold the spring in place until the lower suspension arm is separated from the steering knuckle.**

7. Remove the steering knuckle. Refer to Steering knuckle.
8. Remove the stabilizer link. Refer to Stabilizer Bar Link.
9. Remove the lower control arm support.
10. Tighten the spring compressor tool (2) to collapse the coil spring.

➡**It may necessary to loosen the control arm pivot bolt to allow downward swing.**

11. Loosen the tension on the spring compressor tool (2) slowly allowing the lower suspension arm to pivot downward.
12. Remove the spring compressor tool (2).
13. Remove coil spring (1) and isolator pad from the vehicle.

To install:

14. Tape the isolator pad to the top of the coil spring. Position the spring in the lower suspension arm well. Be sure that the coil spring is seated in the well.
15. Install Front Spring Compressor DD-1278 (2) up through the lower suspension arm, coil spring and shock hole in the frame.
16. Tighten the tool nut to compress the coil spring.
17. Install the steering knuckle. Refer to Steering knuckle.
18. Install the retaining nut on the upper ball joint and tighten to 40 ft. lbs. (54 Nm), then add an additional 200° turn.
19. Remove the spring compressor tool.

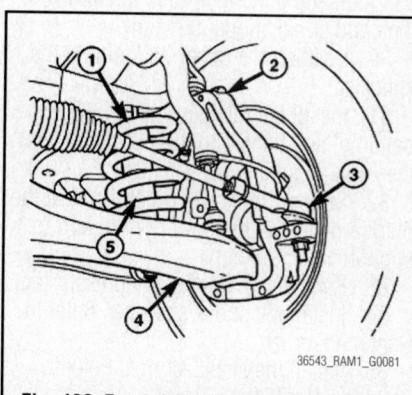

Fig. 136 Front coil spring—2WD models

20. Support the lower control arm at the outboard side of the lower control arm to support vehicle weight.
21. Install the shock absorber.
22. Install the stabilizer link. Refer to Stabilizer Bar Link.
23. Remove the lower control arm support.
24. Install the wheel and tire assembly.
25. Remove the support and lower the vehicle to the floor with vehicle weight. Tighten the front and rear control arm frame pivot bolts if loosened to 155 ft. lbs. (210 Nm).
26. Perform a wheel alignment.

LOWER BALL JOINT

REMOVAL & INSTALLATION

2WD Models

See Figures 137 and 138.

1. Raise and support the vehicle.
2. Remove the knuckle. Refer to Steering Knuckle.

➡**Extreme pressure lubrication must be used on the threaded portions of the tool. This will increase the longevity of the tool and insure proper operation during the removal and installation process.**

3. Press the ball joint from the lower control arm using Ball Joint Press C-4212-F (PRESS) (1), Remover/Installer 8836-6 (DRIVER) (2) and Ball Joint Remover/Installer 8698-2 (RECEIVER) (3).

To install:

➡**Extreme pressure lubrication must be used on the threaded portions of the**

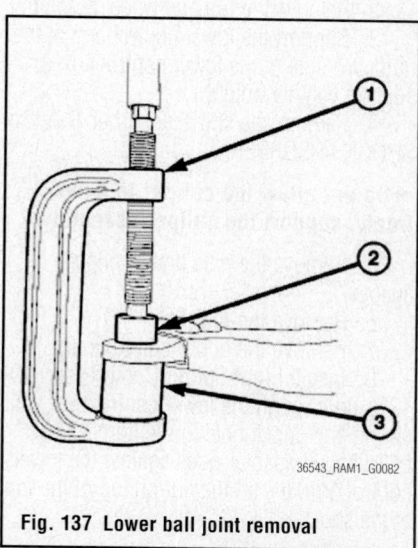

Fig. 137 Lower ball joint removal

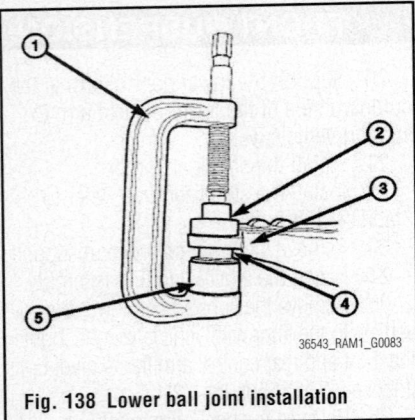

Fig. 138 Lower ball joint installation

tool. This will increase the longevity of the tool and insure proper operation during the removal and installation process .

4. Install the ball joint (3) into the upper control arm (4) and press in using Ball Joint Press C-4212-F (1), Ball Joint Installer 9652 (2) and Installer 8445-1 (5).

5. Install the upper ball joint into the knuckle.

6. Install the upper ball joint retaining nut and tighten to 40 ft. lbs. (54 Nm) then add an additional 90° turn.

7. Install the wheel speed sensor wire to the upper control arm.

8. Install the tire and wheel.

9. Remove the supports and lower the vehicle.

10. Perform a wheel alignment.

LOWER CONTROL ARM

REMOVAL & INSTALLATION

2WD Models

1. Raise and support the vehicle.
2. Remove the tire and wheel assembly.
3. Support the lower control arm at the outboard side of the lower control arm to support vehicle weight.
4. Remove the shock absorber. Refer to SHOCK ABSORBER.

➡ Do not allow the caliper to hang freely, support the caliper assembly.

5. Remove the disc brake caliper adapter.

6. Remove the rotor.

7. Remove the upper ball joint nut.

8. Install Front Spring Compressor DD-1278 up through the lower control arm, coil spring and shock hole in the frame. The bell-shaped adapter goes against the lower control arm. Install the nut on top of the tool at the shock hole.

9. Tighten the spring compressor nut against bell-shaped adapter finger tight then loosen 1/2 turn to hold the spring in place.

10. Separate the upper ball joint from the knuckle using Ball Joint Remover 9360.

11. Remove the knuckle from the vehicle.

12. Remove the lower stabilizer link nut.

13. Remove the lower ball joint nut at the steering knuckle.

14. Separate the ball joint from the knuckle using Ball Joint Remover 8677.

➡ Do not allow the upper control arm to rebound downward, it must be supported.

15. Remove the lower control arm support.

16. Tighten the spring compressor tool to allow clearance for the lower ball joint to be removed out of the knuckle.

17. Loosen the tension on the spring compressor tool slowly allowing the lower control arm to pivot downward.

18. Remove the spring compressor tool.

19. Remove coil spring and isolator pad from the vehicle.

20. Remove the front and rear pivot bolts.

21. Remove the lower control arm.

To install:

22. Install the lower control arm into place on the vehicle.

23. Install the front and rear control arm pivot bolts finger tight.

24. Install the coil spring into the frame pocket. Refer to Coil Spring.

25. Install the Spring Compressor DD-1278 up through the lower suspension arm, coil spring and shock hole in the frame.

26. Tighten the tool nut to compress the coil spring.

27. Install the knuckle to the control arms.

28. Position the lower ball joint into the steering knuckle.

29. Install the retaining nut on the lower ball joint and tighten to 40 ft. lbs. (54 Nm) then add an additional 90° turn.

30. Position the upper ball joint to the knuckle.

31. Install the retaining nut on the upper ball joint and tighten to 40 ft. lbs. (54 Nm) then add an additional 90° turn.

32. Support the lower control arm at the outboard side of the lower control arm to support vehicle weight.

33. Remove the spring compressor tool.

34. Install the shock absorber. Refer to Shock Absorber.

35. Install the stabilizer link. Refer to Stabilizer Bar Link.

36. Remove the lower control arm support.

37. Install the wheel and tire assembly and lower the vehicle.

38. Lower the vehicle to the floor with vehicle weight and Tighten the front and rear pivot bolts to the frame to 150 ft. lbs. (204 Nm).

39. Perform a wheel alignment.

4WD Models

1. Raise and support the vehicle.
2. Remove the wheel and tire assembly.
3. Remove halfshaft nut from the shaft.
4. Compress the disc brake caliper.
5. Remove the caliper adapter bolts.

✳✳ CAUTION

Never allow the disc brake caliper to hang from the brake hose. Damage to the brake hose will result. Provide a suitable support to hang the caliper securely.

6. Remove the disc brake caliper and the caliper adapter as an assembly.

7. Remove the rotor from the hub/bearing.

8. If equipped with ABS, remove the wheel speed sensor wiring clips and disconnect the electrical connector.

9. Remove the upper ball joint nut.

10. Separate the ball joint from the steering knuckle using Ball Joint Remover 9360.

11. Disengage inner C/V joint from axle shaft with two pry bars between the C/V housing and axle housing.

12. Remove the front halfshaft.

13. Remove the shock absorber lower nut/bolt.

14. Remove the stabilizer bar link lower nut.

15. Using a suitable tie strap, support the knuckle. Remove the lower ball joint nut. Separate ball joint from the steering knuckle using Ball Joint Remover 8677.

16. Remove the two control arm pivot bolts and control arm from frame rail brackets.

To install:

17. Position the lower control arm at the frame rail brackets. Install the pivot bolts and nuts. Tighten the nuts finger-tight.

✳✳ CAUTION

The ball joint stud taper must be CLEAN and DRY before installing the knuckle. Clean the stud taper with mineral spirits to remove dirt and grease.

18. Insert the lower ball joint stud into the steering knuckle. Install and tighten the retaining nut to 37.5 ft. lbs. (51 Nm) then add an additional 90° turn.

19. Install shock absorber lower bolt/nut and tighten to 155 ft. lbs. (210 Nm).

20. Install the stabilizer bar link lower nut and tighten to 75 ft. lbs. (102 Nm).

21. Install the front halfshaft to the axle by pushing the inner C/V firmly to engage axle shaft snap ring into the inner C/V housing.

22. Clean hub bearing bore, hub bearing mating surface and halfshaft splines and apply a light coating of grease to the front axle shaft output splines.

23. Install halfshaft into the knuckle.

24. Insert the upper ball joint into the steering knuckle.

25. Install and tighten the upper ball joint retaining nut to 40 ft. lbs. (54 Nm), then add an additional 200° turn.

26. Tighten the lower control arm front pivot nut to 150 ft. lbs. (204 Nm). Tighten rear pivot bolt to 150 ft. lbs. (204 Nm).

27. Install halfshaft hub nut and tighten to 185 ft. lbs. (251 Nm).

28. Install the wheel and tire assembly.

29. Remove the support and lower the vehicle.

30. Perform a wheel alignment.

SHOCK ABSORBERS

REMOVAL & INSTALLATION

2WD Models

1. Raise and support vehicle.

2. Support the lower control arm outboard end.

3. Remove the upper shock absorber nut by using Strut Nut Wrench 9362, retainer and grommet. If necessary, insert 11/32 socket though Wrench onto hex located on end of shock shaft to prevent shaft from turning.

4. Remove the lower bolts and remove the shock absorber.

To install:

➡Upper shock nut must be replaced or use Mopar® Lock 'N Seal or Loctite® 242 on existing nut.

5. Install the lower retainer and grommet on the shock absorber stud. Insert the shock absorber through the frame bracket hole.

6. Install the lower bolts and tighten the bolts to 19 ft. lbs. (26 Nm).

7. Install the upper grommet, retainer and new nut or use Mopar® Lock 'N Seal or Loctite® 242 on existing nut, on the shock

absorber stud. Tighten nut to 40 ft. lbs. (54 Nm). using Strut Nut Wrench 9362.

8. Remove the support from the lower control arm outboard end.

9. Remove the support and lower the vehicle.

STEERING KNUCKLE

REMOVAL & INSTALLATION

See Figure 139.

1. Raise and support the vehicle.

2. Remove the wheel and tire assembly.

3. Remove the ABS wheel speed sensor, disconnecting the electrical harness as necessary to remove knuckle. Refer to Wheel Speed Sensor.

4. Remove the tie rod end nut from the ball stud.

5. Separate the tie rod ball stud (1) from the knuckle with Ball Joint Remover 9360 (2).

6. Remove the halfshaft nut (4X4 only).

7. Remove the upper ball joint nut. Separate the ball joint (4) from the knuckle (6) with Ball Joint Remover 9360 (5)

✳✳ CAUTION

When installing puller 8677 to separate the ball joint, be careful not to damage the ball joint seal.

8. Support the outboard side of the lower control arm to support vehicle weight.

9. Remove the lower ball joint nut. Separate the ball joint from the knuckle with Ball Joint Remover 8677 (2).

10. Remove the steering knuckle (1) from the vehicle.

11. If required, remove the hub/bearing and dust shield from the knuckle (1).

12. Remove the three hub/bearing mounting bolts from the steering knuckle (1).

13. Slide the hub/bearing out of the steering knuckle (1).

14. Remove the brake dust shield.

To install:

✳✳ CAUTION

The ball joint stud tapers must be CLEAN and DRY before installing the knuckle. Clean the stud tapers with mineral spirits to remove dirt and grease.

➡When installing hub/bearing with ABS brakes, position the speed sensor opening towards the front of the vehicle.

15. Install the brake dust shield and hub/bearing to the steering knuckle (1) and tighten the 3 bolts to 120 ft. lbs. (163 Nm).

16. Install the knuckle (1) onto the upper and lower ball joints.

17. Install the upper and lower ball joint nuts. Tighten the upper ball joint nut to 40 ft. lbs. (54 Nm) then add an additional 90° turn, and tighten the lower ball joint nut to 38 ft. lbs. (52 Nm) then add an additional 90° turn.

18. Remove the hydraulic jack from the lower control arm (4).

19. Install the tie rod end and tighten the nut to 45 ft. lbs. (61 Nm).

20. Install the front halfshaft into the hub/bearing (if equipped).

21. Install the halfshaft nut and tighten to 185 ft. lbs. (251 Nm) (if equipped).

22. Install the ABS wheel speed sensor. Refer to Wheel Speed Sensor. Install brake shield, rotor and caliper. Refer to Brakes.

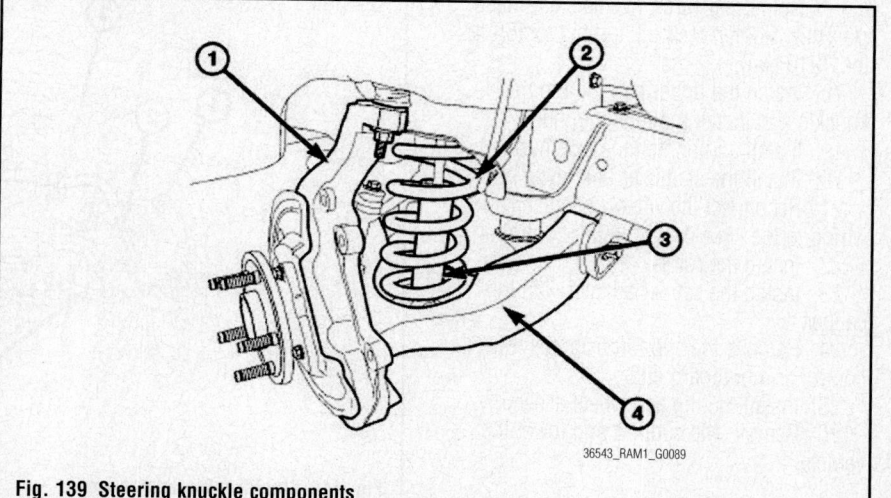

36543_RAM1_G0089

Fig. 139 Steering knuckle components

23. Install the wheel and tire assembly.
24. Remove the support and lower the vehicle.
25. Perform a wheel alignment.

STRUT

REMOVAL & INSTALLATION

4WD Models

1. Raise and support the vehicle.
2. Remove the tire and wheel assembly.
3. Support the lower control arm outboard end.
4. Remove the three upper shock nuts.
5. Remove the lower shock bolt and nut.
6. Remove the caliper adapter with the caliper.
7. Remove the rotor..
8. Disconnect the wheel speed sensor wiring from the knuckle and upper control arm.
9. Remove the upper ball joint retaining nut and separate the upper ball joint from the knuckle using Ball Joint Remover 9360.
10. Remove the stabilizer link lower nut.
11. Remove the axle hub nut.
12. Remove the shock assembly.

To install:

➡**All suspension components should be tighten with the weight of the vehicle on them (curb height).**

13. Install the shock back in place in the vehicle.
14. Install the upper part of the shock into the frame bracket.
15. Install the upper nuts. Tighten to 43.5 ft. lbs. (59 Nm).
16. Install the lower part of the shock into the lower control arm shock bushing.
17. Install and position bolt so head of bolt is facing rearward of vehicle and hand start nut. Tighten the bolt and nut to 155 ft. lbs. (210 Nm).
18. Install the upper ball joint to the knuckle and install the retaining nut.
19. Install and tighten the axle hub nut.
20. Install the stabilizer link lower nut.
21. Reconnect the wheel speed sensor wiring to the knuckle and upper control arm.
22. Install the rotor.
23. Install the caliper adapter with the caliper.
24. Remove the support from the lower control arm outboard end.
25. Install the tire and wheel assembly.
26. Remove the support and lower the vehicle.

STABILIZER BAR

REMOVAL & INSTALLATION

See Figure 140.

➡**To service the stabilizer bar the vehicle should be on a drive on hoist. The vehicle suspension must be at curb height for stabilizer bar installation.**

1. Remove the stabilizer bar link upper nuts and remove the retainers and grommets (4).
2. Remove the stabilizer bar mounting bolts (1) and discard the mounting bolts.
3. Remove the retainers (7) from the frame crossmember and remove the bar (3).
4. If necessary, remove the bushings (2) from the stabilizer bar (3), Do not cut the old bushings off the stabilizer bar use a mixture of soapy water in order to aid in sliding the bushing off.

To install:

➡**To service the stabilizer bar the vehicle must be on a drive on hoist. The vehicle suspension must be at curb height for stabilizer bar installation.**

5. If the bushings were removed, Clean the bar and install the bushings on the stabilizer bar using a mixture of soapy water or equivalent in order to slide the bushing over the bar with ease. Do not cut the new bushing for installation.

➡**Install new mounting bolts Do not reuse old bolts.**

➡**Check the alignment of the bar to ensure there is no interference with the either frame rail or chassis component. Spacing should be equal on both sides.**

6. Position the stabilizer bar (4) on the frame crossmember brackets and install the bracket (3) bolts finger-tight.
7. Install the stabilizer bar (3) to the stabilizer link (5) and install the grommets and retainers.
8. Install the nuts (4) to the stabilizer link (3) and tighten to 20 ft. lbs. (27 Nm).
9. Tighten the brackets to the frame to 43.5 ft. lbs. (59 Nm).

STABILIZER BAR LINK

REMOVAL & INSTALLATION

2WD Models

1. Raise and support the vehicle.
2. Remove the lower nut .
3. Remove the upper nut, retainer and grommets.
4. Remove the stabilizer link from the vehicle .

To install:

5. Install the stabilizer link to the vehicle.
6. Install the lower nut and Tighten to 75 ft. lbs. (102 Nm).
7. Install the retainers, grommets and upper nut and Tighten to 20 ft. lbs. (27 Nm).
8. Remove the support and lower the vehicle.

4WD Models

➡**It may be necessary to remove the other stabilizer link upper nut in order to remove the link being worked on from the vehicle.**

1. Raise and support the vehicle.
2. Remove the lower nut.
3. Remove the upper nut, retainers and grommets.

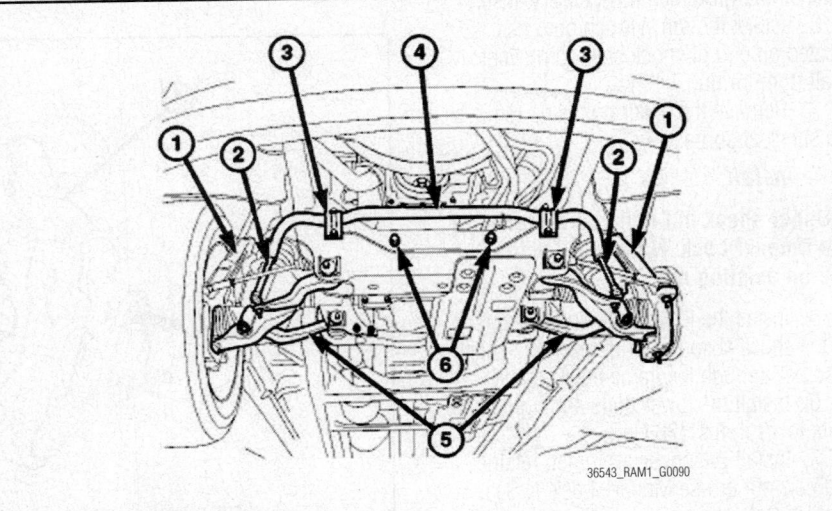

36543_RAM1_G0090

Fig. 140 Stabilizer bar components

4. Remove the stabilizer link from the vehicle.

To install:

5. Install the stabilizer link to the vehicle.

6. Install the lower nut and Tighten to 75 ft. lbs. (102 Nm).

7. Install the retainers, grommets and upper nut and Tighten to 20 ft. lbs. (27 Nm).

8. Remove the support and lower the vehicle.

UPPER BALL JOINT

REMOVAL & INSTALLATION

See Figures 141 through 143.

1. Raise vehicle and support the vehicle.
2. Remove the tire and wheel.
3. Remove the upper ball joint retaining nut.

4. Separate the upper ball joint (4) from the knuckle (6) using Ball Joint Remover 9360 (5).

5. Remove the wheel speed sensor wire from the upper control arm.

6. Move the knuckle out of the way for access to remove the ball joint.

7. Remove the ball joint boot.

➡**It may be necessary to install a block of wood between the control arm and frame bracket to allow clearance for the ball joint press tool.**

➡**Extreme pressure lubrication must be used on the threaded portions of the tool. This will increase the longevity of the tool and insure proper operation during the removal and installation process .**

8. Remove the ball joint (4) from the upper control arm (3) using Ball Joint Press C-4212-F (1), Ball Joint Remover 9770-1 (2) and Ball Joint Remover 9770-2 (5).

To install:

➡**Extreme pressure lubrication must be used on the threaded portions of the tool. This will increase the longevity of the tool and insure proper operation during the removal and installation process.**

9. Install the ball joint (3) into the upper control arm (4) and press in using Ball Joint Press C-4212-F (1), Ball Joint Installer 9652 (2) and Installer 8445-1 (5).

10. Install the upper ball joint into the knuckle.

11. Install the upper ball joint retaining nut and tighten to 40 ft. lbs. (54 Nm) then add an additional 90° turn.

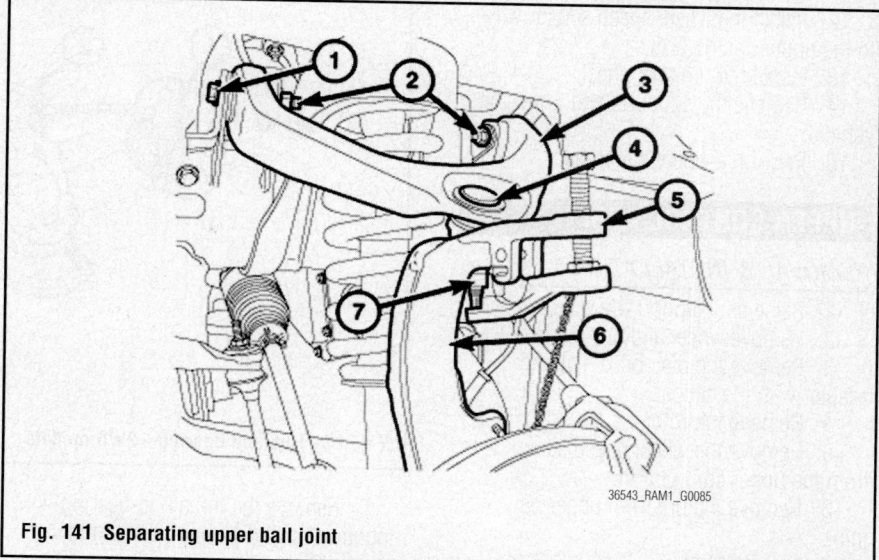

36543_RAM1_G0085

Fig. 141 Separating upper ball joint

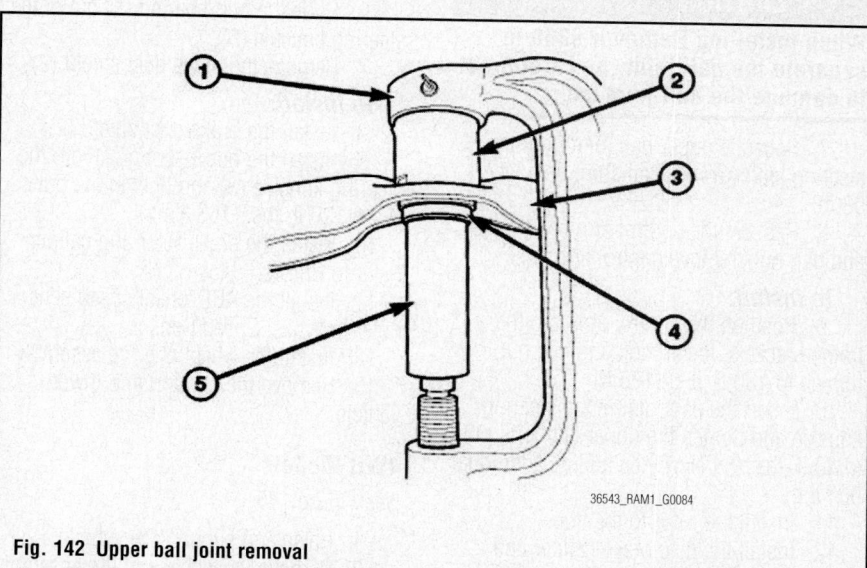

36543_RAM1_G0084

Fig. 142 Upper ball joint removal

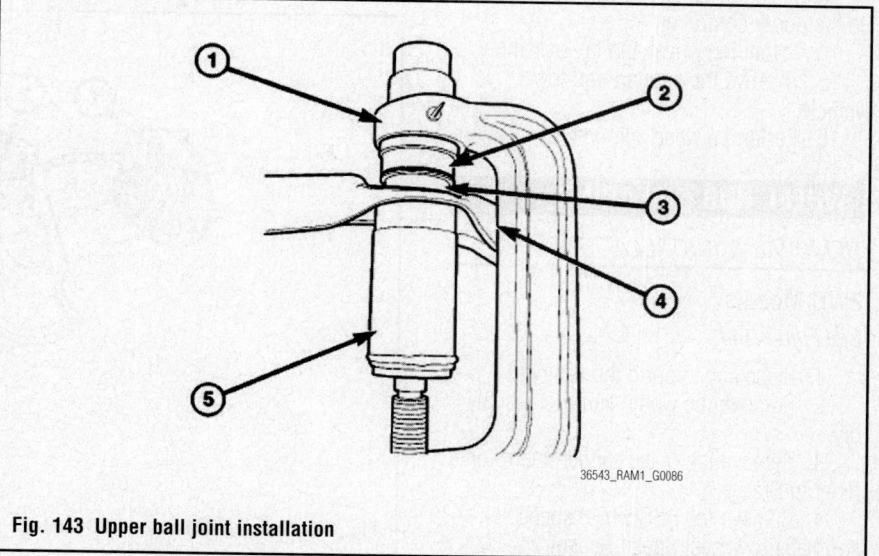

36543_RAM1_G0086

Fig. 143 Upper ball joint installation

12. Install the wheel speed sensor wire to the upper control arm.

13. Install the tire and wheel.

14. Remove the supports and lower the vehicle.

15. Perform a wheel alignment.

UPPER CONTROL ARM

REMOVAL & INSTALLATION

1. Raise and support the vehicle.
2. Remove wheel and tire assembly.
3. Remove the disc brake caliper adapter with the caliper.
4. Remove the rotor.
5. Remove the wheel speed sensor wire from the upper control arm.
6. Remove the nut from upper ball joint.

✳✳ CAUTION

When installing Remover 9360 to separate the ball joint, be careful not to damage the ball joint seal.

7. Separate upper ball joint from the steering knuckle with Ball Joint Remover 9360.

8. Remove the control arm pivot bolts and flag nuts remove control arm.

To install:

9. Position the control arm into the frame brackets. Install bolt and flag nut, tighten to 130 ft. lbs. (176 Nm).

10. Insert the ball joint in the steering knuckle and tighten the upper ball joint nut to 40 ft. lbs. (54 Nm) then add an additional 90° turn.

11. Install the rotor to the hub.

12. Install the disc brake caliper and adapter to the knuckle.

13. Install the wheel speed sensor wire to the upper control arm.

14. Install the wheel and tire assembly.

15. Remove the support and lower vehicle.

16. Perform a wheel alignment.

WHEEL HUB & BEARING

REMOVAL & INSTALLATION

2WD Models

See Figure 144.

1. Raise and support the vehicle.
2. Remove the wheel and tire assembly.
3. Remove the brake caliper and rotor. Refer to Brakes.
4. Remove the ABS wheel speed sensor. Refer to Wheel Speed Sensor.

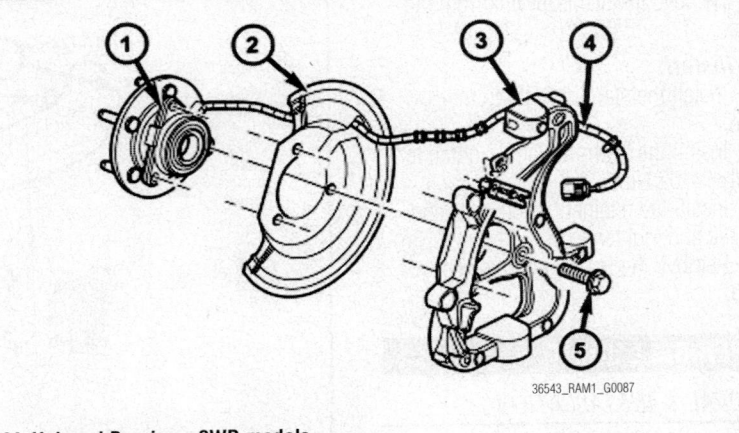

Fig. 144 Hub and Bearing—2WD models

5. Remove the three hub/bearing mounting bolts (5) from the steering knuckle (3).

6. Slide the hub/bearing (1) out of the steering knuckle (3).

7. Remove the brake dust shield (2).

To install:

8. Install the brake dust shield (2).

9. Install the hub/bearing (1) into the steering knuckle (3) and tighten the bolts (5) to 120 ft. lbs. (163 Nm).

10. Install the brake rotor and caliper. Refer to Brakes.

11. Install the ABS wheel speed sensor. Refer to Wheel Speed Sensor.

12. Install the wheel and tire assembly.

13. Remove the support and lower vehicle.

4WD Models

See Figure 145.

1. Raise and support the vehicle.
2. Remove the wheel and tire assembly.

3. Remove the brake caliper and rotor. Refer to Brakes.

4. Remove the ABS wheel speed sensor. Refer to Wheel Speed Sensor.

5. Remove the halfshaft nut.

➡**Do not strike the knuckle with a hammer to remove the tie rod end or the ball joint. Damage to the steering knuckle will occur.**

6. Remove the tie rod end nut and separate the tie rod from the knuckle using Ball Joint Remover 9360.

7. Remove the upper ball joint nut and separate the upper ball joint from the knuckle using Ball Joint Remover 9360.

8. Pull down on the steering knuckle to separate the halfshaft (2) from the hub/bearing.

9. Remove the three hub/bearing mounting bolts (1) from the steering knuckle.

10. Slide the hub/bearing out of the steering knuckle.

11. Remove the brake dust shield.

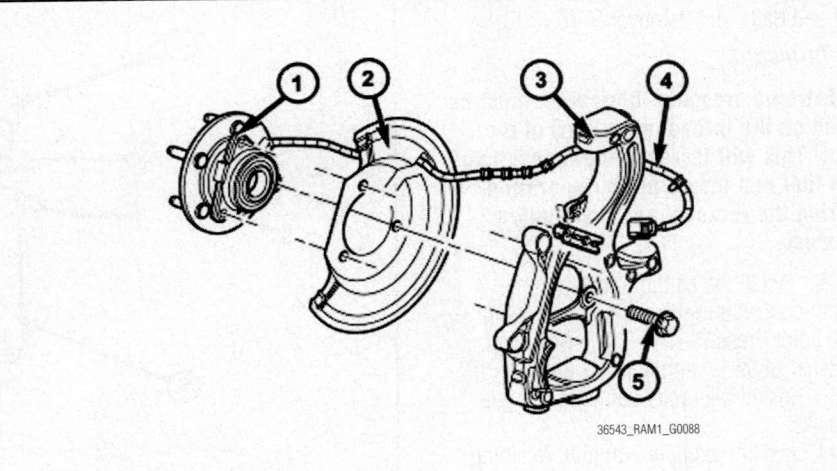

Fig. 145 Hub and Bearing—4WD models

To install:

12. Install the brake dust shield (2).

13. Install the hub/bearing (1) into the steering knuckle (3) and tighten the bolts to 120 ft. lbs. (163 Nm).

14. Install the brake rotor and caliper. Refer to Brakes.

15. Install the ABS wheel speed sensor. Refer to Wheel Speed Sensor.

16. Install the upper ball joint nut to the steering knuckle and tighten to 40 ft. lbs. (54 Nm), then add an additional 90° turn).

17. Install the tie rod end nut to the steering knuckle and tighten to 45 ft. lbs. (61 Nm) then add an additional 90°.

18. Install the halfshaft nut and tighten to 185 ft. lbs. (251 Nm).

19. Install the wheel and tire assembly.

20. Remove the support and lower vehicle.

SUSPENSION

See Figure 146.

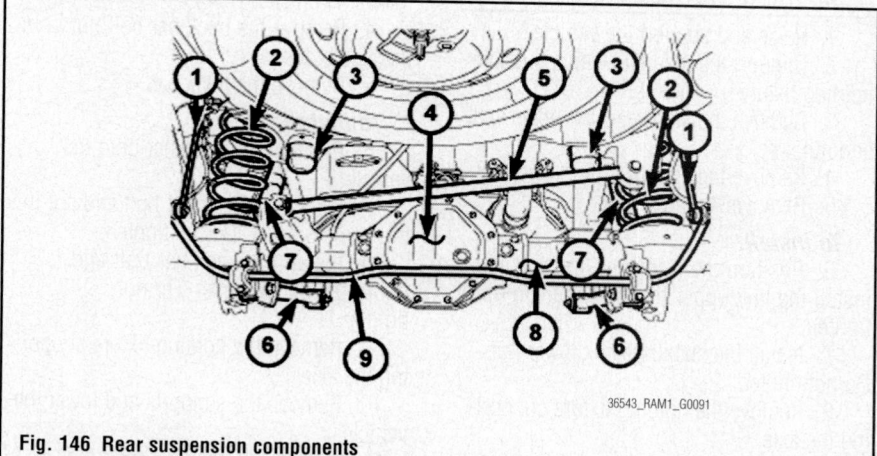

Fig. 146 Rear suspension components

36543_RAM1_G0091

COIL SPRING

REMOVAL & INSTALLATION

1. Raise and support the vehicle.
2. Support the axle with a suitable holding fixture.
3. Remove the shock lower bolt) and nut.
4. Lower the axle carefully and avoid putting stress on the flexible brake line. Lower the axle support and tilt the axel to remove the spring and isolator from the vehicle.

To install:

➡**All torques should be made with the full vehicle weight on the ground being supported by the tires.**

5. Position spring and isolator on the axle and align into the spring upper pocket.
6. Carefully raise the rear axle into place.
7. Install the shock lower bolt and nut, and do not tighten.
8. Remove the holding fixture for the rear axle.
9. Remove the support and lower vehicle.
10. Tighten shock lower bolt and nut to 100 ft. lbs. (136 Nm).

CONTROL ARMS/LINKS

REMOVAL & INSTALLATION

Lower Control Arm

1. Raise and support the vehicle.
2. Support the rear axle with a suitable holding fixture.
3. Remove the parking brake cable guide bolt (Left side only).
4. Remove the lower control arm bolt and nut at the axle.
5. Remove the lower control arm bolt and nut at the frame.
6. Remove the lower control arm from the vehicle.

To install:

➡**The small bushing attaches to the frame and the large bushing to the axle.**

7. Install the lower control arm to the vehicle.
8. Install the lower control arm bolt and nut at the axle. Do not tighten.
9. Install the lower control arm bolt and nut at the frame. Do not tighten.
10. Position the parking brake cable guide, install the guide bolt and tighten to 15 ft. lbs. (20 Nm) (Left side only).
11. Remove the holding fixture supporting the axle.

REAR SUSPENSION

12. Remove the support and lower the vehicle.
13. Tighten the lower control arm bolts to 225 ft. lbs. (305 Nm).

Upper Control Arm

1. Raise and support the vehicle.
2. Support the rear axle with a suitable holding fixture.
3. Remove the upper control arm bolt and nut at the axle.
4. Remove the upper control arm front bolt and nut at the frame.
5. Remove the upper control arm from the vehicle.

To install:

➡**The small bushing attaches to the axel and the large bushing to the frame.**

6. Position the upper control arm to the vehicle.
7. Install the upper control arm bolt and nut at the frame. Do not tighten.
8. Install the upper control arm bolt and nut at the axle. Do not tighten.
9. Remove the holding fixture supporting the axle.
10. Remove the support and lower the vehicle.
11. Tighten the lower control arm nuts to 225 ft. lbs. (305 Nm).

SHOCK ABSORBER

REMOVAL & INSTALLATION

2WD Models

1. Raise and support the vehicle.
2. Support the rear axle with a suitable holding fixture.
3. Remove the shock upper bolt and nut.
4. Remove the shock lower bolt and nut.
5. Remove the shock absorber from the vehicle.

To install:

➡**All torques should be made with the full vehicle weight on the ground being supported by the tires.**

6. Position the shock absorber in the brackets.

7. Install the bolts through the brackets and the shock.

8. Install the nuts on the bolts and do not tighten.

9. Remove the holding fixture supporting the axle.

10. Remove the support and lower the vehicle.

11. Tighten shock bolts and nuts to 100 ft. lbs. (135 Nm).

STABILIZER BAR

REMOVAL & INSTALLATION

1. Raise and support vehicle.

2. Remove both stabilizer bar link lower mounting nuts.

3. Remove stabilizer bar retainer bolts and retainers.

4. Remove stabilizer bar.

5. Remove and transfer the bushings if necessary.

To install:

6. Install stabilizer bar bushings.

7. Install the stabilizer bar and center it with equal spacing on both sides.

8. Install stabilizer bar retainers and bolts. Do not tighten.

9. Install the stabilizer bar links on the stabilizer bar and install link lower mounting nuts. Do not tighten.

10. Remove the support and lower the vehicle.

11. Tighten the stabilizer bar retainer bolts to 37 ft. lbs. (50 Nm).

12. Tighten stabilizer link lower nuts to 79 ft. lbs. (107 Nm).

STABILIZER BAR LINK

REMOVAL & INSTALLATION

1. Raise and support the vehicle.

2. Support the rear axle with a suitable holding fixture.

3. Remove the stabilizer link upper bolt and nut.

4. Remove the stabilizer link lower nut.

5. Remove stabilizer link.

To install:

6. Position the stabilizer link and install the link upper bolt and nut. Do not tighten.

7. Install the stabilizer link lower nut. Do not tighten.

8. Remove the holding fixture supporting the axle.

9. Remove the support and lower the vehicle.

10. Tighten stabilizer link upper nuts to 55 ft. lbs. (75 Nm).

11. Tighten stabilizer link lower nuts to 79 ft. lbs. (107 Nm).

TRACK BAR

REMOVAL & INSTALLATION

1. Raise and support the vehicle.

2. Support the rear axle with a suitable holding fixture.

3. Remove the track bar bolt/nut from the frame bracket.

4. Remove the track bar bolt/nut from the axle bracket.

5. Remove the track bar.

To install:

6. Position the track bar onto the vehicle.

7. Install the track bar bolt and nut in the frame bracket. Do not tighten.

8. Install the track bar bolt and nut in the axle bracket. Do not tighten.

9. Remove the holding fixture supporting the axle.

10. Remove the supports and lower the vehicle.

11. Tighten the track bar mounting bolts/nuts to 129 ft. lbs. (175 Nm).

DODGE

16

Ram 1500 (DH Series) • 2500 • 3500

SPECIFICATIONS AND MAINTENANCE CHARTS

ENGINE AND VEHICLE IDENTIFICATION

Engine							Model Year	
Code ①	Liters (cc)	Cu. In.	Cyl.	Fuel Sys.	Engine Type	Eng. Mfg.	Code ②	Year
T	5.7 (5653)	345	8	SMPI	OHV	Chrysler	9	2009
7	5.9 (5882)	359	6	DSL-24V Turbo	OHV	Cummins		
L	6.7 (6702)	409	6	DSL-24V Turbo	OHV	Cummins		

OHV: Overhead Valve

DSL-24V: Diesel with 24-valve cylinder head

SMFI: Sequential Multi-port Fuel Injection

① 8th position of VIN

② 10th position of VIN

36543_RAM2_C0001

GENERAL ENGINE SPECIFICATIONS

Year	Model	Engine Displacement Liters	Engine Series (ID/VIN)	Net Horsepower @ rpm	Net Torque @ rpm (ft. lbs.)	Bore x Stroke (in.)	Com-pression Ratio	Oil Pressure @ rpm
2009	Ram Truck 1500	5.7	T	345@5400	375@4200	3.92x3.58	10.5:1	25-110@3000
	Ram Truck 2500	5.7	T	345@5400	375@4200	3.92x3.58	10.5:1	25-110@3000
		5.9	7	325@2900	610 @ 1400	4.02x4.72	17.2:1	30@2500
		6.7	L	350@3013	650@1400	4.21x4.88	17.2:1	30@2500
	Ram Truck 3500	5.7	T	345@5400	375@4200	3.92x3.58	10.5:1	25-110@3000
		5.9	7	325@2900	610 @ 1400	4.02x4.72	17.2:1	30@2500
		6.7	L	350@3013	650@1400	4.21x4.88	17.2:1	30@2500

36543_RAM2_C0002

GASOLINE ENGINE TUNE-UP SPECIFICATIONS

Year	Engine Displacement Liters	Engine ID/VIN	Spark Plug Gap (in.)	Ignition Timing (deg.)	Fuel Pump (psi)	Idle Speed (rpm)	Valve Clearance	
							Intake	Exhaust
2009	5.7	T	0.04	①	56-60	②	HYD	HYD

NOTE: The Vehicle Emission Control Information (VECI) label often reflects specification changes made during production.

The label figures must be used if they differ from those in this chart.

HYD: Hydraulic

① Ignition timing is controlled by the PCM and is not adjustable.

② Idle speed is controlled by the PCM and is not adjustable

36543_RAM2_C0003

DIESEL ENGINE TUNE-UP SPECIFICATIONS

Year	Engine Displacement Liters	Engine ID/VIN	Valve Clearance		Intake Valve Opens (deg.)	Injection Pump Setting (deg.)	Injection Nozzle Pressure (psi)		Idle Speed (rpm)	Cranking Compression Pressure (psi)
			Intake (in.)	Exhaust (in.)			New	Used		
2009	5.9	7	0.006-0.015	0.021-0.034	NA	①	4351-23206	NA	①	350 ②
	6.7	L	0.006-0.015	0.021-0.034	NA	①	2900-26107	NA	①	350 ②

NOTE: The Vehicle Emission Control Information (VECI) label often reflects specification changes made during production.

The label figures must be used if they differ from those in this chart

NA: Not Available

① Computer controlled

② Minimum reading

36543_RAM2_C0004

CAPACITIES

Year	Model	Engine Displacement Liters	Engine ID/VIN	Engine Oil with Filter (qts.)	Transmission (pts.)		Transfer Case (pts.)	Drive Axle		Fuel Tank (gal.)	Cooling System (qts.)
					Manual	Auto. ①		Front (pts.)	Rear (pts.)		
2009	Ram Truck 1500	5.7	T	7.0	②	③	④	⑤	⑥	⑦	18.7
	Ram Truck 2500	5.7	T	7.0	②	③	④	⑤	⑥	⑦	18.7
		5.9	7	12.0	②	③	④	⑤	⑥	⑦	28.2
		6.7	L	12.0	②	③	④	⑤	⑥	⑦	22.6
	Ram Truck 3500	5.7	T	7.0	②	③	④	⑤	⑥	⑦	18.7
		5.9	7	12.0	②	③	④	⑤	⑥	⑦	28.2
		6.7	L	12.0	②	③	④	⑤	⑥	⑦	22.6

NOTE: All capacities are approximate. Add fluid gradually and check to be sure a proper fluid level is obtained.

① For fluid drain and filter replacement only.

② Getrag 238: 4.6 pts.
G56: 12.0 pts. Diesel Engines

③ 48RE: 8.0 pts.
45RFE/545RFE:
4x2: 11.0 pts.
4x4: 13.0 pts.
68RFE:
4x2: 11.0 pts.
4x4: 13.0 pts.
AS68RC: 14.4 pts

④ NV241 GEN II: 3.4 pts.
NV243: 3.4 pts.
NV244 GENII: 3.4 pts.
NV 246: 4.0 pts.
NV 271: 4.0 pts.
NV 273: 4.0 pts.

⑤ C200F Open: 3.5 pts.
C200FE Anti-spin: 3.5 pts. W/ 4 oz. friction modifier
C205F Open: 3.5 pts.
Dana 186 FBI Open: 2.1 pts.
Dana 186 FIA Open: 2.6 pts.
Dana 216 FBI Anti-spin: 2.7 pts. W/ 4 oz. friction modifier

⑥ 8.25 Open: 4.4 pts.
8.25 Anti-spin: 4.5 pts. W/ 4 oz. friction modifier
9.25 Open: 4.6 pts.
9.25 Anti-spin: 4.5 pts. W/ 4 oz. friction modifier
C213R Open: 4.3 pts.
C213RE Anti-spin: 4.7 pts. W/ 4 oz. friction modifier
Dana 226 RBI Open: 4.75 pts.
Dana 226 RBI Anti-spin: 4.75 pts. W/ 4 oz. friction modifier
Dana 302 RBI Open: 13.9 pts.
Dana 302 RBI Anti-spin: 13.9 pts.

⑦ 1500 Mega cab: 26.0
2500/3500 Short bed: 34.0
Long bed: 35.0

36543_RAM2_C0005

FLUID SPECIFICATIONS

Year	Model	Engine Displacement Liters	Engine ID/VIN	Engine Oil	Manual Trans. ①	Auto. Trans. ②	Drive Axle ③	Power Steering Fluid	Brake Master Cylinder	Engine Coolant
2009	Ram	5.7	T	5W-20	ATF+4	ATF+4	75W-90 ④	ATF+4	DOT 3	Mopar® (HOAT)
	Truck	5.9	7	15W-40 ⑤	ATF+4	ATF+4	75W-90 ④	ATF+4	DOT 3	Mopar® (HOAT)
	1500-3500	6.7	L	15W-40 ⑤	ATF+4	ATF+4	75W-90 ④	ATF+4	DOT 3	Mopar® (HOAT)

NOTE: Check the engines oil cap or owners manual for specific engine oil grade variations.

DOT: Department Of Transpotation

① G-56 and G238 transmissions

② NVG 246 automatic transfer case only: Mopar® NVG 246 Transmission fluid

③ Ram 1500 Models rear axle: Synthetic 75W-140 plus 4oz limited slip additive

④ Synthetic is recommended

⑤ Oils of the 5W-40 grade are preferred when temperatures consistently fall below -15 degrees

36543_RAM2_C0006

VALVE SPECIFICATIONS

Year	Engine Displacement Liters	Engine ID/VIN	Seat Angle (deg.)	Face Angle (deg.)	Spring Test Pressure (lbs. @ in.)	Spring Installed Height (in.)	Stem-to-Guide Clearance (in.) Intake	Stem-to-Guide Clearance (in.) Exhaust	Stem Diameter (in.) Intake	Stem Diameter (in.) Exhaust
2009	5.7	T	44.5-45	45-45.5	242 @ 1.283	1.810	0.0008-0.0025	0.0009-0.0025	0.3120-0.3130	0.3120-0.3130
	5.9	7	①	NA	NA	NA	NA	NA	0.274-0.276	0.274-0.276
	6.7	L	①	NA	NA	NA	0.002	0.002	0.274-0.276	0.274-0.276

① Intake: 30 degrees
   Exhaust: 45 degrees

36543_RAM2_C0008

CAMSHAFT AND BEARING SPECIFICATIONS CHART

All measurements are given in inches.

Year	Engine Displ. Liters	Engine ID/VIN	Journal Dia.	Brg. Oil Clearance	Shaft End-play	Runout	Journal Bore	Lobe Height Intake	Lobe Height Exhaust
2009	5.7	T	①	②	0.0031-0.0114	NA	NA	NA	NA
	5.9	7	2.0904-2.1278	NA	0.005-0.02	NA	2.1293-2.1318	NA	NA
	6.7	L	2.0904-2.1278	NA	0.005-0.02	NA	2.1293-2.1318	NA	NA

NA: Not Available

① No.1: 2.29
No.2: 2.28
No.3: 2.26
No.4: 2.24
No.5: 1.72

② No.1, 3, 5: (0.0015-.003)
No.2, 4: (0.0019-.0035)

36543_RAM2_C0007

CRANKSHAFT AND CONNECTING ROD SPECIFICATIONS

All measurements are given in inches.

Year	Engine Displacement Liters	Engine ID/VIN	Crankshaft Main Brg. Journal Dia.	Crankshaft Main Brg. Oil Clearance	Crankshaft Shaft End-play	Thrust on No.	Connecting Rod Journal Diameter	Connecting Rod Oil Clearance	Connecting Rod Side Clearance
2009	5.7	T	2.5585-2.5595	0.0007-0.0023	0.0020-0.0110	3	2.1250-2.1260	0.0007-0.0023	0.0030-0.0137
	5.9	7	3.2662-3.2682	0.0020-0.0050	0.0040-0.0017	6	2.7150-2.7170	0.0020-0.0050	0.0040-0.0130
	6.7	L	3.2662-3.2682	0.0020-0.0050	0.0040-0.0017	6	2.7150-2.7170	0.0020-0.0050	0.0040-0.0130

36543_RAM2_C0009

PISTON AND RING SPECIFICATIONS

All measurements are given in inches.

Year	Engine Displacement Liters	Engine ID/VIN	Piston Clearance	Ring Gap Top Compression	Ring Gap Bottom Compression	Ring Gap Oil Control	Ring Side Clearance Top Compression	Ring Side Clearance Bottom Compression	Ring Side Clearance Oil Control
2009	5.7	T	0.012-0.0230	0.015-0.0210	0.009-0.0200	0.0059-0.0259	0.001-0.0035	0.001-0.0031	0.002-0.008
	5.9	7	NA	0.0100-0.0230	0.0330-0.0540	0.0100-0.0300	NA	0.0016-0.0043	0.0016-0.0033
	6.7	L	NA	0.0120-0.0180	0.0320-0.0470	0.0100-0.0230	NA	0.0016-0.0043	0.0016-0.0033

NA - Not available

36543_RAM2_C0010

TORQUE SPECIFICATIONS
All readings in ft. lbs.

Year	Engine Displacement Liters	Engine ID/VIN	Cylinder Head Bolts	Main Bearing Bolts	Rod Bearing Bolts	Crankshaft Damper Bolts	Flywheel Bolts	Manifold Intake	Manifold Exhaust	Spark Plugs	Oil Pan Drain Plug
2009	5.7	T	①	②	③	130	70	④	18	20	25
	5.9	7	⑤	⑥	⑦	⑧	101	18	32	—	37
	6.7	L	⑤	⑨	⑦	⑧	101	18	32	—	37

① Step 1: 1-10 to 25 ft. lbs.

  Step 2: 11-15 to 15 ft. lbs.

  Step 3: 1-10 to 40 ft. lbs.

  Step 4: 11-15 to 15 ft. lbs.

  Step 5: 1-10 plus 90 degrees

  Step 6: 1-10 plus 90 degrees

  Step 7: 11-15 to 25 ft. lbs.

② Step 1: Main bolts to 10 ft. lbs.

  Step 2: Main bolts to 20 ft. lbs.

  Step 3: Main bolts plus 90 degrees

  Step 4: Crossbolts to 21 ft. lbs.

  Step 5: Repeat step 4.

③ 20 ft. lbs. plus 90 degrees

④ 105 inch lbs.

⑤ Step 1: 52 ft. lbs.

  Step 2: Back off 360 degrees

  Step 3: 77 ft. lbs.

  Step 4: Recheck 77 ft. lbs.

  Step 5: Plus 90 degrees

⑥ Step 1: 37 ft. lbs.

  Step 2: 59 ft. lbs.

  Step 3: Plus 90 degrees

⑦ Step 1: 22 ft. lbs.

  Step 2: 44 ft. lbs.

  Step 3: Plus 60 degrees

⑧ Step 1: 30 ft. lbs.

  Step 2: Plus 60 degrees

⑨ Note: Used bolt procedure as follows:

  Step 1: 37 ft. lbs.

  Step 2: 59 ft. lbs.

  Step 3: Plus 90 degrees

Note: New bolt Procedure as follows:

  Step 1: 89 ft. lbs.

  Step 2: Loosen completely

  Step 3: 44 ft. lbs.

  Step 4: 63 ft. lbs.

  Step 5: Plus 120 degrees

36543_RAM2_C0011

WHEEL ALIGNMENT

Year	Model	GVW	Wheel Base (in.)	Caster Range (+/-Deg.)	Caster Preferred Setting (Deg.)	Camber Range (+/-Deg.)	Camber Preferred Setting (Deg.)	Toe-in (in.)
2009	1500 2WD	—	—	①	①	- 0.40 to 0.60	0.10	0.10+/-0.10
	1500 4WD	—	—	②	②	- 0.40 to 0.60	0.10	0.10+/-0.10
	2500 & 3500 2WD	—	—	③	③	-0.50 to +0.050	0.00	0.10+/-0.10
	2500 & 3500 4WD	—	—	④	④	-0.25 to +0.75	0.25	0.10+/-0.10

① Left side range 3.00 to 4.00 Preferred 3.50

  Right side range 3.25 to 4.25 Preferred 3.75

② Left side range 3.00 to 4.00 Preferred 3.50

  Right side range 3.40 to 4.40 Preferred 3.90

① Right side range: +3.05 to 4.05 Preferred +4.00

  Left side range: +3.65 to 4.65 Preferred +4.15

④ Right side range: +4.00 to 5.00 Preferred +4.50

  Left side range: +4.00 to 5.00 Preferred +4.50

36543_RAM2_C0014

TIRE, WHEEL AND BALL JOINT SPECIFICATIONS

| Year | Model | OEM Tires | | Tire Pressures (psi) | | Wheel Size | Lug Nut (ft. lbs.) |
		Standard	Optional	Front	Rear		
2009	1500 Mega 2WD	P265/70R17	None	①	①	8	②
	2500 ST Regular 2WD	P245/70R17	P265/70R17	①	①	7.5	②
	2500 ST Quad 2WD	P245/70R17	P265/70R17	①	①	7.5	②
	2500 ST Regular 4WD	P245/70R17	P265/70R17	①	①	7.5	②
	2500 ST Quad 4WD	P245/70R17	P265/70R17	①	①	7.5	②
	2500 SLT Regular 2WD	P265/70R17	None	①	①	8	②
	2500 SLT Quad 2WD	P265/70R17	None	①	①	8	②
	2500 SLT Mega 2WD	P265/70R17	None	①	①	8	②
	2500 SLT Regular 4WD	P245/70R17	P265/70R17	①	①	8	②
	2500 SLT Quad 4WD	P245/70R17	P265/70R17	①	①	8	②
	2500 SLT Mega 4WD	P265/70R17	None	①	①	8	②
	2500 Laramie Quad 2WD	P265/70R17	None	①	①	8	②
	2500 Laramie Mega 2WD	P265/70R17	None	①	①	8	②
	2500 Laramie Quad 4WD	P245/70R17	P265/70R17	①	①	8	②
	2500 Laramie Mega 4WD	P265/70R17	None	①	①	8	②
	2500 Power Wagon 4WD	P285/70R17	None	①	①	8	②
	3500 ST Regular 2WD	LT235/80R17	None	①	①	6	②
	3500 ST Quad Short 2WD	LT265/70R17	None	①	①	7.5	②
	3500 ST Quad Long 2WD	LT235/80R17	LT265/70R17	①	①	6 or 7.5	②
	3500 ST Regular 4WD	LT235/80R17	None	①	①	6	②
	3500 ST Quad 4WD	LT265/70R17	None	①	①	7.5	②
	3500 ST Quad Long 4WD	LT235/80R17	LT265/70R17	①	①	6 or 8	②
	3500 SLT Regular 2WD	LT235/80R17	None	①	①	6	②
	3500 SLT Quad Short 2WD	LT265/70R17	None	①	①	7.5	②
	3500 SLT Quad Long 2WD	LT235/80R17	LT265/70R17	①	①	6 or 7.5	②
	3500 SLT Mega 2WD	LT235/80R17	LT265/70R17	①	①	6 or 8	②
	3500 SLT Regular 4WD	LT235/80R17	None	①	①	6	②
	3500 SLT Quad Short 4WD	LT265/70R17	None	①	①	8	②
	3500 SLT Quad Long 4WD	LT235/80R17	LT265/70R17	①	①	6 or 8	②
	3500 SLT Mega 4WD	LT235/80R17	LT265/70R17	①	①	6 or 8	②
	3500 Laramie Quad Short 2WD	LT265/70R17	None	①	①	8	②
	3500 Laramie Quad Long 2WD	LT235/80R17	LT265/70R17	①	①	6 or 8	②
	3500 Laramie Mega 2WD	LT235/80R17	LT265/70R17	①	①	6 or 8	②
	3500 Laramie Quad Short 4WD	LT265/70R17	None	①	①	8	②
	3500 Laramie Quad Long 4WD	LT235/80R17	LT265/70R17	①	①	6 or 8	②
	3500 Laramie Mega 4WD	LT235/80R17	LT265/70R17	①	①	6 or 8	②

OEM: Original Equipment Manufacturer

PSI: Pounds Per Square Inch

STD: Standard

OPT: Optional

① See sticker on drivers door

② Single rear wheel: 140 Dual rear wheel: 145

BRAKE SPECIFICATIONS
All measurements in inches unless noted

| Year | Model | | Brake Disc | | | Brake Drum | | | Minimum Lining Thickness | | Brake Caliper | |
			Original Thickness	Minimum Thickness	Maximum Run-out	Original Inside Diameter	Max. Wear Limit	Max. Machine Diameter	Front	Rear	Bracket Bolts (ft. lbs.)	Mounting Bolts (ft. lbs.)
2009	Ram Pick-up HD	F	NA	1.039	0.002	—	—	—	①	①	130	24
	1500 Mega Cab	R	NA	.803	0.002	—	—	—	①	①	50	22
	Ram Pick-up HD	F	1.535	1.47	0.009	—	—	—	①	①	275	24
	2500/3500 SRW	R	1.33	1.27	0.009	—	—	—	①	①	②	22
	Ram Pick-up HD	F	1.535	1.47	0.005	—	—	—	①	①	275	24
	2500/3500 DRW	R	1.33	1.27	0.005	—	—	—	①	①	②	22

NA: Not Available

SRW: Single rear wheel, DRW: Dual rear wheel

① Minimum: 0.04 in.

② Upper: 163

   Lower: 190

SCHEDULED MAINTENANCE INTERVALS
Ram 1500 (DH Style), 2500, 3500 — Gasoline Engines

TO BE SERVICED	TYPE OF SERVICE	VEHICLE MILEAGE INTERVAL (x1000)														
		6	12	18	24	30	36	42	48	54	60	66	72	78	84	90
Engine oil & filter*	R	✓	✓	✓	✓	✓	✓	✓	✓	✓	✓	✓	✓	✓	✓	✓
Front driveshaft fitting (4WD)	L	✓	✓	✓	✓	✓	✓	✓	✓	✓	✓	✓	✓	✓	✓	✓
Tire pressure, battery & terminals ①	I															
CV joints	I		✓		✓		✓		✓		✓		✓		✓	
Drive axle fluid	I			✓			✓			✓			✓			✓
Engine coolant & hoses ①	I															
Lights & other electrical items ①	I															
Brake, P/S & A/T fluid levels	I	✓	✓	✓	✓	✓	✓	✓	✓	✓	✓	✓	✓	✓		✓
Front suspension components	I				✓				✓				✓			
Brake hoses	I	✓	✓	✓	✓	✓	✓	✓	✓	✓	✓	✓	✓	✓		✓
Exhaust system	I		✓		✓		✓		✓		✓		✓		✓	
Brake linings	I		✓		✓		✓		✓		✓		✓		✓	
Air cleaner element	R					✓					✓					✓
Spark plugs	R					✓					✓					✓
Transfer case fluid	I					✓					✓					✓
Tires	Rotate	✓	✓	✓	✓	✓	✓	✓	✓	✓	✓	✓	✓	✓	✓	✓
Engine coolant	R										✓					

R: Replace   S/I: Service or Inspect   Adj: Adjust   L: Lubricate

① Once a month, inspect tires and check pressure. Check battery and tighten terminals if required. Check fluid levels.

FREQUENT OPERATION MAINTENANCE (SEVERE SERVICE)

If a vehicle is operated under any of the following conditions it is considered severe service:

- Extremely dusty areas.
- 50% or more of the vehicle operation is in 32°C (90°F) or higher temperatures, or constant operation in temperatures below 0°C (32°F).
- Prolonged idling (vehicle operation in stop and go traffic.
- Frequent short running periods (engine does not warm to normal operating temperatures).
- Police, taxi, delivery usage or trailer towing usage.

Air filter: change every 12,000 miles.

Front and rear axle fluid: change every 18,000 miles.

Automatic transmission fluid & filter: change every 60,000 miles.

*Oil Change Indicator System

On Electronic Vehicle Information Center (EVIC) equipped vehicles, "Oil Change Require" is displayed in the EVIC and a single chime sounds indicating that an oil change is necessary.

On non-EVIC equipped vehicles, "Change Oil" flashes in the instrument cluster and a single chime sounds indicating that an oil change is necessary.

Illumination of the oil change message is based on the operating conditions of the vehicle. When the message is illuminated, the vehicle must be serviced within 500 miles.

The oil change indicator will not monitor the time since the last oil change. Change the oil if it has been more than 6 months since the last oil change, even if the oil change indicator message is not illuminated.

Under no circumstances should oil change intervals exceed 6,000 miles or 6 months, whichever comes first.

To reset the oil change indicator, refer to the following procedure:

1. Turn the ignition switch to the ON position. Do not start the engine.
2. Fully press the accelerator pedal 3 times within 10 seconds.
3. Turn the ignition switch to the LOCK position.

If the indicator message illuminates when the vehicle is started, repeat the procedure.

36543_RAM2_C0015

SCHEDULED MAINTENANCE INTERVALS
Ram 1500 (DH Style), 2500, 3500 — Turbo Diesel Engines

TO BE SERVICED	TYPE OF SERVICE	6	12	18	24	30	36	42	48	54	60	66	72	78	84	90
Engine oil & filter*	R	✓	✓	✓	✓	✓	✓	✓	✓	✓	✓	✓	✓	✓	✓	✓
Front driveshaft fitting (4WD)	L	✓	✓	✓	✓	✓	✓	✓	✓	✓	✓	✓	✓	✓	✓	✓
Outer tie rod ends	L	✓	✓	✓	✓	✓	✓	✓	✓	✓	✓	✓	✓	✓	✓	✓
Tire pressure, battery & terminals ①	I															
CV joints	I		✓		✓		✓		✓		✓		✓		✓	
Drive axle fluid	R		✓		✓		✓		✓		✓		✓		✓	
Engine coolant & hoses ①	I															
Fuel filter	R		✓		✓		✓		✓		✓		✓		✓	
Brake, P/S & A/T fluid levels	I	✓	✓	✓	✓	✓	✓	✓	✓	✓	✓	✓	✓	✓	✓	✓
Front suspension components	I			✓			✓			✓			✓			✓
Exhaust system	I		✓		✓		✓		✓		✓		✓		✓	
Brake linings	I			✓			✓			✓			✓			✓
EGR valve & cooler	S/I									✓						
Drive belt	I R						✓							✓		
Parking brake	I A						✓							✓		
Tires	Rotate	✓	✓	✓	✓	✓	✓	✓	✓	✓	✓	✓	✓	✓	✓	✓
Power steering fluid (3500 only)	R													✓		
Engine coolant	R										✓					

R: Replace   S/I: Service or Inspect   Adj: Adjust   L: Lubricate

① Once a month, inspect tires and check pressure. Check battery and tighten terminals if required. Check fluid levels.

FREQUENT OPERATION MAINTENANCE (SEVERE SERVICE)

If a vehicle is operated under any of the following conditions it is considered severe service:

- Extremely dusty areas.
- 50% or more of the vehicle operation is in 32°C (90°F) or higher temperatures, or constant operation in temperatures below 0°C (32°F).
- Prolonged idling (vehicle operation in stop and go traffic.
- Frequent short running periods (engine does not warm to normal operating temperatures).
- Police, taxi, delivery usage or trailer towing usage.

Air filter: change every 12,000 miles.

Front and rear axle fluid: change every 18,000 miles.

Automatic transmission fluid & filter: change every 60,000 miles.

*Oil Change Indicator System

On Electronic Vehicle Information Center (EVIC) equipped vehicles, "Oil Change Require" is displayed in the EVIC and a single chime sounds indicating that an oil change is necessary.

On non-EVIC equipped vehicles, "Change Oil" flashes in the instrument cluster and a single chime sounds indicating that an oil change is necessary.

Illumination of the oil change message is based on the operating conditions of the vehicle. When the message is illuminated, the vehicle must be serviced within 500 miles.

The oil change indicator will not monitor the time since the last oil change. Change the oil if it has been more than 6 months since the last oil change, even if the oil change indicator message is not illuminated.

Under no circumstances should oil change intervals exceed 7,5000 miles or 6 months, whichever comes first.

To reset the oil change indicator, see the procedure below the Maintenance Schedule.

Oil Change Indicator Reset Procedure

1. Turn the ignition switch to the ON position. Do not start the engine.
2. Fully press the accelerator pedal 3 times within 10 seconds.
3. Turn the ignition switch to the LOCK position.

If the indicator message illuminates when the vehicle is started, repeat the procedure.

36543_RAM2_C0016

PRECAUTIONS

Before servicing any vehicle, please be sure to read all of the following precautions, which deal with personal safety, prevention of component damage, and important points to take into consideration when servicing a motor vehicle:

• Never open, service or drain the radiator or cooling system when the engine is hot; serious burns can occur from the steam and hot coolant.

• Observe all applicable safety precautions when working around fuel. Whenever servicing the fuel system, always work in a well-ventilated area. Do not allow fuel spray or vapors to come in contact with a spark, open flame, or excessive heat (a hot drop light, for example). Keep a dry chemical fire extinguisher near the work area. Always keep fuel in a container specifically designed for fuel storage; also, always properly seal fuel containers to avoid the possibility of fire or explosion. Refer to the additional fuel system precautions later in this section.

• Fuel injection systems often remain pressurized, even after the engine has been turned **OFF**. The fuel system pressure must be relieved before disconnecting any fuel lines. Failure to do so may result in fire and/or personal injury.

• Brake fluid often contains polyglycol ethers and polyglycols. Avoid contact with the eyes and wash your hands thoroughly after handling brake fluid. If you do get brake fluid in your eyes, flush your eyes with clean, running water for 15 minutes. If eye irritation persists, or if you have taken

brake fluid internally, IMMEDIATELY seek medical assistance.

• The EPA warns that prolonged contact with used engine oil may cause a number of skin disorders, including cancer. You should make every effort to minimize your exposure to used engine oil. Protective gloves should be worn when changing oil. Wash your hands and any other exposed skin areas as soon as possible after exposure to used engine oil. Soap and water, or waterless hand cleaner should be used.

• All new vehicles are now equipped with an air bag system, often referred to as a Supplemental Restraint System (SRS) or Supplemental Inflatable Restraint (SIR) system. The system must be disabled before performing service on or around system components, steering column, instrument panel components, wiring and sensors. Failure to follow safety and disabling procedures could result in accidental air bag deployment, possible personal injury and unnecessary system repairs.

• Always wear safety goggles when working with, or around, the air bag system. When carrying a non-deployed air bag, be sure the bag and trim cover are pointed away from your body. When placing a non-deployed air bag on a work surface, always face the bag and trim cover upward, away from the surface. This will reduce the motion of the module if it is accidentally deployed. Refer to the additional air bag system precautions later in this section.

• Clean, high quality brake fluid from a

sealed container is essential to the safe and proper operation of the brake system. You should always buy the correct type of brake fluid for your vehicle. If the brake fluid becomes contaminated, completely flush the system with new fluid. Never reuse any brake fluid. Any brake fluid that is removed from the system should be discarded. Also, do not allow any brake fluid to come in contact with a painted surface; it will damage the paint.

• Never operate the engine without the proper amount and type of engine oil; doing so WILL result in severe engine damage.

• Timing belt maintenance is extremely important. Many models utilize an interference-type, non-freewheeling engine. If the timing belt breaks, the valves in the cylinder head may strike the pistons, causing potentially serious (also time-consuming and expensive) engine damage. Refer to the maintenance interval charts for the recommended replacement interval for the timing belt, and to the timing belt section for belt replacement and inspection.

• Disconnecting the negative battery cable on some vehicles may interfere with the functions of the on-board computer system(s) and may require the computer to undergo a relearning process once the negative battery cable is reconnected.

• When servicing drum brakes, only disassemble and assemble one side at a time, leaving the remaining side intact for reference.

• Only an MVAC-trained, EPA-certified automotive technician should service the air conditioning system or its components.

BRAKES

GENERAL INFORMATION

PRECAUTIONS

• Certain components within the ABS system are not intended to be serviced or repaired individually.

• Do not use rubber hoses or other parts not specifically specified for and ABS system. When using repair kits, replace all parts included in the kit. Partial or incorrect repair may lead to functional problems and require the replacement of components.

• Lubricate rubber parts with clean, fresh brake fluid to ease assembly. Do not use shop air to clean parts; damage to rubber components may result.

• Use only DOT 3 brake fluid from an unopened container.

• If any hydraulic component or line is

removed or replaced, it may be necessary to bleed the entire system.

• A clean repair area is essential. Always clean the reservoir and cap thoroughly before removing the cap. The slightest amount of dirt in the fluid may plug an orifice and impair the system function. Perform repairs after components have been thoroughly cleaned; use only denatured alcohol to clean components. Do not allow ABS components to come into contact with any substance containing mineral oil; this includes used shop rags.

• The Anti-Lock control unit is a microprocessor similar to other computer units in the vehicle. Ensure that the ignition switch is **OFF** before removing or installing controller harnesses. Avoid static electricity discharge at or near the controller.

ANTI-LOCK BRAKE SYSTEM (ABS)

• If any arc welding is to be done on the vehicle, the control unit should be unplugged before welding operations begin.

WHEEL SPEED SENSOR

REMOVAL & INSTALLATION

With Rear Wheel Anti-lock Brakes (RWAL)

Rear Wheel Sensor

See Figure 1.

1. Raise the vehicle.
2. Remove the brake line mounting nut, if fitted, and remove the brake line from the sensor stud.
3. Remove the mounting stud from the sensor and shield.

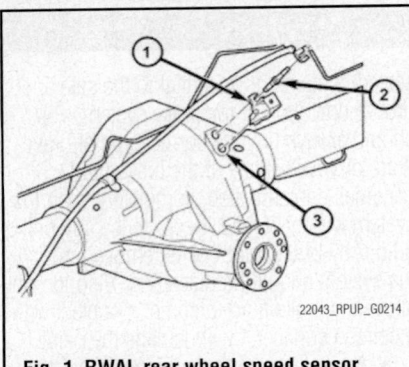

Fig. 1 RWAL rear wheel speed sensor removal shown

4. Remove the sensor and shield from the differential housing.

5. Disconnect the wire and remove the sensor.

To install:

6. Connect harness to sensor. Be sure the seal is securely in place between the sensor and wiring connector.

7. Install O—ring on sensor if removed.

8. Install sensor on differential; housing, sensor shield, mounting stud. Tighten to 18 ft. lbs. (24 Nm).

9. Install the brake line on the sensor stud and install the nut.

➡**Use the original or replacement sensor bolt only. The bolt is special and must not be substituted.**

10. Lower the vehicle.

With 4 Wheel Anti-lock Brakes (4WAL)

Front Wheel Speed Sensor—2WD Vehicles

1. Before servicing the vehicle, refer to the Precautions Section.

2. Raise and support the vehicle.

3. Remove the sensor bolt from the steering knuckle/hub and remove the sensor.

4. Disconnect the ABS wheel speed sensor wire and detach the wire from securing clips.

To install:

5. Tighten the sensor bolt to 17 ft. lbs. (23 Nm).

➡**Use the original or replacement sensor bolt only. The bolt is special and must not be substituted.**

6. The remainder of the procedure is the reverse of removal.

Front Wheel Speed Sensor—4WD Vehicles

See Figure 2.

1. Before servicing the vehicle, refer to the Precautions Section.

2. Raise and support the vehicle.

3. Remove the wheel.

4. Remove the brake caliper.

5. On 8—stud wheels, remove the rotor hub bearing assembly and separate the rotor from the hub bearing.

6. On other wheels, remove the rotor.

7. Remove the sensor attaching bolts.

8. Disconnect the wire and remove the sensor from the vehicle.

To install:

9. Tighten the bolts to 13 ft. lbs. (18 Nm).

➡**Use the original or replacement sensor bolts only. The bolts are special and must not be substituted.**

10. The remainder of the procedure is the reverse of removal.

Rear Wheel Sensor

See Figure 3.

1. Before servicing the vehicle, refer to the Precautions Section.

2. Raise the vehicle on a hoist.

3. Disconnect the wheel speed sensor electrical connector.

4. Remove the mounting bolt from the sensor.

5. Remove the sensor from the brake caliper adapter.

To install:

6. Insert the wheel speed sensor in the brake caliper adapter.

7. Install the sensor mounting bolt and tighten to 17 ft. lbs. (24 Nm).

8. Reconnect the electrical wiring connector to the sensor.

9. Lower the vehicle.

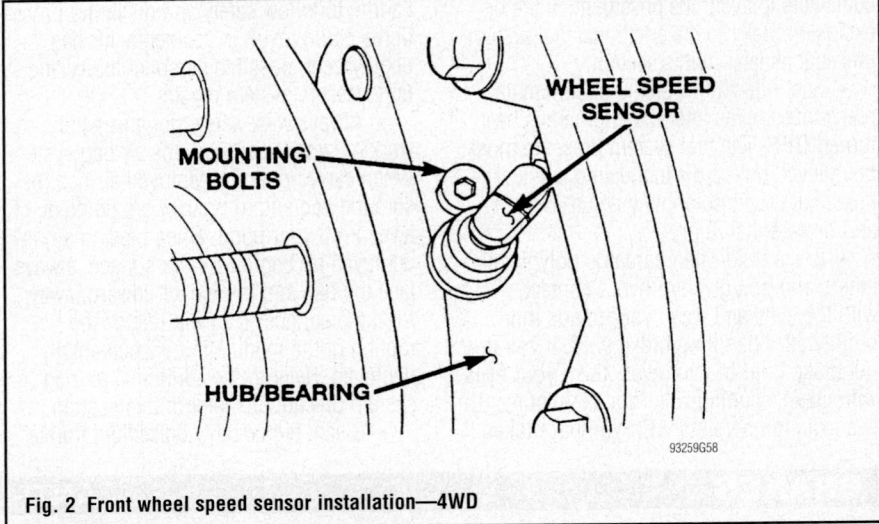

Fig. 2 Front wheel speed sensor installation—4WD

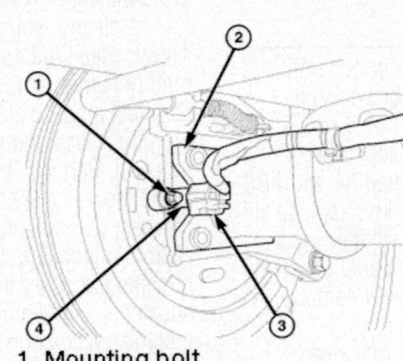

1. Mounting bolt
2. Brake caliper adapter
3. Speed sensor electrical connector
4. Wheel speed sensor

Fig. 3 Rear wheel speed sensor view

BRAKES

BLEEDING THE BRAKE SYSTEM

BLEEDING PROCEDURE

Manual Bleeding

1. Before servicing the vehicle, refer to the Precautions Section.

➡This procedure covers bleeding of the base brakes only. On vehicles equipped with ABS, refer to the bleeding procedure located under the ABS portion of this section.

➡Use Mopar® brake fluid, or an equivalent quality fluid meeting SAE J1703-F and DOT 3 standards only. Use fresh, clean fluid from a sealed container at all times.

2. Remove reservoir filler caps and fill reservoir.

3. If calipers were overhauled, open all caliper bleed screws. Then close each bleed screw as fluid starts to drip from it. Top off master cylinder reservoir once more before proceeding.

4. Attach one end of bleed hose to bleed screw and insert opposite end in glass container partially filled with brake fluid. Be sure end of bleed hose is immersed in fluid.

➡Bleed procedure should be in this order: (1) Right rear (2) Left rear (3) Right front (4) Left front.

5. Open up bleeder, then have a helper press down the brake pedal. Once the pedal is down close the bleeder. Repeat bleeding until fluid stream is clear and free of bubbles. Then move to the next wheel.

6. Before moving the vehicle verify the pedal is firm and not mushy.

7. Top off the brake fluid and install the reservoir cap.

Pressure Bleeding

1. Before servicing the vehicle, refer to the Precautions Section.

➡This procedure covers bleeding of the base brakes only. On vehicles

equipped with ABS, refer to the bleeding procedure located under the ABS portion of this section.

➡Use Mopar® brake fluid, or an equivalent quality fluid meeting SAE J1703-F and DOT 3 standards only. Use fresh, clean fluid from a sealed container at all times.

2. Follow the manufacturer's instructions carefully when using pressure equipment. Do not exceed the tank manufacturers pressure recommendations. Generally, a tank pressure of 15-20 psi is sufficient for bleeding.

3. Fill the bleeder tank with recommended fluid and purge air from the tank lines before bleeding.

4. Do not pressure bleed without a proper master cylinder adapter. The wrong adapter can lead to leakage, or drawing air back into the system.

BRAKES

FRONT DISC BRAKES

✳✳ CAUTION

Dust and dirt accumulating on brake parts during normal use may contain asbestos fibers from production or aftermarket brake linings. Breathing excessive concentrations of asbestos fibers can cause serious bodily harm. Exercise care when servicing brake parts. Do not sand or grind brake lining unless equipment used is designed to contain the dust residue. Do not clean brake parts with compressed air or by dry brushing. Cleaning should be done by dampening the brake components with a fine mist of water, then wiping the brake components clean with a dampened cloth. Dispose of cloth and all residue containing asbestos fibers in an impermeable container with the appropriate label. Follow practices prescribed by the Occupational Safety and Health Administration (OSHA) and the Environmental Protection Agency (EPA) for the handling, processing, and disposing of dust or debris that may contain asbestos fibers.

BRAKE CALIPER

REMOVAL & INSTALLATION

Light Duty

See Figure 4.

1. Raise and support the vehicle.
2. Remove the tire and wheel assembly.
3. Compress the disc brake caliper.
4. Remove the banjo bolt and discard the copper washers.
5. Remove the caliper slide pin bolts.

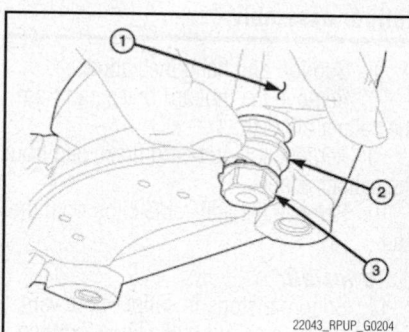

Fig. 4 Caliper adapter (1), boot (2), pin (3)

22043_RPUP_G0204

6. Remove the disc brake caliper from the caliper adapter.

7. Remove the caliper slide pins from the adapter.

To install:

8. Clean slide pin bores thoroughly to remove any old grease.

9. Thoroughly coat the new slide pins on all working surfaces with Dow Corning-807® grease or equivalent.

✳✳ WARNING

Petroleum based grease should not be used on any of the rubber components of the caliper, Use only Non-Petroleum based grease.

10. Install the boot onto the slide pin and then insert into the adapter.

11. Push the pin all the way into the adapter and carefully expel the trapped air by gently pushing on the boot near the slide pin head.

12. Install the disc brake caliper to the brake caliper adapter.

➡Verify brake hose is not twisted or kinked before tightening fitting bolt.

13. Install the banjo bolt with new copper washers to the caliper. Tighten to 21 ft. lbs. (28 Nm).

14. Install the caliper slide pin bolts. Tighten to 24 ft. lbs. (32 Nm).

15. Remove the prop rod.

16. Bleed the area of repair for the brake system.

➡ **If a proper pedal is not felt during bleeding an area of repair then a base bleed system must be performed.**

17. Install the tire and wheel assembly.

18. Lower the vehicle.

Heavy Duty

1. Raise and support the vehicle.

2. Remove the tire and wheel assembly.

3. Compress the disc brake caliper.

4. Remove the banjo bolt and discard the copper washer.

5. Remove the caliper slide bolts.

6. Remove the disc brake caliper.

To install:

7. Install the disc brake caliper.

➡ **Verify brake hose is not twisted or kinked before tightening fitting bolt.**

8. Install the banjo bolt with new copper washers to the caliper. Tighten to 20 ft. lbs. (27 Nm).

9. Install the caliper slide pin bolts. Tighten to 24 ft. lbs. (32 Nm).

10. Remove the prop rod.

11. Bleed the area of repair for the brake system.

➡ **If a proper pedal is not felt during bleeding an area of repair then a base bleed system must be performed.**

12. Install the tire and wheel assembly.

13. Lower the vehicle.

DISC BRAKE PADS

REMOVAL & INSTALLATION

Light Duty

See Figures 5 and 6.

1. Before servicing the vehicle, refer to the Precautions Section.

2. Raise and support vehicle.

3. Remove the wheel and tire assemblies.

4. Compress the caliper.

5. Remove the caliper slide pin bolts.

6. Remove the caliper from the caliper adapter.

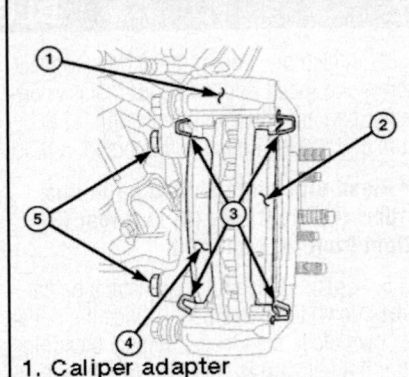

1. Caliper adapter
2. Outboard brake pad
3. Anti-rattle clips
4. Inboard brakepad
5. Caliper adapter mounting bolts

22043_RPUP_G0206

Fig. 5 Brake pad mounting shown

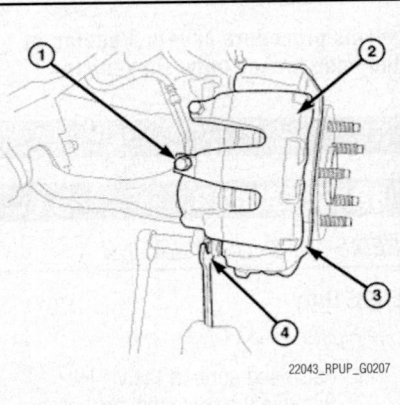

22043_RPUP_G0207

Fig. 6 Caliper slide pin bolt tightening shown

⁂ **WARNING**

Do not allow brake hose to support caliper assembly.

7. Support and hang the caliper.

8. Remove the inboard brake pad from the caliper adapter

9. Remove the outboard brake pad from the caliper adapter.

10. Remove the anti-rattle clips from the pad.

To install:

11. Bottom pistons in caliper bore with C-clamp. Place an old brake shoe between a C-clamp and caliper piston.

12. Clean caliper mounting adapter.

13. Install new anti-rattle clips to the brake pads.

14. Install inboard brake pad in adapter.

15. Install outboard brake pad in adapter.

16. Install the caliper over rotor, Then push the caliper onto the adapter.

17. Install the caliper slide pin bolts. Tighten to 24 ft. lbs. (32 Nm).

18. Install wheel and tire assemblies and lower vehicle.

19. Apply brakes several times to seat caliper pistons and brake shoes and obtain firm pedal.

20. Top off master cylinder fluid level.

Heavy Duty

See Figure 7.

1. Before servicing the vehicle, refer to the Precautions Section.

2. Raise and support vehicle.

3. Remove the wheel and tire assemblies.

4. Compress the caliper.

5. Remove the caliper.

6. Remove the caliper by tilting the top up and off the caliper adapter.

➡ **Do not allow brake hose to support caliper assembly.**

7. Support and hang the caliper.

8. Remove the inboard and outboard brake pads from the caliper adapter.

➡ **Anti-rattle springs are not interchangeable.**

9. Remove the top and bottom anti-rattle springs from the caliper adapter.

To install:

10. Bottom pistons in caliper bore with C-clamp. Place an old brake shoe between a C-clamp and caliper piston.

11. Clean caliper mounting adapter and anti-rattle springs.

12. Lubricate anti-rattle springs with Mopar® brake grease.

13. Install new top and bottom anti-rattle springs.

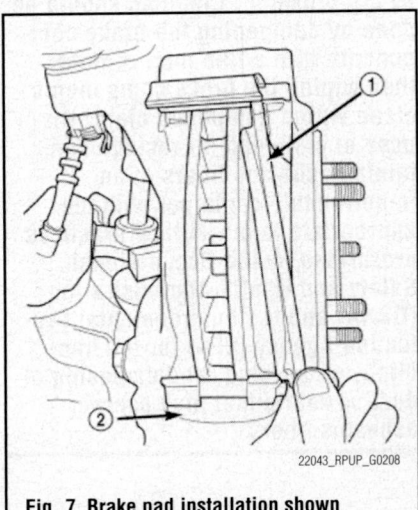

22043_RPUP_G0208

Fig. 7 Brake pad installation shown

14. Install inboard and outboard brake pads in adapter.

15. Tilt the top of the caliper over rotor and under adapter. Then push the bottom of the caliper down onto the adapter.

16. Install brake caliper.

17. Install the caliper slide pin bolts. Tighten to 24 ft. lbs. (32 Nm).

18. Install wheel and tire assemblies and lower vehicle.

19. Apply brakes several times to seat caliper pistons and brake shoes and obtain firm pedal.

20. Top off master cylinder fluid level.

BRAKES

REAR DISC BRAKES

✳✳ CAUTION

Dust and dirt accumulating on brake parts during normal use may contain asbestos fibers from production or aftermarket brake linings. Breathing excessive concentrations of asbestos fibers can cause serious bodily harm. Exercise care when servicing brake parts. Do not sand or grind brake lining unless equipment used is designed to contain the dust residue. Do not clean brake parts with compressed air or by dry brushing. Cleaning should be done by dampening the brake components with a fine mist of water, then wiping the brake components clean with a dampened cloth. Dispose of cloth and all residue containing asbestos fibers in an impermeable container with the appropriate label. Follow practices prescribed by the Occupational Safety and Health Administration (OSHA) and the Environmental Protection Agency (EPA) for the handling, processing, and disposing of dust or debris that may contain asbestos fibers.

BRAKE CALIPER

REMOVAL & INSTALLATION

See Figure 8.

1. Before servicing the vehicle, refer to the Precautions Section.

2. Raise and support the vehicle.

3. Remove the rear wheel and tire assemblies.

4. Compress the caliper.

5. Remove caliper slide bolts.

✳✳ WARNING

Do not allow brake hose to support caliper assembly.

6. Remove the rear brake caliper.

To install:

7. Install caliper to the caliper adapter.

8. Coat the caliper mounting slide pin bolts with silicone grease. Then install and tighten the bolts to 22 ft. lbs. (30 Nm).

9. Install the brake hose to the caliper with new seal washers and tighten banjo bolt to 20 ft. lbs. (27 Nm).

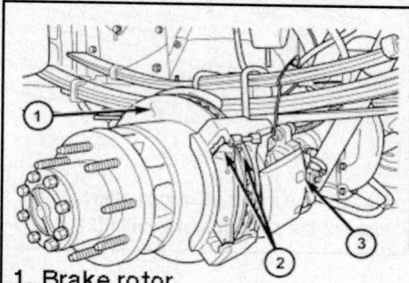

1. Brake rotor
2. Brake pad
3. Brake rotor

22043_RPUP_G0209

Fig. 8 Rear brake caliper shown removed and supported

✳✳ WARNING

Verify brake hose is not twisted or kinked before tightening fitting bolt.

10. Remove the prop rod from the brake pedal.

11. Bleed the area of repair for the brake system.

➡ If a proper pedal is not felt during bleeding an area of repair then a base bleed system must be performed.

12. Install the wheel and tire assemblies.

13. Remove the supports and lower the vehicle.

14. Verify a firm pedal before moving the vehicle.

DISC BRAKE PADS

REMOVAL & INSTALLATION

See Figure 9.

1. Before servicing the vehicle, refer to the Precautions Section.

✳✳ WARNING

Never allow the disc brake caliper to hang from the brake hose. Damage to the brake hose will result. Provide a suitable support to hang the caliper securely.

2. Install prop rod on the brake pedal to keep pressure on the brake system, Holding pedal in this position will isolate master cylinder from hydraulic brake system and

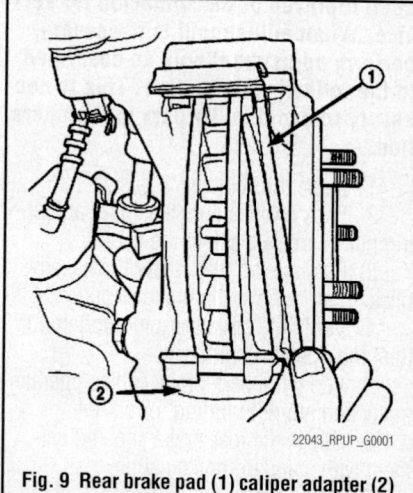

22043_RPUP_G0001

Fig. 9 Rear brake pad (1) caliper adapter (2)

will not allow brake fluid to drain out of brake fluid reservoir while brake lines are open. This will allow you to bleed out the area of repair instead of the entire system.

3. Raise and support vehicle.

4. Remove the wheel and tire assembly.

5. Compress the caliper.

6. Remove caliper slide bolts.

7. Remove the caliper and then tilt the top up and off the caliper adapter.

8. Remove inboard and outboard brake pads from the caliper adapter.

9. Remove the top and bottom anti-rattle spring from the caliper adapter.

To install:

10. Clean caliper mounting adapter and anti-rattle springs.

11. Lubricate anti-rattle springs with Mopar® brake grease.

12. Install new top and bottom anti-rattle spring

13. Install outboard and inboard brake pads in adapter.

14. Tilt the bottom of the caliper over rotor and under adapter. Then push the top of the caliper down onto the adapter.

15. Coat the caliper mounting slide pin bolts with silicone grease. Then install and tighten the bolts to 22 ft. lbs. (30 Nm).

16. Install the wheel and tire assemblies and lower vehicle.

17. Apply brakes several times to seat caliper pistons and brake shoes and obtain firm pedal.

18. Top off master cylinder fluid level.

BRAKES   **PARKING BRAKE**

PARKING BRAKE CABLES

ADJUSTMENT

➡Tensioner adjustment is only necessary when the tensioner, or a cable has been replaced or disconnected for service. When adjustment is necessary, perform adjustment only as described in the following procedure. This is necessary to avoid faulty park brake operation.

1. Raise the vehicle.
2. Back off the cable tensioner adjusting nut to create slack in the cables.
3. Remove the rear wheel/tire assemblies. Then remove the brake rotors.
4. Verify the brakes are in good condition and operating properly.
5. Verify the park brake cables operate freely and are not binding, or seized.
6. Check the rear brake shoe adjustment with standard brake gauge.
7. Install the rotors and verify that the rotors rotate freely without drag.
8. Install the wheel and tire assemblies.
9. Lower the vehicle enough for access to the park brake foot pedal. Then fully apply the park brakes.

➡**Leave park brakes applied until adjustment is complete.**

10. Raise the vehicle again.
11. Mark the tensioner rod ¼ inch. (6.35 mm) from edge of the tensioner.
12. Tighten the adjusting nut on the tensioner rod until the mark is no longer visible.

➡**Do not loosen, or tighten the tensioner adjusting nut for any reason after completing adjustment.**

13. Lower the vehicle until the rear wheels are (15–20 cm) 6–8 inch. off the shop floor.
14. Release the park brake foot pedal and verify that rear wheels rotate freely without drag. Then lower the vehicle.

PARKING BRAKE SHOES

REMOVAL & INSTALLATION

See Figures 10 through 13.

1. Raise and support the vehicle.
2. Remove the tire and wheel assembly.
3. Remove the disc brake caliper and rotor, as outlined in this section.

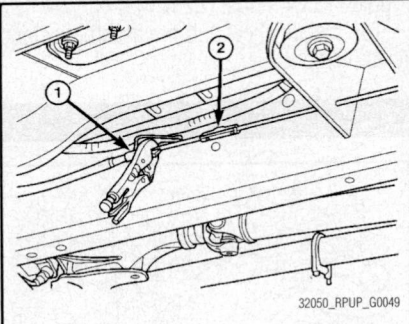

Fig. 10 Use a pair of locking pliers (1) to lock out the parking brake cable (2)

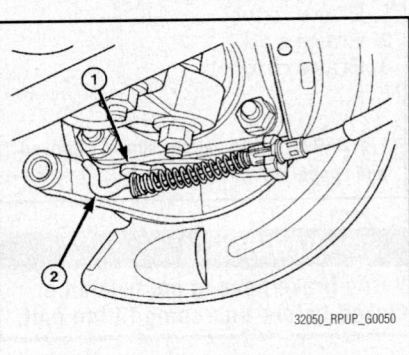

Fig. 11 View of the lever (1) and parking brake cable end (2)

4. Lockout the parking brake cable.
5. Disengage the park brake cable from behind the rotor assembly to allow easier disassembly of the park brake shoes.
6. Disassemble the rear park brake shoes.

To install:

7. Reassemble the rear park brake shoes.
8. Release the parking brake cable.
9. Adjust the rear park brake shoes.
10. Install the disc brake rotor and caliper.
11. Install the tire and wheel assembly.
12. Lower the vehicle.

ADJUSTMENT

Adjustment can be made with a standard brake gauge or with adjusting tool. Adjustment is performed with the complete brake assembly installed on the backing plate.

1. Be sure parking brake lever is fully released.
2. Raise vehicle so rear wheels can be rotated freely.

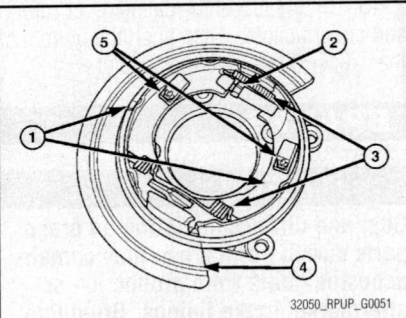

Fig. 12 View of the parking brake shoes (1), adjuster (2), return springs (3), splash shield (4) and hold-downs (5)

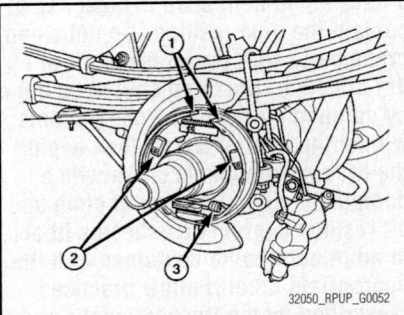

Fig. 13 View of the assembled parking brake shoes (1), hold-downs (2) and return springs (3)

3. Remove plug from each access hole in brake support plates.
4. Loosen parking brake cable adjustment nut until there is slack in front cable.
5. Insert adjusting tool through support plate access hole and engage tool in teeth of adjusting screw star wheel.
6. Rotate adjuster screw star wheel (move tool handle upward) until slight drag can be felt when wheel is rotated.
7. Push and hold adjuster lever away from star wheel with thin screwdriver.
8. Back off adjuster screw star wheel until brake drag is eliminated.
9. Repeat adjustment at opposite wheel. Be sure adjustment is equal at both wheels.
10. Install support plate access hole plugs.
11. Adjust parking brake cable and lower vehicle.
12. Depress park brake pedal and make sure park brakes hold the vehicle stationary.
13. Release park brake pedal.

CHASSIS ELECTRICAL

AIR BAG (SUPPLEMENTAL RESTRAINT SYSTEM)

GENERAL INFORMATION

❋❋ CAUTION

Vehicles are equipped with an air bag system. The system must be disarmed before performing service on, or around, system components, the steering column, instrument panel components, wiring and sensors. Failure to follow the safety precautions and the disarming procedure could result in accidental air bag deployment, possible injury and unnecessary system repairs.

SERVICE PRECAUTIONS

Disconnect and isolate the battery negative cable before beginning any airbag system component diagnosis, testing, removal, or installation procedures. Allow system capacitor to discharge for two minutes before beginning any component service. This will disable the airbag system. Failure to disable the airbag system may result in accidental airbag deployment, personal injury, or death.

Do not place an intact undeployed airbag face down on a solid surface. The airbag will propel into the air if accidentally deployed and may result in personal injury or death.

When carrying or handling an undeployed airbag, the trim side (face) of the airbag should be pointing towards the body to minimize possibility of injury if accidental deployment occurs. Failure to do this may result in personal injury or death.

Replace airbag system components with OEM replacement parts. Substitute parts may appear interchangeable, but internal differences may result in inferior occupant protection. Failure to do so may result in occupant personal injury or death.

Wear safety glasses, rubber gloves, and long sleeved clothing when cleaning powder residue from vehicle after an airbag deployment. Powder residue emitted from a deployed airbag can cause skin irritation. Flush affected area with cool water if irritation is experienced. If nasal or throat irritation is experienced, exit the vehicle for fresh air until the irritation ceases. If irritation continues, see a physician.

Do not use a replacement airbag that is not in the original packaging. This may result in improper deployment, personal injury, or death.

The factory installed fasteners, screws and bolts used to fasten airbag components have a special coating and are specifically designed for the airbag system. Do not use substitute fasteners. Use only original equipment fasteners listed in the parts catalog when fastener replacement is required.

During, and following, any child restraint anchor service, due to impact event or vehicle repair, carefully inspect all mounting hardware, tether straps, and anchors for proper installation, operation, or damage. If a child restraint anchor is found damaged in any way, the anchor must be replaced. Failure to do this may result in personal injury or death.

Deployed and non-deployed airbags may or may not have live pyrotechnic material within the airbag inflator.

Do not dispose of driver/passenger/curtain airbags or seat belt tensioners unless you are sure of complete deployment. Refer to the Hazardous Substance Control System for proper disposal.

Dispose of deployed airbags and tensioners consistent with state, provincial, local, and federal regulations.

After any airbag component testing or service, do not connect the battery negative cable. Personal injury or death may result if the system test is not performed first.

If the vehicle is equipped with the Occupant Classification System (OCS), do not connect the battery negative cable before performing the OCS Verification Test using the scan tool and the appropriate diagnostic information. Personal injury or death may result if the system test is not performed properly.

Never replace both the Occupant Restraint Controller (ORC) and the Occupant Classification Module (OCM) at the same time. If both require replacement, replace one, then perform the Airbag System test before replacing the other.

Both the ORC and the OCM store Occupant Classification System (OCS) calibration data, which they transfer to one another when one of them is replaced. If both are replaced at the same time, an irreversible fault will be set in both modules and the OCS may malfunction and cause personal injury or death.

If equipped with OCS, the Seat Weight Sensor is a sensitive, calibrated unit and must be handled carefully. Do not drop or handle roughly. If dropped or damaged, replace with another sensor. Failure to do so may result in occupant injury or death.

If equipped with OCS, the front passenger seat must be handled carefully as well. When removing the seat, be careful when setting on floor not to drop. If dropped, the sensor may be inoperative, could result in occupant injury, or possibly death.

If equipped with OCS, when the passenger front seat is on the floor, no one should sit in the front passenger seat. This uneven force may damage the sensing ability of the seat weight sensors. If sat on and damaged, the sensor may be inoperative, could result in occupant injury, or possibly death.

DISARMING THE SYSTEM

1. Disconnect and isolate the negative battery cable. Wait 2 minutes for the system capacitor to discharge before performing any service.

2. When repairs are completed, connect the negative battery cable.

ARMING THE SYSTEM

To arm the Supplemental Restraint System (SRS), connect the negative battery cable.

CLOCKSPRING CENTERING

See Figure 14.

❋❋ WARNING

To avoid serious or fatal injury on vehicles equipped with airbags, disable the Supplemental Restraint System (SRS) before attempting any steering wheel, steering column, airbag, seat belt tensioner, impact sensor, or instrument panel component diagnosis or service. Disconnect and isolate the battery negative (ground) cable, then wait two minutes for the system capacitor to discharge before performing further diagnosis or service. This is the only sure way to disable the SRS. Failure to take the proper precautions could result in accidental airbag deployment.

➡Before starting this procedure, be certain to turn the steering wheel until the front wheels are in the straight-ahead position.

1. Place the front wheels in the straight-ahead position.
2. Remove the clockspring from the steering column.

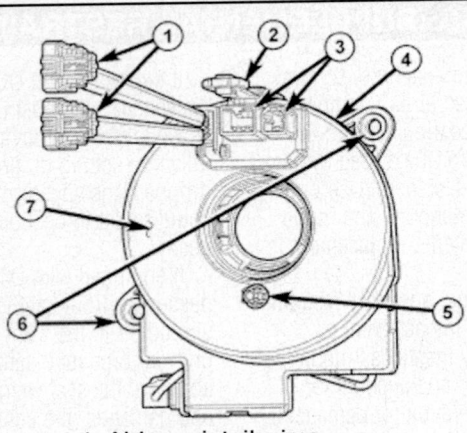

1. Airbag pigtail wires
2. Clockspring locking pin
3. Connector receptacles
4. Clockspring assembly
5. Engagement dowel
6. Mounting holes
7. Clockspring rotor

22043_RPUP_G0002

Fig. 14 Clockspring assembly

3. Rotate the clockspring rotor (7) clockwise to the end of its travel. Do not apply excessive torque.

4. From the end of the clockwise travel, rotate the rotor about two and one-half turns counterclockwise. The engagement dowel (5) should end up at the bottom, and the airbag pigtail wires (1) and connector receptacles (3) should be at the top. Turn the rotor slight19ly clockwise or counterclockwise as necessary so that the slots for the clockspring locking pin (2) are in alignment.

5. The clockspring is now centered. Secure the clockspring rotor to the clockspring case to maintain clockspring centering until it is reinstalled on the steering column.

6. The front wheels should still be in the straight-ahead position. Reinstall the clockspring onto the steering column.

DRIVE TRAIN

AUTOMATIC TRANSMISSION ASSEMBLY

REMOVAL & INSTALLATION

45RFE/545RFE

1. Before servicing the vehicle, refer to the Precautions Section.
2. Disconnect the negative battery cable.
3. Raise and support the vehicle
4. Remove any necessary skid plates.
5. Mark propeller shaft and axle companion flanges for assembly alignment.
6. Remove the rear propeller shaft.
7. Remove the front propeller shaft, if necessary.
8. Remove the engine to transmission structural dust cover.
9. Remove the exhaust support bracket from the rear of the transmission.
10. Disconnect and lower or remove any necessary exhaust components.
11. Remove the starter motor.
12. Rotate crankshaft in clockwise direction until converter bolts are accessible. Then remove bolts one at a time. Rotate crankshaft with socket wrench on dampener bolt.
13. Disengage the output speed sensor connector from the output speed sensor.
14. Disengage the input speed sensor connector from the input speed sensor.
15. Disengage the transmission solenoid/TRS assembly connector from the transmission solenoid/TRS assembly.

16. Disengage the line pressure sensor connector from the line pressure sensor.
17. Disconnect gearshift cable from transmission manual valve lever.
18. Disconnect the transmission vent hose from the transmission.
19. Support rear of engine with safety stand or jack.
20. Raise transmission slightly with service jack to relieve load on crossmember and supports.
21. Remove bolts securing rear support and cushion to transmission and crossmember.
22. Remove transfer case, if necessary.
23. Disconnect transmission fluid cooler lines at transmission fittings and clips.
24. Remove all remaining converter housing bolts.
25. Carefully work transmission and torque converter assembly rearward off engine block dowels.
26. Hold torque converter in place during transmission removal.
27. Lower transmission and remove assembly from under the vehicle.
28. To remove torque converter, carefully slide torque converter out of the transmission.

To install:

29. Check torque converter hub and hub drive flats for sharp edges burrs, scratches, or nicks. Polish the hub and flats with 320/400 grit paper and crocus cloth if nec-

essary. Verify that the converter hub O-ring is properly installed and is free of any debris. The hub must be smooth to avoid damaging pump seal at installation.

30. If a replacement transmission is being installed, transfer any components necessary, such as the manual shift lever and shift cable bracket, from the original transmission onto the replacement transmission.
31. Lubricate oil pump seal lip with transmission fluid.
32. Align converter and oil pump.
33. Carefully insert converter in oil pump. Then rotate converter back and forth until fully seated in pump gears.
34. Check converter seating with steel scale and straightedge. Surface of converter lugs should be at least ½ inch (13mm) to rear of straightedge when converter is fully seated.
35. Temporarily secure converter with C-clamp.
36. Position transmission on jack and secure it with chains.
37. Check condition of converter driveplate. Replace the plate if cracked, distorted or damaged. Also be sure transmission dowel pins are seated in engine block and protrude far enough to hold transmission in alignment.
38. Apply a light coating of Mopar® High Temp Grease to the torque converter hub pocket in the rear pocket of the engine's crankshaft.

39. Raise transmission and align the torque converter with the drive plate and transmission converter housing with the engine block.

40. Move transmission forward. Then raise, lower or tilt transmission to align the converter housing with engine block dowels.

41. Carefully work transmission forward and over engine block dowels until converter hub is seated in crankshaft. Verify that no wires, or the transmission vent hose, have become trapped between the engine block and the transmission.

42. Install two bolts to attach the transmission to the engine.

43. Install remaining torque converter housing to engine bolts. Tighten to 50 ft. lbs. 50 ft. lbs (68 Nm).

44. Install transfer case, if equipped. Tighten transfer case nuts to 26 ft. lbs. (35 Nm).

45. Install rear support to transmission. Tighten bolts to 35 ft. lbs. (47 Nm).

46. Lower transmission onto crossmember and install bolts attaching transmission mount to crossmember. Tighten clevis bracket to crossmember bolts to 35 ft. lbs. (47 Nm). Tighten the clevis bracket to rear support bolt to 50 ft. lbs. (68 Nm).

47. Remove engine support fixture.

48. Connect gearshift cable to transmission.

49. Connect wires to solenoid and pressure switch assembly connector.

50. Connect wires to input and output speed sensors.

51. Connect wires to line pressure sensor.

➡ **Be sure transmission harnesses are properly routed.**

✳✳ WARNING

It is essential that correct length bolts be used to attach the converter to the driveplate. Bolts that are too long will damage the clutch surface inside the converter.

52. Install torque converter-to-driveplate bolts. Tighten bolts to 270 inch lbs. (31 Nm).

53. Install starter motor and cooler line bracket.

54. Connect cooler lines to transmission.

55. Install transmission fill tube.

56. Install exhaust components, if necessary.

57. Install the structural dust cover onto the transmission and the engine.

58. Align and connect propeller shaft(s).

59. Adjust gearshift cable if necessary.

60. Install any skid plates removed previously.

61. Lower the vehicle.

62. Fill transmission with Mopar® ATF +4, Automatic Transmission Fluid.

48RE

➡**The overdrive unit can be removed and serviced separately. It is not necessary to remove the entire transmission assembly to perform overdrive unit repairs.**

1. Before servicing the vehicle, refer to the Precautions Section.

2. Disconnect battery negative cable.

3. Raise the vehicle.

4. Remove the transfer case skid plate if equipped.

5. Disconnect and lower or remove any necessary exhaust components.

6. Remove engine-to-transmission struts.

7. Remove starter motor.

8. Disconnect and remove the crankshaft position sensor.

9. If transmission is being removed for overhaul, remove transmission oil pan, drain fluid and reinstall pan.

10. Remove torque converter access cover.

11. Rotate crankshaft in clockwise direction until converter bolts are accessible. Then remove bolts one at a time. Rotate crankshaft with socket wrench on dampener bolt.

12. Mark propeller shaft and axle yokes for assembly alignment. Then disconnect and remove propeller shaft. On 4WD models, remove both propeller shafts.

13. Disconnect wires from the transmission range sensor and transmission solenoid connector.

14. Disconnect gearshift cable from the transmission manual lever.

15. For vehicles with gas engines, disconnect throttle valve cable from transmission bracket and throttle valve lever.

16. For vehicles with a diesel engine, remove the bolts holding the Transmission Throttle Valve Actuator (TTVA) to the transmission case.

17. Allow the TTVA to rotate clockwise away from the transmission.

18. Remove the wiring connector from the TTVA.

19. Lift the TTVA straight upward and off the throttle valve shaft.

20. On 4WD models, disconnect shift rod from transfer case shift lever.

21. Support rear of engine with safety stand or jack.

22. Raise transmission slightly with service jack to relieve load on crossmember and supports.

23. Remove the nuts securing the rear support to the transmission crossmember.

24. Remove the bolts holding the rear support to the transmission remove the rear support.

25. Remove bolts attaching crossmember to frame and remove crossmember.

26. On 4WD models, remove transfer case.

27. Remove fill tube bracket bolts and pull tube out of transmission. Retain fill tube seal. On 4X4 models, it will also be necessary to remove bolt attaching transfer case vent tube to converter housing.

28. Disconnect fluid cooler lines at transmission.

29. Remove all bolts holding the transmission to the engine adapter, diesel engines.

30. Carefully work transmission and torque converter assembly rearward off engine block dowels.

31. Lower transmission and remove assembly from under the vehicle.

32. To remove torque converter, remove C-clamp from edge of bell housing and carefully slide torque converter out of the transmission.

33. Remove all bolts holding the transmission to the engine adapter, gas engines.

34. Carefully work transmission and torque converter assembly rearward off engine block dowels.

35. Lower transmission and remove assembly from under the vehicle.

36. To remove torque converter, remove C-clamp from edge of bell housing and carefully slide torque converter out of the transmission.

To install:

37. Check torque converter hub inner and outer diameters and hub drive notches for sharp edges burrs, scratches, or nicks. Polish the hub and notches with 320/400 grit paper and crocus cloth if necessary. The hub must be smooth to avoid damaging pump seal at installation

38. Lubricate pocket in the rear oil pump seal lip with transmission fluid.

39. Lubricate converter pilot hub of the crankshaft with a light coating of Mopar® High Temp Grease.

40. Align and install converter in oil pump.

41. Carefully insert converter in oil pump. Then rotate converter back and forth until fully seated in pump gears.

42. Check converter seating with steel scale and straightedge. Surface of converter lugs should be 0.75 inch (19mm) to rear of straightedge when converter is fully seated.

43. Temporarily secure converter with C-clamp.

44. **DIESEL ENGINES** are as follows:

a. Position transmission on jack and secure it with chains.

b. Check condition of converter driveplate. Replace the plate if cracked, distorted or damaged. Also be sure transmission dowel pins are seated in engine block and protrude far enough to hold transmission in alignment.

c. Raise transmission and align converter with drive plate and converter housing with engine block.

d. Move transmission forward. Then raise, lower or tilt transmission to align converter housing with engine block dowels.

e. Carefully work transmission forward and over engine block dowels until converter hub is seated in crankshaft.

f. Install bolts attaching transmission to engine adapter.

45. **GAS ENGINES** are as follows:

a. Position transmission on jack and secure it with chains. Also be sure transmission dowel pins are seated in engine block and protrude far enough to hold transmission in alignment.

b. Raise transmission and align converter with drive plate and converter housing with engine block.

c. Move transmission forward. Then raise, lower or tilt transmission to align converter housing with engine block dowels.

d. Carefully work transmission forward and over engine block dowels until converter hub is seated in crankshaft.

e. Install bolts attaching transmission to engine.

46. Install rear support.

47. Install the rear transmission crossmember.

48. Lower transmission onto crossmember and install bolts attaching transmission mount to crossmember

49. Remove engine support fixture.

50. Install the transfer case, if equipped.

51. Install crankshaft position sensor.

52. Connect gearshift cable and throttle cable (gas engines only) to transmission.

53. For vehicles equipped with a diesel engine, position the Transmission Throttle Valve Actuator (TTVA) over the throttle valve shaft.

54. Align the D-shaped opening in the bottom of the TTVA to the throttle valve shaft and install the TTVA onto the shaft.

55. Install the wiring connector to the TTVA.

56. Rotate the TTVA to the transmission case and install the bolts to hold the TTVA to the transmission.

57. Tighten the bolts to 75 inch lbs. (8.5 Nm).

58. Initialize the TTVA.

59. Connect cooler lines to transmission.

60. Connect wires to the transmission range sensor and transmission solenoid connector. Be sure the transmission harnesses are properly routed.

61. Install torque converter-to-driveplate bolts.

62. Install converter housing access cover.

63. Install starter motor and cooler line bracket.

64. Install transmission fill tube. Install new seal on tube before installation.

65. Install any exhaust components previously removed.

66. Align and connect propeller shaft.

67. Adjust gearshift cable and throttle valve cable, if necessary.

68. Install the transfer case skid plate, if equipped.

69. Lower the vehicle.

70. Fill transmission with Mopar® ATF +4, Automatic Transmission fluid.

68RFE

1. Before servicing the vehicle, refer to the Precautions Section.

2. Disconnect the negative battery cable.

3. Raise and support the vehicle.

4. Remove any necessary skid plates.

➡**Mark propeller shaft and axle companion flanges for assembly alignment.**

5. Remove the rear propeller shaft.

6. Remove the front propeller shaft, if necessary.

7. Remove the exhaust support bracket from the front and rear of the transmission (if equipped).

8. Disconnect and lower or remove any necessary exhaust components.

9. Remove the bolts securing the power bending bracket to the engine block and the transmission case.

10. Remove the power bending bracket.

11. Loosen the inspection cover bolts and remove the inspection cover.

12. Remove the transmission dust shield.

To install:

13. Check torque converter hub and hub drive flats for sharp edges burrs, scratches, or nicks. Polish the hub and flats with 800/1000 grit paper and crocus cloth if necessary. Verify that the converter hub O-ring is properly installed and is free of any debris. The hub must be smooth to avoid damaging pump seal at installation.

14. If a replacement transmission is being installed, transfer any components necessary, such as the manual shift lever and shift cable bracket, from the original transmission onto the replacement transmission.

15. Lubricate oil pump seal lip with transmission fluid.

16. Align converter and oil pump.

17. Carefully insert converter in oil pump. Then rotate converter back and forth until fully seated in pump gears.

18. Check converter seating with steel scale and straightedge. Surface of converter lugs should be in front of the bell housing face about 1 inch, (25 mm).

19. Temporarily secure converter with C-clamp.

20. Position transmission on jack and secure it with chains.

21. Check condition of converter driveplate. Replace the plate if cracked, distorted or damaged. Also be sure transmission dowel pins are seated in engine block and protrude far enough to hold transmission in alignment

22. Apply a light coating of Mopar® High Temp Grease to the torque converter hub pocket in the rear pocket of the engine's crankshaft

23. Raise transmission and align the torque converter with the drive plate and transmission converter housing with the engine block.

24. Move transmission forward. Then raise, lower or tilt transmission to align the converter housing with engine block dowels while positioning filler tube into the filler tube bore.

25. Carefully work transmission forward and over engine block dowels until converter hub is seated in crankshaft. Verify that no wires, or the transmission vent hose, have become trapped between the engine block and the transmission.

26. Install two bolts to attach the transmission to the engine.

27. Install remaining torque converter housing to engine bolts. Tighten to 50 ft. lbs. (68 Nm).

28. Install transfer case, if equipped. Tighten transfer case nuts to 26 ft. lbs. (35 Nm).

29. Install rear support to transmission. Tighten bolts to 35 ft. lbs. (47 Nm).

30. Lower transmission onto crossmember and install bolts attaching transmission mount to crossmember. Tighten clevis bracket to crossmember bolts to 35 ft. lbs. (47 Nm). Tighten the clevis bracket to rear support bolt to 50 ft. lbs. (68 Nm).

31. Remove engine support fixture.

32. Install the transmission inspection cover. Tighten the bolts to 88 inch lbs. (10Nm).

33. Install the power bending bracket.

34. Install the transmission dust shield.

35. Connect gearshift cable to transmission.

36. Connect wires to solenoid and pressure switch assembly connector.

37. Connect wires to input and output speed sensor.

38. Connect wires to line pressure sensor. Be sure transmission harnesses are properly routed.

39. Install the differential pressure sensor bolt (if equipped). Tighten bolt to 88 inch lbs. (10Nm).

✳✳ WARNING

It is essential that correct length bolts be used to attach the converter to the driveplate. Bolts that are too long will damage the clutch surface inside the converter.

40. Install torque converter-to-driveplate bolts. Tighten bolts to 270 inch lbs. (31 Nm).

41. Connect cooler lines to transmission.

42. Install transmission fill tube bolt. Tighten bolt to 88 inch lbs. (10Nm).

43. Install exhaust components, if necessary.

44. Align and connect propeller shaft(s).

45. Adjust gearshift cable if necessary.

46. Install any skid plates removed previously.

47. Lower the vehicle.

48. Fill transmission with Mopar® ATF +4, Automatic Transmission Fluid.

AS68RC

1. Before servicing the vehicle, refer to the Precautions Section.

2. Disconnect the negative battery cable.

3. Raise and support the vehicle.

4. Remove any necessary skid plates.

5. Mark propeller shaft and axle companion flanges for assembly alignment.

6. Remove the rear propeller shaft.

7. Remove the front propeller shaft, if necessary.

8. Remove the engine to transmission inspection cover.

9. Remove the exhaust support bracket from the rear of the transmission.

10. Remove the exhaust particulate filter

11. Rotate crankshaft in clockwise direction until torque converter bolts (4) are accessible. Then remove bolts one at a time. Rotate crankshaft with socket wrench on dampener bolt.

✳✳ WARNING

Tag the orientation of all electrical connectors. Some electrical connectors may be interchangeable, damage to the electrical system may occur if the connectors are reversed.

12. Disconnect the input speed sensor, output speed sensor, electrical connectors and position the harness aside.

13. Disconnect the transmission valve body solenoid and pressure switch electrical connectors and position harness aside.

14. Disconnect the cooler line temperature sensor electrical connector and position harness aside.

15. Disconnect gearshift cable ball socket from transmission manual valve lever.

16. Remove the shift cable from the shift cable bracket.

17. Remove the shift cable bracket bolt and shift cable bracket.

18. Remove the bolt securing the differential pressure sensor to the transmission case, if equipped.

19. Disconnect the transmission vent hose from the transmission.

20. Support rear of engine with safety stand or jack.

➡️**Support the transmission where the transmission oil pan meets the transmission case.**

21. Raise transmission slightly with service jack to relieve load on crossmember and supports.

22. Remove bolts securing rear support and cushion to transmission and crossmember.

23. Remove transfer case, if necessary.

24. Remove the nuts securing the power bending bracket to extension housing, if equipped.

25. Disconnect transmission fluid cooler lines at transmission Jiffy Tite fittings with quick connect tool 9546.

26. Remove all remaining converter housing bolts.

27. Carefully work transmission and

torque converter assembly rearward off engine block dowels.

28. Hold torque converter in place during transmission removal.

29. Lower transmission and remove assembly from under the vehicle.

✳✳ WARNING

Verify that transmission is secure on the lifting device or work surface, the center of gravity of the transmission will shift when the torque converter is removed creating an unstable condition. The torque converter is a heavy unit. Use caution when separating the torque converter from the transmission.

30. To remove torque converter, carefully slide torque converter out of the transmission.

To install:

➡️**After the installation of the transmission, a quick learn must be performed using the scan tool.**

31. Check torque converter hub and hub drive flats for sharp edges burrs, scratches, or nicks. Polish the hub and flats with 320/400 grit paper and crocus cloth if necessary. The hub must be smooth to avoid damaging pump seal at installation.

32. If a replacement transmission is being installed, transfer any components necessary, such as the manual shift lever and shift cable bracket, from the original transmission onto the replacement transmission.

33. Lubricate oil pump seal lip with trans jell or petroleum jelly.

34. Align converter and oil pump.

35. Carefully insert converter in oil pump. Then rotate converter back and forth until fully seated in pump gears.

36. Check converter seating with steel scale (1) and straightedge (2). Surface of converter lugs should be at least 1.12 inch (28.2 mm) to rear of straightedge when converter is fully seated.

37. Temporarily secure converter with C-clamp.

38. Position transmission on jack and secure it with chains.

39. Check condition of converter driveplate. Replace the plate if cracked, distorted or damaged. Also be sure transmission dowel pins are seated in engine block and protrude far enough to hold transmission in alignment.

40. Apply a light coating of MOPAR® High Temp Grease to the torque converter hub pocket in the rear pocket of the engine's crankshaft.

41. Raise transmission and align the torque converter with the drive plate and transmission converter housing with the engine block.

42. Move transmission forward. Then raise, lower or tilt transmission to align the converter housing with engine block dowels.

43. Carefully work transmission forward and over engine block dowels until converter hub is seated in crankshaft. Verify that no wires, or the transmission vent hose, have become trapped between the engine block and the transmission.

44. Install the bolts to attach the transmission to the engine. Tighten the bolts to 47 inch lbs. (64 Nm).

45. It is essential that correct length bolts be used to attach the converter to the driveplate. Failure to follow this caution may result in transmission damage.

46. Rotate crankshaft with socket wrench on dampener bolt in clockwise direction and install NEW torque converter to driveplate bolts. Tighten bolts to 270 inch lbs. (31 Nm).

WARNING

If replacing a engine mount / bracket, be certain to inspect all other engine mounts in the system. Failure to follow this caution may result in damage to the vehicle.

47. Install the power bending bracket onto the extension housing, if equipped. Tighten the power bending bracket nuts to 22 ft. lbs. (30 Nm).

48. Install transfer case, if equipped. Tighten transfer case nuts to 26 ft. lbs. (35 Nm).

49. Install rear support to transmission. Tighten bolts to 35 ft. lbs. (47 Nm).

50. Lower transmission onto crossmember and install bolts attaching transmission mount to crossmember. Tighten clevis bracket to crossmember bolts to 35 ft. lbs. (47 Nm). Tighten the clevis bracket to rear support bolt to 50 ft. lbs. (68 Nm).

51. Remove engine support fixture.

WARNING

Install the electrical connectors correctly. Some electrical connectors may be interchangeable, damage to the electrical system may occur if the connectors are reversed.

52. Connect wire harnesses to solenoids and transmission range sensor assembly.

53. Install shift cable bracket and the shift cable bracket bolt. Tighten bolt to 20 ft. lbs. (27 Nm).

54. Install the shift cable into the shift cable bracket.

55. Connect gearshift cable ball socket from transmission manual valve lever.

56. Connect the wire harness to the input speed sensor and the output speed sensor.

57. Connect the electrical harness to torque converter temperature sensor and be certain transmission harnesses are properly routed.

58. Connect cooler lines to transmission.

59. Install transmission fill tube.

60. Install bolt securing the differential pressure sensor onto the transmission case. Tighten the bolt to 88 inch lbs. (10 Nm).

61. Install exhaust particulate filter.

62. Align and connect propeller shaft(s).

63. Adjust gearshift cable if necessary.

64. Install any skid plates removed previously.

65. Lower the vehicle.

66. Fill transmission with MOPAR® AS68RC Automatic Transmission Fluid.

MANUAL TRANSMISSION ASSEMBLY

REMOVAL & INSTALLATION

G56—Diesel Engines

1. Before servicing the vehicle, refer to the Precautions Section.
2. With vehicle in neutral, position vehicle on hoist.
3. Disconnect battery negative cable.
4. Remove shift boot bezel screws and slide boot upward on shift lever extension.
5. Remove shift lever extension from the shift tower and lever assembly.
6. Remove skid plate, if equipped.
7. Remove drain plug and drain fluid.
8. Mark propeller shaft/shafts and companion flange yoke/yokes for installation reference and remove propeller shaft/shafts.
9. Disconnect harness from clips on transmission housing.
10. Remove transfer case linkage 4x4 equipped.
11. Remove transfer case mounting nuts and remove transfer case 4x4 equipped.
12. Remove slave cylinder mounting nut and remove cylinder.
13. Remove starter motor, 5.7L structural dust cover bolts to clutch housing and dust shield bolts.

WARNING

On 5.7L, do not remove structural dust cover from engine block. If cover is removed clutch housing and structural dust cover must be aligned with the engine.

14. Remove exhaust bracket bolts and remove bracket.
15. Support engine with adjustable jack stand and wood block.
16. Support and secure transmission to a transmission jack with safety chains.
17. Remove transmission mount bolts.
18. Remove rear crossmember bolts and remove crossmember with transmission mount.
19. Remove bolts attaching transmission to the engine.
20. Move transmission rearward until input shaft is clear of clutch disc and pressure plate. Then lower jack and remove transmission from under vehicle.

To install:

21. Clean transmission front housing mounting surface.
22. Apply a light coat of Mopar® high temperature bearing grease or equivalent to contact surfaces of following components:
    - Release fork
    - Release fork ball stud
    - Release bearing slide
    - Input shaft splines
    - Release bearing bore
23. Support and secure transmission to jack.
24. Raise and align transmission input shaft with clutch disc, then slide transmission into place.
25. Install exhaust bracket.
26. Verify front housing is fully seated. Install transmission bolts without washers and tighten bolts into the engine to 30 ft. lbs. (41 Nm). Tighten the bolts with washers into the transmission to 50 ft. lbs. (68 Nm).
27. Install crossmember and tighten nuts to 75 ft. lbs. (102 Nm).
28. Install transmission mount bolts and tighten to 50 ft. lbs. (68 Nm).
29. Install front dust shield tighten bolt to 40 inch lbs. (4.5 Nm). On 5.7L, if structural dust cover was removed, install onto the transmission and engine.
30. Install structural dust cover and tighten the bolts to 40 ft. lbs. (54 Nm).
31. Install starter motor 5.7L.
32. Connect transmission harnesses to clips on case and connect switches.
33. Install slave cylinder and tighten cylinder nuts to 200 inch lbs. (23 Nm).
34. Install transfer case and transfer case linkage 4x4 equipped.
35. Remove transmission jack.

36. Install propeller shaft/shafts with reference marks aligned.

37. Install exhaust on the exhaust manifolds.

38. Fill transmission with lubricant. Correct fill level is to bottom edge of fill plug hole.

GETRAG 238—5.7L engines Engine

1. Before servicing the vehicle, refer to the Precautions Section.

2. With vehicle in neutral, position vehicle on hoist.

3. Disconnect battery negative cable.

4. Remove shift knob, boot, shift lever extension and console.

5. Remove 4WD shift boot if equipped and remove floor console.

6. Remove skid plate, if equipped.

7. Remove drain plug from rear housing and drain fluid.

8. Mark propeller shafts and companion flange yokes for installatio n reference and remove propeller shafts.

9. Disconnect harness from clips on transmission housing.

10. Remove transfer case linkage if equipped.

11. Remove transfer case mounting nuts and remove transfer case if equipped.

12. Remove slave cylinder mounting nut and remove cylinder.

13. Remove starter motor, structural dust cover bolts to clutch housing, dust shield bolt and suspension crossmember.

✳✳ WARNING

Do not remove structural dust cover from engine block. If cover is removed clutch housing and cover must be aligned with the engine.

14. Remove exhaust pipe from the exhaust manifolds.

15. Support engine with adjustable jack stand and wood block.

16. Support and secure transmission to a transmission jack with safety chains.

17. Remove bolts from the rear transmission mount.

18. Remove the rear crossmember and transmission mount.

19. Remove transmission to the engine bolts.

20. Move transmission rearward until input shaft is clear of clutch disc and pressure plate. Then lower jack and remove transmission from under vehicle.

To install:

21. Clean transmission front housing mounting surface.

22. Apply a light coat of Mopar® high temperature bearing grease or equivalent to contact surfaces of following components:
- Release fork
- Release fork ball stud
- Release bearing slide
- Input shaft splines
- Release bearing bore

23. Support and secure transmission to jack.

24. Raise and align transmission input shaft with clutch disc, then slide transmission into place.

25. Verify front housing is fully seated. Install transmission bolts without washers (1) and tighten bolts into the engine to 30 ft. lbs. (41 Nm). Tighten the bolts with washers into the transmission to 50 ft. lbs. (68 Nm).

26. Install rear crossmember and tighten nuts to 75 ft. lbs. (102 Nm).

27. Install transmission rear mount bolts and tighten to 50 ft. lbs. (68 Nm).

28. Install front dust shield tighten bolt to 40 inch lbs. (4.5 Nm).

29. Install structural cover to transmission bolts and tighten to 40 ft. lbs. (54 Nm).

30. Install starter motor.

31. Install suspension crossmember and tighten nuts to 75 ft. lbs. (102 Nm).

32. Connect transmission harnesses to clips on case and connect switches.

33. Install slave cylinder and tighten cylinder nuts to 200 inch lbs. (23 Nm).

34. Install transfer case and transfer case linkage if equipped.

35. Remove transmission jack.

36. Install propeller shafts with reference marks aligned.

37. Install exhaust on the exhaust manifolds.

38. Fill transmission with lubricant. Correct fill level is to bottom edge of fill plug hole.

39. Install inner shift boot, extension lever, console, boot and shift knob.

CLUTCH DRIVEN DISC & PRESSURE PLATE

REMOVAL & INSTALLATION

See Figure 15.

1. Before servicing the vehicle, refer to the Precautions Section.

2. Support engine with wood block and adjustable jack stand, to prevent strain on engine mounts.

3. Remove transmission and transfer case, if equipped.

4. If pressure plate will be reused, mark the position on flywheel with paint or scriber. Also note location marks on the pressure next to the bolt holes. The mark will be a L or a circle with an X in it.

5. Insert clutch alignment tool through pressure plate and into pilot bushing, to hold disc in place while removing bolts.

6. Loosen pressure plate bolts evenly, a few threads at a time and in a diagonal pattern to prevent warping the plate.

7. Remove bolts completely and remove pressure plate, disc and alignment tool.

To install:

✳✳ WARNING

Before installing a clutch disc on the Diesel engine with Dual Mass Flywheel and self-adjusting pressure plate, the pressure plate must be reset. Refer to clutch disc adjustment for procedure. Failure to reset the pressure will result in damage to the clutch disc.

8. Check runout and free operation of new clutch disc.

9. Lubricate crankshaft pilot bearing with a NLGI—2 rated grease.

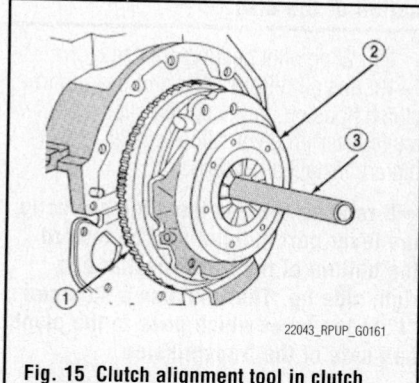

Fig. 15 Clutch alignment tool in clutch disc hub shown

10. Install clutch alignment tool in clutch disc hub with the raised side of hub is facing away from the flywheel.

➡**Flywheel side is imprinted on the disc face.**

11. Install alignment tool in pilot bearing and position disc on the flywheel.

12. Position pressure plate over disc and onto the flywheel.

➡**Over the wear life of a clutch disc the pressure plate will lose some of its clamp load. It is recommended when replacing a worn clutch, the pressure plate is replaced at the same time.**

13. Align and hold pressure plate in position and install bolts finger tight.

14. Tighten bolts evenly and a few threads at a time in a diagonal pattern.

❋❋ WARNING

Bolts must be tightened evenly and to specified torque to avoid warping pressure plate cover.

15. Tighten pressure plate bolts as follows:
- 5.7L—37 ft. lbs. (50 Nm).
- 5.9L & 6.7L Diesel—22 ft. lbs. (30 Nm).

16. Remove release lever and release bearing from clutch housing. Apply Mopar® high temperature bearing grease to bore of release bearing, release lever contact surfaces and release lever pivot stud.

17. Apply light coat of Mopar® high temperature bearing grease to splines of transmission input shaft and to release bearing slide surface of the transmission front bearing retainer.

❋❋ WARNING

Do not over lubricate shaft splines. This can result in grease contamination of the disc.

18. Wipe pilot bearing surface clean.

19. Install release lever and bearing in clutch housing. Verify spring clips that retain lever on pivot ball and release bearing are installed properly.

➡**If release lever is installed correctly, the lever part number will be toward the bottom of the transmission and right side up. There is also a stamped "I" in the lever which goes to the pivot ball side of the transmission.**

20. Install transmission and transfer case if equipped.

21. Check fluid level in clutch master cylinder and depress clutch pedal several time.

ADJUSTMENTS

See Figures 16 and 17.

Perform the following procedure, when replacing only the clutch disc on Diesel vehicles with Dual Mass Flywheel and self-adjusting pressure plate. The pressure plate must be reset before installing a new disc.

1. Support pressure plate flange with press blocks on a press.

2. Center press ram on the pressure plate diaphragm spring fingers.

3. Compress the diaphragm spring fingers, until tension is released from the stepped adjusting ring.

4. Place two screwdrivers against two

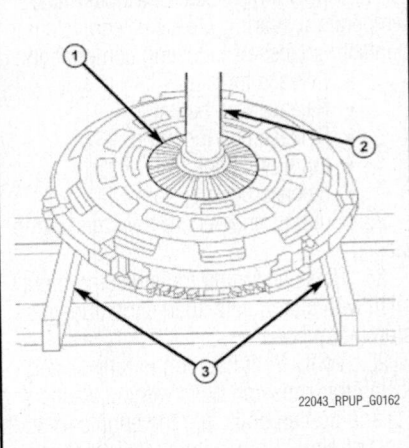

Fig. 16 Compressing the diaphragm spring fingers

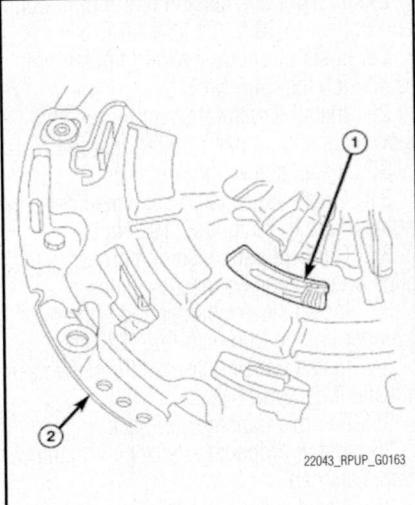

Fig. 17 Rotate stepped adjuster rings counterclockwise

of the three stepped adjusting ring (1) tension spring stops, just ahead of the adjusting ring tension springs on the pressure plate (2).

5. Rotate stepped adjusting ring (1) on the pressure plate (2) counterclockwise until the coil springs are fully compressed. Then hold adjusting ring while releasing the press pressure.

6. Remove the screwdrivers.

7. The pressure plate is now adjusted for a new clutch disc.

CLUTCH MASTER & SLAVE CYLINDER

REMOVAL & INSTALLATION

See Figures 18 and 19.

❋❋ WARNING

The hydraulic linkage has a quick disconnect at the slave cylinder. This fitting should never be disconnected or tampered with. Once the hydraulic line is connected to the slave cylinder, it should never be disconnected.

1. Before servicing the vehicle, refer to the Precautions Section.

2. Raise and support vehicle.

3. Remove nuts attaching slave cylinder to studs on clutch housing.

4. Remove heat shield over hydraulic line.

5. Remove slave cylinder from clutch housing.

6. Remove the plastic clip securing the hydraulic line to the dash panel from the lower dash panel flange.

7. Remove the plastic clip securing hydraulic line to the dash panel from the upper dash panel stud.

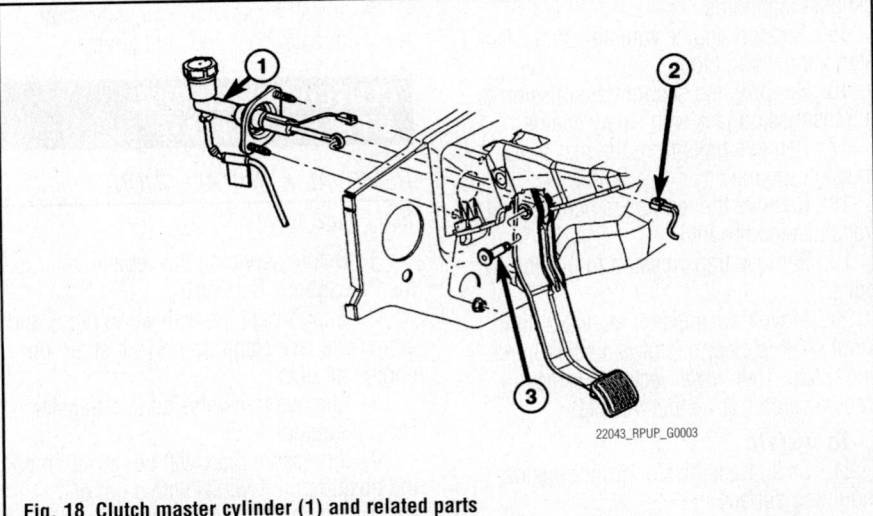

Fig. 18 Clutch master cylinder (1) and related parts

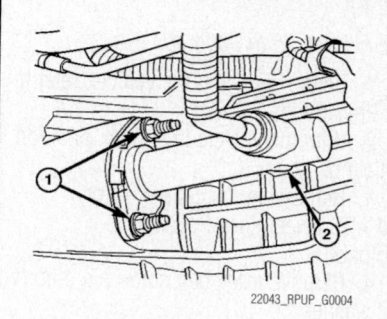

Fig. 19 Clutch slave cylinder and retaining nuts

8. Lower the vehicle.

9. Disconnect clutch pedal interlock switch connector.

10. Remove clutch master cylinder rod pin.

11. Verify that cap on clutch master cylinder reservoir is tight. This will avoid spillage during removal.

12. Remove clutch master cylinder nuts holding cylinder to the dash panel.

13. Remove clutch cylinders, reservoir and connecting lines from vehicle.

To install:

14. Position cylinders and connecting line in vehicle engine compartment. Position the clutch hydraulic line against the dash panel and behind all engine hoses and wiring.

15. Apply a light coating of grease to the inside diameter of the master cylinder push rod eye.

16. Install clutch master cylinder on dash panel and tighten clutch master cylinder nuts to 21 ft. lbs. (28 Nm).

17. Install clutch master cylinder push rod pin.

18. Connect clutch pedal position interlock switch connector.

19. Install the plastic clip securing hydraulic line to the dash panel into the lower dash panel flange.

20. Install the plastic clip securing hydraulic line to the dash panel onto the upper dash panel stud.

21. Raise the vehicle.

22. Install slave cylinder and verify cylinder rod is properly seated in release lever.

23. Install and tighten slave cylinder nuts to 17 ft. lbs. (23 Nm).

24. If new clutch linkage is being installed, connect the clutch hydraulic line to the clutch slave cylinder.

25. Install heat shield over hydraulic line.

26. Operate the linkage several times to verify proper operation.

HYDRAULIC SYSTEM BLEEDING

LINKAGE BLEED

1. Remove the reservoir cap taking care not to damage the diaphragm. If fluid level is not up to the step in the reservoir add D.O.T. 4 brake fluid.

✳✳ WARNING

Use only D.O.T. 4 compatible brake fluid. Substitutes will cause system malfunction.

2. Slowly depressing the clutch pedal while opening the clutch slave cylinder bleed screw.

3. Holding down the clutch pedal and tighten bleed screw to 11–14 ft. lbs. (15–20 Nm).

4. Repeat Step 2 and Step 3 two times then check fluid level in reservoir.

5. Pump clutch pedal rapidly a minimum of 10 times. If clutch pedal still feels spongy, repeat Step 2 through Step 5.

MASTER CYLINDER BLEED

1. Remove the reservoir cap taking care not to damage the diaphragm. If the fluid level is not up to the step in the reservoir, add D.O.T. 4 brake fluid.

✳✳ WARNING

Use only D.O.T. 4 compatible brake fluid. Other than D.O.T 4 will cause system malfunction.

2. Open the male quick connect coupling by depressing the poppet in the coupling while depress the clutch pedal to the floor.

3. Close the quick connect coupling by releasing the poppet while holding the clutch pedal to the floor.

4. Release the pedal.

5. Repeat Step 3 through Step 5 two more times and check fluid level.

6. Couple the system back together. Then pump clutch pedal rapidly a minimum of 10 times.

7. If clutch pedal still feels spongy repeat Step 3 through Step 7.

TRANSFER CASE ASSEMBLY

REMOVAL & INSTALLATION

See Figure 20.

1. Before servicing the vehicle, refer to the Precautions Section.

2. Shift the transfer case into **2WD**.

3. Mark front and rear propeller shafts for alignment reference.

4. Support the transmission with jack stand.

5. Remove the transfer case skid plate, if equipped.

6. Disconnect front and rear propeller shafts at transfer case.

7. Disconnect transfer case shift motor and mode sensor wire connectors.

8. Disconnect transfer case vent hose.

9. Support transfer case with transmission jack.

10. Secure transfer case to jack with chains.

11. Remove nuts attaching the transfer case to transmission.

12. Pull transfer case and jack rearward to disengage transfer case.

13. Remove transfer case from under vehicle.

To install:

14. Mount transfer case on a transmission jack.

15. Secure transfer case to jack with chains.

16. Position transfer case under vehicle.

17. Align transfer case and transmission shafts and install transfer case onto the transmission.

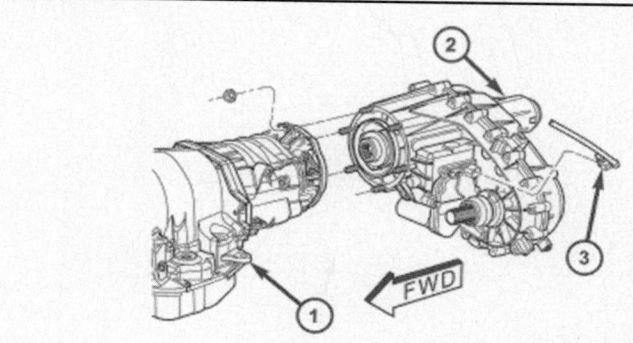

Fig. 20 Transfer case (2) removal from transmission (1) wire connectors (3)

18. Install and tighten transfer case attaching nuts to 23 ft. lbs. (31 Nm).

19. Connect the vent hose.

20. Connect the shift motor and mode sensor wiring connectors. Secure wire harness to clips on transfer case.

21. Align and connect the propeller shafts.

22. Fill transfer case with correct fluid as listed below:

23. Recommended lubricant for the NV241 GENII, NV271, NV243, NV244 GENII, and NV273 transfer cases is MOPAR® ATF +4, Automatic Transmission Fluid.

24. Recommended lubricant for the NV246 transfer case is MOPAR®NVG 246 Automatic Transmission Fluid or equivalent.

25. Install skid plate, if equipped.

26. Remove transmission jack and support stand.

27. Lower vehicle and verify transfer case shift operation.

FRONT AXLE SHAFT, BEARING & SEAL

REMOVAL & INSTALLATION

C205F

See Figures 21 through 23.

1. Before servicing the vehicle, refer to the Precautions Section.

2. Remove halfshaft from vehicle.

3. Clean axle seal area.

4. Remove O-ring and snap ring from axle shaft.

5. Remove axle with remove 8420A (2,3,4) and slide hammer C-3752.

To install:

6. Wipe axle shaft tube bore clean.

7. Install new axle shaft seal with installer 8694.

8. Install axle shaft with new snap ring and verify axle shaft snap ring is seated in side gear.

9. Install O-ring and snap ring on axle shaft.

10. Install halfshaft.

11. Verify differential fluid level and add fluid if necessary.

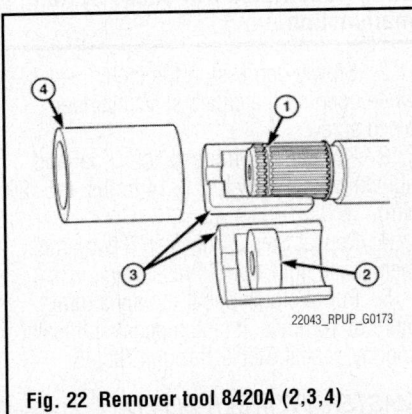

Fig. 22 Remover tool 8420A (2,3,4)

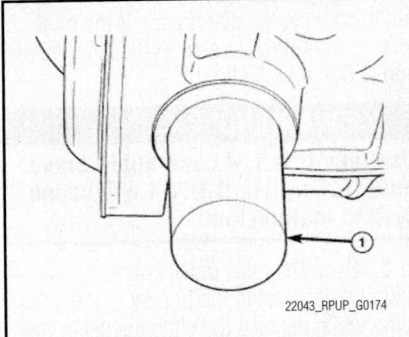

Fig. 23 Axle seal installation with tool 8694

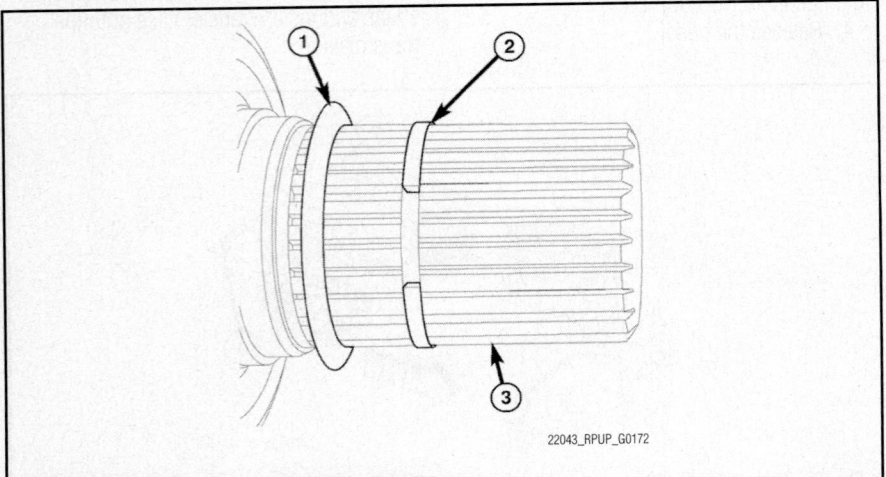

Fig. 21 O-ring (1), snap ring (2), axle shaft (3)

9¼ AA

See Figures 25 through 30.

1. Before servicing the vehicle, refer to the Precautions Section.

2. With the vehicle in neutral, position vehicle on hoist.

3. Remove brake caliper, rotor and ABS wheel speed sensor if equipped.

4. Remove axle shaft cotter pin, hub nut and washer.

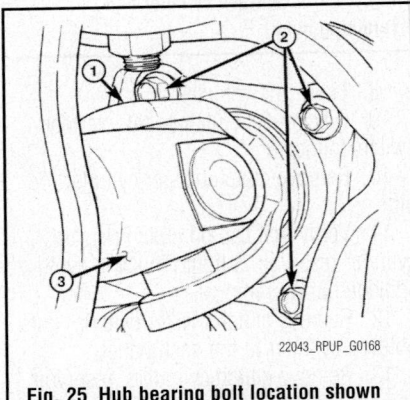

Fig. 25 Hub bearing bolt location shown

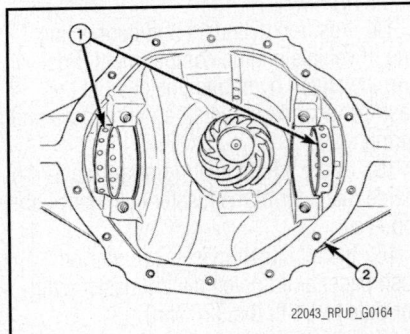

Fig. 26 Differential housing (2), bearing adjusters (1)

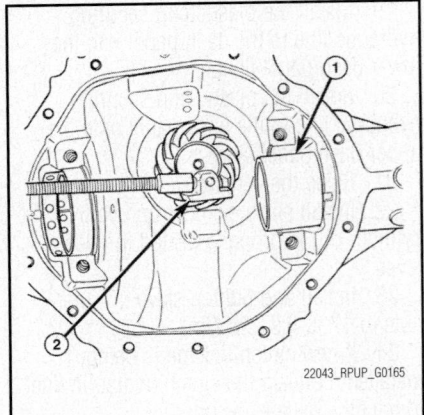

Fig. 27 Extractor rod 6310 with extractor foot 6310-9 shown

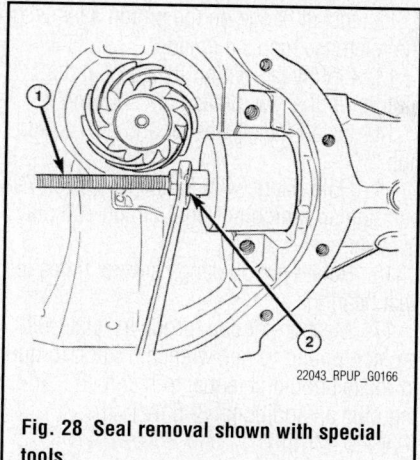

Fig. 28 Seal removal shown with special tools

22043_RPUP_G0166

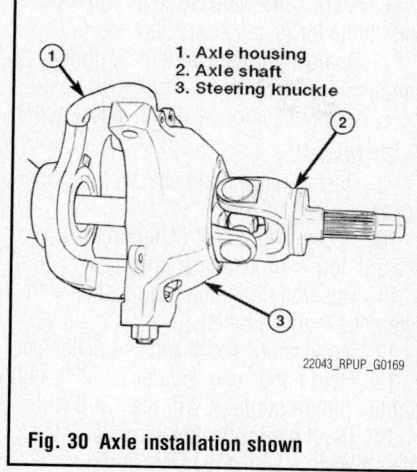

1. Axle housing
2. Axle shaft
3. Steering knuckle

22043_RPUP_G0169

Fig. 30 Axle installation shown

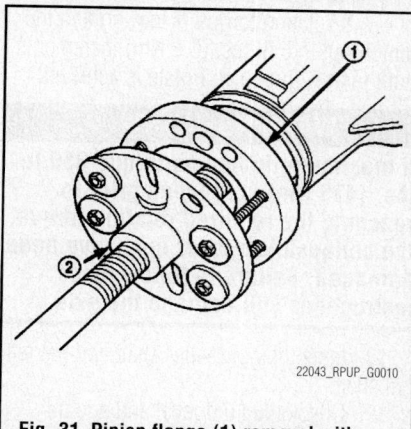

22043_RPUP_G0010

Fig. 31 Pinion flange (1) removal with C—452 (2)

5. Remove four hub bearing bolts from the back of the steering knuckle.

6. Remove hub bearing from the steering knuckle.

7. Remove axle shaft from steering knuckle and axle housing.

8. Remove differential from differential housing.

9. Remove differential bearing adjusters.

10. Remove axle seals located behind adjusters with receiver 8498 and extractor 6310.

11. Install receiver 8498 (1) into the adjuster bore.

12. Install extractor rod 6310 with extractor foot 6310-9 (2) through the receiver and axle seal.

13. Install extractor plate 6310-2 and nut 6310-7 (2) on the extractor rod (1).

14. Tighten nut (2) on extractor rod (1) to pull seal into the receiver.

15. Remove and discard seal.

To install:

16. Install axle seal on Installer Cups 8885-2 (1) (3) and position cups with seals into the housing.

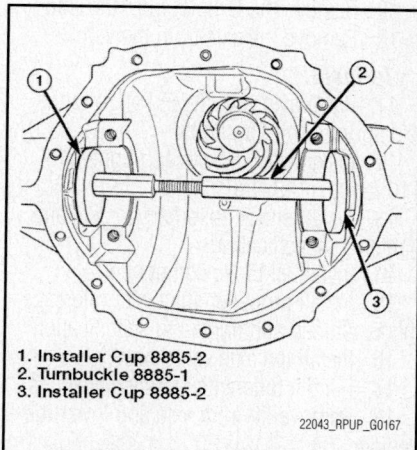

1. Installer Cup 8885-2
2. Turnbuckle 8885-1
3. Installer Cup 8885-2

22043_RPUP_G0167

Fig. 29 Seal installation with special tools

➡**Seals are installed with the axle guide facing outward.**

17. Install Turnbuckle 8885-1(2) into installer cups and expand the turnbuckle until the seals bottom out in the housing.

18. Install adjuster (1) into the differential housing (2).

19. Install differential in housing.

20. Clean axle shaft and apply a thin film of Mopar® wheel bearing grease to the shaft splines and hub bore.

21. Install axle shaft through the steering knuckle and into the differential side gears.

22. Install hub bearing in the knuckle.

23. Install hub bearing bolts and tighten to 149 ft. lbs. (202 Nm).

24. Install ABS wheel speed sensor, brake rotor and caliper.

25. Install axle washer and nut. Tighten axle nut to 132 ft. lbs. (179 Nm).

26. Rotate axle several 5 to 10 times to seat the wheel bearing.

27. Tighten axle nut to final torque of 263 ft. lbs (356 Nm).

28. Align nut to next cotter pin hole and install new cotter pin.

FRONT PINION SEAL

REMOVAL & INSTALLATION

C205FD

See Figure 31.

1. Before servicing the vehicle, refer to the Precautions Section.

2. With axle in **2WD** remove front propeller shaft and left halfshaft.

3. Rotate pinion gear three or four times and verify pinion rotates smoothly.

4. Record pinion torque to rotate with an inch pound torque wrench, for installation reference.

5. Position Holder 6719 against the

companion flange and install a four bolts and washers into the threaded holes and tighten the bolts.

6. Remove pinion nut.

7. Mark a line across the pinion shaft and flange for installation reference.

8. Remove the companion flange with Remover C-452.

9. Remove pinion seal with a seal puller.

To install:

10. Apply a light coating of gear lubricant on the lip of pinion seal

11. Install seal with Installer 8695 and Handle C-4171.

12. Install flange on the pinion shaft with the reference marks aligned.

13. Install companion flange onto the pinion with Installer C-3718 and Holder 6719A.

14. Position holder against the companion flange and install four bolts and washers into the threaded holes. Tighten the bolt and washer so that the holder is held to the flange.

15. Install a new pinion nut onto the pinion shaft and tighten the pinion nut until there is zero bearing end-play

❄❄ WARNING

Do not exceed 200 ft. lbs. (271 Nm) the minimum tightening torque when installing the companion flange at this point. Never loosen pinion nut to decrease pinion bearing rotating torque and never exceed specified preload torque. Failure to follow these instructions will damage the axle.

16. Measure pinion Torque To Rotate with an inch pound torque wrench. Pinion Torque To Rotate should be equal to recorded reading plus an additional 5 inch. lbs. (0.56 Nm).

17. If rotating torque is low, tighten the pinion nut in 5 ft. lbs. (6.8 Nm) increments until pinion Torque To Rotate is achieved.

✳✳ WARNING

If maximum tightening torque 350 ft. lbs. (475 Nm) is reached prior to reaching the required rotating torque, the collapsible spacer may have been damaged. Failure to follow these instructions will damage the axle.

18. Install the propeller shaft and the left halfshaft.

19. Check the fluid level and add as needed.

275FBI

See Figures 32 and 33.

1. Before servicing the vehicle, refer to the Precautions Section.

2. With the vehicle in neutral, position vehicle on hoist.

3. Remove the propeller shaft.

4. Bend the pinion flange nut collar lock out of the pinion shaft keyway.

5. Hold the pinion flange with Holder C-3281 and remove pinion flange nut.

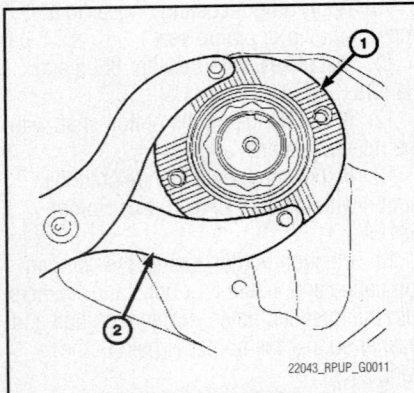

Fig. 32 Pinion flange (1) with Holder C — 3281 (2)

6. Mark a line across the pinion shaft and flange for installation reference.

7. Remove pinion flange with pinion flange puller 8992.

8. Remove pinion seal with a seal puller.

To install:

9. Install new pinion seal with installer 10069.

10. Apply a light coat of Teflon thread sealant, to pinion flange splines.

11. Position flange on pinion shaft with reference marks aligned.

12. Install pinion flange and new pinion nut.

13. Hold flange with Holder C-3281 and tighten pinion nut to 369 ft. lbs. (500 Nm).

14. Bend pinion flange nut collar into pinion keyway with a hammer and punch.

15. Install propeller shaft with reference marks aligned.

16. Check the fluid level and add as needed.

9 ¼ AA

See Figure 33.

1. Before servicing the vehicle, refer to the Precautions Section.

2. Mark propeller shaft and pinion flange for installation reference.

3. Remove the propeller shaft.

4. Remove the hub bearings and axle shafts.

5. Rotate pinion gear three or four times.

6. Record pinion torque to rotate with an inch pound torque wrench for installation reference.

7. Hold pinion flange with flange wrench 8979 and remove pinion flange nut and washer.

8. Mark a line across the pinion shaft and flange for installation reference.

9. Remove pinion flange with pinion flange puller 8992.

10. Remove pinion seal with a seal puller.

To install:

11. Install new pinion seal with Installer 8882 and Handle C-4171.

12. Install flange on the pinion shaft with the reference marks aligned.

13. Lightly tap pinion flange onto the pinion, until a few threads are showing.

14. Install flange washer and new pinion nut.

15. Hold flange with flange wrench 8979 and tighten pinion nut until pinion end play is taken up.

16. Rotate pinion flange several times to seat bearings.

17. Measure pinion torque to rotate with an inch pound torque wrench. Pinion torque to rotate should be equal to recorded reading plus an additional 3–5 inch. lbs. (0.40–0.57 Nm).

18. If torque to rotating is low, tighten the pinion nut in 5 ft. lbs. (6.8 Nm) increments until pinion torque to rotate is achieved.

19. Rotate pinion several times then verify pinion torque to rotate again.

20. Install the axle shafts and hub bearings.

21. Install propeller shaft with reference marks aligned.

REAR AXLE HOUSING

REMOVAL & INSTALLATION

All Axles, Except 302RBI

See Figure 35.

1. Before servicing the vehicle, refer to the Precautions Section.

2. With vehicle in neutral, position vehicle on hoist.

3. Position a lift under axle and secure lift to the axle.

4. Remove all brake components.

5. Mark propeller shaft and companion flange for installation alignment reference.

6. Remove the propeller shaft.

7. Remove the axle vent hose.

8. Remove shock absorbers from axle.

9. Remove the U-bolts from the axle.

10. Remove the axle from the vehicle.

To install:

11. Raise axle with lift and align to the leaf spring centering bolts.

12. Install axle U-bolts and tighten to 110 ft. lbs. (149 Nm).

13. Install shock absorbers to axle and tighten to specification.

14. Install all brake components.

15. Install propeller shaft with reference marks aligned and tighten to specification.

16. Install the axle vent hose.

17. Fill the differential to specifications.

18. Remove lift from axle and lower the vehicle.

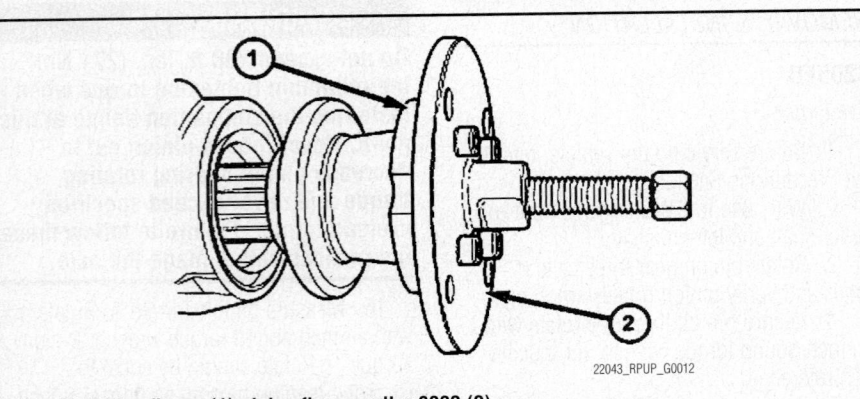

Fig. 33 Pinion flange (1) pinion flange puller 8992 (2)

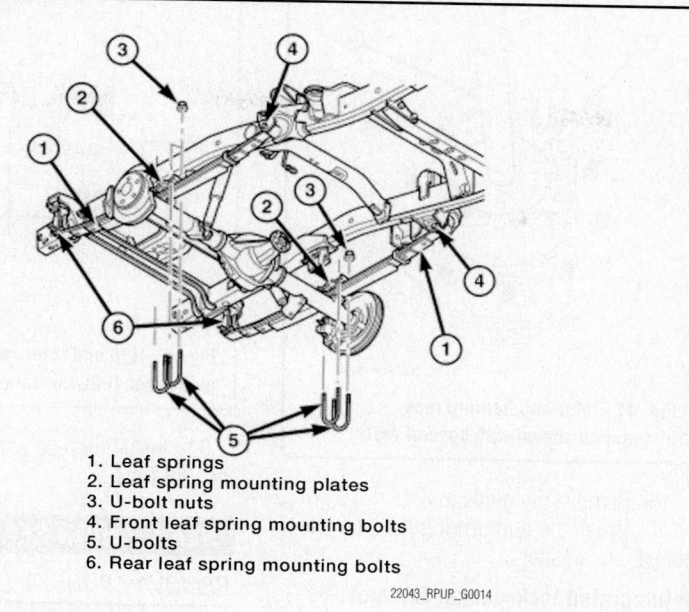

1. Leaf springs
2. Leaf spring mounting plates
3. U-bolt nuts
4. Front leaf spring mounting bolts
5. U-bolts
6. Rear leaf spring mounting bolts

22043_RPUP_G0014

Fig. 35 Rear axle and related parts shown

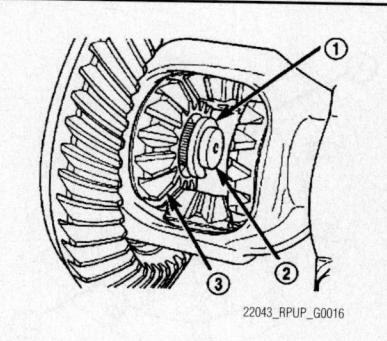

22043_RPUP_G0016

Fig. 37 Remove C-lock (1) from axle shaft (2)

302RBI Axle

1. Before servicing the vehicle, refer to the Precautions Section.

2. With vehicle in neutral, position vehicle on hoist.

3. Position a lift under axle and secure lift to the axle.

4. Mark propeller shaft and companion flange for installation alignment reference.

5. Remove the propeller shaft from pinion flange.

6. Remove axle vent hose axle housing.

7. Remove wiring harness from the brake sensor.

8. Remove brake calipers, rotors, brake lines and park cables from axle housing.

9. Remove shock absorbers and stabilizer bar from the axle.

10. Remove U-bolts nuts from the axle.

11. Remove U-bolts and lower the axle from the vehicle.

To install:

12. Raise axle with lift and align to the leaf spring centering bolts.

13. Install axle U-bolts and tighten nuts to 336 ft. lbs. (455 Nm).

14. Install shock absorbers to axle and tighten nuts to 118 ft. lbs. (160 Nm).

15. Install stabilizer bar to axle and tighten nuts to 48 ft. lbs. (65 Nm).

16. Install rotors, brake calipers, brake lines and park cables to the axle housing.

17. Install the wiring harness to brake sensor.

18. Install the axle vent hose to axle housing.

19. Install propeller shaft to pinion

flange with reference marks aligned and tighten to specification.

20. Fill differential to specifications.

21. Remove lift from axle and lower the vehicle.

REAR AXLE SHAFT, BEARING & SEAL

REMOVAL & INSTALLATION

C-Clip Type

See Figures 36 and 37.

1. Before servicing the vehicle, refer to the Precautions Section.

2. Remove or disconnect the following:
   • Rear wheel
   • Brake drum
   • Differential cover
   • Differential gear shaft retainer
   • Differential gear shaft

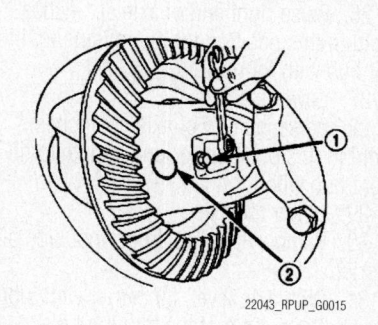

22043_RPUP_G0015

Fig. 36 Differential gear shaft retainer (1) pinion gear shaft (2)

• C-clip
• Axle shaft
• Axle seal
• Axle bearing

To install:

3. Install or connect the following:
   • Axle bearing
   • Axle seal
   • Axle shaft
   • C-clip
   • Differential gear shaft. Use Loctite® and tighten the retainer to 14 ft. lbs. (19 Nm).
   • Differential cover. Tighten the bolts to 30 ft. lbs. (41 Nm).
   • Brake drum
   • Rear wheel

4. Fill the axle assembly with gear oil and check for leaks.

Non C-Clip Type

See Figures 38 through 43.

1. Before servicing the vehicle, refer to the Precautions Section.

2. Remove axle bolts from axle flange.

3. Remove the axle shaft from axle.

4. With Socket 10051 remove hub nut with integrated lock washer from hub spindle.

5. Slide the hub/rotor with bearings off hub spindle with the use of Guide tool 10064.

6. Remove outer bearing from hub.

7. Remove the hub seal from the back of the hub with seal puller.

8. Remove the inner bearing from hub.

9. Remove the outer and inner bearing race from hub with a hammer and brass drift.

To install:

10. Install inner and outer hub bearing race, with seal and race driver kit.

11. Lubricate and install the inner hub bearing into hub.

12. Install the hub seal with seal installer kit.

13. Lubricate and install the outer hub bearing into hub.

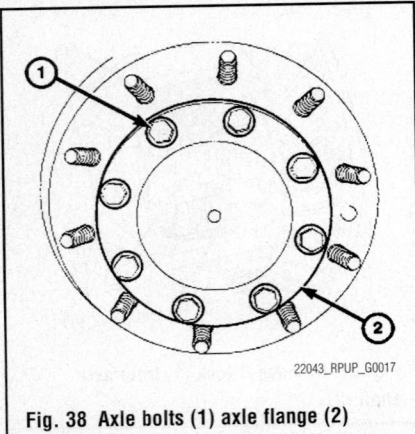

Fig. 38 Axle bolts (1) axle flange (2)

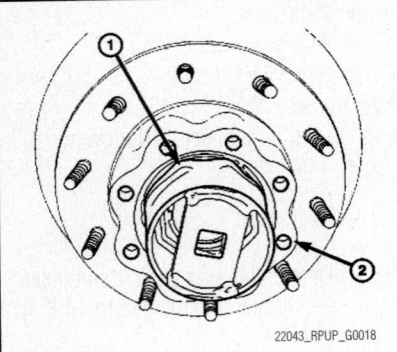

Fig. 39 Hub nut removal shown with socket 10051

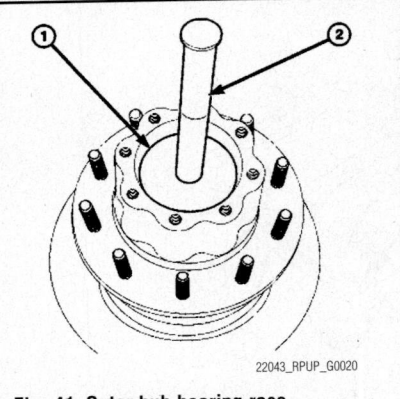

Fig. 41 Outer hub bearing race installation shown with special tools

16. Remove the guide tool.

17. Install the hub bearing nut with integrated lock washer.

➡**Integrated lock washer tab must be aligned with the spindle keyway.**

18. Tighten the hub nut with Socket 10051 to 70 ft. lbs. (95 Nm) while rotating the hub. Then back off nut 90 degrees and retighten nut to 30 ft. lbs. (41 Nm). This will set hub to zero end-play.

19. Install a new O-ring on axle flange.

20. Install the axle shaft.

21. Install axle bolts through axle flange and tighten to 98 ft. lbs. (133 Nm).

22. Remove fill plug, from right side of carrier.

23. With the axle level, fill carrier with lubricant to the bottom of the fill plug hole.

24. Install fill plug and tighten to 50 ft. lbs. (68 Nm).

❊❊ WARNING

Wheel hub cavities must be filled with lubricate before using axle. Failure to follow these instructions will result in hub bearing damage.

25. Wheel hub cavities oil fill instruction are as follows:

26. Raise right end of axle six inches. Hold in this position for one minute to fill left hub with lubricate.

27. Lower the axle.

28. Raise left end of axle six inches. Hold in this position for one minute to fill right hub with lubricate.

29. Lower the axle.

30. Remove fill plug, from right side of carrier.

31. With axle level, fill carrier with lubricant to the bottom of the fill plug hole.

➡**Axle will require approximately 40 oz. (1.18 L) of additional lubricant.**

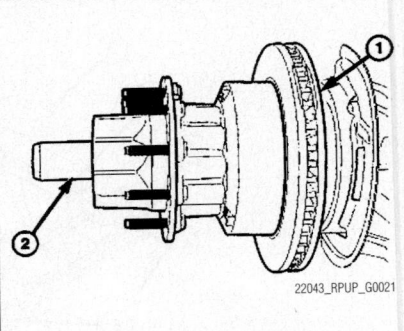

Fig. 42 Hub and rotor installation with guide tool 10064 installed

32. Install fill plug and tighten to 50 ft. lbs. (68 Nm).

REAR PINION SEAL

REMOVAL & INSTALLATION

C-Clip Type

1. Before servicing the vehicle, refer to the Precautions Section.

2. Remove or disconnect the following:
   • Wheels
   • Brake rotors
   • Driveshaft

3. Check the bearing preload with an inch lb. torque wrench.

4. Remove the pinion flange and seal.

To install:

➡**Use a new pinion nut for assembly.**

5. Install the new pinion seal and flange. Tighten the nut to 210 ft. lbs. (285 Nm).

6. Check the bearing preload. The bearing preload should be equal to the reading taken earlier, plus 5 inch lbs.

7. If the preload torque is low, tighten the pinion nut in 5 inch lb. increments until the torque value is reached. Do not exceed 350 ft. lbs. (474 Nm) pinion nut torque.

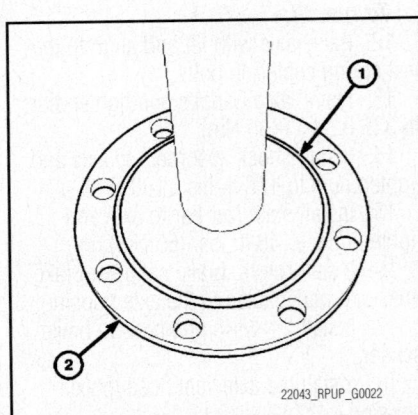

Fig. 43 O-ring (1) and Axle flange (2) shown

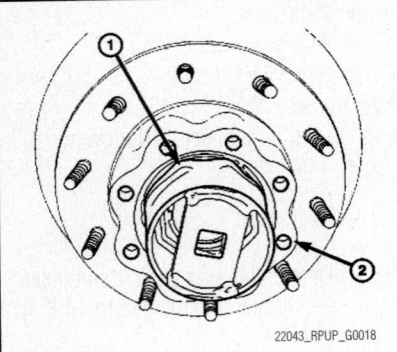

Fig. 40 Inner bearing race (1) removal shown from hub (2)

14. Install the hub and rotor Guide 10064 into the axle spindle.

15. Carefully install the hub and rotor over Guide 10064 onto the axle spindle.

❊❊ WARNING

Never support hub with just the inner bearing and seal. Failure to follow these instructions will result in damaging the hub seal.

8. If the pinion bearing preload torque cannot be attained at maximum pinion nut torque, replace the collapsible spacer.

9. Install or connect the following:
- Driveshaft
- Brake rotors
- Wheels

10. Fill the axle assembly with gear oil and check for leaks.

Non C-Clip Type

1. Before servicing the vehicle, refer to the Precautions Section.

2. Remove or disconnect the following:
- Wheels
- Brake rotors or drums

- Driveshaft

3. Check the bearing preload with an inch lb. torque wrench.

4. Remove the pinion flange and seal.

To install:

➡ **Use a new pinion nut for assembly.**

5. Install the new pinion seal, flange and new pinion nut.

6. Check the bearing preload. The bearing preload should be equal to the reading taken earlier, plus 5 inch lbs.

7. If the preload torque is low, tighten the pinion nut in 5 inch lb. increments until the torque value is reached. Do not exceed 260 ft. lbs. (353 Nm) pinion nut torque.

➡ **For 302RBI axles the pinion nut should be tightened to 689 ft. lbs. (937 Nm) with a torque multiplier (and torque wrench.**

8. If the pinion bearing preload torque cannot be attained at maximum pinion nut torque, remove one or more pinion preload shims.

9. Install or connect the following:
- Driveshaft
- Brake rotors or drums
- Wheels

10. Fill the axle assembly with gear oil and check for leaks.

ENGINE COOLING

ENGINE FAN

REMOVAL & INSTALLATION

5.7L Engine

See Figure 44.

> ❈❈ **WARNING**
>
> **If the viscous fan drive is replaced because of mechanical damage, the cooling fan blades should also be inspected. Inspect for fatigue cracks, loose blades, or loose rivets that could have resulted from excessive vibration. Replace fan blade assembly if any of these conditions are found. Also inspect water pump bearing and shaft assembly for any related damage due to a viscous fan drive malfunction.**

1. Before servicing the vehicle, refer to the Precautions Section.

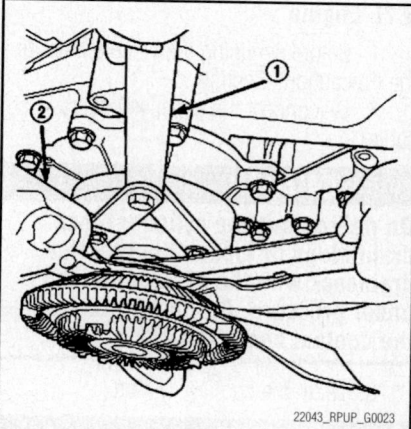

Fig. 44 Viscous fan drive assembly removal

2. Disconnect negative battery cable from battery.

3. Remove coolant reserve/overflow container from fan shroud and lay aside. **Do Not** disconnect the hoses or drain coolant from the container.

4. The thermal viscous fan drive/fan blade assembly is attached (threaded) to the water pump hub shaft. Remove the fan blade/viscous fan drive assembly from the water pump by turning the mounting nut counterclockwise as viewed from the front. Threads on the viscous fan drive are **RIGHT-HAND** A 36 mm fan wrench should be used to prevent pulley from rotating.

➡ **Do not unbolt the fan blade assembly from viscous fan drive at this time.**

5. Remove the fan shroud-to-radiator mounting bolts.

6. Pull the lower shroud mounts out of the radiator tank clips.

7. Remove the fan shroud and fan blade/viscous fan drive assembly as a complete unit from vehicle.

8. After removing the fan blade/viscous fan drive assembly, **do not** place the viscous fan drive in a horizontal position. If stored horizontally, silicone fluid in the viscous fan drive could drain into its bearing assembly and contaminate lubricant.

> ❈❈ **WARNING**
>
> **Do not remove water pump pulley-to-water pump bolts. This pulley is under spring tension**

9. Remove four bolts securing fan blade assembly to viscous fan drive.

> ❈❈ **WARNING**
>
> **Some engines equipped with serpentine drive belts have reverse rotating**

fans and viscous fan drives. They are marked with the word REVERSE to designate their usage. Installation of the wrong fan or viscous fan drive can result in engine overheating.

To install:

➡ **Viscous Fan Drive Fluid Pump Out Requirement: After installing a new viscous fan drive, bring the engine speed up to approximately 2000 rpm and hold for approximately two minutes. This will ensure proper fluid distribution within the drive.**

10. Install fan blade assembly to the viscous fan drive. Tighten the bolts to 18 ft. lbs. (24 Nm).

11. Position the fan shroud and the fan blade/viscous fan drive assembly to the vehicle as a complete unit.

12. Install the fan shroud.

13. Install the fan blade/viscous fan drive assembly to the water pump shaft. Tighten mounting nut to 37 ft. lbs. (50 Nm).

14. Install the coolant reserve/overflow container to the fan shroud.

15. Connect the negative battery cable.

5.9L & 6.7L Diesel Engines

See Figures 45 and 46.

> ❈❈ **WARNING**
>
> **If the electronically controlled viscous fan drive is replaced because of mechanical damage, the cooling fan blades should also be inspected. Inspect for fatigue cracks, or chipped blades that could have resulted from excessive vibration. Replace fan blade assembly if any of these conditions are found. Also inspect wiring harness and connectors for damage.**

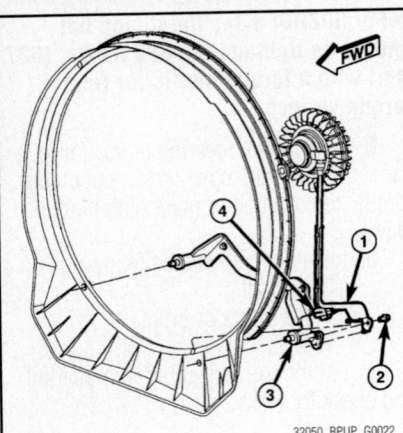

Fig. 45 View of the fan wiring bracket (1), bracket mounting bolts (2), shroud mounting bracket (3), viscous fan connector (4)—5.9L and 6.7L diesel engines

1. Before servicing the vehicle, refer to the Precautions Section.
2. Disconnect the battery negative cables.
3. Remove fan shroud-to-engine bracket nuts.
4. Detach the electronically controlled viscous fan electrical connector from the lower fan shroud bracket if equipped.
5. Remove wiring bracket -to-lower fan shroud bracket mounting bolt.
6. Remove the fan drive wire harness support from fan shroud.

⁂ CAUTION

Do not remove the fan pulley bolts. This pulley is under spring tension.

7. The electronically controlled viscous fan drive/fan blade assembly is attached (threaded) to the fan pulley shaft. Remove the fan blade/fan drive assembly from fan pulley by turning the mounting nut counterclockwise (as viewed from front). Threads on the viscous fan drive are RIGHT-HAND. A 36mm Fan Wrench can be used. Place a bar or screwdriver between the fan pulley bolts to prevent pulley from rotating.

➡ **It may be necessary to loosen the top two fan shroud brackets. Removal of the engine mounted fan shroud brackets is not necessary unless removing or installing the engine.**

8. Collapse fan shroud toward front of vehicle and remove fan drive/fan blade and fan shroud as an assembly.

⁂ WARNING

The electronically controlled viscous fan drive is vibration and impact sensitive, especially at the electrical connectors. Do not drop the unit.

9. Remove the six fan blade-to-viscous fan drive mounting bolts.
10. Inspect the fan for cracked, chipped or damaged fan blades.

To install:

➡**Viscous Fan Drive Fluid Pump Out Requirement: After installing a new viscous fan drive, bring the engine speed up to approximately 2000 rpm and hold for approximately two minutes. This will ensure proper fluid distribution within the drive.**

11. Install fan blade assembly to electrically controlled viscous fan drive. Tighten mounting bolts to 18 ft. lbs. (24 Nm).
12. Loosen both upper engine mounted fan shroud brackets.
13. Make sure lower engine mounted fan shroud bracket bolts are tightened to 18 ft. lbs. (24 Nm).
14. Position fan/fan drive assembly inside fan shroud and lower into position.
15. Install the viscous fan drive assembly onto fan pulley hub shaft. Tighten mounting nut to 85 ft. lbs. (115 Nm).
16. Install the fan drive wire harness support to fan shroud.
17. Install viscous fan wiring bracket onto lower fan shroud bracket. Tighten nut to 18 ft. lbs. (24 Nm).
18. Install fan shroud onto fan shroud brackets.
19. Connect the fan drive wire harness.
20. Install fan shroud to upper engine fan shroud brackets. Tighten nut finger-tight.
21. Tighten upper engine fan shroud bracket bolts to 18 ft. lbs. (24 Nm).
22. Tighten four fan shroud bracket nuts to 18 ft. lbs. (24 Nm).
23. Make sure of fan tip clearance all the way around inside of fan shroud.
24. Connect the battery negative cables.

RADIATOR

REMOVAL & INSTALLATION

5.7L Engine

1. Before servicing the vehicle, refer to the Precautions Section.
2. Disconnect the negative battery cable.

⁂ CAUTION

Do not remove the cylinder block drain plugs or loosen the radiator draincock with the system hot and under pressure. Serious burns from the coolant can occur.

3. Drain the cooling system.

⁂ WARNING

Constant tension hose clamps are used on most cooling system hoses.

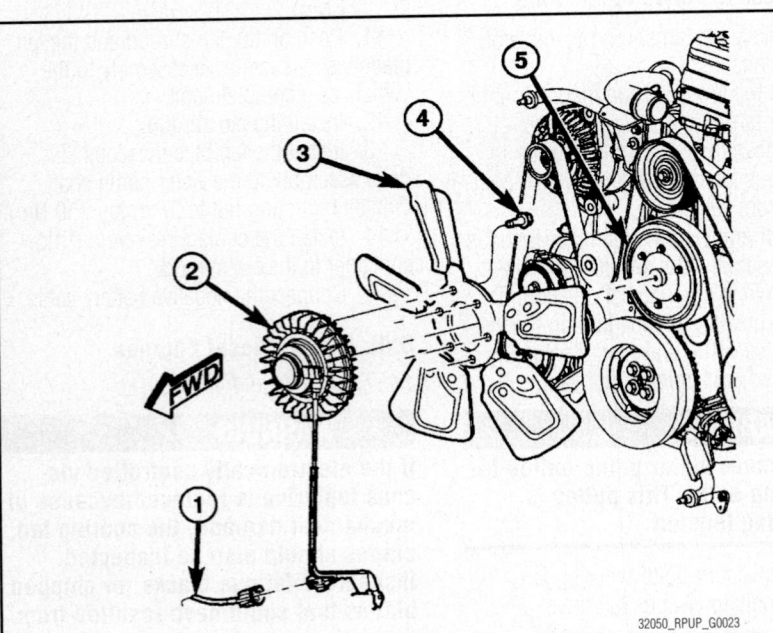

Fig. 46 Exploded view of the electrical connector (1), viscous fan drive (2), fan blade (3), bolts (4) and radiator fan pulley (5)—5.9L and 6.7L diesel engines

When removing or installing, use only tools designed for servicing this type of clamp. Always wear safety glasses when servicing constant tension clamps. A number or letter is stamped into the tongue of constant tension clamps. If replacement is necessary, use only an original equipment clamp with a matching number or letter and the correct width.

4. Remove the hose clamps and hoses from radiator.

5. Remove the coolant reserve/overflow tank hose from the radiator filler neck.

6. Remove the coolant reserve/overflow tank from the fan shroud (pull straight up). The tank slips into slots on the fan shroud.

7. Unclip the power steering hoses from the fan shroud.

8. Disconnect the electrical connectors at the windshield washer reservoir tank and remove the tank.

9. Remove the fan shroud mounting bolts and pull up and out of the radiator tank clips. Position the shroud rearward over the fan blades towards engine.

10. Disconnect the transmission cooler lines from the transmission cooler, then plug the transmission lines and cooler to prevent leakage.

11. Disconnect the power steering lines from the power steering cooler, then plug the power steering lines and cooler to prevent leakage.

12. Remove the two radiator upper mounting bolts.

13. Lift the radiator straight up and out of the engine compartment. Take care not to damage cooling fins or tubes on the radiator and oil coolers when removing.

➡The radiator is equipped with one alignment dowel on the bottom of the outlet tank and one retaining bracket on the front side of the inlet tank. Both features have rubber insulators attached to them that must be present. The alignment dowel fits into a hole at the bottom of the front end sheet metal vertical support post and the support bracket rests on top of the lower radiator closure tube.

To install:

14. Position the fan shroud over the fan blades rearward towards engine.

15. Install the rubber insulators to the lower radiator mounting features (alignment dowel and support bracket at the lower part of the radiator).

16. Lower the radiator into position

while guiding the alignment dowel into the vertical post bracket.

17. Position and seat the lower radiator support bracket onto the lower radiator closure tube.

18. Install the upper radiator mounting bolts. Tighten bolts to 90 inch lbs. (10 Nm).

19. Connect the lower radiator hose and install the clamp in the proper position.

20. Connect the power steering hoses to the power steering oil cooler and install the clamps.

21. Connect the transmission oil cooler lines to the transmission oil cooler and install the secondary latches.

22. Position the fan shroud into the mounting clips on the radiator tanks and secure with bolts. Tighten the bolts to 75 inch lbs. (8.5 Nm).

23. Secure the power steering hoses into the clip on the lower fan shroud.

24. Install the windshield washer reservoir tank and connect the hose and electrical connector.

25. Install coolant reserve/overflow container hose(s) to radiator filler neck and secure properly with clamps.

26. Install coolant reserve/overflow container or degas container to fan shroud and tighten the bolts to 75 inch lbs. (8.5 Nm).

27. Connect upper radiator hose and install clamp.

28. Install the battery negative cable.

29. Fill the cooling system with coolant.

30. Operate the engine until it reaches normal operating temperature. Check cooling system fluid levels.

5.9L & 6.7L Diesel Engines

See Figure 47.

1. Before servicing the vehicle, refer to the Precautions Section.

2. Disconnect both battery negative cables.

3. Drain the cooling system.

4. Disconnect ambient air temperature sensor electrical connector and mass airflow sensor electrical connector (If equipped).

5. Remove air box and turbocharger inlet tube.

6. Remove coolant tank hose, washer bottle hose and the positive battery cable from the fastening clips located on top of the radiator.

7. Remove hose clamps and hoses from radiator.

8. Remove fan shroud mounting nuts from mounting brackets.

9. Pull shroud toward front of vehicle to clear mounting brackets

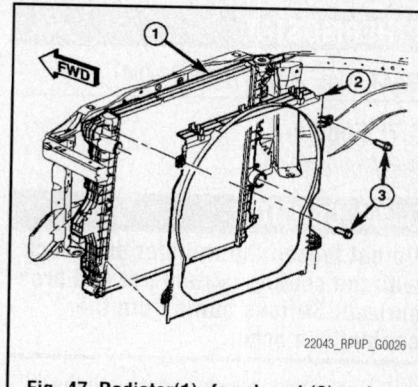

Fig. 47 Radiator(1), fan shroud (2) and bolts (3)

10. Turn shroud slightly and push toward engine to gain clearance for radiator.

To install:

11. Install rubber insulators to alignment dowels at lower part of radiator.

12. Lower the radiator into position while guiding the two alignment dowels into lower radiator support.

➡**Different alignment holes are provided in the lower radiator support for each engine application.**

13. Install two upper radiator mounting bolts. Tighten bolts to 105 inch lbs. (12 Nm).

14. If equipped, connect transmission cooler lines to transmission cooler. Inspect quick connect fittings for debris and install until an audible **click** is heard. Tug on lines to verify connection.

15. Position power steering cooler on the radiator and tighten nuts to 90 inch lbs. (10 Nm).

16. Position fan shroud on brackets.

17. Install fan shroud mounting nut. Tighten nut to 18 ft. lbs. (24 Nm).

18. Install the coolant recovery container.

19. Position coolant recovery tank hose, washer bottle hose and the positive battery cable into the clips located on the top of the radiator.

20. Install the air box and turbocharger inlet hose. Tighten clamps to 35 inch lbs. (4 Nm).

21. Connect mass airflow sensor electrical connector and ambient air temp sensor electrical connector (if equipped).

22. Position the heater controls to the **Full Heat** position.

23. Fill the cooling system with coolant.

24. Operate engine until it reaches normal temperature. Check cooling system and automatic transmission (if equipped) fluid levels.

THERMOSTAT

REMOVAL & INSTALLATION

5.7L Engine

See Figure 48.

✳✳ CAUTION

Do not loosen the radiator draincock with the cooling system hot and pressurized. Serious burns from the coolant can occur.

Do not waste reusable coolant. If the solution is clean, drain the coolant into a clean container for reuse.

If the thermostat is being replaced, be sure that the replacement is the specified thermostat for the vehicle model and engine type.

1. Before servicing the vehicle, refer to the Precautions Section.
2. Disconnect the negative battery cable.
3. Drain the cooling system
4. Remove the radiator hose clamp and radiator hose at the thermostat housing.
5. Remove the thermostat housing mounting bolts, thermostat housing and thermostat.

To install:

6. Position the thermostat and housing on the front cover.
7. Install the thermostat housing bolts. Tighten the bolts to 112 inch lbs. (13 Nm).
8. Install the radiator hose onto the thermostat housing.
9. Fill the cooling system.
10. Connect negative battery cable.
11. Start and warm the engine. Check for leaks.

5.9L Diesel Engine

See Figure 49.

1. Before servicing the vehicle, refer to the Precautions Section.
2. Disconnect the battery negative cables.
3. Drain cooling system until coolant level is below thermostat
4. Remove radiator hose clamp and hose from thermostat housing.
5. Remove the three water thermostat housing bolts and remove thermostat housing.
6. Clean the mating surfaces of thermostat housing and clean the thermostat seat groove at the top of the thermostat housing.

➡**The thermostat for 5.9L and the 6.7L are different and are not interchangeable. Use caution when replacing the thermostat to ensure the proper part number is reinstalled.**

7. Inspect the thermostat seal for cuts or nicks. Replace if damaged.
8. Install the thermostat into the groove in the top of the cylinder head
9. Install the thermostat housing and bolts. Tighten the bolts to 89 inch lbs. (10 Nm).
10. Install the radiator upper hose and clamp.
11. Fill the cooling system.
12. Connect the battery negative cables.

13. Start the engine and check for coolant leaks. Run engine to check for proper thermostat operation.

6.7L Diesel Engine

See Figure 50.

1. Before servicing the vehicle, refer to the Precautions Section.
2. Disconnect the battery negative cables.
3. Remove vent plug near EGR cooler.
4. Drain cooling system until coolant level is below the thermostat.
5. Disconnect exhaust gas pressure sensor electrical connector.
6. Remove exhaust pressure tube from thermostat housing.
7. Remove EGR cooler cross over tube.
8. Remove radiator hose clamp and hose from thermostat housing.
9. Remove heat shield.
10. Remove the three water outlet-to-cylinder head bolts and remove the water outlet connector.
11. Clean the mating surfaces of the thermostat housing and clean the thermostat seat groove at the top of the thermostat housing.

To install:

12. Inspect the thermostat seal for cuts or nicks. Replace if damaged.
13. Install the thermostat into the groove in the top of the cylinder head.
14. Install the thermostat housing and bolts. Tighten the bolts to 89 inch lbs. (10 Nm).
15. Install heat shield. Tighten bolts to 79 inch lbs. (9 Nm).

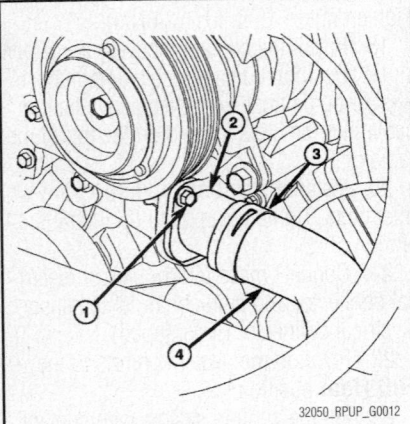

Fig. 48 View of the retaining bolt (1), thermostat housing (2), clamp (3) and radiator hose (4)—5.7L engines engine

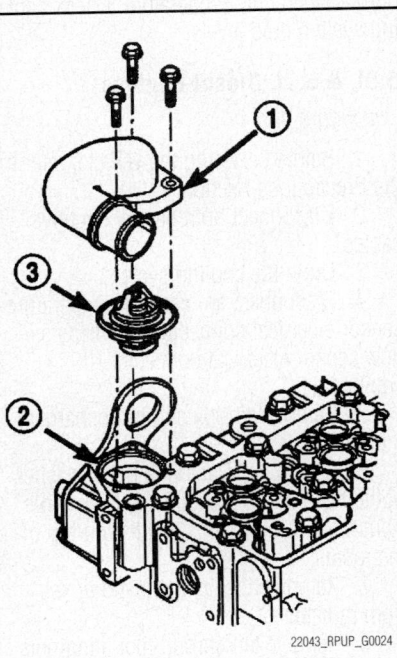

Fig. 49 Engine thermostat, housing, and bolts—5.9L Diesel engine

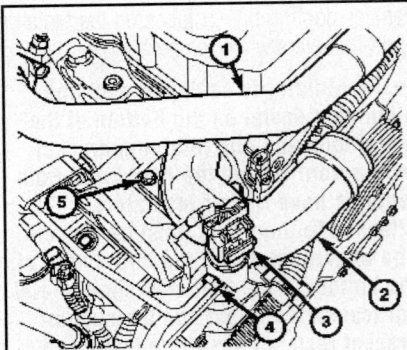

1. EGR cross over tube
2. Thermostat housing
3. Exhaust pressure sensor electrical connector
4. Exhaust pressure tube fitting
5. Thermostat housing bolts

Fig. 50 Engine thermostat housing and related parts—6.7L diesel engine

16. Install exhaust pressure tube. Tighten to 88 inch lbs. (10 Nm).

17. Connect exhaust pressure sensor electrical connector.

18. Install EGR cross over tube.

19. Install the P-clip and bolt. Tighten to 70 inch lbs. (8 Nm).

20. Install the radiator upper hose and clamp.

21. Fill the cooling system with coolant.

22. Connect the battery negative cables.

23. Start the engine and check for coolant leaks. Run engine to check for proper thermostat operation.

WATER PUMP

REMOVAL & INSTALLATION

5.7L Engine

1. Before servicing the vehicle, refer to the Precautions Section.

2. Drain the cooling system.

3. Remove or disconnect the following:
- Negative battery cable
- Accessory drive belt
- Engine cooling fan
- Coolant recovery bottle
- Washer bottle
- Fan shroud
- A/C compressor and alternator brace
- Idler pulleys
- Belt tensioner
- Radiator hoses

- Heater hoses
- Water pump

To install:

4. Install or connect the following:
- Water pump and tighten the bolts to 18 ft. lbs. (24 Nm)
- Heater hoses
- Radiator hoses
- Idler pulleys
- A/C compressor and alternator brace
- Fan shroud
- Washer bottle
- Coolant recovery bottle
- Accessory drive belt
- Negative battery cable
- Negative battery cable

5. Fill the cooling system.

6. Start the engine and check for leaks.

5.9L & 6.7L Diesel Engines

See Figure 51.

1. Before servicing the vehicle, refer to the Precautions Section.

2. Disconnect both negative battery cables.

3. Drain the cooling system.

4. Disconnect ambient air temp sensor electrical connector and mass airflow sensor electrical connector (if equipped).

5. Remove turbocharger inlet tube and air filter housing.

6. Remove the alternator assembly.

7. Remove the accessory drive belt.

8. Remove water pump mounting bolts.

9. Remove O-ring from water pump.

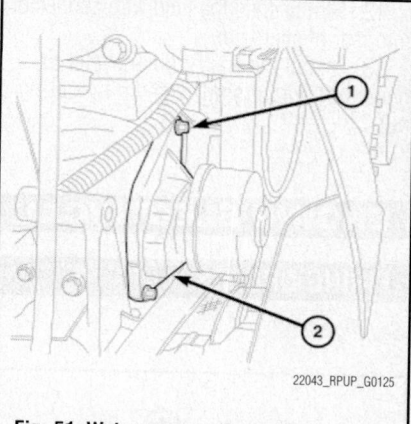

22043_RPUP_G0125

Fig. 51 Water pump and mounting bolt view

To install:

10. Install new O-ring seal in groove on water pump.

11. Install water pump with the weep hole facing downward. Tighten mounting bolts to 18 ft. lbs. (24 Nm).

12. Install the alternator assembly. Tighten mounting bolts and nut to 30 ft. lbs. (41 Nm).

13. Install accessory drive belt.

14. Install air box and tube assembly.

15. Install air filter housing.

16. Fill cooling system.

17. Connect both negative battery cables.

18. Start and warm the engine. Check for leaks.

ENGINE ELECTRICAL

ALTERNATOR

REMOVAL & INSTALLATION

5.7L Engine

1. Before servicing the vehicle, refer to the Precautions Section.

2. Remove or disconnect the following:
- Negative battery cable
- Accessory drive belt
- Alternator harness connectors
- Support bracket nuts and bolt
- Mounting bolts and alternator

➡**The 3.7L and 4.7L engine has 1 vertical and 2 horizontal bolts.**

To install:

3. Before servicing the vehicle, refer to the Precautions Section.

4. Install the alternator and tighten the bolts 30 ft. lbs. (41 Nm). Position support bracket to front of generator and install bolt

and nuts. Tighten bolt/nuts to 30 ft. lbs. (41 Nm).

5. Install or connect the following:
- Alternator harness connectors. Tighten B+ terminal eyelet mounting nut to 8.8 ft. lbs. (12 Nm).
- Accessory drive belt
- Negative battery cable

5.9L & 6.7L Diesel Engines

✳✳ CAUTION

Disconnect both negative battery cables from both batteries before removing battery output wire (b+ wire) from alternator. Failure to do so can result in injury or damage to electrical system.

1. Before servicing the vehicle, refer to the Precautions Section.

CHARGING SYSTEM

2. Disconnect both negative battery cables at both batteries.

3. Remove the alternator drive belt.

4. Remove the upper mounting bracket bolt.

5. Remove the lower mounting bracket bolt and nut.

6. Remove the alternator from engine.

7. Unsnap the plastic insulator cap from B+ output terminal.

8. Remove the B+ terminal mounting nut at rear of generator. Disconnect terminal from alternator.

9. Disconnect field wire connector at rear of alternator by pushing on connector tab.

To install:

10. Position alternator to upper and lower mounting brackets and install upper bolt and lower bolt / nut.

11. Tighten all bolts/nut to 30 ft. lbs. (41 Nm).

12. Firmly snap the field wire connector into rear of alternator.

13. Install the B+ terminal eyelet to generator output stud. Tighten mounting nut.

ENGINE ELECTRICAL

FIRING ORDERS

See Figure 52.

➡ Use dielectric grease on each of the spark plug boots before installing the coil.

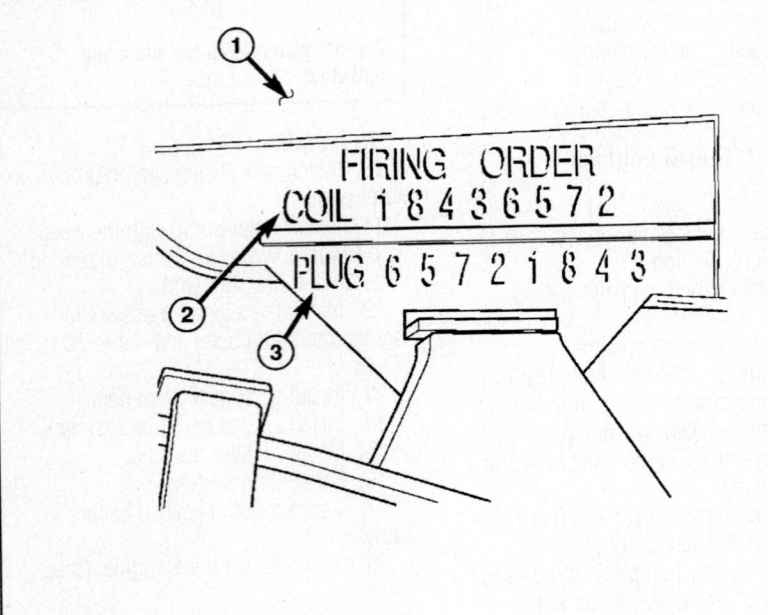

1 - TOP OF INTAKE MANIFOLD
2 - CYLINDER FIRING ORDER (IGNITION COIL NUMBER)
3 - CORRESPONDING SPARK PLUG NUMBER

67189-RAMT-G14

Fig. 52 Engine firing order—5.7L engines Distributorless ignition

IGNITION COIL

REMOVAL & INSTALLATION

5.7L Engine

See Figure 53.

1. Disconnect the electrical connector from coil.

2. Clean area at the base of the coil with compressed air before removal.

3. Remove two mounting bolts (note that mounting bolts are retained to coil).

4. Carefully pull up coil from valve cover.

5. Remove coil from vehicle.

To install:

6. Using compressed air, blow out any dirt or contaminants from around top of spark plug.

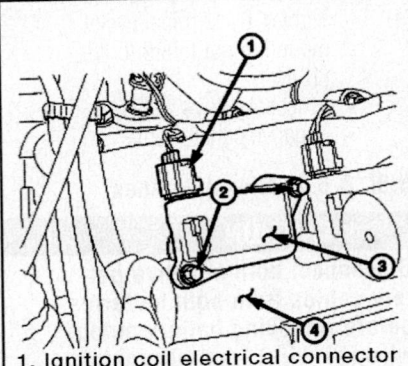

1. Ignition coil electrical connector
2. Mounting bolts
3. Ignition coil
4. Valve cover

22043_RPUP_G0027

Fig. 53 Ignition coil—5.7L engines

WARNING

When installing a serpentine accessory drive belt, the belt MUSTbe routed correctly. The water pump may be rotating in the wrong direc- tion if the belt is installed incorrectly, causing the engine to overheat.

14. Install the alternator drive belt.

15. Install both negative battery cables to both batteries.

IGNITION SYSTEM

7. Position ignition coil into valve cover and push onto spark plugs.

8. Position ignition coil into valve cover and push onto spark plugs.

9. Install 2 coil mounting bolts. Tighten to 62 inch lbs. (7 Nm).

10. Connect the electrical connector to coil by snapping into position.

IGNITION TIMING

ADJUSTMENT

The ignition timing is controlled by the Powertrain Control Module (PCM). No adjustment is necessary or possible.

SPARK PLUGS

REMOVAL & INSTALLATION

5.7L Engine

➡**Each individual spark plug is located under each ignition coil. Each individual ignition coil must be removed to gain access to each spark plug.**

1. Before servicing the vehicle, refer to the Precautions Section.

2. Remove necessary air filter tubing at throttle body.

3. Prior to removing the ignition coil, spray compressed air around coil base at cylinder head.

4. Prior to removing spark plug, spray compressed air into cylinder head opening. This will help prevent foreign material from entering combustion chamber.

5. Remove spark plug from cylinder head using a quality socket with a rubber or foam insert. Also check condition of ignition coil O-ring and replace as necessary.

6. Inspect spark plug condition.

To install:

➡**Special care should be taken when installing spark plugs into the cylinder head spark plug wells. Be sure the plugs do not drop into the plug wells as electrodes can be damaged.**

✳✳ WARNING

Always tighten spark plugs to the specified torque. Over tightening can cause distortion resulting in a change in the spark plug gap or a cracked porcelain insulator.

7. Start the spark plug into the cylinder head by hand to avoid cross threading.

8. The **5.7L** is equipped with torque critical design spark plugs. Do not exceed 15 ft. lbs. Tighten spark plugs to 13 ft. lbs. (18 Nm).

9. Before installing ignition coils, check condition of coil O-ring and replace as necessary. To aid in coil installation, apply silicone to coil O-ring.

10. Install ignition coils.

STARTER

REMOVAL & INSTALLATION

5.7L Engine

1. Before servicing the vehicle, refer to the Precautions Section.

2. Remove or disconnect the following:
   • Negative battery cable

➡**Depending on drivetrain configuration, a support bracket may be used.**

   • Starter mounting bolts
   • Starter solenoid harness connections
   • Starter

To install:

3. Connect the starter solenoid wiring connectors.

4. Install the starter and torque the bolts to 50 ft. lbs. (68 Nm).

5. Install the negative battery cable and check for proper operation.

5.9L Diesel Engine

See Figure 54.

1. Before servicing the vehicle, refer to the Precautions Section.

2. Disconnect and isolate both negative battery cables at both batteries.

3. Raise and support vehicle.

4. Remove 3 starter mounting bolts.

5. Move starter motor towards front of vehicle far enough for nose of starter pinion housing to clear housing. Always support starter motor during this process. Do not let starter motor hang from wire harness.

6. Tilt nose downwards and lower starter motor far enough to access and remove nuts securing starter wiring harness

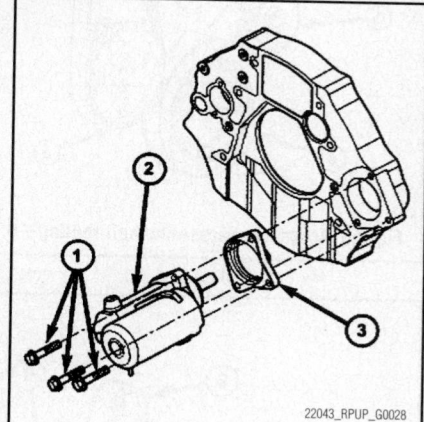

Fig. 54 Starter mounting bolts (1), starter motor (2), and spacer plate (3)

22043_RPUP_G0028

to starter. Do not let starter motor hang from wire harness.

➡**Certain diesel engines use an aluminum spacer. Note position and orientation of spacer before removal.**

7. Remove the starter motor from the engine.

To install:

8. If equipped, position and hold aluminum spacer to rear of starter while positioning starter to engine.

9. Connect solenoid wire to starter motor. Tighten nut to 4.4 ft. lbs. (6 Nm).

10. Position the battery cable to starter stud. Install and tighten battery cable nut to 10.3 ft. lbs. (14 Nm).

➡**Do not allow starter motor to hang from wire harness.**

11. Position the starter motor to transmission.

12. If equipped with automatic transmission, slide cooler tube bracket into position.

13. Install and tighten 3 starter mounting bolts to 32 ft. lbs. (43 Nm).

14. Lower the vehicle.

15. Connect both negative battery cables to both batteries.

6.7L Diesel Engine

1. Before servicing the vehicle, refer to the Precautions Section.

2. Disconnect and isolate both negative battery cables at both batteries.

3. Raise and support vehicle.

4. Disconnect the solenoid electrical connector.

5. Remove the battery cable mounting nut.

6. Remove the battery cable from stud.

7. Remove three starter mounting bolts.

8. Remove the starter motor from engine.

To install:

9. Connect solenoid wire to starter motor. Tighten nut to 4.4 ft. lbs. (6 Nm).

10. Position the battery cable to starter stud. Install and tighten battery cable nut to 10.3 ft. lbs. (14 Nm).

➡**Do not allow starter motor to hang from wire harness.**

11. Position the starter motor to transmission.

12. Install and tighten 3 starter mounting bolts to 32 ft. lbs. (43 Nm).

13. Lower the vehicle.

14. Connect both negative battery cables to both batteries.

ENGINE MECHANICAL

ACCESSORY DRIVE BELTS

ACCESSORY BELT ROUTING

See Figures 55 through 57.

INSPECTION

Inspect the drive belt for signs of glazing or cracking. A glazed belt will be perfectly smooth from slippage, while a good belt will have a slight texture of fabric visible. Cracks will usually start at the inner edge of the belt and run outward. All worn or damaged drive belts should be replaced immediately.

ADJUSTMENT

Belt tension is not adjustable. Belt adjustment is maintained by an automatic (spring load) belt tensioner.

REMOVAL & INSTALLATION

5.7L Engine

1. Remove the air intake tube between intake manifold and air filter assembly.
2. Insert a suitable square drive ratchet into the square hole on belt tensioner arm.
3. Release the belt tension by rotating the tensioner **clockwise**. Rotate belt tensioner until belt can be removed from pulleys.
4. Remove the drive belt.
5. Gently release tensioner.

To install:

➡ **When installing accessory drive belt onto pulleys, make sure that belt is properly routed and all V-grooves make proper contact with pulleys.**

6. Position the drive belt over all pulleys except for the water pump pulley.
7. Rotate tensioner **clockwise** and slip the belt over the water pump pulley.
8. Gently release tensioner.
9. Install the air intake tube between intake manifold and air filter assembly.

5.9L & 6.7L Diesel Engines

1. A ½ inch square hole is provided in the automatic belt tensioner. Attach a suitable tool into this hole.
2. Rotate tensioner assembly clockwise (as viewed from front) until tension has been relieved from belt.
3. Remove belt from water pump pulley first
4. Remove belt from vehicle.

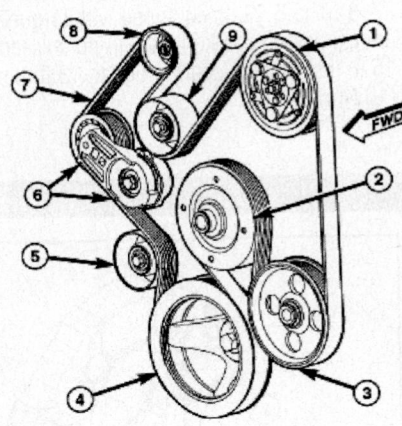

1. A/C COMPRESSOR IDLER PULLEY
2. FAN DRIVE PULLEY
3. POWER STEERING PUMP
4. CRANKSHAFT PULLEY
5. IDLER ASSEMBLY
6. TENSIONER ASSEMBLY
7. ACCESSORY DRIVE BELT
8. Alternator
9. IDLER PULLEY

22043_RPUP_G0031

Fig. 55 Accessory serpentine belt routing—5.7L engines

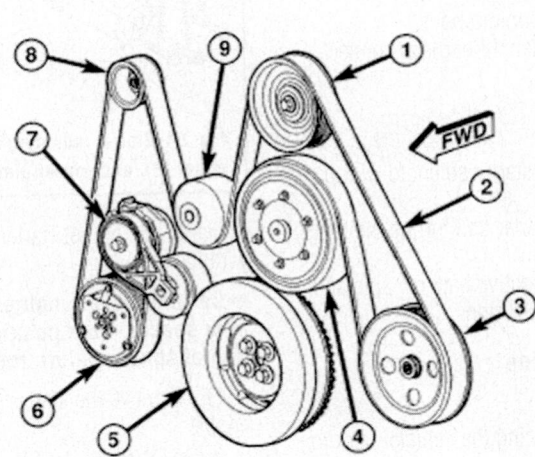

1. Idler pulley
2. Drive belt
3. Power steering pump pulley
4. Radiator fan pulley
5. Crankshaft pulley
6. A/C compressor pulley
7. Automatic belt tensioner
8. Alternator pulley
9. Water pump pulley

22043_RPUP_G0029

Fig. 56 Accessory serpentine belt routing—5.9L and 6.7L diesel engines with A/C

To install:

❊❊ WARNING

When installing the accessory drive belt, the belt must be routed correctly. If not, engine may overheat due to water pump rotating in wrong direction.

5. Position drive belt over all pulleys except water pump pulley.
6. Attach a suitable tool to the accessory drive belt tensioner.
7. Rotate the accessory drive belt tensioner clockwise. Place belt over water pump pulley. Let tensioner rotate back into place. Remove tool.

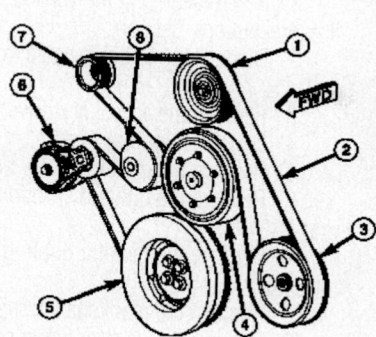

1. Idler pulley
2. Drive belt
3. Power steering pump pulley
4. Radiator fan pulley
5. Crankshaft pulley
6. Automatic belt tensioner
7. Alternator pulley

22043_RPUP_G0030

Fig. 57 Accessory serpentine belt routing—5.9L and 6.7L diesel engines without A/C

Be sure belt is properly seated on all pulleys.

CAMSHAFT AND VALVE LIFTERS

REMOVAL & INSTALLATION

5.7L Engine

1. Before servicing the vehicle, refer to the Precautions Section.
2. Drain the cooling system.
3. Recover the A/C refrigerant, if equipped with air conditioning.
4. Set the crankshaft to Top Dead Center (TDC) of the compression stroke for the No. 1 cylinder.
5. Remove or disconnect the following:
   - Negative battery cable
   - Camshaft rear cam bearing core plug
   - Air cleaner
   - Accessory drive belt
   - Alternator
   - A/C compressor
   - Radiator
   - Intake manifold
   - Cylinder head covers
   - Cylinder heads
   - Oil pan
   - Front cover
   - Oil pickup tube
   - Oil pump
   - Timing chain and sprockets
   - Camshaft thrust plate
   - Hydraulic lifters
   - Camshaft

To install:

6. Install or connect the following:
   - Camshaft
   - Camshaft thrust plate. Tighten the bolts to 21 ft. lbs. (28 Nm).
   - Timing chain and sprockets
   - Oil pump
   - Oil pickup tube

➡ **Lifters must be replaced in their original positions.**

- Hydraulic lifters
- Cylinder heads
- Pushrods
- Rocker arms
- Front cover
- Oil pan
- Cylinder head covers
- Intake manifold
- A/C compressor
- Alternator
- Accessory drive belt
- Radiator
- Air cleaner
- Camshaft rear cam bearing core plug
- Negative battery cable
7. Fill the cooling system.
8. Recharge the A/C system, if equipped.
9. Start the engine and check for leaks.

CRANKSHAFT DAMPER

REMOVAL & INSTALLATION

5.7L Engine

See Figures 58 through 61.

1. Disconnect the negative battery cable.
2. Remove accessory drive belt, as outlined in Engine Mechanical.
3. Drain cooling system.
4. Remove radiator upper hose.
5. Remove upper fan shroud.
6. Using Special Tools 6958 Spanner with Adapter Pins 8346 (1), loosen fan (2) and viscous assembly from water pump.
7. Remove fan and viscous assembly.
8. Disconnect electrical connector for fan mounted inside radiator shroud.

➡ **Transmission cooler line snaps into shroud lower right hand corner.**

9. Remove crankshaft damper bolt.
10. Remove damper using Special Tools 8513 Insert (1) and 1026 Three Jaw Puller (2).

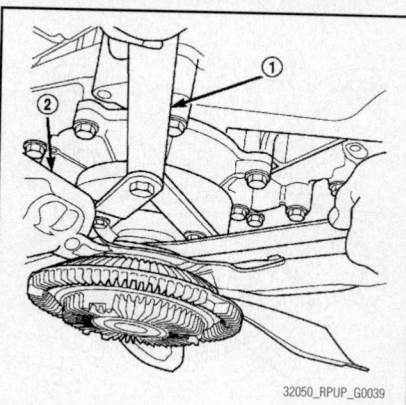

32050_RPUP_G0039

Fig. 58 Using Special Tools 6958 Spanner with Adapter Pins 8346 (1), loosen fan (2) and viscous assembly from water pump

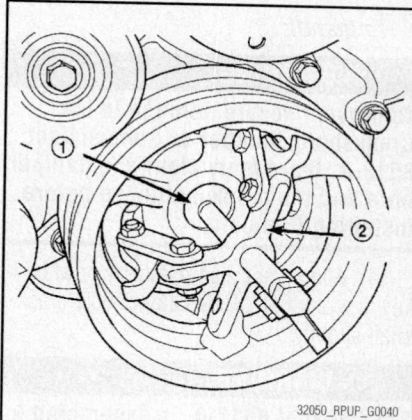

32050_RPUP_G0040

Fig. 59 Remove damper using Special Tools 8513 Insert (1) and 1026 Three Jaw Puller (2)

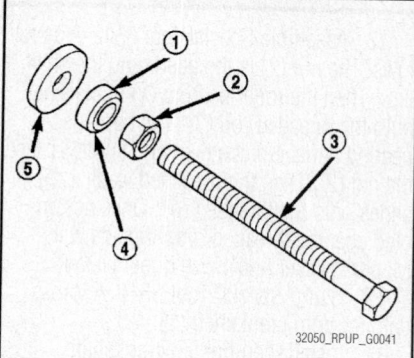

32050_RPUP_G0041

Fig. 60 Assemble Special Tool 8512-A as follows, The nut (2) is threaded onto the shaft first. Then the roller bearing (1) is placed onto the threaded rod (3) (The hardened bearing surface of the bearing (1) MUST face the nut (2). Then the hardened washer (5) slides onto the threaded rod

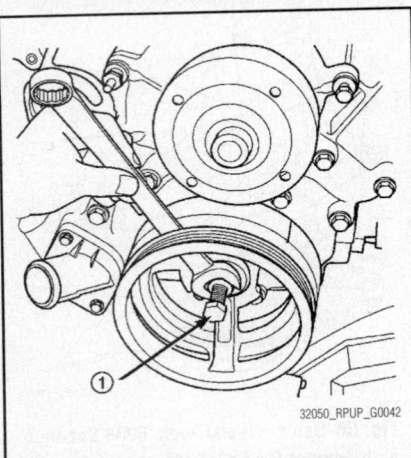

Fig. 61 Using Special Tool 8512-A, press damper onto crankshaft (1)

To install:

⁕⁕ WARNING

To prevent severe damage to the Crankshaft, Damper or Special Tool 8512-A, thoroughly clean the damper bore and the crankshaft nose before installing Damper.

11. Align crankshaft damper slot with key in crankshaft. Slide damper onto crankshaft slightly.

⁕⁕ WARNING

Special Tool 8512-A, is assembled in a specific sequence. Failure to assemble this tool in this sequence can result in tool failure and severe damage to either the tool or the crankshaft.

12. Assemble Special Tool 8512-A as follows, The nut (2) is threaded onto the shaft first. Then the roller bearing (1) is placed onto the threaded rod (3) (The hardened bearing surface of the bearing (1) MUST face the nut (2). Then the hardened washer (5) slides onto the threaded rod. Once assembled coat the threaded rod's threads with Mopar® Nickel Anti-Seize or equivalent.

13. Using Special Tool 8512-A, press damper onto crankshaft (1).

14. Install then tighten crankshaft damper bolt to 130 ft. lbs. (175 Nm).

15. Install fan blade assembly.

16. Install radiator upper shroud and tighten fasteners to 95 inch lbs. (11 Nm).

17. Connect electrical connector for shroud fan.

18. Install radiator upper hose.

19. Install accessory drive belt.

20. Refill cooling system.

21. Connect the negative battery cable.

5.9L & 6.7L Diesel Engines

1. Remove the accessory drive belt, as outlined in this section.

2. Remove the four (4) damper to crankshaft bolts and remove damper and speed indicator ring.

To install:

3. Install speed indicator ring.

➡**The speed indicator ring is located over a dowel pin.**

4. Install the crankshaft damper and bolts. Tighten bolts to 30 ft. lbs. (40 Nm), plus an additional 60° turn.

➡**The damper must be installed so the hole is located over the dowel pin.**

5. Install the accessory drive belt.

CRANKSHAFT FRONT SEAL

REMOVAL & INSTALLATION

5.7L Engine

See Figures 62 and 63.

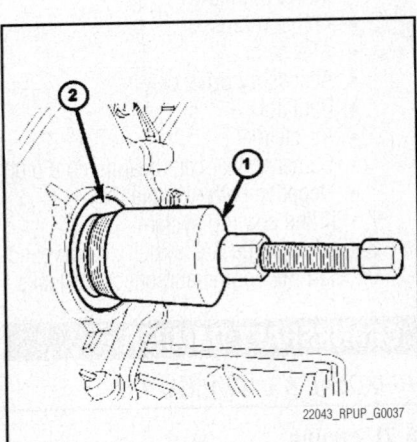

Fig. 62 Using Crankshaft Front Seal Remover 9071 (1), to remove crankshaft front seal (2).

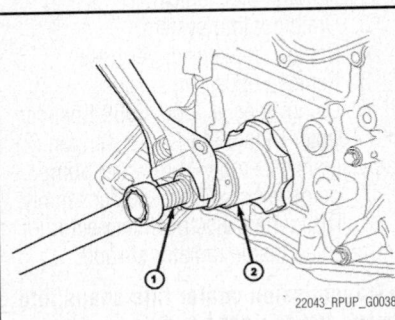

Fig. 63 Using crankshaft front oil seal installer 9072 (2) and damper installer 8512A (1), to install crankshaft front seal.

1. Before servicing the vehicle, refer to the Precautions Section.

2. Disconnect negative cable from battery.

3. Remove the accessory drive belt.

4. Drain the cooling system.

5. Remove the upper radiator hose.

6. Remove the radiator shroud attaching fasteners.

7. Remove the radiator cooling fan and shroud.

8. Remove the crankshaft damper bolt.

9. Remove the damper using crankshaft insert 8513A and three jaw puller 1023.

10. Using crankshaft front seal remover 9071, remove crankshaft front seal.

To install:

⁕⁕ WARNING

The front crankshaft seal must be installed dry. Do not apply lubricant to sealing lip or to outer edge.

11. Using crankshaft front oil seal installer 9072 and damper installer 8512A, install crankshaft front seal.

⁕⁕ WARNING

To prevent severe damage to the Crankshaft or Damper, thoroughly clean the damper bore and the crankshaft nose before installing Damper.

12. Install the vibration damper. Tighten bolt to 129 ft. lbs. (176 Nm).

13. Install radiator cooling fan and shroud.

14. Install the upper radiator hose.

15. Install the accessory drive belt refer

16. Refill the cooling system.

17. Connect negative cable to battery.

5.9L & 6.7L Diesel Engines

See Figure 64.

1. Disconnect both battery negative cables.

2. Raise the vehicle on hoist.

3. Partially drain the engine coolant.

4. Lower the vehicle.

5. Remove the radiator upper hose.

6. Disconnect the coolant recovery bottle hose from the radiator filler neck.

7. Disconnect windshield washer pump supply hose and electrical connections and lift washer bottle off of fan shroud.

8. Remove viscous fan/drive assembly.

9. Remove the cooling fan shroud and fan assembly from the vehicle.

10. Remove the accessory drive belt.

11. Remove the cooling fan support/hub from the front of the engine.

12. Raise the vehicle on hoist.

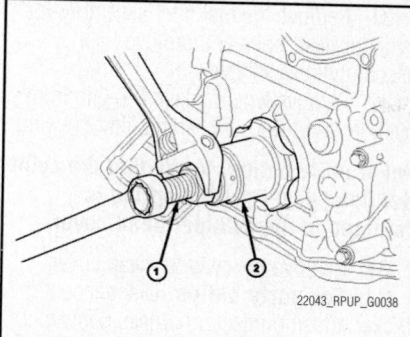

Fig. 64 Diesel engine front seal removal shown

13. Remove the crankshaft damper and speed indicator ring.

14. Remove power steering pump.

15. Remove the accessory drive belt tensioner.

16. Remove the gear cover-to-housing bolts and gently pry the cover away from the housing, taking care not to mar the gasket surfaces. Remove crank seal dust shield with cover.

17. Support the cover on a flat work surface with wooden blocks, and using a suitable punch and hammer, drive the old seal out of the cover from the back side of the cover to the front side.

To install:

✳✳ WARNING

The seal lip and the sealing surface on the crankshaft must be free of all oil residue, to prevent leaks. The crankshaft and seal surface must be completely dry when the seal is installed.

18. Clean cover and housing gasket mating surfaces. Use a suitable scraper and be careful not to damage the gear housing surface. Remove any old sealer from the oil seal bore. Thoroughly clean the front seal area of the crankshaft. Do not sand this surface. The seal lip and the sealing surface on the crankshaft must be free from all oil residue to prevent seal leaks.

19. Inspect the gear housing and cover for cracks and replace if necessary. Carefully straighten any bends or imperfections in the gear cover with a ball-peen hammer on a flat surface. Inspect the crankshaft front journal for any grooves or nicks that would affect the integrity of the new seal.

20. Apply a bead of Mopar® Stud & Bearing Mount to the outside diameter of the seal. Do not lubricate the inside diameter of the new seal.

21. With the cover supported by wood blocks, install the seal into the rear of the cover using crankshaft seal installer special tool 8281 and driver handle C-417

22. Strike the driver handle until the installation tool bottoms out on the inside of the cover.

23. Install the plastic seal pilot (provided with seal kit) into the crankshaft seal.

24. Apply a bead of Mopar® silicone rubber adhesive sealant or equivalent to the gear housing cover sealing surface.

25. Install the cover to the gear housing, aligning the seal pilot with the nose of the crankshaft.

➡ **Failure to follow the cover installation procedure can result in misalignment of the crankshaft seal to the crankshaft, causing an oil leak.**

26. Install the cover bolts and hand snug 2 cap screws at the 3 o'clock and 9 o'clock position, to keep the cover from moving when the first cap screw is tightened. Tighten to 18 ft. lbs. (24 Nm). Remove pilot tool.

27. Install dust shield over nose of crankshaft.

28. Install the crankshaft damper and speed indicator ring. Tighten the bolts to 30 ft. lbs. (40 Nm). Then rotate an additional 60 degrees. Use the engine barring tool to keep the engine from rotating during tightening operation.

29. Install the fan support/hub assembly and tighten the bolts to 24 ft. lbs. (32 Nm).

30. Install power steering pump.

31. Install the accessory drive belt tensioner. Tighten the bolt to 32 ft. lbs. (43 Nm).

32. Install the cooling fan

33. Install the accessory drive belt.

34. Refill the cooling system.

35. Connect the battery negative cables.

36. Start engine and check for oil leaks.

CYLINDER HEAD

REMOVAL & INSTALLATION

5.7L Engine
See Figure 65.

1. Before servicing the vehicle, refer to the Precautions Section.

2. Drain the cooling system.

3. Properly relieve the fuel system pressure.

4. Remove or disconnect the following:
   - Negative battery cable
   - Air cleaner resonator and ducts
   - Alternator
   - Closed crankcase ventilation system
   - EVAP control system
   - Heater hoses
   - Cylinder head covers
   - Intake manifold
   - Rocker arms and pushrods
   - Cylinder heads

To install:

➡ **The head gaskets are not interchangeable. They are marked "L" and "R".**

5. Install the cylinder heads. Use new gaskets and tighten the bolts, in sequence, as follows:

   a. Step 1: 12 mm bolts–25 ft. lbs. (34 Nm); 8mm bolts–15 ft. lbs. (20 Nm)

   b. Step 2: 12mm bolts–40 ft. lbs. (54 Nm); 8mm bolts retorque–15 ft. lbs. (20 Nm)

   c. Step 3: 12mm bolts–plus 90 degrees; 8mm bolts–25 ft. lbs. (34 Nm)

6. Install or connect the following:
   - Rocker arms and pushrods
   - Intake manifold
   - Heater hoses
   - Alternator
   - Cylinder head covers. Torque the studs and bolts to 70 inch lbs. (8 Nm).
   - Air cleaner resonator and ducts
   - Negative battery cable

5.9L & 6.7L Diesel Engines
See Figure 66.

1. Before servicing the vehicle, refer to the Precautions Section.

2. Raise vehicle on hoist.

3. Drain engine coolant.

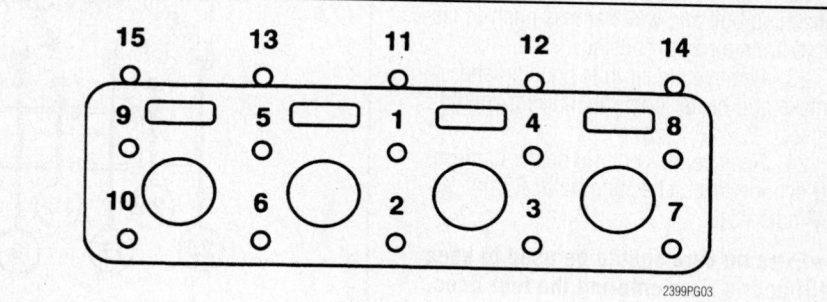

Fig. 65 Cylinder head torque sequence—5.7L engines

4. Disconnect exhaust pipe from turbocharger elbow.

5. Remove turbocharger drain tube bolts at turbocharger. Cap off ports to prevent dirt or foreign material from entering.

6. Lower the vehicle.

7. Disconnect air inlet temperature/pressure sensor.

8. Remove air cleaner housing and snorkel from the vehicle. Cap off turbocharger air inlet to prevent intrusion of dirt or foreign material.

9. Disconnect cab heater core supply and return hoses from the cylinder head and heater pipe.

10. Disconnect turbocharger oil supply line at the turbocharger end. Cap off open ports to prevent intrusion of dirt or foreign material.

11. Remove exhaust manifold-to-cylinder head bolts, spacers, heat shield, retention straps, and cab heater plumbing. Remove exhaust manifold and turbocharger from the vehicle as an assembly.

12. Remove cooling fan/drive/shroud assembly.

13. Remove accessory drive belt.

14. Remove cooling fan support from cylinder block.

15. Remove upper generator bolt, loosen lower generator bolt, and rotate generator away from cylinder head.

16. Disconnect radiator upper hose from the thermostat housing.

17. Disconnect the Intake Air Temperature/Manifold Air Pressure, and Coolant Temperature sensor connectors.

18. Remove the engine harness to cylinder head attaching bolts and P-clips at front of head.

19. Remove the intake air grid heater wires from the grid heater.

20. Remove engine oil level indicator tube attaching bolt at fuel filter housing bracket and inlet air connection.

21. Remove the charge air cooler-to-air inlet housing pipe.

22. Remove the engine wire harness attaching bolt and wire harness push-in fastener from air inlet housing.

23. Remove the air inlet housing and intake grid heater from the intake manifold cover.

24. Remove the two grid heater harness-to-cylinder head attaching bolts at front of cylinder head.

➡ **Extreme care should be used to keep dirt/debris from entering the fuel lines. Plastic caps should be used on the ends of the fuel lines.**

25. Remove the high pressure pump to fuel rail fuel line as follows:

a. Loosen fuel line nuts at fuel pump and at fuel rail.

b. Use a back-up wrench on the fitting at the fuel pump to keep it from loosening.

26. Remove the fuel rail to cylinder head fuel lines as follows:

a. Loosen No. 6 high pressure fuel line shield and position out of way.

b. Loosen the fuel line nuts at the fuel rail and at the cylinder head. Use a back-up wrench on HPC nut.

c. Remove the fuel line bracket bolts at the intake manifold cover.

27. Remove the engine lift bracket from the rear of the cylinder head.

28. Remove the fuel rail as follows:

a. Remove fuel rail pressure sensor connector.

b. Remove banjo fitting at pressure limiting valve.

c. Remove fuel rail bolts and fuel rail.

29. Remove the low pressure lines as follows:

a. Remove the fuel drain banjo fitting on the front side of fuel filter housing.

b. Remove the fuel drain banjo fitting on rear side of fuel filter housing.

c. Remove the fuel drain line support bracket on rear side of filter housing.

d. Disconnect fuel drain hose.

e. Remove banjo fitting at bottom of fuel filter housing.

f. Disconnect fuel supply hose at fuel filter.

30. Disconnect fuel heater, and water in fuel sensor.

31. Remove the fuel filter assembly-to-cylinder head bolts and remove filter assembly from vehicle.

32. Remove wire harness P—clip from cylinder head (located behind filter housing).

➡ **For early builds. Verify that the cylinder head cover ground spring is retained in the cylinder head cover.**

33. Remove the cylinder head cover.

34. **For early builds.** Disconnect the rocker housing injector harness connectors.

35. Remove injector harness nuts from injectors.

36. Remove the rocker levers, cross heads and push rods. Mark each component so they can be installed in their original positions.

➡ **The No. 5 cylinder exhaust and the No. 6 cylinder intake and exhaust push rods are removed by lifting them up and through the provided cowl panel access holes. Remove the rubber plugs to expose these relief holes.**

37. Remove the fuel return line and banjo bolt at the rear of the cylinder head. Be careful not to drop the two sealing washers.

38. Remove the fuel injectors.

39. Remove rocker housing bolts and rocker housing and gasket.

40. Reinstall the engine lift bracket at the rear of cylinder head. Torque to 57 ft. lbs. (77 Nm).

41. Remove twenty six (26) cylinder head-to-block bolts.

42. Attach an engine lift crane to engine lift brackets and lift cylinder head off engine and out of vehicle.

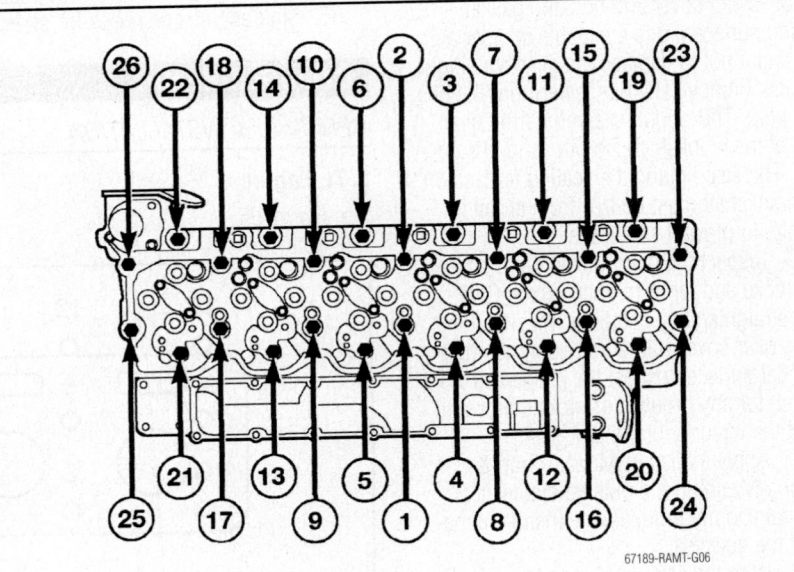

Fig. 66 Cylinder head torque sequence—5.9L Diesel engine

67189-RAMT-G06

43. Remove the head gasket and inspect for failure.

To install:

44. Install a new gasket with the part number side up, and locate the gasket over the dowel sleeves.

45. Using an engine lifting crane, lower the cylinder head onto the engine.

46. Lightly lubricate head bolts under bolt head and on threads, with engine oil and install. Using the sequence shown , tighten bolts in the following steps:
   a. Step 1: 52 ft. lbs. (70 Nm).
   b. Step 2: Back off 360 degrees in sequence.
   c. Step 3: Tighten to 77 ft. lbs. (105 Nm).
   d. Step 4: Recheck all bolts to 77 ft. lbs. (105 Nm).
   e. Tighten all bolts an additional 90 degrees.

47. Install push rods into their original locations.

48. Inspect rocker housing gasket for cuts and proper installation into groove. Replace if damaged.

49. Install rocker housing and bolts. Tighten to 18 ft lbs. (24 Nm).

50. Install the fuel injectors.

51. Lubricate valve stem tips and install the crossheads in their original locations.

52. Lubricate the rocker arms and pedestals and install them in their original locations. Install the bolts and torque them to 27 ft. lbs. (36 Nm).

53. Verify that the valve lash settings are maintained. Refer to valve lash adjustment.

54. Install cylinder head cover gasket onto rocker housing.

55. Install injector harness nuts. Tighten to 11 inch lbs. (1.25 Nm).

56. Connect injector harness connectors at cylinder head cover gasket.

57. Install wire harness P—clip to cylinder head behind filter housing 18 ft. lbs. (24 Nm).

58. Connect the IAT/MAP sensor connector.

59. Install the fuel filter housing assembly and Hand-tighten mounting bolts, Do not torque at this time.

60. Connect WIF sensor, and fuel heater.

✳✳ WARNING

Failure to follow procedure will result in fuel leaks and/or fuel system failure.

61. Install the fuel rail and high pressure fuel lines as follows:

a. Hand-tighten fuel rail bolts.
b. Hand-tighten fuel drain line to pressure limiting valve. Hand-tighten banjo bolt at fuel filter housing.
c. Hand-tighten fuel rail-to-cylinder head high pressure fuel lines.
d. Install fuel line brace bolts-to-intake manifold finger tight for fuel lines No. 2 thru No. 5.
e. Install fuel line brace nut to rear lift bracket stud, finger tight, for fuel line No. 6.
f. Hand-tighten fuel pump to fuel rail line.
g. Tighten fuel line nuts at cylinder head to 22 ft. lbs. (30 Nm).
h. Tighten fuel line nuts at fuel rail to 22 ft. lbs. (30 Nm).
i. Using a back up wrench, torque fuel pump to fuel rail line to 27 ft. lbs. (37 Nm). At injection pump.
j. Tighten fuel pump to fuel rail line to 27 ft. lbs. (37 Nm). at fuel rail.
k. Tighten fuel drain banjo bolt at pressure limiting valve and front of fuel filter housing to 18 ft. lbs. (24 Nm).
l. Tighten fuel line brace bolts to 18 ft. lbs. (24 Nm).
m. Tighten fuel line brace nut to 18 ft. lbs. (24 Nm).
n. Tighten rail bolts to 18 ft. lbs. (24 Nm).
o. Connect fuel pressure sensor.
p. Tighten fuel filter mounting bolts to 18 ft. lbs. (24 Nm).

62. Reposition number 6 fuel line shield and tighten to 32 ft. lbs. (43 Nm).

63. Install the fuel filter to injection pump low pressure line. Inspect and replace sealing washers if necessary. Torque banjo bolts to 18 ft. lbs. (24 Nm).

64. Connect fuel return line at back of cylinder head hand tight.

65. Connect fuel return line at filter housing hand tight.

66. Tighten banjo connections at cylinder head and fuel filter housing to 18 ft. lbs. (24 Nm).

67. Install bracket to rear of filter housing. Torque to 18 ft. lbs. (24 Nm).

68. Using new gaskets, install the intake grid heater and air inlet housing. Tighten bolts to 18 ft. lbs. (24 Nm).

69. Install wire harness P—clip and push on clip to air inlet housing.

70. Connect engine oil level indicator tube at fuel filter housing and at air inlet housing.

71. Install the charge air cooler-to-air inlet housing duct assembly. Tighten all clamps to 100 inch lbs. (11 Nm).

72. Connect intake grid heater wires.

73. Secure engine harness to front of cylinder head with bolt at four locations.

74. Connect engine coolant temperature sensor connector.

75. Connect radiator upper hose to thermostat housing.

76. Rotate generator into position. Install upper bolt and torque upper and lower bolts.

77. Install wire harness push-on clip below bracket.

78. Install wire harness P—clip to top of bracket.

79. Install fan support and torque to 24 ft. lbs. (32 Nm).

80. Install cooling fan/drive.

81. Install accessory drive belt.

82. Install exhaust manifold/turbocharger assembly, using new gaskets. Start all bolts/spacers by hand. Starting from the center bolts out, Tighten bolts to 32 ft. lbs. (43 Nm), then retighten from the center out again.

83. Install exhaust manifold heat shield to exhaust manifold studs. Install retaining nuts. Tighten to 18 ft. lbs. (24 Nm).

84. Install exhaust bolt retention straps across cylinders 5 & 6.

85. Using a new gasket, connect the turbocharger oil drain tube. Tighten to 18 ft. lbs. (24 Nm).

86. **Pre-lube** turbocharger with 1–2 oz. (29.9–59.14 ml) clean engine oil.

87. Connect the turbocharger oil supply line. Tighten to 18 ft. lbs. (24 Nm).

88. Install air cleaner housing and duct.

89. Connect air inlet temperature/pressure sensor.

90. Raise and safely support the vehicle.

➡**Do not reuse the clamp for the exhaust pipe to turbocharger elbow connection.**

91. Install the exhaust pipe to turbocharger elbow using a new clamp. Torque bolts to 100 inch lbs. (11 Nm).

92. Lower the vehicle.

93. Fill engine with coolant.

94. Start engine and check for leaks.

ENGINE ASSEMBLY

REMOVAL & INSTALLATION

5.7L Engine

1. Before servicing the vehicle, refer to the Precautions Section.
2. Drain the cooling system.
3. Drain the engine oil.
4. Relieve the fuel system pressure.
5. Remove or disconnect the following:
   • Negative battery cable
   • Hood
   • Air cleaner and resonator
   • Accessory drive belt

- Engine fan
- Radiator
- Upper crossmember and top core support
- A/C compressor, if equipped
- Alternator
- Intake manifold and IAFM as an assembly
- Heater hoses
- Power steering pump
- Fuel line
- Engine front mount thru-bolt nuts
- Transmission oil cooler lines, if equipped
- Exhaust pipes at the manifolds
- Starter motor
- Structural dust cover and transmission inspection cover
- Torque converter-to-flexplate bolts
- Transmission flange bolts. Support the transmission.
- Engine

To install:

> ### ✳✳ WARNING
> **The structural cover must be held tightly against the engine and bellhousing during tightening. The torque for all bolts is 40 ft. lbs. (54 Nm); the bolts must be tightened in the order shown.**

6. Install or connect the following:
   - Engine. Tighten the engine mount thru-bolt finger-tight.
   - Transmission flange bolts. Tighten the bolts to 40–45 ft. lbs. (54–61 Nm). Then, tighten the mount bolt nuts to 70 ft. lbs. (95 Nm)
   - Transmission oil cooler lines, if equipped
   - Torque converter, if equipped. Tighten the bolts to 23 ft. lbs. (31 Nm).
   - Structural dust cover and transmission inspection cover
   - Starter motor
   - Fuel line
   - Power steering pump
   - Heater hoses
   - Intake manifold and IAFM as an assembly
   - Alternator
   - A/C compressor, if equipped
   - Upper crossmember and top core support
   - Radiator
   - Engine fan
   - Accessory drive belt
   - Air cleaner and resonator
   - Hood
   - Negative battery cable

7. Fill the crankcase to the correct level.
8. Fill the cooling system.
9. Start the engine and check for leaks.

5.9L & 6.7L Diesel Engines

1. Before servicing the vehicle, refer to the Precautions Section.
2. Disconnect both battery negative cables.
3. Disconnect engine grid heater harness at grid heater relays.
4. Disconnect the electrical connections from rear of alternator.
5. Recover the A/C refrigerant.
6. Raise the vehicle on a hoist.
7. Drain engine coolant.
8. Remove engine oil drain plug and drain engine oil. Reinstall drain plug.
9. Lower the vehicle.
10. Remove fan and fan drive.
11. Remove fan shroud mounting bracket and shroud.
12. Remove the radiator upper hose.
13. Disconnect the coolant recovery bottle hose from the radiator fill neck.
14. Disconnect heater core supply and return hoses from the cylinder head fitting and coolant pipe.
15. Raise the vehicle on a hoist.
16. Remove transmission and transfer case (if equipped).
17. Disconnect exhaust pipe from turbocharger extension pipe.
18. Disconnect engine harness to vehicle harness connectors.
19. Remove the starter motor.
20. Remove the flywheel/flexplate.
21. Remove the transmission adapter. (If equipped).
22. Disconnect A/C suction/discharge hose from the rear of the A/C compressor.
23. Lower the vehicle.
24. Disconnect lower radiator hose from radiator outlet.
25. For automatic transmission models, disconnect transmission oil cooler lines from in front of radiator using special tool 6931
26. Remove the radiator.
27. If A/C equipped, disconnect A/C condenser refrigerant lines.
28. Disconnect charge air cooler piping.
29. Remove charge air cooler mounting bolts.
30. Remove charge air cooler from vehicle.
31. Remove the A/C condenser.
32. Remove damper and speed indicator ring from front of engine.
33. Remove the lower fan shroud bracket from engine.
34. Remove upper fan shroud brackets from engine

35. Disconnect engine block heater connector
36. Disconnect A/C compressor and pressure sensor electrical connectors.
37. Remove the passenger battery ground cable from the engine block. Remove the driver side battery ground cable from the engine block.
38. Remove power steering pump from engine by removing 3 bolts.
39. Disconnect the ECM power connector.
40. Disconnect the ECM ground wire from the hydro form screw.
41. Disconnect the fuel supply and return hoses.
42. Remove the cylinder head cover.
43. Disconnect the wire harnesses from the injectors.
44. Remove the cylinder head cover carrier gasket

➡ **Extreme care should be used to keep dirt/debris from entering the fuel lines. Plastic caps should be used on the ends of the fuel lines.**

45. Loosen number 6 fuel line shield bolts and rotate shield out of the way.
46. Remove cylinder number 5 and number 6 high pressure fuel lines.
47. Remove the rear engine lift bracket.
48. Remove cylinder number 4, number 5, and number 6 intake and exhaust rocker arms, pedestals, and push tubes. (Note the original location for reassembly).
49. Remove the fuel connector tube nut and fuel connector tube. Remove cylinder number 5 and number 6 fuel injector.
50. Remove rocker housing.
51. Remove two cylinder head bolts and install tool number 9009. Tighten bolts to 77 ft. lbs. (105 Nm).
52. Loosen but do not remove engine mount through bolts and nuts.
53. Disconnect hood support struts and position hood out of the way.
54. Attach a chain with two hooks to the engine lift brackets.
55. While keeping engine level, lift straight up out of the mounts.
56. Rotate nose of the engine upward and pull out of the chassis.

To install:

57. Remove cylinder head bolts. Install special tool 9009. Tighten bolts to 77 ft. lbs. (105 Nm).
58. Lower engine into the engine compartment and install the engine mount through bolts and nuts.
59. Tighten the mount through bolts and nuts to 65 ft. lbs. (88 Nm).
60. Remove the engine lifting device tool 9009.

61. Check cylinder head cap screw length and install into cylinder head.

62. Tighten in 4 steps as follows:
- Step 1: Tighten to 52 ft. lbs. (70 Nm)
- Step 2: Back off 360 degrees
- Step 3: Tighten to 77 ft. lbs. (105 Nm)
- Step 4: Rotate 90 degrees

63. Install rocker housing. Torque to 18 ft. lbs. (24 Nm).

64. Replace injector O-ring and sealing washer on injector's number 5 and number 6.

65. Install injectors and tighten using the following steps:
- Install injector hold-down cap screws and torque to 44 inch lbs. (5 Nm).
- Loosen injector hold-down cap screws
- Install HPC connector tube and nut. Tighten nut to 11 ft. lbs. (15 Nm).
- Tighten the injector hold-down cap screws to 89 inch lbs. (10 Nm).
- Tighten the HPC connector tube nut to 37 ft. lbs. (50 Nm).

66. Install rear engine lift bracket. Tighten to 57 ft. lbs. (77 Nm).

67. Install number 5 and number 6 high pressure fuel lines.

68. Tighten fuel line fittings to 22 ft. lbs. (30 Nm). Tighten brace cap screw and nut to 18 ft. lbs. (24 Nm).

69. Install push tubes, rocker arms, and pedestals for cylinders number 4, number 5, and number 6. Tighten the mounting bolts to 27 ft. lbs. (36 Nm).

70. Reset valve lash on cylinders number 4, number 5, and number 6. Tighten adjusting nuts to 18 ft. lbs. (24 Nm)

71. Install the injector wiring/gasket.

72. Install cylinder head cover carrier gasket

73. Connect the injector harness nuts to injectors. Tighten to 11 in. lbs (1.25 Nm).

74. Connect the injector wiring harness connectors to injector connections on cylinder head cover carrier gasket.

75. Install cylinder head cover

76. Connect breather tube and lube oil drain tube to cylinder head cover

77. Connect fuel supply and return hoses.

78. Connect ECM ground to hydro form screw. Connect ECM power connector.

79. Install the power steering pump.

80. Install the damper and speed indicator ring. Tighten to 30 ft. lbs. (40 Nm) plus 60 degrees.

81. Install the lower fan shroud bracket. Tighten to 18 ft. lbs. (24 Nm).

82. Install upper fan shroud brackets, but do not tighten fasteners at this time.

83. Connect the engine block heater connection.

84. Connect the A/C compressor and pressure sensor connectors

85. Install the charge air cooler. Install and tighten the charge air cooler mounting bolts to 17 inch lbs. (2 Nm).

86. Connect the charge air cooler tubes. Tighten all clamps to 72 inch lbs. (8 Nm).

87. Install the a/c condenser.

88. Connect the a/c refrigerant lines to the a/c condenser.

89. Install the radiator upper support panel.

90. Install the radiator.

91. Connect the transmission quick-connect oil cooler lines.

92. Raise the vehicle.

93. Connect A/C compressor suction/discharge hose (if equipped).

94. Install the radiator lower hose and clamps.

95. Install the battery negative cables to the engine block on the driver and passenger side.

96. Install the transmission adapter with a new camshaft rectangular ring seal. Tighten to 57 ft. lbs. (77 Nm).

97. Install the flywheel and adapter or flexplate. Tighten to 101 ft. lbs. (137 Nm).

➡️ **If the engine is equipped with a flexplate or crankshaft adapter, a new clamp ring must be used. If the engine has a flywheel with washers, the washers can be reused.**

98. Install the starter motor and tighten to 32 ft. lbs. (43 Nm).

99. Connect engine to vehicle harness connectors.

100. Install transmission and transfer case (if equipped).

101. Connect the exhaust pipe to the turbocharger elbow.

102. Connect the transmission auxiliary oil cooler lines (if equipped).

103. Lower the vehicle.

104. Connect the heater core supply and return hoses.

105. Fill the crankcase to the correct level.

106. Fill the cooling system.

107. Vacuum and recharge the A/C system (if equipped).

108. Start the engine and check for leaks.

EXHAUST MANIFOLD

REMOVAL & INSTALLATION

5.7L Engine

See Figures 67 and 68.

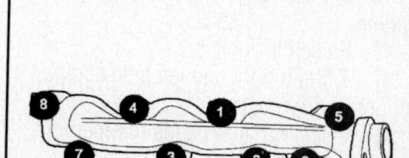

Fig. 67 Left exhaust manifold tighten sequence—5.7L engines engine

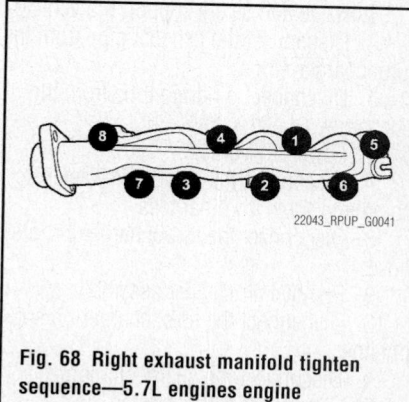

Fig. 68 Right exhaust manifold tighten sequence—5.7L engines engine

1. Before servicing the vehicle, refer to the Precautions Section.

2. Disconnect negative battery cable.

3. Raise the vehicle.

4. Remove exhaust pipe to manifold bolts.

5. Lower the vehicle.

6. Install engine support fixture special tool number 8534.

7. Raise the engine enough to remove manifolds.

✳✳ WARNING

Do not damage the engine harness while raising the engine.

8. Remove heat shield.

9. Remove manifold bolts using sequence provided.

10. Remove the manifold and gasket.

To install:

11. Install manifold gasket and manifold.

12. Install manifold bolts and tighten using sequence provided to 18 ft. lbs. (25 Nm).

13. Install heat shield and tighten nuts to 11 ft. lbs. (15 Nm).

14. Lower the engine.

✳✳ WARNING

Do not damage the engine harness while lowering the engine.

15. Remove engine support fixture from engine.

16. Raise the vehicle.

17. Tighten right and left side engine mount through bolts.

18. Install exhaust flange to pipe bolts.

19. Lower the vehicle.

20. Connect negative battery cable.

5.9L Diesel Engine

See Figure 69.

1. Before servicing the vehicle, refer to the Precautions Section.

2. Disconnect the battery negative cables.

3. Raise and safely support the vehicle.

4. Disconnect the exhaust pipe from the turbocharger elbow.

5. Disconnect oil drain tube from turbocharger.

6. Lower the vehicle.

7. Disconnect the electronic wastegate command valve from harness.

8. Disconnect the turbocharger air inlet hose.

9. Remove air cleaner assembly.

10. Disconnect the turbocharger oil supply line.

11. Disconnect the charge air cooler inlet pipe from the turbocharger.

12. Remove the turbocharger and gasket from the exhaust manifold.

13. Remove the cab heater return pipe nut from the exhaust manifold stud. Position the tube out of the way.

14. Remove heat shield.

15. Remove exhaust manifold bolt lockplates.

16. Remove the exhaust manifold-to-cylinder head bolts and spacers.

17. Remove the exhaust manifold and gaskets.

To install:

18. Using new exhaust manifold gaskets, install the exhaust manifold. Install the bolts and spacers and tighten the bolts in the sequence shown in to 32 ft. lbs. (43 Nm).

19. Retighten the four center bolts.

20. Install heat shield and torque nuts to 18 ft. lbs. (24 Nm).

21. Install cab heater tube.

22. Install exhaust manifold bolt retention straps.

23. Install the cab heater return tube brace to the manifold bolt stud. Tighten the nut to 18 ft. lbs. (24 Nm).

24. Install the turbocharger and a new gasket. Tighten the turbocharger mounting nuts to 32 ft. lbs. (43 Nm).

25. Raise and safely support the vehicle.

26. Install the oil drain tube and a new

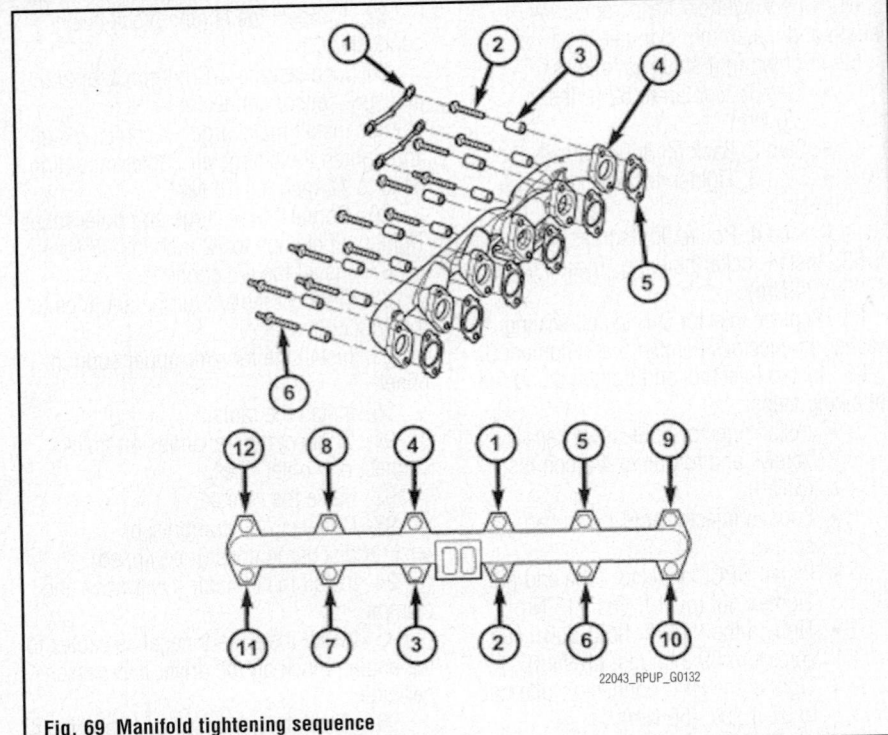

Fig. 69 Manifold tightening sequence

22043_RPUP_G0132

gasket to the turbocharger. Tighten the drain tube bolts to 18 ft. lbs. (24 Nm).

➡️**A new exhaust pipe to turbocharger elbow must be used. Do not reuse clamp.**

27. Connect the exhaust pipe to the turbocharger and tighten the bolts to 100 inch lbs. (11 Nm).

28. Connect the wastegate command valve connector.

29. Lower the vehicle.

30. **Pre-lube the turbocharger.** Pour 2–3 oz. (50–60 cc) clean engine oil in the oil supply line fitting on the turbo. Rotate the turbocharger impeller by hand to distribute the oil thoroughly.

31. Install and tighten the oil supply line fitting nut to18 ft. lbs. (24Nm).

32. Position the charge air cooler inlet pipe to the turbocharger. With the clamp in position, tighten the clamp nut to 95 inch lbs. (11 Nm).

33. Position the air inlet hose to the turbocharger. Tighten the clamp to 35 inch lbs. (4 Nm).

34. Connect the battery negative cables.

35. Start the engine to check for leaks.

6.7L Diesel Engine

See Figure 70.

1. Disconnect the battery negative cables.

2. Drain the coolant.

3. Raise the vehicle on hoist.

4. Remove the EGR cooler.

5. Remove the air filter housing.

6. Remove the air filter inlet hose from the turbo inlet.

7. Remove the delta P line bracket cap screw nuts and remove the delta P line from the exhaust manifold and thermostat housing.

8. Remove the heat shield and noise panel (if equipped) from the exhaust manifold.

9. Remove the four turbo to exhaust manifold nuts (15 mm).

10. Remove the two rear exhaust manifold cap screw lock plates.

11. Remove the Cab Heater tubing/bracket from the exhaust manifold stud (15 mm).

12. Remove the exhaust manifold.

To install:

13. Clean the exhaust manifold gasket surfaces.

14. Clean the cylinder head exhaust port gasket surfaces.

15. Clean the turbo mounting flange on the exhaust manifold.

16. Clean the turbo mounting flange on the turbocharger.

17. Install the exhaust manifold to turbocharger gasket and cap screws.

18. Install the exhaust manifold gasket.

➡️**The five exhaust manifold cap screws with studs are used at the number 1 and number 2 cylinder locations for the heat shield mounting and one**

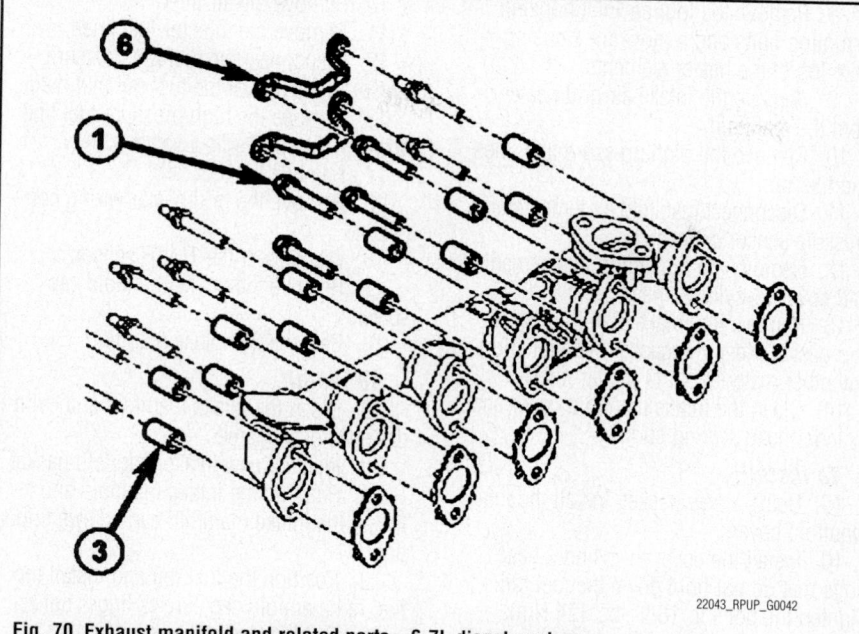

Fig. 70 Exhaust manifold and related parts—6.7L diesel engine

22043_RPUP_G0042

on the rear lower corner of the manifold for the cabin heater tube bracket.

19. Install the exhaust manifold spacers and cap screws.

20. Starting from the center and moving in a pattern outward, torque the exhaust manifold bolts to 32 ft. lbs. (43 Nm).

21. Install the exhaust manifold cap screw lock plates.

22. Install the exhaust manifold heat shields/noise panels. Torque the mounting nuts to 18 ft. lbs. (24 Nm).

23. Torque the turbocharger mounting nuts to 32 ft. lbs. (43 Nm).

24. Attach the mounting tabs and start the delta-P tube to exhaust manifold and thermostat cap screws.

25. Torque the delta-P tube 15 mm nut to 18 ft. lbs. (24 Nm).

26. Torque the delta-P tube 6 mm nut to 89 inch lbs. (10 Nm).

27. Torque the delta-P flare nuts to 89 inch lbs. (10 Nm).

28. Install the EGR cooler.

29. Install the air filter housing.

30. Fill the coolant.

31. Connect the battery negative cables.

32. Start the engine to check for leaks.

FLEXPLATE

REMOVAL & INSTALLATION

See Figure 71.

1. Before servicing the vehicle, refer to the Precautions Section

2. Remove the transmission.

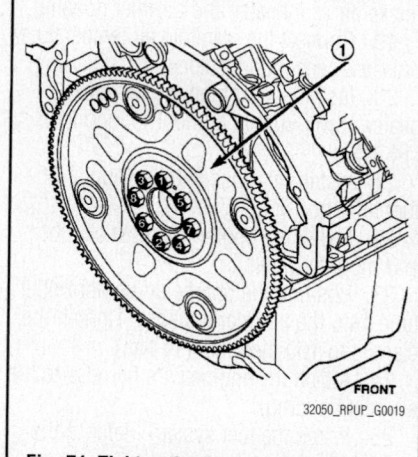

Fig. 71 Tighten the flexplate bolts in the sequence shown

32050_RPUP_G0019

3. Remove the bolts and flexplate.

To install:

4. Position the flexplate onto the crankshaft and install the bolts hand-tight.

5. Tighten the flexplate retaining bolts, in the sequence shown, to 70 ft. lbs. (95 Nm)

6. Install the transmission.

FLYWHEEL

REMOVAL & INSTALLATION

See Figure 72.

➡The Dual Mass Flywheel is used on the diesel engines with G56 transmission. The Dual Mass Flywheel is

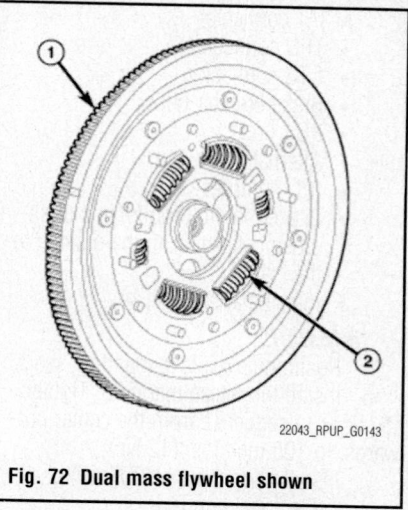

Fig. 72 Dual mass flywheel shown

22043_RPUP_G0143

serviced as an assembly only and should never be taken apart.

1. Before servicing the vehicle, refer to the Precautions Section

2. Remove transmission assembly from the vehicle.

3. Loosen pressure plate bolts evenly, a few threads at a time and in a diagonal pattern to prevent warping the plate.

4. Remove bolts completely and remove pressure plate and disc.

5. Remove flywheel bolts and remove flywheel.

➡Vehicles with Dual Mass Flywheel use an adapter plate between the flywheel and crank. This plate does not need to be removed.

To install:

6. Install flywheel on the crankshaft or adapter plate if vehicle has Dual Mass flywheel.

7. Install flywheel bolts and tighten evenly in sequence to 70 ft. lbs. (95 Nm). Vehicles with Dual Mass Flywheel, tighten adapter plate bolts to 40 ft. lbs. (55 Nm).

8. Install clutch.

9. Install transmission.

INTAKE MANIFOLD

REMOVAL & INSTALLATION

5.7L Engine

1. Before servicing the vehicle, refer to the Precautions Section.

2. Drain the cooling system.

3. Relieve the fuel system pressure.

4. Remove or disconnect the following:
   • Negative battery cable
   • Air cleaner assembly
   • Accessory drive belt
   • MAP connector

- IAT connector
- TPS connector
- CTS connector
- Brake booster hose
- PCV hose
- Alternator
- A/C compressor
- Intake manifold bolts, in a criss-cross pattern, from the outside to the center
- Intake manifold/IAFM

To install:

5. Position new intake manifold seals.

6. Install the intake manifold. Tighten the bolts in sequence from the center outwards, to 105 inch lbs. (12 Nm).

7. Install or connect the following:
- Electrical connectors
- Alternator
- A/C compressor
- Brake booster hose
- PCV hose
- Accessory drive belt
- Negative battery cable
- Air cleaner assembly

5.9L Diesel Engine

See Figure 73.

1. Before servicing the vehicle, refer to the Precautions Section.

2. Disconnect the negative battery cable.

3. Remove the charge air cooler outlet tube from the air inlet housing.

4. Remove the engine oil dipstick tube mounting bolt.

5. Remove dipstick support at fuel filter housing. Position dipstick tube to the side.

6. Disconnect the air grid heater power cables at the cable mounting studs.

7. Remove the engine wiring harness connections at the air inlet housing elbow.

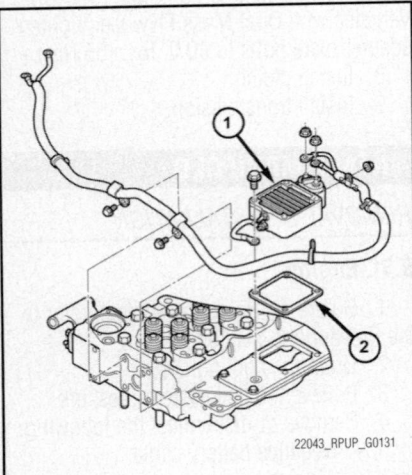

22043_RPUP_G0131

Fig. 73 Intake air grid heater (1), gasket (2)

8. Remove the four air inlet housing mounting bolts and remove the housing from top of the heater elements.

9. Remove the intake air grid heater from the manifold.

10. Remove the high pressure fuel lines and fuel rail.

11. Disconnect manifold air temperature/pressure sensor connector.

12. Remove the remaining intake manifold cover-to-cylinder head bolts.

13. Remove the intake manifold cover and gasket. Keep the gasket material and any other material out of the air intake.

14. Clean the intake manifold cover and cylinder head sealing surface.

To install:

15. Using a new gasket, install the intake manifold cover.

16. Install the cover-to-cylinder head bolts that do not hold down the fuel rail. Tighten the bolts to 18 ft. lbs. (24 Nm).

17. Install the high pressure rail and fuel lines

18. Using two new gaskets, install the intake air grid heater and air inlet housing.

19. Connect the manifold air temperature/pressure sensor connector.

20. Install and tighten the air intake heater power supply nut to 120 inch lbs. (14 Nm).

21. Install oil dipstick tube support at fuel filter housing.

22. Install the engine oil dipstick tube and mounting bolt.

23. Position the charge air cooler outlet tube onto the air inlet housing. Tighten the clamps to 100 inch lbs. (11 Nm).

24. Attach the engine wire harness to the air inlet housing.

25. Prime the fuel system. Refer to the fuel priming procedure.

26. Connect the battery negative cables.

6.7L Diesel Engine

1. Before servicing the vehicle, refer to the Precautions Section.

2. Disconnect the batteries.

3. Disconnect the EGR air transfer tube temperature sensor.

4. Disconnect the EGR valve actuator connector.

5. Disconnect the Engine Oil level tube at the Air Inlet bracket

6. Loosen and remove both v-band clamps at each end of the air transfer tube

7. Remove the P—clip mounting cap screw

8. Remove the air transfer tube.

9. Loosen and remove six air inlet mounting cap screws.

10. Remove the air inlet.

11. Remove the injector fuel lines.

12. Disconnect the fuel rail pressure sensor at the rear of the fuel rail manifold.

13. Remove the high pressure fuel line from the dump/overflow valve.

14. Remove the fuel rail.

15. Remove the grid heater wiring connector.

16. Disconnect the TMAP sensor.

17. Remove the intake manifold cap screws.

18. Remove the intake manifold.

To install:

19. Clean the intake manifold and cylinder head gasket area.

20. Install a new intake manifold gasket.

21. Position the intake manifold and Install the intake manifold cap screws finger tight.

22. Position the fuel rail and install the fuel rail manifold cap screws finger tight.

23. Tighten the intake manifold cap screws to 18 ft. lbs. (24 Nm).

24. Connect the fuel rail pressure sensor.

25. Connect the intake manifold grid heater. Torque the cap screw to 89 inch lbs. (10 Nm).

26. Install the fuel lines.

27. Tighten the fuel rail mounting cap screws to 18 ft. lbs. (24 Nm).

28. Clean the air inlet gasket area.

29. Clean the intake manifold to air inlet area.

30. Install the new air intake connection gasket.

31. Install the air intake connection to the intake manifold.

32. Tighten the intake manifold to 18 ft. lbs. (24 Nm).

33. Install the oil level gauge tube and torque to 18 ft. lbs. (24 Nm).

34. Clean the gasket area of the air transfer Tube (both ends).

35. Clean the EGR cooler and EGR control valve gasket area.

36. Using new gaskets, install the air transfer tube.

37. Install the V—band clamps.

38. Install the P—clip to the bracket. Torque the mounting cap screw to 18 ft. lbs. (24 Nm).

39. Tighten the V-band clamps to 89 lbs. in. (10 Nm).

40. Connect the EGR valve actuator connector.

41. Connect the EGR gas temperature connector.

42. Connect the batteries.

43. Start the engine and check for leaks.

OIL PAN

REMOVAL & INSTALLATION

5.7L Engine

See Figure 74.

1. Before servicing the vehicle, refer to the Precautions Section.
2. Drain the engine oil.
3. Attach an engine crane.
4. Loosen, but don't remove, the left and right mount through-bolts.
5. Remove or disconnect the following:
   - Negative battery cable
   - Structural cover
   - Front crossmember
6. Raise the engine just enough for clearance.
7. Remove or disconnect the following:

➡**Don't pry on the pan. The gasket is integral with the windage tray, and doesn't come out with the pan.**

   - Pan bolts and studs
   - Pan

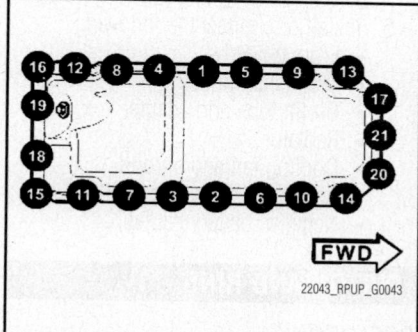

Fig. 74 Oil pan mounting bolt tightening sequence—5.7L engines

➡**The double ended studs must be installed in their original locations.**

To install:

8. Install or connect the following:
   - Oil pan gasket
   - Oil pan. Tighten the bolts, in sequence, to 105 inch lbs. (12 Nm).
   - Front crossmember
   - Structural cover
   - Negative battery cable
9. Fill the crankcase to the proper level with engine oil.
10. Start the engine and check for leaks.

5.9L & 6.7L Diesel Engines

2WD Models

1. Before servicing the vehicle, refer to the Precautions Section.

2. Open the hood.
3. Remove the negative battery cables.
4. Raise and support the vehicle.
5. Remove the transmission oil cooler lines.
6. Remove the propeller shaft.
7. Remove the starter bolts.
8. Support the starter.
9. Remove the torque converter bolts.
10. Remove the exhaust hanger bolts.
11. Remove the gear shift cable.
12. Remove the wiring harness.
13. Remove the transmission mount.
14. Remove the crossover bolts.
15. Position the transmission jack.
16. Remove the bell housing bolts.
17. Remove the transmission.
18. Remove the flywheel housing bolts (8).
19. Remove the flex plate bolts (8).
20. Remove the engine oil dip stick.
21. Drain the oil.
22. Remove the steering rack bolts.
23. Remove the oil pan bolts.
24. Remove the oil pickup bolts.
25. Remove the oil pan.

To install:

26. Clean the sealing surfaces of the cylinder block and oil pan with a suitable cleaner.
27. Clean the oil pan.
28. Clean the oil pan T-joints.
29. Fill the T-joint between the pan rail/gear housing and pan rail/rear seal retainer with sealant. Use Mopar® silicone rubber adhesive sealant or equivalent.
30. Position the new oil pan gasket.
31. Place suction tube in oil pan and guide them into place. Using a new tube-to-block gasket, install and tighten the suction tube bolts by hand. Starting with the oil pump inlet bolts, tighten the bolts to 18 ft. lbs. (24 Nm). Tighten the remaining tube brace bolts to 32 ft. lbs. 43 Nm
32. Starting in the center and working outward, tighten the oil pan bolts to 21 ft. lbs. (28 Nm).
33. Install the steering rack bolts.
34. Install the flex plate.
35. Install the flywheel to crankshaft adapter. Tighten to 101 ft. lbs. (137 Nm).
36. Install the transmission.
37. Install the flywheel housing assembly with the starter motor attached and tighten bolts to 57 ft. lbs. (77 Nm).

➡**A new clamping ring must be used on early or late builds, automatic or manual. Do not reuse clamping ring.**

38. Install the EGR cooler.
39. Install the fan and fan shroud

➡**Make sure that the fan shroud seal is properly seated in the radiator fan shroud and that it is not out of position causing excessive contact with the radiator coolant tubes.**

40. Remove the transmission jack.
41. Install the crossmember bolts.
42. Install the transmission mount.
43. Install the wiring harness.
44. Install the gear shift cable.
45. Install the exhaust hanger bolts.
46. Install the torque converter bolts.
47. Install the starter.
48. Install the starter bolts.
49. Install the transmission oil cooler lines.
50. Connect the negative battery cables.
51. Close the hood

4WD Models

See Figure 75.

1. Before servicing the vehicle, refer to the Precautions Section.
2. Open the hood.
3. Disconnect the battery negative cables.
4. Remove the intake air assembly.
5. Remove the radiator shroud retaining bolts.
6. Install engine support fixture No. 8534B.
7. Raise and support the vehicle.
8. Drain the engine oil.
9. Loosen the front engine mount bolts.
10. Lower the vehicle.
11. Use the engine support fixture No. 8534B to raise engine out of the front mounts.
12. Remove the engine oil dipstick.
13. Raise and support the vehicle.
14. Remove oil pan bolts, break the pan to block seal, and lower pan slightly and remove oil suction tube fasteners.
15. Remove oil pan and suction tube.
16. Remove the 2 bolts from the front of the engine block stiffener.
17. Remove the oil pan.

To install:

18. Clean the sealing surfaces of the cylinder block and oil pan with a suitable cleaner.
19. Clean the oil pan.
20. Clean the oil pan T-joints.
21. Fill the T-joint between the pan rail/gear housing and pan rail/rear seal retainer with sealant. Use Mopar® Silicone rubber adhesive sealant or equivalent.
22. Position the new oil pan gasket.
23. Place suction tube in oil pan and guide them into place. Using a new tube-to-block gasket, install and tighten the suction tube bolts by hand. Starting with the oil pump inlet bolts, tighten the bolts to 18 ft.

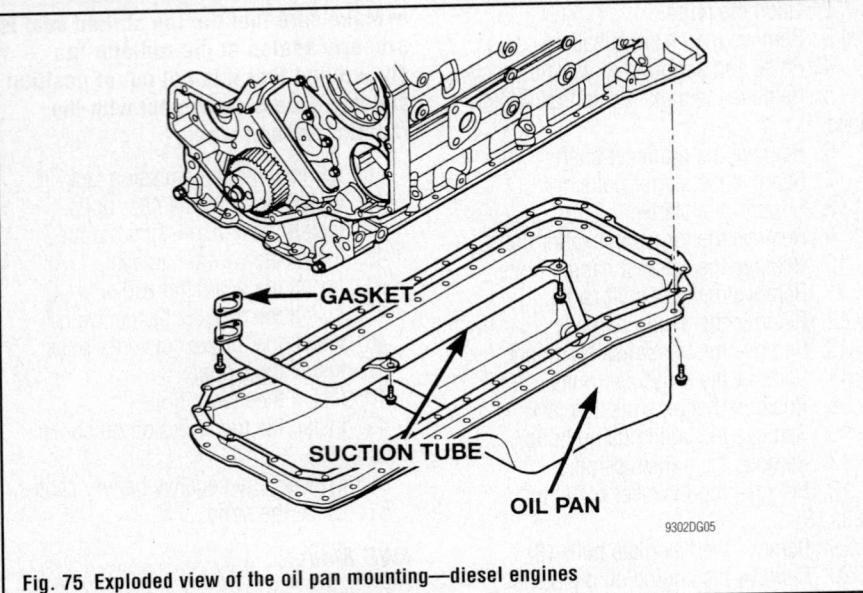

Fig. 75 Exploded view of the oil pan mounting—diesel engines

lbs. (24 Nm). Tighten the remaining tube brace bolts to 32 ft. lbs. (43 Nm).

24. Starting in the center and working outward, tighten the oil pan bolts to 21 ft. lbs. (28 Nm).

25. Install the engine oil dipstick.

26. Install the engine block stiffener.

27. Install the flywheel to crankshaft adapter. Torque to 101 ft. lbs. (137 Nm).

28. Lower the vehicle.

29. Lower the engine into the motor mounts and tighten the through bolts to 64 ft. lbs. (88 Nm).

30. Remove the engine support fixture No. 8534.

31. Install battery negative cables.

32. Fill the crankcase with new engine oil.

33. Start engine and check for leaks. Stop engine, check oil level, and adjust, if necessary.

34. Remove the engine support fixture No. 8534B.

35. Install the fan and fan shroud.

➥Make sure that the fan shroud seal is properly seated in the radiator fan shroud and that it is not out of position causing excessive contact with the radiator coolant tubes.

36. Fill the engine oil.

37. Connect the battery negative cables.

38. Close the hood.

OIL PUMP

REMOVAL & INSTALLATION

5.7L Engine

1. Before servicing the vehicle, refer to the Precautions Section.

2. Drain the engine oil.

3. Remove or disconnect the following:
- Negative battery cable
- Oil pan
- Oil pump pick-up tube
- Timing chains and tensioners
- Oil pump

To install:

4. Install or connect the following:
- Oil pump. Tighten the bolts to 21 ft. lbs. (28 Nm).
- Timing chains and tensioners
- Oil pump pick-up tube
- Oil pan
- Negative battery cable

5. Fill the crankcase to the correct level.

6. Start the engine and check for leaks.

5.9L & 6.7L Diesel Engines

See Figure 76.

1. Before servicing the vehicle, refer to the Precautions Section.

2. Drain the cooling system.

3. Remove or disconnect the following:
- Negative battery cables
- Accessory drive belt
- Cooling fan and shroud
- Radiator
- Oil fill tube and adapter
- Crankshaft pulley
- Front cover
- Oil pump

To install:

➥When the pump is correctly installed, the flange on the pump does not touch the block; the back plate on the pump seats against the bottom of the bore.

4. Install the oil pump. Tighten the bolts in sequence as follows:
   a. Step 1: 71 inch lbs. (8 Nm).
   b. Step 2: 18 ft. lbs. (24 Nm).

5. Install or connect the following:
- Front cover
- Crankshaft pulley
- Oil fill tube and adapter
- Radiator
- Cooling fan and shroud
- Accessory drive belt
- Negative battery cables

PISTON AND RING

POSITIONING

See Figures 77 through 80.

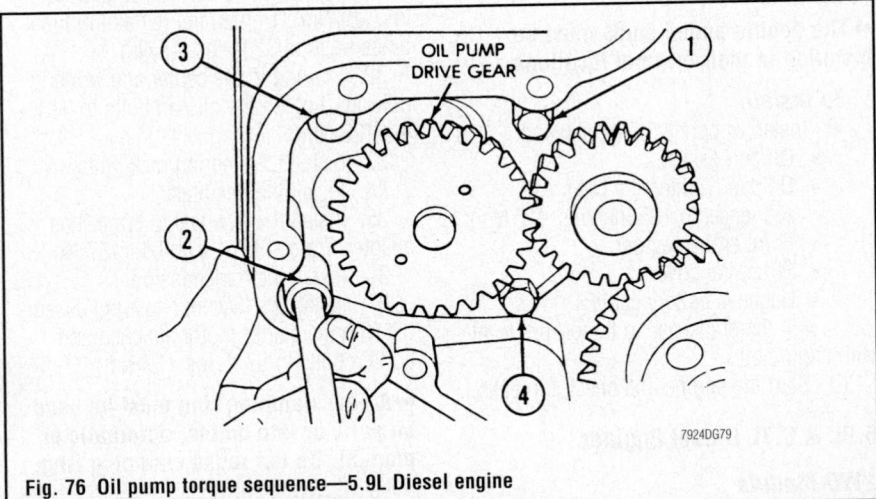

Fig. 76 Oil pump torque sequence—5.9L Diesel engine

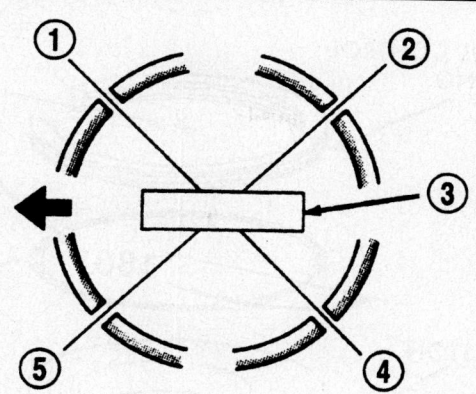

1 - SIDE RAIL UPPER
2 - NO. 1 RING GAP
3 - PISTON PIN
4 - SIDE RAIL LOWER
5 - NO. 2 RING GAP AND SPACER EXPANDER GAP

2399PG02

Fig. 77 Piston ring end-gap spacing—5.7L engines

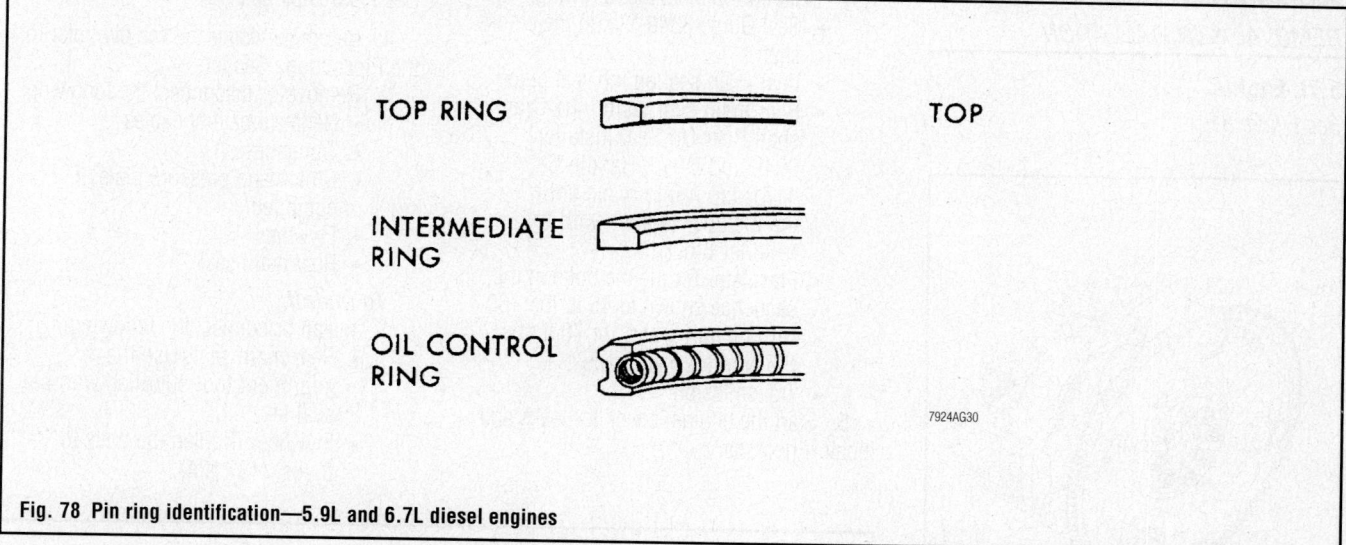

TOP RING

INTERMEDIATE RING

OIL CONTROL RING

TOP

7924AG30

Fig. 78 Pin ring identification—5.9L and 6.7L diesel engines

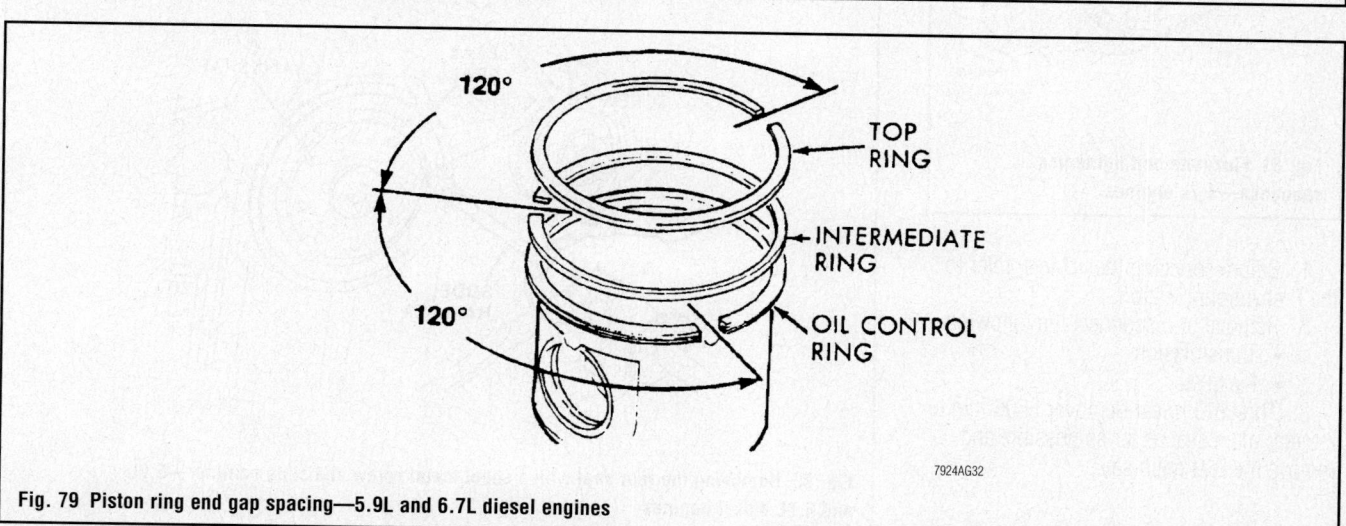

120°

120°

TOP RING

INTERMEDIATE RING

OIL CONTROL RING

7924AG32

Fig. 79 Piston ring end gap spacing—5.9L and 6.7L diesel engines

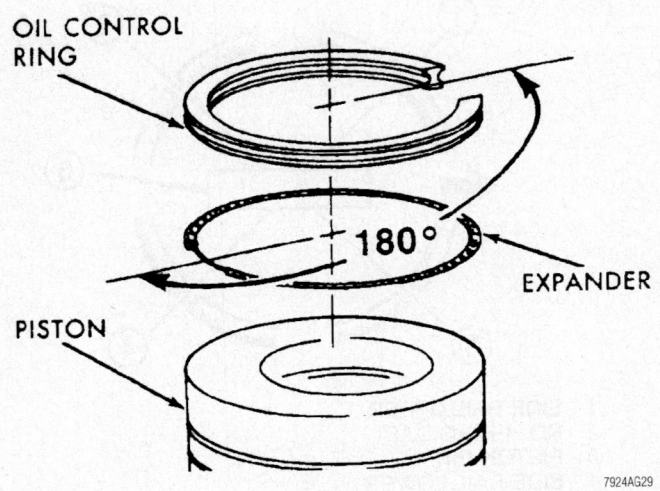

Fig. 80 Oil control ring-to-spacer end gap spacing—5.9L and 6.7L diesel engines

REAR MAIN SEAL

REMOVAL & INSTALLATION

5.7L Engine

See Figure 81.

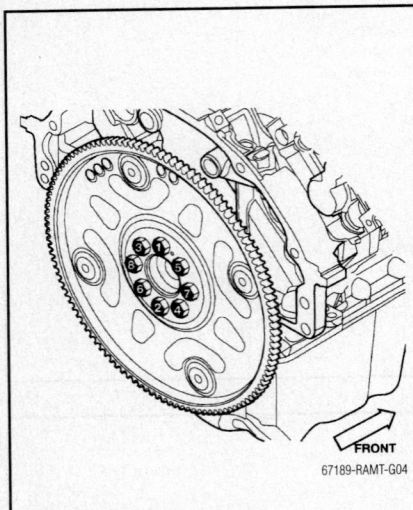

67189-RAMT-G04

Fig. 81 Flexplate bolt tightening sequence—5.7L engines

1. Before servicing the vehicle, refer to the Precautions Section.
2. Remove or disconnect the following:
   • Transmission
   • Flexplate
3. Thread Oil Seal Remover 8506 into the rear main seal as far as possible and remove the rear main seal.

To install:

4. Install or connect the following:
   • Seal Guide 8349-2 onto the crankshaft
   • Rear main seal on the seal guide
   • Rear main seal, using the Crankshaft Rear Oil Seal Installer 8349 and Driver Handle C-4171; tap it into place until the installer is flush with the cylinder block
   • Flexplate. Torque the bolts in the sequence shown to 45 ft. lbs. (60 Nm) on auto trans., or 70 ft. lbs. (95 Nm) for man. trans.
   • Transmission
5. Start the engine, check for leaks and repair if necessary.

5.9L & 6.7L Diesel Engines

See Figures 82 and 83.

1. Before servicing the vehicle, refer to the Precautions Section.
2. Remove or disconnect the following:
   • Negative battery cables
   • Transmission
   • Clutch and pressure plate, if equipped
   • Flywheel
   • Rear main seal

To install:

3. Install or connect the following:
   • Rear main seal. Use the alignment tool supplied with the seal kit.
   • Flywheel. Tighten the bolts to 101 ft. lbs. (137 Nm).

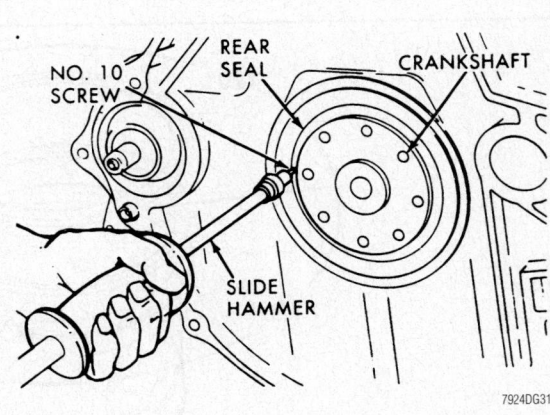

7924DG31

Fig. 82 Removing the rear seal with a sheet metal screw and slide hammer—5.9L and 6.7L diesel engines

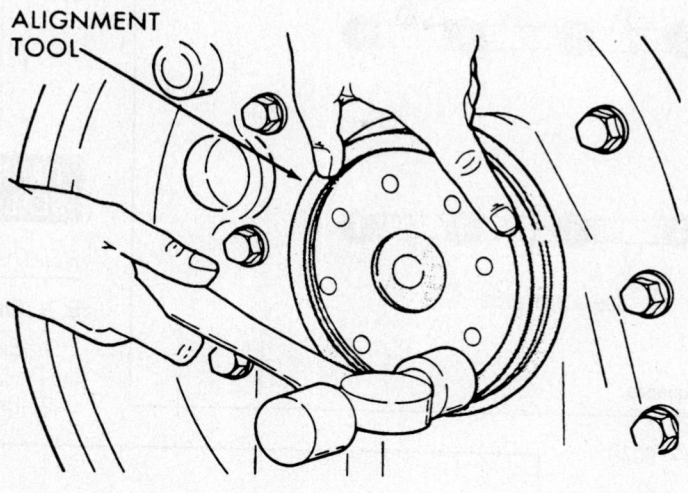

Fig. 83 Place the alignment tool on the seal and tap the seal into place—5.9L and 6.7L diesel engines

- Clutch and pressure plate, if equipped
- Transmission
- Negative battery cables

4. Start the engine and check for leaks.

ROCKER ARMS/SHAFTS

REMOVAL & INSTALLATION

5.7L Engine

See Figures 84 and 85.

1. Before servicing the vehicle, refer to the Precautions Section.
2. Install push rod retainer (1) 9070.
3. Loosen the rocker shafts using the sequence provided.

✸✸ WARNING

The rocker shaft assemblies are not interchangeable between intake and exhaust. The intake rocker arms are marked with an (I).

4. Remove the rocker shafts. Note location for reassembly.

✸✸ WARNING

The longer push rods are for the exhaust side, and the shorter push rods are for intake side.

5. Remove the push rods. Note push rod location for reassembly.

To install:

6. Install the push rods in the same order as removed.
7. Install the push rod retainer (1) 9070.

✸✸ WARNING

Ensure that retainers and rocker arms are not overlapped when tightening bolts or engine damage could result.

✸✸ WARNING

Verify that push rod is installed into rocker arm and tappet correctly while installing rocker shaft assembly or

engine damage could result. Recheck after rocker shaft has been tightened to specification.

8. Install rocker shaft assemblies in the same order as removed.
9. Tighten the rocker shaft bolts to 195 inch. lbs. (22 Nm). Use loosening procedure for tightening sequence.

✸✸ WARNING

DO NOT rotate or crank the engine during or immediately after rocker arm installation. Allow the hydraulic roller tappets adequate time to bleed down (about 5 minutes).

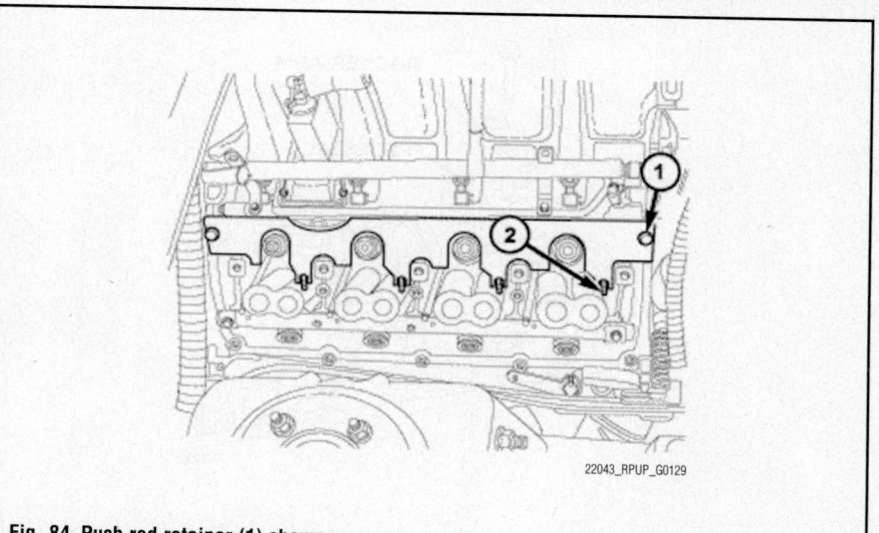

Fig. 84 Push rod retainer (1) shown

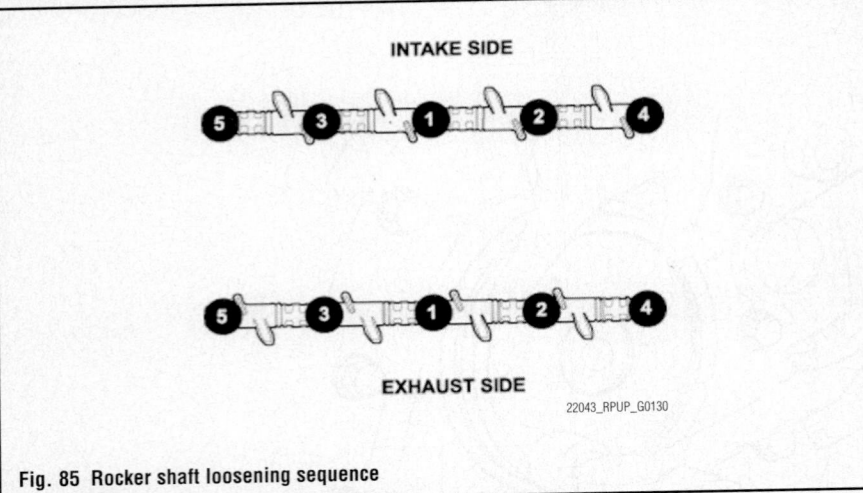

Fig. 85 Rocker shaft loosening sequence

10. Remove push rod retainer (1) 9070.
11. Install cylinder head cover.

5.9L & 6.7L Diesel Engines

See Figures 86 and 87.

1. Before servicing the vehicle, refer to the Precautions Section.
2. Remove or disconnect the following:
   - Negative battery cables
   - Valve cover

❋❋ WARNING

The sockets may fall out of the rocker arms as the rocker arms are lifted from the cylinder head. Do not drop the sockets into the engine.

➡ Keep all valvetrain components in order for assembly.

   - Rocker arms and pedestal assemblies

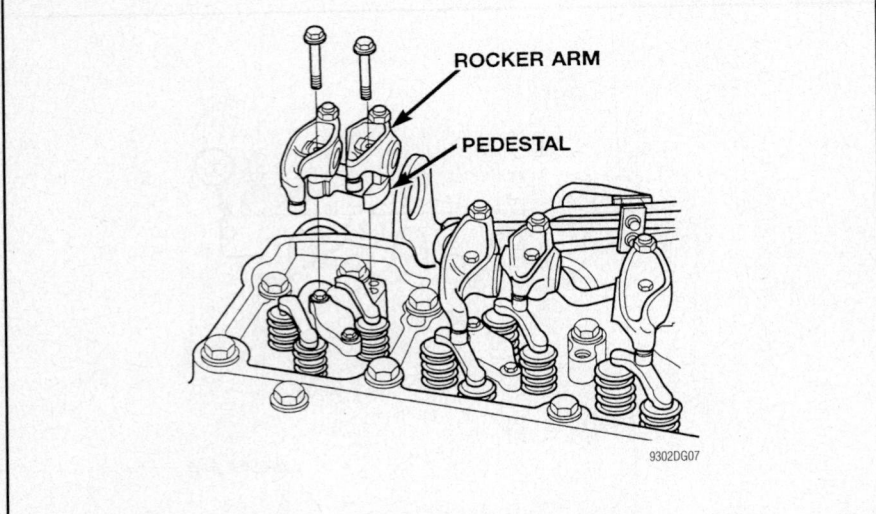

Fig. 86 Exploded view of the rocker arm mounting—5.9L Diesel engine

To install:

3. Install or connect the following:
   - Rocker arm and pedestal assemblies. Tighten the bolts to 27 ft. lbs. (36 Nm).
   - Valve cover. Tighten the bolts to 18 ft. lbs. (24 Nm).
   - Negative battery cables

TIMING CHAIN COVER AND SEAL

REMOVAL & INSTALLATION

5.7L Engine

1. Before servicing the vehicle, refer to the Precautions Section.
2. Drain the cooling system.

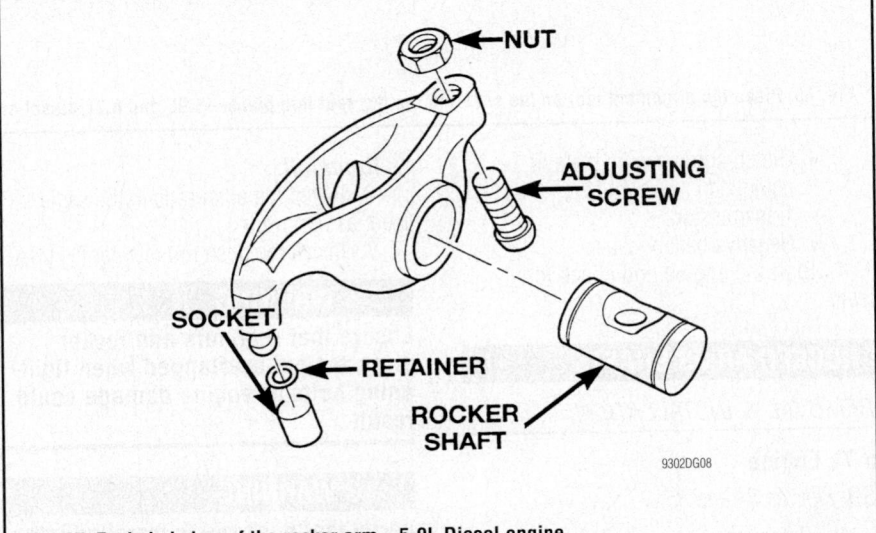

Fig. 87 Exploded view of the rocker arm—5.9L Diesel engine

3. Remove or disconnect the following:
   - Negative battery cable
   - Drive belt
   - Radiator and cooling fan
   - Coolant and washer bottles
   - Fan shroud
   - A/C compressor
   - Alternator
   - Radiator and heater hoses
   - Tensioner and idler pulleys
   - Crankshaft damper
   - Power steering pump
   - Oil pan and pickup tube
   - Timing cover

To install:

4. Install or connect the following:
   - Timing cover. Torque all fasteners to 21 ft. lbs. (28 Nm). Torque the large lifting lug to 40 ft. lbs. (55 Nm).

- Oil pan and pickup tube
- Power steering pump
- Crankshaft damper
- Tensioner and idler pulleys
- Radiator and heater hoses
- Alternator
- A/C compressor
- Fan shroud
- Coolant and washer bottles
- Radiator fan
- Drive belt
- Negative battery cable

5.9L & 6.7L Diesel Engines

1. Before servicing the vehicle, refer to the Precautions Section.
2. Remove or disconnect the following:

- Negative battery cables
- Accessory drive belt
- Cooling fan and shroud
- Accessory drive belt tensioner
- Oil fill tube and adapter
- Crankshaft pulley
- Front cover
- Front crankshaft seal

To install:

3. Install or connect the following:

- Front crankshaft seal
- Front cover. Tighten the bolts to 18 ft. lbs. (24 Nm).
- Crankshaft pulley
- Oil fill tube and adapter. Tighten the bolts to 32 ft. lbs. (43 Nm).
- Accessory drive belt tensioner. Tighten the bolts to 32 ft. lbs. (43 Nm).
- Cooling fan and shroud
- Accessory drive belt. Tighten the crankshaft pulley bolts to 92 ft. lbs. (125 Nm).
- Negative battery cables

4. Start the engine and check for leaks.

TIMING CHAIN AND SPROCKETS

REMOVAL & INSTALLATION

5.7L Engine

See Figure 88.

1. Before servicing the vehicle, refer to the Precautions Section.
2. Drain the cooling system.

3. Remove timing cover. Refer to Timing Chain Cover and Seal.
4. Re-install the damper
5. Rotate the crankshaft so that the camshaft sprocket and crankshaft sprocket timing marks are aligned.

➡ **The camshaft pin and slot in the cam sprocket must be a 12 o'clock, the crankshaft keyway must be at 2 o'clock, and the dots or paint on the crank sprocket must be at 6 o'clock.**

6. Pin back the tensioner shoe.
7. Remove the timing chain and sprockets.

To install:

8. With the timing marks aligned, wrap the chain around the sprockets. The chain must be installed with the single plated link aligned with the dot or paint on the cam sprocket. The dot or paint on the crank sprocket should be aligned between the 2 plated links.
9. Install the assembly and torque the cam sprocket bolt to 90 ft. lbs. (122 Nm).
10. Unpin the tensioner and verify the alignment.

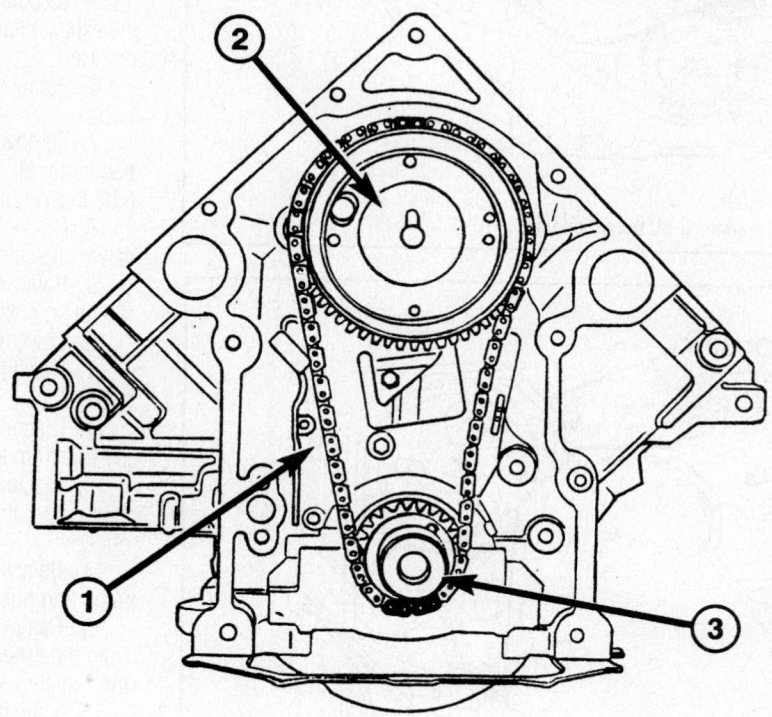

1 - Chain Tensioner
2 - Camshaft Sprocket
3 - Crankshaft Sprocket

Fig. 88 Timing mark alignment—5.7L engines

2399PG01

11. Install timing cover. Refer to Timing Chain Cover and Seal.

5.9L & 6.7L Diesel Engines

See Figures 89 and 90.

1. Before servicing the vehicle, refer to the Precautions Section.
2. Remove or disconnect the following:
   - Negative battery cables
   - Accessory drive belt
   - Cooling fan and shroud
   - Belt tensioner
   - Oil fill tube and adapter
   - Crankshaft pulley

   - Front cover
   - Camshaft
3. Press the camshaft out of the timing gear.

To install:

4. Install the camshaft key.
5. Heat the timing gear in an oven to 350°F (177°C) for 45 minutes.

➡**The camshaft gear will be permanently distorted if overheated. Do not exceed 350°F (177°C).**

6. Install the timing gear to the camshaft with the timing marks facing out and the gear seated on the camshaft shoulder.

7. Install or connect the following:
   - Camshaft with the timing marks aligned
   - Front cover. Tighten the bolts to 18 ft. lbs. (24 Nm).
   - Crankshaft pulley. Tighten the bolt to 92 ft. lbs. (125 Nm).
   - Oil fill tube and adapter. Tighten the mounting bolts to 32 ft. lbs. (43 Nm).
   - Belt tensioner. Tighten the mounting bolts to 32 ft. lbs. (43 Nm).
   - Cooling fan and shroud
   - Accessory drive belt
   - Negative battery cables

TURBOCHARGER

REMOVAL & INSTALLATION

5.9L Diesel Engine

1. Before servicing the vehicle, refer to the Precautions Section.
2. Disconnect the battery negative cables.
3. Raise and safely support the vehicle.
4. Disconnect the exhaust pipe from the turbocharger elbow.
5. Disconnect the exhaust system from the exhaust hangers and move the system rearward.
6. Remove the exhaust elbow from the turbo.
7. Remove the bolts from the turbocharger oil drain tube. Remove oil drain tube from engine.
8. Disconnect wastegate command valve connector.
9. Remove two lower turbocharger mounting nuts.
10. Lower the vehicle.
11. Disconnect the turbocharger air inlet hose.
12. Disconnect the turbocharger oil supply line from the turbocharger.
13. Disconnect the charge air cooler inlet pipe from the turbocharger compressor outlet.
14. Remove two upper turbocharger mounting nuts.
15. Remove the turbocharger and gasket from the exhaust manifold from the top of the vehicle.
16. If the turbocharger is not to be installed immediately, cover the opening to prevent material from entering into the manifold.
17. If replacing the turbocharger, transfer the turbocharger oil supply fitting to the new

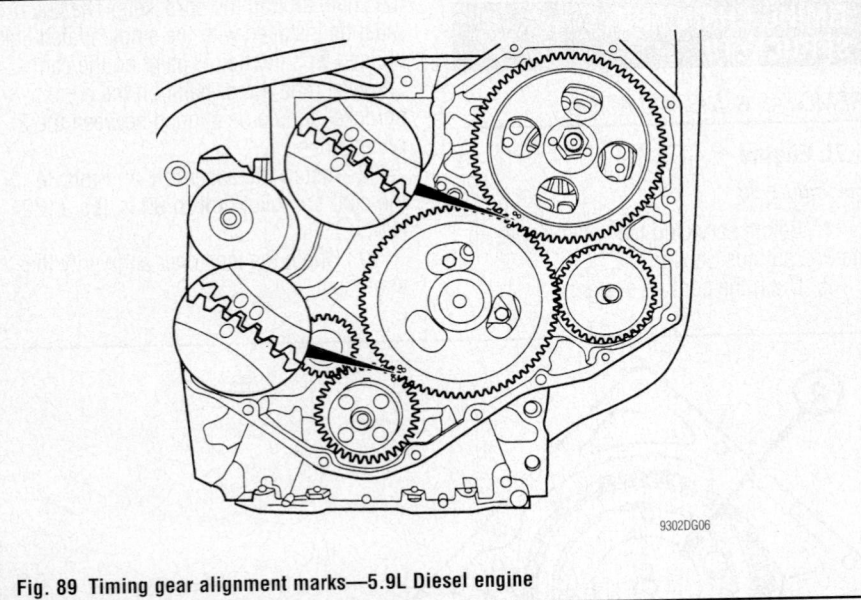

Fig. 89 Timing gear alignment marks—5.9L Diesel engine

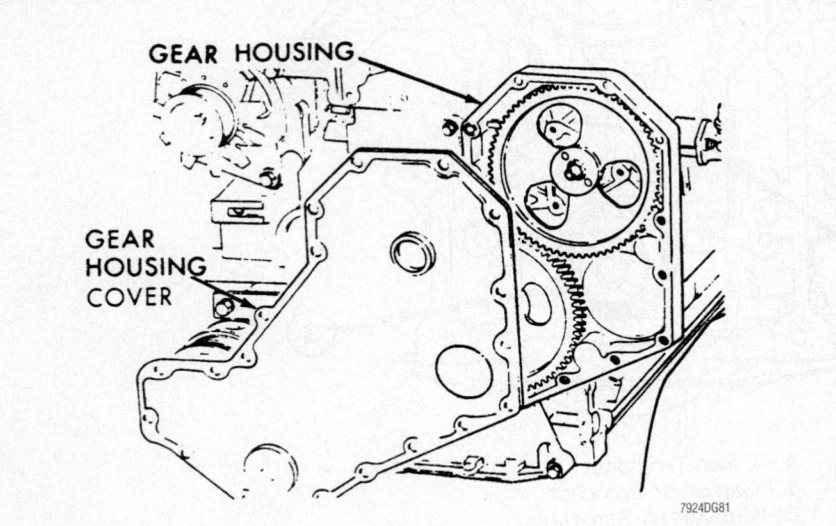

Fig. 90 Remove the gear cover to replace the timing gears—5.9L Diesel engine

assembly. Tighten fitting to 27 ft. lbs. (36 Nm).

18. Clean and inspect the sealing surface.

19. Using a straight edge and feeler gauge, measure the flatness between the two longest sections of the turbocharger mounting flange. Specification is 0.0039 inch. (0.1 mm) maximum.

20. Using a straight edge and feeler gauge, the exhaust manifold flange. Specification is 0.0039 inch (0.1 mm) maximum. The combined measurements of the turbocharger and the exhaust manifold flanges must not exceed the maximum spec of either of the two flanges. Example: if the turbocharger flange measured 0.005 mm and the exhaust manifold flange measures 0.005 mm then the spec.

✳✳ WARNING

The Wastegate Command Valve, and Command Valve O-ring are the only serviceable components on the turbocharger. The turbocharger itself is serviced as a component. Do not attempt to repair the turbocharger as turbocharger and/or engine damage can result.

To install:

✳✳ WARNING

Insure that turbocharger and charge air cooler are free of excess oil and debris. Do not allow any water or solvents to enter the turbocharger inlet or outlet If necessary clean turbocharger.

21. Using a new gasket, install the turbocharger. Tighten the turbocharger mounting nuts to 32 ft. lbs. (43 Nm).

22. Raise and safely support the vehicle.

23. Inspect oil drain tube O-rings for nicks or cuts. Replace if necessary.

24. Using a new gasket, install the oil drain tube to the turbocharger. Tighten the drain tube bolts to18 ft. lbs. (24Nm).

➡**Always use a new clamp when installing the exhaust elbow.**

25. Install the exhaust elbow.

26. Reinstall the exhaust system on the exhaust hangers.

27. Connect the exhaust pipe to the turbocharger and tighten the bolts to 100 inch lbs. (11 Nm).

28. Connect wastegate command valve connector.

29. Lower the vehicle.

30. **Pre-lube the turbocharger**. Pour 50 to 60 cc (2 to 3 oz.) clean engine oil in the oil supply line fitting. Carefully rotate the turbocharger impeller by hand to distribute the oil thoroughly.

31. Install turbocharger oil return tube.

32. Install and tighten the oil supply line to 18 ft. lbs. (24Nm).

33. Position the charge air cooler inlet pipe to the turbocharger. With the clamp in position, tighten the clamp nut to 95 inch lbs. (11 Nm).

34. Position the air inlet hose to the turbocharger. Tighten the clamp to 35 inch lbs. (4 Nm).

35. Connect the battery negative cables.

36. Start the engine to check for leaks.

6.7L Diesel Engine

1. Before servicing the vehicle, refer to the Precautions Section.

2. Disconnect the battery negative cables.

3. Drain cooling system.

4. Remove air filter housing.

5. Remove charge air cooler inlet tube at turbocharger inlet.

6. Disconnect turbocharger speed sensor electrical connector.

7. Disconnect turbocharger actuator electrical connector.

8. Remove turbocharger oil supply line.

9. Remove turbocharger coolant lines at engine block.

10. Remove RH engine mount.

11. Remove exhaust steady rest bracket from transmission.

12. Remove V-clamp from turbocharger exhaust outlet.

13. Remove turbocharger drain tube mounting bolts at turbocharger. Remove tube from cylinder block.

14. Lower the vehicle.

15. Using Tool 9866, remove turbocharger mounting nuts.

16. Remove turbocharger from vehicle

To install:

✳✳ WARNING

Insure that turbocharger and charge air cooler are free of excess oil and debris. Do not allow any water or solvents to enter the turbocharger inlet or outlet If necessary, clean turbocharger

17. Clean turbocharger mounting surface and exhaust manifold flange surface.

18. Using a new gasket, position turbocharger on exhaust manifold studs.

19. Install turbocharger mounting nuts. Using Turbocharger Tool 9866, using across pattern, tighten nuts to 32 ft. lbs. (43Nm).

20. Install turbocharger speed sensor. Tighten bolt to 70 inch lbs. (8 Nm).

21. Install coolant supply and return lines. Tighten banjo fittings 18 ft. lbs. (24 Nm).

22. Inspect oil drain tube O-rings for nicks or cuts. Replace if necessary.

23. Position turbocharger drain tube into engine block.

24. Using a new gasket, install turbocharger drain tube mounting bolts. Tighten to 95 inch lbs. (11 Nm).

25. Install RH engine mount.

26. Using a new V—clamp, connect exhaust pipe to turbocharger exhaust outlet. Tighten clamp to 95 inch lbs. (11 Nm).

27. Lower the vehicle.

28. Install charge air tube to turbocharger inlet. Tighten clamp to 95 inch lbs. (11 Nm).

29. Install oil return line. Tighten fitting to 27 ft. lbs. (36 Nm).

30. **Pre-lube** turbocharger with 1–2 oz. (29.9–59.14 ml) clean engine oil.

31. Install turbocharger oil pressure line. Tighten fitting to 27 ft. lbs. (36 Nm).

32. Connect turbocharger actuator electrical connector.

33. Connect valve cover breather tube.

34. Install the air filter housing.

35. Connect the negative battery cables.

36. Fill the cooling system.

37. Check for leaks and proper operation.

VALVE COVERS

REMOVAL & INSTALLATION

5.7L Engine

See Figure 91.

1. Before servicing the vehicle, refer to the Precautions Section.

2. Disconnect the negative battery cable.

3. Disconnect ignition coil connector.

4. Remove ignition coil retaining bolts.

5. Remove ignition coil.

6. Remove cylinder head cover retaining bolts.

7. Remove cylinder head cover.

To install:

✳✳ WARNING

Do not use harsh cleaners to clean the cylinder head covers. Severe damage to covers may occur.

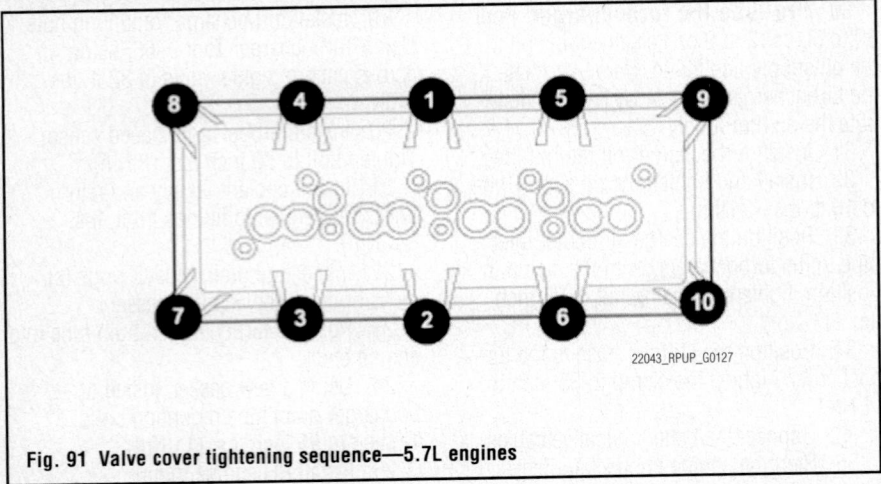

Fig. 91 Valve cover tightening sequence—5.7L engines

8. Clean cylinder head cover and both sealing surfaces. Inspect and replace gasket as necessary.

9. Install cylinder head cover and hand start all fasteners. Verify that all double ended studs are in the correct location.

10. Tighten cylinder head cover bolts and double ended studs to 70 inch lbs. (8Nm). Begin torque sequence in the middle of head cover and tighten bolts moving outward in a crisscross pattern from top to bottom.

11. Before installing coil(s), apply dielectric grease to inside of spark plug boots.

12. Install ignition coils. Tighten fasteners to 62 inch lbs. (7Nm).

13. Connect ignition coil electrical connectors.

14. Install PCV hose.

15. Connect the negative battery cable.

5.9L Diesel Engine

See Figure 92.

1. Before servicing the vehicle, refer to the Precautions Section.

2. Disconnect the negative battery cable.

3. Disconnect the breather tube and breather drain tube from the cylinder head cover.

4. Remove the cylinder head cover bolts.

5. Remove the cylinder head cover

To install:

6. Position cylinder head cover on top of cylinder head cover gasket.

7. Install bolts finger tight.

8. Starting with the center bolt, torque bolts to 18 ft. lbs. (24 Nm).

9. Install breather tube to cylinder head cover.

10. Install breather drain tube to cylinder head cover.

6.7L Diesel Engine

1. Before servicing the vehicle, refer to the Precautions Section.

2. Disconnect both negative battery cables.

3. Remove the breather cover cap screws (8—M6 screws).

4. Remove the CCV breather and filter cover.

5. Disconnect CCV Tube at the CDR valve (one spring clamp) and remove 10mm nut from tube bracket at EGR Cooler support bracket stud.

6. Disconnect CDR valve tube to air inlet silencer (Spring Clamp).

7. Disconnect CDR/Valve cover pressure sensor connector.

8. Remove Oil fill cap.

9. Remove CCV oil drains from valve cover (2 hoses).

10. Disconnect both injector harness connectors.

11. Remove six (6) valve cover caps crews (10mm).

12. Remove the valve cover.

13. Loosen injector wire nuts from the valve cover gasket (8mm)

14. Remove gasket.

To install:

➡**Gasket must be completely dry and free of oil before installation.**

15. Wipe oil from the valve cover gasket, rocker box, and valve cover.

16. Inspect valve cover gasket for tears, or splits. Replace if necessary.

17. Install the valve cover gasket on the rocker box.

18. Install the injector nuts (8 mm) to injector studs. Torque to 11 inch lbs. (1.25 Nm).

19. Install valve cover and valve cover cap screws (10mm). Tighten screws from center out to 18 ft. lbs. (24 Nm).

20. Install the valve cover CCV drain hoses.

21. Remove any oil from the CCV seal area and install the CCV filter.

22. Install the CCV cover and cap screws (6mm). Tighten to 89 inch lbs. (10 Nm).

23. Connect CDR valve tube to Air Inlet Silencer (spring clamps).

24. Connect the Breather/Valve Cover Pressure sensor.

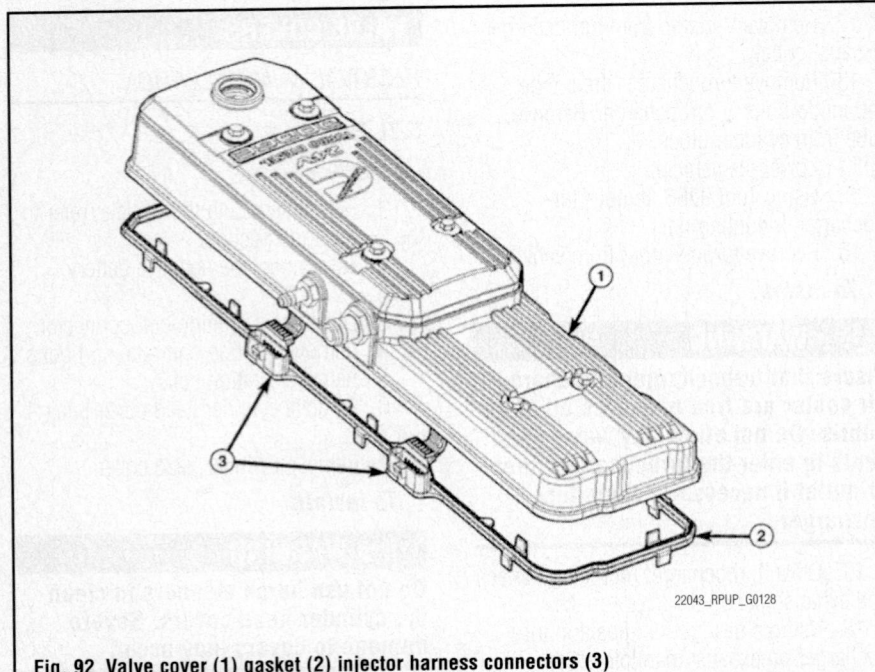

Fig. 92 Valve cover (1) gasket (2) injector harness connectors (3)

25. Install oil fill cap.
26. Connect the batteries.
27. Start the vehicle and check for leaks.

VALVE LASH

ADJUSTMENT

5.7L Engine

The 5.7L engine uses hydraulic lifters. No maintenance or periodic adjustment is required.

5.9L & 6.7L Diesel Engines

See Figures 93 and 94.

1. Before servicing the vehicle, refer to the Precautions Section.
2. Remove or disconnect the following:
   - Negative battery cables
   - Valve cover
   - Fuel pump gear access cover
3. Position the gear as shown and measure the clearance of the indicated valves. No adjustment is necessary if the lash falls within the following specifications:
   - a. Intake—0.006–0.015 inch (0.152–0.381mm).
   - b. Exhaust—0.021–0.034 inch (0.381–0.762mm).
4. Install or connect the following: Fuel pump access cover
   - Valve cover
   - Negative battery cables

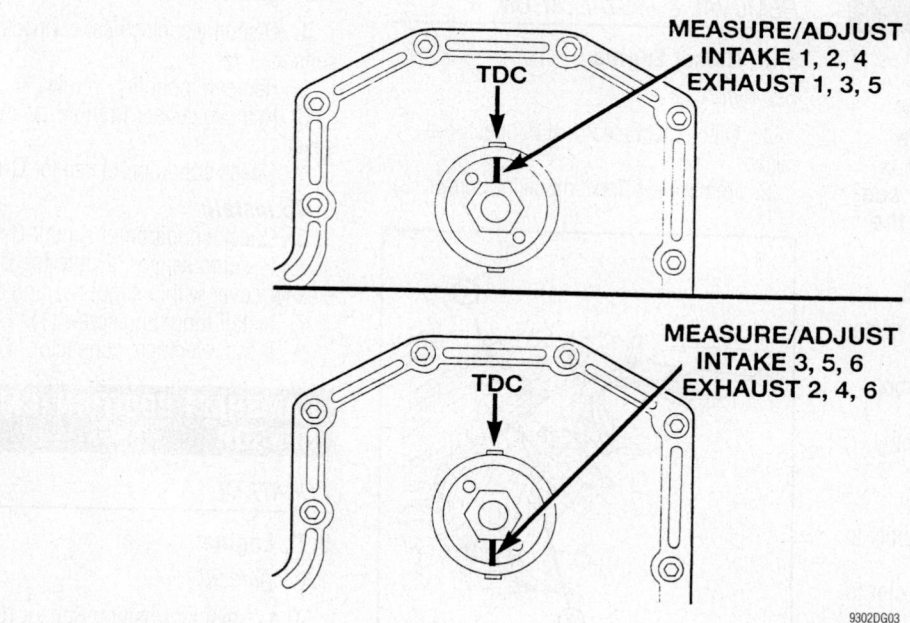

MEASURE/ADJUST
INTAKE 1, 2, 4
EXHAUST 1, 3, 5

TDC

MEASURE/ADJUST
INTAKE 3, 5, 6
EXHAUST 2, 4, 6

TDC

9302DG03

Fig. 93 Adjust the specified valves when the mark on the pump gear is in either of the 2 positions—diesel engines

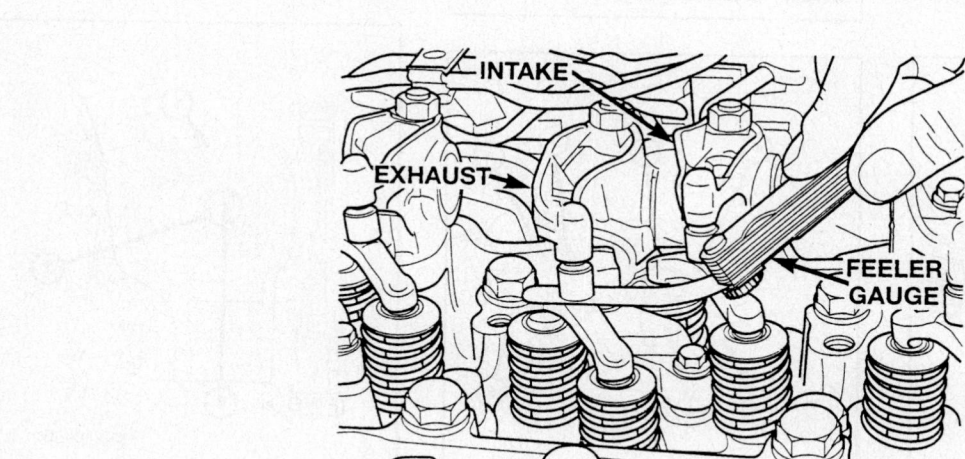

INTAKE

EXHAUST

FEELER GAUGE

9302DG04

Fig. 94 Use a feeler gauge to measure the valve lash—diesel engine

ENGINE PERFORMANCE & EMISSION CONTROLS

ACCELERATOR PEDAL POSITION (APP) SENSOR

LOCATION

See Figure 95.

The APP sensor is located on the accelerator pedal assembly.

REMOVAL & INSTALLATION

See Figure 95.

❊❊ CAUTION

Do not attempt to separate or remove the Accelerator Pedal Position Sensor (APPS) from the accelerator pedal assembly. The APPS and the accelerator pedal is replaced as an assembly. If the sensor is removed from the pedal, the electronic calibration may be destroyed.

1. Disconnect 6-way electrical connector at top of APPS (2).
2. Remove APPS lower mounting bolt (4) and two mounting nuts.
3. Remove pedal and APPS assembly from vehicle.

To install:

4. Position pedal and APPS assembly to its mounting bracket.
5. Connect 6-way electrical connector to top of APPS (2).
6. Install APPS lower mounting bolt (4) and two mounting nuts.
7. If necessary, use a Scan Tool to erase any Diagnostic Trouble Codes (DTC's).

INLET AIR TEMPERATURE/PRESSURE SENSOR

LOCATION

5.9L & 6.7L Diesel Engines

See Figures 96 and 97.

The Inlet Air Temperature/Pressure Sensor is located on the air cleaner cover.

REMOVAL & INSTALLATION

5.9L Diesel Engine

See Figure 96.

1. Disconnect electrical connector at sensor.
2. Remove two Torx® mounting screws (3).

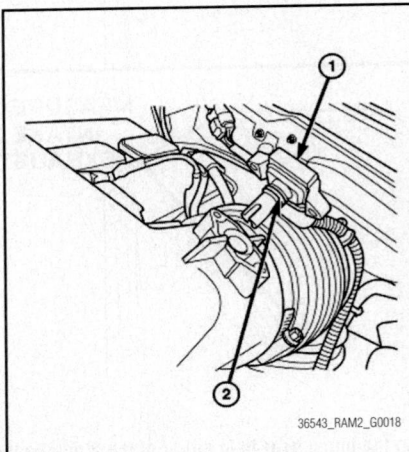

Fig. 96 Inlet Air Temperature/Pressure Sensor—5.9L Diesel engine

3. Remove sensor from air cleaner cover.
4. Check condition of sensor O-ring (2).

To install:

5. Check condition of sensor O-ring.
6. Position sensor into top of air cleaner cover with a slight twisting action.
7. Install 2 mounting screws (3).
8. Install electrical connector (2).

6.7L Diesel Engine

See Figure 97.

1. Disconnect electrical connector (6) at sensor.
2. Remove mounting screw (1).
3. Remove sensor from air cleaner cover.
4. Check condition of sensor O-ring.

To install:

5. Check condition of sensor O-ring.
6. Position sensor (2) into top of air cleaner cover with a slight twisting action.
7. Install mounting screw (1).
8. Install electrical connector (6).

CAMSHAFT POSITION (CMP) SENSOR

LOCATION

5.7L Engine

See Figure 98.

The Camshaft Position Sensor (CMP) (2) is located below the generator on the timing chain / case cover (1) on the right/front side of engine.

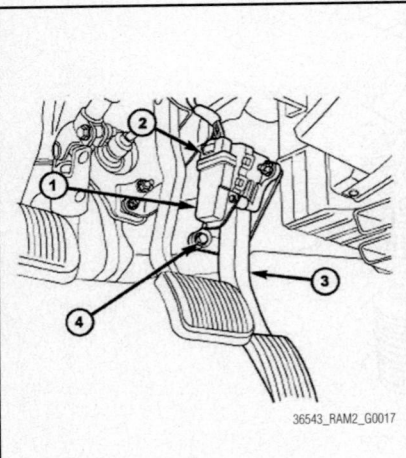

Fig. 95 Accelerator Pedal Position Sensor (APPS)

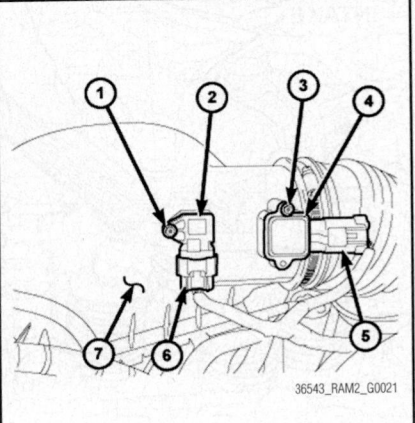

Fig. 97 Inlet Air Temperature/Pressure Sensor—6.7L diesel engine

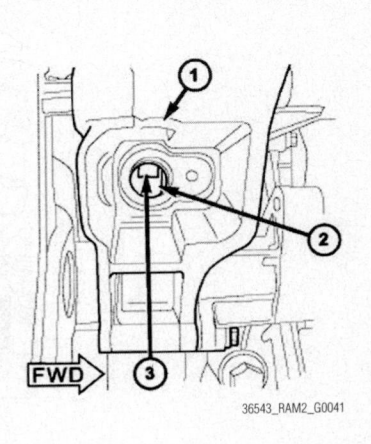

Fig. 98 Camshaft Position (CMP) sensor—5.7L engines

5.9L & 6.7L Diesel Engines

See Figure 99.

The Camshaft Position Sensor (CMP) (1) is located below the fuel injection pump. It is bolted to the back of the timing gear cover.

REMOVAL & INSTALLATION

5.7L Engine

See Figure 98.

1. Disconnect electrical connector (3) at CMP sensor.
2. Remove sensor mounting bolt (3).
3. Carefully twist sensor (2) from timing gear/chain cover.
4. Check condition of sensor O-ring.

To install:

5. Clean out machined hole in timing gear/chain cover.
6. Install sensor (2) into timing gear/chain cover with a slight rocking action. Do not twist sensor into position as damage to O-ring may result.

✳✳ CAUTION

Before tightening sensor mounting bolt, be sure sensor is completely flush to timing gear/chain cover. If sensor is not flush, damage to sensor mounting tang may result.

7. Install mounting bolt (3) and tighten to 106 inch lbs. (12 Nm).
8. Connect electrical connector to sensor.

5.9L & 6.7L Diesel Engines

See Figure 99.

1. Disconnect electrical connector (5) at CMP sensor.
2. Remove sensor mounting bolt (6).

3. Carefully twist sensor from timing gear cover.
4. Check condition of sensor O-ring.

To install:

5. Clean out machined hole in back of timing gear cover.
6. Apply a small amount of engine oil to sensor O-ring.
7. Install sensor into timing gear cover with a slight rocking action. Do not twist sensor into position as damage to O-ring may result.

✳✳ CAUTION

Before tightening sensor mounting bolt, be sure sensor is completely flush to back of timing chain cover. If sensor is not flush, damage to sensor mounting tang may result.

8. Install mounting bolt and tighten to 106 inch lbs. (12 Nm).

CRANKCASE PRESSURE SENSOR

LOCATION

6.7L Diesel Engine

See Figure 100.

The Crankcase Pressure (CP) Sensor (5) is mounted on the valve cover (4).

REMOVAL & INSTALLATION

6.7L Diesel Engine

See Figure 100.

1. Remove mounting screw (6).
2. Disconnect electrical connector (7).
3. Remove sensor (5) from valve cover (4).

4. Check condition of sensor O-ring.

To install:

5. Check condition of sensor O-ring.
6. Install sensor (5) into valve cover (4).
7. Install mounting screw (6). Tighten to 27 inch lbs. (3 Nm) torque.
8. Connect electrical connector (7).

CRANKSHAFT POSITION (CKP) SENSOR

LOCATION

5.7L Engine

See Figure 101.

The Crankshaft Position (CKP) (4) sensor is mounted into the right rear side of the cylinder block. It is positioned and bolted into a machined hole.

5.9L & 6.7L Diesel Engines

The Crankshaft Position Sensor (CKP) on the diesel engine is attached at the front / left side of the engine next to the engine harmonic balancer (crankshaft damper).

REMOVAL & INSTALLATION

5.7L Engine

See Figure 101.

1. Raise vehicle.
2. Disconnect CKP electrical connector at sensor.
3. Remove CKP mounting bolt (3).
4. Carefully twist sensor (4) from cylinder block.
5. Remove sensor from vehicle.
6. Check condition of sensor O-ring.

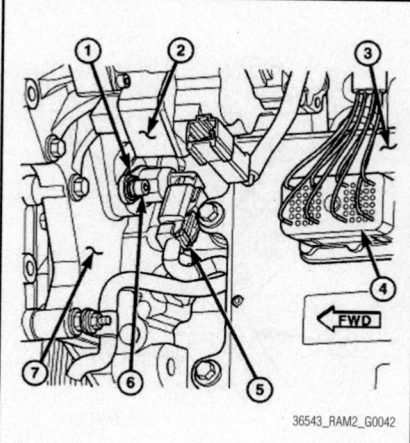

Fig. 99 Camshaft Position (CMP) sensor—5.9L and 6.7L diesel engines

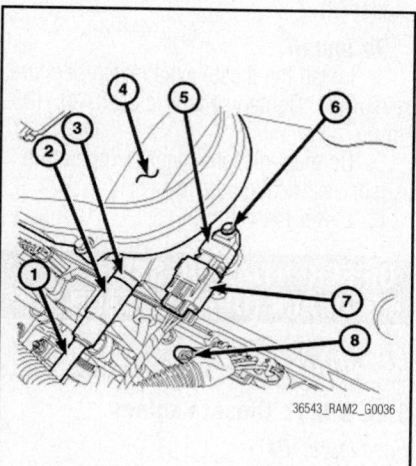

Fig. 100 Crankcase Pressure (CP) Sensor—6.7L diesel engine

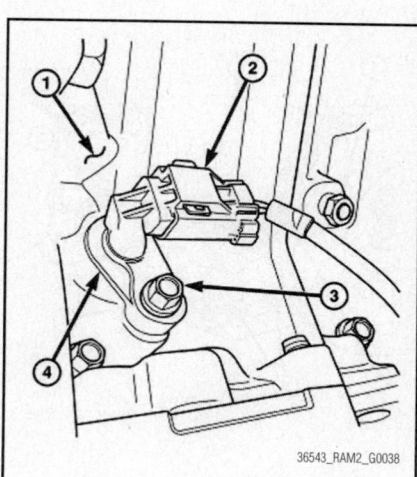

Fig. 101 Crankcase Position (CKP) Sensor—5.7L engines

To install:

7. Clean out machined hole in engine block.

8. Apply a small amount of engine oil to sensor O-ring.

9. Install sensor (4) into engine block with a slight rocking and twisting action.

❊❊ CAUTION

Before tightening the sensor mounting bolt, be sure the sensor is completely flush to the cylinder block. If the sensor is not flush, damage to the sensor mounting tang may result.

10. Install mounting bolt (3) and tighten to 21 ft. lbs. (28 Nm) torque.

11. Connect electrical connector to sensor.

12. Lower the vehicle.

5.9L & 6.7L Diesel Engines

See Figure 102.

1. Raise and support vehicle
2. Disconnect electrical connector (4) at CKP sensor.
3. Remove 1 sensor mounting bolt (3).
4. Remove CKP sensor.

To install:

5. Position and install CKP sensor (5) to engine.
6. Install 1 sensor mounting bolt and tighten to 80 inch lbs. (9 Nm) torque.
7. Install electrical connector (4) to CKP sensor.

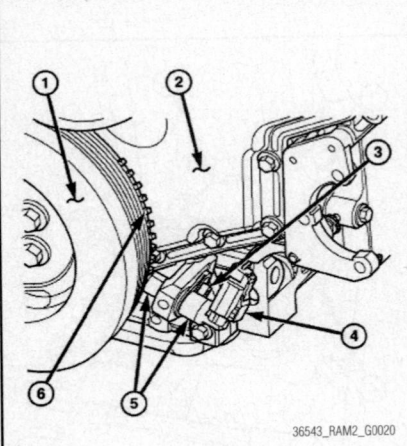

Fig. 102 Crankshaft Position (CKP) Sensor—5.9L and 6.7L diesel engines

DIESEL EXHAUST TEMPERATURE SENSORS

LOCATION

6.7L Diesel Engine

See Figure 103.

The Diesel Exhaust Temperature Sensors are located in the exhaust system.

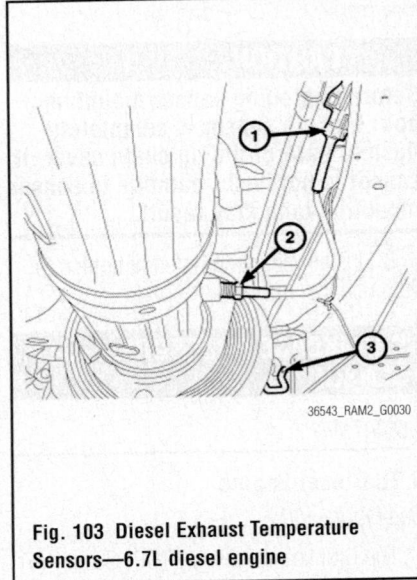

Fig. 103 Diesel Exhaust Temperature Sensors—6.7L diesel engine

REMOVAL & INSTALLATION

6.7L Diesel Engine

See Figure 103.

1. Raise and support vehicle.
2. Disconnect diesel exhaust temperature sensor electrical connector (1).
3. Remove diesel exhaust temperature sensor (2).

To install:

4. Install the diesel exhaust temperature sensor (2). Tighten sensor to 22 ft. lbs. (30 Nm).
5. Connect diesel exhaust temperature sensor electrical connector (1)
6. Lower the vehicle.

DIFFERENTIAL PRESSURE FEEDBACK (DPFE) SENSOR

LOCATION

5.9L & 6.7L Diesel Engines

See Figure 104.

The Exhaust Differential Pressure Sensor is remotely mounted on the transmission housing.

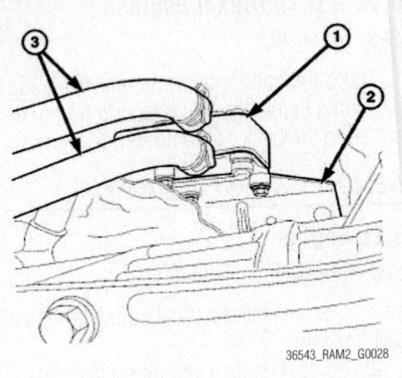

Fig. 104 Exhaust Differential Pressure Sensor—5.9L and 6.7L diesel engines

REMOVAL & INSTALLATION

5.9L & 6.7L Diesel Engines

See Figures 104 and 105.

1. Raise and support vehicle.
2. Disconnect electrical connector.
3. Disconnect hoses at pressure differential pressure sensor.
4. Remove mounting bolt and differential pressure sensor.
5. Remove mounting bolts (1).
6. Remove pressure differential pressure tubing.

To install:

7. Install differential pressure tubing, if removed. Tighten fittings to 22 ft. lbs. (30 Nm).
8. Position differential pressure sensor (1).
9. Install mounting nuts (5) and bolts. Tighten to 89 inch lbs. (10 Nm).

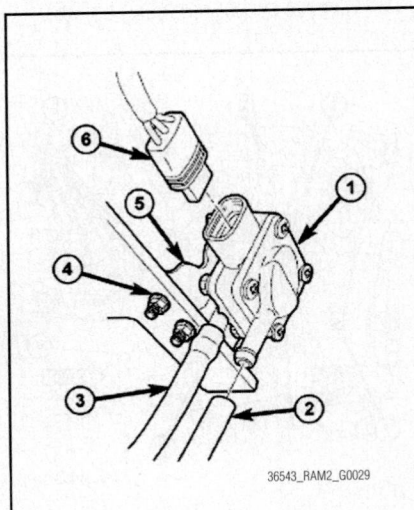

Fig. 105 Exhaust Differential Pressure Sensor components—6.7L diesel engine

➤Before installing, inspect both pressure hoses and make sure there is not any dip across the hoses. In cases where water is frozen, a dip across the hoses can cause condensation which can set a MIL.

10. Install hose (2) to the rear DPF tubing.

11. Install hose (3) to the front DPF tubing.

12. Connect electrical connector (6).

13. Lower the vehicle.

EVAPORATIVE EMISSION (EVAP) CANISTER

REMOVAL & INSTALLATION

Type-1 Canisters

See Figure 106.

A single, vertically mounted EVAP canister (1) is used with Type 1. The ESIM (Emission System Integrity Monitor) switch (3) is mounted to the canister.

1. Raise and support vehicle.

2. If equipped, remove necessary skid plates. Certain models, equipped with a certain fuel tank size, may require the removal of the fuel tank skid plate and/or the transfer case skid plate to gain access to the EVAP canister(s).

3. Disconnect electrical wiring connector from ESIM switch (3).

4. Disconnect vapor line (6) from ESIM switch.

5. Disconnect quick-connect vapor line (5) from canister.

6. Remove canister mounting bracket

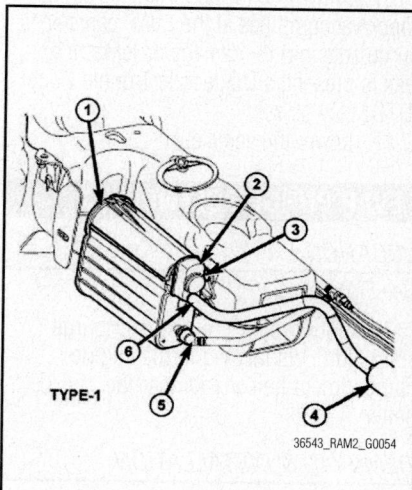

Fig. 106 Evaporative (EVAP) system type 1 canister—5.7L engines

bolt. This is located below and near the ESIM switch.

7. Pull canister from mounting bracket while guiding two canister locating pins from mounting bracket.

To install:

> **❄❄ CAUTION**
>
> **After installing any EVAP canister or ESIM switch, the electrical connector on the switch MUST be in the 3 O'clock position (as viewed from front). This step must be done for proper ESIM switch operation.**

8. Two locating pins are located at rear of canister. Push these two pins into canister mounting bracket.

9. Install canister mounting bracket bolt. This is located below and near the ESIM switch.

10. Connect quick-connect vapor line (5) to canister.

11. Connect vapor line (6) to ESIM switch.

12. Connect electrical wiring connector to ESIM switch (3).

13. If equipped, install necessary skid plates.

14. All vapor/vacuum lines and hoses must be firmly connected. Also check the vapor/vacuum lines at the EVAP canister purge solenoid for damage or leaks. If a leak is present, a Diagnostic Trouble Code (DTC) may be set.

15. Lower the vehicle.

Type-2 Canisters

See Figure 107.

A single, vertically mounted EVAP canister (1) is used with Type 2. The ESIM (Emission System Integrity Monitor) switch (2) is mounted to the canister.

1. Raise and support vehicle.

2. If equipped, remove necessary skid plates. Certain models, equipped with a certain fuel tank size, may require the removal of the fuel tank skid plate and/or the transfer case skid plate to gain access to the EVAP canister(s).

3. Disconnect electrical wiring connector from ESIM switch (3).

4. Disconnect vapor line (7) from ESIM switch.

5. Disconnect quick-connect vapor line (5) at canister.

6. Remove canister mounting bracket bolt (6).

7. Pull canister from mounting bracket while guiding two canister locating pins from mounting bracket.

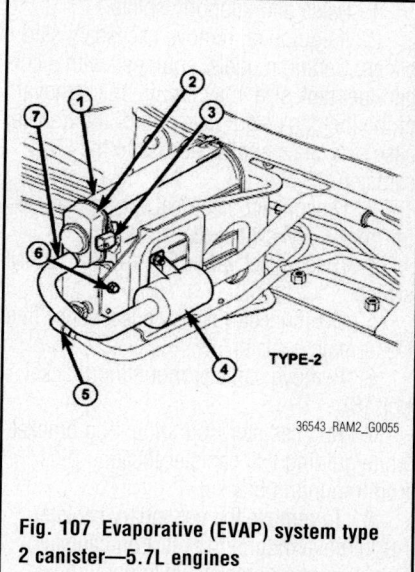

Fig. 107 Evaporative (EVAP) system type 2 canister—5.7L engines

To install:

> **❄❄ CAUTION**
>
> **After installing any EVAP canister or ESIM switch, the electrical connector on the switch MUST be in the 3 O'clock position (as viewed from front). This step must be done for proper ESIM switch operation.**

8. Two locating pins are located at rear of canister. Push these two pins into canister mounting bracket.

9. Install canister mounting bracket bolt (6).

10. Connect quick-connect vapor line (5) to canister.

11. Connect vapor line (7) to ESIM switch.

12. Connect electrical wiring connector to ESIM switch (3).

13. If equipped, install necessary skid plates.

14. All vapor/vacuum lines and hoses must be firmly connected. Also check the vapor/vacuum lines at the EVAP canister purge solenoid for damage or leaks. If a leak is present, a Diagnostic Trouble Code (DTC) may be set.

15. Lower the vehicle.

Type-3 Canisters

See Figure 108.

Dual, vertically mounted EVAP canisters (1) and (4) are used with Type 3. The ESIM (Emission System Integrity Monitor) switch (2) is mounted to the main canister (1). Canister (4) is considered a secondary canister.

1. Raise and support vehicle.

2. If equipped, remove necessary skid plates. Certain models, equipped with a certain fuel tank size, may require the removal of the fuel tank skid plate and/or the transfer case skid plate to gain access to the EVAP canister(s).

3. Disconnect electrical wiring connector from ESIM switch (3).

4. Disconnect vapor line (9) from ESIM switch.

5. Disconnect quick-connect vapor line (7) at main canister.

6. Remove canister mounting bracket bolt (8).

7. Pull canister from mounting bracket while guiding two canister locating pins from mounting bracket.

8. To remove the secondary canister (4), remove mounting bolt. Pull canister from mounting bracket while guiding two canister locating pins (6) from mounting bracket.

To install:

> ❋❋ **CAUTION**
>
> After installing any EVAP canister or ESIM switch, the electrical connector on the switch MUST be in the 3 O'clock position (as viewed from front). This step must be done for proper ESIM switch operation.

9. Push secondary canister (4) into mounting bracket while guiding two canister locating pins (6) into mounting bracket. Install mounting bolt.

10. Push main, primary canister (1) into mounting bracket while guiding two canister locating pins into mounting bracket.

11. Install main canister mounting bracket bolt (8).

12. Connect quick-connect vapor line (7) to main canister.

13. Connect vapor line (9) to ESIM switch.

14. Connect electrical wiring connector to ESIM switch (3).

15. If equipped, install necessary skid plates.

16. All vapor/vacuum lines and hoses must be firmly connected. Also check the vapor/vacuum lines at the EVAP canister purge solenoid for damage or leaks. If a leak is present, a Diagnostic Trouble Code (DTC) may be set.

17. Lower the vehicle.

Type-4 Canisters

See Figure 109.

Dual, horizontally mounted EVAP canisters (1) and (7) are used with Type 4. The ESIM (Emission System Integrity Monitor) switch (3) is mounted to the main, primary canister (1). Canister (7) is considered a secondary canister.

1. Raise and support vehicle.

2. If equipped, remove necessary skid plates. Certain models, equipped with a certain fuel tank size, may require the removal of the fuel tank skid plate and/or the transfer case skid plate to gain access to the EVAP canister(s).

3. Disconnect electrical wiring connector from ESIM switch (4).

4. Disconnect vapor line (5) from ESIM switch.

5. Disconnect quick-connect vapor line (8) at main canister.

6. Remove primary canister mounting bracket nut (9).

7. Pull canister from mounting bracket while guiding two canister locating pins from mounting bracket.

8. To remove the secondary canister (7), remove mounting nut (6). Pull canister from mounting bracket while guiding two canister locating pins from mounting bracket.

To install:

> ❋❋ **CAUTION**
>
> After installing any EVAP canister or ESIM switch, the electrical connector on the switch MUST be in the 3 O'clock position (as viewed from front). This step must be done for proper ESIM switch operation.

9. Position two secondary canister locating pins into mounting bracket. Install mounting nut (6).

10. Position two primary canister locating pins into mounting bracket.

11. Install primary canister mounting bracket nut (9).

12. Connect quick-connect vapor line (8) to main canister.

13. Connect vapor line (5) to ESIM switch.

14. Connect electrical wiring connector to ESIM switch (4).

15. If equipped, install necessary skid plates.

16. All vapor/vacuum lines and hoses must be firmly connected. Also check the vapor/vacuum lines at the EVAP canister purge solenoid for damage or leaks. If a leak is present, a Diagnostic Trouble Code (DTC) may be set.

17. Lower the vehicle.

EVAP PURGE SOLENOID

LOCATION

See Figure 110.

The duty cycle EVAP canister purge solenoid (1) is located in the engine compartment below and near the battery.

REMOVAL & INSTALLATION

See Figure 110.

1. Carefully pull the solenoid assembly straight up from the tongue-type

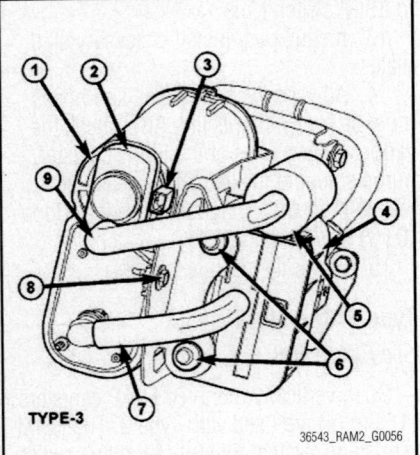

Fig. 108 Evaporative (EVAP) system type 3 canister—5.7L engines

36543_RAM2_G0056

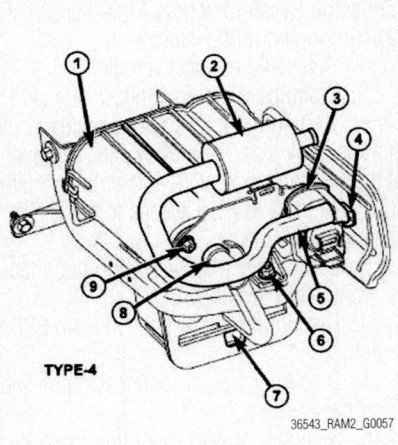

Fig. 109 Evaporative (EVAP) system type 4 canister—5.7L engines

36543_RAM2_G0057

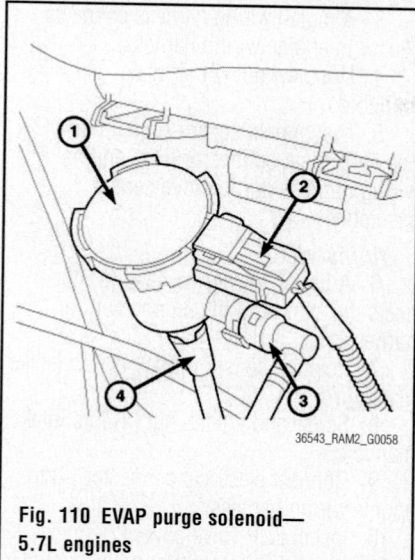

Fig. 110 EVAP purge solenoid—5.7L engines

bracket without bending the two vapor lines.

2. Disconnect electrical wiring connector (2) at solenoid.

3. Disconnect vapor line quick-connect fitting (3) at solenoid.

4. Disconnect vapor line quick-connect fitting (4) at solenoid.

To install:

5. Connect vapor line quick-connect fitting (3) to solenoid.

6. Connect vapor line quick-connect fitting (4) to solenoid.

7. Connect electrical wiring connector (2) to solenoid.

8. Carefully push the solenoid assembly (1) straight down onto the tongue-type bracket without bending the two vapor lines.

EXHAUST GAS PRESSURE SENSOR

LOCATION

6.7L Diesel Engine

See Figure 111.

Refer to the accompanying illustration.

REMOVAL & INSTALLATION

6.7L Diesel Engine

See Figure 111.

1. Disconnect exhaust gas pressure sensor electrical connector (1).

2. Using a 6 point deepwell socket, remove exhaust gas sensor (2).

To install:

3. Using a 6 point deepwell socket, install exhaust gas pressure sensor.

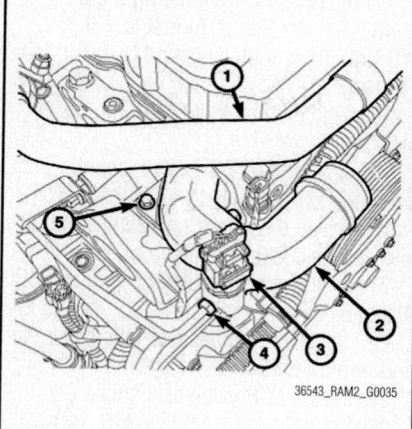

Fig. 111 Exhaust Gas pressure sensor—6.7L diesel engine

4. Tighten sensor to 13 ft. lbs. (18 Nm).

5. Connect exhaust gas pressure sensor electrical connector (3).

EXHAUST GAS RECIRCULATION (EGR) VALVE

LOCATION

5.7L Engine

The electronic EGR valve and solenoid assembly (3) is attached to the front of the right cylinder head (1). An exhaust gas routing tube connects the EGR valve to the intake manifold.

6.7L Diesel Engine

See Figure 112.

Refer to the accompanying illustration.

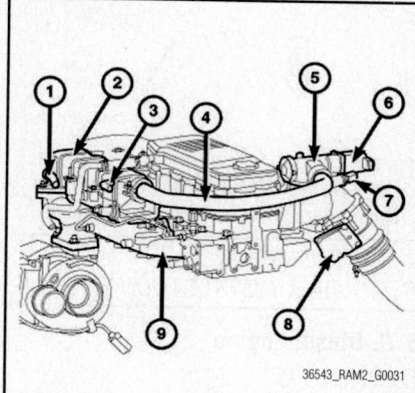

Fig. 112 Exhaust Gas Recirculation (EGR) system components—6.7L diesel engine

See Figure 113.

REMOVAL & INSTALLATION

5.7L Engine

See Figure 113.

1. Use a diagnostic scan tool to record any DTC's (Diagnostic Trouble Codes).

2. Disconnect and isolate the negative battery cable.

3. Disconnect electrical connector (1) from EGR solenoid (2).

4. Remove two bolts (3) connecting EGR tube (4) to valve assembly.

5. Remove gasket located between EGR tube flange and EGR valve assembly.

6. Remove two mounting bolts (2).

7. Separate valve assembly (3) from cylinder head (1).

8. Remove and discard metal gasket located between cylinder head and valve assembly.

To install:

9. Position a new metal gasket between cylinder head (1) and valve assembly (3).

10. Install two mounting bolts (2) and tighten to 20 ft. lbs. (27 Nm).

11. Clean EGR tube where it joins EGR valve.

12. Position new gasket between EGR tube flange and EGR valve assembly.

13. Install two bolts (3) connecting EGR tube (4) to valve assembly (2). Tighten bolts to 20 ft. lbs. (27 Nm).

14. Connect electrical connector (1) to EGR solenoid (2).

15. Connect negative battery cable.

16. Using a diagnostic scan tool, erase any previously recorded DTC's (Diagnostic Trouble Codes).

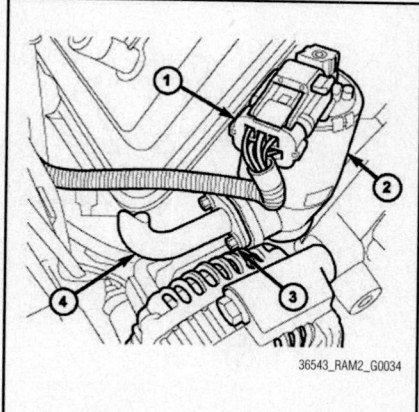

Fig. 113 Exhaust Gas Recirculation (EGR) valve—5.7L engines

6.7L Diesel Engine

See Figure 114.

1. Use a diagnostic scan tool to record any DTC's (Diagnostic Trouble Codes).

2. Disconnect and isolate both negative battery cables at both batteries.

3. Remove four bolts (2) and remove EGR crossover tube cover (1).

4. Remove EGR valve heat shield (2).

5. Loosen (only) clamp (6). Remove clamp (1) at end of EGR Crossover Tube.

6. Remove bolt (3) at center of EGR Crossover Tube.

7. Disconnect electrical connector at end of valve assembly.

8. Remove two EGR valve assembly mounting bolts and two nuts (1).

9. Remove EGR valve assembly (2) from intake connector (3) by prying up.

10. Remove crossover tube doughnut gasket (1) and clean EGR valve. Also clean end of EGR tube of any old gasket material.

11. Remove two gaskets on bottom EGR valve (4). Clean bottom of EGR valve and top of its intake connection point of any old gasket material.

12. To prevent contaminants, cover the exposed opening at intake connection.

To install:

13. Install new gasket (1) to end of EGR tube.

14. Position EGR valve assembly (2) and two new gaskets to intake connection (3).

15. Install two EGR valve mounting bolts (1) and two nuts (1). Tighten four nuts/bolts finger tight only.

16. Install and lightly tighten two clamps (1) and (6) at ends of EGR Crossover Tube.

17. Install bolt (3) finger tight only.

18. Tighten clamp (6) first to 7 ft. lbs. (10 Nm), then tighten clamp (1) to 7 ft. lbs. (10 Nm).

19. Tighten tube bolt (3) to 7 ft. lbs. (10 Nm).

20. Tighten two EGR valve mounting bolts and two nuts (1) to 18 ft. lbs. (25 Nm). Tighten these four nuts/bolts in an alternating, crisscross fashion.

21. Connect electrical connector to EGR Actuator.

22. Install EGR crossover tube cover (1) and four bolts (2).

23. Install EGR valve heat shield (2). Tighten bolts/nuts to 7 ft. lbs. (10 Nm).

24. Connect both negative battery cables to both batteries.

25. Using a diagnostic scan tool, erase any previously recorded DTC's (Diagnostic Trouble Codes).

EXHAUST GAS RECIRCULATION (EGR) TEMPERATURE SENSOR

LOCATION

6.7L Diesel Engine

See Figure 115.

The EGR Temperature Sensor (1) is located on the intake manifold, below, and to the rear of the EGR valve (5).

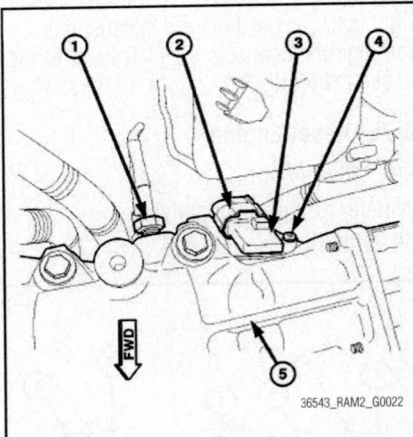

Fig. 115 Exhaust Gas Recirculation (EGR) temperature sensor—6.7L diesel engine

REMOVAL & INSTALLATION

6.7L Diesel Engine

See Figure 115.

1. If equipped, remove four cover bolts (2) and remove EGR crossover tube cover (1).

2. If equipped, remove EGR valve cover (2).

3. A pigtail wiring harness connects sensor to engine wiring harness.

4. Unscrew nut (2) at intake manifold.

5. Disconnect sensor pigtail harness electrical connector from engine wiring harness and remove sensor assembly.

To install:

6. A pigtail wiring harness (3) connects the sensor to the engine wiring harness.

7. Position sensor probe (1) into intake manifold.

8. Screw and tighten nut (2) into intake manifold.

9. Connect electrical connector (4) to engine wiring harness.

10. Install EGR valve cover (2).

11. Install EGR crossover tube cover (1) and four cover bolts (2).

ELECTRONIC CONTROL MODULE (ECM)

LOCATION

The Engine Control Module (ECM) is bolted to the left side of the engine.

REMOVAL & INSTALLATION

5.9L Diesel Engine

See Figure 116.

The Engine Control Module (ECM) (16) is bolted to a support bracket near the fuel filter. The support bracket mounts to the block with four capscrews and vibration isolators. A ground wire is fastened to the bracket. The other end of the wire is fastened to the engine block.

1. Record any Diagnostic Trouble Codes (DTC's) found in the ECM.

➡**To avoid possible voltage spike damage to the ECM, ignition key must be off, and both negative battery cables must be disconnected before unplugging ECM connectors.**

2. Disconnect both negative battery cables at both batteries.

3. Remove the 50—way and 60—way connector bolts at the ECM.

➡**The connector bolt is a female Allen head. As bolt is being removed, very carefully remove connectors from the ECM.**

4. Remove five ECM mounting bolts and remove ECM from vehicle.

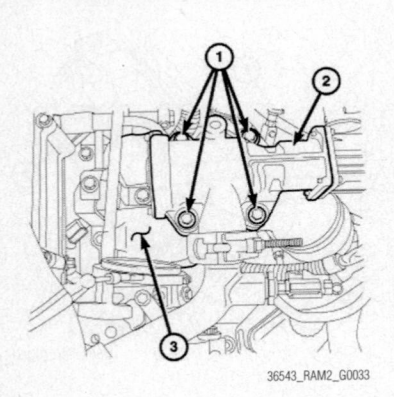

36543_RAM2_G0033

Fig. 114 Exhaust Gas Recirculation (EGR) valve—6.7L diesel engine

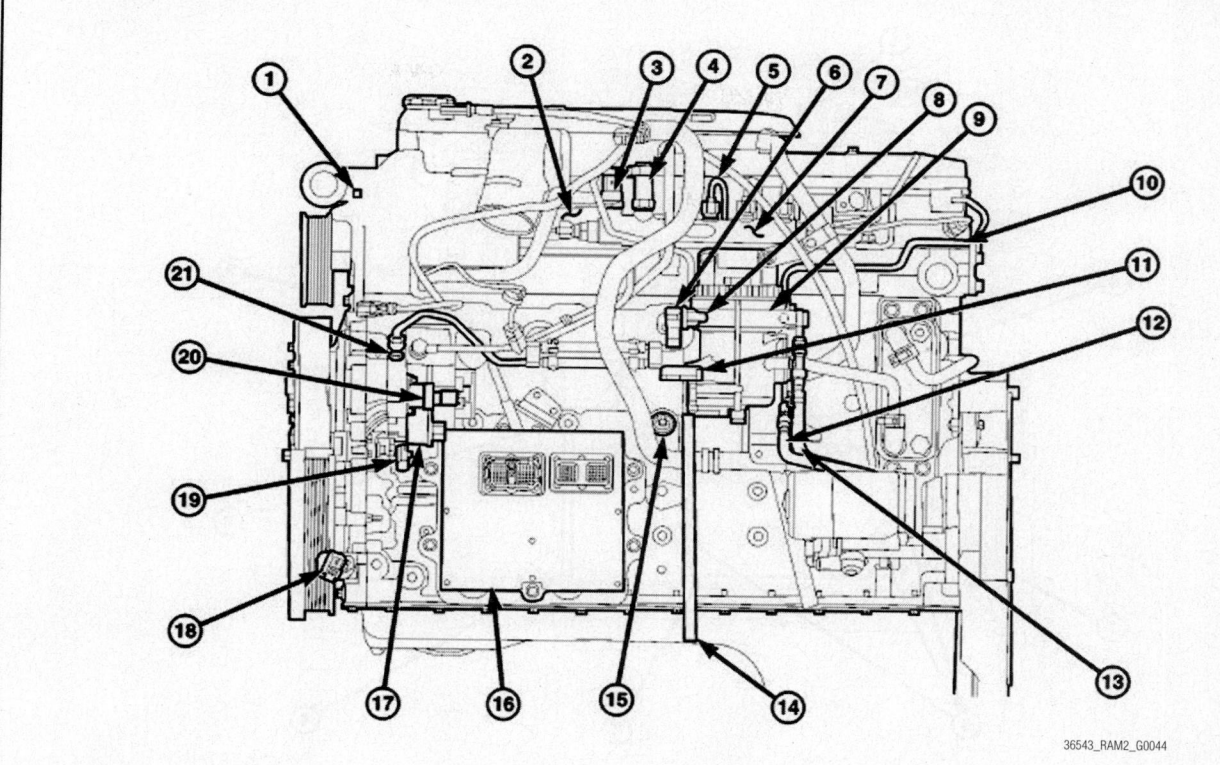

Fig. 116 Engine Control Module (ECM)—5.7L engines Diesel

36543_RAM2_G0044

To install:

➡**Do not apply paint to ECM or a poor ground will result.**

5. Position the ECM (16) to the ECM support bracket and install the five mounting bolts. Tighten bolts to 18 ft. lbs. (25 Nm).

6. Check pin connectors in ECM, 50–way and 60–way connectors for corrosion or damage. Repair as necessary.

7. Clean pins in the 50–way and 60–way electrical connectors with a electrical contact cleaner.

8. Install the 50–way and 60–way connectors to ECM. Tighten connector bolts to 27 inch lbs. (3 Nm).

9. Reconnect both negative battery cables.

10. Reprogram the ECM. Refer to reset procedure.

11. Use a diagnostic scan tool to erase any Diagnostic Trouble Codes (DTC's) from ECM.

6.7L Diesel Engine

See Figure 117.

The Engine Control Module (ECM) (5) is located on the left side of the engine. A support bracket mounts to the block with four

capscrews and vibration isolators. A ground wire is fastened to the bracket. The other end of the wire is fastened to the engine block.

1. Record any Diagnostic Trouble Codes (DTC's) found in the ECM.

➡**To avoid possible voltage spike damage to the ECM, ignition key must be off, and both negative battery cables must be disconnected before unplugging ECM connectors.**

2. Disconnect both negative battery cables at both batteries.

➡**Access to the ECM is easier by working through the left front wheel opening.**

3. Remove left front wheel.
4. Remove plastic left front fender splash shield.
5. Remove electrical connector bolts at ECM.

➡**As each bolt is being removed, very carefully remove connectors from the ECM.**

6. Remove three ECM mounting bolts (6) and remove ECM from engine.

To install:

➡**Do not apply paint to ECM or a poor ground will result.**

7. Position ECM (5) to the ECM support bracket and install mounting bolts. Tighten bolts to 18 ft. lbs. (25 Nm).

8. Check pins in electrical connectors for corrosion, damage or dirt intrusion. Also check all pins for being bent. Repair as necessary. Damaged, dirty, bent or corroded pins could result in poor conductivity, causing intermittent electrical issues or DTC's.

9. Clean pins in electrical connectors with an electrical contact cleaner.

10. Install connectors to ECM. Tighten connector bolts to 27 inch lbs. (3 Nm).

11. Install splash shield.
12. Install left front wheel.
13. Connect both negative battery cables.
14. Program the ECM. Refer to reset procedure.

15. Use a diagnostic scan tool to erase any Diagnostic Trouble Codes (DTC's) from ECM.

RESET PROCEDURE

PCM/ECM Reprogramming—Diesel Engines

PCM/TCM Flash Reprogramming

This procedure will need to be done when one or more of the following situations are true:

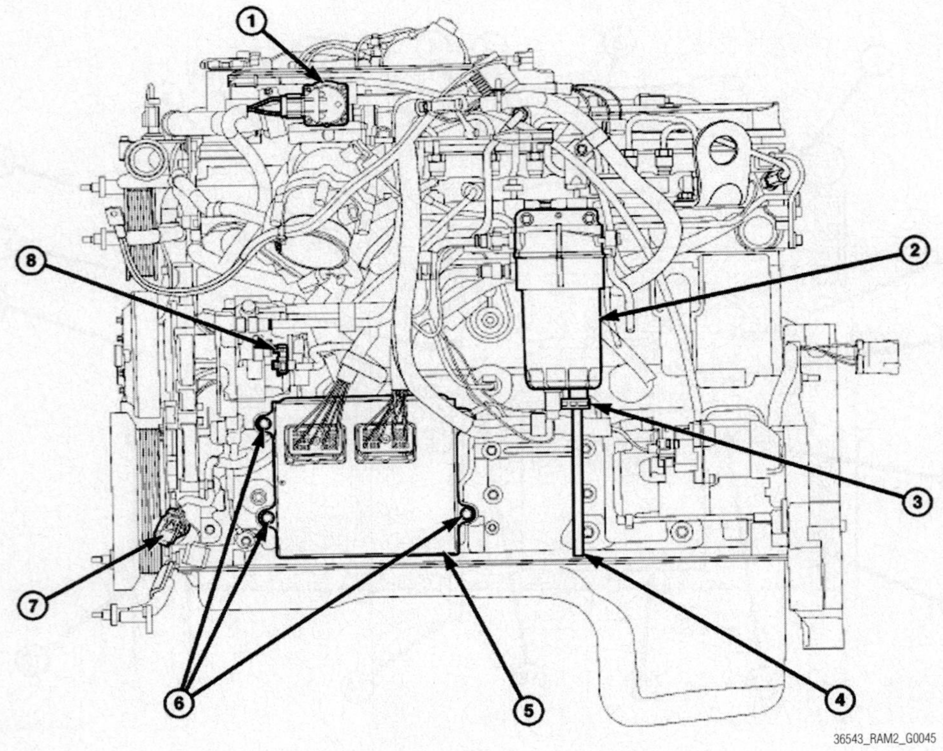

Fig. 117 Engine Control Module (ECM)—6.7L diesel engine

1. A vehicle's Powertrain control module (PCM) has been replaced.

2. A diagnostic trouble code (DTC) is set P1602 - PCM Not Programmed.

3. An updated calibration or software release is available for either the PCM or TCM ECUs.

This procedure assumes that the StarSCAN® and StarMOBILE® devices are configured to your dealership's network with either a wired or wireless connection. The StarSCAN® and StarMOBILE® must also be running at the latest operating system and software release level. For more help on how to network your StarSCAN® or StarMO-BILE® reference the StarSCAN® / StarMO-BILE® Quick Start Networking Guide available on 'DealerCONNECT> Service> StarSCAN® and StarMOBILE® Tools> Online Documentation' or at www.dcctools.com, under the Download Center.

6.7L Diesel Engine

Fuel Injector ID Correction Codes:

See Figure 118.

Each fuel injector has a six-digit alphanumeric correction code. The correction code is printed on the intake side of the fuel injector (1) and is used to identify injector calibration. When replacing any fuel injectors, this code must be entered into the vehicles Engine Control Module (ECM) using a diagnostic scan tool. In addition, if a new ECM is

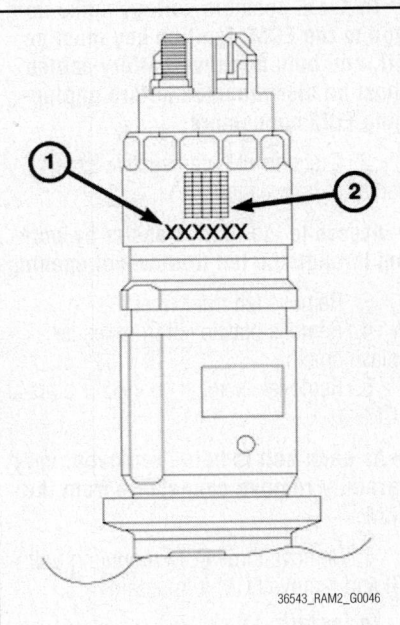

Fig. 118 Fuel injector code location—6.7L diesel engine

installed, use a diagnostic scan tool to program all six of the injector codes from the original fuel injectors into the new ECM.

ENGINE COOLANT TEMPERATURE (ECT) SENSOR

LOCATION

The Engine Coolant Temperature (ECT) sensor protrudes into an engine water jacket.

REMOVAL & INSTALLATION

5.7L Engine

✳✳ CAUTION

Hot, pressurized coolant can cause injury by scalding. Cooling system must be partially drained before removing the Engine Coolant Temperature (ECT) sensor.

1. Before servicing the vehicle, refer to the Precautions Section.

2. Partially drain the cooling system.

3. Remove accessory drive belt

4. Carefully unbolt the air conditioning compressor from front of engine. Do not disconnect any A/C hoses from compressor.

5. Temporarily support the compressor to gain access to ECT sensor.

6. Disconnect the electrical connector from sensor.

7. Remove the ECT sensor from the cylinder block.

To install:

8. Apply thread sealant to ETC sensor threads.

9. Install the ETC sensor into engine.

10. Tighten the sensor to 8 ft. lbs. (11 Nm).

11. Connect the electrical connector to ETC sensor.

12. Install air conditioning compressor onto the front of engine

13. Install the accessory drive belt.

14. Replace any lost engine coolant.

5.9L & 6.7L Diesel Engines

✳✳ CAUTION

Hot, pressurized coolant can cause injury by scalding. Cooling system must be partially drained before removing the Engine Coolant Temperature (ECT) sensor.

1. Before servicing the vehicle, refer to the Precautions Section.

2. Partially drain the cooling system

3. Remove heat shield (if equipped).

4. Disconnect the electrical connector from the ETC sensor.

5. Remove the ETC sensor from the cylinder head.

To install:

6. Install the ECT sensor to the engine.

7. Tighten the ECT sensor to 13 ft. lbs (18 Nm).

8. Connect the electrical connector to the ETC sensor.

9. Install heat shield (if equipped).

10. Replace any lost engine coolant.

EXHAUST TEMPERATURE SENSOR

LOCATION

5.9L Diesel Engine

See Figure 119.

The exhaust temperature sensor is located in the exhaust system, under vehicle.

REMOVAL & INSTALLATION

5.9L Diesel Engine

See Figure 119.

1. Raise and support vehicle.

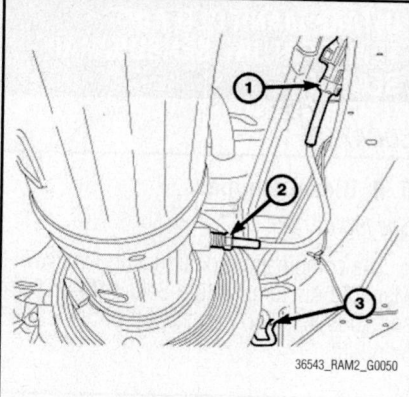

Fig. 119 Exhaust temperature sensor — 5.9L Diesel engine

2. Disconnect diesel exhaust temperature sensor electrical connector (1).

3. Remove diesel exhaust temperature sensor (2).

To install:

4. Install the diesel exhaust temperature sensor (2). Tighten sensor to 22 ft. lbs. (30 Nm).

5. Connect diesel exhaust temperature sensor electrical connector (1)

6. Lower the vehicle.

FUEL RAIL PRESSURE SENSOR

LOCATION

5.9L Diesel Engine

The fuel pressure sensor is mounted vertically near the top/center of the fuel rail.

6.7L Diesel Engine

The fuel pressure sensor is mounted to the rear of the fuel rail.

REMOVAL & INSTALLATION

5.9L Diesel Engine

See Figure 120.

1. Disconnect electrical connector (1) at sensor.

2. Remove sensor from fuel rail.

3. Inspect sensor sealing surface

To install:

4. Inspect fuel pressure sensor sealing surface.

5. Lubricate sensor threads with clean diesel fuel.

6. Install sensor (4) into fuel rail.

7. To prevent leaks, sensor must be tightened to 52 ft. lbs. (70 Nm).

8. Connect electrical connector to sensor.

9. Start engine and check for fuel leaks.

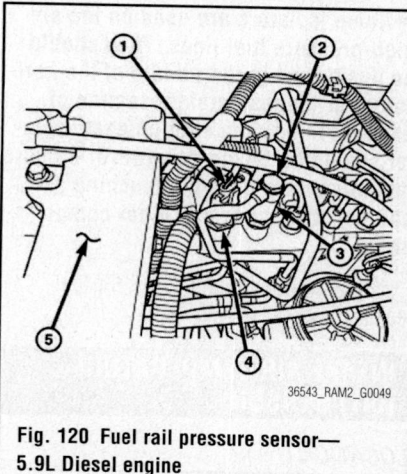

Fig. 120 Fuel rail pressure sensor— 5.9L Diesel engine

6.7L Diesel Engine

See Figure 121.

1. Remove two bolts (3) and bracket (4) at rear of cylinder head.

2. Remove engine oil dipstick tube mounting bolts.

3. Disconnect electrical connector (2) at sensor.

4. Remove sensor (1) from fuel rail.

5. Inspect sensor sealing surface.

To install:

6. Inspect fuel pressure sensor sealing surface.

7. Lubricate sensor threads with clean diesel fuel.

8. Install sensor (1) into fuel rail.

9. To prevent leaks, sensor must be tightened to 52 ft. lbs. (70 Nm).

10. Connect electrical connector (2) to sensor.

11. Install rear engine lift bracket (4) and bolts (3). Tighten to 57 ft. lbs. (77 Nm).

12. Install engine oil dipstick tube mounting bolts.

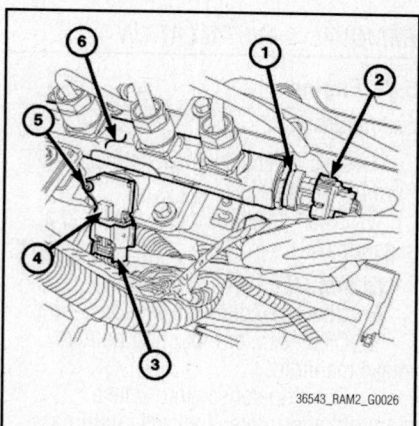

Fig. 121 Fuel rail pressure sensor—6.7L diesel engine

➡Noise isolators are used on the six high-pressure fuel lines. They should be positioned in the middle of the horizontal or longest straight section of each fuel line. The split on each isolator should be facing downward. Be sure the noise isolator is not touching another isolator or any other components.

13. Start engine and check for fuel leaks.

INTAKE AIR TEMPERATURE (IAT) SENSOR

LOCATION

5.7L Engine

See Figure 122.

The intake manifold air temperature (IAT) sensor is installed into the front of the intake manifold air box plenum.

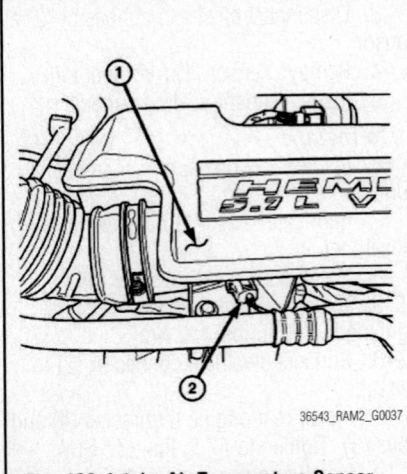

Fig. 122 Intake Air Temperature Sensor (IAT) sensor—5.7L engines

REMOVAL & INSTALLATION

5.7L Engine

See Figure 122.

1. Disconnect electrical connector (2) from IAT sensor.
2. Clean dirt from intake manifold at sensor base.

To install:

3. Check condition of sensor O-ring.
4. Clean sensor mounting hole in intake manifold.
5. Position sensor into intake manifold and rotate clockwise until past release tab.
6. Install electrical connector

INTAKE MANIFOLD AIR TEMPERATURE SENSOR/MAP SENSOR

LOCATION

5.9L Diesel Engine

See Figure 123.

The combination, dual function Intake Manifold Air Temperature Sensor/MAP Sensor (2) is installed into the top of the intake manifold.

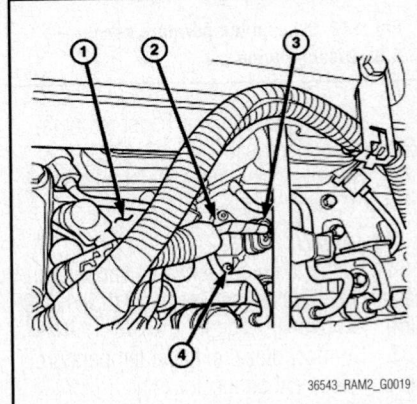

Fig. 123 Intake Manifold Air Temperature Sensor/MAP (IAT/MAP) sensor—5.9L Diesel engine

6.7L Diesel Engine

See Figure 124.

The combination, dual function Intake Manifold Air Temperature Sensor/MAP (IAT/MAP) (3) sensor is installed into the intake air connection manifold, below, and to the rear of the EGR valve (5).

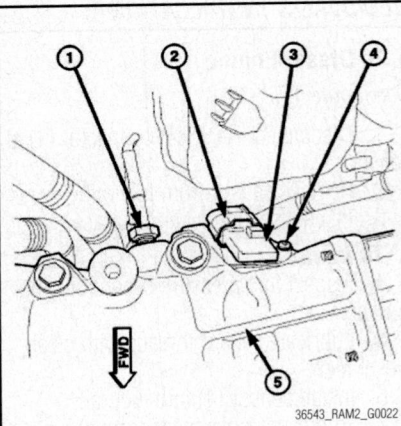

Fig. 124 Intake Manifold Air Temperature Sensor/MAP (IAT/MAP) sensor—6.7L diesel engine

REMOVAL & INSTALLATION

5.9L Diesel Engine

See Figure 123.

1. Clean area around sensor.
2. Disconnect electrical connector (3) from IAT/MAP sensor.
3. Remove two T-15 Torx® headed screws (4).
4. Remove sensor from intake manifold.
5. Check condition of sensor O-ring (2).

To install:

6. Check condition of sensor O-ring.
7. Lubricate sensor O-ring and sensor hole in intake manifold cover with clean engine oil.
8. Clean sensor mounting area at intake manifold (1).
9. Position sensor (2) into intake manifold.
10. Install and tighten 2 sensor mounting screws to 9 inch lbs. (1 Nm) torque.
11. Connect electrical connector to sensor.

6.7L Diesel Engine

See Figure 124.

1. Clean area around sensor.
2. Disconnect electrical connector (2) from IAT/MAP sensor.
3. Remove mounting screw (4).
4. Remove sensor from manifold.
5. Check condition of sensor O-ring.

To install:

6. Check condition of sensor O-ring.
7. Clean sensor mounting area at manifold.
8. Lubricate sensor O-ring and sensor mounting hole in intake manifold with clean engine oil.
9. Position sensor (3) into intake manifold.
10. Install and tighten sensor mounting screw (4) to 9 inch lbs. (1 Nm) torque.
11. Connect electrical connector (2) to sensor.

KNOCK SENSOR (KS)

LOCATION

5.7L Engine

See Figure 125.

Two knock sensors are used. These are bolted into each side of the cylinder block (outside) under the exhaust manifold.

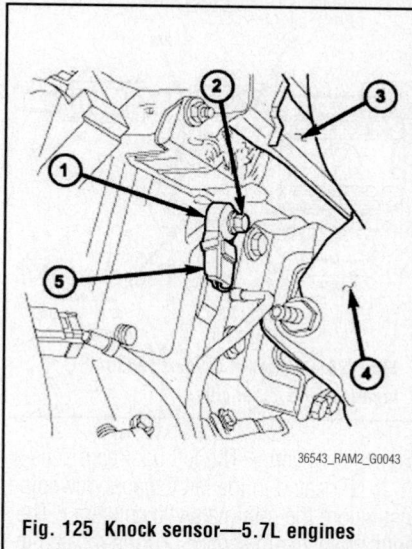

Fig. 125 Knock sensor—5.7L engines

REMOVAL & INSTALLATION

5.7L Engine

See Figure 125.

1. Raise the vehicle.
2. Disconnect the knock sensor electrical connector (5).
3. Remove the knock sensor mounting bolt (2).

➡**Note the foam strip on bolt threads. This foam strip is used only to retain the bolts to the sensors for plant assembly. It is not used as a sealant. Do not apply any adhesive, sealant or thread locking compound to these bolts.**

4. Remove the knock sensor (1) from the engine.

To install:

5. Thoroughly clean knock sensor mounting hole.
6. Install sensor (1) into cylinder block (3).

➡**Over or under tightening the sensor mounting bolts will affect knock sensor performance, possibly causing improper spark control. Always use the specified torque when installing the knock sensors. The torque for the knock sensor bolt is relatively light for an 8 mm bolt (2).**

➡**Note foam strip on bolt threads. This foam is used only to retain the bolts to sensors for plant assembly. It is not used as a sealant. Do not apply any adhesive, sealant or thread locking compound to these bolts.**

7. Install and tighten mounting bolt (2). Tighten to 13–17 ft. lbs. (18–22 Nm).

8. Install electrical connector to sensor (5).

MALFUNCTION INDICATOR LIGHT (MIL)

RESET PROCEDURES

Malfunction Indicator Light and DTCs can be erased anytime with a scan tool or by disconnecting the battery, it also clears all Freeze Frame data.

Erasing the DTC with the scan tool erases all OBD II information. The scan tool automatically displays a warning that erasing the DTC will also erase all OBD II monitor data. This includes all counter information for warm-up cycles, trips and Freeze Frame.

MASS AIR FLOW (MAF) SENSOR

LOCATION

5.9L Diesel Engine

The combination, dual function Intake Manifold Air Temperature Sensor/MAP Sensor (2) is installed into the top of the intake manifold.

6.7L Diesel Engine

The combination, dual function Intake Manifold Air Temperature Sensor/MAP (IAT/MAP) (3) sensor is installed into the intake air connection manifold, below, and to the rear of the EGR valve (5).

REMOVAL & INSTALLATION

5.9L & 6.7L Diesel Engines

See Intake Manifold Air Temperature Sensor/MAP Sensor.

MANIFOLD ABSOLUTE PRESSURE (MAP) SENSOR

LOCATION

5.7L Engine

See Figure 126.

The Manifold Absolute Pressure (MAP) sensor is mounted to the front of the intake manifold air plenum box.

REMOVAL & INSTALLATION

5.7L Engine

See Figure 126.

1. Disconnect electrical connector at sensor by sliding release lock out. Press down on lock tab for removal.

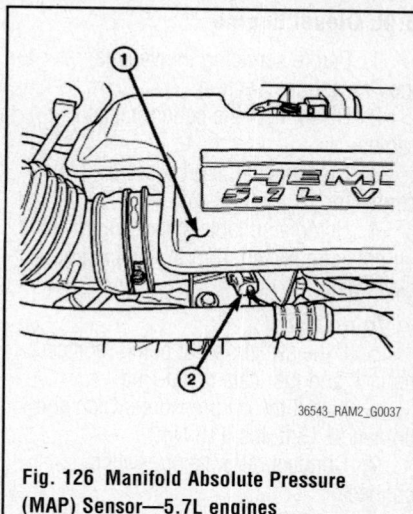

Fig. 126 Manifold Absolute Pressure (MAP) Sensor—5.7L engines

2. Rotate sensor (3) 1/4 turn counterclockwise for removal.
3. Check condition of sensor O-ring

To install:

4. Clean MAP sensor mounting hole at intake manifold.
5. Check MAP sensor O-ring seal for cuts or tears.
6. Position sensor into manifold.
7. Rotate sensor 1/4 turn clockwise for installation.
8. Connect electrical connector.

OIL PRESSURE SENSOR

REMOVAL & INSTALLATION

5.7L Engine

1. Before servicing the vehicle, refer to the precautions in the beginning of this section.
2. Disconnect the negative battery cable.
3. Remove all alternator mounting bolts.
4. Remove the alternator electrical connectors.
5. Disconnect oil pressure sender wire.
6. Remove the pressure sender.

To install:

7. Apply thread sealant to sensor threads.
8. Install oil pressure sender.
9. Connect oil pressure sender wire.
10. Tighten the sensor to 20 ft. lbs. (28 Nm).
11. Connect oil pressure sender wire.
12. Install all alternator mounting bolts.
13. Install the alternator electrical connectors.
14. Connect the negative battery cable.

5.9L Diesel Engine

1. Before servicing the vehicle, refer to the Precautions Section.
2. Disconnect the battery negative cables.
3. Disconnect the oil pressure switch connector.
4. Using a suitable socket, remove the oil pressure switch from the block (counterclockwise).

To install:

5. If the switch is not being replaced, replace and lubricate the O-ring.
6. Install the oil pressure switch and tighten to 13 ft. lbs. (18 Nm).
7. Connect oil pressure switch connector.
8. Connect the battery negative cables.
9. Start engine and check for oil leaks at the switch.

6.7L Diesel Engine

➡**When installing a new oil pressure switch, the kit will include a special 90° fitting that must be installed. Clock the fitting and switch assembly between the 1:00 o'clock and 2:00 o'clock position. Tighten the fitting bolt to 13 ft. lbs. (18 Nm).**

1. Before servicing the vehicle, refer to the Precautions Section.
2. Disconnect the battery negative cables.
3. Disconnect the oil pressure switch connector.
4. Using a suitable socket, remove the oil pressure switch from the block (counterclockwise).
5. Remove the banjo screw from the oil pressure switch mounting block.

To install:

6. Install banjo screw through the oil pressure switch mounting block. The switch mounting block port (oil switch port) should point to the 2 o'clock position. Tighten the banjo screw to or 18 ft lbs. (24 Nm).
7. If the switch is not being replaced, replace and lubricate the O-ring.
8. Install the oil pressure switch and tighten to 13 ft. lbs. (18 Nm).
9. Connect oil pressure switch connector.
10. Connect the battery negative cables.
11. Start engine and check for oil leaks at the switch.

TESTING

1. The oil pressure sensor is threaded into the engine block (see location illustrations). Low oil pressure (less than 10 psi)

will close the switch, creating a circuit which includes the warning light. The light will go on when the switch is closed.

2. Disconnect the harness wire(s) from the sensor. Connect a jumper wire from the harness wire to ground on the engine (if single wire) or across the two harness wires.
3. Turn the ignition switch **ON**. The low oil pressure warning light should go ON. Disconnect the jumper. The light should go **OFF**. If the lamp does not light when the circuit is completed, suspect a burned out bulb or wiring problem.
4. With the engine off and oil pressure "zero", check for continuity across the switch body. On single-terminal switches, check continuity between the switch terminal and ground on the switch body or engine block. On two-terminal switches, check for continuity between the two terminals. In either case, there should be continuity. If not, replace the switch.

OXYGEN (O2) SENSOR

LOCATION

5.7L Engine

See Figures 127 and 128.

Federal Emission Packages : Two sensors are used: upstream (referred to as 1/1) and downstream (referred to as 1/2). With this emission package, the upstream sensor (1/1) is located just before the main catalytic converter. The downstream sensor (1/2) is located just after the main catalytic converter.

California Emission Packages: On this emissions package, 4 sensors are used: 2 upstream (referred to as 1/1 and 2/1) and 2 downstream (referred to as 1/2 and 2/2). With this emission package, the right upstream sensor (2/1) is located in the right exhaust downpipe just before the mini-

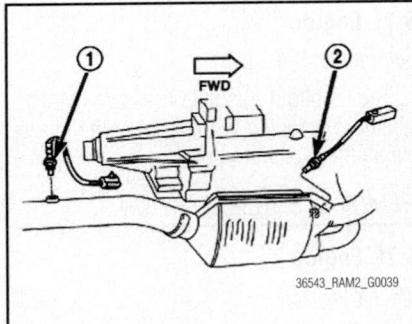

Fig. 127 Federal oxygen sensor locations—5.7L engines

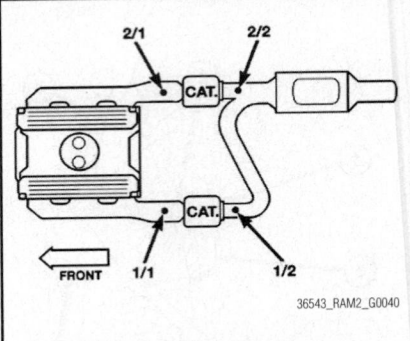

Fig. 128 California oxygen sensor locations—5.7L engines

catalytic converter. The left upstream sensor (1/1) is located in the left exhaust downpipe just before the mini-catalytic converter. The right downstream sensor (2/2) is located in the right exhaust downpipe just after the mini-catalytic converter, and before the main catalytic converter. The left downstream sensor (1/2) is located in the left exhaust downpipe just after the mini-catalytic converter, and before the main catalytic converter.

6.7L Diesel Engine

See Figure 129.

Refer to the accompanying illustration.

REMOVAL & INSTALLATION

5.7L Engine

See Figures 127 and 128.

1. Raise and support vehicle.
2. Disconnect wire connector from O2S sensor.

❋❋ CAUTION

When disconnecting the sensor electrical connector, do not pull directly on the wire going into sensor.

3. Remove O2S sensor with an oxygen sensor removal and installation tool.
4. Clean threads in exhaust pipe using appropriate tap.

To install:

➡**Threads of new oxygen sensors are factory coated with anti-seize compound to aid in removal. DO NOT add any additional anti-seize compound to threads of a new oxygen sensor.**

5. Install O2S sensor. Tighten to 30 ft. lbs. (41 Nm) torque.
6. Connect O2S sensor wire connector.
7. Lower the vehicle.

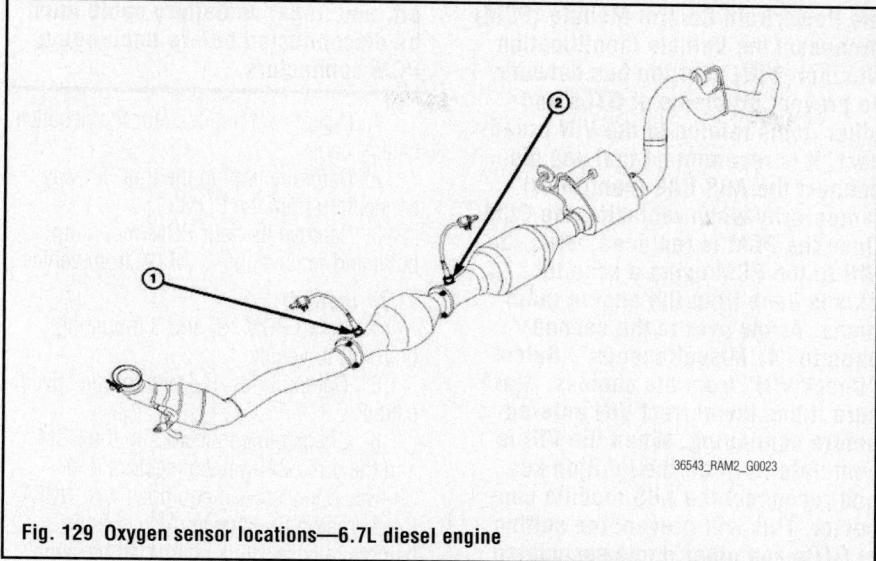

Fig. 129 Oxygen sensor locations—6.7L diesel engine

6.7L Diesel Engine

See Figures 129 and 130.

> ❋❋ **CAUTION**
>
> **Never apply any type of grease to the oxygen sensor electrical connector, or attempt any soldering of the sensor wiring harness.**

> ❋❋ **WARNING**
>
> **The exhaust manifold, exhaust pipes and catalytic converters become very hot during engine operation. Allow engine to cool before removing oxygen sensor.**

1. Raise and support the vehicle.
2. Disconnect the main wire connector from the O2S sensor pigtail harness.

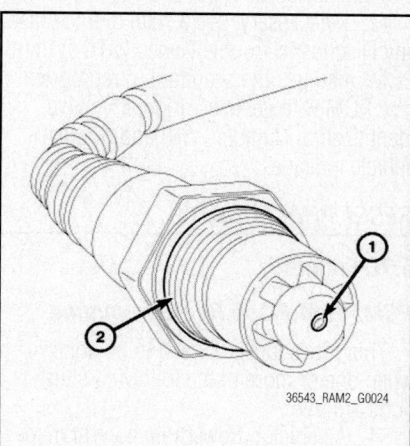

Fig. 130 Oxygen sensor center hole—6.7L diesel engine

> ❋❋ **CAUTION**
>
> **When disconnecting the sensor electrical connector, do not pull directly on the wire going into sensor.**

3. Remove the O2S sensor with an oxygen sensor removal and installation tool.
4. Inspect the O2S sensor wiring boot for cuts, tears or damage.
5. Clean the threads in catalytic converter using the appropriate tap.
6. If the O2S sensor is going to be reinstalled, apply pressurized shop air directly into center hole (1) of O2S sensor.
7. Wipe excess soot off the O2S sensor with a soft cloth.

To install:

➡**Threads of NEW oxygen sensors are factory coated with anti-seize compound to aid in removal. DO NOT add any additional anti-seize compound to threads of a new oxygen sensor. Be careful not to get anti-seize compound on sensor tip.**

8. Inspect the O2S sensor wiring boot for cuts, tears or damage.
9. If the O2S sensor is going to be reinstalled, apply pressurized shop air directly into center hole (1) of O2S sensor.
10. Wipe excess soot off the O2S sensor with a soft cloth.
11. Install the O2S sensor. Tighten to 30 ft. lbs. (41 Nm) torque.
12. Connect the O2S sensor pigtail harness to main wire harness connector.
13. Lower the vehicle.

OXYGEN (O2) SENSOR MODULE

LOCATION

6.7L Diesel Engine

See Figure 131.

The oxygen sensor module (1) is located under the vehicle. It is bolted to the outer side of right frame rail (4).

REMOVAL & INSTALLATION

6.7L Diesel Engine

See Figure 131.

1. Raise and support vehicle.
2. Disconnect electrical connector (2) at module (1).
3. Remove four bolts (3).
4. Remove module from frame rail.

To install:

5. Position module (1) to frame rail (4).
6. Install four bolts (3).
7. Tighten bolts (3) to 53 inch lbs. (6 Nm) torque.
8. Connect electrical connector (2) to module (1).
9. Lower the vehicle.

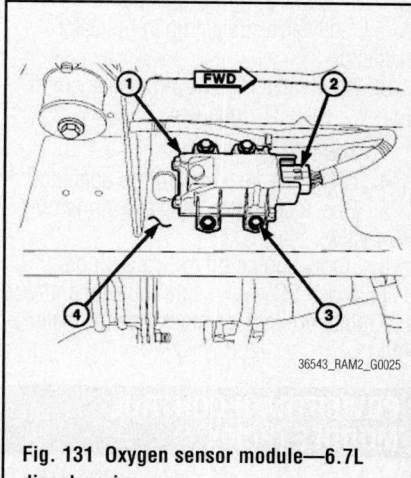

Fig. 131 Oxygen sensor module—6.7L diesel engine

POSITIVE CRANKCASE VENTILATION (PCV) VALVE

LOCATION

5.7L Engine

See Figure 132.

The PCV valve is mounted into the top of the intake manifold. This is located to the right / rear of the throttle body.

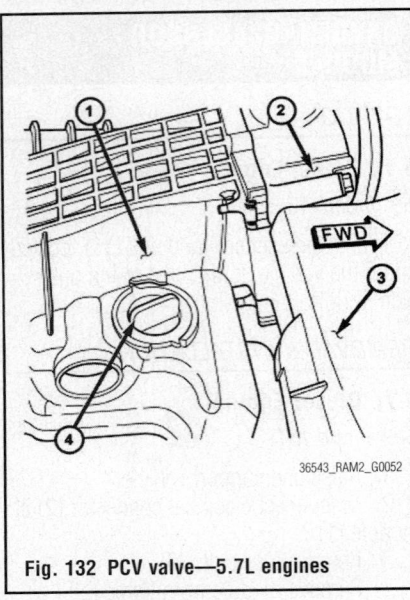

Fig. 132 PCV valve—5.7L engines

REMOVAL & INSTALLATION

5.7L Engine

See Figure 132.

1. The PCV valve is sealed to the intake manifold with 2 O-rings (2).
2. Remove PCV valve by rotating counterclockwise 90 degrees until locating tabs (3) have been freed. After tabs have leared, pull valve straight up from intake manifold.
3. After valve is removed, check condition of 2 valve O-rings (2).

To install:
4. Clean out intake manifold opening.
5. Check condition of two O-rings on PCV valve.
6. Apply engine oil to two O-rings.
7. Place PCV valve into intake manifold and rotate 90 degrees clockwise for installation.

POWERTRAIN CONTROL MODULE (PCM)

LOCATION

5.7L Engine

The PCM is located in the engine compartment attached to the passenger side dash panel.

REMOVAL & INSTALLATION

5.7L Engine

See Figure 133.

❋❋ CAUTION

Certain ABS systems rely on having

the Powertrain Control Module (PCM) broadcast the Vehicle Identification Number (VIN) over the bus network. To prevent problems of DTCs and other items related to the VIN broadcast, it is recommend that you disconnect the ABS CAB (controller) temporarily when replacing the PCM. Once the PCM is replaced, write the VIN to the PCM using a scan tool. This is done from the engine main menu. Arrow over to the second page to "1. Miscellaneous". Select "Check VIN" from the choices. Make sure it has the correct VIN entered before continuing. When the VIN is complete, turn off the ignition key and reconnect the ABS module connector. This will prevent the setting of DTCs and other items associated with the lack of a VIN detected when you turn the key ON after replacing the PCM.

❋❋ CAUTION

Use the scan tool to reprogram the new PCM with the vehicles original identification number (VIN) and the vehicles original mileage. If this step is not done, a Diagnostic Trouble Code (DTC) may be set.

❋❋ CAUTION

To avoid possible voltage spike damage to the PCM, ignition key must be

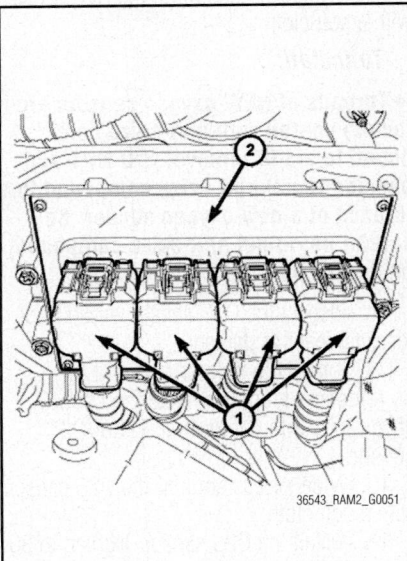

Fig. 133 Powertrain Control Module (PCM) and connectors—5.7L engines

off, and negative battery cable must be disconnected before unplugging PCM connectors.

1. Disconnect and isolator the negative battery cable.
2. Carefully unplug the four 38–way connectors from the PCM (1).
3. Remove the four PCM mounting bolts and remove the PCM (2) from vehicle.

To install:
4. Install PCM (3) and 3 mounting bolts (4) to vehicle.
5. Tighten bolts. Refer to torque specifications.
6. Check pin connectors in the PCM and the three 32–way connectors (four 38–way connectors if equipped with NGC) for corrosion or damage. Also, the pin heights in connectors should all be same. Repair as necessary before installing connectors.
7. Install three 32–way connectors (four 38–way connectors if equipped with NGC).
8. Install cover over electrical connectors. Cover snaps onto PCM.
9. Install negative battery cable.
10. The 5.7L is equipped with a fully electronic accelerator pedal position sensor. Perform the following 3 steps:
   a. Connect negative battery cable to battery.
   b. Turn ignition switch ON, but do not crank engine.
   c. Leave ignition switch ON for a minimum of 10 seconds. This will allow PCM to learn electrical parameters.
   d. The scan tool may also be used to learn electrical parameters. Go to the Miscellaneous menu, and then select ETC Learn.
11. If the previous step is not performed, a Diagnostic Trouble Code (DTC) will be set.
12. If necessary, use a scan tool to erase any Diagnostic Trouble Codes (DTC's) from PCM. Also use the scan tool to reprogram new PCM with vehicles original Vehicle Identification Number (VIN) and original vehicle mileage.

RESET PROCEDURE

5.7L Engine

PCM/ TCM Flash Reprogramming

This procedure will need to be done when one or more of the following situations are true:

1. A vehicle's Powertrain control module (PCM) has been replaced.
2. A diagnostic trouble code (DTC) is set "P1602 - PCM Not Programmed."

3. An updated calibration or software release is available for either the PCM or TCM ECUs.

This procedure assumes that the StarSCAN® and StarMOBILE® devices are configured to your dealership's network with either a wired or wireless connection. The StarSCAN® and StarMOBILE® must also be running at the latest operating system and software release level. For more help on how to network your StarSCAN® or StarMOBILE® reference the StarSCAN® / StarMOBILE® Quick Start Networking Guide available on 'DealerCONNECT> Service> StarSCAN® and StarMOBILE® Tools> Online Documentation' or at www.dcctools.com, under the Download Center.

FUEL

GASOLINE FUEL INJECTION SYSTEM

FUEL SYSTEM SERVICE PRECAUTIONS

Safety is the most important factor when performing not only fuel system maintenance but any type of maintenance. Failure to conduct maintenance and repairs in a safe manner may result in serious personal injury or death. Maintenance and testing of the vehicle's fuel system components can be accomplished safely and effectively by adhering to the following rules and guidelines.

• To avoid the possibility of fire and personal injury, always disconnect the negative battery cable unless the repair or test procedure requires that battery voltage be applied.

• Always relieve the fuel system pressure prior to disconnecting any fuel system component (injector, fuel rail, pressure regulator, etc.), fitting or fuel line connection. Exercise extreme caution whenever relieving fuel system pressure to avoid exposing skin, face and eyes to fuel spray. Please be advised that fuel under pressure may penetrate the skin or any part of the body that it contacts.

• Always place a shop towel or cloth around the fitting or connection prior to loosening to absorb any excess fuel due to spillage. Ensure that all fuel spillage (should it occur) is quickly removed from engine surfaces. Ensure that all fuel soaked cloths or towels are deposited into a suitable waste container.

• Always keep a dry chemical (Class B) fire extinguisher near the work area.

• Do not allow fuel spray or fuel vapors to come into contact with a spark or open flame.

• Always use a back-up wrench when loosening and tightening fuel line connection fittings. This will prevent unnecessary stress and torsion to fuel line piping.

• Always replace worn fuel fitting O-rings with new. Do not substitute fuel hose or equivalent where fuel pipe is installed.

Before servicing the vehicle, make sure to also refer to the precautions in the beginning of this section as well.

RELIEVING FUEL SYSTEM PRESSURE

➡A separate fuel pump relay is no longer used. A circuit within the Totally Integrated Power Module (TIPM) is used to control the electric fuel pump located within the fuel pump module. The TIPM is located in the engine compartment in front of the battery.

1. Remove fuel fill cap.
2. On bottom of vehicle, disconnect fuel pump module electrical connector. This can be accomplished at either of the two connectors.
3. Start and run engine until it stalls.
4. Attempt restarting engine until it will no longer run.
5. Turn ignition key to OFF position.
6. Place a rag or towel below fuel line quick-connect fitting at fuel rail.
7. Disconnect quick-connect fitting at fuel rail.
8. Reconnect fuel pump module electrical connector on bottom of vehicle.
9. One or more Diagnostic Trouble Codes (DTC's) may have been stored in PCM memory due to disconnecting fuel pump module circuit. A diagnostic scan tool must be used to erase a DTC.

FUEL FILTER

REMOVAL & INSTALLATION
See Figure 134.

The fuel filter is located in the fuel tank. If the electrical fuel pump, primary inlet filter, fuel filter or fuel pressure regulator require service, the fuel pump module must be removed.

1. Before servicing the vehicle, refer to the Precautions Section.
2. Relieve the fuel system pressure.
3. Remove or disconnect the following:
   • Negative battery cable
   • Fuel tank
4. Pull the filter/regulator out of the rubber grommet. Cut the hose clamp and remove the fuel line.

To install:
5. Install the filter/regulator with a new clamp and push it into the rubber grommet.
6. Install or connect the following:
   • Fuel tank
   • Negative battery cable
7. Start the engine and check for leaks.

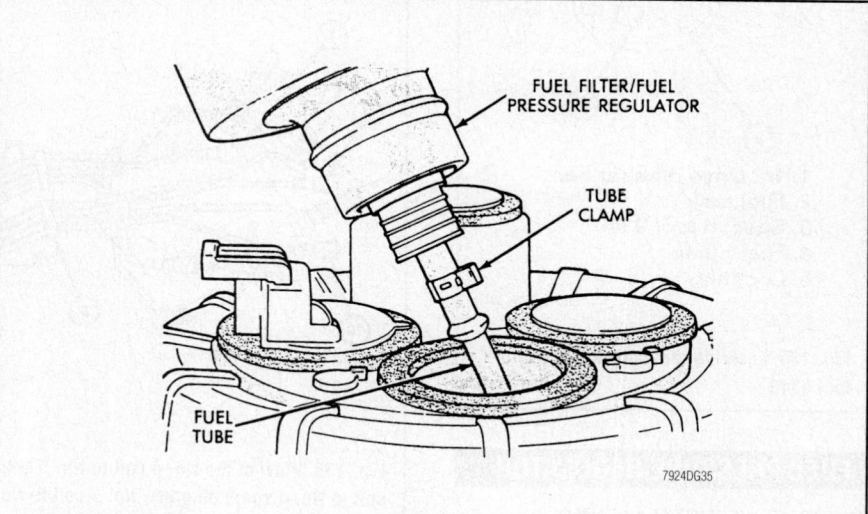

FUEL FILTER/FUEL PRESSURE REGULATOR

TUBE CLAMP

FUEL TUBE

7924DG35

Fig. 134 Pull and twist the filter/regulator to remove it from the top of the fuel pump module

FUEL PUMP

REMOVAL & INSTALLATION

See Figure 135.

✳✳ CAUTION

The fuel system may be under a constant pressure (even with the engine off). Before servicing the fuel pump module, the fuel system pressure must be released.

1. Before servicing the vehicle, refer to the Precautions Section.
2. Drain and remove fuel tank. Refer to Fuel Tank Removal/Installation.
3. Remove plastic fuel pump module cover by pushing pegs outward.
4. Note rotational position of module before attempting removal. An indexing arrow is located on top of module for this purpose.
5. Position special tool 9340 into notches on outside edge of lockring.
6. Install ½ inch drive breaker bar to tool 9340.
7. Rotate breaker bar counter-clockwise to remove lockring.
8. Remove lockring. The module will spring up slightly when lockring is removed.
9. Remove module from fuel tank. Be careful not to bend float arm while removing.

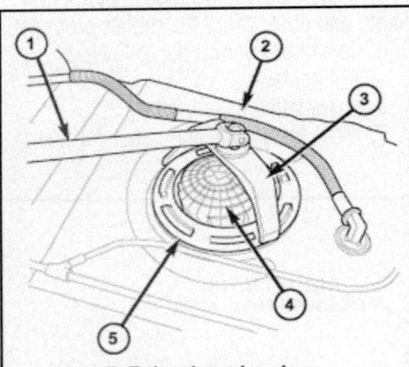

1. 1/2 Drive breaker bar
2. Fuel tank
3. Special tool 9340
4. Fuel pump
5. Lockring

22043_RPUP_G0144

Fig. 135 Lockring removal shown with tool 9340

FUEL PRESSURE REGULATOR

REMOVAL & INSTALLATION

The fuel pressure regulator is located in the fuel pump module assembly.

FUEL RAIL & INJECTORS

REMOVAL & INSTALLATION

5.7L Engine

See Figures 136 and 137.

✳✳ CAUTION

The fuel system is under constant pressure even with engine off. Before servicing fuel rail, fuel system pressure must be released.

✳✳ WARNING

The left and right fuel rails are replaced as an assembly. Do not attempt to separate rail halves at connector tube. Due to design of tube, it does not use any clamps. Never attempt to install a clamping device of any kind to tube. When removing fuel rail assembly for any reason, be careful not to bend or kink tube.

1. Before servicing the vehicle, refer to the Precautions Section.
2. Remove fuel tank filler tube cap.
3. Properly relieve the fuel system pressure, as outlined in this section.
4. Remove negative battery cable at battery.
5. Remove flex tube (air cleaner housing to engine).
6. Remove air resonator box at throttle body.
7. Disconnect all spark plug cables from all spark plugs and ignition coils. Do not remove cables from cable routing tray. Note original cable positions while removing.
8. Remove spark plug cable tray from engine by releasing 4 retaining clips. Remove tray and cables from engine as an assembly.
9. Disconnect electrical connectors at all 8 ignition coils. Refer to Ignition Coil Removal/Installation in Engine Electrical.
10. Disconnect fuel line latch clip and fuel line at fuel rail. A special tool will be necessary for fuel line disconnection.
11. Disconnect electrical connectors at all 8 fuel injectors. To remove connector, push red colored slider away from injector. While pushing slider, depress tab and remove connector from injector. The factory fuel injection wiring harness is numerically tagged (INJ 1, INJ 2, etc.) for injector position identification. If harness is not tagged, note wiring location before removal.
12. Disconnect electrical connectors at all throttle body sensors.
13. Remove 4 fuel rail mounting bolts (2) and hold-down clamps (3).
14. Gently rock and pull left side of fuel rail until fuel injectors just start to clear machined holes in intake manifold. Gently rock and pull right side of rail until injectors just start to clear intake manifold head holes.
15. Repeat this procedure (left/right) until all injectors have cleared machined holes.
16. Remove fuel rail (with injectors attached) from engine.
17. Disconnect clip(s) that retain fuel injector(s) to fuel rail.

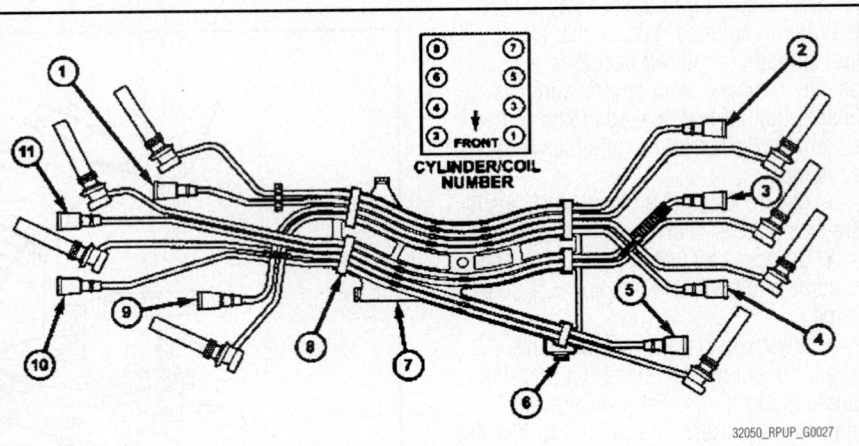

32050_RPUP_G0027

Fig. 136 View of the No. 8 coil to No. 5 spark plug (1), No. 5 coil to No. 8 spark plug (2), No. 7 coil to No. 4 spark plug (3), No. 3 coil to No. 2 spark plug (4), No. 1 coil to No. 6 spark plug (5), clips (6), cable tray (7), clips (8), No. 2 coil to No. 3 spark plug (9), No. 6 coil to No. 1 spark plug (10), No. 4 coil to No. 7 spark plug (11)—5.7L engines

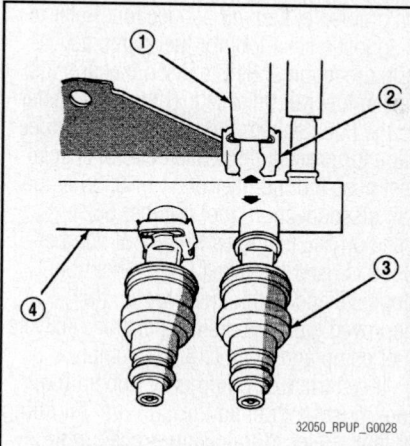

Fig. 137 Typical injector removal—pliers (1), injector clip (2), fuel injector (3) and fuel rail (4)

32050_RPUP_G0028

To install:

18. Install fuel injector(s) into fuel rail assembly and install retaining clip(s).

19. If same injector(s) is being reinstalled, install new O-ring(s).

20. Apply a small amount of clean engine oil to each injector O-ring. This will aid in installation.

21. Position fuel rail/fuel injector assembly to machined injector openings in intake manifold.

22. Guide each injector into intake manifold. Be careful not to tear injector O-rings.

23. Push right side of fuel rail down until fuel injectors have bottomed on shoulders. Push left fuel rail down until injectors have bottomed on shoulders.

24. Install 4 fuel rail hold-down clamps and 4 mounting bolts.

25. Position spark plug cable tray and cable assembly to intake manifold. Snap 4 cable tray retaining clips into intake manifold.

26. Install all cables to spark plugs and ignition coils.

27. Connect electrical connector to throttle body.

28. Install electrical connectors to all 8 ignition coils.

29. Connect electrical connector to throttle body.

30. Attach the electrical connectors at all fuel injectors. To install connector, push connector onto injector and then push and lock red colored slider. Make sure the connector is locked to the injector by lightly tugging on connector.

31. Connect the fuel line latch clip and fuel line to fuel rail.

32. Install air resonator to throttle body (2 bolts).

33. Install flexible air duct to air box.

34. Connect battery cable to battery.

35. Start engine and check for leaks.

FUEL TANK

REMOVAL & INSTALLATION

Rear Mounted Tank

See Figure 138.

1. Before servicing the vehicle, refer to the Precautions Section.

2. Release fuel system pressure.

3. Raise and support vehicle.

4. Drain fuel tank. Refer to Standard Procedure - Draining Fuel Tank.

5. Remove both clamps.

6. Remove ground wire screw and disconnect ground wire.

7. Remove fuel fill hose assembly.

8. Disconnect electrical connector from module.

9. **GAS POWERED** Disconnect fuel supply line and vapor line quick-connect fittings.

10. **DIESEL POWERED** Disconnect fuel return and supply line quick-connect fittings.

11. Support tank with a hydraulic jack.

12. Certain models may have an optional fuel tank skid plate. The same mounting bolts are used to retain both the skid plate and fuel tank. Remove bolts.

13. Lower the tank assembly from vehicle and lift tank from skid plate.

To install:

14. If fuel pump module (gas), or fuel tank module (diesel) is being installed, refer to either Fuel Pump Module Installation, or Fuel Tank Module Installation. This must be done before installing tank.

15. Position fuel tank into fuel tank skid plate.

16. Place assembly to a hydraulic jack.

17. Raise assembly up to frame.

18. Install bolts and tighten to 41 ft. lbs. (55 Nm).

19. **GAS POWERED** Connect quick-connect fittings.

20. **DIESEL POWERED** Connect fuel return and supply line quick-connect fittings.

21. Connect electrical connector to module.

22. Fit fuel fill hose assembly to tank fittings.

23. Install both clamps.

24. Install ground wire screw and ground wire.

25. Fill tank and check for leaks.

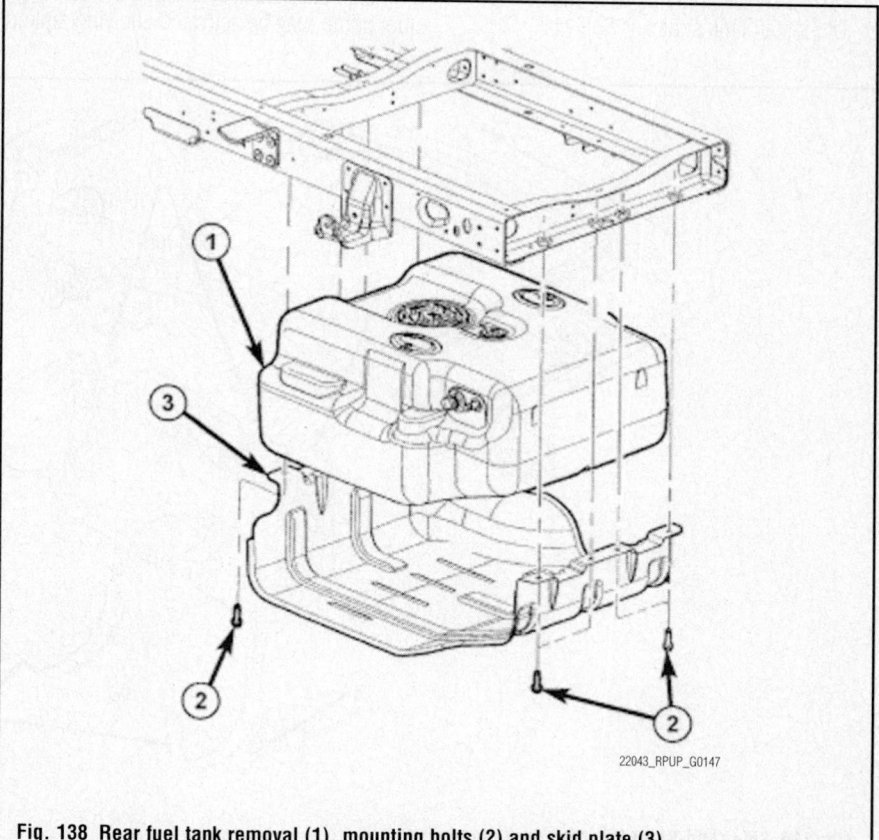

22043_RPUP_G0147

Fig. 138 Rear fuel tank removal (1), mounting bolts (2) and skid plate (3)

Side (Mid-Ship) Mounted Tank

See Figure 139.

1. Before servicing the vehicle, refer to the Precautions Section.
2. Release fuel system pressure.
3. Raise and support vehicle.
4. Drain fuel tank. Refer to Standard Procedure - Draining Fuel Tank.
5. Loosen clamps.
6. Remove hoses and from tank.
7. Disconnect electrical connector at top of module.
8. **GAS POWERED** Disconnect fuel supply line and vapor line quick-connect fittings.
9. **DIESEL POWERED** Disconnect fuel return and supply line quick-connect fittings.
10. Support tank with a hydraulic jack.
11. Remove nuts.
12. Remove both tank straps (4).
13. Lower tank and remove from hydraulic jack.

To install:

14. If fuel pump module (gas), or fuel tank module (diesel) is being installed, refer to either Fuel Pump Module Installation, or Fuel Tank Module Installation. This must be done before installing tank.
15. Place assembly to a hydraulic jack.
16. Raise assembly up to frame.
17. Install tank straps.
18. Install strap nuts and tighten to 30 ft. lbs. (41 Nm).
19. **GAS POWERED** Connect quick-connect fittings.
20. **DIESEL POWERED** Connect fuel return and supply line quick-connect fittings.
21. Position hoses and to tank fittings.
22. Tighten clamps.
23. Connect electrical connector at top of module.
24. Fill tank and check for leaks.

FUEL TANK DRAINING

> **✻✻ WARNING**
>
> **The fuel system may be under constant fuel pressure even with the engine off. This pressure must be released before servicing fuel tank.**

Two different procedures may be used to drain fuel tank: through the fuel fill fitting on tank, or using a diagnostic scan tool to activate the fuel pump relay. Due to a one-way check valve installed into the fuel fill opening fitting at the tank, the tank cannot be drained conventionally at the fill cap.

The quickest draining procedure involves removing the rubber fuel fill hose at the fuel tank.

As an alternative procedure, the electric fuel pump may be activated allowing tank to be drained at fuel rail connection. Refer to diagnostic scan tool for fuel pump activation procedures. Before disconnecting fuel line at fuel rail, release fuel pressure. Refer to the Fuel System Pressure Release Procedure for procedures. Attach end of special test hose tool number 6631 or 6539 at fuel rail disconnection (tool number 6631 is used on 5/16 fuel lines while tool number 6539 is used on 3/8 fuel lines). Position opposite end of this hose tool to an approved gasoline draining station. Activate fuel pump and drain tank until empty.

If electric fuel pump is not operating, fuel must be drained through fuel fill fitting at tank. Refer to following procedures:

1. Release fuel system pressure.
2. Raise the vehicle.
3. Thoroughly clean area around fuel fill fitting and rubber fuel fill hose at tank.
4. If vehicle is equipped with 4 doors and a 6 foot (short) box, remove left-rear tire/wheel.
5. Loosen clamp and disconnect rubber fuel fill hose at tank fitting. Using an approved gas holding tank, drain fuel tank through this fitting.

IDLE SPEED

ADJUSTMENT

Idle speed is maintained by the Powertrain Control Module (PCM). No adjustment is necessary or possible.

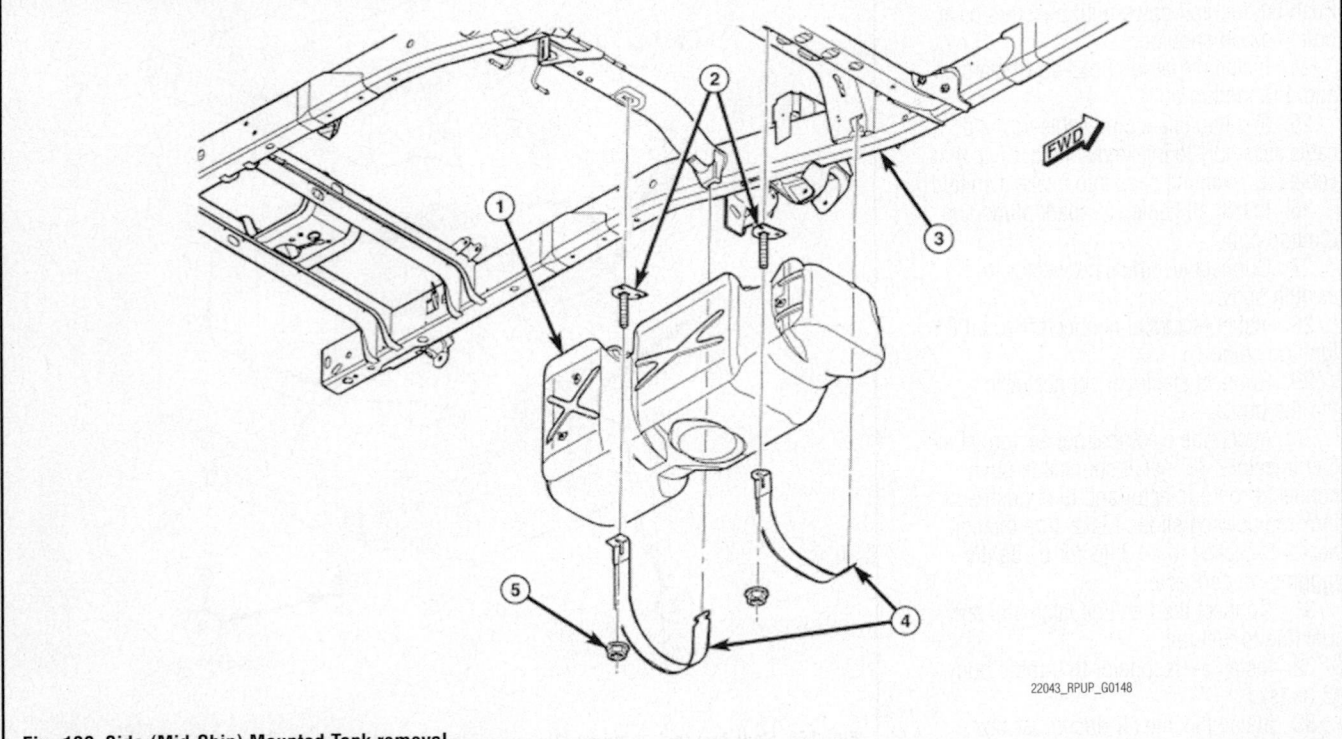

22043_RPUP_G0148

Fig. 139 Side (Mid-Ship) Mounted Tank removal

THROTTLE BODY

REMOVAL & INSTALLATION

5.7L Engine

☀ WARNING

Do not use spray (carb) cleaners on any part of the throttle body. Do not apply silicone lubricants to any part of the throttle body.

1. Before servicing the vehicle, refer to the Precautions Section.
2. Remove air duct and air resonator box at throttle body.
3. Disconnect electrical connector from the throttle body.

4. Remove 4 throttle body mounting bolts.
5. Remove throttle body from intake manifold.
6. Check condition of throttle body O-ring.

To install:

7. Clean and check condition of throttle body-to-intake manifold O-ring.
8. Clean mating surfaces of throttle body and intake manifold.
9. Install the throttle body to the intake manifold by positioning the throttle body to the manifold alignment pins.
10. Install 4 mounting bolts and tighten to 105 inch lbs. (12 Nm).
11. Attach the electrical connector.

12. Install the air plenum.
13. Using the diagnostic scan tool, erase all previous DTC's and perform the ETC Relearn Procedure.

THROTTLE RELEARN PROCEDURE

If the throttle body has been changed, the following procedure must be performed:

1. Disconnect negative battery cable from battery. Leave cable disconnected for approximately 90 seconds.
2. Reconnect cable to battery.
3. Turn ignition switch **ON**, but do not crank engine.
4. Leave ignition switch **ON** for a minimum of 10 seconds. This will allow PCM to learn throttle body electrical parameters.

FUEL

DIESEL FUEL INJECTION SYSTEM

FUEL SYSTEM SERVICE PRECAUTIONS

Safety is the most important factor when performing not only fuel system maintenance but any type of maintenance. Failure to conduct maintenance and repairs in a safe manner may result in serious personal injury or death. Maintenance and testing of the vehicle's fuel system components can be accomplished safely and effectively by adhering to the following rules and guidelines.

• To avoid the possibility of fire and personal injury, always disconnect the negative battery cable unless the repair or test procedure requires that battery voltage be applied.

• Always relieve the fuel system pressure prior to disconnecting any fuel system component (injector, fuel rail, pressure regulator, etc.), fitting or fuel line connection. Exercise extreme caution whenever relieving fuel system pressure to avoid exposing skin, face and eyes to fuel spray. Please be advised that fuel under pressure may penetrate the skin or any part of the body that it contacts.

• Always place a shop towel or cloth around the fitting or connection prior to loosening to absorb any excess fuel due to spillage. Ensure that all fuel spillage (should it occur) is quickly removed from engine surfaces. Ensure that all fuel soaked cloths or towels are deposited into a suitable waste container.

• Always keep a dry chemical (Class B) fire extinguisher near the work area.

• Do not allow fuel spray or fuel vapors to come into contact with a spark or open flame.

• Always use a back-up wrench when loosening and tightening fuel line connection fittings. This will prevent unnecessary stress and torsion to fuel line piping.

• Always replace worn fuel fitting O-rings with new. Do not substitute fuel hose or equivalent where fuel pipe is installed.

Before servicing the vehicle, make sure to also refer to the precautions in the beginning of this section as well.

ACTUATOR FUEL CONTROL

REMOVAL & INSTALLATION

5.9L & 6.7L Diesel Engines

The Fuel Control Actuator (FCA) is located at the rear of the high-pressure, fuel injection pump.

1. Before servicing the vehicle, refer to the Precautions Section.
2. Remove the electrical connector from the FCA.
3. Remove FCA mounting screws.
4. Twist and pull FCA to remove from injection pump.

To install:

5. Lubricate the new Fuel Control Actuator (FCA) O-ring with clean oil before installation.
6. Turn FCA in a clockwise direction while pressing it into machined bore on rear of fuel injection pump. Be sure FCA flange is flush with the mounting surface on fuel injection pump.
7. Install FCA mounting screws (1) by hand.
8. Tighten the FCA mounting screws to 62 inch lbs. (7 Nm).

FUEL FILTER

REMOVAL & INSTALLATION

See Figure 140.

1. Before servicing the vehicle, refer to the Precautions Section.
2. Remove left front tire/wheel.
3. Remove left front wheel splash shield.
4. Clean all debris from around filter canister and canister head.
5. Disconnect the Water In Fuel (WIF) sensor electrical connector.
6. Open the drain valve two complete revolutions. Drain approximately 1 cup of fuel into a waste canister.

➡**Dispose of fuel according to environmental regulations.**

7. Remove drain hose from drain valve.
8. Use an oil filter type wrench to loosen filter. Continue removing filter by hand.
9. After fuel filter removal, also check and clean secondary filter screen. Press button on quick-connect fitting. Disconnect fitting from fitting. Unscrew the fitting from canister head to expose screen.
10. Clean screen and check the condition of O-ring.

To install:

11. Reverse removal procedure for installation.

DRAINING WATER FROM THE SYSTEM

See Figure 141.

1. Before servicing the vehicle, refer to the Precautions Section.

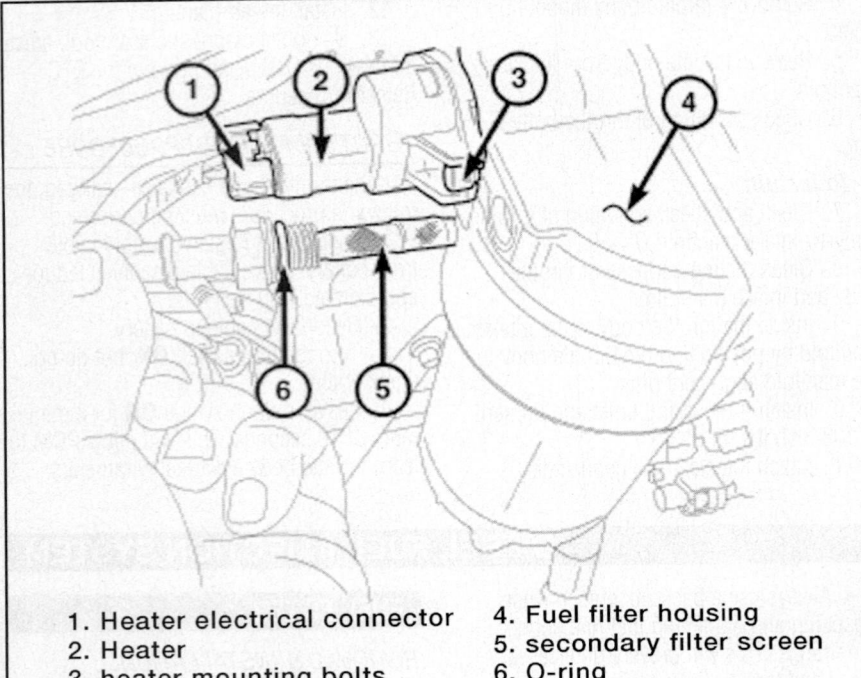

1. Heater electrical connector
2. Heater
3. heater mounting bolts
4. Fuel filter housing
5. secondary filter screen
6. O-ring

22043_RPUP_G0051

Fig. 140 Fuel filter housing and related parts—5.9L and 6.7L diesel engines

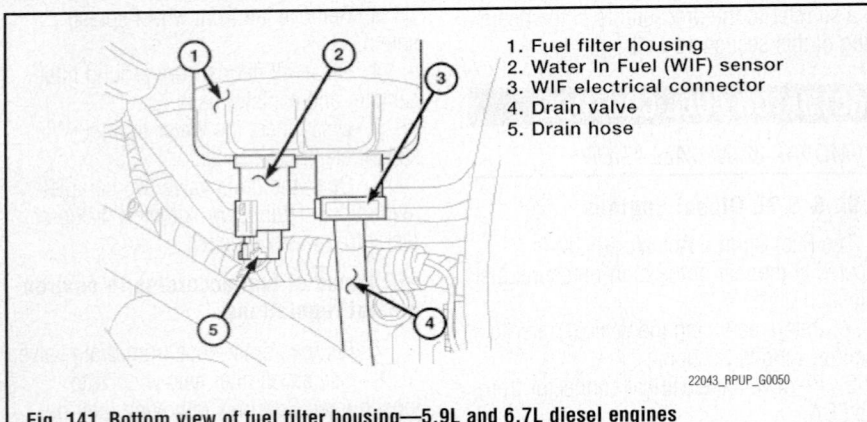

1. Fuel filter housing
2. Water In Fuel (WIF) sensor
3. WIF electrical connector
4. Drain valve
5. Drain hose

22043_RPUP_G0050

Fig. 141 Bottom view of fuel filter housing—5.9L and 6.7L diesel engines

2. A drain hose is located at the bottom of drain valve. Place drain pan under drain hose.

3. With engine not running, rotate drain valve approximately two revolutions to open it. Leave open until all water and contaminants have been removed and clean fuel exits. Hand-tighten drain valve after tightening.

4. After draining operation, close and tighten drain valve.

FUEL TANK DRAINING

Two different procedures may be used to drain fuel tank: through the fuel fill fitting on tank, or using a diagnostic scan tool to activate the fuel pump relay. Due to a one-way check valve installed into the fuel fill opening fitting at the tank, the tank cannot be drained conventionally at the fill cap.

The quickest draining procedure involves removing the rubber fuel fill hose at the fuel tank.

As an alternative procedure, the electric fuel pump may be activated allowing tank to be drained at fuel rail connection. Refer to diagnostic scan tool for fuel pump activation procedures. Before disconnecting fuel line at fuel rail, release fuel pressure. Refer to the Fuel System Pressure Release Procedure for procedures. Attach end of special test hose tool number 6631 or 6539 at fuel rail disconnection (tool number 6631 is used on ⁵⁄₁₆ fuel lines while tool number 6539 is used on ³⁄₈ fuel lines). Position opposite end of this hose tool to an approved gasoline draining station. Activate fuel pump and drain tank until empty.

If electric fuel pump is not operating, fuel must be drained through fuel fill fitting at tank. Refer to following procedures:

1. Release fuel system pressure.
2. Raise the vehicle
3. Thoroughly clean area around fuel fill fitting and rubber fuel fill hose at tank.
4. If vehicle is equipped with 4 doors and a 6 foot (short) box, remove left-rear tire/wheel.
5. Loosen clamp and disconnect rubber fuel fill hose at tank fitting. Using an approved diesel fuel holding tank, drain fuel tank through this fitting.

FUEL PRESSURE LIMITING VALVE

REMOVAL & INSTALLATION

5.9L Diesel Engine

The fuel pressure limiting valve is located on the top of the fuel rail.

✳✳ WARNING

Cleanliness cannot be overemphasized when handling or replacing diesel fuel system components. This especially includes the fuel injectors, high-pressure fuel lines and fuel injection pump. Very tight tolerances are used with these parts. Dirt contamination could cause rapid part wear and possible plugging of fuel injector nozzle tip holes. This in turn could lead to possible engine misfire. Always wash/clean any fuel system component thoroughly before disassembly and then air dry. Cap or cover any open part after disassembly. Before assembly, examine each part for dirt, grease or other contaminants and clean if necessary. When installing new parts, lubricate them with clean engine oil or clean diesel fuel only.

1. Thoroughly clean area at pressure limiting valve.
2. Remove banjo bolt from the banjo fitting.
3. Remove pressure limiting valve from fuel rail.

To install:
4. Be sure both top of manifold and limiting valve are clean.

5. Install valve and torque to 52 ft. lbs. (70 Nm).

6. Assemble the banjo bolt and new sealing washers to limiting valve.

7. Tighten the banjo bolt to 18 ft. lbs. (24 Nm).

6.7L Diesel Engine

See Figure 142.

The fuel pressure limiting valve is screwed into the front of the fuel rail.

The fuel pressure limiting valve drain port is located on the side of the fuel rail next to the limiting valve. The drain port is not serviceable.

1. Before servicing the vehicle, refer to the Precautions Section.

2. Thoroughly clean area at pressure limiting valve.

3. To gain access to the limiting valve, the intake connection/EGR valve assembly must be removed. Loosen clamp securing EGR crossover tube to EGR valve. Also loosen opposite end of EGR crossover tube. Remove clamp from intake connection.

4. Remove six bolts securing intake connection. Lift the entire EGR valve/intake connection up and to the side to gain access to fuel pressure limiting valve.

5. Discard the gasket.

6. Remove pressure limiting valve from fuel rail.

To install:

7. Be sure both end of manifold and limiting valve mounting area are clean.

8. Lubricate O-ring on limiting valve with fresh diesel oil. Also lubricate limiting valve threads with fresh diesel oil.

9. Install valve and tighten to 74 ft. lbs. (100 Nm). To prevent leaks, valve must be tightened to prescribed torque.

10. Install new intake connection gasket.

11. Position EGR valve/intake connection and install six bolts. Tighten bolts to 18 ft. lbs. (24 Nm).

12. Install new EGR crossover tube gasket. Tighten crossover tube clamps to 88 inch lbs. (10 Nm).

13. Using a diagnostic scan tool, reset vale life by using the (Reset Two-Stage Dump Valve Accumulator) function in the PCM portion of the diagnostic scan tool.

14. Start engine and check for leaks.

FUEL SUPPLY PUMP

REMOVAL & INSTALLATION

5.9L & 6.7L Diesel Engines

See Figure 143.

1. Before servicing the vehicle, refer to the Precautions Section.

2. Drain and remove fuel tank. Refer to Fuel Tank Removal/Installation.

3. Note the rotational position of module before attempting removal. An indexing arrow is located on top of module for this purpose.

4. Position special tool 9340 into notches on outside edge of lockring.

5. Install the ½ inch drive breaker bar to tool 9340.

6. Rotate breaker bar counter-clockwise to remove lockring.

7. Remove the lockring. The module will spring up slightly when lockring is removed.

8. Remove the module from fuel tank. Be careful not to bend float arm while removing.

To install:

9. Using a new seal (gasket), position the fuel pump module into opening in fuel tank.

10. Position the lockring over top of fuel pump module.

11. Rotate module until embossed alignment arrow points to center alignment mark.

12. This step must be performed to prevent float from contacting side of fuel tank.

Also be sure fuel fitting on top of pump module is pointed to drivers side of vehicle.

13. Install the special tool 9340 to lockring.

14. Install ½ inch drive breaker into Special Tool 9340.

15. Tighten the lockring (clockwise) until all seven notches have engaged.

16. Install the fuel tank.

FUEL SYSTEM PURGING

BLEEDING

See Figures 144 and 145.

1. Loosen the low pressure bleed bolt.

2. Operate the rubber push-button primer on the fuel transfer pump. Do this until the fuel exiting the bleed screw is free of air. If the primer button feels as if it is not pumping, rotate (crank) the engine approximately 90°, then continue pumping as described.

3. Tighten the low pressure bleed screw to 72 inch lbs. (8 Nm).

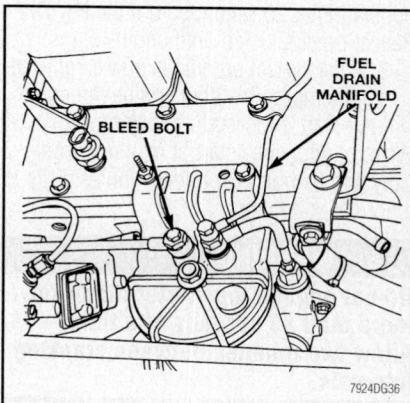

Fig. 144 Location of the low pressure bleed bolt—5.9L Diesel engine

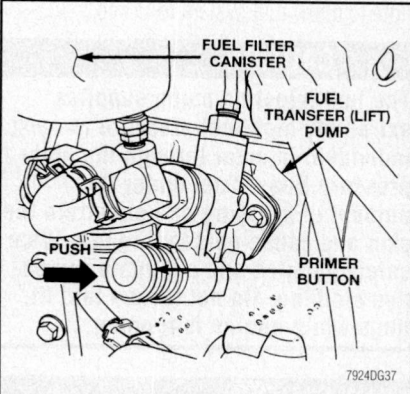

Fig. 145 Operate the push-button primer on the fuel transfer pump until the escaping fuel is free of air

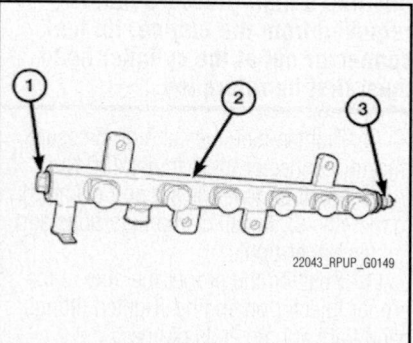

Fig. 142 Fuel pressure limiting valve (1), fuel rail (2) fuel pressure sensor (3)

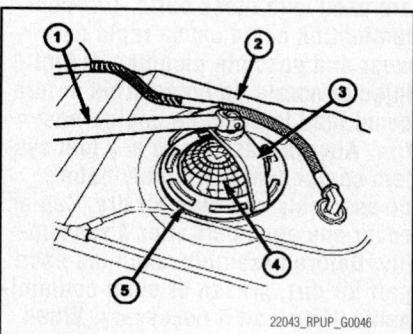

Fig. 143 Special tool 9340 shown in removal of lockring

PRIMING

A certain amount of air becomes trapped in the fuel system when fuel system components on the supply and/or high-pressure side are serviced or replaced. Fuel system priming is accomplished using the electric fuel transfer (lift) pump.

1. Servicing or replacing fuel system components will not require fuel system priming.

2. The fuel transfer (lift) pump is self-priming: When the key is first turned on (without cranking engine), the pump operates for approximately 1 to 2 second and then shuts off. The pump will also operate for up to 25 seconds after the starter is quickly engaged, and then disengaged without allowing the engine to start. The pump shuts off immediately if the key is on and the engine stops running.

3. Turn the key to CRANK position and quickly release key to ON position before engine starts. This will operate fuel transfer pump for approximately 25 seconds.

4. Crank the engine. If the engine does not start after 25 seconds, turn the key OFF. Repeat previous step until engine starts.

5. Fuel system priming is now completed.

6. Attempt to the start engine. If engine will not start, proceed to following steps. When engine does start, it may run erratically and be noisy for a few minutes. This is a normal condition.

✳✳ WARNING

Do not engage the starter motor for more than 30 seconds at a time. Allow two minutes between cranking intervals.

7. Perform previous fuel priming procedure steps using fuel transfer pump. Be sure fuel is present at fuel tank.

8. Crank the engine for 30 seconds at a time to allow fuel system to prime.

✳✳ CAUTION

The fuel injection pump supplies extremely high fuel pressure to each individual injector through the high-pressure lines. Fuel under this amount of pressure can penetrate the skin and cause personal injury. Wear safety goggles and adequate protective clothing. Do not loosen fuel fittings while engine is running.

✳✳ CAUTION

Engine may start while cranking starter motor.

FUEL TRANSFER (LIFT) PUMP

REMOVAL & INSTALLATION

The fuel transfer pump (fuel lift pump) is part of the fuel pump module. The fuel pump module is located in the fuel tank. The 12—volt electric pump is operated and controlled by the Engine Control Module (ECM). The ECM controls a relay in the Intelligent Power Module (IPM) for transfer pump operation. Refer to Fuel Supply Pump.

GLOW PLUGS

REMOVAL & INSTALLATION

The 5.9L and 6.7L diesel engines use an intake manifold air heater instead of glow plugs to preheat the air for improved starting ability. The heater element is located within the intake manifold top cover. Refer to the intake manifold removal and installation procedure to service the intake manifold air heater.

IDLE SPEED

ADJUSTMENT

5.9L Diesel Engine

Idle speed is controlled by the ECM. No adjustment is provided or necessary.

INJECTION LINES

REMOVAL & INSTALLATION

5.9L Diesel Engine

✳✳ WARNING

Cleanliness cannot be overemphasized when handling or replacing diesel fuel system components. This especially includes the fuel injectors, high-pressure fuel lines and fuel injection pump. Very tight tolerances are used with these parts. Dirt contamination could cause rapid part wear and possible plugging of fuel injector nozzle tip holes. This in turn could lead to possible engine misfire. Always wash/clean any fuel system component thoroughly before disassembly and then air dry. Cap or cover any open part after disassembly. Before assembly, examine each part for dirt, grease or other contaminants and clean if necessary. When installing new parts, lubricate them with clean engine oil or clean diesel fuel only.

1. Disconnect both negative battery cables from both batteries. Cover and isolate ends of cables.

2. Thoroughly clean fuel lines at both ends.

3. If removing fuel line at either No. 1 or No. 2 cylinder, the intake manifold air heater elements must first be removed from top of intake manifold.

4. If removing fuel line at No. 6 cylinder, a bracket is located above fuel line connection at cylinder head. Two bolts secure this bracket to rear of cylinder head. The upper bolt hole is slotted. Loosen (but do not remove) these 2 bracket bolts. Tilt bracket down to gain access to No. 6 fuel line connection.

5. Remove engine lift bracket (if necessary).

6. Remove necessary insulated fuel line support clamps and bracket bolts at intake manifold. DO NOT remove insulators from fuel lines.

7. Place shop towels around fuel lines at fuel rail and injectors. If possible, do not allow fuel to drip down side of engine.

✳✳ WARNING

When loosening or tightening high-pressure lines attached to a separate fitting , use a back-up wrench on fitting. Do not allow fitting to rotate. Damage to both fuel line and fitting will result.

8. Carefully remove each fuel line from engine. Note position of each while removing. Do not bend lines while removing.

To install:

➡All high-pressure fuel lines are of the same length and inside diameter. Correct high-pressure fuel line usage and installation is critical to smooth engine operation.

✳✳ WARNING

Anytime a high-pressure line is removed from the engine, its fuel connector nut at the cylinder head must first be retorqued.

9. Tighten fuel lines at high pressure injector connector to 37 ft. lbs. (50 Nm).

10. Position fuel line support clamp(s) to fuel line(s). Install clamp nuts/bolts and tighten finger-tight.

11. Position the proper fuel line to the proper injector on engine. Tighten fittings hand tight at both ends of line.

12. Tighten fuel lines at fuel rail to 27 ft. lbs. (37 Nm).

13. Tighten clamp/support nuts and bolts.

14. Install engine lifting bracket and bolt. Tighten to 56 ft. lbs. 77 (Nm).

15. If fuel line at either Number 1 or Number 2 cylinder has been replaced, install intake manifold air heater elements to top of intake manifold.

16. If fuel line at Number 6 cylinder has been replaced, tilt metal bracket upward and tighten 2 bolts at rear of cylinder head to 32 ft. lbs. (43 Nm).

17. Install remaining fuel line support clamps and bracket bolts at intake manifold.

18. Connect both negative battery cables to both batteries.

19. Prime the fuel system. Refer to Fuel System Priming.

20. Check lines/fittings for leaks.

6.7L Diesel Engine

✳✳ WARNING

Cleanliness cannot be overemphasized when handling or replacing diesel fuel system components. This especially includes the fuel injectors, high-pressure fuel lines and fuel injection pump. Very tight tolerances are used with these parts. Dirt contamination could cause rapid part wear and possible plugging of fuel injector nozzle tip holes. This in turn could lead to possible engine misfire. Always wash/clean any fuel system component thoroughly before disassembly and then air dry. Cap or cover any open part after disassembly. Before assembly, examine each part for dirt, grease or other contaminants and clean if necessary. When installing new parts, lubricate them with clean engine oil or clean diesel fuel only.

➡ **If removing fuel line at either No. 1 or No. 2 cylinder, the air inlet housing/EGR valve assembly must first be removed from the top of the intake manifold.**

1. Before servicing the vehicle, refer to the Precautions Section.

2. Disconnect both negative battery cables from both batteries. Cover and isolate ends of cables.

3. Thoroughly clean fuel lines at both ends.

✳✳ WARNING

When loosening or tightening high—pressure lines attached to a separate

fitting, use a back-up wrench on fitting. Do not allow fittings to rotate. Damage to both fuel line and fitting will result.

4. If removing fuel line at No. 6 cylinder, a bracket (4) is located above fuel line connection at cylinder head. Two bolts (3) secure this bracket to rear of cylinder head. The upper bolt hole is slotted. Loosen (but do not remove) these two bracket bolts. Tilt bracket down to gain access to No. 6 fuel line connection.

5. If removing fuel line at either No. 1 or No. 2 cylinder, the air inlet housing/EGR assembly must first be removed from top of intake manifold. Refer to EGR valve removal for procedures.

6. Place shop towels around fuel lines at fuel rail and injectors. If possible, do not allow fuel to drip down side of engine.

7. Carefully remove each fuel line from engine. Note position of each while removing.

➡ **Do not bend lines while removing.**

To install:

➡ **All high-pressure fuel lines are of the same length and inside diameter. Correct high-pressure fuel line usage and installation is critical to smooth engine operation.**

✳✳ WARNING

Anytime a high-pressure line is removed from the engine, its fuel connector nut at the cylinder head must first be retorqued.

8. Tighten nuts at high pressure injector connector nut at the cylinder head. Tighten nut to 37 ft. lbs. (50 Nm).

9. Position proper fuel line to proper injector on engine. Tighten fittings hand tight at both ends of line.

10. Tighten fuel line at cylinder head. Torque nut to 30 ft. lbs. (40 Nm).

11. Tighten fuel line nuts at fuel rail to 30 ft. lbs. (40 Nm).

12. If fuel line at No. 6 cylinder has been replaced, tilt metal bracket upward and tighten two bolts at rear of cylinder head. Tighten to 32 ft. lbs. (43 Nm).

13. If necessary, install EGR valve/air intake manifold assembly.

14. Connect both negative battery cables to both batteries.

15. Prime fuel system. Refer to Fuel System Priming.

16. Check lines/fittings for leaks.

INJECTION PUMP

REMOVAL & INSTALLATION

5.9L & 6.7L Diesel Engines

See Figure 146.

1. Before servicing the vehicle, refer to the Precautions Section.

2. Remove or disconnect the following:
- Negative battery cables
- Intake air tube
- Drive belt
- Pump wiring harness
- Injection pump supply line
- Fuel lines
- Drive gear access cover
- Drive gear mounting nut

3. Using a gear puller, remove the drive gear and leave it hanging within the timing gear cover.

4. Remove 3 pump mounting nuts and remove the pump.

To install:

5. Install a new O-ring coated with clean engine oil into the machined groove at the pump mounting area.

6. Install the pump to the mounting flange on the gear housing while aligning the pump shaft through the back of the pump gear.

7. Install the 3 pump mounting nuts and finger-tighten.

8. Install the shaft washer and nut and tighten by hand.

9. Tighten the pump mounting nuts to 18 ft. lbs. (25 Nm).

10. Tighten the pump shaft nut to 77 ft. lbs. (105 Nm).

11. Install the drive gear cover and tighten to 71 inch lbs. (8 Nm).

12. Install or connect the following:
- Fuel lines
- Injection pump supply line
- Pump wiring harness
- Drive belt
- Intake air tube
- Negative battery cables

13. Bleed air from the system.

14. Start the engine and check for leaks.

INJECTION TIMING

ADJUSTMENT

5.9L & 6.7L Diesel Engines

See Figures 147 and 148.

1. Perform the following phasing procedure anytime the injection pump has been removed and re-installed.

2. Locate the end of the fuel injection

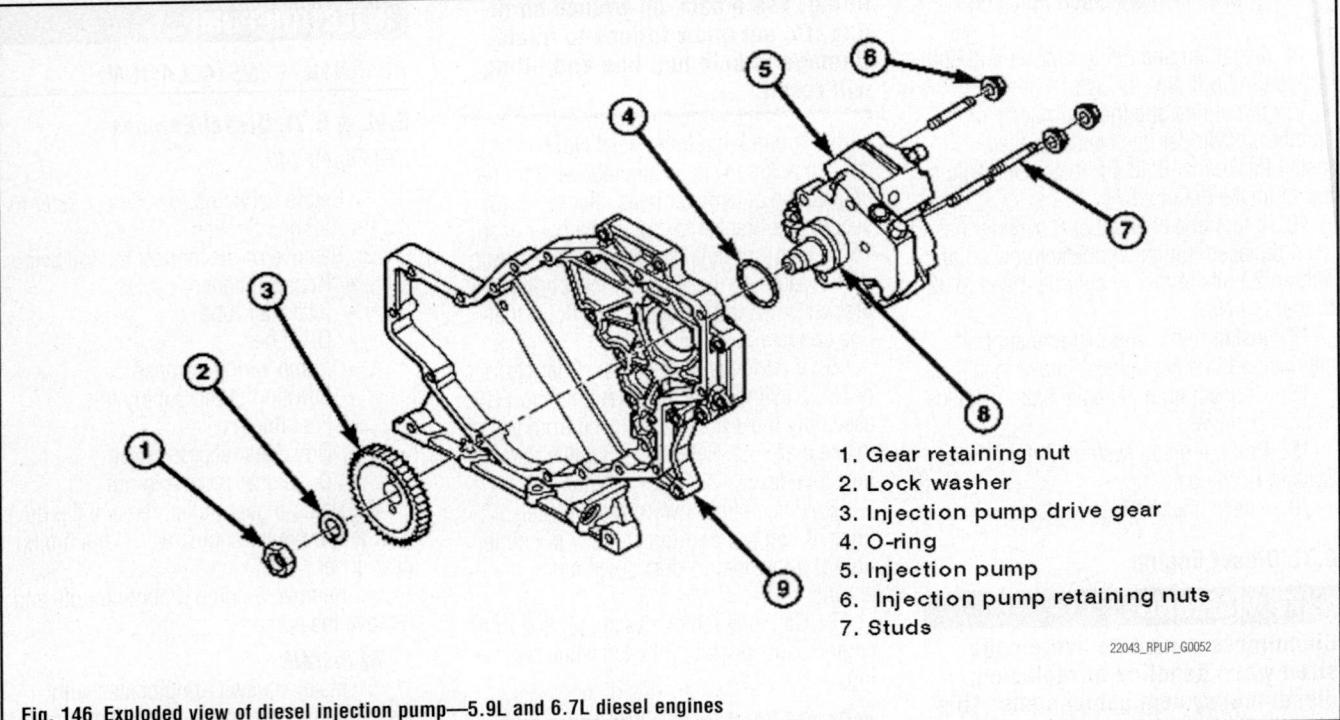

1. Gear retaining nut
2. Lock washer
3. Injection pump drive gear
4. O-ring
5. Injection pump
6. Injection pump retaining nuts
7. Studs

22043_RPUP_G0052

Fig. 146 Exploded view of diesel injection pump—5.9L and 6.7L diesel engines

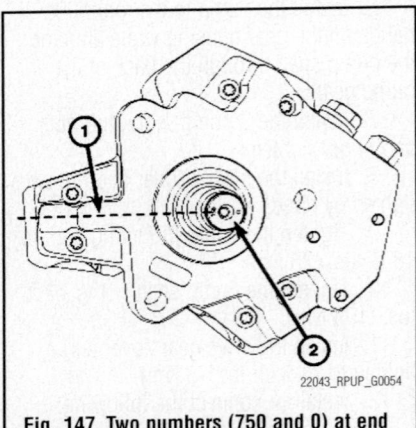

22043_RPUP_G0054

Fig. 147 Two numbers (750 and 0) at end of injection pump shaft shown

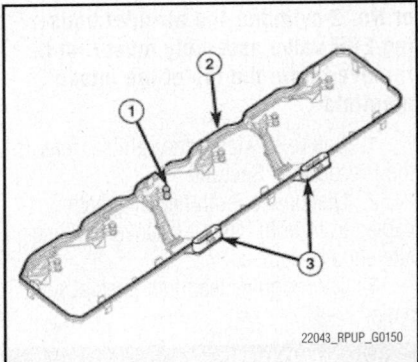

22043_RPUP_G0055

Fig. 148 Number 5 shown at the 9 o'clock position

pump shaft. Two numbers (750 and 0) are stamped into the end of the shaft.

3. Rotate the injection pump shaft until the number 5 (located in the center of number 750) is positioned at 9 o'clock.

4. Position injection pump to mounting flange on gear housing while aligning injection pump shaft through back of injection pump gear. Be sure the number 5 is still at the 9 o'clock position.

5. Bring the engine to TDC position. Do this by rotating the crankshaft until the TDC mark on the crankshaft damper is at 12 o'clock position. It does not matter if cylinder number 1 or number 6 is at TDC. Again, check to be sure the number 5 is still at the 9 o'clock position. Rotate pump shaft accordingly.

INJECTORS

REMOVAL & INSTALLATION

5.9L & 6.7L Diesel Engines

See Figures 149 through 153.

Each fuel injector has a six-digit alphanumeric correction code. The correction code is printed on the intake side of the fuel injector and is used to identify injector calibration. When replacing any fuel injectors, this code must be entered into the vehicles Engine Control Module (ECM) using a diagnostic scan tool. In addition, if a new ECM is installed, use a diagnostic scan tool to pro-

gram all six of the injector codes from the original fuel injectors into the new ECM.

➡The valve cover and valve cover gasket will need to be removed in order to manually record the values from the original injectors. Contact cleaner or brake cleaner may be used to clean the fuel injector.

➡If the fuel injectors are being removed such as for engine teardown or diagnostic purposes, be sure to mark each injector with its corresponding cylinder number. The fuel injectors MUST be reinstalled into the original (same) cylinder due to the fuel injector correction code.

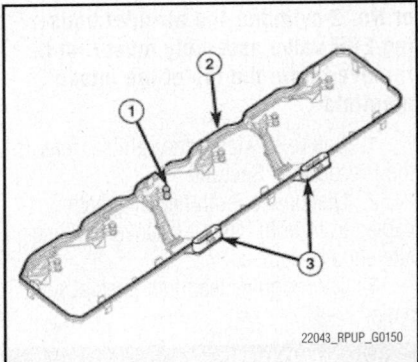

22043_RPUP_G0150

Fig. 149 Integrated fuel injector wire harness / valve cover gasket

1. Before servicing the vehicle, refer to the Precautions Section.

2. Disconnect both negative battery cables from both batteries. Cover and isolate ends of cables.

3. Remove vanity cover.

4. Remove breather assembly and tubes.

5. Remove valve cover.

6. Remove all 12 fuel injector wire harness nuts securing integrated wiring harness to all 6 fuel injectors.

7. An integrated fuel injector wire harness / valve cover gasket is used. After all 12 nuts have been removed, remove this integrated gasket. Before removing gasket, disconnect engine wiring harness at both electrical connectors.

8. Remove necessary high pressure fuel line connecting the necessary fuel injector rail to high pressure connector. Refer to Fuel Line Removal for procedures.

9. A connector retainer (nut) is used on each connector tube. Remove this nut(s) by unthreading from cylinder head. These nuts hold the fuel injector retainers to the fuel injector.

10. Using special high—pressure connector removal tool No. 9015 (4) remove necessary high-pressure connector(s) from cylinder head. Tool No. 9015 threads onto connector tube. Use tool to pry connector tube(s) from cylinder head.

11. Remove 2 fuel injector hold—down clamp bolts at each injector being removed.

12. Remove necessary exhaust rocker arm assembly(s).

13. Remove fuel injector(s) with Special Tool 9010 as follows:

a. Special tool 9010 is equipped with 2 clamshell clamps, a sliding retainer sleeve to retain the clamshell clamps, a

2-piece mounting stud, and a pivoting handle. Do not attempt to remove the fuel injector with any other device. Damage to injector will occur.

b. The rocker housing is bolted to the top of cylinder head. The mounting stud from tool No. 9010 was meant to temporarily replace a rocker housing mounting bolt. Remove the necessary rocker housing mounting bolt. These mounting bolts are located at the center of each of the 5 rocker housing support bridges.

c. Install and tighten 2-piece mounting stud to rocker housing. If removing the No. 6 fuel injector, separate the 2-piece mounting stud. Install lower half of mounting stud to center of rocker housing bridge. Install upper half of mounting stud to lower half.

d. Position tool handle to mounting stud and install handle nut. Leave handle nut loose to allow a pivoting action.

e. Position lower part of clamshell halves to sides of fuel injector (wider shoulder to bottom). The upper part of clamshell halves should also be positioned into machined shoulder on the handles pivoting head.

f. Slide the retainer sleeve over pivoting handle head to lock clamshell halves together.

g. Be sure handle pivot nut is loose.

h. Depress handle downward to remove fuel injector straight up from cylinder head bore.

14. Remove and discard injector sealing washer. This washer should be located on tip of injector, or may have remained in the injector bore.

15. Measure sealing gasket (washer).

➡ **If the fuel injectors are being removed such as for engine teardown**

or diagnostic purposes, be sure to mark each injector with its corresponding cylinder number. The fuel injectors MUST be reinstalled into the original (same) cylinder due to the fuel injector correction code.

➡ **Do not install new fuel injectors unless the alphanumeric codes have been recorded.**

To install:

16. Inspect fuel injector(s) as follows:

a. Look for burrs on injector inlet.

b. Check nozzle holes for hole erosion or plugging.

c. Inspect end of nozzle for burrs or rough machine marks.

d. Look for cracks at nozzle end.

e. If any of these conditions occur, replace injector.

17. Record six—digit alphanumeric correction code located on the side of injector.

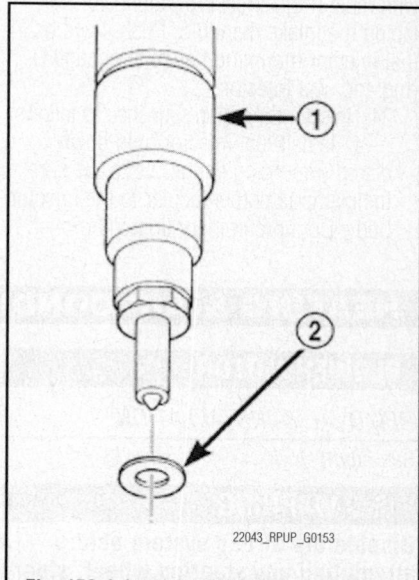

22043_RPUP_G0153

Fig. 152 Injector tip (1), sealing washer (2)

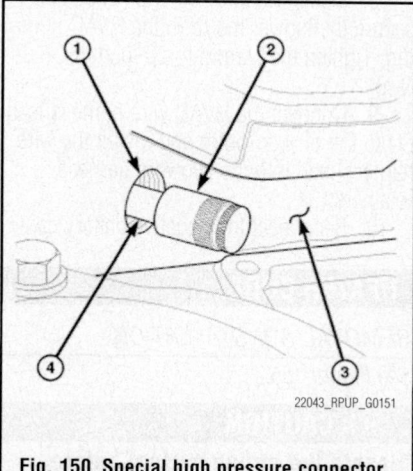

22043_RPUP_G0151

Fig. 150 Special high pressure connector removal tool No. 9015

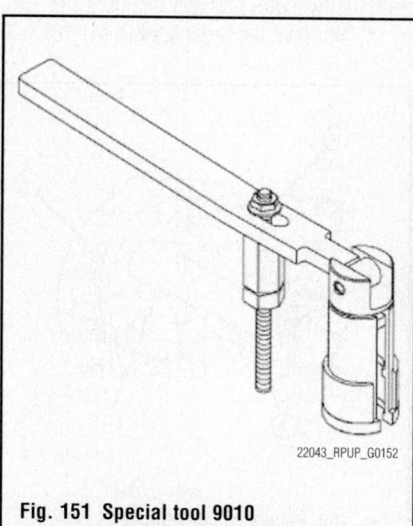

22043_RPUP_G0152

Fig. 151 Special tool 9010

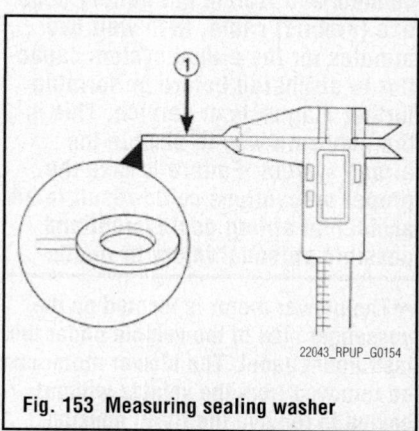

22043_RPUP_G0154

Fig. 153 Measuring sealing washer

18. Inspect high-pressure fuel injector connector(s) as follows:
   a. Damaged tip.
   b. Loose of missing alignment pin.
   c. Cut or missing O-ring.

19. Thoroughly clean fuel injector cylinder head bore. Blow out bore hole with compressed air.

20. The bottom of fuel injector is sealed to cylinder head bore with a copper sealing washer (shim) of a certain thickness. A new shim with correct thickness must always be re-installed after removing injector. Measure thickness of injector shim. Shim thickness:.060 inch (1.5 mm).

21. Install new shim (washer) to bottom of injector. Apply light coating of clean engine oil to washer. This will keep washer in place during installation.

22. Install new O-ring to fuel injector. Apply small amount of clean engine oil to O-ring and injector bore.

23. Install injector into cylinder head with male (high-pressure) connector port facing the intake manifold. Push down on fuel injector mounting flange to engage O-ring and seat injector

24. Injector tightening sequence as follows:
   a. Install fuel injector hold down clamp (mounting flange) bolts. Be sure the clamp is perpendicular to the injector body. Do a preliminary tightening of

these bolts to 44 inch lbs. (5 Nm). This preliminary tightening insures the fuel injector is seated and centered.
   b. After tightening, relieve bolt torque, but leave both bolts threaded in place.
   c. Install high-pressure connector and retaining nut. Do a preliminary tightening of nut to 11 ft. lbs. (15 Nm).
   d. Alternately tighten injector hold down bolts to 71 inch lbs. (8 Nm).
   e. Do a final tightening of the high—pressure connector and retaining nut. Tighten to 37 ft. lbs. (50 Nm).

25. Install integrated gasket.

26. Connect injector solenoid wires and nuts to top of injectors. Tighten connector nuts to 11 inch lbs. (1.25 Nm).Be very careful not to overtighten these nuts as damage to fuel injector will occur.

27. Install exhaust rocker arm assembly.

28. Set exhaust valve lash.

29. Install fuel connector tube nut at cylinder head and tighten to 37 ft. lbs. (50 Nm). Be sure to use a secondary back-up wrench on the connector nut (fitting) while torquing fuel line fitting.

30. Install valve cover.

31. Install breather assembly.

32. Connect negative battery cables to both batteries.

Each fuel injector has a six-digit alphanumeric correction code. The correc-

tion code is printed on the intake side of the fuel injector and is used to identify injector calibration. When replacing any fuel injectors, this code must be entered into the vehicles Engine Control Module (ECM) using a diagnostic scan tool. In addition, if a new ECM is installed, use a diagnostic scan tool to program all six of the injector codes from the original fuel injectors into the new ECM.

FUEL INJECTOR CORRECTION CODE PROGRAMMING

1. Turn ignition switch **ON**.
2. Using a diagnostic scan tool, select ECU view, PCM, Miscellaneous functions.
3. Select injector quantity adjustments and click start.
4. Choose appropriate cylinder number and click next.
5. Click on show keyboard.

➡**A fault code will be set if incorrect serialization codes have been inputted.**

6. Input six-digit Injector Correction Code and click enter.
7. Review code as it was typed, then click Next if correct, or edit if necessary.
8. Repeat the preceding steps for other cylinders if necessary.
9. Once all fuel injector correction codes are entered, cycle the ignition to complete.

HEATING & AIR CONDITIONING SYSTEM

BLOWER MOTOR

REMOVAL & INSTALLATION

See Figure 154.

✳✳ WARNING

Disable the airbag system before attempting any steering wheel, steering column, or instrument panel component diagnosis or service. Disconnect and isolate the battery negative (ground) cable, then wait two minutes for the airbag system capacitor to discharge before performing further diagnosis or service. This is the only sure way to disable the airbag system. Failure to take the proper precautions could result in an accidental airbag deployment and possible personal injury or death.

➡**The blower motor is located on the passenger side of the vehicle under the instrument panel. The blower motor can be removed from the vehicle without having to remove the HVAC housing.**

1. Before servicing the vehicle, refer to the Precautions Section.
2. Disconnect and isolate the negative battery cable.
3. Disconnect the HVAC wire harness lead (1) from the blower motor (2).
4. Remove the HVAC wire harness lead from the two wire harness retainers (3).
5. Remove the three screws (4) that

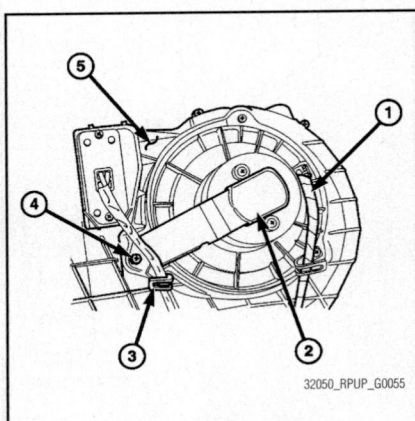

Fig. 154 Blower motor removal

32050_RPUP_G0055

secure the blower motor to the bottom of the HVAC housing (5).
6. Remove the blower motor from the HVAC housing.

To install:

7. Position the blower motor (2) into the bottom of the HVAC housing (5).
8. Install the three screws (4) that secure the blower motor to the HVAC housing. Tighten the screws to 20 inch lbs. (2.2 Nm).
9. Connect the HVAC wire harness lead (1) to the blower motor and install the wire harness lead into the two wire harness retainers (3).
10. Reconnect the negative battery cable.

HEATER CORE

REMOVAL & INSTALLATION

See Figure 155.

✳✳ CAUTION

Disable the airbag system before attempting any steering wheel, steering column, or instrument panel

component diagnosis or service. **Disconnect and isolate the negative battery (ground) cable, then wait two minutes for the airbag system capacitor to discharge before performing further diagnosis or service. This is the only sure way to disable the airbag system. Failure to take the proper precautions could result in accidental airbag deployment and possible personal injury or death.**

➡️**The HVAC housing must be removed from the vehicle and disassembled for service of the A/C evaporator, evaporator temperature sensor, mode-air and blend-air doors.**

1. Before servicing the vehicle, refer to the Precautions Section.

2. Disconnect and isolate the negative battery cable.

3. Recover the refrigerant from the A/C system.

4. Drain the engine cooling system.

5. Disconnect the A/C liquid line and the A/C accumulator from the A/C evaporator.

6. Disconnect the heater hoses from the heater core tubes.

7. Remove the powertrain control module (PCM) to gain access to the two nuts that secure the HVAC housing to the engine compartment side of the dash panel and remove the nuts.

8. On Mega Cab models, remove the floor console duct.

9. Remove the front seat assembly.

10. Remove the left a-pillar trim.

11. Disconnect the headliner wire harness connector located at the a-pillar.

12. Remove the instrument panel top cover.

13. Remove the left cowl trim panel.

14. Remove the steering column.

15. Remove the two bolts that secure the steering column support bracket to the instrument panel.

16. Remove the park brake release handle actuator rod.

17. Disconnect the instrument panel wire harness connector located above the brake pedal from the bulkhead wire harness connector.

18. Using a trim stick C-4755 or equivalent, from the notch on the bottom, remove the left instrument panel side cover.

19. Remove the three bolts that secure the left side of the instrument panel to the dash panel.

20. Remove the air bag control module cover, if equipped.

21. Disconnect the air bag control module electrical connector.

22. Remove the two bolts that secure the instrument panel to the center of the floor panel.

23. Remove the right cowl trim cover.

24. Disconnect the two instrument panel wire harness connectors from the two body wire harness connectors located on the right side of the cowl panel.

25. Disconnect the antenna coaxial cable connector from the radio coaxial cable connector located on the right side of the cowl panel.

26. Remove the one bolt that secures the instrument panel to the HVAC housing below the glove box opening.

27. Remove the right a-pillar trim.

28. Using a trim stick C-4755 or equivalent, from the notch on the bottom, remove the right instrument panel side cover from the instrument panel.

29. Remove the three bolts that secure the right side instrument panel bracket to the dash panel.

30. Remove the four screws that secure the instrument panel to the top of the cowl panel.

31. Remove the two bolts that secure the instrument panel to the top of the cowl panel

32. Pull back the driver's side carpet as necessary to pull the air bag module harness out from under the carpet.

33. With the help of an assistant, lift the instrument panel up and off of the cowl panel and remove the instrument panel from the vehicle.

34. If required, remove the four plastic screws inserts from the top of the cowl panel.

35. Remove the bolt that secures the HVAC housing to the floor bracket.

36. Remove the two nuts that secure the HVAC housing to the passenger compartment side of the dash panel.

37. Pull the HVAC housing assembly rearward and remove the housing assembly from the passenger compartment.

38. If required, remove the fresh air inlet from the dash panel.

39. Remove the foam seal from the heater core tubes.

40. If equipped with the dual zone heating-A/C system, remove the linkage rod (4) to gain access to the heater core.

41. Remove the two screws that secure the heater core tube bracket to the HVAC housing and remove the bracket.

42. Carefully pull the heater core out of the front of the HVAC housing.

43. Inspect all foam seals and replace as required.

To install:

44. Carefully install the heater core into the front of the HVAC housing.

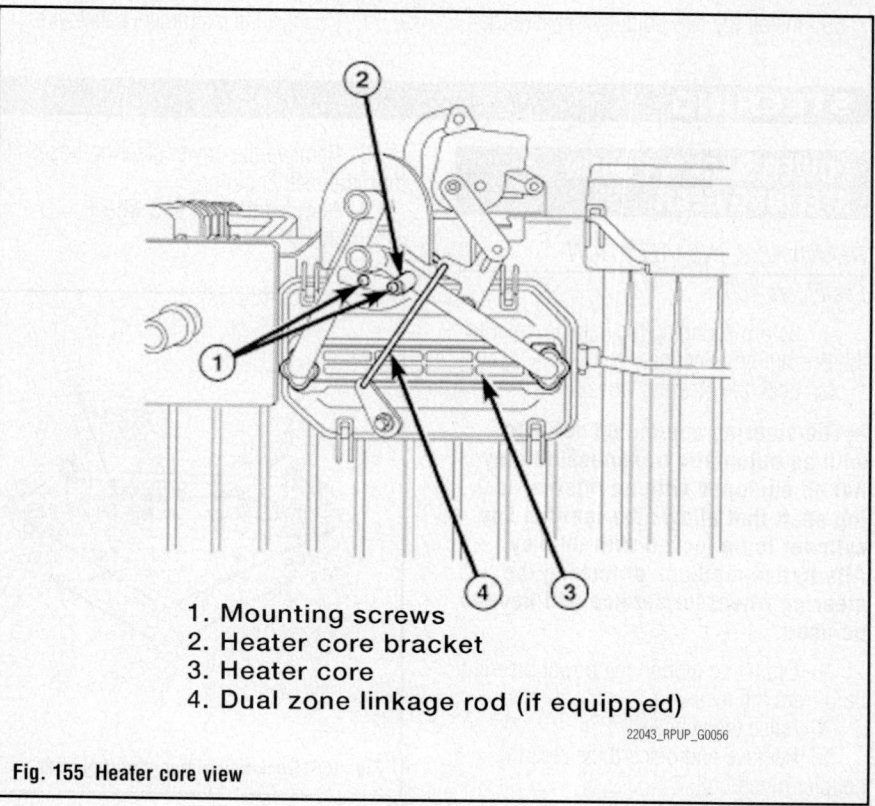

1. **Mounting screws**
2. **Heater core bracket**
3. **Heater core**
4. **Dual zone linkage rod (if equipped)**

22043_RPUP_G0056

Fig. 155 Heater core view

45. Position the heater core tube bracket onto the HVAC housing.

46. Install the two screws (1) that secure the heater core bracket to the HVAC housing. Tighten the screws to 10 inch lbs. (1.1 Nm)

47. If equipped with the dual zone heating and A/C system, install the linkage rod.

48. Install the foam seal onto the heater core tubes.

➡**If the heater core is being replaced, flush the cooling system.**

49. If removed, install the fresh air inlet onto the dash panel

50. Position the HVAC housing assembly into the passenger compartment with the mounting studs and the condensate drain tube in their proper locations in the dash panel.

51. Install the two nuts that secure the HVAC housing to the passenger compartment side of the dash panel. Tighten the nuts to 60 inch lbs. (68 Nm).

52. Install the bolt that secures the HVAC housing to the floor bracket. Tighten the bolt to 60 inch lbs. (68 Nm).

53. If removed, install the four plastic screw inserts into the top of the cowl panel.

54. With the help of an assistant, position the instrument panel into the vehicle and install the right side guide pin and the left side guide hook to the sides of the cowl panel.

55. Install the two bolts that secure the instrument panel to the top of the cowl panel

56. Tighten the bolts to 9 ft. lbs. (12 Nm).

57. Install the four screws that secure the instrument panel to the top of the cowl panel.

58. Tighten the screws to 20 inch lbs. (2 Nm).

59. Install the three bolts that secure the right side instrument panel bracket to the cowl panel.

60. Tighten the bolts to 9 ft. lbs. (12 Nm).

61. Position the air bag module harness under the carpet and position the carpet back.

62. Install the right a-pillar trim.

63. Install the two bolts that secure the instrument panel to the center of the floor panel

64. Tighten the bolts to 9 ft. lbs. (12 Nm).

65. Connect the air bag control module electrical connector.

66. Install the air bag control module cover, if equipped.

67. Install the floor console, if equipped.

68. Install the three bolts that secure the left side of the instrument panel to the dash panel.

69. Tighten the bolts to 9 ft. lbs. (12 Nm).

70. Install the left cowl trim panel.

71. Connect the instrument panel wire harness connector located above the brake pedal to the bulkhead wire harness connector.

72. Install the park brake release handle actuator rod.

73. Install the two bolts that secure the steering column support bracket to the instrument panel.

74. Tighten the bolts to 10 ft. lbs. (14 Nm).

75. Install the steering column.

76. Install the left cowl trim cover.

77. Install the left instrument panel side cover.

78. Connect the headliner wire harness connector located at the a-pillar.

79. Install the instrument panel top cover.

80. Install the left a-pillar trim.

81. Install the front seat assembly.

82. On Mega Cab models, install the floor console duct.

83. Install the two nuts (3) that secure the HVAC housing (1) to the engine compartment side of the dash panel. Tighten the nuts to 60 inch lbs. (6.8 Nm).

84. Install the Powertrain Control Module (PCM).

85. Connect the heater hoses to the heater core tubes.

86. Connect the A/C liquid line and the A/C accumulator to the A/C evaporator.

87. Reconnect the negative battery cable.

88. Refill the engine cooling system.

89. Evacuate the A/C system.

90. Charge the A/C system.

STEERING

POWER RACK & PINION STEERING GEAR

REMOVAL & INSTALLATION

See Figure 156.

1. Before servicing the vehicle, refer to the Precautions Section.

2. Lock the steering wheel.

➡**The steering column on vehicles with an automatic transmission may not be equipped with an internal locking shaft that allows the ignition key cylinder to be locked with the key. Alternative methods of locking the steering wheel for service will have to be used.**

3. Drain and siphon the power steering fluid from the reservoir.

4. Raise the vehicle.

5. Remove and discard the steering coupler pinch bolt.

6. Remove the power steering hoses from the rack & pinion.

7. Remove the tire and wheel assembly.

8. Remove the tie rod end nuts and separate tie rod ends from the knuckles with puller 8677

9. Remove the skid plate.

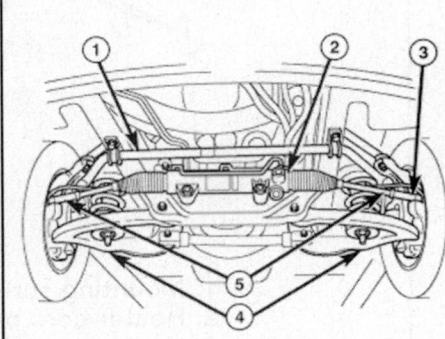

1. Stabilizer bar
2. Rack and pinion steering gear
3. Tie rod sleeve
4. Lower control arms
5. Inner and outer tie rods

22043_RPUP_G0057

Fig. 156 Rack and pinion steering gear

10. Remove the rack & pinion mounting bolts.

11. Remove the rack & pinion from the vehicle.

To install:

➡**Before installing gear inspect bushings and replace if worn or damaged.**

12. Install the gear on the front crossmember and tighten the mounting bolts for light duty trucks to 235 ft. lbs. (319 Nm). Tighten the mounting bolts for heavy duty 4X2 trucks to 185 ft. lbs. (251 Nm).

13. Slide the shaft coupler onto the gear. Install new pinch bolt and tighten to 36 ft. lbs. (49 Nm).

14. Clean and dry the tie rod end studs and the knuckle tapers.

15. Install the tie rod ends into the steering knuckles and tighten the nuts to 45 ft. lbs. (61 Nm). then an additional 90 degrees.

16. Install the pressure power steering hose to the steering gear and tighten to 23 ft. lbs. (32 Nm).

17. Install the return power steering hose to the steering gear and for light duty trucks tighten to 37 ft. lbs (50 Nm). Tighten the mounting bolts for heavy duty 4X2 trucks to 40 ft. lbs. (54 Nm).

18. Install the front skid plate.

19. Install the tire and wheel assembly.

20. Remove the support and lower the vehicle.

21. Fill and bleed the power steering system.

22. Adjust the toe.

POWER RECIRCULATING BALL STEERING GEAR

REMOVAL & INSTALLATION

See Figures 157 through 159.

1. Before servicing the vehicle, refer to the Precautions Section.

2. Place the front wheels in a straight-ahead position.

➡**The steering column on vehicles with an automatic transmission may not be equipped with an internal locking shaft that allows the ignition key cylinder to be locked with the key. Alternative methods of locking the steering wheel for service will have to be used.**

3. Lock the steering wheel.

4. Siphon out as much power steering fluid as possible.

5. Disconnect and cap the fluid hoses from steering gear.

6. Remove coupler pinch bolt at the steering gear and slide shaft off gear.

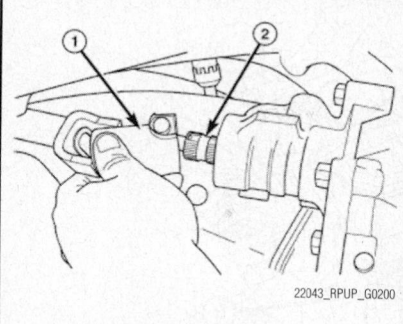

Fig. 157 Coupler pinch bolt (1), steering gear (2)

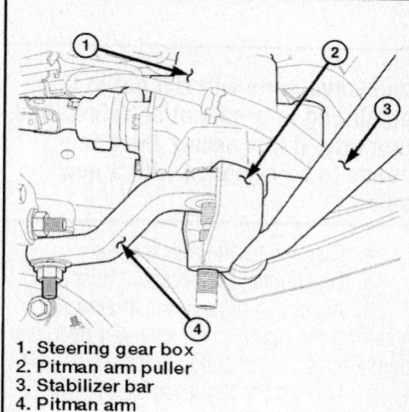

1. Steering gear box
2. Pitman arm puller
3. Stabilizer bar
4. Pitman arm

Fig. 158 Pitman arm removal shown with puller

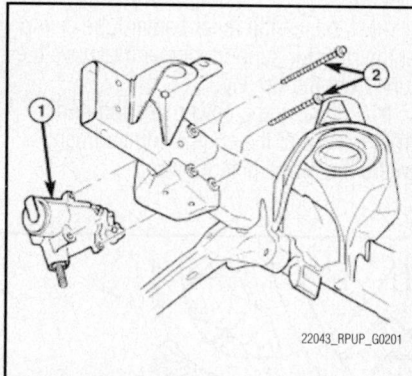

Fig. 159 Steering gear removal shown

7. Mark the pitman shaft and pitman arm for installation reference. Remove the pitman arm from the shaft with pitman arm remover 9615.

8. Remove steering gear three mounting bolts. Remove the steering gear from the vehicle.

To install:

9. Position the steering gear the frame rail and install the three mounting bolts.

Tighten the mounting bolts to 145 ft. lbs. (196 Nm).

10. Align steering coupler on gear shaft. Install pinch bolt and tighten to 36 ft. lbs. (49 Nm).

11. Align and install the pitman arm.

12. Install the washer and retaining nut on the pitman shaft. Tighten the nut to 225 ft. lbs. (305 Nm).

13. Connect fluid hoses to steering gear, tighten to 23 ft. lbs. (32 Nm).

14. Add Mopar® power steering fluid+4 or Mopar® ATF+4 automatic transmission fluid and bleed system.

POWER STEERING PUMP

REMOVAL & INSTALLATION

Gasoline Engines

See Figure 160.

1. Before servicing the vehicle, refer to the Precautions Section.

2. Drain and siphon the power steering fluid from the reservoir.

3. Remove the serpentine belt, as outlined in the Engine Mechanical Section.

✷✷ WARNING

Do not remove the fitting on the pump that the high pressure hose screws into. The fitting may come loose unless it is backed up using another wrench. If the fitting does come loose, it must be retightened to 40–50 ft. lbs. (57–67 Nm) before continuing. If this fitting comes out of the pump body, the internal spring and valve parts will fall out of the pump and they cannot be reinstalled properly. If this occurs the pump needs to be replaced with a new pump.

4. Disconnect the return hose.

5. Disconnect the pressure hose.

6. Access to remove the three bolts securing the pump to the cylinder head can be gained thru the pulley holes.

To install:

7. Align the pump with the mounting holes in the left cylinder head.

8. Install 3 pump mounting bolts through the pulley access holes. Tighten the bolts to 21 ft. lbs. (28 Nm).

9. Reconnect the pressure line and return hose to the pump and reservoir. Tighten the pressure line to 27 ft. lbs. (37 Nm).

10. Install the serpentine drive belt.

Fig. 160 View of the power steering pump pulley (1), fluid reservoir (2), return hose (3) and high pressure hose (4)

11. Fill the reservoir with power steering fluid and perform BLEEDING.

12. Start the engine and check the operation of the brakes.

Diesel Engines

See Figure 161.

1. Before servicing the vehicle, refer to the Precautions Section.

2. Drain and siphon the power steering fluid from the reservoir.

3. Remove the serpentine belt, as outlined in the Engine Mechanical Section.

✱✱ WARNING

Do not remove the fitting on the pump that the high pressure hose screws into. The fitting may come loose unless it is backed up using another wrench. If the fitting does come loose, it must be retightened to 40–50 ft. lbs. (57–67 Nm) before continuing. If this fitting comes out of the pump body, the internal spring and valve parts will fall out of the pump and they cannot be reinstalled properly. If this occurs the pump needs to be replaced with a new pump.

4. Disconnect the return hose.

5. Disconnect the pressure hose.

6. Access to remove the three bolts securing the pump to the cylinder head can be gained thru the pulley holes.

7. Loosen the pump bracket to the block.

8. Remove the 6 intake plenum bolts.

9. Loosen the inner cooler tube clamp at the intake plenum and remove the intake plenum.

10. Loosen the inner cooler tube clamp at the radiator support side and remove the tube from the vehicle.

11. Remove the power steering pump from the top of the engine compartment where the intake plenum was.

To install:

12. Set the power steering pump in place in the engine compartment from the top.

13. Install the inner cooler tube.

14. Tighten the inner cooler tube clamp at the radiator support side.

15. Install the 6 intake plenum bolts.

16. Tighten the inner cooler tube clamp at the intake plenum.

17. Install 3 pump mounting bolts through the pulley access holes. Tighten the bolts to 21 ft. lbs. (28 Nm).

18. Tighten the pump bracket to the block.

19. Reconnect the pressure line and return hose to the pump and reservoir. Tighten the pressure line to 27 ft. lbs. (37 Nm).

20. Install the serpentine drive belt.

21. Fill the reservoir with power steering fluid and perform BLEEDING.

22. Start the engine and check the operation of the brakes.

BLEEDING

✱✱ WARNING

The fluid level should be checked with engine off to prevent injury from moving components.

✱✱ CAUTION

Mopar® Power Steering Fluid + 4 or Mopar® ATF+4 Automatic Transmission Fluid is to be used in the power steering system. Both Fluids have the same material standard specifications (MS-9602). No other power steering or automatic transmission fluid is to be used in the system. Damage may result to the power steering pump and system if another fluid is used. Do not overfill the system.

✱✱ CAUTION

If the air is not purged from the power steering system correctly, pump failure could result.

➡Be sure the vacuum tool used in the following procedure is clean and free of any fluids.

1. Check the fluid level. As measured on the side of the reservoir, the level should indicate between MAX and MIN when the fluid is at normal ambient temperature. Adjust the fluid level as necessary.

2. Tightly insert P/S Cap Adapter 9688 (4) into the mouth of the reservoir (3).

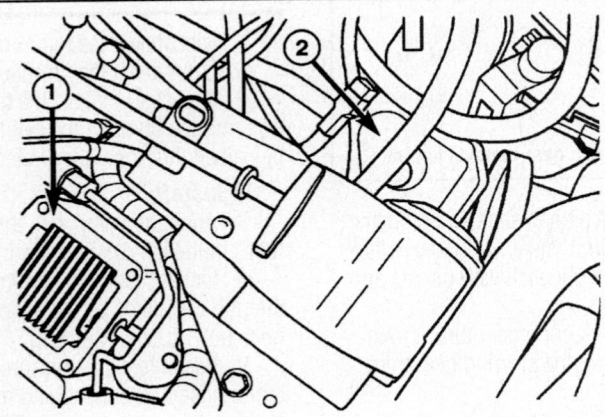

Fig. 161 View of the intake plenum (1) and power steering pump (2) mounting

✳✳ CAUTION

Failure to use a vacuum pump reservoir (1) may allow power steering fluid to be sucked into the hand vacuum pump.

3. Attach Hand Vacuum Pump C-4207-A (2), or equivalent, with reservoir (1) attached, to the P/S Cap Adapter 9688 (4).

✳✳ CAUTION

Do not run the vehicle while vacuum is applied to the power steering system. Damage to the power steering pump can occur.

➡️**When performing the following step make sure the vacuum level is maintained during the entire time period.**

4. Using Hand Vacuum Pump (2), apply 68-85 kpa (20-25 in. Hg) of vacuum to the system for a minimum of three minutes.
5. Slowly release the vacuum and remove the special tools.
6. Adjust the fluid level as necessary. Refer to Step 1.

7. Repeat Step 1 through Step 6 until the fluid no longer drops when vacuum is applied.
8. Start the engine and cycle the steering wheel lock-to-lock three times.

➡️**Do not hold the steering wheel at the stops.**

9. Stop the engine and check for leaks at all connections.
10. Check for any signs of air in the reservoir and check the fluid level. If air is present, repeat the procedure as necessary.

SUSPENSION

COIL SPRING

REMOVAL & INSTALLATION

Coil Spring Suspension—2WD Models

1. Before servicing the vehicle, refer to the Precautions Section.
2. Support the lower control arm on a floor jack.
3. Remove or disconnect the following:
   • Front wheel
   • Shock absorber
4. Compress the spring.
5. Remove or disconnect the following:
   • Stabilizer bar link
   • Lower ball joint

✳✳ WARNING

Support the upper control arm and knuckle.

6. Lower the jack and tighten the compressor to allow coil spring removal. Catch the isolator pad.

To install:

7. Install the coil spring and raise the control arm into position.
8. Install or connect the following:
   • Lower ball joint. Tighten the nut to 38 ft. lbs. (52 Nm), plus a 90 degree turn (1500 Series), or, 100 ft. lbs. (135 Nm) (HD Series)
   • Shock absorber
   • Stabilizer bar link. Tighten the nut to 27 ft. lbs. (37 Nm).
   • Front wheel
9. Lower the vehicle and allow the suspension to take the weight. Tighten the front and rear control arm pivot bolts to 150 ft. lbs. (204 Nm) LD; 210 ft. lbs. (285 Nm) HD

Link/Coil Suspension—4WD Models

1. Before servicing the vehicle, refer to the Precautions Section.

2. Support the axle on a floor jack.
3. Place alignment marks on the lower arm adjuster and axle bracket.
4. Remove or disconnect the following:
   • Front wheel
   • Upper control arm and loosen the lower arm bolts
   • Track bar from the frame rail bracket
   • Drag link from the Pitman arm
   • Stabilizer bar link
   • Shock absorber
5. Lower the jack and remove the coil spring.

To install:

6. Install the coil spring and raise the axle into position.
7. Install or connect the following:
   • Stabilizer bar link. Tighten the nut to 45 ft. lbs. (61 Nm).
   • Shock absorber
   • Track bar
   • Drag link
   • On 4WD, the front driveshaft
   • Upper control arm and lower arm

FRONT SUSPENSION

bolts. Upper arm nuts to 110 ft. lbs. (149 Nm); lower arm nuts to 160 ft. lbs. (217 Nm)

Coil Over Suspension—4WD Models

See Figures 162 and 163.

1. Before servicing the vehicle, refer to the Precautions Section.
2. Remove the shock.
3. Install the shock assembly in the Branick 7200® or equivalent spring removal/installation tool.
4. Compress the spring.
5. Position the shock wrench 9362, on shock shaft retaining nut. Next, insert 8 mm socket though Wrench onto hex located on end of shock shaft. While holding shock shaft from turning, remove nut from shock shaft using Wrench.
6. Remove the upper shock nut.
7. Remove the shock upper mounting plate.
8. Remove and inspect the upper spring isolator.
9. Remove the shock.

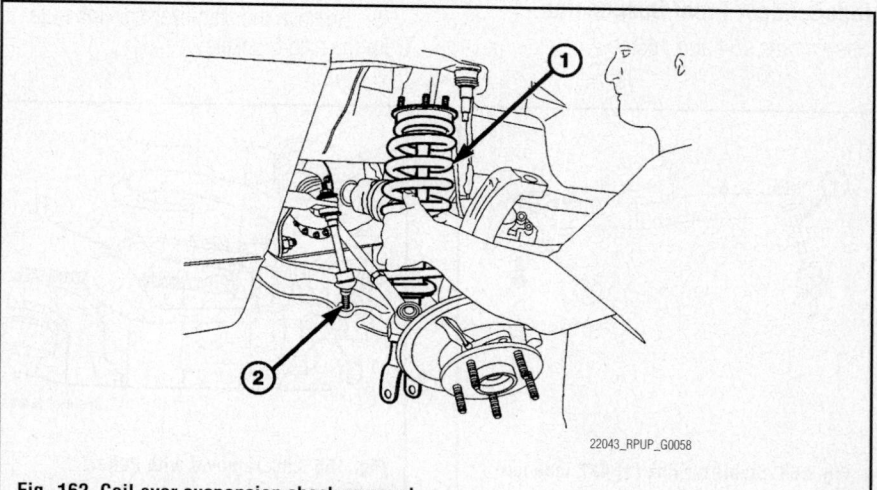

22043_RPUP_G0058

Fig. 162 Coil over suspension shock removal

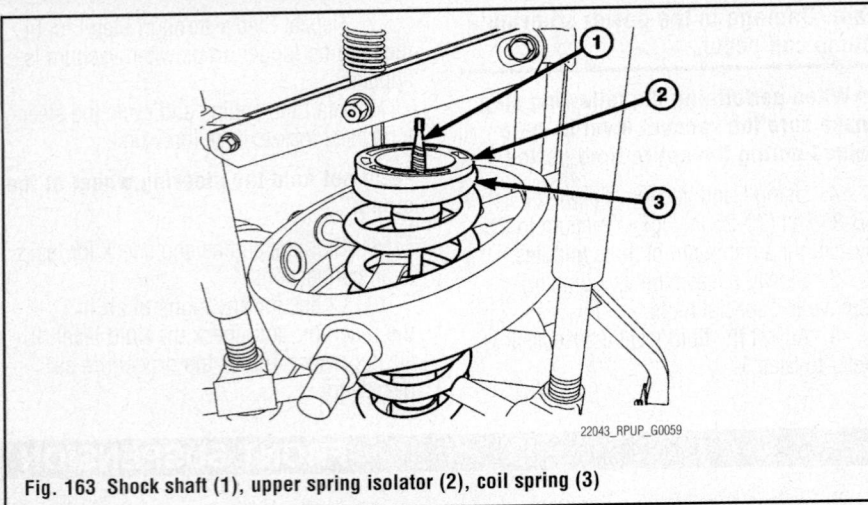

Fig. 163 Shock shaft (1), upper spring isolator (2), coil spring (3)

To install:

10. Position the shock into the coil spring.

11. Install the upper isolator.

12. Install the upper shock mounting plate.

13. Install the shock upper mounting nut.

14. Install the shock wrench 9362 (on end of a torque wrench), on shock shaft retaining nut. Next, insert 8 mm socket though Wrench onto hex located on end of shock shaft. While holding the shock shaft from turning, tighten nut using Wrench to 66 ft. lbs. (90 Nm).

15. Decompress the spring.

16. Remove the shock assembly from the spring compressor tool.

17. Install the shock assembly.

CONTROL LINKS

REMOVAL & INSTALLATION

Independent Front Suspension

See Figures 164 and 165.

1. Before servicing the vehicle, refer to the Precautions Section.

2. Raise and support the vehicle.

3. Remove the lower nut.

4. Remove the upper nut, retainer and grommets.

5. Remove the stabilizer link from the vehicle

6. Install the stabilizer link to the vehicle.

7. Install the lower nut and tighten to 75 ft. lbs. (102 Nm).

8. Install the retainers, grommets and upper nut and tighten to 20 ft. lbs. (27 Nm).

9. Remove the support and lower the vehicle.

Link/Coil Suspension

1. Before servicing the vehicle, refer to the Precautions Section.

2. Raise and support the vehicle.

3. Hold the stabilizer link shafts with a wrench and remove the link nuts at the stabilizer bar.

4. Remove the retainers and grommets from the stabilizer bar links.

5. Remove the stabilizer bar link nuts from the axle brackets.

6. Remove the links from the axle brackets with Puller C-3894-A.

To install:

7. Install links to the axle bracket and tighten nut to 110 ft. lbs. (149 Nm).

8. Install links, retainers, grommets and nuts to the stabilizer bar. Hold the link shaft with a wrench and tighten the nuts to 27 ft. lbs. (38 Nm).

9. Remove the supports and lower the vehicle

LOWER BALL JOINT

REMOVAL & INSTALLATION

Independent Front Suspension

See Figure 166.

1. Before servicing the vehicle, refer to the Precautions Section.

2. Remove or disconnect the following:
- Front wheel
- Brake caliper and rotor
- Outer tie rod ends
- Steering knuckle
- Snapring from the ball joint (HD 2wd)

3. Use tools C-4212-F, 8698-2 and 8698-3 (or equivalents) to remove the lower ball joint.

➡ **Use EP grease on the tool threads.**

To install:

4. Use tools C-4212-F, 8698-1 and 8698-3 (or equivalents) to install the lower ball joint.

5. On 2wd HD models, install a new snapring; on all others, stake the ball joint flange in 4 evenly spaced places.

6. Install or connect the following:
- Knuckle. Torque the ball stud nut to 38 ft. lbs. (52 Nm) plus 90 degrees on all except 2X4 HD; on 2wd HD, torque the nut to 100 ft. lbs. (135 Nm).

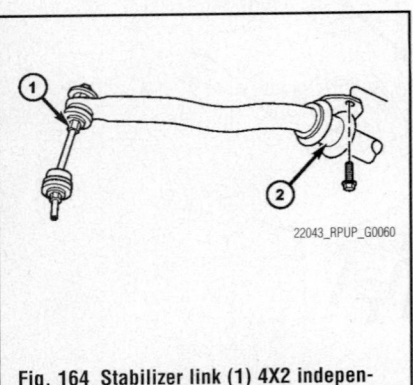

Fig. 164 Stabilizer link (1) 4X2 independent front suspension shown 4X4 similar

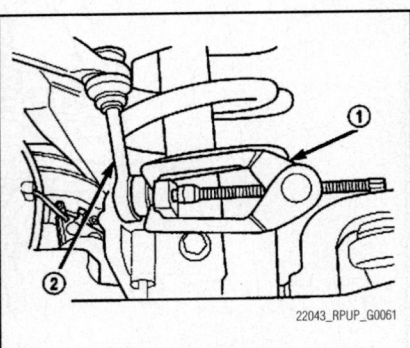

Fig. 165 Link removal with Puller C-3894-A shown

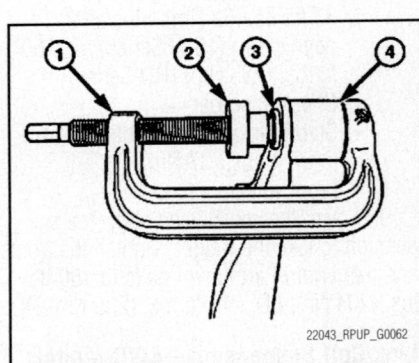

Fig. 166 Lower ball joint removal with tools shown

- Outer tie rod ends
- Axle shaft
- Hub retainer
- Brake caliper and rotor
- Front wheel

Link/Coil Suspension

See Figure 167.

1. Before servicing the vehicle, refer to the Precautions Section.
2. Remove the steering knuckle.
3. Remove the axle shaft from the axle.
4. Remove lower snap ring from the lower ball joint.
5. Remove the lower ball joint, using tool 6761 and 8445-3 with C-4212-F

To install:

6. To install, use driver 8445-2, receiver 8975-5 and tool C-4212-F.
7. Install the axle shaft into the axle.
8. Install the knuckle. Tighten the ball stud nut to 35 ft. lbs. (47 Nm), then tighten it to 70 ft. lbs. (94 Nm) and install the pin.

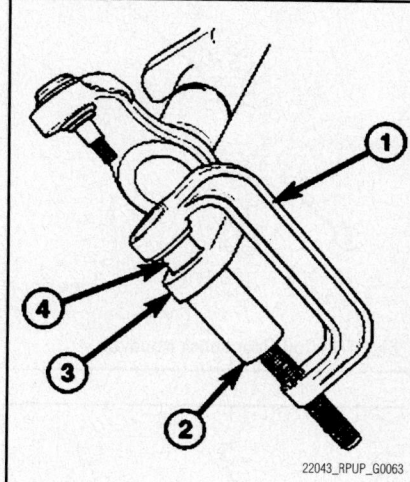

Fig. 167 Link/Coil suspension, lower ball joint removal with tools shown

22043_RPUP_G0063

LOWER CONTROL ARM

REMOVAL & INSTALLATION

Independent Front Suspension—2WD Models

1. Before servicing the vehicle, refer to the Precautions Section.
2. Support the lower control arm with a floor jack.
3. Remove or disconnect the following:
4. Remove or disconnect the following:
   - Front wheel
   - Brake caliper and rotor

- Stabilizer bar link
- Lower ball joint
- Coil spring
- Crossmember nuts
- Lower control arm

To install:

5. Install or connect the following:
   - Lower control arm. Tighten the crossmember nuts to 145 ft. lbs. (196 Nm).
   - Coil spring
   - Lower ball joint. Tighten the nut to 135 ft. lbs. (183 Nm).
   - Stabilizer bar link
   - Brake caliper and rotor
   - Front wheel

Independent Front Suspension—4WD Models

1. Before servicing the vehicle, refer to the Precautions Section.
2. Remove or disconnect the following:
   - Front wheel
   - Upper ball joint from the knuckle
   - Halfshaft
   - Torsion bar
   - Shock absorber lower bolt
   - Stabilizer bar link
   - Lower ball joint from the knuckle
   - Lower control arm

To install:

3. Install or connect the following:
   - Lower control arm. Tighten bolts finger-tight.
   - Torsion bar

➡The ball stud taper must be clean and dry before installation.

   - Lower ball joint. Tighten the nut to 38 ft. lbs. (52 Nm) (on 1500 series, plus 90 degrees).
   - Shock absorber lower bolt. Torque it to 100 ft. lbs. (135 Nm).
   - Halfshaft
   - Upper ball joint. Tighten the nut to 40 ft. lbs. (54 Nm) (on 1500 series, plus 90 degrees).
   - Stabilizer bar link
4. Tighten the pivot bolts to 150 ft. lbs. (204 Nm).
   - Front wheel

Link/Coil Suspension

1. Before servicing the vehicle, refer to the Precautions Section.
2. Paint or scribe matchmarks on the cam adjusters and suspension arm.
3. Remove or disconnect the following:
   - Lower arm nut, cam and cam bolt
   - Nut and bolt from the frame rail
   - Lower arm

To install:

4. Install or connect the following:
   - Lower control arm. Tighten bolts finger-tight. Align the reference marks.
5. Lower the truck to load the suspension
6. Tighten the nuts to 160 ft. lbs. (217 Nm).

Light Duty 4WD Models

See Figure 168.

1. Before servicing the vehicle, refer to the Precautions Section.
2. Raise and support the vehicle.
3. Remove the wheel and tire assembly.
4. Remove the upper ball joint nut. Separate the ball joint from the steering knuckle with remover tool 8677.
5. Remove the front halfshaft.
6. Remove the shock absorber lower nut/bolt.
7. Remove the stabilizer bar link.
8. Remove the lower ball joint nut. Separate ball the joint from the steering knuckle with remover tool 8677.
9. Remove the control arm pivot bolts and suspension arm from frame rail brackets.

To install:

10. Position the lower control arm at the frame rail brackets. Install the pivot bolts and nuts. Tighten the nuts finger-tight.

✳✳ WARNING

The ball joint stud taper must be clean and dry before installing the knuckle. Clean the stud taper with mineral spirits to remove dirt and grease.

11. Insert the lower ball joint stud into the steering knuckle. Install and tighten the retaining nut to 38 ft. lbs. (52 Nm), (on 1500 series only turn an additional 90 degrees).
12. Install shock absorber lower bolt/nut and tighten to 155 ft. lbs. (210 Nm).
13. Install the front halfshaft.
14. Insert the upper ball joint into the steering knuckle. Install and tighten the retaining nut to 40 ft. lbs. (54 Nm), (on 1500 series only an additional 90 degree turn is required).
15. Install the stabilizer bar link.
16. Tighten the lower control arm front pivot nut to 150 ft. lbs. (204 Nm). Tighten rear pivot bolt to 150 ft. lbs. (204 Nm).
17. Install the wheel and tire assembly.
18. Remove the support and lower the vehicle.
19. Perform a wheel alignment.

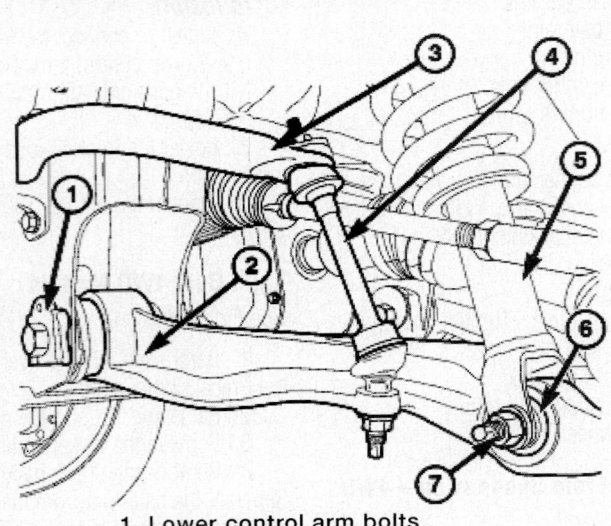

1. Lower control arm bolts
2. Lower control arm
3. Stabilizer bar
4. Stabilizer link
5. Coil/over shock
6. Bushing
7. Coil/over shock mounting nut

22043_RPUP_G0064

Fig. 168 Lower control arm view— LD 4WD

SHOCK ABSORBERS

REMOVAL & INSTALLATION

Coil Spring Suspension—2WD Models

See Figure 169.

1. Before servicing the vehicle, refer to the Precautions Section.
2. Raise and support vehicle.
3. Support the lower control arm outboard end.
4. Remove the upper shock absorber nut by using shock wrench 9362 (1), retainer and grommet (2). If necessary,

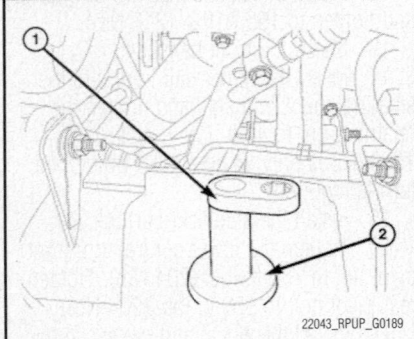

22043_RPUP_G0189

Fig. 169 Upper shock absorber removal using shock wrench 9362

insert ¹¹⁄₃₀ socket though Wrench onto hex located on end of shock shaft to prevent shaft from turning.

5. Remove the lower bolts and remove the shock absorber.

To install:

✳✳ WARNING

Upper shock nut must be replaced or use Mopar® Lock 'N Seal or Loctite® 242 on existing nut.

6. Install the lower retainer and grommet on the shock absorber stud. Insert the shock absorber through the frame bracket hole.
7. Install the lower bolts and tighten the bolts to 25 ft. lbs. (35 Nm).
8. Install the upper grommet, retainer and new nut or use Mopar® Lock 'N Seal or Loctite® 242 on existing nut, on the shock absorber stud. Tighten nut to 40 ft. lbs. (54 Nm) using wrench 9362.
9. Remove the support from the lower control arm outboard end.
10. Lower the vehicle.

Coil Over Suspension—4WD Models

See Figures 170 and 171.

1. Before servicing the vehicle, refer to the Precautions Section.
2. Raise and support the vehicle.

3. Remove the tire and wheel assembly.
4. Support the lower control arm outboard end.
5. Remove the three upper shock nuts.
6. Remove the lower shock bolt and nut.
7. Remove the brake caliper adapter with the caliper
8. Remove the brake rotor.
9. Disconnect the wheel speed sensor wiring from the knuckle and upper control arm.
10. Remove the upper ball joint retaining nut and separate the upper ball joint from the knuckle using separator 9360.
11. Remove the stabilizer link lower nut.
12. Remove the axle hub nut.
13. Remove the shock assembly.

To install:

➡All suspension components should be tighten with the weight of the vehicle on them (curb height).

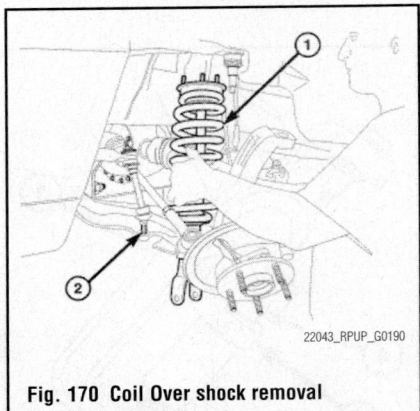

22043_RPUP_G0190

Fig. 170 Coil Over shock removal

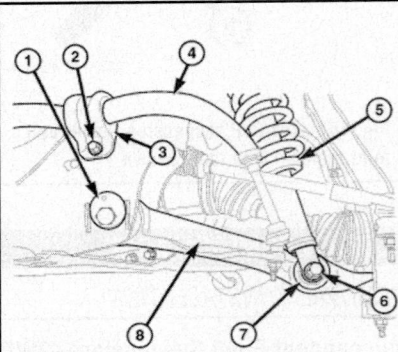

1. Lower control arm eccentric bolt
2. Stabilizer mounting bolt
3. Stabilizer bracket and bushing
4. Stabilizer bar
5. Coil-Over shock
6. Lower shock mounting bolt

22043_RPUP_G0191

Fig. 171 Lower suspension and shock view

14. Install the shock back in place in the vehicle.

15. Install the upper part of the shock into the frame bracket.

16. Install the upper nuts. Tighten to 45 ft. lbs. (61 Nm).

17. Install the lower part of the shock into the lower control arm shock bushing.

18. Install and position bolt so head of bolt is facing rearward of vehicle and hand start nut. Tighten the bolt and nut to 155 ft. lbs. (210 Nm).

19. Install the upper ball joint to the knuckle and install the retaining nut.

20. Install and tighten the axle hub nut.

21. Install the stabilizer link lower nut

22. Reconnect the wheel speed sensor wiring to the knuckle and upper control arm.

23. Install the brake rotor.

24. Install the brake caliper adapter with the caliper.

25. Remove the support from the lower control arm outboard end.

26. Install the tire and wheel assembly.

27. Remove the support and lower the vehicle.

Link/Coil Suspension

See Figures 172 and 173.

1. Before servicing the vehicle, refer to the Precautions Section.

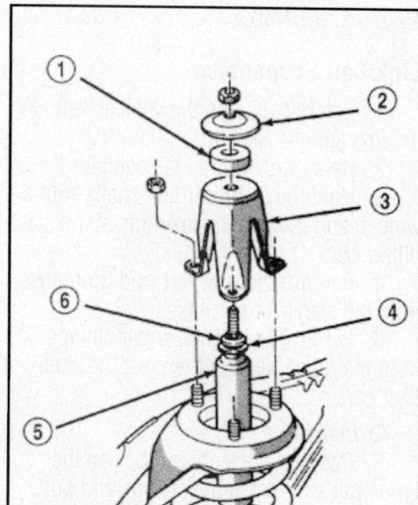

1. **Grommet**
2. **Retainer**
3. **Upper shock bracket**
4. **Retainer**
5. **Shock absorber**
6. **Grommet**

22043_RPUP_G0187

Fig. 172 Upper shock absorber view

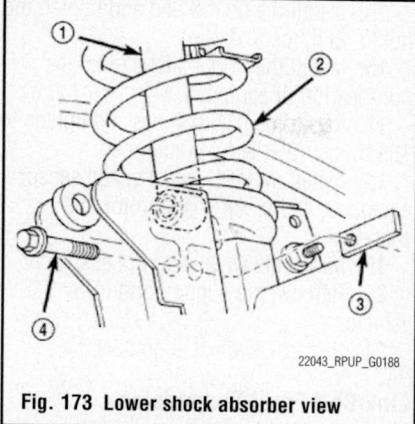

22043_RPUP_G0188

Fig. 173 Lower shock absorber view

2. Remove the nut, retainer and grommet from the upper stud in the engine compartment.

3. Remove three nuts from the upper shock bracket.

4. Remove the lower bolt from the axle bracket. Remove the shock absorber from engine compartment.

To install:

5. Position the lower retainer and grommet on the upper stud. Insert the shock absorber through the spring from engine compartment.

6. Install the lower bolt and tighten to 100 ft. lbs. (135 Nm).

7. Install the upper shock bracket and three nuts. Tighten nuts to 55 ft. lbs. (75 Nm).

8. Install upper grommet and retainer. Install upper shock nut and tighten to 40 ft. lbs. (54 Nm).

STEERING KNUCKLE

REMOVAL & INSTALLATION

Independent Front Suspension

See Figures 174 and 175.

1. Raise and support the vehicle.

2. Remove the wheel.

3. Remove the brake caliper and rotor, shield and ABS wheel speed sensor, if equipped.

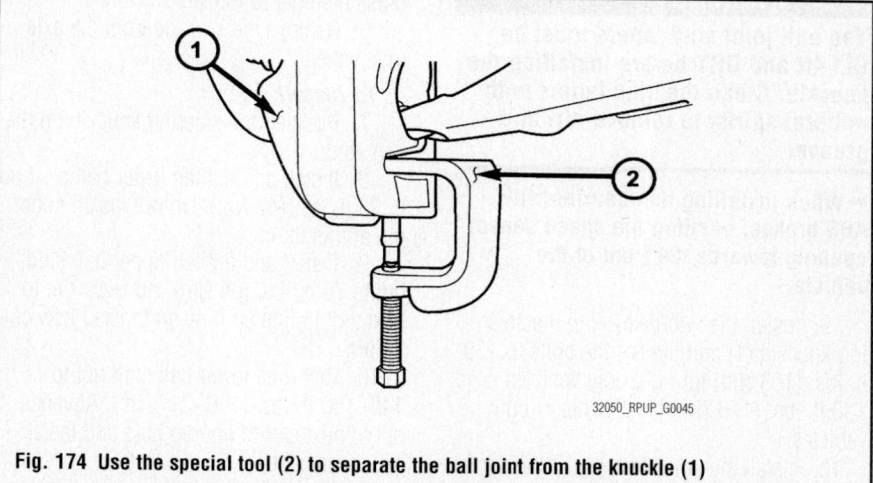

32050_RPUP_G0045

Fig. 174 Use the special tool (2) to separate the ball joint from the knuckle (1)

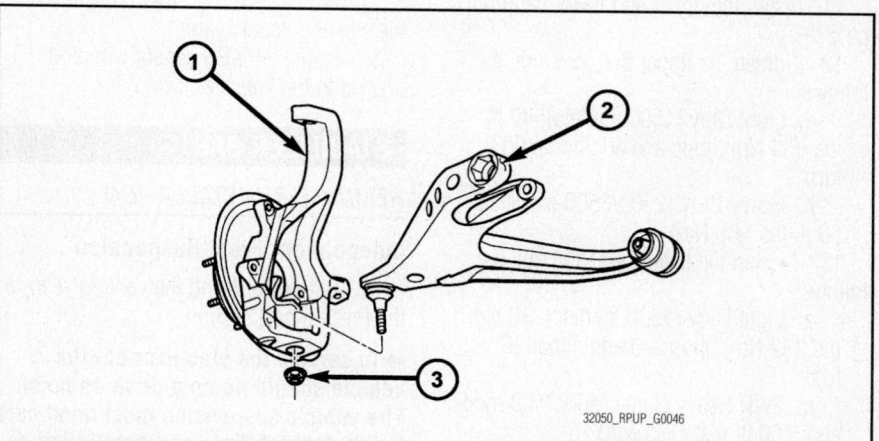

32050_RPUP_G0046

Fig. 175 Exploded view of the steering knuckle (1), lower control arm (2) and lower ball joint nut (3)

4. Remove the front halfshaft nut (if equipped)

5. Remove the cotter pin and nut from the tie rod. Disconnect the tie rod from the steering knuckle with Remover 8677, or equivalent.

✳✳ WARNING

When installing Remover 8677 to separate the ball joint, be careful not to damage the ball joint seal.

6. Remove the lower ball joint nut. Separate the ball joint from the knuckle with Remover 8677 and remove the knuckle.

7. For light duty vehicles, remove the upper ball joint nut. Separate the ball joint from the knuckle with Remover 8677 LD. For heavy duty vehicles, remove the upper ball joint nut. Separate the ball joint from the knuckle with Remover 9360 HD

8. Remove the hub/bearing from the steering knuckle.

To install:

✳✳ WARNING

The ball joint stud tapers must be CLEAN and DRY before installing the knuckle. Clean the stud tapers with mineral spirits to remove dirt and grease.

➡**When installing hub/bearing with ABS brakes, position the speed sensor opening towards the front of the vehicle.**

9. Install the hub/bearing to the steering knuckle (1) and tighten the bolts to 120 ft. lbs. (163 Nm) for light duty vehicles or to 130 ft. lbs. (176 Nm) for 2X4 heavy duty vehicles.

10. Install the knuckle (1) onto the upper and lower ball joints.

11. Install the upper and lower ball joint nuts (3).

12. Tighten the upper ball joint nut, as follows:
   a. Light Duty (1500 models): 40 ft. lbs. (54 Nm), plus and additional 90° turn
   b. Heavy Duty (2500/3500 models): 50 ft. lbs. (68 Nm)

13. Tighten the lower ball joint nut, as follows:
   a. Light Duty (1500 models): 38 ft. lbs. (52 Nm), plus and additional 90° turn
   b. 2WD Heavy Duty (2500/3500 models): 100 ft. lbs. (135 Nm)

14. Remove the hydraulic jack from the lower suspension arm.

15. Install the tie rod end and tighten the nut to 45 ft. lbs. (61 Nm).

16. Install the front halfshaft into the hub/bearing, if equipped.

17. Install the halfshaft nut and tighten to 185 ft. lbs. (251 Nm), if equipped.

18. Install the ABS wheel speed sensor if equipped, and brake shield, rotor and caliper.

19. Install the wheel and tire assembly.

20. Remove the support and lower the vehicle.

21. Perform a wheel alignment.

Link/Coil Front Suspension

1. Remove the hub bearing and axle shaft.

2. Remove the tie rod or drag link end from the steering knuckle arm.

3. Remove the ABS sensor wire and bracket from the knuckle.

4. Remove the cotter pin from the upper ball stud nut. Remove the upper and lower ball stud nuts.

5. Strike the steering knuckle with a brass hammer to loosen.

6. Remove the knuckle from the axle tube yokes.

To install:

7. Position the steering knuckle on the ball studs.

8. Install and tighten lower ball stud nut to 35 ft. lbs. (47 Nm). Do not install cotter pin at this time.

9. Install and tighten upper ball stud nut to 70 ft. lbs. (94 Nm). Advance nut to next slot to line up hole and install new cotter pin.

10. Retorque lower ball stud nut to 140–160 ft. lbs. (190–217 Nm). Advance nut to next slot to line up hole and install new cotter pin.

11. Install the hub bearing.

12. Install tie-rod or drag link end onto the steering knuckle arm.

13. Install the ABS sensor wire and bracket to the knuckle.

STABILIZER BAR

REMOVAL & INSTALLATION

Independent Front Suspension

1. Before servicing the vehicle, refer to the Precautions Section.

➡**To service the stabilizer bar the vehicle should be on a drive on hoist. The vehicle suspension must be at curb height for stabilizer bar installation.**

2. Remove the stabilizer bar link upper

nuts and remove the retainers and grommets.

3. Remove the stabilizer bar mounting bolts and discard the mounting bolts.

4. Remove the retainers from the frame crossmember and remove the bar.

5. If necessary, remove the bushings from the stabilizer bar, Do not cut the old bushings off the stabilizer bar use a mixture of soapy water in order to aid in sliding the bushing off.

To install:

6. If the bushings were removed, Clean the bar and install the bushings on the stabilizer bar using a mixture of soapy water or equivalent in order to slide the bushing over the bar with ease. Do not cut the new bushing for installation.

➡**Install new mounting bolts Do not reuse old bolts.**

7. Position the stabilizer bar on the frame crossmember brackets and install the bracket bolts finger-tight.

8. Check the alignment of the bar to ensure there is no interference with the either frame rail or chassis component. Spacing should be equal on both sides.

9. Install the stabilizer bar to the stabilizer link and install the grommets and retainers.

10. Install the nuts to the stabilizer link and tighten to 20 ft. lbs. (27 Nm).

11. Tighten the brackets to the frame to 45 ft. lbs. (61 Nm).

Link/Coil Suspension

1. Before servicing the vehicle, refer to the Precautions Section.

2. Raise and support the vehicle.

3. Hold the stabilizer link shafts with a wrench and remove the link nuts at the stabilizer bar.

4. Remove the retainers and grommets from the stabilizer bar links.

5. Remove the stabilizer bar clamps from the frame rails and remove the stabilizer bar.

To install:

6. Position the stabilizer bar on the frame rail and install the clamps and bolts. Ensure the bar is centered with equal spacing on both sides.

7. Tighten the clamp bolts to 45 ft. lbs. (61 Nm).

8. Install links, retainers, grommets and nuts to the stabilizer bar. Hold the link shaft with a wrench and tighten the nuts to 27 ft. lbs. (38 Nm).

9. Remove the supports and lower the vehicle

STABILIZER BAR ACTUATOR

REMOVAL & INSTALLATION

The actuator is a motor driven unit that engages and disengages the disconnecting stabilizer bar. This system allows greater front suspension travel in off-road situations. It consists of a disconnecting unit, electronic actuator and stabilizer bar.

✳✳ WARNING

The disconnecting stabilizer bar unit is not serviced separately from the bar. Do not disassemble this unit from the stabilizer bar.

1. Before servicing the vehicle, refer to the Precautions Section.
2. Raise and support the vehicle.

➡️**Before removing the connector from the actuator clean the outside of the connector with a cleaner and compressed air, to remove any dirt or debris.**

3. Disconnect the electronic actuator electrical connector for the disconnecting stabilizer bar.
4. Remove the 3 actuator bolts then remove the actuator.

To install:

5. Install the actuator to the disconnecting unit. Tighten the bolts to 37 ft. lbs. (45 Nm).
6. Reconnect the electronic actuator electrical connector for the disconnecting stabilizer bar.
7. Remove the supports and lower the vehicle.
8. Using a scan tool program the new stabilizer bar to the vehicle.

TRACK BAR

REMOVAL & INSTALLATION

See Figure 176.

1. Before servicing the vehicle, refer to the Precautions Section.
2. Raise and support the axle.
3. Remove the track bar bolts and nuts.
4. Remove the track bar.

To install:

5. Install the track bar.
6. Install the new bolts and nuts.
7. Tighten bolts as follows:
   - M14 fasteners: 150 ft. lbs. (203 Nm).
   - M16 fasteners: 200 ft. lbs. (271 Nm).
8. Remove the supports under the axle and lower the vehicle to the ground.

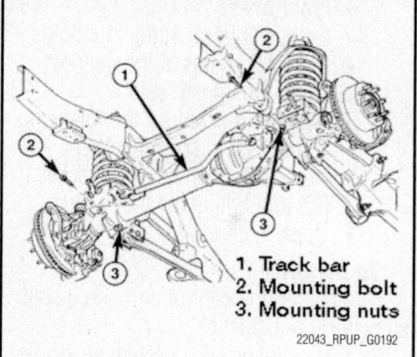

1. Track bar
2. Mounting bolt
3. Mounting nuts

22043_RPUP_G0192

Fig. 176 Track bar removal

UPPER BALL JOINT

REMOVAL & INSTALLATION

Independent Front Suspension

See Figure 177.

1. Before servicing the vehicle, refer to the Precautions Section.
2. Raise vehicle and support the axle.
3. Remove the tire and wheel.
4. Remove the upper ball joint retaining nut.
5. Separate the upper ball joint from the knuckle using separator tool 9360.
6. Remove the wheel speed sensor wire from the knuckle heavy duty models, and from the upper control arm light duty models.
7. Move the knuckle out of the way to allow ball joint removal tool access.
8. Remove the ball joint boot for removal.

➡️**It may be necessary to install a block of wood between the control arm and frame bracket to allow clearance for the ball joint press tool.**

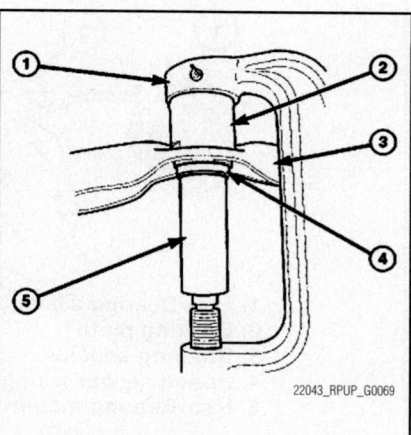

22043_RPUP_G0069

Fig. 177 Upper ball joint removal with special tools

9. Press the ball joint (4) from the upper control arm (3) using special tools C-4212-F (PRESS) (1), 9770-1 (Receiver) (2) and 9770-2 (Driver) (5).
10. Install the upper ball joint with special tools.
11. Install the upper ball joint into the knuckle.
12. Install the upper ball joint retaining nut and tighten to 40 ft. lbs. (54 Nm) (on 1500 series only an additional 90 degree turn is required) or 50 ft. lbs. (68 Nm). Heavy duty models.
13. Install the wheel speed sensor wire to the knuckle heavy duty models, and to the upper control arm light duty models.
14. Install the tire and wheel.
15. Remove the supports and lower the vehicle.
16. Perform a wheel alignment.

Link/Coil Front Suspension

See Figures 178 and 179.

1. Before servicing the vehicle, refer to the Precautions Section.

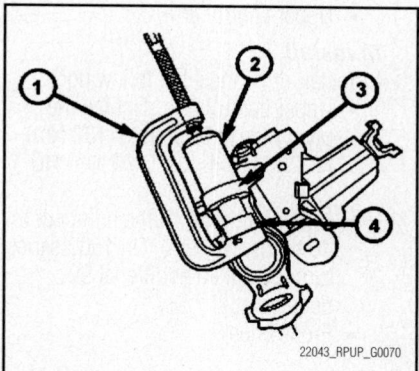

22043_RPUP_G0070

Fig. 178 Upper ball joint removal with special tools

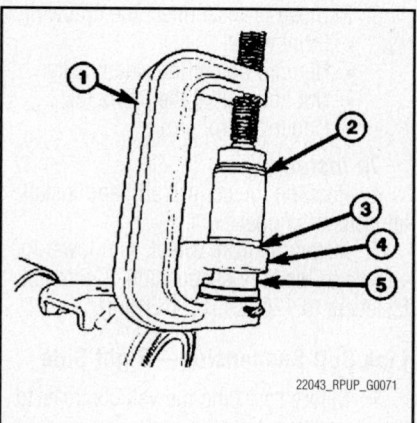

22043_RPUP_G0071

Fig. 179 Upper ball joint Installation with special tools

2. Remove the steering knuckle.

3. Remove the axle shaft from the axle.

4. Position special tool 6761 (RECEIVER) (2) and 8445-3 (DRIVER) (4) with C-4212-F (PRESS)(1) as shown to remove upper ball stud.

To install:

5. Position special tool 8445-2 (DRIVER) (2) and 8975-5 (RECEIVER) (5) with C-42121-F (PRESS)(1) as shown to install upper ball stud (3).

6. Install the axle shaft into the axle.

7. Install the steering knuckle.

UPPER CONTROL ARM

REMOVAL & INSTALLATION

Independent Front Suspension

1. Before servicing the vehicle, refer to the Precautions Section.

2. Support the lower control arm.

3. Remove or disconnect the following:
   - Front wheel
   - Upper ball joint
   - Pivot mounting nuts
   - Upper control arm

To install:

4. Install or connect the following:
   - Upper control arm. Tighten the pivot nuts to 97 ft. lbs. (132 Nm) for LD; 125 ft. lbs. (170 Nm) HD 2X4
   - Upper ball joint. Tighten the nut to 40 ft. lbs. (54 Nm). On 1500 series, turn the nut an additional 90 degrees.
   - Front wheel

Link/Coil Suspension—Left Side

1. Before servicing the vehicle, refer to the Precautions Section.

2. Support the lower control arm.

3. Remove or disconnect the following:
   - Front wheel
   - Nut and bolt at the axle bracket
   - Nut and bolt at the frame rail
   - Upper control arm

To install:

4. Position the control arm and install all fasteners finger-tight.

5. Install the front wheel. And lower the vehicle to load the suspension. Tighten all fasteners to 120 ft. lbs. (163 Nm).

Link/Coil Suspension—Right Side

1. Before servicing the vehicle, refer to the Precautions Section.

2. Support the lower control arm.

3. Remove or disconnect the following:

- Front wheel
- Exhaust system at the manifolds
- Exhaust mounts at the muffler

4. Support the transmission

5. Remove or disconnect the following:
   - Transmission crossmember
   - Nut and bolt at the axle bracket
   - Nut and bolt at the frame rail
   - Upper control arm

To install:

6. Position the control arm and install all fasteners finger-tight.

7. Install the exhaust system and crossmember.

8. Install the front wheel. And lower the vehicle to load the suspension. Tighten all fasteners to 120 ft. lbs. (163 Nm).

WHEEL HUB & BEARING

REMOVAL & INSTALLATION

Independent Front Suspension— 2WD Models

See Figure 180.

1. Before servicing the vehicle, refer to the Precautions Section.

2. Remove or disconnect the following:
   - Front wheel
   - Brake caliper and rotor
   - Wheel speed sensor
   - Hub/bearing mounting bolts
   - Hub/bearing assembly

To install:

3. Install or connect the following:
   - Hub and bearing assembly. Tighten the bolts to 120 ft. lbs. (163 Nm).
   - Wheel speed sensor
   - Brake caliper and rotor
   - Front wheel

Independent Front Suspension— 4WD Models

See Figure 181.

1. Before servicing the vehicle, refer to the Precautions Section.

2. Remove or disconnect the following:
   - Front wheel
   - Brake caliper and rotor
   - Wheel speed sensor
   - Halfshaft nut
   - Tie rod end from the knuckle
   - Upper ball joint from the knuckle
   - Knuckle from the halfshaft
   - Hub/bearing mounting bolts
   - Hub/bearing assembly

To install:

3. Install or connect the following:
   - Hub and bearing assembly. Tighten the bolts to 120 ft. lbs. (163 Nm).
   - Knuckle onto the halfshaft
   - Upper ball joint on the knuckle. Torque the nut to 40 ft. lbs. (54 Nm) (on 1500 series, plus 90 degrees).

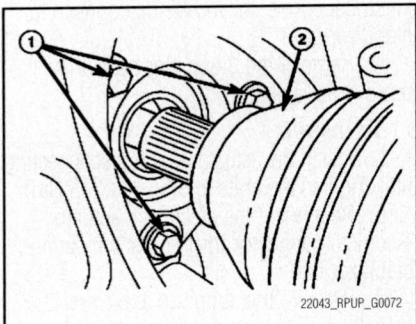

22043_RPUP_G0072

Fig. 181 Hub/bearing (1), mounting bolts (2)

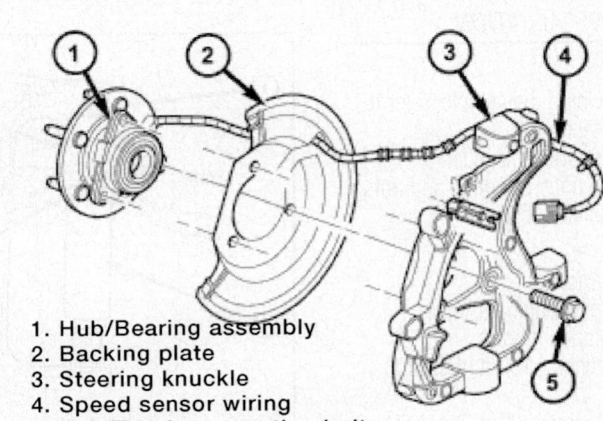

1. Hub/Bearing assembly
2. Backing plate
3. Steering knuckle
4. Speed sensor wiring
5. Hub/Bearing mounting bolt

22043_RPUP_G0073

Fig. 180 Hub/bearing and related parts

- Tie rod end to the knuckle. Tighten the nut to 45 ft. lbs. (61 Nm) plus 90 degrees.
- Halfshaft nut. Torque to 185 ft. lbs. (251 Nm).
- Wheel speed sensor
- Brake caliper and rotor
- Front wheel

Link/Coil Suspension

See Figure 182.

1. Before servicing the vehicle, refer to the Precautions Section.
2. Remove or disconnect the following:
   - Front wheel
   - Hub extension from the rotor, if equipped
   - Brake caliper and rotor
   - Hub nut
   - Wheel speed sensor wiring
   - Hub/bearing mounting bolts ¼ each. Then, tap the bolts with a mallet to loosen the hub/bearing assembly.
   - Hub/bearing assembly, wheel studs/extension studs, rotor, shield and spacer
   - Wheel speed sensor

To install:

3. Install or connect the following:
   - Wheel speed sensor
   - Rotor on the hub/bearing
   - Studs
4. Apply a liberal amount of anti-seize compound on the splines of the front shaft.

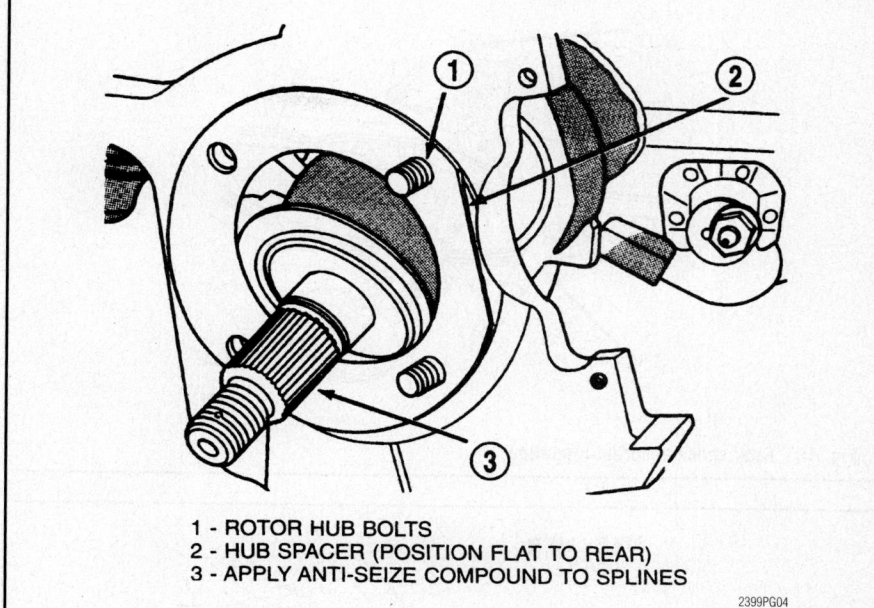

1 - ROTOR HUB BOLTS
2 - HUB SPACER (POSITION FLAT TO REAR)
3 - APPLY ANTI-SEIZE COMPOUND TO SPLINES

2399PG04

Fig. 182 Hub bolt positioning

5. Insert the 2 rearmost, top and bottom rotor hub bolts in the knuckle, so they extend from the front face as shown.
6. Install or connect the following:
   - Spacer and shield
   - Hub assembly onto the shaft
7. Align the bolt holes in the flange with the installed bolts. Thread the bolts onto the flange far enough to hold the unit in place.

8. Install the remaining bolts. Tighten all hub/bearing bolts to 149 ft. lbs. (202 Nm).
9. Install the washer and shaft nut. Tighten the nut to 132 ft. lbs. (179 Nm). Rotate the axle 5 to 10 times to seat the bearings. Tighten the nut to 263 ft. lbs. (356 Nm). Install a new cotter pin, advancing the nut for alignment.
10. The remainder of installation is the reverse of removal.

SUSPENSION

LEAF SPRING

REMOVAL & INSTALLATION

1. Before servicing the vehicle, refer to the Precautions Section.
2. Raise and support the vehicle.
3. Support the axle with a suitable holding fixture.
4. Remove the nuts, spring clamp bolts and the plate that attach the spring to the axle.
5. Remove the nuts and bolts from the spring front and rear shackle.
6. Remove the spring from the vehicle.

To install:

7. Position spring on axle shaft tube so spring center bolt is inserted into the locating hole in the axle tube.
8. Align the front of the spring with the bolt hole in the front bracket. Install the eye pivot bolt and nut.
9. Align the rear of the spring into the shackle and install the bolt and nut.

10. Tighten the spring front and rear eye pivot bolt snug, Do not torque.
11. Install the spring clamp bolts, plate and the retaining nuts.
12. Remove the holding fixture for the rear axle.
13. Remove the supports and lower the vehicle so that the weight is being supported by the tires.
14. Tighten the spring clamp retaining nuts to 110 ft. lbs. (149 Nm).
15. Tighten the spring front and rear pivot bolt nuts to 120 ft. lbs. (163 Nm) for light duty or 170 ft. lbs. (230 Nm) for heavy duty models.

SHOCK ABSORBER

REMOVAL & INSTALLATION

See Figure 183.

1. Before servicing the vehicle, refer to the Precautions Section.

REAR SUSPENSION

2. Support the axle.
3. Remove or disconnect the following:
   - Upper bolt
   - Lower bolt
   - Shock absorber

To install:

4. Install the bolts through the brackets and shock and tighten them as follows:
   - Tighten the upper and lower bolt 100 ft. lbs. (135 Nm)

STABILIZER BAR

REMOVAL & INSTALLATION

See Figure 184.

1. Raise and support the vehicle.
2. Remove the hardware bolting the links to the stabilizer bar. Separate the links with Puller C-3894-A, or equivalent.
3. Remove the hardware bolting the stabilizer bar retainers to the axle.

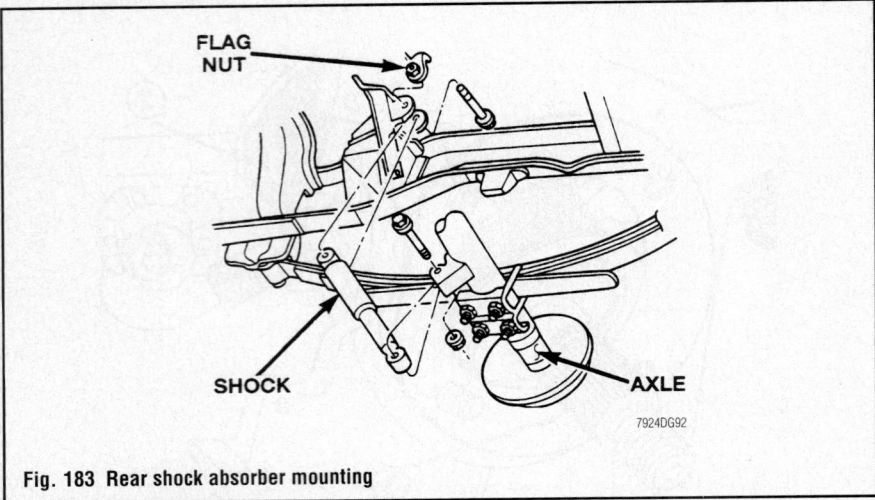

Fig. 183 Rear shock absorber mounting

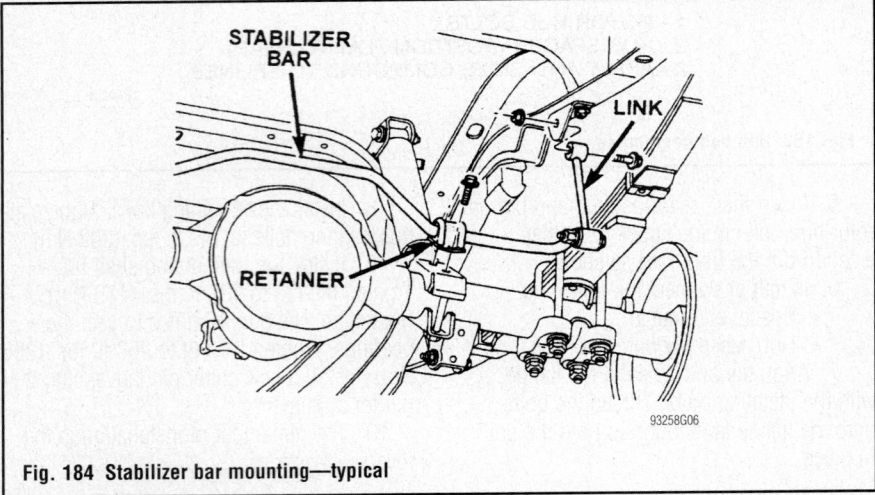

Fig. 184 Stabilizer bar mounting—typical

STABILIZER LINKS

REMOVAL & INSTALLATION

See Figure 185.

1. Before servicing the vehicle, refer to the Precautions Section.
2. Raise and support the vehicle.
3. Remove the upper nut at the frame bracket.
4. Remove the lower link nut at the stabilizer bar.
5. Remove the link from the bar.

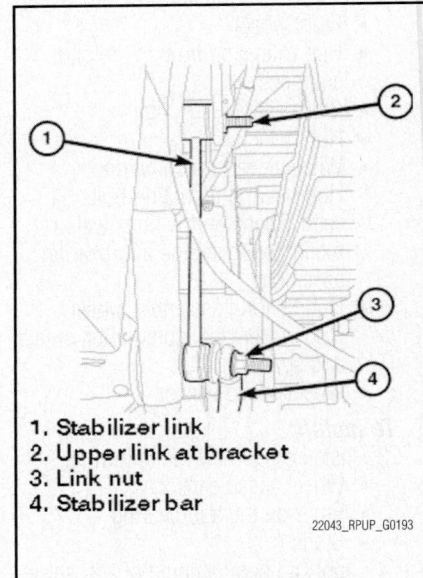

1. Stabilizer link
2. Upper link at bracket
3. Link nut
4. Stabilizer bar

Fig. 185 Stabilizer link and related parts

4. Remove the stabilizer bar.
5. Unbolt and remove the links from the frame, if desired.
6. Replace worn, cracked or distorted bushings.
7. Remove links upper mounting nuts and bolts and remove links.

To install:

8. Install link into frame brackets and install mounting nuts and bolts.

9. Install the stabilizer bar and center it with equal spacing on both sides. Tighten retainer hardware to 100 ft. lbs. (135 Nm).
10. Install the links and tighten the hardware on frame and at the bar hand tight.
11. Lower the vehicle onto the suspension.
12. Tighten the links as follows:
    • Link upper: 100 ft. lbs. (135 Nm)
    • Link lower: 100 ft. lbs. (135 Nm)

To install:

6. Install the link to the bar.
7. Install the lower link nut at the stabilizer bar. Tighten the nuts to 27 ft. lbs. (38 Nm).
8. Install the upper link nut at the frame bracket. Tighten the bolts to 45 ft. lbs. (61 Nm).
9. Lower the vehicle.

DODGE

Sprinter

17

SPECIFICATIONS AND MAINTENANCE CHARTS

ENGINE AND VEHICLE IDENTIFICATION

			Engine				Model Year	
Code ①	Liters	Cu. In.	Cyl.	Fuel Sys.	Engine Type	Eng. Mfg.	Code ②	Year
5	3.0	182	6	CDI	DOHC	DaimlerChrysler	8	2008
6	3.5	NA	6	MFI	DOHC	DaimlerChrysler	9	2009

CDI: Common Rail Direct Injection

MFI: Multi-Port Fuel Injection

DOHC: Dual Overhead Camshaft

① 8th position of VIN

② 10th position of VIN

36543_SPRI_C0001

GENERAL ENGINE SPECIFICATIONS

Year	Model	Engine Displ. Liters	Engine VIN	Net Horsepower @ rpm	Net Torque @ rpm (ft. lbs.)	Bore x Stroke (in.)	Comp. Ratio	Oil Pressure @ rpm
2008	Sprinter	3.0	5	154@3400	280@1200	3.26x3.62	18:1	52@3000
		3.5	6	254@5900	250@2500	NA	NA	NA
2009	Sprinter	3.0	5	154@3400	280@1200	3.26x3.62	18:1	52@3000

NA: Not Available

36543_SPRI_C0002

GASOLINE ENGINE TUNE-UP SPECIFICATIONS

Year	Engine Displacement Liters	Engine VIN	Spark Plug Gap (in.)	Ignition Timing (deg.)	Fuel Pump (psi)	Idle Speed (rpm)	Valve Clearance Intake	Valve Clearance Exhaust
2008	3.5	6	0.031	①	NA	①	HYD	HYD

Note: The information on the Vehicle Emission Control label must be used, if different from the figures in this chart.

HYD: Hydraulic

① Ignition timing and idle speed are controlled by the PCM. No adjustment is necessary.

36543_SPRI_C0003

DIESEL ENGINE TUNE-UP SPECIFICATIONS

Year	Engine Displacement Liters	Engine VIN	Valve Clearance Intake (in.)	Exhaust (in.)	Injection Pump Setting (deg.)	Injection Nozzle Pressure (psi) New	Used	Idle Speed (rpm)	Cranking Compression Pressure (psi)
2008	3.0	5	HYD	HYD	①	②	②	620	392-464
2009	3.0	5	HYD	HYD	①	②	②	620	392-464

NOTE: The Vehicle Emission Control Information label often reflects specification changes made during production.

The label figures must be used if they differ from those in this chart

HYD: Hydraulic

① Driven by camshaft, requires no timing

② 2,900-23,205 psi

36543_SPRI_C0004

CAPACITIES

Year	Model	Engine Displacement Liters	Engine VIN	Engine Oil with Filter	Transmission (pts.) Man.	Auto.**	Transfer Case (pts.)	Drive Axle Front (pts.)	Rear (pts.)	Fuel Tank① (gal.)	Cooling System (qts.)
2008	Sprinter	3.0	5	13.2	—	16.3	—	NA	4.4	25.0	11.0
		3.5	6	10.0	—	16.3	—	NA	4.4	25.0	8.0
2009	Sprinter	3.0	5	13.2	—	16.3	—	NA	4.4	25.0	11.0

① Reserve Tank: 2.8 gal.

**Overhaul

36543_SPRI_C0005

FLUID SPECIFICATIONS

Year	Model	Engine Displacement Liters	Engine ID/VIN	Engine Oil	Auto. Trans.	Rear Axle	Power Steering Fluid	Brake Master Cylinder
2008	Sprinter	3.0	5	①	②	③	④	DOT 4
		3.5	6	①	②	③	④	DOT 4
2009	Sprinter	3.0	5	①	②	③	④	DOT 4

DOT: Department Of Transpotation

① Only use engine oils that are labeled as meeting API designations of quality. The following oils meet Chrysler requirements:

Castrol Syntec 5W-40

Castrol Syntec European Formula 0W-30

Chevron Supreme Synthetic Motor Oil 5W-40

Havoline Ultra S 5W-30

Havoline Ultra S 5W-40

High Star 5W-30

Mobil 1 0W-30

Mobil 15W-30

Mobil 1 ESP Formula MB 5W-40

Mopar Part No. 68001334AA 5W-30

Pennzoil European Formula Ultra 5W-30

Pennzoil Platinum European Formula 5W-40

Q Diesel Plus 5W-30

Q European Engine 5W-40

Q European Engine Ultra 5W-30

Shell Helix Ultra AX 5W-30

Shell Rimula Signia 10W-40

Texaco Havoline Synthetic Motor Oil 5W-40

Valvoline SynPower MST 5W-30

② Shell ATF 3403/M-115 or equivalent

③ Shell Spirax MB90 or Mopar® P/N 05130603AA

④ Mopar® Power Steering Fluid + 4 or Mopar® ATF+4 Automatic Transmission Fluid

36543_SPRI_C0006

VALVE SPECIFICATIONS

Year	Engine Displ. Liters	Engine VIN	Seat Angle (deg.)	Face Angle (deg.)	Spring Test Pressure (lbs. @ in.)	Spring Installed Height (in.)	Stem-to-Guide Clearance (in.) Intake	Stem-to-Guide Clearance (in.) Exhaust	Stem Diameter (in.) Intake	Stem Diameter (in.) Exhaust
2008	3.0	5	44.5-45.5	44.5-45.5	NA	NA	NA	NA	0.234-0.2350	0.234-0.2350
	3.5	6	NA	NA	NA	NA	NA	NA	NA	NA
2009	3.0	5	44.5-45.5	44.5-45.5	NA	NA	NA	NA	0.234-0.2350	0.234-0.2350

NA: Information not available

36543_SPRI_C0007

CAMSHAFT AND BEARING SPECIFICATIONS CHART

All measurements are given in inches.

Year	Engine Displacement Liters	Engine VIN	Journal Diameter	Brg. Oil Clearance	Shaft End-play	Runout	Journal Bore	Lobe Lift	
								Intake	Exhaust
2008	3.0	5	NA	NA	NA	NA	NA	NA	NA
	3.5	6	NA	NA	NA	NA	NA	NA	NA
2009	3.0	5	NA	NA	NA	NA	NA	NA	NA

NA: Information not available

36543_SPRI_C0008

CRANKSHAFT AND CONNECTING ROD SPECIFICATIONS

All measurements are given in inches.

Year	Engine Displ. Liters	Engine VIN	Crankshaft				Connecting Rod		
			Main Brg. Journal Dia.	Main Brg. Oil Clearance	Shaft End-play	Thrust on No.	Journal Diameter	Oil Clearance	Side Clearance
2008	3.0	5	2.9800-2.9900	0.0012-0.0023	0.0040-0.0100	3	NA	NA	NA
	3.5	6	NA	NA	NA	NA	NA	NA	NA
2009	3.0	5	2.9800-2.9900	0.0012-0.0023	0.0040-0.0100	3	NA	NA	NA

NA: Information not available

36543_SPRI_C0009

PISTON AND RING SPECIFICATIONS

All measurements are given in inches.

Year	Engine Displ. Liters	Engine VIN	Piston Clearance	Ring Gap			Ring Side Clearance		
				Top Compression	Bottom Compression	Oil Control	Top Compression	Bottom Compression	Oil Control
2008	3.0	5	NA	0.0048-0.0063	0.0026-0.0044	0.0012-0.0028	NA	NA	NA
	3.5	6	NA	NA	NA	NA	NA	NA	NA
2009	3.0	5	NA	0.0048-0.0063	0.0026-0.0044	0.0012-0.0028	NA	NA	NA

NA: Information not available

36543_SPRI_C0010

TORQUE SPECIFICATIONS

All readings in ft. lbs.

Year	Engine Displ. Liters	Engine VIN	Cylinder Head Bolts	Main Bearing Bolts	Rod Bearing Bolts	Crankshaft Damper Bolts	Flywheel Bolts	Manifold Intake	Manifold Exhaust	Spark Plugs	Oil Pan Drain Plug
2008	3.0	5	①	33	②	③	33	12	18	NA	35
	3.5	6	④	NS	⑤	148	⑥	NS	8	17	22
2009	3.0	5	①	33	②	③	33	12	18	NA	35

NA: Not Applicable

NS: Not Specified

① Refer to procedure for illustration

　Step 1: Tighten bolts 1-8 to 10 ft. lbs. (10 Nm)

　Step 2: Tighten bolts 1-8 to 44 ft. lbs. (60 Nm)

　Step 3: Tighten bolts 9-10 to 15 ft. lbs. (20 Nm)

　Step 4: Tighten bolts 1-8 an addt'l 90 degrees

　Step 5: Verify bolts 9-10 at 15 ft. lbs. (20 Nm)

　Step 6: Tighten bolts 1-8 an addt'l 90 degrees

② Connecting rods must be replaced if removed.

　Step 1: 11 ft. lbs. (15 Nm)

　Step 2: 22 ft. lbs. (30 Nm)

　Step 3: Plus 90 degrees

③ 154 ft. lbs. + 180 degrees

④ Cyl. Head to Timing Cover bolts: 18 ft. lbs. (25Nm) plus 90 degrees.

　Cylinder head to block bolts:

　Step 1: Tighten bolts to 15 ft. lbs. (20 Nm)

　Step 2: Tighten bolts to 30 ft. lbs. (40 Nm)

　Step 3: Verify bolts at 30 ft. lbs. (40 Nm)

　Step 4: Tighten bolts 90 degrees

　Step 5: Tighten bolts an addt'l 90 degrees

⑤ 20 ft. lbs. + 90 degrees

⑥ Step 1: Tighten bolts to 15 ft. lbs. (20 Nm)

　Step 2: Tighten bolts to 33 ft. lbs. (45 Nm)

　Step 3: Tighten bolts an addt'l 90 degrees

36543_SPRI_C0011

WHEEL ALIGNMENT

Year	Model		Caster Range (+/-Deg.)	Caster Preferred Setting (Deg.)	Camber Range (+/-Deg.)	Camber Preferred Setting (Deg.)	Toe-in (deg.)
2008	Sprinter	F	③	③	0.3	1.0	0.20+/-0.10
	①	R	—	—	—	0.00	0.00+/-0.25
	Sprinter	F	③	③	0.3	1.3	0.25+/-0.10
	②	R	—	—	—	0.00	0.00+/-0.25
2009	Sprinter	F	③	③	0.3	1.0	0.20+/-0.10
	①	R	—	—	—	0.00	0.00+/-0.25
	Sprinter	F	③	③	0.3	1.3	0.25+/-0.10
	②	R	—	—	—	0.00	0.00+/-0.25

NA: Not Available

F - Front

R - Rear

① 2500 & 3500 Series without reinforced axle

② 3500 Series with reinforced axle

③ Refer to curb height chart for caster. Caster is not adjustable on these vehicles.

36543_SPRI_C0012

TIRE, WHEEL AND BALL JOINT SPECIFICATIONS

| Year | Model | OEM Tires | | Tire Pressures (psi) | | Wheel Size | Ball Joint Inspection | Lug Nut Torque (ft. lbs.) |
		Standard	Optional	Front	Rear			
2008	Sprinter	LT215/85R16E	none	①	①	16x5.5	NA	②
2009	Sprinter	LT215/85R16E	none	①	①	16x5.5	NA	②

OEM: Original Equipment Manufacturer

NA: Not Available

① See placard on vehicle

② Lug nuts and aluminum wheel lug bolts: 133 ft. lbs.

   Steel wheel lug bolts: 177 ft. lbs.

36543_SPRI_C0013

BRAKE SPECIFICATIONS
All measurements in inches unless noted

| Year | Model | | Brake Disc ① | | | Minimum Lining Thickness | | Brake Caliper | |
			Original Thickness	Minimum Thickness	Maximum Run-out	Front	Rear	Bracket Bolts (ft. lbs.)	Mounting Bolts (ft. lbs.)
2008	Sprinter	F	1.102	0.984	0.0011	NA	—	②	③
		R	④	⑤	0.0011	—	NA	②	③
2009	Sprinter	F	1.102	0.984	0.0011	NA	—	②	③
		R	④	⑤	0.0011	—	NA	②	③

F - Front

R - Rear

① Brake Disc Rotors cannot be resurfaced.

   They must be replaced.

② 59 ft. lbs. plus 40 degrees

③ M8 bolt: 25 ft. lbs. (34 Nm)

   M10 bolt: 48 ft. lbs. (65 Nm)

④ SRW: 0.620

   DRW: 1.102

⑤ SRW: 0.550

   DRW: 0.984

36543_SPRI_C0014

SCHEDULED MAINTENANCE INTERVALS
Sprinter

Maintenance – With ASSYST MAINTENANCE COMPUTER

ASSYST provides you with information on the best possible timing for maintenance work.
When the next maintenance service is due, this will be indicated in the multifunction display with a symbol.
You should have the maintenance performed within the stated period/distance.
The service indicator should be reset after an oil service and/or maintenance service has been performed.
To reset the ASSYST MAINTENANCE COMPUTER, perform the procedure below.

TO BE SERVICED	TYPE OF SERVICE	VEHICLE MILEAGE INTERVAL (x1000)												
		10	20	30	40	50	60	70	80	90	100	110	120	130
Engine oil & filter	R	✓	✓	✓	✓	✓	✓	✓	✓	✓	✓	✓	✓	✓
Tires	Rotate	✓	✓	✓	✓	✓	✓	✓	✓	✓	✓	✓	✓	✓
Power steering fluid	S/I	✓	✓	✓	✓	✓	✓	✓	✓	✓	✓	✓	✓	✓
Windshield washer system	S/I	✓	✓	✓	✓	✓	✓	✓	✓	✓	✓	✓	✓	✓
Brake hoses & linings	S/I			✓			✓			✓			✓	
Engine air filter	I	✓	✓	✓	✓	✓	✓	✓	✓	✓	✓	✓	✓	✓
Engine air filter	R		✓		✓		✓		✓		✓		✓	
Cabin Air Filter	R			✓			✓			✓			✓	
Battery	S/I			✓			✓			✓			✓	
Fuel Filter	R	✓	✓	✓	✓	✓	✓	✓	✓	✓	✓	✓	✓	✓
Parking Brake adjustment	S/I	✓	✓	✓	✓	✓	✓	✓	✓	✓	✓	✓	✓	✓
Chassis & Body bolts	S/I			✓										
Spark Plugs (3.5L)	R						✓						✓	
Accessory drive belt	I/R						✓						✓	
Diesel Particle Filter (3.0L)	R									✓				
Tire pressures	S/I	✓	✓	✓	✓	✓	✓	✓	✓	✓	✓	✓	✓	✓
Automatic trans. fluid and filter	R						✓						✓	
Engine coolant	R	Every 180,000 miles												

R: Replace   S/I: Service or Inspect   C/L: Clean and lubricate   I/R: Inspect and rerplace if necessary

In addition to the above maintenance work, the following should be performed:

Change the brake fluid every 2 years

Engine coolant every 10 years (if 180,000 miles has not already been achieved)

3.5L Engines: Accessory drive belt should be replaced at 60,000 miles

Change the rear axle fluid every 180,000 miles or 10 years

To reset the ASSYST MAINTENANCE COMPUTER, perform the following procedure:

Without Steering Wheel Buttons

1. Turn key to the ON/RUN position.
2. Within one second press the M button repeatedly until the service symbol and the current remaining distance,
the remaining time or service exceeded is displayed.
3. Within 10 seconds turn the key to OFF/LOCK while still holding the M button.
4. Turn the key to ON/RUN again. The present status for days or distance is displayed once more.
Continue to hold the M button.
After approximately 10 seconds, a signal sounds and the display shows 16 000 km (10,000 miles) for approximately 10 seconds.
Release the M button.

With Steering Wheel Buttons

1. Turn key to the ON/RUN position.
Within one second press the service selection button repeatedly until the instrument cluster
display shows the "Total and trip odometer" basic display.
3. Press the scroll forward/back button until the service symbol and the current remaining distance,
the remaining time or service exceeded is displayed.
4. Press reset button on the instrument cluster until display on the instrument cluster shows the message "Reset service interval?"
5. Confirm the message "Reset service interval?" with the reset button on the instrument cluster.
If the reset button on the instrument cluster is pressed again, the message "Service interval was reset" is shown.
If the ASSYST counter was inadvertently reset, have an authorized dealer correct it.

PRECAUTIONS

Before servicing any vehicle, please be sure to read all of the following precautions, which deal with personal safety, prevention of component damage, and important points to take into consideration when servicing a motor vehicle:

• Never open, service or drain the radiator or cooling system when the engine is hot; serious burns can occur from the steam and hot coolant.

• Observe all applicable safety precautions when working around fuel. Whenever servicing the fuel system, always work in a well-ventilated area. Do not allow fuel spray or vapors to come in contact with a spark, open flame, or excessive heat (a hot drop light, for example). Keep a dry chemical fire extinguisher near the work area. Always keep fuel in a container specifically designed for fuel storage; also, always properly seal fuel containers to avoid the possibility of fire or explosion. Refer to the additional fuel system precautions later in this section.

• Fuel injection systems often remain pressurized, even after the engine has been turned **OFF**. The fuel system pressure must be relieved before disconnecting any fuel lines. Failure to do so may result in fire and/or personal injury.

• Brake fluid often contains polyglycol ethers and polyglycols. Avoid contact with the eyes and wash your hands thoroughly after handling brake fluid. If you do get brake fluid in your eyes, flush your eyes with clean, running water for 15 minutes. If eye irritation persists, or if you have taken

brake fluid internally, IMMEDIATELY seek medical assistance.

• The EPA warns that prolonged contact with used engine oil may cause a number of skin disorders, including cancer. You should make every effort to minimize your exposure to used engine oil. Protective gloves should be worn when changing oil. Wash your hands and any other exposed skin areas as soon as possible after exposure to used engine oil. Soap and water, or waterless hand cleaner should be used.

• All new vehicles are now equipped with an air bag system, often referred to as a Supplemental Restraint System (SRS) or Supplemental Inflatable Restraint (SIR) system. The system must be disabled before performing service on or around system components, steering column, instrument panel components, wiring and sensors. Failure to follow safety and disabling procedures could result in accidental air bag deployment, possible personal injury and unnecessary system repairs.

• Always wear safety goggles when working with, or around, the air bag system. When carrying a non-deployed air bag, be sure the bag and trim cover are pointed away from your body. When placing a non-deployed air bag on a work surface, always face the bag and trim cover upward, away from the surface. This will reduce the motion of the module if it is accidentally deployed. Refer to the additional air bag system precautions later in this section.

• Clean, high quality brake fluid from a sealed container is essential to the safe and

proper operation of the brake system. You should always buy the correct type of brake fluid for your vehicle. If the brake fluid becomes contaminated, completely flush the system with new fluid. Never reuse any brake fluid. Any brake fluid that is removed from the system should be discarded. Also, do not allow any brake fluid to come in contact with a painted surface; it will damage the paint.

• Never operate the engine without the proper amount and type of engine oil; doing so WILL result in severe engine damage.

• Timing belt maintenance is extremely important. Many models utilize an interference-type, non-freewheeling engine. If the timing belt breaks, the valves in the cylinder head may strike the pistons, causing potentially serious (also time-consuming and expensive) engine damage. Refer to the maintenance interval charts for the recommended replacement interval for the timing belt, and to the timing belt section for belt replacement and inspection.

• Disconnecting the negative battery cable on some vehicles may interfere with the functions of the on-board computer system(s) and may require the computer to undergo a relearning process once the negative battery cable is reconnected.

• When servicing drum brakes, only disassemble and assemble one side at a time, leaving the remaining side intact for reference.

• Only an MVAC-trained, EPA-certified automotive technician should service the air conditioning system or its components.

BRAKES

ANTI-LOCK BRAKE SYSTEM (ABS)

GENERAL INFORMATION

PRECAUTIONS

• Certain components within the ABS system are not intended to be serviced or repaired individually.

• Do not use rubber hoses or other parts not specifically specified for and ABS system. When using repair kits, replace all parts included in the kit. Partial or incorrect repair may lead to functional problems and require the replacement of components.

• Lubricate rubber parts with clean, fresh brake fluid to ease assembly. Do not use shop air to clean parts; damage to rubber components may result.

• Use only DOT 3 brake fluid from an unopened container.

• If any hydraulic component or line is removed or replaced, it may be necessary to bleed the entire system.

• A clean repair area is essential. Always clean the reservoir and cap thoroughly before removing the cap. The slightest amount of dirt in the fluid may plug an orifice and impair the system function. Perform repairs after components have been thoroughly cleaned; use only denatured alcohol to clean components. Do not allow ABS components to come into contact with any substance containing mineral oil; this includes used shop rags.

• The Anti-Lock control unit is a microprocessor similar to other computer units in the vehicle. Ensure that the ignition switch is **OFF** before removing or installing con-

troller harnesses. Avoid static electricity discharge at or near the controller.

• If any arc welding is to be done on the vehicle, the control unit should be unplugged before welding operations begin.

WHEEL SPEED SENSORS

REMOVAL & INSTALLATION

Front

See Figure 1.

1. Raise and safely support the vehicle.
2. Remove the speed sensor mounting nuts.
3. Remove the speed sensor from the knuckle.

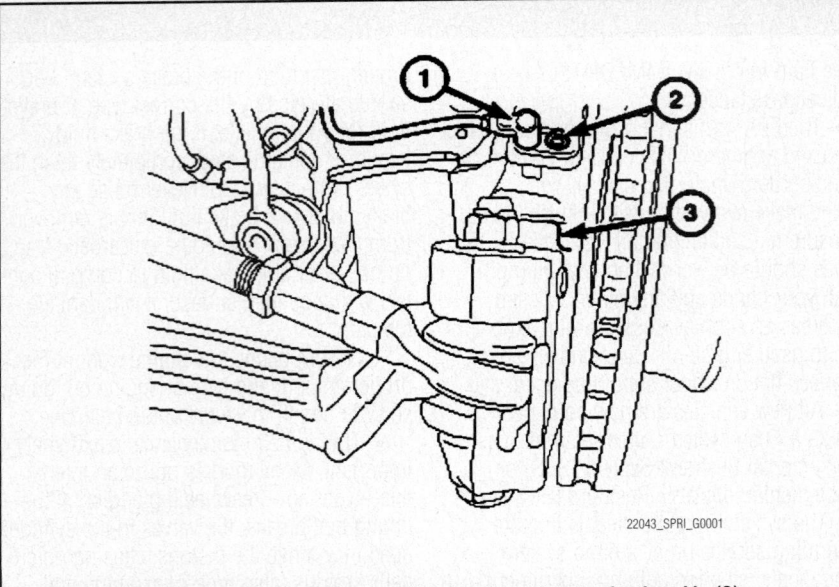

Fig. 1 Remove the nut (2) and pull the speed sensor from the steering knuckle (3)

To install:

4. Install the speed sensor to the steering knuckle and tighten the nut to 71 inch lbs. (8 Nm).
5. Install the front wheel.
6. Lower the vehicle.

Rear

1. Raise and safely support the vehicle.
2. Remove the speed sensor mounting bolt from the axle tube.
3. Remove the speed sensor.
4. Remove the sensor wire from the tie strap and disconnect the electrical connector.

To install:

5. Install the wheel speed sensor in the axle tube and tighten the mounting bolt to 71 inch lbs. (8 Nm).
6. Install the sensor wire into the routing clips and install new tie straps.
7. Reconnect the electrical connector.
8. Lower the vehicle.

BRAKES | BLEEDING THE BRAKE SYSTEM

BLEEDING PROCEDURE

Manual Bleeding

1. Remove reservoir filler caps and fill reservoir.
2. If the calipers or wheel cylinders were overhauled, open all caliper and wheel cylinder bleed screws. Then close each bleed screw as fluid starts to drip from it. Top off master cylinder reservoir once more before proceeding.
3. Attach one end of the bleed hose to the bleed screw and insert opposite end in glass container partially filled with brake fluid. Be sure the end of bleed hose is immersed in fluid.
4. Open up the bleeder, then have a helper press down the brake pedal. Once the pedal is down, close the bleeder. Repeat bleeding until fluid stream is clear and free of bubbles. Then move to the next wheel.

Pressure Bleeding

Use approved brake fluid. Use fresh, clean fluid from a sealed container at all times.

Follow the manufacturer's instructions carefully when using pressure equipment. Do not exceed the tank manufacturer's pressure recommendations. Generally, a tank pressure of 15-20 psi is sufficient for bleeding.

Fill the bleeder tank with recommended fluid and purge air from the tank lines before bleeding.

Do not pressure bleed without a proper master cylinder adapter. The wrong adapter can lead to leakage, or drawing air back into the system.

BRAKES | FRONT DISC BRAKES

✳✳ CAUTION

Dust and dirt accumulating on brake parts during normal use may contain asbestos fibers from production or aftermarket brake linings. Breathing excessive concentrations of asbestos fibers can cause serious bodily harm. Exercise care when servicing brake parts. Do not sand or grind brake lining unless equipment used is designed to contain the dust residue. Do not clean brake parts with compressed air or by dry brushing. Cleaning should be done by dampening the brake components with a fine mist of water, then wiping the brake components clean with a dampened cloth. Dispose of cloth and all residue containing asbestos fibers in an impermeable container with the appropriate label. Follow practices prescribed by the Occupational Safety and Health Administration (OSHA) and the Environmental Protection Agency (EPA) for the handling, processing, and disposing of dust or debris that may contain asbestos fibers.

BRAKE CALIPER

REMOVAL & INSTALLATION

See Figure 2.

1. Unscrew the cap from the brake fluid reservoir.
2. Raise and safely support the vehicle.
3. Remove the front wheels.
4. Remove the wear indicator.
5. Remove the brake hose at the brake caliper.

➡ Cap the ends of the brake lines.

6. Remove the brake caliper guide bolts and remove the brake caliper.

To install:

7. Install the brake caliper to the brake caliper adapter. Tighten the guide pin bolts as follows:
    a. M8 bolts to 24 ft. lbs. (34 Nm).
    b. M10 bolts to 48 ft. lbs. (65 Nm).
8. Install the brake hose to the brake caliper and tighten to 10 ft. lbs. (14 Nm).

➡ Ensure the brake hose is not twisted.

9. Install the wear indicator and tighten the bolt to 71 inch lbs. (8 Nm).

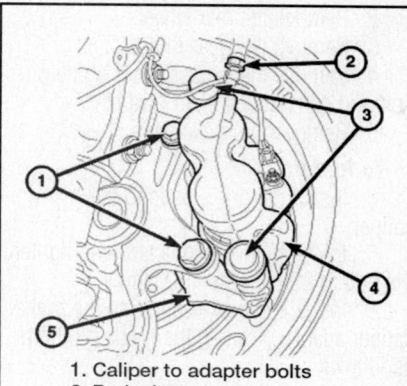

1. Caliper to adapter bolts
2. Brake hose
3. Caliper guide bolts
4. Caliper

36543_SPRI_G0062

Fig. 2 Brake caliper

10. Bleed and brake system and check for leaks.
11. Install the front wheel.
12. Lower the vehicle.

BRAKES

✳✳ CAUTION

Dust and dirt accumulating on brake parts during normal use may contain asbestos fibers from production or aftermarket brake linings. Breathing excessive concentrations of asbestos fibers can cause serious bodily harm. Exercise care when servicing brake parts. Do not sand or grind brake lining unless equipment used is designed to contain the dust residue. Do not clean brake parts with compressed air or by dry brushing. Cleaning should be done by dampening the brake components with a fine mist of water, then wiping the brake components clean with a dampened cloth. Dispose of cloth and all residue containing asbestos fibers in an impermeable container with the appropriate label. Follow practices prescribed by the Occupational Safety and Health Administration (OSHA) and the Environmental Protection Agency (EPA) for the handling, processing, and disposing of dust or debris that may contain asbestos fibers.

BRAKE CALIPER

REMOVAL & INSTALLATION

Single Rear Wheels (SRW)

See Figure 4.

DISC BRAKE PADS

REMOVAL & INSTALLATION

See Figure 3.

1. Unscrew the cap from the brake fluid reservoir.
2. Raise and safely support the vehicle.
3. Remove the front wheel.
4. Remove the wear indicator.
5. Remove the lower brake caliper guide pin bolts and remove the caliper.

✳✳ WARNING

Support the caliper assembly. Do not let the caliper hang by the brake hose.

6. Remove the brake pads from the caliper.

To install:

7. Install the brake pads.
8. Install the brake caliper to the brake

1. Unscrew the cap from the brake fluid reservoir.
2. Raise and safely support the vehicle.
3. Remove the rear wheel.
4. Remove the wear indicator.
5. Remove the brake hose at the brake caliper.

➡ **Cap the ends of the brake lines.**

6. Remove the brake caliper guide bolts and remove the brake caliper.

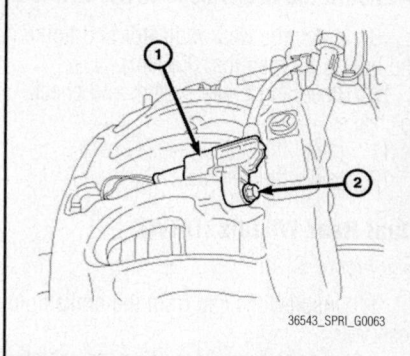

Fig. 3 Wear indicator (1) and bolt (2)

caliper adapter. Tighten the guide pin bolts as follows:

   a. M8 bolts to 24 ft. lbs. (34 Nm).
   b. M10 bolts to 48 ft. lbs. (65 Nm).
9. Install the wear indicator and tighten the bolt to 89 inch lbs. (10 Nm).
10. Install the front wheels.
11. Lower the vehicle.

REAR DISC BRAKES

To install:

7. Install the brake caliper to the brake caliper adapter. Tighten the guide pin bolts as follows:

   a. M8 bolts to 24 ft. lbs. (34 Nm).
   b. M10 bolts to 48 ft. lbs. (65 Nm).
8. Install the brake hose to the brake caliper and tighten to 10 ft. lbs. (14 Nm).

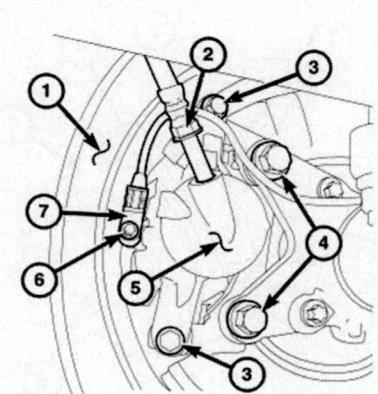

1. Rear wheel
2. Brake hose
3. Caliper guide bolts
4. Caliper to adapter bolts
5. Caliper
6. Wear indicator bolt
7. Wear indicator

36543_SPRI_G0064

Fig. 4 Caliper for Single Rear Wheels (SRW)

➡**Ensure the brake hose is not twisted.**

9. Install the wear indicator and tighten the bolt to 89 inch lbs. (10 Nm).

10. Bleed and brake system and check for leaks.

11. Install the rear wheel.

12. Lower the vehicle.

Dual Rear Wheels (DRW)

See Figure 5.

1. Unscrew the cap from the brake fluid reservoir.

2. Raise and safely support the vehicle.

3. Remove the rear wheel.

4. Remove the wear indicator.

5. Remove the brake hose at the brake caliper.

➡**Cap the ends of the brake lines.**

6. Remove the brake caliper guide bolts and remove the brake caliper.

To install:

7. Install the brake caliper to brake caliper adapter. Tighten the guide pin bolts as follows:

    a. M8 bolts to 18 ft. lbs. (25 Nm).

    b. M10 bolts to 22 ft. lbs. (30 Nm).

➡**Do not install the brake hose twisted and ensure freedom of movement.**

8. Install the brake hose at the brake caliper. Tighten the bolt to 10 ft. lbs. (14 Nm).

9. Install the wear indicator to the caliper. Tighten to 89 in. lbs. (10 Nm).

10. Bleed the brake system.

11. Check the brake system for any leaks.

12. Install the rear wheels.

13. Lower the vehicle.

DISC BRAKE PADS

REMOVAL & INSTALLATION

Single Rear Wheels (SRW)

See Figure 6.

1. Raise and safely support the vehicle.

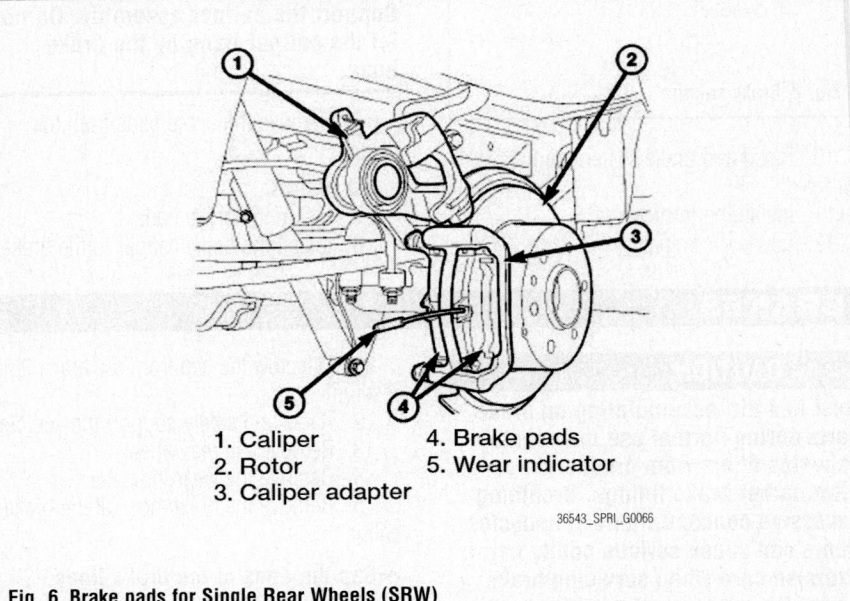

1. Caliper
2. Rotor
3. Caliper adapter
4. Brake pads
5. Wear indicator

36543_SPRI_G0066

Fig. 6 Brake pads for Single Rear Wheels (SRW)

2. Remove the rear wheel.

3. Remove the wear indicator.

4. Remove the caliper lower guide pin bolt and raise the caliper upward.

5. Remove the brake pads.

To install:

6. Install the brake pads to the caliper.

7. Install the wear indicator and tighten the bolt to 89 inch lbs. (10 Nm).

8. Install the brake caliper to the brake caliper adapter. Tighten the guide pin bolts as follows:

    a. M8 bolts to 24 ft. lbs. (34 Nm).

    b. M10 bolts to 48 ft. lbs. (65 Nm).

9. Install the rear wheel.

10. Lower the vehicle.

Dual Rear Wheels (DRW)

See Figure 5.

1. Unscrew the cap from the brake fluid reservoir.

2. Raise and support the vehicle.

3. Remove the rear wheels.

4. Remove the wear indicator cable from the wear indicator.

5. Remove the wear indicator from the brake caliper.

6. Compress the caliper piston.

7. Remove the upper brake caliper guide pin.

8. Pivot the brake caliper downward from the caliper adapter.

9. Remove the pads.

10. Remove the wear indicator sensor from the inboard brake pad.

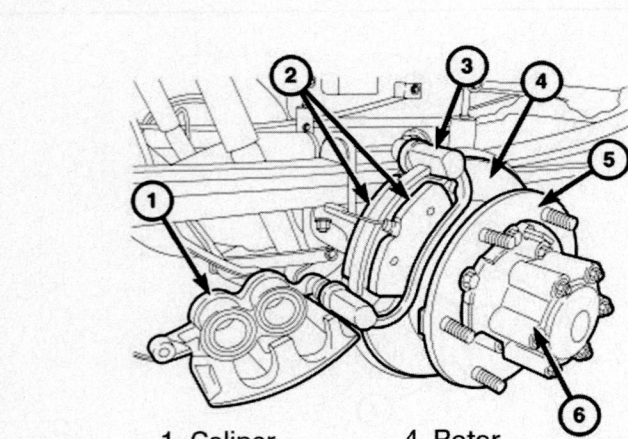

1. Caliper
2. Brake pads
3. Caliper adapter
4. Rotor
5. Wheel adapter
6. Rear hub

36543_SPRI_G0065

Fig. 5 Caliper for Dual Rear Wheels (DRW)

11. Remove the retaining clips.

To install:

12. Install the retaining clips.

13. Install the wear indicator to the inboard brake pad.

14. Install the brake pads.

15. Rotate the brake caliper back up into position.

16. Install the wear indicator to the caliper. Tighten bolt (2) to 89 inch lbs. (10 Nm).

17. Install the wear indicator cable to the wear indicator.

➡**Do not install the brake hose twisted and ensure freedom of movement.**

18. Install the brake caliper pin to brake caliper adapter. Tighten the guide pins as follows:

   a. M8 bolts to 18 ft. lbs. (25 Nm).

   b. M10 bolts to 22 ft. lbs (30 Nm).

19. Install the rear wheels.

20. Lower the vehicle.

BRAKES

PARKING BRAKE

PARKING BRAKE CABLES

ADJUSTMENT

Loosen Adjustment

1. Release the load on the parking brake cables at the adjuster nut.

2. Push the cable adjuster all the way in direction of travel to loosen.

Tighten Adjustment

1. Adjust the parking brake shoes.

2. Actuate the hand brake lever several times with moderate force, then release and actuate to second notch. Tighten the adjusting nut of the cable adjuster until the rear wheels can just be turned by hand.

3. Actuate and release the park brake lever 3 times. The rear wheels must turn freely and without grinding the brake. If the rear wheels do not turn freely, the adjustment must be repeated.

PARKING BRAKE SHOES

REMOVAL & INSTALLATION

Single Rear Wheels (SRW)

See Figure 7.

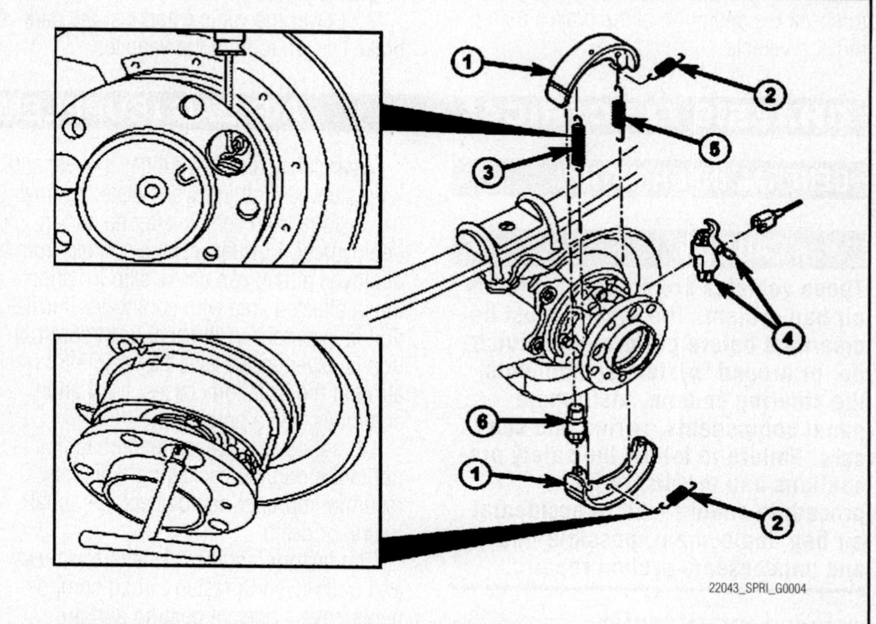

1. Raise and safely support the vehicle.

2. Remove the rear wheel.

3. Remove the caliper adapter

4. Remove the rotor set screw and remove the brake rotor.

5. Disconnect the front park brake cable from the equalizer.

6. Remove the return springs.

7. Remove the hold down springs.

8. Remove the adjuster spring.

9. Remove the adjuster.

10. Remove the rear park brake shoes.

To install:

11. Install the park brake shoes.

12. Install the hold down springs.

13. Install the return spring.

14. Install the adjuster.

15. Install the adjuster spring.

22043_SPRI_G0004

Fig. 7 Exploded view of the parking brake assembly—Brake shoes (1), hold down springs (2), adjuster spring (3), equalizer (4), return springs (5), adjuster (6)

16. Install the park brake cable to the equalizer.

17. Install the disc brake rotor and install the set screw.

18. Install the caliper adapter.

19. Install the rear wheel.

20. Turn the adjusting wheel until it is no longer possible to rotate the rear wheel.

21. Loosen the adjusting wheel 3-4 teeth divisions.

22. Inspect the clearance, or a slight drag when rotating the wheel/rear disc brake rotor.

23. Lower the vehicle.

Dual Rear Wheels (DRW)

1. Raise and support the vehicle.

2. Remove the rear wheels.

3. Remove the wheel flange ring.

4. Remove the disc brake rotor.

5. Remove the hub/bearing assembly.

6. Remove the retracting springs.

7. Remove the hold down springs by depressing with a pair of needle nose pliers and twisting.

8. Remove the rear park brake shoes. Pull the park brake shoes apart at the bottom and remove them together with the top spring.

9. Remove the adjuster.

To install:

10. Lubricate the pads on the support plate that the shoes ride on.

➡**Preassemble the retracting spring with the short hook eye from the inside together with the adjuster wheel at the top. Fit the preassembled park brake shoes on the brake carrier.**

11. Ensure that the cable lock moves easily before installing shoes. Install the park brake shoes.

12. Install the pressure hold down springs by depressing with a pair of needle nose pliers and twisting to lock in place.

13. Install the adjuster between the park brake shoes.

14. Install the lower retracting springs.

15. Install the hub/bearing assembly.

16. Install the disc brake rotor.

17. Install the rear wheel flange ring. Tighten to 148 ft. lbs. (200 Nm).

18. Install the rear wheels.

19. Adjust the parking brakes.

20. Lower the vehicle.

21. Pump the brake pedal several times to check the operation of the brakes before moving vehicle.

ADJUSTMENT

Single Rear Wheels (SRW)

1. Raise and support the vehicle.

2. Remove the rear wheels.

3. Turn the adjusting wheel until it is no longer possible to rotate the rear wheel .

4. Loosen the adjusting wheel 3-4 teeth divisions.

5. Inspect the clearance, or a slight drag when rotating the wheel/rear disc brake rotor.

6. Install rear wheels.

7. Lower the vehicle and test the park brake system to hold the vehicle.

Dual Rear Wheels (DRW)

1. Raise and support the vehicle.

2. Remove the rear wheels.

3. Turn the adjusting wheel until it is no longer possible to rotate the rear wheel.

4. Loosen the adjusting wheel 3-4 teeth divisions.

5. Inspect the clearance, or a slight drag when rotating the wheel/rear disc brake rotor.

6. Install rear wheels.

7. Lower the vehicle and test the park brake system to hold the vehicle.

CHASSIS ELECTRICAL

GENERAL INFORMATION

✳✳ CAUTION

These vehicles are equipped with an air bag system. The system must be disarmed before performing service on, or around, system components, the steering column, instrument panel components, wiring and sensors. Failure to follow the safety precautions and the disarming procedure could result in accidental air bag deployment, possible injury and unnecessary system repairs.

SERVICE PRECAUTIONS

Disconnect and isolate the battery negative cable before beginning any airbag system component diagnosis, testing, removal, or installation procedures. Allow system capacitor to discharge for two minutes before beginning any component service. This will disable the airbag system. Failure to disable the airbag system may result in accidental airbag deployment, personal injury, or death.

Do not place an intact undeployed airbag face down on a solid surface. The airbag will propel into the air if accidentally deployed and may result in personal injury or death.

When carrying or handling an undeployed airbag, the trim side (face) of the airbag should be pointing towards the body to minimize possibility of injury if accidental deployment occurs. Failure to do this may result in personal injury or death.

Replace airbag system components with OEM replacement parts. Substitute parts may appear interchangeable, but internal differences may result in inferior occupant protection. Failure to do so may result in occupant personal injury or death.

AIR BAG (SUPPLEMENTAL RESTRAINT SYSTEM)

Wear safety glasses, rubber gloves, and long sleeved clothing when cleaning powder residue from vehicle after an airbag deployment. Powder residue emitted from a deployed airbag can cause skin irritation. Flush affected area with cool water if irritation is experienced. If nasal or throat irritation is experienced, exit the vehicle for fresh air until the irritation ceases. If irritation continues, see a physician.

Do not use a replacement airbag that is not in the original packaging. This may result in improper deployment, personal injury, or death.

The factory installed fasteners, screws and bolts used to fasten airbag components have a special coating and are specifically designed for the airbag system. Do not use substitute fasteners. Use only original equipment fasteners listed in the parts catalog when fastener replacement is required.

During, and following, any child restraint anchor service, due to impact event or vehicle repair, carefully inspect all mounting hardware, tether straps, and anchors for proper installation, operation, or damage. If a child restraint anchor is found damaged in any way, the anchor must be replaced. Failure to do this may result in personal injury or death.

Deployed and non-deployed airbags may or may not have live pyrotechnic material within the airbag inflator.

Do not dispose of driver/passenger/curtain airbags or seat belt tensioners unless you are sure of complete deployment. Refer to the Hazardous Substance Control System for proper disposal.

Dispose of deployed airbags and tensioners consistent with state, provincial, local, and federal regulations.

After any airbag component testing or service, do not connect the battery negative cable. Personal injury or death may result if the system test is not performed first.

If the vehicle is equipped with the Occupant Classification System (OCS), do not connect the battery negative cable before performing the OCS Verification Test using the scan tool and the appropriate diagnostic information. Personal injury or death may result if the system test is not performed properly.

Never replace both the Occupant Restraint Controller (ORC) and the Occupant Classification Module (OCM) at the same time. If both require replacement, replace one, then perform the Airbag System test before replacing the other.

Both the ORC and the OCM store Occupant Classification System (OCS) calibration data, which they transfer to one another when one of them is replaced. If both are replaced at the same time, an irreversible fault will be set in both modules and the OCS may malfunction and cause personal injury or death.

If equipped with OCS, the Seat Weight Sensor is a sensitive, calibrated unit and must be handled carefully. Do not drop or handle roughly. If dropped or damaged, replace with another sensor. Failure to do so may result in occupant injury or death.

If equipped with OCS, the front passenger seat must be handled carefully as well. When removing the seat, be careful when setting on floor not to drop. If dropped, the sensor may be inoperative, could result in occupant injury, or possibly death.

If equipped with OCS, when the passenger front seat is on the floor, no one should sit in the front passenger seat. This uneven force may damage the sensing ability of the seat weight sensors. If sat on and damaged, the sensor may be inoperative, could result in occupant injury, or possibly death.

DISARMING THE SYSTEM

Disconnect the negative battery cable. Wait at least two minutes for the system capacitor to discharge for servicing the vehicle.

ARMING THE SYSTEM

Connect the negative battery cable.

CLOCKSPRING CENTERING

✳✳ WARNING

To avoid serious or fatal injury on vehicles equipped with airbags, disable the supplemental restraint system before attempting any steering wheel, steering column, airbag, seat belt tensioner, impact sensor, or instrument panel component diagnosis or service. Disconnect and isolate the battery negative (ground) cable, then wait two minutes for the system

capacitor to discharge before performing further diagnosis or service. This is the only sure way to disable the supplemental restraint system. Failure to take the proper precautions could result in accidental airbag deployment.

➡A service replacement clockspring is shipped with the clockspring pre-centered and with a molded plastic locking pin installed. This locking pin should not be removed until the steering wheel has been installed on the steering column. If the locking pin is removed before the steering wheel is installed, the clockspring centering procedure must be performed.

➡Before starting this procedure, be certain to turn the steering wheel until the front wheels are in the straight-ahead position and that the entire

steering system is locked or inhibited from rotation.

1. Place the front wheels in the straight-ahead position.
2. Remove the clockspring from the steering column.
3. Rotate the clockspring rotor counter-clockwise to the end of its travel. Do not apply excessive torque.
4. From the end of the counterclock-wise travel, rotate the rotor about three to three and one-half turns clockwise, until the clearance holes in the clockspring rotor are aligned with the three mounting screw holes in the clockspring case.
5. The clockspring is now centered. Secure the clockspring rotor to the clockspring case using a locking pin, adhesive tape or some similar device to maintain clockspring centering until the unit is reinstalled on the steering column.

DRIVE TRAIN

AUTOMATIC TRANSMISSION ASSEMBLY

REMOVAL & INSTALLATION

See Figures 8 through 10.

1. Disconnect the negative battery cable.
2. Apply the parking brake and move the transmission gear selector into Neutral **(N)**.
3. Remove transmission fill tube bolts from engine.
4. Raise and support the vehicle.
5. Drain the transmission fluid.
6. Remove the starter.
7. Remove the transmission oil filler pipe by removing the mounting bolts from the cylinder head and transmission housing. Guide the oil filler pipe up and out of the engine compartment.
8. Remove the exhaust heat shield.
9. Remove the retaining bracket and disconnect the driveshaft from the transmission. Secure the driveshaft out of the way.
10. Remove the transmission cooler lines mounting bracket and disconnect the transmission cooler lines.
11. Disconnect the transmission wiring harness.
12. Disconnect the transmission shift cable.
13. Remove the steering gear from the crossmember and lower.
14. Remove the plastic torque converter access cover.

15. Rotate engine by hand to access bolts and remove the torque converter bolts.
16. Support the engine assembly with a suitable jack.

➡Use a wooden block between the oil pan and jack to avoid damage to the engine.

17. Remove the vent hose bracket and tie back to one side.
18. Disconnect the ground strap.
19. Remove the bolts on the underside of the transmission. Two bolts on the top of the transmission must remain in the housing.
20. Place a suitable jack under the trans-

mission assembly and raise it slightly. Secure the transmission to the jack with a strap.
21. Remove the rear engine crossmember.
22. Remove the last two transmission mounting bolts.
23. Remove the transmission rearward and then lower. Ensure the torque converter remains in the bellhousing when the transmission is removed.
24. Remove the torque converter.

To install:

25. Coat outside of the torque converter hub with long-term grease, install the torque converter into the transmission.

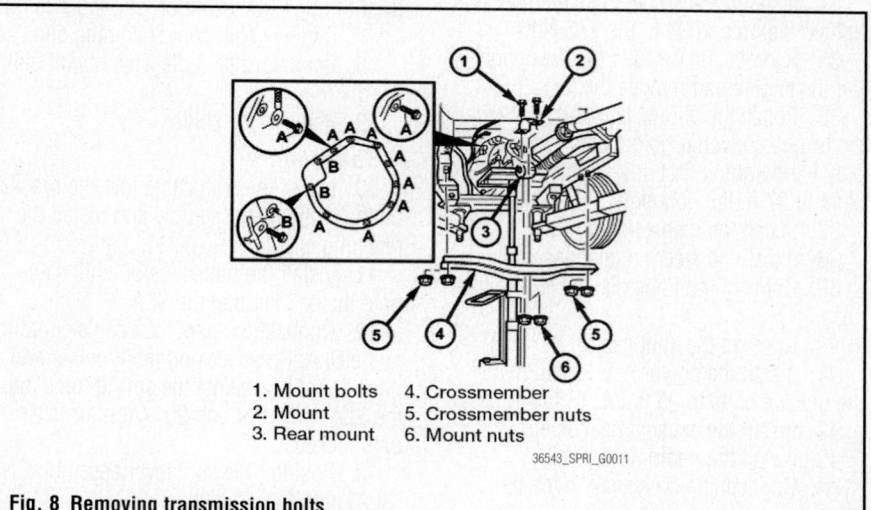

1. Mount bolts
2. Mount
3. Rear mount
4. Crossmember
5. Crossmember nuts
6. Mount nuts

36543_SPRI_G0011

Fig. 8 Removing transmission bolts

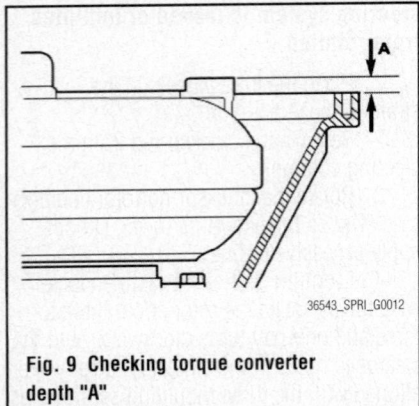

Fig. 9 Checking torque converter depth "A"

26. Measure distance "A" from torque converter to transmission housing. If the torque converter is properly installed, distance "A" will be 55 mm (2.17 in.).

27. Move the torque covert to the position shown to ensure the bottom bolts are accessible through the inspection cover.

28. Ensure the dowel pins are installed in their correct position at the transmission housing flange.

29. Using a suitable jack, raise the transmission into position. Secure transmission on hydraulic jack with a strap or ask an assistant to hold it.

30. Move the transmission into position on the dowel pins and install the two bolts on the top of the transmission. Tighten the bolts to 28 ft. lbs. (38 Nm).

31. Install the vent hose bracket to the transmission and tighten to 28 ft. lbs. (38 Nm).

32. Install the ground strap to the transmission and tighten the bolt to 28 ft. lbs. (38 Nm).

33. Install the remaining transmission mounting bolts and tighten to 28 ft. lbs. (38 Nm).

34. Install rear engine cross member and tighten the nuts to 33 ft. lbs. (45 Nm).

35. Remove the wooden block supporting the engine and remove the jack.

36. Rotate the engine by hand and install the torque converter bolts. Install them all only hand tight at first, then tighten them in pairs to 37 ft. lbs. (50 Nm).

37. Install the inspection cover.

38. Install the steering gear assembly.

39. Connect the transmission wiring harness.

40. Connect the shift cable.

41. Install the cooler lines and tighten the bracket bolts to 25 ft. lbs. (34 Nm).

42. Install the exhaust heat shield.

43. Install the retaining bracket.

44. Connect the driveshaft to the transmission.

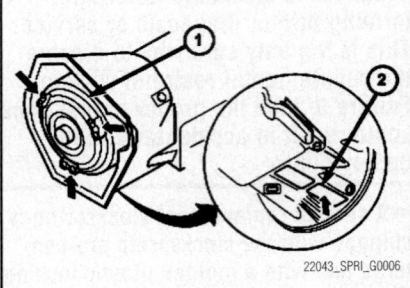

Fig. 10 Check the position of the torque converter through the inspection cover (2) when reinstalling

45. Install the transmission oil fill pipe. Tighten the mounting bolts to 71 inch lbs. (8 Nm) and install the dipstick.

46. Install the transmission oil drain plug and tighten to 15 ft. lbs. (20 Nm).

47. Install the starter, if removed.

48. Lower the vehicle.

49. Refill the transmission with fluid to the correct level.

50. Test drive the vehicle to ensure proper operation and check for leaks.

SHIFTER ASSEMBLY

REMOVAL & INSTALLATION

1. Move selector lever to position "D".

2. Remove top section of the center section of instrument panel.

3. Remove bottom section of the center section of instrument panel.

4. Disconnect all electrical connectors.

5. Remove shift lever assembly mounting bolts.

6. Disconnect the park lock cable coupling from the shift lever assembly (SLA). Press locking tab together and push coupling against the spring force into the SLA, twist through 90° (right or left) and pull off.

7. Remove shift cable retaining clip.

8. Remove shift cable from shifter ball knob.

9. Remove the shifter.

To install:

10. Install the shift cable into the bracket on the shift lever assembly and install the retaining clip .

11. Install the transmission shift cable onto the ball knob at the SLA.

12. Connect the park lock cable coupling to the SLA. Press locking tab together and push coupling against the spring force into the SLA, twist through 90° (right or left) until locked.

13. Position the shift lever assembly (SLA) onto the vehicle.

14. Install the bolts to hold the SLA to the vehicle. Tighten the bolts to 53 inch lbs. (6 Nm).

15. Connect all electrical connectors.

16. Turn on ignition and apply brakes. Move selector lever back to position "D".

17. Install the bottom of the center section of instrument panel.

18. Install the top of the center section of instrument panel.

REAR AXLE HOUSING

REMOVAL & INSTALLATION

See Figure 11.

1. Raise and safely support the vehicle.

2. Position a suitable lifting device under the axle and secure axle to device.

3. Remove the rear wheels.

4. Unplug wear indicator cable.

5. Detach cable connector for brake pad wear indicator.

6. Remove ABS sensor and clamp bushing from mounting bore.

➡**The right-hand ABS sensor cable is labeled at the factory with a white tag.**

7. Remove the cable ties from the park brake cables. Release the connection cable of brake pad wear indicator and ABS sensor cable up to the relay unit of the parking brake.

8. Remove the brake cables.

9. Remove the parking brake cable at relay unit.

10. Remove bracket for brake cables at rear axle tube.

11. Remove the stabilizer bar from axle brackets.

12. Remove the shock absorber mounting bolts from the rear axle.

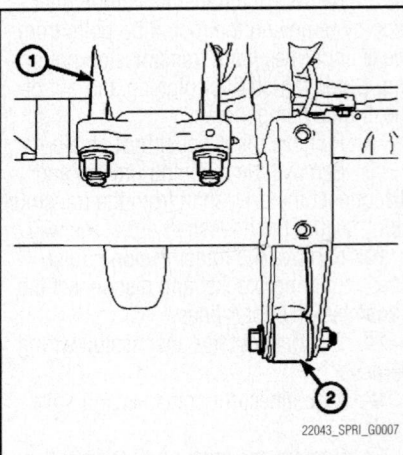

Fig. 11 Remove the lower shock mounting bolts (2) and U-Bolts (1) to remove the rear axle assembly.

13. Remove the ALB lever from the rear axle bracket.

14. Pull the vent line of the rear axle out of the frame.

15. Remove the driveshaft.

16. Remove the brake calipers

17. Remove the U-brackets and plates

18. Remove the axle from the vehicle.

To install:

19. Raise the rear axle into position.

20. Using new nuts, install the plates and U-brackets and tighten the nuts to 125 ft. lbs. (170 Nm).

21. Install the driveshaft.

➡ **When installing the driveshaft, the joint arrows must be flush and must point towards the frame floor. Tighten the driveshaft in this position.**

22. Install the ALB lever to axle bracket using a new nut and tighten to 25 ft. lbs. (34 Nm).

23. Install the shock absorber-to-rear axle mounting bolts.

24. Install the stabilizer bar-to-rear axle mounting bolts.

25. Install the brake calipers with adapters and lines.

26. Install the brake hoses and hold-down clips.

27. Install and adjust the parking brake cables.

28. Install the connection cable of brake pad wear indicator and ABS sensor cable up to the relay unit of the parking brake.

29. Install new cable ties to the park brake cables.

30. Install the ABS sensor and clamp bushing to mounting bore.

31. Attach the connector cable for brake pad wear indicator.

32. Plug in the cable of brake pad wear indicator.

33. Install the rear wheels.

34. Fill the rear axle with fluid to the correct level.

35. Remove the jack from underneath the axle.

36. Lower the vehicle.

REAR AXLE SHAFT, BEARING & SEAL

REMOVAL & INSTALLATION

Single Rear Wheels (SRW)

See Figures 12 through 14.

1. Raise and safely support the vehicle.

2. Drain the rear differential.

3. Remove the brake caliper, rotor and parking brakes. Refer to BRAKES.

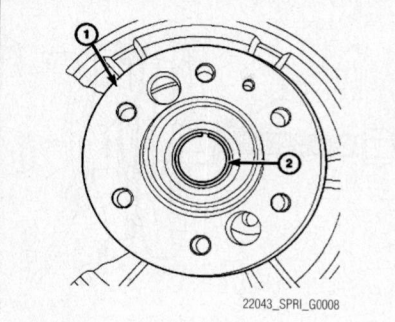

Fig. 12 Remove the axle flange (1) plug snap ring (2)

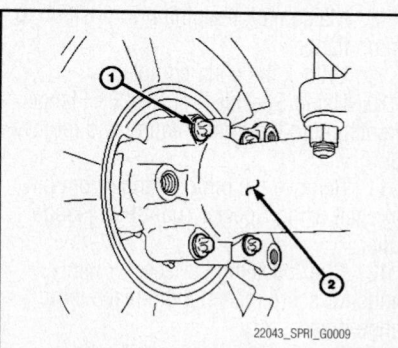

Fig. 13 Remove the axle bearing bolts (1) from the axle (2)

4. Remove the axle flange plug snap ring.

5. Tap the axle end plug loose from the axle flange with a hammer and punch. Pull the plug out of the axle flange.

6. Remove the axle bearing bolts from the axle.

7. Remove the axle shaft assembly from the axle.

8. Press the axle shaft out of the flange and bearing.

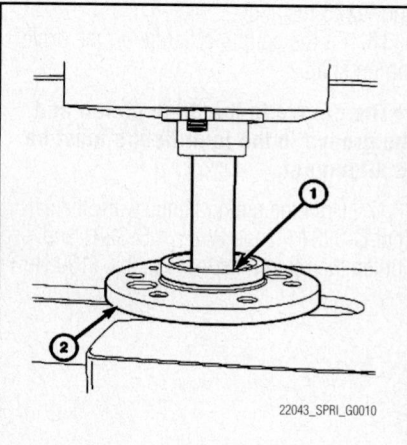

Fig. 14 Press the axle shaft (1) out of the flange (2) and bearing

To install:

9. Coat the axle splines with Mopar® Thread Sealant or equivalent.

10. Press the axle shaft into the bearing and axle flange using a shop press.

11. Install a new plug in the axle flange.

12. Install the axle flange plug snap ring.

13. Install the axle shaft assembly into the vehicle.

14. Install the axle bearing bolts.

15. Install the brake components. Refer to BRAKES.

16. Fill the differential with fluid to the correct level.

Dual Rear Wheels (DRW)

1. Remove brake caliper with support.

2. Remove axle shaft.

3. Back-off parking brakes. Refer to BRAKES.

4. Remove outer hub nut with Wrench 10095.

5. Remove locking plate, inner hub nut and thrust washer.

✳✳ CAUTION

Thrust washer is designed for left or right side and are not interchangeable.

6. Pull hub off axle tube.

7. Remove front hub bearing from hub.

8. Drive out ABS sensor tone ring hub seal and rear bearing from hub.

9. Remove inner and outer bearing cups from hub with a hammer and brass drift.

To install:

10. Install outer hub bearing cup with Installer 9588 and a hammer.

11. Install inner hub bearing cup with Bearing Cup Installer 10099 and Universal Drive Handle C-4171.

12. Clean and thoroughly grease bearings with Multi-purpose grease.

13. Install inner wheel bearing.

14. Coat outer circumference of new seal (2) with Hylomar SQ 32 M sealant.

✳✳ CAUTION

Do not coat seals rubberized sealing surfaces with sealant.

15. Install seal into hub with Seal Installer 10098 and Universal Drive Handle C-4171.

➡ **Seal ring should be flush with wheel hub or a maximum of 3 mm (0.12 in.) deep.**

16. Coat contact surface of ABS sensor ring with Hylomar SQ 32 M sealant.

17. Drive ABS sensor ring in with Tone Ring Installer 10097 and Universal Drive Handle C-4171.

18. Install hub on axle tube.

19. Install outer hub bearing.

20. Install thrust washer.

✳✳ CAUTION

Thrust washer is designed for left or right side and are not interchangeable.

21. Install inner hub nut.

22. Tighten inner hub nut with Hub Nut Socket 10095 to 221 ft. lbs. (300 Nm) while spinning the wheel hub constantly. Turn back inner nut and then tighten until it touches the thrust washer without play. Then tighten 1/8 turn.

23. Install locking plate.

24. Install outer hub nut and tighten with Hub Nut Socket 10095 to 184 ft. lbs. (250 Nm).

25. Install axle shaft.

26. Install brake caliper and support. Refer to BRAKES.

27. Adjust parking brakes. Refer to BRAKES.

REAR PINION SEAL

REMOVAL & INSTALLATION

See Figures 15 and 16.

1. Raise and safely support the vehicle.

2. Remove the rear wheels.

3. Push back brake pads and release hand brake.

4. Drain the rear differential fluid.

➡**On dual rear wheel axle, remove axle shafts.**

5. Remove the driveshaft. Refer to Driveshaft.

6. Spin pinion flange by hand and check axial play of bearing.

➡**There must not be any thrust bearing play. If there excess play or there are particles (shavings) in the drained oil, the rear gear assembly must be replaced.**

7. Measure and record the torque required to rotate the pinion.

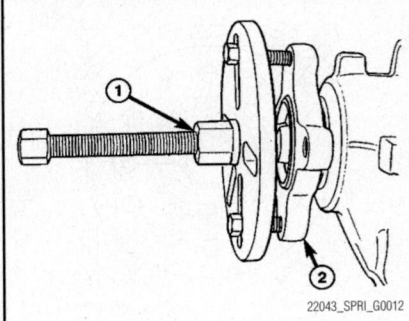

22043_SPRI_G0012

Fig. 15 Remove the pinion flange (2) from the shaft using Special Tool 8992 (1).

8. Matchmark the pinion in position to pinion flange

9. Unlock the collared nut.

10. Using Special Tool C-3281 Flange Wrench, hold the pinion flange and remove nut.

11. Remove the pinion flange from pinion shaft using Special Tool 8992 Flange Puller.

12. Check sealing surfaces of joint flange for score marks and replace joint flange if necessary.

13. Remove the pinion seals.

To install:

14. Pack the space between the dust lip and sealing lip on the seal ring with multipurpose grease.

➡**On seals without rubberized external surface, coat outer circumference with sealant.**

✳✳ WARNING

Do not coat partially rubberized seals with sealant.

15. Drive new pinion seals into the rear axle housing until they stop using Special Tool 9276 Installer.

16. Fit the coupling flange on the drive pinion shaft.

➡**The groove in the drive pinion and the groove in the joint flange must be in alignment.**

17. Hold the pinion flange with Special Tool C-3281 Flange Wrench C-3281 and tighten the pinion nut to 74 ft. lbs. (100 Nm).

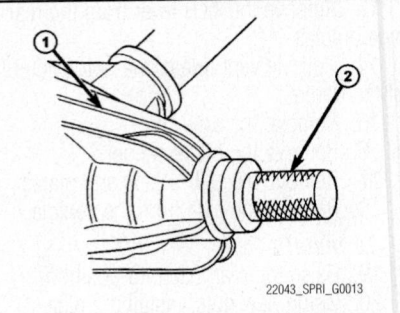

22043_SPRI_G0013

Fig. 17 Drive new pinion seals into the axle housing (1) using Special Tool 9276 (2).

18. Using a dial indicator check free play at the pinion flange.

➡**Should the bearing not be free of play, tighten in increases of 88 inch lbs. (10 Nm) to a maximum of 95 ft. lbs. (130 Nm). If the bearing is not free of play, the collapsible spacer must be replaced.**

19. Identify the position of the pinion to the nut twelve points and mark pinion and nut. Turn the pinion nut 30° (one twelve point). Then rotate the pinion thirty times.

20. Measure the torque required to rotate. The torque to rotate must be 0.9-1.7 in. lbs. (0.1-0.2 Nm) higher then torque recorded during the removal procedure.

➡**If value is below or above collapsible spacer must be replaced.**

21. Cut the collar of the collared nut.

22. Using a hammer and drift, bend the collar nut so it touches the wall of the slot in the pinion shaft.

23. Install the driveshaft.

➡**On dual rear wheel axle, install axle shafts.**

24. Refill the rear differential with fluid to the correct level.

25. Install the wheels.

26. Operate brake pedal several times until brake pads contact brake discs (brake pressure built up).

27. Attach rear brake cables if removed and adjust parking brake. Refer to BRAKES.

ENGINE COOLING

ENGINE FAN

REMOVAL & INSTALLATION

See Figure 17.

1. Disconnect the negative battery cable.
2. Detach the coolant line from the lower radiator shroud.

➡**The radiator fan assembly is threaded to the water pump hub shaft. Remove the fan blade/viscous fan drive assembly from the water pump by turning the mounting nut counterclockwise as viewed from the front. Threads on the radiator fan drive are RIGHT-HAND.**

3. Using Special Tool 8930 Counterholder, remove the radiator fan.
4. Remove the upper air seal. (3.0L Diesel)
5. Remove the upper radiator hose. (3.0L Diesel)
6. Remove the radiator fan shroud and radiator fan.

➡**Store the fan in the upright position. Do not place down flat.**

To install:

7. Install the radiator fan and clutch assembly to the engine.
8. Install the center bolt, and using Special Tool 8930 to hold the fan, tighten the bolt to 33 ft. lbs. (45 Nm).
9. Attach the upper radiator hose and install the air seal. (3.0L Diesel)
10. Attach the coolant line to the lower radiator shroud.
11. Properly align and clip the fan shroud into place.
12. Connect the negative battery cable.

RADIATOR

REMOVAL & INSTALLATION

1. Drain the cooling system.
2. Remove the headlights.
3. Remove the front crossmember together with front grille.
4. Remove the front bumper.
5. Remove the bolts holding the air charge hose to the sheet metal and intercooler.
6. Detach the air intake pipe at the body.
7. Detach both coolant hoses at the coolant reservoir.
8. Unplug the wiring connector at the coolant level sensor.
9. Detach the coolant hose at bottom right of radiator.
10. Detach the transmission cooler lines from the radiator.
11. Remove the left and right radiator trim.
12. Remove the radiator fan. Refer to Engine Fan.
13. Remove the bolts securing the intercooler to the radiator.
14. Remove the screws and upper radiator trim from the radiator.
15. Move the condenser/intercooler/power steering cooler assembly forward.
16. Lift the radiator assembly up and out of the rubber grommets.

To install:

17. Install the radiator assembly into the rubber grommets.
18. Install both right and left side radiator trim panels.
19. Attach the transmission cooler lines.

20. Attach the coolant hose to the bottom right of the radiator.
21. Attach both power steering hydraulic lines.
22. Connect the coolant level sensor electrical connector.
23. Connect the coolant hoses to the coolant reservoir, radiator and water pump.
24. Attach the air intake pipe to the body.
25. Attach the charge air hose to the air intake.
26. Attach the charge air hose to the turbocharger.
27. Install the A/C condenser.
28. Install the front bumper.
29. Install front end crossmember.
30. Refill the power steering reservoir to the correct level.
31. Refill the transmission to the correct level.
32. Refill the cooling system to the correct level.
33. Start the engine and check for leaks.

THERMOSTAT

REMOVAL & INSTALLATION

3.0L Engine

1. Disconnect the negative battery cable.
2. Drain the cooling system.
3. Remove the engine appearance cover.
4. Remove the thermostat mounting bolts.
5. Pull the thermostat housing back and remove the thermostat and discard the sealing ring.

To install:

6. Clean the mounting surfaces of any gasket material.
7. Install the thermostat with a new sealing ring.
8. Position the thermostat housing into place and tighten the mounting bolts to 80 inch lbs. (9 Nm).
9. Refill the cooling system to the correct level.
10. Install the engine appearance cover.
11. Connect the negative battery cable.
12. Start the engine and check for leaks.

3.5L Engine

1. Remove the engine appearance cover.
2. Drain the cooling system.

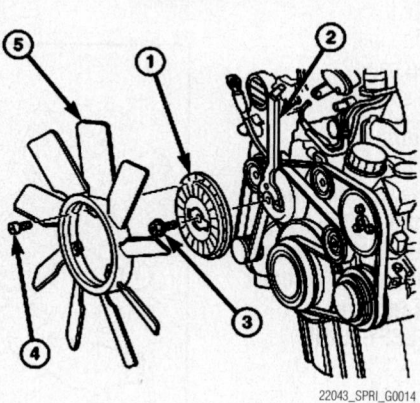

22043_SPRI_G0014

Fig. 18 Use a counterholder (2) to remove the center bolt (3) of the engine fan (1,4) assembly—3.0L Diesel engines

3. Remove the locking ring and remove the coolant hose from the thermostat housing.

4. Disconnect the thermostat electrical connector.

5. Remove the thermostat housing mounting bolts.

6. Remove the thermostat housing and discard the gasket.

7. Remove the thermostat.

To install:

8. Clean the mounting surface of any gasket material.

9. Install the thermostat.

10. Using a new gasket, install the thermostat housing and tighten the mounting bolts to 80 inch lbs. (9 Nm).

11. Connect the coolant hose to the thermostat housing.

12. Refill the cooling system to the correct level.

13. Install the engine appearance cover.

WATER PUMP

REMOVAL & INSTALLATION

3.0L Engine

See Figure 18.

❊❊ WARNING

Risk of injury to skin and eyes from scalding with hot coolant. Risk of poisoning from swallowing coolant. Do not open cooling system unless coolant temperature is below 90°C (194°F)). Open cap slowly to release pressure. store coolant in suitable and appropriately marked container. Wear protective gloves, clothes and eye wear.

➡**Inspect condition of all clamps and hoses, replace as necessary.**

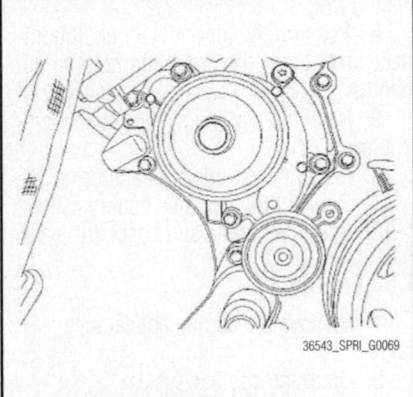

36543_SPRI_G0069

Fig. 18 Water pump—3.0L Engine

1. Disconnect the negative battery cable.

2. Disconnect the AGM starter negative battery cable located inside the vehicle under the instrument panel near the accelerator pedal.

3. Remove the air box assembly. Refer Air Cleaner.

4. Remove the engine cover.

5. Drain the cooling system.

6. Remove the fan and shroud. Refer to Engine Fan.

➡**The radiator fan assembly is attached (threaded) to the fan pulley (1). Remove the fan blade/viscous fan drive assembly from the fan pulley by turning the mounting nut clockwise as viewed from the front. Threads on the radiator cooling fan are REVERSE THREADED (LEFT-HAND THREAD).**

7. Remove the fan drive belt (2).

8. Remove the serpentine belt (1).

9. Remove the oil dipstick retaining bolt.

10. Remove the generator.

11. Remove the lower charge air cooler hose.

12. Remove the EGR airflow valve assembly.

13. Remove water pump retaining bolts, water pump and gasket.

To install:

➡**Clean all mating surfaces.**

14. Properly position water pump with new gasket to the engine and tighten bolts to 10 ft. lbs. (14 Nm).

15. Install the EGR airflow valve assembly.

16. Install the oil dipstick retaining bolt.

17. Install the lower charge air cooler hose.

18. Install the generator.

19. Install the serpentine belt (1).

20. Install the fan drive belt (2).

21. Install the fan and shroud.

➡**The radiator fan assembly is attached (threaded) to the fan pulley (1). Install the fan blade/viscous fan drive assembly to the fan pulley by turning the mounting nut counter-clockwise as viewed from the front. Threads on the radiator cooling fan are REVERSE THREADED (LEFT-HAND THREAD).**

22. Install the engine cover.

23. Install the air box assembly.

24. Connect the AGM starter negative battery cable located inside the vehicle

under the instrument panel near the accelerator pedal.

25. Connect the negative battery cable.

26. Evacuate air and refill the cooling system. Refer to Coolant Air Evacuation.

27. Check cooling system for leaks.

3.5L Engine

See Figure 19.

1. Disconnect the negative battery cable.

2. Drain the cooling system.

3. Remove the viscous fan clutch. Refer to Engine Fan.

4. Detach the fuel lines from the brackets of the water pump.

5. Detach the coolant hoses from the water pump.

6. Remove the accessory drive belt.

7. Press off the cap at the belt guide pulleys.

8. Remove the belt guide pulleys.

9. Remove the water pump retaining bolts and remove the water pump.

To install:

10. Install the water pump with a new gasket and tighten the mounting bolts 10 ft. lbs. (14 Nm) and the M8 bolts to 15 ft. lbs. (20 Nm).

11. Install the belt guide pulleys and tighten the bolts to 26 ft. lbs. (35 Nm).

12. Connect the coolant hoses to the water pump.

13. Attach the fuel lines to the brackets of the water pump.

14. Install the accessory drive belt.

15. Install viscous fan clutch.

16. Refill the cooling system to the correct level.

17. Connect the negative battery cable.

18. Start the engine and check for leaks.

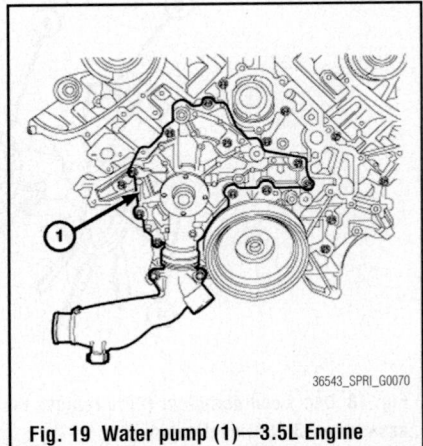

36543_SPRI_G0070

Fig. 19 Water pump (1)—3.5L Engine

COOLANT AIR EVACUATION

EVACUATION PROCEDURE

Evacuating or purging air from the cooling system involves the use of a pressurized air operated vacuum generator. The vacuum created allows for a quick and complete coolant refilling while removing any airlocks present in the system components.

➡ **To avoid damage to the cooling system, ensure that no component would be susceptible to damage when a vacuum is drawn on the system.**

✻✻ WARNING

Antifreeze is an ethylene glycol base coolant and is harmful if swallowed or inhaled. If swallowed, drink two glasses of water and induce vomiting. If inhaled, move to fresh air area. Seek medical attention immediately. Do not store in open or unmarked containers. Wash skin and clothing thoroughly after coming in contact with ethylene glycol. Keep out of reach of children. Dispose of glycol based coolant properly. Contact your dealer or government agency for location of collection center in your area. Do not open a cooling system when the engine is at operating temperature or hot under pressure; personal injury can result. Avoid radiator cooling fan when engine compartment related service is performed; personal injury can result.

✻✻ WARNING

Wear appropriate eye and hand protection when performing this procedure.

➡ **The service area where this procedure is performed should have a minimum shop air requirement of 80 PSI (5.5 bar) and should be equipped with an air dryer system.**

➡ **For best results, the radiator should be empty. The vehicle's heater control**

should be set to the heat position (ignition may need to be turned to the on position but do not start the motor).

1. Refer to the Chrysler Pentastar Service Equipment (Chrysler PSE) Coolant Refiller #85-15-0650 or equivalent tool's operating manual for specific assembly steps.

2. Choose an appropriate adapter cone that will fit the vehicle's radiator filler neck or reservoir tank.

3. Attach the adapter cone to the vacuum gauge.

4. Make sure the vacuum generator/venturi ball valve is closed and attach an airline hose (minimum shop air requirement of 80 PSI/5.5 bar) to the vacuum generator/venturi.

5. Position the adaptor cone/vacuum gauge assembly into the radiator filler neck or reservoir tank. Ensure that the adapter cone is sealed properly.

6. Connect the vacuum generator/venturi to the positioned adaptor cone/vacuum gauge assembly.

7. Open the vacuum generator/venturi ball valve.

➡ **Do not bump or move the assembly as it may result in loss of vacuum. Some radiator overflow hoses may need to be clamped off to obtain vacuum.**

8. Let the system run until the vacuum gauge shows a good vacuum through the cooling system. Refer to the tool's operating manual for appropriate pressure readings.

➡ **If a strong vacuum is being created in the system, it is normal to see the radiator hoses to collapse.**

9. Close the vacuum generator/venturi ball valve.

10. Disconnect the vacuum generator/venturi and airline from the adaptor cone/vacuum gauge assembly.

11. Wait approximately 20 seconds, if the pressure readings do not move, the system has no leaks. If the pressure readings move, a leak could be present in the system and the cooling system should be checked

for leaks and the procedure should be repeated.

12. Place the tool's suction hose into the coolant's container.

➡ **Ensure there is a sufficient amount of coolant, mixed to the required strength/protection level available for use. For best results and to assist the refilling procedure, place the coolant container at the same height as the radiator filler neck. Always draw more coolant than required. If the coolant level is too low, it will pull air into the cooling system which could result in airlocks in the system.**

13. Connect the tool's suction hose to the adaptor cone/vacuum gauge assembly.

14. Open the suction hose's ball valve to begin refilling the cooling system.

15. When the vacuum gauge reads zero, the system is filled.

➡ **On some remote pressurized tanks, it is recommended to stop filling when the proper level is reached.**

16. Close the suction hose's ball valve and remove the suction hose from the adaptor cone/vacuum gauge assembly.

17. Remove the adaptor cone/vacuum gauge assembly from the radiator filler neck or reservoir tank.

18. With heater control unit in the HEAT position, operate engine with container cap in place.

19. After engine has reached normal operating temperature, shut engine off and allow it to cool. When engine is cooling down, coolant will be drawn into the radiator from the pressure container.

20. Add coolant to the recovery bottle/container as necessary. Only add coolant to the container when the engine is cold. Coolant level in a warm engine will be higher due to thermal expansion. Add necessary coolant to raise container level to the COLD MINIMUM mark after each cool down period.

21. Once the appropriate coolant level is achieved, attach the radiator cap or reservoir tank cap.

ENGINE ELECTRICAL

ALTERNATOR

REMOVAL & INSTALLATION

See Figure 20.

1. Disconnect the negative battery cable.
2. Remove accessory drive belt. Refer to Accessory Drive Belt.
3. Raise and safely support the vehicle.
4. Remove the protective plastic cover from battery positive stud at top of the alternator.
5. Remove the nut securing the battery output cable to the battery positive terminal at the top of the alternator.

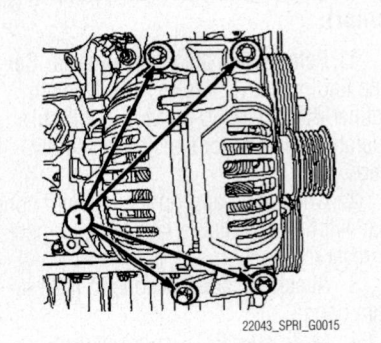

22043_SPRI_G0015

Fig. 20 The mounting bolt (1) for the alternator is Torx® no. 12 size

CHARGING SYSTEM

6. Unplug the ground terminal harness connector at rear of the alternator.
7. Remove the four mounting bolts.
8. Remove the alternator from the lower side of vehicle.

To install:

9. Install the alternator and tighten the mounting bolts to 15 ft. lbs. (20 Nm).
10. Connect the ground terminal to the rear of the alternator.
11. Install the battery positive cable to the top terminal and install the protective plastic cover.
12. Install the accessory drive belt.
13. Lower the vehicle.

ENGINE ELECTRICAL

FIRING ORDERS

3.0L Diesel Engine

Cylinders are numbered front to back, beginning with the right bank. The right bank cylinders are numbered 1, 2, 3. The left bank cylinders 4, 5, 6. The injection order of the engine is 1-4-2-5-3-6.

IGNITION COIL

REMOVAL & INSTALLATION

3.5L Engine

See Figure 21.

1. Disconnect the negative battery cable.
2. Remove the engine appearance cover.
3. Remove the air intake assembly.
4. Disconnect the ignition coil wiring harness.
5. Remove the two ignition coil mounting bolts and remove the ignition coil.

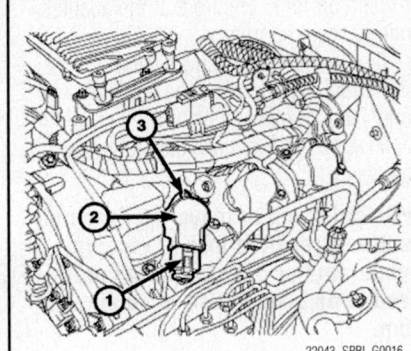

22043_SPRI_G0016

Fig. 21 Disconnect the wiring harness (1) and remove the mounting bolts (3) to remove the ignition coil (2)—3.5L Engine

To install:

6. Install the ignition coil and tighten the mounting bolts to 80 inch lbs. (9 Nm).
7. Connect the ignition coil wiring harness.
8. Install the air intake assembly.

IGNITION SYSTEM

9. Install the engine appearance cover.
10. Connect the negative battery cable.

IGNITION TIMING

ADJUSTMENT

The ignition timing is controlled by the Powertrain Control Module (PCM). No adjustment is necessary or possible.

SPARK PLUGS

REMOVAL & INSTALLATION

3.5L Engine

1. Disconnect the negative battery cable.
2. Remove the ignition coil. Refer to Ignition Coil.
3. Remove the spark plug.

To install:

4. Install the spark plug and tighten to 17 ft. lbs. (23 Nm).
5. Install the ignition coil.
6. Connect the negative battery cable.

ENGINE ELECTRICAL

STARTER

REMOVAL & INSTALLATION

See Figure 22.

1. Disconnect the negative battery cable.
2. Raise and safely support the vehicle.
3. Remove the engine undercover.
4. Remove the bolt securing the starter wiring harness retainer bracket to the transmission bellhousing.
5. Disconnect the battery positive cables and the starter solenoid wire from the starter solenoid.

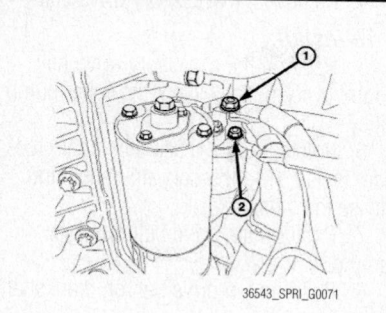

Fig. 22 Starter battery cable nut (1) and solenoid wire nut (2)

STARTING SYSTEM

6. Remove the starter mounting bolts.
7. Remove the starter from transmission bellhousing.

To install:

8. Positing the starter to the transmission bellhousing and tighten the mounting bolts to 30 ft. lbs. (40 Nm).
9. Connect the battery cable and solenoid wiring to the solenoid and tighten the nut to 10 ft. lbs. (14 Nm).
10. Position the wiring harness retainer bracket and install retaining bolt.
11. Lower the vehicle.
12. Connect the negative battery cable.

ENGINE MECHANICAL

ACCESSORY DRIVE BELTS

ACCESSORY BELT ROUTING

See Figures 23 through 27.

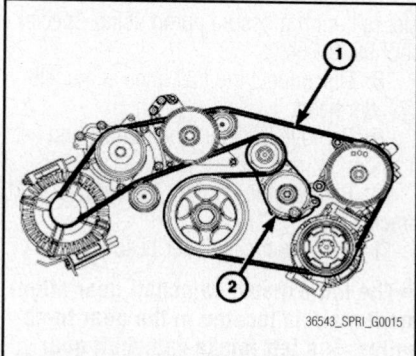

Fig. 23 Accessory Belt Routing—3.0L Engine

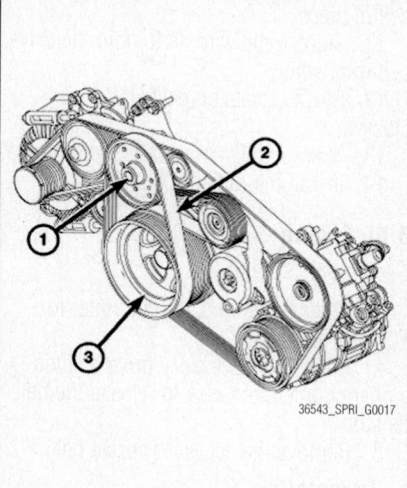

Fig. 25 Cooling fan belt routing—3.0L Engine

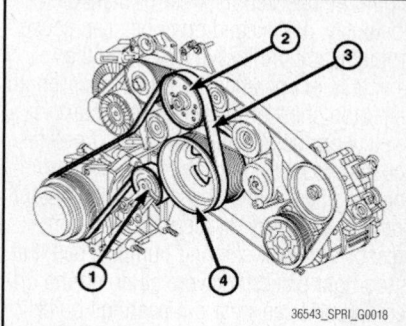

Fig. 26 Cooling fan belt routing with rear A/C—3.0L Engine

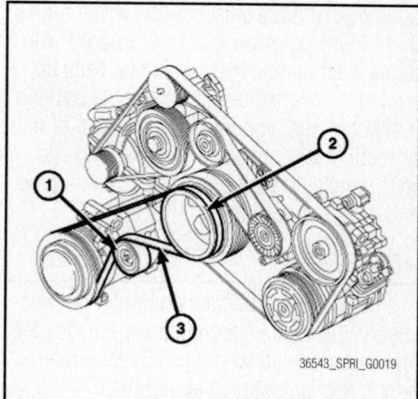

Fig. 27 Cooling fan belt routing with rear A/C—3.5L Engine

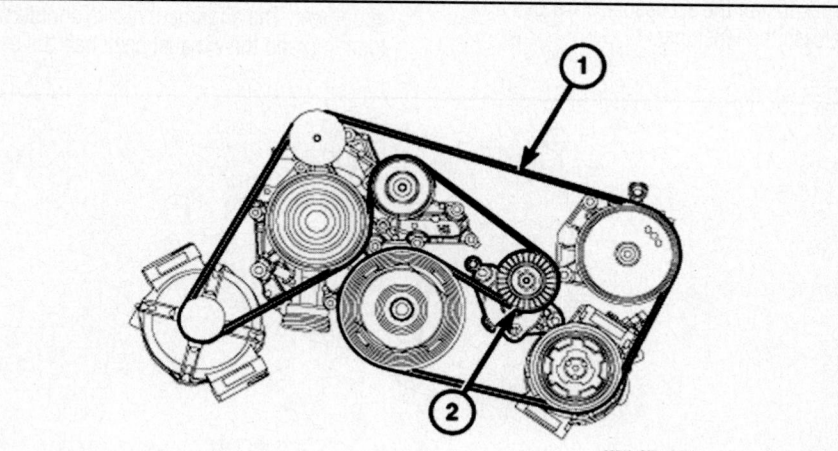

Fig. 24 Accessory Belt Routing—3.5L Engine

INSPECTION

See Figure 28.

Although many manufacturers recommend that the drive belt(s) be inspected every 30,000 miles (48,000 km) or more, it is really a good idea to check them at least once a year, or at every major fluid change.

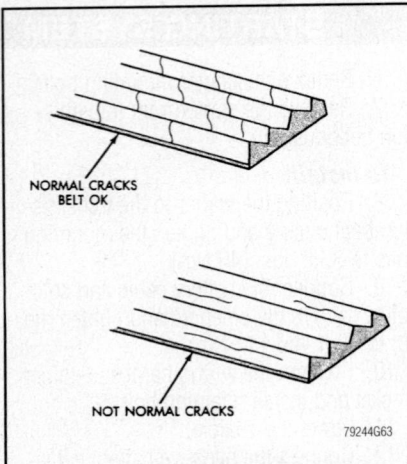

Fig. 28 Inspect the wear patterns for the serpentine drive belt.

Whichever interval you choose, the belts should be checked for wear or damage. Obviously, a damaged drive belt can cause problems should it give way while the vehicle is in operation. But, improper length belts (too short or long), as well as excessively worn belts, can also cause problems. Loose accessory drive belts can lead to poor engine cooling and diminished output from the alternator, air conditioning compressor or power steering pump. A belt that is too tight places a severe strain on the driven unit and can wear out bearings quickly.

Serpentine drive belts should be inspected for rib chunking (pieces of the ribs breaking off), severe glazing, frayed cords or other visible damage. Any belt which is missing sections of 2 or more adjacent ribs which are ½ in. (13mm) or longer must be replaced. You might want to note that serpentine belts do tend to form small cracks across the backing. If the only wear you find is in the form of one or more cracks are across the backing and NOT parallel to the ribs, the belt is still good and does not need to be replaced.

ADJUSTMENT

Periodic drive belt tensioning is not necessary, because an automatic spring-loaded tensioner is used with these belts to maintain proper adjustment at all times.

REMOVAL & INSTALLATION

3.0L Engine

See Figures 23, 25 and 26.

1. Remove the radiator fan. Refer to Engine Fan.
2. Rotate the crankshaft pulley clockwise and walk the fan drive belt off of the crankshaft pulley.
3. Rotate the accessory drive belt ten-

sioner counterclockwise to release the belt tension.
4. Remove the accessory drive belt.

To install:

5. Position the accessory drive belt around every pulley except the water pump pulley.
6. Rotate the drive belt tensioner clockwise, install the accessory drive belt and release the tensioner.
7. Position fan drive belt on water pump pulley.
8. Position fan drive belt on crankshaft pulley.

➡**Use only wire ties with nylon locks, not metal.**

9. Working from the back side of the crankshaft pulley, insert a nylon wire tie through one of the holes in the pulley.
10. Use a nylon wire tie to hold fan drive belt in place.
11. Tighten the wire tie to hold the drive belt in position.
12. Slowly rotate crankshaft pulley clockwise
13. Make sure fan drive belt is fully seated.
14. Install the radiator fan.

3.5L Engine

See Figures 30 and 31.

1. Remove the radiator fan. Refer to Engine Fan.
2. Rotate the accessory drive belt tensioner counterclockwise to release the belt tension.
3. Remove the accessory drive belt.

To install:

4. Position the accessory drive belt around every pulley except one.
5. Rotate the drive belt tensioner clockwise, install the accessory drive belt and release the tensioner.

6. Install the radiator fan.

CAMSHAFT AND VALVE LIFTERS

REMOVAL & INSTALLATION

3.0L Engine

Left Camshafts

See Figure 29.

✷✷ WARNING

Replacement of the camshaft will also require replacement of the finger followers and hydraulic lifters.

1. Disconnect negative battery cable.
2. Remove engine appearance cover.
3. Rotate the engine to Top Dead Center (TDC) using the crankshaft damper bolt.
4. Remove the main engine wiring harness retainers at the rear of the cylinder head cover.
5. Remove the EGR valve.
6. Remove the charge air inlet tube.
7. Disconnect the fuel line hoses at the fuel rail, high pressure pump using Special Tool 9539 Pliers.
8. Disconnect the fuel lines at the left cylinder head.
9. Remove the fuel pipe bundle and set it aside.
10. Remove the oil filter housing support bracket.
11. Remove the cylinder head cover.

➡**The left exhaust camshaft gear alignment mark is located in the gear tooth valley. The left intake camshaft gear mark is located on the outside of the tooth.**

12. Check the camshaft timing gears for alignment. The alignment marks should be touching and the exhaust camshaft drive

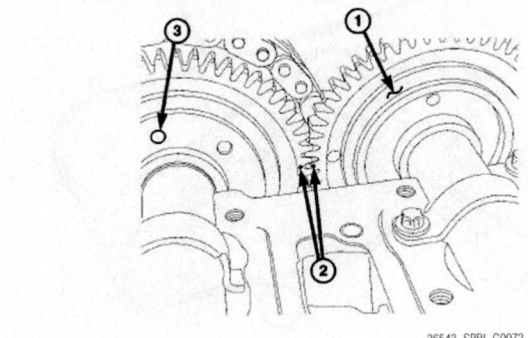

Fig. 29 Intake camshaft gear (1), alignment marks (2) and exhaust cam gear alignment pin (3)—3.0L Engine

gear alignment pin should be located at approximately 12 o'clock, when viewed from the front camshaft seal.

13. Rotate the engine by the vibration damper bolt, past TDC to gain access to the lower camshaft drive gear bolt, and remove the bolt.

14. Rotate the engine back to TDC and check the camshaft gear alignment.

15. Remove the timing chain tensioner.

16. Matchmark the timing chain in relation to the camshaft sprocket.

17. Tie a strap around the timing chain and secure it to the camshaft sprocket.

18. Remove the remaining camshaft drive gear bolts and separate the drive gear from camshaft gear.

19. Remove the intake and exhaust camshaft retainers.

20. Remove the left cylinder head camshafts.

To install:

21. Clean all of the mating surfaces.

22. Lubricate the camshafts with clean engine oil.

23. Carefully install the camshafts onto the cylinder head journals and align the camshaft gear timing marks.

24. Install the camshaft retainers and tighten each retaining bolt to 80 in. lbs. (9 Nm).

25. After the camshafts are properly installed in cylinder head cover check end play of camshafts with a dial indicator.

➡**The left exhaust camshaft gear alignment mark is located in the gear tooth valley. The left intake camshaft gear mark is located on the outside of the tooth.**

➡**The alignment marks should be touching and the exhaust camshaft drive gear alignment pin should be located at approximately 12 o'clock, when viewed from the front camshaft seal.**

26. Ensure the proper positioning of the camshaft gear alignment marks and install the camshaft driven gear onto the exhaust camshaft alignment dowel.

27. Install two of the drive gear bolts and tighten the bolts to 13 ft. lbs. (18 Nm).

28. Ensure the proper positioning of the timing chain to drive gear matchmarks and remove the tie strap.

29. Rotate the engine by the crankshaft damper bolt enough to install the third camshaft drive gear bolt. Tighten the bolt to 13 ft. lbs. (18 Nm).

30. Rotate the engine back to TDC and check camshaft gear alignment.

31. Install the timing chain tensioner.

32. Install the left front camshaft oil seal.

33. Install the left rear camshaft oil seal.

➡**Care must be taken not to get any engine sealant on the camshaft journals of the cylinder head cover.**

34. Install a ⅛ inch bead of Mopar® Engine RTV Gen II sealant to the underside of the cylinder head cover.

✱✱ WARNING

The cylinder head cover bolts are different lengths. Do not use the wrong length bolts or engine damage may result.

35. Carefully position the cylinder head cover and install the bolts into their original position. Refer to Valve Cover.

36. Install the EGR valve.

✱✱ CAUTION

The fuel injector sealing washers MUST be replaced. DO NOT use the old sealing washers or double the sealing washers.

➡**Care must be taken not to apply any lubricant to the fuel injector nozzles.**

37. Install the fuel injectors. Tighten the injector retaining claw bolt to 60 inch lbs. (7 Nm) and then an additional 180°.

38. Re-position and secure the engine harness.

39. Install the left fuel rail. Tighten the fuel rail bolts to 98 inch lbs. (11 Nm).

40. Position the return fuel lines and secure to the injectors. Push down on the release lock tab to secure.

41. Connect the fuel injector electrical connectors.

42. Install the left rear engine cover bracket.

43. Install the high pressure fuel lines from the fuel rail to injectors. Tighten the line connections to 20 ft. lbs. (27 Nm).

44. Install the fuel line from the high pressure pump to the left fuel rail. Tighten the retaining bolt to 22 ft. lbs. (30 Nm).

45. Install the fuel supply line to the fuel filter and high pressure pump.

46. Connect both fuel lines at the high pressure pump.

47. Install the air filter housing and tube.

48. Connect the negative battery cable.

49. Install the engine appearance cover.

50. Start the engine and check for leaks.

Right Camshafts

See Figure 29.

✱✱ WARNING

Replacement of the camshaft will also require replacement of the finger followers and hydraulic lifters.

1. Disconnect the negative battery cable.

2. Remove the engine appearance cover.

3. Rotate the engine to Top Dead Center (TDC) using the crankshaft damper bolt.

4. Remove the intake air resonator.

5. Remove the vacuum pump.

6. Remove the oil level indicator tube retaining bolt at the right cylinder head cover.

7. Remove the crankcase breather assembly from the right cylinder head cover.

8. Remove the cylinder head cover.

➡**The right exhaust camshaft gear alignment mark is located in the gear tooth valley. The left intake camshaft gear mark is located on the outside of the tooth.**

9. Check the camshaft timing gears for alignment. The alignment marks should be touching and the exhaust camshaft drive gear alignment pin should be located at approximately 12 o'clock, when viewed from the front camshaft seal.

10. Rotate the engine by the vibration damper bolt, past TDC to gain access to the lower camshaft drive gear bolt, and remove the bolt.

11. Rotate the engine back to TDC and check camshaft gear alignment.

12. Remove the timing chain tensioner.

13. Matchmark the timing chain in relation to the camshaft drive gear.

14. Tie a strap the timing chain to the drive gear.

15. Remove the remaining camshaft drive gear bolts and separate the drive gear from camshaft gear.

16. Remove the intake and exhaust camshaft retainers.

17. Remove the right cylinder head camshafts.

To install:

18. Clean all mating surfaces and lubricate camshafts with clean engine oil.

19. Carefully install camshafts onto cylinder head journals and align the camshaft gear timing marks.

20. Install the camshaft retainers and tighten each retaining bolt to 80 inch lbs. (9 Nm).

21. After camshafts are properly installed in cylinder head cover check end play of camshafts with a dial indicator.

➡ If the camshaft endplay is not within specification, replace the cylinder head and cylinder head cover.

➡ The right exhaust camshaft gear alignment mark is located in the gear tooth valley. The right intake camshaft gear mark is located on the outside of the tooth. The alignment marks should be touching and the exhaust camshaft drive gear alignment pin should be located at approximately 12 o'clock, when viewed from the front camshaft seal.

22. Ensure the proper positioning of the camshaft gear alignment marks and install the camshaft driven gear onto the exhaust camshaft alignment dowel.

23. Install two of the drive gear bolts and tighten to 13 ft. lbs. (18 Nm).

24. Ensure the proper positioning of the timing chain to drive gear matchmarks and remove the tie strap.

25. Rotate the engine by the crankshaft damper bolt enough to install the third camshaft drive gear bolt. Tighten the bolt to 13 ft. lbs. (18 Nm).

26. Rotate the engine back to TDC and check camshaft gear alignment.

✳✳ WARNING

Turn the engine clockwise only!

27. Install the timing chain tensioner.

➡ Care must be taken not to get any engine sealer on the camshaft journals.

28. Apply a ⅛ inch bead of Mopar® Engine RTV Sealant to the cylinder head cover.

29. Install the camshaft seal into position.

30. Install the cylinder head cover. Tighten the bolts in sequence as follows:
   a. Tighten the bolts to 35 inch lbs. (4 Nm).
   b. Tighten the bolts to 53 inch lbs. (6 Nm).
   c. Then tighten the bolts to 75 inch lbs. (8.4 Nm).

31. Install the oil separator housing adapter with a new camshaft seal and tighten fasteners to 80 inch lbs. (9 Nm).

32. Install the oil separator and tighten fasteners to 80 inch lbs. (9 Nm).

33. Secure the transmission tube fastener to the engine cover bracket.

34. Secure the heater hose bracket to the cylinder head cover.

35. Secure the vacuum pump hose pipe to the cylinder head cover.

36. Install the fuel injectors. Refer to Fuel Injectors.

37. Connect the camshaft position sensor and fuel injector wiring harness connectors.

38. Connect the return fuel hose to each injector.

39. Install the fuel rail, high pressure fuel lines and injector cover.

40. Secure the oil dipstick tube to the cylinder head and tighten the bolt to 98 inch lbs. (11 Nm).

41. Install the vacuum pump.

42. Install the air control valve resonator.

43. Install the air cleaner outlet tube to the turbocharger and secure the air cleaner housing cover.

44. Install the engine appearance cover.

45. Connect the negative battery cable.

46. Start the engine and check for leaks.

3.5L Engine

Left Camshafts

See Figures 32 and 33.

✳✳ WARNING

Replacement of the camshaft will also require replacement of the finger followers and hydraulic lifters.

1. Disconnect the negative battery cable.

2. Disconnect the remote ground cable by the accelerator pedal.

3. Remove the air intake assembly.

4. Remove the left cylinder head cover. Refer to Cylinder Head Cover.

5. Place a drift into the camshaft adjuster to lock it into position.

6. Hold the back of the camshaft with a Torx bit while removing the center valve from the front of the camshaft.

7. Remove the pulse wheel from the camshaft.

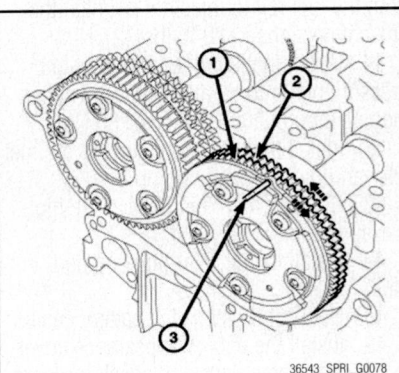

Fig. 30 Locking adjuster (1) to camshaft (2) using Drift (3)—3.5L Engine

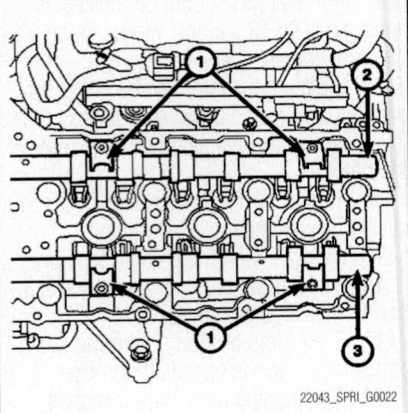

Fig. 31 Remove the camshaft hold downs (1) to remove the camshafts (2,3) from the adjuster—3.5L Engine Left Camshafts

✳✳ CAUTION

Use care not to nick or scratch the journals when removing the camshaft.

8. Remove the camshaft hold downs.

9. Remove the camshafts from the camshaft adjuster.

To install:

10. Install the camshafts into the camshaft adjuster.

11. Install the camshaft hold downs.

12. Install a new pulse wheel onto the camshaft adjusters.

13. Remove the drift from the camshaft adjuster.

14. Hold the back of the camshaft with a Torx® bit while installing the center valve into the front of the camshaft.

15. Install the left cylinder head cover.

16. Install the air intake assembly.

17. Connect the remote ground.

18. Connect the negative battery cable.

19. Start the engine and check for leaks.

Right Camshafts

See Figures 32 through 36.

✳✳ WARNING

Replacement of the camshaft will also require replacement of the finger followers and hydraulic lifters.

1. Disconnect the negative battery cable.

2. Remove the air intake assembly.

3. Turn the engine in the direction of rotation until the engine is set to 40 degrees after Top Dead Center (TDC).

4. Remove the air control valve on the right cylinder head.

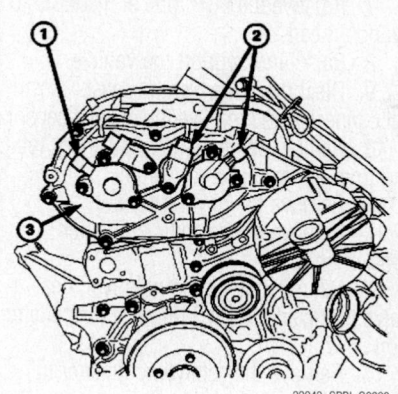

Fig. 32 Disconnect the camshaft position sensors (1,2) and then remove the upper front cover (3)—3.5L Engine Right Camshaft

5. Remove the air control valve gasket and bracket.

6. Remove the centrifugal oil separator cover.

7. Remove the center bolt from the oil separator.

8. Remove the oil separator.

9. Remove the camshaft plug.

10. Disconnect the camshaft position sensors in the right front upper cover.

11. Remove the upper front cover on the right cylinder head.

12. Remove the bolts from the engine wiring harness on the right cylinder head cover.

13. Disconnect the engine wiring harness and secure it out of the way.

14. Disconnect and remove the ignition coils.

15. Remove the cylinder head cover.

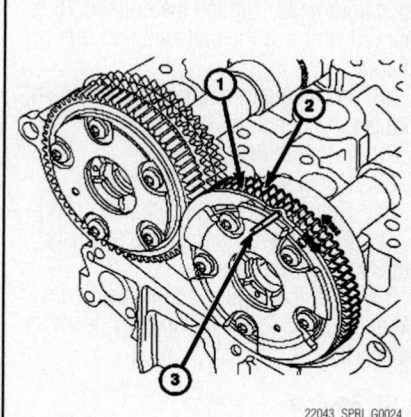

Fig. 33 Install a drift (3) into the camshaft to hold the split gears (1,2) in place—3.5L Engine Right Camshaft

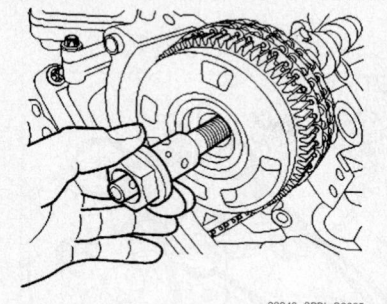

Fig. 34 Use a Torx® bit to the end of the camshaft while removing the center valve from the camshaft adjuster in the exhaust camshaft—3.5L Engine Right Camshaft

16. Install a drift into the camshaft to hold the split gears in place.

17. Use a Torx® bit to the end of the camshaft while removing the center valve from the camshaft adjuster in the intake camshaft.

18. Remove the intake camshaft pulse wheel.

19. Use a Torx® bit to the end of the camshaft while removing the center valve from the camshaft adjuster in the exhaust camshaft.

20. Remove the exhaust camshaft pulse wheel.

21. Support the timing chain to prevent the chain from slipping from the crankshaft sprocket.

22. Remove the exhaust camshaft adjuster.

23. Remove the intake camshaft adjuster.

24. Remove the camshafts.

To install:

25. Make sure that the crankshaft is set to 40 degrees after top dead center.

26. Install the camshafts.

27. Install the camshaft hold downs.

28. Install the intake camshaft adjuster.

29. Install the exhaust camshaft adjuster.

30. Remove the drift from the camshaft adjuster.

31. Make sure that when the timing chain is installed, the camshaft adjuster marks line up as illustrated.

32. Use a Torx® bit to the end of the camshaft while installing the center valve to the camshaft adjuster in the exhaust camshaft.

33. Install the exhaust camshaft pulse wheel.

34. Use a Torx® bit to the end of the camshaft while installing the center valve

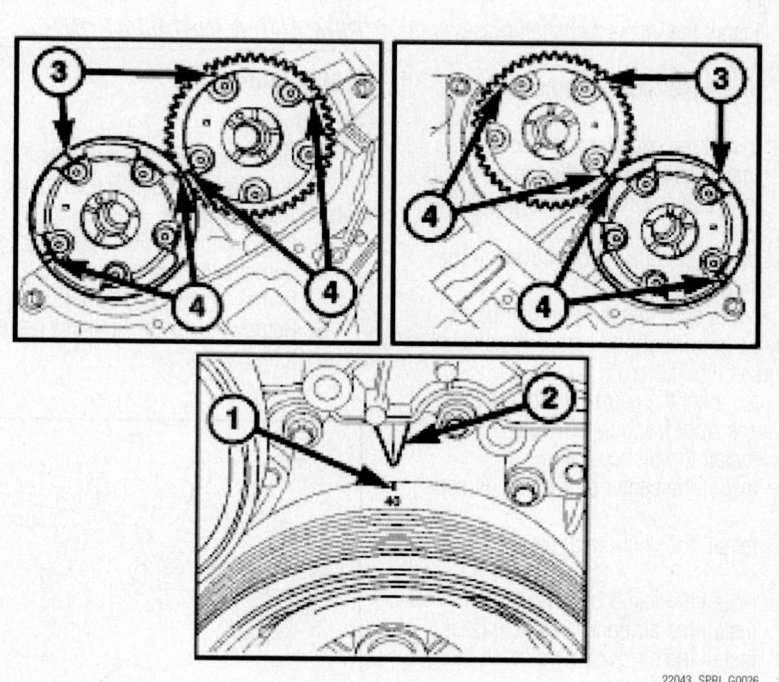

Fig. 35 Make sure that when the timing chain is installed, the camshaft adjuster marks line up as illustrated—3.5L Engine Right Camshaft

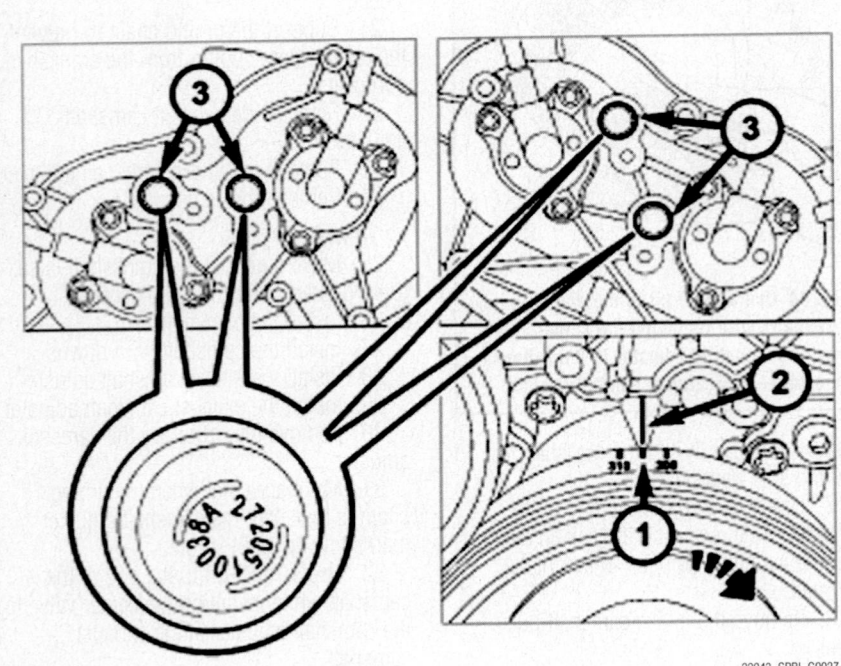

Fig. 36 Make sure that the number stamp can be seen through the camshaft sensor holes (3)—3.5L Engine Right Camshaft

from the camshaft adjuster in the intake camshaft.

35. Install the intake camshaft pulse wheel.

36. Install the camshaft adjuster center bolts.

37. Install the cylinder head cover.

38. Install and connect the ignition coils.

39. Install and connect the engine wiring harness.

40. Install the upper front cover on the right cylinder head.

41. Make sure that the number stamp can be seen through the camshaft sensor holes (see illustration).

42. Connect the camshaft position sensors in the right front upper cover.

43. Install the oil separator.

44. Install the center bolt to the oil separator.

45. Install the centrifugal oil separator cover.

46. Install the camshaft plug.

47. Install the air control valve gasket.

48. Install the air control valve on the right cylinder head.

49. Install the air control valve bracket.

50. Install the air intake assembly.

51. Connect the negative battery cable.

52. Start the engine and check for leaks.

CATALYTIC CONVERTER

REMOVAL & INSTALLATION

3.0L Engine

See Figure 37.

1. Disconnect the negative battery cable.

2. If equipped, disconnect the auxiliary battery negative cable.

3. Remove the air box assembly.

4. Remove the engine cover.

5. Remove the turbocharger heat shield.

6. Remove the catalytic converter elbow to turbocharger bolts.

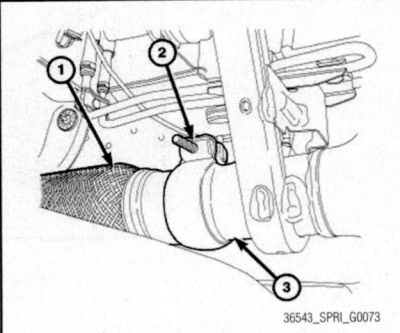

Fig. 37 Catalytic converter (1), clamp (2) and particulate filter (3)—3.0L Engine

7. Remove the EGR tube at manifold to cylinder head.

8. Raise and support the vehicle.

9. Disconnect the oxygen sensor electrical connector and remove the oxygen sensor.

10. Remove the temperature sensor tubing from the catalytic converter.

11. Remove the oxygen sensor.

12. Remove the catalytic converter bracket bolt.

13. Saturate the clamp nuts with heat valve lubricant. Allow 5 minutes for penetration.

14. Remove the catalytic converter to diesel particulate filter clamp.

15. Remove the catalytic converter from diesel particulate filter.

16. Remove the catalytic converter assembly from the vehicle.

To install:

17. Position the catalytic converter into the vehicle.

18. Install the catalytic converter to the diesel particulate filter clamp. Do not tighten at this time.

19. Install the oxygen sensor. Tighten to 36 ft. lbs. (50 Nm).

20. Install the catalytic converter temperature sensor. Tighten to 33 ft. lbs. (45 Nm).

21. Install the turbocharger elbow to the catalytic converter bracket bolt. Do not tighten at this time.

22. Check the exhaust system for contact with the body panels. Make any adjustments, if necessary.

23. Install the catalytic converter bracket bolt. Tighten to 70 inch lbs. (8 Nm).

24. Tighten clamp nuts to 15 ft. lbs. (20 Nm).

25. Lower the vehicle.

26. Install the rear EGR tube.

27. Install the catalytic converter to turbocharger bolts. Tighten the bolts to 15 ft. lbs. (20 Nm) and then add another 90° of rotation.

28. Install the turbocharger heat shield. Tighten to 70 inch lbs. (8 Nm).

29. Install the engine cover.

30. Install the air box assembly.

31. Connect the negative battery cable.

32. If equipped, connect the auxiliary battery negative cable.

33. Start the vehicle and inspect for exhaust leaks. Repair any exhaust leaks as necessary.

3.5L Engine

See Figure 38.

1. Disconnect negative battery cable.

2. Raise and support vehicle.

3. Remove underbody panel.

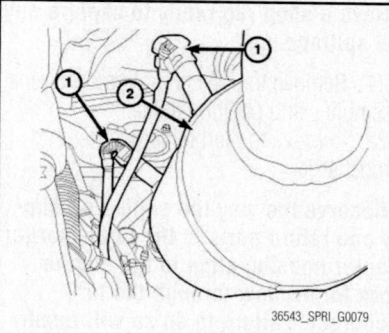

Fig. 38 Oxygen sensors (1) and catalytic converter (2)—3.5L Engine

4. Disconnect LH and RH oxygen sensor electrical connectors.

5. Remove LH and RH upstream oxygen sensors.

6. Remove LH and RH manifold to catalytic converter bolts.

7. Remove catalytic converter to muffler flange bolts.

8. Remove catalytic converter from vehicle.

To install:

9. Position catalytic converter.

10. Install LH and RH catalytic converter to manifold bolts. Do not tighten at this time.

11. Install catalytic converter to muffler flange bolts. Do not tighten at this time.

12. Make sure the muffler/catalytic converter assembly is correctly positioned and the properly aligned. The minimum clearance between components is 25mm (1 inch).

13. Tighten catalytic converter to exhaust manifold bolts to 35 ft. lbs. (47 Nm).

14. Tighten catalytic converter to muffler to 35 ft. lbs. (47 Nm).

15. Install LH and RH oxygen sensors.

16. Connect LH and RH oxygen sensor electrical connectors.

17. Install under body panel.

18. Lower the vehicle.

19. Connect negative battery cable.

20. Start the engine and inspect for exhaust leaks. Repair exhaust leaks as necessary.

CRANKSHAFT DAMPER

REMOVAL & INSTALLATION

3.0L Engine

See Figure 39.

1. Disconnect negative battery cable.
2. Remove the air cleaner assembly.
3. Drain the cooling system.

4. Remove the lower radiator hose.
5. Remove the serpentine belt.
6. Remove the starter blank.
7. Install the Flywheel Locking Tool 9102.
8. Remove the vibration damper bolt.

❊❊ CAUTION

Care must be taken when removing the damper. DO NOT damage or gouge the front crankshaft seal.

9. Using Vibration Damper Puller 9544, remove the vibration damper.

To install:

❊❊ CAUTION

Care must be taken when installing the damper. DO NOT damage or gouge the front crankshaft seal

➡ **To prevent potential oil leaks, DO NOT touch the front crankshaft inner seal.**

10. Align the alignment key in the crankshaft with the key way in the damper and install the vibration damper.

11. Install the vibration bolt (1). Tighten bolt to 154 ft. lbs., plus 180 degrees (210 Nm plus 180 degrees).

12. Remove Flywheel Locking Tool 9102.

13. Install the starter blank.
14. Install the serpentine belt.
15. Fill the cooling system.
16. Install the lower radiator hose.
17. Install the cleaner assembly.
18. Connect negative battery cable.

3.5L Engine

1. Disconnect negative battery cable.
2. Install the crankshaft locking tool.
3. Remove accessory drive belt Refer to Accessory Drive Belt.
4. Raise vehicle on hoist.

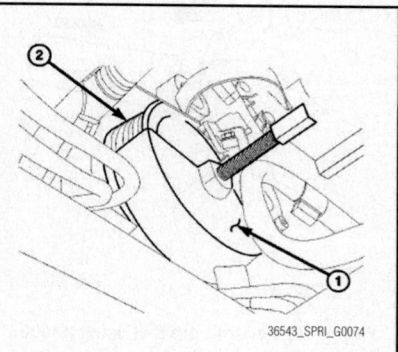

Fig. 39 Puller (1) and Damper (2)

5. Remove vibration damper bolt.
6. Remove crankshaft damper.

To install:

7. Raise vehicle on hoist.

8. Install the vibration damper bolt. Tighten the bolt to 148 ft. lbs. (200 Nm).

9. Install the accessory drive belt. Refer to Accessory Drive Belt.

10. Remove the crankshaft locking tool.

11. Connect negative battery cable.

CRANKSHAFT FRONT SEAL

REMOVAL & INSTALLATION

3.0L Engine

See Figure 40.

1. Disconnect negative battery cable.
2. Raise and safely support the vehicle.
3. Remove both front lower splash shields.

4. Remove the transmission thermal bypass valve and the cooler lines between the block and transmission.

5. Remove the starter blank.

6. Install Special Tool 9102 Flywheel Locking Tool.

7. Release the accessory drive belt tension by resetting the drive belt tensioner and installing a retaining pin.

8. Remove the vibration damper bolt.

9. Install Special Tool 9544 Crankshaft Damper Puller.

10. Remove the vibration damper.

❊❊ WARNING

Use care when removing the crankshaft seal not to damage or gouge the timing chain cover.

11. Using suitable seal puller, remove the front crankshaft seal.

To install:

12. Install crankshaft oil seal using Special Tool 8936A Seal Installer.

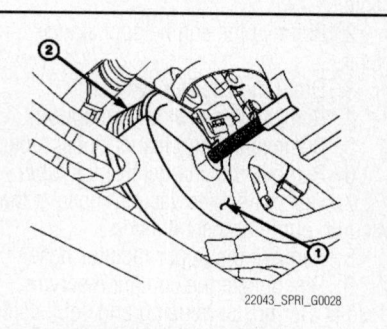

Fig. 40 Use Special Tool 9544 (1) to remove the crankshaft damper (2)—3.0L Diesel Engine shown

13. Align the alignment key in the crankshaft with the key way in the damper and install the crankshaft damper. Tighten the bolt to 224 ft. lbs. (304 Nm) plus 90 degrees.

14. Position the accessory drive belt back onto the pulleys and release the belt tensioner.

15. Remove Special Tool 9102 flywheel locking tool.

16. Install the transmission thermal bypass valve and transmission cooler lines.

17. Install both underbody splash shields.

18. Lower the vehicle.

19. Connect the negative battery cable.

20. Start the engine and check for leaks.

3.5L Engine

1. Remove the front cover. Refer Front Cover.

2. Remove crankshaft seal using an appropriately sized socket.

❊❊ CAUTION

Do not nick shaft seal surface or seal bore.

3. Shaft seal lip surface must be free of varnish, dirt or nicks. Polish with 400 grit paper if necessary.

To install:

4. Install crankshaft seal into the front cover.

5. Install the front cover. Refer to Front Cover.

CYLINDER HEAD

REMOVAL & INSTALLATION

3.0L Engine

Left Side

See Figures 41 through 45.

1. Disconnect the negative battery cable.

2. Remove the engine appearance cover.

3. Drain the cooling system.

4. Remove the strut tower support.

5. Remove the air cleaner outlet tube.

6. Remove the charge air inlet tube.

7. Disconnect the vacuum hose at the vacuum pump and set it aside.

8. Remove the upper radiator hose.

9. Disconnect the coolant reservoir hose at thermostat housing and set it aside.

10. Disconnect the fuel supply and return hose quick connects at the left cylinder head cover.

11. Loosen the high pressure fuel pipes at the fuel rail and disconnect the high pressure fuel pipes at the left injectors.

12. Disconnect the high pressure fuel line at the high pressure pump.

13. Disconnect the fuel rail solenoid wiring harness connector and remove the left fuel rail along with the fuel rail transfer pipe.

14. Remove the low pressure fuel supply and return pipe bundle fasteners.

15. Disconnect the right fuel rail pressure sensor and remove the fuel rail.

16. Disconnect the camshaft position sensor (CMP), the right fuel injector wiring harness connectors, the right return fuel hoses from the injectors.

17. Remove the return fuel bundle fasteners.

18. Disconnect the water in fuel sensor, if equipped, and the turbocharger servo motor harness connectors.

19. Remove the fuel filter bracket fasteners.

20. Disconnect the fuel return hose bundle, engine ground strap, at the right front of the intake manifold.

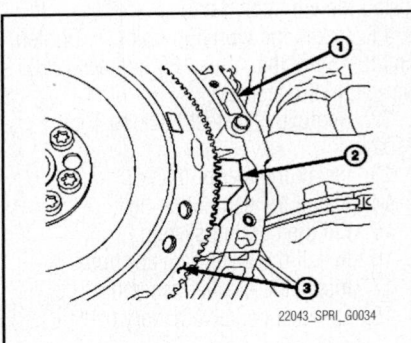

Fig. 41 Install Special Tool 9102 (2) into the starter access blank to lock the ring gear (3) into place—3.0L Engine

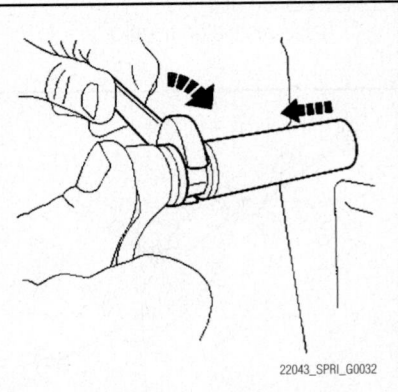

Fig. 42 Make a roll pin tool using a tube, nut, bolt and washer to remove the roll pin—3.0L Engine - Left cylinder head

➡Have a shop rag ready to capture any fuel spillage.

21. Remove the fuel filter, hose and pipe assemblies and position aside.

22. Remove the turbocharger. Refer to Turbocharger.

➡Observe the way the engine oil supply and return ports in the turbocharger adapter housing align to the engine block for oil flow through the turbocharger. Failure to do so will result in immediate turbocharger failure.

23. Remove turbocharger oil housing adapter.

24. Disconnect the swirl valve actuator, glow plugs, EGR pressure sensor and coolant temperature sensor wiring harness connector.

25. Remove the main engine wiring harness fasteners and position the harness out of the way.

26. Disconnect the EGR coolant pipe from the rear of the EGR housing.

27. Remove the EGR valve.

➡The intake manifold is of the split design meaning that there are two halves. Whenever the intake manifold is removed, inspect the shared coolant passage in the front of the intake manifold for leaks, repair as necessary.

28. Remove the intake manifold. Refer to Intake Manifold.

29. Remove the accessory drive belt. Refer to Accessory Drive Belt.

30. Remove the two idler pulleys.

31. Remove the belt tensioner.

32. Rotate the engine by the crankshaft damper bolt until cylinder No. 1 is at Top Dead Center (TDC).

33. Raise and safely support the vehicle.

34. Remove the right side starter blank.

35. Disconnect the hydraulic cooling fan lines and capture the fluid in an approved and clearly marked container.

36. Remove the front oil pan retaining bolts.

37. Lower the vehicle.

38. Remove the left rear heater hose retainer.

39. Remove the left fuel injectors.

40. Disconnect the vacuum supply hose.

41. Remove the oil filter housing bracket.

➡The timing cover is sealed with Mopar® sealant that may be difficult when separating components. If it is difficult to separate, heat the sealed edges or area with a heat gun. DO NOT use any heat source that works with flame.

42. Remove the left cylinder head cover.

43. Observe the left camshaft gear alignment marks on the rear of the camshaft gears. If they are together, continue with the next step. If the left camshaft alignment marks are separated, rotate the engine by the vibration damper another 360 degrees, until camshaft marks align together and the vibration damper reaches TDC.

44. Raise and safely support the vehicle.

45. Install Special Tool 9102 Crankshaft Lock into the starter access blank.

46. Lower the vehicle.

47. Remove the cooling fan module.

48. Remove the vibration damper.

49. Remove the front timing chain cover.

50. Matchmark the balance shaft position to the engine block and timing chain.

51. Matchmark the timing chain to crankshaft gear and camshaft drive gear relation.

52. Raise and safely support the vehicle.

53. Remove Special Tool 9102 Locking Tool.

54. Lower the vehicle.

55. Remove the high pressure fuel pump.

56. Rotate the engine and remove the left camshaft drive gear lower bolt.

➡**The left exhaust camshaft drive gear dowel pin should align at approximately the 12 O'clock position when viewing through the camshaft seal access hole.**

57. Rotate the engine back to TDC and check the alignment marks at the balance shaft, camshaft gear and crankshaft gear.

58. Remove the timing chain tensioner.

59. Remove the remaining left camshaft drive gear retaining bolts.

60. Separate the left camshaft drive gear and chain from camshaft.

61. Remove the left camshaft retainers (1 and 2) and camshafts.

62. Remove the left camshaft drive gear. Make a roll pin tool by using a tube, nut, bolt and washer. Place the nut on the bolt and the bolt through the tube. Thread the bolt into the roll pin and turn the nut to remove the roll pin (as illustrated).

63. Remove the left lower timing chain guide fastener and guide.

64. Remove the left cylinder head glow plugs.

65. Remove the cylinder head and gasket from engine block.

To install:

66. Clean all remaining gasket material from the mating surfaces.

67. Position the cylinder head and gasket on the engine block.

➡**If new cylinder head bolts are used, do not lubricate the new cylinder head bolts. They already are coated with an anti scuff treatment.**

68. Lightly coat the cylinder head bolts with clean engine oil.

69. Tighten the cylinder head mounting bolts as follows:

   a. Tighten the M12 bolts (1-8) in sequence to 44 ft. lbs. (60 Nm).

   b. Tighten the M8 bolts (9-10) to 15 ft. lbs. (20 Nm).

   c. Tighten the M12 bolts in sequence an additional 90 degrees.

   d. Verify the M8 bolts again to 15 ft. lbs. (20 Nm).

   e. Tighten the M12 bolts in sequence an additional 90 degrees.

70. Install the followers and tappets into their original positions.

71. Install the glow plugs and tighten to 11 ft. lbs. (15 Nm).

72. Install the camshafts. Refer to Camshaft.

73. Align the camshaft marks so the alignment marks are facing each other.

74. Insert the timing chain, through the cylinder head, and on to the camshaft drive gear.

75. Align the balance shaft with the matchmark.

76. Once the camshaft drive gear is mated with the timing chain, install the camshaft drive gear on to the camshaft and assure the balance shaft is aligned properly.

77. Install the upper two of the three camshaft drive gear bolts.

78. Install the left lower and upper timing chain guide.

79. Install the timing chain tensioner.

80. Rotate the engine by the crankshaft damper bolt enough to gain access to the third camshaft drive gear bolt hole.

81. Install the third camshaft drive gear retaining bolt and tighten the bolt to 13 ft. lbs. (18 Nm).

✲✲ WARNING

If the camshaft, balance shaft and or crankshaft alignment marks are not aligned properly immediate damage to the engine will occur. If the camshafts, balance shaft and or crankshaft do not align properly after rotating the engine to the original starting point, STOP and begin the alignment procedure again.

82. Rotate the engine back to TDC by the crankshaft damper bolt until the crankshaft, camshaft and balance shaft align TDC again.

✲✲ WARNING

Check that all the timing chain fits properly on all the timing gears. Failure to do so will result in immediate engine damage.

83. Install the timing chain cover and tighten the bolts to 74 inch lbs. (8.4 Nm).

84. Raise and safely support the vehicle.

85. Tighten the five front oil pan-to-timing cover bolts to 15 ft. lbs. (20 Nm).

86. Install Special Tool 9102 Crankshaft Lock into the starter access blank.

87. Lower the vehicle.

88. Install the crankshaft damper and tighten the bolts to 148 ft. lbs. (200 Nm) plus 90°.

89. Apply a 1.5mm continuous bead of Mopar® Engine Sealant RTV around the diameter of the left cylinder head cover, and install the cover with new camshaft seals.

90. Tighten the bolts for the cylinder head cover as follows:

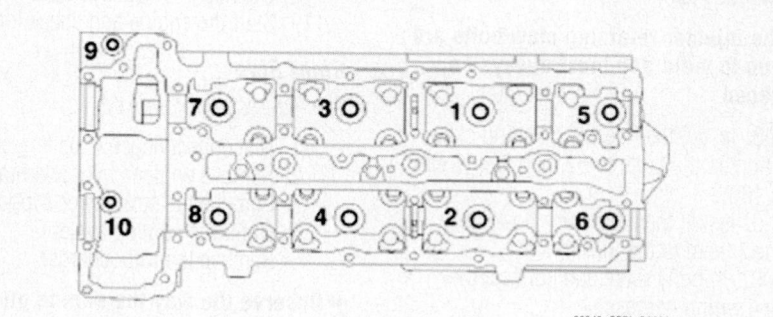

22043_SPRI_G0033

Fig. 43 Left cylinder head torque sequence—3.0L Engine

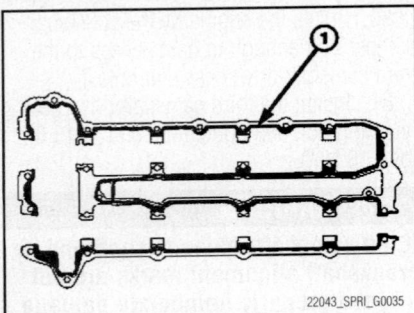

Fig. 44 Apply a bead of RTV (1) around the diameter of the cylinder head cover—3.0L Engine

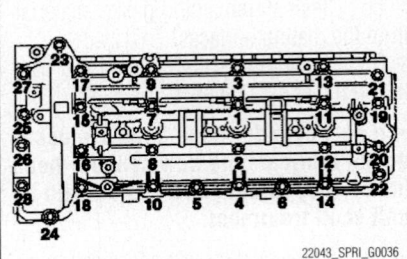

Fig. 45 Left cylinder head cover torque sequence—3.0L Engine

a. Tighten the bolts in sequence to 35 inch lbs. (4 Nm).

b. Tighten the bolts in sequence to 53 inch lbs. (6 Nm).

c. Then tighten the bolts in sequence to 75 inch lbs. (8.4 Nm).

91. Install the oil filter housing bracket and tighten the bolts to 122 inch lbs. (13.8 Nm).

92. Install the high pressure pump and tighten bolts to 120 inch lbs. (13.5 Nm).

93. Install the belt idler pulleys and tighten the bolts to 43 ft. lbs. (58 Nm).

94. Install the drive belt tensioner and tighten the bolts to 43 ft. lbs. (58 Nm).

95. Install the accessory drive belt.

96. Install the intake manifold. Tighten bolts to 12 ft. lbs. (16 Nm), starting in the middle and tightening in a cross pattern outward until reaching the upper thermostat bolts on the right front manifold.

➡ **The right intake manifold upper thermostat housing bolts should be tightened to 74 inch lbs. (8.4 Nm).**

➡ **The fuel injector sealing washers MUST be replaced. DO NOT use the old sealing washers or double the sealing washers.**

97. Lubricate the fuel injector body and install the left fuel injectors and new lower sealing washers.

➡ **The injector retaining claw bolts are torque to yield and must always be replaced.**

98. Install the injector retaining claws and tighten the bolts to 62 inch lbs. (7 Nm) plus 180°.

99. Install the fuel return hoses and connect them to the injectors.

100. Properly route and connect the engine wiring harness.

101. Install the fuel rail. Refer to Fuel Injectors.

➡ **Inspect the fuel lines for wear or damage, look closely around the flange area. Replace as necessary. DO NOT over tighten.**

102. Install the high pressure fuel lines, including the fuel rail equalizing line. Tighten the line nuts to 20 ft. lbs. (27 Nm).

103. Install the fuel filter.

104. Install the turbocharger.

105. Install the air control valve and resonator.

106. Install the charge air cooler inlet pipe and resonator.

107. Install the cooling fan module.

108. Install the heater hose bracket and secure hoses.

109. Connect the vacuum pump supply hose.

110. Raise and safely support the vehicle.

111. Remove Special Tool 9102 and install the starter blank.

112. Connect the cooling fan hydraulic lines.

113. Lower the vehicle.

114. Refill the cooling system to the correct level.

115. Ensure the power steering system is filled to the correct level.

116. Install the strut tower support.

117. Install the engine appearance cover.

118. Connect the negative battery cable.

119. Start the engine and check for leaks.

Right Side

See Figures 46 through 60.

1. Disconnect negative battery cable.
2. Remove engine cover and brackets.
3. Remove the strut tower support.
4. Drain the cooling system.
5. Remove the turbocharger.

➡ **Observe the way the engine oil supply and return ports in the turbocharger adaptor align to the engine block for oil flow through the turbocharger. Failure**

to do so will result in immediate turbocharger failure.

6. Remove the turbocharger oil housing adaptor.

7. Remove the intake manifold.

8. Remove the accessory drive belt.

9. Remove the two idler pulleys.

10. Remove the belt tensioner.

11. Rotate the engine by the vibration damper bolt, to TDC.

12. Raise and support the vehicle.

13. Remove right side starter blank.

14. Disconnect the hydraulic cooling fan lines and capture the fluid in an approved and clearly marked container.

15. Remove the front oil pan retaining bolts.

16. Lower the vehicle.

17. Remove the breather/oil separator (1) assembly from the right cylinder head cover.

18. Remove the right fuel injectors (6).

19. Remove the fuel rail (3).

20. Disconnect the vacuum supply hose from the vacuum pump (4).

21. Remove the vacuum pump (4).

➡ **If the cylinder head cover is difficult to remove, DO NOT PRY or damage the cover. Use a heat gun to warm the sealing surface until the cover can be removed.**

22. Remove the right cylinder head cover.

23. Observe the right camshaft gear alignment marks (2). If they are together, continue with the next step. If the right camshaft alignment marks are separated, rotate the engine by the vibration damper until camshaft marks align together and the vibration damper reaches TDC.

24. Raise and support the vehicle.

25. Install special tool No. 9102 crankshaft lock.

26. Lower the vehicle.

27. Remove the cooling fan module.

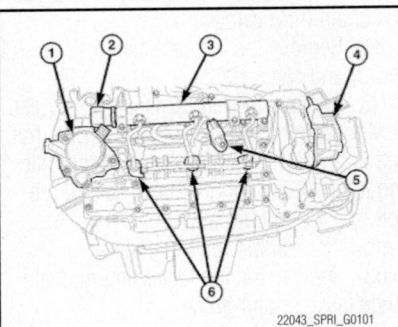

Fig. 46 Removing breather/oil separator, fuel injectors, fuel rail and vacuum pump—3.0L Engine

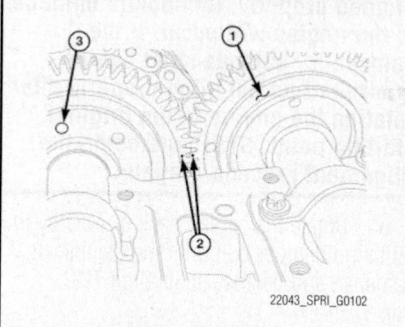

Fig. 47 Camshaft gear alignment marks—3.0L Engine

28. Remove the vibration damper using special tool No. 9944.

29. Remove front timing chain cover.

30. Paint mark or scribe the balance shaft (2) position to the engine block and timing chain.

31. Paint mark or scribe the timing chain to crankshaft gear and camshaft drive gear relation.

32. Raise and support the vehicle.

33. Remove special tool No. 9102 crankshaft locking tool.

34. Lower the vehicle.

35. Rotate the engine and remove the right camshaft drive gear (1) lower bolt.

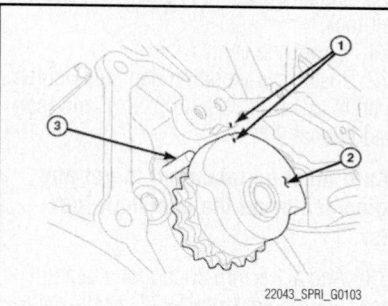

Fig. 48 Marking the balance shaft (2) position to the engine block and timing chain—3.0L Engine

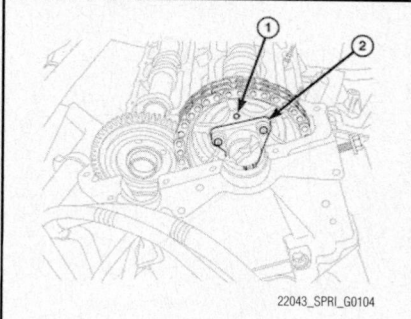

Fig. 49 Right camshaft drive gear (1) lower bolt—3.0L Engine

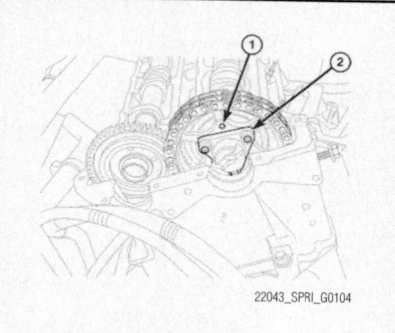

Fig. 50 Right camshaft drive gear (1) retaining bolt—3.0L Engine

36. Rotate the engine back to TDC and check the alignment marks at the balance shaft, camshaft gear and crankshaft gear.

37. Remove the timing chain tensioner.

38. Remove the remaining right camshaft drive gear (1) retaining bolts.

39. Separate the right camshaft drive gear and chain from camshaft.

40. Remove the right camshaft drive gear.

41. Remove the right camshafts retainers (1, 2) and camshafts.

42. Make a roll pin tool by using a tube, nut, bolt and washer. Place the nut on the bolt and the bolt through the tube. Thread the bolt into the roll pin and turn the nut to remove the roll pin (as illustrated).

43. Remove the right upper timing chain upper guide.

44. Remove the right lower timing chain guide (1).

➡Followers and tappets assemblies must be installed in same location as removed.

➡Do not store the cylinder head on the sealing surface. The glow plugs protrude into the cylinder surface area and may be damaged.

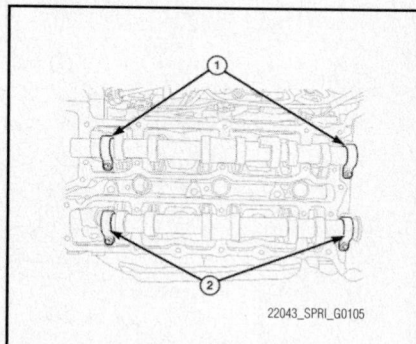

Fig. 51 Right camshafts retainers (1, 2) and camshafts—3.0L Engine

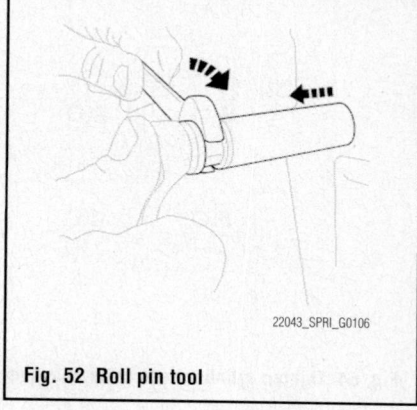

Fig. 52 Roll pin tool

45. Remove the right cylinder head glow plugs.

46. Remove the cylinder head and gasket from engine block.

To install:

✷✷ CAUTION

Inspect and measure all cylinder head bolt lengths. If out of specification, replace as necessary.

47. Clean and inspect gasket mating surfaces.

48. Position head gasket on engine block. Be sure the coolant passages align (part number should be facing up).

49. Place the cylinder head on engine block.

✷✷ CAUTION

Inspect and measure all cylinder head bolt lengths. If out of specification, replace as necessary. Do not lubricate new cylinder head bolts. They already are coated with an anti scuff treatment.

50. Tighten cylinder head bolts following procedure below.

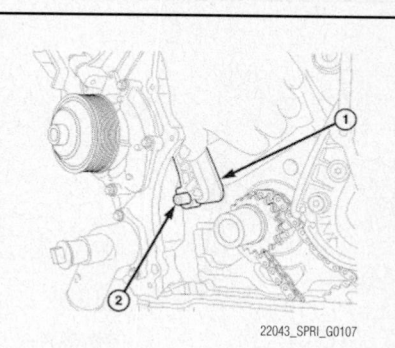

Fig. 53 Right lower timing chain guide (1)—3.0L Engine

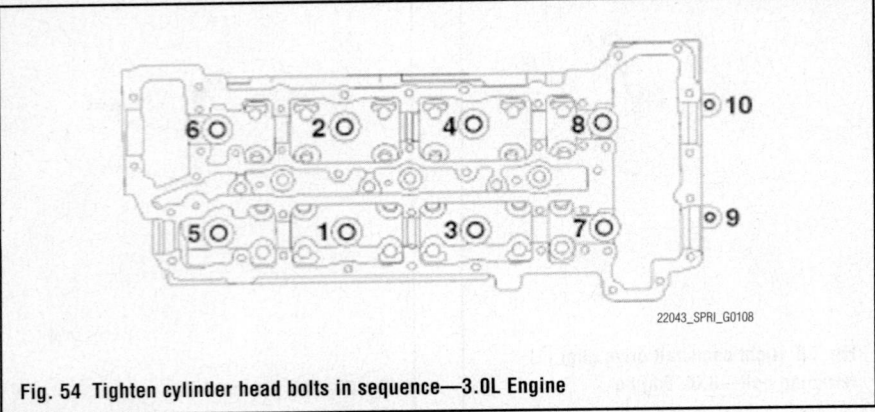

Fig. 54 Tighten cylinder head bolts in sequence—3.0L Engine

- Tighten M12 cylinder head bolts 1 through 8, in the sequence shown to 44 ft. lbs. (60 Nm).
- Tighten bolts 9 and 10 to 177 inch lbs. (20 Nm).
- Tighten 12 mm cylinder head bolts, 1 through 8, in sequence shown an additional 90 degrees.
- Recheck and tighten M8 bolts 9 and 10 to 177 inch lbs. (20 Nm).
- And then again, tighten M12 cylinder head bolts, 1 through 8, in sequence an additional 90 degrees.

➡**Followers and tappets assemblies must be installed in same location as removed.**

51. Install the followers and tappets into their original positions.
52. Install the glow plugs. Tighten glow plugs to 100 inch lbs. (12.5 Nm).
53. Install the right exhaust camshaft. Tighten the retaining fasteners to 71 inch lbs. (8 Nm).
54. Install the right intake camshaft. Tighten the retaining fasteners to 71 inch lbs. (8 Nm).

➡**Care must be taken to assure the proper exhaust camshaft to intake camshaft alignment.**

55. Align the camshaft marks so the alignment marks are facing each other.
56. Insert the timing chain, through the cylinder head, and on to the camshaft drive gear.
57. Align the balance shaft with the scribe or paint mark.
58. Once the camshaft drive gear is mated with the timing chain, install the camshaft drive gear on to the camshaft and assure the balance shaft is aligned properly.
59. Install the upper two of the three camshaft drive gear bolts.
60. Install the right lower timing chain guide, seat the guide pin at the top, and tighten the guide bolt to 9 ft. lbs. (12 Nm).
61. Install the right upper timing chain guide, seat the guide pin at the top, and tighten the guide bolt to 9 ft. lbs. (12 Nm).
62. Install the timing chain tensioner.
63. Rotate the engine by the vibration damper bolt enough to gain access to the third camshaft bolt hole.
64. Install the third camshaft drive gear retaining bolt and tighten the bolt to 13 ft. lbs. (18 Nm).

✳✳ WARNING

If the camshaft, balance shaft and or crankshaft alignment marks are not aligned properly, immediate damage to the engine will occur. If the camshafts, balance shaft and or crankshaft do not align properly after rotating the engine to the original starting point, STOP and begin the alignment procedure again.

65. Rotate the engine back to TDC by the vibration damper bolt until the crankshaft, camshaft and balance shaft align TDC again.
66. Tighten the two remaining camshaft drive gear bolts to 13 ft. lbs. (18 Nm).

✳✳ WARNING

Check that all the timing chain fits properly on all the timing gears. Failure to do so will result in immediate engine damage.

67. Add a 1.5 mm continuous bead of Mopar Engine Sealant RTV (1) to the timing chain cover and the front portion of the oil pan, then install the timing chain cover. Tighten the bolts to 74 inch lbs. (8.5 Nm).
68. Raise and support the vehicle.
69. Install the 5 front oil pan to timing cover bolts. Tighten the bolts to 177 in. lbs. (20 Nm).
70. Install special tool No. 9102 crankshaft lock.
71. Lower the vehicle.
72. Install the vibration damper. Tighten the bolts to 148 ft. lbs. (200 Nm). and then an additional 90°.

➡**Care must be taken not to get any engine sealer on the camshaft journals.**

73. Add a 1.5 mm continuous bead of Mopar Engine Sealant RTV (1) to the cylinder head cover, then install the right cylinder head cover along with a new camshaft seal.

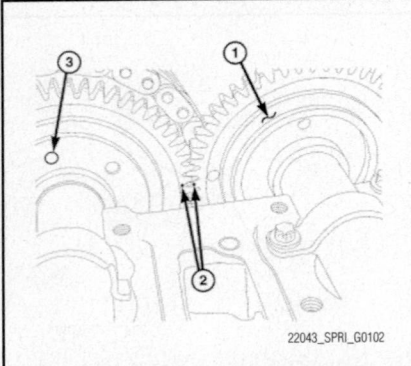

Fig. 55 Camshaft gear alignment marks—3.0L Engine

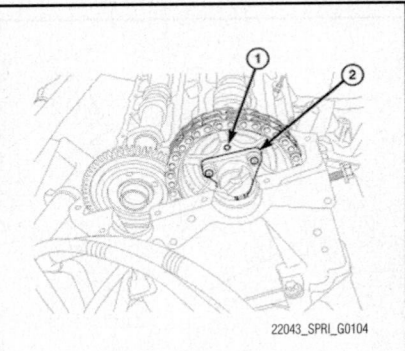

Fig. 56 Right camshaft drive gear (1) retaining bolts—3.0L Engine

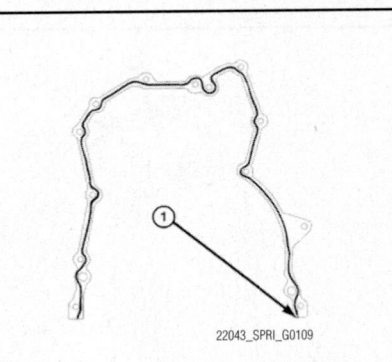

Fig. 57 Continuous bead of Mopar Engine Sealant RTV on timing chain cover (1)

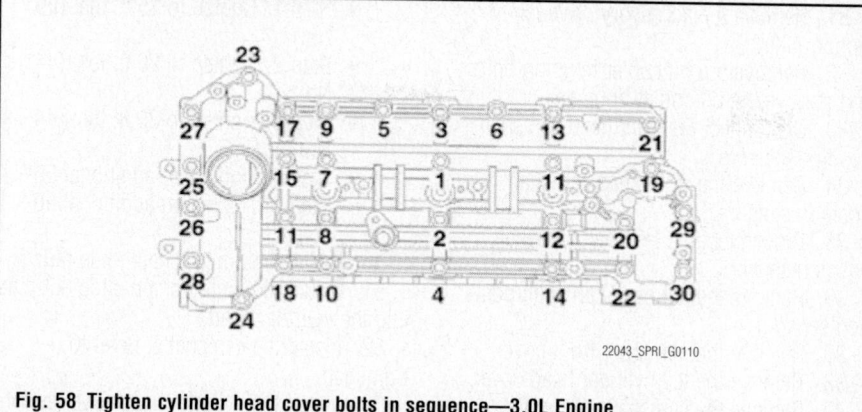

Fig. 58 Tighten cylinder head cover bolts in sequence—3.0L Engine

74. Tighten the bolts in three stages following the sequence provided. First to 35 inch lbs. (4 Nm), then to 53 inch lbs. (6 Nm) and then to 75 inch lbs. (8.5 Nm).

75. Install the oil separator and housing adaptor with new camshaft seal. Tighten the bolts to 97 inch lbs. (11 Nm).

76. Align the pump drive gear (1) with the camshaft drive gear (3) and install the vacuum pump (2) with new gasket. Tighten bolts to 7 ft. lbs. (9 Nm).

77. Install the belt idler pulleys Tighten the bolts to 43 ft. lbs. (58 Nm).

78. Install the accessory drive belt tensioner (2). Tighten the bolts to 43 ft. lbs. (58 Nm).

79. Install the accessory drive belt.

✳✳ CAUTION

The right intake manifold upper thermostat housing bolts should be tightened to 74 inch lbs. (8.5 Nm).

80. Install the intake manifold. Tighten bolts to 142 inch lbs. (16 Nm), starting in the middle and tightening in a cross pattern outward until reaching the upper thermostat bolts on the right front manifold.

81. Tighten the upper thermostat bolts on the right cylinder head to 74 inch lbs. (8.5 Nm).

✳✳ CAUTION

The fuel injector sealing washers MUST be replaced. DO NOT use the old sealing washers or double the sealing washers. DO NOT apply injector body lubricant near the injector nozzles.

82. Lubricate the fuel injector body, install the right fuel injectors and new sealing washers.

✳✳ CAUTION

The fuel injector retaining claw bolts are torque to yield and must always be replaced.

83. Install the injector retaining claws and tighten the bolts to 62 in. lbs., plus 180° (7 Nm, plus 180°).

84. Properly route and install the fuel return hoses and connect them to the injectors.

85. Properly route and connect the engine harness.

86. Install the fuel rail (2). Tighten the bolts to 20 ft. lbs. (27 Nm).

✳✳ CAUTION

Inspect the fuel lines for wear or damage, look closely around the flange area. Replace as necessary. DO NOT over tighten.

87. Install the high pressure fuel lines (3), including the fuel rail transfer line (1). Tighten the line nuts to 24 ft. lbs. (33 Nm).

88. Install the fuel filter and connect the harnesses and hoses using Fuel Line Pliers 9539 Hose Clamp pliers.

✳✳ CAUTION

Care must be taken when installing the turbocharger oil housing adaptor. The gasket MUST be aligned properly with the oil housing passages or immediate damage to the turbocharger will occur.

89. Install the turbocharger oil housing adaptor with the gasket tabs secured to the adaptor. Tighten bolts to 9 ft. lbs. (12 Nm).

90. Install the turbocharger.

91. Install the charge air inlet pipe and resonator.

92. Install the air control valve and resonator.

93. Install the cooling fan module.

94. Connect the vacuum pump supply hose.

95. Raise and support the vehicle.

96. Remove special tool No. 9102 crankshaft lock.

97. Install the starter blank.

98. Connect the cooling fan hydraulic lines.

99. Lower the vehicle.

100. Fill the cooling system.

101. Fill power steering system.

102. Install the strut tower support.

103. Connect the negative battery cable.

104. Start engine, allow to warm, turn engine off and inspect for leaks.

105. Purge the air from the power steering system using the scan tool.

106. Install the engine cover brackets and engine cover.

3.5L Engine

See Figures 62 and 63.

1. Disconnect the negative battery cable.

2. Properly relieve the fuel system pressure.

3. Drain the cooling system.

4. Drain the engine oil.

5. Remove the air intake assembly.

6. Remove the accessory drive belt. Refer to Accessory Drive Belt.

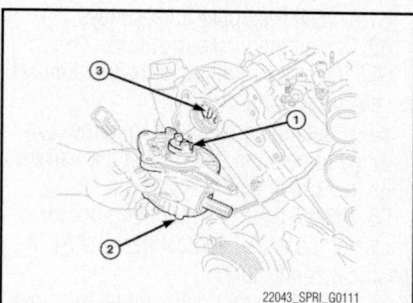

Fig. 59 Align the pump drive gear (1) with the camshaft drive gear (3) and install the vacuum pump (2) with new gasket.

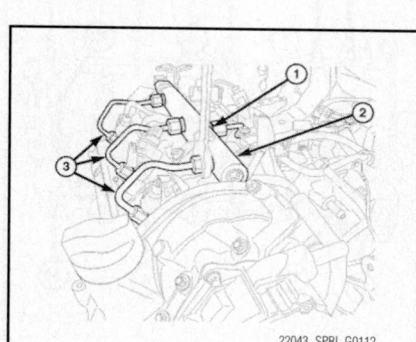

Fig. 60 Install fuel rail (2), high pressure fuel lines (3) and fuel rail transfer line (1)

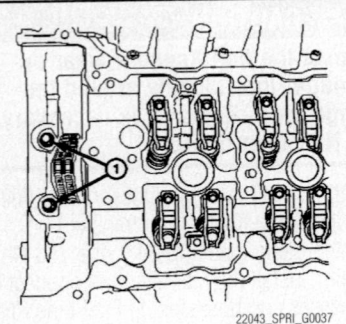

Fig. 62 Install the two cylinder head-to-front cover bolts (1) before the rest of the cylinder head mounting bolts—3.5L Engine

7. Rotate the engine in a clockwise direction until the No. 1 cylinder is at 40 degrees after Top Dead Center (TDC).

8. Raise and safely support the vehicle.

9. Remove the lower sound shield.

10. Remove the catalytic converter to manifold mounting bolts.

11. Remove the timing chain tensioner.

12. Lower the vehicle.

13. Disconnect the upper radiator hose from the engine.

14. Remove the fan and fan shroud assembly.

15. Disconnect the canister purge line from the engine.

16. Remove the air intake housing support.

17. Remove the evaporative emissions vacuum lines.

18. Remove the fuel rail and fuel injectors. Refer to Fuel Injectors.

19. Disconnect and remove the Powertrain Control Module (PCM).

20. Remove the left and right PCM bracket.

21. Position aside the remote battery positive terminal connection.

22. Disconnect the engine wiring harness ground from the cylinder head.

23. Remove the three ignition coils from the cylinder head. Refer to Ignition Coil.

24. Remove the intake manifold. Refer to Intake Manifold.

25. Remove the air injection valve bolts.

26. Remove the air injection adapter bolts.

27. Remove the hoses from the air injection pump.

28. Remove the air injection pump and bracket.

29. Remove the upper idler pulleys.

30. Remove the accessory drive tensioner pulley bolts.

31. Remove the accessory drive tensioner pulley.

32. Remove the oil cooler housing bolts and remove the oil cooler housing.

33. Disconnect the right head camshaft position sensors.

34. Remove the right head camshaft position sensors.

35. Disconnect the left head camshaft position sensors.

36. Remove the left head camshaft position sensors.

37. Remove the left upper front cover.

38. Remove the left cylinder head cover.

39. Remove the camshafts. Refer to Camshaft.

40. Use a slide hammer to remove the timing chain slide rail pins from the cylinder head.

41. Remove the timing chain slide rail.

42. Loosen all of the cylinder head bolts in the reverse order of the tightening sequence.

43. Remove the cylinder head bolts and remove cylinder head.

44. Place the cylinder head on wooden blocks on the bench and remove the exhaust manifold if necessary.

To install:

45. If removed, install the exhaust manifold to the cylinder and tighten the nuts to 12 ft. lbs. (16 Nm).

46. Clean any old gasket material from the mating surfaces.

47. Install the cylinder head with a new gasket.

48. Install the cylinder head-to-timing chain front cover bolts to 18 ft. lbs. (25 Nm) plus 90°

49. Install the cylinder head mounting bolts in a spiral pattern as follows:

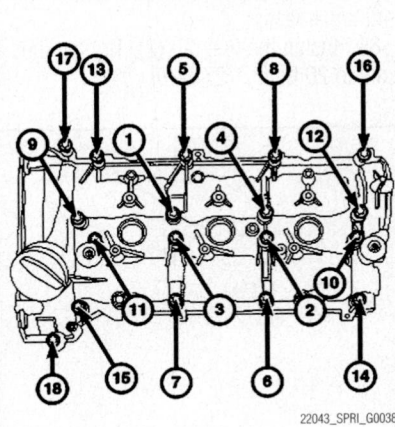

Fig. 63 Cylinder head cover torque sequence—3.5L engine

- Step 1: Tighten to 15 ft. lbs. (20 Nm)
- Step 2: Tighten to 29 ft. lbs. (44 Nm)
- Step 3: Tighten to 29 ft. lbs. (44 Nm) again
- Step 4: Tighten an additional 90°
- Step 5: Tighten an additional 90° again

50. Install the timing chain slide rail.

51. Install the timing chain slide rail pins into the cylinder head.

52. Install the camshafts. Refer to Camshaft.

53. Install the cylinder head cover as follows:

a. Remove any old gasket material from the sealing surfaces of the cylinder head cover.

b. Apply a thin layer of silicone sealant to the cylinder head cover mating surface.

c. Install the cylinder head cover with new bolts and tighten them in the sequence shown to 106 inch lbs. (12 Nm).

d. Tighten all of the bolts in sequence in additional 90°

54. Install the upper front cover as follows:

a. Clean any old gasket material from the mating surfaces.

b. Apply silicone sealant to the upper front cover sealing surface.

c. Install the upper front cover and tighten the mounting bolts to 80 inch lbs. (9 Nm).

55. Install the camshaft position sensors.

56. Install the air injection pump and bracket.

57. Install the air injection valve.

58. Install the hoses to the air injection pump.

59. Install the oil cooler housing and tighten the bolts to 18 ft. lbs. (25 Nm).

60. Install the accessory drive tensioner pulley and tighten the bolts to 26 ft. lbs. (35 Nm)

61. Install the upper idler pulleys.

62. Install the intake manifold.

63. Install the ignition coils and connect the electrical connectors.

64. Route the engine wiring harness in its original position and tighten the harness bolts to 71 inch lbs. (8 Nm).

65. Install the PCM mounting bolts brackets, the install and connect the PCM electrical connectors.

66. Install the fuel rail and fuel injectors.

67. Install the vacuum line to the fuel pressure regulator.

68. Install the intake air housing support.

69. Connect the remote battery positive terminal connection.
70. Connect the canister purge line to the engine.
71. Install the fan assembly.
72. Connect the upper radiator hose to the engine.
73. Install the lower sound shield.
74. Install the accessory drive belt.
75. Lower the vehicle.
76. Refill the engine with oil to the correct level.
77. Refill the cooling system to the correct level.
78. Connect the negative battery cable.
79. Start the engine and check for leaks.

ENGINE ASSEMBLY

REMOVAL & INSTALLATION

3.0L Engine

See Figure 64.

1. Remove the hood.
2. Disconnect the negative battery cable.
3. Drain the cooling system.
4. Remove air intake hose downstream of air filter on air filter housing.
5. Disconnect electrical connectors.
6. Disconnect the jump-starting point on air filter housing and place to one side.
7. Pull out air intake hose upstream of air filter on front module.
8. Lift the air filter housing at front from front module and pull out of the rear guides.
9. Remove the air filter housing bracket from the bulkhead.
10. Disconnect the electrical connector at the intake manifold pressure sensor.
11. Remove the intake manifold pressure sensor.
12. Remove hot film mass air flow sensor.

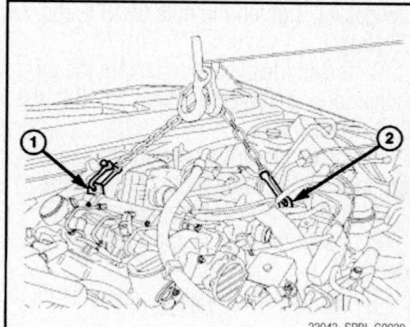

Fig. 64 Attach the engine chains to the lift points (1,2)—3.0L Engine

22043_SPRI_G0039

13. Remove the holder for air filter housing to front plate.
14. Remove the trim panel on right cylinder head cover.
15. Remove the trim panel on left cylinder head cover.
16. Place the gearshift into neutral.
17. Disconnect and remove the auxiliary battery.
18. Remove the battery tray for the auxiliary battery.
19. Raise and safely support the vehicle.
20. Disconnect the speed sensors on transmission.
21. Disconnect the oxygen sensors.
22. Remove the coolant lines from the heater core.
23. Remove the upper and lower radiator hoses from the radiator and position aside.
24. Remove the vacuum line at the vacuum pump.
25. Disconnect the engine ground.
26. Disconnect the Engine Control Module (ECM).
27. Remove the power steering lines at the power steering pump and cap the lines.
28. Remove the clamp and disconnect exhaust system between catalytic converter and diesel particulate filter.
29. Remove the driveshaft center support bearing on frame floor assembly.
30. Detach power take-off connections.
31. Remove the bolts, and remove driveshaft and hang to the side outside the working area.
32. Insert a suitable wooden block between the transmission and crossmember.
33. Attach engine removal chains to the lift points.
34. Remove the bolts from the right engine mount at the front.
35. Remove the bolts from the left engine mount at the front.
36. Using a suitable engine hoist, lift the engine and transmission assembly from the vehicle.

To install:

37. Using a suitable engine hoist, lower the engine and transmission assembly into the vehicle.
38. Install the front right and left engine mount bolts.
39. Remove the engine removal chains.
40. Install the rear engine mount.
41. Connect the driveshaft.
42. Attach the power take-off connections.
43. Install the driveshaft center support bearing on frame floor assembly.
44. Connect the exhaust system between

the catalytic converter and diesel particulate filter.
45. Install the power steering lines at the power steering pump.
46. Connect the ECM and engine ground.
47. Install the vacuum line at the vacuum pump.
48. Connect the upper and lower radiator hoses at the radiator.
49. Connect the coolant lines to the heater core.
50. Connect the oxygen sensors.
51. Connect the speed sensors on transmission.
52. Install the battery tray for auxiliary battery and install the auxiliary battery.
53. Install the trim panel on left cylinder head cover.
54. Install the trim panel on right cylinder head cover.
55. Install the holder for air filter housing to front plate.
56. Install the hot film mass air flow sensor.
57. Install the intake manifold pressure sensor.
58. Connect the electrical connector at intake manifold pressure sensor.
59. Install the air filter housing bracket to the bulkhead.
60. Connect the jump-starting point on air filter housing and place to one side.
61. Install air intake hose downstream of air filter on air filter housing.
62. Refill the engine cooling system to the correct level.
63. Connect the negative battery cable.
64. Install the engine hood

3.5L Engine

1. Disconnect the negative battery cable.
2. Drain the cooling system.
3. Drain the engine oil.
4. Drain the power steering fluid.
5. Remove the air intake assembly.
6. Remove the grill.
7. Remove the headlight trim panel.
8. Raise and safely support the vehicle.
9. Remove the license plate holder and step grip plate.
10. Remove the front fascia assembly.
11. Lower the vehicle.
12. Drain the power steering fluid from the power steering fluid reservoir.
13. Disconnect the power steering fluid lines.
14. Disconnect the A/C pressure sensor.
15. Remove the condenser line bolt.
16. Remove the condenser lines.

17. Remove the transmission cooler lines from the radiator.

18. Remove the heater hose lines from the extension line.

19. Remove the upper and lower radiator hoses.

20. Matchmark the radiator support location on the frame.

21. Disconnect the electric fan connector.

22. Remove the cooling module assembly.

23. Disconnect the canister purge lines and position aside.

24. Disconnect the fuel lines.

25. Disconnect the fuel lines at the fuel rail.

26. Disconnect the Powertrain Control Module (PCM) connectors and remove the PCM

27. Remove the transmission dip stick mounting bolts.

28. Disconnect the engine ground strap.

29. Disconnect the coolant level sensor.

30. Raise and safely support the vehicle.

31. Remove the torque converter bolts.

32. Disconnect the oxygen sensor connectors at the connector bracket.

33. Remove the bolts from the right and left exhaust flange.

34. Remove the starter. Refer to Starter.

35. Disconnect the alternator electrical connectors.

36. Remove all but the top bell housing bolt.

37. Remove the left motor mount bolt.

38. Remove the left motor mount bolt.

39. Lower the vehicle.

40. Support the transmission with a suitable jack.

41. Install a suitable engine lift to the engine.

42. Remove the last bellhousing bolt.

43. Remove the engine assembly from the vehicle.

To install:

44. Using an engine lift, lower the engine assembly into the vehicle.

45. Install a single bellhousing bolt and tighten to 28 ft. lbs. (38 Nm).

46. Install the right motor mount bolt and tighten to 42 ft. lbs. (58 Nm).

47. Install the left motor mount bolt and tighten to 42 ft. lbs. (58 Nm).

48. Remove the jack supporting the transmission assembly and remove the engine lift.

49. Connect the alternator electrical connector.

50. Install the remaining bellhousing bolts and tighten to 28 ft. lbs. (38 Nm).

51. Install the torque converter bolts and tighten to 37 ft. lbs. (50 Nm).

52. Install the starter motor.

53. Install the bolts for the left and right exhaust flanges and tighten to 15 ft. lbs. (20 Nm).

54. Connect the oxygen sensor electrical connectors.

55. Install the front lower sound shield.

56. Connect the coolant level sensor.

57. Connect the engine ground strap.

58. Install the transmission dipstick mounting bolts.

59. Install the PCM and connect the electrical connectors.

60. Connect the fuel lines to the fuel rail.

61. Connect the canister purge lines.

62. Connect the electric fan connector.

63. Install the radiator support. Make sure the radiator support location lines up with the marks made on the frame during the removal process.

64. Install the upper and lower radiator hose.

65. Install the heater hose lines to the extension line.

66. Install the transmission cooler lines to the radiator.

67. Install the condenser lines.

68. Connect the A/C pressure sensor.

69. Connect the power steering fluid lines.

70. Install the front fascia assembly.

71. Install the license plate holder and step grip plate.

72. Install the head lamp trim panel.

73. Install the grill assembly.

74. Install the air intake assembly.

75. Refill the engine with oil to the correct level.

76. Refill the power steering system with fluid to the correct level.

77. Refill the cooling system to the correct level.

78. Connect the negative battery cable.

79. Start the engine and check for leaks.

EXHAUST MANIFOLD

REMOVAL & INSTALLATION

3.0L Engine

See Figures 65 and 66.

1. Disconnect the negative battery cable.

2. Remove the engine appearance cover.

3. Remove the turbo heat shield.

4. Remove the EGR tube, left side only.

5. Remove the exhaust elbow at the turbo.

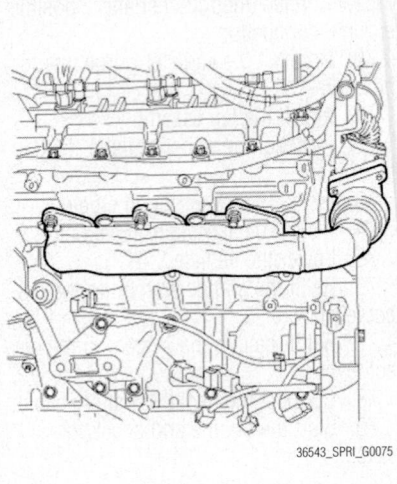

Fig. 65 Left exhaust manifold— 3.0L Engine

36543_SPRI_G0075

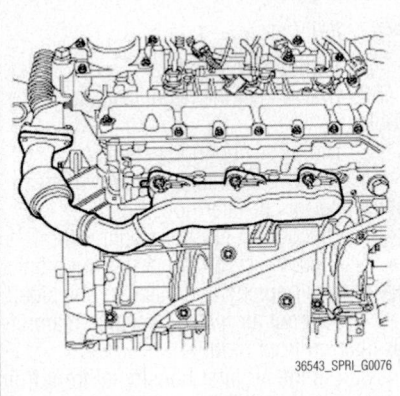

Fig. 66 Right exhaust manifold— 3.0L Engine

36543_SPRI_G0076

6. Remove the exhaust manifold and gasket.

To install:

7. Clean the mating surfaces of any old gasket material.

8. Install the exhaust manifold with a new gasket. Tighten the nuts to 18 ft. lbs. (25 Nm).

9. Install the exhaust elbow to the turbocharger and tighten the bolts to 15 ft. lbs. (20 Nm) plus 90°.

10. Install the turbo heat shield and tighten the bolts to 89 inch lbs. (10 Nm).

11. Install the EGR tube, left side only.

12. Install the engine appearance cover.

13. Connect the negative battery cable.

3.5L Engine

1. Disconnect the negative battery cable.

2. Remove the air intake assembly.

3. Remove the EGR valve, left side only.

4. Disconnect the exhaust back pressure sensor.

5. Remove the exhaust back pressure sensor.

6. Remove the catalytic converter to exhaust manifold bolts.

7. Remove the EGR line, left side only.

8. Remove the exhaust manifold bolts.

9. Remove the exhaust manifold and gasket.

To install:

10. Clean the mating surfaces of any old gasket material.

11. Install the exhaust manifold with a new gasket. Tighten the bolts to 98 inch lbs. (11 Nm).

12. Install the EGR line, left side only.

13. Install the catalytic converter-to-exhaust manifold nuts and tighten to 15 ft. lbs. (20 Nm).

14. Install the battery pressure sensor.

15. Install the EGR valve, left side only.

16. Install the air intake assembly.

17. Connect the negative battery cable.

FLEXPLATE

REMOVAL & INSTALLATION

1. Remove the transmission.

2. Paint mark the flexplate hub to flex plate relation.

3. Remove the flexplate bolts and flex plate.

4. Remove the flexplate backing plate (3.5L engine).

5. Inspect flexplate for damage.

To install:

➡**Do not lubricate new bolts as they are already coated with an anti-scuff treatment. Align the flex plate to hub paint marks, where applicable.**

6. Install the flexplate locating pin.

7. Install the flexplate to the hub and the flex plate backing plate (3.5L engine). Install the fasteners.

   a. On 3.0L engine, tighten the flexplate fasteners in a cross sequence to 32.5 ft. lbs. (44 Nm).

   b. On 3.5L engine, tighten the flex plate fasteners in a cross sequence to 15 ft. lbs. (20 Nm), and then to 33 ft. lbs. (45 Nm), and then tighten the bolts an additional 90 degrees.

8. Install the transmission.

INTAKE MANIFOLD

REMOVAL & INSTALLATION

3.0L Engine

1. Disconnect the negative battery cable.

2. Drain the coolant.

3. Remove air filter housing.

4. Remove the intake air tube.

5. Perform the fuel pressure release procedure.

6. Disconnect the PCM connector.

7. Remove the PCM.

8. Remove the PCM bracket bolts.

9. Remove the PCM bracket.

10. Disconnect the fuel rail electrical connectors.

11. Remove the engine wiring harness bolts.

12. Position aside the engine wiring harness.

13. Remove the power brake booster vacuum line connector.

14. Disconnect the Mass Air Flow sensor.

15. Remove the Mass Air Flow sensor (MAF).

16. Remove the oil separator tube from the oil separator.

17. Disconnect the crankcase ventilation sensor hose.

18. Disconnect the right hand exhaust camshaft position sensor.

19. Disconnect the right hand intake camshaft position sensor.

20. Disconnect the left hand exhaust camshaft position sensor.

21. Disconnect the left hand intake camshaft position sensor.

22. Disconnect the Short Runner connector.

23. Disconnect the throttle sensor connector.

24. Disconnect the Tumbler Valve Solenoid connector.

25. Disconnect the MAP Sensor harness connector.

26. Disconnect the Electronic throttle control solenoid connector.

27. Position the engine harness aside.

28. Disconnect the fuel injector harness connectors.

29. Release the fuel rail pressure.

30. Disconnect the fuel line.

31. Remove the fuel rail bolts.

32. Remove the fuel rail.

33. Disconnect the EVAP purge solenoid hose.

34. Disconnect the power brake booster vacuum line at the intake manifold.

35. Disconnect the air pump solenoid vacuum line.

36. Remove the intake manifold bolts.

37. Remove the intake manifold.

To install:

38. Position the intake manifold.

39. Install the intake manifold bolts.

40. Connect the air pump solenoid vacuum line.

41. Connect the power brake booster vacuum line at the intake manifold.

42. Connect the EVAP purge solenoid hose.

43. Install the fuel rail.

44. Install the fuel rail bolts.

45. Connect the fuel line.

46. Connect the fuel rail electrical connectors.

47. Connect the fuel injector harness connectors.

48. Position the engine harness.

49. Install the engine harness bolts.

50. Connect the Electronic throttle control solenoid connector.

51. Install the Mass Air Flow sensor (MAF).

52. Connect the Mass Air Flow sensor.

53. Connect the MAP Sensor harness connector.

54. Connect the Tumbler Valve Solenoid connector.

55. Connect the throttle sensor connector.

56. Connect the Short Runner connector.

57. Connect the left hand intake camshaft position sensor.

58. Connect the left hand exhaust camshaft position sensor.

59. Connect the right hand intake camshaft position sensor.

60. Connect the right hand exhaust camshaft position sensor.

61. Connect the crankcase ventilation sensor hose.

62. Install the oil separator tube to the oil separator.

63. Install the power brake booster vacuum line connector.

64. Install the PCM brackets.

65. Install the PCM bracket bolts.

66. Install the PCM.

67. Connect the PCM connector.

68. Install the intake air tube.

69. Install the air filter housing.

70. Fill the coolant.

71. Connect the negative battery cable.

3.5L Engine

1. Disconnect the negative battery cable.

2. Drain the cooling system.

3. Properly relieve the fuel system pressure.

4. Remove the air intake assembly.

5. Disconnect the Powertrain Control Module (PCM) and remove the PCM and mounting bracket.

6. Disconnect the fuel rail electrical connectors.

7. Remove the engine wiring harness bolts.

8. Position aside the engine wiring harness.

9. Remove the power brake booster vacuum line connector.

10. Disconnect the Mass Air Flow sensor.

11. Remove the Mass Air Flow sensor (MAF).

12. Remove the oil separator tube from the oil separator.

13. Disconnect the crankcase ventilation sensor hose.

14. Disconnect all four camshaft position sensors.

15. Disconnect the Short Runner connector.

16. Disconnect the throttle sensor connector.

17. Disconnect the Tumbler Valve Solenoid connector.

18. Disconnect the MAP Sensor harness connector.

19. Disconnect the Electronic throttle control solenoid connector.

20. Position the engine harness aside.

21. Disconnect the fuel injector harness connectors.

22. Remove the fuel rail. Refer to Fuel Injectors.

23. Disconnect the EVAP purge solenoid hose.

24. Disconnect the power brake booster vacuum line at the intake manifold.

25. Disconnect the air pump solenoid vacuum line.

26. Remove the intake manifold bolts and remove the intake manifold.

To install:

27. Position the intake manifold into place and install the mounting bolts.

28. Connect the air pump solenoid vacuum line.

29. Connect the power brake booster vacuum line at the intake manifold.

30. Connect the EVAP purge solenoid hose.

31. Install the fuel rail and connect the fuel line and injector electrical connectors.

32. Position the engine harness into place and install the engine harness bolts.

33. Connect the following to the engine wiring harness:
- Electronic throttle control solenoid connector
- MAF sensor
- Tumbler Valve Solenoid connector
- Throttle sensor connector
- Short Runner connector

34. Connect all four camshaft position sensors.

35. Connect the crankcase ventilation sensor hose.

36. Install the oil separator tube to the oil separator.

37. Install the power brake booster vacuum line connector.

38. Install the PCM brackets and install the PCM.

39. Install the air intake assembly.

40. Refill the cooling system to the correct level.

41. Connect the negative battery cable.

OIL FILTER HOUSING

REMOVAL & INSTALLATION

3.5L Engine

See Figure 67.

1. Remove the accessory drive belt.

2. Remove the accessory drive tensioner.

3. Remove the accessory drive idler pulley.

4. Drain the oil.

5. Remove the oil filter from the oil filter housing.

6. Drain the coolant.

7. Remove the air pump (5).

8. Remove the upper radiator hose from the thermostat housing.

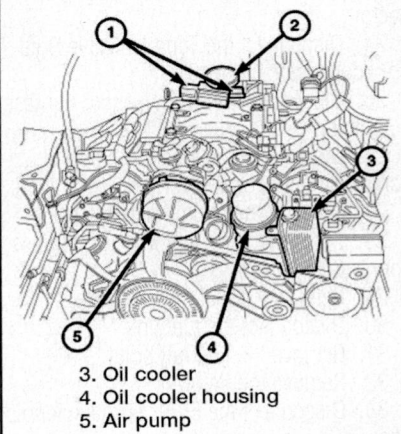

3. Oil cooler
4. Oil cooler housing
5. Air pump

36543_SPRI_G0047

Fig. 67 Oil filter housing—3.5L Engine

9. Remove the thermostat housing.

10. Remove the oil cooler housing.

To install:

11. Install the oil cooler housing gasket.

12. Install the oil cooler housing.

13. Tighten the bolts in a cross pattern to 18 ft. lbs. (25 Nm).

14. Install a new oil filter into the oil filter housing.

15. Install the thermostat gasket.

16. Install the thermostat housing.

17. Tighten the thermostat bolts to 18 ft. lbs. (25 Nm).

18. Install the upper radiator hose onto the thermostat housing.

19. Install the accessory drive idler pulley.

20. Install the accessory drive tensioner.

21. Install the accessory drive belt.

22. Install the air pump (5).

23. Fill the oil.

24. Fill the coolant.

OIL PAN

REMOVAL & INSTALLATION

3.0L Engine

1. Disconnect the negative battery cable.

2. Remove the accessory drive belt. Refer to Accessory Drive Belt.

3. Remove the transmission. Refer to Automatic Transmission Assembly.

4. Remove the flex plate.

5. Remove the five bolts on the bottom of the rear main seal carrier.

6. Remove the oil pan bolts.

7. Remove the oil pan.

To install:

8. Clean the mating surfaces of any old gasket material.

9. Install the oil pan and gasket and install the bolts holding the rear main seal carrier to the oil pan. Tighten the bolts to 80 inch lbs. (9 Nm).

10. Push the oil pan against the transmission and tighten transmission to oil pan bolts first, including the rear main seal carrier bolts.

11. Tighten the oil pan bolts to 106 inch lbs. (12 Nm).

12. Tighten the transmission-to-oil pan bolts to 15 ft. lbs. (20 Nm).

13. Install the flex plate.

14. Install the transmission.

15. Lower the vehicle.

16. Install the accessory drive belt.

17. Refill the engine with oil to the correct level.

18. Connect the negative battery cable.

19. Start the engine and check for leaks.

3.5L Engine

Lower Oil Pan

See Figure 68.

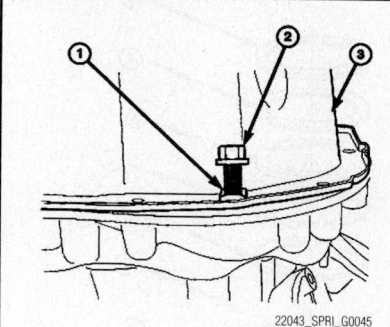

Fig. 68 Use a bolt (2) in the oil pan boss (1) to pull the lower oil pan (3) from the upper oil pan—3.5L Engine

1. Disconnect the negative battery cable.
2. Drain the engine oil.
3. Remove the engine oil dipstick and dipstick tube.
4. Remove the lower oil pan mounting bolts.
5. Use a bolt in the oil pan boss to carefully pull the lower oil pan from the upper oil pan.

To install:

6. Install the oil dipstick tube and tighten the mounting bolt to 80 inch lbs. (9 Nm).
7. Remove any sealant residues with an adhesive and sealant remover. Do not use any sharp-edged tools or abrasive paper as this can damage the sealing surfaces. Make sure the sealing surfaces are clean and dry before applying the RTV.
8. Apply Loctite® 7200 or equivalent to the mating surface of the lower oil pan.
9. Install the lower oil pan and tighten the mounting bolts in a crisscross pattern to 80 inch lbs. (9 Nm).
10. Install the oil dipstick.
11. Install the oil drain plug, if not already installed.
12. Refill the engine with oil to the correct level.
13. Connect the negative battery cable.

Upper Oil Pan

See Figure 69.

1. Disconnect the negative battery cable.
2. Drain the engine oil.
3. Remove the air intake assembly.
4. Remove the lower oil pan.

5. Loosen the hose clamp bolt from the catalytic converter diesel particulate filter device at the connecting flange at the turbocharger.
6. Remove the bracket bolt for the catalytic converter diesel particulate filter unit.
7. Attach a suitable engine supporting shackle.
8. Detach the charge air hose upstream of the charge air cooler.
9. Detach the charge air hose on the engine charge air duct downstream of charge air cooler.
10. Unscrew the bracket for the transmission oil lines on the right side of the oil pan.
11. Remove the transmission with the torque converter. Refer to Automatic Transmission Assembly.
12. Remove the end cover.
13. Remove the bolts that connect the left and right engine mount to the engine support.
14. Using a suitable engine lift, carefully raise the engine.
15. Remove the oil suction pipe.
16. Remove the refrigerant compressor bolt at the top section of the oil pan.
17. Remove the upper oil pan mounting bolts.
18. Remove the upper oil pan.

To install:

19. Install the oil suction pipe.
20. Install the upper oil pan and tighten the mounting bolts.
21. Connect the oil level switch connector.
22. Install the oil dipstick guide tube.

23. Install the bolt from catalytic converter diesel particulate filter unit bracket
24. Tighten the bolt on hose clamp from catalytic converter diesel particulate filter device at connecting flange from turbocharger.
25. Lower the engine into place.
26. Install the bolts connecting the left and right engine mount to the engine support.
27. Remove the engine supporting shackle.
28. Install the charge air hose upstream of charge air cooler.
29. Install the charge air hose on engine charge air duct downstream of charge air cooler.
30. Install the bracket for transmission oil lines on the oil pan on the right.
31. Install the transmission with the torque converter.
32. Install the end cover.
33. Install the refrigerant compressor bolt at oil pan top section.
34. Install the lower oil pan.
35. Install the air intake assembly.
36. Connect negative battery cable.
37. Refill the engine with oil to the correct level.
38. Start the engine and check for leaks.

OIL PUMP

REMOVAL & INSTALLATION

3.0L Engine

See Figure 70.

1. Disconnect the negative battery cable.

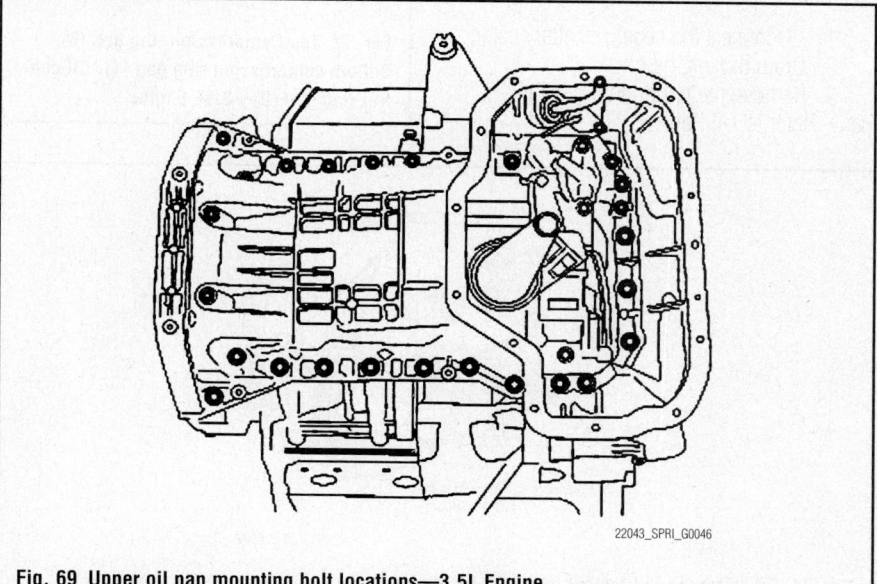

Fig. 69 Upper oil pan mounting bolt locations—3.5L Engine

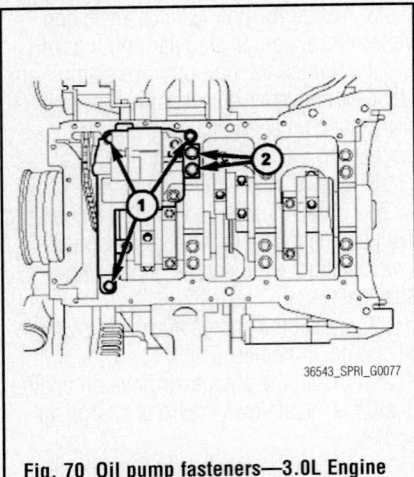

Fig. 70 Oil pump fasteners—3.0L Engine

2. Drain the engine oil.
3. Remove the oil pan. Refer to Oil Pan.
4. Remove the oil pump cover.
5. Remove the mounting bolts and remove the oil pump.

To install:

6. Clean the strainer of the oil pump and replace the sealing ring. Fill the oil pump with engine oil so that oil is delivered when the engine is started.
7. Install the oil pump. Tighten the bolts to 14 ft. lbs. (19 Nm).
8. Install the oil pump cover and tighten the bolts to 9 ft. lbs. (12 Nm).
9. Install the oil pan.
10. Connect the negative battery cable.
11. Fill the engine with oil to the correct level.
12. Start then engine and check for leaks.

3.5L Engine

See Figure 71.

1. Disconnect the negative battery cable.
2. Drain the engine oil.
3. Remove the upper and lower oil pans. Refer to Oil Pan.

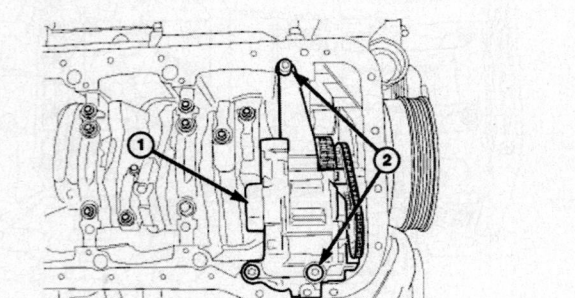

Fig. 71 Oil pump (1) and fasteners (2)—3.5L Engine

4. Remove the oil suction tube bolt.
5. Press the oil pump chain tensioner to completely remove the tension from the oil pump chain.
6. Remove the oil pump chain.
7. Remove the oil pump bolts.
8. Remove the oil pump and suction tube.

To install:

9. Install the oil pump and suction tube.
10. Install the oil suction tube bolt.
11. Pressure the oil pump chain tensioner to completely remove the tension from the oil pump chain.
12. Install the oil pump bolts.
13. Install the upper and lower oil pans.
14. Connect the negative battery.
15. Refill the engine with oil to the correct level.

PISTON AND RING

POSITIONING

3.0L Engine

See Figure 72.

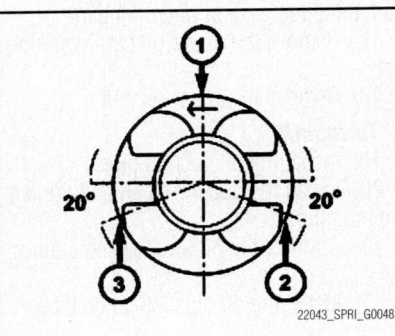

Fig. 72 Top Compression ring gap (3), Bottom compression ring gap (1), Oil control ring gap (2)—3.0L Engine

3.5L Engine

See Figure 73.

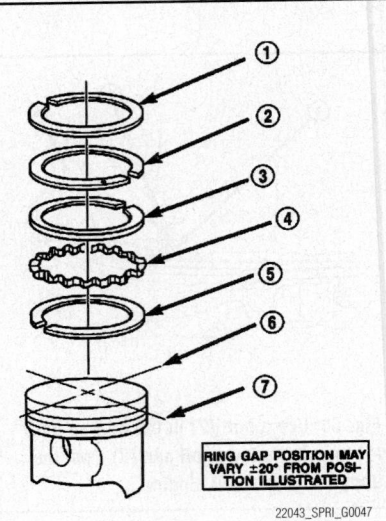

Fig. 73 Correct orientation of the Top Compression ring (1), Bottom Compression ring (2), Top Oil Control Rail (3), Oil Rail Spacer (4), Bottom Oil Control Rail (5), Imaginary Lines to center (6,7)—3.5L Engine

REAR MAIN SEAL

REMOVAL & INSTALLATION

3.0L Engine

See Figure 74.

1. Remove the transmission. Refer to Automatic Transmission Assembly.
2. Remove the flex plate.
3. Remove the bolts holding the rear main seal carrier to the engine block.
4. Remove the rear main seal carrier from the engine block and oil pan.

➡The rear seal is bonded to the retainer and must be replaced as an assembly.

To install:

5. Clean all of the sealing surfaces. The retainer assembly must be replaced if the seal is torn or damaged.
6. Apply Mopar® Engine Sealant RTV Silicone Adhesive to the points where the oil pan and engine block are joined.
7. Install the rear oil seal carrier and tighten the bolts to 70 inch lbs. (8 Nm) and then to 88 inch lbs. (10 Nm).
8. Install the flex plate.
9. Install the transmission.
10. Start the engine and check for leaks.

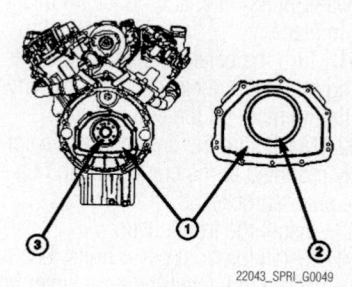

Fig. 74 Location of the rear main seal (2) and rear main seal carrier (1) behind the flex plate—3.0L Engine

3.5L Engine

1. Remove the transmission.
2. Remove the flexplate. Refer to Flexplate.
3. Remove the 7 upper bolts holding the rear main seal carrier (3) to the engine block.
4. Remove 2 lower bolts (2) holding the rear main seal carrier to the engine block
5. Remove the rear main seal carrier from the engine block and oil pan.
6. Clean sealant residue from the engine block and oil pan.

➡Seal retainer gasket is bonded to the retainer and must be replaced as an assembly.

To install:

7. Clean all sealing surfaces. Replace retainer assembly if gasket is torn or damaged.
8. Apply MOPAR Engine Sealant / RTV Silicone Rubber Adhesive to the points where the oil pan and engine block are joined (3).
9. Install the rear oil seal carrier and tighten the bolts to 70 inch lbs. (8 Nm)

✳✳ CAUTION

Make sure that seal is correctly installed on the crankshaft, with the lip of the seal to the lubricant (2).

ROCKER ARMS/SHAFTS

REMOVAL & INSTALLATION

3.0L Engine

1. Remove the appropriate cylinder head cover(s).
2. Remove the appropriate camshaft(s).
3. Remove the rocker arm and lifter assembly.

➡When the hydraulic lifters are removed from the engine, they must be stored upright and in clean conditions.

4. Separate the rocker arm from the lifter.

To install:

5. Assemble the rocker arm to the hydraulic lifter with the retaining clip.
6. Install the rocker arm and lifter assembly onto the cylinder head.
7. Install the camshaft(s).
8. Install the cylinder head cover(s).

TIMING CHAIN COVER AND SEAL

REMOVAL & INSTALLATION

3.0L Engine

1. Disconnect the negative battery cable.
2. Drain the cooling system.
3. Drain the engine oil.
4. Drain the power steering fluid.
5. Remove the engine appearance cover.
6. Remove the front engine cover bracket.
7. Raise and safely support the vehicle.
8. Remove the power steering hose between the pump and cooling fan.
9. Remove the power steering hose between the cooling fan and suspension.
10. Remove the lower cooling fan module retaining bolts.
11. Disconnect the cooling fan wiring harness connector.
12. Remove the power steering line between the retainer and cooling fan module.
13. Remove the front splash shield.
14. Remove the front oil pan to timing cover bolts.
15. Lower the vehicle.
16. Remove the hoses at the power steering reservoir.
17. Remove the cooling fan module upper bolts and remove the fan assembly.
18. Remove the charge air outlet tube.
19. Remove the accessory drive belt.
20. Disconnect the charge air inlet hose at the EGR air control valve.
21. Remove the glow plug module.
22. Remove the EGR air control valve.
23. Remove both accessory drive belt idler pulleys.
24. Remove the accessory drive belt tensioner.
25. Rotate the engine to Top Dead Center (TDC) by the crankshaft bolt.
26. Raise and safely support the vehicle.
27. Remove the starter blank.
28. Install Special Tool 9102 Crankshaft Lock.

29. Lower the vehicle.
30. Remove the vibration damper and pulley.
31. Remove the front timing cover seal.
32. Remove the front timing cover bolts and cover.
33. Pry the front oil seal from the front cover, if necessary.

To install:

34. Install the front crankshaft seal in the timing cover.
35. Install the timing cover and tighten bolts to 80 inch lbs. (9 Nm).
36. Raise and safely support the vehicle.
37. Install the front oil pan bolts and tighten the bolts to 88 inch lbs. (10 Nm).
38. Lower the vehicle.
39. Install the vibration damper and pulley. Tighten the bolt to 154 ft. lbs. (210 Nm) plus 180°.
40. Install the accessory drive belt tensioner. Tighten bolt to 43 ft. lbs. (58 Nm).
41. Install the idler pulleys and tighten the bolts to 20 ft. lbs. (28 Nm).
42. Install the accessory drive belt.
43. Install the EGR air control valve assembly.
44. Install the glow plug module.
45. Install the charge air outlet tube.
46. Install the cooling fan module. Tighten upper bolts to 10 ft. lbs. (14 Nm).
47. Raise and safely support the vehicle.
48. Remove Special Tool 9102 Crankshaft Lock.
49. Install the starter blank.
50. Install the lower cooling fan module bolts and tighten the lower bolts to 10 ft. lbs. (14 Nm).
51. Install the power steering line between the retainer and cooling fan module.
52. Connect the cooling fan wiring harness connector.
53. Install the power steering hose between the cooling fan and suspension.
54. Install the power steering hose between the pump and cooling fan.
55. Install the front skid plate.
56. Lower the vehicle.
57. Install the hoses at the power steering reservoir.
58. Refill the power steering reservoir to the correct level.
59. Install the front engine cover bracket.
60. Install the engine cover.
61. Refill the cooling system to the correct level.
62. Refill the engine with oil to the correct level.
63. Connect the negative battery cable.
64. Purge the air from the power steering

system before starting by raising the vehicle and rotating the steering wheel back and forth 20 times.

65. Start the engine and follow the bleed procedure with the scan tool.

66. Turn engine off and inspect for leaks.

3.5L Engine

See Figures 75 through 78.

1. Open the hood.
2. Remove the engine cover.
3. Disconnect the remote battery ground.
4. Raise and support the vehicle.
5. Turn the engine to 40 degrees after Top Dead Center.
6. Install the crankshaft locking tool.
7. Remove the lower splash shield.
8. Drain the coolant.
9. Drain the engine oil.
10. Remove the lower bolt to the engine oil dipstick tube.
11. Lower the vehicle.
12. Remove the grille.
13. Remove the cooling module.
14. Remove the PCM.
15. Remove the engine harness.
16. Remove the upper oil dipstick tube bolt.
17. Remove the oil dipstick and oil dipstick tube.
18. Remove the intake manifold.
19. Remove the air pump (5).
20. Remove the lower oil pan bolts.
21. Remove the lower oil pan.
22. Remove the upper oil pan bolts.
23. Remove the upper oil pan.
24. Remove the accessory drive belt.
25. Remove the thermostat housing.
26. Remove the thermostat gasket.
27. Remove the accessory drive belt tensioner assembly.
28. Remove the oil filter/cooler housing.
29. Remove the idler pulley.
30. Remove the crankshaft damper bolt.

31. Remove the crankshaft damper pulley.
32. Remove the water pump pulley bolts.
33. Remove the water pump pulley.
34. Remove the water pump.
35. Remove the water pump gasket.
36. Remove the left front cylinder head cover.
37. Remove the right side air control valve bolts.
38. Remove the right side air control valve.
39. Remove the right air control valve gasket.
40. Remove the upper right front cylinder head cover.
41. Remove the left air control valve.
42. Remove the left air control valve gasket.
43. Remove the left air control valve adapter.
44. Remove the left air control valve adapter gasket.
45. Remove and position aside the power steering pump.
46. Remove and position aside the AC compressor.
47. Remove the generator.
48. Remove the left cylinder head cover.
49. Remove the right cylinder head cover.
50. Remove the timing chain tensioner.
51. Install a drift into the camshaft to lock the split gears.
52. Remove the timing chain guide roll pins from the right cylinder head.
53. Remove the center valve bolts from the camshafts.

➡The intake camshaft adjuster bolts are a L.H. thread. The exhaust camshaft bolts are a R.H thread.

54. Remove the CMP plates.

➡Support the timing chain to prevent it from falling off the crankshaft or balance shaft.

55. Remove the camshaft adjusters.
56. Remove the cylinder head to front cover bolts in the left cylinder head.
57. Remove the cylinder head to front cover bolts in the right cylinder head.

➡The front cover bolts have several different sizes. Note the locations of each bolt.

58. Remove the front cover bolts.
59. Remove the front cover.

To install:

➡Make sure that all sealing surfaces on the engine are clean and free of oil.

60. Make sure the front cover O-rings at

the water pump inlet and outlet are intact and in place.

61. Turn the balance shaft so that the timing mark on the balance shaft matches the timing mark on the engine block.

62. Make sure the timing chain is correctly mounted to the crankshaft and balance shaft sprockets.

63. Install the front cover.

64. Install the front cover bolts. Use a cross pattern to tighten the front cover bolts to 15 ft. lbs. (20 Nm).

65. Install the cylinder head to front cover bolts in the right cylinder head.

66. Tighten the cylinder head to front cover bolts to 132 inch lbs. (15 Nm) and then an additional 90 degrees.

67. Install the cylinder head to front cover bolts in the left cylinder head.

68. Tighten the cylinder head to front cover bolts to 132 inch lbs. (15 Nm) and then an additional 90 degrees.

69. Coat the end of the camshafts with a small amount of oil.

70. Line up the pin in the camshaft adjusters with the hole in the camshafts.

71. The camshaft pulse wheel must be replaced every time it is removed. The dimples in the pulse wheel must line up with the depressions in the camshaft adjusters.

72. Make sure that the crankshaft is set to 40° ATDC, and that the crankshaft lock is installed.

73. When the crankshaft adjusters are correctly installed, the timing marks will line up with each other and the top mark will be pointed up.

74. Install the timing chain onto the left cylinder head intake camshaft adjuster.

75. Install the camshaft adjuster to the intake camshaft in the left cylinder head.

76. Install the camshaft adjuster to the exhaust camshaft in the left cylinder head. Make sure the timing marks line up correctly.

36543_SPRI_G0020

Fig. 75 Aligning dimples and depressions—3.5L Engine

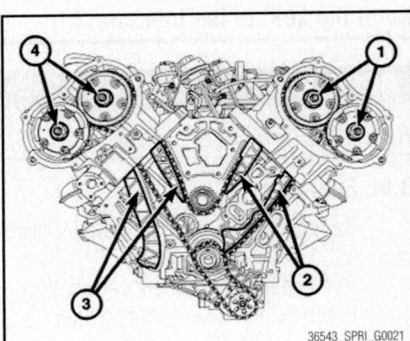

36543_SPRI_G0021

Fig. 76 Center valves (1), tensioners (2), slide rails (3) and center valves (4)—3.5L Engine

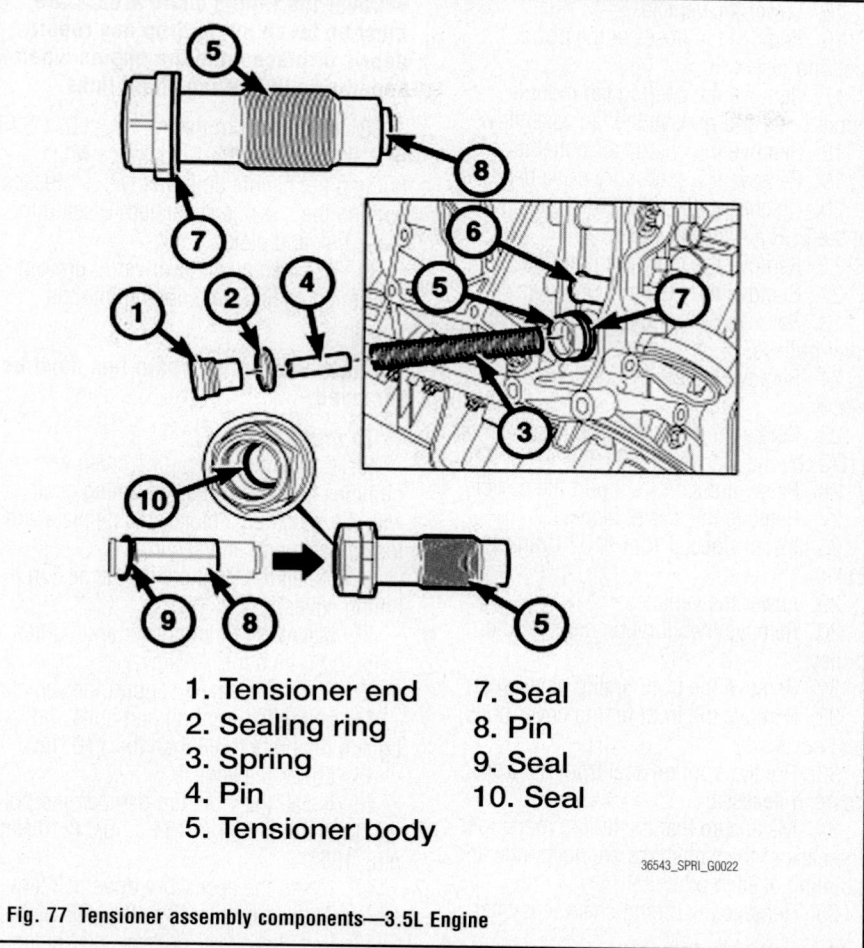

1. Tensioner end
2. Sealing ring
3. Spring
4. Pin
5. Tensioner body
7. Seal
8. Pin
9. Seal
10. Seal

36543_SPRI_G0022

Fig. 77 Tensioner assembly components—3.5L Engine

77. Install the slide rails (3).

78. Install the timing chain on the right cylinder head intake camshaft adjuster.

79. Install the right cylinder head camshaft adjuster to the intake camshaft.

80. Install the right cylinder head exhaust camshaft adjuster.

81. Verify that the intake camshafts are correctly timed to the crankshaft position.

➡**The center valves in the exhaust camshafts are L. H. thread. The center valves in the intake camshafts are R.H. thread.**

82. Install new CMP plates.

83. Install the center valves into the left and right cylinder head camshafts.

84. Tighten the camshaft adjuster center valves to 106 ft. lbs. (145 Nm).

85. Remove the drift from the camshafts.

86. Reset the timing chain tensioner by removing the end of the tensioner assembly.

87. Remove the sealing ring from the tensioner assembly.

88. Remove the spring (3) and (4) pin from the tensioner assembly.

89. Replace the pin (8) into the back of the tensioner assembly, followed by the spring (3), dowel (4), sealing ring (2), and tensioner end (1).

90. Tighten the end of the tensioner to 36 ft. lbs. (50 Nm)

91. Install the timing chain tensioner and tighten to 51 ft. lbs. (70 Nm)

92. Apply silicone to the cylinder head cover sealing surface.

93. Install the right cylinder head cover.

94. Install the left cylinder head cover.

95. Tighten the cylinder head cover bolts to 106 inch lbs. (12 Nm) and then an additional 90 degrees.

96. Install the power steering pump.

97. Install the AC compressor.

98. Install the left air control valve adapter gasket.

99. Install the left air control valve adapter. Tighten the left air control valve adapter bolts to 143 inch lbs. (14 Nm)

100. Install the left air control valve gasket.

101. Install the left air control valve. Tighten the left air control valve bolts to 143 inch lbs. (14 Nm)

102. Apply a bead of silicone to the cylinder head front cover sealing surface.

103. Install the left front cylinder head cover.

104. Tighten the front cover bolts in a cross pattern to 70 inch lbs. (8 Nm).

105. Apply a bead of silicone to the cylinder head front cover sealing surface.

106. Install the upper right front cylinder head cover.

107. Tighten the front cover bolts in a cross pattern to 70 inch lbs. (8 Nm).

108. Install the right air control valve gasket.

109. Install the right side air control valve.

110. Install the right air control valve bolts.

111. Tighten the bolts to 123 inch lbs. (14 Nm).

112. Install the water pump gasket.

113. Install the water pump.

114. Tighten the water pump bolts in a cross pattern to 18 ft. lbs. (25 Nm).

115. Install the water pump pulley.

116. Install the water pump pulley bolts.

117. Tighten the water pump pulley M7 bolts to 88 inch lbs. (10 Nm) and then to 18 ft. lbs. (25 Nm).

118. Tighten the water pump pulley M8 bolts to 44 inch lbs. (5 Nm) and then to 15 ft. lbs. (20 Nm).

119. Install the crankshaft damper pulley.

120. Install the crankshaft damper bolt and tighten to 147 ft. lbs. (200 Nm) and then an additional 90 degrees.

121. Install the idler pulley.

122. Tighten the idler pulley bolts to 26 ft. lbs. (35 Nm)

123. Install the oil filter/cooler housing.

124. Tighten the oil filter/cooler housing bolts to 15 ft. lbs. (20 Nm).

125. Install the thermostat gasket.

126. Install the thermostat housing and tighten the bolts to 18 ft. lbs. (25 Nm).

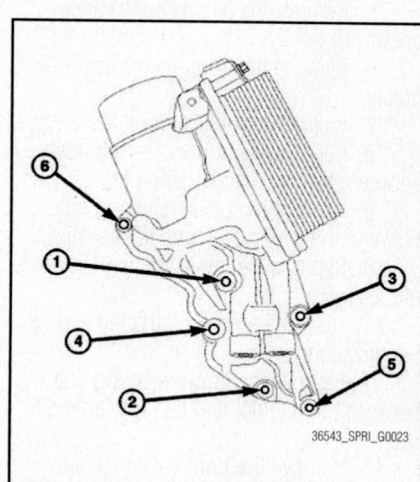

36543_SPRI_G0023

Fig. 78 Oil filter/cooler housing bolt torque sequence—3.5L Engine

127. Install the accessory drive belt tensioner assembly and tighten the bolts to 25 ft. lbs. (35 Nm).

128. Install the accessory drive belt.

129. Install the air pump.

130. Install the intake manifold.

131. Install the engine harness.

132. Install the PCM.

133. Raise the vehicle.

134. Remove the crankshaft lock.

135. Install the starter.

136. Install the generator.

137. Install the upper oil pan. Refer to Oil Pan.

138. Install the lower oil pan.

139. Install the oil dipstick and oil dipstick tube.

140. Install the lower bolt to the engine oil dipstick tube.

141. Install the upper oil dipstick tube bolt and tighten to 80 inch lbs. (9 Nm).

142. Install the lower splash shield.

143. Lower the vehicle.

144. Connect the remote battery ground.

145. Install the cooling module.

146. Install the grille.

147. Fill the coolant.

148. Fill the engine oil.

149. Install the engine cover.

150. Close the hood.

TIMING CHAIN AND SPROCKETS

REMOVAL & INSTALLATION

3.0L Engine

1. Disconnect the negative battery cable.

2. Drain the cooling system.

3. Drain the engine oil.

4. Drain the power steering fluid.

5. Remove the engine appearance cover.

6. Remove the front engine cover bracket.

7. Raise and safely support the vehicle.

8. Remove the power steering hose between the pump and cooling fan.

9. Remove the power steering hose between the cooling fan and suspension.

10. Remove the lower cooling fan module retaining bolts.

11. Disconnect the cooling fan wiring harness connector.

12. Remove the power steering line between the retainer and cooling fan module.

13. Remove the front splash shield.

14. Remove the front oil pan to timing cover bolts.

15. Lower the vehicle.

16. Remove the hoses at the power steering reservoir.

17. Remove the cooling fan module upper bolts and remove the fan assembly.

18. Remove the charge air outlet tube.

19. Remove the accessory drive belt.

20. Disconnect the charge air inlet hose at the EGR air control valve.

21. Remove the glow plug module.

22. Remove the EGR air control valve.

23. Remove both accessory drive belt idler pulleys.

24. Remove the accessory drive belt tensioner.

25. Rotate the engine to Top Dead Center (TDC) by the crankshaft bolt.

26. Raise and safely support the vehicle.

27. Remove the starter blank.

28. Install Special Tool 9102 Crankshaft Lock.

29. Lower the vehicle.

30. Remove the vibration damper and pulley.

31. Remove the front timing cover seal.

32. Remove the front timing cover bolts and cover.

33. Pry the front oil seal from the front cover, if necessary.

34. Make sure that the timing marks on the back of the camshafts are horizontal and pointing at each other.

35. Remove the timing chain tensioner.

➡ **Cover the timing chain area. Care must be taken not to drop any repair debris or pieces into the engine when separating the timing chain links.**

36. Install Special Tool 9554 using two of the cylinder head cover bolts.

37. Assemble Special Tool 9312-1 using 9312-3 and 9312-4. Install Insert 9312-13 and retain with screw provided.

✳✳ CAUTION

Care must be taken not to drop the timing chain plates into the engine once the timing chain is separated.

➡ **When installing Special Tool 9312-1 onto timing chain link, be sure to back off the smaller nut of the Thrust Pin 9312-3 until the pin is recessed inside of the spindle, 9312-4. Screw the Thrust Spindle 9312-4 in until it is seated and aligned properly over the rivet of the timing chain.**

➡ **When fitting the thrust spindle, ensure that the thrust pin is positioned at the left timing chain pin of a chain link.**

➡ **Cover the timing chain area. Care must be taken not to drop any repair debris or pieces into the engine when separating the timing chain links.**

38. Carefully turn the thrust pin 9312-13 of Special Tool 9312-1 clockwise while holding the handle until the rivet is pressed out and the chain is separated. Discard the loose link and plates.

39. Use a small screwdriver to prevent the timing chain from slipping into the engine.

➡ **One whole timing chain link must be removed.**

To install:

40. Connect a new timing chain with the oil holes facing up, and old timing chain with the assembly link, assembly plate and locking element, and secure.

41. Install the front crankshaft seal in the timing cover.

42. Install the timing cover and tighten bolts to 80 inch lbs. (9 Nm).

43. Raise and safely support the vehicle.

44. Install the front oil pan bolts and tighten the bolts to 88 inch lbs. (10 Nm).

45. Lower the vehicle.

46. Install the vibration damper and pulley. Tighten the bolt to 154 ft. lbs. (210 Nm) plus 180°.

47. Install the accessory drive belt tensioner. Tighten bolt to 43 ft. lbs. (58 Nm).

48. Install the idler pulleys and tighten the bolts to 20 ft. lbs. (28 Nm).

49. Install the accessory drive belt.

50. Install the EGR air control valve assembly.

51. Install the glow plug module.

52. Install the charge air outlet tube.

53. Install the cooling fan module. Tighten upper bolts to 10 ft. lbs. (14 Nm).

54. Raise and safely support the vehicle.

55. Remove Special Tool 9102 Crankshaft Lock.

56. Install the starter blank.

57. Install the lower cooling fan module bolts and tighten the lower bolts to 10 ft. lbs. (14 Nm).

58. Install the power steering line between the retainer and cooling fan module.

59. Connect the cooling fan wiring harness connector.

60. Install the power steering hose between the cooling fan and suspension.

61. Install the power steering hose between the pump and cooling fan.

62. Install the front skid plate.

63. Lower the vehicle.

64. Install the hoses at the power steering reservoir.

65. Refill the power steering reservoir to the correct level.

66. Install the front engine cover bracket.

67. Install the engine cover.

68. Refill the cooling system to the correct level.

69. Refill the engine with oil to the correct level.

70. Connect the negative battery cable.

71. Purge the air from the power steering system before starting by raising the vehicle and rotating the steering wheel back and forth 20 times.

72. Start the engine and follow the bleed procedure with the scan tool.

73. Turn engine off and inspect for leaks.

3.5L Engine

See Figures 79 through 81.

1. Disconnect the negative battery cable.

2. Drain the cooling system.

3. Drain the engine oil

4. Remove the engine appearance cover.

5. Raise and safely support the vehicle.

6. Turn the engine to 40 degrees after Top Dead Center (TDC).

7. Install the crankshaft locking tool.

8. Remove the lower splash shield.

9. Remove the lower bolt to the engine oil dipstick tube.

10. Lower the vehicle.

11. Remove the grille.

12. Remove the cooling module.

13. Remove the PCM.

14. Remove the engine harness.

15. Remove the upper oil dipstick tube bolt.

16. Remove the oil dipstick and oil dipstick tube.

17. Remove the intake manifold.

18. Remove the air pump.

19. Remove the lower and upper oil pan.

20. Remove the accessory drive belt.

21. Remove the thermostat housing.

22. Remove the thermostat gasket.

23. Remove the accessory drive belt tensioner assembly.

24. Remove the oil filter/cooler housing.

25. Remove the idler pulley.

26. Remove the crankshaft damper bolt.

27. Remove the crankshaft damper pulley.

28. Remove the water pump and gasket.

29. Remove the left front cylinder head cover.

30. Remove the right side air control valve.

31. Remove the right air control valve gasket.

32. Remove the upper right front cylinder head cover.

33. Remove the left air control valve and gasket.

34. Remove the left air control valve adapter and gasket.

35. Remove and position aside the power steering pump.

36. Remove and position aside the AC compressor.

37. Remove the alternator.

38. Remove the cylinder head covers.

39. Remove the timing chain tensioner.

40. Install a drift into the camshaft to lock the split gears.

41. Remove the timing chain guide (2, 3) roll pins from the right cylinder head.

42. Remove the center valve bolts (1, 4) from the camshafts.

➡ **The intake camshaft adjuster bolts are a left-hand thread. The exhaust camshaft bolts are a right-hand thread.**

➡ **Support the timing chain to prevent it from falling off the crankshaft or balance shaft.**

43. Remove the camshaft adjusters.

44. Remove the cylinder head to front cover bolts in the left cylinder head.

45. Remove the cylinder head to front cover bolts in the right cylinder head.

➡ **The front cover bolts have several different sizes. Note the locations of each bolt.**

46. Remove the front cover bolts.

47. Remove the front cover.

48. Remove the timing chain tensioner.

49. Use a slide hammer to remove the slide rail pins in the left and right cylinder head.

50. Remove the oil pump chain.

51. Remove the timing chain slide rails.

52. Insert a drift into left camshaft adjuster.

22043_SPRI_G0053

Fig. 79 Remove the timing chain guide (2,3) roll pins and center valve bolts (1,4) from the camshafts—3.5L engine

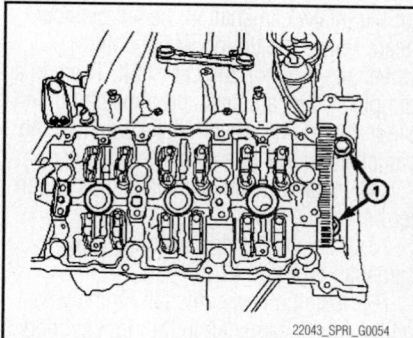

22043_SPRI_G0054

Fig. 80 The cylinder head-to-front cover bolts must be removed in each cylinder head—3.5L Engine

53. Insert a drift into the right camshaft adjuster.

54. Remove the camshaft adjuster from the left cylinder head.

55. Remove the camshaft adjuster from the right cylinder head.

56. Disconnect the timing chain links.

57. Remove the timing chain.

To install:

58. Make sure that the drift is installed into the camshaft adjuster.

59. Align the pin with the hole in the end of the camshaft to install the camshaft adjuster on the intake camshaft.

60. When the camshaft is correctly aligned on the camshaft adjuster, the alignment marks on the back of the camshaft adjuster will be lined up and the camshaft will seat all of the way into the adjuster.

61. Install the intake and exhaust camshafts into the cylinder head so that the horizontal alignment marks line up with the top edge of the cylinder head and the vertical alignment mark is pointed upwards.

62. Align the slot in the balance shaft with the mark on the cylinder head (the mark is at about the 2 o'clock position).

63. Replace any timing chain guides with excessive wear.

64. Install all of the timing chain guides.

65. Install the timing chain guide pins.

66. Feed one end of the timing chain into the left cylinder head.

67. Feed the timing chain through the engine and around the balance shaft.

68. Draw the timing chain up through the right cylinder head and over the right cylinder head intake camshaft.

69. Feed the chain down through the cylinder head to the crankshaft sprocket.

70. Draw the timing chain up through the left cylinder head.

71. Assemble the chain using a new link.

72. Remove the drift from the left camshaft adjuster.

73. Install a new camshaft timing wheel on the intake camshaft in the left cylinder head. Rotate the timing wheel until the wheel sits flush on the camshaft. There is a dimple in the camshaft and a matching dimple in the timing wheel. Make sure that the camshaft timing wheel dimples line up.

74. Install the left camshaft adjuster center bolt finger tight.

75. Remove the drift from the right camshaft adjuster.

76. Install a new camshaft timing wheel on the intake camshaft in the right cylinder head. Rotate the timing wheel until the wheel sits flush on the camshaft. There is a dimple in the camshaft and a matching dim-

ple in the timing wheel. Make sure that the camshaft timing wheel dimples line up.

77. Install the right camshaft adjuster center bolt finger tight.

78. Make sure the front cover O-rings at the water pump inlet and outlet are intact and in place.

79. Turn the balance shaft so that the timing mark on the balance shaft matches the timing mark on the engine block.

80. Make sure the timing chain is correctly mounted to the crankshaft and balance shaft sprockets.

81. Install the front cover and tighten the bolts in a crisscross pattern to 15 ft. lbs. (20 Nm).

82. Tighten the cylinder head-to-front cover bolts to 11 ft. lbs. (15 Nm) plus an additional 90°.

83. Coat the end of the camshafts with a small amount of oil.

84. Line up the pin in the camshaft adjusters with the hole in the camshafts.

85. The camshaft pulse wheel must be replaced every time it is removed. The dimples in the pulse wheel must line up with the depressions in the camshaft adjusters.

86. Make sure that the crankshaft is set to 40° After Top Dead Center (ATDC), and that the crankshaft lock is installed.

87. When the crankshaft adjusters are correctly installed, the timing marks will line up with each other and the top mark will be pointed up.

88. Install the timing chain onto the left cylinder head intake camshaft adjuster.

89. Install the camshaft adjuster to the intake camshaft in the left cylinder head.

90. Install the camshaft adjuster to the exhaust camshaft in the left cylinder head.

Make sure the timing marks line up correctly.

91. Install the slide rails.

92. Install the timing chain on the right cylinder head intake camshaft adjuster.

93. Install the right cylinder head camshaft adjuster to the intake camshaft.

94. Install the right cylinder head exhaust camshaft adjuster.

95. Verify that the intake camshafts are correctly timed to the crankshaft position.

96. Install the center valves into the left and right cylinder head camshafts and tighten to 106 ft. lbs. (145 Nm).

97. Remove the drift from the camshafts.

98. Reset the timing chain tensioner by removing the end of the tensioner assembly.

99. Remove the sealing ring from the tensioner assembly.

100. Remove the spring and pin from the tensioner assembly.

101. Replace the pin into the back of the tensioner assembly, followed by the spring, dowel, sealing ring, and tensioner end.

102. Tighten the end of the tensioner to 36 ft. lbs. (50 Nm).

103. Install the timing chain tensioner and tighten to 51 ft. lbs. (70 Nm).

104. Apply silicone to the cylinder head cover sealing surfaces and install the left and right cylinder head covers. Tighten the cylinder head cover bolts to 106 inch lbs. (12 Nm) plus an additional 90°. Refer to Cylinder Head.

105. Install the power steering pump.

106. Install the AC compressor.

107. Install the left air control valve adapter gasket and adapter. Tighten the left air control valve adapter bolts to 10 ft. lbs. (14 Nm).

108. Install the left air control valve gasket and control valve. Tighten the left air control valve bolts to 10 ft. lbs. (14 Nm).

109. Apply a bead of silicone to the cylinder head front cover sealing surface.

110. Install the left front cylinder head cover and tighten the front cover bolts in a cross pattern to 70 inch lbs. (8 Nm).

111. Apply a bead of silicone to the cylinder head front cover sealing surface.

112. Install the upper right front cylinder head cover and tighten the front cover bolts in a cross pattern to 70 inch lbs. (8 Nm).

113. Install the right air control valve gasket and control valve. Tighten the mounting bolts to 10 ft. lbs. (14 Nm).

114. Install the water pump gasket and water pump. Tighten the mounting bolts to 18 ft. lbs. (25 Nm).

115. Install the water pump pulley. Tighten the water pump pulley M7 bolts to 88 inch lbs. (10 Nm) and then to 18 ft. lbs.

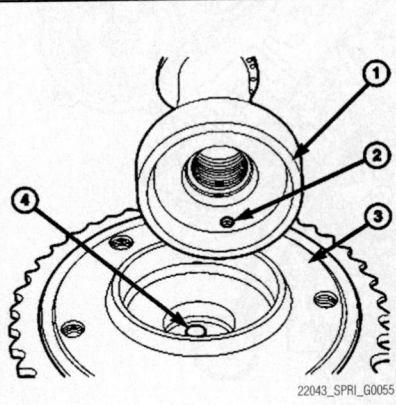

22043_SPRI_G0055

Fig. 81 After coating the end of the camshaft (1) with oil, line up the pin in the camshaft adjusters (4) with the hole in the camshafts (2)—3.5L Engine

(25 Nm). Tighten the water pump pulley M8 bolts to 44 inch lbs. (5 Nm) and then to 15 ft. lbs. (20 Nm).

116. Install the crankshaft damper pulley and tighten to 147 ft. lbs. (200 Nm) plus 90°.

117. Install the idler pulley and tighten the bolts to 26 ft. lbs. (35 Nm).

118. Install the oil filter/cooler housing and tighten the housing bolts to 15 ft. lbs. (20 Nm).

119. Install the thermostat gasket, and install the thermostat housing. Tighten the bolts to 18 ft. lbs. (25 Nm).

120. Install the accessory drive belt tensioner assembly and tighten the bolts to 25 ft. lbs. (35 Nm).

121. Install the accessory drive belt.
122. Install the air pump.
123. Install the intake manifold.
124. Install the engine harness.
125. Install the PCM.
126. Raise and safely support the vehicle.
127. Remove the crankshaft lock.
128. Install the starter.
129. Install the alternator.
130. Install the upper and lower oil pans.
131. Install the oil dipstick and oil dipstick tube. Tighten the mounting bolt to 80 inch lbs. (9 Nm).
132. Install the lower splash shield.
133. Lower the vehicle.
134. Install the cooling module.
135. Install the grille.
136. Refill the cooling system to the correct level.
137. Refill the engine with oil to the correct level.
138. Install the engine appearance cover.
139. Connect the negative battery cable.
140. Start the engine and check for leaks.

TURBOCHARGER

REMOVAL & INSTALLATION

3.0L Engine

See Figures 82 and 83.

1. Disconnect the negative battery cable.
2. Drain the cooling system.
3. Remove the engine appearance cover.
4. Remove the air cleaner to turbo intake tube.
5. Remove the engine cover front bracket.
6. Remove the turbo to cooler air turbo.
7. Remove the turbo heat shield.
8. Remove the elbow-to-converter exhaust clamp.

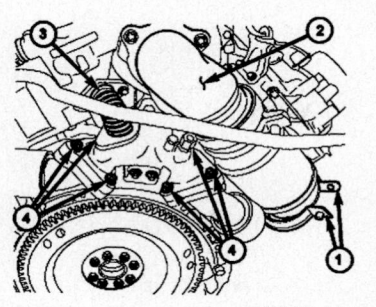

Fig. 82 Remove the exhaust clamp (1), exhaust elbow (2), EGR tube (3) and manifold retaining bolts (4) to access the turbo—3.0L Engine

9. Remove the turbo front bracket retaining bolts.
10. Raise and safely support the vehicle.
11. Remove the front splash shield.
12. Disconnect the downstream catalytic converter at the extension pipe.
13. Disconnect the extension pipe to muffler.
14. Disconnect the O2 sensor wire connector.
15. Reposition the extension pipe and catalytic converter.
16. Lower the vehicle.
17. Disconnect catalytic converter to downstream catalytic converter clamp.
18. Remove upstream catalytic converter.
19. Disconnect the transmission fill tube and trim cover bracket and set aside.
20. Disconnect exhaust elbow at turbo.
21. Disconnect EGR tube at manifold to left cylinder head.
22. Remove left and right exhaust manifold retaining bolts and gaskets.
23. Remove the front turbo retaining bolts.
24. Remove the turbo mount retaining bolts.
25. Remove the turbocharger assembly.

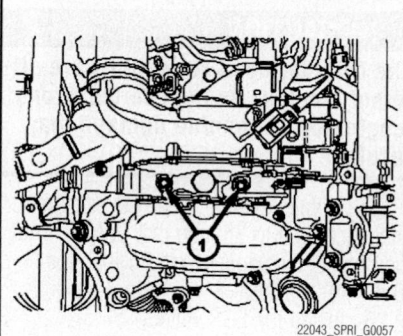

Fig. 83 Remove the front turbo bolts (1) and turbo mount retaining bolts to remove the turbocharger—3.0L Engine

26. Disconnect the turbo boost pressure servo connector.

To install:

27. Reconnect the turbo boost pressure servo connector, if it was disconnected.
28. Position and install the turbocharger on the exhaust manifold, tighten the mount retaining bolts to 22 ft. lbs. (30 Nm).
29. Install the front turbo retaining bolts and gasket.

❊❊ CAUTION

Make sure the gasket is installed properly or the turbo oil feed hole will be blocked.

30. Install left and right exhaust manifold retaining bolts and gaskets (4).
31. Reconnect EGR tube at manifold to left cylinder head (3).
32. Reconnect EGR tube at manifold to left cylinder head (3).
33. Reconnect the transmission fill tube and trim cover bracket.
34. Install the upstream catalytic converter.
35. Raise and safely support the vehicle.
36. Reconnect catalytic converter to downstream catalytic converter clamp.
37. Install the extension pipe and catalytic converter.
38. Reconnect the O2 sensor wire connector.
39. Reconnect the extension pipe to muffler.
40. Reconnect the downstream catalytic converter at the extension pipe.
41. Install the front splash shield.
42. Lower the vehicle.
43. Install the turbo front bracket retaining bolts.
44. Install the exhaust clamp (elbow to converter)
45. Install the turbo heat shield.
46. Install air tube (turbo to cooler).
47. Install the engine cover front bracket.
48. Install the air intake tube (air cleaner to turbo)
49. Install the engine appearance cover.
50. Connect the negative battery cable.

VALVE COVERS

REMOVAL & INSTALLATION

3.0L Engine

Left

See Figures 84 and 85.

1. Disconnect negative battery cable.
2. Remove engine cover and bracket.

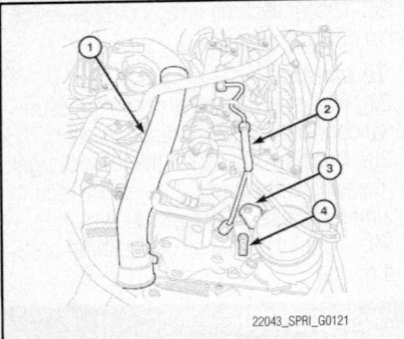

Fig. 84 Remove high pressure fuel line (2), bracket (3), fuel temperature sensor connector (4) and intercooler air inlet tube (1).

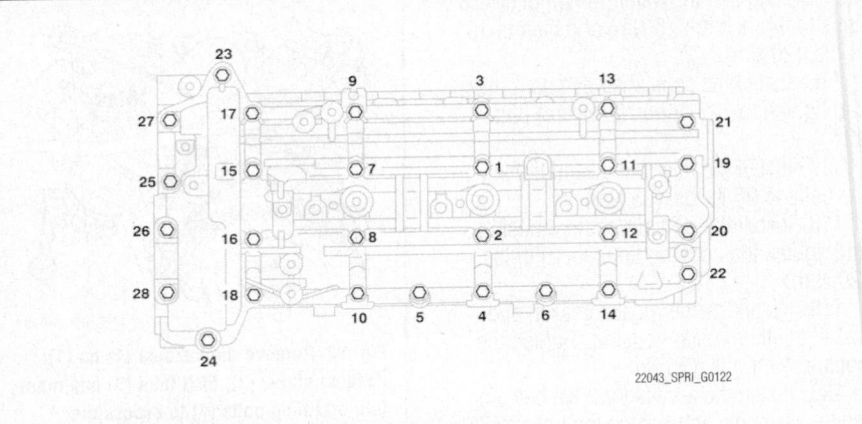

Fig. 85 Tighten left cylinder cover bolts in sequence.

3. Remove air cleaner cover and inlet tube to turbocharger.

4. Remove the high pressure line (2) from the fuel pump and the fuel rail.

5. Remove the bracket (3) from the oil filter housing.

6. Disconnect the fuel temperature sensor connector (4).

7. Disconnect the fuel quantity solenoid connector.

8. Remove the wiring harness retaining bolts and position the engine harness aside.

9. Remove the bolts from the intercooler air chamber.

10. Remove the turbo outlet to intercooler inlet air tube (1).

11. Remove the power brake booster vacuum line from the vacuum pump and position aside.

12. Disconnect the power feed line from the alternator and position aside.

13. Remove the supply and return fuel lines.

14. Disconnect the EGR solenoid connector.

15. Remove the EGR valve.

16. Disconnect the fuel injector electrical connectors.

17. Remove the fuel injector wiring harness from the cylinder head cover and position aside.

18. Remove the left cylinder head fuel return line.

19. Remove the high pressure fuel lines from the fuel injectors.

20. Remove the fuel injectors.

✳✳ CAUTION

Care must be taken when removing the cylinder head cover. The cover is the camshaft retainer and end play interface. Do not pry on the cylinder head cover tabs.

✳✳ CAUTION

The cylinder head cover is sealed with Mopar sealant that may be difficult when separating components. If the component are difficult to separate heat the sealed edges or area with a heat gun. DO NOT use any heat source that works with flame.

➡ **Note the different length cylinder head cover bolts and their position for assembly purposes.**

21. Remove the cylinder head cover fasteners and cover.

To install:

22. Clean and inspect all sealing surfaces.

➡ **Care must be taken not to get any engine sealant on the camshaft journals of the cylinder head cover.**

23. Install a ⅛ inch bead of Mopar® Engine RTV Gen II sealant to the underside of the cylinder head cover

24. Carefully position the cylinder head cover and install the bolts into their original position.

✳✳ CAUTION

The cylinder head cover bolts are different lengths. Do not use the wrong length bolts or engine damage may result.

25. Tighten cylinder head cover bolts in sequence, first to 35 inch lbs. (4 Nm), and then repeat the sequence to 75 inch lbs. (8.4 Nm).

26. Install the EGR valve.

✳✳ CAUTION

The fuel injector sealing washers MUST be replaced. DO NOT use the old sealing washers or double the sealing washers.

➡ **Care must be taken not to apply any lubricant to the fuel injector nozzles.**

27. Install the fuel injectors. Tighten the injector retaining claw bolt to 60 inch lbs. (7 Nm) and then an additional 180°.

28. Re-position and secure the engine harness.

29. Install the left fuel rail. Tighten the fuel rail bolts to 97 inch lbs. (11 Nm).

30. Position the return fuel lines and secure to the injectors. Push down on the release lock tab to secure.

31. Connect the fuel injector electrical connectors.

32. Install the left rear engine cover bracket.

33. Install the high pressure fuel lines from the fuel rail to injectors. Tighten the line connections to 20 ft. lbs. (27 Nm).

34. Install the fuel line from the high pressure pump to the left fuel rail. Tighten the retaining bolt to 22 ft. lbs. (30 Nm).

35. Install the fuel supply line to the fuel filter and high pressure pump.

36. Connect both fuel lines at the high pressure pump.

37. Install the air filter housing and tube.

38. Connect the negative battery cable.

39. Start the engine, run until warm, turn engine off and inspect for leaks.

Right

See Figure 86.

1. Disconnect the negative battery cable.

2. Position the coolant reservoir aside.

3. Remove the strut tower support.

4. Remove engine cover.

5. Remove engine cover front bracket.

6. Remove air cleaner cover and inlet tube to turbocharger.

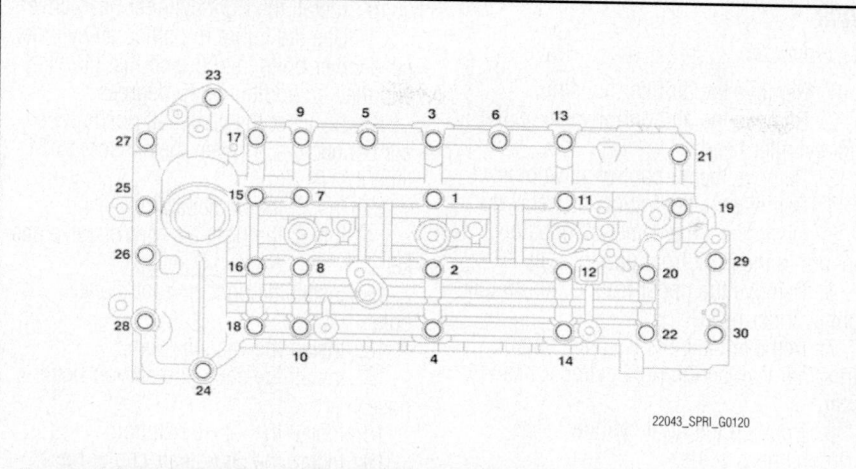

Fig. 86 Tighten right cylinder head cover bolts in sequence.

7. Remove engine cover right rear bracket.

8. Remove the crankcase ventilation valve (CCV) and breather tube.

9. Disconnect the fuel return line.

10. Disconnect the fuel supply and return lines at the right cylinder head cover.

11. Disconnect the camshaft position sensor (CMP) and fuel injector wiring and position the right engine wiring harness aside.

12. Pull out on the fuel injector return fuel hose retainers, disconnect the hoses and position aside.

13. Remove the right fuel injectors.

14. Remove the air conditioning (A/C) heater hose bracket.

15. Remove the oil level indicator tube retaining bolt.

16. Remove the EGR air control valve assembly resonator.

17. Remove the vacuum pump.

18. Remove the cylinder head cover retaining bolts and remove cover.

To install:

19. Clean and inspect all sealing surfaces.

➡ **Care must be taken not to get any engine sealant on the camshaft journals of the cylinder head cover.**

20. Install a ⅛ inch bead of Mopar Engine RTV Gen II sealant to the underside of the cylinder head cover.

✳✳ CAUTION

The cylinder head cover bolts are different lengths. Make sure to install the bolts into their original position.

21. Carefully position the cylinder head cover and install the bolts into their original position.

22. Tighten cylinder head cover bolts in sequence, first to 35 inch lbs. (4 Nm), and then repeat the sequence to 75 inch lbs (8.4 Nm).

✳✳ CAUTION

Make sure to replace the lower copper washer seal on the injector. DO NOT re-use the old seal, DO NOT double the seals.

23. Install the fuel injectors. Tighten the retaining claw bolts to 60 inch lbs. (7 Nm) and then an additional 180°.

24. Install the CCV housing. Tighten the fasteners to 80 inch lbs. (9 Nm).

25. Install the vacuum pump. Tighten the fasteners to 80 inch lbs. (9 Nm).

26. Install the EGR air control valve resonator. Tighten the fasteners to 80 inch lbs. (9 Nm).

27. Install the oil level indicator tube fastener. Tighten the bolt to 97 inch lbs. (11 Nm).

28. Install the A/C heater hose bracket. Tighten the bolts to 80 inch lbs. (9 Nm).

29. Install the fuel rail. Tighten bolts to 80 inch lbs. (9 Nm).

➡ **Inspect all fuel lines for damage or wear. Replace as necessary. DO NOT over tighten the fuel line nuts.**

30. Install the fuel injector high pressure lines. Tighten line nuts to 24 ft. lbs. (33 Nm).

31. Position the engine wiring harness and connect the CMP, fuel rail pressure sensor and fuel injectors.

32. Connect the fuel return hoses to fuel injectors, pushing down on the hose retainers.

33. Install the air cleaner cover and inlet tube.

34. Install the rear engine cover bracket.

35. Connect the CCV hose to air inlet tube and connect the CCV heater wiring harness connector.

36. Install the engine cover.

37. Install the strut tower support.

38. Install the coolant reservoir.

39. Connect the negative battery cable.

40. Start engine, allow to warm, turn engine off and inspect for leaks.

3.5L Engine

Left

See Figure 87.

1. Remove the engine cover.

2. Release the fuel rail pressure.

3. Drain the coolant.

4. Drain the oil.

5. Remove the accessory drive belt.

6. Remove the power steering reservoir.

7. Remove the thermostat.

8. Remove the oil filter housing. Refer to Oil Filter Housing.

9. Remove the air pump.

10. Disconnect the PCM.

11. Remove the PCM.

12. Remove the bolts securing the engine wiring harness.

13. Position aside the engine wiring harness.

14. Remove the left cylinder head oil separator.

15. Disconnect the engine ground wire at the left cylinder head cover.

16. Disconnect the camshaft sensors in the left cylinder head.

17. Disconnect the three ignition coils in the left cylinder head.

18. Remove the three ignition coils from the left cylinder head.

19. Remove the upper front cover from the left cylinder head.

20. Remove the rubber grommets from the left cylinder head cover.

21. Remove the left cylinder head cover bolts.

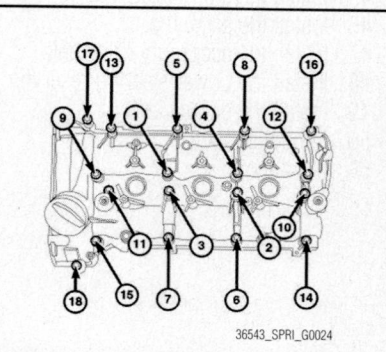

Fig. 87 Cylinder head cover bolt torque sequence—3.5L Engine

22. Use a heat gun and the tabs on the outside of the cylinder head cover to remove the left cylinder head cover.

To install:

23. Remove all debris, gasket material, and oil from the cylinder head cover sealing surface.

24. Apply a thin layer of silicone to the cylinder head cover sealing surface.

25. Install new cylinder head cover bolts.

26. Using the figure, torque the cylinder head cover bolts to 106 inch lbs. (12 Nm)

27. Use a torque angle gauge to turn the cylinder head cover bolts an additional 90°.

28. Install the rubber grommets on the left cylinder head cover.

29. Clean any debris, oil or silicone from the upper front cover sealing surface.

30. Apply silicone to the upper front cover sealing surface

31. Install the upper front cover from the left cylinder head.

32. Install the upper front cover bolts and torque to 80 inch lbs. (9 Nm).

33. Connect the engine ground wire at the left cylinder head cover.

34. Connect the camshaft sensors in the left cylinder head.

35. Install the three ignition coils from the left cylinder head.

36. Connect the three ignition coils in the left cylinder head.

37. Connect the engine ground to the left cylinder head.

38. Install the oil separator.

39. Torque the oil separator bolts to 106 inch lbs. (12 Nm).

40. Install the PCM.

41. Connect the PCM.

42. Install the bolts securing the engine wiring harness.

43. Position and install the engine wiring harness.

44. Install the oil filter housing.

45. Install the thermostat.

46. Install the air pump.

47. Install the accessory drive belt.

48. Install the power steering reservoir.

49. Install the engine cover.

50. Fill the coolant.

51. Fill the oil.

Right

See Figure 88.

1. Remove the air filter housing.

2. Remove the air control valve on the right cylinder head.

3. Remove the air control valve bracket.

4. Remove the centrifugal oil separator.

5. Disconnect the camshaft position sensors in the right front upper cover.

6. Remove the upper front cover on the right cylinder head.

7. Remove the bolts from the engine wiring harness on the right cylinder head cover.

8. Position the right cylinder head wiring harness aside.

9. Remove the cylinder head cover.

To install:

→The sealing compound should only be applied along the sealing area in the form of a bead of sealing compound of 1.0 mm ± 0.2 mm. The sealing compound must be applied within 10 minutes. The sealing compound bead must not be spread. Only the approved sealing compound may be used.

10. Install the right cylinder head cover.

11. Use the figure to tighten all cylinder head cover bolts to 106 inch lbs. (12 Nm) and then an additional 90 degrees.

12. Connect the camshaft position sensor connectors. Tighten the sensors to 71 inch lbs. (9 Nm)

13. Install the oil separator.

14. Install the right air control valve gasket.

15. Install the right air control valve bolts.

16. Install the vacuum pump.

17. Install the coolant reservoir bottle hose.

18. Install the intake manifold.

19. Install the charge air cooler hose.

20. Install the air filter housing.

VALVE LASH

ADJUSTMENT

All of the engines are equipped with hydraulic valve lifters that do not require periodic valve lash adjustment. Adjustment to zero lash is maintained automatically by hydraulic pressure in the lifters.

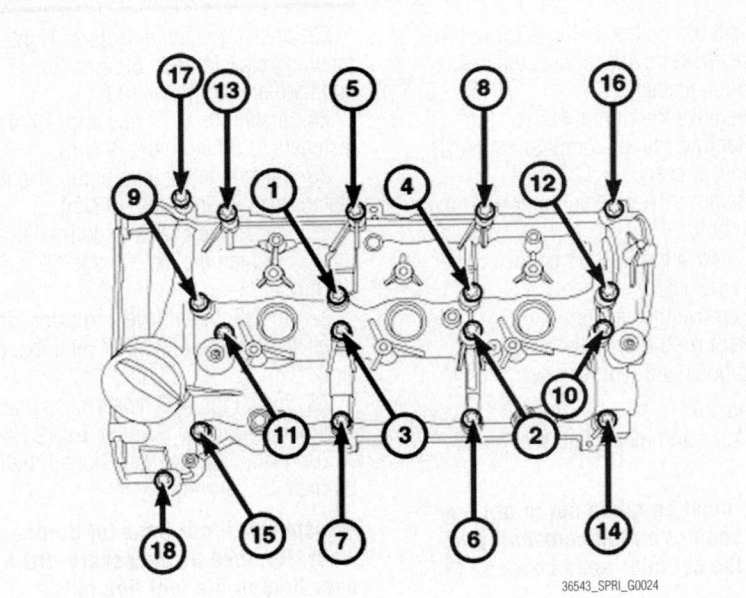

36543_SPRI_G0024

Fig. 88 Cylinder head cover bolt torque sequence—3.5L Engine

ENGINE PERFORMANCE & EMISSION CONTROLS

ACCELERATOR PEDAL POSITION (APP) SENSOR

LOCATION

The Accelerator Pedal Position (APP) sensor is located on the accelerator pedal assembly. The accelerator pedal position sensor is serviced as an assembly with the accelerator pedal assembly.

REMOVAL & INSTALLATION

3.0L Engine

See Figure 89.

1. Disconnect the negative battery cable.
2. Disconnect the APP sensor electrical connectors.
3. Remove the APP sensor fasteners and remove the sensor assembly (1).

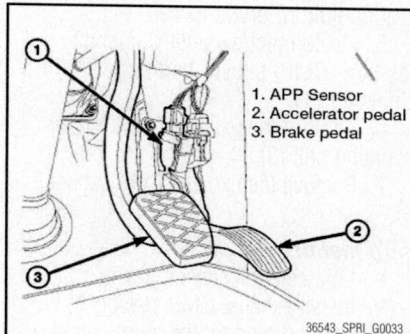

1. APP Sensor
2. Accelerator pedal
3. Brake pedal

36543_SPRI_G0033

Fig. 89 Accelerator Pedal Position (APP) sensor—3.0L Engine

To install:

4. Connect the accelerator pedal position sensor wiring harness connector.
5. Position the sensor assembly and install the fasteners.
6. Connect the negative battery cable.

3.5L Engine

See Figure 90.

1. Disconnect negative battery cable.
2. Disconnect the electrical connector from the module (2).
3. Remove the mounting nuts (1, 3).
4. Remove the Accelerator Pedal Position Sensor assembly (4) from the mounting studs.

To install:

5. Install the Accelerator Pedal Position Sensor module (4).
6. Tighten the mounting nuts and (3). Tighten to 71 inch lbs. (8 Nm).

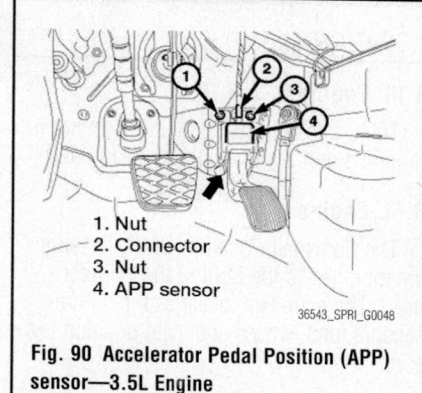

1. Nut
2. Connector
3. Nut
4. APP sensor

36543_SPRI_G0048

Fig. 90 Accelerator Pedal Position (APP) sensor—3.5L Engine

7. Connect the Harness Connector (2).
8. Connect negative battery cable.

AIR CHARGE TEMPERATURE (ACT) SENSOR

LOCATION

3.0L Engine

Air Charge Temperature (ACT) Sensor is located in the air intake duct.

REMOVAL & INSTALLATION

3.0L Engine

1. Disconnect the negative battery cable.
2. Unplug the wiring harness connector at the intake air temperature sensor (1).
3. Press together the sensor locking arms and remove the sensor from the air control valve extension (3).

To install:

4. Position the intake air temperature sensor along side of the air control valve extension (3) access hole.
5. Press together the sensor locking tabs, seat the sensor to the extension (3) and release tabs.
6. Connect negative battery cable.

BOOST PRESSURE SENSOR

LOCATION

3.0L Engine

The boost pressure sensor is mounted to the charge air pipe.

REMOVAL & INSTALLATION

3.0L Engine

See Figure 91.

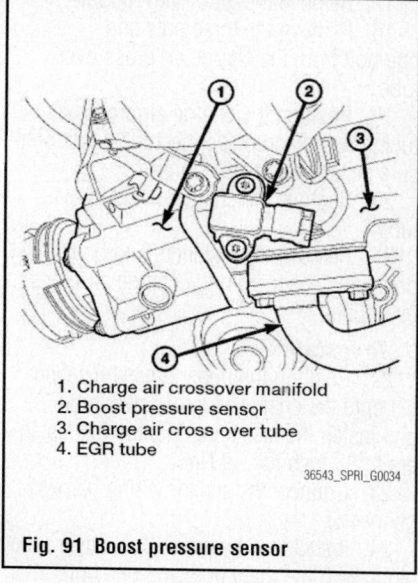

1. Charge air crossover manifold
2. Boost pressure sensor
3. Charge air cross over tube
4. EGR tube

36543_SPRI_G0034

Fig. 91 Boost pressure sensor

1. Disconnect the negative battery cable at battery.
2. Disconnect the negative battery cable located by the accelerator pedal.
   - Take the key out of the ignition lock and wait for approximately 20 seconds.
   - Pull down on the isolating connector locking tab.
   - Pull the connector away from the grounding stud
   - Clamp connector under the accelerator pedal so that it cannot make contact with the ground pin.
3. Disconnect the air cleaner inlet and outlet tubes.
4. Disconnect the MAF sensor electrical connector.
5. Disconnect the air intake air pressure sensor.
6. Remove the air cleaner assembly.
7. Drain the cooling system.
8. Disconnect the CAC outlet tube from CAC.
9. Disconnect and remove the CAC from the EGR air flow control valve.
10. Disconnect coolant hoses from the coolant recovery bottle.
11. Remove the coolant recovery bottle.
12. Remove the upper radiator hose.
13. Remove the cooling fan and shroud assembly.
14. Remove the upper fasteners, lower fasteners, and remove the EGR Tube from the Charge Air Crossover Manifold.
15. Disconnect the IAT sensor electrical connector.

16. Remove the rear IAT Sensor Housing Bracket bolts.

17. Remove the glow plug module.

18. Remove the three nuts and one bolt from the charge air cross over tube.

19. Position the charge air crossover tube forward and disconnect the boost pressure sensor electrical connector.

20. Remove the charge air cross over tube.

21. Remove the fasteners and boost pressure sensor from the charge air cross over tube (3).

To install:

22. Position the boost pressure sensor (2) onto the charge air cross over tube (3) and install the fasteners. Tighten the fasteners to 80 inch lbs. (9 Nm).

23. Connect the sensor wiring harness connector.

24. Install the charge air cross over tube along with the three nuts and one bolt. Tighten to 80 inch lbs. (9 Nm).

25. Install the glow plug module.

26. Install the rear IAT sensor housing bracket bolts. Tighten to 80 inch lbs. (9 Nm).

27. Connect the IAT sensor electrical connector.

28. Install the EGR tube (4) into the charge air crossover manifold and install the upper fasteners, and the lower fasteners. Tighten to 80 inch lbs. (9 Nm).

29. Install the cooling fan and shroud assembly.

30. Install the upper radiator hose

31. Install the coolant recovery bottle. Tighten bolt to 98 inch lbs. (10 Nm).

32. Connect coolant hoses from the coolant recovery bottle.

33. Connect and remove the CAC from the EGR air flow control valve.

34. Connect the CAC outlet tube from CAC.

35. Fill the cooling system.

36. Install the air cleaner assembly (4).

37. Connect the air intake air pressure sensor (3).

38. Connect the MAF sensor electrical connector (2).

39. Connect the air cleaner inlet (5) and outlet tubes.

40. Retrieve the isolating connector from under the accelerator pedal and position it onto the grounding stud.

41. Slide the isolating connector locking tab upward to secure the connector to the stud.

42. Connect the negative battery cable.

CAMSHAFT POSITION (CMP) SENSOR

LOCATION

3.0L Engine

The Camshaft Position (CMP) sensor is mounted on the right cylinder head cover.

3.5L Engine

The Camshaft Position (CMP) sensors are mounted to the front of the cylinder head. There are two intake cam position sensors, and two exhaust cam position sensors.

REMOVAL & INSTALLATION

3.0L Engine

See Figure 92.

1. Disconnect the negative battery cable.
2. Remove engine cover.
3. Disconnect Camshaft Position (CMP) sensor harness connector (1).
4. Remove the CMP sensor retaining bolt (2) and remove camshaft position sensor (3).

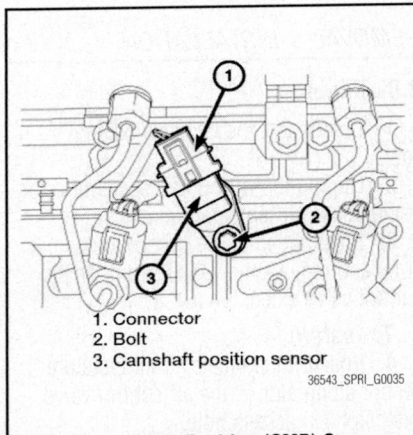

1. Connector
2. Bolt
3. Camshaft position sensor

36543_SPRI_G0035

Fig. 92 Camshaft Position (CMP) Sensor

To install:

5. Install the CMP sensor (3) and tighten the sensor bolt (2) to 71 inch lbs. (8 Nm).
6. Reconnect the CMP sensor harness connector (1).
7. Install engine cover.
8. Reconnect negative battery cable.

3.5L Engine

Exhaust

See Figure 93.

1. Remove the engine cover.
2. Remove the air cleaner and throttle body hose.

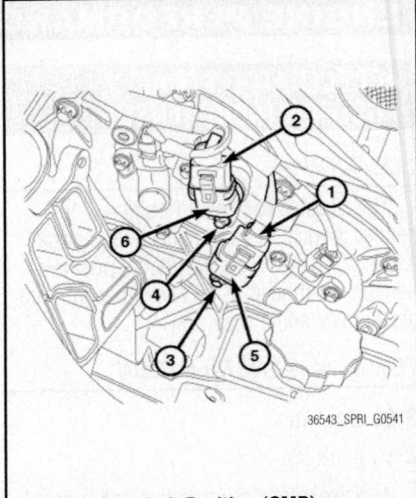

36543_SPRI_G0541

Fig. 93 Camshaft Position (CMP) sensors

3. Disconnect negative battery cable.
4. If necessary, position the power steering fluid reservoir aside.
5. Disconnect exhaust Camshaft Position (CMP) sensor harness connector (1).
6. Remove the exhaust CMP sensor mounting bolt (3).
7. Remove the exhaust CMP sensor (5).

To install:

8. Lubricate the sensor O-ring.
9. Install exhaust CMP sensor (5) so that it is fully seated on the mounting surface.
10. Install exhaust CMP sensor mounting bolt (3). Tighten to 80 inch lbs. (9 Nm).
11. Reconnect the exhaust CMP harness connector (1).
12. If necessary, reinstall the power steering fluid reservoir.
13. Connect the exhaust CMP sensor harness connector.
14. Connect negative battery cable.
15. Install the air cleaner and throttle body hose.

Intake

1. Remove the engine cover.
2. Remove the air cleaner and throttle body hose.
3. Disconnect negative battery cable.
4. Disconnect intake Camshaft Position (CMP) sensor harness connector (2).
5. Remove intake CMP sensor mounting bolt (4).
6. Remove the intake CMP sensor (6).

To install:

7. Lubricate sensor O-ring.

8. Install the intake CMP sensor (5) so that it is fully seated on the mounting surface.

9. Install the intake CMP sensor bolt (3). Tighten to 80 inch lbs. (9 Nm).

10. Reconnect the intake CMP sensor harness connector (1).

11. Reconnect the negative battery cable.

12. Install the air cleaner and throttle body hose.

CRANKSHAFT POSITION (CKP) SENSOR

LOCATION

3.0L Engine

The Crankshaft Position (CKP) sensor is located at the left rear of the engine just above the starter motor.

3.5L Engine

The Crankshaft Position (CKP) sensor mounts to the rear of the engine block near the left front edge of the transmission.

REMOVAL & INSTALLATION

3.0L Engine

See Figure 94.

1. Disconnect the negative battery cable.

2. Raise and support the vehicle.

3. Remove the crankshaft position sensor heat shield.

4. Disconnect the crankshaft position sensor wiring harness connector.

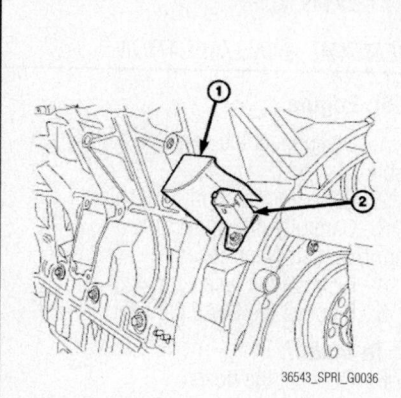

Fig. 94 Crankshaft Position (CKP) sensor(2) and bolt (1)—3.0L Engine

5. Remove the crankshaft position sensor bolt and crankshaft position sensor (2).

To install:

6. Clean the crankshaft sensor bore and install the sensor (2). Tighten the bolt to 80 inch lbs. (9 Nm).

7. Connect the engine harness connector.

8. Install the heat shield.

9. Lower the vehicle.

10. Connect the negative battery cable.

3.5L Engine

See Figure 95.

1. Disconnect the negative battery cable.

2. Raise vehicle and support.

3. Unlock and disconnect the crankshaft position sensor harness connector (1).

4. Remove the crankshaft position sensor bolt (2).

5. Remove the crankshaft position sensor (3).

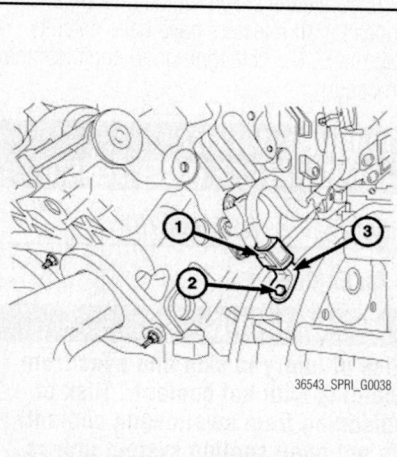

Fig. 95 Crankshaft Position (CKP) sensor (3) bolt (2) and connector (1)—3.5L Engine

To install:

6. Check O-ring for damage and lubricate the O-ring with engine oil before installing the crankshaft position sensor.

7. Install the crankshaft position sensor (3).

8. Install and tighten the crankshaft position sensor bolt (2).

9. Connect the crankshaft position sensor harness connector to the crankshaft position sensor (3).

10. Lower vehicle.

11. Connect the negative battery cable.

ELECTRONIC CONTROL MODULE (ECM)

LOCATION

3.0L Engine

The Engine Control Module (ECM) is located in the left side of engine compartment, and is attached to the top of the left fender behind the battery.

REMOVAL & INSTALLATION

3.0L Engine

➡ If a replacement (new) ECM is installed, a scan tool must be used to program (flash) the new ECM with vehicle specific information.

1. Disconnect the negative battery cable.

2. Disconnect the ECM harness connectors.

3. Grasp ECM and pull up firmly to release ECM from the retaining bracket.

To install:

➡ Any time a new ECM is installed, the injector quantity adjustment procedure, also called injector classification must be performed. Refer to Injector Classification Procedure and Injector Quantity Adjustment in RESET.

4. Position the ECM into the guide of the retaining bracket.

5. Carefully push the ECM in to the bracket.

6. Connect the ECM wiring harness connectors.

7. Connect negative battery cable.

8. Using the scan tool, perform the "ECU Auto Replacement", "Diesel Particulate Filter (New) Initialization", and "Engine ECU Replaced (Drive Authorization)" procedures. Refer to ECM in RESET.

RESET PROCEDURE

ECM

This procedure will need to be done when one or more of the following situations are true:

1. A vehicle's Powertrain control module (PCM) has been replaced.

2. A diagnostic trouble code (DTC) is set P1602 - PCM Not Programmed.

3. An updated calibration or software release is available for either the PCM or TCM ECUs.

This procedure assumes that the StarSCAN® and StarMOBILE® devices are configured to your dealership's network with either a wired or wireless connection. The StarSCAN® and StarMOBILE® must also be running at the latest operating system and software release level. For more help on how to network your StarSCAN® or StarMO-BILE® reference the StarSCAN® / StarMO-BILE® Quick Start Networking Guide available on 'DealerCONNECT> Service> StarSCAN® and StarMOBILE® Tools> Online Documentation' or at www.dcctools.com, under the Download Center.

Injector Quantity Adjustment

The injector quantity adjustment, or classification of injectors describes the quantity, or fuel delivery characteristic of the injector. This will make it possible to match the ECM fuel delivery strategy to the mechanical characteristics of the injector within a more narrowly graduated range. Injector classification can only be performed with a scantool.

The fuel injectors used in this vehicle have a seven digit alphanumeric code, which allows the ECM to determine the fuel quantity characteristic of each injector.

When carrying out service procedures where the injectors are removed from the cylinder head, it is important to observe the original locations of each individual injector, as installing an original injector in the wrong location, vehicle driveability and smoking concerns could result.

If an injector(s) is replaced, or if there is any concern that an injector may not be installed in its original location, the injector quantity adjustment procedure must be performed with the scan tool in order to program the quantity classification (seven digit alphanumeric code) to the corresponding cylinder in the engine control module.

Injector Classification Procedure

➡The engine must not be running for this procedure.

➡If installing a new injector, make a note of the seven digit alphanumeric code. You will need to enter it into the scan tool during the Injector Quantity Adjustment procedure.

➡Before performing this procedure, if the ECU has been replaced, or if any injector has been installed anywhere but its original location, make a note of the seven digit alphanumeric codes

and the physical location of each injector. You will need to enter them into the scan tool during the Injector Quantity Adjustment procedure.

1. Turn ignition switch "ON".
2. Using a scan tool, select ECU View, then MISCELLANEOUS FUNCTIONS.
3. Select Injector Quantity Adjustment, then NEXT.
4. If the ECU was replaced, the Injector EEPROM Location procedure must be performed. Select YES, then NEXT, and follow the directions on the scan tool. Otherwise, go to step 5.
5. Select the injector(s) that has been replaced, access the keyboard function, and type the seven digit alphanumeric code next to the cylinder number that corresponds to the physical location where the injector has been installed.
6. Click NEXT. The scan tool will prompt to turn the ignition switch off for 12 seconds.
7. Repeat step 5 and 6 for any other injectors that are new, or have been moved from their original location. Once injectors are classified, cycle ignition to complete.
8. Once the seven digit alphanumeric codes for all injectors have been entered into the ECU, cycle ignition to complete the procedure.

ENGINE COOLANT TEMPERATURE (ECT) SENSOR

REMOVAL & INSTALLATION

3.0L Engine

❋❋ WARNING

Risk of injury to skin and eyes from scalding with hot coolant . Risk of poisoning from swallowing coolant. Do not open cooling system unless coolant temperature is below 194°F (90°C). Open cap slowly to release pressure. Store coolant in suitable and appropriately marked container. Wear protective gloves, clothes and eye wear.

1. Remove engine cover.
2. Partially drain cooling system.
3. Disconnect electrical connector.
4. Remove clip.
5. Remove Engine Coolant Temperature (ECT) sensor.

To install:

6. Install ECT sensor.
7. Install retaining clip.
8. Connect electrical connector.

9. Fill cooling system.
10. Install engine cover.

3.5L Engine

❋❋ WARNING

Risk of injury to skin and eyes from scalding with hot coolant . Risk of poisoning from swallowing coolant. Do not open cooling system unless coolant temperature is below 194°F (90°C). Open cap slowly to release pressure. Store coolant in suitable and appropriately marked container. Wear protective gloves, clothes and eye wear.

1. Disconnect negative battery cable.
2. Remove engine cover.
3. Partially drain coolant system.
4. Unplug coolant temperature sensor electrical connector.
5. Remove coolant temperature sensor .

To install:

6. Position and install coolant temperature sensor .
7. Connect coolant temperature sensor electrical connector.
8. Refill coolant system.
9. Install engine cover.
10. Connect negative battery cable.
11. Start engine and inspect for leaks.

EVAPORATIVE EMISSIONS (EVAP) CANISTER

LOCATION

3.5L Engine

See Figure 96.

The EVAP Canister is located at the rear of the fuel tank.

REMOVAL & INSTALLATION

3.5L Engine

1. Disconnect the negative battery cable.
2. Raise and support the vehicle.
3. Carefully disconnect the vapor/vacuum/vent hoses.
4. Remove the fasteners.
5. Remove the EVAP canister

To install:

6. Connect the hoses.
7. Install the charcoal canister.
8. Install the fasteners.
9. Connect the negative battery cable.

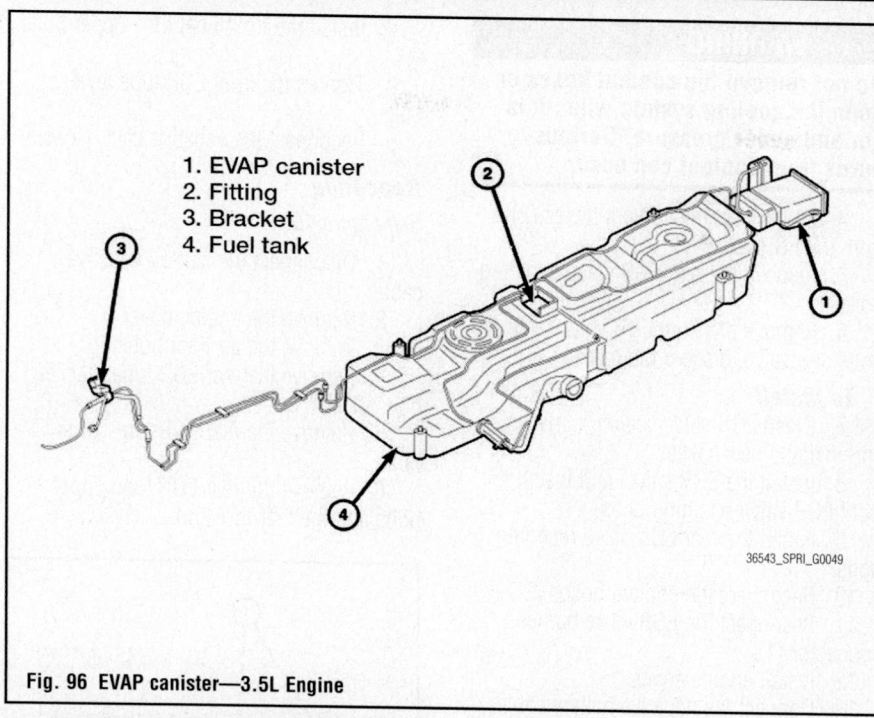

1. EVAP canister
2. Fitting
3. Bracket
4. Fuel tank

36543_SPRI_G0049

Fig. 96 EVAP canister—3.5L Engine

EVAPORATIVE EMISSIONS (EVAP) PURGE CONTROL SOLENOID

LOCATION

3.5L Engine

See Figure 97.

This vehicle uses a pulse-width modulated EVAP Purge Solenoid (8). The solenoid regulates the rate of vapor flow from the EVAP canister (6) to the throttle body. The PCM controls the frequency at which the solenoid open and closes in order to optimize the fuel vapor volume delivered to each cylinder.

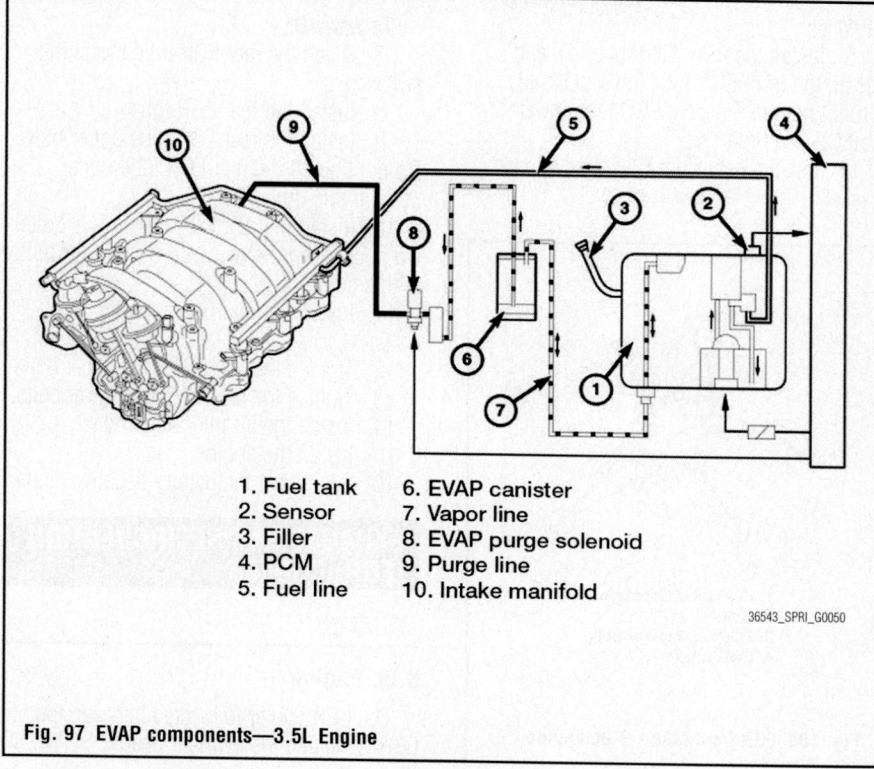

1. Fuel tank
2. Sensor
3. Filler
4. PCM
5. Fuel line
6. EVAP canister
7. Vapor line
8. EVAP purge solenoid
9. Purge line
10. Intake manifold

36543_SPRI_G0050

Fig. 97 EVAP components—3.5L Engine

REMOVAL & INSTALLATION

3.5L Engine

1. Disconnect harness connector from solenoid.
2. Disconnect vapor hoses from solenoid.
3. Remove solenoid from bracket.

To install:

4. Install solenoid.
5. Connect vapor hoses to solenoid.
6. Connect harness connector to solenoid.

FUEL TEMPERATURE SENSOR

LOCATION

3.0L Engine

The fuel temperature sensor is integrated in the high pressure fuel pump next to the fuel quantity valve.

REMOVAL & INSTALLATION

3.0L Engine

See Figure 98.

➡**Capture and properly store all fluid seepage in appropriately marked containers.**

1. Disconnect the negative battery cable.
2. Disconnect the fuel quantity solenoid wiring harness connector.
3. Disconnect the temperature sensor wiring harness connector.
4. Remove the fuel temperature sensor from the high pressure pump.

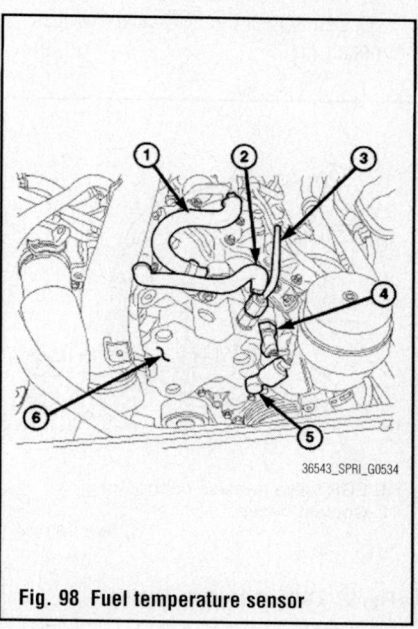

36543_SPRI_G0534

Fig. 98 Fuel temperature sensor

To install:

> ❊❊ **WARNING**
>
> No sparks, open flames or smoking. Risk of poisoning from inhaling and swallowing fuel. Risk of injury to eyes and skin from contact with fuel. Pour fuels only into suitable and appropriately marked containers. Wear protective clothing.

5. Clean sealing surfaces.
6. Install new seal on sensor.
7. Screw the sensor into the high pressure pump and tighten to 18 ft. lbs. (25 Nm).
8. Connect the temperature sensor wiring harness connector.
9. Connect the fuel quantity solenoid wiring harness connector.
10. Connect negative battery cable.
11. Start engine, allow to warm, shut engine off and inspect for leaks.

EXHAUST GAS RECIRCULATION (EGR) VALVE

LOCATION

3.0L Engine

The EGR valve is mounted to the cylinder head.

REMOVAL & INSTALLATION

3.0L Engine

See Figure 99.

1. Disconnect the negative battery cable.
2. Remove engine cover.
3. Disconnect the EGR valve harness connector (1).

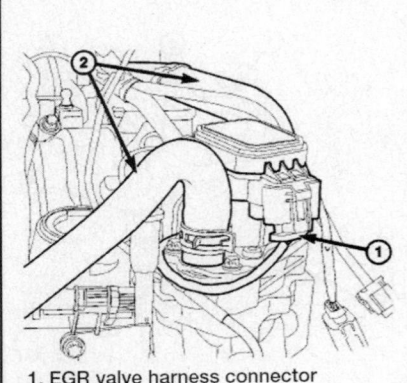

1. EGR valve harness connector
2. Coolant hoses

36543_SPRI_G0056

Fig. 99 EGR valve—3.0L Engine

> ❊❊ **WARNING**
>
> Do not remove the coolant hoses or open the cooling system when it is hot and under pressure. Serious burns from coolant can occur.

4. Disconnect the coolant hoses (2) from the EGR valve.
5. Remove the rear EGR valve retaining bolts.
6. Remove the front EGR valve retaining bolts and valve, discard the gasket.

To install:

7. Clean EGR valve sealing surfaces and install a new gasket.
8. Install the EGR valve, and install the front EGR valve retaining bolts.
9. Install the rear EGR valve retaining bolts.
10. Reconnect the coolant hoses (2).
11. Reconnect the EGR valve harness connector (1).
12. Install engine cover.
13. Connect the negative battery cable.

Front Tube

See Figure 100.

1. Disconnect the negative battery cable.
2. Remove the front EGR tube upper bolts (1).
3. Remove the front EGR tube lower bolts (3), and remove the front EGR tube (4).

To install:

4. Clean all front EGR tube mounting surfaces.
5. Install the front EGR tube (4), and install the front EGR tube lower bolts (3). Do not tighten the front EGR tube lower bolts at this time
6. Install a new front EGR tube upper gasket.

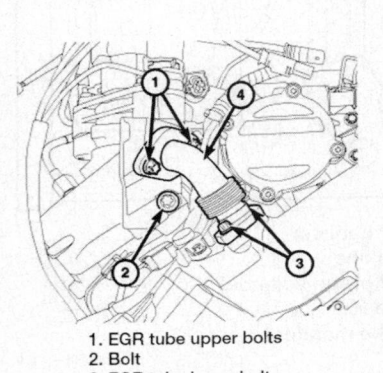

1. EGR tube upper bolts
2. Bolt
3. EGR tube lower bolts
4. EGR tube

36543_SPRI_G0060

Fig. 100 EGR front tube—3.0L Engine

7. Install the front EGR tube upper bolts (1).
8. Tighten the front EGR tube lower bolts.
9. Reconnect the negative battery cable.

Rear Tube

See Figure 101.

1. Disconnect the battery negative cable.
2. Remove the engine cover.
3. Remove the air filter housing.
4. Remove the rear EGR tube bracket bolts (1).
5. Remove the rear EGR tube lower bolts.
6. Remove the rear EGR tube upper bolts and the rear EGR tube.

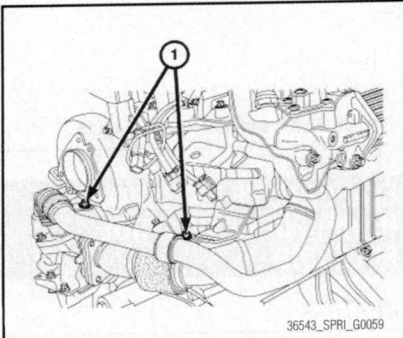

36543_SPRI_G0059

Fig. 101 EGR rear tube bracket bolts (1)—3.0L Engine

To install:

7. Clean the rear EGR tube mounting surfaces.
8. Install the rear EGR tube.
9. Install the rear EGR tube upper bolts. Do not tighten the rear EGR tube upper bolts at this time.
10. Install the rear EGR tube lower bolts. Do not tighten the rear EGR tube lower bolts at this time.
11. Install the rear EGR tube bracket bolts (1).
12. Tighten the rear EGR tube upper bolts.
13. Tighten the rear EGR tube lower bolts.
14. Install the air filter housing.
15. Install the engine cover.
16. Reconnect the battery negative cable.

EXHAUST GAS RECIRCULATION (EGR) COOLER

LOCATION

3.0L Engine

The EGR cooler is located between the EGR valve and the cylinder head.

REMOVAL & INSTALLATION

3.0L Engine

1. Remove the air filter housing and air inlet tube from the EGR throttle body

2. Disconnect the EGR Temperature Sensor harness connector.

3. Remove the rear transmission dipstick tube bolt and disconnect the vacuum line from the EGR Bypass Valve Actuator.

4. Remove the front transmission dipstick tube bolt, and position the transmission dipstick tube aside.

5. Disconnect the front EGR cooler engine coolant hose.

6. Disconnect the rear EGR cooler engine coolant hose.

7. Disconnect the EGR valve actuator harness connector.

8. Disconnect the EGR Backpressure sensor harness connector.

9. Disconnect the EGR bypass valve position sensor harness connector.

10. Remove the 2 Rear throttle body bracket bolts.

11. Remove the 2 upper front EGR tube bolts.

12. Remove the front EGR cooler-to-cylinder head bolt.

13. Remove the 2 upper rear EGR tube bolts.

14. Remove the rear EGR cooler-to-cylinder head bolts.

15. Remove the two front EGR cooler-to-cylinder head bolts, the EGR throttle body bracket, and the EGR cooler.

To install:

16. Clean the front and rear EGR tube gasket mounting surfaces.

17. Install the EGR cooler, the EGR throttle body bracket, and the two front EGR cooler-to-cylinder head bolts. Do not tighten the front EGR cooler-to-cylinder head bolts at this time.

18. Install the rear EGR cooler-to-cylinder head bolts. Do not tighten the rear EGR cooler-to-cylinder head bolts at this time.

19. Install a new rear EGR tube gasket.

20. Install the 2 upper rear EGR tube bolts. Do not tighten the upper rear EGR tube bolts at this time.

21. Install the front EGR cooler-to-cylinder head bolt. Do not tighten the front EGR cooler-to-cylinder head bolts at this time.

22. Install the 2 upper front EGR tube bolts. Do not tighten the front EGR tube bolts at this time.

23. Install the 2 Rear throttle body bracket bolts.

24. Tighten the front EGR cooler-to-cylinder head bolts.

25. Tighten the rear EGR cooler-to-cylinder head bolts.

26. Tighten the upper rear EGR tube bolts.

27. Tighten the front EGR cooler-to-cylinder head bolts.

28. Tighten the front EGR tube bolts.

29. Reconnect the EGR bypass valve position sensor harness connector).

30. Reconnect the EGR Backpressure sensor harness connector.

31. Reconnect the EGR valve actuator harness connector.

32. Reconnect the rear EGR cooler engine coolant hose.

33. Reconnect the front EGR cooler engine coolant hose.

34. Install the transmission dipstick tube, and the front transmission dipstick tube bolt.

35. Install the rear transmission dipstick tube bolt and reconnect the vacuum line to the EGR Bypass Valve Actuator.

36. Reconnect the EGR Temperature Sensor harness connector.

37. Install the air filter housing and the EGR throttle body air inlet tube.

38. Install the engine cover.

39. Reconnect the battery negative cable.

EXHAUST GAS RECIRCULATION (EGR) TEMPERATURE SENSOR

LOCATION

3.0L Engine

The EGR temperature sensor is located in base of the EGR valve.

REMOVAL & INSTALLATION

3.0L Engine

See Figure 102.

1. Disconnect the battery negative cable.

2. Disconnect the EGR temperature sensor harness connector (1).

3. Remove the EGR temperature sensor.

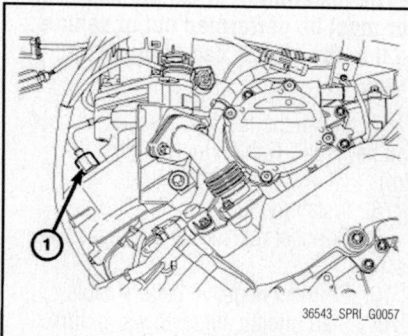

Fig. 102 EGR temperature sensor harness connector (1)—3.0L Engine

To install:

4. Install the EGR temperature sensor.

5. Reconnect the EGR temperature sensor harness connector (1).

6. Reconnect the battery negative cable.

EXHAUST GAS RECIRCULATION (EGR) BACKPRESSURE TRANSDUCER

LOCATION

3.0L Engine

The EGR back pressure sensor is located in the exhaust stream next to the EGR bypass valve.

REMOVAL & INSTALLATION

3.0L Engine

See Figure 103.

1. Disconnect the negative battery cable.

2. Remove the engine cover.

3. Disconnect the EGR Backpressure Sensor harness connector (1).

4. Remove the EGR Backpressure Sensor (2).

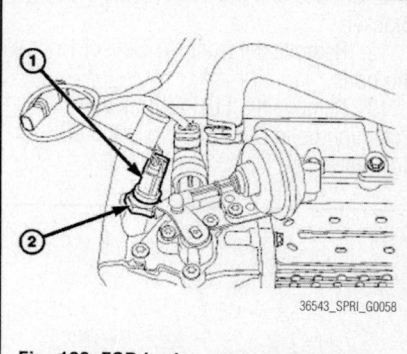

36543_SPRI_G0058

Fig. 103 EGR backpressure sensor (2) and harness connector (1)—3.0L Engine

To install:

5. Install the EGR back pressure sensor (2).

6. Connect the EGR back pressure sensor harness connector (1).

7. Install the engine cover.

8. Connect the negative battery cable.

EXHAUST GAS RECIRCULATION (EGR) AIRFLOW CONTROL VALVE

LOCATION

3.0L Engine

The Exhaust Gas Recirculation (EGR) Air Flow Valve Actuator and Resonator are located in the air intake tube between the turbocharger intercooler and the intake manifold.

REMOVAL & INSTALLATION

3.0L Engine

See Figure 104.

1. Perform the Fuel Pressure Release procedure.
2. Disconnect the Negative Battery Cable.
3. Remove the Engine Cover.
4. Remove the Air Filter Housing and Intake Tube.
5. Remove the Engine Cover Support Brace.
6. Remove the Lower Turbocharger Intercooler Flex Hose.
7. Position the Vacuum Pump aside.
8. Disconnect the EGR Airflow Valve and IAT harness connectors.
9. Disconnect the front EGR Tube from the Charge Air Crossover Manifold, located upstream of the Intake Manifolds.
10. Remove the rear IAT Sensor Housing Bracket bolts.
11. Remove the rear IAT Sensor Housing Bracket bolts and the IAT Sensor Housing Bracket.
12. Remove the front IAT Sensor Housing bolts.
13. Remove the EGR Airflow Valve Retaining bolts (1) and remove the EGR Airflow Valve (2).

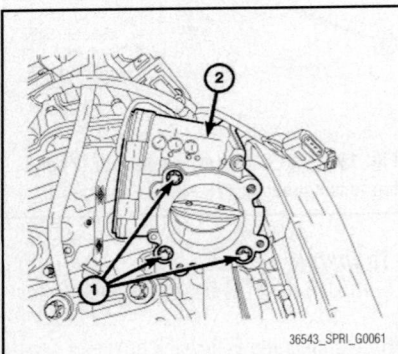

Fig. 104 EGR airflow valve (2) and bolts (2)—3.0L Engine

To install:

14. Install the EGR Airflow Valve (2).
15. Install the EGR Airflow Valve bolts (1).
16. Install the IAT Sensor Housing and the front IAT Sensor Housing retaining bolts.
17. Install the IAT Sensor Housing Bracket and the 2 rear IAT Sensor housing bolts.

18. Install the front EGR Tube.
19. Reconnect the EGR Airflow Valve and IAT harness connectors.
20. Install the Vacuum Pump.
21. Install the Lower Turbocharger Intercooler Flex Hose.
22. Install the Engine Cover Support Brace.
23. Install the Air Filter Housing and Intake Tube.
24. Install the Engine Cover.
25. Reconnect the Negative Battery Cable.

FUEL RAIL PRESSURE SENSOR

LOCATION

3.0L Engine

The fuel rail pressure sensor is located on the fuel rail.

REMOVAL & INSTALLATION

3.0L Engine

✷✷ WARNING

No sparks, open flames or smoking. Risk of poisoning from inhaling and swallowing fuel. Risk of injury to eyes and skin from contact with fuel. Pour fuels only into suitable and appropriately marked containers. Wear protective clothing.

➡ To avoid leakage problems, the rail pressure sensor should not be removed unless it is to be replaced.

1. Disconnect negative battery cable.
2. Remove engine cover.
3. Unplug electrical connector at fuel rail pressure sensor.
4. Remove the right fuel rail.
5. Position the fuel rail in a soft jawed vise.
6. Remove rail pressure sensor.

To install:

➡ The installation of the pressure sensor must be performed out of vehicle so that the sensor can be tightened properly.

7. Install the fuel rail pressure sensor and new seal. Tighten to 16 ft. lbs. (22 Nm).
8. Install the fuel rail.
9. Connect rail sensor electrical connector.
10. Connect negative battery cable.
11. Start engine, allow to warm, turn engine off and inspect for leaks.
12. Install engine cover.

HEATED OXYGEN (HO2S) SENSOR

LOCATION

3.0L Engine

The sensor is mounted in the exhaust pipe at a 30 degree angle to prevent the collection of moisture between the sensor housing and element. The sensor is located close to the turbocharger for a quicker response time.

3.5L Engine

The right and left upstream oxygen sensors are installed in the exhaust pipe upstream of the left and right catalytic converters, and downstream of the left and right exhaust manifolds.

The right and left downstream heated oxygen sensors are installed into the center of the left and right catalytic converters.

REMOVAL & INSTALLATION

3.0L Engine

See Figure 105.

1. Disconnect the negative battery cable.
2. Disconnect the O2 sensor harness connector.
3. Remove the O2 sensor (1).

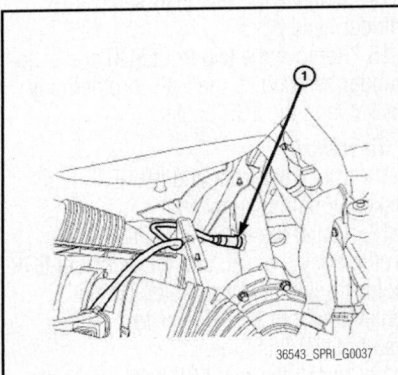

Fig. 105 Heated Oxygen sensor— 3.0L Engine

To install:

4. Install the oxygen sensor (1).
5. Properly position the oxygen sensor wiring harness and connect the electrical connector.
6. Connect the negative battery cable.

3.5L Engine

See Figure 106.

1. Disconnect the negative battery cable.
2. Disconnect electrical connector from O2 sensor.

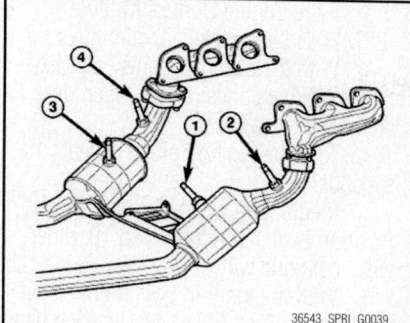

**Fig. 106 Heated Oxygen sensor—
3.5L Engine**

3. Remove sensor using an oxygen sensor crow foot wrench such as Snap-On tool YA8875 or equivalent.

To install:

4. After removing the sensor, the exhaust manifold threads must be cleaned. Use a suitable oxygen sensor thread cleaning tap. If reusing the original sensor, coat the sensor threads with an anti-seize compound. New sensors have compound on the threads and do not require an additional coating.

5. Install sensor using an oxygen sensor crow foot wrench such as Snap-On tool YA8875 or equivalent.

6. Connect electrical connector to oxygen sensor.

7. Connect the negative battery cable.

INTAKE AIR TEMPERATURE (IAT) SENSOR

LOCATION

3.5L Engine

The Intake Air Temperature Sensor (IAT) is integrated into the Mass Airflow (MAF) Sensor.

REMOVAL & INSTALLATION

3.5L Engine

Refer to Mass Airflow (MAF) Sensor.

KNOCK SENSOR (KS)

LOCATION

3.5L Engine

The knock sensors are located below the intake manifold.

REMOVAL & INSTALLATION

3.5L Engine

Left

See Figure 107.

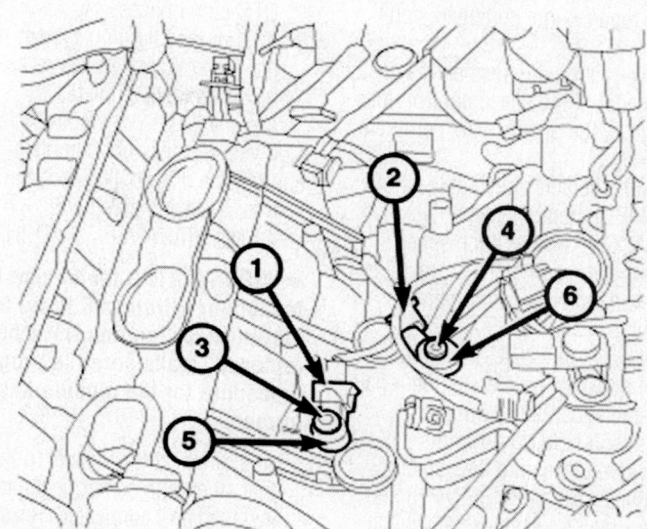

1. Right knock sensor connector
2. Left knock sensor connector
3. Right knock sensor bolt
4. Left knock sensor bolt
5. Right knock sensor
6. Left knock sensor

Fig. 107 Knock sensors—3.5L Engine

1. Disconnect the negative battery cable.
2. Remove the upper intake manifold.
3. Disconnect the Left Knock Sensor harness connector (2).
4. Disconnect the Left Knock Sensor bolt (4).
5. Remove the Left Knock sensor (6).

To install:

6. Install the Left Knock sensor (6).
7. Install the Left Knock Sensor bolt (4). Tighten to 15 ft. lbs. (20 Nm).
8. Reconnect the Left Knock Sensor harness connector (2).
9. Reconnect the negative battery cable.
10. Install the upper intake manifold.

Right

1. Disconnect the negative battery cable.
2. Remove the upper intake manifold.
3. Disconnect the Right Knock Sensor harness connector (1).
4. Disconnect the Right Knock Sensor bolt (3).
5. Remove the Right Knock sensor (5).

To install:

6. Install the Right Knock sensor (5).
7. Install the Right Knock Sensor bolt (3). Tighten to 15 ft. lbs. (20 Nm).
8. Reconnect the Right Knock Sensor harness connector (1).
9. Reconnect the negative battery cable.
10. Install the upper intake manifold.

MALFUNCTION INDICATOR LIGHT (MIL)

RESET PROCEDURE

3.0L Engine

ECM Verification Test

1. SELECT THE PROPER VERIFICATION TEST

Select the verification test for the repair that has been completed:

- Speed Control repair: Go to step 2
- Charging System repair: Go to step 3
- No Start repair: Go to step 4
- DTC and all other repairs: Go to step 5

2. SPEED CONTROL VERIFICATION TEST

a. Inspect the vehicle to make sure that all engine components are properly installed and connected. Reassemble and reconnect components as necessary.

b. With the scan tool, erase all diagnostic trouble codes (DTCs).

c. Road test the vehicle at a speed above 60 km/h (35 MPH).

d. Turn the speed control ON/OFF switch on.

e. Depress and release the SET switch. If the speed control does not engage, the repair is not complete, continue with .

f. Quickly depress and release the RESUME/ACCEL switch. If the vehicle speed does not increase by 3 km/h (2 MPH), the repair is not complete, continue with .

g. Using caution, depress and release the brake pedal. If the speed control does not disengage, the repair is not complete, continue with .

h. With the vehicle speed at least 60 km/h (35 MPH), depress the RESUME/ACCEL switch. If the speed control does not resume at the previously set speed, the repair is not complete, continue with .

i. Hold down the COAST switch. If the vehicle does not decelerate, the repair is not complete, continue with .

j. While still holding down the COAST switch, make sure the vehicle speed is at least 60 km/h (35 MPH) and release the COAST switch. If the vehicle does not adjust and set a new vehicle speed, the repair is not complete, continue with .

k. With the speed control engaged, depress the ON/OFF switch. If the speed control does not disengage, the repair is not complete, continue with .

l. If the vehicle did not successfully perform all of the previous steps, check for Technical Service Bulletins (TSBs) that pertain to this speed control problem and then, if necessary, return to the DTC List.

m. If the vehicle successfully performed all of the previous steps, the speed control system is now functioning as designed. The repair is now complete.
Are any DTCs or symptoms remaining?
If yes, repair is not complete, perform the appropriate diagnostic procedure.
If no, repair is complete.

3. CHARGING SYSTEM VERIFICATION TEST

a. Inspect the vehicle to make sure that all engine components are properly installed and connected. Reassemble and reconnect components as necessary.

b. With the scan tool, erase all diagnostic trouble codes (DTCs).

c. Start the engine.

d. Raise the engine speed to 2000 RPM for at least 30 seconds.

e. Allow the engine to idle.

f. Turn the ignition off for 20 seconds.

g. Turn the ignition on.

h. With the scan tool, read ECM DTCs.

i. If this DTC has set again, or another DTC has set, look for any Technical Service Bulletins (TSBs) that may

relate to this condition. Return to the DTC List if necessary.

j. If the charging system is functioning correctly and there are no DTCs, the repair is now complete.
Are any DTCs or symptoms remaining?
If yes, repair is not complete, perform the appropriate diagnostic procedure.
If no, repair is complete.

4. NO START VERIFICATION TEST

➡ IMPORTANT! If the Engine Control Module or Wireless Control Module/Wireless Ignition Node has been replaced, make sure the programming procedure for the module has been performed.

a. Inspect the vehicle to make sure that all engine components are properly installed and connected. Reassemble and reconnect components as necessary.

b. Inspect the engine oil for contamination. If it is contaminated, change the oil and filter.

c. With the scan tool, erase all diagnostic trouble codes (DTCs).

d. Turn the ignition off for at least 10 seconds.

e. Attempt to start the engine.

f. If the engine is unable to start, look for any Technical Service Bulletins (TSBs) that may relate to this condition. Return to the DTC List if necessary.

g. If the engine starts and continues to run, the repair is now complete.
Are any DTCs or symptoms remaining?
If yes, repair is not complete, perform the appropriate diagnostic procedure.
If no, repair is complete.

5. ROAD TEST VERIFICATION TEST

a. Inspect the vehicle to make sure that all engine components are properly installed and connected. Reassemble and reconnect components as necessary.

b. If this verification procedure is being performed after a non-DTC test, perform steps 3 and 4. If not, proceed to step 5.

c. Check to see if the initial symptom still exists. If there are no trouble codes and the symptom no longer exists, the repair was successful and testing is now complete.

d. If the initial or another symptom exists, the repair is not complete. Check all pertinent Technical Service Bulletins (TSBs) and return to the DTC List if necessary.

e. For previously read DTCs that have not been dealt with, return to the DTC List and follow the diagnostic path for that DTC; otherwise, continue.

f. If the Engine Control Module (ECM) has been replaced, continue.

g. With the scan tool, erase all diagnostic trouble codes (DTCs), then disconnect the scan tool.

h. Turn the ignition off for at least 10 seconds.

i. If equipped with a Transfer Case Position Switch, perform step 10, otherwise, continue with .

j. With the ignition switch on, place the Transfer Case Shift Lever in each gear position, stopping for 15 seconds in each position.

k. Road test the vehicle. For some of the road test, go at least 64 km/h (40 MPH). If this test is for an A/C Relay Control Circuit, drive the vehicle for at least five minutes with the A/C on.

l. At some point, stop the vehicle and turn the engine off for at least 10 seconds, then restart the engine and continue.

m. Upon completion of the road test, turn the engine off and check for DTCs with the scan tool.

n. If the repaired DTC has set again, the repair is not complete. Check for any pertinent Technical Service Bulletins (TSBs) and return to the DTC List. If there are no DTCs, the repair was successful and is now complete.
Are any DTCs or symptoms remaining?
If yes, repair is not complete, perform the appropriate diagnostic procedure.
If no, repair is complete.

3.5L Engine

Powertrain Verification Test

1. VERIFICATION TESTS
Select the verification test for the repair that has been completed:
- Charging System repair: Go to step 2
- No Start repair: Go to step 3
- All other repairs: Go to step 4

2. CHARGING SYSTEM VERIFICATION TEST

a. Inspect the vehicle to verify that all engine components are properly installed and connected. Reassemble and reconnect components as necessary.

b. With the scan tool, erase all diagnostic trouble codes (DTCs).

c. Start the engine.

d. Raise the engine speed to 2000 RPM for at least 30 seconds.

e. Allow the engine to idle.

f. Turn the ignition off for 20 seconds.

g. Turn the ignition on.

h. With the scan tool, read ECM DTCs.

i. If this DTC has set again, or another DTC has set, look for any Technical Service Bulletins (TSBs) that may relate to this condition. Return to the Symptom List if necessary.

j. If the charging system is functioning correctly and there are no DTCs, the repair is now complete.

Are any DTCs or symptoms remaining?

If yes, repair is not complete, perform the appropriate diagnostic procedure.

If no, repair is complete.

3. NO START VERIFICATION TEST

➡**IMPORTANT! If the Powertrain Control Module, Engine Control Module, or Sentry Key Immobilizer Module have been replaced, verify the programming procedure for the module has been performed in accordance with the Service Information.**

a. Inspect the vehicle to verify that all engine components are properly installed and connected. Reassemble and reconnect components as necessary.

b. Inspect the engine oil for contamination. If it is contaminated, the oil and the oil filter must be changed.

c. With the scan tool, erase all diagnostic trouble codes (DTCs).

d. Turn the ignition off for at least 10 seconds.

e. Attempt to start the engine.

f. If the engine will not start, refer to any Technical Service Bulletins (TSBs) that may relate to this condition. Return to the Symptom List if necessary.

g. If the engine starts and continues to run, the repair is now complete.

Are any DTCs or symptoms remaining?

If yes, repair is not complete, perform the appropriate diagnostic procedure.

If no, repair is complete.

4. ROAD TEST VERIFICATION TEST

a. Inspect the vehicle to verify that all engine components are properly installed and connected. Reassemble and reconnect components as necessary.

b. If this verification procedure is being performed after a non-DTC test, perform steps 3 and 4. If not, proceed to step 5.

c. Check to see if the initial symptom still exists. If there are no trouble codes and the symptom no longer exists, the repair was successful and testing is now complete.

d. If the initial or another symptom exists, the repair is not complete. Check all pertinent Technical Service Bulletins (TSBs) and return to the Symptom List if necessary.

e. For previously read DTCs that have not been dealt with, return to the Symptom List and follow the diagnostic path for that DTC; otherwise, continue.

f. If the Engine Control Module (ECM) has been replaced, continue with step 9.

g. With the scan tool, erase all diagnostic trouble codes (DTCs), then disconnect the scan tool.

h. Turn the ignition off for at least 10 seconds.

i. If equipped with a Transfer Case Position Switch, perform step 10, otherwise, continue with step 11.

j. With the ignition switch on, place the Transfer Case Shift Lever in each gear position, stopping for 15 seconds in each position.

k. Road test the vehicle. For some of the road test, go at least 64 km/h (40 MPH). If this test is for an A/C Control condition, drive the vehicle for at least 5 minutes with the A/C on.

l. At some point, stop the vehicle and turn the engine off for at least 10 seconds, then restart the engine and continue.

m. Upon completion of the road test, turn the engine off and check for DTCs with the scan tool.

n. If the repaired DTC has set again, the repair is not complete. Check for any pertinent Technical Service Bulletins (TSBs) and return to the Diagnostic Trouble Code List. If there are no DTCs, the repair was successful and is now complete.

Are any DTCs or symptoms remaining?

If yes, repair is not complete, perform the appropriate diagnostic procedure.

If no, repair is complete.

MASS AIR FLOW (MAF) SENSOR

LOCATION

3.0L Engine

The Mass Air Flow (MAF) Sensor is located in the air intake port between the air filter and the turbocharger .

3.5L Engine

The MAF sensor is located at the back of the intake manifold between the air filter housing and the electronic throttle valve.

REMOVAL & INSTALLATION

3.0L Engine

1. Disconnect the negative battery cable.
2. Detach the air hose at the Manifold Air Flow (MAF) sensor

3. Unplug the MAF wiring harness connector.

4. Remove the screws retaining the MAF sensor to the air cleaner housing, and remove MAF sensor.

To install:

5. Position the MAF sensor to air cleaner housing and install the retaining screws .

6. Connect the air intake hose to the MAF sensor and tighten clamp.

7. connect the MAF wiring harness connector.

8. Connect negative battery cable.

3.5L Engine

See Figure 108.

1. Disconnect the negative battery cable.
2. Remove the engine cover.
3. Remove the air filter housing.
4. Disconnect the MAF sensor harness connector (1).
5. Disengage the right notch (3).
6. Disengage the left notch (2).
7. Disconnect the retaining clip (4).
8. Remove the MAF sensor (5).

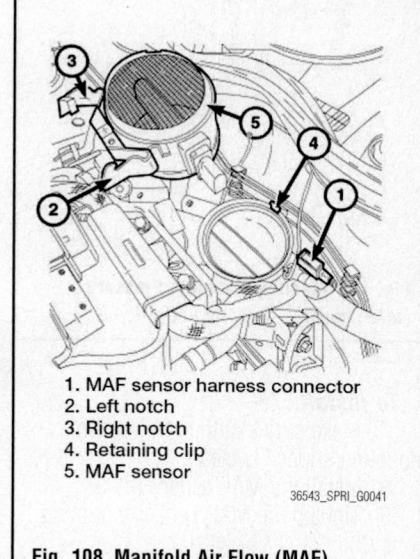

1. MAF sensor harness connector
2. Left notch
3. Right notch
4. Retaining clip
5. MAF sensor

36543_SPRI_G0041

Fig. 108 Manifold Air Flow (MAF) sensor—3.5L Engine

To install:

9. Install the MAF sensor.
10. Reconnect the retaining clip (4).
11. Engage the left notch (2).
12. Engage the right notch (3).
13. Reconnect the MAF sensor harness connector (1).
14. Install the engine cover.
15. Install the air filter housing.
16. Reconnect the negative battery cable.

MANIFOLD ABSOLUTE PRESSURE (MAP) SENSOR

LOCATION

3.5L Engine

The Manifold Absolute Pressure (MAP) sensor is located at the top of the engine on the left cylinder head.

REMOVAL & INSTALLATION

3.5L Engine

See Figure 109.

1. Disconnect the battery negative cable.
2. Remove the engine cover.
3. Remove the air filter housing.
4. Disconnect the MAP sensor harness connector (1).
5. Remove the bolts (3) from the MAP sensor.
6. Remove the MAP sensor (2).

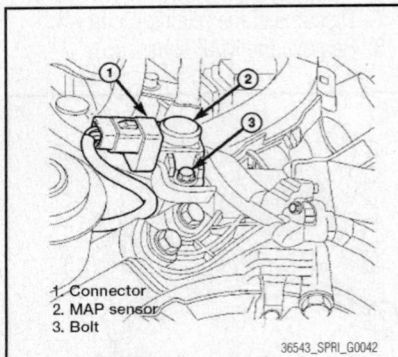

1. Connector
2. MAP sensor
3. Bolt

36543_SPRI_G0042

Fig. 109 Manifold Absolute Pressure (MAP) sensor—3.5L Engine

To install:

7. Make sure that the MAP sensor mounting surface is clean.
8. Install the MAP sensor (2).
9. Tighten the MAP sensor mounting bolts (3).
10. Connect the MAP sensor harness connector (1).
11. Connect the negative battery cable.
12. Install the air filter housing.
13. Install the engine cover.

POSITIVE CRANKCASE VENTILATION (PCV) VALVE

LOCATION

3.0L Engine

Located on the rear of the right cylinder head cover is a Positive Crankcase Ventilation (PCV) valve.

3.5L Engine

See Figure 110.

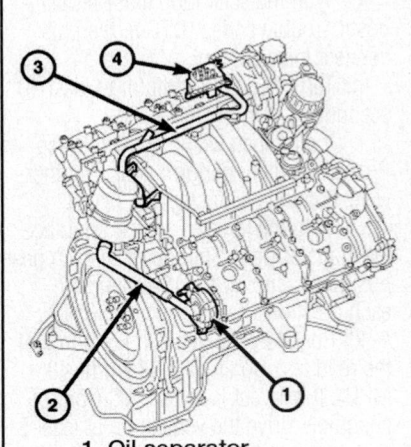

1. Oil separator
2. Tube
3. Tube
4. Oil separator

36543_SPRI_G0043

Fig. 110 Closed Crankcase Ventilation (CCV) system components—3.5L Engine

REMOVAL & INSTALLATION

3.0L Engine

See Figure 111.

1. Remove the engine cover.

➡Inspect the oil drain back access hole in the cylinder head cover to assure that it is free of obstruction.

2. Remove the oil separator fasteners and oil separator.

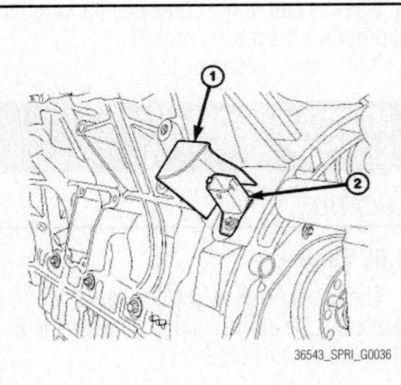

36543_SPRI_G0036

Fig. 111 Positive Crankcase Ventilation (PCV) valve—3.0L Engine

To install:

➡Inspect the oil drain back access hole in the cylinder head cover to assure that it is free of obstruction.

3. Lubricate the Positive Crankcase Ventilation (PCV) O-rings with clean engine oil.
4. Carefully position and push down on the PCV to seat.
5. Install the PCV retaining fasteners. Tighten fasteners to 96 inch lbs. (10.8 Nm).

3.5L Engine

Crankcase Ventilation Restrictor/Oil Separator

1. Disconnect the crankcase vent hose (1).
2. Remove the three crankcase ventilation restrictor/oil separator bolts (2).
3. Remove the crankcase ventilation restrictor/oil separator (3).

To install:

4. Install the crankcase ventilation restrictor/oil separator (3).
5. Install the three crankcase ventilation restrictor/oil separator bolts (2).
6. Reconnect the crankcase vent hose (1).

POWERTRAIN CONTROL MODULE (PCM)

LOCATION

3.5L Engine

The PCM is attached to a bracket that is mounted on top of the intake manifold.

REMOVAL & INSTALLATION

3.5L Engine

➡If a replacement (new) PCM is installed, a scan tool must be used to program (flash) the new PCM with vehicle specific information.

1. Disconnect the negative battery cable.
2. Disconnect the PCM harness connectors.
3. Grasp PCM and pull up firmly to release PCM from the retaining bracket.

To install:

4. Position the PCM into the guide of the retaining bracket.
5. Carefully push the PCM in to the bracket.
6. Connect the PCM wiring harness connectors.
7. Connect the negative battery cable.

SECONDARY AIR INJECTION SWITCHING VALVE

LOCATION

3.5L Engine

See Figure 112.

This vehicle is equipped with a secondary air injection system. The Secondary air injection system consists of an Air Pump that forces air into the exhaust ports of the cylinder head to reduce the emissions during engine warm-up. The air injected into the exhaust will cause the catalytic converters to heat up more quickly. This will improve the emission levels during a cold start. The Air Pump Switchover System incorporates an Air Pump (1) with two Air Pump Switchover Valves (2 and 3), an Air Pump Switchover Solenoid (5), an Air Pump Relay (4), and the PCM.

The Air Pump is mounted to the front of the engine. The Air Pump Switchover valves (2 and 3) are located at the front, top of the engine, mounted just in front of the left and right cylinder covers. The Air Pump Switchover Solenoid (5) is mounted on the right front of the engine, next to the air pump (1).

REMOVAL & INSTALLATION

3.5L Engine

Left

See Figure 113.

1. Disconnect the negative battery cable.
2. Remove the air filter housing.
3. Disconnect the vacuum line (2).
4. Disconnect the air pump switchover tube (1).

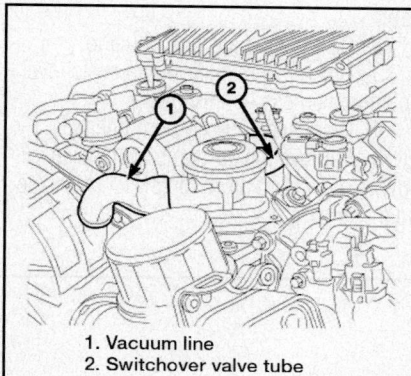

1. Vacuum line
2. Switchover valve tube

36543_SPRI_G0052

Fig. 113 Left air pump switchover valve— 3.5L Engine

5. Remove the air pump switchover valve retaining bolts.
6. Remove the air pump switchover valve and discard the old gasket.

To install:

7. Install the air pump switchover valve and a new gasket.
8. Install the retaining bolts.
9. Connect the vacuum line (2).
10. Connect the air pump switchover tube (1).
11. Install the air filter housing.
12. Connect the negative battery cable.

Right

See Figure 114.

1. Disconnect the negative battery cable.
2. Remove the air cleaner housing.
3. Remove the Air Pump. Refer to Air Pump.
4. Disconnect the vacuum line (2).
5. Disconnect the air pump switchover tube (1).
6. Remove the air pump switchover valve retaining bolts (1).
7. Remove the air pump switchover valve (3) discard the old gasket.

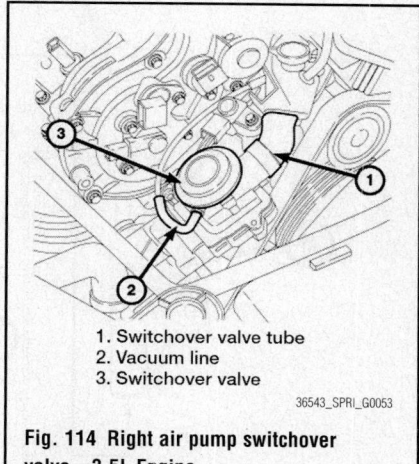

1. Switchover valve tube
2. Vacuum line
3. Switchover valve

36543_SPRI_G0053

Fig. 114 Right air pump switchover valve—3.5L Engine

To install:

8. Install the air pump switchover valve and a new gasket.
9. Install the air pump switchover valve retaining bolts.
10. Reconnect the air pump switchover tube (1).
11. Install the Air Pump. Refer to Air Pump.
12. Reconnect the vacuum line (2).
13. Install the air cleaner housing.
14. Reconnect the negative battery cable.

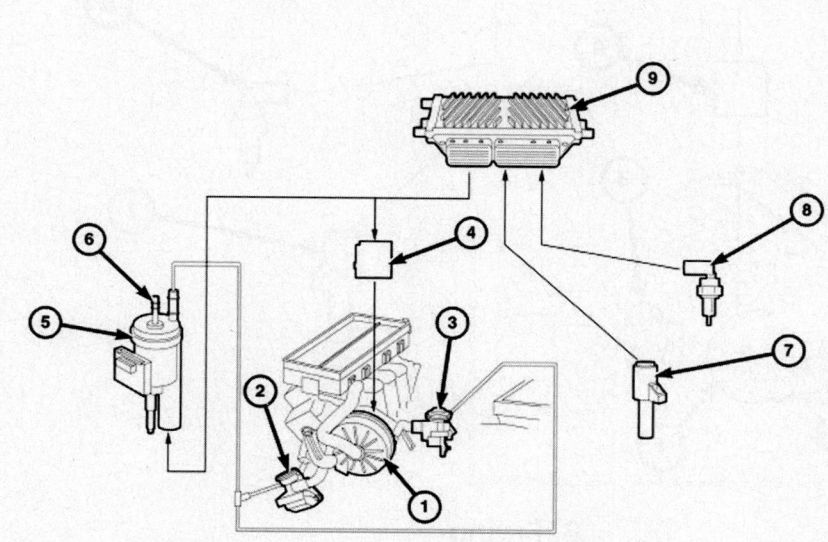

1. **Air pump**
2. **Switchover valve**
3. **Switchover valve**
4. **Air pump relay**
5. **Air pump switchover solenoid**
6. **Fitting**
7. **Engine speed sensor**
8. **Coolant temperature sensor**
9. **PCM**

36543_SPRI_G0051

Fig. 112 Secondary AIR system components—3.5L Engine

SECONDARY AIR INJECTION SWITCHOVER SOLENOID

LOCATION

3.5L Engine

See Figure 115.

This vehicle is equipped with a secondary air injection system. The Secondary air injection system consists of an Air Pump that forces air into the exhaust ports of the cylinder head to reduce the emissions during engine warm-up. The air injected into the exhaust will cause the catalytic converters to heat up more quickly. This will improve the emission levels during a cold start. The Air Pump Switchover System incorporates an Air Pump (1) with two Air Pump Switchover Valves (2 and 3), an Air Pump Switchover Solenoid (5), an Air Pump Relay (4), and the PCM.

The Air Pump is mounted to the front of the engine. The Air Pump Switchover valves (2 and 3) are located at the front, top of the engine, mounted just in front of the left and right cylinder covers. The Air Pump Switch over Solenoid (5) is mounted on the right front of the engine, next to the air pump (1).

REMOVAL & INSTALLATION

3.5L Engine

See Figure 116.

1. Disconnect the negative battery cable.
2. Remove the air filter housing.
3. Disconnect the air pump switchover solenoid harness connector (2).
4. Disconnect the vacuum lines (1).
5. Remove the air pump switchover solenoid (3) from air pump switchover solenoid retaining bracket.

To install:

6. Install the air pump switchover solenoid (3) above air pump switchover solenoid mounting bracket.
7. Connect the vacuum lines (1).
8. Connect the air pump switchover solenoid harness connector (2).
9. Install the air filter housing.
10. Connect the negative battery cable.

SECONDARY AIR INJECTION PUMP

LOCATION

3.5L Engine

See Figure 115.

This vehicle is equipped with a secondary air injection system. The Secondary air injection system consists of an Air Pump

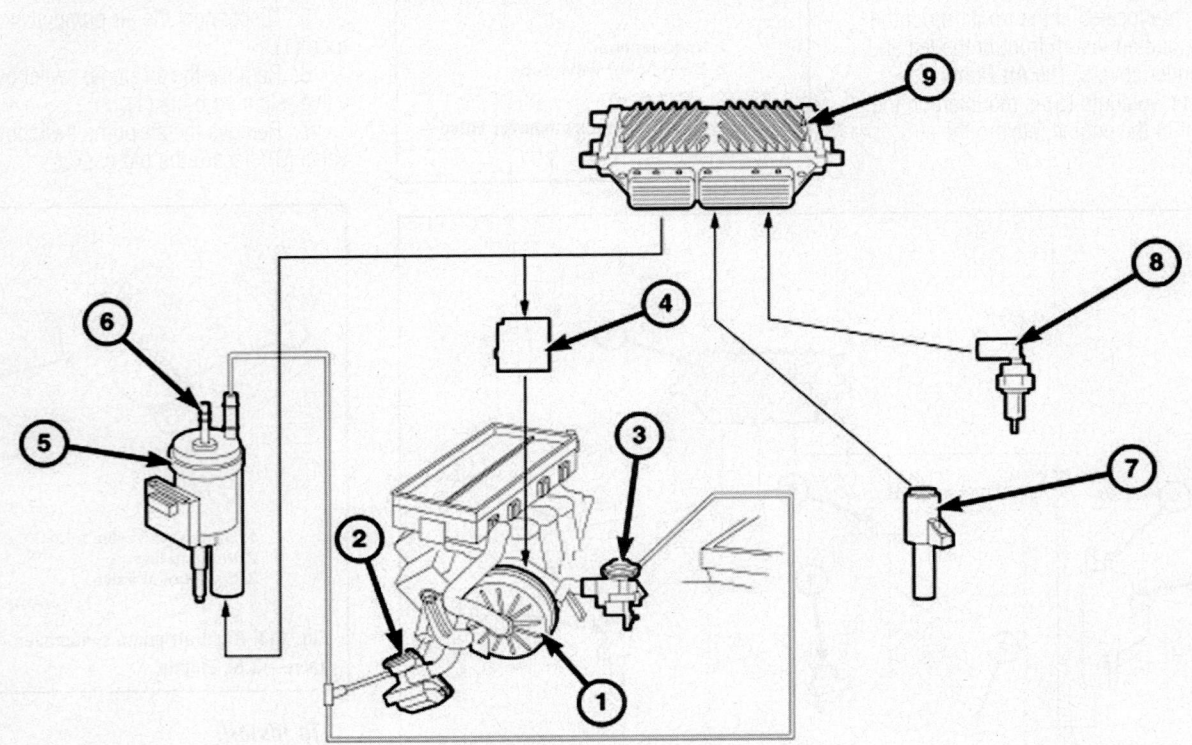

1. Air pump
2. Switchover valve
3. Switchover valve
4. Air pump relay
5. Air pump switchover solenoid
6. Fitting
7. Engine speed sensor
8. Coolant temperature sensor
9. PCM

36543_SPRI_G0051

Fig. 115 Secondary AIR system components—3.5L Engine

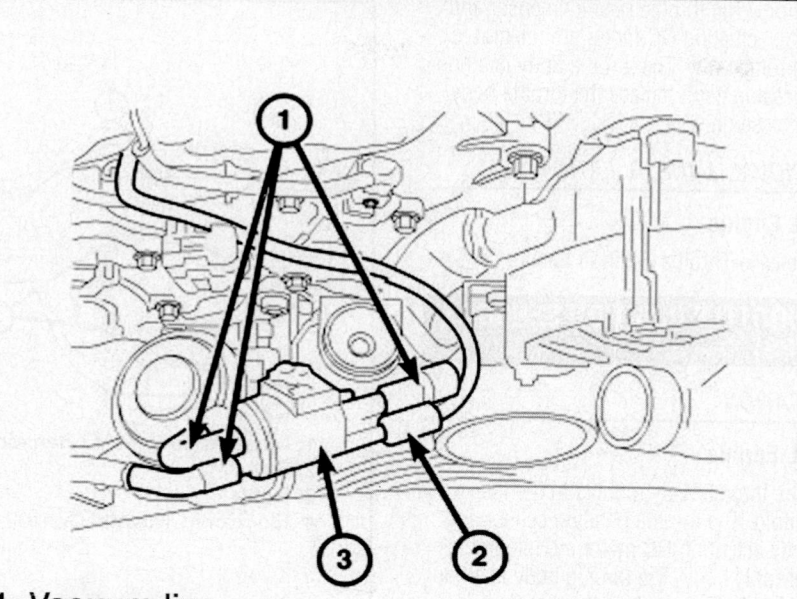

1. **Vacuum line**
2. **Air pump switchover solenoid harness connector**
3. **Air pump switchover solenoid**

36543_SPRI_G0054

Fig. 116 air pump switchover solenoid—3.5L Engine

that forces air into the exhaust ports of the cylinder head to reduce the emissions during engine warm-up. The air injected into the exhaust will cause the catalytic converters to heat up more quickly. This will improve the emission levels during a cold start. The Air Pump Switchover System incorporates an Air Pump (1) with two Air Pump Switchover Valves (2 and 3), an Air Pump Switchover Solenoid (5), an Air Pump Relay (4), and the PCM.

The Air Pump is mounted to the front of the engine. The Air Pump Switchover valves (2 and 3) are located at the front, top of the engine, mounted just in front of the left and right cylinder covers. The Air Pump Switch over Solenoid (5) is mounted on the right front of the engine, next to the air pump (1).

REMOVAL & INSTALLATION

3.5L Engine

See Figure 117.

1. Disconnect the negative battery cable.
2. Remove the air filter housing and disconnect the air inlet hose (1) from the air pump (2).
3. Remove the air pump solenoid. Refer to Secondary Air Injection Switchover Solenoid.

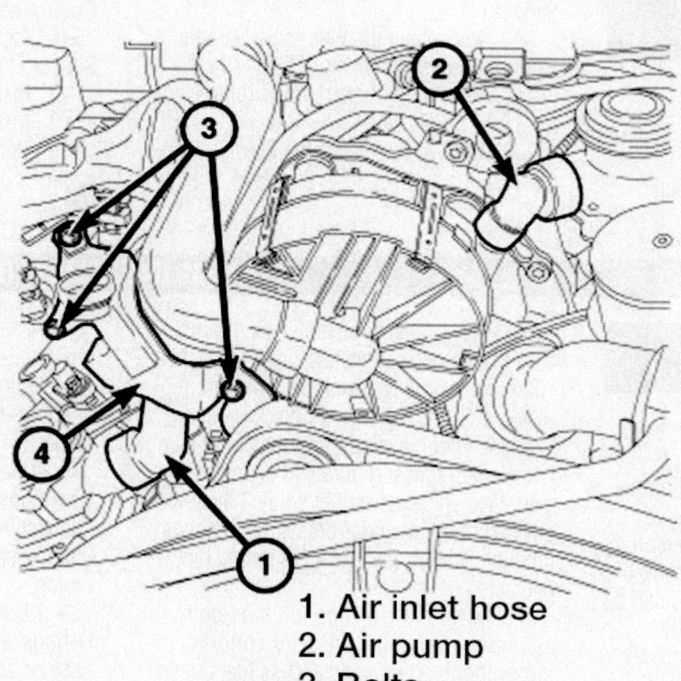

1. **Air inlet hose**
2. **Air pump**
3. **Bolts**
4. **Bracket**

36543_SPRI_G0055

Fig. 117 air pump and solenoid bracket—3.5L Engine

4. Remove the 3 bolts (3) from the air pump solenoid bracket (4), and remove the bracket.

5. Disconnect the right air pump outlet tube (1).

6. Disconnect the left air pump outlet tube (2).

7. Disconnect the air pump harness connector (2).

8. Remove the 3 air pump retaining bolts (1).

9. Remove the air pump (2) from the bracket.

To install:

10. Install the air pump (2).

11. Install the 3 air pump retaining bolts (1).

12. Reconnect the air pump harness connector (2).

13. Reconnect the left air pump outlet tube (2).

14. Reconnect the right air pump outlet tube (1).

15. Install the air pump solenoid bracket, and install the 3 air pump solenoid bracket bolts.

16. Install the air pump solenoid. Refer to Secondary Air Injection Switchover Solenoid.

17. Install the air filter housing and reconnect the air inlet hose (1) to the air pump (2).

18. Connect the negative battery cable.

THROTTLE CONTROL ACTUATOR (TAC)

LOCATION

3.5L Engine

The throttle body mounts to the intake

manifold. The throttle position sensor and throttle actuating DC motor are integral to the throttle body. The throttle body is a non serviceable item, replace the throttle body as an assembly.

REMOVAL & INSTALLATION

3.5L Engine

Refer to Throttle Position Sensor (TPS).

THROTTLE POSITION SENSOR (TPS)

LOCATION

3.5L Engine

The throttle body mounts to the intake manifold. The throttle position sensor and throttle actuating DC motor are integral to the throttle body. The throttle body is a non serviceable item, replace the throttle body as an assembly.

REMOVAL & INSTALLATION

3.5L Engine

See Figure 118.

1. Disconnect the negative battery cable.
2. Remove the engine cover.
3. Remove the air filter housing.
4. Remove the Mass Airflow (MAF) Sensor (1).
5. Disconnect the Electronic Throttle Control harness connector (1).
6. Remove the Electronic Throttle Control bolts (2) and (3).
7. Remove the Electronic Throttle Control (4).

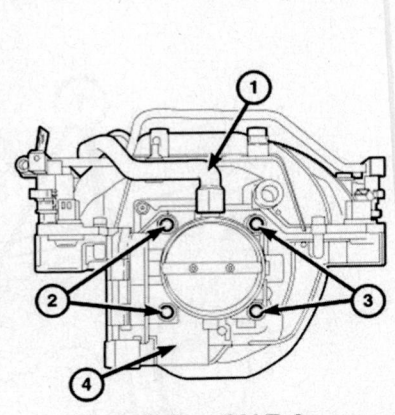

1. Mass Airflow (MAF) Sensor
2. Bolts
3. Bolts
4. Electronic Throttle Control

36543_SPRI_G0044

Fig. 118 Throttle body components— 3.5L Engine

To install:

8. Install the Electronic Throttle Control (4).

9. Install the Electronic Throttle Control bolts (2) and (3). Tighten to 80 inch lbs. (9 Nm).

10. Reconnect the Electronic Throttle Control harness connector (1).

11. Install the Mass Airflow (MAF) Sensor (1).

12. Install the air filter housing.

13. Install the engine cover.

14. Reconnect the negative battery cable.

FUEL

GASOLINE FUEL INJECTION SYSTEM

FUEL SYSTEM SERVICE PRECAUTIONS

Safety is the most important factor when performing not only fuel system maintenance but any type of maintenance. Failure to conduct maintenance and repairs in a safe manner may result in serious personal injury or death. Maintenance and testing of the vehicle's fuel system components can be accomplished safely and effectively by adhering to the following rules and guidelines.

• To avoid the possibility of fire and personal injury, always disconnect the negative battery cable unless the repair or test procedure requires that battery voltage be applied.

• Always relieve the fuel system pressure prior to disconnecting any fuel system component (injector, fuel rail, pressure regulator, etc.), fitting or fuel line connection. Exercise extreme caution whenever relieving fuel system pressure to avoid exposing skin, face and eyes to fuel spray. Please be advised that fuel under pressure may penetrate the skin or any part of the body that it contacts.

• Always place a shop towel or cloth around the fitting or connection prior to loosening to absorb any excess fuel due to spillage. Ensure that all fuel spillage (should it occur) is quickly removed from engine surfaces. Ensure that all fuel soaked cloths or towels are deposited into a suitable waste container.

• Always keep a dry chemical (Class B) fire extinguisher near the work area.

• Do not allow fuel spray or fuel vapors to come into contact with a spark or open flame.

• Always use a back-up wrench when loosening and tightening fuel line connection fittings. This will prevent unnecessary stress and torsion to fuel line piping.

• Always replace worn fuel fitting O-rings with new. Do not substitute fuel hose or equivalent where fuel pipe is installed.

Before servicing the vehicle, make sure to also refer to the precautions in the beginning of this section as well.

RELIEVING FUEL SYSTEM PRESSURE

PROCEDURE

3.5L Engine

1. Disconnect the fuel pump relay.
2. Start and run engine until it stalls.
3. Attempt restarting engine until it will no longer run.
4. Turn the ignition key to the **OFF** position.
5. Disconnect the negative battery cable.
6. One or more Diagnostic Trouble Codes (DTC's) may have been stored in PCM memory. The scan tool must be used to erase a DTC.

FUEL FILTER

REMOVAL & INSTALLATION

3.5L Engine

The fuel filter is not serviceable, it is mounted on the inside of the fuel tank in the fuel pump module. For additional information, refer to Fuel Pump Module.

FUEL PUMP MODULE

REMOVAL & INSTALLATION

3.5L Engine

See Figure 119.

1. Release Fuel System pressure. Refer to Relieving Fuel System Pressure.
2. Drain Fuel Tank.
3. Remove the 2 Fuel Filler Door Fasteners (1), and remove the Gas Cap (2) and Fuel Filler Door (3).
4. Remove the 4 Fuel Filler Tube Panel Fasteners (4) and remove the Fuel Filler Tube Panel (2).

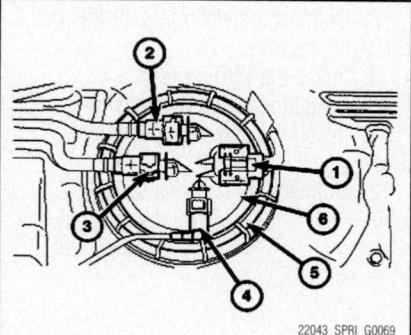

Fig. 119 Harness Connector (1), Return Line (2), Feed Line (3), Lock Ring (5), Fuel Pump (6)—3.5L Fuel Pump Assembly

5. Remove the Fuel Filler Tube Fastener (1).
6. Remove the tie straps (2).
7. Disconnect the harness connector (1).
8. Remove the Fuel Filler Tube Grommet (3).
9. Disconnect the harness connector (1).
10. Disconnect the Fuel Feed line (2) and Fuel Return line (3).
11. Remove the center fuel tank strap (1).
12. Support the fuel tank with a transmission jack.
13. Disconnect the Evaporative Emission Vent Line from the Fuel Tank (2).
14. Lower the Fuel Tank.
15. Disconnect the Fuel Pump Harness Connector (1).
16. Disconnect the Fuel Feed Line (3) and the Fuel Return Line (2) from the Fuel Pump (6).
17. Unscrew Fuel Pump Lock Ring (5).
18. Remove the Fuel Pump Assembly (6).

To install:

19. Install the fuel pump assembly into the tank.
20. Install the Fuel Pump Lock Ring.
21. Reconnect the Fuel Feed Line and the Fuel Return Line to the Fuel Pump.
22. Reconnect the Fuel Pump Harness Connector.
23. Install the fuel tank.
24. Connect the negative battery cable.
25. Start the engine and check for leaks.
26. Install the Fuel Pump Assembly.
27. Install the Fuel Pump Lock Ring (5).
28. Reconnect the Fuel Feed Line (3) and the Fuel Return Line (2) to the Fuel Pump (6).
29. Reconnect the Fuel Pump Harness Connector (1).
30. Using a Transmission Jack, raise the Fuel Tank.
31. Reconnect the Evaporative Emission Vent Line to the Fuel Tank (2).
32. Install the Center Fuel Tank Strap (1).
33. Reconnect the Fuel Feed line (2) and Fuel Return line (3).
34. Reconnect the harness connector (1).
35. Install the Fuel Filler Tube Grommet (3).
36. Reconnect the harness connector (1).
37. Install the tie straps (2).
38. Install the Fuel Filler Tube (2) and the Fuel Filler Tube Fastener (1).
39. Install the Fuel Filler Tube Panel (2) and install the 4 Fuel Filler Tube Panel Fasteners (4).

40. Install the Fuel Filler Door (3) and the Gas Cap (2), then install the 2 Fuel Filler Door Fasteners (1).

FUEL RAIL & INJECTORS

REMOVAL & INSTALLATION

3.5L Engine

See Figure 120.

1. Properly relieve the fuel system pressure.
2. Disconnect the negative battery cable.
3. Remove the air intake assembly.
4. Disconnect the fuel line from the fuel rail.
5. Remove any vacuum lines from the throttle as necessary.
6. Disconnect the electrical connectors from the fuel injectors.
7. Disconnect the electrical connectors from the throttle body and position the wiring harness aside.
8. Remove the four fuel rail mounting bolts.
9. Gently rock and pull left side of fuel rail until fuel injectors just start to clear machined holes in cylinder head. Gently rock and pull right side of rail until injectors just start to clear cylinder head holes. Repeat this procedure (left/right) until all injectors have cleared cylinder head holes.
10. Remove the fuel rail from engine.
11. Release the fuel injector clip and separate the fuel injector from the fuel rail.

To install:

12. Install the fuel injector into the fuel and install the injector clip.
13. Clean out the fuel injector bores in the intake manifold.

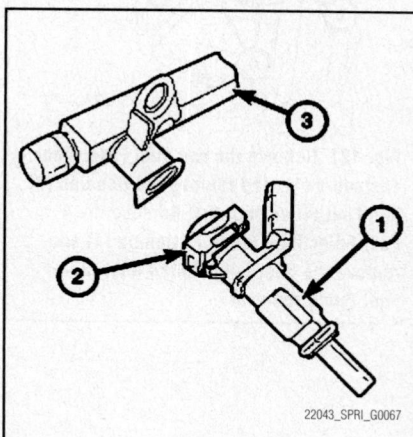

Fig. 120 Release the clip (2) to remove the fuel injector (1) from the fuel rail (3)— 3.5L Engine

14. Apply a small amount of engine oil to each fuel injector O-ring. This will help in fuel rail installation.

15. Position the fuel rail/fuel injector assembly to the injector openings in cylinder head.

16. Guide each injector into cylinder head. Be careful not to tear injector O-rings.

17. Push the right side of the Fuel Rail down until the Fuel Injectors are seated on the Cylinder Head Shoulder. Push the left Fuel Rail Down until the Injectors are seated on the Cylinder Head Shoulder. Install the fuel rail mounting bolts.

18. Install the engine wiring harness and install the electrical connectors to the throttle body and all six injectors.

19. Install any removed vacuum lines to the throttle body.

20. Reconnect the fuel line to the fuel rail.

21. Install the air intake assembly.

22. Install the engine appearance cover.

23. Connect the negative battery cable.

FUEL TANK

REMOVAL & INSTALLATION

3.5L Engine

See Figures 121 and 122.

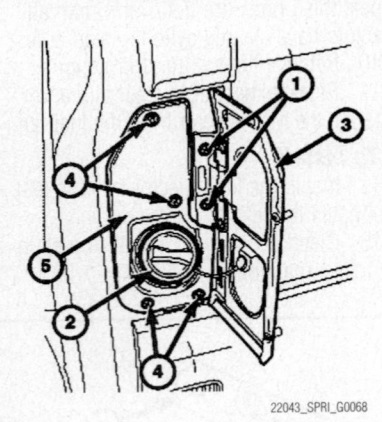

Fig. 121 Remove the two Fuel Filler Door Fasteners (1), and remove the Gas Cap (2) and Fuel Filler Door (3). Remove the 4 Fuel Filler Tube Panel Fasteners (4) and remove the Fuel Filler Tube Panel (2)—Fuel Pump removal

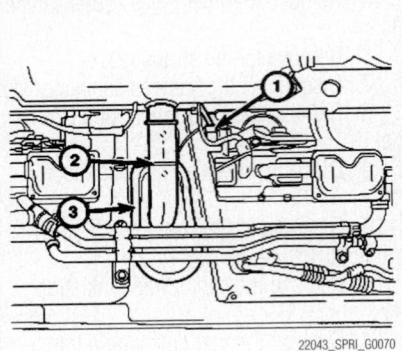

Fig. 122 Remove the tie straps (2), harness connector (1) and Fuel Filler Tube Grommet (3)—3.5L Fuel Tank removal

1. Properly relieve the fuel system pressure.

2. Disconnect the negative battery cable.

3. Drain the fuel tank.

4. Remove the filler door fasteners, then remove the filler door and gas cap.

5. Remove the filler tube panel fasteners, then remove the filler tube panel.

6. Remove the fuel filler tube fastener, located just inside the filler door panel.

7. Remove the tie straps, harness connector and fuel filler grommet.

8. Disconnect the harness connector.

9. Disconnect the Fuel Feed line and Fuel Return line.

10. Remove the front and rear tank straps.

11. Support the fuel tank with a suitable jack.

12. Remove the center fuel tank strap.

13. Disconnect the Evaporative Emission Vent Line from the Fuel Tank (2).

14. Lower the fuel tank from the vehicle.

To install:

15. Raise the fuel tank into position in the vehicle.

16. Reconnect the Evaporative Emission Vent Line to the Fuel Tank (2).

17. Install the Center Fuel Tank Strap and tighten the strap bolt to 41 ft. lbs. (56 Nm).

18. Reconnect the fuel feed and return lines.

19. Reconnect the wiring harness connector.

20. Install the Fuel Filler Tube Grommet, harness connector and tie straps.

21. Install the front and rear Fuel Tank Straps and tighten the strap bolt to 41 ft. lbs. (56 Nm).

22. Install the Fuel Filler Tube and Tube Fastener.

23. Install the Fuel Filler Tube Panel and install the 4 Fuel Filler Tube Panel Fasteners.

24. Install the Fuel Filler Door and the Gas Cap, then install the 2 Fuel Filler Door Fasteners.

IDLE SPEED

ADJUSTMENT

3.5L Engine

Idle speed is controlled by the Powertrain Control Module (PCM). No adjustment is necessary or possible.

THROTTLE BODY

REMOVAL & INSTALLATION

3.5L Engine

1. Disconnect the negative battery cable.

2. Remove the engine appearance cover.

3. Remove the air intake assembly.

4. Remove the Mass Air Flow (MAF) sensor.

5. Disconnect the electronic throttle control wiring harness.

6. Remove the throttle body mounting bolts and remove the throttle body.

To install:

7. Install the throttle body assembly and tighten the mounting bolts to 80 inch lbs. (9 Nm).

8. Connect the electronic throttle control wiring harness.

9. Install the MAF sensor.

10. Install the air intake assembly.

11. Install the engine appearance cover.

12. Connect the negative battery cable.

FUEL   **DIESEL FUEL INJECTION SYSTEM**

FUEL SYSTEM SERVICE PRECAUTIONS

Safety is the most important factor when performing not only fuel system maintenance but any type of maintenance. Failure to conduct maintenance and repairs in a safe manner may result in serious personal injury or death. Maintenance and testing of the vehicle's fuel system components can be accomplished safely and effectively by adhering to the following rules and guidelines.

• To avoid the possibility of fire and personal injury, always disconnect the negative battery cable unless the repair or test procedure requires that battery voltage be applied.

• Always relieve the fuel system pressure prior to disconnecting any fuel system component (injector, fuel rail, pressure regulator, etc.), fitting or fuel line connection. Exercise extreme caution whenever relieving fuel system pressure to avoid exposing skin, face and eyes to fuel spray. Please be advised that fuel under pressure may penetrate the skin or any part of the body that it contacts.

• Always place a shop towel or cloth around the fitting or connection prior to loosening to absorb any excess fuel due to spillage. Ensure that all fuel spillage (should it occur) is quickly removed from engine surfaces. Ensure that all fuel soaked cloths or towels are deposited into a suitable waste container.

• Always keep a dry chemical (Class B) fire extinguisher near the work area.

• Do not allow fuel spray or fuel vapors to come into contact with a spark or open flame.

• Always use a back-up wrench when loosening and tightening fuel line connection fittings. This will prevent unnecessary stress and torsion to fuel line piping.

• Always replace worn fuel fitting O-rings with new. Do not substitute fuel hose or equivalent where fuel pipe is installed.

Before servicing the vehicle, make sure to also refer to the precautions in the beginning of this section as well.

FUEL FILTER

REMOVAL & INSTALLATION

3.0L Engine
See Figure 123.

1. Disconnect the negative battery cable.
2. Disconnect the water in fuel (WIF) sensor electrical connector.

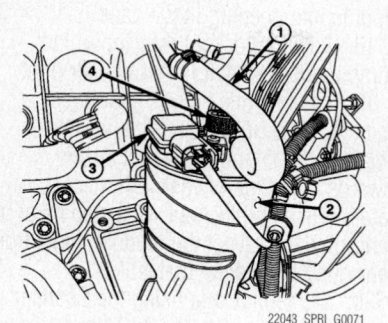

Fig. 123 Fuel supply hose (1), Fuel Filter (2), WIF Sensor (3), Water in Fuel Drain (4)—2.7L Engine, 3.0L Engine similar

3. Using Special Tool 9539, release the fuel hose clamps at the fuel filter.
4. Remove the fuel filter retaining bracket bolt and remove the fuel filter.

To install:

5. Fill new fuel filter with the new diesel fuel.
6. Carefully seat the WIF sensor (if removed) and tighten bolt to 13 inch lbs. (1.5 Nm).
7. Position fuel filter in the bracket and tighten the retaining bolt to 53 inch lbs. (6 Nm).
8. Install the fuel lines and re-crimp clamps using Special Tool no. 9539.
9. Connect the WIF wiring harness connector.
10. Connect the negative battery cable.
11. Cycle the ignition several times to build pressure.
12. Start engine and inspect for leaks.

DRAINING WATER FROM THE SYSTEM

Connect a hose to the Water in Fuel (WIF) drain and place it in a clearly marked and suitable container. Open the WIF drain by turning counterclockwise. Turn the ignition key on for 20 seconds. Repeat the procedure until all water is removed, close the drain and remove the hose.

FUEL LEVEL SENDING UNIT

REMOVAL & INSTALLATION

3.0L Engine

The fuel level sending unit (fuel level sensor) and float assembly is located on the side of the fuel pump module.

1. Remove fuel pump module from fuel tank. Refer to Fuel Pump Module.
2. Unplug sensor's 2-wire harness from pump module electrical connector.
3. Before disconnecting wiring from 2-wire harness electrical connector, note position of each wire in the connector. Record this position.
4. Disconnect wiring from 2-wire harness electrical connector using a terminal pick / removal tool.
5. To remove sending unit from pump module, press on plastic locking tabs while sliding sending unit on its tracks.

To install:

6. Noting their previous positions, connect wires from 2-wire harness into its connector.
7. Plug 2-wire harness connector into pump module electrical connector.
8. Position sending unit (4) to tracks on fuel pump module. Slide and snap into place.
9. Install fuel pump module. Refer to Fuel Pump Module.

FUEL PRESSURE REGULATOR

REMOVAL & INSTALLATION

3.0L Engine

1. Disconnect the negative battery cable.
2. Disconnect the sensor wiring harness connector.

➡**Place a shop towel underneath the sensor to capture any fuel spillage.**

3. Unscrew the sensor and discard the seal.

To install:

4. Install the sealing ring onto the sensor and screw the fuel pressure sensor into the fuel rail.
5. Tighten the senor to 44 ft. lbs. (60 Nm), back it off 90° and retighten to 59 ft. lbs. (80 Nm).
6. Connect the sensor wiring harness connector.

✲✲ CAUTION
Care must be taken when installing the engine cover. Assure the proper routing of the fuel injector return fuel hose to the banjo bolt fitting in the left rear corner of the cover. Failure to do so may pinch or damage the hose causing fuel leakage or a driveability concern.

7. Start engine, allow to run for a few minutes, turn the engine off and inspect for leaks.

FUEL PUMP MODULE

REMOVAL & INSTALLATION

3.0L Engine

> **✳✳ CAUTION**
>
> **To prevent damage to the float rod, the float and float rod must be removed from the pump module. This step must be done before the pump module is removed from the fuel tank.**

1. Drain and remove fuel tank. Refer to Fuel Tank.
2. Thoroughly clean area around pump module at top of tank.
3. Disconnect all fuel lines from pump module fittings.
4. The plastic fuel pump module locknut (lockring) is threaded onto fuel tank. Install Special Tool #6856 to locknut and remove locknut. The fuel pump module will spring up slightly after locknut is removed.
5. Pull module assembly up just a few inches to gain access to float support arm/rod. Be careful not to bend float support rod while removing pump module.
6. Rotate clip to release float rod from fuel level sensor.
7. Twist rod slightly to remove from fuel level sensor. Do not allow float assembly to fall into fuel tank.
8. While holding float rod, remove fuel pump module from fuel tank.
9. Remove float assembly from fuel tank.
10. Remove and discard rubber gasket (seal) from pump module.

To install:

> **✳✳ CAUTION**
>
> **Whenever the fuel pump module is serviced, the rubber gasket must be replaced.**

11. Thoroughly clean locknut (lockring) and locknut threads at top of tank.
12. Position new gasket (seal) to fuel tank opening.
13. Position float rod assembly partially into fuel tank.
14. Position fuel pump module partially into fuel tank.
15. Twist rod into clip on fuel level sensor.

16. Rotate clip to attach rod to clip.
17. After attaching float assembly to fuel level sensor, carefully position fuel pump module into opening in fuel tank.
18. Position locknut over top of fuel pump module. Install locknut finger tight.
19. The fuel line fittings should be pointed to the right side of the vehicle. Rotate and position alignment arrow towards right side of vehicle (if necessary) before tightening locknut. This step must be performed to prevent the module's float from contacting the side of fuel tank.
20. Tighten locknut using the Spanner Wrench 6856 to 44 ft. lbs. (60 Nm).
21. Install fuel tank. Refer to Fuel Tank.

FUEL RAIL & INJECTORS

REMOVAL & INSTALLATION

3.0L Engine

Left Fuel Rail

> **✳✳ WARNING**
>
> **No sparks, open flames or smoking. Risk of poisoning from inhaling and swallowing fuel. Risk of injury to eyes and skin from contact with fuel. Pour fuels only into suitable and appropriately marked containers. Wear protective clothing.**

1. Disconnect negative battery cable.
2. Remove engine cover.
3. Disconnect the fuel rail solenoid.
4. Remove the charge air cooler inlet tube.
5. Unfasten the fuel supply and return hose clamps at the high pressure pump, fuel filter and fuel rail using Fuel Line Pliers 9539.
6. Remove the fuel supply and return pipe bundle and position aside.
7. Remove the main engine wiring harness fasteners at the left rear cylinder head.
8. Loosen the high pressure lines at the left fuel injectors.
9. Disconnect the high pressure lines at the fuel rail.
10. Remove the left fuel rail.

To install:

> **✳✳ CAUTION**
>
> **Inspect sealing cones at the lines. Replace as necessary. Ensure that all fuel pressure lines are exactly located in original position.**

11. Carefully position the fuel rail and hand tighten all of the high pressure fuel lines.
12. Install the fuel rail fasteners and tighten to 97 inch lbs. (11 Nm).
13. Tighten the high pressure line to the fuel rail to 24 ft. lbs. (33 Nm)
14. Tighten the high pressure fuel rail transfer pipe to 19 ft. lbs. (27 Nm).
15. Tighten the high pressure fuel lines at the fuel rail to 19 ft. lbs. (27 Nm).
16. Tighten the high pressure fuel lines at the fuel injectors to 19 ft. lbs. (27 Nm).
17. Reposition the main engine wiring harness and install the fasteners. Tighten fasteners to 97 inch lbs. (11 Nm).
18. Connect the fuel supply and return pipe bundle, connect the fuel hoses to the high pressure pump, fuel filter, fuel rail and clamp with Fuel Line Pliers 9539.
19. Connect the fuel rail pressure solenoid.
20. Install the charge cooler inlet air pipe.
21. Connect the negative battery cable.
22. Start engine, allow to warm, turn engine off and inspect for leaks.
23. Install the strut tower support.
24. Install engine cover.

Right Fuel Rail

> **✳✳ WARNING**
>
> **No sparks, open flames or smoking. Risk of poisoning from inhaling and swallowing fuel. Risk of injury to eyes and skin from contact with fuel. Pour fuels only into suitable and appropriately marked containers. Wear protective clothing.**

1. Disconnect negative battery cable.
2. Remove engine cover.
3. Remove the strut tower support.
4. Loosen the high pressure lines at the fuel injectors.
5. Disconnect the high pressure lines at the fuel rail.
6. Disconnect the fuel rail pressure sensor.
7. Remove the right fuel rail.

To install:

> **✳✳ CAUTION**
>
> **Inspect sealing cones at the lines. Replace as necessary. Ensure that all fuel pressure lines are exactly located in original position.**

8. Carefully position the fuel rail and hand tighten all of the high pressure fuel lines.

9. Install the fuel rail fasteners and tighten to 97 inch lbs. (11 Nm).

10. Tighten the high pressure line to the fuel rail to 24 ft. lbs. (33 Nm)

11. Tighten the high pressure fuel rail transfer pipe to 19 ft. lbs. (27 Nm).

12. Tighten the high pressure fuel lines at the fuel rail to 19 ft. lbs. (27 Nm).

13. Tighten the high pressure fuel lines at the fuel injectors to 19 ft. lbs. (27 Nm).

14. Connect the fuel rail pressure sensor.

15. Connect the negative battery cable.

16. Start engine, allow to warm, turn engine off and inspect for leaks.

17. Install the strut tower support.

18. Install engine cover.

FUEL SUPPLY PUMP

REMOVAL & INSTALLATION

3.0L Engine

See Figures 124 and 125.

1. Drain and remove fuel tank.

2. Thoroughly clean the area around pump module at top of tank.

3. Disconnect all the fuel lines from pump module fittings.

4. The plastic fuel pump module locknut (lockring) is threaded onto fuel tank. Install Special Tool 6856 to locknut and remove locknut. The fuel pump module will spring up slightly after locknut is removed.

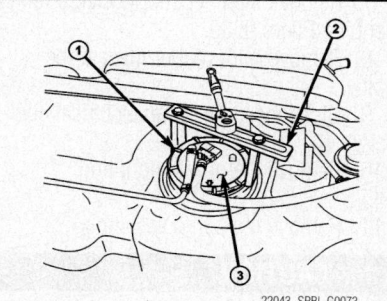

Fig. 124 Use Special Tool 6856 (2) to remove the lockring (1) and remove the fuel supply pump (3)—Typical

5. Pull the fuel pump assembly up just a few inches to gain access to float support arm/rod.

✳✳ WARNING

Be careful not to bend float support rod while removing pump module.

6. Rotate the clip to release float rod from the fuel level sensor.

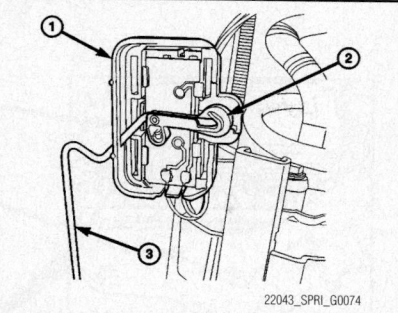

Fig. 125 Rotate the clip (2) to release the float rod (3) from the fuel level sensor (1)— Typical

7. Twist the rod slightly to remove from fuel level sensor. Do not allow float assembly to fall into fuel tank.

8. While holding the float rod, remove the fuel pump module from the fuel tank.

9. Remove float assembly from fuel tank.

10. Remove and discard rubber gasket (seal) from pump module.

To install:

11. Thoroughly clean the locknut (lockring) and locknut threads at top of the tank.

12. Position a new gasket (seal) to the fuel tank opening.

13. Position the float rod assembly partially into the fuel tank.

14. Position the fuel pump module partially into the fuel tank.

15. Twist the rod into the clip on the fuel level sensor.

16. Rotate the clip to attach the rod to the clip.

17. After attaching the float assembly to the fuel level sensor, carefully position the fuel pump module into opening in the fuel tank.

18. Position the locknut over top of fuel pump module. Install locknut finger tight.

19. The fuel line fittings should be pointed to the right side of the vehicle. Rotate and position the alignment arrow towards right side of vehicle (if necessary) before tightening the locknut. This step must be performed to prevent the module's float from contacting the side of fuel tank.

20. Tighten the locknut using Special Tool 6856.

21. Install the fuel tank.

FUEL SYSTEM PURGING

BLEEDING

3.0L Engine

If a diesel engine's fuel supply has been contaminated (with gasoline, water, etc.), the following procedure must be followed:

1. Remove all fuel from the fuel tank. Use an appropriate fuel container. Dispose of the contaminated fuel using the proper procedures.

✳✳ CAUTION

Dispose of petroleum based products in a manner consistent with all applicable Local, State, Federal, and Provincial regulations.

2. Remove and clean fuel tank.

3. Install the fuel tank.

4. Fill fuel tank with fresh diesel fuel.

5. Drain and remove the fuel filter.

6. Install a new fuel filter.

7. Check the engine control module for any diagnostic trouble codes (DTCs). Record and clear any DTCs that are present.

8. Start and run the engine. Run the engine for up to 15 minutes to allow time for any DTCs to reset and shut off the engine.

9. Check the engine control module for any diagnostic trouble codes (DTCs). Record any DTCs that are present. Refer to the appropriate engine electrical diagnostics to diagnose any DTCs that were set.

✳✳ CAUTION

With the high pressure fuel system in this vehicle, any residual contaminated fuel will be removed very quickly. Shut off the engine immediately if signs of engine damage are noted.

The engine should then be evaluated to determine if the contaminated fuel has caused any damage to the fuel system and/or engine. Indicators that the fuel system has been damaged include the following:

• Unstable fuel rail pressure. This can manifest itself as instability of idle speeds, excessive undershoot/overshoot at engine start-up, or excessive undershoot/overshoot when the engine operating conditions change. A typical engine response to a large rail pressure undershoot would be a decrease in engine speed or engine stall.

• Excessive noise from the engine. This could indicate poor rail pressure control or the inability of the injection system to inject the proper amount of fuel.

• Excessive smoke (black or white). This could indicate the inability of the fuel system to inject the proper amount of fuel.

➡**If any of these conditions are exhibited after cleaning the fuel system, proceed to the appropriate engine** electrical diagnostic information. Repair the fuel system and/or engine as necessary.

FUEL TANK

REMOVAL & INSTALLATION

3.0L Engine

1. Drain Fuel Tank.
2. Remove the 2 Fuel Filler Door Fasteners, and remove the Gas Cap and Fuel Filler Door.
3. Remove the 4 Fuel Filler Tube Panel Fasteners and remove the Fuel Filler Tube Panel.
4. Remove the Fuel Filler Tube Fastener.
5. Remove the tie straps.
6. Disconnect the harness connector.
7. Remove the Fuel Filler Tube Grommet.
8. Disconnect the harness connector.
9. Disconnect the Fuel Feed line and Fuel Return line.
10. Remove the center fuel tank strap.
11. Support the fuel tank with a transmission jack.
12. Disconnect the Evaporative Emission Vent Line from the Fuel Tank.
13. Lower the Fuel Tank.

To install:

14. Using a Transmission Jack, raise the Fuel Tank.
15. Reconnect the Evaporative Emission Vent Line to the Fuel Tank.
16. Install the Center Fuel Tank Strap. Tighten strap bolt to 41 ft. lbs. (56 Nm).
17. Reconnect the Fuel Feed line and Fuel Return line.
18. Reconnect the harness connector.
19. Install the Fuel Filler Tube Grommet.
20. Reconnect the harness connector.
21. Install the front and rear Fuel Tank Straps. Tighten strap bolts to 41 ft. lbs. (56 Nm).
22. Install the tie straps.
23. Install the Fuel Filler Tube and the Fuel Filler Tube Fastener.
24. Install the Fuel Filler Tube Panel and install the 4 Fuel Filler Tube Panel Fasteners.
25. Install the Fuel Filler Door and the Gas Cap, then install the Fuel Filler Door Fasteners.

GLOW PLUGS

REMOVAL & INSTALLATION

3.0L Engine
See Figure 126.

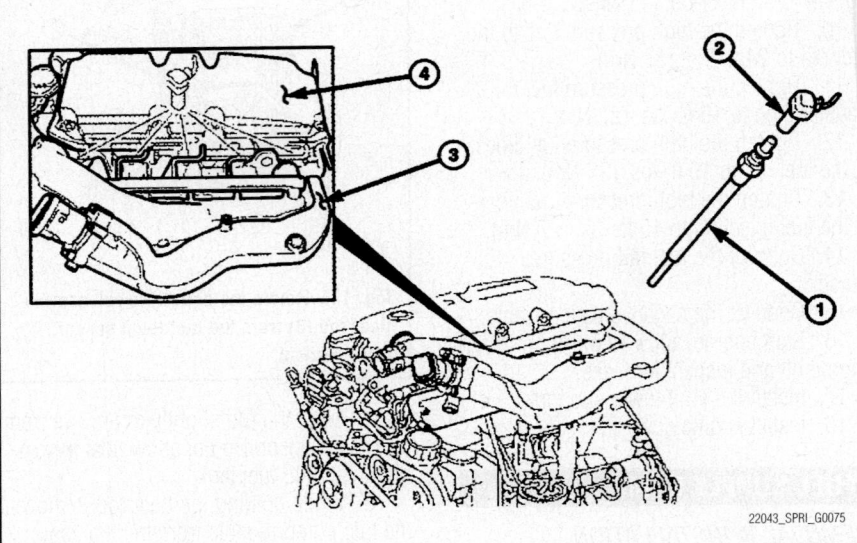

Fig. 126 Remove the engine appearance cover (4) and wiring harness (2) to remove the glow plug (1)—2.7L Engine shown, 3.0L Engine similar

1. Disconnect the negative battery cable.
2. Remove the engine appearance cover.
3. Using Special Tool 9286 Pliers, unplug the glow plug wiring harness connector at the glow plug.
4. Remove the glow plug.

To install:

5. Screw the glow plug into the cylinder head and tighten to 9 ft. lbs. (12 Nm).
6. Connect the glow plug wiring harness connector.
7. Install the engine appearance cover.
8. Connect the negative battery cable.

HIGH PRESSURE OIL PUMP DRIVE GEAR

REMOVAL & INSTALLATION

3.0L Engine

✷✷ WARNING

High pressure fuel lines deliver diesel fuel under extreme pressure from the injection pump to the fuel injectors. This may be as high as 23,200 psi (1600 bar). Use extreme caution when inspecting for high pressure fuel leaks. Fuel under this amount of pressure can penetrate skin causing personal injury or death. Inspect for high pressure fuel leaks with a sheet of cardboard. Wear safety goggles and adequate protective clothing when servicing fuel system.

1. Remove the engine cover.
2. Remove the negative battery cable.
3. Release the fuel pressure.
4. Remove the high pressure line support bracket.
5. Remove the high pressure line retaining nut.
6. Remove the return line clamp using Fuel Line Pliers 9539.
7. Remove the inlet supply clamp using Fuel Line Pliers 9539.
8. Remove both rubber lines at the pump.
9. Disconnect the pump electrical connectors.
10. Remove the pump mounting bolts.
11. Remove the pump assembly.

✷✷ CAUTION

Do not crimp or bend the fuel line. Capture all fluids that flow out of connections.

To install:

12. Install the high pressure pump to the left cylinder head. Torque the mounting bolts to 10 ft. lbs. (14 Nm).
13. Connect the pump electrical connectors.
14. Install the fuel lines at the pump.
15. Install the inlet supply line clamp using Fuel Line Pliers 9539.
16. Install the return line clamp using Fuel Line Pliers 9539.

❊❊ CAUTION

Do not crimp or bend the fuel line. Inspect sealing cone at line; replace the line if compression exists.

17. Install the high pressure fuel line retaining nuts. Torque the nuts to 24 ft. lbs. (33 Nm).
18. Install the high pressure line support bracket.
19. Install the negative battery cable.
20. Install the engine cover.
21. Start engine and check for leaks.

INJECTION LINES

REMOVAL & INSTALLATION

3.0L Engine

1. Disconnect negative battery cable.

❊❊ CAUTION

Counterhold with wrench at threaded connections of injectors. DO NOT EXCEED the tightening torque in order to avoid damaging the threaded connection.

❊❊ CAUTION

DO NOT crimp or bend lines.

➡**After removing injection lines, seal connections and ensure cleanliness.**

2. Unscrew union nuts of injection lines.
3. Remove injection lines.

To install:

4. Loosen the fuel rail mounting bolts to install lines free of stress.

❊❊ CAUTION

Inspect sealing cone at lines. Replace if compression points, kinks, or gouges exist. Ensure lines are correctly positioned in the fitting.

5. Position and install fuel lines. Tighten to 195 inch lbs. (22 Nm) using a wrench to counterhold at threaded connection.
6. Tighten fuel rail to 124 inch lbs. (14 Nm).
7. Connect negative battery cable.

❊❊ CAUTION

Care must be taken when installing the engine cover. Assure the proper routing of the fuel injector return fuel hose to the banjo bolt fitting in the left rear corner of the cover. Failure to do so may pinch or damage the

hose causing fuel leakage or a drive-ability concern.

8. Start engine, run for a few minutes, turn engine off and inspect for leaks.

INJECTION PUMP

REMOVAL & INSTALLATION

3.0L Engine

❊❊ WARNING

High pressure fuel lines deliver diesel fuel under extreme pressure from the injection pump to the fuel injectors. This may be as high as 1600 bar (23,200 psi). Use extreme caution when inspecting for high pressure fuel leaks. Fuel under this amount of pressure can penetrate skin causing personal injury or death. Inspect for high pressure fuel leaks with a sheet of cardboard. Wear safety goggles and adequate protective clothing when servicing fuel system.

1. Remove engine cover.
2. Remove negative battery cable.
3. Release fuel pressure.
4. Remove high pressure line support bracket.
5. Remove high pressure line retaining nut .
6. Remove the return line clamp using Fuel Line Pliers 9539.
7. Remove the inlet supply clamp using Fuel Line Pliers 9539.
8. Remove both rubber lines at the pump.
9. Disconnect the pump electrical connectors.
10. Remove the pump mounting bolts.
11. Remove the pump assembly.

❊❊ CAUTION

Do not crimp or bend fuel line. Capture all fluids that flow out of connections.

To install:

12. Install high pressure pump to the left cylinder head. Tighten mounting bolts to 10 ft. lbs. (14 Nm).
13. Connect the pump electrical connectors.
14. Install fuel lines at pump.
15. Install inlet supply line clamp using Fuel Line Pliers 9539.
16. Install return line clamp using Fuel Line Pliers 9539.

❊❊ CAUTION

Do not crimp or bend fuel line. Inspect sealing cone at line; replace line if compression exists.

17. Install high pressure fuel line retaining nuts. Torque nuts to 24 ft. lbs. (33 Nm).
18. Install high pressure line support bracket.
19. Install negative battery cable.
20. Install the engine cover.
21. Start engine and check for leaks.

INJECTION TIMING

ADJUSTMENT

3.0L Engine

Injection timing is synchronized according to the camshaft signal and the crankshaft signal. The ECM uses the signals sent by the camshaft position sensor (CMP) and the crankshaft position sensor (CKP) to determine injection timing.

INJECTORS

REMOVAL & INSTALLATION

3.0L Engine
See Figure 127.

1. Disconnect the negative battery cable.
2. Remove the engine appearance cover.
3. Remove the fuel return hose locking clamps, and remove the hose.
4. Disconnect the fuel injector high pressure line.

➡**Counterhold injection lines with wrench socket at threaded connections of injectors.**

5. Remove the fuel injector retaining bolt and tension claw, then remove the injector and seal.

➡**If injectors are tight, remove with special tool 9552.**

6. Remove the fuel injectors.

To install:

7. Clean the injector and recesses.
8. Coat the injector body with anti-seize lubricant, then install the injector with new seals.
9. Install the tensioning claws with new screws to the injectors. Tighten the screws to 62 inch lbs. (7 Nm) plus 90°.

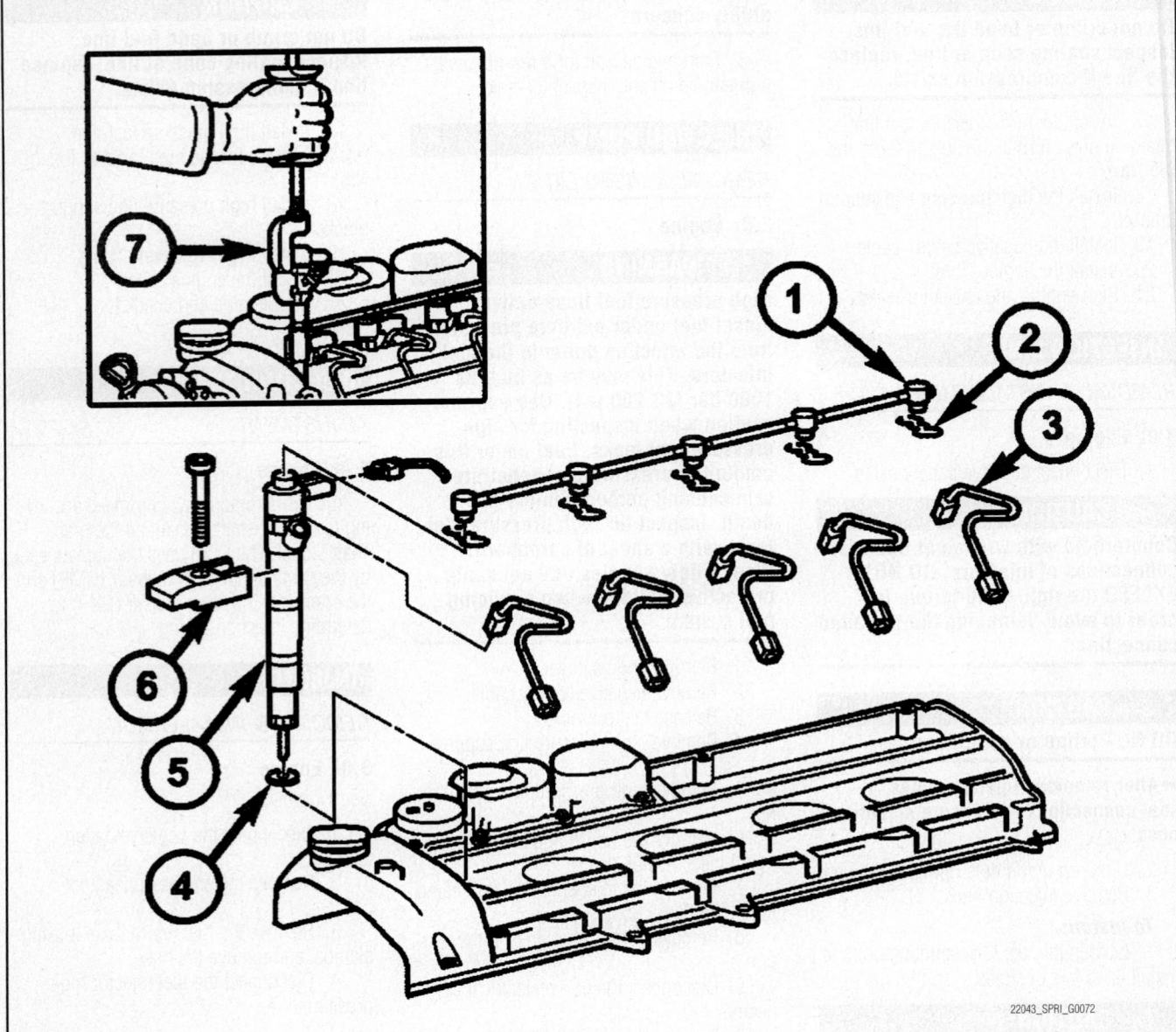

Fig. 127 Remove the locking clamps (2) and return hose (1), disconnect the injector high pressure line (3). Remove the retaining bolt and tension claw (6) and remove the injector (5) and seal (4)—Typical

10. Position the fuel return line to the injectors and secure the locking clamps.

11. Install the high pressure injection lines.

12. Connect the injector electrical connectors.

13. Install the engine appearance cover.

14. Connect the negative battery cable.

15. Program all of the injector codes into the Engine Control Module using a scan tool.

16. Start the engine and check for leaks.

OIL PRESSURE REGULATOR

REMOVAL & INSTALLATION

The oil pressure relief valve is integral to the oil pump and is not serviceable.

HEATING & AIR CONDITIONING SYSTEM

BLOWER MOTOR

REMOVAL & INSTALLATION

1. Disconnect and isolate the negative battery cable.

2. Remove the glove box from the instrument panel as follows:

   a. Remove the trim below the air outlet.

   b. Open the glove box, push up on the two rear stops and fold the box down completely.

   c. Remove the hinge screws and remove the glove box.

   d. Remove the screws and remove the inner compartment liner.

   e. Disconnect the glove box light electrical connector and remove the coolant air hose.

3. Remove the right side floor duct.

4. Remove the screw that secures the instrument panel cover to the lower right portion of instrument panel.

5. Disengage the locking feature and rotate the blower motor counterclockwise until it is loose from the HVAC housing.

6. Gently pull the lower right portion of the instrument panel cover slightly rearward to gain clearance and remove the blower motor from the HVAC housing.

7. Disconnect the wire harness connector from the blower motor and remove the blower motor from the passenger compartment.

To install:

8. Connect the wire harness connector to the blower motor.

9. Gently pull the lower right portion of the instrument panel cover slightly rearward to gain clearance and position the blower motor into the HVAC housing.

10. Rotate the blower motor clockwise until it is fully seated in the HVAC housing. Make sure the blower motor locking feature is fully engaged to the housing.

11. Install the screw that secures the instrument panel cover to the instrument panel. Tighten the screw securely.

12. Install the right side floor duct.

13. Install the glove box as follows:

   a. Install the coolant air hose to the inner glove box liner and connect the glove box light electrical connector.

   b. Install the inner glove box liner and install the screws.

   c. Install the glove box and install the hinge screws.

   d. Position the glove box up into the instrument panel and engage the rear retaining stop tabs.

   e. Install the trim panel below the air outlet.

14. Reconnect the negative battery cable.

HEATER CORE

REMOVAL & INSTALLATION

See Figures 128 through 131.

1. Remove the instrument panel and HVAC housing as an assembly as follows:

   a. Disconnect the negative battery cable.

   b. Recover the refrigerant from the A/C system.

   c. Drain the cooling system.

   d. Remove the air intake assembly.

   e. Remove the nut and disconnect the A/C liquid line and the A/C suction line from the A/C expansion valve and remove and discard the O-ring seals.

   f. Loosen the clamps and disconnect the heater hoses from the heater core.

   g. Cap the expansion valve and heater core openings.

   h. Remove the A-pillar trim.

   i. Remove the sun visors and storage trays.

   j. Remove the dome light.

   k. Remove the headliner

   l. Remove the steering column opening cover.

   m. Remove the trim below the air outlet.

   n. Open the glove box, push up on the two rear stops and fold the box down completely.

   o. Remove the hinge screws and remove the glove box.

   p. Remove the screws and remove the inner compartment liner.

   q. Disconnect the glove box light electrical connector and remove the coolant air hose.

   r. Using a trim stick C-4755 or equivalent, separate the clips and remove the center bezel.

   s. Remove the air outlet covers from the instrument panel center section.

   t. Remove the cover on the gearshift lever.

   u. Remove the gear shifter assembly.

   v. Remove the side air nozzles.

   w. Turn the steering wheel to center position and lock steering.

   x. Remove the airbag module from the steering wheel and remove the steering wheel.

➡**Matchmark the steering wheel to the steering column shaft for proper orientation during installation.**

   y. Disconnect all electrical connectors from wiring harness in area of A-pillar and roof and remove the wiring harness.

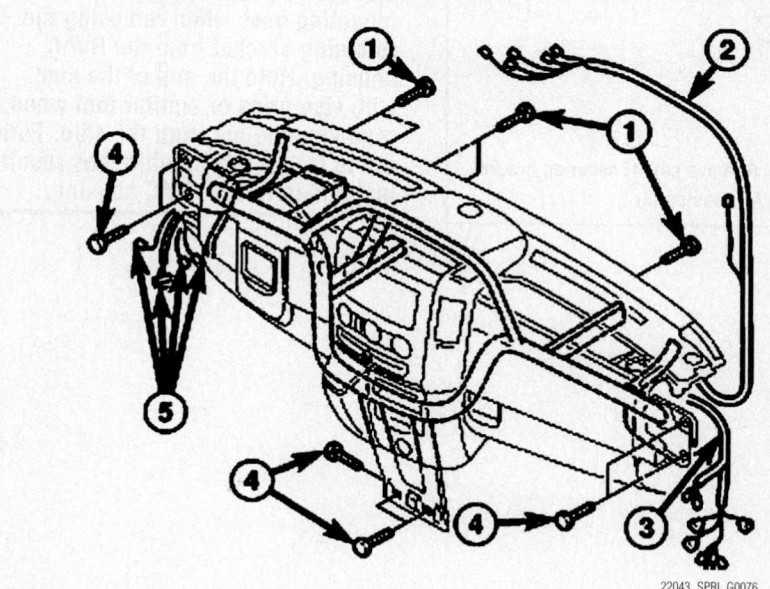

22043_SPRI_G0076

Fig. 128 Disconnect all wiring harnesses (2, 3, 5) and remove the firewall bolts (1) and mounting bolts (4) to remove the instrument panel

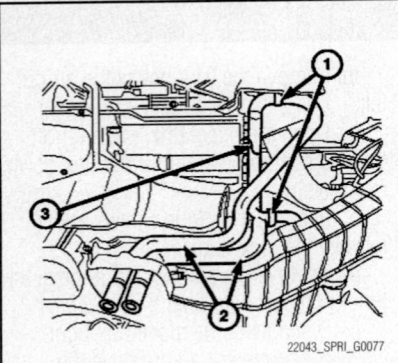

Fig. 129 Remove the retaining clamps (1) that secure the heater core tubes (2) to the heater core (3)

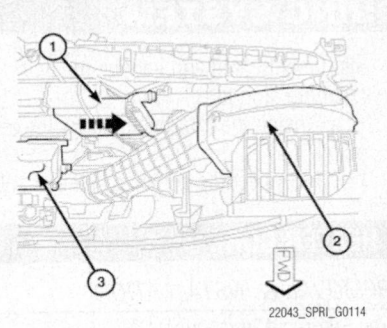

Fig. 131 Position the blower motor portion of the HVAC housing (2) slightly forward for clearance and remove the heater core (1) from the HVAC housing (3))

z. Disconnect all the electrical connectors from wiring harness in passenger footwell.

aa. Disconnect all electrical connectors on instrument panel in driver footwell.

bb. Disconnect the connections and lines of instrument panel in interior compartment.

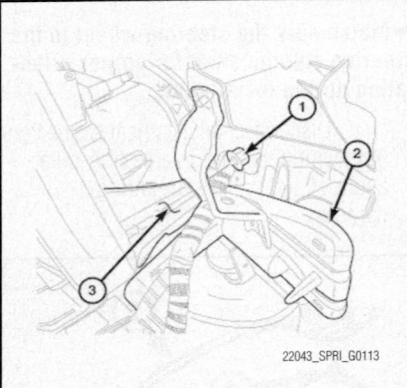

Fig. 130 Remove nut (1) securing bracket (2) to HVAC housing (3)

cc. Remove the air filter housing.

dd. Disconnect the connections and lines of instrument panel in engine compartment.

ee. Remove the bolts from firewall.

ff. Remove the bolts.

gg. Lift out the instrument panel support with instrument panel.

2. Remove the blower motor power module or blower motor resistor (depending on application).

3. Remove the two metal retaining clamps that secure the heater core tubes to the heater core.

4. Disconnect the heater core tubes from the heater core and remove and discard the O-ring seals.

✽✽ CAUTION

Make sure not to damage the stud mounting boss when removing the retaining bracket from the HVAC housing. Hold the end of the stud with vise grips or similar tool when removing the nut from the stud. Failure to follow this caution may result in damage to the HVAC housing.

5. Remove the nut (1) that secures the bracket (2) to the HVAC housing (3) near the blower motor. Hold the end of the stud with vise grips or similar tool when removing the nut from the stud.

6. Carefully position the blower motor portion of the HVAC housing (2) slightly forward for clearance and remove the heater core (1) from the HVAC housing (3) by pulling it straight out of the side of the housing.

To install:

7. Carefully position the blower motor portion of the HVAC housing slightly forward for clearance and install the heater core into the side of the HVAC housing.

8. Install the bracket to the HVAC housing.

9. Install the nut that secures the bracket to the HVAC housing. Tighten the nut securely.

10. Lubricate new rubber O-ring seals with clean engine coolant and install them onto the heater core fittings. Use only the specified O-rings as they are made of a special material compatible to engine coolant. Use only engine coolant of the type recommended for the engine in the vehicle.

11. Install the heater core tubes onto the heater core.

12. Install the two metal retaining clamps that secure the heater core tubes to the heater core.

13. Install the blower motor power module or blower motor resistor (depending on application).

14. The remainder of the installation is the reverse order of removal.

15. Evacuate and recharge the refrigerant system.

16. Refill the cooling system to the correct level.

17. Start the engine and check for leaks.

AUXILIARY HEATING & AIR CONDITIONING SYSTEM

BLOWER MOTOR

REMOVAL & INSTALLATION

See Figures 132 and 133.

1. Disconnect and isolate the negative battery cable.
2. Remove the screws that secure the rear condenser cover to the top of the vehicle and remove the cover.
3. Remove the nut and bolt that secure the rear A/C suction line to the rear condenser cover bracket.

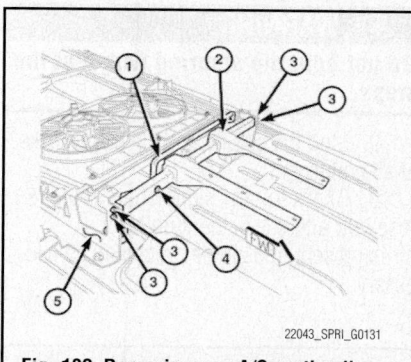

Fig. 132 Removing rear A/C suction line and cover brackets.

4. Remove the four bolts that secure the rear condenser cover bracket to the rear condenser bracket and remove the cover bracket.
5. Remove the screws that secure the rear evaporator cover and insulator to the top of the vehicle and remove the cover and insulator.
6. Disconnect the wire harness connectors from the rear blower motor.

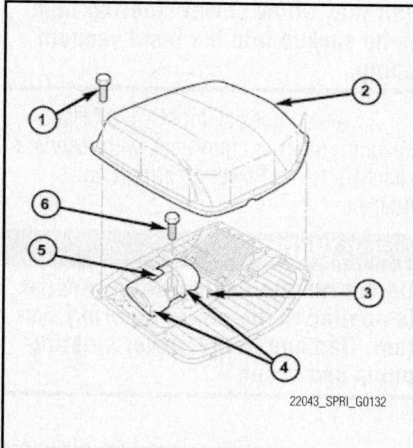

Fig. 133 Removing rear evaporator cover and rear blower motor.

7. Remove the screws that secure the rear blower motor to the rear evaporator housing and remove the blower motor.

To install:

8. Position the rear blower motor to the rear evaporator housing and tighten the retaining screws to 44 inch lbs. (5 Nm).
9. Connect the wire harness connectors to the blower motor.
10. Install the rear evaporator insulator and cover to the top of the vehicle and tighten the retaining screws to 17 inch lbs. (2 Nm).
11. Install the rear condenser cover bracket onto the rear condenser bracket and install the four retaining bolts. Tighten the bolts securely.
12. Install the nut and bolt that secure the rear A/C suction line to the rear condenser cover bracket. Tighten the nut securely.
13. Install the rear condenser cover to the top of the vehicle and tighten the retaining screws to 17 inch lbs. (2 Nm).
14. Reconnect the negative battery cable.

STEERING

POWER RACK & PINION STEERING GEAR

REMOVAL & INSTALLATION

1. Siphon the power steering fluid out of the reservoir.
2. Raise and safely support the vehicle.
3. Remove the front wheels.
4. Remove the stabilizer bar from the upper part of the stabilizer link. Refer to Stabilizer Bar.
5. Using Special Tool C-3894-A, remove the outer tie rod end nuts and separate the tie rods from the steering knuckles.
6. Remove the left outer tie rod end from the steering gear.
7. Remove both spring clamp plates.
8. Remove both the high pressure and return hoses from the steering gear.
9. Remove the steering shaft clamping bolt from the steering gear.
10. Separate the universal joint from the steering gear.
11. Remove the steering gear bolts from the front axle.
12. Remove the steering gear by sliding it toward the passenger's side of the vehicle and then tilt downward on the driver's side and remove from vehicle.

To install:

13. Install the steering gear assembly into the vehicle. Install the steering gear bolts and tighten them as follows:
   - Step 1: Tighten to 18 ft. lbs. (25 Nm)
   - Step 2: Tighten to 33 ft. lbs. (45 Nm).
   - Step 3: Plus 90°
14. Install the universal joint to the steering gear and tighten the fitted bolt to 18 ft. lbs. (24 Nm).

➡ **Make sure to install the steering shaft universal joint onto the steering gear shaft all the way down until the hole lines up with the radial groove in the steering shaft.**

15. Install both the power steering hoses to the steering gear. Tighten the high pressure hose to 27 ft. lbs. (37 Nm).
16. Install the spring clamp plates.
17. Install the left outer tie rod end to the steering gear.

18. Install both the outer tie rod ends to the steering knuckle and tighten to 96 ft. lbs. (130 Nm).
19. Install the upper stabilizer bar link to the stabilizer bar.
20. Install the front wheels.
21. Fill and bleed the power steering system
22. Check and adjust the alignment as necessary.
23. Start the engine and check for leaks.

POWER STEERING PUMP

REMOVAL & INSTALLATION

3.0L Engine

1. Remove the accessory drive belt. Refer to Accessory Drive Belt.
2. Siphon as much power steering fluid as possible out of the reservoir.
3. Remove the pressure and supply line from the pump.
4. Remove the pump mounting bolts and remove the pump.

➡If the pump is being replaced, transfer the front and rear pump brackets and pulley.

To install:

5. Install the power steering pump to the vehicle and tighten the mounting bolts to:
   a. 3.0L Engine: 21 ft. lbs. (28 Nm).
   b. 2.7L Engine: 15 ft. lbs. (21 Nm).
6. Connect the supply hose to the pump.
7. Install the pressure link to the pump and tighten the nut to 35 ft. lbs. (47 Nm).
8. Install the accessory drive belt.
9. Refill the power steering system to the correct level.
10. Start the engine and check for leaks.

3.5L Engine

1. Remove the accessory drive belt from the power steering pump. Refer to Accessory Drive Belt.
2. Remove the washer bottle mounting screws and disconnect the electrical connectors to relocate the bottle out of the way.
3. Siphon as much power steering fluid as possible out of the reservoir.
4. Remove the high pressure power steering hose at the pump.
5. Remove the supply hose from the pump.
6. Remove the bolts securing the power steering pump to the engine.

➡If the pump is being replaced, transfer the front and rear pump brackets and pulley.

To install:

7. Install the power steering pump to the engine and tighten the mounting bolts to 15 ft. lbs. (21 Nm).
8. Replace all O-rings and hose clamps.
9. Install the supply hose to the pump and tighten the clamp.
10. Install the high pressure hose to the pump and tighten to 28 ft. lbs. (38 Nm).
11. Install the accessory drive belt over the power steering pump pulley.
12. Refill the power steering system to the correct level.
13. Install the washer bottle mounting screws and connect the electrical connectors.

BLEEDING

See Figure 134.

1. Check the fluid level. As measured on the side of the reservoir, the level should indicate between MAX and MIN when the fluid is at normal ambient temperature. Adjust the fluid level as necessary.
2. Tightly insert Special Tool 9688 Power Steering Cap Adapter into the mouth of the reservoir.

✳✳ CAUTION

Failure to use a vacuum pump reservoir may allow power steering fluid to be sucked into the hand vacuum pump.

3. Attach Special Tool C-4207 Hand Vacuum Pump or equivalent, with reservoir attached, to the Power Steering Cap Adapter.

✳✳ WARNING

Do not run the engine while vacuum is applied to the power steering system. Damage to the power steering pump can occur.

➡When performing the following step make sure the vacuum level is maintained during the entire time period.

4. Using a Hand Vacuum Pump, apply 20-25 in. Hg (68-85 kPa) of vacuum to the system for a minimum of three minutes.
5. Slowly release the vacuum and remove the special tools.
6. Adjust the fluid level as necessary.
7. Repeat the process until the fluid no longer drops when vacuum is applied.
8. Start the engine and cycle the steering wheel lock-to-lock three times.

✳✳ WARNING

Do not hold the steering wheel at the stops.

9. Stop the engine and check for leaks at all connections.
10. Check for any signs of air in the reservoir and check the fluid level. If air is present, repeat the procedure as necessary.

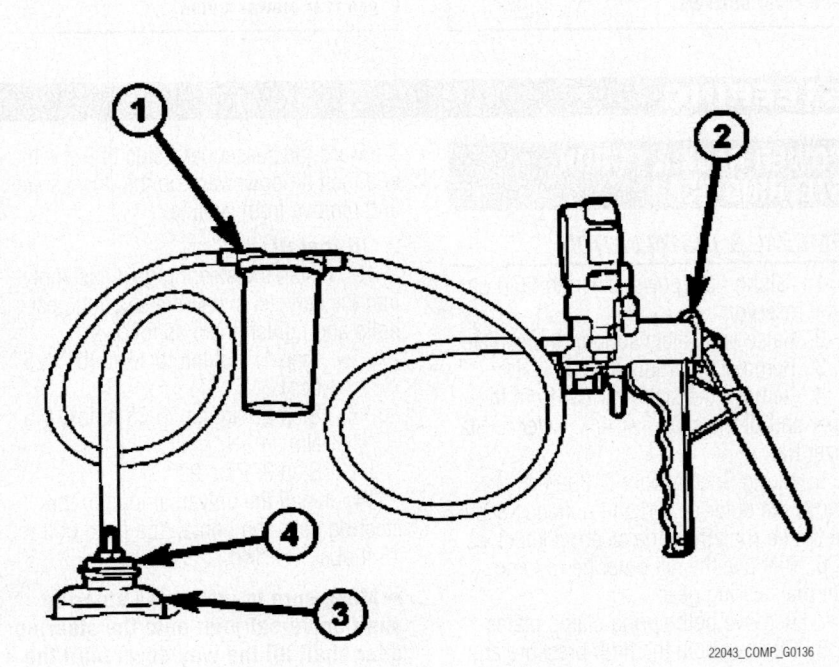

Fig. 134 Bleed the power steering system with a reservoir (1) Hand Vacuum Pump (2), Power Steering Cap Adapter (4) attached to the Power Steering Pump reservoir (3).

22043_COMP_G0136

SUSPENSION

LEAF SPRING

REMOVAL & INSTALLATION
See Figure 135.

1. Raise and safely support the vehicle.
2. Remove the left side front wheel.
3. Remove the left side strut. For additional information, refer to the following section, "MacPherson Strut."
4. Remove the left side outer tie rod end and shield from the steering knuckle.
5. Remove the left side upper spring stop plate.
6. Remove the left side lower control arm. Refer to Lower Control Arm.
7. Using a suitable floor jack, raise the outer edge of the spring slightly in order to remove the lower spring clamp plate.

➡️**To avoid damaging the transverse leaf spring, cushion the pad on the jack accordingly.**

8. Install a jack stand on the outer edge of the spring to apply spring pressure in order to remove the left side lower spring clamp plate.
9. Lower the jack to release the spring pressure.
10. Loosen the right side upper spring stop plate bolts.
11. Remove the right side lower spring clamp plate.
12. Remove the rubber spring blocks.

➡️**The upper and lower spring blocks are different. Keep them in the correct order for proper installation. The blocks are different in sizes to accommodate the weight of the vehicle and driver in order for the vehicle to sit level.**

13. Remove the transverse leaf spring towards the left side of the vehicle.

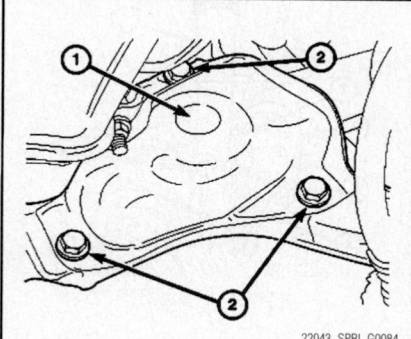

Fig. 135 Remove the bolts (2) to remove the left side upper spring stop plate (1)

To install:

➡️**Hand tighten all bolts until vehicle is on the ground. Failure to do so may cause the bushings to become distorted.**

➡️**The upper spring blocks and lower spring blocks are different, Make sure not to mix the blocks per sides. The blocks are different in sizes to accommodate the weight of the vehicle and driver in order for the vehicle to sit level.**

14. Install the rubber spring block on the right side lower control arm.
15. Install and center the transverse leaf spring from the left side of the vehicle to the right side make sure not to unseat the rubber block in the control arm.
16. Tighten the right side upper spring stop plate bolts. Tighten the M10 bolt to 43 ft. lbs. (58 Nm). Tighten the M2 bolt to 78 ft. lbs. (106 Nm) plus 90°.
17. Install the right side lower spring clamp plate. Tighten the M8 bolt to 21 ft. lbs. (29 Nm). Tighten the M12 bolt to 78 ft. lbs. (106 Nm) plus 90°.
18. Install a jack stand on the outer edge of the spring to apply spring pressure in order to install the left side lower spring clamp plate.

➡️**To avoid damaging the transverse leaf spring, cushion the pad on the jack accordingly.**

19. Install the left side lower spring clamp plate. Tighten the M8 bolt to 21 ft. lbs. (29 Nm). Tighten the M12 bolt to 78 ft. lbs. (106 Nm) plus 90°.
20. Loosen the jack stand to release the spring pressure.
21. Install the left side lower control arm.
22. Install the left side upper spring stop plate. Tighten the M10 bolt to 43 ft. lbs. (58 Nm). Tighten the M2 bolt to 78 ft. lbs. (106 Nm) plus 90°.
23. Install the left side steering knuckle.
24. Install the left side outer tie rod end and shield to the knuckle.
25. Install the left side strut.
26. Lower the vehicle.
27. Tighten the nuts on the lower control arm to the frame to 127 ft. lbs. (172 Nm) Plus an additional 90° turn.
28. Apply brake to actuate brake pressure.
29. Perform a front wheel alignment.

LOWER BALL JOINT

REMOVAL & INSTALLATION
See Figures 136 through 138.

1. Raise and safely support the vehicle.
2. Remove the front wheel.
3. Remove the brake caliper. Refer to Brake Caliper.

➡️**Mark the strut on the knuckle with a scribe for installation.**

4. Remove the front strut bolts from the knuckle
5. Remove the steering knuckle. Refer to Steering Knuckle.
6. Remove the outer tie rod end from the knuckle.
7. Separate the lower ball joint from the knuckle using a suitable ball joint puller.
8. Remove the lower ball joint using Special Tool 10002 Driver and striking the

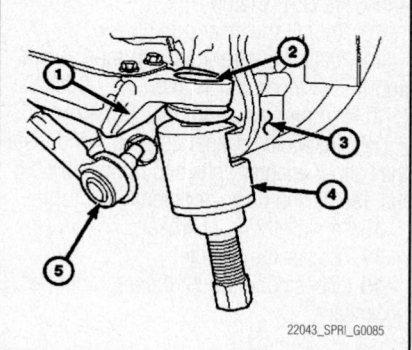

Fig. 136 Remove the outer tie rod end (5) from the knuckle (3), then separate the lower ball joint (2) from the knuckle using a suitable ball joint puller (4)

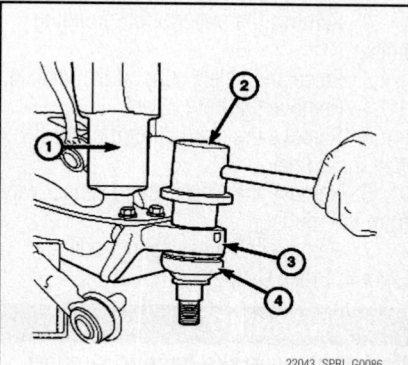

Fig. 137 Use Special Tool 10002 (2) to force the ball joint (4) from the lower control arm (3)

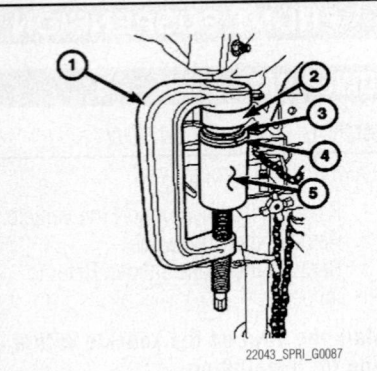

Fig. 138 Install the ball joint (3) into the lower control arm (2) using Special Tool 9294-3 (4) inserted in 9294-2 (5) and C-4212-F (1)

tool to force the ball joint outward from the lower control arm.

To install:

9. Install the ball joint into the lower control arm using Special Tool 9294-3 Installer Ring inserted in 9294-2 Receiver and C-4212-F Clamp.

10. Install the steering knuckle.

11. Install the front strut to the knuckle and install the bolts. Tighten to 103 ft. lbs. (140 Nm) plus an additional 120° turn.

12. Install the caliper assembly and install the caliper adapter bolts and tighten to 59 ft. lbs. (80 Nm) plus an additional 40° turn.

13. Install the front wheel.

14. Lower the vehicle.

15. Check and adjust the alignment as necessary.

LOWER CONTROL ARM

REMOVAL & INSTALLATION

See Figure 139.

1. Remove the floor pan screws.

2. Remove the upper strut mounting bolts.

3. Raise and safely support the vehicle.

4. Remove the front wheel.

5. Remove the rear half of the wheel well inner liner.

6. Remove the wheel speed sensor wire from the routing clip.

7. Remove the brake caliper adapter. Refer to Brake Caliper.

✱✱ WARNING

Do not allow brake hose to support the caliper weight.

8. Remove the brake rotor.

9. Remove the retaining nut holding the tie rod to the steering knuckle.

10. Separate the tie rod off the steering knuckle using Special Tool 9360.

11. Remove the lower bolts from the knuckle.

12. Remove the strut from the steering knuckle.

13. Remove the lower ball joint nut from the steering knuckle.

14. Separate the lower ball joint from the knuckle using special tool 9282.

15. Remove the spring stop plate bolts and rotate the plate upwards with the stabilizer link attached.

16. Remove the lower control arm pivot nuts and bolts from the frame.

17. Remove the lower control arm.

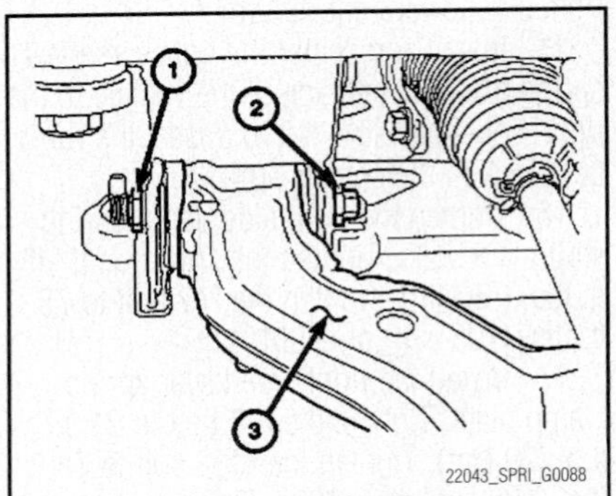

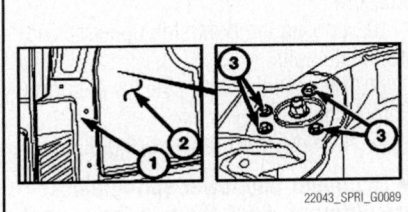

Fig. 139 Remove the pivot nuts (1) and bolts (2) to remove the lower control arm (3)

To install:

18. Install the lower control arm to the frame. Install the pivot nuts and bolts, but only hand tighten at this time.

19. Install the spring stop plate. Tighten the M10 bolt to 43 ft. lbs. (58 Nm). Tighten the M2 bolt to 78 ft. lbs. (106 Nm) plus 90°.

20. Install the steering knuckle to the lower ball joint and tighten the nut to 125 ft. lbs. (170 Nm).

21. Install the strut bolts to the steering knuckle and tighten to 103 ft. lbs. (140 Nm) plus an additional 120°.

22. Attach the tie rod end and shield to the steering knuckle. Tighten the nut to 37 ft. lbs. (50 Nm), then to 103 ft. lbs. (140 Nm) plus an additional 60° turn

23. Install the wheel sensor wire to the routing clip.

24. Install the brake rotor

25. Install the brake caliper adapter to the knuckle. Tighten to 59 ft. lbs. (80 Nm) plus an additional 40° turn.

26. Install the strut into the upper strut mounting hole

27. Install the rear half of the wheel well liner.

28. Lower the vehicle.

29. Install the upper strut bolts and tighten to 21 ft. lbs. (28 Nm).

30. Install the floor pan screws and floor pan.

31. Raise the vehicle.

32. Install the front wheels.

33. Lower the vehicle.

34. Tighten the lower control arm nuts to 125 ft. lbs. (172 Nm) plus an additional 90° with full vehicle weight.

35. Check and adjust the alignment as necessary.

MACPHERSON STRUT

REMOVAL & INSTALLATION

See Figures 140 and 141.

1. Remove the floor pan screws and remove the floor mat.

2. Remove the upper strut mounting bolts.

3. Raise and safely support the vehicle.

4. Remove the front wheels.

5. Remove the rear half of the wheel well liner.

6. Remove the wheel sensor wire from the routing clip.

Fig. 140 Remove the floor pan screws (1) and floor mat (2) to access the upper strut mounting bolts (3)

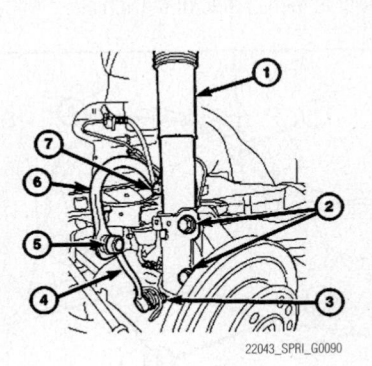

Fig. 141 Remove the sensor wire (7) from the clip then remove the strut mounting bolts (2) to remove the strut (1)

7. Remove the lower bolts from the knuckle.

8. Remove the strut from the steering knuckle.

To install:

9. Install the strut to the steering knuckle. Tighten the lower bolts to 103 ft. lbs. (140 Nm) plus 120°.

10. Raise the lower control arm with a suitable jack to install the upper part of the strut into the upper wheel well.

11. Install the speed sensor to the routing clip.

12. Install the rear half of the wheel well liner.

13. Install the front wheels.

14. Lower the vehicle.

15. Install the upper strut mounting bolts. Tighten the upper strut mounting bolts to 21 ft. (28 Nm).

16. Install the floor pan screws and floor mat.

17. Check and adjust the alignment as necessary.

STABILIZER BAR

REMOVAL & INSTALLATION

1. Raise and safely support the vehicle.

2. Remove the front transverse spring. Refer to Leaf Spring.

3. Remove the stabilizer bar links at the stabilizer bar.

4. Remove the stabilizer bar retainer clamp bolts.

5. Lower the stabilizer bar downwards.

6. Remove the bushings from the bar.

7. Remove the stabilizer bar from the vehicle.

To install:

8. Install the stabilizer bar and install the bushings to the bar.

9. Install the bar clamp and tighten the bolts to 43 ft. lbs. (55 Nm).

10. Install the links to the stabilizer bar and tighten the bolts to 78 ft. lbs. (106 Nm).

11. Install the front transverse spring.

12. Lower the vehicle.

13. Check and adjust the alignment as possible.

STEERING KNUCKLE

REMOVAL & INSTALLATION
See Figure 142.

1. Raise and safely support the vehicle.

2. Remove the front wheel.

3. Remove the outer tie rod end nut.

4. Separate the outer tie rod from the steering knuckle using Special Tool 9360.

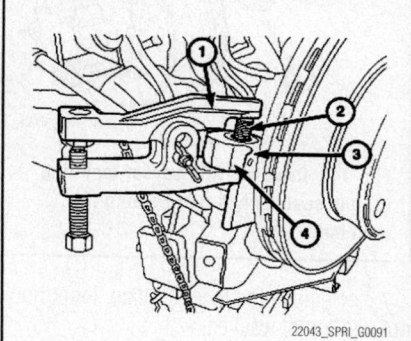

22043_SPRI_G0091

Fig. 142 Separate the outer tie rod (2) from the steering knuckle (4) using Special Tool 9360 (1) and remove the tie rod end shield (3)

5. Remove the tie rod end shield.

6. Remove the brake caliper adapter. Refer to Brake Caliper.

7. Remove the brake rotor.

8. Remove the wheel speed sensor. Refer to Speed Sensor.

9. Remove the lower ball joint nut.

10. Separate the lower ball joint from the steering knuckle using Special Tool 9282.

11. Remove the lower strut bolts from the knuckle.

12. Remove the strut at the knuckle.

13. Remove the steering knuckle.

To install:

14. Install the steering knuckle on the lower ball joint stud. Tighten the ball joint nut to 125 ft. lbs. (170 Nm).

15. Install the strut to the steering knuckle and tighten the bolts to 103 ft. lbs. (140 Nm) plus 120°.

16. Install the brake rotor.

17. Install the wheel speed sensor.

18. Install the brake caliper adapter with the brake caliper assembly and tighten the bolts to 59 ft. lbs. (80 Nm) plus an additional 40° turn.

19. Install the outer tie rod end and shield and tighten the nut to 37 ft. lbs. (50 Nm) plus 60°.

20. Install the front wheel.

21. Lower the vehicle.

22. Check and adjust the alignment as necessary.

WHEEL BEARINGS

The hub/bearing assembly is pressed into the steering knuckle and is not serviceable. The steering knuckle must be replaced if the hub/bearing needs service.

SUSPENSION

LEAF SPRING

REMOVAL & INSTALLATION

1. Raise and safely support the vehicle.

2. Support the rear axle assembly with a suitable jack.

3. Remove the lower shock mounting bolts.

4. Remove the leaf spring U-bolts and spring plate.

5. Remove the mounting nut and bolt from the front spring bracket.

6. Remove the rear spring nut and bolt from the spring shackle.

7. Lower the rear axle and remove the leaf spring.

To install:

8. Install the leaf spring assembly to the vehicle.

9. Install the front spring mounting bolt and nut and tighten as follows:
- Single Rear Wheel (SRW): 70 ft. lbs. (95 Nm).
- Dual Rear Wheels (DRW): 136 ft. lbs. (185 Nm).

10. Install the rear spring mounting bolt and nut and tighten as follows:
- SRW: 63 ft. lbs. (85 Nm)
- DRW: 136 ft. lbs. (185 Nm)

11. Raise the rear axle with a suitable jack and install the spring plate and U-bolts. Tighten the nuts to 125 ft. lbs. (170 Nm).

REAR SUSPENSION

12. Install the lower shock mounting bolt and tighten as follows:
- M12 x 1.5 bolts: 70 ft. lbs. (106 Nm)
- M14 x 1.5 bolts: 100 ft. lbs. (135 Nm)

13. Lower the vehicle.

SHOCK ABSORBER

REMOVAL & INSTALLATION

1. Raise and safely support the vehicle.

2. Support the rear axle with a suitable jack.

3. Remove the shock absorber bolt from the rear axle.

4. Remove the shock absorber bolt from the frame side.

5. Remove the shock absorber.

To install:

6. Install the shock absorber and tighten the frame side bolt to 100 ft. lbs. (135 Nm).

7. Install the shock absorber rear axle mounting bolt as follows:
- M12 x 1.5 bolts: 78 ft. lbs. (106 Nm)
- M14 x 1.5 bolts: 100 ft. lbs. (135 Nm)

8. Remove the jack supporting the rear axle.

9. Lower the vehicle.

WHEEL BEARINGS

REMOVAL & INSTALLATION

See Figures 143 through 145.

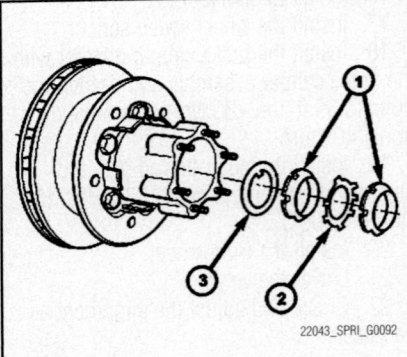

22043_SPRI_G0092

Fig. 143 Using Special Tool 10095 to remove outer hub nut (1), then remove the locking plate (2), inner hub nut (1) and thrust washer (3)

1. Raise and safely support the vehicle.
2. Remove the rear wheel.
3. Remove brake caliper adapter. Refer to Brake Caliper.
4. Remove the axle shaft.
5. Back-off the parking brakes.
6. Remove the outer hub nut with Special Tool 10095 Wrench.

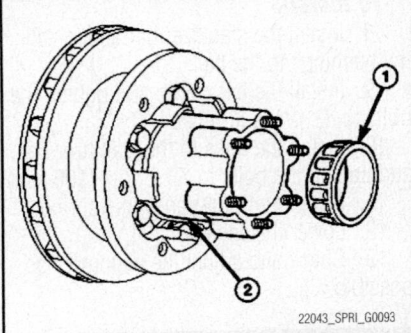

22043_SPRI_G0093

Fig. 144 Remove the front hub bearing (1) from the hub (2)

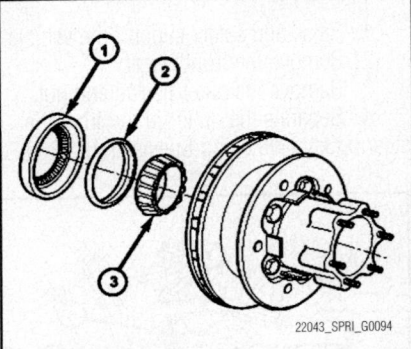

22043_SPRI_G0094

Fig. 145 Drive out ABS sensor tone ring (1) hub seal (2) and rear bearing (3) from hub

7. Remove the locking plate, inner hub nut and thrust washer.

➡**Thrust washer is designed for left or right side and not interchangeable.**

8. Pull the hub off axle tube.
9. Remove front hub bearing from hub.
10. Drive out the ABS sensor tone ring, hub seal and rear bearing from the hub.
11. Remove the inner and outer bearing cups from hub with a hammer and brass drift.

To install:

12. Install the outer hub bearing cup with Special Tool 9588 Installer and a hammer.

13. Install the inner hub bearing cup with Special Tool 10099 Bearing Cup Installer and Universal Drive Handle C-4171.

14. Clean and thoroughly grease bearings with multi-purpose grease.

15. Install the inner wheel bearing.

16. Coat the outer circumference of a new seal with Hylomar SQ 32 M sealant.

✳✳ WARNING

Do not coat the seal's rubberized sealing surfaces with sealant.

17. Install the seal into the hub with Special Tool 10098 Seal Installer and Universal Drive Handle C-4171.

➡**Seal ring should be flush with wheel hub or a maximum of 0.12 inches (3 mm) deep.**

18. Coat contact surface of ABS sensor ring with Hylomar SQ 32 M sealant.

19. Drive the ABS sensor ring in with Special Tool 10097 Tone Ring Installer and Universal Drive Handle C-4171.

20. Install the hub on axle tube.
21. Install the outer hub bearing.
22. Install thrust washer .
23. Install the inner hub nut.
24. Tighten the inner hub nut with Special Tool 10095 Hub Nut Socket to 221 ft. lbs. (300 Nm) while spinning the wheel hub constantly. Turn back inner nut and then tighten until it touches the thrust washer without play. Then tighten an additional ⅛ of a turn.
25. Install the locking plate.
26. Install the outer hub nut and tighten with Special Tool 10095 Hub Nut Socket to 184 ft. lbs. (250 Nm).
27. Install the axle shaft.
28. Install the brake caliper.
29. Adjust the parking brakes and install the rear wheel.
30. Lower the vehicle.

JEEP

Wrangler

18

SPECIFICATIONS AND MAINTENANCE CHARTS

ENGINE AND VEHICLE IDENTIFICATION

			Engine					Model Year	
Code	Liters (cc)	Cu. In.	Cyl.	Fuel Sys.	Engine Type	Eng. Mfg.		Code	Year
1	3.8 (3778)	231	6	MFI	OHV	Chrysler		8	2008
								9	2009

MFI: Multi-port Fuel Injection

OHV: Over Head Valve

36543_WRAN_C0001

GENERAL ENGINE SPECIFICATIONS

Year	Model	Engine Displ. Liters	Engine VIN	Net Horsepower @ rpm	Net Torque @ rpm (ft. lbs.)	Bore x Stroke (in.)	Comp. Ratio	Oil Pressure psi @ rpm
2008	Wrangler	3.8	1	202@5200	237@4000	3.78x3.43	9.6:1	30-80@3000
2009	Wrangler	3.8	1	202@5200	237@4000	3.78x3.43	9.6:1	30-80@3000

36543_WRAN_C0002

GASOLINE ENGINE TUNE-UP SPECIFICATIONS

Year	Displ. Liters	Engine VIN	Gap (in.)	Timing (deg.)	Pump (psi)	Speed (rpm)	Clearance	
							Intake	Exhaust
2008	3.8	1	0.048-0.053	①	56-60	①	HYD	HYD
2009	3.8	1	0.048-0.053	①	56-60	①	HYD	HYD

Note: The information on the Vehicle Emission Control label must be used, if different from the figures in this chart.

HYD: Hydraulic

① Ignition timing and idle speed are controlled by the PCM. No adjustment is necessary.

36543_WRAN_C0003

CAPACITIES

Year	Model	Engine Displ. Liters	Engine VIN	Engine Oil with Filter	Transmission (pts.) Man.	Transmission (pts.) Auto.	Transfer Case (pts.)	Axle Front (pts.)	Axle Rear (pts.)	Fuel Tank (gal.)	Cooling System (qts.)
2008	Wrangler	3.8	1	6.0	3.17	①	4.2	③	4.75	⑤	13
2009	Wrangler	3.8	1	6.0	3.17	①	4.2	③	4.75	⑤	13

NOTE: All capacities are approximate. Add fluid gradually and check to be sure a proper fluid level is obtained.

① Overhaul:
    42RLE: 17.6
    Drain/Refill:
    42RLE: 8.0

③ Model 30: 2.1 pts.
    Model 44: 2.7 pts.

④ Add 3.4 oz. of limited slip additive, where applicable.

⑤ 2 door: 18.5

36543_WRAN_C0004

FLUID SPECIFICATIONS

Year	Model	Engine Displacement Liters (VIN)	Engine Oil	Auto. Trans.	Man. Trans.	Transfer Case	Drive Axle	Power Steering Fluid	Brake Master Cylinder
2008	Wrangler	3.8 (1)	5W-20	Mopar ATF+4	Mopar MT fluid	Mopar ATF+4	①	Mopar ATF+4	DOT-3
2009	Wrangler	3.8 (1)	5W-20	Mopar ATF+4	Mopar MT fluid	Mopar ATF+4	①	Mopar ATF+4	DOT-3

DOT: Department Of Transpotation

NA: Not Applicable.....There is NO NA in the chart

① Mopar Front axle: 80W-90 Gear Lubricant. Rear axle: 80W-90 or Mopar Synthetic Gear Lube 75W-140 for trailer towing

36543_WRAN_C0005

VALVE SPECIFICATIONS

Year	Engine Displ. Liters	Engine VIN	Seat Angle (deg.)	Face Angle (deg.)	Spring Test Pressure (lbs. @ in.)	Spring Installed Height (in.)	Stem-to-Guide Clearance (in.) Intake	Stem-to-Guide Clearance (in.) Exhaust	Stem Diameter (in.) Intake	Stem Diameter (in.) Exhaust
2008	3.8	1	44.5-45	45-45.5	①	1.61-1.68	0.0010-0.0025	0.0020-0.0037	0.2718-0.2725	0.2718-0.2725
2009	3.8	1	44.5-45	45-45.5	①	1.61-1.68	0.0010-0.0025	0.0020-0.0037	0.2718-0.2725	0.2718-0.2725

① Closed: 84.6-95.4 lbs. @ 1.65 in.
    Open: 199.0-221.0 @ 1.22 in

36543_WRAN_C0006

CAMSHAFT AND BEARING SPECIFICATIONS CHART

All measurements are given in inches.

Year	Engine Displacement Liters	Engine VIN	Journal Diameter	Brg. Oil Clearance	Shaft End-play	Runout	Journal Bore	Valve Lift	
								Intake	Exhaust
2008	3.8	1	①	0.0010-0.0040	0.0010-0.0020	NA	NA	0.433	0.433
2009	3.8	1	①	0.0010-0.0040	0.0010-0.0020	NA	NA	0.433	0.433

NA: Not Available

① No 1: 1.997-1.999
  No 2: 1.9809-1.9829
  No 3: 1.9659-1.9679
  No 4: 1.9499-1.9520

36543_WRAN_C0007

CRANKSHAFT AND CONNECTING ROD SPECIFICATIONS

All measurements are given in inches.

Year	Engine Displ. Liters	Engine VIN	Crankshaft				Connecting Rod		
			Main Brg. Journal Dia.	Main Brg. Oil Clearance	Shaft End-play	Thrust on No.	Journal Diameter	Oil Clearance	Side Clearance
2008	3.8	1	2.5192-2.5202	0.0005-0.0022	0.0036-0.0095	2	2.2829-2.2837	0.0007-0.0026	0.005-0.016
2009	3.8	1	2.5192-2.5202	0.0005-0.0022	0.0036-0.0095	2	2.2829-2.2837	0.0007-0.0026	0.005-0.016

36543_WRAN_C0008

PISTON AND RING SPECIFICATIONS

All measurements are given in inches.

Year	Engine Displ. Liters	Engine VIN	Piston Clearance	Ring Gap			Ring Side Clearance		
				Top Compression	Bottom Compression	Oil Control	Top Compression	Bottom Compression	Oil Control
2008	3.8	1	0.0002-0.0015	0.008-0.014	0.012-0.022	0.010-0.030	0.0012-0.0027	0.0016-0.0033	0.0006-0.0089
2009	3.8	1	0.0002-0.0015	0.008-0.014	0.012-0.022	0.010-0.030	0.0012-0.0027	0.0016-0.0033	0.0006-0.0089

36543_WRAN_C0009

TORQUE SPECIFICATIONS

All readings in ft. lbs.

Year	Engine Displ. Liters	Engine VIN	Cylinder Head Bolts	Main Bearing Bolts	Rod Bearing Bolts	Crankshaft Damper Bolts	Flywheel Bolts	Manifold Intake	Manifold Exhaust	Spark Plugs	Oil Pan Drain Plug
2008	3.8	1	①	②	③	40	65	④	⑤	12	20
2009	3.8	1	①	②	③	40	65	④	⑤	12	20

① Step 1: 45 ft. lbs.

   Step 2: 65 ft. lbs.

   Step 3: 65 ft. lbs.

   Step 4: Plus 90 degrees

② Step 1: 30 ft. lbs.

   Step 2: Plus 90 degrees

   Step 3: Cross bolt 45 ft. lbs.

③ Step 1: 60 inch lbs.

   Step 2: 15 ft. lbs.

   Step 3: +90 degrees

④ Lower manifold: Step 1: 10 inch lbs.

   Step 2: 200 inch lbs.

   Step 3: 200 inch lbs.

   Upper manifold: 105 inch lbs.

⑤ Step 1: Center runner bolts 25 inch lbs.

   Step 2: All bolts 17 ft. lbs.

36543_WRAN_C0010

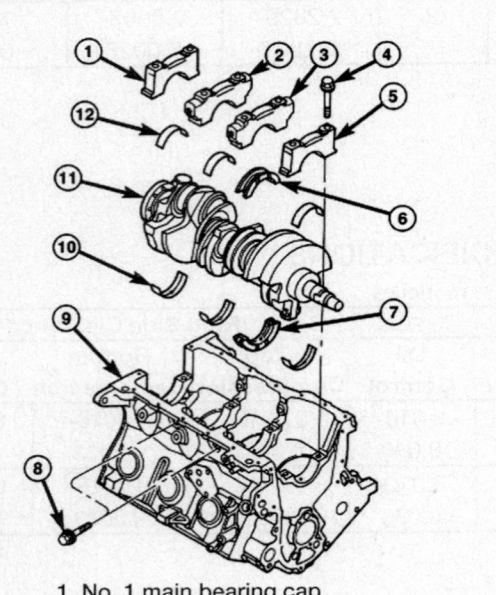

1. No. 1 main bearing cap
2. No. 2 main bearing cap
3. No. 3 main bearing cap
4. Main bearing cap bolt
5. No. 4 main bearing cap
6. Thrust bearing bottom
7. Thrust bearing top
8. Cross bolt

36543_WRAN_G0060

Fig. 1 Main bearing tightening sequence

WHEEL ALIGNMENT

Year	Model		Caster Range (+/-Deg.)	Caster Preferred Setting (Deg.)	Camber Range (+/-Deg.)	Camber Preferred Setting (Deg.)	Total* Toe-in (deg.)
2008	Wrangler	F	0.50	+4.20	0.37	-0.25	0.20 +/- 0.03
		R	—	—	0.50	-0.25	0.25 +/- 0.50
2009	Wrangler	F	1.0	①	0.37	-0.25	0.20 +/- 0.03
		R	—	—	0.25	-0.25	0.25 +/- 0.50

* 0.10 degree at each front wheel

① Left: +4.2 deg.; right: +4.4 deg.

36543_WRAN_C0011

TIRE, WHEEL AND BALL JOINT SPECIFICATIONS

Year	Model	OEM Tires Standard	OEM Tires Optional	Tire Pressures (psi) Front	Tire Pressures (psi) Rear	Wheel Size	Ball Joint Inspection Maximum Movement	Lug Nut Torque (ft. lbs.)
2008	Wrangler	P225/75R16		①	①	①	②	92-132
			P245/75R16	①	①	①		
			P255/75R17	①	①	①		
			P255/70R18	①	①	①		
			LT255/75R17	①	①	①		
			245/75R16	①	①	①		
			255/70R18	①	①	①		
2009	Wrangler	P225/75R16		①	①	①	②	92-132
			P245/75R16	①	①	①		
			P255/75R17	①	①	①		
			P255/70R18	①	①	①		
			LT255/75R17	①	①	①		
			245/75R16	①	①	①		
			255/70R18	①	①	①		

OEM: Original Equipment Manufacturer

① See placard on vehicle

② Lower axial movement: 0.050 in.; Upper radial movement: 0.060 in.

36543_WRAN_C0012

BRAKE SPECIFICATIONS

All measurements in inches unless noted

| Year | Model | | Brake Disc | | | Brake Drum | | | Minimum Lining Thickness | | Caliper Mounting Bolts (ft. lbs.) |
			Original Thickness	Minimum Thickness	Maximum Run-out	Original Inside Diameter	Max. Wear Limit	Maximum Machine Diameter	Front	Rear	
2008	Wrangler	F	1.10	0.8937	0.0039	—	—	—	0.040	—	32
		R	0.472	0.4330	0.004	—	—	—	—	0.040	26
2009	Wrangler	F	1.10	0.8937	0.0039	—	—	—	0.040	—	32
		R	0.472	0.4330	0.004	—	—	—	—	0.040	26

F- Front

R - Rear

36543_WRAN_C0013

SCHEDULED MAINTENANCE INTERVALS
JEEP Wrangler

TO BE SERVICED	TYPE OF SERVICE	VEHICLE MILEAGE INTERVAL (x1000)												
		6	12	18	24	30	36	42	48	54	60	66	72	78
Engine oil & filter ①	R	✓	✓	✓	✓	✓	✓	✓	✓	✓	✓	✓	✓	✓
Tires	Rotate		✓		✓		✓		✓		✓		✓	
Brake linings	I/R						✓		✓		✓		✓	
Brake hoses and lines	I	✓	✓	✓	✓	✓	✓	✓	✓	✓	✓	✓	✓	✓
Manual transmission fluid level	I	✓	✓	✓	✓	✓	✓	✓	✓	✓	✓	✓	✓	✓
Drive axle fluid	R			✓			✓			✓			✓	
Parking brake	Adj					✓					✓			
CV-joints	I								✓					
Air filter	R					✓					✓			
Exhaust system	I								✓					
Transfer case fluid level	I					✓					✓			
Front suspension components	I								✓					
PCV valve	I/R										✓			
Windshield washer fluid	I/F	At every fuel stop												
Tire pressure	I/Adj	Once a month												
Brake fluid level	I/adj	Once a month												
Power Steering fluid	I/adj	Once a month												
Automatic transmission fluid	I/adj	Once a month												
Engine coolant level	I/adj	Once a month												
Transfer case fluid	R	Every 90,000 miles												
Engine coolant	R	Every 102,000 miles												
Ignition cables	I/R	Every 102,000 miles												
Spark plugs	R	Every 102,000 miles												
Automatic trans. Fluid & filter	R	Every 120,000 miles												

R: Replace   S/I: Service or Inspect   I/R: Inspect and replace if necessary   L: Lubricate   I/F Inspect and fill as needed   I/Adj: Inspect and adjust

If driving in dusty or off-road conditions:

...inspect, and if necessary, replace, the air cleaner every 12,000 miles

...inspect the brake pads, replace if necessary every 12,000 miles.

...inspect the CV-joints every 12,000 miles

...inspect the exhaust system every 12,000 miles

...inspect all front suspension components every 24,000 miles

If used for police, taxi, fleet, off-road, or frequent trailer towing:

...change the front and rear axle fluid every 18,000 miles

...change the automatic transmission fluid and filter every 60,000 miles

...change the transfer case fluid every 60,000 miles

If used for any of the following: trailer towing, snow plowing, heavy loading, taxi, police, delivery service above 90°F (32°C):

(commercial service), off-road, desert operation or more then 50% of your driving is at sustained high speeds during hot weather:

...change the manual transmission fluid every 30,000 miles

① Oil Change Indicator System

On Electronic Vehicle Information Center (EVIC) equipped vehicles, "Oil Change Require" is displayed in the EVIC and a single chime sounds indicating that an oil change is necessary. On non-EVIC equipped vehicles, "Change Oil" flashes in the instrument cluster and a single chime sounds indicating that an oil change is necessary. Illumination of the oil change message is based on the operating conditions of the vehicle. When the message is illuminated, the vehicle must be serviced within 500 miles.

The oil change indicator will not monitor the time since the last oil change. Change the oil if it has been more than 6 months since the last oil change, even if the oil change indicator message is not illuminated.

Under no circumstances should oil change intervals exceed 6,000 miles or 6 months, whichever comes first.

To reset the oil change indicator, perform the following procedure:

1. Turn the ignition switch to the ON position. Do not start the engine.

2. Fully press the accelerator pedal 3 times within 10 seconds.

3. Turn the ignition switch to the LOCK position.

If the indicator message illuminates when the vehicle is started, repeat the procedure.

PRECAUTIONS

Before servicing any vehicle, please be sure to read all of the following precautions, which deal with personal safety, prevention of component damage, and important points to take into consideration when servicing a motor vehicle:

• Never open, service or drain the radiator or cooling system when the engine is hot; serious burns can occur from the steam and hot coolant.

• Observe all applicable safety precautions when working around fuel. Whenever servicing the fuel system, always work in a well-ventilated area. Do not allow fuel spray or vapors to come in contact with a spark, open flame, or excessive heat (a hot drop light, for example). Keep a dry chemical fire extinguisher near the work area. Always keep fuel in a container specifically designed for fuel storage; also, always properly seal fuel containers to avoid the possibility of fire or explosion. Refer to the additional fuel system precautions later in this section.

• Fuel injection systems often remain pressurized, even after the engine has been turned **OFF**. The fuel system pressure must be relieved before disconnecting any fuel lines. Failure to do so may result in fire and/or personal injury.

• Brake fluid often contains polyglycol ethers and polyglycols. Avoid contact with the eyes and wash your hands thoroughly after handling brake fluid. If you do get brake fluid in your eyes, flush your eyes with clean, running water for 15 minutes. If eye irritation persists, or if you have taken brake fluid internally, IMMEDIATELY seek medical assistance.

• The EPA warns that prolonged contact with used engine oil may cause a number of skin disorders, including cancer. You should make every effort to minimize your exposure to used engine oil. Protective gloves should be worn when changing oil. Wash your hands and any other exposed skin areas as soon as possible after exposure to used engine oil. Soap and water, or waterless hand cleaner should be used.

• All new vehicles are now equipped with an air bag system, often referred to as a Supplemental Restraint System (SRS) or Supplemental Inflatable Restraint (SIR) system. The system must be disabled before performing service on or around system components, steering column, instrument panel components, wiring and sensors. Failure to follow safety and disabling procedures could result in accidental air bag deployment, possible personal injury and unnecessary system repairs.

• Always wear safety goggles when working with, or around, the air bag system. When carrying a non-deployed air bag, be sure the bag and trim cover are pointed away from your body. When placing a non-deployed air bag on a work surface, always face the bag and trim cover upward, away from the surface. This will reduce the motion of the module if it is accidentally deployed. Refer to the additional air bag system precautions later in this section.

• Clean, high quality brake fluid from a sealed container is essential to the safe and proper operation of the brake system. You should always buy the correct type of brake fluid for your vehicle. If the brake fluid becomes contaminated, completely flush the system with new fluid. Never reuse any brake fluid. Any brake fluid that is removed from the system should be discarded. Also, do not allow any brake fluid to come in contact with a painted surface; it will damage the paint.

• Never operate the engine without the proper amount and type of engine oil; doing so WILL result in severe engine damage.

• Timing belt maintenance is extremely important. Many models utilize an interference-type, non-freewheeling engine. If the timing belt breaks, the valves in the cylinder head may strike the pistons, causing potentially serious (also time-consuming and expensive) engine damage. Refer to the maintenance interval charts for the recommended replacement interval for the timing belt, and to the timing belt section for belt replacement and inspection.

• Disconnecting the negative battery cable on some vehicles may interfere with the functions of the on-board computer system(s) and may require the computer to undergo a relearning process once the negative battery cable is reconnected.

• When servicing drum brakes, only disassemble and assemble one side at a time, leaving the remaining side intact for reference.

• Only an MVAC-trained, EPA-certified automotive technician should service the air conditioning system or its components.

BRAKES

GENERAL INFORMATION

PRECAUTIONS

• Certain components within the ABS system are not intended to be serviced or repaired individually.

• Do not use rubber hoses or other parts not specifically specified for and ABS system. When using repair kits, replace all parts included in the kit. Partial or incorrect repair may lead to functional problems and require the replacement of components.

• Lubricate rubber parts with clean, fresh brake fluid to ease assembly. Do not use shop air to clean parts; damage to rubber components may result.

• Use only DOT 3 brake fluid from an unopened container.

• If any hydraulic component or line is removed or replaced, it may be necessary to bleed the entire system.

• A clean repair area is essential. Always clean the reservoir and cap thoroughly before removing the cap. The slightest amount of dirt in the fluid may plug an orifice and impair the system function. Perform repairs after components have been thoroughly cleaned; use only denatured alcohol

ANTI-LOCK BRAKE SYSTEM (ABS)

to clean components. Do not allow ABS components to come into contact with any substance containing mineral oil; this includes used shop rags.

• The Anti-Lock control unit is a microprocessor similar to other computer units in the vehicle. Ensure that the ignition switch is **OFF** before removing or installing controller harnesses. Avoid static electricity discharge at or near the controller.

• If any arc welding is to be done on the vehicle, the control unit should be unplugged before welding operations begin.

BRAKES

BLEEDING PROCEDURE

➡Add only fresh, clean brake fluid from a sealed container when bleeding the brakes. If pressure bleeding equipment is used, the front brake metering valve will have to be held open to bleed the front brakes. The valve stem is located in the forward end or top of the combination valve. The stem must either be pressed inward or held outward slightly. Follow equipment manufacturer's instructions carefully when using pressure equipment. Do not exceed the maker's pressure recommendations. Generally, a tank pressure of 15—20 psi is sufficient. Do not pressure bleed without the proper master cylinder adapter.

When any part of the hydraulic system has been disconnected for repair or replacement, air may get into the lines and cause spongy pedal action (because air can be compressed and brake fluid cannot). To correct this condition, it is necessary to bleed the hydraulic system so to be sure all air is purged.

Bleeding must start where the lines were disconnected. If lines were disconnected at the master cylinder, for example, bleeding must be done at that point before proceeding downstream.

When bleeding the brake system, bleed one brake bleeder point at a time. Failure to do so may result in more air being drawn into the lines.

If the existing system fluid seems dirty or if the vehicle has covered considerable mileage, it is recommended that the system be completely purged and refilled with fresh, clean fluid. The best way to start is to siphon the old fluid out of the master cylinder reservoir and fill it completely with fresh fluid.

Brake fluid tends to darken over time. This does not necessarily indicate contamination. Examine fluid closely for foreign matter.

The primary and secondary hydraulic brake systems are separate and are bled independently. During the bleeding operation, do not allow the reservoir to run dry. Keep the master cylinder reservoir filled with brake fluid. Never use brake fluid that has been drained from the hydraulic system, no matter how clean it seems.

1. Clean all dirt from around the master cylinder fill cap, remove the cap and fill the master cylinder with brake fluid until the level is within ¼ in. (6mm) of the top edge of the reservoir.

2. Clean the bleeder screws at all 4 wheels. The bleeder screws are located on the back of the brake calipers.

3. Bleeder screws should be protected with rubber caps. If they are missing, the orifice may easily become clogged with road dirt. If the screw refuses to bleed when loosened, remove it and blow clear. After-market caps are readily available.

Manual Bleeding

See Figure 2.

Manual bleeding requires two people and a degree of patience and cooperation. Bleeding should be performed in this order: (1) Right rear, (2) Left rear, (3) Right front, (4) Left front.

1. Follow the preparatory steps, above.
2. Attach a length of rubber hose over the bleeder screw and place the other end of the hose in a glass jar, submerged in brake fluid.
3. Have your assistant press down on the brake pedal, then open the bleeder screw ½–¾ turn.
4. The brake pedal will go to the floor.
5. Close the bleeder screw, preferably before the pedal reaches the floor. Tell your assistant to allow the brake pedal to return slowly.
6. Repeat these steps to purge all air from the system.
7. When bubbles cease to appear at the end of the bleeder hose, close the bleeder

screw and remove the hose. Check that the pedal is firm or at least more firm than it was when you started. If not, continue the procedure.

8. Check the master cylinder fluid level and add fluid accordingly. Do this after bleeding each wheel.
9. Repeat the bleeding operation at the remaining three wheels, ending with the one closet to the master cylinder.
10. Fill the master cylinder reservoir to the proper level.

➡If there is excessive air in the system, it is possible that the stroke of the brake pedal will be insufficient to purge the lines. In this case, a pressure bleeder or vacuum bleeder is the easiest solution.

Vacuum Bleeding

Vacuum bleeding can be carried out by one person. Since a good vacuum bleeder will normally move more fluid than a brake pedal stroke, this procedure is preferred. These tools are inexpensive and readily available at auto parts outlets. Bleeding should be performed in this order: (1) Right rear, (2) Left rear, (3) Right front, (4) Left front.

1. Follow the preparatory steps, above.
2. Attach the vacuum bleeder according to the manufacturer's recommendations.
3. Pump up the unit until maximum vacuum is reached. Loosen the bleeder screw

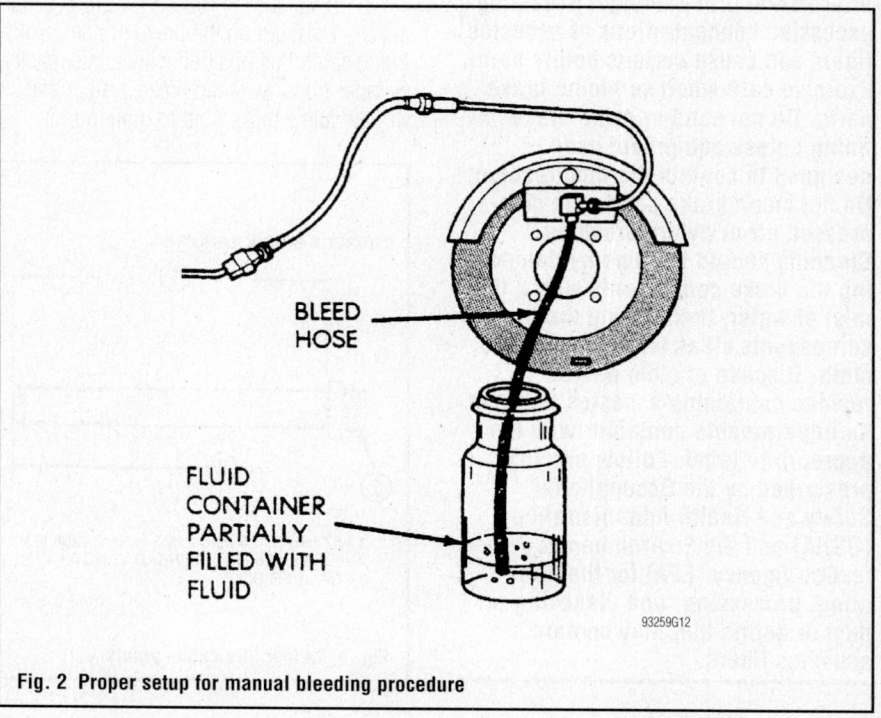

BLEED HOSE

FLUID CONTAINER PARTIALLY FILLED WITH FLUID

93259G12

Fig. 2 Proper setup for manual bleeding procedure

slightly until bubbles and fluid issue forth. Close the screw before the vacuum is equalized.

4. Repeat the procedure until fluid without bubbles issues from the bleeder screw.

5. Keep a close check on master cylinder fluid level during this procedure as vacuum bleeders move considerable amounts of fluid.

BLEEDING THE ABS SYSTEM

The base brake's hydraulic system must be bled anytime air enters the hydraulic system. The ABS must always be bled anytime it is suspected that the HCU has ingested air.

Brake systems with ABS must be bled as two independent braking systems. The non-ABS portion of the brake system with ABS is to be bled the same as any non-ABS system.

The ABS portion of the brake system must be bled separately. Use the following procedure to properly bleed the brake hydraulic system including the ABS.

➡ During the brake bleeding procedure, be sure the brake fluid level remains close to the FULL level in the master cylinder fluid reservoir. Check the fluid level periodically during the bleeding procedure and add Mopar® DOT 3 brake fluid as required.

When bleeding the ABS system, the following bleeding sequence must be followed to insure complete and adequate bleeding.

1. Make sure all hydraulic fluid lines are installed and properly torqued.

2. Connect the scan tool to the diagnostics connector. The diagnostic connector is located under the lower steering column cover to the left of the steering column.

3. Using the scan tool, check to make sure the ABM does not have any fault codes stored. If it does, clear them.

❊❊ WARNING

When bleeding the brake system wear safety glasses. A clear bleed tube (1) must be attached to the bleeder screws and submerged in a clear container filled part way with clean brake fluid (2). Direct the flow of brake fluid away from yourself and the painted surfaces of the vehicle. Brake fluid at high pressure may come out of the bleeder screws when opened.

➡ **Pressure bleeding is recommended to bleed the base brake system to ensure all air is removed from system. Manual bleeding may also be used, but additional time is needed to remove all air from system.**

4. Bleed the base brake system.

5. Using the scan tool, select ECU VIEW, followed by ABS MISCELLANEOUS FUNCTIONS to access bleeding. Follow the instructions displayed. When finished, disconnect the scan tool and proceed.

6. Bleed the base brake system a second time. Check brake fluid level in the reservoir periodically to prevent emptying, causing air to enter the hydraulic system.

7. Fill the master cylinder fluid reservoir to the FULL level.

8. Test drive the vehicle to be sure the brakes are operating correctly and that the brake pedal does not feel spongy.

BRAKES

❊❊ CAUTION

Dust and dirt accumulating on brake parts during normal use may contain asbestos fibers from production or aftermarket brake linings. Breathing excessive concentrations of asbestos fibers can cause serious bodily harm. Exercise care when servicing brake parts. Do not sand or grind brake lining unless equipment used is designed to contain the dust residue. Do not clean brake parts with compressed air or by dry brushing. Cleaning should be done by dampening the brake components with a fine mist of water, then wiping the brake components clean with a dampened cloth. Dispose of cloth and all residue containing asbestos fibers in an impermeable container with the appropriate label. Follow practices prescribed by the Occupational Safety and Health Administration (OSHA) and the Environmental Protection Agency (EPA) for the handling, processing, and disposing of dust or debris that may contain asbestos fibers.

BRAKE CALIPER

REMOVAL & INSTALLATION

See Figures 3 and 4.

1. Install a prop rod on the brake pedal to keep pressure on the brake system, Holding pedal in this position will isolate master cylinder from hydraulic brake system and will not allow brake fluid to drain out of

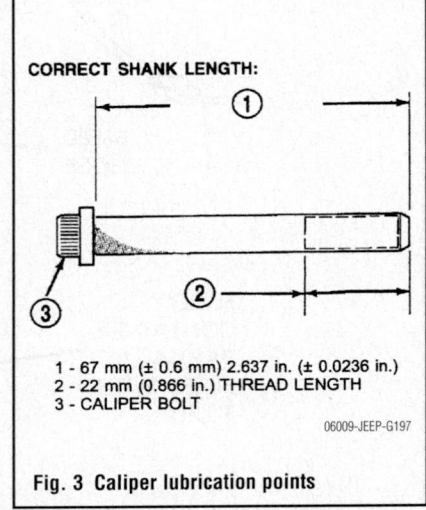

CORRECT SHANK LENGTH:

1 - 67 mm (± 0.6 mm) 2.637 in. (± 0.0236 in.)
2 - 22 mm (0.866 in.) THREAD LENGTH
3 - CALIPER BOLT

06009-JEEP-G197

Fig. 3 Caliper lubrication points

FRONT DISC BRAKES

brake fluid reservoir while brake lines are open. This will allow you to bleed out the area of repair instead of the entire system.

2. Raise and support vehicle.

3. Remove front wheel and tire assembly.

4. Drain small amount of fluid from master cylinder brake reservoir with clean suction gun.

5. Bottom caliper pistons into the caliper by prying the caliper over.

6. Remove brake hose banjo bolt and gasket washers. Discard gasket washers.

7. Remove the caliper slide bolts.

8. Remove the caliper from the adapter.

To install:

9. Connect the brake line to the caliper with new sealing washers and fitting bolt. Hand-tighten the fitting bolt.

10. Position the caliper into place over the rotor.

11. Coat the caliper mounting bolt with silicone grease and torque them to 26 ft. lbs. (35 Nm).

12. Position the brake line clear of all chassis components, untwisted and free of

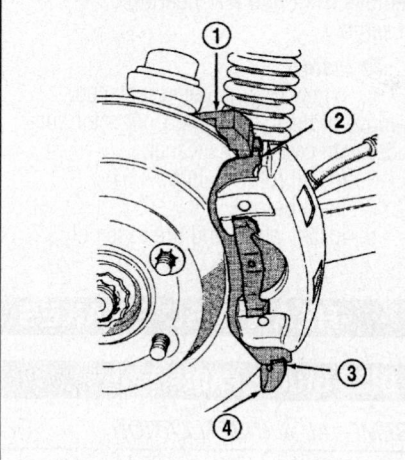

1 - TOP LEDGE
2 - BRAKESHOE TAB ON LEDGE OUTER SURFACE
3 - LEDGE SEATED IN BRAKESHOE NOTCH
4 - BOTTOM LEDGE

06009-JEEP-G198

Fig. 4 Caliper installation

kinks. Torque the fitting bolt to 23 ft. lbs. (31 Nm).

13. Install the wheels.

14. Fill the master cylinder with fluid and bleed the brake system, if necessary.

15. Before driving the vehicle, pump the brakes several times to seat the pads.

DISC BRAKE PADS

REMOVAL & INSTALLATION

See Figures 5 and 6.

1. Before servicing the vehicle, refer to the precautions in the beginning of this section.

2. Raise and support vehicle.

3. Remove wheel and tire assembly.

4. Remove caliper mounting bolts.

5. Compress the caliper and remove from the adaptor.

6. Secure caliper to nearby suspension part with wire. Do not allow brake hose to support caliper weight.

7. Remove the inboard and outboard brake pads from the caliper adapter.

8. Remove the anti-rattle clips from the brake caliper adapter.

9. Wipe caliper off with shop rags or towels.

To install:

10. Install new anti-rattle clips into the caliper adapter.

11. Install the inboard and outboard brake pads onto the caliper adapter.

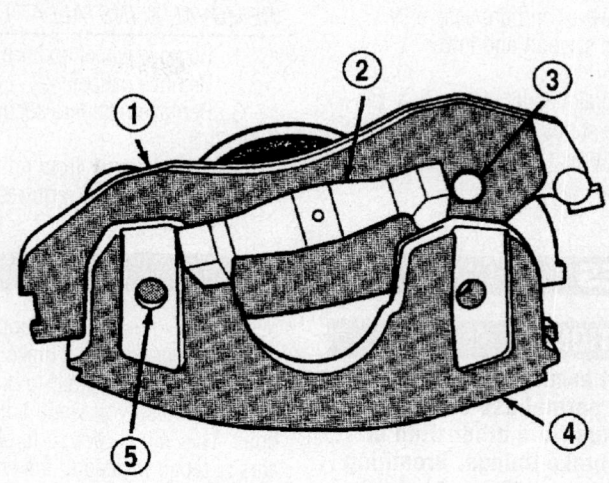

1 - OUTBOARD BRAKESHOE
2 - SHOE SPRING
3 - LOCATING LUG
4 - CALIPER
5 - LOCATING LUG

06009-JEEP-G199

Fig. 5 Outboard front brake pad removal/installation

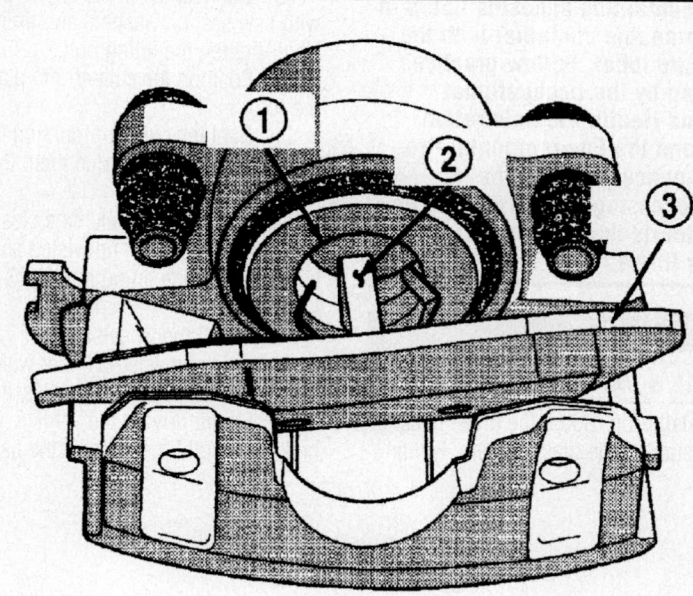

1 - CALIPER PISTON
2 - SHOE SPRINGS
3 - INBOARD BRAKESHOE

06009-JEEP-G200

Fig. 6 Inboard front brake pad removal/installation

12. Install caliper and tighten to 26 ft. lbs. (35 Nm).

13. Install wheel and tire assembly.

14. Remove support and lower vehicle.

15. Pump brake pedal until caliper pistons and brake shoes are seated.

16. Top off brake fluid level, if necessary.

BRAKES

✳✳ CAUTION

Dust and dirt accumulating on brake parts during normal use may contain asbestos fibers from production or aftermarket brake linings. Breathing excessive concentrations of asbestos fibers can cause serious bodily harm. Exercise care when servicing brake parts. Do not sand or grind brake lining unless equipment used is designed to contain the dust residue. Do not clean brake parts with compressed air or by dry brushing. Cleaning should be done by dampening the brake components with a fine mist of water, then wiping the brake components clean with a dampened cloth. Dispose of cloth and all residue containing asbestos fibers in an impermeable container with the appropriate label. Follow practices prescribed by the Occupational Safety and Health Administration (OSHA) and the Environmental Protection Agency (EPA) for the handling, processing, and disposing of dust or debris that may contain asbestos fibers.

BRAKE CALIPER

REMOVAL & INSTALLATION

1. Install prop rod on the brake pedal to keep pressure on the brake system, Holding

ROTOR

REMOVAL & INSTALLATION

1. Remove wheel and tire assemble.

2. Remove caliper.

3. Remove retainers securing rotor to hub studs.

4. Remove rotor from hub.

5. If rotor shield requires service,

pedal in this position will isolate master cylinder from hydraulic brake system and will not allow brake fluid to drain out of brake fluid reservoir while brake lines are open. This will allow you to bleed out the area of repair instead of the entire system.

2. Raise and support vehicle.

3. Remove rear wheel and tire assembly.

4. Drain small amount of fluid from master cylinder brake reservoir with clean suction gun.

5. Bottom caliper pistons into the caliper by prying the caliper over.

6. Remove brake hose banjo bolt and gasket washers. Discard gasket washers.

7. Remove the caliper slide bolts.

8. Remove the caliper from the adapter.

To install:

9. Connect the brake line to the caliper with new sealing washers and fitting bolt. Hand-tighten the fitting bolt.

10. Position the caliper into place over the rotor.

11. Coat the caliper mounting bolt with silicone grease and torque them to 26 ft. lbs. (35 Nm).

12. Position the brake line clear of all chassis components, untwisted and free of kinks. Torque the fitting bolt to 23 ft. lbs. (31 Nm).

13. Install the wheels.

14. Fill the master cylinder with fluid and bleed the brake system, if necessary.

15. Before driving the vehicle, pump the brakes several times to seat the pads.

remove front hub and bearing assembly.

To install:

6. If new rotor is being installed, remove protective coating from rotor surfaces with carburetor cleaner.

7. Install rotor on hub.

8. Install caliper.

9. Install wheel and tire assembly.

REAR DISC BRAKES

DISC BRAKE PADS

REMOVAL & INSTALLATION

1. Before servicing the vehicle, refer to the precautions in the beginning of this section.

2. Raise and support vehicle.

3. Remove wheel and tire assembly.

4. Remove caliper mounting bolts.

5. Compress the caliper and remove from the adaptor.

6. Secure caliper to nearby suspension part with wire. Do not allow brake hose to support caliper weight.

7. Remove the inboard and outboard brake pads from the caliper adapter.

8. Remove the anti-rattle clips from the brake caliper adapter.

9. Wipe caliper off with shop rags or towels.

To install:

10. Install new anti-rattle clips into the caliper adapter.

11. Install the inboard and outboard brake pads onto the caliper adapter.

12. Install caliper and tighten to 26 ft. lbs. (35 Nm).

13. Install wheel and tire assembly.

14. Remove support and lower vehicle.

15. Pump brake pedal until caliper pistons and brake shoes are seated.

16. Top off brake fluid level, if necessary.

BRAKES

PARKING BRAKE

PARKING BRAKE SHOES

REMOVAL & INSTALLATION

See Figures 7 and 8.

1. Raise and support the vehicle.
2. Remove the tire and wheel assembly.
3. Remove the disc brake caliper adapter.
4. Remove the disc brake rotor.
5. Remove the wheel speed sensor.
6. Remove the center floor console.
7. Lock out the park brake system at the lever using a suitable tool and pulling upward on the brake cable.
8. Remove the rear parking brake cables from the equalizer.
9. Remove the parking brake cable from the brake shoe lever at the axle.
10. Remove the axle shaft.
11. Tap the seal plate from the brake support on the axle shaft.
12. Remove the support plate with the brake shoes from the axle shaft.
13. Disassemble the rear park brake shoes.

To install:

14. Reassemble the rear park brake shoes.
15. Install the support plate on the axle shaft.
16. Install the axle shaft to the axle housing.
17. Reconnect the brake cable to the park brake shoe lever behind the support plate.
18. Install the rear wheel speed sensor.
19. Adjust the rear brake shoes.
20. Install the disc brake rotor.
21. Install the disc brake caliper adapter.
22. Install the tire and wheel assembly.
23. Lower the vehicle.
24. Install the rear park brake cables at the equalizer.
25. Remove the lockout on the front park brake lever.
26. Check the operation of the park brake system.
27. Install the center floor console.

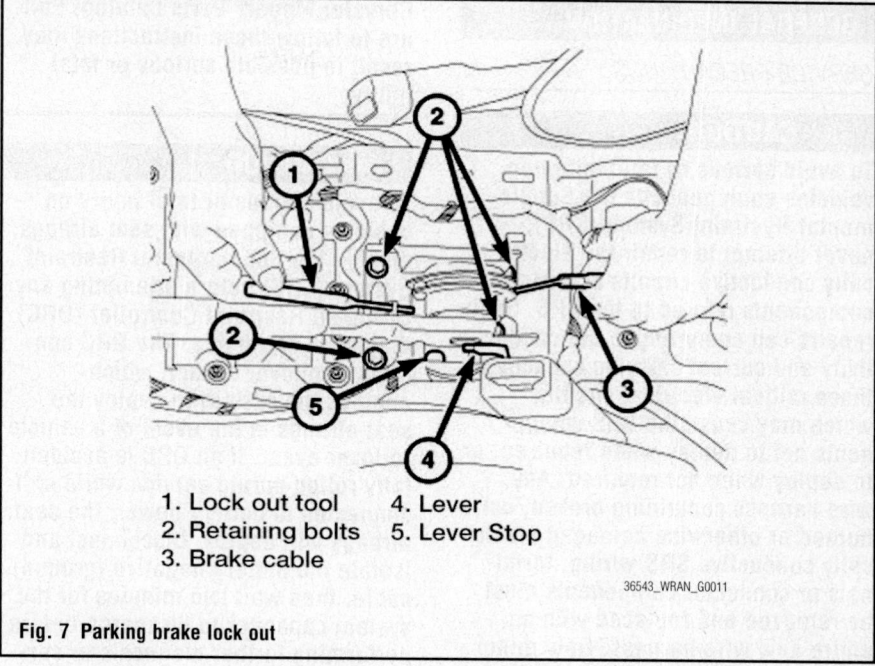

1. Lock out tool
2. Retaining bolts
3. Brake cable
4. Lever
5. Lever Stop

36543_WRAN_G0011

Fig. 7 Parking brake lock out

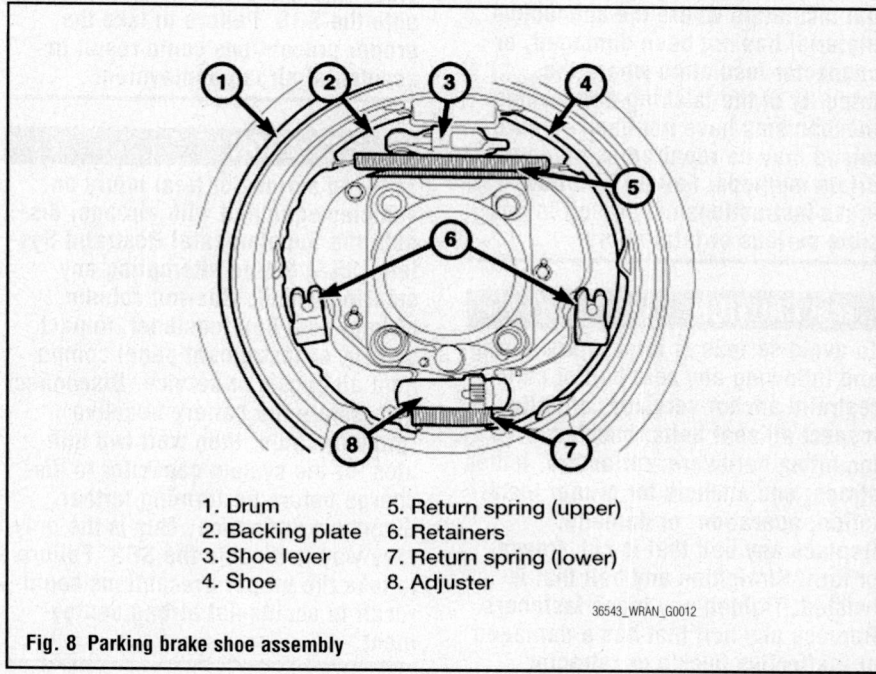

1. Drum
2. Backing plate
3. Shoe lever
4. Shoe
5. Return spring (upper)
6. Retainers
7. Return spring (lower)
8. Adjuster

36543_WRAN_G0012

Fig. 8 Parking brake shoe assembly

CHASSIS ELECTRICAL — AIR BAG (SUPPLEMENTAL RESTRAINT SYSTEM)

GENERAL INFORMATION

SERVICE PRECAUTIONS

✻✻ CAUTION

To avoid serious or fatal injury on vehicles equipped with the Supplemental Restraint System (SRS), never attempt to repair the electrically conductive circuits or wiring components related to the SRS. Such repairs can compromise the conductivity and current carrying capacity of those critical electrical circuits, which may cause the SRS components not to deploy when required, or to deploy when not required. Any wire harness containing broken, cut, burned or otherwise damaged electrically conductive SRS wiring, terminals or connector components must be removed and replaced with an entire new wire harness. Only minor cuts or abrasions of wire and terminal insulation where the conductive material has not been damaged, or connector insulators where the integrity of the latching and locking mechanisms have not been compromised may be repaired using appropriate methods. Failure to follow these instructions may result in possible serious or fatal injury.

✻✻ CAUTION

To avoid serious or fatal injury during and following any seat belt or child restraint anchor service, carefully inspect all seat belts, buckles, mounting hardware, retractors, tether straps, and anchors for proper installation, operation, or damage. Replace any belt that is cut, frayed, or torn. Straighten any belt that is twisted. Tighten any loose fasteners. Replace any belt that has a damaged or ineffective buckle or retractor. Replace any belt that has a bent or damaged latch plate or anchor plate. Replace any child restraint anchor or the unit to which the anchor is integral that has been bent or damaged. Never attempt to repair a seat belt or child restraint component. Always replace damaged or ineffective seat belt and child restraint components with the correct, new and unused replacement parts listed in the Chrysler Mopar® Parts Catalog. Failure to follow these instructions may result in possible serious or fatal injury.

✻✻ CAUTION

To avoid serious or fatal injury on vehicles equipped with seat airbags, disable the Supplemental Restraint System (SRS) before attempting any Occupant Restraint Controller (ORC) diagnosis or service. The ORC contains a rollover sensor, which enables the system to deploy the seat airbags in the event of a vehicle rollover event. If an ORC is accidentally rolled during service while still connected to battery power, the seat airbags will deploy. Disconnect and isolate the battery negative (ground) cable, then wait two minutes for the system capacitor to discharge before performing further diagnosis or service. This is the only sure way to disable the SRS. Failure to take the proper precautions could result in accidental airbag deployment.

✻✻ CAUTION

To avoid serious or fatal injury on vehicles equipped with airbags, disable the Supplemental Restraint System (SRS) before attempting any steering wheel, steering column, airbag, seat belt tensioner, impact sensor, or instrument panel component diagnosis or service. Disconnect and isolate the battery negative (ground) cable, then wait two minutes for the system capacitor to discharge before performing further diagnosis or service. This is the only sure way to disable the SRS. Failure to take the proper precautions could result in accidental airbag deployment.

✻✻ CAUTION

To avoid serious or fatal injury on vehicles equipped with airbags, before performing any welding operations disconnect and isolate the battery negative (ground) cable and disconnect all wire harness connectors from the Occupant Restraint Controller (ORC). Failure to take the proper precautions could result in accidental airbag deployment and other possible damage to the Supplemental Restraint System (SRS) circuits and components.

✻✻ CAUTION

To avoid serious or fatal injury, do not attempt to dismantle an airbag unit or tamper with its inflator. Do not puncture, incinerate or bring into contact with electricity. Do not store at temperatures exceeding 93° C (200° F). An airbag inflator unit may contain sodium azide and potassium nitrate. These materials are poisonous and extremely flammable. Contact with acid, water, or heavy metals may produce harmful and irritating gases (sodium hydroxide is formed in the presence of moisture) or combustible compounds. An airbag inflator unit may also contain a gas canister pressurized to over 17.24 kPa (2500 psi). Failure to follow these instructions may result in possible serious or fatal injury.

✻✻ CAUTION

To avoid serious or fatal injury when handling a seat belt tensioner retractor. Exercise proper care to keep fingers out from under the retractor cover and away from the seat belt webbing where it exits from the retractor cover. Failure to follow these instructions may result in possible serious or fatal injury.

✻✻ CAUTION

To avoid serious or fatal injury, replace all Supplemental Restraint System (SRS) components only with parts specified in the Chrysler Mopar® Parts Catalog. Substitute parts may appear interchangeable, but internal differences may result in inferior occupant protection. Failure to follow these instructions may result in possible serious or fatal injury.

✻✻ CAUTION

To avoid serious or fatal injury, the fasteners, screws, and bolts originally used for the Supplemental Restraint System (SRS) components must never be replaced with any substitutes. These fasteners have special coatings and are specifically designed for the SRS. Anytime a new fastener is needed, replace it with the correct fasteners provided in the service package or specified in the Chrysler Mopar® Parts Catalog. Failure to follow these instructions may result in possible serious or fatal injury.

✳✳ CAUTION

To avoid serious or fatal injury when a steering column has an airbag unit attached, never place the column on the floor or any other surface with the steering wheel or airbag unit face down. Failure to follow these instructions may result in possible serious or fatal injury.

DISARMING THE SYSTEM

Disconnect and isolate the negative battery cable. Wait 2 minutes for the system capacitor to discharge before performing any service.

ARMING THE SYSTEM

To arm the system, connect the negative battery cable.

CLOCKSPRING CENTERING

1. Place the front wheels in the straight-ahead position and inhibit the steering column shaft from rotation.
2. Remove the steering wheel from the steering shaft.

3. Rotate the clockspring rotor clockwise to the end of its travel. Do not apply excessive torque.
4. From the end of the clockwise travel, rotate the rotor about two and one-half turns counterclockwise.
5. Turn the rotor slightly clockwise or counterclockwise as necessary so that the clockspring airbag pigtail wires and connector receptacle are at the top and the dowel or drive pin is at the bottom.
6. The clockspring is now centered. Secure the clockspring rotor to the clockspring case using a locking pin or some similar device to maintain clockspring centering until the steering wheel is reinstalled on the steering column.

DRIVE TRAIN

AUTOMATIC TRANSMISSION ASSEMBLY

REMOVAL & INSTALLATION

1. Disconnect battery negative cable.
2. Raise and support vehicle.
3. Disconnect and lower or remove necessary exhaust components.
4. Remove engine-to-transmission bending braces or engine collar.
5. Remove starter motor.

➡**If transmission is being removed for overhaul, remove transmission oil pan, drain fluid and reinstall pan.**

6. Remove torque converter access structural collar.
7. Rotate crankshaft in clockwise direction until converter bolts are accessible. Then remove bolts one at a time. Rotate crankshaft with socket wrench on dampener bolt.
8. Mark propeller shaft and axle yokes for assembly alignment. Then disconnect and remove propeller shafts.
9. Disconnect wires from the input and output speed sensors.
10. Disconnect wires from the transmission range sensor and the solenoid/pressure switch assembly.
11. Disconnect gearshift cable from transmission manual valve lever.
12. Disconnect shift cable and electrical connector from transfer case.
13. Support rear of engine with safety stand or jack.
14. Raise transmission slightly with service jack to relieve load on skid plate and transmission support.

15. Remove bolts securing rear support and cushion to transmission and skid plate.
16. Remove bolts attaching skid plate to frame and remove skid plate.
17. Disconnect transfer case vent hose.
18. Remove transfer case.
19. Remove fill tube bracket bolts and pull tube and vent hose out of transmission. Retain fill tube seal.
20. Remove the bolt attaching transfer case vent tube to converter housing.
21. Remove the fuel line bracket bolt.
22. Disconnect fluid cooler lines at transmission.
23. Remove crank shaft position sensor.
24. Remove all converter housing bolts.
25. Carefully work transmission and torque converter assembly rearward off engine block dowels.
26. Hold torque converter in place during transmission removal.
27. Lower transmission and remove assembly from under the vehicle.
28. To remove torque converter, carefully slide torque converter out of the transmission.

To install:

➡**Check torque converter hub and hub drive notches for sharp edges burrs, scratches, or nicks. Polish the hub and notches with 320/400 grit paper and crocus cloth if necessary. The hub must be smooth to avoid damaging pump seal at installation.**

29. Lubricate converter drive hub and oil pump seal lip with transmission fluid.
30. Align converter and oil pump.

31. Carefully insert converter in oil pump. Then rotate converter back and forth until fully seated in pump gears.
32. Check converter seating with steel scale and straightedge. Surface of converter lugs should be ½ in. to rear of straightedge when converter is fully seated.
33. Temporarily secure converter with C-clamp.
34. Lightly grease crankshaft flange hole.
35. Position transmission on jack and secure it with safety chains.
36. Check condition of converter driveplate. Replace the plate if cracked, distorted or damaged. Also be sure transmission dowel pins are seated in engine block and protrude far enough to hold transmission in alignment.
37. Raise transmission and align converter with drive plate and converter housing with engine block.
38. Move transmission forward. Then raise, lower or tilt transmission to align converter housing with engine block dowels.
39. Carefully work transmission forward and over engine block dowels until converter hub is seated in crankshaft.
40. Install bolts that attach transmission converter housing to engine block. Tighten bolts to 95 ft. lbs. (129 Nm).

➡**Be sure the converter housing is fully seated on the engine block dowels before tightening any bolts.**

41. Install torque converter attaching bolts. Tighten bolts to 65 ft. lbs. (88 Nm).
42. Install transmission fill tube, new seal, and breather hose.

43. Install fuel line bracket bolt.
44. Install crank shaft position sensor.
45. Connect transmission cooler lines to transmission.
46. Install transfer case onto transmission.
47. Remove engine support fixture.
48. Remove transmission jack.
49. Connect input and output speed sensor wires.
50. Connect wires to the transmission range sensor and the solenoid/pressure switch assembly.
51. Install converter housing support collar.
52. Install exhaust pipes and support brackets, if removed.
53. Install starter motor.
54. Connect transfer case shift cable and electrical connectors.
55. Adjust gearshift linkage, if necessary.
56. Align and connect propeller shaft.
57. Install transmission structural collar.
58. Fill transfer case to bottom edge of fill plug hole.
59. Install all skid plates and attach skid plate to transmission rear support.
60. Lower vehicle and connect battery negative cable.
61. Fill transmission to correct level with Mopar® ATF +4.

MANUAL TRANSMISSION ASSEMBLY

REMOVAL & INSTALLATION

See Figures 9 and 10.

1. Disconnect negative battery cable.
2. With vehicle in neutral, position vehicle on hoist.
3. Slide shift lever boot up and remove shift lever bolt and lever.
4. Remove drain plug and drain fluid.
5. Remove transfer case skid plate.

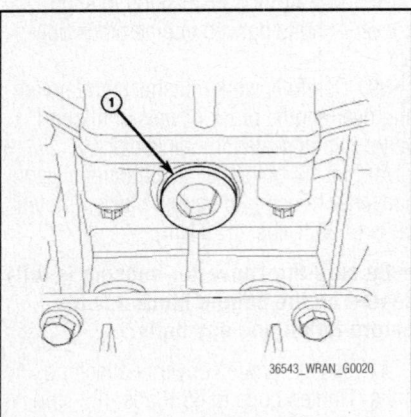

Fig. 9 Transmission drain plug location

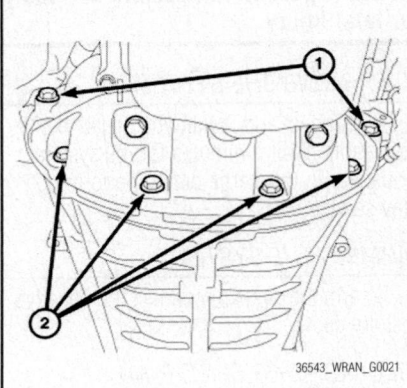

36543_WRAN_G0021

Fig. 10 Transmission and structural cover bolt locations

6. Remove catalyst assembly.
7. Mark installation reference marks on propeller shaft/shafts and remove shafts.
8. Remove transfer case shift linkage, wiring connector, and vent hose, if equipped.
9. Remove transfer case, if equipped.
10. Remove clutch slave cylinder nuts and remove cylinder.
11. Remove backup lamp switch wiring connector.
12. Remove starter bolts and remove starter.
13. Support transmission with jack.
14. Remove transmission mount, crossmember and skid plate bolts. Lower and slide crossmember out left side of the vehicle.
15. Remove transmission bolts from engine and structural cover.

➡ Do not remove the structural cover from the engine. If cover is removed clutch housing and structural dust cover must be aligned with the engine.

To install:

16. Install transmission on engine.
17. Tighten top transmission bolts to 30 ft. lbs. (40 Nm).
18. Tighten two side bolts to 50 ft. lbs. (68 Nm).
19. Tighten four bottom bolts to 40 ft. lbs. (54 Nm).
20. Install backup lamp wiring connector.
21. Install clutch slave cylinder and tighten mounting nuts to 17 ft. lbs. (23 Nm).
22. Install transmission crossmember and tighten bolts to 35 ft. lbs. (47 Nm).
23. Install transmission mount bolts and tighten to 35 ft. lbs. (47 Nm).
24. Install and tighten skid plate bolts.

25. Install transfer case, if equipped.
26. Install propeller shaft/shafts with reference marks aligned.
27. Remove fill plug and fill transmission with lubricant.
28. Install shift lever and tighten bolt to 33 inch lbs. (4 Nm).

TRANSFER CASE ASSEMBLY

REMOVAL & INSTALLATION

NV241 Gen II Transfer Case

See Figure 11.

1. Shift transfer case into NEUTRAL.
2. Raise vehicle.
3. Remove skid plate.
4. Drain transfer case lubricant.
5. Mark front and rear propeller shaft yokes for alignment reference.
6. Remove the front/rear propeller shafts at transfer case.
7. Disconnect transfer case position sensor connector from the position sensor.
8. Disconnect transfer case shift cable at the range lever.
9. Disconnect the transfer case shift cable from the shift cable bracket.
10. Disconnect transfer case vent hose.
11. Support transfer case with transmission jack.
12. Secure transfer case to jack with chains.
13. Remove nuts attaching transfer case to transmission.
14. Pull transfer case and jack rearward to disengage transfer case.
15. Remove transfer case from under vehicle.

To install:

16. Mount transfer case on a transmission jack.
17. Secure transfer case to jack with chains.

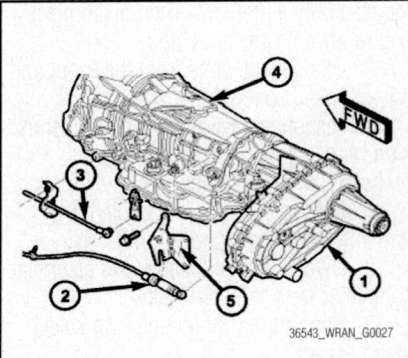

36543_WRAN_G0027

Fig. 11 Transfer case shift cable and shift cable bracket

18. Position transfer case under vehicle.

19. Align transfer case and transmission shafts and install transfer case on transmission.

20. Install and tighten transfer case attaching nuts to 26 ft. lbs. (35 Nm) torque.

21. Connect vent hose.

22. Connect transfer case position sensor connector to sensor.

23. Align and connect propeller shafts.

24. Connect shift cable to transfer case range lever.

25. Fill transfer case with correct fluid. Check transmission fluid level. Correct as necessary.

26. Install skid plate.

27. Remove transmission jack and support stand.

28. Lower vehicle and verify transfer case shift operation.

NV241OR Transfer Case

1. Raise and support vehicle.

2. Remove skid plate, if equipped.

3. Position drain oil container under transfer case.

4. Remove transfer case drain plug and drain lubricant into container.

5. Disconnect vent hose and vacuum harness at transfer case switch.

6. Disconnect shift rod from grommet in transfer case shift lever, or from floor shift arm whichever provides easy access. Use adjustable pliers to press rod out of lever grommet.

7. Support transmission with jack stand.

8. Remove rear crossmember.

9. Mark front and rear propeller shafts for assembly reference.

10. Remove front and rear propeller shafts.

11. Support transfer case with suitable jack. Secure transfer case to jack with safety chains.

12. Remove nuts attaching transfer case to transmission.

13. Move transfer case assembly rearward until free of transmission output shaft.

14. Lower jack and move transfer case from under vehicle.

To install:

15. Align and seat transfer case on transmission.

➡ **Be sure transfer case input gear splines are aligned with transmission output shaft. Align splines by rotating transfer case rear output shaft yoke if necessary. Do not install any transfer case attaching nuts until the transfer case is completely seated against the transmission.**

16. Install and tighten transfer case attaching nuts. Tighten nuts to 20–30 ft. lbs. (30–41 Nm).

17. Install rear crossmember.

18. Remove jack stand from under transmission.

19. Align and connect propeller shafts.

20. Connect vacuum harness and vent hose.

21. Connect shift rod to transfer case lever or floor shift arm. Use channel lock style pliers to press rod back into lever grommet.

22. Adjust shift linkage, if necessary.

23. Fill transfer case with recommended transmission fluid and install fill plug.

24. Install skid plate, if equipped.

25. Lower vehicle.

CLUTCH DRIVEN DISC & PRESSURE PLATE

REMOVAL & INSTALLATION

1. Remove transmission.

2. Mark position of pressure plate (1) on flywheel with paint or a scriber for assembly reference, if clutch is not being replaced.

3. Loosen pressure plate bolts evenly and in rotation to relieve spring tension and avoid warping the plate.

4. Remove pressure plate bolts and pressure plate and disc.

To install:

5. Lightly scuff sand flywheel face with 180 grit emery cloth, then clean with a wax and grease remover.

6. Lubricate pilot bearing with Mopar high temperature bearing grease or equivalent.

7. Check runout and operation of new clutch disc.

➡ **Disc must slide freely on transmission input shaft splines.**

8. With the disc on the input shaft, check face runout with dial indicator. Check runout at disc hub ¼ in. (6 mm) from outer edge of facing. Obtain another clutch disc if runout exceeds 0.020 in. (0.5 mm).

9. Position clutch disc on flywheel with side marked flywheel against the flywheel.

10. If not marked, the flat side of disc hub goes towards the flywheel.

11. Insert clutch alignment tool through the clutch disc and into the pilot bearing.

12. Position clutch pressure plate over disc and on the flywheel.

13. Install pressure plate bolts finger tight.

➡ **Use only the factory bolts to mount the pressure plate. The bolts must be the correct size. If bolts are too short, there isn't enough thread engagement, if too long bolts interfere with the Dual Mass Flywheel.**

14. Tighten pressure plate bolts evenly and in rotation a few threads at a time.

➡ **The bolts must be tightened evenly and to specified torque. Failure to follow these instructions will distort the pressure plate.**

15. Tighten pressure plate bolts 37 ft. lbs. (50 Nm).

16. Apply light coat of Mopar® high temperature bearing grease or equivalent to clutch disc hub and splines of transmission input shaft.

➡ **Do not over lubricate shaft splines. This will result in grease contamination of disc.**

17. Install transmission.

CLUTCH MASTER CYLINDER

REMOVAL & INSTALLATION

1. Pry actuator rod off clutch pedal pin.

2. Remove hose from clutch master cylinder and plug hose to prevent fluid loss.

3. Pull hydraulic line clip and remove line from bottom of clutch master cylinder.

4. Disconnect wiring harness from pedal position switch.

5. Turn clutch master cylinder assembly clockwise a quarter turn and remove from brake booster mounting plate.

To install:

6. Install clutch master cylinder through brake booster mounting plate and turn counter clockwise a quarter turn.

7. Install hose to clutch master cylinder from brake master cylinder reservoir.

8. Install hydraulic line to the bottom of clutch master cylinder.

➡ **Verify O-ring is on hydraulic line.**

9. Connect wiring harness to pedal position switch.

10. Install actuator rod on clutch pedal pin.

11. Bleed clutch hydraulic circuit.

CLUTCH SLAVE CYLINDER

REMOVAL & INSTALLATION

1. With transmission in neutral, position vehicle on hoist.

2. Remove mounting nuts from slave cylinder.

3. Pull hydraulic line clip and the line with bracket from slave cylinder.

4. Remove slave cylinder.

To install:

5. Install slave cylinder in transmission.

6. Install hydraulic line and with bracket to slave cylinder.

➡**Verify O-ring is on hydraulic line.**

7. Install slave cylinder nuts and tighten to 17 ft. lbs. (23 Nm).

8. Bleed hydraulic system

HYDRAULIC SYSTEM BLEEDING

BLEEDING PROCEDURE

Use Mopar® brake fluid, or an equivalent quality fluid meeting SAE J1703-F and DOT 3 standards only. Use fresh, clean fluid from a sealed container at all times.

Do not allow the master cylinder to run out of fluid during bleed operations. An empty cylinder will allow additional air to be drawn into the system. Check the cylinder fluid level frequently and add fluid as needed.

1. Verify fluid level in brake master cylinder, top off brake fluid as necessary.

2. Open bleeder (1) on slave cylinder (2) and install a length of clear hose to divert fluid into suitable container. Push and hold clutch pedal down then close bleeder. Repeat this step several times.

3. Remove slave cylinder from transmission.

4. Hold slave cylinder with actuator rod pointing down and open bleeder. Push cylinder actuator rod in completely then close bleeder. Repeat this step several times.

5. Remove drain hose and replace dust cap on bleeder and install slave cylinder on transmission.

6. Actuate clutch pedal 25 times, then start engine and verify clutch operation and pedal feel.

➡**If pedal feels spongy or clutch does not fully disengage, air is still trapped in the hydraulic circuit and must be bleed again.**

FRONT AXLE SHAFT, BEARING & SEAL

REMOVAL & INSTALLATION

See Figure 12.

1. With transmission in neutral, position vehicle on hoist.

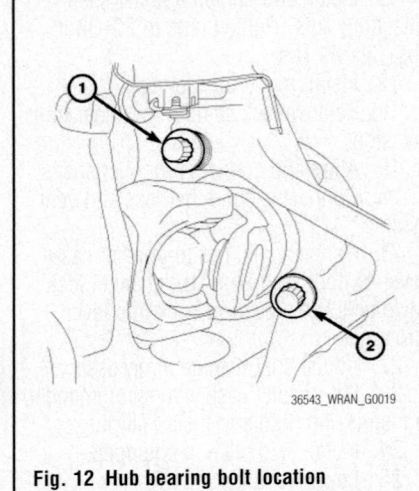

Fig. 12 Hub bearing bolt location

2. Remove brake components.

3. Remove wheel speed sensor from hub bearing.

4. Remove hub nut from axle shaft.

5. Remove three hub bearing bolts from steering knuckle.

6. Remove hub bearing with axle shaft through steering knuckle.

7. Remove brake shield and hub bearing from axle.

To install:

8. Clean axle shaft and apply a thin film of Mopar® Wheel Bearing Grease or equivalent to the shaft splines and seal contact surface.

9. Install hub bearing and brake shield on axle shaft.

10. Install axle shaft with hub bearing through steering knuckle and into differential side gears.

11. Install three hub bearing bolts through steering knuckle and tighten to 75 ft. lbs. (102 Nm).

12. Install hub nut on axle shaft and tighten to 100 ft. lbs. (136 Nm).

13. Install wheel speed sensor.

14. Install brake components.

FRONT PINION SEAL

REMOVAL & INSTALLATION

1. With transmission in neutral, position vehicle on hoist.

2. Remove brake rotors and calipers.

3. Remove propeller shaft.

4. Rotate pinion gear three or four times.

5. Record pinion torque to rotate with an inch pound torque wrench, for installation reference.

6. Hold pinion flange with Flange Wrench C-3281 and remove pinion nut.

7. Mark a reference line across the pinion shaft and flange for installation reference.

8. Remove pinion flange with Puller C-452.

9. Remove seal with a seal puller.

To install:

10. Apply a light coating of gear lubricant on the lip of pinion seal. Install seal with Installer 8681 and Handle C-4171.

11. Install flange on the pinion shaft with the reference marks aligned.

12. Install flange with Installer 8112 and Cup 8109.

13. Install new pinion nut.

14. Hold pinion flange with Flange Wrench C-3281 and tighten pinion nut to 160 ft. lbs. (217 Nm).

15. Measure pinion torque to rotating with an inch pound torque wrench. With a torque wrench set at 400 ft. lbs. (542 Nm), tighten nut in 5 ft. lb. (6.8 Nm) increments until pinion torque to rotating is achieved. Pinion torque to rotating is the recorded reading plus an additional 5 inch lbs. (0.56 Nm).

❊❊ WARNING

For the 186FBI (Dana 33) axle, if maximum tightening torque of 400 ft. lbs. (542 Nm) is reached before torque to rotate is achieved, the collapsible spacer may have been damaged. Never loosen pinion gear nut to decrease pinion gear bearing rotating torque and never exceed specified preload torque. Failure to follow these instruction may result in damage.

❊❊ WARNING

For the 216FBI (Dana 44) axle, if maximum tightening torque of 200 ft. lbs. (271 Nm) is reached before torque to rotate is achieved, the collapsible spacer may have been damaged. Never loosen pinion gear nut to decrease pinion gear bearing rotating torque and never exceed specified preload torque. Failure to follow these instruction may result in damage.

16. Install propeller shaft.

17. Install brake components

REAR AXLE HOUSING

REMOVAL & INSTALLATION

See Figure 13.

1. With vehicle in neutral, position vehicle on hoist.

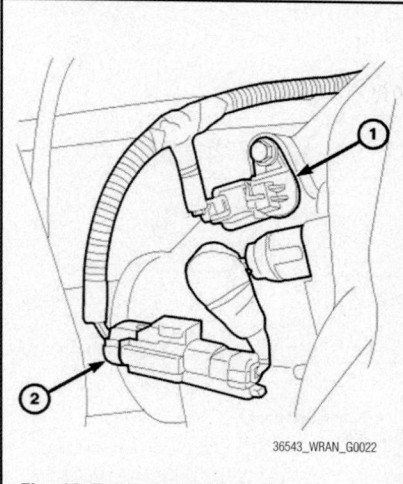

Fig. 13 Transmission Tru-Lok® connector locations

2. Position and secure a lift under the axle.

3. Mark propeller shaft flange and axle pinion flange for installation reference.

4. Remove propeller shaft and suspend under the vehicle.

5. Remove vent hose from the axle tube.

6. Disconnect Tru-Lok® wiring connectors.

7. Remove brake calipers and rotors from axle.

8. Remove park brake cables from axle.

➡**Park brake cables are self adjusting and must be locked out before removal.**

9. Remove brake sensors connector from sensors.

10. Remove track bar from axle bracket.

11. Remove stabilizer bar links from axle brackets.

12. Remove shock absorbers from axle brackets.

13. Remove upper control arms from axle brackets.

14. Loosen lower control arm bolts and lower axle enough to remove coil springs and spring insulators.

15. Remove lower control arm from axle brackets.

16. Lower and remove the axle.

To install:

➡**The weight of the vehicle must be supported by the springs before the control arms and track bar are tightened. Failure to follow these instruction will cause premature bushing failure.**

17. Raise the axle under the vehicle.

18. Install lower control arms onto axle brackets and loosely install mounting bolts and nuts.

19. Install coil spring isolators and springs.

20. Raise axle up until springs are seated.

21. Install upper control arms onto axle brackets and loosely install mounting bolts and nuts.

22. Install shock absorbers onto axle brackets and tighten nuts to 56 ft. lbs. (76 Nm)

23. Install stabilizer links onto axle brackets and tighten nuts to 75 ft. lbs. (102 Nm) with the full weight of the Jeep on the axle.

24. Install track bar onto axle bracket, and loosely install track bar bolt.

25. Install brake sensors connector on sensors.

26. Install park brake cables on axle.

27. Install brake rotors and calipers on axle.

28. Install vent hose on axle tube.

29. Connect Tru-Lok wiring connectors.

30. Install propeller shaft with propeller shaft flange and pinion flange reference marks aligned.

➡**Clean all propeller shaft bolts and apply Mopar® Lock and Seal Adhesive or equivalent to the threads before installation.**

31. Install propeller shaft bolts and tighten to 15 ft. lbs. (20 Nm).

32. Install wheels and tires.

33. Remove lift from axle and lower vehicle.

34. Tighten lower control arms, upper control arms and track bar nuts to 125 ft. lbs. (169 Nm) with vehicle weight.

REAR AXLE SHAFT, BEARING & SEAL

REMOVAL & INSTALLATION

See Figures 14 through 17.

1. With transmission in neutral, position vehicle on hoist.

2. Remove brake caliper with adapter and rotor.

3. Remove park brake cable from support plate.

➡**Park brake cables are self adjusting and must be locked out before removal.**

4. Remove brake sensor harness and remove sensor from support plate.

5. Remove axle retainer plate nuts.

6. Pull axle shaft with support plate, bearing and seal from axle tube.

➡**Axle bearing race is a slip fit in the axle tube. No tool are required.**

7. Remove brake dust shield and support plate from the axle.

8. Bearing retainer, axle bearing, axle shaft seal and axle shaft retainer are removed as an assembly.

9. Remove bearing retainer and bearing with seal from axle with Splitter 1130 and press. Position splitter between axle shaft retainer and tone ring and press assembly off shaft.

➡**Inspect axle shaft retaining plate, if plate is bent or warped replace plate.**

10. Install retaining plate on axle shaft.

11. Apply a coat of multi-purpose grease on sealing surface of axle seal.

12. Install seal on axle shaft with cavity away from axle shaft retaining.

13. Press bearing and bearing retaining ring onto axle shaft with press and press blocks.

14. Install dust shield and support plate on axle shaft retainer.

15. Lubricate bearing with Mopar® Wheel Bearing Grease, or equivalent. Wipe excess grease from outside of bearing.

To install:

16. Install axle assembly into the axle tube.

➡**Never reuse axle retainer nuts. Used torque nuts can loosen up. Failure to follow these instruction may result in personal injury.**

17. Install new axle retainer nuts and tighten to 45 ft. lbs. (61 Nm).

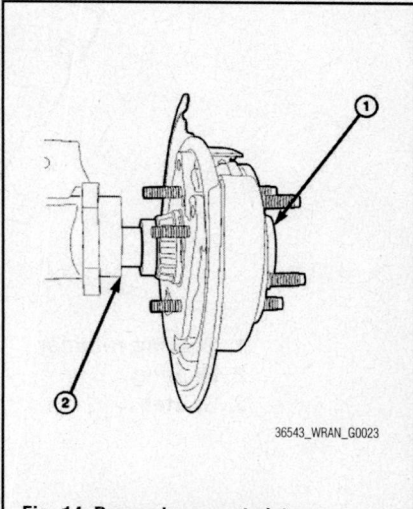

Fig. 14 Rear axle support plate

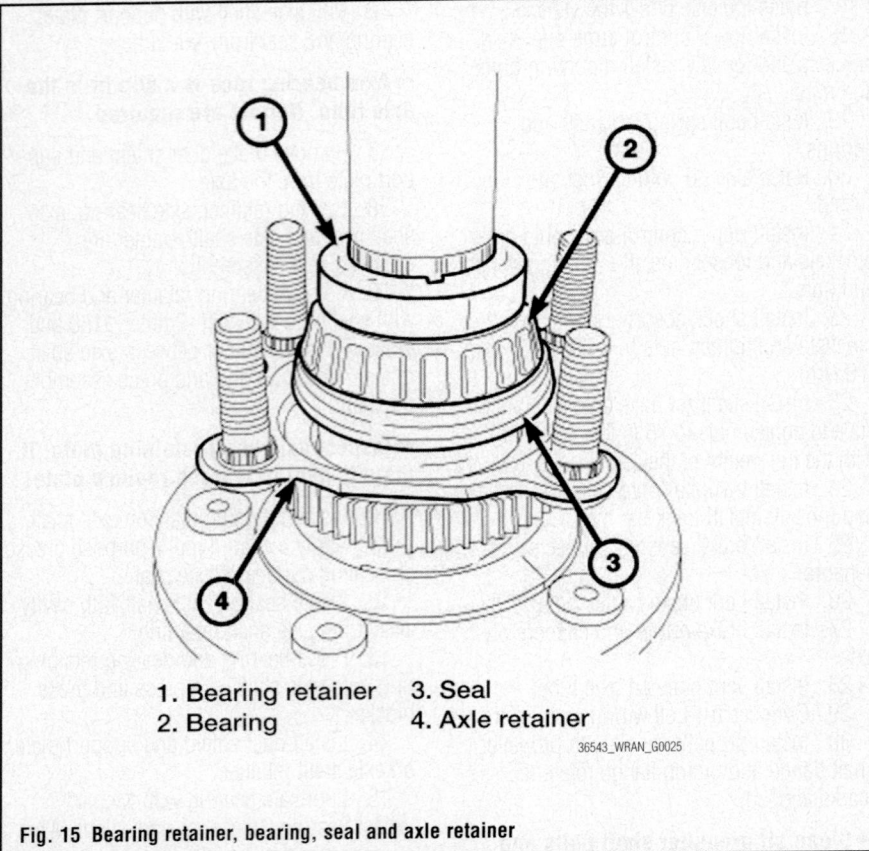

1. Bearing retainer   3. Seal
2. Bearing   4. Axle retainer

36543_WRAN_G0025

Fig. 15 Bearing retainer, bearing, seal and axle retainer

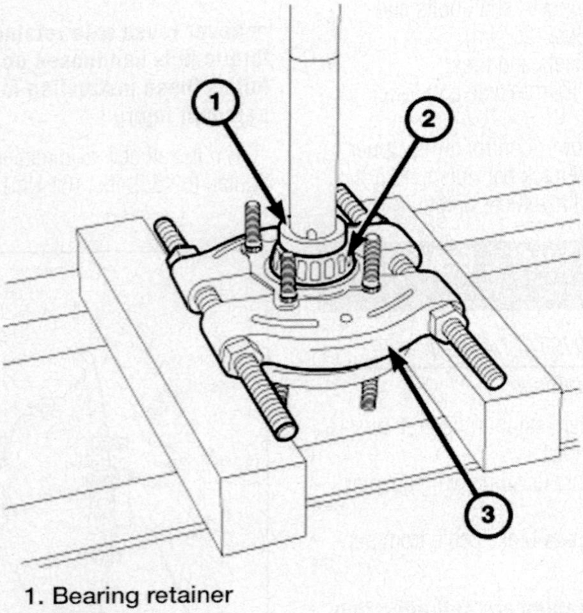

1. Bearing retainer
2. Bearing
3. Spitter

36543_WRAN_G0024

Fig. 16 Bearing retainer and bearing

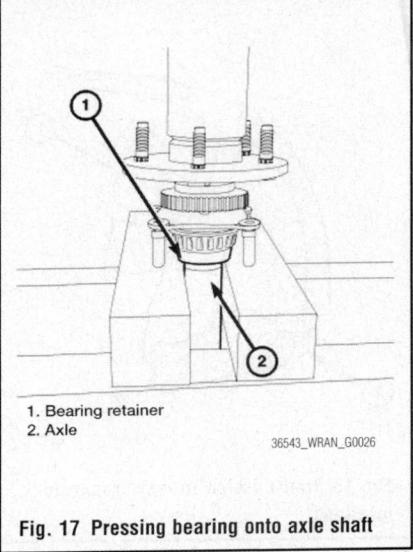

1. Bearing retainer
2. Axle

36543_WRAN_G0026

Fig. 17 Pressing bearing onto axle shaft

18. Install brake and harness.
19. Install park brake cables.

REAR PINION SEAL

REMOVAL & INSTALLATION

1. With transmission in neutral, position vehicle on hoist.
2. Remove brake component to eliminate drag.
3. Remove propeller shaft at pinion flange.
4. Rotate pinion gear three or four times.
5. Record pinion torque to rotate with an inch pound torque wrench.
6. Hold pinion flange with Spanner Wrench 6958 and remove pinion nut and washer.
7. Mark a line across the pinion shaft and flange for installation reference.
8. Remove pinion flange with Puller C-452.
9. Remove pinion seal with a seal puller.

To install:

10. Apply a light coating of gear lubricant on the lip of pinion seal.
11. Install flange on the pinion shaft with the reference marks aligned.
12. Install flange Installer C-3718 on pinion shaft.
13. Hold pinion flange with Spanner Wrench 6958 and tighten Installer C-3718 nut. Tighten nut to remove all end play.
14. Install pinion washer and a new nut on the pinion gear.
15. Hold pinion flange with Spanner Wrench 6958 and tighten pinion nut to 160 ft. lbs. (217 Nm).

16. Measure pinion torque to rotate inch pound torque wrench. Pinion torque to rotate is recorded reading plus 5 inch lbs (0.56 Nm).

17. If pinion rotating torque is low. Hold pinion flange with Spanner Wrench 6958 and tighten pinion nut in 5 ft. lbs. (6.8 Nm)

increments until pinion torque to rotating is achieved.

➡ **If maximum tightening torque of 200 ft. lbs. (271 Nm) is reached before torque to rotate is achieved, the collapsible spacer may have been damaged. Never loosen pinion gear nut to**

decrease pinion gear bearing rotating torque and never exceed specified preload torque. Failure to follow these instruction may result in damage.

18. Install propeller shaft.
19. Install brake components.

ENGINE COOLING

ENGINE FAN

REMOVAL & INSTALLATION

1. Drain cooling system.
2. Remove upper radiator hose.
3. Remove the heater hose.
4. Remove the coolant recovery container and position out of the way.
5. Disconnect the engine fan electrical connector.
6. Remove radiator upper seal.
7. Remove the mounting screws.
8. Remove the cooling fan assembly .

To install:

9. Position the cooling fan assembly.
10. Install mounting screws. Tighten to 50 inch lbs. (5.5 Nm).
11. Install upper radiator hose.
12. Install upper radiator seal.
13. Install the heater hose.
14. Connect the electrical connector.
15. Fill cooling system.

RADIATOR

REMOVAL & INSTALLATION

➡ **When removing the radiator or A/C condenser for any reason, note the location of all radiator-to-body and radiator-to-A/C condenser rubber air seals. These are used at the top, bottom and sides of the radiator and A/C condenser. To prevent overheating, these seals must be installed to their original positions.**

1. Disconnect negative battery cable at battery.
2. Drain cooling system drain coolant into a clean container for reuse.
3. Remove coolant recovery container.
4. Remove radiator upper seal.
5. Remove the electric cooling fan.
6. Remove lower radiator seal.
7. Remove lower radiator hose.
8. Remove front grille.
9. Remove two A/C condenser mounting bolts. Lift A/C condenser out of J-clips.

10. Loosen horn mounting bolt. Rotate horn out of the way.
11. Remove A/C tubing mounting bracket bolt.
12. Remove radiator mounting bolts.

➡ **The lower part of radiator is equipped with two alignment dowel pins. They are located on the bottom of radiator tank and fit into rubber grommets. These rubber grommets are pressed into the radiator lower crossmember.**

13. Lift radiator straight up and out of vehicle taking care not to damage radiator fins.

✳✳ WARNING

When removing radiator, note position of the rubber seals located on the top and bottom of radiator (on certain models only). To prevent possible overheating, these seals must be installed to their original positions.

To install:

✳✳ WARNING

Before installing the radiator or A/C condenser, be sure the radiator-to-body and radiator-to-A/C condenser rubber air seals are properly fastened to their original positions. These are used at the top, bottom and sides of the radiator and A/C condenser. To prevent overheating, these seals must be installed to their original positions.

14. Guide the two radiator alignment dowels into the rubber grommets located in lower radiator crossmember. Install and tighten mounting bolts to 70 inch lbs. (8 Nm) torque.
15. Position combination A/C condenser/transmission oil cooler in J-clips and install mounting bolts.
16. Tighten bolts to 70 inch lbs. (8 Nm).

17. Position evaporator line tapping block and install mounting bolt. Tighten to 70 inch lbs. (8 Nm).
18. Position horn and tighten mounting bolt to 70 inch lbs. (8 Nm).
19. Install the electric cooling fan.
20. Position and install the lower radiator seal.
21. Install upper radiator seal.
22. Install front grille.
23. Connect radiator hoses and install hose clamps.
24. Install coolant recovery container.
25. Fill cooling system with correct coolant.
26. Connect battery negative cable.
27. Start engine and check for leaks.

THERMOSTAT

REMOVAL & INSTALLATION

1. Disconnect negative battery cable.
2. Remove air filter housing.
3. Drain cooling system down below the thermostat level.
4. Disconnect throttle body electrical connector.
5. Remove radiator upper hose at thermostat housing.
6. Remove thermostat housing bolts and thermostat housing.
7. Remove thermostat from thermostat housing.
8. Clean both sealing surfaces and inspect the sealing ring. If reinstalling the original thermostat, make sure the sealing ring is not damaged. New thermostats come with a new sealing ring.

To install:

9. Position thermostat in thermostat housing.
10. Install thermostat housing and thermostat assembly on intake manifold and tighten bolts to 21 ft. lbs. (28 Nm).
11. Install the radiator upper hose to thermostat housing.
12. Connect throttle body electrical connector.

13. Refill the cooling system to the proper level.

14. Connect negative battery cable.

15. Install air filter housing.

WATER PUMP

REMOVAL & INSTALLATION

1. Drain the cooling system.
2. Remove the accessory drive belt shield.
3. Remove the accessory drive belt.
4. Remove water pump pulley bolts.

➡To remove the water pump pulley, it MUST first be positioned between water pump housing and drive hub. The pulley can then be removed with the water pump assembly.

5. Rotate pulley until openings in pulley align with water pump drive hub spokes. Move pulley inward between pump housing and hub.

6. Position pulley to allow access to water pump mounting bolts. Remove water pump mounting bolts.

7. Remove water pump with the pulley loosely positioned between hub and the pump body.

8. Remove and discard the seal.

9. Clean seal groove and sealing surfaces on pump and timing chain case cover. Take care not to scratch or gouge sealing surfaces.

To install:

10. Install new seal into water pump housing groove.

➡The water pump pulley MUST be positioned loosely between the pump housing and drive hub BEFORE water pump installation.

11. Position the water pump pulley loosely between pump housing and drive hub.

12. Install water pump and pulley to the timing chain case cover. Tighten water pump bolts to 105 inch lbs. (12 Nm).

13. Position pulley on water pump hub. Install bolts and tighten to 21 ft. lbs. (28 Nm).

14. Rotate pump by hand to check for freedom of movement.

15. Install the accessory drive belt.

16. Install drive belt shield.

17. Fill the cooling system.

ENGINE ELECTRICAL   CHARGING SYSTEM

ALTERNATOR

REMOVAL & INSTALLATION

See Figure 18.

1. Disconnect negative battery cable at battery.

2. Remove generator drive belt.

3. Remove generator mounting bolts and nut.

4. Unsnap plastic cover from B+ terminal.

5. Remove B+ cable output terminal mounting nut. Disconnect terminal from generator.

6. Disconnect field wire connector at rear of generator by pushing on connector tab.

7. Remove generator from vehicle.

To install:

8. Install generator mounting fasteners and tighten to 40 ft. lbs. (54 Nm).

❋❋ WARNING

Never force a belt over a pulley rim using a screwdriver. The synthetic fiber of the belt can be damaged.

❋❋ WARNING

When installing a serpentine accessory drive belt, the belt MUST be

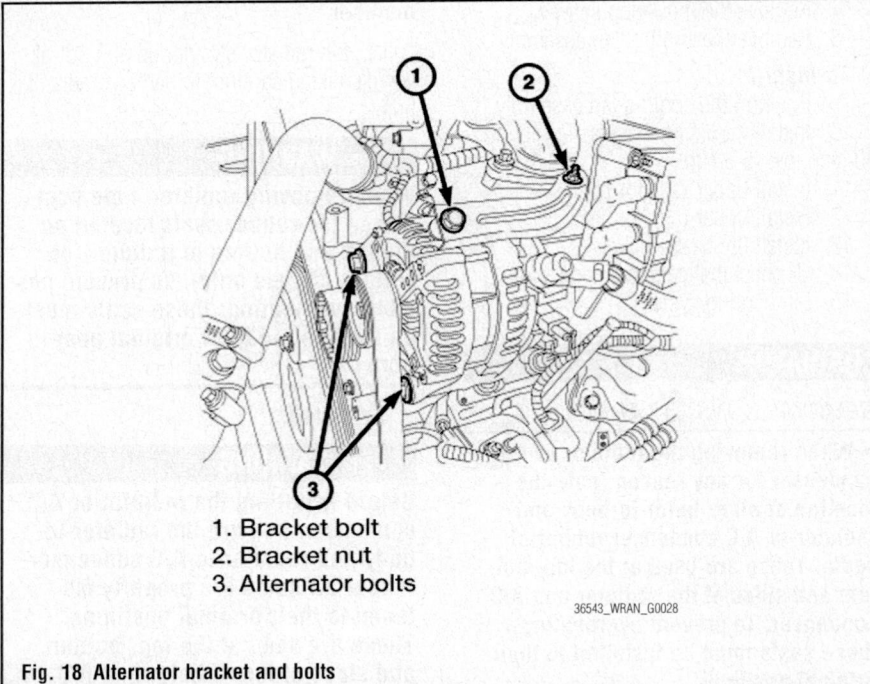

1. Bracket bolt
2. Bracket nut
3. Alternator bolts

36543_WRAN_G0028

Fig. 18 Alternator bracket and bolts

routed correctly. The water pump will be rotating in the wrong direction if the belt is installed incorrectly, causing the engine to overheat. Refer to belt routing label in engine compartment.

9. Install generator drive belt.

10. Snap field wire connector into generator.

11. Install B+ terminal to generator mounting stud. Tighten mounting nut to 9 ft. lbs. (12 Nm).

12. Snap plastic cover to B+ terminal.

13. Install negative battery cable to battery.

ENGINE ELECTRICAL

IGNITION SYSTEM

FIRING ORDERS

See Figure 19.

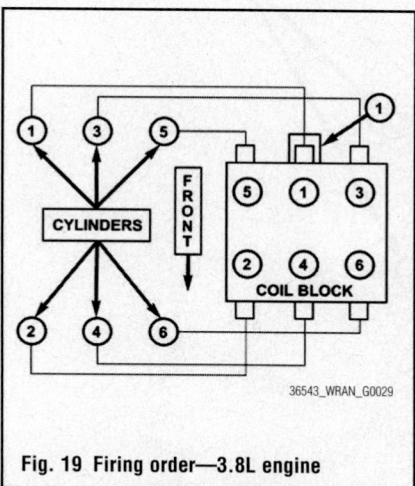

Fig. 19 Firing order—3.8L engine

IGNITION COIL PACK

REMOVAL & INSTALLATION

See Figure 20.

➡ **The ignition coil pack is located above the left valve cover.**

1. Disconnect negative battery cable.
2. Label then disconnect the six spark plug cables.
3. Disconnect electrical connector from ignition coil.
4. Remove two coil mounting nuts.
5. Pull coil pack from mounting studs.

To install:

6. Install coil pack over mounting studs.
7. Install two mounting nuts. Torque the nuts to 105 inch lbs. (12 Nm).

8. Connect electrical connector to ignition coil.
9. Install six ignition cables to ignition coil.
10. Connect negative battery cable.

SPARK PLUGS

REMOVAL & INSTALLATION

➡ **When replacing the spark plugs and spark plug cables, route the cables correctly and secure them in the appropriate retainers. Failure to route the cables properly can cause the radio to reproduce ignition noise, cross ignition of the spark plugs or short circuit the cables to ground.**

➡ **Always remove cables by grasping at the boot, rotating the boot ½ turn, and pulling straight back in a steady motion.**

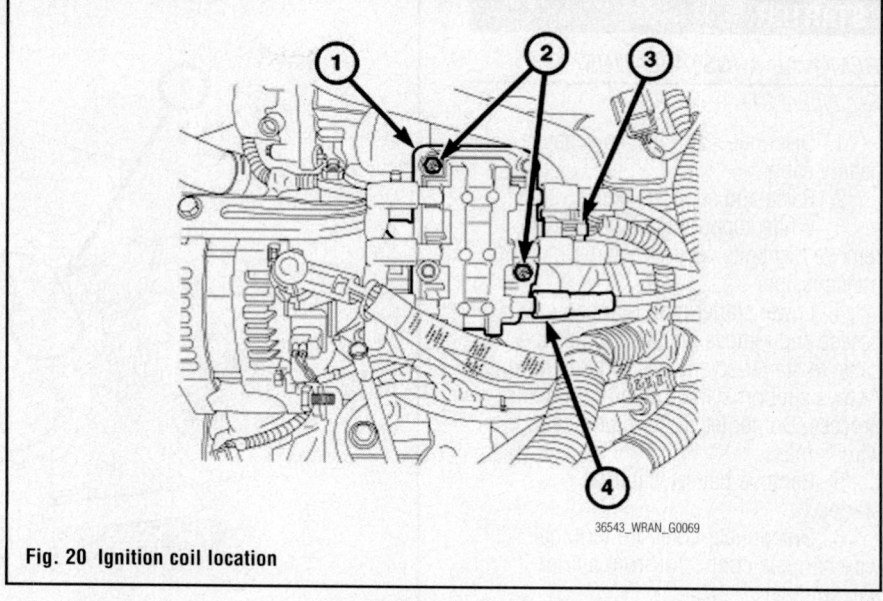

Fig. 20 Ignition coil location

1. Prior to removing the spark plug, make sure the area around the spark plug is clean.
2. Remove the spark plug using a quality socket with a foam insert.
3. Inspect the spark plug condition.

To install:

4. Coat threads of spark plug with an anti-seize compound.

➡ **Be sure not to get anti-seize anywhere but on the threads of the spark plug.**

5. To avoid cross threading, start the spark plug into the cylinder head by hand.
6. Tighten spark plugs to 13 ft. lbs. (17.5 Nm).
7. Install spark plug cables over spark plugs. A click will be heard and felt when the cable properly attaches to the spark plug.

STARTER

REMOVAL & INSTALLATION

See Figure 21.

1. Disconnect and isolate negative battery cable.
2. Raise and support vehicle.
3. While supporting starter motor, remove two bolts securing starter motor to transmission.
4. Lower starter motor far enough to access and remove nut securing battery cable to starter solenoid B(+) terminal stud. Always support starter motor during this process. Do not let starter motor hang from wire harness.
5. Remove battery cable at starter.
6. Disconnect solenoid terminal wire harness connector from starter solenoid.
7. Remove starter motor.

To install:

8. Connect solenoid terminal wire harness connector to starter solenoid. Always support starter motor during this process. Do not let starter motor hang from wire harness.

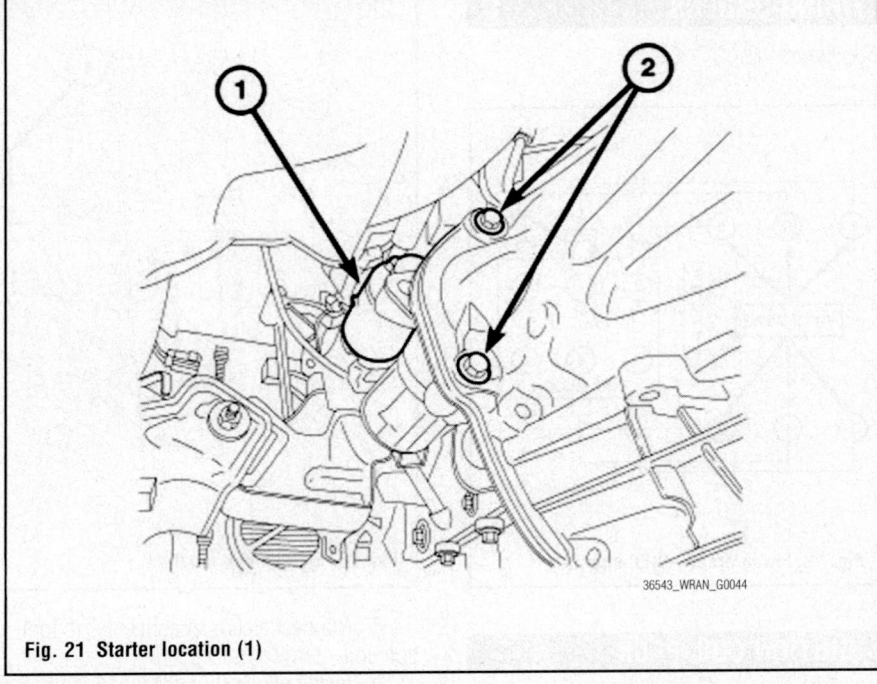

Fig. 21 Starter location (1)

9. Install battery cable eyelet onto starter solenoid stud. Install and tighten nut to 96 inch lbs. (11.3 Nm).
10. Position starter motor to transmis-
sion. Install and tighten two mounting bolts to 40 ft. lbs. (54 Nm).
11. Lower vehicle.
12. Connect negative battery cable.

ENGINE MECHANICAL

ACCESSORY DRIVE BELTS

ACCESSORY BELT ROUTING

See Figure 22.

INSPECTION

See Figure 23.

When diagnosing serpentine accessory drive belts, small cracks that run across the ribbed surface of the belt from rib to rib, are considered normal. These are not a reason to replace the belt. However, cracks running along a rib (not across) are not normal. Any belt with cracks running along a rib must be replaced. Also replace the belt if it has excessive wear, frayed cords or severe glazing.

ADJUSTMENT

There is no adjustment necessary or possible.

REMOVAL & INSTALLATION

See Figure 22.

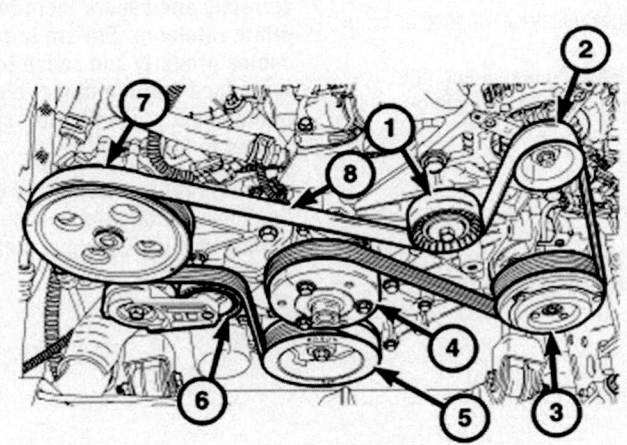

1. Idler pulley
2. Generator
3. A/C compressor
4. Water pump
5. Crankshaft
6. Tensioner pulley
7. Power steering
8. Serpentine belt

Fig. 22 Drive belt routing—3.8L engine

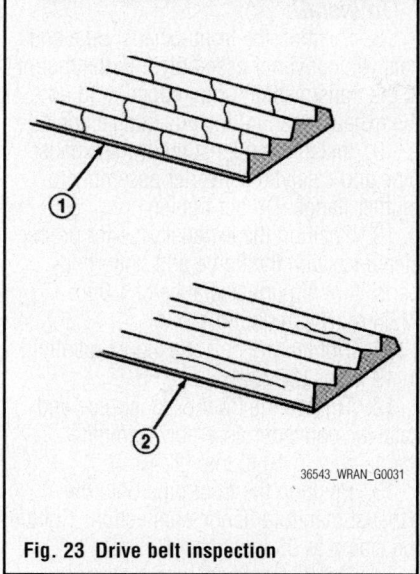

Fig. 23 Drive belt inspection

1. Disconnect negative battery cable from battery.

2. Rotate accessory belt tensioner clockwise until it contacts its stop. Remove accessory drive belt, then slowly rotate the accessory drive belt tensioner into the free arm position.

✷✷ WARNING

Do not let the tensioner arm snap back to the free arm position, severe damage may occur to the tensioner.

To install:

3. Check condition of all pulleys.

4. Route accessory drive belt around all pulleys except the idler pulley. Rotate the accessory drive belt tensioner clockwise until it contacts its stop position. Route the accessory drive belt around the idler pulley and slowly let the tensioner rotate into the belt. Make sure the accessory drive belt is properly seated onto all pulleys.

CAMSHAFT AND VALVE LIFTERS

REMOVAL & INSTALLATION

See Figures 24 through 27.

1. Remove the radiator and cooling fan from the vehicle.

2. Remove the cylinder heads.

3. Remove the timing chain and camshaft sprocket.

4. Remove the yoke retainer.

5. Remove the hydraulic lifters. If necessary use a magnetic or claw-type lifter tool to remove the lifters from the bores. If

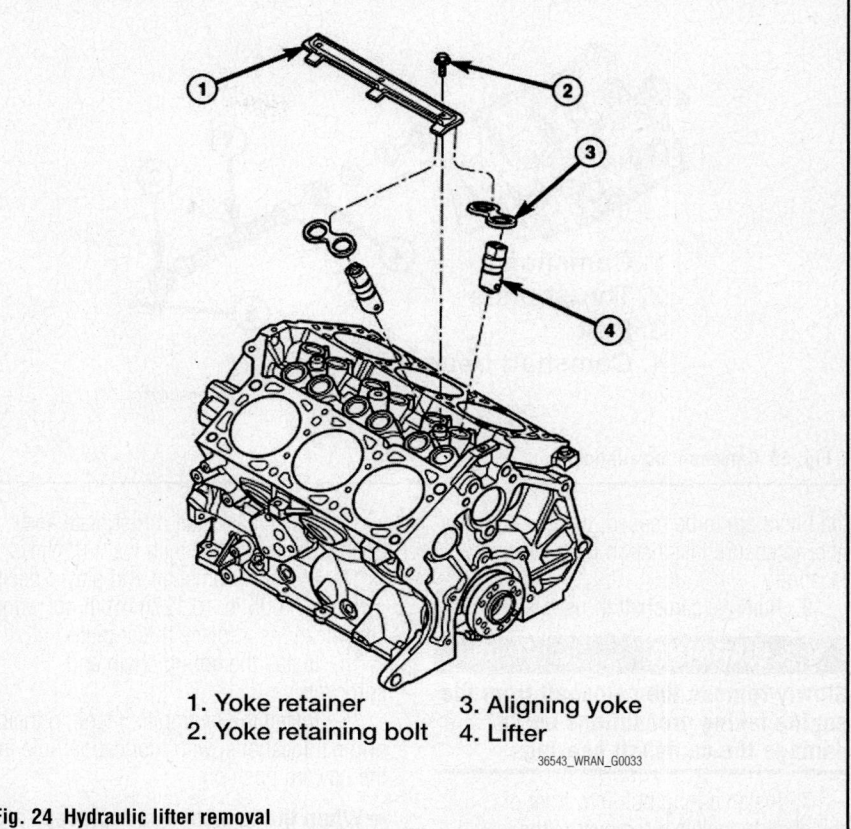

1. Yoke retainer   3. Aligning yoke
2. Yoke retaining bolt   4. Lifter

Fig. 24 Hydraulic lifter removal

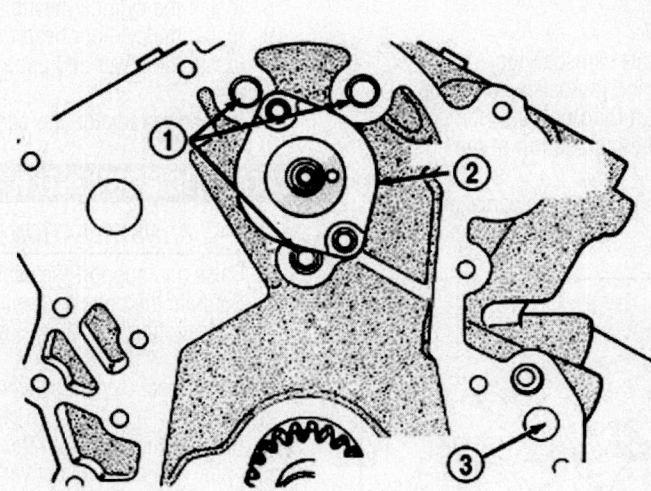

1. Oil galley cup plugs
2. Camshaft thrust plate
3. Oil feed galley from pump

Fig. 25 Camshaft thrust plate

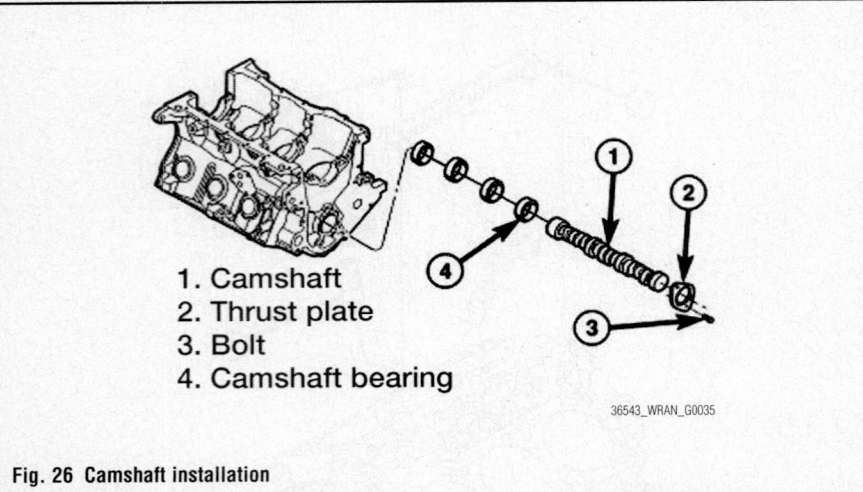

1. Camshaft
2. Thrust plate
3. Bolt
4. Camshaft bearing

36543_WRAN_G0035

Fig. 26 Camshaft installation

the lifters are to be reused, identify each lifter to ensure installation in its original location.

6. Remove camshaft thrust plate.

※※ WARNING

Slowly remove the camshaft from the engine taking precautions not to damage the camshaft bearings.

7. Install a long bolt into front of camshaft to facilitate removal of the camshaft.

8. Carefully remove the camshaft.

➡**The camshaft bearings are serviced with the engine block.**

To install:

9. Lubricate camshaft lobes and camshaft bearing journals with engine oil.

10. Install a long bolt into the camshaft to assist in the installation of the camshaft.

11. Carefully install the camshaft in engine block.

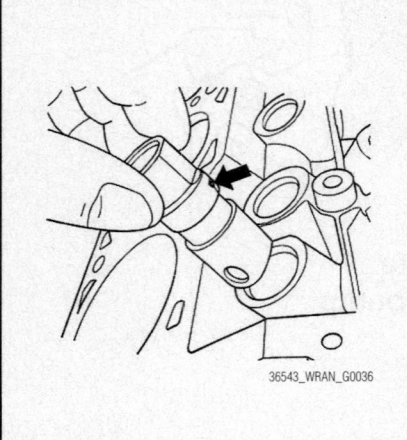

36543_WRAN_G0036

Fig. 27 Hydraulic lifter positioning

12. Install camshaft thrust plate and bolts. Tighten to 105 inch lbs. (12 Nm).

13. Measure camshaft end play. Specification is 0.005 in. (0.127mm). If not within specifications, replace thrust plate.

14. Install the timing chain and sprockets.

15. Install the hydraulic lifters, in their original locations, with lubrication hole in the upward position.

➡**When the camshaft is replaced, all of the hydraulic lifters must be replaced.**

16. Install timing chain and sprockets.

17. Install the timing chain cover.

18. Install the cylinder heads.

19. Install the cylinder head covers.

20. Install the lower and upper intake manifolds.

21. Install the radiator and cooling fan.

CATALYTIC CONVERTER

REMOVAL & INSTALLATION

1. Raise and support the vehicle.

2. Saturate the bolts and nuts with a suitable penetrating oil. Allow 5 minutes for penetration.

3. Disconnect oxygen sensor electrical connectors.

4. Remove the nuts from the front exhaust pipe and catalytic converter assembly to muffler flange.

5. Remove bolts and flanged nuts at the manifold.

6. Lower the front exhaust pipe/catalytic converter assembly and slide out of the mount at the transmission (if equipped).

7. Remove the front exhaust pipe/catalytic converter assembly from the vehicle.

To install:

8. Position the front exhaust pipe and catalytic converter assembly into the mount at the transmission (if equipped) and onto the exhaust manifold flange connection.

9. Install the nuts at the front exhaust pipe and catalytic converter assembly to muffler flange. Do not tighten.

10. Position the exhaust pipe for proper clearance with the frame and underbody parts. A minimum clearance of 1.0 in. (25.4 mm) is required.

11. Tighten the bolt at exhaust manifold to 19 ft. lbs.(27 Nm).

12. Tighten the front exhaust pipe and catalytic converter assembly to muffler flange nuts to 19 ft. lbs. (27 Nm).

13. Position the front pipe onto the exhaust manifold flange connection. Tighten the clamp to 95 inch lbs. (10 Nm).

14. Connect oxygen sensor electrical connectors.

15. Lower the vehicle.

16. Start the vehicle and inspect for exhaust leaks. Repair exhaust leaks as necessary.

17. Check the exhaust system for contact with the body panels. Make adjustments, if necessary.

CRANKSHAFT DAMPER

REMOVAL & INSTALLATION

1. Disconnect negative cable from battery.

2. Raise vehicle on hoist.

3. Remove the accessory drive belt.

4. Remove vibration damper bolt.

5. Insert Special Tool 8450 into crankshaft nose.

6. Position 3-jaw puller Special Tool 1026 on damper. Turn puller forcing screw until damper releases from crankshaft.

7. Remove the crankshaft vibration damper.

To install:

8. Install crankshaft vibration damper using the forcing screw, nut, and thrust bearing/washer from Special Tool 8452.

➡**To minimize friction and prolong tool life, lubricate the threads on the forcing screw of Special Tool 8452.**

9. Position vibration damper on crankshaft.

10. Screw Special Tool 8452 into crankshaft until the bolt seats. Turn the nut to install damper until it seats fully.

11. Remove Special Tool 8452.

12. Install vibration damper bolt. Torque bolt to 40 ft. lbs. (54 Nm).

13. Install the accessory drive belt.
14. Connect negative cable to battery.

CRANKSHAFT FRONT SEAL

REMOVAL & INSTALLATION

See Figure 28.

1. Disconnect negative cable from battery.
2. Remove accessory drive belt.
3. Remove crankshaft damper.
4. Position Special Tool 6341A on crankshaft nose. Carefully screw the tool into the seal until it engages firmly. Be careful not to damage that crankshaft seal surface of cover.
5. Remove oil seal by turning the forcing screw until the seal disengages from the cover.

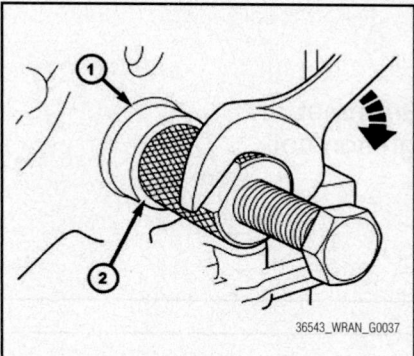

Fig. 28 Crankshaft seal removal

To install:

6. Position Special Tool C-4992-2 Guide, on the crankshaft nose.
7. Position new seal over the guide with the seal spring in the direction of the engine front cover.
8. Install seal using Special Tool C-4992-1 until seal is flush with cover.
9. Install crankshaft damper.
10. Install accessory drive belt.
11. Lower vehicle and connect negative cable to battery.

CYLINDER HEAD

REMOVAL & INSTALLATION

See Figures 29 and 30.

1. Drain the cooling system.
2. Disconnect negative cable from battery.
3. Remove upper and lower intake manifolds.

✳✳ CAUTION

Intake manifold gasket is made of very thin metal and may cause personal injury, handle with care.

4. Remove the valve (cylinder head) covers.
5. Remove the spark plugs from cylinder head.
6. Remove the oil level indicator and tube.
7. Remove exhaust manifold(s).
8. Remove rocker arm and shaft assemblies. Remove push rods and mark positions to ensure installation in original locations.
9. Remove the eight head bolts from each cylinder head and remove cylinder heads.

To install:

10. Clean all sealing surfaces of engine block and cylinder heads.
11. Position new gasket(s) on engine block . The left bank gasket is identified with the "L" stamped in the exposed area of the gasket located at front of engine (shown in). The right bank gasket is identified with a "R" stamped in the exposed area of the gasket also, but is located at the rear of the engine.

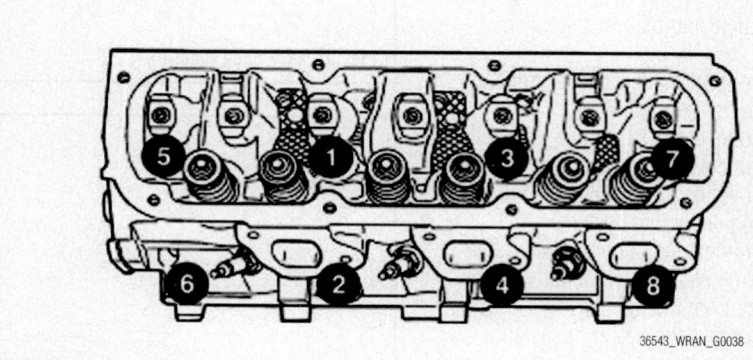

Fig. 29 Cylinder head tightening sequence

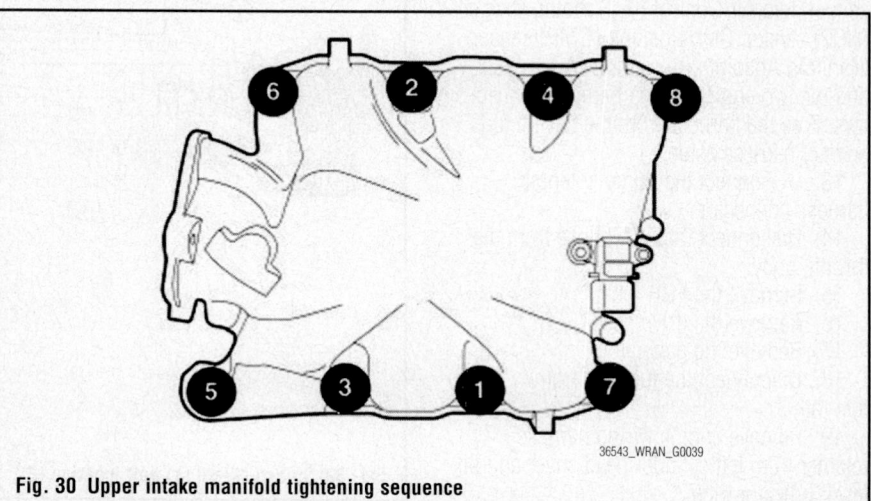

Fig. 30 Upper intake manifold tightening sequence

➡The cylinder head bolts should be examined BEFORE reuse. If the threads are necked down, the bolts must be replaced . Necking can be checked by holding a scale or straight edge against the threads. If all the threads do not contact the scale the bolt should be replaced.

12. Tighten the cylinder head bolts 1-8 in the sequence shown. Using the 4 step torque turn method, tighten according to the following values:

- Step 1: Bolts 1–8 to 45 ft. lbs. (61 Nm)
- Step 2: Bolts 1–8 to 65 ft. lbs. (88 Nm)
- Step 3: Bolts 1–8 (again) to 65 ft. lbs. (88 Nm)
- Step 4: Bolts 1–8 turn an additional ¼ turn. (Do not use a torque wrench for this step.)
- Bolt torque after ¼ turn should be over 90 ft. lbs. (122 Nm) (If not, replace the bolt.)

13. Inspect and replace worn or bent push rods.

14. Install the push rods.

15. Install the rocker arm and shaft assemblies.

16. Install the valve (cylinder head) covers.

17. Install the exhaust manifolds.

18. Install new O-ring on oil level indicator tube. Install oil level indicator tube assembly.

19. Install upper and lower intake manifolds.

20. Fill the cooling system.

21. Connect negative cable to battery.

ENGINE ASSEMBLY

REMOVAL & INSTALLATION

See Figures 31 through 38.

1. Perform fuel pressure release procedure.

2. Disconnect negative battery cable.

3. Disconnect the Inlet Air Temp Sensor (IAT), and remove air cleaner hose and housing.

4. Evacuate and recover the air conditioning.

5. Disconnect the throttle control connectors from the throttle body.

6. Disconnect the PCV hose at the left cylinder head cover.

7. Remove the front splash shield.

8. Drain the cooling system.

9. Disconnect the upper radiator hose from the thermostat housing and the lower radiator hose from the radiator.

10. Disconnect the heater hoses and coolant reservoir hose.

11. Disconnect the generator electrical connectors.

12. Disconnect the Throttle Position (TP) sensor, Idle Air Control (IAC) motor, Oxygen (HO2) sensor, Cam Position (CMP) sensor, Manifold Absolute Pressure (MAP) sensor, and the two engine wiring harness connectors. Free the harness from the cover studs and set harness aside.

13. Disconnect the purge solenoid harness connector.

14. Disconnect the EVAP hose from the throttle body.

15. Remove the EGR tube.

16. Remove the drive belts.

17. Remove the generator.

18. Disconnect the fuel line from fuel rail.

19. Remove engine wiring harness retainer from left cylinder head cover and oil level indicator tube.

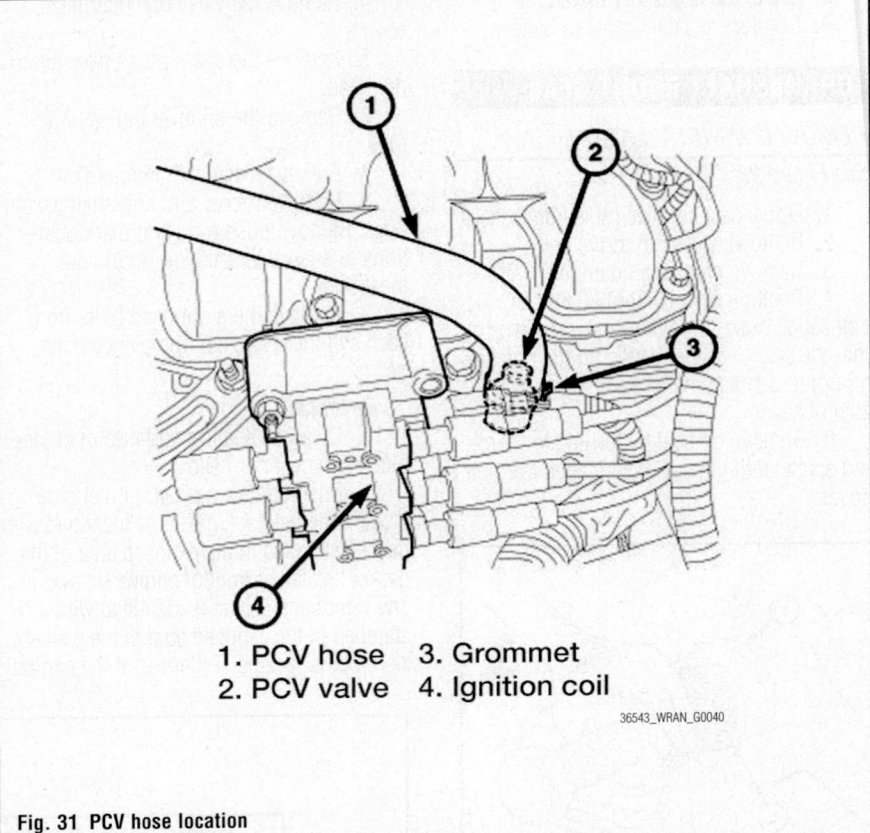

1. PCV hose   3. Grommet
2. PCV valve   4. Ignition coil

36543_WRAN_G0040

Fig. 31 PCV hose location

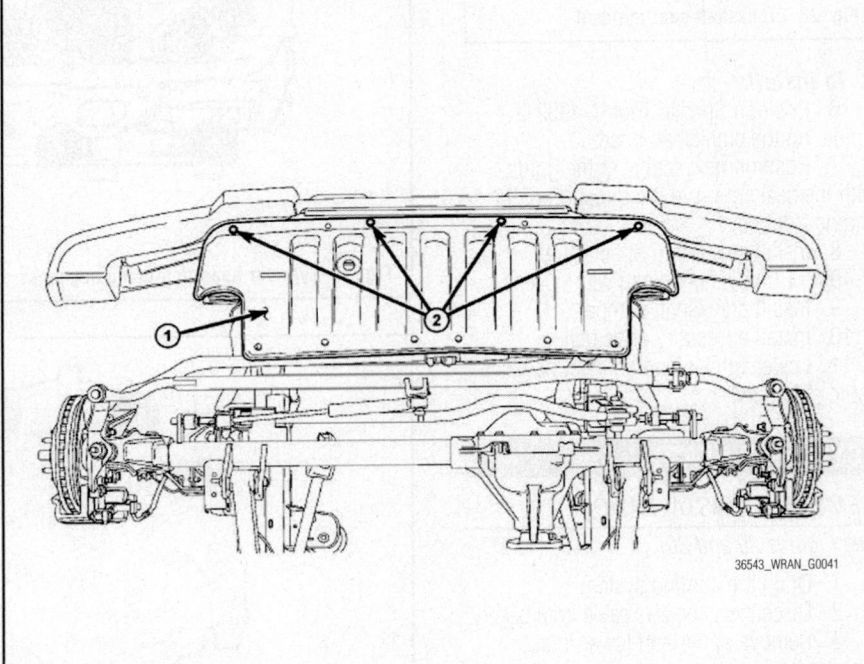

36543_WRAN_G0041

Fig. 32 Splash shield (1) bolt location (2)

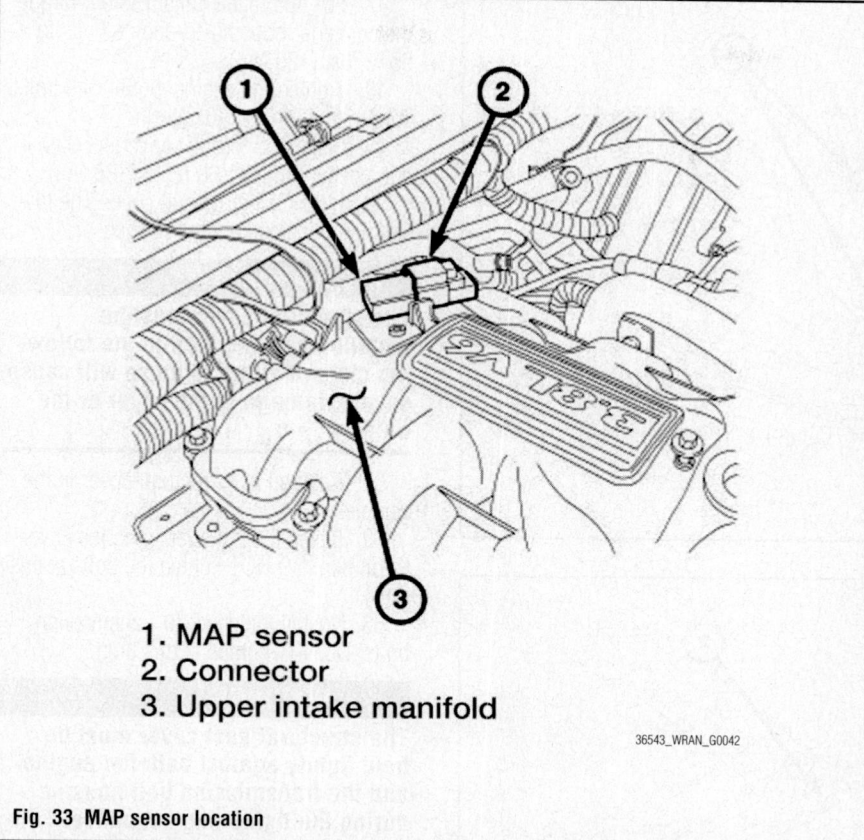

1. MAP sensor
2. Connector
3. Upper intake manifold

36543_WRAN_G0042

Fig. 33 MAP sensor location

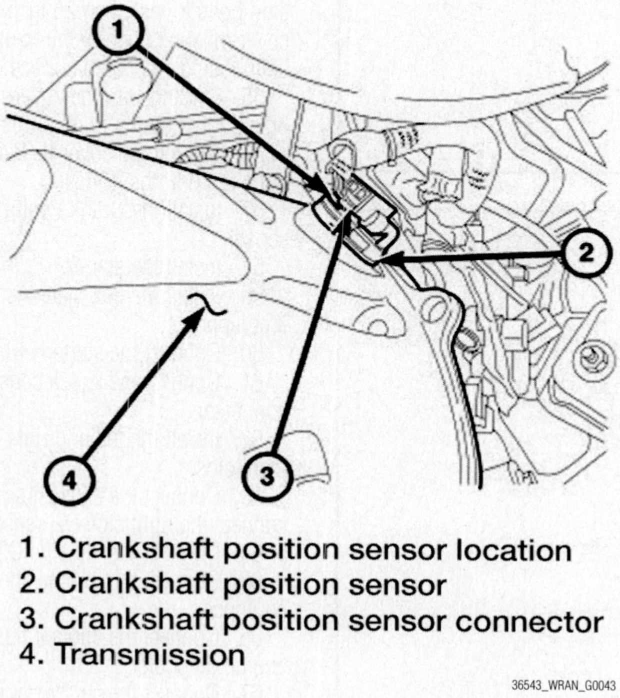

1. Crankshaft position sensor location
2. Crankshaft position sensor
3. Crankshaft position sensor connector
4. Transmission

36543_WRAN_G0043

Fig. 34 Crankshaft Position (CKP) sensor location

20. Disconnect the knock sensor wiring harness connector.
21. Remove the upper intake manifold.
22. Disconnect the A/C electrical connector.
23. Disconnect the A/C discharge line from the compressor. Cover and seal all openings of hoses and compressor.
24. Disconnect the A/C suction line from the compressor. Cover and seal all openings of hoses and compressor.
25. Disconnect the Oil Pressure Sending (OPS) unit.
26. Disconnect the coolant hose at the engine oil cooler.
27. Remove the Crankshaft Position (CKP) sensor.
28. Disconnect the in block heater (if equipped).
29. Disconnect the starter wiring and remove starter.
30. Remove the starter.
31. Remove the flexplate inspection cover, if equipped.
32. Rotate the engine at the crankshaft pulley bolt and remove the torque converter bolts, if equipped.
33. Disconnect the left side oxygen sensors.
34. Disconnect the right side oxygen sensors.
35. Disconnect the exhaust pipes from the manifolds.
36. Remove the left and right exhaust manifolds.
37. Remove the power steering pump mounting bolts and pump, with hoses attached.
38. Remove the engine mount thru bolts.
39. Remove the structural cover mounting bolts, and cover, if equipped.
40. Support the transmission using a suitable jack.
41. Connect engine lifting chain to engine, and lift the engine using a suitable hoist.
42. Lift the engine using a suitable hoist.
43. Separate the transmission from the engine.

To install:
44. Position the engine in the vehicle.
45. Install the transmission bellhousing to engine mounting bolts. The following critical steps were missed:
46. For Manual Transmissions:
   a. Tighten top transmission bolts to 30 ft. lbs. (40 Nm).
   b. Tighten two side bolts to 50 ft. lbs. (68 Nm).
   c. Tighten four bottom bolts to 40 ft. lbs. (50 Nm).

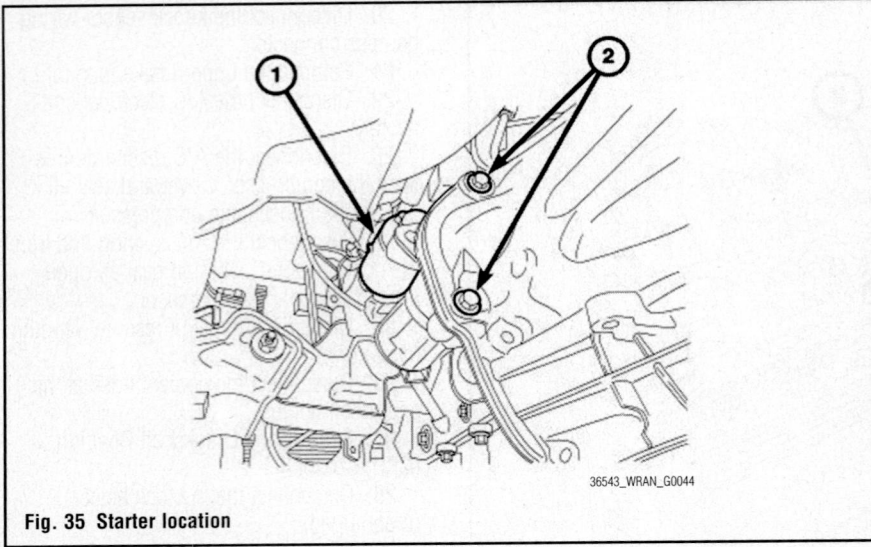

Fig. 35 Starter location

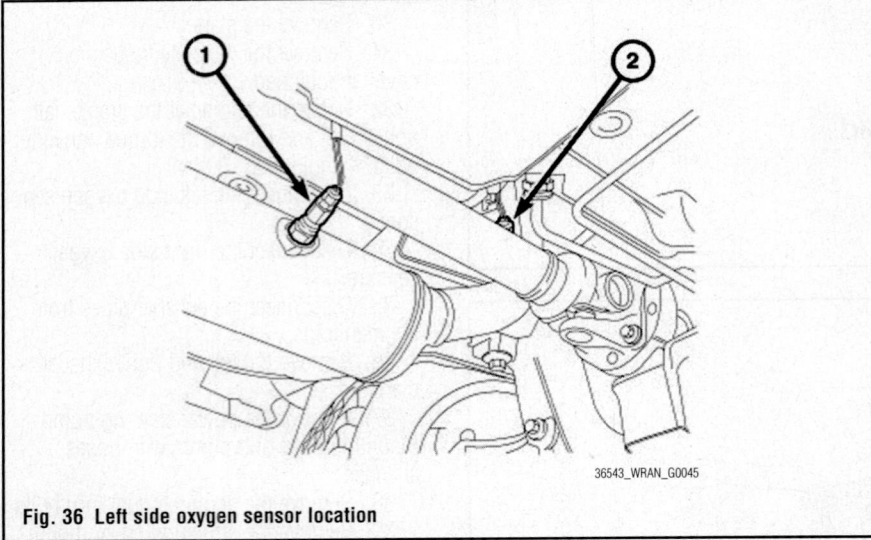

Fig. 36 Left side oxygen sensor location

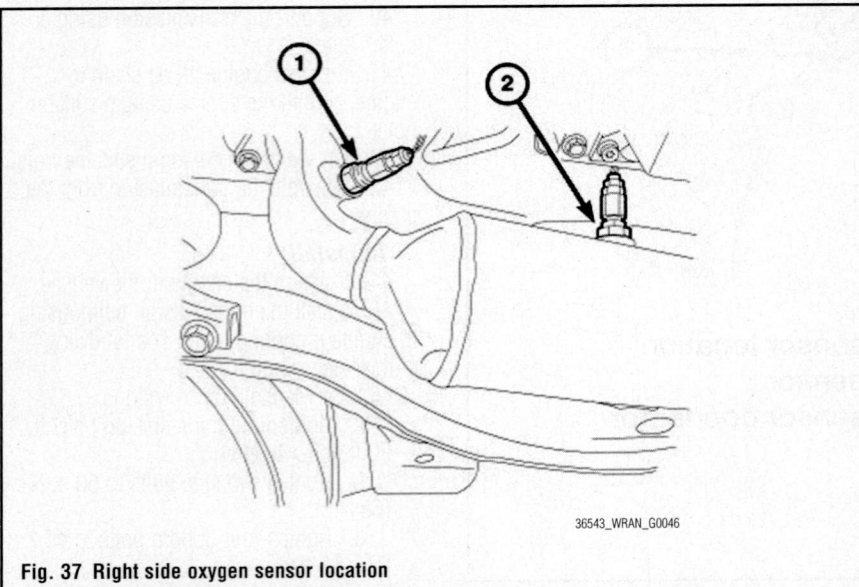

Fig. 37 Right side oxygen sensor location

47. For Automatic transmission, torque the converter housing-to-engine bolts to 95 ft. lbs. (129 Nm).

48. Tighten the engine mount thru bolts. Torque to 45 ft. lbs. (61 Nm).

49. Install the torque converter bolts, if equipped. Torque to 65 ft. lbs. (88 Nm).

50. Install the structural cover. The following critical steps were missed:

✲✲ WARNING

The structural cover must be installed as described in the following steps. Failure to do so will cause severe damage to the cover or the oil pan.

51. Position the structural cover in the vehicle.

52. Install the bolts retaining the cover-to-oil pan. DO NOT tighten the bolts at this time.

53. Install the cover-to-transmission bolts. Do NOT tighten at this time.

✲✲ WARNING

The structural dust cover must be held tightly against both the engine and the transmission bell housing during the tightening sequence. Failure to do so may cause damage to the cover.

54. Tighten the two cover-to-transmission bolts to less than 25 inch lbs. The cover must be flush to the transmission bellhousing machined surface.

55. Starting with the cover-to-oil pan bolts, tighten bolts to 40 ft. lbs. (54 Nm).

56. Tighten the cover-to-transmission bolts to 40 ft. lbs. (54 Nm).

57. Install the Crank Position (CKP) sensor.

58. Install the starter.

59. Install the flex plate inspection cover, if equipped.

60. Connect the starter wiring.

61. Connect the knock sensor electrical connector.

62. Install the left and right exhaust manifolds.

63. Connect the exhaust system and connect the right side O2 sensors.

64. Connect the left side O2 sensors.

65. Connect the in block heater, if equipped.

66. Connect the coolant hose at the engine oil cooler.

67. Connect the Oil Pressure Sending (OPS) unit wiring harness connector.

68. Install the upper intake manifold.

69. Install the EGR tube.

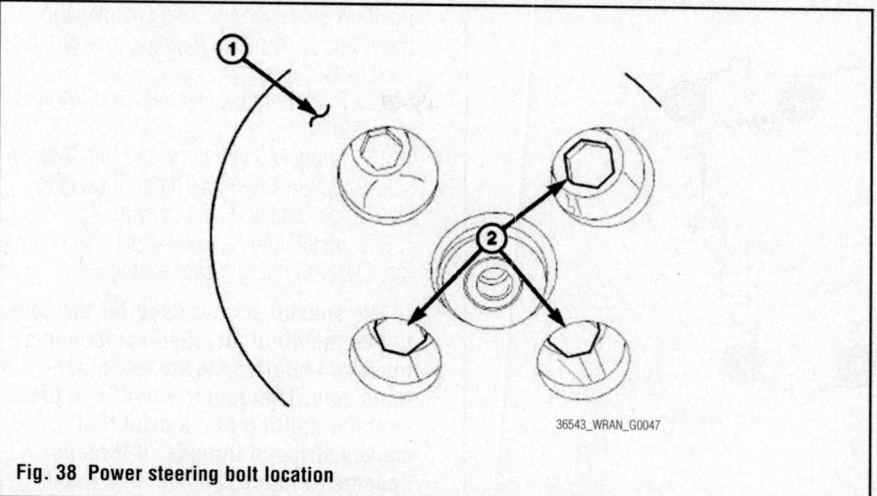

Fig. 38 Power steering bolt location

70. Connect the engine vacuum harnesses.

71. Route the engine harness to the left cylinder head and attach the purge solenoid.

72. Connect the Throttle Position (TP) sensor, Idle Air Control (IAC) motor, Oxygen (HO2) sensor, Cam Position (CMP) sensor, Manifold Absolute Pressure (MAP) sensor, and the engine wiring harness connectors.

73. Connect the A/C discharge line at the compressor.

74. Connect the A/C suction line at the compressor and compressor electrical connector.

75. Install the power steering pump.

76. Connect the fuel line to the fuel rail.

77. Install the generator.

78. Reconnect the generator wiring.

79. Install the drive belt.

80. Connect the radiator, coolant reservoir and heater hoses.

81. Connect the throttle wiring harness (ETC).

82. Install the PCV hose.

83. Fill the cooling system.

84. Install the air cleaner housing, inlet hose and Inlet Air Temp (IAT) sensor.

85. Evacuate and recharge A/C system.

86. Install new oil filter. Fill engine crankcase with proper oil to correct level.

87. Install the front splash shield.

88. Connect negative cable to battery.

89. Start engine and run until operating temperature is reached.

EXHAUST MANIFOLD

REMOVAL & INSTALLATION

Left Side Manifold

1. Disconnect battery negative cable.
2. Remove the fresh air hose.

3. Disconnect cylinder bank spark plug wires.

4. Remove heat shield attaching bolts.

5. Remove bolts attaching exhaust pipe to manifold.

6. Disconnect the left side oxygen sensors.

7. Remove bolts attaching exhaust manifold to cylinder head.

8. Remove the exhaust manifold.

To install:

9. Position exhaust manifold on cylinder head. Install bolts to center runner (cylinder No. 4) and initial tighten to 25 inch lbs. (2.8 Nm).

10. Position heat shield on manifold.

11. Install the remaining manifold attaching bolts. Tighten all bolts to 200 inch lbs. (23 Nm).

12. Install and tighten heat shield attaching nut to 105 inch lbs. (12 Nm).

13. Attach exhaust pipe to exhaust manifold and tighten bolts to 30 ft. lbs. (41 Nm).

14. Connect the left side oxygen sensors.

15. Connect battery negative cable.

Right Side Manifold

1. Disconnect battery negative cable.
2. Separate the exhaust pipe at the exhaust manifold.
3. Remove the air cleaner hose and housing.
4. Disconnect the Throttle Position (TP) sensor, Idle Air Control (IAC) motor, and purge vacuum hose from the throttle body.
5. Disconnect the spark plug wires at the spark plugs.
6. Disconnect the oxygen sensors.
7. Remove bolts attaching exhaust manifold to cylinder head and remove manifold.
8. Inspect and clean manifold.

To install:

9. Position exhaust manifold on cylinder head and install bolts to center runner (cylinder No. 3) and initial tighten to 25 inch lbs. (2.8 Nm).

10. Install the remaining manifold attaching bolts. Tighten all bolts to 200 inch lbs. (23 Nm).

11. Connect the oxygen sensors.

12. Connect the spark plug wires to the spark plugs.

13. Connect the IAC, TPS and the EVAP hose to the throttle body.

14. Attach exhaust pipe to exhaust manifold.

15. Install the air cleaner housing and hose.

16. Connect battery negative cable.

FLEXPLATE

REMOVAL & INSTALLATION

1. Remove the transmission.
2. Remove flexplate attaching bolts.
3. Remove the flexplate

To install:

4. Position flexplate with backing plate on the crankshaft.

5. Apply Mopar® Lock and Seal Adhesive to the flexplate bolts.

6. Install flexplate bolts. Tighten bolts to 60 ft. lbs. (81 Nm).

7. Install the transmission.

FLYWHEEL

REMOVAL & INSTALLATION

1. Remove the transmission.
2. Remove the clutch pressure plate and disc.
3. Remove the flywheel-to-crankshaft bolts and remove the flywheel assembly.

To install:

4. Clean the surfaces of the flywheel and pressure.

5. Install flywheel with new bolts and tighten in a criss-cross pattern. Tighten the bolts to 70 ft. lbs. (95 Nm).

6. Install the clutch disc and pressure plate.

7. Install the transmission.

INTAKE MANIFOLD

REMOVAL & INSTALLATION

Upper

See Figures 39 and 40.

1. Disconnect battery negative cable.

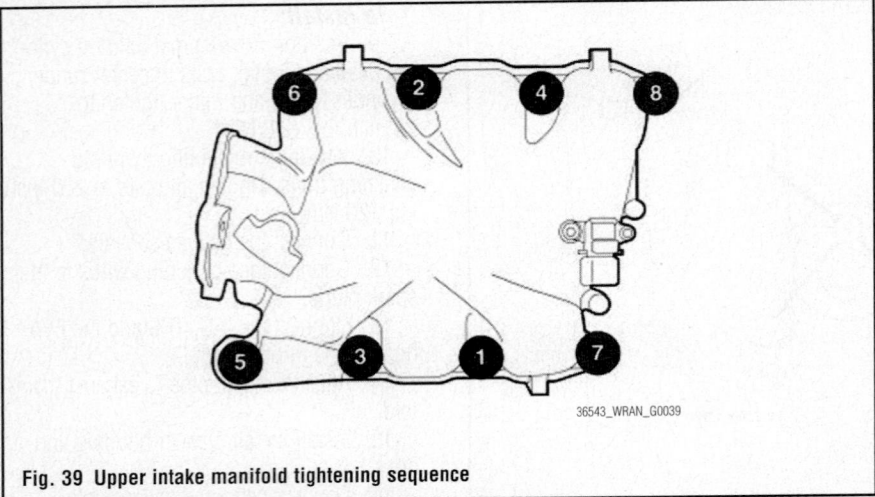

Fig. 39 Upper intake manifold tightening sequence

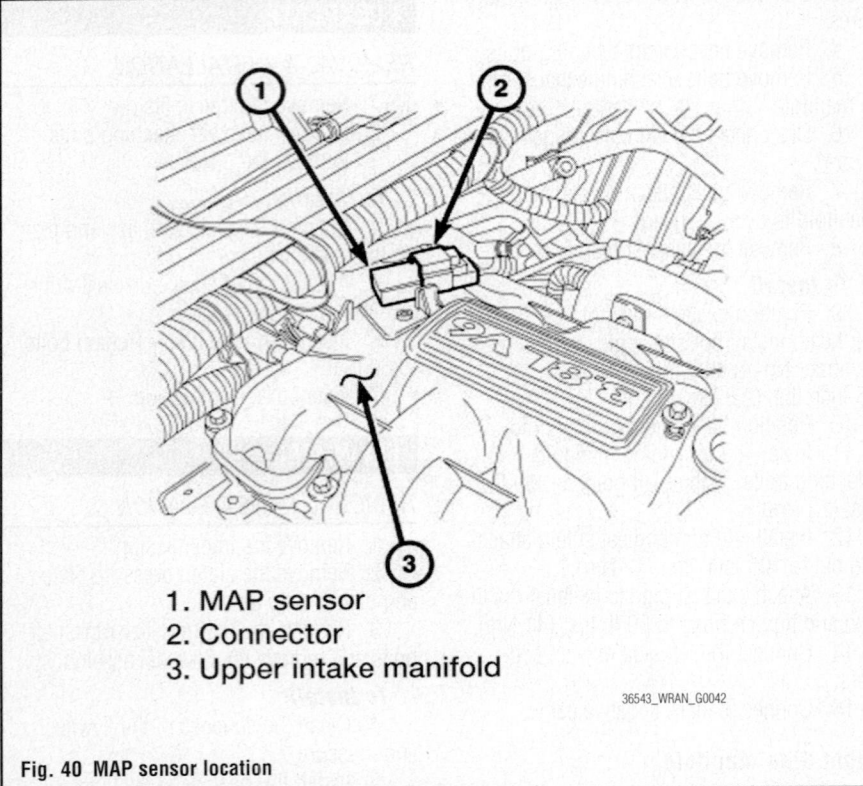

1. MAP sensor
2. Connector
3. Upper intake manifold

Fig. 40 MAP sensor location

Position new gasket in seal channel and press lightly in-place. Repeat procedure for each gasket position.

15. Position upper manifold on lower manifold.

16. Apply Mopar® Lock and Seal Adhesive (Medium Strength Thread locker) to each upper intake manifold bolt.

17. Install and tighten bolts to 105 inch lbs. (12 Nm) using torque sequence.

➡The special screws used for the composite manifold attached components must be installed slowly using hand tools only. This requirement is to prevent the melting of material that causes stripped threads. If threads become stripped, an oversize repair screw is available.

18. Install the MAP sensor, and torque fasteners to 15 inch lbs. (1.7 Nm).

19. Connect the MAP sensor electrical connector.

➡The special screws used for attaching the EGR tube to the manifold must be installed slowly using hand tools only. This requirement is to prevent the melting of material that causes stripped threads. If threads become stripped, an oversize repair screw is available.

20. Install the EGR tube.

21. Connect the throttle (ETC) connector to throttle body.

22. Connect the EVAP hose to the throttle body.

23. Connect the wiring connectors to the TPS and IAC motor.

24. Connect the PCV hose

25. Install air cleaner and air inlet hose assembly.

26. Connect the IAT sensor electrical connector.

27. Connect battery negative cable.

Lower

See Figures 30, 41 through 43.

1. Perform fuel system pressure release procedure.

2. Drain the cooling system.

3. Remove the upper intake manifold.

4. Remove the fuel line.

5. Remove ignition coil and bracket.

6. Disconnect heater supply hose and Engine Coolant Temperature (ECT) sensor.

7. Disconnect the fuel injector wire harness.

8. Remove the fuel injectors and rail assembly.

9. Remove radiator upper hose.

2. Disconnect Inlet Air Temperature (IAT) sensor electrical connector.

3. Remove air inlet resonator to throttle body hose assembly.

4. Disconnect the throttle connectors (ETC) from the throttle body.

5. Disconnect the EVAP hose at the throttle.

6. Remove the EGR tube.

7. Disconnect the Idle Air Control (IAC) motor and Throttle Position sensor (TPS) wiring.

8. Disconnect the manifold absolute pressure (MAP) sensor electrical connector.

9. Disconnect the PCV hose.

10. Remove intake manifold bolts and remove the manifold.

11. Cover the lower intake manifold with a suitable cover while the upper manifold is removed.

12. Clean and inspect the upper intake manifold.

To install:

13. Remove covering on lower intake manifold and clean surfaces.

14. Inspect manifold gasket condition. Gaskets can be re-used, if not damaged.

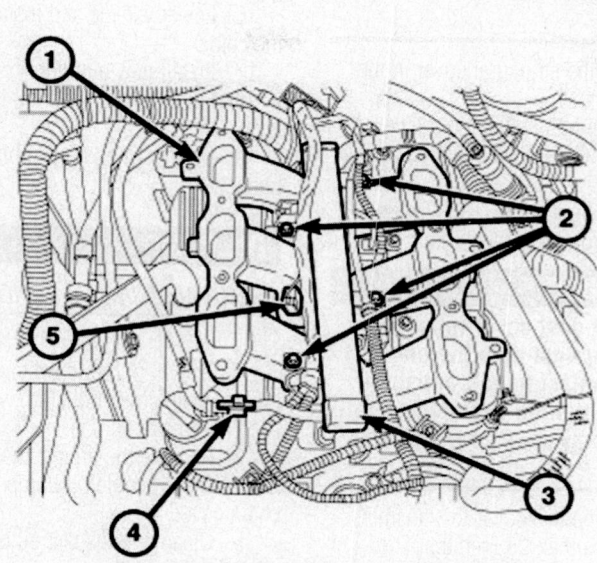

1. Lower intake manifold
2. Fuel rail bolt locations
3. Fuel rail
4. Fuel rail connection
5. Injector connection

36543_WRAN_G0048

Fig. 41 Fuel rail and injector location

10. Remove the intake manifold bolts.
11. Remove lower intake manifold.

⁑ CAUTION

Intake manifold gasket is made of very thin metal and may cause personal injury, handle with care.

12. Remove intake manifold seal retainers screws. Remove intake manifold gasket.

To install:

13. Place a bead (approximately ¼ in. diameter) of Mopar® Engine RTV GEN II onto each of the four manifold to cylinder head gasket corners.

14. Carefully install the new intake manifold gasket. Tighten end seal retainer screws to 105 inch lbs. (12 Nm).

15. Install lower intake manifold. Install the bolts and torque to 10 inch lbs. (1 Nm). Then torque bolts to 17 ft. lbs. (22 Nm) in sequence shown. Then torque again to 17 ft. lbs. (22 Nm). After intake manifold is in place, inspect to make sure seals are in place.

16. Install the fuel injectors and rail assembly.

17. Connect fuel injector electrical harness.

18. Connect the ECT sensor.

19. Connect the heater supply and radiator upper hoses to manifold.

20. Connect the fuel line.

21. Install the upper intake manifold tighten bolts to 105 inch lbs. (12 Nm) using torque sequence.

22. Connect negative battery cable.

23. Fill the cooling system.

24. Connect the negative battery cable.

OIL PAN

REMOVAL & INSTALLATION

See Figures 44 and 45.

1. Disconnect negative cable from battery and remove engine oil level indicator tube.

2. Remove engine oil level indicator tube.

3. Raise vehicle on hoist and drain engine oil, and remove the oil filter.

4. Remove the structural cover fasteners and structural cover.

36543_WRAN_G0050

Fig. 42 Lower intake manifold sealant locations

36543_WRAN_G0049

Fig. 43 Lower intake manifold tightening sequence

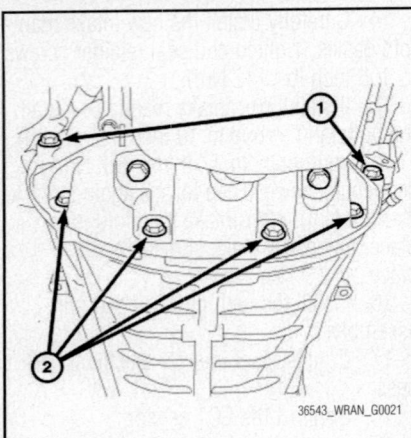

Fig. 44 Transmission and structural cover bolt locations

➡️**Do not remove the lower oil pan bolts. Only remove the upper oil pan-to-engine block bolts.**

5. Remove the oil pan fasteners, oil pan and gasket.

To install:

6. Thoroughly clean sealing surfaces of any oil, dirt, or original sealer, and apply a ⅛ in. bead of Mopar® Engine RTV GEN II at the parting line of the chain case cover and the rear seal retainer.

7. Position a new pan gasket on oil pan.

8. Install oil pan and tighten fasteners to 105 inch lbs. (12 Nm).

9. Install the structural cover and tighten fasteners.

⁂ WARNING

The structural cover must be installed as described in the follow-

---

ing steps. **Failure to do so will cause severe damage to the cover or the oil pan.**

10. Position the structural cover in the vehicle.

11. Install the bolts retaining the cover-to-oil pan. DO NOT tighten the bolts at this time.

12. Install the cover-to-transmission bolts. Do NOT tighten at this time.

⁂ WARNING

The structural dust cover must be held tightly against both the engine and the transmission bell housing during the tightening sequence. Failure to do so may cause damage to the cover.

13. Tighten the two cover-to-transmission bolts to less than 25 inch lbs. The cover must be flush to the transmission bellhousing machined surface.

14. Starting with the cover-to-oil pan bolts, tighten bolts to 40 ft. lbs. (54 Nm).

---

15. Tighten the cover-to-transmission bolts to 40 ft. lbs. (54 Nm).

16. Lower vehicle and install oil level indicator.

17. Install new oil filter.

18. Fill crankcase with oil to proper level.

19. Connect negative cable to battery.

OIL PUMP

REMOVAL & INSTALLATION

See Figure 46.

1. The oil pump is contained within the timing chain cover housing.

2. Remove oil pan.

3. Remove the timing chain cover.

4. Disassemble oil pump from timing chain cover.

5. Clean and Inspect oil pump components.

To install:

6. Install oil pump assembly.

7. Install timing chain cover.

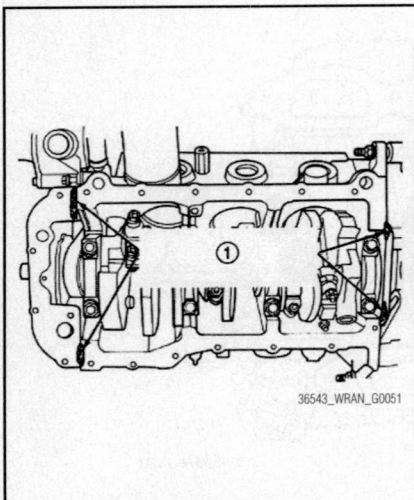

Fig. 45 Sealant locations

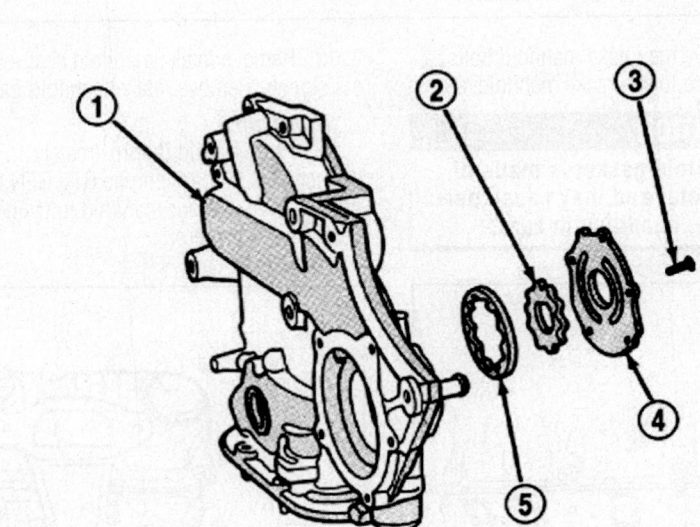

1. Timing chain cover
2. Inner rotor
3. Cover screw
4. Pump cover
5. Outer rotor

Fig. 46 Oil pump exploded view

PISTON AND RING

POSITIONING

See Figure 47.

REAR MAIN SEAL

REMOVAL & INSTALLATION

See Figure 48.

➡Any time the rear crank oil seal has been removed from the engine block, a new seal assembly must be installed. Do not re-use a real crank oil seal assembly once it has been removed.

1. Remove transmission.
2. Remove flex plate or flywheel.
3. Remove oil seal retainer bolts.
4. Remove oil seal retainer.
5. Clean engine block and retainer of oil and gasket material. Make sure surfaces are clean and free of oil.

To install:

➡Before installing a new rear oil seal assembly, ensure that the plastic installation sleeve is present in the seal assembly. The new seal cannot be properly installed without the plastic installation sleeve, and if the seal assembly is installed without it, oil leakage will result.

6. Remove any original sealer, oil, or debris from the rear oil seal retainer assembly mounting area.
7. Place a bead (approximately ¼ in. diameter) of Mopar® Engine RTV GEN II in the lower corners of the rear crankshaft oil seal retainer mounting surface, where the seal retainer meets the oil pan (the T-Joint).
8. Place a bead (approximately ¼ in. diameter) of Mopar® Engine RTV GEN II around the inside edge of the rear crankshaft oil seal retainer assembly recess in the engine block.
9. Place the rear crankshaft oil seal assembly over the rear crankshaft flange. Do not press seal assembly over the rear crankshaft flange at this time.
10. Using both hands, one on each side of the rear crankshaft flange, press the rear crankshaft oil seal over the rear crankshaft flange.
11. Ensure that the extruded dowels in the rear crankshaft oil seal are seated in the locating holes in the rear of the engine block.
12. Install the five rear crankshaft oil seal fasteners. Do not tighten at this time.
13. Remove and discard the plastic installation sleeve.

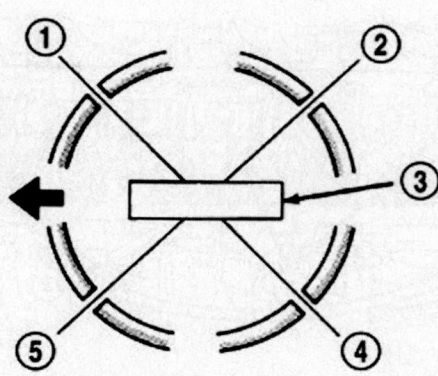

1. Side rail upper
2. No. 1 ring gap
3. Piston pin
4. Side rail lower
5. No. 2 Gap and spacer

36543_WRAN_G0061

Fig. 47 Piston ring positioning

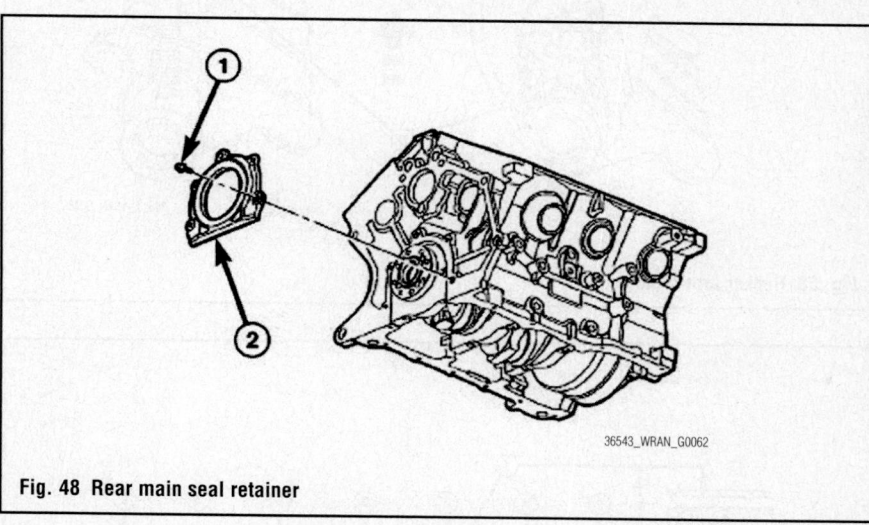

36543_WRAN_G0062

Fig. 48 Rear main seal retainer

14. Tighten the five rear crankshaft oil seal fasteners to 105 inch lbs. (11.8 Nm).
15. Install the flex plate.
16. Install the transmission.

ROCKER ARMS & SHAFTS

REMOVAL & INSTALLATION

See Figures 49 through 51.

1. Remove the cylinder head cover.

➡Rocker arm shaft bolts are captured to the shaft.

2. Loosen the rocker shaft bolts , rotating one turn each, until all valve spring pressure is relieved.

3. Remove the rocker arms and shaft assembly .

✱✱ WARNING

Do not attempt to drive the billeted bolt from the rocker shaft. This can damage the rocker arm retainer and bolt assembly.

4. Remove the rocker arm retainer and bolt by performing the following procedure:

   a. Using adjustable pliers, grip the edges of the retainer.
   b. Apply an upward force with a slight rocking motion until the retainer disengages from shaft.

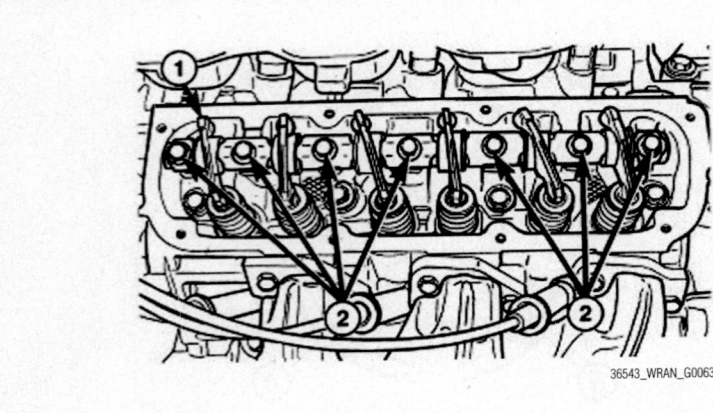

Fig. 49 Rocker shaft bolt locations (2)

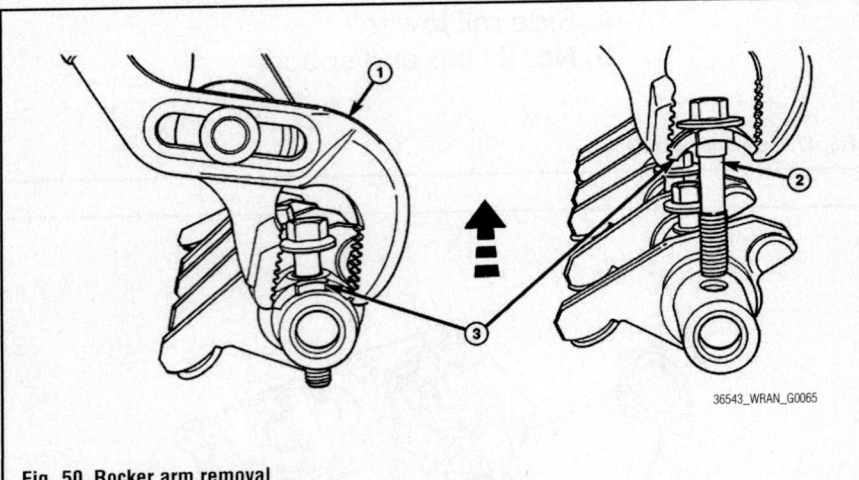

Fig. 50 Rocker arm removal

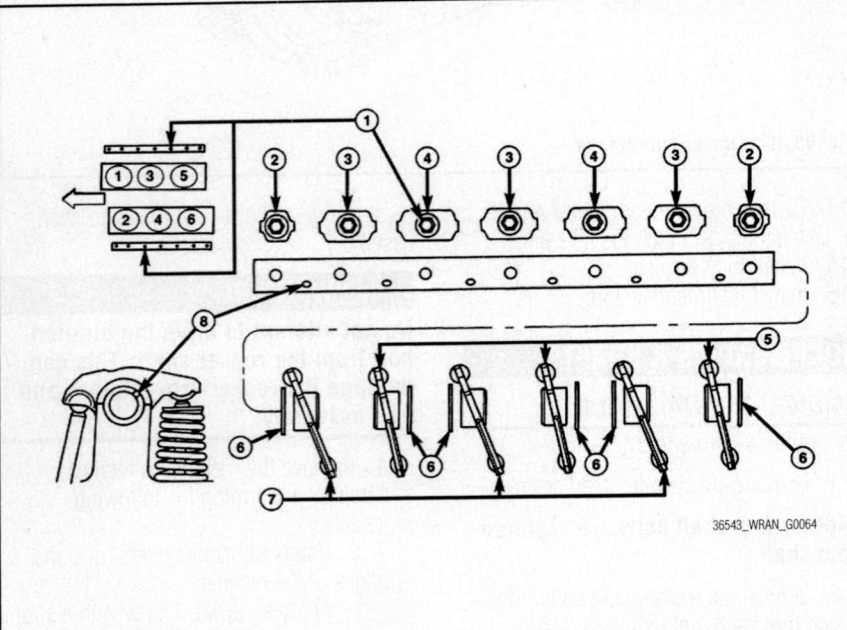

Fig. 51 Rocker arm locations

5. Remove rocker arms . Identify the component locations for reassembly in original locations.

To install:

➡Ensure the longer shaft retaining bolt is installed in the proper location on the rocker shaft Position the rocker arm and shaft assemblies on the pedestal mounts.

➡Ensure all pushrods are properly located on the lifter and the rocker arm socket.

6. Align each rocker arm socket with each pushrod end.

➡The rocker arm shaft should be tightened down slowly, starting with the center bolts. Allow 20 minutes lifter bleed down time after installation of the rocker shafts before engine operation.

7. Slowly tighten rocker shaft bolts evenly until shaft is seated. Tighten bolts to 200 inch lbs. (23 Nm).

8. Install the cylinder head cover.

TIMING CHAIN COVER AND SEAL

REMOVAL & INSTALLATION

See Figures 52 and 53.

1. Perform the fuel pressure relief procedure.
2. Disconnect negative cable from battery.
3. Drain cooling system.
4. Remove the air cleaner hose and housing assembly.
5. Remove the accessory drive belt and belt tensioner.
6. Remove the generator.
7. Remove the oil level indicator tube.
8. Drain engine oil.
9. Remove oil pan.
10. Remove the oil filter.
11. Disconnect the oil pressure switch.
12. Remove power steering pump fasteners and set pump aside.
13. Disconnect the lower radiator hose.
14. Separate the air conditioning compressor from the engine and set aside.
15. Remove crankshaft vibration damper using special tool No. 8454 and insert No. 8450.
16. Remove Camshaft Position (CMP) sensor from timing chain cover.

17. Remove the timing chain cover fasteners and remove timing chain cover.

To install:

➡ **Crankshaft oil seal must be removed to insure correct oil pump engagement.**

18. Be sure mating surfaces of chain case cover and cylinder block are clean and free from burrs.

➡ **Do not use sealer on cover gasket.**

19. Position new gasket on timing cover. Adhere new gasket to chain case cover, making sure that the lower edge of the gasket is 0.020 in. (0.5 mm) beyond the lower edge of the cover.

20. Rotate crankshaft so that the oil pump drive flats are in the vertical position.

21. Position oil pump inner rotor so the mating flats are in the same position as the crankshaft drive flats.

❋❋ WARNING

Make sure the oil pump is engaged on the crankshaft correctly or severe damage may result.

22. Install timing cover.

➡ **Torque the M10 bolts first, then the M8.**

23. Install timing chain cover bolts. Tighten the M10 bolts to 40 ft. lbs. (54 Nm) and M8 bolts to 21 ft. lbs. (28 Nm).

24. Install the oil pan.

25. Install crankshaft front oil seal.

26. Position Special Tool C-4992-2 Guide, or equivalent, on the crankshaft nose.

27. Position a new seal over the guide with the seal spring in the direction of the engine front cover.

28. Install the seal using Special Tool C-4992-1, or equivalent, until the seal is flush with the cover.

29. Install crankshaft vibration damper.

30. Install a new oil filter and connect the oil pressure switch.

31. Connect the coolant hoses.

32. Install Camshaft Position (CMP) sensor.

33. Install A/C compressor.

34. Install the oil level indicator tube.

35. Install the generator.

36. Install the power steering pump.

37. Install the accessory drive belt and idler pulley.

38. Fill crankcase with engine oil to proper level.

39. Install the Air cleaner housing and hose.

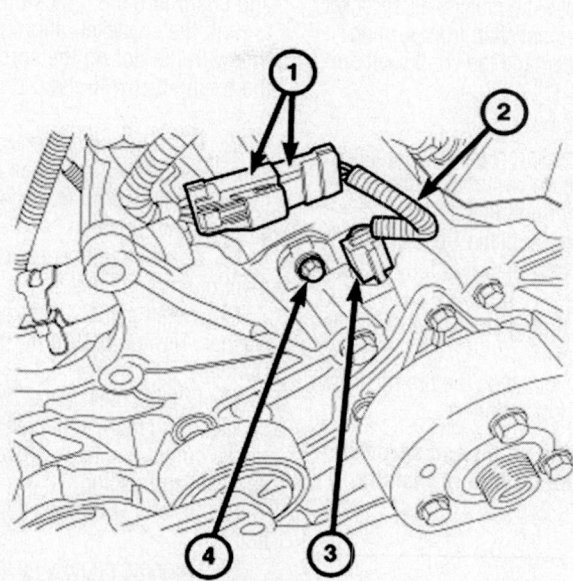

1. Camshaft position sensor
2. Timing chain cover
3. Camshaft position sensor connector
4. Camshaft position sensor retaining bolt

36543_WRAN_G0066

Fig. 52 Camshaft Position (CMP) sensor location

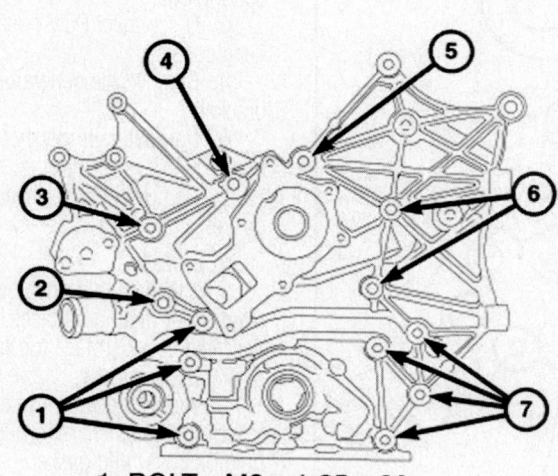

1. BOLT - M8 x 1.25 x 80
2. BOLT - M10 x 1.5 x 85
3. BOLT - M8 x 1.25 x 80
4. BOLT - M10 x 1.5 x 85
5. BOLT - M8 x 1.25 x 80
6. BOLT - M10 x 1.5 x 85
7. BOLT - M8 x 1.25 x 80

36543_WRAN_G0067

Fig. 53 Timing chain cover bolt locations

40. Fill cooling system.
41. Connect negative cable to battery.

TIMING CHAIN AND SPROCKETS

REMOVAL & INSTALLATION

See Figure 54.

1. Disconnect negative cable from battery.
2. Remove the timing chain cover bolt, and timing cover.
3. Rotate engine by turning crankshaft until the timing marks are aligned as shown.
4. Remove camshaft sprocket attaching bolt.
5. Remove the timing chain with camshaft sprocket.

6. Using Special Tools 8539, 5048-6, and 5048-1, remove the crankshaft sprocket while holding the crankshaft from turning. Be careful not to damage the crankshaft surfaces.

To install:

7. Position the sprocket on the crankshaft (timing mark out) with the timing slot aligned with the timing pin.
8. Install sprocket using Special Tool 8452. Install sprocket until it is fully seats on the crankshaft.
9. Install the timing chain and camshaft sprocket.
10. Rotate crankshaft so the timing arrow is to the 12 o'clock position.

➡Lubricate timing chain and sprockets with clean engine oil before installation.

11. While holding camshaft sprocket and chain in hand, place timing chain around the sprocket, aligning the plated link with the dot on the sprocket. Position the timing arrow to the 6 o'clock position.
12. Place timing chain around crankshaft sprocket with the plated link lined up with the dot on the sprocket. Install camshaft sprocket into position.
13. Use a straight edge to check alignment of timing marks.
14. Install camshaft sprocket bolt and washer. Tighten bolt to 40 ft. lbs. (54 Nm).
15. Rotate crankshaft 2 revolutions and check timing mark alignment. If timing marks do not line up, remove camshaft sprocket and realign.
16. Install the timing chain cover, and bolts.
17. Connect negative cable to battery.

VALVE COVERS

REMOVAL & INSTALLATION

Left Side

See Figure 55.

1. Remove the ignition coil pack.
2. Disconnect spark plug wires from spark plugs.
3. Disconnect PCV hose from cylinder head cover.
4. Remove the generator support bracket.
5. Remove cylinder head cover bolts.
6. Remove cylinder head cover and gasket.

To install:

7. Clean cylinder head and cylinder head cover mating surfaces. Inspect cylinder head cover surface for flatness. Replace gasket as necessary.
8. Assemble gasket to cylinder cover by inserting the fasteners through each bolt hole on cover and gasket.
9. Install the cylinder head cover and bolts.
10. Tighten cylinder head cover bolts to 105 inch lbs. (12 Nm).
11. Connect PCV hose.
12. Install the ignition coil pack and plug wires.
13. Install the generator support bracket.
14. Connect spark plug wires to spark plugs.

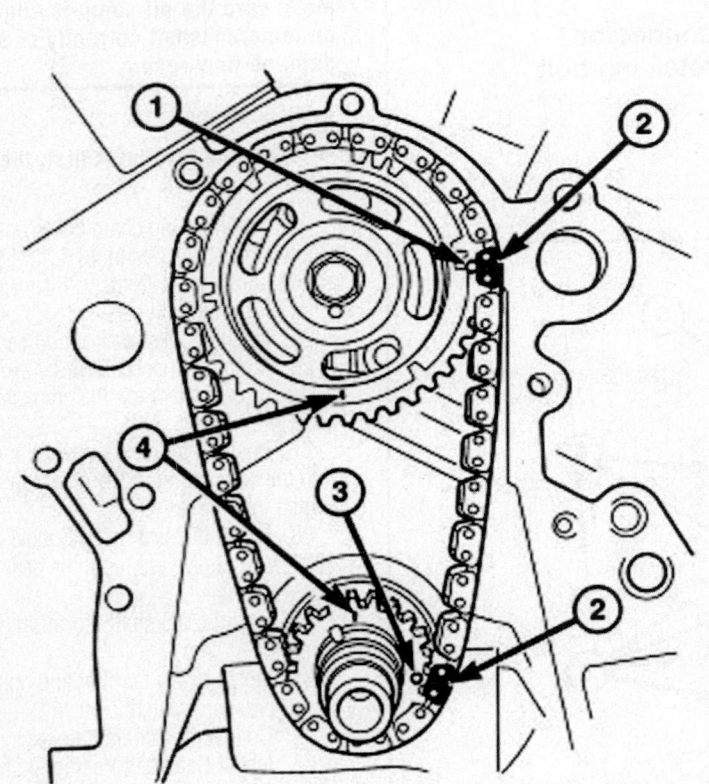

1. Camshaft mark 3. Crankshaft mark
2. Plated links   4. Timing arrows

36543_WRAN_G0068

Fig. 54 Timing chain alignment

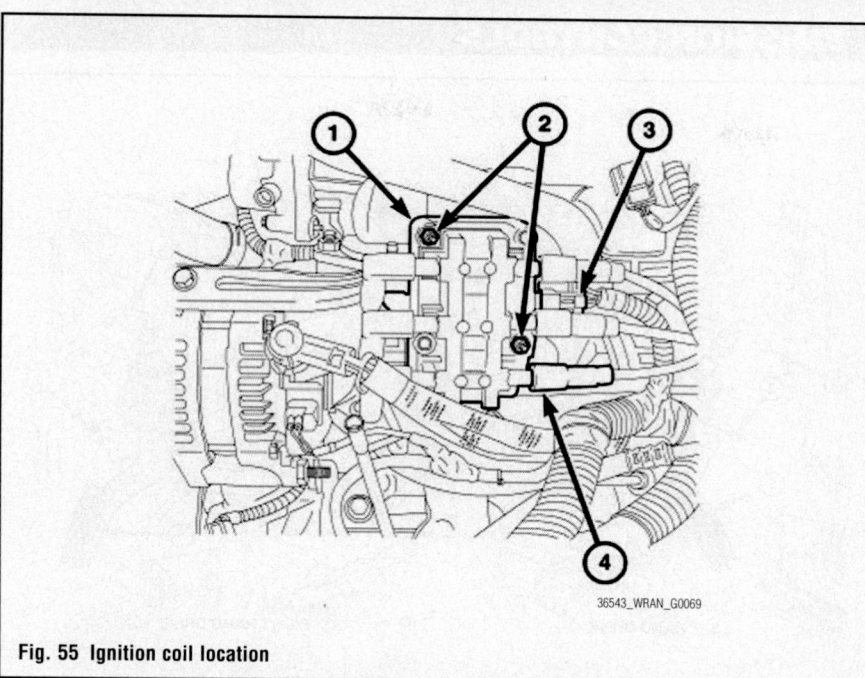

Fig. 55 Ignition coil location

7. Inspect seal on the cover bolt for wear or damage. Replace bolt assembly as necessary.

8. Inspect the PCV hose for damage. replace as necessary.

➡️**The cylinder head cover bolts contain a torque limiter sleeve and a seal. The seal and torque sleeve is replaced with the bolt.**

9. Assemble gasket to cylinder cover by inserting the bolt assemblies through each bolt hole on the cover and gasket.

10. Install cylinder head cover and bolts.

11. Tighten cylinder head cover bolts to 105 inch lbs. (12 Nm).

12. Connect CCV hose to cylinder head cover.

13. Connect spark plug wires to spark plugs.

14. Connect negative cable to battery.

Right Side

See Figure 56.

1. Disconnect negative cable from battery.

2. Disconnect spark plug wires from plugs.

3. Disconnect CCV hose from cylinder head cover.

4. Remove cylinder head cover bolts.

5. Remove cylinder head cover and gasket.

To install:

6. Clean cylinder head and cylinder head cover mating surfaces. Inspect cylinder head cover surface for flatness. Replace gasket as necessary.

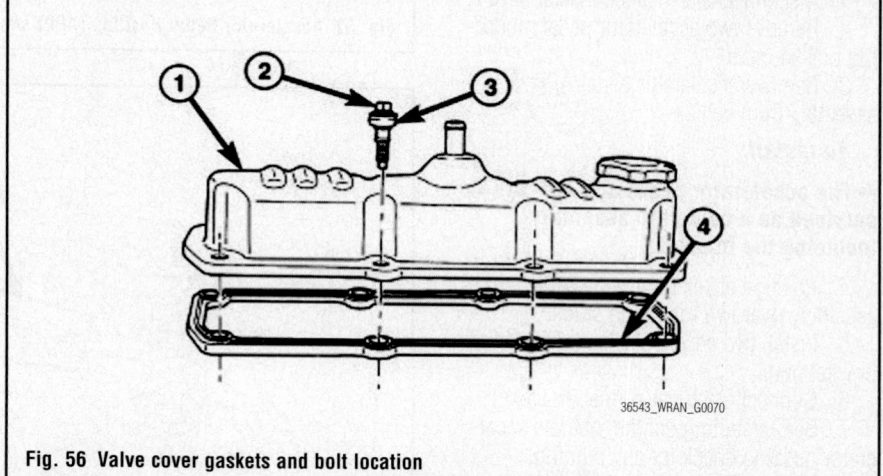

Fig. 56 Valve cover gaskets and bolt location

ENGINE PERFORMANCE & EMISSION CONTROLS

ACCELERATOR PEDAL POSITION (APP) SENSOR

LOCATION

See Figure 57.

Refer to the accompanying illustration for sensor location.

REMOVAL & INSTALLATION

See Figure 57.

➡ Replacement of the Accelerator Pedal Position (APP) sensor requires an Electronic Throttle Control (ETC) relearn procedure to be performed after the APP sensor replacement. A proprietary scan tool is required to perform this procedure.

➡ The accelerator pedal and APP are serviced as a complete assembly including the bracket.

1. Disconnect electrical connector at APP.
2. Remove two accelerator pedal mounting bracket nuts.
3. Remove accelerator pedal/APP assembly from vehicle.

To install:

➡ The accelerator pedal and APP are serviced as a complete assembly including the bracket.

4. Position accelerator pedal/APP assembly over two mounting studs.
5. Install two accelerator pedal mounting bracket nuts.
6. Connect electrical connector at APP.
7. Before starting engine, operate accelerator pedal to check for any binding.

CAMSHAFT POSITION (CMP) SENSOR

LOCATION

See Figure 58.

The Camshaft Position (CMP) sensor is bolted to front of engine. The CMP uses a pigtail wiring harness. This connects the sensor to the engine harness.

REMOVAL & INSTALLATION

See Figure 52.

1. Disconnect negative battery cable.
2. Disconnect electrical connectors.
3. Remove sensor mounting bolt.
4. An O-ring is used to seal the sensor to engine. Remove sensor from engine by pulling while rotating.

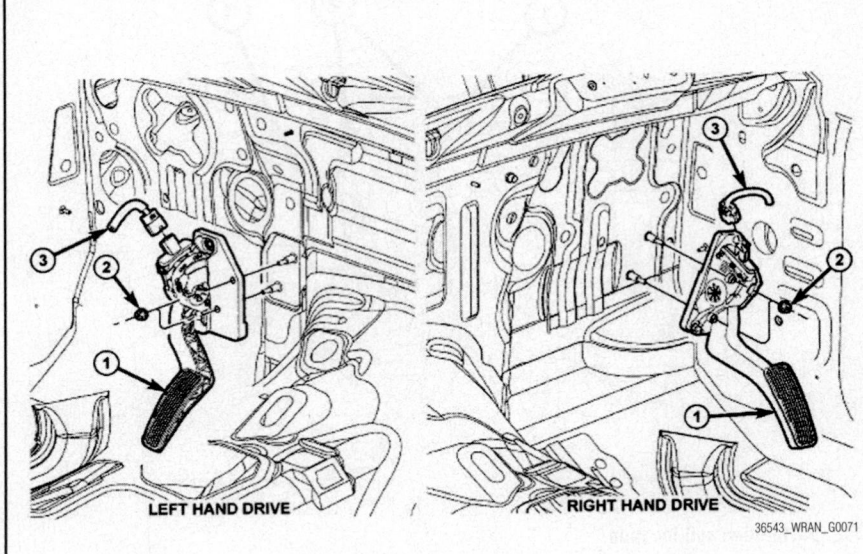

LEFT HAND DRIVE RIGHT HAND DRIVE

36543_WRAN_G0071

Fig. 57 Accelerator Pedal Position (APP) sensor location

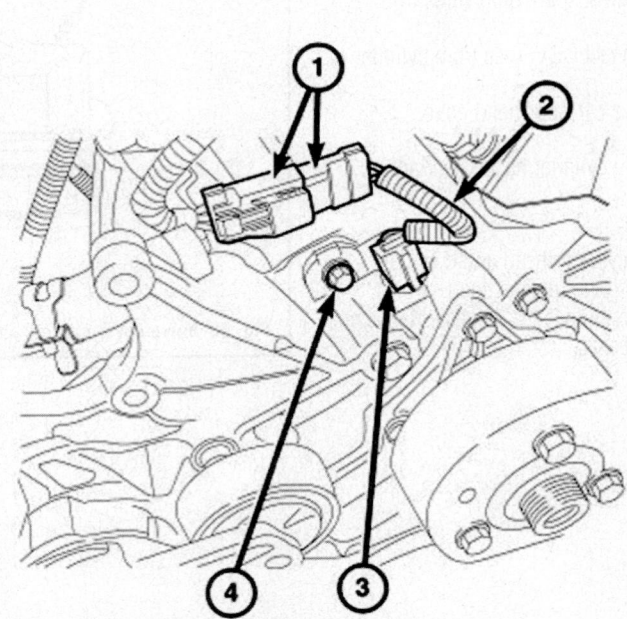

1. Camshaft position sensor
2. Timing chain cover
3. Camshaft position sensor connector
4. Camshaft position sensor retaining bolt

36543_WRAN_G0066

Fig. 58 Camshaft Position (CMP) sensor location

To install:

➡ **If the removed sensor is reinstalled, clean off old spacer on sensor face. A new spacer must be attached to face before installation.**

5. Inspect O-ring for damage, replace if necessary.

➡ **If sensor is being replaced, confirm that paper spacer is attached to face, and O-ring is positioned in groove of new sensor.**

6. Apply a couple drops of clean engine oil to the O-ring prior to installation.

7. Install sensor into engine and rotate into position.

8. Push sensor down until contact is made with camshaft gear. While holding sensor in this position, install and tighten mounting bolt to 125 inch lbs. (14 Nm).

9. Connect sensor pigtail connector to engine harness connector.

10. Connect negative battery cable.

CRANKSHAFT POSITION (CKP) SENSOR

LOCATION

See Figure 59.

The Crankshaft Position (CKP) sensor is mounted into the right side of the transmission bellhousing. It is positioned and bolted into a machined hole.

REMOVAL & INSTALLATION

See Figure 34.

1. Raise vehicle.
2. Disconnect CKP sensor electrical connector.
3. Remove sensor mounting bolt.
4. Carefully twist CKP sensor from cylinder block.
5. Check condition of sensor O-ring.

To install:

6. Clean out machined hole in transmission bellhousing.

7. Apply a small amount of engine oil to sensor O-ring.

8. Install sensor into transmission with a slight rocking and twisting action.

➡ **Before tightening sensor mounting bolt, be sure sensor is completely flush to transmission bellhousing. If sensor is not flush, damage to sensor mounting tang may result.**

9. Install mounting bolt and tighten to 21 ft. lbs. (28 Nm).

10. Connect electrical connector to sensor.

11. Lower vehicle.

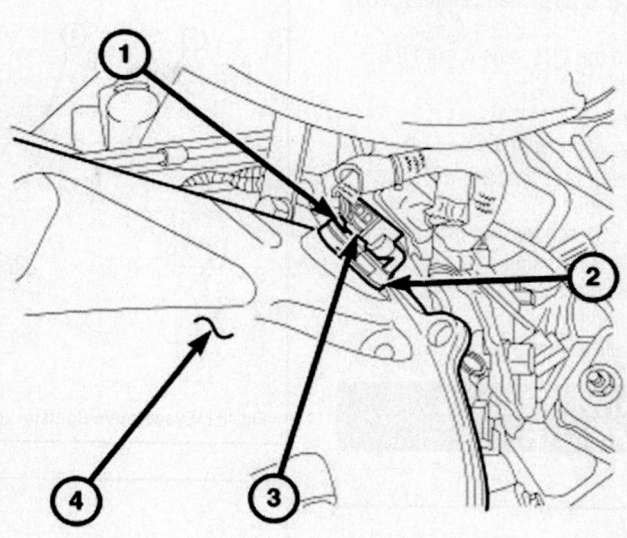

1. Crankshaft position sensor location
2. Crankshaft position sensor
3. Crankshaft position sensor connector
4. Transmission

36543_WRAN_G0043

Fig. 59 Crankshaft Position (CKP) sensor location

ENGINE COOLANT TEMPERATURE (ECT) SENSOR

LOCATION

See Figure 60.

Refer to the accompanying illustration for sensor location.

REMOVAL & INSTALLATION

See Figure 60.

✳✳ WARNING

Hot, pressurized coolant can cause injury by scalding. Cooling system must be partially drained before removing the coolant temperature sensor.

1. Remove air cleaner assembly.
2. Partially drain the cooling system.

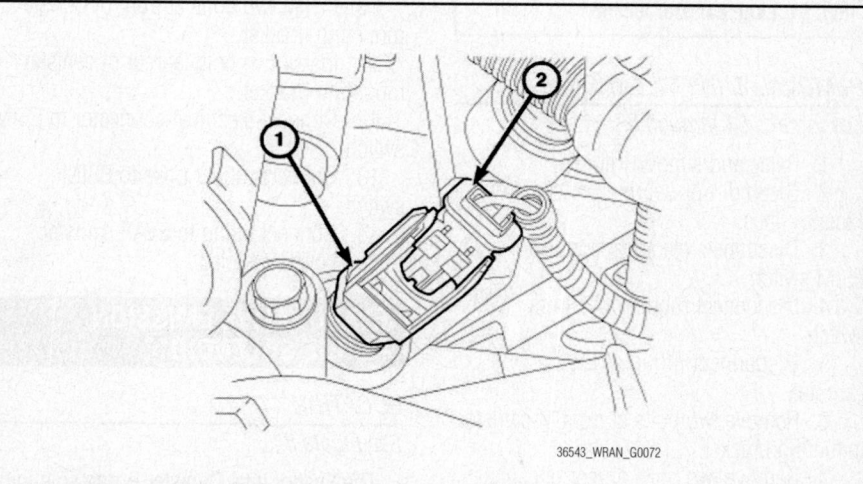

36543_WRAN_G0072

Fig. 60 Engine Coolant Temperature (ECT) sensor location

3. Disconnect the electrical connector from the Engine Coolant Temperature (ECT) sensor.

4. Remove the ECT sensor from the intake manifold.

To install:

5. Apply sealant to ECT sensor threads (new replacement ECT sensors will have sealant already applied).

6. Install ECT sensor into intake manifold. Tighten to 8 ft. lbs. (11 Nm).

7. Connect electrical connector.

8. Fill cooling system.

9. Install air cleaner housing.

EVAPORATIVE EMISSION (EVAP) CANISTER

LOCATION

See Figure 61.

The Evaporative Emission (EVAP) canister is located under the vehicle next to the rear prop shaft. The Evaporative Systems Integrity Monitor (ESIM) switch is attached to the EVAP canister.

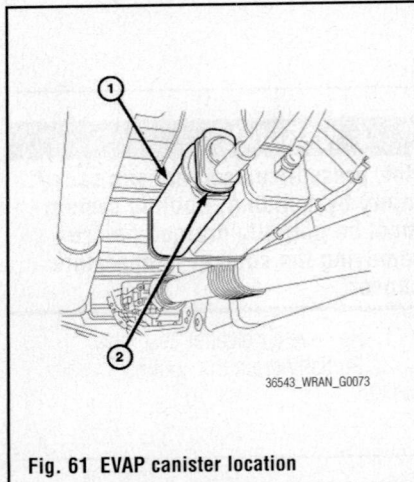

Fig. 61 EVAP canister location

REMOVAL & INSTALLATION

See Figures 61 through 63.

1. Raise and support vehicle.

2. Clean dirt or debris from canister vacuum lines.

3. Disconnect electrical connector at ESIM switch.

4. Disconnect rubber hose from ESIM switch.

5. Disconnect fitting at EVAP canister.

6. Remove two bolts at front of canister mounting bracket.

7. Remove two bolts at rear of canister mounting bracket.

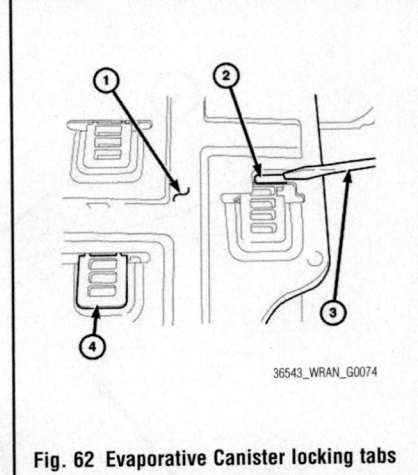

Fig. 62 Evaporative Canister locking tabs

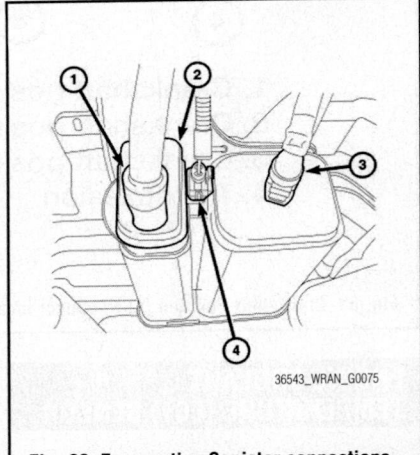

Fig. 63 Evaporative Canister connections

8. To separate EVAP canister from mounting bracket, pry on lock-tab.

To install:

9. Attach canister to mounting bracket. Lock canister to mounting bracket by using lock tab.

10. Install two bolts at front of canister mounting bracket.

11. Install two bolts at rear of canister mounting bracket.

12. Connect electrical connector to ESIM switch.

13. Connect rubber hose to ESIM switch.

14. Connect fitting to EVAP canister.

15. Lower vehicle.

EVAPORATIVE EMISSION PURGE SOLENOID

LOCATION

See Figure 64.

The Evaporative Canister Purge solenoid is located near the battery.

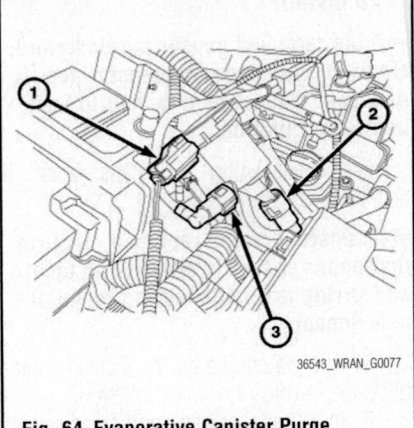

Fig. 64 Evaporative Canister Purge solenoid

REMOVAL & INSTALLATION

See Figure 64.

1. Lift the solenoid assembly from the tongue-type bracket.

2. Disconnect electrical connector.

3. Disconnect quick-connect fittings and from solenoid.

To install:

4. Connect quick-connect fittings and to solenoid.

5. Connect electrical connector.

6. Push solenoid assembly onto the tongue-type bracket.

EXHAUST GAS RECIRCULATION (EGR) VALVE

LOCATION

See Figure 65.

The EGR valve and solenoid assembly is attached to the rear of the right cylinder head.

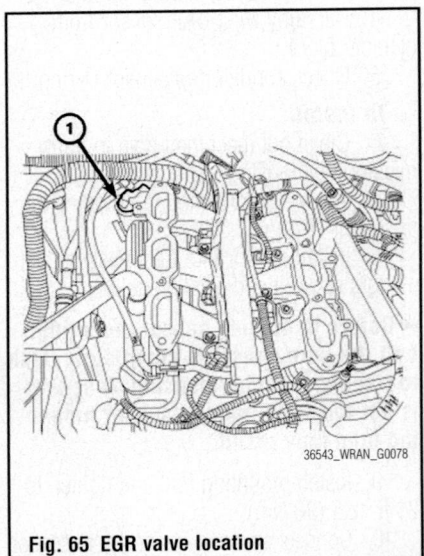

Fig. 65 EGR valve location

REMOVAL & INSTALLATION

See Figures 65 and 66.

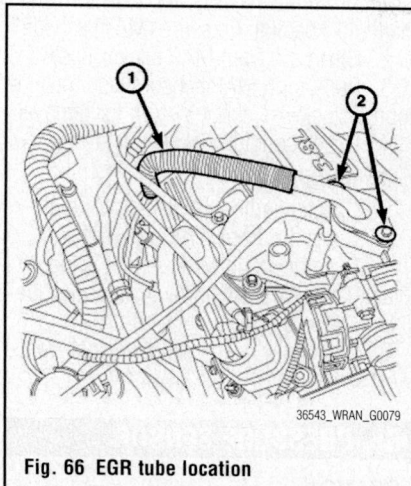

Fig. 66 EGR tube location

1. Use a diagnostic scan tool to record any DTC's (Diagnostic Trouble Codes).
2. Disconnect and isolate the negative battery cable.

➡**A metal gasket is used between the EGR valve/solenoid assembly, and the right cylinder head.**

➡**A metal tube connects the EGR valve/solenoid assembly to the intake manifold.**

3. Remove the upper (plastic) half of the intake manifold.
4. Disconnect electrical connector at EGR valve.
5. Remove tube mounting bolt.
6. Remove two tube mounting bolts at EGR valve end of tube.
7. Remove and discard gasket and O-ring.
8. Remove two EGR valve mounting bolts.
9. Discard gasket.

To install:

10. Clean gasket mounting area at rear of cylinder head and EGR valve.
11. Install new gasket.
12. Position EGR valve to rear of cylinder head and install two EGR valve mounting bolts.
13. Clean gasket mounting areas at both ends of EGR tube.
14. Install new gasket and new O-ring to EGR tube.
15. Install two tube mounting bolts at EGR valve end of tube.
16. Install tube mounting bolt.
17. Connect electrical connector to EGR valve.

18. Install the upper (plastic) half of the intake manifold.
19. Install two tube flange bolts at intake manifold.
20. Connect negative battery cable.
21. Using a diagnostic scan tool, erase any previously recorded DTC's

HEATED OXYGEN (HO2S) SENSOR

LOCATION

See Figures 67 and 68.

1. Refer to the accompanying illustrations for sensor location.

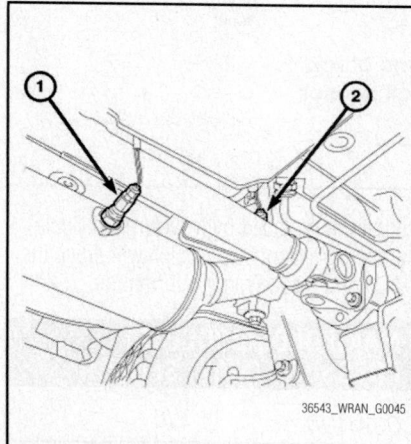

Fig. 67 Left side Oxygen sensor location

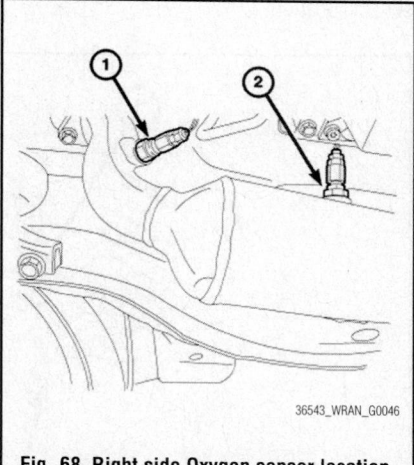

Fig. 68 Right side Oxygen sensor location

REMOVAL & INSTALLATION

See Figures 36 and 37.

✳✳ CAUTION

Never apply any type of grease to the oxygen sensor electrical connector, or attempt any soldering of the sensor wiring harness.

➡**Sensor (1) is referred to as the 1/1 sensor. Sensor (2) is referred to as the 1/2 Sensor.**

1. Raise and support vehicle.
2. Disconnect wire connector from Heated Oxygen (HO2S) sensor.

✳✳ CAUTION

When disconnecting the sensor electrical connector, do not pull directly on the wire going into the sensor.

3. Remove HO2S sensor with an oxygen sensor removal and installation tool.
4. Clean threads in exhaust pipe using appropriate size tap.

To install:

5. The threads of new oxygen sensors are factory coated with anti-seize compound to aid in removal. DO NOT add any additional anti-seize compound to threads of a new oxygen sensor.
6. Install HO2S sensor. Tighten to 30 ft. lbs. (41 Nm).
7. Connect HO2S sensor wire connector.
8. Lower vehicle.

INTAKE AIR TEMPERATURE (IAT) SENSOR

LOCATION

The 2-wire Intake Manifold Air Temperature (IAT) sensor is installed in the rubber air intake tube near the throttle body with the sensor element extending into the air stream.

REMOVAL & INSTALLATION

1. Disconnect electrical connector from Intake Air Temperature (IAT) sensor.
2. Clean dirt from intake manifold at IAT sensor base.
3. Gently lift on small plastic release tab and rotate sensor about ¼ turn counterclockwise for removal.
4. Check condition of sensor O-ring.

To install:

5. Check condition of sensor O-ring.
6. Clean sensor mounting hole in intake manifold.
7. Position sensor into intake manifold and rotate clockwise until past release tab.
8. Install electrical connector.

KNOCK SENSOR (KS)

LOCATION

See Figure 69.

Refer to the accompanying illustration for sensor location.

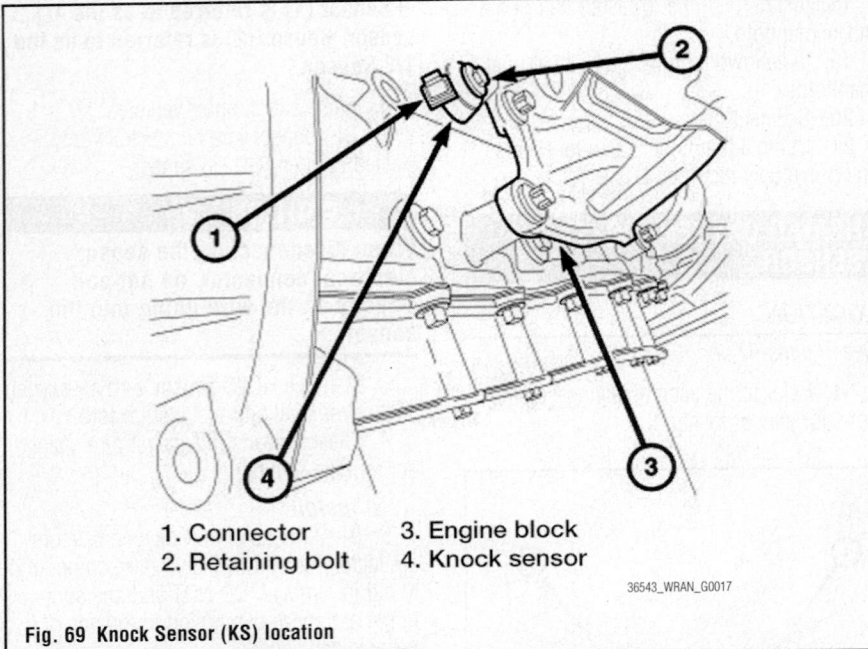

1. Connector
2. Retaining bolt
3. Engine block
4. Knock sensor

36543_WRAN_G0017

Fig. 69 Knock Sensor (KS) location

REMOVAL & INSTALLATION

See Figure 69.

➡**Only one Knock Sensor (KS) is used. It is located on the right side of engine block, to the rear of right engine mount.**

1. Disconnect negative battery cable.
2. Raise vehicle and support.
3. Disconnect electrical connector from KS.
4. Remove mounting bolt.
5. Remove sensor from engine.

To install:

6. Thoroughly clean KS mounting hole.
7. Position sensor to engine.

➡**Over or under tightening the sensor mounting bolts will affect knock sensor performance, possibly causing improper spark control. Always use the specified torque when installing the knock sensors. The torque for the KS bolt is relatively light for an 8 mm bolt.**

8. Install and tighten mounting bolt and tighten to 176 inch lbs. (20 Nm).
9. Attach electrical connector to knock sensor.
10. Lower vehicle.
11. Connect negative cable.

MALFUNCTION INDICATOR LIGHT (MIL)

RESET PROCEDURES

After 3 consecutive "Good Trips", the MIL is extinguished and the good trip counter is replaced by a "Warm Up Cycle" counter. 40 Warm-Up Cycles will erase the DTC and Freeze Frame information.

MANIFOLD ABSOLUTE PRESSURE (MAP) SENSOR

LOCATION

See Figure 70.

Refer to the accompanying illustration for sensor location.

REMOVAL & INSTALLATION

See Figure 33.

1. Disconnect electrical connector from Manifold Absolute Pressure (MAP) sensor.
2. Clean dirt from MAP sensor base.
3. Pull up on MAP sensor while rotating counterclockwise about ¼ turn for removal.
4. Check condition of sensor O-ring.

To install:

5. Check condition of sensor O-ring.
6. Clean dirt from MAP sensor base.
7. Push down on MAP sensor while rotating clockwise about ¼ turn for installation.
8. Disconnect electrical connector from MAP sensor.

OIL PRESSURE SENSOR

LOCATION

See Figure 71.

Refer to the accompanying illustration for sensor location.

REMOVAL & INSTALLATION

See Figure 71.

1. Raise vehicle on hoist.
2. Disconnect electrical connector from switch.
3. Remove oil pressure switch.

To install:

4. Install oil pressure switch and tighten to 200 inch lbs. (23 Nm).

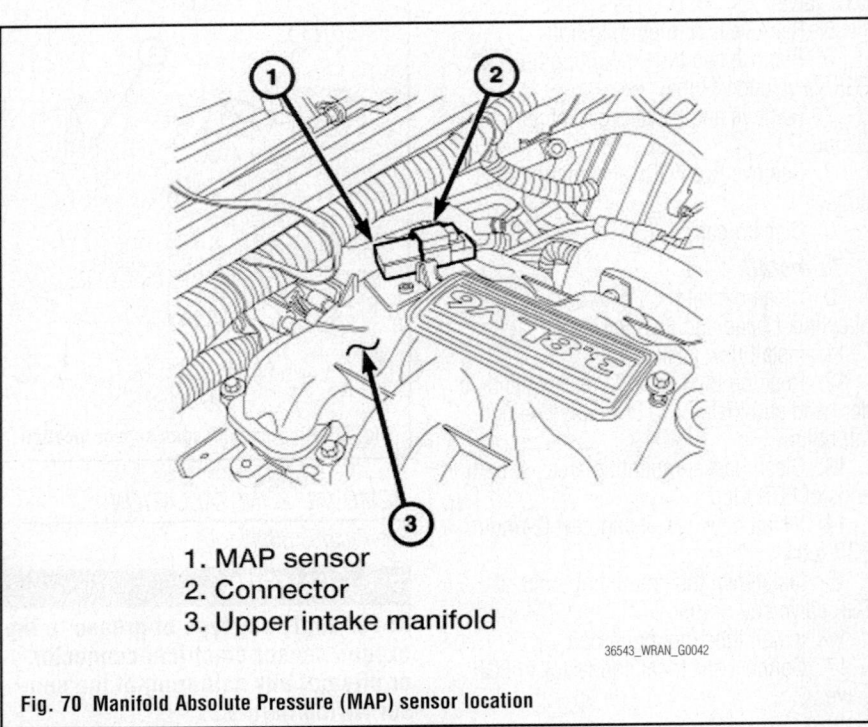

1. MAP sensor
2. Connector
3. Upper intake manifold

36543_WRAN_G0042

Fig. 70 Manifold Absolute Pressure (MAP) sensor location

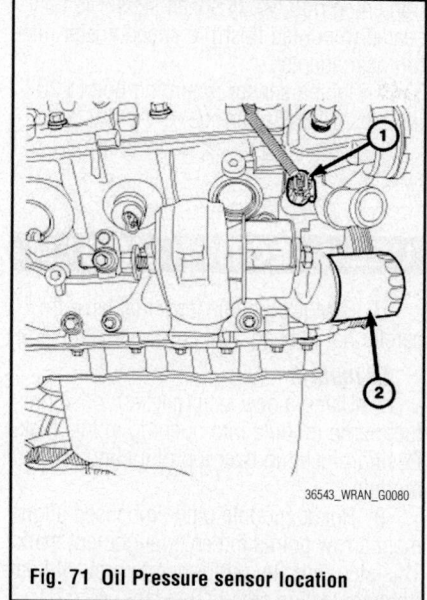

Fig. 71 Oil Pressure sensor location

36543_WRAN_G0080

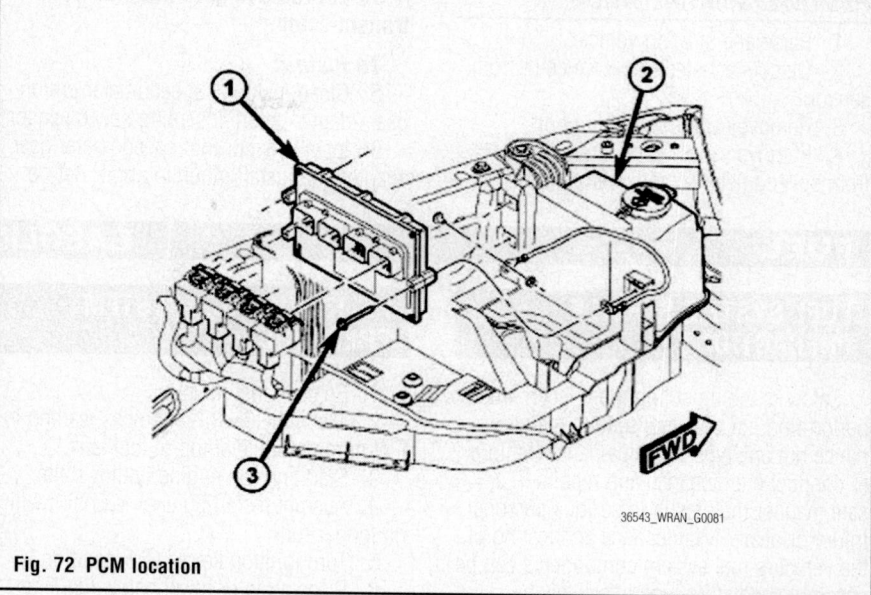

Fig. 72 PCM location

36543_WRAN_G0081

5. Connect electrical connector to switch.

6. Lower the vehicle.

7. Start engine and check for leaks.

8. Check engine oil level. Adjust as necessary.

POSITIVE CRANKCASE VENTILATION (PCV) VALVE

LOCATION

The PCV valve is located in the left valve cover near the ignition coil.

REMOVAL & INSTALLATION

1. Remove clamp.

2. Disconnect hose, then remove the PCV valve.

To install:

3. Clean the mounting hold in the valve cover.

4. Install the PCV valve into the valve cover.

5. Install the hose and clamp.

POWERTRAIN CONTROL MODULE (PCM)

LOCATION

See Figure 72.

Refer to the accompanying illustration for PCM location.

REMOVAL & INSTALLATION

See Figure 72.

1. Disconnect negative battery cable at battery.

2. Remove plastic shields from over four electrical connectors. Shields snap to connectors.

3. Carefully unplug four electrical connectors from PCM.

4. Remove three PCM mounting bolts or and remove PCM from vehicle.

To install:

5. Install PCM and three mounting screws to vehicle and tighten screws to 35 inch lbs. (4 Nm).

6. Check pin connectors in PCM and four electrical connectors for corrosion or damage. Also check pin heights in connectors. Pin heights should all be the same. Repair as necessary before installing electrical connectors.

7. Install four electrical connectors to PCM.

8. Install plastic shield to electrical connectors. Shields snap to connectors.

9. Install battery cable.

10. Use a scan tool to reprogram new PCM with vehicles original Vehicle Identification Number (VIN) and original vehicle mileage.

RESET PROCEDURE

→**Use the scan tool to reprogram the new powertrain control module (PCM) with the vehicles original identification number (VIN) and the vehicles original mileage. If this step is not done, a diagnostic trouble code (DTC) may be set. To avoid possible voltage spike damage to the PCM, ignition key must be off, and negative battery cable must be disconnected before unplugging PCM connectors.**

THROTTLE POSITION SENSOR (TPS)

LOCATION

The 3-wire Throttle Position sensor (TPS) is mounted on the throttle body and is connected to the throttle blade.

REMOVAL & INSTALLATION

1. Disconnect Throttle Position sensor (TPS) electrical connector.

2. Remove 2 TPS mounting screws.

3. Remove TPS.

To install:

→**The throttle shaft end of the throttle body slides into a socket in the TPS. The TPS must be installed so that it can be rotated a few degrees. (If sensor will not rotate, install sensor with throttle shaft on other side of socket tangs). The TPS will be under slight tension when rotated.**

4. Install TPS and retaining screws and tighten to 60 inch lbs. (7 Nm).

5. Connect TPS electrical connector to TPS.

6. Manually operate throttle (by hand) to check for any TPS binding before starting engine.

7. Install air cleaner tube to throttle body.

VEHICLE SPEED SENSOR (VSS)

LOCATION

Refer to the accompanying illustration for VSS location.

REMOVAL & INSTALLATION

1. Raise and support vehicle.
2. Disconnect electrical connector from sensor.
3. Remove sensor mounting bolt.
4. Remove sensor (pull straight out) from speedometer pinion gear adapter.

➡**Do not remove gear adapter from transmission.**

To install:

5. Clean inside of speedometer pinion gear adapter before installing speed sensor.
6. Install sensor into speedometer gear adapter and install mounting bolt. Before tightening bolt, verify speed sensor is fully seated (mounted flush) to speedometer pinion gear adapter.
7. Tighten sensor mounting bolt to 20 inch lbs. (2.2 Nm) torque.
8. Connect electrical connector to sensor.

FUEL   GASOLINE FUEL INJECTION SYSTEM

FUEL SYSTEM SERVICE PRECAUTIONS

Safety is the most important factor when performing not only fuel system maintenance but any type of maintenance. Failure to conduct maintenance and repairs in a safe manner may result in serious personal injury or death. Maintenance and testing of the vehicle's fuel system components can be accomplished safely and effectively by adhering to the following rules and guidelines.

• To avoid the possibility of fire and personal injury, always disconnect the negative battery cable unless the repair or test procedure requires that battery voltage be applied.

• Always relieve the fuel system pressure prior to disconnecting any fuel system component (injector, fuel rail, pressure regulator, etc.), fitting or fuel line connection. Exercise extreme caution whenever relieving fuel system pressure to avoid exposing skin, face and eyes to fuel spray. Please be advised that fuel under pressure may penetrate the skin or any part of the body that it contacts.

• Always place a shop towel or cloth around the fitting or connection prior to loosening to absorb any excess fuel due to spillage. Ensure that all fuel spillage (should it occur) is quickly removed from engine surfaces. Ensure that all fuel soaked cloths or towels are deposited into a suitable waste container.

• Always keep a dry chemical (Class B) fire extinguisher near the work area.

• Do not allow fuel spray or fuel vapors to come into contact with a spark or open flame.

• Always use a back-up wrench when loosening and tightening fuel line connection fittings. This will prevent unnecessary stress and torsion to fuel line piping.

• Always replace worn fuel fitting O-rings with new. Do not substitute fuel hose or equivalent where fuel pipe is installed.

Before servicing the vehicle, make sure to also refer to the precautions in the beginning of this section as well.

RELIEVING FUEL SYSTEM PRESSURE

1. Remove fuel fill cap.
2. Disconnect wiring harness leading to fuel pump module at top of fuel tank.
3. Start and run engine until it stalls.
4. Attempt restarting engine until it will no longer run.
5. Turn ignition key to OFF position.
6. Place a rag or towel below fuel line quick-connect fitting at fuel rail.
7. Disconnect quick-connect fitting at fuel rail.
8. After performing service procedure, reconnect fuel pump module.
9. One or more Diagnostic Trouble Codes (DTC's) may have been stored in PCM memory due to the disconnection of fuel pump module. A diagnostic scan tool must be used to erase a DTC.

FUEL FILTER

REMOVAL & INSTALLATION

Two fuel filters are used. One is located at the bottom of the fuel pump module. The other is located inside the module. Both fuel filters are designed for extended service. They do not require normal scheduled maintenance. Filters should only be replaced if a diagnostic procedure indicates to do so.

FUEL PUMP MODULE

REMOVAL & INSTALLATION

1. Drain and remove fuel tank.

➡**Note rotational position of module before attempting removal. An indexing arrow is located on top of module for this purpose.**

2. Position Lockring Remover/Installer 9340 into notches on outside edge of lockring.
3. Install ½ inch drive breaker bar.
4. Rotate breaker bar counter-clockwise to remove lockring.
5. Remove lockring. The module will spring up slightly when lockring is removed.

6. Remove module from fuel tank. Be careful not to bend float arm while removing.

To install:

7. Using a new seal (gasket), position fuel pump module into opening in fuel tank. Position lockring over top of fuel pump module.
8. Rotate module until embossed alignment arrow points to center alignment mark. This step must be performed to prevent float from contacting side of fuel tank. Also be sure fuel fitting on top of pump module is pointed to front of vehicle.
9. Install Lockring Remover/Installer 9340 to lockring.
10. Install 1/2 inch drive breaker into Lockring Remover/Installer 9340.
11. Tighten lockring (clockwise) until all seven notches have engaged.
12. Install fuel tank.

FUEL PRESSURE REGULATOR

REMOVAL & INSTALLATION

The fuel pressure regulator is located within the fuel pump module. It is serviced by replacing the fuel pump module assembly.

FUEL TANK

REMOVAL & INSTALLATION

See Figure 73.

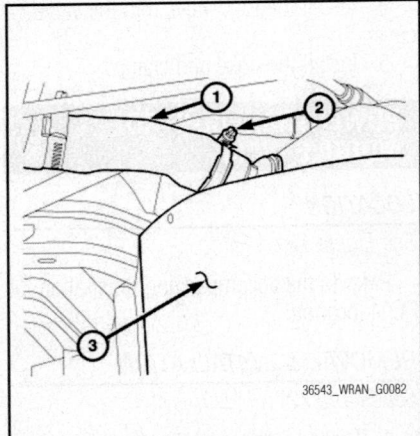

36543_WRAN_G0082

Fig. 73 Fuel tank connections

1. Remove fuel tank filler tube cap.
2. Perform Fuel System Pressure Release Procedure.
3. Remove fuel fill cap.
4. Raise and support vehicle.
5. Remove fuel fill hose clamp at rear of tank.
6. Remove fuel fill hose from fuel tank.
7. Position a drain hose into the fuel fill hose opening. Note that a small flapper valve is installed into the opening.
8. Drain fuel tank using an approved gasoline fuel draining station.
9. Disconnect quick-connect fittings.
10. Remove hose clamp and disconnect hose at tank.
11. Support tank with a hydraulic jack.
12. Disconnect quick-connect fittings at front of tank.
13. Remove two tank mounting bolts at rear of fuel tank.
14. Remove three tank mounting bolts at right side of fuel tank.
15. Remove three tank mounting bolts at left side of fuel tank.
16. Partially lower tank to gain access to pump module electrical connector.
17. Disconnect electrical connector at fuel pump module.
18. Continue lowering tank for removal.
19. Lift fuel tank from skid plate.
20. If fuel tank is to be replaced, remove fuel pump module from tank.

To install:

➡ **The fuel tank skid plate and the fuel tank assembly are installed at the same. They share common fasteners.**

21. If fuel pump module had been removed, install module to tank.
22. Position fuel tank into skid plate.
23. Support tank with a hydraulic jack.
24. Partially raise tank to allow connections at top of tank.
25. Connect electrical connector to fuel pump module.
26. Continue raising tank snugly to body.
27. Connect the quick-connect fittings.
28. Install hose to tank and install clamp.
29. Connect quick-connect fittings at front of tank.
30. Install two tank mounting bolts at rear of fuel tank.
31. Install three tank mounting bolts at right side of fuel tank.
32. Install three tank mounting bolts at left side of fuel tank.
33. Install all mounting bolts to 30 ft. lbs. (41 Nm).

FUEL RAIL & INJECTORS

REMOVAL & INSTALLATION

See Figures 74 and 75.

1. Remove fuel tank filler tube cap.
2. Perform Fuel System Pressure Release Procedure
3. Remove negative battery cable at battery.
4. Remove upper half of intake manifold.
5. Disconnect electrical connectors at all six fuel injectors. Push red colored slider away from injector. While pushing slider, depress tab and remove connector from injector.

➡ **The factory fuel injection wiring harness is numerically tagged (INJ 1, INJ 2, etc.) for injector position identification. If harness is not tagged, note wiring location before removal.**

6. Disconnect fuel line latch clip and fuel line at fuel rail.
7. Remove four fuel rail mounting bolts.
8. Gently rock and pull left side of fuel rail until fuel injectors just start to clear machined holes in cylinder head. Gently rock and pull right side of rail until injectors just start to clear cylinder head holes. Repeat this procedure (left/right) until all injectors have cleared cylinder head holes.

9. Remove fuel rail (with injectors attached) from engine.
10. Disconnect injector wiring connector from each injector.
11. Rotate injector and pull out of fuel rail. The clip will stay on injector.
12. Check injector O-ring for damage. If O-ring is damaged, it must be replaced. If injector is reused, a protective cap must be installed on injector tip to prevent damage. Replace injector clip if it is damaged.
13. Repeat procedures for remaining injectors.

To install:

14. If same injectors are being reinstalled, install new O-ring(s).
15. Apply a small amount of clean engine oil to each injector O-ring. This will aid in installation.
16. Push fuel injector(s) into fuel rail assembly until clip has latched.
17. Clean out fuel injector machined bores in intake manifold.

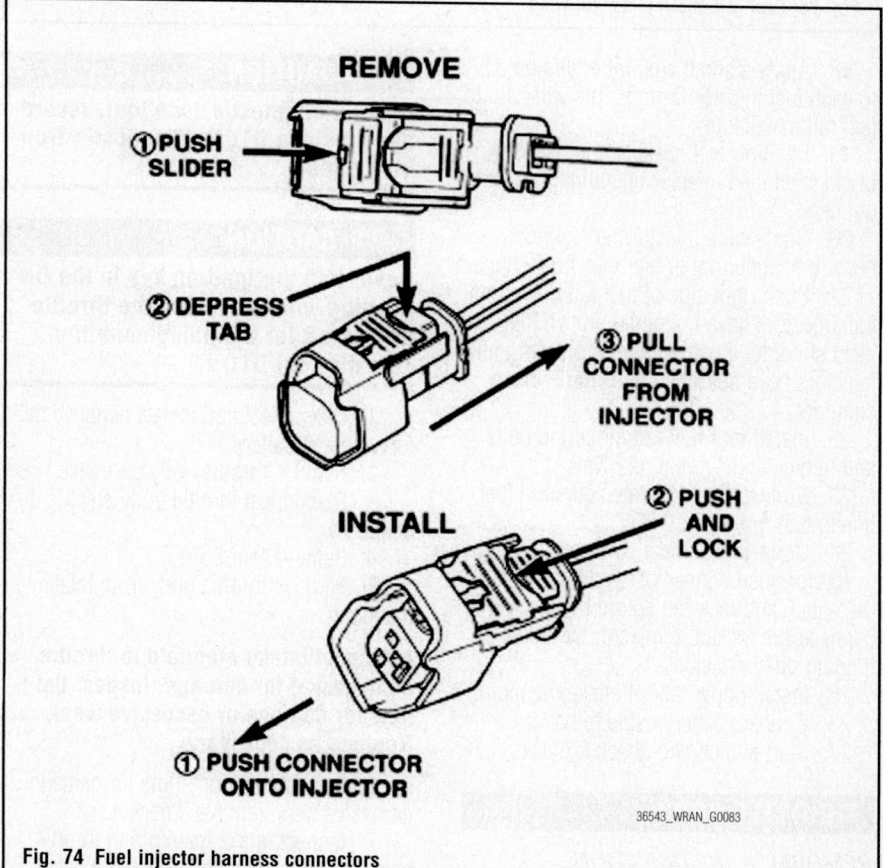

Fig. 74 Fuel injector harness connectors

36543_WRAN_G0083

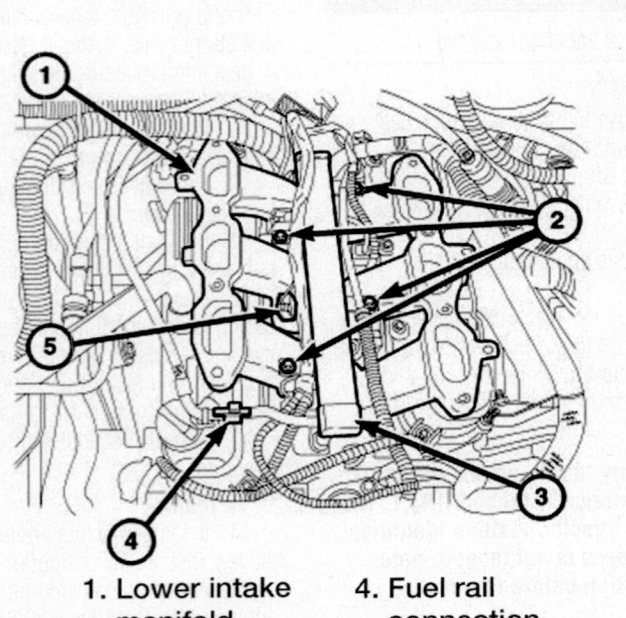

1. Lower intake manifold
2. Fuel rail bolt locations
3. Fuel rail
4. Fuel rail connection
5. Injector connection

36543_WRAN_G0048

Fig. 75 Fuel rail and injector location

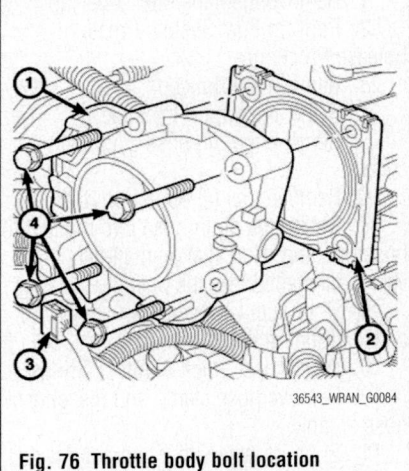

36543_WRAN_G0084

Fig. 76 Throttle body bolt location

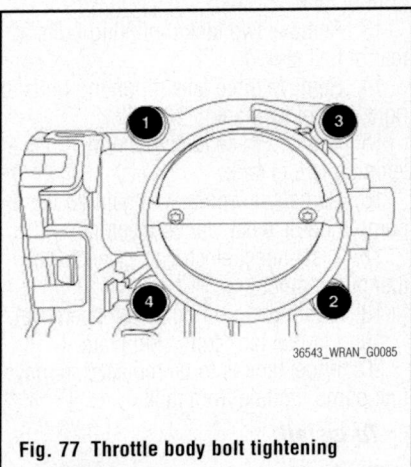

36543_WRAN_G0085

Fig. 77 Throttle body bolt tightening sequence

18. Apply a small amount of engine oil to each fuel injector O-ring. This will help in fuel rail installation.

19. Position fuel rail/fuel injector assembly to machined injector openings in cylinder head.

20. Guide each injector into cylinder head. Be careful not to tear injector O-rings.

21. Push right side of fuel rail down until fuel injectors have bottomed on cylinder head shoulder. Push left fuel rail down until injectors have bottomed on cylinder head shoulder.

22. Install four fuel rail mounting bolts and tighten to 17 ft. lbs. (22 Nm)

23. Connect fuel line latch clip and fuel line to fuel rail.

24. Connect electrical connectors at fuel injectors. Push connector onto injector and then push and lock red colored slider. Verify connector is locked to injector by lightly tugging on connector.

25. Install upper half of intake manifold.

26. Connect battery cable to battery.

27. Start engine and check for leaks.

THROTTLE BODY

REMOVAL & INSTALLATION

See Figures 76 and 77.

✵✵ CAUTION

Using a diagnostic scan tool, record any previous DTC's (Diagnostic Trouble Codes).

✵✵ CAUTION

Never had the ignition key in the ON position when checking the throttle body shaft for a binding condition. This may set DTC's.

1. Disconnect and isolate negative battery cable at battery.

2. Remove throttle body air intake hose.

3. Disconnect throttle body electrical connector.

4. Remove four bolts.

5. Remove throttle body from intake manifold.

➡Inspect intake manifold to throttle body gasket for damage. Inspect the j-nuts for damage or excessive wear. Replace as necessary.

6. Inspect the four j-nuts for damage or excessive wear, remove if necessary.

7. Inspect intake manifold to throttle body gasket for damage, remove if necessary.

To install:

8. Install a new intake manifold to throttle body gasket, if replacement was necessary.

9. Install four new four j-nuts, if replacement was necessary.

➡The throttle body mounting bolts MUST be tightened to specifications. Over tightening can cause damage to the throttle body or the intake manifold.

10. Install throttle body to intake manifold.

11. Install four bolts and hand tighten.

12. Connect throttle body electrical connector.

13. Obtain a torque wrench. Tighten mounting bolts (as shown) in a mandatory torque crossed pattern sequence to 65 inch lbs. (7.5 Nm).

14. Install clean air hose and tighten clamps to 35 inch lbs. (4 Nm).

15. Connect negative battery cable, tighten nut to 45 inch lbs. (5 Nm).

16. Using the diagnostic scan tool, erase all previous DTC's and perform the ETC Relearn function.

HEATING & AIR CONDITIONING SYSTEM

BLOWER MOTOR

REMOVAL & INSTALLATION

See Figure 78.

> ✳✳ **CAUTION**
>
> **Disable the airbag system before attempting any steering wheel, steering column, or instrument panel component diagnosis or service. Failure to take the proper precautions could result in accidental airbag deployment and possible personal injury or death.**

→The blower motor is located on the passenger side of the vehicle under the instrument panel. The blower motor can be removed without having to remove the instrument panel or the HVAC housing.

1. Disconnect and isolate the negative battery cable.
2. Disconnect the wire harness connector from the blower motor.
3. Release the three screws that secures the blower motor to the HVAC housing and rotate blower motor counterclockwise.
4. Rotate and tilt the blower motor as needed for clearance to remove the blower motor and wheel from the HVAC housing.

To install:

→Failure to install the blower motor assembly correctly could result in an air leak or the blower motor assembly becoming completely disengaged from the HVAC housing.

5. Align and install the blower motor into the HVAC housing.

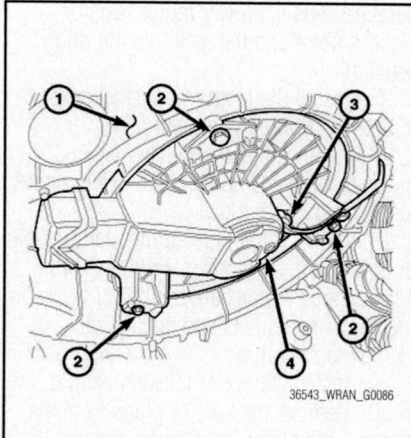

Fig. 78 Blower motor connections

6. Rotate the blower motor until all of the holes align and install the three retaining screws attaching the motor assembly to the HVAC housing.
7. Connect the wire harness connector to the blower motor.
8. Reconnect the battery negative cable.
9. Test the blower motor for proper installation by turning the blower motor speed to its fastest position and checking around the outer edges of the blower assembly for air leaks. If any air leaks are found, remove and reinstall the blower motor.

HEATER CORE

REMOVAL & INSTALLATION

See Figures 79 and 80.

> ✳✳ **CAUTION**
>
> **Disable the airbag system before attempting any steering wheel, steering column or instrument panel component diagnosis or service. Disconnect and isolate the negative battery (ground) cable, then wait two minutes for the airbag system capacitor to discharge before performing further diagnosis or service. This is the only sure way to disable the airbag system. Failure to follow these instructions may result in accidental airbag deployment and possible serious or fatal injury.**

> ✳✳ **WARNING**
>
> **Refer to the applicable warnings and cautions for this system before performing the following operation. Failure to follow these instructions may result in possible serious or fatal injury**

1. Remove the HVAC housing assembly and place it on a workbench.
2. Remove the floor distribution duct from the passenger side of the air distribution housing.
3. Remove the foam seal from the flange located on the front of the HVAC housing.
4. Remove the screw that secures the flange to the HVAC housing and remove the flange.
5. Remove the screw that secures the bracket retaining the heater core tubes to the passenger side of the air

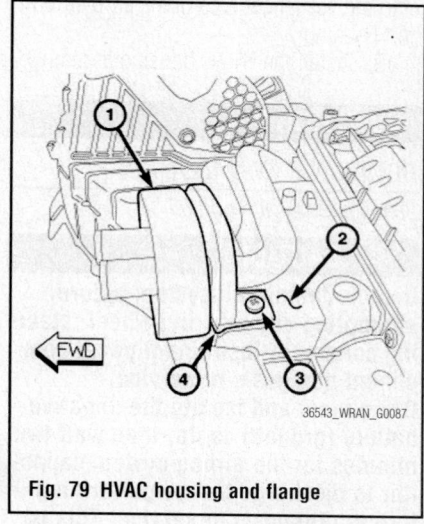

Fig. 79 HVAC housing and flange

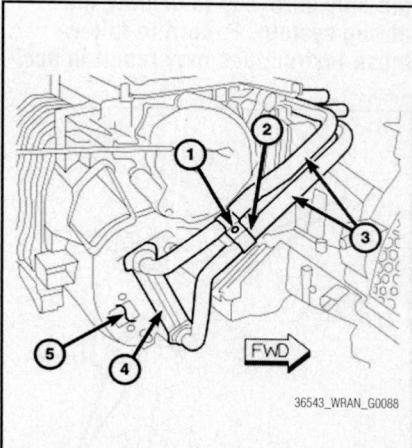

Fig. 80 Heater core and core tube locations

distribution housing and remove the bracket.
6. Carefully pull the heater core out of the side of the air distribution housing.

To install:

7. Carefully install the heater core into the passenger side of the air distribution housing.
8. Install the retaining bracket and the screw that secures the heater core tubes to the air distribution housing. Tighten the screw to 10 inch lbs. (1.2 Nm).
9. Position the flange to the front of the HVAC housing.
10. Install the screw that secures the flange to the HVAC housing. Tighten the screw to 10 inch lbs. (1.2 Nm).

→If the foam seal for the flange is deformed or damaged, it must be replaced.

11. Install the foam seal onto the flange.

12. Install the floor distribution duct onto the passenger side of the air distribution housing.

13. Install the HVAC housing assembly.

HVAC HOUSING

REMOVAL & INSTALLATION

See Figures 81 through 83.

✱✱ CAUTION

Disable the airbag system before attempting any steering wheel, steering column or instrument panel component diagnosis or service. Disconnect and isolate the negative battery (ground) cable, then wait two minutes for the airbag system capacitor to discharge before performing further diagnosis or service. This is the only sure way to disable the airbag system. Failure to follow these instructions may result in acci-

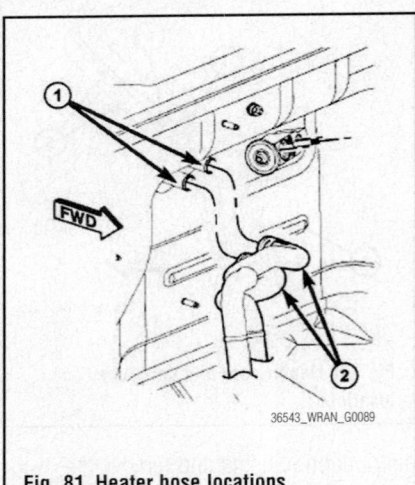

Fig. 81 Heater hose locations

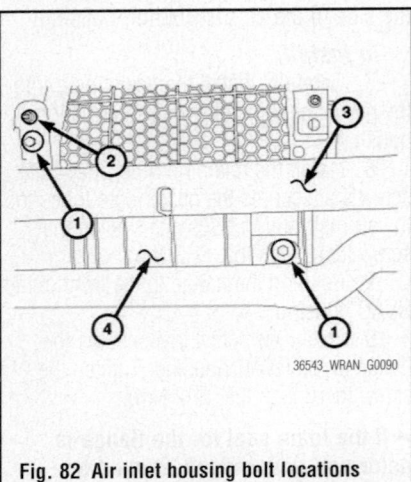

Fig. 82 Air inlet housing bolt locations

dental airbag deployment and possible serious or fatal injury.

➡ **Refer to the applicable warnings and cautions for this system before performing the following operation.**

➡ **The HVAC housing and instrument panel must be removed from the vehicle as an assembly.**

➡ **The HVAC housing must be removed from the instrument panel and disassembled for service of the A/C evaporator, air intake housing, mode-air and blend-air doors and the heater core.**

1. Disconnect and isolate the negative battery cable.

2. Recover the refrigerant from the refrigerant system.

3. Partially drain the engine cooling system.

4. Remove the nut that secures the A/C liquid line and A/C suction line to the A/C expansion valve.

5. Disconnect the A/C liquid and suction lines from the A/C expansion valve and remove and discard the O-ring seals.

6. Install plugs in, or tape over the opened refrigerant line fittings and the expansion valve ports.

7. Remove the upper intake manifold to help gain access to the hose clamps that secure the heater hoses to the heater core.

8. Using cable-type spring clamp pliers or equivalent, release the hose clamps that secure the heater hoses to the heater core tubes and disconnect the hoses from the tubes. Install plugs in, or tape over the opened heater core tubes to prevent coolant spillage during HVAC housing assembly removal.

9. Remove the instrument panel and place it on a workbench.

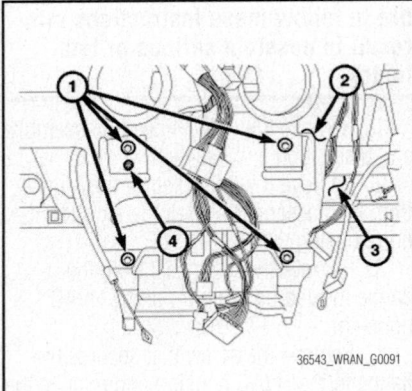

Fig. 87 HVAC housing removal from instrument panel

10. Remove the instrument panel cover.

11. Disconnect the instrument panel wire harness connectors from the evaporator temperature sensor, blower motor resistor, blower motor and the recirculation door actuator.

12. Remove the two bolts that secure the air inlet housing to the passenger side of the instrument panel support. Use caution not to damage the housing alignment pin during removal of the HVAC housing assembly from the support.

13. Remove the demister ducts.

14. Remove the defroster duct.

15. Remove the instrument panel ducts.

16. Remove the four bolts that secure the HVAC housing assembly to the center of the instrument panel support and remove the housing from the support. Use caution not to damage the housing alignment pin during removal of the housing from the support.

To install:

17. Position the HVAC housing assembly into the instrument panel support. Be certain that the housing alignment pin is correctly located.

18. Install the four bolts that secure the HVAC housing assembly to the center of instrument panel support. Tighten the bolts to 35 inch lbs. (4 Nm).

19. Install the instrument panel ducts.

20. Install the defroster duct.

21. Install the demister ducts.

22. Verify that the housing alignment pin is correctly located in the passenger side of the instrument panel support.

23. Install the two bolts that secure the air inlet housing to the instrument panel support. Tighten the bolts to 35 inch lbs. (4 Nm).

24. Connect the instrument panel wire harness connectors to the evaporator temperature sensor, blower motor resistor, blower motor and the recirculation door actuator.

25. Install the instrument panel cover.

26. Install the instrument panel.

27. Remove the previously installed plugs or caps and connect the heater hoses to the heater core tubes.

28. Using cable-type spring clamp pliers or equivalent, correctly position the two hose clamps that secure the heater hoses to the heater core tubes and engage the clamps to the tubes.

29. Install the upper intake manifold.

30. Remove the tape or plugs from the opened refrigerant line fittings and the expansion valve ports.

31. Lubricate new O-ring seals with clean refrigerant oil and install them onto the refrigerant line fittings.

32. Use only the specified O-rings as they are made of special materials compatible to the R-134a system.

33. Use only refrigerant oil of the type recommended for the A/C compressor in the vehicle.

34. Connect the A/C liquid line and A/C suction line onto the A/C expansion valve.

35. Install the nut that secures the A/C liquid and suction lines to the A/C expansion valve. Tighten the nut to 70 inch lbs. (8 Nm).

36. Reconnect the negative battery cable.

37. If the heater core is being replaced, flush the cooling system.

38. Refill the engine cooling system.

39. Evacuate and charge the refrigerant system.

STEERING

POWER RECIRCULATING BALL STEERING GEAR

REMOVAL & INSTALLATION

➡The steering column on vehicles with an automatic transmission may not be equipped with an internal locking shaft that allows the ignition key cylinder to be locked with the key. Alternative methods of locking the steering wheel for service will have to be used.

1. Place the front wheels in the straight ahead position with the steering wheel centered and locked.

2. Siphon out as much power steering fluid as possible.

3. Move the coolant bottle to the side out of the way.

4. Remove the lower column pinch bolt at the gear.

5. Remove the lower column coupler shaft from the gear.

6. Remove power steering hoses/tubes from steering gear.

7. Raise and support the vehicle.

8. Remove the track bar bolt at the frame and lower the track bar.

9. Matchmark the Pitman arm and gear. Remove the nut. Separate the pitman arm from the gear using special tool 9615 puller, or equivalent.

10. Remove pitman arm from gear.

11. Remove the steering gear retaining bolts and remove the gear.

To install:

12. Install steering gear on the frame rail and tighten bolts to 70 ft. lbs. (95 Nm).

13. Align and install the pitman arm and tighten nut to 185 ft. lbs. (251 Nm).

14. It may be necessary to pry the axle assembly over to install the track bar at the frame rail. Install track bar at the frame rail bracket. Install the nut and bolt at the frame rail bracket.

15. Tighten the bolt at the frame bracket to 125 ft. lbs. (169 Nm).

16. Install the track bar back into position at the frame.

17. Remove the support and lower the vehicle.

18. Align the column coupler shaft to steering gear. Install a new coupler pinch bolt and tighten to 36 ft. lbs. (49 Nm).

POWER STEERING PUMP

REMOVAL & INSTALLATION

See Figure 84.

1. Remove cap from power steering fluid reservoir.

2. Siphon as much fluid as possible from the power steering fluid reservoir.

3. Remove the air box assembly.

4. Remove the pressure hose at the pump.

5. Remove the supply hose from the pump.

6. Remove the drive belt.

7. Remove the three front mounting bolts through the pulley.

8. Remove the pump (with pulley).

✳✳ WARNING

Do not reuse the old power steering pump pulley it is not intended for reuse. A new pulley must be installed if removed.

9. Remove the pulley from the pump using a tool such as OTC 7185, or equivalent.

To install:

10. Install pulley on pump (if removed), using OTC 7771, or equivalent, making sure it's flush with the end of the shaft.

➡After the pump installation is complete, run the engine about 5 minutes and note any belt chirp. If chirp exists, move the pulley outward about 0.020 in. (0.5mm). If noise increases, press the pulley on about 0.040 in. (1.0mm). Take care that the pulley doesn't contact the mounting bolts.

11. Install pump on the engine.

12. Install 3 pump mounting bolts and tighten to 19 ft. lbs. (26 Nm).

13. Install the pressure line on the pump and tighten to 23 ft. lbs. (31 Nm).

14. Install supply hose on pump.

15. Install drive belt.

16. Fill and bleed the power steering system.

17. Check for leaks.

18. Install the air box assembly.

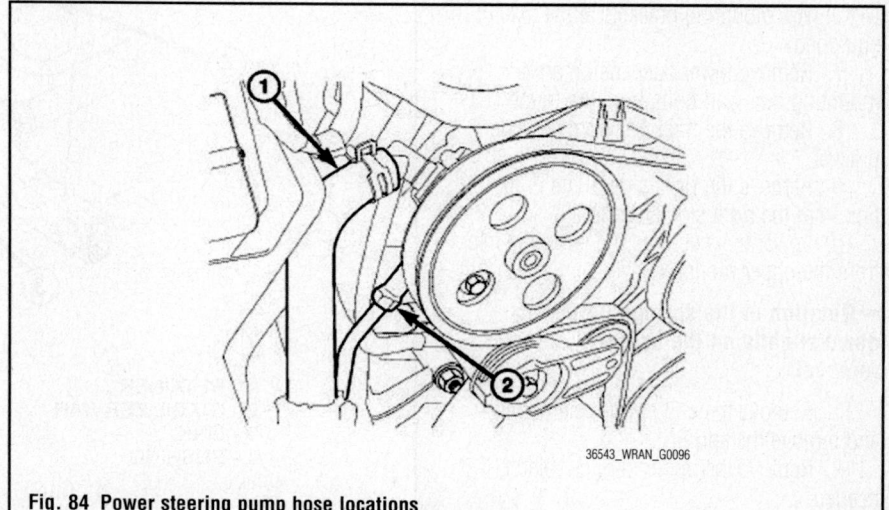

36543_WRAN_G0096

Fig. 84 Power steering pump hose locations

BLEEDING

➡ **Mopar® Power Steering Fluid + 4 or Mopar® ATF+4 Automatic Transmission Fluid is to be used in the power steering system. Both Fluids have the same material standard specifications (MS-9602). No other power steering or automatic transmission fluid is to be used in the system. Damage may result to the power steering pump and system if another fluid is used. Do not overfill the system. If the air is not purged from the power steering system correctly, pump failure could result.**

1. Check the fluid level. The power steering fluid level can be viewed through the side of the power steering fluid reservoir. Compare the fluid level to the markings on the side of the reservoir. When the fluid is at normal ambient temperature, approximately 70°–80° F (21°–27° C) the fluid level should read between the MAX and MIN markings. When the fluid is hot, fluid level is allowed to read up to the MAX line.

2. Remove the cap from the fluid reservoir and fill the power steering fluid reservoir up to the MAX marking with Mopar® Power Steering Fluid + 4 or Mopar® ATF+4 Automatic Transmission Fluid.

3. Tightly insert Power Steering Cap Adapter, Special Tool 9688, into the mouth of the reservoir.

➡ **Failure to use a vacuum pump reservoir may allow power steering fluid to be sucked into the hand vacuum pump.**

4. Attach Hand Vacuum Pump, Special Tool C-4207 or equivalent, with reservoir attached, to the Power Steering Cap Adapter.

➡ **When performing the following step make sure the vacuum level is maintained during the entire time period.**

5. Using Hand Vacuum Pump, apply 20-25 inch Hg (68-85 kPa) of vacuum to the system for a minimum of three minutes.

6. Slowly release the vacuum and remove the special tools.

7. Adjust the fluid level as necessary.

8. Repeat Step No. 5 through Step No. 7 until the fluid no longer drops when vacuum is applied.

9. Start the engine and cycle the steering wheel lock-to-lock three times.

10. Do not hold the steering wheel at the stops.

11. Stop the engine and check for leaks at all connections.

12. Check for any signs of air in the reservoir and check the fluid level. If air is present, repeat the procedure as necessary.

SUSPENSION

COIL SPRING

REMOVAL & INSTALLATION

See Figures 85 through 87.

1. Before servicing the vehicle, refer to the precautions in the beginning of this section.

2. Raise and support the vehicle.

3. Remove the wheel and tire assemblies.

4. Position a hydraulic jack under the axle to support it.

5. Remove the front shocks at the lower mountings.

6. Remove the Anti-lock Brake System (ABS) wire mounting brackets at the axle, if equipped.

7. Remove lower suspension arms mounting nuts and bolts from the frame.

8. Remove the track bar from the axle bracket.

9. Remove the right side of the drag link from the right side knuckle.

10. Lower the axle until the spring is free from the upper mount.

➡ **Rotation of the spring and prying down slightly on the axle will aid in removal.**

11. Remove the coil spring retainer clip and remove the spring.

12. Remove the upper spring isolator, if needed.

13. Pull jounce bumper out of mount, if needed.

To install:

14. Install jounce bumper into mount.

15. Install the spring isolator.

➡ **Rotation of the spring and prying down slightly on the axle will aid in installation.**

FRONT SUSPENSION

16. Position the coil spring on the axle pad. It may be necessary to rotate the spring while installing.

17. Install the spring retainer clip and bolt. Tighten bolt to 16 ft. lbs. (21 Nm).

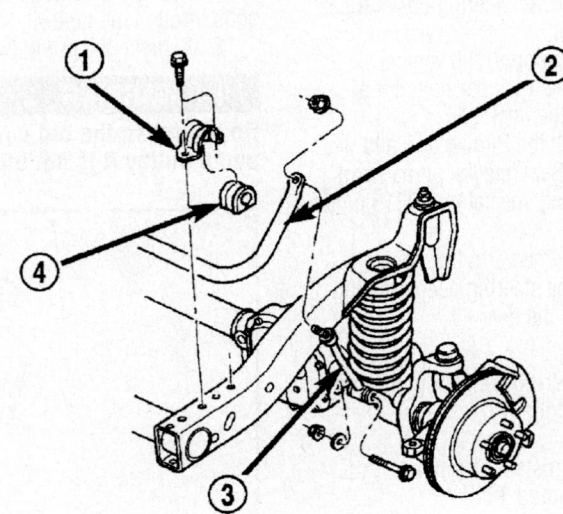

1 - RETAINER
2 - STABILIZER BAR
3 - LINK
4 - BUSHING

06009-JEEP-G183

Fig. 85 Stabilizer bar

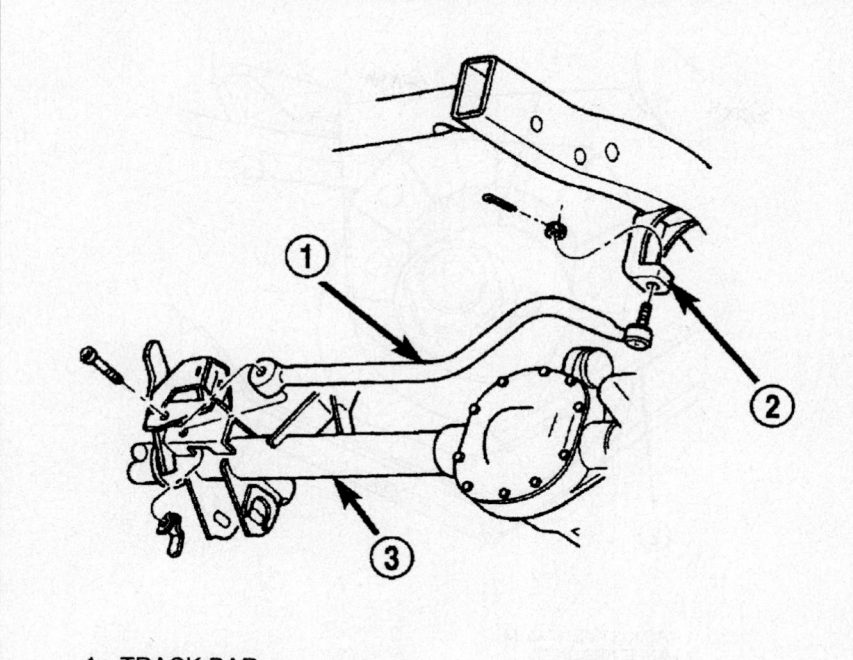

1 - TRACK BAR
2 - FRAME BRACKET
3 - FRONT AXLE

06009-JEEP-G184

Fig. 86 Track bar

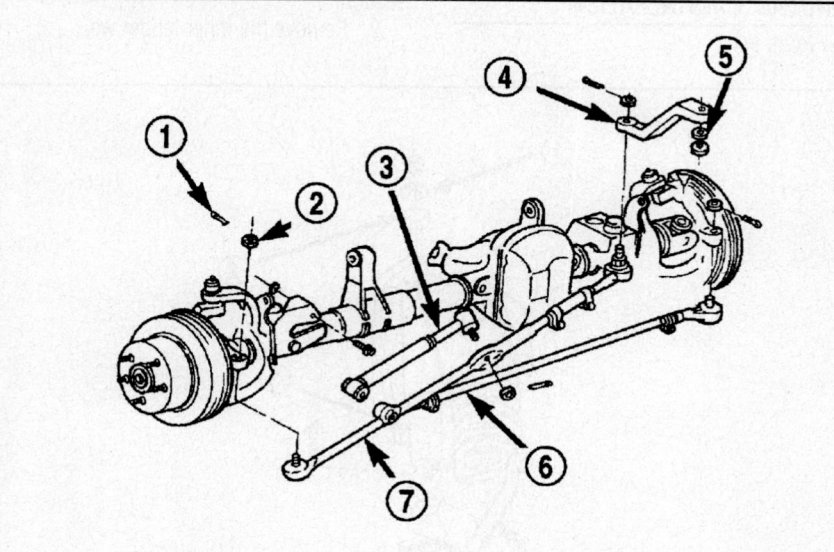

1 - COTTER PIN
2 - NUT
3 - DAMPENER
4 - PITMAN ARM
5 - WASHER
6 - TIE ROD
7 - DRAG LINK

06009-JEEP-G185

Fig. 87 Steering linkage

18. Raise the axle into position until the spring seats in the upper mount.

19. Install the shock at the axle and tighten to 56 ft. lbs. (76 Nm).

20. Install the ABS wire mounting brackets at the axle, if equipped.

21. Install the track bar to the axle bracket. Torque to 125 ft. lbs. (169 Nm).

22. Install the lower suspension arms to the frame. Install mounting bolts and nuts finger tight.

23. Install the drag link to the right side knuckle. Torque to 63 ft. lbs. (85 Nm). Use new cotter pins.

24. Remove the hydraulic jack from under the axle.

25. Install the wheel and tire assemblies.

26. Remove the supports and lower the vehicle.

27. Tighten the lower suspension arms nuts to 125 ft. lbs. (169 Nm) at normal ride height with the vehicle weight.

LOWER BALL JOINT

REMOVAL & INSTALLATION

See Figure 88.

1. Before servicing the vehicle, refer to the precautions in the beginning of this section.

2. Remove hub/bearing and axle shaft.

3. Disconnect the tie-rod or drag link from the steering knuckle arm.

4. Remove the cotter pins from the upper and lower ball studs.

5. Remove the upper and lower ball stud nuts.

6. Using special tool and separate the ball joints from the steering knuckle. Remove knuckle from ball studs.

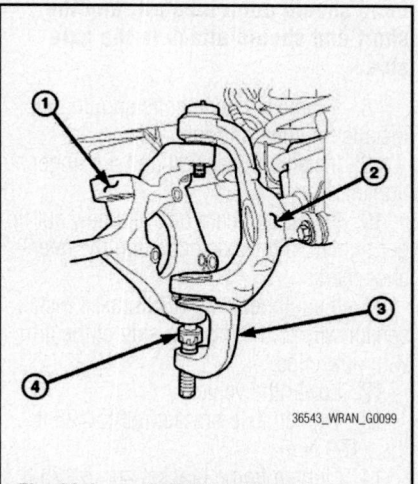

36543_WRAN_G0099

Fig. 88 Lower ball joint removal

To install:

7. Position special tool 9950 (DRIVER) and 6289-12 (RECEIVER) with C4212-F (PRESS) as shown to install lower ball stud.

8. Position the steering knuckle on the ball studs.

9. Install and tighten the bottom retaining nut to 70 ft. lbs. (95 Nm) torque. Install new cotter pin.

10. Install and tighten the top retaining nut to 70 ft. lbs. (95 Nm) torque. Install new cotter pin.

11. Install the hub bearing and axle shaft.

12. Connect the tie-rod or drag link end to the steering knuckle arm. Torque to 63 ft. lbs. (85 Nm).

LOWER CONTROL ARM

REMOVAL & INSTALLATION

See Figure 89.

1. Before servicing the vehicle, refer to the precautions in the beginning of this section.

2. Raise and support the vehicle.

3. If equipped with ABS brakes remove sensor wire from the inboard side of the arm.

4. If the vehicle is equipped with a cam bolt service package paint or scribe alignment marks on the cam adjusters and suspension arm for installation reference.

5. Remove the lower suspension arm nut and bolt from the axle.

6. Remove the nut and bolt/cam bolt from the frame rail bracket and remove the lower suspension arm.

To install:

7. Position the lower suspension arm in the axle bracket and frame rail bracket.

➥**Position the paint dot located on the control arm toward the axle and facing outboard. If paint dot is not visible, the bend should point inboard, and the short end should attach to the axle side.**

8. Frame and axle bolts should be installed outboard to inboard

9. Install the rear bolt and nut finger tighten.

10. Install bolt/cam bolt and new nut finger tighten in the axle and align the reference marks.

11. If equipped with ABS brakes install sensor wire to the inboard side of the arm with new clips.

12. Lower the vehicle.

13. Tighten axle bracket nut to 125 ft. lbs. (169 Nm).

14. Tighten frame bracket nut to 125 ft. lbs. (169 Nm).

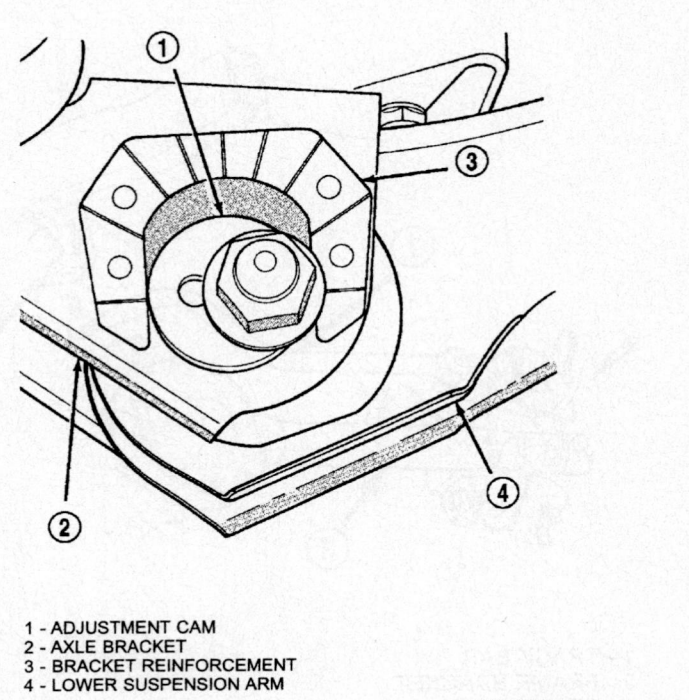

1 - ADJUSTMENT CAM
2 - AXLE BRACKET
3 - BRACKET REINFORCEMENT
4 - LOWER SUSPENSION ARM

06009-JEEP-G193

Fig. 89 Cam bolt service package

SHOCK ABSORBERS

REMOVAL & INSTALLATION

See Figure 90.

1. Before servicing the vehicle, refer to the precautions in the beginning of this section.

2. Remove the inner fender well.

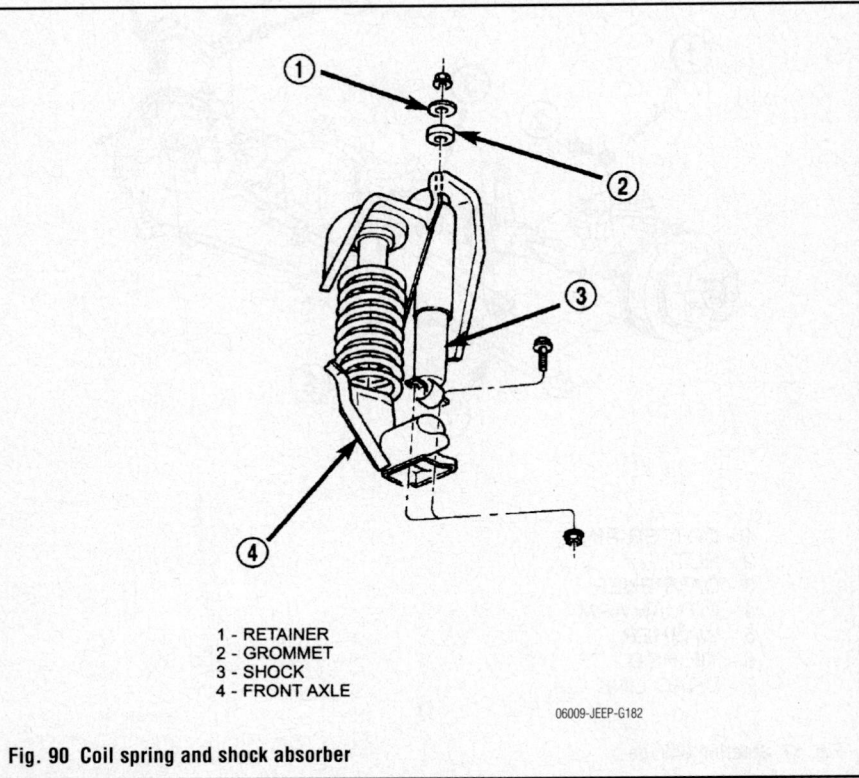

1 - RETAINER
2 - GROMMET
3 - SHOCK
4 - FRONT AXLE

06009-JEEP-G182

Fig. 90 Coil spring and shock absorber

3. Remove or disconnect the following:
- Upper nut, washer and grommet from the upper stud
- Lower bolt
- Shock absorber

To install:

4. Install or connect the following:
- Shock absorber. Torque the lower fasteners to 56 ft. lbs (76 Nm).
- Upper grommet, washer, and nut to the stud. Torque it to 20 ft. lbs. (27 Nm).

5. Install the inner fender well.

STEERING KNUCKLE

REMOVAL & INSTALLATION

Ball stud service procedures below require removal of the hub bearing and axle shaft. Removal and installation of upper and lower ball studs require the use of a special tool.

1. Remove hub bearing and axle shaft.
2. Disconnect the tie-rod or drag link from the steering knuckle arm.
3. Remove the cotter pins from the upper and lower ball studs.
4. Remove the upper and lower ball stud nuts.
5. Using special tool, separate the ball joints from the steering knuckle. Remove knuckle from ball studs.

To install:

6. Position the steering knuckle on the ball studs.
7. Install and tighten the bottom retaining nut to 70 ft. lbs. (95 Nm) torque. Install new cotter pin.
8. Install and tighten the top retaining nut to 70 ft. lbs. (95 Nm) torque. Install new cotter pin.
9. Install the hub bearing and axle shaft.
10. Connect the tie-rod or drag link end to the steering knuckle arm.

STABILIZER BAR

REMOVAL & INSTALLATION

1. Remove upper link nuts and separate the links from the stabilizer bar with special tool.
2. Remove the splash shield, if necessary.
3. Remove stabilizer retainer bolts and remove retainers.
4. Remove stabilizer bar.
5. Remove lower link nuts and bolts and remove links

To install:

➡ **The stabilizer bar link-to-axle bolt should be tightening with the vehicle sitting on its tires.**

6. Center stabilizer bar on top of the frame rails and install retainers and bolts. Tighten bolts to 75 ft. lbs. (102 Nm).
7. Position links on axle brackets and into the stabilizer bar. Install lower link bolts and nuts and tighten to 75 ft. lbs. (102 Nm).
8. Install upper link nuts and tighten to 75 ft. lbs. (102 Nm).
9. Install the splash shield, if removed.

TRACK BAR

REMOVAL & INSTALLATION
See Figure 91.

1. Raise and support the vehicle.
2. Remove the cotter pin and nut from the ball stud end at the frame rail bracket.
3. Use a universal puller tool to separate the track bar ball stud from the frame rail bracket.
4. Remove the bolt and flag nut from the axle bracket.
5. Remove the track bar

To install:

6. Install the track bar at axle tube bracket. Loosely install the retaining bolt and flag nut.

➡ **The frame bolt must be installed from front to rear.**

7. It may be necessary to pry the axle assembly over to install the track bar at the frame rail. Install track bar at the frame rail bracket. Install the retaining nut on the stud.
8. Tighten the ball stud nut to 125 ft. lbs. (169 Nm). and install a new cotter pin.
9. Remove the supports and lower the vehicle.
10. Tighten the bolt at the axle bracket to 125 ft. lbs. (169 Nm).
11. Check alignment if a new track bar was installed.

UPPER BALL JOINT

REMOVAL & INSTALLATION
See Figures 92 and 93.

1. Before servicing the vehicle, refer to the precautions in the beginning of this section.
2. Remove hub/bearing and axle shaft.
3. Disconnect the tie-rod or drag link from the steering knuckle arm.
4. Remove the cotter pins from the upper and lower ball studs.
5. Remove the upper and lower ball stud nuts.

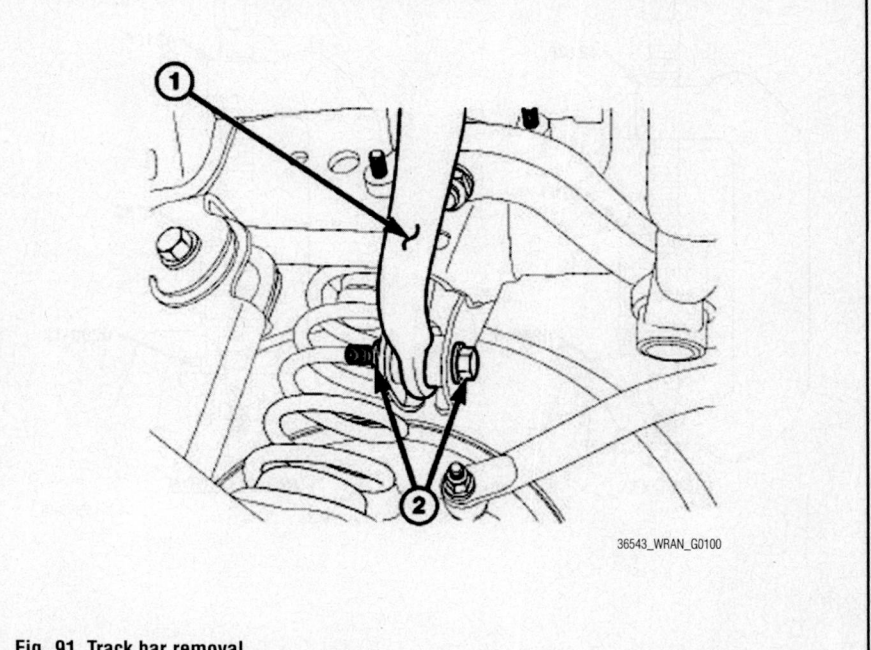

Fig. 91 Track bar removal

36543_WRAN_G0100

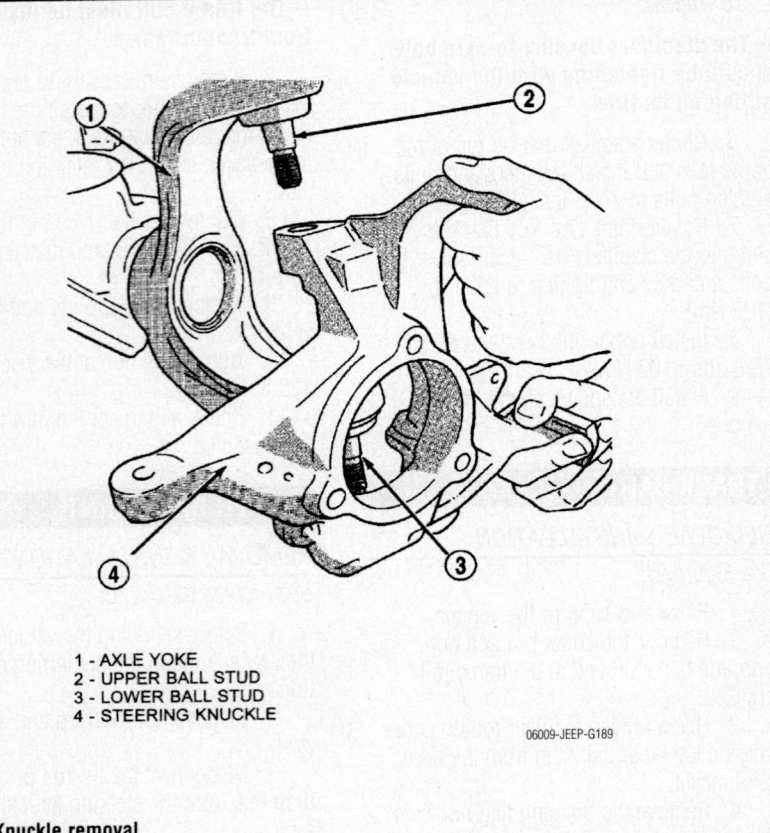

1 - AXLE YOKE
2 - UPPER BALL STUD
3 - LOWER BALL STUD
4 - STEERING KNUCKLE

06009-JEEP-G189

Fig. 92 Knuckle removal

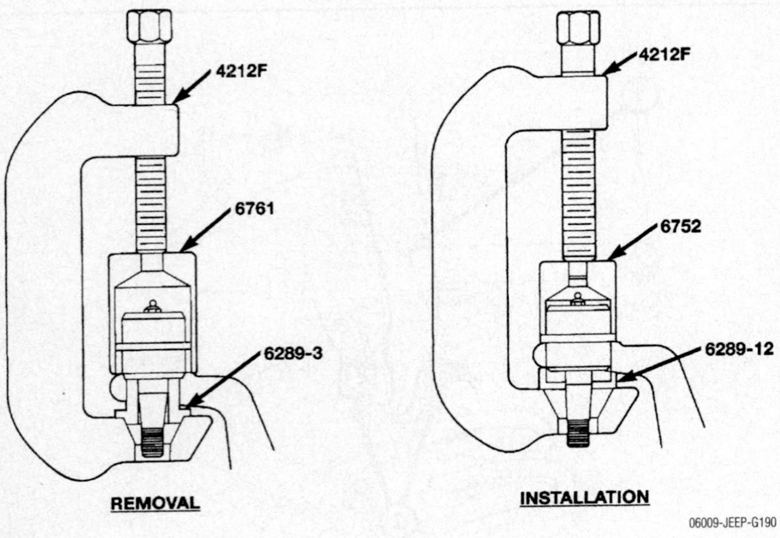

4212F

6761

6289-3

REMOVAL

4212F

6752

6289-12

INSTALLATION

06009-JEEP-G190

Fig. 93 Upper ball joint removal/installation

6. Using special tool separate the ball joints from the steering knuckle. Remove knuckle from ball studs.

To install:

7. Position the steering knuckle on the ball studs.

8. Install and tighten the bottom retaining nut to 70 ft. lbs. (95 Nm) torque. Install new cotter pin.

9. Install and tighten the top retaining nut to 70 ft. lbs. (95 Nm) torque. Install new cotter pin.

10. Install the hub bearing and axle shaft.

11. Connect the tie-rod or drag link end to the steering knuckle arm. Torque to 63 ft. lbs. (85 Nm).

UPPER CONTROL ARM

REMOVAL & INSTALLATION

See Figure 94.

1. Before servicing the vehicle, refer to the precautions in the beginning of this section.

2. Raise and support the vehicle.

3. Remove the electrical clip from the control arm clevis bracket if equipped.

4. Remove the upper suspension arm nut and bolt at the axle bracket.

5. Remove the nut and bolt at the frame rail and remove the upper suspension arm.

To install:

6. Position the upper suspension arm at the axle and frame rail.

➡ **The axle bolt must be installed from the inboard to outboard.**

7. Install the bolts and finger tighten the nuts.

8. Remove the supports and lower the vehicle.

9. Tighten the nut at the axle and frame brackets to 75 ft. lbs. (102 Nm).

WHEEL HUB & BEARING

REMOVAL & INSTALLATION

See Figure 95.

1. Before servicing the vehicle, refer to the precautions in the beginning of this section.

2. Raise and support the vehicle.

3. Remove the wheel and tire assembly.

4. Remove the brake caliper, rotor and ABS wheel speed sensor.

5. Remove the cotter pin, nut retainer and axle hub nut.

6. Remove the hub bearing mounting bolts from the back of the steering knuckle.

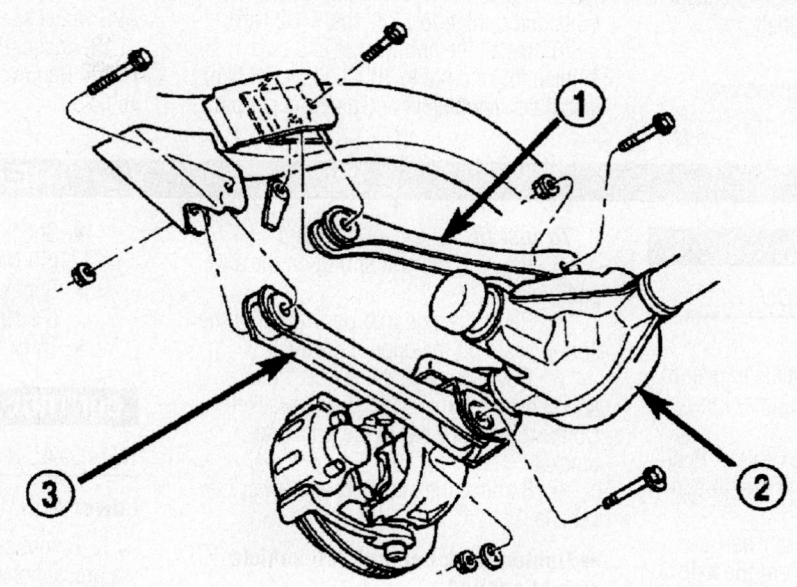

1 - UPPER SUSPENSION ARM
2 - FRONT AXLE
3 - LOWER SUSPENSION ARM

06009-JEEP-G192

Fig. 94 Upper and lower front control arms

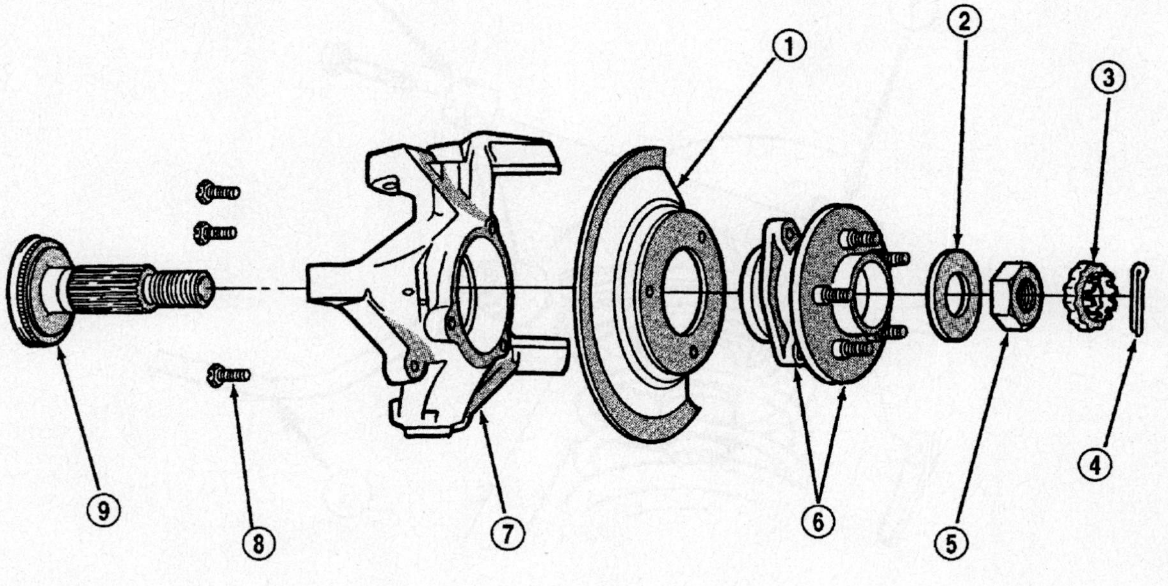

1 - BRAKE SHIELD
2 - WASHER
3 - RETAINER
4 - COTTER PIN
5 - NUT

6 - HUB AND BEARING ASSEMBLY
7 - STEERING KNUCKLE
8 - BOLT
9 - TONE WHEEL (ABS)

06009-JEEP-G195

Fig. 95 Hub/bearing and knuckle

7. Remove hub bearing from the steering knuckle and off the axle shaft.

To install:

8. Install the hub bearing and brake dust shield to the knuckle.

9. Install the hub bearing to knuckle bolts and tighten to 75 ft. lbs. (102 Nm).

10. Install the hub washer and nut. Tighten the hub nut to 100 ft. lbs. (136 Nm). Install the nut retainer and a new cotter pin.

11. Install the brake rotor, caliper and ABS wheel speed sensor.

12. Install the wheel and tire assembly.

13. Remove support and lower the vehicle.

SUSPENSION

COIL SPRING

REMOVAL & INSTALLATION

See Figures 96 through 98.

1. Before servicing the vehicle, refer to the precautions in the beginning of this section.

2. Raise and support the vehicle. Position a hydraulic jack under the axle to support it.

3. Disconnect the stabilizer bar links and shock absorbers from the axle brackets.

4. Disconnect the track bar from the frame rail bracket.

5. Lower the axle until the spring is free from the upper mount seat and remove the spring.

To install:

6. Position the coil spring on the axle pad isolator.

7. Raise the axle into position until the spring seats on the upper isolator.

8. Connect the stabilizer bar links and shock absorbers to the axle bracket. Connect the track bar to the frame rail bracket.

9. Remove the supports and lower the vehicle.

➡**Tighten track bar with full vehicle weight applied.**

10. Observe the following torques:
- Stabilizer bar links top: 66 ft. lbs. (90 Nm)
- Stabilizer bar links bottom: 75 ft. lbs. (102 Nm)

REAR SUSPENSION

- Shock absorbers top: 37 ft. lbs. (50 Nm)
- Shock absorbers bottom: 56 ft. lbs. (76 Nm)
- Track bar: 125 ft. lbs. (169 Nm).

CONTROL ARMS/LINKS

REMOVAL & INSTALLATION

Lower Arm

1. Before servicing the vehicle, refer to the precautions in the beginning of this section.

2. Support the axle with a jackstand.

3. Unbolt and remove the lower control arm.

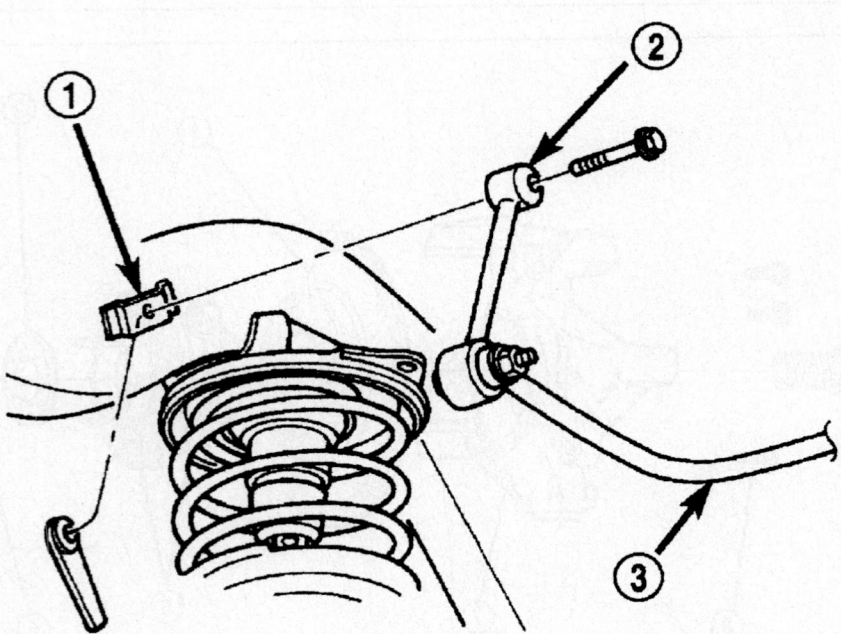

1 - FRAME MOUNT
2 - LINK
3 - STABILIZER BAR

06009-JEEP-G187

Fig. 96 Rear stabilizer bar link

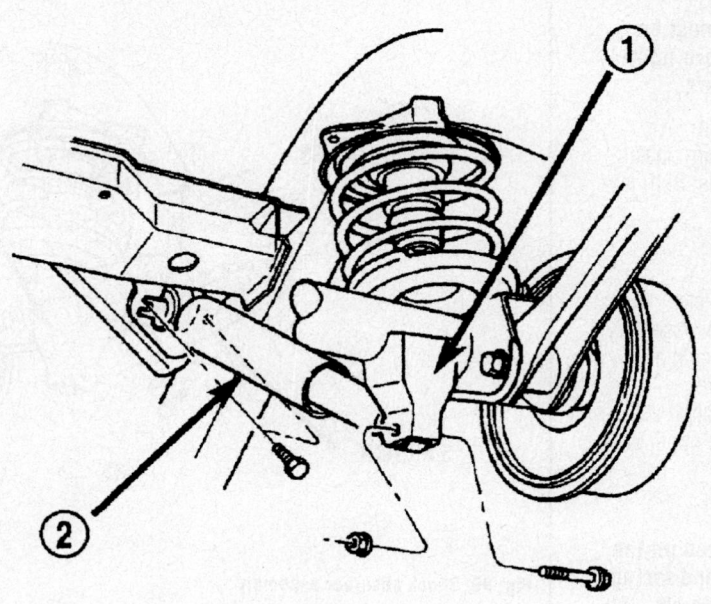

1 - AXLE BRACKET
2 - SHOCK

06009-JEEP-G186

Fig. 97 Rear spring and shock absorber

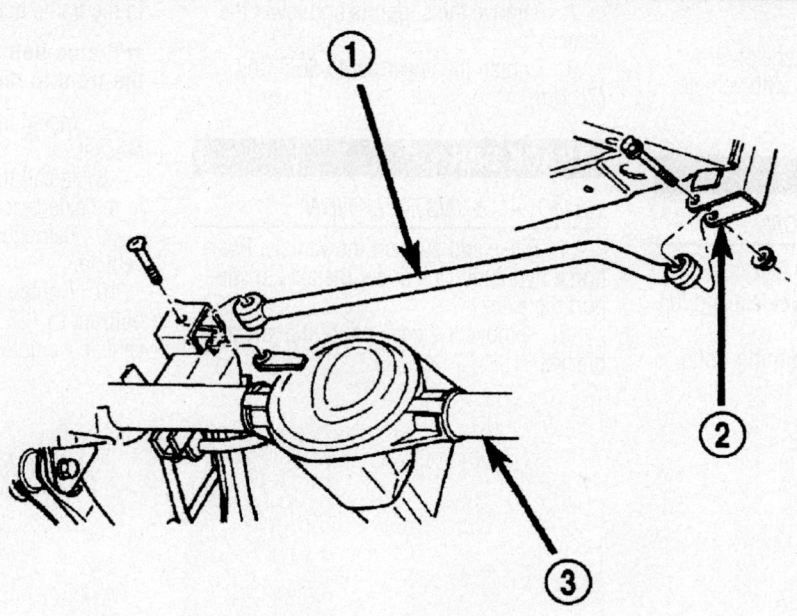

1 - TRACK BAR
2 - FRAME BRACKET
3 - REAR AXLE

06009-JEEP-G188

Fig. 98 Rear track bar

To install:

➡ **The weight of the vehicle must be supported by the springs before tightening the control arm fasteners.**

4. Install the lower control arm.

5. Tighten the lower control arm fasteners to the following specifications: Both fasteners to 125 ft. lbs. (169 Nm)

Upper Arm

1. Raise and support the vehicle.

2. Remove the tire and wheel assembly.

3. Remove the upper suspension arm flagnut and bolt at the axle bracket.

4. Remove the flagnut and bolt at the frame rail mount and remove the upper suspension arm.

To install:

➡ **Position the paint dot located on the control arm toward the axle and facing outboard. If paint dot is not visible, the bend should point inboard, and the short end should attach to the axle side.**

5. Position the upper suspension arm in the axle bracket and frame rail mount.

6. Install the mounting bolt and finger tighten.

7. Remove the supports and lower the vehicle.

8. Tighten the upper suspension arm bolts to 125 ft. lbs. (169 Nm) with vehicle weight on the wheels.

SHOCK ABSORBER

REMOVAL & INSTALLATION

See Figure 99.

1. Raise and support the vehicle and the axle.

2. Remove the upper mounting bolts.

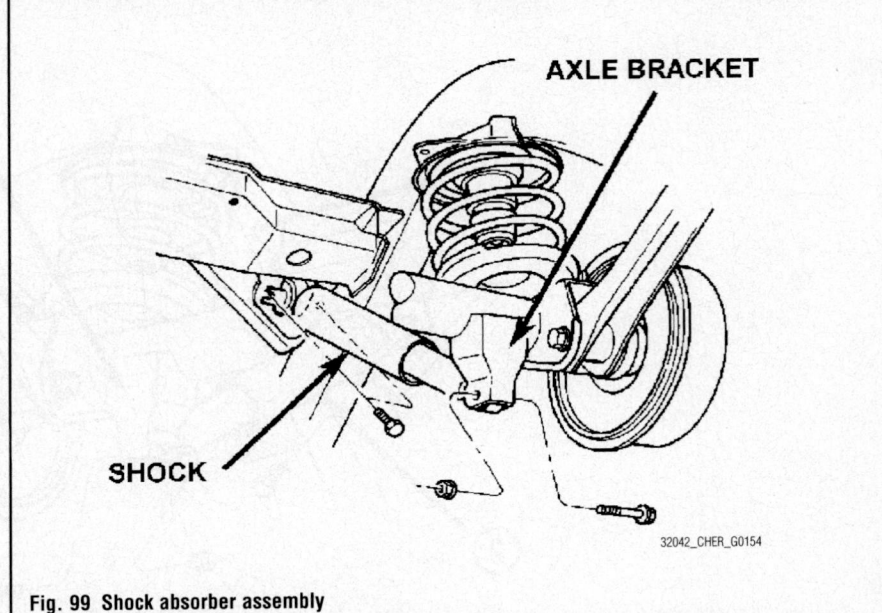

Fig. 99 Shock absorber assembly

3. Remove the lower nut and bolt from the axle bracket. Remove the shock absorber.

To install:

4. Install the shock absorber on the upper frame rail and install mounting bolts.

5. Tighten the upper bolts to 37 ft. lbs. (50 Nm).

6. Install lower bolt and nut finger tight.

7. Remove the supports and lower the vehicle.

8. Tighten the lower nut to 56 ft. lbs. (76 Nm).

TRACK BAR

REMOVAL & INSTALLATION

1. Raise and support the vehicle. Position a hydraulic jack under the axle to support the axle.

2. Remove the track bar bolt at the axle bracket.

3. Remove the track bar bolt and nut from the frame bracket.

4. Remove the track bar from the vehicle.

To install:

5. Install the track bar to the vehicle.

6. Install the track bar bolt and flagnut in the frame bracket.

➡ **Frame bolt must be installed from the front to the rear of the vehicle.**

7. Install the track bar into the axle bracket.

8. Install the track bar bolt and flagnut in the axle bracket.

9. Remove the supports and lower the vehicle.

10. Tighten the frame and axle mounting bolt/nut to 125 ft. lbs. (169 Nm) with full vehicle weight on the wheels.

CHRYSLER, DODGE AND JEEP

Diagnostic Trouble Codes

DIAGNOSTIC TROUBLE CODES

OBD II VEHICLE APPLICATIONS

CHRYSLER CORP

Dakota
2008
- 3.7L ....VIN K
- 4.7L ....VIN N
2009
- 3.7L ....VIN K
- 4.7L ....VIN P

Grand Cherokee
2008
- 3.0L Diesel ....VIN M
- 3.7L ....VIN K
- 4.7L ....VIN N
- 5.7L ....VIN 2
- 6.1L ....VIN 3
2009
- 3.0L Diesel ....VIN M
- 3.7L ....VIN K
- 4.7L ....VIN P
- 5.7L ....VIN T
- 6.1L ....VIN W

Journey
2009
- 2.0L Diesel ....VIN Y
- 2.4L ....VIN B

- 2.7L ....VIN D
- 3.5L ....VIN V

Liberty
2008
- 2.8L Diesel ....VIN 9
- 3.7L ....VIN K
2009
- 2.8L Diesel ....VIN 5
- 3.7L ....VIN K

Nitro
2008
- 3.7L ....VIN K
- 4.0L ....VIN 6
2009
- 3.7L ....VIN K
- 4.0L ....VIN X

Pacifica
2008
- 3.8L ....VIN L
- 4.0L ....VIN X

PT Cruiser
2008
- 2.4L ....VIN B
- 2.4L Turbo ....VIN 8
2009
- 2.4L ....VIN 9
- 2.4L Turbo ....VIN 8

Ram Truck
2008
- 3.7L ....VIN K
- 4.7L ....VIN N
- 5.7L Magnum ....VIN D
- 5.7L HEMI ....VIN 2
- 5.9L Diesel ....VIN C
- 6.7L Diesel ....VIN A
2009
- 3.7L ....VIN K
- 4.7L ....VIN P
- 5.7L HEMI ....VIN T
- 5.9L Diesel ....VIN 7
- 6.7L Diesel ....VIN L

Wrangler
2008
- 2.8L Diesel ....VIN 9
- 3.8L ....VIN 1
2009
- 2.8L Diesel ....VIN 5
- 3.8L ....VIN 1

OBD II Trouble Code List (P0xxx Codes)

DTC	Trouble Code Title, Conditions & Possible Causes
DTC: P000B **2T CCM** **Years:** 2008, 2009 **Models:** Dakota, Grand Cherokee, Nitro, Pacifica, Ram Truck **Engines:** All **Transmissions:** All	**Bank 1 Camshaft 2 Position Slow Response** The actual measured camshaft phase does not match the desired camshaft phasing set point. **Possible Causes:** • Engine oil dirty or contaminated • Incorrect engine oil viscosity • Insufficient engine oil pressure • CMP control circuit open or shorted • Solenoid ground circuit excessive resistance or open • Camshaft position solenoid (variable cam timing solenoid) • Camshaft phaser • Improper assembly of camshaft/crankshaft timing chain and sprockets • Engine oil pressure sensor or circuit • Engine oil temperature sensor or circuit • High friction in camshaft or other valvetrain components
DTC: P0013 **2T CCM** **Years:** 2008, 2009 **Models:** Dakota, Grand Cherokee, Journey, Nitro, Pacifica, Ram Truck, Wrangler **Engines:** All **Transmissions:** All	**Bank 1 Camshaft 2 Position Actuator Circuit Open** The PCM detects that the actual voltage of the Variable Cam Timing (VCT) Solenoid Control circuit does not match the intended state. Three good trips required to turn off the MIL. **Possible Causes:** • VCT control circuit open or high resistance • VCT control circuit shorted to ground • VCT control circuit shorted to voltage • Ground circuit open or high resistance • Variable cam timing (VCT) solenoid • Powertrain Control Module (PCM)
DTC: P0014 **2T CCM** **Years:** 2008, 2009 **Models:** Dakota, Grand Cherokee, Journey, Nitro, Pacifica, Ram Truck, Wrangler **Engines:** All **Transmissions:** All	**Bank 1 Camshaft 2 Position Target Performance** The actual camshaft phasing position is not moving towards the desired camshaft phasing position during steady state operation. **Possible Causes:** • Engine oil dirty or contaminated • Incorrect oil viscosity or low oil pressure • Fused main relay output circuit open of high resistance • CMP1/1 control circuit open or high resistance • Camshaft 1/2 position solenoid • Camshaft 1/2 phaser • Powertrain Control Module (PCM)
DTC: P0016 **1T CCM** **Years:** 2008, 2009 **Models:** Dakota, Grand Cherokee, Journey, Liberty, Nitro, Pacifica, PT Cruiser, Ram Truck, Wrangler **Engines:** All **Transmissions:** All	**Crankshaft/Camshaft Timing Misalignment** Engine cranking or running; and the PCM detected the camshaft was out of phase with the crankshaft during the CCM test period. **Possible Causes:** • Base engine problem (i.e., the camshaft timing is not correct) • Intermittent condition • CKP or CMP Sensor signal is erratic (check with lab scope) • Tone wheel or pulse wheel is damaged or contains debris • CKP or CMP Sensor, harness or connector has failed • PCM has failed
DTC: P0030 **1T CCM** **Years:** 2008, 2009 **Models:** Ram Truck **Engines:** All **Transmissions:** All	**O2 (B1 S1) Heater Circuit Fault** Engine started; system voltage over 10.6v, and the PCM detected a fault in the O2 heater element feedback sense circuit. **Possible Causes:** • O2 assembly is damaged or it has failed • O2 heater control circuit is open, shorted to ground or B+ • O2 heater ground circuit is open • O2 heater element is damaged or has failed • PCM has failed
DTC: P0031 **1T CCM** **Years:** 2008, 2009 **Models:** Dakota, Grand Cherokee, Journey, Liberty, Nitro, Pacifica, PT Cruiser, Ram Truck, Wrangler **Engines:** All **Transmissions:** All	**O2 (B1 S1) Heater Circuit Low** Key on; system voltage over 10.6v; ASD relay on; O2 heater "on". The PCM detected the O2 Heater circuit is out of acceptable range low. **Possible Causes:** • O2 assembly is damaged or it has failed • O2 heater element is damaged or has failed • O2 heater control circuit is shorted to ground • PCM has failed

DTC	Trouble Code Title, Conditions & Possible Causes
DTC: P0032 **1T CCM** **Years:** 2008, 2009 **Models:** Dakota, Grand Cherokee, Journey, Liberty, Nitro, Pacifica, PT Cruiser, Ram Truck, Wrangler **Engines:** All **Transmissions:** All	**O2 (B1 S1) Heater Circuit High** Key on; system voltage over 10.6v; ASD relay on; O2 heater "off". The PCM detected the O2 Heater circuit is out of range high. **Possible Causes:** • O2 heater element is damaged or the heater has failed • O2 heater control circuit is open or it is shorted to power • O2 heater ground circuit is open • PCM has failed
DTC: P0033 **1T CCM** **Years:** 2008, 2009 **Models:** Dakota, Grand Cherokee, Journey, Nitro, Pacifica, PT Cruiser, Ram Truck, Wrangler **Engines:** All **Transmissions:** All	**Surge Valve Solenoid Circuit Fault** Key on or engine running; system voltage over 10v. The PCM detected the Actual state of the Surge Valve solenoid circuit did not match the Intended state during the CCM test. **Possible Causes:** • Surge valve power supply is open (test power from ASD relay) • Surge valve solenoid circuit is open • Surge valve solenoid circuit is shorted to ground or power (B+) • Surge valve solenoid is damaged or it has failed • PCM has failed
DTC: P0036 **1T CCM** **Years:** 2008, 2009 **Models:** Dakota, Grand Cherokee, Journey, Nitro, Pacifica, PT Cruiser, Ram Truck, Wrangler **Engines:** All **Transmissions:** All	**O2 (B1 S2) Heater Circuit Fault** Engine started; system voltage over 10.8v and the PCM detected a problem in the Heater Relay circuit. **Possible Causes:** • O2 assembly is damaged or it has failed • O2 heater control circuit is open, shorted to ground or B+ • O2 heater ground circuit is open • O2 heater element is damaged or has failed • PCM has failed
DTC: P0037 **1T CCM** **Years:** 2008, 2009 **Models:** Dakota, Grand Cherokee, Journey, Liberty, Nitro, Pacifica, PT Cruiser, Ram Truck, Wrangler **Engines:** All **Transmissions:** All	**O2 (B1 S2) Heater Circuit Low** Key on; system voltage over 10.6v; ASD relay on; O2 heater "on". The PCM detected the O2 Heater circuit is out of acceptable range (i.e., below 0.0926v). **Possible Causes:** • O2 assembly is damaged or it has failed • O2 heater element is damaged or has failed • O2 heater control circuit is shorted to ground • PCM has failed
DTC: P0038 **1T CCM** **Years:** 2008, 2009 **Models:** Dakota, Grand Cherokee, Journey, Liberty, Nitro, Pacifica, PT Cruiser, Ram Truck, Wrangler **Engines:** All **Transmissions:** All	**O2 (B1 S2) Heater Circuit High** Key on; system voltage over 10.6v; ASD relay on; O2 heater "off". The PCM detected the O2 heater voltage is out of range high. **Possible Causes:** • O2 Sensor failed or improper operation • O2 heater element is damaged or failed • O2 heater control circuit is open or it is shorted to power • O2 heater ground circuit is open • PCM has failed
DTC: P0045 **1T CCM** **Years:** 2008, 2009 **Models:** Liberty **Engines:** 2.8L Diesel **Transmissions:** All	**Boost Pressure Solenoid Excessive Current** Ignition on; ECM Boost Pressure Solenoid commanded ON. The ECM detects excessive current on the BP Solenoid Control circuit. **Possible Causes:** • Intermittent condition • Boost Pressure Solenoid has failed • BP Solenoid control circuit is shorted to voltage • ECM has failed
DTC: P0045 **1T CCM** **Years:** 2008, 2009 **Models:** Liberty **Engines:** 2.8L Diesel **Transmissions:** All	**Boost Pressure Solenoid Open Circuit** Ignition on; ECM Boost Pressure Solenoid commanded OFF. The ECM did not detect voltage on the BP Solenoid Control circuit. **Possible Causes:** • Intermittent condition • ASD relay output circuit is open • BP Solenoid control circuit is open or is shorted to ground • Boost Pressure Solenoid has failed • ECM has failed

DTC	Trouble Code Title, Conditions & Possible Causes
DTC: P0047 **1T CCM** **Years:** 2008, 2009 **Models:** Liberty **Engines:** 2.8L Diesel **Transmissions:** All	**Boost Pressure Solenoid Short To Ground Circuit** Ignition on; ECM Boost Pressure Solenoid commanded OFF. The ECM did not detect voltage on the BP Solenoid Control circuit. **Possible Causes:** • Intermittent condition • ASD relay output circuit is open • BP Solenoid control circuit is open or is shorted to ground • Boost Pressure Solenoid has failed • ECM has failed
DTC: P0048 **1T CCM** **Years:** 2008, 2009 **Models:** Liberty **Engines:** 2.8L Diesel **Transmissions:** All	**Boost Pressure Solenoid Short Circuit** Ignition on; ECM Boost Pressure Solenoid commanded ON. The ECM detects excessive current on the BP Solenoid Control circuit. **Possible Causes:** • Intermittent condition • Boost Pressure Solenoid has failed • BP Solenoid control circuit is shorted to voltage • ECM has failed
DTC: P0050 **1T CCM** **Years:** 2008, 2009 **Models:** Dakota, Grand Cherokee, Journey, Liberty, Nitro, Pacifica, Ram Truck, Wrangler **Engines:** All **Transmissions:** All	**O2 (B2 S1) Heater Relay Circuit Low** Key on, system voltage over 10.6v, ASD relay on, O2 heater "on", and the PCM detected the Heater Relay circuit Actual state did not match the Desired state (low circuit). **Possible Causes:** • O2 assembly is damaged, or the O2 heater element is damaged or has failed • O2 heater control circuit is shorted to ground • PCM has failed
DTC: P0051 **1T CCM** **Years:** 2008, 2009 **Models:** Dakota, Grand Cherokee, Journey, Liberty, Nitro, Pacifica, Ram Truck, Wrangler **Engines:** All **Transmissions:** All	**O2 (B2 S1) Heater Relay Circuit Low** Key on, system voltage over 10.6v, ASD relay on, O2 heater "on", and the PCM detected the Heater Relay circuit Actual state did not match the Desired state (low circuit). 3 good trips are required to turn off the MIL. **Possible Causes:** • O2 assembly is damaged or it has failed • O2 heater element is damaged or has failed • O2 heater control circuit is shorted to ground • PCM has failed
DTC: P0052 **1T CCM** **Years:** 2008, 2009 **Models:** Dakota, Grand Cherokee, Journey, Liberty, Nitro, Pacifica, Ram Truck, Wrangler **Engines:** All **Transmissions:** All	**O2 (B2 S1) Heater Relay Circuit High** Key on, system voltage over 10.6v, ASD relay on, O2 heater "off", and the PCM detected the Heater Relay circuit Actual state did not match the Desired state (high circuit). **Possible Causes:** • O2 heater element is damaged or the heater has failed • O2 heater control circuit is open or it is shorted to power • O2 heater ground circuit is open • PCM has failed
DTC: P0056 **1T CCM** **Years:** 2008, 2009 **Models:** Dakota, Grand Cherokee, Journey, Liberty, Nitro, Pacifica, Ram Truck, Wrangler **Engines:** All **Transmissions:** All	**O2 (B2 S1) Heater Relay Circuit Low** Key on, system voltage over 10.6v, ASD relay on, O2 heater "on", and the PCM detected the Heater Relay circuit Actual state did not match the Desired state (low circuit). **Possible Causes:** • O2 assembly is damaged or it has failed • O2 heater element is damaged or has failed • O2 heater control circuit is shorted to ground • PCM has failed
DTC: P0057 **1T CCM** **Years:** 2008, 2009 **Models:** Dakota, Grand Cherokee, Journey, Liberty, Nitro, Pacifica, Ram Truck, Wrangler **Engines:** All **Transmissions:** All	**O2 (B2 S2) Heater Relay Circuit Low** Key on, system voltage over 10.6v, ECT input under test condition value, and the PCM detected the Heater Relay signal was too low. **Possible Causes:** • O2 assembly is damaged or it has failed • O2 heater element is damaged or has failed • O2 heater control circuit is shorted to ground • PCM has failed

DTC	Trouble Code Title, Conditions & Possible Causes
DTC: P0058 **1T CCM** **Years:** 2008, 2009 **Models:** Dakota, Grand Cherokee, Journey, Liberty, Nitro, Pacifica, Ram Truck, Wrangler **Engines:** All **Transmissions:** All	**O2 (B2 S2) Heater Relay Circuit High** Key on, system voltage over 10.6v, ASD powered up, and O2 heater is off. ECT input under test condition value and the PCM detected the Heater Relay signal was too high. **Possible Causes:** • O2 heater element is damaged or the heater has failed • O2 heater control circuit is open or it is shorted to power • O2 heater ground circuit is open • PCM has failed
DTC: P0068 **1T CCM** **Years:** 2008, 2009 **Models:** Dakota, Grand Cherokee, Journey, Liberty, Nitro, Pacifica, PT Cruiser, Ram Truck, Wrangler **Engines:** All **Transmissions:** All	**MAP Sensor/TP Sensor Correction – High Flow/Vacuum Leak** Engine started; engine speed over 2000 RPM, and the PCM detected the Manifold Air Pressure (MAP) value dropped to less than 1.5" Hg with the throttle closed during the test. **Possible Causes:** • An engine vacuum leak present • High resistance in the MAP ground circuit, MAP Sensor signal or VREF (5V) circuit • High resistance in the TP ground, TP circuit or the TP Sensor VREF (5V) circuit • MAP Sensor is damaged or it has failed • TP Sensor is damaged or it has failed • PCM has failed
DTC: P0068 **1T CCM** **Years:** 2008, 2009 **Models:** Ram Truck **Engines:** All **Transmissions:** All	**MAP Sensor/TP Sensor Correlation** Condition is monitored during all drive modes. This DTC will set when an unexpectedly high intake manifold airflow condition exists that can lead to increased engine speed and which then puts the Next Generation Controller into a High Airflow Protection Limiting Mode. This feature includes RPM limits whenever a TP and/or MAP Sensor limp-in fault is present. If vacuum drops below 1.5 in. Hg, with engine speed greater than 2000 RPM and closed throttle, this DTC will set. **Possible Causes:** • An engine vacuum leak present • High resistance in the 5V supply circuit • 5V supply circuit is shorted to ground • High resistance in the MAP signal circuit or the TP signal circuit • TP signal circuit is shorted to ground • High resistance in the Sensor ground circuit • MAP Sensor is damaged or it has failed • TP Sensor is damaged or it has failed • PCM has failed
DTC: P0070 **1T CCM** **Years:** 2008, 2009 **Models:** Dakota, Grand Cherokee, Journey, Nitro, Pacifica, PT Cruiser, Ram Truck, Wrangler **Engines:** All **Transmissions:** All	**Ambient Temperature Sensor Circuit Stuck** Engine started 4 times, 4 warm-up cycles completed, vehicle driven for 200 miles, and the PCM did not detect more than a 6°F change in the Ambient Air Temperature (AAT) Sensor signal in the test. **Possible Causes:** • AAT Sensor signal circuit shorted to power (VREF) • AAT Sensor ground circuit is open • AAT Sensor signal circuit is open • AAT Sensor signal circuit is shorted to ground • PCM High or Low circuit is damaged or it has failed
DTC: P0070 **1T CCM** **Years:** 2008, 2009 **Models:** Liberty **Engines:** 2.8L Diesel **Transmissions:** All	**Ambient Air Temperature Signal Voltage Too High** Ignition on; Ambient Air Temp. Sensor signal is above 4.82v. **Possible Causes:** • Intermittent condition • AAT Sensor signal circuit is open or is shorted to voltage • AAT Sensor ground circuit is open • AAT Sensor has failed • ECM has failed
DTC: P0070 **1T CCM** **Years:** 2008, 2009 **Models:** Liberty **Engines:** 2.8L Diesel **Transmissions:** All	**Ambient Air Temperature Signal Voltage Too Low** Ignition on; Ambient Air Temp. Sensor signal is below 0.068v. **Possible Causes:** • Intermittent condition • AAT Sensor signal circuit is shorted to ground or to sensor ground • AAT Sensor has failed • ECM has failed

DTC	Trouble Code Title, Conditions & Possible Causes
DTC: P0071 **2T CCM** **Years:** 2008, 2009 **Models:** Dakota, Grand Cherokee, Journey, Liberty, Nitro, Pacifica, PT Cruiser, Ram Truck, Wrangler **Engines:** All **Transmissions:** All	**Ambient Temperature Sensor Performance** Engine "off" time over 8 hours; DTC P0072 and P0073 not set; ambient temperature more than 38°F (4°C). The PCM determined the Ambient Air Temperature (AAT) Sensor was not within calibrated temperature of the ECT and IAT Sensor signals after a cool down period. **Possible Causes:** • AAT Sensor circuit open, shorted to ground or VREF • AAT Sensor voltage below 1.0v • AAT signal circuit is open or is shorted to ground, to battery voltage or to Sensor ground • AAT Sensor ground circuit is open • AAT Sensor is damaged or it has failed • PCM High or Low circuit is damaged or it has failed
DTC: P0072 **1T CCM** **Years:** 2008, 2009 **Models:** Dakota, Grand Cherokee, Journey, Liberty, Nitro, Pacifica, PT Cruiser, Ram Truck, Wrangler **Engines:** All **Transmissions:** All	**Ambient Temperature Sensor Circuit Low Input** Related DTCs not set, key on or engine running; system voltage over 10.5V, at least 5 warm-up cycles completed, odometer mileage change at least 196.6 miles, and the PCM detected the AAT Sensor signal was less than 0.3v (0.78v: Jeep) at PCM. 3 good trips required to turn off MIL. **Possible Causes:** • AAT Sensor internal failure • AAT signal circuit shorted to ground • AAT signal circuit shorted to Sensor ground • PCM has failed
DTC: P0072 **1T CCM** **Years:** 2008, 2009 **Models:** Liberty **Engines:** All **Transmissions:** All	**Ambient Temperature Sensor Circuit Low Input** Ignition is on. When the Ambient Temperature Sensor is less than 0.039v for 4.2 seconds this DTC with set. 3 good trips required to turn off MIL. **Possible Causes:** • AAT Sensor internal failure • AAT signal circuit shorted to ground • AAT signal circuit shorted to Sensor ground • Front Control Module has failed
DTC: P0073 **1T CCM** **Years:** 2008, 2009 **Models:** Dakota, Grand Cherokee, Journey, Liberty, Nitro, Pacifica, PT Cruiser, Ram Truck, Wrangler **Engines:** All **Transmissions:** All	**Ambient Temperature Sensor Circuit High Input** Key on or engine running; system voltage over 10.0v and the PCM detected the Ambient Air Temperature (AAT) Sensor signal was more than 4.9v for more than 2.8 seconds. Note that this code can be set due to an intermittent failure. 3 good trips are required to turn off the MIL. **Possible Causes:** • AAT Sensor signal shorted to VREF (5V) or battery voltage • AAT Sensor signal circuit or Sensor ground circuit is open • AAT Sensor is damaged (it may be open) • PCM has failed
DTC: P0087 **1T CCM** **Years:** 2008, 2009 **Models:** Liberty **Engines:** 2.8L Diesel **Transmissions:** All	**Fuel Rail Pressure Too Low Malfunction** Engine running; ECM determines that the fuel rail pressure is too low for a given engine speed. **Possible Causes:** • Air in fuel system • Fuel injector problems • Fuel Pressure Solenoid has failed • Fuel Pump has malfunctioned or failed • Fuel system has contamination • Fuel system has a leak • Intermittent condition
DTC: P0088 **1T CCM** **Years:** 2008, 2009 **Models:** Liberty **Engines:** 2.8L Diesel **Transmissions:** All	**Fuel Rail Pressure Too High Malfunction** Engine running; ECM detects the fuel rail pressure is above 23,000 psi. **Possible Causes:** • Air in fuel system • Fuel injector problems • Fuel Pressure Solenoid has failed • Fuel Pump has malfunctioned or failed • Fuel system has contamination • Fuel system has a leak • Intermittent condition

DTC	Trouble Code Title, Conditions & Possible Causes
DTC: P0089 **1T CCM** **Years:** 2008, 2009 **Models:** Liberty **Engines:** 2.8L Diesel **Transmissions:** All	**Fuel Pressure Solenoid After-Run Plausibility** Engine running; ECM determines that fuel rail pressure is too low for a given engine speed. **Possible Causes:** • Air in fuel system • Fuel injector problems • Fuel Pressure Solenoid has failed • Fuel Pump has malfunctioned or failed • Fuel system has contamination • Fuel system has a leak • Intermittent condition
DTC: P0090 **1T CCM** **Years:** 2008, 2009 **Models:** Liberty **Engines:** 2.8L Diesel **Transmissions:** All	**Fuel Quality Solenoid Open Circuit** Ignition on; ECM Fuel Quality Solenoid commanded OFF; ECM detects an open in the Fuel Quality Solenoid circuit. **Possible Causes:** • FQ Solenoid circuit(s) are open, shorted to ground, shorted to voltage, or shorted together • Intermittent condition • FQ Solenoid has failed • ECM has failed
DTC: P0091 **1T CCM** **Years:** 2008, 2009 **Models:** Liberty **Engines:** 2.8L Diesel **Transmissions:** All	**Fuel Quality Solenoid Short To Ground Circuit** Ignition on; ECM Fuel Quality Solenoid commanded OFF; ECM detects short to ground on the Fuel Quality Solenoid circuit. **Possible Causes:** • FQ Solenoid circuit(s) are open, shorted to ground, shorted to voltage, or shorted together • Intermittent condition • FQ Solenoid has failed • ECM has failed
DTC: P0092 **1T CCM** **Years:** 2008, 2009 **Models:** Liberty **Engines:** 2.8L Diesel **Transmissions:** All	**Fuel Quality Solenoid Short Circuit** Ignition on; ECM Fuel Quality Solenoid commanded ON; ECM detects excessive current on the Fuel Quality Solenoid circuit. **Possible Causes:** • FQ Solenoid circuit(s) are open, shorted to ground, shorted to voltage, or shorted together • Intermittent condition • FQ Solenoid has failed • ECM has failed
DTC: P0100 **1T CCM** **Years:** 2008, 2009 **Models:** Liberty **Engines:** 2.8L Diesel **Transmissions:** All	**MAF Sensor Signal Voltage Too Low Or Too High** Engine running between 500-5000 RPM; ECM detects the MAF Sensor signal is blow 15 kg/h for 0.5 seconds, or is above 800 kg/h for 0.5 seconds. **Possible Causes:** • ASD relay output circuit is open • ECM 5V supply circuit problem • MAF Sensor ground circuit is open • MAF Sensor has failed • Intermittent condition • MAF Sensor signal circuit is open or is shorted to ground or shorted to MAF Sensor ground • MAF Sensor 5V supply circuit is shorted to MAF Sensor ground circuit or shorted to ground • MAF Sensor ground circuit is open • MAF Sensor 5V supply circuit is shorted to voltage • MAF Sensor circuit is shorted to voltage • ECM has failed
DTC: P0101 **1T CCM** **Years:** 2008, 2009 **Models:** Liberty **Engines:** 2.8L Diesel **Transmissions:** All	**MAF Sensor Signal Negative Or Positive Deviation** Engine running; engine coolant temperature between (60-100°C); IAT Sensor reading is steady; atmospheric pressure is below 21.8 psi (1500 kPa); boost pressure is between 10.9-34.8 psi (750-2400 kPa). ECM detects the MAF Sensor reading is below (negative) or above (positive) the calibrated value for more than 2 seconds. **Possible Causes:** • Air filer problem • Air restriction in intake system • Air leak(s) in intake system • MAF Sensor has failed • Intermittent condition

DTC	Trouble Code Title, Conditions & Possible Causes
DTC: P0105 **1T CCM** **Years:** 2008, 2009 **Models:** Liberty **Engines:** 2.8L Diesel **Transmissions:** All	**Inlet Pressure Sensor Signal Plausibility** Engine running below 800 RPM; no other IAT DTCs are present. The difference between Inlet Pressure Sensor signal and Atmospheric Pressure Sensor signal is 50.8 psi for 5 seconds. **Possible Causes:** • Air filer problem • Air restriction in intake system • Intermittent condition • High resistance in Inlet Pressure Sensor signal circuit, ground circuit, or 5V supply circuit • ECM has failed
DTC: P0105 **1T CCM** **Years:** 2008, 2009 **Models:** Liberty **Engines:** 2.8L Diesel **Transmissions:** All	**Inlet Pressure Sensor Signal Voltage Too High** Ignition on; ECM detects the Inlet Pressure Sensor signal is above 4.75V for 2 seconds. **Possible Causes:** • Intermittent condition • Inlet Pressure Sensor ground circuit is open, or shorted to voltage • Inlet Pressure Sensor signal circuit is shorted to voltage • Inlet Pressure Sensor has failed • ECM has failed
DTC: P0105 **1T CCM** **Years:** 2008, 2009 **Models:** Liberty **Engines:** 2.8L Diesel **Transmissions:** All	**Inlet Pressure Sensor Signal Voltage Too Low** Ignition on; ECM detects the Inlet Pressure Sensor signal is below 0.25V for 2 seconds. **Possible Causes:** • Intermittent condition • Inlet Pressure Sensor 5V supply circuit problem • Inlet Pressure Sensor has failed • Inlet Pressure Sensor signal circuit is shorted to ground • Inlet Pressure Sensor signal circuit and ground circuit are shorted together • ECM has failed • Inlet Pressure Sensor signal circuit is open
DTC: P0106 **1T CCM** **Years:** 2008, 2009 **Models:** Dakota, Grand Cherokee, Journey, Nitro, Pacifica, PT Cruiser, Ram Truck, Wrangler **Engines:** All **Transmissions:** All	**BARO Out-Of-Range at Key On / MAP Sensor Low** Key on for less than 350 ms; engine speed less than 255 RPM, and the PCM detected the MAP Sensor input was less than 2.196v but more than 0.019v during a 300 ms period. **Possible Causes:** • Loss of 5-volt supply from PCM (internal failure) • Sensor 5-volt supply circuit is shorted, open or grounded • Sensor signal circuit is open or shorted to ground • Sensor has failed • PCM has failed
DTC: P0107 **1T CCM** **Years:** 2008, 2009 **Models:** Dakota, Grand Cherokee, Journey, Liberty, Nitro, Pacifica, PT Cruiser, Ram Truck, Wrangler **Transmissions:** All	**MAP Sensor Circuit Low Input** Engine speed from 416-1470 RPM; TP Sensor input less than 1v, and the PCM detected the MAP Sensor input was less than 2.35V at startup, or was less than 0.20v with the engine running (conditions met for 1.76 seconds). **Possible Causes:** • Loss of 5-volt supply from PCM (internal failure) • Sensor 5-volt supply circuit is open or shorted to ground • Sensor signal circuit is shorted to ground • Sensor or PCM has failed
DTC: P0108 **1T CCM** **Years:** 2008, 2009 **Models:** Dakota, Grand Cherokee, Journey, Liberty, Nitro, Pacifica, PT Cruiser, Ram Truck, Wrangler **Engines:** All **Transmissions:** All	**MAP Sensor Circuit High Input** Ignition on or engine speed from 600-3500 RPM; TP Sensor input more than 1.2v, for more than 1.7 seconds; battery voltage over 10.0v. The PCM detected the MAP Sensor signal voltage (input) was over 4.92v. **Possible Causes:** • MAP Sensor signal circuit is open • MAP Sensor ground circuit is open • MAP Sensor signal circuit shorted to 5-volt supply circuit or to battery voltage • MAP Sensor has failed or it has failed (possible open circuit) • MAP Sensor has failed • PCM has failed

DTC	Trouble Code Title, Conditions & Possible Causes
DTC: P0110 **1T CCM** **Years:** 2008, 2009 **Models:** Liberty, Pacifica, PT Cruiser **Engines:** All **Transmissions:** All	**IAT Sensor Circuit High or Low Input** Key on for 60 seconds or right after startup; and the PCM detected an IAT Sensor input of 4.6v or less than 0.2v for 4 seconds. **Possible Causes:** • IAT Sensor signal circuit is open, shorted to ground or to VREF • IAT Sensor signal circuit has a high resistance condition • IAT Sensor is damaged or it has failed • PCM has failed
DTC: P0110 **1T CCM** **Years:** 2008, 2009 **Models:** Liberty **Engines:** 2.8L Diesel **Transmissions:** All	**IAT Sensor Signal Voltage Too Low Or Too High** Ignition on; ECM detects the IAT Sensor signal is either below 0.45V (too low) or above 4.95V (too high). **Possible Causes:** • Intermittent condition • IAT Sensor signal circuit is open or is shorted to voltage (too high) • IAT Sensor signal circuit is shorted to ground or to Sensor ground (too low) • IAT Sensor ground circuit is open (too high) • Boost Pressure/IAT Sensor has failed • ECM has failed
DTC: P0111 **2T CCM** **Years:** 2008, 2009 **Models:** Dakota, Grand Cherokee, Journey, Liberty, Nitro, Pacifica, PT Cruiser, Ram Truck, Wrangler **Engines:** All **Transmissions:** All	**IAT Sensor Performance** Engine off. After calibrated amount of cool down (over 8 hours). PCM detects IAT Sensor is not within calibrated temperature amount of ECT Sensor and AAT Sensor. Engine time off when monitored is more than 8 hours and ambient temperature is more than 38°F (4°C). 3 good trips are required to turn off the MIL. **Possible Causes:** • IAT Sensor signal circuit is open, shorted to ground, to Sensor ground, or to battery voltage • IAT Sensor voltage is below 1.0v • IAT Sensor ground circuit is open • IAT Sensor is damaged or has failed • PCM High or Low circuit is damaged or has failed
DTC: P0112 **1T CCM** **Years:** 2008, 2009 **Models:** Dakota, Grand Cherokee, Journey, Liberty, Nitro, Pacifica, PT Cruiser, Ram Truck, Wrangler **Engines:** All **Transmissions:** All	**IAT Sensor Circuit Low Input** Ignition on or engine started; battery voltage greater than 10v. If the PCM detected an IAT Sensor input of less than 0.078v (Ram Truck, Grand Cherokee) for 3 seconds, less than 0.8v (), or less than 0.5V (Liberty) this DTC will set. **Possible Causes:** • IAT Sensor signal circuit is shorted to chassis ground • IAT Sensor signal circuit is shorted to Sensor ground • IAT Sensor is damaged or it has failed (an internal short circuit) • PCM has failed
DTC: P0113 **1T CCM** **Years:** 2008, 2009 **Models:** Dakota, Grand Cherokee, Journey, Liberty, Nitro, Pacifica, PT Cruiser, Ram Truck, Wrangler **Engines:** All **Transmissions:** All	**IAT Sensor Circuit High Input** Check with ignition on or engine running; battery voltage more than 10v; The PCM detected the IAT Sensor input was over 4.90v (exc. Ram) or 4.98v (Ram) for 3 seconds. **Possible Causes:** • IAT Sensor signal circuit shorted to VREF (5V) • IAT Sensor signal circuit is open, or the ground circuit is open • IAT Sensor is damaged or it has failed (an internal open circuit) • PCM has failed
DTC: P0115 **1T CCM** **Years:** 2008, 2009 **Models:** Liberty **Engines:** 2.8L Diesel **Transmissions:** All	**ECT Sensor Signal Voltage Too Low Or Too High** Ignition on; ECM detects the ECT Sensor signal is either below 0.12v (too low) or above 4.95V (too high). **Possible Causes:** • Intermittent condition • ECT Sensor signal circuit is open or is shorted to voltage (too high) • ECT Sensor signal circuit is shorted to ground or to Sensor ground (too low) • ECT Sensor ground circuit is open (too high) • Boost Pressure/IAT Sensor has failed • ECM has failed
DTC: P0116 **1T CCM** **Years:** 2008, 2009 **Models:** Dakota, Grand Cherokee, Journey, Liberty, Nitro, Pacifica, PT Cruiser, Ram Truck, Wrangler **Engines:** All **Transmissions:** All	**ECT Sensor Circuit Performance** Engine started; engine runtime over 10 minutes, and the PCM detected the ECT Sensor did not reach a calibrated level during the test period (i.e., it failed the CCM rationality test). **Possible Causes:** • ECT Sensor signal circuit is open or it is shorted to ground • ECT Sensor signal circuit is shorted to VREF (5V) • ECT Sensor ground circuit is open • ECT Sensor is damaged or it has failed • PCM High or Low circuit is damaged or has failed

DTC	Trouble Code Title, Conditions & Possible Causes
DTC: P0117 **1T CCM** **Years:** 2008, 2009 **Models:** Dakota, Grand Cherokee, Journey, Liberty, Nitro, Pacifica, PT Cruiser, Ram Truck, Wrangler **Engines:** All **Transmissions:** All	**ECT Sensor Circuit Low Input** Ignition on or engine started. The PCM detected the ECT Sensor input voltage was below 0.51v (95-03) or 0.1v (04-05, exc. Grand Cherokee, Liberty), less than 0.5V (04-05Liberty), less than 0.78v (Grand Cherokee) for 3 seconds. **Possible Causes:** • ECT Sensor signal circuit is shorted to chassis ground • ECT Sensor signal circuit is shorted to Sensor ground • ECT Sensor is damaged or it has failed (it may be shorted) • PCM has failed
DTC: P0118 **1T CCM** **Years:** 2008, 2009 **Models:** Dakota, Grand Cherokee, Journey, Liberty, Nitro, Pacifica, PT Cruiser, Ram Truck, Wrangler **Engines:** All **Transmissions:** All	**ECT Sensor Circuit High Input** Ignition on or engine started and the PCM detected the ECT Sensor input was over 4.9v for 3 seconds. If equipped, the ETC lamp will illuminate with the MIL. 3 good trips are required to turn off the MIL. **Possible Causes:** • ECT Sensor signal circuit is shorted to VREF (5V) • ECT Sensor signal circuit is open • ECT Sensor ground circuit is open • ECT Sensor is damaged or it has failed (possible open circuit) • PCM has failed
DTC: P0120 **1T CCM** **Years:** 2008, 2009 **Models:** PT Cruiser **Engines:** All **Transmissions:** All	**Throttle Position Sensor Circuit** Engine started; and the TCM detected an unexpected change in the throttle angle, or that the throttle angle went out-of-range abruptly. **Possible Causes:** • TP Sensor signal circuit is open or shorted to ground • TP Sensor ground circuit is open • TP Sensor signal circuit to TCM is open or shorted to ground • TP Sensor is damaged or it has failed • PCM has failed
DTC: P0121 **1T CCM** **Years:** 2008, 2009 **Models:** Dakota, Grand Cherokee, Journey, Liberty, Nitro, Pacifica, PT Cruiser, Ram Truck, Wrangler **Engines:** All **Transmissions:** All	**TP Sensor No. 1 Does Not Agree With MAP** Ignition is on and no MAP Sensor DTCs are set. The PCM determines the TP Sensor signals do not correlate with the MAP Sensor signal. The ECT light will illuminate. DTC P2135 should also set with this DTC. **Possible Causes:** • TP Sensor No. 1 signal circuit shorted to battery voltage • Resistance in either TP Sensor No. 1 or 2 signal circuit, 5V supply circuit or TP Sensor return circuit • TP Sensor No. 1 signal circuit shorted to group or to TP Sensor No. 2 signal circuit • 5V supply circuit shorted to ground • TP Sensor or throttle body damaged or failed • PCM has failed
DTC: P0122 **1T CCM** **Years:** 2008, 2009 **Models:** Dakota, Grand Cherokee, Journey, Liberty, Nitro, Pacifica, PT Cruiser, Ram Truck, Wrangler **Engines:** All **Transmissions:** All	**TP Sensor No. 1 Circuit Low Input** Key on; system voltage over 10v; and the PCM detected the TP Sensor indicated less than minimum value. 3 good trips are required to turn off the MIL. If equipped, the ETC light will illuminate. **Possible Causes:** • TP Sensor sweep • Intermittent condition • 5V supply circuit open or shorted to ground • TP Sensor No. 1 signal circuit shorted to ground or to Sensor return circuit • TP Sensor or throttle body damaged or has failed • PCM has failed
DTC: P0122 **1T CCM** **Years:** 2008, 2009 **Models:** Liberty **Engines:** 2.8L Diesel **Transmissions:** All	**TP Sensor/APP Sensor Circuit Low Input** Engine running. If the monitored APP Sensor voltage drops below 0.078v for 0.48 second, this DTC will set. **Possible Causes:** • TP Sensor sweep • Intermittent condition • 5V supply circuit open or shorted to ground • TP Sensor No. 1 signal circuit shorted to ground or to Sensor return circuit • TP Sensor or throttle body damaged or has failed • PCM has failed

DTC	Trouble Code Title, Conditions & Possible Causes
DTC: P0123 **1T CCM** **Years:** 2008, 2009 **Models:** Dakota, Grand Cherokee, Journey, Liberty, Nitro, Pacifica, PT Cruiser, Ram Truck, Wrangler **Engines:** All **Transmissions:** All	**TP Sensor/APPS Circuit High Input** Key on or engine running; system voltage over 10v. The PCM detected the TP Sensor indicated more than 4 4.94v for 0.48 second. If equipped, ETC light will illuminate. **Possible Causes:** • Related TP Sensor engine DTCs present • Intermittent wiring or connector problem • TP signal circuit is open or is shorted to battery voltage or to 5V supply circuit • TP sensor has failed • TP sensor ground circuit is open • PCM has failed
DTC: P0123 **1T CCM** **Years:** 2008, 2009 **Models:** Dakota, Grand Cherokee, Ram Truck **Engines:** All **Transmissions:** All	**Throttle Position Sensor No. 1 Circuit High** Ignition is on; battery voltage is more than 10.4v. The PCM detected the TP Sensor voltage is more than 4.47v for 1.3 seconds (3.7L, 4.7L) or more than 4.8v for 25ms (5.7L). If equipped, the ETC light will illuminate. **Possible Causes:** • TP Sensor No. 1 circuit is open, or is shorted to battery voltage • TP Sensor No. 1 signal circuit is shorted to 5V supply circuit • TP Sensor ground circuit is open • TP Sensor has failed • Throttle body is damaged (5.7L) • Throttle plate is jammed against the maximum stop (5.7L) • PCM has failed
DTC: P0123 **1T CCM** **Years:** 2008, 2009 **Models:** Liberty **Engines:** 2.8L Diesel **Transmissions:** All	**TP Sensor/APP Sensor Circuit High Input** Engine running. If the monitored APP Sensor voltage rises above 4.94v for 0.48 second, this DTC will set. **Possible Causes:** • Speed Sensor ground circuit open or shorted to voltage • 5V supply circuit shorted to voltage • APP Sensor has failed • TCM has failed • Intermittent wiring and connector problems
DTC: P0124 **1T CCM** **Years:** 2008, 2009 **Models:** Dakota, Grand Cherokee, Journey, Liberty, Nitro, Pacifica, PT Cruiser, Ram Truck, Wrangler **Engines:** All **Transmissions:** All	**TP Sensor/APPS Circuit Intermittent** Key on or engine running; system voltage over 10.5V. This DTC will set if the monitored TP Sensor angle between 6-120 and the degree change is greater than 5 within a period of less than 7.0 ohms. **Possible Causes:** • Related TP Sensor engine DTCs present • TP Sensor has failed • Intermittent wiring or connector problem • PCM has failed
DTC: P0124 **1T CCM** **Years:** 2008, 2009 **Models:** Liberty **Engines:** 2.8L Diesel **Transmissions:** All	**TP Sensor/APP Sensor Intermittent Circuit** Engine running. This DTC will set with a throttle angle between 6 and 120.6 with a 5 or higher change under 7ms. Related DTCs may be present. **Possible Causes:** • Intermittent wiring and connector problems • APP Sensor has failed • TCM has failed
DTC: P0125 **2T CCM** **Years:** 2008, 2009 **Models:** Dakota, Grand Cherokee, Journey, Liberty, Nitro, Pacifica, PT Cruiser, Ram Truck, Wrangler **Engines:** All **Transmissions:** All	**Closed Loop Temperature Not Reached** Engine running; battery over 10v. Engine temperature does not enable closed loop. Failure time depends on start-up coolant temperature and ambient temperature (i.e., 2 minutes for a start temperature of 50°F (10°C), or up to 10 minutes for a vehicle with start-up temperature of −18°F (−28°C). **Possible Causes:** • Low coolant level • Improper thermostat operation or thermostat failure • ECT has failed
DTC: P0128 **1T CCM** **Years:** 2008, 2009 **Models:** Pacifica, PT Cruiser **Engines:** All **Transmissions:** All	**Thermostat Rationality Test** DTC P0117, P0118, P1492 and P1493 not set, ECT Sensor between 20°F and 130°F at startup, and the PCM detected the ECT Sensor did not exceed 170°F after 10-32 minutes of sustained engine operation (the actual time depends on the ECT Sensor at startup). **Possible Causes:** • Check the operation of the thermostat (it may be stuck open) • ECT Sensor is contaminated, damaged or it has failed • Inspect for low coolant level or for an incorrect coolant mixture

DTC	Trouble Code Title, Conditions & Possible Causes
DTC: P0128 **2T CCM** **Years:** 2008, 2009 **Models:** Dakota, Grand Cherokee, Journey, Liberty, Nitro, Ram Truck, Wrangler **Engines:** All **Transmissions:** All	**Thermostat Rationality Test** With engine running after cold start. PCM predicts a coolant temperature value that it will compare to the actual coolant temperature. If the 2 coolant temperature values are not within 50°F (10°C) of each other, an error is detected. **Possible Causes:** <ul><li>Low coolant level</li><li>Thermostat has failed</li><li>Signal circuit shorted to battery voltage</li><li>ECT Sensor has failed or voltage is below 1.0v</li><li>Signal circuit is open, shorted to ground or shorted to Sensor ground</li><li>ECT Sensor ground circuit or signal circuit is open</li><li>PCM has failed</li></ul>
DTC: P0128 **1T CCM** **Years:** 2008, 2009 **Models:** Liberty **Engines:** 2.8L Diesel **Transmissions:** All	**ECT Sensor: Engine Is Cold Too Long** Ignition on; With engine running and engine temperature is below 40C, this DTC will set. **Possible Causes:** <ul><li>Intermittent condition</li><li>Cooling system problems</li><li>ECT Sensor has failed</li><li>ECM has failed</li></ul>
DTC: P0129 **1T CCM** **Years:** 2008, 2009 **Models:** Dakota, Grand Cherokee, Journey, Liberty, Nitro, Pacifica, PT Cruiser, Ram Truck, Wrangler **Engines:** All **Transmissions:** All	**Barometric Pressure Out-Of-Range** Engine cranking at less than 250 RPM; no CKP or CMP Sensor signals within 75ms. The PCM detected the MAP/BARO Sensor signal range was 0.04-2.2v for 300ms during testing. If equipped, the ETC lamp will be illuminated. 3 good trips are required to turn off the MIL. **Possible Causes:** <ul><li>IAC motor control low or control high circuit has failed</li><li>MAP Sensor VREF (5V) circuit is open or shorted to ground</li><li>MAP Sensor signal circuit is open or shorted to ground</li><li>MAP Sensor is damaged or it has failed</li><li>May be an intermittent condition</li><li>PCM has failed</li></ul>
DTC: P0130 **1T CCM** **Years:** 2008, 2009 **Models:** Dakota, Grand Cherokee, Journey, Liberty, Nitro, Pacifica, PT Cruiser, Ram Truck, Wrangler **Engines:** All **Transmissions:** All	**O2 (B1 S1) Circuit Fault** Key on or engine running; system voltage over 10.5V and the PCM detected the state of the O2 relay coil circuit (between the PCM and the relay) did not match the expected state. **Possible Causes:** <ul><li>Fused ignition feed (power) circuit open</li><li>Heater relay control circuit open</li><li>Heater relay has failed (an internal winding is open)</li><li>PCM has failed</li></ul>
DTC: P0131 **2T CCM** **Years:** 2008, 2009 **Models:** Dakota, Grand Cherokee, Journey, Liberty, Nitro, Pacifica, PT Cruiser, Ram Truck, Wrangler **Engines:** All **Transmissions:** All	**O2 (B1 S1) Circuit Short to Ground** Engine running; cold start. O2 Sensor signal voltage is below 2.402v for 9 seconds. **Possible Causes:** <ul><li>O2 signal circuit is shorted to chassis or Sensor ground</li><li>O2 return circuit is shorted to ground or to signal circuit</li><li>O2 signal circuit is shorted to O2 return upstream circuit</li><li>O2 may be contaminated or it has failed</li><li>PCM has failed</li></ul>
DTC: P0132 **1T CCM** **Years:** 2008, 2009 **Models:** Pacifica, PT Cruiser **Engines:** All **Transmissions:** All	**O2 (B1 S1) Circuit Short to Voltage** Engine started; engine runtime over 119 seconds, system voltage over 10.5V, ECT Sensor more than 176°F, and the PCM detected the O2 signal was more than 1.29v for 3 seconds. **Possible Causes:** <ul><li>O2 signal circuit shorted to heater B+ circuit (inspect the connector for oil or moisture inside the terminal area)</li><li>O2 signal circuit is open</li><li>PCM has failed</li></ul>
DTC: P0132 **1T CCM** **Years:** 2008, 2009 **Models:** Dakota, Grand Cherokee, Journey, Liberty, Nitro, Ram Truck, Wrangler **Engines:** All **Transmissions:** All	**O2 (B1 S1) Circuit Short to Voltage** Engine started; engine runtime over 119 seconds, system voltage over 10.99v, O2 heater temperature over 1085°F and the PCM detected the O2 input was over 3.70v for 1 minute. **Possible Causes:** <ul><li>O2 signal tracking (wet/oily) in connector causing a short between the signal and heater power circuits</li><li>O2 ground circuit is open</li><li>O2 signal circuit is open</li><li>PCM has failed</li></ul>

DTC	Trouble Code Title, Conditions & Possible Causes
DTC: P0133 **2T O2** **Years:** 2008, 2009 **Models:** Dakota, Grand Cherokee, Journey, Liberty, Nitro, Pacifica, PT Cruiser, Ram Truck, Wrangler **Engines:** All **Transmissions:** All	**O2 (B1 S1) Slow Response** Engine runtime over 2 minutes, ECT Sensor more than 147°F, VSS over 10 MPH, A/C and PSPS indicating off, then at idle speed in Drive (A/T) or Neutral (M/T), and the PCM detected the O2 signal did not switch enough times from 270-620 mV in the test period. **Possible Causes:** • Exhaust leak present in the exhaust manifold or exhaust pipes • O2 element is fuel contaminated • O2 element is deteriorated or it has failed
DTC: P0134 **2T O2** **Years:** 2008, 2009 **Models:** Dakota, Grand Cherokee, Journey, Liberty, Nitro, Pacifica, PT Cruiser, Ram Truck, Wrangler **Engines:** All **Transmissions:** All	**O2 (B1 S1) Remains At Center** The PCM detected the O2 signal remained fixed in a range between 350-580 mV, condition met for 60 seconds. **Possible Causes:** • Exhaust leak present in exhaust manifold or exhaust pipes • O2 element is fuel contaminated or has deteriorated • O2S signal circuit or ground circuit has high resistance • PCM has failed
DTC: P0135 **2T CCM** **Years:** 2008, 2009 **Models:** Dakota, Grand Cherokee, Journey, Liberty, Nitro, Pacifica, PT Cruiser, Ram Truck, Wrangler **Engines:** All **Transmissions:** All	**O2 (B1 S1) Heater Circuit** No Sensor output is received when the PCM powers up the Sensor heater. 3 good trips are required to turn off the MIL. **Possible Causes:** • O2 heater ground circuit open or O2 signal circuit is open • O2 heater element has failed • PCM has failed
DTC: P0137 **1T CCM** **Years:** 2008, 2009 **Models:** Dakota, Grand Cherokee, Journey, Liberty, Nitro, Pacifica, PT Cruiser, Ram Truck, Wrangler **Engines:** All **Transmissions:** All	**O2 (B1 S2) Sensor Circuit Low** Engine running; battery voltage over 10.9v; O2 heater temperature below 484°F (251°C) or ECT above 170F from previous key off. The PCM detected the O2 Sensor signal voltage was less than minimum value. **Possible Causes:** • O2 return circuit is shorted to ground • O2 signal circuit is shorted to ground, or to O2 return circuit, or O2 heater ground circuit • O2 Sensor has failed • PCM has failed
DTC: P0138 **2T CCM** **Years:** 2008, 2009 **Models:** Dakota, Grand Cherokee, Journey, Liberty, Nitro, Pacifica, PT Cruiser, Ram Truck, Wrangler **Engines:** All **Transmissions:** All	**O2 (B1 S2) Sensor Voltage High Condition:** Engine runtime for 119 seconds; O2 Sensor heater temperature is more than 662°F (350°C); Battery voltage more than 10.99v. O2 Sensor voltage is above maximum value. **Possible Causes:** • O2 Sensor signal circuit or return circuit shorted to voltage • O2 Sensor has failed • O2 Sensor signal circuit or return circuit open • PCM has failed
DTC: P0139 **2T O2** **Years:** 2008, 2009 **Models:** Pacifica **Engines:** All **Transmissions:** All	**O2 (B1 S2) Slow Response** Engine started; vehicle driven at 20-60 MPH with the throttle open for 2 minutes; ECT Sensor more than 158°F (70°C); engine is between 1200-2000 RPM; vacuum is between 28-56 kPa. PCM-compared differences (state of change) between front and rear O2 Sensors indicate difference is greater than calibrated amount. **Possible Causes:** • Exhaust leak present in the exhaust manifold or exhaust pipes • O2 element is contaminated, deteriorated or it has failed • O2 signal circuit or return circuit has failed
DTC: P0139 **2T O2** **Years:** 2008, 2009 **Models:** Dakota, Grand Cherokee, Journey, Liberty, Nitro, PT Cruiser, Ram Truck, Wrangler **Engines:** All **Transmissions:** All	**O2 (B1 S2) Slow Response** Engine started; vehicle driven at 20-55 MPH with the throttle open for 2 minutes; ECT at more than 158°F (70°C); catalytic converter temperature is more than 1112°F (600°C); and EVAP purge is active. O2 Sensor signal voltage switches less than 16 times from lean to rich within 20 seconds during monitoring, or will compare the state of change between the front and rear O2 Sensors and if the differences are greater than a calibrated amount, the DTC will set. 3 good trips are required to turn off the MIL. **Possible Causes:** • Exhaust leak • O2 element is contaminated, deteriorated or it has failed • O2 signal circuit or return circuit has failed

DTC	Trouble Code Title, Conditions & Possible Causes
DTC: P013A **2T O2** **Years:** 2008, 2009 **Models:** Dakota, Grand Cherokee, Journey, Liberty, Nitro, Pacifica, PT Cruiser, Ram Truck, Wrangler **Engines:** All **Transmissions:** All	**O2 (B1 S2) Slow Response – Rich To Lean** The Powertrain Control Module (PCM) detects that the oxygen sensor signal switches from lean to rich less than 16 times within 20 seconds during monitoring. Three good trips required to turn off the MIL. **Possible Causes:** • Exhaust leak • O2 element is contaminated, deteriorated or it has failed • O2 signal circuit or return circuit has failed
DTC: P013C **2T O2** **Years:** 2008, 2009 **Models:** Dakota, Grand Cherokee, Journey, Liberty, Nitro, Pacifica, PT Cruiser, Ram Truck, Wrangler **Engines:** All **Transmissions:** All	**O2 (B2 S2) Slow Response – Rich To Lean** The Powertrain Control Module (PCM) detects that the oxygen sensor signal switches from lean to rich less than 16 times within 20 seconds during monitoring. Three good trips required to turn off the MIL. **Possible Causes:** • Exhaust leak • O2 element is contaminated, deteriorated or it has failed • O2 signal circuit or return circuit has failed
DTC: P0140 **2T O2** **Years:** 2008, 2009 **Models:** Dakota, Grand Cherokee, Journey, Liberty, Nitro, Pacifica, PT Cruiser, Ram Truck, Wrangler **Engines:** All **Transmissions:** All	**O2 (B1 S2) Remains At Center** Engine started; system voltage over 10.5V, ECT Sensor over 150.8°F, engine running in closed loop, and the PCM detected the O2 signal was fixed at 350-580 mV for 60 seconds. **Possible Causes:** • Exhaust leak present in exhaust manifold or exhaust pipes • O2 element is fuel contaminated or has deteriorated • O2 signal circuit or ground circuit has high resistance • PCM has failed
DTC: P0141 **2T CCM** **Years:** 2008, 2009 **Models:** Dakota, Grand Cherokee, Journey, Liberty, Nitro, Pacifica, PT Cruiser, Ram Truck, Wrangler **Engines:** All **Transmissions:** All	**O2 (B1 S2) Heater Circuit** Engine running; O2 heater duty cycle is greater than 0%; ASD relay is energized; battery voltage is greater than 10.4v. No sensor output is received when the PCM powers up the sensor heater. The O2 heater is out of control for 128 seconds after it has reached 662°F (350°C). **Possible Causes:** • O2 heater ground circuit open or O2 signal circuit is open • O2 heater element has failed • PCM has failed
DTC: P0151 **1T CCM** **Years:** 2008, 2009 **Models:** Dakota, Grand Cherokee, Journey, Liberty, Nitro, Pacifica, Ram Truck, Wrangler **Engines:** All **Transmissions:** All	**O2 (B2 S1) Circuit Short to Ground** Engine runtime under 30 seconds, system voltage over 10.99v, O2 heater temperature below 484°F. The PCM detected the O2 signal was below minimum value after engine start. **Possible Causes:** • O2 upstream circuit is shorted to ground • O2 signal circuit is shorted to ground or to O2 upstream return circuit • O2 signal circuit is shorted to the heater ground circuit • O2 may be contaminated or it has failed • PCM has failed
DTC: P0152 **1T CCM** **Years:** 2008, 2009 **Models:** Dakota, Grand Cherokee, Journey, Liberty, Nitro, Pacifica, Ram Truck, Wrangler **Engines:** All **Transmissions:** All	**O2 (B2 S1) Circuit High** O2 Sensor heater temperature is more than 925°F (496°C); battery voltage is more than 10.99v. O2 Sensor voltage is more than maximum value. **Possible Causes:** • O2 signal circuit is open or is shorted to battery voltage. • O2 upstream return circuit is open or is shorted to battery voltage • O2 Sensor is damaged or has failed • PCM has failed
DTC: P0153 **2T CCM** **Years:** 2008, 2009 **Models:** Dakota, Grand Cherokee, Journey, Liberty, Nitro, Pacifica, Ram Truck, Wrangler **Engines:** All **Transmissions:** All	**O2 (B2 S1) Slow Response** Engine started; vehicle driven at a steady speed of 20-55 MPH with the throttle open for at least 2 minutes, ECT Sensor more than 158°F (70°C), Catalytic Converter temperature more than 1112°F (600°C), EVAP purge is active, and the PCM detected the O2 signal switched from lean to rich less than minimum value. 3 good trips are required to turn off MIL. **Possible Causes:** • Exhaust leak • O2 signal circuit has an open or grounded condition • O2 upstream return circuit has an open or grounded condition • O2 element is deteriorated or it has failed

DTC	Trouble Code Title, Conditions & Possible Causes
DTC: P0155 **2T CCM** **Years:** 2008, 2009 **Models:** Dakota, Grand Cherokee, Journey, Liberty, Nitro, Pacifica, Ram Truck, Wrangler **Engines:** All **Transmissions:** All	**O2 (B2 S1) Heater Circuit** Engine running and heater duty cycle is greater than 0%; battery voltage is more than 11v. O2 heater temperature does not reach 959°F (575°C) within 90 seconds, or no Sensor output is received when the PCM powers up the Sensor heater. 3 good trips required to turn off MIL. **Possible Causes:** • O2 heater control circuit is open • O2 heater ground circuit is open • O2 heater element is damaged or has failed • PCM has failed
DTC: P0157 **1T CCM** **Years:** 2008, 2009 **Models:** Dakota, Grand Cherokee, Journey, Liberty, Nitro, Pacifica, Ram Truck, Wrangler **Engines:** All **Transmissions:** All	**O2 (B2 S2) Circuit Low** Engine runtime under 30 seconds; system voltage over 10.99v; O2 heater temperature below 484°F (251°C); O2 Sensor signal was less than minimum value after engine start. 3 good trips are required to turn off the MIL. **Possible Causes:** • O2 signal circuit is shorted to chassis or Sensor ground • O2 is damaged or it has failed • PCM has failed
DTC: P0158 **1T CCM** **Years:** 2008, 2009 **Models:** Dakota, Grand Cherokee, Journey, Liberty, Nitro, Pacifica, Ram Truck, Wrangler **Engines:** All **Transmissions:** All	**O2 (B2 S2) Circuit High** Engine is running; system voltage over 10.99v; O2 heater temperature more than 925°F (496°C). The PCM detected the O2 signal was more than maximum value. 3 good trips required to turn off MIL. **Possible Causes:** • O2 signal circuit is open or is shorted to battery • O2 downstream return circuit is open or is shorted to battery • O2 is damaged or it has failed • PCM has failed
DTC: P0159 **2T O2** **Years:** 2008, 2009 **Models:** Dakota, Grand Cherokee, Journey, Liberty, Nitro, Pacifica, Ram Truck, Wrangler **Engines:** All **Transmissions:** All	**O2 (B2 S2) Slow Response** Engine is driven at 20-55 MPH with throttle open for 2 minutes; ECT Sensor over 158°F (70°C); catalytic converter temperature over 1112°F (600°C); EVAP purge is active. The O2 Sensor signal voltage switches less than 16 times or 11 times (2.7L exc. Liberty) from lean to rich with 20 seconds during monitoring. 3 good trips required to turn off MIL. **Possible Causes:** • Exhaust leak • O2 signal circuit is open or shorted • O2 downstream return circuit is open or shorted • O2 Sensor is damaged or has failed
DTC: P0161 **2T CCM** **Years:** 2008, 2009 **Models:** Dakota, Grand Cherokee, Journey, Liberty, Nitro, Pacifica, PT Cruiser, Ram Truck, Wrangler **Engines:** All **Transmissions:** All	**O2 (B1 S1) Heater Circuit** Engine running; O2 heater duty cycle is more than 0%; ASD relay is energized; battery voltage is over 10.4v. No sensor output is received when the PCM powers up the sensor heater. The O2 heater is out of control for 2 minutes after it has reached 662°F (350°C). **Possible Causes:** • O2 heater ground circuit open or O2 signal circuit is open • O2 heater element or PCM has failed
DTC: P0171 **2T Fuel** **Years:** 2008, 2009 **Models:** Dakota, Grand Cherokee, Journey, Liberty, Nitro, Pacifica, PT Cruiser, Ram Truck, Wrangler **Engines:** All **Transmissions:** All	**Fuel System Lean (B1 S1)** Engine running in closed loop. AAT Sensor signal over 20°F (-7°C). Altitude less than 8,500 feet. Fuel level greater than 15%. If PCM multiplies short-term compensation by long-term adaptive and a certain percentage is exceeded for 2 trips, a freeze frame is stored, the MIL illuminates, and a DTC is stored. **Possible Causes:** • Restricted fuel supply line • Fuel pump inlet strainer plugged or fuel pump has failed • O2 Sensor has failed • O2 signal circuit or return circuit has failed • O2 Sensor heater operation is faulty • TP Sensor sweep has failed • MAP Sensor operation has failed • ECT Sensor operation has failed • Engine mechanical problem is present • Fuel is contaminated • Exhaust leak exists

DTC	Trouble Code Title, Conditions & Possible Causes
DTC: P0172 **2T Fuel** **Years:** 2008, 2009 **Models:** Dakota, Grand Cherokee, Journey, Liberty, Nitro, Pacifica, PT Cruiser, Ram Truck, Wrangler **Engines:** All **Transmissions:** All	**Fuel System (S1 B1) Rich** Engine running in closed loop. IAT Sensor signal over 20°F (−7°C). Altitude less than 8,500 feet. PCM multiplies short-term compensation by long-term adaptive, as well as a purge fuel multiplier, and the result is below a certain value for 30 seconds over 2 trips, a freeze frame is stored. MIL illuminates and DTC is stored. **Possible Causes:** • O2 Sensor heater or O2 Sensor has failed • EVAP purge solenoid failed or improper operation • O2 signal circuit or return circuit has failed • MAP Sensor has failed or circuit malfunction • ECT Sensor has failed or circuit malfunction • Engine mechanical problem • Fuel filter/pressure regulator has failed or needs repair • PCM has failed
DTC: P0174 **2T Fuel** **Years:** 2008, 2009 **Models:** Dakota, Grand Cherokee, Journey, Liberty, Nitro, Pacifica, PT Cruiser, Ram Truck, Wrangler **Engines:** All **Transmissions:** All	**Fuel System (S2 B1) Lean** Engine running in closed loop. IAT Sensor signal over 20°F (−7°C). Altitude less than 8,500 feet. PCM multiplies short-term compensation by long-term adaptive, and a certain percentage is exceeded in 2 trips, a freeze frame is stored. MIL illuminates and DTC is stored. 3 good trips required to turn off MIL. **Possible Causes:** • Restricted fuel supply line • Fuel pump inlet strainer plugged • Fuel pump is damaged or has failed • O2 signal circuit or return circuit has failed • MAP Sensor has failed or circuit malfunction • ECT Sensor has failed or circuit malfunction • Engine mechanical problem • Fuel filter/pressure regulator has failed or needs repair • O2 Sensor has failed • PCM has failed
DTC: P0175 **2T Fuel** **Years:** 2008, 2009 **Models:** Dakota, Grand Cherokee, Journey, Liberty, Nitro, Pacifica, PT Cruiser, Ram Truck, Wrangler **Engines:** All **Transmissions:** All	**Fuel System (S2 B1) Rich** Engine running in closed loop. IAT Sensor signal over 20°F (−7°C). Altitude less than 8,500 feet. If the PCM multiplies short-term compensation by long-term adaptive, and a purge fuel multiplier, and the result is below a certain value for 30 seconds in 2 trips, a freeze frame is stored. MIL illuminates and DTC is stored. 3 good trips required to turn off MIL. **Possible Causes:** • Restricted fuel supply line • Fuel pump inlet strainer plugged • Fuel pump is damaged or has failed • O2 signal circuit or return circuit has failed • MAP Sensor has failed or circuit malfunction • ECT Sensor has failed or circuit malfunction • Engine mechanical problem • Fuel filter/pressure regulator has failed or needs repair • O2 Sensor has failed • PCM has failed
DTC: P0180 **1T CCM** **Years:** 2008, 2009 **Models:** Liberty **Engines:** 2.8L Diesel **Transmissions:** All	**Fuel Temperature Sensor Signal Voltage Too Low Or Too High** Ignition on; Fuel Temperature Sensor signal is below 0.12v or above 4.95V for 0.5 seconds. **Possible Causes:** • Intermittent condition • Fuel Temp. Sensor signal circuit is open or is shorted to voltage (too high) • Fuel Temp. Sensor signal circuit is shorted to ground (too low) • Fuel Temp. Sensor signal and ground circuits are shorted together • Fuel Temp. Sensor has failed • ECM has failed
DTC: P0181 **1T CCM** **Years:** 2008, 2009 **Models:** Liberty **Engines:** 2.8L Diesel **Transmissions:** All	**Fuel Temperature Sensor Circuit Malfunction** ECT Sensor from 14-97°F and IAT Sensor within 5°F of the ECT at startup, ECT Sensor over 140°F during testing, engine running with the VSS less than 17 MPH, and the PCM detected the difference between the Fuel Temperature and ECT Sensor signals was more than 27°F. **Possible Causes:** • Fuel Temperature Sensor connector is damaged or loose • Fuel Temperature Sensor is damaged or it has failed • PCM has failed

DTC	Trouble Code Title, Conditions & Possible Causes
DTC: P0190 **1T CCM** **Years:** 2008, 2009 **Models:** Liberty **Engines:** 2.8L Diesel **Transmissions:** All	**Fuel Pressure Sensor Signal Voltage Too Low Or Too High** Ignition on; Fuel Pressure Sensor signal is below 0.2v or above 4.8v for 0.5 second. **Possible Causes:** • Fuel Pressure Sensor signal circuit is open or is shorted to voltage (too high) • Fuel Pressure Sensor signal circuit is shorted to ground (too low) • Fuel Pressure Sensor ground circuit is open (too high) • Fuel Pressure Sensor signal circuit is shorted to Sensor ground (too low) • Intermittent condition • Fuel Pressure Sensor 5V supply circuit is open (too high) • Fuel Pressure Sensor ground circuit is shorted to voltage (too high) • Fuel Pressure Sensor has failed • ECM has failed
DTC: P0191 **1T CCM** **Years:** 2008, 2009 **Models:** Liberty **Engines:** 2.8L Diesel **Transmissions:** All	**Fuel Pressure Sensor After-Run Negative Or Positive Plausibility** At ignition shut off during After-Run; Fuel Pressure Sensor signal is below 0.415V or above 0.615V for 1.0 second. **Possible Causes:** • Fuel Pressure Sensor has failed • Intermittent condition
DTC: P0196 **1T CCM** **Years:** 2008, 2009 **Models:** Dakota, Grand Cherokee, Journey, Liberty, Nitro, Pacifica, PT Cruiser, Ram Truck, Wrangler **Engines:** All **Transmissions:** All	**Engine Oil Temperature Sensor Circuit Performance** Engine off time is more than 8 hours; ambient temperature is more than 38°F (4°C). If the PCM detects the engine oil temperature value is incorrect, by comparing it with other engine inputs, then the DTC will set. 3 good trips required to turn off MIL. **Possible Causes:** • Engine oil temp signal circuit is open or is shorted to ground or to battery voltage • Engine oil temp Sensor ground circuit is open • Engine oil temp signal circuit is shorted to Sensor ground • Engine oil temp Sensor has failed • PCM has failed
DTC: P0197 **1T CCM** **Years:** 2008, 2009 **Models:** Dakota, Grand Cherokee, Journey, Liberty, Nitro, Pacifica, PT Cruiser, Ram Truck, Wrangler **Engines:** All **Transmissions:** All	**Engine Oil Temperature Sensor Circuit Low** Ignition is on; battery voltage is more than 10.4v. The engine oil temperature Sensor circuit voltage at the PCM is less than the calibrated amount. 3 good trips required to turn off MIL. **Possible Causes:** • Engine oil temp signal circuit is shorted to ground • Engine oil temp signal circuit is shorted to Sensor ground • Engine oil temp Sensor has failed • PCM has failed
DTC: P0198 **1T CCM** **Years:** 2008, 2009 **Models:** Dakota, Grand Cherokee, Journey, Liberty, Nitro, Pacifica, PT Cruiser, Ram Truck, Wrangler **Engines:** All **Transmissions:** All	**Engine Oil Temperature Sensor Circuit High** Ignition is on; battery voltage is more than 10.4v. The engine oil temperature Sensor circuit voltage at the PCM is higher than the calibrated amount. 3 good trips required to turn off MIL. **Possible Causes:** • Engine oil temp signal circuit is open or is shorted to battery voltage • Engine oil temp Sensor ground circuit is open • Engine oil temp Sensor has failed • PCM has failed
DTC: P0201-P0204 **1T CCM** **Years:** 2008, 2009 **Models:** PT Cruiser **Engines:** 4 **Transmissions:** All	**Fuel Injector 1, 2, 3 or 4 Control Circuit Open** Ignition on. The PCM tests the injector circuit internally for more than 27 injector pulses and has determined that the circuit is open. **Possible Causes:** • Intermittent condition • Fuel injector 1-4 control circuit is open • Fuel injector 1-4 ASD relay output circuit is open • Fuel injector driver circuit is open • Fuel injector is clogged or has failed • PCM has failed

DTC	Trouble Code Title, Conditions & Possible Causes
DTC: P0201-P0204 **1T CCM** **Years:** 2008, 2009 **Models:** Liberty **Engines:** 2.8L Diesel **Transmissions:** All	**Fuel Injector 1, 2, 3 or 4 Injector Circuit Load Drop Or Overcurrent High Side Or Low Side** Engine running. The ECM detects insufficient current through the injector driver when commanded ON (circuit load drop), or the ECM detects excessive current on the high side driver circuit or on the low side driver circuit. **Possible Causes:** • ECM has failed • Intermittent condition • Fuel injector control circuit is open or is shorted to ground or to voltage • Fuel injector control circuits are shorted together • Fuel injector has failed
DTC: P0201-P0210 **1T CCM** **Years:** 2008, 2009 **Models:** Ram Truck **Engines:** V10 **Transmissions:** All	**Injector 1, 2, 3, 4, 5, 6, 7, 8, 9 or 10 Control** ASD relay "on", engine speed under 3000 RPM, injector pulse width under 10 ms, system voltage over 12v, and the PCM did not detect any inductive spike from the injector for 0.18 ms after it is turned off. **Note: This code takes 0.64-10 seconds to set once the injector is off.** **Possible Causes:** • Fuel injector 1-10 control circuit is open or grounded • Fuel injector 1-10 power circuit from the ASD relay is open • Fuel injector 1-10 has failed • PCM injector 1-10 driver has failed
DTC: P0201-P0206 **1T CCM** **Years:** 2008, 2009 **Models:** Dakota, Grand Cherokee, Journey, Liberty, Nitro, Pacifica, Ram Truck, Wrangler **Engines:** 6 Cylinder **Transmissions:** All	**Injector 1, 2, 3, 4, 5, or 6 Control** ASD relay "on"; engine speed under 3000 RPM; battery voltage greater than 10v (11.9981v: Liberty). No inductive spike is detected after injector turns off. **Possible Causes:** • ASD relay output circuit failure • Fuel injector has malfunctioned or failed • Fuel injector control circuit is open or shorted to ground • PCM has failed
DTC: P0201-P0208 **1T CCM** **Years:** 2008, 2009 **Models:** Dakota, Grand Cherokee, Ram Truck **Engines:** 8 Cylinder **Transmissions:** All	**Injector 1, 2, 3, 4, 5, 6, 7 or 8 Control** ASD relay "on", engine speed under 3000 RPM, battery voltage greater than 10v. No inductive spike is detected after injector turn off. **Possible Causes:** • ASD relay output circuit failure • Fuel injector has malfunctioned or failed • Fuel injector control circuit is open or shorted to ground • PCM has failed
DTC: P0218 **1T CCM** **Years:** 2008, 2009 **Models:** Journey, Pacifica, PT Cruiser, Wrangler **Engines:** All **Transmissions:** All	**A/T High Temperature Operation Activated** Engine started; vehicle driven in gear, and the TCM indicated the Overheat shift schedule was activated (i.e., the TCM had detected a transmission oil temperature of more than 240°F). **Note: This is an informational DTC, designed to aid the technician in diagnosing shift quality complaints.** **Possible Causes:** • Engine cooling system malfunction present • High temperature operations activated • Transmission oil pump flow is too low or it is restricted
DTC: P0218 **1T CCM** **Years:** 2008, 2009 **Models:** Liberty **Engines:** 2.8L Diesel **Transmissions:** All	**Transmission High Temperature Operation Activated** Engine running. This DTC is an informational code and does not necessarily indicate that a failure exists. It merely flags the fact that the transmission sump oil temperature reached 240°F (116°C). This temperature level can be reached when operating under a heavy load in hot weather. This causes the transmission controller to use an overheat shift schedule, which changes the shift patterns in an attempt to control the temperature. Customers may notice a different feeling or response under these conditions. The Owners Manual includes an explanation of this Over Temperature Mode for information purposes. The DTC sets immediately when the Overheat Shift Schedule is activation with a transmission oil temperature above 240°F (116°C). **Possible Causes:** • Sever operation: trailer towing in hot weather • Engine cooling system problem • Oil pump volume check • Torque converter failure • High temperature operations activated

DTC	Trouble Code Title, Conditions & Possible Causes
DTC: P0221 **1T CCM** **Years:** 2008, 2009 **Models:** Dakota, Grand Cherokee, Journey, Liberty, Nitro, Pacifica, PT Cruiser, Ram Truck, Wrangler **Engines:** All **Transmissions:** All	**Throttle Position Sensor No. 2 Performance** Ignition on; No MAP Sensor DTCs are set. TP Sensor signals Do NOT correlate to the MAP Sensor signal. If equipped, ETC light will illuminate. P2135 should also set. **Possible Causes:** • TP Sensor No. 1 or 2 signal circuit is shorted to battery voltage or to ground • TP Sensor No. 1 or 2 signal circuit has high resistance • 5V supply circuit is shorted to ground • TP Sensor return circuit has high resistance • TP Sensor No. 1 signal circuit shorted to TP Sensor No. 2 signal circuit • TP Sensor or throttle body damaged or has failed • PCM has failed
DTC: P0222 **1T CCM** **Years:** 2008, 2009 **Models:** Liberty **Engines:** 2.8L Diesel **Transmissions:** All	**Throttle Position Sensor No. 2 Circuit Low** Ignition on; battery voltage is more than 10v. TP Sensor voltage at the PCM is less than 0.16v for 0.7 second. 3 good trips required to turn off MIL. **Possible Causes:** • 5V supply circuit is open or shorted to ground • TP Sensor No. 2 signal circuit shorted to ground or to Sensor return circuit • TP Sensor or throttle body damaged or has failed • Throttle plate jammed against the maximum stop • PCM has failed
DTC: P0223 **1T CCM** **Years:** 2008, 2009 **Models:** Dakota, Grand Cherokee, Journey, Liberty, Nitro, Pacifica, PT Cruiser, Ram Truck, Wrangler **Engines:** All **Transmissions:** All	**Throttle Position Sensor No. 2 Circuit High** Ignition on; battery voltage is more than 10v. TP Sensor voltage at the PCM is more than 4.9v for 25ms. If equipped, ETC light will illuminate. **Possible Causes:** • TP Sensor No. 2 signal circuit shorted to battery voltage or to 5V supply circuit • TP Sensor return circuit is open • TP Sensor or throttle body is damaged or has failed • PCM has failed
DTC: P0234 **1T CCM** **Years:** 2008, 2009 **Models:** Liberty **Engines:** 2.8L Diesel **Transmissions:** All	**Turbo Boost Pressure Negative Deviation Performance** Engine running. Actual boost pressure differs from the boost pressure set point by more than 14.5 psi (1000 kPa). **Possible Causes:** • Air filter is clogged or malfunctioning • Air restrictions exist in intake or boost components • Air leaks exist in intake or boost components • Boost control vacuum supply is insufficient • Boost pressure actuator is malfunctioning or has failed • Turbocharger is malfunctioning or has failed
DTC: P0235 **1T CCM** **Years:** 2008, 2009 **Models:** Liberty **Engines:** 2.8L Diesel **Transmissions:** All	**Turbo Boost Pressure Sensor Plausibility** Engine running at less than 850 RPM; no other Boost Pressure Sensor DTCs are present; No Atmospheric Pressure DTCs are present. The Boost Pressure Sensor signal differs from the Atmospheric Pressure signal by 2.18 (150 kPa) or more for at least 2 seconds. **Possible Causes:** • Intermittent condition • High resistance in Boost Pressure Sensor signal circuit, ground circuit or 5V supply circuit • Boost Pressure/Intake Air Temperature Sensor has failed • ECM has failed
DTC: P0235 **1T CCM** **Years:** 2008, 2009 **Models:** Liberty **Engines:** 2.8L Diesel **Transmissions:** All	**Turbo Boost Pressure Sensor Signal Voltage Too High Or Too Low** Ignition on. The Boost Pressure Sensor signal voltage is above 4.79v for 0.5 second (too high) or is below 0.29v for 0.5 second (too low). **Possible Causes:** • Intermittent condition • BP Sensor ground circuit is shorted to voltage or is open (too high) • BP Sensor 5V supply circuit is open (too low) • BP Sensor signal circuit is shorted to voltage (too high) • BP Sensor signal circuit is shorted to ground or is open (too low) • BP Sensor signal and ground circuits are shorted together (too low) • BP/IAT Sensor has failed • Poor connector terminal contact (too high) • ECM has failed

DTC	Trouble Code Title, Conditions & Possible Causes

DTC: P0243
1T CCM
Years: 2008, 2009
Models:
Engines: All
Transmissions: All
	Wastegate Solenoid Circuit Malfunction
	Key on or engine running; system voltage over 10.5V. The PCM detected an unexpected voltage condition on the Wastegate Solenoid control circuit during the CCM test period.
	Possible Causes:
	  • Wastegate solenoid control circuit is open or shorted to ground
	  • Wastegate solenoid control circuit is shorted to system power
	  • Wastegate solenoid is damaged or it has failed
	  • PCM has failed

DTC: P0251
1T CCM
Years: 2008, 2009
Models: Liberty
Engines: 2.8L Diesel
Transmissions: All
	Fuel Quality Solenoid Open Or Short Circuit
	Ignition on; ECM detects an open or short in the Fuel Quality Solenoid circuit.
	Possible Causes:
	  • FQ Solenoid circuit(s) are open, shorted to ground, shorted to voltage, or shorted together
	  • Intermittent condition
	  • FQ Solenoid or ECM has failed

DTC: P0252
1T CCM
Years: 2008, 2009
Models: Liberty
Engines: 2.8L Diesel
Transmissions: All
	Fuel Quality Solenoid Circuit Malfunction
	Engine running; ECM detects a malfunction with the Fuel Quality Solenoid circuit.
	Possible Causes:
	  • FQ Solenoid circuit(s) are open, shorted to ground, shorted to voltage, or shorted together
	  • Intermittent condition
	  • FQ Solenoid or ECM has failed

DTC: P0253
1T CCM
Years: 2008, 2009
Models: Liberty
Engines: 2.8L Diesel
Transmissions: All
	Fuel Quality Solenoid Short To Ground Circuit
	Ignition on; ECM detects a short to ground in the Fuel Quality Solenoid circuit(s).
	Possible Causes:
	  • FQ Solenoid circuit(s) are open, shorted to ground, shorted to voltage, or shorted together
	  • Intermittent condition
	  • FQ Solenoid has failed
	  • ECM has failed

DTC: P0254
1T CCM
Years: 2008, 2009
Models: Liberty
Engines: 2.8L Diesel
Transmissions: All
	Fuel Quality Solenoid Short Circuit
	Ignition on; ECM detects a short in the Fuel Quality Solenoid circuit.
	Possible Causes:
	  • FQ Solenoid circuit(s) are open, shorted to ground, shorted to voltage, or shorted together
	  • Intermittent condition
	  • FQ Solenoid has failed
	  • ECM has failed

DTC: P0261
1T CCM
Years: 2008, 2009
Models: PT Cruiser
Engines: All
Transmissions: All
	Injector No. 1 Control Circuit Low
	Ignition is on. The PCM tests the injector circuit internally for more than 27 injector pulses and has determined that the circuit is shorted to ground. MIL is illuminated.
	Possible Causes:
	  • Intermittent condition
	  • Fuel injector has malfunctioned or failed
	  • ASD relay output circuit is open
	  • Fuel injector driver circuit is shorted to ground
	  • PCM has failed

DTC: P0262
1T CCM
Years: 2008, 2009
Models: PT Cruiser
Engines: All
Transmissions: All
	Injector No. 1 Control Circuit High
	Ignition is on. The PCM tests the injector circuit internally for more than 27 injector pulses and has determined that the circuit is shorted to voltage. MIL is illuminated.
	Possible Causes:
	  • Intermittent condition
	  • Fuel injector has malfunctioned or failed
	  • ASD relay output circuit is open
	  • Fuel injector driver circuit is shorted to ASD relay output circuit or to battery voltage
	  • PCM has failed

DTC	Trouble Code Title, Conditions & Possible Causes
DTC: P0264 **1T CCM** **Years:** 2008, 2009 **Models:** PT Cruiser **Engines:** All **Transmissions:** All	**Injector No. 2 Control Circuit Low** Ignition is on. The PCM tests the injector circuit internally for more than 27 injector pulses and has determined that the circuit is shorted to ground. MIL is illuminated. **Possible Causes:** • Intermittent condition • Fuel injector has malfunctioned or failed • ASD relay output circuit is open • Fuel injector driver circuit is shorted to ground • PCM has failed
DTC: P0265 **1T CCM** **Years:** 2008, 2009 **Models:** PT Cruiser **Engines:** All **Transmissions:** All	**Injector No. 2 Control Circuit High** Ignition is on. The PCM tests the injector circuit internally for more than 27 injector pulses and has determined that the circuit is shorted to voltage. MIL is illuminated. **Possible Causes:** • Intermittent condition • Fuel injector has malfunctioned or failed • ASD relay output circuit is open • Fuel injector driver circuit is shorted to ASD relay output circuit or to battery voltage • PCM has failed
DTC: P0267 **1T CCM** **Years:** 2008, 2009 **Models:** PT Cruiser **Engines:** All **Transmissions:** All	**Injector No. 3 Control Circuit Low** Ignition is on. The PCM tests the injector circuit internally for more than 27 injector pulses and has determined that the circuit is shorted to ground. MIL is illuminated. **Possible Causes:** • Intermittent condition • Fuel injector has malfunctioned or failed • ASD relay output circuit is open • Fuel injector driver circuit is shorted to ground • PCM has failed
DTC: P0268 **1T CCM** **Years:** 2008, 2009 **Models:** PT Cruiser **Engines:** All **Transmissions:** All	**Injector No. 3 Control Circuit High** Ignition is on. The PCM tests the injector circuit internally for more than 27 injector pulses and has determined that the circuit is shorted to voltage. MIL is illuminated. **Possible Causes:** • Intermittent condition • Fuel injector has malfunctioned or failed • ASD relay output circuit is open • Fuel injector driver circuit is shorted to ASD relay output circuit or to battery voltage • PCM has failed
DTC: P0270 **1T CCM** **Years:** 2008, 2009 **Models:** PT Cruiser **Engines:** All **Transmissions:** All	**Injector No. 4 Control Circuit Low** Ignition is on. The PCM tests the injector circuit internally for more than 27 injector pulses and has determined that the circuit is shorted to ground. MIL is illuminated. **Possible Causes:** • Intermittent condition • Fuel injector has malfunctioned or failed • ASD relay output circuit is open • Fuel injector driver circuit is shorted to ground • PCM has failed
DTC: P0271 **1T CCM** **Years:** 2008, 2009 **Models:** PT Cruiser **Engines:** All **Transmissions:** All	**Injector No. 4 Control Circuit High** Ignition is on. The PCM tests the injector circuit internally for more than 27 injector pulses and has determined that the circuit is shorted to voltage. MIL is illuminated. **Possible Causes:** • Intermittent condition • Fuel injector has malfunctioned or failed • ASD relay output circuit is open • Fuel injector driver circuit is shorted to ASD relay output circuit or to battery voltage • PCM has failed

DTC	Trouble Code Title, Conditions & Possible Causes
DTC: P0299 **1T CCM** **Years:** 2008, 2009 **Models:** Liberty **Engines:** 2.8L Diesel **Transmissions:** All	**Turbo Boost Pressure Positive Deviation Performance** Engine running. Actual boost pressure differs from the boost pressure set point by more than 14.5 psi (1000 kPa). **Possible Causes:** <ul><li>Air filter is clogged or malfunctioning</li><li>Air restrictions exist in intake or boost components</li><li>Air leaks exist in intake or boost components</li><li>Boost control vacuum supply is insufficient</li><li>Boost pressure actuator is malfunctioning or has failed</li><li>Turbocharger is malfunctioning or has failed</li></ul>
DTC: P0300 **2T CCM** **Years:** 2008, 2009 **Models:** Dakota, Grand Cherokee, Journey, Liberty, Nitro, Pacifica, PT Cruiser, Ram Truck, Wrangler **Engines:** All **Transmissions:** All	**Multiple Cylinder Misfire** Engine is running; atmospheric pressure, fuel level, battery voltage, engine speed, engine load are above minimal predetermined specifications; the engine is not in fuel cutoff and intake air temperature and coolant temperature are within normal operating ranges; there are no DTCs relating to MAP, ECT, CMP, CKP or IAT Sensor, to Crank rationality, to Crank Sensor Learn invalid, or to System Voltage. If total misfires detected are greater than 8.5% during the first 1000 RPM, or are 40% during any 200 RPM, with no single cylinder or multiple cylinder misfire counters above 80%, this DTC will set. The MIL will flash after first trip occurrence and will be steady after second trip. **Possible Causes:** <ul><li>ASD relay output circuit fault</li><li>Injector control circuit fault</li><li>Coil control circuit fault</li><li>Ignition wiring, coil control circuit or coil fault</li><li>Fuel pump inlet strainer plugged</li><li>Restricted fuel supply line</li><li>Fuel pump module is damaged</li><li>Fuel pressure leakdown fault</li><li>Fuel injector damaged or has failed</li><li>Engine mechanical problems exist</li><li>PCM has failed</li></ul>
DTC: P0300 **1T CCM** **Years:** 2008, 2009 **Models:** Liberty **Engines:** 2.8L Diesel **Transmissions:** All	**Misfire** Engine running. The ECM detects multiple misfires from one or more cylinders. **Possible Causes:** <ul><li>Engine compression problems exist</li><li>Fuel injector quantity is insufficient</li><li>Fuel injector leaking</li><li>Intermittent condition</li></ul>
DTC: P0301-P0304 **2T CCM** **Years:** 2008, 2009 **Models:** Journey, PT Cruiser **Engines:** All **Transmissions:** All	**Cylinder No. 1, 2, 3 or 4 Misfire Detected** Engine is running; atmospheric pressure, fuel level, battery voltage, engine speed, engine load are above minimal predetermined specifications; the engine is not in fuel cutoff and intake air temperature and coolant temperature are within normal operating ranges; there are no DTCs relating to ECT, CMP, CKP, MAP or IAT Sensor, to Crank rationality, to Crank Sensor Learn invalid, or to System Voltage. If total misfires detected are greater than 7% during the first 1000 RPM, or are over 3% after the first 1000 RPM, or are 25% during any 200 RPM with suspect cylinder misfire counter more than 80% and no other cylinder misfire counters above 80%, this DTC will set. The MIL will flash after first trip occurrence and will be steady after second trip. **Possible Causes:** <ul><li>Fuel system problems exist</li><li>Erratic CMP or CKP Sensor signals</li><li>Ignition system problems exist</li><li>Engine mechanical problems exist</li><li>PCM has failed</li></ul>
DTC: P0301-P0304 **1T CCM** **Years:** 2008, 2009 **Models:** Liberty **Engines:** 2.8L Diesel **Transmissions:** All	**Misfire Detected In Specific Cylinder** Engine running. The ECM detects multiple misfires from cylinder No. 1 (P0301), No. 2 (P0302), No. 3 (P0303) or No. 4 (P0304). **Possible Causes:** <ul><li>Engine compression problems exist</li><li>Fuel injector quantity is insufficient</li><li>Fuel injector leaking</li><li>Intermittent condition</li></ul>

DTC	Trouble Code Title, Conditions & Possible Causes
DTC: P0301-P0306 **2T Catalyst** **2T CCM** **Years:** 2008, 2009 **Models:** Dakota, Grand Cherokee, Journey, Liberty, Nitro, Pacifica, Ram Truck, Wrangler **Engines:** 6 & 8 Cylinder **Transmissions:** All	**Cylinder 1-6 Misfire Detected** Any time engine is running and Target Learning Coefficient (TLC) has been successfully updated, if more than 1.0% (Pacifica), 2% (Ram Truck, Liberty), 2.5% (LEV, Ram LEV, Liberty LEV), misfire rate is measured during 2 trips or with 10-30% misfire rate during one trip. **Possible Causes:** • Intermittent misfire • Base engine mechanical fault that affects only 1 cylinder • Ignition wiring, coil control circuit or coil fault • ASD relay output circuit (coil or injector) problem • Spark plug malfunction or failure on 1 cylinder • CMP Sensor, Sensor wiring harness or tone wheel is damaged • Fuel delivery component fault that affects only 1 cylinder (e.g., a dirty fuel injector) • Injector or control circuit failure • PCM has failed
DTC: P0301-P0308 **2T Catalyst** **Years:** 2008, 2009 **Models:** Dakota, Grand Cherokee, Ram Truck **Engines:** All 8 Cylinder **Transmissions:** All	**Cylinder 1-8 Misfire Detected** Any time engine is running and the adaptive numerator has been successfully updated. When more than 2% (Ram), 2.5% (LEV, Ram LEV), misfire rate is measured during 2 trips, or with 10-30% misfire during 1 trip. 3 good trips required to turn off MIL. **Possible Causes:** • ASD relay output 2 circuit fault • Injector control 1 circuit fault • Coil control 1 circuit fault • Ignition wiring, spark plug, or ignition coil fault • Fuel pump inlet strainer plugged • Restricted fuel supply line • Fuel pump module fault • Fuel pressure leakdown fault • Fuel injector is damaged or has failed • Engine mechanical problems exist • PCM has failed
DTC: P0315 **1T CCM** **Years:** 2008, 2009 **Models:** Dakota, Grand Cherokee, Journey, Liberty, Nitro, Pacifica, PT Cruiser, Ram Truck, Wrangler **Engines:** All **Transmissions:** All	**No Crankshaft Position Sensor Learned** Engine started; engine runtime more than 50 seconds under closed throttle conditions; A/C off; ECT Sensor more than 167°F (75°C). The PCM detected that one of the CKP Sensor windows had too much variance (e.g., over 2.86%) from its calibrated reference point. **Possible Causes:** • Crankshaft tone wheel flex plate is damaged • Tone wheel/pulse ring may be damaged • Erratic CKP Sensor signals (wiring/connector problem) • CKP Sensor has failed • PCM has failed
DTC: P0325 **1T CCM** **Years:** 2008, 2009 **Models:** Dakota, Grand Cherokee, Journey, Nitro, Pacifica, PT Cruiser, Ram Truck, Wrangler **Engines:** All **Transmissions:** All	**Knock Sensor No. 1 Circuit** Engine running at idle or in deceleration mode, and the PCM detected the Knock Sensor signal was below a minimum value (value depends on engine speed), or if Sensor voltage was about 5.0v with engine within idle range. **Possible Causes:** • Knock Sensor connector is damaged or shorted • Knock Sensor signal circuit open or grounded • Knock Sensor signal circuit shorted to return circuit • Knock Sensor return circuit is open • Knock Sensor not tightened properly • Knock Sensor damaged or has failed (it may be open internally) • PCM has failed
DTC: P0325 **1T CCM** **Years:** 2008, 2009 **Models:** Liberty **Engines:** All **Transmissions:** All	**Knock Sensor No. 1 Circuit** Engine running at higher than 1312 RPM; coolant temperature greater than 150°F (65°C); MAF signal greater than 250 mg/tdc; no MAF, ECT or CMP Sensor DTCs present. The Knock Sensor error program internal to the PCM is on; KS voltage was less than 0.49v and the value of the KS changes less than 0.06v every 11 or more seconds. 3 good trips required to turn off MIL. **Possible Causes:** • Knock Sensor signal circuit open or is shorted to ground or to voltage • Knock Sensor return circuit is open • Knock Sensor signal circuit is short to KS return circuit • Knock Sensor damaged or has failed • PCM has failed

DTC	Trouble Code Title, Conditions & Possible Causes
DTC: P0330 **1T CCM** **Years:** 2008, 2009 **Models:** Dakota, Grand Cherokee, Nitro, Pacifica, Ram Truck, Wrangler **Engines:** All **Transmissions:** All	**Knock Sensor No. 2 Circuit** Engine running. The Knock Sensor circuit voltage falls below a minimum value at idle or deceleration. The minimum value is from a lookup table internal to the PCM and is based on engine RPM. This DTC will also set if the Sensor voltage goes above 5V. 3 good trips required to turn off MIL. **Possible Causes:** • Knock Sensor No. 2 signal circuit shorted to battery voltage or to KS 2 return circuit • Knock Sensor No. 2 signal circuit or return circuit is open • Knock Sensor No. 2 signal circuit is shorted to KS 2 return circuit or to ground • Knock Sensor damaged or has failed • PCM has failed
DTC: P0330 **1T CCM** **Years:** 2008, 2009 **Models:** Liberty **Engines:** All **Transmissions:** All	**Knock Sensor No. 2 Circuit** Engine running at higher than 1312 RPM; coolant temperature greater than 150°F (65°C); MAF signal greater than 250 mg/tdc; no MAF, ECT or CMP Sensor DTCs present. The Knock Sensor error program internal to the PCM is on; KS voltage was less than 0.49v and the value of the KS changes less than 0.06v every 11 or more seconds. 3 good trips required to turn off MIL. **Possible Causes:** • Knock Sensor signal circuit open or is shorted to ground or to voltage • Knock Sensor return circuit is open • Knock Sensor signal circuit is short to KS return circuit • Knock Sensor damaged or has failed • PCM has failed
DTC: P0335 **1T CCM** **Years:** 2008, 2009 **Models:** Dakota, Grand Cherokee, Journey, Liberty, Nitro, Pacifica, Ram Truck, Wrangler **Engines:** All **Transmissions:** All	**Crankshaft Position Sensor Circuit** Engine cranking with at least 8 CMP Sensor signals detected. The PCM did not detect any CKP Sensor signals for 2 seconds. **Possible Causes:** • Intermittent CKP signal • CKP Sensor signal circuit is open or it is shorted to ground or voltage • CKP Sensor 5V supply circuit is open or shorted to ground or voltage • CKP Sensor ground circuit is open • CKP Sensor or CMP Sensor is damaged or has failed • PCM has failed
DTC: P0335 **1T CCM** **Years:** 2008, 2009 **Models:** PT Cruiser **Engines:** All **Transmissions:** All	**No Crankshaft Position Sensor Signal At PCM** Engine running and no CMP Sensor DTCs are present. If the PCM did not detect any CKP Sensor pulses when synchronization is attempted with the CMP signal, this DTC will set. **Possible Causes:** • Intermittent CKP signal • 5V supply circuit open, or shorted to ground or voltage • CKP Sensor signal circuit is open or shorted to ground or voltage • CKP Sensor signal circuit is shorted to 5V supply circuit • CKP Sensor ground circuit is open • CKP Sensor or PCM has failed
DTC: P0335 **1T CCM** **Years:** 2008, 2009 **Models:** Liberty **Engines:** 2.8L Diesel **Transmissions:** All	**Crankshaft Position Sensor Circuit Incorrect Or Missing Signal** Engine running at less than 6000 RPM. The ECM does not receive a CKP Sensor signal or receives an incorrect signal. **Possible Causes:** • CKP Sensor is damaged, improperly positioned or has failed • ECM has failed • Intermittent condition • CKP Sensor signal circuit(s) shorted to ground or shorted together • CKP Sensor signal circuits open or shorted to voltage
DTC: P0336 **1T CCM** **Years:** 2008, 2009 **Models:** PT Cruiser **Engines:** All **Transmissions:** All	**Crankshaft Position Sensor Incorrect Performance** Engine running and no CMP Sensor DTCs are present. If the PCM detects an incorrect amount of CKP Sensor pulses when compared to CMP Sensor pulse, this DTC will set. **Possible Causes:** • Intermittent CMP signal • Wiring harness problems exist • Tone wheel/pulse ring damaged or has failed • CKP Sensor is damaged or has failed • CMP Sensor has failed

DTC	Trouble Code Title, Conditions & Possible Causes
DTC: P0339 **1T CCM** **Years:** 2008, 2009 **Models:** Dakota, Grand Cherokee, Journey, Liberty, Nitro, Pacifica, PT Cruiser, Ram Truck, Wrangler **Engines:** All **Transmissions:** All	**Crankshaft Position Sensor Circuit Intermittent** Engine cranking or running; CMP Sensor signals detected. The PCM detected an intermittent loss of the CKP Sensor signal. The Failure counter must reach 20 before this code will set. **Possible Causes:** • Check the tone wheel/pulse ring for damage or debris collection • CKP Sensor signal circuit is open or shorted to ground • CKP Sensor 5V supply circuit is open or shorted to ground • CKP Sensor is damaged or it has failed • PCM has failed
DTC: P0339 **1T CCM** **Years:** 2008, 2009 **Models:** Liberty **Engines:** 2.8L Diesel **Transmissions:** All	**Crankshaft Position Sensor Circuit Intermittent Or Missing Signal** Engine running at less than 6000 RPM. The ECM does not receive a CKP Sensor signal or receives an incorrect signal. **Possible Causes:** • CKP Sensor is damaged, improperly positioned or has failed • ECM has failed • Intermittent condition • CKP Sensor signal circuit(s) shorted to ground or shorted together • CKP Sensor signal circuits open or shorted to voltage
DTC: P0340 **1T CCM** **Years:** 2008, 2009 **Models:** Dakota, Grand Cherokee, Journey, Liberty, Nitro, Pacifica, Ram Truck, Wrangler **Engines:** All **Transmissions:** All	**No Camshaft Position Sensor Circuit Failure** Engine cranking or running, system voltage over 10v. The PCM detected CKP pulses without detecting any CMP Sensor pulses for 5 seconds or 2.5 engine revolutions. **Possible Causes:** • CMP Sensor connector is damaged, open or it is shorted • CMP Sensor signal circuit is open or shorted to ground or to battery voltage or 5V supply circuit • CMP Sensor 5V supply circuit is open or shorted to ground or to battery voltage • CMP Sensor ground circuit is open • CMP Sensor is damaged or has failed • CKP Sensor is damaged or has failed • PCM has failed
DTC: P0340 **1T CCM** **Years:** 2008, 2009 **Models:** PT Cruiser **Engines:** All **Transmissions:** All	**No CMP Sensor Signal** Engine cranking or running; no CKP Sensor DTCs present. At least 10 engine revolutions have elapsed, with CKP Sensor signals present, but no CMP Sensor signal polarity change. **Possible Causes:** • Intermittent CMP signal • 5V supply circuit open or is shorted to ground or to voltage • CMP Sensor signal circuit is open or shorted to ground or to battery voltage or 5V supply circuit • CMP Sensor ground circuit is open • 5V supply has failed • CMP Sensor is damaged or has failed
DTC: P0340 **1T CCM** **Years:** 2008, 2009 **Models:** Liberty **Engines:** 2.8L Diesel **Transmissions:** All	**Camshaft Position Sensor Circuit Incorrect Or Missing Signal** Engine running at less than 6000 RPM. The ECM does not receive a CMP Sensor signal or receives an incorrect signal. **Possible Causes:** • 5V supply circuit is open • CMP Sensor signal circuit shorted to voltage • CMP Sensor is damaged, improperly positioned or has failed • ECM has failed
DTC: P0344 **1T CCM** **Years:** 2008, 2009 **Models:** Dakota, Grand Cherokee, Journey, Liberty, Nitro, Pacifica, PT Cruiser, Ram Truck, Wrangler **Engines:** All **Transmissions:** All	**Camshaft Position Sensor Circuit Intermittent** Engine cranking or running; system voltage over 10.5V. The PCM detected an intermittent loss of the CMP Sensor signal during the period of 2.5 complete engine revolutions. The failure counter must reach 20 before this code matures and a code is set. **Possible Causes:** • Wiring harness fault • 5V supply circuit open or shorted to ground • Tone wheel/pulse ring is damaged or corroded • CMP Sensor has failed • CMP Sensor signal circuit is open, shorted to ground or battery voltage or 5V supply • CMP Sensor ground circuit is open • PCM has failed

DTC	Trouble Code Title, Conditions & Possible Causes
DTC: P0344 **1T CCM** **Years:** 2008, 2009 **Models:** Liberty **Engines:** 2.8L Diesel **Transmissions:** All	**Camshaft Position Sensor Circuit Intermittent Or Missing Signal** Engine running at less than 6000 RPM. The ECM does not receive a CMP Sensor signal or receives an intermittent signal. **Possible Causes:** • 5V supply circuit is open or is shorted to ground or to Sensor ground circuit • CMP Sensor signal circuit is open or is shorted to voltage or to ground • CMP Sensor is damaged, improperly positioned or has failed • ECM has failed • CMP Sensor ground circuit open • Intermittent condition
DTC: P0346 **1T CCM** **Years:** 2008, 2009 **Models:** PT Cruiser **Engines:** All **Transmissions:** All	**Camshaft Position Sensor Bank 1 Sensor 1 Performance** The PCM receives either no signal or an incorrect signal from the Camshaft 1/1 Position Sensor. **Possible Causes:** • CMP Sensor connector is damaged, open or it is shorted • CMP Sensor signal circuit is open or shorted to ground or to battery voltage or 5V supply circuit • CMP Sensor 5V supply circuit is open or shorted to ground or to battery voltage • CMP Sensor ground circuit is open • CMP Sensor is damaged or has failed • PCM has failed
DTC: P0351 **1T CCM** **Years:** 2008, 2009 **Models:** PT Cruiser **Engines:** All **Transmissions:** All	**Ignition Coil 1 Circuit** The PCM detects that the actual state of Ignition Coil 1 does not match the intended state. **Possible Causes:** • Fused main relay output circuit open or high resistance • Coil control circuit open or high resistance • Ignition coil • PCM
DTC: P0352 **1T CCM** **Years:** 2008, 2009 **Models:** PT Cruiser **Engines:** All **Transmissions:** All	**Ignition Coil 2 Circuit** The PCM detects that the actual state of Ignition Coil 2 does not match the intended state. **Possible Causes:** • Fused main relay output circuit open or high resistance • Coil control circuit open or high resistance • Ignition coil • PCM
DTC: P0353 **1T CCM** **Years:** 2008, 2009 **Models:** PT Cruiser **Engines:** All **Transmissions:** All	**Ignition Coil 3 Circuit** The PCM detects that the actual state of Ignition Coil 3 does not match the intended state. **Possible Causes:** • Fused main relay output circuit open or high resistance • Coil control circuit open or high resistance • Ignition coil • PCM
DTC: P0354 **1T CCM** **Years:** 2008, 2009 **Models:** PT Cruiser **Engines:** All **Transmissions:** All	**Ignition Coil 4 Circuit** The PCM detects that the actual state of Ignition Coil 4 does not match the intended state. **Possible Causes:** • Fused main relay output circuit open or high resistance • Coil control circuit open or high resistance • Ignition coil • PCM
DTC: P0365 **1T CCM** **Years:** 2008, 2009 **Models:** PT Cruiser **Engines:** All **Transmissions:** All	**Camshaft Position Sensor Bank 1 Sensor 2** The PCM receives either no signal or an incorrect signal from the Camshaft 1/2 Position Sensor. **Possible Causes:** • CMP Sensor connector is damaged, open or it is shorted • CMP Sensor signal circuit is open or shorted to ground or to battery voltage or 5V supply circuit • CMP Sensor 5V supply circuit is open or shorted to ground or to battery voltage • CMP Sensor ground circuit is open • CMP Sensor is damaged or has failed • PCM has failed

DTC	Trouble Code Title, Conditions & Possible Causes
DTC: P0366 **1T CCM** **Years:** 2008, 2009 **Models:** PT Cruiser **Engines:** All **Transmissions:** All	**Camshaft Position Sensor Bank 1 Sensor 2** The PCM receives either no signal or an incorrect signal from the Camshaft 1/2 Position Sensor. **Possible Causes:** • CMP Sensor connector is damaged, open or it is shorted • CMP Sensor signal circuit is open or shorted to ground or to battery voltage or 5V supply circuit • CMP Sensor 5V supply circuit is open or shorted to ground or to battery voltage • CMP Sensor ground circuit is open • CMP Sensor is damaged or has failed • PCM has failed
DTC: P0369 **1T CCM** **Years:** 2008, 2009 **Models:** PT Cruiser **Engines:** All **Transmissions:** All	**Camshaft Position Sensor Intermittent Bank 1 Sensor 2** The PCM detects an intermittent signal error from the Camshaft 1/2 Position Sensor. **Possible Causes:** • CMP Sensor connector is damaged, open or it is shorted • CMP Sensor signal circuit is open or shorted to ground or to battery voltage or 5V supply circuit • CMP Sensor 5V supply circuit is open or shorted to ground or to battery voltage • CMP Sensor ground circuit is open • CMP Sensor is damaged or has failed • PCM has failed
DTC: P0401 **2T EGR** **Years:** 2008, 2009 **Models:** Dakota, Grand Cherokee, Journey, Liberty, Nitro, Pacifica, PT Cruiser, Ram Truck, Wrangler **Engines:** All **Transmissions:** All	**EGR System Fault** Engine running for more than 2 minutes with ECT more than 158°F (70°C). EGR is active. Vehicle is at less than 8500 feet altitude. Ambient temperature more than 20°F (−6°C). PCM closes EGR valve while monitoring O2 Sensor signal. Once a closed EGR fueling sample has been established, PCM then ramps in EGR and additional fueling, while monitoring the O2 Sensor signal in the open state. A fueling sample is again established. The PCM then compares the 2 different O2 Sensor signal readings (fueling samples). If a larger than expected variation is detected, a soft failure is recorded. Three soft failures set a one-trip (1T) failure. After 2 failed trips (2T), a DTC is set and the MIL illuminated. **Possible Causes:** • EGR valve is open at idle • EGR solenoid ground circuit is open • EGR solenoid control circuit is open, shorted to ground or to voltage • ASD relay power circuit open to the EGR solenoid • EGR valve or solenoid is damaged or has failed • PCM has failed (EGR open or EGR closed)
DTC: P0402 **1T CCM** **Years:** 2008, 2009 **Models:** Liberty **Engines:** 2.8L Diesel **Transmissions:** All	**EGR Solenoid Circuit Deviation** Engine running. The ECM detects the EGR flow is less than the requested flow (negative deviation) or is greater than the requested flow (positive deviation). **Possible Causes:** • Air filter is restricted or damaged • Air restrictions in intake air system or EGR system • Air leaks in intake air system or EGR system • EGR valve has malfunctioned or failed • Intermittent condition
DTC: P0403 **1T CCM** **Years:** 2008, 2009 **Models:** Dakota, Grand Cherokee, Journey, Liberty, Nitro, Pacifica, PT Cruiser, Ram Truck, Wrangler **Engines:** All **Transmissions:** All	**EGR Solenoid Circuit** Engine started; system voltage over 10.5V. The EGR solenoid control circuit was not in its expected state when requested to operate by the PCM. **Possible Causes:** • EGR solenoid ground circuit is open • EGR solenoid control circuit is open or shorted to ground or to voltage • EGR solenoid power circuit is open • EGR solenoid is damaged or has failed • PCM has failed
DTC: P0403 **1T CCM** **Years:** 2008, 2009 **Models:** Liberty **Engines:** 2.8L Diesel **Transmissions:** All	**EGR Solenoid Circuit Excessive Current** Ignition on; ECM commands EGR Solenoid on. The ECM detects excessive current on the EGR Solenoid control circuit. **Possible Causes:** • Intermittent condition • EGR Solenoid has malfunctioned • EGR Solenoid control circuit is shorted to voltage • EMC has internal short to voltage

DTC	Trouble Code Title, Conditions & Possible Causes
DTC: P0403 **1T CCM** **Years:** 2008, 2009 **Models:** Liberty **Engines:** 2.8L Diesel **Transmissions:** All	**EGR Solenoid Circuit Open** Ignition on; ECM commands EGR Solenoid off. The ECM does not detect voltage on the EGR Solenoid control circuit. **Possible Causes:** • Intermittent condition • ASD Relay output circuit is open • EGR Solenoid control circuit is open or is shorted to ground • EGR Solenoid has malfunctioned • EMC has failed
DTC: P0404 **1T CCM** **Years:** 2008, 2009 **Models:** Dakota, Grand Cherokee, Journey, Liberty, Nitro, Pacifica, PT Cruiser, Ram Truck, Wrangler **Engines:** All **Transmissions:** All	**EGR Position Sensor Signal Performance** Engine started; system voltage over 10.5V and the PCM detected that the EGR flow (or valve movement) was not what was expected during the test period. **Possible Causes:** • EGR Sensor signal circuit is open or shorted to ground • EGR Sensor 5V supply circuit is open or has high resistance • EGR Sensor ground circuit is open • EGR solenoid control circuit has a problem • EGR valve actuator loose, sticking, blocked or improperly grounded • EGR Sensor is damaged or has failed • Intermittent condition • PCM has failed
DTC: P0405 **1T CCM** **Years:** 2008, 2009 **Models:** Dakota, Grand Cherokee, Journey, Liberty, Nitro, Pacifica, PT Cruiser, Ram Truck, Wrangler **Engines:** All **Transmissions:** All	**EGR Position Sensor Circuit Low Input** Key on or engine running; system voltage over 10v. The PCM detected that the EGR Sensor signal indicated less than 0.1v. **Possible Causes:** • EGR Sensor signal circuit is shorted to ground or open • EGR Sensor VREF (5V) circuit is open or shorted to ground • EGR Sensor is damaged (shorted internally) or it has failed • EGR position internal failure • PCM has failed
DTC: P0406 **1T CCM** **Years:** 2008, 2009 **Models:** Dakota, Grand Cherokee, Journey, Liberty, Nitro, Pacifica, PT Cruiser, Ram Truck, Wrangler **Engines:** All **Transmissions:** All	**EGR Position Sensor Circuit High Input** Key on or engine running; system voltage over 10.5V. The PCM detected the EGR Sensor indicated more than 4.89v for 6 seconds. **Possible Causes:** • Intermittent condition • EGR Sensor signal is shorted to VREF (5V) supply circuit or to battery voltage • EGR Sensor ground circuit is open • EGR Sensor signal circuit is open • EGR Sensor is damaged (it may have an internal open circuit) • EGR solenoid failure • PCM has failed
DTC: P0420 **2T Catalyst** **Years:** 2008, 2009 **Models:** Dakota, Grand Cherokee, Journey, Liberty, Nitro, Pacifica, PT Cruiser, Ram Truck, Wrangler **Engines:** All **Transmissions:** All	**Catalyst Efficiency Below Normal (Bank 1)** Engine speed at 1200-1700 RPM in closed loop with the throttle open for over 2 minutes, ECT Sensor more than 147°F, MAP Sensor signal from 15.0-21.0 in. Hg, and the PCM detected the switch rate of the rear O2 reached 70% of the switch rate of the front O2. **Possible Causes:** • Air leaks in at the exhaust manifold or exhaust pipes • Base engine problems (high coolant or engine oil consumption) • Catalytic converter damaged or has failed • Front O2 older (aged) than the rear O2 (O2 is lazy)
DTC: P0430 **1T Catalyst** **Years:** 2008, 2009 **Models:** Dakota, Grand Cherokee, Journey, Liberty, Nitro, Pacifica, PT Cruiser, Ram Truck, Wrangler **Engines:** All **Transmissions:** All	**Catalyst (2/1) Efficiency Below Normal** After engine warm-up, ECT Sensor more than 170°F for 180 seconds of open throttle operation and over 20 MPH (engine between 1200-1700 RPM and MAP vacuum between 15-20 in. Hg). As catalyst efficiency deteriorates, the switch rate of the downstream O2 Sensor approaches that of the upstream O2 Sensor. If, at any point during the test, the switch ratio reaches a predetermined value, a counter is incremented by one. 3 good trips required to turn off MIL. **Possible Causes:** • Exhaust leaks • Base engine problems • Catalytic converter damaged or has failed • Front O2 older (aged) than the rear O2 (O2 is lazy)

DTC	Trouble Code Title, Conditions & Possible Causes
DTC: P0432 **2T Catalyst** **Years:** 2008, 2009 **Models:** Dakota, Grand Cherokee, Journey, Liberty, Nitro, Pacifica, Ram Truck, Wrangler **Engines:** All **Transmissions:** All	**Catalyst Efficiency Below Normal (Bank 2)** Engine speed at 1200-1700 RPM in closed loop with the throttle open for over 2 minutes, ECT Sensor more than 147°F, MAP Sensor signal from 15.0-21.0" Hg, and the PCM detected the switch rate of the rear O2 reached 70% of the switch rate of the front O2. **Possible Causes:** • Air leaks in at the exhaust manifold or exhaust pipes • Base engine problems (high coolant or engine oil consumption) • Catalytic converter damaged or has failed • Front O2 older (aged) than the rear O2 (O2 is lazy)
DTC: P0440 **2T EVAP** **Years:** 2008, 2009 **Models:** Dakota, Grand Cherokee, Journey, Liberty, Nitro, Pacifica, PT Cruiser, Ram Truck, Wrangler **Engines:** All **Transmissions:** All	**EVAP Purge System Fault** Ambient Air Temperature from 39-89°F (4-32°C); engine running; Fuel level over 12%. The PCM detected that the NVLD switch did not close during medium/large leak test. Once this event occurs, the PCM will increase the amount of vacuum in the system that flows past the purge valve. If the NVLD switch does not close under these conditions, the PCM will set this code. **Possible Causes:** • EVAP purge valve vacuum supply is leaking or clogged • EVAP purge valve is stuck closed • EVAP purge solenoid has failed • NVLD assembly (leak detection) is damaged or has failed • NVLD switch circuit is open or the NVLD switch has failed • Ground circuit is open • PCM has failed
DTC: P0441 **2T EVAP** **Years:** 2008, 2009 **Models:** Dakota, Grand Cherokee, Journey, Liberty, Nitro, Pacifica, PT Cruiser, Ram Truck, Wrangler **Engines:** All **Transmissions:** All	**EVAP Purge System Performance** Check with cold start test. Engine running. Small leak test passed. The PCM activates the EVAP purge solenoid and it gradually increases to maximum flow. During flow, the PCM looks for the NVLD switch to close. If the PCM does not see the NVLD switch close at maximum flow, an error is detected. **Possible Causes:** • Intermittent condition • EVAP purge solenoid functioning improperly • EVAP purge solenoid vacuum supply leaking or clogged
DTC: P0442 **2T EVAP** **Years:** 2008, 2009 **Models:** Dakota, Grand Cherokee, Journey, Liberty, Nitro, Pacifica, PT Cruiser, Ram Truck, Wrangler **Engines:** All **Transmissions:** All	**EVAP System Medium Leak Detected** Monitor with engine running. Cold start test. Fuel level more than 12%. Ambient temperature between 39-89°F (4-32°C). Closed loop fuel system. Test runs when small leak test is maturing. The PCM activates EVAP purge solenoid to pull EVAP system into a vacuum to close the NVLD switch. Once this switch is closed, the PCM turns the EVAP purge solenoid off to seal the EVAP system. If the NVLD switch re-opens before the calibrated amount of time for a Medium leak, an error is detected. **Possible Causes:** • Intermittent condition • Vacuum hoses, connections or switches have come loose or malfunctioned • EVAP emission system has a leak • EVAP purge solenoid operation has malfunctioned • NVLD switch operation has malfunctioned
DTC: P0443 **1T CCM** **Years:** 2008, 2009 **Models:** Dakota, Grand Cherokee, Journey, Liberty, Nitro, Pacifica, PT Cruiser, Ram Truck, Wrangler **Engines:** All **Transmissions:** All	**EVAP Purge Solenoid Circuit Fault** Ignition on or engine running. Battery voltage more than 10v. The PCM will set a trouble code if the actual state of the solenoid does not match the intended state. **Possible Causes:** • EVAP purge solenoid control circuit open or shorted to ground • EVAP purge solenoid return circuit open or shorted to ground • EVAP purge solenoid is damaged or it has failed • PCM has failed
DTC: P0444 **1T CCM** **Years:** 2008, 2009 **Models:** PT Cruiser **Engines:** All **Transmissions:** All	**EVAP Purge Solenoid Circuit Open** Any time key is on, if the PCM detects an open circuit in the purge solenoid or in the circuit for more than 280ms, a one-trip fault is set and the MIL is illuminated. **Possible Causes:** • Intermittent condition • 12V supply circuit is open • EVAP purge solenoid control circuit open • EVAP purge solenoid is open • PCM has failed

DTC	Trouble Code Title, Conditions & Possible Causes
DTC: P0445 **2T EVAP** **Years:** 2008, 2009 **Models:** Pacifica **Engines:** All **Transmissions:** All	**EVAP System Large Leak Detected** Monitor with engine running. Cold start test. Fuel level more than 12%. Ambient temperature between 39-89°F (4-32°C). Closed loop fuel system. Test runs when small leak test is maturing. The PCM activates EVAP purge solenoid to pull EVAP system into a vacuum to close the NVLD switch. Once this switch is closed, the PCM turns the EVAP purge solenoid off to seal the EVAP system. If the NVLD switch re-opens before the calibrated amount of time for a Large leak, an error is detected. **Possible Causes:** • Intermittent condition • Vacuum hoses, connections or switches have come loose or malfunctioned • EVAP emission system has a leak • EVAP purge solenoid operation has malfunctioned • NVLD switch operation has malfunctioned
DTC: P0452 **1T CCM** **Years:** 2008, 2009 **Models:** Dakota, Grand Cherokee, Journey, Liberty, Nitro, Pacifica, PT Cruiser, Ram Truck, Wrangler **Engines:** All **Transmissions:** All	**NVLD Pressure Switch Sense Circuit Low Input** Engine started; and immediately after the engine is running. The PCM activates the NVLD solenoid to test the NVLD switch circuit. If the switch is not open, the PCM sets this code. **Possible Causes:** • EVAP purge solenoid control circuit is shorted to ground • EVAP purge solenoid is leaking or it is stuck in open position • NVLD assembly or NVLD switch is damaged or it has failed • NVLD switch signal circuit is shorted to ground • PCM has failed
DTC: P0453 **1T CCM** **Years:** 2008, 2009 **Models:** Dakota, Grand Cherokee, Journey, Liberty, Nitro, Pacifica, PT Cruiser, Ram Truck, Wrangler **Engines:** All **Transmissions:** All	**NVLD Pressure Switch Sense Circuit High Input** Engine started; and immediately after the engine is running, the PCM activates the NVLD solenoid to test the NVLD switch circuit. If the switch does not close under these conditions, this code is set. **Possible Causes:** • NVLD assembly ground circuit is open • NVLD switch signal circuit is open or shorted to power (B+) or to NVLD solenoid control circuit • NVLD assembly or switch is damaged or it has failed • PCM has failed
DTC: P0455 **2T EVAP** **Years:** 2008, 2009 **Models:** Dakota, Grand Cherokee, Journey, Liberty, Nitro, Pacifica, PT Cruiser, Ram Truck, Wrangler **Engines:** All **Transmissions:** All	**EVAP Large Leak Detected** Ambient Air Temperature from 39-89°F at engine startup, engine running under closed loop conditions, Fuel Level over 12%, then with the EVAP purge solenoid enabled (to pull vacuum into the system to close the NVLD switch) and the EVAP "small leak" test maturing, the PCM turns "off" the EVAP purge solenoid once the NVLD switch closes. If the NVLD switch reopens before a calibrated amount of time expires, a "large" leak in the system is detected (larger than 0.080 in.). **Possible Causes:** • EVAP purge solenoid is damaged or it has failed • Fuel tank cap is damaged, missing or the wrong part number • NVLD switch is damaged or it has failed
DTC: P0456 **2T EVAP** **Years:** 2008, 2009 **Models:** Dakota, Grand Cherokee, Journey, Liberty, Nitro, Pacifica, PT Cruiser, Ram Truck, Wrangler **Engines:** All **Transmissions:** All	**EVAP System Small Leak Detected** Ambient Air Temperature from 39-109°F at engine startup, engine running under closed loop conditions, Fuel Level below 88%, then with the EVAP system sealed, the PCM monitors the NVLD switch. If the NVLD switch does not close within a calibrated amount of time expires, a "small" leak in the EVAP system was detected. **Possible Causes:** • Fuel tank cap is damaged, loose or the wrong part number • Small leak present somewhere in the EVAP system
DTC: P0457 **2T EVAP** **Years:** 2008, 2009 **Models:** Dakota, Grand Cherokee, Journey, Liberty, Nitro, Pacifica, PT Cruiser, Ram Truck, Wrangler **Engines:** All **Transmissions:** All	**Loose Fuel Cap Condition:** Monitor with ignition on. Ambient temperature should be between 39-109°F (4-43°C). Vehicle should be in closed loop fuel system. The PCM has detected an EVAP system leak after a fuel level increase. If the NVLD switch reopens before the calibrated amount of time after a fuel tank fill, an error is detected. MIL will illuminate. Condition requires 3 good trips to turn off MIL. **Possible Causes:** • Loose or missing fuel fill cap • Intermittent condition • NVLD system or switch malfunction • EVAP system leaking • EVAP purge solenoid malfunction

DTC	Trouble Code Title, Conditions & Possible Causes
DTC: P0458 **1T EVAP** **Years:** 2008, 2009 **Models:** PT Cruiser **Engines:** All **Transmissions:** All	**EVAP Purge Solenoid Low Condition:** Monitor with ignition on. If PCM detected an open in the purge solenoid of in the circuit for more than 280ms, a one-trip fault is set and the MIL is illuminated. **Possible Causes:** • Intermittent condition • EVAP purge solenoid connector problems • EVAP purge solenoid control circuit is shorted to ground • EVAP purge solenoid leaks, stuck open, or stuck closed • PCM has failed
DTC: P0459 **1T EVAP** **Years:** 2008, 2009 **Models:** PT Cruiser **Engines:** All **Transmissions:** All	**EVAP Purge Solenoid High Condition:** Monitor with ignition on. If PCM detected a short to ground in the purge solenoid of in the circuit for more than 280ms, a one-trip fault is set and the MIL is illuminated. **Possible Causes:** • Intermittent condition • EVAP purge solenoid connector problems • EVAP purge solenoid control circuit is shorted to battery voltage • EVAP purge solenoid leaks, stuck open, or stuck closed • PCM has failed
DTC: P0460 **1T CCM** **Years:** 2008, 2009 **Models:** Liberty **Engines:** 2.8L Diesel **Transmissions:** All	**Fuel Level Sensor Circuit Signal Voltage Too High Or Too Low** Ignition on. The Fuel Level Sensor signal voltage is above 4.51v for 0.6 second (too high) or is below 0.19v for 0.6 second (too low). **Possible Causes:** • Intermittent condition • Fuel Level Sensor signal circuit is open or is shorted to voltage (too high) • Fuel Level Sensor ground circuit is open (too high) • Fuel Level Sensor signal circuit is short to ground (too low) • Fuel Level Sensor signal circuit and ground circuit are shorted together (too low) • Fuel Level Sensor has failed • FCM has failed
DTC: P0461 **1T CCM** **Years:** 2008, 2009 **Models:** PT Cruiser **Engines:** All **Transmissions:** All	**Fuel Level Sensor Malfunction** With engine running and under partial load, the fuel level must be above 0%, and there must not be any fuel level Sensor electrical DTCs. If the PCM detects the fuel level change is less than 2% over 2 hours, this DTC will set. **Possible Causes:** • Intermittent condition • Fuel tank or component damage • Fuel level Sensor signal circuit open or shorted to ground • Ground circuit is open • Fuel level Sensor malfunction
DTC: P0462 **1T CCM** **Years:** 2008, 2009 **Models:** Dakota, Grand Cherokee, Journey, Liberty, Nitro, Pacifica, Ram Truck, Wrangler **Engines:** All **Transmissions:** All	**Fuel Level Sensor No. 1 Low Input** Key on. Battery voltage over 10.4v. Fuel level Sensor signal goes below 0.1961v (exc. Ram) for more than 5 seconds, or below 0.4v for more than 90 seconds (Ram). DTC is recorded. **Possible Causes:** • Intermittent condition • Fuel level sending unit signal circuit shorted to Sensor or chassis ground • Fuel level sensing unit is damaged or the fuel tank is damaged • Instrument cluster problem
DTC: P0462 **1T CCM** **Years:** 2008, 2009 **Models:** PT Cruiser **Engines:** All **Transmissions:** All	**Fuel Level Sending Unit Low Voltage** Key on. If the PCM detects the fuel level as more than 100% for more than 4.5 minutes, this DTC will set. **Possible Causes:** • Intermittent condition
DTC: P0463 **1T CCM** **Years:** 2008, 2009 **Models:** Dakota, Grand Cherokee, Journey, Liberty, Nitro, Pacifica, Ram Truck, Wrangler **Engines:** All **Transmissions:** All	**Fuel Level Sensor No. 1 High Input** Key on. Battery voltage over 10.4v. If Fuel Level Sensor signal goes above 4.7v for more than 5 seconds (exc. Ram Truck, Liberty), above 4.9v for more than 90 seconds (Ram Truck, Liberty), this DTC is recorded. **Possible Causes:** • Fuel level sending unit signal circuit is open or is shorted to battery voltage • Fuel level Sensor ground circuit is open • Fuel level Sensor is damaged or the fuel tank is damaged • Instrument cluster is faulty • BCM or PCM has failed

DTC	Trouble Code Title, Conditions & Possible Causes
DTC: P0480 **1T CCM** **Years:** 2008, 2009 **Models:** Dakota, Grand Cherokee, Journey, Liberty, Nitro, Pacifica, PT Cruiser, Ram Truck, Wrangler **Engines:** All **Transmissions:** All	**Low Speed (No.1) Fan Control Relay Circuit** Key on. Battery voltage over 10v. An open or shorted circuit is detected in the Low Speed Fan Relay control circuit system. **Possible Causes:** • Fan relay intermittent condition • Ground circuit is open • Fused B+ output circuit malfunction • Fan relay control circuit is open or shorted to battery voltage or ground • Fan relay is damaged or has failed • PCM has failed
DTC: P0480 **1T CCM** **Years:** 2008, 2009 **Models:** Liberty **Engines:** 2.8L Diesel **Transmissions:** All	**Fan No. 1 Control Circuit Excessive Current Or Short Circuit** Ignition on; Low Speed Radiator Fan Relay commanded OFF (excessive current) or commanded ON (short circuit). The ECM detects excessive current on Low Speed Radiator Fan Relay control circuit. **Possible Causes:** • Intermittent condition • Low Speed Radiator Fan Relay has failed • Low Speed Radiator Fan control circuit is shorted to voltage • ECM has failed
DTC: P0480 **1T CCM** **Years:** 2008, 2009 **Models:** Liberty **Engines:** 2.8L Diesel **Transmissions:** All	**Fan No. 1 Control Circuit Open Or Short-to-Ground** Ignition on; Low Speed Radiator Fan Relay commanded OFF. The ECM does not detect voltage on Low Speed Radiator Fan Relay control circuit. **Possible Causes:** • Intermittent condition • ASD Relay output circuit is open • Low Speed Radiator Fan Relay has failed • Low Speed Radiator Fan control circuit is open or is shorted to ground • ECM has failed
DTC: P0481 **1T CCM** **Years:** 2008, 2009 **Models:** Dakota, Grand Cherokee, Journey, Liberty, Nitro, Pacifica, PT Cruiser, Ram Truck, Wrangler **Engines:** All **Transmissions:** All	**High Speed (No. 2) Fan Relay Control Circuit** Key on or engine running; and the PCM detected an unexpected low or high voltage condition (open or shorted condition) on the High Speed Fan Relay circuit. **Possible Causes:** • HFAN relay power circuit is open from the relay to fused power • HFAN relay control circuit is open or shorted to chassis ground • Fan relay(s) failed • PCM has failed.
DTC: P0489 **1T CCM** **Years:** 2008, 2009 **Models:** Liberty **Engines:** 2.8L Diesel **Transmissions:** All	**EGR Solenoid Circuit Short-To-Ground** Ignition on; ECM commands EGR Solenoid off. The ECM does not detect voltage on the EGR Solenoid control circuit. **Possible Causes:** • Intermittent condition • ASD Relay output circuit is open • EGR Solenoid control circuit is open or is shorted to ground • EGR Solenoid has malfunctioned • EMC has failed
DTC: P0490 **1T CCM** **Years:** 2008, 2009 **Models:** Liberty **Engines:** 2.8L Diesel **Transmissions:** All	**EGR Solenoid Circuit Short** Ignition on; ECM commands EGR Solenoid on. The ECM detects excessive current on the EGR Solenoid control circuit. **Possible Causes:** • Intermittent condition • EGR Solenoid has malfunctioned • EGR Solenoid control circuit is shorted to voltage • EMC has internal short to voltage
DTC: P0498 **1T CCM** **Years:** 2008, 2009 **Models:** Dakota, Grand Cherokee, Journey, Liberty, Nitro, Pacifica, PT Cruiser, Ram Truck, Wrangler **Engines:** All **Transmissions:** All	**NVLD Canister Vent Solenoid Circuit Low** Key on or engine running; and the PCM detected an unexpected low voltage condition on the Natural Vacuum Leak Detection (NVLD) control circuit during the CCM test period. **Possible Causes:** • NVLD canister vent solenoid control circuit is shorted to ground • NVLD canister vent solenoid is damaged or it has failed • PCM has failed

DTC	Trouble Code Title, Conditions & Possible Causes
DTC: P0499 **1T CCM** **Years:** 2008, 2009 **Models:** Dakota, Grand Cherokee, Journey, Liberty, Nitro, Pacifica, PT Cruiser, Ram Truck, Wrangler **Engines:** All **Transmissions:** All	**NVLD Canister Vent Solenoid Circuit High** Key on or engine running. The PCM detected an open or unexpected high voltage condition on the Natural Vacuum Leak Detection (NVLD) circuit. **Possible Causes:** • NVLD canister vent solenoid control circuit is open or is shorted to power • NVLD canister vent solenoid ground circuit is open • NVLD canister vent solenoid is damaged or it has failed • PCM has failed
DTC: P0500 **1T CCM** **Years:** 2008, 2009 **Models:** PT Cruiser **Engines:** All **Transmissions:** All	**No Vehicle Speed Sensor Signal** Engine started; if the PCM did not detect a VSS signal for over 6 seconds, this DTC will set. **Possible Causes:** • Intermittent condition • 5V supply circuit open • VSS circuit is open or is shorted to ground • VSS ground circuit is open • VSS has failed • PCM has failed
DTC: P0501 **2T CCM** **Years:** 2008, 2009 **Models:** Dakota, Grand Cherokee, Journey, Liberty, Nitro, Pacifica, PT Cruiser, Ram Truck, Wrangler **Engines:** All **Transmissions:** All	**Vehicle Speed Sensor Performance** Engine started; vehicle driven at over 1500 RPM for 10 seconds, gear selector not in Park or Neutral (or clutch is not depressed on M/T); brakes not applied. The PCM (or ECM: Liberty with Diesel) did not receive any VSS signals from the TCM (BCM: Liberty) for 11 seconds for 2 consecutive trips. 3 good trips required to turn off MIL. **Possible Causes:** • Check for any ABS/RWAL or TCM codes related to the VSS • VSS connector is damaged, open or it is shorted • VSS signal is open, shorted to ground or shorted to power • Incorrect tire circumference • ABS/RWAL controller, BCM, ECM, TCM or PCM has failed
DTC: P0503 **1T or 2T CCM** **Years:** 2008, 2009 **Models:** Dakota, Grand Cherokee, Journey, Liberty, Nitro, Pacifica, PT Cruiser, Ram Truck, Wrangler **Engines:** All **Transmissions:** All	**Vehicle Speed Sensor No. 1 Erratic Performance** Ignition is on; battery voltage over 10v; transmission in Drive or Reverse; brakes not applied. Vehicle speed signal is erratic during road load conditions. One-trip fault for ETC vehicles; Two-trip fault for ETC vehicles. 3 good trips required to turn off MIL. **Possible Causes:** • Check for active Bus or Communication DTCs • Incorrect Tire Circumference • PCM has failed
DTC: P0504 **1T CCM** **Years:** 2008, 2009 **Models:** Liberty **Engines:** 2.8L Diesel **Transmissions:** All	**Brake Switch Signal Circuits Plausibility With Redundant Contact** Ignition is on. The Primary Brake Switch signal and the Secondary Brake Switch signal inputs to the ECM do not agree. **Possible Causes:** • Intermittent condition • Brake Lamp Switch sense circuit is open or shorted to ground • Brake Switch sense circuit is open or shorted to ground • Brake Lamp Switch output circuit is open or shorted to voltage • ECM has failed
DTC: P0505 **2T IAC** **Years:** 2008, 2009 **Models:** Cherokee, Grand Cherokee, PT Cruiser, Ram Truck, Wrangler **Engines:** All **Transmissions:** All	**Idle Air Control Motor Circuit** Engine started; system voltage over 11.5V and the PCM detected an unexpected voltage condition on one or more of the IAC motor circuits for 2.75 seconds with the IAC motor active. **Possible Causes:** • Stepper motor Coil No. 1, 2, 3 or 4 circuit open or shorted to ground • Stepper motor coil circuit(s) shorted to system power (B+) • Stepper motor is damaged or has failed • PCM has failed

DTC	Trouble Code Title, Conditions & Possible Causes
DTC: P0506 **2T CCM** **Years:** 2008, 2009 **Models:** Pacifica **Engines:** All **Transmissions:** All	**Idle Speed Low Performance** Engine running at idle speed in closed loop. If engine RPM does not come within a calibratable low limit of the target idle speed, a failure timer will increment. When the appropriate failure timer reaches its maximum threshold without sign of RPM trending toward control, a soft-fail is generated. When a calibratable number of the soft-fails is reached, a 1-trip fault is set. When two 1-trip faults occur in a row, the DTC is set and the MIL illuminates. **Possible Causes:** • PCV system malfunction • Air induction system restrictions (clogged air filter, etc.) • Idle air control passage is clogged or dirty (clean and retest) • Air induction system malfunction • Throttle body or linkage is binding, damaged or sticking
DTC: P0506 **1T CCM** **Years:** 2008, 2009 **Models:** Dakota, Grand Cherokee, Journey, Liberty, Nitro, PT Cruiser, Ram Truck, Wrangler **Engines:** All **Transmissions:** All	**Idle Speed Low Performance** Engine running at idle speed; MAF is less than 250 mg/tdc; air temperature is greater than 0°F (−18°C) and less than 19°F (−7°C) enable after coolant temperature is greater than 158°F (70°C) or air temperature is greater than 19°F (−7°C); coolant temperature is between 19 to 266°F (−7 to 130°C); canister purge is less than 100% duty cycle; no DTCs are present for VSS, MAF/MAP, ECT, TPS, ECT and CKP Sensors; also no fuel system or injector related DTCs are present. If the DTC detects that engine speed is 100 RPM or more below the normal idle speed for 7 seconds, this DTC will set. **Possible Causes:** • Air induction system restrictions • Throttle body or linkage is binding, damaged or sticking • Intermittent condition • PCM has failed
DTC: P0507 **2T CCM** **Years:** 2008, 2009 **Models:** Dakota, Grand Cherokee, Journey, Liberty, Nitro, Pacifica, PT Cruiser, Ram Truck, Wrangler **Engines:** All **Transmissions:** All	**Idle Speed High Performance** Engine running at idle speed in closed loop. If engine RPM does not come within a calibratable high limit of the target idle speed, a failure timer will increment. When the appropriate failure timer reaches its maximum threshold without sign of RPM trending toward control, a soft-fail is generated. When a calibratable number of the soft-fails are reached, a 1-trip fault is set. When two 1-trip faults occur in a row, the DTC is set and the MIL illuminates. **Possible Causes:** • PCV system malfunction • Air induction system restrictions (clogged air filter, etc.) • Idle air control passage is clogged or dirty (clean and retest) • Air induction system malfunction • Throttle body or linkage is binding, damaged or sticking
DTC: P0508 **2T CCM** **Years:** 2008, 2009 **Models:** Dakota, Grand Cherokee, Journey, Liberty, Nitro, Pacifica, PT Cruiser, Ram Truck, Wrangler **Engines:** All **Transmissions:** All	**Idle Air Control Motor Sense Circuit Low Input** Engine started; system voltage over 10.5V; IAC motor operating. The PCM detected the IAC Motor Sense circuit current was less than 175mA during the CCM test period. **Possible Causes:** • IAC motor driver circuit is open or shorted to ground • IAC motor sense circuit is open or shorted to ground • IAC motor is damaged or it has failed • PCM has failed
DTC: P0509 **2T CCM** **Years:** 2008, 2009 **Models:** Dakota, Grand Cherokee, Journey, Liberty, Nitro, Pacifica, PT Cruiser, Ram Truck, Wrangler **Engines:** All **Transmissions:** All	**Idle Air Control Motor Circuit High** Engine started; system voltage over 10.5V, IAC motor activated, and the PCM detected a high voltage on one or more of the IAC motor circuits (over 980mA) during the CCM test period. **Possible Causes:** • IAC motor driver circuit is shorted to power • IAC motor sense circuit is shorted to power • IAC motor is damaged or it has failed • PCM has failed
DTC: P0509 **1 CCM** **Years:** 2008, 2009 **Models:** Grand Cherokee, Ram Truck, Wrangler **Engines:** All **Transmissions:** All	**Idle Air Control Motor Sense Circuit High** Engine running; system voltage over 10v; IAC motor operating. The PCM senses a short-to-power on any of the Linear Idle Air Control (LIAC) control circuits for 2.75 seconds while the IAC motor is active. 3 good trips are required to turn off the MIL. **Possible Causes:** • IAC motor control circuit is shorted to battery power • IAC motor signal circuit is open or shorted to battery power • IAC control circuit is shorted to IAC return circuit • IAC motor is damaged or it has failed • PCM has failed

DTC	Trouble Code Title, Conditions & Possible Causes
DTC: P050B **2T CCM** **Years:** 2008, 2009 **Models:** Dakota, Grand Cherokee, Journey, Liberty, Nitro, Pacifica, PT Cruiser, Ram Truck, Wrangler **Engines:** All **Transmissions:** All	**Cold Start Ignition Timing Performance** The PCM detects that engine speed is 50 RPM or more (depending on vehicle specifications) below target idle speed for more than 3 seconds, and the average spark advance is above the failure threshold for more than the specified limit. Three good trips required to turn off the MIL. **Possible Causes:** • Restricted intake air system • Low battery voltage • Fuel contamination • Excessive resistance in the ETC motor • Throttle body • PCM has failed
DTC: P050D **2T CCM** **Years:** 2008, 2009 **Models:** Dakota, Grand Cherokee, Journey, Liberty, Nitro, Pacifica, PT Cruiser, Ram Truck, Wrangler **Engines:** All **Transmissions:** All	**Cold Start Rough Idle** The PCM detects that engine speed is 50 RPM or more (depending on vehicle specifications) below target idle speed for more than 3 seconds, and the average spark advance is above the failure threshold for more than the specified limit. Three good trips required to turn off the MIL. **Possible Causes:** • Restricted intake air system • Low battery voltage • Fuel contamination • Excessive resistance in the ETC motor • Throttle body • PCM has failed
DTC: P0513 **1T PCM** **Years:** 2008, 2009 **Models:** Dakota, Grand Cherokee, Journey, Liberty, Nitro, Pacifica, PT Cruiser, Ram Truck, Wrangler **Engines:** All **Transmissions:** All	**Invalid SKIM Key Detected** Key on, and the PCM detected an invalid Sentry Key Immobilizer key had been inserted into the ignition key assembly. **Possible Causes:** • Incorrect VIN in the PCM • No communication between the PCM and the SKIM • SKIM trouble codes present (check for any SKIM codes) • Valid SKIM key not present • VIN not programmed into the PCM • PCM has failed
DTC: P0516 **1T CCM** **Years:** 2008, 2009 **Models:** Dakota, Grand Cherokee, Journey, Liberty, Nitro, Pacifica, PT Cruiser, Ram Truck, Wrangler **Engines:** All **Transmissions:** All	**Battery Temperature Sensor Circuit Low Input** Key on or engine running; and the PCM detected a Battery Temperature Sensor signal that indicated less than 0.10v (exc. Ram Truck, Liberty) or less than 0.039v (Ram Truck, Liberty). 3 good trips required to turn off MIL. **Possible Causes:** • BTS signal circuit is shorted to Sensor or chassis ground • BTS assembly is damaged or it has failed • PCM has failed
DTC: P0517 **1T CCM** **Years:** 2008, 2009 **Models:** Dakota, Grand Cherokee, Journey, Liberty, Nitro, Pacifica, PT Cruiser, Ram Truck, Wrangler **Engines:** All **Transmissions:** All	**Battery Temperature Sensor Circuit High Input** Key on or engine running; and the PCM detected a Battery Temperature Sensor signal that indicated more than 4.8v (exc. Ram Truck, Liberty) or more than 4.94v (Ram Truck, Liberty). **Possible Causes:** • BTS signal circuit is shorted to VREF (5V) • BTS signal circuit is open or the BTS ground circuit is open • BTS assembly is damaged or it has failed • PCM has failed
DTC: P0519 **2T IAC** **Years:** 2008, 2009 **Models:** Dakota, Grand Cherokee, Journey, Liberty, Nitro, Pacifica, PT Cruiser, Ram Truck, Wrangler **Engines:** All **Transmissions:** All	**Idle Air Performance** DTC P0106, P0107, P0108, P0121, P0122 and P0123 not set, engine started, engine running with the gear selector indicating Drive position, and the PCM detected the engine idle speed was not within 200 RPM of the high idle limit or within 100 RPM of the low idle limit when compared to the Target Idle Speed limit for 40 seconds. **Possible Causes:** • Idle air control passage is clogged or dirty (clean and retest) • Throttle body or linkage is binding, damaged or sticking • Vacuum leaks in the engine or PCV system components

DTC	Trouble Code Title, Conditions & Possible Causes
DTC: P0520 **1T CCM** **Years:** 2008, 2009 **Models:** Dakota, Grand Cherokee, PT Cruiser, Ram Truck, Wrangler **Engines:** All **Transmissions:** All	**Engine Oil Pressure Sensor Out of Range** Key on (engine not started). The PCM detected an engine oil pressure reading out of the calibrated range. **Possible Causes:** <ul><li>Oil pressure Sensor signal circuit is open or shorted to ground</li><li>Oil pressure Sensor signal circuit has high resistance</li><li>5V supply circuit has high resistance</li><li>5V supply circuit is shorted to ground</li><li>Oil pressure Sensor ground circuit has high resistance</li><li>Oil pressure Sensor is damaged or has failed</li><li>PCM has failed</li></ul>
DTC: P0504 **1T CCM** **Years:** 2008, 2009 **Models:** Liberty **Engines:** 2.8L Diesel **Transmissions:** All	**Engine Oil Pressure Sensor Circuit Too Low Or Too High** Engine running at start up. The Oil Pressure signal is below the lower limit for 8 seconds after engine startup. After the engine is running, the OP Sensor signal is above 4.8v for 0.5 seconds or it may be below 0.19v for 0.5 second. **Possible Causes:** <ul><li>5V supply circuit is open</li><li>Front Control Module (FCM) Oil Pressure Sensor signal circuit is shorted to ground or to voltage</li><li>Engine mechanical problem exists</li><li>Oil Pressure Sensor has failed</li><li>Oil Pressure Sensor signal circuit is open, shorted to voltage or to ground</li><li>Oil Pressure Sensor signal circuit is shorted to Sensor ground</li><li>Oil Pressure Sensor ground circuit is open</li><li>Intermittent condition</li></ul>
DTC: P0521 **1T CCM** **Years:** 2008, 2009 **Models:** Dakota, Grand Cherokee, PT Cruiser, Ram Truck, Wrangler **Engines:** All **Transmissions:** All	**Engine Oil Pressure Sensor Does Not Reach Range** Engine running. The PCM detected an engine oil pressure reading never reaches the calibrated specification when engine is at 1250 RPM. **Possible Causes:** <ul><li>Engine oil or engine mechanical fault</li><li>Oil pressure Sensor signal circuit is shorted to battery</li><li>Oil pressure Sensor signal circuit has high resistance</li><li>5V supply circuit has high resistance</li><li>5V supply circuit is shorted to ground</li><li>Oil pressure Sensor return circuit has high resistance</li><li>Oil pressure Sensor is damaged or has failed</li><li>PCM has failed</li></ul>
DTC: P0522 **1T CCM** **Years:** 2008, 2009 **Models:** Dakota, Grand Cherokee, Journey, Liberty, Nitro, Pacifica, PT Cruiser, Ram Truck, Wrangler **Engines:** All **Transmissions:** All	**Engine Oil Pressure Sensor Rationality** Engine running; battery voltage over 10.4v. If the PCM detected an engine oil pressure voltage reading of less than 0.1v for 0.5 second (Ram), or less that 0.942v (Liberty), this DTC will set. **Possible Causes:** <ul><li>5V supply circuit is open or is shorted to ground</li><li>Oil pressure Sensor signal circuit is shorted to ground or to sensor ground</li><li>Oil pressure Sensor is damaged or has failed</li><li>PCM has failed</li></ul>
DTC: P0523 **1T CCM** **Years:** 2008, 2009 **Models:** Dakota, Grand Cherokee, Journey, Liberty, Nitro, Pacifica, PT Cruiser, Ram Truck, Wrangler **Engines:** All **Transmissions:** All	**Engine Oil Pressure Sensor Circuit High** Key on (engine not started). The PCM detected an engine oil pressure reading greater than the calibrated amount. **Possible Causes:** <ul><li>Oil pressure Sensor signal circuit is open or shorted to battery voltage or to 5V supply circuit</li><li>Oil pressure Sensor ground circuit is open</li><li>Oil pressure Sensor is damaged or has failed</li><li>PCM has failed</li></ul>
DTC: P0524 **1T CCM** **Years:** 2008, 2009 **Models:** Dakota, Grand Cherokee, Journey, Liberty, Nitro, Pacifica, PT Cruiser, Ram Truck, Wrangler **Engines:** All **Transmissions:** All	**Engine Oil Pressure Low** Engine running. The PCM detected that the engine oil pressure never reaches the calibrated specification to allow the MDS activation. **Possible Causes:** <ul><li>Engine oil system or engine mechanical faults</li><li>Oil pressure Sensor signal circuit is shorted to battery voltage or to ground</li><li>Oil pressure Sensor signal circuit has high resistance</li><li>5V supply circuit has high resistance</li><li>5V supply circuit is shorted to ground</li><li>Oil pressure Sensor return circuit has high resistance</li><li>Oil pressure Sensor is damaged or has failed</li><li>PCM has failed</li></ul>

DTC	Trouble Code Title, Conditions & Possible Causes
DTC: P0530 **1T CCM** **Years:** 2008, 2009 **Models:** Liberty **Engines:** 2.8L Diesel **Transmissions:** All	**A/C Pressure Sensor Circuit Too Low Or Too High** Ignition on. An error occurs with the A/C Pressure CAN Bus message from the Front Control Module (FCM) to the ECM, or the signal is below 0.06v or above 4.74v for 0.6 second. **Possible Causes:** • Intermittent condition • A/C Pressure Sensor signal circuit is shorted to 5V supply or to voltage • A/C Pressure Sensor ground circuit is shorted to voltage • 5V supply circuit is open • A/C Pressure Sensor has failed • A/C Pressure Sensor signal circuit is open • A/C Pressure Sensor signal circuit is shorted to ground or to Sensor ground circuit • FCM to 5V supply circuit problem
DTC: P0532 **1T CCM** **Years:** 2008, 2009 **Models:** Dakota, Grand Cherokee, Journey, Liberty, Nitro, Pacifica, PT Cruiser, Ram Truck, Wrangler **Engines:** All **Transmissions:** All	**Air Conditioning Pressure Sensor Circuit Low Input** Engine running with the A/C relay energized. The PCM detected the signal from the A/C Pressure Sensor indicated less than 0.58v for over 2.6 seconds during the CCM test period. **Possible Causes:** • A/C pressure Sensor 5V power supply (VREF) circuit is open or is shorted to ground • A/C pressure Sensor signal circuit is shorted to ground or to Sensor ground circuit • A/C pressure Sensor is damaged or it has failed • Front A/C control module damaged or has failed • PCM has failed
DTC: P0533 **1T CCM** **Years:** 2008, 2009 **Models:** Dakota, Grand Cherokee, Journey, Liberty, Nitro, Pacifica, PT Cruiser, Ram Truck, Wrangler **Engines:** All **Transmissions:** All	**Air Conditioning Pressure Sensor Circuit High Input** Engine running with the A/C relay energized, and the PCM detected the signal from the A/C Pressure Sensor indicated less than 4.92v for over 2.6 seconds during the CCM test period. **Possible Causes:** • A/C pressure Sensor signal circuit is shorted to 5V VREF power • A/C pressure Sensor signal circuit or ground circuit is open • A/C pressure Sensor is damaged or it has failed • Front A/C control module is damaged or has failed • PCM has failed
DTC: P0551 **1T CCM** **Years:** 2008, 2009 **Models:** Grand Cherokee, Pacifica, Ram Truck, Wrangler **Engines:** All **Transmissions:** All	**Power Steering Pressure Switch Circuit Failure** Engine running and vehicle driven at more than 40 MPH for 30 seconds. If the PCM detected the PSPS signal remains open for 2 consecutive trips, this DTC will set. 3 good trips required to turn off MIL. **Possible Causes:** • PSPS sense circuit is open between the switch and the PCM • PSPS ground circuit is open between the switch and ground • PSPS is damaged or it has failed • PCM has failed
DTC: P0551 **1T CCM** **Years:** 2008, 2009 **Models:** PT Cruiser **Engines:** All **Transmissions:** All	**Power Steering Pressure Switch Circuit Failure** Engine running and vehicle driven at more than 30 MPH for 60 seconds; no VSS DTC is present. If the PCM detected the PSPS signal remains high after 60 seconds, this DTC will set. **Possible Causes:** • PSPS sense circuit is open or is shorted to ground • PSPS ground circuit is open • PSPS is damaged or it has failed • PCM has failed
DTC: P0562 **1T CCM** **Years:** 2008, 2009 **Models:** Dakota, Grand Cherokee, Journey, Liberty, Nitro, Pacifica, Ram Truck, Wrangler **Engines:** All **Transmissions:** All	**Battery Voltage Low Input** Engine running at a speed over 1000 RPM. If battery voltage is 1v less than desired voltage for a set period of time, this DTC will set. The ETC light is flashing. **Possible Causes:** • Resistance in battery positive circuit • Resistance in the generator case ground • Generator field ground circuit is open or shorted to ground • Generator is damaged or it has failed • Ground circuit is open • PCM has failed

DTC	Trouble Code Title, Conditions & Possible Causes
DTC: P0562 **1T CCM** **Years:** 2008, 2009 **Models:** PT Cruiser **Engines:** All **Transmissions:** All	**Charging System Voltage Low** PCM: Engine is running for over 30 sec. If the PCM detects battery voltage is under 11.5V for more than 5 sec., this DTC will set. Other charging system DTCs may be present. TCM w/NGC: Engine is running and PCM has closed the Transmission Control Relay. If battery voltage of the TC Relay output sense circuit is less than 10v for 15 seconds, this DTC will set. **Note: P0562 usually indicates failing battery voltage or resistive connection to the PCM. This DTC also sets if battery voltage sensed at PCM is less than 6.5V for 200ms or when the TC Relay output circuit is less than 7.2v for 200ms.** **Possible Causes:** • Resistance is high in battery positive circuit or in generator case ground • Ground circuit is open or has high resistance • Fused B+ circuit to TC relay or to PCM has high resistance • Intermittent wiring or connector condition • TC relay output to TCM is open or has high resistance • TC relay has failed • Generator field driver circuit is open • ASD relay output circuit is open • Generator has failed • PCM has failed
DTC: P0563 **1T CCM** **Years:** 2008, 2009 **Models:** Dakota, Grand Cherokee, Journey, Liberty, Nitro, Pacifica, PT Cruiser, Ram Truck, Wrangler **Engines:** All **Transmissions:** All	**Battery Sense Circuit High Input** Engine running at a speed over 380 RPM, and the PCM detected the Battery Sense circuit voltage indicated 1v higher than the Charging system "goal" during the CCM test. **Possible Causes:** • Generator field control circuit is shorted to system power (B+) • Generator is damaged or it has failed • PCM has failed
DTC: P0564 **1T CCM** **Years:** 2008, 2009 **Models:** Liberty **Engines:** 2.8L Diesel **Transmissions:** All	**Speed Control Switch No. 1 Circuit Plausibility, Signal Too High, Too Low Or Stuck Switch** Ignition is on. ECM detects Speed Control (S/C) Switch circuit signal is not in agreement with expected result. **Possible Causes:** • ECM to S/C signal circuit is open or shorted to ground • ECM to S/C Sensor ground is open • S/C Switch signal circuit is open or shorted to voltage or to ground • S/C Sensor ground is open • S/C switch is damaged or has failed
DTC: P0571 **1T CCM** **Years:** 2008, 2009 **Models:** Dakota, Grand Cherokee, Journey, Liberty, Nitro, Pacifica, PT Cruiser, Ram Truck, Wrangler **Engines:** All **Transmissions:** All	**Brake Switch No. 1 No Output Signal** Ignition is on. If output of BS 1 to PCM looks like brake is not applied, while BS 2 circuit is applied, the fault will mature in 60ms. **Possible Causes:** • BS 1 signal open or shorted to ground • BS 2 signal open or shorted to ground • Ground circuit is open • Fused ignition switch output is open • Stop lamp switch is damaged or has failed • PCM has failed
DTC: P0572 **1T CCM** **Years:** 2008, 2009 **Models:** Dakota, Grand Cherokee, Journey, Liberty, Nitro, Pacifica, Ram Truck, Wrangler **Engines:** All **Transmissions:** All	**Brake Switch Signal No. 1 Circuit Low** Ignition is on. When PCM recognizes that brake switch is mechanically stuck in the low/on position, a DTC will set. Three global good trips are necessary to turn off MIL. **Possible Causes:** • Brake switch signal circuit is shorted to ground • BS No. 2 signal open (5.7L) • Brake switch is damaged or has failed • PCM has failed
DTC: P0572 **1T CCM** **Years:** 2008, 2009 **Models:** PT Cruiser **Engines:** All **Transmissions:** All	**Brake Switch Circuit Low** Engine is running and vehicle speed is above 31 MPH; battery voltage is more than 9.5V; no other brake switch DTCs are present. If the PCM detects no change from the brake switch sense circuit input after coming to a complete stop, it will increment a counter. If the counter increments 10 times, the DTC will set and the MIL will illuminate. **Possible Causes:** • Intermittent condition • Fused B+ circuit problem • Brake switch sense circuit is shorted to ground • Brake switch is closed • PCM has failed

DTC	Trouble Code Title, Conditions & Possible Causes
DTC: P0573 **1T CCM** **Years:** 2008, 2009 **Models:** Dakota, Grand Cherokee, Journey, Liberty, Nitro, Pacifica, Ram Truck, Wrangler **Engines:** All **Transmissions:** All	**Brake Switch No. 1 Stuck High/Off** Ignition is on. If PCM recognizes BS No. 11 is mechanically stuck in the high/off position, this DTC will set. **Possible Causes:** • BS No. 2 signal open or shorted to ground • BS No. 1 signal shorted to ground or to voltage • Ground circuit is open • Fused ignition switch output is open • Stop lamp switch is damaged or has failed • PCM has failed
DTC: P0573 **1T CCM** **Years:** 2008, 2009 **Models:** Liberty, PT Cruiser, Wrangler **Engines:** All **Transmissions:** All	**Brake Switch Circuit High** Engine is running and vehicle speed is above 31 MPH; accelerator pedal position is more than 25%; battery voltage is more than 9.5V; no other brake switch DTCs are present. If the PCM detects a high brake switch sense circuit input, it will increment a counter. If the counter increments 10 times, the DTC will set and the MIL will illuminate. **Possible Causes:** • Intermittent condition • Fused B+ circuit problem • Brake switch sense circuit is open or is shorted to voltage • Ground circuit is open • Brake switch lamp operation has failed • PCM has failed
DTC: P0579 **1T CCM** **Years:** 2008, 2009 **Models:** Dakota, Grand Cherokee, Journey, Liberty, Nitro, Pacifica, PT Cruiser, Ram Truck, Wrangler **Engines:** All **Transmissions:** All	**Speed Control Switch No. 1 Performance** Ignition on. The PCM detected the cruise switch voltage output is not out of range, but it does not equal any of the values for any of the button positions. **Possible Causes:** • S/C switch No. 1 signal circuit is open or shorted to battery voltage • S/C switch No. 1 signal circuit is shorted to ground or to switch return circuit • S/C switch No. 1 switch return circuit is open • Clockspring or S/C switch is damaged or it has failed • PCM has failed
DTC: P0580 **1T CCM** **Years:** 2008, 2009 **Models:** Dakota, Grand Cherokee, Journey, Liberty, Nitro, Pacifica, PT Cruiser, Ram Truck, Wrangler **Engines:** All **Transmissions:** All	**Speed Control Switch No. 1 Circuit Low Input** Key on or engine started; system voltage over 10.0v and the PCM detected the Speed Control Switch No. 1 signal indicated less than 0.43v (exc. Liberty) or 0.60v (Liberty) for 2 minutes. 3 good trips required to turn off MIL. **Possible Causes:** • Intermittent condition • S/C switch signal circuit is shorted to chassis or Sensor ground • S/C On/Off switch is damaged or it has failed • S/C Resume/Accel switch is damaged or it has failed • PCM has failed.
DTC: P0581 **1T CCM** **Years:** 2008, 2009 **Models:** Dakota, Grand Cherokee, Journey, Liberty, Nitro, Pacifica, PT Cruiser, Ram Truck, Wrangler **Engines:** All **Transmissions:** All	**Speed Control Switch No. 1 Circuit High Input** Engine started; system voltage over 10v and the PCM detected an open or shorted condition, or above maximum acceptable S/C switch voltage, in the Speed Control Switch signal circuit. **Possible Causes:** • S/C switch No.1 signal circuit is shorted to system power (B+) • S/C switch ground circuit is open • S/C switch signal circuit is open between PCM and clockspring • S/C Sensor ground circuit is open between PCM and clockspring or clockspring and S/C switch • Clockspring has failed • S/C switch (one or more) is damaged or has failed • PCM has failed
DTC: P0582 **1T CCM** **Years:** 2008, 2009 **Models:** Liberty, PT Cruiser, Wrangler **Engines:** All **Transmissions:** All	**Speed Control Vacuum Solenoid Circuit Malfunction** Ignition on or engine started; Speed Control (S/C) system activated, and the PCM detected an open or short to voltage condition on the S/C Vacuum solenoid circuit during the CCM test period. **Possible Causes:** • S/C supply circuit is open or is short to ground or to battery voltage • S/C vacuum solenoid control circuit is open • S/C vacuum solenoid control circuit is shorted to ground • S/C vacuum solenoid is damaged or has failed • PCM has failed

DTC	Trouble Code Title, Conditions & Possible Causes
DTC: P0585 **1T CCM** **Years:** 2008, 2009 **Models:** Dakota, Grand Cherokee, Journey, Liberty, Nitro, Pacifica, PT Cruiser, Ram Truck, Wrangler **Engines:** All **Transmissions:** All	**Speed Control Switch Plausibility Between Switch No. 1 & Switch No. 2** Ignition is on. ECM detects a discrepancy between S/C switch No. 1 and No. 2 signals. **Possible Causes:** • Intermittent condition • High resistance in the S/C Switch signal circuit or ground circuit • S/C switch is damaged or has failed • ECM has failed
DTC: P0586 **1T CCM** **Years:** 2008, 2009 **Models:** Liberty, PT Cruiser, Wrangler **Engines:** All **Transmissions:** All	**Speed Control Vent Solenoid Circuit Malfunction** Engine started; battery voltage over 10v; Speed Control (S/C) system activated. The PCM detected an unexpected voltage condition on the S/C Vent solenoid circuit during the CCM test period. **Possible Causes:** • S/C supply circuit is open or is short to ground • S/C vent solenoid control circuit is open • S/C vent solenoid control circuit is shorted to ground • S/C vent solenoid is damaged or has failed • PCM has failed
DTC: P0589 **1T CCM** **Years:** 2008, 2009 **Models:** Liberty, PT Cruiser, Wrangler **Engines:** All **Transmissions:** All	**Speed Control Switch No. 2 Plausibility, Voltage Too High Or Too Low, Or Switch Stuck** Ignition is on. ECM detects a discrepancy in the S/C switch No. 2 circuit signals. **Possible Causes:** • ECM to S/C signal circuit is open or shorted to voltage • ECM to S/C Sensor ground is open • S/C Switch signal circuit is open or shorted to voltage or to ground • S/C Sensor ground is open • S/C switches damaged or failed
DTC: P0591 **1T CCM** **Years:** 2008, 2009 **Models:** Dakota, Grand Cherokee, Journey, Liberty, Nitro, Pacifica, PT Cruiser, Ram Truck, Wrangler **Engines:** All **Transmissions:** All	**Speed Control Switch No. 2 Malfunction** Ignition on; Speed Control (S/C) system activated. The PCM detected S/C switch No. 2 output voltage is not out of range, but it does not equal any of the values for any of the button positions. **Possible Causes:** • S/C switch No. 2 signal circuit is open or is shorted to ground or to battery voltage • S/C return circuit is open • S/C switch No. 2 signal circuit is shorted to switch return circuit • S/C switch No. 2 has failed • Clockspring has failed • PCM has failed
DTC: P0592 **1T CCM** **Years:** 2008, 2009 **Models:** Dakota, Grand Cherokee, Journey, Liberty, Nitro, Pacifica, PT Cruiser, Ram Truck, Wrangler **Engines:** All **Transmissions:** All	**Speed Control Switch No. 2 Circuit Low** Ignition on; Speed Control (S/C) system activated. The PCM detected S/C switch No. 2 input voltage is below minimum acceptable voltage at the PCM. **Possible Causes:** • S/C switch No. 2 signal circuit is shorted to ground or to switch return circuit • S/C switch No. 2 has failed • Clockspring has failed • PCM has failed
DTC: P0593 **1T CCM** **Years:** 2008, 2009 **Models:** Dakota, Grand Cherokee, Journey, Liberty, Nitro, Pacifica, PT Cruiser, Ram Truck, Wrangler **Engines:** All **Transmissions:** All	**Speed Control Switch No. 2 Circuit High** Ignition on; Speed Control (S/C) system activated. The PCM detected S/C switch No. 2 input voltage is above maximum acceptable voltage at the PCM. **Possible Causes:** • S/C switch No. 2 signal circuit shorted to voltage or open between PCM and clockspring • S/C switch No. 2 signal circuit is open between the clockspring and S/C switch • S/C switch return circuit is open between PCM and clockspring or S/C switch • S/C switch No. 2 or clockspring has failed • PCM has failed

DTC	Trouble Code Title, Conditions & Possible Causes
DTC: P0594 **1T CCM** **Years:** 2008, 2009 **Models:** Dakota, Grand Cherokee, Journey, Liberty, Nitro, Pacifica, PT Cruiser, Ram Truck, Wrangler **Engines:** All **Transmissions:** All	**Speed Control Servo Power Circuit Malfunction** Engine started; Speed Control (S/C) system activated. The PCM detected an unexpected voltage condition on the S/C Vent solenoid circuit during the CCM test period. **Possible Causes:** • S/C solenoid or vent solenoid has failed • Brake switch is damaged or it has failed • S/C brake switch circuit is open or it is shorted to ground • S/C power circuit is open or it is shorted to ground • PCM has failed
DTC: P0600 **1T PCM** **Years:** 2008, 2009 **Models:** Dakota, Grand Cherokee, Journey, Liberty, Nitro, Pacifica, PT Cruiser, Ram Truck, Wrangler **Engines:** All **Transmissions:** All	**Serial Communication Link Malfunction** Ignition on. Internal Bus communication failure is recognized between engine and transmission processors. **Possible Causes:** • PCM or SPI failure
DTC: P0600 **1T ECM** **Years:** 2008, 2009 **Models:** Liberty **Engines:** 2.8L Diesel **Transmissions:** All	**ECM Communication Error** Ignition on. ECM detects an internal failure. **Possible Causes:** • ECM has failed • Intermittent condition
DTC: P0601 **1T PCM** **Years:** 2008, 2009 **Models:** Dakota, Grand Cherokee, Journey, Liberty, Nitro, Pacifica, PT Cruiser, Ram Truck, Wrangler **Engines:** All **Transmissions:** All	**PCM Internal Controller Failure** Ignition on. Internal CHECKSUM (or Bus communication) for software has failed; no communication between processors; cannot match calculated value. **Possible Causes:** • PCM or SPI failure
DTC: P0602 **1T PCM** **Years:** 2008, 2009 **Models:** Dakota, Grand Cherokee, Journey, Liberty, Nitro, Pacifica, PT Cruiser, Ram Truck, Wrangler **Engines:** All **Transmissions:** All	**Control Module Programming Error** Condition is monitored continuously. This DTC will always illuminate the MIL and is designed to signal the technician that the controller still has generic software installed. **Possible Causes:** • Control module needs updated programming
DTC: P0602 **1T ECM** **Years:** 2008, 2009 **Models:** Liberty **Engines:** 2.8L Diesel **Transmissions:** All	**ECM Invalid Code Word** Ignition on. ECM detects an internal failure. **Possible Causes:** • ECM has failed • Intermittent condition
DTC: P0604 **1T PCM** **Years:** 2008, 2009 **Models:** Dakota, Grand Cherokee, Journey, Liberty, Nitro, Pacifica, PT Cruiser, Ram Truck, Wrangler **Engines:** All **Transmissions:** All	**Internal TCM Error** Condition is monitored continuously. This DTC will always illuminate the MIL and is designed to signal the technician that there is a PCM internal error. **Possible Causes:** • PCM needs to be replaced, and then reprogrammed
DTC: P0604 **1T ECM** **Years:** 2008, 2009 **Models:** Liberty **Engines:** 2.8L Diesel **Transmissions:** All	**TCM Internal Problem** Ignition on. TCM detects an internal controller problem **Possible Causes:** • TCM has failed

DTC	Trouble Code Title, Conditions & Possible Causes
DTC: P0605 **1T PCM** **Years:** 2008, 2009 **Models:** Dakota, Grand Cherokee, Journey, Liberty, Nitro, Pacifica, PT Cruiser, Ram Truck, Wrangler **Engines:** All **Transmissions:** All	**Internal TCM Error** Condition is monitored continuously. This DTC will always illuminate the MIL and is designed to signal the technician that there is a PCM internal error. **Possible Causes:** • PCM needs to be replaced, and then reprogrammed
DTC: P0605 **1T ECM** **Years:** 2008, 2009 **Models:** Liberty **Engines:** 2.8L Diesel **Transmissions:** All	**TCM Internal Problem** Ignition on. TCM detects an internal controller problem **Possible Causes:** • TCM has failed
DTC: P0606 **1T PCM** **Years:** 2008, 2009 **Models:** Dakota, Grand Cherokee, Journey, Liberty, Nitro, Pacifica, PT Cruiser, Ram Truck, Wrangler **Engines:** All **Transmissions:** All	**Engine Control Module Processor Malfunction** Engine running. When the PCM detected an internal failure to communicate with the ECM, or the CMP and CKP Sensor count periods are too short, the DTC will set. The ETC light will be flashing. **Possible Causes:** • PCM has failed
DTC: P0606 **1T ECM** **Years:** 2008, 2009 **Models:** Liberty **Engines:** 2.8L Diesel **Transmissions:** All	**ECM CHECKSUM Error Or Deviation Error** Ignition on. ECM detects an internal failure. **Possible Causes:** • ECM has failed • Intermittent condition
DTC: P0607 **1T ECM** **Years:** 2008, 2009 **Models:** Liberty **Engines:** 2.8L Diesel **Transmissions:** All	**ECM Internal Error** Ignition on. ECM detects an internal failure. **Possible Causes:** • ECM has failed • Intermittent condition
DTC: P060B **1T PCM** **Years:** 2008, 2009 **Models:** Dakota, Grand Cherokee, Journey, Liberty, Nitro, Pacifica, PT Cruiser, Ram Truck, Wrangler **Engines:** All **Transmissions:** All	**Electronic Throttle Control A-D Ground Malfunction** When throttle motor is powered, if A to D reading does not return to ground within a set period of time from the test activation, this DTC will set. The test typically runs a couple of times per second, and is the reason why the APP2 signal spikes to ground a couple of times per second in normal running. Reprogramming the module may not always fix this fault. The ETC lamp will flash. **Possible Causes:** • PCM need to be reprogrammed • PCM has failed
DTC: P060D **1T PCM** **Years:** 2008, 2009 **Models:** Dakota, Grand Cherokee, Journey, Liberty, Nitro, Pacifica, PT Cruiser, Ram Truck, Wrangler **Engines:** All **Transmissions:** All	**Electronic Throttle Control Level 2 Performance** When throttle motor is powered and no matured faults related to APP Sensors are present. When secondary software determines that APPS 1 and APPS 2 signals do not match for a period of time, this DTC will set. The ETC lamp will flash. **Possible Causes:** • PCM need to be reprogrammed • PCM has failed
DTC: P060E **1T PCM** **Years:** 2008, 2009 **Models:** Dakota, Grand Cherokee, Journey, Liberty, Nitro, Pacifica, PT Cruiser, Ram Truck, Wrangler **Engines:** All **Transmissions:** All	**Electronic Throttle Control Level 2 TPS Performance** When throttle motor is powered and no matured faults related to TP Sensors are present. When secondary software determines that TP Sensor No. 1 and TP Sensor No. 2 signals do not match for a period of time, this DTC will set. The ETC lamp will flash. **Possible Causes:** • PCM need to be reprogrammed • PCM has failed

DTC	Trouble Code Title, Conditions & Possible Causes
DTC: P060F **1T PCM** **Years:** 2008, 2009 **Models:** Dakota, Grand Cherokee, Journey, Liberty, Nitro, Pacifica, PT Cruiser, Ram Truck, Wrangler **Engines:** All **Transmissions:** All	**Electronic Throttle Control Level 2 ETC Performance** When throttle motor is powered and no matured faults related to ETC Sensor is present. When secondary software determines that ETC Sensor signal is implausible for a period of time, this DTC will set. The ETC lamp will flash. **Possible Causes:** • PCM need to be reprogrammed • PCM has failed
DTC: P0610 **1T ECM** **Years:** 2008, 2009 **Models:** Liberty **Engines:** 2.8L Diesel **Transmissions:** All	**A/T Or M/T Miscoding Error** Ignition on. ECM detects an automatic transmission has been programmed as a manual transmission, or it detects a manual transmission has been programmed as an automatic transmission. **Possible Causes:** • ECM needs to be reprogrammed • ECM has failed
DTC: P0611 **1T ECM** **Years:** 2008, 2009 **Models:** Liberty **Engines:** 2.8L Diesel **Transmissions:** All	**ECM Capacitor Voltage 1 Error** Engine running; capacitor monitored during every 180 degrees of engine rotation. ECM determines that the capacitor voltage is greater than 100v. **Possible Causes:** • ECM has failed • Intermittent condition
DTC: P0613 **1T PCM** **Years:** 2008, 2009 **Models:** Dakota, Grand Cherokee, Journey, Liberty, Nitro, Pacifica, PT Cruiser, Ram Truck, Wrangler **Engines:** All **Transmissions:** All	**Internal TCM Error** Condition is monitored continuously. This DTC will always illuminate the MIL and is designed to signal the technician that there is a PCM internal error. **Possible Causes:** • PCM needs to be replaced, and then reprogrammed
DTC: P0613 **1T ECM** **Years:** 2008, 2009 **Models:** Liberty **Engines:** 2.8L Diesel **Transmissions:** All	**TCM Internal Problem** Ignition on. TCM detects an internal controller problem **Possible Causes:** • Ground circuit is open • TCM has failed
DTC: P0615 **1T ECM** **Years:** 2008, 2009 **Models:** Liberty **Engines:** 2.8L Diesel **Transmissions:** All	**Starter Relay Circuit Excessive Current Or Open Circuit** Ignition on and ECM Starter Relay commanded ON (excessive current), or commanded OFF (open circuit). ECM detects excessive current or does not detect voltage on the Starter Relay control circuit. **Possible Causes:** • Intermittent condition • Starter Relay has failed • Ignition Switch Start output is open • Starter Relay control circuit is open, or is shorted to ground or to voltage • ECM has failed
DTC: P0616 **1T ECM** **Years:** 2008, 2009 **Models:** Liberty **Engines:** 2.8L Diesel **Transmissions:** All	**Starter Relay Circuit Short-To-Ground** Ignition on and ECM Starter Relay commanded OFF. ECM does not detect voltage on the Starter Relay control circuit. **Possible Causes:** • Intermittent condition • Starter Relay has failed • Ignition Switch Start output is open • Starter Relay control circuit is open, or is shorted to ground or to voltage • ECM has failed
DTC: P0617 **1T ECM** **Years:** 2008, 2009 **Models:** Liberty **Engines:** 2.8L Diesel **Transmissions:** All	**Starter Relay Circuit Short** Ignition on and ECM Starter Relay commanded ON. ECM detects excessive current on the Starter Relay control circuit. **Possible Causes:** • Intermittent condition • Starter Relay has failed • Ignition Switch Start output is open • Starter Relay control circuit is open, or is shorted to ground or to voltage • ECM has failed

DTC	Trouble Code Title, Conditions & Possible Causes
DTC: P061A **1T PCM** **Years:** 2008, 2009 **Models:** Dakota, Grand Cherokee, Journey, Liberty, Nitro, Pacifica, PT Cruiser, Ram Truck, Wrangler **Engines:** All **Transmissions:** All	**ETC Level 2 RPM Performance** When secondary software determines that the customer requested output is not being achieved by the engine for a period of time. One trip fault. ETC lamp will flash. **Possible Causes:** • PCM need to be reprogrammed • PCM has failed
DTC: P061C **1T PCM** **Years:** 2008, 2009 **Models:** Dakota, Grand Cherokee, Journey, Liberty, Nitro, Pacifica, PT Cruiser, Ram Truck, Wrangler **Engines:** All **Transmissions:** All	**Engine Temperature Control Level 2 RPM Performance** When throttle motor is powered, and no CMP or CKP electrical signal related DTCs are set, if the secondary software determines that the engine speed is implausible for a period of time, this DTC will set. The ETC lamp will flash. **Possible Causes:** • PCM need to be reprogrammed • PCM has failed
DTC: P0622 **1T CCM** **Years:** 2008, 2009 **Models:** Dakota, Grand Cherokee, Journey, Liberty, Nitro, Pacifica, PT Cruiser, Ram Truck, Wrangler **Engines:** All **Transmissions:** All	**Generator Field Control Circuit Malfunction** Engine running. The PCM detected the Generator Field control circuit had malfunctioned (PCM tries to regulate the generator field with no result). **Possible Causes:** • Generator field control circuit is open or is shorted to ground • Generator field control circuit is shorted to system power (B+) • Generator field ground circuit is open • Generator is damaged or PCM has failed • PCM has failed
DTC: P0625 **1T CCM** **Years:** 2008, 2009 **Models:** PT Cruiser **Engines:** All **Transmissions:** All	**Generator Field Control Circuit Low** Engine running for more than 25 seconds. The PCM detected the Generator Field circuit is open or is shorted to ground. **Possible Causes:** • Wiring harness intermittent problem • Generator field driver circuit is open or is shorted to ground • Generator field has malfunctioned • Generator field coil is open • PCM has failed
DTC: P0626 **1T CCM** **Years:** 2008, 2009 **Models:** PT Cruiser **Engines:** All **Transmissions:** All	**Generator Field Control Circuit High** Engine running for more than 25 seconds. The PCM detected the Generator Field circuit is shorted B+. **Possible Causes:** • Wiring harness intermittent problem • Generator field circuit is shorted to voltage • Generator has malfunctioned
DTC: P0627 **1T CCM** **Years:** 2008, 2009 **Models:** Dakota, Grand Cherokee, Journey, Liberty, Nitro, Pacifica, PT Cruiser, Ram Truck, Wrangler **Engines:** All **Transmissions:** All	**Fuel Pump Relay Control Circuit Malfunction** Engine started; system voltage over 10.5V. The PCM detected an unexpected voltage condition (open or short) on the Fuel Pump relay control circuit during the CCM test period. **Possible Causes:** • Fuel pump relay control circuit is open or is shorted to ground • Fuel pump relay control circuit is shorted to system power (B+) • Fuel pump relay power circuit (fused ignition) circuit is open • Fuel pump relay is damaged or it has failed • PCM has failed
DTC: P0628 **1T CCM** **Years:** 2008, 2009 **Models:** PT Cruiser **Engines:** All **Transmissions:** All	**Fuel Pump Relay Control Circuit Low** Ignition is on. If the PCM detects no voltage on the fuel pump relay control circuit for more than 3 seconds, this DTC will set. **Possible Causes:** • Fuel pump relay intermittent operation • Fuel system/circuit intermittent operation • Fused ignition switch output circuit problem • Fuel pump relay has failed • Fuel pump relay control circuit is open or shorted to ground • PCM has failed

DTC	Trouble Code Title, Conditions & Possible Causes
DTC: P0629 **1T CCM** **Years:** 2008, 2009 **Models:** PT Cruiser **Engines:** All **Transmissions:** All	**Fuel Pump Relay Control Circuit High** Ignition is on. If the PCM detects high voltage on the fuel pump relay control circuit for more than 3 seconds, this DTC will set. **Possible Causes:** • Fuel pump relay intermittent operation • Fuel system/circuit intermittent operation • Fuel pump relay has failed • Fuel pump relay control circuit is shorted to battery voltage • PCM has failed
DTC: P062C **1T PCM** **Years:** 2008, 2009 **Models:** Dakota, Grand Cherokee, Journey, Liberty, Nitro, Pacifica, PT Cruiser, Ram Truck, Wrangler **Engines:** All **Transmissions:** All	**Engine Temperature Control Level 2 MPH Performance** When throttle motor is powered, and no vehicle speed related DTCs are set, if the secondary software determines that the vehicle speed is implausible for a period of time, this DTC will set. The ETC lamp will flash. **Possible Causes:** • PCM need to be reprogrammed • PCM has failed
DTC: P0630 **1T CCM** **Years:** 2008, 2009 **Models:** Dakota, Grand Cherokee, Journey, Liberty, Nitro, Pacifica, PT Cruiser, Ram Truck, Wrangler **Engines:** All **Transmissions:** All	**VIN Not Programmed Into The PCM** Key on, and the PCM determined that the Vehicle Identification Number (VIN) had not been programmed into its memory. **Possible Causes:** • Reprogram the correct VIN into the PCM • PCM has failed
DTC: P0632 **1T CCM** **Years:** 2008, 2009 **Models:** Dakota, Grand Cherokee, Journey, Liberty, Nitro, Pacifica, PT Cruiser, Ram Truck, Wrangler **Engines:** All **Transmissions:** All	**Odometer Not Programmed Into The PCM** Key on, and the PCM detected the vehicle mileage had not been programmed into memory. **Possible Causes:** • Reprogram the correct mileage into the PCM • PCM has failed
DTC: P0633 **1T CCM** **Years:** 2008, 2009 **Models:** Dakota, Grand Cherokee, Journey, Liberty, Nitro, Pacifica, PT Cruiser, Ram Truck, Wrangler **Engines:** All **Transmissions:** All	**SKIM Key Not Programmed Into The PCM** Key on, and the PCM determined that the Security Key Immobilizer (SKIM) information had not been programmed into its memory. **Possible Causes:** • Reprogram the SKIM key into the PCM • PCM has failed
DTC: P0641 **1T ECM** **Years:** 2008, 2009 **Models:** Liberty **Engines:** 2.8L Diesel **Transmissions:** All	**Sensor Supply No. 1 Voltage Too High Or Too Low** Ignition on. ECM detects a short-to-voltage (too high) or no voltage (too low) on the Sensor Supply No. 1 circuit, which supplies 5V to the CMP Sensor and the APP Sensor No. 1. **Possible Causes:** • Intermittent condition • Wiring problem in either circuit • APP Sensor No. 1 5V supply circuit is shorted to voltage (too high) • CMP Sensor 5V supply circuit is shorted to voltage (too high) • APP Sensor No. 1 5V supply circuit is shorted to ground (too low) • CMP Sensor 5V supply circuit is shorted to ground (too low) • APP Sensor or CMP Sensor has failed (too low) • ECM has failed
DTC: P0642 **1T CCM** **Years:** 2008, 2009 **Models:** Dakota, Grand Cherokee, Journey, Liberty, Nitro, Pacifica, PT Cruiser, Ram Truck, Wrangler **Engines:** All **Transmissions:** All	**Sensor Reference Voltage 1 Circuit Low** Ignition is on. When the PCM recognizes the primary 5V supply circuit voltage is too low, this DTC will set. The ETC light is flashing. **Possible Causes:** • Primary 5V supply shorted to ground • Sensor is shorted to ground • 5V Sensor has failed • PCM has failed

DTC	Trouble Code Title, Conditions & Possible Causes
DTC: P0643 **1T CCM** **Years:** 2008, 2009 **Models:** Dakota, Grand Cherokee, Journey, Liberty, Nitro, Pacifica, PT Cruiser, Ram Truck, Wrangler **Engines:** All **Transmissions:** All	**Sensor Reference Voltage 1 Circuit High** Ignition is on. When the PCM recognizes the primary 5V supply circuit voltage is too high, this DTC will set. The ETC light is flashing. **Possible Causes:** • Primary 5V supply shorted to battery voltage • PCM has failed
DTC: P0645 **1T CCM** **Years:** 2008, 2009 **Models:** Dakota, Grand Cherokee, Journey, Liberty, Nitro, Pacifica, PT Cruiser, Ram Truck, Wrangler **Engines:** All **Transmissions:** All	**A/C Clutch Relay Circuit Malfunction** Engine started; system voltage over 10.0v, A/C switch "on". The PCM detected an unexpected voltage condition (open or shorted condition) on the A/C Clutch relay control circuit during the CCM test. **Possible Causes:** • Internally fused ignition switch output circuit is faulty • A/C relay clutch control circuit is open or it is shorted to ground • A/C relay clutch power supply (fused ignition) circuit is open • A/C relay is damaged or it has failed • PCM has failed
DTC: P0645 **1T ECM** **Years:** 2008, 2009 **Models:** Liberty **Engines:** 2.8L Diesel **Transmissions:** All	**A/C Clutch Relay Circuit Malfunction** Ignition on and A/C Clutch Relay commanded ON. If the ECM detects an excessive current on the A/C Clutch Relay control circuit (excessive current or short circuit), or if the A/C Clutch Relay is commanded OFF, and the ECM does not detect voltage on the A/C Clutch Relay control circuit (open circuit or short-to-ground), this DTC will set. **Possible Causes:** • Intermittent condition • A/C Clutch Relay has failed • A/C Clutch Relay control circuit is shorted to voltage • Fused ASD Relay output circuit is open • A/C Clutch Relay control circuit is open or is shorted to ground • ECM has failed
DTC: P0646 **1T CCM** **Years:** 2008, 2009 **Models:** PT Cruiser **Engines:** All **Transmissions:** All	**A/C Clutch Relay Control Circuit Low** Ignition is on. If the PCM detects low voltage on the A/C clutch relay control circuit for more than 2.73 seconds, this DTC will set. **Possible Causes:** • A/C relay intermittent operation • Fused B+ circuit problem • A/C clutch relay has failed • A/C clutch relay control circuit is open or is shorted to ground • PCM has failed
DTC: P0647 **1T CCM** **Years:** 2008, 2009 **Models:** PT Cruiser **Engines:** All **Transmissions:** All	**A/C Clutch Relay Control Circuit High** Ignition is on. If the PCM detects high voltage on the A/C clutch relay control circuit for more than 2.73 seconds, this DTC will set. **Possible Causes:** • A/C relay intermittent operation • A/C system intermittent condition • A/C clutch relay has failed • A/C clutch relay control circuit is shorted to battery voltage • PCM has failed
DTC: P0651 **1T ECM** **Years:** 2008, 2009 **Models:** Liberty **Engines:** 2.8L Diesel **Transmissions:** All	**Sensor Supply No. 2 Voltage Too High Or Too Low** Ignition on. If the ECM detects a short-to-voltage (current too high), or if a low voltage (too low) is detected on the Sensor Supply No. 2 circuit, which supplies 5V to the MAF Sensor, Fuel Pressure Sensor, and Boost Pressure Sensor, this DTC will set. **Possible Causes:** • Intermittent condition • Boost Pressure Sensor 5V supply circuit is shorted to voltage (too high) • Fuel Pressure Sensor 5V supply circuit is shorted to voltage (too high) • MAF Sensor 5V supply circuit is shorted to voltage (too high) • Boost Pressure Sensor 5V supply circuit is shorted to ground (too low) • Fuel Pressure Sensor 5V supply circuit is shorted to ground (too low) • MAF Sensor 5V supply circuit is shorted to ground (too low) • FP Sensor, BP Sensor or MAF Sensor has failed • ECM has failed

DTC	Trouble Code Title, Conditions & Possible Causes
DTC: P0652 **1T CCM** **Years:** 2008, 2009 **Models:** Dakota, Grand Cherokee, Journey, Liberty, Nitro, Pacifica, PT Cruiser, Ram Truck, Wrangler **Engines:** All **Transmissions:** All	**Sensor Reference Voltage 2 Circuit Low** Ignition is on. When the PCM recognizes the auxiliary 5V supply circuit voltage is too low, this DTC will set. The ETC light is flashing. **Possible Causes:** • Auxiliary 5V supply shorted to ground • Sensor is shorted to ground • CMP Sensor has failed • PCM has failed
DTC: P0653 **1T CCM** **Years:** 2008, 2009 **Models:** Dakota, Grand Cherokee, Journey, Liberty, Nitro, Pacifica, PT Cruiser, Ram Truck, Wrangler **Engines:** All **Transmissions:** All	**Sensor Reference Voltage 2 Circuit High** Ignition is on. When the PCM recognizes the auxiliary 5V supply circuit voltage is too high, this DTC will set. The ETC light is flashing. **Possible Causes:** • Auxiliary 5V supply shorted to battery voltage • PCM has failed
DTC: P0657 **1T TCM** **Years:** 2008, 2009 **Models:** Dakota, Grand Cherokee, Journey, Liberty, Nitro, Pacifica, PT Cruiser, Ram Truck, Wrangler **Engines:** All **Transmissions:** All	**Solenoid Supply Voltage Circuit** When the monitored supply voltage and battery voltage differ by 3.6 volts. **Possible Causes:** • Solenoid supply voltage circuit open • Solenoid supply voltage circuit short to ground • Solenoid supply voltage circuit short to voltage • Solenoid supply voltage circuit short to another circuit • TCM has failed
DTC: P0660 **1T CCM** **Years:** 2008, 2009 **Models:** Dakota, Grand Cherokee, Journey, Liberty, Pacifica, Ram Truck, Sprinter **Engines:** All **Transmissions:** All	**Manifold Tune Valve Solenoid Circuit Malfunction** Engine started; ASD relay "on", system voltage over 10.0v, and the PCM detected an unexpected voltage condition on the Manifold Tune Valve (MTV) solenoid control circuit. **Possible Causes:** • Fused B+ circuit has failed • MTV solenoid/relay circuit is open or it is shorted to ground • MTV solenoid/relay circuit is shorted to power • MTV solenoid/relay ground circuit is open • MTV solenoid/relay is damaged or it has failed • PCM has failed
DTC: P0670 **1T ECM** **Years:** 2008, 2009 **Models:** Liberty **Engines:** 2.8L Diesel **Transmissions:** All	**Glow Plug Controller Circuit Malfunction** Ignition on. If the ECM detects an open or shorted condition on the glow plug module signal/control circuit, this DTC will set. **Possible Causes:** • Glow Plug Module has failed • Glow Plug Module signal/control circuit is open or is shorted to ground or to voltage • Intermittent condition • ECM has failed
DTC: P0671-P0674 **1T ECM** **Years:** 2008, 2009 **Models:** Liberty **Engines:** 2.8L Diesel **Transmissions:** All	**Glow Plug Failure Or Short Circuit** Ignition on and Glow Plug Module Glow Plug commanded ON. If the ECM detects no current or excessive current on the respective Glow Plug output circuit, this DTC will set. **Possible Causes:** • Glow Plug has failed • Glow Plug control circuit is open or is shorted to ground or to voltage • Glow Plug Module has failed • Intermittent condition
DTC: P0683 **1T ECM** **Years:** 2008, 2009 **Models:** Liberty **Engines:** 2.8L Diesel **Transmissions:** All	**Glow Plug Module Signal Circuit Malfunction** Ignition on. If the ECM detects an open or shorted condition on the glow plug module signal/control circuit, this DTC will set. **Possible Causes:** • Glow Plug Module has failed • Glow Plug Module signal/control circuit is open or is shorted to ground or to voltage • Intermittent condition • ECM has failed

DTC	Trouble Code Title, Conditions & Possible Causes
DTC: P0685 **1T CCM** **Years:** 2008, 2009 **Models:** Dakota, Grand Cherokee, Journey, Liberty, Nitro, Pacifica, PT Cruiser, Ram Truck, Wrangler **Engines:** All **Transmissions:** All	**ASD Relay Control Circuit Malfunction** Key on; system voltage over 10.0v. The PCM detected an unexpected voltage condition (open or short) on the Automatic Shutdown (ASD) relay control circuit during the CCM test period (ASD actual state is not equal to the desired state). 3 good trips are required to turn off MIL. P0688 may also set. **Possible Causes:** • Fused B+ circuit faults • ASD relay connector is damaged, loose or shorted • ASD relay control circuit is open or it is shorted to ground • ASD power supply (fused B+) circuit is open • ASD relay is damaged, has high resistance, or it has failed • PCM has failed
DTC: P0685 **1T ECM** **Years:** 2008, 2009 **Models:** Liberty **Engines:** 2.8L Diesel **Transmissions:** All	**ASD Relay Control Circuit Shuts Off Malfunction** During after-run. The internal ECM timer determines that the ASD Relay has shut off before the After-Run mode of operation has been completed, or remains on too long when the After-Run mode of operation has been completed. Other DTCs may be present. **Possible Causes:** • Intermittent condition • Replace ASD Relay and retest • ASD Relay control circuit is open intermittently (shut off too soon) • ASD Relay control circuit is shorted to ground intermittently (shut off too late) • ASD Relay control circuit is shorted to voltage (shut off too late) • ECM has failed
DTC: P0686 **1T CCM** **Years:** 2008, 2009 **Models:** PT Cruiser **Engines:** All **Transmissions:** All	**ASD Relay Control Circuit Low** Ignition is on. If the PCM detects no voltage on the ASD relay control circuit for more than 3.5 seconds, this DTC will set. **Possible Causes:** • ASD relay intermittent operation • ASD system intermittent condition • Fused B+ circuit problem • ASD relay has failed • ASD relay control circuit is open or is shorted to ground • PCM has failed
DTC: P0687 **1T CCM** **Years:** 2008, 2009 **Models:** PT Cruiser **Engines:** All **Transmissions:** All	**ASD Relay Control Circuit High** Ignition is on. If the PCM detects high voltage on the ASD relay control circuit for more than 3.5 seconds, this DTC will set. **Possible Causes:** • ASD relay intermittent operation • ASD system intermittent condition • ASD relay has failed • ASD relay control circuit is shorted to battery voltage • PCM has failed
DTC: P0688 **1T CCM** **Years:** 2008, 2009 **Models:** Dakota, Grand Cherokee, Journey, Liberty, Nitro, Pacifica, PT Cruiser, Ram Truck, Wrangler **Engines:** All **Transmissions:** All	**ASD Relay Sense Circuit Low** Key on, ASD relay energized, system voltage over 10.0v, and the PCM did not detect any voltage on the Automatic Shutdown (ASD) Sense circuit during the CCM test period. **Possible Causes:** • ASD relay output circuit is open • ASD power supply (fused B+) circuit is open • ASD relay is damaged or it has failed • Problem in fuse/relay center • PCM no start condition • PCM has failed
DTC: P0689 **1T CCM** **Years:** 2008, 2009 **Models:** Dakota, Grand Cherokee, Journey, Liberty, Nitro, Pacifica, PT Cruiser, Ram Truck, Wrangler **Engines:** All **Transmissions:** All	**ASD Relay Sense Circuit Low** Key on; ASD relay energized; system voltage 9-16v. The ASD output circuit voltage drops below an acceptable value at the Front Control Module (FCM). This circuit is continuously monitored. **Possible Causes:** • ASD power supply (fused B+) problem • ASD relay output circuit is open or is shorted to ground • ASD relay has failed • PCM has failed

DTC	Trouble Code Title, Conditions & Possible Causes
DTC: P0690 **1T CCM** **Years:** 2008, 2009 **Models:** Dakota, Grand Cherokee, Journey, Liberty, Nitro, Pacifica, PT Cruiser, Ram Truck, Wrangler **Engines:** All **Transmissions:** All	**ASD Relay Sense Circuit High** Key on, ASD relay energized, system voltage over 10.0v, and the PCM detects high voltage on the Automatic Shutdown (ASD) Sense circuit during the CCM test period. **Possible Causes:** • Intermittent condition • ASD relay output circuit is shorted to voltage • ASD relay is damaged or it has failed • PCM internal short to voltage • PCM has failed
DTC: P0691 **1T CCM** **Years:** 2008, 2009 **Models:** Dakota, Grand Cherokee, Journey, Liberty, Nitro, Pacifica, PT Cruiser, Ram Truck, Wrangler **Engines:** All **Transmissions:** All	**Low Speed Fan (Fan No. 1) Relay Control Circuit Low** Key on; No. 1 cooling fan relay is actuated. If the PCM detects no voltage (open or shorted to ground) on the Radiator Fan Relay control circuit for more than 3 seconds, this DTC will set. **Possible Causes:** • Intermittent condition • Fused ignition switch output circuit problems • Radiator fan relay has failed • Radiator fan control circuit is open or is shorted to ground • PCM has failed
DTC: P0692 **1T CCM** **Years:** 2008, 2009 **Models:** Dakota, Grand Cherokee, Journey, Liberty, Nitro, Pacifica, PT Cruiser, Ram Truck, Wrangler **Engines:** All **Transmissions:** All	**Low Speed Fan (Fan No. 1) Relay Control Circuit High** Key on; radiator fan commanded ON. If the PCM detects an open or high voltage on the Radiator Fan Relay circuit for more than 3 seconds, this DTC will set. **Possible Causes:** • Intermittent condition • Radiator fan relay has failed • Radiator fan control circuit is shorted to battery voltage • PCM has failed
DTC: P0693 **1T CCM** **Years:** 2008, 2009 **Models:** Dakota, Grand Cherokee, Journey, Liberty, Nitro, Pacifica, PT Cruiser, Ram Truck, Wrangler **Engines:** All **Transmissions:** All	**High Speed Fan (Fan No. 2) Relay Control Circuit Low** Key on; fan relay is powered on. If the PCM (PT Cruiser) detects no voltage (open or shorted) on the Radiator Fan Relay control circuit for more than 3 seconds, this DTC will set. Circuit is continuously monitored. **Possible Causes:** • Intermittent condition • Fused ignition switch output circuit problems • Radiator fan relay has failed • Radiator fan control circuit is open or is shorted to ground • PCM has failed
DTC: P0694 **1T CCM** **Years:** 2008, 2009 **Models:** Dakota, Grand Cherokee, Journey, Liberty, Nitro, Pacifica, PT Cruiser, Ram Truck, Wrangler **Engines:** All **Transmissions:** All	**High Speed Fan (Fan No. 2) Relay Control Circuit High** Key on; radiator fan commanded ON. If the PCM (PT Cruiser) detects an open, short or high voltage on the Radiator Fan Relay circuit for more than 3 seconds, this DTC will set. This circuit is continuously monitored. **Possible Causes:** • Intermittent condition • Radiator fan relay has failed • Radiator fan control circuit is open or shorted to battery voltage • PCM has failed
DTC: P0697 **1T ECM** **Years:** 2008, 2009 **Models:** Liberty **Engines:** 2.8L Diesel **Transmissions:** All	**Sensor Supply No. 3 Voltage Too High Or Too Low** Ignition on. If the ECM detects a short-to-voltage (current too high), or if a low voltage (too low) is detected on the Sensor Supply No. 3 circuit, which supplies 5V to the Inlet Pressure Sensor and the APP Sensor No. 2, this DTC will set. **Possible Causes:** • Intermittent condition • 5V supply circuit(s) shorted to voltage • APP Sensor has failed (too low) • Inlet Pressure Sensor has failed (too low) • ECM has failed
DTC: P0700 **2T TCM** **Years:** 2008, 2009 **Models:** Dakota, Grand Cherokee, Journey, Liberty, Nitro, Pacifica, PT Cruiser, Ram Truck, Wrangler **Engines:** All **Transmissions:** All	**Automatic Transmission Control System Malfunction** Ignition on or engine started. The PCM received a message over the CCD Bus from the Transmission Control Module (TCM) that it had detected a problem and set a trouble code in memory. **Possible Causes:** • The presence of this code means the TCM detected a problem • TCM related Sensor has solenoid is damaged or has failed • This code is for information only - check for other TCM codes • TCM or PCM has failed

DTC	Trouble Code Title, Conditions & Possible Causes
DTC: P0700 **1T ECM** **Years:** 2008, 2009 **Models:** Liberty **Engines:** 2.8L Diesel **Transmissions:** All	**TCM DTC** Ignition on. If the ECM detects a CAN Bus message indicating the presences of a TCM-related DTC, this code will set. **Possible Causes:** • Verify presence of any DTCs
DTC: P0703 **1T CCM** **Years:** 2008, 2009 **Models:** Dakota, Grand Cherokee, Journey, Liberty, Nitro, Pacifica, Ram Truck, Wrangler **Engines:** All **Transmissions:** All	**A/T Brake Switch No. 2 Performance Malfunction** Ignition is on. When the PCM recognizes brake switch No.2 voltage is not equal to applied value at the PCM when brake switch No. 1 is applied, this DTC will set. **Note: This could be a normal condition; however, if this condition is seen repeatedly by the PCM, the DTC will be set. Cruise control will not work for the rest of the key cycle.** **Possible Causes:** • Fused B+ circuit malfunction • Brake switch output circuit is open or is shorted to battery voltage or to ground • Brake switch 1 signal circuit is open • Brake switch has failed • PCM has failed
DTC: P0703 **1T CCM** **Years:** 2008, 2009 **Models:** PT Cruiser **Engines:** All **Transmissions:** All	**Brake Lamp Switch No. 2 Performance Malfunction** Engine is running; battery voltage is more than 9.5V; no other brake switch DTCs are present. When Brake Switch 1 output is the same as Brake Switch No. 2 output for more than 25 seconds, this DTC will set. **Possible Causes:** • Intermittent condition • Fused B+ circuit malfunction • Brake switch output circuit is open or is shorted to battery voltage or to ground • Ground circuit is open • Brake switch or PCM has failed
DTC: P0706 **1T CCM** **Years:** 2008, 2009 **Models:** Dakota, Grand Cherokee, Journey, Liberty, Nitro, Pacifica, PT Cruiser, Ram Truck, Wrangler **Engines:** All **Transmissions:** All	**A/T Check Shifter Signal Circuit Malfunction** Key on. After 3 occurrences in one ignition cycle of an invalid PRNDL DDTC which last for more than 0.1 second. **Note: All indicator lights on the instrument cluster will illuminate boxed when the vehicle engine is not running, ignition on, or engine running in Park or Neutral if a problem exists.** **Possible Causes:** • Shifter out of adjustment • TRS T1, T3, T41 or T42 sense circuit is open, shorted to ground or to voltage • TRS Sensor has failed • Intermittent wiring or connector problems • PCM has failed
DTC: P0706 **1T ECM** **Years:** 2008, 2009 **Models:** Liberty **Engines:** 2.8L Diesel **Transmissions:** All	**Check Shifter Signal** Ignition on. This DTC will set with 3 occurrences in one ignition start with an invalid PRNDL code, which lasts more than 0.1 second. **Possible Causes:** • Shifter out of adjustment • TRS T1, T2 or T3 sense circuit is open, shorted to ground or to voltage • T41 or T42 sense circuit is open, shorted to ground or to voltage • Transmission Range Sensor (TRS) has failed • TCM has failed • Intermittent wiring and connector problems
DTC: P0711 **1T CCM** **Years:** 2008, 2009 **Models:** Dakota, Grand Cherokee, Journey, Liberty, Nitro, Pacifica, PT Cruiser, Ram Truck, Wrangler **Engines:** All **Transmissions:** All	**A/T Transmission Fluid Temperature Sensor Signal - No Rise After Startup** Engine started. This DTC will set when the desired transmission temperature does not reach a normal operation temperature within a given time frame. Time is variable due to ambient temperature at cold engine start: from 35 minutes at 40°F (−40°C) to 10 minutes at 60°F (15°C). **Possible Causes:** • Related DTCs will be present • Transmission temperature Sensor has failed • Intermittent wiring or connector problems • PCM has failed

DTC	Trouble Code Title, Conditions & Possible Causes
DTC: P0711 **1T ECM** **Years:** 2008, 2009 **Models:** Liberty **Engines:** 2.8L Diesel **Transmissions:** All	**Transmission Temperature Sensor Performance** Ignition on and engine running. This DTC will set when the desired transmission temperature does not reach a normal operating temperature within a given time frame. Time is variable due to ambient temperature. At 60°F (16°C) ambient temperature, warmup time is approximately 10 minutes. Related DTCs may be present. **Possible Causes:** • Transmission Temperature Sensor (TTS) has failed • TCM has failed • Intermittent wiring and connector problems
DTC: P0712 **1T CCM** **Years:** 2008, 2009 **Models:** Dakota, Grand Cherokee, Journey, Liberty, Nitro, Pacifica, PT Cruiser, Ram Truck, Wrangler **Engines:** All **Transmissions:** All	**A/T Transmission Fluid Temperature Sensor Low Input** Engine started and the PCM detected the TFT Sensor signal was under 0.078v for 0.45 second. **Possible Causes:** • Related DTCs are present • TFT Sensor signal circuit is shorted to ground • TFT Sensor is damaged or has failed (it may be shorted) • Intermittent wiring or connector problems • PCM has failed
DTC: P0712 **1T ECM** **Years:** 2008, 2009 **Models:** Liberty **Engines:** 2.8L Diesel **Transmissions:** All	**Transmission Temperature Sensor Low** Ignition on and engine running. This DTC will set when the monitored transmission temperature drops below 0.78v for 0.45 second. Related DTCs may be present. **Possible Causes:** • Transmission Temperature Sensor (TTS) signal circuit is shorted to ground • TTS has failed • TCM has failed • Intermittent wiring and connector problems
DTC: P0713 **1T CCM** **Years:** 2008, 2009 **Models:** Dakota, Grand Cherokee, Journey, Liberty, Nitro, Pacifica, PT Cruiser, Ram Truck, Wrangler **Engines:** All **Transmissions:** All	**A/T Transmission Fluid Temperature Sensor High Input** Engine started and the PCM detected the TFT Sensor signal was over 4.94v for 0.45 second. **Possible Causes:** • Related DTCs are present • TFT Sensor signal circuit is open or is shorted to voltage • TFT Sensor is damaged or has failed (it may be shorted) • Intermittent wiring or connector problems • PCM has failed
DTC: P0713 **1T ECM** **Years:** 2008, 2009 **Models:** Liberty **Engines:** 2.8L Diesel **Transmissions:** All	**Transmission Temperature Sensor High** Ignition on and engine running. This DTC will set when the monitored Transmission Temperature Sensor signal rises above 4.94v for 0.45 second. **Possible Causes:** • Transmission Temperature Sensor (TTS) signal circuit is open or is shorted to voltage • TTS has failed • TCM has failed • Intermittent wiring and connector problems
DTC: P0714 **1T CCM** **Years:** 2008, 2009 **Models:** Dakota, Grand Cherokee, Journey, Liberty, Nitro, Pacifica, PT Cruiser, Ram Truck, Wrangler **Engines:** All **Transmissions:** All	**A/T Transmission Fluid Temperature Sensor Intermittent** Engine started and the PCM detected the TFT Sensor signal was fluctuating or changes abruptly within a predetermined period of time. **Possible Causes:** • Related DTCs are present • TFT Sensor is damaged or has failed (it may be shorted) • Intermittent wiring or connector problems • PCM has failed
DTC: P0714 **1T ECM** **Years:** 2008, 2009 **Models:** Liberty **Engines:** 2.8L Diesel **Transmissions:** All	**Transmission Temperature Sensor Intermittent** Ignition on and engine running. This DTC will set when the monitored Transmission Temperature Sensor voltage fluctuates or changes abruptly within a predetermined period. Related DTCs may be present. **Possible Causes:** • TTS has failed • TCM has failed • Intermittent wiring and connector problems

DTC	Trouble Code Title, Conditions & Possible Causes
DTC: P0715 **1T CCM** **Years:** 2008, 2009 **Models:** Dakota, Grand Cherokee, Journey, Liberty, Nitro, Pacifica, PT Cruiser, Ram Truck, Wrangler **Engines:** All **Transmissions:** All	**TCM Input Speed Sensor Circuit Malfunction** Engine started; the transmission gear ratio is monitored continuously while the transmission is in gear. This DTC will set if there is an excessive change in the Input RPM in any gear. **Possible Causes:** • ISS ground circuit is open or is shorted to voltage • ISS signal circuit is open, shorted to ground or to power • ISS Sensor is damaged or it has failed • Intermittent wiring or connector problems • PCM has failed
DTC: P0719 **1T CCM** **Years:** 2008, 2009 **Models:** PT Cruiser **Engines:** All **Transmissions:** All	**Brake Lamp Switch Circuit Low** Vehicle is driven over 31 MPH; battery over 9.5V. If the PCM detects no change from Brake Lamp Switch circuit input, after a complete stop, it will increment a counter. If the counter increments 10 times, this DTC will set and the MIL will illuminate. **Possible Causes:** • Intermittent condition • Fused B+ circuit problems • Brake lamp switch sense circuit is open or is shorted to ground • Ground circuit is open • Brake lamp switch has failed • PCM has failed
DTC: P0720 **1T CCM** **Years:** 2008, 2009 **Models:** Dakota, Grand Cherokee, Journey, Liberty, Nitro, Pacifica, PT Cruiser, Ram Truck, Wrangler **Engines:** All **Transmissions:** All	**TCM Output Speed Sensor Circuit Malfunction** Engine started; the transmission gear ratio is monitored continuously while the transmission is in gear. This DTC will set if there is an excessive change in the Output RPM in any gear. On some models, this DTC can take up to 5 minutes of problem identification before lighting the MIL. **Possible Causes:** • OSS ground circuit is open or is shorted to voltage or to ground • Speed Sensor ground circuit is open, shorted to ground or to voltage • OSS Sensor is damaged or it has failed • Intermittent wiring or connector problems • PCM or TCM has failed
DTC: P0724 **1T CCM** **Years:** 2008, 2009 **Models:** PT Cruiser **Engines:** All **Transmissions:** All	**Brake Lamp Switch Circuit High** Vehicle is driven at speeds over 31 MPH; accelerator pedal position is more than 25%; battery voltage over 9.5V. If the PCM detects a high Brake Lamp Switch circuit input, it will increment a counter. If the counter increments 10 times, this DTC will set and the MIL will illuminate. **Possible Causes:** • Intermittent condition • Brake lamp switch sense circuit is shorted to battery voltage • Brake lamp switch has failed • PCM has failed
DTC: P0725 **1T CCM** **Years:** 2008, 2009 **Models:** Dakota, Grand Cherokee, Journey, Liberty, Nitro, Pacifica, PT Cruiser, Ram Truck, Wrangler **Engines:** All **Transmissions:** All	**A/T Engine Speed Sensor Circuit Malfunction** Engine running; and the PCM detected an Engine Speed Sensor reading of less than 390 RPM or more than 8000 RPM occurred for 2 seconds during the CCM test. **Possible Causes:** • Check for trouble codes related to the CKP Sensor • CKP Sensor signal circuit open, shorted to ground or to power • CKP Sensor is damaged or has failed (open or shorted) • Intermittent wiring or connector problems • PCM has failed
DTC: P0725 **1T ECM** **Years:** 2008, 2009 **Models:** Liberty **Engines:** 2.8L Diesel **Transmissions:** All	**Engine Speed Sensor Circuit Malfunction** Engine running. This DTC will set when the TCM senses an engine RPM less than 400 RPM, with engine running for at least 2 seconds. Engine RPM information is transferred over the communication Bus from the ECM. This DTC can take up to 5 minutes of problem identification before lighting the MIL. **Possible Causes:** • Engine speed signal circuit is open, or is shorted to ground or to voltage • TCM has failed • ECM has failed • Intermittent wiring and connector problems

DTC	Trouble Code Title, Conditions & Possible Causes
DTC: P0731 **1T CCM** **Years:** 2008, 2009 **Models:** Dakota, Grand Cherokee, Journey, Liberty, Nitro, Pacifica, PT Cruiser, Ram Truck, Wrangler **Engines:** All **Transmissions:** All	**A/T Additional Gear Ratio Error In First Gear** The transmission gear ratio is monitored continuously while the transmission is in gear. If the ratio of the Input RPM to the Output RPM does not match the current gear ratio, this DTC will set. **Possible Causes:** • Related DTCs will be present • Internal transmission mechanical problems may exist • Intermittent gear ratio errors are present
DTC: P0732 **1T CCM** **Years:** 2008, 2009 **Models:** Dakota, Grand Cherokee, Journey, Liberty, Nitro, Pacifica, PT Cruiser, Ram Truck, Wrangler **Engines:** All **Transmissions:** All	**A/T Additional Gear Ratio Error In Second Gear** The transmission gear ratio is monitored continuously while the transmission is in gear. If the ratio of the Input RPM to the Output RPM does not match the current gear ratio, this DTC will set. **Possible Causes:** • Related DTCs will be present • Transmission solenoid/pressure switch assembly has malfunctioned or failed • Internal transmission mechanical problems may exist • Intermittent gear ratio errors are present
DTC: P0733 **1T CCM** **Years:** 2008, 2009 **Models:** Dakota, Grand Cherokee, Journey, Liberty, Nitro, Pacifica, PT Cruiser, Ram Truck, Wrangler **Engines:** All **Transmissions:** All	**A/T Additional Gear Ratio Error In Third Gear** The transmission gear ratio is monitored continuously while the transmission is in gear. If the ratio of the Input RPM to the Output RPM does not match the current gear ratio, this DTC will set. **Possible Causes:** • Related DTCs will be present • Transmission solenoid/pressure switch assembly has malfunctioned or failed • Internal transmission mechanical problems may exist • Intermittent gear ratio errors are present
DTC: P0734 **1T CCM** **Years:** 2008, 2009 **Models:** Dakota, Grand Cherokee, Journey, Liberty, Nitro, Pacifica, PT Cruiser, Ram Truck, Wrangler **Engines:** All **Transmissions:** All	**A/T Additional Gear Ratio Error In Fourth Gear** The transmission gear ratio is monitored continuously while the transmission is in gear. If the ratio of the Input RPM to the Output RPM does not match the current gear ratio, this DTC will set. **Possible Causes:** • Related DTCs will be present • Transmission solenoid/pressure switch assembly has malfunctioned or failed • Internal transmission mechanical problems may exist • Intermittent gear ratio errors are present
DTC: P0735 **1T CCM** **Years:** 2008, 2009 **Models:** Dakota, Grand Cherokee, Journey, Liberty, Nitro, Pacifica, PT Cruiser, Ram Truck, Wrangler **Engines:** All **Transmissions:** All	**A/T Gear Ratio Error Fourth Prime** Vehicle driven any forward Gear, and the TCM detected the ratio of the Input speed to the Output Speed did not match the current Gear Ratio (this test can take up to 5 minutes). **Possible Causes:** • Related Gear Ratio trouble codes may be stored (note that some of these Gear Ratio trouble codes may be intermittent) • Transmission has internal problems or damage present
DTC: P0736 **1T CCM** **Years:** 2008, 2009 **Models:** Dakota, Grand Cherokee, Journey, Liberty, Nitro, Pacifica, PT Cruiser, Ram Truck, Wrangler **Engines:** All **Transmissions:** All	**A/T Additional Gear Ratio Error In Reverse Gear** The transmission gear ratio is monitored continuously while the transmission is in gear. If the ratio of the Input RPM to the Output RPM does not match the current gear ratio, this DTC will set. **Possible Causes:** • Related DTCs will be present • Internal transmission mechanical problems may exist • Intermittent gear ratio errors are present
DTC: P0740 **1T CCM** **Years:** 2008, 2009 **Models:** Dakota, Grand Cherokee, Journey, Liberty, Nitro, Pacifica, PT Cruiser, Ram Truck, Wrangler **Engines:** All **Transmissions:** All	**A/T Torque Converter Clutch System Out of Range** The TCC is in FEMCC or PEMCC, transmission temperature is hot, engine temperature is more than 100°F (38°C), transmission input speed is more than 1750 RPM, with TPS less than 30. The TCC is modulated by controlling the duty cycle of the L/R solenoid, until the difference between the engine and transmission input speed RPM or duty cycle is within desired range. The DTC is set after the period of 10 seconds and 3 occurrences of either: FEMCC with slip greater than 100 RPM or PEMCC duty cycle is more than 85%. **Possible Causes:** • Related DTCs will be present • Internal transmission mechanical problems may exist • Intermittent gear ratio errors are present

DTC	Trouble Code Title, Conditions & Possible Causes
DTC: P0740 **1T ECM** **Years:** 2008, 2009 **Models:** Liberty **Engines:** 2.8L Diesel **Transmissions:** All	**A/T Torque Converter Clutch System Out of Range** System is monitored during Electronically Modulated Converter Clutch (EMCC) operation. Transmission must be in EMCC, with input speed of more than 1750 RPM. This DTC will set when the TCC-L/R Solenoid achieves the maximum duty cycle and cannot pull engine speed within 60 RPM of input speed. Also, it will set when the transmission is in EMCC and the engine slips TCC more than 100 RPM for 10 seconds. This DTC can take up to 5 minutes of problem identification before lighting the MIL. **Possible Causes:** • Related DTC 0750 is present • Internal transmission problem • Transmission Solenoid/TRS Assembly has failed • Intermittent wiring and connector problems
DTC: P0750 **1T CCM** **Years:** 2008, 2009 **Models:** Dakota, Grand Cherokee, Journey, Liberty, Nitro, Pacifica, PT Cruiser, Ram Truck, Wrangler **Engines:** All **Transmissions:** All	**A/T Low/Reverse Solenoid Circuit Failure** Solenoids are tested initially at power-up, then every 10 seconds thereafter, the solenoids will also be tested immediately after a gear ratio or pressure switch error is detected. 3 consecutive solenoid continuity test failures, or one failure if test is run in response to a gear ratio or pressure switch error. **Possible Causes:** • Related relay DTCs present • Transmission control relay output circuit open • L/R solenoid control circuit open or shorted to ground or to voltage • L/R solenoid/pressure switch assembly has malfunctioned or failed • Intermittent wiring and connectors • PCM has failed
DTC: P0755 **1T CCM** **Years:** 2008, 2009 **Models:** Dakota, Grand Cherokee, Journey, Liberty, Nitro, Pacifica, PT Cruiser, Ram Truck, Wrangler **Engines:** All **Transmissions:** All	**A/T 2/4 Solenoid Circuit Failure** 2/4 solenoid in monitored initially at power-up, then every 10 seconds thereafter. Also, immediately after a gear ratio or pressure switch error is detected. 3 consecutive solenoid continuity test failures, or one failure if test is run in response to a gear ratio or pressure switch error. **Possible Causes:** • Related DTCs present • Transmission control relay output circuit open • 2/4 Solenoid control circuit is open or shorted to ground • 2/4 Solenoid control circuit is shorted to system power • 2/4 Solenoid is damaged or has failed • Intermittent wiring or connector problems • PCM has failed
DTC: P0755 **1T ECM** **Years:** 2008, 2009 **Models:** Liberty **Engines:** 2.8L Diesel **Transmissions:** All	**A/T 2C Solenoid Circuit Malfunction** System is monitored initially at powerup and every 10 seconds thereafter. It will also be tested immediately after a gear ratio or pressure switch error is detected. After 3 consecutive solenoid continuity test failures, or after one failure if a test is run in response to a gear ratio or pressure switch error, this DTC will set. **Possible Causes:** • Related Relay DTCs are present • Transmission Control Relay output circuit is open • 2C Solenoid control circuit is open or is shorted to ground or to voltage • Transmission Solenoid/TRS Assembly has failed • TCM has failed • Intermittent wiring and connector problems
DTC: P0760 **1T CCM** **Years:** 2008, 2009 **Models:** Dakota, Grand Cherokee, Journey, Liberty, Nitro, Pacifica, PT Cruiser, Ram Truck, Wrangler **Engines:** All **Transmissions:** All	**A/T Overdrive Solenoid Circuit Failure** O/D solenoid in monitored initially at power-up, then every 10 seconds thereafter. Also, immediately after a gear ratio or pressure switch error is detected. 3 consecutive solenoid continuity test failures, or one failure if test is run in response to a gear ratio or pressure switch error. **Possible Causes:** • Related DTCs present • Transmission control relay output circuit open • O/D Solenoid control circuit is open or shorted to ground • O/D Solenoid control circuit is shorted to system power • O/D Solenoid is damaged or has failed • PCM has failed

DTC	Trouble Code Title, Conditions & Possible Causes
DTC: P0765 **1T CCM** **Years:** 2008, 2009 **Models:** Dakota, Grand Cherokee, Journey, Liberty, Nitro, Pacifica, PT Cruiser, Ram Truck, Wrangler **Engines:** All **Transmissions:** All	**A/T Underdrive Solenoid Circuit Failure** U/D solenoid in monitored initially at power-up, then every 10 seconds thereafter. Also, immediately after a gear ratio or pressure switch error is detected. 3 consecutive solenoid continuity test failures, or one failure if test is run in response to a gear ratio or pressure switch error. **Possible Causes:** • Related DTCs present • Transmission control relay output circuit open • U/D Solenoid control circuit is open or shorted to ground • U/D Solenoid control circuit is shorted to system power • U/D Solenoid is damaged or has failed • Intermittent wiring or connector problems • PCM has failed
DTC: P0770 **1T ECM** **Years:** 2008, 2009 **Models:** Liberty **Engines:** 2.8L Diesel **Transmissions:** All	**A/T 4C Solenoid Circuit Malfunction** System is monitored initially at powerup and every 10 seconds thereafter. It will also be tested immediately after a gear ratio or pressure switch error is detected. After 3 consecutive solenoid continuity test failures, or after one failure if a test is run in response to a gear ratio or pressure switch error, this DTC will set. **Possible Causes:** • Related Relay DTCs are present • Transmission Control Relay output circuit is open • 4C Solenoid control circuit is open or is shorted to ground or to voltage • Transmission Solenoid/TRS Assembly has failed • TCM has failed • Intermittent wiring and connector problems
DTC: P0781 **1T CCM** **Years:** 2008, 2009 **Models:** PT Cruiser **Engines:** All **Transmissions:** All	**A/T Low/Reverse Pressure Switch Circuit Failure** Monitored whenever engine is running. If one of the pressure switches are open or closed at the wrong time, this DTC will set. **Possible Causes:** • Related DTCs present • Loss of Prime P0944 DTC present • L/R pressure switch sense circuit is open or is shorted to ground or to voltage • L/R pressure switch has failed • Intermittent wiring or connector problems • PCM has failed
DTC: P0833 **1T CCM** **Years:** 2008, 2009 **Models:** PT Cruiser **Engines:** All **Transmissions:** All	**Clutch Pedal Position Switch Circuit Malfunction** Condition is monitored with the engine running; battery voltage over 9v; vehicle speed is less than 0 MPH, then more than 27 MPH; MAP is greater than 90mbar; and engine speed is over 3200 RPM. If the Clutch Switch status did not change for more than 15 seconds, this DTC will set. **Possible Causes:** • Intermittent condition • CPP switch signal circuit is open or shorted to ground • CPP switch ground circuit is open • Clutch pedal is damaged or has failed • PCM has failed
DTC: P0836 **1T ECM** **Years:** 2008, 2009 **Models:** Liberty **Engines:** 2.8L Diesel **Transmissions:** All	**Transfer Case Position Sensor Plausibility Or Improper Voltage Signal** Ignition on. If the ECM detects a voltage signal from the Transfer Case Switch that does not fall into a valid switch position voltage range, or if the Position Sensor signal is above 4.8v or below 0.14v for 0.5 second, this DTC will set. **Possible Causes:** • Transfer Case Position Sensor has failed • Intermittent wiring and/or connector problems • Transfer Case Position Sensor signal circuit is open, shorted to ground, shorted to voltage or shorted to Sensor ground circuit • ECM has failed

DTC	Trouble Code Title, Conditions & Possible Causes
DTC: P0841 **1T CCM** **Years:** 2008, 2009 **Models:** Dakota, Grand Cherokee, Journey, Liberty, Nitro, Pacifica, PT Cruiser, Ram Truck, Wrangler **Engines:** All **Transmissions:** All	**Low/Reverse Pressure Switch Sense Circuit Malfunction** Switches are monitored whenever engine is running. This DTC will set if one of the pressure switches in open or closed at the wrong time in a given gear. **Possible Causes:** • Related DTCs present • Loss of Prime P0944 DTC present • Transmission control relay output circuit open • L/R switch sense circuit is open or is shorted to ground or to voltage • L/R pressure switch is damaged or has failed • Intermittent wiring or connector problems • PCM has failed
DTC: P0845 **1T CCM** **Years:** 2008, 2009 **Models:** Dakota, Grand Cherokee, Journey, Liberty, Nitro, Pacifica, PT Cruiser, Ram Truck, Wrangler **Engines:** All **Transmissions:** All	**A/T 2/4 Hydraulic Pressure Test Malfunction** Engine speed over 1000 RPM, then immediately after a shift event, the PCM detected a failure in one or more of the Pressure Switch circuits (i.e., it tests switches that are not operating). **Possible Causes:** • 2/4 pressure is incorrect, or internal transmission faults exist • 2/4 pressure switch circuit is open, shorted to ground or power • 2/4 pressure switch is damaged or it has failed • Transmission solenoids/TRS assembly is damaged or have failed • TCM relay power circuit to 2/4 switch is open (loss of B+) • Intermittent wiring or connector problems exist • PCM or TCM has failed
DTC: P0845 **1T ECM** **Years:** 2008, 2009 **Models:** Liberty **Engines:** 2.8L Diesel **Transmissions:** All	**A/T 2C Hydraulic Pressure Test Failure** System hydraulic pressure is monitored in any forward gear with engine speed above 1000 RPM, shortly after a shift, and every minute thereafter. After a shift into a forward gear, with engine speed above 1000 RPM, the TCM momentarily turns ON element pressure to the Clutch circuits that don't have pressure, in order to identify the correct Pressure Switch closes. If the Pressure Switch does not close 2 times, the DTC will set. **Possible Causes:** • Related Relay DTCs are present • Transmission Solenoid/TRS Assembly has failed • 2C Pressure Switch sense circuit is open or is shorted to ground or to voltage • 5V supply circuit is open or is shorted to ground • Pressure Sensor has poor line connection • Transmission Control Relay output circuit is open • Excessive debris in oil pan • Line Pressure Sensor has failed • Internal transmission problems • TCM has failed • Intermittent wiring and connector problems
DTC: P0846 **1T CCM** **Years:** 2008, 2009 **Models:** Dakota, Grand Cherokee, Journey, Liberty, Nitro, Pacifica, PT Cruiser, Ram Truck, Wrangler **Engines:** All **Transmissions:** All	**A/T 2/4 Pressure Switch Circuit Malfunction** Engine started; vehicle driven in a forward gear, and the PCM detected that the 2/4 Pressure Switch circuit indicated open or closed at the wrong time. Related relay DTCs may be present. **Possible Causes:** • 2/4 pressure is incorrect, or internal transmission faults exist • 2/4 pressure switch circuit is open, shorted to ground or power • 2/4 pressure switch is damaged or it has failed • TCM relay power circuit to L/R switch is open (loss of B+) • PCM/TCM has failed
DTC: P0846 **1T ECM** **Years:** 2008, 2009 **Models:** Liberty **Engines:** 2.8L Diesel **Transmissions:** All	**A/T 2C Pressure Switch Sense Circuit Malfunction** Pressure Switch circuit is monitored whenever engine is running. The appropriate DTC is set if one of the Pressure Switches is open or closed at the wrong time for a given gear. **Possible Causes:** • Related Relay DTCs are present • Transmission Solenoid/TRS Assembly has failed • 2C Pressure Switch sense circuit is open or is shorted to ground or to voltage • 2C Pressure Switch has failed • TCM has failed • Intermittent wiring and connector problems

DTC	Trouble Code Title, Conditions & Possible Causes
DTC: P0850 **2T CCM** **Years:** 2008, 2009 **Models:** Dakota, Grand Cherokee, Journey, Liberty, Nitro, Pacifica, PT Cruiser, Ram Truck, Wrangler **Engines:** All **Transmissions:** All	**A/T Park/Neutral Switch Performance** Engine running; gearshift selector in Park, Neutral or Drive position (not Limp-In mode). The PCM detected an invalid Park/Neutral switch state during vehicle operation. **Possible Causes:** • Check for any TCM related codes stored in the TCM controller • PCM has failed
DTC: P0864 **1T ECM** **Years:** 2008, 2009 **Models:** Liberty **Engines:** 2.8L Diesel **Transmissions:** All	**TCM Torque Reduction Signal Error** Ignition on or engine running. If the TCM receives an improper or implausible Torque Management Request signal, this DTC will set. **Possible Causes:** • ECM has failed • Torque Management Request signal circuit is open, shorted to ground, shorted to voltage • TCM has failed • Intermittent condition
DTC: P0868 **1T ECM** **Years:** 2008, 2009 **Models:** Liberty **Engines:** 2.8L Diesel **Transmissions:** All	**A/T Line Pressure Low** Line pressure is monitored whenever driving in a forward gear. The TCM continuously monitors the Transducer Line Pressure output and compares it to a desired line pressure. If the actual pressure is more than 10 psi below the desired line pressure, the DTC will set in about 2.1 seconds. **Possible Causes:** • Related Relay DTCs may be present • 5V supply circuit is open or is shorted to ground or to voltage • Poor Line Pressure Sensor connection • Pressure Control Solenoid control circuit is shorted to voltage • Internal transmission problems • Line Pressure Sensor has failed • Plugged filter • TCM has failed • Intermittent wiring and connector problems
DTC: P0869 **1T ECM** **Years:** 2008, 2009 **Models:** Liberty **Engines:** 2.8L Diesel **Transmissions:** All	**A/T Line Pressure High** Line pressure is monitored whenever driving in a forward gear. The TCM continuously monitors the Transducer Line Pressure output and compares it to a desired line pressure. If the actual pressure is more than the highest desired line pressure ever used in the current gear, while the Pressure Control Solenoid duty cycle is at or near its maximum value (which should result in minimum line pressure), the DTC will set. **Possible Causes:** • Related Relay DTCs may be present • 5V supply circuit is open or is shorted to ground • Poor Line Pressure Sensor connection • Pressure Control Solenoid control circuit is open or is shorted to ground • Internal transmission problems (line pressure high) • Line Pressure Sensor has failed • TCM has failed • Intermittent wiring and connector problems
DTC: P0870 **1T CCM** **Years:** 2008, 2009 **Models:** Dakota, Grand Cherokee, Journey, Liberty, Nitro, Pacifica, PT Cruiser, Ram Truck, Wrangler **Engines:** All **Transmissions:** All	**A/T Hydraulic Pressure Line Malfunction** Engine started; vehicle driven at over 1000 RPM, then immediately after a shift, the PCM detected a malfunction in one or more of the Pressure Switch circuits (it detected the switch did not close twice). DTC P0944 may be present. **Possible Causes:** • Check for related line pressure trouble codes • Check for related speed ratio and pressure switch codes • 5V supply circuit is open or is shorted to ground • Transmission Control Relay output circuit is open • OD Pressure Switch sense circuit is shorted to ground or to voltage • Excessive debris in the oil pan • Line pressure Sensor connector is loose or damaged • Oil pressure switch is damaged or has failed • Intermittent wiring or connector problems exist • PCM or TCM has failed

DTC	Trouble Code Title, Conditions & Possible Causes
DTC: P0871 **1T CCM** **Years:** 2008, 2009 **Models:** Dakota, Grand Cherokee, Journey, Liberty, Nitro, Pacifica, PT Cruiser, Ram Truck, Wrangler **Engines:** All **Transmissions:** All	**A/T O/D Pressure Switch Circuit Malfunction** Engine started; vehicle driven in a forward gear, and the PCM detected that the O/D Pressure Switch circuit indicated open or closed at the wrong time. **Possible Causes:** • Related DTCs may be present • O/D pressure is incorrect, or internal transmission faults exist • O/D pressure switch circuit is open, shorted to ground or power • O/D pressure switch is damaged or it has failed • TCM relay power circuit to O/D switch is open (loss of B+) • Intermittent wiring or connector problems exist • PCM or TCM has failed
DTC: P0875 **1T CCM** **Years:** 2008, 2009 **Models:** Dakota, Grand Cherokee, Journey, Liberty, Nitro, Pacifica, PT Cruiser, Ram Truck, Wrangler **Engines:** All **Transmissions:** All	**A/T U/D Hydraulic Pressure Test Malfunction** Engine speed over 1000 RPM, then immediately after a shift event, the TCM/PCM detected a fault in one or more of the Pressure Switch circuits (it detected the switch did not close twice). **Possible Causes:** • Check for related line pressure trouble codes • Check for related speed ratio and pressure switch codes • 5V supply circuit is open or shorted to ground • U/D Pressure switch sense circuit is open or shorted to ground or to voltage • Excessive debris in the oil pan • Line pressure Sensor connector is loose or damaged • U/D Oil Pressure Switch is damaged or it has failed • TCM has failed • Intermittent wiring and connector problems
DTC: P0876 **1T CCM** **Years:** 2008, 2009 **Models:** Dakota, Grand Cherokee, Journey, Liberty, Nitro, Pacifica, PT Cruiser, Ram Truck, Wrangler **Engines:** All **Transmissions:** All	**A/T U/D Pressure Switch Sense Malfunction** Engine started; vehicle driven in a forward gear, and the PCM detected that the U/D Pressure Switch Sense circuit indicated open or closed at the wrong time during the CCM test period. **Possible Causes:** • U/D pressure is incorrect, or internal transmission faults exist • U/D pressure switch circuit is open, shorted to ground or power • U/D pressure switch is damaged or it has failed • TCM relay power circuit to L/R switch is open (loss of B+) • TCM has failed
DTC: P0884 **1T CCM** **Years:** 2008, 2009 **Models:** Dakota, Grand Cherokee, Journey, Liberty, Nitro, Pacifica, PT Cruiser, Ram Truck, Wrangler **Engines:** All **Transmissions:** All	**Power-Up Automatic Transmission Speed Malfunction** Engine started, TCM relay enabled; and the TCM detected a valid forward gear PNDRL signal with the Output Speed more than 800 RPM indicating a vehicle speed of over 20 MPH. **Note: The TCM has separate powers and grounds specifically to its portion of the PCM.** **Possible Causes:** • TCM power supply circuit to direct battery is open • TCM power supply circuit to the ignition switch is open • TCM power ground circuit is open or the connector is loose • TCM has failed
DTC: P0888 **1T CCM** **Years:** 2008, 2009 **Models:** Dakota, Grand Cherokee, Journey, Liberty, Nitro, Pacifica, PT Cruiser, Ram Truck, Wrangler **Engines:** All **Transmissions:** All	**A/T Relay Output Malfunction** Engine started, TCM relay enabled and monitored continuously. This DTC sets when less than 3v are present at the relay output circuits at the TCM when the TCM is energizing the relay. **Note: Due to the integration of the PCM and TCM, the transmission part of the PCM has its own specific power and ground circuits.** **Possible Causes:** • Fused B+ circuit is open • TC relay output circuit is open or is shorted to ground • TC relay control circuit is open or is shorted to ground • TC relay ground circuit is open • TC relay has failed • Intermittent wiring or connector problems exist • Transmission solenoid/pressure switch assembly has malfunctioned or failed • PCM/TCM has failed

DTC	Trouble Code Title, Conditions & Possible Causes
DTC: P0890 **1T CCM** **Years:** 2008, 2009 **Models:** Dakota, Grand Cherokee, Journey, Liberty, Nitro, Pacifica, PT Cruiser, Ram Truck, Wrangler **Engines:** All **Transmissions:** All	**A/T TCM Switched Battery Circuit Malfunction** Ignition switch position is changed from one position to another. TCM relay "not" energized, and the TCM detected voltage present at any of the Pressure Switch input circuits. **Note: Due to the integration of the PCM and TCM, the transmission part of the PCM has its own specific power and ground circuits.** **Possible Causes:** • 2/4 switch circuit is shorted to system power (B+) • L/R switch circuit is shorted to system power (B+) • O/D switch circuit is shorted to system power (B+) • TCM switched battery circuit is damaged • Intermittent wiring or connector problems exist • PCM/TCM has failed
DTC: P0891 **1T CCM** **Years:** 2008, 2009 **Models:** Dakota, Grand Cherokee, Journey, Liberty, Nitro, Pacifica, PT Cruiser, Ram Truck, Wrangler **Engines:** All **Transmissions:** All	**A/T TCM Relay Always On** Key on or engine cranking; TCM relay "not" energized, and the TCM detected voltage present at the TCM output circuit during the test. **Note: Due to the integration of the PCM and TCM, the transmission part of the PCM has its own specific power and ground circuits.** **Possible Causes:** • TCM relay output circuit is shorted to system power (B+) • TCM relay control circuit is shorted to system power (B+) • TCM relay is damaged or it has failed (it may be stuck closed) • Intermittent wiring or connector problems exist • PCM/TCM has failed
DTC: P0897 **1T CCM** **Years:** 2008, 2009 **Models:** Dakota, Grand Cherokee, Journey, Liberty, Nitro, Pacifica, PT Cruiser, Ram Truck, Wrangler **Engines:** All **Transmissions:** All	**A/T Transmission Fluid Burnt Or Worn Out** Engine started; vehicle driven, and immediately after a transition from full TCC lockup to partial TCC engagement (for A/C bump prevention), the TCM detected vehicle shutter during engagement. **Possible Causes:** • Automatic transmission fluid is burnt or contaminated • Automatic transmission fluid is worn out
DTC: P0932 **1T CCM** **Years:** 2008, 2009 **Models:** Liberty **Engines:** 2.8L Diesel **Transmissions:** All	**A/T Line Pressure Sensor Malfunction** Sensor is monitored continuously while driving in a forward gear. T PCM continuously monitors actual line pressure and compares it to desired line pressure. If the actual pressure is more than 25 psi higher than the desire line pressure, but is less than the highest line pressure ever used in the current gear, this DTC will set. Related DTCs may be present. **Possible Causes:** • Poor line pressure connection • Poor wiring connection • Internal transmission problems • TCM has failed • Intermittent wiring and connector problems
DTC: P0934 **1T CCM** **Years:** 2008, 2009 **Models:** Liberty **Engines:** 2.8L Diesel **Transmissions:** All	**A/T Line Pressure Sensor Low** Sensor is monitored continuously while engine is running and Output Speed is more than 390 RPM. This DTC will set when the Line Pressure Sensor output signal is less than 0.35V for 1.4 seconds. **Possible Causes:** • 5V supply circuit is open or is shorted to ground • Line Pressure Sensor signal circuit is shorted to ground • Line Pressure Sensor has failed • TCM has failed • Intermittent wiring and connector problems
DTC: P0935 **1T CCM** **Years:** 2008, 2009 **Models:** Liberty **Engines:** 2.8L Diesel **Transmissions:** All	**A/T Line Pressure Sensor High** Sensor is monitored continuously while engine is running and Output Speed is more than 390 RPM and desired line pressure is less than 200 psi. This DTC will set when the Line Pressure Sensor output signal is more than 4.75V for 1.4 seconds. **Possible Causes:** • Line Pressure Sensor ground circuit is open • Line Pressure Sensor signal circuit is open or is shorted to voltage • Line Pressure Sensor has failed • TCM has failed • Intermittent wiring and connector problems

DTC	Trouble Code Title, Conditions & Possible Causes
DTC: P0944 **1T CCM** **Years:** 2008, 2009 **Models:** Dakota, Grand Cherokee, Journey, Liberty, Nitro, Pacifica, PT Cruiser, Ram Truck, Wrangler **Engines:** All **Transmissions:** All	**A/T Loss Of Prime Pressure** Engine started; vehicle driven, and immediately after a slipping condition is detected with the pressure switches "not" indicating pressure, the PCM detected a loss of prime pressure. In effect, the TCM turns "on" available elements to detect if prime pressure exists. The DTC sets if no pressure switches respond. **Possible Causes:** • A/T pressure switch connector is damaged, loose or shorted • Invalid PRNDL code (shift lever position error) • Automatic transmission fluid level is too low • Transmission oil filter is clogged or severely restricted • Transmission oil pump is damaged or weak • Intermittent wiring or connector problems exist
DTC: P0952 **1T CCM** **Years:** 2008, 2009 **Models:** Dakota, Grand Cherokee, Journey, Liberty, Nitro, Pacifica, PT Cruiser, Ram Truck, Wrangler **Engines:** All **Transmissions:** All	**A/T AutoStick Sensor Circuit Malfunction** Engine started; vehicle driven, transmission not in AutoStick position, and the TCM that either the Upshift or Downshift switch was closed (below 0.3v), or if both the Upshift and Downshift switches are closed at the same time. **Possible Causes:** • AutoStick assembly is damaged or has failed • Intermittent wiring or connector problems exist • Downshift sense or Upshift sense circuit is shorted to ground • PCM/TCM has failed
DTC: P0953 **1T CCM** **Years:** 2008, 2009 **Models:** Dakota, Grand Cherokee, Journey, Liberty, Nitro, Pacifica, PT Cruiser, Ram Truck, Wrangler **Engines:** All **Transmissions:** All	**A/T AutoStick Sensor Circuit High** The AutoStick circuit is checked every .007 second, with the ignition on and in both AutoStick and non-AutoStick modes. If the TCM detects circuit voltage rises above 4.8v, this DTC will set. **Possible Causes:** • AutoStick assembly is damaged or has failed • Intermittent wiring or connector problems exist • Downshift sense or Upshift sense circuit is shorted to ground • PCM/TCM has failed
DTC: P0987 **1T CCM** **Years:** 2008, 2009 **Models:** Dakota, Grand Cherokee, Journey, Liberty, Nitro, Pacifica, PT Cruiser, Ram Truck, Wrangler **Engines:** All **Transmissions:** All	**A/T 4C Hydraulic Pressure Test Malfunction** Engine started; vehicle driven at over 1000 RPM, then immediately after a shift and every minute thereafter. After a shift into a forward gear, with engine speed more than 1000 RPM, the TCM momentarily turns on element pressure to the clutch circuits that don't have pressure to identify the correct pressure switch that closes. If the pressure switch does not close 2 times, this DTC will set. Related line pressure DTCs are present. **Possible Causes:** • Check for related speed ratio and pressure switch codes • Excessive debris in the oil pan • 5V supply circuit is open or is shorted to ground • Transmission Control Relay output circuit is open • 4C Pressure Switch sense circuit is shorted to ground or to voltage • Line Pressure Sensor connector is loose or damaged • 4C Line Pressure Sensor has failed • Transmission Solenoid/TRS Assembly has failed • Internal transmission problems • TCM has failed • Intermittent wiring and connector problems
DTC: P0988 **1T CCM** **Years:** 2008, 2009 **Models:** Dakota, Grand Cherokee, Journey, Liberty, Nitro, Pacifica, PT Cruiser, Ram Truck, Wrangler **Engines:** All **Transmissions:** All	**A/T 4C Pressure Switch Sense Circuit Malfunction** Engine started; vehicle driven in any forward gear, and the PCM detected that the 4C Pressure Switch circuit indicated open or closed at the wrong time during the CCM test. Related Relay DTCs are present. **Possible Causes:** • 4C pressure is incorrect, or internal transmission faults exist • 4C Pressure Switch sense circuit is open, shorted to ground or power • 4C Pressure Switch is damaged or it has failed • TCM Relay power circuit to L/R switch is open (loss of B+) • PCM/TCM has failed • Intermittent wiring and connector problems

DTC	Trouble Code Title, Conditions & Possible Causes
DTC: P0992 **1T CCM** **Years:** 2008, 2009 **Models:** Dakota, Grand Cherokee, Journey, Liberty, Nitro, Pacifica, PT Cruiser, Ram Truck, Wrangler **Engines:** All **Transmissions:** All	**A/T 2/4 & O/D Hydraulic Pressure Test Malfunction** Engine started; vehicle driven at over 1000 RPM, then immediately after a shift, the PCM detected a malfunction in one or more of the Pressure Switch circuits (it tests the switches that are not operating). If the pressure switch does not close 2 times, the DTC will set. **Possible Causes:** • 2/4 pressure switch circuit is open, shorted to ground or power • 2/4 pressure switch is damaged or it has failed • O/D pressure switch circuit is open, shorted to ground or power • O/D pressure switch is damaged or it has failed • Internal transmission faults exist • TCM relay power circuit to 2/4 or O/D switch open (loss of B+) • PCM/TCM has failed

OBD II Trouble Code List (P1XXX Codes)

DTC	Trouble Code Title, Conditions & Possible Causes
DTC: P1004 **1T CCM** **Years:** 2008, 2009 **Models:** Dakota, Grand Cherokee, Journey, Liberty, Nitro, Pacifica, PT Cruiser, Ram Truck, Wrangler **Engines:** All **Transmissions:** All	**Short Runner Valve Control Performance** The Powertrain Control Module (PCM) compares the circuit feedback to a calibrated closed range when the circuit is de-energized or to a calibrated open range when the circuit is energized. If the value is determined to be out of the calibrated range in either the de-energized or energized state for more than a calibrated amount of time, this DTC will set. **Possible Causes:** • ASD relay output circuit open or high resistance • 5 volt supply circuit open or high resistance • SRV signal circuit open or high resistance • SRV control circuit shorted to ground • SRV control circuit open or high resistance • Sensor ground circuit open or high resistance • Short Runner Valve (SRV) assembly • Powertrain Control Module (PCM)
DTC: P1005 **1T CCM** **Years:** 2008, 2009 **Models:** Dakota, Grand Cherokee, Journey, Liberty, Nitro, Pacifica, PT Cruiser, Ram Truck, Wrangler **Transmissions:** All	**Manifold Tuning Valve Control Performance** The Powertrain Control Module (PCM) compares the circuit feedback to a calibrated closed range when the circuit is de-energized or to a calibrated open range when the circuit is energized. If the value is determined to be out of the calibrated range in either the de-energized or energized state for more than a calibrated amount of time, this DTC will set. **Possible Causes:** • MTV control circuit shorted to voltage • MTV control circuit shorted to ground • MTV control circuit open or high resistance • Ground circuit open or high resistance • manifold tune valve assembly • Powertrain Control Module (PCM)
DTC: P1101 **1T ECM** **Years:** 2008, 2009 **Models:** Liberty **Engines:** 2.8L Diesel **Transmissions:** All	**ACM Crash Signal Received** Ignition on. If crash signal is received from Airbag Control Module, this DTC will set. **Possible Causes:** • Clear DTC • Examine airbag system integrity • Check connections and grounds
DTC: P1102 **1T ECM** **Years:** 2008, 2009 **Models:** Liberty **Engines:** 2.8L Diesel **Transmissions:** All	**Viscous/Cabin Heater Relay Error** Ignition on. ECM Viscous/Cabin Heater Relay is commanded on (excessive current or short circuit), or is commanded OFF (open circuit or short-to-ground). If the ECM detects excessive current or no voltage signal on the Viscous/Cabin Heater Relay control circuit, this DTC will set. **Possible Causes:** • ASD Relay output circuit is open • Cabin Heater Relay has failed • Cabin Heater Relay control circuit is open, shorted to voltage, or to ground • ECM has failed

DTC	Trouble Code Title, Conditions & Possible Causes
DTC: P1105 **2T CCM** **Years:** 2008, 2009 **Models:** PT Cruiser Turbo **Engines:** All **Transmissions:** All	**Throttle Inlet Pressure Sensor Solenoid Circuit Malfunction** Engine started, system voltage over 10.5V, Turbo Boost mode enabled, and the PCM detected the Actual and Intended state of the Throttle Inlet Pressure Sensor solenoid did not match. **Possible Causes:** • ASD output circuit to the TIP solenoid is open • Throttle inlet pressure Sensor solenoid is damaged or has failed • TIP solenoid control circuit is open, shorted to ground or power • PCM has failed
DTC: P1106 **2T CCM** **Years:** 2008, 2009 **Models:** PT Cruiser Turbo **Engines:** All **Transmissions:** All	**Throttle Inlet Pressure Sensor Solenoid Circuit Malfunction** Engine started; battery over 10.5V; Turbo Boost mode enabled. The PCM did not detect enough difference between BARO Sensor and TIP Sensor values during boost. **Possible Causes:** • Check the vacuum supply to the turbo surge solenoid unit • Inspect the hoses and tubing to the turbo charger assembly • Review results of Solenoid Tests (Test 1, 2, 3 and 4 results) • Turbocharger assembly is damaged or it has failed • Wastegate actuator has failed (due to a mechanical failure)
DTC: P1115 **1T CCM** **Years:** 2008, 2009 **Models:** Dakota, Grand Cherokee, Journey, Liberty, Nitro, Pacifica, PT Cruiser, Ram Truck, Wrangler **Engines:** All **Transmissions:** All	**General Temperature Sensor Performance** Engine "off" more than 8 hours, then engine started, ambient temperature above −10°F; and after a calibrated amount of cool-down time, the PCM compares the values from the Ambient Air Temperature (AAT), Engine Coolant Temperature (ECT) and Intake Air Temperature (IAT) Sensors. If the PCM detects that the value of any combination of these Sensors (AAT-IAT, AAT-ECT or ECT-IAT) is less than a calibrated value, it will set this trouble code. **Possible Causes:** • Sensor signal circuit is open or shorted to ground • Sensor ground circuit is open or shorted to VREF (5V) • One or more of the identified Sensors is out-of-calibration • Ambient air temperature Sensor is damaged or it has failed • PCM High or Low circuit is damaged or it has failed
DTC: P1128 **2T CCM** **Years:** 2008, 2009 **Models:** Dakota, Grand Cherokee, Journey, Liberty, Nitro, Pacifica, PT Cruiser, Ram Truck, Wrangler **Engines:** All **Transmissions:** All	**Closed Loop Fueling Not Achieved - Bank 1** The Powertrain Control Module (PCM) detects a condition where the vehicle has remained in open loop fuel control, from a start-up condition, longer than a calibrated amount of time, when conditions would have otherwise expected closed loop operation. Two Trip Fault. Three good trips required to turn off the MIL. **Possible Causes:** • Fuel delivery system • ECT sensor, wiring or connectors • MAP sensor, wiring or connectors • O2 sensor, wiring or connectors • Engine mechanical • PCM
DTC: P1129 **2T CCM** **Years:** 2008, 2009 **Models:** Dakota, Grand Cherokee, Journey, Liberty, Nitro, Pacifica, Ram Truck, Wrangler **Engines:** All **Transmissions:** All	**Closed Loop Fueling Not Achieved - Bank 2** The Powertrain Control Module (PCM) detects a condition where the vehicle has remained in open loop fuel control, from a start-up condition, longer than a calibrated amount of time, when conditions would have otherwise expected closed loop operation. Two Trip Fault. Three good trips required to turn off the MIL. **Possible Causes:** • Fuel delivery system • ECT sensor, wiring or connectors • MAP sensor, wiring or connectors • O2 sensor, wiring or connectors • Engine mechanical • PCM
DTC: P1131 **1T ECM** **Years:** 2008, 2009 **Models:** Liberty **Engines:** 2.8L Diesel **Transmissions:** All	**Glow Plug Module Voltage Supply** Ignition on or engine running. If the ECM detects an improper voltage supply signal, this DTC will set. **Possible Causes:** • Battery supply circuit is open • Ground circuit is open • Intermittent condition • Glow Plug Control Module has failed

DTC	Trouble Code Title, Conditions & Possible Causes
DTC: P1132 **1T ECM** **Years:** 2008, 2009 **Models:** Liberty **Engines:** 2.8L Diesel **Transmissions:** All	**Glow Plug Module Internal Fault** Ignition on or engine running. If the ECM detects an improper voltage supply signal, this DTC will set. **Possible Causes:** • Battery supply circuit is open • Ground circuit is open • Intermittent condition • Glow Plug Control Module has failed
DTC: P1135 **1T ECM** **Years:** 2008, 2009 **Models:** Liberty **Engines:** 2.8L Diesel **Transmissions:** All	**Glow Plug Module Control Circuit Fault** Ignition on or engine running. If the ECM detects a no-signal or improper current signal on the control circuit, this DTC will set. **Possible Causes:** • ECM has failed • Glow Plug Module has failed • Glow Plug Module control circuit is open or is shorted to voltage or to ground • Intermittent condition
DTC: P1135 **1T CCM** **Years:** 2008, 2009 **Models:** PT Cruiser **Engines:** All **Transmissions:** All	**O2 (B1 S1) Heater Element Resistance Out-Of-Range** Monitored with engine running; O2 (B1 S1) Sensor has reached 98% of duty cycle at least once since cranking; vehicle speed is between 20-93 MPH; catalyst temperature is between 1112-1706°F (600-930°C); battery voltage is 9-16v; and no O2 Sensor electrical DTCs are present. If the PCM determines the O2 Sensor resistance is less than 2 ohms for more than 30 seconds, this DTC will set. **Possible Causes:** • O2 heater element has failed • O2 Sensor heater ground circuit is open • ASD relay output circuit is open • Intermittent condition • PCM has failed
DTC: P1136 **1T CCM** **Years:** 2008, 2009 **Models:** PT Cruiser **Engines:** All **Transmissions:** All	**O2 (B1 S2) Heater Element Resistance Out-Of-Range** Monitored with engine running; O2 Sensor has reached 98% of duty cycle at least once since cranking; vehicle speed is between 20-93 MPH; catalyst temperature is between 1112-1706°F (600-930°C); battery voltage is 9-16v; and no O2 Sensor electrical DTCs are present. If the PCM determines the B1 S2 O2 Sensor resistance is less than 2 ohms for more than 30 seconds, this DTC will set. **Possible Causes:** • O2 heater element has failed • O2 Sensor heater ground circuit is open • ASD relay output circuit is open • Intermittent condition • PCM has failed
DTC: P1140 **1T ECM** **Years:** 2008, 2009 **Models:** Liberty **Engines:** 2.8L Diesel **Transmissions:** All	**Vacuum Reservoir Solenoid Open Or Short-To-Ground** Ignition on; Vacuum Reservoir Solenoid commanded OFF. If the ECM does not detect a voltage signal or a change in voltage on the control circuit, this DTC will set. **Possible Causes:** • Intermittent condition • ASD Relay output circuit is open • Vacuum Reservoir Solenoid control circuit is open or is shorted to ground • Vacuum Reservoir Solenoid has failed • ECM has failed
DTC: P1142 **1T ECM** **Years:** 2008, 2009 **Models:** Liberty **Engines:** 2.8L Diesel **Transmissions:** All	**Fuel Pressure Solenoid Open Or Short-To-Ground Circuit** Ignition on; ECM Fuel Pressure Solenoid commanded OFF. If the ECM does not detect a voltage signal or detects excessive current in voltage on the control circuit, this DTC will set. **Possible Causes:** • FP Solenoid circuit(s) open, shorted to voltage, shorted to ground, or shorted together • Intermittent condition • FP Solenoid has failed • ECM has failed

DTC	Trouble Code Title, Conditions & Possible Causes
DTC: P1155 **1T CCM** **Years:** 2008, 2009 **Models:** Liberty **Engines:** 2.8L Diesel **Transmissions:** All	**Fuel Rail Pressure Too High Malfunction** Engine running; ECM determines that the fuel rail pressure exceeds 1700 bar. **Possible Causes:** • Air in fuel system • Fuel injector problems • Fuel Pressure Solenoid has failed • Fuel Pump has malfunctioned or failed • Fuel system has contamination • Fuel system has a leak • Intermittent condition
DTC: P1159 **1T ECM** **Years:** 2008, 2009 **Models:** Liberty **Engines:** 2.8L Diesel **Transmissions:** All	**Improper Start Attempt** Engine running; vehicle drive at less than 2 MPH. If the ECM detects engine speed above 100 RPM without activating the starter relay control, this DTC will set. Verify the active DTCs. **Possible Causes:** • ECM has failed
DTC: P1160 **1T ECM** **Years:** 2008, 2009 **Models:** Liberty **Engines:** 2.8L Diesel **Transmissions:** All	**Ignition Voltage Improper Signal** Engine running. If the ECM detects an improper ignition voltage at any time, this DTC will set. **Possible Causes:** • ECM power and/or ground connection problems • ECM has failed • Intermittent condition
DTC: P1167 **1T ECM** **Years:** 2008, 2009 **Models:** Liberty **Engines:** 2.8L Diesel **Transmissions:** All	**Capacitor Voltage Problem** Engine cranking or running. If the ECM detects a capacitor voltage problem during injector actuation, this DTC will set. Verify any other injector-related DTCs. **Possible Causes:** • ECM has failed • Intermittent condition
DTC: P1168 **1T ECM** **Years:** 2008, 2009 **Models:** Liberty **Engines:** 2.8L Diesel **Transmissions:** All	**ECM Communication Error** Ignition on. ECM detects an internal failure. **Possible Causes:** • ECM has failed • Intermittent condition
DTC: P1169 **1T ECM** **Years:** 2008, 2009 **Models:** Liberty **Engines:** 2.8L Diesel **Transmissions:** All	**ECM A/D Converter Error** Ignition on. ECM detects an internal failure. **Possible Causes:** • ECM has failed • Intermittent condition
DTC: P1188 **2T CCM** **Years:** 2008, 2009 **Models:** PT Cruiser Turbo **Engines:** All **Transmissions:** All	**Throttle Inlet Pressure Sensor Signal Range/Performance** Engine started, engine running in Turbo Boost or Non-Boost mode, and the PCM detected a significant difference between the BARO Sensor and TIP Sensor signals (i.e., the TIP Sensor cannot read the signal correctly). **Possible Causes:** • ASD output circuit to the TIP solenoid is open • Throttle inlet pressure Sensor solenoid is damaged or has failed • TIP solenoid control circuit is open, shorted to ground or power • PCM has failed
DTC: P1189 **2T CCM** **Years:** 2008, 2009 **Models:** PT Cruiser Turbo **Engines:** All **Transmissions:** All	**Throttle Inlet Pressure Sensor Circuit Low Input** Engine started, TP Sensor less than 1.2v, system voltage over 10.5V, and the PCM detected the Throttle Inlet Pressure (TIP) Sensor was less than 0.0782v for a period of 1-7 seconds. **Possible Causes:** • TIP Sensor VREF circuit is open • TIP Sensor signal circuit is open • TIP Sensor signal circuit is shorted to chassis or Sensor ground • TIP Sensor is damaged or it has failed • PCM has failed

DTC	Trouble Code Title, Conditions & Possible Causes
DTC: P1190 **2T CCM** **Years:** 2008, 2009 **Models:** PT Cruiser Turbo **Engines:** All **Transmissions:** All	**Throttle Inlet Pressure Sensor Circuit High Input** Engine started, TP Sensor less than 1.2v, system voltage over 10.5V, and the PCM detected the Throttle Inlet Pressure (TIP) Sensor was more than 4.92v for a period of 1-7 seconds. **Possible Causes:** • TIP Sensor VREF circuit is open • TIP Sensor signal circuit is open • TIP Sensor signal circuit is shorted to chassis or Sensor ground • TIP Sensor is damaged or it has failed • PCM has failed
DTC: P1196 **1T CCM** **Years:** 2008, 2009 **Models:** Dakota, Grand Cherokee, Journey, Liberty, Nitro, Pacifica, PT Cruiser, Ram Truck, Wrangler **Engines:** All **Transmissions:** All	**O2 (B2 S1) Circuit Insufficient Activity** Engine started, vehicle driven with the throttle open at a speed over 18-55 MPH at light engine load for over 5 minutes, ECT Sensor more than 170°F, and the PCM detected the O2 signal switched from 0.39v to 0.60v too few times in the Oxygen Sensor Monitor test. **Possible Causes:** • Base engine mechanical fault affecting more than one cylinder • Exhaust leak present in exhaust manifold or exhaust pipes • O2 element fuel contamination or has deteriorated • O2 signal circuit or ground circuit has high resistance
DTC: P1250 **1T ECM** **Years:** 2008, 2009 **Models:** Liberty **Engines:** 2.8L Diesel **Transmissions:** All	**Vacuum Reservoir Solenoid Open Circuit** Ignition on; solenoid commanded ON. If the ECM does not detect a voltage signal on the Vacuum Reservoir Solenoid control circuit, this DTC will set. **Possible Causes:** • Intermittent condition • ASD Relay output circuit is open • VR Solenoid control circuit is open or is shorted to ground • VR Solenoid or ECM has failed
DTC: P1251 **1T ECM** **Years:** 2008, 2009 **Models:** Liberty **Engines:** 2.8L Diesel **Transmissions:** All	**Vacuum Reservoir Solenoid Short-To-Ground Circuit** Ignition on; solenoid commanded ON. If the ECM does not detect a voltage signal on the Vacuum Reservoir Solenoid control circuit, this DTC will set. **Possible Causes:** • Intermittent condition • ASD Relay output circuit is open • VR Solenoid control circuit is open or shorted to ground • VR Solenoid or ECM has failed
DTC: P1252 **1T ECM** **Years:** 2008, 2009 **Models:** Liberty **Engines:** 2.8L Diesel **Transmissions:** All	**Vacuum Reservoir Solenoid Short Circuit** Ignition on; solenoid commanded ON. If the ECM detects excessive voltage signal on the Vacuum Reservoir Solenoid control circuit, this DTC will set. **Possible Causes:** • Intermittent condition • ASD Relay output circuit is open • VR Solenoid control circuit is open or shorted to ground • VR Solenoid or ECM has failed
DTC: P1281 **2T ECT** **Years:** 2008, 2009 **Models:** Dakota, Grand Cherokee, Journey, Liberty, Nitro, Pacifica, PT Cruiser, Ram Truck, Wrangler **Engines:** All **Transmissions:** All	**Engine Is Cold Too Long** Engine started, engine runtime more than 20 minutes, and the PCM detected the engine temperature did not exceed 176°F in the period. **Possible Causes:** • Check the operation of the thermostat (it may be stuck open) • ECT Sensor signal circuit has high resistance • ECT Sensor is damaged or it has failed • Inspect for low coolant level or an incorrect coolant mixture
DTC: P1282 **1T CCM** **Years:** 2008, 2009 **Models:** Dakota, Grand Cherokee, Journey, Liberty, Nitro, Pacifica, PT Cruiser, Ram Truck, Wrangler **Engines:** All **Transmissions:** All	**Fuel Pump Relay Control Circuit Malfunction** Key on or engine started, system voltage over 10.5V, and the PCM detected an unexpected voltage condition on the Fuel Pump Relay control circuit during the CCM test period. **Possible Causes:** • Fuel pump relay control circuit is open or shorted to ground • Fuel pump relay power circuit is open (test power from Ignition) • Fuel pump relay is damaged or has failed • PCM has failed

DTC	Trouble Code Title, Conditions & Possible Causes
DTC: P1294 **1T CCM** **Years:** 2008, 2009 **Models:** Dakota, Grand Cherokee, Journey, Liberty, Nitro, Pacifica, PT Cruiser, Ram Truck, Wrangler **Engines:** All **Transmissions:** All	**Target Idle Speed Not Reached** DTC P0106, P0107, P0108, P0121, P0122 and P0123 not set, engine started, running at idle in Drive or Neutral, and the PCM detected the Actual idle speed was more than 200 RPM over or more than 100 RPM less than the Target speed for over 14 seconds. **Possible Causes:** • Engine vacuum leak in a hose, brake booster or in the engine • IAC motor control circuits open or grounded in the wire harness • Throttle body dirty or restricted (trying cleaning it and retesting) • Throttle linkage or throttle plate not in the correct position • PCM has failed
DTC: P1296 **1T CCM** **Years:** 2008, 2009 **Models:** Dakota, Grand Cherokee, Journey, Liberty, Nitro, Pacifica, PT Cruiser, Ram Truck, Wrangler **Engines:** All **Transmissions:** All	**5-Volt VREF Supply Not Present** Key on, altitude indicating zero feet above seal level, then the PCM detected the MAP Sensor was near 101 kPa; or with altitude at 1200 feet above sea level, the MAP Sensor was near 88 kPa. **Possible Causes:** • MAP Sensor VREF circuit open between the Sensor and PCM • MAP Sensor ground circuit open between the Sensor and PCM • MAP Sensor is damaged or has failed • PCM has failed
DTC: P1297 **1T CCM** **Years:** 2008, 2009 **Models:** Dakota, Grand Cherokee, Journey, Liberty, Nitro, Pacifica, PT Cruiser, Ram Truck, Wrangler **Engines:** All **Transmissions:** All	**No Change In MAP Signal From Start To Run Transition** Engine started, and with the engine speed within 64 RPM of the Target idle speed, the PCM detected too small a difference between the BARO and MAP Sensor signals for 8.80 seconds. **Possible Causes:** • Engine vacuum port to MAP Sensor clogged, dirty or restricted • MAP Sensor signal is skewed or the Sensor is out-of-calibration • MAP Sensor VREF circuit open or grounded (intermittent fault) • PCM has failed
DTC: P1388 **1T CCM** **Years:** 2008, 2009 **Models:** Dakota, Grand Cherokee, Journey, Liberty, Nitro, Pacifica, PT Cruiser, Ram Truck, Wrangler **Engines:** All **Transmissions:** All	**Auto Shutdown Relay Control Circuit Malfunction** Key on or engine cranking; and the PCM detected an unexpected voltage condition on the ASD Relay Control circuit. The ASD Relay coil resistance is 95-105ohms at 68°F. **Possible Causes:** • ASD relay control circuit is open between the relay and PCM • ASD relay control circuit is shorted to ground • ASD relay power circuit is open (test power from Fused B+) • ASD relay is damaged or has failed • PCM has failed
DTC: P1389 **1T CCM** **Years:** 2008, 2009 **Models:** Dakota, Grand Cherokee, Journey, Liberty, Nitro, Pacifica, PT Cruiser, Ram Truck, Wrangler **Engines:** All **Transmissions:** All	**No Auto Shutdown Relay Output Voltage To PCM** Engine cranking; and the PCM did not detect any voltage on the ASD Relay Output circuit to the PCM during the CCM test. **Possible Causes:** • ASD relay connector is damaged, loose or shorted • ASD relay output circuit is open between the relay and PCM • ASD relay power circuit is open (test power from Fused B+) • ASD relay is damaged or has failed • PCM has failed
DTC: P1391 **1T CCM** **Years:** 2008, 2009 **Models:** Dakota, Grand Cherokee, Journey, Liberty, Nitro, Pacifica, PT Cruiser, Ram Truck, Wrangler **Engines:** All **Transmissions:** All	**CKP Or CMP Sensor Signal Intermittent** Engine started, engine running, and after every 69-degree CKP Sensor leading edge and trailing signal edge is determined, the PCM updates this data and compares it to the true CMP Sensor port level. If the PCM detects a disagreement between these two values 20 times in succession, this trouble code is set. **Possible Causes:** • Camshaft Sensor is not installed properly • Engine valve timing is not within specifications • Perform a CKP and CMP Sensor relearn with the scan tool • Tone wheel or pulse ring is damaged

DTC	Trouble Code Title, Conditions & Possible Causes
DTC: P1398 **1T CCM** **Years:** 2008, 2009 **Models:** Dakota, Grand Cherokee, Journey, Liberty, Nitro, Pacifica, PT Cruiser, Ram Truck, Wrangler **Engines:** All **Transmissions:** All	**Misfire Adaptive Numerator At Limit** Engine started; ECT Sensor under 75°F; engine runtime over 50 sec.; A/C "OFF"; vehicle speed over 36 MPH in 1st gear, or over 65 MPH in high gear, followed by a closed throttle decel period. This code sets if the PCM detects one of the CKP Sensor target windows varies more than 2.86% from the reference window. Background - PCM needs to learn any variation in engine machining to detect when a misfire is present. CKP Sensor has 2 40 windows that are 180 apart. The window for Cylinders 1 and 4 is the reference window. It is checked against the window for Cylinders 2 and 3. The PCM checks for any variation to make engine speed adjustments. **Possible Causes:** • Base engine problem (i.e., low cylinder compression) • CKP Sensor crankshaft target variation too large • CKP Sensor improperly installed or the CKP Sensor has failed • CKP Sensor signal circuit open or shorted (intermittent fault) • Tone wheel or pulse ring is damaged
DTC: P1404 **2T CCM** **Years:** 2008, 2009 **Models:** Dakota, Grand Cherokee, Journey, Liberty, Nitro, Pacifica, PT Cruiser, Ram Truck, Wrangler **Engines:** All **Transmissions:** All	**EGR Close Position Performance** The EGR flow or valve movement is not what is expected. A rationality error has been detected for the EGR Open Position Performance. Two trip fault. **Possible Causes:** • 5 volt supply circuit high resistance • EGR signal circuit high resistance • Sensor ground circuit high resistance • Ground circuit high resistance • EGR control circuit high resistance • EGR signal circuit shorted to ground • Exhaust gas recirculation valve
DTC: P1486 **2T EVAP** **Years:** 2008, 2009 **Models:** Dakota, Grand Cherokee, Journey, Liberty, Nitro, Pacifica, PT Cruiser, Ram Truck, Wrangler **Engines:** All **Transmissions:** All	**EVAP Leak Detection Monitor Pinched Hose Detected** BTS from 40-96°F and ECT Sensor within 20°F of the BTS signal at startup (cold engine), engine started, and after the EVAP Leak Detection test was enabled, the PCM detected the LDP switch did not reach 3 closures (i.e., a "no flow" condition was present). **Possible Causes:** • EVAP vapor hose blocked between the fuel tank and the LDP (i.e., in the OLFV, rollover or vapor hose) • EVAP canister is clogged or full of dirt or moisture • EVAP ventilation solenoid is damaged or has failed • Purge line is loose, damaged or incorrectly routed • PCM has failed
DTC: P1492 **1T CCM** **Years:** 2008, 2009 **Models:** Dakota, Grand Cherokee, Journey, Liberty, Nitro, Pacifica, PT Cruiser, Ram Truck, Wrangler **Engines:** All **Transmissions:** All	**Battery Temperature Sensor Circuit High Input** Key on or engine running; and the PCM detected the BTS signal indicated more than 4.90v for 3 seconds during the CCM test. **Possible Causes:** • BTS signal circuit is open between the Sensor and the PCM • BTS ground circuit is open between the Sensor and the PCM • BTS (Sensor) is damaged or the PCM has failed
DTC: P1493 **1T CCM** **Years:** 2008, 2009 **Models:** Dakota, Grand Cherokee, Journey, Liberty, Nitro, Pacifica, PT Cruiser, Ram Truck, Wrangler **Engines:** All **Transmissions:** All	**Battery Temperature Sensor Circuit Low Input** Key on or engine running; and the PCM detected the BTS signal indicated less than 0.30v for 3 seconds during the CCM test. **Possible Causes:** • BTS circuit is shorted to ground between Sensor and the PCM • BTS (Sensor) is damaged or has failed • PCM has failed
DTC: P1494 **1T CCM** **Years:** 2008, 2009 **Models:** Dakota, Grand Cherokee, Journey, Liberty, Nitro, Pacifica, PT Cruiser, Ram Truck, Wrangler **Engines:** All **Transmissions:** All	**EVAP Leak Detection Pump Switch Or Mechanical Fault** BTS from 40-96°F and ECT Sensor within 10°F of the BTS signal at startup (cold engine), engine started, and the PCM detected the LDP switch was not in its expected state at key "on" or engine running. **Possible Causes:** • LDP switch signal circuit is open or shorted to ground • LDP switch power circuit is open (test power to Fused Ignition) • LDP vacuum hose is clogged, loose or restricted • LDP assembly is damaged or has failed (the switch has failed)

DTC	Trouble Code Title, Conditions & Possible Causes
DTC: P1495 **1T CCM** **Years:** 2008, 2009 **Models:** Dakota, Grand Cherokee, Journey, Liberty, Nitro, Pacifica, PT Cruiser, Ram Truck, Wrangler **Engines:** All **Transmissions:** All	**Leak Detection Pump Solenoid Circuit Malfunction** Engine started, ECT Sensor from 40-90°F and within 10°F of the Battery Temperature Sensor signal, engine running, and the PCM detected the Actual state of the Leak Detection Pump solenoid did not match the Intended state of the solenoid during the test period. **Possible Causes:** • LDP power supply circuit from the ignition switch is open • LDP solenoid control circuit is open or shorted to ground • LDP assembly is damaged or it has failed • PCM has failed
DTC: P1499 **1T CCM** **Years:** 2008, 2009 **Models:** Grand Cherokee, Wrangler **Engines:** All **Transmissions:** All	**Radiator (Hydraulic) Fan Solenoid Circuit Failure** Key on or engine running; and the PCM detected an unexpected voltage condition on the Radiator Fan Solenoid Control circuit. **Possible Causes:** • Radiator fan solenoid control circuit is open • Radiator fan solenoid ground circuit is open • Radiator fan solenoid power circuit is open • Radiator fan solenoid is damaged or has failed • PCM has failed
DTC: P1501 **1T CCM** **Years:** 2008, 2009 **Models:** Dakota, Grand Cherokee, Journey, Liberty, Nitro, Pacifica, PT Cruiser, Ram Truck, Wrangler **Engines:** All **Transmissions:** All	**Vehicle Speed Sensor No. 1/2 Drive Wheel Correlation** Engine is running and vehicle is moving. Speed control is learned and the speed control is trying to be activated. If the PCM recognizes the rear wheel speed is greater than the front wheel speed, this DTC will set. **Possible Causes:** • Other active Bus or Communication DTCs • Incorrect tire circumference • PCM has failed
DTC: P1502 **1T CCM** **Years:** 2008, 2009 **Models:** Dakota, Grand Cherokee, Journey, Liberty, Nitro, Pacifica, PT Cruiser, Ram Truck, Wrangler **Engines:** All **Transmissions:** All	**Vehicle Speed Sensor No. 1/2 Non-Drive Wheel Correlation** Engine is running and vehicle is moving; brake pedal must not be applied. If the PCM recognizes the rear wheel speed is greater than the front wheel speed, this DTC will set. **Possible Causes:** • Other active Bus or Communication DTCs • Incorrect tire circumference • PCM has failed
DTC: P1572 **1T CCM** **Years:** 2008, 2009 **Models:** Dakota, Grand Cherokee, Journey, Liberty, Nitro, Pacifica, PT Cruiser, Ram Truck, Wrangler **Engines:** All **Transmissions:** All	**Brake Switch Stuck ON** Ignition is on. The PCM recognizes that brake switch 1 is mechanically stuck in the Low/On position. **Possible Causes:** • Brake switch 1 signal is shorted to ground • Brake switch 2 signal is open • Stop lamp switch has failed • PCM has failed
DTC: P1573 **1T CCM** **Years:** 2008, 2009 **Models:** Dakota, Grand Cherokee, Journey, Liberty, Nitro, Pacifica, PT Cruiser, Ram Truck, Wrangler **Engines:** All **Transmissions:** All	**Brake Switch Stuck ON** Ignition is on. The PCM recognizes that brake switch 1 is mechanically stuck in the High/Off position. **Possible Causes:** • Brake switch 1 signal is shorted to ground or to voltage • Brake switch 2 signal is open or is shorted to ground • Ground circuit is open • Fused ignition switch output is open • Stop lamp switch has failed • PCM has failed
DTC: P1593 **1T CCM** **Years:** 2008, 2009 **Models:** Dakota, Grand Cherokee, Journey, Liberty, Nitro, Pacifica, PT Cruiser, Ram Truck, Wrangler **Engines:** All **Transmissions:** All	**Speed Control Switch Stuck Operation** Ignition on. Either S/C switch is mechanically stuck in On/Off, Resume/Accel or Set position for too long. **Possible Causes:** • Intermittent speed control switch 1/2 stuck DTC • S/C switches or Steering Column Control Module malfunctioning • S/C signal circuit open or shorted ground or to battery voltage • S/C switch signal circuit shorted to switch return circuit • S/C Sensor ground open • PCM has failed

DTC	Trouble Code Title, Conditions & Possible Causes
DTC: P1594 **1T CCM** **Years:** 2008, 2009 **Models:** Grand Cherokee, Wrangler **Engines:** All **Transmissions:** All	**Charging System Voltage Too High** Engine started, engine running, and the PCM detected the Charging System voltage was too high even after it tried to lower the generator output by controlling the Field control circuit (Generator Lamp is on). **Possible Causes:** • Battery temperature Sensor is damaged or has failed (skewed) • Generator field driver circuit is shorted to ground • Generator has an internal short circuit condition • PCM has failed
DTC: P1594 **1T CCM** **Years:** 2008, 2009 **Models:** PT Cruiser **Engines:** All **Transmissions:** All	**Charging System Voltage Too High** Engine is running at more than 380 RPM. If the battery voltage is 1v greater than the desired voltage, this DTC will set. **Possible Causes:** • Intermittent condition • Generator field driver circuit is shorted to ground • Generator field is damaged or has failed • PCM has failed
DTC: P1598 **1T CCM** **Years:** 2008, 2009 **Models:** Dakota, Grand Cherokee, Journey, Liberty, Nitro, Pacifica, PT Cruiser, Ram Truck, Wrangler **Engines:** All **Transmissions:** All	**A/C Pressure Sensor Circuit High Input** Engine started, engine running, A/C Relay is "on", and the PCM detected the A/C Pressure Sensor indicated more than 4.90v. **Possible Causes:** • A/C pressure Sensor circuit is open or shorted to VREF (5V) • A/C pressure Sensor ground circuit is open • A/C pressure Sensor is damaged or has failed • PCM has failed
DTC: P1599 **1T CCM** **Years:** 2008, 2009 **Models:** Dakota, Grand Cherokee, Journey, Liberty, Nitro, Pacifica, PT Cruiser, Ram Truck, Wrangler **Engines:** All **Transmissions:** All	**A/C Pressure Sensor Circuit Low Input** Engine started, engine running, A/C Relay is "on", and the PCM detected the A/C Pressure Sensor indicated less than 0.70v. **Possible Causes:** • A/C pressure Sensor circuit is shorted to ground • A/C pressure Sensor power circuit is open • A/C pressure Sensor is damaged or has failed • PCM has failed
DTC: P1602 **1T PCM** **Years:** 2008, 2009 **Models:** Dakota, Grand Cherokee, Journey, Liberty, Nitro, Pacifica, PT Cruiser, Ram Truck, Wrangler **Engines:** All **Transmissions:** All	**PCM Not Programmed** Key on. The PCM detected that it had not been programmed. **Possible Causes:** • Program the PCM and then retest for this same trouble code • PCM has failed
DTC: P1603 **1T PCM** **Years:** 2008, 2009 **Models:** Dakota, Grand Cherokee, Journey, Liberty, Nitro, Pacifica, PT Cruiser, Ram Truck, Wrangler **Engines:** All **Transmissions:** All	**Powertrain Control Module Internal Dual-Port Ram Communication** Key on; and the PCM detected an error message that indicated that it had not been programmed or that it was programmed properly. **Possible Causes:** • Fused ignition switch output is missing (off-start-run circuit) • PCM is damaged or it has an internal failure
DTC: P1604 **1T PCM** **Years:** 2008, 2009 **Models:** Dakota, Grand Cherokee, Journey, Liberty, Nitro, Pacifica, PT Cruiser, Ram Truck, Wrangler **Engines:** All **Transmissions:** All	**PCM Internal Dual-Port Ram Read/Write Integrity Failure** Key on; and the PCM detected an error message that indicated it had not been programmed, or it was not programmed properly. **Possible Causes:** • Fused ignition switch output is missing (off-start-run circuit) • PCM is damaged or it has an internal failure

DTC	Trouble Code Title, Conditions & Possible Causes

DTC: P1607
1T PCM
Years: 2008, 2009
Models: Dakota, Grand Cherokee, Journey, Liberty, Nitro, Pacifica, PT Cruiser, Ram Truck, Wrangler
Engines: All
Transmissions: All
	Powertrain Control Module Internal Shutdown Timer Rationality
	Cold engine startup, and after the PCM compared the coolant temperature to the shutdown time, it detected a rationality fault.
	Possible Causes:
	  • Fused ignition switch output is missing (off-start-run circuit)
	  • PCM is damaged or it has an internal failure

DTC: P1616
1T PCM
Years: 2008, 2009
Models: PT Cruiser
Engines: All
Transmissions: All
	Primary 5V Sensor Reference Voltage Low
	Key on. If the PCM detects a voltage of less than 4.75V on the primary 5V supply circuit for at least 100ms, this DTC will set.
	Possible Causes:
	  • Intermittent condition
	  • Primary 5V supply circuit shorted to ground
	  • PCM has failed

DTC: P1617
1T PCM
Years: 2008, 2009
Models: PT Cruiser
Engines: All
Transmissions: All
	Primary 5V Sensor Reference Voltage High
	Key on. If the PCM detects a voltage of more than 5.25V on the primary 5V supply circuit for at least 100ms, this DTC will set.
	Possible Causes:
	  • Intermittent condition
	  • Primary 5V supply circuit is open or is shorted to voltage
	  • PCM has failed

DTC: P1618
1T PCM
Years: 2008, 2009
Models: PT Cruiser
Engines: All
Transmissions: All
	Primary 5V Sensor Reference Voltage Unstable
	Key on. If the PCM detects a voltage variance of more than 0.25V on the primary 5V supply circuit for more than 100ms, this DTC will set.
	Possible Causes:
	  • Primary 5V supply circuit open or shorted to ground or to battery voltage
	  • 5V Sensor has failed
	  • PCM has failed

DTC: P1618
1T PCM
Years: 2008, 2009
Models: Dakota, Grand Cherokee, Journey, Liberty, Nitro, Pacifica, PT Cruiser, Ram Truck, Wrangler
Engines: All
Transmissions: All
	Primary 5V Sensor Reference Voltage Malfunction
	Key on. The PCM recognizes the primary 5V supply circuit voltage is varying too much too quickly. ETC light is flashing.
	Possible Causes:
	  • Primary 5V supply circuit open or shorted to ground or to battery voltage
	  • 5V Sensor has failed
	  • PCM has failed

DTC: P1626
1T PCM
Years: 2008, 2009
Models: PT Cruiser
Engines: All
Transmissions: All
	Secondary 5V Sensor Reference Voltage Low
	Key on. If the PCM detects a voltage of less than 4.75V on the secondary 5V supply circuit for more than 100ms, this DTC will set.
	Possible Causes:
	  • Intermittent condition
	  • 5V supply circuit shorted to ground
	  • 5V Sensor has failed
	  • PCM has failed

DTC: P1627
1T PCM
Years: 2008, 2009
Models: PT Cruiser
Engines: All
Transmissions: All
	Secondary 5V Sensor Reference Voltage High
	Key on. If the PCM detects a voltage of more than 5.25V on the secondary 5V supply circuit for more than 100ms, this DTC will set.
	Possible Causes:
	  • Intermittent condition
	  • 5V supply circuit is open or is shorted to voltage
	  • 5V Sensor has failed
	  • PCM has failed

DTC: P1628
1T PCM
Years: 2008, 2009
Models: PT Cruiser
Engines: All
Transmissions: All
	Secondary 5V Sensor Reference Voltage Unstable
	Key on. If the PCM detects a voltage variance of more than 0.25V on the secondary 5V supply circuit for more than 100ms, this DTC will set.
	Possible Causes:
	  • Intermittent condition
	  • ETC assembly has failed
	  • 5V supply circuit has high resistance
	  • PCM has failed

DTC	Trouble Code Title, Conditions & Possible Causes
DTC: P1628 **1T PCM** **Years:** 2008, 2009 **Models:** Dakota, Grand Cherokee, Journey, Liberty, Nitro, Pacifica, Ram Truck, Wrangler **Engines:** All **Transmissions:** All	**Auxiliary 5V Sensor Reference Voltage Malfunction** Key on. The PCM recognizes the auxiliary 5V supply circuit voltage is varying too much too quickly. ETC light is flashing. **Possible Causes:** • Auxiliary 5V supply circuit open or shorted to ground or to battery voltage • 5V Sensor has failed • PCM has failed
DTC: P1652 **1T CCM** **Years:** 2008, 2009 **Models:** Dakota, Grand Cherokee, Journey, Liberty, Nitro, Pacifica, PT Cruiser, Ram Truck, Wrangler **Engines:** All **Transmissions:** All	**Serial Communication Link Malfunction** Engine started; and after the TCM did not detect any signals on the Serial Communication Line for more than 20 seconds. **Note: Due to the integration of the PCM and TCM, Bus communication between the modules is internal.** **Possible Causes:** • TCM cannot communicate with the Instrument Cluster (MIC) • TCM cannot communicate with the Powertrain Control Module • PCM/TCM is damaged or it has an internal failure
DTC: P1653 **1T PCM** **Years:** 2008, 2009 **Models:** PT Cruiser **Engines:** All **Transmissions:** All	**PCI Bus Shorted To Ground** Key on. If the PCM detects a short to ground on the PCI Bus for more than 5 seconds, this DTC will set. **Possible Causes:** • Intermittent condition • Internal controller short to ground • PCI Bus short to ground
DTC: P1654 **1T PCM** **Years:** 2008, 2009 **Models:** PT Cruiser **Engines:** All **Transmissions:** All	**PCI Bus Shorted To Voltage** Key on. If the PCM detects a short to voltage on the PCI Bus for more than 5 seconds, this DTC will set. **Possible Causes:** • Intermittent condition • Internal controller short to battery voltage • PCI Bus short to voltage
DTC: P1654 **1T PCM** **Years:** 2008, 2009 **Models:** PT Cruiser **Engines:** All **Transmissions:** All	**PCI Bus Not Available** Key on. If the PCM detects the PCI Bus is not available for more than 5 seconds, this DTC will set. **Possible Causes:** • Intermittent condition • PCI Bus circuit is open • PCM has failed
DTC: P1682 **1T CCM** **Years:** 2008, 2009 **Models:** Dakota, Grand Cherokee, Journey, Liberty, Nitro, Pacifica, PT Cruiser, Ram Truck, Wrangler **Engines:** All **Transmissions:** All	**Charging System Voltage Too Low** Engine started; engine speed over 1152 RPM, and the PCM detected the Battery Sense circuit was 1.0v less than the Charging System circuit for 25 seconds during the CCM test (Generator Lamp is "on"). **Possible Causes:** • Battery positive or Fused Ignition circuit has high resistance • Generator drive belt out-of-adjustment or worn out • Generator field circuit has a high resistance condition • PCM has failed
DTC: P1684 **1T PCM** **Years:** 2008, 2009 **Models:** Dakota, Grand Cherokee, Journey, Liberty, Nitro, Pacifica, PT Cruiser, Ram Truck, Wrangler **Engines:** All **Transmissions:** All	**Battery Has Been Disconnected** Key on, and the TCM detected that it had been disconnected from the Battery Direct (B+) circuit or its Power Ground circuit. This DTC will also set during the scan tool Quick Battery Disconnect procedure. **Note: Due to the integration of the PCM and TCM, the transmission part of the PCM has its own specific power and ground circuits.** **Possible Causes:** • Quick Learn procedure was performed with scan tool • TCM battery direct (B+) circuit is open or disconnected • TCM power ground circuit is open • PCM/TCM was disconnected or it has been replaced
DTC: P1686 **1T PCM** **Years:** 2008, 2009 **Models:** PT Cruiser **Engines:** All **Transmissions:** All	**No SKIM Bus Message Received** Key on. If the PCM does not receive a Bus message from the SKIM when expected, this DTC will set. **Possible Causes:** • Intermittent condition • SKIM/PCM has failed • Loss of SKIM communication link • PCI Bus circuit open from PCM to SKIM

DTC	Trouble Code Title, Conditions & Possible Causes
DTC: P1687 **1T PCM** **Years:** 2008, 2009 **Models:** Dakota, Grand Cherokee, Journey, Liberty, Nitro, Pacifica, PT Cruiser, Ram Truck, Wrangler **Engines:** All **Transmissions:** All	**No Cluster Bus Messages** Key on or engine running; and the PCM determined that it did not receive any Security Key Bus Messages over the Data Bus line for 20 seconds. This malfunction may be an intermittent problem. **Possible Causes:** • Data Bus circuit from SKIM to PCM is damaged or it is open • PCM unable to communicate with the Body Control Module • PCM has failed, or the SKIM is damaged or has failed
DTC: P1687 **1T PCM** **Years:** 2008, 2009 **Models:** Dakota, Grand Cherokee, Journey, Liberty, Nitro, Pacifica, PT Cruiser, Ram Truck, Wrangler **Engines:** All **Transmissions:** All	**No Communication with MIC** Communications are monitored continuously with engine running. The DTC sets in about 25 seconds if no Bus messages are received from the MIC. **Possible Causes:** • Other Bus problems exist • Intermittent wiring or connector problems exist • PCM has failed
DTC: P1694 **1T PCM** **Years:** 2008, 2009 **Models:** Dakota, Grand Cherokee, Journey, Liberty, Nitro, Pacifica, PT Cruiser, Ram Truck, Wrangler **Engines:** All **Transmissions:** All	**No PCM Bus Messages** Ignition on or engine started; system voltage over 10.5V and the PCM determined that it did not receive any Bus messages for 10 seconds. **Note: Due to the integration of the PCM and TCM, Bus communication between the modules is internal.** **Possible Causes:** • Data Bus circuit connector is damaged, open or it is shorted • Data Bus circuit to the PCM is damaged or it is open • PCM unable to communicate with the body control module • Intermittent wiring or connector problems exist • PCM has failed
DTC: P1695 **1T PCM** **Years:** 2008, 2009 **Models:** Dakota, Grand Cherokee, Journey, Liberty, Nitro, Pacifica, PT Cruiser, Ram Truck, Wrangler **Engines:** All **Transmissions:** All	**No BCM Bus Messages** Engine started; system voltage over 10.5V and the TCM determined that it did not receive any BCM messages for 20 seconds. **Possible Causes:** • Data Bus circuit from BCM to the PCM is damaged or it is open • BCM is damaged or has failed • TCM unable to communicate with the TCM • TCM has failed
DTC: P1696 **1T PCM** **Years:** 2008, 2009 **Models:** Dakota, Grand Cherokee, Journey, Liberty, Nitro, Pacifica, PT Cruiser, Ram Truck, Wrangler **Engines:** All **Transmissions:** All	**PCM EEPROM Write Operation Denied/Invalid** Engine started or ignition on continuously. PCM detected an unsuccessful attempt to program/write to the internal EEPROM. Occurred at initialization or shutdown. **Possible Causes:** • DRB or scan tool displays a "write" failure occurred • DRB or scan tool displays "write" refused a second time • DRB or scan tool displays SRI mileage invalid (compare the SRI mileage reading to the reading on the odometer) • PCM has failed
DTC: P1697 **1T PCM** **Years:** 2008, 2009 **Models:** Dakota, Grand Cherokee, Journey, Liberty, Nitro, Pacifica, PT Cruiser, Ram Truck, Wrangler **Engines:** All **Transmissions:** All	**PCM Failure (EMR/SRI Mileage Not Stored)** Key on, and the PCM detected an unsuccessful attempt to "write" the Service Reminder Indicator (SRI) or Emission Mileage Request (EMR) mileage to an EEPROM located occurred during initialization. **Possible Causes:** • Clear the trouble codes and retest for the same trouble code. If DTC P1697 resets, replace the PCM and then reprogram it.
DTC: P1715 **1T CCM** **Years:** 2008, 2009 **Models:** Liberty **Engines:** 2.8L Diesel **Transmissions:** All	**Restricted Port in T3 Range** Monitored whenever the PRNDL code indicates Temp 3. This DTC will set whenever the conditions for a code P1776 are satisfied with the shifter in the Temp 3 zone. This causes a restricted port. Related transmission DTCs are present. **Possible Causes:** • Improper customer driving habits • Misadjusted shifter

DTC	Trouble Code Title, Conditions & Possible Causes
DTC: P1719 **1T CCM** **Years:** 2008, 2009 **Models:** **Engines:** All **Transmissions:** All	**A/T Skip Shift Solenoid Control Circuit Malfunction** Engine started; vehicle driven to a speed of 12-18 MPH in 1st Gear at light to moderate engine load at an engine speed over 608 RPM, and the PCM detected an unexpected "low" or high voltage condition on the Reverse Gear Lockout solenoid circuit. **Possible Causes:** • Skip Shift solenoid control circuit is open • Skip Shift solenoid control circuit shorted to ground • Skip Shift solenoid is damaged or has failed • PCM has failed
DTC: P1736 **1T CCM** **Years:** 2008, 2009 **Models:** Dakota, Grand Cherokee, Liberty, Nitro, Ram Truck **Engines:** 3.7L **Transmissions:** All	**A/T Gear Ratio Error In Second Prime** Transmission gear ratio is monitored whenever the transmission is in gear. If the ratio of the Input Speed (RPM) to the Output Speed did not match the current gear ratio, this DTC will set. This DTC can take up to 5 minutes of problem identification before lighting the MIL. Related DTCs are present. **Possible Causes:** • Internal transmission problems • Transmission intermittent gear ratio malfunction
DTC: P1775 **1T CCM** **Years:** 2008, 2009 **Models:** Dakota, Grand Cherokee, Journey, Liberty, Nitro, Pacifica, PT Cruiser, Ram Truck, Wrangler **Engines:** All **Transmissions:** All	**A/T Solenoid Switch Latched In TCC Position** Engine started; vehicle driven to over 15 MPH and the TCM detected the Transmission did not shift into 1st Gear (test must fail 3 times). **Possible Causes:** • Related DTC P0841 may be present. • Intermittent wiring or connector problems • Extremely low battery (system) voltage • L/R Solenoid pressure switch circuit is open or switch has failed • Transmission solenoid pack is damaged or has failed • Transmission control relay circuit is shorted to L/R solenoid • Valve body engine idle too high • Valve body solenoid switch stuck in "lockup" position • PCM has failed
DTC: P1776 **2T CCM** **Years:** 2008, 2009 **Models:** Dakota, Grand Cherokee, Journey, Liberty, Nitro, Pacifica, PT Cruiser, Ram Truck, Wrangler **Engines:** All **Transmissions:** All	**A/T Solenoid Switch Latched In Low/Reverse Position** Engine started; vehicle driven to over 30 MPH and the TCM detected the L/R switch was closed while performing partial or full PEMCC or FEMCC. **Possible Causes:** • Related DTC P0841 may be present. • Intermittent wiring or connector problems • L/R pressure switch sense circuit is open, shorted to ground or to voltage • Extremely low battery (system) voltage • Transmission pan has debris caused by valve body damage • Transmission internal problems, SSV sticking, or valve body damage • PCM has failed
DTC: P1790 **1T CCM** **Years:** 2008, 2009 **Models:** Dakota, Grand Cherokee, Journey, Liberty, Nitro, Pacifica, PT Cruiser, Ram Truck, Wrangler **Engines:** All **Transmissions:** All	**A/T Malfunction Immediately After Shift Event** Engine started; vehicle driven to a speed over 10 MPH in Drive, and the TCM detected a Speed Ratio error within 1.3 seconds of a shift. **Possible Causes:** • Transmission internal mechanical problem
DTC: P1794 **1T CCM** **Years:** 2008, 2009 **Models:** Dakota, Grand Cherokee, Journey, Liberty, Nitro, Pacifica, PT Cruiser, Ram Truck, Wrangler **Engines:** All **Transmissions:** All	**A/T Speed Sensor Ground Circuit Malfunction** Engine started; gear selector position indicating Neutral, and the PCM an error in the Output Speed Sensor signal during the test. **Possible Causes:** • Extremely low battery (system) voltage • TCM "reset" function has just been performed

DTC	Trouble Code Title, Conditions & Possible Causes
DTC: P1794 **1T CCM** **Years:** 2008, 2009 **Models:** Liberty **Engines:** 2.8L Diesel **Transmissions:** All	**A/T Speed Sensor Ground Error** The gear ratio is monitored whenever the transmission is in gear. After a TCM reset in Neutral and a ratio for Input to Output is 1 to 2, this DTC will set. This DTC can take up to 5 minutes of problem identification to light the MIL. **Possible Causes:** • Speed Sensor ground circuit is open or is shorted to ground or to voltage • TCM has failed • Intermittent wiring or connector problems
DTC: P1797 **1T CCM** **Years:** 2008, 2009 **Models:** Dakota, Grand Cherokee, Journey, Liberty, Nitro, Pacifica, PT Cruiser, Ram Truck, Wrangler **Engines:** All **Transmissions:** All	**A/T Manual Shift Overheat Malfunction** Whenever the engine is running and the transmission is in the AutoStick mode, if the engine temperature exceeds 275°F (135°C), this DTC will set. **Note: Aggressive driving or driving in Low for extended periods in AutoStick mode will set this DTC.** **Possible Causes:** • ATF fluid level too high (transmission may be overfilled) • Engine Cooling System or engine cooling fan malfunction • Excessive drive time in low gear, or aggressive drive patterns • Transmission oil cooler is clogged or restricted
DTC: P1854 **2T CCM** **Years:** 2008, 2009 **Models:** PT Cruiser **Engines:** All **Transmissions:** All	**Throttle Inlet Pressure BARO Reading Out Of Range** Engine started. The PCM detected the BARO Sensor indicated an incorrect reading. On MAP Sensor voltage is greater than 4.9v or below 2.28v (non-Turbo) or greater than 2.4v or below 1.2v (Turbo) for 400ms. **Possible Causes:** • Inspect the hoses and tubing to the turbo charger assembly • Review results of Solenoid Tests (Test 1, 2, 3 and 4 results) • TIP signal circuit is open (may be an intermittent fault) • TIP ground circuit is open (may be an intermittent fault) • PCM has failed
DTC: P1861 **1T PCM** **Years:** 2008, 2009 **Models:** Pacifica **Engines:** All **Transmissions:** All	**Siphon Line Disconnected** Ignition on. PCM compares the primary tank level with the secondary tank level. If the PCM detects the primary side is lower than the secondary side, by a calibrated amount, the DTC will set. **Possible Causes:** • Damage to fuel tank • Fuel level signal circuit is open or shorted to ground • Ground circuit is open • Internal tank components or siphon hose damaged • Fuel level Sensor has failed

OBD II Trouble Code List (P2XXX Codes)

DTC	Trouble Code Title, Conditions & Possible Causes
DTC: P2008 **1T CCM** **Years:** 2008, 2009 **Models:** Pacifica **Engines:** All **Transmissions:** All	**Short Runner Solenoid Circuit Malfunction** Engine started. ASD relay energized. PCM detected the Short Runner solenoid circuit was not in its expected voltage state. **Possible Causes:** • S/R solenoid control circuit is open • S/R solenoid control circuit is shorted to ground or power (B+) • S/R solenoid power supply circuit is open to the ASD relay • Short runner solenoid is damaged or it has failed • PCM has failed
DTC: P2066 **2T CCM** **Years:** 2008, 2009 **Models:** Pacifica **Engines:** All **Transmissions:** All	**Fuel Level Sensor No. 2 Malfunction** Test No. 1: With ignition on, fuel level is compared to the previous key-down after a 20-second delay. If the PCM does not see a difference in the fuel level of more than 0.1v, the test will fail. Test No. 2: The PCM monitors the fuel level with ignition on. If the PCM does not see a change in the fuel level of 0.1765 in. over a set amount of miles, the test will fail. **Possible Causes:** • Fuel tank or internal siphon hose damage • Fuel level signal circuit open or shorted to ground • Ground circuit is open • Fuel level Sensor malfunction

DTC	Trouble Code Title, Conditions & Possible Causes
DTC: P2067 **1T CCM** **Years:** 2008, 2009 **Models:** Pacifica **Engines:** All **Transmissions:** All	**Fuel Level Sensor No. 2 Low Input** Key on. Battery voltage over 10.4v. Fuel level Sensor signal goes below 0.1961v for more than 5 seconds. DTC is recorded. **Possible Causes:** • Intermittent condition • Fuel level sending unit signal circuit shorted to Sensor or chassis ground • Fuel level sensing unit is damaged or the fuel tank is damaged • BCM or PCM has failed
DTC: P2068 **1T CCM** **Years:** 2008, 2009 **Models:** Pacifica **Engines:** All **Transmissions:** All	**Fuel Level Sensor No. 2 High Input** Key on. Battery voltage over 10.4v. Fuel level Sensor signal goes above 4.7v for more than 5 seconds. DTC is recorded. **Possible Causes:** • Fuel level sending unit signal circuit shorted to Sensor or chassis ground • Fuel level sensing unit is damaged or the fuel tank is damaged • Instrument cluster module faulty • BCM or PCM has failed
DTC: P2072 **1T CCM** **Years:** 2008, 2009 **Models:** Dakota, Grand Cherokee, Journey, Liberty, Nitro, Pacifica, PT Cruiser, Ram Truck, Wrangler **Engines:** All **Transmissions:** All	**Electronic Throttle Control System Malfunction** Key on. The PCM recognizes the throttle plate is stuck during extremely cold ambient temperature conditions. The throttle plate goes through a de-icing procedure, but if the throttle plate still does not move, this DTC will set. The MIL will not illuminate. The vehicle will be in the Limp Home mode, limiting RPM and vehicle speed. **Possible Causes:** • Throttle plate frozen
DTC: P2074 **1T CCM** **Years:** 2008, 2009 **Models:** Dakota, Grand Cherokee, Journey, Liberty, Nitro, Pacifica, PT Cruiser, Ram Truck, Wrangler **Engines:** All **Transmissions:** All	**Manifold Pressure/Throttle Position Correlation; High Flow/Vacuum Leak** Engine running in all drive modes. The relationship between the MAP Sensor and TP Sensor exceeds a predetermined value for a given engine speed. If vacuum drops below 1.5 in. Hg with engine RPM at more than 2000 RPM at closed throttle, or if an unexpectedly high intake manifold airflow exists that can lead to increased engine speed and puts the NGC (Ram) into a High Airflow Protection Limiting mode; in this case, RPM limits for when a TP Sensor and/or MAP Sensor limp-in fault is present. **Possible Causes:** • Vacuum leak in hoses or component connections • High resistance or resistance to ground in MAP 5V supply or signal circuit • MAP Sensor has failed • High resistance in MAP ground circuit • TP Sensor has failed or is improperly adjusted • High resistance or resistance to ground in TP Sensor 5V supply or signal circuit • High resistance in TP Sensor ground circuit • PCM has failed
DTC: P2096 **2T CCM** **Years:** 2008, 2009 **Models:** Dakota, Grand Cherokee, Journey, Liberty, Nitro, Pacifica, PT Cruiser, Ram Truck, Wrangler **Engines:** All **Transmissions:** All	**Downstream Fuel System 1/2 Lean** Engine running in closed loop mode. Ambient/battery temperature above 20°F (-7°C). Altitude below 8500 feet. Fuel level is more than 15%. If the PCM adds downstream short-term compensation to long-term adaptive, and a certain percentage is exceeded for 2 trips, a freeze frame is stored, the MIL illuminates and a DTC is set. **Possible Causes:** • Exhaust leak • Engine mechanical problem • O2 Sensor has failed • O2 Sensor signal circuit or return circuit problem • Fuel contamination
DTC: P2097 **2T CCM** **Years:** 2008, 2009 **Models:** Dakota, Grand Cherokee, Journey, Liberty, Nitro, Pacifica, PT Cruiser, Ram Truck, Wrangler **Engines:** All **Transmissions:** All	**Downstream Fuel System 1/2 Rich** Engine running in closed loop mode. Ambient/battery temperature above 20°F (-7°C). Altitude below 8500 feet. Fuel level is more than 15%. If the PCM adds downstream short-term compensation to long-term adaptive, and a certain percentage is exceeded for 2 trips, a freeze frame is stored, the MIL illuminates and a DTC is set. **Possible Causes:** • Exhaust leak • Engine mechanical problem • O2 Sensor No. 1/2 has failed • O2 Sensor No. 1/2 signal circuit or return circuit problem • Fuel contamination

DTC	Trouble Code Title, Conditions & Possible Causes
DTC: P2098 **2T CCM** **Years:** 2008, 2009 **Models:** Dakota, Grand Cherokee, Journey, Liberty, Nitro, Pacifica, Ram Truck, Wrangler **Engines:** All **Transmissions:** All	**Downstream Fuel System 2/2 Lean** Engine running in closed loop mode. Ambient/battery temperature above 20°F (-7°C). Altitude below 8500 feet. Fuel level is more than 15%. If the PCM adds downstream short-term compensation to long-term adaptive, and a certain percentage is exceeded for 2 trips, a freeze frame is stored, the MIL illuminates and a DTC is set. **Possible Causes:** • Exhaust leak • Engine mechanical problem • O2 Sensor No. 2/2 has failed • O2 Sensor No. 2/2 signal circuit or return circuit problem • Fuel contamination
DTC: P2099 **2T CCM** **Years:** 2008, 2009 **Models:** Dakota, Grand Cherokee, Journey, Liberty, Nitro, Pacifica, Ram Truck, Wrangler **Engines:** All **Transmissions:** All	**Downstream Fuel System 2/2 Rich** Engine running in closed loop mode. Ambient/battery temperature above 20°F (−7°C). Altitude below 8500 feet. Fuel level is more than 15%. If the PCM adds downstream short-term compensation to long-term adaptive, and a certain percentage is exceeded for 2 trips, a freeze frame is stored, the MIL illuminates and a DTC is set. **Possible Causes:** • Exhaust leak • Engine mechanical problem • O2 Sensor No. 2/2 has failed • O2 Sensor No. 2/2 signal circuit or return circuit problem • Fuel contamination
DTC: P2100 **1T CCM** **Years:** 2008, 2009 **Models:** Dakota, Grand Cherokee, Journey, Liberty, Nitro, Pacifica, PT Cruiser, Ram Truck, Wrangler **Engines:** All **Transmissions:** All	**Electronic Throttle Control Motor Circuit Malfunction** Ignition on and the ETC motor is not is Limp Home mode. When the PCM detects an internal error or a short between the ETC Motor and the ETC Motor positive circuit in the ETC Motor Driver, this DTC will set. The ETC light will be flashing. **Possible Causes:** • Intermittent condition • Throttle plate or bore may have foreign object blockage • ETC positive circuit is open or is shorted to battery voltage, to ground, or to ETC negative circuit • ETC negative circuit is open or is shorted to battery voltage or to ground • Low battery voltage • ETC Motor or Throttle Body has failed • PCM has failed
DTC: P2101 **1T CCM** **Years:** 2008, 2009 **Models:** Dakota, Grand Cherokee, Journey, Liberty, Nitro, Pacifica, Ram Truck, Wrangler **Engines:** All **Transmissions:** All	**Electronic Throttle Control Motor Malfunction** With vehicle running and ETC motor is not is Limp Home mode, and the TPS adaptation is complete. The PCM recognizes too large of an error between the actual position of the throttle plate and the set point position. This DTC will set within 5 seconds. 3 good trips required to turn off MIL. The ETC light will be flashing. **Possible Causes:** • Throttle body assembly may have failed • Low battery voltage • PCM has failed
DTC: P2101 **1T CCM** **Years:** 2008, 2009 **Models:** PT Cruiser **Engines:** All **Transmissions:** All	**Electronic Throttle Control Motor Malfunction** With vehicle running and ETC motor is not is Limp Home mode, and the TPS adaptation is complete. If the PCM recognizes the difference between the TPS set point and the TPS actual setting is 8 for more than 405ms, this DTC will set. **Possible Causes:** • Intermittent condition • Electronic throttle control motor operation has failed • Throttle position is out of adjustment or has malfunctioned
DTC: P2101 **1T ECM** **Years:** 2008, 2009 **Models:** Liberty **Engines:** 2.8L Diesel **Transmissions:** All	**EGR Airflow Control Valve Excessive Current Or Open Circuit** Ignition on; EGR Airflow Control Valve commanded ON (excessive current) or OFF (open circuit). If the ECM detects excessive voltage signal or no voltage signal (open) on the EGR Airflow Control Valve control circuit, this DTC will set. **Possible Causes:** • Intermittent condition • ASD Relay Output circuit is open • EGR Airflow Control Valve has failed • EGR Airflow Control Valve control circuit is open, shorted to voltage or to ground • ECM has failed

DTC	Trouble Code Title, Conditions & Possible Causes
DTC: P2107 **1T CCM** **Years:** 2008, 2009 **Models:** Dakota, Grand Cherokee, Journey, Liberty, Nitro, Pacifica, PT Cruiser, Ram Truck, Wrangler **Engines:** All **Transmissions:** All	**Electronic Throttle Control Module Processor Malfunction** Ignition is on. This condition is caused by an internal PCM failure. The module will attempt to reset, so you will be able to hear the throttle relearning. If the condition is continuous, the vehicle may not be drivable. The ETC light will be flashing. **Possible Causes:** • PCM requires reprogramming
DTC: P2108 **1T CCM** **Years:** 2008, 2009 **Models:** Dakota, Grand Cherokee, Journey, Liberty, Nitro, Pacifica, PT Cruiser, Ram Truck, Wrangler **Engines:** All **Transmissions:** All	**Electronic Throttle Control Module Processor Malfunction** Ignition is on. This condition is caused by an internal PCM failure. Customer may experience an extended cranking condition, with limited driving and a rough idle. This code will set within 5 seconds. The ETC light will be flashing. **Possible Causes:** • PCM requires reprogramming
DTC: P2110 **1T CCM** **Years:** 2008, 2009 **Models:** Dakota, Grand Cherokee, Journey, Liberty, Nitro, Pacifica, PT Cruiser, Ram Truck, Wrangler **Engines:** All **Transmissions:** All	**Electronic Throttle Control Forced Limited RPM** Ignition is on and ETC motor is working. When the PCM requests to limit engine speed, if the PWM is too high for 20.5 seconds and before P2118 sets. This one-trip fault will set within 5 seconds. The ETC light will be illuminated. **Possible Causes:** • Throttle plate stuck • ETC positive circuit is open or is shorted to ground • ETC negative circuit is open or is shorted to ground • ETC motor has failed • PCM has failed
DTC: P2111 **1T CCM** **Years:** 2008, 2009 **Models:** Dakota, Grand Cherokee, Journey, Liberty, Nitro, Pacifica, PT Cruiser, Ram Truck, Wrangler **Engines:** All **Transmissions:** All	**Electronic Throttle Control Forced Limited RPM** Ignition is on and battery voltage is more than 10v. If the TP Sensor does not return to Limp Home position at the end of this test, the DTC will set. This one-trip fault will set within 5 seconds. The ETC light will be flashing. **Possible Causes:** • Throttle plate stuck above Limp Home position • TP Sensors 1 & 2 both read 2.5V • ETC positive circuit is open or is shorted to ground or to battery voltage • ETC negative circuit is open or is shorted to ground • PCM has failed
DTC: P2112 **1T CCM** **Years:** 2008, 2009 **Models:** Dakota, Grand Cherokee, Journey, Liberty, Nitro, Pacifica, PT Cruiser, Ram Truck, Wrangler **Engines:** All **Transmissions:** All	**Electronic Throttle Control Unable To Open** Ignition is on and battery voltage is more than 10v. Just after the ignition is turned on, the throttle is opened and closed to test the system. If the TP Sensor does not return to Limp Home position at the end of this test, the DTC will set. This one-trip fault will set within 5 seconds. The ETC light will be flashing. **Possible Causes:** • Throttle plate stuck at or below Limp Home position • ETC positive circuit is open or is shorted to ground • ETC negative circuit is open or is shorted to ground or to battery voltage • PCM has failed
DTC: P2115 **1T CCM** **Years:** 2008, 2009 **Models:** Dakota, Grand Cherokee, Journey, Liberty, Nitro, Pacifica, PT Cruiser, Ram Truck, Wrangler **Engines:** All **Transmissions:** All	**Accelerator Pedal Position Sensor No. 1 Minimum Stop Performance** Ignition is on. During in-plant mode the APP Sensors need to be checked to make sure that idle and full pedal travel can be reached on both Sensors. The test for this DTC is enabled once the test for DTC P2166 has passed. This DTC will set if the APP Sensor No. 1 has failed to achieve the required minimum value during in-plant testing. This one-trip fault will set within 5 seconds. The engine will only idle. **Possible Causes:** • APP Sensors must be reprogrammed to relearn
DTC: P2116 **1T CCM** **Years:** 2008, 2009 **Models:** Dakota, Grand Cherokee, Journey, Liberty, Nitro, Pacifica, PT Cruiser, Ram Truck, Wrangler **Engines:** All **Transmissions:** All	**Accelerator Pedal Position Sensor No. 2 Minimum Stop Performance** Ignition is on. During in-plant mode the APP Sensors need to be checked to make sure that idle and full pedal travel can be reached on both Sensors. The test for this DTC is enabled once the test for DTC P2167 has passed. This DTC will set if the APP Sensor No. 2 has failed to achieve the required minimum value during in-plant testing. This one-trip fault will set within 5 seconds. The engine will only idle. **Possible Causes:** • APP Sensors must be reprogrammed to relearn

DTC	Trouble Code Title, Conditions & Possible Causes
DTC: P2118 **1T CCM** **Years:** 2008, 2009 **Models:** Dakota, Grand Cherokee, Journey, Liberty, Nitro, Pacifica, PT Cruiser, Ram Truck, Wrangler **Engines:** All **Transmissions:** All	**Electronic Throttle Control Motor Circuit Malfunction** Ignition is on and ETC motor is not in limp-home mode. When the PCM detects an internal error or short between the ETC motor and ETC motor positive circuits in the ETC motor driver. The ETC light will be flashing. **Possible Causes:** • Throttle plate or bore malfunctions • ETC positive circuit is open or is shorted to ground, battery voltage or ETC negative circuit • ETC negative circuit is open or is shorted to ground or to battery voltage • ETC motor has malfunctioned • PCM has failed
DTC: P2120 **1T ECM** **Years:** 2008, 2009 **Models:** Liberty **Engines:** 2.8L Diesel **Transmissions:** All	**APP Sensor No. 1 Circuit Plausibility Or Signal Voltage Too High Or Too Low** Ignition on. If the APP Sensor No. 1 and No. 2 signals do not agree (plausibility) or if Sensor No. 1 voltage signal is above 4.8v (too high) or below 0.29v (too low), this DTC will set. **Possible Causes:** • APP Sensor has failed • APP Sensor No. 1 5V supply circuit is open, shorted to ground, to voltage, or shorted to Sensor ground • APP Sensor ground circuit or signal circuit is open • Intermittent condition • APP Sensor signal circuit is shorted to the Sensor ground circuit • ECM has failed
DTC: P2122 **1T CCM** **Years:** 2008, 2009 **Models:** Dakota, Grand Cherokee, Journey, Liberty, Nitro, Pacifica, Ram Truck, Wrangler **Engines:** All **Transmissions:** All	**Accelerator Pedal Position Sensor No. 1 Circuit Low** Ignition is on and no other APP Sensor No. 1 DTCs are present. When APP Sensor No. 1 voltage is too low, the engine will additionally idle, if the brake pedal is pressed or has failed. Acceleration rate and engine output are limited. This one-trip fault will set within 5 seconds. The ETC light will be flashing. **Possible Causes:** • 5V supply circuit is open or shorted to ground • APP Sensor No. 1 signal circuit is open, shorted to ground or to Sensor return circuit • APP Sensor No. 1 has failed • PCM has failed
DTC: P2122 **1T CCM** **Years:** 2008, 2009 **Models:** PT Cruiser **Engines:** All **Transmissions:** All	**Accelerator Pedal Position Sensor No. 1 Circuit Low** Ignition is on. When APP Sensor No. 1 voltage is less than 0.2444v, or the circuit is shorted to ground or open for more than 120msec, this DTC will set. **Possible Causes:** • APP Sensor sweep • Intermittent condition • 5V supply circuit is open or shorted to ground • APP Sensor No. 1 signal circuit is open, shorted to ground or to Sensor return circuit • APP Sensor No. 1 has failed • PCM 5V supply circuit problem • PCM has failed
DTC: P2123 **1T CCM** **Years:** 2008, 2009 **Models:** Dakota, Grand Cherokee, Journey, Liberty, Nitro, Pacifica, PT Cruiser, Ram Truck, Wrangler **Engines:** All **Transmissions:** All	**Accelerator Pedal Position Sensor No. 1 Circuit High** Ignition is on and no other APP Sensor No. 1 DTCs are present. When APP Sensor No. 1 voltage is too high, the engine will additionally idle, if the brake pedal is pressed or has failed. Acceleration rate and engine output are limited. This one-trip fault will set within 5 seconds. The ETC light will be flashing. **Possible Causes:** • APP Sensor No. 1 return circuit is open • APP Sensor No. 1 signal circuit is shorted to either 5V supply circuit • APP Sensor No. 1 has failed • PCM has failed
DTC: P2123 **1T CCM** **Years:** 2008, 2009 **Models:** PT Cruiser **Engines:** All **Transmissions:** All	**Accelerator Pedal Position Sensor No. 1 Circuit High** Ignition is on. When APP Sensor No. 1 voltage is more than 4.8192v, because of a short to voltage, this DTC will set. **Possible Causes:** • Intermittent condition • 5V supply circuit is shorted to battery voltage • APP Sensor No. 1 signal circuit is shorted to battery voltage or to 5V circuit • APP Sensor sweep • PCM has failed

DTC	Trouble Code Title, Conditions & Possible Causes
DTC: P2125 **1T ECM** **Years:** 2008, 2009 **Models:** Liberty **Engines:** 2.8L Diesel **Transmissions:** All	**APP Sensor No. 2 Circuit Plausibility Or Signal Voltage Too High Or Too Low** Ignition on. If the APP Sensor No. 1 and No. 2 signals do not agree (plausibility) or if Sensor No. 1 voltage signal is above 2.4v (too high) or below 0.15V (too low), this DTC will set. **Possible Causes:** • APP Sensor has failed • APP Sensor No. 1 5V supply circuit is open, shorted to ground, to voltage, or shorted to Sensor ground • APP Sensor ground circuit or signal circuit is open • Intermittent condition • APP Sensor signal circuit is shorted to the Sensor ground circuit • ECM has failed
DTC: P2127 **1T CCM** **Years:** 2008, 2009 **Models:** Dakota, Grand Cherokee, Journey, Liberty, Nitro, Pacifica, Ram Truck, Wrangler **Engines:** All **Transmissions:** All	**Accelerator Pedal Position Sensor No. 2 Circuit Low** Ignition is on and no other APP Sensor No. 2 DTCs are present. When APP Sensor No. 2 voltage is too high, the engine will additionally idle, if the brake pedal is pressed or has failed. Acceleration rate and engine output are limited. This one-trip fault will set within 5 seconds. The ETC light will be flashing. **Possible Causes:** • 5V supply circuit is open or shorted to ground • APP Sensor No. 2 signal circuit is open, shorted to ground or to Sensor return circuit • APP Sensor No. 2has failed • PCM has failed
DTC: P2127 **1T CCM** **Years:** 2008, 2009 **Models:** PT Cruiser **Engines:** All **Transmissions:** All	**Accelerator Pedal Position Sensor No. 2 Circuit Low** Ignition is on. When APP Sensor No. 2 voltage is less than 0.2444v, or the circuit is shorted to ground or open for more than 120msec, this DTC will set. **Possible Causes:** • APP Sensor sweep • Intermittent condition • 5V supply circuit is open or shorted to ground • APP Sensor No. 2 signal circuit is open, shorted to ground or to Sensor return circuit • APP Sensor No. 2 has failed • PCM 5V supply circuit problem • PCM has failed
DTC: P2128 **1T CCM** **Years:** 2008, 2009 **Models:** Dakota, Grand Cherokee, Journey, Liberty, Nitro, Pacifica, Ram Truck, Wrangler **Engines:** All **Transmissions:** All	**Accelerator Pedal Position Sensor No. 2 Circuit High** Ignition is on and no other APP Sensor No. 2 DTCs are present. When APP Sensor No. 2 voltage is too high, the engine will additionally idle, if the brake pedal is pressed or has failed. Acceleration rate and engine output are limited. This one-trip fault will set within 5 seconds. The ETC light will be flashing. **Possible Causes:** • APP Sensor No. 2 return circuit is open • APP Sensor No. 2 signal circuit is shorted to either 5V supply circuit • APP Sensor No. 2 has failed • PCM has failed
DTC: P2128 **1T CCM** **Years:** 2008, 2009 **Models:** PT Cruiser **Engines:** All **Transmissions:** All	**Accelerator Pedal Position Sensor No. 2 Circuit High** Ignition is on. When APP Sensor No. 2 voltage is more than 4.8192v, because of a short to voltage, this DTC will set. **Possible Causes:** • Intermittent condition • 5V supply circuit is shorted to battery voltage • APP Sensor No. 1 signal circuit is shorted to battery voltage or to 5V circuit • APP Sensor sweep • PCM has failed
DTC: P2135 **1T CCM** **Years:** 2008, 2009 **Models:** Dakota, Grand Cherokee, Journey, Liberty, Nitro, Pacifica, Ram Truck, Wrangler **Engines:** All **Transmissions:** All	**Throttle Position Sensors 1 & 2 Correlation** Ignition is on and no other TP Sensor DTCs are present. The PCM recognizes that TP Sensors 1 and 2 are not coherent, this one-trip fault will set within 5 seconds. The ETC light will be illuminated. **Possible Causes:** • TP Sensor No. 1 or 2 signal circuit is shorted to ground or to battery voltage • TP Sensor No. 1 or 2 signal circuit has high resistance • 5V supply circuit has high resistance • 5V supply circuit shorted to ground • TP Sensor ground circuit has high resistance • TP Sensor No. 1 signal circuit is shorted to Sensor No. 2 signal circuit • TP Sensor has failed • PCM has failed

DTC	Trouble Code Title, Conditions & Possible Causes
DTC: P2135 **1T CCM** **Years:** 2008, 2009 **Models:** PT Cruiser **Engines:** All **Transmissions:** All	**Throttle Position Sensors 1 & 2 Voltage Correlation** Ignition is on. When the difference between TP Sensor No. 1 degrees and TP Sensor No. 2 degrees is more than 1.995 degrees, this DTC will set. **Possible Causes:** • Intermittent condition • 5V supply circuit has high resistance • TP Sensor signal circuit has high resistance • Ground signal circuit shows high resistance • TP Sensors 1 & 2 require lab scope check • PCM has failed
DTC: P2138 **1T CCM** **Years:** 2008, 2009 **Models:** Dakota, Grand Cherokee, Journey, Liberty, Nitro, Pacifica, Ram Truck, Wrangler **Engines:** All **Transmissions:** All	**Accelerator Pedal Position Sensors 1 & 2 Correlation** Ignition is on and no other APP Sensor DTCs are present. The PCM recognizes that APP Sensors 1 and 2 are not coherent. Acceleration rate and engine output are limited. This one-trip fault will set within 5 seconds. The ETC light will be flashing. **Possible Causes:** • APP Sensor No. 1 or 2 signal circuit has high resistance • APP Sensor No. 1 or 2 return circuit has high resistance • 5V supply circuit has high resistance • APP Sensor has failed • PCM has failed
DTC: P2138 **1T CCM** **Years:** 2008, 2009 **Models:** PT Cruiser **Engines:** All **Transmissions:** All	**Accelerator Pedal Position Sensors 1 & 2 Voltage Correlation** Ignition is on. DTCs P2122, 2123, 2127 and 2128 are not present. When APP Sensor No. 1 voltage is 1.7 times the APP Sensor No. 2 voltage, and this equals more than 0.2v for 120msec, this DTC will set. **Possible Causes:** • Intermittent condition • 5V supply circuit is open or is shorted to ground • APP Sensor signal circuit has high resistance • 5V supply circuit has high resistance • Ground signal circuit shows high resistance • APP Sensors 1 & 2 require lab scope check • PCM has failed
DTC: P2141 **1T ECM** **Years:** 2008, 2009 **Models:** Liberty **Engines:** 2.8L Diesel **Transmissions:** All	**EGR Airflow Control Valve Short-To-Ground Circuit** Ignition on; EGR Airflow Control Valve commanded OFF. If the ECM detects no voltage signal on the EGR Airflow Control Valve control circuit, this DTC will set. **Possible Causes:** • Intermittent condition • ASD Relay Output circuit open • EGR Airflow Control Valve has failed • EGR Airflow Control Valve control circuit is open, shorted to ground • ECM has failed
DTC: P2142 **1T ECM** **Years:** 2008, 2009 **Models:** Liberty **Engines:** 2.8L Diesel **Transmissions:** All	**EGR Airflow Control Valve Short Circuit** Ignition on; EGR Airflow Control Valve commanded ON. If the ECM detects excessive voltage signal on the EGR Airflow Control Valve control circuit, this DTC will set. **Possible Causes:** • Intermittent condition • EGR Airflow Control Valve has failed • EGR Airflow Control Valve control circuit is shorted to voltage • ECM has failed
DTC: P2147 **1T CCM** **Years:** 2008, 2009 **Models:** Liberty **Engines:** 2.8L Diesel **Transmissions:** All	**Fuel Injector Bank 1 Open Circuit** Engine running. ECM detects unexpected current flow through injector control circuit. **Possible Causes:** • Intermittent condition • Fuel injector control circuit is open or is shorted to ground • Fuel injector has failed • ECM has failed

DTC	Trouble Code Title, Conditions & Possible Causes
DTC: P2148 **1T CCM** **Years:** 2008, 2009 **Models:** Liberty **Engines:** 2.8L Diesel **Transmissions:** All	**Fuel Injector Bank 1 Short Circuit** Engine running. The ECM detects unexpected current flow through the injector control circuit. **Possible Causes:** • Intermittent condition • Fuel injector control circuit is shorted to ground or to voltage • Fuel injector control circuits are shorted together • Fuel injector has failed • ECM has failed
DTC: P2150 **1T CCM** **Years:** 2008, 2009 **Models:** Liberty **Engines:** 2.8L Diesel **Transmissions:** All	**Fuel Injector Bank 2 Open Circuit** Engine running. The ECM detects unexpected current flow through the injector control circuit. **Possible Causes:** • Intermittent condition • Fuel injector control circuit is open or is shorted to ground • Fuel injector has failed • ECM has failed
DTC: P2148 **1T CCM** **Years:** 2008, 2009 **Models:** Liberty **Engines:** 2.8L Diesel **Transmissions:** All	**Fuel Injector Bank 2 Short Circuit** Engine running. The ECM detects unexpected current flow through the injector control circuit. **Possible Causes:** • Intermittent condition • Fuel injector control circuit is shorted to ground or to voltage • Fuel injector control circuits are shorted together • Fuel injector has failed • ECM has failed
DTC: P2161 **1T CCM** **Years:** 2008, 2009 **Models:** Dakota, Grand Cherokee, Journey, Liberty, Nitro, Pacifica, PT Cruiser, Ram Truck, Wrangler **Engines:** All **Transmissions:** All	**Vehicle Speed Sensor No. 2 Erratic** Ignition is on and battery voltage is greater than 10v. Transmission is in Drive or Reverse. The PCM recognizes the VSS 2 speed signal is erratic or high. No MIL and no ETC light. The cruise control is disabled. **Possible Causes:** • Active Bus or Communications DTCs • Incorrect tire circumference • PCM has failed
DTC: P2166 **1T CCM** **Years:** 2008, 2009 **Models:** Dakota, Grand Cherokee, Journey, Liberty, Nitro, Pacifica, PT Cruiser, Ram Truck, Wrangler **Engines:** All **Transmissions:** All	**Accelerator Pedal Position Sensor No. 1 Maximum Stop Performance** Ignition is on. During in-plant mode the APP Sensors need to be checked to make sure that idle and full pedal travel can be reached on both Sensors. This DTC will set if the APP Sensor No. 1 has failed to achieve the required maximum value during in-plant testing. This one-trip fault will set within 5 seconds. The engine will only idle. **Possible Causes:** • In-Plant test failure • APP Sensors must be reprogrammed to relearn
DTC: P2167 **1T CCM** **Years:** 2008, 2009 **Models:** Dakota, Grand Cherokee, Journey, Liberty, Nitro, Pacifica, PT Cruiser, Ram Truck, Wrangler **Engines:** All **Transmissions:** All	**Accelerator Pedal Position Sensor No. 2 Maximum Stop Performance** Ignition is on. During in-plant mode the APP Sensors need to be checked to make sure that idle and full pedal travel can be reached on both Sensors. This DTC will set if the APP Sensor No. 2 has failed to achieve the required maximum value during in-plant testing. This one-trip fault will set within 5 seconds. The engine will only idle. **Possible Causes:** • In-Plant test failure • APP Sensors must be reprogrammed to relearn

DTC	Trouble Code Title, Conditions & Possible Causes
DTC: P2172 **1T CCM** **Years:** 2008, 2009 **Models:** Dakota, Grand Cherokee, Journey, Liberty, Nitro, Pacifica, PT Cruiser, Ram Truck, Wrangler **Engines:** All **Transmissions:** All	**High Airflow/Vacuum Leak Detected (Instantaneous Accumulation)** Ignition is on and engine running with no MAP Sensor DTCs present. A large vacuum leak has been detected or both of the TP Sensors have failed, based on their position being 2.5V and the calculated MAP value is less than the actual MAP, minus an Offset value. This one-trip fault will set within 5 seconds. The ETC light will flash. **Possible Causes:** • Vacuum leak • 5V supply circuit has high resistance or is shorted to ground • MAP signal circuit has high resistance or is shorted to ground • TP Sensor ground circuit has high resistance • TP Sensor signal circuit is shorted to ground • TP Sensor return circuit has high resistance • MAP Sensor has failed • TP Sensor has failed • PCM has failed
DTC: P2173 **1T CCM** **Years:** 2008, 2009 **Models:** Dakota, Grand Cherokee, Journey, Liberty, Nitro, Pacifica, PT Cruiser, Ram Truck, Wrangler **Engines:** All **Transmissions:** All	**High Airflow/Vacuum Leak Detected (Slow Accumulation)** Ignition is on and engine running with no MAP Sensor DTCs present. A large vacuum leak has been detected or both of the TP Sensors have failed, based on their position being 2.5V and the calculated MAP value is less than the Gas Flow Adaptation value. This one-trip fault will set within 5 seconds. The ETC light will flash. **Possible Causes:** • Vacuum leak • 5V supply circuit has high resistance or is shorted to ground • MAP signal circuit has high resistance or is shorted to ground • TP Sensor ground circuit has high resistance • TP Sensor signal circuit is shorted to ground • TP Sensor return circuit has high resistance • MAP Sensor has failed • TP Sensor has failed • PCM has failed
DTC: P2174 **1T CCM** **Years:** 2008, 2009 **Models:** Dakota, Grand Cherokee, Journey, Liberty, Nitro, Pacifica, PT Cruiser, Ram Truck, Wrangler **Engines:** All **Transmissions:** All	**Low Airflow/Vacuum Leak Detected (Instantaneous Accumulation)** Ignition is on and engine running with no MAP Sensor DTCs present. The PCM calculated the MAP value is greater than actual MAP value, plus an Offset value. 3 good trips required to turn off MIL. The ETC light will flash. **Possible Causes:** • Restricted air inlet system • 5V supply circuit has high resistance or is shorted to ground • MAP signal circuit has high resistance or is shorted to ground • TP Sensor ground circuit has high resistance • TP Sensor signal circuit is shorted to ground • TP Sensor return circuit has high resistance • MAP Sensor has failed • TP Sensor has failed • PCM has failed
DTC: P2175 **1T CCM** **Years:** 2008, 2009 **Models:** Dakota, Grand Cherokee, Journey, Liberty, Nitro, Pacifica, PT Cruiser, Ram Truck, Wrangler **Engines:** All **Transmissions:** All	**Low Airflow/Vacuum Leak Detected (Slow Accumulation)** Ignition is on and engine running with no MAP Sensor DTCs present. The PCM calculated the MAP value is greater than actual MAP value, plus an Offset value. This DTC will set in 5 seconds after occurrence. 3 good trips required to turn off MIL. The ETC light will flash. **Possible Causes:** • Restricted air inlet system • 5V supply circuit has high resistance or is shorted to ground • MAP signal circuit has high resistance or is shorted to ground • TP Sensor ground circuit has high resistance • TP Sensor signal circuit is shorted to ground • TP Sensor return circuit has high resistance • MAP Sensor has failed • TP Sensor has failed • PCM has failed

DTC	Trouble Code Title, Conditions & Possible Causes
DTC: P2181 **2T CCM** **Years:** 2008, 2009 **Models:** Dakota, Grand Cherokee, Journey, Liberty, Nitro, Pacifica, PT Cruiser, Ram Truck, Wrangler **Engines:** All **Transmissions:** All	**Cooling System Performance** Ignition is on and engine running with no ECT Sensor DTCs present. The PCM recognizes that the ECT has failed its self-coherence test. The coolant temperature should only change at a certain rate. If this rate is too slow or too fast, this DTC will set. 3 good trips required to turn off MIL. The ETC light will illuminate on first trip failure. **Possible Causes:** • Low coolant level • ECT signal circuit is open or shorted to ground, Sensor ground, or battery voltage • ECT Sensor ground circuit is open • Thermostat has failed • ECT Sensor has failed • PCM has failed
DTC: P2226 **1T ECM** **Years:** 2008, 2009 **Models:** Liberty **Engines:** 2.8L Diesel **Transmissions:** All	**ECM Barometric Pressure Error** Ignition on. ECM detects an internal failure. **Possible Causes:** • ECM has failed • Intermittent condition
DTC: P2264 **1T ECM** **Years:** 2008, 2009 **Models:** Liberty **Engines:** 2.8L Diesel **Transmissions:** All	**Water In Fuel Voltage Above Upper Limit Or Below Lower Limit** Ignition on. If the ECM detects high voltage (above upper limit) or low voltage (below lower limit) on the Water In Fuel Sensor signal circuit, this DTC will set. **Possible Causes:** • Intermittent condition • WIF Sensor signal circuit is open or is shorted to voltage (high) or to ground (low) • WIF Sensor ground circuit is open • WIF Sensor signal and ground circuits are shorted together (low) • WIF Sensor has failed • FCM has failed (low) • ECM has failed (high)
DTC: P2294 **1T ECM** **Years:** 2008, 2009 **Models:** Liberty **Engines:** 2.8L Diesel **Transmissions:** All	**Fuel Pressure Solenoid Short-To-Ground Circuit** Ignition on; ECM Fuel Pressure Solenoid commanded OFF. If the ECM detects a short-to-ground on the control circuit, this DTC will set. **Possible Causes:** • FP Solenoid circuit(s) open, shorted to voltage, shorted to ground, or shorted together • Intermittent condition • FP Solenoid has failed • ECM has failed
DTC: P2296 **1T ECM** **Years:** 2008, 2009 **Models:** Liberty **Engines:** 2.8L Diesel **Transmissions:** All	**Fuel Pressure Solenoid Short Circuit** Ignition on; ECM Fuel Pressure Solenoid commanded ON. If the ECM detects excessive current on the control circuit, this DTC will set. **Possible Causes:** • FP Solenoid circuit(s) open, shorted to voltage, shorted to ground, or shorted together • Intermittent condition • FP Solenoid has failed • ECM has failed
DTC: P2299 **1T CCM** **Years:** 2008, 2009 **Models:** Dakota, Grand Cherokee, Journey, Liberty, Nitro, Pacifica, PT Cruiser, Ram Truck, Wrangler **Engines:** All **Transmissions:** All	**Brake Pedal Position/Accelerator Pedal Position Incompatible** Ignition is on and no Brake or APPS DTCs present. The PCM recognizes that a brake application following the APPS showing a fixed pedal opening. Temporary or permanent in nature. Internally, the PCM will reduce throttle opening below driver demand. This one-trip fault code will set in 5 seconds. The ETC light will illuminate and will only stay on while the DTC is active. **Possible Causes:** • Customer pressing accelerator pedal, then pressing brake pedal and holds both down at the same time • Stop lamp switch has failed • APP Sensor has failed
DTC: P2300 **1T CCM** **Years:** 2008, 2009 **Models:** PT Cruiser **Engines:** All **Transmissions:** All	**Ignition Coil No. 1 Secondary Circuit Low** Ignition is on. If the PCM detects an open or short to ground on the Ignition Coil No. 1 control circuit for more than 15 coil change requests, it will set this DTC. **Possible Causes:** • Ignition Coil No. 1 is damaged or it has failed • ASD relay output circuit problems • Ignition coil driver circuit is shorted to ground • PCM has failed

DTC	Trouble Code Title, Conditions & Possible Causes
DTC: P2301 **1T CCM** **Years:** 2008, 2009 **Models:** PT Cruiser **Engines:** All **Transmissions:** All	**Ignition Coil No. 1 Secondary Circuit High** Ignition is on. If the PCM detects a short to voltage on the Ignition Coil No. 1 control circuit for more than 15 coil change requests, it will set this DTC. **Possible Causes:** • ASD relay output circuit problems • Ignition coil driver circuit is open • Ignition Coil No. 1 is damaged or it has failed • Ignition coil driver circuit is shorted to ASD output circuit • PCM has failed • Intermittent condition
DTC: P2302 **1T CCM** **Years:** 2008, 2009 **Models:** Dakota, Grand Cherokee, Journey, Liberty, Nitro, Pacifica, PT Cruiser, Ram Truck, Wrangler **Engines:** All **Transmissions:** All	**Ignition Coil No. 1 Secondary Circuit Insufficient Ionization** Engine started; and the PCM detected the Ignition Coil No. 1 secondary "burn time" was insufficient, or it was missing. **Possible Causes:** • Intermittent condition • Cylinder No. 1 spark plug or wire is damaged or it has failed • Ignition Coil No. 1 is damaged or it has failed • Ignition coil control circuit is open or shorted to ground • ASD relay output circuit problems • PCM has failed
DTC: P2303 **1T CCM** **Years:** 2008, 2009 **Models:** PT Cruiser **Engines:** All **Transmissions:** All	**Ignition Coil No. 2 Secondary Circuit Low** Ignition is on. If the PCM detects an open or short to ground on the Ignition Coil No. 2 control circuit for more than 15 coil change requests, it will set this DTC. **Possible Causes:** • Ignition Coil No. 2 is damaged or it has failed • ASD relay output circuit problems • Ignition coil driver circuit is shorted to ground • PCM has failed
DTC: P2304 **1T CCM** **Years:** 2008, 2009 **Models:** PT Cruiser **Engines:** All **Transmissions:** All	**Ignition Coil No. 2 Secondary Circuit High** Ignition is on. If the PCM detects a short to voltage on the Ignition Coil No. 2 control circuit for more than 15 coil change requests, it will set this DTC. **Possible Causes:** • ASD relay output circuit problems • Ignition coil driver circuit is open • Ignition Coil No. 2 is damaged or it has failed • Ignition coil driver circuit is shorted to ASD output circuit • PCM has failed • Intermittent condition
DTC: P2305 **1T CCM** **Years:** 2008, 2009 **Models:** Dakota, Grand Cherokee, Journey, Liberty, Nitro, Pacifica, PT Cruiser, Ram Truck, Wrangler **Engines:** All **Transmissions:** All	**Ignition Coil No. 2 Secondary Circuit Insufficient Ionization** Engine started; and the PCM detected the Ignition Coil No. 2 secondary "burn time" was insufficient, or it was missing. **Possible Causes:** • Intermittent condition • Cylinder No. 2 spark plug or wire is damaged or it has failed • Ignition Coil No. 2 is damaged or it has failed • Ignition coil control circuit is open or shorted to ground • ASD relay output circuit problems • PCM has failed
DTC: P2308 **1T CCM** **Years:** 2008, 2009 **Models:** Dakota, Grand Cherokee, Journey, Liberty, Nitro, Pacifica, PT Cruiser, Ram Truck, Wrangler **Engines:** All **Transmissions:** All	**Ignition Coil No. 3 Secondary Circuit Insufficient Ionization** Engine started; and the PCM detected the Ignition Coil No. 3 secondary "burn time" was insufficient, or it was missing. **Possible Causes:** • Intermittent condition • Cylinder No. 3 spark plug or wire is damaged or it has failed • Ignition Coil No. 3 is damaged or it has failed • Ignition coil control circuit is open or shorted to ground • ASD relay output circuit problems • PCM has failed

DTC	Trouble Code Title, Conditions & Possible Causes
DTC: P2311 **1T CCM** **Years:** 2008, 2009 **Models:** Dakota, Grand Cherokee, Journey, Liberty, Nitro, Pacifica, PT Cruiser, Ram Truck, Wrangler **Engines:** All **Transmissions:** All	**Ignition Coil No. 4 Secondary Circuit Insufficient Ionization** Engine started; and the PCM detected the Ignition Coil No. 4 secondary "burn time" was insufficient, or it was missing. **Possible Causes:** • Intermittent condition • Cylinder No. 4 spark plug or wire is damaged or it has failed • Ignition Coil No. 4 is damaged or it has failed • Ignition coil control circuit is open or shorted to ground • ASD relay output circuit problems • PCM has failed
DTC: P2314 **1T CCM** **Years:** 2008, 2009 **Models:** Dakota, Grand Cherokee, Journey, Liberty, Nitro, Pacifica, Ram Truck, Wrangler **Engines:** All **Transmissions:** All	**Ignition Coil No. 5 Secondary Circuit Insufficient Ionization** Engine started; and the PCM detected the Ignition Coil No. 5 secondary "burn time" was insufficient, or it was missing. **Possible Causes:** • Intermittent condition • Cylinder No. 5 spark plug or wire is damaged or it has failed • Ignition Coil No. 5 is damaged or it has failed • Ignition coil control circuit is open or shorted to ground • ASD relay output circuit problems • PCM has failed
DTC: P2317 **1T CCM** **Years:** 2008, 2009 **Models:** Dakota, Grand Cherokee, Journey, Liberty, Nitro, Pacifica, Ram Truck, Wrangler **Engines:** All **Transmissions:** All	**Ignition Coil No. 6 Secondary Circuit Insufficient Ionization** Engine started; and the PCM detected the Ignition Coil No. 6 secondary "burn time" was insufficient, or it was missing. **Possible Causes:** • Intermittent condition • Cylinder No. 6 spark plug or wire is damaged or it has failed • Ignition Coil No. 6 is damaged or it has failed • Ignition coil control circuit is open or shorted to ground • ASD relay output circuit problems • PCM has failed
DTC: P2320 **1T CCM** **Years:** 2008, 2009 **Models:** Dakota, Grand Cherokee, Ram Truck **Engines:** All **Transmissions:** All	**Ignition Coil No. 7 Secondary Circuit Insufficient Ionization** Engine started; and the PCM detected the Ignition Coil No. 7 secondary "burn time" was insufficient, or it was missing. **Possible Causes:** • Cylinder No. 7 spark plug or wire is damaged or it has failed • Ignition Coil No. 7 is damaged or it has failed • Ignition coil control circuit is open or shorted to ground • PCM has failed
DTC: P2323 **1T CCM** **Years:** 2008, 2009 **Models:** Dakota, Grand Cherokee, Ram Truck **Engines:** All **Transmissions:** All	**Ignition Coil No. 8 Secondary Circuit Insufficient Ionization** Engine started; and the PCM detected the Ignition Coil No. 8 secondary "burn time" was insufficient, or it was missing. **Possible Causes:** • Cylinder No. 8 spark plug or wire is damaged or it has failed • Ignition Coil No. 8 is damaged or it has failed • Ignition coil control circuit is open or shorted to ground • PCM has failed
DTC: P2503 **1T CCM** **Years:** 2008, 2009 **Models:** Dakota, Grand Cherokee, Journey, Liberty, Nitro, Pacifica, PT Cruiser, Ram Truck, Wrangler **Engines:** All **Transmissions:** All	**Charging System Voltage Low** Engine started; engine speed over 1157 RPM; PCM detected the Battery Sense voltage was 1v less than the Charging system voltage "goal" for 13.47 seconds during the CCM test. The PCM senses the battery voltage turns off the field driver and then senses the battery voltage again. If the voltages are the same, the DTC is set. **Possible Causes:** • Battery sense circuit has a high resistance condition • Generator ground circuit has a high resistance condition • Generator field ground circuit is open • Generator field control circuit is open or shorted to ground • Generator is damaged or it has failed
DTC: P2525 **1T ECM** **Years:** 2008, 2009 **Models:** Liberty **Engines:** 2.8L Diesel **Transmissions:** All	**Vacuum Reservoir Solenoid Open Circuit** Ignition on; Vacuum Reservoir Solenoid commanded OFF. If the ECM does not detect a voltage signal on the control circuit, this DTC will set. **Possible Causes:** • Intermittent condition • ASD Relay output circuit is open • Vacuum Reservoir Solenoid control circuit is open or is shorted to ground • Vacuum Reservoir Solenoid has failed • ECM has failed

DTC	Trouble Code Title, Conditions & Possible Causes
DTC: P2527 **1T ECM** **Years:** 2008, 2009 **Models:** Liberty **Engines:** 2.8L Diesel **Transmissions:** All	**Vacuum Reservoir Solenoid Short-To-Ground** Ignition on; Vacuum Reservoir Solenoid commanded OFF. If the ECM does not detect a voltage signal on the control circuit, this DTC will set. **Possible Causes:** • Intermittent condition • ASD Relay output circuit is open • Vacuum Reservoir Solenoid control circuit is open or is shorted to ground • Vacuum Reservoir Solenoid has failed • ECM has failed
DTC: P2700 **1T CCM** **Years:** 2008, 2009 **Models:** Dakota, Grand Cherokee, Journey, Liberty, Nitro, Pacifica, PT Cruiser, Ram Truck, Wrangler **Engines:** All **Transmissions:** All	**A/T L/R Inadequate Element Volume Detected** Engine started; transmission fluid temperature more than 110°F, vehicle driven, and the PCM updated the L/R volume (during a 3-1 or 2-1 Manual downshift) with the throttle angle less than 5 degrees, and it detected that the L/R volume fell below 16 during the test. **Possible Causes:** • L/R volume clutch index is too low • TCM L/R volume clutch circuit is damaged or has failed
DTC: P2701 **1T CCM** **Years:** 2008, 2009 **Models:** Dakota, Grand Cherokee, Journey, Liberty, Nitro, Pacifica, PT Cruiser, Ram Truck, Wrangler **Engines:** All **Transmissions:** All	**A/T 2C Inadequate Element Volume Detected** Engine started; transmission fluid temperature more than 110°F, vehicle driven, then after the PCM updated the 2C volume (during a 3-2 kickdown event) with the throttle angle from 10-54 degrees, the PCM detected that the 2C volume fell below 5 during the CCM test. **Possible Causes:** • 2C volume clutch index is too low • TCM 2C volume clutch circuit is damaged or has failed
DTC: P2702 **1T CCM** **Years:** 2008, 2009 **Models:** Dakota, Grand Cherokee, Journey, Liberty, Nitro, Pacifica, PT Cruiser, Ram Truck, Wrangler **Engines:** All **Transmissions:** All	**A/T O/D Inadequate Element Volume Detected** Engine started; transmission fluid temperature more than 110°F, vehicle driven, then after he PCM updated the O/D volume (during a 2-3 Upshift event) with the throttle angle from 10-54 degrees, the PCM detected that the O/D volume fell below 5 during the CCM test. **Possible Causes:** • O/D volume clutch index is too low • TCM O/D volume clutch circuit is damaged or has failed
DTC: P2703 **1T CCM** **Years:** 2008, 2009 **Models:** Dakota, Grand Cherokee, Journey, Liberty, Nitro, Pacifica, PT Cruiser, Ram Truck, Wrangler **Engines:** All **Transmissions:** All	**A/T U/D Inadequate Element Volume Detected** Engine started; transmission fluid temperature more than 110°F, vehicle driven, and the TCM updated the U/D volume (during a 4-3 kickdown) with the throttle angle from 10-54 degrees, and it detected that the U/D volume fell below 11 during the test. **Possible Causes:** • U/D volume clutch index is too low • TCM U/D volume clutch circuit is damaged or has failed
DTC: P2704 **1T CCM** **Years:** 2008, 2009 **Models:** Dakota, Grand Cherokee, Journey, Liberty, Nitro, Pacifica, PT Cruiser, Ram Truck, Wrangler **Engines:** All **Transmissions:** All	**A/T 4C Inadequate Element Volume Detected** Engine started; transmission fluid temperature more than 110°F, vehicle driven, then after the TCM updated the 4C volume (during a 3-4 Upshift event) with the throttle angle from 10-54 degrees, the PCM detected that the 4C volume fell below 5 during the CCM test. **Possible Causes:** • 4C volume clutch index is too low • TCM 4C volume clutch circuit is damaged or has failed
DTC: P2706 **1T CCM** **Years:** 2008, 2009 **Models:** Dakota, Grand Cherokee, Journey, Liberty, Nitro, Pacifica, PT Cruiser, Ram Truck, Wrangler **Engines:** All **Transmissions:** All	**A/T MS Solenoid Circuit Malfunction** Engine started; vehicle driven in a forward gear, and immediately after a gear ratio or pressure switch change, the TCM detected a detected a MS solenoid error. The PCM sets this code when it detects three consecutive solenoid continuity test faults; or 1 failure if the test is run in response to a gear ratio of pressure switch fault. **Possible Causes:** • Check for a loose connector to the MS solenoid (intermittent) • MS solenoid control circuit is open or shorted to ground • MS solenoid control circuit is shorted to system power (B+) • MS solenoid is damaged or it has failed • Transmission control relay output supply circuit is open • TCM MS solenoid circuit is damaged or it has failed

OBD II Trouble Code List (UXXXX Codes)

DTC	Trouble Code Title, Conditions & Possible Causes
DTC: U0001 **1T TCM** **Years:** 2008, 2009 **Models:** Dakota, Grand Cherokee, Journey, Liberty, Nitro, Pacifica, PT Cruiser, Ram Truck, Wrangler **Engines:** All **Transmissions:** All	**CAN C Bus Circuit Malfunction** Ignition is on and battery voltage is 9-16v. Engine is running for more than 3 seconds. The PCM loses communication over the CAN C Bus circuit. The circuit is continuously monitored. **Possible Causes:** • CAN C Bus failure open or shorted • PCM has failed
DTC: U0101 **1T TCM** **Years:** 2008, 2009 **Models:** Dakota, Grand Cherokee, Journey, Liberty, Nitro, Pacifica, PT Cruiser, Ram Truck, Wrangler **Engines:** All **Transmissions:** All	**No TCM Bus Message** Engine running. Battery voltage more than 10v. No Bus messages are received from the TCM for 20 seconds. 2 trips required. **Possible Causes:** • PCI Bus unable to communicate with (DRBIII) scan tool • Fused ignition switch output incorrect (off-run-start) • Intermittent condition • PCM has failed
DTC: U0103 **1T TCM** **Years:** 2008, 2009 **Models:** Dakota, Grand Cherokee, Journey, Liberty, Nitro, Pacifica, PT Cruiser, Ram Truck, Wrangler **Engines:** All **Transmissions:** All	**Lost Communication With Electric Gear Shift Module** Ignition is on and battery voltage is 9-16v. Engine is running for more than 3 seconds. The PCM does not receive an Electric Gear Shift Module message over the CAN C circuit. The circuit is continuously monitored. **Possible Causes:** • CAN C Bus failure open or shorted • Electric gear shift module has failed • PCM has failed
DTC: U0104 **1T ACC** **Years:** 2008, 2009 **Models:** Dakota, Grand Cherokee, Journey, Liberty, Nitro, Pacifica, PT Cruiser, Ram Truck, Wrangler **Engines:** All **Transmissions:** All	**Lost Communication With ACC Module** The Powertrain Control Module (PCM) doesn't receive a bus message from the ACC Module for a specific amount of time.. **Possible Causes:** • CAN C Bus failure open or shorted • PCM has failed
DTC: U0121 **1T PCM** **Years:** 2008, 2009 **Models:** Dakota, Grand Cherokee, Journey, Liberty, Nitro, Pacifica, PT Cruiser, Ram Truck, Wrangler **Engines:** All **Transmissions:** All	**Lost Communication With ABS Module** Ignition is on and battery voltage is 9-16v. Engine is running for more than 3 seconds. The PCM does not receive an ABS message over the CAN C circuit for 7 consecutive seconds. The circuit is continuously monitored. **Possible Causes:** • CAN C Bus failure open or shorted • ABS module has failed • PCM has failed
DTC: U0140 **1T BCM** **Years:** 2008, 2009 **Models:** Dakota, Grand Cherokee, Journey, Liberty, Nitro, Pacifica, PT Cruiser, Ram Truck, Wrangler **Engines:** All **Transmissions:** All	**No Body Bus Message** Engine running. Battery voltage more than 10v. No Bus messages are received from the BCM for 20 seconds. **Possible Causes:** • Communication link with BCM has failed • PCI Bus circuit open • PCM has failed
DTC: U0155 **1T MIC** **Years:** 2008, 2009 **Models:** Dakota, Grand Cherokee, Journey, Liberty, Nitro, Pacifica, PT Cruiser, Ram Truck, Wrangler **Engines:** All **Transmissions:** All	**No Cluster Bus Message** Engine running. Battery voltage more than 10v. No Bus messages are received from the MIC (instrument cluster) for 20 seconds. **Possible Causes:** • Communication link with instrument cluster has failed • Instrument cluster operation improper or has failed • PCM has failed

DTC	Trouble Code Title, Conditions & Possible Causes
DTC: U0168 **1T MIC** **Years:** 2008, 2009 **Models:** Dakota, Grand Cherokee, Journey, Liberty, Nitro, Pacifica, PT Cruiser, Ram Truck, Wrangler **Engines:** All **Transmissions:** All	**No SKIM Bus Message** Engine running or ignition on. Battery voltage more than 10v. No Bus or J1850 messages are received from the SKIM for 20 seconds. **Possible Causes:** • Intermittent operation • PCI Bus circuit open or shorted from PCM to SKIM • Loss of communication between PCM and SKIM • SKIM or PCM has failed
DTC: U110A **1T TCM** **Years:** 2008, 2009 **Models:** Dakota, Grand Cherokee, Journey, Liberty, Nitro, Pacifica, PT Cruiser, Ram Truck, Wrangler **Engines:** All **Transmissions:** All	**Lost Communication With Steering Control Module (SCCM)** Ignition is on and battery voltage is 9-16v. Engine is running for more than 3 seconds. Bus message not received from the SCCM from about 2-5 seconds. **Possible Causes:** • CAN C Bus failure open or shorted • SCCM module has failed • PCM has failed
DTC: U110C **1T MIC** **Years:** 2008, 2009 **Models:** Dakota, Grand Cherokee, Journey, Liberty, Nitro, Pacifica, PT Cruiser, Ram Truck, Wrangler **Engines:** All **Transmissions:** All	**No Fuel Level Bus Message** Ignition on. Battery voltage more than 10v. No fuel level Bus messages are received from the PCM for 20 seconds. **Possible Causes:** • PCI Bus circuit open between PCM and BCM • Fuel level Bus message circuit failure • BCM has failed

GLOSSARY

ABS: Anti-lock braking system. An electro-mechanical braking system which is designed to minimize or prevent wheel lock-up during braking.

ABSOLUTE PRESSURE: Atmospheric (barometric) pressure plus the pressure gauge reading.

ACCELERATOR PUMP: A small pump located in the carburetor that feeds fuel into the air/fuel mixture during acceleration.

ACCUMULATOR: A device that controls shift quality by cushioning the shock of hydraulic oil pressure being applied to a clutch or band.

ACTUATING MECHANISM: The mechanical output devices of a hydraulic system, for example, clutch pistons and band servos.

ACTUATOR: The output component of a hydraulic or electronic system.

ADVANCE: Setting the ignition timing so that spark occurs earlier before the piston reaches top dead center (TDC).

ADAPTIVE MEMORY (ADAPTIVE STRATEGY): The learning ability of the TCM or PCM to redefine its decision-making process to provide optimum shift quality.

AFTER TOP DEAD CENTER (ATDC): The point after the piston reaches the top of its travel on the compression stroke.

AIR BAG: Device on the inside of the car designed to inflate on impact of crash, protecting the occupants of the car.

AIR CHARGE TEMPERATURE (ACT) SENSOR: The temperature of the airflow into the engine is measured by an ACT sensor, usually located in the lower intake manifold or air cleaner.

AIR CLEANER: An assembly consisting of a housing, filter and any connecting ductwork. The filter element is made up of a porous paper, sometimes with a wire mesh screening, and is designed to prevent airborne particles from entering the engine through the carburetor or throttle body.

AIR INJECTION: One method of reducing harmful exhaust emissions by injecting air into each of the exhaust ports of an engine. The fresh air entering the hot exhaust manifold causes any remaining fuel to be burned before it can exit the tailpipe.

AIR PUMP: An emission control device that supplies fresh air to the exhaust manifold to aid in more completely burning exhaust gases.

AIR/FUEL RATIO: The ratio of air-to-gasoline by weight in the fuel mixture drawn into the engine.

ALDL (assembly line diagnostic link): Electrical connector for scanning ECM/PCM/TCM input and output devices.

ALIGNMENT RACK: A special drive-on vehicle lift apparatus/measuring device used to adjust a vehicle's toe, caster and camber angles.

ALL WHEEL DRIVE: Term used to describe a full time four wheel drive system or any other vehicle drive system that continuously delivers power to all four wheels. This system is found primarily on station wagon vehicles and SUVs not utilized for significant off road use.

ALTERNATING CURRENT (AC): Electric current that flows first in one direction, then in the opposite direction, continually reversing flow.

ALTERNATOR: A device which produces AC (alternating current) which is converted to DC (direct current) to charge the car battery.

AMMETER: An instrument, calibrated in amperes, used to measure the flow of an electrical current in a circuit. Ammeters are always connected in series with the circuit being tested.

AMPERAGE: The total amount of current (amperes) flowing in a circuit.

AMPLIFIER: A device used in an electrical circuit to increase the voltage of an output signal.

AMP/HR. RATING (BATTERY): Measurement of the ability of a battery to deliver a stated amount of current for a stated period of time. The higher the amp/hr. rating, the better the battery.

AMPERE: The rate of flow of electrical current present when one volt of electrical pressure is applied against one ohm of electrical resistance.

ANALOG COMPUTER: Any microprocessor that uses similar (analogous) electrical signals to make its calculations.

ANODIZED: A special coating applied to the surface of aluminum valves for extended service life.

ANTIFREEZE: A substance (ethylene or propylene glycol) added to the coolant to prevent freezing in cold weather.

ANTI-FOAM AGENTS: Minimize fluid foaming from the whipping action encountered in the converter and planetary action.

ANTI-WEAR AGENTS: Zinc agents that control wear on the gears, bushings, and thrust washers.

ANTI-LOCK BRAKING SYSTEM: A supplementary system to the base hydraulic system that prevents sustained lock-up of the wheels during braking as well as automatically controlling wheel slip.

ANTI-ROLL BAR: See stabilizer bar.

ARC: A flow of electricity through the air between two electrodes or contact points that produces a spark.

ARMATURE: A laminated, soft iron core wrapped by a wire that converts electrical energy to mechanical energy as in a motor or relay. When rotated in a magnetic field, it changes mechanical energy into electrical energy as in a generator.

ATDC: After Top Dead Center.

ATF: Automatic transmission fluid.

ATMOSPHERIC PRESSURE: The pressure on the Earth's surface caused by the weight of the air in the atmosphere. At sea level, this pressure is 14.7 psi at 32°F (101 kPa at 0°C).

ATOMIZATION: The breaking down of a liquid into a fine mist that can be suspended in air.

AUXILIARY ADD-ON COOLER: A supplemental transmission fluid cooling device that is installed in series with the heat exchanger (cooler), located inside the radiator, to provide additional support to cool the hot fluid leaving the torque converter.

AUXILIARY PRESSURE: An added fluid pressure that is introduced into a regulator or balanced valve system to control valve movement. The auxiliary pressure itself can be either a fixed or a variable value. (See balanced valve; regulator valve.)

AWD: All wheel drive.

AXIAL FORCE: A side or end thrust force acting in or along the same plane as the power flow.

AXIAL PLAY: Movement parallel to a shaft or bearing bore.

AXLE CAPACITY: The maximum load-carrying capacity of the axle itself, as specified by the manufacturer. This is usually a higher number than the GAWR.

AXLE RATIO: This is a number (3.07:1, 4.56:1, for example) expressing the ratio between driveshaft revolutions and wheel revolutions. A low numerical ratio allows the engine to work easier because it doesn't have to turn as fast. A high numerical ratio means that the engine has to turn more rpm's to move the wheels through the same number of turns.

BACKFIRE: The sudden combustion of gases in the intake or exhaust system that results in a loud explosion.

BACKLASH: The clearance or play between two parts, such as meshed gears.

BACKPRESSURE: Restrictions in the exhaust system that slow the exit of exhaust gases from the combustion chamber.

BAKELITE®: A heat resistant, plastic insulator material commonly used in printed circuit boards and transistorized components.

BALANCED VALVE: A valve that is positioned by opposing auxiliary hydraulic pressures and/or spring force. Examples include mainline regulator, throttle, and governor valves. (See regulator valve.)

BAND: A flexible ring of steel with an inner lining of friction material. When tightened around the outside of a drum, a planetary member is held stationary to the transmission/transaxle case.

BALL BEARING: A bearing made up of hardened inner and outer races between which hardened steel balls roll.

BALL JOINT: A ball and matching socket connecting suspension components (steering knuckle to lower control arms). It permits rotating movement in any direction between the components that are joined.

BARO (BAROMETRIC PRESSURE SENSOR): Measures the change in the intake manifold pressure caused by changes in altitude.

BAROMETRIC MANIFOLD ABSOLUTE PRESSURE (BMAP) SENSOR: Operates similarly to a conventional MAP sensor; reads intake manifold pressure and is also responsible for determining altitude and barometric pressure prior to engine operation.

BAROMETRIC PRESSURE: (See atmospheric pressure.)

BALLAST RESISTOR: A resistor in the primary ignition circuit that lowers voltage after the engine is started to reduce wear on ignition components.

BATTERY: A direct current electrical storage unit, consisting of the basic active materials of lead and sulfuric acid, which converts chemical energy into electrical energy. Used to provide current for the operation of the starter as well as other equipment, such as the radio, lighting, etc.

BEAD: The portion of a tire that holds it on the rim.

BEARING: A friction reducing, supportive device usually located between a stationary part and a moving part.

BEFORE TOP DEAD CENTER (BTDC): The point just before the piston reaches the top of its travel on the compression stroke.

BELTED TIRE: Tire construction similar to bias-ply tires, but using two or more layers of reinforced belts between body plies and the tread.

BEZEL: Piece of metal surrounding radio, headlights, gauges or similar components; sometimes used to hold the glass face of a gauge in the dash.

BIAS-PLY TIRE: Tire construction, using body ply reinforcing cords which run at alternating angles to the center line of the tread.

BI-METAL TEMPERATURE SENSOR: Any sensor or switch made of two dissimilar types of metal that bend when heated or cooled due to the different expansion rates of the alloys. These types of sensors usually function as an on/off switch.

BLOCK: See Engine Block.

BLOW-BY: Combustion gases, composed of water vapor and unburned fuel, that leak past the piston rings into the crankcase during normal engine operation. These gases are removed by the PCV system to prevent the buildup of harmful acids in the crankcase.

BOOK TIME: See Labor Time.

BOOK VALUE: The average value of a car, widely used to determine trade-in and resale value.

BOOST VALVE: Used at the base of the regulator valve to increase mainline pressure.

BORE: Diameter of a cylinder.

BRAKE CALIPER: The housing that fits over the brake disc. The caliper holds the brake pads, which are pressed against the discs by the caliper pistons when the brake pedal is depressed.

BRAKE HORSEPOWER (BHP): The actual horsepower available at the engine flywheel as measured by a dynamometer.

BRAKE FADE: Loss of braking power, usually caused by excessive heat after repeated brake applications.

BRAKE HORSEPOWER: Usable horsepower of an engine measured at the crankshaft.

BRAKE PAD: A brake shoe and lining assembly used with disc brakes.

BRAKE PROPORTIONING VALVE: A valve on the master cylinder which restricts hydraulic brake pressure to the wheels to a specified amount, preventing wheel lock-up.

BREAKAWAY: Often used by Chrysler to identify first-gear operation in D and 2 ranges. In these ranges, first-gear operation depends on a one-way roller clutch that holds on acceleration and releases (breaks away) on deceleration, resulting in a freewheeling coast-down condition.

BRAKE SHOE: The backing for the brake lining. The term is, however, usually applied to the assembly of the brake backing and lining.

BREAKER POINTS: A set of points inside the distributor, operated by a cam, which make and break the ignition circuit.

BRINNELLING: A wear pattern identified by a series of indentations at regular intervals. This condition is caused by a lack of lube, overload situations, and/or vibrations.

BTDC: Before Top Dead Center.

BUMP: Sudden and forceful apply of a clutch or band.

BUSHING: A liner, usually removable, for a bearing; an anti-friction liner used in place of a bearing.

CALIFORNIA ENGINE: An engine certified by the EPA for use in California only; conforms to more stringent emission regulations than Federal engine.

CALIPER: A hydraulically activated device in a disc brake system,

which is mounted straddling the brake rotor (disc). The caliper contains at least one piston and two brake pads. Hydraulic pressure on the piston(s) forces the pads against the rotor.

CAPACITY: The quantity of electricity that can be delivered from a unit, as from a battery in ampere-hours, or output, as from a generator.

CAMBER: One of the factors of wheel alignment. Viewed from the front of the car, it is the inward or outward tilt of the wheel. The top of the tire will lean outward (positive camber) or inward (negative camber).

CAMSHAFT: A shaft in the engine on which are the lobes (cams) which operate the valves. The camshaft is driven by the crankshaft, via a belt, chain or gears, at one half the crankshaft speed.

CAPACITOR: A device which stores an electrical charge.

CARBON MONOXIDE (CO): A colorless, odorless gas given off as a normal byproduct of combustion. It is poisonous and extremely dangerous in confined areas, building up slowly to toxic levels without warning if adequate ventilation is not available.

CARBURETOR: A device, usually mounted on the intake manifold of an engine, which mixes the air and fuel in the proper proportion to allow even combustion.

CASTER: The forward or rearward tilt of an imaginary line drawn through the upper ball joint and the center of the wheel. Viewed from the sides, positive caster (forward tilt) lends directional stability, while negative caster (rearward tilt) produces instability.

CATALYTIC CONVERTER: A device installed in the exhaust system, like a muffler, that converts harmful byproducts of combustion into carbon dioxide and water vapor by means of a heat-producing chemical reaction.

CENTRIFUGAL ADVANCE: A mechanical method of advancing the spark timing by using flyweights in the distributor that react to centrifugal force generated by the distributor shaft rotation.

CENTRIFUGAL FORCE: The outward pull of a revolving object, away from the center of revolution. Centrifugal force increases with the speed of rotation.

CETANE RATING: A measure of the ignition value of diesel fuel. The higher the cetane rating, the better the fuel. Diesel fuel cetane rating is roughly comparable to gasoline octane rating.

CHECK VALVE: Any one-way valve installed to permit the flow of air, fuel or vacuum in one direction only.

CHOKE: The valve/plate that restricts the amount of air entering an engine on the induction stroke, thereby enriching the air/fuel ratio.

CHUGGLE: Bucking or jerking condition that may be engine related and may be most noticeable when converter clutch is engaged; similar to the feel of towing a trailer.

CIRCLIP: A split steel snapring that fits into a groove to hold various parts in place.

CIRCUIT BREAKER: A switch which protects an electrical circuit from overload by opening the circuit when the current flow exceeds a pre-determined level. Some circuit breakers must be reset manually, while most reset automatically.

CIRCUIT: Any unbroken path through which an electrical current can flow. Also used to describe fuel flow in some instances.

CIRCUIT, BYPASS: Another circuit in parallel with the major circuit through which power is diverted.

CIRCUIT, CLOSED: An electrical circuit in which there is no interruption of current flow.

CIRCUIT, GROUND: The non-insulated portion of a complete circuit used as a common potential point. In automotive circuits, the ground is composed of metal parts, such as the engine, body sheet metal, and frame and is usually a negative potential.

CIRCUIT, HOT: That portion of a circuit not at ground potential. The hot circuit is usually insulated and is connected to the positive side of the battery.

CIRCUIT, OPEN: A break or lack of contact in an electrical circuit, either intentional (switch) or unintentional (bad connection or broken wire).

CIRCUIT, PARALLEL: A circuit having two or more paths for current flow with common positive and negative tie points. The same voltage is applied to each load device or parallel branch.

CIRCUIT, SERIES: An electrical system in which separate parts are connected end to end, using one wire, to form a single path for current to flow.

CIRCUIT, SHORT: A circuit that is accidentally completed in an electrical path for which it was not intended.

CLAMPING (ISOLATION) DIODES: Diodes positioned in a circuit to prevent self-induction from damaging electronic components.

CLEARCOAT: A transparent layer which, when sprayed over a vehicle's paint job, adds gloss and depth as well as an additional protective coating to the finish.

CLUTCH: Part of the power train used to connect/disconnect power to the rear wheels.

CLUTCH, FLUID: The same as a fluid coupling. A fluid clutch or coupling performs the same function as a friction clutch by utilizing fluid friction and inertia as opposed to solid friction used by a friction clutch. (See fluid coupling.)

CLUTCH, FRICTION: A coupling device that provides a means of smooth and positive engagement and disengagement of engine torque to the vehicle powertrain. Transmission of power through the clutch is accomplished by bringing one or more rotating drive members into contact with complementing driven members.

COAST: Vehicle deceleration caused by engine braking conditions.

COEFFICIENT OF FRICTION: The amount of surface tension between two contacting surfaces; identified by a scientifically calculated number.

COIL: Part of the ignition system that boosts the relatively low voltage supplied by the car's electrical system to the high voltage required to fire the spark plugs.

COMBINATION MANIFOLD: An assembly which includes both the intake and exhaust manifolds in one casting.

COMBINATION VALVE: A device used in some fuel systems that routes fuel vapors to a charcoal storage canister instead of venting them into the atmosphere. The valve relieves fuel tank pressure and allows fresh air into the tank as the fuel level drops to prevent a vapor lock situation.

COMBUSTION CHAMBER: The part of the engine in the cylinder head where combustion takes place.

COMPOUND GEAR: A gear consisting of two or more simple gears with a common shaft.

COMPOUND PLANETARY: A gearset that has more than the three elements found in a simple gearset and is constructed by combining members of two planetary gearsets to create additional gear ratio possibilities.

COMPRESSION CHECK: A test involving removing each spark plug and inserting a gauge. When the engine is cranked, the gauge will record a pressure reading in the individual cylinder. General operating condition can be determined from a compression check.

COMPRESSION RATIO: The ratio of the volume between the piston and cylinder head when the piston is at the bottom of its stroke (bottom dead center) and when the piston is at the top of its stroke (top dead center).

COMPUTER: An electronic control module that correlates input data according to prearranged engineered instructions; used for the management of an actuator system or systems.

CONDENSER: An electrical device which acts to store an electrical charge, preventing voltage surges.

2. A radiator-like device in the air conditioning system in which refrigerant gas condenses into a liquid, giving off heat.

CONDUCTOR: Any material through which an electrical current can be transmitted easily.

CONNECTING ROD: The connecting link between the crankshaft and piston.

CONSTANT VELOCITY JOINT: Type of universal joint in a halfshaft assembly in which the output shaft turns at a constant angular velocity without variation, provided that the speed of the input shaft is constant.

CONTINUITY: Continuous or complete circuit. Can be checked with an ohmmeter.

CONTROL ARM: The upper or lower suspension components which are mounted on the frame and support the ball joints and steering knuckles.

CONVENTIONAL IGNITION: Ignition system which uses breaker points.

CONVERTER: (See torque converter.)

CONVERTER LOCKUP: The switching from hydrodynamic to direct mechanical drive, usually through the application of a friction element called the converter clutch.

COOLANT: Mixture of water and anti-freeze circulated through the engine to carry off heat produced by the engine.

CORROSION INHIBITOR: An inhibitor in ATF that prevents corrosion of bushings, thrust washers, and oil cooler brazed joints.

COUNTERSHAFT: An intermediate shaft which is rotated by a mainshaft and transmits, in turn, that rotation to a working part.

COUPLING PHASE: Occurs when the torque converter is operating at its greatest hydraulic efficiency. The speed differential between the impeller and the turbine is at its minimum. At this point, the stator freewheels, and there is no torque multiplication.

CRANKCASE: The lower part of an engine in which the crankshaft and related parts operate.

CRANKSHAFT: Engine component (connected to pistons by connecting rods) which converts the reciprocating (up and down) motion of pistons to rotary motion used to turn the driveshaft.

CURB WEIGHT: The weight of a vehicle without passengers or payload, but including all fluids (oil, gas, coolant, etc.) and other equipment specified as standard.

CURRENT: The flow (or rate) of electrons moving through a circuit. Current is measured in amperes (amp).

CURRENT FLOW CONVENTIONAL: Current flows through a circuit from the positive terminal of the source to the negative terminal (plus to minus).

CURRENT FLOW, ELECTRON: Current or electrons flow from the negative terminal of the source, through the circuit, to the positive terminal (minus to plus).

CV-JOINT: Constant velocity joint.

CYCLIC VIBRATIONS: The off-center movement of a rotating object that is affected by its initial balance, speed of rotation, and working angles.

CYLINDER BLOCK: See engine block.

CYLINDER HEAD: The detachable portion of the engine, usually fastened to the top of the cylinder block and containing all or most of the combustion chambers. On overhead valve engines, it contains the valves and their operating parts. On overhead cam engines, it contains the camshaft as well.

CYLINDER: In an engine, the round hole in the engine block in which the piston(s) ride.

DATA LINK CONNECTOR (DLC): Current acronym/term applied to the federally mandated, diagnostic junction connector that is used to monitor ECM/PC/TCM inputs, processing strategies, and outputs including diagnostic trouble codes (DTCs).

DEAD CENTER: The extreme top or bottom of the piston stroke.

DECELERATION BUMP: When referring to a torque converter clutch in the applied position, a sudden release of the accelerator pedal causes a forceful reversal of power through the drivetrain (engine braking), just prior to the apply plate actually being released.

DELAYED (LATE OR EXTENDED): Condition where shift is expected but does not occur for a period of time, for example, where clutch or band engagement does not occur as quickly as expected during part throttle or wide open throttle apply of accelerator or when manually downshifting to a lower range.

DETENT: A spring-loaded plunger, pin, ball, or pawl used as a holding device on a ratchet wheel or shaft. In automatic transmissions, a detent mechanism is used for locking the manual valve in place.

DETENT DOWNSHIFT: (See kickdown.)

DETERGENT: An additive in engine oil to improve its operating characteristics.

DETONATION: An unwanted explosion of the air/fuel mixture in the combustion chamber caused by excess heat and compression, advanced timing, or an overly lean mixture. Also referred to as "ping".

DEXRON®: A brand of automatic transmission fluid.

DIAGNOSTIC TROUBLE CODES (DTCs): A digital display from the control module memory that identifies the input, processor, or output device circuit that is related to the powertrain emission/driveability malfunction detected. Diagnostic trouble codes can be read by the MIL to flash any codes or by using a handheld scanner.

DIAPHRAGM: A thin, flexible wall separating two cavities, such as in a vacuum advance unit.

DIESELING: The engine continues to run after the car is shut off; caused by fuel continuing to be burned in the combustion chamber.

DIFFERENTIAL: A geared assembly which allows the transmission of motion between drive axles, giving one axle the ability to rotate faster than the other, as in cornering.

DIFFERENTIAL AREAS: When opposing faces of a spool valve are acted upon by the same pressure but their areas differ in size, the face with the larger area produces the differential force and valve movement. (See spool valve.)

DIFFERENTIAL FORCE: (See differential areas)

DIGITAL READOUT: A display of numbers or a combination of numbers and letters.

DIGITAL VOLT OHMMETER: An electronic diagnostic tool used to measure voltage, ohms and amps as well as several other functions, with the readings displayed on a digital screen in tenths, hundredths and thousandths.

DIODE: An electrical device that will allow current to flow in one direction only.

DIRECT CURRENT (DC): Electrical current that flows in one direction only.

DIRECT DRIVE: The gear ratio is 1:1, with no change occurring in the torque and speed input/output relationship.

DISC BRAKE: A hydraulic braking assembly consisting of a brake disc, or rotor, mounted on an axle shaft, and a caliper assembly containing, usually two brake pads which are activated by hydraulic pressure. The pads are forced against the sides of the disc, creating friction which slows the vehicle.

DISPERSANTS: Suspend dirt and prevent sludge buildup in a liquid, such as engine oil.

DOUBLE BUMP (DOUBLE FEEL): Two sudden and forceful applies of a clutch or band.

DISPLACEMENT: The total volume of air that is displaced by all pistons as the engine turns through one complete revolution.

DISTRIBUTOR: A mechanically driven device on an engine which is responsible for electrically firing the spark plug at a pre-determined point of the piston stroke.

DOHC: Double overhead camshaft.

DOUBLE OVERHEAD CAMSHAFT: The engine utilizes two camshafts mounted in one cylinder head. One camshaft operates the exhaust valves, while the other operates the intake valves.

DOWEL PIN: A pin, inserted in mating holes in two different parts allowing those parts to maintain a fixed relationship.

DRIVELINE: The drive connection between the transmission and the drive wheels.

DRIVE TRAIN: The components that transmit the flow of power from the engine to the wheels. The components include the clutch, transmission, driveshafts (or axle shafts in front wheel drive), U-joints and differential.

DRUM BRAKE: A braking system which consists of two brake shoes and one or two wheel cylinders, mounted on a fixed backing plate, and a brake drum, mounted on an axle, which revolves around the assembly.

DRY CHARGED BATTERY: Battery to which electrolyte is added when the battery is placed in service.

DVOM: Digital volt ohmmeter

DWELL: The rate, measured in degrees of shaft rotation, at which an electrical circuit cycles on and off.

DYNAMIC: An application in which there is rotating or reciprocating motion between the parts.

EARLY: Condition where shift occurs before vehicle has reached proper speed, which tends to labor engine after upshift.

EBCM: See Electronic Control Unit (ECU).

ECM: See Electronic Control Unit (ECU).

ECU: Electronic control unit.

ELECTRODE: Conductor (positive or negative) of electric current.

ELECTROLYSIS: A surface etching or bonding of current conducting transmission/transaxle components that may occur when grounding straps are missing or in poor condition.

ELECTROLYTE: A solution of water and sulfuric acid used to activate the battery. Electrolyte is extremely corrosive.

ELECTROMAGNET: A coil that produces a magnetic field when current flows through its windings.

ELECTROMAGNETIC INDUCTION: A method to create (generate) current flow through the use of magnetism.

ELECTROMAGNETISM: The effects surrounding the relationship between electricity and magnetism.

ELECTROMOTIVE FORCE (EMF): The force or pressure (voltage) that causes current movement in an electrical circuit.

ELECTRONIC CONTROL UNIT: A digital computer that controls engine (and sometimes transmission, brake or other vehicle system) functions based on data received from various sensors. Examples used by some manufacturers include Electronic Brake Control Module (EBCM), Engine Control Module (ECM), Powertrain Control Module (PCM) or Vehicle Control Module (VCM).

ELECTRONIC IGNITION: A system in which the timing and firing of the spark plugs is controlled by an electronic control unit, usually called a module. These systems have no points or condenser.

ELECTRONIC PRESSURE CONTROL (EPC) SOLENOID: A specially designed solenoid containing a spool valve and spring assembly to control fluid mainline pressure. A variable current flow, controlled by the ECM/PCM, varies the internal force of the solenoid on the spool valve and resulting mainline pressure. (See variable force solenoid.)

ELECTRONICS: Miniaturized electrical circuits utilizing semiconductors, solid-state devices, and printed circuits. Electronic circuits utilize small amounts of power.

ELECTRONIFICATION: The application of electronic circuitry to a mechanical device. Regarding automatic transmissions, electrification is incorporated into converter clutch lockup, shift scheduling, and line pressure control systems.

ELECTROSTATIC DISCHARGE (ESD): An unwanted, high-voltage electrical current released by an individual who has taken on a static charge of electricity. Electronic components can be easily damaged by ESD.

ELEMENT: A device within a hydrodynamic drive unit designed with a set of blades to direct fluid flow.

ENAMEL: Type of paint that dries to a smooth, glossy finish.

END BUMP (END FEEL OR SLIP BUMP): Firmer feel at end of shift when compared with feel at start of shift.

END-PLAY: The clearance/gap between two components that allows for expansion of the parts as they warm up, to prevent binding and to allow space for lubrication.

ENERGY: The ability or capacity to do work.

ENGINE: The primary motor or power apparatus of a vehicle, which converts liquid or gas fuel into mechanical energy.

ENGINE BLOCK: The basic engine casting containing the cylinders, the crankshaft main bearings, as well as machined surfaces for the mounting of other components such as the cylinder head, oil pan, transmission, etc.

ENGINE BRAKING: Use of engine to slow vehicle by manually downshifting during zero-throttle coast down.

ENGINE CONTROL MODULE (ECM): Manages the engine and incorporates output control over the torque converter clutch solenoid. (Note: Current designation for the ECM in late model vehicles is PCM.)

ENGINE COOLANT TEMPERATURE (ECT) SENSOR: Prevents converter clutch engagement with a cold engine; also used for shift timing and shift quality.

EP LUBRICANT: EP (extreme pressure) lubricants are specially formulated for use with gears involving heavy loads (transmissions, differentials, etc.).

ETHYL: A substance added to gasoline to improve its resistance to knock, by slowing down the rate of combustion.

ETHYLENE GLYCOL: The base substance of antifreeze.

EXHAUST MANIFOLD: A set of cast passages or pipes which conduct exhaust gases from the engine.

FAIL-SAFE (BACKUP) CONTROL: A substitute value used by the PCM/TCM to replace a faulty signal from an input sensor. The temporary value allows the vehicle to continue to be operated.

FAST IDLE: The speed of the engine when the choke is on. Fast idle speeds engine warm-up.

FEDERAL ENGINE: An engine certified by the EPA for use in any of the 49 states (except California).

FEEDBACK: A circuit malfunction whereby current can find another path to feed load devices.

FEELER GAUGE: A blade, usually metal, of precisely predetermined thickness, used to measure the clearance between two parts.

FILAMENT: The part of a bulb that glows; the filament creates high resistance to current flow and actually glows from the resulting heat.

FINAL DRIVE: An essential part of the axle drive assembly where final gear reduction takes place in the powertrain. In RWD applications and north-south FWD applications, it must also change the power flow direction to the axle shaft by ninety degrees. (Also see axle ratio).

FIRING ORDER: The order in which combustion occurs in the cylinders of an engine. Also the order in which spark is distributed to the plugs by the distributor.

FIRM: A noticeable quick apply of a clutch or band that is considered normal with medium to heavy throttle shift; should not be confused with harsh or rough.

FLAME FRONT: The term used to describe certain aspects of the fuel explosion in the cylinders. The flame front should move in a controlled pattern across the cylinder, rather than simply exploding immediately.

FLARE (SLIPPING): A quick increase in engine rpm accompanied by momentary loss of torque; generally occurs during shift.

FLAT ENGINE: Engine design in which the pistons are horizontally opposed. Porsche, Subaru and some old VW are common examples of flat engines.

FLAT RATE: A dealership term referring to the amount of money paid to a technician for a repair or diagnostic service based on that particular service versus dealership's labor time (NOT based on the actual time the technician spent on the job).

FLAT SPOT: A point during acceleration when the engine seems to lose power for an instant.

FLOODING: The presence of too much fuel in the intake manifold and combustion chamber which prevents the air/fuel mixture from firing, thereby causing a no-start situation.

FLUID: A fluid can be either liquid or gas. In hydraulics, a liquid is used for transmitting force or motion.

FLUID COUPLING: The simplest form of hydrodynamic drive, the fluid coupling consists of two look-alike members with straight radial varies referred to as the impeller (pump) and the turbine. Input torque is always equal to the output torque.

FLUID DRIVE: Either a fluid coupling or a fluid torque converter. (See hydrodynamic drive units.)

FLUID TORQUE CONVERTER: A hydrodynamic drive that has the ability to act both as a torque multiplier and fluid coupling. (See hydrodynamic drive units; torque converter.)

FLUID VISCOSITY: The resistance of a liquid to flow. A cold fluid (oil) has greater viscosity and flows more slowly than a hot fluid (oil).

FLYWHEEL: A heavy disc of metal attached to the rear of the crankshaft. It smoothes the firing impulses of the engine and keeps the crankshaft turning during periods when no firing takes place. The starter also engages the flywheel to start the engine.

FOOT POUND (ft. lbs., lbs. ft. or sometimes, ft. lb.): The amount of energy or work needed to raise an item weighing one pound, a distance of one foot.

FREEZE PLUG: A plug in the engine block which will be pushed out if the coolant freezes. Sometimes called expansion plugs, they protect the block from cracking should the coolant freeze.

FRICTION: The resistance that occurs between contacting surfaces. This relationship is expressed by a ratio called the coefficient of friction (CL).

FRICTION, COEFFICIENT OF: The amount of surface tension between two contacting surfaces; expressed by a scientifically calculated number.

FRONT END ALIGNMENT: A service to set caster, camber and toe-in to the correct specifications. This will ensure that the car steers and handles properly and that the tires wear properly.

FRICTION MODIFIER: Changes the coefficient of friction of the fluid between the mating steel and composition clutch/band surfaces during the engagement process and allows for a certain amount of intentional slipping for a good "shift-feel".

FRONTAL AREA: The total frontal area of a vehicle exposed to air flow.

FUEL FILTER: A component of the fuel system containing a porous paper element used to prevent any impurities from entering the engine through the fuel system. It usually takes the form of a canister-like housing, mounted in-line with the fuel hose, located anywhere on a vehicle between the fuel tank and engine.

FUEL INJECTION: A system replacing the carburetor that sprays fuel into the cylinder through nozzles. The amount of fuel can be more precisely controlled with fuel injection.

FULL FLOATING AXLE: An axle in which the axle housing extends through the wheel giving bearing support on the outside of the housing. The front axle of a four-wheel drive vehicle is usually a full floating axle, as are the rear axles of many larger (1 ton and over) pick-ups and vans.

FULL-TIME FOUR-WHEEL DRIVE: A four-wheel drive system that continuously delivers power to all four wheels. A differential between the front and rear driveshafts permits variations in axle speeds to control gear wind-up without damage.

FULL THROTTLE DETENT DOWNSHIFT: A quick apply of accelerator pedal to its full travel, forcing a downshift.

FUSE: A protective device in a circuit which prevents circuit overload by breaking the circuit when a specific amperage is present. The device is constructed around a strip or wire of a lower amperage rating than the circuit it is designed to protect. When an amperage higher than that stamped on the fuse is present in the circuit, the strip or wire melts, opening the circuit.

FUSIBLE LINK: A piece of wire in a wiring harness that performs the same job as a fuse. If overloaded, the fusible link will melt and interrupt the circuit.

FWD: Front wheel drive.

GAWR: (Gross axle weight rating) the total maximum weight an axle is designed to carry.

GCW: (Gross combined weight) total combined weight of a tow vehicle and trailer.

GARAGE SHIFT: initial engagement feel of transmission, neutral to reverse or neutral to a forward drive.

GARAGE SHIFT FEEL: A quick check of the engagement quality and responsiveness of reverse and forward gears. This test is done with the vehicle stationary.

GEAR: A toothed mechanical device that acts as a rotating lever to transmit power or turning effort from one shaft to another. (See gear ratio.)

GEAR RATIO: A ratio expressing the number of turns a smaller gear will make to turn a larger gear through one revolution. The ratio is found by dividing the number of teeth on the smaller gear into the number of teeth on the larger gear.

GEARBOX: Transmission

GEAR REDUCTION: Torque is multiplied and speed decreased by the factor of the gear ratio. For example, a 3:1 gear ratio changes an input torque of 180 ft. lbs. and an input speed of 2700 rpm to 540 Ft. lbs. and 900 rpm, respectively. (No account is taken of frictional losses, which are always present.)

GEARTRAIN: A succession of intermeshing gears that form an assembly and provide for one or more torque changes as the power input is transmitted to the power output.

GEL COAT: A thin coat of plastic resin covering fiberglass body panels.

GENERATOR: A device which produces direct current (DC) necessary to charge the battery.

GOVERNOR: A device that senses vehicle speed and generates a hydraulic oil pressure. As vehicle speed increases, governor oil pressure rises.

GROUND CIRCUIT: (See circuit, ground.)

GROUND SIDE SWITCHING: The electrical/electronic circuit control switch is located after the circuit load.

GVWR: (Gross vehicle weight rating) total maximum weight a vehicle is designed to carry including the weight of the vehicle, passengers, equipment, gas, oil, etc.

HALOGEN: A special type of lamp known for its quality of brilliant white light. Originally used for fog lights and driving lights.

HARD CODES: DTCs that are present at the time of testing; also called continuous or current codes.

HARSH(ROUGH): An apply of a clutch or band that is more noticeable than a firm one; considered undesirable at any throttle position.

HEADER TANK: An expansion tank for the radiator coolant. It can be located remotely or built into the radiator.

HEAT RANGE: A term used to describe the ability of a spark plug to carry away heat. Plugs with longer nosed insulators take longer to carry heat off effectively.

HEAT RISER: A flapper in the exhaust manifold that is closed when the engine is cold, causing hot exhaust gases to heat the intake manifold providing better cold engine operation. A thermostatic spring opens the flapper when the engine warms up.

HEAVY THROTTLE: Approximately three-fourths of accelerator pedal travel.

HEMI: A name given an engine using hemispherical combustion chambers.

HERTZ (HZ): The international unit of frequency equal to one cycle per second (10,000 Hertz equals 10,000 cycles per second).

HIGH-IMPEDANCE DVOM (DIGITAL VOLT-OHMMETER): This styled device provides a built-in resistance value and is capable of limiting circuit current flow to safe milliamp levels.

HIGH RESISTANCE: Often refers to a circuit where there is an excessive amount of opposition to normal current flow.

HORSEPOWER: A measurement of the amount of work; one horsepower is the amount of work necessary to lift 33,000 lbs. one foot in one minute. Brake horsepower (bhp) is the horsepower delivered by an engine on a dynamometer. Net horsepower is the power remaining (measured at the flywheel of the engine) that can be used to turn the wheels after power is consumed through friction and running the engine accessories (water pump, alternator, air pump, fan etc.)

HOT CIRCUIT: (See circuit, hot; hot lead.)

HOT LEAD: A wire or conductor in the power side of the circuit. (See circuit, hot.)

HOT SIDE SWITCHING: The electrical/electronic circuit control switch is located before the circuit load.

HUB: The center part of a wheel or gear.

HUNTING (BUSYNESS): Repeating quick series of up-shifts and downshifts that causes noticeable change in engine rpm, for example, as in a 4-3-4 shift pattern.

HYDRAULICS: The use of liquid under pressure to transfer force of motion.

HYDROCARBON (HC): Any chemical compound made up of hydrogen and carbon. A major pollutant formed by the engine as a by-product of combustion.

HYDRODYNAMIC DRIVE UNITS: Devices that transmit power solely by the action of a kinetic fluid flow in a closed recirculating path. An impeller energizes the fluid and discharges the high-speed jet stream into the turbine for power output.

HYDROMETER: An instrument used to measure the specific gravity of a solution.

HYDROPLANING: A phenomenon of driving when water builds up under the tire tread, causing it to lose contact with the road. Slowing down will usually restore normal tire contact with the road.

HYPOID GEARSET: The drive pinion gear may be placed below or above the centerline of the driven gear; often used as a final drive gearset.

IDLE MIXTURE: The mixture of air and fuel (usually about 14:1) being fed to the cylinders. The idle mixture screw(s) are sometimes adjusted as part of a tune-up.

IDLER ARM: Component of the steering linkage which is a geometric duplicate of the steering gear arm. It supports the right side of the center steering link.

IMPELLER: Often called a pump, the impeller is the power input (drive) member of a hydrodynamic drive. As part of the torque converter cover, it acts as a centrifugal pump and puts the fluid in motion.

INCH POUND (inch lbs.; sometimes in. lb. or in. lbs.): One twelfth of a foot pound.

INDUCTANCE: The force that produces voltage when a conductor is passed through a magnetic field.

INDUCTION: A means of transferring electrical energy in the form of a magnetic field. Principle used in the ignition coil to increase voltage.

INITIAL FEEL: A distinct firmer feel at start of shift when compared with feel at finish of shift.

INJECTOR: A device which receives metered fuel under relatively low pressure and is activated to inject the fuel into the engine under relatively high pressure at a predetermined time.

INPUT: In an automatic transmission, the source of power from the engine is absorbed by the torque converter, which provides the power input into the transmission. The turbine drives the input(turbine)shaft.

INPUT SHAFT: The shaft to which torque is applied, usually carrying the driving gear or gears.

INTAKE MANIFOLD: A casting of passages or pipes used to conduct air or a fuel/air mixture to the cylinders.

INTERNAL GEAR: The ring-like outer gear of a planetary gearset with the gear teeth cut on the inside of the ring to provide a mesh with the planet pinions.

ISOLATION (CLAMPING) DIODES: Diodes positioned in a circuit to prevent self-induction from damaging electronic components.

IX ROTARY GEAR PUMP: Contains two rotating members, one shaped with internal gear teeth and the other with external gear teeth. As the gears separate, the fluid fills the gaps between gear teeth, is pulled across a crescent-shaped divider, and then is forced to flow through the outlet as the gears mesh.

IX ROTARY LOBE PUMP: Sometimes referred to as a gerotor type pump. Two rotating members, one shaped with internal lobes and the other with external lobes, separate and then mesh to cause fluid to flow.

JOURNAL: The bearing surface within which a shaft operates.

JUMPER CABLES: Two heavy duty wires with large alligator clips used to provide power from a charged battery to a discharged battery mounted in a vehicle.

JUMPSTART: Utilizing the sufficiently charged battery of one vehicle to start the engine of another vehicle with a discharged battery by the use of jumper cables.

KEY: A small block usually fitted in a notch between a shaft and a hub to prevent slippage of the two parts.

KICKDOWN: Detent downshift system; either linkage, cable, or electrically controlled.

KILO: A prefix used in the metric system to indicate one thousand.

KNOCK: Noise which results from the spontaneous ignition of a portion of the air-fuel mixture in the engine cylinder caused by overly advanced ignition timing or use of incorrectly low octane fuel for that engine.

KNOCK SENSOR: An input device that responds to spark knock, caused by over advanced ignition timing.

LABOR TIME: A specific amount of time required to perform a certain repair or diagnostic service as defined by a vehicle or after-market manufacturer .

LACQUER: A quick-drying automotive paint.

LATE: Shift that occurs when engine is at higher than normal rpm for given amount of throttle.

LIGHT-EMITTING DIODE (LED): A semiconductor diode that emits light as electrical current flows through it; used in some electronic display devices to emit a red or other color light.

LIGHT THROTTLE: Approximately one-fourth of accelerator pedal travel.

LIMITED SLIP: A type of differential which transfers driving force to the wheel with the best traction.

LIMP-IN MODE: Electrical shutdown of the transmission/ transaxle output solenoids, allowing only forward and reverse gears that are hydraulically energized by the manual valve. This permits the vehicle to be driven to a service facility for repair.

LIP SEAL: Molded synthetic rubber seal designed with an outer sealing edge (lip) that points into the fluid containing area to be sealed. This type of seal is used where rotational and axial forces are present.

LITHIUM-BASE GREASE: Chassis and wheel bearing grease using lithium as a base. Not compatible with sodium-base grease.

LOAD DEVICE: A circuit's resistance that converts the electrical energy into light, sound, heat, or mechanical movement.

LOAD RANGE: Indicates the number of plies at which a tire is rated. Load range B equals four-ply rating; C equals six-ply rating; and, D equals an eight-ply rating.

LOAD TORQUE: The amount of output torque needed from the transmission/transaxle to overcome the vehicle load.

LOCKING HUBS: Accessories used on part-time four-wheel drive systems that allow the front wheels to be disengaged from the drive train when four-wheel drive is not being used. When four-wheel drive is desired, the hubs are engaged, locking the wheels to the drive train.

LOCKUP CONVERTER: A torque converter that operates hydraulically and mechanically. When an internal apply plate (lockup plate) clamps to the torque converter cover, hydraulic slippage is eliminated.

LOCK RING: See Circlip or Snapring

MAGNET: Any body with the property of attracting iron or steel.

MAGNETIC FIELD: The area surrounding the poles of a magnet that is affected by its attraction or repulsion forces.

MAIN LINE PRESSURE: Often called control pressure or line pressure, it refers to the pressure of the oil leaving the pump and is controlled by the pressure regulator valve.

MALFUNCTION INDICATOR LAMP (MIL): Previously known as a check engine light, the dash-mounted MIL illuminates and signals the driver that an emission or driveability problem with the powertrain has been detected by the ECM/PCM. When this occurs, at least one diagnostic trouble code (DTC) has been stored into the control module memory.

MANIFOLD ABSOLUTE PRESSURE (MAP) SENSOR: Reads the amount of air pressure (vacuum) in the engine's intake manifold system; its signal is used to analyze engine load conditions.

MANIFOLD VACUUM: Low pressure in an engine intake manifold formed just below the throttle plates. Manifold vacuum is highest at idle and drops under acceleration.

MANIFOLD: A casting of passages or set of pipes which connect the cylinders to an inlet or outlet source.

MANUAL LEVER POSITION SWITCH (MLPS): A mechanical switching unit that is typically mounted externally to the transmission/transaxle to inform the PCM/ECM which gear range the driver has selected.

MANUAL VALVE: Located inside the transmission/transaxle, it is directly connected to the driver's shift lever. The position of the manual valve determines which hydraulic circuits will be charged with oil pressure and the operating mode of the transmission.

MANUAL VALVE LEVER POSITION SENSOR (MVLPS): The input from this device tells the TCM what gear range was selected.

MASS AIR FLOW (MAF) SENSOR: Measures the airflow into the engine.

MASTER CYLINDER: The primary fluid pressurizing device in a hydraulic system. In automotive use, it is found in brake and hydraulic clutch systems and is pedal activated, either directly or, in a power brake system, through the power booster.

MacPherson STRUT: A suspension component combining a shock absorber and spring in one unit.

MEDIUM THROTTLE: Approximately one-half of accelerator pedal travel.

MEGA: A metric prefix indicating one million.

MEMBER: An independent component of a hydrodynamic unit such as an impeller, a stator, or a turbine. It may have one or more elements.

MERCON: A fluid developed by Ford Motor Company in 1988. It contains a friction modifier and closely resembles operating characteristics of Dexron.

METAL SEALING RINGS: Made from cast iron or aluminum, their primary application is with dynamic components involving pressure sealing circuits of rotating members. These rings are designed with either butt or hook lock end joints.

METER (ANALOG): A linear-style meter representing data as lengths; a needle-style instrument interfacing with logical numerical increments. This style of electrical meter uses relatively low impedance internal resistance and cannot be used for testing electronic circuitry.

METER (DIGITAL): Uses numbers as a direct readout to show values. Most meters of this style use high impedance internal resistance and must be used for testing low current electronic circuitry.

MICRO: A metric prefix indicating one-millionth (0.000001).

MILLI: A metric prefix indicating one-thousandth (0.001).

MINIMUM THROTTLE: The least amount of throttle opening required for upshift; normally close to zero throttle.

MISFIRE: Condition occurring when the fuel mixture in a cylinder fails to ignite, causing the engine to run roughly.

MODULE: Electronic control unit, amplifier or igniter of solid state or integrated design which controls the current flow in the ignition primary circuit based on input from the pick-up coil. When the module opens the primary circuit, high secondary voltage is induced in the coil.

MODULATED: In an electronic-hydraulic converter clutch system (or shift valve system), the term modulated refers to the pulsing of a solenoid, at a variable rate. This action controls the buildup of oil pressure in the hydraulic circuit to allow a controlled amount of clutch slippage.

MODULATED CONVERTER CLUTCH CONTROL (MCCC): A pulse width duty cycle valve that controls the converter lockup apply pressure and maximizes smoother transitions between lock and unlock conditions.

MODULATOR PRESSURE (THROTTLE PRESSURE): A hydraulic signal oil pressure relating to the amount of engine load, based on either the amount of throttle plate opening or engine vacuum.

MODULATOR VALVE: A regulator valve that is controlled by engine vacuum, providing a hydraulic pressure that varies in relation to engine torque. The hydraulic torque signal functions to delay the shift pattern and provide a line pressure boost. (See throttle valve.)

MOTOR: An electromagnetic device used to convert electrical energy into mechanical energy.

MULTIPLE-DISC CLUTCH: A grouping of steel and friction lined plates that, when compressed together by hydraulic pressure acting upon a piston, lock or unlock a planetary member.

MULTI-WEIGHT: Type of oil that provides adequate lubrication at both high and low temperatures.

needed to move one amp through a resistance of one ohm.

MUSHY: Same as soft; slow and drawn out clutch apply with very little shift feel.

MUTUAL INDUCTION: The generation of current from one wire circuit to another by movement of the magnetic field surrounding a current-carrying circuit as its ampere flow increases or decreases.

NEEDLE BEARING: A bearing which consists of a number (usually a large number) of long, thin rollers.

NITROGEN OXIDE (NOx): One of the three basic pollutants found in the exhaust emission of an internal combustion engine. The amount of NOx usually varies in an inverse proportion to the amount of HC and CO.

NONPOSITIVE SEALING: A sealing method that allows some minor leakage, which normally assists in lubrication.

O2 SENSOR: Located in the engine's exhaust system, it is an input device to the ECM/PCM for managing the fuel delivery and ignition system. A scanner can be used to observe the fluctuating voltage readings produced by an O2 sensor as the oxygen content of the exhaust is analyzed.

O-RING SEAL: Molded synthetic rubber seal designed with a circular cross-section. This type of seal is used primarily in static applications.

OBD II (ON-BOARD DIAGNOSTICS, SECOND GENERATION): Refers to the federal law mandating tighter control of 1996 and newer vehicle emissions, active monitoring of related devices, and standardization of terminology, data link connectors, and other technician concerns.

OCTANE RATING: A number, indicating the quality of gasoline based on its ability to resist knock. The higher the number, the better the quality. Higher compression engines require higher octane gas.

OEM: Original Equipment Manufactured. OEM equipment is that furnished standard by the manufacturer.

OFFSET: The distance between the vertical center of the wheel and the mounting surface at the lugs. Offset is positive if the center is outside the lug circle; negative offset puts the center line inside the lug circle.

OHM'S LAW: A law of electricity that states the relationship between voltage, current, and resistance. Volts = amperes x ohms

OHM: The unit used to measure the resistance of conductor-to-electrical flow. One ohm is the amount of resistance that limits current flow to one ampere in a circuit with one volt of pressure.

OHMMETER: An instrument used for measuring the resistance, in ohms, in an electrical circuit.

ONE-WAY CLUTCH: A mechanical clutch of roller or sprag design that resists torque or transmits power in one direction only. It is used to either hold or drive a planetary member.

ONE-WAY ROLLER CLUTCH: A mechanical device that transmits or holds torque in one direction only.

OPEN CIRCUIT: A break or lack of contact in an electrical circuit, either intentional (switch) or unintentional (bad connection or broken wire).

ORIFICE: Located in hydraulic oil circuits, it acts as a restriction. It slows down fluid flow to either create back pressure or delay pressure buildup downstream.

OSCILLOSCOPE: A piece of test equipment that shows electric impulses as a pattern on a screen. Engine performance can be analyzed by interpreting these patterns.

OUTPUT SHAFT: The shaft which transmits torque from a device, such as a transmission.

OUTPUT SPEED SENSOR (OSS): Identifies transmission/transaxle output shaft speed for shift timing and may be used to calculate TCC slip; often functions as the VSS (vehicle speed sensor).

OVERDRIVE: (1.) A device attached to or incorporated in a transmission/transaxle that allows the engine to turn less than one full revolution for every complete revolution of the wheels. The net effect is to reduce engine rpm, thereby using less fuel. A typical overdrive gear ratio would be .87:1, instead of the normal 1:1 in high gear. (2.) A gear assembly which produces more shaft revolutions than that transmitted to it.

OVERDRIVE PLANETARY GEARSET: A single planetary gearset designed to provide a direct drive and overdrive ratio. When coupled to a three-speed transmission/transaxle configuration, a four-speed/overdrive unit is present.

OVERHEAD CAMSHAFT (OHC): An engine configuration in which the camshaft is mounted on top of the cylinder head and operates the valve either directly or by means of rocker arms.

OVERHEAD VALVE (OHV): An engine configuration in which all of the valves are located in the cylinder head and the camshaft is located in the cylinder block. The camshaft operates the valves via lifters and pushrods.

OVERRUNCLUTCH: Another name for a one-way mechanical clutch. Applies to both roller and sprag designs.

OVERSTEER: The tendency of some vehicles, when steering into a turn, to over-respond or steer more than required, which could result in excessive slip of the rear wheels. Opposite of under-steer.

OXIDATION STABILIZERS: Absorb and dissipate heat. Automatic transmission fluid has high resistance to varnish and sludge buildup that occurs from excessive heat that is generated primarily in the torque converter. Local temperatures as high as 6000F (3150C) can occur at the clutch plates during engagement, and this heat must be absorbed and dissipated. If the fluid cannot withstand the heat, it burns or oxidizes, resulting in an almost immediate destruction of friction materials, clogged filter screen and hydraulic passages, and sticky valves.

OXIDES OF NITROGEN: See nitrogen oxide (NOx).

OXYGEN SENSOR: Used with a feedback system to sense the presence of oxygen in the exhaust gas and signal the computer which can use the voltage signal to determine engine operating efficiency and adjust the air/fuel ratio.

PARALLEL CIRCUIT: (See circuit, parallel.)

PARTS WASHER: A basin or tub, usually with a built-in pump mechanism and hose used for circulating chemical solvent for the purpose of cleaning greasy, oily and dirty components.

PART-TIME FOUR WHEEL DRIVE: A system that is normally in the two wheel drive mode and only runs in four-wheel drive when the system is manually engaged because more traction is desired. Two or four wheel drive is normally selected by a lever to engage the front axle, but if locking hubs are used, these must also be manually engaged in the Lock position. Otherwise, the front axle will not drive the front wheels.

PASSIVE RESTRAINT: Safety systems such as air bags or automatic seat belts which operate with no action required on the part of the driver or passenger. Mandated by Federal regulations on all vehicles sold in the U.S. after 1990.

PAYLOAD: The weight the vehicle is capable of carrying in addition to its own weight. Payload includes weight of the driver, passengers and cargo, but not coolant, fuel, lubricant, spare tire, etc.

PCM: Powertrain control module.

PCV VALVE: A valve usually located in the rocker cover that vents crankcase vapors back into the engine to be reburned.

PERCOLATION: A condition in which the fuel actually "boils," due to excessive heat. Percolation prevents proper atomization of the fuel causing rough running.

PICK-UP COIL: The coil in which voltage is induced in an electronic ignition.

PING: A metallic rattling sound produced by the engine during acceleration. It is usually due to incorrect ignition timing or a poor grade of gasoline.

PINION: The smaller of two gears. The rear axle pinion drives the ring gear which transmits motion to the axle shafts.

PINION GEAR: The smallest gear in a drive gear assembly.

PISTON: A disc or cup that fits in a cylinder bore and is free to move. In hydraulics, it provides the means of converting hydraulic pressure into a usable force. Examples of piston applications are found in servo, clutch, and accumulator units.

PISTON RING: An open-ended ring which fits into a groove on the outer diameter of the piston. Its chief function is to form a seal between the piston and cylinder wall. Most automotive pistons have three rings: two for compression sealing; one for oil sealing.

PITMAN ARM: A lever which transmits steering force from the steering gear to the steering linkage.

PLANET CARRIER: A basic member of a planetary gear assembly that carries the pinion gears.

PLANET PINIONS: Gears housed in a planet carrier that are in constant mesh with the sun gear and internal gear. Because they have their own independent rotating centers, the pinions are capable of rotating around the sun gear or the inside of the internal gear.

PLANETARY GEAR RATIO: The reduction or overdrive ratio developed by a planetary gearset.

PLANETARY GEARSET: In its simplest form, it is made up of a basic assembly group containing a sun gear, internal gear, and planet carrier. The gears are always in constant mesh and offer a wide range of gear ratio possibilities.

PLANETARY GEARSET (COMPOUND): Two planetary gearsets combined together.

PLANETARY GEARSET (SIMPLE): An assembly of gears in constant mesh consisting of a sun gear, several pinion gears mounted in a carrier, and a ring gear. It provides gear ratio and direction changes, in addition to a direct drive and a neutral.

PLY RATING: A. rating given a tire which indicates strength (but not necessarily actual plies). A two-ply/four-ply rating has only two plies, but the strength of a four-ply tire.

POLARITY: Indication (positive or negative) of the two poles of a battery.

PORT: An opening for fluid intake or exhaust.

POSITIVE SEALING: A sealing method that completely prevents leakage.

POTENTIAL: Electrical force measured in volts; sometimes used interchangeably with voltage.

POWER: The ability to do work per unit of time, as expressed in horsepower; one horsepower equals 33,000 ft. lbs. of work per minute, or 550 ft. lbs. of work per second.

POWER FLOW: The systematic flow or transmission of power through the gears, from the input shaft to the output shaft.

POWER-TO-WEIGHT RATIO: Ratio of horsepower to weight of car.

POWERTRAIN: See Drivetrain.

POWERTRAIN CONTROL MODULE (PCM): Current designation for the engine control module (ECM). In many cases, late model vehicle control units manage the engine as well as the transmission. In other settings, the PCM controls the engine and is interfaced with a TCM to control transmission functions.

Ppm: Parts per million; unit used to measure exhaust emissions.

PREIGNITION: Early ignition of fuel in the cylinder, sometimes due to glowing carbon deposits in the combustion chamber. Preignition can be damaging since combustion takes place prematurely.

PRELOAD: A predetermined load placed on a bearing during assembly or by adjustment.

PRESS FIT: The mating of two parts under pressure, due to the inner diameter of one being smaller than the outer diameter of the other, or vice versa; an interference fit.

PRESSURE: The amount of force exerted upon a surface area.

PRESSURE CONTROL SOLENOID (PCS): An output device that provides a boost oil pressure to the mainline regulator valve to control line pressure. Its operation is determined by the amount of current sent from the PCM.

PRESSURE GAUGE: An instrument used for measuring the fluid pressure in a hydraulic circuit.

PRESSURE REGULATOR VALVE: In automatic transmissions, its purpose is to regulate the pressure of the pump output and supply the basic fluid pressure necessary to operate the transmission. The regulated fluid pressure may be referred to as mainline pressure, line pressure, or control pressure.

PRESSURE SWITCH ASSEMBLY (PSA): Mounted inside the transmission, it is a grouping of oil pressure switches that inputs to the PCM when certain hydraulic passages are charged with oil pressure.

PRESSURE PLATE: A spring-loaded plate (part of the clutch) that transmits power to the driven (friction) plate when the clutch is engaged.

PRIMARY CIRCUIT: The low voltage side of the ignition system which consists of the ignition switch, ballast resistor or resistance wire, bypass, coil, electronic control unit and pick-up coil as well as the connecting wires and harnesses.

PROFILE: Term used for tire measurement (tire series), which is the ratio of tire height to tread width.

PROM (PROGRAMMABLE READ-ONLY MEMORY): The heart of the computer that compares input data and makes the engineered program or strategy decisions about when to trigger the appropriate output based on stored computer instructions.

PULSE GENERATOR: A two-wire pickup sensor used to produce a fluctuating electrical signal. This changing signal is read by the controller to determine the speed of the object and can be used to measure transmission/transaxle input speed, output speed, and vehicle speed.

PSI: Pounds per square inch; a measurement of pressure.

PULSE WIDTH DUTY CYCLE SOLENOID (PULSE WIDTH MODULATED SOLENOID): A computer-controlled solenoid that turns on and off at a variable rate producing a modulated oil pressure; often referred to as a pulse width modulated (PWM) solenoid. Employed in many electronic automatic transmissions and transaxles, these solenoids are used to manage shift control and converter clutch hydraulic circuits.

PUSHROD: A steel rod between the hydraulic valve lifter and the valve rocker arm in overhead valve (OHV) engines.

PUMP: A mechanical device designed to create fluid flow and pressure buildup in a hydraulic system.

QUARTER PANEL: General term used to refer to a rear fender. Quarter panel is the area from the rear door opening to the tail light area and from rear wheel well to the base of the trunk and roof-line.

RACE: The surface on the inner or outer ring of a bearing on which the balls, needles or rollers move.

RACK AND PINION: A type of automotive steering system using a pinion gear attached to the end of the steering shaft. The pinion meshes with a long rack attached to the steering linkage.

RADIAL TIRE: Tire design which uses body cords running at right angles to the center line of the tire. Two or more belts are used to give tread strength. Radials can be identified by their characteristic sidewall bulge.

RADIATOR: Part of the cooling system for a water-cooled engine, mounted in the front of the vehicle and connected to the engine with rubber hoses. Through the radiator, excess combustion heat is dissipated into the atmosphere through forced convection using a water and glycol based mixture that circulates through, and cools, the engine.

RANGE REFERENCE AND CLUTCH/BAND APPLY CHART: A guide that shows the application of clutches and bands for each gear, within the selector range positions. These charts are extremely useful for understanding how the unit operates and for diagnosing malfunctions.

RAVIGNEAUX GEARSET: A compound planetary gearset that features matched dual planetary pinions (sets of two) mounted in a single planet carrier. Two sun gears and one ring mesh with the carrier pinions.

REACTION MEMBER: The stationary planetary member, in a planetary gearset, that is grounded to the transmission/transaxle case through the use of friction and wedging devices known as bands, disc clutches, and one-way clutches.

REACTION PRESSURE: The fluid pressure that moves a spool valve against an opposing force or forces; the area on which the opposing force acts. The opposing force can be a spring or a combination of spring force and auxiliary hydraulic force.

REACTOR, TORQUE CONVERTER: The reaction member of a fluid torque converter, more commonly called a stator. (See stator.)

REAR MAIN OIL SEAL: A synthetic or rope-type seal that prevents oil from leaking out of the engine past the rear main crankshaft bearing.

RECIRCULATING BALL: Type of steering system in which recirculating steel balls occupy the area between the nut and worm wheel, causing a reduction in friction.

RECTIFIER: A device (used primarily in alternators) that permits electrical current to flow in one direction only.

REDUCTION: (See gear reduction.)

REGULATOR VALVE: A valve that changes the pressure of the oil in a hydraulic circuit as the oil passes through the valve by bleeding off (or exhausting) some of the volume of oil supplied to the valve.

REFRIGERANT 12 (R-12) or 134 (R-134): The generic name of the refrigerant used in automotive air conditioning systems.

REGULATOR: A device which maintains the amperage and/or voltage levels of a circuit at predetermined values.

RELAY: A switch which automatically opens and/or closes a circuit.

RELAY VALVE: A valve that directs flow and pressure. Relay valves simply connect or disconnect interrelated passages without restricting the fluid flow or changing the pressure.

RELIEF VALVE: A spring-loaded, pressure-operated valve that limits oil pressure buildup in a hydraulic circuit to a predetermined maximum value.

RELUCTOR: A wheel that rotates inside the distributor and triggers the release of voltage in an electronic ignition.

RESERVOIR: The storage area for fluid in a hydraulic system; often called a sump.

RESIN: A liquid plastic used in body work.

RESIDUAL MAGNETISM: The magnetic strength stored in a material after a magnetizing field has been removed.

RESISTANCE: The opposition to the flow of current through a circuit or electrical device, and is measured in ohms. Resistance is equal to the voltage divided by the amperage.

RESISTOR SPARK PLUG: A spark plug using a resistor to shorten the spark duration. This suppresses radio interference and lengthens plug life.

RESISTOR: A device, usually made of wire, which offers a preset amount of resistance in an electrical circuit.

RESULTANT FORCE: The single effective directional thrust of the fluid force on the turbine produced by the vortex and rotary forces acting in different planes.

RETARD: Set the ignition timing so that spark occurs later (fewer degrees before TDC).

RHEOSTAT: A device for regulating a current by means of a variable resistance.

RING GEAR: The name given to a ring-shaped gear attached to a differential case, or affixed to a flywheel or as part of a planetary gear set.

ROADLOAD: grade.

ROCKER ARM: A lever which rotates around a shaft pushing down (opening) the valve with an end when the other end is pushed up by the pushrod. Spring pressure will later close the valve.

ROCKER PANEL: The body panel below the doors between the wheel opening.

ROLLER BEARING: A bearing made up of hardened inner and outer races between which hardened steel rollers move.

ROLLER CLUTCH: A type of one-way clutch design using rollers and springs mounted within an inner and outer cam race assembly.

ROTARY FLOW: The path of the fluid trapped between the blades of the members as they revolve with the rotation of the torque converter cover (rotational inertia).

ROTOR: (1.) The disc-shaped part of a disc brake assembly, upon which the brake pads bear; also called, brake disc. (2.) The device mounted atop the distributor shaft, which passes current to the distributor cap tower contacts.

ROTARY ENGINE: See Wankel engine.

RPM: Revolutions per minute (usually indicates engine speed).

RTV: A gasket making compound that cures as it is exposed to the atmosphere. It is used between surfaces that are not perfectly machined to one another, leaving a slight gap that the RTV fills and in which it hardens. The letters RTV represent room temperature vulcanizing.

RUN-ON: Condition when the engine continues to run, even when the key is turned off. See dieseling.

SEALED BEAM: A automotive headlight. The lens, reflector and filament from a single unit.

SEATBELT INTERLOCK: A system whereby the car cannot be started unless the seatbelt is buckled.

SECONDARY CIRCUIT: The high voltage side of the ignition system, usually above 20,000 volts. The secondary includes the ignition coil, coil wire, distributor cap and rotor, spark plug wires and spark plugs.

SELF-INDUCTION: The generation of voltage in a current-carrying wire by changing the amount of current flowing within that wire.

SEMI-CONDUCTOR: A material (silicon or germanium) that is neither a good conductor nor an insulator; used in diodes and transistors.

SEMI-FLOATING AXLE: In this design, a wheel is attached to the axle shaft, which takes both drive and cornering loads. Almost all solid axle passenger cars and light trucks use this design.

SENDING UNIT: A mechanical, electrical, hydraulic or electromagnetic device which transmits information to a gauge.

SENSOR: Any device designed to measure engine operating conditions or ambient pressures and temperatures. Usually electronic in nature and designed to send a voltage signal to an on-board computer, some sensors may operate as a simple on/off switch or they may provide a variable voltage signal (like a potentiometer) as conditions or measured parameters change.

SERIES CIRCUIT: (See circuit, series.)

SERPENTINE BELT: An accessory drive belt, with small multiple v-ribs, routed around most or all of the engine-powered accessories such as the alternator and power steering pump. Usually both the front and the back side of the belt comes into contact with various pulleys.

SERVO: In an automatic transmission, it is a piston in a cylinder assembly that converts hydraulic pressure into mechanical force and movement; used for the application of the bands and clutches.

SHIFT BUSYNESS: When referring to a torque converter clutch, it is the frequent apply and release of the clutch plate due to uncommon driving conditions.

SHIFT VALVE: Classified as a relay valve, it triggers the automatic shift in response to a governor and a throttle signal by directing fluid to the appropriate band and clutch apply combination to cause the shift to occur.

SHIM: Spacers of precise, predetermined thickness used between parts to establish a proper working relationship.

SHIMMY: Vibration (sometimes violent) in the front end caused by misaligned front end, out of balance tires or worn suspension components.

SHORT CIRCUIT: An electrical malfunction where current takes the path of least resistance to ground (usually through damaged insulation). Current flow is excessive from low resistance resulting in a blown fuse.

SHUDDER: Repeated jerking or stick-slip sensation, similar to chuggle but more severe and rapid in nature, that may be most noticeable during certain ranges of vehicle speed; also used to define condition after converter clutch engagement.

SIMPSON GEARSET: A compound planetary gear train that integrates two simple planetary gearsets referred to as the front planetary and the rear planetary.

SINGLE OVERHEAD CAMSHAFT: See overhead camshaft.

SKIDPLATE: A metal plate attached to the underside of the body to protect the fuel tank, transfer case or other vulnerable parts from damage.

SLAVE CYLINDER: In automotive use, a device in the hydraulic clutch system which is activated by hydraulic force, disengaging the clutch.

SLIPPING: Noticeable increase in engine rpm without vehicle speed increase; usually occurs during or after initial clutch or band engagement.

SLUDGE: Thick, black deposits in engine formed from dirt, oil, water, etc. It is usually formed in engines when oil changes are neglected.

SNAP RING: A circular retaining clip used inside or outside a shaft or part to secure a shaft, such as a floating wrist pin.

SOFT: Slow, almost unnoticeable clutch apply with very little shift feel.

SOFTCODES: DTCs that have been set into the PCM memory but are not present at the time of testing; often referred to as history or intermittent codes.

SOHC: Single overhead camshaft.

SOLENOID: An electrically operated, magnetic switching device.

SPALLING: A wear pattern identified by metal chips flaking off the hardened surface. This condition is caused by foreign particles, overloading situations, and/or normal wear.

SPARK PLUG: A device screwed into the combustion chamber of a spark ignition engine. The basic construction is a conductive core inside of a ceramic insulator, mounted in an outer conductive base. An electrical charge from the spark plug wire travels along the conductive core and jumps a preset air gap to a grounding point or points at the end of the conductive base. The resultant spark ignites the fuel/air mixture in the combustion chamber.

SPECIFIC GRAVITY (BATTERY): The relative weight of liquid (battery electrolyte) as compared to the weight of an equal volume of water.

SPLINES: Ridges machined or cast onto the outer diameter of a shaft or inner diameter of a bore to enable parts to mate without rotation.

SPLIT TORQUE DRIVE: In a torque converter, it refers to parallel paths of torque transmission, one of which is mechanical and the other hydraulic.

SPONGY PEDAL: A soft or spongy feeling when the brake pedal is depressed. It is usually due to air in the brake lines.

SPOOLVALVE: A precision-machined, cylindrically shaped valve made up of lands and grooves. Depending on its position in the valve bore, various interconnecting hydraulic circuit passages are either opened or closed.

SPRAG CLUTCH: A type of one-way clutch design using cams or contoured-shaped sprags between inner and outer races. (See one-way clutch.)

SPRUNG WEIGHT: The weight of a car supported by the springs.

SQUARE-CUT SEAL: Molded synthetic rubber seal designed with a square- or rectangular-shaped cross-section. This type of seal is used for both dynamic and static applications.

SRS: Supplemental restraint system

STABILIZER (SWAY) BAR: A bar linking both sides of the suspension. It resists sway on turns by taking some of added load from one wheel and putting it on the other.

STAGE: The number of turbine sets separated by a stator. A turbine set may be made up of one or more turbine members. A three-element converter is classified as a single stage.

STALL: In fluid drive transmission/transaxle applications, stall refers to engine rpm with the transmission/transaxle engaged and the vehicle stationary; throttle valve can be in any position between closed and wide open.

STALL SPEED: In fluid drive transmission/transaxle applications, stall speed refers to the maximum engine rpm with the transmission/transaxle engaged and vehicle stationary, when the throttle valve is wide open. (See stall; stall test.)

STALL TEST: A procedure recommended by many manufacturers to help determine the integrity of an engine, the torque converter stator, and certain clutch and band combinations. With the shift lever in each of the forward and reverse positions and with the brakes firmly applied, the accelerator pedal is momentarily pressed to the wide open throttle (WOT) position. The engine rpm reading at full throttle can provide clues for diagnosing the condition of the items listed can above.

STALL TORQUE: The maximum design or engineered torque ratio of a fluid torque converter, produced under stall speed conditions. (See stall speed.)

STARTER: A high-torque electric motor used for the purpose of starting the engine, typically through a high ratio geared drive connected to the flywheel ring gear.

STATIC: A sealing application in which the parts being sealed do not move in relation to each other.

STATOR (REACTOR): The reaction member of a fluid torque converter that changes the direction of the fluid as it leaves the turbine to enter the impeller vanes. During the torque multiplication phase, this action assists the impeller's rotary force and results in an increase in torque.

STEERING GEOMETRY: Combination of various angles of suspension components (caster, camber, toe-in); roughly equivalent to front end alignment.

STRAIGHT WEIGHT: Term designating motor oil as suitable for use within a narrow range of temperatures. Outside the narrow temperature range its flow characteristics will not adequately lubricate.

STROKE: The distance the piston travels from bottom dead center to top dead center.

SUBSTITUTION: Replacing one part suspected of a defect with a like part of known quality.

SUMP: The storage vessel or reservoir that provides a ready source of fluid to the pump. In an automatic transmission, the sump is the oil pan. All fluid eventually returns to the sump for recycling into the hydraulic system.

SUN GEAR: In a planetary gearset, it is the center gear that meshes with a cluster of planet pinions.

SUPERCHARGER: An air pump driven mechanically by the engine through belts, chains, shafts or gears from the crankshaft. Two general types of supercharger are the positive displacement and centrifugal type, which pump air in direct relationship to the speed of the engine.

SUPPLEMENTAL RESTRAINT SYSTEM: See air bag.

SURGE: Repeating engine-related feeling of acceleration and deceleration that is less intense than chuggle.

SWITCH: A device used to open, close, or redirect the current in an electrical circuit.

SYNCHROMESH: A manual transmission/transaxle that is equipped with devices (synchronizers) that match the gear speeds so that the transmission/transaxle can be downshifted without clashing gears.

SYNTHETIC OIL: Non-petroleum based oil.

TACHOMETER: A device used to measure the rotary speed of an engine, shaft, gear, etc., usually in rotations per minute.

TDC: Top dead center. The exact top of the piston's stroke.

TEFLON SEALING RINGS: Teflon is a soft, durable, plastic-like material that is resistant to heat and provides excellent sealing. These rings are designed with either scarf-cut joints or as one-piece rings. Teflon sealing rings have replaced many metal ring applications.

TERMINAL: A device attached to the end of a wire or cable to make an electrical connection.

TEST LIGHT, CIRCUIT-POWERED: Uses available circuit voltage to test circuit continuity.

TEST LIGHT, SELF-POWERED: Uses its own battery source to test circuit continuity.

THERMISTOR: A special resistor used to measure fluid temperature; it decreases its resistance with increases in temperature.

THERMOSTAT: A valve, located in the cooling system of an engine, which is closed when cold and opens gradually in response to engine heating, controlling the temperature of the coolant and rate of coolant flow.

THERMOSTATIC ELEMENT: A heat-sensitive, spring-type device that controls a drain port from the upper sump area to the lower sump. When the transaxle fluid reaches operating temperature, the port is closed and the upper sump fills, thus reducing the fluid level in the lower sump.

THROTTLE POSITION (TP) SENSOR: Reads the degree of throttle opening; its signal is used to analyze engine load conditions. The ECM/PCM decides to apply the TCC, or to disengage it for coast or load conditions that need a converter torque boost.

THROTTLE PRESSURE/MODULATOR PRESSURE: A hydraulic signal oil pressure relating to the amount of engine load, based on either the amount of throttle plate opening or engine vacuum.

THROTTLE VALVE: A regulating or balanced valve that is controlled mechanically by throttle linkage or engine vacuum. It sends a hydraulic signal to the shift valve body to control shift timing and shift quality. (See balanced valve; modulator valve.)

THROW-OUT BEARING: As the clutch pedal is depressed, the throwout bearing moves against the spring fingers of the pressure plate, forcing the pressure plate to disengage from the driven disc.

TIE ROD: A rod connecting the steering arms. Tie rods have threaded ends that are used to adjust toe-in.

TIE-UP: Condition where two opposing clutches are attempting to apply at same time, causing engine to labor with noticeable loss of engine rpm.

TIMING BELT: A square-toothed, reinforced rubber belt that is driven by the crankshaft and operates the camshaft.

TIMING CHAIN: A roller chain that is driven by the crankshaft and operates the camshaft.

TIRE ROTATION: Moving the tires from one position to another to make the tires wear evenly.

TOE-IN (OUT): A term comparing the extreme front and rear of the front tires. Closer together at the front is toe-in; farther apart at the front is toe-out.

TOP DEAD CENTER (TDC): The point at which the piston reaches the top of its travel on the compression stroke.

TORQUE: Measurement of turning or twisting force, expressed as foot-pounds or inch-pounds.

TORQUE CONVERTER: A turbine used to transmit power from a driving member to a driven member via hydraulic action, providing changes in drive ratio and torque. In automotive use, it links the driveplate at the rear of the engine to the automatic transmission.

TORQUE CONVERTER CLUTCH: The apply plate (lockup plate) assembly used for mechanical power flow through the converter.

TORQUE PHASE: Sometimes referred to as slip phase or stall phase, torque multiplication occurs when the turbine is turning at a slower speed than the impeller, and the stator is reactionary (stationary). This sequence generates a boost in output torque.

TORQUE RATING (STALL TORQUE): The maximum torque multiplication that occurs during stall conditions, with the engine at wide open throttle (WOT) and zero turbine speed.

TORQUE RATIO: An expression of the gear ratio factor on torque effect. A 3:1 gear ratio or 3:1 torque ratio increases the torque input by the ratio factor of 3. Input torque (100 ft. lbs.) x 3 = output torque (300 ft. lbs.)

TRACTION: The amount of usable tractive effort before the drive wheels slip on the road contact surface.

TORSION BAR SUSPENSION: Long rods of spring steel which take the place of springs. One end of the bar is anchored and the other arm (attached to the suspension) is free to twist. The bars' resistance to twisting causes springing action.

TRACK: Distance between the centers of the tires where they contact the ground.

TRACTION CONTROL: A control system that prevents the spinning of a vehicle's drive wheels when excess power is applied.

TRACTIVE EFFORT: The amount of force available to the drive wheels, to move the vehicle.

TRANSAXLE: A single housing containing the transmission and differential. Transaxles are usually found on front engine/front wheel drive or rear engine/rear wheel drive cars.

TRANSDUCER: A device that changes energy from one form to another. For example, a transducer in a microphone changes sound energy to electrical energy. In automotive air-conditioning controls used in automatic temperature systems, a transducer changes an electrical signal to a vacuum signal, which operates mechanical doors.

TRANSMISSION: A powertrain component designed to modify torque and speed developed by the engine; also provides direct drive, reverse, and neutral.

TRANSMISSION CONTROL MODULE (TCM): Manages transmission functions. These vary according to the manufacturer's product design but may include converter clutch operation, electronic shift scheduling, and mainline pressure.

TRANSMISSION FLUID TEMPERATURE (TFT) SENSOR: Originally called a transmission oil temperature (TOT) sensor, this input device to the ECM/PCM senses the fluid temperature and provides a resistance value. It operates on the thermistor principle.

TRANSMISSION INPUT SPEED (TIS) SENSOR: Measures turbine shaft (input shaft) rpm's and compares to engine rpm's to determine torque converter slip. When compared to the transmission output speed sensor or VSS, gear ratio and clutch engagement timing can be determined.

TRANSMISSION OIL TEMPERATURE (TOT) SENSOR: (See transmission fluid temperature (TFT) sensor.)

TRANSMISSION RANGE SELECTOR (TRS) SWITCH: Tells the module which gear shift position the driver has chosen.

TRANSFER CASE: A gearbox driven from the transmission that delivers power to both front and rear driveshafts in a four-wheel drive system. Transfer cases usually have a high and low range set of gears, used depending on how much pulling power is needed.

TRANSISTOR: A semi-conductor component which can be actuated by a small voltage to perform an electrical switching function.

TREAD WEAR INDICATOR: Bars molded into the tire at right angles to the tread that appear as horizontal bars when 1/16 in. of tread remains.

TREAD WEAR PATTERN: The pattern of wear on tires which can be "read" to diagnose problems in the front suspension.

TUNE-UP: A regular maintenance function, usually associated with the replacement and adjustment of parts and components in the electrical and fuel systems of a vehicle for the purpose of attaining optimum performance.

TURBINE: The output (driven) member of a fluid coupling or fluid torque converter. It is splined to the input (turbine) shaft of the transmission.

TURBOCHARGER: An exhaust driven pump which compresses intake air and forces it into the combustion chambers at higher than atmospheric pressures. The increased air pressure allows more fuel to be burned and results in increased horsepower being produced.

TURBULENCE: The interference of molecules of a fluid (or vapor) with each other in a fluid flow.

TYPE F: Transmission fluid developed and used by Ford Motor Company up to 1982. This fluid type provides a high coefficient of friction.

TYPE 7176: The preferred choice of transmission fluid for Chrysler automatic transmissions and transaxles. Developed in 1986, it closely resembles Dexron and Mercon. Type 7176 is the recommended service fill fluid for all Chrysler products utilizing a lockup torque converter dating back to 1978.

U-JOINT (UNIVERSAL JOINT): A flexible coupling in the drive train that allows the driveshafts or axle shafts to operate at different angles and still transmit rotary power.

UNDERSTEER: The tendency of a car to continue straight ahead while negotiating a turn.

UNIT BODY: Design in which the car body acts as the frame.

UNLEADED FUEL: Fuel which contains no lead (a common gasoline additive). The presence of lead in fuel will destroy the functioning elements of a catalytic converter, making it useless.

UNSPRUNG WEIGHT: The weight of car components not supported by the springs (wheels, tires, brakes, rear axle, control arms, etc.).

UPSHIFT: A shift that results in a decrease in torque ratio and an increase in speed.

VACUUM: A negative pressure; any pressure less than atmospheric pressure.

VACUUM ADVANCE: A device which advances the ignition timing in response to increased engine vacuum.

VACUUM GAUGE: An instrument used for measuring the existing vacuum in a vacuum circuit or chamber. The unit of measure is inches (of mercury in a barometer).

VACUUM MODULATOR: Generates a hydraulic oil pressure in response to the amount of engine vacuum.

VALVES: Devices that can open or close fluid passages in a hydraulic system and are used for directing fluid flow and controlling pressure.

VALVE BODY ASSEMBLY: The main hydraulic control assembly of the transmission/transaxle that contains numerous valves, check balls, and other components to control the distribution of pressurized oil throughout the transmission.

VALVE CLEARANCE: The measured gap between the end of the valve stem and the rocker arm, cam lobe or follower that activates the valve.

VALVE GUIDES: The guide through which the stem of the valve passes.

The guide is designed to keep the valve in proper alignment.

VALVE LASH (clearance): The operating clearance in the valve train.

VALVE TRAIN: The system that operates intake and exhaust valves, consisting of camshaft, valves and springs, lifters, pushrods and rocker arms.

VAPOR LOCK: Boiling of the fuel in the fuel lines due to excess heat. This will interfere with the flow of fuel in the lines and can completely stop the flow. Vapor lock normally only occurs in hot weather.

VARIABLE DISPLACEMENT (VARIABLE CAPACITY) VANE PUMP: Slipper-type vanes, mounted in a revolving rotor and contained within the bore of a movable slide, capture and then force fluid to flow. Movement of the slide to various positions changes the size of the vane chambers and the amount of fluid flow. **Note:** GM refers to this pump design as variable displacement, and Ford terms it variable capacity.

VARIABLE FORCE SOLENOID (VFS): Commonly referred to as the electronic pressure control (EPC) solenoid, it replaces the cable/linkage style of TV system control and is integrated with a spool valve and spring assembly to control pressure. A variable computer-controlled current flow varies the internal force of the solenoid on the spool valve and resulting control pressure.

VARIABLE ORIFICE THERMAL VALVE: Temperature-sensitive hydraulic oil control device that adjusts the size of a circuit path opening. By altering the size of the opening, the oil flow rate is adapted for cold to hot oil viscosity changes.

VARNISH: Term applied to the residue formed when gasoline gets old and stale.

VCM: See Electronic Control Unit (ECU).

VEHICLE SPEED SENSOR (VSS): Provides an electrical signal to the computer module, measuring vehicle speed, and affects the torque converter clutch engagement and release.

VESPEL SEALING RINGS: Hard plastic material that produces excellent sealing in dynamic settings. These rings are found in late versions of the 4T60 and in all 4T60-E and 4T80-E transaxles.

VISCOSITY: The ability of a fluid to flow. The lower the viscosity rating, the easier the fluid will flow. 10 weight motor oil will flow much easier than 40 weight motor oil.

VISCOSITY INDEX IMPROVERS: Keeps the viscosity nearly constant with changes in temperature. This is especially important at low temperatures, when the oil needs to be thin to aid in shifting and for cold-weather starting. Yet it must not be so thin that at high temperatures it will cause excessive hydraulic leakage so that pumps are unable to maintain the proper pressures.

VISCOUS CLUTCH: A specially designed torque converter clutch apply plate that, through the use of a silicon fluid, clamps smoothly and absorbs torsional vibrations.

VOLT: Unit used to measure the force or pressure of electricity. It is defined as the pressure needed to move one amp through the resistance of one ohm.

VOLTAGE: The electrical pressure that causes current to flow. Voltage is measured in volts (V).

VOLTAGE, APPLIED: The actual voltage read at a given point in a circuit. It equals the available voltage of the power supply minus the losses in the circuit up to that point.

VOLTAGE DROP: The voltage lost or used in a circuit by normal loads such as a motor or lamp or by abnormal loads such as a poor (high-resistance) lead or terminal connection.

VOLTAGE REGULATOR: A device that controls the current output of the alternator or generator.

VOLTMETER: An instrument used for measuring electrical force in units called volts. Voltmeters are always connected parallel with the circuit being tested.

VORTEX FLOW: The crosswise or circulatory flow of oil between the blades of the members caused by the centrifugal pumping action of the impeller.

WANKEL ENGINE: An engine which uses no pistons. In place of pistons, triangular-shaped rotors revolve in specially shaped housings.

WATER PUMP: A belt driven component of the cooling system that mounts on the engine, circulating the coolant under pressure.

WATT: The unit for measuring electrical power. One watt is the product of one ampere and one volt (watts equals amps times volts). Wattage is the horsepower of electricity (746 watts equal one horsepower).

WHEEL ALIGNMENT: Inclusive term to describe the front end geometry (caster, camber, toe-in/out).

WHEEL CYLINDER: Found in the automotive drum brake assembly, it is a device, actuated by hydraulic pressure, which, through internal pistons, pushes the brake shoes outward against the drums.

WHEEL WEIGHT: Small weights attached to the wheel to balance the wheel and tire assembly. Out-of-balance tires quickly wear out and also give erratic handling when installed on the front.

WHEELBASE: Distance between the center of front wheels and the center of rear wheels.

WIDE OPEN THROTTLE (WOT): Full travel of accelerator pedal.

WORK: The force exerted to move a mass or object. Work involves motion; if a force is exerted and no motion takes place, no work is done. Work per unit of time is called power. Work = force x distance = ft. lbs. 33,000 ft. lbs. in one minute = 1 horsepower

ZERO-THROTTLE COAST DOWN: A full release of accelerator pedal while vehicle is in motion and in drive range.

Commonly Used Abbreviations

2

2WD	Two Wheel Drive

4

4WD	Four Wheel Drive

A

A/C	Air Conditioning
ABDC	After Bottom Dead Center
ABS	Anti-lock Brakes
AC	Alternating Current
ACL	Air cleaner
ACT	Air Charge Temperature
AIR	Secondary Air Injection
ALCL	Assembly Line Communications Link
ALDL	Assembly Line Diagnostic Link
AT	Automatic Transaxle/Transmission
ATDC	After Top Dead Center
ATF	Automatic Transmission Fluid
ATS	Air Temperature Sensor
AWD	All Wheel Drive

B

BAP	Barometric Absolute Pressure
BARO	Barometric Pressure
BBDC	Before Bottom Dead Center
BCM	Body Control Module
BDC	Bottom Dead Center
BPT	Backpressure Transducer
BTDC	Before Top Dead Center
BVSV	Bimetallic Vacuum Switching Valve

C

CAC	Charge Air Cooler
CARB	California Air Resources Board
CAT	Catalytic Converter
CCC	Computer Command Control
CCCC	Computer Controlled Catalytic Converter
CCCI	Computer Controlled Coil Ignition
CCD	Computer Controlled Dwell
CDI	Capacitor Discharge Ignition
CEC	Computerized Engine Control
CFI	Continuous Fuel Injection
CIS	Continuous Injection System
CIS-E	Continuous Injection System - Electronic
CKP	Crankshaft Position
CL	Closed Loop
CMP	Camshaft Position
CPP	Clutch Pedal Position
CTOX	Continuous Trap Oxidizer System
CTP	Closed Throttle Position
CVC	Constant Vacuum Control
CYL	Cylinder

D

DBC	Dual Bed Catalyst
DC	Direct Current
DFI	Direct Fuel Injection
DIS	Distributorless Ignition System
DLC	Data Link Connector
DMM	Digital Multimeter
DOHC	Double Overhead Camshaft
DRB	Diagnostic Readout Box
DTC	Diagnostic Trouble Code
DTM	Diagnostic Test Mode
DVOM	Digital Volt/Ohmmeter

E

EBCM	Electronic Brake Control Module
ECM	Engine Control Module
ECT	Engine Coolant Temperature
ECU	Engine Control Unit or Electronic Control Unit
EDIS	Electronic Distributorless Ignition System
EEC	Electronic Engine Control
EEPROM	Electrically Erasable Programmable Read Only Memory
EFE	Early Fuel Evaporation
EGR	Exhaust Gas Recirculation
EGRT	Exhaust Gas Recirculation Temperature
EGRVC	EGR Valve Control
EPROM	Erasable Programmable Read Only Memory
EVAP	Evaporative Emissions
EVP	EGR Valve Position

F

FBC	Feedback Carburetor
FEEPROM	Flash Electrically Erasable Programmable Read Only Memory
FF	Flexible Fuel
FI	Fuel Injection
FT	Fuel Trim
FWD	Front Wheel Drive

G

GND	Ground

H

HAC	High Altitude Compensation
HEGO	Heated Exhaust Gas Oxygen sensor
HEI	High Energy Ignition
HO2 Sensor	Heated Oxygen Sensor

I

IAC	Idle Air Control
IAT	Intake Air Temperature
ICM	Ignition Control Module
IFI	Indirect Fuel Injection
IFS	Inertia Fuel Shutoff
ISC	Idle Speed Control
IVSV	Idle Vacuum Switching Valve

Commonly Used Abbreviations

K

KOEO	Key On, Engine Off
KOER	Key ON, Engine Running
KS	Knock Sensor

M

MAF	Mass Air Flow
MAP	Manifold Absolute Pressure
MAT	Manifold Air Temperature
MC	Mixture Control
MDP	Manifold Differential Pressure
MFI	Multiport Fuel Injection
MIL	Malfunction Indicator Lamp or Maintenance
MST	Manifold Surface Temperature
MVZ	Manifold Vacuum Zone

N

NVRAM	Nonvolatile Random Access Memory

O

O2 Sensor	Oxygen Sensor
OBD	On-Board Diagnostic
OC	Oxidation Catalyst
OHC	Overhead Camshaft
OL	Open Loop

P

P/S	Power Steering
PAIR	Pulsed Secondary Air Injection
PCM	Powertrain Control Module
PCS	Purge Control Solenoid
PCV	Positive Crankcase Ventilation
PIP	Profile Ignition Pick-up
PNP	Park/Neutral Position
PROM	Programmable Read Only Memory
PSP	Power Steering Pressure
PTO	Power Take-Off
PTOX	Periodic Trap Oxidizer System

R

RABS	Rear Anti-lock Brake System
RAM	Random Access Memory
ROM	Read Only Memory
RPM	Revolutions Per Minute
RWAL	Rear Wheel Anti-lock Brakes
RWD	Rear Wheel Drive

S

SBC	Single Bed Converter
SBEC	Single Board Engine Controller
SC	Supercharger
SCB	Supercharger Bypass
SFI	Sequential Multiport Fuel Injection
SIR	Supplemental Inflatible Restraint
SOHC	Single Overhead Camshaft
SPL	Smoke Puff Limiter
SPOUT	Spark Output
SRI	Service Reminder Indicator
SRS	Supplemental Restraint System
SRT	System Readiness Test
SSI	Solid State Ignition
ST	Scan Tool
STO	Self-Test Output

T

TAC	Thermostatic Air Clearner
TBI	Throttle Body Fuel Injection
TC	Turbocharger
TCC	Torque Converter Clutch
TCM	Transmission Control Module
TDC	Top Dead Center
TFI	Thick Film Ignition
TP	Throttle Position
TR Sensor	Transaxle/Transmission Range Sensor
TVV	Thermal Vacuum Valve
TWC	Three-way Catalytic Converter

V

VAF	Volume Air Flow, or Vane Air Flow
VAPS	Variable Assist Power Steering
VRV	Vacuum Regulator Valve
VSS	Vehicle Speed Sensor
VSV	Vacuum Switching Valve

W

WOT	Wide Open Throttle
WU-TWC	Warm Up Three-way Catalytic Converter

ENGLISH TO METRIC CONVERSION: TORQUE

To convert foot-pounds (ft. lbs.) to Newton-meters (Nm), multiply the number of ft. lbs. by 1.36

To convert Newton-meters (Nm) to foot-pounds (ft. lbs.), multiply the number of Nm by 0.7376

ft. lbs.	Nm	ft. lbs.	Nm	ft. lbs.	Nm	ft. lbs.	Nm
0.1	0.1	34	46.2	76	103.4	118	160.5
0.2	0.3	35	47.6	77	104.7	119	161.8
0.3	0.4	36	49.0	78	106.1	120	163.2
0.4	0.5	37	50.3	79	107.4	121	164.6
0.5	0.7	38	51.7	80	108.8	122	165.9
0.6	0.8	39	53.0	81	110.2	123	167.3
0.7	1.0	40	54.4	82	111.5	124	168.6
0.8	1.1	41	55.8	83	112.9	125	170.0
0.9	1.2	42	57.1	84	114.2	126	171.4
1	1.4	43	58.5	85	115.6	127	172.7
2	2.7	44	59.8	86	117.0	128	174.1
3	4.1	45	61.2	87	118.3	129	175.4
4	5.4	46	62.6	88	119.7	130	176.8
5	6.8	47	63.9	89	121.0	131	178.2
6	8.2	48	65.3	90	122.4	132	179.5
7	9.5	49	66.6	91	123.8	133	180.9
8	10.9	50	68.0	92	125.1	134	182.2
9	12.2	51	69.4	93	126.5	135	183.6
10	13.6	52	70.7	94	127.8	136	185.0
11	15.0	53	72.1	95	129.2	137	186.3
12	16.3	54	73.4	96	130.6	138	187.7
13	17.7	55	74.8	97	131.9	139	189.0
14	19.0	56	76.2	98	133.3	140	190.4
15	20.4	57	77.5	99	134.6	141	191.8
16	21.8	58	78.9	100	136.0	142	193.1
17	23.1	59	80.2	101	137.4	143	194.5
18	24.5	60	81.6	102	138.7	144	195.8
19	25.8	61	83.0	103	140.1	145	197.2
20	27.2	62	84.3	104	141.4	146	198.6
21	28.6	63	85.7	105	142.8	147	199.9
22	29.9	64	87.0	106	144.2	148	201.3
23	31.3	65	88.4	107	145.5	149	202.6
24	32.6	66	89.8	108	146.9	150	204.0
25	34.0	67	91.1	109	148.2	151	205.4
26	35.4	68	92.5	110	149.6	152	206.7
27	36.7	69	93.8	111	151.0	153	208.1
28	38.1	70	95.2	112	152.3	154	209.4
29	39.4	71	96.6	113	153.7	155	210.8
30	40.8	72	97.9	114	155.0	156	212.2
31	42.2	73	99.3	115	156.4	157	213.5
32	43.5	74	100.6	116	157.8	158	214.9
33	44.9	75	102.0	117	159.1	159	216.2

METRIC TO ENGLISH CONVERSION: TORQUE

To convert foot-pounds (ft. lbs.) to Newton-meters (Nm), multiply the number of ft. lbs. by 1.36
To convert Newton-meters (Nm) to foot-pounds (ft. lbs.), multiply the number of Nm by 0.7376

Nm	ft. lbs.	Nm	ft. lbs.	Nm	ft. lbs.	Nm	ft. lbs.	Nm	ft. lbs.
0.1	0.1	34	25.0	76	55.9	118	86.8	160	117.6
0.2	0.1	35	25.7	77	56.6	119	87.5	161	118.4
0.3	0.2	36	26.5	78	57.4	120	88.2	162	119.1
0.4	0.3	37	27.2	79	58.1	121	89.0	163	119.9
0.5	0.4	38	27.9	80	58.8	122	89.7	164	120.6
0.6	0.4	39	28.7	81	59.6	123	90.4	165	121.3
0.7	0.5	40	29.4	82	60.3	124	91.2	166	122.1
0.8	0.6	41	30.1	83	61.0	125	91.9	167	122.8
0.9	0.7	42	30.9	84	61.8	126	92.6	168	123.5
1	0.7	43	31.6	85	62.5	127	93.4	169	124.3
2	1.5	44	32.4	86	63.2	128	94.1	170	125.0
3	2.2	45	33.1	87	64.0	129	94.9	171	125.7
4	2.9	46	33.8	88	64.7	130	95.6	172	126.5
5	3.7	47	34.6	89	65.4	131	96.3	173	127.2
6	4.4	48	35.3	90	66.2	132	97.1	174	127.9
7	5.1	49	36.0	91	66.9	133	97.8	175	128.7
8	5.9	50	36.8	92	67.6	134	98.5	176	129.4
9	6.6	51	37.5	93	68.4	135	99.3	177	130.1
10	7.4	52	38.2	94	69.1	136	100.0	178	130.9
11	8.1	53	39.0	95	69.9	137	100.7	179	131.6
12	8.8	54	39.7	96	70.6	138	101.5	180	132.4
13	9.6	55	40.4	97	71.3	139	102.2	181	133.1
14	10.3	56	41.2	98	72.1	140	102.9	182	133.8
15	11.0	57	41.9	99	72.8	141	103.7	183	134.6
16	11.8	58	42.6	100	73.5	142	104.4	184	135.3
17	12.5	59	43.4	101	74.3	143	105.1	185	136.0
18	13.2	60	44.1	102	75.0	144	105.9	186	136.8
19	14.0	61	44.9	103	75.7	145	106.6	187	137.5
20	14.7	62	45.6	104	76.5	146	107.4	188	138.2
21	15.4	63	46.3	105	77.2	147	108.1	189	139.0
22	16.2	64	47.1	106	77.9	148	108.8	190	139.7
23	16.9	65	47.8	107	78.7	149	109.6	191	140.4
24	17.6	66	48.5	108	79.4	150	110.3	192	141.2
25	18.4	67	49.3	109	80.1	151	111.0	193	141.9
26	19.1	68	50.0	110	80.9	152	111.8	194	142.6
27	19.9	69	50.7	111	81.6	153	112.5	195	143.4
28	20.6	70	51.5	112	82.4	154	113.2	196	144.1
29	21.3	71	52.2	113	83.1	155	114.0	197	144.9
30	22.1	72	52.9	114	83.8	156	114.7	198	145.6
31	22.8	73	53.7	115	84.6	157	115.4	199	146.3
32	23.5	74	54.4	116	85.3	158	116.2	200	147.1
33	24.3	75	55.1	117	86.0	159	116.9	201	147.8

ENGLISH/METRIC CONVERSION: TEMPERATURE

To convert Fahrenheit (F°) to Celsius (C°), take F° temperature and subtract 32, multiply the result by 5 and divide the result by 9
To convert Celsius (C°) to Fahrenheit (F°), take C° temperature and multiply it by 9, divide the result by 5 and add 32

F°	C°	F°	C°	C°	F°	C°	F°
-40	-40.0	150	65.6	-38	-36.4	46	114.8
-35	-37.2	155	68.3	-36	-32.8	48	118.4
-30	-34.4	160	71.1	-34	-29.2	50	122
-25	-31.7	165	73.9	-32	-25.6	52	125.6
-20	-28.9	170	76.7	-30	-22	54	129.2
-15	-26.1	175	79.4	-28	-18.4	56	132.8
-10	-23.3	180	82.2	-26	-14.8	58	136.4
-5	-20.6	185	85.0	-24	-11.2	60	140
0	-17.8	190	87.8	-22	-7.6	62	143.6
1	-17.2	195	90.6	-20	-4	64	147.2
2	-16.7	200	93.3	-18	-0.4	66	150.8
3	-16.1	205	96.1	-16	3.2	68	154.4
4	-15.6	210	98.9	-14	6.8	70	158
5	-15.0	212	100.0	-12	10.4	72	161.6
10	-12.2	215	101.7	-10	14	74	165.2
15	-9.4	220	104.4	-8	17.6	76	168.8
20	-6.7	225	107.2	-6	21.2	78	172.4
25	-3.9	230	110.0	-4	24.8	80	176
30	-1.1	235	112.8	-2	28.4	82	179.6
35	1.7	240	115.6	0	32	84	183.2
40	4.4	245	118.3	2	35.6	86	186.8
45	7.2	250	121.1	4	39.2	88	190.4
50	10.0	255	123.9	6	42.8	90	194
55	12.8	260	126.7	8	46.4	92	197.6
60	15.6	265	129.4	10	50	94	201.2
65	18.3	270	132.2	12	53.6	96	204.8
70	21.1	275	135.0	14	57.2	98	208.4
75	23.9	280	137.8	16	60.8	100	212
80	26.7	285	140.6	18	64.4	102	215.6
85	29.4	290	143.3	20	68	104	219.2
90	32.2	295	146.1	22	71.6	106	222.8
95	35.0	300	148.9	24	75.2	108	226.4
100	37.8	305	151.7	26	78.8	110	230
105	40.6	310	154.4	28	82.4	112	233.6
110	43.3	315	157.2	30	86	114	237.2
115	46.1	320	160.0	32	89.6	116	240.8
120	48.9	325	162.8	34	93.2	118	244.4
125	51.7	330	165.6	36	96.8	120	248
130	54.4	335	168.3	38	100.4	122	251.6
135	57.2	340	171.1	40	104	124	255.2
140	60.0	345	173.9	42	107.6	126	258.8
145	62.8	350	176.7	44	111.2	128	262.4

LENGTH CONVERSION

To convert inches (in.) to millimeters (mm), multiply the number of inches by 25.4

To convert millimeters (mm) to inches (in.), multiply the number of millimeters by 0.04

Inches	Millimeters	Inches	Millimeters	Inches	Millimeters	Inches	Millimeters
0.0001	0.00254	0.005	0.1270	0.09	2.286	4	101.6
0.0002	0.00508	0.006	0.1524	0.1	2.54	5	127.0
0.0003	0.00762	0.007	0.1778	0.2	5.08	6	152.4
0.0004	0.01016	0.008	0.2032	0.3	7.62	7	177.8
0.0005	0.01270	0.009	0.2286	0.4	10.16	8	203.2
0.0006	0.01524	0.01	0.254	0.5	12.70	9	228.6
0.0007	0.01778	0.02	0.508	0.6	15.24	10	254.0
0.0008	0.02032	0.03	0.762	0.7	17.78	11	279.4
0.0009	0.02286	0.04	1.016	0.8	20.32	12	304.8
0.001	0.0254	0.05	1.270	0.9	22.86	13	330.2
0.002	0.0508	0.06	1.524	1	25.4	14	355.6
0.003	0.0762	0.07	1.778	2	50.8	15	381.0
0.004	0.1016	0.08	2.032	3	76.2	16	406.4

ENGLISH/METRIC CONVERSION: LENGTH

To convert inches (in.) to millimeters (mm), multiply the number of inches by 25.4

To convert millimeters (mm) to inches (in.), multiply the number of millimeters by 0.04

Inches		Millimeters	Inches		Millimeters	Inches		Millimeters
Fraction	Decimal	Decimal	Fraction	Decimal	Decimal	Fraction	Decimal	Decimal
1/64	0.016	0.397	11/32	0.344	8.731	11/16	0.688	17.463
1/32	0.031	0.794	23/64	0.359	9.128	45/64	0.703	17.859
3/64	0.047	1.191	3/8	0.375	9.525	23/32	0.719	18.256
1/16	0.063	1.588	25/64	0.391	9.922	47/64	0.734	18.653
5/64	0.078	1.984	13/32	0.406	10.319	3/4	0.750	19.050
3/32	0.094	2.381	27/64	0.422	10.716	49/64	0.766	19.447
7/64	0.109	2.778	7/16	0.438	11.113	25/32	0.781	19.844
1/8	0.125	3.175	29/64	0.453	11.509	51/64	0.797	20.241
9/64	0.141	3.572	15/32	0.469	11.906	13/16	0.813	20.638
5/32	0.156	3.969	31/64	0.484	12.303	53/64	0.828	21.034
11/64	0.172	4.366	1/2	0.500	12.700	27/32	0.844	21.431
3/16	0.188	4.763	33/64	0.516	13.097	55/64	0.859	21.828
13/64	0.203	5.159	17/32	0.531	13.494	7/8	0.875	22.225
7/32	0.219	5.556	35/64	0.547	13.891	57/64	0.891	22.622
15/64	0.234	5.953	9/16	0.563	14.288	29/32	0.906	23.019
1/4	0.250	6.350	37/64	0.578	14.684	59/64	0.922	23.416
17/64	0.266	6.747	19/32	0.594	15.081	15/16	0.938	23.813
9/32	0.281	7.144	39/64	0.609	15.478	61/64	0.953	24.209
19/64	0.297	7.541	5/8	0.625	15.875	31/32	0.969	24.606
5/16	0.313	7.938	41/64	0.641	16.272	63/64	0.984	25.003
21/64	0.328	8.334	21/32	0.656	16.669	1/1	1.000	25.400
			43/64	0.672	17.066